Hoover's Handbook of Emerging Companies 2023

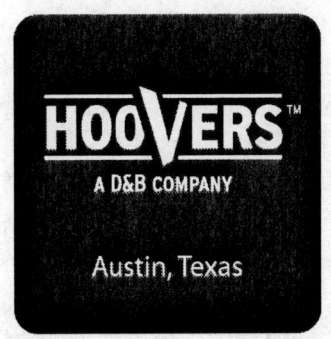

HOOVERS™
A D&B COMPANY

Austin, Texas

Hoover's Handbook of Emerging Companies 2023 is intended to provide readers with accurate and authoritative information about the enterprises covered in it. Hoover's researched all companies and organizations profiled, and in many cases contacted them directly so that companies represented could provide information. The information contained herein is as accurate as we could reasonably make it. In many cases we have relied on third-party material that we believe to be trustworthy, but were unable to independently verify. We do not warrant that the book is absolutely accurate or without error. Readers should not rely on any information contained herein in instances where such reliance might cause financial loss. The publisher, the editors, and their data suppliers specifically disclaim all warranties, including the implied warranties of merchantability and fitness for a specific purpose. This book is sold with the understanding that neither the publisher, the editors, nor any content contributors are engaged in providing investment, financial, accounting, legal, or other professional advice.

The financial data (Historical Financials sections) in this book are from a variety of sources. Mergent Inc., provided selected data for the Historical Financials sections of publicly traded companies. For private companies and for historical information on public companies prior to their becoming public, we obtained information directly from the companies or from trade sources deemed to be reliable. Hoover's, Inc., is solely responsible for the presentation of all data.

Many of the names of products and services mentioned in this book are the trademarks or service marks of the companies manufacturing or selling them and are subject to protection under US law. Space has not permitted us to indicate which names are subject to such protection, and readers are advised to consult with the owners of such marks regarding their use. Hoover's is a trademark of Hoover's, Inc.

Copyright © 2023 by Dun & Bradstreet. All rights reserved. No part of this book may be reproduced or transmitted in any form or by any means, electronic or mechanical, including by photocopying, facsimile transmission, recording, rekeying, or using any information storage and retrieval system, without permission in writing from Hoover's, except that brief passages may be quoted by a reviewer in a magazine, in a newspaper, online, or in a broadcast review.

10 9 8 7 6 5 4 3 2 1

Publishers Cataloging-in-Publication Data

Hoover's Handbook of Emerging Companies 2023

   Includes indexes.

   ISBN: 978-1-68525-305-9

   ISSN 1073-6433

   1. Business enterprises — Directories. 2. Corporations — Directories.

HF3010 338.7

U.S. AND WORLD BOOK SALES
Mergent Inc.

580 Kingsley Park Drive
Fort Mill, SC 29715
Phone: 704-559-6961
e-mail: skardon@ftserussell.com
Web: www.mergentbusinesspress.com

Mergent Inc.

Executive Managing Director: John Pedernales

Publisher and Managing Director of Print Products: Thomas Wecera

Director of Print Products: Charlot Volny

Quality Assurance Editor: Wayne Arnold

Production Research Assistant: Davie Christna

Data Manager: Allison Shank

MERGENT CUSTOMER SERVICE-PRINT
Support and Fulfillment Manager: Stephanie Kardon Phone: 704-559-6961
email: skardon@ftserussell.com

ABOUT MERGENT INC.

For over 100 years, Mergent, Inc. has been a leading provider of business and financial information on public and private companies globally. Mergent is known to be a trusted partner to corporate and financial institutions, as well as to academic and public libraries. Today we continue to build on a century of experience by transforming data into knowledge and combining our expertise with the latest technology to create new global data and analytical solutions for our clients. With advanced data collection services, cloud-based applications, desktop analytics and print products, Mergent and its subsidiaries provide solutions from top down economic and demographic information, to detailed equity and debt fundamental analysis. We incorporate value added tools such as quantitative Smart Beta equity research and tools for portfolio building and measurement. Based in the U.S., Mergent maintains a strong global presence, with offices in New York, Charlotte, San Diego, London, Tokyo, Kuching and Melbourne. Mergent, Inc. is a member of the London Stock Exchange plc group of companies. The Mergent business forms part of LSEG's Information Services Division, which includes FTSE Russell, a global leader in indexes.

Abbreviations

AFL-CIO – American Federation of Labor and Congress of Industrial Organizations
AMA – American Medical Association
AMEX – American Stock Exchange
ARM – adjustable-rate mortgage
ASP – application services provider
ATM – asynchronous transfer mode
ATM – automated teller machine
CAD/CAM – computer-aided design/computer-aided manufacturing
CD-ROM – compact disc – read-only memory
CD-R – CD-recordable
CEO – chief executive officer
CFO – chief financial officer
CMOS – complementary metal oxide silicon
COO – chief operating officer
DAT – digital audiotape
DOD – Department of Defense
DOE – Department of Energy
DOS – disk operating system
DOT – Department of Transportation
DRAM – dynamic random-access memory
DSL – digital subscriber line
DVD – digital versatile disc/digital video disc
DVD-R – DVD-recordable
EPA – Environmental Protection Agency
EPS – earnings per share
ESOP – employee stock ownership plan
EU – European Union
EVP – executive vice president
FCC – Federal Communications Commission
FDA – Food and Drug Administration
FDIC – Federal Deposit Insurance Corporation
FTC – Federal Trade Commission
FTP – file transfer protocol
GATT – General Agreement on Tariffs and Trade
GDP – gross domestic product
HMO – health maintenance organization
HR – human resources
HTML – hypertext markup language
ICC – Interstate Commerce Commission
IPO – initial public offering
IRS – Internal Revenue Service
ISP – Internet service provider
kWh – kilowatt-hour
LAN – local-area network
LBO – leveraged buyout
LCD – liquid crystal display
LNG – liquefied natural gas
LP – limited partnership
Ltd. – limited
mips – millions of instructions per second
MW – megawatt
NAFTA – North American Free Trade Agreement
NASA – National Aeronautics and Space Administration
NASDAQ – National Association of Securities Dealers Automated Quotations
NATO – North Atlantic Treaty Organization
NYSE – New York Stock Exchange
OCR – optical character recognition
OECD – Organization for Economic Cooperation and Development
OEM – original equipment manufacturer
OPEC – Organization of Petroleum Exporting Countries
OS – operating system
OSHA – Occupational Safety and Health Administration
OTC – over-the-counter
PBX – private branch exchange
PCMCIA – Personal Computer Memory Card International Association
P/E – price to earnings ratio
RAID – redundant array of independent disks
RAM – random-access memory
R&D – research and development
RBOC – regional Bell operating company
RISC – reduced instruction set computer
REIT – real estate investment trust
ROA – return on assets
ROE – return on equity
ROI – return on investment
ROM – read-only memory
S&L – savings and loan
SEC – Securities and Exchange Commission
SEVP – senior executive vice president
SIC – Standard Industrial Classification
SOC – system on a chip
SVP – senior vice president
USB – universal serial bus
VAR – value-added reseller
VAT – value-added tax
VC – venture capitalist
VoIP – Voice over Internet Protocol
VP – vice president
WAN – wide-area network

Contents

Companies Profiled vi
About *Hoover's Handbook of Emerging Companies 2023* x
Using Hoover's Handbooks xi
A List-Lover's Compendium 1a
    The 300 Largest Companies by Sales in *Mergents*
    Data Base for 2023 .... 2a
    The 300 Largest Employers in *Mergents*
    Data Base for 2023 .... 4a
    Top 300 Companies by Net Income in *Mergents*
    Data Base for 2023 .... 6a
The Companies 1
The Indexes 549
    Index of Companies by Headquarters Location 551
    Index of Company Executives 581

Companies Profiled

Company	Page
1-800 Flowers.com, Inc.	1
ABIOMED, Inc.	2
ACM Research Inc	3
ACNB Corp	3
Addus HomeCare Corp	4
Advanced Drainage Systems Inc	5
Advanced Energy Industries Inc	5
AeroVironment, Inc.	7
Agree Realty Corp.	8
Air Lease Corp	9
Air Transport Services Group, Inc.	10
Akamai Technologies Inc	11
Alamo Group, Inc.	12
Alarm.com Holdings Inc	13
Alerus Financial Corp	14
Alexandria Real Estate Equities Inc	14
Align Technology Inc	15
Allegiance Bancshares Inc	17
AllianceBernstein Holding LP	17
Allied Motion Technologies Inc	17
Alpine Banks of Colorado	19
Alpine Income Property Trust Inc	19
Amalgamated Financial Corp	19
Amedisys, Inc.	20
Ameresco Inc	21
America's Car-Mart Inc	22
American Bank Inc (PA)	23
American Business Bank (Los Angeles, CA)	24
American National Bankshares, Inc. (Danville, VA)	24
American Outdoor Brands Inc	25
American Riviera Bancorp	25
American Vanguard Corp.	26
American Woodmark Corp.	27
Ameris Bancorp	28
Ames National Corp.	29
Amneal Pharmaceuticals Inc	30
Ansys Inc.	31
Antares Pharma Inc.	32
Antero Midstream Corp	33
Apollo Medical Holdings Inc	33
AppFolio Inc	33
Arbor Realty Trust Inc	34
Ares Management Corp	34
Arista Networks Inc	35
ARKO Corp	35
Armada Hoffler Properties Inc	35
Arrow Financial Corp.	36
ASGN Inc	37
Aspen Technology Inc	38
Atkore Inc	39
Atlantic Union Bankshares Corp	40
Atlanticus Holdings Corp	41
AtriCure Inc	42
Aura Minerals Inc (British Virgin Islands)	43
Autodesk Inc	43
Avid Bioservices Inc	45
Avidbank Holdings Inc	46
Axcelis Technologies Inc	46
Axos Financial Inc	47
AZEK Co Inc (The)	48
B Riley Financial Inc	49
B&G Foods Inc	50
BancFirst Corp. (Oklahoma City, Okla)	51
Bank First Corp	52
Bank Of Princeton (The)	53
Bank OZK	53
Bank7 Corp	54
BankFirst Capital Corp.	54
Bar Harbor Bankshares	55
Barnwell Industries, Inc.	56
BayCom Corp	56
BCB Bancorp Inc	56
Beauty Health Co (The)	57
BellRing Brands Inc	57
BEO Bancorp, Heppner OR	57
Bio-Techne Corp	58
BioDelivery Sciences International Inc	60
BioMarin Pharmaceutical Inc	61
Bioqual Inc	61
Blackhawk Bancorp Inc	61
Blackstone Mortgage Trust Inc	62
Blue Ridge Bankshares Inc (Luray, VA)	62
Bluerock Residential Growth REIT Inc	62
BNCCORP Inc	63
BOK Financial Corp	63
Boomer Holdings Inc	64
Boot Barn Holdings Inc	64
Boston Beer Co Inc (The)	65
Bridgewater Bancshares Inc	66
BrightView Holdings Inc	66
Broadmark Realty Capital Inc	67
Broadstone Net Lease Inc	67
Brown & Brown Inc	67
Business First Bancshares Inc	69
BV Financial Inc	69
BWX Technologies inc	69
Byline Bancorp Inc	71
Cable One Inc	71
Cactus Inc	72
Cadence Bank	72
Cadence Design Systems Inc	73
California First Leasing Corp	75
Calloway's Nursery, Inc.	76
Cambium Networks Corp	77
Cambridge Bancorp	77
Canandaigua National Corp.	78
Capital Bancorp Inc (MD)	78
Capital City Bank Group, Inc.	79
CapStar Financial Holdings Inc	79
Cara Therapeutics Inc	80
Cardinal Ethanol LLC	81
CareTrust REIT Inc	81
CarGurus Inc	81
Casella Waste Systems, Inc.	82
Cashmere Valley Bank Washington (New)	83
Catalent Inc	83
Cathay General Bancorp	83
Cavco Industries Inc (DE)	84
Cboe Global Markets Inc	86
Celsius Holdings Inc	88
Central Garden & Pet Co	88
Central Valley Community Bancorp	90
Cerence Inc	91
CF Bankshares Inc	91
ChampionX Corp	91
ChannelAdvisor Corp	92
Charles & Colvard Ltd	93
Charles River Laboratories International Inc.	93
Chart Industries Inc	95
ChoiceOne Financial Services, Inc.	96
CIB Marine Bancshares Inc	97
Citizens & Northern Corp	97
Citizens Community Bancorp Inc (MD)	98
Citizens Financial Services Inc	99
City Holding Co.	99
Civista Bancshares Inc	100
Civitas Resources Inc	100
Clearfield Inc	101
CNB Bank Shares Inc	102
CNB Community Bancorp Inc	102
CNB Financial Corp. (Clearfield, PA)	102
Coastal Financial Corp (WA)	103
CoastalSouth Bancshares Inc	104
Cognex Corp	104
Cohen & Company Inc (New)	105
Coherus BioSciences Inc	106
Cohu Inc	106
Collegium Pharmaceuticals Inc	107
Colony Bankcorp, Inc.	108
Columbia Banking System Inc	108
Columbia Financial Inc	109
Comfort Systems USA Inc	110
Communities First Financial Corp	111
Community Bank System Inc	111
Community Financial Corp (The)	113
Community Healthcare Trust Inc	114
Community West Bancshares	114
Compass Diversified	114
ConnectOne Bancorp Inc (New)	115
Consolidated Communications Holdings Inc	116
Construction Partners Inc	117
Consumers Bancorp, Inc. (Minerva, OH)	117
Cooper Companies, Inc. (The)	117
Copart Inc	119
Corcept Therapeutics Inc	121
CoreCard Corp	122
CoStar Group, Inc.	122
Cousins Properties Inc	124
Cowen Inc	125
CRA International Inc	126
Crawford United Corp	127
Credit Acceptance Corp (MI)	127
Crescent Capital BDC Inc	129
Crexendo Inc	129
Crocs Inc	129
CrossFirst Bankshares Inc	131
Crossroads Systems Inc (New)	131
CSB Bancorp Inc (OH)	132
Customers Bancorp Inc	132
CVB Financial Corp	133
CW Bancorp	134
CyrusOne Inc	134
Dart Financial Corp	134
Davey Tree Expert Co. (The)	135
Deckers Outdoor Corp.	136
DexCom Inc	137
Digi International Inc	138
Digital Realty Trust Inc	140
Digital Turbine Inc	141
Diodes, Inc.	142
DLH Holdings Corp	143
Dorian LPG Ltd.	144
Dorman Products Inc	144
Dropbox Inc	145
Duke Realty Corp	146
Duluth Holdings Inc	146
Dynatrace Inc	147
EACO Corp	147
Eagle Bancorp Inc (MD)	148
Eagle Bancorp Montana, Inc.	148
Eagle Financial Services, Inc.	149
East West Bancorp, Inc	149
Easterly Government Properties Inc	150
EastGroup Properties Inc	151
Ebix Inc	152
Educational Development Corp.	153

Companies Profiled (continued)

Company	Page
eHealth Inc	154
Ellington Residential Mortgaging Real Estate Investment Trust	155
Embassy Bancorp Inc	156
Emclaire Financial Corp.	156
Emergent BioSolutions Inc	156
ENB Financial Corp	158
Encore Capital Group Inc	158
Encore Wire Corp.	159
Energizer Holdings Inc (New)	160
Energy Recovery Inc	161
Enerkon Solar International Inc	162
Enova International Inc	162
Enphase Energy Inc.	162
Ensign Group Inc	163
Entegris Inc	165
Enterprise Bancorp, Inc. (MA)	166
Enterprise Financial Services Corp	167
Envela Corp	168
Enviva Inc	169
Epam Systems, Inc.	169
Equitrans Midstream Corp	171
Erie Indemnity Co.	171
Escalade, Inc.	172
Esquire Financial Holdings Inc	173
Essential Properties Realty Trust Inc	173
Essential Utilities Inc	174
Etsy Inc	175
Evans Bancorp, Inc.	175
Evercore Inc	175
EVI Industries Inc	176
Exelixis Inc	177
ExlService Holdings Inc	178
eXp World Holdings Inc	179
Extra Space Storage Inc	180
Exxe Group Inc	181
F & M Bank Corp.	181
Fair Isaac Corp	181
Farmers & Merchants Bancorp (Lodi, CA)	183
Farmers & Merchants Bancorp Inc (OH)	184
Farmers National Banc Corp. (Canfield,OH)	184
Farmland Partners Inc	185
FB Financial Corp	185
FCN Banc Corp	185
Federal Agricultural Mortgage Corp	186
Federal Home Loan Bank New York	186
Federal Home Loan Bank Of Dallas	187
Federal Signal Corp.	187
Fentura Financial Inc	189
FFD Financial Corp	189
Fidelity D&D Bancorp Inc	190
Finance of America Companies Inc	190
Finemark Holdings Inc	190
Finward Bancorp	191
First Bancorp (NC)	191
First Bancorp Inc (ME)	192
First Bancshares Inc (MS)	193
First Bank (Williamstown, NJ)	193
First Busey Corp	193
First Commonwealth Financial Corp (Indiana, PA)	195
First Community Corp (SC)	195
First Farmers Financial Corp	196
First Financial Bancorp (OH)	196
First Financial Bankshares, Inc.	197
First Financial Northwest Inc	198
First Foundation Inc	199
First Guaranty Bancshares, Inc.	199
First Horizon Corp	200
First Internet Bancorp	201
First Interstate BancSystem Inc	201
First Merchants Corp	203
First Mid Bancshares Inc	204
First Northwest Bancorp	204
First Ottawa Bancshares Inc	204
First Reliance Bancshares Inc	205
First Republic Bank (San Francisco, CA)	205
First Savings Financial Group Inc	206
First Western Financial Inc	206
FirstCash Holdings Inc	207
Five Below Inc	208
Flagstar Bancorp, Inc.	209
Floor & Decor Holdings Inc	210
FNB Corp	211
Focus Financial Partners Inc	212
Forestar Group Inc (New)	212
FormFactor Inc	213
Forrester Research Inc.	214
Fortinet Inc	216
Founders Bay Holdings	217
Four Corners Property Trust Inc	217
Fox Factory Holding Corp	217
Franchise Group Inc	218
Franklin Wireless Corp	220
Friedman Industries, Inc.	220
FRMO Corp.	221
Frontdoor Inc	221
FRP Holdings Inc	222
FS Bancorp (Indiana)	222
FS Bancorp Inc (Washington)	223
FTI Consulting Inc.	223
Fulgent Genetics Inc	224
Fuller (HB) Company	225
FVCBankcorp Inc	227
Gaming & Leisure Properties, Inc	227
Generac Holdings Inc	227
Genie Energy Ltd	229
German American Bancorp Inc	229
Glacier Bancorp, Inc.	230
Gladstone Commercial Corp	231
Global Net Lease Inc	232
Globus Medical Inc	232
GMS Inc	234
GoDaddy Inc	234
Goldman Sachs BDC Inc	234
Good Times Restaurants Inc.	235
Goosehead Insurance Inc	235
GrafTech International Ltd	235
Granite Falls Energy LLC	236
Gray Television Inc	236
Green Brick Partners Inc	238
Green Dot Corp	238
Green Thumb Industries Inc	239
Greene County Bancorp Inc	240
GreenSky Inc	240
Griffon Corp.	240
Grocery Outlet Holding Corp	242
Guaranty Bancshares Inc	243
Guaranty Federal Bancshares Inc (Springfield, MO)	243
Halozyme Therapeutics Inc	243
Hamilton Lane Inc.	244
Hannon Armstrong Sustainable Infrastructure Capital Inc	245
HarborOne Bancorp Inc (New)	246
Hawthorn Bancshares Inc	246
Healthcare Trust Of America Inc	247
HealthEquity Inc	247
Heartland BancCorp	247
Heartland Financial USA, Inc. (Dubuque, IA)	248
Helios Technologies Inc	249
Helix Energy Solutions Group Inc	250
Heritage Commerce Corp	251
Heritage Financial Corp (WA)	252
Hess Midstream LP	253
Hibbett Inc	253
Hillenbrand Inc	254
Hingham Institution for Savings	256
Home Bancorp Inc	257
Home BancShares Inc	257
HomeTrust Bancshares Inc.	258
Hope Bancorp Inc	258
Horizon Bancorp Inc	259
Hostess Brands Inc	260
Houlihan Lokey Inc	260
HV Bancorp Inc	260
IAC/InterActiveCorp (New)	261
Ichor Holdings Ltd	261
ICU Medical Inc	261
Idexx Laboratories, Inc.	262
IES Holdings Inc	264
II-VI Inc	265
Incyte Corporation	266
Independence Realty Trust Inc	268
Independent Bank Corp (MA)	268
Independent Bank Corporation (Ionia, MI)	269
Independent Bank Group Inc.	269
Industrial Logistics Properties Trust	270
InfuSystem Holdings Inc	271
Innovative Industrial Properties Inc	271
Innoviva Inc	271
Inotiv Inc	272
Installed Building Products Inc	273
Insteel Industries, Inc.	275
Insulet Corp	276
Integra LifeSciences Holdings Corp	277
Interactive Brokers Group Inc	278
Investar Holding Corp	279
Investors Title Co.	280
Invitation Homes Inc	280
iRobot Corp	280
Ironwood Pharmaceuticals Inc	282
Janus International Group Inc	283
John Marshall Bancorp Inc	283
Johnson Outdoors Inc	283
Joint Corp (New)	285
Kadant Inc	285
Kearny Financial Corp (MD)	286
Kilroy Realty L.P.	287
Kimball Electronics Inc	287
Kinsale Capital Group Inc	287
Kish Bancorp Inc.	288
KKR Real Estate Finance Trust Inc	288
Lakeland Bancorp, Inc.	288
Lakeland Financial Corp	289
Lakeland Industries, Inc.	290
Landmark Bancorp Inc	291
Lazydays Holdings Inc	292
LCI Industries	292
LCNB Corp	293
Ledyard Financial Group Inc	294
Lee Enterprises, Inc.	294
Legacy Housing Corp	296
LeMaitre Vascular Inc	296
Leslie's Inc	297
Level One Bancorp Inc	298
LGI Homes, Inc.	298
LHC Group Inc	299
Liberty Broadband Corp	300
LICT Corp	300
Limbach Holdings Inc	301
Limestone Bancorp Inc	301
Lincoln Educational Services Corp	302
Littelfuse Inc	302
Live Oak Bancshares Inc	304
Live Ventures Inc	304
Lovesac Co	305
Lumentum Holdings Inc	305
Luther Burbank Corp	305
Lyons Bancorp Inc.	306
M/I Homes Inc	306
Magnolia Oil & Gas Corp	307
MainStreet Bancshares Inc	307
Malibu Boats Inc	308
ManTech International Corp	308
MarineMax Inc	309
MarketAxess Holdings Inc.	310
Marquette National Corp (IL)	311
Masimo Corp.	312
Mastech Digital Inc	313
MasterCraft Boat Holdings Inc	313

vii

Companies Profiled (continued)

Company	Page
MaxLinear Inc	313
Maxus Realty Trust Inc	314
Medical Properties Trust Inc	315
Medifast Inc	316
Medpace Holdings Inc	317
Mercantile Bank Corp.	317
Merchants Bancorp (Indiana)	318
Mercury Systems Inc	318
Meridian Bioscience Inc.	320
Meridian Corp	321
Meritage Hospitality Group Inc	321
Mesabi Trust	322
Meta Financial Group Inc	322
MetroCity Bankshares Inc	323
Metropolitan Bank Holding Corp	323
Mettler-Toledo International, Inc.	324
Mid Penn Bancorp Inc	325
Middlefield Banc Corp.	326
Midland States Bancorp Inc	326
MidWestOne Financial Group, Inc.	327
Mitek Systems, Inc.	328
MKS Instruments Inc	329
Moelis & Co	330
Monolithic Power Systems Inc	330
Morningstar Inc	331
Morris St Bancshares Inc	333
Mountain Commerce Bancorp Inc	333
MP Materials Corp	334
Mr Cooper Group Inc	334
MSCI Inc	335
Muncy Bank Financial, Inc. (Muncy, PA)	336
MVB Financial Corp	336
MYR Group Inc	337
NASB Financial Inc	338
National Bank Holdings Corp	339
National Rural Utilities Cooperative Finance Corp	340
National Storage Affiliates Trust	340
National Vision Holdings Inc	341
Natural Alternatives International, Inc.	341
Natural Grocers By Vitamin Cottage Inc	342
Nautilus Inc	343
Nelnet Inc	344
Neurocrine Biosciences, Inc.	346
New Residential Investment Corp	346
Newmark Group Inc	347
Newtek Business Services Corp	347
NexPoint Residential Trust Inc	348
NI Holdings Inc	348
Nicolet Bankshares Inc	349
NMI Holdings Inc	349
Northeast Bank (ME)	350
NorthEast Community Bancorp Inc (MD)	351
Northern Technologies International Corp.	351
Northrim BanCorp Inc	352
Northwest Pipe Co.	353
Norwood Financial Corp.	354
Novanta Inc	354
Nuvera Communications Inc	355
NV5 Global Inc	356
Oak Valley Bancorp (Oakdale, CA)	357
Oakworth Capital Inc	358
Ocean Bio-Chem, Inc.	358
OceanFirst Financial Corp	358
Old Second Bancorp., Inc. (Aurora, Ill.)	359
Ollie's Bargain Outlet Holdings Inc	360
OneMain Finance Corp	361
OneWater Marine Inc	361
Onto Innovation Inc	361
OP Bancorp	362
Oppenheimer Holdings Inc	363
Orange County Bancorp Inc	364
Origin Bancorp	364
Orion Energy Systems Inc	364
Orrstown Financial Services, Inc.	365
OTC Markets Group Inc	366
Otter Tail Corp.	366
Overstock.com Inc (DE)	367
Pacific Premier Bancorp Inc	368
Pacira BioSciences Inc	369
Palomar Holdings Inc	370
Pangaea Logistics Solutions Ltd.	370
Parade Technologies Ltd.	370
Park National Corp (Newark, OH)	371
Parke Bancorp Inc	371
Parkway Acquisition Corp	372
Pathfinder Bancorp Inc. (MD)	372
Patrick Industries Inc	372
Paycom Software Inc	374
Paylocity Holding Corp	374
PBF Logistics LP	374
PCB Bancorp	375
Peapack-Gladstone Financial Corp.	375
Pennant Group Inc	376
PennyMac Financial Services Inc (New)	376
Pennymac Mortgage Investment Trust	377
People's United Financial Inc	378
PerkinElmer, Inc.	379
PGT Innovations Inc	381
Phillips 66 Partners LP	382
Phillips Edison & Co Inc	382
Photronics, Inc.	383
Physicians Realty Trust	384
Pinnacle Financial Partners Inc	385
Pinterest Inc	386
Piper Sandler Companies	386
PJT Partners Inc	387
Plumas Bancorp Inc	388
Pool Corp	388
PotlatchDeltic Corp	389
Power Integrations Inc.	391
Preferred Bank (Los Angeles, CA)	392
Preformed Line Products Co.	393
Premier Financial Corp	394
Primerica Inc	395
Primis Financial Corp	395
Primoris Services Corp	396
Private Bancorp Of America Inc	397
Professional Holding Corp	397
Progyny Inc	398
Prosperity Bancshares Inc.	398
Proto Labs Inc	399
Provident Bancorp Inc (MD)	400
Prudential Bancorp Inc (New)	401
PTC Inc	401
Pure Cycle Corp.	402
QCR Holdings Inc	403
Quaker Houghton	404
Qualys, Inc.	404
Quidel Corp.	405
QuinStreet, Inc.	406
R1 RCM Inc	407
Rand Worldwide Inc.	409
Randolph Bancorp Inc	409
Rattler Midstream LP	409
RBB Bancorp	409
Re/Max Holdings Inc	410
Ready Capital Corp	410
Realty Income Corp	411
Red River Bancshares Inc	412
Regional Management Corp	413
Renasant Corp	413
Repligen Corp.	414
Republic Bancorp, Inc. (KY)	415
ResMed Inc.	416
Retractable Technologies Inc	418
Revolve Group Inc	418
Rexford Industrial Realty Inc	419
RF Industries Ltd.	420
Rhinebeck Bancorp Inc	420
Ribbon Communications Inc	420
Richmond Mutual Bancorporation Inc	421
Risk George Industries Inc	421
River City Bank	421
River Financial Corp	422
RLI Corp	422
RMR Group Inc (The)	423
Roku Inc	423
Rollins, Inc.	423
Royalty Pharma plc	425
Sachem Capital Corp	425
Safehold Inc	426
Saia Inc	426
Sandy Spring Bancorp Inc	427
Santa Cruz County Bank (CA)	428
SB Financial Group Inc	428
Schnitzer Steel Industries Inc	428
SciPlay Corp	430
Scripps (EW) Company (The)	430
Seacoast Banking Corp. of Florida	432
Security Federal Corp (SC)	433
Security National Financial Corp	434
Selective Insurance Group Inc	434
SelectQuote Inc	435
Semler Scientific Inc	436
ServisFirst Bancshares Inc	436
Sharps Compliance Corp.	437
Shell Midstream Partners LP	437
Shutterstock Inc	437
Sierra Bancorp	438
SIGA Technologies Inc	439
Signature Bank (New York, NY)	440
Sila Realty Trust Inc	441
Silvergate Capital Corp	441
Simmons First National Corp	441
Simply Good Foods Company (The)	443
Simpson Manufacturing Co., Inc. (DE)	443
Simulations Plus Inc	444
SiteOne Landscape Supply Inc	445
SJW Group	445
Skyline Champion Corp	446
Sleep Number Corp	447
SLM Corp.	448
Smart Sand Inc	450
SmartFinancial Inc	451
SolarWinds Corp	451
Solera National Bancorp Inc	451
Sonos Inc	452
Sound Financial Bancorp Inc	452
South Atlantic Bancshares Inc	452
South Jersey Industries Inc	453
South Plains Financial Inc	454
Southern First Bancshares, Inc.	454
Southern Michigan Bancorp Inc (United States)	454
Southern Missouri Bancorp, Inc.	455
SouthState Corp	455
Spirit of Texas Bancshares Inc	456
Sportsman's Warehouse Holdings Inc	456
SPS Commerce, Inc.	457
SStarTrade Tech Inc	458
St. Joe Co. (The)	458
Staar Surgical Co.	460
STAG Industrial Inc	461
Starwood Property Trust Inc.	462
StepStone Group Inc	462
Sterling Construction Co Inc	463
Stifel Financial Corp	463
Stock Yards Bancorp Inc	465
STORE Capital Corp	466
Strategic Education Inc	466
Stride Inc	467
Sturgis Bancorp Inc	468
Summit Financial Group Inc	469
Summit Materials Inc	469
Summit State Bank (Santa Rosa, CA)	470
Sun Communities Inc	470
Sun Country Airlines Holdings Inc	471
Super Micro Computer Inc	472
Superior Group of Companies Inc	473
Supernus Pharmaceuticals Inc	474

Companies Profiled (continued)

Company	Page
Surface Oncology Inc	475
SVB Financial Group	475
Switch Inc	477
Synovus Financial Corp	477
Take-Two Interactive Software, Inc.	479
Teb Bancorp Inc	480
Techpoint Inc	481
TechTarget Inc	481
Teledyne Technologies Inc	482
Teleflex Incorporated	483
Teradyne, Inc.	484
Terreno Realty Corp	486
Texas Pacific Land Corp	487
The Bancorp Inc	487
The Trade Desk Inc	489
Thomasville Bancshares, Inc.	489
Timberland Bancorp, Inc.	489
TopBuild Corp	490
Toro Company (The)	490
Touchmark Bancshares Inc	492
TowneBank	492
Tradeweb Markets Inc	493
TransUnion	493
Trex Co Inc	493
Tri Pointe Homes Inc	495
TriCo Bancshares (Chico, CA)	495
Trimble Inc	496
TriState Capital Holdings Inc	498
Triumph Bancorp Inc	499
TTEC Holdings Inc	499
Turning Point Brands Inc	501
Turtle Beach Corp	501
Tyler Technologies, Inc.	501
U&I Financial Corp	503
Ubiquiti Inc	503
Ultra Clean Holdings Inc	503
UMB Financial Corp	505
Union Bankshares, Inc. (Morrisville, VT)	506
United Bancorp, Inc. (Martins Ferry, OH)	506
United Bancshares Inc. (OH)	507
United Bankshares Inc	507
United Community Banks Inc (Blairsville, GA)	508
United States 12 Month Oil Fund LP	509
United States Brent Oil Fund L.P.	509
United States Gasoline Fund LP	510
Unity Bancorp, Inc.	510
Universal Display Corp	511
Universal Insurance Holdings Inc	511
University Bancorp Inc. (MI)	512
Univest Financial Corp	512
Upstart Holdings Inc	513
US Global Investors Inc	514
USA Compression Partners LP	514
USA Truck, Inc.	514
Uwharrie Capital Corp.	515
Valley National Bancorp (NJ)	516
Valley Republic Bancorp	517
Valvoline Inc	517
Vanda Pharmaceuticals Inc	517
Veeva Systems Inc	519
Veritex Holdings Inc	520
Veritex Holdings Inc	521
Veru Inc	521
Viavi Solutions Inc	522
VICI Properties Inc	524
Vicor Corp	524
Victory Capital Holdings Inc (DE)	525
Viemed Healthcare Inc	526
Village Bank & Trust Financial Corp	526
Virginia National Bankshares Corp	526
VirnetX Holding Corp	527
Virtu Financial Inc	527
Virtus Investment Partners Inc	528
Vital Farms Inc	529
Vitesse Energy Inc	529
Voyager Therapeutics Inc	529
W.P. Carey Inc	530
Walker & Dunlop Inc	530
Waterstone Financial Inc (MD)	532
Weber Inc	532
WesBanco Inc	532
West Bancorporation, Inc.	533
West Pharmaceutical Services, Inc.	534
Western Alliance Bancorporation	535
Western Midstream Partners LP	536
Western New England Bancorp Inc	537
WidePoint Corp	537
Willis Lease Finance Corp.	538
Wilson Bank Holding Co.	539
Wingstop Inc	539
Winnebago Industries, Inc.	539
Wintrust Financial Corp (IL)	540
World Wrestling Entertainment Inc	542
WSFS Financial Corp	543
XOMA Corp	545
XPEL Inc	546
Xperi Holding Corp	546
Zedge Inc	547
Ziff Davis Inc	547
Zoom Video Communications Inc	547
Zynex Inc	547

About Hoover's Handbook of Emerging Companies 2023

Hoover's Handbook of Emerging Companies enters its 28th year as one of America's premier sources of business information on younger, growth-oriented enterprises. Given our current economic realities, finding value in the marketplace becomes ever more difficult, and so we are particularly pleased to present this edition of Hoover's Handbook of Emerging Companies 2023 — the result of a search of our extensive database of business information for companies with demonstrated growth and the potential for future gains.

The 600 companies in this book were chosen from the universe of public US companies with sales between $10 million and $2.5 billion. Their selection was based primarily on sales growth and profitability, although in a few cases we made some rather subjective decisions about which companies we chose to include. They all have reported at least three years of sales and have sustained annualized sales growth of at least 7% during that time. Also, they are profitable (through year-end December 2022).

In addition to the companies featured in our handbooks, comprehensive coverage of more than 40,000 business enterprises is available in electronic format on our website, Hoover's Online (www.hoovers.com). Our goal is to provide one site that offers authoritative, updated intelligence on US and global companies, industries, and the people who shape them. Hoover's has partnered with other prestigious business information and service providers to bring you all the right business information, services, and links in one place.

Hoover's Handbook of Emerging Companies is one of our four-title series of handbooks that covers, literally, the world of business. The series is available as an indexed set, and also includes Hoover's Handbook of American Business, Hoover's Handbook of World Business, and Hoover's Handbook of Private Companies. This series brings you information on the biggest, fastest-growing, and most influential enterprises in the world.

We believe that anyone who buys from, sells to, invests in, lends to, competes with, interviews with, or works for a company should know as much as possible about that enterprise. Taken together, Hoover's Handbook of Emerging Companies 2023 and the other Hoover's products represent the most complete source of basic corporate information readily available to the general public.

How to use this book

This book has four sections:

1. "Using Hoover's Handbooks" describes the contents of our profiles.

2. "A List-Lover's Compendium" contains lists of the fastest-growing and most profitable companies. The lists are based on the information in our profiles, or compiled from well-known sources.

3. The company profiles section makes up the largest and most important part of the book — 600 profiles arranged alphabetically. Each profile features an overview of the company; some larger and more visible companies have an additional History section. All companies have up to five years of financial information, product information where available, and a list of company executives and key competitors.

4. At the end of this volume are the combined indexes from our 2023 editions of all Hoover's Handbooks. The information is organized into three separate sections. The first sorts companies by industry groups, the second by headquarters location. The third index is a list of all the executives found in the Executives section of each company profile. For a more thorough description of our indexing style, see page xii.

Using Hoover's Handbooks

ORGANIZATION

The profiles in this volume are presented in alphabetical order. This alphabetization is generally word by word, which means that Bridge Bancorp precedes Bridgepoint Education. You will find the commonly used name of the enterprise at the beginning of the profile; the full, legal name is found in the Locations section. If a company name starts with initials, such as BJ's Restaurants or U.S. Physical Therapy, look for it under the combined initials (in the above example, BJ or US, respectively).

Basic financial data is listed under the heading Historical Financials; also included is the exchange on which the company's stock is traded, the ticker symbol used by the stock exchange, and the company's fiscal year-end. The annual financial information contained in the profiles is current through fiscal year-ends occurring as late as January 2021. We have included certain nonfinancial developments, such as officer changes, through December 2022.

OVERVIEW

In the first section of the profile, we have tried to give a thumbnail description of the company and what it does. The description will usually include information on the company's strategy, reputation, and ownership. We recommend that you read this section first.

HISTORY

This extended section, which is available for some of the larger and more well-known companies, reflects our belief that every enterprise is the sum of its history and that you have to know where you came from in order to know where you are going. While some companies have limited historical awareness, we think the vast majority of the enterprises in this book have colorful backgrounds. We have tried to focus on the people who made the enterprises what they are today. We have found these histories to be full of twists and ironies; they make fascinating reading.

EXECUTIVES

Here we list the names of the people who run the company, insofar as space allows. In the case of public companies, we have shown the ages and pay of key officers. The published data is for the previous fiscal year, although the company may have announced promotions or retirements since year-end. The pay represents cash compensation, including bonuses, but excludes stock option programs.

Although companies are free to structure their management titles any way they please, most modern corporations follow standard practices. The ultimate power in any corporation lies with the shareholders, who elect a board of directors, usually including officers or "insiders," as well as individuals from outside the company. The chief officer, the person on whose desk the buck stops, is usually called the chief executive officer (CEO). Often, he or she is also the chairman of the board.

As corporate management has become more complex, it is common for the CEO to have a "right-hand person" who oversees the day-to-day operations of the company, allowing the CEO plenty of time to focus on strategy and long-term issues. This right-hand person is usually designated the chief operating officer (COO) and is often the president of the company. In other cases one person is both chairman and president.

A multitude of other titles exists, including chief financial officer (CFO), chief administrative officer, and vice chairman. We have always tried to include the CFO, the chief legal officer, and the chief human resources or personnel officer. Our best advice is that officers' pay levels are clear indicators of who the board of directors thinks are the most important members of the management team.

The people named in the Executives section are indexed at the back of the book.

The Executives section also includes the name of the company's auditing (accounting) firm, where available.

LOCATIONS

Here we include the company's full legal name and its headquarters, street address, telephone and fax numbers, and website, as available. The back of the book includes an index of companies by headquarters locations.

In some cases we have also included information on the geographic distribution of the company's business, including sales and profit data. Note that these profit numbers, like those in the Products/Operations section below, are usually operating or pretax profits rather than net profits. Operating profits are generally those before financing costs (interest income and payments) and before taxes, which are considered costs attributable to the whole company rather than to one division or part of the world. For this reason the net income figures (in the Historical Financials section) are usually much lower, since they are after interest and taxes. Pretax profits are after interest but before taxes.

PRODUCTS/OPERATIONS

This section lists as many of the company's products, services, brand names, divisions, subsidiaries, and joint ventures as we could fit. We have tried to include all its major lines and all familiar brand names. The nature of this section varies by company and the amount of information available. If the company publishes sales and profit information by type of business, we have included it.

COMPETITORS

In this section we have listed companies that compete with the profiled company. This feature is included as a quick way to locate similar companies and compare them. The universe of competitors includes all public companies and all private companies with sales in excess of $500 million. In a few instances we have identified smaller private companies as key competitors.

HISTORICAL FINANCIALS

Here we have tried to present as much data about each enterprise's financial performance as we could compile in the allocated space. Although the information varies somewhat from industry to industry, the following is generally present.

A five-year table, with relevant annualized compound growth rates, covers:

- Sales — fiscal year sales (year-end assets for most financial companies)
- Net income — fiscal year net income (before accounting changes)
- Net profit margin — fiscal year net income as a percent of sales (as a percent of assets for most financial firms)
- Employees — fiscal year-end or average number of employees
- Stock price — the fiscal year closing price
- P/E — high and low price/earnings ratio
- Earnings per share — fiscal year earnings per share (EPS)
- Dividends per share — fiscal year dividends per share
- Book value per share — fiscal year-end book value (common shareholders' equity per share)

The information on the number of employees is intended to aid the reader interested in knowing whether a company has a long-term trend of increasing or decreasing employment. As far as we know, we are the only company that publishes this information in print format.

The numbers on the left in each row of the Historical Financials section give the month and the year in which the company's fiscal year actually ends. Thus, a company with a September 30, 2022, year-end is shown as 9/22.

In addition, we have provided in graph form a stock price history for each company. The graphs, covering up to five years, show the range of trading between the high and the low price, as well as the closing price for each fiscal year.

Key year-end statistics in this section generally show the financial strength of the enterprise, including:

- Debt ratio (long-term debt as a percent of shareholders' equity)
- Return on equity (net income divided by the average of beginning and ending common shareholders' equity)
- Cash and cash equivalents
- Current ratio (ratio of current assets to current liabilities)
- Total long-term debt (including capital lease obligations)
- Number of shares of common stock outstanding
- Dividend yield (fiscal year dividends per share divided by the fiscal year-end closing stock price)
- Dividend payout (fiscal year dividends divided by fiscal year EPS)
- Market value at fiscal year-end (fiscal year-end closing stock price multiplied by fiscal year-end number of shares outstanding)

Per-share data has been adjusted for stock splits. The data for public companies has been provided to us by Morningstar, Inc. Other public company information was compiled by Hoover's, which takes full responsibility for the content of this section.

Hoover's Handbook of Emerging Companies

A List-Lover's Compendium

The 300 Largest Public Global Companies by Sales in Mergent's Database

Rank	Company	Sales ($mil.)
1	Walmart Inc	$611,289
2	Amazon.com Inc	$513,983
3	China Petroleum & Chemical Corp	$431,727
4	Exxon Mobil Corp	$413,680
5	PetroChina Co Ltd	$411,796
6	Apple Inc	$394,328
7	UnitedHealth Group Inc	$324,162
8	CVS Health Corp	$322,467
9	Berkshire Hathaway Inc	$302,089
10	Volkswagen AG	$283,192
11	Alphabet Inc	$282,836
12	Shell plc	$272,657
13	McKesson Corp	$263,966
14	Toyota Motor Corp	$257,976
15	Chevron Corporation	$246,252
16	AmerisourceBergen Corp.	$238,587
17	Samsung Electronics Co Ltd	$235,340
18	Costco Wholesale Corp	$226,954
19	Industrial and Commercial Ba	$220,629
20	Hon Hai Precision Industry C	$216,488
21	Glencore PLC	$203,751
22	China Construction Bank Corp	$203,166
23	Microsoft Corporation	$198,270
24	TotalEnergies SE	$184,634
25	Cardinal Health, Inc.	$181,364
26	The Cigna Group	$180,516
27	Marathon Petroleum Corp.	$179,952
28	Valero Energy Corp	$176,383
29	Phillips 66	$175,702
30	Stellantis NV	$169,121
31	BP PLC	$162,319
32	Ford Motor Co. (DE)	$158,057
33	Home Depot Inc	$157,403
34	General Motors Co	$156,735
35	Elevance Health Inc	$156,595
36	JPMorgan Chase & Co	$154,792
37	Mercedes-Benz AG	$151,548
38	JD.com, Inc.	$149,888
39	China Railway Group Ltd	$149,038
40	Centene Corp	$144,547
41	Mitsubishi Corp	$141,937
42	China Railway Construction Corp Ltd	$139,188
43	Kroger Co (The)	$137,888
44	Verizon Communications Inc	$136,835
45	Alibaba Group Holding Ltd	$134,496
46	China Mobile Limited	$133,612
47	Walgreens Boots Alliance Inc	$132,703
48	Fortum OYJ	$127,221
49	Bayerische Motoren Werke AG	$125,907
50	AXA SA	$125,789
51	Deutsche Telekom AG	$123,139
52	Federal Reserve System	$122,368
53	Fannie Mae	$121,596
54	Comcast Corp	$121,427
55	Allianz SE	$121,285
56	AT&T Inc	$120,741
57	Honda Motor Co Ltd	$119,640
58	Rosneft Oil Co OJSC (Moscow)	$116,673
59	Meta Platforms Inc	$116,609
60	CITIC Ltd	$116,053
61	Bank of America Corp	$115,053
62	SAIC Motor Corp Ltd	$113,471
63	Assicurazioni Generali S.p.A	$111,010
64	Target Corp	$109,120
65	China Communications Constructions Group Ltd	$107,997
66	Credit Agricole SA	$103,322
67	Archer Daniels Midland Co.	$101,556
68	Dell Technologies Inc	$101,197
69	Citigroup Inc	$101,078
70	ITOCHU Corp (Japan)	$101,065
71	United Parcel Service Inc	$100,338
72	Pfizer Inc	$100,330
73	Nippon Telegraph & Telephone Corp (Japan)	$99,940
74	Enel SpA	$99,610
75	Hyundai Motor Co., Ltd.	$98,991
76	PTT Public Co Ltd	$97,464
77	Reliance Industries Ltd	$97,241
78	Mitsui & Co., Ltd.	$96,661
79	Lowe's Companies Inc	$96,250
80	Nestle SA	$95,823
81	Johnson & Johnson	$94,943
82	FedEx Corp	$93,512
83	Humana, Inc.	$92,870
84	Japan Post Holdings Co Ltd	$92,609
85	Deutsche Post AG	$92,526
86	Equinor ASA	$90,924
87	Energy Transfer LP	$89,876
88	Eneos Holdings Inc	$89,789
89	BASF SE	$88,962
90	E.ON SE	$88,444
91	Tencent Holdings Ltd.	$88,226
92	ENI S.p.A.	$88,026
93	Freddie Mac	$86,717
94	PepsiCo Inc	$86,392
95	Koninklijke Ahold Delhaize N	$85,569
96	PJSC Gazprom	$84,926
97	Hitachi, Ltd.	$84,387
98	Petroleo Brasileiro SA	$83,966
99	BNP Paribas (France)	$83,162
100	Wells Fargo & Co (New)	$82,859
101	Disney (Walt) Co. (The)	$82,722
102	ConocoPhillips	$82,156
103	Tesco PLC	$82,123
104	Sony Group Corp	$81,566
105	Tesla Inc	$81,462
106	HSBC Holdings Plc	$80,376
107	Procter & Gamble Co (The)	$80,187
108	T-Mobile US Inc	$79,571
109	Munich Re Group	$77,374
110	ArcelorMittal SA	$76,571
111	General Electric Co	$76,555
112	Seven & i Holdings Co. Ltd.	$75,733
113	Brookfield Corp	$75,731
114	Aeon Co Ltd	$75,440
115	Mexican Petroleum	$73,147
116	LVMH Moet Hennessy Louis Vuitton	$72,697
117	Banco Santander SA	$72,156
118	Roche Holding AG	$72,138
119	Albertsons Companies Inc	$71,887
120	Lenovo Group Ltd	$71,618
121	Country Garden Holdings Co L	$70,770
122	Siemens AG (Germany)	$70,164
123	Marubeni Corp.	$69,950
124	MetLife Inc	$69,898
125	Zurich Insurance Group AG	$69,867
126	Shanghai Jinfeng Investment C	$69,731
127	Nissan Motor Co., Ltd.	$69,260
128	Goldman Sachs Group Inc	$68,711
129	Sysco Corp	$68,636
130	Federal Reserve Bank Of New Y	$67,807
131	Bunge Ltd.	$67,232
132	Raytheon Technologies Corp	$67,074
133	Boeing Co.	$66,608
134	Xiamen C & D Inc	$66,197
135	Toyota Tsusho Corp	$65,999
136	Lockheed Martin Corp	$65,984
137	Morgan Stanley	$65,936
138	StoneX Group Inc	$65,855
139	Engie SA	$65,496
140	BHP Group Ltd	$65,098
141	Dai-ichi Life Holdings Inc	$64,360
142	China Vanke Co Ltd	$64,081
143	China Pacific Insurance (Group) Co., Ltd.	$64,059
144	POSCO Holdings Inc	$63,976
145	Legend Holdings Ltd	$63,845
146	Rio Tinto Plc (United Kingdom)	$63,495
147	Intel Corp	$63,054
148	HP Inc	$62,983
149	JBS S.A.	$62,930
150	LG Electronics Inc	$62,892
151	Alimentation Couche-Tard Inc	$62,809
152	TD SYNNEX Corp	$62,343
153	A.P. Moller - Maersk A/S	$61,787
154	Zhejiang Material Industrial	$61,766
155	Accenture plc	$61,594
156	Legal & General Group PLC (U	$61,252
157	Metallurgical Corp China Ltd	$61,177
158	Panasonic Holdings Corp	$60,744
159	International Business Machines Corp.	$60,530
160	HCA Healthcare Inc	$60,233
161	China Telecom Corp Ltd	$60,175
162	Prudential Financial Inc	$60,050
163	Rio Tinto Ltd	$59,617
164	Caterpillar Inc.	$59,427
165	Unilever Plc (United Kingdom)	$59,359
166	Merck & Co Inc	$59,283
167	World Fuel Services Corp.	$59,043
168	Airbus SE	$59,025
169	Enterprise Products Partners L.P.	$58,186
170	AbbVie Inc	$58,054
171	Plains GP Holdings LP	$57,342
172	Plains All American Pipeline LP	$57,342
173	Taiwan Semiconductor Manufacturing Co., Ltd.	$57,331
174	Lloyds Banking Group Plc	$57,304
175	Societe Generale	$57,262
176	Repsol S.A.	$57,163
177	Dow Inc	$56,902
178	Vinci SA	$56,867
179	American International Group Inc	$56,437
180	Nippon Steel Corp (New)	$55,977
181	American Express Co.	$55,625
182	Xiamen Xiangyu Co Ltd	$55,076
183	Idemitsu Kosan Co Ltd	$54,973
184	Publix Super Markets, Inc.	$54,942
185	Vale SA	$54,502
186	Anheuser Busch InBev SA/NV	$54,304
187	Charter Communications Inc (New)	$54,022
188	State Bank Of India	$53,836
189	Xiamen International Trade Gr	$53,681
190	Tyson Foods Inc	$53,282
191	Novartis AG Basel	$52,877
192	China Shenhua Energy Co., Lt	$52,801

SOURCE: MERGENT INC., DATABASE, APRIL 2023

The 300 Largest Public Global Companies by Sales in Mergent's Database (continued)

Rank	Company	Sales ($mil.)
193	Deere & Co.	$52,577
194	AEGON NV	$52,535
195	Japan Post Insurance Co Ltd	$52,487
196	Renault S.A. (France)	$52,306
197	Cisco Systems Inc	$51,557
198	Tianjin Tianhai Investment C	$51,480
199	Allstate Corp	$51,412
200	SoftBank Group Corp	$51,148
201	Performance Food Group Co	$50,894
202	Vodafone Group Plc	$50,596
203	Delta Air Lines Inc (DE)	$50,582
204	Wilmar International Ltd	$50,526
205	LyondellBasell Industries NV	$50,451
206	Korea Electric Power Corp KEPCO	$50,428
207	Compagnie de Saint-Gobain	$50,041
208	Bayer AG	$49,893
209	Sberbank Russia	$49,628
210	Progressive Corp. (OH)	$49,610
211	Royal Bank of Canada (Montreal, Quebec)	$49,058
212	American Airlines Group Inc	$48,971
213	Jiangxi Copper Co., Ltd.	$48,708
214	TJX Companies, Inc.	$48,549
215	Orange	$48,132
216	CHS Inc	$47,791
217	AIA Group Ltd.	$47,514
218	Tokio Marine Holdings Inc	$47,484
219	PBF Energy Inc	$46,830
220	SoftBank Corp (New)	$46,783
221	Swiss Re AG	$46,739
222	NIKE Inc	$46,710
223	Toronto Dominion Bank	$46,616
224	Brookfield Business Partners LP	$46,587
225	China United Network Communi	$46,456
226	China Unicom (Hong Kong) Ltd	$46,456
227	Best Buy Inc	$46,298
228	Bristol Myers Squibb Co.	$46,159
229	GSK plc	$45,974
230	Denso Corp	$45,344
231	Sumitomo Corp.	$45,175
232	Intesa Sanpaolo S.P.A.	$45,078
233	United Airlines Holdings Inc	$44,955
234	Thermo Fisher Scientific Inc	$44,915
235	KDDI Corp	$44,778
236	Aviva Plc (United Kingdom)	$44,721
237	Compal Electronics Inc	$44,628
238	Telefonica SA	$44,456
239	Sanofi	$44,340
240	Iberdrola SA	$44,271
241	Qualcomm Inc	$44,200
242	Imperial Oil Ltd	$44,120
243	Tokyo Electric Power Company	$43,653
244	Abbott Laboratories	$43,653
245	Baoshan Iron & Steel Co Ltd	$43,490
246	Chubb Ltd	$43,166
247	Coca-Cola Co (The)	$43,004
248	Bouygues S.A.	$42,607
249	Aluminum Corp of China Ltd.	$42,489
250	Fresenius SE & Co KGaA	$42,467
251	Oracle Corp	$42,440
252	George Weston Ltd	$42,200
253	Woolworths Group Ltd	$41,986
254	America Movil SAB de CV	$41,842
255	Loblaw Companies Ltd	$41,746
256	Anglo American Plc (United K	$41,554
257	Nucor Corp.	$41,512
258	MS&AD Insurance Group Holdin	$41,296
259	Volvo AB	$41,084
260	Gazprom Neft PJSC	$40,863
261	UBS Group AG	$40,638
262	OMV AG (Austria)	$40,243
263	ThyssenKrupp AG	$40,103
264	Banco Bilbao Vizcaya Argentaria S.A. (BBVA)	$39,997
265	J.Sainsbury PLC	$39,719
266	Enbridge Inc	$39,417
267	General Dynamics Corp	$39,407
268	CNOOC Ltd	$38,765
269	Suning.com Co Ltd	$38,575
270	Capital One Financial Corp	$38,373
271	Continental AG (Germany, Fed	$38,217
272	HF Sinclair Corp	$38,204
273	China Life Insurance Co Ltd	$38,135
274	Exor NV	$38,049
275	Magna International Inc	$37,840
276	AstraZeneca Plc	$37,417
277	Poly Developments and Holdings Group Co Ltd	$37,186
278	Barclays PLC	$37,159
279	Arrow Electronics, Inc.	$37,124
280	Occidental Petroleum Corp	$37,095
281	Travelers Companies Inc (The)	$36,884
282	Mitsubishi Electric Corp	$36,804
283	Northrop Grumman Corp	$36,602
284	L'Oreal S.A.	$36,545
285	Tata Motors Ltd	$36,512
286	Daiwa House Industry Co Ltd	$36,498
287	Cenovus Energy Inc	$36,397
288	Prudential Plc	$36,187
289	CK Hutchison Holdings Ltd	$36,014
290	Wal-Mart de Mexico S.A.B. de	$35,998
291	Power Corp. of Canada	$35,980
292	Kuehne & Nagel International	$35,933
293	Imperial Brands PLC	$35,927
294	JFE Holdings Inc	$35,886
295	Jardine Matheson Holdings Ltd.	$35,862
296	Honeywell International Inc	$35,466
297	Mitsubishi UFJ Financial Gro	$35,426
298	Shanghai Construction Group	$35,369
299	Deutsche Bank AG	$35,308
300	Casino Guichard Perrachon S.	$35,147

SOURCE: MERGENT INC., DATABASE, APRIL 2023

The 300 Largest Public Global Companies by Employees in Mergent's Database

Rank	Company	Employees
1	Walmart Inc	2,100,000
2	Amazon.com Inc	1,541,000
3	Hon Hai Precision Industry C	826,608
4	Accenture plc	721,000
5	Volkswagen AG	672,800
6	Randstad NV	603,480
7	Deutsche Post AG	592,263
8	United Parcel Service Inc	536,000
9	Compass Group PLC (United Ki	513,707
10	Home Depot Inc	471,600
11	PJSC Gazprom	467,000
12	China Mobile Limited	449,934
13	Target Corp	440,000
14	Industrial and Commercial Ba	434,089
15	Sodexo	421,991
16	Kroger Co (The)	420,000
17	Teleperformance SA	418,742
18	Starbucks Corp.	402,000
19	UnitedHealth Group Inc	400,000
20	Jardine Matheson Holdings Ltd.	400,000
21	JD.com, Inc.	385,357
22	Berkshire Hathaway Inc	383,000
23	Marriott International, Inc.	377,000
24	Toyota Motor Corp	372,817
25	Hitachi, Ltd.	368,247
26	Rosneft Oil Co OJSC (Moscow)	355,900
27	Cognizant Technology Solutions Corp.	355,300
28	China Construction Bank Corp	351,252
29	Reliance Industries Ltd	342,982
30	TJX Companies, Inc.	340,000
31	X5 Retail Group NV	339,716
32	Nippon Telegraph & Telephone Corp (Japan)	333,840
33	Fomento Economico Mexicano, S.A.B. de C.V.	320,752
34	Fresenius SE & Co KGaA	316,078
35	Magnit PJSC	316,001
36	PepsiCo Inc	315,000
37	Concentrix Corp	315,000
38	Infosys Ltd.	314,015
39	International Business Machines Corp.	311,300
40	Siemens AG (Germany)	311,000
41	Costco Wholesale Corp	304,000
42	CVS Health Corp	300,000
43	JPMorgan Chase & Co	293,723
44	Albertsons Companies Inc	290,000
45	Sberbank Russia	287,866
46	Stellantis NV	281,595
47	Sumitomo Electric Industries	281,075
48	China Telecom Corp Ltd	280,747
49	Nestle SA	276,000
50	Koninklijke Ahold Delhaize N	259,000
51	Alibaba Group Holding Ltd	254,941
52	China Unicom (Hong Kong) Ltd	254,702
53	JBS S.A.	250,000
54	Jabil Inc	250,000
55	Aramark	245,700
56	State Bank Of India	244,250
57	Publix Super Markets, Inc.	242,000
58	Panasonic Holdings Corp	240,198
59	Jardine Cycle & Carriage Ltd	240,000
60	Wipro Ltd	240,000
61	Citigroup Inc	240,000
62	Wells Fargo & Co (New)	238,000
63	Japan Post Holdings Co Ltd	232,112
64	Wal-Mart de Mexico S.A.B. de	231,271
65	Tesco PLC	231,223
66	Country Garden Services Holdings Co Ltd	223,667
67	Microsoft Corporation	221,000
68	Deutsche Telekom AG	220,840
69	Disney (Walt) Co. (The)	220,000
70	Dairy Farm International Hol	220,000
71	HSBC Holdings Plc	219,697
72	Vinci SA	219,400
73	Bank of America Corp	217,000
74	Yamato Holdings Co., Ltd.	216,873
75	George Weston Ltd	215,000
76	Loblaw Companies Ltd	215,000
77	HCA Healthcare Inc	207,000
78	Honda Motor Co Ltd	204,035
79	Lowe's Companies Inc	200,000
80	Walgreens Boots Alliance Inc	200,000
81	Woolworths Group Ltd	198,000
82	Banco Santander SA	197,070
83	Casino Guichard Perrachon S.	196,307
84	FedEx Corp	191,000
85	Continental AG (Germany, Fed	190,875
86	Alphabet Inc	190,234
87	BNP Paribas (France)	189,765
88	Hyatt Hotels Corp	189,000
89	Comcast Corp	186,000
90	Canon Inc	184,034
91	EssilorLuxottica	182,684
92	Raytheon Technologies Corp	182,000
93	America Movil SAB de CV	181,205
94	Brookfield Corp	180,000
95	Darden Restaurants, Inc. (United States)	178,956
96	Ford Motor Co. (DE)	173,000
97	Flex Ltd	172,648
98	Mercedes-Benz AG	172,425
99	General Electric Co	172,000
100	Renault S.A. (France)	170,158
101	Engie SA	170,000
102	Anheuser Busch InBev SA/NV	169,339
103	Lear Corp.	168,700
104	Denso Corp	167,950
105	Compagnie de Saint-Gobain	167,816
106	Apple Inc	164,000
107	Dollar General Corp	163,000
108	AT&T Inc	160,700
109	Aptiv PLC	160,000
110	International Distributions Services Plc	159,819
111	Hilton Worldwide Holdings Inc	159,000
112	Accor SA	158,604
113	Magna International Inc	158,000
114	LVMH Moet Hennessy Louis Vuitton	157,953
115	ArcelorMittal SA	157,909
116	Boeing Co.	156,000
117	Aeon Co Ltd	155,465
118	Allianz SE	155,411
119	Johnson & Johnson	152,700
120	NTT Data Corp	151,991
121	McDonald's Corp	150,000
122	Unilever Plc (United Kingdom)	149,000
123	Prosegur Compania De Seguridad SA	147,231
124	Mitsubishi Electric Corp	145,696
125	Yum China Holdings Inc	145,000
126	Industria De Diseno Textil	144,116
127	Oracle Corp	143,000
128	Shoprite Holdings, Ltd.	142,602
129	Tyson Foods Inc	142,000
130	HDFC Bank Ltd	141,579
131	Atento SA	140,553
132	Orange	139,698
133	CITIC Ltd	136,637
134	Grupo Bimbo SAB de CV (Mexic	136,559
135	Bridgestone Corp. (Japan)	135,636
136	Glencore PLC	135,000
137	Nissan Motor Co., Ltd.	134,114
138	Dell Technologies Inc	133,000
139	Associated British Foods Plc	132,273
140	Intel Corp	131,900
141	ICICI Bank Ltd (India)	130,542
142	Empire Co Ltd	130,000
143	Thermo Fisher Scientific Inc	130,000
144	DXC Technology Co	130,000
145	American Airlines Group Inc	129,700
146	Mitsubishi UFJ Financial Gro	129,700
147	Zug Estates Holding AG	128,100
148	Tesla Inc	127,855
149	Barrett Business Services, Inc.	127,141
150	ABM Industries, Inc.	127,000
151	Airbus SE	126,495
152	Bouygues S.A.	124,651
153	Fujitsu Ltd	124,216
154	Societe Generale	124,089
155	Jeronimo Martins S.G.P.S. SA	123,458
156	Fresenius Medical Care AG & Co KGaA	122,909
157	Bidvest Group Ltd	121,344
158	ACS Actividades de Construcc	120,827
159	Mexican Petroleum	120,798
160	Wesfarmers Ltd.	120,000
161	Bayerische Motoren Werke AG	118,909
162	Genpact Ltd	118,900
163	Cie Generale des Etablissements Michelin SCA	118,414
164	Cencosud SA	117,638
165	NEC Corp	117,418
166	Aisin Corporation	117,177
167	Verizon Communications Inc	117,100
168	TDK Corp	116,808
169	Toshiba Corp	116,224
170	Lockheed Martin Corp	116,000
171	BASF SE	115,973
172	ITOCHU Corp (Japan)	115,124
173	Abbott Laboratories	115,000
174	CBRE Group Inc	115,000
175	Valeo SE	114,700
176	Nidec Corp	114,371
177	Surgutneftegas PJSC	113,000
178	Tencent Holdings Ltd.	112,771
179	AutoZone, Inc.	112,000
180	Faurecia SE (France)	111,140
181	China Pacific Insurance (Group) Co., Ltd.	110,940
182	Banco Bilbao Vizcaya Argentaria S.A. (BBVA)	110,432
183	KE Holdings Inc	110,082
184	WPP Plc (New)	109,382
185	Caterpillar Inc.	109,100
186	Sony Group Corp	108,900
187	TELUS Corp	108,500
188	Lufthansa AG (Germany, Fed. Rep.)	107,643
189	SAP SE	107,415
190	Grupo Aval Acciones Y Valores SA	107,076

SOURCE: MERGENT INC., DATABASE, APRIL 2023

The 300 Largest Public Global Companies by Employees in Mergent's Database (continued)

Rank	Company	Employees
191	WH Group Ltd	107,000
192	Nippon Steel Corp (New)	106,528
193	General Dynamics Corp	106,500
194	Procter & Gamble Co (The)	106,000
195	Chipotle Mexican Grill Inc	104,958
196	Elior SCA	104,566
197	Atos Origin	104,430
198	ABB Ltd	104,400
199	Novartis AG Basel	104,323
200	Telefonica SA	104,150
201	Jones Lang LaSalle Inc	103,300
202	Royal Caribbean Group	102,500
203	Tenet Healthcare Corp.	102,400
204	Elevance Health Inc	102,300
205	Johnson Controls International plc	102,000
206	Charter Communications Inc (New)	101,700
207	Ericsson	101,322
208	TotalEnergies SE	101,309
209	Sumitomo Mitsui Financial Group Inc Tokyo	101,000
210	Roche Holding AG	100,920
211	BRF S.A.	100,176
212	Ross Stores Inc	100,000
213	Wilmar International Ltd	100,000
214	Itau Unibanco Holding S.A.	99,598
215	Bayer AG	99,572
216	Schlumberger Ltd	99,000
217	BT Group Plc	98,400
218	Danone	98,105
219	Intesa Sanpaolo S.P.A.	97,698
220	Metro AG (New)	97,639
221	Honeywell International Inc	97,000
222	Vodafone Group Plc	96,941
223	ThyssenKrupp AG	96,494
224	SGS SA	96,216
225	Falabella SA	96,111
226	Volvo AB	95,850
227	Shenzhou International Group	95,820
228	ASE Technology Holding Co Ltd	95,727
229	Sanofi	95,442
230	Delta Air Lines Inc (DE)	95,000
231	Northrop Grumman Corp	95,000
232	Gap Inc	95,000
233	Medtronic PLC	95,000
234	Toronto Dominion Bank	94,945
235	Leoni AG	94,690
236	Country Garden Holdings Co L	93,899
237	Universal Health Services, Inc.	93,800
238	Outsourcing Inc, Shizuoka	93,028
239	United Airlines Holdings Inc	92,800
240	AXA SA	92,398
241	Lufax Holding Ltd	92,380
242	Chinasoft International Ltd	92,039
243	Eaton Corp plc	92,000
244	3M Co	92,000
245	TE Connectivity Ltd	92,000
246	Royal Bank of Canada (Montreal, Quebec)	91,427
247	Mondelez International Inc	91,000
248	Amphenol Corp.	91,000
249	Bank Nova Scotia Halifax	90,979
250	GSK plc	90,096
251	En+ Group Plc	90,000
252	Best Buy Inc	90,000
253	Pick 'n Pay Stores Ltd.	90,000
254	Kyndryl Holdings Inc	90,000
255	Brookfield Business Partners LP	90,000
256	GXO Logistics Inc	89,000
257	Macy's Inc	88,857
258	Daikin Industries Ltd	88,698
259	Publicis Groupe S.A.	88,531
260	Ramsay Health Care Ltd. (Aus	88,000
261	Nokia Corp	87,927
262	Banco Bradesco SA	87,274
263	Unicredit SpA	87,165
264	Bloomin' Brands Inc	87,000
265	Meta Platforms Inc	86,482
266	BAE Systems Plc	86,200
267	IQVIA Holdings Inc	86,000
268	Emerson Electric Co.	85,500
269	L'Oreal S.A.	85,412
270	A.P. Moller - Maersk A/S	85,375
271	Marsh & McLennan Companies Inc.	85,000
272	Legend Holdings Ltd	84,000
273	Coca-Cola FEMSA SAB de CV	83,754
274	Seven & i Holdings Co. Ltd.	83,635
275	Cisco Systems Inc	83,300
276	Schaeffler AG	83,297
277	AstraZeneca Plc	83,100
278	Kyocera Corp	83,001
279	Pfizer Inc	83,000
280	Deutsche Bank AG	82,969
281	Gazprom Neft PJSC	82,960
282	British American Tobacco Plc (United Kingdom)	82,868
283	Coca-Cola Co (The)	82,500
284	Heineken Holding NV (Netherl	82,257
285	Heineken NV (Netherlands)	82,257
286	Deere & Co.	82,200
287	Air France-KLM	82,132
288	Shell plc	82,000
289	Kingfisher PLC	82,000
290	Morgan Stanley	82,000
291	Texas Roadhouse Inc	82,000
292	Standard Chartered Plc	81,957
293	Minebea Mitsumi Inc	81,659
294	Olam International Ltd.	81,600
295	Barclays PLC	81,600
296	Arcos Dorados Holdings Inc	81,256
297	Thales	81,098
298	General Motors Co	81,000
299	Lewis (John) Plc (United Kingd	80,800
300	Mitsubishi Corp	80,728

SOURCE: MERGENT INC., DATABASE, APRIL 2023

The 300 Largest Public Global Companies by Net Income in Mergent's Database

Rank	Company	Net Income ($mil.)
1	Apple Inc	$99,803
2	Microsoft Corporation	$72,738
3	Alphabet Inc	$59,972
4	Exxon Mobil Corp	$55,740
5	Industrial and Commercial Ba	$54,868
6	China Construction Bank Corp	$47,872
7	JPMorgan Chase & Co	$37,676
8	Chevron Corporation	$35,465
9	Tencent Holdings Ltd.	$35,412
10	Samsung Electronics Co Ltd	$33,031
11	Pfizer Inc	$31,372
12	BHP Group Ltd	$30,900
13	Vivendi SE	$27,947
14	Bank of America Corp	$27,528
15	Mercedes-Benz AG	$26,039
16	Novartis AG Basel	$24,021
17	Toyota Motor Corp	$23,431
18	Meta Platforms Inc	$23,200
19	Vale SA	$22,445
20	Taiwan Semiconductor Manufacturing Co., Ltd.	$21,544
21	Verizon Communications Inc	$21,256
22	Rio Tinto Ltd	$21,094
23	UnitedHealth Group Inc	$20,120
24	Shell plc	$20,101
25	Petroleo Brasileiro SA	$19,875
26	Prosus N V	$18,733
27	ConocoPhillips	$18,680
28	Nestle SA	$18,519
29	China Mobile Limited	$18,294
30	A.P. Moller - Maersk A/S	$17,942
31	Johnson & Johnson	$17,941
32	Home Depot Inc	$17,105
33	Volkswagen AG	$16,800
34	Sberbank Russia	$16,656
35	Stellantis NV	$16,072
36	TotalEnergies SE	$16,032
37	Ping An Insurance (Group) Co	$16,006
38	Roche Holding AG	$15,260
39	Visa Inc	$14,957
40	ArcelorMittal SA	$14,956
41	Citigroup Inc	$14,845
42	Procter & Gamble Co (The)	$14,742
43	iShares III Plc	$14,710
44	Merck & Co Inc	$14,519
45	PetroChina Co Ltd	$14,516
46	Marathon Petroleum Corp.	$14,516
47	Bayerische Motoren Werke AG	$14,014
48	HSBC Holdings Plc	$13,910
49	LVMH Moet Hennessy Louis Vuitton	$13,623
50	Occidental Petroleum Corp	$13,304
51	Wells Fargo & Co (New)	$13,182
52	Qualcomm Inc	$12,936
53	Fannie Mae	$12,923
54	Toronto Dominion Bank	$12,564
55	Tesla Inc	$12,556
56	Naspers Ltd	$12,223
57	Bank of Japan	$11,932
58	AbbVie Inc	$11,836
59	Cisco Systems Inc	$11,812
60	Rosneft Oil Co OJSC (Moscow)	$11,759
61	Walmart Inc	$11,680
62	BioNTech SE	$11,649
63	Royal Bank of Canada (Montreal, Quebec)	$11,557
64	United Parcel Service Inc	$11,548
65	Valero Energy Corp	$11,528
66	Broadcom Inc (DE)	$11,495
67	Goldman Sachs Group Inc	$11,261
68	China Petroleum & Chemical Corp	$11,216
69	CNOOC Ltd	$11,076
70	Morgan Stanley	$11,029
71	Phillips 66	$11,024
72	BNP Paribas (France)	$10,739
73	American International Group Inc	$10,276
74	General Motors Co	$9,934
75	Surgutneftegas PJSC	$9,930
76	Mastercard Inc	$9,930
77	Bank of Montreal (Quebec)	$9,906
78	Alibaba Group Holding Ltd	$9,814
79	Nippon Telegraph & Telephone Corp (Japan)	$9,709
80	Barclays PLC	$9,674
81	Coca-Cola Co (The)	$9,542
82	America Movil SAB de CV	$9,410
83	Freddie Mac	$9,327
84	Telefonica SA	$9,209
85	Banco Santander SA	$9,195
86	British American Tobacco Plc (United Kingdom)	$9,165
87	Philip Morris International Inc	$9,048
88	CITIC Ltd	$9,004
89	PepsiCo Inc	$8,910
90	Texas Instruments, Inc.	$8,749
91	Micron Technology Inc.	$8,687
92	Evergreen Marine Corp Taiwan	$8,632
93	Equinor ASA	$8,563
94	Anglo American Plc (United K	$8,562
95	Sinovac Biotech Ltd	$8,467
96	Lowe's Companies Inc	$8,442
97	Moderna Inc	$8,362
98	Nippon Yusen Kabushiki Kaisha	$8,296
99	AXA SA	$8,255
100	Corebridge Financial Inc	$8,149
101	China Life Insurance Co Ltd	$8,020
102	Reliance Industries Ltd	$8,014
103	Intel Corp	$8,014
104	Novo-Nordisk AS	$7,974
105	China Shenhua Energy Co., Lt	$7,918
106	Pioneer Natural Resources Co	$7,845
107	Lloyds Banking Group Plc	$7,794
108	EOG Resources, Inc.	$7,759
109	Mitsubishi Corp	$7,707
110	Nucor Corp.	$7,607
111	BP PLC	$7,565
112	Mitsui & Co., Ltd.	$7,520
113	American Express Co.	$7,514
114	Allianz SE	$7,481
115	UBS Group AG	$7,457
116	AIA Group Ltd.	$7,427
117	Commonwealth Bank of Australia	$7,410
118	Capital One Financial Corp	$7,360
119	Sony Group Corp	$7,252
120	Danaher Corp	$7,209
121	Charles Schwab Corp	$7,183
122	Oxbridge Acquisition Corp	$7,175
123	Kweichow Moutai Co., Ltd.	$7,139
124	Deere & Co.	$7,131
125	Bank Nova Scotia Halifax	$7,066
126	Sanofi	$7,043
127	UBS AG London Branch	$7,032
128	Union Pacific Corp	$6,998
129	Thermo Fisher Scientific Inc	$6,950
130	Abbott Laboratories	$6,933
131	Accenture plc	$6,877
132	Unilever Plc (United Kingdom)	$6,846
133	ITOCHU Corp (Japan)	$6,743
134	ING Groep NV	$6,735
135	Oracle Corp	$6,717
136	Caterpillar Inc.	$6,705
137	Gazprom Neft PJSC	$6,704
138	The Cigna Group	$6,668
139	ASML Holding NV	$6,658
140	Mercantil Servicios Financie	$6,658
141	Credit Agricole SA	$6,614
142	ENI S.p.A.	$6,588
143	Amgen Inc	$6,552
144	Applied Materials, Inc.	$6,525
145	MMC Norilsk Nickel PJSC	$6,512
146	Investor AB	$6,461
147	Societe Generale	$6,384
148	China Vanke Co Ltd	$6,347
149	Bristol Myers Squibb Co.	$6,327
150	Truist Financial Corp	$6,260
151	BASF SE	$6,251
152	Eli Lilly & Co	$6,244
153	Fortescue Metals Group Ltd	$6,197
154	McDonald's Corp	$6,177
155	NIKE Inc	$6,046
156	PNC Financial Services Group (The)	$6,041
157	Elevance Health Inc	$6,025
158	Canadian Natural Resources Ltd	$6,017
159	Devon Energy Corp.	$6,015
160	YangMing Marine Transport Co	$5,968
161	SAP SE	$5,949
162	CaixaBank SA	$5,915
163	GSK plc	$5,909
164	DuPont de Nemours Inc	$5,868
165	DR Horton Inc	$5,857
166	Costco Wholesale Corp	$5,844
167	Mitsui OSK Lines Ltd	$5,827
168	U.S. Bancorp (DE)	$5,825
169	Honda Motor Co Ltd	$5,812
170	3M Co	$5,777
171	Novatek Joint Stock Co	$5,765
172	Altria Group Inc	$5,764
173	Lockheed Martin Corp	$5,732
174	Deutsche Post AG	$5,719
175	Jackson Financial Inc	$5,697
176	Thomson Reuters Corp	$5,689
177	HCA Healthcare Inc	$5,643
178	Dell Technologies Inc	$5,563
179	Barclays Bank Plc	$5,561
180	POSCO Holdings Inc	$5,560
181	KDDI Corp	$5,528
182	Enterprise Products Partners L.P.	$5,490
183	Woolworths Group Ltd	$5,474
184	Segro PLC REIT	$5,471
185	Imperial Oil Ltd	$5,427
186	Manulife Financial Corp	$5,393
187	Comcast Corp	$5,370
188	Country Garden Holdings Co L	$5,354
189	Chubb Ltd	$5,313
190	E.ON SE	$5,309
191	Tata Steel Ltd	$5,300
192	Kawasaki Kisen Kaisha Ltd	$5,281

SOURCE: MERGENT INC., DATABASE, APRIL 2023

The 300 Largest Public Global Companies by Net Income in Mergent's Database (continued)

Rank	Company	Net Income ($mil.)
193	Banco Bilbao Vizcaya Argentaria S.A. (BBVA)	$5,266
194	3i Group Plc	$5,266
195	Anhui Conch Cement Co Ltd	$5,240
196	Nippon Steel Corp (New)	$5,239
197	L'Oreal S.A.	$5,203
198	Zurich Insurance Group AG	$5,202
199	Raytheon Technologies Corp	$5,197
200	BlackRock Inc	$5,178
201	Porsche Automobil Holding SE	$5,168
202	China Resources Land Ltd	$5,103
203	HDFC Bank Ltd	$5,095
204	Charter Communications Inc (New)	$5,055
205	DBS Group Holdings Ltd.	$5,041
206	Medtronic PLC	$5,039
207	Cathay Financial Holding Co	$5,038
208	Novolipetsk Steel	$5,036
209	Hon Hai Precision Industry C	$5,031
210	Glencore PLC	$4,974
211	Honeywell International Inc	$4,966
212	Prudential Annuities Life As	$4,965
213	Anglo American Platinum Ltd	$4,953
214	Chesapeake Energy Corp.	$4,936
215	Kinnevik AB	$4,929
216	Northrop Grumman Corp	$4,896
217	Principal Financial Group Inc	$4,811
218	Itau Unibanco Holding S.A.	$4,801
219	Hitachi, Ltd.	$4,796
220	Airbus SE	$4,768
221	Adobe Inc	$4,756
222	Energy Transfer LP	$4,756
223	SPDR S&P 500 ETF Trust	$4,748
224	Intesa Sanpaolo S.P.A.	$4,736
225	Deutsche Telekom AG	$4,726
226	Schibsted ASA	$4,684
227	Anheuser Busch InBev SA/NV	$4,670
228	State Bank Of India	$4,669
229	ZIM Integrated Shipping Services Ltd	$4,640
230	Lennar Corp	$4,614
231	Lam Research Corp	$4,605
232	Australia & New Zealand Banking Group Ltd	$4,601
233	Gilead Sciences Inc	$4,592
234	Dow Inc	$4,582
235	Canadian Imperial Bank Of Commerce	$4,551
236	ABB Ltd	$4,546
237	Roper Technologies Inc	$4,544
238	Netflix Inc	$4,491
239	National Australia Bank Ltd.	$4,454
240	Poly Developments and Holdings Group Co Ltd	$4,426
241	Eneos Holdings Inc	$4,415
242	Iberdrola SA	$4,397
243	Discover Financial Services	$4,392
244	Diamondback Energy, Inc.	$4,386
245	NatWest Group PLC	$4,378
246	NVIDIA Corp	$4,368
247	Public Storage	$4,349
248	Archer Daniels Midland Co.	$4,340
249	Regeneron Pharmaceuticals, Inc.	$4,338
250	Walgreens Boots Alliance Inc	$4,337
251	JSC VTB Bank	$4,332
252	Nordea Bank ABp	$4,306
253	CK Hutchison Holdings Ltd	$4,293
254	SoftBank Corp (New)	$4,254
255	London Stock Exchange Group Plc	$4,216
256	AFLAC Inc.	$4,201
257	CSX Corp	$4,166
258	Hyundai Motor Co., Ltd.	$4,159
259	Banco Bradesco SA	$4,158
260	CVS Health Corp	$4,149
261	NextEra Energy Inc	$4,147
262	Linde PLC (New)	$4,147
263	Engie SA	$4,143
264	Japan Post Holdings Co Ltd	$4,124
265	Shin-Etsu Chemical Co., Ltd.	$4,111
266	Sumitomo Mitsui Financial Group Inc Tokyo	$4,107
267	Severstal PAO	$4,074
268	Coterra Energy Inc	$4,065
269	China Yangtze Power Co Ltd	$4,020
270	SSE PLC	$3,978
271	Brookfield Corp	$3,966
272	Vonovia SE	$3,962
273	MPLX LP	$3,944
274	Diageo Plc	$3,934
275	Nintendo Co., Ltd.	$3,927
276	LyondellBasell Industries NV	$3,889
277	Steel Dynamics. Inc.	$3,862
278	China Railway Group Ltd	$3,851
279	Ecopetrol SA	$3,844
280	SSGA SPDR ETFs Europe II PLC	$3,844
281	FedEx Corp	$3,826
282	Ternium S A	$3,825
283	Sumitomo Corp.	$3,812
284	Canadian National Railway Co	$3,784
285	National Westminster Bank Plc	$3,764
286	Heineken NV (Netherlands)	$3,762
287	China Pacific Insurance (Group) Co., Ltd.	$3,758
288	NN Group NV (Netherlands)	$3,710
289	Florida Power & Light Co.	$3,701
290	Westpac Banking Corp	$3,680
291	JBS S.A.	$3,676
292	Light & Wonder Inc	$3,675
293	APA Corp	$3,674
294	Ovintiv Inc	$3,637
295	Siemens AG (Germany)	$3,629
296	Industria De Diseno Textil I	$3,619
297	Volvo AB	$3,618
298	Marathon Oil Corp.	$3,612
299	Enel SpA	$3,609
300	Kering SA	$3,594

SOURCE: MERGENT INC., DATABASE, APRIL 2023

Hoover's Handbook of Emerging Companies

The Companies

1-800 Flowers.com, Inc.

1-800-FLOWERS.COM is a leading provider of gifts designed to help customers express, connect and celebrate. sells fresh-cut flowers, floral arrangements, and plants through its toll-free number and websites; it also markets gifts via catalogs, TV and radio ads, and online affiliates. Through subsidiaries, the company offers gourmet foods (Harry & David), popcorn (The Popcorn Factory), baked goods (Cheryl's), fruit arrangements (FruitBouquets.com), and a host of other products. Its BloomNet service provides products and services to florists. Founder and chairman James McCann launched the company in 1976. In 2020, the company has completed its acquisition of PersonalizationMall.com.

Operations

1-800-FLOWERS operates through three segments: Gourmet Foods & Gift Baskets, Consumer Floral & Gifts, and BloomNet.

Gourmet Foods & Gift Baskets generates just about 50% its revenue from premium food items and gift boxes and containers. Businesses in this segment include Simply Chocolates (artisan chocolates and confections) and Harry & David (fruit baskets, gourmet food, gifts); other brands include Wolferman's, Cushman's, and MooseMunch.

The company's traditional cut flowers and plants business -- offered through its namesake business as well as Flowerama, Goodsey, and others -- accounts for about 45% of revenue.

Services for florists (clearinghouse, marketing, communications) account for over 5% of revenue and are provided through 1-800-FLOWERS' BloomNet business.

Geographic Reach

1-800-FLOWERS, headquartered in New York, operates almost completely in the US.

Sales and Marketing

1-800-FLOWERS aims to reach customers through online and offline media, direct marketing, public relations, and strategic online and digital relationship. Advertising expense was $307.9 million, $171.4 million, and $147.8 million, for the years ended 2021, 2020, and 2019, respectively. E-commerce represents about 90% of total revenue.

Financial Performance

Despite a slight fall in revenue in 2018, the company performance was generally on an upward swing in the last five years.

In fiscal 2021, the company revenue saw an increase of $633 million to $2.1 billion as compared to 2020's revenue of $1.5 billion.

Net income for fiscal year ended 2021 increased by almost double at $59.6 million to $118.6 million as compared to the prior year's net income of $59.0 million.

Cash at the end of fiscal 2021 was at $173.6 million. Cash from operations contributed $173.3 million to the coffers. Investing activities used $307.9 million while financing activities provided $67.7 million. Main cash uses for the year were for the acquisition of PersonalizationMall.

Company Background

Social worker Jim McCann bought a New York City florist shop in 1976 to supplement his income from St. John's Home for Boys. By 1986 he had expanded his Flora Plenty chain to 14 shops in the New York metropolitan area and made the floral business his full-time job.

The next year McCann paid $9 million for 1-800-FLOWERS, a young, struggling Dallas-based floral-delivery company that had been founded by John Davis and Jim Poage. McCann's shops had worked with 1-800-FLOWERS, but he had to sell most of his Flora Plenty stores to keep the telemarketing business from wilting altogether. By 1990, however, business was blossoming and 1-800-FLOWERS was profitable.

It went public in 1999.

HISTORY

Social worker Jim McCann bought a New York City florist shop in 1976 to supplement his income from St. John's Home for Boys. By 1986 he had expanded his Flora Plenty chain to 14 shops in the New York metropolitan area and made the floral business his full-time job.

The next year McCann paid $9 million for 1-800-FLOWERS, a young, struggling Dallas-based floral-delivery company that had been founded by John Davis and Jim Poage. McCann's shops had worked with 1-800-FLOWERS, but he had to sell most of his Flora Plenty stores to keep the telemarketing business from wilting altogether. By 1990, however, business was blossoming and 1-800-FLOWERS was profitable.

In 1992 the company began selling flowers online through Compuserve. 1-800-FLOWERS launched its own website three years later and teamed with online providers such as America Online (now Time Warner Inc.) and Microsoft Network.

1-800-FLOWERS added home and garden merchandise to its offerings -- and picked up catalog expertise -- when it bought an 80% stake in Plow & Hearth in 1998 (it acquired the remainder in 1999). In May 1999 the company received more than $100 million from Benchmark Capital, Japanese technology firm SOFTBANK, and luxury goods kingpin LVMH. 1-800-FLOWERS then added ".COM" to its name and went public in August 1999.

In late 1999 the company bought online gourmet foods retailer GreatFood.com for $18.5 million. It added jewelry to its offerings by teaming up with retailer Finlay Enterprises in 2000. It also launched its Spanish language Web site -- 1-800-LASFLORES.COM. New additions in 2001 included a partnership with Touchpoint, allowing customers to create personalized cards and photos, and the addition of children's gifts, dolls, crafts, and other toys and games with the acquisition of The Children's Group.

1-800-FLOWERS.COM continued its acquisitive ways in 2002 by acquiring The Popcorn Factory (direct marketing of premium popcorn, chocolates, and other food gift products packaged in decorative tins and baskets). That year the firm agreed to cross-promote its goods with American Greetings; under the agreement, 1-800-FLOWERS.COM became the exclusive provider of flowers on several American Greetings Web sites. And in 2004 it got into the wine distribution business with its purchase of The Winetasting Network, which is now a subsidiary.

In March 2005 the company acquired cookie-and-baked-gifts-maker Cheryl & Co. for an undisclosed price. The company moved its corporate headquarters to Carle Place, New York, the next year. In mid-2006 the Internet flower company acquired candy maker Fannie May Confections Brands for $85 million.

1-800-FLOWERS.COM bought gourmet gift basket maker DesignPac Gifts in May 2008 for about $36 million. It also purchased Napco Marketing, which wholesales and markets products for the floral industry, for $9 million.

In March 2009 the company acquired certain assets of online wine seller Geerlings & Wade, Inc. for about $2 million to complement its Winetasting Network business. It also launched 1-800-BASKETS.com that year.

To focus on its core floral and food units, 1-800-FLOWERS.COM sold its home dÃ©cor and children's gift brands to PH International, a Virginia-based home dÃ©cor distributor, in January 2010. The deal, which was worth $17 million, included the brands of HearthSong, Magic Cabin, Plow & Hearth, Problem Solvers, and Wind & Weather.

EXECUTIVES

Executive Chairman, Director, James F. McCann, $975,000 total compensation
President, Chief Executive Officer, Director, Christopher G. McCann, $775,000 total compensation
Senior Vice President, Chief Financial Officer, Treasurer, William E. Shea, $492,308 total compensation
Senior Vice President, Corporate Secretary, General Counsel, Michael R. Manley
Senior Vice President, Chief Information Officer, Arnold P. (Arnie) Leap
Business Affairs Senior Vice President, Gerard M. Gallagher, $443,333 total compensation
Division Officer, Thomas G. Hartnett, $421,154 total compensation
Division Officer, Mark L. Nance
Director, Geralyn R. Breig
Director, Celia R. Brown
Director, James A. Cannavino
Director, Eugene F. DeMark

Director, Leonard J. Elmore
Director, Adam Hanft
Director, Sean P. Hegarty
Director, Katherine Oliver
Director, Larry Zarin
Auditors : BDO USA, LLP

LOCATIONS

HQ: 1-800 Flowers.com, Inc.
Two Jericho Plaza, Suite 200, Jericho, NY 11753
Phone: 516 237-6000
Web: www.1800flowers.com

PRODUCTS/OPERATIONS

2018 Sales

	$ mil.	% of total
1-800-Flowers.com consumer floral	457	40
Gourmet food & gift baskets	606	52
BloomNet Wire Service	90	8
Corporate	1	-
Adjustments	(2)	-
Total	1,152	100

2018 Sales

	$ mil.	% of total
E-commerce	922	80
Other	230	20
Total	1,152	100

Selected Brands

1-800-Flowers.com
1-800-Baskets
Celebrations
Cheryl's
Cushman's
DesignPac
Flowerama
Goodsey
GreatFoods.com
Harry & David
MooseMunch
Mrs. Beasley's
Napco
Personalization Universe
Simply Chocolate
The Popcorn Factory
Wolferman's

COMPETITORS

AMAZON.COM, INC.
BED BATH & BEYOND INC.
HARRY & DAVID HOLDINGS, INC.
L. L. BEAN, INC.
LANDS' END, INC.
NEW LOOK RETAILERS LIMITED
Otto (GmbH & Co KG)
PARTYLITE, INC.
SIERRA TRADING POST, INC.
WILLIAMS-SONOMA, INC.

HISTORICAL FINANCIALS

Company Type: Public

Income Statement — FYE: June 27

	REVENUE ($mil)	NET INCOME ($mil)	NET PROFIT MARGIN	EMPLOYEES
06/21	2,122.2	118.6	5.6%	4,800
06/20	1,489.6	58.9	4.0%	4,300
06/19*	1,248.6	34.7	2.8%	4,095
07/18	1,151.9	40.7	3.5%	4,785
07/17	1,193.6	44.0	3.7%	4,633
Annual Growth	15.5%	28.1%	—	0.9%

*Fiscal year change

2021 Year-End Financials

Debt ratio: 16.9%
Return on equity: 26.1%
Cash ($ mil.): 173.5
Current Ratio: 1.50
Long-term debt ($ mil.): 161.5
No. of shares ($ mil.): 65.0
Dividends
  Yield: —
  Payout: —
Market value ($ mil.): 2,189.0

	STOCK PRICE ($) FY Close	P/E High/Low		PER SHARE ($) Earnings	Dividends	Book Value
06/21	33.68	21	11	1.78	0.00	7.83
06/20	19.87	27	12	0.89	0.00	6.22
06/19*	18.88	39	19	0.52	0.00	5.32
07/18	12.55	21	13	0.61	0.00	4.87
07/17	9.75	16	13	0.65	0.00	4.33
Annual Growth	36.3%	—	—	28.6%	—	15.9%

*Fiscal year change

ABIOMED, Inc.

ABIOMED is a provider of medical devices that provide circulatory support and oxygenation. The company has developed a range of cardiac assist devices and is developing a self-contained artificial heart. Its Impella micro heart pumps can temporarily take over blood circulation during surgery or catheterization. Its Impella CP device provides blood flow of approximately one liter more per minute than the Impella 2.5 device and is primarily used by either interventional cardiologists to support patients in the cath lab or by cardiac surgeons in the heart surgery suite. About 80% of the company's revenue generates from the US.

Operations

ABIOMED's products include Impella 2.5, Impella CP, Impella 5.0 and Impella LD, Impella 5.5, as well as Impella RP, Impella SmartAssist, Abiomed Beethe OXY-1 System and Impella Connect. ABIOMED's product pipeline includes Impella ECP, Impella XR Sheath, preCARDIA and Impella BTR.

The company generates about 95% of total revenue from Impella products, while service and other provide the remaining.

Geographic Reach

Headquartered in Danvers, Massachusetts, ABIOMED markets and sells its products in certain parts of Europe, Asia, South America and the Middle East. The company manufactures its products in Danvers, Massachusetts and Aachen, Germany. Its Aachen facility performs final assembly and manufactures most of the company's disposable Impella devices.

In addition to its locations in Massachusetts and Germany, the company has regulatory and clinical affairs, marketing, and distribution center in Japan.

The US provides about 80% of total revenue, while outside the US accounts for the remaining 15%.

Sales and Marketing

ABIOMED primarily sells its products to hospitals and distributors. No customer accounts for more than 10% of total revenues.

Financial Performance

The company had revenue of $1 billion in 2021, a 22% increase from the previous year's revenue of $847.5 million.

In 2021, the company had a net income of $136.5 million, a 39% decrease from the previous year's net income of $225.5 million.

The company's cash at the end of 2021 was $132.8 million. Operating activities generated $285.4 million, while investing activities used $381 million, primarily for purchases of marketable securities. Financing activities used another $2.2 million, mainly for taxes paid related to net share settlement upon vesting of stock awards.

Strategy

The company's strategic focus and the driver of its revenue growth is the market penetration of its family of Impella heart pumps. The Impella device portfolio, which includes the Impella 2.5, Impella CP, Impella 5.0, Impella LD, Impella 5.5 and Impella RP devices, has supported thousands of patients worldwide. The company expects that most of its product and service revenue in the near future will be from the company's Impella devices. Its Impella 2.5, Impella CP, Impella 5.0, Impella LD, Impella 5.5 and Impella RP devices have U.S Food and Drug Administration or FDA and CE Mark, which allows the company to market these devices in the U.S. and European Union.

Mergers and Acquisitions

In 2021, ABIOMED acquired preCARDIA, developer of a proprietary catheter and controller that will complement Abiomed's product portfolio to expand options for patients with acute decompensated heart failure (ADHF). This acquisition aligns with ABIOMED's principles of leading in technology and innovation and putting patients first.

HISTORY

David Lederman founded ABIOMED in 1981 to make products he had designed (such as artificial heart pumps and valves), as well as dental diagnostic products. ABIOMED went public in 1987. In 1988 it got about $1 million from the National Institutes of Health for heart replacement device (HRD) research and development. In 1990 it began working with Canada's World Heart on HRD technology. In 1992 ABIOMED launched BVS-5000.

In 1990 the company formed ABIODENT to consolidate its dental operations. It received FDA clearance to market the PerioTemp device in 1994. In 1996 it voluntarily recalled some of its BVS-5000 blood pumps, citing component irregularities (it said no patients were affected).

To fund product development, ABIOMED accepted government funding to finish testing its battery-powered HRD (1996) and to develop a laser-based tissue-welding system (1998). Biotech firm Genzyme invested about $15 million in ABIOMED that year, acquiring 14% of the firm.

In 1998, ABIOMED again recalled some lots of BVS-5000, this time for electrical problems. The company attributed 1998's losses to an increase in self-funding on the HRD project, as well as to red ink in its now-discontinued dental business.

ABIOMED received funding from the National Heart, Lung and Blood Institutes in 2000 to support the testing of its AbioCor product, an implantable heart replacement device. The following year AbioCor became the first artificial heart implanted in a patient.

The FDA approved the use of the artificial hearts in five patients in 2001, all of whom were considered too sick to receive heart transplants. The first patient died the same year, but the cause of death was not attributed to AbioCor.

The fifth patient to receive the device died early in 2002. By late 2002 seven patients had been fitted with the device, but only one was living. A moratorium on recruiting new patients was imposed. ABIOMED wanted patients that were healthy enough to live long past the time of implantation, but only patients that were extremely ill would be considered candidates for the device.

By January of 2003 the moratorium had been lifted and three more patients had received implants by March. Because of the troubles with finding qualified recipients for its AbioCor product, the company began focusing on other products to sustain revenues. It got good news on that front that same year when the FDA approved ABIOMED's AB5000 Circulatory Support System Console, a device that temporarily pumps the patient's blood when the heart has failed.

EXECUTIVES

Healthcare Solutions Executive Vice President, Healthcare Solutions Chief Commercial Officer, Andrew J. Greenfield, $329,909 total compensation
Director, Susan Morano
Director, Vincent Sommella
Director, David Fortunat
Auditors : DELOITTE & TOUCHE LLP

LOCATIONS

HQ: ABIOMED, Inc.
22 Cherry Hill Drive, Danvers, MA 01923
Phone: 978 646-1400 **Fax:** 978 777-8411
Web: www.abiomed.com

2015 Sales

	% of total
US	90
Other countries	10
Total	100

PRODUCTS/OPERATIONS

2015 Revenues

	$ mil.	% of total
Impella products	212.7	92
Service & other revenue	13.8	6
Other products	3.5	2
Funded research & development	0.3	-
Total	230.3	100

COMPETITORS

CRYOLIFE, INC.
DELTEX MEDICAL GROUP PLC
Gambro AB
HOLOGIC, INC.
LIVANOVA USA, INC.
NXSTAGE MEDICAL, INC.
RESHAPE LIFESCIENCES INC.
STEREOTAXIS, INC.
THORATEC LLC
VOLCANO CORPORATION

HISTORICAL FINANCIALS
Company Type: Public

Income Statement — FYE: March 31

	REVENUE ($mil)	NET INCOME ($mil)	NET PROFIT MARGIN	EMPLOYEES
03/21	847.5	225.5	26.6%	1,725
03/20	840.8	203.0	24.1%	1,536
03/19	769.4	259.0	33.7%	1,371
03/18	593.7	112.1	18.9%	1,143
03/17	445.3	52.1	11.7%	908
Annual Growth	17.5%	44.2%	—	17.4%

2021 Year-End Financials

Debt ratio: — No. of shares ($ mil.): 45.2
Return on equity: 18.8% Dividends
Cash ($ mil.): 232.7 Yield: —
Current Ratio: 6.11 Payout: —
Long-term debt ($ mil.): — Market value ($ mil.): 14,429.0

	STOCK PRICE ($) FY Close	P/E High/Low		PER SHARE ($) Earnings	Dividends	Book Value
03/21	318.73	71	28	4.94	0.00	29.37
03/20	145.16	63	29	4.43	0.00	23.67
03/19	285.59	78	48	5.61	0.00	20.76
03/18	290.99	116	76	2.45	0.00	15.54
03/17	125.20	109	78	1.17	0.00	10.35
Annual Growth	26.3%	—		43.3%	—	29.8%

ACM Research Inc

EXECUTIVES

Chairman, Chief Executive Officer, President, Director, David H. Wang, $189,373 total compensation
Chief Financial Officer, Treasurer, Secretary, Mark McKechnie
Chief Financial Officer, Treasurer, Min Xu, $144,472 total compensation
Development Vice President, Research Vice President, Development Subsidiary Officer, Research Subsidiary Officer, Jian Wang, $140,059 total compensation
Manufacturing Vice President, Manufacturing Subsidiary Officer, Sotheara Cheav, $139,824 total compensation
Sales Vice President, Sales Subsidiary Officer, Fufa Chen, $156,554 total compensation
Subsidiary Officer, Lisa Feng
Lead Director, Director, Haiping Dun
Director, Tracy Liu
Director, Yinan Xiang
Director, Chenming C. Hu
Director, Zhengfan Yang
Auditors : BDO China Shu Lun Pan Certified Public Accountants LLP

LOCATIONS

HQ: ACM Research Inc
42307 Osgood Road, Suite I, Fremont, CA 94539
Phone: 510 445-3700
Web: www.acmrcsh.com

HISTORICAL FINANCIALS
Company Type: Public

Income Statement — FYE: December 31

	REVENUE ($mil)	NET INCOME ($mil)	NET PROFIT MARGIN	EMPLOYEES
12/20	156.6	18.7	12.0%	543
12/19	107.5	18.8	17.6%	361
12/18	74.6	6.5	8.8%	273
12/17	36.5	(0.3)	—	191
12/16	27.3	1.0	3.8%	187
Annual Growth	54.7%	106.6%	—	30.5%

2020 Year-End Financials

Debt ratio: 13.4% No. of shares ($ mil.): 18.7
Return on equity: 15.7% Dividends
Cash ($ mil.): 71.7 Yield: —
Current Ratio: 2.53 Payout: —
Long-term debt ($ mil.): 17.9 Market value ($ mil.): 1,519.0

	STOCK PRICE ($) FY Close	P/E High/Low		PER SHARE ($) Earnings	Dividends	Book Value
12/20	81.25	109	17	0.89	0.00	7.55
12/19	18.45	19	8	0.99	0.00	5.39
12/18	10.88	36	11	0.37	0.00	3.27
12/17	5.25	—	—	(0.05)	0.00	2.60
Annual Growth	149.2%	—	—	—	—	42.7%

ACNB Corp

Seven score and a few years ago, ACNB Corporation's fathers brought forth a small-town bank. Now ACNB is dedicated to the proposition of being the holding company for Adams County National Bank, operating more than 20 branches in the Gettysburg and Newville areas of Pennsylvania. It is altogether fitting and proper that the bank offers traditional retail banking services. The world may long note and remember that the bank also provides residential mortgage (about 60% of the portfolio), commercial real estate, consumer, and business loans. In addition, ACNB gives a full measure of devotion to insurance products; provides trust services; and hopes that community banking shall not perish from the earth.

EXECUTIVES

Chairman, Subsidiary Officer, Director, Alan J. Stock
Subsidiary Officer, Director, Frank Elsner
Subsidiary Officer, Vice-Chairman, Director, Todd L. Herring
President, Chief Executive Officer, Subsidiary Officer, Director, James P. Helt, $400,000 total compensation
Executive Vice President, Chief Financial Officer, Treasurer, Subsidiary Officer, Jason H. Weber
Director, James J. Lott
Director, Donna M. Newell
Director, Douglas Arthur Seibel, $230,000 total compensation
Director, Kimberly S. Chaney
Director, Scott L. Kelley
Director, Daniel W. Potts
Auditors : RSM US LLP

LOCATIONS

HQ: ACNB Corp
16 Lincoln Square, Gettysburg, PA 17325
Phone: 717 334-3161
Web: www.acnb.com

COMPETITORS

BANK OF SOUTH CAROLINA CORPORATION
BURKE & HERBERT BANK & TRUST COMPANY
HIGHLANDS BANKSHARES, INC.
M&F BANCORP, INC.
SYNOVUS FINANCIAL CORP.

HISTORICAL FINANCIALS

Company Type: Public

Income Statement — FYE: December 31

	ASSETS ($mil)	NET INCOME ($mil)	INCOME AS % OF ASSETS	EMPLOYEES
12/20	2,555.3	18.3	0.7%	396
12/19	1,720.2	23.7	1.4%	374
12/18	1,647.7	21.7	1.3%	361
12/17	1,595.4	9.7	0.6%	358
12/16	1,206.3	10.8	0.9%	303
Annual Growth	20.6%	14.1%	—	6.9%

2020 Year-End Financials

Return on assets: 0.8%
Return on equity: 8.1%
Long-term debt ($ mil.): —
No. of shares ($ mil.): 8.7
Sales ($ mil.): 105.2
Dividends
Yield: 4.0%
Payout: 49.0%
Market value ($ mil.): 218.0

	STOCK PRICE ($) FY Close	P/E High/Low	PER SHARE ($) Earnings	Dividends	Book Value
12/20	25.00	17 9	2.13	1.00	29.62
12/19	37.82	12 10	3.36	0.98	26.77
12/18	39.25	13 9	3.09	0.89	23.86
12/17	29.55	21 17	1.50	0.80	21.92
12/16	31.25	18 12	1.80	0.80	19.80
Annual Growth	(5.4%)	— —	4.3%	5.7%	10.6%

Addus HomeCare Corp

Addus HomeCare is a provider of home care services that primarily include personal care services that assist with activities of daily living, as well as hospice and home health services. Addus HomeCare's consumers are primarily persons who, without these services, are at risk of hospitalization or institutionalization, such as the elderly, chronically ill and disabled. Addus HomeCare's payor clients include federal, state and local governmental agencies, managed care organizations, commercial insurers and private individuals. Addus HomeCare currently provides home care services to approximately 44,500 consumers through more than 205 locations across some 20 US states.

Operations

The company operates three segments: personal care, hospice, and home health.

Personal care segment provides non-medical assistance with activities of daily living, primarily to persons who are at increased risk of hospitalization or institutionalization, such as the elderly, chronically ill or disabled. The services include assistance with bathing, grooming, oral care, feeding and dressing, medication reminders, meal planning and preparation, housekeeping and transportation services. The segment accounts the largest for about 80% of total revenue.

The hospice segment (nearly 20%) provides physical, emotional and spiritual care for people who are terminally ill as well as related services for their families. The hospice services include palliative nursing care, social work, spiritual counseling, homemaker services and bereavement counseling.

Home health segment provides services that are primarily medical in nature to individuals who may require assistance during an illness or after hospitalization and include skilled nursing and physical, occupational and speech therapy. It generally provides home health services on a short-term, intermittent or episodic basis to individuals, typically to assist patients recovering from an illness or injury. The segment accounts a small portion of the revenue.

Geographic Reach

Headquartered in Frisco, Texas, Addus HomeCare has support centers in Downers Grove, Illinois and Frisco, Texas. It derives a significant amount of its revenue from its operations in Illinois, New Mexico, and New York.

Sales and Marketing

Addus HomeCare's payor clients include federal, state and local governmental agencies, managed care organizations, commercial insurers and private individuals. Addus derives about 60% of its revenue from state and local governmental agencies, primarily through Medicaid state programs. The Illinois Department on Aging is its largest customer (accounted for about 20% revenue).

Financial Performance

Net service revenues increased by 13.0% to $864.5 million for the year ended December 31, 2021 compared to $764.8 million in 2020.

Net service revenue increased by $38.6 million and $51.0 million in its personal care and hospice segments, respectively, for the year ended December 31, 2021, compared to 2020.

Net income for fiscal 2021 increased to $45.1 million compared from the prior year with $33.1 million. Cash held by the company at the end of fiscal 2021 increased to $168.9 million. Cash provided by operations and financing activities were $39.5 million and $26.3 million, respectively. Cash used for investing activities was $42.0 million, mainly for acquisitions of businesses.

Strategy

The growth of its revenues is closely correlated with the number of consumers to whom the company provide its services. Addus Homecare's continued growth depends on its ability to provide consistently high quality care, maintain its existing payor relationships, establish relationships with new payors, increase our referral sources and its ability to attract and retain caregivers. Addus Homecare continued growth is also dependent upon the authorization by state agencies of new consumers to receive its services. The company believe there are several market opportunities for growth as the population ages. Moreover, the company believe that individuals generally prefer to receive care in their homes.

The company plan to continue its revenue growth and margin improvement and enhance our competitive positioning by executing on the following growth strategies: consistently provide high-quality care; drive organic growth in existing markets; market to managed care organizations; and grow through acquisition.

Mergers and Acquisitions

In 2022, Addus HomeCare completed the acquisition of substantially all the assets of JourneyCare, Inc. (JourneyCare) for a cash purchase price of approximately $85 million, after customary purchase price adjustments. Based in Glenview, Illinois, JourneyCare serves an average daily adult census of approximately 750 patients in a surrounding 13 county territory. The acquisition enables Addus to provide all three levels of home care in Illinois, consistent with its broader growth strategy.

In late 2021, Addus HomeCare acquired Summit Home Health (Summit). Based in Bolingbrook, Illinois, a suburb of Chicago, Summit currently serves an average daily census of approximately 240 patients for skilled home health services, with primary coverage in the 14 counties in and around Chicago. The acquisition advances Addus' goal of adding clinical services in geographic markets where it currently has a strong personal care presence and opens further opportunities in value-based care.

In 2021, Addus HomeCare acquired Armada Skilled Home Health of New Mexico, LLC, Armada Hospice of New Mexico, LLC and Armada Hospice of Santa Fe, LLC, ("Armada") for a cash purchase price of approximately $29.8 million. Based in Albuquerque, New Mexico, Armada currently serves an average daily census of approximately 1,100 patients for home health services and 100 patients for hospice care, with primary coverage across Bernalillo County and surrounding counties. With the purchase of Armada, the company expanded its home health and hospice services in the state of New Mexico.

EXECUTIVES

Chief Executive Officer, Chairman, Director, R. Dirk Allison, $588,701 total compensation
President, Chief Operating Officer, W. Bradley Bickham, $383,846 total compensation
Executive Vice President, Chief Financial Officer, Treasurer, Secretary, Brian Poff, $369,614 total compensation
Executive Vice President, Chief Legal Officer, Sean Gaffney
Executive Vice President, Chief Government Relations Officer, Darby Anderson, $323,462 total compensation
Executive Vice President, Chief Information Officer, Michael D. Wattenbarger
Executive Vice President, Chief Strategy Officer, David W. Tucker
Executive Vice President, Chief Human Resources Officer, Roberton James Stevenson
Executive Vice President, Chief Compliance Officer, Chief Quality Officer, Monica Raines
Executive Vice President, Chief Development Officer, Cliff Donald Blessing
Lead Director, Director, Steven I. Geringer
Director, Heather Brianne Dixon
Director, Esteban Lopez
Director, Jean Rush
Director, Susan T. Weaver
Director, Michael M. Earley
Director, Veronica Hill-Milbourne
Director, Mark L. First
Director, Darin J. Gordon
Auditors : PricewaterhouseCoopers LLP

LOCATIONS

HQ: Addus HomeCare Corp
6303 Cowboys Way, Suite 600, Frisco, TX 75034
Phone: 469 535-8200
Web: www.addus.com

COMPETITORS

AMEY UK PLC
CORDANT GROUP PLC
DIVERSICARE HEALTHCARE SERVICES, INC.
DOMESTIC & GENERAL GROUP LIMITED
GENTIVA HEALTH SERVICES, INC.
MITIE GROUP PLC
RES-CARE, INC.
RYDON GROUP LIMITED
SPOTLESS GROUP LIMITED
SYNERGY HEALTH LIMITED

HISTORICAL FINANCIALS
Company Type: Public

Income Statement — FYE: December 31

	REVENUE ($mil)	NET INCOME ($mil)	NET PROFIT MARGIN	EMPLOYEES
12/20	764.7	33.1	4.3%	35,139
12/19	648.7	25.2	3.9%	33,238
12/18	518.1	17.5	3.4%	33,153
12/17	425.7	13.6	3.2%	26,097
12/16	400.6	12.0	3.0%	23,070
Annual Growth	17.5%	28.8%	—	11.1%

2020 Year-End Financials
Debt ratio: 21.8%
Return on equity: 6.6%
Cash ($ mil.): 145.0
Current Ratio: 2.00
Long-term debt ($ mil.): 193.9
No. of shares ($ mil.): 15.8
Dividends
Yield: —
Payout: —
Market value ($ mil.): 1,853.0

	STOCK PRICE ($) FY Close	P/E High/Low		PER SHARE ($) Earnings	Dividends	Book Value
12/20	117.09	55	23	2.08	0.00	32.77
12/19	97.22	53	32	1.77	0.00	30.45
12/18	67.88	53	24	1.41	0.00	20.99
12/17	34.80	34	25	1.17	0.00	15.05
12/16	35.05	34	15	1.06	0.00	13.79
Annual Growth	35.2%	—	—	18.4%	—	24.2%

Advanced Drainage Systems Inc

EXECUTIVES

Chairman, Director, Robert M. Eversole
President, Chief Executive Officer, Director, D. Scott Barbour, $825,000 total compensation
Executive Vice President, Chief Financial Officer, Treasurer, Secretary, Scott A. Cottrill, $500,000 total compensation
Market Management Executive Vice President, Robert M. Klein, $375,000 total compensation
Executive Vice President, Roy E. Moore
Executive Vice President, Chief Administrative Officer, Kevin C. Talley, $370,000 total compensation
Supply Chain Executive Vice President, Darin S. Harvey
Marketing Executive Vice President, Product Management Executive Vice President, Brian W. King
International Senior Vice President, Thomas J. Waun
Sales Senior Vice President, Michael G. Huebert
Director, Anesa T. Chaibi
Director, Alexander R. Fischer
Director, Kelly S. Gast
Director, Mark A. Haney
Director, Ross M. Jones
Director, Anil Seetharam
Director, Manuel J. Perez de la Mesa
Director, Michael B. Coleman
Director, Tanya D. Fratto
Director, Carl A. Nelson
Auditors : DELOITTE & TOUCHE LLP

LOCATIONS

HQ: Advanced Drainage Systems Inc
4640 Trueman Boulevard, Hilliard, OH 43026
Phone: 614 658-0050
Web: www.ads-pipe.com

HISTORICAL FINANCIALS
Company Type: Public

Income Statement — FYE: March 31

	REVENUE ($mil)	NET INCOME ($mil)	NET PROFIT MARGIN	EMPLOYEES
03/21	1,982.7	224.2	11.3%	5,000
03/20	1,673.8	(193.1)	—	4,950
03/19	1,384.7	77.7	5.6%	4,400
03/18	1,330.3	62.0	4.7%	4,400
03/17	1,257.2	32.9	2.6%	4,500
Annual Growth	12.1%	61.5%	—	2.7%

2021 Year-End Financials
Debt ratio: 34.9%
Return on equity: 24.6%
Cash ($ mil.): 195.0
Current Ratio: 2.33
Long-term debt ($ mil.): 815.1
No. of shares ($ mil.): 71.5
Dividends
Yield: 0.3%
Payout: 14.5%
Market value ($ mil.): 7,400.0

	STOCK PRICE ($) FY Close	P/E High/Low		PER SHARE ($) Earnings	Dividends	Book Value
03/21	103.39	43	10	2.59	0.36	14.67
03/20	29.44	—	—	(3.21)	1.36	11.15
03/19	25.77	27	19	1.22	0.32	8.46
03/18	25.90	27	18	0.99	0.28	7.39
03/17	21.90	55	37	0.50	0.24	6.06
Annual Growth	47.4%	—	—	50.9%	10.7%	24.7%

Advanced Energy Industries Inc

Advanced Energy Industries designs, manufactures, sells, and supports precision power products that transform, refine, and modify the raw electrical power coming from either the utility or the building facility and convert it into various types of highly controllable, usable power that is predictable, repeatable, and customizable to meet the necessary requirements for powering a wide range of complex equipment. Semiconductor and solar manufacturing equipment maker Applied Materials is its top customer. Advanced Energy's OEM customers design equipment utilizing its process power technologies in a variety of industrial production applications including glass coating, glass manufacturing, flat panel displays, photovoltaics solar cell manufacturing, and similar thin film manufacturing. The company gets about 40% of its sales from the US.

Operations
Advanced Energy provides highly engineered, mission-critical, precision power conversion, measurement, and control solutions to its global customers. Semiconductor equipment generates nearly 50% of the company's revenue, followed by industrial and medical (about 25%), data center computing (around 20%), and telecom and networking (roughly 10%).

Overall, product sales bring in about 90% of the company's revenue, while services account for the rest.

Geographic Reach
Advanced Energy, based in Denver, Colorado, has facilities throughout the US, North America, Europe, and Asia.

Customers in the US generate about 40% of the company's revenue, followed by Asia (nearly 40%), Europe (more than 10%), and North America (excluding US) and other (account for the rest).

Sales and Marketing
Advanced Energy sells to OEMs, integrators, distributors and directly to end users. It uses a direct sales force as well as independent sales representatives, channel partners and distributors. The company's 10 largest customers account for about 60% of sales. Advanced Energy relies on two customers for about 50% of its sales with Applied Materials accounting for approximately 20% and LAM Research supplying about 10%.

Financial Performance
Company's revenue for fiscal 2021 increased by 3% to $1.5 billion compared from the prior year with $1.4 billion. The increase in sales was primarily due to increased demand and shipments in the Semiconductor Equipment and Industrial and Medical markets.

Net income for fiscal 2021 increased to $134.8 million compared from the prior year with $134.7 million.

Cash held by the company at the end of fiscal 2021 increased to $544.4 million. Cash provided by operations was $140.2 million while cash used for investing and financing activities were $47.3 million and $25.4 million, respectively. Main uses of cash were for purchases of property and equipment; and purchase and retirement of common stock.

Strategy
Advanced Energy's business strategy for many of its product lines has been focused on product performance and technology innovation to provide enhanced efficiencies and productivity.

Mergers and Acquisitions
In mid-2022 Advanced Energy acquired SL Power Electronics Corporation from Steel Partners Holdings L.P. The acquisition adds complementary products to the company's medical power offerings and extends its presence in several advanced industrial markets.

Company Background
Douglas Schatz (chairman), a veteran of Applied Materials, and Brent Backman, who had worked for Hughes Aircraft, founded Advanced Energy Industries in 1981. The company's first product replaced a refrigerator-sized power source with one the size of a bread box. Also during the 1980s the company introduced its first direct-current system for use in semiconductor deposition processes.

HISTORY
Douglas Schatz (chairman), a veteran of Applied Materials, and Brent Backman, who had worked for Hughes Aircraft (sold to General Motors in 1986), founded Advanced Energy Industries in 1981. The company's first product replaced a refrigerator-sized power source with one the size of a bread box. Also during the 1980s the company introduced its first direct-current system for use in semiconductor deposition processes.

The company went public in 1995. The following year, sales growth slowed as the chip industry went through one of its periodic slumps. To cushion its dependence on the volatile semiconductor market, in 1997 and 1998 Advanced Energy acquired power supply firms Tower Electronics (products used in the telecommunications, medical, and non-impact printing industries) and MIK Physics (power supplies used in industrial vacuum coating), among others. Advanced Energy also bought one of its main rivals, RF Power Products. In 2000 Advanced Energy bought Noah Holding, a privately held maker of temperature control systems.

In 2001 the company acquired Engineering Measurements Company (EMCO), a maker of flow meters and other precision measurement equipment. During 2001 the company twice cut its workforce -- by a total of one-fourth -- in response to a sharp decline in the worldwide electronics industry.

In 2002 Advanced Energy acquired Aera Japan (mass flow controllers) for about $80 million in cash and debt assumption. Later that year it acquired Germany-based Dressler HF Technik (power systems for plasma-based production equipment), and the e-diagnostics applications of privately held Symphony Systems (Web-based software used to control wafer manufacturing processes).

In 2005 Doug Schatz said he would retire as president and CEO once a successor could be found. Hans-Georg Betz, CEO of West STEAG Partners (a German venture capital firm) and a director of Advanced Energy since 2004, was named president and CEO later that year. Schatz remained as nonexecutive chairman of the company.

Later that year, Advanced Energy raised around $92 million in a secondary stock offering. The company marked its 25th anniversary in business during 2006.

The company closed its plant in Stolberg, Germany, in 2007. Manufacturing was shifted to Advanced Energy's high-volume plant in Shenzhen, China, and to its advanced manufacturing facility in Fort Collins, Colorado. The company said the decision came down to deciding whether to expand the plants in Stolberg and Shenzhen, with the Chinese facility getting the nod. Advanced Energy acquired the Stolberg location through the acquisition of Dressler HF Technik in 2002. The German plant employed about 65 people.

Bolstering its power conversion products for the solar market, in 2010 Advanced Energy acquired PV Powered, a maker solar inverters for the commercial, residential, and utility-scale markets. Later the same year, the company sold its Aera mass flow control and related product lines to Hitachi Metals for about $44 million, in order to focus on its core power product lines.

EXECUTIVES

Chairman, Director, Grant H. Beard
President, Chief Executive Officer, Director, Stephen Douglas Kelley
Executive Vice President, Chief Financial Officer, Paul Oldham, $267,397 total compensation
Executive Vice President, Chief Operating Officer, Eduardo Bernal Acebedo
Executive Vice President, Corporate Secretary, General Counsel, Thomas O. McGimpsey, $350,000 total compensation
Director, Frederick A. Ball
Director, Tina M. Donikowski
Director, David W. Reed
Director, Ronald C. Foster
Director, Edward C. Grady
Director, Thomas M. Rohrs
Director, John A. Roush
Director, Anne T. DelSanto
Director, Lanesha T. Minnix
Auditors : Ernst & Young LLP

LOCATIONS
HQ: Advanced Energy Industries Inc
1595 Wynkoop Street, Suite 800, Denver, CO 80202
Phone: 970 407-6626
Web: www.advancedenergy.com

2018 Sales

	$ mil.	% of total
North America		
US	370.8	52
Canada	2	-
Asia/Pacific		
Republic of Korea	74.6	10
China	61.9	9
Other countries	114.1	16
Europe		
Germany	39.7	5
Other countries	55.1	8
Other countries	0.7	-
Total	718.9	100

AeroVironment, Inc.

AeroVironment (AV) designs, develops, produces, delivers and supports a technologically-advanced portfolio of intelligent, multi-domain robotic systems and related services for government agencies and businesses. The company designs and manufactures a line of small unmanned aircraft systems (UAS), tactical missile systems (TMS), unmanned ground vehicles (UGV) and related services primarily for the Department of Defense (DoD). The business addresses the increasing economic and security value of distributed, network-centric intelligence, surveillance and reconnaissance (ISR), communications, remote sensing and effects delivery with innovative UAS and tactical missile system solutions. Dr. Paul B. MacCready, Jr. founded AeroVironment in July 1971. The company generates around 60% of total sales domestically.

Operations
AV operates its business into four main reportable segment: Small UAS; MUAS; TMS; and HAPS.

Small UAS, including Raven, Wasp AE, Puma AE, Puma LE, VAPOR and Quantix Recon are designed to operate reliably at very low altitudes in a wide range of environmental conditions, providing a vantage point from which to collect and deliver valuable information. Military forces employ the company's small UAS to deliver ISR and communications. The segment generates some 40% of total revenue.

MUAS (about 20%) provides similar capabilities to its small UAS, its field-deployable MUAS, including T-20 and JUMP 20, deliver extended endurance and expanded payload capacity to support a broader set of missions that benefit from aerial surveillance and the use of specialized payloads.

TMS accounts for more than 15% of revenue and consists of tube-launched aircraft that deploy with the push of a button, fly at higher speeds than its small UAS, and perform either effects delivery or reconnaissance missions.

In HAPS, AV has existing solutions such as terrestrial cellular towers and communications. In addition, AV provides comprehensive training services to support all of the small UAS and tactical missile systems for defense applications. The segment brings in some 10% of revenue.

Overall, the business focuses primarily on the design, development, production, marketing, support and operation of innovative UAS, TMS and UGV that provide situational awareness, remote sensing, multi-band communications, force protection and other information and mission effects to increase the safety and effectiveness of its customers' operations.

Geographic Reach
Based in Arlington, Virginia, AV has facilities located in California, Alabama, Kansas, Massachusetts, Pennsylvania, Minnesota, Virginia and Stuttgart, Germany. Its domestic sales account for around 60%, while international sales accounted for about 40% of its revenue.

Sales and Marketing
AV sells the majority of its UAS and services to organizations within the DoD, including the US Army, Marine Corps, Special Operations Command, Air Force and Navy, and to allied governments. It sells tactical missile systems to organizations within the US government. It sells its UGV and services to US and allied government military and public safety agencies as well as to commercial entities. It also develops High Altitude Pseudo-Satellite (HAPS) systems for SoftBank Corp., HAPS Mobile Inc., a commercial joint venture of which the company owns over 5%. The US Army and other US government agencies generate about 65% of its total sales. Non-US government is responsible for the remaining 35%.

AV's advertising expenses were approximately $451,000, $675,000 and $934,000 for the years 2022, 2021 and 2020, respectively.

Financial Performance
Revenue for the fiscal year ended April 30, 2022 was $445.7 million, as compared to $394.9 million for the fiscal year ended April 30, 2021, representing an increase of $50.8 million, or 13%. The increase in revenue was due to an increase in service revenue of $89 million, partially offset by a decrease in product revenue of $38.2 million.

In 2021, the company had a net loss of $4.2 million, an 82% drop from the previous year's net income of $23.3 million. The decrease was primarily due to the cost of contract services more than doubling for the year.

The company's cash for the year ended 2022 was $77.2 million. Operating activities used $9.6 million. Investing and financing activities used $52.3 million and $16.6 million, respectively. Cash uses were mainly for acquisitions.

Strategy
AeroVironment intends to grow its business by preserving a leadership position in its core UAS and tactical missile systems markets, and by creating new solutions that enable it to create and establish leadership positions in new markets. Key components of this strategy include the following:

Expand the market penetration of existing products and services. The company intends to increase the penetration of its small and medium UAS and UGV products and services within the U.S. military, the military forces of allied nations, other government agencies and non-government organizations, including commercial entities, and to increase the penetration of its TMS within the U.S. military

PRODUCTS/OPERATIONS

2018 Sales

	$ mil.	% of total
Semiconductor capital equipment	443.1	62
Industrial technology capital equipment	167.2	23
Global Support	108.6	15
Total	718.9	100

Selected Products
Inductively coupled plasma sources
Ion sources
Optical fiber thermometers
Photovoltaic (PV) power inverters
    Bipolar, transformerless inverters (Solaron)
    Grid-tie PV inverters (PV Powered)
Power control and conversion systems (used with wafer etching and vapor deposition equipment)
    AC power supply
    Direct-current (DC) products
    High-power products
    Low-frequency products
    Mid-frequency power supplies
    Radio-frequency generators
Radio-frequency power systems (cables, generators, instrumentation, power supplies, power delivery systems, and variable frequency generators)

COMPETITORS
AMERICAN SUPERCONDUCTOR CORPORATION
BEL FUSE INC.
IXYS, LLC
Infineon Technologies AG
MTS SYSTEMS CORPORATION
PULSE ELECTRONICS CORPORATION
RENESAS ELECTRONICS AMERICA INC.
SL INDUSTRIES, INC.
SOITEC
VICOR CORPORATION

HISTORICAL FINANCIALS
Company Type: Public

Income Statement — FYE: December 31

	REVENUE ($mil)	NET INCOME ($mil)	NET PROFIT MARGIN	EMPLOYEES
12/20	1,415.8	134.6	9.5%	10,000
12/19	788.9	64.9	8.2%	10,917
12/18	718.8	147.0	20.5%	2,259
12/17	671.0	137.8	20.5%	1,876
12/16	483.7	127.4	26.3%	1,558
Annual Growth	30.8%	1.4%	—	59.2%

2020 Year-End Financials
Debt ratio: 19.5%
Return on equity: 18.0%
Cash ($ mil.): 480.3
Current Ratio: 3.31
Long-term debt ($ mil.): 304.5
No. of shares ($ mil.): 38.2
Dividends
Yield: —
Payout: —
Market value ($ mil.): 3,713.0

	STOCK PRICE ($) FY Close	P/E High/Low		Earnings	Dividends	Book Value
12/20	96.97	29	10	3.50	0.00	21.28
12/19	71.20	42	24	1.69	0.00	17.64
12/18	42.93	21	10	3.74	0.00	15.90
12/17	67.48	27	16	3.43	0.00	13.15
12/16	54.75	18	8	3.18	0.00	9.87
Annual Growth	15.4%	—	—	2.4%	—	21.2%

and within the military forces of allied nations.

Deliver innovative new solutions into existing and new markets. Customer-focused innovation is the primary driver of its growth. AeroVironment's plan to continue investing in internally-funded research and development projects while expanding its pursuit of customer-funded research and development projects to generate revenue and develop better, more capable products, services and business models, both in response to and in anticipation of emerging customer needs.

Foster its entrepreneurial culture and continue to attract, develop and retain highly-skilled personnel. AeroVironment's company culture encourages innovation and entrepreneurialism, which helps to attract and retain highly-skilled professionals. AeroVironment intend to preserve this culture to encourage the development of the innovative, highly technical system solutions and business models that give the company its competitive advantage.Preserve its agility and flexibility. AeroVironment respond rapidly to evolving markets, solve complicated customer problems, and strive to deliver new products, services and capabilities quickly, efficiently and affordably relative to available alternatives.

Effectively manage its growth portfolio for long-term value creation. AeroVironment's production and development programs and services present numerous investment opportunities that the company believe will deliver long-term growth by providing its customers with valuable new capabilities.

Mergers and Acquisitions

In 2021, AeroVironment was granted clearance from the German government and completed the previously announced acquisition of Telerob Gesellschaft fÃ¼r Fernhantierungstechnik mbH (Telerob), in a $45.4 million. Telerob now operates as a wholly-owned subsidiary of AeroVironment. Telerob offers one of the industry's most advanced and comprehensive turn-key unmanned ground robotics solutions, including the telemax and tEODor EVO family of UGVs, fully-equipped transport vehicles and training, repair and support services. Its acquisition of Telerob marks a significant expansion to its portfolio of intelligent, multi-domain robotic systems, from small and medium unmanned aircraft systems, to tactical missile systems and now, unmanned ground vehicles.

In early 2021, AeroVironment has acquired Progeny Systems Corporation's Intelligent Systems Group (ISG), a leader in the development of artificial intelligence-enabled computer vision, machine learning and perceptive autonomy technologies and provider of related services to United States government customers. The acquisition will significantly accelerate AeroVironment's development of advanced autonomy capabilities for the company's growing portfolio of intelligent, multi-domain robotic systems, increase customer-funded research and development revenue and broaden its advanced engineering services offering to defense and commercial customers. Under the terms of the transaction, AeroVironment acquired ISG for $30 million in cash.

Also in early 2021, AeroVironment has completed its acquisition of California-based, Arcturus UAV, Inc. a leading designer and manufacturer of high-performance unmanned aircraft systems (UAS) for approximately $405 million. The acquisition of Arcturus UAV enables the company to accelerate its growth strategy and expand its reach into the more valuable Group 2 and 3 UAS segments.

EXECUTIVES

President, Chief Executive Officer, Director, Wahid Nawabi, $534,628 total compensation
Senior Vice President, Chief Financial Officer, Kevin McDonnell
Vice President, General Counsel, Corporate Secretary, Melissa Brown, $241,935 total compensation
Vice President, Chief Accounting Officer, Corporate Controller, Brian Shackley
Lead Independent Director, Director, Charles Thomas Burbage
Director, Catharine Merigold
Director, Stephen F. Page
Director, Edward R. Muller
Director, Cindy K. Lewis
Auditors : Deloitte & Touche LLP

LOCATIONS

HQ: AeroVironment, Inc.
241 18th Street, Suite 415, Arlington, VA 22202
Phone: 805 520-8350
Web: www.avinc.com

PRODUCTS/OPERATIONS

2015 Sales

	$ mil.	% of total
Product sales	205.0	79
Contract services	54.4	21
Total	259.4	100

2015 Sales

	$ mil.	% of total
UAS	221.0	85
EES	38.4	15
Total	259.4	100

Selected Products Efficient Energy Systems Electric Vehicle Charging Solutions: Passenger and Fleet Electric Vehicle Charging Systems, Installation Service and Data Communications PosiCharge Industrial Electric Vehicle Fast Charge System Power Cycling and Test Systems Unmanned Aircraft Systems Digital Data Link (DDL) Mantis line of gimbaled sensor payloads Public Safety UAS: QubeSmall UAS: Raven, Wasp AE, Puma AE, Shrike VTOLUAS Services: Mission services, training, repairs and spare parts UAS under development: Global Observer, Switchblade

COMPETITORS

APTIV PLC
BAE SYSTEMS PLC
EXELIS INC.
FLIR SYSTEMS, INC.
GENERAL ATOMICS AERONAUTICAL SYSTEMS, INC.
GENERAL DYNAMICS CORPORATION
KAMAN CORPORATION
LEONARDO SPA
TEXTRON INC.
THE BOEING COMPANY

HISTORICAL FINANCIALS

Company Type: Public

Income Statement FYE: April 30

	REVENUE ($mil)	NET INCOME ($mil)	NET PROFIT MARGIN	EMPLOYEES
04/21	394.9	23.3	5.9%	1,177
04/20	367.2	41.0	11.2%	828
04/19	314.2	47.4	15.1%	699
04/18	271.0	20.0	7.4%	697
04/17	264.8	12.4	4.7%	661
Annual Growth	10.5%	16.9%	—	15.5%

2021 Year-End Financials

Debt ratio: 21.3% No. of shares ($ mil.): 24.7
Return on equity: 4.1% Dividends
Cash ($ mil.): 148.7 Yield: —
Current Ratio: 4.18 Payout: —
Long-term debt ($ mil.): 187.5 Market value ($ mil.): 2,735.0

	STOCK PRICE ($) FY Close	P/E High/Low		PER SHARE ($) Earnings	Dividends	Book Value
04/21	110.37	142	61	0.96	0.00	24.70
04/20	60.26	42	27	1.71	0.00	21.19
04/19	68.56	58	26	1.97	0.00	19.32
04/18	54.50	68	33	0.84	0.00	17.15
04/17	28.57	60	41	0.54	0.00	16.16
Annual Growth	40.2%	—	—	15.5%	—	11.2%

Agree Realty Corp.

Shopping sprees really agree with Agree Realty. The self-managed real estate investment trust (REIT) owns, develops, and manages retail real estate. It owns around 820 retail properties spanning approximately 14.6 million square feet of leasable space across 45-plus states. Most of its tenants are national retailers, with its largest tenants being Sherwin-Williams, Wal-Mart, and TJX Companies. The REIT typically acquires either property portfolios or single-asset, net lease retail properties worth approximately $702.9 million with creditworthy tenants. It was founded in 1971 by CEO Richard Agree.

Operations

Agree Realty's portfolio is made up of over 820 properties. Approximately all of it are leased and has a weighted average remaining lease term of approximately 10 years. Virtually all of the REIT's revenue is from rental income.

Geographic Reach

Bloomfields hills, Michigan-based, Agree Realty had properties in about 45 US states.

About 10% of its rental revenue came from properties in Michigan, while more than 15% came from properties based in Florida, Ohio, and Texas. All other regions each accounted for less than 5% of its revenue.

Sales and Marketing

The REIT mostly leases properties to retailers such as pharmacies, restaurants, general merchandisers, apparel retailers, grocery stores, warehouse clubs, sporting goods stores, health & fitness centers, convenience stores, and dollar stores, among others.

Agree Realty's largest tenant by revenue is Sherwin-Williams, which contributed about 5% to the REIT's total rental income during 2019. Its four next largest tenants that year were Wal-Mart (nearly 5% of rental income), TJX (roughly 5%), Walgreens (less than 5%), and Best Buy (less than 5%).

Financial Performance

Agree Realty's annual revenues have almost tripled since 2015, as net income doubled for the same period.

The REIT's revenue climbed 37% to $187.5 million during 2019 mostly as its real estate investment portfolio grew to approximately $2.2 billion in gross investment amount representing 821 properties with 14.6 million square feet of gross leasable space.

Net income increased $22 million, or 38%, to $80.1 million for fiscal 2019, compared to $58.2 million for 2018. Higher revenues and higher gains on asset mainly contributed to the increase.

Cash at the end of fiscal 2019 was $42.2 million. Net cash provided by operating activities was $126.7 million, and financing activities added another $529 million to the coffers. Investing activities used $667.5 million for acquisition of real estate investments and developments.

Strategy

The company's primary business objective is to generate consistent shareholder returns by primarily investing in and actively managing a diversified portfolio of retail properties net leased to industry-leading tenants.

Its investment strategy is to expand and enhance its portfolio by identifying the best risk-adjusted investment opportunities across its development, Partner Capital Solutions (PCS) and acquisition platforms. It believes that development and PCS projects have the potential to generate superior risk-adjusted returns on investment in properties that are substantially similar to those it acquires.

Its financing strategy is to maintain a capital structure that provides it with the flexibility to manage its business and pursue its growth strategies while allowing it to service its debt requirements and generate appropriate risk-adjusted returns for its shareholders. The company believes these objectives are best achieved by a capital structure that consists primarily of common equity and prudent amounts of debt financing. However, it may raise capital in any form and under terms that it deemed acceptable and in the best interest of its shareholders.

Company Background

In 1971, Richard Agree, Executive Chairman of the Board of Directors founded Agree Development Company, the predecessor to Agree Realty Corporation. Over its 23 year history, Agree developed over 40 community shopping centers primarily throughout the Midwestern and Southeast United States.

With an Initial Public Offering of 2.5 million shares in 1994, Agree Realty Corporation commenced operations as a publicly traded Real Estate Investment Trust (REIT). Agree Realty is listed on the New York Stock Exchange under the ticker symbol ADC.

EXECUTIVES

Executive Chairman, Richard Agree, $149,967 total compensation
President, Chief Executive Officer, Director, Joel (Joey) N. Agree, $609,712 total compensation
People and Culture Executive Vice President, People and Culture Chief of Staff, Nicole Witteveen
Chief Financial Officer, Secretary, Peter Coughenou
Chief Operating Officer, Craig Erlich
Deputy Chief Accounting Officer, Stephen Breslin
General Counsel, Danielle Spehar
Lead Independent Director, Director, Gregory Lehmkuhl
Director, Michael Judlowe
Director, Jerome R. Rossi
Director, Merrie S. Frankel
Director, John Rakolta
Director, Karen J. Dearing
Director, Michael Hollman
Auditors : Grant Thornton LLP

LOCATIONS

HQ: Agree Realty Corp.
  70 E. Long Lake Road, Bloomfield Hills, MI 48304
Phone: 248 737-4190 **Fax:** 248 737-9110
Web: www.agreerealty.com

PRODUCTS/OPERATIONS

2015 sales

	in mil.	%of total
Minimum rents	64.3	92
operating cost reimbursement	5.3	8
Percentage rents	0.2	-
other income	0.2	-
Total	70.0	100

COMPETITORS

A & J MUCKLOW GROUP LIMITED
INVESTORS REAL ESTATE TRUST
KITE REALTY GROUP TRUST
LEXINGTON REALTY TRUST
REALTY INCOME CORPORATION

HISTORICAL FINANCIALS

Company Type: Public

Income Statement FYE: December 31

	REVENUE ($mil)	NET INCOME ($mil)	NET PROFIT MARGIN	EMPLOYEES
12/20	248.5	91.3	36.8%	49
12/19	187.4	80.0	42.7%	41
12/18	148.1	58.1	39.3%	36
12/17	116.5	58.1	49.9%	32
12/16	91.5	45.1	49.3%	24
Annual Growth	28.4%	19.3%	—	19.5%

2020 Year-End Financials
Debt ratio: 31.3%   No. of shares ($ mil.): 60.0
Return on equity: 4.3%   Dividends
Cash ($ mil.): 7.9   Yield: 3.6%
Current Ratio: 0.43   Payout: 138.2%
Long-term debt ($ mil.): 1,218.2   Market value ($ mil.): 3,996.0

	STOCK PRICE ($) FY Close	P/E High	P/E Low	PER SHARE ($) Earnings	PER SHARE ($) Dividends	PER SHARE ($) Book Value
12/20	66.58	45	28	1.74	2.41	42.06
12/19	70.17	40	29	1.93	2.28	37.07
12/18	59.12	35	25	1.78	2.16	32.92
12/17	51.44	25	21	2.08	2.03	29.31
12/16	46.05	26	16	1.97	1.92	26.10
Annual Growth	9.7%	—	—	(3.1%)	5.8%	12.7%

Air Lease Corp

Air Lease doesn't really lease air, unless of course you include the air inside the cabins of its fleet of airplanes. An aircraft leasing company, Air Lease buys new and used commercial aircraft from manufacturers and airlines and then leases to airline carriers in Europe, the Asia-Pacific region, and the Americas. It owns a fleet of almost 240 aircraft comprised of 181 single-aisle narrowbody jet aircraft, 40 twin-aisle widebody jet aircraft, and 19 turboprop aircraft. In addition to leasing, Air Lease also offers fleet management services such as lease management and sales.

Geographic Reach

Air Lease is based in Los Angeles and has airline customers throughout the world. Europe accounted for 32% of its net sales in 2015. Other markets included China (22%); Asia excluding China (19%); Central America, South America and Mexico (10%); the Middle East and Africa (8%); the US and Canada (5%); and the Pacific, Australia, and New Zealand (4%).

Sales and Marketing

Its customers have included Air Canada; Sunwing Airlines; WestJet; AeroMexico; Aeromar; Interjet; Volaris; Hawaiian Airlines; Southwest Airlines; Spirit Airlines; Sun Country; United Continental Holdings; Liat Airline; and Caribbean-Airlines.

Financial Performance

Air Lease has experienced explosive growth over the years, with revenues reaching a record-setting $1.22 billion in 2015. Profits also remained consistent, hovering around the $255 million mark, for both 2014 and 2015. The static profits for 2015 was attributed to about $72 million it paid in litigation settlement expenses. The company's cash from operating activities has gradually increased the last five years, climbing by 9% from 2014 to 2015.

The historic growth for 2015 was fueled by an 18% spike in the rental of flight equipment. This was aided by the delivery of 51 additional aircraft, all of which were leased at the time of delivery. Air Lease also enjoyed major growth in the key markets of the Middle East and Africa (89%); the Pacific, Australia, and New Zealand (52%), and China (21%).

Strategy

Although the largest portion of its fleet is leased to customers in Western Europe, Air Lease is setting its sights on markets in the Asia-Pacific region, Eastern Europe, South America, and the Middle East, where it predicts the travel industry will grow the fastest in coming years. It has also targeted carriers in stable, but slower-growing, travel markets such as North America.

One way Air Lease has achieved impressive revenue growth over the years is by adding to its fleet size. In 2015 it purchased and took delivery of 51 aircraft and sold 24 aircraft, ending the year with a total of 240 owned aircraft. During 2015, it increased its managed fleet by 12 aircraft, ending the year with 29 aircraft in its managed fleet portfolio. (The company typically sells aircraft that are currently operated by an airline with multiple years of lease term remaining on the contract.)

Company Background

Air Lease went public in 2011. Udvar-Házy and other Air Lease used a significant portion of the proceeds raised to acquire additional aircraft and for general corporate purposes. With sufficient capital and financing already in place, Air Lease has placed orders for some 150 new aircraft to be delivered by 2017. While most of its fleet will consist of Boeing and Airbus passenger airplanes, the company has ordered similar aircraft manufactured by Embraer and turboprops from Avions de Transport Régional (ATR).

Udvar-Házy had co-founded ILFC, now one of the largest aircraft leasing companies in the industry, in the 1970s. He stayed on after AIG bought ILFC in the 1990s and continued to head the company until 2010, when he retired in the wake of the ongoing financial trouble that hit AIG in 2008. Udvar-Házy subsequently founded Air Lease with the help of institutional investors, including some that were large shareholders prior to the IPO's filing (Ares Management, which held an 11% stake; Leonard Green & Partners, 11%; and Commonwealth Bank of Australia, 10%). Udvar-Házy maintained a 7% stake in Air Lease in 2013.

EXECUTIVES

Executive Chairman, Director, Steven F. Udvar-Hazy, $1,800,000 total compensation
President, Chief Executive Officer, Director, John L. Plueger, $1,000,000 total compensation
Commercial Affairs Executive Vice President, Marketing Executive Vice President, Grant A. Levy, $820,000 total compensation
Finance Executive Vice President, Finance Chief Financial Officer, Gregory B. Willis, $626,667 total compensation
Marketing Executive Vice President, Kishore Korde
Executive Vice President, Chief Compliance Officer, General Counsel, Corporate Secretary, Carol H. Forsyte
Director, Yvette Hollingsworth Clark
Director, Matthew J. Hart
Director, Cheryl Gordon Krongard
Director, Marshall O. Larsen
Director, Susan McCaw
Director, Robert A. Milton
Director, Ian M. Saines
Auditors : KPMG LLP

LOCATIONS

HQ: Air Lease Corp
2000 Avenue of the Stars, Suite 1000N, Los Angeles, CA 90067
Phone: 310 553-0555
Web: www.airleasecorp.com

PRODUCTS/OPERATIONS

2015 Sales

	$ mil.	% of total
Rental of flight equipment	1,174.5	96
Aircraft sales, trading and other	48.3	4
Total	1,222.8	100

COMPETITORS

AIRCASTLE LIMITED
ASHTEAD GROUP PUBLIC LIMITED COMPANY
ATLAS AIR WORLDWIDE HOLDINGS, INC.
CAI INTERNATIONAL, INC.
FLYBE GROUP LIMITED
HARSCO CORPORATION
HERC HOLDINGS INC.
SKYWEST, INC.
TRITON CONTAINER INTERNATIONAL, INCORPORATED OF NORTH AMERICA
WILLIS LEASE FINANCE CORPORATION

HISTORICAL FINANCIALS

Company Type: Public

Income Statement   FYE: December 31

	REVENUE ($mil)	NET INCOME ($mil)	NET PROFIT MARGIN	EMPLOYEES
12/21	2,088.3	436.6	20.9%	129
12/20	2,015.4	516.2	25.6%	120
12/19	2,016.9	587.1	29.1%	117
12/18	1,679.7	510.8	30.4%	97
12/17	1,516.3	756.1	49.9%	87
Annual Growth	8.3%	(12.8%)	—	10.3%

2021 Year-End Financials

Debt ratio: 63.1% No. of shares ($ mil.): 113.9
Return on equity: 6.6% Dividends
Cash ($ mil.): 1,086.5 Yield: 1.5%
Current Ratio: 1.47 Payout: 20.4%
Long-term debt ($ mil.): 17,022.4 Market value ($ mil.): 5,042.0

	STOCK PRICE ($) FY Close	P/E High/Low		PER SHARE ($) Earnings	Dividends	Book Value
12/21	44.23	15	10	3.57	0.67	61.49
12/20	44.42	11	2	4.39	0.61	53.33
12/19	47.52	9	6	5.09	0.54	49.61
12/18	30.21	10	6	4.60	0.43	43.32
12/17	48.09	7	5	6.82	0.33	39.83
Annual Growth	(2.1%)	—	—	(14.9%)	19.6%	11.5%

Air Transport Services Group, Inc.

Air Transport Services Group (ATSG) leases aircraft and provides airline operations, ground handling services, aircraft modification and maintenance services, and other support services to the air transportation and logistics industries. It is a leading provider of aircraft leasing and air cargo transportation services in the United States and internationally. In addition, it is a provider of passenger charter service to the United States Department of Defense ("DoD"). ATSG's Cargo Aircraft Management (CAM) subsidiary leases Boeing 777, 767, and 757 aircraft and aircraft engines. The company was founded in 1980.

Operations

The company has two reportable segments: ACMI Services (nearly 60%), which includes the airlines' operations and "CAM" (about 20% of the total sales).

CAM offers aircraft leasing and related services to external customers and also leases aircraft internally to the company's airlines. CAM acquires passenger aircraft and manages the modification of the aircraft into freighters. The follow-on aircraft leases normally cover a term of five to ten years. CAM currently leases Boeing 767, 757 and 777 aircraft and aircraft engines.

ACMI Services includes the cargo and passenger transportation operations of our three airlines. ATSG's airlines operate under contracts to provide a combination of aircraft, crews, maintenance, insurance and aviation fuel.

Geographic Reach

Based in Ohio, the company has its presence in Illinois, Florida and Oklahoma.

Sales and Marketing

The business development and marketing activities of its operating subsidiaries are supported by its Airborne Global Solutions, Inc. (AGS). The company have long-standing, strategic customer relationships with ASI, the

DoD, and DHL.

The DoD accounts for around 25% of sales, Amazon with around 35%, and DHL with over 10%.

Financial Performance

External customer revenues from continuing operations increased by $163.7 million, or 10%, to $1.7 billion during 2021 compared to 2020. Customer revenues increased in 2021 for contracted airline services, charter flights, aircraft leasing and aviation fuel sales, compared to the previous year periods.

Net income for fiscal 2021 increased to $229.0 million compared from the prior year with $25.1 million.

Cash held by the company at the end of fiscal 2021 increased to $69.5 million. Cash provided by operations was $583.6 million while cash used for investing and financing activities were $487.5 million and $66.3 million, respectively. Main uses of cash were expenditures for property and equipment; principal payments on long term obligations.

Strategy

ASTG's primary business segment is aircraft leasing. It acquires used medium wide-body and narrow-body passenger aircraft, manage their conversion into a freighter configuration leveraging its experience as an airline and lease the converted freighters to customers under long-term contracts. The aircraft the company target for conversion are ideal for express and e-commerce driven regional air networks. As a result, its aircraft can be deployed into regional markets more economically than larger capacity aircraft, newly built aircraft or other competing alternatives.

ATSG's business development and marketing efforts leverage the entire portfolio of its capabilities to create a customized bundled solution to meet its customers' needs. The company's ability to offer its customers differentiated services, including aircraft leasing, airline express operations, line and heavy maintenance, and ground handling services makes the company unique from other providers in its industry.

Company Background

ATSG was formed as a holding company in late 2007 from the reorganization of ABX.

EXECUTIVES

Chairman, Director, Joseph C. Hete, $750,000 total compensation
President, Chief Executive Officer, Director, Richard Francis Corrado, $484,615 total compensation
Chief Legal Officer, Secretary, W. Joseph Payne, $366,538 total compensation
Chief Operating Officer, Edward J. Koharik
Chief Strategy Officer, Michael L. Berger, $258,750 total compensation
Chief Financial Officer, Quint O. Turner, $414,231 total compensation
Chief Commercial Officer, Paul Chase
Lead Independent Director, Director, Randy D. Rademacher
Director, Phyllis J. Campbell
Director, Raymond E. Johns
Director, Laura J. Peterson
Director, John Christopher Teets
Director, Jeffrey J. Vorholt
Director, Paul S. Williams
Director, Jeffrey A. Dominick
Auditors: DELOITTE & TOUCHE LLP

LOCATIONS

HQ: Air Transport Services Group, Inc.
145 Hunter Drive, Wilmington, OH 45177
Phone: 937 382-5591
Web: www.atsginc.com

PRODUCTS/OPERATIONS

2014 Sales

	$ mil.	% of total
ACMI Services	439.9	59
CAM	166.3	22
Other	142.3	19
Adjustments	(158.9)	-
Total	589.6	100

Services
Aircraft leasing
ACMI services
Support services

COMPETITORS

ANA HOLDINGS INC.
ASTAR USA LLC
ATLAS AIR WORLDWIDE HOLDINGS, INC.
DHL EXPRESS (USA), INC.
Express ehf.
FEDEX CORPORATION
Flugfelagid Atlanta ehf.
HAECO AMERICAS, LLC
KALITTA AIR, L.L.C.
UNITED PARCEL SERVICE, INC.

HISTORICAL FINANCIALS

Company Type: Public

Income Statement — FYE: December 31

	REVENUE ($mil)	NET INCOME ($mil)	NET PROFIT MARGIN	EMPLOYEES
12/20	1,570.5	32.1	2.0%	5,305
12/19	1,452.1	61.2	4.2%	4,380
12/18	892.3	69.2	7.8%	3,830
12/17	1,068.2	18.4	1.7%	3,010
12/16	768.8	23.4	3.1%	3,230
Annual Growth	19.6%	8.1%	—	13.2%

2020 Year-End Financials

Debt ratio: 49.3%
Return on equity: 4.8%
Cash ($ mil.): 39.7
Current Ratio: 0.90
Long-term debt ($ mil.): 1,465.3
No. of shares ($ mil.): 59.5
Dividends
Yield: —
Payout: —
Market value ($ mil.): 1,867.0

	STOCK PRICE ($) FY Close	P/E High/Low		PER SHARE ($)		
				Earnings	Dividends	Book Value
12/20	31.34	59	26	0.54	0.00	14.36
12/19	23.46	25	19	0.79	0.00	7.76
12/18	22.81	23	15	0.91	0.00	7.38
12/17	23.14	82	48	0.31	0.00	6.69
12/16	15.96	45	24	0.37	0.00	5.58
Annual Growth	18.4%	—	—	9.9%	—	26.7%

Akamai Technologies Inc

Akamai Technologies provides solutions for securing and delivering content and business applications over the internet. The company's cloud services help its customers ? corporations and government agencies ? deliver digital content over the internet at optimal speeds and security. It also offers applications that supply network data feeds and website analytics to customers. With its software working from a network of more than 350,000 servers in over 130 countries, Akamai analyzes and manages web traffic, transmitting content from servers that are geographically closest to end users. Customers include IKEA, Sony Interactive Entertainment, Toshiba, WarnerMedia, the Coca-Cola Company, and PayPal. About 55% of the company's total revenue comes from the US.

Operations

At the heart of Akamai business is its Intelligent Edge Platform, which connects nearly 1,400 networks ranging from large, backbone network providers to medium and small internet service providers to cable modem and satellite providers to universities and other networks.

Akamai offers products and services that include cloud and enterprise security, web and mobile performance, media delivery, edge compute, carrier, and services and support.

The company reports revenue in two divisions according to the customers they serve. The Edge Technology Group accounts for nearly 60% of revenue and the Security Technology Group account for about 40% of revenue.

Geographic Reach

Akamai is based in Cambridge, Massachusetts and has several other sites in the US. Overseas, the company has operations in Santa Clara, California; Bangalore, India; and Krakow, Poland.

The share of international revenue has grown to more than 45% of Akamai's revenue with about 55% from the US customers.

Sales and Marketing

Akamai sells its products through a direct sales force as well as channel partners, such as AT&T, IBM, Orange Business Services,

Deutsche Telecom, and Spain's top telco, Telefonica. It also does business with public sector customers.

Other Akamai customers include many of the world's leading corporations, such as Autodesk, eBay, Electronic Arts, FedEx, Honda, Rabobank, Spotify, Toshiba, the US Department of Labor, the US Department of State, the US Department of Transportation and the US Department of the Treasury, the US Census Bureau, and the US Department of Defense.

Financial Performance

Akamai's revenue has been rising in the last five years. It has an overall increase of 39% between 2017 and 2021. Net income follows a similar trend with an overall increase of 192%.

The company's revenue for 2021 increased 8% to $3.5 billion. The increase in revenue in 2021 as compared to 2020 was primarily the result of continued strong growth in sales of solutions offered by the company's Security Technology Group.

In 2021, the company had a net income of $651.6 million, a 17% increase from the previous year's net income of $557.1 million.

The company's cash at the end of 2021 totaled $537.8 million, a 52% increase from the previous year's cash of $353.5 million. Operating activities generated $1.4 billion, while investing activities used $646.9 million, mainly for purchases of short-and long-term marketable securities. Financing activities used another $562 million, mainly for repurchases of common stock.

Strategy

Akamai regularly evaluates its portfolio of solutions and potential strategic acquisitions. It plans to continue to pursue potential strategic acquisitions that complement existing business, represent a strong strategic fit and are consistent with its overall growth strategy. The company may also target future acquisitions to expand or add functionality and capabilities to its existing portfolio of solutions.

Mergers and Acquisitions

In early 2022, Akamai acquired Linode, one of the easiest-to-use and most trusted infrastructure-as-a-service (IaaS) platform providers, for approximately $900 million. Linode's developer-friendly cloud computing capabilities combined with Akamai's market-leading edge platform and security services will provide businesses with a massively distributed platform to build, run and secure applications.

In late 221, Akamai acquired Tel Aviv, Israel-based Guardicore for approximately $600 million. By adding Guardicore's micro-segmentation solution into Akamai's extensive Zero Trust security portfolio, Akamai will be uniquely suited to provide comprehensive protections to the enterprise, defending against threat actors and the spread of malware and ransomware.

In early 2021, Akamai acquired Montreal-based Inverse for approximately $17.1 million. Inverse provides a robust data repository and world class algorithms capable of identifying an expansive universe of IoT, mobile and other device types. The acquisition is intended to enhance Akamai's enterprise security capabilities and expand its portfolio of zero trust and secure access service edge solutions for IoT.

Company Background

Tom Leighton, a mathematics professor at MIT, developed algorithms to help move traffic in the early days o the World Wide Web. In 1997, Leighton and his partners entered an entrepreneurship contest at MIT and finished in the top six. In 1998, they incorporated Akamai, licensing intellectual property from MIT. Most of the company's early employees were students who had worked on the project at MIT.

EXECUTIVES

Chairman, Frederic V. Salerno, $55,000 total compensation
Chief Executive Officer, Director, F. Thomson Leighton, $1 total compensation
Executive Vice President, General Counsel, Corporate Secretary, Aaron S. Ahola
Executive Vice President, Chief Financial Officer, Edward J. McGowan, $450,000 total compensation
Executive Vice President, Chief Marketing Officer, Kim Salem-Jackson
Executive Vice President, Division Officer, Mani Sundaram
Executive Vice President, Chief Human Resources Officer, Anthony Williams
Chief Operating Officer, Division Officer, Adam Karon, $425,000 total compensation
Chief Technology Officer, Robert Blumofe, $505,000 total compensation
Principal Financial Officer, Laura F. Howell
Division Officer, Paul C. Joseph
Director, Sharon Y. Bowen
Director, Marianne C. Brown
Director, Monte E. Ford
Director, Daniel R. Hesse
Director, Peter Thomas Killalea
Director, Jonathan Frank Miller
Director, Madhu Ranganathan
Director, Bernardus Johannes Maria Verwaayen
Director, William R. Wagner
Director, Jill A. Greenthal, $29,167 total compensation
Auditors : PricewaterhouseCoopers LLP

LOCATIONS

HQ: Akamai Technologies Inc
145 Broadway, Cambridge, MA 02142
Phone: 617 444-3000   **Fax:** 617 444-3001
Web: www.akamai.com

2017 Sales

	$ mil.	% of total
U.S.	1,648	66
International	855	34
Total	2,503	100

PRODUCTS/OPERATIONS

2018 Sales

	$ mil.	% of total
Web Division	1,446.1	53
Media Delivery Solutions	1,268.4	47
Total	2,714.5	100

PRODUCTS
Security
Media Delivery
Network Operator
Services
Web Performance

COMPETITORS

BROADSOFT, INC.
CA, INC.
CIENA CORPORATION
FIVE9, INC.
LIMELIGHT NETWORKS, INC.
MARKETO, INC.
MULESOFT, INC.
OKTA, INC.
SERVICENOW, INC.
SPLUNK INC.

HISTORICAL FINANCIALS

Company Type: Public

Income Statement — FYE: December 31

	REVENUE ($mil)	NET INCOME ($mil)	NET PROFIT MARGIN	EMPLOYEES
12/20	3,198.1	557.0	17.4%	8,368
12/19	2,893.6	478.0	16.5%	7,724
12/18	2,714.4	298.3	11.0%	7,519
12/17	2,502.9	218.3	8.7%	7,650
12/16	2,340.0	316.1	13.5%	6,490
Annual Growth	8.1%	15.2%	—	6.6%

2020 Year-End Financials
Debt ratio: 24.6%
Return on equity: 14.0%
Cash ($ mil.): 352.9
Current Ratio: 2.54
Long-term debt ($ mil.): 1,906.7
No. of shares ($ mil.): 162.7
Dividends
Yield: —
Payout: —
Market value ($ mil.): 17,083.0

	STOCK PRICE ($) FY Close	P/E High/Low		PER SHARE ($)		
		High	Low	Earnings	Dividends	Book Value
12/20	104.99	35	23	3.37	0.00	26.13
12/19	86.38	31	20	2.90	0.00	22.58
12/18	61.08	46	33	1.76	0.00	19.59
12/17	65.04	56	35	1.26	0.00	19.49
12/16	66.68	39	22	1.79	0.00	18.61
Annual Growth	12.0%	—	—	17.1%	—	8.9%

Alamo Group, Inc.

Alamo Group is a leader in the design and manufacture of high quality agricultural equipment and infrastructure maintenance equipment for governmental and industrial use. Its branded lines, Alamo Industrial and Tiger hydraulically powered tractor-mounted mowers, serve US government agencies.

Rhino Products and M&W Gear subsidiaries sell rotary cutters and other equipment to farmers for pasture upkeep. UK McConnel and Bomford, and France's S.M.A. subsidiaries market vegetation maintenance equipment, such as hydraulic boom-mounted hedge and grass mowers. The company generates the majority of revenue domestically.

Operations
Alamo has two reportable segments: the Vegetation Division and the Industrial Equipment Division.

The Vegetation Management Division includes all of the operations of the former Agricultural Division plus the mowing and forestry/tree care operations that were previously part of the former Industrial Division. The Industrial Equipment Division includes the Company's vocational truck business and other industrial operations such as excavators, vacuum trucks, street sweepers, and snow removal equipment.

Geographic Reach
Alamo operates about 30 plants in North America, South America, Europe, and Australia. The US generates more than 70% of its sales. Other major markets include France (over 5%), the UK (approximately 5%), Canada (some 5%), and Australia. The company is headquartered in Seguin, Texas.

Sales and Marketing
Alamo sells its products primarily through a network of independent dealers and distributors to governmental end-users, related independent contractors, as well as to the agricultural and commercial turf markets.

Advertising and marketing expense related to operations for fiscal years 2021, 2020, and 2019 was approximately $10.2 million, $10.1 million and $12.2 million, respectively.

Financial Performance
The company's net sales in 2021 were $1.3 billion, an increase of $170.7 million or 15% compared to $1.2 billion in 2020. The increase in sales was attributable to the continued strong recovery in customer demand for its products in both the Vegetation Management and the Industrial Equipment Divisions.

Net income in 2021 increased to $80.2 million compared with $57.8 million in the prior year, primarily due to a strong recovery in customer demand for its products compared to the prior year where demand for its products was materially impacted as a result of the onset of the COVID-19 pandemic.

Cash held by the company at the end of fiscal 2021 decreased to $42.1 million. Cash provided by operations was $49.7 million while investing and financing activities used $33.4 million and $23.0 million, respectively. Main cash were purchase of property, plant and equipment; and repayment on bank revolving credit facility.

Mergers and Acquisitions
In late 2021, Alamo acquired 100% of the outstanding capital shares of Timberwolf Limited (Timberwolf), a manufacturer a broad range of commercial wood chippers primarily serving markets in the UK and the European Union. Jeff Leonard, Alamo Group's President and Chief Executive Officer commented, "We are delighted to have completed our acquisition of Timberwolf. The company offers a full range of gravity fed, towed, track mounted and PTO-driven chippers for arboriculture, horticulture, private estates and infrastructure management. Timberwolf builds upon, and complements our existing range of tree care products and strengthens our presence in the U.K. and European forestry and tree care markets. We are pleased that Timberwolf's management team will remain with the company and we look forward to working closely with them to drive the company's future growth."

EXECUTIVES

Chairman, Director, Roderick R. Baty
President, Chief Executive Officer, Director, Jeffery A. Leonard, $368,846 total compensation
Executive Vice President, Chief Financial Officer, Richard J. Wehrle, $160,746 total compensation
Executive Vice President, General Counsel, Secretary, Edward T. Rizzuti
Executive Vice President, Chief Sustainability Officer, Dan E. Malone, $314,077 total compensation
Division Officer, Richard H. Raborn, $329,115 total compensation
Division Officer, Michael A. Haberman
Director, Ronald A. Robinson, $695,254 total compensation
Director, Robert P. Bauer
Director, Eric P. Etchart
Director, Nina C. Grooms
Director, Tracy C. Jokinen
Director, Richard W. Parod
Director, Lorie L. Tekorius
Auditors : KPMG LLP

LOCATIONS

HQ: Alamo Group, Inc.
1627 East Walnut, Seguin, TX 78155
Phone: 830 379-1480   Fax: 830 372-9683
Web: www.alamo-group.com

2014 Sales

	$ mil.	% of total
USA	571.8	68
France	93.7	11
UK	59.0	7
Canada	54.1	6
Australia	13.7	2
Other regions	46.8	6
Total	839.1	100

PRODUCTS/OPERATIONS

2014 Sales

	$ mil.	% of total
North American		
Industrial	436.0	52
Agricultural	214.4	26
European	188.7	22
Total	839.1	100

Selected Products
Boom mowers/power arms
Excavators
Flail mowers
Loader/backhoes
Rotary mowers
Snow removal equipment
Street sweepers
Vacuum trucks

COMPETITORS

ALLIANCE LAUNDRY HOLDINGS LLC
ASTEC INDUSTRIES, INC.
BLOUNT INTERNATIONAL, INC.
CATERPILLAR INC.
CNH INDUSTRIAL N.V.
DEERE & COMPANY
DOUGLAS DYNAMICS, INC.
GENCOR INDUSTRIES, INC.
HITACHI CONSTRUCTION MACHINERY CO., LTD.
KOBELCO CONSTRUCTION MACHINERY AMERICA LLC

HISTORICAL FINANCIALS

Company Type: Public

Income Statement — FYE: December 31

	REVENUE ($mil)	NET INCOME ($mil)	NET PROFIT MARGIN	EMPLOYEES
12/20	1,163.4	56.6	4.9%	3,990
12/19	1,119.1	62.9	5.6%	4,270
12/18	1,008.8	73.4	7.3%	3,470
12/17	912.3	44.3	4.9%	3,280
12/16	844.7	40.0	4.7%	2,900
Annual Growth	8.3%	9.0%	—	8.3%

2020 Year-End Financials

Debt ratio: 25.7%
Return on equity: 9.4%
Cash ($ mil.): 50.2
Current Ratio: 3.20
Long-term debt ($ mil.): 270.3
No. of shares ($ mil.): 11.8
Dividends
Yield: 0.3%
Payout: 10.8%
Market value ($ mil.): 1,629.0

	STOCK PRICE ($) FY Close	P/E High/Low		PER SHARE ($) Earnings	Dividends	Book Value
12/20	137.95	30	16	4.78	0.52	52.98
12/19	125.55	24	14	5.33	0.48	48.48
12/18	77.32	19	12	6.25	0.44	43.50
12/17	112.87	31	19	3.79	0.40	38.79
12/16	76.10	22	14	3.46	0.36	33.95
Annual Growth	16.0%	—	—	8.4%	9.6%	11.8%

Alarm.com Holdings Inc

EXECUTIVES

Chairman, Director, Timothy McAdam
Chief Executive Officer, Director, Stephen Trundle, $210,000 total compensation

Corporate Development Chief Legal Officer, Corporate Development Chief Compliance Officer, Corporate Development Division Officer, Daniel Ramos, $300,000 total compensation
Chief Financial Officer, Steve Valenzuela, $341,667 total compensation
Division Officer, Jeffrey A. Bedell, $304,167 total compensation
Division Officer, Daniel Kerzner, $288,333 total compensation
Director, Donald E. Clarke
Director, Timothy J. Whall
Director, Simone Wu
Director, Stephen C. Evans
Director, Darius G. Nevin
Auditors : PricewaterhouseCoopers LLP

LOCATIONS

HQ: Alarm.com Holdings Inc
  8281 Greensboro Drive, Suite 100, Tysons, VA 22102
Phone: 877 389-4033
Web: www.alarm.com

HISTORICAL FINANCIALS
Company Type: Public

Income Statement — FYE: December 31

	REVENUE ($mil)	NET INCOME ($mil)	NET PROFIT MARGIN	EMPLOYEES
12/20	618.0	77.8	12.6%	1,404
12/19	502.3	53.5	10.7%	1,160
12/18	420.4	21.5	5.1%	884
12/17	338.9	29.2	8.6%	784
12/16	261.1	10.1	3.9%	607
Annual Growth	24.0%	66.4%	—	23.3%

2020 Year-End Financials
Debt ratio: 15.0%
Return on equity: 18.8%
Cash ($ mil.): 253.4
Current Ratio: 4.40
Long-term debt ($ mil.): 110
No. of shares ($ mil.): 49.4
Dividends
  Yield: —
  Payout: —
Market value ($ mil.): 5,119.0

	STOCK PRICE ($) FY Close	P/E High/Low		PER SHARE ($) Earnings	Dividends	Book Value
12/20	103.45	65	22	1.53	0.00	9.45
12/19	42.97	64	37	1.06	0.00	7.30
12/18	51.87	130	78	0.43	0.00	5.77
12/17	37.75	78	43	0.59	0.00	4.93
12/16	27.83	150	65	0.21	0.00	4.14
Annual Growth	38.9%	—	—	64.3%	—	22.9%

Alerus Financial Corp

EXECUTIVES

President, Chief Executive Officer, Subsidiary Officer, Chairman, Director, Randy L. Newman
Executive Vice President, Chief Financial Officer, Dan J. Cheever
Executive Vice President, Division Officer, Karl A. Bollingberg
Corporate Development Executive Vice President, Corporate Development Director, Corporate Development General Counsel, Jay Kim
Market Management Executive Vice President, David Latta
Executive Vice President, Chief Shared Services Officer, Ann M. McConn
Consumer Segment Chief Information Officer, Consumer Segment Division Officer, Jon N. Hendry
Senior Wealth Management Advisor, Sandy Korbel
Chief Operating Officer, Kris E. Compton
Division Officer, Dan Doeden
Division Officer, Jan Fitzer
Division Officer, David Norris
Division Officer, Deb Otto
Division Officer, Brian Overby
Division Officer, Rob Schwister
Division Officer, Chris Wolf
Division Officer, Sara Ausman
Division Officer, Nels Carlson
Division Officer, John G. Flesch
Chief Lending Officer, Dan Jacobson
Securities Head, Brian Kraft
Chief Deposit Officer, Karna Loyland
Director, Daniel E. Coughlin
Director, Michael S. Mathews
Director, Kevin D. Lemke
Director, James J. Karley
Director, Harold A. Gershman
Director, Karen M. Bohn
Director, Lloyd G. Case
Director, Sally J. Smith
Director, A. Bart Holaday
Director, Galen G. Vetter
Auditors : CliftonLarsonAllen LLP

LOCATIONS

HQ: Alerus Financial Corp
  401 Demers Avenue, Grand Forks, ND 58201
Phone: 701 795-3200   **Fax:** 701 795-3378
Web: www.alerus.com

HISTORICAL FINANCIALS
Company Type: Public

Income Statement — FYE: December 31

	ASSETS ($mil)	NET INCOME ($mil)	INCOME AS % OF ASSETS	EMPLOYEES
12/20	3,013.7	44.6	1.5%	851
12/19	2,356.8	29.5	1.3%	789
12/18	2,179.0	25.8	1.2%	0
12/17	2,137.0	15.4	0.7%	0
12/16	2,050.5	14.0	0.7%	0
Annual Growth	10.1%	33.6%	—	—

2020 Year-End Financials
Return on assets: 1.6%
Return on equity: 14.4%
Long-term debt ($ mil.): —
No. of shares ($ mil.): 17.1
Sales ($ mil.): 245.4
Dividends
  Yield: 2.1%
  Payout: 25.4%
Market value ($ mil.): 469.0

	STOCK PRICE ($) FY Close	P/E High/Low		PER SHARE ($) Earnings	Dividends	Book Value
12/20	27.37	11	6	2.52	0.60	19.28
12/19	22.85	12	10	1.91	0.57	16.76
12/18	19.25	14	10	1.84	0.53	14.30
12/17	20.45	18	15	1.10	0.48	13.18
12/16	17.00	19	16	1.00	0.44	12.47
Annual Growth	12.6%	—	—	26.0%	8.1%	11.5%

Alexandria Real Estate Equities Inc

Alexandria Real Estate Equities owns, develops, and operates offices and labs to life science tenants including biotech and pharmaceutical companies, universities, research institutions, medical office developers, and government agencies. A real estate investment trust (REIT), Alexandria owns approximately 415 specialized properties with approximately 43.7 million sq. ft. of rentable space in the US and Canada. Its portfolio is largely located in high-tech hotbeds such as Boston, greater New York City, the San Francisco Bay area, San Diego, Seattle, and Research Triangle. The company was founded in 1994.

Operations
The company engaged in the business of providing space for lease to the life science, technology, and agtech industries. Its properties are similar in that they provide space for lease to the aforementioned industries, consist of improvements that are generic and reusable, are primarily located in AAA urban innovation cluster locations, and have similar economic characteristics. Most of its revenues came from rentals.

Geographic Reach
The company has about 415 properties in North America containing approximately 38.8 million RSF of operating properties and development and redevelopment of new Class A properties (under construction), including about 55 properties that are held by consolidated real estate joint ventures and four properties that are held by unconsolidated real estate joint ventures. Greater Boston consists about 85 properties and is the highest in terms of annual rental which accounts for more than 35%.

Its corporate headquarters is located in Pasadena, California.

Sales and Marketing
Bristol-Myers, Takeda, Moderna, Illumina, and Sanofi are among the REIT's top largest tenants (though none account for more than 5% of its overall rental revenues).

Financial Performance
For the year ended 2021, the company had a total revenue of $2.1 billion, an 11% increase from the previous year's total revenue

of $1.9 million. The increase was primarily due to a higher sales volume in the company's income from rentals.

In 2021, the company had a net income of $654.3 million, a 21% decrease from the previous year's net income of $827.2 million.

The company's cash at the end of 2021 was $415.2 million. Operating activities generated $1 billion, while investing activities used $7.1 billion, primarily for purchases of real estate. Financing activities provided another $5.9 billion.

Strategy

The company's primary business objective is to maximize long-term asset value and shareholder returns based on a multifaceted platform of internal and external growth. A key element of its strategy is its unique focus on Class A properties clustered in urban campuses located in AAA innovation cluster locations. These key urban campus locations are characterized by high barriers to entry for new landlords, high barriers to exit for tenants, and a limited supply of available space. They represent highly desirable locations for tenancy by life science, technology, and agtech entities because of their close proximity to concentrations of specialized skills, knowledge, institutions, and related businesses.

Its strategy also includes drawing upon its deep and broad real estate, life science, technology, and agtech relationships in order to identify and attract new and leading tenants and to source additional value-creation real estate.

EXECUTIVES

Executive Chairman, Director, Joel S. Marcus, $1,010,000 total compensation
Co-President, Chief Financial Officer, Dean A. Shigenaga, $595,000 total compensation
Co-President, Region Officer, Thomas J. Andrews, $595,000 total compensation
Co-Chief Executive Officer, Stephen A. Richardson, $625,000 total compensation
Co-Chief Executive Officer, Co-Chief Investment Officer, Peter M. Moglia, $625,000 total compensation
Finance Executive Vice President, Finance Treasurer, Marc E. Binda
Executive Vice President, Region Officer, Terezia C. Nemeth
Executive Vice President, Region Officer, John H. Cunningham
Legal Affairs Senior Vice President, Real Estate Senior Vice President, Legal Affairs Secretary, Real Estate Secretary, Legal Affairs General Counsel, Real Estate General Counsel, Jackie Clem
Chief Development Officer, Vincent R. Ciruzzi, $247,500 total compensation
Chief Strategic Transactions Officer, Co-Chief Operating Officer, Joseph Hakman
Chief Accounting Officer, Andres R. Gavinet
Co-Chief Investment Officer, Region Officer, Daniel J. Ryan, $595,000 total compensation
Co-Chief Operating Officer, Region Officer, Lawrence J. Diamond
Lead Director, Director, Steven R. Hash
Director, John L. Atkins
Director, James P. Cain
Director, Maria C. Freire
Director, Jennifer Friel Goldstein
Director, Richard H. Klein
Director, James H. Richardson, $67,904 total compensation
Director, Michael A. Woronoff
Auditors : Ernst & Young LLP

LOCATIONS

HQ: Alexandria Real Estate Equities Inc
26 North Euclid Avenue, Pasadena, CA 91101
Phone: 626 578-0777
Web: www.are.com

2015 Properties

	No.
US	
San Diego	51
Greater Boston	44
San Francisco Bay	29
Maryland	28
North Carolina - Research Triangle Park	15
Seattle	11
New York City	2
Asia	8
Canada	4
Held for sale	1
Other	6
Total	199

PRODUCTS/OPERATIONS

2015 Sales

	$ mil.	% of total
Rental	608.8	72
Tenant recoveries	209.1	25
Other	25.6	3
Total	843.5	100

2015 Client Tenant Mix by ABR

	% of total
Public Biotechnology	26
Multinational Pharmaceutical	22
Life Science Product, Service, and Device	22
Institutional	20
Private Biotechnology	7
Office & Tech Office	3
Total	100

COMPETITORS

BIOMED REALTY TRUST, INC.
CENTERPOINT PROPERTIES TRUST
FEDERAL REALTY INVESTMENT TRUST
FRANKLIN STREET PROPERTIES CORP.
JBG SMITHPROPERTIES
LINCOLN PROPERTY COMPANY
MEREDITH ENTERPRISES, INC.
PERKINS EASTMAN ARCHITECTS, D.P.C.
PIEDMONT OFFICE REALTY TRUST, INC.
THE INTERGROUP CORPORATION

HISTORICAL FINANCIALS

Company Type: Public

Income Statement — FYE: December 31

	REVENUE ($mil)	NET INCOME ($mil)	NET PROFIT MARGIN	EMPLOYEES
12/21	2,114.1	571.2	27.0%	559
12/20	1,885.6	770.9	40.9%	470
12/19	1,531.2	363.1	23.7%	439
12/18	1,327.4	379.3	28.6%	386
12/17	1,128.0	169.0	15.0%	323
Annual Growth	17.0%	35.6%	—	14.7%

2021 Year-End Financials

Debt ratio: 29.1% No. of shares ($ mil.): 158.0
Return on equity: 4.0% Dividends
Cash ($ mil.): 415.2 Yield: 2.0%
Current Ratio: 0.18 Payout: 66.5%
Long-term debt ($ mil.): 8,791.8 Market value ($ mil.): 35,237.0

	STOCK PRICE ($) FY Close	P/E High/Low		PER SHARE ($) Earnings	Dividends	Book Value
12/21	222.96	58	41	3.82	4.48	102.44
12/20	178.22	29	19	6.01	4.24	85.78
12/19	161.58	52	36	3.12	4.00	73.39
12/18	115.24	37	31	3.52	3.73	66.14
12/17	130.59	84	68	1.58	3.45	59.63
Annual Growth	14.3%	—	—	24.7%	6.7%	14.5%

Align Technology Inc

Align Technology is a global medical device company engaged in the design, manufacture and marketing of Invisalign clear aligners and iTero intraoral scanners and services for dentistry, and exocad computer-aided design and computer-aided manufacturing (CAD/CAM) software for dental laboratories and dental practitioners. Its products are intended primarily for the treatment of malocclusion or the misalignment of teeth and are designed to help dental professionals achieve the clinical outcomes that they expect and the results patients' desire. To date, over 12 million people worldwide have been treated with Invisalign System. Most of the company's revenue comes from the US.

Operations

Align operates into two reportable segments: Clear Aligner segment and Imaging Systems and CAD/CAM services (Systems and Services) segment.

Clear Aligner segment consists of comprehensive products (Invisalign Comprehensive and Invisalign First), non-comprehensive products (Invisalign Moderate, Lite and Express packages and Invisalign Go) and non-case (Vivera retainers along with its training and ancillary products for treating malocclusion). The segment accounts for about 80% of total revenue.

The Systems and Services segment consists of its iTero intraoral scanning systems, which includes a single hardware platform and restorative or orthodontic software options, OrthoCAD services and ancillary products, as well as exocad's CAD/CAM software solution that integrates workflows to dental labs and dental practices. The segment generates roughly 20% of total revenue.

Geographic Reach

Tempe, Arizona-based Align has Americas regional headquarters in Raleigh, North Carolina; EMEA regional headquarters in Rotkreuz, Switzerland; and Asia Pacific regional headquarters in Singapore.

Manufacturing facilities are located in Juarez, Mexico, and Ziyang, China, where it conducts aligner fabrication, distributes and repairs scanners, and performs CAD/CAM services. In addition, Align produces its handheld intraoral scanner wand, perform final scanner assembly and repair its scanners at its facilities in Or Yehuda, Israel and Ziyang, China. It also performs digital treatment planning and interpretation for restorative cases based on digital scans generated by its iTerointraoral scanners. The digital treatment planning facilities are located worldwide, including in Costa Rica, China, Germany, Spain, Poland, and Japan, among other international locations.

About 45% of revenue comes from the US, while some 35% are generated from Switzerland and more than 20% of revenue from China and other countries.

Sales and Marketing

Align sells the majority of its products directly through a dedicated and specialized sales force to its customers: orthodontists, general practitioner dentists (GPs), restorative and aesthetic dentists, including prosthodontists, periodontists, and oral surgeons, and dental laboratories. It also sells through non-inventory carrying sales agents and distributors in certain countries. In addition, Align sells directly to Dental Support Organizations (DSOs) who contract with dental practices to provide critical business management and support including non-clinical operations, and it sell products used by dental laboratories who manufacture or customize a variety of products used by licensed dentists to provide oral health care. Align sells its consumer products online through its corporate website and large e-commerce websites.

Because the teenage and younger market makes up to about 75% of the approximately 21million total orthodontic case starts each year, the company continues to target teenage and younger patients through sales and marketing programs. Align has approximately 122,500 active Invisalign trained doctors, which the company defines as having submitted at least one case in the prior 12-month period.

The cost of advertising and media for 2021, 2020, and 2019 was $325.6 million, $161.0 million, and $119.1 million, respectively.

Financial Performance

Company's revenue for fiscal 2021 increased by 60% to $4.0 billion compared from the prior year with $2.5 billion.

Net income for fiscal 2021 decreased to $772.0 million compared from the prior year with $1.8 billion.

Cash held by the company at the end of fiscal 2021 increased to $1.1 billion. Cash provided by operations was $1.2 billion while cash used for investing and financing activities were $563.4 million and $458.3 million, respectively. Main uses of cash were purchase of property, plant and equipment; and common stock repurchases.

Strategy

Align's technology and innovations are designed to meet the demands of today's patients with treatment options that are convenient, comfortable, and affordable, while helping to improve overall oral health. The company strive to help doctors and lab technicians move their businesses forward by connecting them with new patients, providing digital solutions that increase operational speed and efficiency and provide solutions that allow them to deliver the best possible treatment outcomes and experiences to millions of people around the world. Align achieve this by focusing on and executing to its strategic growth drivers: international expansion; GP adoption; patient demand & conversion; and orthodontist utilization.

Company Background

In 1997, five employees in a small duplex in Redwood City, California, founded Align Technology with a single concept in mind ? how to leverage technology to straighten teeth. In 1999, Align Technology introduced the Invisalign system and sublaunched a large US national advertising campaign. The company went public in 2001, at which point it had manufactured one million unique aligners and trained more than ten thousand doctors.

EXECUTIVES

Chairman, Director, C. Raymond Larkin
President, Chief Executive Officer, Joseph (Joe) M. Hogan, $1,130,000 total compensation
Finance Senior Vice President, Finance Chief Financial Officer, John F. Morici, $500,000 total compensation
Business Development Senior Vice President, Product Senior Vice President, Business Development Chief Marketing Officer, Product Chief Marketing Officer, Raj Pudipeddi
Senior Vice President, Region Officer, Julie Tay
Senior Vice President, Division Officer, Jennifer Olson
Senior Vice President, Region Officer, Simon M. Beard
Senior Vice President, Chief Legal Officer, Chief Regulatory Officer, Julie Coletti
Legal Affairs Senior Vice President, Corporate Affairs Senior Vice President, Legal Affairs Chief Legal Officer, Corporate Affairs Chief Legal Officer, Legal Affairs Chief Regulatory Officer, Corporate Affairs Chief Regulatory Officer, Roger E. George, $410 total compensation
Research Senior Vice President, Development Senior Vice President, Research Chief Technology Officer, Development Chief Technology Officer, Zelko Relic, $423,077 total compensation
Information Technology Senior Vice President, Sreelakshmi Kolli
Global Human Resources Senior Vice President, Stuart A. Hockridge, $420,000 total compensation
Operations Senior Vice President, Emory M. Wright, $438,462 total compensation
Director, Kevin Dallas
Director, Joseph S. Lacob
Director, George J. Morrow
Director, Anne Myong
Director, Thomas M. Prescott, $705,000 total compensation
Director, Andrea Lynn Saia
Director, Greg J. Santora
Director, Susan E. Siegel
Director, Warren S. Thaler
Auditors : PricewaterhouseCoopers LLP

LOCATIONS

HQ: Align Technology Inc
410 North Scottsdale Road, Suite 1300, Tempe, AZ 85281
Phone: 602 742-2000
Web: www.aligntech.com

2017 Sales

	$ mil.	% of total
US	836.2	57
Netherlands	456.1	31
Other	181.1	12
Total	1,473.4	100

PRODUCTS/OPERATIONS

2017 Sales by Segment

	$ mil.	% of total
Clear Align	1,309.3	89
Scanner	164.1	11
Total	1,473.4	100

COMPETITORS

ACCURAY INCORPORATED
ASENSUS SURGICAL, INC.
BIOLASE, INC.
DENTSPLY SIRONA INC.
HU-FRIEDY MFG. CO., LLC
MILESTONE SCIENTIFIC INC.
ORMCO CORPORATION
SYBRON DENTAL SPECIALTIES, INC.
TRIVASCULAR TECHNOLOGIES, INC.
YOUNG INNOVATIONS, INC.

HISTORICAL FINANCIALS
Company Type: Public

Income Statement — FYE: December 31

	REVENUE ($mil)	NET INCOME ($mil)	NET PROFIT MARGIN	EMPLOYEES
12/20	2,471.9	1,775.8	71.8%	18,070
12/19	2,406.7	442.7	18.4%	14,530
12/18	1,966.4	400.2	20.4%	11,660
12/17	1,473.4	231.4	15.7%	8,715
12/16	1,079.8	189.6	17.6%	6,060
Annual Growth	23.0%	74.9%	—	31.4%

2020 Year-End Financials
Debt ratio: —
Return on equity: 77.3%
Cash ($ mil.): 960.8
Current Ratio: 1.40
Long-term debt ($ mil.): —
No. of shares ($ mil.): 78.8
Dividends
Yield: —
Payout: —
Market value ($ mil.): 42,141.0

	STOCK PRICE ($) FY Close	P/E High/Low		PER SHARE ($) Earnings	Dividends	Book Value
12/20	534.38	24	6	22.41	0.00	41.01
12/19	279.04	59	31	5.53	0.00	17.16
12/18	209.43	79	39	4.92	0.00	15.70
12/17	222.19	91	31	2.83	0.00	14.37
12/16	96.13	42	25	2.33	0.00	12.51
Annual Growth	53.5%	—	—	76.1%	—	34.5%

Allegiance Bancshares Inc

Auditors: Crowe LLP

LOCATIONS
HQ: Allegiance Bancshares Inc
8847 West Sam Houston Parkway, N., Suite 200,
Houston, TX 77040
Phone: 281 894-3200
Web: www.allegiancebank.com

HISTORICAL FINANCIALS
Company Type: Public

Income Statement — FYE: December 31

	ASSETS ($mil)	NET INCOME ($mil)	INCOME AS % OF ASSETS	EMPLOYEES
12/20	6,050.1	45.5	0.8%	598
12/19	4,992.6	52.9	1.1%	588
12/18	4,655.2	37.3	0.8%	569
12/17	2,860.2	17.6	0.6%	375
12/16	2,450.9	22.8	0.9%	327
Annual Growth	25.3%	18.8%	—	16.3%

2020 Year-End Financials
Return on assets: 0.8%
Return on equity: 6.1%
Long-term debt ($ mil.): —
No. of shares ($ mil.): 20.2
Sales ($ mil.): 249.9
Dividends
Yield: 1.1%
Payout: 19.0%
Market value ($ mil.): 690.0

	STOCK PRICE ($) FY Close	P/E High/Low		PER SHARE ($) Earnings	Dividends	Book Value
12/20	34.13	17	10	2.22	0.40	37.54
12/19	37.60	16	12	2.47	0.00	34.59
12/18	32.37	19	12	2.37	0.00	32.04
12/17	37.65	30	23	1.31	0.00	23.20
12/16	36.15	21	9	1.75	0.00	21.59
Annual Growth	(1.4%)	—	—	6.1%	—	14.8%

AllianceBernstein Holding LP

The raison d'etre of AllianceBernstein Holding is its more than 35% stake in investment manager AllianceBernstein. (French insurer AXA, through its AXA Financial unit, owns a majority of the subsidiary.) AllianceBernstein, which has more than $420 million of client assets under management, administers about 200 mutual funds invested in growth and value equities, fixed-income securities, and index and blended strategies. The subsidiary also offer separately managed accounts, closed-end funds, structured financial products, and alternative investments such as hedge funds. It mainly serves institutional clients such as pension funds, corporations, and not-for-profits, in addition to retail investors.

EXECUTIVES
Chairman, Joan M. Lamm-Tennant
President, Chief Executive Officer, Director, Seth P. Bernstein, $500,000 total compensation
Interim Chief Financial Officer, Chief Accounting Officer, Controller, William R. Siemers
Human Capital Chief Operating Officer, Kate C. Burke, $300,000 total compensation
Global Technology and Operations Head, Karl Sprules
Director, Nella L. Domenici
Director, Jeffrey J. Hurd
Director, Daniel G. Kaye
Director, Nicholas Lane
Director, Kristi Matus
Director, Das Narayandas
Director, Mark Pearson
Director, Charles G. T. Stonehill
Director, Todd Walthall
Auditors: PricewaterhouseCoopers LLP

LOCATIONS
HQ: AllianceBernstein Holding LP
501 Commerce Street, Nashville, TN 37203
Phone: 615 622-0000
Web: www.alliancebernstein.com

HISTORICAL FINANCIALS
Company Type: Public

Income Statement — FYE: December 31

	REVENUE ($mil)	NET INCOME ($mil)	NET PROFIT MARGIN	EMPLOYEES
12/21	416.3	385.8	92.7%	4,118
12/20	308.4	279.3	90.6%	3,929
12/19	266.2	238.5	89.6%	3,811
12/18	270.6	242.3	89.6%	3,641
12/17	232.3	207.4	89.3%	3,466
Annual Growth	15.7%	16.8%	—	4.4%

2021 Year-End Financials
Debt ratio: —
Return on equity: —
Cash ($ mil.): —
Current Ratio: —
Long-term debt ($ mil.): —
No. of shares ($ mil.): 99.2
Dividends
Yield: 7.3%
Payout: 100.9%
Market value ($ mil.): 4,848.0

	STOCK PRICE ($) FY Close	P/E High/Low		PER SHARE ($) Earnings	Dividends	Book Value
12/21	48.84	15	9	3.88	3.58	16.34
12/20	33.77	12	5	2.88	2.79	16.32
12/19	30.26	13	11	2.49	2.32	15.81
12/18	27.32	12	9	2.50	2.88	15.42
12/17	25.05	12	9	2.19	2.13	16.00
Annual Growth	18.2%	—	—	15.4%	13.9%	0.5%

Allied Motion Technologies Inc

Allied Motion Technologies is a global company that designs, manufactures and sells precision and specialty controlled motion components and systems. The company makes specialized brush and brushless DC (BLDC) motors, and brushless drives used in broad range of industries. Its products are incorporated into a number of end products, including high-definition printers, scanners, surgical tools and equipment, surgical robots, diagnostic equipment, test equipment, patient mobility and rehabilitation equipment, hospital beds and mobile equipment carts. Allied Motion's target markets include vehicle, aerospace and defense, industrial, and medical. The company was incorporated in 1962. The US was responsible for about 60% of the total sales.

Operations
The company operates in one segment for the manufacture and marketing of controlled motion products for OEM and end user applications. Its target markets are vehicle (a third of the total sales), industrial (a third), medical (around 20%), and aerospace and defense (around 10%).

In vehicles, it focuses on electronic power steering and drive-by-wire applications to electrically replace, or provide power-assist to a variety of mechanical linkages, traction / drive systems and pumps, automated and remotely guided power steering systems. It includes HVAC systems, LPG and others.

In medical, it centers on surgical robots, prosthetics, electric powered surgical hand pieces, programmable pumps to meter and administer infusions associated with chemotherapy, pain control and antibiotics.

In Aerospace & Defense, it includes inertial guided missiles, mid-range smart munitions systems, weapons systems on armed personnel carriers, unmanned vehicles, security and access control, camera systems, door access control, airport screening and scanning devices.

Lastly, Industrial products are used in factory automation, specialty equipment, material handling equipment, commercial grade floor polishers and cleaners, commercial building equipment such as welders, cable pullers and assembly tools, the handling, inspection, and testing of components and final products such as PCs, gaming equipment and cell phone.

Geographic Reach

The company manufactures its products in the US, Canada, China, Germany, Portugal, Mexico, Czech Republic, the Netherlands, and Great Britain. The US accounts for nearly 60% sales, followed by Europe with some 35%, and Asia Pacific with around 10%.

The company is headquartered in Amherst, New York.

Sales and Marketing

The company sells the products and solutions globally to a broad spectrum of customers through direct sales force and authorized manufacturers' representatives and distributors. The customers include end users and original equipment manufacturers (OEMs). The target markets include Vehicle, Medical, Aerospace & Defense (A&D), and Industrial.

Financial Performance

The company's revenue in 2021 increased by 10% to $403.5 million compared with $366.7 million in the prior year. The increase in revenues in 2021 reflects improved sales in certain markets the company serve, specifically Vehicle and Industrial.

Net income in 2021 increased by 77% to $24.1 million compared with $13.6 million in the prior year. These increases reflect the impact of increased revenue along with the effect of a $7,373 discrete tax benefit in the first quarter of 2021.

Cash held by the company at the end of 2021 decreased to $22.5 million. Operating and financing activities provided $25.4 million and $35.8 million, respectively. Investing activities used $61.0 million, mainly for consideration paid for acquisitions.

Strategy

Allied Motion growth strategy is focused on becoming a leading global controlled motion solution provider in its selected target markets by further developing our products and services platform to utilize multiple Allied Motion technologies which create increased value solutions for its customers. The company's strategy further defines Allied Motion as being a "technology/know-how" driven company and to be successful, Allied continue to invest in its areas of excellence.

Mergers and Acquisitions

In 2021, Allied Motion acquired Washington-based Spectrum Controls, Inc. (Spectrum), an innovator and manufacturer of a wide variety of Industrial I/O and Universal Communications Gateway products, for a purchase price of $70 million. This acquisition is an excellent strategic fit and provides us with a tremendous opportunity to enhance our position as a value-added solutions supplier to the industrial automation and industrial controls market," commented Dick Warzala, Chairman and CEO. "In addition, Spectrum enhances our customer base, adds significant engineering resources and has the technology and know-how to provide solutions that meet the system requirements of Functional Safety."

In late 2021, Allied Motion acquired Colorado-based ALIO Industries (ALIO), an innovator and manufacturer of advanced linear and rotary motion systems for nano-precision applications, for a purchase price of $20 million. Equally important is ALIO's culture and passion for innovation, customer service and product quality, all traits that align well with what we have built at Allied. We expect that the business can grow rapidly as we leverage our joint channels to market and bring scale to their operations," commented Dick Warzala, Chairman and CEO.

Also in late 2021, Allied Motion acquired New York-based ORMEC Systems Corp. (ORMEC), a developer and manufacturer of mission critical electro-mechanical automation solutions and motion control products including multi-axis controls, electronic drives and actuators for the automation and aerospace industries. The acquisition is expected to be accretive to both EPS and the gross margin profile of Allied.

Company Background

Allied Motion was originally incorporated as a public company in 1962.

EXECUTIVES

Chairman, President, Chief Executive Officer, Director, Richard S. Warzala, $486,667 total compensation

Marketing Vice President, Kenneth R. Wyman, $162,500 total compensation

Operational Excellence Vice President, Robert P. Maida, $210,250 total compensation

Chief Financial Officer, Michael R. Leach, $266,667 total compensation

Director, Linda P. Duch

Director, Robert B. Engel

Director, Richard D. Federico

Director, Gerald J. Laber

Director, Richard D. Smith, $320,833 total compensation

Director, James J. Tanous

Director, Michael R. Winter

Auditors: DELOITTE & TOUCHE LLP

LOCATIONS

HQ: Allied Motion Technologies Inc
495 Commerce Drive, Amherst, NY 14228
Phone: 716 242-8634
Web: www.alliedmotion.com

Selected Distributors Locations

Austria
Belgium
Finland
France
Germany
Israel
Italy
Netherlands
Norway
Sweden
United Kingdom
USA

PRODUCTS/OPERATIONS

Selected Products

Brushless DC motors
Brushless drives
Encoders
Gearmotors
Permanent magnet DC motors
Servo motors
Small precision motors
Torque motors
Transaxles

COMPETITORS

BWX TECHNOLOGIES, INC.
FRANKLIN ELECTRIC CO., INC.
GENERAC HOLDINGS INC.
LENNOX INTERNATIONAL INC.
LINEAR TECHNOLOGY LLC
MITSUBISHI ELECTRIC CORPORATION
MTS SYSTEMS CORPORATION
NIDEC CORPORATION
PARKER-HANNIFIN CORPORATION
REGAL BELOIT CORPORATION

HISTORICAL FINANCIALS

Company Type: Public

Income Statement — FYE: December 31

	REVENUE ($mil)	NET INCOME ($mil)	NET PROFIT MARGIN	EMPLOYEES
12/20	366.6	13.6	3.7%	1,770
12/19	371.0	17.0	4.6%	1,700
12/18	310.6	15.9	5.1%	1,600
12/17	252.0	8.0	3.2%	1,250
12/16	245.8	9.0	3.7%	1,220
Annual Growth	10.5%	10.7%	—	9.7%

2020 Year-End Financials

Debt ratio: 34.4%
Return on equity: 10.3%
Cash ($ mil.): 23.1
Current Ratio: 2.71
Long-term debt ($ mil.): 120
No. of shares ($ mil.): 14.6
Dividends
Yield: 0.2%
Payout: 8.3%
Market value ($ mil.): 748.0

	STOCK PRICE ($) FY Close	P/E High/Low		PER SHARE ($) Earnings	Dividends	Book Value
12/20	51.10	53	21	0.95	0.08	9.78
12/19	48.50	39	26	1.20	0.08	8.28
12/18	44.69	47	26	1.13	0.08	7.16
12/17	33.09	57	33	0.58	0.07	6.18
12/16	21.39	39	24	0.67	0.07	5.14
Annual Growth	24.3%	—	—	9.4%	4.7%	17.4%

Alpine Banks of Colorado

EXECUTIVES

Chairman, Chief Executive Officer, Subsidiary Officer, Director, J. Robert Young
Vice-Chairman, President, Subsidiary Officer, Director, Glen Jammaron
Chief Administration Officer, Subsidiary Officer, Director, Thomas H. Kenning
Chief Operations Officer, Chief Credit Officer, Rachel Gerlach
Chief Retail Officer, Subsidiary Officer, Director, Glenn Davis
Chief Digital Officer, Andrew Karow
President, Front Range Region Region Officer, Director, Norman Franke
Regional President, Roaring Fork Valley Region Officer, Director, Stephen Briggs
Director, Raymond T. Baker
Director, Linda S. Childears
Director, John W. Cooper
Director, Wally Dallenbach
Director, Terry Farina
Director, L. Kristine Gardner
Director, Peter N. Guy
Director, Stan Kornasiewicz
Director, Steve Parker
Director, R. Bruce Robinson
Director, H. David Scruby
Director, Rodney E. Slifer
Director, Margo Young-Gardey
Auditors : Dalby Wendland & Co., P.C.

LOCATIONS

HQ: Alpine Banks of Colorado
  2200 Grand Avenue, Glenwood Springs, CO 81601
Phone: 970 384-3257 **Fax:** 970 945-2214
Web: www.alpinebank.com

HISTORICAL FINANCIALS
Company Type: Public

Income Statement				FYE: December 31
	REVENUE ($mil)	NET INCOME ($mil)	NET PROFIT MARGIN	EMPLOYEES
12/20	214.5	51.1	23.8%	0
12/19	207.4	58.0	28.0%	0
12/18	188.1	54.8	29.2%	730
12/17	163.3	33.6	20.6%	0
12/16	144.1	33.4	23.2%	0
Annual Growth	10.5%	11.2%	—	—

2020 Year-End Financials
Debt ratio: 2.3%
Return on equity: 14.1%
Cash ($ mil.): 864.1
Current Ratio: 0.19
Long-term debt ($ mil.): 119.1
No. of shares ($ mil.): 7.6
Dividends
  Yield: 291.8%
  Payout: 16.4%
Market value ($ mil.): 211.0

	STOCK PRICE ($) FY Close	P/E High/Low		PER SHARE ($) Earnings	Dividends	Book Value
12/20	27.75	1524	8	3.28	81.00	49.50
12/19	4,950.00	10	9	553.00	87.00	3,272
Annual Growth	(99.4%)	—	—	(99.4%)	(6.9%)	(98.5%)

Alpine Income Property Trust Inc

EXECUTIVES

Chairman, Director, Andrew C. Richardson
President, Chief Executive Officer, Director, John P. Albright
Senior Vice President, General Counsel, Corporate Secretary, Daniel E. Smith
Investments Senior Vice President, Steven R. Greathouse
Senior Vice President, Chief Financial Officer, Treasurer, Matthew M. Partridge
Director, Mark O. Decker
Director, Jeffrey S. Yarckin
Director, M. Carson Good
Auditors : Grant Thornton LLP

LOCATIONS

HQ: Alpine Income Property Trust Inc
  1140 North Williamson Blvd. Suite 140, Daytona Beach, FL 32114
Phone: 386 274-2202
Web: www.alpinereit.com

HISTORICAL FINANCIALS
Company Type: Public

Income Statement				FYE: December 31
	REVENUE ($mil)	NET INCOME ($mil)	NET PROFIT MARGIN	EMPLOYEES
12/21	30.1	9.9	33.1%	0
12/20	19.2	0.9	5.1%	0
12/19*	1.3	(0.0)	—	0
11/19	11.8	3.6	30.7%	0
12/18	11.7	4.0	34.3%	0
Annual Growth	37.0%	35.4%	—	—

*Fiscal year change

2021 Year-End Financials
Debt ratio: 53.0%
Return on equity: 6.1%
Cash ($ mil.): 9.5
Current Ratio: 2.16
Long-term debt ($ mil.): 267.7
No. of shares ($ mil.): 11.4
Dividends
  Yield: 5.0%
  Payout: 597.0%
Market value ($ mil.): 230.0

	STOCK PRICE ($) FY Close	P/E High/Low		PER SHARE ($) Earnings	Dividends	Book Value
12/21	20.04	20	14	0.89	1.02	17.16
12/20	14.99	151	60	0.11	0.82	16.99
12/19*	19.03	—	—	0.00	0.06	17.40
11/19	18.65	—	—	0.00	0.00	0.00
Annual Growth	3.7%	—	—	—	—	—

*Fiscal year change

Amalgamated Financial Corp

EXECUTIVES

Chairman, Director, Lynne P. Fox
President, Chief Executive Officer, Subsidiary Officer, Director, Priscilla Sims Brown
Senior Executive Vice President, Chief Financial Officer, Subsidiary Officer, Jason Darby
Executive Vice President, Sam Brown
Executive Vice President, Chief Information Officer, Bruce Rucinski
Executive Vice President, General Counsel, Mandy Tenner
Executive Vice President, Chief Risk Officer, Sherry Williams
Executive Vice President, Chief Accounting Officer, Leslie Veluswamy
Subsidiary Officer, Sean Searby
Director, Meredith Miller
Director, Donald E. Bouffard
Director, Maryann Bruce
Director, Mark A. Finser
Director, Darrell Jackson
Director, Julie Kelly
Director, JoAnn Sannasardo Lilek
Director, John McDonagh
Director, Robert G. Romasco
Director, Edgar Romney
Auditors : Crowe LLP

LOCATIONS

HQ: Amalgamated Financial Corp
  275 Seventh Avenue, New York, NY 10001
Phone: 212 255-6200
Web: www.amalgamatedbank.com

HISTORICAL FINANCIALS
Company Type: Public

Income Statement				FYE: December 31
	REVENUE ($mil)	NET INCOME ($mil)	NET PROFIT MARGIN	EMPLOYEES
12/20	231.0	46.1	20.0%	370
12/19	215.1	47.2	21.9%	398
12/18	192.2	44.6	23.2%	421
12/17	166.4	6.1	3.7%	401
12/16	158.4	10.5	6.7%	0
Annual Growth	9.9%	44.6%	—	—

2020 Year-End Financials

Debt ratio: —
Return on equity: 8.9%
Cash ($ mil.): 38.7
Current Ratio: 0.01
Long-term debt ($ mil.): —
No. of shares ($ mil.): 31.0
Dividends
Yield: —
Payout: 21.6%
Market value ($ mil.): 427.0

	STOCK PRICE ($) FY Close	P/E High/Low		PER SHARE ($) Earnings	Dividends	Book Value
12/20	13.74	13	5	1.48	0.32	17.25
12/19	19.45	13	10	1.47	0.26	15.56
12/18	19.50	180	11	1.46	0.00	13.82
Annual Growth	(16.1%)	—	—	0.7%	—	11.7%

Amedisys, Inc.

Through nearly 530 home health care agencies located throughout the US, Amedisys is a leading healthcare services company committed to helping its patients age in place by providing clinically excellent care and support in the home. It provides skilled nursing and home health services, primarily to geriatric patients covered by Medicare. It is also a post-acute care partner to over 3,000 hospitals and some 90,000 physicians across the country. In addition to home health services, Amedisys owns or manages some 175 hospice centers that offer palliative care to terminally ill patients. Amedisys provides home health, hospice care, personal care, and high acuity care services to more than 445,000 patients annually.

Operations

Amedisys operates four reportable business segments: Home Health, Hospice, Personal Care, and High Acuity Care.

Home health segment account for around 60% of total revenue, delivers a wide range of services in the homes of individuals who may be recovering from surgery, have a chronic disability or terminal illness or need assistance with completing important tasks.

The Hospice segment accounts for nearly another around 35% of revenue, provides care that is designed to provide comfort and support for those who are facing a terminal illness.

The Personal Care segment provides patients with assistance with the essential activities of daily living. It brings less than 5% of total revenue.

The High Acuity Care segment delivers the essential elements of inpatient hospital and skilled nursing facility (SNF) care to patients in their homes.

The company owns and operates around 330 Medicare-certified home health centers, some 175 Medicare-certified hospice care centers, around 15 personal care centers, and nearly 10 high acuity care joint ventures. Due to the demographics of its patient base, its services are primarily paid by Medicare.

Geographic Reach

Amedisys operates in about 40 states, with the heaviest concentration of home health and hospice operations in the Georgia, South Carolina, Tennessee, South Carolina, and Alabama.

Its executive office is located in Nashville, Tennessee, and its corporate headquarters is located in Baton Rouge, Louisiana.

Sales and Marketing

Because Amedisys serves predominantly older patients, some 75% of its revenue is derived from Medicare. Advertising expense was $7.4 million, $6.5 million, and $7.0 million for the year 2021, 2020, and 2019, respectively.

Financial Performance

The company had a revenue of $2.2 billion, a 7% increase from the previous year's revenue of $2.1 billion. These results were impacted by the acquisition of Contessa on August 1, 2021, which contributed $4 million in revenue and an operating loss of $10 million, which is inclusive of $1 million of amortization associated with our technology intangible asset. The year-over-year increases in operating income and net service revenue are primarily related to the impact of COVID-19 on prior year's results.

In 2021, the company had a net income of $210.2 million, a 13% increase from the previous year's net income of $185.2 million.

The company's cash at the end of 2021 was $45.8 million. Operating activities generated $188.9 million, while investing activities used $281.6 million, mainly for acquisitions of businesses. Financing activities provided another $55.1 million.

Strategy

Amedisys' strategy is to be the best choice for care wherever its patients call home. The company accomplishes this by providing clinically distinct care, being the employer of choice and delivering operational excellence and efficiency, which when combined, drive growth. Amedisys' mission is to provide best-in-class home health, hospice and personal care services allowing its patients to maintain a sense of independence, quality of life and dignity while delivering industry leading outcomes. The company believes that its unwavering dedication to clinical quality and constant focus on both patients and employees differentiates it from its competitors.

Mergers and Acquisitions

In early 2022, Amedisys has signed a definitive agreement to acquire certain home health assets from AssistedCare Home Health, Inc., and RH Homecare Services, LLC, doing business as AssistedCare Home Health and AssistedCare of the Carolinas, respectively. Once the agreement is complete, this acquisition will increase Amedisys' home health access to more than 1.5 million Medicare enrollees and more than 540,000 Medicare Advantage enrollees in North Carolina. Post-closing, Amedisys will be able to provide both home health and hospice services to more communities across North Carolina, including those in and around Wilmington and Greenville, furthering our strategy to become the solution for those who want to age in place in North Carolina. Terms were not disclosed.

Also in early 2022, Amedisys has signed a definitive agreement to acquire Evolution Health, LLC, a division of Envision Healthcare, doing business as Guardian Healthcare, Gem City, and Care Connection of Cincinnati, headquartered in Dallas, Texas. Once complete, this will increase Amedisys' home health access to more than 1.9 million Medicare enrollees and more than 690,000 Medicare Advantage enrollees in Texas, and more than 800,000 Medicare enrollees and more than 350,000 Medicare Advantage enrollees in Ohio. Terms were not disclosed.

In mid-2021, Amedisys has closed on its Asset Purchase with Visiting Nurse Association (VNA), a 125-year-old nonprofit that allows Amedisys to conduct home health and hospice operations in Omaha, Neb. and Council Bluffs, Iowa. Under the terms of the agreement, home health and hospice services will be provided by Amedisys Home Health and AseraCare Hospice, an Amedisys Company. Terms were not disclosed.

Also in mid-2021, Amedisys has signed a definitive agreement to acquire Tennessee-based, Contessa Health, a leader in hospital-at-home and skilled nursing facility (SNF) at-home services. The acquisition will add higher acuity, home-based care to Amedisys' current service offering, allowing Amedisys to create a premier home-based health system. Terms were not disclosed.

EXECUTIVES

Chairman, Director, Paul B. K. Kusserow, $875,000 total compensation
President, Chief Executive Officer, Director, Richard Ashworth
Accounting Executive Vice President, Finance Executive Vice President, Accounting Chief Financial Officer, Finance Chief Financial Officer, Accounting Acting Chief Operating Officer, Finance Acting Chief Operating Officer, Scott G. Ginn, $464,904 total compensation
Chief Strategy Officer, Nick Muscato
Chief Compliance Officer, Denise M. Bohnert
Chief Information Officer, Michael P. North
Lead Independent Director, Director, Julie D. Klapstein
Director, Ivanetta Davis Samuels
Director, Vickie L. Capps
Director, Molly J. Coye
Director, Teresa L. Kline
Director, Bruce D. Perkins
Director, Jeffrey A. Rideout
Auditors : KPMG LLP

LOCATIONS

HQ: Amedisys, Inc.
3854 American Way, Suite A, Baton Rouge, LA 70816

Phone: 225 292-2031
Web: www.amedisys.com

PRODUCTS/OPERATIONS

2017 Sales by Segment

	$ mil.	% of total
Home Health	1,101.8	72
Hospice	371.0	24
Personal Care	60.9	4
Total	1,533.7	100

2017 Centers

	No.
Georgia	68
Alabama	37
Massachusetts	29
South Carolina	26
Florida	21
Kentucky	17
West Virginia	17
Louisiana	14
North Carolina	14
Virginia	14
Pennsylvania	13
Maryland	10
Mississippi	9
Indiana	6
Maine	6
Missouri	6
New Hampshire	6
Oklahoma	6
Arkansas	5
Connecticut	5
New York	5
Arizona	4
California	4
Oregon	4
Illinois	3
New Jersey	3
Ohio	3
Rhode Island	3
Delaware	2
Kansas	2
Texas	2
Washington	1
Wisconsin	1
Washington, DC	1
Total	421

COMPETITORS

ADDUS HOMECARE CORPORATION
ALMOST FAMILY, INC.
ENCOMPASS HEALTH CORPORATION
GENTIVA HEALTH SERVICES, INC.
LEGACY LIFEPOINT HEALTH, INC.
LHC GROUP, INC.
OPTION CARE HEALTH, INC.
STEWARD HEALTH CARE SYSTEM LLC
TIVITY HEALTH, INC.
VISITING NURSE SERVICE OF NEW YORK

HISTORICAL FINANCIALS

Company Type: Public

Income Statement — FYE: December 31

	REVENUE ($mil)	NET INCOME ($mil)	NET PROFIT MARGIN	EMPLOYEES
12/20	2,105.8	183.6	8.7%	21,000
12/19	1,955.6	126.8	6.5%	21,300
12/18	1,662.5	119.3	7.2%	21,000
12/17	1,533.6	30.3	2.0%	17,900
12/16	1,437.4	37.2	2.6%	16,000
Annual Growth	10.0%	49.0%	—	7.0%

2020 Year-End Financials

Debt ratio: 13.7%
Return on equity: 25.2%
Cash ($ mil.): 81.8
Current Ratio: 0.79
Long-term debt ($ mil.): 204.5
No. of shares ($ mil.): 32.8
Dividends
  Yield: —
  Payout: —
Market value ($ mil.): 9,625.0

	STOCK PRICE ($) FY Close	P/E High/Low		PER SHARE ($) Earnings	Dividends	Book Value
12/20	293.33	52	24	5.52	0.00	24.66
12/19	166.92	42	27	3.84	0.00	19.84
12/18	117.11	39	14	3.55	0.00	15.06
12/17	52.71	73	47	0.88	0.00	15.17
12/16	42.63	49	28	1.10	0.00	13.70
Annual Growth	62.0%	—	—	49.7%	—	15.8%

Ameresco Inc

Primarily serving commercial and industrial customers, along with municipal and federal government agencies, Ameresco provides designing, engineering, and installation services to clients seeking to upgrade and improve the efficiency of their heating and air conditioning, ventilation, lighting, and other building systems. Other services include developing and constructing small-scale, on-site (or near-site) renewable energy plants for customers, as well as installing solar panels, wind turbines, and other alternative energy sources. Ameresco has approximately 65 regional offices in the US, Canada, and the UK. The US accounts for about 95% of company's revenues.

Operations

Ameresco operates through US Regions (roughly 45% of revenue), US Federal (more than 30%), Canada (around 5%), Non-Solar Distributed Generation (about 10%), and All Other (some 10% of revenue).

The company's US Regions, US Federal, and Canada segments offer energy efficiency products and services which include the design, engineering, and installation of equipment and other measures to improve the efficiency and control the operation of a facility's energy infrastructure, renewable energy solutions and services which include the construction of small-scale plants that the company owns or develops for customers that produce electricity, gas, heat or cooling from renewable sources of energy and O&M services.

The company's Non-Solar DG segment sells electricity, processed renewable gas fuel, heat or cooling, produced from renewable sources of energy, other than solar, and generated by small-scale plants that the company owns and O&M services for customer-owned small-scale plants.

The All Other category offers enterprise energy management services, consulting services and the sale of solar PV energy products and systems which the company refers to as integrated-PV.

By product and services line, Projects generate the majority of its revenue, followed by energy assets, O&M, Integrated-PV, and other services.

Geographic Reach

Headquartered in Framingham, Massachusetts, Ameresco occupies nine regional offices in Arizona, New York, Illinois, Maryland, North Carolina, Tennessee, Texas, Washington, and Ontario. In addition, it also has about 55 offices throughout North America and in the UK and about 145 small-scale renewable energy plants in North America and one in Ireland.

Majority of its revenue came from the US.

Sales and Marketing

The sales, design and construction process for energy efficiency and renewable energy projects recently has been averaging from 18 to 54 months. The company identifies project opportunities through referrals, requests for proposals (RFPs), conferences and events, website, online campaigns, telemarketing and repeat business from existing customers. The company's direct sales force develops and follows up on customer leads and had about 180 employees in direct sales.

More than 65% of revenue were derived from federal, state, provincial or local government entities, including public housing authorities and public universities. The US federal government, which is considered a single customer for reporting purposes. Its largest 20 customers accounted for about 65% of total revenues.

Financial Performance

Total revenues increased 18% to $1.2 billion primarily due to a $139.4 million increase in the company's project revenue attributed to the timing of revenue recognized as a result of the phase of active projects versus the prior year, including its SCE battery storage project, a $33.1 million, or 28%, increase in our energy asset revenue attributed to the continued growth of Ameresco's operating portfolio, strong renewable gas production and higher pricing on RINs generated from certain non-solar distributed generation assets in operation, and a $6.3 million increase in O&M revenue.

Net income for fiscal 2021 increased 30% to $70.5 million compared from the prior year with $54.1 million.

Cash held by the company at the end of fiscal 2021 increased to $87.1 million. Cash provided by financing activities was $365.5 million while cash used for operations and investing activities were $172.3 million and $205.3 million, respectively. Main cash uses for the year was capital investment in energy assets.

Strategy

Ameresco's growth is driven by staying ahead of the curve and at the leading edge of innovation taking place in the energy sector, offering new products and services to new and existing customers. In 2020, the company launched its first owned and operated wind power project in Ireland, that became its first renewable energy asset outside of North America. Strategic acquisitions of complementary businesses and assets have been an important part of the company's growth enabling it to broaden its service offerings and expand its geographical reach.

Mergers and Acquisitions

In 2022, Ameresco acquired Plug Smart, an Ohio-based energy services company that specializes in the development and implementation of budget neutral capital improvement projects including building controls and building automation systems. With this acquisition, Ameresco expands its existing pipeline and solution offerings in the smart buildings sector. Financial terms of the transaction are undisclosed.

EXECUTIVES

Chairman, President, Chief Executive Officer, George P. Sakellaris, $733,333 total compensation
Executive Vice President, General Counsel, Secretary, Director, David J. Corrsin
Executive Vice President, Division Officer, Nicole A. Bulgarino, $334,090 total compensation
Executive Vice President, Region Officer, Louis P. Maltezos, $336,075 total compensation
Human Resources Senior Vice President, Operations Senior Vice President, Lauren K. Todd
Senior Vice President, Chief Financial Officer, Principal Financial Officer, Spencer Doran Hole
Finance Senior Vice President, Finance Chief Accounting Officer, Mark A. Chiplock, $241,863 total compensation
Renewable Energy Division Officer, Michael T. Bakas, $314,087 total compensation
Region Officer, Britta MacIntosh
Region Officer, Robert Georgeoff
Director, Claire Hughes Johnson
Director, Frank V. Wisneski
Director, Joseph W. Sutton
Director, Nickolas Stavropoulos
Director, Jennifer L. Miller
Auditors : RSM US LLP

LOCATIONS

HQ: Ameresco Inc
111 Speen Street, Suite 410, Framingham, MA 01701
Phone: 508 661-2200
Web: www.ameresco.com

2018 Sales

	$ mil.	% of total
United States	734.7	93
Canada	36.7	5
Other	15.7	2
Total	787.1	100

PRODUCTS/OPERATIONS

2018 Sales by Segment

	$ mil.	% of total
US Region	334.3	42
US Federal	246.3	31
Canada	39	5
Non-Solar DG	82.7	11
All Other	84.8	11
Total	787.1	100

2018 Sales

	$ mil.	% of total
Project Revenue	545.1	69
Energy Assets	95.8	12
O&M Revenue	65.3	8
Other	81.1	10
Total	787.2	100

Selected Subsidiaries

Ameresco Canada Inc.
Ameresco CEPEO Solar Inc.
Ameresco Duffering Solar Inc.
Ameresco Enertech, Inc.
Ameresco Federal Solutions, Inc.
Ameresco Geothermal, Inc.
Ameresco Langstaff Solar Inc.
Ameresco Myles Solar Inc.
Ameresco Planergy Housing, Inc.
Ameresco Quantum, Inc.
Ameresco Select, Inc.
Ameresco Solar - Solutions, Inc.
Ameresco Vasco Road LLC
AmerescoSolutions, Inc.
EI Fund, One, Inc.

COMPETITORS

AECOM
ALLETE, INC.
CH2M HILL COMPANIES, LTD.
COSTAIN GROUP PLC
PIKE CORPORATION
PRIMORIS SERVICES CORPORATION
RENEW HOLDINGS PLC.
SNC-Lavalin Group Inc
Stantec Inc
WILLDAN GROUP, INC.

HISTORICAL FINANCIALS

Company Type: Public

Income Statement — FYE: December 31

	REVENUE ($mil)	NET INCOME ($mil)	NET PROFIT MARGIN	EMPLOYEES
12/20	1,032.2	54.0	5.2%	1,141
12/19	866.9	44.4	5.1%	1,127
12/18	787.1	37.9	4.8%	1,116
12/17	717.1	37.4	5.2%	1,049
12/16	651.2	12.0	1.8%	1,038
Annual Growth	12.2%	45.6%	—	2.4%

2020 Year-End Financials

Debt ratio: 21.8%
Return on equity: 11.6%
Cash ($ mil.): 66.4
Current Ratio: 1.28
Long-term debt ($ mil.): 311.6
No. of shares ($ mil.): 48.2
Dividends
Yield: —
Payout: —
Market value ($ mil.): 2,519.0

	STOCK PRICE ($) FY Close	P/E High/Low		PER SHARE ($) Earnings	Dividends	Book Value
12/20	52.24	47	13	1.10	0.00	10.22
12/19	17.50	19	14	0.93	0.00	9.08
12/18	14.10	20	9	0.81	0.00	8.14
12/17	8.60	11	6	0.82	0.00	7.39
12/16	5.50	24	15	0.26	0.00	6.44
Annual Growth	75.6%	—	—	43.4%	—	12.2%

America's Car-Mart Inc

No Credit? Bad Credit? No problem. America's Car-Mart targets car buyers with poor or limited credit histories. The company's subsidiaries operate about 150 used car dealerships in more than 10 states, primarily in smaller urban and rural markets throughout the US South Central region. Dealerships focus on selling basic and affordable transportation, with an average selling price of about $11,795 in 2020. It has facilities in Alabama, Tennessee, and Mississippi, among others. While the company's business plan has focused on cities with up to 50,000 in population (about 75% of sales), it sees better collection results among the smaller communities it serves. America's Car-Mart was founded in 1981 as the Crown Group. Most of the company's stores are located in Arkansas.

Operations

America's Car-Mart operates its business through two subsidiaries: one that sells cars (America's Car Mart, Inc., also known as Car-Mart of Arkansas) and one that finances them (Colonial Auto Finance, Inc.). Substantially all of its customers take advantage of financing offered by Colonial Auto Finance. The company's dealerships operate within a decentralized model. For instance, dealers conduct their own collections with support from corporate management.

Nearly 90% of total revenue came from the company's sales, while interest income and others accounts for the rest.

Geographic Reach

Arkansas-based, Car-Mart has about 150 locations in Alabama, Arkansas, Georgia, Indiana, Kentucky, Mississippi, Missouri, Oklahoma, Tennessee, Illinois, Iowa and Texas.

Sales and Marketing

Selling is done predominantly by the dealership manager, assistant manager, manager trainee or sales associate. The Company uses an outside marketing firm and has recently hired a director of digital experience in order to broaden and increase the company's usage of digital and social media channels. The company estimates that approximately 10% to 15% of the company's sales result from customer referrals.

Car-Mart spent $3.1 million, $3.1 million and $3.8 million for fiscal year 2020, 2019 and 2018, respectively for advertising consists of radio, print media and digital marketing.

Financial Performance

Total revenues increased $75.5 million, or 11%, in fiscal 2020, as compared to revenue growth of 9% in fiscal 2019, principally as a result of revenue growth from dealerships that operated a full twelve months in both fiscal years ($61.5 million), and revenue from stores opened or acquired during or after the year ended April 30, 2019 ($17.0 million), partially offset by decreased revenue from dealerships closed during or after the year ended April 30, 2019 ($3.0 million). The increase in revenue for fiscal 2020 is attributable to a 6% increase in average retail sales price, a 5% increase in retail units sold and an 11% increase in interest and other income.

The company's net income increased by $3.7 million to $51.3 million in 2020 compared to $47.6 million in prior year. The increase was due to higher revenues.

Cash held by the company at the end of 2020 increased by $1.8 million to $59.6 million compared to $57.8 million in prior year. Cash provided by operations and financing activities were $20.9 million and $46.8 million, respectively. Cash used for investing activities was $10.0 million, primarily for purchase of investments and purchases of property and equipment.

Strategy

In general, it is the company's objective to continue to expand its business using the same business model that has been developed and used by Car-Mart for over 38 years. This business strategy focuses on collecting customer accounts, maintaining a decentralized operation, expanding through controlled organic growth and strategic acquisitions, selling basic transportation, operating in smaller communities, enhanced management talent and experience, and cultivating customer relationships.

The company focuses on selling basic and affordable transportation to its customers. The company's average retail sales price was $11,793 per unit in fiscal 2020. By selling vehicles at this price point, the company can keep the terms of its instalment sales contracts relatively short (overall portfolio weighted average of 33.3 months), while requiring relatively low payments.

Mergers and Acquisitions

In late 2019, Car-Mart entered an agreement to acquire dealership assets of Taylor Motor Company and Auto Credit of Southern Illinois for an undisclosed amount. The company will be gaining three dealership locations in Marion, Benton and Mount Vernon, Illinois, as well as a vehicle reconditioning location in Benton, Illinois after this acquisition. Illinois will represent the company's 12th state and these locations are near existing Car-Mart dealerships in surrounding states.

Company Background

Car-Mart was started in 1981, when the company's first used-car dealership opened in Rogers, Arkansas. The basis of the company's business strategy from the start was to sell automobiles to customers with limited or poor credit. In 1999, Car-Mart was acquired by Crown Group, Inc. In 2002, Crown Group changes its name to America's Car-Mart, Inc.

EXECUTIVES

Chairman, Director, Joshua G. Welch
President, Douglas Campbell
Field Operations Senior Vice President, Leonard L. Walthall
Accounting Chief Financial Officer, Vickie D. Judy, $232,308 total compensation
Finance Chief Executive Officer, Director, Jeffrey A. Williams, $440,962 total compensation
Director, Ann G. Bordelon
Director, Julia K. Davis
Director, Daniel J. Englander
Director, William H. (Hank) Henderson, $328,274 total compensation
Director, Dawn C. Morris
Auditors : Grant Thornton LLP

LOCATIONS

HQ: America's Car-Mart Inc
  1805 North 2nd Street, Suite 401, Rogers, AR 72756
Phone: 479 464-9944
Web: www.car-mart.com

2015 Stores

	No.
Arkansas	38
Oklahoma	26
Missouri	18
Alabama	15
Texas	14
Kentucky	12
Tennessee	6
Georgia	6
Mississippi	5
Indiana	1
Total	141

PRODUCTS/OPERATIONS

2015 Sales

	$ mil.	% of total
Sales	472.6	89
Interest income & other	57.7	11
Total	530.3	100

Selected Subsidiaries

Auto Finance Investors, Inc.
Colonial Auto Finance, Inc.
Colonial Underwriting, Inc.
Crown Delaware Investments Corp.
Crown Group of Nevada, Inc.
Texas Car-Mart, Inc.

COMPETITORS

AUTONATION, INC.
AUTOTRADER.COM, INC.
CAR GIANT LIMITED
CARMAX, INC.
CARVANA CO.
DRIVETIME AUTOMOTIVE GROUP, INC.
DUVAL MOTOR COMPANY INC
MOTORPOINT GROUP PLC
NICHOLAS FINANCIAL, INC.
THE PROGRESSIVE CORPORATION

HISTORICAL FINANCIALS

Company Type: Public

Income Statement — FYE: April 30

	REVENUE ($mil)	NET INCOME ($mil)	NET PROFIT MARGIN	EMPLOYEES
04/21	918.6	104.1	11.3%	1,850
04/20	744.6	51.3	6.9%	1,750
04/19	669.1	47.6	7.1%	1,600
04/18	612.2	36.5	6.0%	1,504
04/17	587.7	20.2	3.4%	1,460
Annual Growth	11.8%	50.7%	—	6.1%

2021 Year-End Financials

Debt ratio: 27.5%
Return on equity: 29.3%
Cash ($ mil.): 2.8
Current Ratio: 6.70
Long-term debt ($ mil.): 225.9
No. of shares ($ mil.): 6.6
Dividends
Yield: —
Payout: —
Market value ($ mil.): 999.0

	STOCK PRICE ($) FY Close	P/E High/Low		PER SHARE ($) Earnings	Dividends	Book Value
04/21	150.83	11	4	14.95	0.00	61.39
04/20	65.95	17	5	7.39	0.00	45.78
04/19	99.05	15	8	6.73	0.00	38.93
04/18	53.30	11	7	4.90	0.00	33.70
04/17	37.30	18	8	2.49	0.00	30.66
Annual Growth	41.8%	—	—	56.5%	—	19.0%

American Bank Inc (PA)

American Bank Incorporated is the holding company for American Bank, which operates a single branch in Allentown, Pennsylvania. It serves customers throughout the US via its pcbanker.com Web site. The bank's products and services include checking and savings accounts, money market accounts, CDs, credit cards, and discount brokerage. It primarily originates real estate loans although it also offers commercial mortgages and residential mortgages. The Jaindl family, including company president and CEO Mark Jaindl, owns a majority of American Bank Incorporated.

EXECUTIVES

President, Chief Executive Officer, Subsidiary Officer, Chairman, Mark W. Jaindl, $239,351 total compensation
Senior Vice President, Chief Financial Officer, Treasurer, Subsidiary Officer, Toney C. Horst
Senior Vice President, Chief Operating Officer, Secretary, Subsidiary Officer, Sandra A. Berg
Senior Vice President, Chief Lending Officer, Subsidiary Officer, Chris J. Persichetti, $115,027 total compensation
Senior Vice President, Chief Information Officer, Subsidiary Officer, Robert W. Turner, $102,470 total compensation
Director, John F. Eureyecko
Director, John W. Galuchie

Director, Zachary J. Jaindl
Director, Michael D. Molewski
Director, Phillip S. Schwartz
Director, Martin F. Spiro
Director, Donald J. Whiting
Auditors : S. R. Snodgrass, P.C.

LOCATIONS

HQ: American Bank Inc (PA)
   4029 West Tilghman Street, Allentown, PA 18104
Phone: 610 366-1800   **Fax:** 610 366-1900
Web: www.ambk.com

COMPETITORS

COMMUNITY SHORES BANK CORPORATION
EASTERN VIRGINIA BANKSHARES, INC.
FIRST KEYSTONE CORPORATION
FIRST NATIONAL CORPORATION
FIRST US BANCSHARES, INC.

HISTORICAL FINANCIALS
Company Type: Public

Income Statement   FYE: December 31

	ASSETS ($mil)	NET INCOME ($mil)	INCOME AS % OF ASSETS	EMPLOYEES
12/20	734.2	8.7	1.2%	0
12/19	641.5	7.8	1.2%	0
12/18	621.9	6.8	1.1%	0
12/17	580.8	5.5	1.0%	0
12/16	557.1	4.4	0.8%	0
Annual Growth	7.1%	18.3%	—	—

2020 Year-End Financials
Return on assets: 1.2%   Dividends
Return on equity: 13.6%   Yield: 4.0%
Long-term debt ($ mil.): —   Payout: 35.0%
No. of shares ($ mil.): 5.5   Market value ($ mil.): 67.0
Sales ($ mil.): 29

	STOCK PRICE ($) FY Close	P/E High/Low		PER SHARE ($) Earnings	Dividends	Book Value
12/20	12.00	8	7	1.37	0.48	11.90
12/19	12.00	9	8	1.24	0.46	10.83
12/18	12.50	10	9	1.08	0.40	9.82
12/17	11.45	12	11	0.87	0.36	9.05
12/16	12.40	16	12	0.70	0.36	8.74
Annual Growth	(0.8%)	—	—	18.3%	7.5%	8.0%

American Business Bank (Los Angeles, CA)

EXECUTIVES

President, Chief Executive Officer, Director,
Leon I. Blankstein
Auditors : RSM US LLP

LOCATIONS

HQ: American Business Bank (Los Angeles, CA)
   400 South Hope Street, Suite 300, Los Angeles, CA 90071

Phone: 213 430-4000
Web: www.americanbb.bank

HISTORICAL FINANCIALS
Company Type: Public

Income Statement   FYE: December 31

	ASSETS ($mil)	NET INCOME ($mil)	INCOME AS % OF ASSETS	EMPLOYEES
12/20	3,454.2	28.7	0.8%	0
12/19	2,401.9	22.0	0.9%	0
12/18	2,157.4	16.3	0.8%	0
12/17	1,873.5	8.3	0.4%	0
12/16	1,843.1	12.7	0.7%	0
Annual Growth	17.0%	22.6%	—	—

2020 Year-End Financials
Return on assets: 0.9%   Dividends
Return on equity: 12.6%   Yield: —
Long-term debt ($ mil.): —   Payout: —
No. of shares ($ mil.): 8.7   Market value ($ mil.): 278.0
Sales ($ mil.): 98.7

	STOCK PRICE ($) FY Close	P/E High/Low		PER SHARE ($) Earnings	Dividends	Book Value
12/20	31.83	11	6	3.22	0.00	28.37
12/19	35.65	15	12	2.48	0.00	23.93
12/18	31.55	22	16	1.90	0.00	19.47
12/17	39.40	42	35	0.97	0.00	18.42
12/16	34.95	22	18	1.56	0.00	16.60
Annual Growth	(2.3%)	—	—	19.8%	—	14.3%

American National Bankshares, Inc. (Danville, VA)

American National Bankshares, with total assets of around $2.5 billion, is the holding company for American National Bank and Trust. Founded in 1909, the bank operates some 30 branches that serve southern and central Virginia and north central North Carolina. Operating through two segments -- Community Banking and Trust and Investment Services -- it offers checking and savings accounts, CDs, IRAs, and insurance. Lending activities primarily consist of real estate loans: Commercial mortgages account for about 40% of its loan portfolio while residential mortgages bring in another 20%. American National Bankshares' trust and investment services division manages nearly $610 million in assets.

Operations

American National Bankshares operates through two segments: Community Banking, which accounts for more than 80% of the company's total revenue and offers deposit accounts and loans to individuals and small and middle-market businesses; and Trust and Investment Services, which provides estate planning, trust account administration, investment management, and retail brokerage services.

The bank makes more than 80% of its revenue from interest income. About 68% of its total revenue came from loan interest during 2015, while another 13% came from interest income on investment securities. The rest of its revenue came from trust fees (6% of revenue), deposit account service charges (3%), mortgage banking income (2%), brokerage fees (1%), and other miscellaneous income sources.

Geographic Reach

Danville, Virginia-based American National Bankshares has 25 branches mostly in southern Virginia and in North Carolina (including in Alamance and Guilford Counties). It also has two loan production offices in Roanoke, Virginia and Raleigh, North Carolina.

Sales and Marketing

American National Bankshares has been cutting back on its advertising and marketing spend in recent years. It spent $356,000 on advertising and marketing in 2015, up from $453,000 and $607,000 in 2014 and 2013, respectively.

Financial Performance

The bank group has struggled to consistently grow its revenues and profits over the past several years despite steadily increasing loan business, mostly due to shrinking interest margins on loans stemming from the low-interest environment.

American National had a breakthrough year in 2015, however, as its revenue jumped 17% to $68.46 million almost entirely thanks to its acquisition of MainStreet BankShares, which boosted its loan and other interest-earning assets by double digits and increased its non-interest income by 19% with newly acquired deposit and other fee related income.

Double-digit revenue growth in 2015 drove the group's net income up 18% to $15.04 million. The bank's operating cash levels climbed 16% to $19.26 million for the year thanks to the boost in cash-denominated earnings.

Strategy

American National Bankshares grows its branch reach as well as its loan and deposit business by opening new branch locations or by buying other branches or banks.

The bank continues to have the largest deposit market share in the Dannville, Virginia metro area, boasting a 32.8% market share in the region as of mid-2015. It also had the second-largest market share in Pittsylvania County, Virginia with a 21.1% share.

Mergers and Acquisitions

In 2019 American National Bankshares acquired Roanoke, Virginia-based Hometown Bankshares for about $85 million. The acquisition expands American National's network to around 30 branches. The combined company has about $2.5 billion in assets.

Company Background

In 2011, American National acquired bank holding company MidCarolina Financial, expanding its presence in North Carolina, specifically in both Alamance and Guilford counties.

EXECUTIVES

Chairman, Subsidiary Officer, Charles H. Majors, $240,000 total compensation

President, Chief Executive Officer, Subsidiary Officer, Director, Jeffrey V. Haley, $514,039 total compensation

Executive Vice President, Chief Financial Officer, Chief Operating Officer, Subsidiary Officer, Jeffrey W. Farrar

Executive Vice President, Chief Administrative Officer, Division Officer, Subsidiary Officer, Edward C. Martin, $235,817 total compensation

Executive Vice President, Subsidiary Officer, Division Officer, John H. Settle, $216,057 total compensation

Lead Independent Director, Director, Michael P. Haley

Director, Nancy Howell Agee
Director, John H. Love
Director, Ronda M. Penn
Director, Dan M. Pleasant
Director, Joel R. Shepherd
Director, Tammy M. Finley
Director, Charles S. Harris
Director, F. D. Hornaday
Director, J. Nathan Duggins
Director, William J. Farrell
Auditors : Yount, Hyde & Barbour, P.C.

LOCATIONS

HQ: American National Bankshares, Inc. (Danville, VA)
  628 Main Street, Danville, VA 24541
Phone: 434 792-5111
Web: www.amnb.com

PRODUCTS/OPERATIONS

2015 Sales

	$ mil.	% of total
Interest and Dividend Income		
Interest and fees on loans	46.9	69
Taxable	4.2	6
Tax-exempt	3.9	5
Other	0.1	1
Non-interest income		
Trust fees	3.9	7
Service charges on deposit accounts	2.1	3
Other fees and commissions	2.4	3
Other	4.9	6
Total	68.4	100

Selected Subsidiaries
American National Bank and Trust Company
AMNB Statutory Trust I, A Delaware Statutory Trust
MidCarolina Trust I, A Delaware Statutory Trust
MidCarolina Trust II, A Delaware Statutory Trust

Selected Services
Business Banking
  Cash Management
  Checking
  Loans
  Savings
Personal Banking
  Checking
  Loans
  Savings
Insurance
  Business
  Personal

COMPETITORS

CAMDEN NATIONAL CORPORATION
CITY HOLDING COMPANY
FIRSTMERIT CORPORATION
MIDSOUTH BANCORP, INC.
NATIONAL BANK HOLDINGS CORPORATION

HISTORICAL FINANCIALS
Company Type: Public

Income Statement — FYE: December 31

	ASSETS ($mil)	NET INCOME ($mil)	INCOME AS % OF ASSETS	EMPLOYEES
12/20	3,050.0	30.0	1.0%	342
12/19	2,478.5	20.9	0.8%	355
12/18	1,862.8	22.5	1.2%	305
12/17	1,816.0	15.2	0.8%	328
12/16	1,678.6	16.3	1.0%	320
Annual Growth	16.1%	16.5%	—	1.7%

2020 Year-End Financials
Return on assets: 1.0%
Return on equity: 9.1%
Long-term debt ($ mil.): —
No. of shares ($ mil.): 10.9
Sales ($ mil.): 112.6
Dividends
  Yield: 4.1%
  Payout: 41.3%
Market value ($ mil.): 288.0

	STOCK PRICE ($) FY Close	P/E High/Low		PER SHARE ($) Earnings	Dividends	Book Value
12/20	26.21	14	7	2.73	1.08	30.77
12/19	39.57	20	15	1.98	1.04	28.93
12/18	29.31	16	11	2.59	1.00	25.52
12/17	38.30	24	20	1.76	0.97	24.13
12/16	34.80	19	12	1.89	0.96	23.37
Annual Growth	(6.8%)	—	—	9.6%	3.0%	7.1%

American Outdoor Brands Inc

EXECUTIVES

Chairman, Director, Barry M. Monheit
President, Chief Executive Officer, Director, Brian Daniel Murphy
Sales Vice President, Mark A. Reasoner
Operations Vice President, Analytics Vice President, Brent A. Vulgamott
Product Development Vice President, James E. Tayon
Investor Relations Vice President, Elizabeth A. Sharp
Chief Financial Officer, H. Andrew Fulmer
Chief Counsel, Corporate Secretary, Douglas V. Brown
Corporate Controller, Assistant Secretary, Kyle M. Carter
Director, Mary E. Gallagher
Director, Gregory J. Gluchowski
Director, I. Marie Wadecki
Director, Luis G. Marconi
Director, Bradley T. Favreau

LOCATIONS

HQ: American Outdoor Brands Inc
  1800 North Route Z, Suite A, Columbia, MO 65202
Phone: 800 338-9585
Web: www.aob.com

HISTORICAL FINANCIALS
Company Type: Public

Income Statement — FYE: April 30

	REVENUE ($mil)	NET INCOME ($mil)	NET PROFIT MARGIN	EMPLOYEES
04/21	276.6	18.4	6.7%	317
04/20	167.3	(96.2)	—	262
04/19	177.3	(9.5)	—	0
04/18	171.6	8.1	4.8%	0
Annual Growth	17.2%	31.1%	—	—

2021 Year-End Financials
Debt ratio: —
Return on equity: 7.3%
Cash ($ mil.): 60.8
Current Ratio: 4.95
Long-term debt ($ mil.): —
No. of shares ($ mil.): 14.0
Dividends
  Yield: —
  Payout: —
Market value ($ mil.): 363.0

	STOCK PRICE ($) FY Close	P/E High/Low		PER SHARE ($) Earnings	Dividends	Book Value
04/21	25.85	22	10	1.29	0.00	19.91
Annual Growth	—	—	—	—	—	—

American Riviera Bancorp

LOCATIONS

HQ: American Riviera Bancorp
  1033 Anacapa Street, Santa Barbara, CA 93101
Phone: —

HISTORICAL FINANCIALS
Company Type: Public

Income Statement — FYE: December 31

	ASSETS ($mil)	NET INCOME ($mil)	INCOME AS % OF ASSETS	EMPLOYEES
12/21	1,306.5	11.8	0.9%	0
12/20	971.6	7.3	0.8%	0
12/19	718.9	6.3	0.9%	0
12/18	616.5	5.8	1.0%	0
Annual Growth	28.4%	26.2%	—	—

2021 Year-End Financials
Return on assets: 1.0%
Return on equity: 13.0%
Long-term debt ($ mil.): —
No. of shares ($ mil.): 5.6
Sales ($ mil.): 43.6
Dividends
  Yield: —
  Payout: —
Market value ($ mil.): 115.0

	STOCK PRICE ($) FY Close	P/E High/Low		PER SHARE ($) Earnings	Dividends	Book Value
12/21	20.29	10	8	2.09	0.00	17.04
12/20	16.50	15	9	1.33	0.00	15.19
12/19	19.80	17	14	1.19	0.00	13.75
12/18	17.85	16	14	1.21	0.00	12.41
Annual Growth	4.4%	—	—	20.0%	—	11.2%

American Vanguard Corp.

American Vanguard Corporation (AVD) is a specialty chemical manufacturer that develops and markets products for agricultural, commercial and consumer uses. The company sells products to protect crops, turf and ornamental plants, as well as human and animal health. Products include insecticides, fungicides, herbicides, molluscicides, growth regulators, and soil fumigants. The company conducts its business through its principle operating subsidiaries, including AMVAC Chemical Corporation (AMVAC) for its domestic business and AMVAC Netherlands BV (AMVAC BV) for its international business. The company generates about 60% of sales from the US.

Operations
AVD sells products in two categories: crop (more than 45% of total sales) and non-crop (about 15%).

Geographic Reach
In the US, AVD has currently owns and operates five manufacturing facilities which are located in Los Angeles, California; Axis, Alabama; Hannibal, Missouri; Marsing, Idaho; Clackamas, Oregon; and Etchojoa, Mexico. Internationally, it operates in Australia, Costa Rica, the Netherlands, Brazil, Hong Kong, and Singapore. The US accounts for about 60% of annual sales.

AVD is headquartered in Newport Beach, California.

Sales and Marketing
The company delivers its products through "closed delivery systems" like SmartBox, Lock 'n Load and EZ Load systems, and is commercializing a precision application technology known as SIMPAS which permits the delivery of multiple products (from AMVAC and/or other companies) at variable rates in a single pass.

AVD primarily sells its products to distribution companies, buying groups or co-operatives.

AVD's advertising costs were $5.2 million, $4.8 million, and $5.5 million 2021, 2020, and 2019, respectively.

Financial Performance
In 2021, the company had net sales of $556.9 million, a 21% increase from the previous year's net sales of $458.7 million.

The company had a net income of $18.6 million, a 22% increase from the previous year's net income of $15.2 million. The higher volume of net sales for the year overpowered the higher volume of cost of sales.

The company's cash at the end of 2021 was $16.3 million. Operating activities generated $86.4 million, while investing activities used $20 million, mainly for acquisitions of businesses and product lines. Financing activities used another $65.9 million, mainly for payments of borrowings under line of credit agreement.

Strategy
The company has had a history of investing in technological innovation, including with respect to product delivery systems, essential oil technology and biologicals, as one of its core strategies. These investments are based upon the premise that new technology will allow for safer handling or lower overall toxicity profile of the company's product portfolio, appeal to regulatory agencies and the market it serves, gain commercial acceptance and command a return that is sufficiently in excess of the investment.

Mergers and Acquisitions
In mid-2021, AVD's subsidiary, AMVAC Chemical, has entered into agreements with Syngenta Crop Protection, to acquire rights to Envoke herbicide. The acquisition includes end-use product registrations and trademarks for Envoke herbicide in the US. Syngenta and AMVAC will work together over the next several months until the US Environmental Protection Agency registration has officially transferred to facilitate an orderly transition to maintain quality customer service in all domestic geographies. The financial terms of the transaction were not disclosed.

EXECUTIVES

Chief Executive Officer, Chairman, Director, Eric G. Wintemute, $651,519 total compensation
Vice President, Chief Financial Officer, Treasurer, David T. Johnson, $369,255 total compensation
Chief Administrative Officer, Secretary, General Counsel, Timothy J. Donnelly, $312,298 total compensation
Subsidiary Officer, Ulrich G. Trogele, $387,317 total compensation
Subsidiary Officer, Peter E. Eilers, $266,500 total compensation
Region Officer, Anthony S. Hendrix, $279,831 total compensation
Lead Independent Director, Director, John L. Killmer
Director, Scott D. Baskin
Director, Lawrence S. Clark
Director, Debra F. Edwards
Director, Morton D. Erlich
Director, Emer OBroin Gunter
Director, Alfred F. Ingulli
Director, M. Esmail Zirakparvar
Auditors : BDO USA, LLP

LOCATIONS

HQ: American Vanguard Corp.
4695 MacArthur Court, Newport Beach, CA 92660
Phone: 949 260-1200
Web: www.american-vanguard.com

2015 Sales
	$ mil.	% of total
US	212.1	73
Other countries	77.3	27
Total	289.4	100

2016 Sales
	$ mil.	% of total
US	228.8	73
Other countries	83.3	27
Total	312.1	100

PRODUCTS/OPERATIONS

2016 Sales
	$ mil.	% of total
Crops		
Insecticides	119.2	38
Herbicides	123.6	40
Other	29.4	9
Non-crop	39.9	13
Total	312.1	100

COMPETITORS

ADAMA AGRICULTURAL SOLUTIONS LTD
Agrium Inc
Bayer CropScience AG
E. I. DU PONT DE NEMOURS AND COMPANY
MARRONE BIO INNOVATIONS, INC.
MONSANTO COMPANY
SYNGENTA CORPORATION
THE CHEMOURS COMPANY
UNIVAR SOLUTIONS INC.
ZOETIS INC.

HISTORICAL FINANCIALS

Company Type: Public

Income Statement — FYE: December 31

	REVENUE ($mil)	NET INCOME ($mil)	NET PROFIT MARGIN	EMPLOYEES
12/20	458.7	15.2	3.3%	771
12/19	468.1	13.6	2.9%	671
12/18	454.2	24.1	5.3%	624
12/17	355.0	20.2	5.7%	605
12/16	312.1	12.7	4.1%	395
Annual Growth	10.1%	4.5%	—	18.2%

2020 Year-End Financials
Debt ratio: 15.8%
Return on equity: 4.3%
Cash ($ mil.): 15.9
Current Ratio: 1.94
Long-term debt ($ mil.): 107.4
No. of shares ($ mil.): 30.8
Dividends
Yield: 0.2%
Payout: 10.8%
Market value ($ mil.): 479.0

	STOCK PRICE ($) FY Close	P/E High/Low		PER SHARE ($) Earnings	Dividends	Book Value
12/20	15.52	38	22	0.51	0.04	11.69
12/19	19.47	42	27	0.46	0.08	11.41
12/18	15.19	29	17	0.81	0.08	11.03
12/17	19.65	34	22	0.68	0.06	10.24
12/16	19.15	45	23	0.44	0.03	9.61
Annual Growth	(5.1%)	—	—	3.8%	7.5%	5.0%

American Woodmark Corp.

American Woodmark offers a wide variety of products that fall into product lines including kitchen cabinetry, bath cabinetry, office cabinetry, home organization and hardware. Its cabinetry products are available in a variety of designs, finishes and finish colors and door styles. Styles vary by finish (plywood, cherry, beech lumber, hard maple, as well as laminate) and door design. Brands include American Woodmark, Shenandoah Cabinetry, Timberlake, and Waypoint. Targeting the remodeling and new home construction markets, American Woodmark sells its lineup through home centers and independent dealers and distributors; it also sells directly to major builders. American Woodmark was established through a leveraged buyout of Boise Cascade's cabinet division.

Operations
Business is divided between two markets ? remodeling and new home construction. Products are distributed directly from the company's assembly plants and a third-party logistics network.

Through its eight service centers nationwide, American Woodmark offers complete turnkey installation services to its direct builder customers.

The company offers products in two categories: made-to-order and stock. Made-to-order products typically utilize higher grade materials with more options as compared to stock and are all special ordered and shipped directly to the home from the factory. Its home organization products are exclusively stock products. Kitchen cabinetry and bath cabinetry are offered across all product categories (made-to-order and stock) and office cabinetry is offered as stock.

Geographic Reach
Virginia-based American Woodmark presently operates more than 15 manufacturing facilities located in Maryland, Indiana, West Virginia, Georgia, Arizona, Kentucky, Virginia, California, Texas, North Carolina and Tijuana, Mexico and eight primary service centers across the country and Mexico.

Sales and Marketing
Through three primary channels ? home centers (about 50% of sales), builders (nearly 40%), and independent dealers and distributors (more than 10%) ? American Woodmark services the remodeling and new home construction markets. Its brand names include American Woodmark, Timberlake (sold to major home builders), Shenandoah Cabinetry (Lowe's), Waypoint Living Spaces and others.

Together, Lowe's and Home Depot accounted for about 50% of the company's sales.

Advertising expenses were approximately $32.6 million, $34.1 million, and $33.9 million in 2022, 2021, and 2020, respectively.

Financial Performance
The company's revenue for fiscal 2021 increased by 7% to $1.9 billion compared from the prior year with $1.7 billion. The company experienced growth in the home center, builder and independent dealers and distributors channels.

Net loss for fiscal 2022 was $29.7 million compared from the prior year with a net income of $61.2 million.

Cash held by the company at the end of fiscal 2021 decreased to $22.3 million. Cash provided by operations was $24.4 million while cash used for investing and financing activities were $51.6 million and $41.6 million, respectively. Main uses of cash were payments to acquire property, plant and equipment; and payments of long-term debt.

Strategy
The company strategy has been to develop long-term strategic relationships with both Home Depot and Lowe's to distribute its products. Products for R&R projects are predominately purchased through home centers such as Home Depot and Lowe's. The market presence, store network and customer reach of these large home centers are why the company wants to maintain its strategic relationship with them.

Company Background
American Woodmark Corporation was incorporated by the four principal managers of the Boise Cascade Cabinet Division executives, Bill Brandt, Al Graber, Jeff Holcomb and Don Mathias, through a leveraged buyout of that division in 1980. The company operated privately until it went public in 1986, and moved to a new corporate headquarters in Winchester, Virginia, and operated a limited-product-line, high-inventory business model for rapid order fulfillment. In 2017, American Woodmark acquired RSI, a company known for creating exceptional value for customers. This is the largest acquisition in industry history, adding more than 10 brands and nearly 4,500 employees to the American Woodmark family.

HISTORY

Alvin Goldhush in 1951 started cabinet company Form Laminates, which lumber giant Boise Cascade acquired two decades later. Four senior managers of Boise Cascade's cabinet division -- William Brandt, Jeff Holcomb, Al Graber, and Donald Mathias -- engineered an LBO of the unit in 1980 and named it American Woodmark after a popular line of cabinets. The company started selling cabinets nationwide through distribution centers and went public in 1986.

American Woodmark spent the first half of the 1990s diversifying its product and brands. In 1990 it introduced Timberlake, a cabinet line for the construction industry. Other brands, including Coventry and Case, Crestwood, and Scots Pine, were added and quintupled its product line.

President and COO Jake Gosa became CEO in 1996. The sales cupboard was rather bare that year from a downturn in the closely linked home centers industry. The market surged in 1997, causing American Woodmark's profits to nearly triple, and new equipment and manufacturing techniques boosted output. In 1998 the company began offering hickory cabinets (its first new wood species in a decade), kitchen accessories, and high-quality ready-to-assemble framed cabinets (Flat Pack).

In 1999 American Woodmark expanded its hickory cabinet offerings (adding the Newport and Charleston brands). The company began operations at its new assembly facility in Gas City, Indiana, in 2000. To both preserve and increase market share in a slow-growth economy, in 2001 American Woodmark initiated plans to expand two plants and open two more in Kentucky and Oklahoma.

EXECUTIVES

President, Chief Executive Officer, Director, Michael Scott Culbreth, $426,004 total compensation
Senior Vice President, Chief Marketing Officer, Teresa M. May
Vice President, Chief Financial Officer, Paul Joachimczyk
Division Officer, Robert J. Adams, $324,464 total compensation
Non-Executive Chairman, Director, Vance W. Tang
Director, Latasha Akoma
Director, James G. Davis
Director, Daniel T. Hendrix
Director, Andrew B. Cogan
Director, Martha M. Hayes
Director, David Rodriquez
Director, Emily Videtto
Auditors : KPMG LLP

LOCATIONS

HQ: American Woodmark Corp.
561 Shady Elm Road, Winchester, VA 22602
Phone: 540 665-9100
Web: www.americanwoodmark.com

Selected Manufacturing Facilities
Allegany County, MD
Gas City, IN
Hardy County, WV
Humboldt, TN
Jackson, GA
Kingman, AZ
Monticello, KY
Orange, VA
Toccoa, GA

Selected Service Centers
Berryville, VA
Coppell, TX
Houston, TX
Huntersville, NC
Kennesaw, GA
Montgomeryville, PA

Orlando, FL
Phoenix, AZ
Raleigh, NC
Rancho Cordova, CA
Tampa, FL

PRODUCTS/OPERATIONS

Selected Brands
American Woodmark
Potomac
Shenandoah Cabinetry
Timberlake
Waypoint Living Spaces

COMPETITORS

BJT PROPERTIES, INC.
BOISE CASCADE COMPANY
FLEXSTEEL INDUSTRIES, INC.
KIMBALL INTERNATIONAL, INC.
KREAMER CABINET COMPANY
MASTERBRAND CABINETS, INC.
NORCRAFT HOLDINGS, L.P.
REPUBLIC NATIONAL CABINET CORPORATION
WELLBORN CABINET, INC.
WOODCRAFT INDUSTRIES, INC.

HISTORICAL FINANCIALS
Company Type: Public

Income Statement — FYE: April 30

	REVENUE ($mil)	NET INCOME ($mil)	NET PROFIT MARGIN	EMPLOYEES
04/21	1,744.0	58.7	3.4%	10,000
04/20	1,650.3	74.8	4.5%	9,900
04/19	1,645.3	83.6	5.1%	9,300
04/18	1,250.2	63.1	5.1%	9,400
04/17	1,030.2	71.1	6.9%	5,808
Annual Growth	14.1%	(4.7%)	—	14.5%

2021 Year-End Financials

Debt ratio: 31.9%
Return on equity: 8.1%
Cash ($ mil.): 91.0
Current Ratio: 1.78
Long-term debt ($ mil.): 513.4
No. of shares ($ mil.): 16.8
Dividends
Yield: —
Payout: —
Market value ($ mil.): 1,671.0

	STOCK PRICE ($) FY Close	P/E High/Low		PER SHARE ($) Earnings	Dividends	Book Value
04/21	99.46	31	13	3.45	0.00	44.22
04/20	51.41	26	8	4.42	0.00	41.39
04/19	89.93	22	11	4.83	0.00	36.82
04/18	82.20	37	21	3.77	0.00	33.23
04/17	91.90	21	14	4.34	0.00	21.71
Annual Growth	2.0%	—	—	(5.6%)	—	19.5%

Ameris Bancorp

Ameris Bancorp is a financial holding company whose business is conducted primarily through its wholly owned banking subsidiary, Ameris Bank, which provides a full range of banking services to its retail and commercial customers who are primarily concentrated in select markets in in Alabama, Georgia, South Carolina, and northern Florida. It operates some 165 full-service domestic banking offices. Loans secured by commercial real estate and farmland accounted for about 45% of the company's loan portfolio. Ameris Bank opened its doors as American Banking company on 1971.

Operations
The company has five reportable segments; the Banking Division (around 50% of sales), the Retail Mortgage Division (some 35%), the Warehouse Lending Division, the SBA Division and the Premium Finance Division, which generated about 15% combined.

The Banking Division derives its revenues from the delivery of full-service financial services to include commercial loans, consumer loans and deposit accounts. The Retail Mortgage Division derives its revenues from the origination, sales and servicing of one-to-four family residential mortgage loans. The Warehouse Lending Division derives its revenues from the origination and servicing of warehouse lines to other businesses that are secured by underlying one-to-four family residential mortgage loans and residential mortgage servicing rights. The SBA Division derives its revenues from the origination, sales and servicing of SBA loans. The Premium Finance Division derives its revenues from the origination and servicing of commercial insurance premium finance loans.

Overall, interest and fees on loans generated about 65% of sales, while mortgage banking activity generated more than 25%. In addition, its loan portfolio includes real estate - commercial and farmland (about 45% of sales), real estate ? residential (nearly 20%), and commercial, financial and agricultural and real estate - construction and development (around 10% each).

Geographic Reach
Headquartered in Atlanta, Georgia, the company's markets are concentrated primarily in Georgia, Alabama, Florida and South Carolina. Ameris operates roughly 165 office or branch locations.

Sales and Marketing
Through an acquisition-oriented growth strategy, Ameris seeks to grow its brand and presence in the markets it currently serves in Georgia, Alabama, Florida and South Carolina, as well as in neighboring communities.

The company spent $8.4 million, $8.0 million, and $7.9 million for the years 2021, 2020, and 2019, respectively.

Financial Performance
The company's revenue for fiscal 2021 decreased to $1.0 billion compared from the prior year with $1.1 billion.

Net income for fiscal 2021 increased to $376.9 million compared from the prior year with $262.0 million.

Cash held by the company at the end of fiscal 2021 increased to $4.1 billion. Cash provided by operations and financing activities were $9.1 million and $2.4 billion, respectively. Cash used for investing activities was $421.0 million, mainly for net increase in loans.

Strategy
The company seek to increase its presence and grow the "Ameris" brand in the markets that it currently serves in Georgia, Alabama, Florida, North Carolina and South Carolina and in neighboring communities that present attractive opportunities for expansion. Management has pursued this objective through an acquisition-oriented growth strategy and a prudent operating strategy.

Ameris have maintained its focus on a long-term strategy of expanding and diversifying its franchise in terms of revenues, profitability and asset size. Company's growth over the past several years has been enhanced significantly by bank acquisitions. Ameris expect to continue to take advantage of the consolidation in the financial services industry and enhance its franchise through future acquisitions. The company intend to grow within its existing markets, to branch into or acquire financial institutions in existing markets as well as financial institutions in other markets consistent with its capital availability and management abilities.

Mergers and Acquisitions
In late 2021, Ameris Bancorp announced that its banking subsidiary, Ameris Bank, has acquired Balboa Capital Corporation, an online provider of business lending solutions to small and mid-sized businesses nationwide based in Costa Mesa, California. The acquisition of Balboa Capital and its technology accelerates Ameris Bank's small business and C&I lending initiatives and increases its presence in the fast-growing point-of-sale financing market. The addition of Balboa Capital also diversifies Ameris Bank's already robust portfolio of nationwide lending platforms, which includes its premium finance, mortgage banking, and warehouse lending businesses. Terms were not disclosed.

Company Background
In addition to acquiring several troubled and failing banks with help from the FDIC, Ameris merged with Prosperity Bank in 2013, which broadened its reach into Florida through Prosperity's branches in St. Augustine, Jacksonville, Panama City, Lynn Haven, Palatka and Ormand Beach.

Georgia's economy was one of the hardest hit in the US during the recession, and Ameris has taken advantage of the plethora of banks seized by regulators in the state. Since 2009, the company has acquired about 10 failed banks in Georgia though FDIC-assisted transactions, adding some 20 branches to its network. Ameris also snagged the failed First Bank of Jacksonville in Florida, which had two locations.

EXECUTIVES

Chief Executive Officer, H. Palmer Procter
President, Chief Executive Officer, Dennis J. Zember, $500,000 total compensation

Banking Group President, Banking Subsidiary Officer, Lawton E. Bassett, $400,000 total compensation
Executive Vice President, Chief Administrative Officer, Corporate Secretary, Cindi H. Lewis, $170,000 total compensation
Executive Vice President, Chief Information Officer, Joseph B. Kissel, $310,000 total compensation
Executive Vice President, Chief Risk Officer, Subsidiary Officer, William D. McKendry
Executive Vice President, Chief Financial Officer, Nicole S. Stokes, $300,000 total compensation
Credit Administration Executive Vice President, Credit Administration Director, Jon S. Edwards, $320,000 total compensation
Executive Vice President, General Counsel, Subsidiary Officer, Stephen A. Melton, $280,000 total compensation
Executive Vice President, Chief Strategy Officer, James A. LaHaise, $320,000 total compensation
Executive Vice President, Region Officer, Johnny R. Myers, $160,417 total compensation
Banking Chief Banking Executive Officer, Banking Subsidiary Officer, Andrew B. Cheney, $400,000 total compensation
Division Officer, C. Johnson Hipp, $225,000 total compensation
Director, Elizabeth (Beth) A. McCague
Director, William Millard Choate
Director, Rodney D. Bullard
Director, Gloria A. O'Neal
Director, Robert Dale Ezzell
Director, William I. Bowen
Director, Edwin W. Hortman, $466,667 total compensation
Director, Daniel B. Jeter
Director, James Miller
Director, Robert P. Lynch
Director, Jimmy D. Veal
Director, Johnny W. Floyd
Director, Leo J. Hill
Director, William H. Stern
Auditors : KPMG LLP

LOCATIONS

HQ: Ameris Bancorp
 3490 Piedmont Rd N.E., Suite 1550, Atlanta, GA 30305
Phone: 404 639-6500
Web: www.amerisbank.com

PRODUCTS/OPERATIONS

2016 sales chart

	$ mil.	% of total
Interest income:		
Interest and fees on loans	218.7	64
Interest on taxable securities	17.9	5
Interest on nontaxable securities	1.8	-
Interest on deposits in other banks	0.9	-
Interest on federal funds sold	-	-
Non Interest income:		
Service charges on deposit accounts	42.8	13
Mortgage banking activity	48.2	14
Other service charges, commissions and fees	3.5	1
Net gains on sales of securities	-	-
Gain on sale of SBA loans	3.9	1
Other noninterest income	7.1	2
Total	**344.8**	**100**

2016 sales chart

	% of total
Banking Division	91
Retail Mortgage Division	5
Warehouse Lending Division	3
SBA Division	1
Total	**100**

Selected Acquisitions
American United Bank
Central Bank of Georgia
Darby Bank & Trust
First Bank of Jacksonville
High Trust Bank
Montgomery Bank & Trust
One Georgia Bank
Satilla Community Bank
Tifton Banking Company
United Security Bank

COMPETITORS

CASCADE BANCORP
CENTERSTATE BANK CORPORATION
CLIFTON BANCORP INC.
FLAGSTAR BANCORP, INC.
LEGACYTEXAS FINANCIAL GROUP, INC.
NATIONAL BANK HOLDINGS CORPORATION
OLD LINE BANCSHARES, INC.
SEACOAST BANKING CORPORATION OF FLORIDA
SOUTHSIDE BANCSHARES, INC.
TRUSTCO BANK CORP N Y

HISTORICAL FINANCIALS

Company Type: Public

Income Statement — FYE: December 31

	ASSETS ($mil)	NET INCOME ($mil)	INCOME AS % OF ASSETS	EMPLOYEES
12/20	20,438.6	261.9	1.3%	2,671
12/19	18,242.5	161.4	0.9%	2,722
12/18	11,443.5	121.0	1.1%	1,804
12/17	7,856.2	73.5	0.9%	1,460
12/16	6,892.0	72.1	1.0%	1,298
Annual Growth	31.2%	38.1%	—	19.8%

2020 Year-End Financials
Return on assets: 1.3%
Return on equity: 10.2%
Long-term debt ($ mil.): —
No. of shares ($ mil.): 69.5
Sales ($ mil.): 1,173
Dividends Yield: 1.5%
Payout: 17.9%
Market value ($ mil.): 2,647.0

	STOCK PRICE ($) FY Close	P/E High/Low		PER SHARE ($) Earnings	Dividends	Book Value
12/20	38.07	12	5	3.77	0.60	38.06
12/19	42.54	16	12	2.75	0.50	35.53
12/18	31.67	21	11	2.80	0.40	30.66
12/17	48.20	26	21	1.98	0.40	21.59
12/16	43.60	23	12	2.08	0.30	18.51
Annual Growth	(3.3%)	—	—	16.0%	18.9%	19.7%

Ames National Corp.

This company aims to please citizens of Ames... and central Iowa. Ames National Corporation is the multi-bank holding company for flagship subsidiary First National Bank, Ames, Iowa, as well as Boone Bank & Trust, Reliance State, State Bank & Trust, and United Bank & Trust. Boasting over $1 billion in assets and 15 branches, the banks provide area individuals and businesses with standard services such as deposit accounts, IRAs, and credit and debit cards. Commercial-related loans account for about 50% of Ames' loan portfolio, while agricultural loans make up another 20%. The banks also write residential, construction, consumer, and business loans, and offer trust and financial management services.

Operations
Ames National's five banking subsidiaries consists of two national banks (First National Bank and United Bank & Trust) and three state-chartered banks (Reliance State Bank, Boone Bank & Trust Co. and State Bank & Trust Co.).

About 54% of Ames National's total revenue came from loan interest (including fees) in 2014, while another 28% came from interest on its taxable and tax-exempt investment securities. The rest of its revenue came from wealth management income (5%), service fees (3%), merchant and card fees (2%) and other miscellaneous income sources. The bank had a staff of roughly 220 employees at the end of 2014.

Geographic Reach
The company's five commercial banks serve central and north central Iowa through 16 branches in the counties of Boone, Hancock, Marshall, Polk, and Story counties.

Financial Performance
Ames National's revenues and profits have been rising over the past few years largely thanks to growing loan business and lower interest expenses on deposits in the low-interest environment.

The company's revenue jumped 9% to $50.22 million in 2014 mostly thanks to real estate loan business growth and higher yields on its taxable investment securities. Its non-interest income rose by 20% largely due to gains made on the sale of some of its property and equipment and higher wealth management fee income.

Higher revenue, a continued decline in interest expenses, and lower loan loss provisions drove Ames National's net income higher by 9% to $15.3 million. The bank's operating cash levels fell by 17% to $19.5 million after adjusting its cash for non-cash items mostly related to amortization of mortgage-backed securities, asset changes, and gains on property and equipment sales.

Strategy

The bank (through its banking subsidiaries) focuses on serving small-to-medium size businesses that traditionally wish to develop and maintain an exclusive relationship with a single bank. It sometimes pursues bank or branch acquisitions in its target markets in Iowa to strengthen its market share, expand its reach, and grow its loan and deposit business.

Mergers and Acquisitions

In August 2014, subsidiary First National Bank continued to strengthen and expand its market share in Des Moines, Iowa after purchasing three bank branches of First Bank located in West Des Moines and Johnston for $4.1 million. The deal added $80 million in new deposits and $49 million in new loan business to First National's books.

Growing its customer base and increasing its presence in north central Iowa, in 2012 Ames National's Reliance State Bank (formerly known as Randall-Story State Bank) purchased two bank offices in Garner and Klemme, Iowa from Liberty Bank FSB.

EXECUTIVES

Chairman, Director, Thomas H. Pohlman, $221,533 total compensation

President, Chief Executive Officer, Director, John P. Nelson, $320,540 total compensation

Innovation & Corporate Services Executive Vice President, Michael A. Wilson

Vice President, Technology Director, Kevin G. Deardorff

Chief Financial Officer, Secretary, Director, John L. Pierschbacher

Subsidiary Officer, Kathy L. Baker

Subsidiary Officer, Scott T. Bauer, $219,080 total compensation

Subsidiary Officer, Stephen C. McGill, $161,560 total compensation

Subsidiary Officer, Jeffrey K. Putzier, $167,520 total compensation

Subsidiary Officer, Richard J. Schreier, $152,100 total compensation

Subsidiary Officer, Terrill L. Wycoff, $102,772 total compensation

Director, David W. Benson
Director, Jeffery C. Baker
Director, Michelle R. Cassabaum
Director, Lisa M. Eslinger
Director, Betty A. Baudler Horras
Director, Steven D. Forth
Director, Patrick G. Hagan
Director, James R. Larson
Director, Kevin L. Swartz
Auditors : CliftonLarsonAllen LLP

LOCATIONS

HQ: Ames National Corp.
405 5th Street, Ames, IA 50010
Phone: 515 232-6251 **Fax:** 515 663-3033
Web: www.amesnational.com

PRODUCTS/OPERATIONS

2014 Sales

	$ mil.	% of total
Interest income	41.0	82
Non-interest income	9.2	18
Total	50.2	100

COMPETITORS

AMERICAN NATIONAL BANKSHARES INC.
CAMDEN NATIONAL CORPORATION
CAPITAL BANK FINANCIAL CORP.
CITY HOLDING COMPANY
OLD NATIONAL BANCORP

HISTORICAL FINANCIALS

Company Type: Public

Income Statement FYE: December 31

	ASSETS ($mil)	NET INCOME ($mil)	INCOME AS % OF ASSETS	EMPLOYEES
12/20	1,975.6	18.8	1.0%	265
12/19	1,737.1	17.1	1.0%	133
12/18	1,455.6	17.0	1.2%	138
12/17	1,375.0	13.6	1.0%	221
12/16	1,366.4	15.7	1.2%	202
Annual Growth	9.7%	4.6%	—	7.0%

2020 Year-End Financials

Return on assets: 1.0%
Return on equity: 9.4%
Long-term debt ($ mil.): —
No. of shares ($ mil.): 9.1
Sales ($ mil.): 73.5
Dividends
Yield: 4.1%
Payout: 50.5%
Market value ($ mil.): 219.0

	STOCK PRICE ($) FY Close	P/E High/Low		PER SHARE ($) Earnings	Dividends	Book Value
12/20	24.02	13	8	2.06	0.99	22.96
12/19	28.06	16	13	1.86	0.95	20.34
12/18	25.42	17	14	1.83	1.16	18.60
12/17	27.85	23	18	1.47	0.87	18.34
12/16	33.00	21	13	1.69	0.83	17.73
Annual Growth	(7.6%)	—	—	5.1%	4.5%	6.7%

Amneal Pharmaceuticals Inc

Impax Laboratories is betting that its pharmaceuticals will make a positive impact on the world's health. The company makes specialty generic pharmaceuticals, which it markets through its Impax Generics division and through marketing alliances with other pharmaceutical firms. It concentrates on controlled-release versions of various generic versions of branded and niche pharmaceuticals that require difficult-to-obtain raw materials or specialized expertise. Additionally, the company's branded pharmaceuticals business (Impax Specialty Pharma) is developing and improving upon previously approved drugs that target Parkinson's disease, multiple sclerosis, and other central nervous system disorders. In 2018 Impax merged with Amneal Pharmaceuticals to create a top generics firm.

Operations

Prior to the merger with Amneal Pharmaceuticals, Impax earned the majority (more than 70%) of its revenue through its Impax Generics division, which produces dosage variations of about 75 generic compounds including fenofibrate (generic Lofibra for high cholesterol), midodrine HCl (generic ProAmatine), and generic Adderall XR (for attention-deficit hyperactivity disorder, or ADHD).

The smaller Impax Pharmaceuticals division, which brought in about 30% of revenue, develops, sells, and distributes branded drugs. Its portfolio includes central nervous system products, other specialty drugs, and development-stage candidates.

Geographic Reach

Impax is headquartered in New Jersey; it has administrative offices in Pennsylvania. The company has other locations in the US, India, Ireland, Germany, Switzerland, and the UK.

Sales and Marketing

Impax Generics sells the group's generic products to wholesalers, chain drug stores, and mail order pharmacies. Impax also works through strategic alliances that include co-promotion, licensing, third-party marketing, or manufacturing and supply agreements with other generic and branded pharmaceutical manufacturers.

The company's top three customers are wholesalers Cardinal (about one-third of revenue), McKesson (some 30%), and AmerisourceBergen (about 25%).

Strategy

To expand the operations of its main Impax Generics division, Impax works to develop new generic versions of drugs that have lost (or are about to lose) patent protection, with a focus on controlled-release and specialty products. It also develops medicines that come in alternative-dosage forms, such as nasal sprays, inhalers, ointments, injectables, and patches. The company's generic development programs are conducted both independently and through research or licensing partnerships with other drug makers. Impax seeks to gain first-to-file and first-to market status with its new products, and in some cases, Impax enters agreements with branded pharmaceutical firms to make authorized generic versions of off-patent drugs.

Revenues for the unit fluctuate from year to year due to competitive conditions (how many additional generic versions of a product are on the market) and shifts in consumer demand for certain medications.

The Impax Pharmaceuticals division has products in clinical stages of development, including treatments for multiple sclerosis and Parkinson's disease. The division also focuses its development efforts on other central nervous system disorders such as Alzheimer's disease, depression, epilepsy, and migraines. The company hopes to build its portfolio of branded products through internal development, acquisitions, and licensing agreements, with the ultimate goal of selling some products commercially.

Mergers and Acquisitions

In 2018 Impax merged with another generics drug maker, Amneal Pharmaceuticals. The combined firm, which is 75%-owned by Amneal shareholders, is now be the nation's fifth-largest generics manufacturer. It has some 150 pending Abbreviated New Drug Applications.

In 2016, Impax bought a portfolio of generic drugs from Teva and Allergan for $586 million. The deal included about 20 marketed, pending, and development products, as well as the commercial rights to the generic equivalent to Concerta.

EXECUTIVES

Chairman, Director, Paul M. Meister
President, Co-Chief Executive Officer, Director, Chirag Patel
Co-Chief Executive Officer, Director, Chintu Patel
Generics Executive Vice President, Generics Chief Commercial Officer, Andrew Boyer, $412,500 total compensation
Executive Vice President, Chief Human Resources Officer, Strategic Planning Officer, Nikita Shah, $246,132 total compensation
Executive Vice President, Chief Financial Officer, Anastasios G. Konidaris
Senior Vice President, General Counsel, Corporate Secretary, Stephen J. Manzano
Director, Emily Peterson Alva
Director, Jeffrey P. George
Director, John J. Kiely
Director, Ted C. Nark
Director, Shiomo Yanai
Director, Gautam Patel
Auditors : Ernst & Young LLP

LOCATIONS

HQ: Amneal Pharmaceuticals Inc
400 Crossing Boulevard, Bridgewater, NJ 08807
Phone: 908 947-3120
Web: www.amneal.com

COMPETITORS

ADARE PHARMACEUTICALS, INC.
Apotex Inc
DR.REDDY'S LABORATORIES LIMITED
HIKMA PHARMACEUTICALS PUBLIC LIMITED COMPANY
HOSPIRA, INC.
LANNETT COMPANY, INC.
MYLAN PHARMACEUTICALS INC.
NOVEN PHARMACEUTICALS, INC.
PAR PHARMACEUTICAL COMPANIES, INC.
SANDOZ INC.

HISTORICAL FINANCIALS

Company Type: Public

Income Statement   FYE: December 31

	REVENUE ($mil)	NET INCOME ($mil)	NET PROFIT MARGIN	EMPLOYEES
12/20	1,992.5	91.0	4.6%	6,000
12/19	1,626.3	(361.9)	—	5,500
12/18	1,662.9	(169.7)	—	6,000
12/17	775.7	(469.2)	—	1,257
12/16	824.4	(472.0)	—	1,495
Annual Growth	24.7%	—	—	41.5%

2020 Year-End Financials

Debt ratio: 71.8%   No. of shares ($ mil.): 299.7
Return on equity: 33.9%   Dividends
Cash ($ mil.): 341.3   Yield: —
Current Ratio: 2.29   Payout: —
Long-term debt ($ mil.): 2,831.8   Market value ($ mil.): 1,370.0

	STOCK PRICE ($) FY Close	P/E High/Low		PER SHARE ($) Earnings	Dividends	Book Value
12/20	4.57	9	4	0.61	0.00	1.01
12/19	4.82	—	—	(2.74)	0.00	0.78
12/18	13.53	—	—	(0.16)	0.00	1.69
Annual Growth	(41.9%)	—	—	—	—	(22.6%)

Ansys Inc.

ANSYS develops and globally markets engineering simulation software and services widely used by engineers, designers, researchers and student across a broad spectrum of industries and academia, including aerospace and defense, automotive, electronics, semiconductors, energy, consumer products, healthcare and more. The company focus on development and flexible solutions that enable users to analyze and designs directly to desktop, providing a common platform for fast, efficient and cost-conscious product development, from design concept to final-stage testing and validation. The company products consist of platform, structures, fluids, electronics, semiconductors, embedded software, and more.

Operations

ANSYS revenue is derived principally from the licensing of computer software products and from maintenance contracts. About half of the company's revenue comes from maintenance and services and the rest comes from licensing.

Geographic Reach

ANSYS is based in Canonsburg, Pennsylvania. The company has office facility Lebanon, New Hampshire, Pune, India, Livermore California, and Apex North Carolina. The US accounts for about 45% revenue and Japan about 10% and Germany for about 10% of revenue each. European countries other than Germany supply about 20% of revenue.

Sales and Marketing

ANSYS distributes and supports its products through its own direct sales offices, as well as a global network of independent channel partners. It also has a direct sales organization to develop an enterprise-wide, focused sales approach and to implement a worldwide go-to-market account strategy. The sales management organization also functions as a focal point for requests from the channel partners and provides additional support in strategic locations through the presence of direct sales offices. In total, its direct sales and marketing organization comprised 2,500.

The company derives some 25% of total revenue through the indirect sales channel.

Financial Performance

Company's revenue for fiscal 2021 increased by 13% to $1.9 billion compared from the prior year with $1.7 billion. The growth rate was favorably impacted by our continued investments in its global sales, support and marketing organizations, the timing and duration of its multi-year lease contracts, strong perpetual license sales off a relatively lower 2020 compare, sales to its small- and medium-sized businesses, and its recent acquisitions.

Net income for fiscal 2021 increased to $454.6 million compared with $433.9 million in the prior year.

Cash held by the company at the end of fiscal 2021 decreased to $667.7 million. Cash provided by operations was $549.5 million while investing and financing activities used $536.8 million and $245.9 million, respectively. Main cash uses were acquisitions and purchase of treasury stock.

Strategy

ANSYS' strategy of Pervasive Engineering Simulation seeks to deepen the use of simulation in its core, to inject simulation throughout the product lifecycle and to embed simulation into its partners' ecosystems. The engineering software simulation market is strong and growing. The market growth is driven by customers' need for rapid, quality innovation in a cost efficient manner, enabling faster time to market new products and lower warranty costs. We are investing in solutions to help engineers deal with increasing product complexity in electrification, including electric vehicles; autonomy, including self-driving vehicles; 5G and telecommunications; and the industrial internet of things (IIoT).

EXECUTIVES

Chairman, Director, Ronald W. Hovsepian
President, Chief Executive Officer, Director, Ajei S. Gopal, $768,750 total compensation
Senior Vice President, Chief Financial Officer, Nicole Anasenes
Products Senior Vice President, Shane R. Emswiler, $266,864 total compensation
Vice President, General Counsel, Secretary, Janet Lee, $316,975 total compensation

Worldwide Sales Senior Vice President, Customer Excellence Senior Vice President, Richard S. Mahoney, $378,325 total compensation
Finance Senior Vice President, Administration Senior Vice President, Maria T. Shields, $396,700 total compensation
Director, Jim Frankola
Director, Alec D. Gallimore
Director, Robert M. Calderoni
Director, Glenda M. Dorchak
Director, Barbara V. Scherer
Director, Ravi K. Vijayaraghavan
Director, Anil Chakravarthy
Auditors : DELOITTE & TOUCHE LLP

LOCATIONS

HQ: Ansys Inc.
2600 ANSYS Drive, Canonsburg, PA 15317
Phone: 844 462-6797
Web: www.ansys.com

2018 Sales

	$ mil.	% of total
United States	506.3	39
Japan	146	11
Germany	140.5	11
South Korea	72.7	6
France	67.6	5
Canada	57.6	5
Other European	193.3	15
Other international	109.6	8
Total	1,293.6	100

PRODUCTS/OPERATIONS

2018 Sales

	$ mil.	% of total
Software licenses:		
Lease licenses	275.6	21
Perpetual licenses	301.1	23
Maintenance & service:		
Maintenance	676.9	53
Service	40	3
Total	1,293.6	100

COMPETITORS

ALTERYX, INC.
CDK GLOBAL, INC.
FIREEYE, INC.
FIVE9, INC.
NETSCOUT SYSTEMS, INC.
PTC INC.
RAPID7, INC.
SPLUNK INC.
SYNOPSYS, INC.
VERINT SYSTEMS INC.

HISTORICAL FINANCIALS

Company Type: Public

Income Statement — FYE: December 31

	REVENUE ($mil)	NET INCOME ($mil)	NET PROFIT MARGIN	EMPLOYEES
12/21	1,906.7	454.6	23.8%	5,100
12/20	1,681.2	433.8	25.8%	4,800
12/19	1,515.8	451.2	29.8%	4,100
12/18	1,293.6	419.3	32.4%	3,400
12/17	1,095.2	259.2	23.7%	2,900
Annual Growth	14.9%	15.1%	—	15.2%

2021 Year-End Financials

Debt ratio: 11.9%
Return on equity: 10.5%
Cash ($ mil.): 667.6
Current Ratio: 2.10
Long-term debt ($ mil.): 753.5
No. of shares ($ mil.): 87.0
Dividends
 Yield: —
 Payout: —
Market value ($ mil.): 34,929.0

	STOCK PRICE ($) FY Close	P/E High/Low		PER SHARE ($) Earnings	Dividends	Book Value
12/21	401.12	79	56	5.16	0.00	51.49
12/20	363.80	72	40	4.97	0.00	47.33
12/19	257.41	48	26	5.25	0.00	40.28
12/18	142.94	38	27	4.88	0.00	31.68
12/17	147.59	50	31	2.98	0.00	26.68
Annual Growth	28.4%	—	—	14.7%	—	17.9%

Antares Pharma Inc.

Antares Pharma understands antagonism towards needles. The company develops needle-free systems for administering injectable drugs. Its Medi-Jector Vision system, for instance, injects a thin, high-pressure stream of liquid, eliminating the need for a needle. The Vision system is used primarily for the delivery of insulin and of human growth hormones (hGH) and Vibex disposable pen injectors carry epinephrine and other products. The products are available in the US and overseas. In addition to its needle-free systems, the company develops other drug-delivery platforms, including topical gels, orally administered disintegrating tablets, and mini-needle injection systems.

Operations

Much of the company's revenue, particularly for its injection devices, comes via agreements with pharmaceutical partners, which sell its needle-free injectors along with their drugs. Antares' multi-product deal with manufacturer Teva Pharmaceutical includes hGH and epinephrine delivery systems. Dutch drug firm Ferring, which distributes Antares' needle-free device for use with its hGH hormone, is another key customer. Teva and Ferring each account for a third of Antares' sales.

Its first topical gel product, the Elestrin treatment for menopausal symptoms, is marketed by Meda Pharma. Gelnique, another menopause-related treatment, is marketed by Actavis.

Geographic Reach

Antares has two facilities in the US; it markets its products in the US, Canada, Europe, and Asia through partners. The US accounts for about three-quarters of revenue.

Financial Performance

For 2012 revenue jumped nearly 40% on the strength of its agreements with Teva, milestone payments from undisclosed development projects, and other partner payouts. R&D spending, however, lead to an $11 million net loss as the company works on a rheumatoid arthritis treatment. The company issued stock during the year and finished with positive cash flow. Though Antares has been experiencing revenue growth, continued R&D and marketing expenses have it operating at an accumulated deficit of $152 million.

Strategy

Going forward, Antares just has to keep developing products and finding marketing partners to help sell them. To cut the risk a bit, it usually partners with others for R&D, which keeps the money flowing in the form of milestone payments.

Company Background

Antares was formed in 2001 when Medi-Ject (the company's former name) completed a reverse acquisition of Permatec, a Swiss company with expertise in topical and oral drug delivery technologies. Director Jacques Gonella, the founder of Permatec, owns about 15% of Antares Pharma.

EXECUTIVES

Chairman, Director, Leonard S. Jacob
President, Chief Executive Officer, Chief Financial Officer, Robert F. Apple, $550,000 total compensation
Executive President, Chief Financial Officer, Fred M. Powell, $365,525 total compensation
Executive Vice President, General Counsel, Chief Compliance Officer, Human Resources, Secretary, Peter J. Graham, $382,940 total compensation
Vice President, Corporate Controller, Keith Muckenhirn, $261,092 total compensation
Division Officer, Dario Carrara, $346,023 total compensation
Division Officer, Peter Sadowski, $278,000 total compensation
Director, Thomas J. Garrity
Director, Peter S. Greenleaf
Director, Anton G. Gueth
Director, Robert P. Roche
Director, Marvin S Samson
Director, Karen L. Smith
Auditors : KPMG LLP

LOCATIONS

HQ: Antares Pharma Inc.
100 Princeton South, Suite 300, Ewing, NJ 08628
Phone: 609 359-3020
Web: www.antarespharma.com

2015 Sales

	$ mil.	% of total
US	39.3	86
Europe	6.0	13
Other	0.4	1
Total	45.7	100

PRODUCTS/OPERATIONS

2015 Sales

	$ mil.	% of total
Product sales	27.5	60
Development revenue	8.9	19
Licensing fees	7.3	16
Royalties	2.0	4
Total	45.7	100

Selected Products
Elestrin estradiol gel (Meda)
Gelnique 3% (Oxybutynin Gel 3%) (Actavis)
Otrexup (McKesson)
Twin-Jector EZ II (JCR Pharmaceuticals)
ZOMA-Jet for ZOMACTON brand human growth hormone. (Ferring)
ZomaJet 2 Vision (Ferring)

COMPETITORS
ACURA PHARMACEUTICALS, INC.
ADARE PHARMACEUTICALS, INC.
ALLERGAN LIMITED
AMPHASTAR PHARMACEUTICALS, INC.
CUTERA, INC.
LANNETT COMPANY, INC.
MANNKIND CORPORATION
NOVEN PHARMACEUTICALS, INC.
VECTURA GROUP SERVICES LIMITED
ZOGENIX, INC.

HISTORICAL FINANCIALS
Company Type: Public

Income Statement — FYE: December 31

	REVENUE ($mil)	NET INCOME ($mil)	NET PROFIT MARGIN	EMPLOYEES
12/20	149.5	56.2	37.6%	185
12/19	123.8	(2.0)	—	178
12/18	63.5	(6.5)	—	165
12/17	54.5	(16.7)	—	111
12/16	52.2	(24.3)	—	110
Annual Growth	30.1%	—	—	13.9%

2020 Year-End Financials
Debt ratio: 19.2%
Return on equity: 64.5%
Cash ($ mil.): 53.1
Current Ratio: 2.00
Long-term debt ($ mil.): 24.6
No. of shares ($ mil.): 166.8
Dividends
 Yield: —
 Payout: —
Market value ($ mil.): 666.0

STOCK PRICE ($) FY Close	P/E High/Low		PER SHARE ($) Earnings Dividends Book Value		
12/20 3.99	13	5	0.33	0.00	0.71
12/19 4.70	—	—	(0.01)	0.00	0.33
12/18 2.72	—	—	(0.04)	0.00	0.24
12/17 1.99	—	—	(0.11)	0.00	0.21
12/16 2.33	—	—	(0.16)	0.00	0.29
Annual Growth 14.4%			—	—	25.1%

Antero Midstream Corp

EXECUTIVES

Chairman, President, Chief Executive Officer, Subsidiary Officer, Director, Paul M. Rady, $858,000 total compensation
Legal Senior Vice President, Legal Chief Compliance Officer, Legal General Counsel, Legal Secretary, Yvette K. Schultz
Finance Senior Vice President, Finance Subsidiary Officer, Director, Michael N. Kennedy, $384,375 total compensation
Reserves, Planning & Midstream Senior Vice President, W. Patrick Ash
Regional Senior Vice President, Subsidiary Officer, Alvyn A. Schopp, $442,800 total compensation
Vice President, Chief Financial Officer, Treasurer, Brendan E. Krueger
Director, Nancy E. Chisholm
Director, Peter A. Dea
Director, W. Howard Keenan
Director, Janine J. McArdle
Director, Brooks J. Klimley
Director, John C. Mollenkopf
Director, David H. Keyte
Director, Rose M. Robeson
Auditors : KPMG LLP

LOCATIONS
HQ: Antero Midstream Corp
 1615 Wynkoop Street, Denver, CO 80202
Phone: 303 357-7310
Web: www.anteromidstream.com

HISTORICAL FINANCIALS
Company Type: Public

Income Statement — FYE: December 31

	REVENUE ($mil)	NET INCOME ($mil)	NET PROFIT MARGIN	EMPLOYEES
12/21	898.2	331.6	36.9%	519
12/20	900.7	(122.5)	—	522
12/19	792.5	(355.1)	—	547
12/18	142.9	66.6	46.6%	0
12/17	69.7	2.3	3.3%	0
Annual Growth	89.5%	245.6%	—	—

2021 Year-End Financials
Debt ratio: 56.3%
Return on equity: 14.0%
Cash ($ mil.): —
Current Ratio: 0.74
Long-term debt ($ mil.): 3,122.9
No. of shares ($ mil.): 477.5
Dividends
 Yield: 10.1%
 Payout: 142.3%
Market value ($ mil.): 4,622.0

STOCK PRICE ($) FY Close	P/E High/Low		PER SHARE ($) Earnings Dividends Book Value		
12/21 9.68	17	11	0.69	0.98	4.79
12/20 7.71	—	—	(0.26)	1.23	5.07
12/19 7.59	—	—	(0.80)	0.92	6.49
12/18 11.18	67	32	0.33	0.54	0.17
12/17 19.72	752	559	0.03	0.00	0.08
Annual Growth (16.3%)			— 119.0%		— 174.9%

Apollo Medical Holdings Inc

EXECUTIVES

Subsidiary Officer, Executive Chairman, Director, Kenneth Sim, $950,000 total compensation
President, Co-Chief Executive Officer, Subsidiary Officer, Director, Thomas S. Lam, $950,000 total compensation
Engineering Co-Chief Executive Officer, Brandon Sim
Interim Chief Financial Officer, Chan Basho
Chief Administrative Officer, Subsidiary Officer, Wai Chow (Albert) Young
Chief Accounting Officer, John Vong
Subsidiary Officer, Director, Linda Marsh
Lead Independent Director, Director, Mitchell W. Kitayama
Director, David G. Schmidt
Director, Michael F. Eng
Director, Ernest A. Bates
Director, John Chiang
Director, Matthew Mazdyasni
Director, J. Lorraine Estradas
Director, Weili Dai
Director, Mark Fawcett
Auditors : Ernst and Young, LLP

LOCATIONS
HQ: Apollo Medical Holdings Inc
 1668 S. Garfield Avenue, 2nd Floor, Alhambra, CA 91801
Phone: 626 282-0288
Web: www.apollomed.net

HISTORICAL FINANCIALS
Company Type: Public

Income Statement — FYE: December 31

	REVENUE ($mil)	NET INCOME ($mil)	NET PROFIT MARGIN	EMPLOYEES
12/20	687.1	37.8	5.5%	630
12/19	560.6	14.1	2.5%	555
12/18	519.9	10.8	2.1%	575
12/17*	357.7	25.8	7.2%	613
03/17	57.4	(8.9)	—	1,149
Annual Growth	86.0%	—	—	(13.9%)

*Fiscal year change

2020 Year-End Financials
Debt ratio: 29.5%
Return on equity: 14.4%
Cash ($ mil.): 193.4
Current Ratio: 2.94
Long-term debt ($ mil.): 230.5
No. of shares ($ mil.): 42.2
Dividends
 Yield: —
 Payout: —
Market value ($ mil.): 772.0

STOCK PRICE ($) FY Close	P/E High/Low		PER SHARE ($) Earnings Dividends Book Value		
12/20 18.27	19	9	1.01	0.00	7.83
12/19 18.41	52	34	0.39	0.00	5.33
12/18 19.85	91	40	0.29	0.00	5.22
12/17* 24.00	24	6	0.90	0.00	4.95
03/17 9.00	—	—	(1.49)	0.00	(0.06)
Annual Growth 19.4%	—	—	—	—	—

*Fiscal year change

AppFolio Inc

EXECUTIVES

Chairperson, Andreas von Blottnitz

Real Estate President, Real Estate Chief Executive Officer, Director, Shane Trigg
Chief Financial Officer, Principal Accounting Officer, Fay Sien Goon
Chief Technology Officer, Jonathan Walker, $250,000 total compensation
Chief Legal Officer, Corporate Secretary, Matt Mazza
Director, Timothy Bliss
Director, Winifred Webb
Director, Agnes Bundy Scanlan
Director, Janet E. Kerr
Director, Olivia Nottebohm
Director, Alex Wolf
Auditors : PricewaterhouseCoopers LLP

LOCATIONS

HQ: AppFolio Inc
50 Castilian Drive, Santa Barbara, CA 93117
Phone: 805 364-6093

HISTORICAL FINANCIALS
Company Type: Public

Income Statement — FYE: December 31

	REVENUE ($mil)	NET INCOME ($mil)	NET PROFIT MARGIN	EMPLOYEES
12/20	310.0	158.4	51.1%	1,335
12/19	256.0	36.2	14.2%	1,240
12/18	190.0	19.9	10.5%	916
12/17	143.8	9.7	6.8%	672
12/16	105.5	(8.2)	—	626
Annual Growth	30.9%	—	—	20.8%

2020 Year-End Financials
Debt ratio: —
Return on equity: 75.6%
Cash ($ mil.): 140.2
Current Ratio: 4.00
Long-term debt ($ mil.): —
No. of shares ($ mil.): 34.3
Dividends
 Yield: —
 Payout: —
Market value ($ mil.): 6,191.0

	STOCK PRICE ($) FY Close	P/E High/Low		PER SHARE ($) Earnings	Dividends	Book Value
12/20	180.04	40	18	4.44	0.00	8.31
12/19	109.95	108	53	1.02	0.00	3.86
12/18	59.22	154	66	0.56	0.00	2.71
12/17	41.50	178	76	0.28	0.00	2.50
12/16	23.85	—	—	(0.25)	0.00	2.07
Annual Growth	65.8%	—	—	—	—	41.6%

Arbor Realty Trust Inc

Money doesn't grow on trees, so Arbor Realty Trust invests in real estate-related assets. The real estate investment trust (REIT) buys structured finance assets in the commercial and multifamily real estate markets. It primarily invests in bridge loans (short-term financing) and mezzanine loans (large and usually unsecured loans), but also invests in discounted mortgage notes and other assets. The REIT targets lending and investment opportunities where borrowers seek interim financing until permanent financing is attained. Arbor Realty Trust is managed by financing firm Arbor Commercial Mortgage, though in early 2016 the REIT agreed to buy Arbor Commercial Mortgage for $250 million to expand into the government-sponsored, multi-family real estate loan origination business.

EXECUTIVES

Chairman, President, Chief Executive Officer, Director, Ivan Kaufman, $1,000,000 total compensation
Chief Financial Officer, Treasurer, Paul Elenio, $500,000 total compensation
Structured Finance Executive Vice President, Fred Weber, $500,000 total compensation
Structured Securitization Executive Vice President, Gene Kilgore, $500,000 total compensation
Executive Vice President, Corporate Secretary, Senior Counsel, General Counsel, John J. Bishar, $256,986 total compensation
Executive Vice President, General Counsel, Malvina Iannone
Managing Director, Chief Accounting Officer, Thomas J. Ridings
Division Officer, John Natalone
Division Officer, Danny van der Reis
Division Officer, Andrew Guziewicz, $322,917 total compensation
Division Officer, John Caulfield, $500,000 total compensation
Lead Director, Director, William C. Green
Director, Melvin F. Lazar
Director, Kenneth J. Bacon
Director, Elliot Schwartz
Director, Joseph A. Martello
Director, Edward J. Farrell
Director, Caryn Effron
Auditors : Ernst & Young LLP

LOCATIONS

HQ: Arbor Realty Trust Inc
333 Earle Ovington Boulevard, Suite 900, Uniondale, NY 11553
Phone: 516 506-4200
Web: www.arbor.com

COMPETITORS

ANWORTH MORTGAGE ASSET CORPORATION
ARBOR COMMERCIAL MORTGAGE, LLC
BLACKSTONE MORTGAGE TRUST, INC.
CHERRY HILL MORTGAGE INVESTMENT CORPORATION
EASTERN LIGHT CAPITAL, INCORPORATED
ELLINGTON FINANCIAL INC.
JER INVESTORS TRUST INC
PETRA REAL ESTATE OPPORTUNITY TRUST
STARWOOD PROPERTY TRUST, INC.
TIS MORTGAGE INVESTMENT COMPANY

HISTORICAL FINANCIALS
Company Type: Public

Income Statement — FYE: December 31

	REVENUE ($mil)	NET INCOME ($mil)	NET PROFIT MARGIN	EMPLOYEES
12/21	799.2	339.3	42.5%	579
12/20	603.7	170.9	28.3%	522
12/19	535.7	128.6	24.0%	532
12/18	484.8	180.2	37.2%	468
12/17	346.6	121.6	35.1%	445
Annual Growth	23.2%	29.2%	—	6.8%

2021 Year-End Financials
Debt ratio: 80.0%
Return on equity: 18.0%
Cash ($ mil.): 404.5
Current Ratio: 0.19
Long-term debt ($ mil.): 7,575.1
No. of shares ($ mil.): 151.3
Dividends
 Yield: 7.5%
 Payout: 57.7%
Market value ($ mil.): 2,773.0

	STOCK PRICE ($) FY Close	P/E High/Low		PER SHARE ($) Earnings	Dividends	Book Value
12/21	18.32	9	6	2.28	1.38	15.98
12/20	14.18	11	3	1.41	1.23	10.91
12/19	14.35	12	8	1.27	1.29	10.80
12/18	10.07	8	5	1.50	1.13	10.66
12/17	8.64	8	6	1.12	0.72	11.27
Annual Growth	20.7%	—	—	19.4%	17.7%	9.1%

Ares Management Corp

EXECUTIVES

President, Chief Executive Officer, Associate/Affiliate Company Officer, Director, Michael J. Arougheti
Executive Vice President, Chief Legal Officer, Secretary, Associate/Affiliate Company Officer, Michael D. Weiner
Chief Operating Officer, Chief Financial Officer, Executive Vice President, Associate/Affiliate Company Officer, Michael R. McFerran, $1,200,000 total compensation
Chief Marketing Officer, Chief Strategy Officer, Associate/Affiliate Company Officer, Ryan Berry
Partner, Associate/Affiliate Company Officer, Director, David B. Kaplan
Executive Chairman, Chairman, Director, Antony P. Ressler
Partner, Associate/Affiliate Company Officer, John H. Kissick
Partner, Associate/Affiliate Company Officer, Director, Bennett Rosenthal
Partner, Associate/Affiliate Company Officer, R. Kipp deVeer
Director, Antoinette Bush
Director, Paul G. Joubert
Director, Michael M. Lynton
Director, Judy D. Olian
Auditors : Ernst & Young LLP

LOCATIONS

HQ: Ares Management Corp
2000 Avenue of the Stars, 12th Floor, Los Angeles, CA 90067
Phone: 310 201-4100
Web: www.aresmgmt.com

HISTORICAL FINANCIALS

Company Type: Public

Income Statement — FYE: December 31

	REVENUE ($mil)	NET INCOME ($mil)	NET PROFIT MARGIN	EMPLOYEES
12/20	1,764.0	152.1	8.6%	1,450
12/19	1,765.4	148.8	8.4%	1,200
12/18	958.4	57.0	5.9%	1,100
12/17	1,415.4	76.1	5.4%	1,000
12/16	1,199.2	111.8	9.3%	925
Annual Growth	10.1%	8.0%	—	11.9%

2020 Year-End Financials
Debt ratio: 70.7%   No. of shares ($ mil.): 259.6
Return on equity: 15.4%   Dividends
Cash ($ mil.): 1,062.1   Yield: 3.4%
Current Ratio: 8.39   Payout: 296.2%
Long-term debt ($ mil.): 10,722.9   Market value ($ mil.): 12,216.0

	STOCK PRICE ($) FY Close	P/E High/Low		PER SHARE ($) Earnings	Dividends	Book Value
12/20	47.05	56	26	0.87	1.60	4.60
12/19	35.69	32	15	1.06	1.28	6.67
12/18	17.78	84	56	0.30	1.33	5.79
12/17	20.00	38	28	0.62	1.13	6.97
12/16	19.20	16	9	1.20	0.83	7.32
Annual Growth	25.1%	—	—	(7.7%)	17.8%	(11.0%)

Arista Networks Inc

EXECUTIVES

Chairman, Chief Development Officer, Andreas Bechtolsheim, $300,000 total compensation
President, Chief Executive Officer, Director, Jayshree Ullal, $300,000 total compensation
Senior Vice President, Chief Financial Officer, Ita M. Brennan, $300,000 total compensation
Software Engineering Senior Vice President, Software Engineering Chief Technology Officer, Kenneth Duda, $280,769 total compensation
Engineering Senior Vice President, Operations Senior Vice President, Engineering Chief Platform Officer, Operations Chief Platform Officer, John McCool, $236,538 total compensation
Senior Vice President, General Counsel, Marc Taxay, $256,154 total compensation
Chief Operating Officer, Anshul Sadana, $290,385 total compensation
Lead Independent Director, Director, Daniel Scheinman
Director, Kelly Battles
Director, Charles H. Giancarlo
Director, Mark B. Templeton
Director, Nikos Theodosopoulos
Director, Lewis Chew
Auditors : Ernst & Young LLP

LOCATIONS

HQ: Arista Networks Inc
5453 Great America Parkway, Santa Clara, CA 95054
Phone: 408 547-5500
Web: www.arista.com

HISTORICAL FINANCIALS

Company Type: Public

Income Statement — FYE: December 31

	REVENUE ($mil)	NET INCOME ($mil)	NET PROFIT MARGIN	EMPLOYEES
12/21	2,948.0	840.8	28.5%	2,993
12/20	2,317.5	634.5	27.4%	2,613
12/19	2,410.7	859.8	35.7%	2,300
12/18	2,151.3	328.1	15.3%	2,300
12/17	1,646.1	423.2	25.7%	1,800
Annual Growth	15.7%	18.7%	—	13.6%

2021 Year-End Financials
Debt ratio: —   No. of shares ($ mil.): 307.6
Return on equity: 23.0%   Dividends
Cash ($ mil.): 620.8   Yield: —
Current Ratio: 4.34   Payout: —
Long-term debt ($ mil.): —   Market value ($ mil.): 44,229.0

	STOCK PRICE ($) FY Close	P/E High/Low		PER SHARE ($) Earnings	Dividends	Book Value
12/21	143.75	194	44	2.63	0.00	12.93
12/20	290.57	139	75	2.00	0.00	10.90
12/19	203.40	117	66	2.66	0.00	9.47
12/18	210.70	281	172	1.02	0.00	7.08
12/17	235.58	167	60	1.34	0.00	5.64
Annual Growth	(11.6%)	—	—	18.4%	—	23.1%

ARKO Corp

EXECUTIVES

Chairman, President, Chief Executive Officer, Director, Arie Kotler
Chief Financial Officer, Donald Bassell
General Counsel, Secretary, Maury Bricks
Director, Steven J. Heyer
Director, Michael J. Gade
Director, Sherman K. Edmiston
Director, Morris Willner
Director, Starlette B. Johnson
Director, Andrew R. Heyer

LOCATIONS

HQ: ARKO Corp
8565 Magellan Parkway, Suite 400, Richmond, VA 23227-1150
Phone: 804 730-1568
Web: www.arkocorp.com

HISTORICAL FINANCIALS

Company Type: Public

Income Statement — FYE: December 31

	REVENUE ($mil)	NET INCOME ($mil)	NET PROFIT MARGIN	EMPLOYEES
12/20	3,910.7	13.1	0.3%	10,380
12/19	4,128.6	(43.5)	—	10,102
12/18	4,064.8	10.9	0.3%	0
12/17	3,041.1	(5.8)	—	0
Annual Growth	8.7%	—	—	—

2020 Year-End Financials
Debt ratio: 35.9%   No. of shares ($ mil.): 124.1
Return on equity: 6.8%   Dividends
Cash ($ mil.): 293.6   Yield: —
Current Ratio: 1.57   Payout: —
Long-term debt ($ mil.): 935.2   Market value ($ mil.): 1,117.0

	STOCK PRICE ($) FY Close	P/E High/Low		PER SHARE ($) Earnings	Dividends	Book Value
12/20	9.00	67	56	0.14	0.00	2.56
Annual Growth	—	—	—	—	—	—

Armada Hoffler Properties Inc

EXECUTIVES

Executive Chairman, Director, Daniel A. Hoffler
Vice-Chairman, President, Chief Executive Officer, Director, Louis S. Haddad, $779,738 total compensation
Finance Chief Financial Officer, Finance Treasurer, Finance Corporate Secretary, Matthew Barnes-Smith
Chief Operating Officer, Shawn J. Tibbetts
Division Officer, Eric E. Apperson, $352,996 total compensation
Division Officer, Shelly R. Hampton, $301,809 total compensation
Lead Independent Director, Independent Director, James C. Cherry
Director, A. Russell Kirk
Independent Director, John W. Snow
Independent Director, George F. Allen
Independent Director, James A. Carroll
Independent Director, Eva S. Hardy
Auditors : Ernst & Young LLP

LOCATIONS

HQ: Armada Hoffler Properties Inc
222 Central Park Avenue, Suite 2100, Virginia Beach, VA 23462
Phone: 757 366-4000
Web: www.armadahoffler.com

HISTORICAL FINANCIALS
Company Type: Public

Income Statement   FYE: December 31

	REVENUE ($mil)	NET INCOME ($mil)	NET PROFIT MARGIN	EMPLOYEES
12/20	383.6	29.1	7.6%	158
12/19	257.1	24.0	9.4%	169
12/18	193.3	17.2	8.9%	156
12/17	302.7	21.0	7.0%	160
12/16	258.3	28.0	10.9%	151
Annual Growth	10.4%	0.9%	—	1.1%

2020 Year-End Financials
Debt ratio: 51.2%   No. of shares ($ mil.): 59.0
Return on equity: 6.2%   Dividends
Cash ($ mil.): 41.0   Yield: 3.9%
Current Ratio: 2.76   Payout: 115.7%
Long-term debt ($ mil.): 981.7   Market value ($ mil.): 663.0

	STOCK PRICE ($) FY Close	P/E High/Low		PER SHARE ($) Earnings	Dividends	Book Value
12/20	11.22	50	19	0.38	0.44	8.86
12/19	18.35	46	34	0.41	0.84	7.26
12/18	14.06	45	36	0.36	0.80	5.48
12/17	15.53	32	25	0.50	0.76	5.04
12/16	14.57	18	12	0.85	0.72	3.95
Annual Growth	(6.3%)	—	—	(18.2%)	(11.6%)	22.4%

Arrow Financial Corp.

Arrow Financial has more than one shaft in its quiver. It's the holding company for two banks: $2 billion-asset Glens Falls National Bank operates 30 branches in eastern upstate New York, while $400 million-asset Saratoga National Bank and Trust Company has around 10 branches in Saratoga County. Serving local individuals and businesses, the banks offer standard deposit and loan products as well as retirement, trust, and estate planning services and employee benefit plan administration. Its subsidiaries include: McPhillips Insurance Agency and Upstate Agency, which offer property and casualty insurance; Capital Financial Group, which sells group health plans; and North Country Investment Advisors, which provides financial planning services.

Operations
Arrow Financial's loan portfolio consisted of residential real estate mortgages and home equity loans (40% of loan assets), commercial and commercial real estate loans (31%), and indirect auto loans (29%) at the end of 2015.

The banking group makes more than 70% of its revenue from interest income. About 58% of Arrow Financial's total revenue came from loan interest (including fees) during 2015, while another 14% came from interest on taxable and tax-exempt investment securities. The rest of its revenue came from insurance commissions (9% of revenue), customer service fees (9%), fiduciary activity income (8%), and other miscellaneous income sources.

Geographic Reach
Glens Falls National Bank has 30 branches in eastern upstate New York (in Warren, Washington, Saratoga, Essex, and Clinton Counties). Saratoga Springs-based Saratoga National Bank operates nine branches in Saratoga, Albany, and Rensselaer Counties.

Financial Performance
Arrow Financial Corporation's revenues and profits have been slowly rising since 2013 mostly as steady -- and more creditworthy -- loan growth has spurred more interest income.

The group's revenue climbed 4% to $98.86 million during 2015 mostly as 7%-plus growth in loan and other interest-earning assets continued to spur additional interest income.

Revenue growth in 2015 pushed Arrow Financial's net income up 6% to $24.66 million. The banking group's operating cash levels dipped 6% to $28.93 million despite earnings growth, mostly due to unfavorable working capital changes.

Strategy
Arrow Financial has been working its loan portfolio quality by implementing smarter lending strategies with stronger underwriting and collateral control procedures and credit review systems.

It's also slowly expanding its business and branch network in the Capital District of New York, which has been a key market for the bnak's growth. In September 2015, its Saratoga National Bank subsidiary opened its ninth branch in Troy. In June 2014, it opened a new branch in Colonie after opening two new branches in Queensbury and Clifton Park in 2013.

EXECUTIVES
Chairman, Director, Thomas L. Hoy, $415,000 total compensation
President, Chief Executive Officer, Subsidiary Officer, Director, Thomas J. Murphy, $490,000 total compensation
Senior Vice President, Chief Financial Officer, Treasurer, Subsidiary Officer, Edward J. Campanella, $235,000 total compensation
Senior Vice President, Chief Operating Officer, Andrew J. Wise, $195,000 total compensation
Senior Vice President, Subsidiary Officer, Director, David S. DeMarco, $290,000 total compensation
Senior Vice President, Subsidiary Officer, David D. Kaiser, $235,000 total compensation
Director, Mark L. Behan
Director, Tenee R. Casaccio
Director, Michael B. Clarke
Director, Gary C. Dake
Director, David G. Kruczlnicki
Director, Elizabeth Miller
Director, Raymond F. O'Conor
Director, William L. Owens
Director, Colin L. Read
Director, Richard J. Reisman
Auditors: KPMG LLP

LOCATIONS
HQ: Arrow Financial Corp.
250 Glen Street, Glens Falls, NY 12801
Phone: 518 745-1000
Web: www.arrowfinancial.com

PRODUCTS/OPERATIONS
2015 Sales

	$ mil.	% of total
Interest and dividend income		
Interest and Fees on Loans	56.9	58
Fully Taxable	8.0	8
Exempt from Federal Taxes	5.7	6
Non-interest income		
Fees for Other Services to Customers	9.2	9
Insurance Commissions	9.0	9
Income From Fiduciary Activities	7.8	8
Other	2.2	2
Total	98.8	100

Selected Subsidiaries
Glens Falls National Bank and Trust Company
    Arrow Properties, Inc. (real estate investment trust)
    Capital Financial Group, Inc.
    Glens Falls National Community Development Corporation
    Glens Falls National Insurance Agencies, LLC (dba McPhillips Agency)
    Loomis & LaPann, Inc.
    NC Financial Services, Inc.
    North Country Investment Advisers, Inc.
    Upstate Agency, LLC
Saratoga National Bank and Trust Company

COMPETITORS
AMERICAN NATIONAL BANKSHARES INC.
AMES NATIONAL CORPORATION
CITY HOLDING COMPANY
COMMUNITY BANK SYSTEM, INC.
FIRST HORIZON CORPORATION

HISTORICAL FINANCIALS
Company Type: Public

Income Statement   FYE: December 31

	ASSETS ($mil)	NET INCOME ($mil)	INCOME AS % OF ASSETS	EMPLOYEES
12/20	3,688.6	40.8	1.1%	517
12/19	3,184.2	37.4	1.2%	520
12/18	2,988.3	36.2	1.2%	516
12/17	2,760.4	29.3	1.1%	533
12/16	2,605.2	26.5	1.0%	524
Annual Growth	9.1%	11.4%	—	(0.3%)

2020 Year-End Financials
Return on assets: 1.1%   Dividends
Return on equity: 12.8%   Yield: 3.5%
Long-term debt ($ mil.): —   Payout: 39.6%
No. of shares ($ mil.): 15.9 Market value ($ mil.): 478.0
Sales ($ mil.): 144.5

	STOCK PRICE ($)	P/E	PER SHARE ($)		
	FY Close	High/Low	Earnings	Dividends	Book Value
12/20	29.91	15 9	2.56	1.02	20.92
12/19	37.80	16 13	2.36	0.99	18.96
12/18	32.02	17 13	2.29	0.94	17.04
12/17	33.95	22 17	1.87	0.87	15.91
12/16	40.50	24 15	1.70	0.84	14.88
Annual Growth	(7.3%)	— —	10.8%	4.8%	8.9%

ASGN Inc

ASGN Incorporated (formerly known as On Assignment) is a specialist staffing agency that places professionals, from IT consultants to lab assistants, with clients in need of temporary (or permanent) help. The firm offers its services to both commercial and federal government customers. Its largest segment caters to companies in Fortune 1000 clients as well as mid-market companies. The company generated majority of its sales in domestic operations. The company has about 30 branch offices across the US.

Operations

ASGN has reorganized after selling its Oxford Global Resources segment in 2021. The company now has two operating segments: Commercial (more than 70%) and Federal Government (about 30%).

The company's Commercial segment provides consulting, creative digital marketing, and permanent placement services primarily to Fortune 1000 clients and mid-market companies. The Federal Government segment provides mission-critical solutions to the Department of Defense, intelligence agencies, and civilian agencies.

Geographic Reach

Headquartered in Virgina, ASGN operates from about 130 branch offices in US, Canada, UK, and Spain. The Apex Systems Headquarters is also located at Richmond, Virginia, the ESC Headquarters at Fairfax, Virginia, and its Delivery Centers in Mexico and India.

Sales and Marketing

ASGN provides staffing services and solutions to several markets, including Fortune 1000 companies and mid-market clients, and the federal, state, and local government.

Financial Performance

ASGN's performance for the past five years has fluctuated with decrease from 2018 to 2019, but has recovered annually after that ending with 2021 as the company's strongest performing year over the period.

In 2021, the company's revenues for the year were $4.0 billion, up 14.5% from 2020 primarily as a result of double-digit organic growth of its Commercial Segment and the contribution of $124.4 million from acquired businesses.

ASGN reported an increase in net income of $209 million to $409.9 million in 2021 compared to the prior year's $200.3 million.

ASGN's cash balance at the end of 2021 amounted to $529.6 million. The company generated $193.7 million from its operating activities. Investing activities and financing activities used $246.5 million and $529.6 million, respectively. Main cash uses were for aquisitions, purchases of property and equipment, and repurchases of common stock.

Strategy

The company is focused on high-margin work with high-volume scalable clients and projects, at large commercial enterprise accounts and federal government customers.

ASGN strategic innovation efforts and technology investments focus on putting the best productivity tools in the hands of its recruiters, candidates and clients, making it easy for clients and consultants to work with ASGN. The company respond to emerging trends in digitization and candidate sourcing to better position its businesses and improve how it serve clients and consultants.

Mergers and Acquisitions

In 2022, ASGN agreed to acquire Massachusetts-based GlideFast Consulting LLC (GlideFast), an elite ServiceNow Partner and leading IT consulting, implementation and development company, for $350 million in cash. Upon the close of the acquisition, ASGN will become a major player in the large and growing ServiceNow marketplace.

In 2021, ASGN acquired Virginia-based Enterprise Resource Performance, Inc. (ERPi), a premier healthcare consulting and data analytics firm that delivers federal healthcare transformation services. ERPi's team of 250 consultants will become part of the Enterprise Solutions business unit within ECS, ASGN's Federal Government Segment. "The acquisition of ERPi deepens ECS' capabilities across a number of exciting solution areas and provides key contract vehicles that will bolster our current healthcare industry offerings. We are thrilled to bring their team's experience to new and existing customers across industry and government," said George Wilson, President of ECS.

Also in 2021, ASGN acquired Virgina-based IndraSoft Inc., a leading cybersecurity and digital transformation solutions provider to the federal government. IndraSoft's team of more than 220 highly skilled consultants will be integrated into the ECS Missions Solutions business unit. "The acquisition of IndraSoft deepens our footprint at key customers, including the U.S. Air Force, Army Intelligence, DISA, and other defense agencies," said George Wilson, President of ECS.

Company Background

ASGN Incorporated was founded in 1985. Since its IPO in 1992, the company has grown steadily, with multiple offices throughout North America and Europe.

HISTORY

Chemists Bruce Culver and Raf Dahlquist concocted the company in 1985. Lab Support (its original name) got off to a good start, but the founders were scientists, not business strategists; by 1989 the company was losing steam. The firm's venture investors took over, installing new management under Tom Buelter, who had developed Kelly Services' home care division. He refocused operations to temporary scientific services and turned the company around. It went public in 1992 as On Assignment.

In 1994 On Assignment bought 1st Choice Personnel and Sklar Resource Group, which specialized in temporary placement of financial professionals. The next year it started its Advanced Science Professionals unit to place temps in highly skilled scientific positions. With the 1996 purchase of Minneapolis-based EnviroStaff, On Assignment also began providing temporary workers in environmental fields. On Assignment crossed the border and started operations in Canada in 1997. In 1999 it established Clinical Lab Staff as its fourth division. Also by 1999 the company had opened the first three of several planned European offices in the UK.

In 2001 Buelter relinquished the CEO position to Joe Peterson. (Buelter resigned as chairman early the following year.) Also in 2002 the company acquired Health Personnel Options Corporation, a provider of temporary travel nurses and other health care professionals. The end of 2003 saw the appointment of Peter Dameris as the president and CEO of On Assignment.

In 2007 On Assignment reached new levels of growth with the key acquisitions of IT and engineering staffing provider Oxford Global Resources and physician staffing firm VISTA Staffing Solutions.

As with most players in the staffing sector, On Assignment felt the painful effects of the global recession in 2008 and 2009 as it was hurt by high unemployment rates and shrinking demand for its staffing services.

As the economy began to pick up, in 2010 On Assignment bought The Cambridge Group Ltd., a staffing services firm placing physicians, clinical and scientific personnel, and IT professionals. Also that year the company acquired Sharpstream, a firm with expertise in search services for executive to middle managers residing in the life sciences sector. The deal added offices in the US, the UK, and Shanghai.

Continuing its string of acquisitions, in 2011 On Assignment obtained Valesta, a provider of clinical research specialized staffing services with headquarters in Belgium and additional offices in Spain and The Netherlands. The company next acquired Apex Systems, the sixth largest staffing firm and one of the fastest growing IT staffing firms in the US, in 2012.

EXECUTIVES

Chairman, Director, Arshad Matin
President, Chief Executive Officer, Director, Theodore S. Hanson, $630,000 total compensation
Executive Vice President, Chief Financial Officer, Marie L. Perry
Senior Vice President, Chief Legal Officer, Secretary, Jennifer Hankes Painter, $378,000 total compensation
Finance Senior Vice President, Finance Chief Administrative Officer, Finance Treasurer, James L. Brill, $335,564 total compensation
Chief Accounting Officer, Rose Cunningham
Subsidiary Officer, Randolph C. Blazer, $790,079 total compensation
Director, Brian J. Callaghan
Director, Maria R. Hawthorne
Director, Edwin A. Sheridan
Director, Mark A. Frantz
Director, Jonathan S. Holman
Director, Joseph W. Dyer
Director, Mariel A. Joliet
Director, Marty R. Kittrell
Director, Carol Lindstrom
Auditors: DELOITTE & TOUCHE LLP

LOCATIONS

HQ: ASGN Inc
4400 Cox Road, Suite 110, Glen Allen, VA 23060
Phone: 888 482-8068
Web: www.asgn.com

2016 Sales

	$ mil.	% of total
US	2,324.7	95
Other countries	115.7	5
Total	2,440.4	100

PRODUCTS/OPERATIONS

2018 Sales

	$ mil.	% of total
Assignment	2,760.5	81
Permanent Placement	146.3	5
ECS	439.0	14
Total	3,399.8	100

2018 Sales

	$ mil.	% of total
Apex	2,300.3	68
Oxford	606.5	18
ECS	493.0	14
Total	3,399.8	100

Selected Divisions and Operating Units
Apex (IT staffing)
On Assignment Clinical Research
On Assignment Engineering
On Assignment Healthcare Staffing
On Assignment Health Information Management
On Assignment Lab Support
Oxford Global Resources (IT and engineering staffing)

COMPETITORS

CAPITA PLC
CTPARTNERS EXECUTIVE SEARCH INC.
DHI GROUP, INC.
EMPRESARIA GROUP PLC
HAYS PLC
IGATE CORP.
IMPELLAM GROUP PLC
MANPOWERGROUP INC.
PARITY GROUP PUBLIC LIMITED COMPANY
ROBERT WALTERS PLC

HISTORICAL FINANCIALS

Company Type: Public

Income Statement — FYE: December 31

	REVENUE ($mil)	NET INCOME ($mil)	NET PROFIT MARGIN	EMPLOYEES
12/20	3,950.6	200.3	5.1%	55,200
12/19	3,923.9	174.7	4.5%	67,700
12/18	3,399.7	157.7	4.6%	66,200
12/17	2,625.9	157.6	6.0%	59,200
12/16	2,440.4	97.2	4.0%	55,880
Annual Growth	12.8%	19.8%	—	(0.3%)

2020 Year-End Financials

Debt ratio: 31.5%
Return on equity: 13.4%
Cash ($ mil.): 274.4
Current Ratio: 2.39
Long-term debt ($ mil.): 1,033.4
No. of shares ($ mil.): 52.9
Dividends
Yield: —
Payout: —
Market value ($ mil.): 4,419.0

	STOCK PRICE ($) FY Close	P/E High/Low		PER SHARE ($) Earnings	Dividends	Book Value
12/20	83.53	23	8	3.76	0.00	30.00
12/19	70.97	22	15	3.28	0.00	26.02
12/18	54.50	31	17	2.98	0.00	22.51
12/17	64.27	22	14	2.97	0.00	19.01
12/16	44.16	25	16	1.81	0.00	16.48
Annual Growth	17.3%	—		20.1%	—	16.2%

Aspen Technology Inc

Aspen Technology (AspenTech) is a global leader in asset optimization software that enables industrial manufacturers to design, operate, and maintain their operations for maximum performance. It provides supply chain, manufacturing, and engineering process optimization software to companies in the energy, chemical, construction, and pharmaceutical industries, among others. The company's software ? which includes supplier collaboration, inventory management, production planning, and collaborative engineering functions ? is offered under its aspenONE subscription service. AspenTech, which generates most of its sales outside the US, also provides related technical and professional services such as technical support, training, and systems implementation and integration.

Operations

AspenTech reports in three segments: Heritage AspenTech, OSI Inc., and Subsurface Science and Engineering Solutions (SSE).

Heritage AspenTech is a global leader in asset optimization software that optimizes asset design, operations and maintenance in complex, industrial environments. The segment generates nearly 45% of revenue.

OSI Inc. offers operational technology (OT) solutions that enable utilities to control generation, transmission, and distribution of power and ultimately ensure supply equals demand in the power grid. OSI Inc.'s energy management systems also provide efficient and holistic modeling, monitoring and controlling of complex transmission networks and generation fleets to manage grid stability and ensure security and regulatory compliance. The segment accounts for about 35% of total revenue.

SSE is a leading developer of software solutions to the global energy and alternative energy, carbon capture and storage, and minerals and mining industries. SSE provides geological simulation software that characterizes subsurface geological formations from seismic interpretation to dynamic simulation, connecting reservoirs to operational activities to optimize production and utilization. The segment brings in more than 20% of revenue.

In addition, AspenTech's revenue by type of product and service is divided into three types ? License and Solutions, Maintenance, and Services ? which generates around 70%, approximately 25%, and some 5% of total sales, respectively.

Geographic Reach

AspenTech is headquartered in Bedford, Massachusetts and has offices in the UK, Shanghai, Mexico City, Canada, Australia, Singapore, Beijing, India, Moscow, Tokyo, Oslo and Bahrain. It also leases office space in Medina, Minnesota and in Houston, Texas to accommodate sales, services, product development functions, marketing, operations, finance and administrative functions.

The US is the company's largest geographic segment, accounting for almost 45% of revenue. Europe contributes around 20% of revenue. Other markets served include the Asia-Pacific region, Middle East and Africa.

Sales and Marketing

AspenTech sells directly through Field Sales organization and by licensing to universities to encourage future demand. Using webinars, digital communities, social media, videos, email and other digital means, the company seeks to engage its extensive user base with targeted messages intended to address the specific needs of each market, customer and user.

Financial Performance

The company's revenue for fiscal 2022 increased to $300.6 million compared to $130.5 million in the prior year.

Net loss for fiscal 2022 increased to $20.6 million compared to $20.3 million in the prior year.

Cash held by the company at the end of fiscal 2022 increased to $25.7 million. Cash provided by operations and financing activities were $54.8 million and $1.6 billion, respectively. Cash used for investing activities was $1.6 billion, mainly for payments for business acquisitions, net of cash acquired.

Strategy

Aspen seek to maintain and extend its position as a leading global provider of industrial software to capital-intensive industries. The company have introduced a new strategy to its scope of optimization from the production units in a facility to the process and equipment, or entire asset. The company have expanded its reach in optimization from conceptualization and design, operations, and supply chain to the maintenance aspects of the facility. Aspen plan to continue to build on its expertise in process optimization, its installed base, and long-term customer relationships to further expand its reach in the maintenance area. By focusing on asset optimization, Aspen will be able to optimize the design and operations of a facility considering the performance and constraints of equipment to optimize the full asset lifecycle.

Aspen also expect to be well-positioned to further develop its business through the pursuit of organic and inorganic growth initiatives, which the company expect will be an important element of its growth strategy.

Aspen's primary growth strategy is to expand organically within its core verticals by leveraging its market leadership position and driving increased usage and product adoption of the broad capabilities in its solution offerings.

Additionally, the company seek acquisitions to accelerate its overall growth in the design, operation, optimization, and maintenance of industrial assets; product acquisitions that expand its footprint and relevance to these industries in their pursuit of operational excellence and greater sustainability, or acquisitions that introduce Aspen to or allow the company to further penetrate new industries with a focus on industrial operations.

Mergers and Acquisitions

In 2022, AspenTech agreed to acquire Micromine - a global leader in design and operational management solutions for the mining industry, from private equity firm Potentia Capital and other sellers for AU$900 million in cash (approximately $623 million USD). The transaction complements AspenTech's existing asset optimization solutions and positions the company in a leadership role to deliver the "Digital Mine of the Future," in support of excellence in operations with a focus on safety, sustainability, reliability, and efficiency. In addition, AspenTech is now uniquely positioned to help mining customers address the dual challenge of meeting the demands of a growing population with an increasing standard of living, while reaching sustainability goals. AspenTech's innovation and unique expertise in digitally transforming the chemicals and oil and gas industries will be critical to the mining industry as it embarks on rapid digitalization.

HISTORY

Lawrence Evans was a chemical engineering professor at MIT in 1976 when he became the principal investigator for the Energy Department's ASPEN (Advanced System for Process Engineering) project to develop synthetic fuels. He was joined by Joseph Boston and Herbert Britt (both chemical engineers) in 1977. Four years later they formed Aspen Technology to develop and market computer-aided chemical engineering software for process manufacturers.

The company launched its first product in 1982 and introduced process simulation software the following year. Boston became AspenTech's president, and Evans became chairman and CEO in 1984.

The company went public in 1994. A series of acquisitions followed -- including the purchases of Industrial Systems in 1995 and Dynamic Matrix Control and Setpoint in 1996 -- which gave the company operation control software. In 1997 it bought consultant Special Analysis & Simulation Technologies and intelligent software expert NeuralWare.

EXECUTIVES

Field Operations President, Field Operations Chief Executive Officer, Director, Antonio J. Pietri, $600,000 total compensation
Operations Executive Vice President, John W. Hague
Senior Vice President, Chief Financial Officer, Chantelle Breithaupt
Senior Vice President, General Counsel, Secretary, Frederic G. Hammond, $360,000 total compensation
Director, Robert M. Whelan
Director, Jill D. Smith
Director, Karen M. Golz
Director, Adriana Karaboutis
Director, Amarpreet Hanspal
Director, Thomas Michael Bradicich
Director, Georgia Keresty
Director, R. Halsey Wise
Director, Donald P. Casey
Auditors : KPMG LLP

LOCATIONS

HQ: Aspen Technology Inc
 20 Crosby Drive, Bedford, MA 01730
Phone: 781 221-6400
Web: www.aspentech.com

2015 Sales

	% of total
US	35
Europe	31
Other	34
Total	100

PRODUCTS/OPERATIONS

2015 Sales

	$ mil.	% of total
Subscription & software	405.6	92
Services	34.8	8
Total	440.4	100

Selected Products

Aspen Plus
Aspen HYSYS
Aspen Exchanger Design and Rating
Aspen Economic Evaluation
Aspen Basic Engineering
Aspen Info Plus.21
Aspen DMCplus
Aspen Collaborative Demand Manager
Aspen Petroleum Scheduler
Aspen PIMS
Aspen Plant Scheduler
Aspen Supply Chain Planner
Aspen Inventory Management & Operations Scheduling
Aspen Petroleum Supply Chain Planner
Aspen Fleet Optimizer

COMPETITORS

AMERICAN SOFTWARE, INC.
CALLIDUS SOFTWARE INC.
COGNIZANT TECHNOLOGY SOLUTIONS CORPORATION
ENEL X NORTH AMERICA, INC.
INFOR, INC.
LOGILITY, INC.
PERFICIENT, INC.
PROGRESS SOFTWARE CORPORATION
SYNOPSYS, INC.
Software AG

HISTORICAL FINANCIALS

Company Type: Public

Income Statement				FYE: June 30
	REVENUE ($mil)	NET INCOME ($mil)	NET PROFIT MARGIN	EMPLOYEES
06/21	709.3	319.8	45.1%	1,897
06/20	598.7	229.6	38.4%	1,710
06/19	598.3	262.7	43.9%	1,600
06/18	499.5	148.6	29.8%	1,466
06/17	482.9	162.1	33.6%	1,419
Annual Growth	10.1%	18.5%	—	7.5%

2021 Year-End Financials

Debt ratio: 20.2% No. of shares ($ mil.): 67.9
Return on equity: 50.4% Dividends
Cash ($ mil.): 379.8   Yield: —
Current Ratio: 5.43   Payout: —
Long-term debt ($ mil.): 273.1 Market value ($ mil.): 9,341.0

	STOCK PRICE ($) FY Close	P/E High/Low		PER SHARE ($) Earnings	Dividends	Book Value
06/21	137.54	34	20	4.67	0.00	11.79
06/20	103.61	42	23	3.34	0.00	6.89
06/19	124.28	33	20	3.71	0.00	5.73
06/18	92.74	48	27	2.04	0.00	(3.99)
06/17	55.26	30	19	2.11	0.00	(3.55)
Annual Growth	25.6%	—	—	22.0%	—	—

Atkore Inc

EXECUTIVES

Chairman, Director, Michael V. Schrock
President, Chief Executive Officer, Director, William E. Waltz, $490,385 total compensation

Vice President, Chief Financial Officer, Chief Accounting Officer, David P. Johnson, $63,942 total compensation
Vice President, General Counsel, Corporate Secretary, Daniel S. Kelly, $344,500 total compensation
Global Human Resources Vice President, LeAngela W. Lowe
Division Officer, John W. Pregenzer
Division Officer, Mark F. Lamps
Director, Betty R. Johnson
Director, A. Mark Zeffiro
Director, Jeri L. Isbell
Director, Wilbert W. James
Director, Justin A. Kershaw
Director, Scott H. Muse
Director, B. Joanne Edwards
Auditors : DELOITTE & TOUCHE LLP

LOCATIONS

HQ: Atkore Inc
16100 South Lathrop Avenue, Harvey, IL 60426
Phone: 708 339-1610
Web: www.atkore.com

HISTORICAL FINANCIALS

Company Type: Public

Income Statement — FYE: September 30

	REVENUE ($mil)	NET INCOME ($mil)	NET PROFIT MARGIN	EMPLOYEES
09/21	2,928.0	587.8	20.1%	4,000
09/20	1,765.4	152.3	8.6%	3,700
09/19	1,916.5	139.0	7.3%	3,900
09/18	1,835.1	136.6	7.4%	3,500
09/17	1,503.9	84.6	5.6%	3,500
Annual Growth	18.1%	62.3%	—	3.4%

2021 Year-End Financials

Debt ratio: 34.3%
Return on equity: 94.5%
Cash ($ mil.): 576.2
Current Ratio: 2.71
Long-term debt ($ mil.): 758.3
No. of shares ($ mil.): 46.0
Dividends
Yield: —
Payout: —
Market value ($ mil.): 3,998.0

	STOCK PRICE ($) FY Close	P/E High/Low		PER SHARE ($) Earnings	Dividends	Book Value
09/21	86.92	8	2	12.19	0.00	18.80
09/20	22.73	14	4	3.10	0.00	7.98
09/19	30.35	11	6	2.83	0.00	4.96
09/18	26.53	11	7	2.48	0.00	2.59
09/17	19.51	20	12	1.27	0.00	5.70
Annual Growth	45.3%	—	—	76.0%	—	34.8%

Atlantic Union Bankshares Corp

Atlantic Union Bankshares (formerly Union Bankshares Corporation) is a financial holding company and a bank holding company committed to the delivery of financial services through its subsidiary Atlantic Union Bank and non-bank financial services affiliates. The bank also provides banking, trust, and wealth management services through some 130 branches and approximately 150 ATMs located throughout Virginia, and portions of Maryland and North Carolina. Certain non-bank affiliates include: Atlantic Union Equipment Finance, Inc., which provides equipment financing; Dixon, Hubard, Feinour & Brown, Inc., which provide investment advisory services; Atlantic Union Financial Consultants LLC, which provides brokerage services; and Union Insurance Group, LLC, which offers various lines of insurance products.

Operations

Atlantic Union Bankshares generates income from interest and fees on loan (around 70% of sales) and interest and dividends on securities (around 10%). The company loan portfolio include Commercial real estate, which accounts for about 45% of the company's loan portfolio followed by Residential real estate at some 15%. The bank's loan portfolio also includes Commercial and Industrial (about 20%), Construction and Land Development (over 5%), and Multifamily Real Estate (more than 5%).

It has one reportable segment: its traditional full-service community banking business. It is a full-service bank offering consumers and businesses a wide range of banking and related financial services, including checking, savings, certificates of deposit, and other depository services, as well as loans for commercial, industrial, residential mortgage, and consumer purposes. It also offers mobile and internet banking services and online bill payment for all customers, whether retail or commercial. Additionally, it also offers a full array of Treasury Management and related working capital services to its commercial clients.

Geographic Reach

The company is headquarters in Richmond, Virginia. The bank provides banking, trust, and wealth management services through about 130 branches and approximately 150 ATMs located throughout Virginia, and portions of Maryland and North Carolina.

Sales and Marketing

The company used about $9.9 million and $11.6 million in 2021 and 2020 for marketing and advertising, respectively.

Financial Performance

The company's revenue in 2021 decreased to $689.7 million compared with $698.3 million in the prior year. Net interest income in 2021 totaled $551.3 million, which was a decrease of $4.0 million or 0.7% compared to the prior year, primarily reflecting the impact of a decline in overall earning asset yields of 52 bps for 2021, offset by a decline in cost of funds of 35 bps for 2021 and increased loan accretion recognized on PPP loans.

Net income in 2021 increased to $252.0 million compared with $152.6 million in the prior year. The increase primarily reflects the decrease in the provision for credit losses, by $148.0 million from 2020 to a negative $60.9 million for 2021, primarily due to decreases to the company's ACL estimates driven by ongoing economic improvements, benign credit quality metrics since the COVID-19 pandemic began and a positive macroeconomic outlook.

Cash held by the company at the end of fiscal 2021 increased to $802.5 million. Cash provided by operations and financing activities were $337.8 million and $316.9 million, respectively. Cash used for investing activities was $345.4 million, mainly for purchases of AFS securities, restricted stock, and other investments.

Strategy

The company expands its market area and increases its market share through organic growth (internal growth and de novo expansion) and strategic acquisitions. Strategic acquisitions by the company to date have included whole bank acquisitions, branch and deposit acquisitions, purchases of existing branches from other banks, and registered investment advisory firms. The company generally considers acquisitions of companies in strong growth markets or with unique products or services that will benefit the entire organization.

EXECUTIVES

Vice-Chairman, Director, Ronald L. Tillett, $13,550 total compensation
President, Chief Executive Officer, Subsidiary Officer, Director, John C. Asbury, $674,375 total compensation
Executive Vice President, Chief Financial Officer, Subsidiary Officer, Robert Michael Gorman, $383,425 total compensation
Executive Vice President, Subsidiary Officer, Maria P. Tedesco, $114,375 total compensation
Executive Vice President, Division Officer, David V. Ring, $369,000 total compensation
Senior Vice President, General Counsel, Corporate Secretary, Rachael R. Lape
Director, Patrick E. Corbin
Director, Frank Russell Ellett
Director, Daniel I. Hansen
Director, Jan S. Hoover
Director, Patrick J. McCann, $12,175 total compensation
Director, Thomas P. Rohman
Director, Linda V. Schreiner
Director, Keith L. Wampler
Director, Thomas G. Snead
Director, F. Blair Wimbush
Auditors : Ernst & Young LLP

LOCATIONS

HQ: Atlantic Union Bankshares Corp
1051 East Cary Street, Suite 1200, Richmond, VA 23219
Phone: 804 633-5031

Web: www.bankatunion.com

PRODUCTS/OPERATIONS

2015 Sales

	$ mil.	% of total
Interest		
Loans, including fees	247.5	72
Other	29.3	9
Noninterest		
Other service charges commission and fees	15.6	5
Service charges on deposit accounts	18.9	5
others	30.8	9
Adjustments	(0.3)	-
Total	341.8	100

Selected Subsidiaries
Union First Market Bank
Union Insurance Group, LLC
Union Investment Services, Inc.
Union Mortgage Group, Inc.

COMPETITORS

C&F FINANCIAL CORPORATION
CENTRAL BANCORP, INC.
CLOVER COMMUNITY BANK
D. L. EVANS BANK
FIRST FEDERAL BANK CORPORATION
FIRST UNITED CORPORATION
LIMESTONE BANCORP, INC.
OCEANFIRST FINANCIAL CORP.
TWO RIVER BANCORP
UNITY BANCORP, INC.

HISTORICAL FINANCIALS

Company Type: Public

Income Statement FYE: December 31

	ASSETS ($mil)	NET INCOME ($mil)	INCOME AS % OF ASSETS	EMPLOYEES
12/20	19,628.4	158.2	0.8%	1,879
12/19	17,562.9	193.5	1.1%	1,989
12/18	13,765.5	146.2	1.1%	1,609
12/17	9,315.1	72.9	0.8%	1,149
12/16	8,426.7	77.4	0.9%	1,416
Annual Growth	23.5%	19.5%	—	7.3%

2020 Year-End Financials

Return on assets: 0.8%
Return on equity: 6.0%
Long-term debt ($ mil.): —
No. of shares ($ mil.): 78.7
Sales ($ mil.): 784.9
Dividends
Yield: 3.0%
Payout: 52.3%
Market value ($ mil.): 2,593.0

	STOCK PRICE ($) FY Close	P/E High/Low		PER SHARE ($) Earnings	Dividends	Book Value
12/20	32.94	20	10	1.93	1.00	34.40
12/19	37.55	16	12	2.41	0.96	31.41
12/18	28.23	19	12	2.22	0.88	29.17
12/17	36.17	23	18	1.67	0.81	23.92
12/16	35.74	21	12	1.77	0.77	22.95
Annual Growth	(2.0%)	—	—	2.2%	6.8%	10.6%

Atlanticus Holdings Corp

Atlanticus is a financial technology company powering more inclusive financial solutions for everyday Americans. The company leverages data, analytics, and innovative technology to unlock access to financial solutions for the millions of Americans who would otherwise be underserved. Using its infrastructure and technology, Atlanticus provides loan servicing, including risk management and customer service outsourcing, for third parties. Also through its CaaS segment, the company engages in testing and limited investment in consumer finance technology platforms as it seeks to capitalize on its expertise and infrastructure. In auto finance segment, Atlanticus purchase auto loans at a discount and with dealer retentions or holdbacks that provide risk protection. It also provides certain installment lending products in addition to its traditional loans secured by automobiles.

Operations

Atlanticus operates in two reportable segments: Credit as a Service (CaaS) and Auto Finance.

Within the Credit as a Services segment, the company offers private label credit and general purpose credit cards originated by lenders through multiple channels, including retailers and healthcare providers, direct mail solicitation, digital marketing and partnerships with third parties. The segment accounts for about 95% of total revenue.

The operations of Auto Finance segment (some 5%) are principally conducted through CAR platform, which purchases and/or services loans secured by automobiles from or for a pre-qualified network of independent automotive dealers and automotive finance companies in the buy-here, pay-here used car business. It has expanded these operations to also include certain installment lending products in addition to its traditional loans secured by automobiles both in the US and US territories.

Overall, consumer loans (including past due fees) account for about 70% of revenue, while fees and other revenue account for the remaining 30% of revenue.

Geographic Reach

Altanticus has office space in Atlanta, Georgia for its executive offices and the primary operations of its CaaS segment. Its Auto Finance segment has office space in Lake Mary, Florida, with additional offices and branch location in various states and territories.

Financial Performance

The company reported a revenue of $748.1 million, a 33% increase from the previous year's revenue of $563.4 million. The increase was primarily due to a higher volume of sales across all of the company's segments.

In 2021, the company had a net income of $177.8 million, an 89% increase from the previous year's net income of $93.9 million.

The company's cash at the end of 2021 was $506.6 million. Operating activities generated $212.4 million, while investing activities used $475 million, mainly for investments in earning assets. Financing activities provided another $510.3 million.

Company Background

Atlanticus sold its 300 US microloan retail locations -- which provided payday loans under such banners as First American Cash Advance and First Southern Cash Advance -- to Advance America for more than $46 million in 2011. Prior to selling off its retail stores, the company planned to spin them off as a publicly traded company called Purpose Financial Holdings. The proposed transaction would allow Atlanticus to focus on its core operations. The company chose instead to sell in order to raise capital.

In 2011 Atlanticus also sold its UK payday loan operations. The sales came in the midst of a difficult period for the company. The credit crunch hampered its ability to raise funds to fuel its lending activities, and new regulations passed in the US outlawed many of the high-fee products that the company marketed.

The move also followed other restructurings at the company. It has exited several lines of business since 2007, including its stored-value cards and investment in and servicing of loans secured by motorcycles, personal watercraft, and other "big boy toys." Atlanticus ceased writing new auto loans in 2009 and, as with its credit card accounts, is focusing on servicing that portfolio. Also that year Atlanticus sold its marketing unit to Las Vegas-based Selling Source shortly after it settled the FDIC lawsuit. The company additionally laid off hundreds of employees and closed a number of office locations.

As a way to diversify its holdings, the company has invested in international credit card receivables. Lending abroad might be in the cards, if the regulatory environment allows. Subprime lending in the US proved a risky affair, though: In 2008 the company agreed to a $116 million settlement with the FDIC and FTC. As part of an broader investigation of the subprime credit industry, federal regulators had looked into allegations that Atlanticus provided inadequate policy disclosures to customers. Most of the settlement funds were credited to certain accounts opened between 2001 and 2005.

Chairman David Hanna and his brother Frank, a director, together own more than half of Atlanticus; each holds an equal stake, around 27% apiece.

EXECUTIVES

Chief Executive Officer, Chairman, David G. Hanna, $600,000 total compensation

Chief Financial Officer, Treasurer, William R. McCamey, $450,000 total compensation

President, Director, Jeffrey A. Howard, $600,000 total compensation

Chief Accounting Officer, Controller, Mitchell C. Saunders

Division Officer, Krishnakumar Srinivasan, $262,935 total compensation

Director, Deal W. Hudson
Director, Mack F. Mattingly
Director, Thomas G. Rosencrants
Auditors : BDO USA, LLP

LOCATIONS

HQ: Atlanticus Holdings Corp
Five Concourse Parkway, Suite 300, Atlanta, GA 30328
Phone: 770 828-2000
Web: www.atlanticus.com

PRODUCTS/OPERATIONS

Selected Products & Services
Auto Lending
Credit Card Lending
Loan Servicing and Portfolio Acquisitions
Retail Finance

COMPETITORS

AMERICAN EXPRESS COMPANY
CAPITAL ONE FINANCIAL CORPORATION
CONSUMER PORTFOLIO SERVICES, INC.
CREDIT ACCEPTANCE CORPORATION
DISCOVER FINANCIAL SERVICES
FIRST INVESTORS FINANCIAL SERVICES GROUP, INC.
GENERAL MOTORS FINANCIAL COMPANY, INC.
GREEN DOT CORPORATION
NICHOLAS FINANCIAL, INC.
WORLD ACCEPTANCE CORPORATION

HISTORICAL FINANCIALS

Company Type: Public

Income Statement — FYE: December 31

	REVENUE ($mil)	NET INCOME ($mil)	NET PROFIT MARGIN	EMPLOYEES
12/20	563.4	94.1	16.7%	327
12/19	458.1	26.4	5.8%	319
12/18	233.5	7.8	3.4%	310
12/17	135.4	(40.7)	—	297
12/16	113.6	(6.3)	—	292
Annual Growth	49.2%	—	—	2.9%

2020 Year-End Financials
Debt ratio: 75.4%
Return on equity: 61.2%
Cash ($ mil.): 258.9
Current Ratio: 0.27
Long-term debt ($ mil.): 24.3
No. of shares ($ mil.): 16.1
Dividends
 Yield: —
 Payout: —
Market value ($ mil.): 397.0

	STOCK PRICE ($) FY Close	P/E High/Low		PER SHARE ($) Earnings	Dividends	Book Value
12/20	24.63	5	1	3.95	0.00	13.44
12/19	9.01	6	2	1.66	0.00	5.66
12/18	3.64	8	3	0.56	0.00	(1.40)
12/17	2.40	—	—	(2.93)	0.00	(2.36)
12/16	2.84	—	—	(0.46)	0.00	0.38
Annual Growth	71.6%	—	—	—	—	144.4%

AtriCure Inc

AtriCure, Inc. provides innovative technologies for the treatment of Afib and related conditions. Afib affects more than 33 million people worldwide. AtriCure's Isolator Synergy Ablation System is the first medical device to receive FDA approval for the treatment of persistent Afib. AtriCure's AtriClip Left Atrial Appendage Exclusion System products are the most widely sold LAA management devices worldwide. AtriCure's Hybrid AF Therapy is a minimally invasive procedure that provides a lasting solution for long-standing persistent Afib patients. AtriCure's cryoICE cryoSPHERE probe is cleared for temporary ablation of peripheral nerves to block pain, providing pain relief in cardiac and thoracic procedures. Its US markets account for about 85% of revenue.

Operations

The company develops, manufactures and sells devices designed primarily for the surgical ablation of cardiac tissue, systems designed for the exclusion of the left atrial appendage and devices designed to block pain by temporarily ablating peripheral nerves.

Ablation and Appendage accounts for almost all of the company's revenue.

Geographic Reach

Headquartered in Ohio, AtriCure has offices in Minnesota and California as well as in the Netherlands.

US sales account for about 85% of the company's revenue, while Europe, Asia, and other international countries accounts for the rest.

Sales and Marketing

In the US, AtriCure sell its products to medical centers through direct sales in more than 55 sales territories. Its international sales team includes sales representatives focused on its direct markets, such as Germany, France, the UK and the Benelux region. It also maintain a network of distributors in Asia, South America and Canada, as well as certain countries in Europe, who market and sell its products. Over 10% of revenue were generated from the company's top ten customers.

Advertising expense was $907, $655, and $635 in 2021, 2020, and 2019, respectively.

Financial Performance

Total revenue increased 33% to $50.2 million, reflecting a recovery of cardiac surgery procedure volumes during 2021 from the significant impact of COVID-19 during 2020 within each franchise and across its key markets globally, as well as further adoption of the company's products. Revenue from customers in the United States increased across all product categories.

Net loss for fiscal 2020 increased to $48.2 million compared from the prior year with $35.2 million.

Cash held by the company at the end of fiscal 2021 increased to $43.7 million. Cash provided by investing activities was $23.5 million, while cash used for operations and investing activities were $13.8 million and $7.6 million, respectively. Main cash use for the year was for shares repurchased for payment of taxes on stock awards.

Strategy

The key elements of AtriCure's strategy include:

New product innovation by developing new and innovative products, including those that allow it to enter new market opportunities or expand its growth in existing markets;

Investing in clinical science by investing in landmark clinical trials and making clinical research grants to support its product development efforts and expand the body of clinical evidence;

Building physician and societal relationships to provide insight regarding treatment trends, input on future product direction, and education for providers involved in treating the disease;

Providing training and education by instituting a program to train providers on the use of the Isolator Synergy System to treat persistent and long-standing persistent Afib in patients undergoing open-heart surgery; and

Evaluating acquisition opportunities on a variety of factors, including investment in clinical science, product innovation, and strategic and financial considerations.

Expanding adoption of its minimally invasive products. Atricure believes that the catalysts for expanded adoption of its minimally invasive products include completing clinical trials, including the CONVERGE, aMAZE IDE and DEEP AF IDE clinical trials, procedural advancements, such as the hybrid or multi-disciplinary procedure, continued innovation and product development, and the publication of additional scientific evidence supporting the safety and efficacy of hybrid treatments for persistent and long-standing persistent Afib.

Evaluating acquisition opportunities. The company expects to continue to be opportunistic with respect to acquisitions.

Company Background

Michael Hooven and his wife, Sue Spies, co-founded ENABLE Medical Corporation. ENABLE Medical's first product was a pair of radio frequency energized surgical scissors designed to harvest saphenous veins in cardiac bypass procedures, IMA harvesting, and general surgical applications. In 2000, AtriCure was established as an independent business focused on atrial fibrillation. ENABLE Medical provided contract development and manufacturing services to AtriCure.

EXECUTIVES

Chairman, Richard M. Johnston
President, Chief Executive Officer, Director, Michael H. Carrel, $714,375 total compensation
Vice President, Chief Operating Officer, Andrew L. Lux, $305,799 total compensation
Finance Chief Financial Officer, Finance Senior Vice President, M. Andrew Wade, $329,569 total compensation
Product Development Chief Technology Officer, Engineering Chief Technology Officer, Salvatore Privitera, $348,958 total compensation

Business Development Senior Vice President, Marketing Senior Vice President, Justin J. Noznesky, $342,109 total compensation

Sales Senior Vice President, Marketing Senior Vice President, Sales Chief Operating Officer, Marketing Chief Operating Officer, Douglas J. Seith, $435,998 total compensation

Quality Assurance Vice President, Regulatory Affairs Vice President, James L. Lucky, $210,000 total compensation

Operations Vice President, Frederick Preiss

Product Development Vice President, Jonathon A. Sherman

International Vice President, International General Manager, Patricia J. Kennedy, $237,162 total compensation

Division Officer, Stewart W. Strong, $165,000 total compensation

Director, Mark A. Collar
Director, Scott William Drake
Director, Daniel P. Florin
Director, Regina E. Groves
Director, B. Kristine Johnson
Director, Mark R. Lanning
Director, Karen N. Prange
Director, Sven A. Wehrwein
Director, Robert S. White
Auditors : DELOITTE & TOUCHE LLP

LOCATIONS

HQ: AtriCure Inc
7555 Innovation Way, Mason, OH 45040
Phone: 513 755-4100
Web: www.atricure.com

2014 Sales by Region

	$ mil.	% of total
US	80.2	75
Europe	18.2	17
Asia	8.6	8
Other international	0.5	-
Total	107.5	100

PRODUCTS/OPERATIONS

2014 Sales

	$ mil.	% of total
Open-heart	61.1	57
Minimally invasive	23.9	22
AtriClip	18.9	18
Valve tools	3.6	3
Total	107.5	100

Selected Products
Cardiac Ablation Devices
Left Atrial Appendage Exclusion Devices
Maze Testing
Soft Tissue Dissection System

COMPETITORS
ANGIODYNAMICS, INC.
ARTHROCARE CORPORATION
BOSTON SCIENTIFIC CORPORATION
CRYOLIFE, INC.
EDWARDS LIFESCIENCES CORPORATION
MEDTRONIC PUBLIC LIMITED COMPANY
NUVASIVE, INC.
SPECTRANETICS LLC
STRYKER CORPORATION
TELEFLEX INCORPORATED

HISTORICAL FINANCIALS
Company Type: Public

Income Statement — FYE: December 31

	REVENUE ($mil)	NET INCOME ($mil)	NET PROFIT MARGIN	EMPLOYEES
12/21	274.3	50.1	18.3%	875
12/20	206.5	(48.1)	—	750
12/19	230.8	(35.1)	—	730
12/18	201.6	(21.1)	—	620
12/17	174.7	(26.8)	—	570
Annual Growth	11.9%	—	—	11.3%

2021 Year-End Financials
Debt ratio: 11.3%
Return on equity: 11.2%
Cash ($ mil.): 43.6
Current Ratio: 3.47
Long-term debt ($ mil.): 69.8
No. of shares ($ mil.): 46.0
Dividends
  Yield: —
  Payout: —
Market value ($ mil.): 3,199.0

	STOCK PRICE ($) FY Close	P/E High	P/E Low	PER SHARE ($) Earnings	PER SHARE ($) Dividends	PER SHARE ($) Book Value
12/21	69.53	79	48	1.09	0.00	10.51
12/20	55.67	—	—	(1.14)	0.00	9.09
12/19	32.51	—	—	(0.94)	0.00	6.24
12/18	30.60	—	—	(0.62)	0.00	6.46
12/17	18.24	—	—	(0.83)	0.00	4.66
Annual Growth	39.7%	—	—	—	—	22.6%

Aura Minerals Inc (British Virgin Islands)

Aura Minerals digs deep to make a profit. The mid-tier producer of gold and copper owns operating projects in Honduras, Mexico, and Brazil. The company's diversified portfolio of precious metal assets include the San Andres producing gold mine in Honduras, the Sao Francisco producing gold mine in Brazil, and the copper-gold-silver Aranzazu mine in Mexico (where operations were temporarily suspended in late 2015 due to disruptions caused by unauthorized persons entering the company mine). Aura Minerals' core development asset is the copper-gold-iron Serrote project in Brazil. In early 2018, the company acquired fellow gold miner Rio Novo.

EXECUTIVES

Chief Executive Officer, President, Director, James Bannantine
Chief Financial Officer, Rory Taylor
Technical Services Vice President, Bruce Butcher
Human Resources Vice President, Keith Harris-Lowe
Corporate Responsibility Vice President, Gonzalo Rios
Projects Vice President, Dale Tweed
Corporate Development Vice President, Alex Penha
Chairman, Patrick J. Mars
Director, Tom Ogryzlo
Director, Stephen Keith
Director, Elizabeth Martin
Director, William Murray
Director, Ian Stalker
Auditors : PricewaterhouseCoopers

LOCATIONS

HQ: Aura Minerals Inc (British Virgin Islands)
78 SW 7th Street, Suite # 7144, Miami, FL 33130
Phone: 305 239-9499
Web: www.auraminerals.com

COMPETITORS
Eldorado Gold Corporation
Endeavour Silver Corp
GOLD RESOURCE CORPORATION
INTERNATIONAL MINERALS CORPORATION
PARAMOUNT GOLD NEVADA CORP.

HISTORICAL FINANCIALS
Company Type: Public

Income Statement — FYE: December 31

	REVENUE ($mil)	NET INCOME ($mil)	NET PROFIT MARGIN	EMPLOYEES
12/20	299.8	68.4	22.8%	1,102
12/19	226.2	24.8	11.0%	863
12/18	157.7	51.9	33.0%	863
12/17	157.7	10.1	6.5%	783
12/16	146.2	19.0	13.0%	1,170
Annual Growth	19.7%	37.7%	—	(1.5%)

2020 Year-End Financials
Debt ratio: 13.1%
Return on equity: 26.8%
Cash ($ mil.): 117.7
Current Ratio: 1.80
Long-term debt ($ mil.): 41.9
No. of shares ($ mil.): 70.7
Dividends
  Yield: —
  Payout: —
Market value ($ mil.): 0.0

Autodesk Inc

Autodesk is a global leader in 3D design, engineering, and entertainment software and services, offering customers productive business solutions through powerful technology products and services. The AutoCAD, AutoCAD Civil3D, and Revit software programs are used by architects, engineers, and structural designers to design, draft, and make models of products, buildings, and other objects. The company also provides product and manufacturing software for manufacturers in automotive, transportation, industrial machinery, consumer products, and building product industries with comprehensive digital design, engineering, manufacturing, and production solutions. The company's digital media and entertainment products provide tools for digital sculpting, modeling, animation, effects, rendering, and compositing for design visualization, visual effects, and games production. Customers in the US account for nearly 35% sales.

Operations
Autodesk's biggest operating segment is

Architecture, Engineering, and Construction (AEC), which generates approximately 45% of revenue. It develops software for designing, building, and managing buildings, civil infrastructure, and manufacturing plants. The segment's BIM 360 product helps manage construction projects. BIM stands for building information modeling.

The AutoCAD and AutoCAD LT business, which accounts for close to 30% of revenue, is the home of Autodesk's flagship product and biggest revenue producer, AutoCAD. The companion product, AutoCAD LT, allows sharing of documents. The Manufacturing segment, which generates approximately 20% of revenue, makes prototyping software.

The Media and Entertainment segment, around 5% of revenue, offers computer animation programs such as Autodesk Maya, for design visualization, visual effects, and games production.

Overall, subscription revenue generates approximately 95%. Maintenance and other account for the rest.

Geographic Reach

Autodesk's revenue is spread among its major geographic regions. The US is Autodesk's biggest single market, accounting for about 35% sales, but the Europe, Middle East, and Africa region generates 40% of sales and the Asia Pacific region accounts for about 20% of sales. The company's products are translated and localized for users who speak German, French, Italian, Spanish, Russian, Japanese, Korean, and simplified and traditional Chinese. Autodesk is based in San Rafael, California.

Sales and Marketing

Autodesk relies significantly upon major distributors and resellers in both the US and international regions, including Tech Data Corporation and its global affiliates and Ingram Micro Inc. Total sales to Tech Data and Ingram Micro accounted for about 35% and 10% of Autodesk's total revenue, respectively.

Autodesk sells directly to enterprise and named account customers as well as those who buy from its online store. The company has a network of approximately 1,500 resellers and distributors worldwide.

Total advertising expenses incurred were approximately $80.5 million in fiscal 2022, $60.4 million in fiscal 2021, and $42.2 million in fiscal 2020.

Financial Performance

Total net revenue was $4.39 billion during fiscal 2022, an increase of 16% compared to the prior fiscal year, primarily due to a 19% increase in subscription revenue, partially offset by a 58% decrease in maintenance revenue.

In 2022, the company had a net income of $497 million, a 59% decrease from the previous year's net income of $1.2 billion.

The company's cash at the end of 2022 was $1.5 billion. Operating activities generated $1.5 billion, while investing activities used $1.6 billion, mainly for business combinations. Financing activities generated another $1.5 billion.

Strategy

Autodesk's strategy is to build enduring relationships with customers, delivering innovative technology that provides valuable automation and insight into their design and makes the process. To drive the execution of this strategy, the company is focused on three strategic priorities: delivering on the promise of subscription, digitizing the company, and reimagining construction, manufacturing, and production.

As part of the company's strategy in manufacturing, it continues to attract both global manufacturing leaders and disruptive startups with its generative design and cloud-based Fusion 360 technology enhancements. A fiscal 2021 acquisition included a leading provider of post-processing and machine simulation solutions. In fiscal 2022, the company acquired Upchain, an instant-on, cloud-based data management technology that allows product design and manufacturing customers to collaborate in the cloud across their value chains and bring products to market faster.

Mergers and Acquisitions

In early 2022, Autodesk agreed to acquire The Wild, a cloud-connected, extended reality (XR) platform, which includes its namesake solutions, The Wild and IrisVR. The Wild enables architecture, engineering, and construction (AEC) professionals to present, collaborate and review projects together in immersive and interactive experiences, from anywhere and at any time. This acquisition enables Autodesk to meet increasing needs for augmented reality (AR) and virtual reality (VR) technology advancements within the AEC industry and further support AEC customers throughout the project delivery lifecycle.

In late 2021, Autodesk announced its acquisition of ProEst, a cloud-based estimating solution that enables construction teams to create estimates, perform digital takeoffs, generate detailed reports and proposals and manage bid-day processes. Autodesk plans to integrate ProEst with Autodesk Construction Cloud, a comprehensive construction management platform connecting teams, data and workflows across the entire building lifecycle. The acquisition will strengthen Autodesk Construction Cloud's preconstruction offerings and empower construction teams to manage all their critical preconstruction and construction workflows on one platform.

In early 2021, Autodesk acquired Innovyze, Inc., a global leader in water infrastructure software, for approximately $1 billion net of cash subject to working capital and tax closing adjustments. The acquisition positions Autodesk as a leading global provider of end-to-end digital solutions from design to operations of water infrastructure, accelerates Autodesk's digital twin strategy, and creates a clearer path to a more sustainable and digitized water industry.

Company Background

John Walker founded Autodesk in 1982 as a diversified PC software supplier, and when he bought the software rights to AutoCAD from inventor Michael Riddle, Autodesk took off. While competitors went after more complex computer systems, Autodesk focused on PC software. When PC sales boomed in the early 1980s, the firm was there to take advantage of a growing market. Autodesk went public in 1985.

HISTORY

John Walker founded Autodesk in 1982 as a diversified PC software supplier, and when he bought the software rights to AutoCAD from inventor Michael Riddle, Autodesk took off. While competitors went after more complex computer systems, Autodesk focused on PC software. When PC sales boomed in the early 1980s, the firm was there to take advantage of a growing market. Autodesk went public in 1985.

The company established a multimedia unit and released its first animation tool, 3D Studio, in 1990. In 1993 Autodesk acquired 3-D graphics specialist Ithaca Software. That year Autodesk lost a trade secret lawsuit to Vermont Microsystems and was ordered to pay $25.5 million; the fine was later lowered to $7.8 million.

In 1996 the company spun off its multimedia unit as Kinetix, geared toward 3-D PC and Web applications. Continuing its acquisition drive, Autodesk bought interior decorating software developer Creative Imaging Technologies in 1996 and rival CAD software developer Softdesk in 1997.

In an effort to expand its presence in the entertainment software realm, the company bought digital video effects and editing tools maker Discreet Logic for $520 million in 1999. Later that year Autodesk bolstered its geographic information systems division by acquiring Canadian mapping software company VISION*Solutions from WorldCom for $26 million. Product delays helped prompt Autodesk that year to reorganize into four divisions, and cut 350 jobs -- about 10% of its workforce.

EXECUTIVES

Marketing President, Industry Strategy President, Marketing Chief Executive Officer, Industry Strategy Chief Executive Officer, Director, Andrew Anagnost, $819,711 total compensation

Executive Vice President, Chief Legal Officer, Ruth Ann Keene

Executive Vice President, Chief Financial Officer, Deborah L. Clifford

Worldwide Sales and Services Executive Vice President, Worldwide Sales and Services Chief Operating Officer, Steven M. Blum, $569,915 total compensation
Non-Executive Chairman, Director, Stacy J. Smith
Director, Rami Rahim
Director, Karen Blasing
Director, R. Reid French
Director, Ayanna Howard
Director, Blake J. Irving
Director, Mary T. McDowell
Director, Stephen D. Milligan
Director, Lorrie M. Norrington
Director, Elizabeth (Betsy) Rafael
Auditors : Ernst & Young LLP

LOCATIONS

HQ: Autodesk Inc
  111 McInnis Parkway, San Rafael, CA 94903
Phone: 415 507-5000
Web: www.autodesk.com

2019 Sales

	$ mil.	% of total
Americas		
United States	874.6	34
Americas	175.3	7
Europe, Middle East, and Africa	1,034.3	40
Asia Pacific	485.6	19
Total	2,569.8	100

PRODUCTS/OPERATIONS

2019 Sales

	$ mil.	% of total
Architecture, Engineering, and Construction	1,021.6	40
AutoCAD and AutoCAD LT	731.8	28
Manufacturing	616.2	24
Media and Entertainment	182	7
Other	18.2	1
Total	2,569.8	100

2019 Sales

	$ mil.	% of total
Subscription	1,802.3	70
Subscription	635.1	25
Other	132.4	5
Total	2,569.8	100

COMPETITORS

ADOBE INC.
AVID TECHNOLOGY, INC.
CA, INC.
DASSAULT SYSTEMES
DATAWATCH CORPORATION
MENTOR GRAPHICS CORPORATION
MICROSOFT CORPORATION
PROGRESS SOFTWARE CORPORATION
PTC INC.
SYNOPSYS, INC.

HISTORICAL FINANCIALS
Company Type: Public

Income Statement — FYE: January 31

	REVENUE ($mil)	NET INCOME ($mil)	NET PROFIT MARGIN	EMPLOYEES
01/21	3,790.4	1,208.2	31.9%	11,500
01/20	3,274.3	214.5	6.6%	10,100
01/19	2,569.8	(80.8)	—	9,600
01/18	2,056.6	(566.9)	—	8,800
01/17	2,031.0	(582.1)	—	9,000
Annual Growth	16.9%	—	—	6.3%

2021 Year-End Financials

Debt ratio: 22.5%
Return on equity: —
Cash ($ mil.): 1,772.2
Current Ratio: 0.83
Long-term debt ($ mil.): 1,637.2
No. of shares ($ mil.): 219.6
Dividends
  Yield: —
  Payout: —
Market value ($ mil.): 60,924.0

	STOCK PRICE ($) FY Close	P/E High	P/E Low	Earnings	Dividends	Book Value
01/21	277.43	58	25	5.44	0.00	4.40
01/20	196.85	204	143	0.96	0.00	(0.63)
01/19	147.20	—	—	(0.37)	0.00	(0.96)
01/18	115.62	—	—	(2.58)	0.00	(1.17)
01/17	81.34	—	—	(2.61)	0.00	3.33
Annual Growth	35.9%	—	—	—	—	7.2%

Avid Bioservices Inc

Peregrine Pharmaceuticals is spreading its wings and taking flight to attack and kill its prey: cancer and viral infections. While nearly all its revenue comes from its Avid Bioservices subsidiary, which provides contract antibody and protein manufacturing to drug companies, Peregrine is focused on shepherding its own candidates through clinical trials. Up first is bavituximab, a monoclonal antibody candidate being tested to treat lung, pancreatic, and liver cancers, as well as for other oncology and infectious disease applications. Next is Cotara, being tested to treat glioblastoma multiforme, a deadly brain cancer. The company also has development programs for potential diagnostic imaging agents.

Operations
The company supports its development activities with revenues earned by Avid Bioservices subsidiary, which accounts for nearly all of Peregrine's revenues.

The company also seeks out licensing and development partnerships to bring in additional funding for its research operations. For instance, it has licensed some of its development technologies to the likes of Affitech and Merck KGaA. It also had a collaboration with the Department of Defense to develop antibodies to treat viral hemorrhagic fever infections that brought in revenues for several years until 2012, when the contract ended.

Geographic Reach
Peregrine conducts its research programs at facilities in the US, which accounts for nearly all revenue. Avid Bioservices serves customers primarily located in North America and Europe.

Financial Performance
As a development-stage drug company, Peregrine Pharmaceuticals' revenues fluctuate each year, depending on how much the company earns from its licensing, development, and contract manufacturing agreements. Revenues increased by 42% in 2012 due to increased contract manufacturing activities at the Avid Biosciences unit. Like many pharmaceutical R&D firms, Peregrine Pharmaceuticals has yet to turn a profit as its research expenses outweigh earnings. Its net loss for 2013 did decrease by 29% as R&D expense dropped.

Strategy
Peregrine is focused on the development of its two core drug candidates, with the ultimate goal of commercializing the drugs in the US and international markets. It als seeks to license the core technologies used in its candidates to additional partners. Bavituximab uses its PS-targeting (phosphatidylserine-targeting) technology, which works by turning off natural immune suppression, allowing the body to fight off infections with more vigor. Cotara uses Peregrine's TNT (tumor necrosis therapy), which uses radioisotopes to attack tumor cells without harming healthy tissue.

Once Peregrine's products gain regulatory approval, the company plans to market the drugs through collaborative partners or via a direct sales force.

EXECUTIVES

Chairman, Director, Joseph Carleone
President, Chief Executive Officer, Director, Nicholas Stewart Green
Vice President, General Counsel, Corporate Secretary, Mark R. Ziebell, $361,920 total compensation
Chief Financial Officer, Daniel R. Hart, $385,000 total compensation
Director, Esther M. Alegria
Director, Richard B. Hancock
Director, Catherine J. Mackey
Director, Gregory P. Sargen
Director, Jeanne A. Thoma
Auditors : Ernst & Young LLP

LOCATIONS

HQ: Avid Biosciences Inc
  2642 Michelle Drive, Suite 200, Tustin, CA 92780
Phone: 714 508-6100
Web: www.avidbio.com

PRODUCTS/OPERATIONS

2015 Sales

	$ mil.	% of total
Contract manufacturing	44.4	99
Licensing	0.3	1
Total	44.7	100

COMPETITORS

ADVAXIS, INC.
CELLDEX THERAPEUTICS, INC.
CHIMERIX, INC.
CURIS, INC.
INFINITY PHARMACEUTICALS, INC.
INNATE PHARMA
MACROGENICS, INC.
TRANSGENE
VERASTEM, INC.
XOMA CORPORATION

HISTORICAL FINANCIALS
Company Type: Public

Income Statement   FYE: April 30

	REVENUE ($mil)	NET INCOME ($mil)	NET PROFIT MARGIN	EMPLOYEES
04/21	95.8	11.2	11.7%	257
04/20	59.7	(10.4)	—	227
04/19	53.6	(4.2)	—	215
04/18	53.6	(21.8)	—	186
04/17	57.6	(28.1)	—	323
Annual Growth	13.6%	—	—	(5.6%)

2021 Year-End Financials
Debt ratio: 36.5%
Return on equity: 18.7%
Cash ($ mil.): 169.9
Current Ratio: 2.93
Long-term debt ($ mil.): 96.9
No. of shares ($ mil.): 61.0
Dividends
  Yield: —
  Payout: —
Market value ($ mil.): 1,307.0

	STOCK PRICE ($) FY Close	P/E High	P/E Low	PER SHARE ($) Earnings	PER SHARE ($) Dividends	PER SHARE ($) Book Value
04/21	21.41	364	88	0.06	0.00	1.27
04/20	6.10	—	—	(0.27)	0.00	0.74
04/19	4.79	—	—	(0.16)	0.00	0.95
04/18	3.67	—	—	(0.56)	0.00	1.00
04/17	0.62	—	—	(0.88)	0.00	1.22
Annual Growth	142.8%	—	—	—	—	1.1%

Avidbank Holdings Inc

EXECUTIVES

Chief Executive Officer, Chairman, Director, Mark D. Mordell
President, Chief Credit Officer, Ronald E. Oliveira
Executive Vice President, Chief Financial Officer, Steve Leen
Strategic Relationships Head, Director, Kenneth D. Brenner
Executive Vice President, Chief Banking Officer, Dori Hamilton
Corporate Finance Executive Vice President, Larry LaCroix
Banking Subsidiary Officer, Chris Greene
Subsidiary Officer, Nicole L. Bader
Subsidiary Officer, Greg J. Hickel
Relationship Manager Subsidiary Officer, Jon Krogstad
Commercial Real Estate Lending Subsidiary Officer, Joe Maleti
Banking Subsidiary Officer, Sarah Wesner
Subsidiary Officer, Geoffrey E. Butner
Construction Lending Subsidiary Officer, Fergal J. O'Boyle
Subsidiary Officer, Gina Stephens
Director, Bryan C. Polster
Director, Kristofer W. Biorn
Director, Lisa B. Hendrickson
Director, Roxy H. Rapp
Director, Michael F. Rosinus
Director, Daniel P. Vetras
Director, Robert H. Scott
Auditors: Crowe LLP

LOCATIONS

HQ: Avidbank Holdings Inc
400 Emerson Street, Palo Alto, CA 94301
Phone: 650 843-2265   **Fax:** 650 289-9192
Web: www.the-private-bank.com

HISTORICAL FINANCIALS
Company Type: Public

Income Statement   FYE: December 31

	ASSETS ($mil)	NET INCOME ($mil)	INCOME AS % OF ASSETS	EMPLOYEES
12/20	1,430.6	9.6	0.7%	0
12/19	1,131.5	12.8	1.1%	0
12/18	916.9	11.1	1.2%	0
12/17	782.9	5.6	0.7%	0
12/16	646.6	7.2	1.1%	0
Annual Growth	22.0%	7.3%	—	—

2020 Year-End Financials
Return on assets: 0.7%
Return on equity: 7.8%
Long-term debt ($ mil.): —
No. of shares ($ mil.): 6.1
Sales ($ mil.): 53.5
Dividends
  Yield: —
  Payout: —
Market value ($ mil.): 108.0

	STOCK PRICE ($) FY Close	P/E High	P/E Low	PER SHARE ($) Earnings	PER SHARE ($) Dividends	PER SHARE ($) Book Value
12/20	17.50	15	8	1.61	0.00	20.74
12/19	24.75	11	9	2.17	0.00	19.12
12/18	21.00	14	11	1.90	0.00	16.84
12/17	23.95	22	16	1.08	0.00	15.12
12/16	18.10	12	9	1.56	0.00	13.50
Annual Growth	(0.8%)	—	—	0.8%	—	11.3%

Axcelis Technologies Inc

Axcelis Technologies designs, manufactures and services ion implantation and other processing equipment used in the fabrication of semiconductor chips. Axcelis Technologies manufactures its ion implantation devices in house at its plant in Beverly, Massachusetts. In addition to equipment, it offers aftermarket service and support, including used tools, spare parts, equipment upgrades, and maintenance services. While the company sells its products around the world, the US accounts for some third-quarter of sales. Axcelis' business commenced in 1978.

Operations
The company operates in one business segment, which is the manufacture of capital equipment for the semiconductor chip manufacturing industry. Ion implantation systems and services surrounding them account for 95% of Axcelis Technologies' revenue. The other 5% comes from other systems and services.

Product revenue, which includes new system sales, sales of spare parts, product upgrades and used system sales was about 95% of revenue in 2021. And the remaining revenue was from Services revenue, which includes the labor component of maintenance and service contracts and fees for service hours provided by on-site service personnel.

Geographic Reach
Massachusetts-based, Axcelis Technologies has about 40 other properties, of which around 10 are located in the United States and the remainder are located in Asia and Europe, including offices in Taiwan, Singapore, South Korea, China, Japan, Italy, and Germany. The US is its largest market with more than 75% of sales, while sales to customers in Asia make some 15% of revenues and Europe accounts for around 5%.

The company has field offices serving customers in approximately 30 countries.

Sales and Marketing
Axcelis Technologies sells equipment and services through a direct sales force from offices in the United States, Taiwan, South Korea, China, Singapore, Japan, Germany and Italy.

For the year ended December 31, 2021, revenues from Samsung Electronics Co, Ltd. and Semiconductor Manufacturing International Corporation represented 10% or more of consolidated revenues.

Sales and marketing expense was $47.5 million in 2021, an increase of $8.8 million, or 23%, compared with $38.7 million in 2020.

Financial Performance
The company's revenue for fiscal 2021 increased to 40% to $662.4 million compared from the prior year with $474.6 million.

Net income for fiscal 2021 increased to $98.7 million compared from the prior year with $50.0 million.

Cash held by the company at the end of fiscal 2021 increased to $295.7 million. Cash provided by operations was $150.2 million while cash used for investing and financing activities were $8.7 million and $52.5 million, respectively. Main uses of cash were expenditures for property, plant and equipment and capitalized software; and repurchase of common stock.

Strategy
Axcelis' 2022 strategic goals are to: achieve its $850M revenue model run rate in 2022, positioning Axcelis to achieve its $1 billion revenue model in future years; execute a capital strategy that funds appropriate investments in the business and enables the potential for return of cash to shareholders; and prepare for a post-COVID-19 business environment.

Axcelis continue to invest in research and development to ensure its products meet the needs of its customers.

Company Background
Axcelis' business commenced in 1978 and

its current corporate entity was incorporated in Delaware in 1995.

HISTORY

Axcelis Technologies began as part of the Semiconductor Equipment Operations of industrial manufacturer Eaton. In 2000, Eaton spun off the operations as a wholly owned subsidiary, and Axcelis completed an IPO that year, selling less than 20% of the company's shares to the public. Brian Bachman, Eaton SVP and group executive for hydraulics, semiconductor equipment, and specialty controls, was named vice chairman and CEO of the spinoff.

At the end of 2000 Eaton distributed the remaining 82% ownership it held in Axcelis as a stock dividend to its shareholders, fully ending its involvement in the semiconductor production equipment market.

Bachman resigned as vice chairman and CEO in 2002. Mary Puma, the company's president and COO, was elevated to the chief executive's post to succeed him. A former General Electric executive, Puma worked at Eaton for four years before the Axcelis spinoff, including two years in leadership positions with the Semiconductor Equipment Operations. Puma added the title of chairman of the Axcelis board in 2005.

EXECUTIVES

Chairman, Director, Patrick H. Nettles
President, Chief Executive Officer, Director, Mary G. Puma, $585,000 total compensation
Manufacturing Operations Executive Vice President, Operations Executive Vice President, Manufacturing Operations Chief Financial Officer, Operations Chief Financial Officer, Kevin J. Brewer, $387,423 total compensation
Product Development Executive Vice President, William Bintz, $330,000 total compensation
Engineering Executive Vice President, Russell J. Low, $325,384 total compensation
Division Officer, John E. Aldeborgh, $355,385 total compensation
Legal Executive Vice President, Human Resources Executive Vice President, Legal Secretary, Human Resources Secretary, Legal General Counsel, Human Resources General Counsel, Lynnette C. Fallon, $320,000 total compensation
Senior Vice President, Chief Information Officer, Craig Halterman
Lead Director, Stephen R. Hardis
Director, Tzu-Yin Chiu
Director, Richard J. Faubert
Director, R. John Fletcher
Director, Arthur L. George
Director, Joseph P. Keithley
Director, John T. Kurtzweil
Director, Thomas St. Dennis
Director, Jorge Titinger
Auditors : Ernst & Young LLP

LOCATIONS

HQ: Axcelis Technologies Inc
108 Cherry Hill Drive, Beverly, MA 01915
Phone: 978 787-4000   **Fax:** 978 787-3000
Web: www.axcelis.com

2014 Sales

	$ mil.	% of total
US	126.3	63
Asia/Pacific	47.7	23
Europe	29.1	14
Total	203.1	100

PRODUCTS/OPERATIONS

2014 Sales

	$ mil.	% of total
Ion implantation systems, services & royalties	183.2	90
Other products, services & royalties	19.9	10
Total	203.1	100

2014 Sales

	$mil.	% of total
Product	179.3	88
Services	23.8	12
Total	203.1	100

COMPETITORS

APPLIED MATERIALS, INC.
BROOKS AUTOMATION, INC.
BTU INTERNATIONAL, INC.
Celestica Inc
FEDERAL-MOGUL LLC
FLEX LTD.
INTEVAC, INC.
ULTRATECH, INC.
VEECO INSTRUMENTS INC.
XCERRA CORPORATION

HISTORICAL FINANCIALS

Company Type: Public

Income Statement   FYE: December 31

	REVENUE ($mil)	NET INCOME ($mil)	NET PROFIT MARGIN	EMPLOYEES
12/20	474.5	49.9	10.5%	1,004
12/19	342.9	17.0	5.0%	1,009
12/18	442.5	45.8	10.4%	1,079
12/17	410.5	126.9	30.9%	985
12/16	266.9	11.0	4.1%	845
Annual Growth	15.5%	46.0%	—	4.4%

2020 Year-End Financials

Debt ratio: 7.7%   No. of shares ($ mil.): 33.6
Return on equity: 11.0%   Dividends
Cash ($ mil.): 203.4   Yield: —
Current Ratio: 5.58   Payout: —
Long-term debt ($ mil.): 47.3   Market value ($ mil.): 979.0

	STOCK PRICE ($) FY Close	P/E High/Low		PER SHARE ($) Earnings	Dividends	Book Value
12/20	29.12	21	9	1.46	0.00	14.32
12/19	24.10	48	27	0.50	0.00	12.87
12/18	17.80	22	11	1.35	0.00	12.54
12/17	28.70	9	3	3.80	0.00	11.03
12/16	14.55	38	6	0.36	0.00	6.82
Annual Growth	18.9%	—	—	41.9%	—	20.4%

Axos Financial Inc

Formerly BofI Holding, Axos Financial is the holding company for Axos Bank, which provides consumers and businesses a variety of deposit and loan products via the internet. It has designed its online banking platform and its workflow processes to handle traditional banking functions with elimination of duplicate and unnecessary paperwork and human intervention. Axos Bank has deposit and loan customers nationwide including consumer and business checking, savings and time deposit accounts and financing for single family and multifamily residential properties, small-to-medium size businesses in target sectors, and selected specialty finance receivables. Founded in 2000, the company holds over $17.4 billion in assets, and a total portfolio of net loans and leases of about $14 billion.

Operations

Axos Financial operates through two segments: Banking Business (about 90% of the company's sales) and Securities Business (around 10%).

The Banking Business includes a broad range of banking services including online banking, concierge banking, and mortgage, vehicle and unsecured lending through online and telephonic distribution channels to serve the needs of consumers and small businesses nationally. In addition, the Banking Business focuses on providing deposit products nationwide to industry verticals (Title and Escrow), cash management products to a variety of businesses, and commercial & industrial and commercial real estate lending to clients. The Banking Business also includes a bankruptcy trustee and fiduciary service that provides specialized software and consulting services to Chapter 7 bankruptcy and non-Chapter 7 trustees and fiduciaries.

The Securities Business includes the Clearing Broker-Dealer, Registered Investment Advisor custody business, Registered Investment Advisor, and Introducing Broker-Dealer lines of businesses. These lines of business offer products independently to their own customers as well as to Banking Business clients. The products offered by the lines of business in the Securities Business primarily generate net interest and non-banking service fee income.

Some 85% of Axos' revenue is generated by net interest income; non-interest income is derived mostly from banking and service fees. The bank's net loan and lease portfolio is dominated by single-family real estate: nearly 30% of its value is represented by mortgages. Some 20% is secured by multifamily real estate, and another roughly 35% is made up of commercial and real estate loans.

Geographic Reach

Las Vegas, Nevada-based Axos Financial holds deposits from customers in every US state, with large sources of balances in Florida, and the Mid-Atlantic states. Some 35% of its mortgage portfolio is secured by real estate in California. Its next largest geographic segments by loan principal are New York and Florida, which comprises about 25% and some 5%, respectively.

Sales and Marketing

The bank creates brand awareness through direct mail, email, digital marketing, personal sales, and print advertising. It also garners deposits through financial advisory companies and affinity partnerships.

Its advertising and promotional expenses for the years 2022 and 2021 were $13.6 and $14.2 million, respectively.

Financial Performance

The company's revenue for fiscal 2022 (ended June) increased to $720.5 million compared to $644.0 million in the prior fiscal year. Net interest income increased $68.4 million for fiscal 2022 compared to the fiscal 2021. The growth of net interest income is primarily due to an increase in average earning assets mainly due to net loan portfolio growth, reduced rates on interest-bearing deposits and an increase in non-interest bearing demand deposits.

Net income for fiscal 2022 (ended June) increased to $240.7 million compared to $215.5 million in the prior fiscal year. Growth in its interest earning assets, particularly the loan and lease portfolio, reduced cost of interest-bearing liabilities and growth in non-interest bearing deposits were the primary reasons for the increase in its net income from fiscal 2021 to fiscal 2022.

Cash held by the company at the end of fiscal 2022 increased to $1.6 billion. Cash provided by operations and financing activities were $210.3 million and $3.1 billion, respectively. Cash used for investing activities was $2.8 billion, mainly for origination of loans held for investment.

Strategy

The company's long-term business plan includes the following principal objectives: maintain an annualized return on average common stockholders' equity of 17.0% or better; annually increase average interest-earning assets by 12% or more; and maintain an annualized efficiency ratio at the Bank to a level 40% or lower.

The company's business strategy is to grow its loan originations and its deposits to achieve increased economies of scale and reduce the cost of products and services to its customers by leveraging its distribution channels and technology.

Mergers and Acquisitions

In mid-2021, Axos Financial, Inc. has closed its acquisition of E*TRADE Advisor Services ("EAS"), the registered investment advisor ("RIA") custody business Morgan Stanley acquired in its acquisition of E*TRADE Financial Corporation. Axos will fund the $55 million cash purchase price with existing capital at Axos Financial, Inc. The addition of a turnkey technology platform serving 200 RIA custody relationships with approximately $25 billion of combined assets under custody significantly accelerates its time-to-scale in this business.

Company Background

Axos Financial launched in 2000 as Bank of Internet USA as a digital bank offering checking accounts. The company went public in 2005 as BofI Holding. In 2018, after launching its Universal Digital Bank Platform, BofI changed its name to Axos Financial in tandem with a listing on the NYSE.

EXECUTIVES

Chairman, Subsidiary Officer, Director, Paul J. Grinberg
Subsidiary Officer, Vice-Chairman, Director, Nicholas A. Mosich
President, Chief Executive Officer, Subsidiary Officer, Director, Geogory Garrabrants, $700,000 total compensation
Strategic Partnerships Executive Vice President, Strategic Partnerships Chief Legal Officer, Strategic Partnerships Subsidiary Officer, Eshel Bar-Adon, $275,000 total compensation
Executive Vice President, Chief Credit Officer, Thomas M. Constantine, $250,000 total compensation
Executive Vice President, Chief Operating Officer, Raymond Matsumoto
Finance Executive Vice President, Finance subsidiary Officer, Andrew J. Micheletti, $245,000 total compensation
Commercial Banking and Treasury Management Executive Vice President, David X. Park
Executive Vice President, Division Officer, Brian Swanson, $255,000 total compensation
Executive Vice President, Chief Governance Officer, Chief Risk Officer, Chief Compliance Officer, Subsidiary Officer, John Tolla
Executive Vice President, Chief Financial Officer, Subsidiary Officer, Derrick K. Walsh
Securities and Digital Assets Senior Vice President, Securities and Digital Assets Head, Ron Pitters
Director, James S. Argalas
Director, James John Court
Director, Stefani D. Carter
Director, Roque A. Santi
Director, Tamara N. Bohlig
Director, Edward J. Ratinoff
Director, Uzair Dada
Auditors : BDO USA, LLP

LOCATIONS

HQ: Axos Financial Inc
9205 West Russell Road, STE 400, Las Vegas, NV 89148
Phone: 858 649-2218
Web: www.axosfinancial.com

PRODUCTS/OPERATIONS

2018 Sales

	$ mil.	% of total
Interest and dividend income:		
Loans and leases, including fees	447	79
Investments	28.1	5
Interest expense	(106.6)	-
Non-interest income:		
Banking and service fees	47.8	11
Mortgage banking income	13.7	3
Gain on sale - other	5.7	1
Prepayment penalty fee income	3.9	1
Gain (loss) on sale of securities	(0.2)	-
Total	455.3	100

COMPETITORS

BANKUNITED, INC.
COMMERCE BANCSHARES, INC.
FLAGSTAR BANCORP, INC.
LEGACYTEXAS FINANCIAL GROUP, INC.
M&T BANK CORPORATION
META FINANCIAL GROUP, INC.
PEOPLE'S UNITED FINANCIAL, INC.
PROVIDENT FINANCIAL SERVICES, INC.
THE SOUTHERN BANC COMPANY INC
TIAA FSB HOLDINGS, INC.

HISTORICAL FINANCIALS

Company Type: Public

Income Statement — FYE: June 30

	ASSETS ($mil)	NET INCOME ($mil)	INCOME AS % OF ASSETS	EMPLOYEES
06/21	14,265.5	215.7	1.5%	1,165
06/20	13,851.9	183.4	1.3%	1,099
06/19	11,220.2	155.1	1.4%	1,007
06/18	9,539.5	152.4	1.6%	801
06/17	8,501.6	134.7	1.6%	681
Annual Growth	13.8%	12.5%	—	14.4%

2021 Year-End Financials

Return on assets: 1.5%
Return on equity: 16.3%
Long-term debt ($ mil.): —
No. of shares ($ mil.): 59.3
Sales ($ mil.): 723.1
Dividends
Yield: —
Payout: —
Market value ($ mil.): 2,752.0

	STOCK PRICE ($) FY Close	P/E High/Low		PER SHARE ($) Earnings	Dividends	Book Value
06/21	46.39	14	5	3.56	0.00	23.62
06/20	22.08	10	5	2.98	0.00	20.65
06/19	27.25	17	10	2.48	0.00	17.55
06/18	40.91	19	10	2.37	0.00	15.32
06/17	23.72	16	7	2.07	0.00	13.13
Annual Growth	18.3%	—	—	14.5%	—	15.8%

AZEK Co Inc (The)

When it comes to CPG's building products, appearance is key. Through its AZEK, Scranton, and Vycom operating segments, CPG is a leading manufacturer of synthetic building products and other materials used in residential remodeling and construction, as well as by commercial and industrial clients, in the US and Canada. Its core AZEK unit manufactures PVC-based residential products such as trim, deck, rail, moulding, and porch materials made to look like wood and other natural materials. CPG's Scranton unit makes polyurethane bathroom partitions and lockers for commercial and institutional end-users, while Vycom makes PVC plastic sheeting for industrial uses. CPG's TimberTech unit makes decking and railings.

Operations

The company operates through three business units: Residential, Commercial, and Industrial.

CPG International offers high-performance residential building products (including trim, decking, moulding, railing, porch, lighting).

Subsidiary Scranton Products offers a line of synthetic commercial building products, including locker systems, bathroom partitions, counter tops, shower stalls, and other products.

Vycom makes and markets PVC and Olefin industrial products for the marine, graphic display, saferoom, food processing, playground equipment, and semiconductor industries.

Geographic Reach

CPG owns and operates five manufacturing facilities in Scranton, Pennsylvania. In addition, it manufactures its AZEK deck products at its facility in Foley, Alabama, and Timbertech products in Wilmington, Ohio. The Boise Cascade Building Material Distribution branch in Lathrop, California supplies Northern California and the Carson City area of Nevada; the Riverside, California branch serves Southern California.

Sales and Marketing

The company sells its products through distributors, dealers, and retail outlets. CPG's brands include AZEK Trim and Moulding, AZEK Deck, AZEK Rail, TimberTech, TuffTec, Duralife Lockers, Seaboard, Hiny Hider, and Celtec.

Strategy

CPG is focused on capitalizing on the economic and functional advantages of its products relative to wood, metal, and other synthetic products. It grows its product offerings partly through acquisitions of (and partnerships with) complementary businesses.

In 2013 the company formed a partnership with Boise Cascade Building Materials Distribution to distribute TimberTech products throughout California and the Carson City area of Nevada.

Mergers and Acquisitions

In 2012 it acquired TimberTech, a decking and railing manufacturer and a subsidiary of Ohio-based Crane Group Co. CPG combined TimberTech with its AZEK business to boost its strength as a leading manufacturer in the trim, decking, and railing market. Both have strong distribution channels in the US and Canada.

Company Background

CPG filed to go public in 2011. The company intended to use a significant portion of the proceeds that it raised in its IPO (up to $150 million) to repay debt and for general corporate purposes. However, the IPO never went through and the company was acquired in 2013. Prior to this deal CPG was majority owned by AEA Investors, which acquired its stake in 2005.

The company got its start in the mid-1980s as a plastic sheet manufacturer; it subsequently expanded its product offerings during the 1990s to include bathroom partitions and, later in the decade, residential building products.

EXECUTIVES

Chairman, Director, Gary E. Hendrickson
President, Chief Executive Officer, Director, Jesse G. Singh
Senior Vice President, Chief Financial Officer, Principal Accounting Officer, Peter G. Clifford
Senior Vice President, Chief Human Resources Officer, Sandra Lamartine
Senior Vice President, Chief Legal Officer, Secretary, Morgan Walbridge
Senior Vice President, Chief Marketing Officer, Samara Toole
Operations Senior Vice President, Christopher Latkovic
Vice President, Chief Information Officer, Michelle Kasson
Division Officer, Amanda Cimaglia
Strategy Division Officer, Execution Division Officer, Jonathan Skelly
Director, Howard C. Heckes
Director, Bennett Rosenthal
Director, Sallie B. Bailey
Director, Fumbi Chima
Director, Vernon J. Nagel
Director, Natasha Li
Director, Ashfaq Qadri
Director, Brian A. Spaly

LOCATIONS

HQ: AZEK Co Inc (The)
1330 W. Fulton Street, Suite 350, Chicago, IL 60607
Phone: 877 275-2935
Web: www.azekco.com

PRODUCTS/OPERATIONS

Selected Brands
AZEK
Acacia
Arbor Collection
Celtec
Cobre
Corrtec
Fawn
Flametec
Harvest Collection
Hiny Hiders
Kona
Morado
Playboard
Procell
Redland Rose
Resistall
Sanatec
Scranton Products
Seaboard
Sedona
Silver Oak
Tahoe
TimberTech
TuffTec Lockers
Vycom

COMPETITORS

BEMIS MANUFACTURING COMPANY
CRH AMERICAS, INC.
DAVIS-STANDARD, LLC
DAYTON SUPERIOR CORPORATION
JL REALISATIONS 2020 LIMITED
MEDPLAST GROUP, INC.
MILGARD MANUFACTURING LLC
MOLDED FIBER GLASS COMPANIES
Royal Group, Inc
TNEMEC COMPANY, INC.

HISTORICAL FINANCIALS

Company Type: Public

Income Statement — FYE: September 30

	REVENUE ($mil)	NET INCOME ($mil)	NET PROFIT MARGIN	EMPLOYEES
09/21	1,178.9	93.1	7.9%	2,072
09/20	899.2	(122.2)	—	1,663
09/19	794.2	(20.1)	—	1,540
09/18	681.8	6.7	1.0%	0
Annual Growth	20.0%	139.9%	—	—

2021 Year-End Financials

Debt ratio: 21.2%
Return on equity: 6.8%
Cash ($ mil.): 250.5
Current Ratio: 3.12
Long-term debt ($ mil.): 464.7
No. of shares ($ mil.): 154.8
Dividends
Yield: —
Payout: —
Market value ($ mil.): 5,657.0

	STOCK PRICE ($) FY Close	P/E High/Low		PER SHARE ($)		
				Earnings	Dividends	Book Value
09/21	36.53	83	55	0.59	0.00	9.22
09/20	34.81	—	—	(1.01)	0.00	8.43
Annual Growth	4.9%	—	—	—	—	9.3%

B Riley Financial Inc

EXECUTIVES

Chairman, Co-Chief Executive Officer, Director, Bryant R. Riley, $600,000 total compensation
Co-Chief Executive Officer, Thomas J. Kelleher, $545,769 total compensation
Chief Financial Officer, Chief Operating Officer, Phillip J. Ahn, $412,500 total compensation
President, Subsidiary Officer, Kenneth Young, $519,039 total compensation
Executive Vice President, General Counsel, Alan N. Forman
Subsidiary Officer, Andrew Gumaer, $500,000 total compensation
Subsidiary Officer, Andrew Moore, $283,077 total compensation
Retail Services Executive Vice President, Scott K. Carpenter, $278,801 total compensation
Senior Vice President, Chief Accounting Officer, Howard Weitzman
Senior Vice President, Secretary, General Counsel, Subsidiary Officer, Mark P. Naughton

Chief Investment Officer, Subsidiary Officer, Daniel Shribman
Subsidiary Officer, Lester M. Friedman
Subsidiary Officer, Michael Jerbich
Subsidiary Officer, Mark Weitz
Director, Robert D'Agostino
Director, Robert L. Antin
Director, Michael J. Sheldon
Director, Todd D. Sims
Director, Richard L. Todaro
Director, Mimi K. Walters
Director, Mikel H. Williams
Director, Gary K. Wunderlich
Auditors : Marcum LLP

LOCATIONS

HQ: B Riley Financial Inc
11100 Santa Monica Blvd., Suite 800, Los Angeles, CA 90025
Phone: 310 966-1444
Web: www.brileyfin.com

HISTORICAL FINANCIALS

Company Type: Public

Income Statement — FYE: December 31

	REVENUE ($mil)	NET INCOME ($mil)	NET PROFIT MARGIN	EMPLOYEES
12/20	902.7	205.1	22.7%	996
12/19	652.1	81.6	12.5%	982
12/18	422.9	15.5	3.7%	1,071
12/17	322.1	11.5	3.6%	833
12/16	190.3	21.5	11.3%	388
Annual Growth	47.6%	75.7%	—	26.6%

2020 Year-End Financials

Debt ratio: 66.1%
Return on equity: 46.8%
Cash ($ mil.): 103.6
Current Ratio: 1.90
Long-term debt ($ mil.): 962.3
No. of shares ($ mil.): 25.7
Dividends
 Yield: 2.9%
 Payout: 84.3%
Market value ($ mil.): 1,140.0

	STOCK PRICE ($) FY Close	P/E High/Low		PER SHARE ($) Earnings	Dividends	Book Value
12/20	44.22	6	2	7.56	1.33	19.88
12/19	25.18	10	4	2.95	1.49	13.37
12/18	14.20	38	24	0.58	0.74	9.70
12/17	18.10	43	27	0.48	0.67	10.01
12/16	18.45	16	7	1.17	0.28	7.80
Annual Growth	24.4%	—	—	59.4%	47.5%	26.3%

B&G Foods Inc

B&G Foods makes, markets, and distributes a wide variety of shelf-stable foods, frozen foods, and household goods. Many of B&G's products are regional or national best-sellers, including B&M and B&G (beans, condiments), Clabber Girl (baking), Green Giant (frozen and canned foods), Spice Islands (seasonings), McCann's (oatmeal), Ortega (Mexican foods), Grandma's and Brer Rabbit (molasses), Snackwell's (snacks), and Underwood (meat spread). They are sold through B&G's subsidiaries to supermarkets, mass merchants, warehouse clubs, and drug store chains, as well as institutional and food service operators in the US, Canada, and Puerto Rico.

Operations

B&G Foods operates in a single industry segment. It offers a diverse portfolio of more than 50 brands that include Green Giant (frozen) which generates more than 15% of the company's total revenue, Crisco (about 15%), Spices & Seasonings (nearly 15%), Ortega and Green Giant ? shelf stable (more than 5% each), Maple Grove Farms of Vermont, Cream of Wheat, Dash, and Clabber Girl (nearly 5% each), all other brands generate more than 25%.

Geographic Reach

Headquartered in Four Gatehall Drive, Parsippany, B&G Foods operates nearly a dozen of manufacturing facilities including in Ontario, Iowa, Maryland, Mexico, Wisconsin, and Indiana.

Sales and Marketing

B&G Foods sells, markets and distributes its products through a multiple-channel sales, marketing and distribution system to all major US food channels, including sales and shipments to supermarkets, mass merchants, warehouse clubs, wholesalers, foodservice distributors and direct accounts, specialty food distributors, military commissaries and non-food outlets such as drug, dollar store chains and e-tailers. The company primarily sells its products through broker sales networks that handle the sale of B&G Foods' products at the retail level.

Financial Performance

The company's revenue increased $88.4 million, or 5%, to $2.1 billion from $2.0 billion in 2020. The increase was primarily due to the Crisco acquisition, largely offset by comparisons against the extraordinary demand resulting from the COVID-19 pandemic during fiscal 2020, one fewer reporting week in fiscal 2021 compared to fiscal 2020, and supply chain disruptions in the fourth quarter of 2021 resulting from the COVID-19 Omicron variant.

Net income in 2021 decreased to $67.4 million compared to $132.0 million in the prior year.

Cash held by the company at the end of 2021 decreased to $33.7 million. Cash provided by operations was $93.9 million while, investing and financing activities used $42.8 million and $69.8 million, respectively. Main cash uses were capital expenditures and repayments of borrowings under revolving credit facility.

Strategy

B&G's company has been built upon a successful track record of acquisition-driven growth. The company's goal is to continue to increase sales, profitability and cash flows through strategic acquisitions, new product development and organic growth. The company intends to implement its growth strategy through the following initiatives: expanding its brand portfolio with disciplined acquisitions of complementary branded businesses, continuing to develop new products and delivering them to market quickly, leveraging its multiple channel sales and distribution system and continuing to focus on higher growth customers and distribution channels.

EXECUTIVES

Chairman, Director, Stephen C. Sherrill
President, Chief Executive Officer, Director, Kenneth C. ("Casey") Keller
Executive Vice President, Chief Commercial Officer, Jordan E. Greenberg
Human Resources Executive Vice President, Human Resources Chief Human Resources Officer, Eric H. Hart
Executive Vice President, Chief Compliance Officer, General Counsel, Secretary, Scott E. Lerner, $467,900 total compensation
Executive Vice President, Chief Customer Officer, Ellen M. Schum
Finance Executive Vice President, Finance Chief Financial Officer, Bruce C. Wacha, $425,000 total compensation
Director, DeAnn L. Brunts
Director, Debra Martin Chase
Director, Charles F. Marcy
Director, Robert D. Mills
Director, Dennis M. Mullen
Director, Cheryl M. Palmer
Director, Alfred Poe
Director, David L. Wenner, $675,000 total compensation
Auditors : KPMG LLP

LOCATIONS

HQ: B&G Foods Inc
Four Gatehall Drive, Parsippany, NJ 07054
Phone: 973 401-6500
Web: www.bgfoods.com

Selected Locations
Corporate Headquarters
 Parsippany, New Jersey
Distribution Centers
 Antioch, Tennessee
 Houston, Texas
 Easton, Pennsylvania
Manufacturing/Warehouse
 Hurlock, Maryland
 Portland, Maine
 Stoughton, Wisconsin
 St. Johnsbury, Vermont
 Williamstown, New Jersey
 Yadkinville, North Carolina
 Roseland, New Jersey
 Irapuato, Mexico
Sales Office
 Bentonville, Arkansas
 Chicago, Illinois
Storage Facility
 St. Evariste, Quebec
 Sharptown, Maryland

PRODUCTS/OPERATIONS

2016 Sales

	$ mil.	% of total
Green Giant	506.7	36
Ortega	142	10
Pirate Brands	84.9	6
Maple Grove Farms of Vermont	72.8	5
Cream of Wheat	62.2	4
Mrs. Dash	60.6	4
Bear Creek Country Kitchens	52.9	4
Las Palmas	39.1	3
Mama Mary's	35.8	2
Polaner	34.3	2
New York Style	33.1	2
Spices & Seasonings	28.2	2
All other brands	238.6	17
Total	1,391.3	100

Selected Products

Bagel chips
Canned meats and beans
Dry soups
Frozen and canned vegetables
Fruit spreads
Hot cereals
Hot sauces
Maple syrup
Mexican-style sauces
Molasses
Nut clusters
Peppers
Pickles
Pizza crusts
Puffed corn
Rice snacks
Salad dressings
Salsas
Seasonings
Spices
Taco shells and kits
Wine vinegar

Selected Brands

Ac'cent
B&G
B&M
Baker's Joy
Brer Rabbit
Cream of Rice
Cream of Wheat
Devonsheer
Don Pepino
Emeril's (licensed)
Grandma's Molasses
JJ Flats
Joan of Arc
Kleen Guard (sells and distributes)
Las Palmas
Maple Grove Farms of Vermont
Molly McButter
Mrs. Dash
New York Style
Old London
Ortega
Polaner
Red Devil
Regina
Sa-son
Sclafani
Static Guard (sells and distributes)
Sugar Twin
Trappey's
TrueNorth
Underwood
Vermont Maid
Wright's

COMPETITORS

ADVANCEPIERRE FOODS, INC.
FRESH MARK, INC.
JTM PROVISIONS COMPANY, INC
KEYSTONE FOODS LLC
OBERTO SNACKS INC.
PATRICK CUDAHY, LLC
PERFORMANCE FOOD GROUP COMPANY
PINNACLE FOODS INC.
SMITHFIELD FOODS, INC.
TREEHOUSE FOODS, INC.

HISTORICAL FINANCIALS

Company Type: Public

Income Statement — FYE: January 2

	REVENUE ($mil)	NET INCOME ($mil)	NET PROFIT MARGIN	EMPLOYEES
01/21*	1,967.9	131.9	6.7%	3,207
12/19	1,660.4	76.3	4.6%	2,899
12/18	1,700.7	172.4	10.1%	2,675
12/17	1,668.0	217.4	13.0%	2,680
12/16	1,391.2	109.4	7.9%	2,590
Annual Growth	9.1%	4.8%	—	5.5%

*Fiscal year change

2021 Year-End Financials

Debt ratio: 62.0%
Return on equity: 15.7%
Cash ($ mil.): 52.1
Current Ratio: 3.00
Long-term debt ($ mil.): 2,334
No. of shares ($ mil.): 64.2
Dividends
Yield: 0.1%
Payout: 116.4%
Market value ($ mil.): 1,782.0

	STOCK PRICE ($) FY Close	P/E High	P/E Low	PER SHARE ($) Earnings	PER SHARE ($) Dividends	PER SHARE ($) Book Value
01/21*	27.73	15	6	2.04	2.38	12.95
12/19	18.22	26	13	1.17	1.43	12.69
12/18	29.96	14	8	2.60	1.89	13.71
12/17	35.15	15	9	3.26	1.86	13.25
12/16	43.80	30	19	1.73	1.73	11.83
Annual Growth	(10.8%)	—	—	4.2%	8.3%	2.3%

*Fiscal year change

BancFirst Corp. (Oklahoma City, Okla)

This Oklahoma bank wants to be more than OK. It wants to be super . BancFirst Corporation is the holding company for BancFirst, a super-community bank that emphasizes decentralized management and centralized support. BancFirst operates more than 100 branches in more than 50 Oklahoma communities. It serves individuals and small to midsized businesses, offering traditional deposit products such as checking and savings accounts, CDs, and IRAs. Commercial real estate lending (including farmland and multifamily residential loans) makes up more than a third of the bank's loan portfolio, while one-to-four family residential mortgages represent about 20%. The bank also issues business, construction, and consumer loans.

Operations

The company operates three core units: metropolitan banks, community banks, and other financial service. Metropolitan and community banks offer traditional banking products such as commercial and retail lending, and a full line of deposit accounts in the metropolitan Oklahoma City and Tulsa areas. Community banks consist of banking locations in communities throughout Oklahoma. Other financial services are specialty product business units including guaranteed small business lending, residential mortgage lending, trust services, securities brokerage, electronic banking and insurance.

The company's BancFirst Insurance Services arm sells property/casualty coverage, while the bank's trust and investment management division oversees some $1.21 billion of assets on behalf of clients. Bank subsidiaries Council Oak Investment Corporation and Council Oak Real Estate focus on small business and property investments, respectively.

Like other retail banks, BancFirst makes the bulk of its money from interest income. More than 60% of its total revenue came from loan interest (including fees) during 2015, while another 2% came from interest on taxable securities. The rest of its revenue came from service charges on deposits (19% of revenue), insurance commissions (5%), trust revenue (3%), securities transactions (3%), and loan sales (1%).

Geographic Reach

BancFirst has 95 banking locations serving more than 52 communities across Oklahoma.

Sales and Marketing

The bank customers are generally small to medium-sized businesses engaged in light manufacturing, local wholesale and retail trade, commercial and residential real estate development and construction, services, agriculture, and the energy industry.

BancFirst spent about $6.9 million for advertising and promotion during 2015, compared to $6.6 million in each of 2014 and 2013.

Financial Performance

BancFirst's annual revenues have risen 20% since 2011 thanks to continued loan asset and deposit growth (partly thanks to branch expansion). The company's annual profits have grown more than 40% over the same period as it's kept a lid on operating expenses and loan loss provisions.

BancFirst's revenue climbed 6% to $306.85 million during 2015 thanks to a combination of loan asset growth and gains on the sales of some of its securities.

Revenue growth in 2015 drove the company's net income up nearly 4% to $66.17 million. The bank's operating cash levels increased by almost 2% to $78.1 million with the rise in cash-based earnings.

Strategy

BancFirst's strategy focuses on providing a full range of commercial banking services to retail customers and small to medium-sized businesses in both the non-metropolitan trade centers and cities in the metropolitan statistical areas of Oklahoma. It operates as a 'super community bank', managing its community banking offices on a decentralized basis, which permits them to be responsive to local customer needs. Underwriting, funding, customer service and pricing decisions are made by presidents in each market within the company's strategic parameters.

Mergers and Acquisitions

In October 2015, BancFirst purchased $196 million-asset CSB Banchsares and its Bank of Commerce branches in Yukon, Mustang, and El Reno in Oklahoma. The deal also added $148 million in new loan business and $170 million in deposits.

Company Background

The company has been buying smaller banks to expand in Oklahoma. In 2011 it acquired FBC Financial Corporation and its subsidiary bank, 1st Bank Oklahoma, with about five branches throughout the state. In 2010 BancFirst acquired Union Bank of Chandler, Okemah National Bank, and Exchange National Bank of Moore, adding about another five branches. It acquired First State Bank, Jones in 2009 to expand in eastern Oklahoma.

President and CEO David Rainbolt owns some 40% of BancFirst.

EXECUTIVES

Executive Chairman, Subsidiary Officer, Director, David E. Rainbolt, $400,000 total compensation
Vice-Chairman, Director, Dennis L. Brand, $400,000 total compensation
Vice-Chairman, Subsidiary Officer, William O. Johnstone, $200,000 total compensation
Chief Executive Officer, President, Director, David R. Harlow, $500,000 total compensation
Executive Vice President, Chief Financial Officer, Treasurer, Kevin Lawrence, $275,000 total compensation
Executive Vice President, Subsidiary Officer, Scott Copeland
Executive Vice President, Subsidiary Officer, Roy C. Ferguson
Executive Vice President, Chief Risk Officer, Secretary, Randy P. Foraker, $174,423 total compensation
Executive Vice President, Chief Compliance Officer, Subsidiary Officer, Kelly Foster
Community Banking Subsidiary Officer, Director, Darryl Schmidt, $500,000 total compensation
Subsidiary Officer, Dara Wanzer
Subsidiary Officer, Director, Joe R. Goyne
Chairman Emeritus, H. E. Rainbolt, $410,000 total compensation
Director, F. Ford Drummond
Director, Joseph Ford
Director, Mautra Staley Jones
Director, Francis (Frank) A. Keating
Director, Bill G. Lance
Director, David R. Lopez
Director, William Scott Martin
Director, Tom H. McCasland
Director, Robin Roberson
Director, Natalie Shirley
Director, Michael K. Wallace
Director, Gregory G. Wedel
Director, G. Rainey Williams
Auditors: BKD, LLP

LOCATIONS

HQ: BancFirst Corp. (Oklahoma City, Okla)
101 N. Broadway, Oklahoma City, OK 73102-8405
Phone: 405 270-1086 **Fax:** 405 270-1089
Web: www.bancfirst.com

PRODUCTS/OPERATIONS

2015 Sales

	$ mil.	% of total
Interest		
Loans, including fees	190.3	63
Securities	6.5	2
Interest-bearing deposit	4.23	1
Noninterest		
Service charges on deposits	57.7	18
Insurance commissions	14.8	5
Security transactions	9.3	3
Trust revenue	9.1	3
Income from sale of loans	2.0	1
Cash management	7.5	2
Other	5.5	2
Total	306.9	100

Selected Subsidiaries
BancFirst
    BancFirst Agency, Inc. (credit life insurance)
    BancFirst Community Development Corporation
    Council Oak Investment Corporation (small business investments)
    Council Oak Real Estate, Inc. (real estate investments)
Council Oak Partners, LLC
BancFirst Insurance Services, Inc.

COMPETITORS

CITIZENS & NORTHERN CORPORATION
CITY HOLDING COMPANY
COMMERCE BANCSHARES, INC.
COMMUNITY BANK SYSTEM, INC.
EAGLE BANCORP, INC.
FINANCIAL INSTITUTIONS, INC.
GUARANTY BANCORP
M&T BANK CORPORATION
PRIVATEBANCORP, INC.
WINTRUST FINANCIAL CORPORATION

HISTORICAL FINANCIALS

Company Type: Public

Income Statement				FYE: December 31
	ASSETS ($mil)	NET INCOME ($mil)	INCOME AS % OF ASSETS	EMPLOYEES
12/20	9,212.3	99.5	1.1%	2,036
12/19	8,565.7	134.8	1.6%	1,948
12/18	7,574.2	125.8	1.7%	1,906
12/17	7,253.1	86.4	1.2%	1,782
12/16	7,018.9	70.6	1.0%	1,773
Annual Growth	7.0%	9.0%	—	3.5%

2020 Year-End Financials

Return on assets: 1.1%   Dividends
Return on equity: 9.5%   Yield: 2.2%
Long-term debt ($ mil.): —   Payout: 43.8%
No. of shares ($ mil.): 32.7   Market value ($ mil.): 1,921.0
Sales ($ mil.): 464.3

	STOCK PRICE ($) FY Close	P/E High/Low		PER SHARE ($) Earnings	Dividends	Book Value
12/20	58.70	21	9	3.00	1.32	32.64
12/19	62.44	15	12	4.05	1.24	30.74
12/18	49.90	17	13	3.76	1.02	27.69
12/17	51.15	40	18	2.65	0.80	24.32
12/16	93.05	42	23	2.22	0.74	22.49
Annual Growth	(10.9%)	—	—	7.8%	15.6%	9.8%

Bank First Corp

EXECUTIVES

Chairman, Subsidiary Officer, Director, Michael G. Ansay
President, Chief Executive Officer, Subsidiary Officer, Director, Michael B. Molepske, $425,015 total compensation
Subsidiary Officer, Director, Michael P. Dempsey, $295,665 total compensation
Chief Financial Officer, Subsidiary Officer, Kevin M. LeMahieu, $206,000 total compensation
Corporate Secretary, General Counsel, Subsidiary Officer, Kelly M. Dvorak
Director, Judy L. Heun
Director, Stephen E. Johnson
Director, Robert W. Holmes
Director, Donald R. Brisch
Director, Mary-Kay H. Bourbulas
Director, Robert D. Gregorski
Director, Katherine M. Reynolds
Director, David R. Sachse
Director, Peter J. Van Sistine
Director, Robert J. Wagner
Auditors: Dixon Hughes Goodman LLP

LOCATIONS

HQ: Bank First Corp
402 North 8th Street, Manitowoc, WI 54220
Phone: 920 652-3100 **Fax:** 920 652-3182
Web: www.bankfirstnational.com

HISTORICAL FINANCIALS

Company Type: Public

Income Statement				FYE: December 31
	ASSETS ($mil)	NET INCOME ($mil)	INCOME AS % OF ASSETS	EMPLOYEES
12/20	2,718.0	38.0	1.4%	314
12/19	2,210.1	26.6	1.2%	284
12/18	1,793.1	25.4	1.4%	253
12/17	1,753.4	15.3	0.9%	249
12/16	1,315.9	14.9	1.1%	173
Annual Growth	19.9%	26.4%	—	16.1%

2020 Year-End Financials

Return on assets: 1.5%   Dividends
Return on equity: 14.4%   Yield: 1.2%
Long-term debt ($ mil.): —   Payout: 17.6%
No. of shares ($ mil.): 7.7   Market value ($ mil.): 500.0
Sales ($ mil.): 120.9

	STOCK PRICE ($)	P/E		PER SHARE ($)		
	FY Close	High/Low		Earnings	Dividends	Book Value
12/20	64.82	14	9	5.07	0.81	38.25
12/19	70.01	19	12	3.87	0.80	32.49
12/18	46.60	15	11	3.81	0.68	26.37
12/17	44.70	18	14	2.44	0.64	23.76
12/16	33.33	14	11	2.40	0.59	20.53
Annual Growth	18.1%	—	—	20.6%	8.2%	16.8%

Bank Of Princeton (The)

EXECUTIVES

Chairman, Richard Gillespie
Vice-Chairman, Stephen Distler
President, Director, Edward J. Dietzler
Executive Vice President, Chief Financial Officer, George S. Rapp
Director, Ross Wishnick
Director, Judith A. Giacin
Director, Stephen Shueh
Director, Robert N. Ridolfi
Auditors : BDO USA, LLP

LOCATIONS

HQ: Bank Of Princeton (The)
  183 Bayard Lane, Princeton, NJ 08540
Phone: 609 921-1700
Web: www.thebankofprinceton.com

HISTORICAL FINANCIALS

Company Type: Public

Income Statement — FYE: December 31

	ASSETS ($mil)	NET INCOME ($mil)	INCOME AS % OF ASSETS	EMPLOYEES
12/20	1,602.8	13.8	0.9%	176
12/19	1,454.8	10.1	0.7%	178
12/18	1,251.5	14.7	1.2%	151
12/17	1,200.5	11.0	0.9%	146
12/16	1,025.9	11.8	1.2%	135
Annual Growth	11.8%	3.9%	—	6.9%

2020 Year-End Financials

Return on assets: 0.9%
Return on equity: 6.8%
Long-term debt ($ mil.): —
No. of shares ($ mil.): 6.7
Sales ($ mil.): 66.4
Dividends
  Yield: 1.7%
  Payout: 21.0%
Market value ($ mil.): 159.0

	STOCK PRICE ($)	P/E		PER SHARE ($)		
	FY Close	High/Low		Earnings	Dividends	Book Value
12/20	23.41	16	9	2.01	0.40	30.75
12/19	31.49	22	17	1.47	0.19	28.98
12/18	27.90	16	12	2.14	0.03	27.69
12/17	34.34	19	15	1.90	0.00	25.69
12/16	30.00	12	11	2.36	0.00	22.01
Annual Growth	(6.0%)	—	—	(3.9%)	—	8.7%

Bank OZK

Bank of the Ozarks is the holding company for the bank of the same name, which has about 260 branches in Alabama, Arkansas, California, the Carolinas, Florida, Georgia, New York, and Texas. Focusing on individuals and small to midsized businesses, the $12-billion bank offers traditional deposit and loan services, in addition to personal and commercial trust services, retirement and financial planning, and investment management. Commercial real estate and construction and land development loans make up the largest portion of Bank of the Ozarks' loan portfolio, followed by residential mortgage, business, and agricultural loans. Bank of the Ozarks grows its loan and deposit business by acquiring smaller banks and opening branches across the US.

Operations

The bank makes three-fourths of its total revenue from interest income, while the rest comes from fee-based sources. About 43% of Bank of the Ozark's total revenue came from non-purchased loan interest in 2014, while another 26% came from interest on purchased loans, and a further 8% came from interest on its investment securities. The rest of its revenue came from service charges on deposit accounts (8% of revenue), mortgage lending income (1%), trust income (1%), and other non-recurring sources.

Geographic Reach

Bank of the Ozarks had 174 branches in eight states at the end of 2014, with 81 of them in Alabama and another 75 branches split among Georgia, North Carolina, and Texas. It has two loan offices in Houston and Manhattan that serve as an extension of the bank's Dallas-based Real Estate Specialties Group.

Sales and Marketing

The bank spent $3.03 million on advertising and public relations expenses in 2014, compared to $2.2 million and $4.09 million in 2013 and 2012, respectively.

Financial Performance

Bank of the Ozarks' annual revenues and profits have doubled since 2010, mostly as its loan assets have doubled from recent bank acquisitions, spawning higher interest income.

The bank's revenue jumped 31% to $376 million during 2014 mostly thanks to strong purchased and non-purchased loan asset growth during the year from recent bank acquisitions. Its non-interest income grew 12% thanks to a 20% increase in deposit account service charges stemming from newly acquired deposit customers.

Strong revenue growth in 2014 boosted Bank of the Ozarks' net income by 30% to $119 million for the year. Its operating cash levels jumped 22% to $61 million during the year mostly thanks to higher cash earnings.

Strategy

Bank of the Ozarks continues its strategy of loan and deposit volume growth by acquiring smaller banks in new and existing geographic markets. It has also opened new branches and loan offices sparingly. During 2014, for example, the bank opened retail branches in Bradenton, Florida; Cornelius, North Carolina; and Hilton Head Island, South Carolina, along with a new loan production office in Asheville, North Carolina.

Mergers and Acquisitions

In July 2016, Bank of the Ozarks acquired Georgia-based Community & Southern Holdings and its Community & Southern Bank subsidiary. Adding some 45 branch locations in Georgia plus another in Florida, it was the company's largest acquisition to-date.

Also in July 2016, the bank purchased C1 Financial, along with its 32 CI Bank branches on the west coast of Florida and in Miami-Dade and Orange Counties. The deal added $1.7 billion in total assets, $1.4 billion in loans, and $1.3 billion in deposits. This transaction was the bank's fifteenth acquisition in the past six years.

In August 2015, the bank purchased Bank of the Carolinas Corporation (BCAR) -- and its eight Bank of the Carolinas branches in North Carolina, $345 million in total assets, $277 million in loans, and $296 million in deposits -- for a total price of $65.4 million.

In February 2015, Bank of the Ozarks bought Intervest Bancshares Corporation and its seven Intervest National Bank branches in (five in Clearwater, Florida and two more in New York City and Pasadena Florida) for $238.5 million. The deal added $1.5 billion in assets, including $1.1 billion in loans and $1.2 billion in deposits.

In May 2014, it bought Arkansas-based Summit Bancorp, Inc. and its 23 Summit Bank branches across Arkansas for $42.5 million, though it closed more than a handful of them later in the year.

In March 2014, the company acquired Houston-based Bancshares, Inc. and its subsidiary Omnibank, N.A. for $21.5 million, adding three branches in Houston, Texas and a branch each in Austin, Cedar Park, Lockhart, and San Antonio.

Company Background

The expansion strategy of Bank of the Ozarks - which had a mere five branches in Arkansas 20 years ago -- centered on opening new locations in smaller communities in Arkansas. But with the financial crash, the bank was able to expand to more states through a series of FDIC-assisted transactions to take over failed banks. It bought Chestatee State Bank, First Choice Community Bank, Horizon Bank, Oglethorpe Bank, Park Avenue Bank, Unity National, and Woodlands Bank.

Chairman and CEO George Gleason initially bought the bank more than three decades ago at age 25.

EXECUTIVES

President, Chief Executive Officer, Subsidiary Officer, Chairman, Director, George Gleason, $1,000,000 total compensation
Chief Financial Officer, Chief Accounting Officer, Subsidiary Officer, Greg McKinney, $594,615 total compensation
Chief Operating Officer, Chief Banking Officer, Subsidiary Officer, Tyler A. Vance, $594,615 total compensation
Executive Vice President, Chief of Staff, Tim Hicks
Subsidiary Officer, Brannon Hamblen
Chief Credit Officer, John Carter
Chief Banking Officer, Cindy Wolfe
Chief Lending Officer, Alan Jessup
Subsidiary Officer, Jennifer Junker
Regulatory and Government Relations Executive Vice President, Regulatory and Government Relations Director, Dennis James
Chief Audit Executive, Subsidiary Officer, Brad Rebel
Chief Risk Officer, Subsidiary Officer, Edward J. Wydock
Director, Nicholas A. Brown
Director, Paula H. J. Cholmondeley
Director, Richard Cisne
Director, Robert East
Director, Catherine Blanton Freedberg
Director, Linda Gleason
Director, William A. Koefoed
Director, Walter Jack Mullen
Director, Robert L. Proost
Director, John B. Reynolds
Director, Ross M. Whipple
Auditors : PricewaterhouseCoopers LLP

LOCATIONS

HQ: Bank OZK
 18000 Cantrell Road, Little Rock, AR 72223
Phone: 501 978-2265   **Fax:** 501 978-2224
Web: www.bankozarks.com

PRODUCTS/OPERATIONS

2014 Sales

	$ mil.	% of total
Interest income		
Non-purchased loans and leases	162.5	43
Purchased loans	98.2	26
Investment securities	30.7	8
Non-interest income		
Service charges on deposit accounts	26.6	8
Other income from purchased loans, net	14.8	4
Others	43.5	11
Total	376.3	100

Selected Services
Personal Banking
Apple PayChecking AccountsCredit CardsFree Bill PayFREE Debit CardsCustom Debit CardsEMV Chip CardsMobile BankingMortgage LoansMy Change KeeperOnline BankingOverdraft ProtectionPersonal LoansReloadable Spending CardsRetirement PlanningReorder ChecksSafe Deposit BoxSavings, CDs & Money MarketsVISA Gift CardsCustomer ServiceCustomer Service Center

Business Banking
Business ProductsApple Pay for BusinessDebit CardEMV Chip CardsBusiness Credit CardsChecking & Money MarketCommercial LoansExpress DepositMerchant ProcessingOnline BankingOverdraft ProtectionReorder ChecksTreasury Management Services
Online & Mobile Banking
Online BankingMobile BankingMobile DepositOnline Bill Pay
Wealth Management Services
Investment ProgramsFinancial PlanningCustomer Service

COMPETITORS

F.N.B. CORPORATION
MAINSOURCE FINANCIAL GROUP, INC.
MIDLAND STATES BANCORP, INC.
PARK STERLING CORPORATION
WILSHIRE BANCORP, INC.

HISTORICAL FINANCIALS
Company Type: Public

Income Statement   FYE: December 31

	ASSETS ($mil)	NET INCOME ($mil)	INCOME AS % OF ASSETS	EMPLOYEES
12/20	27,162.5	291.8	1.1%	2,652
12/19	23,555.7	425.9	1.8%	2,774
12/18	22,388.0	417.1	1.9%	2,563
12/17	21,275.6	421.8	2.0%	2,400
12/16	18,890.1	269.9	1.4%	2,315
Annual Growth	9.5%	2.0%	—	3.5%

2020 Year-End Financials
Return on assets: 1.1%   Dividends
Return on equity: 6.9%   Yield: 3.4%
Long-term debt ($ mil.): —   Payout: 47.6%
No. of shares ($ mil.): 129.3   Market value ($ mil.): 4,045.0
Sales ($ mil.): 1,185.3

	STOCK PRICE ($) FY Close	P/E High/Low		PER SHARE ($) Earnings	Dividends	Book Value
12/20	31.27	14	7	2.26	1.08	33.03
12/19	30.51	10	7	3.30	0.94	32.19
12/18	22.83	16	7	3.24	0.80	29.32
12/17	48.45	17	12	3.35	0.37	26.98
12/16	52.59	21	13	2.58	0.63	23.02
Annual Growth	(12.2%)	—	—	(3.3%)	14.4%	9.4%

Bank7 Corp

EXECUTIVES

Founder, Chairman, subsidiary Officer, William B. Haines, $434,615 total compensation
President, Chief Executive Officer, Subsidiary Officer, Director, Thomas L. Travis, $330,800 total compensation
Senior Executive Vice President, Chief Operating Officer, Secretary, Subsidiary Officer, Director, John T. Phillips, $225,039 total compensation
Executive Vice President, Chief Credit Officer, Subsidiary Officer, Jason E. Estes
Senior Vice President, Chief Financial Officer, Subsidiary Officer, Kelly J. Harris
Subsidiary Officer, Douglas A. Haines
Subsidiary Officer, Lisa K. Haines
Region Officer, Andrew J. Levinson
Director, Bobby J. Alexander
Director, Charles W. Brown
Director, William M. Buergler
Director, J. Michael Sanner
Director, Gary D. Whitcomb
Director, Lonny D. Wilson
Auditors : BKD, LLP

LOCATIONS

HQ: Bank7 Corp
 1039 N.W., 63rd Street, Oklahoma City, OK 73116-7361
Phone: 405 810-8600
Web: www.bank7.com

HISTORICAL FINANCIALS
Company Type: Public

Income Statement   FYE: December 31

	ASSETS ($mil)	NET INCOME ($mil)	INCOME AS % OF ASSETS	EMPLOYEES
12/20	1,016.6	19.2	1.9%	0
12/19	866.3	8.2	0.9%	78
12/18	770.5	25.0	3.2%	72
12/17	703.5	23.7	3.4%	74
12/16	613.7	16.8	2.7%	0
Annual Growth	13.4%	3.5%	—	—

2020 Year-End Financials
Return on assets: 2.0%   Dividends
Return on equity: 18.5%   Yield: 2.8%
Long-term debt ($ mil.): —   Payout: 20.8%
No. of shares ($ mil.): 9.0   Market value ($ mil.): 128.0
Sales ($ mil.): 54.9

	STOCK PRICE ($) FY Close	P/E High/Low		PER SHARE ($) Earnings	Dividends	Book Value
12/20	14.20	9	3	2.05	0.41	11.87
12/19	18.96	24	16	0.81	0.60	9.96
12/18	13.35	6	4	3.03	7.71	8.68
Annual Growth	3.1%	—	—	(17.7%)	(76.9%)	16.9%

BankFirst Capital Corp.

Auditors : T. E. Lott & Company

LOCATIONS

HQ: BankFirst Capital Corp.
 900 Main Street, Columbus, MS 39701
Phone: 662 328-2345
Web: www.bankfirstfs.com

HISTORICAL FINANCIALS
Company Type: Public

Income Statement   FYE: December 31

	REVENUE ($mil)	NET INCOME ($mil)	NET PROFIT MARGIN	EMPLOYEES
12/20	81.5	13.4	16.5%	0
12/19	65.5	11.8	18.0%	0
12/18	48.7	9.8	20.1%	0
12/17	43.6	6.1	14.0%	0
Annual Growth	23.1%	30.0%	—	—

2020 Year-End Financials

Debt ratio: 3.2%
Return on equity: 10.2%
Cash ($ mil.): 128.9
Current Ratio: 0.09
Long-term debt ($ mil.): 54.7
No. of shares ($ mil.): 5.2
Dividends
Yield: —
Payout: 18.1%
Market value ($ mil.): 104.0

	STOCK PRICE ($) FY Close	P/E High/Low		PER SHARE ($) Earnings	Dividends	Book Value
12/20	19.75	9	5	2.76	0.50	27.89
12/19	23.85	10	9	2.72	0.50	25.62
Annual Growth	(17.2%)	—	—	1.5%	0.0%	8.9%

Bar Harbor Bankshares

Bar Harbor Bankshares which holds Bar Harbor Bank & Trust, is a Maine -stay. Boasting $1.6 billion in assets, the bank offers traditional deposit and retirement products, trust services, and a variety of loans to individuals and businesses through 15 branches in the state's Hancock, Knox, and Washington counties. Commercial real estate and residential mortgages loans make up nearly 80% of the bank's loan portfolio, though it also originates business, construction, agricultural, home equity, and other consumer loans. About 10% of its loans are to the tourist industry, which is associated with nearby Acadia National Park. Subsidiary Bar Harbor Trust Services offers trust and estate planning services.

Operations

Around 80% of the bank's loan assets are tied to real estate. About 41% of its loan portfolio was made up of residential real estate mortgages at the end of 2015 while another 37% was made up of commercial real estate mortgages. The rest of the portfolio was tied to commercial and industrial loans (8% of loan assets), home equity loans (5%), agricultural and farming loans (3%), commercial construction (3%), and other consumer loans (1%).

More than 80% of Bar Harbor's revenue comes from interest income. About 61% of its total revenue came from loan interest (including fees) during 2015, while another 25% came from interest income on investment securities. The remainder of its revenue came from trust and other financial services (6% of revenue), debit card service charges and fees (3%), deposit account service charges (1%), and other miscellaneous income sources.

Geographic Reach

The Bar Harbor, Maine-based group operates 15 branches across the downeast, midcoast, and central regions of Maine, more specifically in Bar Harbor, Northeast Harbor, Southwest Harbor, Somesville, Deer Isle, Blue Hill, Ellsworth, Rockland, Topsham, South China, Augusta, Winter Harbor, Milbridge, Machias, and Lubec.

Sales and Marketing

Bar Harbor serves individuals and retirees, non-profits, municipalities, as well as businesses that are vital to Maine's coastal economy, including retailers, restaurants, seasonal lodging, bio research laboratories.

Financial Performance

The group's annual revenues have risen more than 10% since 2011 as its loan assets have swelled over 35% to $990 million. Its profits have grown more than 30% over the same period as Bar Harbor has kept a lid on rising operating costs and as it's enjoyed low interest rates.

Bar Harbor's revenue climbed 4% to $64.2 million during 2015 mostly as its loan and other interest earning assets grew by more than 7%.

Revenue growth in 2015 drove the bank's net income up 4% to $15.15 million. Bar Harbor's operating cash levels spiked 31% to $20.33 million for the year mainly thanks to favorable working capital changes related to changes in other assets.

Strategy

Bar Harbor Bankshares looks to grow its loan and deposit business organically and through strategic bank acquisitions, targeting the downeast, midcoast, and central Maine markets. It also continued in 2016 to focus on managing its operating expenses, building upon its strong efficient ratio of 56.3% in 2015.

EXECUTIVES

Chairman, Director, David B. Woodside
President, Chief Executive Officer, Subsidiary Officer, Director, Curtis C. Simard, $605,000 total compensation
Executive Vice President, Chief Financial Officer, Treasurer, Subsidiary Officer, Josephine Iannelli, $390,000 total compensation
Retail Delivery Executive Vice President, Retail Delivery Director, Retail Delivery Subsidiary Officer, Marion Colombo, $245,385 total compensation
Executive Vice President, Chief Lending Officer, Subsidiary Officer, John M. Mercier, $290,000 total compensation
Subsidiary Officer, Jason Edgar
Subsidiary Officer, Jennifer Svenson
Subsidiary Officer, Josep P. Scully
Senior Vice President, Chief Risk Officer, John M. Williams
Director, Diana H. Belair
Director, Matthew L. Caras
Director, David M. Colter
Director, Steven H. Dimick
Director, Martha T. Dudman
Director, Lauri E. Fernald
Director, Debra B. Miller
Director, Brendan J. O'Halloran
Director, Kenneth E. Smith
Director, Scott G. Toothaker
Director, Stephen R. Theroux
Auditors : RSM US LLP

LOCATIONS

HQ: Bar Harbor Bankshares
P.O. Box 400, 82 Main Street, Bar Harbor, ME 04609-0400
Phone: 207 288-3314
Web: www.barharbor.bank

PRODUCTS/OPERATIONS

2015 sales

	$ mil.	% of total
Interest and dividend income		
Interest and fees on loans	39.3	61
Interest on securities	15.3	24
Dividends on FHLB stock	0.6	1
Non-interest income		
Trust and other financial services	3.9	6
Debit card service charges and fees	1.7	3
Net securities gains	1.3	2
Other operating income	1.2	2
Service charges on deposit accounts	0.9	1
Total	64.2	100

Selected Services
Retail Products and Services
Retail Brokerage Services
Electronic Banking Services
Commercial Products and Services

COMPETITORS

CITIZENS & NORTHERN CORPORATION
OLD SECOND BANCORP, INC.
STOCK YARDS BANCORP, INC.
UNIVEST FINANCIAL CORPORATION
WESTERN ALLIANCE BANCORPORATION

HISTORICAL FINANCIALS

Company Type: Public

Income Statement — FYE: December 31

	ASSETS ($mil)	NET INCOME ($mil)	INCOME AS % OF ASSETS	EMPLOYEES
12/20	3,725.7	33.2	0.9%	531
12/19	3,669.1	22.6	0.6%	460
12/18	3,608.4	32.9	0.9%	445
12/17	3,565.1	25.9	0.7%	423
12/16	1,755.3	14.9	0.9%	186
Annual Growth	20.7%	22.1%	—	30.0%

2020 Year-End Financials

Return on assets: 0.8%
Return on equity: 8.2%
Long-term debt ($ mil.): —
No. of shares ($ mil.): 14.9
Sales ($ mil.): 169
Dividends
Yield: 3.8%
Payout: 40.3%
Market value ($ mil.): 337.0

	STOCK PRICE ($) FY Close	P/E High/Low		PER SHARE ($) Earnings	Dividends	Book Value
12/20	22.59	12	6	2.18	0.88	27.58
12/19	25.39	19	15	1.45	0.86	25.48
12/18	22.43	14	10	2.12	0.79	23.87
12/17	27.01	28	15	1.70	0.75	22.96
12/16	47.33	30	18	1.63	0.73	17.19
Annual Growth	(16.9%)	—	—	7.5%	4.9%	12.5%

Barnwell Industries, Inc.

Barnwell Industries has more than a barnful of assets, which range from oil and gas production, contract well drilling, and Hawaiian land and housing investments. Barnwell Industries explores for and produces oil and natural gas primarily in Alberta. In 2009 it reported proved reserves of 1.3 million barrels of oil and 20.6 billion cu. ft. of gas. Subsidiary Water Resources International drills water and geothermal wells and installs and repairs water pump systems in Hawaii. The company also owns a 78% interest in Kaupulehu Developments, which owns leasehold rights to more than 1,000 acres in Hawaii, and is engaged in other real estate activities.

EXECUTIVES

Vice-Chairman, Director, Kenneth S. Grossman
President, Chief Executive Officer, Chief Operating Officer, General Counsel, Director, Alexander C. Kinzler, $380,000 total compensation
Executive Vice President, Chief Financial Officer, Treasurer, Secretary, Subsidiary Officer, Russell M. Gifford, $380,000 total compensation
Director, Philip J. McPherson
Director, Laurance E. Narbut
Director, Peter J. O'Malley
Director, Bradley M. Tirpak
Director, Joshua S. Horowitz
Director, Douglas N. Woodrum
Director, Francis J. Kelly
Auditors : Weaver and Tidwell, L.L.P.

LOCATIONS

HQ: Barnwell Industries, Inc.
  1100 Alakea Street, Suite 2900, Honolulu, HI 96813-2840
Phone: 808 531-8400
Web: www.brninc.com

PRODUCTS/OPERATIONS

Subsidiaries
Barnwell of Canada, Ltd. (oil and natural gas)
Kaupulehu Developments (78%, land investment)
Kaupulehu 2007, LLLP (80%, real estate development)
Water Resources International, Inc. (contract drilling)

COMPETITORS

CAMBER ENERGY, INC.
ISRAMCO, INC.
NOBLE ENERGY, INC.
OCCIDENTAL PETROLEUM CORPORATION OF CALIFORNIA
QEP RESOURCES, INC.

HISTORICAL FINANCIALS
Company Type: Public

Income Statement — FYE: September 30

	REVENUE ($mil)	NET INCOME ($mil)	NET PROFIT MARGIN	EMPLOYEES
09/21	18.1	6.2	34.5%	36
09/20	18.3	(4.7)	—	43
09/19	12.0	(12.4)	—	43
09/18	9.3	(1.7)	—	31
09/17	13.0	1.1	9.0%	29
Annual Growth	8.6%	52.0%	—	5.6%

2021 Year-End Financials

Debt ratio: 0.2%
Return on equity: —
Cash ($ mil.): 11.2
Current Ratio: 3.06
Long-term debt ($ mil.): —
No. of shares ($ mil.): 9.4
Dividends
  Yield: —
  Payout: —
Market value ($ mil.): 29.0

	STOCK PRICE ($) FY Close	P/E High/Low		PER SHARE ($) Earnings	Dividends	Book Value
09/21	3.03	8	1	0.73	0.00	1.01
09/20	0.85	—	—	(0.57)	0.00	(0.25)
09/19	0.52	—	—	(1.50)	0.00	0.15
09/18	1.78	—	—	(0.21)	0.00	1.94
09/17	1.80	18	11	0.14	0.00	2.08
Annual Growth	13.9%	—	—	51.1%	—	(16.7%)

BayCom Corp

EXECUTIVES

Chairman, Director, Lloyd W. Kendall
President, Chief Executive Officer, George J. Guarini, $495,000 total compensation
Executive Vice President, Chief Operating Officer, Janet L. King, $357,500 total compensation
Executive Vice President, Chief Financial Officer, Secretary, Keary L. Colwell, $357,500 total compensation
Director, James S. Camp
Director, Harpreet S. Chaudhary
Director, Rocco Davis
Director, Malcolm F. Hotchkiss
Director, Robert G. Laverne
Director, Syvia L. Magid
Director, David M. Spatz
Auditors : Moss Adams LLP

LOCATIONS

HQ: BayCom Corp
  500 Ygnacio Valley Road, Suite 200, Walnut Creek, CA 94596
Phone: 925 476-1800
Web: www.unitedbusinessbank.com

HISTORICAL FINANCIALS
Company Type: Public

Income Statement — FYE: December 31

	ASSETS ($mil)	NET INCOME ($mil)	INCOME AS % OF ASSETS	EMPLOYEES
12/20	2,195.6	13.7	0.6%	315
12/19	1,994.1	17.3	0.9%	304
12/18	1,478.3	14.4	1.0%	214
12/17	1,245.7	5.2	0.4%	0
12/16	675.2	5.9	0.9%	0
Annual Growth	34.3%	23.4%	—	—

2020 Year-End Financials

Return on assets: 0.6%
Return on equity: 5.4%
Long-term debt ($ mil.): —
No. of shares ($ mil.): 11.3
Sales ($ mil.): 95.9
Dividends
  Yield: —
  Payout: —
Market value ($ mil.): 171.0

	STOCK PRICE ($) FY Close	P/E High/Low		PER SHARE ($) Earnings	Dividends	Book Value
12/20	15.17	20	9	1.15	0.00	22.36
12/19	22.74	17	14	1.47	0.00	20.43
12/18	23.09	18	13	1.50	0.00	18.47
12/17	19.45	24	18	0.81	0.00	15.82
12/16	14.86	14	11	1.09	0.00	14.26
Annual Growth	0.5%	—	—	1.3%	—	11.9%

BCB Bancorp Inc

BCB Bancorp be the holding company for BCB Community Bank, which opened its doors in late 2000. The independent bank serves Hudson County and the surrounding area from about 15 offices in New Jersey's Bayonne, Hoboken, Jersey City, and Monroe. The bank offers traditional deposit products and services, including savings accounts, money market accounts, CDs, and IRAs. Funds from deposits are used to originate mortgages and loans, primarily commercial real estate and multi-family property loans (which together account for more than half of the bank's loan portfolio). BCB agreed to acquire IA Bancorp in a $20 million deal in 2017.

EXECUTIVES

Chairman, Subsidiary Officer, Director, Mark D. Hogan
President, Chief Executive Officer, Subsidiary Officer, Director, Thomas Michael Coughlin, $455,400 total compensation
Senior Vice President, Chief Operating Officer, Corporate Secretary, Subsidiary Officer, Ryan Blake
Senior Vice President, Chief Financial Officer, Subsidiary Officer, Jawad Chaudhry
Senior Vice President, Chief Strategy Officer, Chief Risk Officer, Subsidiary Officer, Kenneth G. Emerson
Subsidiary Officer, David Rogue Garcia
Subsidiary Officer, Sandra L. Sievewright, $169,308 total compensation

Subsidiary Officer, Wing Siu
Director, Robert Ballance
Director, James G. Rizzo
Director, Judith Q. Bielan
Director, James E. Collins, $79,237 total compensation
Director, Vincent DiDomenico
Director, Joseph Lyga
Director, John Pulomena
Director, Spencer B. Robbins
Auditors : Wolf & Company, P.C.

LOCATIONS

HQ: BCB Bancorp Inc
  104-110 Avenue C, Bayonne, NJ 07002
Phone: 201 823-0700
Web: www.bcb.bank

COMPETITORS

BCSB BANCORP, INC.
COMMUNITY SHORES BANK CORPORATION
FIRSTFED BANCORP, INC.
OCEANFIRST FINANCIAL CORP.
UNION BANKSHARES, INC.

HISTORICAL FINANCIALS
Company Type: Public

Income Statement — FYE: December 31

	ASSETS ($mil)	NET INCOME ($mil)	INCOME AS % OF ASSETS	EMPLOYEES
12/20	2,821.0	20.8	0.7%	302
12/19	2,907.4	21.0	0.7%	365
12/18	2,674.7	16.7	0.6%	365
12/17	1,942.8	9.9	0.5%	314
12/16	1,708.2	8.0	0.5%	353
Annual Growth	13.4%	27.1%	—	(3.8%)

2020 Year-End Financials
Return on assets: 0.7%
Return on equity: 8.5%
Long-term debt ($ mil.): —
No. of shares ($ mil.): 17.1
Sales ($ mil.): 125.9
Dividends
  Yield: 5.0%
  Payout: 54.9%
Market value ($ mil.): 189.0

	STOCK PRICE ($) FY Close	P/E High/Low		PER SHARE ($) Earnings	Dividends	Book Value
12/20	11.07	12	7	1.14	0.56	14.57
12/19	13.79	12	9	1.20	0.56	13.67
12/18	10.47	16	10	1.01	0.56	12.60
12/17	14.50	22	16	0.75	0.56	11.73
12/16	13.00	21	16	0.63	0.56	11.63
Annual Growth	(3.9%)	—	—	16.0%	0.0%	5.8%

Beauty Health Co (The)

EXECUTIVES

Executive Chairman, Director, Brenton L. Saunders
President, Chief Executive Officer, Director, Andrew Roy Stanleick
Executive Vice President, Chief Financial Officer, Liyuan Woo
Chief Revenue Officer, Daniel E. Watson
Director, Michael D. Capellas
Director, Julius Few
Director, Brian Miller
Director, Doug K. Schillinger
Director, Michelle C. Kerrick
Director, Desiree Gruber
Director, Marla Malcolm Beck

LOCATIONS

HQ: Beauty Health Co (The)
  2165 Spring Street, Long Beach, CA 90806
Phone: 800 603-4996
Web: www.beautyhealth.com

HISTORICAL FINANCIALS
Company Type: Public

Income Statement — FYE: December 31

	REVENUE ($mil)	NET INCOME ($mil)	NET PROFIT MARGIN	EMPLOYEES
12/22	365.8	44.3	12.1%	1,034
12/21	260.0	(375.1)	—	704
12/20*	0.0	(1.1)	—	2
08/20	0.0	(0.0)	—	2
12/19	166.6	(1.6)	—	0
Annual Growth	30.0%	—	—	—

*Fiscal year change

2022 Year-End Financials
Debt ratio: 72.8%
Return on equity: 18.7%
Cash ($ mil.): 568.2
Current Ratio: 10.79
Long-term debt ($ mil.): 734.1
No. of shares ($ mil.): 132.2
Dividends
  Yield: —
  Payout: —
Market value ($ mil.): 1,203.0

	STOCK PRICE ($) FY Close	P/E High/Low		PER SHARE ($) Earnings	Dividends	Book Value
12/22	9.10	80	28	(0.23)	0.00	1.30
12/21	24.16	—	—	(3.67)	0.00	2.01
12/20*	11.31	—	—	(0.09)	0.00	7.78
Annual Growth	(10.3%)	—	—	—	—	(59.2%)

*Fiscal year change

BellRing Brands Inc

EXECUTIVES

Executive Chairman, Subsidiary Officer, Director, Robert V. Vitale
President, Chief Executive Officer, Subsidiary Officer, Director, Darcy Horn Davenport
Senior Vice President, General Counsel, Secretary, Craig L. Rosenthal
Chief Financial Officer, Treasurer, Subsidiary Officer, Paul A. Rode
Subsidiary Officer, Robert Lee Partin
Subsidiary Officer, Robin Singh
Subsidiary Officer, Douglas J. Cornille
Director, Chonda J. Nwamu
Director, Thomas P. Erickson
Director, Jennifer Kuperman
Director, Elliot H. Stein
Auditors : PricewaterhouseCoopers LLP

LOCATIONS

HQ: BellRing Brands Inc
  2503 S. Hanley Road, St. Louis, MO 63144
Phone: 314 644-7600
Web: www.bellringbrands.com

HISTORICAL FINANCIALS
Company Type: Public

Income Statement — FYE: September 30

	REVENUE ($mil)	NET INCOME ($mil)	NET PROFIT MARGIN	EMPLOYEES
09/21	1,247.1	27.6	2.2%	355
09/20	988.3	23.5	2.4%	390
09/19	854.4	123.1	14.4%	400
09/18	827.5	96.1	11.6%	380
09/17	713.2	35.2	4.9%	0
Annual Growth	15.0%	(5.9%)	—	—

2021 Year-End Financials
Debt ratio: 85.8%
Return on equity: —
Cash ($ mil.): 152.6
Current Ratio: 1.54
Long-term debt ($ mil.): 481.2
No. of shares ($ mil.): 39.5
Dividends
  Yield: —
  Payout: 89.1%
Market value ($ mil.): 1,215.0

	STOCK PRICE ($) FY Close	P/E High/Low		PER SHARE ($) Earnings	Dividends	Book Value
09/21	30.75	49	26	0.70	0.00	(77.52)
09/20	20.74	40	24	0.60	0.00	(55.36)
Annual Growth	48.3%	—	—	16.7%	—	—

BEO Bancorp, Heppner OR

EXECUTIVES

Chairman, E. George Koffler
Vice-Chairman, Director, Joel Peterson
President, Chief Executive Officer, Subsidiary Officer, Director, Jeff L. Bailey
Executive Vice President, Chief Financial Officer, Mark D. Lemmon
Executive Vice President, Chief Operating Officer, Gary L. Propheter
Operations Senior Vice President, Becky Kindle
Senior Vice President, Senior Loan Officer, John Qualls
Senior Vice President, Edward C. Rollins
Vice President, John Bailey
Vice President, James Gardner
Vice President, Mike Short
Vice President, Russell Seewald
Vice President, Kristy Perry
Vice President, Kevin Sakamoto
Vice President, Jill Parker
Vice President, Robert Quinton
Vice President, Robert Williams
Vice President, Janet Dezellem

Vice President, Tricia Gunderson
Assistant Vice President, Chief Compliance Officer, Dawna Dougherty
Assistant Vice President, Christy Correa
Assistant Vice President, Janice Provencher
Assistant Vice President, Jennifer LD Smith
Assistant Vice President, Karen Cossitt
Vice President, Rhonda Shaffer
Assistant Vice President, Justin Miller
Assistant Vice President, Lucy Gonzalez
Assistant Vice President, Anita Orem
Director, Brad Anderson
Director, Robert M. Armstrong
Director, Joe Gonzalez
Director, Gary D. Neal
Auditors : Eide Bailly LLP

LOCATIONS

HQ: BEO Bancorp, Heppner OR
279 N. Main, P.O. Box 39, Heppner, OR 97836
Phone: 541 676-0201   Fax: 541 646-5541
Web: www.beobank.com

HISTORICAL FINANCIALS
Company Type: Public

Income Statement				FYE: December 31
	ASSETS ($mil)	NET INCOME ($mil)	INCOME AS % OF ASSETS	EMPLOYEES
12/21	821.5	6.9	0.8%	0
12/20	666.6	5.5	0.8%	0
12/19	492.2	4.2	0.9%	0
12/18	414.3	3.9	1.0%	0
12/17	414.5	3.0	0.7%	0
Annual Growth	18.7%	22.3%	—	—

2021 Year-End Financials
Return on assets: 0.9%
Return on equity: 15.3%
Long-term debt ($ mil.): —
No. of shares ($ mil.): 1.2
Sales ($ mil.): 33.5
Dividends
Yield: —
Payout: 18.5%
Market value ($ mil.): 49.0

	STOCK PRICE ($) FY Close	P/E High/Low		PER SHARE ($)		
				Earnings	Dividends	Book Value
12/21	41.00	7	6	5.38	1.00	39.80
12/20	43.40	9	5	4.34	0.95	34.96
12/19	35.00	10	8	3.62	0.90	31.90
12/18	28.35	9	8	3.33	0.85	29.21
12/17	31.04	12	10	2.60	0.80	26.67
Annual Growth	7.2%	—		19.9%	5.7%	10.5%

Bio-Techne Corp

Bio-Techne develops, manufactures and sells life science reagents, instruments and services for the research, diagnostics and bioprocessing markets worldwide. With its broad product portfolio and application expertise, it sells integral components of scientific investigations into biological processes and molecular diagnostics, revealing the nature, diagnosis, etiology and progression of specific diseases. Through subsidiaries including Research and Diagnostic Systems (R&D Systems), Boston Biochem, Bionostics, and Tocris, the company makes and distributes life science reagents, instruments and services for the research, diagnostics and bioprocessing markets worldwide. It also makes hematology controls and calibrators for blood analysis systems and sells them to equipment makers. The US accounts the largest for about 55% of total revenue.

Operations
Bio-Techne operates through two reportable segments: Protein Sciences segment and Diagnostics and Genomics segment.

The Protein Sciences segment is comprised of divisions with complementary product offerings serving many of the same customers ? the Reagent Solutions division and the Analytical Solutions division. Reagent Solutions division consists of specialized proteins, such as cytokines and growth factors, antibodies, small molecules, tissue culture sera and cell selection technologies while the Analytical Solutions division includes manual and automated protein analysis instruments and immunoassays that are used in quantifying proteins in a variety of biological fluids. The segment accounts about 75% of total revenue.

The Diagnostics and Genomics segment (about 25%) also includes three divisions focused primarily in the diagnostics market and includes spatial biology, liquid biopsy, molecular diagnostics kits and products, and diagnostics reagents. The Spatial Biology division products sold under the Advanced Cell Diagnostics, or ACD, brand, are novel in-situ hybridization (ISH) assays for transcriptome, DNA copy, and structural variation analysis within intact cells, providing highly sensitive and specific spatial information at single cell resolution. The Molecular Diagnostics division markets and sells products and services under the Exosome Diagnostics and Asuragen brands. The Exosome Diagnostics brand is based on exosome-based liquid biopsy techniques that analyze genes or their transcripts. It also sells products for genetic carrier screening, oncology diagnostics, molecular controls, and research under the Asuragen brand. The Diagnostic Reagents division consists of regulated products traditionally used as calibrators and controls in the clinical setting. Also included are instrument and process control products for hematology, blood chemistry, blood gases, coagulation controls and reagents used in various diagnostic applications.

Overall, consumables accounts about 80% of total sales, instruments approximately 10%, while services and royalty revenues accounts the remainder.

Geographic Reach
Headquartered in Minneapolis, Minnesota, Bio-Techne has operations in Canada, China, France, Ireland, the US and the UK.

The US market accounts for about 55% of Bio-Techne's sales. EMEA (excluding the UK) is the second-largest region, accounting for some 20% of sales; the company also conducts sales in Asia Pacific and other regions.

Sales and Marketing
Bio-Techne's protein sciences segment customers include researchers in academia, government and industry (chiefly pharmaceutical and biotech companies), as well as diagnostic/companion diagnostic and therapeutic customers, especially customers engaged in the development of cell and gene based therapies. Diagnostic and genomics customers include physicians prescribing such tests for the patients.

Advertising expenses were $4.6 million, $4.7 million, and $4.2 million for fiscal 2022, 2021, and 2020 respectively.

Financial Performance
For fiscal 2022, consolidated net sales increased 19% to $1.1 billion as compared to fiscal 2021. Organic growth was 17%, with acquisitions having a favorable impact of 3% and foreign currency translation having an unfavorable impact of 1%. Organic revenue growth was broad based and driven by overall execution of the company's long-term growth strategy.

In 2022, the company had a net income of $272.1 million, a 94% increase from the previous year's net income of $140.4 million.

The company's cash for the year ended 2022 was $172.6 million. Operating activities generated $325.3 million, while investing activities used $96.9 million, mainly for purchases of available-for-sale investments. Financing activities used another $242.9 million, primarily for payments on line-of-credit.

Strategy
Over the last ten years, the company has been implementing a disciplined strategy to accelerate growth in part by acquiring businesses and product portfolios that leveraged and diversified its existing product lines, filled portfolio gaps with differentiated high growth businesses, and expanded its geographic scope. From fiscal years 2013 through 2022, it has acquired sixteen companies that have expanded the product offerings and geographic footprint of both operating segments. Recognizing the importance of an integrated, global approach to meeting its mission and accomplishing its strategies, it has maintained many of the brands of the companies it has acquired, but unified under a single global brand -- Bio-Techne.

Mergers and Acquisitions
In 2022, Bio-Techne announced it has completed the acquisition of Namocell, a leading provider of fast and easy to use single cell sorting and dispensing platforms that are gentle to cells, and preserve cell viability and

integrity. The Namocell acquisition adds easy-to-use single cell sorting and dispensing platforms that are gentle to cells and preserve cell viability and integrity. Namocell's instruments and consumables are critical technologies in various workflows in both biotherapeutics and diagnostics, including cell and gene therapy development and commercialization, cell engineering, cell line development, single cell genomics, antibody discovery, synthetic biology, and rare cell isolation.

In early 2021, Bio-Techne acquired the Texas-based Asuragen, a leader in the development, manufacturing and commercialization of genetic carrier screening and oncology testing kits. Its products leverage proprietary chemistries which can be used on widely available platforms including, PCR, qPCR, capillary electrophoresis, and next-generation sequencing instruments. The transaction included initial consideration of $215 million in cash plus contingent consideration of up to $105 million upon the achievement of certain future milestones. The Asuragen acquisition adds a leading portfolio of best-in-class molecular diagnostic and research products, including genetic screening and oncology testing kits, molecular controls, a Good Manufacturing Practice (GMP)-compliant 50,000 square foot manufacturing facility and a CLIA-certified laboratory, plus a team with deep expertise navigating products through the global diagnostic regulatory environment.

HISTORY

David Mundschenk founded biological products maker Research and Diagnostics Systems in 1976. In 1983 Mundschenk made a disastrous move, buying heavily indebted French hematology instrument maker Hycel. R&D System's disgruntled board named Thomas Oland (at the time a consultant) CEO.

Enter TECHNE. Founded in 1981 by George Kline and Peter Peterson to pursue profitable acquisitions, it went public in 1983 and in 1985 bought R&D Systems (which became an operating subsidiary of TECHNE), a sign of their confidence in Oland. TECHNE formed a biotechnology division in 1986 to produce and market human cytokines. In 1988 Kline resigned following a failed acquisition attempt by medical test kit maker Incstar.

In 1991 TECHNE bought Amgen's research reagent and diagnostic assay kit business and began selling Quantikine cytokine diagnostic kits. In 1993 it acquired what would become the company's R&D Europe unit.

In 1995 the company debuted 10 new Quantikine immunoassay kits. TECHNE restructured its European research operation in 1997, pulling underperforming molecular biology products from the market and refocusing on TECHNE's core cytokine-related products. The next year TECHNE bought Genzyme's research products business (antibodies, proteins, and research kits) for about $65 million.

As drug and biotechnology research became growth markets in the late 1990s and early 21st century, TECHNE expanded through purchases. In 1999 it bought the reagent business and immunoassay patents of partner Cistron. The next year the firm increased its ownership in drug developer ChemoCentryx to almost 50% (reduced in 2001 to about 25% and then again in 2004 to 20%). TECHNE also acquired research and diagnostic market rights to all products developed by the firm. A similar deal was made in 2001 with functional genomics firm Discovery Genomics; that investment was not realized to TECHNE's satisfaction, so it wrote off the investment in 2004.

It didn't wait long to fill the gap when it acquired the operations of Fortron Bio Science and Biospacific in 2005. The makers of antibodies and reagents had been partners since 1992 before they were integrated into TECHNE's R&D Systems division.

In 2007 the company set up a sales and distribution subsidiary in Shanghai to capitalize on the growing Chinese market. In 2007 TECHNE acquired minority stakes in two additional companies: diagnostics developer Nephromics and biotechnology firm ACTGen.

EXECUTIVES

Chairman, Director, Robert V. Baumgartner
President, Chief Executive Officer, Director, Charles R. Kummeth, $957,000 total compensation
Finance Executive Vice President, Finance Chief Financial Officer, James T. Hippel, $514,188 total compensation
Senior Vice President, General Counsel, Corporate Secretary, Shane Bohnen
Division Officer, William Alexander Geist
Division Officer, Kim Kelderman, $452,400 total compensation
Director, Julie L. Bushman
Director, John L. Higgins
Director, Joseph D. Keegan
Director, Roeland Nusse
Director, Alpna Seth
Director, Randolph C. Steer
Director, Rupert Vessey
Auditors : KPMG LLP

LOCATIONS

HQ: Bio-Techne Corp
   614 McKinley Place N.E., Minneapolis, MN 55413
Phone: 612 379-8854
Web: www.bio-techne.com

2015 Sales

	$ mil.	% of total
US	245.2	54
Europe	134.1	30
China	26.1	6
Other Asia	23.8	5
Rest of world	23.0	5
Total	452.2	100

PRODUCTS/OPERATIONS

2015 Sales by Segment

	$ mil.	% of total
Biotechnology	325.9	72
Protein Platforms	66.2	15
Clinical Controls	60.4	13
Adjustments	(0.3)	-
Total	452.2	100

Selected Products and Services

R&D Systems
   Activity assays and reagents
   Antibodies
   Biomarker testing service
   ELISAs
   ELISpot kits & FluoroSpot kits
   Flow cytometry and cell selection/detection
   General laboratory reagents
   Multiplex assays/arrays
   Proteins
   Stem cell and cell culture products
Tocris
   Caged compounds
   Controlled substances
   Fluorescent probes
   Ligand sets
   Peptides
   Screening libraries
   Small molecules
   Toxins
Boston Biochem
   Affinity matrices/proteins
   Antibodies
   Buffers, solutions, and standards
   Fractions
   Inhibitors
   Kits
   Proteasome
   Substrate Proteins
   Ubiquitin

COMPETITORS

ABBOTT LABORATORIES
AKERS BIOSCIENCES, INC.
IMMUCOR, INC.
LIFE TECHNOLOGIES CORPORATION
LUMINEX CORPORATION
MERIDIAN BIOSCIENCE, INC.
PERKINELMER, INC.
QUIDEL CORPORATION
REPLIGEN CORPORATION
SERACARE LIFE SCIENCES, INC.

HISTORICAL FINANCIALS

Company Type: Public

Income Statement — FYE: June 30

	REVENUE ($mil)	NET INCOME ($mil)	NET PROFIT MARGIN	EMPLOYEES
06/21	931.0	140.4	15.1%	2,600
06/20	738.6	229.2	31.0%	2,300
06/19	714.0	96.0	13.5%	2,250
06/18	642.9	126.1	19.6%	2,000
06/17	563.0	76.0	13.5%	1,800
Annual Growth	13.4%	16.6%	—	9.6%

2021 Year-End Financials

Debt ratio: 15.1%
Return on equity: 9.5%
Cash ($ mil.): 199.0
Current Ratio: 3.35
Long-term debt ($ mil.): 328.8
No. of shares ($ mil.): 38.9
Dividends
 Yield: 0.2%
 Payout: 27.8%
Market value ($ mil.): 17,540.0

	STOCK PRICE ($) FY Close	P/E High/Low		PER SHARE ($) Earnings	Dividends	Book Value
06/21	450.26	124	64	3.47	1.28	40.12
06/20	264.07	47	27	5.82	1.28	35.92
06/19	208.49	85	52	2.47	1.28	30.73
06/18	147.95	49	34	3.31	1.28	28.69
06/17	117.50	58	48	2.03	1.28	25.42
Annual Growth	39.9%	—	—	14.3%	0.0%	12.1%

BioDelivery Sciences International Inc

BioDelivery Sciences International (BDSI) is a specialty pharmaceutical firm that takes already approved drugs to patients living with chronic pain and associated conditions. Drugs delivered via its BEMA (BioErodible MucoAdhesive) systems focus on the areas of pain management and opioid-induced constipation. Its BEMA fentanyl product ONSOLIS is a buccally delivered polymer film used for the treatment of cancer pain. Other FDA-approved product includes BUNAVAIL, for the treatment of opioid dependence, and BELBUCA, for chronic severe pain management.

Operations

The company also include FDA approved product Symproic (naldemedine) for the treatment of OIC in adult patients with chronic non-cancer pain, including patients with chronic pain related to prior cancer or its treatment who do not require frequent (weekly) opioid dosage escalation. It licenses its product, ONSOLIS, to TTY Biopharm, which markets the product as PAINKYL in Taiwan, and to Mylan which markets the product as BREAKYL in Europe.

The company generates revenue from its product sales that account for more than 95% of total revenues, while a small portion comes from product royalties.

Geographic Reach

The company commercializes its products around the world, but primarily in North America as well as in Taiwan and South Korea.

Sales and Marketing

The company commercializes its products in the US through its own sales force, its about 120 sales representatives, and nearly 15 regional sales managers that support its BELBUCA and Symproic products. It works in partnership with third parties to commercialize its products outside the US.

Reflecting the increased activity around product approvals, BDSI spent $11 million, $10.8 million, and $4.5 million on advertising for the FY 2020, 2019, and 2018, respectively.

Financial Performance

The company revenue for the last five years has been fluctuating but still registered positive growth, with 2020 as its highest performing year.

BDSI's revenue decreased by about $45 million to $156.4 million in 2020 as compared to 2019's revenue of about $111.4 million

In 2020, the company had a net income of $25.7 million compared to the prior year's net loss of $15.3 million.

Cash and cash equivalents at the end of the year were $111.6 million. Net cash flows provided by operating activities was $24.9 million. Investing activities used $13,000, primarily for acquisition of equipment. On the other hand, financing activities was able to provide $22.7 million to the coffers.

Strategy

The company strategy is evolving with the establishment of its commercial footprint in the management of chronic pain. It seeks to continue to build a well-balanced, diversified, high-growth specialty pharmaceutical company. Through its industry-leading commercialization infrastructure, it is executing the commercialization of its existing products. As part of its corporate growth strategy, it has licensed, and will continue to explore opportunities to acquire or license, additional products that meet the needs of patients living with debilitating chronic conditions and treated primarily by therapeutic specialists. As it gains access to these drugs and technologies, it will employ its commercialization experience to bring them to the marketplace. With a strong commitment to patient access and a focused business-development approach for transformative acquisitions or licensing opportunities, it will leverage its experience and apply it to developing new partnerships that enable it to commercialize novel products that can change the lives of people suffering from debilitating chronic conditions.

Its commercial strategy for BELBUCA is to further drive continued adoption in the large long-acting opioid (LAO) market based on its unique profile coupled with growing physician interest, policy tailwinds, and expanding payer access. It aims to leverage the specialized commercial infrastructure it established for BELBUCA as a vehicle to enable commercial growth in Symproic, which is being increasingly seen as a complementary asset.

Mergers and Acquisitions

In 2021, BDSI has completed the acquisition of U.S. and Canadian rights to ELYXYB (celecoxib oral solution) from Dr. Reddy's Laboratories Limited. ELYXYB is the first and only FDA-approved ready-to-use oral solution for the acute treatment of migraine, with or without aura, in adults. BDSI intends to launch ELYXYB in the first quarter of 2022. Additionally, BDSI plans to conduct an ELYXYB pediatric study, which will have the potential to address the significant unmet needs of pediatric and adolescent patients suffering from migraine attacks. The acquisition of ELYXYB represents a critical step to building its presence in Neurology which is an excellent strategic adjacency to its pain franchise.

EXECUTIVES

President, Chief Executive Officer, Holding/Parent Company Officer, Director, Joseph Ciaffoni
Chief Financial Officer, Treasurer, Holding/Parent Company Officer, Director, Colleen Tupper
Auditors: Ernst & Young LLP

LOCATIONS

HQ: BioDelivery Sciences International Inc
4131 ParkLake Avenue, Suite 225, Raleigh, NC 27612
Phone: 919 582-9050
Web: www.bdsi.com

PRODUCTS/OPERATIONS

2014 Sales

	$ mil.	% of total
Contract revenue	22.7	58
Research & development reimbursement	12.7	33
Product royalty	3.4	9
Product sales	0.1	-
Total	38.9	100

Selected Products
BELBUCA
BUNAVAIL
ONSOLIS

COMPETITORS

ASSERTIO THERAPEUTICS, INC.
BIOCRYST PHARMACEUTICALS, INC.
EXELIXIS, INC.
FLEXION THERAPEUTICS, INC.
LEXICON PHARMACEUTICALS, INC.
LUMOS PHARMA, INC.
SUCAMPO PHARMACEUTICALS, INC.
SUPERNUS PHARMACEUTICALS, INC.
VANDA PHARMACEUTICALS INC.
VIVUS, INC.

HISTORICAL FINANCIALS

Company Type: Public

Income Statement — FYE: December 31

	REVENUE ($mil)	NET INCOME ($mil)	NET PROFIT MARGIN	EMPLOYEES
12/20	156.4	25.7	16.4%	176
12/19	111.3	(15.3)	—	178
12/18	55.6	(33.8)	—	164
12/17	61.9	5.2	8.5%	116
12/16	15.5	(67.1)	—	99
Annual Growth	78.1%	—	—	15.5%

2020 Year-End Financials

Debt ratio: 32.7%
Return on equity: 28.8%
Cash ($ mil.): 111.5
Current Ratio: 3.44
Long-term debt ($ mil.): 78.4
No. of shares ($ mil.): 101.3
Dividends
 Yield: —
 Payout: —
Market value ($ mil.): 426.0

	STOCK PRICE ($) FY Close	P/E High/Low		PER SHARE ($) Earnings	Dividends	Book Value
12/20	4.20	24	12	0.24	0.00	1.07
12/19	6.32	—	—	(0.18)	0.00	0.73
12/18	3.70	—	—	(0.73)	0.00	0.42
12/17	2.95	35	16	0.09	0.00	0.16
12/16	1.75	—	—	(1.25)	0.00	(0.33)
Annual Growth	24.5%	—	—	—	—	—

BioMarin Pharmaceutical Inc

EXECUTIVES

Chairman, Chief Executive Officer, Director, Jean-Jacques Bienaime, $1,149,423 total compensation
Commercial Operations Executive Vice President, Commercial Operations Chief Commercial Officer, Jeffrey Robert Ajer, $554,232 total compensation
Executive Vice President, General Counsel, Secretary, G. Eric Davis, $409,593 total compensation
Division Officer, Henry J. Fuchs, $668,269 total compensation
Finance Executive Vice President, Finance Chief Financial Officer, Brian R. Mueller
Executive Vice President, Chief Technical Officer, C. Stephen Guyer
Group Vice President, Chief Accounting Officer, Andrea Acosta
Lead Independent Director, Director, Richard A. Meier
Director, Maykin Ho
Director, Elizabeth McKee Anderson
Director, Willard H. Dere
Director, Michael G. Grey
Director, Elaine J. Heron
Director, Robert J. Hombach
Director, V. Bryan Lawlis
Director, David E. I. Pyott
Director, Dennis J. Slamon
Auditors : KPMG LLP

LOCATIONS

HQ: BioMarin Pharmaceutical Inc
770 Lindaro Street, San Rafael, CA 94901
Phone: 415 506-6700
Web: www.bmrn.com

HISTORICAL FINANCIALS
Company Type: Public

Income Statement — FYE: December 31

	REVENUE ($mil)	NET INCOME ($mil)	NET PROFIT MARGIN	EMPLOYEES
12/20	1,860.4	859.1	46.2%	3,059
12/19	1,704.0	(23.8)	—	3,001
12/18	1,491.2	(77.2)	—	2,849
12/17	1,313.6	(117.0)	—	2,581
12/16	1,116.8	(630.2)	—	2,293
Annual Growth	13.6%	—	—	7.5%

2020 Year-End Financials
Debt ratio: 18.4%
Return on equity: 23.7%
Cash ($ mil.): 649.1
Current Ratio: 4.76
Long-term debt ($ mil.): 1,075.1
No. of shares ($ mil.): 181.7
Dividends
Yield: —
Payout: —
Market value ($ mil.): 15,937.0

	STOCK PRICE ($) FY Close	P/E High/Low		PER SHARE ($) Earnings	Dividends	Book Value
12/20	87.69	28	15	4.53	0.00	22.59
12/19	84.55	—	—	(0.13)	0.00	17.36
12/18	85.15	—	—	(0.44)	0.00	16.65
12/17	89.17	—	—	(0.67)	0.00	15.97
12/16	82.84	—	—	(3.81)	0.00	16.02
Annual Growth	1.4%	—	—	—	—	9.0%

Bioqual Inc

EXECUTIVES

Chmn., Pres., C.E.O., John C. Landon
Chief Financial Officer, David A. Newcomer
C.O.O., Sec., Michael P. O'flaherty
Vice President, Marisa St. claire
Vice President, Leanne Denenno
Vice President, Jerry R. Reel
Chairman, John C. Landon
Director, Chander P. Sarma
Director, Mark G. Lewis
Auditors : Aronson LLC

LOCATIONS

HQ: Bioqual Inc
9600 Medical Center Drive, Suite 101, Rockville, MD 20850
Phone: 240 404-7654
Web: www.bioqual.com

HISTORICAL FINANCIALS
Company Type: Public

Income Statement — FYE: May 31

	REVENUE ($mil)	NET INCOME ($mil)	NET PROFIT MARGIN	EMPLOYEES
05/21	57.6	6.3	11.0%	0
05/20	46.3	4.2	9.1%	0
05/19	39.4	2.8	7.2%	0
05/18	35.8	3.6	10.2%	0
05/17	36.6	3.9	10.8%	0
Annual Growth	12.0%	12.4%	—	—

2021 Year-End Financials
Debt ratio: —
Return on equity: 20.5%
Cash ($ mil.): 7.7
Current Ratio: 3.44
Long-term debt ($ mil.): —
No. of shares ($ mil.): 0.8
Dividends
Yield: —
Payout: 15.5%
Market value ($ mil.): 73.0

	STOCK PRICE ($) FY Close	P/E High/Low		PER SHARE ($) Earnings	Dividends	Book Value
05/21	81.10	13	9	7.08	1.10	37.49
05/20	60.00	16	6	4.73	0.70	31.51
05/19	36.00	13	9	3.17	0.60	27.46
05/18	33.45	11	8	4.10	0.60	24.65
05/17	36.50	8	5	4.44	0.45	21.17
Annual Growth	22.1%	—	—	12.4%	25.0%	15.4%

Blackhawk Bancorp Inc

This Blackhawk's mission is to increase your bottom line. Blackhawk Bancorp is the holding company for Blackhawk State Bank (aka Blackhawk Bank), which has nearly 10 locations in south-central Wisconsin and north-central Illinois. Serving area consumers and businesses, the bankÂ offersÂ standard financial services, such as checking,Â savings, andÂ money marketÂ accounts, CDs, credit cards, and wealth management. ItÂ also caters to the Hispanic community by offering bilingualÂ services atÂ some of its branches. Blackhawk Bank maintains a somewhat diverse loan portfolio, withÂ residential mortgages, commercial and industrial loans, and commercial real estate loans accounting for the bulk of its lending activities.

EXECUTIVES

Chairman, President, Chief Executive Officer, Todd J. James, $100,883 total compensation
Technology Executive Vice President, Operations Executive Vice President, Phyllis Oldenburg
Chief Operating Officer, Subsidiary Officer, Director, Dave K. Adkins
Human Resources Senior Vice President, Jeanine Woyner
Senior Vice President, Chief Financial Officer, Matthew McDonnell
Marketing Senior Vice President, Communications Senior Vice President, Stephanie Meier
Executive Vice President, Chief Credit Officer, Todd L. Larson
Division Officer, Tammy Zurfluh
Division Officer, Mathew Reynolds
Division Officer, Andy Williams
Director, April Glosser
Director, Bruce Ware
Director, Todd Buehl
Director, Eric Anderberg
Director, Steven A. Ceroni
Director, Lucas Derry
Director, Paul L. Palmby
Auditors : Plante & Moran, PLLC

LOCATIONS

HQ: Blackhawk Bancorp Inc
400 Broad Street, Beloit, WI 53511
Phone: 608 364 8911   **Fax:** 608 363 6186
Web: www.blackhawkbank.com

COMPETITORS

BCSB BANCORP, INC.
CENTRAL VIRGINIA BANKSHARES, INC.
OXFORD BANK
PACIFIC FINANCIAL CORPORATION
UNITY BANCORP, INC.

HISTORICAL FINANCIALS
Company Type: Public

Income Statement   FYE: December 31

	ASSETS ($mil)	NET INCOME ($mil)	INCOME AS % OF ASSETS	EMPLOYEES
12/20	1,141.5	10.8	1.0%	0
12/19	963.8	9.6	1.0%	0
12/18	817.2	8.1	1.0%	0
12/17	720.6	6.2	0.9%	0
12/16	665.7	5.9	0.9%	0
Annual Growth	14.4%	16.1%	—	—

2020 Year-End Financials
Return on assets: 1.0%
Return on equity: 10.3%
Long-term debt ($ mil.): —
No. of shares (mil.): 3.3
Sales ($ mil.): 61.1
Dividends
Yield: 1.5%
Payout: 14.8%
Market value ($ mil.): 94.0

	STOCK PRICE ($) FY Close	P/E High/Low		PER SHARE ($) Earnings	Dividends	Book Value
12/20	28.00	10	6	3.25	0.44	33.14
12/19	27.85	10	9	2.90	0.40	29.54
12/18	26.60	12	11	2.47	0.38	25.76
12/17	27.05	13	11	2.01	0.28	24.02
12/16	23.00	9	7	2.59	0.16	21.68
Annual Growth	5.0%	—	—	5.8%	28.8%	11.2%

Blackstone Mortgage Trust Inc

Capital Trust thinks investing in commercial mortgages is a capital idea. The self-managed real estate investment trust (REIT) originates, underwrites, and invests in commercial real estate assets on its own behalf and for other investors. Its portfolio includes first mortgage and bridge loans, mezzanine loans, and collateralized mortgage-backed securities. Subsidiary CT Investment Management, which the company is selling, manages five private equity funds and a separate account for third parties. Most Capital Trust's assets are related to US properties, but the REIT does make occasional investments in international instruments.

EXECUTIVES

Executive Chairman, Director, Michael B. Nash
President, Chief Executive Officer, Director, Katharine A. Keenan
Investments Executive Vice President, Austin Pena
Finance Vice President, Courtney Cheng
Chief Financial Officer, Treasurer, Assistant Secretary, Anthony F. Marone, $0 total compensation
Chief Legal Officer, Managing Director, Secretary, Subsidiary Officer, Leon Volchyok
Investor Relations Senior Managing Director, Investor Relations Head, Weston Tucker

Asset Management Managing Director, Asset Management Head, Robert Sitman
Director, Leonard W. Cotton
Director, Thomas E. Dobrowski
Director, Henry N. Nassau
Director, Jonathan Lee Pollack
Director, Lynne B. Sagalyn
Director, Nnenna Lynch
Director, Gilda Perez-Alvarado
Auditors: DELOITTE & TOUCHE LLP

LOCATIONS

HQ: Blackstone Mortgage Trust Inc
345 Park Avenue, 24th Floor, New York, NY 10154
Phone: 212 655-0220
Web: www.blackstonemortgagetrust.com

COMPETITORS

ARBOR REALTY TRUST, INC.
EASTERN LIGHT CAPITAL, INCORPORATED
JER INVESTORS TRUST INC
MADISON SQUARE CAPITAL, INC.
STARWOOD PROPERTY TRUST, INC.

HISTORICAL FINANCIALS
Company Type: Public

Income Statement   FYE: December 31

	REVENUE ($mil)	NET INCOME ($mil)	NET PROFIT MARGIN	EMPLOYEES
12/21	854.6	419.1	49.0%	0
12/20	779.6	137.6	17.7%	0
12/19	882.6	305.5	34.6%	0
12/18	756.1	285.0	37.7%	0
12/17	537.9	217.6	40.5%	0
Annual Growth	12.3%	17.8%	—	—

2021 Year-End Financials
Debt ratio: 76.9%
Return on equity: 9.8%
Cash ($ mil.): 551.1
Current Ratio: 3.60
Long-term debt ($ mil.): 17,459.3
No. of shares ($ mil.): 168.1
Dividends
Yield: 8.0%
Payout: 96.4%
Market value ($ mil.): 5,150.0

	STOCK PRICE ($) FY Close	P/E High/Low		PER SHARE ($) Earnings	Dividends	Book Value
12/21	30.62	12	9	2.77	2.48	27.28
12/20	27.53	42	13	0.97	2.48	26.48
12/19	37.22	16	13	2.35	2.48	27.87
12/18	31.86	14	12	2.50	2.48	27.25
12/17	32.18	14	13	2.27	2.48	26.98
Annual Growth	(1.2%)	—	—	5.1%	0.0%	0.3%

Blue Ridge Bankshares Inc (Luray, VA)

EXECUTIVES

Chairman, Director, Larry Dees
President, Chief Executive Officer, Subsidiary Officer, Director, Brian K. Plum
Executive Vice President, Chief Financial Officer, Subsidiary Officer, Judy C. Gavant
Chief Accounting Officer, Subsidiary Officer, Brett E. Raynor
Corporate Secretary, Amanda G. Story
General Counsel, Director, Robert S. Janney
Subsidiary Officer, LaNell DeLoach
Director, Hunter H. Bost
Director, Mensel D. Dean
Director, Julien G. Patterson
Director, Randolph N. Reynolds
Director, Elizabeth Hinton Crowther
Director, Vance H. Spilman
Director, Carolyn J. Woodruff
Director, Richard A. Farmar
Director, Andrew C. Holzwarth
Director, William W. Stokes

LOCATIONS

HQ: Blue Ridge Bankshares Inc (Luray, VA)
1807 Seminole Trail, Charlottesville, VA 22835
Phone: 540 743-6521   **Fax:** 540 743-5536
Web: www.mybrb.com

HISTORICAL FINANCIALS
Company Type: Public

Income Statement   FYE: December 31

	ASSETS ($mil)	NET INCOME ($mil)	INCOME AS % OF ASSETS	EMPLOYEES
12/20	1,498.2	17.6	1.2%	386
12/19	960.8	4.5	0.5%	271
12/18	539.5	4.5	0.8%	196
12/17	424.1	3.3	0.8%	0
Annual Growth	52.3%	74.1%	—	—

2020 Year-End Financials
Return on assets: 1.4%
Return on equity: 17.6%
Long-term debt ($ mil.): —
No. of shares ($ mil.): 8.5
Sales ($ mil.): 111.2
Dividends
Yield: 4.8%
Payout: 27.4%
Market value ($ mil.): 153.0

	STOCK PRICE ($) FY Close	P/E High/Low		PER SHARE ($) Earnings	Dividends	Book Value
12/20	17.81	11	6	2.07	0.57	12.59
12/19	20.95	31	23	0.73	0.57	10.85
12/18	17.25	25	15	1.09	0.54	9.41
12/17	17.00	28	19	0.81	0.21	8.74
Annual Growth	1.6%	—	—	36.6%	38.8%	12.9%

Bluerock Residential Growth REIT Inc

EXECUTIVES

Chairman, Chief Executive Officer, Director, R. Ramin Kamfar, $400,000 total compensation
President, Chief Operating Officer, Jordan B. Ruddy, $300,000 total compensation
Operations Executive President, Michael DiFranco, $39,231 total compensation

Chief Financial Officer, Treasurer, Christopher J. Vohs, $250,000 total compensation
Chief Investment Officer, Ryan S. MacDonald, $250,000 total compensation
Chief Strategy Officer, James G. Babb, $325,000 total compensation
Chief Legal Officer, Secretary, Michael L. Konig, $300,000 total compensation
Lead Director, Director, I. Bobby Majumder
Director, Romano Tio
Director, Kamal Jafarnia
Director, Elizabeth Harrison
Auditors : Grant Thornton LLP

LOCATIONS

HQ: Bluerock Residential Growth REIT Inc
1345 Avenue of the Americas, 32nd Floor, New York, NY 10105
Phone: 212 843-1601
Web: www.bluerockresidential.com

HISTORICAL FINANCIALS
Company Type: Public

Income Statement				FYE: December 31
	REVENUE ($mil)	NET INCOME ($mil)	NET PROFIT MARGIN	EMPLOYEES
12/20	219.8	30.6	13.9%	0
12/19	209.9	36.7	17.5%	0
12/18	184.7	(1.1)	—	0
12/17	123.1	(15.6)	—	0
12/16	77.0	(4.3)	—	0
Annual Growth	30.0%	—	—	—

2020 Year-End Financials
Debt ratio: 61.2%
Return on equity: 3.6%
Cash ($ mil.): 83.8
Current Ratio: 4.65
Long-term debt ($ mil.): 1,490.9
No. of shares ($ mil.): 22.1
Dividends
Yield: 5.1%
Payout: —
Market value ($ mil.): 280.0

	STOCK PRICE ($) FY Close	P/E High/Low		PER SHARE ($) Earnings	Dividends	Book Value
12/20	12.67	—	—	(1.91)	0.65	38.88
12/19	12.05	—	—	(0.91)	0.65	34.30
12/18	9.02	—	—	(1.82)	0.65	26.81
12/17	10.11	—	—	(1.79)	1.16	23.86
12/16	13.72	—	—	(0.91)	1.16	23.26
Annual Growth	(2.0%)	—	—	—	(13.5%)	13.7%

BNCCORP Inc

BNCCORP is the holding company for BNC National Bank, which has about 20 branches in Arizona, North Dakota, and Minnesota. Serving individuals and small and midsized businesses, the bank offers deposit accounts, credit cards, and wealth management services. It also has residential mortgage banking operations in Iowa, Kansas, and Missouri. Real estate loans account for nearly half of the company's portfolio; commercial, industrial, construction, agricultural, and consumer loans make up most of the remainder. BNCCORP sold BNC Insurance Services to Hub International in 2007 for more than $37 million. It arranged to sell some of its operations in Arizona and Minnesota to Alerus Financial in 2010.

EXECUTIVES

Chairman, Subsidiary Officer, Director, Michael M. Vekich
President, Chief Executive Officer, Subsidiary Officer, Timothy J. Franz, $140,672 total compensation
Chief Operating Officer, Subsidiary Officer, Goll Shawn Cleveland
Chief Legal Officer, Subsidiary Officer, Cheryl A. Stanton
Subsidiary Officer, Mark E. Peiler, $120,000 total compensation
Subsidiary Officer, Scott Spillman
Subsidiary Officer, Dave Hoekstra
Subsidiary Officer, Director, Daniel J. Collins
Director, Tracy J. Scott, $250,000 total compensation
Director, Tom Redmann
Director, Nathan P. Brenna
Director, Gaylen Ghylin
Director, John W. Palmer
Auditors : CliftonLarsonAllen LLP

LOCATIONS

HQ: BNCCORP Inc
322 East Main Avenue, Bismarck, ND 58501
Phone: 701 250-3040   Fax: 701 222-3653
Web: www.bnccorp.com

COMPETITORS

BANC OF CALIFORNIA, INC.
HANMI FINANCIAL CORPORATION
TRUIST FINANCIAL CORPORATION
VALLEY NATIONAL BANCORP
WOODFOREST FINANCIAL GROUP, INC.

HISTORICAL FINANCIALS
Company Type: Public

Income Statement				FYE: December 31
	ASSETS ($mil)	NET INCOME ($mil)	INCOME AS % OF ASSETS	EMPLOYEES
12/20	1,074.1	44.6	4.2%	0
12/19	966.7	10.2	1.1%	0
12/18	971.0	6.8	0.7%	0
12/17	946.1	4.8	0.5%	0
12/16	910.4	7.1	0.8%	0
Annual Growth	4.2%	58.0%	—	—

2020 Year-End Financials
Return on assets: 4.3%
Return on equity: 41.4%
Long-term debt ($ mil.): —
No. of shares ($ mil.): 3.5
Sales ($ mil.): 122.5
Dividends
Yield: 17.6%
Payout: 84.6%
Market value ($ mil.): 160.0

	STOCK PRICE ($) FY Close	P/E High/Low		PER SHARE ($) Earnings	Dividends	Book Value
12/20	45.25	4	1	12.52	8.00	33.39
12/19	34.65	12	7	2.88	0.00	27.39
12/18	20.50	16	10	1.93	0.00	22.26
12/17	31.00	22	18	1.38	0.00	22.40
12/16	26.05	13	7	2.03	0.00	21.47
Annual Growth	14.8%	—	—	57.6%	—	11.7%

BOK Financial Corp

BOK Financial began in 1910 as a regional source of capital for the energy industry. It has seven principal banking divisions in Oklahoma, Texas, New Mexico, Northwest Arkansas, Colorado, Arizona, and Kansas/Missouri. Its primary focus is to provide a comprehensive range of nationally competitive financial products and services in a personalized and responsive manner. Products and services include loans and deposits, cash management services, fiduciary and insurance services, mortgage banking and brokerage and trading services to middle-market businesses, financial institutions and consumers. About 35% of total loan portfolio are in Texas, while Oklahoma has around 15%.

Operations

BOK Financial operates through three primary segments: Commercial Banking, Consumer Banking, and Wealth Management.

The Commercial Banking segment brings in nearly 55% of BOK's total revenue with offerings including lending, treasury and cash management, and risk management products for small, midsized, and large companies.

The Wealth Management segment (about 25%) engages in brokerage and trading activities, mainly related to providing liquidity to the mortgage markets through trading of US government agency mortgage-backed securities and related derivative contracts.

The Consumer Banking segment, which brings in some 5% of total revenue, is the retail arm providing lending and deposit services and all mortgage activities.

Funds Management and other generated the rest.

Its commercial loans generated over 60% of total loan portfolio, and about 20% each from commercial real estate and loans to individual.

Geographic Reach

Most of Tulsa-based BOK Financial's locations are located in and around Tulsa, Oklahoma City, Dallas/Fort Worth, Houston, Albuquerque, New Mexico, Denver, Phoenix, and Kansas City in Kansas and Missouri. The company's primary operations facilities are in Tulsa, Oklahoma City, Dallas, and Albuquerque, New Mexico.

The bank's loans to businesses and individuals with collateral primarily located in Texas totaled $8.3 billion or around 40% of the total loan portfolio. Loans to businesses and individuals with collateral primarily located in Oklahoma totaled $5.3 billion or around 25% of its total loan portfolio. Loans to businesses and individuals with collateral primarily located in Colorado totaled $2.7 billion or nearly 15% of its total loan portfolio.

Financial Performance

Company's revenue for fiscal 2021 increased to $2.6 billion compared from the prior year with $2.5 billion.

Net income for fiscal 2021 increased to $616.3 million compared from the prior year with $435.1 million.

Cash held by the company at the end of fiscal 2021 increased to $2.8 billion. Cash used for operations was $3.7 billion while cash provided by investing and financing activities were $2.6 billion and $2.7 billion, respectively.

Strategy

Company's overall strategic objective is to emphasize growth in long-term value by building on its leadership position in Oklahoma through expansion into other high-growth markets in contiguous states.

EXECUTIVES

Chairman, Director, George B. Kaiser
Vice-Chairman, Director, Stanley A. Lybarger, $864,410 total compensation
President, Chief Executive Officer, Director, Stacy C. Kymes, $456,125 total compensation
Executive Vice President, Chief Credit Officer, James A. Dietz
Executive Vice President, Chief Information Officer, Joseph A. Gottron
Executive Vice President, Chief Risk Officer, Martin E. Grunst
Executive Vice President, Chief Auditor, Rebecca D. Keesling
Executive Vice President, Chief Financial Officer, Subsidiary Officer, Director, Steven E. Nell, $529,375 total compensation
Executive Vice President, Chief Human Resources Officer, Kelley E. Weil
Chief Accounting Officer, Mike Rogers
Division Officer, Marc C. Maun
Subsidiary Officer, Division Officer, Norman P. Bagwell, $454,075 total compensation
Division Officer, Brad A. Vincent
Subsidiary Officer, Division Officer, Scott B. Grauer, $509,847 total compensation
Division Officer, Derek Martin
Director, Alan S. Armstrong
Director, C. Fred Ball, $300,000 total compensation
Director, Steven Bangert
Director, Chester Cadieux
Director, John W. Coffey
Director, Joseph W. Craft
Director, David F. Griffin
Director, V. Burns Hargis, $285,000 total compensation
Director, Douglas D. Hawthorne
Director, Kimberley D. Henry
Director, E. Carey Joullian
Director, Steven J. Malcolm
Director, Emmet C. Richards
Director, Claudia San Pedro
Director, Peggy I. Simmons
Director, Michael C. Turpen
Director, Rose M. Washington
Auditors: Ernst & Young LLP

LOCATIONS

HQ: BOK Financial Corp
Bank of Oklahoma Tower, Boston Avenue at Second Street, Tulsa, OK 74172
Phone: 918 588-6000
Web: www.bokf.com

PRODUCTS/OPERATIONS

2017 Sales

	% of total
Commercial Banking	76
Consumer Banking	7
Wealth Management	17
Total	100

Selected Banking Subsidiaries
Bank of Albuquerque, National Association
Bank of Arizona, National Association
Bank of Arkansas, National Association
Bank of Oklahoma, National Association
Bank of Texas, National Association
Colorado State Bank & Trust
Mobank

COMPETITORS

BOKF MERGER CORPORATION NUMBER SIXTEEN
CITY HOLDING COMPANY
FIRST HORIZON CORPORATION
FIRST MIDWEST BANCORP, INC.
UMB FINANCIAL CORPORATION

HISTORICAL FINANCIALS
Company Type: Public

Income Statement				FYE: December 31
	ASSETS ($mil)	NET INCOME ($mil)	INCOME AS % OF ASSETS	EMPLOYEES
12/20	46,671.0	435.0	0.9%	4,915
12/19	42,172.0	500.7	1.2%	5,107
12/18	38,020.5	445.6	1.2%	5,313
12/17	32,272.1	334.6	1.0%	4,930
12/16	32,772.2	232.6	0.7%	4,884
Annual Growth	9.2%	16.9%	—	0.2%

2020 Year-End Financials
Return on assets: 0.9%
Return on equity: 8.5%
Long-term debt ($ mil.): —
No. of shares ($ mil.): 69.6
Sales ($ mil.): 2,112.9
Dividends
Yield: 2.9%
Payout: 36.9%
Market value ($ mil.): 4,769.0

	STOCK PRICE ($) FY Close	P/E High/Low		PER SHARE ($) Earnings	Dividends	Book Value
12/20	68.48	14	6	6.19	2.05	75.62
12/19	87.40	13	10	7.03	2.01	68.80
12/18	73.33	16	11	6.63	1.90	61.45
12/17	92.32	18	15	5.11	1.77	53.45
12/16	83.04	24	13	3.53	1.73	50.12
Annual Growth	(4.7%)	—	—	15.1%	4.3%	10.8%

Boomer Holdings Inc

EXECUTIVES

Chairman, President, Treasurer, Secretary, Director, Daniel Capri
Chief Executive Officer, Director, Michael Quaid
Director, Giang Thi Hoang
Auditors: Benjamin & Ko

LOCATIONS

HQ: Boomer Holdings Inc
8670 W. Cheyenne Avenue, Las Vegas, NV 89129
Phone: 888 266-6370
Web: www.boomernaturals.com

HISTORICAL FINANCIALS
Company Type: Public

Income Statement				FYE: January 31
	REVENUE ($mil)	NET INCOME ($mil)	NET PROFIT MARGIN	EMPLOYEES
01/21*	45.1	7.3	16.2%	120
07/20	11.4	(15.5)	—	80
07/19	0.0	(0.0)	—	0
07/18	0.0	(0.0)	—	0
07/17	0.0	(0.0)	—	0
Annual Growth	605.6%	—	—	—

*Fiscal year change

2021 Year-End Financials
Debt ratio: 22.2%
Return on equity: —
Cash ($ mil.): 1.1
Current Ratio: 0.74
Long-term debt ($ mil.): 0.3
No. of shares ($ mil.): 155.2
Dividends
Yield: —
Payout: —
Market value ($ mil.): 108.0

	STOCK PRICE ($) FY Close	P/E High/Low		PER SHARE ($) Earnings	Dividends	Book Value
01/21*	0.70	86	12	0.05	0.00	(0.03)
07/20	2.75	—	—	(0.12)	0.00	(0.09)
Annual Growth	(74.7%)	—	—	—	—	—

*Fiscal year change

Boot Barn Holdings Inc

EXECUTIVES

Chairman, Director, Peter M. Starrett
President, Chief Executive Officer, Director, James G. Conroy, $745,827 total compensation
Executive Vice President, Chief Operating Officer, Gregory V. Hackman, $375,000 total compensation
Finance Senior Vice President, Investor Relations Senior Vice President, Finance Chief Financial Officer, Investor Relations Chief Financial Officer, Finance Secretary, Investor Relations Secretary, Finance Principal Financial Officer, Investor Relations Principal Financial Officer, Finance Principal Accounting Officer, Investor Relations Principal Accounting Officer, James M. Watkins
Stores Senior Vice President, Michael A. Love, $277,114 total compensation
Chief Merchandising Officer, Laurie Grijalva, $364,290 total compensation
Chief Digital Officer, John Hazen, $375,000 total compensation
Director, Gregory M. Bettinelli
Director, Christopher Bruzzo
Director, Gene Eddie Burt
Director, Lisa G. Laube

Director, Anne MacDonald
Director, Brenda I. Morris
Director, Bradley Morgan Weston
Auditors : DELOITTE & TOUCHE LLP

LOCATIONS

HQ: Boot Barn Holdings Inc
 15345 Barranca Pkwy., Irvine, CA 92618
Phone: 949 453-4400
Web: www.bootbarn.com

HISTORICAL FINANCIALS
Company Type: Public

Income Statement   FYE: March 27

	REVENUE ($mil)	NET INCOME ($mil)	NET PROFIT MARGIN	EMPLOYEES
03/21	893.4	59.3	6.6%	4,900
03/20	845.5	47.9	5.7%	3,200
03/19	776.8	39.0	5.0%	4,000
03/18*	677.9	28.8	4.3%	3,500
04/17	629.8	14.1	2.3%	3,000
Annual Growth	9.1%	43.0%	—	13.0%

*Fiscal year change

2021 Year-End Financials
Debt ratio: 11.8%   No. of shares ($ mil.): 29.2
Return on equity: 16.6%   Dividends
Cash ($ mil.): 73.1   Yield: —
Current Ratio: 1.69   Payout: —
Long-term debt ($ mil.): 109.7   Market value ($ mil.): 1,852.0

	STOCK PRICE ($) FY Close	P/E High/Low		PER SHARE ($) Earnings	Dividends	Book Value
03/21	63.30	32	5	2.01	0.00	13.50
03/20	13.37	28	6	1.64	0.00	11.17
03/19	29.44	23	11	1.35	0.00	9.32
03/18*	17.73	18	6	1.05	0.00	7.86
04/17	9.89	31	11	0.53	0.00	6.77
Annual Growth	59.1%	—	—	39.6%	—	18.8%

*Fiscal year change

Boston Beer Co Inc (The)

The Boston Beer Company, Inc. is a high-end alcoholic beverage company and one of the largest craft brewers in the United States. In fiscal 2020, Boston Beer sold approximately 7.4 million barrels of its proprietary products. The company's brands include Truly Hard Seltzer, Twisted Tea, Samuel Adams, Angry Orchard Hard Cider and Dogfish Head Craft Brewery, as well as other local craft beer brands. Boston Beer produces alcohol beverages, including hard seltzer, malt beverages (beers), and hard cider at company-owned breweries and its cidery and under contract arrangements at other brewery locations.

Geographic Reach
Headquartered in Boston, The Boston Beer Company owns breweries in Cincinnati; Breinigsville, Pennsylvania; and Milton, Delaware. The company distributes its brews primarily in the US, but they are also sold in Canada, Europe, Israel, Australia, New Zealand, the Caribbean, the Pacific Rim, Mexico, and Central and South America.

Subsidiary A&S Brewing has breweries in LA, Miami, and Brooklyn.

Sales and Marketing
The company sells its beverages in various packages. Sleek cans, standard cans and bottles are sold primarily for off-premise retailers, which include grocery stores, club stores, convenience stores and liquor stores. Kegs are sold primarily for on-premise retailers, which include bars, restaurants, stadiums and other venues.

The company's media campaigns include TV, digital and social, radio, billboards, and print. The brewer complements is media buying by sponsoring which currently include such as National Hockey League, The Boston Red Sox, the Boston Marathon, local concert and festivals, industry-related trade shows and promotional events at local establishments, to the extent permitted under local laws and regulations.

Total advertising and sales promotional expenditures of $477.6 million, $355.6 million, and $304.9 million were included in advertising, promotional and selling expenses in the accompanying consolidated statements of comprehensive income for fiscal years 2020, 2019 and 2018, respectively.

Financial Performance
Net revenue increased by $486.6 million, or 39%, to $1.7 billion in 2020, as compared to $1.2 billion in 2019, due primarily to increased shipments.

Net income for fiscal 2020 increased to $192.0 million compared with $110.0 million in the prior year.

Cash held by the company at the end of fiscal 2021 increased to $163.3 million. Cash provided by operations and financing activities were $253.4 million and $12.3 million, respectively. Investing activities used $139.1 million, mainly for purchases of property, plant and equipment.

Strategy
The company continues to pursue a production strategy that includes production at breweries owned by the company and breweries and packaging facilities owned by others. During 2019 and 2020, the company brewed, fermented and packaged approximately 74% and 65% of its volume at breweries owned by the company, respectively. The company made capital investments in 2020 of approximately $140.0 million, most of which represented investments in the company's breweries. These investments were made to increase production, drive efficiencies and cost reductions and support product innovation and future growth. Based on its current estimates of future volumes and mix, the company expects to invest between $300 million and $400 million in 2021 to meet those estimates. Because actual capital investments are highly dependent on meeting demand, the actual amount spent may well be significantly different from the company's current expectations.

Company Background
Management consultant James Koch started The Boston Beer Company with his former secretary, Rhonda Kallman, in 1983. With Koch's $100,000 in life savings plus $300,000 raised from family and friends, the company contracted with Pittsburgh Brewing to make beer using Koch's great-great-grandfather's recipe. (Louis Koch had brewed beer in Germany before opening a St. Louis brewery in 1860.)

EXECUTIVES

Chairman, Director, C. James Koch, $412,692 total compensation
President, Chief Executive Officer, Director, David A. Burwick, $562,500 total compensation
Legal Vice President, Legal Deputy General Counsel, Tara L. Heath
Sales Chief Sales Officer, John C. Geist, $516,538 total compensation
Chief Marketing Officer, Lesya Lysyj
Interim Chief Financial Officer, Chief Accounting Officer, Interim Treasurer, Matthew D. Murphy
Chief People Officer, Carolyn L. O'Boyle
Associate General Counsel, Corporate Secretary, Michael G. Andrews
Division Officer, David L. Grimnell
Subsidiary Officer, Director, Samuel A. Calagione, III
Lead Director, Director, Jean-Michel Valette
Director, Meghan V. Joyce
Director, Michael Spillane
Director, Cynthia A. Fisher
Director, Michael M. Lynton
Director, Julio N. Nemeth
Auditors : DELOITTE & TOUCHE LLP

LOCATIONS

HQ: Boston Beer Co Inc (The)
 One Design Center Place, Suite 850, Boston, MA 02210
Phone: 617 368-5000   **Fax:** 617 368-5500
Web: www.bostonbeer.com

PRODUCTS/OPERATIONS

Selected Brands and Year Introduced
Barrel Room Collection
  Samuel Adams American Kriek, 2009
  Samuel Adams New World Tripel, 2009
  Samuel Adams Stony Brook Red, 2009
  Samuel Adams Thirteenth Hour, 2011
Brewmaster's Collection
  Samuel Adams Black Lager, 2005
  Samuel Adams Blackberry Witbier, 2009
  Samuel Adams Boston Ale, 1987
  Samuel Adams Cherry Wheat, 1995
  Samuel Adams Coastal Wheat, 2009
  Samuel Adams Cranberry Lambic, 1990
  Samuel Adams Cream Stout, 1993
  Samuel Adams Irish Red, 2008
  Samuel Adams Latitude 48 IPA, 2010
  Samuel Adams Pale Ale, 1999
Core Focus Beers

Samuel Adams Boston Lager, 1984
Sam Adams Light, 2001
Flavored Malt Beverages
Twisted Tea Backyard Batch Hard Iced Tea, 2009
Twisted Tea Half Hard Iced Tea & Half Hard Lemonade, 2003
Twisted Tea Hard Iced Tea, 2001
Twisted Tea Light Hard Iced Tea, 2007
Twisted Tea Peach Hard Iced Tea, 2005
Twisted Tea Raspberry Hard Iced Tea, 2001
Twisted Tea Blueberry Hard Iced Tea, 2011
Hard Cider
Angry Orchard Crisp Apple, 2011
Angry Orchard Apple Ginger, 2011
HardCore Crisp Hard Cider, 1997
Imperial Series
Samuel Adams Double Bock, 1988
Samuel Adams Imperial Stout, 2009
Samuel Adams Imperial White, 2009
Samuel Adams Wee Heavy, 2011
Limited Edition Beers
Infinium, 2010
Samuel Adams Utopias, 2001
Seasonal Beers
Samuel Adams Octoberfest, 1989
Samuel Adams Summer Ale, 1996
Samuel Adams Winter Lager, 1989
Samuel Adams Alpine Spring, 2011

COMPETITORS

ANHEUSER-BUSCH COMPANIES, LLC
Anheuser-Busch InBev
Anheuser-Busch InBev
CRAFT BREW ALLIANCE, INC.
DIAGEO PLC
FOSTER'S GROUP PTY LTD
Heineken N.V.
MAGIC HAT BREWING COMPANY & PERFORMING ARTS CENTER, INC.
MOLSON COORS BEVERAGE COMPANY
NEW BELGIUM BREWING COMPANY, INC.

HISTORICAL FINANCIALS

Company Type: Public

Income Statement — FYE: December 26

	REVENUE ($mil)	NET INCOME ($mil)	NET PROFIT MARGIN	EMPLOYEES
12/20	1,736.4	191.9	11.1%	2,423
12/19	1,249.8	110.0	8.8%	2,128
12/18	995.6	92.6	9.3%	1,543
12/17	862.9	99.0	11.5%	1,439
12/16	906.4	87.3	9.6%	1,505
Annual Growth	17.6%	21.8%	—	12.6%

2020 Year-End Financials

Debt ratio: —
Return on equity: 22.7%
Cash ($ mil.): 163.2
Current Ratio: 1.59
Long-term debt ($ mil.): —
No. of shares ($ mil.): 12.1
Dividends
  Yield: —
  Payout: —
Market value ($ mil.): 12,365.0

	STOCK PRICE ($) FY Close	P/E High/Low		PER SHARE ($) Earnings	Dividends	Book Value
12/20	1,014.93	69	19	15.53	0.00	78.55
12/19	378.75	48	25	9.16	0.00	61.08
12/18	238.82	41	21	7.82	0.00	40.03
12/17	191.10	24	16	8.09	0.00	36.44
12/16	169.85	29	21	6.79	0.00	36.11
Annual Growth	56.3%	—	—	23.0%	—	21.4%

Bridgewater Bancshares Inc

EXECUTIVES

President, Chief Executive Officer, Subsidiary Officer, Chairman, Director, Jerry J. Baack, $526,250 total compensation
Executive Vice President, Chief Operating Officer, Mary Jayne Crocker, $350,000 total compensation
Executive Vice President, Chief Credit Officer, Secretary, Director, Jeffrey D. Shellberg, $337,500 total compensation
Senior Vice President, Chief Financial Officer, Joseph M. Chybowski
Senior Vice President, Chief Lending Officer, Nick L. Place
Chief Deposit Officer, Lisa M. Salazar
Chief Technology Officer, Mark E. Hokanson
Lead Independent Director, Director, David B. Juran
Director, Douglas J. Parish
Director, Lisa M. Brezonik
Director, Mohammed Lawal
Director, Thomas P. Trutna
Director, Todd B. Urness
Director, James S. Johnson
Director, David J. Volk
Auditors : CliftonLarsonAllen LLP

LOCATIONS

HQ: Bridgewater Bancshares Inc
4450 Excelsior Boulevard, Suite 100, St. Louis Park, Bloomington, MN 55416
Phone: 952 893-6868
Web: www.bridgewaterbankmn.com

HISTORICAL FINANCIALS

Company Type: Public

Income Statement — FYE: December 31

	ASSETS ($mil)	NET INCOME ($mil)	INCOME AS % OF ASSETS	EMPLOYEES
12/20	2,927.3	27.1	0.9%	185
12/19	2,268.8	31.4	1.4%	160
12/18	1,973.7	26.9	1.4%	140
12/17	1,616.6	16.8	1.0%	114
12/16	1,260.3	13.2	1.0%	0
Annual Growth	23.5%	19.8%	—	—

2020 Year-End Financials

Return on assets: 1.0%
Return on equity: 10.6%
Long-term debt ($ mil.): —
No. of shares ($ mil.): 28.1
Sales ($ mil.): 120.6
Dividends
  Yield: —
  Payout: —
Market value ($ mil.): 352.0

	STOCK PRICE ($) FY Close	P/E High/Low		PER SHARE ($) Earnings	Dividends	Book Value
12/20	12.49	15	9	0.93	0.00	9.43
12/19	13.78	13	9	1.05	0.00	8.45
12/18	10.55	14	11	0.91	0.00	7.34
Annual Growth	8.8%	—	—	1.1%	—	13.3%

BrightView Holdings Inc

EXECUTIVES

President, Chief Executive Officer, Director, Andrew V. Masterman, $850,000 total compensation
Executive Vice President, Chief Legal Officer, Corporate Secretary, Jonathan M. Gottsegen, $540,000 total compensation
Executive Vice President, Chief Human Resources Officer, Amanda Orders
Chief Financial Officer, Brett Urban
Division Officer, Jeffery R. Herold, $485,000 total compensation
Division Officer, Thomas C. Donnelly, $465,000 total compensation
Division Officer, Michael J. Dozier
Division Officer, Jamie C. Gollotto
Director, James R. Abrahamson
Director, Frank Lopez
Director, Paul E. Raether
Director, Richard W. Roedel
Director, Jane Okun Bomba
Director, William L. Cornog
Director, Mara E. Swan
Auditors : DELOITTE & TOUCHE LLP

LOCATIONS

HQ: BrightView Holdings Inc
980 Jolly Road, Blue Bell, PA 19422
Phone: 484 567-7204
Web: www.brightview.com

HISTORICAL FINANCIALS

Company Type: Public

Income Statement — FYE: September 30

	REVENUE ($mil)	NET INCOME ($mil)	NET PROFIT MARGIN	EMPLOYEES
09/21	2,553.6	46.3	1.8%	20,500
09/20	2,346.0	(41.6)	—	19,700
09/19	2,404.6	44.4	1.8%	21,500
09/18	2,353.6	(15.0)	—	20,000
09/17	1,713.5	(13.9)	—	19,000
Annual Growth	10.5%	—	—	1.9%

2021 Year-End Financials

Debt ratio: 35.2%
Return on equity: 3.5%
Cash ($ mil.): 123.7
Current Ratio: 1.43
Long-term debt ($ mil.): 1,130.6
No. of shares ($ mil.): 105.2
Dividends
  Yield: —
  Payout: —
Market value ($ mil.): 1,553.0

	STOCK PRICE ($) FY Close	P/E High/Low		PER SHARE ($) Earnings	Dividends	Book Value
09/21	14.76	43	27	0.44	0.00	12.76
09/20	11.40	—	—	(0.40)	0.00	12.12
09/19	17.15	46	22	0.43	0.00	12.29
09/18	16.05	—	—	(0.18)	0.00	11.75
Annual Growth	(2.8%)	—	—	—	—	2.8%

	STOCK PRICE ($) FY Close	P/E High/Low		PER SHARE ($) Earnings	Dividends	Book Value
12/20	10.20	19	9	0.68	0.78	8.86
12/19*	12.75	318	273	0.04	0.12	8.97
Annual Growth	(20.0%)	—	—	1600.0%	550.0%	(1.2%)

*Fiscal year change

2020 Year-End Financials

Debt ratio: 36.2%   No. of shares ($ mil.): 145.6
Return on equity: 2.5%   Dividends
Cash ($ mil.): 100.4   Yield: —
Current Ratio: 2.59   Payout: 187.5%
Long-term debt ($ mil.): 1,541.1   Market value ($ mil.): 2,851.0

	STOCK PRICE ($) FY Close	P/E High/Low		PER SHARE ($) Earnings	Dividends	Book Value
12/20	19.58	45	37	0.44	0.83	15.79
Annual Growth	—	—	—	—	—	—

Broadmark Realty Capital Inc

EXECUTIVES

Chairman, Director, Jeffrey B. Pyatt
Chief Executive Officer, Director, Brian P. Ward
Executive Vice President, Chief Legal Officer, Secretary, Nevin Singh Boparai
Chief Financial Officer, Principal Financial Officer, Principal Accounting Officer, Treasurer, David Schneider
Chief Operating Officer, Assistant Secretary, Linda D. Koa
Chief Credit Officer, Daniel Hirsty
Lead Independent Director, David A. Karp
Director, Pinkie D. Mayfield
Director, Stephen G. Haggerty
Director, Daniel J. Hirsch
Director, Norma J. Lawrence
Director, Kevin M. Luebbers

LOCATIONS

HQ: Broadmark Realty Capital Inc
1420 Fifth Avenue, Suite 2000, Seattle, WA 98101
Phone: 206 971-0800
Web: www.broadmark.com

HISTORICAL FINANCIALS

Company Type: Public

Income Statement — FYE: December 31

	REVENUE ($mil)	NET INCOME ($mil)	NET PROFIT MARGIN	EMPLOYEES
12/20	122.3	90.2	73.7%	54
12/19*	15.9	5.3	33.3%	41
11/19	115.0	69.9	60.8%	0
12/18	95.8	81.7	85.3%	0
12/17	52.2	45.3	86.9%	0
Annual Growth	32.8%	25.7%	—	—

*Fiscal year change

2020 Year-End Financials

Debt ratio: —   No. of shares ($ mil.): 132.5
Return on equity: 7.6%   Dividends
Cash ($ mil.): 223.3   Yield: 7.6%
Current Ratio: 18.43   Payout: 114.7%
Long-term debt ($ mil.): —   Market value ($ mil.): 1,352.0

Broadstone Net Lease Inc

EXECUTIVES

Chairman, Director, Laurie A. Hawkes
President, Chief Operating Officer, Ryan M. Albano
Chief Executive Officer, Director, John D. Moragne
Capital Markets and Credit Risk Executive Vice President, Capital Markets and Credit Risk Chief Financial Officer, Kevin M. Fennell
Senior Vice President, General Counsel, Secretary, John D. Callan
Corporate Finance Senior Vice President, Investor Relations Senior Vice President, Michael B. Caruso
Human Resources Senior Vice President, Molly Kelly Wiegel
Senior Vice President, Chief Administrative Officer, Kristen Duckles
Senior Vice President, Chief Accounting Officer, Treasurer, Timothy D. Dieffenbacher
Property Management Senior Vice President, Andrea T. Wright
Acquisitions Senior Vice President, Roderick A. Pickney
Asset Management Senior Vice President, Laurier James Lessard
Director, Denise Brooks-Williams
Director, Michael A. Coke
Director, David M. Jacobstein
Director, Shekar Narasimhan
Director, Geoffrey H. Rosenberger
Director, James H. Watters

LOCATIONS

HQ: Broadstone Net Lease Inc
800 Clinton Square, Rochester, NY 14604
Phone: 585 287-6500

HISTORICAL FINANCIALS

Company Type: Public

Income Statement — FYE: December 31

	REVENUE ($mil)	NET INCOME ($mil)	NET PROFIT MARGIN	EMPLOYEES
12/20	321.6	51.1	15.9%	71
12/19	298.8	79.3	26.6%	71
12/18	237.4	69.3	29.2%	0
12/17	181.5	54.7	30.2%	0
Annual Growth	21.0%	(2.3%)	—	—

Brown & Brown Inc

Insurance agency Brown & Brown is one of largest independent insurance brokerages in the US. The company provides property/casualty, life, and health insurance plus risk management services through its Retail segment, mainly to commercial clients. Its National Programs division designs customized programs for such niche clients as dentists, lawyers, and optometrists. Brown & Brown's Wholesale Brokerage unit distributes excess and surplus commercial insurance, as well as reinsurance, to retail agents, while the company's Services segment provides self-insured and third-party administrator services. The company has more than 330 offices in about 45 states and Canada, the UK, the Cayman Islands, and Bermuda.

Operations

Brown & Brown's business is divided into four reportable segments: Retail, National Programs, Wholesale Brokerage, and Services.

The company's Retail segment accounts for about 60% company's total revenue. The segment provides property/casualty and employee benefit offerings to commercial, public, professional, and individual customers. Products include commercial packages, property risk, general liability, workers' compensation, and group medical. It also offers ancillary products for groups and individuals including life, accident, disability, health, hospitalization, and dental.

The National Programs segment, roughly 25% of revenue, provides managing general agency services in five categories: Professional Programs (profession-specific liability), Personal Lines Programs (personal property, auto, earthquake, and marine coverage via Arrowhead subsidiary), Commercial Programs (industry, trade, and market niches), Public Entity-Related Programs (insurance trusts for cities, counties, and other government agencies), and Specialty Programs (flood insurance, all-risk commercial property and sovereign native-American nations and parcel insurance, among others).

The Wholesale Brokerage segment (nearly 15% of revenue) sells excess and surplus commercial insurance policies to retail insurance agencies (including the Retail segment's offices).

The Services segment (around 5% of revenue) provides third-party claims administration and comprehensive medical utilization management services in both the workers' compensation and all-lines liability arenas, as well as Medicare Set-aside services, Social Security disability and Medicare benefits advocacy services and claims adjusting services.

Geographic Reach

Based in Florida, Brown & Brown operates more than 330 locations in about 45 states, and around 20 international locations in Canada, Ireland, the UK, Bermuda and the Cayman Islands. Its largest market is Florida, where it operates more than 50 agency locations, followed by California, Massachusetts, Georgia, New York, and Michigan.

Sales and Marketing

Brown & Brown's network of agency offices sells insurance policies that are underwritten by third-party carriers. The Retail division receives commission fees on policy sales to customers including commercial businesses, government agencies, professionals, and individual consumers. The National Programs division sells niche policies to businesses and professionals through a nationwide network of independent agents and through the Retail segment's offices. The Wholesale Brokerage division sells commercial policies to independent brokers and agents (as well as some Retail segment offices).

Financial Performance

The company's revenue for fiscal 2021 increased by 17% to $3.1 billion compared from the prior year with $2.6 billion.

Net income for fiscal 2021 increased by 22% to $587.1 million compared from the prior year with $480.5 million.

Cash held by the company at the end of fiscal at the end of fiscal 2021 increased to $1.5 billion. Cash provided by operations was $942.5 million while cash used for investing activities and financing activities were $396.7 million and $343.9 million, respectively. Main uses of cash were payments for businesses acquired and cash dividends paid.

Strategy

Brown & Brown's growth strategy partially includes the acquisition of other insurance intermediaries. Company's ability to successfully identify suitable acquisition candidates, complete acquisitions, integrate acquired businesses into its operations, and expand into new markets requires the company to implement and continuously improve its operations and its financial and management information systems.

Mergers and Acquisitions

In 2022, Brown & Brown agreed to acquire Global Risk Partners Limited (GRP), one of the top independent insurance intermediaries in the UK, servicing nearly half a million personal and commercial customers.

GRP's position as an industry leader in the UK, their experience in international markets and generation of new market segments will allow us to further expand our international footprint and broaden the scope of our global capabilities," said J. Powell Brown, president and chief executive officer of Brown & Brown.

In early 2022, Brown & Brown Lone Star Insurance Services, Inc., a subsidiary of Brown & Brown, Inc., has acquired substantially all of the assets of HARCO. HARCO is a full-service, independent retail insurance agency serving businesses and individuals throughout Texas. Following the acquisition, the HARCO team will continue operating from their existing Houston, Texas office as a branch location of Brown & Brown's Houston, Texas retail operations. The combined offices will operate under the leadership of Ryan Beavers, executive vice president of Brown & Brown Lone Star Insurance Services, Inc.

In late 2021, Brown & Brown acquired the assets of Heacock Insurance, a fifth-generation, family-owned agency providing risk management solutions for its central Florida customers since 1922. The acquisition of Heacock Insurance strengthens Brown & Brown's operations in central Florida.

Company Background

Brown & Brown traces its roots to 1939, when Metropolitan Life insurance agent Adrian Brown partnered with his cousin, Charles "Cov" Owen, to open their own agency (named Brown & Owen) in Daytona Beach, Florida. Adrian's son Hyatt Brown joined in 1959, creating Brown & Brown, and still serves as Chairman.

In 1993 the company merged with Poe & Associates (founded in 1958) and operated as Poe & Brown until 1999, when the Brown & Brown name was revived. Throughout its history the company has embarked on a steady growth strategy to buy middle-market insurance brokers across the US.

EXECUTIVES

Chairman, Director, J. Hyatt Brown, $1,000,000 total compensation

Vice-Chairman, Director, James C. Hays

President, Chief Executive Officer, Director, J. Powell Brown, $1,000,000 total compensation

Executive Vice President, Chief Financial Officer, Treasurer, R. Andrew Watts, $500,000 total compensation

Executive Vice President, Division Officer, P. Barrett Brown

Executive Vice President, Chief Acquisitions Officer, J. Scott Penny, $500,000 total compensation

Executive Vice President, Division Officer, Chris L. Walker, $500,000 total compensation

Executive Vice President, Corporate Secretary, General Counsel, Robert W. Lloyd

Lead Independent Director, Director, H. Palmer Proctor

Director, Hugh M. Brown

Director, Lawrence L. Gellerstedt
Director, Theodore J. Hoepner
Director, James S. Hunt
Director, Toni Jennings
Director, Timothy R.M. Main
Director, Wendell S. Reilly
Director, Chilton D. Varner
Director, Jaymin B. Patel
Auditors: Deloitte & Touche LLP

LOCATIONS

HQ: Brown & Brown Inc
300 North Beach Street, Daytona Beach, FL 32114
Phone: 386 252-9601
Web: www.bbinsurance.com

PRODUCTS/OPERATIONS

2015 Sales

	$ mil	% of total
Core commissions and fees	1,595.2	96
Profit-sharing contingent commissions	51.7	3
Guaranteed supplemental commissions	10.0	1
Investment income	1.0	-
Other income, net	2.6	-
Total	1,660.5	100

2015 Sales

	$ mil	% of total
Retail	870.3	52
National Programs	428.7	26
Wholesale Brokerage	217.0	13
Services	145.4	9
Other	(0.9)	-
Total	1,660.5	100

Selected Products and Services
Personal Insurance
Business Insurance
Employee Benefits
Wholesale Brokerage
Services Division
Financial Services
Trade Credit
Surety Bonds
Risk Management

COMPETITORS

AMERITRUST GROUP, INC.
AMTRUST FINANCIAL SERVICES, INC.
AMWINS GROUP, INC.
ARTHUR J. GALLAGHER & CO.
ASSURANT, INC.
HALLMARK FINANCIAL SERVICES, INC.
NATIONAL GENERAL HOLDINGS CORP.
SECURA INSURANCE, A MUTUAL COMPANY
SECURIAN FINANCIAL GROUP, INC.
SELECTIVE INSURANCE GROUP, INC.

HISTORICAL FINANCIALS

Company Type: Public

Income Statement — FYE: December 31

	REVENUE ($mil)	NET INCOME ($mil)	NET PROFIT MARGIN	EMPLOYEES
12/21	3,051.3	587.1	19.2%	12,023
12/20	2,613.3	480.4	18.4%	11,136
12/19	2,392.1	398.5	16.7%	10,083
12/18	2,014.2	344.2	17.1%	1,281
12/17	1,881.3	399.6	21.2%	8,491
Annual Growth	12.9%	10.1%	—	9.1%

2021 Year-End Financials

Debt ratio: 20.7%
Return on equity: 14.7%
Cash ($ mil.): 887.0
Current Ratio: 1.25
Long-term debt ($ mil.): 1,980.4
No. of shares ($ mil.): 282.5
Dividends
　Yield: 0.5%
　Payout: 18.5%
Market value ($ mil.): 19,854.0

	STOCK PRICE ($) FY Close	P/E High/Low		PER SHARE ($) Earnings	Dividends	Book Value
12/21	70.28	34	21	2.07	0.38	14.86
12/20	47.41	29	19	1.69	0.35	13.27
12/19	39.48	28	19	1.40	0.33	11.89
12/18	27.56	43	20	1.22	0.31	10.73
12/17	51.46	36	29	1.45	0.28	9.35
Annual Growth	8.1%	—	—	9.3%	8.2%	12.3%

Business First Bancshares Inc

EXECUTIVES

Chairman, Subsidiary Officer, Director, Robert S. Greer

President, Chief Executive Officer, Subsidiary Officer, Director, David R. Melville, $460,000 total compensation

Executive Vice President, Subsidiary Officer, Director, Mark P. Folse

Chief Financial Officer, Treasurer, Subsidiary Officer, Gregory Robertson, $261,363 total compensation

Subsidiary Officer, Philip Jordan, $261,363 total compensation

Subsidiary Officer, Margaret Singer Lee

Subsidiary Officer, Donald A. Hingle

Subsidiary Officer, Keith Mansfield

Subsidiary Officer, Alicia Robertson

Director, Keith Tillage

Director, Carol Calkins

Director, Vernon J. Johnson

Director, Ricky D. Day

Director, James J. Buquet

Director, John A. Graves

Director, Rolfe Hood McCollister

Director, Andrew D. McLindon

Director, Patrick E. Mockler

Director, David A. Montgomery

Director, Arthur J. Price

Director, Kenneth Wm. Smith

Director, Steve G. White

Auditors : Hannis T. Bourgeois, LLP

LOCATIONS

HQ: Business First Bancshares Inc
500 Laurel Street, Suite 101, Baton Rouge, LA 70801
Phone: 225 248-7600
Web: www.b1bank.com

HISTORICAL FINANCIALS
Company Type: Public

Income Statement　　　　　　　　　　　　FYE: December 31

	ASSETS ($mil)	NET INCOME ($mil)	INCOME AS % OF ASSETS	EMPLOYEES
12/20	4,160.3	29.9	0.7%	590
12/19	2,273.8	23.7	1.0%	355
12/18	2,094.8	14.0	0.7%	333
12/17	1,321.2	4.8	0.4%	219
12/16	1,105.8	5.1	0.5%	208
Annual Growth	39.3%	55.6%	—	29.8%

2020 Year-End Financials

Return on assets: 0.9%
Return on equity: 8.6%
Long-term debt ($ mil.): —
No. of shares ($ mil.): 20.6
Sales ($ mil.): 171.3
Dividends
　Yield: 1.9%
　Payout: 30.0%
Market value ($ mil.): 420.0

	STOCK PRICE ($) FY Close	P/E High/Low		PER SHARE ($) Earnings	Dividends	Book Value
12/20	20.36	16	6	1.64	0.40	19.88
12/19	24.93	14	13	1.74	0.38	21.47
12/18	24.23	23	17	1.22	0.24	19.68
Annual Growth	(8.3%)	—	—	15.9%	29.1%	0.5%

BV Financial Inc

EXECUTIVES

Chairman, Chief Financial Officer, Subsidiary Officer, Edmund T. Leonard, $149,000 total compensation

President, Chief Executive Officer, Subsidiary Officer, Director, Carolyn M. Mroz, $149,000 total compensation

Senior Vice President, Security Officer, Subsidiary Officer, Director, Daniel J. Gallagher, $115,000 total compensation

Subsidiary Officer, Michele J. Kelly

Subsidiary Officer, Jeffrey S. Collier

Director, Jerry S. Sopher

Director, Brian K. McHale, $6,400 total compensation

Director, Anthony J. Narutowicz

Director, Michael J. Birmingham, $7,900 total compensation

Director, Catherine M. Staszak

Director, Robert R. Kern

Director, Frank W. Dingle

LOCATIONS

HQ: BV Financial Inc
7114 North Point Road, Edgemere, MD 21219
Phone: 410 477-5000　**Fax:** 410 477-3869
Web: www.bayvanguard.com

HISTORICAL FINANCIALS
Company Type: Public

Income Statement　　　　　　　　　　　　FYE: December 31

	ASSETS ($mil)	NET INCOME ($mil)	INCOME AS % OF ASSETS	EMPLOYEES
12/21	815.1	9.4	1.2%	0
12/20	815.5	7.6	0.9%	0
12/19*	294.1	2.4	0.8%	0
06/09	154.5	(2.7)	—	36
06/08	164.0	(0.3)	—	35
Annual Growth	12.1%	—	—	—

*Fiscal year change

2021 Year-End Financials

Return on assets: 1.1%
Return on equity: 11.9%
Long-term debt ($ mil.): —
No. of shares ($ mil.): 7.1
Sales ($ mil.): 31.7
Dividends
　Yield: —
　Payout: —
Market value ($ mil.): 143.0

	STOCK PRICE ($) FY Close	P/E High/Low		PER SHARE ($) Earnings	Dividends	Book Value
12/21	20.10	16	12	1.32	0.00	11.69
12/20	17.00	18	10	1.07	0.00	10.43
12/19*	17.25	50	36	0.38	0.00	9.29
06/09	3.60	—	—	(1.17)	0.20	5.67
06/08	5.50	—	—	(0.14)	0.20	6.86
Annual Growth	9.7%	—	—	—	—	3.9%

*Fiscal year change

BWX Technologies inc

BWX Technologies is a specialty manufacturer of nuclear components, a developer of nuclear technologies and a service provider with an operating history of more than 100 years. Its core businesses focus on the design, engineering and manufacture of precision naval nuclear components, reactors and nuclear fuel for the US government. It also provides precision manufactured components, nuclear fuel and services to the commercial nuclear industry and provides special nuclear materials processing, environmental site restoration services, and a variety of products and services to customers in the critical medical radioisotopes and radiopharmaceuticals industries. US government agencies are its largest customers. Additionally, the US is responsible for around 85% of the sales. The company was founded in 1867.

Operations

BWX operates in three reportable segments: Nuclear Operations Group (accounts for some 75%), Nuclear Power Group (about 20%) and Nuclear Services Group (around 5%).

Nuclear Operations Group segment specializes in the design and manufacture of close-tolerance and high-quality equipment for nuclear applications.

The Nuclear Power Group designs and manufactures commercial nuclear steam generators, heat exchangers, pressure vessels, reactor components and other auxiliary equipment, including containers for the storage of spent nuclear fuel and other high-level nuclear waste. BWX has supplied the nuclear industry with more than 1,300 large, heavy components worldwide.

Nuclear Services Group provides special nuclear materials processing, environmental site restoration services and management and operating services.

Among its product and service lines are government programs (around 70% of sales), and nuclear manufacturing (approximately 10%), and nuclear services and engineering (about 10%).

Geographic Reach

Headquartered in Virginia, BWX owns and operates manufacturing plants in Lynchburg, Virginia; Mount Vernon, Indiana; Euclid, Ohio; Barberton, Ohio; and Erwin, Tennessee. In addition, the company has plants in Canada.

The US accounts for roughly 85% of BWX's revenues while Canada generates some 15%.

Sales and Marketing

The company provides its products and services to a diverse customer base, including the US Government, utilities and other customers in the nuclear power and radiopharmaceutical industries. The US government is BWX's largest customer, accounting for around 75% of net sales. Additionally, it serves the US Department of Energy (DOE)/National Nuclear Security Administration's (NNSA) Naval Nuclear Propulsion Program and perform development and fabrication activities for missile launch tubes for US Navy submarines.

Financial Performance

Consolidated revenues increased slightly to $2.124 billion in the year ended December 31, 2021 compared to $2.123 billion in 2020, due to an increase in its Nuclear Power Group segment revenues of $35.8 million, which was partially offset by decreases in revenues in its Nuclear Operations Group and Nuclear Services Group segments of $23.7 million and $13.0 million, respectively.

Net income for fiscal 2021 increased to $306.3 million compared from the prior year with $279.2 million.

Cash held by the company at the end of fiscal 2021 decreased to $39.8 million. Cash provided by operations was $386.0 million while cash used for investing and financing activities were $304.7 million and $90.1 million, respectively. Main uses of cash were for purchases of property, plant and equipment; and repayments of long-term debt.

Strategy

BWX are currently exploring growth strategies across its segments through strategic investments and acquisitions to expand and complement its existing businesses. The company would expect to fund these opportunities with cash generated from operations or by raising additional capital through debt, equity or some combination thereof.

HISTORY

Stephen Wilcox patented the water tube boiler in 1856, and two year later Wilcox and George Babcock established Babcock, Wilcox & Company. At the turn of the century, B&W boilers powered New York's first subway and President Roosevelt's Great White Fleet. In the mid-1940s the company provided components and materials for the Manhattan Project and designed components for the world's first nuclear powered submarine, the USS Nautilus , a decade later.

Babcock & Wilcox became a subsidiary of engineering and construction giant McDermott International in 1978. As a result of mounting asbestos liability costs, B&W filed for bankruptcy in 2000. McDermott deconsolidated B&W's operations from its own financial statements at that time. Emergence from Chapter 11 in early 2006 returned B&W to full reporting status.

To further its ambitions in government operations, in 2007 the company bought Marine Mechanical Corporation for $71.5 million. MMC manufactures and supplies electro-mechanical equipment for the US Navy. The next year it acquired three companies, first paying $20 million for the Intech group of companies (Intech, Inc., Ivey-Cooper Services, L.L.C. and Intech International Inc.), a provider of nuclear inspection and maintenance services in the US and Canada. Delta Power Services, LLC, which serves the US power generation industry, complements the company's fossil fuel and biomass markets and will help it to expand into the natural gas-fired power generation market. Delta Power was bought for $13.5 million. Specialty nuclear fuels and service provider Nuclear Fuel Services, bought for $157 million, brought experience in converting highly-enriched uranium into fuel for commercial nuclear reactors. Its fuel production facility is where the US military's submarines and aircraft carriers get their nuclear fill-up.

The company made two acquisitions in late 2009 and early 2010 to boost its international presence. First it bought Instrumentacion y Mantenimiento de Calderas, S.A., a boiler manufacturer in Mexico. A few months later it purchased GÃ¶taverken MiljÃ¶, a Swedish company specializing in flue gas cleaning and energy recovery, giving the company an entrÃ©e to the international energy market. The acquisition was made a part of B&W's Volund unit, which creates thermal energy through byproducts such as household waste and biofuels.

EXECUTIVES

President, Chief Executive Officer, Director, Rex D. Geveden, $850,000 total compensation
Human Resources Senior Vice President, Human Resources Chief Administrative Officer, Richard W. Loving
Senior Vice President, Chief Financial Officer, Robb A. LeMasters
Senior Vice President, General Counsel, Chief Compliance Officer, Secretary, Thomas E. McCabe, $231,510 total compensation
Vice President, Chief Accounting Officer, Jason S. Kerr
Lead Independent Director, Director, Kenneth J. Krieg
Director, Jan A. Bertsch
Director, Gerhard F. Burbach
Director, James M. Jaska
Director, Leland D. Melvin
Director, Robert L. Nardelli
Director, Barbara A. Niland
Director, John M. Richardson
Auditors : DELOITTE & TOUCHE LLP

LOCATIONS

HQ: BWX Technologies inc
800 Main Street, 4th Floor, Lynchburg, VA 24504
Phone: 980 365-4300

2016 Sales

	$ mil.	% of total
US	1,397.5	90
Canada	125	8
China	13	1
Romania	10.7	1
Argentina	1.5	-
All Other countries	2.8	-
Total	1,550.5	100

PRODUCTS/OPERATIONS

2016 Sales

	$ in mil.	% of total
Nuclear Operations	1,269.2	82
Technical Services	97.2	6
Nuclear Energy	189.1	12
Adjustments and Eliminations	(5)	-
Total	1,550.5	100

COMPETITORS

ALLIED MOTION TECHNOLOGIES INC.
Chicago Bridge & Iron Company N.V.
ENERGYSOLUTIONS, INC.
FRANKLIN ELECTRIC CO., INC.
GENERAC HOLDINGS INC.
LENNOX INTERNATIONAL INC.
MATRIX SERVICE COMPANY
NIDEC CORPORATION
Nordex SE
REGAL BELOIT CORPORATION

HISTORICAL FINANCIALS

Company Type: Public

Income Statement				FYE: December 31
	REVENUE ($mil)	NET INCOME ($mil)	NET PROFIT MARGIN	EMPLOYEES
12/20	2,123.5	278.6	13.1%	6,700
12/19	1,894.9	244.1	12.9%	6,450
12/18	1,799.8	226.9	12.6%	6,250
12/17	1,687.7	147.8	8.8%	6,100
12/16	1,550.5	183.0	11.8%	5,900
Annual Growth	8.2%	11.1%	—	3.2%

2020 Year-End Financials

Debt ratio: 37.6%
Return on equity: 54.3%
Cash ($ mil.): 42.6
Current Ratio: 1.46
Long-term debt ($ mil.): 862.7
No. of shares ($ mil.): 95.3
Dividends
 Yield: 1.2%
 Payout: 26.5%
Market value ($ mil.): 5,745.0

	STOCK PRICE ($) FY Close	P/E High/Low		PER SHARE ($) Earnings	Dividends	Book Value
12/20	60.28	24	14	2.91	0.76	6.48
12/19	62.08	25	15	2.55	0.68	4.24
12/18	38.23	31	16	2.27	0.64	2.47
12/17	60.49	42	26	1.47	0.42	2.87
12/16	39.70	23	15	1.76	0.36	1.51
Annual Growth	11.0%	—	—	13.4%	20.5%	43.9%

Byline Bancorp Inc

EXECUTIVES

Executive Chairman, Chief Executive Officer, Subsidiary Officer, Roberto R. Herencia
President, Subsidiary Officer, Director, Alberto J. Paracchini, $491,667 total compensation
Executive Vice President, General Counsel, Subsidiary Officer, Donald J. Gibson
Executive Vice President, Chief Financial Officer, Subsidiary Officer, Lindsay Y. Corby, $301,667 total compensation
Chief Credit Officer, Subsidiary Officer, Mark Fucinato
Subsidiary Officer, John M. Barkidjija
Subsidiary Officer, Thomas J. Bell
Subsidiary Officer, Megan Biggam
Subsidiary Officer, Michelle Lynn Johnson
Subsidiary Officer, Brogan M. Ptacin
Division Officer, Thomas Abraham
Director, Phillip R. Cabrera
Director, Antonio del Valle Perochena
Director, Mary Jo S. Herseth
Director, Steven P. Kent
Director, William G. Kistner
Director, Steven M. Rull
Director, Robert R. Yohanan
Auditors : Moss Adams LLP

LOCATIONS

HQ: Byline Bancorp Inc
180 North LaSalle Street, Suite 300, Chicago, IL 60601
Phone: 773 244-7000
Web: www.bylinebancorp.com

HISTORICAL FINANCIALS
Company Type: Public

Income Statement				FYE: December 31
	ASSETS ($mil)	NET INCOME ($mil)	INCOME AS % OF ASSETS	EMPLOYEES
12/20	6,390.6	37.4	0.6%	931
12/19	5,521.8	57.0	1.0%	1,001
12/18	4,942.5	41.1	0.8%	943
12/17	3,366.1	21.6	0.6%	844
12/16	3,295.8	66.7	2.0%	791
Annual Growth	18.0%	(13.4%)	—	4.2%

2020 Year-End Financials

Return on assets: 0.6%
Return on equity: 4.8%
Long-term debt ($ mil.): —
No. of shares ($ mil.): 38.6
Sales ($ mil.): 301.2
Dividends
 Yield: 0.7%
 Payout: 11.3%
Market value ($ mil.): 597.0

	STOCK PRICE ($) FY Close	P/E High/Low		PER SHARE ($) Earnings	Dividends	Book Value
12/20	15.45	21	9	0.96	0.12	20.86
12/19	19.57	14	11	1.48	0.03	19.61
12/18	16.66	20	13	1.18	0.00	17.90
12/17	22.97	59	50	0.38	0.00	15.64
Annual Growth	(12.4%)	—	—	36.2%	—	10.1%

Cable One Inc

Sparklight (formerly Cable ONE) gives small-town folk CNN and The Cartoon Network. The company provides cable television service primarily to non-metropolitan, secondary, and tertiary markets. Its core service areas are the Gulf Coast region and Boise, Idaho. Approximately 1.1 million subscribers receive data services, some 261,000 subscribers to video services, and around 149,000 subscribers to voice services. The company also offers voice-over-Internet-protocol (VoIP) computer telephony and digital video services. Quarter-fifth of revenue comes from Residential. In 2019, the company rebrand its business as Sparklight.

Operations

Sparklight has its four primary product lines: Residential data, Residential video, Residential voice, and Business services. Residential data services represent over 50% of the company's total revenues. It offers simplified data plans with lower pricing and higher speeds across its premium tiers. The product line also offers its customers the option to purchase an unlimited data plan and advanced Wi-Fi service.

Residential video services offer a broad variety of residential video services including: basic video service that consists of governmental and public access network and weather, shopping and religious channels; and digital video service includes music channels and an interactive, electronic programming guide with parental controls. It also offers premium channels such as HBO, Showtime, Starz and Cinemax. The product line generates nearly 20% of revenue.

Business services (produce around 20% of revenue) offer services for businesses ranging in size from small to mid-market, in addition to enterprise, wholesale, and carrier customers. The offer for its small businesses are generally provided over the company's coaxial network. It offers delivery of data and voice services over EPON technology primarily for mid-market customers with Piranha Fiber. Furthermore, it also offers dedicated bandwidth and Enterprise Wi-Fi in addition to multiple voice services via fiber optic technology for its enterprise and wholesale customers.

Residential voice services account for less than 5% of revenue. The majority of its residential voice service offerings transmit digital voice signals over its network and are interconnected Voice over Internet Protocol ("VoIP") services. Sparklight also offer traditional telecommunications services through some of its subsidiaries.

Geographic Reach

Sparklight has operations in about 25 states throughout the midwestern, southern, and western US.

The company's headquarters is located in Phoenix, Arizona. It has customers in Arizona, Idaho, Mississippi, Missouri, Oklahoma, South Carolina, and Texas.

Sales and Marketing

Sparklight has about 75% of its customers located in seven states. In addition, its biggest customer concentrations are in the Mississippi Gulf Coast region and in the greater Boise, Idaho region.

The total amount of such advertising expense recorded was $40.1 million, $31.6 million, and $34.3 million in 2021, 2020, and 2019, respectively.

Financial Performance

The company's revenue for fiscal 2021 increased by 21% to $1.6 billion compared from the prior year with $1.3 billion.

Net income for fiscal 2021 decreased to $291.8 million compared from the prior year with $304.4 million.

Cash held by the company at the end of fiscal 2021 decreased to $388.8 million. Cash provided by operations and financing activities were $704.3 million and $1.6 billion, respectively. Cash used for investing activities was $2.5 million, mainly for purchase of businesses, net of cash acquired.

Strategy

The company have made significant investments in its business consistent with its strategic focus to enhance sales of residential data services and business services. Since completing significant, multi-year plant and product enhancements in existing Cable One markets in 2017, Sparklight have continued to make ongoing investments in its acquired systems, which has increased its broadband capacity and reliability. The company have invested nearly $950 million over the last three years to bring fast, reliable high-speed data service to its markets. Sparklight expect to continue to invest in strategic capital projects, including around newly acquired operations and market expansions

Company Background

In 1986, The Washington Post Company (former corporate parent, Graham Holdings Company) acquired 53 cable television systems with approximately 350,000 subscribers in 15 Western, Midwestern and Southern states. Since then, the company completed over 30 acquisitions and dispositions of cable systems, both through cash sales and system trades. In the process, they substantially reshaped their original geographic footprint and resized their typical system, including exiting a number of metropolitan markets and acquiring cable systems in non-metropolitan markets that fit their business model. In mid-2015, they became an independent company traded under the ticker symbol "CABO" on the New York Stock Exchange after completion of its spin-off from GHC.

EXECUTIVES

Senior Vice President, James A. Obermeyer
Chairman, President, Chief Executive Officer, Director, Julia M. Laulis, $575,000 total compensation
Senior Vice President, Eric Michael Lardy, $220,000 total compensation
Senior Vice President, Chief Network Officer, Stephen A. Fox, $299,000 total compensation
Senior Vice President, Chief Financial Officer, Steven S. Cochran, $131,781 total compensation
Senior Vice President, General Counsel, Secretary, Peter N. Witty, $236,466 total compensation
Chief Operating Officer, Michael E. Bowker, $360,000 total compensation
Division Officer, Charles B. McDonald, $210,000 total compensation
Lead Independent Director, Thomas S. Gayner
Director, Brad D. Brian
Director, Deborah J. Kissire
Director, Mary E. Meduski
Director, Thomas O. Might, $450,000 total compensation
Director, Kristine E. Miller
Director, Sherrese M. Smith
Director, Wallace R. Weitz
Director, Katharine B. Weymouth
Auditors : PricewaterhouseCoopers LLP

LOCATIONS

HQ: Cable One Inc
210 E. Earll Drive, Phoenix, AZ 85012
Phone: 602 364-6000
Web: www.cableone.net

Locations
Alabama
Arizona
Arkansas
Idaho
Iowa
Kansas
Louisiana
Minnesota
Mississippi
Missouri
Nebraska
New Mexico
North Dakota
Oklahoma
Oregon
South Dakota
Tennessee
Texas
Washington

PRODUCTS/OPERATIONS

2014 Sales

	$ mil.	% of total
Video	361.0	44
Data	265.7	33
Business Sales	72.7	9
Voice	62.4	8
Advertising sales	35.4	4
Others	17.6	2
Total	814.8	100

COMPETITORS

CHARTER COMMUNICATIONS, INC.
Cogeco Communications Inc
DISH NETWORK CORPORATION
FAIRPOINT COMMUNICATIONS LLC
FORMER CHARTER COMMUNICATIONS PARENT, INC.
GRIZZLY MERGER SUB 1, LLC
TIVO SOLUTIONS INC.
Telesat Canada
VIRGIN MEDIA INC.
WIDEOPENWEST, INC.

HISTORICAL FINANCIALS

Company Type: Public

Income Statement — FYE: December 31

	REVENUE ($mil)	NET INCOME ($mil)	NET PROFIT MARGIN	EMPLOYEES
12/20	1,325.2	304.3	23.0%	2,716
12/19	1,167.9	178.5	15.3%	2,751
12/18	1,072.2	164.7	15.4%	2,224
12/17	960.0	234.0	24.4%	2,310
12/16	819.6	98.9	12.1%	1,877
Annual Growth	12.8%	32.4%	—	9.7%

2020 Year-End Financials

Debt ratio: 48.5%
Return on equity: 25.9%
Cash ($ mil.): 574.9
Current Ratio: 3.04
Long-term debt ($ mil.): 2,148.7
No. of shares ($ mil.): 6.0
Dividends
  Yield: 0.4%
  Payout: 22.1%
Market value ($ mil.): 13,428.0

	STOCK PRICE ($) FY Close	P/E High/Low		PER SHARE ($) Earnings	Dividends	Book Value
12/20	2,227.72	44	22	51.27	9.50	248.07
12/19	1,488.47	49	26	31.12	8.50	147.25
12/18	820.10	32	21	28.77	7.50	135.95
12/17	703.35	19	14	40.72	6.50	117.15
12/16	621.73	36	23	17.14	6.00	79.62
Annual Growth	37.6%	—	—	31.5%	12.2%	32.9%

Cactus Inc

EXECUTIVES

Chairman, Director, Bruce Rothstein
President, Chief Executive Officer, Director, Scott Bender, $300,000 total compensation
Senior Vice President, Chief Operating Officer, Director, Joel Bender, $300,000 total compensation
Administration Vice President, Administration General Counsel, Administration Secretary, William Marsh
Operations Vice President, Steven Bender, $222,793 total compensation
Corporate Services Vice President, Corporate Services Chief Financial Officer, Corporate Services Treasurer, Stephen Tadlock, $250,000 total compensation
Director, Melissa Law
Director, Michael Y. McGovern
Director, John Andy O'Donnell
Director, Gary L. Rosenthal
Director, Alan G. Semple
Director, Tymothi O. Tombar
Auditors : PricewaterhouseCoopers LLP

LOCATIONS

HQ: Cactus Inc
920 Memorial City Way, Suite 300, Houston, TX 77024
Phone: 713 626-8800
Web: www.cactuswhd.com

HISTORICAL FINANCIALS

Company Type: Public

Income Statement — FYE: December 31

	REVENUE ($mil)	NET INCOME ($mil)	NET PROFIT MARGIN	EMPLOYEES
12/20	348.5	34.4	9.9%	660
12/19	628.4	85.6	13.6%	1,100
12/18	544.1	51.6	9.5%	1,200
12/17	341.1	66.5	19.5%	880
12/16	155.0	(8.1)	—	880
Annual Growth	22.4%	—	—	(6.9%)

2020 Year-End Financials

Debt ratio: 0.7%
Return on equity: 10.0%
Cash ($ mil.): 288.6
Current Ratio: 8.69
Long-term debt ($ mil.): 2.2
No. of shares ($ mil.): 75.3
Dividends
  Yield: 1.3%
  Payout: 35.2%
Market value ($ mil.): 1,965.0

	STOCK PRICE ($) FY Close	P/E High/Low		PER SHARE ($) Earnings	Dividends	Book Value
12/20	26.07	48	12	0.72	0.36	4.68
12/19	34.32	21	13	1.88	0.09	4.36
12/18	27.41	25	13	1.58	0.00	2.37
Annual Growth	(2.5%)	—	—	(32.5%)	—	40.5%

Cadence Bank

Like Elvis Presley, BancorpSouth has grown beyond its Tupelo roots. It's the holding company for BancorpSouth Bank, which operates some 290 branches in nine southern and midwestern states. Catering to consumers and small and midsized businesses, the bank offers checking and savings accounts, loans, credit cards, and commercial banking services. BancorpSouth also sells insurance and provides brokerage, investment advisory, and asset management services throughout most of its market area. Real estate loans, including consumer and commercial mortgages and home equity, construction, and agricultural loans, comprise approximately three-quarters of its loan portfolio. BancorpSouth has assets of $13 billion.

Geographic Reach
Mississippi-based BancorpSouth Bank operates in Alabama, Arkansas, Florida, Illinois, Louisiana, Mississippi, Missouri, Tennessee, and Texas. BancorpSouth's insurance and financial advisory businesses also operate in Illinois and Florida, respectively.

Financial Performance
BancorpSouth reported net income of $94.1 million in 2013, an increase of 12% versus 2012. The decreased provision for credit losses was the primary factor contributing to the rise. Net interest revenue -- the bank's primary source of revenue -- fell 4% year over year to $$398.9 million, the fourth consecutive year of decline. Net interest revenue declined because the decrease in interest expense was more than offset by the decrease in interest revenue as the yield on earning assets declined by a greater amount than that of interest-bearing liabilities. Noninterest income also declined on lower mortgage origination revenue in 2013 versus 2012.

Strategy
The regional bank has grown via the acquisition of other banks and insurance agencies and by opening new branches, most recently in Texas and Louisiana. To reduce its reliance on interest-related revenue, BancorpSouth hopes to diversify its revenue stream by increasing the amount it generates from mortgage lending, insurance, brokerage, and securities activities. To this end, subsidiary BancorpSouth Insurance Services has acquired small insurance agencies in Arkansas, Missouri, and Texas.

Mergers and Acquisitions
In 2014 BancorpSouth agreed to acquire Central Community Corp., the holding company for First State Bank Central Texas, headquartered in Austin, Texas. First State Bank operates 31 branches in Austin, Round Rock, Killeen, and several other Central Texas communities. BancorpSouth has also agreed to purchase Ouachita Bancshares Corp. with a dozen branches in Louisiana. Both deals were announced in January 2014 and were expected to close promptly. However, they've been delayed because BancorpSouth needs more time to get regulatory approvals and to meet "closing conditions necessary to complete" the mergers.

EXECUTIVES

Chairman, Chief Executive Officer, Subsidiary Officer, Director, James D. Rollins, $840,000 total compensation
President, Chief Operating Officer, Subsidiary Officer, Christopher A. Bagley, $495,000 total compensation
Senior Executive Vice President, Chief Financial Officer, Treasurer, John G. Copeland
Senior Executive Vice President, Chief Information Officer, Jeffrey W. Jaggers
Community Lending Senior Executive Vice President, Community Lending Chief Banking Officer, Community Lending Director, Michael J. Meyer
Senior Executive Vice President, General Counsel, Charles J. Pignuolo
Senior Executive Vice President, Chief Administrative Officer, Secretary, Subsidiary Officer, Cathy S. Freeman
First Vice President, Division Officer, Charlotte Pratt
Senior Vice President, Division Officer, Robert Harris
Chief Risk Officer, Ty Lambert
Director, Gus J. Blass
Director, Shannon A. Brown
Director, James E. Campbell
Director, Deborah M. Cannon
Director, Donald R. Growbowsky
Director, Warren A. Hood
Director, Keith J. Jackson
Director, Larry G. Kirk
Director, Guy W. Mitchell
Director, Alan W. Perry
Director, Thomas R. Stanton
Director, William G. "Skipper" Holliman
Auditors : BKD, LLP

LOCATIONS
HQ: Cadence Bank
One Mississippi Plaza, 201 South Spring Street, Tupelo, MS 38804
Phone: 662 680-2000
Web: www.bancorpsouth.com

PRODUCTS/OPERATIONS
2016 Sales

	$ mil.	% of total
Interest		
Loans & leases	440.7	58
Securities	41.5	5
Deposits with other banks	1.1	-
Noninterest		
Insurance commissions	115.9	15
Deposit service charges	43.4	6
Mortgage lending	41.8	5
Credit card, debit card and merchant fees	37.0	5
Wealth management	21.1	3
Other	19.7	3
Total	762.2	100

Selected Subsidiaries
BancorpSouth Bank
    BancorpSouth Insurance Services, Inc.
    BancorpSouth Investment Services, Inc.
    BancorpSouth Municipal Development Corporation
    Century Credit Life Insurance Company
    Personal Finance Corporation

COMPETITORS
EAGLE BANCORP, INC.
FIRST CITIZENS BANCSHARES, INC.
FIRST COMMUNITY BANCSHARES, INC.
S&T BANCORP, INC.
WASHINGTON FEDERAL, INC.

HISTORICAL FINANCIALS
Company Type: Public

Income Statement — FYE: December 31

	ASSETS ($mil)	NET INCOME ($mil)	INCOME AS % OF ASSETS	EMPLOYEES
12/20	24,081.1	228.0	0.9%	4,596
12/19	21,052.5	234.2	1.1%	4,693
12/18	18,001.5	221.3	1.2%	4,445
12/17	15,298.5	153.0	1.0%	3,947
12/16	14,724.3	132.7	0.9%	3,998
Annual Growth	13.1%	14.5%	—	3.5%

2020 Year-End Financials
Return on assets: 1.0%
Return on equity: 8.2%
Long-term debt ($ mil.): —
No. of shares ($ mil.): 102.5
Sales ($ mil.): 1,135.9
Dividends
Yield: 2.7%
Payout: 35.1%
Market value ($ mil.): 2,814.0

	STOCK PRICE ($) FY Close	P/E High/Low		PER SHARE ($) Earnings	Dividends	Book Value
12/20	27.44	15	8	2.12	0.75	27.52
12/19	31.41	14	11	2.30	0.71	25.69
12/18	26.14	16	11	2.23	0.62	22.10
12/17	31.45	20	16	1.67	0.14	18.97
12/16	31.05	22	13	1.41	0.45	18.40
Annual Growth	(3.0%)	—	—	10.7%	13.4%	10.6%

Cadence Design Systems Inc

Cadence Design Systems is a leader in electronic design, building upon more than 30 years of computational software expertise. Customers use Cadence products to design integrated circuits (ICs), printed circuit boards (PCBs), smartphones, laptop computers, gaming systems, and more. The company offer software, hardware, services and reusable IC design blocks, which are commonly referred to as intellectual property (IP). The company also provides maintenance and support, and design and methodology consulting services. International customers account for nearly 60% of the company's sales.

Operations
Cadence Design Systems has five product areas, each making a robust contribution to total revenue.

Digital IC Design and Signoff delivers some 30% of the company's revenue. Digital IC design and Signoff offerings are used to create logical representations of a digital circuit or an IC that can be verified for correctness prior to implementation.

Its logic design offering is comprised of logic synthesis, test and equivalence checking capabilities. Functional verification products are used by customers to verify that the circuitry or the software they have designed will perform as intended.

Verification takes place during and after custom and analog design, and before manufacturing the circuitry, significantly reducing the risk of discovering a costly error in the completed product. Its Verification Suite includes four primary verification engines, starting with the JasperGold, Formal Verification Platform, and Xcelium. This segment generates about 25% of the company's revenue.

Custom IC design and simulation offerings are used by customers to create schematic and physical representations of circuits down to the transistor level for analog, mixed-signal, custom digital, memory and RF designs. These representations are verified using simulation tools optimized for each type of design, including the design capture environment, simulation and IC layout within the Virtuoso custom design platform. This segment accounts for some 25% of the company's sales.

Other segment includes System design and analysis (10% of the company's sales) and IP (about 15% of the company's sales).

The company's emulation and prototyping hardware, including all individual PCBs, custom ICs and Field-Programmable Gate Array (FPGA)-based prototyping components, is manufactured, assembled and tested by subcontractors before delivery to its customers.

Geographic Reach

With its main headquarters in California, Cadence Design Systems has placed regional headquarters near customers in China, India, UK, and Japan.

The US is Cadence's largest single market, accounting for more than 40% of sales. Customers in Asia (including Japan and China) account more than 30% of sales, and European customers, including Middle East and Africa account for about 20%.

Sales and Marketing

Cadence market its products and provide services to existing and prospective customers through a direct sales force consisting of sales people and applications engineers. The company also promote products and services through advertising, marketing automation, trade shows, public relations and the internet. Internationally, the company market its products and services through subsidiaries as well as third-party distributor to license their products and services to certain customers in Japan.

The company's advertising expenses were $7.5 million, $7.1 million, and $8.4 million in 2021, 2020, and 2019 and, respectively.

Financial Performance

Cadence Design Systems' revenue has been rising consistently year-over-year with 2021 as its highest performing year over the period.

In 2021, Cadence's revenue grew by $306 million to $2.9 billion compared to $2.6 billion in the prior year. The increase was due to revenue growth that exceeded the growth of its costs and expenses; increased product and maintenance revenue, primarily from growth in its software and hardware product offerings; continued investment in research and development activities focused on expanding and enhancing its product portfolio; and higher selling costs, including additional investment in technical sales support in response to its customers' increasing technological requirements.

Net income also increased by $105.3 million to $695.9 million as compared to the prior year's net income of $590,6 million.

Cash and cash equivalents totaled $1 billion at the end of 2021. Operating activities generated $1.1 billion. Investing activities and financing activities used $292.9 million and $643.8 million, respectively. Main cash uses were for cash paid in business combinations and asset acquisitions and payments for repurchases of common stock.

Strategy

Cadence's strategy, which it calls Intelligent System Design, provides the technologies necessary for customers to develop and optimize a complete and functional electronic product. The company addresses the challenges posed by the needs and trends of electronic systems companies as well as semiconductor companies delivering greater portions of these systems. The development of electronic products, or their sub-components, is complex and requires many engineers using its solutions with specialized knowledge and skill.

The second layer of Cadence's strategy centers on system innovation. It includes tools and services used for system design of the packages that encapsulate the ICs and the PCBs, system simulation which includes electromagnetic, electro-thermal and other multi-physics analysis necessary as part of optimizing the full system's performance, Radio Frequency ("RF") and microwave systems, and embedded software.

The third layer of the company's strategy is enabling pervasive intelligence in new electronics. It starts with providing solutions and services to develop AI-enhanced systems and includes machine learning and deep learning capabilities being added to the Cadence technology portfolio to make IP and tools more automated and to produce optimized results faster, supported by cloud access to address the growing computation needs of customers.

Mergers and Acquisitions

In 2021, Cadence acquired all of the outstanding equity of Pointwise, Inc. (Pointwise), a leader in mesh generation for CFD for cash consideration of approximately $31.4 million, net of cash acquired. The addition of Pointwise's technologies and experienced team supports Cadence's Intelligent System Design strategy and further broadens its System Design and Analysis portfolio, complementing its acquisition of NUMECA.

In early 2021, Cadence acquired all of the outstanding equity of Belgium-based Numerical Mechanics Applications International SA (NUMECA). The addition of NUMECA's technologies and talent supports Cadence's Intelligent System Design strategy, servicing the computational fluid dynamics (CFD) market segment as part of System Design and Analysis. The aggregate cash consideration for Cadence's acquisition of NUMECA, net of cash acquired of $9.6 million, was $188.6 million. .

Company Background

Cadence Design Systems arose from the 1988 merger of software firms ECAD (formed in 1982) and SDA Systems (founded 1983). The stock market crash of 1987 helped propel SDA Systems, an EDA company that gave up its planned IPO in the wake of the crash, into its merger with ECAD, which was publicly held, to form Cadence Design. Private venture capital investor and SDA chairman Donald Lucas became chairman of Cadence. Joe Costello, the young, charismatic, and tall (6-foot-7) president and COO of SDA, was named president and CEO of Cadence. It became the world's leading electronic design automation (EDA) software supplier by enlarging and improving the range of software it developed in-house and via such acquisitions as Tangent Systems (1989) and Valid Logic Systems (1991).

The company grew through a series of acquisitions. Cadence concluded long-running litigation with Avant! (after Avant! was acquired by Synopsys) with a $265 million payment to Cadence.

HISTORY

Cadence Design Systems arose from the 1988 merger of software firms ECAD (formed in 1982) and SDA Systems (founded 1983). The stock market crash of 1987 helped propel SDA Systems, an EDA company that gave up its planned IPO in the wake of the crash, into its merger with ECAD, which was publicly held, to form Cadence Design. Private venture capital investor and SDA chairman Donald Lucas became chairman of Cadence. Joe Costello, the young, charismatic, and tall (6-foot-7) president and COO of SDA, was named president and CEO of Cadence. It became the world's leading electronic design automation (EDA) software supplier by enlarging and improving the range of software it developed in-house and via such acquisitions as Tangent Systems (1989) and Valid Logic Systems (1991).

The company grew through a series of acquisitions. Cadence concluded long-running litigation with Avant! (after Avant! was acquired by Synopsys) with a $265 million payment to Cadence.

EXECUTIVES

Chairman, Lead Independent Director, Director, John B. Shoven
Development President, Research President, Development Chief Executive Officer, Research Chief Executive Officer, Director, Anirudh Devgan, $500,000 total compensation
Research & Development Senior Vice President, Chin-Chi Teng
Finance Senior Vice President, Operations Senior Vice President, Finance Chief Financial Officer, Operations Chief Financial Officer, John M. Wall, $375,000 total compensation
Senior Vice President, Chief Revenue Officer, Division Officer, Neil Zaman, $400,000 total compensation
Senior Vice President, Chief Legal Officer, Corporate Secretary, Alinka Flaminia
Development Division Officer, Research Division Officer, Thomas P. Beckley, $375,000 total compensation
Director, Mark W. Adams
Director, Ita M. Brennan
Director, Lewis Chew
Director, Julia Liuson
Director, Mary Louise Krakauer
Director, James D. Plummer
Director, Alberto Sangiovanni-Vincentelli
Director, Young K. Sohn
Auditors : PricewaterhouseCoopers LLP

LOCATIONS

HQ: Cadence Design Systems Inc
2655 Seely Avenue, Building 5, San Jose, CA 95134
Phone: 408 943-1234
Web: www.cadence.com

Selected Acquisitions
FY 2010
Denali Software (software, $315 million)
FY 2011
Altos Design Automation (software)
Azuro (software)
FY 2012
Sigrity
FY 2013
Cosmic Circuits
Tensilica

2017 Sales

	% of total
US	42
Other Americas	2
Asia	27
EMEA	20
Japan	9
Total	100

PRODUCTS/OPERATIONS

Selected Software
Analog simulators (Spectre)
Cycle-based simulators (SpeedSim)
Deep submicron design (Envisia)
Digital IC design (Encounter platform, including First Encounter, SoC Encounter, and Nano Encounter)
Digital simulators (NC-simulator, NC-Verilog, NC-VHDL)
Editing and synthesis, compaction, device-level editing (Virtuoso family)
Equivalence checking (Affirma)
Hardware emulators (CoBALT, Mercury)
Model checking (Affirma Formalcheck)
Place and routing (Envisia Silicon Ensemble)
Printed circuit board design and packaging (Allegro, SPECCTRA)
Synthesis (Envisia Ambit, BuildGates)
Verification (Assura line, including Diva and Dracula; Incisive platform; Palladium)

Selected Services
Education
IC design services (Cadence Design Foundry)
IC implementation
Intellectual property (IP Gallery)
Methodology
Wireless design

2017 Sales

	% of total
Functional verification & design IP	22
Digital IC design and Signoff	29
Custom IC design	27
System interconnect and Analysis	10
IP	12
Total	100

2017 Sales

	$ mil.	% of total
Product and Maintenance	1,814	93
Services	129	7
Total	1,943	100

COMPETITORS

EXAR CORPORATION
FALCONSTOR SOFTWARE, INC.
MENTOR GRAPHICS CORPORATION
NATIONAL INSTRUMENTS CORPORATION
NUANCE COMMUNICATIONS, INC.
PHOENIX TECHNOLOGIES LTD.
PROGRESS SOFTWARE CORPORATION
RADISYS CORPORATION
SYNOPSYS, INC.
WIND RIVER SYSTEMS, INC.

HISTORICAL FINANCIALS

Company Type: Public

Income Statement — FYE: January 1

	REVENUE ($mil)	NET INCOME ($mil)	NET PROFIT MARGIN	EMPLOYEES
01/22	2,988.2	695.9	23.3%	9,300
01/21*	2,682.8	590.6	22.0%	8,800
12/19	2,336.3	988.9	42.3%	8,100
12/18	2,138.0	345.7	16.2%	7,500
12/17	1,943.0	204.1	10.5%	7,200
Annual Growth	11.4%	35.9%	—	6.6%

*Fiscal year change

2022 Year-End Financials

Debt ratio: 7.9%
Return on equity: 26.6%
Cash ($ mil.): 1,088.9
Current Ratio: 1.77
Long-term debt ($ mil.): 347.5
No. of shares ($ mil.): 276.8
Dividends
  Yield: —
  Payout: —
Market value ($ mil.): 51,581.0

	STOCK PRICE ($) FY Close	P/E High/Low		PER SHARE ($) Earnings	Dividends	Book Value
01/22	186.35	75	47	2.50	0.00	9.90
01/21*	136.43	63	25	2.11	0.00	8.94
12/19	70.29	21	11	3.53	0.00	7.51
12/18	43.34	38	28	1.23	0.00	4.60
12/17	41.82	61	34	0.73	0.00	3.51
Annual Growth	45.3%	—	—	36.0%	—	29.6%

*Fiscal year change

California First Leasing Corp

California First National Bancorp (CFNB) is a leasing company and a bank. Its California First Leasing (CalFirst Leasing) subsidiary leases equipment for a wide variety of industries including computers and software. Other leases include retail point-of-sale systems, office furniture, and manufacturing, telecommunications, and medical equipment. The bank holding company also operates California First National Bank (CalFirst Bank), a branchless FDIC-insured retail bank that conducts business mainly over the Internet, but also by mail and phone. About three-quarters of its revenue comes from interest.

Operations
About 68% of CalFirst's revenue comes from finance and loan income. Another major source of revenue, 9%, comes from the sale of leases, loans, and leased property.

Geographic Reach
CalFirst is based in Irvine, California and does business throughout the US.

Sales and Marketing
CalFirst's 10 largest customers accounted for 19% of the lease and loan portfolio in 2015, compared to 24% in 2014.

Financial Performance
In 2015 sales increased 25% from 2014 driven by higher interest income from finance and lending.

The company's net income rose 28% in 2015 from 2014 on the higher revenue.

Strategy
CalFirst maintains diversification in geography and customers to spreading risk across its portfolio.

HISTORY

Lured by the profit margins of the leasing business, Patrick Paddon and Dion Cairns founded Amplicon in California in 1977. The two disagreed over how to run the business, and Cairns soon moved on. Paddon had previously been manager of corporate planning and budgets at Business Systems Technologies, an IBM-compatible peripherals maker.

Early customers of Amplicon included Borden, Campbell Soup, SANYO Manufacturing, and Wherehouse Entertainment. The company implemented its centralized telemarketing operations in 1981. Amplicon went public in 1987, and by the end of the 1980s, its sales had topped $100 million.

Amplicon actually thrived in the recession of the early 1990s, as the economy prompted companies to lease rather than buy capital equipment. Sales dipped in 1992, but after an overhaul of the company's recruiting, training, and sales management processes,

Amplicon rebounded.

Rapidly changing technology also boosted Amplicon's business because many companies chose to lease rather than buy equipment that would quickly become outdated. Sales increased by 11% in 1994 and by 14% in 1995.

Amplicon introduced a Web site for online sales in 1998. The following year it announced plans to sponsor the creation of a national bank to fund the purchase of equipment to be leased to Amplicon's customers. In 2001 the company changed its name to California First National Bancorp and became a bank holding company after it organized California First National Bank.

EXECUTIVES

President, Chief Executive Officer, Director, Patrick E. Paddon, $180,000 total compensation

Chief Financial Officer, S. Leslie Jewett, $275,000 total compensation

Chief Operating Officer, Secretary, Director, Glen T. Tsuma, $180,000 total compensation

Director, Michael H. Lowry

Director, Harris Ravine

Director, Danilo Cacciamatta

Director, Robert W. Kelley

Auditors : Eide Bailly LLP

LOCATIONS

HQ: California First Leasing Corp
5000 Birch Street, Suite 500, Newport Beach, CA 92660
Phone: 949 255-0500   **Fax:** 949 255-0501
Web: www.calfirstlease.com

PRODUCTS/OPERATIONS

2015 sales

	$ mil	% of total
Interest income		
Finance and loan income	21.5	68
Investment interest income	1.5	5
Non-interest income		
Operating and sales-type lease income	0.3	1
Gain on sale of leases, loans and leased property	4.8	14
Realized gain on sale of investment securities	0.5	2
Recovery realized on TFT-LCD settlement	2.7	9
Other fee income	0.4	1
Total	**31.7**	**100**

Products & Services
ATM Cards
Certificates of Deposit
Check Orders
Interest Checking
Money Market Checking
Online Bill Paying
Premium Savings

Selected Items for Lease
Accounting systems (hardware, software, installation, training)
Broadcasting equipment
Exercise training equipment
Furniture, fixtures, and related equipment
Internet-related software, hardware
Laboratory equipment
Imaging equipment
Internet-related software, hardware
LAN/WAN and telecommunications equipment
Medical equipment
Network cabling/routers
Network servers
Personal and laptop computers
Point-of-sale equipment
Printers/copiers
Printing presses
Security equipment
Sports field improvements and scoreboards
Video recording and editing equipment

COMPETITORS

COMERICA INCORPORATED
HUNTINGTON BANCSHARES INCORPORATED
KEYCORP
MUFG AMERICAS HOLDINGS CORPORATION
U.S. BANCORP

HISTORICAL FINANCIALS

Company Type: Public

Income Statement   FYE: June 30

	ASSETS ($mil)	NET INCOME ($mil)	INCOME AS % OF ASSETS	EMPLOYEES
06/21	242.9	36.2	14.9%	0
06/20	267.7	(2.3)	—	0
06/19	304.9	7.3	2.4%	0
06/18	389.2	12.5	3.2%	0
06/17	715.5	11.1	1.6%	98
Annual Growth	(23.7%)	34.3%	—	—

2021 Year-End Financials

Return on assets: —
Return on equity: —
Long-term debt ($ mil.): —
No. of shares ($ mil.): 10.2
Sales ($ mil.): 51
Dividends
 Yield: 2.9%
 Payout: 200.0%
Market value ($ mil.): 188.0

	STOCK PRICE ($) FY Close	P/E High/Low		PER SHARE ($)		
				Earnings	Dividends	Book Value
06/21	18.31	5	4	3.52	0.54	22.39
06/20	15.30	—	—	(0.23)	0.52	19.41
06/19	15.80	25	20	0.71	0.50	20.16
06/18	15.80	15	11	1.22	0.48	19.93
06/17	18.85	18	13	1.08	0.46	19.07
Annual Growth	(0.7%)	—	—	34.4%	4.1%	4.1%

Calloway's Nursery, Inc.

Calloway's Nursery babies its customers with green-thumb know-how -- about half of its employees are certified nursery professionals. The company owns and operates about 20 nurseries under the Calloway's name in the Dallas/Fort Worth area and San Antonio and under the Cornelius Nurseries banner in Houston. The company also sells plants online. Offerings include trees, shrubs, flowers, landscaping materials, soil, fertilizer, and Christmas goods. Christmas merchandise includes trees, poinsettias, wreaths, and garlands.

EXECUTIVES

Chairman, Chief Executive Officer, James C. Estill, $225,000 total compensation

President, Chief Executive Officer, Director, Marce E. Ward

Vice President, Director, George J. Wechsler

Vice President, Chief Financial Officer, Secretary, Daniel G. Reynolds, $125,000 total compensation

Vice President, Director, John S. Peters, $175,000 total compensation

Merchandising Vice President, David S. Weger, $125,000 total compensation

Director, Stanley Block

Director, Timothy J. McKibben

Director, Peter H. Kamin

Auditors : Whitley Penn LLP

LOCATIONS

HQ: Calloway's Nursery, Inc.
9003 Airport Freeway, Suite G350, North Richland Hills, TX 76180
Phone: 817 222-1122
Web: www.calloways.com

PRODUCTS/OPERATIONS

Selected Products
Annuals
Bedding plants
Blooming tropicals
Christmas merchandise
 Garlands
 Poinsettias
 Trees
 Wreaths
Clay pots (Malaysian, Chinese, Mexican)
Gardening accessories
 Gloves
 Hats
 Kneelers
Gardening tools and equipment
Gifts
Grasses
Ground covers
Natural dog and cat food
Perennials
Potted plants
Seeds and bulbs
Shrubs
Soil amendments and fertilizers, including organic
Trees

COMPETITORS

ARMSTRONG GARDEN CENTERS, INC.
ENGLISH GARDENS & FAIRLANE FLORISTS, INC.
MEADOWS FARMS, INC.
PETITTI ENTERPRISES, INC.
WHITE FLOWER FARM, INC.

HISTORICAL FINANCIALS

Company Type: Public

Income Statement   FYE: December 31

	REVENUE ($mil)	NET INCOME ($mil)	NET PROFIT MARGIN	EMPLOYEES
12/20	73.7	9.7	13.2%	0
12/19	58.7	3.0	5.1%	0
12/18	56.6	4.3	7.7%	0
12/17	55.4	5.0	9.1%	0
12/16	50.8	1.9	3.8%	0
Annual Growth	9.8%	49.6%	—	—

2020 Year-End Financials

Debt ratio: 25.5%
Return on equity: 40.4%
Cash ($ mil.): 11.8
Current Ratio: 1.67
Long-term debt ($ mil.): 13.7
No. of shares ($ mil.): 7.3
Dividends
 Yield: 10.3%
 Payout: 75.1%
Market value ($ mil.): 71.0

	STOCK PRICE ($) FY Close	P/E High/Low		PER SHARE ($) Earnings	Dividends	Book Value
12/20	9.63	8	3	1.33	1.00	3.44
12/19	6.10	21	14	0.41	0.00	3.11
12/18	8.00	15	12	0.60	0.50	2.70
12/17	8.30	12	5	0.69	0.50	2.57
12/16	3.84	15	10	0.26	0.00	2.76
Annual Growth	25.8%	—	—	50.4%	—	5.6%

Cambium Networks Corp

EXECUTIVES

Chairman, Director, Robert Amen
President, Chief Executive Officer, Director, Atul Bhatnagar, $500,000 total compensation
Operations Senior Vice President, Raymond de Graaf
Production Senior Vice President, Vibhu Vivek
Product Management Senior Vice President, Scott Imhoff
Sales Senior Vice President, Bryan Sheppeck, $276,230 total compensation
Chief Financial Officer, Andrew Bronstein
General Counsel, Sally Rau
Division Officer, Ronald Ryan, $182,461 total compensation
Director, Vikram Verma
Director, Bruce C. Felt
Director, Kevin J. Lynch
Director, Alexander R. Slusky
Auditors : KPMG LLP

LOCATIONS

HQ: Cambium Networks Corp
3800 Golf Road, Suite 360, Rolling Meadows, IL 60008
Phone: 345 943-3100
Web: www.cambiumnetworks.com

HISTORICAL FINANCIALS
Company Type: Public

Income Statement — FYE: December 31

	REVENUE ($mil)	NET INCOME ($mil)	NET PROFIT MARGIN	EMPLOYEES
12/20	278.4	18.5	6.7%	512
12/19	267.0	(17.6)	—	533
12/18	241.7	(1.5)	—	516
12/17	216.6	9.1	4.2%	0
12/16	181.4	2.2	1.3%	0
Annual Growth	11.3%	69.0%	—	—

2020 Year-End Financials
Debt ratio: 26.3%
Return on equity: 35.8%
Cash ($ mil.): 62.4
Current Ratio: 1.53
Long-term debt ($ mil.): 24.9
No. of shares ($ mil.): 26.0
Dividends
  Yield: —
  Payout: —
Market value ($ mil.): 0.0

Cambridge Bancorp

Cambridge Bancorp is the nearly $2 billion-asset holding company for Cambridge Trust Company, a community bank serving Cambridge and the Greater Boston area through about a dozen branch locations in Massachusetts. It offers standard retail products and services including checking and savings accounts, CDs, IRAs, and credit cards. Residential mortgages, including home equity loans, account for about 50% of the company's loan portfolio, while commercial real estate loans make up more than 40%. The company also offers commercial, industrial, and consumer loans. Established in 1892, the bank also offers trust and investment management services.

Operations
The commercial bank operates a traditional retail banking line focused on lending as well as its Wealth Management Group, which investment management and trust business. The bank had $1.8 billion in total assets and $2.4 billion in client assets under management at the end of 2015.

As with other retail banks, Cambridge Bancorp makes the bulk of its revenue from interest income. About 58% of its total revenue came from loan interest during 2015, while another 10% came from interest on taxable and tax-exempt investment securities. The rest of its revenue came from wealth management income (24% of revenue), deposit account fees (3%), ATM/Debit card income (1%), and other non-interest income sources.

Geographic Reach
Cambridge Bancorp has 12 branches in Massachusetts in Cambridge, Boston, Belmont, Concord, Lexington, Lincoln, and Weston. It also has wealth management offices in Boston, as well as in New Hampshire in Concord, Manchester, and Portsmouth.

Sales and Marketing
The company spent $2.38 million on marketing during 2015, up from $2.12 million in 2014.

Financial Performance
Cambridge's annual revenues and profits have been steadily rising over the past several years thanks to continued commercial real estate mortgage growth, and as its Wealth Management business has nearly doubled its managed assets since 2011, spurring higher fee revenue.

The bank's revenue climbed 7% to $80.2 million during 2015 on 10% loan growth mostly driven by commercial real estate loans, which spurred higher interest income. The company's wealth management business income grew 7% as its client assets continued to grow with new investor inflows.

Revenue growth in 2015 drove Cambridge Bancorp's net income up 5% to $15.7 million. The bank's operating cash levels rose 24% to $20 million for the year with an increase in cash-based earnings and favorable changes in working capital mostly related to a change in accrued interest receivable, deferred taxes, and other assets and liabilities.

Strategy
Cambridge Bancorp continued in 2016 to lean on the success of its commercial mortgage business, though it plans to pivot more to commercial and industrial lending to diversify its commercial lending portfolio.

To better prepare for rising interest rates, Cambridge Bancorp in 2015 and 2016 modified its commercial loan strategy from long-term, fixed-rate loans (which are vulnerable to interest rate risk) to a new interest rate derivative product to offer an alternative long-term financing for its customers while helping the bank earn a variable rate of interest on its loans. For its consumer banking unit, the bank in 2015 began a plan to sell the majority of its long-term residential mortgage production, including secondary loans, to the secondary market.

EXECUTIVES

Chairman, Chief Executive Officer, Subsidiary Officer, Director, Denis K. Sheahan, $493,000 total compensation
Chief Financial Officer, Secretary, Subsidiary Officer, Michael F. Carotenuto, $250,000 total compensation
Chief Commercial Banking Officer, Subsidiary Officer, Steven J. Mead
Chief Credit Officer, Subsidiary Officer, Peter Halberstadt
Subsidiary Officer, Kerri A. Mooney
Subsidiary Officer, Director, Daniel Morrison
Subsidiary Officer, Puneet Nevatia
Subsidiary Officer, Pilar Pueyo
Subsidiary Officer, John J. Sullivan
Subsidiary Officer, Danielle Remis Hackel
Director, Leon A. Palandjian
Director, Cathleen A. Schmidt
Director, Thalia Meehan
Director, Jody A. Rose
Director, Christine Fuchs
Director, Pamela A. Hamlin
Director, Laila S. Partridge
Director, Jeanette G. Clough
Director, Hambleton Lord
Director, R. Gregg Stone
Director, Simon R. Gerlin
Director, Kathryn M. Hinderhofer
Director, Jane C. Walsh
Director, Andargachew S. Zelleke
Auditors : KPMG LLP

LOCATIONS

HQ: Cambridge Bancorp
1336 Massachusetts Avenue, Cambridge, MA 02138
Phone: 617 876-5500

Web: www.cambridgetrust.com

PRODUCTS/OPERATIONS

2015 Sales

	% of total
Interest Income	
Interest on loans	58
Interest on taxable investment securities	7
Interest on tax exempt investment securities	3
Non-Interest Income	
Wealth Management Income	24
Deposits accounts fee	3
ATM/Debit card income	1
Bank Owned life insurance income	1
Gain on disposition on investment securities	1
Gain on loans held of sale	1
Other income	1
Loan related derivative income	-
Total	100

Products/Services
Personal Banking
Checking
Savings, CDs, & IRAs
Online Banking
Mobile Banking
Mortgages
Home Equity
Credit Cards
Personal Loans
More Services
Business Banking
Checking & Savings
Commercial Lending
Commercial Real Estate
Cash Management
Remote Deposit Capture
Online Banking
Mobile Banking
Professional Services Program
More Services
Wealth Management
Investment Process
Investment Management
Fiduciary & Planning Services
Estate Settlement
Wealth Management Personnel
Forums
Online Access

COMPETITORS

ASSOCIATED BANC-CORP
ENTERPRISE BANCORP, INC.
FIRST FINANCIAL BANCORP.
INDEPENDENT BANK CORP.
OFG BANCORP

HISTORICAL FINANCIALS

Company Type: Public

Income Statement — FYE: December 31

	ASSETS ($mil)	NET INCOME ($mil)	INCOME AS % OF ASSETS	EMPLOYEES
12/20	3,949.2	31.9	0.8%	383
12/19	2,855.5	25.2	0.9%	321
12/18	2,101.3	23.8	1.1%	262
12/17	1,949.9	14.8	0.8%	247
12/16	1,848.9	16.8	0.9%	0
Annual Growth	20.9%	17.3%	—	—

2020 Year-End Financials

Return on assets: 0.9%
Return on equity: 9.2%
Long-term debt ($ mil.): —
No. of shares ($ mil.): 6.9
Sales ($ mil.): 168.9
Dividends
Yield: 3.0%
Payout: 48.2%
Market value ($ mil.): 483.0

	STOCK PRICE ($) FY Close	P/E High/Low		PER SHARE ($) Earnings	Dividends	Book Value
12/20	69.75	15	9	5.03	2.12	58.00
12/19	80.15	16	13	5.37	2.04	53.06
12/18	83.25	16	13	5.77	1.96	40.67
12/17	79.80	24	17	3.61	1.86	36.24
12/16	62.29	15	11	4.15	1.84	33.36
Annual Growth	2.9%	—	—	4.9%	3.6%	14.8%

Canandaigua National Corp.

Canandaigua National can undoubtedly stake its claim as the holding company for Canandaigua National Bank and Trust, which operates more than two dozen branches in the Finger Lakes region of upstate New York. In addition to traditional deposits and loans, the bank also offers online brokerage, insurance, and wealth management services, including corporate retirement plan management and individual financial planning. The company also owns Genesee Valley Trust Company and the recently formed Canandaigua National Trust Company of Florida. Canandaigua National's loan portfolio is composed largely of commercial mortgages, other business loans, and residential mortgages.

Geographic Reach

The company has also slowly expanded its branch network by opening new locations in Monroe and Ontario counties.

Strategy

Although the tepid economy has impacted community banks with lower yields, Canandaigua's presence in the relatively stable Rochester region has helped keep things from looking too grim. The quality of the company's loan portfolio has been improving, so it has had to dip in to less of its loan loss reserves.

EXECUTIVES

Chairman, Trust Officer, Subsidiary Officer, George W. Hamlin, $422,640 total compensation
Vice-Chairman, Director, Daniel P. Fuller
President, Chief Executive Officer, Subsidiary Officer, Director, Frank H. Hamlin, $225,000 total compensation
Finance Executive Vice President, Operations Executive Vice President, Finance Chief Financial Officer, Operations Chief Financial Officer, Finance Subsidiary Officer, Operations Subsidiary Officer, Lawrence A. Heilbronner, $231,088 total compensation
Corporate Risk Operations/Security Executive Vice President, Corporate Risk Operations/Security Secretary, Corporate Risk Operations/Security General Counsel, Corporate Risk Operations/Security Subsidiary Officer, Steven H. Swartout, $217,896 total compensation
Retail services Executive Vice President, Retail services Cashier, Retail services Subsidiary Officer, Director, Robert G. Sheridan, $206,409 total compensation
Customer Value Management Subsidiary Officer, Joseph L. Dugan, $228,701 total compensation
Senior Vice President, Treasurer, Subsidiary Officer, Gregory S. MacKay, $165,494 total compensation
Director, Richard C. Fox
Director, Stephen D. Hamlin
Director, Richard P. Miller
Director, Caroline C. Shipley
Director, Sue S. Stewart
Director, Alan J. Stone

LOCATIONS

HQ: Canandaigua National Corp.
72 South Main Street, Canandaigua, NY 14424
Phone: 585 394-4260 **Fax:** 585 394-4001
Web: www.cnbank.com

COMPETITORS

FARMERS CAPITAL BANK CORPORATION
FNBH BANCORP, INC.
KEYCORP
PLAINSCAPITAL CORPORATION
VALLEY NATIONAL BANCORP

HISTORICAL FINANCIALS

Company Type: Public

Income Statement — FYE: December 31

	ASSETS ($mil)	NET INCOME ($mil)	INCOME AS % OF ASSETS	EMPLOYEES
12/20	3,635.3	42.2	1.2%	580
12/19	3,015.6	39.1	1.3%	572
12/18	2,862.4	35.9	1.3%	556
12/17	2,661.7	22.0	0.8%	541
12/16	2,476.1	22.4	0.9%	533
Annual Growth	10.1%	17.1%	—	2.1%

2020 Year-End Financials

Return on assets: 1.2%
Return on equity: 15.0%
Long-term debt ($ mil.): —
No. of shares ($ mil.): 1.8
Sales ($ mil.): 184.9
Dividends
Yield: —
Payout: 31.2%
Market value ($ mil.): 352.0

	STOCK PRICE ($) FY Close	P/E High/Low		PER SHARE ($) Earnings	Dividends	Book Value
12/20	188.00	10	6	22.43	7.00	158.09
12/19	202.25	10	8	20.77	5.70	142.18
12/18	175.00	10	8	18.97	4.80	124.85
12/17	152.00	15	12	11.58	4.30	111.11
12/16	140.00	15	11	11.84	3.87	103.87
Annual Growth	7.6%	—	—	17.3%	16.0%	11.1%

Capital Bancorp Inc (MD)

EXECUTIVES

Chairman, Director, Steven J. Schwartz
Chief Executive Officer, Subsidiary Officer, Director, Edward F. Barry, $400,000 total compensation
Subsidiary Officer, Director, Scott R. Browning, $309,000 total compensation
Chief Operating Officer, Subsidiary Officer, Steven M. Poynot
Principal Financial Officer, Principal Accounting Officer, Subsidiary Officer, Connie Egan
Subsidiary Officer, Sandeep Uthra
Subsidiary Officer, Gary M. Kausmeyer
Subsidiary Officer, Eric M. Suss
Subsidiary Officer, Kathy Yamada
Subsidiary Officer, Director, James F. Whalen
Subsidiary Officer, Karl Dicker
Director, Jerome R. Bailey
Director, Joshua B. Bernstein
Director, Randall J. Levitt
Director, Deborah Ratner-Salzberg
Director, C. Scott Brannan
Director, Fred J. Lewis
Auditors : Elliott Davis, PLLC

LOCATIONS

HQ: Capital Bancorp Inc (MD)
2275 Research Boulevard, Suite 600, Rockville, MD 20850
Phone: 301 468-8848
Web: www.capitalbankmd.com

HISTORICAL FINANCIALS
Company Type: Public

Income Statement — FYE: December 31

	ASSETS ($mil)	NET INCOME ($mil)	INCOME AS % OF ASSETS	EMPLOYEES
12/20	1,876.5	25.8	1.4%	247
12/19	1,428.4	16.8	1.2%	230
12/18	1,105.0	12.7	1.2%	204
12/17	1,026.0	7.1	0.7%	195
12/16	905.6	9.4	1.0%	0
Annual Growth	20.0%	28.6%	—	—

2020 Year-End Financials
Return on assets: 1.5%
Return on equity: 17.5%
Long-term debt ($ mil.): —
No. of shares ($ mil.): 13.7
Sales ($ mil.): 158.3
Dividends
Yield: —
Payout: —
Market value ($ mil.): 192.0

	STOCK PRICE ($) FY Close	P/E High/Low		PER SHARE ($) Earnings	Dividends	Book Value
12/20	13.93	8	4	1.87	0.00	11.58
12/19	14.89	12	9	1.21	0.00	9.60
12/18	11.41	13	11	1.02	0.00	8.38
Annual Growth	10.5%	—	—	35.4%	—	17.6%

Capital City Bank Group, Inc.

Capital City Bank Group is the holding company for Capital City Bank (CCB). The bank provides traditional deposit and credit services, mortgage banking, asset management, trust, merchant services, bank cards, data processing, and securities brokerage services through some 60 banking offices in Florida, Georgia, and Alabama. Through Capital City Home Loans, the company has about 30 additional offices in mortgage banking in the Southeast. In addition to CCB, other assets include Capital City Trust Company and Capital City Investments. The bank was founded in 1895.

EXECUTIVES

President, Chief Executive Officer, Subsidiary Officer, Chairman, Director, William G. Smith, $400,000 total compensation
Executive Vice President, Chief Financial Officer, Jep Larkin
Treasurer, Subsidiary Officer, Director, Thomas A. Barron, $350,000 total compensation
Lead Director, Director, Stanley W. Connally
Director, Robert Antoine
Director, William F. Butler
Director, Marshall M. Criser
Director, Kimberly Crowell
Director, Bonnie Davenport
Director, J. Everitt Drew
Director, Eric Grant
Director, Laura L. Johnson
Director, John G. Sample
Director, Ashbel C. Williams
Auditors : BKD, LLP

LOCATIONS

HQ: Capital City Bank Group, Inc.
217 North Monroe Street, Tallahassee, FL 32301
Phone: 850 402-7821
Web: www.ccbg.com

PRODUCTS/OPERATIONS

2015 Sales

	$ Mil.	% of Total
Interest		
Loans, including fees	73.2	55
Investment securities	5.9	5
Funds sold	0.6	-
Noninterest income		
Deposit fee	22.6	17
Bank card fees	11.3	8
Wealth management fees	7.5	6
Mortgage Banking fees	4.5	3
Data processing fees	1.5	1
Other	6.6	5
Total	133.7	100

COMPETITORS

ASSOCIATED BANC-CORP
CAPITAL BANK FINANCIAL CORP.
CITY HOLDING COMPANY
CVB FINANCIAL CORP.
ENTERPRISE FINANCIAL SERVICES CORP
FIRST FINANCIAL BANCORP.
FIRST FINANCIAL CORPORATION
S&T BANCORP, INC.
SHINSEI BANK, LIMITED
WASHINGTON FEDERAL, INC.

HISTORICAL FINANCIALS
Company Type: Public

Income Statement — FYE: December 31

	ASSETS ($mil)	NET INCOME ($mil)	INCOME AS % OF ASSETS	EMPLOYEES
12/20	3,798.0	31.5	0.8%	773
12/19	3,088.9	30.8	1.0%	815
12/18	2,959.1	26.2	0.9%	819
12/17	2,898.7	10.8	0.4%	825
12/16	2,845.1	11.7	0.4%	853
Annual Growth	7.5%	28.0%	—	(2.4%)

2020 Year-End Financials
Return on assets: 0.9%
Return on equity: 9.4%
Long-term debt ($ mil.): —
No. of shares ($ mil.): 16.7
Sales ($ mil.): 217.3
Dividends
Yield: 2.3%
Payout: 29.5%
Market value ($ mil.): 413.0

	STOCK PRICE ($) FY Close	P/E High/Low		PER SHARE ($) Earnings	Dividends	Book Value
12/20	24.58	16	9	1.88	0.57	20.42
12/19	30.50	17	12	1.83	0.48	19.50
12/18	23.21	17	14	1.54	0.32	18.07
12/17	22.94	41	28	0.64	0.24	16.73
12/16	20.48	32	19	0.69	0.17	16.34
Annual Growth	4.7%	—	—	28.5%	35.3%	5.7%

CapStar Financial Holdings Inc

EXECUTIVES

President, Chief Executive Officer, Subsidiary Officer, Director, Timothy K. Schools
Chief Risk Officer, General Counsel, Steve Groom
Executive Vice President, Chief Financial Officer, Michael J. Fowler
Chief Risk Officer, Corporate Secretary, Amy C. Goodin
Subsidiary Officer, Jennie O'Bryan
Subsidiary Officer, Christopher G. Tietz, $288,548 total compensation
Subsidiary Officer, John A. Davis
Subsidiary Officer, Jeffrey L. Cunningham
Non-Executive Chairman, Director, James S. Turner
Director, L. Earl Bentz
Director, Sam DeVane
Director, Thomas R. Flynn
Director, Louis A. Green
Director, Valora Gurganious
Director, Myra NanDora Jenne
Director, Joelle J. Phillips

HOOVER'S HANDBOOK OF EMERGING COMPANIES 2023

Director, Stephen B. Smith
Director, Toby S. Wilt
Auditors : Elliot Davis Decosimo, LLC

LOCATIONS

HQ: CapStar Financial Holdings Inc
1201 Demonbreun Street, Suite 700, Nashville, TN 37203
Phone: 615 732-6400
Web: www.capstarbank.com

HISTORICAL FINANCIALS
Company Type: Public

Income Statement   FYE: December 31

	ASSETS ($mil)	NET INCOME ($mil)	INCOME AS % OF ASSETS	EMPLOYEES
12/20	2,987.0	24.6	0.8%	380
12/19	2,037.2	22.4	1.1%	289
12/18	1,963.8	9.6	0.5%	295
12/17	1,344.4	1.5	0.1%	175
12/16	1,333.6	9.0	0.7%	170
Annual Growth	22.3%	28.4%	—	22.3%

2020 Year-End Financials

Return on assets: 0.9%   Dividends
Return on equity: 7.9%   Yield: 1.3%
Long-term debt ($ mil.): —   Payout: 16.3%
No. of shares ($ mil.): 21.9   Market value ($ mil.): 324.0
Sales ($ mil.): 135.1

	STOCK PRICE ($) FY Close	P/E High/Low		PER SHARE ($)		
				Earnings	Dividends	Book Value
12/20	14.75	14	6	1.22	0.20	15.62
12/19	16.65	14	11	1.20	0.19	14.87
12/18	14.73	30	19	0.67	0.08	14.35
12/17	20.77	169	125	0.12	0.00	12.69
12/16	21.96	22	16	0.81	0.00	12.42
Annual Growth	(9.5%)	—	—	10.8%	—	5.9%

Cara Therapeutics Inc

Cara Therapeutics cares about pain therapy. The clinical-stage biopharmaceutical company focuses on developing and commercializing new chemical products designed to alleviate pain by selectively targeting kappa opioid receptors. Its proprietary class of product candidates targets the body's peripheral nervous system. In a test with patients with moderate-to-severe pain, they have demonstrated efficacy without inducing many of the undesirable side effects often associated with pain therapeutics. Cara's most advanced product candidates are KORSUVA (CR845/difelikefalin) injection and Oral KORSUVA (CR845/difelikefalin). Founded in 2004, the company is based in Stamford, Connecticut.

Operations

Its product candidate, CR845/difelikefalin, is a new chemical entity, which is designed to selectively stimulate kappa, rather than mu, and delta opioid receptors. CR845/difelikefalin has been designed with specific chemical characteristics to restrict its entry into the CNS and further limit its mechanism of action to KORs in the peripheral nervous system and on immune cells. Activation of kappa receptors in the CNS is known to result in some undesirable effects, including dysphoria. Since CR845/difelikefalin modulates kappa receptor signals peripherally without any significant activation of opioid receptors in the CNS, it is generally not expected to produce the CNS-related side effects of mu opioid agonists (such as addiction and respiratory depression) or centrally-active kappa opioid agonists (such as dysphoria and hallucinations).

Sales and Marketing

Cara Therapeutics plan to have its own specialty sales force, to launch KORSUVA (CR845/difelikefalin) injection in the hemodialysis setting in the US, as well as through collaborations with other pharmaceutical or biotechnology companies or third-party manufacturing and sales organizations. If approved for marketing outside the US, the existing or new partners will commercialize KORSUVA (CR845/difelikefalin) injection with its own, or its collaborators', sales force.

Financial Performance

In the last five years, the company reported increased revenue as a License, and milestone fee starts to trickle in.

In 2019, revenue increased by 48% to $19.9 million, primarily due to a $6.3 million increase in License and milestone fees.

Net loss for 2019 increased by $32.4 million to $106.4 million, mainly due to high operating expenses.

Cash and cash equivalents at the end of the period were $18.7 million. Net cash used in operating activities was $109.2 million and investing activities used another $30.5 million. Financing activities provided $142.6 million to the company coffers.

Strategy

The company strategy is to develop and commercialize a novel and first-in-class portfolio of peripherally-acting kappa opioid receptor agonists, with KORSUVA (CR845/difelikefalin) injection and Oral KORSUVA (CR845/difelikefalin) as its lead candidates. It has designed and is developing product candidates that have clearly defined clinical development programs and target significant commercial market opportunities. The key elements of its strategy are as follows:

Advance KORSUVA (CR845/difelikefalin) injection for the treatment of moderate-to-severe CKD-aP in patients undergoing hemodialysis to support regulatory approval;

Build a specialty sales and marketing organization to commercialize KORSUVA (CR845/difelikefalin) injection for the treatment of CKD-aP in hemodialysis patients in the United States, if approved;

Expand the use of Oral KORSUVA (CR845/difelikefalin) in other pruritic indications by establishing proof-of-concept in clinical conditions such as non-dialysis stage III-V CKD-aP, CLD-aP and AD; and

Establish partnerships for further development and commercialization of I.V. CR845/difelikefalin for the treatment of moderate-to-severe acute pain and/or PONV in acute care settings in the United States

EXECUTIVES

President, Chief Executive Officer, Director, Derek T. Chalmers, $542,100 total compensation
Development Senior Vice President, Research Senior Vice President, Development Chief Scientific Officer, Research Chief Scientific Officer, Frédérique Menzaghi, $400,000 total compensation
Accounting Vice President, Accounting Head, Accounting Controller, Richard Makara
Chief Financial Officer, Thomas Reilly
Chief Medical Officer, Joana Goncalves, $82,639 total compensation
Chief Compliance Officer, Secretary, General Counsel, Scott M. Terrillion
Director, Susan Shiff
Director, Martin Vogelbaum
Director, Harrison M. Bains
Director, Jeffrey L. Ives
Director, Christopher Posner
Auditors : Ernst & Young LLP

LOCATIONS

HQ: Cara Therapeutics Inc
4 Stamford Plaza, 107 Elm Street, 9th Floor, Stamford, CT 06902
Phone: 203 406-3700
Web: www.caratherapeutics.com

PRODUCTS/OPERATIONS

2015 Sales

	$ mil.	% of total
Collaborative revenue	2.1	55
License and milestone fee	1.7	45
Total	3.8	100

COMPETITORS

CHIMERIX, INC.
CORCEPT THERAPEUTICS INCORPORATED
ENDOCYTE, INC.
ESPERION THERAPEUTICS, INC.
HERON THERAPEUTICS, INC.
INSMED INCORPORATED
OMEROS CORPORATION
RECRO PHARMA, INC.
XENOPORT, INC.
ZOGENIX, INC.

HISTORICAL FINANCIALS
Company Type: Public

Income Statement				FYE: December 31
	REVENUE ($mil)	NET INCOME ($mil)	NET PROFIT MARGIN	EMPLOYEES
12/20	135.0	8.4	6.2%	80
12/19	19.8	(106.3)	—	67
12/18	13.4	(74.0)	—	55
12/17	0.9	(58.1)	—	37
12/16	0.0	(57.2)	—	34
Annual Growth	529.5%	—	—	23.9%

2020 Year-End Financials
Debt ratio: —
Return on equity: 3.8%
Cash ($ mil.): 31.6
Current Ratio: 10.55
Long-term debt ($ mil.): —
No. of shares ($ mil.): 49.8
Dividends
Yield: —
Payout: —
Market value ($ mil.): 755.0

	STOCK PRICE ($) FY Close	P/E High/Low		PER SHARE ($) Earnings Dividends		Book Value
12/20	15.13	100	51	0.18	0.00	4.99
12/19	16.11	—	—	(2.49)	0.00	4.00
12/18	13.00	—	—	(2.06)	0.00	3.38
12/17	12.24	—	—	(1.86)	0.00	2.66
12/16	9.29	—	—	(2.10)	0.00	1.86
Annual Growth	13.0%	—	—	—	—	28.0%

Cardinal Ethanol LLC

EXECUTIVES

Chairman, Director, Robert Davis
Vice-Chairman, Thomas Chalfant
President, Chief Executive Officer, Jeff Painter, $252,212 total compensation
Chief Financial Officer, Treasurer, William Dartt, $142,335 total compensation
Plant Manager, Jeremey Herlyn, $147,988 total compensation
Commodity Manager, Casey Bruns
Director, Thomas Chronister
Director, Danny Huston
Director, Cyril LeFevre
Director, Dale Schwieterman
Director, Steven Snider
Director, J. Philip Zicht
Director, Robert Baker
Director, David Dersch
Director, Gerald Forsythe
Director, William Garth
Director, Lewis M. Roch
Director, C. Alan Rosar
Director, Daniel Sailer
Auditors : Boulay PLLP

LOCATIONS

HQ: Cardinal Ethanol LLC
1554 N. County Road 600 E., Union City, IN 47390
Phone: 765 964-3137
Web: www.cardinalethanol.com

HISTORICAL FINANCIALS
Company Type: Public

Income Statement				FYE: September 30
	REVENUE ($mil)	NET INCOME ($mil)	NET PROFIT MARGIN	EMPLOYEES
09/21	404.0	27.1	6.7%	58
09/20	244.7	(1.1)	—	57
09/19	260.6	(6.5)	—	59
09/18	266.8	7.6	2.9%	56
09/17	228.4	13.4	5.9%	55
Annual Growth	15.3%	19.2%	—	1.3%

2021 Year-End Financials
Debt ratio: —
Return on equity: 23.2%
Cash ($ mil.): 33.9
Current Ratio: 3.22
Long-term debt ($ mil.): —
No. of shares ($ mil.): 0.0
Dividends
Yield: 0.1%
Payout: 41.7%
Market value ($ mil.): 106.0

	STOCK PRICE ($) FY Close	P/E High/Low		PER SHARE ($) Earnings Dividends		Book Value
09/21	7,230.00	4		31,856.00	775.00	8,540
09/20	5,000.00	—		(78.00)	150.00	7,459
09/19	7,102.00	—		(452.00)	100.00	7,687
09/18	9,985.00	27	18	522.00	950.00	8,239
09/17	5,500.00	17	15	919.00	1,175.00	8,667
Annual Growth	(17.4%)	—	—	19.2%	(9.9%)	(0.4%)

CareTrust REIT Inc

EXECUTIVES

Chairman, Director, Diana M. Laing
Operations President, Operations Chief Executive Officer, Director, David M. Sedgwick, $315,000 total compensation
Executive Vice President, Chief Investment Officer, Secretary, James Callister
Chief Financial Officer, Treasurer, Principal Accounting Officer, William M. Wagner, $342,000 total compensation
Director, Spencer G. Plumb
Director, Careina D. Williams
Auditors : DELOITTE & TOUCHE LLP

LOCATIONS

HQ: CareTrust REIT Inc
905 Calle Amanecer, Suite 300, San Clemente, CA 92673
Phone: 949 542-3130
Web: www.caretrustreit.com

HISTORICAL FINANCIALS
Company Type: Public

Income Statement				FYE: December 31
	REVENUE ($mil)	NET INCOME ($mil)	NET PROFIT MARGIN	EMPLOYEES
12/21	192.3	71.9	37.4%	16
12/20	178.3	80.8	45.3%	15
12/19	163.4	46.3	28.4%	52
12/18	156.9	57.9	36.9%	57
12/17	132.9	25.8	19.5%	50
Annual Growth	9.7%	29.1%	—	(24.8%)

2021 Year-End Financials
Debt ratio: 41.0%
Return on equity: 7.8%
Cash ($ mil.): 19.9
Current Ratio: 0.43
Long-term debt ($ mil.): 673.3
No. of shares ($ mil.): 96.3
Dividends
Yield: 4.6%
Payout: 137.6%
Market value ($ mil.): 2,198.0

	STOCK PRICE ($) FY Close	P/E High/Low		PER SHARE ($) Earnings Dividends		Book Value
12/21	22.83	34	27	0.74	1.06	9.51
12/20	22.18	28	9	0.85	1.00	9.60
12/19	20.63	52	37	0.49	0.90	9.75
12/18	18.46	28	18	0.72	0.82	8.95
12/17	16.76	56	42	0.35	0.74	7.88
Annual Growth	8.0%	—	—	20.6%	9.4%	4.8%

CarGurus Inc

EXECUTIVES

Chairman, Executive Chairman, Director, Langley Steinert, $325,000 total compensation
President, Chief Operating Officer, Samuel Zales, $380,000 total compensation
International Chief Executive Officer, Director, Jason Trevisan, $348,129 total compensation
Product Chief Products Officer, Thomas Caputo, $242,959 total compensation
Chief People Officer, Andrea Eldridge
Chief Financial Officer, Treasurer, Secretary, Scot Fredo
Chief Technology Officer, Matthew Quinn
Chief Marketing Officer, Dafna Sarnoff
Director, Lori A. Hickok
Director, Greg M. Schwartz
Director, Steven Conine
Director, Stephen Kaufer
Director, Ian G. Smith
Auditors : Ernst & Young LLP

LOCATIONS

HQ: CarGurus Inc
2 Canal Park, 4th Floor, Cambridge, MA 02141
Phone: 617 354-0068
Web: www.cargurus.com

HISTORICAL FINANCIALS
Company Type: Public

Income Statement				FYE: December 31
	REVENUE ($mil)	NET INCOME ($mil)	NET PROFIT MARGIN	EMPLOYEES
12/20	551.4	77.5	14.1%	827
12/19	588.9	42.1	7.2%	921
12/18	454.0	65.1	14.4%	732
12/17	316.8	13.1	4.2%	549
12/16	198.1	6.4	3.3%	514
Annual Growth	29.2%	85.9%	—	12.6%

2020 Year-End Financials
Debt ratio: —
Return on equity: 24.5%
Cash ($ mil.): 190.3
Current Ratio: 4.99
Long-term debt ($ mil.): —
No. of shares ($ mil.): 113.3
Dividends
Yield: —
Payout: —
Market value ($ mil.): 3,598.0

	STOCK PRICE ($) FY Close	P/E High/Low		Earnings	PER SHARE ($) Dividends	Book Value
12/20	31.73	55	23	0.68	0.00	3.29
12/19	35.18	113	75	0.37	0.00	2.29
12/18	33.73	93	49	0.57	0.00	1.76
12/17	29.98	251	212	0.12	0.00	1.20
Annual Growth	1.9%	—	—	78.3%	—	40.1%

Casella Waste Systems, Inc.

The wasteful habits of Americans are big business for Casella Waste Systems, which operates regional waste-hauling businesses mainly in the northeastern US. The company serves residential, commercial, industrial, and municipal customers. In 2022, it owned and/or operated about 50 solid waste collection operations, about 65 transfer stations, about 25 recycling facilities, more than eight Subtitle D landfills, three landfill gas-to-energy facilities and one landfill permitted to accept construction and demolition materials. The company was founded in 1975.

Operations
The company operates in three segments: Western (about 45%), Eastern (around 30%), and Resource Solutions (about 25%).Eastern region consists of wastesheds located in Maine, northern, central and southeastern New Hampshire, central and eastern Massachusetts, and northeastern Connecticut.

Western region includes wastesheds located in Vermont, southwestern New Hampshire, eastern, western and upstate New York, northwestern Massachusetts, and in Pennsylvania around its Subtitle D landfill located in Mount Jewett, Pennsylvania ("McKean Landfill").

Resource Solutions operating segment, which includes its larger-scale recycling and commodity brokerage operations along with its organics services and large scale commercial and industrial services, from its historical lines-of-service of recycling, organics and customer solutions into two lines-of-service: processing and non-processing.

Geographic Reach
The company provides integrated solid waste services in seven states: Vermont, New Hampshire, New York, Massachusetts, Connecticut, Maine, and Pennsylvania. Its corporate headquarters is located in Vermont.

Sales and Marketing
The waste services company serves commercial, industrial, municipal, and residential customers. The name and logo, or, where appropriate, that of the divisional operations, are displayed on all of containers and trucks. The company attend and make presentations at municipal and state meetings, and advertise in a variety of media throughout their service footprint.

Financial Performance
The company's revenue for fiscal 2021 increased by $114.6 million to $889.2 million compared from the prior year with $774.6 million.

Net income for fiscal 2021 decreased to $41.1 million compared from the prior year with $91.1 million.

Cash held by the company at the end of fiscal 2021 decreased to $33.8 million. Cash provided by operations was $182.7 million while cash used for investing and financing activities were $293.2 million and $10.1 million, respectively. Main uses of cash were acquisitions and principal payments on debt.

Strategy
The 2021 plan was focused on enhancing shareholder returns by improving cash flows and reducing debt leverage by advancing efforts in five key areas: increasing landfill returns; driving additional profitability in collection operations; creating incremental value through Resource Solutions; using technology to drive profitable growth and efficiencies; and allocating capital to balance delivering with smart growth.

Company Background
The company was founded in 1975 with one truck.

EXECUTIVES

Chief Executive Officer, Chairman, Director, John W. Casella, $535,500 total compensation
Vice-Chairman, Subsidiary Officer, Director, Douglas R. Casella
President, Chief Operating Officer, Edwin D. Johnson, $413,100 total compensation
Investor Relations Senior Vice President, Finance Senior Vice President, Investor Relations Chief Financial Officer, Finance Chief Financial Officer, Investor Relations Treasurer, Finance Treasurer, Edmond R. Coletta, $341,700 total compensation
Vice President, General Counsel, Shelley Sayward
Lead Director, Director, Joseph G. Doody
Director, Michael Louis Battles
Director, Gary Sova
Director, Emily Nagle Green
Director, William P. Hulligan
Director, Michael K. Burke
Director, Rose Stuckey Kirk
Auditors : RSM US LLP

LOCATIONS

HQ: Casella Waste Systems, Inc.
25 Greens Hill Lane, Rutland, VT 05701
Phone: 802 775-0325
Web: www.casella.com

2015 Sales
	$ mil.	% of total
Western	231.9	43
Eastern	167.5	31
Recycling	46.3	8
Other	100.7	18
Total	546.4	100

PRODUCTS/OPERATIONS
2015 Sales
	$ mil.	% of total
Solid Waste Operations		
Collection	238.3	44
Disposal	156.5	29
Power generation	6.8	1
Processing	6.1	1
Customer Solutions	53.3	10
Recycling	46.3	8
Organics	39.1	7
Total	546.4	100

COMPETITORS
A2A SPA
ADVANCED DISPOSAL SERVICES, INC.
BIFFA GROUP HOLDINGS (UK) LIMITED
CLEAN HARBORS, INC.
COVANTA HOLDING CORPORATION
RENTECH, INC.
SELECT ENERGY SERVICES, LLC
STERICYCLE, INC.
US ECOLOGY HOLDINGS, INC.
WASTE CONNECTIONS US, INC.

HISTORICAL FINANCIALS
Company Type: Public

Income Statement — FYE: December 31

	REVENUE ($mil)	NET INCOME ($mil)	NET PROFIT MARGIN	EMPLOYEES
12/21	889.2	41.1	4.6%	2,900
12/20	774.5	91.1	11.8%	2,500
12/19	743.2	31.6	4.3%	2,500
12/18	660.6	6.4	1.0%	2,300
12/17	599.3	(21.7)	—	2,000
Annual Growth	10.4%	—	—	9.7%

2021 Year-End Financials
Debt ratio: 43.0% No. of shares ($ mil.): 51.4
Return on equity: 10.4% Dividends
Cash ($ mil.): 33.8 Yield: —
Current Ratio: 0.96 Payout: —
Long-term debt ($ mil.): 542.5 Market value ($ mil.): 4,392.0

	STOCK PRICE ($) FY Close	P/E High/Low		Earnings	PER SHARE ($) Dividends	Book Value
12/21	85.42	112	68	0.80	0.00	8.22
12/20	61.95	34	19	1.86	0.00	7.09
12/19	46.03	71	41	0.66	0.00	2.57
12/18	28.49	225	149	0.15	0.00	(0.37)
12/17	23.02	—	—	(0.52)	0.00	(0.90)
Annual Growth	38.8%	—	—	—	—	—

Cashmere Valley Bank Washington (New)

EXECUTIVES

Chairman, Subsidiary Officer, Brian Charles Nelson
Executive Vice President, Chief Loan Officer, Steve Vradenburg
Vice-Chairman, Director, Lyman Boyd
President, Chief Executive Officer, Subsidiary Officer, Director, Greg Oakes
Vice President, Chief Retail Operations Officer, Connie Fritz
Vice President, Chief Information Officer, Sue Ozburn
Human Resources Assistant Vice President, Human Resources Subsidiary Officer, Director, Annie Horey
Executive Vice President, Chief Financial Officer, David E. Hooston
Director, John Doyle
Director, Judy Conner
Director, Bill Dronen
Director, Keith Wiggins
Auditors : BDO USA, LLP

LOCATIONS

HQ: Cashmere Valley Bank Washington (New)
117 Aplets Way, Cashmere, WA 98815
Phone: 509 782-2092 **Fax:** 509 782-1643
Web: www.cashmerevalleybank.com

HISTORICAL FINANCIALS
Company Type: Public

Income Statement — FYE: December 31

	ASSETS ($mil)	NET INCOME ($mil)	INCOME AS % OF ASSETS	EMPLOYEES
12/20	1,994.2	25.5	1.3%	0
12/19	1,651.4	23.3	1.4%	0
12/18	1,520.7	21.7	1.4%	0
12/17	1,516.0	18.4	1.2%	0
12/16	1,454.2	17.5	1.2%	0
Annual Growth	8.2%	9.9%	—	—

2020 Year-End Financials

Return on assets: 1.3%
Return on equity: 11.4%
Long-term debt ($ mil.): —
No. of shares ($ mil.): 3.9
Sales ($ mil.): 74.6
Dividends
 Yield: —
 Payout: 52.9%
Market value ($ mil.): 209.0

	STOCK PRICE ($) FY Close	P/E High/Low		PER SHARE ($) Earnings	Dividends	Book Value
12/20	52.61	10	6	6.42	3.40	60.09
12/19	63.00	11	10	5.69	1.30	51.78
12/18	54.01	14	10	5.27	2.70	45.54
12/17	58.00	13	11	4.47	1.08	43.90
12/16	47.25	11	9	4.27	0.98	40.50
Annual Growth	2.7%	—	—	10.7%	36.5%	10.4%

Catalent Inc

EXECUTIVES

Chairman, Chief Executive Officer, Director, John R. Chiminski, $1,025,000 total compensation
Chief Commercial Officer, Karen Flynn
President, Chief Operating Officer, Alessandro Maselli, $450,266 total compensation
Senior Vice President, Chief Human Resources Officer, Ricardo Pravda
Senior Vice President, Chief Financial Officer, Wetteny Joseph, $498,489 total compensation
Senior Vice President, Corporate Secretary, General Counsel, Steven L. Fasman, $550,000 total compensation
Regulatory Affairs Senior Vice President, Quality Assurance Senior Vice President, Scott Gunther
Division Officer, Kay Schmidt
Division Officer, Jonathan Arnold, $387,095 total compensation
Division Officer, Barry B. Littlejohns, $448,571 total compensation
Division Officer, Aristippos Gennadios
Division Officer, Paul Hegwood
Division Officer, Manja Boerman
Division Officer, Peter L. Buzy, $49,253 total compensation
Region Officer, Mario Gargiulo
Director, Madhavan Balachandran
Director, J. Martin Carroll
Director, Rolf A. Classon
Director, Rosemary A. Crane
Director, John J. Greisch
Director, Christa Kreuzburg
Director, Gregory T. Lucier
Director, Donald Eugene Morel
Lead Director, Director, Jack L. Stahl
Director (frmr), Peter Zippelius
Auditors : Ernst & Young LLP

LOCATIONS

HQ: Catalent Inc
14 Schoolhouse Road, Somerset, NJ 08873
Phone: 732 537-6200
Web: www.catalent.com

HISTORICAL FINANCIALS
Company Type: Public

Income Statement — FYE: June 30

	REVENUE ($mil)	NET INCOME ($mil)	NET PROFIT MARGIN	EMPLOYEES
06/21	3,998.0	585.0	14.6%	17,300
06/20	3,094.3	220.7	7.1%	13,900
06/19	2,518.0	137.4	5.5%	12,300
06/18	2,463.4	83.6	3.4%	10,700
06/17	2,075.4	109.8	5.3%	10,800
Annual Growth	17.8%	51.9%	—	12.5%

2021 Year-End Financials

Debt ratio: 35.6%
Return on equity: 15.0%
Cash ($ mil.): 896.0
Current Ratio: 2.44
Long-term debt ($ mil.): 3,166
No. of shares ($ mil.): 170.5
Dividends
 Yield: —
 Payout: —
Market value ($ mil.): 18,434.0

	STOCK PRICE ($) FY Close	P/E High/Low		PER SHARE ($) Earnings	Dividends	Book Value
06/21	108.12	40	23	3.11	0.00	25.07
06/20	73.30	68	32	1.14	0.00	21.53
06/19	54.21	59	32	0.90	0.00	15.70
06/18	41.89	74	53	0.63	0.00	8.14
06/17	35.10	43	25	0.87	0.00	5.79
Annual Growth	32.5%	—	—	37.5%	—	44.3%

Cathay General Bancorp

Cathay General Bancorp is the holding company for Cathay Bank, which mainly serves Chinese and Vietnamese communities from more than 35 branches in California, and about 20 in New York, Washington, Illinois, Texas, Maryland, Massachusetts, Nevada, New Jersey. It also has a branch in Hong Kong, and offices in Beijing, Shanghai, and Taipei. Catering to small to medium-sized businesses and individual consumers, the bank offers standard deposit services and loans. Commercial mortgage loans account for about half of the bank's portfolio; residential mortgage loans comprise nearly 30%. The bank's Cathay Wealth Management unit offers stocks, bonds, mutual funds, insurance, annuities, and advisory services.

Operations

Through its branch network and lending units, Cathay Bank provides a broad range of financial services to individuals and companies. These services include demand, time and savings deposits; and commercial and industrial, real estate and consumer lending.

Overall, the bank makes up some 90% of its total revenue from interest income on loan receivable, with roughly 5% of total revenue coming from interest income on the bank's investment securities. About 5% of total revenue comes from service charges on depository services, credit commission and other operating income.

Geographic Reach

California-based Cathay Bank operates about 30 branches in Southern California, about 15 branches in Northern California, ten branches in New York State, four branches in Washington State, two branches in Illinois, two branches in Texas, one branch in each of Maryland, Massachusetts, Nevada, and New Jersey, one branch in Hong Kong, and a representative office in Beijing, in Shanghai, and in Taipei.

Financial Performance

Net interest income increased $45.6 million, or 8.3%, from $552.1 million in 2020 to $597.8 million in 2021. The increase in net interest income was due primarily to the decrease in interest expense from time deposits partially offset by lower interest income from loans.

In 2021, the company had a net income of $298.3 million, a 30% increase from the previous year's net income of $228.9 million.

The company's cash at the end of 2021 was $2.4 billion. Operating activities generated $334.3 million, while investing activities used $859.9 million, mainly for net increase in loans, and purchase of investment securities available-for-sale. Financing activities provided another $1.6 billion.

EXECUTIVES

Subsidiary Officer, Executive Chairman, Director, Dunson K. Cheng, $800,000 total compensation

Subsidiary Officer, Vice-Chairman, Director, Anthony M. Tang, $231,428 total compensation

Subsidiary Officer, Vice-Chairman, Director, Peter Wu, $789,104 total compensation

President, Chief Executive Officer, Subsidiary Officer, Director, Pin Tai, $783,750 total compensation

Executive Vice President, Chief Financial Officer, Treasurer, Subsidiary Officer, Heng W. Chen, $473,800 total compensation

Executive Vice President, Secretary, General Counsel, Subsidiary Officer, Lisa L. Kim

Subsidiary Officer, Irwin Wong, $450,000 total compensation

Subsidiary Officer, Kim R. Bingham, $353,294 total compensation

Subsidiary Officer, Chang M. Liu, $380,806 total compensation

Subsidiary Officer, Mark H. Lee

Director, Kelly L. Chan

Director, Joseph C.H. Poon

Director, Nelson Chung

Director, Felix S. Fernandez

Director, Ting Y. Liu

Director, Richard Sun

Director, Michael M.Y. Chang

Director, Jane H. Jelenko

Auditors: KPMG LLP

LOCATIONS

HQ: Cathay General Bancorp
777 North Broadway, Los Angeles, CA 90012
Phone: 213 625-4700
Web: www.cathaybank.com

2015 Branch offices

	No.
Southern California Branches	21
Northern California Branches	12
New York Branches	12
Illinois Branches	4
Washington Branches	3
Texas Branches	2
Massachusetts Branch	1
Nevada Branch	1
New Jersey Branch	1
Maryland Branch	1
Overseas Branch	1
Total	59

PRODUCTS/OPERATIONS

2015 sales

	$ mil.	% of total
Interest and Dividend income		
Loan receivable	427.6	88
Investment securities- taxable	21.5	4
Federal Home Loan Bank stock	3.2	1
Deposits with banks	1.4	-
Non-Interest income		
Securities losses, net	(3.3)	-
Letters of credit commissions	5.6	1
Depository service fees	5.3	1
Other operating income	25.1	5
Total	486.4	100

Products/Services
Personal
Accounts
Checking Accounts
Savings Accounts
CDs
IRA CD
Debit Cards
Loans
Mortgage Loan
Home Equity Financing
Auto Loan
Credit Cards
Cathay Online Banking
Mobile Banking
Business/Commercial
Business Accounts
Business Checking Account
Business Savings Account
CDs
Cash Management Services
Merchant Deposit Capture
Zero Balance Account
Lockbox Service
Merchant Bankcard Services
Courier Deposit Service
Armored Transport Services
Cash Vault Services
Business Online Banking
Loans
Commercial Financing
Real Estate & Construction Financing
International Banking & Financing
Smart Capital Line
SBA Guaranteed Loan Program
Credit Cards

COMPETITORS

BANK OF HAWAII CORPORATION
BANNER CORPORATION
EAST WEST BANCORP, INC.
FB CORPORATION
HOMESTREET, INC.
MIDLAND FINANCIAL CO.
NEW YORK COMMUNITY BANCORP, INC.
REGIONS FINANCIAL CORPORATION
WASHINGTON TRUST BANCORP, INC.
WILSHIRE BANCORP, INC.

HISTORICAL FINANCIALS

Company Type: Public

Income Statement
FYE: December 31

	ASSETS ($mil)	NET INCOME ($mil)	INCOME AS % OF ASSETS	EMPLOYEES
12/20	19,043.1	228.8	1.2%	1,205
12/19	18,094.1	279.1	1.5%	1,219
12/18	16,784.7	271.8	1.6%	1,277
12/17	15,640.1	176.0	1.1%	1,271
12/16	14,520.7	175.0	1.2%	1,129
Annual Growth	7.0%	6.9%	—	1.6%

2020 Year-End Financials

Return on assets: 1.2%
Return on equity: 9.6%
Long-term debt ($ mil.): —
No. of shares ($ mil.): 79.5
Sales ($ mil.): 743.3
Dividends
Yield: 3.8%
Payout: 43.9%
Market value ($ mil.): 2,559.0

	STOCK PRICE ($) FY Close	P/E High/Low		PER SHARE ($) Earnings	Dividends	Book Value
12/20	32.19	13	6	2.87	1.24	30.41
12/19	38.05	11	9	3.48	1.24	28.78
12/18	33.53	13	10	3.33	1.03	26.36
12/17	42.17	20	16	2.17	0.87	24.39
12/16	38.03	17	12	2.19	0.75	22.97
Annual Growth	(4.1%)	—	—	7.0%	13.4%	7.3%

Cavco Industries Inc (DE)

Cavco Industries designs and produces factory-built housing products primarily distributed through a network of independent and company-owned retailers. It is one of the largest producers of manufactured and modular homes in the US, based on reported wholesale shipments. Its products are marketed under a variety of brand names including Cavco, Fleetwood, Palm Harbor, Nationwide, Fairmont, Friendship, Chariot Eagle, Destiny, Commodore, Colony, Pennwest, R-Anell, Manorwood and MidCountry. It is also a leading producer of park model RVs, vacation cabins and factory-built commercial structures. Its insurance subsidiary, Standard Casualty, provides property and casualty insurance to owners of manufactured homes. Cavco was founded in 1965.

Operations

Cavco operates two business segments: factory-built housing, which includes wholesale and retail factory-built housing operations and accounts for about 95% of sales, and a finance and insurance segment (some 5% of sales), which includes manufactured housing consumer finance and insurance.

Cavco's mortgage subsidiary, CountryPlace, is an approved Fannie Mae and Freddie Mac, seller and servicer, and a Ginnie Mae mortgage-backed securities offering mortgages to buyers of the company's homes. Its insurance subsidiary, Standard Casualty, provides property and casualty insurance to owners of manufactured homes.

Its factory-built houses are marketed under brand names such as Cavco Homes, Nationwide Homes, Fleetwood Homes, Palm Harbor Homes, Fairmont Homes, Friendship Homes, Chariot Eagle, Destiny, Destiny, Commodore, Colony, Pennwest, R-Anell, Manorwood and MidCountry.

Geographic ReachBased in Phoenix, Arizona, Cavco operates about 25 homebuilding facilities located throughout the US.

Sales and Marketing Cavco distributes its homes through about 45 company-owned US retail outlets and a network of independent distributors in nearly 50 states, Canada. Texas is Cavco's biggest market with more than 30 company-owned stores. Advertising costs are expensed as incurred and were $1.4 million in fiscal year 2022, $807,000 in fiscal year 2021 and $900,000 in fiscal year 2020.

Financial Performance

Net revenue for 2021 was $1.6 billion, a 47% increase from the previous year's revenue of $1.1 billion.

In 2021, the company had a net income of $197.7 million, a 158% increase from the previous year's net income of $76.6 million.

The company's cash at the end of 2021 was $259.3 million. Operating activities generated $144.2 million, while investing activities used $159.1 million, mainly for payments for acquisitions. Financing activities used another $65.1 million, primarily for payments for common stock repurchases.

Strategy

The company's marketing efforts are focused on providing manufactured homes that are customizable and appeal to a wide range of home buyers, on a regional basis, in the markets it serves. The primary demographics for its products are entry-level and move-up buyers and persons age 55 and older. The company also markets to special niches such as subdivision developers and vacation home buyers.

It focuses on developing and maintaining the resources necessary to meet its customer's desire for varied and unique specifications in an efficient factory production environment. This enables the company to attract distributors and consumers who desire the flexibility the custom home building process provides but who also seek the value and affordability created by building a home on a factory production line.

Mergers and Acquisitions

In 2022, Cavco agreed to acquire a 184,000 square-foot manufacturing facility in Hamlet, North Carolina, which will be modified to produce homes built under the standards of the US Department of Housing and Urban Development (HUD code). With the addition of this new facility, which will bring its total number of homebuilding production lines to 27, the company is expanding its access to much-needed affordable housing solutions and strengthening its position in the region. The seller, Volumetric Building Companies (VBC), currently produces multi-family residential and commercial projects in the facility and intends to move that production closer to their markets in the Northeast.

In late 2021, Cavco acquired the business and certain assets and liabilities of The Commodore Corporation (Commodore), the largest independent builder of manufactured and modular housing in the US, operating under a variety of brand names and with two wholly owned retail stores. Bill Boor, Cavco President and Chief Executive Officer, said, "We are excited to welcome the Commodore employees to the Cavco family and look forward to building on the strong reputation and success that Commodore has developed over their long history." The purchase price totals $153 million, before certain adjustments at and following closing of the transaction. The acquisition is being funded with cash on hand.

Company Background

Alfred Ghelfi and partner Bob Curtis began a part-time business in 1965 making pickup truck camper shells. The business, Roadrunner Manufacturing, became Cavalier Manufacturing in 1966, incorporated in 1968, and went public in 1969. The Cavalier name was already in use, so in 1974 the company's name was changed to Cavco. After the 1970s oil crisis nearly wiped out the firm, Ghelfi bought out Curtis' share and began making mobile homes. In time, Cavco began leasing movable storage buildings, but the only successful part of that business was the security container segment (the rest was sold in 1994). A mid-1980s housing market crash in Arizona spurred Cavco to enter a totally-new field -- health care utilization management -- in 1987.

In 1995, Cavco partnered with Japan's Auto Berg Enterprises to begin selling modular housing in Japan. The next year Cavco teamed up with Arizona Public Service to develop solar-powered manufactured housing, and it also sold its health care business. Centex acquired nearly 80% of Cavco for $75 million in 1997. The next year Cavco moved into Texas (one of the biggest markets for factory-built homes), acquiring Texas retailer Boerne Homes.

HISTORY

Alfred Ghelfi and partner Bob Curtis began a part-time business in 1965 making pickup truck camper shells. The business, Roadrunner Manufacturing, became Cavalier Manufacturing in 1966, incorporated in 1968, and went public in 1969. The Cavalier name was already in use, so in 1974 the company's name was changed to Cavco. After the 1970s oil crisis nearly wiped out the firm, Ghelfi bought out Curtis' share and began making mobile homes. In time Cavco began leasing movable storage buildings, but the only successful part of that business was the security container segment (the rest was sold in 1994). A mid-1980s housing market crash in Arizona spurred Cavco to enter a totally new field -- health care utilization management -- in 1987.

In 1995 Cavco partnered with Japan's Auto Berg Enterprises to begin selling modular housing in Japan. The next year Cavco teamed up with Arizona Public Service to develop solar-powered manufactured housing, and it also sold its health care business. Centex acquired nearly 80% of Cavco for $75 million in 1997. The next year Cavco moved into Texas (one of the biggest markets for factory-built homes), acquiring Texas retailer Boerne Homes.

With demand shrinking and surplus inventory building up, the company closed its Belen, New Mexico, factory in 2000 and moved its production to plants in Phoenix and Seguin, Texas. That fall Centex tapped manufactured housing veteran Joseph Stegmayer as chairman of its manufactured housing segment.

In 2001 the company launched Factory Liquidators, a new retail concept focusing on repossessed homes.

Centex's board of directors approved the tax-free distribution to its shareholders of all of Cavco's outstanding common stock in 2003. The spin-off was completed in June of that year. Continued weakness within the industry forced Cavco to close eight of its company-owned retail outlets in fiscal 2004 and seven more in 2005.

EXECUTIVES

Chairman, Director, Steven G. Bunger, $200,000 total compensation

President, Chief Executive Officer, Director, William C. Boor

Executive Vice President, Chief Compliance Officer, Corporate Secretary, General Counsel, Mickey R. Dragash, $325,000 total compensation

Senior Vice President, Steven K. Like, $145,000 total compensation

Chief Accounting Officer, Joshua J. Barsetti, $200,000 total compensation

Secretary, General Counsel, James P. Glew

Subsidiary Officer, Charles E. Lott, $250,000 total compensation

Subsidiary Officer, Larry H. Keener, $240,000 total compensation

Director, Susan L. Blount

Director, David A. Greenblatt

Director, Richard A. Kerley

Director, Steven W. Moster

Director, Julia W. Sze

Auditors : RSM US LLP

LOCATIONS

HQ: Cavco Industries Inc (DE)
3636 North Central Ave., Ste. 1200, Phoenix, AZ 85012
Phone: 602 256-6263
Web: www.cavco.com

PRODUCTS/OPERATIONS

2017 Sales

	$ mil.	% of total
Factory-built housing	815.5	94
Financial Services	55.7	6
Total	871`.2	100

Selected Products
Manufactured Homes

Modular Homes
Park Model RVs and Cabins
Commercial Structures
Mortgage Lending
Insurance

Selected Brands
Cavco Homes
Chariot Eagle
Fleetwood Homes
Palm Harbor Homes
Fairmont Homes
Friendship Homes
Lexington Homes

COMPETITORS

CENTURY COMMUNITIES, INC.
CHAMPION ENTERPRISES HOLDINGS, LLC
CLAYTON HOMES, INC.
D.R. HORTON, INC.
DELTEC HOMES, INC.
HOVNANIAN ENTERPRISES, INC.
KB HOME
NVR, INC.
PULTEGROUP, INC.
TOLL BROTHERS, INC.

HISTORICAL FINANCIALS
Company Type: Public

Income Statement
FYE: April 3

	REVENUE ($mil)	NET INCOME ($mil)	NET PROFIT MARGIN	EMPLOYEES
04/21*	1,108.0	76.6	6.9%	4,700
03/20	1,061.7	75.0	7.1%	5,000
03/19	962.7	68.6	7.1%	4,650
03/18	871.2	61.5	7.1%	4,500
04/17	773.7	37.9	4.9%	4,300
Annual Growth	9.4%	19.2%	—	2.2%

*Fiscal year change

2021 Year-End Financials

Debt ratio: 1.1%
Return on equity: 11.6%
Cash ($ mil.): 322.2
Current Ratio: 2.75
Long-term debt ($ mil.): 10.3
No. of shares ($ mil.): 9.2
Dividends
  Yield: —
  Payout: —
Market value ($ mil.): 2,146.0

	STOCK PRICE ($) FY Close	P/E High/Low		PER SHARE ($) Earnings	Dividends	Book Value
04/21*	232.41	28	13	8.25	0.00	74.03
03/20	148.47	28	14	8.10	0.00	66.23
03/19	117.53	34	15	7.40	0.00	58.21
03/18	173.75	26	16	6.68	0.00	50.54
04/17	116.40	28	20	4.17	0.00	43.85
Annual Growth	18.9%	—	—	18.6%	—	14.0%

*Fiscal year change

Cboe Global Markets Inc

Cboe Global Markets, Inc., a leading provider of market infrastructure and tradable products, delivers cutting-edge trading, clearing, and investment solutions to market participants around the world. The company is committed to operating a trusted, inclusive global marketplace, and to providing leading products, technology and data solutions that enable participants to define a sustainable financial future. The company offers trading across a diverse range of products in multiple asset classes and geographies, including options, futures, US, Canadian, and European equities, exchange-traded products (ETPs), global foreign exchange (FX) and volatility products based on the Cboe Volatility Index (VIX Index), recognized as the world's premier gauge of US equity market volatility. In addition, the company operates one of the largest stock exchanges by value traded in Europe, and owns EuroCCP, a leading Pan-European equities clearing house.

Operations

Cboe Global Markets operates through five segments: North American Equities, Options, Europe and Asia Pacific, Futures, and Global FX.

Its North American Equities segment includes trading of listed cash equities and ETP transaction services that occur on BZX, BYX, EDGX, and EDGA and Canadian equities and other transaction services that occur on or through the MATCHNow ATS. It also includes the listing business where ETPs and the company are listed on BZX. It accounts for some 45% of total revenue.

The Options segment includes trading of listed market indeces, mostly on an exclusive basis, as well as on non-exclusive "multi-listed" options, such as on the stock of individual corporation and options on other exchange-traded products (ETP options), such as exchange ? traded funds (ETF options) and exchange ? traded notes (ETN options) that occur on Cboe Options, C2, BZX and EDGX, all US national security exchanges. The options segment accounts for roughly 45% of revenue.

Its European and Asia Pacific segment includes trading of Pan-European listed equities transaction services, ETPs, exchange-traded commodities, and international depository receipts that are hosted on MTFs operated by Cboe Europe Equities. It also includes the ETP listings business on RMs and clearing activities of EuroCCP. Cboe Europe Equities operates lit and dark pools, a periodic auctions book, and a Large-in-Scale (LIS) trading negotiation facility. Cboe Europe Equities also includes revenue generated from the licensing of proprietary market data and from access and capacity services. It accounts for over 5% of revenue.

The Futures segment includes transaction services provided by the company's fully electronic futures exchange, CFE, which includes offerings for trading of VIX futures and other futures products, the licensing of proprietary market data, as well as access and capacity services. The futures segment accounts for about 5% of revenue.

Its Global FX segment includes institutional FX services on the Cboe FX platform, as well as non-deliverable forward FX transactions executed on Cboe SEF and Cboe Swiss, as well as revenue generated from the licensing of proprietary market data and from access and capacity services. It accounts for less than 5% of revenue.

Overall, transaction and clearing fees account for over 75% of revenue, while access and capacity fees generated about 10%, market data and regulatory fees with around 5% each, and other revenues accounting for the rest.

Geographic Reach

Cboe Global Markets is headquartered in Chicago with a network of domestic and global offices across the Americas, Europe and Asia, including main hubs in New York, London, Kansas City, and Amsterdam.

Sales and Marketing

Cboe Global Markets advertises through advertising, costs for special events, sponsorship of industry conferences, options education seminars.

Travel and promotional expenses increased in 2021 compared to the same period in 2020, primarily due to an increase in marketing and advertising expenses attributable to promotional efforts.. Travel and Promotional Expenses were $9.7 million, $6.6 million, and $11.9 million in 2021, 2020, and 2019, respectively.

Its customers include financial institutions, trading platforms, institutional and individual investors and professional traders.

Financial Performance

The company's revenue for fiscal 2021 increased to $3.5 billion compared from the prior year with $3.4 billion. The increase was primarily due to increases in subscribers which results in an increase in logical port revenue across the Options, Europe and Asia Pacific, and North American Equities segments, coupled with an increase in physical port revenue in the North American Equities and Options segments.

Net income for fiscal 2021 increased to $529.0 million compared from the prior year with $468.2 million.

Cash held by the company at the end of fiscal 2021 increased to $1.1 billion. Cash provided by operations was $596.8 million while cash used for investing and financing activities were $352.7 million and $200.3 million, respectively. Main uses of cash were contributions to investments and cash dividends on common stock.

Strategy

Cboe's strategy is to build one of the world's largest global derivatives and securities networks to create value and drive growth by: innovating to capture growing demand for trading products and data services, globally; integrating across ecosystems to increase efficiency and better serve customers; and growing by accessing untapped addressable markets.

Mergers and Acquisitions

Early 2022, Cboe Global Markets has completed the acquisition of Eris Digital

Holdings, LLC (ErisX), an operator of a U.S. based digital asset spot market, a regulated futures exchange and a regulated clearinghouse. Ownership of ErisX allows Cboe to enter the digital asset spot and derivatives marketplaces through a digital-first platform developed with industry partners to focus on robust regulatory compliance, data and transparency. With Cboe, ErisX aims to be a digital asset market rooted in the exchange principles of transparency and regulatory compliance, supported by a network of intermediaries, providing client-driven solutions that help institutions fully embrace this emerging asset class. Terms were not disclosed.

In late 2021, Cboe Global Markets has entered into a definitive agreement to acquire Aequitas Innovations, Inc., more commonly known as NEO1, a fintech organization that comprises of a fully registered Tier-1 Canadian securities exchange with a diverse product and services set ranging from corporate listings to cash equity trading. Adding NEO to the Cboe network better enables to create a first-class equities offering in Canada, bolstering its global markets in North America, Europe and Asia Pacific, and bringing it one step closer to its vision of building one of the world's largest global derivatives and securities trading networks. Terms were not disclosed.

Also in late 2021, Cboe Global Markets has entered into an agreement as a limited partner to invest in the planned acquisition of Trading Technologies International, Inc. (TT), a global provider of next-generation professional trading software, connectivity and data solutions. Trading Technologies, based in Chicago, has an expansive and highly engaged customer base with thousands of users, including the top futures commission merchants (FCM) and brokers globally, as well as many of the world's leading buy-side institutions. Terms were not disclosed.

In mid-2021, Cboe Global Markets has completed the acquisition of Chi-X Asia Pacific Holdings, Ltd. (Chi-X Asia Pacific), an alternative market operator and provider of innovative market solutions, from J.C. Flowers & Co. LLC. This acquisition will provide Cboe with a single point of entry into two key capital markets ? Australia and Japan ? to help enable it to expand its global equities business into Asia Pacific, bring other products and services to the region, and further expand access to its unique proprietary product suite in the region. Terms of the deal were not disclosed.

In early 2021, Cboe Global Markets completed its acquisition of BIDS Trading, a registered broker-dealer and the operator of the BIDS Alternative Trading System (ATS), the largest block-trading ATS by volume in the US. Through ownership of BIDS Trading, Cboe gains a competitive foothold in the off-exchange segment of the US equities market, which now accounts for more than 40% of overall US equities trading volume. The acquisition of BIDS Trading also provides Cboe with the opportunity to expand its global footprint and diversify its product and service offerings in markets beyond US equities and options. Terms of the deal were not disclosed.

Company Background

In early 2012 the company bought the fully electronic National Stock Exchange. The move boosted the exchange's stock market presence by about half. In 2010 CBOE launched C2, an all-electronic options market capable of trading all of CBOE's products electronically.

CBOE went public in 2010 to better compete in the highly competitive options industry. As a corporation, CBOE had better access to capital markets and was able to more easily enter joint ventures or other business combinations. The long-delayed IPO was also part of CBOE's restructuring efforts and a shift from being member-owned to a for-profit corporation.

The company was founded in 1973 by the Chicago Board of Trade (now part of CME Group).

HISTORY

The company was founded in 1973 by the Chicago Board of Trade (now part of CME Group).

CBOE went public in 2010 to better compete in the highly competitive options industry. As a corporation, CBOE has better access to capital markets and is able to more easily enter joint ventures or other business combinations. CBOE raised $339 million in a 2010 initial public offering (IPO). The long-delayed IPO was part of CBOE's restructuring efforts and a shift from being member-owned to a for-profit corporation. CBOE allotted funds raised in its IPO for general corporate purposes and for the issuance of common stock shares to existing members.

CBOE launched an all-electronic options market in 2010. Named C2, the new platform was capable of trading all of CBOE's products electronically.

In 2011 the CBOE Stock Exchange moved its trading operations from Chicago to the East Coast to better compete with other stock exchanges and better serve its primarily East Coast-based clientele.

In early 2012 the company bought the fully electronic National Stock Exchange, which it continues to run as a separate entity. The move boosted the exchange's stock market presence by about half.

EXECUTIVES

Chairman, Chief Executive Officer, Subsidiary Officer, Director, Edward T. Tilly, $1,265,000 total compensation
President, David Howson
Executive Vice President, Chief Financial Officer, Treasurer, subsidiary Officer, Brian N. Schell, $521,000 total compensation
Executive Vice President, Chief Operating Officer, Christopher A. Isaacson, $540,000 total compensation
Executive Vice President, General Counsel, Secretary, John Patrick Sexton
Senior Vice President, Chief Accounting Officer, Jill Griebenow, $275,000 total compensation
Lead Director, Director, Eugene S. Sunshine
Director, William M. Farrow
Director, Edward J. Fitzpatrick
Director, Ivan K. Fong
Director, Janet P. Froetscher
Director, Jill R. Goodman
Director, Alexander J. Matturri
Director, Jennifer J. McPeek
Director, Roderick A. Palmore
Director, James E. Parisi
Director, Joseph (Joe) P. Ratterman
Director, Fredric J. Tomczyk
Auditors : KPMG LLP

LOCATIONS

HQ: Cboe Global Markets Inc
433 West Van Buren Street, Chicago, IL 60607
Phone: 312 786-5600
Web: www.cboe.com

PRODUCTS/OPERATIONS

Sales 2015

	$ mil.	% of total
Transaction fees	456.0	72
Access fees	53.3	8
Exchange services and other fees	42.2	7
Market data fees	30.0	5
Regulatory fees	33.5	5
Other revenue	19.5	3
Total	634.5	100

COMPETITORS

CME GROUP INC.
INTERACTIVE BROKERS GROUP, INC.
LIQUIDNET HOLDINGS, INC.
MARKETAXESS HOLDINGS INC.
MATSUI SECURITIES CO., LTD.
NASDAQ, INC.
STONEX GROUP INC.
VIRTU FINANCIAL, INC.
VIRTU ITG HOLDINGS LLC
VIRTU KNIGHT CAPITAL GROUP LLC

HISTORICAL FINANCIALS

Company Type: Public

Income Statement — FYE: December 31

	REVENUE ($mil)	NET INCOME ($mil)	NET PROFIT MARGIN	EMPLOYEES
12/21	3,494.8	529.0	15.1%	1,196
12/20	3,427.1	468.2	13.7%	1,010
12/19	2,496.1	374.9	15.0%	823
12/18	2,768.8	426.5	15.4%	842
12/17	2,229.1	401.7	18.0%	889
Annual Growth	11.9%	7.1%	—	7.7%

2021 Year-End Financials

Debt ratio: 19.1%
Return on equity: 15.2%
Cash ($ mil.): 341.9
Current Ratio: 1.31
Long-term debt ($ mil.): 1,299.3
No. of shares ($ mil.): 106.6
Dividends
Yield: —
Payout: 36.5%
Market value ($ mil.): 13,907.0

	STOCK PRICE ($) FY Close	P/E High/Low		PER SHARE ($) Earnings	Dividends	Book Value
12/21	130.40	27	18	4.92	1.80	33.80
12/20	93.12	30	18	4.27	1.56	31.21
12/19	120.00	37	27	3.34	1.34	30.32
12/18	97.83	36	24	3.76	1.16	29.04
12/17	124.59	34	20	3.69	1.04	27.59
Annual Growth	1.1%	—	—	7.5%	14.7%	5.2%

Celsius Holdings Inc

Celsius Holdings wants consumers to enjoy the taste of burning calories. The company develops, markets, and distributes nutritional drinks that claim to burn calories, raise metabolism, and boost energy. Its first product, Celsius, is a canned sparkling beverage that comes in a variety of flavors and is marketed as an alternative to soda, coffee, and traditional energy drinks. Although it has undergone independent clinical studies, results have not been US FDA approved. Its products, which also include non-carbonated Celsius green tea drinks and single-serving powder mix packets that can be added to water, are manufactured by third-party co-packers. Celsius Holdings was founded in 2004 under the name Elite FX.

EXECUTIVES

Chairman, President, Chief Executive Officer, Director, John Fieldly, $410,000 total compensation
Chief Financial Officer, Jarrod Langhans
Lead Director, Director, Hal Kravitz
Director, Caroline Levy
Director, Nicholas (Nick) A Castaldo
Director, Alexandre Ruberti
Director, Cheryl S. Miller
Director, Damon DeSantis
Director, Joyce Russell
Director, James Lee
Auditors : Ernst & Young LLP

LOCATIONS

HQ: Celsius Holdings Inc
2424 N. Federal Highway, Suite 208, Boca Raton, FL 33431
Phone: 561 276-2239
Web: www.celsius.com

COMPETITORS

CHARLIE'S HOLDINGS, INC
ENERGY BRANDS INC.
HORNELL BREWING CO., INC.
MONSTER BEVERAGE CORPORATION
ODWALLA, INC.
REED'S, INC.
SNAPPLE BEVERAGE CORP (DEL)
SUNNY DELIGHT BEVERAGES CO.
SWEET GREEN FIELDS LLC
THE JOLT COMPANY INC

HISTORICAL FINANCIALS
Company Type: Public

Income Statement   FYE: December 31

	REVENUE ($mil)	NET INCOME ($mil)	NET PROFIT MARGIN	EMPLOYEES
12/20	130.7	8.5	6.5%	154
12/19	75.1	9.9	13.3%	120
12/18	52.6	(11.2)	—	50
12/17	36.1	(8.2)	—	39
12/16	22.7	(3.0)	—	39
Annual Growth	54.8%	—	—	41.0%

2020 Year-End Financials
Debt ratio: 0.2%
Return on equity: 10.1%
Cash ($ mil.): 43.2
Current Ratio: 3.53
Long-term debt ($ mil.): —
No. of shares ($ mil.): 72.2
Dividends
  Yield: —
  Payout: —
Market value ($ mil.): 3,636.0

	STOCK PRICE ($) FY Close	P/E High/Low		PER SHARE ($) Earnings	Dividends	Book Value
12/20	50.31	370	27	0.11	0.00	1.44
12/19	4.83	32	20	0.16	0.00	0.92
12/18	3.47	—	—	(0.23)	0.00	0.21
12/17	5.25	—	—	(0.19)	0.00	0.38
12/16	0.42	—	—	(0.09)	0.00	0.27
Annual Growth	230.8%	—	—	—	—	51.7%

Central Garden & Pet Co

Central Garden & Pet is among the leading US producers and distributors of consumer lawn, garden, and pet supplies, providing its products to retailers, home improvement centers, nurseries, and mass merchandisers. Central Garden & Pet operates about 55 manufacturing plants and nearly 70 sales and distribution centers throughout the US. The company sells private label brands as well as brands from other manufacturers. It offers product lines such as AMDRO fire ant bait, Four Paws animal products, Kaytee bird seed, Nylabone dog chews, and TFH pet books. The company was founded by Bill Brown in 1980 as Central Garden Supply.

Operations

Central Garden & Pet operates two primary business lines, Pet and Garden.

The Pet segment generates more than 55% of revenue by producing, distributing, marketing, and selling a wide variety of pet related products for the US. This segment includes: products for dogs and cats, including edible bones, premium healthy edible and non-edible chews, rawhide, toys, pet beds, pet carriers, grooming supplies and other accessories; products for birds, small animals and specialty pets, including cages and habitats, toys, chews, and related accessories; animal and household health and insect control products; products for fish, reptiles and other aquarium-based pets, including aquariums, furniture and lighting fixtures, pumps, filters, water conditioners and supplements, and information and knowledge resources; and products for horses and livestock.

The Garden segment accounts for about 45% of total revenue. It produces and markets proprietary and non-proprietary grass seed; wild bird feed, bird feeders, bird houses and other birding accessories; weed, grass, and other herbicides, insecticide and pesticide products; fertilizers; and decorative outdoor lifestyle products including pottery.

While the company relies on its sales and logistics network to promote its proprietary brands to thousands of independent specialty stores, other garden products account for over 25% of Central Garden & Pet's total revenue. Other pet products and other manufacturers' products provide about 25% each, dog and cat products bring in over 15%, and wild bird represent approximately 10%.

Geographic Reach

Central Garden & Pet is headquartered in Walnut Creek, California. The company operates nearly 55 manufacturing facilities and about 70 sales and logistics facilities, including office and warehouse space. In addition, its garden segment leases approximately 150 acres of land in Oregon, New Jersey, and Virginia used in its grass seed and live plant operations and owns approximately 430 acres of land in Virginia, North Carolina, Maryland, and Ohio for live plant operations. Although most operations are in the US, the company operates facilities in the UK, Canada and China.

Sales and Marketing

Central Garden & Pet relies heavily on just a few national retail chains for much of its sales. Walmart, its largest customer, represents about 15% of total sales while Home Depot, its second largest, accounts for approximately 15%. Lowe's, Costco, and Petco are also significant customers, and together with Walmart and Home Depot generate around half of sales. The company relies on a domestic and international distribution network to deliver its proprietary brands to thousands of independent specialty stores and mass market customers.

Central Garden & Pet advertising costs were approximately $54.6 million, $37.0 million and $27.5 million in fiscal 2021, 2020 and 2019, respectively.

Financial Performance

Net sales for fiscal 2021 increased $608.2 million, or 23%, to $3.3 billion, with organic net sales increasing $335.3 million and sales from its four recent acquisitions of $272.9 million. The company's Pet segment sales increased 13%, and its Garden segment sales increased 39%.

In 2021, the company had a net income of $152.8 million, a 26% increase from the previous year's net income of $121.5 million.

The company's cash at the end of 2021

was $439.2 million. Operating activities generated $250.8 million, while investing activities used $899.4 million, mainly for businesses acquired. Financing activities provided another $420.5 million.

Strategy

The company's Central to Home strategy reinforces its unique purpose to nurture happy and healthy homes and its ambition to lead the future of the pet and garden industries. The company's objective is to grow net sales, operating income and cash flows by developing new products, increasing market share, acquiring businesses and working in partnership with customers to grow the categories in which it participates. It runs its business with a long-term perspective, and we believe the successful delivery of its strategy will enable it to create long-term value for its shareholders. To achieve its objective, the company plans to capitalize on strengths and favorable industry trends by executing on five key strategic pillars to drive growth:

Consumer: Build and Grow Brands that Consumers Love; Customer: Win with Winning Customers and Channels; Central: Fortify the Central Portfolio; Cost: Reduce Cost to Improve Margins and Fuel Growth; and Culture: Strengthen Our Entrepreneurial Business-Unit Led Growth Culture.

Mergers and Acquisitions

In mid-2021, Central Garden & Pet acquired D&D Commodities (D&D). Headquartered in Stephen, Minnesota, D&D is a provider of high-quality, premium bird feed. The addition of D&D's brands will expand Central's portfolio in the bird feed category and further deepen the company's relationship with major retailers.

In early 2021, Central Garden & Pet closed the previously announced acquisition of Green Garden Products (Green Garden), formerly known as Plantation Products, for approximately $532 million from private equity firm Freeman Spogli & Co and other shareholders. Green Garden, headquartered in Norton, Massachusetts, is a leading provider of vegetable, herb and flower seed packets, seed starters and plant nutrients in North America, shipping over 250 million seed packets annually. Under the terms of the merger agreement, the company paid a total of $532 million, subject to certain post-closing adjustments.

Company Background

Central Garden & Pet Company's roots go back to 1955, when it was founded as a small California distributor of lawn and garden supplies. After nearly three decades of unremarkable growth, it was purchased in 1980 by William Brown, a former VP of finance at camera maker Vivitar. The company acquired small distributors but let them operate autonomously. By 1987 Central had sales of $25 million with distribution in California.

The company's first major acquisition was the result of a restructuring of forestry giant Weyerhaeuser, which had diversified into insurance, home building, and diapers, among other products, but was selling noncore divisions to focus solely on timber. It sold Weyerhaeuser Garden Supply to Central in 1990 for $32 million.

Overnight, Central became a national powerhouse with 25 distribution centers serving 38 states. In 1991 sales reached $280 million, of which acquired operations accounted for nearly 70%. The purchase also gave Central 10 high-volume retail customers -- including Costco, Kmart, and Wal-Mart -- which accounted for half of its business. That year the company also acquired a pet distributor, its first move into pet supplies.

To pay down debt associated with the Weyerhaeuser acquisition, the company (then officially known as Central Garden & Pet Company) went public in 1993 (a 1992 IPO was withdrawn when a warehouse fire damaged inventory). With the capital for growth, Central continued to acquire other distributors (from early 1993 to early 1994, it acquired six distributors with about $70 million in sales).

HISTORY

Central Garden & Pet Company's roots go back to 1955, when it was founded as a small California distributor of lawn and garden supplies. After nearly three decades of unremarkable growth, it was purchased in 1980 by William Brown, a former VP of finance at camera maker Vivitar. The company acquired small distributors but let them operate autonomously. By 1987 Central had sales of $25 million with distribution in California.

The company's first major acquisition was the result of a restructuring of forestry giant Weyerhaeuser, which had diversified into insurance, home building, and diapers, among other products, but was selling noncore divisions to focus solely on timber. It sold Weyerhaeuser Garden Supply to Central in 1990 for $32 million.

Overnight, Central became a national powerhouse with 25 distribution centers serving 38 states. In 1991 sales reached $280 million, of which acquired operations accounted for nearly 70%. The purchase also gave Central 10 high-volume retail customers -- including Costco, Kmart, and Wal-Mart -- which accounted for half of its business. That year the company also acquired a pet distributor, its first move into pet supplies.

To pay down debt associated with the Weyerhaeuser acquisition, the company (then officially known as Central Garden & Pet Company) went public in 1993 (a 1992 IPO was withdrawn when a warehouse fire damaged inventory). With the capital for growth, Central continued to acquire other distributors (from early 1993 to early 1994, it acquired six distributors with about $70 million in sales).

In 1994 the company's largest supplier, Solaris (then a unit of Monsanto and maker of Ortho and Roundup products), decided to bypass Central as its distributor and sell products directly. Solaris products accounted for nearly 40% of the company's sales, and revenues dipped in 1995. However, that year Solaris decided that self-distribution was too difficult and made Central its exclusive distributor. Total sales increased about 65% in 1996.

Broadening its pet supply distribution network, in 1996 Central paid $33 million for Kenlin Pet Supply, the East Coast's largest pet distributor, and Longhorn Pet Supply in Texas. The following year the company bought Four Paws Products and Sandoz Agro.

In 1997 Central paid $132 million for TFH Publications, one of the nation's largest producers of pet books and maker of Nylabone dog snacks, and Kaytee Products, a maker of bird seed. It added Pennington Seed, a maker of grass and bird seed, in 1998.

The company broadened its scope in 1999 with the purchase of Norcal Pottery Products. It also tried to buy Solaris, but that year Monsanto sold its Solaris unit to grass firm The Scotts Company (now Scotts Miracle-Gro). In a familiar refrain for Central, Scotts then decided to shift partially toward self-distribution, costing Central between $200 million and $250 million in annual sales; Scotts would completely sever distribution ties with Central the following year, leading to countering lawsuits.

Central said in early 2000 it would spin off its lawn and garden distribution business to shareholders, but the company abandoned the plan less than a year later. In March 2000 the company acquired AMDRO fire ant killer and IMAGE, a weed herbicide, from American Home Products (now Wyeth) for $28 million. Later that year Central purchased All-Glass Aquarium Company, a manufacturer and marketer of aquariums and related products.

As a result of no longer being the distributor of Scotts products, Central closed 13 of its distribution centers in 2001. Central announced the next year that it would restate its financial results for 1998 through 2002. The company said the changes would improve fiscal 2001 net results by $2 million, but decrease net results by $1.7 million in 2000, $0.3 million in 1999, and $0.1 million in 1998. Also that year Mars' Kal Kan Division and Arch Chemicals stopped using Central as a distributor.

In 2003 Central acquired a 49% stake in E. M. Matson, a lawn and garden manufacturer in the western US.

In 2004 the company completed a menagerie's worth of acquisitions: Kent Marine, an aquarium supplements maker; New England Pottery, which sells decorative pottery and Christmas items (from Heritage Partners); Lawrence plc's pet products division, Interpet; KRB Seed, which does business as Budd Seed (Rebel and Palmer's Pride grass-seed brands); and Energy Savers Unlimited, which distributes aquarium lighting systems and related environmental controls and conditioners.

It continued along the same path throughout the rest of the decade, acquiring Gulfstream Home & Garden (garden products), Pets International (small animal and specialty pet supplies), Farnam Companies (animal health products), and the assets of family-owned pet food maker Breeder's Choice. The firm also increased its stakes in insect control products supplier Tech Pac (from 20% to 80%) and garden controls manufacturer Matson (from 50% to full ownership).

EXECUTIVES

Chairman, Director, William E. Brown, $176,618 total compensation
Chief Executive Officer, Director, Timothy (Tim) P. Cofer
Chief Financial Officer, Nicholas (Niko) Lahanas, $387,308 total compensation
Division Officer, John Hanson
Division Officer, John D. Walker
Lead Independent Director, Director, Mary Beth Springer
Director, Courtnee A. Chun
Director, Lisa Coleman
Director, Brendan P. Dougher
Director, Michael J. Griffith
Director, Christopher T. Metz
Director, Daniel P. Myers
Director, Brooks M. Pennington, $360,072 total compensation
Director, John R. Ranelli, $778,846 total compensation
Auditors : DELOITTE & TOUCHE LLP

LOCATIONS

HQ: Central Garden & Pet Co
1340 Treat Boulevard, Suite 600, Walnut Creek, CA 94597
Phone: 925 948-4000
Web: www.central.com

PRODUCTS/OPERATIONS

2018 Sales

	$ mil.	% of total
Pet Products		
Dog and cat products	444.4	20
Other pet products	896.5	40
Garden Products		
Garden controls and fertilizer products	345.7	16
Other garden supplies	528.8	24
Total	2,215.4	100

Selected Products and Brands
Pet products
    Aquatics
    All-Glass Aquarium
    Kent Marine
    Bird and small animal
    Kaytee
    Dog and cat
    Four Paws
    Interpet
    Nylabone
    Pet Select
    TFH
    Insect control and animal health
    Strike
    Zodiac
Garden products
    Garden decor and pottery
    New England Pottery
    Grass seed
    Lofts Seed
    Pennington
    Rebel
    Weed, insect, and pest control
    AMDRO
    IMAGE
    Lilly Miller
    Over'n Out
    Sevin
    Wild bird
    Kaytee
    Pennington

COMPETITORS

GRAHAM PACKAGING COMPANY, L.P.
Kesko Oyj
MCBRIDE PLC
SMITHS GROUP PLC
SOCIETE INTERNATIONALE DE PLANTATIONS D'HEVEAS
SPECTRUM BRANDS HOLDINGS, INC.
SPECTRUM BRANDS LEGACY, INC.
THE SCOTTS MIRACLE-GRO COMPANY
TRAVIS PERKINS PLC
TRIFAST PLC

HISTORICAL FINANCIALS

Company Type: Public

Income Statement   FYE: September 25

	REVENUE ($mil)	NET INCOME ($mil)	NET PROFIT MARGIN	EMPLOYEES
09/21	3,303.6	151.7	4.6%	7,000
09/20	2,695.5	120.6	4.5%	6,300
09/19	2,383.0	92.7	3.9%	5,800
09/18	2,215.3	123.5	5.6%	5,400
09/17	2,054.4	78.8	3.8%	4,100
Annual Growth	12.6%	17.8%	—	14.3%

2021 Year-End Financials

Debt ratio: 38.0%   No. of shares ($ mil.): 55.2
Return on equity: 13.2%   Dividends
Cash ($ mil.): 439.5   Yield: —
Current Ratio: 2.96   Payout: —
Long-term debt ($ mil.): 1,184.6   Market value ($ mil.): 2,327.0

	STOCK PRICE ($) FY Close	P/E High/Low		PER SHARE ($) Earnings	Dividends	Book Value
09/21	42.14	19	12	2.75	0.00	22.13
09/20	34.23	18	10	2.20	0.00	19.65
09/19	27.95	22	13	1.61	0.00	17.73
09/18	33.14	17	14	2.32	0.00	16.49
09/17	37.19	24	14	1.52	0.00	12.26
Annual Growth	3.2%	—	—	16.0%	—	15.9%

Central Valley Community Bancorp

Central Valley Community Bancorp is the holding company for Central Valley Community Bank, which offers individuals and businesses traditional banking services through about 25 offices in California's San Joaquin Valley. Deposit products include checking, savings, and money market accounts; IRAs; and CDs. The bank, founded in 1979, offers credit card services and originates a variety of loans, including residential and commercial mortgage, Small Business Administration, and agricultural loans. Through Central Valley Community Insurance Services, it markets health, property, and casualty insurance products primarily to business customers.

EXECUTIVES

Chairman, Subsidiary Officer, Director, Daniel J. Doyle, $38,634 total compensation
Subsidiary Officer, Vice-Chairman, Director, Daniel N. Cunningham
President, Chief Executive Officer, Subsidiary Officer, Director, James J. Kim
Executive Vice President, Chief Financial Officer, Subsidiary Officer, Shannon R. Avrett
Executive Vice President, Principal Accounting Officer, Subsidiary Officer, Dawn P. Crusinberry
Executive Vice President, Chief Administrative Officer, Subsidiary Officer, Teresa Gilio
Executive Vice President, Chief Credit Officer, Subsidiary Officer, Patrick A. Luis
Secretary, Subsidiary Officer, Director, Steven D. McDonald
Subsidiary Officer, Blaine C. Lauhon
Subsidiary Officer, A Kenneth Ramos
Subsidiary Officer, Jeff M. Martin
Director, Andriana D. Majarian
Director, Louis C. McMurray
Director, Karen Musson
Director, Dorothea D. Silva
Director, William S. Smittcamp
Independent Director, Frank Tommy Elliott
Independent Director, Robert J. Flautt
Independent Director, Gary D. Gall
Auditors : Crowe LLP

LOCATIONS

HQ: Central Valley Community Bancorp
7100 N. Financial Dr., Suite 101, Fresno, CA 93720
Phone: 559 298-1775
Web: www.cvcb.com

COMPETITORS

FREMONT BANCORPORATION
MBANK
OAK VALLEY BANCORP.
SOUTHEASTERN BANKING CORPORATION
SOUTHERN COMMUNITY FINANCIAL CORPORATION

HISTORICAL FINANCIALS
Company Type: Public

Income Statement — FYE: December 31

	ASSETS ($mil)	NET INCOME ($mil)	INCOME AS % OF ASSETS	EMPLOYEES
12/20	2,004.0	20.3	1.0%	287
12/19	1,596.7	21.4	1.3%	288
12/18	1,537.8	21.2	1.4%	290
12/17	1,661.6	14.0	0.8%	316
12/16	1,443.3	15.1	1.1%	287
Annual Growth	8.6%	7.6%	—	0.0%

2020 Year-End Financials
Return on assets: 1.1%
Return on equity: 8.5%
Long-term debt ($ mil.): —
No. of shares ($ mil.): 12.5
Sales ($ mil.): 79.8
Dividends
Yield: 2.9%
Payout: 27.1%
Market value ($ mil.): 186.0

	STOCK PRICE ($) FY Close	P/E High/Low		PER SHARE ($) Earnings	Dividends	Book Value
12/20	14.89	13	7	1.62	0.44	19.59
12/19	21.67	14	11	1.59	0.43	17.48
12/18	18.87	14	11	1.54	0.31	15.98
12/17	20.18	21	16	1.10	0.24	15.30
12/16	19.96	15	8	1.33	0.24	13.51
Annual Growth	(7.1%)	—	—	5.1%	16.4%	9.7%

Cerence Inc

EXECUTIVES

Chairman, Director, Arun Sarin
President, Chief Executive Officer, Director, Stefan Ortmanns, $315,944 total compensation
Executive Vice President, Chief Financial Officer, Director, Thomas L. Beaudoin
Executive Vice President, Chief Technology Officer, Prateek Kathpal
Senior Vice President, Division Officer, Christophe Couvreur
Director, Marianne N. Budnik
Director, Douglas Davis
Director, Sanjay K. Jha
Director, Kristi Ann Matus
Director, Alfred A. Nietzel
Auditors: BDO USA, LLP

LOCATIONS
HQ: Cerence Inc
1 Burlington Woods Drive, Suite 301A, Burlington, MA 01803
Phone: 857 362-7300
Web: www.cerence.com

HISTORICAL FINANCIALS
Company Type: Public

Income Statement — FYE: September 30

	REVENUE ($mil)	NET INCOME ($mil)	NET PROFIT MARGIN	EMPLOYEES
09/21	387.1	45.8	11.9%	1,700
09/20	329.6	(20.6)	—	1,500
09/19	303.3	100.2	33.1%	1,400
09/18	276.9	5.8	2.1%	1,300
09/17	244.7	47.2	19.3%	0
Annual Growth	12.2%	(0.7%)	—	—

2021 Year-End Financials
Debt ratio: 15.9%
Return on equity: 4.6%
Cash ($ mil.): 128.4
Current Ratio: 1.74
Long-term debt ($ mil.): 265
No. of shares ($ mil.): 38.0
Dividends
Yield: —
Payout: —
Market value ($ mil.): 3,655.0

	STOCK PRICE ($) FY Close	P/E High/Low		PER SHARE ($) Earnings	Dividends	Book Value
09/21	96.11	109	40	1.17	0.00	27.14
09/20	48.87	—	—	(0.57)	0.00	26.00
Annual Growth	96.7%	—	—	—	—	4.4%

CF Bankshares Inc

Central Federal Corporation is the holding company for CFBank. Traditionally a retail-focused savings and loan, CFBank has added business banking, commercial real estate, and business lending to its foundation. It now serves not only local individuals, but also businesses through five branches in eastern Ohio and the state capital, Columbus. Its deposit products include checking, savings, NOW, and money market accounts, as well as CDs. Commercial, commercial real estate, and multifamily residential mortgages represent nearly 80% of the company's loan portfolio. Single-family mortgages make up about 13% of loans. CFBank traces its roots to 1892.

EXECUTIVES

Chairman, Subsidiary Officer, Director, Robert E. Hoeweler
Chief Executive Officer, Subsidiary Officer, Director, Timothy T. O'Dell, $300,000 total compensation
Executive Vice President, Chief Financial Officer, Subsidiary Officer, John W. Helmsdoerfer, $237,500 total compensation
Director, James H. Frauenberg
Director, Thomas P. Ash
Director, Edward W. Cochran
Director, Robert H. Milbourne
Director, John Pietrzak
Director, David L. Royer
Auditors: BKD, LLP

LOCATIONS
HQ: CF Bankshares Inc
7000 North High Street, Worthington, OH 43085

Phone: 614 334-7979   **Fax:** 614 334-7980
Web: www.cfbankonline.com

COMPETITORS
EASTERN VIRGINIA BANKSHARES, INC.
LIBERTY BANCORP, INC.
THE COMMUNITY FINANCIAL CORPORATION
UNION BANKSHARES, INC.
UNITY BANCORP, INC.

HISTORICAL FINANCIALS
Company Type: Public

Income Statement — FYE: December 31

	ASSETS ($mil)	NET INCOME ($mil)	INCOME AS % OF ASSETS	EMPLOYEES
12/20	1,476.9	29.6	2.0%	177
12/19	880.5	9.6	1.1%	125
12/18	665.0	4.2	0.6%	95
12/17	481.4	1.3	0.3%	66
12/16	436.1	1.6	0.4%	64
Annual Growth	35.7%	106.5%	—	29.0%

2020 Year-End Financials
Return on assets: 2.5%
Return on equity: 30.9%
Long-term debt ($ mil.): —
No. of shares ($ mil.): 6.5
Sales ($ mil.): 102.3
Dividends
Yield: 0.1%
Payout: 0.7%
Market value ($ mil.): 116.0

	STOCK PRICE ($) FY Close	P/E High/Low		PER SHARE ($) Earnings	Dividends	Book Value
12/20	17.69	4	2	4.47	0.03	16.79
12/19	13.95	7	6	2.03	0.00	15.00
12/18	11.69	16	2	1.00	0.00	10.51
12/17	2.75	14	7	0.22	0.00	9.48
12/16	1.75	7	4	0.28	0.00	13.26
Annual Growth	78.3%	—	—	100.8%	—	6.1%

ChampionX Corp

EXECUTIVES

Chairman, Director, Daniel W. Rabun
President, Chief Executive Officer, Director, Sivasankaran Somasundaram, $644,314 total compensation
Executive Vice President, Chief Financial Officer, Kenneth M. Fisher
Senior Vice President, Chief Operating Officer, Division Officer, Deric Bryant
Senior Vice President, General Counsel, Secretary, Julia Wright, $324,461 total compensation
Division Officer, Paul E. Mahoney, $413,815 total compensation
Director, Elaine Pickle
Director, Carlos A. Fierro
Director, Heidi S. Alderman
Director, Mamatha Chamarthi
Director, Gary P. Luquette
Director, Stuart Porter
Director, Stephen M. Todd
Auditors: PricewaterhouseCoopers LLP

LOCATIONS

HQ: ChampionX Corp
 2445 Technology Forest Blvd., Building 4, 12th Floor,
 The Woodlands, TX 77381
Phone: 281 403-5772
Web: www.apergy.com

HISTORICAL FINANCIALS
Company Type: Public

Income Statement — FYE: December 31

	REVENUE ($mil)	NET INCOME ($mil)	NET PROFIT MARGIN	EMPLOYEES
12/21	3,074.9	113.2	3.7%	7,000
12/20	1,899.9	(743.9)	—	6,600
12/19	1,131.2	52.1	4.6%	3,000
12/18	1,216.6	94.0	7.7%	3,300
12/17	1,009.5	110.6	11.0%	3,100
Annual Growth	32.1%	0.6%	—	22.6%

2021 Year-End Financials
Debt ratio: 20.5%
Return on equity: 6.6%
Cash ($ mil.): 251.6
Current Ratio: 1.82
Long-term debt ($ mil.): 697.6
No. of shares ($ mil.): 202.9
Dividends
Yield: —
Payout: —
Market value ($ mil.): 4,101.0

	STOCK PRICE ($) FY Close	P/E High/Low		PER SHARE ($) Earnings	Dividends	Book Value
12/21	20.21	53	27	0.54	0.00	8.73
12/20	15.30	—	—	(5.01)	0.00	8.11
12/19	33.78	64	36	0.67	0.00	13.33
12/18	27.08	37	22	1.21	0.00	12.65
Annual Growth	(9.3%)	—	—	(23.6%)	—	(11.6%)

ChannelAdvisor Corp

ChannelAdvisor is a leading provider of cloud-based e-commerce solutions whose mission is to connect and optimize the world's commerce. Its multichannel commerce platform allows its customers to connect to hundreds of global channels, market to consumers on those channels, sell products, manage fulfillment processes, and analyze and optimize channel performance. The company offers software and support services for brands and retailer worldwide looking for greater product visibility and brand management in marketplaces (such as eBay, Amazon, and Google), comparison shopping sites (Google Shopping), search engines (Google and Bing), and their own Web stores. Founded in 2001, the company generates around 70% of sales domestically.

Operations
ChannelAdvisor offers SaaS solutions that enable clients to integrate, manage and optimize the merchandise sales across disparate online channels. In addition, the company facilitates improved collaboration between brands and the authorized resellers through solutions that deliver high value leads from brands to the resellers. It generates the majority of revenue from clients' usage of its SaaS solutions, which are organized into modules. Each module integrates with a particular type of channel, such as third-party marketplaces, digital marketing websites and authorized reseller websites.

Overall, ChannelAdvisor generates over 70% of total revenue from Marketplaces, some 15% from Digital Marketing, and over 10% from other.

Geographic Reach
Headquartered in Morrisville, North Carolina, ChannelAdvisor maintains sales, service, support and research and development offices in various domestic and international locations. International sales account for about 30% of revenue; the rest is from the US.

Sales and Marketing
ChannelAdvisor sells services to brands and retailers, as well as advertising agencies that use its solutions on behalf of their clients. The retailers generated about 55% of sales, brands with some 40%, while others account for the rest of sales.

ChannelAdvisor's advertising costs for the year 2021, 2020, and 2019 were $4.8 million, $3.5 million, and $4.2 million, respectively.

Financial Performance
Revenue increased by 16%, or $22.7 million, to $167.7 million in 2021 compared with $145.1 million in the prior year. The change was primarily due to a $24.2 million increase in subscription revenue compared to the prior year, driven by strong net bookings, particularly from brands customers.

Net income for fiscal 2021 increased to $47.2 million compared with $18.8 million, driven primarily by the current year release of the valuation allowance recorded against deferred tax assets.

Cash held by the company at the end of 2021 increased to $100.6 million. Cash provided by operations was $34.3 million while investing and financing activities used $5.0 million and $16 thousand, respectively. Main cash uses were payment of software development costs and payment of statutory tax withholding related to net-share settlement of restricted stock units.

Strategy
Given the rapidly evolving e-commerce landscape and increased demand for its proprietary SaaS cloud platform, particularly driven by the effects of the COVID-19 pandemic on consumer shopping habits, in 2020 and 2021, the company achieved substantial growth in revenue, especially from its brands customers, as well as adjusted EBITDA and cash flow. ChannelAdvisor intends to continue making incremental strategic investments focused on driving revenue growth, maintaining strong margin performance and building shareholder value. The company expects its financial performance in the future to be driven by its ability to: increase penetration and expansion opportunities with new and existing brands customers; maintain an appropriate number of sales representatives to address anticipated increases in demand for its platform; enhance its services organization with investments in people and technology to better serve its customers; expand the number of marketplaces with which ChannelAdvisor integrate to further enhance transaction volume from marketplaces; and execute on strategic investments in product innovation targeted to expand and optimize its platform and drive new revenue streams.

EXECUTIVES
Chairman, Director, Timothy J. Buckley
Chief Financial Officer, Treasurer, Richard F. Cornetta
Chief Executive Officer, Director, David J. Spitz, $411,000 total compensation
Service Chief Operating Officer, Elizabeth Segovia
Director, M. Scot Wingo, $125,000 total compensation
Director, Himanshu Palsule
Director, Joseph L. Cowan
Director, Timothy V. Williams
Director, Janet R. Cowell
Director, Marshall A. Heinberg
Director, Linda M. Crawford
Auditors: Ernst & Young LLP

LOCATIONS
HQ: ChannelAdvisor Corp
 3025 Carrington Mill Boulevard, Morrisville, NC 27560
Phone: 919 228-4700
Web: www.channeladvisor.com

2015 Sales

	% of total
US	77
International	23
Total	100

PRODUCTS/OPERATIONS
Selected Products & Services
Products
 ChannelAdvisor stores (inventory management)
 MarketplaceAdvisor (product listing and tracking across marketplace sites)
 RichFX (rich media design and management)
 SearchAdvisor (keyword and bid management across search engine sites)
 ShoppingAdvisor (product performance and reporting across comparison shopping sites for retail marketing managers)
Services
 CAGuided (e-commerce campaign training for any-sized retailer)
 CAManaged (outsourced e-commerce campaign management for large retailers)
 CASelect (outsourced e-commerce campaign management for small to mid-sized retailers)

COMPETITORS
BAZAARVOICE, INC.
BOX, INC.
DEMANDWARE, INC.
LIMELIGHT NETWORKS, INC.
MOBILEIRON, INC.
MULESOFT, INC.
OKTA, INC.
RAPID7, INC.
SENDGRID, INC.
YEXT, INC.

HISTORICAL FINANCIALS
Company Type: Public

Income Statement — FYE: December 31

	REVENUE ($mil)	NET INCOME ($mil)	NET PROFIT MARGIN	EMPLOYEES
12/21	167.7	47.2	28.1%	846
12/20	145.0	18.8	13.0%	725
12/19	129.9	3.4	2.7%	642
12/18	131.2	(7.6)	—	730
12/17	122.5	(16.5)	—	737
Annual Growth	8.2%	—		3.5%

2021 Year-End Financials
Debt ratio: —
Return on equity: 29.6%
Cash ($ mil.): 100.5
Current Ratio: 2.97
Long-term debt ($ mil.): —
No. of shares ($ mil.): 30.1
Dividends
Yield: —
Payout: —
Market value ($ mil.): 745.0

	STOCK PRICE ($) FY Close	P/E High	P/E Low	PER SHARE ($) Earnings	Dividends	Book Value
12/21	24.68	18	10	1.50	0.00	6.23
12/20	15.98	33	7	0.63	0.00	4.48
12/19	9.04	113	70	0.12	0.00	3.55
12/18	11.35	—	—	(0.28)	0.00	3.28
12/17	9.00	—	—	(0.63)	0.00	3.08
Annual Growth	28.7%	—	—	—		19.3%

Charles & Colvard Ltd

Charles & Colvard hopes that it isn't just some shooting star. The company makes gemstones made from moissanite, a diamond substitute created in laboratories. Composed of silicon and carbon, moissanite (aka silicon carbide or SiC) is typically found in meteorites. Charles & Colvard makes its gemstones from SiC crystals purchased primarily from Cree, Inc.Â and Swedish companyÂ Norstel.Â Charles & Colvard markets its gemstones through two distributors (Stuller and Rio Grande) andÂ jewelry manufacturers such as K&G Creations, Reeves Park, and Samuel Aaron International.

EXECUTIVES

Chairman, Director, Neal I. Goldman
Supply Chain President, Supply Chain Chief Executive Officer, Director, Don O'Connell, $137,500 total compensation
Chief Financial Officer, Treasurer, Clint J. Pete, $120,000 total compensation
Director, Anne B. Butler
Director, Benedetta I. Casamento
Director, Ollin B. Sykes
Auditors : BDO USA, LLP

LOCATIONS

HQ: Charles & Colvard Ltd
170 Southport Drive, Morrisville, NC 27560
Phone: 919 468-0399
Web: www.charlesandcolvard.com

COMPETITORS

AARON GROUP, LLC
D. Swarovski KG
PRANDA JEWELRY PUBLIC COMPANY LIMITED
RICHLINE GROUP, INC.
ROSY BLUE, INC.

HISTORICAL FINANCIALS
Company Type: Public

Income Statement — FYE: June 30

	REVENUE ($mil)	NET INCOME ($mil)	NET PROFIT MARGIN	EMPLOYEES
06/21	39.2	12.8	32.7%	51
06/20	29.1	(6.1)	—	48
06/19	32.2	2.2	7.1%	63
06/18*	13.1	(1.2)	—	60
12/17	27.0	(0.4)	—	76
Annual Growth	13.2%	—	—	(12.5%)

*Fiscal year change

2021 Year-End Financials
Debt ratio: —
Return on equity: 26.3%
Cash ($ mil.): 21.4
Current Ratio: 6.36
Long-term debt ($ mil.): —
No. of shares ($ mil.): 29.9
Dividends
Yield: —
Payout: —
Market value ($ mil.): 89.0

	STOCK PRICE ($) FY Close	P/E High	P/E Low	PER SHARE ($) Earnings	Dividends	Book Value
06/21	2.98	8	2	0.42	0.00	1.86
06/20	0.73	—	—	(0.22)	0.00	1.43
06/19	1.58	24	8	0.10	0.00	1.63
06/18*	1.07	—	—	(0.06)	0.00	1.56
12/17	1.35	—	—	(0.02)	0.00	1.62
Annual Growth	30.2%	—	—	—		4.8%

*Fiscal year change

Charles River Laboratories International Inc.

Charles River Laboratories International provides early-stage contract research organization (CRO) services to pharmaceutical firms and other manufacturers and institutions. The company provides contract drug discovery services, including target identification and toxicology, through its Discovery and Safety Assessment segment. Its Research Models and Services (RMS) segment is a leading global provider of research models (lab rats and mice) bred specifically for use in medical testing. The Manufacturing Support unit offers biologics testing and chicken eggs for vaccines. Charles River has operations in over 20 countries, but generates around 55% of sales in the US. Charles River began operating in 1947 and went public in 2000.

Operations

Charles River operates through three reportable segments: Discovery and Safety Assessment (DSA), Research Models and Services (RMS), and Manufacturing Support.

Its DSA reportable segment (about 60% of total revenue) includes services required to take a drug through the early development process including discovery services, which are non-regulated services to assist clients with the identification, screening, and selection of a lead compound for drug development, and regulated and non-regulated (GLP and non-GLP) safety assessment services.

Manufacturing reportable segment (around 20%) includes Microbial Solutions, which provides in vitro (non-animal) lot-release testing products, microbial detection products, and species identification services; Biologics Testing Services (Biologics), which performs specialized testing of biologics; and Avian Vaccine Services (Avian), which supplies specific-pathogen-free chicken eggs and chickens.

The RMS reportable segment (some 20%) includes the Research Models, Research Model Services, and Research Products businesses. Research Models includes the commercial production and sale of small research models, as well as the supply of large research models. Research Model Services includes: Genetically Engineered Models and Services (GEMS), which performs contract breeding and other services associated with genetically engineered models; Research Animal Diagnostic Services (RADS), which provides health monitoring and diagnostics services related to research models; and Insourcing Solutions (IS), which provides colony management of its clients' research operations (including recruitment, training, staffing, and management services). Research Products supplies controlled, consistent, customized primary cells and blood components derived from normal and mobilized peripheral blood, bone marrow, and cord blood.

Overall, its services account roughly 80% of total revenue while products accounts the remainders.

Geographic Reach

Based in Wilmington, Massachusetts, Charles River has operations over 110 locations in over 20 countries. While the US accounts for around 55% of its revenue, the company is growing its operations in other key markets including Europe (nearly 30% of revenue), Canada (about 10%), and the Asia/Pacific region (around 5%).

Sales and Marketing

Charles River provides its products and services directly to customers around the globe. Clients include small, midsized, and large pharmaceutical, biotechnology, agricultural, chemical, and life science companies, as well as educational, health care, and government institutions. It also supplies research models to other CROs.

The company primarily sells its products and services through a direct sales force and business development professionals in North America, Europe, and the Asia/Pacific region. In some markets, sales are assisted by international distributors and agents. Marketing efforts include organizing scientific conferences, publishing scientific papers, conducting webinars, and presenting at trade shows. It also participates in online and direct mail marketing.

Financial Performance

Revenue for fiscal year 2021 was $3.5 billion compared to $2.9 billion in fiscal year 2020. The 2021 increase as compared to the corresponding period in 2020 was $616.3 million, or 21%, and was primarily due to the increased demand across all of its reporting segments, principally within DSA and the impact of RMS recovering from the effects of the COVID-19 pandemic in the prior period.

Net income attributable to common shareholders increased to $391.0 million in fiscal year 2021, from $364.3 million in the corresponding period of 2020.

Cash held by the company at the end of fiscal 2021 increased to $246.3 million. Cash provided by operations and financing activities were $760.8 million and $672.6 million, respectively. Cash used for investing activities was $1.4 billion, mainly for acquisition of businesses and assets.

Strategy

Charles River's objective is to be the preferred strategic global partner for its clients. Company's strategy is to deliver a comprehensive and integrated portfolio of drug discovery and non-clinical development products, services and solutions to support its clients' discovery and early-stage drug research, process development, scale up and manufacturing efforts, and enable them to bring new and improved therapies to market faster and more cost effectively. Separately, through its various Manufacturing segment businesses, the company aim to be the premier provider of products and services that ensure its clients produce and release their products safely.

The company believe it has certain competitive advantages in executing this strategy because of its continuing focus on the following: integrated early-stage portfolio; comprehensive biopharmaceutical manufacturing portfolio; deep scientific expertise; commitment to animal welfare; superior quality and client support; flexible and customized environment to provide the right solutions; and large, global partner.

Mergers and Acquisitions

In mid-2021, Charles River acquired Vigene Biosciences, Inc. for $292.5 million in cash. In addition to the initial purchase price, the transaction includes additional payments of up to $57.5 million, contingent on future performance. Based in Rockville, Maryland, Vigene Biosciences is a premier, gene therapy contract development and manufacturing organization (CDMO), providing viral vector-based gene delivery solutions. The acquisition complements Charles River's existing cell and gene therapy contract manufacturing capabilities and establishes an end-to-end, gene-modified cell therapy solution in the US. In addition, the acquisition enables clients to seamlessly conduct analytical testing, process development, and manufacturing for advanced modalities with the same scientific partner, facilitating their goal of driving greater efficiency and accelerating their speed to market.

Also, in 2021, Charles River completed the acquisition of Tennessee-based Cognate BioServices, Inc. for approximately $875 million. Cognate BioServices is a premier, cell and gene therapy contract development and manufacturing organization (CDMO) offering comprehensive manufacturing solutions for cell therapies, as well as for production of plasmid DNA and other inputs in the CDMO value chain. The acquisition establishes Charles River as a premier scientific partner for cell and gene therapy development, testing, and manufacturing, providing clients with an integrated solution from basic research and discovery through CGMP production.

In early 2021, Charles River acquired California-based Distributed Bio, a next-generation antibody discovery company, for $83 million in cash. The acquisition marks the culmination of an exclusive partnership between these companies that was initiated in October 2018. The acquisition of Distributed Bio expands Charles River's scientific capabilities with an innovative, large-molecule discovery platform. The transaction combines Distributed Bio's antibody libraries and immuno-engineering platform with Charles River's extensive drug discovery and non-clinical development expertise to create an integrated, end-to-end platform for therapeutic antibody and cell and gene therapy discovery and development.

Company Background

The company was founded in 1947 as Charles River Breeding Laboratories in Boston, Massachusetts, by Dr. Henry Foster. It began commercial pathogen-free rodent production in 1955 at its new headquarters in Wilmington, Massachusetts. In 1966, it expanded overseas by opening an animal production facility in France.

The company was acquired by Bausch & Lomb in 1984. In 1997 Jim Foster purchased Charles River back from Bausch & Lomb. The company went public on the NYSE in 2000.

Acquisitions over the years included Argenta, BioFocus, Agilux Labs, and Brains On-Line.

EXECUTIVES

Chairman, President, Chief Executive Officer, Director, James C. Foster, $1,225,473 total compensation
Corporate Vice-President, Chief Financial Officer, Flavia H. Pease
Corporate Executive Vice President, Chief Commercial Officer, William D. Barbo, $461,509 total compensation
Corporate Development Executive Vice President, Strategy Executive Vice President, Joseph LaPlume
Discovery & Safety Assessment Chief Operating Officer, Birgit Girshick, $397,040 total compensation
Legal Compliance Senior Vice President, Legal Compliance Chief Compliance Officer, Legal Compliance General Counsel, Legal Compliance Corporate Secretary, Matthew L. Daniel
Director, Nancy C. Andrews
Director, Robert J. Bertolini
Director, Deborah T. Kochevar
Director, George Llado
Director, Martin W. Mackay
Director, George E. Massaro
Director, C. Richard Reese
Director, Richard F. Wallman
Director, Virginia M. Wilson
Auditors: PricewaterhouseCoopers LLP

LOCATIONS

HQ: Charles River Laboratories International Inc.
251 Ballardvale Street, Wilmington, MA 01887
Phone: 781 222-6000
Web: www.criver.com

2016 Sales

	$ mil.	% of total
US	850.4	51
Europe	521.0	31
Canada	194.2	11
Japan	46.8	3
Other countries	69.0	4
Total	1,681.4	100

PRODUCTS/OPERATIONS

2016 Sales

	$ mil.	% of total
Discovery and safety assessment	836.6	50
Research Models & Services	494.0	29
Manufacturing support	350.8	21
Total	1,681.4	100

Selected Services

Agrochemical & veterinary services
Antibody production services
Avian products & services
Biopharmaceutical services
Clinical trial services
Consulting & staffing services
Discovery & imaging services
Endotoxin & microbial detection
Equipment & instrumentation
Facilities design & management services
Genetic testing services
Genetically engineered models & services
In Vitro services
Pathology associates
Preclinical services
Program management
Regulatory navigator services
Research animal diagnostic services
Research animal models
Surgical model services

COMPETITORS

ARCADIA BIOSCIENCES, INC.
BIOANALYTICAL SYSTEMS, INC.
COVANCE INC.
KBR WYLE SERVICES, LLC
LANDAUER, INC.
LFI1 LIMITED
NEOGENOMICS, INC.
PRECIPIO, INC.
SYNEOS HEALTH, INC.
UNDERWRITERS LABORATORIES INC.

HISTORICAL FINANCIALS
Company Type: Public

Income Statement — FYE: December 25

	REVENUE ($mil)	NET INCOME ($mil)	NET PROFIT MARGIN	EMPLOYEES
12/21	3,540.1	390.9	11.0%	20,000
12/20	2,923.9	364.3	12.5%	18,400
12/19	2,621.2	252.0	9.6%	17,100
12/18	2,266.0	226.3	10.0%	14,700
12/17	1,857.6	123.3	6.6%	11,800
Annual Growth	17.5%	33.4%	—	14.1%

2021 Year-End Financials

Debt ratio: 38.0%
Return on equity: 16.8%
Cash ($ mil.): 241.2
Current Ratio: 1.23
Long-term debt ($ mil.): 2,663.5
No. of shares ($ mil.): 50.4
Dividends
Yield: —
Payout: —
Market value ($ mil.): 18,637.0

	STOCK PRICE ($) FY Close	P/E High/Low		PER SHARE ($) Earnings	Dividends	Book Value
12/21	369.20	59	32	7.60	0.00	50.21
12/20	251.71	34	13	7.20	0.00	42.49
12/19	151.93	29	20	5.07	0.00	33.40
12/18	111.72	29	21	4.62	0.00	27.33
12/17	109.45	45	29	2.54	0.00	22.05
Annual Growth	35.5%	—	—	31.5%	—	22.8%

Chart Industries Inc

Chart Industries is a leading independent global manufacturer of highly engineered equipment servicing multiple applications in the Energy and Industrial Gas markets. Its unique product portfolio is used in every phase of the liquid gas supply chain, including upfront engineering, service and repair. Being at the forefront of the clean energy transition, Chart is a leading provider of technology, equipment and services related to liquefied natural gas, hydrogen, biogas and CO2 Capture amongst other applications. Chart's customers are mainly large, multinational producers and distributors of hydrocarbon and industrial gases. The company generates about half its sales in North America.

Operations
The company's reportable segments are Cryo Tank Solutions, Heat Transfer Systems, Specialty Products and Repair Service & Leasing.

Chart Industries' Cryo Tank Solutions segment accounts for about 35% of total sales, it designs and manufactures cryogenic solutions for the storage and delivery of cryogenic liquids used in industrial gas and LNG applications. Products include bulk, microbulk and mobile equipment used in the storage, distribution, vaporization, and application of industrial gases and certain hydrocarbons.

Heat Transfer Systems segment supplies mission critical engineered equipment and systems used in the separation, liquefaction, and purification of hydrocarbon and industrial gases that span gas-to-liquid applications. Products include brazed aluminum heat exchangers, Core-in-Kettle heat exchangers, cold boxes, air cooled heat exchangers, shell & tube heat exchangers, axial cooling fans, high pressure reactors and vessels along with associated process technologies.

Specialty Products segment (around a third) supplies highly-engineered equipment used in specialty end-market applications including hydrogen, LNG, biogas, CO2 Capture, food and beverage, aerospace, lasers, cannabis and water treatment, among others.

Its Repair, Service & Leasing segment (nearly 15%) provides installation, service, repair, maintenance, and refurbishment of cryogenic products globally in addition to providing equipment leasing solutions.

Geographic Reach
Headquartered in Ball Ground, GA, Chart Industries has over 25 locations from the US to Asia, Australia, India, Europe and South America.

The company's largest single market is North America with about half of company's revenue followed by EMEA & India with about a third of revenue.

Sales and Marketing
Chart Industries' primary customers are large, multinational producers and distributors of hydrocarbon and industrial gases?the company has more than 2,500 customers worldwide. The company developed relationships with leading companies in the gas production, gas distribution, gas processing, liquefied natural gas or LNG, petroleum refining, chemical, industrial gas, spaceflight, over the road trucking manufacturing and hydrogen, CO2 capture and other clean energy industries, including Linde, Air Liquide, IVECO, Air Products, Shell, Chevron, ExxonMobil, New Fortress Energy, Samsung, Plug Power, SpaceX, and Blue Origin.

Chart Industries markets its products and services through direct sales personnel and independent sales representatives and distributors. The company use independent sales representatives and distributors to market its products and services in certain foreign countries and in certain North American regions. These independent sales representatives supplement its direct sales force in dealing with language and cultural matters. Its domestic and foreign independent sales representatives earn commissions on sales, which vary by product type.

The company's advertising costs of $3.9 million, $2.7 million, and $4.0 million for the years 2021, 2020 and 2019, respectively.

Financial Performance
Sales in 2021 increased by $140.6 million, from $1.2 billion to a record $1.3 billion, or 12%. This increase was primarily driven by growth in its Specialty Products segment on favorable sales in hydrogen and helium applications, HLNG vehicle tanks, water treatment equipment sales and food & beverage applications, within its Cryo Tank Solutions segment on favorable sales in mobile equipment, engineered tanks and storage systems, and within its Repair, Service & Leasing segment on favorable sales in its leasing business.

Net income for fiscal 2021 decreased to $60.9 million compared with $309.5 million in the prior year.

Cash held by the company at the end of fiscal 2021 decreased to $122.4 million. Cash provided by financing activities was $381.9 million while operating and investing activities used $21.3 million and $361.2 million, respectively. Main cash uses were unbilled contract revenue and other assets; and acquisition of businesses.

Mergers and Acquisitions
In late 2021, Chart Industries completes the acquisition of 85% of Earthly Labs for $62 million. Earthly Labs is the leading provider of small-scale carbon capture systems offering an affordable, small footprint technology platform called "CiCi" to capture, recycle, reuse, track and sell CO2. "Earthly Labs' small-scale carbon capture solution is a natural fit for our portfolio given the complementary end markets, sustainable portfolio and customers that need CO2 in the production and packaging of beer, wine, cannabis and food," stated Jill Evanko, CEO and President of Chart.

In 2021, Chart Industries acquired AdEdge Holdings, a water treatment technology and solution provider specializing in the design, development, fabrication and supply of water treatment solutions, specialty medias, legacy and innovative technologies that remove a wide range of contaminants from water, for a purchase price of $40 million in cash. Its technologies, solutions, and expertise strengthen Chart's position in the growing water treatment space as it continues to invest in sustainable solutions for a wide variety of industries and applications.

In early 2021, Chart Industries acquired Cryogenic Gas Technologies for $55 million in cash. Cryo Technologies is a global leader in custom engineered process systems to separate, purify, refrigerate, liquefy and distribute high value industrial gases such as hydrogen, helium, argon and hydrocarbons with design capabilities for cold boxes for hydrogen and helium use. The combination of Chart and Cryo Technologies offers the market a unique one-stop shop for customers who want to liquefy and market the hydrogen molecule, regardless of plant capacity, but need an experienced and reliable equipment and process supplier for liquefaction and storage.

HISTORY

In 1986 Arthur Holmes teamed up with his brother Charles to purchase ALTEC International, a struggling maker of brazed aluminum heat exchangers that dated to 1949. The brothers turned ALTEC around and used it to acquire undervalued companies. From 1986 to 1991, they purchased storage and transportation equipment for liquefied gases and high-pressure cryogenic equipment, including Greenville Tube Corporation (stainless steel tubing, 1987); Process Engineering, Inc. (cryogenic tanks, 1990); and Process Systems International (cold boxes, 1991). The Holmes brothers finally established a public holding company in 1992, and named it Chart Industries (for CHarles and ARThur).

EXECUTIVES

Chair, Director, Singleton B. McAllister
President, Chief Executive Officer, Director, Jillian C. Evanko, $591,163 total compensation
Vice President, Chief Financial Officer, Joseph R. Brinkman
Vice President, General Counsel, Secretary, Herbert G. Hotchkiss
Vice President, Chief Human Resources Officer, Gerald F. Vinci, $324,450 total compensation
Chief Commercial Officer, Joseph A. Belling
Chief Technology Officer, Brian Bostrom
Director, Paula M. Harris
Director, Linda A. Harty
Director, Michael L. Molinini
Director, David M. Sagehorn
Director, Roger A. Strauch
Auditors : DELOITTE & TOUCHE LLP

LOCATIONS

HQ: Chart Industries Inc
3055 Torrington Drive, Ball Ground, GA 30107
Phone: 770 721-8800
Web: www.chartindustries.com

2017 Sales

	$ mil.	% of total
United States	526.7	53
China	110.0	11
Other foreign countries	352.1	36
Total	988.8	100

PRODUCTS/OPERATIONS

2017 sales

	$ mil.	% of total
Distribution & Storage	540.3	55
Energy & Chemical	225.6	23
BioMedical	222.9	22
Total	988.8	100

Selected Products

Products for Energy
    Air cooled heat exchangers
    Brazed aluminum heat exchangers
    Nitrogen rejection units
    LNG equipment and systems
Products for Industry
    Bulk storage tanks
    AirSep commercial products
    Bulk CO2 carbonation
    Flow measurement products
    Vacuum insulation pipe (VIP)
    Packaged gases
    Nitrogen dosing
    Vaporizers
Products for Life Sciences
    Aluminum dewars
    Stainless steel cryogenic freezers
Products for Respiratory Health
    CAIRE Inc. (subsidiary)
    SeQual oxygen products
    AirSep oxygen products

COMPETITORS

AMTROL INC.
COLFAX CORPORATION
CONNELL LIMITED PARTNERSHIP
ENERFAB, INC.
GRAHAM CORPORATION
MODINE MANUFACTURING COMPANY
NORTHWEST PIPE COMPANY
RPC GROUP LIMITED
SPX CORPORATION
SPX FLOW, INC.

HISTORICAL FINANCIALS

Company Type: Public

Income Statement   FYE: December 31

	REVENUE ($mil)	NET INCOME ($mil)	NET PROFIT MARGIN	EMPLOYEES
12/20	1,177.1	308.1	26.2%	4,318
12/19	1,299.1	46.4	3.6%	5,743
12/18	1,084.3	88.0	8.1%	4,605
12/17	988.8	28.0	2.8%	4,424
12/16	859.1	28.2	3.3%	4,050
Annual Growth	8.2%	81.7%	—	1.6%

2020 Year-End Financials

Debt ratio: 17.2%
Return on equity: 21.9%
Cash ($ mil.): 125.1
Current Ratio: 1.11
Long-term debt ($ mil.): 221.6
No. of shares ($ mil.): 36.1
Dividends
  Yield: —
  Payout: —
Market value ($ mil.): 4,262.0

	STOCK PRICE ($) FY Close	P/E High/Low		PER SHARE ($) Earnings	Dividends	Book Value
12/20	117.79	14	2	8.45	0.00	43.46
12/19	67.49	69	38	1.32	0.00	34.29
12/18	65.03	28	16	2.73	0.00	28.20
12/17	46.86	53	35	0.89	0.00	26.04
12/16	36.02	44	15	0.91	0.00	22.78
Annual Growth	34.5%	—	—	74.6%	—	17.5%

ChoiceOne Financial Services, Inc.

One choice for a place to park your money is ChoiceOne Financial Services. The institution is the holding company for ChoiceOne Bank, which has more than a dozen offices in the western part of Michigan's Lower Peninsula. The bank serves consumers and area businesses, offering checking and savings accounts, CDs, investment planning, and other services. Real estate loans, including residential and commercial mortgages, constitute more than two-thirds of the company's loan portfolio. Agricultural, consumer, and business loans help to round out the bank's lending activities. ChoiceOne Financial Services sells life, health, and disability coverage through its ChoiceOne Insurance Agencies subsidiaries.

EXECUTIVES

Chairman, Director, Jack G. Hendon
President, Subsidiary Officer, Director, Michael J. Burke
Chief Executive Officer, Subsidiary Officer, Director, Kelly J. Potes, $255,000 total compensation
Chief Financial Officer, Secretary, Treasurer, Subsidiary Officer, Adom J. Greenland, $151,162 total compensation
Subsidiary Officer, Robert M. Jamula
Subsidiary Officer, Peter Batistoni
Subsidiary Officer, Steven M. DeVolder
Subsidiary Officer, Bradley A. Henion, $163,019 total compensation
Subsidiary Officer, Lee A. Braford
Subsidiary Officer, Shelly M. Childers
Subsidiary Officer, Heather D. Brolick
Director, Bruce J. Essex
Director, Greg L. Armock
Director, Bradley F. McGinnis
Director, Keith D. Brophy
Director, Roxanne M. Page
Director, Nels W. Nyblad
Director, Gregory A. McConnell
Director, Eric E. Burrough
Director, Harold J. Burns
Director, Patrick A. Cronin
Director, David J. Churchill
Auditors : Plante & Moran, PLLC

LOCATIONS

HQ: ChoiceOne Financial Services, Inc.
109 East Division Street, Sparta, MI 49345
Phone: 616 887-7366
Web: www.choiceone.com

COMPETITORS

CITIZENS FINANCIAL SERVICES, INC.
COMMUNITY SHORES BANK CORPORATION
MACKINAC FINANCIAL CORPORATION
SVB & T CORPORATION
TOUCHSTONE BANK

HISTORICAL FINANCIALS

Company Type: Public

Income Statement   FYE: December 31

	ASSETS ($mil)	NET INCOME ($mil)	INCOME AS % OF ASSETS	EMPLOYEES
12/20	1,919.3	15.6	0.8%	359
12/19	1,386.1	7.1	0.5%	339
12/18	670.5	7.3	1.1%	174
12/17	646.5	6.1	1.0%	173
12/16	607.3	6.0	1.0%	160
Annual Growth	33.3%	26.5%	—	22.4%

CIB Marine Bancshares Inc

CIB Marine Bancshares is semper fi to its banking strategy. The company owns CIBM Bank, which operates in the Indianapolis, Milwaukee, and Phoenix markets. Through some 20 branches, the bank caters to individuals and small-and midsized-business customers, offering checking and savings accounts, ATM and debit cards, CDs, and IRAs. The company's loan portfolio mainly consists of commercial mortgages, business loans, and commercial real estate construction loans. CIB Marine Bancshares emerged from Chapter 11 bankruptcy protection in early 2010.

EXECUTIVES

Chairman, President, Chief Executive Officer, Subsidiary Officer, Director, John P. Hickey, $134,532 total compensation
Senior Vice President, J. Brian Chaffin
Senior Vice President, Mark V. Wilmington
Senior Vice President, David R. Pendley
Senior Vice President, Joanne M. P. Blaesing
Executive Vice President, General Counsel, Secretary, Daniel J. Rasmussen
Executive Vice President, Chief Credit Officer, Subsidiary Officer, Paul C. Melnick, $154,231 total compensation
Chief Financial Officer, Principal Accounting Officer, Subsidiary Officer, Patrick J. Straka, $174,481 total compensation
Subsidiary Officer, John T. Bean
Director, Gary L. Longman
Director, Charles E. Baker
Director, Ronald E. Rhoades
Director, Charles D. Mires
Director, Willard Bunn
Director, Mark A. Elste
Auditors: Crowe LLP

LOCATIONS

HQ: CIB Marine Bancshares Inc
19601 West Bluemound Road, Brookfield, WI 53045
Phone: 262 695-6010 **Fax:** 630 735-2841
Web: www.cibmarine.com

COMPETITORS

CAPITAL BANK CORPORATION
CENTRAL VIRGINIA BANKSHARES, INC.
DCB FINANCIAL CORP
FREMONT BANCORPORATION
PACIFIC FINANCIAL CORPORATION

HISTORICAL FINANCIALS

Company Type: Public

Income Statement — FYE: December 31

	ASSETS ($mil)	NET INCOME ($mil)	INCOME AS % OF ASSETS	EMPLOYEES
12/20	750.9	8.1	1.1%	0
12/19	703.7	2.0	0.3%	0
12/18	721.2	3.3	0.5%	0
12/17	662.3	26.9	4.1%	183
12/16	653.5	4.0	0.6%	171
Annual Growth	3.5%	19.1%	—	—

2020 Year-End Financials
Return on assets: 1.1%
Return on equity: 8.2%
Long-term debt ($ mil.): —
No. of shares ($ mil.): 1.2
Sales ($ mil.): 48.7
Dividends
Yield: —
Payout: —
Market value ($ mil.): 20.0

	STOCK PRICE ($) FY Close	P/E High/Low		PER SHARE ($) Earnings	Dividends	Book Value
12/20	15.80	3	0	3.79	0.00	81.77
12/19	1.39	1	1	1.05	0.00	75.09
12/18	1.54	0	0	2.25	0.00	74.85
12/17	1.42	0	0	11.10	0.00	80.12
12/16	1.08	0	0	1.65	0.00	57.50
Annual Growth	95.6%	—	—	23.1%	—	9.2%

Citizens & Northern Corp

Citizens & Northern Corp. is the holding company for Citizens & Northern (C&N) Bank, Citizens & Northern Investment Corp., and Bucktail Life Insurance Company. Its primary business and largest subsidiary is C&N Bank, a community bank that serves individuals and commercial customers in Pennsylvania and New York. The bank operates more than 25 branches and offers online and telebanking services. The firm's other subsidiaries are Citizens & Northern Investment Corp., which provides investment services, and Bucktail Life Insurance, a provider of credit, life, and property/casualty reinsurance. The bank holding company has assets of more than $1.3 billion.

Operations

C&N Bank offers standard deposit and loan products including savings accounts, IRAs, and mortgages. Its loan portfolio includes residential mortgages (more than half of total loans), commercial loans (more than 40%), and consumer loans (less than 5%).

Citizens & Northern Corporation also has a trust division which provides 401(k) plans, retirement and estate planning, and asset management services. Another arm offers personal and commercial insurance coverage as well as mutual funds, annuities, and other investment products.

Geographic Reach

Wellsboro, Pennsylvania-based C&N Bank operates in nine counties in Pennsylvania and New York. Full-service branch offices are located in Bradford, Cameron, Lycoming, McKean, Potter, Sullivan, and Tioga counties in Pennsylvania, and Steuben and Chemung counties in New York.

Financial Performance

Citizens & Northern revenue has remained relatively flat for the past few years, primarily due to ongoing low interest rates and a slowdown of natural gas activities (which had boomed between 2009 and 2011) in the company's service area. Net income has been creeping downward over the same time period.

In 2017, revenue increased 2% to $58.4 million. Net interest income rose 4% that year as total outstanding loans increased, while non-interest income rose 4% as assets under management increased by 13%. Debit card processing revenue also rose with a higher volume of transactions. However, other revenue sources declined, including net gains from sales of loans and interest on long-term borrowings.

Net income fell 15% to $13.4 million in 2017. This decline was largely due to an additional income tax provision of $2.2 million related to the 2017 Tax Act, but operating expenses also increased that year, further impacting the bottom line.

The company ended 2017 with $37 million in net cash, $8.4 million more than it had at the end of 2016. Operating activities provided $19.4 million and financing activities provided $19.9 million. Investing activities used $30.9 million.

Strategy

These days, bank customers make fewer (or no) trips to physical branch locations in favor of online and mobile banking, and Citizens & Northern is investing in better serving its customers' changing behaviors. As such, the company has made improvements to its brick-and-mortar banking locations while also enhancing its technological capabilities. For example, in 2017 it upgraded its business banking platform, allowing commercial customers to originate same-day Automated Clearing House electronic money transfer credits. The firm also tweaks or introduces new products, such as the specialty package for not-for-profit organizations in launched in 2017. These efforts help Citizens & Northern to build its business by attracting new

---

2020 Year-End Financials (CIB Marine, top of page)
Return on assets: 0.9%
Return on equity: 7.4%
Long-term debt ($ mil.): —
No. of shares ($ mil.): 7.8
Sales ($ mil.): 78.4
Dividends
Yield: 2.6%
Payout: 39.6%
Market value ($ mil.): 240.0

	STOCK PRICE ($) FY Close	P/E High/Low		PER SHARE ($) Earnings	Dividends	Book Value
12/20	30.81	16	8	2.07	0.82	29.15
12/19	31.96	21	16	1.58	1.40	26.52
12/18	25.00	15	11	2.02	0.71	22.25
12/17	23.80	14	13	1.70	0.64	21.14
12/16	23.75	14	13	1.68	0.62	19.84
Annual Growth	6.7%	—	—	5.4%	7.4%	10.1%

customers, while deepening its relationships with existing customers.

The company also has geographic expansion in its sights, as evidenced by the pending acquisition of Monument Bank in Bucks County, Pennsylvania.

Mergers and Acquisitions

In 2018 Citizens & Northern agreed to buy Monument Bank for $42.7 million. Monument Bank operates two branches and a loan production office in Bucks County, Pennsylvania, which will bring Citizens & Northern's operations closer to Philadelphia.

Company Background

Citizens & Northern Bank was formed in 1971 following the consolidation of Northern National Bank of Wellsboro and Citizens National Bank of Towanda.

EXECUTIVES

Chairman, Subsidiary Officer, Director, Terry L. Lehman

President, Chief Executive Officer, Subsidiary Officer, Director, J. Bradley Scovill, $416,160 total compensation

Treasurer, Subsidiary Officer, Mark A. Hughes, $270,000 total compensation

Executive Vice President, Chief Credit Officer, Subsidiary Officer, Stan R. Dunsmore, $170,000 total compensation

Executive Vice President, Subsidiary Officer, John M. Reber

Executive Vice President, Subsidiary Officer, Blair T. Rush

Executive Vice President, Subsidiary Officer, Tracy E. Watkins

Subsidiary Officer, Alexander Balagour

Subsidiary Officer, Matthew L. Bower

Subsidiary Officer, Harold F. Hoose, $215,000 total compensation

Subsidiary Officer, Shelley L. D'Haene

Subsidiary Officer, Thomas L. Rudy, $163,500 total compensation

Director, Susan E. Hartley

Director, Leo F. Lambert

Director, Helen S. Santiago

Director, Katherine W. Shattuck

Director, Stephen M. Dorwart

Director, Aaron K. Singer

Director, Bobbi J. Kilmer

Director, Robert G. Loughery

Director, Frank G. Pellegrino

Auditors : Baker Tilly US, LLP

LOCATIONS

HQ: Citizens & Northern Corp
90-92 Main Street, Wellsboro, PA 16901
Phone: 570 724-3411
Web: www.cnbankpa.com

PRODUCTS/OPERATIONS

2017 Sales

	$ mil.	% of total
Interest		
Interest & fees on loans	37.0	59
Income from available-for-sale securities	8.7	14
Interest on balances with depository institutions	0.2	-
Non-interest		
Trust & financial management	5.4	9
Service charges on deposit accounts	4.5	7
Interchange revenue on debit card transactions	2.2	4
Realized gains on available-for-sale securities, net	0.3	1
Other	4.0	6
Adjustments	(3.9)	-
Total	58.4	100

COMPETITORS

BANCFIRST CORPORATION
EAGLE BANCORP, INC.
PEOPLES FINANCIAL SERVICES CORP.
WESTERN ALLIANCE BANCORPORATION
WINTRUST FINANCIAL CORPORATION

HISTORICAL FINANCIALS

Company Type: Public

Income Statement — FYE: December 31

	ASSETS ($mil)	NET INCOME ($mil)	INCOME AS % OF ASSETS	EMPLOYEES
12/21	2,327.6	30.5	1.3%	0
12/20	2,239.1	19.2	0.9%	0
12/19	1,654.1	19.5	1.2%	336
12/18	1,290.8	22.0	1.7%	299
12/17	1,276.9	13.4	1.1%	296
Annual Growth	16.2%	22.8%	—	—

2021 Year-End Financials

Return on assets: 1.3%
Return on equity: 10.1%
Long-term debt ($ mil.): —
No. of shares ($ mil.): 15.7
Sales ($ mil.): 110.3
Dividends
 Yield: 4.2%
 Payout: 58.4%
Market value ($ mil.): 412.0

	STOCK PRICE ($) FY Close	P/E High/Low		PER SHARE ($) Earnings	Dividends	Book Value
12/21	26.12	14	10	1.92	1.11	19.13
12/20	19.84	22	12	1.30	1.08	18.84
12/19	28.25	20	16	1.46	1.18	17.82
12/18	26.43	16	12	1.79	1.08	16.02
12/17	24.00	24	20	1.10	1.04	15.43
Annual Growth	2.1%	—	—	14.9%	1.6%	5.5%

Citizens Community Bancorp Inc (MD)

Citizens Community Bancorp is the holding company for Citizens Community Federal, a community bank with about 20 branches in Wisconsin, southern Minnesota, and northern Michigan. Serving consumers and businesses, the bank offers standard deposit services such as savings, checking, money market, and retirement accounts, as well as a variety of loan products. The bank focuses its lending activities on one- to four-family mortgages, which represent more than half of its loan portfolio. The bank also offers consumer loans such as auto and personal loans; it does not routinely make commercial loans. Founded in 1938, Citizens Community was a state-chartered credit union until 2001.

EXECUTIVES

Chairman, Director, Richard McHugh

President, Chief Executive Officer, Subsidiary Officer, Stephen M. Bianchi, $315,000 total compensation

Executive Vice President, Principal Accounting Officer, Subsidiary Officer, Mark C. Oldenberg, $175,000 total compensation

Chief Financial Officer, James S. Broucek, $165,922 total compensation

Treasurer, Brian R. Schilling

Director, Kristina Bourget

Director, Francis E. Felber

Director, James R. Lang

Director, James D. Moll

Director, Tim Olson

Director, Michael L. Swenson

Auditors : Eide Bailly LLP

LOCATIONS

HQ: Citizens Community Bancorp Inc (MD)
2174 EastRidge Center, Eau Claire, WI 54701
Phone: 715 836-9994
Web: www.ccf.us

COMPETITORS

FIRST NILES FINANCIAL, INC.
HFB FINANCIAL CORPORATION
NORTHEAST COMMUNITY BANCORP, INC.
UNITED COMMUNITY BANCORP
YAKIMA FEDERAL SAVINGS & LOAN ASSOCIATION

HISTORICAL FINANCIALS

Company Type: Public

Income Statement — FYE: December 31

	ASSETS ($mil)	NET INCOME ($mil)	INCOME AS % OF ASSETS	EMPLOYEES
12/20	1,649.0	12.7	0.8%	251
12/19	1,531.2	9.4	0.6%	288
12/18*	1,287.9	1.2	0.1%	265
09/18	975.4	4.2	0.4%	282
09/17	940.6	2.4	0.3%	224
Annual Growth	20.6%	72.0%	—	3.9%

*Fiscal year change

2020 Year-End Financials

Return on assets: 0.7%
Return on equity: 8.1%
Long-term debt ($ mil.): —
No. of shares ($ mil.): 11.0
Sales ($ mil.): 82.9
Dividends
 Yield: 1.9%
 Payout: 18.4%
Market value ($ mil.): 120.0

	STOCK PRICE ($) FY Close	P/E High/Low		PER SHARE ($) Earnings	Dividends	Book Value
12/20	10.89	11	5	1.14	0.21	14.52
12/19	12.22	15	12	0.85	0.20	13.36
12/18*	10.90	117	88	0.12	0.36	12.62
09/18	14.00	20	18	0.58	0.20	12.45
09/17	13.95	30	23	0.46	0.16	12.48
Annual Growth	(7.9%)	—	—	35.3%	9.5%	5.2%

*Fiscal year change

Citizens Financial Services Inc

Citizens Financial Services is an upstanding resident of the financial community. The holding company for First Citizens National Bank serves north-central Pennsylvania's Tioga, Potter, and Bradford counties and southern New York. Through some 15 branches, the bank offers checking, savings, time, and deposit accounts as well as real estate, commercial, industrial, residential, and consumer loans. Residential mortgage loans account for more than half of the bank's total loan portfolio. The Trust and Investment division offers investment advice and employee benefits coordination, as well as estate and retirement planning services. Insurance is offered through the First Citizen's Insurance Agency subsidiary.

EXECUTIVES

Chairman, Director, R. Lowell Coolidge
Vice-Chairman, Director, R. Joseph Landy
President, Chief Executive Officer, Subsidiary Officer, Director, Randall E. Black, $425,000 total compensation
Executive Vice President, Subsidiary Officer, Jeffrey L. Wilson, $162,000 total compensation
Executive Vice President, Chief Operating Officer, Treasurer, Assistant Secretary, Subsidiary Officer, Director, Mickey L. Jones, $260,000 total compensation
Senior Vice President, Subsidiary Officer, Robert B. Mosso
Senior Vice President, Subsidiary Officer, Amy C. Wood
Senior Vice President, Subsidiary Officer, Kathleen M. Campbell, $103,247 total compensation
Senior Vice President, Chief Financial Officer, Subsidiary Officer, Stephen J. Guillaume
Senior Vice President, Subsidiary Officer, Jeffrey B. Carr, $145,000 total compensation
Subsidiary Officer, Gregory J. Anna
Subsidiary Officer, Zerick D. Cook
Subsidiary Officer, Christopher S. Landis
Subsidiary Officer, Sean P. McKinney
Subsidiary Officer, Director, David Z. Richards, $210,000 total compensation
Director, Robert W. Chappell
Director, Roger C. Graham
Director, E. Gene Kosa
Director, Thomas E. Freeman
Director, Christopher W. Kunes
Director, Alletta M. Schadler
Director, Rinaldo A. DePaola
Director, Janie Hilfiger
Auditors : S.R. Snodgrass, P.C.

LOCATIONS

HQ: Citizens Financial Services Inc
15 South Main Street, Mansfield, PA 16933
Phone: 570 662-2121
Web: www.firstcitizensbank.com

COMPETITORS

CHOICEONE FINANCIAL SERVICES, INC.
COMMUNITY SHORES BANK CORPORATION
MBT FINANCIAL CORP.
SVB & T CORPORATION
VOLUNTEER BANCORP, INC

HISTORICAL FINANCIALS
Company Type: Public

Income Statement				FYE: December 31
	ASSETS ($mil)	NET INCOME ($mil)	INCOME AS % OF ASSETS	EMPLOYEES
12/20	1,891.6	25.1	1.3%	306
12/19	1,466.3	19.4	1.3%	268
12/18	1,430.7	18.0	1.3%	274
12/17	1,361.8	13.0	1.0%	273
12/16	1,223.0	12.6	1.0%	270
Annual Growth	11.5%	18.7%	—	3.2%

2020 Year-End Financials
Return on assets: 1.4%
Return on equity: 14.3%
Long-term debt ($ mil.): —
No. of shares ($ mil.): 3.9
Sales ($ mil.): 81.7
Dividends
  Yield: 3.4%
  Payout: 29.4%
Market value ($ mil.): 222.0

	STOCK PRICE ($) FY Close	P/E High/Low		PER SHARE ($)		
				Earnings	Dividends	Book Value
12/20	56.00	10	6	6.52	1.92	49.04
12/19	61.50	12	10	5.42	1.76	43.04
12/18	55.55	13	11	4.99	1.71	38.56
12/17	63.00	18	14	3.59	1.60	35.56
12/16	53.00	15	14	3.46	1.52	33.98
Annual Growth	1.4%	—	—	17.2%	6.0%	9.6%

City Holding Co.

City Holding conducts its principal activities through its wholly owned subsidiary City National Bank of West Virginia. City National offers full range of commercial banking services to corporation and other business customers, and provides banking services to consumers, including checking, savings and money market accounts as well as certificates of deposit and individual retirement accounts. It also provides mortgage banking services and offers specialized services and expertise in the areas of wealth management, trust, investment and custodial services for commercial and individual customers. City Nationals operates more than 90 branches along the I-64 corridor from Lexington, Kentucky through Lexington, Virginia and along the I-81 corridor through the Shenandoah Valley from Lexington, Virginia to Martinsburg, West Virginia.

EXECUTIVES

Chairman, Director, C. Dallas Kayser
President, Chief Executive Officer, Subsidiary Officer, Director, Charles R. Hageboeck, $618,550 total compensation
Branch Banking Executive Vice President, Retail Banking Executive Vice President, Branch Banking Subsidiary Officer, Retail Banking Subsidiary Officer, Michael T. Quinlan, $173,409 total compensation
Division Officer, Subsidiary Officer, John A. DeRito, $285,000 total compensation
Executive Vice President, Chief Financial Officer, Subsidiary Officer, David L. Bumgarner, $255,000 total compensation
Executive Vice President, Chief Administrative Officer, Chief Information Officer, Subsidiary Officer, Jeffrey Dale Legge, $245,000 total compensation
Director, Thomas L. Burnette
Director, Robert D. Fisher
Director, Jay C. Goldman
Director, John R. Elliot
Director, J. Thomas Jones
Director, James L. Rossi
Director, Diane W. Strong-Treister
Director, Charles W. Fairchilds
Director, William H. File
Director, Tracy W. Hylton
Director, Sharon H. Rowe
Auditors : Crowe LLP

LOCATIONS

HQ: City Holding Co.
25 Gatewater Road, Charleston, WV 25313
Phone: 304 769-1100
Web: www.bankatcity.com

PRODUCTS/OPERATIONS

2014 Sales

	$ mil.	% of total
Interest		
Loans, including fees	116.6	62
Investment securities & other	13.0	7
Noninterest		
Service charges	26.5	14
Bankcard revenue	15.1	8
Other	17.1	9
Total	188.3	100

COMPETITORS

CAPITAL BANK FINANCIAL CORP.
CVB FINANCIAL CORP.
EAGLE BANCORP, INC.
FIRST COMMONWEALTH FINANCIAL CORPORATION
FIRST HORIZON CORPORATION
FIRST MIDWEST BANCORP, INC.
FIRSTMERIT CORPORATION
OLD NATIONAL BANCORP
S&T BANCORP, INC.
WSFS FINANCIAL CORPORATION

HISTORICAL FINANCIALS
Company Type: Public

Income Statement				FYE: December 31
	ASSETS ($mil)	NET INCOME ($mil)	INCOME AS % OF ASSETS	EMPLOYEES
12/20	5,758.6	89.5	1.6%	926
12/19	5,018.7	89.3	1.8%	918
12/18	4,899.0	70.0	1.4%	891
12/17	4,132.2	54.3	1.3%	839
12/16	3,984.4	52.1	1.3%	847
Annual Growth	9.6%	14.5%	—	2.3%

2020 Year-End Financials

Return on assets: 1.6%
Return on equity: 13.1%
Long-term debt ($ mil.): —
No. of shares ($ mil.): 15.7
Sales ($ mil.): 260.9
Dividends
Yield: 3.2%
Payout: 41.2%
Market value ($ mil.): 1,097.0

	STOCK PRICE ($) FY Close	P/E High/Low		PER SHARE ($) Earnings	Dividends	Book Value
12/20	69.55	15	10	5.55	2.28	44.47
12/19	81.95	15	12	5.42	2.16	40.36
12/18	67.59	18	14	4.49	1.91	36.29
12/17	67.47	21	17	3.48	1.75	32.17
12/16	67.60	20	12	3.45	1.71	29.25
Annual Growth	0.7%	—	—	12.6%	7.5%	11.0%

Civista Bancshares Inc

First Citizens Banc Corp. is the holding company for The Citizens Banking Company and its Citizens Bank and Champaign Bank divisions, which together operate more than 30 branches in northern Ohio. The banks offer such deposit products as checking and savings accounts and CDs, in addition to trust services. They concentrate on real estate lending, with residential mortgages and commercial mortgages each comprising approximately 40% of the company's loan portfolio. The Citizens Banking Company's Citizens Wealth Management division provides financial planning, brokerage, insurance, and investments through an agreement with third-party provider UVEST (part of LPL Financial).

EXECUTIVES

President, Chief Executive Officer, Dennis G. Shaffer, $350,000 total compensation
Senior Vice President, Secretary, General Counsel, Subsidiary Officer, James E. McGookey, $202,105 total compensation
Senior Vice President, Controller, Subsidiary Officer, Todd A. Michel, $165,401 total compensation
Senior Vice President, Subsidiary Officer, Richard J. Dutton, $249,183 total compensation
Senior Vice President, Subsidiary Officer, Charles A. Parcher, $217,692 total compensation
Senior Vice President, Subsidiary Officer, Paul J. Stark
Non-Executive Chairman, Director, James O. Miller, $415,926 total compensation
Lead Independent Director, Director, Dennis E. Murray
Director, Harry Singer
Director, Allen R. Nickles
Director, Thomas A. Depler
Director, William F. Ritzmann
Director, Julie A. Mattlin
Director, Daniel J. White
Director, Mary Patricia Oliver
Auditors: BKD, LLP

LOCATIONS

HQ: Civista Bancshares Inc
100 East Water Street, Sandusky, OH 44870
Phone: 419 625-4121

COMPETITORS

CBT BANK
CITIZENS HOLDING COMPANY
COMMUNITY SHORES BANK CORPORATION
EMCLAIRE FINANCIAL CORP.
GUARANTY BANK AND TRUST COMPANY

HISTORICAL FINANCIALS

Company Type: Public

Income Statement — FYE: December 31

	ASSETS ($mil)	NET INCOME ($mil)	INCOME AS % OF ASSETS	EMPLOYEES
12/20	2,762.9	32.1	1.2%	459
12/19	2,309.5	33.8	1.5%	457
12/18	2,138.9	14.1	0.7%	432
12/17	1,525.8	15.8	1.0%	350
12/16	1,377.2	17.2	1.3%	337
Annual Growth	19.0%	16.9%	—	8.0%

2020 Year-End Financials

Return on assets: 1.2%
Return on equity: 9.4%
Long-term debt ($ mil.): —
No. of shares ($ mil.): 15.9
Sales ($ mil.): 128
Dividends
Yield: 2.5%
Payout: 24.0%
Market value ($ mil.): 279.0

	STOCK PRICE ($) FY Close	P/E High/Low		PER SHARE ($) Earnings	Dividends	Book Value
12/20	17.53	12	6	2.00	0.44	22.02
12/19	24.00	11	8	2.01	0.42	19.78
12/18	17.42	23	15	1.02	0.32	19.16
12/17	22.00	16	13	1.28	0.25	18.09
12/16	19.43	10	5	1.57	0.22	16.49
Annual Growth	(2.5%)	—	—	6.2%	18.9%	7.5%

Civitas Resources Inc

Bonanza Creek Energy searches for a treasure of black gold. The independent oil and natural gas company has exploration and production assets in Arkansas, California, Colorado, and Texas. Unlike many in the industry, it operates nearly all of its projects and has an 89% working interest in its holdings. The company reported a 32% increase in proved reserves in 2013 to 69.8 million barrels of oil equivalent, resulting primarily from the development of the Wattenberg Field in Colorado. Most of the company's proved reserves are in its Rocky Mountains (Niobara oil shale) and Arkansas (Cotton Valley sands) holdings. Bonanza Creek Energy filed for and emerged from Chapter 11 bankruptcy protection in 2017.

Operations

In 2013 the company drilled 134 wells and completed 121 productive operated wells and participated in drilling 12 and completing 4 productive non-operated wells. The resulting production rates achieved by the drilling program boosted sales volumes by 72% over 2012, to 16,219 barrels of oil equivalent per day (of which 72% was crude oil and natural gas liquids-NGLs).

In 2013, Bonanza Creek produced about 3.9 million barrels of oil, 20 billion cu. ft. of natural gas, and 352,800 barrels of natural gas liquids.

That year the company reported about 73,889 gross (62,003 net) leasehold acres and 684 gross (616.2 net) productive wells.

Geographic Reach

The company's assets and operations are focused in the Rocky Mountains in the Wattenberg Field (primarily the Niobrara oil shale), and in Dorcheat Macedonia Field in southern Arkansas (Cotton Valley sands).

The Rocky Mountain region contributed 66% if the company's total production in 2013; the Mid-Continent region, 34%.

Bonanza Creek also has field offices in Houston, Texas; Bakersfield, California; Stamps, Arkansas; and Kersey, Colorado.

Sales and Marketing

Though Bonanza Creek sells crude oil, natural gas, and associated NGLs, the majority of sales come from oil. The marketing arm of Plains All American Pipeline accounted for 37% of the company's revenues in 2013; petroleum marketer Lion Trading & Transportation, 29%; and Sierra Crude Oil & Marketing 15%.

Financial Performance

The company's revenues increased by 82% in 2013, fueled by higher crude oil, natural gas, and NGL production, and higher crude oil and natural gas prices, partially offset by lower NGL prices. Oil, natural gas, and NGL production increased as a direct result of the $447 million expended for drilling and completion during 2013.

Bonanza Creek's net income grew by 49% in 2013, thanks to higher revenues, offset by an increase in lease operating expense, related to the increased production volumes attributable to the drilling program and the operation of an additional gas plant (constructed during 2012). The increase in depreciation, depletion, and amortization expenses is due to a 55% rise in depreciable assets and a loss incurred on derivative contracts during 2013.

The company has seen year over year growth in revenues since 2010, primarily due to its continuous investment in drilling activity, which triggered the volume growth and as well through the expansion of its properties and by acquisitions.

Strategy

The company is concentrating on increasing production from existing unconventional assets in its core areas while making complementary acquisitions.

Bonanza Creek capital expenditures for 2014 arein the range of $575 million to $625 million. It is focused on the horizontal development of significant resource potential from the Niobrara and Codell formations in the Wattenberg Field, expecting to invest approximately 85% of its 2014 capital budget in this project. The remaining 15% of its 2014 budget is allocated primarily to the vertical development of the Dorcheat Macedonia and McKamie Patton Fields in southern Arkansas, targeting oil-rich Cotton Valley sands.

It invested 82% of its 2013 capital budget in the horizontal development in the Niobrara and Codell formations in the Wattenberg Field. While it has focused on the Niobrara B bench, primarily using 4,000 foot laterals, it has begun to develop the Niobrara C bench and Codell formation as well as to test extended reach lateral drilling in the Wattenberg Field and down-spacing concepts in both of its core areas.

It also intends to pursue bolt-on acquisitions in the Wattenberg Field and in southern Arkansas where it can take advantage of its core operational and engineering competencies.

In 2013 Bonanza Creek increased its 2013 capital budget to drill a "super-section" test of stacked laterals in multiple zones from multi-well pads in the Wattenberg Field and to drill additional wells in southern Arkansas during the fourth quarter. In addition, the expanded budget accommodated increasing non-operated activity and infrastructure projects in the Wattenberg Field. It spent about $472 million in 2013.

In order to focus on its core areas, in 2012 the company sold most of its non-core properties in California, for $9 million.

Mergers and Acquisitions

In 2012 Bonanza Creek bought leases in the Wattenberg Field from the State of Colorado, State Board of Land Commissioners, for $60 million.

Company Background

The company went public in 2011. It used its $251 million in IPO proceeds to repay debt and to fund the exploration and development of oil producing assets.

Bonanza Creek was formed in 2006.

EXECUTIVES

Chairman, Director, Wouter T. van Kempen
President, Chief Executive Officer, Director, M. Christopher Doyle
Business Development Senior Vice President, Corporate Planning Senior Vice President, Brian T. Kuck
Asset Development Senior Vice President, Clinton Bradley Johnson
Vice President, Chief Accounting Officer, Treasurer, Sandra K. Garbiso, $230,769 total compensation
Chief Financial Officer, Marianella Foschi
Chief Sustainability Officer, Brian Cain
Chief Operating Officer, Matthew R. Owens
Chief Legal Officer, Secretary, Travis L. Counts
Director, Deborah Byers
Director, Morris R. Clark
Director, Carrie M. Fox
Director, Carrie L. Hudak
Director, James M. Trimble
Director, Howard A. Willard
Director, Jeffrey E. Wojahn
Auditors : DELOITTE & TOUCHE LLP

LOCATIONS

HQ: Civitas Resources Inc
  410 17th Street, Suite 1400, Denver, CO 80202
Phone: 720 440-6100   **Fax:** 720 305-0804
Web: www.bonanzacrk.com

PRODUCTS/OPERATIONS

2015 Sales

	$ mil.	% of total
Oil	248.9	85
Natural gas	26.5	9
Natural gas liquids	17.3	6
CO2	-	-
Total	292.7	100

COMPETITORS

AMPLIFY ENERGY CORP.
CALLON PETROLEUM COMPANY
CONTINENTAL RESOURCES, INC.
DENBURY INC.
PETROQUEST ENERGY, INC.
REX ENERGY CORPORATION
SARATOGA RESOURCES INC
SM ENERGY COMPANY
SRC ENERGY INC.
VAALCO ENERGY, INC.

HISTORICAL FINANCIALS

Company Type: Public

Income Statement   FYE: December 31

	REVENUE ($mil)	NET INCOME ($mil)	NET PROFIT MARGIN	EMPLOYEES
12/20	218.0	103.5	47.5%	109
12/19	313.2	67.0	21.4%	125
12/18	276.6	168.1	60.8%	144
12/17*	123.5	(5.0)	—	156
04/17	68.5	2.6	3.9%	0
Annual Growth	33.5%	149.8%	—	—

*Fiscal year change

2020 Year-End Financials

Debt ratio: —
Return on equity: 10.4%
Cash ($ mil.): 24.7
Current Ratio: 1.24
Long-term debt ($ mil.): —
No. of shares ($ mil.): 20.8
Dividends
Yield: —
Payout: —
Market value ($ mil.): 403.0

	STOCK PRICE ($) FY Close	P/E High/Low		PER SHARE ($) Earnings	Dividends	Book Value
12/20	19.33	5	2	4.95	0.00	50.16
12/19	23.34	8	5	3.24	0.00	45.37
12/18	20.67	5	2	8.16	0.00	42.05
12/17*	27.59	—	—	(0.25)	0.00	33.65
Annual Growth	(11.2%)	—	—	—	—	14.2%

*Fiscal year change

Clearfield Inc

Broadband providers can get all the fiber they need from Clearfield Inc. The company designs, manufactures and distributes fiber protection, fiber management and fiber delivery solutions to enable rapid and cost-effective fiber-fed deployment throughout the broadband service provider space across North America. Products include a series of panels, cabinets, wall boxes and other enclosures that house the Clearfield components; optical components integrated for signal coupling, splitting, termination, and multiplexing among others for a seamless integration within their fiber management platform; fiber management and fiber pathway and protection method. More than 95% of Clearfield's revenue comes from customers in the US.

EXECUTIVES

Chairman, Director, Ronald G. Roth
President, Chief Executive Officer, Director, Cheryl Beranek Podzimek, $322,217 total compensation
Administration Chief Financial Officer, Daniel R. Herzog, $200,193 total compensation
Chief Operating Officer, John P. Hill, $322,217 total compensation
Director, Patrick Goepel
Director, Roger G. Harding
Director, Charles N. Hayssen
Director, Donald R. Hayward
Director, Walter Jones
Director, Carol Ann Wirsbinski
Auditors : Baker Tilly US, LLP

LOCATIONS

HQ: Clearfield Inc
  7050 Winnetka Avenue North, Suite 100, Brooklyn Park, MN 55428
Phone: 763 476-6866
Web: www.clearfieldconnection.com

2015 Sales

	$ mil.	% of total
United States	55.3	92
All Other Countries	5.0	8
Total	60.3	100

PRODUCTS/OPERATIONS

Selected products
Accessories
Boxes
Cabinets
Cassettes
Copper Assemblies
Fiber Assemblies
Frames
Optical Components
Panels
Patch Cords
Pedestal Inserts
Pedestals
Pushable Fiber and Microduct
Splice-On Connectors
Terminals
Test Access Points
Vaults
Wall Boxes

COMPETITORS

ACACIA COMMUNICATIONS, INC.

ADTRAN, INC.
CIENA CORPORATION
DZS INC.
FINISAR CORPORATION
Fabrinet
INFINERA CORPORATION
NETGEAR, INC.
OPTICAL CABLE CORPORATION
WESTELL TECHNOLOGIES, INC.

HISTORICAL FINANCIALS
Company Type: Public

Income Statement   FYE: September 30

	REVENUE ($mil)	NET INCOME ($mil)	NET PROFIT MARGIN	EMPLOYEES
09/21	140.7	20.3	14.4%	250
09/20	93.0	7.2	7.8%	230
09/19	85.0	4.5	5.4%	240
09/18	77.6	4.2	5.5%	225
09/17	73.9	3.8	5.2%	230
Annual Growth	17.5%	51.6%	—	2.1%

2021 Year-End Financials
Debt ratio: —   No. of shares ($ mil.): 13.7
Return on equity: 21.7%   Dividends
Cash ($ mil.): 13.2   Yield: —
Current Ratio: 3.49   Payout: —
Long-term debt ($ mil.): —   Market value ($ mil.): 606.0

	STOCK PRICE ($) FY Close	P/E High/Low		PER SHARE ($) Earnings	Dividends	Book Value
09/21	44.15	31	14	1.47	0.00	7.56
09/20	20.17	42	17	0.53	0.00	6.06
09/19	11.85	47	26	0.34	0.00	5.49
09/18	13.45	46	33	0.32	0.00	5.05
09/17	13.60	77	41	0.28	0.00	4.67
Annual Growth	34.2%	—	—	51.4%	—	12.8%

CNB Bank Shares Inc

Auditors : Anders Minkler Huber & Helm LLP

LOCATIONS
HQ: CNB Bank Shares Inc
  450 West Side Square, Carlinville, IL 62626
Phone: 217 854 2674
Web: www.cnbil.com

HISTORICAL FINANCIALS
Company Type: Public

Income Statement   FYE: December 31

	REVENUE ($mil)	NET INCOME ($mil)	NET PROFIT MARGIN	EMPLOYEES
12/20	70.7	14.7	20.8%	0
12/19	69.6	13.5	19.4%	0
12/18	57.6	9.4	16.3%	0
12/17	44.6	8.1	18.3%	0
12/16	41.2	8.2	20.0%	0
Annual Growth	14.4%	15.5%	—	—

2020 Year-End Financials
Debt ratio: 4.3%   No. of shares ($ mil.): 5.3
Return on equity: 10.2%   Dividends
Cash ($ mil.): 116.8   Yield: —
Current Ratio: 0.10   Payout: 19.3%
Long-term debt ($ mil.): 27.8   Market value ($ mil.): 97.0

	STOCK PRICE ($) FY Close	P/E High/Low		PER SHARE ($) Earnings	Dividends	Book Value
12/20	18.00	—	—	0.00	0.45	28.16
12/19	17.89	—	—	0.00	0.41	25.42
12/18	18.80	—	—	0.00	0.13	22.45
Annual Growth	(2.2%)	—	—	—	86.1%	12.0%

CNB Community Bancorp Inc

EXECUTIVES
Chairman, Director, Craig S. Connor
President, Chief Executive Officer, Director, John R. Waldron
Human Resources Vice President, Becky Wiley
Vice President, Chief Risk Officer, Stacey Clemens
Assistant Vice President, Controller, Abba Reeve
Chief Financial Officer, Erik A. Lawson
Chief Operating Officer, Karena Mills
Subsidiary Officer, Barry Malek
Subsidiary Officer, Kelly Lantis
Subsidiary Officer, David Kreger
Subsidiary Officer, Mike Jors
Subsidiary Officer, Lois Howard
Subsidiary Officer, Bill Jors
Subsidiary Officer, Eric Potes
Subsidiary Officer, David J. Arnett
Subsidiary Officer, Tony Baker
Subsidiary Officer, Marcy Brown
Subsidiary Officer, Holleigh Baker
Subsidiary Officer, Christopher Clarke
Subsidiary Officer, Mark Dingee
Subsidiary Officer, Karla Enboy
Subsidiary Officer, Roger Ferguson
Subsidiary Officer, Ron Haber
Subsidiary Officer, Christopher Phillips
Subsidiary Officer, Robert Wrozek
Director, John E. Barrett
Director, Joseph B. Dunigan
Director, Judy R. Gabriele
Director, John P. Lovinger
Director, Stephen J. Maddalena
Director, Steven A. Wells
Director, Joseph R. Williams
Auditors : Rehmann Robson LLC

LOCATIONS
HQ: CNB Community Bancorp Inc
  One South Howell Street, Hillsdale, MI 49242
Phone: 517 439-0401   **Fax:** 517 439-0403
Web: www.countynationalbank.com

HISTORICAL FINANCIALS
Company Type: Public

Income Statement   FYE: December 31

	REVENUE ($mil)	NET INCOME ($mil)	NET PROFIT MARGIN	EMPLOYEES
12/20	46.3	10.1	21.8%	0
12/19	39.7	9.1	23.1%	0
12/18	34.8	8.4	24.3%	0
12/17	31.1	6.0	19.4%	3
12/16	28.7	4.7	16.5%	0
Annual Growth	12.7%	20.8%	—	—

2020 Year-End Financials
Debt ratio: 2.3%   No. of shares ($ mil.): 2.1
Return on equity: 14.8%   Dividends
Cash ($ mil.): 100.4   Yield: 3.0%
Current Ratio: 0.12   Payout: 26.2%
Long-term debt ($ mil.): 21.2   Market value ($ mil.): 76.0

	STOCK PRICE ($) FY Close	P/E High/Low		PER SHARE ($) Earnings	Dividends	Book Value
12/20	35.00	9	6	4.77	1.25	33.30
12/19	39.15	10	7	4.37	1.22	29.69
12/18	32.00	9	6	4.06	1.11	26.61
12/17	23.60	8	8	2.93	0.40	23.81
12/16	19.50	—	—	2.32	0.90	21.88
Annual Growth	15.7%	—	—	19.7%	8.6%	11.1%

CNB Financial Corp. (Clearfield, PA)

CNB Financial is the holding company for CNB Bank, ERIEBANK, and FCBank. The banks and subsidiaries provide traditional deposit and loan services as well as wealth management, merchant credit card processing, and life insurance through nearly 30 CNB Bank- and ERIEBANK-branded branches in Pennsylvania and nine FCBank branches in central Ohio. Commercial, industrial, and agricultural loans make up more than one-third of the bank's loan portfolio, while commercial mortgages make up another one-third. It also makes residential mortgages, consumer, and credit card loans. The company's non-bank subsidiaries include CNB Securities Corporation, Holiday Financial Services Corporation, and CNB Insurance Agency.

Operations
Commercial, industrial, and agricultural loans made up 36% of the bank's $16.74 billion loan portfolio at the end of 2015, while commercial mortgages made up another 33%. The rest of the portfolio was made up of residential mortgages (15% of loan assets), consumer (14%), overdrafts (less than 1%), and credit card loans (less than 1%).

The group makes more than 80% of its revenue from interest income. About 70% of its revenue came from loan interest during 2015, while another 15% came from interest income from taxable and tax-exempt securities. The remainder of its revenue came from deposit account service charges (4% of revenue), wealth and asset management fees (3%), and other miscellaneous income sources.

Geographic Reach
Clearfield, Pennsylvania-based CNB Financial serves clients in its home state, as well as in Ohio. CNB Financial serves a specific market area, such as the Pennsylvania counties of Cambria, Cameron, Centre, Clearfield, Crawford Elk, Erie, Indiana, Jefferson, McKean, and Warren.

Sales and Marketing
The group serves individuals, businesses, government, and institutional customers.

CNB Financial has been increasing its advertising spend in recent years. It spent $1.6 million during 2015, up from $1.5 million and $1 million in 2014 and 2013, respectively.

Financial Performance
CNB Financial's revenues have risen more than 30% since 2011 as its loan assets have nearly doubled to $1.58 billion. The firm's profits have grown nearly 50% over the same period as low-interest rates and declining loan loss provisions have lowered operating costs.

The group's revenue climbed 1% to $102 million during 2015 thanks to a modest rise in interest income stemming mostly from 16% loan asset growth.

Despite revenue growth in 2015, CNB Financial's net income dipped 4% to $22.2 million mostly due to nearly 10% rise in salary and employee benefit costs from new hires and more expensive benefits. The group's operating cash levels jumped 16% to $34 million for the year thanks to favorable working capital changes related to accrued interest payables and other liabilities.

Strategy
CNB Financial has been acquiring other banks and opening branches in new geographic markets in recent years to boost its loan and deposit business. As a sign of success, the bank noted that its assets have nearly doubled in size since 2009, from $1.16 billion to $2.29 billion at the end of 2015.

Toward its branch expansion plans, the group's ERIEBANK brand entered Ohio by opening a loan production office there in 2014 with plans to open another by the end of 2016. After opening an FCBank branch in Dublin, Ohio in 2014, the group in 2016 also continued to push its FCBank brand, which has been enjoying double-digit loan and deposit business growth, in the Columbus and Lancaster regions in Ohio. It plans to open a new FCBank branch in Worthington, Ohio by the end of 2016.

Mergers and Acquisitions
In 2016 CNB looked expanded into Northeast Ohio after buying Mentor, Ohio-based Lake National Bank -- and its $152 million in assets -- for nearly $25 million. Lake National Bank's operations were folded into ERIEBANK's operations when the transaction closed.

In 2013, extending its reach in Ohio, CNB Financial acquired FC Banc Corp. for $41.6 million. The deal gave CNB Financial Farmers Citizens Bank, which serves the northern Ohio communities of Bucyrus, Cardington, Fredericktown, Mount Hope, and Shiloh, as well as the greater Columbus, Ohio, area.

Company Background
In 2012 CNB Financial acquired an Ebensburg, Pennsylvania-based consumer discount company, which brought with it a loan portfolio valued at about $1 million.

EXECUTIVES

Chairman, Director, Peter F. Smith, $33,250 total compensation

President, Chief Executive Officer, Subsidiary Officer, Director, Joseph B. Bower, $572,000 total compensation

Community Banking Senior Executive Vice President, Community Banking Chief, Community Banking Subsidiary Officer, Martin T. Griffith

Senior Executive Vice President, Chief Support Officer, Secretary, Subsidiary Officer, Director, Richard Lee Greslick, $283,000 total compensation

Executive Vice President, Chief Financial Officer, Treasurer, Subsidiary Officer, Tito L. Lima

Executive Vice President, Chief Risk Officer, Gregory M. Dixo

Executive Vice President, Mary Ann Conaway

Division Officer, Leanne D. Kassab

Division Officer, Steven R. Shilling

Director, Joel E. Peterson

Director, Richard B. Seager

Director, Jeffrey S. Powell, $34,725 total compensation

Director, Francis X. Straub

Director, Peter C. Varischetti

Director, Deborah Dick Pontzer, $30,675 total compensation

Director, Nicholas N. Scott

Director, Michael Obi

Director, Julie M. Young

Auditors : Crowe LLP

LOCATIONS

HQ: CNB Financial Corp. (Clearfield, PA)
  1 South Second Street, P.O. Box 42, Clearfield, PA 16830
Phone: 814 765-9621
Web: www.cnbbank.bank

PRODUCTS/OPERATIONS

2015 Sales

	$ mil	% of total
Interest and Dividend Income		
Loans including fees	71.8	70
Securities		
Taxable	11.0	10
Tax-exempt	3.8	4
Dividends	0.6	1
Non-Interest Income		
Wealth and asset management fees	3.0	3
Service charges on deposit accounts	4.4	4
Other service charges and fees	3.1	3
Other revenues	4.3	5
Total	102.0	100

Selected Services
Checking
Credit cards
Loans
Savings

COMPETITORS
FIRST FINANCIAL BANCORP.
FIRST FINANCIAL CORPORATION
GREAT SOUTHERN BANCORP, INC.
MAINSOURCE FINANCIAL GROUP, INC.
UNIVEST FINANCIAL CORPORATION

HISTORICAL FINANCIALS
Company Type: Public

Income Statement				FYE: December 31
	ASSETS ($mil)	NET INCOME ($mil)	INCOME AS % OF ASSETS	EMPLOYEES
12/20	4,729.3	32.7	0.7%	651
12/19	3,763.6	40.0	1.1%	559
12/18	3,221.5	33.7	1.0%	556
12/17	2,768.7	23.8	0.9%	528
12/16	2,573.8	20.5	0.8%	507
Annual Growth	16.4%	12.4%	—	6.4%

2020 Year-End Financials
Return on assets: 0.7%   Dividends
Return on equity: 9.0%   Yield: 3.1%
Long-term debt ($ mil.): —   Payout: 29.9%
No. of shares ($ mil.): 16.8   Market value ($ mil.): 358.0
Sales ($ mil.): 195.2

	STOCK PRICE ($) FY Close	P/E High/Low		PER SHARE ($) Earnings	Dividends	Book Value
12/20	21.29	17	7	1.97	0.68	24.72
12/19	32.68	13	9	2.63	0.68	20.00
12/18	22.95	15	10	2.21	0.67	17.28
12/17	26.24	19	13	1.57	0.66	15.98
12/16	26.74	20	12	1.42	0.66	14.64
Annual Growth	(5.5%)	—	—	8.5%	0.7%	14.0%

Coastal Financial Corp (WA)

EXECUTIVES

Chairman, Director, Andrew P. Skotdal

President, Chief Executive Officer, Chief Operating Officer, Director, Eric M. Sprink, $360,000 total compensation

Vice-Chairman, Director, Christopher D. Adams

Executive Vice President, Chief Financial Officer, Subsidiary Officer, Joel G. Edwards, $257,500 total compensation

Executive Vice President, Chief Operating Officer, Subsidiary Officer, John J. Dickson
Executive Vice President, Chief Lending Officer, Subsidiary Officer, Russ A. Keithley, $196,730 total compensation
Director, Sadhana Akella-Mishra
Director, Andrew R. Dale
Director, John M. Haugen
Director, Steven D. Hovde
Director, Stephan Klee
Director, Thomas D. Lane
Director, Gregory A. Tisdel
Auditors : Moss Adams LLP

LOCATIONS

HQ: Coastal Financial Corp (WA)
5415 Evergreen Way, Everett, WA 98203
Phone: 425 257-9000
Web: www.coastalbank.com

HISTORICAL FINANCIALS
Company Type: Public

Income Statement — FYE: December 31

	ASSETS ($mil)	NET INCOME ($mil)	INCOME AS % OF ASSETS	EMPLOYEES
12/20	1,766.1	15.1	0.9%	250
12/19	1,128.5	13.2	1.2%	195
12/18	952.1	9.7	1.0%	183
12/17	805.7	5.4	0.7%	159
12/16	740.6	5.0	0.7%	0
Annual Growth	24.3%	31.9%	—	—

2020 Year-End Financials
Return on assets: 1.0%
Return on equity: 11.4%
Long-term debt ($ mil.): —
No. of shares ($ mil.): 11.9
Sales ($ mil.): 71.2
Dividends
  Yield: —
  Payout: —
Market value ($ mil.): 251.0

	STOCK PRICE ($) FY Close	P/E High/Low		PER SHARE ($) Earnings	Dividends	Book Value
12/20	21.00	18	7	1.24	0.00	11.73
12/19	16.47	16	13	1.08	0.00	10.42
12/18	15.23	19	13	0.91	0.00	9.18
Annual Growth	17.4%	—	—	16.7%	—	13.0%

CoastalSouth Bancshares Inc

Auditors : Elliott Davis, LLC

LOCATIONS

HQ: CoastalSouth Bancshares Inc
5 Bow Circle, Hilton Head Island, SC 29928
Phone: 843 341-9958
Web: www.coastalstatesbank.com

HISTORICAL FINANCIALS
Company Type: Public

Income Statement — FYE: December 31

	REVENUE ($mil)	NET INCOME ($mil)	NET PROFIT MARGIN	EMPLOYEES
12/20	44.1	6.3	14.4%	0
12/19	36.7	2.6	7.1%	0
12/18	26.9	(0.1)	—	0
12/17	22.5	(11.8)	—	0
12/16	30.9	1.4	4.6%	0
Annual Growth	9.2%	45.1%	—	—

2020 Year-End Financials
Debt ratio: 12.7%
Return on equity: 6.5%
Cash ($ mil.): 157.0
Current Ratio: 0.18
Long-term debt ($ mil.): 146
No. of shares ($ mil.): 7.9
Dividends
  Yield: —
  Payout: —
Market value ($ mil.): 97.0

	STOCK PRICE ($) FY Close	P/E High/Low		PER SHARE ($) Earnings	Dividends	Book Value
12/20	12.10	16	11	0.80	0.00	12.76
12/19	12.55	39	32	0.36	0.00	11.60
12/18	10.11	—	—	(0.03)	0.00	10.60
12/17	1.85	—	—	(3.59)	0.00	10.02
Annual Growth	87.0%	—	—	—	—	8.4%

Cognex Corp

Cognex is a leading worldwide provider of machine vision products that capture and analyze visual information in order to automate manufacturing and distribution tasks where vision is required. Manufacturers of consumer electronics and vehicles, as well as logistics companies use the company's machine vision and industrial identification systems to position and identify products, gauge sizes, and locate defects. It also offers a full range of machine vision systems and sensors, vision software, and industrial image-based barcode readers designed to meet customer needs at different performance and price points. Sales to customers based in the US account for more than 40% of sales.

Operations

Cognex operates in one segment, machine vision technology.

Its Vision software offers customers the flexibility of the Cognex vision tools library to use with the cameras, frame grabbers, and peripheral equipment of their choice. Cognex VisionPro software offers an extensive suite of patented vision tools for advanced programming, while QuickBuild prototyping environment allows customers to build complete vision applications with the simplicity of a graphical, flowchart-based programming interface.

Vision Systems combine smart cameras and software to perform a wide range of inspection tasks including part location, identification, measurement, assembly verification, and robotic guidance. Vision Sensors deliver an easy-to-use, low-cost, reliable solution for simple pass/fail inspections, such as checking the presence and size of parts. In-Sight vision systems and sensors, which includes 2D, 3D, alignment, and deep learning models, meet various price and performance requirements for factory automation customers.

The company's industrial image-based barcode readers, which includes the DataMan line, offers bar code readers for use in automotive, consumer products, medical-related, and logistics.

Overall, nearly 85% of sales were generated from the company's standard products and services, while application-specific customer solutions account for the rest.

Geographic Reach

Customers in US account for more than 40% of Cognex's sales while Europe customers supply around 25%, customers in China generate some 20% of sales, and other regions account for the rest. The company's products are assembled by a contract manufacturer in Indonesia. Testing and shipping is done from its Natick, Massachusetts facility for US customers and from its Ireland facility for customers outside the US.

The company is headquartered in Massachusetts.

Sales and Marketing

Cognex sells through a worldwide direct sales force, and via a global network of integration and distribution partners.

The company's customers are in the consumer electronics, automotive, consumer products, food and beverage, and medical-related industries. Approximately 70% of revenue is from consumer electronics, logistics, and automotive industries.

The company's advertising cost totaled some $1,965,000 in 2021, $1,443,000 in 2020, and $1,385,000 in 2019.

Financial Performance

Revenue in 2021 totaled $1 billion, representing an increase of 28% from 2020. The increase was due in part to significantly higher revenue from the logistics industry, which was the company's largest market in 2021, as well as the impact of a broader recovery in industries that were adversely affected by the COVID-19 pandemic in 2020, most notably the automotive industry.

The company's net income in 2021 increased to $279.9 million compared to $176.2 million.

Cash held by the company at the end of 2021 decreased to $186.2 million. Cash provided by operations were $314.1 million, while investing activities used $252.5 million, mainly for purchases of investments. Cash used for financing activities was $141.6 million, mainly for payment of dividends.

Strategy

Cognex's goal is to expand its position as a leading worldwide provider of machine vision products for industrial customers. The company are selective in choosing growth opportunities that it believe will maintain its historically high gross margin percentages, which have ranged in the mid 70% range for the past several years and reflect the value its customers place on its innovative products. The company's high gross margins have the potential to provide it with strong operating leverage in its financial model, as any incremental revenue at such margins falls through to operating income at a high ratio. Cognex's strong and unique corporate culture reinforces its values of customer first and innovation, and enables the company to attract and retain smart, highly educated, experienced talent who are motivated to solve the most challenging vision tasks.

The company invests heavily in research and development in order to maintain its position as a technology leader in machine vision. Cognex invests in technology that makes vision easier to use and more affordable, and therefore, available to a broader base of customers, such as its vision sensor products that enable customers with a lower budget to use machine vision without the help of sophisticated engineers. The company also invests in technology that addresses the most challenging vision applications, such as its 3D vision products that solve applications where a height or volume measurement is requ+++ired and its deep learning vision software that solves complex applications with unpredictable defects and deviations.

HISTORY

Robert Shillman and two MIT colleagues, Marilyn Matz and William Silver, started Cognex (short for "cognition experts") in 1981 to create vision replacement machines for factories. Competition and inadequate technology forced the firm to reevaluate its distribution strategy in 1986. Cognex began supplying machine vision technology to original equipment manufacturers. The company introduced the first custom vision chip in 1988 and went public the next year.

Cognex found success where human vision fails -- in the high-speed, detailed, repetitive processes required in making semiconductors. The company expanded by purchasing Acumen, a developer of machine vision systems for semiconductor wafer identification (1995); Isys Controls, a maker of quality control systems (1996); and Mayan Automation, a maker of surface inspection systems (1997).

Low demand for semiconductor and printed circuit board manufacturing equipment in Asia hurt sales in 1998. Nonetheless, the company boosted R&D by 10% and acquired some of Rockwell Automation's machine vision operations, also becoming the preferred global supplier to Rockwell's plants. Orders picked up in early 1999 and Cognex invested $1 million in upstart Avalon Imaging (machine vision for the plastics industry), its first investment in such a company.

A series of acquisitions and in-house innovations enabled Cognex to expand into factory automation inspection, which accounts for more than 90% of its business.

EXECUTIVES

Chairman, Director, Anthony Sun
President, Chief Executive Officer, Director, Robert J. Willett, $376,442 total compensation
Finance Senior Vice President, Finance Chief Financial Officer, Paul D. Todgham
Corporate Employee Services Chief Culture Officer, Corporate Employee Services Division Officer, Sheila M. DiPalma, $245,942 total compensation
Senior Vice President, Director, Patrick A. Alias, $94,376 total compensation
Division Officer, Carl W. Gerst
Director, Marjorie T. Sennett
Director, Theodor Krantz
Director, Dianne M. Parrotte
Director, Sachin S. Lawande
Director, John T.C. Lee
Auditors : Grant Thornton LLP

LOCATIONS

HQ: Cognex Corp
One Vision Drive, Natick, MA 01760-2059
Phone: 508 650-3000
Web: www.cognex.com

2017 Sales

	$ mil.	% of total
Europe	323.9	43
United States	179.9	24
Greater China	103.4	14
Other	140.7	19
Total	747.9	100

PRODUCTS/OPERATIONS

Selected ProductsIn-Sight 8000 SeriesIn-Sight 7000 SeriesIn-Sight Laser Profiler3D Vision SystemsVisionProCognex Designer

COMPETITORS

AMETEK, INC.
APPLIED MATERIALS, INC.
FORTIVE CORPORATION
HURCO COMPANIES, INC.
KEYSIGHT TECHNOLOGIES, INC.
MKS INSTRUMENTS, INC.
OMRON CO.,LTD.
SANMINA CORPORATION
SYNOPSYS, INC.
Siemens AG

HISTORICAL FINANCIALS
Company Type: Public

Income Statement
FYE: December 31

	REVENUE ($mil)	NET INCOME ($mil)	NET PROFIT MARGIN	EMPLOYEES
12/21	1,037.0	279.8	27.0%	2,257
12/20	811.0	176.1	21.7%	2,055
12/19	725.6	203.8	28.1%	2,267
12/18	806.3	219.2	27.2%	2,124
12/17	747.9	177.1	23.7%	1,771
Annual Growth	8.5%	12.1%	—	6.2%

2021 Year-End Financials
Debt ratio: —
Return on equity: 20.7%
Cash ($ mil.): 186.1
Current Ratio: 3.39
Long-term debt ($ mil.): —
No. of shares ($ mil.): 175.4
Dividends
Yield: 2.8%
Payout: 136.0%
Market value ($ mil.): 13,645.0

	STOCK PRICE ($) FY Close	P/E High/Low		PER SHARE ($) Earnings	Dividends	Book Value
12/21	77.76	59	46	1.56	2.25	8.15
12/20	80.29	81	37	1.00	2.23	7.18
12/19	56.04	48	30	1.16	0.21	7.86
12/18	38.67	55	28	1.24	0.19	6.65
12/17	61.16	142	60	0.99	0.17	6.31
Annual Growth	6.2%	—	—	12.0%	91.3%	6.6%

Cohen & Company Inc (New)

Institutional Financial Markets Inc. (IFMI) believes in the institution of the markets. Formerly a real estate investment trust named Alesco Financial (and later Cohen & Company), the company now manages and trades financial investments, specializing in credit-related fixed income assets. The company serves institutional investors. IFMI's asset management arm offers funds, separately managed accounts, collateralized debt obligations, international hybrid securities, and other investment products; it manages some $10 billion in assets. The firm also has a capital markets division, which sells, trades, and issues corporate and securitized products. IFMI has about 10 offices in the US and London.

EXECUTIVES

Chairman, Subsidiary Officer, Division Officer, Director, Daniel G. Cohen, $630,000 total compensation
Vice-Chairman, Director, Jack J. DiMaio
Chief Executive Officer, Subsidiary Officer, Lester Raymond Brafman, $630,000 total compensation
Executive Vice President, Chief Financial Officer, Treasurer, Subsidiary Officer, Joseph W. Pooler, $441,000 total compensation
Director, G. Steven Dawson
Director, Jack Haraburda

Director, Diana Louise Liberto
Auditors : Grant Thornton LLP

LOCATIONS
HQ: Cohen & Company Inc (New)
Cira Centre, 2929 Arch Street, Suite 1703, Philadelphia, PA 19104
Phone: 215 701-9555
Web: www.cohenandcompany.com

COMPETITORS
BRC MERGER SUB, LLC
COWEN INC.
KBW, LLC
MESIROW FINANCIAL HOLDINGS, INC
National Bank Financial & Co Inc

HISTORICAL FINANCIALS
Company Type: Public

Income Statement				FYE: December 31
	REVENUE ($mil)	NET INCOME ($mil)	NET PROFIT MARGIN	EMPLOYEES
12/20	130.1	14.2	10.9%	87
12/19	49.6	(2.0)	—	94
12/18	49.3	(2.4)	—	88
12/17	47.5	2.0	4.3%	88
12/16	55.3	2.2	4.1%	79
Annual Growth	23.8%	58.2%	—	2.4%

2020 Year-End Financials
Debt ratio: 0.8%
Return on equity: 36.6%
Cash ($ mil.): 42.0
Current Ratio: 0.02
Long-term debt ($ mil.): 47.1
No. of shares ($ mil.): 1.3
Dividends
  Yield: —
  Payout: 0.1%
Market value ($ mil.): 22.0

	STOCK PRICE ($) FY Close	P/E High/Low		PER SHARE ($) Earnings	Dividends	Book Value
12/20	16.34	2	0	7.66	0.00	33.13
12/19	3.95	—	—	(1.81)	0.80	27.91
12/18	8.43	—	—	(2.14)	0.80	29.71
12/17	8.02	7	1	1.60	0.20	32.87
12/16	1.19	1	0	1.90	0.80	32.08
Annual Growth	92.5%	—	—	41.7%	—	0.8%

Coherus BioSciences Inc

EXECUTIVES
Chairman, President, Chief Executive Officer, Director, Dennis M. Lanfear, $702,322 total compensation
Accounting Senior Vice President, Accounting Corporate Controller, Accounting Principal Accounting Officer, Bryan McMichael
Chief Financial Officer, McDavid Stilwell
Lead Independent Director, Director, Mats Wahlstrom
Director, Lee N. Newcomer
Director, Kimberly J. Tzoumakas
Director, Ali J. Satvat
Director, Mark D. Stolper

Director, Jill O'Donnell-Tormey
Director, Charles Newton
Auditors : Ernst & Young LLP

LOCATIONS
HQ: Coherus BioSciences Inc
333 Twin Dolphin Drive, Suite 600, Redwood City, CA 94065
Phone: 650 649-3530
Web: www.coherus.com

HISTORICAL FINANCIALS
Company Type: Public

Income Statement				FYE: December 31
	REVENUE ($mil)	NET INCOME ($mil)	NET PROFIT MARGIN	EMPLOYEES
12/20	475.8	132.2	27.8%	317
12/19	356.0	89.8	25.2%	291
12/18	0.0	(209.3)	—	232
12/17	1.5	(238.1)	—	122
12/16	190.1	(127.3)	—	152
Annual Growth	25.8%	—	—	20.2%

2020 Year-End Financials
Debt ratio: 48.0%
Return on equity: 68.2%
Cash ($ mil.): 541.1
Current Ratio: 5.27
Long-term debt ($ mil.): 404
No. of shares ($ mil.): 72.5
Dividends
  Yield: —
  Payout: —
Market value ($ mil.): 1,260.0

	STOCK PRICE ($) FY Close	P/E High/Low		PER SHARE ($) Earnings	Dividends	Book Value
12/20	17.38	12	6	1.62	0.00	3.87
12/19	18.01	18	6	1.23	0.00	1.50
12/18	9.05	—	—	(3.22)	0.00	(0.57)
12/17	8.80	—	—	(4.48)	0.00	0.53
12/16	28.15	—	—	(3.04)	0.00	0.45
Annual Growth	(11.4%)	—	—	—	—	71.5%

Cohu Inc

Cohu is a leading supplier of semiconductor test and inspection handlers, micro-electromechanical system (MEMS) test modules, test contactors, thermal sub-systems, and semiconductor automated test equipment used by global semiconductor and electronics manufacturers and semiconductor test subcontractor. Customers include semiconductor integrated, device manufacturers, fabless design houses, PCB manufacturers, and test subcontractors around the world. China is the California-based company's single biggest market. Cohu was founded in 1957.

Operations
The company's Semiconductor Test & Inspection provides more than 95% of the company's revenue. It currently sells Semiconductor Test (Semiconductor Automated Test Equipment (ATE) used both for wafer level and device package testing), Semiconductor Handlers (used in conjunction with semiconductor ATE to automate the testing of packaged semiconductor devices), Interface Products (comprised of test contactors, probe heads and probe pins), Spares and Kits (design and manufacture a wide range of device dedication kits that enable handlers to process different semiconductor packages), Services (performs installations and necessary maintenance of systems sold), and Data Analytics (a comprehensive software suite used to optimize Cohu equipment performance).

Sales by product line includes semiconductor test & inspection systems (including kits), account for about 60%, interface products, spares, kits (not as part of systems sales) and services, more than 35%, and PCB test systems (less than 5%).

Geographic Reach
The company's corporate headquarters is located in San Diego, California, its Asian sales and service headquarters are located in Singapore and Taiwan, and the majority of its sales are made to destinations in Asia. In addition, it has Asia-based manufacturing plants in Malaysia, Philippines, and Japan.

About 25% of sales were generated in China, the Philippines with more than 15%, Taiwan with approximately 10%, and Malaysia and the US with nearly 10%, each. The rest of the sales were generated from other countries.

Sales and Marketing
The company markets its products worldwide through a combination of a direct sales force and independent sales representatives. Its customers include semiconductor integrated device manufacturers, fabless design houses, PCB manufacturers, and test subcontractors.

Financial Performance
Cohu's consolidated net sales increased 40% from $636 million in 2020 to $887.2 million in 2021. In 2020, the global semiconductor market was impacted by US and China trade tensions which impacted our customers' ability to supply product to certain end users. During the first half of 2020 Cohu's net sales were also negatively impacted by the rapid and global spread of COVID-19 which led to supply disruptions impacting the company's ability to ship product.

In 2021, the company had a net income of $167.3 million, a $181.1 million increase from the previous year's net loss of $13.8 million.

Cash held by the company at the end of 2021 increased to $290.2 million. Operating, investing, and financing activities generated $97.7 million, $39.9 million, and $6.7 million, respectively.

HISTORY
Kalbfell Laboratories was incorporated in 1947, an outgrowth of a research and development partnership founded in 1945. The company originally made electronic devices for government agencies. It shifted its emphasis to power supply units in 1952 and a year later expanded into closed-circuit television (CCTV) equipment. The company

was renamed Kay Lab in 1954 and Cohu Electronics (after chairman La Motte Cohu) in 1957. It became Cohu Inc. in 1972.

During the 1980s CEO James Barnes directed Cohu's entry into semiconductor test handling equipment. The company acquired microwave equipment maker Broadcast Microwave Services in 1984.

Chip handling gear became Cohu's primary business during the chip boom of the early 1990s. The company established its Singapore subsidiary in 1993. The next year it acquired Daymarc, a maker of gravity-feed semiconductor handling equipment, to complement its Delta Design pick-and-place machines.

EXECUTIVES

President, Chief Executive Officer, Director, Luis A. Muller, $585,769 total compensation
Finance Vice President, Finance Chief Financial Officer, Jeffrey D. Jones, $340,652 total compensation
Corporate Development Vice President, Corporate Development Secretary, Corporate Development General Counsel, Thomas D. Kampfer, $292,235 total compensation
Region Officer, Hock Woo Chiang, $236,043 total compensation
Division Officer, Pascal Ronde, $94,997 total compensation
Division Officer, Christopher G. Bohrson, $266,925 total compensation
Division Officer, Stephen R. Wigley
Division Officer, Ian von Fellenberg, $173,780 total compensation
Non-Executive Chairman, Director, James A. Donahue, $210,000 total compensation
Director, William E. Bendush
Director, Steven J. Bilodeau
Director, Andrew M. Caggia
Director, Lynne J. Camp
Director, Robert L. Ciardella
Director, Nina L. Richardson
Director, Jorge L. Titinger
Auditors : Ernst & Young LLP

LOCATIONS

HQ: Cohu Inc
  12367 Crosthwaite Circle, Poway, CA 92064-6817
Phone: 858 848-8100
Web: www.cohu.com

2018 Sales

	$ mil.	% of total
China	90.3	20
Malaysia	61.8	14
US	61.2	14
Philippines	46.4	10
Other countries	192.1	42
Total	451.8	100

PRODUCTS/OPERATIONS

2018 Sales

	$ in mil.	% of total
Semiconductor Test & Inspection	443.3	98
PCB Test	8.5	2
Total	451.8	100

Operations and Selected Products

Semiconductor Equipment
    Delta Design (semiconductor test handling equipment and thermal technology)
        Automated test handlers
        Burn-in board loaders and unloaders
        Device kits
        Docking interfaces
        Environmental chambers
        Rasco (semiconductor test handling)
        Gravity-feed and test-on-strip systems
Cohu Electronics (closed-circuit television systems)
    Cameras and control equipment
    Control systems
    Design services
    Lenses
    Software
Broadcast Microwave Services (microwave communications equipment)
    Antenna systems
    Microwave radio equipment

COMPETITORS

ANALOGIC CORPORATION
FLEX LTD.
IXIA
OCLARO, INC.
QORVO, INC.
RADISYS CORPORATION
SANMINA CORPORATION
Sandvine Ltd
TERADYNE, INC.
XCERRA CORPORATION

HISTORICAL FINANCIALS

Company Type: Public

Income Statement — FYE: December 25

	REVENUE ($mil)	NET INCOME ($mil)	NET PROFIT MARGIN	EMPLOYEES
12/21	887.2	167.3	18.9%	3,240
12/20	636.0	(13.8)	—	3,250
12/19	583.3	(69.7)	—	3,200
12/18	451.7	(32.1)	—	3,500
12/17	352.7	32.8	9.3%	1,800
Annual Growth	25.9%	50.2%		15.8%

2021 Year-End Financials

Debt ratio: 9.4%
Return on equity: 24.0%
Cash ($ mil.): 290.2
Current Ratio: 3.90
Long-term debt ($ mil.): 103.3
No. of shares ($ mil.): 48.7
Dividends
  Yield: —
  Payout: —
Market value ($ mil.): 1,853.0

	STOCK PRICE ($) FY Close	P/E High/Low		PER SHARE ($) Earnings	Dividends	Book Value
12/21	38.01	14	8	3.45	0.00	18.10
12/20	38.75	—	—	(0.33)	0.06	12.14
12/19	22.30	—	—	(1.69)	0.24	11.67
12/18	15.81	—	—	(1.01)	0.24	13.40
12/17	21.95	22	11	1.14	0.24	10.15
Annual Growth	14.7%	—	—	31.9%	—	15.6%

Collegium Pharmaceuticals Inc

EXECUTIVES

Chairman, Director, Michael Thomas Heffernan, $502,767 total compensation
President, Chief Executive Officer, Director, Joseph Ciaffoni, $535,577 total compensation
Executive Vice President, Chief Commercial Officer, Scott Dreyer, $356,692 total compensation
Executive Vice President, General Counsel, Shirley Kuhlmann, $297,114 total compensation
Executive Vice President, Chief Medical Officer, Richard Malamut
Technical Operations Executive Vice President, Scott Sudduth
Executive Vice President, Chief Financial Officer, Colleen Tupper
Lead Independent Director, Director, Gino Santini
Director, Rita Balice-Gordon
Director, Garen G. Bohlin
Director, Gwen A. Melincoff
Director, John A. Fallon
Director, John G. Freund
Auditors : DELOITTE & TOUCHE LLP

LOCATIONS

HQ: Collegium Pharmaceuticals Inc
  100 Technology Center Drive, Stoughton, MA 02072
Phone: 781 713-3699
Web: www.collegiumpharma.com

HISTORICAL FINANCIALS

Company Type: Public

Income Statement — FYE: December 31

	REVENUE ($mil)	NET INCOME ($mil)	NET PROFIT MARGIN	EMPLOYEES
12/20	310.0	26.7	8.6%	234
12/19	296.7	(22.7)	—	255
12/18	280.4	(39.1)	—	266
12/17	28.4	(74.8)	—	250
12/16	1.7	(94.1)	—	234
Annual Growth	266.9%	—	—	0.0%

2020 Year-End Financials

Debt ratio: 39.9%
Return on equity: 19.5%
Cash ($ mil.): 174.1
Current Ratio: 1.16
Long-term debt ($ mil.): 209.5
No. of shares ($ mil.): 34.6
Dividends
  Yield: —
  Payout: —
Market value ($ mil.): 693.0

	STOCK PRICE ($) FY Close	P/E High/Low		PER SHARE ($) Earnings	Dividends	Book Value
12/20	20.03	33	18	0.76	0.00	5.37
12/19	20.58	—	—	(0.68)	0.00	2.60
12/18	17.17	—	—	(1.19)	0.00	2.75
12/17	18.46	—	—	(2.47)	0.00	3.18
12/16	15.57	—	—	(3.88)	0.00	4.59
Annual Growth	6.5%	—	—	—	—	4.0%

Colony Bankcorp, Inc.

Colony Bankcorp seems to be colonizing Georgia. The multibank holding company owns seven financial institutions doing business under variations of the Colony Bank name throughout central and southern portions of the state. The banks operate more than 25 branches in all. They offer traditional fare such as checking and savings accounts, NOW and IRA accounts, and CDs. Real estate loans, including residential and commercial mortgages and construction and farmland loans, make up the largest portion of the company's loan portfolio, at more than 80%. The banks also issue business and consumer loans.

EXECUTIVES

Chairman, Director, Mark H. Massee
Executive Vice-Chairman, Subsidiary Officer, Director, Brian D. Schmitt
President, Roy Dallis Copeland
Chief Executive Officer, Director, T. Heath Fountain, $121,514 total compensation
Executive Vice President, Chief Sales Officer, General Counsel, Corporate Secretary, Subsidiary Officer, Edward Lee Bagwell, $140,000 total compensation
Executive Vice President, Chief Credit Officer, Subsidiary Officer, Leonard H. Bateman
Executive Vice President, Chief Administrative Officer, Kimberly C. Dockery
Executive Vice President, Chief Banking Officer, Subsidiary Officer, M. Eddie Hoyle, $171,539 total compensation
Director, Harold W. Wyatt, III
Director, Scott Lowell Downing
Director, Michael Frederick Dwozan
Director, Edward P. Loomis, $216,959 total compensation
Director, Meagan M. Mowry
Director, Matthew D. Reed
Director, Jonathan W.R. Ross
Director, Audrey Hollingsworth
Auditors : Mauldin & Jenkins, LLC

LOCATIONS

HQ: Colony Bankcorp, Inc.
  115 South Grant Street, Fitzgerald, GA 31750
Phone: 229 426-6000
Web: www.colonybank.com

COMPETITORS

BANK OF SOUTH CAROLINA CORPORATION
CENTRAL BANCORP, INC.
CITIZENS BANK INC
HENRY COUNTY BANCSHARES, INC.
PEOPLES FINANCIAL CORPORATION

HISTORICAL FINANCIALS
Company Type: Public

Income Statement   FYE: December 31

	ASSETS ($mil)	NET INCOME ($mil)	INCOME AS % OF ASSETS	EMPLOYEES
12/20	1,763.9	11.8	0.7%	376
12/19	1,515.3	10.2	0.7%	370
12/18	1,251.8	11.9	1.0%	330
12/17	1,232.7	7.7	0.6%	326
12/16	1,210.4	8.6	0.7%	333
Annual Growth	9.9%	8.0%	—	3.1%

2020 Year-End Financials
Return on assets: 0.7%
Return on equity: 8.5%
Long-term debt ($ mil.): —
No. of shares ($ mil.): 9.5
Sales ($ mil.): 87.3
Dividends
  Yield: 2.7%
  Payout: 39.2%
Market value ($ mil.): 139.0

	STOCK PRICE ($) FY Close	P/E High/Low		PER SHARE ($) Earnings	Dividends	Book Value
12/20	14.65	13	7	1.24	0.40	15.21
12/19	16.50	16	13	1.12	0.30	13.74
12/18	14.60	14	10	1.40	0.23	11.33
12/17	14.60	17	14	0.87	0.10	10.70
12/16	13.20	16	10	0.84	0.00	11.07
Annual Growth	2.6%	—	—	10.2%	—	8.3%

Columbia Banking System Inc

Columbia Banking System (CBS) is the roughly $16.6 billion-asset holding company for Columbia Bank. The regional community bank has some 145 branches in Washington, from Puget Sound to the timber country in the southwestern part of the state, as well as in northern Oregon and Idaho. Targeting retail and small to medium-sized business customers, the bank offers standard retail services such as checking and savings accounts, CDs, IRAs, credit cards, loans, and mortgages. Commercial real estate loans make up about 45% of the company's loan portfolio, while business loans make up another nearly 40%. Most of its branches were generated in Washington.

Operations

The company's products and services include Personal Banking, which offers an assortment of account products including noninterest and interest-bearing checking, savings, money market and certificate of deposit accounts; Business Banking, which includes a variety of checking, savings, interest-bearing money market and certificate of deposit accounts are offered to business banking customers to satisfy all their banking needs; and Wealth Management, which offers tailored solutions to individuals, families and professional businesses in the areas of financial services and private banking, as well as trust and investment services.

The company segmented our loan portfolio into two portfolio segments: Commercial, which includes Commercial real estate (about 45% of sales), Commercial business (about 40%), and Construction (less than 5%); and Consumer, which includes One-to-four family residential real estate (over 5%), and other.

The Commercial segment two-factor models utilize a mix of seven macroeconomic factors, including the four most commonly used factors: Real GDP, National Unemployment Rate, Home Price Index and Commercial Real Estate Index. The three additional factors are Nominal GDP, Producer Price Index and Core Consumer Price Index. The Consumer segment two-factor models utilize a mix of three macroeconomic factors: National Unemployment Rate, Home Price Index and Prime Rate.

Overall, about 85% of sales were generated from its net interest income which includes loans (about 70%), taxable securities (nearly 15%), and tax-exempt securities, while Non-interest income accounts for the rest.

Geographic Reach

Headquartered in Tacoma, Washington, the company has two operations facilities in Pierce County, Washington, one operations facility in Vancouver, Washington, and one operations facility in Wilsonville, Oregon. It also has some 145 branches, of which 70 were in Washington, some 60 in Oregon, and Idaho with some 15.

Sales and Marketing

The company provides a full range of banking services to small and medium-sized businesses, professionals and individuals. Advertising and promotion expenses were $4.5 million, $4.9 million, and $5.6 million for the years 2020, 2019, and 2018, respectively.

Financial Performance

The company's revenue for fiscal 2020 increased to $604.6 million compared from the prior year with $590.6 million.

Net income for fiscal 2020 decreased by 21% to $154.2 million compared from the prior year with $194.5 million.

Cash held by the company at the end of fiscal 2020 increased to $653.8 million. Cash provided by operations and financing activities were $192.3 million and $2.1 billion, respectively. Cash used for investing activities was $1.9 billion, mainly for Debt securities available for sale.

Strategy

CBS' business strategy is to provide its customers with the financial sophistication and product depth of a regional banking company while retaining the appeal and service level of a community bank. The company continually evaluates its existing business processes while focusing on maintaining asset quality and a diversified loan and deposit portfolio. The company continues to build its strong deposit base, expanding total revenue and controlling expenses in an effort to gain operational efficiencies and increase its return on average tangible equity. As a result of its strong commitment to highly personalized, relationship-oriented customer service, its diverse products, its strategic branch locations and the long-standing community presence of its managers and staff, the company believes CBS are well positioned to attract and retain new customers and to increase its market share of loans, deposits, investments and other financial services. The company is dedicated to increasing market share in the communities it serves by continuing to leverage its existing branch network and considering business combinations that are consistent with its expansion strategy throughout the Northwest and beyond. The company has grown its franchise over the past decade through a combination of acquisitions and organic growth.

Mergers and Acquisitions

In 2021, Columbia Banking System, Inc., the holding company for Columbia State Bank, and Bank of Commerce Holdings, announced the signing of a definitive agreement to merge Bank of Commerce into Columbia in an all-stock transaction valued at approximately $266.0 million. Bank of Commerce Holdings is a bank holding company headquartered in Sacramento, California is an FDIC-insured California banking corporation providing community banking and financial services in northern California along the Interstate 5 corridor from Sacramento to Yreka and in the wine region north of San Francisco. This transaction is expected to be accretive to Columbia's earnings with 3% accretion to earnings per share in 2022 and 4% accretion in 2023.

Company Background

Columbia Banking System took advantage of the rash of bank failures in past years to increase its presence in the Pacific Northwest region. It added more than 30 branches in 2010 when it acquired most of the deposits and assets of failed banks Columbia River Bank and American Marine Bank a week apart. In similar transactions in 2011, it acquired most of the operations of the failed institutions Summit Bank, First Heritage Bank, and Bank of Whitman. Those deals added more than a dozen branches in Washington.

EXECUTIVES

Chairman, Director, Craig D. Eerkes

President, Chief Executive Officer, Subsidiary Officer, Director, Clint E. Stein, $423,077 total compensation

Executive Vice President, General Counsel, Corporate Secretary, Subsidiary Officer, Kumi Y. Baruffi, $283,269 total compensation

Executive Vice President, Chief Financial Officer, Subsidiary Officer, Aaron J. Deer

Executive Vice President, Chief Risk Officer, Subsidiary Officer, Lisa K. Dow

Executive Vice President, Chief Digital & Technology Officer, Subsidiary Officer, Eric J. Eid

Executive Vice President, Chief Human Resources Officer, Subsidiary Officer, David C. Lawson, $287,308 total compensation

Executive Vice President, Chief Credit Officer, Subsidiary Officer, Andrew L. McDonald, $333,500 total compensation

Executive Vice President, Chief Operating Officer, Subsidiary Officer, Christopher M. Merrywell

Executive Vice President, Chief Marketing & Experience Officer, Subsidiary Officer, David Moore Devine

Director, Mark A. Finkelstein

Director, Eric S. Forrest

Director, Randal L. Lund

Director, S. Mae Fujita Numata

Director, Elizabeth Whitehead Seaton

Director, Laura Alvarez Schrag

Director, Tracy Mack-Askew

Director, Michelle M. Lantow

Director, Janine T. Terrano

Director, Ford Elsaesser

Director, Thomas M. Hulbert

Auditors : DELOITTE & TOUCHE LLP

LOCATIONS

HQ: Columbia Banking System Inc
 1301 A Street, Tacoma, WA 98402-2156
Phone: 253 305-1900
Web: www.columbiabank.com

2018 Branches

	No.
Washington	74
Oregon	62
Idaho	14
Total	150

PRODUCTS/OPERATIONS

2018 Revenue

	% of total
Net Interest Income	
Loans	73
Taxable securities	10
Tax-exempt securities	2
Non-interest Income	15
Total	100

COMPETITORS

CENTERSTATE BANK CORPORATION
F.N.B. CORPORATION
HERITAGE FINANCIAL CORPORATION
NATIONAL BANK HOLDINGS CORPORATION
OLD LINE BANCSHARES, INC.
OLD NATIONAL BANCORP
PACIFIC CONTINENTAL CORPORATION
STATE BANK FINANCIAL CORPORATION
WILSHIRE BANCORP, INC.
WINTRUST FINANCIAL CORPORATION

HISTORICAL FINANCIALS

Company Type: Public

Income Statement — FYE: December 31

	ASSETS ($mil)	NET INCOME ($mil)	INCOME AS % OF ASSETS	EMPLOYEES
12/20	16,584.7	154.2	0.9%	2,091
12/19	14,079.5	194.4	1.4%	2,162
12/18	13,095.1	172.8	1.3%	2,137
12/17	12,716.8	112.8	0.9%	2,120
12/16	9,509.6	104.8	1.1%	1,819
Annual Growth	14.9%	10.1%	—	3.5%

2020 Year-End Financials

Return on assets: 1.0%
Return on equity: 6.8%
Long-term debt ($ mil.): —
No. of shares ($ mil.): 71.6
Sales ($ mil.): 622.3
Dividends
Yield: 3.7%
Payout: 61.7%
Market value ($ mil.): 2,570.0

	STOCK PRICE ($) FY Close	P/E High/Low		PER SHARE ($) Earnings	Dividends	Book Value
12/20	35.90	19	9	2.17	1.34	32.79
12/19	40.69	15	12	2.68	1.40	29.95
12/18	36.29	20	14	2.36	1.14	27.76
12/17	43.44	25	19	1.86	0.88	26.70
12/16	44.68	25	15	1.81	1.53	21.55
Annual Growth	(5.3%)	—	—	4.6%	(3.3%)	11.1%

Columbia Financial Inc

EXECUTIVES

Chairman, Subsidiary Officer, Director, Noel R. Holland

President, Chief Executive Officer, Subsidiary Officer, Holding/Parent Company Officer, Director, Thomas J. Kemly, $745,000 total compensation

Senior Executive Vice President, Chief Operating Officer, Subsidiary Officer, Edward Thomas Allen, $445,000 total compensation

Executive Vice President, Chief Financial Officer, Subsidiary Officer, Dennis E. Gibney, $382,000 total compensation

Executive Vice President, Chief Risk Officer, Subsidiary Officer, John Klimowich

Executive Vice President, Division Officer, Allyson Schlesinger

Executive Vice President, Division Officer, Oliver E. Lewis

Human Resources Executive Vice President, Human Resources Subsidiary Officer, Geri M. Kelly

Operations Executive Vice President, Operations Subsidiary Officer, Brian William Murphy

Executive Vice President, Chief Lending Officer, Subsidiary Officer, Mark S. Krukar

Director, Robert Van Dyk

Director, Lucy Sorrentini

Director, James M. Kuiken

Director, Elizabeth Ellen Randall
Director, Frank Czerwinski
Director, Michael Massood
Director, Daria Stacy-Walls Torres
Director, Paul Van Ostenbridge
Auditors : KPMG LLP

LOCATIONS

HQ: Columbia Financial Inc
19-01 Route 208 North, Fair Lawn, NJ 07410
Phone: 800 522-4167
Web: www.columbiabankonline.com

HISTORICAL FINANCIALS
Company Type: Public

Income Statement — FYE: December 31

	ASSETS ($mil)	NET INCOME ($mil)	INCOME AS % OF ASSETS	EMPLOYEES
12/20	8,798.5	57.6	0.7%	628
12/19	8,188.6	54.7	0.7%	698
12/18	6,691.6	22.7	0.3%	663
12/17	5,766.5	3.6	0.1%	0
09/17	5,429.3	31.0	0.6%	679
Annual Growth	17.5%	22.8%	—	(2.6%)

2020 Year-End Financials
Return on assets: 0.6%
Return on equity: 5.7%
Long-term debt ($ mil.): —
No. of shares ($ mil.): 110.9
Sales ($ mil.): 326.9
Dividends
Yield: —
Payout: —
Market value ($ mil.): 1,726.0

	STOCK PRICE ($) FY Close	P/E High/Low		PER SHARE ($) Earnings	Dividends	Book Value
12/20	15.56	33	21	0.52	0.00	9.12
12/19	16.94	35	30	0.49	0.00	8.64
12/18	15.29	88	74	0.20	0.00	8.39
Annual Growth	0.9%	—	—	61.2%	—	4.2%

Comfort Systems USA Inc

Established in 1997, Comfort Systems USA builds, installs, maintains, repairs and replaces mechanical, electrical and plumbing (MEP) systems throughout its some 40 operating units with about 170 locations in more than 125 cities throughout the US. The company operates primarily in the commercial, industrial and institutional MEP markets and perform most of its services, including mechanical, electrical, process piping, modular construction and building automation controls in industrial, healthcare, education, office, technology, retail and government facilities.

Operations
Comfort Systems USA operates in two business segments: mechanical and electrical.

In mechanical business segment, customers hire the company to ensure HVAC systems deliver specified or generally expected heating, cooling, conditioning and circulation of air in a facility. This entails installing core system equipment such as packaged heating and air conditioning units, or in the case of larger facilities, separate core components such as chillers, boilers, air handlers, and cooling towers. It also typically installs connecting and distribution elements such as piping and ducting. The segment accounts for roughly 85% of company's revenue.

In electrical business segment, its principal business activity is electrical construction and engineering in the commercial and industrial field. It also performs electrical logistics services, electrical service work, and electrical construction and engineering services. The segment accounts for more than 15% of revenue.

About 55% of revenue was attributable to renovation, expansion, maintenance, repair and replacement services in existing buildings and the remaining some 45% was attributable to installation services in newly constructed facilities.

Geographic Reach
Houston-based, Comfort Systems USA operates through nearly 170 locations spanning more than 25 US states.

Sales and Marketing
Comfort Systems USA customers include building owners and developers and property managers, as well as general contractors, architects, and consulting engineers. Major customers come from categories including industrial (nearly 45% of revenue), healthcare (about 15%), education (roughly 15%), office buildings (about 10%), government, retail & restaurants, and entertainment, and multi-family and residential.

Financial Performance
Revenue increased $217.0 million, or 8%, to $3.1 billion in 2021 compared to 2020. The increase included an 8% increase primarily related to the North Carolina electrical contractor, TAS, TEC, Amteck and Ivey acquisitions, partially offset by a 0.4% decrease in revenue related to same-store activity.

In 2021, the company had a net income of $143.3 million, a 5% decrease from the previous year's net income of $150.1 million.

The company's cash at the end of 2021 was $58.8 million. Operating activities generated $180.2 million, while investing activities used $246.7 million, primarily for acquisitions. Financing activities provided another $70.5 million.

Strategy
The company focuses on strengthening core operating competencies, leading in sustainability, efficiency and technological improvement, and on increasing profit margins. The key objectives of its strategy are to improve profitability and generate growth in its operations, to enable sustainable and efficient building environments, to improve the productivity of its workforce, and to acquire complementary businesses.

In order to accomplish these objectives, it is currently focused on the following elements:

Achieve excellence in core competencies in safety, customer service, design and build expertise, effective pre-construction processes, job and cost tracking, leadership in energy efficient and sustainable design, and best-in-class servicing of existing building systems;

Achieve operating efficiencies through purchasing economies, adopting operational "best practices," and focusing on job management to deliver services in a cost-effective and efficient manner;

Develop and adopt leading technologies by the increasing use of innovative techniques in prefabrication, project design, and planning, as well as in coordination and production methods. It has invested in the refinement and adoption of prefabrication practices;

Seek growth through acquisitions by continuing to opportunistically enter new markets or service lines through acquisition. It has dedicated a significant portion of its cash flow on an ongoing basis to seek opportunities to acquire businesses that have strong assembled workforces, excellent historical safety performance, leading design and energy efficiency capabilities, attractive market positions, a record of consistent positive cash flow, and desirable market locations.

Mergers and Acquisitions
In early 2022, Comfort Systems USA acquired MEP Holding Co., Inc., and its related subsidiaries, including Edwards Electrical & Mechanical, Inc. (collectively, "Edwards"), headquartered in Indianapolis, Indiana. Comfort Systems USA also announced that it has acquired a service and controls business headquartered in Richmond, Kentucky and a temporary staffing company based in Indiana. Comfort Systems USA further announced that it has acquired Thermal Service, LLC and TES Controls, LLC (together, "Thermal") headquartered in Richmond, Kentucky. Thermal provides complex HVAC service and automation solutions in the state of Kentucky. Finally, Comfort Systems USA announced that it has acquired Kodiak Labor Solutions, LLC ("Kodiak"). Kodiak is a temporary staffing agency that recruits and provides skilled labor, primarily in the Midwest and Eastern United States. Kodiak was acquired to augment labor resources and is not expected to make a material contribution to revenue on a stand-alone basis.

In mid-2021, Comfort Systems USA acquired Kentucky-based Ameteck, LLC family of companies (Amteck), a provider of electrical contracting solutions and services, including design and build, pre-fabrication and installation for core electric and low-voltage systems, as well as services for planned maintenance, retrofit and emergency work.

Amteck brings an exceptional set of capabilities and relationships, and a strong reputation for electrical contracting and related services in industrial markets such as food processing.

In 2021, Comfort Systems USA agreed to acquire Tennessee Electric Company, Inc. dba T E C Industrial Construction and Maintenance (T E C) headquartered in Kingsport, Tennessee. T E C provides multidisciplined construction and industrial services including electrical, mechanical and other plant services. The acquisition is expected to make a neutral to slightly accretive contribution to earnings per share in 2021 and 2022.

Company Background

Comfort Systems went public in June 1997 with the intention of becoming a nationwide provider of building systems installation and maintenance.

Its growth came from successfully expanding services to existing customers and attracting companies into its network of subsidiary companies. Many of them have been operating for 60 years or more.

EXECUTIVES

Chairman, Director, Franklin Myers
President, Chief Executive Officer, Director, Brian E. Lane, $715,000 total compensation
Executive Vice President, Chief Financial Officer, William George, $451,000 total compensation
Senior Vice President, Chief Accounting Officer, Julie S. Shaeff, $286,500 total compensation
Vice President, General Counsel, Corporate Secretary, Laura F. Howell
Chief Operating Officer, Trent T. McKenna, $361,500 total compensation
Director, Darcy G. Anderson
Director, Herman E. Bulls
Director, Alan P. Krusi
Director, Pablo G. Mercado
Director, William J. Sandbrook
Director, Constance E. Skidmore
Director, Vance W. Tang
Auditors : DELOITTE & TOUCHE LLP

LOCATIONS

HQ: Comfort Systems USA Inc
675 Bering Drive, Suite 400, Houston, TX 77057
Phone: 713 830-9600 **Fax:** 713 830-9696
Web: www.comfortsystemsusa.com

PRODUCTS/OPERATIONS

2015 Sales

	% of total
HVAC	77
Plumbing	14
Building automation control systems	5
Other	4
Total	100

2015 Sales

	% of total customers
Manufacturing	21
Education	15
Health care	11
Office buildings	13
Government	10
Retail & restaurants	7
Multi-family	5
Lodging & entertainment	5
Distribution	2
Technology	7
Religious/non-profit	1
Residential	1
Other	2
Total	100

SOLUTIONS & SERVICES
Construction Services
Retrofit & Replacement
Building Automation Systems
Energy Services

COMPETITORS

ABM INDUSTRIES INCORPORATED
EMCOR GROUP, INC.
IES HOLDINGS, INC.
LARSEN AND TOUBRO LIMITED
MISTRAS GROUP, INC.
MITIE GROUP PLC
PIKE CORPORATION
QUANTA SERVICES, INC.
SUNRUN INC.
UNITEK GLOBAL SERVICES, INC.

HISTORICAL FINANCIALS

Company Type: Public

Income Statement				FYE: December 31
	REVENUE ($mil)	NET INCOME ($mil)	NET PROFIT MARGIN	EMPLOYEES
12/20	2,856.6	150.1	5.3%	11,100
12/19	2,615.2	114.3	4.4%	12,000
12/18	2,182.8	112.9	5.2%	9,900
12/17	1,787.9	55.2	3.1%	8,700
12/16	1,634.3	64.8	4.0%	7,700
Annual Growth	15.0%	23.3%	—	9.6%

2020 Year-End Financials

Debt ratio: 13.4%
Return on equity: 23.3%
Cash ($ mil.): 54.9
Current Ratio: 1.17
Long-term debt ($ mil.): 235.7
No. of shares ($ mil.): 36.1
Dividends
 Yield: 0.8%
 Payout: 10.3%
Market value ($ mil.): 1,906.0

	STOCK PRICE ($) FY Close	P/E High/Low		PER SHARE ($) Earnings	Dividends	Book Value
12/20	52.66	14	7	4.09	0.43	19.24
12/19	49.85	19	12	3.08	0.40	15.97
12/18	43.68	20	13	3.00	0.33	13.50
12/17	43.65	30	22	1.47	0.30	11.24
12/16	33.30	20	14	1.72	0.28	10.12
Annual Growth	12.1%	—	—	24.2%	11.5%	17.4%

Communities First Financial Corp

EXECUTIVES

Chairman, Subsidiary Officer, Director, David N. Price
President, Chief Executive Officer, Subsidiary Officer, Director, Steven Miller
Executive Vice President, Chief Credit Officer, Subsidiary Officer, Robert Lee Reed
Executive Vice President, Chief Financial Officer, Subsidiary Officer, Steven R. Canfield
Director, Jack Holt
Director, Sheila Frowsing
Director, Robert G. Kubo
Director, Lorrie Lorenz
Director, Jared Martin
Director, Mark D. Saleh
Director, Joel H. Slonski
Director, Alvin L. Smith
Director, Daniel R. Suchy
Auditors : Crowe LLP

LOCATIONS

HQ: Communities First Financial Corp
7690 N. Palm Avenue, Suite 101, Fresno, CA 93711
Phone: 559 439-0200
Web: www.fresnofirstbank.com

HISTORICAL FINANCIALS

Company Type: Public

Income Statement				FYE: December 31
	ASSETS ($mil)	NET INCOME ($mil)	INCOME AS % OF ASSETS	EMPLOYEES
12/20	871.8	11.5	1.3%	0
12/19	538.3	9.2	1.7%	0
12/18	467.2	6.2	1.3%	0
12/17	407.4	3.6	0.9%	0
12/16	363.5	3.0	0.8%	0
Annual Growth	24.4%	39.1%	—	—

2020 Year-End Financials

Return on assets: 1.6%
Return on equity: 19.0%
Long-term debt ($ mil.): —
No. of shares ($ mil.): 3.0
Sales ($ mil.): 35.8
Dividends
 Yield: —
 Payout: —
Market value ($ mil.): 93.0

	STOCK PRICE ($) FY Close	P/E High/Low		PER SHARE ($) Earnings	Dividends	Book Value
12/20	31.01	9	5	3.79	0.00	22.82
12/19	28.75	10	6	3.09	0.00	17.67
12/18	19.80	12	9	2.14	0.00	14.24
12/17	19.55	17	9	1.28	0.00	12.19
12/16	11.50	10	9	1.12	0.00	10.96
Annual Growth	28.1%	—	—	35.6%	—	20.1%

Community Bank System Inc

With assets of over $15.5 billion. Community Bank System is among the country's 125 largest banking institutions. In addition to a full range of retail, business, and municipal banking services, the company offers comprehensive financial planning, insurance and wealth management services through its Community Bank Wealth

Management Group and OneGroup NY, Inc. operating units. The company's Benefit Plans Administrative Services, Inc. subsidiary is a leading provider of employee benefits administration, trust services, collective investment fund administration and actuarial consulting services to customers on a national scale.

Operations

Community Bank System operates three business segments: Banking, Employee Benefit Services, and All Other.

The Banking segment provides a wide array of lending and depository-related products and services to individuals, businesses and municipal enterprises. In addition to these general intermediation services, the Banking segment provides treasury management solutions and payment processing services. The segment makes up around 70% of total revenue.

Employee Benefit Services, consisting of BPAS and its subsidiaries, provides the following on a national basis: retirement plans, health & welfare plans, fund administration, institutional trust services, collective investment funds, VEBA/115 trusts, fiduciary services, actuarial & pension services, and healthcare consulting services. BPAS services more than 4,200 benefit plans with approximately 510,000 plan participants and holds more than $110 billion in employee benefit trust assets and $1.3 trillion in fund administration. The segment generates some 20% of revenue.

The All Other segment is comprised of wealth management and insurance services. Wealth management activities include trust services provided by the personal trust unit of CBNA, investment products and services provided by CISI, The Carta Group and OneGroup Wealth Partners, Inc. (Wealth Partners), as well as asset management provided by Nottingham. The insurance services activities include the offerings of personal and commercial lines of insurance and other risk management products and services provided by OneGroup. The segment accounts for about 10% of revenue.

More than 60% of the company's revenue comes from net interest income. About 50% of its revenue comes from loan interest, while another 15% came from interest on taxable and nontaxable investments. The rest of its revenue comes from deposit service fees (about 10% of revenue), employee benefit services (some 20%), wealth management (around 5% of revenue) and insurance services (about 5%).

Geographic Reach

Based in New York, Community Bank System has some 265 properties, of which more than 165 are owned and around 100 are under lease arrangements. With respect to the Banking segment, the company operates about 205 full-service branches, more than 10 drive-thru only facilities and nearly 20 facilities for back office banking operations. With respect to the Employee Benefit Services segment, the company operates over 10 customer service facilities and one facility for back office operations, all of which are leased. With respect to the All Other segment, the company operates around 15 customer service facilities.

BPAS employs about 395 professionals serving clients in every US state plus the Commonwealth of Puerto Rico, and occupies nearly 15 offices located in New York, Pennsylvania, Massachusetts, New Jersey, Texas, Minnesota, South Dakota and Puerto Rico.

Sales and Marketing

Advertising costs totaled approximately $5.2 million, $6.1 million, and $7.1 million for 202, 2020, and 2019, respectively.

Financial Performance

The company reported a net interest income of $374.4 million, a 2% increase from the previous year's net interest income of $368.4 million.

In 2021, the company had a net income of $189.7 million, a 15% increase from the previous year's net income of $164.7 million.

The company's cash at the end of 2021 was $1.9 billion. Operating activities generated $202.5 million, while investing activities used $1.5 billion, mainly for purchases of available-for-sale investment securities. Financing activities provided another $1.6 billion.

Strategy

The company's core operating objectives are: (i) optimize the branch network and digital banking delivery systems, primarily through disciplined acquisition strategies and divestitures/consolidations, (ii) build profitable loan and deposit volume using both organic and acquisition strategies, (iii) manage an investment securities portfolio to complement the company's loan and deposit strategies and optimize interest rate risk, yield and liquidity, (iv) increase the noninterest component of total revenues through development of banking-related fee income, growth in existing financial services business units, and the acquisition of additional financial services and banking businesses, and (v) utilize technology to deliver customer-responsive products and services and improve efficiencies.

Mergers and Acquisitions

In 2022, Community Bank, a subsidiary of Community Bank Systems, announced it completed its merger with Elmira Savings Bank, a New York state chartered savings bank. Community Bank acquired Elmira in an all cash transaction representing total consideration valued at approximately $82.8 million. The merger added eight branch locations across a five-county area in the Central New York and Southern Tier markets. With completion of the merger, Community Bank System has over $16.2 billion in assets and over $13.8 billion in deposits.

In 2021, Community Bank System announced that it acquired the assets of the Thomas Gregory Associates Insurance Brokers, Inc. (TGA), a specialty-lines insurance broker based in the Boston marketplace. TGA's assets were acquired by OneGroup, a wholly-owned subsidiary of Community Bank System. The TGA acquisition not only provides OneGroup with a New England presence, but also brings additional specialty-lines expertise to the organization that management expects to leverage across the broader Community Bank System customer base. TGA is expected to give OneGroup a profile of approximately $35 million in annual revenues.

Also in 2021, Community Bank System announced that it acquired Fringe Benefits Design of Minnesota, Inc. (FBD), a provider of retirement plan administration and benefit consulting services with offices in Minnesota and South Dakota. FBD will become a subsidiary of Benefit Plans Administrative Services, Inc. (BPAS), a wholly-owned subsidiary of Community Bank System. The acquisition of FBD is expected to give BPAS a profile of over $110 million in annual revenues, administration of more than 510,000 retirement plan participant accounts, 4,200 employer clients, approximately $13 billion in defined contribution plan assets on its daily valuation system, and approximately $110 billion of total assets in trust.

Company Background

In mid-2012, the bank purchased about 20 branches in upstate New York from HSBC. The deal, which was made to satisfy antitrust concerns regarding First Niagara's purchase of 195 branches in New York from HSBC, strengthened Community Bank Systems' geographic footprint.

In 2011, the company bought bank holding company The Wilber Corporation, adding about 20 locations in the Catskills Mountains region of central New York.

In 2011, expanding its trust and benefits administration business, it bought retirement plan administrator CAI Benefits, which has offices in New York and Northern New Jersey.

EXECUTIVES

Chairman, Subsidiary Officer, Director, Eric E. Stickels

President, Chief Executive Officer, Subsidiary Officer, Director, Mark E. Tryniski, $800,000 total compensation

Executive Vice President, Chief Financial Officer, Subsidiary Officer, Joseph E. Sutaris, $299,769 total compensation

Executive Vice President, Chief Human Resources Officer, Maureen Gillan-Myer

Corporate Development Executive Vice President, Financial Services Executive Vice President, Corporate Development Chief Operating Officer, Financial Services Chief Operating Officer, Corporate Development Subsidiary Officer, Financial Services Subsidiary Officer, Dimitar A. Karaivanov

Executive Vice President, General Counsel, Subsidiary Officer, Michael N. Abdo

Secretary, Danielle M. Cima

Division Officer, Jeffrey M. Levy

Lead Director, Director, Sally A. Steele

Director, Brian R. Ace

Director, Mark J. Bolus

Director, Jeffrey L. Davis

Director, Neil E. Fesette

Director, Jeffery J. Knauss

Director, Kerrie D. MacPherson

Director, John Parente

Director, Raymond C. Pecor

Director, Susan E. Skerritt

Director, John F. Whipple

Auditors : PricewaterhouseCoopers LLP

LOCATIONS

HQ: Community Bank System Inc
5790 Widewaters Parkway, DeWitt, NY 13214-1883
Phone: 315 445-2282
Web: www.communitybankna.com

PRODUCTS/OPERATIONS

2015 Sales

	$ mil.	% of total
Interest Income:		
Interest and fees on loans	187.7	49
Taxable investments	52.9	14
Nontaxable investments	19.0	5
Noninterest		
Deposit service fees	52.7	14
Employee benefit services	45.4	12
Wealth management	20.2	5
Other	5.0	1
Total	382.9	100

Selected Subsidiaries & Affiliates

Benefit Plans Administrative Services, Inc.
Benefit Plans Administrative Services LLC
Brilie Corporation
CBNA Insurance Agency, Inc.
CBNA Preferred Funding Corp.
CBNA Treasury Management Corporation
Community Bank, N.A. (also dba First Liberty Bank & Trust)
Community Investment Services, Inc.
First of Jermyn Realty Company
First Liberty Service Corporation
Flex Corporation
Hand Benefit & Trust Company
Hand Securities, Inc.
Harbridge Consulting Group LLP
Nottingham Advisors, Inc.
Town & Country Agency LLC
Western Catskill Realty, Inc.

COMPETITORS

AMERICAN NATIONAL BANKSHARES INC.
BANCFIRST CORPORATION
CITIZENS & NORTHERN CORPORATION
CITY HOLDING COMPANY
FINANCIAL INSTITUTIONS, INC.
FIRST HORIZON CORPORATION
FIRST MIDWEST BANCORP, INC.
FIRSTMERIT CORPORATION
WINTRUST FINANCIAL CORPORATION
WSFS FINANCIAL CORPORATION

HISTORICAL FINANCIALS

Company Type: Public

Income Statement
FYE: December 31

	ASSETS ($mil)	NET INCOME ($mil)	INCOME AS % OF ASSETS	EMPLOYEES
12/20	13,931.0	164.6	1.2%	3,047
12/19	11,410.2	169.0	1.5%	3,038
12/18	10,607.2	168.6	1.6%	2,933
12/17	10,746.1	150.7	1.4%	2,874
12/16	8,666.4	103.8	1.2%	2,499
Annual Growth	12.6%	12.2%	—	5.1%

2020 Year-End Financials

Return on assets: 1.2%
Return on equity: 8.2%
Long-term debt ($ mil.): —
No. of shares ($ mil.): 53.5
Sales ($ mil.): 617.6
Dividends
Yield: 2.6%
Payout: 54.7%
Market value ($ mil.): 3,339.0

	STOCK PRICE ($) FY Close	P/E High	P/E Low	PER SHARE ($) Earnings	PER SHARE ($) Dividends	PER SHARE ($) Book Value
12/20	62.31	23	16	3.08	1.66	39.26
12/19	70.94	22	17	3.23	1.58	35.82
12/18	58.30	20	16	3.24	1.44	33.43
12/17	53.75	20	16	3.03	1.32	32.26
12/16	61.79	27	15	2.32	1.26	26.96
Annual Growth	0.2%	—	—	7.3%	7.1%	9.9%

Community Financial Corp (The)

Tri-County Financial is trying to create some interest in the Old Line State. The financialÂ institution is the holding company for Community Bank of Tri-County, which operatesÂ about 10Â branches in Calvert, Charles, and St. Mary's counties in southern Maryland. The bank, which was first organized as a savings and loan associationÂ in 1950,Â offers standard retail products and services, including checking and savings accounts, IRAs, and CDs. It uses funds from deposits to write a variety of loans, including commercial mortgages (about 40% of its loan book), residential mortgages, and business loans. Home equity, construction, equipment, and consumer loans round out its loan portfolio.

EXECUTIVES

Chairman, Subsidiary Officer, Director, Austin J. Slater

Vice-Chairman, President, Chief Executive Officer, Subsidiary Officer, Director, James M. Burke, $336,000 total compensation

Executive Vice President, Chief Administrative Officer, Lacey A. Pierce

Executive Vice President, Subsidiary Officer, Patrick D. Pierce

Executive Vice President, Chief Financial Officer, Subsidiary Officer, Todd L. Capitani, $285,000 total compensation

Executive Vice President, Chief Operating Officer, Subsidiary Officer, Christy M. Lombardi

Subsidiary Officer, John A. Chappelle

Subsidiary Officer, B. Scot Ebron

Subsidiary Officer, Talal Tay

Director, Rebecca Middleton McDonald

Director, Kimberly C. Briscoe-Tonic

Director, James F. Di Misa, $294,000 total compensation

Director, Michael Adams

Director, Mohammad Arshed Javaid

Director, Louis P. Jenkins

Director, Mary Todd Peterson

Director, E. Lawrence Sanders

Director, Gregory C. Cockerham, $320,000 total compensation

Director, Joseph V. Stone

Director, Katheryn M. Zabriskie

Auditors : Dixon Hughes Goodman LLP

LOCATIONS

HQ: Community Financial Corp (The)
3035 Leonardtown Road, Waldorf, MD 20601
Phone: 301 645-5601
Web: www.cbtc.com

COMPETITORS

BCSB BANCORP, INC.
GREAT FLORIDA BANK
KS BANCORP, INC.
SB ONE BANCORP
SOUTHCOAST FINANCIAL CORPORATION

HISTORICAL FINANCIALS

Company Type: Public

Income Statement
FYE: December 31

	ASSETS ($mil)	NET INCOME ($mil)	INCOME AS % OF ASSETS	EMPLOYEES
12/20	2,026.4	16.1	0.8%	191
12/19	1,797.5	15.2	0.8%	194
12/18	1,689.2	11.2	0.7%	189
12/17	1,405.9	7.2	0.5%	165
12/16	1,334.2	7.3	0.5%	162
Annual Growth	11.0%	21.8%	—	4.2%

2020 Year-End Financials

Return on assets: 0.8%
Return on equity: 8.4%
Long-term debt ($ mil.): —
No. of shares ($ mil.): 5.9
Sales ($ mil.): 79.4
Dividends
Yield: 1.8%
Payout: 20.4%
Market value ($ mil.): 156.0

	STOCK PRICE ($) FY Close	P/E High	P/E Low	PER SHARE ($) Earnings	PER SHARE ($) Dividends	PER SHARE ($) Book Value
12/20	26.48	13	7	2.74	0.50	33.54
12/19	35.57	13	10	2.75	0.50	30.76
12/18	29.24	19	13	2.02	0.40	27.70
12/17	38.30	26	18	1.56	0.40	23.65
12/16	29.00	19	12	1.59	0.40	22.54
Annual Growth	(2.2%)	—	—	14.6%	5.7%	10.5%

Community Healthcare Trust Inc

EXECUTIVES

Chairman, President, Chief Executive Officer, Timothy G. Wallace, $458,167 total compensation
Executive Vice President, Chief Financial Officer, David H. Dupuy, $350,000 total compensation
Financial Reporting Executive Vice President, Financial Reporting Chief Accounting Officer, Leigh Ann Stach, $220,500 total compensation
Asset Management Executive Vice President, Timothy L. Meyer
Director, Cathrine Cotman
Lead Director, Director, Alan Gardner
Director, Claire Gulmi
Director, Robert Z. Hensley
Director, R. Lawrence Van Horn
Auditors : BDO USA, LLP

LOCATIONS

HQ: Community Healthcare Trust Inc
3326 Aspen Grove Drive, Suite 150, Franklin, TN 37067
Phone: 615 771-3052
Web: www.chct.reit

HISTORICAL FINANCIALS

Company Type: Public

Income Statement				FYE: December 31
	REVENUE ($mil)	NET INCOME ($mil)	NET PROFIT MARGIN	EMPLOYEES
12/21	90.5	22.4	24.8%	30
12/20	75.6	19.0	25.2%	28
12/19	60.8	8.3	13.8%	25
12/18	48.6	4.4	9.1%	16
12/17	37.3	3.5	9.4%	16
Annual Growth	24.8%	59.1%	—	17.0%

2021 Year-End Financials

Debt ratio: 35.6%
Return on equity: 5.0%
Cash ($ mil.): 2.3
Current Ratio: 0.37
Long-term debt ($ mil.): 268.5
No. of shares ($ mil.): 24.9
Dividends
Yield: 3.6%
Payout: 205.3%
Market value ($ mil.): 1,181.0

	STOCK PRICE ($)	P/E		PER SHARE ($)		
	FY Close	High	Low	Earnings	Dividends	Book Value
12/21	47.27	60	49	0.87	1.73	18.50
12/20	47.11	65	28	0.80	1.69	18.00
12/19	42.86	132	76	0.37	1.65	16.51
12/18	28.83	170	118	0.19	1.61	14.58
12/17	28.10	151	113	0.19	1.57	15.67
Annual Growth	13.9%	—	—	46.3%	2.5%	4.2%

Community West Bancshares

Community West Bancshares is the holding company for Community West Bank, which serves individuals and small to midsized businesses through five branches along California's Central Coast. Services include checking and savings accounts and CDs, as well as health savings accounts. Approximately 40% of the bank's loan portfolio is secured by manufactured housing loans; real estate mortgages account for more than 30%. A preferred Small Business Administration lender, Community West also writes SBA loans through offices in about a dozen other states.

EXECUTIVES

Chairman, Director, William R. Peeples, $0 total compensation
President, Chief Executive Officer, Subsidiary Officer, Director, Martin E. Plourd, $391,667 total compensation
Executive Vice President, Chief Financial Officer, Subsidiary Officer, Richard Pimentel
Secretary, Director, John D. Illgen
Subsidiary Officer, William F. Filippin, $238,209 total compensation
Subsidiary Officer, Timothy J. Stronks
Subsidiary Officer, Director, Robert H. Bartlein
Director, Martin P. Alwin
Director, Dana L. Boutain
Director, Suzanne M. Chadwick
Director, Tom L. Dobyns
Director, James W. Lokey
Director, Shereef Moharram
Director, Christopher R. Raffo
Director, Kirk B. Stovesand
Director, Celina L. Zacarias
Auditors : RSM US LLP

LOCATIONS

HQ: Community West Bancshares
445 Pine Avenue, Goleta, CA 93117
Phone: 805 692-5821   **Fax:** 805 692-5835
Web: www.communitywest.com

Branches
Goleta, California
Santa Barbara, California
Santa Maria, California
Ventura, California
Westlake Village, California
SBA Lending Offices
Alabama
California
Colorado
Florida
Georgia
Maryland
North Carolina
Ohio
Oregon
South Carolina
Tennessee
Washington

PRODUCTS/OPERATIONS

2008 Sales	$ mil.	% of total
Interest		
Loans	43.0	85
Investment securities	2.2	4
Other	0.3	1
Non-interest		
Loan fees	2.1	4
Loan sales	1.0	2
Other fees	1.7	3
Other	0.3	1
Total	50.6	100

COMPETITORS

CENTRAL BANCORP, INC.
COMMUNITY SHORES BANK CORPORATION
FIRST KEYSTONE CORPORATION
FIRST US BANCSHARES, INC.
UNITY BANCORP, INC.

HISTORICAL FINANCIALS

Company Type: Public

Income Statement				FYE: December 31
	ASSETS ($mil)	NET INCOME ($mil)	INCOME AS % OF ASSETS	EMPLOYEES
12/20	975.4	8.2	0.8%	128
12/19	913.8	7.9	0.9%	133
12/18	877.2	7.4	0.8%	139
12/17	833.3	4.9	0.6%	128
12/16	710.5	5.2	0.7%	120
Annual Growth	8.2%	12.1%	—	1.6%

2020 Year-End Financials

Return on assets: 0.8%
Return on equity: 9.6%
Long-term debt ($ mil.): —
No. of shares ($ mil.): 8.4
Sales ($ mil.): 47.7
Dividends
Yield: 2.1%
Payout: 20.1%
Market value ($ mil.): 77.0

	STOCK PRICE ($)	P/E		PER SHARE ($)		
	FY Close	High	Low	Earnings	Dividends	Book Value
12/20	9.08	12	6	0.97	0.20	10.50
12/19	11.10	12	10	0.93	0.22	9.68
12/18	10.03	14	11	0.88	0.19	8.92
12/17	10.65	18	15	0.57	0.16	8.55
12/16	9.24	15	11	0.62	0.14	8.07
Annual Growth	(0.4%)	—	—	11.8%	9.6%	6.8%

Compass Diversified

Compass Diversified Holdings helps niche companies navigate their way toward profitability. The holding company owns controlling stakes in and manages promising middle-market businesses throughout North America. Its strategy is two-fold: help its portfolio firms grow and increase their profits, and increase the size of its own portfolio. Compass invests in niche businesses across a variety of industries, including furniture maker AFM Holdings (sold in 2015) and home and gun safes maker Liberty Safe and Security Products. Its arsenal includes helping its holdings make strategic acquisitions, enter new business arenas, or improve operations to increase profitability.

Strategy

When evaluating acquisition candidates Compass looks for established, US-based companies with significant market share in a niche industry with a low risk of technological or product obsolescence. Other investment criteria include a proven management team, diversified customer and supplier base, and a minimum EBITDA (earnings before interest, taxes, depreciation and amortization) of $8 million.

To that end, in late 2014 Compass spent $163 million to acquire the California-based Candle Lamp Company ("SternoCandleLamp"), a leading manufacturer and marketer of portable food warming fuel and creative table lighting solutions for the food service industry. Also in 2014, the company purchased Clean Earth, which provides environmental services for contaminated soils, dredged materials, hazardous waste, and other contaminated materials. Shortly after that deal, Clean Earth acquired AES Environmental, allowing it deepen its presence in the Midwest and Mid-Atlantic.

In late 2015, Compass sold AFM Holdings for some $24 million; it had acquired the firm in 2007 for $93 million. The company reported a loss on the sale of approximately $14 million.

EXECUTIVES

Chairman, C. Sean Day
Chief Executive Officer, Subsidiary Officer, Director, Elias J. Sabo, $0 total compensation
Chief Financial Officer, Co-Compliance Officer, Subsidiary Officer, Ryan J. Faulkingham, $410,000 total compensation
Secretary, Carrie W. Ryan
Lead Director, Director, D. Eugene Ewing
Director, Alex Bhathal
Director, Harold S. Edwards
Director, Sarah (Sally) Gaines McCoy
Auditors : Grant Thornton LLP

LOCATIONS

HQ: Compass Diversified
   301 Riverside Avenue, Second Floor, Westport, CT 06880
Phone: 203 221-1703
Web: www.compassdiversifiedholdings.com

COMPETITORS

BERWIND CORPORATION
FENWAY PARTNERS, LLC
FIRST ATLANTIC CAPITAL, LTD.
MARKETAXESS HOLDINGS INC.
MITIE GROUP PLC
OCTOPUS INVESTMENTS LIMITED
RIVERSIDE PARTNERS L.L.C.
THE GORES GROUP LLC
VERONIS, SUHLER & ASSOCIATES, INC.
VIRTU ITG HOLDINGS LLC

HISTORICAL FINANCIALS
Company Type: Public

Income Statement   FYE: December 31

	REVENUE ($mil)	NET INCOME ($mil)	NET PROFIT MARGIN	EMPLOYEES
12/20	1,560.7	22.7	1.5%	4,598
12/19	1,450.2	301.8	20.8%	3,456
12/18	1,691.6	(5.7)	—	2,416
12/17	1,269.7	27.9	2.2%	837
12/16	978.3	54.6	5.6%	655
Annual Growth	12.4%	(19.7%)	—	62.8%

2020 Year-End Financials
Debt ratio: 34.6%   No. of shares ($ mil.): 64.9
Return on equity: 2.0%   Dividends
Cash ($ mil.): 70.7   Yield: 7.4%
Current Ratio: 2.40   Payout: 394.4%
Long-term debt ($ mil.): 899.4 Market value ($ mil.): 1,262.0

	STOCK PRICE ($) FY Close	P/E High	P/E Low	PER SHARE ($) Earnings	Dividends	Book Value
12/20	19.45	—	—	(0.34)	1.44	16.95
12/19	24.86	7	4	3.64	1.44	18.62
12/18	12.45	—	—	(0.42)	1.44	14.35
12/17	16.95	—	—	(0.44)	1.44	14.58
12/16	17.90	38	28	0.51	1.44	14.30
Annual Growth	2.1%	—	—	—	0.0%	4.3%

ConnectOne Bancorp Inc (New)

ConnectOne Bancorp (formerly Center Bancorp) is the holding company for ConnectOne Bank, which operates some two dozen branches across New Jersey. Serving individuals and local businesses, the bank offers such deposit products as checking, savings, and money market accounts; CDs; and IRAs. It also performs trust services. Commercial loans account for about 60% of the bank's loan portfolio; residential mortgages account for most of the remainder. It also has a subsidiary that sells annuities and property/casualty, life, and health coverage. The former Center Bancorp acquired rival community bank ConnectOne Bancorp in 2014 and took that name.

Geographic Reach
ConnectOne has 24 branches in Bergen, Essex, Hudson, Manhattan, Mercer, Monmouth, Morris, and Union Counties in New Jersey.

Mergers and Acquisitions
In 2019 ConnectOne Bancorp agreed to acquire online business lending marketplace company BoeFly. BoeFly connects franchisors and small business owners with lenders and loan brokers in the US and has facilitated more than $5 billion in financing transactions. BoeFly's online platform and client network will enhance and expand ConnectOne's Small Business Adminstration (SBA) line of business.

EXECUTIVES

President, Chief Executive Officer, Subsidiary Officer, Chairman, Frank Sorrentino, $800,000 total compensation
Executive Vice President, Chief Financial Officer, Subsidiary Officer, William S. Burns, $411,000 total compensation
Executive Vice President, Chief Operating Officer, Subsidiary Officer, Christopher J. Ewing, $340,000 total compensation
First Senior Vice President, Chief Credit Officer, Subsidiary Officer, Joseph T. Javitz
Subsidiary Officer, Elizabeth Magennis, $385,000 total compensation
Lead Independent Director, Director, Stephen T. Boswell
Director, Frank W. Baier
Director, Frank Huttle
Director, Michael W. Kempner
Director, Nicholas Minoia
Director, Anson M. Moise
Director, Katherin Nukk-Freeman
Director, Joseph Parisi
Director, Daniel M. Rifkin
Director, Mark Sokolich
Director, William A. Thompson
Auditors : Crowe LLP

LOCATIONS

HQ: ConnectOne Bancorp Inc (New)
   301 Sylvan Avenue, Englewood Cliffs, NJ 07632
Phone: 201 816-8900
Web: www.centerbancorp.com

COMPETITORS

COMMUNITY TRUST BANCORP, INC.
FIRST US BANCSHARES, INC.
SB ONE BANCORP
THE FIRST BANK AND TRUST COMPANY
UNITY BANCORP, INC.

HISTORICAL FINANCIALS
Company Type: Public

Income Statement   FYE: December 31

	ASSETS ($mil)	NET INCOME ($mil)	INCOME AS % OF ASSETS	EMPLOYEES
12/20	7,547.3	71.2	0.9%	413
12/19	6,174.0	73.3	1.2%	0
12/18	5,462.0	60.3	1.1%	0
12/17	5,108.4	43.2	0.8%	0
12/16	4,426.3	31.0	0.7%	0
Annual Growth	14.3%	23.1%	—	—

2020 Year-End Financials
Return on assets: 1.0%   Dividends
Return on equity: 8.6%   Yield: 1.8%
Long-term debt ($ mil.): —   Payout: 20.1%
No. of shares ($ mil.): 39.7   Market value ($ mil.): 787.0
Sales ($ mil.): 322.6

	STOCK PRICE ($) FY Close	P/E High/Low		PER SHARE ($) Earnings	Dividends	Book Value
12/20	19.79	14	5	1.79	0.36	23.01
12/19	25.72	13	9	2.07	0.35	20.85
12/18	18.47	17	9	1.86	0.30	18.99
12/17	25.75	21	16	1.34	0.30	17.63
12/16	25.95	26	15	1.01	0.30	16.62
Annual Growth	(6.6%)	—	—	15.4%	4.7%	8.5%

Consolidated Communications Holdings Inc

Consolidated Communications is just what its name implies. The rural local exchange carrier operates systems in Illinois, Kansas, Missouri, Pennsylvania, Texas, and California, providing voice and data telecommunications to business and residential customers. The company offers local access and long-distance, internet and TV, business phone systems, and related services through about 63,450 video connections, 328,850 voice connections, and 384,550 data and Internet connections. It also offers directory publishing and carrier services. The company founded in 1894 as the Mattoon Telephone Company.

Operations
The company's source of revenue were: Commercial and carrier (about 45%); Consumer (about 40%); Subsidies (around 5%); Network access (about 10%); and other products and services (less than 5%).

Commercial and carrier is divided in three segments: Data and Transport Services; Voice Services; and others. Data and transport services provide a variety of business communication solutions to commercial customers of all sizes, including voice and data services over its advanced fiber network. Voice services include basic local phone and long-distance service packages for business customers. Other services include business equipment sales and related hardware and maintenance support, video services and other miscellaneous revenues, including 911 service revenues.

Consumer is divided in three segments: Broadband Services; Video Services; and Voice Services. Broadband services include revenues from residential customers for subscriptions to its VoIP and data products. Video services range from limited basic service to advanced digital television, which includes several plans, each with hundreds of local, national and music channels including premium and Pay-Per-View channels as well as video on-demand service. Voice services offer several different basic local phone service packages and long-distance calling plans, including unlimited flat-rate calling plans.

Subsidies consist of both federal and state subsidies, which are designed to promote widely available, quality broadband services at affordable prices with higher data speeds in rural areas.

Network access services include interstate and intrastate switched access, network special access and end user access.

Other products and services include revenues from telephone directory publishing, video advertising, billing and support services and other miscellaneous revenues such as revenue from its Public Private Partnership arrangements.

Geographic Reach
In its home base of Illinois (the headquarters is in Mattoon), Consolidated offers its services in over 20 state. It also has operations in East Texas, western Pennsylvania, around Sacramento, Calif., and around Kansas City in Missouri and Kansas.

Sales and Marketing
Consolidated currently offer its services through customer service call centers, its website, commissioned sales representatives and third-party sales agents. The company's customer service call centers and dedicated sales teams serve as the primary sales channels for consumer, commercial and carrier services. The company's sales efforts are supported by digital media, direct mail, bill inserts, radio, television and internet advertising, public relations activities, community events and customer promotions. Consolidated sell its Gigabit consumer fiber broadband service using the brand known as Fidium Fiber, which was launched in November 2021 in select markets.

Advertising expense was $18.8 million, $11.1 million, and $11.5 million in 2021, 2020, and 2019, respectively.

Financial Performance
The company's revenue for fiscal 2021 decreased by 2% to $1.3 billion compared from the prior year with $1.3 billion.

Net loss for fiscal 2021 was $106.7 million compared from the prior year with a net income of $37.3 million.

Cash held by the company at the end of fiscal 2021 decreased to $99.6 million. Cash provided by operations and financing were $318.9 million and $211.7 million, respectively. Cash used for investing activities was $586.4 million, mainly for purchases of property, plant and equipment.

Strategy
In addition to its focus on organic growth in its commercial and carrier channels, Consolidated has achieved business growth and diversification of revenue and cash flow streams that have created a strong platform for future growth through our acquisitions over the last 15 years. Through this strategic expansion, the company has positioned its business to provide competitive services in rural, suburban and metropolitan markets spanning the country. Marking a pivotal moment for Consolidated.

In 2020, Consolidated entered into a strategic investment with an affiliate of Searchlight Capital Partners L.P. ("Searchlight"). The company also completed a global debt refinancing concurrently with the strategic investment, which in combination provides Consolidated with greater flexibility to support our fiber expansion and growth plans. The strategic investment offered an immediate capital infusion, delivering significant benefits to the customers and communities we serve, and creating a stronger and more resilient company that is well-positioned to further expand and grow broadband services to meet ever-evolving customer needs.

EXECUTIVES

Chairman, Director, Robert J. Currey, $300,000 total compensation
President, Chief Executive Officer, Director, C. Robert Udell, $541,000 total compensation
Chief Financial Officer, Treasurer, Steven L. Childers, $331,000 total compensation
Chief Legal Officer, Secretary, J. Garrett Van Osdell
Director, David G. Fuller
Director, Marissa Solis
Director, Maribeth S. Rahe
Director, Thomas A. Gerke
Director, Roger H. Moore
Director, Andrew Frey
Auditors : Ernst & Young LLP

LOCATIONS

HQ: Consolidated Communications Holdings Inc
2116 South 17th Street, Mattoon, IL 61938
Phone: 217 235-3311
Web: www.consolidated.com

PRODUCTS/OPERATIONS

2014 Sales

	$ mil.	% of total
Telephone		
Data, Internet & video	287.5	45
Local calling	108.3	17
Network access	106.3	17
Subsidies	53.2	8
Long distance	19.6	3
Other services	60.8	10
Total	635.7	100

COMPETITORS

ELECTRIC LIGHTWAVE COMMUNICATIONS, INC.
FAIRPOINT COMMUNICATIONS LLC
FRONTIER COMMUNICATIONS CORPORATION
LEVEL 3 PARENT, LLC
LUMEN TECHNOLOGIES, INC.
LUMOS NETWORKS CORP.
NORTH STATE COMMUNICATIONS, LLC
SHENANDOAH TELECOMMUNICATIONS COMPANY
TELEPHONE AND DATA SYSTEMS, INC.
ZAYO GROUP HOLDINGS, INC.

HISTORICAL FINANCIALS
Company Type: Public

Income Statement   FYE: December 31

	REVENUE ($mil)	NET INCOME ($mil)	NET PROFIT MARGIN	EMPLOYEES
12/20	1,304.0	36.9	2.8%	3,200
12/19	1,336.5	(20.3)	—	3,400
12/18	1,399.0	(50.8)	—	3,600
12/17	1,059.5	64.9	6.1%	3,930
12/16	743.1	14.9	2.0%	1,676
Annual Growth	15.1%	25.4%	—	17.5%

2020 Year-End Financials
Debt ratio: 55.6%
Return on equity: 10.1%
Cash ($ mil.): 155.5
Current Ratio: 1.26
Long-term debt ($ mil.): 1,932.6
No. of shares ($ mil.): 79.2
Dividends
  Yield: —
  Payout: —
Market value ($ mil.): 387.0

	STOCK PRICE ($) FY Close	P/E High	P/E Low	PER SHARE ($) Earnings	Dividends	Book Value
12/20	4.89	18	8	0.47	0.00	4.83
12/19	3.88	—	—	(0.29)	1.55	4.74
12/18	9.88	—	—	(0.73)	1.55	5.76
12/17	12.19	26	11	1.07	1.55	8.03
12/16	26.85	102	64	0.29	1.55	3.38
Annual Growth	(34.7%)	—	—	12.8%	—	9.3%

Construction Partners Inc

EXECUTIVES

Executive Chairman, Ned N. Fleming
Vice-Chairman, Director, Charles E. Owens, $450,000 total compensation
Executive Vice President, Chief Financial Officer, R. Alan Palmer, $310,000 total compensation
President, Chief Executive Officer, Director, Fred Julius Smith, $400,000 total compensation
Senior Vice President, Subsidiary Officer, M. Brett Armstrong
Legal Senior Vice President, J. Ryan Brooks
Senior Vice President, Subsidiary Officer, Robert P. Flowers
Senior Vice President, Subsidiary Officer, John L. Harper
Senior Vice President, John A. Walker
Chief Accounting Officer, Todd K. Andrews
Director, Craig Jennings
Director, Mark R. Matteson
Director, Michael H. McKay
Director, Stefan L. Shaffer
Director, Noreen E. Skelly
Auditors : RSM US LLP

LOCATIONS

HQ: Construction Partners Inc
  290 Healthwest Drive, Suite 2, Dothan, AL 36303
Phone: 334 673-9763
Web: www.constructionpartners.net

HISTORICAL FINANCIALS
Company Type: Public

Income Statement   FYE: September 30

	REVENUE ($mil)	NET INCOME ($mil)	NET PROFIT MARGIN	EMPLOYEES
09/21	910.7	20.1	2.2%	2,960
09/20	785.6	40.2	5.1%	2,289
09/19	783.2	43.1	5.5%	2,289
09/18	680.0	50.7	7.5%	2,154
09/17	568.2	26.0	4.6%	1,856
Annual Growth	12.5%	(6.2%)	—	12.4%

2021 Year-End Financials
Debt ratio: 26.8%
Return on equity: 5.0%
Cash ($ mil.): 57.2
Current Ratio: 1.90
Long-term debt ($ mil.): 206.1
No. of shares ($ mil.): 52.2
Dividends
  Yield: —
  Payout: —
Market value ($ mil.): 1,745.0

	STOCK PRICE ($) FY Close	P/E High	P/E Low	PER SHARE ($) Earnings	Dividends	Book Value
09/21	33.37	92	47	0.39	0.00	7.82
09/20	18.20	28	16	0.78	0.00	7.44
09/19	15.58	20	10	0.84	0.00	6.63
09/18	12.10	13	10	1.11	0.00	5.82
Annual Growth	40.2%	—	—	(29.4%)	—	10.3%

Consumers Bancorp, Inc. (Minerva, OH)

You don't have to be a consumer to do business with Consumers -- it's happy to serve businesses, as well. Consumers Bancorp is the holding company for Consumers National Bank, which has about 10 branches in eastern Ohio. The bank offers standard services, such as savings and checking accounts, CDs, and NOW accounts. Business loans make up more than half of the bank's loan portfolio; real estate, consumer, and construction loans round out its lending activities. CNB Investment Services, a division of the bank, offers insurance, brokerage, financial planning, and wealth management services through a third-party provider, UVEST. Chairman Laurie McClellan owns more than 20% of Consumers Bancorp.

EXECUTIVES

Chairman, Subsidiary Officer, Director, Laurie L. McClellan
President, Chief Executive Officer, Subsidiary Officer, Director, Ralph J. Lober, $225,251 total compensation
Subsidiary Officer, Vice-Chairman, Director, John P. Furey
Executive Vice President, Senior Loan Officer, Scott E. Dodds, $162,682 total compensation
Executive Vice President, Chief Financial Officer, Treasurer, Renee K. Wood, $147,049 total compensation
Senior Vice President, Chief Credit Officer, Suzanne Mikes

Sales Senior Vice President, Retail Operations Senior Vice President, Derek G. Williams
Secretary, Theresa Linder
Director, Bradley Goris
Director, Harry W. Schmuck
Director, Richard T. Kiko
Director, Thomas M. Kishman
Director, John W. Parkinson
Director, Frank L. Paden
Auditors : Plante & Moran, PLLC

LOCATIONS

HQ: Consumers Bancorp, Inc. (Minerva, OH)
  614 East Lincoln Way, P.O. Box 256, Minerva, OH 44657
Phone: 330 868-7701
Web: www.consumers.bank

COMPETITORS

ANNAPOLIS BANCORP, INC.
LYONS NATIONAL BANK
PRINCETON NATIONAL BANCORP, INC.
THE NATIONAL BANK OF INDIANAPOLIS CORPORATION
WOODFOREST FINANCIAL GROUP, INC.

HISTORICAL FINANCIALS
Company Type: Public

Income Statement   FYE: June 30

	ASSETS ($mil)	NET INCOME ($mil)	INCOME AS % OF ASSETS	EMPLOYEES
06/21	833.8	8.9	1.1%	176
06/20	740.8	5.5	0.7%	172
06/19	553.9	5.5	1.0%	144
06/18	502.6	3.5	0.7%	139
06/17	457.8	2.9	0.7%	128
Annual Growth	16.2%	31.6%	—	8.3%

2021 Year-End Financials
Return on assets: 1.1%
Return on equity: 13.5%
Long-term debt ($ mil.): —
No. of shares ($ mil.): 3.0
Sales ($ mil.): 32.9
Dividends
  Yield: 2.9%
  Payout: 20.1%
Market value ($ mil.): 59.0

	STOCK PRICE ($) FY Close	P/E High	P/E Low	PER SHARE ($) Earnings	Dividends	Book Value
06/21	19.50	7	5	2.98	0.58	23.08
06/20	14.19	10	7	1.92	0.41	20.97
06/19	18.50	12	8	2.04	0.52	18.72
06/18	24.00	19	14	1.31	0.50	16.03
06/17	19.00	18	14	1.10	0.48	15.98
Annual Growth	0.7%	—	—	28.3%	4.6%	9.6%

Cooper Companies, Inc. (The)

The Cooper Companies specializes in eye care and, to a lesser extent, lady care. The global company makes specialty medical devices in two niche markets: vision care and gynecology. Its CooperVision subsidiary makes specialty contact lenses, including toric lenses for astigmatism, multifocal lenses for presbyopia, and cosmetic lenses. The company also offers spherical lenses for more common vision problems such as nearsightedness and farsightedness. Subsidiary CooperSurgical specializes in women's health care; its wide range of products that are based on the point of health care delivery used in medical office and surgical procedures primarily by Obstetricians/Gynecologists (OB/GYN) as well as fertility products and genetic testing services used primarily in fertility clinics and laboratories. Cooper's products are sold in more than 100 countries. The company primarily earns about 45% of revenue from its domestic sales.

Operations

The Cooper Companies operates through two business units: CooperVision and CooperSurgical.

CooperVision, accounts for some 75% of annual sales, is one of the largest contact lens manufacturers in the world. Toric lenses account for about 25% of the company's net sales, while single-use sphere lens accounts for more than 20%. The segment also makes multifocal lenses, which represent about 10% of sales. The segment's non-single-use sphere & other products accounts for more than 20%.

CooperSurgical accounts for about 25% of total sales. It provides diagnostic and therapeutic products used by obstetricians and gynecologists. Fertility products used in office and surgical procedures account for the rest.

Geographic Reach

California-based Cooper Companies rings about 45% of its sales in the US and nearly 30% in Europe. The company's primary manufacturing and distribution facilities for optical products are in the Australia, Japan, US, Puerto Rico, the UK, Hungary, Denmark, Belgium, Spain, and Costa Rica. Its medical device and surgical instrument products are primarily manufactured and distributed from facilities in Costa Rica, Spain, the Netherlands, the UK, and the US.

Sales and Marketing

CooperVision markets its products through its own field sales representative, who call on optometrists, ophthalmologists, opticians, optical chains and distributors. CooperVision also sells to distributors and to mass merchandisers who offer care services. The segment also engages in various activities and offers a variety of services. These include clinical training, digital marketing for the customer, e-commerce, telemarketing, social media, and journal advertisements.

CooperSurgical's products are marketed by a network of dedicated field representatives, independent agents and distributors. The segment augments its sales and marketing activities by participating in national and regional industry trade shows, professional educational programs and internet promotions, including e-commerce, social media and collaborative efforts with professional organizations, telemarketing, direct mail and advertising professional journals. With the addition of PARAGARD, CooperSurgical expanded its awareness campaigns to include direct to consumer elements, including print, internet/social media, radio and television.

Financial Performance

The company had net sales of $2.9 billion in 2021, a 20% increase from the previous year's net sales of $2.4 billion. This was primarily due to a higher sales volume in the company's segments throughout the year.

In 2021, the company had a net income of $2.9 billion, a $2.7 billion increase from the previous year's net income of $238.4 million.

The company's cash at the end of 2021 was $96.6 million. Operating activities generated $738.6 million, while investing activities used $450.3 million, primarily for purchases of property, plant and equipment, as well as acquisitions of businesses and assets. Financing activities used another $311.4 million, primarily for repayments of long-term debt.

Strategy

CooperVision believes that its key accounts which include optical chains, global retailers, certain buying groups and mass merchandisers are growing faster than the overall market. The company is focused on supporting the growth of all its customers by investing in selling, promotional and advertising activities. Further, it is increasing investment in its distribution and packaging capabilities to support the growth of business and to continue providing quality service with its industry leading SKU range and customized offerings.

CooperVision believes that myopia management opens up an attractive new market for contact lenses. With MiSight, CooperVision offers the only FDA approved and first Chinese NMPA approved product to control the progression of myopia in children. CooperVision is investing to create this new market by educating eye care practitioners, patients and their families which increases awareness.

Mergers and Acquisitions

Cooper has been building up both of its segments through acquisitions.

In late 2021, CooperCompanies agreed to acquire Generate Life Sciences, a leading provider of donor egg and sperm for fertility treatments, fertility cryopreservation services and newborn stem cell storage (cord blood & cord tissue), for a purchase price of approximately $1.6 billion. By adding Generate to CooperSurgical, the company is able to provide fertility clinics and Ob/Gyns an even stronger offering.

In mid-2021, CooperCompanies has acquired obp Medical Corporation, a US based medical device company that develops and markets differentiated products including single-use vaginal speculums with integrated LED illumination, for a purchase price of $60 million. The acquisition is a great strategic fit that builds upon CooperSurgical's strong family of OB/GYN medical devices. obp Medical's differentiated products will integrate seamlessly into the company's business and support its mission of advancing women's healthcare.

In 2021, CooperCompanies has acquired Safe Obstetric Systems, a privately held manufacturer of the medical device, Fetal Pillow, for acquisition price of approximately £37.5 million in cash. This FDA approved product is used to elevate the fetal head during a fully dilated cesarean section making the delivery easier and less traumatic for the mother and baby. The acquisition is an excellent strategic fit for CooperSurgical as it aligns perfectly with its mission of advancing women's healthcare.

Also, in 2021, EssilorLuxottica and CooperCompanies have entered into an agreement to create a 50/50 joint venture for the acquisition of SightGlass Vision, a US based life sciences company focused on developing innovative spectacle lenses to reduce the progression of myopia in children. EssilorLuxottica and CooperCompanies will leverage their shared expertise and global leadership in myopia management to accelerate the commercialization of SightGlass Vision spectacle lenses. Through this partnership, they will further strengthen innovation opportunities and go-to-market capabilities to grow the myopia control category. SightGlass Vision's technology will complement both companies' existing solutions, including Essilor's Stellest lens and CooperVision's MiSight and Orthokeratology contact lenses.

Company Background

Parker G. Montgomery founded Martin H. Smith Co. in 1958. The company changed its name to Cooper Tinsley Laboratories in 1961 and went public the following year.

HISTORY

Cooper Labs (medical devices, founded in 1958 and dissolved 1985) created CooperVision as a subsidiary in 1980. CooperVision diversified into diagnostic equipment and drugs; by 1987 (when it was renamed The Cooper Companies), debt had increased sixfold and creditors came knocking.

Two scandal-tainted families (the Sturmans and the Singers -- fraud/organized crime and Medicaid fraud, respectively) then bought their way onto the board. Proxy fights, cronyism, nepotism, indictments, and lawsuits ensued. Meanwhile, cash-strapped Cooper sold most of its international and part of its US contact lens business, as well as its ophthalmic surgical products and medical diagnostics businesses. Co-chairman Gary Singer took a leave of absence after being indicted in 1992.

Cooper bought Hospital Group of America and its hospitals that year. Singer resigned shortly before being convicted on 21 counts, including racketeering, mail and wire fraud, and money laundering in 1994. Pharmaceutical industry veteran Thomas Bender joined the board that year and was named CEO in 1995. He was elected chairman in 2002.

Cooper rebuilt its contact business and turned to the women's health field in the early 1990s. In 1996 it bought a line of disposable gynecological products and worked to boost lens-making capacity. The next year it bought a line of colored contact lenses, a minimally invasive gynecological surgical and disposable products company, and a UK lens maker.

In 1998 The Cooper Companies discontinued its Hospital Group of America operations. It sold the group's hospitals, treatment centers, and clinics to Universal Health Services in 1999. In 2000 the company made three acquisitions, including two makers of gynecological instruments. In 2002 The Cooper Companies bought Biocompatibles Eye Care, one of the world's largest contact lens manufacturers.

The company's acquisitions in 2003 included Avalon Medical Corporation (distributor of female sterilization system) and Prism Enterprises (manufacturer of medical devices for the women's health care markets). The Cooper Companies bought gynecology products manufacturer Milex Products in 2004.

It nearly doubled its revenue with the 2005 acquisition of leading contact lens maker Ocular Sciences. The purchase strengthened its presence in the spheric (non-specialty) lens market; it also opened up new geographic markets, particularly Germany and Japan. It also purchased NeoSurg Technologies and Inlet Medical in 2005, both of which made devices used in laparoscopic surgeries.

In 2006 it purchased Lone Star Medical Products, adding a line of gynecological surgical products. The following year it added medical instrument maker Wallach Surgical Devices.

EXECUTIVES

Chairman, Director, Robert S. Weiss, $925,000 total compensation
Vice-Chairman, Lead Director, William A. Kozy
Investor Relations President, Investor Relations Chief Executive Officer, President, Chief Executive Officer, Albert G. (Al) White, $925,000 total compensation
CooperVision Executive Vice President, CooperVision Chief Operating Officer, CooperVision President, Daniel G. McBride, $700,000 total compensation
Executive Vice President, Chief Financial Officer, Treasurer, Brian G. Andrews, $425,000 total compensation

Vice President, Secretary, General Counsel, Mark J. Drury
Finance & Tax Chief Accounting Officer, Finance & Tax Senior Vice President, Agostino Ricupati, $327,202 total compensation
Subsidiary Officer, Holly R. Sheffield, $525,000 total compensation
Subsidiary Officer, Gerard ("Jerry") H. Warner
Director, Colleen E. Jay
Director, Teresa S. Madden
Director, Gary S. Petersmeyer
Director, Maria Rivas
Director, Cynthia L. Lucchese
Auditors : KPMG LLP

LOCATIONS

HQ: Cooper Companies, Inc. (The)
6101 Bollinger Canyon Road, Suite 500, San Ramon, CA 94583
Phone: 925 460-3600   **Fax:** 925 460-3648
Web: www.coopercos.com

2018 Sales

	$ mil.	% of total
US	1,162.2	46
Europe	846.5	33
Rest of world & corporate	524.1	21
Total	2,532.8	100

PRODUCTS/OPERATIONS

2018 Sales by Segment

	$ mil.	% of total
CooperVision		
Toric lens	591.4	23
Single-use sphere lens	520.1	20
Multifocal lens	196.6	8
Non-single-use sphere & other	573.9	23
CooperSurgical	650.8	26
Total	2,352.8	100

COMPETITORS

BAUSCH & LOMB INCORPORATED
CONMED CORPORATION
COOPERVISION, INC.
DENTSPLY SIRONA INC.
ESSILOR OF AMERICA, INC.
ESSILORLUXOTTICA
NATIONAL VISION HOLDINGS, INC.
OLYMPUS CORPORATION
SIGNET ARMORLITE, INC.
STAAR SURGICAL COMPANY

HISTORICAL FINANCIALS

Company Type: Public

Income Statement
FYE: October 31

	REVENUE ($mil)	NET INCOME ($mil)	NET PROFIT MARGIN	EMPLOYEES
10/21	2,922.5	2,944.7	100.8%	12,000
10/20	2,430.9	238.4	9.8%	12,000
10/19	2,653.4	466.7	17.6%	12,000
10/18	2,532.8	139.9	5.5%	12,000
10/17	2,139.0	372.9	17.4%	11,800
Annual Growth	8.1%	67.6%	—	0.4%

2021 Year-End Financials

Debt ratio: 15.4%   No. of shares ($ mil.): 49.3
Return on equity: 54.7%   Dividends
Cash ($ mil.): 95.9   Yield: —
Current Ratio: 2.00   Payout: 0.1%
Long-term debt ($ mil.): 1,396.1   Market value ($ mil.): 20,554.0

	STOCK PRICE ($) FY Close	P/E High/Low		PER SHARE ($) Earnings	Dividends	Book Value
10/21	416.92	8	5	59.16	0.06	140.81
10/20	319.05	74	50	4.81	0.06	77.89
10/19	291.00	36	25	9.33	0.06	73.90
10/18	258.31	98	76	2.81	0.06	67.23
10/17	240.26	33	21	7.52	0.06	65.08
Annual Growth	14.8%	—	—	67.5%	0.0%	21.3%

Copart Inc

Copart is one of the leading provider of online auctions and vehicle remarketing services. It takes those vehicles and auctions them for insurers as well as auto dealers, fleet operations, charities, and banks. The buyers are mostly rebuilders, licensed dismantlers, and used-car dealers and exporters. The company has replaced live auctions with internet auctions using a platform known as Virtual Bidding Third Generation (VB3 for short). It also provides services such as towing and storage to buyers and other salvage companies. Copart serves customers in the US, Canada, the UK, Brazil, Ireland, Germany, Finland, the UAE, Oman, Bahrain, and Spain, although the US accounts for about 85% of sales.

Operations

Copart offers vehicle sellers a full range of vehicle services, which expedite each stage of the vehicle sales process, minimize administrative and processing costs, and maximize the ultimate sales price through the online auction process. The company offers online seller access, salvage estimation, estimating services, end-of-life vehicle processing, intelliSeller, and transportation services among other.

Overall, Copart generates about 80% of its revenue from services it offers and the rest of the revenue comes from vehicle sales.

Geographic Reach

Dallas-based, Copart has facilities in every state except Vermont. It also has facilities in Canada, the UK, Brazil, Ireland, Germany, UAE, Spain, Oman, Bahrain, and Finland. The US generates about 85% of total revenue, and the rest comes from the international market.

Sales and Marketing

The company's advertising expenses were approximately $15.4 million, $13.7 million, and $7.7 million, for the years ended 2022, 2021, and 2020, respectively.

Financial Performance

Copart's performance for the past five years have grown year-over-year with 2022 as its highest performing year.

The company's revenue increased $808.4 million to $3.5 billion for 2022 as compared to 2021's revenue of $2.7 billion.

Copart's net income increased to $1.1 billion in fiscal year end 2022 as compared to the prior year's net income of $936.5 million.

The company's cash at the end of 2022 was $1.4 billion. Operating activities generated $1.2 billion. Investing activities and financing activities used $442.3 million and $382.7 million, respectively. Main cash uses were for held purchases to maturity securities and principal payments on long-term debt.

Strategy

Copart's growth strategy is to increase revenues and profitability by, among other things, acquiring and developing additional vehicle storage facilities in key markets, including foreign markets; pursuing global, national and regional vehicle seller agreements; increasing its service offerings; and expanding the application of VB3 into new markets. In addition, the company implement its pricing structure and auction procedures, and attempt to introduce cost efficiencies at each of its acquired facilities by implementing its operational procedures, integrating its management information systems, and redeploying personnel, when necessary.

As part of its overall expansion strategy, its objective is to increase its revenues, operating profits, and market share in the vehicle remarketing industry. To implement its growth strategy, it intends to continue to: acquire and develop new vehicle storage facilities in key markets including foreign markets; pursue global, national, and regional vehicle supply agreements; and expand its service offerings to sellers and members.

HISTORY

Copart was co-founded in 1982 by Willis Johnson, who had owned and operated an auto dismantling business for more than 10 years. After buying out his partner in 1986, he became CEO and used his own money to expand the company into a network of four California salvage yards by 1991. In the next two years, Copart nearly tripled the number of salvage operations it owned by acquiring companies throughout the US. HPB Associates, a private investor group, came on board in 1993, buying 26% of the firm for $10 million, and the company went public the next year.

Copart doubled its total facilities in 1995 with the acquisition of NER Auction Systems, the largest privately held salvage auction company in the US. The firm acquired or opened more than 30 facilities between 1995 and 1997. In 1998 the company started an online auction site; expanded through acquisitions into Alabama, Iowa, Michigan, and South Carolina; and opened new locations in California and Minnesota. The next year rival Insurance Auto Auctions spurned its merger overtures.

In 2000 Copart opened three new salvage vehicle auction facilities and acquired eight more. That year the company also signed an agreement to sell Keystone Automotive Industries' parts through its Web site. In 2001 and 2002 the company acquired or opened 13 new locations. Continuing its acquisition strategy, the company opened or acquired five more facilities in 2004.

In 2005 the company made two acquisitions for about $4.5 million: Kentucky Auto Salvage Pool, a 25-acre salvage facility in Lexington, Kentucky; and Insurance Auctions of Missouri. In November Copart acquired the salvage pool assets of Central Penn Sales, a vehicle salvage disposal company with four sites in Pennsylvania and Maryland, totaling 255 acres. In December the company opened a second salvage facility in Michigan.

In June 2007 Copart acquired Universal Salvage, the operator of about 10 salvage yards in the UK and a vehicle remarketer to the insurance and automotive industries, for about $120 million. Adding to its UK holdings, in August Copart purchased Century Salvage Sales Limited, which has three salvage yards, and AG Watson, which has four salvage yards in England and Scotland.

During 2008 the company launched CopartDirect. The service allows Copart to sell cars to the general public, using its VB 2 application, so that individuals can avoid the inconvenience of selling a vehicle themselves.

In February 2010, Willis Johnson relinquished the CEO's title to A. Jayson Adair, who formerly served as president of Copart. Johnson continued as chairman of the company.

In 2011, Copart acquired the Indiana-based auto auction firm Barodge Auto Pool, expanding its presence in Indiana and surrounding states. The company also broadened its existing range of farming equipment in the UK when it acquired Hewitt International, an auctioneer of agricultural vehicles and equipment based in central England, in 2011.

In 2012, the company made several acquisitions in international markets, including Brazil, Canada, Germany, and Dubai, UAE. That year Copart expanded into Germany (the world's fourth largest auto market) with the purchase of WOM Wreck Online Marketing, a leading European salvage vehicle auction platform there. Earlier in the year it bought Canada's Diamond Auto Bids and Disposals, a privately-held automotive auction that gives Copart a foothold in Western Canada, specifically Calgary and Edmonton. It also extended the reach of its business into South America through its purchase of Central de Leiloes LTDA, based in Sao Paulo, Brazil.

EXECUTIVES

Chairman, Director, Willis J. Johnson, $1 total compensation

President, Co-Chief Executive Officer, Region Officer, Jeffrey Liaw, $341,550 total compensation

Chief Executive Officer, Director, A. Jayson Adair, $1 total compensation

Senior Vice President, General Counsel, Secretary, Gregory R. DePasquale

Director, Matt Blunt

Director, Steven D. Cohan

Director, Daniel J. Englander

Director, James E. Meeks, $375,000 total compensation

Director, Thomas N. Tryforos

Director, Diane M. Morefield

Director, Stephen Fisher

Director, Cherylyn Harley LeBon

Director, Carl D. Sparks

Auditors : Ernst & Young LLP

LOCATIONS

HQ: Copart Inc
14185 Dallas Parkway, Suite 300, Dallas, TX 75254
Phone: 972 391-5000
Web: www.copart.com

2018 Sales

	$ mil.	% of total
US	1,491.0	83
International	314.7	17
Total	1,805.7	100

PRODUCTS/OPERATIONS

2018 Sales

	$ mil.	% of total
Services	1,578.5	86
Vehicles	227.2	14
Total	1,805.7	100

Selected Services
Copart Access (online vehicle information retrieval)
Copart Dealer Services (online trade-in vehicle sales)
Copart Direct (online used car sales)
CoPartfinder (online used-parts search engine)
DMV processing (title document processing)
Monthly reporting (summary of all vehicles processed by company for suppliers)
Online bidding (online auctions)
Salvage brokerage network (coordination of vehicle disposal outside areas of current operation)
Salvage Lynk (software providing online information on vehicles being processed)
Transportation services (fleet of transport trucks)
Vehicle inspection stations (central locations for insurance companies to inspect vehicles)
Vehicle preparation and merchandising (cleaning and weather protection, direct mailings to buyers)

COMPETITORS

ADESA CORPORATION, LLC
AUTONATION, INC.
AVIS BUDGET GROUP, INC.
BRP Inc
COLUMBUS FAIR AUTO AUCTION, INC.
HERC HOLDINGS INC.
INSURANCE AUTO AUCTIONS, INC.
KAR AUCTION SERVICES, INC.
PENNSYLVANIA AUTO DEALERS' EXCHANGE, INC.
RUSH ENTERPRISES, INC.

HISTORICAL FINANCIALS
Company Type: Public

Income Statement   FYE: July 31

	REVENUE ($mil)	NET INCOME ($mil)	NET PROFIT MARGIN	EMPLOYEES
07/21	2,692.5	936.4	34.8%	8,600
07/20	2,205.5	699.9	31.7%	7,600
07/19	2,041.9	591.6	29.0%	7,327
07/18	1,805.6	417.8	23.1%	6,026
07/17	1,447.9	394.2	27.2%	5,323
Annual Growth	16.8%	24.1%	—	12.7%

2021 Year-End Financials
Debt ratio: —   No. of shares ($ mil.): 237.0
Return on equity: 31.1%   Dividends
Cash ($ mil.): 1,048.2   Yield: —
Current Ratio: 4.04   Payout: —
Long-term debt ($ mil.): —   Market value ($ mil.): 34,841.0

	STOCK PRICE ($) FY Close	P/E High	P/E Low	PER SHARE ($) Earnings	Dividends	Book Value
07/21	147.00	37	24	3.90	0.00	14.89
07/20	93.25	35	20	2.93	0.00	10.58
07/19	77.53	31	17	2.46	0.00	7.74
07/18	57.39	33	17	1.73	0.00	6.76
07/17	31.49	36	17	1.66	0.00	4.76
Annual Growth	47.0%	—	—	23.8%	—	33.0%

Corcept Therapeutics Inc

Corcept Therapeutics is a commercial-stage firm exploring treatments that regulate the presence of cortisol, a steroid hormone associated with some psychiatric and metabolic disorders. Its sole commercial product, Korlym, is a version of the compound mifepristone (commonly known as RU-486 or the "abortion pill") used to regulate release patterns of cortisol. The drug is approved in the US for use in patients with Cushing's Syndrome, a metabolic disorder caused by high levels of cortisol in the blood. The company's lead compounds have other potential treatments for weight gain caused by antipsychotic medications.

Operations
Corcept has discovered more than 1,000 proprietaries, selective cortisol modulators in four structurally distinct series. These novel molecules share Korlym's affinity for the glucocorticoid receptor (GR) but, unlike Korlym, do not bind to the progesterone receptor (PR) and therefore do not cause effects arising from antagonism of progesterone activity, such as termination of pregnancy, endometrial thickening and vaginal bleeding. The composition of these compounds and their methods of use in a wide range of indications are covered by US and foreign patents. Its lead compounds have entered the clinic as potential treatments for a variety of serious disorders - Cushing's syndrome, solid tumors (including advanced, high-grade serous ovarian cancer, metastatic pancreatic cancer and castration-resistant prostate cancer), weight gain caused by antipsychotic medications, and non-alcoholic steatohepatitis (NASH).

The company does not manufacture Korlym or its drug candidates but rather relies on contract manufacturer Produits Chimiques Auxiliaires et de Synthese ("PCAS")

Geographic Reach
Based in Menlo Park, California, Corcept sells Korlym in the US.

Sales and Marketing
Corcept markets Korlym in the US through sales representatives, health care providers, and via medical science liaisons.

Financial Performance
Corcept's revenues have been rising rapidly over the past five years, with 2020 as its highest performing year over the period.

The company's revenue increased by $47.4 million to $353.9 million compared to $306.5 million. The increase in revenue was due to an increase in Korlym's price for the year ended December 31, 2020, was due to a relative decrease in the number of patients covered by Medicaid (which reimburses Korlym at a lower rate), a statutorily-mandated increase in the price paid by other government programs.

Net income also increased by $12 million to $106 million compared to the prior year's net income of $94.2 million.

Cash and cash equivalents at the end of the period were $76.2 million. Net cash provided by operating activities was $151.9 million. Investing activities used $119.3 million, while financing activities provided $12.2 million. Main cash uses were for purchases of marketable securities and property and equipment.

Strategy
The company is dependent on revenue from the sale of Korlym and its cash reserves to fund its commercial operations and development programs. If Korlym revenue declines, it may need to raise funds to support its plans. It may also choose to raise funds for strategic reasons. It cannot be certain funding will be available on acceptable terms or at all. In any event, equity financing would cause dilution and debt financing, if available, may involve restrictive covenants.

If the company obtains funds through collaborations with other companies, it may have to relinquish rights to Korlym or its product candidates. If adequate funds are not available, it may have to delay, reduce the scope of, or eliminate one or more of its development programs or even discontinue operations.

EXECUTIVES

Chairman, Director, James N. Wilson
President, Chief Executive Officer, Director, Joseph K. Belanoff, $679,792 total compensation
Commercial Senior Vice President, Sean Maduck, $436,667 total compensation
Chief Accounting Officer, Joseph Douglas Lyon
Chief Business Officer, Secretary, Gary Charles Robb, $436,667 total compensation
Chief Medical Officer, Andreas Grauer
Chief Financial Officer, Atabak Mokari
Director, Gillian M. Cannon
Director, Kimberly Park
Director, Gregg H. Alton
Director, G. Leonard Baker
Director, David L. Mahoney
Director, Daniel N. Swisher
Auditors: Ernst & Young LLP

LOCATIONS
HQ: Corcept Therapeutics Inc
149 Commonwealth Drive, Menlo Park, CA 94025
Phone: 650 327-3270
Web: www.corcept.com

COMPETITORS
ACHILLION PHARMACEUTICALS, INC.
ALEXION PHARMACEUTICALS, INC.
AMAG PHARMACEUTICALS, INC.
BIOSPECIFICS TECHNOLOGIES CORP.
CHEMOCENTRYX, INC.
DURECT CORPORATION
ENDOCYTE, INC.
ESPERION THERAPEUTICS, INC.
LEXICON PHARMACEUTICALS, INC.
STEMLINE THERAPEUTICS, INC.

HISTORICAL FINANCIALS
Company Type: Public

Income Statement   FYE: December 31

	REVENUE ($mil)	NET INCOME ($mil)	NET PROFIT MARGIN	EMPLOYEES
12/21	365.9	112.5	30.7%	238
12/20	353.8	106.0	30.0%	236
12/19	306.4	94.1	30.7%	206
12/18	251.2	75.4	30.0%	166
12/17	159.2	129.1	81.1%	136
Annual Growth	23.1%	(3.4%)	—	15.0%

2021 Year-End Financials
Debt ratio: —   No. of shares ($ mil.): 105.9
Return on equity: 25.0%   Dividends
Cash ($ mil.): 77.6   Yield: —
Current Ratio: 5.60   Payout: —
Long-term debt ($ mil.): —   Market value ($ mil.): 2,098.0

	STOCK PRICE ($) FY Close	P/E High	P/E Low	PER SHARE ($) Earnings	Dividends	Book Value
12/21	19.80	32	18	0.89	0.00	3.55
12/20	26.16	30	11	0.85	0.00	4.48
12/19	12.10	21	12	0.77	0.00	3.24
12/18	13.36	39	17	0.60	0.00	2.40
12/17	18.06	18	6	1.04	0.00	1.66
Annual Growth	2.3%	—	—	(3.8%)	—	20.8%

CoreCard Corp

Intelligent Software Solutions (ISS) is no dummy when it comes to software development and IT systems analysis. The privately-held company develops and integrates custom software for data visualization and analysis, pattern detection, and mission planning for the aerospace, defense, and maritime industries. Its products include a software tool that counters improvised explosive devices (Dfuze) and public safety management software tool (WebTAS). The company provides on-site product and development support and training. Customers include government military, intelligence agencies, and local law enforcement in the US and abroad.

Operations

With expertise in counter-terrorism, homeland security, intelligence, and special operations, the company has about 100 projects under dozens of contracts. In 2013, ISS was selected as the lead contractor on a $250 million project with a US Air Force unit to replace a system for planning and carrying out military missions. ISS products include Combined Information Data Network Exchange (CIDNE), a web-enabled database that enables users such as agencies in different countries to collect, manage, and share data through a web-browser to support operations, and C2Core, database software for planning and carrying out missions.

The company's subsidiary, ISS Global, works with the Dfuze product and works with military, public safety and law enforcement agencies in more than 40 countries.

Geographic Reach

ISS has facilities in Colorado, Florida, Massachusetts, Virginia, and Washington, DC. The company keeps in close contact with key clients by placing offices nearby. Its Tampa, Florida facility houses part of the company's combat systems division that supports the US Central Command (CENTCOM).

Sales and Marketing

The company's customers include the US Department of Defense and Department of Homeland Security, national intelligence organizations and other US, NATO and government customers. Its international public sector customers include the Hong Kong Police Force, the Hungarian National Police Mine Disposal Service, New Scotland Yard, and the Police Service of Northern Ireland. ISS works with technology companies including Adobe, Oracle, and RedHat.

Strategy

ISS often used open source software and government off-the-shelf (GOTS) products to make it easier for agencies to integrate its products into their networks. It has taken that expertise to start an open source consulting business, Springblox, to provide open source software integration, education, and support to private and public sector customers.

Springblox formed a partnership with MuleSoft, which develops software integrating systems. Together they will offer customers programs to effectively organize data.

EXECUTIVES

Chairman, President, Chief Executive Officer, J. Leland Strange, $300,000 total compensation
Chief Financial Officer, Secretary, Matthew A. White
Vice President, J. William Goodhew
Director, A. Russell Chandler
Director, Philip H. Moise
Auditors : Nichols, Cauley and Associates, LLC

LOCATIONS

HQ: CoreCard Corp
4355 Shackleford Road, Norcross, GA 30093
Phone: 770 381-2900
Web: www.intelsys.com

PRODUCTS/OPERATIONS

Selected Portfolio Companies
Alliance Technology Ventures
ChemFree Corporation
CoreCard Software, Inc.
NKD Enterprises, LLC (dba CoreXpand, 26%)

COMPETITORS

ACTUATE CORPORATION
ANALYTICAL GRAPHICS, INC.
ATHOC, INC.
ID TECHNOLOGIES, LLC
INFORMATICA LLC

HISTORICAL FINANCIALS

Company Type: Public

Income Statement — FYE: December 31

	REVENUE ($mil)	NET INCOME ($mil)	NET PROFIT MARGIN	EMPLOYEES
12/20	35.8	8.1	22.7%	570
12/19	34.3	10.9	32.0%	530
12/18	20.1	6.2	31.1%	430
12/17	9.3	0.4	5.1%	350
12/16	8.1	(1.1)	—	286
Annual Growth	44.7%	—	—	18.8%

2020 Year-End Financials

Debt ratio: —
Return on equity: 19.9%
Cash ($ mil.): 37.9
Current Ratio: 4.22
Long-term debt ($ mil.): —
No. of shares ($ mil.): 8.8
Dividends
Yield: —
Payout: —
Market value ($ mil.): 356.0

	STOCK PRICE ($) FY Close	P/E High/Low		PER SHARE ($) Earnings	Dividends	Book Value
12/20	40.11	49	27	0.91	0.00	4.97
12/19	39.94	45	11	1.22	0.00	4.18
12/18	12.92	21	6	0.70	0.00	2.94
12/17	4.56	95	70	0.05	0.00	2.22
12/16	4.24	—	—	(0.13)	0.35	2.51
Annual Growth	75.4%	—	—	—	—	18.6%

CoStar Group, Inc.

CoStar is the leading provider of information, analytics and online marketplace services through its comprehensive, proprietary database of commercial real estate information in the US, Canada, the UK, France, Spain, and Germany. Its hundreds of data points include location, ownership, and tenant names. Clients include government agencies, real estate brokerages, real estate investment trusts (REITs), and property owners and managers who stand to benefit from insight on property values, market conditions, and current availabilities. The company was founded in 1987. Majority of the company's sales were generated from the North America.

Operations

CoStar has nine flagship brands: CoStar, LoopNet, Apartments.com, STR, Ten-X, BizBuySell, LandsofAmerica, Homes.com and HomeSnap.

CoStar is its subscription-based integrated platform for commercial real estate intelligence, which includes information about office, industrial, retail, multifamily, hospitality and student housing properties, properties for sale, comparable sales, tenants, space available for lease, industry professionals and their business relationships, industry news and market and lease analytical capabilities.

Apartments.com is the flagship brand in CoStar's network of apartment marketing sites, which also includes ApartmentFinder.comTM, ForRent.com, ApartmentHomeLiving.comTM, WestsideRentals.com, AFTER55.com, CorporateHousing.comTM, ForRentUniversity.com, Apartamentos.comTM, which is its apartment-listing site offered exclusively in Spanish, and Off Campus Partners, which provides student housing marketplace content and powers off campus housing sites for many universities across the US.

LoopNet is the flagship brand in its network of commercial real estate marketing sites, which also includes CityFeet.com, Showcase.com.

The acquisitions of Homes.com and Homesnap enabled us to expand our offerings to the residential for sale market. Homes.com is a homes for sale listings site. Homesnap is an online and mobile software platform that provides subscription-based access to applications that manage residential real estate agent workflow and marketing campaigns delivered on third-party platforms. Homesnap also receives transaction-based revenue for short-term advertising delivered on third-party platforms.

Ten-X operates an online auction platform for commercial real estate.

CoStar's BizBuySell services, which include BizQuest and FindaFranchise, provide an online marketplace for businesses and franchises for-sale. The company's LandsofAmerica services, which include LandAndFarm and LandWatch.com, provide an online marketplace for rural lands for-sale and are also accessible via our Land.com domain.

Geographic Reach

Washington, DC-based CoStar Group manages its business geographically in two operating segments, with primary areas of measurement and decision-making being North America, which includes the US and Canada, and International, which primarily includes Europe, Asia-Pacific and Latin America. While the company continues its international expansion, North America still accounts for nearly all revenue.

The company operates its research functions out of leased office spaces in Richmond, Virginia; San Diego, California; and Atlanta, Georgia. Additionally, its lease office space in a variety of other metropolitan areas. These locations include, among others, the following: Hendersonville, Tennessee; Irvine, California; Boston, Massachusetts; San Francisco, California; Ontario, California; and Los Angeles, California.

Sales and Marketing

CoStar's clients come from across the commercial real estate sector and related businesses and include real estate brokers, owners, developers, landlords, property managers, financial institutions, retailers, appraisers, investment banks, government agencies, and other parties involved in commercial real estate.

To generate brand awareness and site traffic, CoStar uses a multi-channel marketing campaign, including television and radio advertising, online/digital advertising, social media and out-of-home ads, and search engine marketing.

Advertising costs were approximately $312 million, $270 million and $168 million for the years ended 2021, 2020 and 2019, respectively.

Financial Performance

Revenues increased to $1.9 billion in 2021, from $1.7 billion in 2020. The $285 million increase was attributable to increases across all of its primary service offerings, led by an $80 million, or 13%, increase in multifamily revenue. The multifamily increase was due to higher sales volume and upgrades of existing customers to higher value advertising packages earlier in 2021.

Net income in 2021 increased by 29% to $292.6 million compared to $1.7 billion in the prior year.

Cash held by the company at the end of fiscal 2021 increased to $3.8 billion. Operating activities contributed $469.7 million investing and financing activities used $381.3 million and $15.7 million, respectively. Main cash uses were purchase of Richmond assets and other intangibles; and repurchase of restricted stock to satisfy tax withholding obligations.

Strategy

The company's strategy is to provide real estate industry professionals and consumers with critical knowledge to explore and complete transactions by offering the most comprehensive, timely, and standardized information on real estate and the right tools to be able to effectively utilize that information. Over time, CoStar has expanded and continues to expand its services for real estate information, analytics, and online marketplaces to continue to meet the needs of the industry as it grows and evolves.

Mergers and Acquisitions

In late 2021, CoStar acquired COMREAL INFO, the owner and operator of BureauxLocaux.com. Based in Paris, BureauxLocaux is one of the largest specialized property portals for buying and leasing commercial real estate in France, with over 60,000 for sale and lease listings and over 425,000 visits to its website each month. "The acquisition of BureauxLocaux is an important step in continuing our international expansion," said Andrew C. Florance, Founder and Chief Executive Officer of CoStar Group.

In 2021, CoStar completed the acquisition of Homes.com, for $156 million in cash. Homes.com is a well-recognized residential property listing and marketing portal that supports over 500,000 residential agents and brokers in the home sale process. "The combination of Homes.com and Homesnap, which we acquired in December 2020, sets the stage for us to offer sellers, buyers, and real estate agents a better, more collaborative online home sale and purchase experience," said Andrew C. Florance, Founder and Chief Executive Officer of CoStar Group.

Also in late 2021, CoStar acquired France's premier commercial real estate news service, Business Immo. The acquisition of Business Immo is an important addition to CoStar Group's growing global news team, which offers daily coverage across the US, Canada, the UK, Germany and through Hotel News Now, CoStar's international hospitality industry news service.

Company Background

Andrew C. Florance founded CoStar Group in 1987 as a company that collected and sold data on office buildings. Over the years, it has expanded into industrial, retail, and rental apartments, partly through acquisitions. The company filed an IPO in 1998. CoStar grew significantly when it acquired rival service LoopNet in 2012.

EXECUTIVES

Chairman, Director, Michael R. Klein
President, Chief Executive Officer, Director, Andrew C. Florance, $750,000 total compensation
Global Research Senior Vice President, Lisa C. Ruggles, $385,539 total compensation
Chief Financial Officer, Scott T. Wheeler, $469,231 total compensation
Chief Technology Officer, Frank A. Simuro
Chief Human Resources Officer, Michael Desmarais
Secretary, General Counsel, Gene Boxer
Division Officer, Frederick (Fred) G. Saint
Director, Laura Cox Kaplan
Director, Michael J. Glosserman
Director, John W. Hill
Director, Robert W. Musslewhite
Director, Christopher J. Nassetta
Director, Louise S. Sams
Auditors: Ernst & Young LLP

LOCATIONS

HQ: CoStar Group, Inc.
1331 L Street, N.W., Washington, DC 20005
Phone: 202 346-6500 **Fax:** 877 739-0486
Web: www.costargroup.com

2015 Sales

	$ mil.	% of total
North America	686.6	96
External customers	25.2	4
Intersegment revenue		0.04
Intersegment eliminations	(0.04)	-
Total	711.8	100

PRODUCTS/OPERATIONS

Selected Subscription Products
CoStar COMPS Professional (comparable sales information)
CoStar Property Professional (flagship real estate database)
CoStar Tenant (tenant information)
FOCUS (UK real estate information)

Selected Data
Building characteristics
Contact information
Demographic information
For-sale information
Historical trends
Income and expense histories
Lease expirations
Mortgage and deed information
Number of retail stores
Ownership
Retail sales per square foot
Sales and lease comparables
Site and zoning information
Space availability
Tax assessments
Tenant names

COMPETITORS

ACXIOM LLC
CORELOGIC, INC.
CORESITE REALTY CORPORATION
COSTAR UK LIMITED
ELAVON, INC.
TECHTARGET, INC.
VERISK ANALYTICS, INC.
YELP INC.
YEXT, INC.
ZAPLABS, LLC

HISTORICAL FINANCIALS
Company Type: Public

Income Statement   FYE: December 31

	REVENUE ($mil)	NET INCOME ($mil)	NET PROFIT MARGIN	EMPLOYEES
12/20	1,659.0	227.1	13.7%	4,753
12/19	1,399.7	314.9	22.5%	4,337
12/18	1,191.8	238.3	20.0%	3,705
12/17	965.2	122.6	12.7%	3,711
12/16	837.6	85.0	10.2%	3,064
Annual Growth	18.6%	27.8%	—	11.6%

2020 Year-End Financials
Debt ratio: 14.3%   No. of shares ($ mil.): 394.1
Return on equity: 5.1%   Dividends
Cash ($ mil.): 3,755.9   Yield: —
Current Ratio: 11.75   Payout: —
Long-term debt ($ mil.): 986.7   Market value ($ mil.): 364,296.0

	STOCK PRICE ($) FY Close	P/E High/Low	PER SHARE ($) Earnings	Dividends	Book Value
12/20	924.28	1574 877	0.59	0.00	13.64
12/19	598.30	732 377	0.86	0.00	9.29
12/18	337.34	676 449	0.65	0.00	8.29
12/17	296.95	838 503	0.37	0.00	7.34
12/16	188.49	849 564	0.26	0.00	5.07
Annual Growth	48.8%	—	22.7%	—	28.0%

Cousins Properties Inc

Cousins Properties, a real estate investment trust (REIT) which buys, develops, and manages Class-A office properties mainly in high-growth markets in the Sunbelt region of the US. Its portfolio includes 19.7 million sq. ft. of office space and 310,000 square feet of mixed-use space in Atlanta, Austin, Dallas, and Charlotte. The company conducts its operations through Cousins Properties, LP ("CPLP"). Its other subsidiary, Cousins TRS Services LLC ("CTRS"), also manages its own real estate portfolio and also provides real estate related services for other parties.

Operations
Cousin Properties' segments are categorized based on both property type and geographical area. The company's segments by property type are Office properties and Mixed-Use properties. The segments by geographical region are Atlanta, Austin, Charlotte, Dallas, Phoenix, Tampa, and Other.

Majority of the company's revenues came from rentals which accounts for more than 95% of sales.

Geographic Reach
The Atlanta-based REIT owns properties in its Atlanta; Austin, Texas; Phoenix, and Charlotte. More than 35% of the company's net operating income came from its office properties in Atlanta during 2020, while another 20% came from its office properties in Austin. The rest came from its properties in Charlotte (more than 10% of net operating income), Phoenix (nearly 10%), and the remaining accounts for Tampa, Dallas, and others.

Sales and Marketing
Reflecting a broad tenant base, the REIT's top 20 tenants made up of more than 30% of its annualized base rental income during 2020, with no single tenant accounting for more than 5% of its rental income.

Some of the REIT's tenants include the NCR Corporation, Amazon, Facebook, Expedia and Bank of America, among others.

Financial Performance
Cousins Properties' performance over the past five years has seen an increase year-over-year, with 2020 as its highest performing year.

REIT's revenue increased by 13% or about $82.8 million to $740.3 million in 2020 compared to $657.5 million in the prior year.

The company's net income also increased by $85.4 million to $238.1 million compared to the prior year's net income of $152.6 million.

Cash held by the company at the end of 2020 amounted to $6.1 million. The company's operating activities provided $351 million to the coffers. Investing and financing activities used $132.4 million and $230 million, respectively. Main cash uses were for property acquisition, development and tenant asset expenditures as well as for repayment of credit facility.

Strategy
The company's strategy is centered on creating value for its stockholders through ownership of the premier office portfolio in the Sun Belt markets of the US. Cousins Properties focuses on Atlanta, Austin, Charlotte, Phoenix, Tampa, and Dallas. The company leverages its strong local operating platforms in its major markets in order to implement this strategy.

Company Background
Cousins Properties experienced challenges from the depressed economy and the downturn in the real estate markets following the financial crisis. The REIT responded by restructuring, reducing headcount, selling non-core assets, and curtailing new development projects. It sold all of its industrial properties to focus on Class-A office properties. It also continues to wind down its multifamily residential portfolio.

Institutional investors own about a third of Cousins Properties' stock. Morgan Stanley holds the largest stake, at more than 10%, followed by BlackRock, Inc. and The Vanguard Group. Chairman Emeritus, Thomas G. Cousins, owns about 10% of the firm's shares.

EXECUTIVES

Chairman, Director, Robert M. Chapman
President, Chief Executive Officer, Director, Michael Colin Connolly, $430,000 total compensation
Executive Vice President, Chief Financial Officer, Gregg D. Adzema, $430,000 total compensation
Operations Executive Vice President, Richard G. Hickson
Investments Executive Vice President, Investments Managing Director, Kennedy Jane Hicks
Development Executive Vice President, John S. McColl, $371,315 total compensation
Executive Vice President, General Counsel, Corporate Secretary, Pamela F. Roper, $344,793 total compensation
Director, Dionne Nelson
Director, Charles T. Cannada
Director, Scott W. Fordham
Director, Lillian C. Giornelli
Director, R. Kent Griffin
Director, Donna W. Hyland
Director, R. Dary Stone
Auditors: Deloitte & Touche LLP

LOCATIONS

HQ: Cousins Properties Inc
3344 Peachtree Road NE, Suite 1800, Atlanta, GA 30326-4802
Phone: 404 407-1000
Web: www.cousins.com

PRODUCTS/OPERATIONS

2011 Sales

	$ mil.	% of total
Rental property	135.6	76
Third-party management & leasing	19.4	11
Fee income	13.8	8
Multifamily residential unit sales	4.7	3
Residential & outparcel	3.0	2
Other	2.0	-
Total	178.5	100

COMPETITORS

ARMADA/HOFFLER PROPERTIES, L.L.C.
Allied Properties Real Estate Investment Trust
ESSEX PROPERTY TRUST, INC.
GOV NEW OPPTY REIT
HIGHWOODS PROPERTIES, INC.
INVESTORS REAL ESTATE TRUST
KIMCO REALTY CORPORATION
KITE REALTY GROUP TRUST
SELECT INCOME REIT
WASHINGTON REAL ESTATE INVESTMENT TRUST

HISTORICAL FINANCIALS
Company Type: Public

Income Statement   FYE: December 31

	REVENUE ($mil)	NET INCOME ($mil)	NET PROFIT MARGIN	EMPLOYEES
12/21	755.0	278.5	36.9%	294
12/20	740.3	237.2	32.0%	316
12/19	657.5	150.4	22.9%	331
12/18	475.2	79.1	16.7%	257
12/17	466.1	216.2	46.4%	261
Annual Growth	12.8%	6.5%	—	3.0%

2021 Year-End Financials
Debt ratio: 30.6%   No. of shares ($ mil.): 148.6
Return on equity: 6.1%   Dividends
Cash ($ mil.): 8.9   Yield: 3.0%
Current Ratio: 0.59   Payout: 148.1%
Long-term debt ($ mil.): 2,237.5   Market value ($ mil.): 5,989.0

	STOCK PRICE ($) FY Close	P/E High/Low		PER SHARE ($) Earnings	Dividends	Book Value
12/21	40.28	22	17	1.87	1.23	30.71
12/20	33.50	27	14	1.60	1.20	30.07
12/19	41.20	35	7	1.17	0.58	29.70
12/18	7.90	13	10	0.76	1.04	26.32
12/17	9.25	5	4	2.08	1.20	26.40
Annual Growth	44.5%	—	—	(2.6%)	0.6%	3.9%

Cowen Inc

Cowen, along with its subsidiaries, offers investment banking, research, sales and trading, prime brokerage, global clearing and commission management services and investment management through its business segments the operating company and the asset company. It provides services primarily to companies and institutional investor clients, as well as media and telecommunications, consumer, and industrials sectors in the US and Europe. Some of its subsidiaries includes UK broker-dealer Cowen International Limited, Cowen Execution Services Limited, and Cowen and Company (Asia) Limited.

Operations

Cowen operates two main business segments: the Operating Company (Op Co) and the Asset Company (Asset Co).

The Op Co segment consists of four divisions: investment banking division, markets division and research division (collectively as its investment banking businesses); Cowen Investment Management (CIM) division, which offers advisers to investment funds (including private equity structures and privately placed hedge funds); and registered funds. Op Co's investment banking businesses offer advisory and global capital markets origination and domain knowledge-driven research, sales and trading platforms for institutional investors, global clearing and commission management services and also a comprehensive suite of prime brokerage services. The segment accounted for 100% of total revenue.

The Asset Co segment consists of the company's private investments, private real estate investments, and other legacy investment strategies. The focus of Asset Co is to drive future monetization of the invested capital of the segment.

Overall, Cowen generates more than 50% of its total revenue from its investment banking, while brokerage services for nearly 30% of revenue. Interest and dividends for about 10%, while insurance premiums, management fees, incentive income, reimbursement, consolidated funds, and other revenues accounts the remainder.

Geographic Reach

Based in New York, Cowen has principal offices in Boston, San Francisco, Stamford and the UK. It provides brokerage services to companies and institutional investor clients in Europe through its broker-dealers located in the UK, Cowen International Limited and Cowen Execution Services Limited and Cowen and Company (Asia) Limited or Cowen Asia.

Sales and Marketing

Cowen's investment banking businesses provides services primarily to companies and institutional investor clients. It also includes sectors from healthcare, technology, media and telecommunications, consumer, industrials, information and technology services, and energy. It provides research and brokerage services to over 6,000 domestic and international clients. It also offers prime brokerage services targeting emerging private fund managers.

Financial Performance

The company, in 2021, had a total revenue of $2.1 billion, a 20% increase from the previous year's total revenue of $1.8 billion. Investment banking revenues increased for the year ended December 31, 2021. During the year ended December 31, 2021, the company completed 190 underwriting transactions, 159 strategic advisory transactions and 20 debt capital markets transactions.

In 2021, the company had a net income of $304 million, a 47% increase from the previous year's net income of $207.1 million. This was mainly due to a higher sales volume for the year.

The company's cash at the end of 2021 was $1.2 billion. Operating activities generated $306.6 million, while financing activities used $15.7 million, mainly for repayments on notes and other debt. Investing activities used $75.5 million, mainly for purchases of other investments.

Strategy

The company intends to continually evaluate potential acquisitions, investments and strategic alliances to expand its business. In the future, it may seek additional acquisitions.

Mergers and Acquisitions

In late 2021, Cowen completes its acquisition of Portico Capital Advisors (Portico), a leading M&A advisory firm focused on the Verticalized Software, Data, and Analytics sector. This transaction adds momentum to Cowen's growing investment banking platform, further differentiating its advisory capabilities in high-growth industries. In addition, Portico clients now have access to the full breadth of Cowen's capital markets, advisory, and research capabilities. All consideration is comprised of 75% cash and 25% stock. Other terms of the deal were not disclosed.

EXECUTIVES

Chairman, President, Chief Executive Officer, Subsidiary Officer, Jeffrey M. Solomon, $950,000 total compensation

Chief Operating Officer, John J. Holmes, $500,000 total compensation

Chief Financial Officer, Stephen A. Lasota, $500,000 total compensation

General Counsel, Secretary, Owen S. Littman, $500,000 total compensation

Auditors : KPMG LLP

LOCATIONS

HQ: Cowen Inc
599 Lexington Avenue, New York, NY 10022
Phone: 646 562-1010
Web: www.cowen.com

PRODUCTS/OPERATIONS

2014 Sales

	$ mil.	% of total
Investment Banking	170.5	40
Brokerage	140.1	33
Interest and dividend income	48.9	11
Management fees	40.6	9
Reimbursement from affiliates	12.5	3
Incentive income	2.8	1
Other revenues	9.5	2
Consolidated Funds revenues	2.9	1
Total	427.8	100

Selected Subsidiaries

Cowen Alternative Investments, LLC
Cowen Asia Limited (Hong Kong)
Cowen Capital LLC
Cowen Capital Partners II, LLC
Cowen and Company, LLC
Cowen and Company (Asia) Limited (Hong Kong)
Cowen Financial Technology LLC
Cowen Healthcare Royalty Management, LLC
Cowen Holdings, Inc.
Cowen International Limited (UK)
Cowen International Trading Limited (UK)
Cowen Latitude Capital Group, LLC
Cowen Latitude China Holdings Limited
Cowen Latitude Investment Consulting Co., Ltd. (China)
Cowen Overseas Investment, LP
Cowen Services Company, LLC
Cowen Structured Holdings Inc.
Cowen Structured Holdings LLC (Hong Kong)
Cowen Structured Products Specialists, LLC
October, LLC
Ramius Advisors, LLC
Ramius Alternative Solutions, LLC
Ramius Asia LLC
Raimus Enterprise Master Fund Ltd (Cayman Islands)
Ramius Japan Ltd.
Ramius, LLC
Ramius Optimum Investments LLC
Ramius Securities LLC
Ramius Structured Credit Group LLC

COMPETITORS

BGC PARTNERS, INC.
BLACKROCK, INC.
BRC MERGER SUB, LLC
BROWN BROTHERS HARRIMAN & CO.
CCMP CAPITAL ADVISORS, LP
EVERCORE INC.
KBW, LLC
MESIROW FINANCIAL HOLDINGS, INC
OPPENHEIMER HOLDINGS INC.
PIPER SANDLER COMPANIES

HISTORICAL FINANCIALS
Company Type: Public

Income Statement
FYE: December 31

	REVENUE ($mil)	NET INCOME ($mil)	NET PROFIT MARGIN	EMPLOYEES
12/20	1,623.3	216.3	13.3%	1,364
12/19	1,049.4	24.6	2.3%	1,325
12/18	966.9	42.8	4.4%	1,212
12/17	658.7	(60.8)	—	1,124
12/16	471.5	(19.2)	—	843
Annual Growth	36.2%	—		12.8%

2020 Year-End Financials
Debt ratio: 37.6%
Return on equity: 24.2%
Cash ($ mil.): 830.9
Current Ratio: 0.43
Long-term debt ($ mil.): 80.8
No. of shares ($ mil.): 26.8
Dividends
Yield: 0.7%
Payout: 30.1%
Market value ($ mil.): 698.0

	STOCK PRICE ($) FY Close	P/E High	P/E Low	Earnings	Dividends	Book Value
12/20	25.99	4	1	7.10	0.20	36.11
12/19	15.75	30	23	0.57	1.94	28.31
12/18	13.34	14	10	1.17	0.99	27.93
12/17	13.65	—	—	(2.29)	0.00	25.24
12/16	15.50	—	—	(0.97)	0.00	28.90
Annual Growth	13.8%	—	—	—		5.7%

CRA International Inc

CRA International, doing business as Charles River Associates, employs around 860 consultants offering economic, financial, and management counsel to corporate clients, attorneys, government agencies, and other clients. Practices are organized into two areas. Litigation, Regulatory, and Financial Consulting advises on topics such as antitrust and competition, damages, valuation financial accounting, and insurance economics. Management Consulting focus areas include auctions and competitive bidding, business strategy, and enterprise risk management. Most business is conducted in the US. The firm was founded in 1965.

Operations
Charles River Associates' litigation, regulatory, and financial consulting arm typically works with law firms working for companies involved in antitrust, damages, or labor disputes. Its consultants help to develop theory and prepare testimony of expert witnesses. The company also provide general litigation support such as legal brief reviews and appeals support.

The management consulting arm provides expertise of its own to companies seeking organizational, operational, and/or strategic changes. Its specialties include transaction advisory services, organization and performance improvement, enterprise risk management, and corporate strategy.

Geographic Reach
Headquartered in Boston, Massachusetts, Charles River Associates have offices throughout North America and Europe, including in New York, San Francisco, Chicago, and London. The US accounts for some 80% of revenue, UK accounts for about 15% and other countries accounts for the remaining revenues.

Sales and Marketing
Charles River Associates' clients include domestic and foreign corporations; federal, state, and local domestic government agencies; governments of foreign countries; public and private utilities; accounting firms; and national and international trade associations. Frequently, it works with major law firms on behalf of their clients.

Existing clients are an important source of repeat business and referrals. Charles River Associates supplements referrals with direct marketing to new clients through conferences, seminars, publications, presentations, and direct solicitations.

Charles River Associates derived approximately 25% of its revenue from fixed-price contracts in fiscal 2021.

Financial Performance
Revenues increased by $57.5 million, or 11%, to $565.9 million for fiscal 2021 from $508.4 million for fiscal 2020. The increase in net revenue was a result of an increase in gross revenues of $57.2 million as compared to fiscal 2020, coupled with a decrease in write-offs and reserves of $0.3 million as compared to fiscal 2020.

Net income for fiscal 2021 increased to $41.7 million compared from the prior year with $24.5 million.

Cash held by the company at the end of fiscal 2021 increased to $66.1 million. Cash provided by operations was $75.7 million while cash used for investing and financing activities were $2.6 million and $52.0 million, respectively. Main uses of cash were purchases of property and equipment; and repurchase of common stock.

Company Background
Charles River Associates was founded in 1965 and filed an initial public offering in 1998. The company has expanded through organic growth and strategic acquisitions. Its purchase of Marakon Associates in 2009 significantly strengthened the company's management consulting capabilities.

EXECUTIVES
Chairman, Rowland T. Moriarty
President, Chief Executive Officer, Paul A. Maleh, $710,000 total compensation
Executive Vice President, Chief Financial Officer, Treasurer, Chad M. Holmes, $375,000 total compensation
Executive Vice President, General Counsel, Jonathan D. Yellin, $375,000 total compensation
Chief Accounting Officer, Douglas C. Miller
Director, Thomas A. Avery
Director, William F. Concannon
Director, Nancy Hawthorne
Director, Robert W. Holthausen
Director, Robert A. Whitman
Auditors : Grant Thornton LLP

LOCATIONS
HQ: CRA International Inc
200 Clarendon Street, Boston, MA 02116-5092
Phone: 617 425-3000   **Fax:** 617 425-3132
Web: www.crai.com

2017 Sales
	$ mil.	% of total
US	295.2	80
UK	53.7	14
Other countries	21.2	6
Total	370.1	100

PRODUCTS/OPERATIONS
Selected Practice Areas
Litigation, regulatory, and financial consulting
- Antitrust and competition
- Damages and valuation
- Financial accounting and valuation
- Financial economics
- Forensic and cyber investigations
- Insurance economics
- Intellectual property
- International arbitration
- Labor and employment
- Mergers and acquisitions
- Regulatory economics and compliance
- Securities and financial markets
- Transfer pricing

Management consulting
- Auctions and competitive bidding
- Corporate and business strategy
- Enterprise risk management
- Environmental and energy strategy
- Intellectual property and technology management
- Organization and performance improvement
- Transaction advisory services

Selected Industries Served
Agriculture
Banking and capital markets
Chemicals
Communications and media
Consumer products
Energy
Entertainment
Financial services
Health care
Insurance
Life sciences
Manufacturing
Metals, mining, and materials
Oil and gas
Real estateRetail
Sports
Telecommunications
Transportation
Technology

COMPETITORS
CBIZ, INC.
CLIFTONLARSONALLEN LLP
EDELMAN FINANCIAL ENGINES, LLC
EXAMWORKS GROUP, INC.
FTI CONSULTING, INC.
GUIDEHOUSE INC.
HURON CONSULTING GROUP INC.
INSPERITY, INC.
MAXIMUS, INC.
STIFEL FINANCIAL CORP.

HISTORICAL FINANCIALS
Company Type: Public

Income Statement				FYE: January 2
	REVENUE ($mil)	NET INCOME ($mil)	NET PROFIT MARGIN	EMPLOYEES
01/21*	508.3	24.5	4.8%	831
12/19	451.3	20.7	4.6%	779
12/18	417.6	22.4	5.4%	687
12/17	370.0	7.6	2.1%	631
12/16	324.7	12.8	4.0%	540
Annual Growth	11.9%	17.4%	—	11.4%

*Fiscal year change

2021 Year-End Financials
Debt ratio: —
Return on equity: 11.8%
Cash ($ mil.): 45.6
Current Ratio: 1.10
Long-term debt ($ mil.): —
No. of shares ($ mil.): 7.6
Dividends
  Yield: —
  Payout: 30.9%
Market value ($ mil.): 392.0

	STOCK PRICE ($) FY Close	P/E High/Low		PER SHARE ($) Earnings	Dividends	Book Value
01/21*	50.93	18	7	3.07	0.95	27.17
12/19	53.57	21	13	2.53	0.83	25.30
12/18	40.92	21	15	2.61	0.71	24.53
12/17	44.95	52	36	0.89	0.59	24.94
12/16	36.60	25	11	1.49	0.14	24.86
Annual Growth	8.6%	—	—	19.8%	61.4%	2.2%

*Fiscal year change

Crawford United Corp

Like "Wild Bill" of Wild West lore, Hickok is quite comfortable shooting it out with competitors on its own measured road to success. The company manufactures testing equipment used by automotive technicians to repair cars. Hickok also makes instruments, indicators, and gauges for manufacturers of aircraft and locomotives. While Ford and General Motors traditionally were the company's largest customers, its biggest customer now is Environmental Systems Products (ESP), at 53% of sales. Hickok sells products primarily in the US. In 2019, Hickok bought Data Genomix, which develops social media marketing applications for political, legal, and recruiting campaigns. The companies are based in Cleveland, Ohio.

HISTORY

Robert D. Hickok founded Hickok Electrical Instrument in Atlanta in 1910 and moved it to Cleveland in 1913. The company introduced the first AC/DC radio tube tester in 1920 and began making electrical instrumentation for aircraft during the mid-1930s. In 1950, after his father's death, Robert D. Hickok Jr. took over the firm; he took it public in 1959. During the 1960s the company acquired a number of firms and Robert Bauman became chief engineer. In 1969 Robert D. Hickok Jr. retired. Hickok began its relationship with Ford Motor in 1981, moving into automotive diagnostic tools. Bauman became president in 1991 and later CEO (1992) and chairman (1993).

To expand its product line, Hickok acquired Allen-Bradley Co. (fastening systems) in 1994. Hickok's name was changed to Hickok Incorporated the next year. Diversification efforts in 1996 included acquiring Maradyne's Beacon Gage Division (railroad and transit car pressure gauges). Sales and earnings suffered in 1997 when Ford and General Motors delayed purchasing automotive diagnostic and fastening systems.

Transitioning to the aftermarket business, Hickok bought automotive diagnostic and specialty toolmaker Waekon Industries (renamed Waekon Corp.) in 1998. The acquisition fit into the company's long-term plan to decrease its dependence on a few large, occasional orders from carmakers and to increase its presence in the more stable automotive aftermarket. Hickok recorded a loss in fiscal 1999, in part because of its change to a lower-margin product mix.

In 2000 Hickok closed its Kirkwood, Pennsylvania, plant and moved production to the firm's Greenwood, Mississippi, factory to reduce costs. The company's line of DIGILOG aircraft instruments was approved by the FAA in fiscal 2002; since that time, other models, which had potential in the aircraft retrofit market, also were certified.

Hickock unsuccessfully attempted to buy out enough of its outstanding shares to enable it to go private in 2004. The company's intention to end its obligations for SEC registration was to eliminate expenses related to compliance with the Sarbanes-Oxley Act and to focus on its operations.

EXECUTIVES

Chairman, President, Chief Executive Officer, Director, Brian E. Powers, $210,833 total compensation
Vice President, Kelly J. Marek, $120,417 total compensation
Chief Financial Officer, Jay Daly
Director, Luis E. Jimenez
Director, Matthew V. Crawford
Director, Steven H. Rosen
Director, Kirin M. Smith
Auditors: Meaden & Moore, Ltd.

LOCATIONS

HQ: Crawford United Corp
10514 Dupont Avenue, Cleveland, OH 44108
Phone: 216 243-2614
Web: www.crawfordunited.com

Hickok operates facilities in Cleveland and in Greenwood, Mississippi.

PRODUCTS/OPERATIONS

Selected Subsidiaries
Supreme Electronics Corp.
Waekon Corp.

COMPETITORS

AMETEK, INC.
COGNEX CORPORATION
KEITHLEY INSTRUMENTS, LLC
Siemens AG
THERMO KING CORPORATION

HISTORICAL FINANCIALS
Company Type: Public

Income Statement				FYE: December 31
	REVENUE ($mil)	NET INCOME ($mil)	NET PROFIT MARGIN	EMPLOYEES
12/20	85.0	5.8	6.9%	260
12/19	89.6	6.9	7.8%	271
12/18	66.3	3.6	5.4%	275
12/17*	11.7	0.5	4.3%	200
09/17	23.8	1.4	5.9%	180
Annual Growth	52.9%	60.7%	—	13.0%

*Fiscal year change

2020 Year-End Financials
Debt ratio: 39.5%
Return on equity: 23.7%
Cash ($ mil.): 6.1
Current Ratio: 2.00
Long-term debt ($ mil.): 26.9
No. of shares ($ mil.): 3.3
Dividends
  Yield: —
  Payout: —
Market value ($ mil.): 62.0

	STOCK PRICE ($) FY Close	P/E High/Low		PER SHARE ($) Earnings	Dividends	Book Value
12/20	18.74	13	7	1.76	0.00	8.27
12/19	19.75	9	4	2.13	0.00	6.52
12/18	10.50	10	6	1.14	0.00	4.69
12/17*	10.49	62	39	0.16	0.00	3.60
09/17	9.40	19	3	0.46	0.00	3.42
Annual Growth	25.9%	—	—	56.4%	—	34.2%

*Fiscal year change

Credit Acceptance Corp (MI)

Credit Acceptance Corporation (CAC) offers financing programs that enable automobile dealers to sell vehicles to consumers. CAC makes the effort a reality. Working with approximately 60,000 independent and franchised automobile dealers in the US, CAC provides financing programs through a nationwide network of automobile dealers who benefit from sales of vehicles to consumers who otherwise could not obtain financing; from repeat and referral sales generated by these same customers; and from sales to customers responding to advertisements for the company's financing programs. CAC, which concentrates its operations in a handful of US states, typically funds about 3.2 million auto loans per year.

Operations

CAC derives its revenues from finance charges (about 95% of sales), which are comprised of interest income earned on loans; administrative fees earned from ancillary products; program fees charged to dealers under the Portfolio Program; Consumer Loan assignment fees charged to dealers; and direct origination costs incurred on Dealer Loans. Premiums earned on the reinsurance of vehicle service contracts and other income generate the remaining. It primarily consists of ancillary product profit sharing, remarketing fees, dealer enrollment fees, interest, dealer support products and services.

In addition, the company offers two programs: the Portfolio Program and the Purchase Program. Under the Portfolio Program, the company advances money to Dealers (Dealer Loan) in exchange for the right to service the underlying Consumer Loans. Under the Purchase Program, the company buys the Consumer Loans from the Dealers (Purchased Loan) and keep all amounts collected from the consumer. Dealer Loans and Purchased Loans are collectively referred to as "Loans". Portfolio Program accounts more than 65% of unit volume while Purchase Program accounts the remainder.

Geographic Reach

Michigan-based CAC serves consumers nationwide. In addition to Michigan, its largest markets include Ohio, New York, Texas, and Tennessee.

Sales and Marketing

CAC caters to and partners with approximately 60,000 independent and franchised automobile dealers throughout the US.

Advertising expenses were approximately $0.3 million, $0.1 million, and $0.3 million for 2021, 2020, and 2019, respectively.

Financial Performance

CAC's revenue has been rising consistently in the last five years with a 67% overall increase between 2017 and 2021. Its net income follows a similar patter with the exception of 2020, when it declined 36%.

The company had a total revenue of $1.9 billion in 2021, an 11% increase from the previous year's revenue of $1.7 billion. The increase was primarily due to a higher sales volume in the company's finance charges segment.

For the year ended December 31, 2021, consolidated net income was $958.3 million. The increase in consolidated net income was primarily due to a decrease in provision for credit losses and an increase in finance charges. The decrease in provision for credit losses was primarily due to an improvement in Consumer Loan performance and a decrease in new Consumer Loan assignment volume.

The company's cash at the end of 2021 was $434.2 million. Operating activities generated $1.1 billion, while financing activities used $1.5 billion, mainly for repayments under revolving secured line of credit, as well as repayments of secured financing. Investing activities generated another $437.3 million.

Strategy

CAC's strategy for accessing capital on acceptable terms needed to maintain and grow the business is to: maintain consistent financial performance; maintain modest financial leverage; and maintain multiple funding sources. The company funded debt to equity ratio was 2.5 to 1 as of December 31, 2021. It currently utilizes the following primary forms of debt financing: a revolving secured line of credit; Warehouse facilities; Term ABS financings; and senior notes.

HISTORY

Donald Foss was a used-car dealer in Detroit, where, to make sales, he sometimes financed cars out of his own pocket. As Foss' chain of dealerships grew, so did his financing business. In 1972 he established it as a separate company and 20 years later took it public.

For most of its history CAC stood alone in the field of subprime auto lending, but stagnating salaries made it a competitive growth business in the early 1990s. At mid-decade, the company entered Canada and the UK to tap similar markets there. In 1996 CAC acquired Montana Investment Group, a credit reporting service.

Even as rising consumer debt and bad credit continued to pump buyers into CAC's loan pipeline, the economic boom of the mid-1990s paradoxically made used cars less desirable. The soft used-car market squeezed several of CAC's competitors out of business; a staggering default rate -- nearing 40% -- also pressured CAC, whose auditors insisted it increase reserves to cover losses. The subsequent earnings dive spurred a shareholder lawsuit accusing CAC of hiding its poor fiscal health. Although bad loans had damaged its bottom line, the company adopted more stringent lending policies to reduce risk. Consumers filed class-action suits alleging unethical practices in 1998, but many claims were dismissed.

To pay off debt acquired through bad loans, CAC sold Montana Investment Group in 1999. In 2000 it launched CAC Leasing to further offset losses from a decrease in subprime lending, but in 2002 the company exited that line, deciding the lending field was more profitable. CAC stopped originating new loans in the UK and Canada in 2003.

In 2005 the SEC investigated CAC's accounting methods, specifically related to its loan portfolio, and the company restated portions of its past financial results.

The company found itself in hot water again in 2008 when it agreed to pay some 15,000 Missouri customers to settle a class action lawsuit. The lawsuit, filed more than a decade prior, alleged that CAC overcharged customers for fees and interest on their loans. As part of the settlement, CAC said it would write off $39 million in outstanding accounts and distribute another $13 million to customers.

EXECUTIVES

President, Chief Operating Officer, Steven M. Jones, $723,074 total compensation
Chief Executive Officer, Brett A. Roberts, $1,025,000 total compensation
Loan Servicing Senior Vice President, Michael W. Knoblauch, $391,923 total compensation
Operations Improvement Senior Vice President, Operations Improvement Chief Information Officer, John P. Neary, $500,000 total compensation
Vice President, Chief Legal Officer, Secretary, General Counsel, Charles A. Pearce, $539,240 total compensation
Chief Analytics Officer, Arthur L. Smith, $539,240 total compensation
Chief Financial Officer, Kenneth S. Booth, $539,240 total compensation
Chief Human Resources Officer, Steven M. Dion
Chief Technology Officer, Michael P. Miotto, $315,000 total compensation
Chief Sales Officer, Daniel A. Ulatowski, $539,240 total compensation
Treasurer, Division Officer, Douglas W. Busk
Director, Glenda J. Flanagan
Director, Thomas N. Tryforos
Director, Scott J. Vassalluzzo
Auditors : Grant Thornton LLP

LOCATIONS

HQ: Credit Acceptance Corp (MI)
25505 West Twelve Mile Road, Southfield, MI 48034-8339
Phone: 248 353 2700

PRODUCTS/OPERATIONS

2016 Sales

	$ mil.	% of total
Finance charges	874.3	90
Premiums earned	43.0	5
Other	51.9	5
Total	969.2	100

Selected Subsidiaries
Buyers Vehicle Protection Plan, Inc.
CAC Leasing, Inc.
CAC Reinsurance, Ltd.
CAC Warehouse Funding Corp. II, III, IV
Credit Acceptance Wholesale Buyers Club, Inc.
Vehicle Remarketing Services, Inc.
VSC Re Company

COMPETITORS

ATLANTICUS HOLDINGS CORPORATION
CIT GROUP INC.
COGNITION FINANCIAL CORPORATION
CONSUMER PORTFOLIO SERVICES, INC.
FIRST INVESTORS FINANCIAL SERVICES GROUP, INC.
GENERAL MOTORS FINANCIAL COMPANY, INC.
NICHOLAS FINANCIAL, INC.
PARAGON BANKING GROUP PLC
SLM CORPORATION
WORLD ACCEPTANCE CORPORATION

HISTORICAL FINANCIALS
Company Type: Public

Income Statement   FYE: December 31

	REVENUE ($mil)	NET INCOME ($mil)	NET PROFIT MARGIN	EMPLOYEES
12/21	1,856.0	958.3	51.6%	2,073
12/20	1,669.3	421.0	25.2%	2,033
12/19	1,489.0	656.1	44.1%	2,016
12/18	1,285.8	574.0	44.6%	2,040
12/17	1,110.0	470.2	42.4%	1,817
Annual Growth	13.7%	19.5%	—	3.4%

2021 Year-End Financials
Debt ratio: 65.5%   No. of shares ($ mil.): 14.1
Return on equity: 46.4%   Dividends
Cash ($ mil.): 23.3   Yield: —
Current Ratio: 3.46   Payout: —
Long-term debt ($ mil.): 4,616.3   Market value ($ mil.): 9,728.0

	STOCK PRICE ($) FY Close	P/E High/Low		PER SHARE ($) Earnings	Dividends	Book Value
12/21	687.68	12	5	59.52	0.00	128.96
12/20	346.14	22	9	23.47	0.00	134.71
12/19	442.33	14	11	34.57	0.00	128.33
12/18	381.76	16	10	29.39	0.00	104.94
12/17	323.48	14	8	24.04	0.00	79.53
Annual Growth	20.7%	—	—	25.4%	—	12.8%

Crescent Capital BDC Inc

EXECUTIVES

President, Chief Executive Officer, Jason A. Breaux
Chief Financial Officer, Gerhard Lombard
Senior Vice President, Chief Compliance Officer, Erik Barrios
Secretary, George P. Hawley
President, Jonathan R. Insull
Controller, Kirill Bouek
Managing Director, Raymond Barrios
Director, Kathleen S. Briscoe
Director, George G. Strong
Director, Michael S. Segal
Director, Steven F. Strandberg
Director, Elizabeth E. Ko
Director, Susan Yun Lee

LOCATIONS

HQ: Crescent Capital BDC Inc
11100 Santa Monica Blvd., Suite 2000, Los Angeles, CA 90025
Phone: 310 235-5900
Web: www.crescentbdc.com

HISTORICAL FINANCIALS
Company Type: Public

Income Statement   FYE: December 31

	REVENUE ($mil)	NET INCOME ($mil)	NET PROFIT MARGIN	EMPLOYEES
12/20	77.1	49.8	64.7%	0
12/19	53.4	31.6	59.2%	0
12/18	33.2	17.7	53.2%	0
12/17	22.2	9.9	44.4%	0
Annual Growth	51.2%	71.4%	—	—

2020 Year-End Financials
Debt ratio: 44.8%   No. of shares ($ mil.): 28.1
Return on equity: 10.2%   Dividends
Cash ($ mil.): 14.8   Yield: 11.2%
Current Ratio: 0.91   Payout: 103.1%
Long-term debt ($ mil.): 471.9   Market value ($ mil.): 410.0

	STOCK PRICE ($) FY Close	P/E High/Low		PER SHARE ($) Earnings	Dividends	Book Value
12/20	14.57	9	3	1.98	1.64	19.88
Annual Growth	—	—	—	—	—	—

Crexendo Inc

Crexendo (formerly iMergent) would like to help increase the volume on your e-commerce business. Catering to home-based, small, and medium-sized businesses, the company's cloud-based software helps merchants create, manage, and promote their e-commerce website and process orders. Premium services include site and logo design, supplier integration, and search engine optimization. The company has primarily used training seminars around the country to sell its products to aspiring e-commerce mavens, but hopes to open more sales channels. More than 90% of sales come from customers in North America (US and Canada). Chairman and CEO Steven Mihaylo, founder and former CEO of Inter-Tel, owns more than a third of Crexendo.

EXECUTIVES

Chief Executive Officer, Chairman, Steven G. Mihaylo, $3,543 total compensation
President, Chief Operating Officer, Doug Gaylor, $207,692 total compensation
Chief Strategy Officer, Director, Anand Buch
Senior Vice President, Secretary, Jeffrey G. Korn, $155,769 total compensation
Chief Financial Officer, Ronald Vincent, $155,769 total compensation
Chief Revenue Officer, Jon D. Brinton
Chief Technology Officer, David Wang
Director, Todd A. Goergen
Director, Anil K. Puri
Director, Jeffrey Parr Bash
Director, David R. Williams
Auditors: Urish Popeck & Co., LLC

LOCATIONS

HQ: Crexendo Inc
1615 South 52nd Street, Tempe, AZ 85281
Phone: 602 714-8500
Web: www.crexendo.com

PRODUCTS/OPERATIONS

Selected Software and Services
E-commerce seminars
Search engine optimization
StoresOnline (e-commerce development platform)
Web hosting
Website development and design
Hosted telecommunications

COMPETITORS

ASPECT SOFTWARE GROUP HOLDINGS LTD.
BLUETIE INC.
IT GLOBALSECURE INC.
Q-MATIC CORPORATION
THE TRIPLE-I CORPORATION

HISTORICAL FINANCIALS
Company Type: Public

Income Statement   FYE: December 31

	REVENUE ($mil)	NET INCOME ($mil)	NET PROFIT MARGIN	EMPLOYEES
12/20	16.3	7.9	48.5%	58
12/19	14.4	1.1	7.9%	56
12/18	11.9	(0.2)	—	56
12/17	10.3	(1.0)	—	54
12/16	9.1	(2.7)	—	53
Annual Growth	15.8%	—	—	2.3%

2020 Year-End Financials
Debt ratio: 6.6%   No. of shares ($ mil.): 17.9
Return on equity: 52.5%   Dividends
Cash ($ mil.): 17.5   Yield: —
Current Ratio: 7.72   Payout: —
Long-term debt ($ mil.): 1.9   Market value ($ mil.): 125.0

	STOCK PRICE ($) FY Close	P/E High/Low		PER SHARE ($) Earnings	Dividends	Book Value
12/20	6.93	23	6	0.46	0.00	1.43
12/19	4.25	58	22	0.07	0.00	0.29
12/18	2.00	—	—	(0.02)	0.00	0.14
12/17	2.10	—	—	(0.07)	0.00	0.09
12/16	1.45	—	—	(0.21)	0.00	0.04
Annual Growth	47.9%	—	—	—	—	147.9%

Crocs Inc

Crocs is one of the world's largest footwear companies. Its shoe collection has grown by leaps and bounds from its ubiquitous classic slip-on clog to a range of trainers, sandals, and boots. Branded as Crocs, its shoes are made of proprietary closed-cell resin and designed for men, women, and children. Jibbitz are the company's decorative add-on charms. It reaches customers via nearly 375 owned stores, first- and third-party e-commerce sites, and third-party retailers. Sold approximately 103.0 million pairs of shoes worldwide, the company has customers in more than 85 countries and earns most of its sales in the US. Every pair of Crocs is manufactured by other companies, mostly in Vietnam and China.

Operations

Crocs has three reportable operating segments based on the geographic nature of its operations: the Americas (approximately 70%), Asia Pacific (approximately 15%), and Europe, Middle East, and Africa (some 15%).

The company offers a broad portfolio of all-season products, while remaining true to its core molded footwear heritage. The vast majority of Crocs shoes feature Croslite material, a proprietary, revolutionary technology that gives each pair of shoes the soft, comfortable, lightweight, non-marking, and odor-resistant. It also uses Croslite material formulations in connection with material technologies used in its visible comfort collections, such as its LiteRide products. LiteRide features comfort-focused, proprietary foam insoles which are soft, lightweight, and resilient.

By channel, the company's wholesale channel accounts for about 50% of sales. It includes domestic and international, multi-brand, brick-and-mortar retailers, e-tailers, and distributors in certain countries, including partner store operators. Brick-and-mortar customers typically include family footwear retailers, national and regional retail chains, sporting goods stores, and independent footwear retailers. The company's direct-to-consumer channel accounts for the rest.

Geographic Reach

Headquartered in Broomfield, Colorado, Crocs has offices and distribution centers worldwide and also leases about 375 retail locations worldwide. Operating in more than 85 countries, the company generates approximately 65% of sales from the US while international sales account for the remaining. It prioritizes five core markets including: US, Japan, China, South Korea, and Western Europe.

Sales and Marketing

Crocs markets its products through media advertising (television, radio, print, social, digital), tactical advertising (signs, banners, point-of-sale materials) and promotional costs.

The company's total marketing expenses, inclusive of advertising, production, promotion, and agency expenses, including variable marketing expenses, were approximately $172.7 million, $101.0 million, and $83.2 million for the years ended 2021, 2020, and 2019, respectively.

Financial Performance

Revenues were $2.3 billion in 2021, a 67% increase compared to 2020. The increase in 2021 revenues compared to 2020 revenues was due to the net effects of higher sales volumes, which increased revenues by $637.4 million, or 46.0%, driven by continued increased consumer demand for its products, some of which was due to improved sales in its DTC businesses as the pandemic subsided; higher average selling prices, which increased revenues by $265.9 million, or 19.2%, as a result of increased prices and reduced promotions and discounts; and favorable changes in exchange rates, which increased revenues by $24.2 million, or 1.7%.

Net income in 2021 increased to $725.7 million compared with $312.9 million in the prior year.

Cash held by the company at the end of fiscal 2021 increased to $216.9 million. Operating activities provided $567.2 million while investing and financing activities provided $55.9 million and $429.6 million, respectively. Main cash uses were purchases of property, equipment, and software; and repurchases of common stock.

Strategy

The company's growth framework is driven by four strategic areas of focus: growing digital sales, gaining market share in sandals, growth opportunities in Asia, and ongoing product and marketing innovation.

Mergers and Acquisitions

In early 2022, Crocs acquired HEYDUDE, a privately-owned casual footwear brand. The acquisition of HEYDUDE adds a second high-growth, highly profitable brand to the Crocs portfolio. The company intends to leverage its global presence, innovative marketing and scale infrastructure to grow HEYDUDE and create significant shareholder value. The acquisition was funded by approximately $2.05 billion in cash and 2,852,280 shares issued to HEYDUDE's founder.

EXECUTIVES

Chairman, Director, Thomas J. Smach, $0 total compensation
President, Chief Executive Officer, Andrew Rees, $950,000 total compensation
Executive Vice President, Chief Financial Officer, Anne Mehlman, $181,923 total compensation
Executive Vice President, Chief Administrative Officer, Chief Legal Officer, Daniel P. Hart, $523,688 total compensation
Director, Ian Martin Bickley
Director, Ronald L. Frasch
Director, William Gray
Director, Prakash A. Melwani
Director, Douglas J. Treff
Director, Doreen A. Wright
Auditors : DELOITTE & TOUCHE LLP

LOCATIONS

HQ: Crocs Inc
  13601 Via Varra, Broomfield, CO 80020
Phone: 303 848-7000
Web: www.crocs.com

2018 Sales

	$ mil.	% of total
Footwear		
Americas	520.2	48
Asia/Pacific	344.6	32
Europe	220.3	20
Other	3.1	--
Total	1,088.2	100

PRODUCTS/OPERATIONS

2018 Sales

	% of total
Wholesale	53
Retail	30
Internet	17
Total	100

2018 Stores

	No.
Retail	120
Outlet	195
Kiosk	68
Total	383

COMPETITORS

Grendene S/A
HANESBRANDS INC.
K-SWISS INC.
NEW BALANCE ATHLETICS, INC.
NIKE, INC.
Pegasus International Holdings Limited
SKECHERS U.S.A., INC.
TAPESTRY, INC.
VANS, INC.
YUE YUEN INDUSTRIAL (HOLDINGS) LIMITED

HISTORICAL FINANCIALS

Company Type: Public

Income Statement — FYE: December 31

	REVENUE ($mil)	NET INCOME ($mil)	NET PROFIT MARGIN	EMPLOYEES
12/21	2,313.4	725.6	31.4%	5,770
12/20	1,385.9	312.8	22.6%	4,600
12/19	1,230.5	119.4	9.7%	3,803
12/18	1,088.2	50.4	4.6%	3,901
12/17	1,023.5	10.2	1.0%	4,382
Annual Growth	22.6%	190.2%	—	7.1%

2021 Year-End Financials

Debt ratio: 49.9%
Return on equity: —
Cash ($ mil.): 213.2
Current Ratio: 1.72
Long-term debt ($ mil.): 771.3
No. of shares ($ mil.): 58.3
Dividends
  Yield: —
  Payout: —
Market value ($ mil.): 7,475.0

	STOCK PRICE ($) FY Close	P/E High	P/E Low	PER SHARE ($) Earnings	Dividends	Book Value
12/21	128.22	16	5	11.39	0.00	0.24
12/20	62.66	14	2	4.56	0.00	4.41
12/19	41.89	24	10	1.66	0.00	1.93
12/18	25.98	—	—	(1.01)	0.00	2.05
12/17	12.64	—	—	(0.07)	0.00	5.35
Annual Growth	78.5%	—	—	—	—	(53.9%)

CrossFirst Bankshares Inc

EXECUTIVES

Chairman, Director, Rodney K. Brenneman
President, Chief Executive Officer, Subsidiary Officer, Director, Michael J. Maddox, $346,875 total compensation
Chief Accounting Officer, Principal Accounting Officer, Subsidiary Officer, Michael John Daley
Chief Financial Officer, Principal Financial Officer, Benjamin R. Clouse
Chief Banking Officer, Steve Peterson
Subsidiary Officer, W. Randall Rapp
Director, Lance Humphreys
Director, Michael Robinson
Director, Stephen K. Swinson
Director, George Bruce
Director, Steven W. Caple
Director, Ron Geist
Director, Jennifer M. Grigsby
Director, George E. Hansen
Director, Mason King
Director, James W. Kuykendall
Director, Kevin S. Rauckman
Director, Grey Stogner
Auditors : BKD, LLP

LOCATIONS

HQ: CrossFirst Bankshares Inc
11440 Tomahawk Creek Parkway, Leawood, KS 66211
Phone: 913 312-6822
Web: www.crossfirstbankshares.com

HISTORICAL FINANCIALS
Company Type: Public

Income Statement				FYE: December 31
	ASSETS ($mil)	NET INCOME ($mil)	INCOME AS % OF ASSETS	EMPLOYEES
12/20	5,659.3	12.6	0.2%	328
12/19	4,931.2	28.4	0.6%	357
12/18	4,107.2	19.5	0.5%	360
12/17	2,961.1	5.8	0.2%	0
Annual Growth	24.1%	29.2%	—	—

2020 Year-End Financials
Return on assets: 0.2%   Dividends
Return on equity: 2.0%   Yield: —
Long-term debt ($ mil.): —   Payout: —
No. of shares ($ mil.): 51.6   Market value ($ mil.): 556.0
Sales ($ mil.): 215.1

	STOCK PRICE ($) FY Close	P/E High/Low		PER SHARE ($) Earnings Dividends		Book Value
12/20	10.75	60	24	0.24	0.00	12.08
12/19	14.42	25	21	0.58	0.00	11.58
Annual Growth	(25.5%)	—	—	(58.6%)	—	4.4%

Crossroads Systems Inc (New)

Crossroads Systems sets up shop where business and information intersect. The company provides storage networking equipment and data archiving systems used to manage and protect critical data. Its products include StrongBox (network attached storage appliance that uses linear tape file system technology), RVA (monitoring tape media and the condition of disk drives), and SPHiNX (protecting data by working as a network attached storage device or virtual tape library). Crossroads Systems sells directly to manufacturers, such as HP (45% of sales) and EMC, and through distributors. The company was founded in 1996.

Geographic Reach
Headquartered in Austin, TX, Crossroads Systems also has a sales office in Germany. International sales account for less than 10% of revenues.

Sales and Marketing
Crossroads relies on a small number of distributors that offer its products as part of an overall data protection package, since many of its tape and disk products are incorporated into larger storage systems, such as those sold by Fujifilm. These distributors can also install and support its products on behalf of Crossroads; its internal sales force is only responsible for managing the OEM and strategic partner relationships.

The company counts on a small number of customers; its top three account for more than two-thirds of sales. End users include small businesses, large corporations, and government agencies.

Financial Performance
Crossroads has also been at a financial crossroads, with a history of losses and declining sales. Revenue was down 10% in 2013 to $12.6 million. Sales from its RVA and SPHiNX product lines experienced decreases, while its StrongBox product grew $2 million in its first full year of sales.

Products account for about 60% of sales, and the other 40% comes from companies that license its intellectual property. Crossroads has a software license and distribution agreement with HP where the computer giant pays Crossroads royalties and support fees; the deal makes up a huge chunk of Crossroads' revenues every year.

Strategy
Crossroads presents itself as a cost-effective storage company, compared with the likes of IBM and Hitachi Data Systems. The markets for its products are characterized by significant price competition and it anticipates that its products will continue to face price pressure.

HISTORY

Crossroads delisted its shares from the Nasdaq National Market in 2006. The company cited the increased costs of operating as a publicly held company, especially those associated with complying with Section 404 of the federal Sarbanes-Oxley Act, as the reason for the listing change. Trading of the company's shares shifted to the Pink Sheets.

In 2007 Crossroads Systems purchased assets of Grau Data Storage, namely its hierarchical storage management (HSM) software product called FileMigrator Agent, for less than $1 million in cash. That same year, the company cut its workforce (primarily in product development) by about 8% in order to reduce expenses.

In September 2011 Crossroads Systems began trading on the Nasdaq Capital Market.

EXECUTIVES

President, Chief Executive Officer, Richard Kenneth Coleman, $300,000 total compensation
Chief Financial Officer, Jennifer Ray Crane
Division Officer, Mark C. Hood
Director, Robert G. Pearse
Director, Don Pearce
Director, Hannah M. Bible
Auditors : Baker Tilly US, LLP

LOCATIONS

HQ: Crossroads Systems Inc (New)
4514 Cole Avenue, Suite 1600, Dallas, TX 75205
Phone: 214 999-0149
Web: www.crossroads.com

COMPETITORS

ACACIA RESEARCH CORPORATION
CEVA, INC.
ICONIX BRAND GROUP, INC.
TIVO CORPORATION
VIRNETX HOLDING CORPORATION

HISTORICAL FINANCIALS
Company Type: Public

Income Statement				FYE: October 31
	REVENUE ($mil)	NET INCOME ($mil)	NET PROFIT MARGIN	EMPLOYEES
10/21	930.6	194.7	20.9%	34
10/20	36.6	3.0	8.2%	27
10/19	37.7	1.7	4.6%	0
10/18	28.4	23.8	83.8%	0
10/17	0.0	(1.6)	—	0
Annual Growth	970.0%	—	—	—

2021 Year-End Financials
Debt ratio: 91.3%   No. of shares ($ mil.): 5.9
Return on equity: —   Dividends
Cash ($ mil.): 589.0   Yield: 1.4%
Current Ratio: 1.70   Payout: —
Long-term debt ($ mil.): 3,176.2   Market value ($ mil.): 111.0

	STOCK PRICE ($) FY Close	P/E High/Low		PER SHARE ($) Earnings Dividends		Book Value
10/21	18.60	—	—	0.00	40.00	(1.91)
10/20	9.00	—	—	0.00	0.00	5.43
10/19	8.50	—	—	0.00	0.00	8.55
10/18	6.90	—	—	0.00	0.00	4.61
10/17	3.30	—	—	(1.51)	0.00	0.85
Annual Growth	54.1%	—	—	—	—	—

CSB Bancorp Inc (OH)

EXECUTIVES

Chairman, Director, Robert K. Baker
President, Chief Executive Officer, Associate/Affiliate Company Officer, Director, Eddie L. Steiner, $250,000 total compensation
Senior Vice President, Chief Financial Officer, Paula J. Meiler, $153,800 total compensation
Senior Vice President, Chief Operating Officer, Chief Information Officer, Associate/Affiliate Company Officer, Brett A. Gallion, $136,885 total compensation
Director, Vikki G. Briggs
Director, Julian L. Coblentz
Director, Cheryl M. Kirkbride
Director, Jeffrey A. Robb
Auditors : S.R. Snodgrass, P.C.

LOCATIONS

HQ: CSB Bancorp Inc (OH)
91 North Clay Street, P.O. Box 232, Millersburg, OH 44654
Phone: 330 674-9015
Web: www.csb1.com

HISTORICAL FINANCIALS

Company Type: Public

Income Statement   FYE: December 31

	ASSETS ($mil)	NET INCOME ($mil)	INCOME AS % OF ASSETS	EMPLOYEES
12/20	1,031.6	10.5	1.0%	187
12/19	818.6	10.4	1.3%	187
12/18	731.7	9.4	1.3%	190
12/17	707.0	7.1	1.0%	187
12/16	669.9	6.7	1.0%	182
Annual Growth	11.4%	11.9%	—	0.7%

2020 Year-End Financials

Return on assets: 1.1%
Return on equity: 11.7%
Long-term debt ($ mil.): —
No. of shares ($ mil.): 2.7
Sales ($ mil.): 38

Dividends
 Yield: —
 Payout: 29.3%
Market value ($ mil.): 96.0

	STOCK PRICE ($) FY Close	P/E High/Low		PER SHARE ($) Earnings Dividends		Book Value
12/20	35.00	11	7	3.85	1.13	34.23
12/19	40.97	11	10	3.80	1.08	31.17
12/18	38.50	13	10	3.43	0.98	27.91
12/17	33.11	13	11	2.59	0.84	25.72
12/16	31.00	14	9	2.46	0.78	23.85
Annual Growth	3.1%	—	—	11.8%	9.7%	9.4%

Customers Bancorp Inc

Boasting some $20.3 billion in assets, Customers Bancorp, is the bank holding company engaged in banking activities through its wholly owned subsidiary, Customers Bank, which operates about 10 branches across Florida, Illinois, Massachusetts, New Hampshire, New Jersey, New York, North Carolina, Pennsylvania, Rhode Island and Texas. It offers traditional loan and deposit banking products and financial services, and non-traditional products and services such as CBIT, to its commercial and consumer customers. Customers also offers traditional deposit products, including commercial and consumer checking accounts, non-interest-bearing demand accounts, MMDA, savings accounts, time deposit accounts and cash management services. Around 85% of the bank's loan portfolio is made up of commercial loans, while the rest consists of consumer loans.

Operations

Customers Bancorp operates two main business lines: Commercial Lending and Consumer Lending. Its Commercial Lending business provides commercial and industrial loans, including small and middle-market business banking and small business administration (SBA) loans, multi-family and commercial real estate loans, and commercial loans to mortgage originators. Its Consumer Lending business mostly makes local market mortgage loans and home equity loans. Around 95% of the bank's loan portfolio was made up of commercial loans.

Broadly speaking, the bank makes roughly 90% of its revenue from interest income. The remainder of its revenue comes from mortgage warehouse transactional fees, commercial lease, deposit fees, bank-owned life insurance and other miscellaneous and non-recurring sources.

Geographic Reach

Customers Bancorp and its wholly owned subsidiaries, Customers Bank, and non-bank subsidiaries, serve residents and businesses in Southeastern Pennsylvania (Bucks, Berks, Chester, Philadelphia and Delaware Counties); Harrisburg, Pennsylvania (Dauphin County); Rye Brook, New York (Westchester County); Hamilton, New Jersey (Mercer County); Boston, Massachusetts; Providence, Rhode Island; Portsmouth, New Hampshire (Rockingham County); Manhattan and Melville, New York; Washington, D.C.; Chicago, Illinois; Dallas, Texas; Orlando, Florida; Wilmington, North Carolina; and nationally for certain loan and deposit products. In addition, Customers Bank has offices in Boston, Massachusetts; Providence, Rhode Island; Portsmouth, New Hampshire; Manhattan and Melville, New York; Philadelphia and Lancaster, Pennsylvania; Chicago, Illinois; Dallas, Texas; Orlando, Florida; Wilmington, North Carolina; and other locations.

Sales and Marketing

Customers Bancorp's customers include private businesses, business customers, non-profits, and consumers. Services and products are available through mobile-first apps, online portals, and a network of offices and branches. Customers Bank provides blockchain-based digital payments via the Customers Bank Instant Token (CBITT) which allows clients to make real-time payments in US dollars, 24 hours a day, 7 days a week, 365 days a year.

Financial Performance

Net interest income increased $281.4 million for the year ended December 31, 2021 compared to the year ended December 31, 2020 as average interest-earning assets increased by $3.6 billion, and NIM increased by 99 basis points to 3.70% for the year ended December 31, 2021 from 2.71% for the year ended December 31, 2020. The increase in interest-earning assets was primarily driven by increases in the origination and purchases of the latest round of PPP loans, investment securities, commercial and industrial loans and leases, commercial loans to mortgage companies and consumer installment loans, offset in part by decreases in multi-family loans.

In 2021, the company had a net income of $314.6 million, a 137% increase from the previous year's net income of $132.6 million.

The company's cash at the end of 2021 was $518 million. Operating activities generated $295.5 million, while investing activities used 1.2 billion, mainly for origination of mortgage warehouse loans. Financing activities generated another $754.8 million.

Strategy

The company's organic growth strategy focuses on, among other things, expanding market share through is "high-tech" model, which includes remote account opening, remote deposit capture, mobile and digital banking. These technological advances are intended to allow the company to generate additional core deposits at a lower cost than generating deposits through opening and operating branch locations.

Company Background

In late 2011 Customers purchased Berkshire Bancorp and picked up five branches in Berks County, Pennsylvania for about $11.3 million.

EXECUTIVES

Chairman, Chief Executive Officer, Subsidiary Officer, Director, Jay S. Sidhu, $680,932 total compensation
Executive Vice President, Chief Administrative Officer, Jennifer L. Frost

Executive Vice President, Chief Financial Officer, Controller, Subsidiary Officer, Carla A. Leibold

Corporate Finance Head, Corporate Finance Subsidiary Officer, Samvir S. Sidhu

Lead Independent Director, Director, Daniel K. Rothermel

Director, Andrea Allon
Director, Robert J. Buford
Director, Rick B. Burkey
Director, T. Lawrence Way
Director, Bernard B. Banks
Director, Robert N. Mackay
Director, Steven J. Zuckerman
Auditors: DELOITTE & TOUCHE LLP

LOCATIONS

HQ: Customers Bancorp Inc
701 Reading Avenue, West Reading, PA 19611
Phone: 610 933-2000
Web: www.customersbank.com

PRODUCTS/OPERATIONS

2015

	$ mil	% of total
Interest income		
Loans receivable, including fees	182.3	66
Loans held for sale	51.6	19
Investment securities	10.4	4
Other	5.6	2
Non interest income		
Mortgage warehouse transnational fees	10.4	4
Bank-owned life insurance	7.0	3
Gains on sales of loans	4.1	1
Deposit fees	0.9	0
Mortgage loan and banking income	0.7	0
Gain (loss) on sale of investment securities	(0.09)	0
Other	4.7	1
Total	277.6	100

Products include
Equipment Loans
Mortgage Warehouse Loans
Multi-Family And Commercial Real Estate Loans
Residential Mortgage Loans
Small Business Loans

COMPETITORS

CENTERSTATE BANK CORPORATION
CENTURY BANCORP, INC.
CITY HOLDING COMPANY
EAGLE BANCORP, INC.
FLAGSTAR BANCORP, INC.
MIDDLESEX SAVINGS BANK
OLD LINE BANCSHARES, INC.
REPUBLIC BANCORP, INC.
REPUBLIC FIRST BANCORP, INC.
WILSHIRE BANCORP, INC.

HISTORICAL FINANCIALS

Company Type: Public

Income Statement — FYE: December 31

	ASSETS ($mil)	NET INCOME ($mil)	INCOME AS % OF ASSETS	EMPLOYEES
12/20	18,439.2	132.5	0.7%	830
12/19	11,520.7	79.3	0.7%	867
12/18	9,833.4	71.6	0.7%	827
12/17	9,839.5	78.8	0.8%	765
12/16	9,382.7	78.7	0.8%	739
Annual Growth	18.4%	13.9%	—	2.9%

2020 Year-End Financials

Return on assets: 0.8%
Return on equity: 12.1%
Long-term debt ($ mil.): —
No. of shares ($ mil.): 31.7
Sales ($ mil.): 645
Dividends Yield: —
Payout: —
Market value ($ mil.): 576.0

	STOCK PRICE ($) FY Close	P/E High	P/E Low	PER SHARE ($) Earnings	Dividends	Book Value
12/20	18.18	6	2	3.74	0.00	35.23
12/19	23.81	12	8	2.05	0.00	33.60
12/18	18.20	18	9	1.78	0.00	30.86
12/17	25.99	17	12	1.97	0.00	29.35
12/16	35.82	15	9	2.31	0.00	28.26
Annual Growth	(15.6%)	—	—	12.8%	—	5.7%

CVB Financial Corp

CVB Financial is the holding company of Citizens Business Bank (CBB), which offers community banking services to primarily small and mid-sized businesses, but also to consumers through nearly 60 banking centers and office locations across central and southern California. Boasting more than $7.82 billion in assets, the bank offers checking, money market, CDs and savings accounts, trust and investment services, and a variety of loans. Commercial real estate loans account for about 75% of the bank's loan portfolio, which is rounded out by business, consumer, and construction loans; residential mortgages; dairy and livestock loans; and municipal lease financing.

Operations

Through its network of banking centers, the bank provides relationship-based banking products, services and solutions, including loans for commercial businesses, commercial real estate, multi-family, construction, land, dairy & livestock and agribusiness, consumer and government-guaranteed small business loans. It also provides business deposit products and treasury cash management services, as well as deposit products to the owners and employees of the businesses it serves.

Overall, the bank makes up some 75% of its total revenue from interest income on loans and leases, with roughly 15% of total revenue coming from interest income on the bank's investment income. About 5% of total revenue comes from service charges on deposit accounts, and less than 5% comes from trust and investment services income.

Geographic Reach

CBB has about 60 banking centers located in the Inland Empire, Los Angeles County, Orange County, San Diego County, Ventura County, Santa Barbara County, and the Central Valley area of California. It also has three trust offices located in Ontario, Newport Beach and Pasadena.

Sales and Marketing

CBB provides services to companies from a variety of industries, including: industrial and manufacturing, dairy and livestock, agriculture, education, nonprofit, entertainment, medical, professional services, title and escrow, government, and property management.

Financial Performance

Net interest income of $414.6 million for 2021 decreased $1.5 million, compared to $416.1 million for 2020. The decrease in earning asset yield was impacted by a change in asset mix with average loan balances declining to 57% of earning assets for 2021, compared to 69% for 2020, as well as lower loan and investment yields.

In 2021, the company had a net income of $212.5 million, a 20% increase from the previous year's net income of $177.2 million.

The company's cash at the end of 2021 was $1.7 billion. Operating activities generated $195.2 million, while investing activities used $1.7 billion, mainly for purchases of investment securities available-for-sale, as well as purchases of investment securities held-to-maturity.

Mergers and Acquisitions

In 2022, CBB, a subsidiary of CVB Financial, completed the acquisition of Suncrest Bank, Visalia, California, had approximately $1.3 billion in total assets, $0.9 billion in gross loans and $1.2 billion in total deposits as of March 31, 2021. Suncrest has seven branch locations and two loan production offices throughout California's Central Valley. The acquisition of Suncrest will deliver important benefits to the bank's combined customers through its increased presence in the Central Valley and expansion into Sacramento, a sizable and important new market for Citizens Business Bank that presents significant growth opportunities going forward.

Company Background

In 2009, CVB Financial, healthier than most California banks, acquired the failed San Joaquin Bank after the FDIC took it over. The deal added five branches banking centers in the Bakersfield area.

EXECUTIVES

Chairman, Director, Raymond Vincent O'Brien
Vice-Chairman, Director, George A. Borba
President, Chief Executive Officer, Subsidiary Officer, Director, David A. Brager, $345,769 total compensation
Executive Vice President, Chief Financial Officer, Subsidiary Officer, E. Allen Nicholson, $324,423 total compensation
Executive Vice President, General Counsel, Subsidiary Officer, Richard H. Wohl
Senior Vice President, Chief Accounting Officer, Francene LaPoint
Subsidiary Officer, David F. Farnsworth, $289,038 total compensation
Subsidiary Officer, David C. Harvey, $345,769 total compensation

Director, Stephen A. Del Guercio
Director, Rodrigo Guerra
Director, Anna Kan
Director, Jane Olvera
Director, Hal W. Oswalt
Auditors: KPMG LLP

LOCATIONS

HQ: CVB Financial Corp
 701 North Haven Ave., Suite 350, Ontario, CA 91764
Phone: 909 980-4030
Web: www.cbbank.com

Selected Branch Locations
Fresno County
Kern County
Los Angeles County
Madera County
Orange County
Riverside County
San Bernardino County
Tulare County

PRODUCTS/OPERATIONS

2014 Sales

	$ mil.	% of total
Interest		
Loans, including fees	181.6	62
Investment securities	68.4	24
Other	2.9	1
Noninterest		
Service charges on deposit accounts	15.8	5
Trust & investment services	8.1	3
Bankcard services	3.4	1
BOLI income	2.4	1
Other	10.3	3
Adjustments	(3.6)	-
Total	289.3	100

COMPETITORS

BANCFIRST CORPORATION
CENTRAL PACIFIC FINANCIAL CORP.
CITY HOLDING COMPANY
EAGLE BANCORP, INC.
FIRST HORIZON CORPORATION
GUARANTY BANCORP
PACWEST BANCORP
PRIVATEBANCORP, INC.
S&T BANCORP, INC.
SIGNATURE BANK

HISTORICAL FINANCIALS

Company Type: Public

Income Statement — FYE: December 31

	ASSETS ($mil)	NET INCOME ($mil)	INCOME AS % OF ASSETS	EMPLOYEES
12/20	14,419.3	177.1	1.2%	1,052
12/19	11,282.4	207.8	1.8%	0
12/18	11,529.1	152.0	1.3%	0
12/17	8,270.5	104.4	1.3%	0
12/16	8,073.7	101.4	1.3%	0
Annual Growth	15.6%	15.0%	—	—

2020 Year-End Financials
Return on assets: 1.3%
Return on equity: 8.8%
Long-term debt ($ mil.): —
No. of shares ($ mil.): 135.6
Sales ($ mil.): 480.2
Dividends
 Yield: 3.6%
 Payout: 55.3%
Market value ($ mil.): 2,644.0

	STOCK PRICE ($) FY Close	P/E High/Low		PER SHARE ($) Earnings	Dividends	Book Value
12/20	19.50	17	12	1.30	0.72	14.81
12/19	21.58	16	14	1.48	0.68	14.23
12/18	20.23	20	15	1.24	0.56	13.22
12/17	23.56	26	21	0.95	0.52	9.70
12/16	22.93	25	15	0.94	0.36	9.15
Annual Growth	(4.0%)	—	—	8.4%	18.9%	12.8%

CW Bancorp

EXECUTIVES

Chairman, President, Chief Executive Officer, Director, Ivo A. Tjan
Executive Vice President, Chief Financial Officer, Secretary, Leeann M. Cochran
Director, Christopher J. Deering
Director, David L. Gaba
Director, Gregory R. Games
Director, Roseanne Luth
Director, Kenneth A. Shelton

LOCATIONS

HQ: CW Bancorp
 2111 Business Center Drive, Irvine, CA 92612
Phone: 949 251-6959 **Fax:** 949 251-6958
Web: www.cwbk.com

HISTORICAL FINANCIALS

Company Type: Public

Income Statement — FYE: December 31

	ASSETS ($mil)	NET INCOME ($mil)	INCOME AS % OF ASSETS	EMPLOYEES
12/20	1,318.8	9.0	0.7%	0
12/19	883.3	8.2	0.9%	60
12/18	798.1	5.9	0.7%	0
12/17	769.3	5.0	0.7%	0
Annual Growth	19.7%	22.0%	—	—

2020 Year-End Financials
Return on assets: 0.8%
Return on equity: 13.4%
Long-term debt ($ mil.): —
No. of shares ($ mil.): 3.5
Sales ($ mil.): 35.1
Dividends
 Yield: 3.9%
 Payout: 32.2%
Market value ($ mil.): 71.0

	STOCK PRICE ($) FY Close	P/E High/Low		PER SHARE ($) Earnings	Dividends	Book Value
12/20	20.10	9	6	2.48	0.80	19.88
12/19	24.00	11	9	2.14	0.68	17.86
12/18	19.95	17	13	1.47	0.68	16.26
12/17	23.00	18	13	1.22	0.68	16.04
Annual Growth	(4.4%)	—	—	26.7%	5.6%	7.4%

CyrusOne Inc

EXECUTIVES

Chairman, Lead Independent Director, Director, Alex Shumate
Interim President, Interim Chief Executive Officer, Director, David H. Ferdman, $360,433 total compensation
Executive Vice President, Chief Financial Officer, Katherine Motlagh
Executive Vice President, Chief Operating Officer, John P. Hatem
Executive Vice President, General Counsel, Secretary, Robert M. Jackson, $344,616 total compensation
Director, John W. Gamble
Director, T. Tod Nielsen
Director, Denise A. Olsen
Director, William E. Sullivan
Director, Lynn A. Wentworth
Director, Michael A. Klayko
Auditors: DELOITTE & TOUCHE LLP

LOCATIONS

HQ: CyrusOne Inc
 2850 N. Harwood Street, Suite 2200, Dallas, TX 75201
Phone: 972 350-0060
Web: www.cyrusone.com

HISTORICAL FINANCIALS

Company Type: Public

Income Statement — FYE: December 31

	REVENUE ($mil)	NET INCOME ($mil)	NET PROFIT MARGIN	EMPLOYEES
12/21	1,205.7	25.3	2.1%	456
12/20	1,033.5	41.4	4.0%	441
12/19	981.3	41.4	4.2%	452
12/18	821.4	1.2	0.1%	448
12/17	672.0	(83.5)	—	416
Annual Growth	15.7%	—	—	2.3%

2021 Year-End Financials
Debt ratio: 46.9%
Return on equity: 0.9%
Cash ($ mil.): 346.3
Current Ratio: 1.15
Long-term debt ($ mil.): 3,492.9
No. of shares ($ mil.): 129.5
Dividends
 Yield: 2.2%
 Payout: 490.4%
Market value ($ mil.): 11,624.0

	STOCK PRICE ($) FY Close	P/E High/Low		PER SHARE ($) Earnings	Dividends	Book Value
12/21	89.72	451	311	0.20	2.06	22.57
12/20	73.15	247	129	0.35	2.02	21.24
12/19	65.43	220	138	0.36	1.92	21.21
12/18	52.88	—	—	0.00	1.84	20.55
12/17	59.53	—	—	(0.95)	1.68	17.83
Annual Growth	10.8%	—	—	—	5.2%	6.1%

Dart Financial Corp

Auditors: Doeren Mayhew

LOCATIONS

HQ: Dart Financial Corp
 368 S. Park Street, Mason, MI 48854
Phone: 517 676-3661
Web: www.dartbank.com

HISTORICAL FINANCIALS

Company Type: Public

Income Statement — FYE: December 31

	REVENUE ($mil)	NET INCOME ($mil)	NET PROFIT MARGIN	EMPLOYEES
12/20	59.7	9.8	16.4%	0
12/19	37.1	3.1	8.5%	0
12/18	31.4	3.7	12.0%	0
12/17	28.8	3.5	12.4%	0
12/16	26.4	2.8	10.8%	0
Annual Growth	22.6%	36.1%	—	—

2020 Year-End Financials

Debt ratio: 10.9%
Return on equity: 21.5%
Cash ($ mil.): 29.3
Current Ratio: 0.07
Long-term debt ($ mil.): 67.4
No. of shares ($ mil.): 1.1
Dividends
Yield: —
Payout: 14.6%
Market value ($ mil.): 0.0

Davey Tree Expert Co. (The)

The Davey Tree Expert Company's roots extend back to 1880 and provides a wide range of arboricultural, horticultural services, environmental and consulting firm, which branched into residential, commercial, utility, and other natural resource management services. With offices in the US and Canada, Davey's services include treatment, preservation, maintenance, and removal of trees, shrubs, and other plants; landscaping; grounds maintenance; tree surgery; tree feeding and tree spraying; the application of fertilizers, herbicides, and insecticides. It also natural resource management and consulting, forestry research and development, and environmental planning. Davey has been employee-owned since 1979. The US generates some 95% of Davey's total revenue.

Operations

Davey operates through two main segments: Utility Services, and Residential & Commercial Services. Other services include natural resource management and consulting, forestry research, and technical support.

The Utility segment accounts around 55% of revenue, provide services to its utility customers--investor-owned, municipal utilities, and rural electric cooperatives--including: the practice of line-clearing and vegetation management around power lines, rights-of-way and chemical brush control; and natural resource management and consulting, forestry research and development and environmental planning.

The Residential and Commercial segment generates about 45% of company's total revenue. The segment provides services to residential and commercial customers including: the treatment, preservation, maintenance, removal and planting of trees, shrubs and other plant life; the practice of landscaping, grounds maintenance, tree surgery, tree feeding and tree spraying; the application of fertilizer, herbicides and insecticides; and natural resource management and consulting, forestry research and development, and environmental planning.

Overall, tree and plant care products generated about 65% of sales, followed by consulting and other with roughly 25%, and the rest were generated from grounds maintenance and storm damage services.

Geographic Reach

The company corporate headquarters campus is located in Kent, Ohio together with The Davey Institute's research, technical support and laboratory diagnostic facilities.

Davey has administrative functions in Livermore, California (Utility Services). Their Canadian operations' administrative functions are located in the provinces of Ontario and British Columbia. The company has also about 215 properties in roughly 35 states and five provinces.

About 95% of Davey's total revenue were generated from US operations.

Sales and Marketing

Davey gets business from residential customers principally through referrals, direct mail programs, and through the placement of advertisements in national magazines, trade journals, local newspapers, and telephone directories. Davey also employs online marketing and lead generation strategies, including email marketing campaigns, search engine optimization, search engine marketing, and social media communication. Business from utility and commercial customers is obtained principally through negotiated contracts and competitive bidding. The company carries out all of its sales and services through its employees.

Pacific Gas and Electric accounts for about 15% of sales, the company's largest customer.

Financial Performance

Revenues of $1.4 billion increased $90.5 million compared with the $1.3 billion reported in 2020. The increase was primarily attributable to additional revenues from increased work year-over-year on existing accounts, rate increases and new accounts.

In 2021, the company had a net income of $65.7 million, an 8% increase from the previous year's net income of $60.9 million.

The company's cash at the end of 2021 was $19.5 million. Operating activities generated $76 million, while investing activities used $87.2 million, mainly for capital expenditures. Financing activities provided another $14.4 million.

Strategy

The company solicits business from residential customers principally through referrals, direct mail programs and to a lesser extent through the placement of advertisements in national magazines and trade journals, local newspapers and telephone directories. It also employs online marketing and lead generation strategies, including email marketing campaigns, search engine optimization, search engine marketing, and social media communication. Business from utility and commercial customers is obtained principally through negotiated contracts and competitive bidding. The company carries out all of its sales and services through employees. The company generally does not use agents, and does not franchise its name or business.

Mergers and Acquisitions

In mid-2022, The Davey Tree Expert Company is pleased to announce the addition of ClearWater Services of Nashville, Tennessee, to its family of brands. ClearWater provides installation and maintenance of residential and commercial irrigation systems and landscape lighting to customers in Nashville and the surrounding area. Joining Davey Tree will give ClearWater and its clients the advantage of Davey's additional service offerings, extensive knowledge of the industry and added support from the Davey team. Terms were not disclosed.

Also in mid-2022, Davey Resource Group, Inc., (DRG) a subsidiary of The Davey Tree Expert Company announced the addition of BDY Environmental of Nashville, Tennessee. DY has provided wetland, stream delineations and permitting; wetland and stream restoration and mitigation services; surface and groundwater consulting; National Environmental Policy Act (NEPA) services; endangered species surveys and consultation; and comprehensive groundwater assessment and remedial site services. Terms were not disclosed.

In 2022, The Davey Tree Expert Company announce the addition of Floral City Tree Service of Monroe, Michigan, to its family of brands. Floral City provides residential and commercial tree and plant health care services in Monroe, Michigan, located between Detroit, Michigan, and Toledo, Ohio. Terms were not disclosed.

In late 2021, Davey Tree Expert Co. of Canada, Limited, a subsidiary, announced the addition of Antler Services Inc., of Brantford, Ontario, to its family of brands. Antler Services Inc. has provided comprehensive landscape, lawn care, snow removal, equipment maintenance, and pest control services. The addition of Antler is Davey Canada's entry into the Commercial Landscape Services (CLS) sector. The company will initially service Brantford and the surrounding areas, but it plans to expand its service area in the future. Terms were not disclosed.

EXECUTIVES

Chairman, Director, Karl J. Warnke, $427,269 total compensation

Operations President, Operations Chief Executive Officer, Director, Patrick M. Covey, $578,692 total compensation

Executive Vice President, Subsidiary Officer, James E. Doyle
Executive Vice President, Division Officer, Dan A. Joy, $255,281 total compensation
Executive Vice President, Chief Financial Officer, Secretary, Joseph R. Paul, $338,362 total compensation
Vice President, Division Officer, Mark J. Vaughn
Vice President, Controller, Thea R. Sears
Vice President, Treasurer, Christopher J. Bast
General Counsel, Vice President, Assistant Secretary, Erika J. Schoenberger
Region Officer, Division Officer, Brent R. Repenning, $244,750 total compensation
Region Officer, Joseph E. Day
Subsidiary Officer, Gregory M. Ina
Subsidiary Officer, Lawrence S. Abernathy
Director, Thomas A. Haught
Director, Donald C. Brown
Director, William J. Ginn
Director, Douglas K. Hall
Director, Alejandra Evans
Director, Charles D. Stapleton
Director, Catherine M. Kilbane
Auditors : DELOITTE & TOUCHE LLP

LOCATIONS

HQ: Davey Tree Expert Co. (The)
1500 North Mantua Street, P.O. Box 5193, Kent, OH 44240
Phone: 330 673-9511
Web: www.davey.com

2016 Sales

	$ mil.	% of total
US	775.9	92
Canada	69.8	8
Total	845.7	100

PRODUCTS/OPERATIONS

2016 Sales

	$ mil.	% of total
Utility Services	433.4	51
Residential & Commercial Services	410.9	49
Other	1.4	0
Total	845.7	100

Selected Mergers and AcquisitionsSelected Tree Care Services
Cabling and bracing
Hazardous tree assessment
Insect and disease management
Large tree moving
Lightning protection
Root collar excavation
Removals and stump grinding
Shrub pruning
Tree cavity treatment
Tree pruning
Tree and shrub fertilization
Tree and shrub planting

COMPETITORS

ARBOR TREE SURGERY
ASPLUNDH TREE EXPERT, LLC
BEAUTIFUL CHINA HOLDINGS COMPANY LIMITED
COSTAIN GROUP PLC
ENVIRONMENTAL RESOURCES MANAGEMENT LIMITED
FURMANITE, LLC
LEWIS TREE SERVICE INC.
RENTOKIL INITIAL PLC
Stantec Inc
TRC COMPANIES, INC.

HISTORICAL FINANCIALS

Company Type: Public

Income Statement — FYE: December 31

	REVENUE ($mil)	NET INCOME ($mil)	NET PROFIT MARGIN	EMPLOYEES
12/20	1,287.5	60.9	4.7%	9,600
12/19	1,143.7	40.7	3.6%	9,700
12/18	1,024.7	27.9	2.7%	8,900
12/17	915.9	22.1	2.4%	8,200
12/16	845.6	22.2	2.6%	8,000
Annual Growth	11.1%	28.6%	—	4.7%

2020 Year-End Financials

Debt ratio: 16.1%
Return on equity: 28.9%
Cash ($ mil.): 16.2
Current Ratio: 1.39
Long-term debt ($ mil.): 83.5
No. of shares ($ mil.): 45.6
Dividends
 Yield:
 Payout: 3.7%
Market value ($ mil.): 0.0

Deckers Outdoor Corp.

Deckers Outdoor is a global leader in designing, marketing, and distributing innovative footwear, apparel, and accessories developed for both everyday casual lifestyle use and high-performance activities. It designs and markets the iconic UGG brand of luxury sheepskin footwear in addition to Teva sports sandals ? a cross between a hiking boot and a flip-flop used for walking, hiking, and rafting, among other pursuits. Other product lines include Sanuk, HOKA UGGpure, and Koolaburra. Deckers Outdoor, which generates most of its revenue in the US, sells its footwear through about 150 retail stores worldwide, independent distributors, and e-commerce sites such as Amazon.com, Zappos.com, and Zalando.com.

Operations

Deckers Outdoor's six reportable operating segments include the worldwide wholesale operations of the UGG brand, HOKA brand, Teva brand, Sanuk brand, and Other brands, as well as DTC.

The UGG brand, accounts for approximately 35% of the company's revenue, is one of the most iconic and recognized brands in the industry, which highlights the company's successful track record of building niche brands into lifestyle and fashion market leaders.

Deckers Outdoor's six reportable operating segments include the worldwide wholesale operations of the UGG brand, HOKA brand, Teva brand, Sanuk brand, and Other brands, as well as DTC. The UGG brand, accounts for approximately 35% of the company's revenue, is one of the most iconic and recognized brands in the industry, which highlights the company's successful track record of building niche brands into lifestyle and fashion market leaders.

On the other hand, the Teva brand has grown into a multi-category modern outdoor lifestyle brand offering a range of performance, casual, and trail lifestyle products, and has emerged as a leader in footwear sustainability observed through recent growth fueled by young and diverse consumers passionate for the outdoors and the planet. The Sanuk brand originated in Southern California surf culture and has emerged into a lifestyle brand with a presence in the relaxed casual shoe and sandal categories with a focus on innovation in comfort and sustainability. The segments provide approximately 5% of the company's revenue.

In addition, Direct-to-Consumer and other brands wholesale represent the remaining sales. Other brands consist primarily of the Koolaburra by UGG brand, while the company's DTC business for all its brands is comprised of retail stores and e-commerce websites which, in an omni-channel marketplace, are intertwined and interdependent.

Geographic Reach

California-based Deckers Outdoor boasts a global presence with operations in the US, Canada, Australia, Vietnam, Japan, the Netherlands, France, Switzerland, China, as well as Europe. However, it is a lot more dependent on the US, which accounts for about 70% of sales, than many of its competitors.

Sales and Marketing

Deckers Outdoor sells its products through a strong network of domestic and international retailers and international distributors as well as directly to consumers worldwide. It also uses approximately 75 retail concept stores, and nearly 75 retail outlet stores to get its products in consumers' hands. The company also has an operated e-commerce business through its company-owned websites and mobile platforms.

The company advertise its business through media advertising such as television, radio, print, social, digital, as well as tactical advertising which includes signs, banners and point-of-sale materials.

Customers have included such big names as Nordstrom, Dillard's, Zappos.com, REI, Dick's Sporting Goods, Macy's, and DSW, among others. The company's 10 largest customers account for more than 25% of total sales.

The company's wholesale channel accounts for nearly 60% of the company's revenue, while direct-to-consumer represents about 40%.

The company's advertising expenses were approximately $255,881, $188,345, and $144,948 for the years ended 2022, 2021, and 2020, respectively.

Financial Performance

The company's revenue in 2021 increased by 24% to $3.2 billion compared to $2.5 billion in the prior. Total revenue increased primarily due to higher HOKA, UGG, and Teva brand sales across all channels, despite impacts from supply chain constraints, including extended transit lead times. Further, the company experienced an increase of 22.2% in total volume of pairs sold to 51,200 from 41,900 compared to the prior period.

Net income in 2021 increased to $443.7 million compared to $391.4 million in the prior year. The increase in net income, compared to the prior period, was due to higher net sales, partially offset by lower gross margin.

Cash held by the company at the end of 2021 decreased to $843.5 million. Cash provided by operations was $172.4 million while cash used for investing and financing activities were $61.0 million and $367.5 million, respectively. Main cash uses were purchases of property and equipment; and repurchases of common stock.

Strategy

Deckers Outdoor remains focused on accelerating consumer adoption of the HOKA brand globally to execute its long-term growth strategy, including through an optimized digital marketing strategy. The HOKA brand's growth has been balanced across its ecosystem of access points, with all geographic regions and distribution channels experiencing significant year-round growth, which has positively impacted its seasonality trends. In its next fiscal year, the company intends to focus its efforts to drive HOKA brand performance on distribution management to drive new consumer acquisitions in key markets and launch innovative product offerings to increase category adoption and market share gains with existing consumers. For example, Deckers Outdoors is looking at volume expansion with new and existing global strategic wholesale partners to drive new consumer acquisition. Further, the company recently opened the HOKA brand's first owned and operated retail stores in Asia and launched pop-up stores in North America to build upon its retail strategy and define the optimal consumer experience and concept for the HOKA brand. The company plans to open additional retail stores for the HOKA brand and to continue exploring opportunities to strategically expand its HOKA brand retail store fleet.

Company Background

Douglas Otto and his former partner, Karl Lopker, founded Styled Steers in 1973. But the small, obscure maker of leather sandals gained prominence with a line of multicolored rubber sandals. Surfers in Hawaii called them "deckers," and the company soon adopted the name. In 1985 Deckers Outdoor licensed Teva from river guide Mark Thatcher, who invented the Teva strapping system for rafters to ensure sandals remained attached in turbulent waters. Teva sport sandals became a popular form of casual footwear, largely through word of mouth.

A continuing rise in UGG sales has extended debates over whether the name is generic or a trademark that could possibly be defended over international boundaries. Australian makers of the sheepskin boots, traditionally called uggs, contend that the name is generic, akin to trying to protect the name "sneaker" as a trademark.

EXECUTIVES

Chairman, Director, Michael F. Devine
President, Chief Executive Officer, Director, David Powers, $1,100,000 total compensation
Planning Chief Financial Officer, Investor Relations Chief Financial Officer, Corporate Strategy Chief Financial Officer, Steven J. Fasching, $600,000 total compensation
Chief Administrative Officer, Thomas Garcia
Chief Supply Chain Officer, Angela Ogbechie
Division Officer, Wendy W. Yang
Division Officer, Stefano Caroti, $650,000 total compensation
Director, Maha Ibrahim
Director, Nelson C. Chan
Director, Cynthia L. Davis
Director, Juan R. Figuereo
Director, Victor Luis
Director, Lauri M. Shanahan
Director, Bonita C. Stewart
Director, David A. Burwick
Auditors : KPMG LLP

LOCATIONS

HQ: Deckers Outdoor Corp.
250 Coromar Drive, Goleta, CA 93117
Phone: 805 967-7611
Web: www.deckers.com

2019 Sales

	$ mil.	% of total
US	1,278.3	63
International	742.1	37
Total	2,020.4	100

PRODUCTS/OPERATIONS

2019 Sales

	$ mil.	% of total
Wholesale		
UGG brand	888.3	44
HOKA brand	185.1	9
Teva brand	119.4	6
Sanuk brand	69.8	4
Other brands	42.8	2
Direct-to-Consumer		
UGG brand	644.5	32
HOKA brand	38.1	2
Teva brand	18.0	1
Sanuk brand	12.8	-
Other brands	1.6	-
Total	2,020.4	100

COMPETITORS

APP WINDDOWN, LLC
COHEN & WILKS INTERNATIONAL LIMITED
DICK'S SPORTING GOODS, INC.
EMILIO PUCCI SRL
NIKE, INC.
SCHUH LIMITED
SELFRIDGES RETAIL LIMITED
SKECHERS U.S.A., INC.
SUPERIOR GROUP OF COMPANIES, INC.
SWANK, INC.

HISTORICAL FINANCIALS

Company Type: Public

Income Statement FYE: March 31

	REVENUE ($mil)	NET INCOME ($mil)	NET PROFIT MARGIN	EMPLOYEES
03/21	2,545.6	382.5	15.0%	3,400
03/20	2,132.6	276.1	12.9%	3,600
03/19	2,020.4	264.3	13.1%	3,500
03/18	1,903.3	114.3	6.0%	3,500
03/17	1,790.1	5.7	0.3%	3,300
Annual Growth	9.2%	186.1%	—	0.7%

2021 Year-End Financials

Debt ratio: —   No. of shares ($ mil.): 27.9
Return on equity: 29.6%   Dividends
Cash ($ mil.): 1,089.3   Yield: —
Current Ratio: 3.52   Payout: —
Long-term debt ($ mil.): —   Market value ($ mil.): 9,222.0

	STOCK PRICE ($) FY Close	P/E High/Low		PER SHARE ($) Earnings	Dividends	Book Value
03/21	330.42	25	9	13.47	0.00	51.75
03/20	134.00	21	9	9.62	0.00	40.72
03/19	146.99	17	10	8.84	0.00	35.86
03/18	90.03	27	15	3.58	0.00	30.90
03/17	59.73	381	250	0.18	0.00	29.83
Annual Growth	53.4%	—	—	194.1%	—	14.8%

DexCom Inc

DexCom is a medical device company that develops and markets continuous glucose monitoring, or CGM, systems for the management of diabetes by patients, caregivers, and clinicians around the world. It develops and manufactures continuous glucose monitoring systems such as its G7, features are 60% reduction in size of the on-body wearable, fully disposable and reduced packaging. DexCom launched its latest generation system, the Dexcom G6 integrated Continuous Glucose Monitoring System, or G6, in 2018. DexCom's products are marketed to physicians, endocrinologists, and diabetes educators in the US and selected international markets. The company's largest geographic market is the US.

Operations

DexCom is working with partners to develop combined glucose monitoring and insulin delivery systems. Among these partners are Eli Lilly, Insulet, Novo Nordisk, Tandem Diabetes and The Ypsomed Group.

Geographic Reach

Although the majority of DexCom's revenue has been generated in the US, the company expanded its operations to include certain countries in Africa, Asia, Europe, Latin America, and the Middle East, as well as Australia, Canada, and New Zealand.

DexCom's corporate headquarters is located in San Diego, California.

Sales and Marketing

DexCom has its own sales force that targets endocrinologists, doctors, and diabetes educators in the US, Canada, and some parts of Europe. DexCom also uses third-party distributors.

Broadly speaking, revenue by sales channel, Distributor accounts for about 85%, and Direct accounts for around 15%.

Advertising expenses were approximately $126.4 million, $76.5 million, and $31.8 million for the years 2021, 2020, and 2019, respectively.

Financial Performance

The company had a revenue of $2.4 billion in 2021, a 27% increase from the previous year's revenue of $1.3 billion. This was primarily due to a higher sales volume from the company's distributor sales channel.

In 2021, the company had a net income of $154.7 million, a 69% decrease from the previous year's net income of $493.6 million. This was primarily due to a higher selling, general and administrative expenses for the year.

The company's cash at the end of 2021 was $1.1 billion. Operating activities generated $442.5 million, while investing activities used $216.1 million, mainly for purchase of marketable securities. Financing activities provided another $10.4 million.

Strategy

DexCom's objective is to remain a leading provider of CGM systems and related products to enable people with diabetes to more effectively and conveniently manage their disease. It is also developing and commercializing products that integrate its CGM technologies into the insulin delivery systems or data platforms of its respective partners. Also, it continues to pursue development partnerships with other insulin delivery companies, including automated insulin delivery systems.

To achieve these objectives, it is focusing on the following business strategies: Establishing and maintaining its technology platform as the leading approach to CGM and leveraging its development expertise to rapidly bring products to market, including for expanded indications; Driving the adoption of its ambulatory products through a direct sales and marketing effort, as well as key distribution arrangements; Driving additional adoption through technology integration partnerships such as its current partnerships with Eli Lilly, Insulet, Novo Nordisk, Tandem Diabetes and others; Seeking broad coverage policies and reimbursement for its products from private third-party payors and national health systems; Driving increased utilization and adoption of its products through a cloud-based data repository platform that enables people with diabetes to aggregate and analyze data from numerous diabetes devices and share the data with their healthcare providers and other individuals involved in their diabetes management and care; Expanding the use of its products to other patient care settings and patient demographics, including use in the hospital setting, people with Type 2 diabetes and people who are pregnant; Providing a high level of customer support, service and education; and Pursuing the highest safety and quality levels for its products.

Company Background

Dexcom was founded based on the groundbreaking research of Dr. Stuart J. Updike and George P. Hicks in 1967? implantable, long-performing glucose sensors that the body would not reject. Dr. Updike joined Dexcom that year to continue CGM innovation. In 2004, Short-term sensor program was created.

EXECUTIVES

Regulatory Affairs Executive Vice President, Global Business Services, IT, Quality Executive Vice President, Donald M. Abbey, $199,641 total compensation
Regulatory Strategy, Clinical Affairs, and Strategic Partnership Development Executive Vice President, Andrew K. Balo, $365,959 total compensation
Executive Vice President, Chief Legal Officer, Patrick M. Murphy
Corporate Development Division Officer, Corporate Affairs Division Officer, Strategy Division Officer, Steven R. Pacelli, $365,959 total compensation
Global Marketing Executive Vice President, Chad M. Patterson
Global Operations Executive Vice President, Barry J. Regan
Information Technology Senior Vice President, Shelly R. Selvaraj
Senior Vice President, Chief Risk Officer, Sumi Shrishrimal
Executive Vice President, Chief Human Resources Officer, Sadie M. Stern
Finance Chief Financial Officer, Finance Chief Accounting Officer, Jereme Sylvain
Division Officer, Paul Flynn
Lead Independent Director, Director, Mark G. Foletta
Director, Nicholas Augustinos
Director, Bridgette P. Heller
Director, Steven R. Altman
Director, Barbara E. Kahn
Director, Kyle Malady
Director, Jay S. Skyler
Director, Richard A. Collins
Director, Karen M. Dahut
Director, Eric J. Topol
Auditors : Ernst & Young LLP

LOCATIONS

HQ: DexCom Inc
6340 Sequence Drive, San Diego, CA 92121
Phone: 858 200-0200
Web: www.dexcom.com

2017 Sales

	$ mil.	% of total
US	596.2	83
Other	122.3	17
Total	718.5	100

COMPETITORS

ACCURAY INCORPORATED
DELTEX MEDICAL GROUP PLC
GENMARK DIAGNOSTICS, INC.
HAEMONETICS CORPORATION
IMMUCOR, INC.
INSULET CORPORATION
MASIMO CORPORATION
MGC DIAGNOSTICS CORPORATION
NUVASIVE, INC.
TANDEM DIABETES CARE, INC.

HISTORICAL FINANCIALS

Company Type: Public

Income Statement — FYE: December 31

	REVENUE ($mil)	NET INCOME ($mil)	NET PROFIT MARGIN	EMPLOYEES
12/21	2,448.5	154.7	6.3%	7,000
12/20	1,926.7	493.6	25.6%	6,400
12/19	1,476.0	101.1	6.8%	5,200
12/18	1,031.6	(127.1)	—	3,900
12/17	718.5	(50.2)	—	2,990
Annual Growth	35.9%	—	—	23.7%

2021 Year-End Financials

Debt ratio: 36.2%
Return on equity: 7.5%
Cash ($ mil.): 1,052.6
Current Ratio: 5.11
Long-term debt ($ mil.): 1,759.7
No. of shares ($ mil.): 97.0
Dividends
Yield: —
Payout: —
Market value ($ mil.): 52,084.0

	STOCK PRICE ($) FY Close	P/E High/Low		PER SHARE ($) Earnings	Dividends	Book Value
12/21	536.95	407	202	1.55	0.00	23.21
12/20	369.72	86	37	5.06	0.00	19.01
12/19	218.74	206	100	1.10	0.00	9.64
12/18	119.80	—	—	(1.44)	0.00	7.37
12/17	57.39	—	—	(0.58)	0.00	4.82
Annual Growth	74.9%	—	—	—	—	48.1%

Digi International Inc

Digi International is a global provider of business and mission-critical Internet of Things (IoT) connectivity products, services and solutions. The IoT Products & Services segment provides its customers with a device management platform and other professional services to enable customers to capture and manage data from devices they connect to networks. Digi serves over 81,000 customer including industries such as food service, retail, healthcare (primarily pharmacies) and supply chain. The company sells directly and through resellers and distributors. About 75% of company's total revenue comes from North America.

Operations

Digi International operates in two reportable segments: IoT Products & Services segment (about 85%); and IoT Solutions segment (some 15%).

IoT Products & Services segment offers hardware products such as cellular routers and gateways, cellular remote management, radio frequency, embedded, and network. Its services include Digi Remote Manager (centralized remote device management solution), Lighthouse Management Software (recurring revenue cloud-based service), and Technical Services (professional services, data plan subscriptions and enhanced technical support offers to customers).

The IoT Solutions segment offers wireless temperature and other condition-based monitoring services as well as employee task management services. These solutions are focused on the following vertical markets: food service, retail, healthcare (primarily pharmacies), transportation/logistics and education. These solutions are marketed as SmartSense by Digi.

Geographic Reach

Digi International gets nearly 75% of its sales in North America. The Europe, Middle East, and Africa region accounts for about 15% while other countries accounts for the rest.

Based in Hopkins, Minnesota, Digi International has locations in Massachusetts, Florida, Utah, New Jersey and Indiana. Internationally, it has facilities in Australia and Germany.

Sales and Marketing

The company sells through distributors, value-added resellers, and systems integrators, as well as directly to original equipment manufacturers (OEMs). Digi's marketing strategy has seen it place increasing emphasis on distribution channel sales, which account for more than 35% of sales. Large enterprise customers and other end user customers which accounted nearly 55% total revenue. Its largest distributors include Arrow Electronics, Avnet, Bressner Technology GmbH, Digi-Key, Express Systems & Peripherals, Ingram Micro, Mouser Electronics, Solid State Supplies, Symmetry Electronics, Synnex, Tech Data, Tokyo Electron Device and Venco ElectrÃ³nica SA. Digi International also has strategic alliances with several corporations, including Bell Mobility, NXP, Orange, Rogers, Silicon Laboratories and AT&T.

Financial Performance

The company's revenue for fiscal 2021 increased by 11% to $308.6 million compared from the prior year's $279.3 million.

Net income for fiscal 2021 increased to $10.4 million compared from the prior year with $8.4 million.

Cash held by the company at the end of fiscal 2021 increased to $152.4 million. Cash provided by operations and financing activities were $57.7 million and $62.2 million, respectively. Cash used for investing activities was $21.4 million, mainly for acquisition of businesses.

Strategy

The company remains focused on taking steps that it believes will deliver consistent, long-term growth with higher levels of profitability. Over the last six years, acquisitions have helped significantly advance its strategy for growth and profitability, in both business segments. Over time Digi International expects to continue to be active in making further acquisitions.

Mergers and Acquisitions

In late 2021, Digi International has acquired Connecticut-based Ventus Holdings, a leader in Managed Network-as-a-Service (MNaaS) solutions that simplify the complexity of enterprise wide area network (WAN) connectivity. The acquisition will enable the company to provide software and subscription service plans along with its award-winning hardware, thereby strengthening its position as a supplier of complete, high-value networking solutions. Digi acquired Ventus for $347.4 million in cash.

In 2021, Digi International has acquired Ctek, Inc., a company specializing in solutions for remote monitoring and industrial controls. Terms of the transaction were not immediately disclosed. Through the acquisition of Ctek, Digi is uniquelypositioned to provide customers with both battery and hardwired options for the control and monitoring of critical infrastructure, from complex off-shore oil rig locations to localized deployments such as municipal park lighting. In addition, Ctek's offering and existing client portfolio is set to further Digi's reach in a rapidly expanding market.

Also, in 2021, Digi International has acquired Dallas-based Haxiot, an industry leader in end-to-end LoRaWAN-based solutions. Terms of the acquisition were not immediately disclosed. Haxiot is a leading provider of low power wide area (LPWA) wireless technology and has an extensive LoRaWAN product portfolio that includes high performance client modules, intelligent industrial devices, gateways and the highly scalable X-ON cloud IoT platform. The acquisition of Haxiot significantly enhances Digi's embedded systems portfolio and immediately extends the company's market reach with a complete LoRaWAN offering including embedded modules, gateways, network server solution, and SaaS offering.

HISTORY

John Schinas was working for a computer company that stopped making digital circuit boards in 1985. He quit that year, mortgaged his home, bought the company's inventory, and started selling under the name DigiBoard. The enterprise became Digi International and went public in 1989. Digi's quality engineering and strong network of distributors fostered growth.

Digi began buying companies in 1991 with the purchase of competitor Arnet. It expanded into the LAN market, buying connectivity device maker MiLAN in 1993. In 1995 Digi bought LAN Access and began developing network and remote-access products. But the acquisitions resulted in drastically lower earnings and a management shakeup in 1996. The following year CEO Ervin Kamm was replaced by consultant Jerry Dusa. Shareholders filed suit against Digi, alleging it misrepresented the financial results of a soured investment in development-stage company AetherWorks.

Losses in 1997 caused the company to take a restructuring charge, consolidate operations, reduce its workforce by 33%, and write off its remaining AetherWorks stake. Digi pursued the growing Internet telephony market with the 1998 purchase of ITK International. Losses resulted that year, leading to Dusa's resignation in 1999. Later in 1999 former Lucent executive Joseph Dunsmore was named CEO.

In 2000 the company exited the Internet telephony market when it wrote off its NetBlazer line. That year the company also restructured its European operations, moving all product development and manufacturing to its US facilities. The following year Digi cut about 13% of its workforce.

In 2002 the company acquired networking equipment maker NetSilicon for about $55 million. Digi sold its MiLAN subsidiary, which made local-area networking devices, to Communications Systems for $8.5 million. In 2003 Digi repurchased all shares held in the company by Sorrento Networks. Sorrento received the shares through its equity ownership in NetSilicon.

The company grew its embedded product line when it acquired Rabbit Semiconductor, a supplier of microprocessors, MPU modules, and single-board computers, for $49 million in cash in 2005. Such products were used in building security, point of sale, parking systems, telecommunications, vehicle and ship systems, and container tracking. In addition to acquiring Rabbit Semi, Digi also bought FS Forth-Systeme and Sistemas Embebidos from Embedded Solutions AG, adding to its portfolio of modules and software for the embedded networking market.

Digi purchased MaxStream, a developer of radio-frequency (RF) modules and modems used in wireless networking, in 2006.

In 2008 the company acquired Sarian Systems, a UK-based developer of IP routers and other networking equipment, for about $31 million. Sarian primarily markets to customers in the finance, lottery, remote access, retail, and telemetry markets.

Digi purchased wireless development services provider Spectrum Design Solutions in 2008. In 2009 it bought MobiApps, an Indian developer of machine-to-machine (M2M) technology, including mixed-signal ASICs. The acquisition moved Digi into the satellite communications market and increased its presence in India and Singapore.

The global recession dampened sales and profitability in fiscal 2009. Digi reacted by restructuring operations, closing two facilities in California and reducing its workforce by about 13%. The company added more than 60 employees with the acquisition of MobiApps following the restructuring.

Internationally, the company discontinued manufacturing at its Breisach, Germany, facility and consolidated the facility's operations into its Minnesota location.

The company moved into the cloud with the 2009 introduction of iDigi, an M2M (machine-to-machine) cloud-based Internet platform for monitoring and controlling electronic devices.

EXECUTIVES

President, Chief Executive Officer, Director, Ronald E. Konezny, $465,000 total compensation

Executive Vice President, Chief Financial Officer, Treasurer, James J. Loch

Corporate Development Executive Vice President, Corporate Development Corporate Secretary, Corporate Development General Counsel, David H. Sampsell, $270,000 total compensation

Senior Vice President, Chief Information Officer, Radha R. Chavali

Supply Chain Management Senior Vice President, Terrence G. Schneider

Non-Executive Chairman, Director, Satbir Khanuja

Director, Christopher D. Heim

Director, Sally J. Smith

Director, Spiro C. Lazarakis

Director, Hatem H. Naguib

Auditors : Grant Thornton LLP

LOCATIONS

HQ: Digi International Inc
9350 Excelsior Blvd., Suite 700, Hopkins, MN 55343
Phone: 952 912-3444
Web: www.digi.com

2015 Sales

	$ mil.	% of total
North America	136.6	64
Europe, Middle East, & Africa	47.5	22
Asia	23.0	11
Latin America	5.8	3
Total	212.9	100

PRODUCTS/OPERATIONS

2015 Sales

	$ mil.	% of total
Cellular routers and gateways	58.7	50
RF	34.4	16
Embedded	51.1	24
Network	51.3	24
Service	17.4	8
Total	212.9	100

2015 Sales

	$ mil.	% of total
Growth hardware products and all services	133.6	63
Mature hardware products	79.3	37
Total	212.9	100

2015 Sales

	$ mil.	% of total
Hardware products	195.5	92
Service	17.4	8
Total	212.9	100

Selected Products

Non-embedded
    Cameras and sensors
    Cellular routers
    Console servers
    Gateways
    Network management software
    Remote display products
    Serial cards
    Serial servers
    USB connected products
    Wireless communications adapters
Embedded
    Chips
    Modules
    Network interface cards
    Single-board computers
    Software and development tools
    Wireless solutions

COMPETITORS

ADTRAN, INC.
ARISTA NETWORKS, INC.
BLACK BOX CORPORATION
BROCADE COMMUNICATIONS SYSTEMS LLC
CISCO SYSTEMS, INC.
LANTRONIX, INC.
NETWORK EQUIPMENT TECHNOLOGIES, INC.
RADISYS CORPORATION
SCANSOURCE, INC.
ZEBRA TECHNOLOGIES CORPORATION

HISTORICAL FINANCIALS

Company Type: Public

Income Statement
FYE: September 30

	REVENUE ($mil)	NET INCOME ($mil)	NET PROFIT MARGIN	EMPLOYEES
09/21	308.6	10.3	3.4%	659
09/20	279.2	8.4	3.0%	656
09/19	254.2	9.9	3.9%	543
09/18	228.3	1.3	0.6%	516
09/17	181.6	9.3	5.2%	514
Annual Growth	14.2%	2.6%	—	6.4%

2021 Year-End Financials

Debt ratio: 7.4%
Return on equity: 2.4%
Cash ($ mil.): 152.4
Current Ratio: 4.18
Long-term debt ($ mil.): 45.7
No. of shares ($ mil.): 34.2
Dividends
  Yield: —
  Payout: —
Market value ($ mil.): 720.0

Stock History

	STOCK PRICE ($) FY Close	P/E High/Low		PER SHARE ($) Earnings	Dividends	Book Value
09/21	21.02	79	46	0.31	0.00	13.79
09/20	15.63	64	22	0.28	0.00	12.74
09/19	13.62	40	26	0.35	0.00	12.36
09/18	13.45	282	189	0.05	0.00	12.04
09/17	10.60	40	25	0.35	0.00	12.01
Annual Growth	18.7%	—	—	(3.0%)	—	3.5%

Digital Realty Trust Inc

One of the largest publicly traded Real Estate Investment Trust (REIT), Digital Realty Trust owns or leases more than 285 data center and technology properties with around 45.5 million sq. ft. of rentable space. Active in around 50 metropolitan areas across some two dozen countries on six continents, the company provides data center, colocation, and interconnection services for tenants in fields such as financial services, cloud and IT tech, manufacturing, energy, healthcare, and consumer products. It also holds some 50 properties with approximately 35.6 million rentable square feet as investments. The company operates through Digital Realty Trust LP.

Operations

Operating through a single reporting segment, Digital Realty Trust owns approximately 45.5 million sq. ft. of rentable space. It also has approximately 7.2 million sq. ft. under active development and some 2.7 million sq. ft. held for future development.

The REIT's interconnection services include cross connects, campus connect, metro connect, Interxion Cloud Connect, internet exchange, IP Bandwidth, pathway, and service exchange. Its portfolio of high-quality data centers provides secure, highly connected and continuously available environments for the exchange, processing and storage of critical data. Data centers are used for digital communication, disaster recovery purposes, transaction processing and housing mission-critical corporate IT applications. Its internet gateway data centers are highly interconnected, network-dense facilities that serve as hubs for internet and data communications within and between major metropolitan areas.

Vast majority of the revenue comes from rents and other services.

Geographic Reach

Austin, Texas-based Digital Realty Trust has regional US offices in Boston, Chicago, Dallas, Los Angeles, New York, Northern Virginia, Phoenix and San Francisco and regional international offices in Amsterdam, Dublin, London, Singapore, Sydney, Tokyo and Hong Kong.

Northern Virginia provides roughly 20% of the company's revenue, and Chicago brings in around 10%.

Sales and Marketing

Digital Realty Trust's occupancy rate is around 85%. The company's top 20 tenants account for some 50% of revenue. It has more than 4,000 customers?the largest of which provides roughly 10% of its rental income.

The REIT's tenants come from a wide array of global market sectors, including energy, financial services, consumer products, life sciences, cloud and IT services, gaming, and manufacturing. Its largest tenants by rental revenue include Fortune 50 Software, IBM, Facebook, Oracle America, Equinix and Fortune 25 Investment Grade-Rated Company, among others.

Financial Performance

The company's revenue for fiscal 2021 increased to $4.4 billion compared from the prior year with $3.9 billion. Total operating revenues increased by approximately $524.3 million for the year ended December 31, 2021 compared to the same period in 2020 driven primarily by growth in non-stabilized rental and other services revenue.

Net income for fiscal 2021 increased to $1.7 billion compared from the prior year with $362.7 million.

Cash held by the company at the end of fiscal 2021 increased to $151.5 million. Cash provided by operations was $1.7 billion while cash used for investing and financing activities were $1.1 billion and $590.6 million, respectively. Main uses of cash were improvements to investments in real estate and payments of dividends and distributions.

Strategy

Through strategic investments, Digital Realty have expanded its footprint into Latin America, enhanced its data center offerings in strategic and complementary US metropolitan areas, established our colocation and interconnection platform in the U.S. and expanded its colocation and interconnection platform in Europe and Africa, with each transaction enhancing its presence in top-tier locations throughout North America, Europe, Latin America and Africa.

Through investments and strategic partnerships, Digital Realty have significantly expanded its capabilities as a leading provider of interconnection and cloud-enablement services globally. The company believe interconnection is an attractive line of business that would be difficult to build organically and enhances the overall value proposition of its data center product offerings.

Mergers and Acquisitions

In 2022, Digital Realty agreed to acquire a majority stake in Teraco, Africa's leading carrier-neutral colocation provider, from a consortium of investors, including Berkshire Partners and Permira, in a transaction valuing Teraco at approximately $3.5 billion. Transaction immediately establishes Digital Realty as the leading colocation and interconnection provider on the high-growth African continent. After closing, Digital Realty will own approximately 55% of the total equity interests in Teraco, while the remaining 45% will be held by a consortium of existing investors, including management, Berkshire Partners LLC, Permira, van Rooyen Group, Columbia Capital, Stepstone Ventures and the Teraco Connect Trust.

Company Background

Digital Realty Trust acquired 15 properties in 2010 (the busiest that the company had been since 2007), including some in new markets. The REIT added its first property in Asia when it bought a data center in Singapore. It entered Massachusetts and Connecticut with the acquisition of three data centers there.

Digital Realty Trust purchased more than a dozen properties in 2011 and 2012, including some in new markets such as London and Sydney. The latter deals added to the company's international presence in Dublin, Melbourne, Paris, and Singapore.

EXECUTIVES

Chairman, Director, Laurence A. Chapman
President, Chief Executive Officer, Director, Andrew P. Power, $600,000 total compensation
Executive Vice President, General Counsel, Secretary, Jeannie Lee
Strategic Advisor Executive Vice President, David C. Ruberg
Finance Chief Financial Officer, Accounting Chief Financial Officer, Matthew Mercier
Chief Human Resources Officer, Cindy A. Fiedelman
Interim Chief Accounting Officer, Peter Olson
Chief Revenue Officer, Corey Dyer
Chief Technology Officer, Christopher Sharp, $460,769 total compensation
Chief Investment Officer, Gregory S. Wright
Director Emeritus, Dennis E. Singleton
Director, Alexis Black Bjorlin
Director, VeraLinn Jamieson
Director, Kevin J. Kennedy
Director, William G. LaPerch
Director, Jean F.H.P. Mandeville
Director, Afshin Mohebbi
Director, Mark R. Patterson
Director, Mary Hogan Preusse
Auditors : KPMG LLP

LOCATIONS

HQ: Digital Realty Trust Inc
5707 Southwest Parkway, Building 1, Suite 275, Austin, TX 78735
Phone: 737 281-0101 **Fax:** 415 738-6501
Web: www.digitalrealty.com

PRODUCTS/OPERATIONS

2018 Sales

	$ mil.	% of total
Rental and other services	2,412.1	79
Tenant reimbursements	624.6	21
Fee income and other	9.8	-
Total	3,046.5	100

COMPETITORS

CAPGEMINI NORTH AMERICA, INC.
CORESITE REALTY CORPORATION
DUPONT FABROS TECHNOLOGY, INC.
DYNTEK, INC.
FIDESSA GROUP HOLDINGS LIMITED
INSIGHT ENTERPRISES, INC.
PROLOGIS, INC.
RIGBY GROUP (RG) PLC
SERVICENOW, INC.
STEEL CONNECT, INC.

HISTORICAL FINANCIALS

Company Type: Public

Income Statement — FYE: December 31

	REVENUE ($mil)	NET INCOME ($mil)	NET PROFIT MARGIN	EMPLOYEES
12/20	3,903.6	356.3	9.1%	2,878
12/19	3,209.2	579.7	18.1%	1,550
12/18	3,046.4	331.2	10.9%	1,530
12/17	2,457.9	248.2	10.1%	1,436
12/16	2,142.2	426.1	19.9%	1,345
Annual Growth	16.2%	(4.4%)	—	20.9%

2020 Year-End Financials

Debt ratio: 36.9%
Return on equity: 2.5%
Cash ($ mil.): 108.5
Current Ratio: 0.65
Long-term debt ($ mil.): 13,304.7
No. of shares ($ mil.): 280.2
Dividends
Yield: 3.2%
Payout: 448.0%
Market value ($ mil.): 39,103.0

	STOCK PRICE ($) FY Close	P/E High/Low		PER SHARE ($) Earnings	Dividends	Book Value
12/20	139.51	160	107	1.00	4.48	63.36
12/19	119.74	57	43	2.35	4.32	47.49
12/18	106.55	103	81	1.21	4.04	47.84
12/17	113.90	127	100	0.99	3.72	50.63
12/16	98.26	51	33	2.20	3.52	32.05
Annual Growth	9.2%	—	—	(17.9%)	6.2%	18.6%

Digital Turbine Inc

When it comes to mobile digital content, Digital Turbine (formerly Mandalay Digital) doesn't play games (but it does make them). Through its Twistbox and AMV subsidiaries, the company develops content for 3G mobile phones, including games, images, chat services, and other products. Its content is targeted to users aged 18 to 40 and covers a variety of themes, including mature entertainment. The company distributes its products in 40 European, North American, Latin American, and Asian countries through agreements with major mobile phone operators, including Verizon, Virgin Mobile, T-Mobile, and Vodafone.

EXECUTIVES

Chairman, Director, Robert M. Deutschman

Diodes, Inc.

Chief Executive Officer, Director, William Gordon Stone, $500,000 total compensation
Executive Vice President, Chief Financial Officer, Barrett Garrison, $313,542 total compensation
Chief Technology Officer, Christine Collins, $275,000 total compensation
Chief Accounting Officer, Michael B. Miller
Controller, David Wesch, $150,000 total compensation
Director, Roy H. Chestnutt
Director, Holly Hess Groos
Director, Mohan S. Gyani
Director, Jeffrey Karish
Director, Michelle M. Sterling
Auditors: Grant Thornton LLP

LOCATIONS

HQ: Digital Turbine Inc
110 San Antonio Street, Suite 160, Austin, TX 78701
Phone: 512 387-7717
Web: www.digitalturbine.com

COMPETITORS

ACTIVEVIDEO NETWORKS, LLC
ATTACHMATE CORPORATION
CINCOM SYSTEMS, INC.
DADA ENTERTAINMENT, INC.
ENTERTAINMENT DIGITAL NETWORK
HANDS-ON MOBILE, INC.
HARMAN CONNECTED SERVICES HOLDING CORP.
QWIKKER, INC.
THEPLATFORM FOR MEDIA, INC.
TIM WE - SGPS, S.A.

HISTORICAL FINANCIALS

Company Type: Public

Income Statement — FYE: March 31

	REVENUE ($mil)	NET INCOME ($mil)	NET PROFIT MARGIN	EMPLOYEES
03/21	313.5	54.8	17.5%	280
03/20	138.7	13.9	10.0%	207
03/19	103.5	(6.0)	—	161
03/18	74.7	(52.8)	—	161
03/17	91.5	(24.2)	—	146
Annual Growth	36.0%	—	—	17.7%

2021 Year-End Financials

Debt ratio: 5.6%
Return on equity: 49.3%
Cash ($ mil.): 30.7
Current Ratio: 0.88
Long-term debt ($ mil.): —
No. of shares ($ mil.): 89.9
Dividends
Yield: —
Payout: —
Market value ($ mil.): 7,228.0

	STOCK PRICE ($) FY Close	P/E High	P/E Low	PER SHARE ($) Earnings	PER SHARE ($) Dividends	PER SHARE ($) Book Value
03/21	80.36	153	6	0.57	0.00	1.61
03/20	4.31	52	20	0.16	0.00	0.89
03/19	3.50	—	—	(0.08)	0.00	0.45
03/18	2.01	—	—	(0.75)	0.00	0.36
03/17	0.94	—	—	(0.36)	0.00	0.93
Annual Growth	204.1%	—	—	—	—	14.7%

Diodes Incorporated is a leading global manufacturer and supplier of high-quality application-specific standard products within the broad discrete, logic, analog, and mixed-signal semiconductor markets. The company serves the consumer electronics, computing, communications, industrial, and automotive markets. Diodes' products include diodes, transistors, amplifiers, comparators, and rectifiers; they are used by computer and consumer electronics manufacturers in products such as notebooks, LCD monitors, smartphones, and game consoles. Other applications include power supplies, climate control systems, GPS devices, and networking gear. The company's products are sold throughout Asia (accounts for some 80% of sales; the largest among its geographic regions), Europe, and the Americas.

Operations

Diodes operate in a single segment, standard semiconductor products, through its various design, manufacturing and distribution facilities. Semiconductors are critical components used to manufacture a broad range of electronic products and systems. The company's product portfolio addresses the design needs of advanced electronic equipment, including high-volume consumer electronic devices such as LCD and LED televisions and LCD panels, set-top boxes and consumer portables such as smartphones, tablets and notebooks.

Most of the company's sales were generated from distribution sales accounting for around 65% of sales, while direct sales accounted for nearly 35% of total sales.

Geographic Reach

Asia is the Texas-based Diodes' largest market, accounting for about 80% of its total sales, followed by Europe with more than 10% of sales, and the Americas with the rest.

Its design, marketing, and engineering centers are located in Plano; Milpitas; Taipei, Taoyuan City, Zhubei City, Taiwan; Shanghai, Yangzhou, China; Oldham, England; and Neuhaus, Germany. Diodes' wafer fabrication facilities are located in South Portland, Maine, US; Oldham, Greenock, UK; Shanghai and Wuxi, China; and Keelung and Hsinchu, Taiwan. Diodes has assembly and test facilities located in Shanghai, Jinan, Chengdu, and Wuxi, China; Neuhaus, Germany; and Jhongli and Keelung, Taiwan. Additional engineering, sales, warehouse, and logistics offices are located in Taipei, Taiwan; Hong Kong; Oldham, UK; Shanghai, Shenzhen, Wuhan, and Yangzhou, China; Seongnam-si, South Korea; and Munich, Frankfurt, Germany; with support offices throughout the world.

Sales and Marketing

The company markets and sells its products worldwide through direct sales and marketing personnel, independent sales representatives, and distributors in the US, Europe, and Asia. Its customers are comprised of leading direct sales customers as well as major electronic manufacturing services (EMS) providers. Diodes serves over 50,000 customers worldwide. Although some of these customers are direct, the majority of its customers are served by its more than 50 distributors.

The company's direct sales and EMS customers together accounted for roughly 35% of the company's net sales. One customer, a broad-based distributor serving thousands of customers, accounted for 10% of total sales.

End users for the company's semiconductors include computing (about 30% of sales); industrial (about 25% of sales); consumer (some 20%), communications (around 15% of sales); and automotive industries (more than 10% of sales).

Financial Performance

The company's net sales increased approximately $575.9 million, or 47%, in 2021, compared to the prior year, due primarily to its content expansion initiatives, improvements in product mix, overall strong demand for its products (especially in comparison to the negative effect of Covid-19 in 2020), and record revenue in the automotive, industrial, communication and consumer end-user markets.

In 2021, net income was $236.3 million compared to $99.2 million in 2020.

Cash held by the company at the end of fiscal 2021 increased to $366.8 million. Cash provided by operations was $338.5 million while cash used for investing and financing activities were $144.2 million and $158.4 million, respectively. Main cash uses were purchases of property, plant and equipment; and repayments of long-term debt.

Strategy

Diodes' strategy is to continue to enhance its position as a leading global designer, manufacturer and supplier of high-quality application-specific standard semiconductor products, utilizing the company's innovative and cost-effective assembly and test (packaging) technology and leveraging its process expertise and design excellence to achieve above-market growth in profitability.

The principal elements of Diodes' strategy include the following:

Continue to rapidly introduce innovative discrete, logic and analog and mixed-signal semiconductor products; Expand its available market opportunities; Maintain intense customer focus; Enhance cost competitiveness; as well as Pursue selective strategic acquisitions.

Mergers and Acquisitions

In 2022, Diodes acquired onsemi's wafer fabrication facility and operations located in South Portland, Maine (SPFAB). "This US-based facility, together with our existing facilities in Asia and Europe, further enhances our global manufacturing footprint and greatly increases Diodes' internal capacity and competitive advantage in this supply constrained environment, while also supporting our future long-term growth. With the transaction now closed, we aim to aggressively ramp new wafer fab processes and capabilities at SPFAB in alignment with Diodes' strategic growth plan," said Diodes' chairman, president and chief executive officer, Dr. Keh-Shew Lu. Diodes plans to utilize the facility to qualify and manufacture CMOS and BiCMOS processes to support multiple analog product lines including power management ICs, signal chain and standard products as well as several high-performance discrete product lines. Terms of the agreement were not disclosed.

EXECUTIVES

Chairman, President, Chief Executive Officer, Director, Keh-Shew Lu, $689,320 total compensation
Chief Financial Officer, Brett R. Whitmire
Chief Operating Officer, Gary Yu
Division Officer, Francis Tang, $369,624 total compensation
Lead Director, Director, Michael Kuo-Chih Tsai
Director, Angie Chen Button
Director, Warren Chen
Director, Michael R Giordano
Director, Peter M. Menard
Director, Christina Wen-chi Sung
Auditors : Moss Adams LLP

LOCATIONS

HQ: Diodes, Inc.
4949 Hedgcoxe Road, Suite 200, Plano, TX 75024
Phone: 972 987-3900
Web: www.diodes.com

2015 Sales

	$ mil.	% of total
Asia	675.5	79
Europe	90.4	11
North America	82.9	10
Total	848.8	100

2015 Sales by Customer Location

	$ mil.	% of total
China	507.8	60
US	76.9	9
Korea	66.6	8
Germany	57.0	7
Singapore	51.7	6
Taiwan	30.1	3
Other countries	58.7	7
Total	848.8	100

PRODUCTS/OPERATIONS

2015 Sales by Market

	% of total
Consumer electronics	32
Computing	18
Industrial	21
Communications	24
Automotive	5
Total	100

Selected Products

Diodes
   Schottky diodes
   Switching diodes
   Zener diodes
High-density arrays
Metal oxide semiconductor field-effect transistors (MOSFETs)
Rectifiers
   Bridge rectifiers
   Schottky rectifiers
   Standard, fast, superfast, and ultrafast recovery rectifiers
Transient voltage suppressors
   Thyristor surge protection devices
   Zener transient-voltage suppressors
Transistors
   Bipolar transistors
   Darlington transistors
   Prebiased transistors

COMPETITORS

APPLIED OPTOELECTRONICS, INC.
BEL FUSE INC.
ENTEGRIS, INC.
EXAR CORPORATION
FINISAR CORPORATION
IXYS, LLC
MACOM TECHNOLOGY SOLUTIONS HOLDINGS, INC.
ON SEMICONDUCTOR CORPORATION
SILICON LABORATORIES INC.
SKYWORKS SOLUTIONS, INC.

HISTORICAL FINANCIALS

Company Type: Public

Income Statement — FYE: December 31

	NET REVENUE ($mil)	NET INCOME ($mil)	NET PROFIT MARGIN	EMPLOYEES
12/21	1,805.1	228.7	12.7%	8,921
12/20	1,229.2	98.0	8.0%	8,939
12/19	1,249.1	153.2	12.3%	7,271
12/18	1,213.9	104.0	8.6%	7,710
12/17	1,054.2	(1.8)	—	8,586
Annual Growth	14.4%	—	—	1.0%

2021 Year-End Financials

Debt ratio: 13.7%
Return on equity: 20.7%
Cash ($ mil.): 363.6
Current Ratio: 2.52
Long-term debt ($ mil.): 265.7
No. of shares ($ mil.): 45.0
Dividends
   Yield: —
   Payout: —
Market value ($ mil.): 4,943.0

	STOCK PRICE ($) FY Close	P/E High	P/E Low	PER SHARE ($) Earnings	Dividends	Book Value
12/21	109.81	22	14	5.00	0.00	27.48
12/20	70.50	38	17	1.88	0.00	21.77
12/19	56.37	18	10	2.96	0.00	21.61
12/18	32.26	19	13	2.04	0.00	18.55
12/17	28.67	—	—	(0.04)	0.00	16.92
Annual Growth	39.9%	—	—	—	—	12.9%

DLH Holdings Corp

Dlh Holdings provides temporary and permanent medical, office administration, and technical staffing services to US government facilities nationwide. Its services on behalf of government agencies include case management, healthcare IT systems and tools, physical and behavioral health examinations; health and nutritional support for children and adults, biological research, disaster and emergency response staffing, among others. The company has contracts with the Department of Defense, Health and Human Services, and Veterans Affairs. It traces its roots back to 1969.

HISTORY

In 1969 Sheldon Kass founded Digital Solutions to provide payroll services to clients in construction. He took the company public in 1989. Kass agreed to resign in 1990 following a lawsuit by board members Raymond Skiptunis and Steven Levine over Kass' employment contract that included a loan for more than $1 million. Skiptunis became CEO.

Skiptunis moved the firm into the professional employer organization (PEO) industry during the 1990s. Digital Solutions expanded through acquisitions of assets from Staff-Rx in 1994 and the employee leasing assets of Texas-based Turnkey Services in 1995. George Eklund became CEO in 1996.

Losses in 1997 prompted Digital Solutions to implement a cost-cutting drive. Later that year Donald Kappauf was appointed CEO. In 1999 the company doubled in size when it acquired 10 human resources services firms operating under the TeamStaff Companies trade name, prompting Digital Solutions' name change. In 2000 it bought PEO Synadyne from Outsource International (later Tandem Staffing Solutions).

The following year the company made several acquisitions, including the purchase of BrightLane, a Georgia-based provider of online payroll and procurement services. In 2002 TeamStaff bought PEO Corporate Staffing Concepts.

HoneyBaked Ham presidentÂ Kent Smith was named CEO of TeamStaff in 2003, replacing Kappauf. To focus on medical staffing, TeamStaff sold two noncore units to Gevity HR: human resource outsourcing (2003) and PEO (2004). The company bought nursing staffing firm Nursing Innovations in 2004, and the next year it acquired Georgia-based RS Staffing, a provider of health care and other staffing services to the federal government.

Smith left the company in 2007 amid a management shake-up, and CFO Rick Filipelli was named president and CEO. A few years later, in early 2010, Filipelli resigned.

In 2008 TeamStaff sold its Nursing Innovations Per Diem unit, which offered temporary and permanent nursing placement services,Â to Temps, Inc., in order to focus on its core business.

EXECUTIVES

Chairman, Director, Frederick Gerald Wasserman
President, Chief Executive Officer, Director, Zachary C. Parker, $465,000 total compensation
Chief Financial Officer, Kathryn M. JohnBull, $318,750 total compensation

Chief Human Resources Officer, Galeel Maliek Ferebee
Subsidiary Officer, Jeanine M. Christian
Subsidiary Officer, Helene Loraine Fisher, $240,058 total compensation
Director, Stephen J. Zelkowicz
Director, Judith L. Bjornaas
Director, Martin J. Delaney
Director, Elder Granger
Director, Frances M. Murphy
Director, Austin J. Yerks
Auditors : WithumSmith+Brown, PC

LOCATIONS

HQ: DLH Holdings Corp
3565 Piedmont Road, Building 3, Suite 700, Atlanta, GA 30305
Phone: 770 554-3545
Web: www.dlhcorp.com

COMPETITORS

KELLY SERVICES, INC.
RIGHT MANAGEMENT INC.
TEAM HEALTH HOLDINGS, INC.
TECHNISOURCE, INC.
TRC COMPANIES, INC.

HISTORICAL FINANCIALS
Company Type: Public

Income Statement — FYE: September 30

	REVENUE ($mil)	NET INCOME ($mil)	NET PROFIT MARGIN	EMPLOYEES
09/21	246.0	10.1	4.1%	2,300
09/20	209.1	7.1	3.4%	2,200
09/19	160.3	5.3	3.3%	1,900
09/18	133.2	1.8	1.4%	1,500
09/17	115.6	3.2	2.8%	1,400
Annual Growth	20.8%	32.5%	—	13.2%

2021 Year-End Financials
Debt ratio: 22.6%
Return on equity: 17.0%
Cash ($ mil.): 24.0
Current Ratio: 0.93
Long-term debt ($ mil.): 44.6
No. of shares ($ mil.): 12.7
Dividends
Yield: —
Payout: —
Market value ($ mil.): 156.0

	STOCK PRICE ($) FY Close	P/E High/Low		PER SHARE ($) Earnings	Dividends	Book Value
09/21	12.30	17	9	0.75	0.00	5.16
09/20	7.25	19	5	0.54	0.00	4.31
09/19	4.46	15	9	0.41	0.00	3.79
09/18	5.76	45	35	0.14	0.00	3.31
09/17	6.48	25	15	0.27	0.00	3.05
Annual Growth	17.4%	—	—	29.1%	—	14.1%

Dorian LPG Ltd.

EXECUTIVES

President, Chief Executive Officer, Subsidiary Officer, Chairman, Director, John C. Hadjipateras, $550,000 total compensation
Business Development Executive Vice President, Alexander C. Hadjipateras
Chief Financial Officer, Treasurer, Principal Accounting Officer, Principal Financial Officer, Subsidiary Officer, Theodore B. Young, $400,000 total compensation
Chief Commercial Officer, Tim T. Hansen
Subsidiary Officer, Director, John C. Lycouris, $450,000 total compensation
Lead Independent Director, Director, Thomas J. Coleman
Director, Marit Lunde
Director, Ted Kalborg
Director, Oivind Lorentzen
Director, Christina Tan
Director, Malcolm McAvity
Auditors : Deloitte Certified Public Accountants S.A.

LOCATIONS

HQ: Dorian LPG Ltd.
c/o Dorian LPG (USA) LLC, 27 Signal Road, Stamford, CT 06902
Phone: 203 674-9900
Web: www.dorianlpg.com

HISTORICAL FINANCIALS
Company Type: Public

Income Statement — FYE: March 31

	REVENUE ($mil)	NET INCOME ($mil)	NET PROFIT MARGIN	EMPLOYEES
03/21	315.9	92.5	29.3%	602
03/20	333.4	111.8	33.5%	585
03/19	158.0	(50.9)	—	564
03/18	159.3	(20.4)	—	69
03/17	167.4	(1.4)	—	69
Annual Growth	17.2%	—	—	71.9%

2021 Year-End Financials
Debt ratio: 37.4%
Return on equity: 9.6%
Cash ($ mil.): 79.3
Current Ratio: 1.87
Long-term debt ($ mil.): 539.6
No. of shares ($ mil.): 41.4
Dividends
Yield: —
Payout: —
Market value ($ mil.): 0.0

Dorman Products Inc

Marketing approximately 118,000 unique parts, Dorman Products is one of the leading suppliers of replacement parts and fasteners for passenger cars and light-, medium-, and heavy-duty trucks in the automotive aftermarket industry. About 75% of the company's products are sold under brands that the company owns. Dorman sells to auto aftermarket retailers and warehouse distributors (such as Advance, AutoZone, and O'Reilly) as well as to parts manufacturers for resale under private labels. The company services over 4,500 active accounts. Dorman distributes its products primarily into Canada and Mexico, Europe, the Middle East, and Australia. About 95% of the company's total sales is generated from the US.

Operations

The company markets its products under the DORMAN and Dayton Parts brand names and several sub-brands, which identify products that address specific segments of the automotive aftermarket industry. In addition, across all of its sub-brands, customers can find a subset of products that have been branded DORMAN OE Fix products.

Its OE FIX products solve common problems with the original equipment manufacturer (OEM) repair alternative. The company's DORMAN OE Solutions is a wide variety of replacement parts the company introduced to the automotive aftermarket, covering many product categories across all areas of the vehicle, including fluid reservoirs, variable value timing components, complex electronics, and integrated door lock actuators. The DORMAN Conduct-Tite is a wide array of electrical components for common repairs as well as for enthusiasts to customize and upgrade their vehicles. In addition, DORMAN HELP! is a broad assortment of small automotive replacement parts that are primarily sold in retail store fronts such as door handles, keyless remotes and cases and door hinge repair parts. Lastly, DORMAN HD Solutions include lighting, cooling, engine management, wheel hardware, air tanks and cab products. Dayton Parts' product offering includes brake, spring, steering, suspension, driveline and hitch and coupling product lines.

The company's major products are grouped into four: powertrain, which generates approximately 40% of sales; chassis, which generates around 35% of sales; automotive body, which accounts for more than 20%; and hardware, which accounts less than 5% of sales.

Geographic Reach

Pennsylvania-based Dorman Products has about 30 warehouse and office facilities throughout the US, Canada, China, Taiwan, and India. Dorman purchases about 75% of its products from international suppliers, primarily in China. About 95% of the company's sale come from customers in US.

Sales and Marketing

Dorman's products are sold primarily in the US through automotive aftermarket retailers, including through their online platforms; national, regional and local warehouse distributors; and specialty markets, and salvage yards. About 55% of its net sales was generated from sales to automotive aftermarket retailers, including major chains such as Advance, AutoZone and O'Reilly; nearly 35% of the company's net sales was generated from sales to warehouse distributors, such as NAPA, which may be local, regional or national in scope, and which also may engage in retail sales; and around 10% was generated from its heavy-duty channel including through national, regional, and local warehouse distributors, such as FleetPride, and specialty service shops, and sales to other markets, which include, among others, salvage yards and the parts distribution systems of OE parts manufacturers as well as mass merchants, such as Walmart, for the company's home electrical wiring components.

Financial Performance

Net sales increased 23% to $1.3 billion in fiscal 2021 from $1.1 billion in fiscal 2020. The increase in net sales reflected the addition of Dayton Parts as well as robust customer demand across all the company's product channels.

In 2021, the company had a net income of $131.5 million, a 23% increase from the previous year's net income of $106.9 million.

The company's cash at the end of 2021 was $58.8 million. Operating activities generated $100.3 million, while investing activities used $365.3 million, mainly for acquisitions. Financing activities provided another $168.2 million.

Strategy

Product development and continuous innovation are central to Dorman's business. The development of a broad range of products, many of which are not conveniently or economically available elsewhere, has enabled it to grow to its present size and is an important driver for its future growth. Its product strategy has been to design and engineer products, many of which it believes are better and easier to install and/or use than the original parts they replace, and to commercialize automotive parts for the broadest possible range of uses. New product ideas are reviewed by its product management staff and a cross-functional in-house team.

Mergers and Acquisitions

In mid-2021, Dorman acquired Dayton Parts (Dayton) for a total cash consideration of approximately $338 million, subject to customary purchase price adjustments. The transaction was financed with $100 million from cash on hand, with the balance financed from borrowings under the company's new revolving credit facility. The addition of Dayton accelerates Dorman's heavy-duty growth strategy by adding large and complementary offerings of undercarriage components in the commercial vehicle aftermarket, a vast distribution network and a trusted brand with over 100 years of experience.

Company Background

In late 1978, Dorman Products, Inc. was incorporated in Pennsylvania.

EXECUTIVES

Executive Chairman, Secretary, Treasurer, Steven L. Berman, $360,000 total compensation
Senior Vice President, David Hession
Senior Vice President, Joseph P. Braun
Sales & Marketing Senior Vice President, Jeffrey L. Darby, $384,303 total compensation
Commercial Operations Executive Vice President, Michael B. Kealey, $437,404 total compensation
Executive Vice President, Chief Financial Officer, Principal Financial Officer, Principal Accounting Officer, Kevin M. Olsen, $437,404 total compensation
Corporate Controller, Michael P. Ginnetti, $232,221 total compensation
Director, John J. Gavin
Director, Paul R. Lederer
Director, Richard T. Riley
Director, Kelly A. Romano
Director, G. Michael Stakias
Auditors: KPMG LLP

LOCATIONS

HQ: Dorman Products Inc
3400 East Walnut Street, Colmar, PA 18915
Phone: 215 997-1800
Web: www.dormanproducts.com

PRODUCTS/OPERATIONS

2014 Sales

	% of total
Power-train	37
Automotive body	29
Chassis	26
Hardware	8
Total	100

Selected Subsidiaries
Allparts, Inc.
RB Distribution, Inc.
RB Management, Inc.
RB Vest, Inc.

COMPETITORS

ADVANCE AUTO PARTS, INC.
AMERICAN AXLE & MANUFACTURING HOLDINGS, INC.
BORGWARNER INC.
CARPARTS.COM, INC.
COOPER-STANDARD HOLDINGS INC.
LKQ CORPORATION
MANN+HUMMEL FILTRATION TECHNOLOGY INTERMEDIATE HOLDINGS INC.
MOTORCAR PARTS OF AMERICA, INC.
STANDARD MOTOR PRODUCTS, INC.
TENNECO INC.

HISTORICAL FINANCIALS

Company Type: Public

Income Statement — FYE: December 25

	REVENUE ($mil)	NET INCOME ($mil)	NET PROFIT MARGIN	EMPLOYEES
12/21	1,345.2	131.5	9.8%	3,360
12/20	1,092.7	106.8	9.8%	2,681
12/19	991.3	83.7	8.4%	2,742
12/18	973.7	133.6	13.7%	2,370
12/17	903.2	106.5	11.8%	2,061
Annual Growth	10.5%	5.4%	—	13.0%

2021 Year-End Financials

Debt ratio: 14.3% No. of shares ($ mil.): 31.6
Return on equity: 14.7% Dividends
Cash ($ mil.): 58.7 Yield: —
Current Ratio: 1.62 Payout: —
Long-term debt ($ mil.): — Market value ($ mil.): 3,364.0

	STOCK PRICE ($) FY Close	P/E High/Low		PER SHARE ($) Earnings	Dividends	Book Value
12/21	106.42	30	21	4.12	0.00	29.51
12/20	89.56	30	14	3.30	0.00	26.53
12/19	75.11	37	27	2.56	0.00	23.76
12/18	88.35	22	15	4.02	0.00	22.05
12/17	61.14	27	19	3.13	0.00	18.91
Annual Growth	14.9%	—	—	7.1%	—	11.8%

Dropbox Inc

EXECUTIVES

Chief Executive Officer, Chairman, Director, Andrew W. Houston, $675,000 total compensation
Chief Financial Officer, Timothy Regan
Chief Legal Officer, Bart E. Volkmer, $445,833 total compensation
Lead Independent Director, Director, Donald W. Blair
Director, Lisa M. Campbell
Director, Paul E. Jacobs
Director, Sara Mathew
Director, Abhay Parasnis
Director, Karen Peacock
Director, Michael Seibel
Auditors: Ernst & Young LLP

LOCATIONS

HQ: Dropbox Inc
1800 Ownes Street, San Francisco, CA 94158
Phone: 415 857-6800
Web: www.dropbox.com

HISTORICAL FINANCIALS

Company Type: Public

Income Statement — FYE: December 31

	REVENUE ($mil)	NET INCOME ($mil)	NET PROFIT MARGIN	EMPLOYEES
12/21	2,157.9	335.8	15.6%	2,667
12/20	1,913.9	(256.3)	—	2,760
12/19	1,661.3	(52.7)	—	2,801
12/18	1,391.7	(484.9)	—	2,323
12/17	1,106.8	(111.7)	—	1,858
Annual Growth	18.2%	—		9.5%

2021 Year-End Financials

Debt ratio: 53.6% No. of shares ($ mil.): 375.5
Return on equity: — Dividends
Cash ($ mil.): 533.0 Yield: —
Current Ratio: 1.57 Payout: —
Long-term debt ($ mil.): 1,538 Market value ($ mil.): 9,215.0

	STOCK PRICE ($) FY Close	P/E High/Low		PER SHARE ($) Earnings	Dividends	Book Value
12/21	24.54	37	25	0.85	0.00	(0.78)
12/20	22.19	—	—	(0.62)	0.00	0.82
12/19	17.91	—	—	(0.13)	0.00	1.94
12/18	20.43	—	—	(1.35)	0.00	1.65
Annual Growth	6.3%	—	—	—	—	—

Duke Realty Corp

Duke Realty is a self-managed and self-administered real estate investment trust (REIT). It owns and develops industrial properties, primarily in major cities that are key logistics markets. In addition to about 550 properties totaling more than 162.7 million sq. ft. of rentable space, the company owns some 431 acres of land and control an additional 925 acres through purchase options. The REIT leases its properties to a variety of tenants including e-commerce, manufacturing, retail, wholesale, and distribution firms. Duke's service operations include construction and development, asset and property management, and leasing. The company was founded in 1972.

Operations

The company's business operations primarily consist of two reportable operating segments: rental operations of industrial properties (roughly 95% of total revenue) and service operations (more than 95%). Rental operations of industrial properties represent the ownership and development of industrial properties and is the primary component of its revenues and earnings. Service operations generate additional revenues from providing various real estate services primarily relating to development, construction management and property management services to customers, unconsolidated joint ventures and third-party owners.

It has about 30 properties with some 8.5 million sq. ft. of space under development and two unconsolidated joint venture property under development with 1.2 million sq. ft.

Geographic Reach

Based in Indianapolis, Duke Realty has regional offices or significant operations in about 20 states. Its properties in Southern California, Chicago, Atlanta and Dallas combined account for about 40% of overall rentable area. Other primary markets include Southern California, South Florida, New Jersey, and Cincinnati.

Financial Performance

The company had a $1.1 billion revenue in 2021. The 11% increase from the previous year was primarily due to higher sales volume in the company's segments.

In 2021, the company had a net income of $852.9 million, a 184% increase from the previous year's net income of $299.9 million.

The company's cash at the end of 2021 was $103.2 million. Operating activities generated $642.4 million, while investing activities used $832.4 million, mainly for acquisition of land and other real estate assets. Financing activities provided another $225.9 million.

Strategy

Duke Realty's overall strategy is to continue to increase its investment in quality industrial properties primarily through development, on both a speculative and build-to-suit basis, supplemented with acquisitions in higher barrier markets with the highest growth potential.

Its operational focus is to drive profitability by maximizing cash from operations and earnings through maintaining property occupancy, increasing rental rates and prioritizing timely collection of monthly rental payments, while also keeping lease-related capital costs contained, by effectively managing portfolio of existing properties and providing a broad line of real estate services to tenants and to third parties.

Company Background

Duke Realty launched its business in 1972 with the development of an industrial building in Indianapolis. With $40,000 in capital and limited knowledge of commercial real estate, John Rosebrough, Phil Duke, and John Wynne embarked on their first industrial development in Park 100 on the northwest side of the city. Over the years, Duke Realty transformed Park 100 into one of the country's largest industrial parks, eventually encompassing 1,500 acres.

EXECUTIVES

Chief Executive Officer, Chairman, Director, James B. Connor, $846,154 total compensation
Executive Vice President, Chief Financial Officer, Mark A. Denien, $536,923 total compensation
Executive Vice President, Chief Operating Officer, Steven W. Schnur, $485,000 total compensation
Executive Vice President, Chief Investment Officer, Nicholas C. Anthony, $457,692 total compensation
Executive Vice President, General Counsel, Corporate Secretary, Ann Colussi Dee, $438,846 total compensation
Lead Independent Director, Director, David P. Stockert
Director, John P. Case
Director, Tamara D. Fischer
Director, Norman K. Jenkins
Director, Kelly T. Killingsworth
Director, Melanie R. Sabelhaus
Director, Peter M. Scott
Director, Chris T. Sultemeier
Director, Warren M. Thompson
Director, Lynn C. Thurber
Director, Scott Anderson
Auditors: KPMG LLP

LOCATIONS

HQ: Duke Realty Corp
8711 River Crossing Boulevard, Indianapolis, IN 46240
Phone: 317 808-6000
Web: www.dukerealty.com

Selected Markets
Atlanta
Baltimore
Central Florida
Chicago
Cincinnati
Columbus, Ohio
Dallas
Houston
Indianapolis
Minneapolis
Nashville, Tennessee
New Jersey
Northern California
Pennsylvania
Raleigh, North Carolina
Savannah, Georgia
Seattle, Washington
South Florida
Southern California
Washington, DC

PRODUCTS/OPERATIONS

2017 Sales

	$ mil.	% of total
Rental Operations		
Industrial	661.2	85
Non-reportable	24.1	3
Service Operations	94.4	12
Other	1.2	-
Total	780.9	100

COMPETITORS

ARMADA/HOFFLER PROPERTIES, L.L.C.
EQUITY RESIDENTIAL
FIRST INDUSTRIAL REALTY TRUST, INC.
ISTAR INC.
KENNEDY-WILSON HOLDINGS, INC.
LIBERTY PROPERTY TRUST
PROLOGIS, INC.
THE CONYGAR INVESTMENT COMPANY PLC
WASHINGTON REAL ESTATE INVESTMENT TRUST
WEINGARTEN REALTY INVESTORS

HISTORICAL FINANCIALS

Company Type: Public

Income Statement — FYE: December 31

	REVENUE ($mil)	NET INCOME ($mil)	NET PROFIT MARGIN	EMPLOYEES
12/21	1,105.9	852.8	77.1%	340
12/20	993.1	299.9	30.2%	350
12/19	973.7	428.9	44.1%	400
12/18	947.8	383.7	40.5%	400
12/17	780.9	1,634.4	209.3%	400
Annual Growth	9.1%	(15.0%)	—	(4.0%)

2021 Year-End Financials

Debt ratio: 35.3%
Return on equity: 15.2%
Cash ($ mil.): 69.7
Current Ratio: 1.15
Long-term debt ($ mil.): 3,689.2
No. of shares ($ mil.): 382.5
Dividends
Yield: 1.5%
Payout: 43.0%
Market value ($ mil.): 25,108.0

	STOCK PRICE ($) FY Close	P/E High	P/E Low	PER SHARE ($) Earnings	Dividends	Book Value
12/21	65.64	29	17	2.25	1.05	15.80
12/20	39.97	51	32	0.80	0.96	13.83
12/19	34.67	30	21	1.18	0.88	13.64
12/18	25.90	27	23	1.07	0.82	12.98
12/17	27.21	7	5	4.56	1.62	12.72
Annual Growth	24.6%	—	—	(16.2%)	(10.4%)	5.6%

Duluth Holdings Inc

EXECUTIVES

Chairman, Director, Stephen L. Schlecht, $321,923 total compensation
President, Chief Executive Officer, Director, Samuel M. Sato
Senior Vice President, Chief Financial Officer, Secretary, David Loretta, $334,385 total compensation
Human Resources Senior Vice President, Store Operations and Asset Protection Senior Vice President, Talent, DE&I, and Retail Operations Senior Vice President, David S. Homolka
Visual Merchandise and Creative Senior Vice President, Product Development Senior Vice President, Richard W. Schlecht
Director, Susan J. Riley
Director, Francesca Maher Edwardson
Director, David C. Finch
Director, Brett L. Paschke
Director, Scott K. Williams
Auditors: KPMG LLP

LOCATIONS

HQ: Duluth Holdings Inc
201 East Front Street, Mount Horeb, WI 53572
Phone: 608 424-1544
Web: www.duluthtrading.com

HISTORICAL FINANCIALS

Company Type: Public

Income Statement				FYE: January 31
	REVENUE ($mil)	NET INCOME ($mil)	NET PROFIT MARGIN	EMPLOYEES
01/21*	638.7	13.5	2.1%	2,977
02/20	615.6	18.9	3.1%	3,004
02/19	568.1	23.1	4.1%	2,794
01/18	471.4	23.3	5.0%	2,172
01/17	376.1	21.3	5.7%	1,627
Annual Growth	14.2%	(10.7%)	—	16.3%

*Fiscal year change

2021 Year-End Financials
Debt ratio: 23.7%
Return on equity: 7.3%
Cash ($ mil.): 47.2
Current Ratio: 2.20
Long-term debt ($ mil.): 116.2
No. of shares ($ mil.): 32.8
Dividends
  Yield: —
  Payout: —
Market value ($ mil.): 410.0

	STOCK PRICE ($) FY Close	P/E High/Low		PER SHARE ($)		
				Earnings	Dividends	Book Value
01/21*	12.47	40	8	0.42	0.00	5.89
02/20	8.45	45	13	0.58	0.00	5.48
02/19	23.48	48	23	0.72	0.00	4.92
01/18	18.68	32	21	0.72	0.00	4.19
01/17	22.97	55	21	0.66	0.00	3.43
Annual Growth	(14.2%)	—	—	(10.7%)	—	14.4%

*Fiscal year change

Dynatrace Inc

EXECUTIVES

Chairperson, Director, Jill A. Ward
Senior Vice President, Chief Technology Officer, Bernd Greifeneder
Global Sales Senior Vice President, Global Sales Chief Revenue Officer, Stephen J. Pace, $375,000 total compensation
Chief Executive Officer, Director, Rick M. McConnell
Chief Financial Officer, Principal Financial Officer, James M. Benson
Director, Kirsten O. Wolberg
Director, Ambika Kapur Gadre
Director, Stephen Eric Rowland
Director, Kenneth Virnig
Director, Michael L. Capone
Director, Stephen J. Lifshatz
Director, Seth Boro
Auditors: BDO USA, LLP

LOCATIONS

HQ: Dynatrace Inc
1601 Trapelo Road, Suite 116, Waltham, MA 02451
Phone: 617 530-1000
Web: www.dynatrace.com

HISTORICAL FINANCIALS

Company Type: Public

Income Statement				FYE: March 31
	REVENUE ($mil)	NET INCOME ($mil)	NET PROFIT MARGIN	EMPLOYEES
03/21	703.5	75.7	10.8%	2,779
03/20	545.8	(418.0)	—	2,243
03/19	430.9	(116.1)	—	1,981
03/18	398.0	9.2	2.3%	0
03/17	406.3	0.7	0.2%	0
Annual Growth	14.7%	212.3%	—	—

2021 Year-End Financials
Debt ratio: 17.4%
Return on equity: 7.2%
Cash ($ mil.): 324.9
Current Ratio: 1.05
Long-term debt ($ mil.): 391.9
No. of shares ($ mil.): 283.1
Dividends
  Yield: —
  Payout: —
Market value ($ mil.): 13,658.0

	STOCK PRICE ($) FY Close	P/E High/Low		PER SHARE ($)		
				Earnings	Dividends	Book Value
03/21	48.24	208	76	0.26	0.00	3.93
03/20	23.84	—	—	(1.58)	0.00	3.42
Annual Growth	102.3%	—	—	—	—	14.9%

EACO Corp

EACO Corporation lost its appetite for the buffet business. For a half-dozen years after selling its restaurant operations to pursue a new line of business, the company generated revenues from a handful of rental properties including restaurant and industrial properties. (Tenant NES Rentals accounts for about half of its rental revenues.) In 2010 the company acquired Bisco Industries, which distributes electronics components in the US and Canada. EACO was once the sole franchisee of Ryan's Restaurant Group restaurants in Florida; it also owned a chain of 16 Whistle Junction and Florida Buffet locations. CEO Glen Ceiley owns 98.9% of EACO.

EXECUTIVES

Chairman, Chief Executive Officer, Subsidiary Officer, Director, Glen F. Ceiley, $206,200 total compensation
Controller, Principal Accounting Officer, Subsidiary Officer, Michael Narikawa
Subsidiary Officer, Donald S. Wagner, $215,092 total compensation
Subsidiary Officer, Zachary Ceiley, $130,206 total compensation
Director, William L. Means, $103,274 total compensation
Director, Stephen Catanzaro
Auditors: Haskell & White LLP

LOCATIONS

HQ: EACO Corp
5065 East Hunter Avenue, Anaheim, CA 92807
Phone: 714 876-2490
Web: www.eacocorp.com

COMPETITORS

AVNET, INC.
BRIGHTPOINT, INC.
ELECTROCOMPONENTS PUBLIC LIMITED COMPANY
HOST HOTELS & RESORTS, INC.
JACO ELECTRONICS, INC.
KANEMATSU CORPORATION
N. F. SMITH & ASSOCIATES, L.P.
RAVE RESTAURANT GROUP, INC.
RETAIL PROPERTIES OF AMERICA, INC.
RICHARDSON ELECTRONICS, LTD.

HISTORICAL FINANCIALS

Company Type: Public

Income Statement				FYE: August 31
	REVENUE ($mil)	NET INCOME ($mil)	NET PROFIT MARGIN	EMPLOYEES
08/20	225.2	7.7	3.5%	525
08/19	221.2	9.4	4.3%	489
08/18	193.2	6.9	3.6%	464
08/17	156.9	4.0	2.6%	407
08/16	148.5	4.0	2.8%	414
Annual Growth	11.0%	17.5%	—	6.1%

2020 Year-End Financials
Debt ratio: 9.3%
Return on equity: 14.1%
Cash ($ mil.): 6.0
Current Ratio: 2.51
Long-term debt ($ mil.): 4.8
No. of shares ($ mil.): 4.8
Dividends
  Yield: —
  Payout: —
Market value ($ mil.): 84.0

	STOCK PRICE ($) FY Close	P/E High/Low		PER SHARE ($)		
				Earnings	Dividends	Book Value
08/20	17.38	15	8	1.59	0.00	12.10
08/19	19.55	10	6	1.92	0.00	10.53
08/18	14.00	10	4	1.41	0.00	8.62
08/17	6.32	11	7	0.82	0.00	7.16
08/16	5.96	7	6	0.83	0.00	6.34
Annual Growth	30.7%	—	—	17.6%	—	17.5%

Eagle Bancorp Inc (MD)

For those nest eggs that need a little help hatching, holding company Eagle Bancorp would recommend its community-oriented EagleBank subsidiary. The bank serves businesses and individuals through more than 20 branches in Maryland, Virginia, and Washington, DC, and its suburbs. Deposit products include checking, savings, and money market accounts; certificates of deposit; and IRAs. Commercial real estate loans represent more than 70% of its loan portfolio, while construction loans make up another more than 20%. The bank, which has significant expertise as a Small Business Administration lender, also writes business, consumer, and home equity loans. EagleBank offers insurance products through an agreement with The Meltzer Group.

Operations

Like other retail banks, Eagle Bancorp makes the bulk of its money from loan interest. About 86% of its total revenue came from loan interest (including fees) during 2015, while another 4% came from interest on investment securities. The rest of its revenue came from deposit account service charges (2% of revenue) and non-recurring income sources.

The bank has two direct subsidiaries: Bethesda Leasing, LLC, which holds the bank's foreclosed real estate (owned and acquired); and Eagle Insurance Services, LLC, which provides commercial and retail insurance products through a referral arrangement with insurance broker The Meltzer Group.

Geographic Reach

The Bethesda, Maryland-based bank operates 21 branches in Maryland, Virginia, and Washington DC (as of mid-2016), including nine in Northern Virginia, seven in Montgomery County, and five in the District of Columbia.

Sales and Marketing

Eagle Bancorp serves local businesses, professional clients, individuals, sole proprietors, small and medium-sized businesses, non-profits, and investors. Other clients are from the healthcare, accountant, and attorney markets.

The bank spent $2.7 million on marketing and advertising during 2015, up 38% from the $2 million it spent in 2014, mostly due to higher digital and print advertising and sponsorship costs.

Financial Performance

Eagle Bancorp's annual revenue has more than doubled since 2011 mostly thanks to strong loan growth with the addition of new branches. Meanwhile, its net income has more than tripled as the bank has kept a lid on credit loss provisions and overhead costs.

The bank's revenue jumped 33% to $279.8 million during 2015 largely thanks to a rise in interest income as its loan assets grew 16%.

Strong revenue growth in 2015 coupled with an absence of merger expenses drove Eagle Bancorp's net income up 55% to $84.1 million. The bank's operating cash levels spiked 66% to $98.5 million for the year thanks to a strong rise in cash-based earnings.

Strategy

The company has been focused on growing within its existing markets. Its strategy for further growth includes continuing to seek opportunities to open or acquire new banking locations while waiting out record low interest rates. Eagle's strict loan underwriting standards -- it didn't write subprime residential mortgages and didn't buy securities backed by subprime mortgages -- has helped it have fewer problem loans, the downfall for many banks.

Beyond its core lending and deposit businesses, Eagle Bancorp continues to expand its other product offerings as well. In 2015, it introduced a Full Service Equipment Leasing program, which provided alternative and convenient financing for all types of business equipment for customers.

Mergers and Acquisitions

In November 2014, Eagle Bancorp significantly expanded its presence in Northern Virginia after it purchased Fairfax County-based Virginia Heritage. The deal added six Virginia Heritage Bank branches (renamed as EagleBank) in northern Virginia, along with $917.4 million in assets -- including $715 million in loans and $737 million in deposits.

EXECUTIVES

President, Chief Executive Officer, Subsidiary Officer, Susan G. Riel, $527,883 total compensation
Executive Vice President, Chief Operating Officer, Subsidiary Officer, Michael T. Flynn, $236,080 total compensation
Executive Vice President, Chief Financial Officer, Subsidiary Officer, Charles D. Levingston, $342,000 total compensation
Executive Vice President, Chief Lending Officer, Subsidiary Officer, Martha Foulon-Tonat, $243,100 total compensation
Executive Vice President, Division Officer, Lindsey S Rheaume
Division Officer, Antonio F. Marquez, $421,350 total compensation
Subsidiary Officer, Division Officer, Thomas D. Murphy, $297,876 total compensation
Subsidiary Officer, Janice L. Williams, $423,725 total compensation
Director, Theresa G LaPlaca
Director, Mathew D Brockwell
Director, A Lesile Ludwig
Director, Norman R. Pozez
Director, Kathy A. Raffa
Director, James A Soltesz
Director, Benjamin M Soto
Auditors : Crowe LLP

LOCATIONS

HQ: Eagle Bancorp Inc (MD)
7830 Old Georgetown Road, Third Floor, Bethesda, MD 20814
Phone: 301 986-1800
Web: www.eaglebankcorp.com

PRODUCTS/OPERATIONS

Selected Subsidiaries
EagleBank
    Bethesda Leasing LLC
    Eagle Insurance Services, LLC
    Fidelity Mortgage, Inc.
Eagle Commercial Ventures, LLC

COMPETITORS

BANCFIRST CORPORATION
CENTERSTATE BANK CORPORATION
CITY HOLDING COMPANY
CUSTOMERS BANCORP, INC.
F.N.B. CORPORATION
FIRST COMMONWEALTH FINANCIAL CORPORATION
FIRST MIDWEST BANCORP, INC.
HERITAGE FINANCIAL CORPORATION
S&T BANCORP, INC.
WESTERN ALLIANCE BANCORPORATION

HISTORICAL FINANCIALS

Company Type: Public

Income Statement				FYE: December 31
	ASSETS ($mil)	NET INCOME ($mil)	INCOME AS % OF ASSETS	EMPLOYEES
12/20	11,117.8	132.2	1.2%	515
12/19	8,988.7	142.9	1.6%	492
12/18	8,389.1	152.2	1.8%	470
12/17	7,479.0	100.2	1.3%	466
12/16	6,890.0	97.7	1.4%	469
Annual Growth	12.7%	7.9%	—	2.4%

2020 Year-End Financials
Return on assets: 1.3%   Dividends
Return on equity: 10.8%   Yield: 2.1%
Long-term debt ($ mil.): —   Payout: 21.5%
No. of shares ($ mil.): 31.7   Market value ($ mil.): 1,313.0
Sales ($ mil.): 435.6

	STOCK PRICE ($) FY Close	P/E High/Low		PER SHARE ($) Earnings	Dividends	Book Value
12/20	41.30	12	6	4.09	0.88	39.05
12/19	48.63	14	9	4.18	0.44	35.82
12/18	48.71	15	10	4.42	0.00	32.25
12/17	57.90	23	17	2.92	0.00	27.80
12/16	60.95	22	15	2.86	0.00	24.77
Annual Growth	(9.3%)	—	—	9.4%	—	12.0%

Eagle Bancorp Montana, Inc.

Eagle Bancorp Montana hopes to swoop down on every potential account holder in its home state. The holding company owns

American Federal Savings Bank, a thrift that serves businesses and residents of southwestern Montana through six branches and seven ATMs. American Federal primarily writes mortgages on one- to four-family residences (these comprise almost half of its loan book); the rest of its portfolio consists of commercial mortgages (25%), home equity (about 20%), and consumer, business, and construction loans. The bank's deposit products include checking, money market, and savings accounts; CDs; IRAs; and Visa debit cards. Eagle Bancorp Montana is buying seven branches from Sterling Financial.

EXECUTIVES

Chairman, Director, Rick F. Hays
President, Chief Executive Officer, Subsidiary Officer, Director, Laura F. Clark, $170,000 total compensation
Senior Vice President, Chief Credit Officer, Dale F. Field
Senior Vice President, Chief Operations Officer, Subsidiary Officer, Rachel R. Amdahl
Senior Vice President, Chief Risk Officer, Chantelle R. Nash
Senior Vice President, Chief Lending Officer, Mark A. O'Neill
Senior Vice President, Chief Information Officer, Patrick D. Rensmon, $148,000 total compensation
Senior Vice President, Chief Financial Officer, Subsidiary Officer, Miranda J. Spaulding
Subsidiary Officer, Linda M. Chilton
Subsidiary Officer, Alana M. Binde
Division Officer, Director, Benjamin G. Ruddy
Director, Samuel D. Waters
Director, Cynthia A. Utterback
Director, Corey Jensen
Director, Tanya J. Chemodurow
Director, Kenneth M. Walsh
Director, Shavon R. Cape
Director, Thomas J. McCarvel
Director, Maureen J. Rude
Auditors: Moss Adams LLP

LOCATIONS

HQ: Eagle Bancorp Montana, Inc.
1400 Prospect Avenue, Helena, MT 59601
Phone: 406 442-3080
Web: www.opportunitybank.com

COMPETITORS

CENTRAL BANCORP, INC.
COMMERCIAL BANCSHARES, INC.
FIRST US BANCSHARES, INC.
FIRSTFED BANCORP, INC.
UNITED BANCSHARES, INC.

HISTORICAL FINANCIALS
Company Type: Public

Income Statement — FYE: December 31

	ASSETS ($mil)	NET INCOME ($mil)	INCOME AS % OF ASSETS	EMPLOYEES
12/20	1,257.6	21.2	1.7%	354
12/19	1,054.2	10.8	1.0%	298
12/18	853.9	4.9	0.6%	249
12/17	716.7	4.1	0.6%	207
12/16	673.9	5.1	0.8%	200
Annual Growth	16.9%	42.6%	—	15.3%

2020 Year-End Financials
Return on assets: 1.8%
Return on equity: 15.4%
Long-term debt ($ mil.): —
No. of shares ($ mil.): 6.7
Sales ($ mil.): 98.7
Dividends
Yield: 1.8%
Payout: 14.1%
Market value ($ mil.): 144.0

	STOCK PRICE ($) FY Close	P/E High	P/E Low	PER SHARE ($) Earnings	Dividends	Book Value
12/20	21.22	7	4	3.11	0.39	22.57
12/19	21.39	13	9	1.69	0.38	18.94
12/18	16.50	24	17	0.91	0.37	17.31
12/17	20.95	22	17	0.99	0.34	16.68
12/16	21.10	16	8	1.32	0.32	15.60
Annual Growth	0.1%	—	—	23.9%	5.1%	9.7%

Eagle Financial Services, Inc.

EXECUTIVES

Chairman, Subsidiary Officer, Director, Thomas T. Gilpin
President, Chief Executive Officer, Subsidiary Officer, Director, Brandon Craig Lorey
Executive Vice President, Chief Financial Officer, Subsidiary Officer, Kathleen J. Chappell, $212,000 total compensation
Executive Vice President, Chief Banking Officer, Subsidiary Officer, Joseph T. Zmitrovich
Secretary, Subsidiary Officer, Kaley P. Crosen
Subsidiary Officer, Carl A. Esterhay
Subsidiary Officer, Aaron M. Poffinberger
Director, Scott M. Hamberger
Director, John R. Milleson, $390,000 total compensation
Director, Tanya Matthews
Director, Edward Hill
Director, Mary Bruce Glaize
Director, Cary R. Nelson
Director, Thomas T. Byrd
Director, Douglas C. Rinker
Director, John D. Stokely
Director, Robert W. Smalley
Auditors: Yount, Hyde & Barbour, P.C.

LOCATIONS

HQ: Eagle Financial Services, Inc.
2 East Main Street, P.O. Box 391, Berryville, VA 22611

Phone: 540 955-2510
Web: www.bankofclarke.com

HISTORICAL FINANCIALS
Company Type: Public

Income Statement — FYE: December 31

	ASSETS ($mil)	NET INCOME ($mil)	INCOME AS % OF ASSETS	EMPLOYEES
12/20	1,130.1	11.1	1.0%	204
12/19	877.3	9.7	1.1%	191
12/18	799.6	9.0	1.1%	184
12/17	765.7	7.7	1.0%	181
12/16	700.1	6.3	0.9%	189
Annual Growth	12.7%	15.1%	—	1.9%

2020 Year-End Financials
Return on assets: 1.1%
Return on equity: 11.0%
Long-term debt ($ mil.): —
No. of shares ($ mil.): 3.4
Sales ($ mil.): 47.4
Dividends
Yield: 3.5%
Payout: 30.9%
Market value ($ mil.): 100.0

	STOCK PRICE ($) FY Close	P/E High	P/E Low	PER SHARE ($) Earnings	Dividends	Book Value
12/20	29.50	10	7	3.27	1.04	30.86
12/19	31.05	12	10	2.84	1.00	28.08
12/18	30.99	15	11	2.60	0.94	25.42
12/17	32.00	15	11	2.24	0.88	24.30
12/16	25.75	14	13	1.81	0.82	22.90
Annual Growth	3.5%	—	—	15.9%	6.1%	7.7%

East West Bancorp, Inc

East West Bancorp is the holding company for East West Bank, which provides standard banking services and loans, operating in more than 120 locations in the US and China. Boasting $60.9 billion in assets, East West Bank focuses on making commercial and industrial real estate loans, which account for the majority of the company's loan portfolio. Catering to the Asian-American community, it also provides international banking and trade financing. The company commenced business on 1998 when, pursuant to a reorganization, it acquired all of the voting stock of East West Bank, which became its principal asset.

Operations

East West Bancorp operates three business segments. Commercial Banking (around 50% of sales), Consumer and Business Banking (roughly 45%), and Other operations (some 5%).

The Commercial Banking segment primarily offers commercial loan and deposit products. Commercial loan products include commercial real estate lending, construction finance, working capital lines of credit, trade finance, letters of credit, commercial business lending, affordable housing lending, asset-based lending, asset-backed finance, project finance and equipment financing. Commercial deposit products and other financial services include treasury management, foreign exchange services, and interest rate and commodity risk hedging.

The Consumer and Business Banking segment primarily provides financial products and services to consumer and commercial customers through the company's domestic branch network. The segment offers consumer and commercial deposits, mortgage and home equity loans and other products and services.

The bank's Other segment centralizes functions including the corporate treasury activities of the company and elimination of inter-segment amounts have been aggregated to this segment. The segment also provides broad administrative support to the company's two core segments.

Overall, the company generated some 75% of sales from loans, including fees. Its loan portfolio includes commercial real estate (about 40%), commercial and industrial (roughly 35%), and residential (over 25%).

Geographic Reach

East West's bank network in the US is mainly in California, Texas, New York, Washington, Georgia, Massachusetts, Nevada, and Illinois. Internationally, the bank has branches in Hong Kong and Greater China (Shanghai, Shantou, and Shenzhen), and five representative offices in Beijing, Chongqing, Guangzhou, Xiamen, and Taiwan.

It is headquartered in Pasadena, California.

Sales and Marketing

The Consumer and Business Banking segment primarily provides financial products and services to consumer and commercial customers through the company's domestic branch network and digital banking platform.

Financial Performance

The company's revenue for fiscal 2021 increased to $1.8 billion compared from the prior year with $1.6 billion.

Net income for fiscal 2021 increased to $873.0 million compared from the prior year with $567.8 million.

Cash held by the company at the end of fiscal 2021 decreased to $3.9 billion. Cash provided by operations and financing activities were $1.2 billion and $7.8 billion, respectively. Cash used for investing was $9.1 billion, mainly for AFS debt securities.

Strategy

The company's strategy focuses on seeking out and deepening client relationships that meet its risk/return parameters. This guides its decision-making across every aspect of its operations: the products it develops, the expertise East West cultivate, and the infrastructure the company build to help its customers conduct their businesses. The company expect its relationship-focused business model to continue to generate organic growth from existing customers and to expand its targeted customer bases. East West constantly invest in technology to improve the customer user experience, strengthen critical business infrastructure, and streamline core processes, while properly managing operating expenses. The company's risk management activities are focused on ensuring that the bank identifies and manages risks to sustain safety and soundness while maximizing profitability.

Company Background

East West Bancorp was founded in 1998.

In 2009 the company acquired more than 60 branches and most of the banking operations of larger rival United Commercial Bank, which had been seized by regulators. The deal gave East West Bank about 40 more California branches, plus some 20 additional US locations beyond the state.

EXECUTIVES

Chairman, Chief Executive Officer, Subsidiary Officer, Director, Dominic Ng, $1,200,000 total compensation

Vice-Chairman, Chief Corporate Officer, Subsidiary Officer, Douglas P. Krause, $469,615 total compensation

Executive Vice President, Chief Financial Officer, Subsidiary Officer, Irene H. Oh, $534,423 total compensation

Executive Vice President, Chief Operating Officer, Subsidiary Officer, Parker L. Shi

Corporate Secretary, Lisa L. Kim

Lead Independent Director, Director, Rudolph I. Estrada

Director, Sabrina Kay

Director, Serge Dumont

Director, Manuel P. Alvarez

Director, Molly C. Campbell

Director, Archana Deskus

Director, Paul H. Irving

Director, Jack C. Liu

Director, Lester M. Sussman

Auditors : KPMG LLP

LOCATIONS

HQ: East West Bancorp, Inc
135 North Los Robles Ave., 7th Floor, Pasadena, CA 91101
Phone: 626 768-6000
Web: www.eastwestbank.com

PRODUCTS/OPERATIONS

2011 Sales

	$ mil.	% of total
Commercial lending	619.8	57
Retail banking	358.8	33
Other & adjustments	112.8	10
Total	1,091.4	100

COMPETITORS

CATHAY GENERAL BANCORP
F.N.B. CORPORATION
FIRST HORIZON CORPORATION
HERITAGE FINANCIAL CORPORATION
PROSPERITY BANCSHARES, INC.
REGIONS FINANCIAL CORPORATION
SOUTHWEST BANCORP, INC.
VALLEY NATIONAL BANCORP
WESTERN ALLIANCE BANCORPORATION
WILSHIRE BANCORP, INC.

HISTORICAL FINANCIALS

Company Type: Public

Income Statement   FYE: December 31

	ASSETS ($mil)	NET INCOME ($mil)	INCOME AS % OF ASSETS	EMPLOYEES
12/20	52,156.9	567.7	1.1%	3,200
12/19	44,196.0	674.0	1.5%	3,300
12/18	41,042.3	703.7	1.7%	3,200
12/17	37,150.2	505.6	1.4%	3,000
12/16	34,788.8	431.6	1.2%	2,873
Annual Growth	10.7%	7.1%	—	2.7%

2020 Year-End Financials

Return on assets: 1.1%
Return on equity: 11.0%
Long-term debt ($ mil.): —
No. of shares ($ mil.): 141.5
Sales ($ mil.): 1,830.5
Dividends
  Yield: 2.1%
  Payout: 27.7%
Market value ($ mil.): 7,179.0

	STOCK PRICE ($) FY Close	P/E High/Low		PER SHARE ($) Earnings	Dividends	Book Value
12/20	50.71	13	6	3.97	1.10	37.22
12/19	48.70	12	8	4.61	1.06	34.46
12/18	43.53	15	8	4.81	0.86	30.52
12/17	60.83	18	14	3.47	0.80	26.58
12/16	50.83	17	9	2.97	0.80	23.78
Annual Growth	(0.1%)	—	—	7.5%	8.3%	11.9%

Easterly Government Properties Inc

EXECUTIVES

Chairman, Director, Darrell W. Crate, $325,000 total compensation

Development Vice-Chairman, Acquisitions Vice-Chairman, Development Executive Vice President, Acquisitions Executive Vice President, Vice-Chairman, Michael P. Ibe, $325,000 total compensation

President, Chief Executive Officer, Director, William C. Trimble, $525,000 total compensation

Executive President, Chief Operating Officer, Chief Financial Officer, Meghan G. Baivier, $425,000 total compensation

Executive Vice President, Chief Accounting Officer, Alison M. Bernard, $225,000 total compensation

Government Relations Executive Vice President, Ronald E. Kendall

Lead Independent Director, Director, William H. Binnie

Director, Cynthia A. Fisher

Director, Scott D. Freeman

Director, Tara S. Innes

Director, Emil W. Henry

Auditors : PricewaterhouseCoopers LLP

LOCATIONS

HQ: Easterly Government Properties Inc
2001 K Street NW, Suite 775 North, Washington, DC 20006
Phone: 202 595-9500
Web: www.easterlyreit.com

HISTORICAL FINANCIALS

Company Type: Public

Income Statement — FYE: December 31

	REVENUE ($mil)	NET INCOME ($mil)	NET PROFIT MARGIN	EMPLOYEES
12/20	245.0	11.9	4.9%	45
12/19	221.7	7.2	3.3%	37
12/18	160.5	5.7	3.6%	32
12/17	130.6	4.4	3.4%	30
12/16	104.6	3.4	3.3%	27
Annual Growth	23.7%	36.8%	—	13.6%

2020 Year-End Financials

Debt ratio: 39.8%
Return on equity: 1.0%
Cash ($ mil.): 8.4
Current Ratio: 4.69
Long-term debt ($ mil.): 978.2
No. of shares ($ mil.): 82.1
Dividends
 Yield: 4.5%
 Payout: 693.3%
Market value ($ mil.): 1,860.0

	STOCK PRICE ($) FY Close	P/E High/Low		PER SHARE ($) Earnings	Dividends	Book Value
12/20	22.65	195	129	0.15	1.04	14.06
12/19	23.73	235	154	0.10	1.30	14.20
12/18	15.68	238	170	0.08	1.04	14.69
12/17	21.34	201	175	0.10	1.00	14.91
12/16	20.02	187	150	0.10	0.92	15.17
Annual Growth	3.1%	—	—	10.7%	3.1%	(1.9%)

EastGroup Properties Inc

EastGroup Properties points its compass all across the Sunbelt. The self-administered real estate investment trust (REIT) invests in, develops, and manages industrial properties, with a particular emphasis on Florida, Texas, Arizona, and California. EastGroup's distribution space properties are typically multitenant buidings. Its distribution space for location sensitive customers ranges from about 15,000 to 70,000 sq. ft. in size, located near major transportation hubs. Its portfolio includes some 360 industrial properties and an office building, totaling more than 40 million sq. ft. of leasable space.

Operations

EastGroup has one reportable segment ? industrial properties. All of its revenues came from real estate rentals.

Geographic Reach

Ridgeland, Mississippi-based EastGroup Properties has regional offices in Orlando, Miami, Houston, and Phoenix. Although its portfolio is focused on the Sun Belt (Arizona, California, Florida, North Carolina, and Texas), the REIT also owns properties in Colorado, Louisiana, Mississippi, and Nevada.

Sales and Marketing

EastGroup's operating portfolio was about 95% leased to approximately 1,500 tenants, with no single tenant accounting for approximately 1.0% of the company's income from real estate operations.

Financial Performance

The company revenue for the last five years saw a 41% increase since 2015. Net income also reported an increasing trend for the same period.

The REIT reported revenue of $331.4 million in 2019, an increase of 10% from 2018. Real estate revenue increased $31.8 million offset by a $0.8 million, decrease in Other revenue.

Net income rose by 37% to $121.7 million in 2019. The increase was due to higher total revenue and a gain of $41 million from sale of real estate investments.

Cash and cash equivalents at the end of the year were $224,000. Net cash provided by operations was $195.9 million and financing activities added another $247.3 million. Investing activities used $443.3 million for development and value-add properties and Purchases of real estate.

Strategy

EastGroup's strategy for growth is based on ownership of premier distribution facilities generally clustered near major transportation features in supply-constrained submarkets.

EastGroup's goal is to maximize shareholder value by being a leading provider in its markets of functional, flexible and quality business distribution space for location sensitive customers (primarily in the 15,000 to 70,000 square foot range). The company develops, acquires and operates distribution facilities, the majority of which are clustered around major transportation features in supply-constrained submarkets in major Sunbelt regions. The company's core markets are in the states of Florida, Texas, Arizona, California and North Carolina.

During 2019, EastGroup increased its holdings in real estate properties through its acquisition and development programs. The company purchased 1,774,000 square feet of operating and value-add properties and 188 acres of land for a total of $269 million. Also, during 2019, the company began construction of 18 development projects containing 2.7 million square feet and transferred 13 projects, which contain 1.8 million square feet and had costs of $156.7 million at the date of transfer, from its development and value-add program to real estate properties. And also during that time, EastGroup completed dispositions including 617,000 square feet of operating properties and 0.2 acres of land, which generated gross proceeds of $68.7 million.

HISTORY

New York-based Third ICM Realty was founded in 1969 and went public two years later as ICM Realty. The company specialized in sale/leaseback transactions. Mississippi investor Leland Speed became a director of the company in 1978; two years later, Speed staged a management coup through his Eastover Corp. and Citizens Growth Properties, taking over the company and moving it to Mississippi. The company was renamed EastGroup Properties in 1983.

Speed continued to divide his time among his various companies. Eastover was at first trying to sell, then to find a joint venture partner for, a golf course development in 1989 and 1990. In the 1990s Speed began consolidating his holdings under EastGroup Properties, merging Eastover into it in 1994. The company also bought Copley Properties that year. These transactions left the company in possession of a wide variety of properties, including hotels, stores, and apartments.

EastGroup Properties started to reposition its portfolio by selling off the noncore properties. As it gained capital from these sales, it began making more acquisitions, both of individual sites and property portfolios. In 1997 EastGroup Properties bought into Meridian Point Realty Trust, completing the purchase the next year and, with it, adding some 2.6 million sq. ft. of property to its portfolio. Also in 1998, the company bought Ensign Properties, an industrial developer in the Orlando, Florida, area.

In 1999 EastGroup Properties announced that it planned to make $50-60 million worth of investments, financed through the sale of existing properties. In 2000 the company expanded its industrial portfolio in Tempe, Arizona; and in Houston, Dallas, and El Paso, Texas, through acquisitions and new developments. The company disposed of its last remaining apartment property, a 240-unit site in Atlanta, the same year. By 2005 it had one last office property in its portfolio.

EXECUTIVES

Chairman, Director, David H. Hoster, $623,000 total compensation
Chairman Emeritus, Leland R. Speed
President, Chief Executive Officer, Director, Marshall A. Loeb, $650,000 total compensation
Executive Vice President, Chief Financial Officer, Treasurer, Brent W. Wood, $407,000 total compensation
Executive Vice President, John F. Coleman, $403,000 total compensation
Senior Vice President, Ryan M. Collins, $325,000 total compensation
Senior Vice President, R. Reid Dunbar, $371,000 total compensation
Senior Vice President, Chief Accounting Officer, Secretary, Staci H. Tyler
Lead Director, Director, H. Eric Bolton
Director, Mary E. McCormick

Director, D. Pike Aloian
Director, H. C. Bailey
Director, Donald F. Colleran
Director, Hayden C. Eaves
Director, Katherine M. Sandstrom
Auditors : KPMG LLP

LOCATIONS

HQ: EastGroup Properties Inc
400 W Parkway Place, Suite 100, Ridgeland, MS 39157
Phone: 601 354-3555
Web: www.eastgroup.net

Selected Property Locations
San Francisco Area
Fresno, CA
Santa Barbara, CA
Los Angeles, CA
San Diego, CA
Phoenix, AZ
Tucson, AZ
Las Vegas, NV
El Paso, TX
San Antonio, TX
Houston, TX
Dallas, TX
Tampa, FL
Fort Myers, FL
Orlando, FL
Jacksonville, FL
South Florida
Charlotte, NC
Denver, CO
Oklahoma City, OK
New Orleans, LA
Jackson, MS

PRODUCTS/OPERATIONS

2016 Sales

	$ mil.	% of total
Income from Real estate operations	252.2	100
Other	0.8	-
Total	253	100

COMPETITORS

BOSTON PROPERTIES, INC.
PIEDMONT OFFICE REALTY TRUST, INC.
RETAIL OPPORTUNITY INVESTMENTS CORP.
RETAIL PROPERTIES OF AMERICA, INC.
THE HOWARD HUGHES CORPORATION

HISTORICAL FINANCIALS

Company Type: Public

Income Statement — FYE: December 31

	REVENUE ($mil)	NET INCOME ($mil)	NET PROFIT MARGIN	EMPLOYEES
12/21	409.4	157.5	38.5%	82
12/20	363.0	108.3	29.9%	80
12/19	331.3	121.6	36.7%	77
12/18	300.3	88.5	29.5%	75
12/17	274.1	83.1	30.3%	71
Annual Growth	10.6%	17.3%	—	3.7%

2021 Year-End Financials

Debt ratio: 45.2%
Return on equity: 11.0%
Cash ($ mil.): 4.3
Current Ratio: 0.65
Long-term debt ($ mil.): 1,451.7
No. of shares ($ mil): 41.2
Dividends
 Yield: 1.5%
 Payout: 116.2%
Market value ($ mil.): 9,403.0

	STOCK PRICE ($) FY Close	P/E High/Low		PER SHARE ($) Earnings	Dividends	Book Value
12/21	227.85	58	34	3.90	3.58	38.04
12/20	138.06	53	32	2.76	3.08	32.00
12/19	132.67	42	27	3.24	2.94	30.84
12/18	91.73	41	31	2.49	2.72	24.74
12/17	88.38	39	28	2.44	2.52	21.56
Annual Growth	26.7%	—	—	12.4%	9.2%	15.3%

Ebix Inc

Ebix Inc. is a leading international supplier of on-demand infrastructure exchanges to the insurance, financial services, travel, and healthcare industries. Its EbixCash Exchange (EbixCash) is primarily derived from the sales of prepaid gift cards and consideration paid by customers for financial transaction services, including services like transferring or exchanging money. It also offers several other services, including payment services and ticketing and travel services for which revenue is impacted by varying factors. Ebix also Software-as-a-Service (SaaS) enterprise solutions in the area of customer relationship management (CRM), front-end & back-end systems, outsourced administrative and risk compliance. The company has domestic and international operations spread across approximately 200 offices and serves thousands of customers in over 70 countries across six continents. Ebix generated majority of its sales in India.

Operations

Ebix reports as a single segment. Its revenues are derived from three product/service groups: EbixCash Exchanges (about 75% of sales), Insurance Exchanges (roughly 20%), and Risk Compliance Solutions (more than 5%).

EbixCash revenues are primarily derived from the sales of prepaid gift cards and consideration paid by customers for financial transaction services, including services like transferring or exchanging money. It also offers several other services, including payment services and ticketing and travel services.

Insurance Exchanges revenues are primarily derived from consideration paid by customers related to its SaaS platforms, related services and the licensing of software. A typical contract for its SaaS platform will also include services for setup, customization, transaction processing, maintenance, and/or hosting.

Risk Compliance Services revenues consist of two revenue streams - Certificates of Insurance (COI) and Consulting Services. COI revenues are derived from consideration paid by customers for the creation and tracking of certificates of insurance. These are transactional-based revenues. Consulting Services revenues are driven by distinct consulting service engagements rendered to customers for which revenues are recognized using the output method on a time and material basis as the services are performed.

Geographic Reach

Georgia-based Ebix's largest market is the India, accounting for around 75% of its sales, followed by US and Australia accounting for about 15% and some 5%, respectively. It has office space, primarily for sales and operations support, in Salt Lake City, Utah, and Pasadena, California. The company leases office space in New Zealand, Australia, Singapore, Dubai, Brazil, Canada, Indonesia, the Philippines, and the UK for support, operations and sales offices. The company also leases approximately 100 facilities across India, while owning six facilities in India.

Sales and Marketing

Ebix employs skilled technology and business professionals who provide products, services, support and consultancy services to thousands of customers. The company's advertising costs were approximately $6.3 million, $4.8 million, and $9.7 million in 2021, 2020, and 2019, respectively.

Financial Performance

In 2021, Ebix' total revenue increased $369.3 million, or 59%, to $994.9 million compared to $625.6 million in 2020. The growth in revenues was due primarily to strong demand for the company's payment solutions business in India (primarily prepaid gift cards). The company also experienced year-over-year increases in revenues in international insurance exchange revenues and the EbixCash BPO business, offset, in part, by declines in the COVID-19 affected business areas of travel, remittance, e-learning, financial technologies and global product consulting businesses. The payment solutions revenues increased year-over-year by approximately $374 million year-over-year to approximately $630 million, or 146% year-over-year growth.

Net income in 2021 decreased to $68.2 million compared to $92.4 million in the prior year.

Cash held by the company at the end of fiscal 2021 decreased to $114.8 million. Operating activities provided $69.5 million, while investing and financing activities used $4.6 million and $63.2 million, respectively. Main cash uses were for capital expenditure and principal payments of term loan obligation.

Strategy

The company seeks to acquire businesses that complement Ebix's existing products and services. Any acquisition made by Ebix typically will fall into one of two different categories: the acquired company has products and/or services that are competitive to its existing products and services; or the acquired company's products and services are either a complement to or an extension of its existing products and services or its core business competencies.

The company's integration strategies are targeted at improving the efficiency of its business, centralizing key functions, exercising better control over its operations, and providing consistent technology and product vision across all functions, entities and products. This is a key part of Ebix's business philosophy designed to enable Ebix to operate at a high level of efficiency and facilitate a consistent end-to-end strategic vision for the industries it serves.

EXECUTIVES

Chairman, President, Chief Executive Officer, Director, Robin Raina, $2,400,000 total compensation
Corporate Executive Vice President, Chief Financial Officer, Steven M. Hamil
Executive Vice President, Division Officer, Leon Royden Thomas d'Apice, $224,400 total compensation
Division Officer, James Scott Senge, $225,000 total compensation
Region Officer, Ash Sawhney
Director, Priyanka Kaul
Director, Pavan Bhalla, $19,000 total compensation
Director, Hans Ueli Keller, $19,000 total compensation
Director, Hanz U. Benz, $19,000 total compensation
Director, Neil D. Eckert, $14,000 total compensation
Director, Rolf Herter, $14,000 total compensation
Director, George W. Hebard
Auditors : KG Somani & Co.

LOCATIONS

HQ: Ebix Inc
1 Ebix Way, Johns Creek, GA 30097
Phone: 678 281-2020
Web: www.ebix.com

2017 Sales

	$ mil.	% of total
US	211,895	58
India	61,857	17
Australia	34,366	9
Latin America	21,128	6
Europe	17,062	5
Canada	7,522	2
Singapore	6,330	2
Other countries	2,757	1
Total	363,971	100

Selected Subsidiaries
Ebix.com, International, Inc., a Delaware corporation
Ebix International, LLC, a Delaware limited liability company
Ebix BPO Division - San Diego, a California corporation
Jenquest, Inc., a California corporation
FACTS Services Inc., a Florida corporation
E-Z Data, Acquisition Sub, LLC, a California limited liability company
Peak Performance Solutions, Inc., a Delaware limited liability company
ADAM, Inc., a Georgia corporation
Agency Solutions.com, LLC (d.b.a. HealthConnect Systems), a Delaware limited liability company
Benefit Software, Incorporated, a California corporation
PlanetSoft Holdings, Inc., a Delaware corporation
Ebix Software India Private Limited
Ebix Software India SEZ, Private Limited
Premier Ebix Exchange Software Private Ltd.
Ebix Australia Pty,. Ltd.
Ebix Australia (VIC) Pty. Ltd.
Ebix Exchange-Australia PTY LTD
Ebix New Zealand
Ebix New Zealand Holdings

PRODUCTS/OPERATIONS

2017 Sales

	$ mil.	% of total
Exchanges	259,470	71
Risk Compliance Solutions	86,832	24
Broker systems	14,672	4
Carrier systems	2,995	1
Total	363,971	100

COMPETITORS

APPIAN CORPORATION
ATOS SYNTEL INC.
CGI Inc
COMPUTER TASK GROUP, INCORPORATED
IMPERVA, INC.
N MODEL INC
SECUREWORKS CORP.
TTEC HOLDINGS, INC.
VIRTUSA CORPORATION
VISA PAYMENTS LIMITED

HISTORICAL FINANCIALS

Company Type: Public

Income Statement — FYE: December 31

	REVENUE ($mil)	NET INCOME ($mil)	NET PROFIT MARGIN	EMPLOYEES
12/20	625.6	92.3	14.8%	9,802
12/19	580.6	96.7	16.7%	7,975
12/18	497.8	93.1	18.7%	9,263
12/17	363.9	100.6	27.6%	4,515
12/16	298.2	93.8	31.5%	2,988
Annual Growth	20.3%	(0.4%)	—	34.6%

2020 Year-End Financials
Debt ratio: 44.3%
Return on equity: 15.8%
Cash ($ mil.): 105.0
Current Ratio: 1.89
Long-term debt ($ mil.): 671.5
No. of shares ($ mil.): 30.5
Dividends
Yield: 0.7%
Payout: 9.9%
Market value ($ mil.): 1,159.0

	STOCK PRICE ($) FY Close	P/E High/Low		PER SHARE ($) Earnings	Dividends	Book Value
12/20	37.97	13	3	3.02	0.30	20.09
12/19	33.41	19	10	3.16	0.30	18.04
12/18	42.56	29	14	2.95	0.30	15.64
12/17	79.25	26	17	3.19	0.30	15.62
12/16	57.05	22	10	2.86	0.30	13.30
Annual Growth	(9.7%)	—	—	1.4%	0.0%	10.9%

Educational Development Corp.

Educational Development Corporation (EDC) likes being in a bind, as long as the cover appeals to youngsters. The company is the exclusive US distributor of a line of aboutÂ 1,500 children's books published by the UK's Usborne Publishing Limited. EDC's Home BusinessÂ Division markets the books to individuals using independent sales reps who sell through personalÂ websites, home parties, direct sales, and book fairs; this division also distributes books to public and school libraries. EDC's Publishing Division distributes the Usborne line to a network of book, toy, and other retail stores. EDCÂ bought multi-cultural children's book publisher Kane/Miller in 2008 to complement its product offerings.

EXECUTIVES

Executive Chairman, Director, Randall W. White, $263,100 total compensation
Information Technology President, Information Technology Chief Executive Officer, Director, Craig M. White, $156,100 total compensation
Chief Financial Officer, Corporate Secretary, Dan E. O'Keefe, $199,600 total compensation
Chief Sales Officer, Chief Marketing Officer, Heather N. Cobb
Director, Brad Stoots
Director, John A. Clerico
Director, Joshua J. Peters
Director, Kara Gae Neal
Auditors : HoganTaylor LLP

LOCATIONS

HQ: Educational Development Corp.
5402 South 122nd East Avenue, Tulsa, OK 74146
Phone: 918 622-4522
Web: www.edcpub.com

COMPETITORS

BAKER & TAYLOR HOLDINGS, LLC
GL GROUP, INC.
INGRAM BOOK GROUP LLC
MEDIA SOURCE, INC.
NIPPAN GROUP HOLDINGS, INC.

HISTORICAL FINANCIALS

Company Type: Public

Income Statement — FYE: February 28

	REVENUE ($mil)	NET INCOME ($mil)	NET PROFIT MARGIN	EMPLOYEES
02/21	204.6	12.6	6.2%	214
02/20	113.0	5.6	5.0%	201
02/19	118.8	6.6	5.6%	178
02/18	111.9	5.2	4.7%	193
02/17	106.6	2.8	2.7%	202
Annual Growth	17.7%	44.9%	—	1.5%

2021 Year-End Financials
Debt ratio: 18.3%
Return on equity: 36.2%
Cash ($ mil.): 1.8
Current Ratio: 1.53
Long-term debt ($ mil.): 10.4
No. of shares ($ mil.): 8.3
Dividends
Yield: —
Payout: 21.3%
Market value ($ mil.): 130.0

	STOCK PRICE ($) FY Close	P/E High/Low		PER SHARE ($) Earnings	Dividends	Book Value
02/21	15.61	13	2	1.50	0.32	4.82
02/20	5.16	13	8	0.68	0.20	3.52
02/19	8.05	33	9	0.81	0.20	3.16
02/18	19.35	36	11	0.64	0.05	2.49
02/17	9.55	42	20	0.35	0.18	1.86
Annual Growth	13.1%	—	—	43.9%	15.5%	26.9%

eHealth Inc

eHealth is a leading health insurance marketplace with a technology and service platform that provides consumer engagement, education and health insurance enrollment solutions. The company created a marketplace that offers consumers a broad choice of insurance products that includes thousands of Medicare Advantage, Medicare Supplement, Medicare Part D prescription drug, individual and family, small business and other ancillary health insurance products. Licensed to sell insurance policies throughout the US, the company has partnerships with more than 200 health insurance carriers, for which it processes and delivers potential members' applications in return for commission on policy sales. It lets consumers compare products online ? including health, dental, and vision insurance products from the likes of Aetna, Humana, and UnitedHealth.

Operations

The company manages its business into two business segments: Medicare segment (about 90% of sales); and Individual, Family, and Small Business Segment (over 10%).

The Medicare segment, through a combination of demand generation strategies, actively market a large selection of Medicare-related health insurance plans and, to a lesser extent, ancillary products such as dental and vision insurance and indemnity plans, to its Medicare-eligible consumers. Its Medicare ecommerce platform, which can be accessed through its websites (www.eHealthMedicare.com, www.PlanPrescriber.com and www.GoMedigap.com), and telephonic enrollment capabilities enable consumers to research, compare and purchase Medicare-related health insurance plans, including Medicare Advantage, Medicare Supplement and Medicare Part D prescription drug plans.

The Individual, Family and Small Business Segment actively markets individual and family health insurance and small business health insurance plans through its ecommerce platform, which can be accessed through its websites (www.eHealth.com and www.eHealthInsurance.com), and generate revenue as a result of commissions it receives from health insurance carriers whose health insurance plans are purchased through the company, as well as commission override payments it receives for achieving sales volume thresholds or other objectives.

Most of its revenues came from commissions which accounts for more than 90% and the remaining sales accounts for others. In terms of sales by product, Medicare generated about 80%.

Geographic Reach

A portion of technology and content group is located at their wholly-owned subsidiary in China, where technology development costs are generally lower than in the US. Its corporate office is located in Santa Clara, California. In addition, it also has offices in Utah, Texas, China, and Indiana.

Sales and Marketing

eHealth focus on building brand awareness, increasing Medicare, individual, family and small business customer visits to its websites, and telephonic sales centers and converting these visitors into members. Its four top clients Humana, UnitedHealthcare, Aetna, and Centene represent some 25%, about 25%, over 15%, and some 10% of total revenue, respectively.

Its online advertising member acquisition channel consists of consumers who access the company's website or call centers through paid keyword search advertising from search engines such as Google, Bing and Yahoo!, paid social platforms like Facebook, as well as various Internet marketing programs such as display advertising and retargeting campaigns. Its online advertising programs are delivered across all internet-enabled devices, including desktop computers, tablet computers and smart phones.

Marketing and advertising expense were $240.4 million, $178.9 million, and $122.6 million for the years ended 2021, 2020, and 2019, respectively.

Financial Performance

The company's revenue for fiscal 2021 decreased to $538.2 million compared from the prior year with $582.8 million.

Net loss for fiscal 2021 was $104.4 million compared from the prior year with a net income of $45.5 million.

Cash held by the company at the end of fiscal 2021 increased to $85.2 million. Cash provided by financing activities was $213.2 million while cash used for operations and investing activities were $162.6 million and $12.6 million, respectively.

Strategy

The company believes its consumer engagement platform and approach to bringing value to consumers is unique in the health insurance market and creates significant opportunities for growth in its core Medicare business and in other areas of the health insurance market. It intends to pursue the following strategies to further advance its business: pursue deliberate Medicare membership and revenue growth; focus on the enrollment quality; focus on the enrollment quality; improve effectiveness of its telesales organization; extend market leadership position in online enrollment; accelerate customer affinity strategy; and create new revenue streams and support growth of ancillary and individual and family plan products.

Company Background

eHealth was founded in 1997.

It began actively marketing Medicare policies through its eHealthMedicare and PlanPrescriber websites following the 2010 acquisition of privately held PlanPrescriber for roughly $30 million. PlanPrescriber provides online and pharmacy-based tools to help seniors navigate Medicare health insurance options. The acquisition has helped accelerate eHealth's penetration of the large and steadily growing senior market. eHealth intends to continue to expand its online Medicare enrollment capabilities as the baby boomer generation continues to shift into the Medicare bracket.

EXECUTIVES

Chairman, Director, Dale B. Wolf
Chief Executive Officer, Director, Francis S. Soistman
Senior Vice President, Chief Financial Officer, John J. Stelben
Chief Accounting Officer, Principal Accounting Officer, John Joseph Dolan
Chief Operating Officer, Chief Transformation Officer, Roman V. Rariy
Operations Interim Chief Revenue Officer, Sales Interim Chief Revenue Officer, Robert S. Hurley, $325,000 total compensation
Interim General Counsel, Julian Hwang
Director, A. John Hass
Director, Aaron C. Tolson
Director, Andrea C. Brimmer
Director, Beth A. Brooke
Director, Erin L. Russell
Director, Cesar M. Soriano
Auditors : Ernst & Young LLP

LOCATIONS

HQ: eHealth Inc
2625 Augustine Drive, Second Floor, Santa Clara, CA 95054
Phone: 650 584-2700
Web: www.ehealth.com

PRODUCTS/OPERATIONS

2015 Sales

	$ mil.	% of total
Commissions	171.3	90
Other	18.2	10
Total	189.5	10

Selected Insurance Carriers

Aetna
Altius
Anthem Blue Cross and Blue Shield
Assurant Health
BlueCross BlueShield of Texas
Blue Shield of California
CareFirst BlueCross BlueShield
Celtic Insurance Company
CIGNA
ConnectiCare
Coventry Health Care
Delta Dental
EmblemHealth
HealthNet
Highmark
Humana
IHC Group
Kaiser Permanente
LifeWise Health Plans
Regence BlueCross BlueShield
Scott & White Health Plan
Security Life Insurance Company of America

UniCare
UnitedHealth
WellPath Select
WellPoint

Selected Products
Health Insurance
Medicare
Maternity Coverage
PPO Plans
HMO Plans
Individual and Family
Individual Health Insurance
Family Health Insurance
Medicare
Short-term Health Insurance
Student Health Insurance
Health Savings Accounts
International Health Insurance
Individual Dental Insurance
Discount Cards
Vision Insurance
Life Insurance
Accident Insurance
Critical Illness Insurance
Travel Health Insurance
FSmall Business
Group Health Insurance
Group Dental Insurance
Group Vision Insurance
Medicare
Medicare Insurance Plans
Medicare Supplement
Medicare Advantage
Medicare Part D
Short Term
Short-term Health Insurance
Dental
Individual Dental Insurance
Group Dental Insurance
Vision
Individual Vision Insurance
Group Vision Insurance
Life
Life Insurance
Other
Travel Health Insurance
International Health Insurance
Pet Insurance
Prescription Discount Card
Telemedicine

COMPETITORS

A ACUITY MUTUAL INSURANCE COMPANY
ATHENAHEALTH, INC.
BENEFITFOCUS.COM, INC.
BENEFITMALL INC.
EXTEND HEALTH, INC.
FORTEGRA FINANCIAL CORPORATION
PARKER, SMITH & FEEK, INC.
SECURIAN FINANCIAL GROUP, INC.
SELECTIVE INSURANCE GROUP, INC.
TIVITY HEALTH, INC.

HISTORICAL FINANCIALS
Company Type: Public

Income Statement — FYE: December 31

	REVENUE ($mil)	NET INCOME ($mil)	NET PROFIT MARGIN	EMPLOYEES
12/20	582.7	45.4	7.8%	1,960
12/19	506.2	66.8	13.2%	1,500
12/18	251.3	0.2	0.1%	1,079
12/17	172.3	(25.4)	—	1,079
12/16	186.9	(4.8)	—	944
Annual Growth	32.9%	—	—	20.0%

2020 Year-End Financials
Debt ratio: —
Return on equity: 6.6%
Cash ($ mil.): 43.7
Current Ratio: 3.92
Long-term debt ($ mil.): —
No. of shares ($ mil.): 25.9
Dividends
Yield: —
Payout: —
Market value ($ mil.): 1,830.0

	STOCK PRICE ($) FY Close	P/E High/Low		PER SHARE ($) Earnings	Dividends	Book Value
12/20	70.61	83	35	1.68	0.00	32.31
12/19	96.08	38	12	2.73	0.00	22.79
12/18	38.42	401	21365	0.01	0.00	15.60
12/17	17.37	—	—	(1.37)	0.00	3.28
12/16	10.65	—	—	(0.27)	0.00	4.23
Annual Growth	60.5%	—	—	—	—	66.3%

Ellington Residential Mortgaging Real Estate Investment Trust

Ellington Financial LLC is ready to double its money. The investment firm formed Ellington Residential Mortgage REIT, a real estate residential trust (REIT), to invest in agency residential mortgage-backed securities (Agency RMBS), or those guaranteed by federally sponsored entities Fannie Mae, Freddie Mac, and Ginnie Mae. (Agency RMBS carry less risk than privately issued mortgage securities.) The trust's portfolio is balanced out with about 10% non-Agency RMBS such as residential whole mortgage loans, mortgage servicing rights (MSRs), and residential real properties. (Non-Agency RMBS carry more risk but might offer better returns.) The trust went public in 2013.

IPO
The trust plans to spend at least 80% of the proceeds from its $129 million IPO to invest in Agency RMBS backed by 15-year and 30-year fixed rate mortgages. The remaining 20% will be used to invest in Agency RMBS backed by hybrid and adjustable rate mortgages and non-Agency RMBS backed by Alt-A, prime, and subprime mortgages.

Operations
Ellington Residential Mortgage REIT formed in August 2012 by affiliates of Ellington Financial and investment firm The Blackstone Group. As a REIT, it is exempt from paying federal income tax as long as it makes a quarterly distribution to shareholders. And as a trust, Ellington Residential Mortgage does not have any employees. It is externally managed and advised by Ellington Residential Mortgage Management LLC.

Strategy
The company's investment philosophy revolves around pursuing various types of mortgage-backed securities and related assets without any restriction as to ratings, structure, or position in the capital structure. Of course, there are risks associated with mortgage investments, but Ellington believes balancing its portfolio with agency-backed securities somewhat levels its risk.

EXECUTIVES

Chairman, Thomas F. Robards
Co-Chief Investment Officer, Trustee, Michael W. Vranos
President, Chief Executive Officer, Trustee, Laurence Penn
Co-Chief Investment Officer, Mark Tecotzky
Chief Financial Officer, Christopher Smernoff, $40,000 total compensation
Chief Operating Officer, Treasurer, John R. (J.R.) Herlihy, $41,600 total compensation
General Counsel, Daniel Margolis
Trustee, Ronald I. Simon
Trustee, Robert B. Allardice
Trustee, David J. Miller
Trustee, Menes O. Chee
Auditors : PricewaterhouseCoopers LLP

LOCATIONS

HQ: Ellington Residential Mortgaging Real Estate Investment Trust
53 Forest Avenue, Old Greenwich, CT 06870
Phone: 203 698-1200
Web: www.earnreit.com

COMPETITORS

ANWORTH MORTGAGE ASSET CORPORATION
CHERRY HILL MORTGAGE INVESTMENT CORPORATION
HUNT COMPANIES FINANCE TRUST, INC.
TWO HARBORS INVESTMENT CORP.
WESTERN ASSET MORTGAGE CAPITAL CORPORATION

HISTORICAL FINANCIALS
Company Type: Public

Income Statement — FYE: December 31

	ASSETS ($mil)	NET INCOME ($mil)	INCOME AS % OF ASSETS	EMPLOYEES
12/20	1,194.8	20.1	1.7%	150
12/19	1,489.1	22.2	1.5%	0
12/18	1,675.5	(11.2)	—	150
12/17	1,887.0	10.7	0.6%	160
12/16	1,429.1	11.9	0.8%	160
Annual Growth	(4.4%)	14.0%	—	(1.6%)

2020 Year-End Financials
Return on assets: 1.4%
Return on equity: 12.2%
Long-term debt ($ mil.): —
No. of shares ($ mil.): 12.3
Sales ($ mil.): 35.9
Dividends
Yield: 8.5%
Payout: 68.7%
Market value ($ mil.): 161.0

	STOCK PRICE ($) FY Close	P/E High/Low		PER SHARE ($) Earnings	Dividends	Book Value
12/20	13.04	8	2	1.63	1.12	13.48
12/19	10.85	7	5	1.79	1.18	12.91
12/18	10.23	—	—	(0.88)	1.45	12.30
12/17	12.04	17	13	0.93	1.57	14.45
12/16	13.01	11	8	1.31	1.65	15.52
Annual Growth	0.1%	—	—	5.6%	(9.2%)	(3.5%)

	STOCK PRICE ($) FY Close	P/E High/Low		PER SHARE ($) Earnings	Dividends	Book Value
12/20	14.60	11	6	1.70	0.22	14.90
12/19	18.50	13	10	1.44	0.20	13.32
12/18	14.95	13	10	1.34	0.17	11.69
12/17	16.00	16	13	0.97	0.14	10.71
12/16	13.00	14	11	0.96	0.13	9.84
Annual Growth	2.9%	—	—	15.4%	14.1%	10.9%

FIRST KEYSTONE CORPORATION
IDAHO INDEPENDENT BANK
PINNACLE BANCSHARES, INC.
SVB & T CORPORATION

HISTORICAL FINANCIALS
Company Type: Public

Income Statement FYE: December 31

	ASSETS ($mil)	NET INCOME ($mil)	INCOME AS % OF ASSETS	EMPLOYEES
12/20	1,032.3	6.7	0.7%	160
12/19	915.2	7.9	0.9%	162
12/18	898.8	4.2	0.5%	164
12/17	750.0	4.2	0.6%	137
12/16	692.1	3.9	0.6%	131
Annual Growth	10.5%	14.1%	—	5.1%

2020 Year-End Financials
Return on assets: 0.6%
Return on equity: 7.5%
Long-term debt ($ mil.): —
No. of shares ($ mil.): 2.7
Sales ($ mil.): 41.5
Dividends
Yield: 3.9%
Payout: 49.7%
Market value ($ mil.): 83.0

	STOCK PRICE ($) FY Close	P/E High/Low		PER SHARE ($) Earnings	Dividends	Book Value
12/20	30.63	14	7	2.41	1.20	33.62
12/19	32.53	13	10	2.86	1.16	31.70
12/18	30.34	22	17	1.72	1.12	29.65
12/17	30.35	16	13	1.93	1.08	26.02
12/16	29.25	16	12	1.85	1.04	25.12
Annual Growth	1.2%	—	—	6.8%	3.6%	7.6%

Embassy Bancorp Inc

EXECUTIVES

Chairman, President, Chief Executive Officer, Subsidiary Officer, David M. Lobach, $599,994 total compensation

Executive Vice President, Assistant Secretary, Subsidiary Officer, Lynne M. Neel

Executive Vice President, Chief Financial Officer, Diane M. Cunningham

Executive Vice President, Subsidiary Officer, James R. Bartholomew, $315,313 total compensation

Chief Financial Officer, Chief Operating Officer, Subsidiary Officer, Judith A. Hunsicker, $415,539 total compensation

Director, Geoffrey F. Boyer
Director, Frank Banko
Director, Patti Gates Smith
Director, John T. Yurconic
Director, John G. Englesson
Director, Bernard M. Lesavoy
Director, John C. Pittman
Auditors : Baker Tilly US, LLP

LOCATIONS

HQ: Embassy Bancorp Inc
One Hundred Gateway Drive, Suite 100, Bethlehem, PA 18017
Phone: 610 882-8800
Web: www.embassybank.com

HISTORICAL FINANCIALS
Company Type: Public

Income Statement FYE: December 31

	ASSETS ($mil)	NET INCOME ($mil)	INCOME AS % OF ASSETS	EMPLOYEES
12/20	1,442.0	12.8	0.9%	96
12/19	1,176.1	10.8	0.9%	95
12/18	1,099.3	10.0	0.9%	91
12/17	996.9	7.3	0.7%	84
12/16	924.2	7.1	0.8%	83
Annual Growth	11.8%	15.7%	—	3.7%

2020 Year-End Financials
Return on assets: 0.9%
Return on equity: 12.0%
Long-term debt ($ mil.): —
No. of shares ($ mil.): 7.5
Sales ($ mil.): 46.7
Dividends
Yield: 1.5%
Payout: 12.9%
Market value ($ mil.): 110.0

Emclaire Financial Corp.

Emclaire Financial is the holding company for the Farmers National Bank of Emlenton, which operates about a dozen branches in northwestern Pennsylvania. Serving area consumers and businesses, the bank offers standard deposit products and services, including checking and savings accounts, money market accounts, and CDs. The bank is mainly a real estate lender, with commercial mortgages, residential first mortgages, and home equity loans and lines of credit making up most of its loan portfolio. Emclaire Financial also owns title insurance and real estate settlement services provider Emclaire Settlement Services.

EXECUTIVES

Chairman, President, Chief Executive Officer, Subsidiary Officer, William C. Marsh, $357,797 total compensation

Chief Financial Officer, Treasurer, Subsidiary Officer, Amanda L. Engles

Secretary, Subsidiary Officer, Jennifer A. Roxbury, $179,520 total compensation

Subsidiary Officer, Robert A. Vernick, $168,100 total compensation

Director, Milissa S. Bauer
Director, David L. Cox, $173,000 total compensation
Director, James M. Crooks
Director, Henry H. Deible
Director, Henry H. Deible
Director, Robert W. Freeman
Director, Mark A. Freemer
Director, Robert L. Hunter
Director, John B. Mason
Director, Deanna K. McCarrier
Director, Nicholas D. Varischetti
Auditors : BKD, LLP

LOCATIONS

HQ: Emclaire Financial Corp.
612 Main Street, Emlenton, PA 16373
Phone: 844 767-2311
Web: www.emclairefinancial.com

COMPETITORS

COMMUNITY SHORES BANK CORPORATION

Emergent BioSolutions Inc

Emergent BioSolutions a global life sciences company focused on providing innovative preparedness and response solutions addressing accidental, deliberate and naturally occurring public health threats (PHTs). Primary product BioThrax is the only FDA-approved anthrax vaccine. Most BioThrax revenue comes from direct sales to US federal agencies including the Department of Defense (DOD) and the Department of Health and Human Services (HHS). Its commercial business line includes Vivotif (typhoid fever), and Vaxchora (cholera); and opioid overdose drug Narcan. Emergent also has contract manufacturing and research operations.

Operations

The company is focused on products and solutions that address the following five distinct PHT categories: Chemical, Biological, Radiological, Nuclear and Explosives (CBRNE); emerging infectious diseases (EID); travel health; emerging health crises; and acute/emergency care.

Its product portfolio comprises about 10 marketed products (vaccines, therapeutics, and drug-device combination products) that are sold to government and commercial customers. Its product portfolio also includes two product candidates, designated AV7909 (vaccine) and Trobigard Auto-Injector (drug-device combination), that are not approved by the FDA or any other regulatory health authority, but which are procured under special circumstances by certain government agencies.

The company's product development pipeline portfolio consists of a diversified mix of both pre-clinical and clinical-stage product candidates, encompassing a mix of vaccines, therapeutics and drug-device combination products. In some cases, certain candidates are supported by external, non-dilutive funding sources (government agencies, non-governmental organizations, pharma/biotech innovators). Certain other candidates are supported solely by internal funding sources.

Emergent's portfolio of CDMO services consists of three distinct but interrelated service pillars: development services (process and analytical development); drug substance manufacturing; and drug product manufacturing (fill/finish). These services, which refers to as molecule-to-market offerings, employ diverse technology platforms (mammalian, microbial, viral, plasma and gene therapy) across a network of nine geographically distinct development and manufacturing sites operated by the company for its internal products and pipeline and CDMO services, for both clinical-stage projects and commercial-stage projects. It directs these CDMO services for a variety of third-party customers, including innovative pharmaceutical companies, government agencies and non-government organizations.

Emergent's revenues are derived from a combination of the sale and procurement of its product portfolio and the provision of is CDMO services to external customers, and the securing of non-dilutive contract and grant funding for research and development (R&D) projects by us from various third-party sources.

Geographic Reach

Headquartered in Gaithersburg, Maryland, Emergent has manufacturing, laboratories, fill/finish facility services, offices and warehouse in about 25 locations in North America and Europe. Some of its main location are in Michigan, Maryland, Massachusetts, California, and Canada, as well as in Switzerland.

Sales and Marketing

The company serves the pharma and biotech industry and government agencies, as well as non-government organizations. The US Government is largest customer and also provides the company with substantial funding for the development of a number of product candidates.

The US Government and Non-US Government accounts for an evenly split of revenue.

Some of other customers for it specific products are state health departments, local law enforcement agencies, community-based organizations, substance abuse centers, federal agencies and consumers through pharmacies fulfilling physician-directed or standing order prescriptions.

Financial Performance

The company's revenue for 2021 was $1.8 billion, a 15% increase from the previous year's revenue of $1.6 billion.

In 2021, the company had a net income of $230.9 million, a 24% decrease from the previous year's net income of $305.1 million.

The company's cash at the end of 2021 was $576.3 million. Operating activities generated $321.1 million, while investing activities used $225 million, mainly for purchases of property, plant and equipment. Financing activities used another $141 million.

Strategy

Emergent's ongoing five-year strategic plan, 2020-2024, is focused on leveraging core competencies, relationships and operating systems Emergent has developed over the last 23 years and driving growth across various segments of the PHT market. The strategic plan specifies employing five core strategies. They are:

Execute Core Business ? Emergent is focused on continuing to build its leadership positions across several markets in the PHT space.

Grow Through Mergers and Acquisitions (M&A) ? The company has successfully executed and integrated several product and facility acquisitions that have increased Emergent's diversification, allowed expansion into new markets, and provided a differentiated R&D pipeline. Emergent plans to continue to leverage its M&A and partnering strengths not only to solidify its leadership positions in the MCM market.

Strengthen R&D Portfolio ? Emergent continues to focus on expanding and advancing its pipeline of vaccines and therapeutic product candidates, with the aim of developing differentiated products that address unmet needs in the PHT space.

Build Scalable Capabilities ? Achieving its 2024 strategic objectives requires an investment in infrastructure, internal governance and capabilities that help us realize the benefits of scale. This includes investing new capital into our development and manufacturing facilities, strengthening the company's global sales and procurement models, upgrading our technology and growing our commercial infrastructure.

Evolve the Culture ? Emergent is committed to attracting, developing, and retaining the best talent reflecting a diversity of ideas, backgrounds, and perspectives and seek to demonstrate that commitment through its talent development strategy, processes and company-wide programs.

Company Background

Emergent BioSolutions was founded in 1998 in Michigan and was reorganized as Delaware corporation in 2004.

In 2014, Emergent acquired Cangene, gaining treatments BAT (botulism), Anthrasil (anthrax infection), and VIGIV (adverse vaccine reactions).

In 2016 the firm spun off its biosciences division, which worked on therapies for leukemia and lymphoma and vaccines for such infectious diseases as influenza, as the new public company Aptevo Therapeutics.

In 2017 Emergent acquired smallpox vaccine ACAM2000 from Sanofi. It also purchased raxibacumab, an antibody product for treatment of inhaled anthrax, from Human Genome Sciences GlaxoSmithKline.

EXECUTIVES

Chairman, Director, Zsolt Harsanyi
Administration President, Administration Chief Executive Officer, Director, Robert G. Kramer, $549,047 total compensation
Executive Vice President, Chief Financial Officer, Treasurer, Richard S. Lindahl, $365,393 total compensation
Executive Vice President, Chief Operating Officer, Division Officer, Adam R. Havey, $480,728 total compensation
External Affairs Executive Vice President, External Affairs General Counsel, External Affairs Corporate Secretary, Jennifer Fox
Corporate Development Executive Vice President, External Affairs Executive Vice President, Corporate Development Chief Development Officer, External Affairs Chief Development Officer, Corporate Development Chief Strategy Officer, External Affairs Chief Strategy Officer, Atul Saran, $488,730 total compensation
Communications Executive Vice President, Human Resources Executive Vice President, Human Resources Chief Human Resources Officer, Communications Chief Human Resources Officer, Katherine Strei
Commercial Operations Executive Vice President, Coleen Glessner
Director, Keith A. Katkin
Director, Kathryn C. Zoon
Director, George A. Joulwan
Director, Louis W. Sullivan
Director, Jerome M. Hauer
Director, Marvin L. White
Lead Director, Director, Ronald B. Richard
Auditors : Ernst & Young LLP

LOCATIONS

HQ: Emergent BioSolutions Inc
400 Professional Drive Suite 400, Gaithersburg, MD 20879
Phone: 240 631-3200
Web: www.emergentbiosolutions.com

PRODUCTS/OPERATIONS

2014 Sales

	$ mil.	% of total
Products	308.3	68
Contracts & grants	110.9	25
Contract manufacturing	30.9	7
Total	450.1	100

2014 Sales

	$ mil	% of total
Biodefense	370.5	82
Biosciences	79.6	18
Total	450.1	100

Selected Acquisitions and Ventures

2014
   Cangene Corporation ($222 million, a biopharmaceutical company)
2013
   Bracco Diagnostics' Healthcare Protective products Division ($26 million, Reactive Skin Decontamination Lotion)
2011
   TenX BioPharma ($2.5 million, late-stage biopharmaceutical candidate zanolimumab)
2010
   Trubion Pharmaceuticals ($135 million, biopharmaceutical development)
   EPIC Bio Pte Limited (joint venture with Temasek Life Sciences, influenza vaccine development)

Selected Products & Candidates

Licensed
   BioThrax (Anthrax Vaccine Adsorbed)
Investigational
   Infectious Disease
     Anthrivig
     NuThrax
     PreviThrax
     Thravixa
   Oncology
     Zanolimumab (T-cell lymphoma)

COMPETITORS

ABBVIE INC.
ASTELLAS PHARMA INC.
ASTELLAS PHARMA US, INC.
Advanz Pharma Corp
BIOMARIN PHARMACEUTICAL INC.
INNOVIVA, INC.
IONIS PHARMACEUTICALS, INC.
KYOWA KIRIN CO., LTD.
NAVIDEA BIOPHARMACEUTICALS, INC.
UNITED THERAPEUTICS CORPORATION

HISTORICAL FINANCIALS

Company Type: Public

Income Statement — FYE: December 31

	REVENUE ($mil)	NET INCOME ($mil)	NET PROFIT MARGIN	EMPLOYEES
12/20	1,555.4	305.1	19.6%	700
12/19	1,106.0	54.5	4.9%	1,834
12/18	782.4	62.7	8.0%	1,705
12/17	560.8	82.5	14.7%	1,256
12/16	488.7	51.7	10.6%	1,098
Annual Growth	33.6%	55.8%	—	(10.6%)

2020 Year-End Financials

Debt ratio: 30.3%
Return on equity: 24.0%
Cash ($ mil.): 621.3
Current Ratio: 3.11
Long-term debt ($ mil.): 841
No. of shares ($ mil.): 53.1
Dividends
  Yield: —
  Payout: —
Market value ($ mil.): 4,758.0

	STOCK PRICE ($) FY Close	P/E High/Low		PER SHARE ($) Earnings	Dividends	Book Value
12/20	89.60	23	9	5.67	0.00	27.25
12/19	53.95	62	38	1.04	0.00	21.05
12/18	59.28	59	36	1.22	0.00	19.74
12/17	46.47	24	14	1.71	0.00	18.47
12/16	32.84	34	19	1.13	0.00	14.69
Annual Growth	28.5%	—	—	49.7%	—	16.7%

ENB Financial Corp

EXECUTIVES

Chairman, President, Chief Executive Officer, Subsidiary Officer, Director, Jeffrey S Stauffer
Senior Executive Vice President, Subsidiary Officer, William J. Kitsch
Senior Executive Vice President, Chief Strategy Officer, Interim Chief Operating Officer, Subsidiary Officer, Division Officer, Chad E. Neiss
Executive Vice President, Chief Human Resources Officer, Cindy L. Hoffman
Executive Vice President, Chief Financial Officer, Treasurer, Subsidiary Officer, Rachel G. Bitner
Subsidiary Officer, Nicholas D. Klein
Subsidiary Officer, Barry E. Miller, $199,269 total compensation
Director, Brian K. Reed
Director, Willis R. Lefever
Director, Jay S. Martin
Director, Judith A. Weaver
Director, Roger L. Zimmerman
Director, Joshua E. Hoffman
Director, Susan Y. Nicholas
Director, Mark C. Wagner
Auditors : S.R. Snodgrass, P.C.

LOCATIONS

HQ: ENB Financial Corp
31 E. Main St., Ephrata, PA 17522-0457
Phone: 717 733-4181
Web: www.enbfc.com

HISTORICAL FINANCIALS

Company Type: Public

Income Statement — FYE: December 31

	ASSETS ($mil)	NET INCOME ($mil)	INCOME AS % OF ASSETS	EMPLOYEES
12/20	1,462.3	12.2	0.8%	276
12/19	1,171.7	11.3	1.0%	280
12/18	1,097.8	9.7	0.9%	294
12/17	1,033.6	6.3	0.6%	285
12/16	984.2	7.5	0.8%	270
Annual Growth	10.4%	13.0%		0.6%

2020 Year-End Financials

Return on assets: 0.9%
Return on equity: 9.9%
Long-term debt ($ mil.): —
No. of shares ($ mil.): 5.5
Sales ($ mil.): 57.4
Dividends
  Yield: —
  Payout: 29.0%
Market value ($ mil.): 104.0

	STOCK PRICE ($) FY Close	P/E High/Low		PER SHARE ($) Earnings	Dividends	Book Value
12/20	18.60	11	8	2.20	0.64	23.39
12/19	20.75	20	10	2.01	0.62	20.69
12/18	34.55	22	20	1.71	0.58	18.02
12/17	34.25	32	29	1.12	0.56	17.50
12/16	34.40	26	24	1.33	0.55	16.65
Annual Growth	(14.2%)	—	—	13.5%	4.1%	8.9%

Encore Capital Group Inc

Encore Capital Group is an international specialty finance company that provides debt recovery solutions and other related services across a broad range of financial assets. Encore Capital purchase portfolios of defaulted consumer receivables at deep discounts to face value and manage them by working with individuals as they repay their obligations and work toward financial recovery. Defaulted receivables are consumers' unpaid financial commitments to credit originators, including banks, credit unions, consumer finance companies and commercial retailers. Defaulted receivables may also include receivables subject to bankruptcy proceedings. The company also provide debt servicing and other portfolio management services to credit originators for non-performing loans in Europe. Around 70% of total revenue comes from domestic operation.

Operations

Encore Capital provides debt recovery solutions and other related services for consumers across a broad range of financial assets. It also provides debt servicing and other portfolio management services to credit originators for non-performing loans. Overall, revenues from receivable portfolios accounts more than 90%, while services and others accounts the remainder of total revenue.

Encore Capital has primary business units: Midland Credit Management (MCM) and its and domestic affiliates; Cabot Credit Management Limited (CCM) and its subsidiaries and European affiliates, Cabot. Through MCM, Encore Capital is a market leader in portfolio purchasing and recovery in the US, including Puerto Rico. Cabot's primary business of portfolio purchasing and recovery, also provides a range of debt servicing offerings such as early stage collections, business process outsourcing (BPO), including through Wescot Credit Services Limited (Wescot), a leading UK contingency debt collection and BPO services company.

Geographic Reach

The San Diego-headquartered Encore Capital operates in US, Europe and Latin America. Encore Capital maintain domestic collection call centers in Phoenix, Arizona; St. Cloud, Minnesota; Troy, Michigan; and Roanoke, Virginia and international call centers in Gurgaon, India and San Jose, Costa Rica.

Its largest market is the US, where it generated around 70% of its revenue, while Europe accounted for roughly 35% and other countries accounts for the remaining revenue.

Sales and Marketing

Encore Capital maintain relationships with various financial service providers such as banks, credit unions, consumer finance companies, retailers, utilities companies and government agencies. It markets services through direct mail, call centers, legal action, third-party collection agencies, and digital collections.

Financial Performance

The company reported a total revenue of $1.6 billion in 2021, an 8% increase from the previous year's total revenue of $1.5 billion.

In 2021, the company had a net income of $350.8 million, a 66% increase from the previous year's net income of $212.5 million. This was primarily due to the lower volume of interest expense and loss on extinguishment of debt for the year.

The company's cash at the end of 2021 was $189.6 million. Operating activities generated $303.1 million, while financing activities used $655.7 million. Investing activities generated $339.9 million.

Strategy

Competitive Advantage. The company strives to enhance its competitive advantages through innovation, which the company expects will result in collections growth and improved productivity. To continue generating strong risk-adjusted returns, the company intends to continue investing in analytics and technology, risk management and compliance. Encore will also continue investing in initiatives that enhance relationships with consumers, expand digital capabilities and collections, improve liquidation rates on the company's portfolios or reduce costs.

Market Focus. The company continues to concentrate on its core portfolio purchasing and recovery business in the US and the UK markets, where scale helps the company generate its highest risk-adjusted returns.

Balance Sheet Strength. Encore is focused on strengthening its balance sheet while delivering strong financial and operational results. This includes increasing the company's cash flow generation through efficient collection operations. Depending on its relative leverage, the company may apply excess cash toward reducing debt or, in circumstances in which it is operating within or below the lower end of the company's target leverage range, Encore may allocate capital toward share repurchases.

Company Background

In early 2016, the company sold its San Antonio, Texas-based Propel Acquisition LLC subsidiary, which acquired and serviced residential and commercial tax liens on property. The firm was the largest tax lien company in Texas.

EXECUTIVES

Chairman, Director, Michael P. Monaco
U.S. Debt Purchasing and Operations President, U.S. Debt Purchasing and Operations Chief Executive Officer, Director, Ashish Masih, $733,562 total compensation
Executive Vice President, Chief Financial Officer, Treasurer, Subsidiary Officer, Principal Accounting Officer, Jonathan C. Clark, $544,944 total compensation
Senior Vice President, General Counsel, Subsidiary Officer, Andrew Asch
Subsidiary Officer, Ryan B. Bell
Subsidiary Officer, Craig A. Buick
Director, Ash Gupta
Director, Wendy G. Hannam
Director, Jeffrey A. Hilzinger
Director, Angela A. Knight
Director, Laura Newman Olle
Director, William C. Goings
Director, Richard P. Stovsky
Auditors : BDO USA, LLP

LOCATIONS

HQ: Encore Capital Group Inc
350 Camino De La Reina, Suite 100, San Diego, CA 92108
Phone: 877 445-4581
Web: www.encorecapital.com

2015 Sales

	$ mil.	% of total
United States	741.0	64
Europe	376.1	32
Other geographies	44.5	4
Total	1,161.6	100

PRODUCTS/OPERATIONS

2015 Sales

	$ mil.	% of total
Portfolio purchasing and recovery	1,130.0	97
Tax lien business	31.6	3
Total	1,161.6	100

Selected Subsidiaries

Ascension Capital Group, Inc.
Cabot Financial (UK, Ireland)
Grove Financial (UK)
Marlin Financial Group (UK)
MCM Midland Management Costa Rica, S.r.l.
Midland Credit Management, Inc.
Midland Credit Management India Private Limited
Midland Funding LLC
Midland Funding NCC-2 Corporation
Midland India LLC
Midland International LLC
Midland Portfolio Services, Inc.
MRC Receivables Corporation
Propel Financial Services (US)
Refinancia S.A. (Colombia, Peru)

COMPETITORS

ALLY COMMERCIAL FINANCE LLC
CHASE PAYMENTECH SOLUTIONS, LLC
CREDIT SAISON CO., LTD.
HITACHI CAPITAL (UK) PLC
HSBC USA, INC.
NEWTEK BUSINESS SERVICES CORP.
NICHOLAS FINANCIAL, INC.
PRA GROUP, INC.
PRIVATEBANCORP, INC.
PURPOSE FINANCIAL, INC.

HISTORICAL FINANCIALS

Company Type: Public

Income Statement — FYE: December 31

	REVENUE ($mil)	NET INCOME ($mil)	NET PROFIT MARGIN	EMPLOYEES
12/20	1,501.4	211.8	14.1%	7,725
12/19	1,397.6	167.8	12.0%	7,300
12/18	1,362.0	115.8	8.5%	7,900
12/17	1,187.0	83.2	7.0%	8,200
12/16	1,029.2	76.5	7.4%	6,700
Annual Growth	9.9%	29.0%	—	3.6%

2020 Year-End Financials

Debt ratio: 67.5%
Return on equity: 18.8%
Cash ($ mil.): 189.1
Current Ratio: 1.18
Long-term debt ($ mil.): 3,281.6
No. of shares ($ mil.): 31.3
Dividends
Yield: —
Payout: —
Market value ($ mil.): 1,221.0

	STOCK PRICE ($) FY Close	P/E High/Low		PER SHARE ($) Earnings	Dividends	Book Value
12/20	38.95	7	2	6.68	0.00	38.85
12/19	35.36	7	5	5.33	0.00	32.87
12/18	23.50	11	5	4.06	0.00	26.49
12/17	42.10	15	9	3.15	0.00	22.55
12/16	28.65	10	6	2.96	0.00	21.85
Annual Growth	8.0%	—	—	22.6%	—	15.5%

Encore Wire Corp.

A low-cost manufacturer of copper electrical building wire and cable, Encore Wire produces NM-B cable, a sheathed cable used to wire homes, apartments, and manufactured housing, and UF-B. Its inventory of stock-keeping units include THWN-2 cable, an insulated feeder, circuit, and branch wiring for commercial and industrial buildings, and other wires including SEU, SER, Photovoltaic, URD, tray cable, metal-clad and armored cable. The company's principal customers are wholesale electrical distributors that sells its products to electrical contractors. The company was founded in 1989.

Operations

The company conducts its business in one segment ? the manufacture of electric building wire, principally NM-B cable, for use primarily as interior wiring in homes, apartments, and manufactured housing, and THHN/THWN-2 cable and metal-clad and armored cable for use primarily as wiring in commercial and industrial buildings. It also offers UF-B cable, XHHW-2, USE-2, RHH/RHW-2 and other types of wire products, including SEU, SER, Photovoltaic, URD, tray cable, metal-clad and armored cable. All of these products are manufactured with copper or aluminum as the current-carrying component of the conductor.

Geographic Reach
Encore primarily maintains its headquarters and manufacturing plants in McKinney, Texas.

Sales and Marketing
Encore mainly provides interior electrical wiring in commercial and industrial buildings, homes, apartments, manufactured housing, and data centers. The principal customers for Encore's wire are wholesale electrical distributors, who sell building wire and a variety of other products to electrical contractors. It sells its products primarily through independent manufacturers' representatives located throughout US and, to a lesser extent, through its own direct in-house marketing efforts.

Financial Performance
Net sales for the twelve months ended December 31, 2021 were $2.6 billion compared to $1.3 billion during the same period in 2020 and $1.3 billion during the same period in 2019. The 103.0% increase in net sales dollars in 2021 versus 2020 is primarily the result of a 105% increase in copper wire sales. Sales dollars were driven higher by an 85% increase in average selling price of copper wire, coupled with a 11% increase in copper wire pounds shipped.

In 2021, the company had a net income of $541.4 million, a 612% increase from the previous year's net income of $76.1 million.

The company's cash at the end of 2021 was $439 million. Operating activities generated $418.4 million, while investing activities used $118.2 million, mainly for purchases of property, plant and equipment. Financing activities used another $44.4 million, primarily for purchase of treasury stock.

Strategy
Encore's strategy is to further expand its share of the building wire market primarily by emphasizing a high level of customer service and the addition of new products that complement its current product line, while maintaining and enhancing its low-cost production capabilities. Encore's low-cost production capability features an efficient plant design incorporating highly automated manufacturing equipment, an integrated production process and a highly-motivated work force. Encore's plants are all located on one large campus. This single-site campus enables and enhances low-cost manufacturing, distribution and administration, as well as helping to build and maintain a cohesive company culture.

Customer Service: Encore is highly focused on responding to customer needs, with an emphasis on building and maintaining strong customer relationships. Encore seeks to establish customer loyalty by achieving an industry-leading order fill rate and rapidly handling customer orders, shipments, inquiries and returns. The company maintains product inventories sufficient to meet anticipated customer demand and believes that the speed and completeness with which it fills orders are key competitive advantages critical to marketing its products.

Product Innovation: Encore has been a leader in bringing new ideas to a commodity product. Encore pioneered the widespread use of color feeder sizes of commercial wire and colors in residential non-metallic cable. The colors have improved on-the-job safety, reduced installation times for contractors and enabled building inspectors to rapidly and accurately inspect construction projects. Encore Wire's patented SmartColor ID system for metal-clad and armor-clad cables allows for quick and accurate identification of gauge, number of conductors, wire and jacket type.

Low-Cost Production: Encore's low-cost production capability features an efficient plant design and an incentivized work force.

Company Background
Industry veterans Vincent Rego and Donald Spurgin founded Encore Wire in 1989 to make wire for residential use after their previous company, Capital Wire, was bought out by Penn Central in 1988. Encore rolled through the home-building recession of the early 1990s, gathering market share along the way. The company went public in 1992.

EXECUTIVES

Chairman, President, Chief Executive Officer, Director, Daniel L. Jones, $850,000 total compensation

Finance Vice President, Bret J. Eckert, $400,000 total compensation

Lead Independent Director, Director, John H. Wilson

Director, Gregory J. Fisher

Director, Gina A. Norris

Director, William R. Thomas

Director, Scott D. Weaver

Auditors : Ernst & Young LLP

LOCATIONS

HQ: Encore Wire Corp.
  1329 Millwood Road, McKinney, TX 75069
Phone: 972 562-9473   **Fax:** 972 562-4744
Web: www.encorewire.com

PRODUCTS/OPERATIONS

Selected Products
Armored Cable (multiple conductors insulated with PVC and coated with nylon used primarily as feeder, circuit, and branch wiring in commercial and industrial buildings)
NM-B Cable (non-metallic sheathed cable for interior wiring in homes)
Photovoltaic Cable (used by the solar industry, providing connections between PV panels, colllector boxes and inverters)
THWN-2 Cable (single conductor insulated with PVC and coated with nylon used primarily as feeder, circuit, and branch wiring in commercial and industrial buildings)
UF-B Cable (underground feeder cable for conducting power underground to outside lighting and other remote residential applications)
USE-2 Cable (general purpose applications; conduit or installed in underground sites, or in recognized raceways for service, feeders, and branch-circuit wiring)
XHHW-2 Cable (used as feeder, circuit and branch wiring in commercial and industrial buildings)

COMPETITORS

AMERCABLE INCORPORATED
BELDEN INC.
GENERAL CABLE CORPORATION
INTERNATIONAL WIRE GROUP, INC.
KALAS MFG. INC.
L. B. FOSTER COMPANY
OLYMPIC STEEL, INC.
OPTICAL CABLE CORPORATION
SUPERIOR ESSEX INC.
THE OKONITE COMPANY INC

HISTORICAL FINANCIALS

Company Type: Public

Income Statement — FYE: December 31

	REVENUE ($mil)	NET INCOME ($mil)	NET PROFIT MARGIN	EMPLOYEES
12/21	2,592.7	541.4	20.9%	1,440
12/20	1,276.9	76.0	6.0%	1,289
12/19	1,274.9	58.1	4.6%	1,380
12/18	1,288.6	78.1	6.1%	1,278
12/17	1,164.2	67.0	5.8%	1,235
Annual Growth	22.2%	68.6%	—	3.9%

2021 Year-End Financials
Debt ratio: —   No. of shares ($ mil.): 20.1
Return on equity: 49.7%   Dividends
Cash ($ mil.): 438.9   Yield: —
Current Ratio: 6.72   Payout: 0.3%
Long-term debt ($ mil.): —   Market value ($ mil.): 2,882.0

	STOCK PRICE ($) FY Close	P/E High/Low		PER SHARE ($) Earnings	Dividends	Book Value
12/21	143.10	6	2	26.22	0.08	66.49
12/20	60.57	16	10	3.68	0.08	40.75
12/19	57.40	22	18	2.77	0.08	37.26
12/18	50.18	15	11	3.74	0.08	34.51
12/17	48.65	15	12	3.21	0.08	30.79
Annual Growth	31.0%	—	—	69.1%	0.0%	21.2%

Energizer Holdings Inc (New)

EXECUTIVES

Chairman, Director, Patrick J. Moore

President, Chief Executive Officer, Chief Operating Officer, Director, Mark S. LaVigne, $570,897 total compensation

Executive Vice President, Chief Financial Officer, John J. Drabik

Chief Human Resources Officer, Susan K. Drath

Division Officer, Michael A. Lampman

Division Officer, Robin W Vauth

Director, Carlos Abrams- Rivera

Director, Cynthia J. Brinkley

Director, Rebecca Frankiewicz

Director, Kevin J. Hunt

Director, James C. Johnson
Director, Donal L. Mulligan
Director, Nneka Louise Rimmer
Director, Robert V. Vitale
Auditors : PricewaterhouseCoopers LLP

LOCATIONS

HQ: Energizer Holdings Inc (New)
533 Maryville University Drive, St. Louis, MO 63141
Phone: 314 985-2000
Web: www.energizerholdings.com

HISTORICAL FINANCIALS

Company Type: Public

Income Statement   FYE: September 30

	REVENUE ($mil)	NET INCOME ($mil)	NET PROFIT MARGIN	EMPLOYEES
09/21	3,021.5	160.9	5.3%	6,000
09/20	2,744.8	(93.3)	—	5,900
09/19	2,494.5	51.1	2.0%	7,500
09/18	1,797.7	93.5	5.2%	4,000
09/17	1,755.7	201.5	11.5%	4,400
Annual Growth	14.5%	(5.5%)	—	8.1%

2021 Year-End Financials

Debt ratio: 69.0%   No. of shares ($ mil.): 66.8
Return on equity: 48.4%   Dividends
Cash ($ mil.): 238.9   Yield: 3.0%
Current Ratio: 1.52   Payout: 857.1%
Long-term debt ($ mil.): 3,333.4 Market value ($ mil.): 2,611.0

	STOCK PRICE ($) FY Close	P/E High	P/E Low	PER SHARE ($) Earnings	Dividends	Book Value
09/21	39.05	24	18	2.11	1.20	5.32
09/20	39.14	—	—	(1.58)	1.20	4.51
09/19	43.58	104	57	0.58	1.20	7.89
09/18	58.65	42	27	1.52	1.16	0.41
09/17	46.05	18	13	3.22	1.10	1.40
Annual Growth	(4.0%)	—	—	(10.0%)	2.2%	39.6%

Energy Recovery Inc

Desalination makes seawater potable; Energy Recovery (ERI) makes desalination practical. The company designs, develops, and manufactures energy recovery devices used in sea water reverse osmosis (SWRO) desalination plants. The SWRO process is energy intensive, using high pressure to drive salt water through membranes to produce fresh water. The company's main product, the PX Pressure Exchanger, helps recapture and recycle up to 98% of the energy available in the high-pressure reject stream, a by-product of the SWRO process. The PX can reduce the energy consumption of a desalination plant by up to 60% compared with a plant lacking an energy recovery device. Subsidiary Pump Engineering also makes high pressure pumps.

Geographic Reach

ERI has its headquarters and main manufacturing center located in California. Other offices reside in Shanghai and Dubai.

Sales and Marketing

Primary customers for ERI consist of international engineering, procurement, and construction firms that build large desalination plants. Energy Recovery also sells its products and services to OEMs of pumps and other water-related equipment for small to mid-size plants used in hotels, cruise ships, farm operations, and power plants. Major customers have included IDE Technologies Ltd, Thiess Degremont J.V., Hydrochem, Acciona Agua, and UTE Mostaganem.

Financial Performance

ERI's revenues decreased 29% from 2013 to 2014. The decrease was primarily due to significantly lower mega-project (MPD) shipments as well as lower OEM shipments. The decreases in MPD and OEM sales were offset by higher aftermarket shipments and revenue attributable to an oil and gas operating lease and lease buy-out.

ERI has suffered five straight years of net losses. Its $19 million net loss in 2014 was fueled by higher sales and marketing expenses coupled with the lower net revenue. Research and development expenses also spiked during 2014.

Strategy

Going forward, ERI intends to benefit from a significant presence in Spain and other countries. Energy Recovery's lineup, for example, supports most of Spain's desalination plants. ERI also plans to enter into the material science and manufacturing of ceramics -- a key component of its PX devices. The strategy aims to boost device production, cut costs, and improve product quality.

EXECUTIVES

Chairman, President, Chief Executive Officer, Director, Robert Yu Lang Mao
Manufacturing Vice President, Nocair Bensalah, $265,202 total compensation
Division Officer, Rodney Clemente, $265,202 total compensation
Operations Senior Vice President, Corporate Development Senior Vice President, Emily C. Smith
Chief Financial Officer, Jashua Ballard, $118,750 total compensation
Chief Technology Officer, Farshad Ghasripoor
Chief Legal Officer, General Counsel, William Chu Kwong Yeung
Lead Independent Director, Director, Pamela L. Tondreau
Director, Alexander Jon Buehler, $207,690 total compensation
Director, Sherif Foda
Director, Olav Fjell
Director, Arve Hanstveit
Auditors : DELOITTE & TOUCHE LLP

LOCATIONS

HQ: Energy Recovery Inc
1717 Doolittle Drive, San Leandro, CA 94577
Phone: 510 483-7370
Web: www.energyrecovery.com

2014 Sales

	% of total
International	96
Domestic	4
Total	100

PRODUCTS/OPERATIONS

2014 Sales

	$ mil.	% of total
PX devices & related products & services	20.9	69
Turbochargers & pumps	8.7	29
Oil and gas product operating lease	0.8	2
Total	30.4	100

PRODUCTS
VorTeq
IsoBoost
IsoGen
IsoBoost for Syngas & Ammonia
PX Pressure Exchanger
Turbochargers
Pumping Systems

Selected Products
Energy recovery devices
   PX pressure exchanger devices (PX-300, the 65 series, the 4S series, and brackish PX devices)
   Turbochargers (HTCAT series, the HALO line, and the LPT series for brackish water desalination)
High pressure and circulation pumps (AquaBold series, the AquaSpire series, and a line of small circulation pumps)
Technical support and replacement parts

COMPETITORS

AMTECH SYSTEMS, INC.
APPLIED MATERIALS, INC.
Andritz AG
BTU INTERNATIONAL, INC.
CHAMPIONX LLC
FUELCELL ENERGY, INC.
INTEVAC, INC.
PMFG, INC.
TRICORN GROUP PLC
ULTRATECH, INC.

HISTORICAL FINANCIALS

Company Type: Public

Income Statement   FYE: December 31

	REVENUE ($mil)	NET INCOME ($mil)	NET PROFIT MARGIN	EMPLOYEES
12/20	118.9	26.3	22.2%	216
12/19	86.9	10.9	12.6%	188
12/18	74.5	22.0	29.6%	143
12/17	63.1	12.3	19.6%	133
12/16	54.7	1.0	1.9%	120
Annual Growth	21.4%	124.8%	—	15.8%

2020 Year-End Financials

Debt ratio: —   No. of shares ($ mil.): 56.3
Return on equity: 17.1%   Dividends
Cash ($ mil.): 94.2   Yield: —
Current Ratio: 9.10   Payout: —
Long-term debt ($ mil.): —   Market value ($ mil.): 769.0

	STOCK PRICE ($) FY Close	P/E High	P/E Low	PER SHARE ($) Earnings	Dividends	Book Value
12/20	13.64	29	14	0.47	0.00	3.05
12/19	9.79	59	34	0.19	0.00	2.46
12/18	6.73	24	16	0.40	0.00	2.10
12/17	8.75	49	27	0.22	0.00	1.53
12/16	10.35	818	268	0.02	0.00	1.23
Annual Growth	7.1%	—	—	120.2%	—	25.6%

Enerkon Solar International Inc

EXECUTIVES

President, Chief Executive Officer, Chief Financial Officer, Director, Benjamin Ballout
Division Officer, Ibrahim EL Nattar, $250,000 total compensation
Treasurer, Secretary, Director, Michael T. Studer
Auditors : Massella Rubenstein LLP

LOCATIONS

HQ: Enerkon Solar International Inc
477 Madison Avenue, 6th Floor - #6834, New York, NY 10022
Phone: 877 573-7797
Web: www.enerkoninternational.com

HISTORICAL FINANCIALS

Company Type: Public

Income Statement				FYE: September 30
	REVENUE ($mil)	NET INCOME ($mil)	NET PROFIT MARGIN	EMPLOYEES
09/20	65.1	13.1	20.2%	0
09/19	76.0	14.2	18.8%	0
09/18	18.9	1.8	9.7%	0
09/17	0.0	(0.0)	—	0
09/16	0.0	(0.2)	—	0
Annual Growth	838.7%	—	—	—

2020 Year-End Financials

Debt ratio: 8.6%
Return on equity: 38.7%
Cash ($ mil.): 24.0
Current Ratio: 1.85
Long-term debt ($ mil.): 8.3
No. of shares ($ mil.): 65.6
Dividends
  Yield: —
  Payout: —
Market value ($ mil.): 3.0

	STOCK PRICE ($) FY Close	P/E High/Low		PER SHARE ($) Earnings	Dividends	Book Value
09/20	0.04	—	—	0.00	0.00	0.74
09/19	0.17	—	—	0.00	0.00	0.42
09/18	0.10	—	—	0.00	0.00	0.11
09/17	0.05	—	—	0.00	0.00	0.00
09/16	0.05	—	—	(0.01)	0.00	0.01
Annual Growth	(2.9%)	—	—	—	—	247.3%

Enova International Inc

EXECUTIVES

Chairman, President, Chief Executive Officer, Director, David A. Fisher, $760,385 total compensation
Chief Financial Officer, Steven E. Cunningham, $457,115 total compensation
Chief Marketing Officer, Kirk Chartier, $378,269 total compensation
Chief Compliance Officer, General Counsel, Secretary, Sean Rahilly, $329,673 total compensation
Chief Accounting Officer, Controller, James J. Lee
Lead Independent Director, Director, James A. Gray
Director, Ellen Carnahan
Director, Daniel R. Feehan
Director, William M. Goodyear
Director, Gregg A. Kaplan
Director, Mark P. McGowan
Director, Mark A. Tebbe
Director, Linda Johnson Rice
Auditors : PricewaterhouseCoopers LLP

LOCATIONS

HQ: Enova International Inc
175 West Jackson Blvd., Chicago, IL 60604
Phone: 312 568-4200
Web: www.enova.com

HISTORICAL FINANCIALS

Company Type: Public

Income Statement				FYE: December 31
	REVENUE ($mil)	NET INCOME ($mil)	NET PROFIT MARGIN	EMPLOYEES
12/20	1,083.7	377.8	34.9%	1,549
12/19	1,174.7	36.6	3.1%	1,325
12/18	1,114.0	70.0	6.3%	1,218
12/17	843.7	29.2	3.5%	1,109
12/16	745.5	34.6	4.6%	1,099
Annual Growth	9.8%	81.8%	—	9.0%

2020 Year-End Financials

Debt ratio: 44.9%
Return on equity: 58.2%
Cash ($ mil.): 369.2
Current Ratio: 3.23
Long-term debt ($ mil.): 946.4
No. of shares ($ mil.): 35.7
Dividends
  Yield: —
  Payout: —
Market value ($ mil.): 886.0

	STOCK PRICE ($) FY Close	P/E High/Low		PER SHARE ($) Earnings	Dividends	Book Value
12/20	24.77	2	1	11.70	0.00	25.65
12/19	24.06	28	18	1.06	0.00	11.42
12/18	19.46	19	8	1.99	0.00	10.35
12/17	15.20	19	13	0.86	0.00	8.41
12/16	12.55	13	5	1.03	0.00	7.26
Annual Growth	18.5%	—	—	83.6%	—	37.1%

Enphase Energy Inc.

Enphase Energy is a global energy technology company that designs, develops, manufactures, and sells home energy solutions that manage energy generation, energy storage, and control and communications on one intelligent platform. The company currently offers solutions targeting the residential and commercial markets in the US, Canada, Mexico, Europe, Australia, New Zealand, India, Brazil, South Africa, and certain other Central American and Asian markets. Enphase Energy has shipped more than 42 million microinverters, and approximately 1.9 million Enphase residential and commercial systems have been deployed in more than 130 countries. The company generates the majority of its revenue in the US.

Operations

Enphase Energy generates revenue from sales of its solutions, which include microinverter units and related accessories, an Envoy communications gateway, the cloud-based Enlighten monitoring service, storage solutions, Electric Vehicle (EV) charging solutions beginning in the first quarter of 2022, design, proposal and permitting services, as well as a platform matching cleantech asset owners to a local and on-demand workforce of service providers, to distributors, large installers, OEMs and strategic partners. The company has sold more than 42 million microinverters.

Overall, products delivered at a point in time bring in around 95% of the company's revenue, while products and services delivered over time account for nearly 5%.

Geographic Reach

California-based Enphase Energy rings up approximately 80% of its sales in the US. International markets include Australia, Brazil, Canada, China, Europe, Mexico, France, India, New Zealand, South Africa, and Asian markets.

Sales and Marketing

Enphase Energy targets the residential and commercial markets. OEM customers include solar module manufacturers who integrate the company's microinverters with their solar module products and resell to both distributors and installers. It also sells certain products and services to homeowners, primarily in support of its warranty services and legacy product upgrade programs, via the company's online store.

In 2021, one customer accounts for about 35% of total net revenues. The company also sell directly to large installers, OEMs, and strategic partners.

Financial Performance

Net revenues increased by 78% or $607.6 million to $1.4 billion in 2021, as compared to the same period in 2020, driven primarily by a 53% increase in microinverter units volume shipped and a 351% increase in Enphase IQ Battery storage systems MWh shipped.

In 2021, the company had a net income of $145.4 million, a 9% increase from the previous year's net income of $134 million.

The company's cash at the end of 2021 was $119.3 million. Operating activities generated $352 million, while investing activities used $1.2 billion, mainly for purchases of marketable securities. Financing activities generated another $309.4 million.

Strategy

Enphase's objective is to build best-in-class home energy systems and deliver them to homeowners through its installer and distribution partners, enabled by a comprehensive digital platform. Key elements of its strategy include:

Best-in-class customer experience. The

company's value proposition is to deliver products that are productive, reliable, smart, simple and safe, and superior customer service, to enable homeowners' storage and energy independence. On the service front, its installer, distributor and module partners are the company's first line of association with its ultimate customer, the homeowner and business user. Enphase's goals are to partner better with these service providers so that it can provide exceptional high quality service to its homeowner. The company is convinced that continued reinforcement of customer experience improvements can be a competitive advantage for the company.

Grow market share worldwide. Enphase intends to capitalize on its market leadership in the microinverter category and its momentum with installers and owners to expand the company's market share position in its core markets. In addition, Enphase intends to further increase its market share in Europe, Asia Pacific and Latin America regions. Further, the company intends to expand into new markets, including emerging markets, with new and existing products and local go-to-market capabilities.

Expand the company's product offerings. Enphase distinguishes itself from other inverter companies with its systems-based and high technology approach as it continues to invest in research and development to develop all components of its energy management solution and remains committed to providing customers and partners with best-in-class power electronics, storage solutions, communications, and load control all managed by a cloud-based energy management system.

Mergers and Acquisitions

In early 2022, Enphase Energy acquired SolarLeadFactory, a best-in-class solar lead generation engine on the web. SolarLeadFactory has joined Enphase with the objective of substantially increasing lead volumes and conversion rates to help drive down the customer acquisition costs for installers.

Also in early 2022, Enphase Energy completed the previously announced acquisition of Auburn, California-based ClipperCreek. The company offers electric vehicle (EV) charging solutions for residential and commercial customers in the US. The acquisition provides Enphase distributors and installers globally with EV charging solutions that can be sold alongside solar and battery systems and it accelerates the Enphase roadmap to enable bi-directional charging capability for vehicle-to-home and vehicle-to-grid applications.

In late 2021, Enphase Energy announced the closing of its acquisition of Scottsdale, Arizona-based 365 Pronto, a predictive software platform dedicated to simplifying the cleantech service landscape by matching cleantech asset owners to a local and on-demand workforce of service providers. "We are pleased to welcome 365 Pronto's customers, service providers, and employees to Enphase," said Badri Kothandaraman, president and CEO at Enphase Energy. "The company's software platform will provide our installers the ability to service their own O&M contracts with an on-demand network of service providers. We are excited about this opportunity to improve the installer experience as we continue to expand our digital platform."

In early 2021, Enphase Energy completed the previously announced acquisition of Noida, India-based Solar Design Services business of DIN Engineering Services, a leading provider of outsourced proposal drawings and permit plan sets for residential solar installers in North America. "We are pleased to welcome DIN's customers and employees to Enphase," said Badri Kothandaraman, president and CEO of Enphase Energy. "We are also excited about the opportunity to add significant capabilities to our digital platform through this acquisition. By offering high quality services to our network of installers, we aim to simplify the sales and installation process, while helping to reduce soft costs and providing an enhanced buying experience for homeowners."

In a separate transaction in early 2021, Enphase Energy acquired Montreal, Canada-based Sofdesk, an industry-leading organization that builds intuitive sales acceleration software for everyday use by solar and roofing companies. Sofdesk's Solargraf integrated software platform offers the industry's leading digital tools and services designed to simplify and accelerate the end-to-end sales process across the residential solar industry. "This acquisition supercharges Enphase's digital transformation efforts," said Jayant Somani, vice president of digital transformation at Enphase Energy. "With these tools, residential installers can drive the industry towards better customer journeys, create happier customers, and help accelerate the transition to clean energy."

EXECUTIVES

President, Chief Executive Officer, Director, Badrinarayanan Kothandaraman, $450,000 total compensation
Executive Vice President, Chief Financial Officer, Eric Branderiz, $232,051 total compensation
Executive Vice President, Chief Commercial Officer, David A. Ranhoff, $400,000 total compensation
Executive Vice President, Chief Operating Officer, Jeffrey McNeil, $316,260 total compensation
Chief Products Officer, Raghuveer R. Belur
Lead Independent Director, Director, Steven J. Gomo
Director, Jamie E. Haenggi
Director, Benjamin John Kortlang
Director, Joseph I. Malchow
Director, Richard S. Mora
Director, Thurman John Rodgers
Auditors : DELOITTE & TOUCHE LLP

LOCATIONS

HQ: Enphase Energy Inc.
47281 Bayside Parkway, Fremont, CA 94538
Phone: 877 774-7000
Web: www.enphase.com

2015 Sales

	$ mil.	% of total
US	303.2	85
International	54.0	15
Total	357.2	100

COMPETITORS

AMERICAN SUPERCONDUCTOR CORPORATION
BTU INTERNATIONAL, INC.
FIRST SOLAR, INC.
IXYS, LLC
POWER INTEGRATIONS, INC.
SOLAREDGE TECHNOLOGIES, INC.
SUNEDISON, INC.
SUNPOWER CORPORATION
ULTRA CLEAN HOLDINGS, INC.
WATERFURNACE RENEWABLE ENERGY, INC.

HISTORICAL FINANCIALS

Company Type: Public

Income Statement — FYE: December 31

	REVENUE ($mil)	NET INCOME ($mil)	NET PROFIT MARGIN	EMPLOYEES
12/21	1,382.0	145.4	10.5%	2,260
12/20	774.4	133.9	17.3%	850
12/19	624.3	161.1	25.8%	577
12/18	316.1	(11.6)	—	427
12/17	286.1	(45.1)	—	336
Annual Growth	48.2%	—	—	61.0%

2021 Year-End Financials
Debt ratio: 49.9%   No. of shares ($ mil.): 133.8
Return on equity: 31.8%   Dividends
Cash ($ mil.): 119.3   Yield: —
Current Ratio: 3.33   Payout: —
Long-term debt ($ mil.): 951.5   Market value ($ mil.): 24,495.0

	STOCK PRICE ($) FY Close	P/E High/Low		PER SHARE ($) Earnings	Dividends	Book Value
12/21	182.94	246	105	1.02	0.00	3.21
12/20	175.47	170	22	0.95	0.00	3.75
12/19	26.13	25	3	1.23	0.00	2.21
12/18	4.73	—	—	(0.12)	0.00	0.07
12/17	2.41	—	—	(0.54)	0.00	(0.11)
Annual Growth	195.2%	—	—	—	—	—

Ensign Group Inc

The Ensign Group offers skilled nursing, senior living and rehabilitative care services through nearly 230 senior living facilities as well as other ancillary businesses (including mobile diagnostics and medical transportation), in about a dozen of states. In addition, it acquires, leases and owns healthcare real estate in addition to servicing the post-acute care continuum through accretive acquisition and investment opportunities in healthcare properties. Its transitional and skilled services companies provided skilled nursing care at around 235 operations, with more than 25,030 operational beds. It provides short and long-term nursing care services for patients with chronic conditions, prolonged illness, and the elderly.

Operations

The company has now two reportable segments: Skilled Services (accounts for nearly 95% of total revenue), which includes the operation of skilled nursing facilities and rehabilitation therapy services; and real estate (less than 5%), which is primarily comprised of properties owned by the company and leased to skilled nursing and senior living operations, including its own operating subsidiaries and third-party operators and are subject to triple-net long-term leases.

Other business (about 5% of total revenue) includes operating results from its senior living operations, mobile diagnostics, transportation and other ancillary operations.

Almost all of its sales were generated from its services.

Geographic Reach

California-based Ensign has facilities in around a dozen states: Arizona, California, Colorado, Idaho, Iowa, Kansas, Nebraska, Nevada, South Carolina, Texas, Utah, Washington and Wisconsin.

Sales and Marketing

Ensign generates around 75% of its revenue from Medicaid and Medicare programs. Managed care companies account for more than 15% of sales, with private payers and others accounting for the rest of revenue.

Financial Performance

The company's revenue in 2021 increased to $2.6 billion compared to $2.4 billion in 2020. The increase in revenue from same facility and transitioning operations was primarily driven by the increase in skilled service revenue per patient day, along with the impact of acquisitions.

Net income for fiscal 2021 increased to $194.7 million compared from the prior year with $171.4 million.

Cash held by the company at the end of fiscal 2021 increased to $262.2 million. Operating activities provided $275.7 million while investing and financing activities used $173.9 million and $76.1 million, respectively. Main cash uses were asset acquisitions and repayments of CARES Act Provider Relief Fund and Medicare Advance Payment Program.

Strategy

To continue with its growth strategy on its real estate portfolio, in early 2022, Engsin formed Standard Bearer REIT. Standard Bearer REIT owns and manages its real estate business. Ensign believes the REIT structure will allow the company to better demonstrate the growing value of its owned real estate and provide the company with an efficient vehicle for future acquisitions of properties that could be operated by Ensign affiliates or other third parties.

Mergers and Acquisitions

Ensign regularly boosts its facility portfolio through purchases of both struggling and well-performing businesses.

In early 2022, Ensign acquired the real estate and operations of The Waterton Healthcare and Rehabilitation, a 74-bed skilled nursing facility located in Tyler, Texas. In a separate transaction on the same day, Ensign announced that its affiliates acquired the operations of Amarsi Assisted Living, a 103-bed assisted living facility located in Glendale, Arizona and Citadel Assisted Living Facility, a 180-unit independent living and 150-bed assisted living facility located in Mesa, Arizona. These acquisitions bring Ensign's growing portfolio to 250 healthcare operations, 23 of which also include senior living operations, across thirteen states. Terms were not disclosed.

In 2021, Ensign acquired the real estate and operations of Windsor Rehabilitation and Healthcare, a 108-bed skilled nursing facility, located in Terrell, TX. This acquisition brings Ensign's growing portfolio to 236 healthcare operations, 22 of which also include senior living operations, across thirteen states. Ensign owns 95 real estate assets.

Also, in 2021, Ensign acquired Boulder Canyon Health and Rehabilitation, a 140-bed skilled nursing facility located in Boulder, CO; Berthoud Care and Rehabilitation, a 76-bed skilled nursing facility located in Berthoud, CO; and South Valley Post Acute Rehabilitation, a 106-bed skilled nursing facility located in Denver, CO.

In early 2021, Ensign acquired Golden Hill Post Acute, a skilled nursing facility with 99 skilled nursing beds located in San Diego, CA; St. Catherine Healthcare, a skilled nursing facility with 99 skilled nursing beds located in Fullerton, CA; and Camino Healthcare, a skilled nursing facility with 99 skilled nursing beds located in Hawthorne, CA.

Ensign acquired the operations of San Pedro Manor, a 150-bed skilled nursing facility located in San Antonio, Texas, in 2021. This acquisition is a perfect fit with its existing facilities in Texas and for the continued growth in the San Antonio area.

Company Background

Ensign Group was founded in 1999. The company spun off some of its assets into CareTrust REIT in 2014.

EXECUTIVES

Chairman Emeritus, Roy E. Christensen
Executive Chairman, Chairman, Director, Christopher R. Christensen, $505,198 total compensation
Chief Executive Officer, Barry R. Port, $356,477 total compensation
Executive Vice President, Secretary, Chad A. Keetch, $309,915 total compensation
Vice President, General Counsel, Beverly B. Wittekind, $439,627 total compensation
Organizational Development Vice President, David M. Sedgwick, $227,103 total compensation
Chief Financial Officer, Suzanne D. Snapper, $336,014 total compensation
Subsidiary Officer, Spencer W. Burton
Subsidiary Officer, Cory R. Monette
Subsidiary Officer, John P. Albrechtsen
Subsidiary Officer, Michael C. Dalton, $183,849 total compensation
Director, Daren J. Shaw
Director, Barry M. Smith
Director, Lee A. Daniels
Director, Ann S. Blouin
Auditors : DELOITTE & TOUCHE LLP

LOCATIONS

HQ: Ensign Group Inc
29222 Rancho Viejo Road, Suite 127, San Juan Capistrano, CA 92675
Phone: 949 487-9500
Web: www.ensigngroup.net

PRODUCTS/OPERATIONS

2016 Sales

	$ mil.	% of total
Medicaid	558.0	34
Medicare	477.0	29
Private & other	266.9	16
Managed care	265.5	16
Medicaid - skilled	87.5	5
Total	1,654.9	100

2016 Sales

	$ mil.	% of total
Transitional and Skilled Services	1,377.7	83
Assisted and Independent Living Services	123.7	7
Home Health and Hospice Services	115.8	7
All Other	42.8	3
Elimination	-5.1	-
Total	1,341.8	100

COMPETITORS

BROOKDALE SENIOR LIVING INC.
CAPITAL SENIOR LIVING CORPORATION
DIVERSICARE HEALTHCARE SERVICES, INC.
FIVE STAR SENIOR LIVING INC.
GENESIS HEALTHCARE, INC.
LHC GROUP, INC.
MANOR CARE, INC.
NATIONAL HEALTHCARE CORPORATION
ODYSSEY HEALTHCARE, INC.
THE EVANGELICAL LUTHERAN GOOD SAMARITAN SOCIETY

HISTORICAL FINANCIALS

Company Type: Public

Income Statement — FYE: December 31

	REVENUE ($mil)	NET INCOME ($mil)	NET PROFIT MARGIN	EMPLOYEES
12/21	2,627.4	194.6	7.4%	25,900
12/20	2,402.5	170.4	7.1%	24,400
12/19	2,036.5	110.5	5.4%	24,500
12/18	2,040.6	92.3	4.5%	23,463
12/17	1,849.3	40.4	2.2%	21,301
Annual Growth	9.2%	48.1%	—	5.0%

2021 Year-End Financials

Debt ratio: 5.5%
Return on equity: 21.1%
Cash ($ mil.): 262.2
Current Ratio: 1.22
Long-term debt ($ mil.): 152.8
No. of shares ($ mil.): 55.1
Dividends
Yield: 0.2%
Payout: 6.2%
Market value ($ mil.): 4,634.0

	STOCK PRICE ($) FY Close	P/E High	P/E Low	PER SHARE ($) Earnings	Dividends	Book Value
12/21	83.96	27	19	3.42	0.21	18.50
12/20	72.92	24	8	3.06	0.20	14.98
12/19	45.37	29	18	1.97	0.19	12.23
12/18	38.79	27	13	1.70	0.18	11.24
12/17	22.20	31	22	0.77	0.17	9.59
Annual Growth	39.5%	—	—	45.2%	5.4%	17.9%

Entegris Inc

Entegris is a leading supplier of advanced materials and process solutions for the semiconductor and other high-technology industries. It makes products integral to the manufacture of semiconductors and computer disk drives. The company makes more than 20,000 standard and custom products used to transport and protect semiconductor and disk drive materials during processing. Its products include filtration, wafer carriers, storage boxes, and chip trays as well as chemical delivery systems, such as pipes, fittings, and valves. Its disk drive offerings include shippers, stamper cases, and transport trays. Entegris gets more than 75% of revenue from international customers. In late 2021, Entegris will acquire CMC Materials in a cash and stock transaction with an enterprise value of approximately $6.5 billion.

Operations

Entegris' business is organized and operated in three segments which align with the key elements of the advanced semiconductor manufacturing ecosystem: Microcontamination Control, or MC; Specialty Chemicals and Engineered Materials, or SCEM; and Advanced Materials Handling, or AMH.

The Microcontamination Control segment offers products and processes that filter and purify critical liquid chemistries and process gases used in manufacturing processes for semiconductors and other complex products. The segment accounts for nearly 40% of the company's revenue.

The Specialty Chemicals and Engineered Materials segment, about 30% of revenue, provides high-performance and high-purity process chemistries, gases, and materials and efficient delivery systems for semiconductor and other advanced manufacturing processes.

The Advanced Materials Handling segment's products monitor, protect, transport, and deliver critical liquid chemistries, wafers, and other substrates for a broad set of applications in manufacturing. It generates approximately 30% of the company's revenue.

Entegris operates manufacturing plants that meet critical purity standards and use processes such as 3D printing for production prototypes of products. The company also uses contract manufacturers to make some of its gas purification systems and electronic materials products.

Geographic Reach

Entegris, based in Billerica, Massachusetts, has manufacturing and research and development facilities in US, Canada, China, Germany, France, Israel, Japan, Malaysia, Singapore, South Korea and Taiwan. It also has sales and service offices throughout Asia and Europe.

The North America generates about 25% of the company's revenue, followed by Taiwan, bringing in approximately 20%, China, South Korea, and Japan, each providing around 15% of Entegris' revenue. Overall, customers in Asia account for about 70% of the company's revenue.

Sales and Marketing

Entegris sells its products through a direct sales force and strategic distributors serving a range of markets, including semiconductor, flat panel display manufacturing, compound semiconductor, disk data storage, aerospace, solar/clean energy, life sciences, emerging technologies, and water treatment industries. The company's most significant customers include logic and memory semiconductor device manufacturers, semiconductor equipment makers, gas and chemical manufacturing companies and wafer grower companies serving the global semiconductor industry. It also sells its products to flat panel display equipment makers, panel manufacturers, manufacturers of hard disk drive components and devices and their related ecosystems.

It relies on its 10 biggest for about 45% of revenue. Taiwan Semiconductor Manufacturing Company Limited accounts for more than 10% of sales.

Financial Performance

Entegris' revenue has been rising in the last five years with an overall increase of 71% from 2017 to 2021. Its net income follows a similar trend with an increase of 381%.

Total net sales for 2021 were $2.3 billion, up $439.6 million, or 24%, from sales of $1,859.3 million for 2020. The increase was primarily the result of an increase in overall demand for the company's products from semiconductor industry customers, particularly in the sale of liquid filtration, advanced deposition materials, selective etch and other areas of increasing importance to customers.

In 2021, the company had a net income of $409.1 million, a 39% increase from the previous year's net income of $295 million.

The company's cash at the end of 2021 was $402.6 million. Operating activities generated $400.5 million, while investing activities used $298.1 million, mainly for acquisition of property and equipment. Financing activities used another $276.5 million, primarily for payments of long-term debt.

Strategy

Entegris intends to build upon its position as a leading supplier of advanced materials and process solutions for the semiconductor and other high-technology industries to expand its core business and to grow in other high value-added manufacturing process markets. The company's strategy includes the following key elements.

Commitment to Technology Leadership. Entegris seeks to continuously improve products and develop new products as its customers' needs evolve;

Leveraging Its Expertise. The company leverages its broad expertise across its portfolio of advanced materials, materials handling and purification capabilities to create innovative and new solutions to address unmet customer needs;

Operational Excellence. The company's strategy is to continue to develop its advanced manufacturing capabilities into a competitive advantage with customers by conducting its manufacturing operations in a manner that ensures the safety of Entegris' employees and of the individuals using its products and by continuing to focus on the other priorities; as well as

Strategic Acquisitions, Partnerships and Related Transactions. Entegris will continue to pursue strategic acquisitions and business partnerships that enable the company to address gaps in its product offerings, secure new customers, diversify into complementary product markets, broaden its technological capabilities and product offerings, access local or regional markets and achieve benefits of increased scale.

Mergers and Acquisitions

In late 2021, Entegris and CMC Materials announced a definitive merger agreement under which Entegris will acquire CMC Materials, a leading supplier of advanced materials primarily for the semiconductor industry, in a cash and stock transaction with an enterprise value of approximately $6.5 billion. The addition of CMC Materials' leading CMP portfolio will broaden Entegris' solutions set, creating a comprehensive electronic materials offering.

EXECUTIVES

Chairman, Director, Paul L.H. Olson
President, Chief Executive Officer, Director, Bertrand Loy, $844,808 total compensation
Senior Vice President, Secretary, General Counsel, Peter W. Walcott, $171,492 total compensation
Human Resources Senior Vice President, John J. Murphy, $258,622 total compensation

Senior Vice President, Chief Technology Officer, Chief Innovation Officer, John Goodman, $195,371 total compensation

Human Resources Senior Vice President, Dame Susan Rice, $360,000 total compensation

Specialty Chemicals & engineered Materials Senior Vice President, Specialty Chemicals & engineered Materials General Manager, Stuart Tison

Senior Vice President, Division Officer, Clinton M. Haris, $304,981 total compensation

Standing Vice President, William Shaner, $326,058 total compensation

Vice President, Chief Accounting Officer, Controller, Michael D. Sauer

Director, Michael A. Bradley

Director, Rodney Clark

Director, James F. Gentilcore

Director, James P. Lederer

Director, Yvette Kanouff

Director, Azita Saleki-Gerhardt

Director, James Robert Anderson

Auditors : KPMG LLP

LOCATIONS

HQ: Entegris Inc
129 Concord Road, Billerica, MA 01821
Phone: 978 436-6500
Web: www.entegris.com

2018 Sales

	$ mil.	% of total
US	347	22
Taiwan	289.9	19
South Korea	242.4	16
Japan	210.7	13
China	204.4	13
Europe	138.1	9
Southeast Asia	118	8
Total	1,550.5	100

PRODUCTS/OPERATIONS

2018 Sales

	$ mil.	% of total
Specialty Chemicals and Engineered Materials	530.2	34
Microcontamination Control	552.9	36
Advanced Materials Handling	467.4	30
Total	1,550.5	100

COMPETITORS

APPLIED MATERIALS, INC.
APTARGROUP, INC.
ASSOCIATED MATERIALS, LLC
BERRY GLOBAL GROUP, INC.
ILLINOIS TOOL WORKS INC.
JL REALISATIONS 2020 LIMITED
MYERS INDUSTRIES, INC.
ONTO INNOVATION INC.
PROTO LABS, INC.
ULTRA CLEAN HOLDINGS, INC.

HISTORICAL FINANCIALS

Company Type: Public

Income Statement FYE: December 31

	REVENUE ($mil)	NET INCOME ($mil)	NET PROFIT MARGIN	EMPLOYEES
12/21	2,298.8	409.1	17.8%	6,850
12/20	1,859.3	294.9	15.9%	5,800
12/19	1,591.0	254.8	16.0%	5,300
12/18	1,550.4	240.7	15.5%	4,900
12/17	1,342.5	85.0	6.3%	3,900
Annual Growth	14.4%	48.1%	—	15.1%

2021 Year-End Financials

Debt ratio: 29.4%
Return on equity: 26.4%
Cash ($ mil.): 402.5
Current Ratio: 3.47
Long-term debt ($ mil.): 937
No. of shares ($ mil.): 135.5
Dividends
 Yield: 0.2%
 Payout: 11.5%
Market value ($ mil.): 18,780.0

	STOCK PRICE ($) FY Close	P/E High/Low		PER SHARE ($) Earnings	Dividends	Book Value
12/21	138.58	51	31	3.00	0.32	12.65
12/20	96.10	45	18	2.16	0.32	10.22
12/19	50.09	27	15	1.87	0.30	8.65
12/18	27.90	23	14	1.69	0.28	7.44
12/17	30.45	55	30	0.59	0.07	7.03
Annual Growth	46.1%	—	—	50.2%	46.2%	15.8%

Enterprise Bancorp, Inc. (MA)

Enterprise Bancorp caters to more customers than just entrepreneurs. The holding company owns Enterprise Bank and Trust, which operates more than 20 branches in north-central Massachusetts and southern New Hampshire. The $2 billion-asset bank offers traditional deposit and loan products, specializing in lending to businesses, professionals, high-net-worth individuals, and not-for-profits. About half of its loan portfolio is tied to commercial real estate, while another one-third is tied to commercial and industrial and commercial construction loans. Subsidiaries Enterprise Investment Services and Enterprise Insurance Services provide investments and insurance geared to the bank's target business customers.

Operations

More than 50% of Enterprise Bancorp's $1.86 billion loan portfolio was tied to commercial real estate loans at the end of 2015, while commercial and industrial and commercial construction loans made up another 25% and 11% of the bank's loan assets. The rest of the bank's portfolio was tied to residential mortgages (9% of loan assets), home equity loans and lines of credit (4%), and consumer loans (less than 1%).

Nearly 80% of the bank's total revenue comes from loan interest, while investment advisory fees and deposit and interchange fees each make up another 5%.

Geographic Reach

The Lowell, Massachusetts-based bank operated 23 branches mostly located in the greater Merrimack Valley and North Central regions of Massachusetts and Southern New Hampshire at the end of 2015.

Sales and Marketing

Enterprise spent $2.7 million on advertising and public relations during 2015, down from $2.9 million in 2014.

Financial Performance

The bank's annual revenues have risen more than 40% since 2011 as its loan assets have swelled by 50% to $1.86 billion. Meanwhile, its net income has grown more than 50% as it's kept a lid on loan loss provisions and operating costs.

Enterprise Bancorp's revenue climbed 8% to $98.4 million during 2015 thanks to 11% loan asset growth driven by a "seasoned" lending team, a sales and service culture, and geographic market expansion. Commercial construction loans grew the fastest rate during the year, though all loans grew albeit at a slightly slower rate.

Revenue growth in 2015 drove the bank's net income up 10% to $16.1 million despite higher salary and employee benefit expenses. Enterprise Bancorp's operating cash levels nearly doubled to $25.7 million for the year largely thanks to positive changes in working capital mainly related to prepaid expenses and other assets.

Strategy

Enterprise Bancorp has traditionally expanded its loan and deposit business by opening new branches rather than by acquiring other banks. Enterprise hopes to take advantage of the trend to switch from larger banks to smaller, community-oriented institutions. The company has also invested in upgrading its branches and operations systems.

EXECUTIVES

Executive Chairman, Subsidiary Officer, Director, George L. Duncan, $412,000 total compensation

Vice-Chairman, Lead Director, Director, James F. Conway

President, Subsidiary Officer, Director, Richard W. Main, $309,000 total compensation

Chief Executive Officer, Subsidiary Officer, Director, John P. Clancy, $489,250 total compensation

Executive Vice President, Treasurer, Chief Financial Officer, Subsidiary Officer, Joseph R. Lussier

Executive Vice President, Chief Commercial Lending Officer, Subsidiary Officer, Brian H. Bullock

Operations Executive Vice President, Operations Director, Brian M. Collins

Executive Vice President, Branch Administration Director, Subsidiary Officer, Susan Covey

Executive Vice President, Regional Commercial Lending Manager, Subsidiary Officer, Ryan C. Dunn

Executive vice President, Chief Human Resources Officer, Subsidiary Officer, Jamie L. Gabriel

Executive Vice President, Chief Risk Officer, Subsidiary Officer, Michael J. Gallagher

Executive Vice President, Construction Lending Director, Subsidiary Officer, Marlene P. Hoyt

Executive Vice President, Chief Operating Officer, Subsidiary Officer, Stephen J. Irish, $326,069 total compensation

Executive Vice President, Chief Banking Officer, Subsidiary Officer, Steven R. Larochelle

Executive Vice President, Subsidiary Officer, Peter J. Rayno

Executive Vice President, Chief Lending Officer, Chief Mortgage Officer, Subsidiary Officer, Diane J. Silva

Executive Vice President, Chief Information Officer, Subsidiary Officer, Keith N. Soucie

Executive Vice President, Chief Community and Customer Relationship Officer, Subsidiary Officer, Chief Sales Officer, Chester J. Szablak

Director, Nickolas Stavropoulos
Director, Anita R. Worden
Director, John R. Clementi
Director, Carole A. Cowan
Director, Normand E. Deschene
Director, John A. Koutsos
Director, Joseph C. Lerner
Director, Gino J. Baroni
Director, John T. Grady
Director, Mary Jane King
Director, Shelagh E. Mahoney
Director, Kenneth S. Ansin
Director, Jacqueline F. Moloney
Director, Luis M. Pedroso
Director, Michael T. Putziger
Director, Carol L. Reid
Auditors : RSM US LLP

LOCATIONS

HQ: Enterprise Bancorp, Inc. (MA)
222 Merrimack Street, Lowell, MA 01852
Phone: 978 459-9000
Web: www.enterprisebanking.com

PRODUCTS/OPERATIONS

2015 Sales

	$ mil.	% of total
Interest and dividend income:		
Loans and loans held for sale	77.9	79
Investment securities	5.3	5
Other interest-earning assets	0.2	-
Non-interest income:		
Investment advisory fees	4.8	5
Deposit and interchange fees	4.9	5
Net gains on sales of investment securities	1.8	2
Income on bank-owned life insurance, net	0.5	1
Gains on sales of loans	0.5	1
Other income	2.5	3
Total	**98.4**	**100**

Products and Services
Lending Products:
Residential Loans
Home Equity Loans and Lines of Credit
Consumer Loans
Credit Risk and Allowance for Loan Losses
Deposit Products:
Cash Management Services
Product Delivery Channels
Investment Services
Insurance Services

COMPETITORS

CAMBRIDGE BANCORP
CENTURY BANCORP, INC.
INDEPENDENT BANK CORP.
LAKELAND FINANCIAL CORPORATION
LEGACYTEXAS FINANCIAL GROUP, INC.

HISTORICAL FINANCIALS

Company Type: Public

Income Statement — FYE: December 31

	ASSETS ($mil)	NET INCOME ($mil)	INCOME AS % OF ASSETS	EMPLOYEES
12/20	4,014.3	31.4	0.8%	527
12/19	3,235.0	34.2	1.1%	538
12/18	2,964.3	28.8	1.0%	508
12/17	2,817.5	19.3	0.7%	482
12/16	2,526.2	18.7	0.7%	468
Annual Growth	12.3%	13.8%	—	3.0%

2020 Year-End Financials
Return on assets: 0.8%
Return on equity: 9.9%
Long-term debt ($ mil.): —
No. of shares ($ mil.): 11.9
Sales ($ mil.): 162
Dividends
Yield: 2.7%
Payout: 26.5%
Market value ($ mil.): 305.0

	STOCK PRICE ($) FY Close	P/E High/Low		PER SHARE ($) Earnings	Dividends	Book Value
12/20	25.55	13	8	2.64	0.70	28.01
12/19	33.87	12	9	2.89	0.64	25.09
12/18	32.16	17	12	2.46	0.58	21.80
12/17	34.05	23	18	1.66	0.54	19.97
12/16	37.56	22	12	1.70	0.52	18.72
Annual Growth	(9.2%)	—	—	11.6%	7.7%	10.6%

Enterprise Financial Services Corp

Enterprise Financial Services wants you to boldly bank where many have banked before. It's the holding company for Enterprise Bank & Trust, which mostly targets closely-held businesses and their owners, but also serves individuals in the St. Louis, Kansas City, and Phoenix metropolitan areas. Boasting $3.8 billion in assets and 16 branches, Enterprise offers standard products such as checking, savings, and money market accounts and CDs. Commercial and industrial loans make up over half of the company's lending activities, while real estate loans make up another 45%. The bank also writes consumer, and residential mortgage loans. Bank subsidiary Enterprise Trust offers wealth management services.

Operations

Enterprise Trust, the company's wealth management unit, targets business owners, wealthy individuals, and institutional investors, providing financial planning, business succession planning, and related services. The unit also invests in Missouri state tax credits from funds for affordable housing development, which it then sells to clients and others.

About 82% of Enterprise Financial's total revenue came from loan interest (including fees) in 2014, while another 7% came from interest on its taxable and tax-exempt investment securities. The rest of its revenue came from wealth management income (4%), service fees (3%), gains on state tax credits (1%), and other miscellaneous income sources. The bank had a staff of 452 full-time employees at the end of 2014.

Geographic Reach

Enterprise Bank & Trust operates eight banking locations in or around Kansas City, six banking locations and a support center in the St. Louis area, and two banking locations in the Phoenix metro area.

Financial Performance

The company has struggled to consistently grow its revenues in recent years mostly due to shrinking interest margins on its loans amidst the low-interest environment. Its profits, however, have mostly trended higher thanks to declining loan loss provisions as its loan portfolio's credit quality has improved with higher property valuations in the strengthened economy.

Enterprise Financials' revenue fell by 9% to $148.4 million in 2014 mostly due to double-digit declines in interest income as its purchased credit-impaired (PCI) loan balances and accelerated payments declined, and as interest margins on its loans continued to shrink. The bank's portfolio loan balances increased, however, helping to offset some of its interest income decline.

Lower revenue and higher loan loss provisions (it received a loan loss benefit of $642 thousand in 2013) in 2014 caused the bank's net income to dive 18% to $27.2 million. Enterprise Financial's operating cash levels rose by 7% to $31.5 million despite lower earnings for the year, mostly thanks to favorable changes in its working capital related to a $12-million change in other asset balances.

Strategy

Enterprise Financial Services planned in 2015 to continue its long-term strategy of keeping a "relationship-oriented distribution and sales approach"; growing its fee income and niche businesses; practicing "prudent" credit and interest rate risk management; and using advanced technology and controlled-expense growth. The company added that it planned on "operating branches with larger average deposits, and employing experienced staff who are compensated on the basis of performance and customer service."

Though it just had two branches in Phoenix in 2015, the bank believes the fast-growing Phoenix market offers long-term growth opportunities for the company with its underlying demographic and geographic factors. Indeed, at the end of 2014, the market had over 90,000 privately-held businesses and 80,000-plus households each with investable assets of more than $1 million.

Mergers and Acquisitions

In 2017, Enterprise Financial Services completed the acquisition of Jefferson County Bancshares, the holding company of Eagle Bank and Trust Company in Missouri. The deal added 13 branches in metropolitan St. Louis and Perry County, Missouri. The acquisition expanded EFS's assets to nearly $5 billion.

Company Background

In a restructuring move, Enterprise Financial Services sold life insurance arm Millennium Brokerage in 2010, five years after investing in the company.

EXECUTIVES

Chairman, Director, Michael A. DeCola
President, Chief Executive Officer, Director, James Brian Lally, $491,667 total compensation
Executive Vice President, Chief Financial Officer, Keene S. Turner, $359,508 total compensation
Executive Vice President, Subsidiary Officer, Scott R. Goodman, $330,285 total compensation
Subsidiary Officer, Mark G. Ponder, $212,500 total compensation
Corporate Secretary, Subsidiary Officer, Nicole M. Iannacone, $221,041 total compensation
Subsidiary Officer, Douglas N. Bauche, $265,525 total compensation
Director, Robert E. Guest
Director, James M. Havel
Director, Michael R. Holmes
Director, Nevada A. Kent
Director, Stephen P. Marsh
Director, Daniel A. Rodrigues
Director, Richard M. Sanborn
Director, Eloise E. Schmitz
Director, Sandra A. Van Trease
Director, Lyne B. Andrich
Director, Marcela Manjarrez
Director, Lina A. Young
Auditors : Deloitte & Touche LLP

LOCATIONS

HQ: Enterprise Financial Services Corp
150 North Meramec, Clayton, MO 63105
Phone: 314 725-5500
Web: www.enterprisebank.com

PRODUCTS/OPERATIONS

2011 Sales

	$ mil.	% of total
Interest		
Loans, including fees	130.1	79
Securities	11.8	7
Other	0.9	1
Noninterest		
Wealth management	6.8	4
Service charges on deposit accounts	5.1	3
Gain on state tax credits, net	3.7	2
Other service charges and fee income	1.7	1
Other	4.7	3
Adjustments	(3.5)	-
Total	161.3	100

Selected Acquisitions

2011
    Legacy Bank (Scottsdale, AZ; community bank)
    The First National Bank of Olathe (Olathe, KS; community bank)
    BankLiberty (Liberty, MO; single branch)
2010
    Home National Bank (AZ operations; community bank)
2009
    Valley Capital Bank (Mesa, AZ; community bank)

COMPETITORS

BANCFIRST CORPORATION
BOKF MERGER CORPORATION NUMBER SIXTEEN
CITIZENS FINANCIAL GROUP, INC.
COMMERCE BANCSHARES, INC.
FIRST BUSINESS FINANCIAL SERVICES, INC.
M&T BANK CORPORATION
PEOPLES FINANCIAL SERVICES CORP.
PRIVATEBANCORP, INC.
RESONA HOLDINGS, INC.
ZIONS BANCORPORATION

HISTORICAL FINANCIALS

Company Type: Public

Income Statement   FYE: December 31

	ASSETS ($mil)	NET INCOME ($mil)	INCOME AS % OF ASSETS	EMPLOYEES
12/20	9,751.5	74.3	0.8%	0
12/19	7,333.7	92.7	1.3%	805
12/18	5,645.6	89.2	1.6%	650
12/17	5,289.2	48.1	0.9%	635
12/16	4,081.3	48.8	1.2%	479
Annual Growth	24.3%	11.1%	—	

2020 Year-End Financials

Return on assets: 0.8%   Dividends
Return on equity: 7.6%   Yield: 2.0%
Long-term debt ($ mil.): —   Payout: 26.0%
No. of shares ($ mil.): 31.2   Market value ($ mil.): 1,091.0
Sales ($ mil.): 359.2

	STOCK PRICE ($) FY Close	P/E High	P/E Low	PER SHARE ($) Earnings	PER SHARE ($) Dividends	PER SHARE ($) Book Value
12/20	34.95	18	9	2.76	0.72	34.57
12/19	48.21	14	11	3.55	0.62	32.67
12/18	37.63	15	10	3.83	0.47	26.47
12/17	45.15	22	18	2.07	0.44	23.76
12/16	43.00	18	10	2.41	0.41	19.31
Annual Growth	(5.1%)	—	—	3.4%	15.1%	15.7%

Envela Corp

Attracted to things gold and shiny? If so, DGSE is for you. The company buys and sells jewelry, bullion, rare coins, fine watches, and collectibles to retail and wholesale customers across the US through its various websites and 30-plus retail stores in California, Texas, and South Carolina. The company's eight e-commerce sites let customers buy and sell jewelry and bullion interactively, and obtain current precious-metal prices. In all, more than 7,500 items are available for sale on DGSE websites, including $2 million in diamonds. DGSE also owns Fairchild Watches, a leading vintage watch wholesaler, and the rare coin dealer Superior Galleries. The company sold its pair of pawn shops in Dallas in 2009.

EXECUTIVES

Chairman, President, Chief Executive Officer, Director, John Richardson Loftus
Chief Financial Officer, Bret Allen Pedersen, $150,000 total compensation
Chief Information Officer, Joel S. Friedman
Director, Alexandra C. Griffin
Director, James R. (Jim) Ruth
Director, Allison M. DeStefano
Auditors : Whitley Penn LLP

LOCATIONS

HQ: Envela Corp
1901 Gateway Drive, Ste 100, Irving, TX 75038
Phone: 972 587-4049   **Fax:** 972 674-2596
Web: www.envela.com

COMPETITORS

BULOVA CORPORATION
Pandora A/S
RICHLINE GROUP, INC.
STULLER, INC.
SUPERIOR GALLERIES, INC.

HISTORICAL FINANCIALS

Company Type: Public

Income Statement   FYE: December 31

	REVENUE ($mil)	NET INCOME ($mil)	NET PROFIT MARGIN	EMPLOYEES
12/20	113.9	6.3	5.6%	152
12/19	82.0	2.7	3.4%	135
12/18	54.0	0.6	1.2%	52
12/17	61.9	1.8	3.0%	54
12/16	48.3	(4.0)	—	77
Annual Growth	23.9%	—		18.5%

2020 Year-End Financials

Debt ratio: 38.0%   No. of shares ($ mil.): 26.9
Return on equity: 44.2%   Dividends
Cash ($ mil.): 9.2   Yield: —
Current Ratio: 3.88   Payout: —
Long-term debt ($ mil.): 13.2   Market value ($ mil.): 140.0

	STOCK PRICE ($) FY Close	P/E High	P/E Low	PER SHARE ($) Earnings	PER SHARE ($) Dividends	PER SHARE ($) Book Value
12/20	5.20	25	6	0.24	0.00	0.65
12/19	1.35	16	4	0.10	0.00	0.42
12/18	0.46	53	19	0.02	0.00	0.31
12/17	0.93	25	12	0.07	0.00	0.29
12/16	1.24	—	—	(0.30)	0.00	0.22
Annual Growth	43.1%	—		—	—	31.3%

Enviva Inc

EXECUTIVES

President, Chief Executive Officer, Director, Thomas Meth

Executive Vice President, Chief Financial Officer, Principal Financial Officer, Shai S. Even

Executive Vice President, Chief Human Resources Officer, Roxanne B. Klein

Communications, Public and Environmental Affairs Executive Vice President, Yanina A. Kravtsova

Corporate Development Executive Vice President, Corporate Development General Counsel, Corporate Development Holding/Parent Company Officer, William H. Schmidt

Operations Executive Vice President, Operations Holding/Parent Company Officer, Edward Royal Smith

Senior Vice President, Deputy General Counsel, Secretary, Jason E. Paral

Vice President, Chief Accounting Officer, Michael A. Johnson

Director, Eva T. Zlotnicka
Director, Martin N. Davidson
Director, David M. Leuschen
Director, Pierre F. Lapeyre
Director, Ralph C. Alexander
Director, John C. Bumgarner
Director, Jim H. Derryberry
Director, Gerrit L. Lansing
Director, Jeffrey W. Ubben
Director, Gary L Whitlock
Director, Janet S. Wong

Auditors : Ernst & Young LLP

LOCATIONS

HQ: Enviva Inc
7272 Wisconsin Ave., Suite 1800, Bethesda, MD 20814
Phone: 301 657-5560
Web: www.envivabiomass.com

HISTORICAL FINANCIALS

Company Type: Public

Income Statement — FYE: December 31

	REVENUE ($mil)	NET INCOME ($mil)	NET PROFIT MARGIN	EMPLOYEES
12/20	875.0	17.0	2.0%	0
12/19	684.3	(2.9)	—	0
12/18	573.7	6.9	1.2%	0
12/17	543.2	17.5	3.2%	0
12/16	464.2	21.3	4.6%	0
Annual Growth	17.2%	(5.5%)	—	—

2020 Year-End Financials

Debt ratio: 64.8%
Return on equity: —
Cash ($ mil.): 10.0
Current Ratio: 1.21
Long-term debt ($ mil.): 912.7
No. of shares ($ mil.): 39.8
Dividends
  Yield: —
  Payout: —
Market value ($ mil.): 1,808.0

	STOCK PRICE ($) FY Close	P/E High/Low		PER SHARE ($) Earnings	Dividends	Book Value
12/20	45.42	—	—	(0.36)	2.90	8.15
12/19	37.31	—	—	(0.54)	2.62	8.39
12/18	27.75	825	628	0.04	2.51	5.54
12/17	27.65	48	38	0.61	2.28	7.99
12/16	26.80	30	15	0.91	2.03	11.90
Annual Growth	14.1%	—	—	—	9.3%	(9.0%)

Epam Systems, Inc.

EPAM is the world's leading provider of digital platform engineering, software development and other IT services to customers primarily in North America, Europe and Russia. The company provides software development, product engineering services, and other business processes. Its key service offerings and solutions include five practice areas, such as engineering, operations, optimization, consulting, and design. The company has delivery locations in Russia, Belarus, Ukraine, Hungary, Poland, India, and the US that employ approximately 42,890 professionals. Approximately 60% of sales come from North America. EPAM was founded in 1993.

Operations

The company's operations consist of three reportable segments: North America (approximately 60% of sales), Europe (about 35%), and Russia (about 5%).

EPAM has operations in five practice areas: engineering, operations, optimization, consulting, and design.

Through its engineering services, the company builds enterprise technologies that improve business processes, offer smarter analytics and result in greater operational excellence through requirements analysis and platform selection, deep and complex customization, cross-platform migration, implementation and integration. It has deep expertise and the ability to offer a comprehensive set of software product development services including product research, customer experience design and prototyping, program management, component design and integration, full lifecycle software testing, product deployment and end-user customization, performance tuning, product support and maintenance, managed services, as well as porting and cross-platform migration.

EPAM also offers proprietary platforms and engineering practices in order to turn customers' operations into intelligent enterprise hubs.

A key optimization service is implementing automation, transforming legacy processes to increase customers' revenues and reduce costs.

The company's consulting services drive deeper relationships as it helps its customers with larger and more complex challenges. Its digital and service design practice provides strategy, design, creative and program management services for customers looking to improve the user experience. Overall, the company generates approximately 85% of sales from time-and-material. Fixed-price and licensing account for the rest.

Geographic Reach

EPAM is based in Newtown, Pennsylvania. North America is the company's biggest market, accounting for about 60% of revenue. European customers provide about 40%.

The company has nearly 12,390 delivery professionals located in Ukraine, about 9,415 delivery professionals located in Belarus and around 8,935 delivery professionals located in Russia. Its other significant locations with delivery professionals are India with about 4,350, Poland with approximately 3,055, the US with over 2,755, Hungary with around 1,990 and Mexico with about 1,020.

EPAM has additional key operations in the US, Hungary, Poland, India, and Russia.

The company also offers the EPAM E-KIDS program in about 15 countries.

Sales and Marketing

The company markets and sells its services through its senior management, sales and business development teams, account managers, and professional staff.

EPAM maintains industry specialization and markets its services to six industry groups: Financial Services (about 25%), Travel & Consumer, Business Information & Media, and Software & Hi-Tech (about 20% each), Life Sciences & Healthcare and Emerging Verticals (about 10% each).

The company has established relationships with many of its customers, with nearly 55% and about 25% of revenue comes from customers that had used its services for at least five and ten years, respectively. Its top five customers accounted for about 20% of revenue while its top ten customers accounted for nearly 30%.

Financial Performance

The company's revenue for fiscal 2021 increased by 41% to $3.8 billion compared from the prior year with $2.7 billion. This growth resulted from its ability to retain existing customers and increase the level of services EPAM provide to them and its ability to produce revenues from new customer relationships.

Net income for fiscal 2021 increased to $481.7 million compared from the prior year with $327.2 million.

Cash held by the company at the end of fiscal 2021 increased to $1.4 billion. Cash provided by operations was $572.3 million while cash used for investing and financing activities were $368.9 million and $59.6 million, respectively. Main uses of cash were acquisition of businesses; and payments of withholding taxes related to net share settlements of restricted stock units.

Strategy

The company's service offerings continuously evolve to provide more customized and integrated solutions to its customers where EPAM combine best-in-class software engineering with customer experience design, business consulting and technology innovation services. EPAM is continually expanding its service capabilities, moving beyond traditional services into business consulting, design and physical product development and areas such as artificial intelligence, robotics and virtual reality.

Mergers and Acquisitions

In late 2021, EPAM acquired Optiva Media, a niche professional services firm that provides product development and digital services to leading media companies. "We're pleased to welcome Optiva Media to EPAM. The combination of EPAM's digital technology and product engineering expertise with Optiva Media's platforms and accelerators will create a complete and valuable end-to-end delivery capability in the media and entertainment space," said Balazs Fejes, President of EU and APAC Markets at EPAM.

Also in late 2021, EPAM acquired Emakina Group, a multi-award-winning digital agency. Headquartered in Belgium with more than 1,100 employees and a strong presence across Central and Western Europe, the Middle East, Asia, Africa, and North America, Emakina Group will enhance EPAM's digital experience practice.

In mid-2021, EPAM acquired CORE SE, a professional service provider specializing in IT strategy and technology-driven transformations. Following the recent announcement of a new Berlin office, EPAM's acquisition of CORE SE will further expand its Western European footprint within the DACH region.

In early 2021, EPAM acquired Just-BI to further expand their comprehensive portfolio of data and analytics services. Just-BI is a niche consultancy firm specializing in Data and Analytics. Based in the Netherlands, the acquisition brings expanded, EU, APAC and global advisory capabilities around the full SAP ecosystem as well as extending EPAM's already rich Data, BI and Advanced Analytics capabilities.

Also in early 2021, EPAM acquired White-Hat, a leading cybersecurity services company, to expand its comprehensive cybersecurity expertise portfolio and diversifying their EMEA delivery capabilities. White-Hat, headquartered in Tel Aviv, Israel, safeguards its customers' businesses using innovative methodologies and an in-depth understanding of the attacker's mindset and landscape.

In a separate transaction in 2021, EPAM acquired PolSource, an expert Salesforce Consulting Partner with more than 350 experienced Salesforce specialists across the Americas and Europe. PolSource brings a reputation for industry innovation ? delivering successful multi-cloud end-to-end solutions across many key industries, including consumer goods, retail, manufacturing, automotive, technology, healthcare, and life sciences.

Company Background

Arkadily Dobkin and Leo Lozner founded EPAM in Princeton, New Jersey and Minsk, Belarus, respectively, in 1993. The company's first significant product development client was SAP. EPAM debuted as the first company with Belarusian engineering roots on the NYSE in 2012.

EXECUTIVES

Chairman, President, Chief Executive Officer, Arkadiy Dobkin, $537,500 total compensation
Global Head Executive Vice President, Global Head Division Officer, Balazs Fejes, $366,710 total compensation
Senior Vice President, Division Officer, Viktar Dvorkin, $293,750 total compensation
Senior Vice President, Chief Financial Officer, Treasurer, Jason Peterson, $357,500 total compensation
Senior Vice President, General Counsel, Corporate Secretary, Edward Rockwell
Senior Vice President, Chief Marketing Officer, Elaina Shekhter, $273,400 total compensation
Senior Vice President, Division Officer, Boris Shnayder, $257,500 total compensation
Senior Vice President, Chief People Officer, Lawrence F. Solomon, $311,250 total compensation
Senior Vice President, Division Officer, Sergey Yezhkov
Vice President, Chief Accounting Officer, Corporate Controller, Gary C. Abrahams
Lead Independent Director, Director, Ronald P. Vargo
Director, Robert E. Segert
Director, Helen Shan
Director, Richard Michael Mayoras
Director, Karl Robb, $823 total compensation
Director, Eugene Roman
Director, Jill B. Smart
Auditors : DELOITTE & TOUCHE LLP

LOCATIONS

HQ: Epam Systems, Inc.
41 University Drive, Suite 202, Newtown, PA 18940
Phone: 267 759-9000
Web: www.epam.com

2014 Sales by Customer Location

	$ mil.	% of total
North America	367.5	50
Europe		
UK	141.4	19
Switzerland	87.1	12
Other countries	56.4	8
CIS		
Russia	48.9	7
Other countries	6.9	1
APAC	13.4	2
Reimbursable expenses & other revenues	8.4	1
Total	730	100

PRODUCTS/OPERATIONS

2014 Sales

	$ mil.	% of total
Software development	504.6	69
Application testing services	140.4	19
Application maintenance & support	58.8	8
Infrastructure services	14.2	2
Licensing	3.6	1
Reimbursable expenses & other revenues	8.4	1
Total	730	100

2014 Sales by Industry

	$ mil.	% of total
Banking & financial services	215.4	29
Independent software vendors & technology	157.9	22
Travel & hospitality	157.8	22
Business information & media	91.7	13
Other verticals	98.8	13
Reimbursable expenses & other revenues	8.4	1
Total	730	100

Selected Services

Application development
Application maintenance and support
Application testing
Business intelligence
Business process management
Content management
Customer Relationship Management (CRM)
Data warehousing and business intelligence
E-commerce
Enterprise application integration
Enterprise resource planning
Infrastructure and hosting
Knowledge management
Localization
Offshore software development
Quality assurance consulting and testing strategy transformation
Server and network management

COMPETITORS

BLACKLINE, INC.
CALLIDUS SOFTWARE INC.
COGNIZANT TECHNOLOGY SOLUTIONS CORPORATION
IMPERVA, INC.
INFOR (US), LLC
INFOR, INC.
LARSEN & TOUBRO INFOTECH LIMITED
MICROSTRATEGY INCORPORATED
NEURONES
PEGASYSTEMS INC.

HISTORICAL FINANCIALS

Company Type: Public

Income Statement — FYE: December 31

	REVENUE ($mil)	NET INCOME ($mil)	NET PROFIT MARGIN	EMPLOYEES
12/20	2,659.4	327.1	12.3%	41,168
12/19	2,293.7	261.0	11.4%	36,739
12/18	1,842.9	240.2	13.0%	30,156
12/17	1,450.4	72.7	5.0%	25,962
12/16	1,160.1	99.2	8.6%	22,383
Annual Growth	23.0%	34.7%	—	16.5%

2020 Year-End Financials

Debt ratio: 0.9%
Return on equity: 18.2%
Cash ($ mil.): 1,322.1
Current Ratio: 4.11
Long-term debt ($ mil.): 25

No. of shares ($ mil.): 56.1
Dividends
  Yield: —
  Payout: —
Market value ($ mil.): 20,106.0

	STOCK PRICE ($) FY Close	P/E High/Low		PER SHARE ($) Earnings	Dividends	Book Value
12/20	358.35	61	27	5.60	0.00	35.34
12/19	212.16	45	24	4.53	0.00	28.92
12/18	116.01	32	23	4.24	0.00	23.35
12/17	107.43	78	45	1.32	0.00	18.40
12/16	64.31	40	29	1.87	0.00	15.29
Annual Growth	53.6%	—	—	31.5%	—	23.3%

Equitrans Midstream Corp

EXECUTIVES

Chief Executive Officer, Chairman, Director, Thomas F. Karam, $212,308 total compensation
President, Chief Operating Officer, Director, Diana M. Charletta, $283,167 total compensation
Senior Vice President, Chief Financial Officer, Kirk R. Oliver, $134,616 total compensation
Senior Vice President, General Counsel, Stephen M Moore
Vice President, Chief Human Resources Officer, Anne M. Naqi
Vice President, Chief Accounting Officer, Brian P. Pietrandrea
Corporate Secretary, Deputy General Counsel, Nathaniel D. DeRose
Lead Independent Director, Director, Robert F. Vagt
Director, Sarah M. Barpoulis
Director, D. Mark Leland
Director, Vicky A. Bailey
Director, Kenneth M. Burke
Director, Norman J. Szydlowski
Auditors : Ernst & Young LLP

LOCATIONS

HQ: Equitrans Midstream Corp
2200 Energy Drive, Canonsburg, PA 15317
Phone: 724 271-7600
Web: www.equitransmidstream.com

HISTORICAL FINANCIALS
Company Type: Public

Income Statement   FYE: December 31

	REVENUE ($mil)	NET INCOME ($mil)	NET PROFIT MARGIN	EMPLOYEES
12/20	1,510.8	423.1	28.0%	771
12/19	1,630.2	(203.7)	—	800
12/18	1,495.0	218.3	14.6%	0
12/17	895.5	(27.1)	—	0
12/16	732.2	65.1	8.9%	0
Annual Growth	19.8%	59.6%	—	—

2020 Year-End Financials
Debt ratio: 56.8%
Return on equity: 18.4%
Cash ($ mil.): 208.0
Current Ratio: 0.94
Long-term debt ($ mil.): 6,928.3
No. of shares ($ mil.): 432.4
Dividends
Yield: 11.1%
Payout: 84.9%
Market value ($ mil.): 3,477.0

	STOCK PRICE ($) FY Close	P/E High/Low		PER SHARE ($) Earnings	Dividends	Book Value
12/20	8.04	13	4	1.06	0.90	9.00
12/19	13.36	—	—	(0.80)	1.76	2.64
12/18	20.02	27	22	0.86	0.41	1.80
Annual Growth	(36.6%)	—	—	11.0%	48.2%	123.6%

Erie Indemnity Co.

Founded in 1925 as an auto insurer, Erie Indemnity now provides management services that relate to the sales, underwriting, and issuance of policies of one customer: Erie Insurance Exchange. The Exchange is a reciprocal insurance exchange that pools the underwriting of several property/casualty insurance firms. The principal personal lines products are private passenger automobile and homeowners. The principal commercial lines products are commercial multi-peril, commercial automobile and workers compensation. Erie Indemnity charges a management fee of some 25% of all premiums written or assumed by the Exchange.

Operations
Management fees (consist of policy issuance and renewal services and administrative services) account for nearly 75% of Erie Indemnity's revenue; service agreements and administrative services reimbursement revenue accounts for the remainder.

The Exchange and its subsidiaries (Erie Insurance, Erie Insurance Company of New York, Erie Insurance Property and Casualty, and Flagship City Insurance) together operate as a property/casualty insurer. The group also owns Erie Family Life Insurance and the Exchange, and its wholly owned subsidiaries, meet the definition of an insurance holding company system.

Personal lines ? primarily private passenger automobile and homeowners ? comprise some 70% of the direct and assumed premiums written; commercial lines ? primarily multi-peril, workers' compensation, and commercial automobile ? make up the rest.

Geographic Reach
Headquartered in Erie, Pennsylvania, Indemnity and the Exchange also operate 25 field offices in around a dozen states to perform primarily claims-related activities. The Exchange owns seven field offices and the remaining field offices are leased from third parties. Commitments for properties leased from other parties expire periodically through 2027. They expect that most leases will be renewed or replaced upon expiration. Rental costs of shared facilities are allocated based upon usage or square footage occupied.

Sales and Marketing
The Exchange is represented by independent agencies that serve as its sole distribution channel. In addition to their principal role as salespersons, the independent agents play a significant role as underwriting and service providers and are an integral part of the Exchange's success.

The company's advertising expenses were $52.5 million, $53.2 million, and $52.4 million in years 2021, 2020, and 2019, respectively.

Financial Performance
The company had a revenue of $2.6 billion, a 4% increase from the previous year's revenue of $2.5 billion.

In 2021, the company had a net income of $297.9 million, a 2% increase from the previous year's net income of $293.3 million.

The company's cash at the end of 2021 was $183.7 million. Operating activities generated $402.8 million, while investing activities used $185.5 million, mainly for available-for-sale securities. Financing activities used another $194.8 million, primarily for dividends paid to shareholders.

Strategy
The Exchange's strategic focus as a reciprocal insurer is to employ a disciplined underwriting philosophy and to leverage its strong surplus position to generate higher risk adjusted investment returns. The goal is to produce acceptable returns, on a long-term basis, through careful risk selection, rational pricing and superior investment returns. This focus allows the Exchange to accomplish its mission of providing as near perfect protection, as near perfect service as is humanly possible at the lowest possible costs.

Company Background
Erie Indemnity's structure and relationship to other parts of the larger Erie Insurance Group are complex, to say the least. The company operated as a property/casualty insurer through its wholly-owned subsidiaries, Erie Insurance Co., Erie New York, and Erie Insurance Property and Casualty throughout 2010. At year-end, however, Erie Indemnity sold all of its outstanding capital stock and voting shares of these subsidiaries to the Exchange. As a result, now all of its former property/casualty insurance operations are owned by the Exchange and Erie Indemnity serves as the management company. The sale of the subsidiaries did not affect its pooling agreement. The company also sold its approximate 22% ownership in Erie Family Life to the Exchange, which became Erie's' full parent.

EXECUTIVES

Chairman, Director, Thomas B. Hagen
President, Chief Executive Officer, Timothy G. NeCastro
Claims & Customer Service Executive Vice President, Lorianne Feltz
Sales and Products Executive Vice President, Douglas E. Smith

Executive Vice President, Chief Information Officer, Parthasarathy Srinivasa
Corporate Services Executive Vice President, Human Resources Executive Vice President, Sean Dugan
Executive Vice President, Chief Financial Officer, Julie Marie Pelkowski
Executive Vice President, General Counsel, Corporate Secretary, Brian W. Bolash
Senior Vice President, Controller, Jorie L. Novacek
Director, Jonathan Hirt Hagen
Director, J. Ralph Borneman
Director, Eugene C. Connell
Director, Salvatore Correnti
Director, LuAnn Datesh
Director, C. Scott Hartz
Director, Brian Arden Hudson
Director, George R. Lucore, $93,750 total compensation
Director, Thomas W. Palmer
Director, Elizabeth Hirt Vorsheck
Auditors : Ernst & Young LLP

LOCATIONS

HQ: Erie Indemnity Co.
100 Erie Insurance Place, Erie, PA 16530
Phone: 814 870-2000
Web: www.erieinsurance.com

PRODUCTS/OPERATIONS

2017 Sales

	$ mil.	% of total
Operating revenue		
Net management fees	1,662.6	97
Service agreements	29.1	2
Investment income	28.6	1
Total	1,720.3	100

COMPETITORS

AMERITRUST GROUP, INC.
ARBELLA SERVICE COMPANY, INC.
CINCINNATI FINANCIAL CORPORATION
FEDNAT HOLDING COMPANY
HCI GROUP, INC.
MAIN STREET AMERICA GROUP, INC.
PROTECTIVE INSURANCE CORPORATION
SELECTIVE INSURANCE GROUP, INC.
THE HANOVER INSURANCE GROUP INC
UNIVERSAL INSURANCE HOLDINGS, INC.

HISTORICAL FINANCIALS

Company Type: Public

Income Statement — FYE: December 31

	ASSETS ($mil)	NET INCOME ($mil)	INCOME AS % OF ASSETS	EMPLOYEES
12/20	2,117.1	293.3	13.9%	5,914
12/19	2,016.2	316.8	15.7%	5,700
12/18	1,778.3	288.2	16.2%	5,500
12/17	1,665.8	196.9	11.8%	5,300
12/16	1,548.9	210.3	13.6%	5,000
Annual Growth	8.1%	8.7%	—	4.3%

2020 Year-End Financials

Return on assets: 14.1%
Return on equity: 25.2%
Long-term debt ($ mil.): —
No. of shares ($ mil.): 46.1
Sales ($ mil.): 2,569.3
Dividends
Yield: 1.9%
Payout: 87.2%
Market value ($ mil.): 11,345.0

	STOCK PRICE ($) FY Close	P/E High/Low		PER SHARE ($) Earnings	Dividends	Book Value
12/20	245.60	40	21	5.61	4.90	25.72
12/19	166.00	40	19	6.06	3.60	24.53
12/18	133.31	22	18	5.51	3.36	21.08
12/17	121.84	30	26	3.76	3.13	18.56
12/16	112.45	25	20	4.01	2.19	17.69
Annual Growth	21.6%	—	—	8.8%	22.3%	9.8%

Escalade, Inc.

Escalade is the world's largest producer of tables for table tennis, residential in-ground basketball goals and archery bows. Its other sporting goods include hockey and soccer tables, play systems, archery, darts, and fitness equipment. Products are sold under the STIGA, Ping-Pong, Goalrilla, Silverback, USWeight, and Woodplay names, as well as private labels. The company manufactures, imports, and distributes widely recognized products through major sporting goods retailers, specialty dealers, key on-line retailers, traditional department stores and mass merchants. Escalade operates through more than five manufacturing and distribution facilities across North America. Almost all of Escalade's revenue comes from the North America.

Operations

Escalade operates in one business segment: the Sporting Goods segment which consists of home entertainment products such as table tennis tables and accessories; basketball goals; pool tables and accessories; outdoor playsets; soccer and hockey tables; archery equipment and accessories; and fitness, arcade and darting products.

Geographic Reach

Based in Indiana, Escalade operates over five manufacturing and distribution facilities across North America in Indiana, Illinois, Florida, and abroad operations in Mexico, and China.

The company manufactures its products in the US, Mexico, and imports products from Asian contract manufacturers. North America accounts almost all of net revenue.

Sales and Marketing

Escalade sells its products through retailers, sporting goods stores, specialty dealers, key on-line retailers, traditional department stores and mass merchants. Amazon.com contributed about 25% of Escalade's total revenues.

The company's sales channels include key on-line retailers or e-commerce (around 35% of sales), mass merchants (nearly 35%), specialty dealers (about 25%), and international (less than 5%). Customers include retailers, dealers and wholesalers.

Financial Performance

In 2020, Escalade's revenue increased by 52% to $273.6 million compared to $180.5 million in 2019. The increase was primarily due to factory utilization, changes in sales mix and supply chain improvements made throughout the year.

Net income in 2020 increased to $25.9 million compared to $7.3 billion in the prior year.

Cash held by the company at the end of 2020 decreased to $3.5 million. Cash provided by operations and financing activities were $2.6 million and $16.0 million, respectively. Cash used for investing activities was $21.0 million, mainly for acquisitions.

Strategy

Core components of Escalade's business development and growth strategy have been, and continue to be, making strategic acquisitions, developing strong brand names, and investing in product innovation.

Within the sporting goods industry, the company has successfully built a robust market presence in several niche markets. This strategy is heavily dependent on expanding the company's customer base, barriers to entry, strong brands, excellent customer service and a commitment to innovation. A key strategic advantage is the company's established relationships with major customers that allow the company to bring new products to market in a cost-effective manner while maintaining a diversified portfolio of products to meet the demands of consumers.

To enhance growth opportunities, the company has focused on promoting new product innovation and development and brand marketing. In addition, the company has embarked on a strategy of acquiring companies or product lines that complement or expand the company's existing product lines or provide expansion into new or emerging categories in sporting goods.

Mergers and Acquisitions

In late 2020, Escalade Sports, a wholly owned subsidiary of Escalade, has acquired substantially all of the business and assets of Revel Match, dba RAVE Sports, a brand known for its innovative and high-quality water recreation products. Adding this business to Escalade's existing portfolio expands its powerful stable of recreational brands and positions the company for continued revenue and profit growth.

Also in late 2020, Escalade Sports, a wholly owned subsidiary of Escalade, has acquired the assets of the billiard table, game room, and recreational product lines of American Heritage Billiards, including the related intellectual property. Escalade agreed to pay a gross purchase price of $1.55 million, which was paid in cash at closing.

EXECUTIVES

Chairman, President, Chief Executive Officer, Director, Walter P. Glazer

Finance Vice President, Finance Chief Financial Officer, Finance Secretary, Stephen R. Wawrin, $218,360 total compensation

Corporate Development Vice President, Investor Relations Vice President, Director, Patrick J. Griffin, $154,500 total compensation

Director, Edward E. Williams

Director, Richard F. Baalmann

Director, Katherine F. Franklin

Auditors : BKD, LLP

LOCATIONS

HQ: Escalade, Inc.
817 Maxwell Ave., Evansville, IN 47711
Phone: 812 467-1358
Web: www.escaladeinc.com

2015 Sales

	$ mil.	% of total
North America	152.9	98
Europe	1.2	1
Other	1.4	1
Total	155.5	100

PRODUCTS/OPERATIONS

Selected Brands

Accudart
American Legend
Arachnid
Atomic
Bear Archery
Cajun Bowfishing
Childlife
Goaliath
Goalrilla
Goalsetter
Hoopstar
Lucasi
Minnesota Fats
Mizerak
Nodor
Onix
Pickleball Now
Ping-Pong
Players
Prince
PureX
Rage
Redline
Silverback
STIGA
The STEP
Trophy Ridge
Unicorn
USWeight
Viva Sol
Whisker Biscuit
Winmau
Woodplay
Zume Games

COMPETITORS

ACCO BRANDS CORPORATION
FRASERS GROUP PLC
Francotyp-Postalia GmbH
KONICA MINOLTA, INC.
PARTYLITE WORLDWIDE, LLC
PITNEY BOWES INC.
QUADIENT, INC.
RICOH COMPANY,LTD.
TELLERMATE LIMITED
TSI, INCORPORATED

HISTORICAL FINANCIALS

Company Type: Public

Income Statement — FYE: December 25

	REVENUE ($mil)	NET INCOME ($mil)	NET PROFIT MARGIN	EMPLOYEES
12/21	313.6	24.4	7.8%	676
12/20	273.6	25.9	9.5%	704
12/19	180.5	7.2	4.0%	468
12/18	175.7	20.4	11.6%	531
12/17	177.3	14.0	7.9%	501
Annual Growth	15.3%	14.8%	—	7.8%

2021 Year-End Financials

Debt ratio: 22.9%
Return on equity: 17.1%
Cash ($ mil.): 4.3
Current Ratio: 3.55
Long-term debt ($ mil.): 50.3
No. of shares ($ mil.): 13.4
Dividends
  Yield: —
  Payout: 31.8%
Market value ($ mil.): 212.0

	STOCK PRICE ($) FY Close	P/E High	P/E Low	Earnings	Dividends	Book Value
12/21	15.69	14	9	1.76	0.56	10.87
12/20	21.69	12	3	1.82	0.53	10.00
12/19	9.79	26	19	0.50	0.50	8.88
12/18	11.44	11	8	1.41	0.50	8.89
12/17	12.30	14	12	0.98	0.46	7.77
Annual Growth	6.3%	—	—	15.8%	5.0%	8.7%

Esquire Financial Holdings Inc

EXECUTIVES

Chairman, Subsidiary Officer, Director, Anthony L. Coelho

President, Chief Executive Officer, Subsidiary Officer, Director, Andrew C. Sagliocca, $525,046 total compensation

Executive Vice President, Chief Operating Officer, Corporate Secretary, Subsidiary Officer, Eric S. Bader, $425,036 total compensation

Sales Executive Vice President, Sales Director, Sales Subsidiary Officer, Ari P. Kornhaber, $425,036 total compensation

Senior Vice President, Chief Financial Officer, Subsidiary Officer, Michael Lacapria

Director, Selig A. Zises

Director, Todd Deutsch

Director, Russ M. Herman

Director, Robert J. Mitzman

Director, Kevin C. Waterhouse

Director, Marc D. Grossman

Director, Janet M. Hill

Director, Richard T. Powers

Auditors : Crowe LLP

LOCATIONS

HQ: Esquire Financial Holdings Inc
100 Jericho Quadrangle, Suite 100, Jericho, NY 11753
Phone: 516 535-2002
Web: www.esquirebank.com

HISTORICAL FINANCIALS

Company Type: Public

Income Statement — FYE: December 31

	ASSETS ($mil)	NET INCOME ($mil)	INCOME AS % OF ASSETS	EMPLOYEES
12/20	936.7	12.6	1.3%	99
12/19	798.0	14.1	1.8%	86
12/18	663.8	8.7	1.3%	74
12/17	533.6	3.6	0.7%	61
12/16	424.8	2.8	0.7%	52
Annual Growth	21.9%	45.4%	—	17.5%

2020 Year-End Financials

Return on assets: 1.4%
Return on equity: 10.6%
Long-term debt ($ mil.): —
No. of shares ($ mil.): 7.7
Sales ($ mil.): 53.2
Dividends
  Yield: —
  Payout: —
Market value ($ mil.): 150.0

	STOCK PRICE ($) FY Close	P/E High	P/E Low	Earnings	Dividends	Book Value
12/20	19.19	15	7	1.65	0.00	16.18
12/19	26.07	14	11	1.82	0.00	14.51
12/18	21.70	23	16	1.13	0.00	12.32
12/17	19.74	36	25	0.58	0.00	11.38
Annual Growth	(0.9%)	—	—	41.7%	—	12.4%

Essential Properties Realty Trust Inc

EXECUTIVES

Chairman, Director, Paul T. Bossidy

President, Chief Executive Officer, Peter M. Mavoides, $300 total compensation

Executive Vice President, Chief Operating Officer, Gregg A. Seibert, $250 total compensation

Senior Vice President, Chief Financial Officer, Hillary P. Hai, $250 total compensation

Division Officer, Daniel P. Donlan

Director, Joyce DeLucca

Director, Anthony K. Dobkin

Director, Scott A. Estes

Director, Lawrence J. Minich

Director, Heather L. Neary

Director, Stephen D. Sautel

Director, Janaki Sivanesan

Auditors : Grant Thornton LLP

LOCATIONS

HQ: Essential Properties Realty Trust Inc
902 Carniege Center Blvd., Suite 520, Princeton, NJ 08540
Phone: 609 436-0619
Web: www.essentialproperties.com

HISTORICAL FINANCIALS
Company Type: Public

Income Statement   FYE: December 31

	REVENUE ($mil)	NET INCOME ($mil)	NET PROFIT MARGIN	EMPLOYEES
12/21	230.2	95.7	41.6%	37
12/20	164.0	42.2	25.8%	33
12/19	139.3	41.8	30.0%	27
12/18	96.2	15.6	16.2%	18
12/17	54.4	6.2	11.6%	19
Annual Growth	43.4%	97.5%	—	18.1%

2021 Year-End Financials
Debt ratio: 35.3%
Return on equity: 5.3%
Cash ($ mil.): 59.7
Current Ratio: 1.82
Long-term debt ($ mil.): 1,165.7
No. of shares ($ mil.): 124.6
Dividends
Yield: 3.4%
Payout: 161.2%
Market value ($ mil.): 3,594.0

	STOCK PRICE ($) FY Close	P/E High/Low		PER SHARE ($) Earnings	Dividends	Book Value
12/21	28.83	40	25	0.82	1.00	16.34
12/20	21.20	66	17	0.44	0.93	14.81
12/19	24.81	41	21	0.63	0.88	14.26
12/18	13.84	56	51	0.26	0.43	12.85
Annual Growth	27.7%	—	—	46.6%	32.1%	8.3%

Essential Utilities Inc

Essential Utilities (Essential), formerly Aqua America, provides water or wastewater services to five million customers in Pennsylvania, Ohio, Texas, Illinois, North Carolina, New Jersey, Indiana, and Virginia. It is the holding company for several regulated utilities, the largest being Aqua Pennsylvania. Additionally, the company provides non-utility water supply services for the natural gas drilling industry, manages a water system operating and maintenance contracts, as well as sewer line protection solutions and repair service to households. The company was formed in 1968. Over 70% of Essential's total sales comes from Pennsylvania.

Operations
The company has identified twelve operating segments and has two reportable segments, the Regulated Water segment and the Regulated Natural Gas segment. The Regulated Water segment is comprised of eight operating segments for its water and wastewater regulated utility companies, aligned with the states where Essential provide these services.

The Regulated Natural Gas segment is comprised of one operating segment representing natural gas utility companies, acquired in the Peoples Gas Acquisition, for which the Company provides natural gas distribution services.

Geographic Reach
Primarily serving Pennsylvania (headquarters), Essential provides services in Ohio, Texas, Illinois, North Carolina, New Jersey, Indiana, and Virginia. Over 25% of company revenue comes from over 25 counties in Pennsylvania and major areas around Philadelphia.

Sales and Marketing
Essential's customers are mostly residential and commercial customers. It also serves fire protection departments, industries, wastewater clients and other utility customers. Residential water and commercial customers bring in about 70% of annual revenue.

Financial Performance
The company's revenue for fiscal 2021 increased by 29% to $1.9 billion compared from the prior year with $1.5 billion.

Net income for fiscal 2021 increased to $431.6 million compared from the prior year with $284 million.

Cash held by the company at the end of fiscal 2021 increased to $10.6 million. Cash provided by operations and financing activities were $644.7 million and $417.1 million, respectively. Cash used for investing activities was $1.1 billion, mainly for repayments of long-term debt.

Mergers and Acquisitions
In August 2021, the Company acquired the water utility system assets of The Commons Water Supply, Inc., which serves 992 customers in Harris County, Texas, and the wastewater utility system assets of the Village of Bourbonnais, which serves approximately 6,500 customers in Kankakee County, Illinois. The total cash purchase prices for these utility systems were $4.0 million and $32.1 million, respectively.

EXECUTIVES

Public Affairs; Customer Operations Chairman, Public Affairs; Customer Operations Chief Executive Officer, Chairman, Director, Christopher H. Franklin, $749,321 total compensation

Executive Vice President, Chief Operating Officer, Richard Scott (Rick) Fox, $373,257 total compensation

Corporate Development Division Officer, Corporate Development Executive Vice President, Strategy Division Officer, Strategy Executive Vice President, Corporate Development Chief Financial Officer, Strategy Chief Financial Officer, Daniel J. Schuller, $392,384 total compensation

Executive Vice President, Chief Strategy Officer, Corporate Development Officer, Matthew (Matt) Rhodes, $203,019 total compensation

Corporate Development Executive Vice President, Corporate Development Secretary, Corporate Development General Counsel, Christopher Paul Luning, $339,732 total compensation

Non-Executive Chairman, Chairman Emeritus, Director, Nicholas DeBenedictis, $573,985 total compensation

Lead Independent Director, Director, Daniel J. Hilferty

Director, Elizabeth B. Amato

Director, Wendy A. Franks
Director, Francis O. Idehen
Director, Ellen T. Ruff
Director, Lee C. Stewart
Director, Christopher C. Womack
Auditors : PricewaterhouseCoopers LLP

LOCATIONS
HQ: Essential Utilities Inc
762 W Lancaster Avenue, Bryn Mawr, PA 19010-3489
Phone: 610 527-8000
Web: www.essential.co

2015 Sales
	% of total
Pennsylvania	52
Ohio	12
Texas	9
Illinois	7
North Carolina	6
Other states	10
Other and eliminations	4
Total	100

PRODUCTS/OPERATIONS
2015 Sales
	$ mil.	% of total
Regulated		
Residential water	477.8	59
Commercial water	126.8	16
Fire protection	29.7	4
Industrial water	28.0	3
Other water	27.2	3
Wastewater	79.4	10
Other utility	10.7	1
Other and eliminations	34.6	4
Total	814.2	100

Selected Subsidiaries
Aqua Illinois, Inc.
Aqua Indiana, Inc.
Aqua New Jersey, Inc.
Aqua North Carolina, Inc.
Aqua Ohio, Inc.
Aqua Pennsylvania, Inc.
Aqua Resources, Inc.
Aqua Services, Inc.
Aqua Texas, Inc.
Aqua Utilities, Inc.
Aqua Virginia, Inc.

COMPETITORS
AMERICAN STATES WATER COMPANY
AMERICAN WATER WORKS COMPANY, INC.
ARTESIAN RESOURCES CORPORATION
CLEAN HARBORS, INC.
CONNECTICUT WATER SERVICE, INC.
NEW JERSEY RESOURCES CORPORATION
ORLANDO UTILITIES COMMISSION (INC)
SJW GROUP
SOUTHWEST GAS HOLDINGS, INC.
THE EMPIRE DISTRICT ELECTRIC COMPANY

HISTORICAL FINANCIALS
Company Type: Public

Income Statement   FYE: December 31

	REVENUE ($mil)	NET INCOME ($mil)	NET PROFIT MARGIN	EMPLOYEES
12/20	1,462.6	284.8	19.5%	3,180
12/19	889.6	224.5	25.2%	1,583
12/18	838.0	191.9	22.9%	1,570
12/17	809.5	239.7	29.6%	1,530
12/16	819.8	234.1	28.6%	1,551
Annual Growth	15.6%	5.0%	—	19.7%

Etsy Inc

2020 Year-End Financials
Debt ratio: 41.4%
Return on equity: 6.6%
Cash ($ mil.): 4.8
Current Ratio: 0.63
Long-term debt ($ mil.): 5,507.7
No. of shares ($ mil.): 245.3
Dividends
Yield: 2.0%
Payout: 97.9%
Market value ($ mil.): 11,605.0

	STOCK PRICE ($) FY Close	P/E High/Low		PER SHARE ($) Earnings	Dividends	Book Value
12/20	47.29	47	29	1.12	0.97	19.09
12/19	46.94	45	32	1.04	0.91	17.58
12/18	34.19	36	30	1.08	0.85	11.28
12/17	39.23	29	22	1.35	0.79	11.02
12/16	30.04	27	22	1.32	0.74	10.43
Annual Growth	12.0%	—	—	(4.0%)	7.1%	16.3%

EXECUTIVES

Chairman, Director, Frederick R. Wilson
President, Chief Executive Officer, Director, Joshua (Josh) Silverman, $395,833 total compensation
Product Senior Vice President, Kruti Patel Goyal
Service Senior Vice President, People Senior Vice President, Strategy Senior Vice President, Raina Moskowitz
Chief Financial Officer, Rachel C. Glaser, $375,000 total compensation
Chief Legal Officer, Corporate Secretary, General Counsel, Jill Simeone, $325,000 total compensation
Chief Marketing Officer, Ryan Scott
Chief Technical Officer, Mike Fisher, $325,000 total compensation
Director, M. Michele Burns
Director, Jonathan D. Klein
Director, Gary S. Briggs
Director, Melissa Reiff
Director, Margaret M. Smyth
Director, C. Andrew Ballard
Auditors: PricewaterhouseCoopers LLP

LOCATIONS

HQ: Etsy Inc
117 Adams Street, Brooklyn, NY 11201
Phone: 718 880-3660
Web: www.etsy.com

HISTORICAL FINANCIALS
Company Type: Public

Income Statement				FYE: December 31
	REVENUE ($mil)	NET INCOME ($mil)	NET PROFIT MARGIN	EMPLOYEES
12/20	1,725.6	349.2	20.2%	1,414
12/19	818.3	95.8	11.7%	1,240
12/18	603.6	77.4	12.8%	874
12/17	441.2	81.8	18.5%	744
12/16	364.9	(29.9)	—	1,043
Annual Growth	47.5%	—	—	7.9%

Evans Bancorp, Inc.

2020 Year-End Financials
Debt ratio: 46.4%
Return on equity: 60.6%
Cash ($ mil.): 1,244.1
Current Ratio: 4.17
Long-term debt ($ mil.): 1,107.2
No. of shares ($ mil.): 125.8
Dividends
Yield: —
Payout: —
Market value ($ mil.): 22,387.0

	STOCK PRICE ($) FY Close	P/E High/Low		PER SHARE ($) Earnings	Dividends	Book Value
12/20	177.91	69	11	2.69	0.00	5.90
12/19	44.30	91	51	0.76	0.00	3.44
12/18	47.57	90	28	0.61	0.00	3.35
12/17	20.45	32	14	0.68	0.00	3.26
12/16	11.78	—	—	(0.26)	0.00	2.97
Annual Growth	97.1%	—	—	—	—	18.7%

Evans National Bank wants to take care of Buffalo's bills. The subsidiary of Evans Bancorp operates about a dozen branches in western New York (including Buffalo). The bank primarily uses funds gathered from deposits to originate commercial and residential real estate loans (more than 70% of its loan portfolio) and to invest in securities. Subsidiaries include ENB Insurance Agency, which sells property/casualty insurance; ENB Associates, offering mutual funds and annuities to bank customers; and Evans National Leasing, which provides financing for business equipment throughout the US. In 2009 Evans Bancorp acquired the assets and single branch of the failed Waterford Village Bank in Clarence, New York.

EXECUTIVES

Chairman, Director, John R. O'Brien
Vice-Chairman, Director, Lee C. Wortham
President, Chief Executive Officer, Subsidiary Officer, Director, David J. Nasca, $484,231 total compensation
Senior Vice President, Principal Accounting Officer, Controller, Nicholas John Snyder
Treasurer, Subsidiary Officer, John B. Connerton, $224,231 total compensation
Secretary, Subsidiary Officer, Director, Robert G. Miller, $278,543 total compensation
Subsidiary Officer, Aaron M. Whitehouse
Director, Kimberley A. Minkel
Director, Christina P. Orsi
Director, Michael A. Battle
Director, James E. Biddle
Director, Jody L. Lomeo
Director, Nora B. Sullivan
Director, Oliver H. Sommer
Director, David R. Pfalzgraf
Director, Michael John Rogers
Director, Thomas H. Waring
Auditors: Crowe LLP

LOCATIONS

HQ: Evans Bancorp, Inc.
6460 Main St, Williamsville, NY 14221
Phone: 716 926-2000
Web: www.evansbancorp.com

COMPETITORS

COMMUNITYONE BANCORP
LCNB CORP.
LYONS NATIONAL BANK
VALLEY NATIONAL BANCORP
ZIONS BANCORPORATION, NATIONAL ASSOCIATION

HISTORICAL FINANCIALS
Company Type: Public

Income Statement				FYE: December 31
	ASSETS ($mil)	NET INCOME ($mil)	INCOME AS % OF ASSETS	EMPLOYEES
12/20	2,044.1	11.2	0.6%	309
12/19	1,460.2	17.0	1.2%	250
12/18	1,388.2	16.3	1.2%	237
12/17	1,295.6	10.4	0.8%	271
12/16	1,100.7	8.2	0.8%	254
Annual Growth	16.7%	8.0%	—	5.0%

2020 Year-End Financials
Return on assets: 0.6%
Return on equity: 7.0%
Long-term debt ($ mil.): —
No. of shares ($ mil.): 5.4
Sales ($ mil.): 86.4
Dividends
Yield: 4.2%
Payout: 54.4%
Market value ($ mil.): 149.0

	STOCK PRICE ($) FY Close	P/E High/Low		PER SHARE ($) Earnings	Dividends	Book Value
12/20	27.54	19	10	2.13	1.16	31.21
12/19	40.10	12	9	3.42	1.04	30.12
12/18	32.51	14	9	3.32	0.92	27.13
12/17	41.90	20	15	2.16	0.80	24.74
12/16	31.55	19	12	1.90	0.76	22.50
Annual Growth	(3.3%)	—	—	2.9%	11.2%	8.5%

Evercore Inc

Evercore is the leading independent investment banking advisory firm in the world based on the dollar volume of announced worldwide merger and acquisition (M&A) transactions. The company provides advisory services on mergers and mergers and acquisitions, strategic shareholder advisory, restructurings, and capital structure to corporate clients. Boasting some $12.2 billion in assets under management, the company's investment management business principally manages and invests capital for clients including institutional investors and private equity businesses. Evercore also makes private equity investments. Beyond the US, the company operates globally through subsidiaries such as Evercore Partners in the UK. About 80% of the company's revenue comes from its domestic operations. Evercore was founded in 1995.

Operations

Evercore operates through two business segments: Investment Banking, which accounts for almost all of its sales, and

Investment Management.

The Investment Banking segment is further divided into four categories. The first is the strategic corporate advisory business, which offers strategic and financial consulting for public and private companies across a range of industries and geographies. The second is the capital markets advisory business in which Evercore acts as an independent advisor, capital placement agent, or underwriter based on each client's needs. The institution equities business is known as Evercore ISI and comprises about 40 senior trading professionals that support customers' money management needs. The fourth category ? Other ? under Investment Banking represents the company's interest in Luminis Partners, an independent corporate advisory firm based in Australia.

The Investment Management segment includes wealth management and trust services through Evercore Wealth Management, as well as private equity through investments in entities that manage private equity funds.

Geographic Reach

While Evercore operates globally, the US accounts for about 80% of the firm's revenue. Europe and other countries make up over 20% and Latin America. Evercore operates from its offices in about 30 cities around the globe and through its affiliates worldwide. Its principal offices are in New York and London.

Sales and Marketing

Evercore serves companies in financial transition, creditors, shareholders, and potential acquirers.

Financial Performance

Total revenues for 2021 was $3.3 billion, a 45% increase from the previous year's revenue of $2.3 billion. The increase in revenues from 2020 was primarily driven by an increase of $996.7 million, or 57%, in Advisory Fees, reflecting an increase in the number of Advisory fees earned and growth in fee size during 2021.

In 2021, the company had a net income of 868.6 million, a 110% increase from the previous year's net income of $412.7 million.

The company's cash at the end of 2021 was $587.3 million. Operating activities generated $1.4 billion, while investing activities used $705.9 million, mainly for purchases of investment securities and futures contracts activity. Financing activities used another $925.3 million, mainly for purchase of treasury stock and non-controlling interests.

Strategy

Evercore intends to continue to grow and diversify its businesses, and to further enhance the company's profile and competitive position, through the following strategies:

Add and Promote Highly Qualified Investment Banking Professionals. The company hired 10 new Senior Managing Directors in 2021, expanding its capabilities in its Capital Markets Advisory practice and Equities business, as well as strengthening the company's coverage of the Healthcare, FinTech, Infrastructure and Renewables and Basic Materials sectors and coverage of Financial Sponsors; and

Achieve Organic Growth and Improved Profitability in Investment Management. Evercore are focused on managing its current Investment Management business effectively. The company also continues to selectively evaluate opportunities to expand Wealth Management.

Company Background

Some of Evercore's past high-profile transactions include the 2012 breakup of Kraft Foods (now Mondelez International), the recapitalizations of GM and CIT Group, and the acquisition of Lubrizol by Berkshire Hathaway.

Evercore was launched in 1996 (it went public 10 years later) by Roger Altman, who formerly led investment banking and merger advisory practices at Lehman Brothers and The Blackstone Group.

EXECUTIVES

Senior Chairman, Director, Roger C. Altman, $500,000 total compensation
Co-Chief Executive Officer, Co-Chairman, John S. Weinberg, $500,000 total compensation
Co-Chairman, Co-Chief Executive Officer, Director, Ralph L. Schlosstein, $500,000 total compensation
Vice-Chairman, Subsidiary Officer, Edward S. Hyman
Chief Financial Officer, Senior Managing Director, Celeste Mellet Brown
General Counsel, Corporate Secretary, Jason Klurfeld
Lead Director, Director, Gail B. Harris
Director, Richard I. Beattie
Director, Pamela G. Carlton
Director, Ellen V. Futter
Director, Robert B. Millard
Director, Willard J. Overlock
Director, Simon M. Robertson
Director, William J. Wheeler
Director, Sarah K. Williamson
Director, Kendrick R. Wilson
Auditors : DELOITTE & TOUCHE LLP

LOCATIONS

HQ: Evercore Inc
55 East 52nd Street, New York, NY 10055
Phone: 212 857-3100 **Fax:** 212 857-3101
Web: www.evercore.com

2018 Sales

	$ mil.	% of total
United States	1,591.9	77
Europe and Other	438.6	21
Latin America	32.9	2
Total (excluding Other Revenue and Interest Expense)	2,063.4	100

PRODUCTS/OPERATIONS

2018 Sales

	$ mil.	% of total
Investment banking		
Advisory fees	1,743.5	84
Commissions and related fees	200.0	10
Underwriting fees	71.7	3
Asset management and administration fees	48.2	2
Other	19.1	1
Interest Expense	(17.8)	-
Total	2,064.7	100

COMPETITORS

ALLIANCEBERNSTEIN HOLDING L.P.
COWEN INC.
Canaccord Genuity Group Inc
GREENHILL & CO., INC.
HOULIHAN LOKEY, INC.
INVESTEC PLC
OPPENHEIMER HOLDINGS INC.
SCHRODERS PLC
STIFEL FINANCIAL CORP.
THE ZIEGLER COMPANIES INC

HISTORICAL FINANCIALS

Company Type: Public

Income Statement   FYE: December 31

	REVENUE ($mil)	NET INCOME ($mil)	NET PROFIT MARGIN	EMPLOYEES
12/20	2,263.9	350.5	15.5%	1,800
12/19	2,008.6	297.4	14.8%	1,900
12/18	2,064.7	377.2	18.3%	1,700
12/17	1,704.3	125.4	7.4%	1,600
12/16	1,440.0	107.5	7.5%	1,475
Annual Growth	12.0%	34.4%	—	5.1%

2020 Year-End Financials

Debt ratio: 11.2%
Return on equity: 33.2%
Cash ($ mil.): 829.6
Current Ratio: 2.23
Long-term debt ($ mil.): 338.5
No. of shares ($ mil.): 40.7
Dividends
Yield: 2.1%
Payout: 28.5%
Market value ($ mil.): 4,468.0

	STOCK PRICE ($) FY Close	P/E High/Low		PER SHARE ($) Earnings	Dividends	Book Value
12/20	109.64	13	4	8.22	2.35	30.21
12/19	74.76	13	10	6.89	2.24	22.20
12/18	71.56	12	7	8.33	1.90	19.07
12/17	90.00	29	21	2.80	1.42	13.91
12/16	68.70	26	15	2.43	1.27	13.45
Annual Growth	12.4%	—	—	35.6%	16.6%	22.4%

EVI Industries Inc

EnviroStar (formerly DRYCLEAN USA) is anything but hard pressed. The firm franchises and licenses more than 400 retail dry cleaners in three US states, the Caribbean, and Latin America through its DRYCLEAN USA unit. However, most of its sales are generated by subsidiary Steiner-Atlantic, which sells coin-operated laundry machines, steam boilers, and other laundry equipment; most are sold under the Aero-Tech, Green-Jet, and Multi-Jet names to some 750 customers and include independent dry cleaners, hotels, cruise lines, and hospitals. The company was founded in 1963 under the name Metro-Tel

Corp. It changed its name to DRYCLEAN USA in 1999.

EXECUTIVES

Chairman, President, Chief Executive Officer, Director, Henry M. Nahmad, $550,000 total compensation
Executive Vice President, Director, Dennis Mack, $300,000 total compensation
Business Development Executive Vice President, Business Development Region Officer, Tom Marks, $300,000 total compensation
Finance Vice President, Finance Chief Financial Officer, Finance Chief Accounting Officer, Robert H. Lazar, $175,000 total compensation
Director, David Blyer
Director, Glen Kruger
Director, Timothy P. LaMacchia
Director, Hal M. Lucas
Auditors : BDO USA, LLP

LOCATIONS

HQ: EVI Industries Inc
4500 Biscayne Blvd., Suite 340, Miami, FL 33137
Phone: 305 402-9300
Web: www.evi-ind.com

COMPETITORS

BROOKS EQUIPMENT COMPANY, LLC
GOLD MEDAL PRODUCTS CO.
HD SUPPLY HOLDINGS, INC.
I SUPPLY CO.
JACUZZI BRANDS LLC
LAGASSE, INC.
PWS, INC.
RED DOT CORPORATION
TINGUE, BROWN & CO.
TWEEZERMAN INTERNATIONAL, LLC

HISTORICAL FINANCIALS

Company Type: Public

Income Statement — FYE: June 30

	NET REVENUE ($mil)	NET INCOME ($mil)	NET PROFIT MARGIN	EMPLOYEES
06/21	242.0	8.3	3.5%	526
06/20	235.8	0.7	0.3%	493
06/19	228.3	3.7	1.6%	475
06/18	150.0	3.9	2.6%	264
06/17	93.9	3.1	3.4%	138
Annual Growth	26.7%	27.6%	—	39.7%

2021 Year-End Financials

Debt ratio: 6.7%
Return on equity: 8.6%
Cash ($ mil.): 6.0
Current Ratio: 1.32
Long-term debt ($ mil.): 11.8
No. of shares ($ mil.): 12.2
Dividends
Yield: —
Payout: —
Market value ($ mil.): 349.0

	STOCK PRICE ($) FY Close	P/E High/Low		PER SHARE ($) Earnings	Dividends	Book Value
06/21	28.40	70	32	0.61	0.00	8.69
06/20	21.71	625	234	0.06	0.00	7.36
06/19	38.27	158	91	0.29	0.13	6.93
06/18	40.30	126	65	0.33	0.12	5.10
06/17	27.05	101	12	0.31	0.10	3.08
Annual Growth	1.2%	—	—	18.4%	—	29.6%

Exelixis Inc

Exelixis is an oncology-focused biotechnology company that strives to accelerate the discovery, development and commercialization of new medicines for difficult-to-treat cancers. Its flagship molecule, cabozantinib, is the origin of two commercial products, CABOMETYX, a tablets approved for advanced renal cell carcinoma and COMETRIQ, capsules approved for progressive, metastatic medullary thyroid cancer. It also include COTELLIC (cobimetinib), a treatment for advanced melanoma and marketed under a collaboration with Genentech. It also has other drug development candidates against multiple target classes for oncology, inflammation and metabolic diseases. The US accounts for about 75% of total revenue.

Operations

Exelixis offers four product from its clinical development and established a commercial presence in various location worldwide. Its first FDA approved products include, CABOMETYX a tablets approved for advanced renal cell carcinoma (RCC) and previously treated hepatocellular carcinoma (HCC); and COMETRI capsules approved for progressive, metastatic medullary thyroid cancer (MTC).

Outside the US, the company relies on collaboration partners for the commercialization of CABOMETYX and COMETRIQ; Ipsen is responsible for all territories outside of the US and Japan, and Takeda is responsible for the Japanese market. The other two products: COTELLIC (cobimetinib), an inhibitor of MEK approved as part of a combination regimen to treat advanced melanoma and marketed under a collaboration with Genentech (a member of the Roche Group); and MINNEBRO (esaxerenone), an oral, non-steroidal, selective blocker of the mineralocorticoid receptor (MR) approved for the treatment of hypertension in Japan and licensed to Daiichi Sankyo.

Overall, its net product accounts about 75% of total revenue, while license for more than 15% and collaboration accounts around 10%.

Geographic Reach

Exelixis is headquartered in Alameda, California. The US accounts for about 75% of total revenue, Europe for about 20%, while Japan accounts for less than 5% of total revenue.

Sales and Marketing

Its largest customer, Ipsen accounts about 20% of revenue, while around 15% each from affiliates of CVS Health Corporation, affiliates of McKesson and affiliates of AmerisourceBergen and about 10% from affiliates of Optum Specialty Pharmacy. It has contracts with a third-party logistics provider, with multiple distribution locations, to provide shipping and warehousing services for its commercial supply of both CABOMETYX and COMETRIQ in the US.

To facilitate its commercial activities in the US, the company employs various third parties, such as advertising agencies, market research firms and vendors providing other sales-support related services as needed, including digital marketing and other non-personal promotion.

Financial Performance

Company's revenue for fiscal 2021 increased by 45% to $1.4 billion compared from the prior year with $987.5 million.

Net income for fiscal 2021 increased to $231.1 million compared from the prior year with $111.8 million.

Cash held by the company at the end of fiscal 2021 increased to $663.9 million. Cash provided by operations was $400.8 million while cash used for investing and financing activities were $42.9 million and $14.8 million, respectively. Main uses of cash were for purchases of investments and taxes paid related to net share settlement of equity awards.

Strategy

Exelxis group its research and development expenses into three categories: development; drug discovery; and other. Company's development group leads the development and implementation of its clinical and regulatory strategies and prioritizes disease indications in which its compounds are being or may be studied in clinical trials. Exelxis' drug discovery group utilizes a variety of technologies, including in-licensed technologies, to enable the rapid discovery, optimization and extensive characterization of lead compounds and biotherapeutics such that the company are able to select development candidates with the best potential for further evaluation and advancement into clinical development.

EXECUTIVES

Chairman, Director, Stelios Papadopoulos
Research & Development President, Research & Development Chief Executive Officer, Director, Michael M. Morrissey, $945,080 total compensation
Executive Vice President, Chief Financial Officer, Christopher J. Senner, $594,740 total compensation
Product Development Executive Vice President, Medical Affairs Executive Vice President, Product Development Chief Medical Officer, Medical Affairs Chief Medical Officer, Vicki L. Goodman
Commercial Executive Vice President, Patrick J. Haley
Executive Vice President, General Counsel, Jeffrey J. Hessekiel, $531,880 total compensation
Scientific Strategy Executive Vice President, Discovery Reasearch Executive Vice President, Peter Lamb, $493,570 total compensation

HOOVER'S HANDBOOK OF EMERGING COMPANIES 2023

Discovery and Translational Research Executive Vice President, Discovery and Translational Research Chief Scientific Officer, Dana T. Aftab
Director, Carl B. Feldbaum
Director, Maria C. Freire
Director, Alan M. Garber
Director, Vincent T. Marchesi
Director, George Poste
Director, Julie Anne Smith
Director, Lance Willsey
Director, Jacqueline Wright
Director, Jack L. Wyszomierski
Auditors: Ernst & Young LLP

LOCATIONS
HQ: Exelixis Inc
1851 Harbor Bay Parkway, Alameda, CA 94502
Phone: 650 837-7000
Web: www.exelixis.com

COMPETITORS
ALNYLAM PHARMACEUTICALS, INC.
ARENA PHARMACEUTICALS, INC.
DYAX CORP.
IMMUNOMEDICS, INC.
INCYTE CORPORATION
LEXICON PHARMACEUTICALS, INC.
LIGAND PHARMACEUTICALS INCORPORATED
MEDIVATION, INC.
PROGENICS PHARMACEUTICALS, INC.
SUCAMPO PHARMACEUTICALS, INC.

HISTORICAL FINANCIALS
Company Type: Public

Income Statement — FYE: December 31

	REVENUE ($mil)	NET INCOME ($mil)	NET PROFIT MARGIN	EMPLOYEES
12/21*	1,434.9	231.0	16.1%	954
01/21	987.5	111.7	11.3%	773
01/20	967.7	321.0	33.2%	617
12/18	853.8	690.0	80.8%	484
12/17	452.4	154.2	34.1%	372
Annual Growth	33.4%	10.6%	—	26.5%

*Fiscal year change

2021 Year-End Financials
Debt ratio: —
Return on equity: 11.3%
Cash ($ mil.): 647.1
Current Ratio: 5.43
Long-term debt ($ mil.): —
No. of shares ($ mil.): 318.8
Dividends
 Yield: —
 Payout: —
Market value ($ mil.): 5,828.0

	STOCK PRICE ($) FY Close	P/E High/Low		PER SHARE ($) Earnings	Dividends	Book Value
12/21*	18.28	35	22	0.72	0.00	6.93
01/21	20.07	76	40	0.35	0.00	6.03
01/20	17.01	23	14	1.02	0.00	5.53
12/18	19.44	14	6	2.21	0.00	4.29
12/17	30.40	59	28	0.49	0.00	0.96
Annual Growth	(11.9%)	—	—	10.1%	—	63.8%

*Fiscal year change

ExlService Holdings Inc

ExlService Holdings, known as EXL, offers business process management (BPM), research and analytics, and consulting services through its operating segments. EXL's BPM offerings, which generate most of its sales, include claims processing, clinical operations, and finance and accounting services. Customers come mainly from the banking, financial services, and insurance industries, as well as from the utilities and telecommunications sectors. EXL operates around the world but generates around 85% of revenue from the US. The company was established in 1999.

Operations
EXL's reportable segments are Insurance, Healthcare, Analytics and Emerging Business.

Insurance strategic business unit serves property and casualty insurance, life insurance, disability insurance, insurance brokers, reinsurers, annuity and retirement services companies. The company provide digital operations and solutions and analytics-driven services across the insurance industry in areas such as claims processing, premium and benefit administration, agency management, account reconciliation, policy research, underwriting support, new business acquisition, policy servicing, premium audit, surveys, billing and collection, commercial and residential survey, and customer service using digital technology, AI, ML and advanced automation.

Healthcare strategic business unit primarily serves US-based healthcare payers, providers, pharmacy benefit managers and life sciences organizations. ExlService combine deep healthcare domain expertise with data-driven insights and technology-enabled services to transform how care is delivered, managed and paid.

Emerging Business strategic business unit provides data-driven and digital enterprise solutions in the areas of revenue enhancement, finance & accounting and customer experience management to clients primarily in the banking and capital markets, utilities, travel, transportation and logistics, media and communications, manufacturing and retail and business services industries.

Analytics strategic business unit, the company help its clients build data-led businesses. By leveraging its suite of end-to-end analytics capabilities, its analytics services focus on driving improved business outcomes for its clients by unlocking deep insights from data and creating data-driven solutions across all parts of its clients' businesses.

Geographic Reach
Headquartered in New York City, EXL operates through multiple offices in the US, more than 50 offices in India, in the Philippines, and an operations center in each of Australia, the UK, South Africa, Colombia, Bulgaria, Romania, and the Czech Republic.

The US generates about 85% of company's revenue, followed by UK (about 10%).

Sales and Marketing
The company provides services through its sales and client management teams. Sales teams, which operate out of the US, Europe, Australia, and South Africa, are aligned by industry verticals including finance and accounting and consulting.

EXL has about 460 clients, with its top three clients generating over 15% of its revenue (Its top ten customers represent more than 35% of revenue).

Financial Performance
The company's revenue in 2021 increased to $1.1 billion compared to $958.4 million in the prior year. This was due to increase in all segment.

Net income increased from $89.5 million in 2020 to $114.7 million in 2021, primarily due to increase in income from operations of $45.9 million, lower interest expense of $3.6 million, partially offset by loss on settlement of the Notes of $12.8 million, lower other income, net of $5.2 million and higher income tax expense of $6.3 million. As a percentage of revenues, net income increased from 9.3% in 2020 to 10.2% in 2021.

Cash held by the company at the end of fiscal 2021 decreased to $143.8 million. Operating activities provided $184.4 million while investing and financing activities used $114.3 million and $146.9 million, respectively. Main cash uses were purchases of investments and repayments of borrowings.

Strategy
EXL is a leading data analytics and digital operations and solutions company and is a key strategic partner for data-led businesses. The company drives business outcomes for its clients through advanced analytics and AI/ML-powered digital solutions on the cloud. The company does this through its data-led value creation framework to enable better and faster decision making and orchestrate the re-designing of operating models to integrate advanced technology into operational workflows. Some of its strategically focused considerations: expanding its services in large addressable markets; integrating its capabilities; cultivating long-term relationships and expanding its client base; optimizing its global delivery footprint and operational Infrastructure in the countries and regions in which the company operates; and pursuing strategic acquisitions and relationships.

Mergers and Acquisitions
In 2021, EXL acquired Clairvoyant, a global data, AI, and cloud services firm. The acquisition strengthens EXL's capabilities by adding additional expertise in data engineering and cloud enablement, further

supporting its clients in insurance, healthcare, banking and financial services, and retail. With the acquisition, Clairvoyant will become part of EXL's fast-growing analytics business, which helps clients make sense of data to drive better decision-making across the enterprise and rapidly adapt business strategies in response to market changes.

EXECUTIVES

Chairman, Director, Vikram S. Pandit
Vice-Chairman, Chief Executive Officer, Director, Rohit Kapoor, $720,000 total compensation
Executive Vice President, Chief Growth Officer, Anita Mahon
Executive Vice President, Chief Digital Officer, Ankor Rai
Executive Vice President, Chief Financial Officer, Maurizio Nicolelli
Executive Vice President, Division Officer, Vivek Jetley
Senior Vice President, General Counsel, Corporate Secretary, Ajay Ayyappan
Executive Vice President, Division Officer, Vikas Bhalla
Executive Vice President, Chief Human Resources Officer, Nalin Miglani, $440,137 total compensation
Executive Vice President, Division Officer, Narasimha Kini, $192,520 total compensation
Director, Nitin Sahney
Director, Kristy M. Pipes
Director, Som Mittal
Director, Jaynie M. Studenmund
Director, Andreas Fibig
Auditors : DELOITTE & TOUCHE LLP

LOCATIONS

HQ: ExlService Holdings Inc
320 Park Avenue, 29th Floor, New York, NY 10022
Phone: 212 277-7100
Web: www.exlservice.com

2018 Sales

	$ mil.	% of total
US	732.6	83
UK	114.5	13
Other countries	36.0	4
Total	883.1	100

PRODUCTS/OPERATIONS

2018 Sales

	$ mil.	% of total
Analytics	285.3	32
BPM and related services		
Insurance	258.2	29
F&A	97.9	11
Healthcare	84.4	10
TT&L	70.2	8
All Other	87.1	10
Total	883.1	100

COMPETITORS

AVAYA INC.
BANCTEC, INC.
CBIZ, INC.
CONDUENT INCORPORATED
CORCENTRIC, LLC
ENVESTNET, INC.
FIDELITY NATIONAL INFORMATION SERVICES, INC.
IDOX PLC
VERISK ANALYTICS, INC.
WORLDPAY, INC.

HISTORICAL FINANCIALS

Company Type: Public

Income Statement — FYE: December 31

	REVENUE ($mil)	NET INCOME ($mil)	NET PROFIT MARGIN	EMPLOYEES
12/20	958.4	89.4	9.3%	31,900
12/19	991.3	67.6	6.8%	31,700
12/18	883.1	56.7	6.4%	29,100
12/17	762.3	48.8	6.4%	27,800
12/16	685.9	61.7	9.0%	26,000
Annual Growth	8.7%	9.7%	—	5.2%

2020 Year-End Financials

Debt ratio: 18.2%
Return on equity: 12.8%
Cash ($ mil.): 402.8
Current Ratio: 2.76
Long-term debt ($ mil.): 202.2
No. of shares ($ mil.): 33.5
Dividends
 Yield: —
 Payout: —
Market value ($ mil.): 2,857.0

	STOCK PRICE ($) FY Close	P/E High/Low		PER SHARE ($) Earnings	Dividends	Book Value
12/20	85.13	33	16	2.59	0.00	21.43
12/19	69.46	36	26	1.95	0.00	19.60
12/18	52.62	40	30	1.62	0.00	18.06
12/17	60.35	43	31	1.39	0.00	17.70
12/16	50.44	29	23	1.79	0.00	15.82
Annual Growth	14.0%	—	—	9.7%	—	7.9%

eXp World Holdings Inc

eXp World Holdings, Inc. owns and operates a cloud-based real estate brokerage and a technology platform business that enables a variety of businesses to operate remotely. Its real estate brokerage is now one of the largest and fastest-growing real estate brokerage companies in the US and is rapidly expanding internationally. The company's technology platform business develops and uses immersive technologies that enable and support virtual workplaces. This unique enabling platform helps businesses increase their effectiveness and reduce costs from operating in traditional brick and mortar office spaces. Through various operating subsidiaries, the company primarily operates a cloud-based real estate brokerage operating throughout the US, most of the Canadian provinces, and in approximately 15 others countries. The company generates the majority of its revenue in the US.

Operations

eXp primarily operates as a cloud-based real estate brokerage. The real estate brokerage business represents the vast majority of the company's total revenue. In addition, the company offers software subscriptions to customers to access its virtual reality software platform. It also offers professional services for implementation and consulting services.

The company's portfolio of companies include eXp Realty, a leading global, cloud-based real estate brokerage powered by more than 84,000 agents and cutting-edge technology; Virbela, the first virtual world platform built specifically to solve the challenges of remote collaboration; SUCCESS, one of the world's most revered professional and personal development media platforms, including SUCCESS magazine, SUCCESS.com, newsletters, podcasts, digital training courses, and more; and Showcase IDX, the leading IDX plug-in for WordPress, helping top agents generate leads, improve their websites, and stand out from other agents.

Geographic Reach

Headquartered in Washington, the company has brokerages in all 50 states in the US. In addition to most of the Canadian provinces, it also has brokerages in some parts of the UK, Australia, South Africa, India, France, Italy, and Germany, among other countries.

Sales and Marketing

eXp's clients are primarily residential homeowners and homebuyers in the markets in which it operates as serviced by the company's international network of independent agents and brokers. These customers are sellers or purchasers of new or existing homes and engage the company to aid in the facilitation of the closing of the real estate transaction, including, but not limited to, searching, listing, application processing and other pre- and post-close support. Its experienced agents and brokers are well suited to support the company's customers' needs with a high level of professionalism, knowledge and support as they endeavor on one of the largest transactions they will most likely experience.

The company's incurred advertising and marketing expenses were approximately $12,180, $5,223, and $3,799 for the years ended 2021, 2020, and 2019, respectively.

Financial Performance

The company reported a 110% increase from 2020 revenue of $1.8 billion to 2021's revenue of $3.8 billion.

In 2021, the company had a net income of $81.2 million, a 161% increase from the previous year's net income of $31.1 million. This was primarily due to a higher volume of sales for the year.

The company's cash at the end of 2021 was $175.9 million. Operating activities generated $246.9 million, while investing activities used $18.9 million, mainly for purchases of property, plant and equipment. Financing activities used another $179.9 million, primarily for repurchase of common stock.

Strategy

As part of its business and growth strategy, eXp World evaluates acquisitions of, or investments in, a wide array of potential strategic opportunities, including third-party technologies and businesses, as well as other real estate brokerages. The company will continue to look for opportunities to acquire technologies or operations that it believes will contribute to its growth and development, including eXp World's July 2020 acquisition of Showcase Web Sites, L.L.C., December 2020 acquisition of SUCCESS Enterprises LLC, and July 2021 launch of the SUCCESS Lending joint venture.

Mergers and Acquisitions

In mid-2022, eXp World acquired Toronto-based Zoocasa Realty Inc., an award-winning consumer real estate search portal and brokerage, and its key property, Zoocasa.com. The deal will expand eXp Realty's online lead generation, home search and listings portal capabilities for its agents and brokers as well as for home buying and selling consumers across North America.

EXECUTIVES

Chairman, Chief Executive Officer, Treasurer, Secretary, Subsidiary Officer, Director, Glenn Darrel Sanford, $49,500 total compensation
Vice-Chairman, Director, Randall D. Miles
Chief Industry Relations Officer, Division Officer, Director, Jason Gesing, $146,104 total compensation
Chief Financial Officer, Chief Collaboration Officer, Jeff Whiteside
Chief Legal Officer, General Counsel, Corporate Secretary, James H. Bramble
Chief Information Officer, Shoeb Ansari
Chief Marketing Officer, Courtney Chakarun
Chief Accounting Officer, Controller, Jian Cheng
Division Officer, Michael Valdes
Director, Peggie J. Pelosi
Director, Eugene Frederick
Director, Dan Cahir
Director, Darren Lee Jacklin
Director, Felicia J. Gentry
Auditors : DELOITTE & TOUCHE LLP

LOCATIONS

HQ: eXp World Holdings Inc
2219 Rimland Drive, Suite 301, Bellingham, WA 98226
Phone: 360 685-4206
Web: www.exprealty.com

HISTORICAL FINANCIALS
Company Type: Public

Income Statement   FYE: December 31

	REVENUE ($mil)	NET INCOME ($mil)	NET PROFIT MARGIN	EMPLOYEES
12/20	1,798.2	31.1	1.7%	900
12/19	979.9	(9.5)	—	634
12/18	500.1	(22.4)	—	15,854
12/17	156.1	(22.1)	—	6,695
12/16	54.1	(26.0)	—	94
Annual Growth	140.0%	—	—	75.9%

2020 Year-End Financials
Debt ratio: 1.8%
Return on equity: 32.0%
Cash ($ mil.): 100.1
Current Ratio: 2.20
Long-term debt ($ mil.): 2.8
No. of shares ($ mil.): 144.1
Dividends
  Yield: —
  Payout: —
Market value ($ mil.): 9,098.0

	STOCK PRICE ($) FY Close	P/E High/Low		PER SHARE ($) Earnings	Dividends	Book Value
12/20	63.12	371	32	0.21	0.00	0.98
12/19	11.33	—	—	(0.08)	0.00	0.40
12/18	7.08	—	—	(0.20)	0.00	0.25
12/17	7.60	—	—	(0.21)	0.00	0.04
12/16	4.05	—	—	(0.26)	0.00	0.02
Annual Growth	98.7%	—	—	—	—	152.5%

Extra Space Storage Inc

Extra Space Storage is a self-administered and self-managed real estate investment trust (REIT) that owns roughly 2,100 self-storage properties, which comprise approximately 1.5 million units and approximately 160.9 million square feet of rentable storage space offering customers conveniently located and secure storage units across the country, including boat storage, RV storage, and business storage. Extra Space is the second largest owner and/or operator of self-storage properties in the US. Founded in 1977, Extra Space Storage went public in 2004.

Operations

Extra Space Storage operates through two segments: self-storage operations and tenant reinsurance.

Its self-storage segment accounts for about 85% of total revenue and include rental operations of wholly-owned stores. Tenant reinsurance segment (some 10%) include the reinsurance of risks relating to the loss of goods stored by tenants in its stores.

Geographic Reach

Utah-based Extra Space Storage operates its business in about 40 US states and Washington, DC.

Sales and Marketing

Approximately 1.2 million tenants were leasing storage units at the operating stores that the company owns and/or manages, primarily on a month-to-month basis, providing the flexibility to increase rental rates over time as market conditions permit.

Extra Space Storage's advertising costs were $18,793, $28,336, and $25,106 for the years 2021, 2020, and 2019 respectively.

Financial Performance

Company's revenue for fiscal 2021 increased by 16% to $1.6 billion compared from the prior year with $1.4 billion.

Net income for fiscal 2021 increased to $877.8 million compared from the prior year with $517.6 million.

Cash held by the company at the end of fiscal 2021 decreased to $76.2 million. Cash provided by operations was $952.4 million while cash used for investing and financing activities were $837.5 million and $166.7 million, respectively. Main uses of cash were acquisition of real estate assets and principal payments on notes payable and revolving lines of credit.

Strategy

Extra Space's primary business objectives are to maximize cash flow available for distribution to its stockholders and to achieve sustainable long-term growth in cash flow per share in order to maximize long-term stockholder value both at acceptable levels of risk. The company continue to evaluate a range of growth initiatives and opportunities. Extra Space's primary strategies include the following: maximize the performance of its stores through strategic, efficient and proactive management; acquire self-storage stores; grow its management business; expand its bridge loan program; and invest in other self-storage businesses selectively.

EXECUTIVES

Chairman, Kenneth M. Woolley, $450,000 total compensation
chief Legal Officer, Matthew Herrington
Chief Executive Officer, Joseph D. (Joe) Margolis, $750,000 total compensation
Operations Executive Vice President, Operations Chief Operating Officer, Operations Chief Marketing Officer, Samrat Sondhi, $400,000 total compensation
Executive Vice President, Chief Financial Officer, P. Scott Stubbs, $475,000 total compensation
Executive Vice President, Chief Legal Officer, Gwyn G. McNeal, $375,000 total compensation
Lead Director, Director, Roger B. Porter
Director, Joseph J. Bonner
Director, Gary L. Crittenden
Director, Spencer F. Kirk, $750,000 total compensation
Director, Dennis J. Letham
Director, Diane Olmstead
Director, Julia Vander Ploeg
Auditors : Ernst & Young LLP

LOCATIONS

HQ: Extra Space Storage Inc
2795 East Cottonwood Parkway, Suite 300, Salt Lake City, UT 84121
Phone: 801 365-4600
Web: www.extraspace.com

PRODUCTS/OPERATIONS

2015 Sales

	$ mil.	% of total
Property rental	676.1	87
Tenant reinsurance	72.0	9
Management & franchise fees	34.2	4
Total	782.3	100

COMPETITORS

AMERICOLD REALTY TRUST
CUBESMART, L.P.
LANDSTAR SYSTEM, INC.
LIFE STORAGE, INC.
MOBILE MINI, INC.
NATIONAL STORAGE AFFILIATES TRUST
NORISH LIMITED
PUBLIC STORAGE
SAFESTORE HOLDINGS PLC
WEIS MARKETS, INC.

HISTORICAL FINANCIALS

Company Type: Public

Income Statement — FYE: December 31

	REVENUE ($mil)	NET INCOME ($mil)	NET PROFIT MARGIN	EMPLOYEES
12/20	1,356.2	481.7	35.5%	4,013
12/19	1,308.4	419.9	32.1%	4,048
12/18	1,196.6	415.2	34.7%	3,624
12/17	1,105.0	479.0	43.3%	3,380
12/16	991.8	366.1	36.9%	3,287
Annual Growth	8.1%	7.1%	—	5.1%

2020 Year-End Financials

Debt ratio: 61.2% No. of shares ($ mil.): 131.3
Return on equity: 18.8% Dividends
Cash ($ mil.): 109.1 Yield: 3.1%
Current Ratio: 0.12 Payout: 97.0%
Long-term debt ($ mil.): 4,797.3 Market value ($ mil.): 15,219.0

	STOCK PRICE ($) FY Close	P/E High	P/E Low	PER SHARE ($) Earnings	Dividends	Book Value
12/20	115.86	32	20	3.71	3.60	19.40
12/19	105.62	38	27	3.24	3.56	19.61
12/18	90.48	31	24	3.27	3.36	18.99
12/17	87.45	23	19	3.76	3.12	18.66
12/16	77.24	32	24	2.91	2.93	17.83
Annual Growth	10.7%	—	—	6.3%	5.3%	2.1%

Exxe Group Inc

EXECUTIVES

Chairman, President, Chief Executive Officer, Chief Financial Officer, Director, Eduard Nazmiev
Chief Administrative Officer, Boris Matsokhin
Chief Marketing Officer, Anna Ivanchenko
Director, Darla Gullons
Director, Peter Sallade
Director, Joanna Karolina Filipowska

LOCATIONS

HQ: Exxe Group Inc
1345 Avenue of The Americas, 2nd Floor, New York, NY 10105
Phone: 855 285-2235
Web: www.exxegroup.com

HISTORICAL FINANCIALS

Company Type: Public

Income Statement — FYE: March 31

	REVENUE ($mil)	NET INCOME ($mil)	NET PROFIT MARGIN	EMPLOYEES
03/21	33.9	6.6	19.6%	0
03/20	15.3	3.5	23.2%	0
03/19	2.1	1.6	80.2%	0
03/18	0.0	0.1	221.1%	0
Annual Growth	654.8%	236.6%	—	—

2021 Year-End Financials

Debt ratio: 31.4% No. of shares ($ mil.): 526.9
Return on equity: 18.4% Dividends
Cash ($ mil.): 0.2 Yield: —
Current Ratio: 0.98 Payout: —
Long-term debt ($ mil.): 66.2 Market value ($ mil.): 38.0

	STOCK PRICE ($) FY Close	P/E High	P/E Low	PER SHARE ($) Earnings	Dividends	Book Value
03/21	0.07	10	0	0.01	0.00	0.08
03/20	0.01	3	1	0.01	0.00	0.07
03/19	0.01	33	0	0.01	0.00	0.10
Annual Growth	291.1%	—	—	—	—	—

F & M Bank Corp.

F & M Bank has deep roots in Virginia's Shenandoah Valley. Founded in 1908, the holding company operates about 10 Farmers & Merchants Bank branches in the northern Virginia counties of Rockingham and Shenandoah. Farmers & Merchants caters to individuals and businesses. It provides typical deposit products, including checking and savings accounts, CDs, and IRAs. Some 40% of its loans are mortgages; it also writes agricultural, business, construction, and consumer loans. The company offers insurance, brokerage, and financial services through TEB Life Insurance and Farmers & Merchants Financial Services.

EXECUTIVES

Chairman, Director, Michael W. Pugh
Subsidiary Officer, Vice-Chairman, Director, Dean W. Withers, $182,539 total compensation
President, Chief Executive Officer, Subsidiary Officer, Director, Mark C. Hanna, $338,015 total compensation
Executive Vice President, Chief Operating Officer, Subsidiary Officer, Barton E. Black
Executive Vice President, Chief Financial Officer, Subsidiary Officer, Lisa F. Campbell
Executive Vice President, Chief Credit Officer, Paul E. Eberly
Executive Vice President, Chief Human Resources Officer, Melody Emswiler
Executive Vice President, Division Officer, Subsidiary Officer, Kevin Russell
Executive Vice President, Farmers & Merchants Bank, Subsidiary Officer, Stephanie E Shillingburg
Executive Vice President, Chief Lending Officer, Subsidiary Officer, Aubrey Michael (Mike) Wilkerson
Director, Edward Ray Burkholder
Director, Larry A. Caplinger, $225,000 total compensation
Director, Christopher S. Runion
Director, Hannah W. Hutman
Director, John A. Willingham
Director, Daphyne S. Thomas
Director, Daniel J. Harshman
Director, Peter H. Wray
Director, Anne B Keeler
Auditors : Yount, Hyde & Barbour, P.C.

LOCATIONS

HQ: F & M Bank Corp.
P.O. Box 1111, Timberville, VA 22853
Phone: 540 896-8941
Web: www.fmbankva.com

COMPETITORS

BANK OF OAK RIDGE
CENTRAL VALLEY COMMUNITY BANCORP
MBANK
SOUTHEASTERN BANKING CORPORATION
VOLUNTEER BANCORP, INC

HISTORICAL FINANCIALS

Company Type: Public

Income Statement — FYE: December 31

	ASSETS ($mil)	NET INCOME ($mil)	INCOME AS % OF ASSETS	EMPLOYEES
12/20	966.9	8.7	0.9%	151
12/19	813.9	4.5	0.6%	173
12/18	780.2	9.0	1.2%	172
12/17	753.2	9.0	1.2%	178
12/16	744.8	9.5	1.3%	173
Annual Growth	6.7%	(2.1%)	—	(3.3%)

2020 Year-End Financials

Return on assets: 0.9% Dividends
Return on equity: 9.3% Yield: 4.5%
Long-term debt ($ mil.): — Payout: 45.4%
No. of shares ($ mil.): 3.2 Market value ($ mil.): 74.0
Sales ($ mil.): 49

	STOCK PRICE ($) FY Close	P/E High	P/E Low	PER SHARE ($) Earnings	Dividends	Book Value
12/20	23.01	11	6	2.56	1.04	29.85
12/19	29.00	27	19	1.30	1.01	28.34
12/18	30.00	15	11	2.53	1.20	28.43
12/17	33.10	13	10	2.48	0.91	27.86
12/16	26.05	10	8	2.57	0.80	26.29
Annual Growth	(3.1%)	—	—	(0.1%)	6.8%	3.2%

Fair Isaac Corp

Fair Isaac, also known as FICO, is a company that provides credit scores and risk management tools for businesses worldwide, including banks, credit card issuers, mortgage and auto lenders, retailers, insurance firms, and health care providers. It also serve consumers through online services that enable people to access and understand their FICO Scores, the standard measure in the US of consumer credit risk, empowering them to manage their financial health. While the Americas accounts for some 80% of its revenue, the company operates globally in more than 120 countries. FICO was founded by Engineer Bill Fair and mathematician Earl Isaac in 1956.

Operations

FICO operates in two operating segments: Scores and Software, which account for an evenly split of revenue.

The Scores segment includes its business-to-business (B2B) scoring solutions and services which give its clients access to predictive credit and other scores that can be easily integrated into their transaction streams and decision-making processes. This segment also includes its business-to-consumer (B2C) scoring solutions, including its myFICO.com subscription offerings.

The Software segment includes pre-configured analytic and decision management solutions designed for a specific type of business need or process ? such as account origination, customer management, customer engagement, fraud detection, financial crimes compliance, and marketing ? as well as associated professional services. This segment also includes FICO Platform, a modular software offering designed to support advanced analytic and decision use cases, as well as stand-alone analytic and decisioning software that can be configured by its customers to address a wide variety of business use cases. Its offerings are available to its customers as software-as-a-service (SaaS) or as on-premises software.

Overall, Scores generate some half of revenue, while on-premises and SaaS software accounts for around 40% and professional services, with about 10%.

Geographic Reach

Montana-based FICO operates in some 45 locations in the US, Canada, Latin America, the Caribbean, Europe, the Middle East and Africa, and the Asia Pacific region.

About 80% of revenue comes from the Americas region, while some 15% of revenue comes from the Europe, Middle East and Africa. The remaining revenue comes from Asia Pacific.

Sales and Marketing

FICO's client base includes more than 600 insurers, 300 retailers and general merchandisers, more than 200 government or public sector agencies, and more than 200 health and pharmaceutical companies. End users of its products include 96 of the 100 largest financial institutions in the US and two-thirds of the largest 100 banks in the world.

About 40% of FICO's revenue is concentrated in Experian, TransUnion, and Equifax.

The company markets its software products and services through its own direct sales division that is organized around its vertical markets. Outside of the US, FICO markets through subsidiary sales organizations that promote FICO products in their local countries not reached by its direct marketing. FICO also markets through indirect channels that include alliance partners and other resellers.

Advertising and promotion costs totaled $6.9 million, $8.7 million, and $3.6 million in the years ended November 2021, 2020, and 2019, respectively.

Financial Performance

The company's revenue for fiscal 2021 increased by 2% to $1.32 billion compared from the prior year with $1.29 billion.

Net income for fiscal 2021 increased to $392.1 million compared from the prior year with $236.4 million.

Cash held by the company at the end of fiscal 2021 increased to $195.4 million. Cash provided by operations and investing activities were $423.8 million and $137.9 million, respectively. Cash used for financing activities were $523.6 million, mainly for repurchases of common stock.

Strategy

During fiscal 2021, the company continued to advance its platform-first, cloud delivered strategy in its Software segment. This led Fair Isaac to exit less strategic areas of its business in order to facilitate incremental investment in higher value, more strategic areas. As part of this process, the company divested the non-platform-based Collections and Recovery ("C&R") business, sold all assets related to our cyber risk score operations, and sold certain assets related to its Software operations to an affiliated joint venture in China.

Company Background

Mathematician William Fair and electrical engineer Earl Isaac founded Fair, Isaac as a management consulting firm in 1956. They sought a means for analyzing consumer behavior patterns to help in decision-making, and came up with the credit scorecard.

The company flourished over the next three decades. It enjoyed a symbiotic relationship with the evolving credit industry, which could not have grown as it did without Fair, Isaac's tools. The firm began selling overseas in the 1970s. Earl Isaac died in 1983. Fair, Isaac went public in 1987. William Fair retired in 1992 and died in 1996.

In 1992 Fair, Isaac bought consumer database management company DynaMark. Three years later the company introduced the Small Business Scoring Service, an automated system for small-business loan approval. Fair, Isaac in 1995 co-developed a marketing relational database with credit card processor Total System Services.

The company acquired Risk Management Technologies in 1997. It began CreditFYI, an Internet business credit-report provider, in 1998 with Web business adviser Net Earnings and credit bureau Experian Information Solutions. In 1999 the firm merged DynaMark into its own operations to hasten its move into online services.

In 2000 the company launched several products and services over the Internet, in order to position itself as an application service provider (ASP). Fair, Isaac also continued to strengthen its customer relationship management (CRM) offerings through the acquisition of smaller CRM businesses. Fair, Isaac teamed up with Experian in 2001 on a product to sell consumers their FICO scores. The next year it began offering more consumer-targeted services, including tips on improving one's score.

Fair, Isaac acquired HNC Software in 2002. The Fair, Isaac executive suite was revamped to include leaders from HNC, which was absorbed into its new parent. The acquisition was part of a growth strategy that had Fair, Isaac looking outside its traditional top market (the financial services industry) and beyond the borders of the US.

The company dropped the comma from its name in 2003 to become Fair Isaac Corporation.

In 2004 the company acquired UK-based London Bridge Software Holdings, thereby adding clients and financial services software that focuses on customer, credit, and mortgage management. Later in the year, Fair Isaac acquired Braun Consulting, a marketing strategy and technology consulting firm.

Fair Isaac rebranded itself as FICO in 2009, underscoring the importance of its flagship FICO Score. Though it retained its legal name, it added "FICO" to the names of most of its products and changed its website and brand logo to follow suit. The company also streamlined operations to cut costs by discontinuing some businesses, selling others, closing some facilities, and cutting staff. It sold its noncore LiquidCredit for Telecom and RoamEx units and exited its Fast Panel and Cortonics product lines.

HISTORY

Mathematician William Fair and electrical engineer Earl Isaac founded Fair, Isaac as a management consulting firm in 1956. They sought a means for analyzing consumer behavior patterns to help in decision-making, and came up with the credit scorecard.

The company flourished over the next three decades. It enjoyed a symbiotic relationship with the evolving credit industry, which could not have grown as it did without Fair, Isaac's tools. The firm began selling overseas in the 1970s. Earl Isaac died in 1983. Fair, Isaac went public in 1987. William Fair retired in 1992 and died in 1996.

In 1992 Fair, Isaac bought consumer database management company DynaMark. Three years later the company introduced the

Small Business Scoring Service, an automated system for small-business loan approval. Fair, Isaac in 1995 co-developed a marketing relational database with credit card processor Total System Services.

The company acquired Risk Management Technologies in 1997. It began CreditFYI, an Internet business credit-report provider, in 1998 with Web business adviser Net Earnings and credit bureau Experian Information Solutions. In 1999 the firm merged DynaMark into its own operations to hasten its move into online services.

In 2000 the company launched several products and services over the Internet, in order to position itself as an application service provider (ASP). Fair, Isaac also continued to strengthen its customer relationship management (CRM) offerings through the acquisition of smaller CRM businesses. Fair, Isaac teamed up with Experian in 2001 on a product to sell consumers their FICO scores. The next year it began offering more consumer-targeted services, including tips on improving one's score.

Fair, Isaac acquired HNC Software in 2002. The Fair, Isaac executive suite was revamped to include leaders from HNC, which was absorbed into its new parent. The acquisition was part of a growth strategy that had Fair, Isaac looking outside its traditional top market (the financial services industry) and beyond the borders of the US.

The company dropped the comma from its name in 2003 to become Fair Isaac Corporation.

In 2004 the company acquired UK-based London Bridge Software Holdings, thereby adding clients and financial services software that focuses on customer, credit, and mortgage management. Later in the year, Fair Isaac acquired Braun Consulting, a marketing strategy and technology consulting firm.

Fair Isaac rebranded itself as FICO in 2009, underscoring the importance of its flagship FICO Score. Though it retained its legal name, it added "FICO" to the names of most of its products and changed its website and brand logo to follow suit. The company also streamlined operations to cut costs by discontinuing some businesses, selling others, closing some facilities, and cutting staff. It sold its noncore LiquidCredit for Telecom and RoamEx units and exited its Fast Panel and Cortonics product lines.

EXECUTIVES

Chairman, Director, Braden R. Kelly
Chief Executive Officer, Director, William J. Lansing, $750,000 total compensation
Marketing Executive Vice President, Sales Executive Vice President, Marketing Division Officer, Sales Division Officer, Stephanie Covert
Executive Vice President, Secretary, General Counsel, Mark R. Scadina, $400,000 total compensation

Scores Executive Vice President, James M. Wehmann, $500,000 total compensation
Vice President, Interim Chief Financial Officer, Steven P. Weber
Director, Fabiola R. Arredondo
Director, James D. Kirsner
Director, Eva Manolis
Director, Marc F. Mcmorris
Director, Joanna Rees
Director, David A. Rey
Auditors: Deloitte & Touche LLP

LOCATIONS

HQ: Fair Isaac Corp
5 West Mendenhall, Suite 105, Bozema, MT 59715
Phone: 406 982-7276
Web: www.fico.com

2017 Sales

	$ mil.	% of total
United States	598.8	64
United Kingdom	72	8
Other countries	261.4	28
Total	932.2	100

PRODUCTS/OPERATIONS

2017 Sales

	$ mil.	% of total
Transactional & maintenance	652.7	70
Professional services	179.6	19
License	99.9	11
Total	932.2	100

2017 Sales by Segment

	$ mil.	% of total
Applications	553.2	59
Scores	266.4	29
Decision Management Software	112.6	12
Total	932.2	100

Selected Products and Services
FICO Xpress Optimization
FICO Decision Management Suite
FICO Score
FICO Score Open Access
FICO Payment Integrity Platform
FICO TONBELLER Siroon AML
FICO TONBELLER Siron KYC
FICO Debt Manager Solution
FICO Falcon Fraud Manager
FICO Originator Manager
FICO TRIAD Customer Manager
FICO Blaze Advisor Decision Rules Manager
FICO Blaze Strategy Directory for Deposit Manager

COMPETITORS
ACXIOM LLC
CERIDIAN LLC
EDMENTUM, INC.
ELCOM INTERNATIONAL, INC.
EQUIFAX INC.
IPREO HOLDINGS LLC
SYMPHONY TECHNOLOGY GROUP, L.L.C.
TSYS ACQUIRING SOLUTIONS, L.L.C.
VENTERA CORPORATION
WIPFLI LLP

HISTORICAL FINANCIALS
Company Type: Public

Income Statement — FYE: September 30

	REVENUE ($mil)	NET INCOME ($mil)	NET PROFIT MARGIN	EMPLOYEES
09/21	1,316.5	392.0	29.8%	3,662
09/20	1,294.5	236.4	18.3%	4,003
09/19	1,160.0	192.1	16.6%	4,009
09/18	1,032.4	142.4	13.8%	3,668
09/17	932.1	128.2	13.8%	3,299
Annual Growth	9.0%	32.2%	—	2.6%

2021 Year-End Financials
Debt ratio: 80.3%
Return on equity: —
Cash ($ mil.): 195.3
Current Ratio: 0.99
Long-term debt ($ mil.): 1,009
No. of shares ($ mil.): 27.5
Dividends
 Yield: —
 Payout: —
Market value ($ mil.): 10,970.0

	STOCK PRICE ($) FY Close	P/E High/Low		PER SHARE ($) Earnings	Dividends	Book Value
09/21	397.93	41	29	13.40	0.00	(4.02)
09/20	425.38	55	26	7.90	0.00	11.38
09/19	303.52	56	26	6.34	0.00	10.01
09/18	228.55	50	30	4.57	0.00	9.09
09/17	140.50	35	27	3.98	0.04	14.10
Annual Growth	29.7%	—	—	35.5%	—	—

Farmers & Merchants Bancorp (Lodi, CA)

EXECUTIVES

President, Chief Executive Officer, Subsidiary Officer, Chairman, Kent A. Steinwert, $811,369 total compensation
Executive Vice President, Subsidiary Officer, Deborah E. Skinner, $332,538 total compensation
Executive Vice President & Senior Credit Officer, Richard S. Erichson, $245,183 total compensation
Executive Vice President, Subsidiary Officer, Kenneth W. Smith, $347,000 total compensation
Executive Vice President, Chief Financial Officer, Stephen W. Haley, $335,000 total compensation
Subsidiary Officer, Jay J. Colombini, $285,000 total compensation
SUbsidiary Officer, Ryan J. Misasi, $280,008 total compensation
Subsidiary Officer, David M. (Dave) Zitterow, $292,000 total compensation
Director, Stephenson K. Green
Director, Edward Corum
Director, Terrance A. Young
Director, Kevin Sanguinetti
Director, Calvin Suess
Director, Gary J. Long
Auditors: Moss Adams LLP

LOCATIONS

HQ: Farmers & Merchants Bancorp (Lodi, CA)
111 W. Pine Street, Lodi, CA 95240
Phone: 209 367-2300
Web: www.fmbonline.com

HISTORICAL FINANCIALS
Company Type: Public

Income Statement				FYE: December 31
	ASSETS ($mil)	NET INCOME ($mil)	INCOME AS % OF ASSETS	EMPLOYEES
12/20	4,550.4	58.7	1.3%	366
12/19	3,721.8	56.0	1.5%	365
12/18	3,434.2	45.5	1.3%	376
12/17	3,075.4	28.3	0.9%	330
12/16	2,922.1	29.7	1.0%	339
Annual Growth	11.7%	18.6%	—	1.9%

2020 Year-End Financials
Return on assets: 1.4%
Return on equity: 14.7%
Long-term debt ($ mil.): —
No. of shares ($ mil.): 0.7
Sales ($ mil.): 174.3
Dividends
Yield: 1.9%
Payout: 19.9%
Market value ($ mil.): 600.0

	STOCK PRICE ($) FY Close	P/E High/Low		PER SHARE ($) Earnings	Dividends	Book Value
12/20	760.00	11	9	74.03	14.75	536.53
12/19	768.10	13	10	71.18	14.20	465.68
12/18	700.00	13	11	56.82	13.90	397.10
12/17	676.00	20	17	35.03	13.55	368.90
12/16	640.00	17	13	37.44	13.10	346.80
Annual Growth	4.4%	—	—	18.6%	3.0%	11.5%

Farmers & Merchants Bancorp Inc (OH)

EXECUTIVES

Chairman, Director, Jack C. Johnson
Vice-Chairman, Vice President, Director, Kevin J. Sauder
President, Chief Executive Officer, Subsidiary Officer, Director, Lars B. Eller
Executive Vice President, Chief Financial Officer, Subsidiary Officer, Barbara J. Britenriker, $209,091 total compensation
Executive Vice President, Chief Operating Officer, Subsidiary Officer, Edward A. Leininger, $184,681 total compensation
Chief Lending Officer, Subsidiary Officer, Rex D. Rice, $178,000 total compensation
Corporate Secretary, Subsidiary Officer, Lydia A. Huber
Director, Simon R. Frank
Director, Andrew J. Briggs
Director, Eugene N. Burkholder
Director, Jo Ellen Hornish
Director, Lori A. Johnston
Director, Marcia Sloan Latta
Director, Steven J. Planson
Director, K. Brad Stamm
Auditors : BKD, LLP

LOCATIONS

HQ: Farmers & Merchants Bancorp Inc (OH)
307 North Defiance Street, Archbold, OH 43502
Phone: 419 446-2501
Web: www.fm-bank.com

HISTORICAL FINANCIALS
Company Type: Public

Income Statement				FYE: December 31
	ASSETS ($mil)	NET INCOME ($mil)	INCOME AS % OF ASSETS	EMPLOYEES
12/20	1,909.5	20.0	1.1%	367
12/19	1,607.3	18.4	1.1%	357
12/18	1,116.1	14.9	1.3%	288
12/17	1,107.0	12.7	1.1%	275
12/16	1,055.8	11.6	1.1%	273
Annual Growth	16.0%	14.6%	—	7.7%

2020 Year-End Financials
Return on assets: 1.1%
Return on equity: 8.3%
Long-term debt ($ mil.): —
No. of shares ($ mil.): 11.2
Sales ($ mil.): 86.9
Dividends
Yield: 2.8%
Payout: 36.6%
Market value ($ mil.): 258.0

	STOCK PRICE ($) FY Close	P/E High/Low		PER SHARE ($) Earnings	Dividends	Book Value
12/20	23.00	17	10	1.80	0.66	22.25
12/19	30.15	24	15	1.66	0.61	20.68
12/18	38.49	30	22	1.61	0.56	15.43
12/17	40.80	63	25	1.38	0.50	14.48
12/16	35.00	32	21	1.27	0.46	13.59
Annual Growth	(10.0%)	—	—	9.2%	9.7%	13.1%

Farmers National Banc Corp. (Canfield,OH)

Farmers National Banc is willing to help even nonfarmers grow their seed income into thriving bounties of wealth. The bank provides commercial and personal banking from nearly 20 branches in Ohio. Founded in 1887, Farmers National Banc offers checking and savings accounts, credit cards, and loans and mortgages. Farmers' lending portfolio is composed of real estate mortgages, consumer loans, and commercial loans. The company also includes Farmers National Insurance and Farmers Trust Company, a non-depository trust bank that offers wealth management and trust services.

Geographic Reach

Farmers National Banc operates 19 branches located throughout Mahoning, Trumbull, Columbiana, Stark and Cuyahoga Counties. Farmers Trust Company operates two offices located in Boardman and Howland, Ohio.

Financial Performance

The company's revenues have ranged from $40 million to $60 million in the past decade. In 2013 overall sales fell 1% to $54 million; the slight dip was due to lessened interest income on loans and taxable securities. (Financial institutions make their money on interest income from loans and non-interest income from fees.) Its non-interest income experienced growth from service charges, insurance agency commissions, and consulting fees for retirement planning.

Profits decreased by 22% to $8 million in 2013 due to increase in a provision for loan losses and non-interest expenses such as salary and employee benefits.

Mergers and Acquisitions

In 2013 the bank added retirement planning services to their portfolio with the acquisition of Cleveland-based National Associates, Inc. for $4.4 million. The acquisition was part of its plan to boost noninterest income and complement its existing retirement services.

EXECUTIVES

Vice-Chairman, Director, David Z. Paull
President, Chief Executive Officer, Subsidiary Officer, Director, Kevin J. Helmick, $432,693 total compensation
Executive Vice President, Chief Financial Officer, Secretary, Subsidiary Officer, Troy Adair
Executive Vice President, Subsidiary Officer, Timothy H. Shaffer
Executive Vice President, Chief Marketing Officer, Subsidiary Officer, Amber B. Wallace Soukenik, $143,895 total compensation
Executive Vice President, Chief Wealth Management Officer, Mark Wenick
Subsidiary Officer, Joseph W. Sabat
Director, Ralph D. Macali
Director, Frank J. Monaco
Director, Edward W Muransky
Director, Richard B. Thompson
Director, Gregory C. Bestic
Director, Neil J. Kaback
Director, Terry A. Moore
Director, Anne Frederick Crawford
Auditors : CliftonLarsonAllen LLP

LOCATIONS

HQ: Farmers National Banc Corp. (Canfield,OH)
20 South Broad Street, Canfield, OH 44406
Phone: 330 533-3341
Web: www.farmersbankgroup.com

PRODUCTS/OPERATIONS

Selected Products
Personal
Certificate of DepositChecking AccountsChildren's AccountsConsumer LoansHome Equity Loans & LinesMortgage LoansOnline BankingPersonal Credit

CardPersonal Debit CardPhone BankingRetirementSavings Accounts Business Business Credit CardBusiness Debit CardBusiness DepositsBusiness LoansCash ManagementRemote Deposit Capture Wealth Management and Insurance Farmers Trust CompanyFarmers National InvestmentsFarmers National Insurance On-line banking

COMPETITORS

CVB FINANCIAL CORP.
INDEPENDENT BANK CORP.
MACATAWA BANK CORPORATION
PEOPLES FINANCIAL SERVICES CORP.
STATE BANK FINANCIAL CORPORATION

HISTORICAL FINANCIALS
Company Type: Public

Income Statement — FYE: December 31

	ASSETS ($mil)	NET INCOME ($mil)	INCOME AS % OF ASSETS	EMPLOYEES
12/20	3,071.1	41.8	1.4%	445
12/19	2,449.1	35.7	1.5%	450
12/18	2,328.8	32.5	1.4%	453
12/17	2,159.0	22.7	1.1%	445
12/16	1,966.1	20.5	1.0%	441
Annual Growth	11.8%	19.5%	—	0.2%

2020 Year-End Financials
Return on assets: 1.5%
Return on equity: 12.8%
Long-term debt ($ mil.): —
No. of shares ($ mil.): 28.1
Sales ($ mil.): 149.2
Dividends
  Yield: 3.3%
  Payout: 29.9%
Market value ($ mil.): 374.0

	STOCK PRICE ($) FY Close	P/E High/Low		PER SHARE ($) Earnings	Dividends	Book Value
12/20	13.27	11	7	1.47	0.44	12.42
12/19	16.32	13	10	1.28	0.38	10.82
12/18	12.74	14	10	1.16	0.30	9.44
12/17	14.75	19	15	0.82	0.22	8.79
12/16	14.20	20	11	0.76	0.16	7.88
Annual Growth	(1.7%)	—	—	17.9%	28.8%	12.0%

Farmland Partners Inc

EXECUTIVES

Executive Chairman, Director, Paul A. Pittman, $477,000 total compensation
President, Chief Executive Officer, Director, Luca Fabbri, $275,000 total compensation
Chief Financial Officer, Treasurer, James Gilligan
General Counsel, Secretary, Christine M. Garrison
Subsidiary Officer, Director, Murray R. Wise
Lead Independent Director, Director, Chris A. Downey
Director, Danny D. Moore
Director, Joseph W. Glauber
Director, John A. Good
Director, Thomas P. Heneghan
Auditors : Plante & Moran, PLLC

LOCATIONS

HQ: Farmland Partners Inc
4600 South Syracuse Street, Suite 1450, Denver, CO 80237-2766
Phone: 720 452-3100
Web: www.farmlandpartners.com

HISTORICAL FINANCIALS
Company Type: Public

Income Statement — FYE: December 31

	REVENUE ($mil)	NET INCOME ($mil)	NET PROFIT MARGIN	EMPLOYEES
12/20	50.6	7.1	14.0%	14
12/19	53.5	13.8	25.9%	13
12/18	56.0	12.2	21.9%	13
12/17	46.2	7.9	17.1%	16
12/16	31.0	4.3	13.9%	18
Annual Growth	13.1%	13.4%	—	(6.1%)

2020 Year-End Financials
Debt ratio: 46.4%
Return on equity: 1.6%
Cash ($ mil.): 27.2
Current Ratio: 1.79
Long-term debt ($ mil.): 506.6
No. of shares ($ mil.): 30.5
Dividends
  Yield: 2.2%
  Payout: —
Market value ($ mil.): 266.0

	STOCK PRICE ($) FY Close	P/E High/Low		PER SHARE ($) Earnings	Dividends	Book Value
12/20	8.70	—	—	(0.18)	0.20	14.06
12/19	6.78	176	127	0.04	0.20	14.60
12/18	4.54	—	—	(0.01)	0.36	14.33
12/17	8.68	381	274	0.03	0.51	14.06
12/16	11.16	133	111	0.09	0.51	9.33
Annual Growth	(6.0%)	—	—	—	(20.9%)	10.8%

FB Financial Corp

EXECUTIVES

President, Chief Executive Officer, Subsidiary Officer, Director, Christopher (Chris) T. Holmes, $433,333 total compensation
Chief Financial Officer, Subsidiary Officer, Michael M. Mettee
Chief Credit Officer, Subsidiary Officer, J. Gregory (Greg) Bowers
Chief Banking Officer, Subsidiary Officer, Travis K. Edmondson
Division Officer, Wilburn J. Evans, $225,000 total compensation
Chief Risk Officer, Subsidiary Officer, Aimee T. Hamilton
Chief Administrative Officer, Subsidiary Officer, R. Wade Peery
General Counsel, Corporate Secretary, Subsidiary Officer, Beth W. Sims
Chief Accounting Officer, Subsidiary Officer, Keith S. Rainwater
Director, Jimmy E. Allen
Director, J. Jonathan (Jon) Ayers
Director, William (Bill) F. Carpenter
Director, Agenia W. Clark
Director, James W. Cross
Director, James (Jimmy) L. Exum

Director, Orrin H. Ingram
Director, Raja J. Jubran
Director, Emily J. Reynolds
Director, Melody J. Sullivan
Auditors : Crowe LLP

LOCATIONS

HQ: FB Financial Corp
211 Commerce Street, Suite 300, Nashville, TN 37201
Phone: 615 564-1212
Web: www.firstbankonline.com

HISTORICAL FINANCIALS
Company Type: Public

Income Statement — FYE: December 31

	ASSETS ($mil)	NET INCOME ($mil)	INCOME AS % OF ASSETS	EMPLOYEES
12/20	11,207.3	63.6	0.6%	1,852
12/19	6,124.9	83.8	1.4%	1,399
12/18	5,136.7	80.2	1.6%	1,356
12/17	4,727.7	52.3	1.1%	1,386
12/16	3,276.8	40.5	1.2%	1,108
Annual Growth	36.0%	11.9%	—	13.7%

2020 Year-End Financials
Return on assets: 0.7%
Return on equity: 6.1%
Long-term debt ($ mil.): —
No. of shares ($ mil.): 47.2
Sales ($ mil.): 616.4
Dividends
  Yield: 1.0%
  Payout: 21.5%
Market value ($ mil.): 1,640.0

	STOCK PRICE ($) FY Close	P/E High/Low		PER SHARE ($) Earnings	Dividends	Book Value
12/20	34.73	23	9	1.67	0.36	27.35
12/19	39.59	15	11	2.65	0.32	24.56
12/18	35.02	17	13	2.55	0.20	21.87
12/17	41.99	23	13	1.86	0.00	19.54
12/16	25.95	12	9	2.10	4.03	13.71
Annual Growth	7.6%	—	—	(5.6%)	(45.3%)	18.8%

FCN Banc Corp

EXECUTIVES

Chairman, Subsidiary Officer, Director, Kenenth T. Wanstrath
President, Chief Executive Officer, Subsidiary Officer, Director, Thomas D. Horninger
Chief Financial Officer, Treasurer, April A. Berne
Chief Technology Officer, Kimmerly D. Johnson
Chief Lending Officer, Roger Potraffke
Chief Risk Officer, Secretary, Raymond Gruner
President, Director, Arthur K. Hildebrand
Director Emeritus, Donald R. Smith
Director Emeritus, Keith Tebbe
Director Emeritus, Jane C. Ludwig
Director Emeritus, Fred Chappelow
Director Emeritus, James A. Hyde
Director, David P. Lorey
Director, Dennis Richter
Director, Devin W. Listerman
Director, Ronald J. Knueven
Director, Kevin D. Lyons

Director, Brad M. Tebbe
Director, Kevin Andrew Yaryan

LOCATIONS

HQ: FCN Banc Corp
501 Main Street, Brookville, IN 47012
Phone: 765 647-4116   Fax: 765 647-2680
Web: www.fcnbank.com

HISTORICAL FINANCIALS

Company Type: Public

Income Statement — FYE: December 31

	ASSETS ($mil)	NET INCOME ($mil)	INCOME AS % OF ASSETS	EMPLOYEES
12/20	683.2	6.9	1.0%	0
12/19	474.0	5.7	1.2%	110
12/18	443.5	5.7	1.3%	0
12/17	442.3	3.9	0.9%	0
12/16	432.3	3.9	0.9%	0
Annual Growth	12.1%	15.1%	—	—

2020 Year-End Financials

Return on assets: 1.1%
Return on equity: 10.7%
Long-term debt ($ mil.): —
No. of shares ($ mil.): 1.7
Sales ($ mil.): 27.9
Dividends
Yield: —
Payout: 33.3%
Market value ($ mil.): 69.0

	STOCK PRICE ($) FY Close	P/E High/Low		PER SHARE ($) Earnings	Dividends	Book Value
12/20	39.66	20	9	4.08	1.36	41.91
12/19	40.20	10	8	3.83	1.35	37.68
12/18	30.50	9	7	3.84	1.22	33.08
12/17	29.50	11	10	2.66	1.12	31.07
12/16	29.50	11	10	2.63	1.08	29.34
Annual Growth	7.7%	—	—	11.6%	5.9%	9.3%

Federal Agricultural Mortgage Corp

Farmer Mac (Federal Agricultural Mortgage Corporation) is stockholder-owned, federally chartered corporation that combines private capital and public sponsorship to serve a public purpose. The company provides a secondary market for a variety of loans made to borrowers in rural America. The company's market activities include purchasing eligible loans directly from lenders and more. Farmer Mac is an institution of the Farm Credit System (FCS) which is composed of the banks, associations, and related entities including Farmer Mac and its subsidiaries. Farmer Mac was chartered by Congress in 1987 and established under federal legislation first enacted in 1988.

EXECUTIVES

Chairman, Director, LaJuana S. Wilcher
Vice-Chairman, Director, Lowell L. Junkins, $227,077 total compensation
President, Chief Executive Officer, Bradford T. Nordholm, $160,275 total compensation
Executive Vice President, Chief Financial Officer, Treasurer, Aparna Ramesh
Executive Vice President, Chief Business Officer, Zachary N Carpenter
Executive Vice President, General Counsel, Secretary, Stephen P. Mullery, $415,000 total compensation
Senior Vice President, Chief Human Resources Officer, Kerry T. Willie
Senior Vice President, Chief Credit Officer, Marc J. Cardy
Business Strategy and Financial Research Senior Vice President, Business Strategy and Financial Research Enterprise Risk Officer, Brian M. Brinch, $285,000 total compensation
Operations Senior Vice President, Robert J. Maines
Director, Chester J. Culver
Director, Dennis L. Brack
Director, Charles A. Stones
Director, Roy H. Tiarks
Director, Amy H. Gales
Director, Eric T. McKissack
Director, James R. Engebretsen
Director, Mitchell A. Johnson
Director, Todd P. Ware
Director, Richard H. Davidson
Director, Everett M. Dobrinski
Director, Robert F. Sexton
Director, Daniel L. Shaw
Director, Sara L. Faivre
Director, Myles James Watts
Auditors: PricewaterhouseCoopers LLP

LOCATIONS

HQ: Federal Agricultural Mortgage Corp
1999 K Street, N.W., 4th Floor, Washington, DC 20006
Phone: 202 872-7600

PRODUCTS/OPERATIONS

2015 Sales

	$ mil	% of total
Interest income		
Farmer Mac Guaranteed Securities and USDA Securities	134.4	47
Loans	117.0	41
Investments and cash equivalents	13.4	5
Noninterest income		
Guarantee and commitment fees	14.1	5
Gains on financial derivatives and hedging activities	2.5	1
Other	3.6	1
Total	285.0	100

2015 Sales

	% of total
Farm & Ranch	39
USDA Guarantees	28
Rural Utilities	18
Institutional Credit	10
Corporate	4
Reconciling Adjustments	1
Total	100

Selected Operations
Farm & Ranch (Farmer Mac I)
USDA Guarantees (Farmer Mac II)
Rural Utilities

COMPETITORS

AGFIRST FARM CREDIT BANK
ASSOCIATED BANC-CORP
BOKF MERGER CORPORATION NUMBER SIXTEEN
CAMBRIDGE BANCORP
COBANK, ACB
FARM CREDIT EAST, ACA
FEDERAL HOME LOAN BANK OF DALLAS
FEDERAL HOME LOAN BANK OF NEW YORK
FEDERAL HOME LOAN BANK OF PITTSBURGH
NORINCHUKIN BANK, THE

HISTORICAL FINANCIALS

Company Type: Public

Income Statement — FYE: December 31

	ASSETS ($mil)	NET INCOME ($mil)	INCOME AS % OF ASSETS	EMPLOYEES
12/20	24,355.5	108.6	0.4%	121
12/19	21,709.3	109.5	0.5%	103
12/18	18,694.3	108.0	0.6%	103
12/17	17,792.2	84.4	0.5%	88
12/16	15,606.0	77.3	0.5%	81
Annual Growth	11.8%	8.9%		10.6%

2020 Year-End Financials

Return on assets: 0.4%
Return on equity: 12.0%
Long-term debt ($ mil.): —
No. of shares ($ mil.): 10.7
Sales ($ mil.): 519.5
Dividends
Yield: 4.3%
Payout: 38.6%
Market value ($ mil.): 797.0

	STOCK PRICE ($) FY Close	P/E High/Low		PER SHARE ($) Earnings	Dividends	Book Value
12/20	74.25	10	5	8.27	3.20	92.44
12/19	83.50	10	7	8.69	2.80	74.62
12/18	60.44	11	6	8.83	2.32	70.54
12/17	78.24	12	8	6.60	1.44	66.69
12/16	57.27	10	4	5.97	1.04	61.05
Annual Growth	6.7%	—	—	8.5%	32.4%	10.9%

Federal Home Loan Bank New York

Federal Home Loan Bank of New York (FHLBNY) provides funds for residential mortgages and community development to more than 310 financial institutions in New York, New Jersey, Puerto Rico, and the US Virgin Islands. One of a dozen Federal Home Loan Banks in the US, it is cooperatively owned by its member institutions and supervised by the Federal Housing Finance Agency.

Operations

The company's primary business is making collateralized loans or advances to members and is also the principal factor that impacts its financial condition. It also serves the public through its mortgage programs, which enable its members to liquefy certain mortgage loans by selling them to the bank. The company also provide members with such correspondent services as safekeeping, wire transfers, depository, and settlement services.

Geographic Reach

Based in New York, FHLBNY serves not only New York, but New Jersey, Puerto Rico, and the US Virgin Islands.

Sales and Marketing
FHLBNY caters to more than 310 financial institutions.

Financial Performance
Net interest income was $540.6 million in 2021, a decrease of $212.4 million, or 28% compared to 2020.

In 2021, the company had a net income of $265.5 million, a 40% decline from the previous year's net income of $442.4 million.

The company's cash at the end of 2021 was $21.7 million. Operating activities generated $899.7 million, while financing activities used $31.4 billion, primarily for payments for maturing. Investing activities provided another $28.6 billion.

EXECUTIVES

Chairman, Michael M. Horn
Vice-Chairman, Director, Joseph R. Ficalora
President, Chief Executive Officer, José Ramón González
Senior Vice President, Deputy Chief Risk Officer, Acting Chief Risk Officer, Melody Feinberg
Bank Relations Senior Vice President, Bank Relations Director, Eric P. Amig
Support Services Senior Vice President, Technology Senior Vice President, Support Services Chief Information Officer, Technology Chief Information Officer, Support Services Head, Technology Head, G. Robert Fusco
Sales Senior Vice President, Marketing Senior Vice President, Sales Head, Marketing Head, Adam D. Goldstein
Member Services Senior Vice President, Member Services Head, Paul B. Heroux, $343,713 total compensation
Strategy Senior Vice President, Business Development Senior Vice President, Strategy Chief Financial Officer, Business Development Chief Financial Officer, Kevin M. Neylan, $364,129 total compensation
Vice President, Controller, Backer Ali
Director, Larry E. Thompson
Director, Anne Evans Estabrook
Director, James W. Fulmer
Director, Katherine J. Liseno
Director, Kevin J. Lynch
Director, Jay M. Ford
Director, Thomas L. Hoy
Director, Monte N. Redman
Director, Christopher Martin
Director, John R. Buran
Director, David J. Nasca
Director, Richard S. Mroz
Director, Carlos J. Vazquez
Director, Kevin Cummings
Independent Director, Caren S. Franzini
Independent Director, C. Cathleen Raffaeli
Independent Director, Edwin C. Reed
Independent Director, DeForest Blake Soaries
Director, Gerald H. Lipkin
Director, Kenneth J. Mahon
Auditors : PricewaterhouseCoopers LLP

LOCATIONS
HQ: Federal Home Loan Bank New York
101 Park Avenue, New York, NY 10178
Phone: 212 681-6000
Web: www.fhlbny.com

PRODUCTS/OPERATIONS
2013 Sales

	$ mil.	% of total
Interest		
Advances	444.5	55
Long-term securities	244.0	30
Mortgage loans held for portfolio	68.3	9
Available-for-sale securities	16.6	2
Other	14.3	2
Non-interest	13.3	2
Total	801	100

COMPETITORS
AGFIRST FARM CREDIT BANK
EAGLE BANCORP, INC.
EXPORT-IMPORT BANK OF THE UNITED STATES
FARM CREDIT EAST, ACA
FEDERAL AGRICULTURAL MORTGAGE CORPORATION
FEDERAL HOME LOAN BANK OF BOSTON
FEDERAL HOME LOAN BANK OF DALLAS
FEDERAL HOME LOAN BANK OF PITTSBURGH
FEDERAL HOME LOAN MORTGAGE CORPORATION
REPUBLIC FIRST BANCORP, INC.

HISTORICAL FINANCIALS
Company Type: Public

Income Statement				FYE: December 31
	ASSETS ($mil)	NET INCOME ($mil)	INCOME AS % OF ASSETS	EMPLOYEES
12/20	136,996.0	442.3	0.3%	354
12/19	162,062.0	472.5	0.3%	342
12/18	144,381.0	560.4	0.4%	314
12/17	158,918.0	479.4	0.3%	308
12/16	143,606.0	401.1	0.3%	280
Annual Growth	(1.2%)	2.5%	—	6.0%

2020 Year-End Financials
Return on assets: 0.2%
Return on equity: 5.9%
Long-term debt ($ mil.): —
No. of shares ($ mil.): 53.6
Sales ($ mil.): 1,883
Dividends
Yield: —
Payout: 79.5%
Market value ($ mil.): 0.0

Federal Home Loan Bank Of Dallas

EXECUTIVES

Chairman, Director, Robert M. Rigby
President, Chief Executive Officer, Sanjay Bhasin
Vice-Chairman, Director, Margo S. Scholin
Executive Vice President, Chief Administrative Officer, Corporate Secretary, Brehan Chapman
Executive Vice President, General Counsel, Sandra Damholt, $260,000 total compensation
Executive Vice President, Chief Risk Officer, Kelly Davis
Executive Vice President, Chief Financial Officer, Tom Lewis, $291,490 total compensation
Executive Vice President, Chief Business Officer, Kalyan Madhavan
Executive Vice President, Chief Banking Operations Officer, Gustavo Molina
Capital Markets Executive Vice President, Capital Markets Head, Jibo Pan
Executive Vice President, Chief Information Officer, Jeff Yeager
Executive Vice President, Chief Credit Officer, Michael Zheng
Independent Director, Mary E. Ceverha
Director, Christopher G. Palmer
Director, A. Fred Miller
Director, Tim H. Carter
Director, Albert C. Christman
Director, Rufus Cormier
Director, James D. Goudge
Director, W. Wesley Hoskins
Director, Stephen Panepinto
Director, Michael C. Hutsell
Director, Ron G. Wiser
Independent Director, Dianne W. Bolen
Independent Director, Lorraine Palacios
Independent Director, Dorsey L. Baskin
Independent Director, Sally I. Nelson
Independent Director, Felipe A. Rael
Independent Director, John P. Salazar
Auditors : PricewaterhouseCoopers LLP

LOCATIONS
HQ: Federal Home Loan Bank Of Dallas
8500 Freeport Parkway South, Suite 600, Irving, TX 75063-2547
Phone: 214 441-8500
Web: www.fhlb.com

HISTORICAL FINANCIALS
Company Type: Public

Income Statement				FYE: December 31
	ASSETS ($mil)	NET INCOME ($mil)	INCOME AS % OF ASSETS	EMPLOYEES
12/20	64,912.5	198.7	0.3%	203
12/19	75,381.6	227.2	0.3%	203
12/18	72,773.2	198.7	0.3%	197
12/17	68,524.3	150.2	0.2%	205
12/16	58,212.0	79.4	0.1%	218
Annual Growth	2.8%	25.8%	—	(1.8%)

2020 Year-End Financials
Return on assets: 0.2%
Return on equity: 5.3%
Long-term debt ($ mil.): —
No. of shares ($ mil.): 21.0
Sales ($ mil.): 823.4
Dividends
Yield: —
Payout: 19.4%
Market value ($ mil.): 0.0

Federal Signal Corp.

Federal Signal designs, manufactures, and supplies a suite of products and integrated solutions for municipal, governmental, industrial, and commercial customers. Offerings include street sweepers, vacuum- and hydro-excavation trucks, and water blasters for general alarm/public address systems; industrial communications and public warning systems for public safety. In addition, the company engages in the sale of parts, service and repair, equipment rentals, and training as part of a comprehensive aftermarket offering to its customers. The company operates some 20 principal manufacturing facilities in five countries and provides products and integrated solutions to customers in all regions of the world. Federal Signal generates the majority of sales from the US market.

Operations

Federal Signal divides its operations across two segments. Environmental Solutions Group accounts for around 85% of revenue. It is a leading manufacturer and supplier of a full range of street sweepers, sewer cleaners, industrial vacuum loaders, safe-digging trucks, high-performance waterblasting equipment, road-marking and line-removal equipment, dump truck bodies, and trailers. It manufactures vehicles and equipment that are sold under the Elgin, Vactor, Guzzler, TRUVAC, Westech, Jetstream, Mark Rite Lines, Ox Bodies, Crysteel, J-Craft, Duraclass, Rugby, and Travis brand names.

The Safety and Security Systems Group, more than 15% of revenue, is a leading manufacturer and supplier of comprehensive systems and products that law enforcement, fire rescue, emergency medical services, campuses, military facilities and industrial sites use to protect people and property. Offerings include systems for community alerting, emergency vehicles, first responder interoperable communications, and industrial communications. Products are sold under the Federal Signal, Federal Signal VAMA, and Victor brand names.

Geographic Reach

The majority of the company's sales (about 75%) are made in the US, about 15% in Canada, and nearly 10% in Europe/Other.

Headquartered at Oak Brook, Illinois, the company utilized approximately 15 principal manufacturing plants located throughout the US, as well as two in Europe, two in Canada, and one in South Africa.

Sales and Marketing

The Environmental Solutions Group uses either a dealer network or direct sales to serve customers. Its direct sales channel concentrates primarily on the industrial, utility, and construction market segments. It also engages in the sale of parts, service and repair, equipment rentals and training through its service centers located across North America. The Safety and Security Systems Group sells to industrial customers through wholesalers and distributors who are supported by company sales personnel or independent manufacturer representatives. Products are also sold to municipal and governmental customers through active independent distributors, as well as through original equipment manufacturers and the direct sales force.

Financial Performance

Company's revenue for fiscal 2021 increased by $82.4 million to $1.2 billion compared from the prior year with $1.1 billion.

Net income for fiscal 2021 increased to $100.6 million compared from the prior year with $96.1 million.

Cash held by the company at the end of fiscal 2021 decreased to $40.5 million. Cash provided by operations and financing activities were $101.8 million and $26.4 million, respectively. Cash used for investing activities was $168.7 million, mainly for payments for acquisition-related activity.

Strategy

Federal Signal's long-term strategy includes exploring acquisitions of companies or businesses to facilitate its growth, enhance its global market position and broaden its product offerings. Such acquisitions may help Federal Signal expand into adjacent markets, add complementary products and services or allow the company to leverage its distribution channels.

Mergers and Acquisitions

In late 2021, Federal Signal acquired substantially all the assets and operations of each of Deist Industries, Inc., Bucks Fabricating, LLC, Roll-Off Parts, LLC and Switch-N-Go, LLC (collectively Deist), all of which are located in Pennsylvania. Deist designs, manufactures and sells interchangeable truck body systems for class 3-7 vehicles in the work truck industry and a full line of waste hauling products, including front/rear loading containers and specialty roll-off containers. "We are thrilled to complete the Deist acquisition, which not only represents another attractive product line extension, but also expands our presence in certain end-markets such as landscaping and waste hauling," said Jennifer L. Sherman, President and Chief Executive Officer.

Also in late 2021, Federal Signal acquired substantially all the assets and operations of Idaho-based Ground Force Worldwide (Ground Force), a leading manufacturer of specialty material handling vehicles that support the extraction of metals. The transaction involves cash consideration of $45.0 million, subject to post-closing adjustments. "We are thrilled to complete the Ground Force acquisition, which further strengthens our position as an industry leading diversified industrial manufacturer of specialized vehicles for maintenance and infrastructure markets," said Jennifer L. Sherman, President and Chief Executive Officer.

In early 2021, Federal Signal Corporation announced the completion of the acquisition of OSW Equipment and Repair, LLC (OSW) for cash consideration of $52.5 million. OSW is a leading manufacturer of dump truck bodies and custom upfitter of truck equipment and trailers, and is headquartered in Snohomish, Washington, with an upfitting location in Tempe, Arizona. The acquisition of OSW represents a highly strategic transaction, adding three premier brands that serve attractive infrastructure, construction and other industrial end-markets on the West Coast, in Arizona and in parts of Canada.

EXECUTIVES

Chairman, Director, Dennis J. Martin, $600,000 total compensation

Human Resources President, Human Resources Chief Executive Officer, Director, Jennifer L. Sherman, $702,975 total compensation

Senior Vice President, Chief Operating Officer, Mark D. Weber, $432,981 total compensation

Senior Vice President, Chief Financial Officer, Ian A. Hudson, $360,000 total compensation

Vice President, General Counsel, Secretary, Daniel A. DuPre, $298,378 total compensation

Vice President, Treasurer, Corporate Development, Svetlana Vinokur

Vice President, Corporate Controller, Lauren B. Elting

Subsidiary Officer, Robert E. Fines, $400,000 total compensation

Lead Independent Director, Director, Brenda L. Reichelderfer

Director, Eugene J. Lowe

Director, Richard R. Mudge

Director, William F. Owens

Director, John L. Workman

Auditors : DELOITTE & TOUCHE LLP

LOCATIONS

HQ: Federal Signal Corp.
1415 West 22nd Street, Oak Brook, IL 60523
Phone: 630 954-2000 **Fax:** 630 954-2030
Web: www.federalsignal.com

2015 Sales

	$ mil.	% of total
US	577	75
Europe/Other	115	15
Canada	76	10
Total	768	100

PRODUCTS/OPERATIONS

2015 Sales

	$ mil.	% of total
Environmental Solutions	534.1	70
Safety and Security Systems	233.9	30
Total	768.0	100

Selected Products

Alerting systems
Hydro-excavators
Industrial vacuum loaders
Mining systems
Parking systems
Sewer cleaners
Sirens
Street sweepers
Truck-mounted aerial platforms
Water blasters

COMPETITORS

ACUITY BRANDS, INC.
DIALIGHT PLC
HONEYWELL INTERNATIONAL INC.
ICHIKOH INDUSTRIES,LTD.
KOITO MANUFACTURING CO., LTD.
LUMINESCENT SYSTEMS, INC.
MARELLI EUROPE SPA
NORTH AMERICAN LIGHTING, INC.
PETERSON MANUFACTURING COMPANY
STREET GLOW INC

HISTORICAL FINANCIALS
Company Type: Public

Income Statement — FYE: December 31

	REVENUE ($mil)	NET INCOME ($mil)	NET PROFIT MARGIN	EMPLOYEES
12/20	1,130.8	96.2	8.5%	3,500
12/19	1,221.3	108.5	8.9%	3,600
12/18	1,089.5	94.0	8.6%	3,300
12/17	898.5	61.6	6.9%	3,100
12/16	707.9	43.8	6.2%	2,200
Annual Growth	12.4%	21.7%	—	12.3%

2020 Year-End Financials
Debt ratio: 17.4%
Return on equity: 14.2%
Cash ($ mil.): 81.7
Current Ratio: 2.73
Long-term debt ($ mil.): 209.8
No. of shares ($ mil.): 60.5
Dividends
  Yield: 0.9%
  Payout: 20.5%
Market value ($ mil.): 2,007.0

	STOCK PRICE ($) FY Close	P/E High/Low		PER SHARE ($) Earnings	Dividends	Book Value
12/20	33.17	22	15	1.56	0.32	11.60
12/19	32.25	19	11	1.76	0.32	10.60
12/18	19.90	18	12	1.54	0.31	8.81
12/17	20.09	22	13	1.02	0.28	7.62
12/16	15.61	23	16	0.71	0.28	6.61
Annual Growth	20.7%	—	—	21.7%	3.4%	15.1%

Fentura Financial Inc

It just makes cents to say that Fentura Financial has its hands full. Fentura Financial is the holding company for Michigan community banks The State Bank, Davison State Bank, West Michigan Community Bank, and Community Bancorp. From about 20 branch locations, the banks provide commercial and consumer banking services and products, including checking and savings accounts and loans. Commercial loans account for some two-thirds of the bank's combined loan portfolio. The State Bank, Fentura's first subsidiary, traces its origins to 1898. Fentura acquired St. Charles-based Community Bancorp in late 2016.

EXECUTIVES

Chairman, Director, Thomas P. McKenney
Vice-Chairman, Director, Brian P. Petty
President, Chief Executive Officer, Subsidiary Officer, Director, Ronald L. Justice, $160,000 total compensation
Director, Steven T. Krause
Director, William H. Dery
Director, Frederick P. Dillingham
Director, Donald L. Grill, $171,430 total compensation
Director, Randy D. Hicks
Director, Ronald K. Rybar
Auditors: Rehmann Robson LLC

LOCATIONS

HQ: Fentura Financial Inc
P.O. Box 725, Fenton, MI 48430-0725
Phone: 810 629-2263
Web: www.fentura.com

COMPETITORS

COMMUNITY SHORES BANK CORPORATION
COMMUNITY TRUST BANCORP, INC.
FB CORPORATION
UNITED BANCSHARES, INC.
VOLUNTEER BANCORP, INC

HISTORICAL FINANCIALS
Company Type: Public

Income Statement — FYE: December 31

	ASSETS ($mil)	NET INCOME ($mil)	INCOME AS % OF ASSETS	EMPLOYEES
12/20	1,251.4	15.4	1.2%	0
12/19	1,034.7	11.5	1.1%	0
12/18	926.4	10.1	1.1%	0
12/17	781.4	8.6	1.1%	0
12/16	703.3	4.4	0.6%	0
Annual Growth	15.5%	36.6%	—	—

2020 Year-End Financials
Return on assets: 1.3%
Return on equity: 14.1%
Long-term debt ($ mil.): —
No. of shares ($ mil.): 4.6
Sales ($ mil.): 65.6
Dividends
  Yield: 1.3%
  Payout: 10.4%
Market value ($ mil.): 103.0

	STOCK PRICE ($) FY Close	P/E High/Low		PER SHARE ($) Earnings	Dividends	Book Value
12/20	22.00	8	4	3.31	0.30	24.68
12/19	25.23	10	8	2.49	0.28	21.75
12/18	21.00	8	7	2.65	0.24	19.31
12/17	18.88	8	6	2.39	0.20	16.37
12/16	16.00	9	8	1.70	0.40	14.00
Annual Growth	8.3%	—	—	18.1%	(6.9%)	15.2%

FFD Financial Corp

FFD Financial is the holding company for First Federal Community Bank, which serves Tuscarawas County and contiguous portions of eastern Ohio through about five branches. Founded in 1898, the bank offers a full range of retail products, including checking and savings accounts, CDs, IRAs, and credit cards. The bank mainly uses these funds to originate one- to four-family residential mortgages, nonresidential real estate loans, and land loans. First Federal Community Bank also originates business, consumer, and multifamily residential real estate loans. In 2012, First Federal Community Bank converted its charter from a savings bank to a national commercial bank.

EXECUTIVES

Chairman, Subsidiary Officer, Director, Stephen G. Clinton
President, Chief Executive Officer, Subsidiary Officer, Director, Trent B. Troyer, $156,000 total compensation
Executive Vice President, Secretary, Subsidiary Officer, Scott C. Finnell, $118,450 total compensation
Senior Vice President, Chief Financial Officer, Treasurer, Subsidiary Officer, Gregory W. Dorris
Senior Vice President, Subsidiary Officer, Michele L. Larkin
Subsidiary Officer, Suzanne Moore
Subsidiary Officer, Kathy Norman
Subsidiary Officer, Matt Stein
Subsidiary Officer, Angela Delong
Subsidiary Officer, Twyla McCartney
Subsidiary Officer, Stephenie M. Wilson
Subsidiary Officer, Tiffany A. Kail
Subsidiary Officer, Alex Geers
Subsidiary Officer, Kerry Egler-Whytsell
Subsidiary Officer, Leslie A. Riker
Subsidiary Officer, Carol L. Slemmer
Subsidiary Officer, Matthew A. Miller
Subsidiary Officer, Kristofer A. Kreinbihl
Subsidiary Officer, Scott Heil
Director Emeritus, Enos L. Loader
Director Emeritus, Robert D. Sensel
Director, Douglas G. Bambeck
Director, Matthew L. Beachy
Director, Richard A. Brinkman
Director, Leonard L. Gundy
Director, David W. Kaufman
Auditors: Clark, Schaefer, Hackett & Co.

LOCATIONS

HQ: FFD Financial Corp
321 North Wooster Avenue, Dover, OH 44622
Phone: 330 364-7777
Web: www.firstfed.com

COMPETITORS

HERITAGE SOUTHEAST BANCORPORATION, INC.
PEOPLES BANCORP
PIEDMONT FEDERAL SAVINGS BANK
PVF CAPITAL CORP.
UNITED COMMUNITY BANCORP

HISTORICAL FINANCIALS
Company Type: Public

Income Statement — FYE: June 30

	ASSETS ($mil)	NET INCOME ($mil)	INCOME AS % OF ASSETS	EMPLOYEES
06/21	591.5	8.8	1.5%	0
06/20	522.2	6.9	1.3%	0
06/19	413.9	6.3	1.5%	0
06/18	382.1	4.8	1.3%	72
06/17	341.4	4.1	1.2%	0
Annual Growth	14.7%	20.6%	—	—

HOOVER'S HANDBOOK OF EMERGING COMPANIES 2023

Fidelity D&D Bancorp Inc

Fidelity D & D Bancorp has loyal banking customers. The institution is the holding company for The Fidelity Deposit and Discount Bank, serving Lackawanna and Luzerne counties in northeastern Pennsylvania through about a dozen locations and about the same number of ATM locations. The bank attracts local individuals and business customers by offering such products and services as checking and savings accounts, certificates of deposit, investments, and trust services. Commercial real estate loans account for the bulk of the company's loan portfolio, followed by consumer loans, business and industrial loans, and residential mortgages. The bank also writes construction loans and direct financing leases.

EXECUTIVES

Chairman, Director, Brian J. Cali
President, Chief Executive Officer, Subsidiary Officer, Director, Daniel J. Santaniello, $281,385 total compensation
Vice President, Chief Operating Officer, Subsidiary Officer, Eugene J. Walsh, $195,865 total compensation
Chief Financial Officer, Treasurer, Subsidiary Officer, Salvatore R. DeFrancesco, $209,079 total compensation
Subsidiary Officer, Michael J. Pacyna, $187,308 total compensation
Subsidiary Officer, Timothy P. O'Brien, $200,923 total compensation
Director, John T. Cognetti
Director, Richard J. Lettieri
Director, Michael J. McDonald
Director, HelenBeth Garofalo Vilcek
Director, William J. Joyce
Director, Kristin Dempsey O'Donnell
Director, Alan H. Silverman
Director, Richard M. Hotchkiss
Director, Paul C. Woelkers
Auditors: RSM US LLP

2021 Year-End Financials
Return on assets: 1.5%
Return on equity: 18.5%
Long-term debt ($ mil.): —
No. of shares ($ mil.): 2.9
Sales ($ mil.): 23.8
Dividends
  Yield: —
  Payout: 68.0%
Market value ($ mil.): 214.0

	STOCK PRICE ($) FY Close	P/E High/Low		PER SHARE ($) Earnings	Dividends	Book Value
06/21	72.60	26	21	2.99	2.04	17.36
06/20	62.05	32	22	2.33	0.95	14.89
06/19	52.70	25	22	2.12	1.52	13.08
06/18	47.06	29	24	1.63	1.25	11.26
06/17	39.15	28	21	1.40	1.12	10.13
Annual Growth	16.7%	—	—	20.9%	16.2%	14.4%

LOCATIONS

HQ: Fidelity D&D Bancorp Inc
Blakely & Drinker Streets, Dunmore, PA 18512
Phone: 570 342-8281
Web: www.bankatfidelity.com

COMPETITORS

KISH BANCORP, INC.
LYONS NATIONAL BANK
PINNACLE BANKSHARES CORPORATION
QNB CORP.
THE COMMERCE BANK OF WASHINGTON

HISTORICAL FINANCIALS
Company Type: Public

Income Statement — FYE: December 31

	ASSETS ($mil)	NET INCOME ($mil)	INCOME AS % OF ASSETS	EMPLOYEES
12/20	1,699.5	13.0	0.8%	265
12/19	1,009.9	11.5	1.1%	189
12/18	981.1	11.0	1.1%	181
12/17	863.6	8.7	1.0%	175
12/16	792.9	7.6	1.0%	167
Annual Growth	21.0%	14.1%	—	12.2%

2020 Year-End Financials
Return on assets: 0.9%
Return on equity: 9.5%
Long-term debt ($ mil.): —
No. of shares ($ mil.): 4.9
Sales ($ mil.): 64.1
Dividends
  Yield: 1.7%
  Payout: 40.4%
Market value ($ mil.): 320.0

	STOCK PRICE ($) FY Close	P/E High/Low		PER SHARE ($) Earnings	Dividends	Book Value
12/20	64.36	24	11	2.82	1.14	33.48
12/19	62.21	22	18	3.03	1.06	28.25
12/18	64.18	25	15	2.90	0.98	24.89
12/17	41.30	25	14	2.33	0.88	23.40
12/16	36.10	18	15	2.09	0.83	21.91
Annual Growth	15.6%	—	—	7.8%	8.4%	11.2%

Finance of America Companies Inc

EXECUTIVES

Chairman, Brian L. Libman
President, Interim Chief Executive Officer, Graham A. Fleming
Chief Financial Officer, Johan Gericke
Chief Investment Officer, Jeremy E. Prahm
Chief Legal Officer, General Counsel, Corporate Secretary, Lauren E. Richmond
Director, Norma Corio
Director, Robert W. Lord
Director, Tyson A. Pratcher
Director, Lance N. West
Director, Patricia L. Cook

LOCATIONS

HQ: Finance of America Companies Inc
909 Lake Carolyn Parkway, Suite 1550, Irving, TX 75039
Phone: 972 999-1833
Web: www.financeofamerica.com

HISTORICAL FINANCIALS
Company Type: Public

Income Statement — FYE: December 31

	REVENUE ($mil)	NET INCOME ($mil)	NET PROFIT MARGIN	EMPLOYEES
12/20	1,797.0	518.3	28.8%	5,900
12/19	894.0	54.4	6.1%	5,600
12/18	789.2	32.0	4.1%	0
12/17	778.4	52.6	6.8%	0
Annual Growth	32.2%	114.3%	—	—

2020 Year-End Financials
Debt ratio: 43.9%
Return on equity: 93.0%
Cash ($ mil.): 233.1
Current Ratio: 0.05
Long-term debt ($ mil.): 8,568
No. of shares ($ mil.): 0.0
Dividends
  Yield: —
  Payout: —
Market value ($ mil.): 0.0

Finemark Holdings Inc

EXECUTIVES

Chairman, Chief Executive Officer, Subsidiary Officer, Director, Joseph R. Catti
Vice-Chairman, Lead Director, Director, Scott A. Edmonds
Executive Vice President, Chief Financial Officer, Subsidiary Officer, Director, Brian J. Eagleston
Executive Vice President, Region Officer, Subsidiary Officer, David A. Highmark
Subsidiary Officer, Malinda L. Schneider
Subsidiary Officer, Robert M. Arnall
Subsidiary Officer, Diana L. Kizer
Subsidiary Officer, Tiffany A. Williams
Subsidiary Officer, Jennifer L. Stevens
Subsidiary Officer, Christopher T. Battifarano
Subsidiary Officer, Robert A. Parimore
Subsidiary Officer, Jeffrey B. Moes
Subsidiary Officer, Jason L. Manwell
Region Officer, Harlan C. Parrish
Region Officer, Adria D. Starkey
Region Officer, Michael E. Drohan
Region Officer, David H. Scaff
Chairman, Director, David H. Lucas
Director, Martin E. Adams
Director, Aurelia J. Bell
Director, Michael J. Carron
Director, Thomas D. Case
Director, Tracey U. Galloway
Director, William N. Horowitz
Director, Clive Lubner
Director, Vito S. Manone
Director, Alan D. Reynolds
Director, Lee J. Seidler
Director, Martin M. Wasmer
Director Emeritus, John F. Blais

Director Emeritus, Hale S. Irwin
Director Emeritus, William H. Turner
Auditors: Hacker, Johnson & Smith P.A.

LOCATIONS

HQ: Finemark Holdings Inc
12681 Creekside Lane, Fort Myers, FL 33919
Phone: 239 461-3850
Web: www.finemarkbank.com

HISTORICAL FINANCIALS
Company Type: Public

Income Statement — FYE: December 31

	REVENUE ($mil)	NET INCOME ($mil)	NET PROFIT MARGIN	EMPLOYEES
12/20	104.3	21.9	21.0%	0
12/19	95.5	15.2	15.9%	0
12/18	81.4	15.1	18.6%	0
12/17	65.4	9.6	14.7%	178
12/16	54.5	7.9	14.6%	0
Annual Growth	17.6%	28.8%	—	—

2020 Year-End Financials
Debt ratio: 13.7%
Return on equity: 11.2%
Cash ($ mil.): 227.9
Current Ratio: 0.11
Long-term debt ($ mil.): 384.9
No. of shares ($ mil.): 8.9
Dividends
Yield: —
Payout: —
Market value ($ mil.): 210.0

	STOCK PRICE ($) FY Close	P/E High/Low		PER SHARE ($) Earnings	Dividends	Book Value
12/20	23.41	10	8	2.42	0.00	23.57
12/19	25.10	17	14	1.69	0.00	20.15
Annual Growth	(6.7%)	—	—	43.2%	—	17.0%

Finward Bancorp

NorthWest Indiana Bancorp is the holding company for Peoples Bank, which serves individuals and businesses customers through about 10 branches in northwest Indiana's Lake County. The savings bank offers traditional deposit services such as checking and savings accounts, money market accounts, and CDs. It primarily uses the funds collected to originate loans secured by single-family residences and commercial real estate; it also makes construction, consumer, and business loans. The bank's Wealth Management Group provides retirement and estate planning, investment accounts, land trusts, and profit-sharing and 401(k) plans.

EXECUTIVES

Executive Chairman, Subsidiary Officer, Director, David A. Bochnowski, $255,852 total compensation
President, Chief Executive Officer, Subsidiary Officer, Director, Benjamin J. Bochnowski, $319,815 total compensation
Executive Vice President, Chief Banking Officer, Todd M. Scheub, $216,920 total compensation
Executive Vice President, Chief Financial Officer, Treasurer, Subsidiary Officer, Peymon S. Torabi
Executive Vice President, Chief Operating Officer, Robert T. Lowry, $214,817 total compensation
Interim Chief Risk Officer, Lynette M. Klemm
Director, Joel Gorelick, $238,821 total compensation
Director, Amy W. Han
Director, Robert W. Youman
Director, Donald P. Fesko
Director, Danette Garza
Director, Robert E. Johnson
Director, Kenneth V. Krupinski
Director, Anthony M. Puntillo
Director, James L. Wieser
Auditors: Plante & Moran, PLLC

LOCATIONS

HQ: Finward Bancorp
9204 Columbia Avenue, Munster, IN 46321
Phone: 219 836-4400
Web: www.ibankpeoples.com

COMPETITORS

AMB FINANCIAL CORP.
ASB FINANCIAL CORP
FIDELITY FEDERAL BANCORP
LIBERTY CAPITAL, INC.
PEOPLES BANCORP

HISTORICAL FINANCIALS
Company Type: Public

Income Statement — FYE: December 31

	ASSETS ($mil)	NET INCOME ($mil)	INCOME AS % OF ASSETS	EMPLOYEES
12/20	1,497.5	16.6	1.1%	263
12/19	1,328.7	12.0	0.9%	290
12/18	1,096.1	9.3	0.9%	276
12/17	927.2	8.9	1.0%	217
12/16	913.6	9.1	1.0%	216
Annual Growth	13.1%	16.1%	—	5.0%

2020 Year-End Financials
Return on assets: 1.1%
Return on equity: 11.5%
Long-term debt ($ mil.): —
No. of shares ($ mil.): 3.4
Sales ($ mil.): 69.7
Dividends
Yield: —
Payout: 25.8%
Market value ($ mil.): 125.0

	STOCK PRICE ($) FY Close	P/E High/Low		PER SHARE ($) Earnings	Dividends	Book Value
12/20	36.10	10	6	4.80	1.24	44.16
12/19	45.90	13	12	3.53	1.23	38.85
12/18	43.00	15	13	3.17	1.19	33.50
12/17	44.50	14	12	3.13	1.15	32.14
12/16	38.85	12	9	3.20	1.11	29.41
Annual Growth	(1.8%)	—	—	10.7%	2.8%	10.7%

First Bancorp (NC)

Don't confuse this First Bancorp with Virginia's First Bancorp or First BanCorp in Puerto Rico. This one is the holding company for First Bank, which operates about 100 branch locations in east-central North Carolina, east South Carolina, and western Virginia (where it operates under the name First Bank of Virginia). In addition to offering standard commercial banking services such as deposit accounts and lending, the bank offers investment products and discount brokerage services. Another subsidiary, First Bank Insurance Services, offers property/casualty products. First Bank focuses its lending on mortgages, which account for more than half of its loan portfolio.

EXECUTIVES

Chairman, Subsidiary Officer, Director, James C. Crawford
President, Chief Executive Officer, Subsidiary Officer, Director, Richard H. Moore, $400,000 total compensation
President, Subsidiary Officer, Director, Michael G. Mayer, $487,500 total compensation
Executive Vice President, Chief Financial Officer, Subsidiary Officer, Eric P. Credle, $346,250 total compensation
Executive Vice President, Secretary, Elizabeth B. Bostian
Director, Daniel T. Blue
Director, Dexter V. Perry
Director, Mary Clara Capel
Director, Suzanne S. DeFerie
Director, Abby Donnelly
Director, John B. (Chip) Gould
Director, O. Temple Sloan
Director, Frederick L. Taylor
Director, Virginia C. Thomasson
Director, Dennis A. Wicker
Auditors: BDO USA, LLP

LOCATIONS

HQ: First Bancorp (NC)
300 S.W. Broad St., Southern Pines, NC 28387
Phone: 910 246-2500
Web: www.localfirstbank.com

PRODUCTS/OPERATIONS

2016 Sales

	$ mil.	% of total
Interest Income	130.9	84
Non-interest Income	25.6	16
Total	156.5	100

COMPETITORS

AMERICAN BANK INCORPORATED
COMMUNITY FIRST BANCORPORATION
FIRST HAWAIIAN BANK
FIRST PLACE BANK
FIRST SOUTH BANCORP, INC.
FIRST SOUTH BANK
FIRST US BANCSHARES, INC.
GEORGIA-CAROLINA BANCSHARES, INC.
SOUTHEASTERN BANK FINANCIAL CORPORATION
THE FIRST BANK AND TRUST COMPANY

HISTORICAL FINANCIALS
Company Type: Public

Income Statement   FYE: December 31

	ASSETS ($mil)	NET INCOME ($mil)	INCOME AS % OF ASSETS	EMPLOYEES
12/20	7,289.7	81.4	1.1%	1,118
12/19	6,143.6	92.0	1.5%	1,111
12/18	5,864.1	89.2	1.5%	1,098
12/17	5,547.0	45.9	0.8%	1,166
12/16	3,614.8	27.5	0.8%	861
Annual Growth	19.2%	31.2%	—	6.7%

2020 Year-End Financials
Return on assets: 1.2%
Return on equity: 9.3%
Long-term debt ($ mil.): —
No. of shares ($ mil.): 28.5
Sales ($ mil.): 318.4
Dividends
Yield: 2.1%
Payout: 25.6%
Market value ($ mil.): 967.0

	STOCK PRICE ($) FY Close	P/E High/Low		PER SHARE ($) Earnings	Dividends	Book Value
12/20	33.83	14	7	2.81	0.72	31.26
12/19	39.91	13	10	3.10	0.54	28.80
12/18	32.66	14	10	3.01	0.40	25.71
12/17	35.31	21	15	1.82	0.32	23.38
12/16	27.14	21	13	1.33	0.32	17.66
Annual Growth	5.7%	—	—	20.6%	22.5%	15.3%

First Bancorp Inc (ME)

It may not actually be the first bank, but The First Bancorp (formerly First National Lincoln) was founded over 150 years ago. It is the holding company for The First, a regional bank serving coastal Maine from more than 15 branches. The bank offers traditional retail products and services, including checking and savings accounts, CDs, IRAs, and loans. Residential mortgages make up about 40% of the company's loan portfolio; business loans account for another 40%; and home equity and consumer loans comprise the rest. Bank subsidiary First Advisors offers private banking and investment management services. Founded in 1864, the bank now boasts more than $1.4 billion in assets.

Operations
Subsidiary First Advisors acts as the bank's Trust and Investment services division, which managed some $740 million in investor assets as of late 2014.

The First Bancorp generated 57% of its total revenue from interest income on loans (including fees), while another 25% came from interest and dividends on its investments. Service charges on deposit accounts (4%), Fiduciary and investment management income (3%), mortgage origination (2%) and net securities gains (2%) made up most of the rest of its total revenue.

Geographic Reach
The Damariscotta-based bank boasts more than 15 branches in Mid-Coast, Eastern, and Down East regions of Maine, in Lincoln, Knox, Hancock, Washington, and Penobscot counties.

Sales and Marketing
The community-oriented bank concentrates on marketing to small businesses and individuals within its local markets.

Financial Performance
The First Bancorp's revenues have slowly declined over the past few years mostly with as its loan business has stagnated and as its interest margins on loans and investments have been shrinking in the low-interest rate environment. Its profits, however, have been steadily rising thanks to declining loan loss provisions as its loan portfolio's credit quality has improved with the strengthened economy.

The company's revenue inched up by less than one-tenth of a percent to $62.07 million in 2014, mostly as the bank carried more interest-earning investment assets during the year. The bank's non-interest income, however, declined by 9% as it collected less from the origination and sale of refinanced mortgage loans into the secondary market.

The First Bancorp's net income jumped by 13% to $14.7 million in 2014, thanks primarily to a continued decline in loan loss provisions as its portfolio's credit quality improved. Slightly higher revenue and lower interest expenses on deposits also helped pad the company's bottom line. The bank's operating cash levels fell by 18% to $20.5 million after adjusting its earnings for non-cash items related to its loan loss provisions and its net proceeds from the sale of its mortgage loans held for sale.

Strategy
As management reiterated in early 2015, remaining well capitalized "remains a top priority for The First Bancorp," and has been key to its profit growth over the past several years. Indeed, its de-risking initiatives for its loan portfolio assets have taken the bank's risk-based capital ratio from 11.13% in 2008 to 16.27% at the end of 2014, well above the FDIC's suggested threshold of 10%. As a result, the bank's loan loss provisions have declined over the period and its profits have blossomed despite a lack of revenue growth.

Company Background
First National Lincoln acquired competitor FNB Bankshares and its First National Bank of Bar Harbor subsidiary in 2005. It merged that bank into its own subsidiary The First National Bank of Damariscotta, which was renamed The First.

EXECUTIVES

Chairman, Director, David B. Soule

President, Chief Executive Officer, Subsidiary Officer, Director, Tony C. McKim, $520,000 total compensation

Executive Vice President, Chief Financial Officer, Subsidiary Officer, Director, F. Stephen Ward, $262,700 total compensation

Executive Vice President, Clerk, Subsidiary Officer, Charles A. Wootton, $256,000 total compensation

Senior Vice President, Carrie H. Kiser

Subsidiary Officer, Tammy L. Plummer

Subsidiary Officer, Steven N. Parady

Subsidiary Officer, Sarah J. Tolman, $182,000 total compensation

Subsidiary Officer, Susan A. Norton, $225,000 total compensation

Subsidiary Officer, Richard M. Elder, $200,000 total compensation

Director, Stuart G. Smith

Director, Renee W. Kelly

Director, Katherine M. Boyd

Director, Bruce B. Tindal

Director, Robert B. Gregory

Director, Mark N. Rosborough

Director, Cornelius J. Russell

Auditors : Berry Dunn McNeil & Parker, LLC

LOCATIONS

HQ: First Bancorp Inc (ME)
  223 Main Street, Damariscotta, ME 04543
Phone: 207 563-3195
Web: www.thefirstbancorp.com

PRODUCTS/OPERATIONS

2007 Sales

	$ mil.	% of total
Interest		
Loans, including fees	60.6	74
Investments & other	11.1	14
Noninterest		
Service charges on deposit accounts	2.7	3
Fiduciary & investment management income	1.1	1
Other	6.4	8
Total	81.9	100

COMPETITORS

CAPITAL BANK FINANCIAL CORP.
FIRST COMMONWEALTH FINANCIAL CORPORATION
FIRST HORIZON CORPORATION
THE FIRST OF LONG ISLAND CORPORATION
WESTAMERICA BANCORPORATION

HISTORICAL FINANCIALS
Company Type: Public

Income Statement   FYE: December 31

	ASSETS ($mil)	NET INCOME ($mil)	INCOME AS % OF ASSETS	EMPLOYEES
12/20	2,361.2	27.1	1.1%	255
12/19	2,068.7	25.5	1.2%	245
12/18	1,944.5	23.5	1.2%	239
12/17	1,842.9	19.5	1.1%	235
12/16	1,712.8	18.0	1.1%	235
Annual Growth	8.4%	10.8%	—	2.1%

First Bancshares Inc (MS)

Hoping to be first in the hearts of its customers, The First Bancshares is the holding company for The First, a community bank with some two dozen branch locations in southern Mississippi's Hattiesburg, Alabama, and Louisiana. The company provides such standard deposit products as checking and savings accounts, NOW and money market accounts, and IRAs. Real estate loans account for about 80% of the bank's lending portfolio, including about equal portions of residential mortgages, commercial mortgages, and construction loans. The bank also writes business loans and consumer loans. The bank, which has expanded beyond Mississippi through several acquisitions, has approximately $970 million in assets.

Mergers and Acquisitions

In April 2013, The First Bancshares acquired First National Bank (FNB) of Baldwin Country, a community bank in Alabama with five branches along the Gulf Coast. The purchase of FNB marked The First's entry into the Alabama market. In 2011, The First expanded into Louisiana and strengthened its hold on southern Mississippi with the acquisition of seven branch banks from Whitney National Bank and one branch from Hancock Bank of Louisiana for an undisclosed amount.

EXECUTIVES

Chairman, Director, E. Ricky Gibson
President, Chief Executive Officer, Subsidiary Officer, Director, M. Ray Cole, $413,063 total compensation
Executive Vice President, Chief Financial Officer, Subsidiary Officer, Donna T. Lowery, $198,687 total compensation
Director, Rodney D. Bennett
Director, David W. Bomboy
Director, Thomas E. Mitchell
Director, Renee Moore
Director, Charles R. Lightsey
Director, Fred A. McMurry
Director, Ted E. Parker
Director, J. Douglas Seidenburg
Director, Andrew D. Stetelman
Auditors: Crowe LLP

LOCATIONS

HQ: First Bancshares Inc (MS)
6480 U.S. Highway 98 West, Suite A, Hattiesburg, MS 39402
Phone: 601 268-8998
Web: www.thefirstbank.com

COMPETITORS

HOME BANCORP, INC.
OLD NATIONAL BANCORP
SIMMONS FIRST NATIONAL CORPORATION
SOUTHWEST BANCORP, INC.
TRUIST FINANCIAL CORPORATION

HISTORICAL FINANCIALS

Company Type: Public

Income Statement — FYE: December 31

	ASSETS ($mil)	NET INCOME ($mil)	INCOME AS % OF ASSETS	EMPLOYEES
12/20	5,152.7	52.5	1.0%	744
12/19	3,941.8	43.7	1.1%	697
12/18	3,003.9	21.2	0.7%	641
12/17	1,813.2	10.6	0.6%	487
12/16	1,277.3	10.1	0.8%	315
Annual Growth	41.7%	50.9%	—	24.0%

2020 Year-End Financials

Return on assets: 1.1%
Return on equity: 8.8%
Long-term debt ($ mil.): —
No. of shares ($ mil.): 21.1
Sales ($ mil.): 221.2
Dividends Yield: 1.3%
Payout: 16.6%
Market value ($ mil.): 652.0

	STOCK PRICE ($) FY Close	P/E High	P/E Low	PER SHARE ($) Earnings	Dividends	Book Value
12/20	30.88	14	6	2.52	0.42	30.54
12/19	35.52	14	11	2.55	0.31	28.91
12/18	30.25	25	17	1.62	0.20	24.49
12/17	34.20	31	24	1.11	0.15	19.92
12/16	27.50	15	8	1.64	0.15	17.19
Annual Growth	2.9%	—	—	11.3%	29.4%	15.5%

First Bank (Williamstown, NJ)

EXECUTIVES

Chairman, Patrick M. Ryan
Vice-Chairman, Leslie E. Goodman
President, Chief Executive Officer, Director, Patrick L. Ryan
Executive Vice President, Chief Financial Officer, Treasurer, Stephen F. Carman
Executive Vice President, Chief Lending Officer, Peter J. Cahill
Director, Elbert G. Basolis
Director, Samuel D. Marrazzo
Director, Gary S. Hofing
Director, Deborah Hanson Imperatore
Director, Anthony J. Cimino
Director, Peter D. Halstead
Director, Maria K. Jinks
Director, Glenn M. Josephs
Director, Raymond Nisivoccia
Director, John E. Strydesky
Auditors: RSM US LLP

LOCATIONS

HQ: First Bank (Williamstown, NJ)
2465 Kuser Road, Hamilton, NJ 08690
Phone: 877 821-2265
Web: www.firstbanknj.com

HISTORICAL FINANCIALS

Company Type: Public

Income Statement — FYE: December 31

	ASSETS ($mil)	NET INCOME ($mil)	INCOME AS % OF ASSETS	EMPLOYEES
12/20	2,346.2	19.4	0.8%	207
12/19	2,011.5	13.4	0.7%	221
12/18	1,711.1	17.5	1.0%	188
12/17	1,452.3	6.9	0.5%	153
12/16	1,073.2	6.4	0.6%	110
Annual Growth	21.6%	32.0%	—	17.1%

2020 Year-End Financials

Return on assets: 0.8%
Return on equity: 8.3%
Long-term debt ($ mil.): —
No. of shares ($ mil.): 19.7
Sales ($ mil.): 95.5
Dividends Yield: 1.2%
Payout: 12.3%
Market value ($ mil.): 185.0

	STOCK PRICE ($) FY Close	P/E High	P/E Low	PER SHARE ($) Earnings	Dividends	Book Value
12/20	9.38	11	6	0.97	0.12	12.08
12/19	11.05	17	15	0.69	0.12	11.07
12/18	12.12	15	12	0.95	0.12	10.43
12/17	13.85	30	23	0.48	0.08	9.36
12/16	11.60	20	10	0.61	0.00	7.78
Annual Growth	(5.2%)	—	—	12.3%	—	11.6%

First Busey Corp

First Busey conducts banking, related banking services, asset management, brokerage, and fiduciary services through its wholly-owned bank subsidiary, Busey Bank, which boasts approximately $10.2 billion in assets and about 70 branches across Illinois, Florida, Missouri, and Indiana. The bank offers a range of diversified financial products and services for consumers and businesses, including online and mobile banking capabilities. Its primary sources of income are interest and fees on loans and investments, wealth management fees and service fees. Subsidiary FirsTech provides retail payment processing services. Most of Busey Bank's branches are located in downstate Illinois.

Operations

2020 Year-End Financials (top-left continuation)

Return on assets: 1.2%
Return on equity: 12.4%
Long-term debt ($ mil.): —
No. of shares ($ mil.): 10.9
Sales ($ mil.): 95.2
Dividends Yield: 4.8%
Payout: 49.1%
Market value ($ mil.): 278.0

	STOCK PRICE ($) FY Close	P/E High	P/E Low	PER SHARE ($) Earnings	Dividends	Book Value
12/20	25.40	12	7	2.48	1.22	20.43
12/19	30.23	13	10	2.34	1.18	19.50
12/18	26.30	14	11	2.17	1.06	17.63
12/17	27.23	18	14	1.81	1.06	16.74
12/16	33.10	20	11	1.66	0.90	15.98
Annual Growth	(6.4%)	—	—	10.6%	7.9%	6.3%

First Busey manages its operations through three operating segments consisting of Banking, Remittance Processing, and Wealth Management. The Banking operating segment (about 95%) provides a full range of banking services to individual and corporate customers through its banking center network in Illinois; the St. Louis, Missouri metropolitan area; southwest Florida; and through its banking center in Indianapolis, Indiana. The Remittance Processing operating segment (nearly 5%) provides solutions for online bill payments, lockbox, and walk-in payments. The Wealth Management operating segment (about 5%) provides a full range of asset management, investment, and fiduciary services to individuals, businesses, and foundations, tax preparation, philanthropic advisory services, and farm and brokerage services.

The company's lending can be summarized into five primary areas: commercial loans, commercial real estate loans, real estate construction loans, retail real estate loans, and retail other loans. Commercial loans typically comprise working capital loans or business expansion loans, including loans for asset purchases and other business loans. Commercial real estate loans are subject to underwriting standards and guidelines similar to commercial loans. Real estate construction loans are primarily commercial in nature. Retail real estate loans are comprised of direct consumer loans that include residential real estate, home equity lines of credit, and home equity loans. Retail other loans consist of installment loans to individuals, including automotive loans.

Busey Bank's commercial services include commercial, commercial real estate, real estate construction, and agricultural loans, as well as commercial depository services such as cash management. Retail banking services include residential real estate, home equity lines of credit and consumer loans, customary types of demand and savings deposits, money transfers, safe deposit services, and IRA and other fiduciary services through our banking center, ATM, and technology-based networks. Brokerage-related services are offered by Busey Investment Services, a division of Busey Bank, through a third-party arrangement with Raymond James Financial Services. In addition, Busey Bank provides professional farm management and brokerage services to the agricultural industry.

About 70% of First Busey's total revenue came from net interest income. The rest of its revenue came from non-interest income (nearly 30%).

Geographic Reach
Busey Bank has nearly 55 branches in Illinois, four locations in southwest Florida, 10 in Missouri, and another office in Indianapolis. Its FirsTech subsidiary accepts payments from its approximately 5,800 agent locations across the US.

Sales and Marketing
First Busey serves individuals, businesses and foundations.

Financial Performance
The company's net interest income for the year 2020 was $282.9 million, a 1% decrease from the previous year's net interest income of $287.2 million.

In 2020, the company had a net income of $100.3 million, a 3% decline from the previous year's net income of $103 million. Decline in net income were due to lower performances from the Banking and Wealth Management segments.

The company's cash at the end of 2020 was $529.3 million. Operating activities generated $169.3 million, while investing activities used $735.7 million, primarily for purchases of debt securities available for sale. Financing activities provided another $725.6 million.

Mergers and Acquisitions
In mid-2021, First Busey acquired Cummins-American, the holding company for Glenview State Bank. This partnership benefits the company's clients through enhanced capabilities and products while a growing, dynamic organization presents more professional growth opportunities for associates. It enhances Busey's existing deposit, commercial banking and wealth management presence in the Chicago-Naperville-Elgin, IL-IN-WI Metropolitan Statistical Area (MSA). Each share of CAC common stock was converted into the right to receive 444.4783 First Busey common stock shares and $14,173.96 in cash. The transaction carried an aggregate value of nearly $187 million.

EXECUTIVES
Vice-Chairman, Gregory B. Lykins
President, Chief Executive Officer, Subsidiary Officer, Director, Van A. Dukeman, $634,423 total compensation
Executive Vice President, Chief Credit Officer, Subsidiary Officer, Region Officer, Robert F. Plecki, $319,808 total compensation
Executive Vice President, Chief Accounting Officer, Jennifer L. Simons
Chief Information Officer, Leanne C. Kopischke, $219,615 total compensation
Chief Financial Officer, Jeffrey D. Jones
General Counsel, John J. Powers, $248,500 total compensation
Subsidiary Officer, Region Officer, Christopher M. Shroyer, $319,808 total compensation
Division Officer, Amy L. Randolph, $284,422 total compensation
Subsidiary Officer, Howard F. Mooney, $250,000 total compensation
Director, George R. Barr
Director, Stanley J. Bradshaw
Director, Michael D. Cassens
Director, David J. Downey
Director, Karen M. Jensen
Director, Frederic L. Kenney
Director, Stephen V. King
Director, George T. Shapland
Director, Thomas G. Sloan
Auditors : RSM US LLP

LOCATIONS
HQ: First Busey Corp
100 W. University Avenue, Champaign, IL 61820
Phone: 217 365-4544

PRODUCTS/OPERATIONS
2014 Sales

	$ mil.	% of total
Interest		
Loans, including fees	92.4	55
Interest & dividends on securities	15.7	10
Noninterest		
Trust fees	19.6	11
Service charges on deposit accounts	12.0	7
Remittance processing	9.4	6
Gain on sales of loans	4.7	3
Commissions and broker's fees, net	2.7	2
Other	10.5	6
Total	167	100

COMPETITORS
ASSOCIATED BANC-CORP
BOKF MERGER CORPORATION NUMBER SIXTEEN
CENTRAL PACIFIC FINANCIAL CORP.
COMMERCE BANCSHARES, INC.
FIRSTMERIT CORPORATION
FIRSTRUST SAVINGS BANK
INDEPENDENT BANK CORP.
MACATAWA BANK CORPORATION
STOCK YARDS BANCORP, INC.
UNIVEST FINANCIAL CORPORATION

HISTORICAL FINANCIALS
Company Type: Public

Income Statement — FYE: December 31

	ASSETS ($mil)	NET INCOME ($mil)	INCOME AS % OF ASSETS	EMPLOYEES
12/20	10,544.0	100.3	1.0%	1,346
12/19	9,695.7	102.9	1.1%	1,531
12/18	7,702.3	98.9	1.3%	1,270
12/17	7,860.6	62.7	0.8%	1,347
12/16	5,425.1	49.6	0.9%	1,295
Annual Growth	18.1%	19.2%	—	1.0%

2020 Year-End Financials
Return on assets: 0.9%
Return on equity: 8.0%
Long-term debt ($ mil.): —
No. of shares ($ mil.): 54.4
Sales ($ mil.): 444.8
Dividends
Yield: 4.0%
Payout: 48.0%
Market value ($ mil.): 1,172.0

	STOCK PRICE ($) FY Close	P/E High	P/E Low	Earnings	Dividends	Book Value
12/20	21.55	15	8	1.83	0.88	23.34
12/19	27.50	15	13	1.87	0.84	22.28
12/18	24.54	16	12	2.01	0.80	20.36
12/17	29.94	22	19	1.45	0.72	19.21
12/16	30.78	22	13	1.40	0.68	15.54
Annual Growth	(8.5%)	—	—	6.9%	6.7%	10.7%

First Commonwealth Financial Corp (Indiana, PA)

First Commonwealth Financial is the holding company for First Commonwealth Bank, which provides consumer and commercial banking services about 120 bank offices throughout central and western Pennsylvania counties as well as in Columbus, Ohio. The bank's loan portfolio mostly consists of commercial and industrial loans, including real estate, operating, agricultural, and construction loans. It also issues consumer loans such as automobile, and home equity loans, and offers wealth management, insurance, financial planning, retail brokerage, and trust services. The company has total assets of some $9.1 billion with deposits of roughly $7.4 billion.

EXECUTIVES

Chairman, Subsidiary Officer, Lead Director, Director, David S. Dahlmann
President, Chief Executive Officer, Subsidiary Officer, Director, T. Michael Price, $471,667 total compensation
Executive Vice President, Chief Financial Officer, Treasurer, Subsidiary Officer, James R. Reske, $387,667 total compensation
Executive Vice President, Chief Revenue Officer, Subsidiary Officer, Director, Jane Grebenc, $435,667 total compensation
Executive Vice President, Chief Risk Officer, General Counsel, Secretary, Matthew C. Tomb, $314,167 total compensation
Human Resources Executive Vice President, Carrie L. Riggle
Executive Vice President, Chief Audit Executive, Leonard V. Lombardi
Executive Vice President, Chief Credit Officer, Subsidiary Officer, Brian G. Karrip, $365,667 total compensation
Subsidiary Officer, Norman J. Montgomery, $287,334 total compensation
Director, Julie A. Caponi
Director, Ray T. Charley
Director, Gary R. Claus
Director, Johnston A. Glass, $370,000 total compensation
Director, Jon L. Gorney
Director, David W. Greenfield
Director, Bart E. Johnson
Director, Luke A. Latimer
Director, Aradhna M. Oliphant
Director, Robert J. Ventura
Director, Stephen A. Wolfe
Auditors : Ernst & Young LLP

LOCATIONS

HQ: First Commonwealth Financial Corp (Indiana, PA)
601 Philadelphia Street, Indiana, PA 15701
Phone: 724 349-7220
Web: www.fcbanking.com

PRODUCTS/OPERATIONS

2014 Sales

	$ mil.	% of total
Interest		
Loans, including fees	171.2	65
Taxable investments	31.0	12
Noninterest		
Service charges on deposit accounts	15.7	7
Insurance & retail brokerage commissions	6.5	2
Trust income	6.0	2
Others	32.6	12
Total	263	100

Selected Subsidiaries
First Commonwealth Bank
    First Commonwealth Insurance Agency
    First Commonwealth Home Mortgage, LLC (49.9%)
First Commonwealth Financial Advisors Incorporated

COMPETITORS

CAMDEN NATIONAL CORPORATION
CAPITAL BANK FINANCIAL CORP.
CITY HOLDING COMPANY
EAGLE BANCORP, INC.
FIRST FINANCIAL BANCORP.
FIRST HORIZON CORPORATION
FIRST MIDWEST BANCORP, INC.
FIRSTMERIT CORPORATION
OLD NATIONAL BANCORP
S&T BANCORP, INC.

HISTORICAL FINANCIALS
Company Type: Public

Income Statement — FYE: December 31

	ASSETS ($mil)	NET INCOME ($mil)	INCOME AS % OF ASSETS	EMPLOYEES
12/20	9,068.1	73.4	0.8%	1,393
12/19	8,308.7	105.3	1.3%	1,571
12/18	7,828.2	107.4	1.4%	1,512
12/17	7,308.5	55.1	0.8%	1,476
12/16	6,684.0	59.5	0.9%	1,376
Annual Growth	7.9%	5.4%	—	0.3%

2020 Year-End Financials
Return on assets: 0.8%
Return on equity: 6.8%
Long-term debt ($ mil.): —
No. of shares ($ mil.): 96.1
Sales ($ mil.): 395.6
Dividends
Yield: 4.0%
Payout: 58.6%
Market value ($ mil.): 1,052.0

	STOCK PRICE ($) FY Close	P/E High	P/E Low	PER SHARE ($) Earnings	Dividends	Book Value
12/20	10.94	19	9	0.75	0.44	11.12
12/19	14.51	14	11	1.07	0.40	10.74
12/18	12.08	16	10	1.08	0.35	9.90
12/17	14.32	26	21	0.58	0.32	9.11
12/16	14.18	21	12	0.67	0.28	8.43
Annual Growth	(6.3%)	—	—	2.9%	12.0%	7.2%

First Community Corp (SC)

Putting first things first, First Community is the holding company for First Community Bank, which serves individuals and smaller businesses in central South Carolina. Through about a dozen offices, the bank, which was founded in 1995, offers such products and services as checking and savings accounts, money market accounts, CDs, IRAs, credit cards, insurance, and investment services. Commercial mortgages make up about 60% of First Community Bank's loan portfolio, which also includes residential mortgages and business, consumer, and construction loans. The company's First Community Financial Consultants division offers asset management and estate planning. First Community is merging with Cornerstone Bancorp, expanding its presence in upstate SC.

EXECUTIVES

Chairman, Subsidiary Officer, Director, J. Thomas Johnson, $142,786 total compensation
Vice-Chairman, Subsidiary Officer, Director, Chimin J. Chao
President, Chief Executive Officer, Subsidiary Officer, Director, Michael C. Crapps, $410,117 total compensation
Executive Vice President, Chief Financial Officer, Subsidiary Officer, Donald Shawn Jordan
Chief Human Resources Officer, Chief Marketing Officer, Subsidiary Officer, Robin D. Brown
Chief Commercial Officer, Chief Retail Banking Officer, Subsidiary Officer, John Ted Nissen, $238,000 total compensation
Chief Risk Officer, Chief Operation Officer, Subsidiary Officer, Tanya A. Butts
Chief Credit Officer, Subsidiary Officer, John F. Walker
Director, Ray E. Jones
Director, Jan H. Hollar
Director, E. Leland Reynolds
Director, Alexander Snipe
Director, Mickey E Layden
Director, Jane S. Sosebee
Director, Thomas C. Brown
Director, Edward J. Tarver
Director, Roderick M. Todd
Director, W. James Kitchens
Auditors : Elliott Davis, LLC

LOCATIONS

HQ: First Community Corp (SC)
5455 Sunset Boulevard, Lexington, SC 29072
Phone: 803 951-2265
Web: www.firstcommunitysc.com

COMPETITORS

CHOICEONE FINANCIAL SERVICES, INC.
COMMUNITY SHORES BANK CORPORATION
EASTERN VIRGINIA BANKSHARES, INC.
FIRST NATIONAL CORPORATION
SOUTHCOAST FINANCIAL CORPORATION

HISTORICAL FINANCIALS
Company Type: Public

Income Statement — FYE: December 31

	ASSETS ($mil)	NET INCOME ($mil)	INCOME AS % OF ASSETS	EMPLOYEES
12/20	1,395.3	10.0	0.7%	244
12/19	1,170.2	10.9	0.9%	242
12/18	1,091.5	11.2	1.0%	226
12/17	1,050.7	5.8	0.6%	224
12/16	914.7	6.6	0.7%	202
Annual Growth	11.1%	10.9%	—	4.8%

2020 Year-End Financials
Return on assets: 0.7%
Return on equity: 7.8%
Long-term debt ($ mil.): —
No. of shares ($ mil.): 7.5
Sales ($ mil.): 57.5
Dividends
 Yield: 2.8%
 Payout: 35.5%
Market value ($ mil.): 127.0

	STOCK PRICE ($) FY Close	P/E High/Low		PER SHARE ($) Earnings	Dividends	Book Value
12/20	16.99	16	9	1.35	0.48	18.18
12/19	21.61	15	12	1.45	0.44	16.16
12/18	19.43	18	13	1.45	0.40	14.73
12/17	22.60	29	21	0.83	0.36	13.93
12/16	18.05	19	13	0.98	0.32	12.20
Annual Growth	(1.5%)	—	—	8.3%	10.7%	10.5%

First Farmers Financial Corp

EXECUTIVES
Subsidiary Officer, Director, Mark A. Holt
President, Chief Executive Officer, Subsidiary Officer, Director, Gene E. Miles
Auditors : BKD, LLP

LOCATIONS
HQ: First Farmers Financial Corp
 123 North Jefferson Street, Converse, IN 46919
Phone: 765 395-3316
Web: www.ffbt.com

HISTORICAL FINANCIALS
Company Type: Public

Income Statement — FYE: December 31

	REVENUE ($mil)	NET INCOME ($mil)	NET PROFIT MARGIN	EMPLOYEES
12/20	108.0	30.4	28.2%	0
12/19	103.5	29.5	28.5%	0
12/18	94.5	27.7	29.3%	0
12/17	82.3	21.7	26.4%	0
12/16	74.9	17.0	22.7%	0
Annual Growth	9.6%	15.6%	—	—

2020 Year-End Financials
Debt ratio: 9.4%
Return on equity: 14.4%
Cash ($ mil.): 191.3
Current Ratio: 0.11
Long-term debt ($ mil.): 208.5
No. of shares ($ mil.): 7.0
Dividends
 Yield: 2.9%
 Payout: 31.6%
Market value ($ mil.): 309.0

	STOCK PRICE ($) FY Close	P/E High/Low		PER SHARE ($) Earnings	Dividends	Book Value
12/20	43.71	11	10	4.29	1.29	31.30
12/19	47.01	11	10	4.13	1.22	27.78
12/18	42.00	22	11	3.87	1.02	24.03
12/17	71.50	26	20	3.04	0.69	21.44
12/16	65.00	27	27	2.38	0.65	18.94
Annual Growth	(9.4%)	—	—	15.9%	18.9%	13.4%

First Financial Bancorp (OH)

The holding company's flagship subsidiary, First Financial Bank, operates about 140 banking centers in Ohio, Indiana, Kentucky, and Illinois. Founded in 1863, the banking services provided by the bank include commercial lending, real estate lending and consumer financing. Real estate loans are loans secured by a mortgage lien on the real property of the borrower, which may either be residential property (one to four family residential housing units) or commercial property (owner-occupied and/or investor income producing real estate, such as apartments, shopping centers, or office buildings). Commercial loans, including real estate and construction loans, make up more than 50% of First Financial's total loan portfolio; the bank also offers residential mortgage and commercial and industrial loans. First Financial Bancorp boasts some $16.3 billion in assets, including nearly $9.2 billion in loans.

Operations
The company's private banking business, First Financial Wealth Management, had some $16.3 billion in assets under management in 2021.

First Financial provides banking and financial services products to business and retail clients through its six lines of business: Commercial, Retail Banking, Mortgage Banking, Wealth Management, Investment Commercial Real Estate and Commercial Finance. Commercial Finance provides equipment and leasehold improvement financing for franchisees in the quick service and casual dining restaurant sector and commission-based financing, primarily to insurance agents and brokers, throughout the United States. Wealth Management had $3.4 billion in assets under management and provides the following services: financial planning, investment management, trust administration, estate settlement, brokerage services and retirement planning.

Overall, net interest income generates about 75% of company's total revenue. Its loan portfolio includes commercial real estate (some 45%), commercial & industrial (about 30%), and residential real estate (some 10%).

Geographic Reach
The company operates some 140 full service banking centers. Its core banking operating markets are located within the four state region of Ohio, Indiana, Kentucky and Illinois. First Financial's executive office is a leased facility located in Cincinnati, Ohio and it operates over 60 banking centers in Ohio, three banking centers in Illinois, more than 60 banking centers in Indiana and over 10 banking centers in Kentucky.

In addition, the company operates its Commercial Finance division, responsible for its insurance lending business and franchise lending business, from a non-banking center location in Indiana.

Sales and Marketing
First Financial spent $8.0 million, $6.4 million, and $6.9 million on marketing in fiscal years 2021, 2020, and 2019, respectively.

Financial Performance
Net interest income decreased $4.4 million, or 1%, from $456.5 million in 2020 to $452.1 million in 2021, as interest rates declined and purchase accounting accretion moderated during 2021.

In 2021, the company had a net income of $205.2 million, a 32% increase from the previous year's net income of $155.8 million.

The company's cash at the end of 2021 was $220 million. Operating activities generated $390.5 million, while investing activities used $512.3 million, mainly for purchases of securities available-for-sale. Financing activities provided another $110.8 million.

Strategy
First Financial aims to develop a competitive advantage by utilizing a local market focus to provide superior service and build long-term relationships with clients while helping them achieve greater financial success. First Financial serves a combination of metropolitan and community markets in Ohio, Indiana, Kentucky and Illinois through its full-service banking centers, and provides financing to franchise owners and clients within the financial services industry throughout the United States. First Financial's investment in community markets is an important part of the Bank's core funding base and has historically provided stable, low-cost funding sources.

First Financial intends to concentrate plans for future growth and capital investment within its current metropolitan markets, and will continue to evaluate additional growth opportunities in metropolitan markets located within, or in close proximity to, the company's current geographic footprint. Additionally, First Financial may assess strategic acquisitions that provide product line extensions or additional industry verticals that complement its existing business and diversify its product suite and revenue streams.

Company Background

In the past, the bank acquired 16 branches in western Ohio from Liberty Savings Bank and bought 22 Indianapolis-area branches from Flagstar Bank in 2011. Together the two acquisitions furthered the bank's growth strategy for the key markets of Dayton and Indianapolis.

EXECUTIVES

Chairman, Subsidiary Officer, Director, Claude E. Davis, $776,899 total compensation
President, Chief Executive Officer, Subsidiary Officer, Director, Archie M. Brown, $588,312 total compensation
Chief Financial Officer, Subsidiary Officer, James M. Anderson, $273,846 total compensation
Chief Operating Officer, Subsidiary Officer, Division Officer, John M. Gavigan, $310,539 total compensation
General Counsel, Chief Risk Officer, Subsidiary Officer, Karen B. Woods, $240,846 total compensation
Chief Corporate Banking Officer, Division Officer, Richard S. Dennen, $399,900 total compensation
Division Officer, Andy Hauck
Director, William G. Barron
Director, Vincent A. Berta
Director, Cynthia O. Booth
Director, Susan L. Knust
Director, William J. Kramer
Director, Thomas M. O'Brien
Director, Maribeth S. Rahe
Auditors: Crowe LLP

LOCATIONS

HQ: First Financial Bancorp (OH)
255 East Fifth Street, Suite 800, Cincinnati, OH 45202
Phone: 877 322-9530
Web: www.bankatfirst.com

PRODUCTS/OPERATIONS

2014 Sales

	$ mil.	% of total
Interest		
Loans, including fees	208.8	66
Investment securities	44.5	14
(Adjustment)	(5.5)	-
Noninterest		
Service charges on deposit accounts	20.3	7
Trust and wealth management fees	13.6	5
Bankcard income	10.7	3
Net gains from sales on loans	4.4	1
Accelerated discount on covered/formerly covered loans	4.2	1
Others	10.8	3
Total	311.8	100

COMPETITORS

CAPITAL BANK FINANCIAL CORP.
CENTERSTATE BANK CORPORATION
CNB FINANCIAL CORPORATION
FIRST COMMONWEALTH FINANCIAL CORPORATION
FIRST FINANCIAL CORPORATION
FIRST MIDWEST BANCORP, INC.
MAINSOURCE FINANCIAL GROUP, INC.
OLD LINE BANCSHARES, INC.
S&T BANCORP, INC.
STATE BANK FINANCIAL CORPORATION

HISTORICAL FINANCIALS

Company Type: Public

Income Statement — FYE: December 31

	ASSETS ($mil.)	NET INCOME ($mil.)	INCOME AS % OF ASSETS	EMPLOYEES
12/21	16,329.1	205.1	1.3%	2,010
12/20	15,973.1	155.8	1.0%	2,107
12/19	14,511.6	198.0	1.4%	2,123
12/18	13,986.6	172.5	1.2%	2,131
12/17	8,896.9	96.7	1.1%	1,366
Annual Growth	16.4%	20.7%	—	10.1%

2021 Year-End Financials

Return on assets: 1.2%
Return on equity: 9.0%
Long-term debt ($ mil.): —
No. of shares ($ mil.): 94.1
Sales ($ mil.): 654.7
Dividends
Yield: 3.7%
Payout: 43.3%
Market value ($ mil.): 2,295.0

	STOCK PRICE ($) FY Close	P/E High	P/E Low	Earnings	Dividends	Book Value
12/21	24.38	12	8	2.14	0.92	23.99
12/20	17.53	16	7	1.59	0.92	23.28
12/19	25.44	14	11	2.00	0.90	22.82
12/18	23.72	17	11	1.93	0.78	21.23
12/17	26.35	19	15	1.56	0.68	14.99
Annual Growth	(1.9%)	—	—	8.2%	7.8%	12.5%

First Financial Bankshares, Inc.

First Financial Bankshares is a financial holding company that through its subsidiary, First Financial Bank (the bank), operates multiple banking regions with around 80 locations in Texas. The bank provides general commercial banking services, which include accepting and holding checking, savings and time deposits, making loans, offering automated teller machines (ATMs), drive-in and night deposit services, safe deposit facilities, remote deposit capture, internet banking, mobile banking, payroll cards, transmitting funds, and performing other customary commercial banking services. The company also provide full-service trust and wealth management activities through its trust company, First Financial Trust & Asset Management. First Financial has a total assets of $13.3 billion.

Operations

First Financial's banking arm, First Financial Bank, provides general commercial banking services, which include accepting and holding checking, savings and time deposits, making loans, offering automated teller machines (ATMs), drive-in and night deposit services, safe deposit facilities, remote deposit capture, internet banking, mobile banking, payroll cards, transmitting funds, and performing other customary commercial banking services. In addition, it provide securities brokerage services through an arrangement with an unrelated third-party in its Abilene and San Angelo regions.

The company also provide full-service trust and wealth management activities through its trust company, First Financial Trust & Asset Management. It offer personal trust services, which include wealth management, the administration of estates, testamentary trusts, revocable and irrevocable trusts and agency accounts. It also administer all types of retirement and employee benefit accounts, which include 401(k) profit sharing plans and IRAs.

Broadly speaking, First Financial gets more than 70% of its revenue from interest income (about 50% from loan interest and fees and around 20% from investment securities). The rest of its revenue comes from trust fee income, ATM, interchange and credit card fees, deposit account service charges, mortgage banking sales, and other miscellaneous income sources.

Geographic Reach

Texas-based First Financial owns some 80 banking, trust and mortgage facilities, some of which are detached drive-ins, and also lease around 15 banking facilities and 15 ATM locations.

Financial Performance

The company reported a net interest income of $370.4 million, a 6% increase from the previous year's net interest income of $349.9 million. This was primarily due to a higher volume of interest and fees on loans for the year.

In 2021, the company had a net income of $227.6 million, a 13% increase from the previous year's net income of $164.8 million.

The company's cash at the end of 2021 was $528.6 million. Operating activities generated $353.2 million, while investing activities used $2.6 billion, mainly for purchases of available-for-sale securities and other investments. Financing activities provided another $2.1 billion.

EXECUTIVES

President, Chief Executive Officer, Subsidiary Officer, Chairman, Director, F. Scott Dueser, $920,833 total compensation
Executive Vice President, Chief Accounting Officer, Subsidiary Officer, J. Kyle McVey
Executive Vice President, Chief Risk Officer, Subsidiary Officer, Randy Roewe
Executive Vice President, Chief Information Officer, Subsidiary Officer, John J. Ruzicka
Executive Vice President, Chief Administrative Officer, Subsidiary Officer, Ronald David Butler, $446,667 total compensation
Executive Vice President, Chief Financial Officer, Michelle S. Hickox

Executive Vice President, Chief Lending Officer, Chief Credit Officer, Subsidiary Officer, T. Luke Longhofer
Subsidiary Officer, Kirk W. Thaxton, $466,667 total compensation
Division Officer, David W. Bailey
Lead Independent Director, Director, Murray Edwards
Director, April Anthony
Director, Vianei Lopez Braun
Director, David L. Copeland
Director, Mike B. Denny
Director, Eli Jones
Director, Kade L. Matthews
Director, Robert C. Nickles
Director, Johnny E. Trotter
Director, Ivan Tim Lancaster
Auditors : Ernst & Young LLP

LOCATIONS

HQ: First Financial Bankshares, Inc.
400 Pine Street, Abilene, TX 79601
Phone: 325 627-7155
Web: www.ffin.com

PRODUCTS/OPERATIONS

2015 sales

	$ mil.	% of total
Interest Income		
Interest and fees on loans	151.7	51
Interest on investment securities	69.7	24
Interest on federal funds sold and interest-bearing deposits in banks	0.2	—
Non-Interest Income		
ATM, interchange and credit card fees	21.9	7
Trust fees	19.2	6
Service charges on deposit accounts	17.2	6
Real estate mortgage operations	10.4	4
Net gain on sale of available-for-sale securities	0.5	—
Net gain on sale of foreclosed assets	0.5	—
Net loss on sale of assets	(0.8)	—
Other	4.6	2
Total	**295.1**	**100**

Products/ServicesPersonal
Learn
Online Banking
Mobile Banking
Consumer Education
FAQS
Privacy & Security Information
Resources
Testimonials
Tools
Bank
Checking
Savings
Invest
CDS & IRAS
Broker Services
Borrow
Mortgage Loans
Mortgage Lenders
Auto Loans
Recreational Loans
Home Equity Loans
Personal Line of Credit
CD Secured Loans
Banking with First Financial
Mobile Banking
Online Banking
Pay Bills
Get Cash
Make Deposit

Move Money
Keep Track
Business
Learn
Online Banking
Mobile Banking
Business Education
Starting your Business
Growing your Business
Tools
Business Banking Services
Manage Cash
Send Payments
Receive Payments
Manage Fraud and Risk
Other Services
Trust & Wealth Management
Investment Management
Trust Management
Estate Management
Oil & Gas Management
Real Estate and Property Management
Company Retirement Plans

Selected Subsidiaries

First Financial Bank, National Association, Abilene, Texas.
First Technology Services, Inc., Abilene, Texas (wholly owned subsidiary of First Financial Bank, National Association, Abilene, Texas).
First Financial Trust & Asset Management Company, National Association, Abilene, Texas.
First Financial Insurance Agency, Inc., Abilene, Texas.
First Financial Investments, Inc., Abilene, Texas.

COMPETITORS

AIG RETIREMENT SERVICES
BENEFITMALL INC.
Baillie Gifford & Co
CADENCE BANCORP LLC
CIVISTA BANCSHARES, INC.
FIFTH THIRD BANCORP
NORTHERN TRUST CORPORATION
SB FINANCIAL GROUP, INC.
SYNOVUS FINANCIAL CORP.
THE BANK OF NEW YORK MELLON CORPORATION

HISTORICAL FINANCIALS

Company Type: Public

Income Statement   FYE: December 31

	ASSETS ($mil)	NET INCOME ($mil)	INCOME AS % OF ASSETS	EMPLOYEES
12/21	13,102.4	227.5	1.7%	1,500
12/20	10,904.5	202.0	1.9%	1,500
12/19	8,262.2	164.8	2.0%	1,345
12/18	7,731.8	150.6	1.9%	1,350
12/17	7,254.7	120.3	1.7%	1,300
Annual Growth	15.9%	17.3%	—	3.6%

2021 Year-End Financials

Return on assets: 1.8%
Return on equity: 13.2%
Long-term debt ($ mil.): —
No. of shares ($ mil.): 141.6
Sales ($ mil.): 518.5
Dividends
Yield: 1.1%
Payout: 36.0%
Market value ($ mil.): 7,199.0

	STOCK PRICE ($) FY Close	P/E High/Low		PER SHARE ($) Earnings	Dividends	Book Value
12/21	50.84	34	22	1.59	0.58	12.42
12/20	36.18	25	17	1.42	0.51	11.88
12/19	35.10	53	24	1.21	0.47	9.09
12/18	57.69	60	40	1.11	0.41	7.83
12/17	45.05	53	41	0.91	0.38	7.02
Annual Growth	3.1%	—	—	15.1%	11.5%	15.4%

First Financial Northwest Inc

Searching for green in The Evergreen State, First Financial Northwest is the holding company for First Financial Northwest Bank (formerly First Savings Bank Northwest). The small community bank offers deposit services like checking and savings accounts, and a variety of lending services to customers in western Washington. Almost 40% of First Savings Bank's loan portfolio consists of one- to four-family residential loans, while commercial real estate loans made up another 35%. Because the bank focuses almost exclusively on real estate loans, it writes very few unsecured consumer and commercial loans.

Operations

About 17% of First Financial Northwest Bank's loan portfolio was comprised of multi-family mortgage loans, while construction/land development loans made up 7%. Less than 2% of the bank's portfolio was made up of business and consumer loans.

The bank generated 93% of its total revenue from loan interest (including fees) in 2014, and another 6% came from interest on its investments available-for-sale.

Geographic Reach

Renton-based First Financial Northwest Bank's one branch office primarily serves King county, as well as Pierce, Snohomish, and Kitsap counties (to a lesser extent) in the western part of Washington State.

Financial Performance

First Financial Northwest's revenues have been in decline in recent years due to shrinking interest margins on loans amidst the low-interest environment. The firm's profits, however, have trended thanks to declining loan loss provisions as its loan portfolio's credit quality has improved with the strengthened housing market and overall economy.

The company's revenue remained mostly flat around $39.2 million in 2014 with slightly higher interest income as it grew its loan business, but with slightly lower non-interest income as it had sold an investment property for a $325,000 gain in 2013.

First Financial's net income plummeted by 56% to $10.7 million despite stable revenue in 2014, mostly because it had collected a (non-recurring) $13.5 million tax benefit in 2013 (compared to a tax expense of $5.9 million in 2014) after a reversal of its deferred tax asset valuation allowance. Not counting this event, the company's before-tax profit grew by more than 50% as its operational expenses fell and its loan loss provisions continued to decline. First Financial's operating levels rose by 22% to $18.6 million thanks to higher cash earnings.

Strategy

First Financial Northwest's long-term business strategy is to grow First Financial Northwest Bank "as a well-capitalized and profitable community bank" with continued focus on one-to-four family residential loans and commercial real estate loans. It also planned in 2015 to promote its "diversified array" of deposit, loan, and other products and services to individuals and businesses, highlighting its locality in its target Puget Sound regional market.

To ensure low-cost funding sources, the bank in 2015 planned to continue using wholesale funding sources from Federal Home Loan Bank advances, and acquired deposits in the national brokered certificate of deposit market. To minimize risk, it would continue to diversify its loan types and manage its loss-invoking credit risk and diminish interest rate risk to keep its interest margins up.

The bank in 2015 also expected to improve profitability through "disciplined pricing, expense control, and balance sheet management, while continuing to provide excellent customer service."

Company Background

First Financial Northwest changed the name of its subsidiary bank to First Financial Northwest Bank from First Savings Bank Northwest in July 2015 to reflect that it was "more than just a savings bank," according to the company's CEO.

EXECUTIVES

Chairman, Director, Daniel L. Stevens
President, Chief Executive Officer, Subsidiary Officer, Director, Joseph W. Kiley, $450,882 total compensation
Executive Vice President, Chief Financial Officer, Chief Operating Officer, Subsidiary Officer, Director, Richard P. Jacobson, $300,000 total compensation
Senior Vice President, Chief Risk Officer, Subsidiary Officer, Ronnie J. Clariza, $195,000 total compensation
Senior Vice President, Chief Deposit Officer, Subsidiary Officer, Dalen D. Harrison, $196,650 total compensation
Senior Vice President, Chief Lending Officer, Subsidiary Officer, Simon Soh, $245,000 total compensation
Vice President, Controller, Subsidiary Officer, Christine A. Huestis
Secretary, Subsidiary Officer, Director, Joann E. Lee
Director, Roger H. Molvar
Director, Richard M. Riccobono
Director, Ralph C. Sabin
Auditors : Moss Adams LLP

LOCATIONS

HQ: First Financial Northwest Inc
201 Wells Avenue South, Renton, WA 98057
Phone: 425 255-4400

PRODUCTS/OPERATIONS

2014 Sales

	$mil.	% of total
Interest income		
Loans(including fees)	36.3	93
Investments available-for-sale	2.3	6
Interest-earning deposits with banks	0.1	-
Non-interest income	0.5	1
Total	39.2	100

COMPETITORS

BANK MUTUAL CORPORATION
FIRST CONNECTICUT BANCORP, INC.
HOMESTREET, INC.
NORTHWEST BANCORP, INC.
UNITED COMMUNITY FINANCIAL CORP.

HISTORICAL FINANCIALS

Company Type: Public

Income Statement — FYE: December 31

	ASSETS ($mil)	NET INCOME ($mil)	INCOME AS % OF ASSETS	EMPLOYEES
12/20	1,387.6	8.5	0.6%	151
12/19	1,341.8	10.3	0.8%	158
12/18	1,252.4	14.8	1.2%	156
12/17	1,210.2	8.4	0.7%	145
12/16	1,037.5	8.8	0.9%	121
Annual Growth	7.5%	(1.0%)	—	5.7%

2020 Year-End Financials

Return on assets: 0.6%
Return on equity: 5.4%
Long-term debt ($ mil.): —
No. of shares ($ mil.): 9.7
Sales ($ mil.): 60.5
Dividends
Yield: 3.5%
Payout: 45.4%
Market value ($ mil.): 111.0

	STOCK PRICE ($) FY Close	P/E High/Low		PER SHARE ($) Earnings	Dividends	Book Value
12/20	11.40	17	9	0.88	0.40	16.05
12/19	14.94	16	13	1.03	0.35	15.25
12/18	15.47	14	10	1.43	0.31	14.35
12/17	15.51	26	18	0.81	0.27	13.27
12/16	19.74	27	17	0.74	0.24	12.63
Annual Growth	(12.8%)	—	—	4.4%	13.6%	6.2%

First Foundation Inc

EXECUTIVES

Subsidiary Officer, Executive Chairman, Director, Ulrich E. Keller, $575,000 total compensation
Vice-Chairman, President, Chief Executive Officer, Interim Chief Financial Officer, Subsidiary Officer, Director, Scott F. Kavanaugh, $706,000 total compensation
Senior Vice President, Chief Credit Officer, Lillian Gavin
Senior Vice President, Chief Risk Officer, Marsha Vick
Interim Chief Financial Officer, Subsidiary Officer, Amy Djou
Subsidiary Officer, Hugo J. Nuno
Subsidiary Officer, Christopher M. Naghibi
Subsidiary Officer, Gary L. Tice
Subsidiary Officer, Director, John Hakopian, $425,000 total compensation
Director, Max Briggs
Director, Elizabeth Pagliarini
Director, Diane Rubin
Director, David G. Lake
Director, Mitchell M. Rosenberg
Director, Jacob Sonenshine
Auditors : Eide Bailly LLP

LOCATIONS

HQ: First Foundation Inc
200 Crescent Court, Suite 1400, Dallas, TX 75201
Phone: 469 638-9636
Web: www.ff-inc.com

HISTORICAL FINANCIALS

Company Type: Public

Income Statement — FYE: December 31

	ASSETS ($mil)	NET INCOME ($mil)	INCOME AS % OF ASSETS	EMPLOYEES
12/20	6,957.1	84.3	1.2%	502
12/19	6,314.4	56.2	0.9%	485
12/18	5,840.4	42.9	0.7%	482
12/17	4,541.1	27.5	0.6%	394
12/16	3,975.4	23.3	0.6%	335
Annual Growth	15.0%	37.9%	—	10.6%

2020 Year-End Financials

Return on assets: 1.2%
Return on equity: 12.8%
Long-term debt ($ mil.): —
No. of shares ($ mil.): 44.6
Sales ($ mil.): 298.5
Dividends
Yield: 1.6%
Payout: 17.5%
Market value ($ mil.): 893.0

	STOCK PRICE ($) FY Close	P/E High/Low		PER SHARE ($) Earnings	Dividends	Book Value
12/20	20.00	11	4	1.88	0.33	15.58
12/19	17.40	14	10	1.25	0.20	13.74
12/18	12.86	20	12	1.01	0.00	12.57
12/17	18.54	36	17	0.78	0.00	10.34
12/16	28.50	41	28	0.70	0.00	8.69
Annual Growth	(8.5%)	—	—	28.0%	—	15.7%

First Guaranty Bancshares, Inc.

EXECUTIVES

Chairman, Subsidiary Officer, Director, Marshall T. Reynolds
Vice-Chairman, President, Chief Executive Officer, Director, Alton B. Lewis, $332,500 total compensation
Chief Financial Officer, Treasurer, Secretary, Subsidiary Officer, Eric J. Dosch, $146,835 total compensation
Director, William K. Hood
Director, Jack Rossi
Director, Edgar R. Smith
Auditors : Castaing, Hussey & Lolan, LLC

LOCATIONS

HQ: First Guaranty Bancshares, Inc.
400 East Thomas Street, Hammond, LA 70401

Phone: 985 345-7685
Web: www.eguaranty.com

HISTORICAL FINANCIALS
Company Type: Public

Income Statement   FYE: December 31

	ASSETS ($mil)	NET INCOME ($mil)	INCOME AS % OF ASSETS	EMPLOYEES
12/20	2,473.0	20.3	0.8%	453
12/19	2,117.2	14.2	0.7%	457
12/18	1,817.2	14.2	0.8%	373
12/17	1,750.4	11.7	0.7%	349
12/16	1,500.9	14.0	0.9%	304
Annual Growth	13.3%	9.6%	—	10.5%

2020 Year-End Financials
Return on assets: 0.8%
Return on equity: 11.7%
Long-term debt ($ mil.): —
No. of shares ($ mil.): 10.7
Sales ($ mil.): 124.4
Dividends
  Yield: 3.9%
  Payout: 33.6%
Market value ($ mil.): 190.0

	STOCK PRICE ($) FY Close	P/E High/Low		PER SHARE ($) Earnings	Dividends	Book Value
12/20	17.77	12	6	1.90	0.64	16.67
12/19	21.77	18	14	1.34	0.60	15.50
12/18	23.21	21	15	1.33	0.58	13.82
12/17	25.00	26	20	1.13	0.54	13.51
12/16	23.93	17	11	1.39	0.53	12.28
Annual Growth	(7.2%)	—	—	8.1%	4.9%	7.9%

First Horizon Corp

The bank holding company provides diversified financial services primarily through its principal subsidiary. Boasting some $89 billion in total assets, it offers traditional banking services like loans, deposit accounts, and credit cards, as well as trust, asset management, financial advisory, and investment services. It provides services through subsidiaries and divisions such as general banking services for consumers, businesses, financial institutions, and governments and fixed income sales and trading; underwriting of bank-eligible securities and other fixed-income securities eligible for underwriting by financial subsidiaries; loan sales; advisory services; and derivative sales. The Bank was founded in 1864 as First National Bank of Memphis.

Operations
First Horizon operates three core business segments: Regional Banking (about 65% of sales, Specialty banking (around 35), and Corporate.

Regional Banking provides traditional banking products and services to retail and commercial customers mostly in Southern US banking. The division also provides investments, financial planning, trust services, and asset management, as well as correspondent banking services such as credit, depository, and other banking related services for financial institutions.

Specialty banking consists of businesses that deliver product offerings and services with specialized industry knowledge. The segment offers asset-based ending, mortgage warehouse lending, commercial real estate, franchise finance, correspondent banking, equipment finance, mortgage, and title insurance. In addition, the segment also has a business line that focuses on fixed income securities sales, trading, underwriting, and strategies for institutional clients in the US.

The corporate segment provide risk management, audit, accounting, finance, executive office, and corporate communications. The segment also includes centralized management of capital and funding to support the business activities of the company including management of wholesale funding, liquidity, and capital management and allocation.

Vast majority of its sales were generated from loans which generated some 60%. In all, its loan portfolio is composed of commercial loans with about 80%, while consumer loans generated the rest.

Geographic Reach
First Horizon Bank is headquartered in Memphis, Tennessee. Nearly 30% of the branches are in Tennessee, while the remaining are in the states of Georgia (northwestern area), Mississippi (northwestern area), North Carolina, Virginia, South Carolina, Texas, and Florida.

Sales and Marketing
The company spent $37 million, $18 million, and $34 million on advertising and public relations in 2021, 2020, and 2019, respectively.

Financial Performance
The company's revenue in 2021 increased to $3.4 billion compared to $2.7 billion in the prior year. Net interest income of $2.0 billion increased $332 million from 2020 driven by an increase in average interest-earning assets as a result of the IBKC merger. Results also reflect the benefit of lower deposit costs, which helped to partially offset the impact of lower interest rates on earning assets.

Net income in 2021 increased to $1.0 billion compared from $857 million in 2020.

Cash held by the company at the end of 2021 increased to $1.8 billion. Cash provided by operations and financing activities were $741 million and $4.0 billion, respectively. Cash used for investing activities was $4.6 billion, mainly for purchases of securities available for sale.

Strategy
Over the past five years, First Horizon's strategic priorities have focused on: targeted and opportunistic expansion of consumer and commercial banking products and markets; targeted and opportunistic expansion of commercial lending, mainly through strategic and tactical transactions, talent development, and talent acquisitions; rigorous expense management with continued investment in revenue generating initiatives; managing business units and products with a strong emphasis on risk-adjusted returns on invested capital; providing exceptional client service and experience as a primary means to differentiate them from competitors; and investment in scalable technology and other infrastructure to attract and retain clients and to support expansion.

Company Background
Frank S. Davis submitted a national charter to establish First National Bank of Memphis in 1864. The bank continued to grow over the years, and in 1977 First National changed its name to First Tennessee to reflect the bank's expansion beyond Memphis.

In 2004 the company changed its name to First Horizon National Corporation. In 2020, as a result of a merger of equals with IBERIABANK Corporation, the company changed its name from First Horizon National Corporation to First Horizon Bank.

EXECUTIVES

President, Chief Executive Officer, Subsidiary Officer, Director, D. Bryan Jordan, $896,827 total compensation
Senior Executive Vice President, Chief Financial Officer, Subsidiary Officer, Hope Dmuchowski
Senior Executive Vice President, Chief Operating Officer, T. S. LoCascio
Senior Vice President, Corporate Secretary, Assistant General Counsel, Clyde A. Billings
Division Officer, Anthony J. Restel
Division Officer, Subsidiary Officer, David T. Popwell, $543,654 total compensation
Director, R. Eugene Taylor
Lead Director, Director, Colin V. Reed
Director, Harry V. Barton
Director, John N. Casbon
Director, John C. Compton
Director, Wendy P. Davidson
Director, William H. Fenstermaker
Director, J. Michael Kemp
Director, Rick E. Maples
Director, Vicki R. Palmer
Director, E. Stewart Shea
Director, Cecelia D. Stewart
Director, Rosa Sugrañes
Auditors: KPMG LLP

LOCATIONS

HQ: First Horizon Corp
165 Madison Avenue, Memphis, TN 38103
Phone: 901 523-4444
Web: www.firsthorizon.com

PRODUCTS/OPERATIONS

First Internet Bancorp

2014 Sales

	$ mil.	% of total
Interest		
Loans, including fees	571.8	45
Investment securities	93.2	7
Trading securities	32.0	3
Loans held for sale	11.2	1
Other	1.1	-
Noninterest		
Capital markets	200.5	16
Deposit transactions & cash management	112.0	9
Mortagage banking	71.3	6
Brokerage management fees & commissions	49.1	4
Trust services and investment management	27.7	2
Bankcard income	23.7	2
Bank owned life insurance	16.4	1
Other	49.3	4
Total	1,259.3	100

COMPETITORS

CAPITAL BANK FINANCIAL CORP.
CITY HOLDING COMPANY
F.N.B. CORPORATION
FIRST COMMONWEALTH FINANCIAL CORPORATION
FIRST COMMUNITY BANCSHARES, INC.
FIRST MIDWEST BANCORP, INC.
MIDSOUTH BANCORP, INC.
NEWBRIDGE BANCORP
OLD NATIONAL BANCORP
SOUTHWEST BANCORP, INC.

HISTORICAL FINANCIALS
Company Type: Public

Income Statement — FYE: December 31

	ASSETS ($mil)	NET INCOME ($mil)	INCOME AS % OF ASSETS	EMPLOYEES
12/20	84,209.0	845.0	1.0%	6,802
12/19	43,310.9	440.9	1.0%	5,017
12/18	40,832.2	545.0	1.3%	5,577
12/17	41,423.3	165.5	0.4%	5,984
12/16	28,555.2	227.0	0.8%	4,288
Annual Growth	31.0%	38.9%	—	12.2%

2020 Year-End Financials
Return on assets: 1.3%
Return on equity: 13.1%
Long-term debt ($ mil.): —
No. of shares ($ mil.): 555.0
Sales ($ mil.): 3,390
Dividends
Yield: 4.7%
Payout: 31.7%
Market value ($ mil.): 7,082.0

	STOCK PRICE ($) FY Close	P/E High	P/E Low	PER SHARE ($) Earnings	PER SHARE ($) Dividends	PER SHARE ($) Book Value
12/20	12.76	9	4	1.89	0.60	14.44
12/19	16.56	12	10	1.38	0.56	15.35
12/18	13.16	12	7	1.65	0.48	14.09
12/17	19.99	31	24	0.65	0.36	13.11
12/16	20.01	22	12	0.94	0.28	10.31
Annual Growth	(10.6%)	—	—	19.1%	21.0%	8.8%

First Internet Bancorp was formed in 2006 to be the holding company for First Internet Bank of Indiana (First IB). Launched in 1999, the bank was the first state-chartered, FDIC-insured institution to operate solely via the Internet. It now operates two locations in Indianapolis after adding one via its 2007 purchase of Landmark Financial (the parent of Landmark Savings Bank), a deal that also brought aboard residential mortgage brokerage Landmark Mortgage. First IB offers traditional checking and savings accounts in addition to CDs, IRAs, credit and check cards, consumer installment and residential mortgage loans, and lines of credit. It serves customers in all 50 states.

EXECUTIVES

Chairman, Chief Executive Officer, Subsidiary Officer, Director, David B. Becker, $700,000 total compensation
Vice-Chairman, Director, David R. Lovejoy
President, Chief Operating Officer, Nicole S. Lorch, $285,000 total compensation
Executive Vice President, Chief Financial Officer, Kenneth J. Lovik, $292,000 total compensation
Director, Aasif M. Bade
Director, John K. Keach
Director, Jean L. Wojtowicz
Director, Michael L. Smith
Director, Justin P. Christian
Director, Ann Colussi Dee
Auditors : BKD, LLP

LOCATIONS

HQ: First Internet Bancorp
11201 USA Parkway, Fishers, IN 46037
Phone: 317 532-7900
Web: www.firstinternetbancorp.com

COMPETITORS

FB CORPORATION
FIRST SAVINGS FINANCIAL GROUP, INC.
GUARANTY BANK AND TRUST COMPANY
INVESTAR HOLDING CORPORATION
THE FIRST BANK AND TRUST COMPANY

HISTORICAL FINANCIALS
Company Type: Public

Income Statement — FYE: December 31

	ASSETS ($mil)	NET INCOME ($mil)	INCOME AS % OF ASSETS	EMPLOYEES
12/20	4,246.1	29.4	0.7%	257
12/19	4,100.0	25.2	0.6%	231
12/18	3,541.6	21.9	0.6%	201
12/17	2,767.6	15.2	0.6%	206
12/16	1,854.3	12.0	0.7%	192
Annual Growth	23.0%	25.0%	—	7.6%

2020 Year-End Financials
Return on assets: 0.7%
Return on equity: 9.2%
Long-term debt ($ mil.): —
No. of shares ($ mil.): 9.8
Sales ($ mil.): 173.1
Dividends
Yield: 0.8%
Payout: 9.2%
Market value ($ mil.): 282.0

	STOCK PRICE ($) FY Close	P/E High	P/E Low	PER SHARE ($) Earnings	PER SHARE ($) Dividends	PER SHARE ($) Book Value
12/20	28.74	10	4	2.99	0.24	33.77
12/19	23.71	10	7	2.51	0.24	31.30
12/18	20.44	18	8	2.30	0.24	28.39
12/17	38.15	19	12	2.13	0.24	26.65
12/16	32.00	14	10	2.30	0.24	23.76
Annual Growth	(2.7%)	—	—	6.8%	0.0%	9.2%

First Interstate BancSystem Inc

First Interstate BancSystem (FIB) is a financial and bank holding company focused on community banking that operates over 145 banking offices, including detached drive-up facilities, in communities across six states? Idaho, Montana, Oregon, South Dakota, Washington, and Wyoming. Through the company's bank subsidiary, First Interstate Bank, they deliver a comprehensive range of banking products and services?including online and mobile banking?to individuals, businesses, municipalities, and others throughout their market areas. The company's principal business activity is lending to, accepting deposits from, and conducting financial transactions with and for individuals, businesses, municipalities, and other entities.

Operations

FIB operates through one segment: community banking. The segment encompasses commercial and consumer banking services provided through its bank are primarily the acceptance of deposits, extensions of credit, mortgage loan origination and servicing, and trust, employee benefit, investment, and insurance services.

Through lending activities, the company offers offer real estate, consumer, commercial, agricultural, and other loans to individuals and businesses in their market areas. Its deposit products include checking, savings, and time deposits. The company also offers repurchase agreements primarily to commercial and municipal depositors. Under repurchase agreements, FIB sells investment securities held by the bank to their clients under an agreement to repurchase the investment securities at a specified time or on demand.

Through their wealth management services, FIB provides a wide range of trust, employee benefit, investment management, insurance, agency, and custodial services to individuals, businesses, and nonprofit organizations. These services include the administration of estates and personal trusts, management of investment accounts for individuals, employee benefit plans and charitable foundations, and insurance planning.

FIB's centralized operational activities generally support their banking offices in the delivery of products and services to clients and include marketing, credit review, loan servicing, credit card issuance and servicing, mortgage loan sales and servicing, loan collections, among others.

The Real estate loans (commercial, construction, residential, and agricultural) account for over 70% of the company's loan portfolio, followed by commercial loans (around 15%), consumer loans (some 10%), and agricultural loans (less than 5%). In all, interest income generated over 75% of its total sales.

Geographic Reach

Billings, Montana-based, FIB provides banking services at over 145 locations in Idaho, Montana, Oregon, South Dakota, Washington, and Wyoming, of which some 35 properties are leased from independent third parties and about 110 properties are owned by the company. After the acquisition of Great Western and GWB, it now operates an additional about 175 banking offices in eight new states?Arizona, Colorado, Iowa, Kansas, Minnesota, Missouri, Nebraska, and North Dakota?and the state of South Dakota.

Sales and Marketing

FIB delivers a comprehensive range of banking products and services?including online and mobile banking?to individuals, businesses, municipalities, and others. It provides lending opportunities to clients that participate in a wide variety of industries, including agriculture, construction, education, energy, governmental services, healthcare, hospitality, housing, mining, real estate development, and retail, among others.

Advertising expense was $2.6 million, $2.8 million, and $4.2 million in 2021, 2020, and 2019, respectively.

Financial Performance

The company, in 2021 had a net interest income of $488.2 million, a 2% decrease from the previous year's net interest income of $497 million.

In 2021, the company had a net income of $192.1 million, a 19% increase from the previous year's net income of $161.2 million.

The company's cash at the end of 2021 was $2.3 billion. Operating activities generated $282.3 million, while investing activities used $2.1 billion, mainly for purchases of investment securities. Financing activities provided another $1.9 billion.

Strategy

FIB's business model is strategically aligned around four key pillars, which help them align, organize, and prioritize business strategies. These pillars guide the company's actions related to their employees, clients, and operations, ultimately leading to their financial success and creating value for their shareholders.

Through the first pillar, "Our People, Our Priority," the company is building a diverse company, attracting the right people, retaining them in the right jobs, and developing them to meet our long-term needs. The second pillar, "Relentless Client Focus," enables the company to connect their clients' goals and dreams to the right products and services by listening to them and learning their needs. The third pillar is "Future Ready, Today" in which the company is focused on adapting its products and processes to be scalable and sustainable. The fourth pillar is "Financial Vitality" in which the company strategically focuses on balance sheet management and goal-oriented financial rigor the keep the company a top-performing bank.

The company's long-term perspective emphasizes providing high-quality financial products and services, delivering exceptional client service, influencing business leadership within their communities through professional and dedicated bankers, supporting their communities through financial contributions and socially responsible leadership, and cultivating a strong corporate culture. FIB plans to continue its business in a disciplined and prudent manner, fueled by organic growth in their existing market areas and expansion into new and complementary markets when appropriate acquisition and other opportunities arise.

EXECUTIVES

Chairman, Director, David L. Jahnke
President, Chief Executive Officer, Director, Kevin P. Riley, $741,106 total compensation
Executive Vice President, Chief Information Officer, Scott E. Erkonen
Executive Vice President, General Counsel, Kirk D. Jensen, $314,539 total compensation
Executive Vice President, Chief Risk Officer, Subsidiary Officer, Karlyn M. Knieriem
Executive Vice President, Chief Financial Officer, Marcy D. Mutch, $379,616 total compensation
Chief Operating Officer, Kristina Robbins
Chief Banking Officer, Ashley Hayslip
Director, James R. Scott
Director, Stephen B. Bowman
Director, James P. Brannen
Director, Alice S. Cho
Director, Frances Pallas Grieb
Director, Thomas Edward Henning
Director, John M. Heyneman
Director, Dennis L. Johnson
Director, Patricia L. Moss
Director, Daniel A. Rykhus
Director, Joyce Ann Phillips
Director, Jonathan R. Scott
Director, Stephen M. Lacy
Auditors: RSM US LLP

LOCATIONS

HQ: First Interstate BancSystem Inc
401 North 31st Street, Billings, MT 59116-0918
Phone: 406 255-5390
Web: www.fibk.com

PRODUCTS/OPERATIONS

Selected ServicesBanking
Checking Accounts
Credit Cards
Debit Cards
Escrow Services
Foreign Currency
Overdraft Protection
Personal Resources
Prepaid Cards
Savings Accounts
Borrowing
AdvanceLine
Auto & Recreation
Debt Consolidation
Home Equity
Home Mortgage
Personal Loans
Create & Build Wealth
Long-Term Planning
Planning for the Unexpected
Saving for College
Saving for Retirement
Wealth Resources
Protect & Preserve Wealth
Asset Management
Employee Exit Strategies
Health Concerns
Investment Services
Retirement Plan Services

Sales 2015

Interest income	70
Non-interest income	30
Total	100

COMPETITORS

AMERIS BANCORP
CARDINAL FINANCIAL CORPORATION
CASCADE BANCORP
HUDSON VALLEY HOLDING CORP.
RENASANT CORPORATION
SEACOAST BANKING CORPORATION OF FLORIDA
TRUSTCO BANK CORP N Y
VIRGINIA COMMERCE BANCORP, INC.
WESBANCO, INC.
WEST BANCORPORATION, INC.

HISTORICAL FINANCIALS

Company Type: Public

Income Statement — FYE: December 31

	ASSETS ($mil)	NET INCOME ($mil)	INCOME AS % OF ASSETS	EMPLOYEES
12/20	17,648.7	161.2	0.9%	2,462
12/19	14,644.2	181.0	1.2%	2,473
12/18	13,300.2	160.2	1.2%	2,330
12/17	12,213.2	106.5	0.9%	2,207
12/16	9,063.8	95.6	1.1%	1,721
Annual Growth	18.1%	13.9%	—	9.4%

2020 Year-End Financials
Return on assets: 0.9%
Return on equity: 8.0%
Long-term debt ($ mil.): —
No. of shares ($ mil.): 62.1
Sales ($ mil.): 680.3
Dividends
Yield: 4.9%
Payout: 79.0%
Market value ($ mil.): 2,532.0

	STOCK PRICE ($)	P/E		PER SHARE ($)		
	FY Close	High/Low		Earnings	Dividends	Book Value
12/20	40.77	16	10	2.53	2.00	31.56
12/19	41.92	15	13	2.83	1.24	30.87
12/18	36.56	17	13	2.75	1.12	27.94
12/17	40.05	22	16	2.05	0.96	25.28
12/16	42.55	20	12	2.13	0.88	21.87
Annual Growth	(1.1%)	—	—	4.4%	22.8%	9.6%

First Merchants Corp

First Merchants is the holding company that owns First Merchants Bank, which operates some 120 branches in Indiana, Illinois, and western Ohio. Through its Lafayette Bank & Trust and First Merchants Private Wealth Advisors divisions, the bank provides standard consumer and commercial banking services, including checking and savings accounts, CDs, check cards, and consumer, commercial, agricultural, and real estate mortgage loans. First Merchants also provides trust and asset management services. Founded in 1982, First Merchants has nearly $9.4 billion worth of consolidated assets.

Operations
Real estate loans made up about 70% of First Merchants's loan portfolio, while commercial and industrial, agricultural, and consumer loans account for the remainder of the bank's lending activity.

Geographic Reach
Muncie, Indiana-based First Merchants's 120-plus bank branches are located across Indiana, and in two counties each in Illinois and Ohio.

Sales and Marketing
First Merchants's marketing expense was $3.73 million in 2017, $3 million (2016), and $3.5 million (2015).

Financial Performance
Revenue jumped by 19% to $348.2 million in 2017, driven by higher interest income from more organic and inorganic loan business and more investment security income, following the bank's recent acquisitions. The bank also collected significantly more non-interest income from deposit account service charges, electronic card fees, and insurance-related gains as it grew its customer base through acquisitions. Higher revenue drove the bank's net income up 18% to $96 million.

Total cash on hand at the end of fiscal 2017 stood at $154.9 million, which was $27 million higher than cash at the start of the year. Cash from operations contributed $126 million and cash generated through financing activities added $535.8, while investments in securities and other uses used $635.3 million.

Strategy
A key part of the First Merchants's growth strategy is to expand geographically through acquisitions of small community banks operating in its key Indiana, Illinois, and western Ohio markets.

In 2017 and 2018, First Merchants added more nearly 3 dozen branches to its banking network after acquiring Michigan-based Monroe Bank & Trust, Ohio-based Arlington Bank, and Independent Alliance Banks, located in Indiana. The bank has, in recent years, acquired 1-2 community banks operating in these states each year, often adding a handful of branches, as well as loans and other assets, through each transaction.

Mergers and Acquisitions
In 2018 First Merchants acquired MBT Financial Corporation, the holding company for Monroe Bank & Trust and its 20 branches serving Monroe, Michigan and the southeastern Michigan area.

In 2017 First Merchants bought Columbus, Ohio-based Arlington Bank. for $82.6 million. The same year it spent $238.8 million to acquire a majority stake in Independent Alliance Banks and IAB's 16 banking centers located in and around Fort Wayne, Indiana.

EXECUTIVES

Chairman, Charles E. Schalliol
President, Chief Executive Officer, Director, Michael C. Reichin, $548,853 total compensation
Chief Operating Officer, Chief Financial Officer, Executive Vice President, Mark K. Hardwick, $372,206 total compensation
Executive Vice President, Chief Banking Officer, Michael J. Stewart, $334,110 total compensation
Senior Vice President, Chief Credit Officer, Executive Vice President, John J. Martin, $267,664 total compensation
Senior Vice President, Chief Accounting Officer, Jami L. Bradshaw, $119,878 total compensation
Senior Vice President, Chief Risk Officer, Jeffery B. Lorenston, $124,466 total compensation
Human Resources Senior Vice President, Human Resources Director, Kimberly J. Ellington, $94,300 total compensation
Senior Vice President, Chief Credit Officer, David W. Spade, $179,823 total compensation
Senior Vice President, Chief Information Officer, Stephan H. Fluhler, $238,680 total compensation
Division Officer, Robert R. Connors, $185,772 total compensation
Director, Michael R. Becher
Director, Michael J. (Jud) Fisher
Director, F. Howard Halderman
Director, William L. Hoy
Director, Gary J. Lehman
Director, Michael C. Marhenke
Director, Clark C. Kellogg
Director, Patrick A. Sherman
Director, Terry L. Walker
Director, Jean L. Wojtowicz
Director, H. Douglas Chaffin

Auditors: BKD, LLP

LOCATIONS

HQ: First Merchants Corp
200 East Jackson Street, Muncie, IN 47305-2814
Phone: 765 747-1500
Web: www.firstmerchants.com

PRODUCTS/OPERATIONS

2017 Sales

	$ mil.	% of total
Interest		
Loans	274.4	71
Investment Securities	38.9	10
Federal Reserve and Federal Home Loan Bank stock	.9	-
Interest Expense/Other	(36.9)	-
Non-interest		
Service charges on deposits	18.7	5
Fiduciary activities	11.6	3
Other customer fees	20.9	5
Earnings on cash surrender value of life insurance	3.9	1
Net gains and fees on sales of loans	7.6	2
Net realized gains on sales of available for sale securities	2.6	1
Others	5.7	2
Total	348.3	100

COMPETITORS

ALLEGHANY CORPORATION
AMERICAN FINANCIAL GROUP, INC.
AMTRUST FINANCIAL SERVICES, INC.
BERKSHIRE HATHAWAY INC.
F.N.B. CORPORATION
HEARTLAND FINANCIAL USA, INC.
MERCURY GENERAL CORPORATION
OLD NATIONAL BANCORP
STATE AUTO FINANCIAL CORPORATION
WEST BEND MUTUAL INSURANCE COMPANY

HISTORICAL FINANCIALS

Company Type: Public

Income Statement — FYE: December 31

	ASSETS ($mil)	NET INCOME ($mil)	INCOME AS % OF ASSETS	EMPLOYEES
12/20	14,067.2	148.6	1.1%	1,907
12/19	12,457.2	164.4	1.3%	1,891
12/18	9,884.7	159.1	1.6%	1,702
12/17	9,367.4	96.0	1.0%	1,684
12/16	7,211.6	81.0	1.1%	1,449
Annual Growth	18.2%	16.4%	—	7.1%

2020 Year-End Financials
Return on assets: 1.1%
Return on equity: 8.0%
Long-term debt ($ mil.): —
No. of shares ($ mil.): 53.9
Sales ($ mil.): 558.4
Dividends
Yield: 2.7%
Payout: 37.9%
Market value ($ mil.): 2,017.0

	STOCK PRICE ($)	P/E		PER SHARE ($)		
	FY Close	High/Low		Earnings	Dividends	Book Value
12/20	37.41	15	8	2.74	1.04	34.78
12/19	41.59	13	10	3.19	1.00	32.26
12/18	34.27	15	10	3.22	0.84	28.54
12/17	42.06	21	17	2.12	0.69	26.52
12/16	37.65	19	11	1.98	0.54	22.04
Annual Growth	(0.2%)	—	—	8.5%	17.8%	12.1%

First Mid Bancshares Inc

Money doesn't grow on trees, so when farmers in Illinois need a little cash, they turn to First Mid-Illinois Bank & Trust. The primary subsidiary of First Mid-Illinois Bancshares is a major supplier of farm credit (including real estate, machinery, and production loans; inventory financing; and lines of credit) in its market area. In addition to agricultural loans, the bank offers commercial, consumer, and real estate lending. It also provides deposit products such as savings and checking accounts, plus trust and investment services through a partnership with Raymond James. First Mid-Illinois Bank & Trust has about 40 branches. Other subsidiaries provide data processing services and insurance products and services.

EXECUTIVES

Chairman, President, Chief Executive Officer, Subsidiary Officer, Director, Joseph R. Dively, $413,591 total compensation
Senior Executive Vice President, Chief Operating Officer, Michael L. Taylor, $287,348 total compensation
Finance Executive Vice President, Finance Chief Financial Officer, Matthew K. Smith, $213,673 total compensation
Executive Vice President, Chief Lending Officer, Eric S. McRae, $260,580 total compensation
Executive Vice President, Chief Wealth Management Officer, Bradley L. Beesley, $161,051 total compensation
Director, Mary J. Westerhold
Director, James Kyle McCurry
Director, Holly B. Adams
Director, Zachary I. Horn
Director, Robert S. Cook
Director, Gisele A. Marcus
Director, James E. Zimmer
Auditors : BKD, LLP

LOCATIONS

HQ: First Mid Bancshares Inc
1421 Charleston Avenue, Mattoon, IL 61938
Phone: 217 234-7454   **Fax:** 217 258-0485
Web: www.firstmid.com

PRODUCTS/OPERATIONS

Selected Subsidiaries
The Checkley Agency, Inc. (dba First Mid Insurance Group)
First Mid-Illinois Bank & Trust, N.A.
First Mid-Illinois Statutory Trust I, II
Mid-Illinois Data Services, Inc.

COMPETITORS

FOUR OAKS FINCORP, INC.
GREAT FLORIDA BANK
SB ONE BANCORP
THE FIRST BANK AND TRUST COMPANY

UNITED FINANCIAL BANKING COMPANIES, INC.

HISTORICAL FINANCIALS
Company Type: Public

Income Statement — FYE: December 31

	ASSETS ($mil)	NET INCOME ($mil)	INCOME AS % OF ASSETS	EMPLOYEES
12/20	4,726.3	45.2	1.0%	824
12/19	3,839.4	47.9	1.2%	827
12/18	3,839.7	36.6	1.0%	818
12/17	2,841.5	26.6	0.9%	592
12/16	2,884.5	21.8	0.8%	598
Annual Growth	13.1%	20.0%	—	8.3%

2020 Year-End Financials
Return on assets: 1.0%   Dividends
Return on equity: 8.2%   Yield: 2.4%
Long-term debt ($ mil.): —   Payout: 30.0%
No. of shares ($ mil.): 16.7   Market value ($ mil.): 564.0
Sales ($ mil.): 203.6

	STOCK PRICE ($) FY Close	P/E High/Low		PER SHARE ($) Earnings	Dividends	Book Value
12/20	33.66	13	7	2.70	0.81	33.94
12/19	35.25	13	11	2.87	0.76	31.58
12/18	31.92	17	12	2.52	1.04	28.59
12/17	38.54	20	14	2.13	0.66	24.32
12/16	34.00	17	11	2.05	0.62	22.51
Annual Growth	(0.3%)	—	—	7.1%	6.9%	10.8%

First Northwest Bancorp

EXECUTIVES

Chairman, Subsidiary Officer, Director, Stephen E. Oliver
President, Chief Executive Officer, Subsidiary Officer, Director, Matthew P. Deines
Executive Vice President, Chief Financial Officer, Principal Accounting Officer, Geri Bullard
Executive Vice President, Chief Credit Officer, Subsidiary Officer, Terry A. Anderson
Executive Vice President, Chief Operating Officer, General Counsel, Corporate Secretary, Christopher J. Riffle
Director, Sherilyn G. Anderson
Director, Dana D. Behar
Director, Craig A. Curtis
Director, Cindy H. Finnie
Director, Gabriel S. Galanda
Director, Norman J. Tonina
Director, Jennifer Zaccardo
Auditors : Moss Adams LLP

LOCATIONS

HQ: First Northwest Bancorp
105 West 8th Street, Port Angeles, WA 98362
Phone: 360 457-0461
Web: www.ourfirstfed.com

HISTORICAL FINANCIALS
Company Type: Public

Income Statement — FYE: December 31

	ASSETS ($mil)	NET INCOME ($mil)	INCOME AS % OF ASSETS	EMPLOYEES
12/20	1,654.3	10.3	0.6%	230
12/19	1,307.3	9.0	0.7%	197
12/18	1,258.7	7.1	0.6%	210
12/17	1,215.6	1.6	0.1%	204
06/17	1,087.6	5.1	0.5%	204
Annual Growth	11.1%	19.2%	—	3.0%

2020 Year-End Financials
Return on assets: 0.6%   Dividends
Return on equity: 5.6%   Yield: 1.3%
Long-term debt ($ mil.): —   Payout: 19.0%
No. of shares ($ mil.): 10.2   Market value ($ mil.): 160.0
Sales ($ mil.): 67.5

	STOCK PRICE ($) FY Close	P/E High/Low		PER SHARE ($) Earnings	Dividends	Book Value
12/20	15.60	16	8	1.10	0.21	18.19
12/19	18.13	20	16	0.91	0.13	16.48
12/18	14.83	26	20	0.68	0.03	15.42
12/17*	16.30	114	95	0.16	0.00	15.02
06/17	15.77	37	28	0.46	0.00	14.93
Annual Growth	(0.3%)	—	—	24.4%	—	5.1%

*Fiscal year change

First Ottawa Bancshares Inc

EXECUTIVES

Chairman, Subsidiary Officer, Bradley Armstrong
President, Chief Executive Officer, Subsidiary Officer, Director, Joachim J. Brown, $260,582 total compensation
Executive Vice President, Chief Operating Officer, Director, Donald J. Harris, $138,569 total compensation
Chief Financial Officer, Subsidiary Officer, Vincent G. Easi, $86,422 total compensation
Chief Trust Officer, Mark D. Dunavan
Corporate Secretary, Cheryl D. Gage
Subsidiary Officer, Steven M. Gonzalo, $118,589 total compensation
Director, Brian P. Zabel
Director, John L. Cantlin
Director, William J. Walsh
Director, Patty P. Godfrey
Director, Thomas P. Rooney
Director, Erika L. Schmidt

LOCATIONS

HQ: First Ottawa Bancshares Inc
701 LaSalle Street, Ottawa, IL 61350
Phone: 815 434-0044
Web: www.firstottawa.com

HISTORICAL FINANCIALS

Company Type: Public

Income Statement — FYE: December 31

	ASSETS ($mil)	NET INCOME ($mil)	INCOME AS % OF ASSETS	EMPLOYEES
12/21	970.8	11.5	1.2%	0
12/20	905.5	2.9	0.3%	0
12/19	453.1	2.3	0.5%	0
12/18	290.4	3.5	1.2%	0
12/17	286.3	3.4	1.2%	0
Annual Growth	35.7%	35.6%	—	—

2021 Year-End Financials

Return on assets: 1.2%
Return on equity: 19.8%
Long-term debt ($ mil.): —
No. of shares ($ mil.): 0.8
Sales ($ mil.): 48.5
Dividends
Yield: —
Payout: 11.0%
Market value ($ mil.): 69.0

	STOCK PRICE ($) FY Close	P/E High	P/E Low	PER SHARE ($) Earnings	Dividends	Book Value
12/21	80.00	6	5	13.61	1.50	74.34
12/20	61.00	21	14	3.54	1.50	63.06
12/19	71.05	38	21	3.10	1.50	59.93
12/18	70.00	13	10	5.68	1.75	56.36
12/17	55.00	10	9	5.54	1.13	52.68
Annual Growth	9.8%	—	—	25.2%	7.3%	9.0%

First Reliance Bancshares Inc

EXECUTIVES

President, Chief Executive Officer, subsidiary Officer, Director, F. R. Saunders, $282,000 total compensation
Auditors : Elliott Davis, LLC

LOCATIONS

HQ: First Reliance Bancshares Inc
2170 West Palmetto Street, Florence, SC 29501
Phone: 843 656-5000
Web: www.firstreliance.com

HISTORICAL FINANCIALS

Company Type: Public

Income Statement — FYE: December 31

	ASSETS ($mil)	NET INCOME ($mil)	INCOME AS % OF ASSETS	EMPLOYEES
12/20	710.1	10.6	1.5%	0
12/19	661.6	4.0	0.6%	0
12/18	584.9	2.4	0.4%	0
12/17	458.6	(0.6)	—	0
12/16	408.1	3.5	0.9%	0
Annual Growth	14.9%	31.8%	—	—

2020 Year-End Financials

Return on assets: 1.5%
Return on equity: 16.8%
Long-term debt ($ mil.): —
No. of shares ($ mil.): 8.5
Sales ($ mil.): 50.3
Dividends
Yield: —
Payout: —
Market value ($ mil.): 0.0

First Republic Bank (San Francisco, CA)

Founded in 1985, First Republic Bank offers private banking, real estate lending, wealth management, trust, and custody services for businesses and high-net-worth clients through nearly 95 offices. Its main geographic focus is on urban markets such as San Francisco, Los Angeles, New York, Portland, and San Diego, among others. The bank generates most of its revenue from commercial banking operations. It also offers investment advice and brokerage and trust services through its wealth management division. First Republic Bank has total assets of $181.1 billion, total deposits of $156.3 billion, total equity of $15.9 billion, and wealth management assets under management or administration of approximately $279.4 billion.

Operations

First Republic Bank currently operates its business through two business segments: Commercial Banking and Wealth Management.

The principal business activities of the Commercial Banking segment are gathering deposits (retail deposit gathering and private banking activities), originating and servicing loans (primarily real estate secured mortgage loans), and investing in investment securities. The primary sources of revenue for this segment are: interest earned on loans and investment securities, fees earned in connection with loan and deposit services, and income earned on loans serviced for investors. The segment brings in approximately 80% of the bank's revenue.

First Republic Bank's Wealth Management segment generates some 20% of revenue. Its services are conducted via subsidiaries: First Republic Investment Management (investment advice), First Republic Securities Company (brokerage services), and First Republic Trust Company (trust services). The primary sources of revenue for this segment are investment management fees, brokerage and investment fees, insurance fees, trust fees, and foreign exchange fee income.

The interest income accounts for more than 80% of the bank's total sales. Investment management fees, trust fees, investments in life insurance, foreign exchange fee income, brokerage and investment fees, deposit fees, loan and related fees, and other income account for the rest.

Geographic Reach

First Republic Bank operates about 95 offices, more than 80 of which are licensed deposit-taking offices primarily located in San Francisco (headquarters), Palo Alto, Los Angeles, Santa Barbara, Newport Beach and San Diego, California; Portland, Oregon; Boston, Massachusetts; Palm Beach, Florida; Greenwich, Connecticut; New York, New York; and Jackson, Wyoming.

Sales and Marketing

First Republic Bank advertises via digital media, newspaper, television, and radio ads; its primary marketing goal is to attract deposits in its Preferred Banking offices, wealth management sweep deposits, and others.

Its advertising and marketing expenses were approximately $64.0 million, $43.0 million, and $66.0 million in 2021, 2020, and 2019, respectively.

Financial Performance

Company's revenue for fiscal 2021 increased to $5.0 billion compared from the prior year with $3.9 billion.

Net income for fiscal 2021 increased to $1.5 billion compared from the prior year with $1.1 billion.

Cash held by the company at the end of fiscal 2021 increased to $12.9 billion. Cash provided by operations and financing activities were $1.2 billion and $35.8 billion, respectively. Cash used for investing activities was $29.1 billion, mainly for loan originations.

Strategy

First Republic's core business principles and service-based culture have successfully guided its efforts over the past 36 years. The company believes focusing on these principles will enable it to expand its capabilities for providing value added services to its urban, coastal client base and generate steady, long-term growth. The company focuses on delivering superior client service, originating high quality loans, growing core deposits, growing its wealth management business, and attracting, retain and develop diverse talented professionals.

Mergers and Acquisitions

In 2016 First Republic acquired Gradifi, a Boston-based company that helps employers offer student-loan repayment as an employee perk.

Company Background

First Republic was founded in 1985 by CEO Jim Herbert.

EXECUTIVES

Chief Executive Officer, Chairman, Director, James H. Herbert
Acting Chairman, Director, George G. C. Parker
Vice-Chairman, Director, Katherine August-deWilde
President, Co-Chief Executive Officer, Director, Michael J. Roffler
Executive Vice President, Chief Financial Officer, Chief Accounting Officer, Olga Tsokova
Director, Frank J. Fahrenkopf
Director, Boris Groysberg
Director, Sandra R. Hernández
Director, Pamela J. Joyner
Director, Reynold Levy
Director, Duncan L. Niederauer

Auditors : KPMG LLP

LOCATIONS

HQ: First Republic Bank (San Francisco, CA)
111 Pine Street, 2nd Floor, San Francisco, CA 94111
Phone: 415 392-1400
Web: www.firstrepublic.com

PRODUCTS/OPERATIONS

2018 Sales

	% of total
Commercial Banking	82
Wealth Management	18
Total	100

COMPETITORS

BANCFIRST CORPORATION
COMMUNITY BANK OF THE BAY
EAGLE BANCORP, INC.
FULTON FINANCIAL CORPORATION
HSBC USA, INC.
Industrial and Commercial Bank of China Limited
PRIVATEBANCORP, INC.
QATAR NATIONAL BANK (Q.P.S.C.)
SHINSEI BANK, LIMITED
TURKIYE GARANTI BANKASI ANONIM SIRKETI

HISTORICAL FINANCIALS

Company Type: Public

Income Statement — FYE: December 31

	ASSETS ($mil)	NET INCOME ($mil)	INCOME AS % OF ASSETS	EMPLOYEES
12/20	142,502.0	1,064.1	0.7%	5,483
12/19	116,264.0	930.3	0.8%	4,812
12/18	99,205.2	853.8	0.9%	4,480
12/17	87,780.5	757.6	0.9%	4,025
12/16	73,277.7	673.4	0.9%	3,566
Annual Growth	18.1%	12.1%	—	11.4%

2020 Year-End Financials

Return on assets: 0.8%
Return on equity: 9.8%
Long-term debt ($ mil.): —
No. of shares ($ mil.): 174.1
Sales ($ mil.): 4,506.9
Dividends
Yield: 0.5%
Payout: 13.5%
Market value ($ mil.): 25,584.0

	STOCK PRICE ($) FY Close	P/E High/Low		PER SHARE ($) Earnings	Dividends	Book Value
12/20	146.93	25	13	5.81	0.79	67.48
12/19	117.45	22	16	5.20	0.75	58.42
12/18	86.90	22	16	4.81	0.71	52.62
12/17	86.64	24	20	4.31	0.67	48.35
12/16	92.14	23	14	3.93	0.63	44.78
Annual Growth	12.4%	—	—	10.3%	5.8%	10.8%

First Savings Financial Group Inc

First Savings Financial Group was formed in 2008 to be the holding company for First Savings Bank, a community bank serving consumers and small businesses in southern Indiana. Through more than a dozen branches, the bank offers standard deposit services like savings, checking, and retirement accounts, as well as a variety of lending services. One- to four- family residential loans make up about 60% of First Savings Bank's loan portfolio; other loans in the bank's portfolio include commercial real estate, construction, consumer, and commercial business. In 2012 First Savings Financial expanded its footprint by acquiring the four Indiana branches of First Financial Service Corporation.

EXECUTIVES

Chairman, Subsidiary Officer, Director, John E. Colin
President, Chief Executive Officer, Subsidiary Officer, Director, Larry W. Myers, $268,523 total compensation
Chief Financial Officer, Corporate Secretary, Subsidiary Officer, Anthony A. Schoen, $170,727 total compensation
Chief Operating Officer, Subsidiary Officer, Jacqueline R. Journell
Director, L. Chris Fordyce
Director, Troy D. Hanke
Director, Pamela Bennett-Martin
Director, Martin A. Padgett
Director, Samuel E. Eckart, $205,488 total compensation
Director, Douglas A. York
Director, John P. Lawson, $178,227 total compensation
Director, Frank N. Czeschin
Director, Steven R. Stemler
Auditors : Monroe Shine & Co., Inc.

LOCATIONS

HQ: First Savings Financial Group Inc
702 North Shore Drive, Suite 300, Jeffersonville, IN 47130
Phone: 812 283-0724
Web: www.fsbbank.net

COMPETITORS

CHOICEONE FINANCIAL SERVICES, INC.
COMMUNITY SHORES BANK CORPORATION
EMCLAIRE FINANCIAL CORP.
FB CORPORATION
OCEANFIRST FINANCIAL CORP.

HISTORICAL FINANCIALS

Company Type: Public

Income Statement — FYE: September 30

	ASSETS ($mil)	NET INCOME ($mil)	INCOME AS % OF ASSETS	EMPLOYEES
09/21	1,720.5	29.5	1.7%	590
09/20	1,764.6	33.3	1.9%	696
09/19	1,222.5	16.1	1.3%	473
09/18	1,034.4	10.9	1.1%	364
09/17	891.1	9.3	1.0%	201
Annual Growth	17.9%	33.5%	—	30.9%

2021 Year-End Financials

Return on assets: 1.6%
Return on equity: 17.5%
Long-term debt ($ mil.): —
No. of shares ($ mil.): 7.1
Sales ($ mil.): 185.6
Dividends
Yield: 1.0%
Payout: 5.2%
Market value ($ mil.): 199.0

	STOCK PRICE ($) FY Close	P/E High/Low		PER SHARE ($) Earnings	Dividends	Book Value
09/21	27.96	21	7	4.12	0.29	25.31
09/20	54.34	14	6	4.68	0.22	22.07
09/19	63.22	29	19	2.27	0.21	17.17
09/18	68.28	46	33	1.53	0.20	14.37
09/17	53.40	39	25	1.32	0.18	13.84
Annual Growth	(14.9%)	—	—	32.8%	12.5%	16.3%

First Western Financial Inc

EXECUTIVES

President, Chief Executive Officer, Subsidiary Officer, Chairman, Scott C. Wylie, $450,000 total compensation
Chief Financial Officer, Treasurer, Subsidiary Officer, Julie A. Courkamp, $242,500 total compensation
Subsidiary Officer, Scott J. Lawley
Subsidiary Officer, Gary B. Lutz
Subsidiary Officer, John E. Sawyer, $240,000 total compensation
Subsidiary Officer, Josh M. Wilson
Subsidiary Officer, Daniel C. Thompson
Lead Director, Director, Joseph C. Zimlich
Director, Julie A. Caponi
Director, David R. Duncan
Director, Thomas A. Gart
Director, Patrick H. Hamill
Director, Luke A. Latimer
Director, Eric D. Sipf
Director, Mark L. Smith
Auditors : Crowe LLP

LOCATIONS

HQ: First Western Financial Inc
1900 16th Street, Suite 1200, Denver, CO 80202
Phone: 303 531-8100
Web: www.myfw.com

HISTORICAL FINANCIALS

Company Type: Public

Income Statement — FYE: December 31

	ASSETS ($mil)	NET INCOME ($mil)	INCOME AS % OF ASSETS	EMPLOYEES
12/20	1,973.6	24.5	1.2%	305
12/19	1,251.6	8.0	0.6%	255
12/18	1,084.3	5.6	0.5%	245
12/17	969.6	2.0	0.2%	263
12/16	915.9	2.3	0.3%	0
Annual Growth	21.2%	80.7%	—	—

2020 Year-End Financials

Return on assets: 1.5%
Return on equity: 17.3%
Long-term debt ($ mil.): —
No. of shares ($ mil.): 7.9
Sales ($ mil.): 104.5
Dividends
Yield: —
Payout: —
Market value ($ mil.): 156.0

	STOCK PRICE ($) FY Close	P/E High/Low		PER SHARE ($) Earnings	Dividends	Book Value
12/20	19.57	6	4	3.08	0.00	19.49
12/19	16.47	17	11	1.01	0.00	16.08
12/18	11.71	31	17	0.63	0.00	14.67
Annual Growth	29.3%	—	—	121.1%	—	15.3%

FirstCash Holdings Inc

FirstCash operates some 2,825 pawnshops and cash advance stores in the US, Colombia, Mexico, El Salvador, and Guatemala. The company lends money secured by such personal property as jewelry, electronics, tools, sporting goods, and musical equipment. The company also melts certain quantities of non-retailable scrap jewelry and sells the gold, silver and diamonds in the commodity markets. Pawn stores provide a quick and convenient source of small, secured consumer loans, also known as pawn loans, to unbanked, under-banked and credit-constrained customers. Pawn loans are safe and affordable non-recourse loans for which the customer has no legal obligation to repay. The US operations generate some 65% of total revenue. The company changed in name to FirstCash Holdings, Inc. from FirstCash, Inc. in late 2021.

Operations

The company organizes its operations into three reportable segments: US Pawn (about 65% of sales), Latin America Pawn (some 35%), and Retail POS Payment Solutions (generates the rest).

The US pawn segment consists of all pawn operations in the US and the Latin America pawn segment consists of all pawn operations in Mexico, Guatemala, Colombia and El Salvador. The retail POS payment solutions segment consists of AFF operations in the US and Puerto Rico. Its primary business line continues to be the operation of retail pawn stores, also known as pawnshops, which focus on serving cash and credit-constrained consumers. Pawn stores help customers meet small short-term cash needs by providing non-recourse pawn loans and buying merchandise directly from customers.

Overall, retail merchandise generated over 65% of sales, pawn loan fees with about 30%, while leased merchandise income, interest and fees on finance receivables, and wholesale scrap jewelry generated the rest.

Geographic Reach

Fort Worth, Texas-based FirstCash operated some 2,825 pawn store locations composed of around 1,080 stores in some 25 US states and the District of Columbia, around 1,655 stores in over 30 states in Mexico, some 60 stores in Guatemala, approximately 15 stores in Colombia and nearly 15 stores in El Salvador. The company generated some 65% of its revenue from its shops in the US, and some 35% generated from Latin America, with most of that coming from Mexico.

Sales and Marketing

Advertising expenses in 2021, 2020, and 2019, was $1.0 million, $1.1 million, and $1.2 million, respectively.

Financial Performance

The company's revenue for fiscal 2021 increased to $1.7 billion compared from the prior year with $1.6 billion.

Net income for fiscal 2021 increased to $124.9 million compared from the prior year with $106.6 million.

Cash held by the company at the end of fiscal 2021 increased to $120.0 million. Cash provided by operations and financing activities were $223.3 million and $577.0 million, respectively. Cash used for investing activities was $744.6 million, mainly for portion of AFF acquisition paid in cash.

Strategy

The company's business strategy is to continue growing pawn revenues and income by opening new ("de novo") retail pawn locations, acquiring existing pawn stores in strategic markets and increasing revenue and operating profits in existing stores. Over the last five years, 1,021 pawn stores have been opened or acquired with the net store count growing at a compound annual store growth rate of 6% over this period. The company intends to open or acquire additional stores in locations where management believes appropriate consumer demand and other favorable conditions exist.

Mergers and Acquisitions

In late 2021, FirstCash Holdings, Inc. has closed its previously announced acquisition of American First Finance (AFF), a rapidly growing, technology-driven virtual lease-to-own ("LTO") and retail finance provider focused on underserved, non-prime customers. Under the terms of the agreement, the total consideration payable at closing is valued at approximately $1.17 billion. The completion of the acquisition establishes FirstCash's entry into the large and growing lease to own and point-of-sale payment space. The addition of American First Finance launches FirstCash into the large and growing point-of-sale ("POS") and buy now pay later payment space, which is estimated to have a $600 billion total addressable market.

Company Background

The company first expanded its presence into Mexico in 2008 with the acquisition of Presta Max, a chain of 16 pawn shops in southern Mexico.

HISTORY

First Cash grew from a single pawnshop in Dallas. John Payne traded some land in Colorado for the store after selling his Dallas bank in 1979. He and his wife ran the shop until 1985, when they sold it and built a new shop in the suburbs, aiming to achieve the ambience of a video store.

It was an opportune moment: The Texas economy, particularly the banking industry, was just beginning its slide. Payne (who later left the company) incorporated First Cash in 1988 and brought in professional management under former banker Rick Powell in 1990.

Eight-store First Cash went public in 1991. Acquisitions and expansions included the 1994 purchase of a Baltimore/Washington, DC, area chain. The next year First Cash upgraded its computers to improve inventory control and loan valuations, and became the first major pawn chain to stop selling or making loans on handguns.

In 1996 and 1997 First Cash added stores in Maryland and Texas. The next year it bought 10-store chain JB Pawn (from a brother of First Cash director Richard Burke) and about 20 individual shops. First Cash also moved into check-cashing, buying 11-store Miraglia.

To reflect the diversification, the company changed its name to First Cash Financial Services in early 1999. That year First Cash joined other pawnbrokers and short-term lenders in moving into Mexico. In 2000 First Cash partnered with Pawnbroker.com to provide online financial and support services to pawn shops.

First Cash discontinued its auto loan operations in 2008, two years after purchasing dealer and lender Auto Master. In the midst of a worldwide credit crunch, First Cash sold Auto Master to Minneapolis-based Interstate Auto Group (dba CarHop).

The company first expanded its presence into Mexico in 2008 with the acquisition of Presta Max, a chain of 16 pawn shops in southern Mexico.

EXECUTIVES

Chairman, Daniel R. Feehan

Vice-Chairman, Chief Executive Officer, Director, Rick L. Wessel, $1,175,000 total compensation

President, Chief Operating Officer, T. Brent Stuart, $725,000 total compensation

Executive Vice President, Chief Financial Officer, Treasurer, Secretary, R. Douglas Orr, $675,000 total compensation

Region Officer, Raul R. Ramos, $420,000 total compensation

Lead Independent Director, Director, Mikel D. Faulkner

Director, Daniel E. Berce

Director, Paula K. Garrett

Director, James H. Graves

Director, Randel G. Owen

Auditors : RSM US LLP

LOCATIONS

HQ: FirstCash Holdings Inc
1600 West 7th Street, Fort Worth, TX 76102
Phone: 817 335-1100
Web: www.firstcash.com

2015 Sales

	$ in mil.	% of total
Latin America	367.8	48
US	336.8	52
Total	704.6	100

2015 Locations

	No.
Mexico	705
Gautemala	32
US	
Texas	180
Colorado	31
Maryland	29
South Carolina	21
North Carolina	24
Indiana	10
Kentucky	15
Missouri	8
Oklahoma	4
Virginia	6
Tennessee	3
Wyoming	3
District of Columbia	3
Nebraska	1
Total	1,075

PRODUCTS/OPERATIONS

2015 Sales

	$ mil.	% of total
Retail merchandise	449.3	63
Pawn loan fees	195.4	28
Wholesale Scrap jewelry	32.0	5
Consumer loan and credit services fees	27.9	4
Total	704.6	100

Selected Subsidiaries

All Access Special Events, LLC
American Loan Employee Services, S.A. de C.V. (Mexico)
Cardplus, Inc.
College Park Jewelers, Inc.
Famous Pawn, Inc.
FCFS MO, Inc.
FCFS OK, Inc.
FCFS SC, Inc.
First Cash Corp.
First Cash Credit, Ltd.
First Cash, Inc.
First Cash Credit Management, LLC
First Cash, Ltd.
First Cash Management, LLC
First Cash, S.A. de C.V. (Mexico)
King Pawn, Inc.
King Pawn II, Inc.
Maryland Precious Metals, Inc.
SHAC, LLC
T.J. Unlimited, LLC

COMPETITORS

399 STRAND LIMITED
CHRISTIE'S INTERNATIONAL PLC
EZCORP, INC.
FRONTIER MERGER SUB LLC
PRICESMART, INC.
SAVERS, INC.
TARGET CORPORATION
VALUE FINANCIAL SERVICES, INC.
WALMART INC.
XPONENTIAL, INC.

HISTORICAL FINANCIALS

Company Type: Public

Income Statement — FYE: December 31

	REVENUE ($mil)	NET INCOME ($mil)	NET PROFIT MARGIN	EMPLOYEES
12/20	1,631.2	106.5	6.5%	17,000
12/19	1,864.4	164.6	8.8%	21,000
12/18	1,780.8	153.2	8.6%	19,000
12/17	1,779.8	143.8	8.1%	17,000
12/16	1,088.3	60.1	5.5%	16,200
Annual Growth	10.6%	15.4%	—	1.2%

2020 Year-End Financials

Debt ratio: 26.0%
Return on equity: 8.0%
Cash ($ mil.): 65.8
Current Ratio: 3.03
Long-term debt ($ mil.): 615.9
No. of shares ($ mil.): 41.0
Dividends
  Yield: —
  Payout: 42.1%
Market value ($ mil.): 2,874.0

	STOCK PRICE ($) FY Close	P/E High/Low		PER SHARE ($) Earnings	Dividends	Book Value
12/20	70.04	34	20	2.56	1.08	31.28
12/19	80.63	28	18	3.81	1.02	31.89
12/18	72.35	28	20	3.41	0.91	30.23
12/17	67.45	23	14	3.00	0.77	31.45
12/16	47.00	31	18	1.72	0.57	29.89
Annual Growth	10.5%	—	—	10.5%	17.6%	1.1%

Five Below Inc

Five Below is a leading high-growth value retailer offering trend-right, high-quality products loved by tweens, teens and beyond. Operating a fast-growing chain of specialty retail stores, it sells a broad range of trend-right products, most priced at $5 and below. The company operates approximately 1,190 stores in shopping centers in some 40 US states; it also operates an e-commerce site. Core merchandise includes fun but inexpensive items meant to entice teens, such as jewelry and accessories, novelty t-shirts, novelty socks, sports gear, decor and crafts, and mobile phone accessories. Five Below was founded in 2002.

Operations

Five Below has three categories of youth-oriented merchandise: leisure, fashion and home, and party and snack.

Leisure is the largest segment, accounting for about 50% of revenue, and includes games, tech, books, electronics accessories, and sporting goods, among other products. Fashion and home (approximately 30%) includes "attitude" t-shirts, personal accessories, home goods, storage options, and beauty offerings, while party and snack (more than 20%) includes candy, beverages, greeting cards, other snacks, and party and seasonal goods.

The company works with approximately 1,000 vendors, with no single vendor representing more than 5% of its purchase.

Its typical store features in excess of 4,000 stock-keeping units, or SKUs, across a number of the company's category worlds including Style, Room, Sports, Tech, Create, Party, Candy and New & Now.

Geographic Reach

From its base in the Northeast (the company is headquartered in Philadelphia), Five Below has a significant number of stores in the Northeastern and Midwestern regions of the US. The company operates in approximately 40 states that include Arizona, California, Florida, Georgia, North Carolina, Texas and Virginia.

The company has distribution centers in Pedricktown, New Jersey, Olive Branch, Mississippi, Forsyth, Georgia, Conroe, Texas, Buckeye, Arizona and Cincinnati, Ohio.

Sales and Marketing

Five Below markets its products through traditional advertising in newspapers and on television, as well as digital advertising, commercial and a growing social media presence. For new store openings, the company seeks to create community awareness and consumer excitement predominantly through digital advertising, public relations and community outreach promoting the grand opening and by creating an engaging grand opening event that includes contests, and giveaways. Its stores are often located in community and lifestyle shopping centers in urban, suburban, and semi-rural markets.

As its geography and store count has increased so has Five Below's spending on advertising. It spent approximately $31.3 million, $31.6 million and $48.1 million in fiscal 2021, fiscal 2020 and fiscal 2019, respectively.

Financial Performance

Net sales increased to $2.8 billion in the fiscal year 2021 from $2 billion in the fiscal year 2020, an increase of $886.3 million, or 45%. The increase was the result of a comparable sales increase of $566.6 million and a non-comparable sales increase of $319.7 million.

In 2021, the company had a net income of $278.8 million, a 126% increase from the previous year's net income of $123.4 million.

The company's cash at the end of 2021 was $65 million. Operating activities generated $327.9 million, while investing activities used $465.6 million, mainly for purchases of investment securities and other investments. Financing activities used another $66.1 million, primarily for the repurchase and retirement of common stock.

Strategy

Five Below believes it can grow its net sales and earnings by executing on its strategies. The company aims to grow its store base; drive comparable sales; increase brand awareness; and enhance operating margins.

Grow Its Store Base. The company analyzes the demographics of the surrounding trade areas and the performance of adjacent retailers, as well as traffic and specific site characteristics and other variables. As of January 29, 2022, it has executed lease agreements for the opening of 89 new stores in fiscal 2022.

Drive Comparable Sales. The company intends to increase brand awareness through cost-effective marketing efforts and enthusiastic customer engagement.

Increase Brand Awareness. The company's strategy predominantly includes the use of digital marketing, streaming video, television, philanthropic and local community marketing to support existing and new market entries. It leverages its growing e-mail database, mobile website and social media presence to drive brand engagement and increased store visits within existing and new markets.

Enhance Operating Margins. A primary driver of the company's expected margin expansion will come from leveraging cost structure as it continues to increase store base and drive its average net sales per store. The company intends to capitalize on opportunities across its supply chain as it grows its business and achieve further economies of scale.

Company Background

Five Below was founded in 2002 as Cheap Holdings by former CEO Thomas Vellios and David Schlessinger. The company changed its name to Five Below later in 2002 and went public in 2012.

EXECUTIVES

Chairman, Director, Thomas G. Vellios
President, Chief Executive Officer, Director, Joel D. Anderson, $815,385 total compensation
Merchandising Chief Merchandising Officer, Michael F. Romanko, $481,154 total compensation
Operations Executive Vice President, Operations Chief Retail Officer, George S. Hill, $481,154 total compensation
Chief Financial Officer, Treasurer, Kenneth R. Bull, $495,192 total compensation
Chief Administrative Officer, Eric M. Specter, $523,077 total compensation
Secretary, Ronald James Masciantonio
Director, Catherine Elizabeth Buggeln
Director, Michael F. Devine
Director, Bernard Kim
Director, Ronald L. Sargent
Director, Kathleen S. Barclay
Director, Thomas M. Ryan
Director, Dinesh S. Lathi
Director, Richard L. Markee
Director, Zuhairah Scott Washington
Auditors : KPMG LLP

LOCATIONS

HQ: Five Below Inc
701 Market Street, Suite 300, Philadelphia, PA 19106
Phone: 215 546-7909
Web: www.fivebelow.com

2018 Locations

	No.
Texas	80
Pennsylvania	64
Florida	62
New York	55
Illinois	43
Michigan	41
New Jersey	39
Ohio	37
California	33
Virginia	31
Other states	265
Total	750

PRODUCTS/OPERATIONS

2018 Sales

	% of total
Leisure	51
Fashion & home	31
Party & snack	18
Total	100

COMPETITORS

BIG LOTS, INC.
DICK'S SPORTING GOODS, INC.
DOLLAR GENERAL CORPORATION
DOLLAR TREE, INC.
ESSELUNGA SPA
FAMILY DOLLAR STORES, INC.
FRED'S, INC.
OLLIE'S BARGAIN OUTLET HOLDINGS, INC.
RTW RETAILWINDS, INC.
TILLY'S, INC.

HISTORICAL FINANCIALS

Company Type: Public

Income Statement — FYE: January 30

	REVENUE ($mil)	NET INCOME ($mil)	NET PROFIT MARGIN	EMPLOYEES
01/21*	1,962.1	123.3	6.3%	19,000
02/20	1,846.7	175.0	9.5%	16,600
02/19	1,559.5	149.6	9.6%	13,900
02/18	1,278.2	102.4	8.0%	12,100
01/17	1,000.4	71.8	7.2%	9,500
Annual Growth	18.3%	14.5%	—	18.9%

*Fiscal year change

2021 Year-End Financials

Debt ratio: —
Return on equity: 15.0%
Cash ($ mil.): 268.7
Current Ratio: 1.73
Long-term debt ($ mil.): —
No. of shares ($ mil.): 55.9
Dividends
Yield: —
Payout: —
Market value ($ mil.): 9,829.0

	STOCK PRICE ($) FY Close	P/E High/Low		PER SHARE ($) Earnings	Dividends	Book Value
01/21*	175.73	88	24	2.20	0.00	15.77
02/20	113.22	47	33	3.12	0.00	13.64
02/19	124.73	50	23	2.66	0.00	11.03
02/18	62.94	39	20	1.84	0.00	8.27
01/17	37.60	40	25	1.30	0.00	6.04
Annual Growth	47.0%	—	—	14.1%	—	27.1%

*Fiscal year change

Flagstar Bancorp, Inc.

Flagstar Bancorp is the holding company for Flagstar Bank, which operates about 160 branches mostly in Michigan. Beyond offering traditional deposit and loan products, Flagstar's mortgages originations specializes in originating, purchasing, and servicing one-to-four family residential mortgage loans across roughly 30 states through a network of brokers and correspondents. Some 65% of the Flagstar's revenue is linked to mortgage origination and servicing, while another some 35% comes from its community banking business. Boasting some $25.5billion in assets, Flagstar is 6th largest bank mortgage originator in the nation and the 6th largest sub-servicer of mortgage loans nationwide.

Operations

Flagstar Bancorp operates three business segments: Mortgage Originations, Community Banking, and Mortgage Servicing.

Mortgage Originations, which made up over 50% of its total revenue and acquires and sells one-to-four family residential mortgage loans; Community Banking (some 35%), which provides originates loans, deposit and fee based services to businesses, individuals, government entities, and mortgage customers; and Mortgage Servicing (nearly 15% of revenue), which charges a fee to service and sub-service mortgage loans for others through scalable servicing platform.

About 45% of its revenue came from interest income (mostly from loans), while most of the rest came from gains on loan sales (some 35% of revenue), loan fees and charges (less than 10%), loan administration income for over 5%, and other non-interest income for over 5%.

Its loan portfolio is consist of consumer loans, which includes residential first mortgage (around 10%), home equity (some 5%), and others (roughly 10%); and commercial loans including warehouse lending (over 35%), commercial real estate (roughly 25%), and commercial and industrial (about 25%).

Geographic Reach

The Troy, Michigan-based company has nearly 160 branches in Michigan, Indiana, California, Wisconsin, and Ohio. It also has about 115 retail mortgage locations, three wholesale lending offices, and nearly 15 commercial lending offices. These locations are primarily leased and located in about 30 states.

Sales and Marketing

The company offers a full set of banking products to the consumer, commercial, and government customers.

Flagstar's advertising expenses totaled $26 million, $22 million, and $25 million for the years ended 2021, 2020, and 2019, respectively.

Financial Performance

Net interest income grew $62 million, or 9% to $747 million compared to the prior year, driven by growth in average interest-earning assets of $1.2 billion, or 5%, and the net interest margin improvement of 12 basis points. Asset growth was led by the company's warehouse lending portfolio, which increased $0.9 billion, or 19%, and growth in its loans held-for-sale portfolio of $1.6 billion, or 29%.

In 2021, the company had a net income of $533 million, a 1% decrease from the previous year's net income of $538 million.

The company's cash at the end of 2021 was $1.1 billion. Investing activities generated $6 billion, while investing operating activities used $1.2 billion. Financing activities used another $4.4 billion, primarily for net change in short-term FHLB borrowings and other short-term debt.

Strategy

As a part of the company's risk management strategy, it uses derivative financial instruments to minimize fluctuation in earnings caused by market risk. The company uses forward sales commitments to hedge its unclosed mortgage closing pipeline and funded mortgage LHFS. All of the company's derivatives and mortgage loan production originated for sale are accounted for at fair market value.

Company Background

In 2011, to raise capital after suffering the effects of the housing bust, the company sold 27 bank branches in the suburbs north of Atlanta, along with their deposits, to PNC. The company also sold its 22 Indiana branches to First Financial Bancorp later that year. In addition to bringing in some cash, the divestitures help Flagstar focus on its Michigan operations.

MP Thrift, an affiliate of private equity firm MatlinPatterson Global Advisors, assumed a controlling stake of Flagstar in 2009. Today it owns 64% of the company.

EXECUTIVES

President, Chief Executive Officer, Subsidiary Officer, Director, Alessandro P. Dinello, $950,000 total compensation

Executive Vice President, Chief Financial Officer, Subsidiary Officer, James K. Ciroli, $480,577 total compensation

Executive Vice President, Chief Risk Officer, Subsidiary Officer, Stephen V. Figliuolo, $403,750 total compensation

Executive Vice President, General Counsel, Subsidiary Officer, Patrick M. McGuirk, $294,245 total compensation

Executive Vice President, Division Officer, Andrew W. Ottaway, $371,634 total compensation

Division Officer, Lee Matthew Smith, $712,500 total compensation

Non-Executive Chairman, Director, John D. Lewis

Lead Independent Director, Director, David L. Treadwell

Director, Jay J. Hansen

Director, Bruce E. Nyberg

Director, James A. Ovenden

Director, Peter Schoels

Director, Jennifer R. Whip

Director, Lori Jordan

Director, Toan Huynh

Auditors: PricewaterhouseCoopers LLP

LOCATIONS

HQ: Flagstar Bancorp, Inc.
5151 Corporate Drive, Troy, MI 48098-2639
Phone: 248 312-2000
Web: www.flagstar.com

PRODUCTS/OPERATIONS

2015 Sales

	$ mil.	% of total
Interest income		
Loans	295	36
Investment securities	59	7
Interest-earning deposits and other	1	—
Non interest income		
Net gain on loan sales	288	36
Loan fees & charges	67	8
Deposit fees and charges	25	3
Loan administration income	26	3
Net return on mortgage serving assets	28	3
Net (loss) gain on sale of assets	(1)	—
Representation and warranty benefit (provision)	19	2
Other non-interest income	18	2
Total	825	100

2015 Sales

	% of total
Mortgage origination	58
Community Banking	24
Mortgage Servicing	12
Others	6
Total	100

Selected Products/Services

Personal Banking
Banking
Checking Accounts
Checking
Savings Accounts
Savings Accounts: Personal
Banking Goals
View All Rates
Online Banking Login: Personal Accounts
Mobile Banking
Detroit Red Wings Partnership
Foreign Currency
Loans
Home Loans
Refinance
Home Equity Solutions
Credit Cards
Money Market
Investment Accounts: Personal

COMPETITORS

ASTORIA FINANCIAL CORPORATION
BANKFINANCIAL CORPORATION
BEAR STATE FINANCIAL, INC.
FIRST FEDERAL SAVINGS AND LOAN ASSOCIATION OF LAKEWOOD
LEGACYTEXAS FINANCIAL GROUP, INC.
PEOPLE'S UNITED FINANCIAL, INC.
PROVIDENT FINANCIAL SERVICES, INC.
REPUBLIC FIRST BANCORP, INC.
THE SOUTHERN BANC COMPANY INC
TRUSTCO BANK CORP N Y

HISTORICAL FINANCIALS

Company Type: Public

Income Statement — FYE: December 31

	ASSETS ($mil)	NET INCOME ($mil)	INCOME AS % OF ASSETS	EMPLOYEES
12/20	31,038.0	538.0	1.7%	5,214
12/19	23,266.0	218.0	0.9%	4,453
12/18	18,531.0	187.0	1.0%	3,938
12/17	16,912.0	63.0	0.4%	3,525
12/16	14,053.0	171.0	1.2%	2,886
Annual Growth	21.9%	33.2%	—	15.9%

2020 Year-End Financials

Return on assets: 1.9%   Dividends
Return on equity: 26.9%   Yield: 0.4%
Long-term debt ($ mil.): —   Payout: 2.1%
No. of shares ($ mil.): 52.6   Market value ($ mil.): 2,146.0
Sales ($ mil.): 2,144

	STOCK PRICE ($) FY Close	P/E High/Low		PER SHARE ($)		
		High	Low	Earnings	Dividends	Book Value
12/20	40.76	4	2	9.52	0.20	41.80
12/19	38.25	10	7	3.80	0.16	31.57
12/18	26.40	12	8	3.21	0.00	27.19
12/17	37.42	35	23	1.09	0.00	24.41
12/16	26.94	11	6	2.66	0.00	23.51
Annual Growth	10.9%	—	—	37.5%	—	15.5%

Floor & Decor Holdings Inc

EXECUTIVES

Chairman, Director, Norman H. Axelrod

Vice-Chairman, Director, George Vincent West

Chief Executive Officer, Director, Thomas V. Taylor, $927,885 total compensation

Executive Vice President, Chief Financial Officer, Bryan Langley

Executive Vice President, Chief Financial Officer, Trevor S. Lang, $432,558 total compensation

Strategy Executive Vice President, Supply Chain Executive Vice President, Business Development Executive Vice President, Brian K. Robbins, $392,368 total compensation

Executive Vice President, General Counsel, Secretary, David V. Christopherson, $340,454 total compensation

Store Operations Executive Vice President, Steven A. Denny

Merchandising Executive Vice President, Ersan Sayman

Chief Accounting Officer, Luke Olson

Director, Charles D. Young

Director, Dwight James

Director, Peter M. Starrett

Director, William T. Giles

Director, Ryan R. Marshall

Director, Richard L. Sullivan

Director, Felicia D. Thornton

Auditors : Ernst & Young LLP

LOCATIONS
HQ: Floor & Decor Holdings Inc
2500 Windy Ridge Parkway SE, Atlanta, GA 30339
Phone: 404 471-1634
Web: www.flooranddecor.com

HISTORICAL FINANCIALS
Company Type: Public

Income Statement — FYE: December 31

	REVENUE ($mil)	NET INCOME ($mil)	NET PROFIT MARGIN	EMPLOYEES
12/20	2,425.7	194.9	8.0%	8,790
12/19	2,045.4	150.6	7.4%	7,317
12/18	1,709.8	116.1	6.8%	6,566
12/17	1,384.7	102.7	7.4%	5,534
12/16	1,050.7	43.0	4.1%	4,391
Annual Growth	23.3%	45.9%	—	18.9%

2020 Year-End Financials
Debt ratio: 7.2%
Return on equity: 21.7%
Cash ($ mil.): 307.7
Current Ratio: 1.49
Long-term debt ($ mil.): 207.1
No. of shares ($ mil.): 104.3
Dividends
 Yield: —
 Payout: —
Market value ($ mil.): 9,691.0

	STOCK PRICE ($) FY Close	P/E High/Low		PER SHARE ($) Earnings	Dividends	Book Value
12/20	92.85	53	14	1.84	0.00	9.56
12/19	50.30	34	17	1.44	0.00	7.53
12/18	26.01	48	20	1.11	0.00	5.99
12/17	49.59	43	28	1.03	0.00	4.64
Annual Growth	23.3%	—	—	21.3%	—	27.3%

FNB Corp

F.N.B. Corporation is a bank holding company and a financial holding company. Through the company's largest subsidiary, it provides a full range of financial services, principally to consumers, corporations, governments and small- to medium-sized businesses in its market areas through its subsidiary network. The company has nearly 335 banking offices throughout Pennsylvania, Ohio, Maryland, West Virginia, North Carolina, South Carolina, Washington, DC, and Virginia. In addition to community banking and consumer finance, FNB also has segments devoted to insurance and wealth management. It also offers leasing and merchant banking services.

Operations
FNB operates in three business segments, with the largest being the Community Banking segment consisting of a regional community bank. The Wealth Management segment consists of a trust company, a registered investment advisor and a subsidiary that offers broker-dealer services through a third-party networking arrangement with a non-affiliated licensed broker-dealer entity. The Insurance segment consists of an insurance agency and a reinsurer.

Community Banking segment consists of FNBPA, which offers commercial and consumer banking services. Commercial banking solutions include corporate banking, small business banking, investment real estate financing, business credit, capital markets and lease financing. Consumer banking products and services include deposit products, mortgage lending, consumer lending and a complete suite of mobile and online banking services. Additionally, Bank Capital Services, LLC, a subsidiary of FNBPA, offers commercial loans and leases to customers in need of new or used equipment.

Wealth Management segment delivers wealth management services to individuals, corporations and retirement funds, as well as existing customers of the Community Banking segment, located primarily within the company's geographic markets.

Insurance segment operates principally through FNIA, which is a subsidiary of FNB. FNIA is a full-service insurance brokerage agency offering numerous lines of commercial and personal insurance through major carriers to businesses and individuals primarily within FNB's geographic markets. This segment also includes a reinsurance subsidiary, Penn-Ohio.

The majority of the company's revenue comes from loans and leases.

Geographic Reach
FNB, headquartered in Pittsburgh, Pennsylvania operates in seven states and the District of Columbia. Its market coverage spans several major metropolitan areas including: Pittsburgh, Pennsylvania; Baltimore, Maryland; Cleveland, Ohio; Washington, DC; and Charlotte, Raleigh, Durham and the Piedmont Triad (Winston-Salem, Greensboro and High Point) in North Carolina.

Sales and Marketing
Marketing expense totaled $14.3 million for 2021 and $12.6 million for 2020.

Financial Performance
The company's revenue for fiscal 2021 increased to $1.24 billion compared from the prior year with $1.22 billion.

Net income for fiscal 2021 increased by 42% to $404.6 million compared from the prior year with $286.0 million.

Cash held by the company at the end of fiscal 2021 increased to $3.5 billion. Cash provided by operations and financing activities were $530 million and $1.7 billion, respectively. Cash used for investing activities was $153 million, mainly for purchases debt securities available for sale.

Strategy
F.N.B. Corporation's business strategy focuses primarily on providing quality, consumer- and commercial-based financial services adapted to the needs of each of the markets it serves. F.N.B. seeks to maintain its community orientation by providing local management with certain autonomy in decision making, enabling them to respond to customer requests more quickly and to concentrate on transactions within their market areas. The company seeks to preserve some decision making at a local level, however, it has centralized legal, loan review, credit underwriting, accounting, investment, audit, loan operations, deposit operations and data processing functions. The centralization of these processes enables FNB to maintain consistent quality of these functions and to achieve certain economies of scale.

Mergers and Acquisitions
In mid-2022, FNB and UB Bancorp announced the signing of a definitive merger agreement for FNB to acquire Greenville, North Carolina-based UB Bancorp, including its wholly-owned banking subsidiary, Union Bank, in an all-stock transaction valued at $19.56 per share, or a fully diluted market value of approximately $117 million. This merger further increases FNB's presence in North Carolina, moving its proforma deposit market share to eighth in the state, while also adding low-cost granular deposits, which will continue to be value accretive in a rising rate environment.

In early 2022, FNB successfully completed its merger with Baltimore, Maryland-based Howard Bancorp, Inc. (Howard). The acquisition was valued at approximately $443 million. As a result of the merger with Howard, FNB has approximately $42 billion in total assets, $27 billion in total loans and $33 billion in total deposits. The company also has assumed the number six retail deposit share for banks in the Baltimore metropolitan statistical area. Upon completion of the system integration in early 2022, all Howard customers will have access to FNB's enhanced online and mobile banking technology, including its award-winning mobile banking app and proprietary eStore. FNB's new customers also will enjoy a more expansive suite of products and services, such as Capital Markets and Debt Capital Markets capabilities, Insurance, Wealth Management, Private Banking, Treasury Management and Mortgage Banking.

Company Background
Founded in 1864, F.N.B. provides a full range of commercial banking, consumer banking and wealth management solutions through its subsidiary network which is led by its largest affiliate, First National Bank of Pennsylvania The company trades on the New York Stock Exchange under the ticker symbol "FNB."

EXECUTIVES

President, Chief Executive Officer, Subsidiary Officer, Chairman, Director, Vincent J. Delie, $1,075,500 total compensation

Chief Financial Officer, Vincent J. Calabrese, $491,769 total compensation

Chief Credit Officer, Gary L. Guerrieri, $450,789 total compensation

Principal Accounting Officer, Corporate Controller, James L. Dutey
Chief Legal Officer, Corporate Secretary, James G. Orie, $165,000 total compensation
Chief Consumer Banking Officer, Barry C. Robinson, $383,827 total compensation
Chief Wholesale Banking Officer, Bryant Mitchell
Lead Director, Director, William B. Campbell
Director, Pamela A. Bena
Director, James D. Chiafullo
Director, Mary Jo Dively
Director, Robert A. Hormell
Director, David J. Malone
Director, Frank C. Mencini
Director, David L. Motley
Director, Heidi A. Nicholas
Director, John S. Stanik
Director, William J. Strimbu
Auditors : Ernst & Young LLP

LOCATIONS

HQ: FNB Corp
One North Shore Center, 12 Federal Street, Pittsburgh, PA 15212
Phone: 800 555-5455
Web: www.fnb-online.com

PRODUCTS/OPERATIONS

2015 Sales by Segment

	$ mil.	% of total
Community banking	616.2	87
Consumer finance	42.8	6
Wealth management	35.2	5
Insurance	13.1	2
parent & other	1.8	-
Total	709.1	100

2015 Sales

	$ mil.	% of total
Interest		
Loans, including fees	482.1	68
Securities, including dividends	64.6	9
Other	0.1	-
Non-interest		
Service charges	70.7	10
Trust Services	20.8	3
Insurance commissions & fees	16.3	2
Securities commissions & fees	13.6	2
Other	40.9	6
Total	709.1	100

Selected Subsidiaries

F.N.B. Capital Corporation (merchant banking)
First National Bank of Pennsylvania
    Bank Capital Services, LLC (also dba F.N.B. Commercial Leasing)
    First National Trust Company
    F.N.B. Investment Advisors
    First National Investment Services Company
First National Insurance Agency, LLC
Regency Finance Company
    Citizens Financial Services, Inc.
    F.N.B. Consumer Discount Company
    Finance and Mortgage Acceptance Corporation

COMPETITORS

EAGLE BANCORP, INC.
FIRST CITIZENS BANCSHARES, INC.
FIRST HORIZON CORPORATION
MAINSOURCE FINANCIAL GROUP, INC.
NORTHWEST BANCORP, INC.
OLD NATIONAL BANCORP

S&T BANCORP, INC.
UNITED BANKSHARES, INC.
WILSHIRE BANCORP, INC.
WINTRUST FINANCIAL CORPORATION

HISTORICAL FINANCIALS

Company Type: Public

Income Statement — FYE: December 31

	ASSETS ($mil)	NET INCOME ($mil)	INCOME AS % OF ASSETS	EMPLOYEES
12/20	37,354.0	286.0	0.8%	4,197
12/19	34,615.0	387.0	1.1%	4,223
12/18	33,102.0	373.0	1.1%	4,420
12/17	31,417.6	199.2	0.6%	4,748
12/16	21,844.8	170.8	0.8%	3,821
Annual Growth	14.4%	13.7%	—	2.4%

2020 Year-End Financials

Return on assets: 0.7%
Return on equity: 5.7%
Long-term debt ($ mil.): —
No. of shares ($ mil.): 321.6
Sales ($ mil.): 1,424
Dividends
  Yield: 5.0%
  Payout: 56.4%
Market value ($ mil.): 3,055.0

	STOCK PRICE ($) FY Close	P/E High/Low		PER SHARE ($) Earnings	Dividends	Book Value
12/20	9.50	15	7	0.85	0.48	15.42
12/19	12.70	11	8	1.16	0.48	15.02
12/18	9.84	13	8	1.12	0.48	14.21
12/17	13.82	26	19	0.63	0.48	13.63
12/16	16.03	21	14	0.78	0.48	12.18
Annual Growth	(12.3%)	—	—	2.2%	0.0%	6.1%

Focus Financial Partners Inc

EXECUTIVES

Chairman, Chief Executive Officer, Subsidiary Officer, Director, Ruediger Adolf, $831,960 total compensation
Chief Financial Officer, Subsidiary Officer, James Shanahan, $489,250 total compensation
Chief Operating Officer, Subsidiary Officer, Director, Rajini Sundar Kodialam, $545,900 total compensation
General Counsel, Corporate Secretary, Subsidiary Officer, J. Russell McGranahan
Mergers & Acquisitions Senior Managing Director, Mergers & Acquisitions Head, Mergers & Acquisitions Subsidiary Officer, Leonard R. Chang
Director, James D. Carey
Director, Joseph Feliciani
Director, Kristine M. Mashinsky
Director, Greg S. Morganroth
Director, Elizabeth R. Neuhoff
Director, Fayez S. Muhtadie
Director, George S. LeMieux
Auditors : DELOITTE & TOUCHE LLP

LOCATIONS

HQ: Focus Financial Partners Inc
875 Third Avenue, 28th Floor, New York, NY 10022

Phone: 646 519-2456
Web: www.focusfinancialpartners.com

HISTORICAL FINANCIALS

Company Type: Public

Income Statement — FYE: December 31

	REVENUE ($mil)	NET INCOME ($mil)	NET PROFIT MARGIN	EMPLOYEES
12/21	1,797.9	10.4	0.6%	4,400
12/20	1,361.3	28.0	2.1%	3,600
12/19	1,218.3	(12.8)	—	3,400
12/18	910.8	(0.5)	—	2,600
12/17	662.8	(48.3)	—	2,000
Annual Growth	28.3%	—	—	21.8%

2021 Year-End Financials

Debt ratio: 50.8%
Return on equity: 1.4%
Cash ($ mil.): 310.6
Current Ratio: 2.54
Long-term debt ($ mil.): 2,393.6
No. of shares ($ mil.): 76.7
Dividends
  Yield: —
  Payout: —
Market value ($ mil.): 4,584.0

	STOCK PRICE ($) FY Close	P/E High/Low		PER SHARE ($) Earnings	Dividends	Book Value
12/21	59.72	379	230	0.18	0.00	11.34
12/20	43.50	80	24	0.57	0.00	7.52
12/19	29.47	—	—	(0.28)	0.00	6.97
12/18	26.33	—	—	(0.01)	0.00	6.80
Annual Growth	31.4%	—	—	—	—	18.6%

Forestar Group Inc (New)

A majority-owned subsidiary of D.R. Horton?which is one of the largest homebuilders in the US?residential lot development company Forestar Group owns or controls over 38,300 residential lots. Most of those are under contract are either under contract to sell to D.R. Horton or are assigned to D.R. Horton for right of first offer. The company owns approximately 4,400 developed lots. Forestar operates in about 50 markets across about 20 states, and while it sometimes develops land for commercial properties?including apartments, retail centers, and offices?Forestar primarily sells lots to homebuilders and developers for single-family homes.

Operations

Forestar Group manage their operations through one real estate reporting segment.

The real estate segment primarily acquires land and develops infrastructure for single-family residential communities. The company's real estate segment generates its revenues principally from sales of residential single-family finished lots to local, regional and national homebuilders. Forestar generates most of its revenue?more than 80%--from sales of residential lots. Approximately 12,800 lots it owns or controls are under contract to sell to D.R. Horton. D.R. Horton also has the right of first offer on almost another 10,600 of the majority-owned subsidiaries lots. Additionally, Forestar makes short-term investments in finished lots and undeveloped land which it then sells to D.R. Horton. Forestar owns around 4,400 developed lots.

Geographic Reach

Arlington, Texas-based Forestar Group operates in about 50 markets across about 20 US states. The company leases office space in Atlanta, Georgia; Dallas, Texas; and Houston, Texas.

Sales and Marketing

Beyond its relationship with D.R. Horton, Forestar group targets its lot sales to local, regional, and national homebuilders.

Financial Performance

In 2019, the company's revenue increased by about $314 million to $428.3 million, from the prior year. Residential lots sold and residential lot sales revenues have increased as they have grown their business primarily through their strategic relationship with D.R. Horton. In fiscal 2019, the company sold 3,728 residential lots to D.R. Horton for $311.7 million. In the nine months ended September 30, 2018, Forestar sold 642 residential lots to D.R. Horton for $43.6 million.

Net income in 2019 decreased by 52% to $33 million, from $68.8 million in 2018. The decrease was due to the great increase on their cost of sales by about $313.2 million even though with the increase of revenue for about $350 million.

Forestar's cash increased by $47.8 million in 2019. Operations used $391.2 million, mostly for net expenditures on real estate development and acquisitions. Due to the loss of their proceeds from sales of assets the company's investing activities used $0.9 million. Additions to debt drove gains from financing activities to $439.8 million.

Strategy

The company's strategy is focused on making investments in land acquisition and development to expand their residential lot development business across a geographically diversified national platform. They are primarily investing in short duration, phased development projects that generate returns similar to production-oriented homebuilders. This strategy is a unique, lower-risk business model that they expect will produce more consistent returns than other public and private land developers.

Forestar's business strategy has changed substantially over the last few years. They divested their non-core assets in the oil and gas, lodging, multifamily and timberland sectors and began to refocus on residential single-family lot development.

Mergers and Acquisitions
Company Background

In 2017 US homebuilding giant D.R. Horton acquired a 75% stake in Forestar Group for more than $550 million.

EXECUTIVES

Executive Chairman, Director, Donald J. Tomnitz, $225,000 total compensation
Chief Executive Officer, Daniel C. Bartok, $225,000 total compensation
Executive Vice President, Chief Operating Officer, Mark S. Walker
Executive Vice President, Chief Financial Officer, Principal Financial Officer, Principal Accounting Officer, James D. Allen
Director, Samuel R. Fuller
Director, Elizabeth Parmer
Director, G.F. (Rick) Ringler
Director, Lisa H. Jamieson
Auditors : Ernst & Young LLP

LOCATIONS

HQ: Forestar Group Inc (New)
2221 E. Lamar Blvd., Suite 790, Arlington, TX 76006
Phone: 817 769-1860
Web: www.forestargroup.com

PRODUCTS/OPERATIONS

2018 Sales

	$ mil.	% of total
Real estate	75.6	96
Commercial real estate	2.0	3
Other	0.7	1
Total	78.3	100

COMPETITORS

Colliers International Group Inc
DAITO TRUST CONSTRUCTION CO.,LTD.
FIRST PROPERTY GROUP PLC
INVITATION HOMES INC.
MAPELEY ESTATES LIMITED
MARCUS & MILLICHAP COMPANY
MCKAY SECURITIES P L C
PROLOGIS, INC.
REALOGY HOLDINGS CORP.
THE MACERICH COMPANY

HISTORICAL FINANCIALS

Company Type: Public

Income Statement — FYE: September 30

	REVENUE ($mil)	NET INCOME ($mil)	NET PROFIT MARGIN	EMPLOYEES
09/21	1,325.8	110.2	8.3%	250
09/20	931.8	60.8	6.5%	143
09/19	428.3	33.0	7.7%	78
09/18*	78.3	68.8	87.9%	41
12/17	114.3	50.2	44.0%	34
Annual Growth	84.5%	21.7%	—	64.7%

*Fiscal year change

2021 Year-End Financials

Debt ratio: 33.5%
Return on equity: 11.6%
Cash ($ mil.): 153.6
Current Ratio: 0.52
Long-term debt ($ mil.): 704.5
No. of shares ($ mil.): 49.5
Dividends
Yield: —
Payout: —
Market value ($ mil.): 924.0

	STOCK PRICE ($) FY Close	P/E High/Low		PER SHARE ($) Earnings	Dividends	Book Value
09/21	18.63	11	7	2.25	0.00	20.47
09/20	17.70	18	8	1.26	0.00	18.12
09/19	18.28	27	16	0.79	0.00	16.84
09/18*	21.20	16	12	1.64	0.00	16.06
12/17	22.00	19	11	1.19	0.00	14.41
Annual Growth	(4.1%)	—	—	17.3%	—	9.2%

*Fiscal year change

FormFactor Inc

FormFactor is a leading provider of test and measurement technologies. It provides a broad range of high-performance probe cards, analytical probes, probe stations, metrology systems, thermal systems and cryogenic systems to both semiconductor companies and scientific institutions. FormFactor designs probe cards to provide for a precise match with the thermal expansion characteristics of the wafer under test across the range of test operating temperatures. Its customers can use the same probe card for both low and high temperature testing. The majority of sales are to customers in Taiwan, its largest single market. FormFactor began life in 1993 when former IBM researcher, Igor Khandros, began developing products for the semiconductor industry in a tiny New York lab.

Operations

FormFactor operates in two reportable segments consisting of the Probe Cards Segment (generates about 85% of company's total revenue) and the Systems Segment (more than 15% of revenue). Sales of the company's probe cards and analytical probes are included in the Probe Cards Segment, while sales of their probe stations, metrology systems, and thermal sub-systems are included in the Systems Segment.

Geographic Reach

FormFactor primarily manufactures its products in Livermore, San Jose, Carlsbad, and Baldwin Park, California; Beaverton, Oregon; Boulder, Colorado in the US; and in Thiendorf, Germany, but it also has smaller manufacturing facilities in Munich and Bergisch Gladbach, Germany; Suzhou, China; and Yokohama, Japan. It also has sales offices in China, Germany, Japan, Singapore, South Korea, and Taiwan. Outside US, Taiwan is the biggest market for FormFactor products, accounting for some 25% of revenue, followed by China with around 20%, and about 15% from South Korea. Around 15% of sales come from customers in the US.

Sales and Marketing

FormFactor sell their products worldwide through a global direct sales force and a combination of manufacturers' representatives and distributors.

The company's customers include companies, universities and institutions that design or make semiconductor, and semiconductor related products in the Foundry & Logic (about 55% of sales), DRAM (around 20%), Flash (some 5%), Display and Sensor markets. Sales to its largest customer, Intel, accounted for about 20% of 2020 sales. Another top customer, Samsung Electronics, accounted for around 10% of sales.

Financial Performance
The company's revenue in fiscal 2021 increased by 11% to $769.7 million compared with $693.6 million in the prior year. The increase in Flash product revenue in fiscal 2021 compared to fiscal 2020 was driven by increased sales resulting from the acquisition of the probe card assets of Advantest Corporation (Baldwin Park). The increase in Systems product revenue in fiscal 2021 compared to fiscal 2020 was driven by increased sales of cryogenic systems due to the acquisition of High Precision Devices, Inc. ("HPD") and increased sales of thermal sub-systems and metrology systems.

Net income in fiscal 2021 increased to $83.9 million compared with $78.5 million in the prior year. The increase in net income in fiscal 2021 compared to fiscal 2020 was primarily due to increased revenue in both of its reportable segments, partially offset by slightly lower margins driven primarily by product mix and a higher tax rate due to significant one-time tax benefits during fiscal 2020 that did not recur.

Cash held by the company at the end of fiscal 2021 decreased to $155.3 million. Operating activities provided $139.4 million while investing and financing activities used $124.7 million and $47.2 million, respectively. Main cash uses were purchases of marketable securities and purchase of common stock through stock repurchase program.

Strategy
FormFactor has invested and intends to continue to invest considerable resources in proprietary probe card design tools and processes. These tools and processes are intended to enable the rapid and accurate customization of products required to meet customer requirements, including automated routing and trace length adjustment within our probe cards, to rapidly design complex structures.

Through ongoing investments in both its technology and operations, the company continues to innovate and improve so that its products will meet customers' future technical roadmap performance, quality, and commercial requirements. FormFactor also focuses on leveraging these ongoing investments across all advanced probe card markets to realize synergies and economies of scale to benefit our competitiveness, time-to-market and overall profitability.

Company Background
FormFactor was incorporated in 1993, and introduced its first product in 1995. In late-2012, the company acquired Astria Semiconductor Holdings, Inc., including its subsidiary Micro-Probe Incorporated (MicroProbe), in mid- 2016, they acquired Cascade Microtech, Inc. (CMI), and in late-2019, they acquired FRT GmbH.

EXECUTIVES

Chairperson, Director, Thomas St. Dennis, $237,077 total compensation
Chief Executive Officer, Director, Michael D. Slessor, $500,000 total compensation
Chief Financial Officer, Shai Shahar
Secretary, General Counsel, Christy Robertson
Director, Brian C. White
Director, Lothar Maier
Director, Rebeca Obregon-Jimenez
Director, Kelley Steven-Waiss
Director, Jorge Luis Titinger, $165,123 total compensation
Director, Sheri Rhodes
Auditors: KPMG LLP

LOCATIONS

HQ: FormFactor Inc
  7005 Southfront Road, Livermore, CA 94551
Phone: 925 290-4000
Web: www.formfactor.com

2012 Sales

	$ mil.	% of total
Asia/Pacific		
South Korea	58.5	32
Taiwan	37.0	21
Japan	21.3	12
Other countries	22.6	13
North America	27.5	15
Europe	11.6	7
Total	178.5	100

PRODUCTS/OPERATIONS

2014 Sales by Market

	$ mil.	% of total
System-on-a-Chip (SoC)	142.3	53
DRAM	110.8	41
Flash memory devices	15.4	6
Total	268.5	100

Selected Products
DRAM
  Harmony eXP
  PH150XP and PH Series
Flash
  Harmony OneTouch
Known good die (KGD)
  HFTAP (K1, K3, K5)
Logic/SoC
  BladeRunner 175
  TrueScale PP40
MicroSpring interconnect technology
Probe cards
Probe heads (PH50, PH75, PH100, PH150 models)
Special Products
  Parametric
  Takumi Pico
  Takumi Femto
TRE test technology

COMPETITORS

AMKOR TECHNOLOGY, INC.
KOPIN CORPORATION
LAM RESEARCH CORPORATION
MATTSON TECHNOLOGY, INC.
MULTI-FINELINE ELECTRONIX, INC.
OCLARO, INC.
OMNIVISION TECHNOLOGIES, INC.
PHOTRONICS, INC.
RENESAS ELECTRONICS AMERICA INC.
ULTRATECH, INC.

HISTORICAL FINANCIALS
Company Type: Public

Income Statement — FYE: December 25

	NET REVENUE ($mil)	NET INCOME ($mil)	NET PROFIT MARGIN	EMPLOYEES
12/21	769.6	83.9	10.9%	2,293
12/20	693.6	78.5	11.3%	2,166
12/19	589.4	39.3	6.7%	1,836
12/18	529.6	104.0	19.6%	1,676
12/17	548.4	40.9	7.5%	1,685
Annual Growth	8.8%	19.7%	—	8.0%

2021 Year-End Financials
Debt ratio: 2.4%
Return on equity: 10.7%
Cash ($ mil.): 151.0
Current Ratio: 3.52
Long-term debt ($ mil.): 15.4
No. of shares ($ mil.): 78.2
Dividends
  Yield: —
  Payout: —
Market value ($ mil.): 3,482.0

	STOCK PRICE ($) FY Close	P/E High/Low		PER SHARE ($) Earnings	Dividends	Book Value
12/21	44.51	47	31	1.06	0.00	10.43
12/20	42.58	44	16	0.99	0.00	9.61
12/19	26.04	50	25	0.51	0.00	8.46
12/18	14.01	12	8	1.38	0.00	7.83
12/17	15.65	32	19	0.55	0.00	6.32
Annual Growth	29.9%	—	—	17.8%	—	13.3%

Forrester Research Inc.

Forrester is one of the leading research and advisory firms in the world. The firm works closely with business and technology leaders to develop strategies for driving growth. Forrester gains powerful insights through its annual surveys of more than 700,000 consumers and business leaders worldwide. The firm's reports and briefs provide insight into market forces, industry trends, and consumer behavior. Through proprietary research, data and analytics, custom consulting, exclusive executive peer groups, certification, and events, Forrester is revolutionizing how businesses grow in an era of powerful customers.

Operations
In 2021, Forrester realigned its management structure into Research (around 65% of sales), Consulting (over 30%), and Events (less than 5%).

The Research segment includes revenues from Research products and the cost of the organizations responsible for developing and delivering the research products (excluding SiriusDecisions). In addition, the segment includes consulting revenues primarily from the delivery of advisory services (such as workshops, speeches and advisory days) delivered by the research analysts.

Forrester's Consulting products include consulting projects and advisory services and leverage its Research, Technographics, and CX Index data, as well as its proprietary consulting frameworks, to deliver focused insights and recommendations that assist clients with their challenges in developing and executing technology and business strategy, including customer experience, digital strategy, marketing, informing critical decisions, and reducing business risk.

The company host multiple events in various locations in North America, Europe, and the Asia-Pacific region throughout the year. Events bring together executives and other participants serving or interested in the particular subject matter or professional role(s) on which an event focuses.

Geographic Reach

Headquartered in Cambridge, Massachusetts, Forrester has offices in San Francisco, New York City, Dallas, McLean, Virginia, Nashville, Austin, Amsterdam, Frankfurt, London, Paris, New Delhi, Singapore, Lausanne, Switzerland, and Sydney. The firm's products are present in various locations including North America, Europe, and Asia Pacific.

Sales and Marketing

Forrester sells its products and services through its direct sales force. The firm's products and services were delivered to more than 3,000 client companies.

Advertising expenses for the years 2021, 2020 and 2019 were $2.1 million, $0.7 million, and $1.3 million, respectively.

Financial Performance

The company's revenue in 2021 increased by 10% to $494.3 million compared to $449.0 million. The increase in revenues attributable to customers outside of the US was primarily due to an increase in revenues in Europe, the UK, the Asia Pacific region, and Canada.

Net income in 2021 increased to $24.8 million compared with $10.0 million in the prior year.

Cash held by the company at the end of 2021 increased to $118.0 million. Operating activities provided $101.1 million while investing and financing activities used $29.3 million and $49.1 million, respectively. Main cash uses were purchases of marketable investments; and payments on borrowings.

Strategy

The foundation of its business model is its ability to help business and technology leaders tackle their most pressing priorities and drive growth through customer obsession. Forrester helps clients solve problems, make decisions, and take action to deliver results. With its proprietary research, consulting, and events, its business model provides multiple sources of value to its clients and creates a system to expand contract value (CV), which Forrester Research view as its most significant business metric.

The foundation of its business model is its ability to help business and technology leaders tackle their most pressing priorities and drive growth through customer obsession. Forrester helps clients solve problems, make decisions, and take action to deliver results. With its proprietary research, consulting, and events, its business model provides multiple sources of value to its clients and creates a system to expand contract value (CV), which Forrester Research view as its most significant business metric.

HISTORY

George Forrester Colony started Forrester Research (named after his grandmother) in 1983, initially offering a research service called Computing Strategy. New services followed at regular intervals, including advisories on networks (1986), software (1990), people and technology (1994), interactive technology (1996, the year it went public), and entertainment and technology (1997).

The company staked its claim in Europe in 1998, opening Amsterdam's Forrester European Research Center, which conducts research on the European market for high technology. The next year Forrester launched initiatives to deliver more of its products online, cut costs, and increase margins. Forrester furthered its reputation for candor with a 1999 report asserting that HDTV (high definition television) will fail to get off the ground as a viable commercial technology. That year it extended its reach into the UK when it bought Fletcher Research.

In 2000 Forrester Research formed Netquity, a joint venture with Information Resources, to deliver Internet-branding research. The following year the company partnered with firms such as NetRatings and Experian to launch new products and services. It also cut about 15% of its workforce (around 110 jobs) and sold online ad product InternetAdWatch in response to the poor economy. The company cut more jobs in 2002.

The following year, Forrester acquired rival market research firm Giga Information Group for about $62 million. Giga provided answers on day-to-day information technology issues, a complementary feature to Forrester's core industry-focused information.

Forrester has also taken advantage of cost-cutting and redundancy measures. It sold off its Ultimate Consumer Panel operations (credit card, financial statements, and transaction data analysis) to research panelist Lightspeed Online in October 2006.

Forrester purchased New Strategic Oxygen, a company that sold tools to marketing professionals, back in 2009. In 2011 the company acquired Springboard Research, a research and advisory firm with expertise in the Asia/Pacific markets. The acquisition laid the groundwork for Forrester to market its products and services in China.

EXECUTIVES

Chairman, President, Chief Executive Officer, Director, George F. Colony, $407,500 total compensation
Chief Financial Officer, L. Christian Finn
Chief Accounting Officer, Treasurer, Scott Chouinard
Chief Legal Officer, Secretary, Ryan D. Darrah
Chief Research Officer, Carrie Johnson
Director, Warren N. Romine
Director, Jean M. Birch
Director, David Boyce
Director, Neil Bradford, $250,000 total compensation
Director, Anthony J. Friscia
Director, Robert M. Galford
Director, Gretchen G. Teichgraeber
Director, Yvonne Wassenaar
Auditors : PricewaterhouseCoopers LLP

LOCATIONS

HQ: Forrester Research Inc.
60 Acorn Park Drive, Cambridge, MA 02140
Phone: 617 613-6000
Web: www.forrester.com

COMPETITORS

ACXIOM LLC
FACTSET RESEARCH SYSTEMS INC.
GARTNER, INC.
GFK U.K. LIMITED
IDC RESEARCH, INC.
IPSOS PAN AFRICA HOLDINGS LTD
NIELSEN CONSUMER INSIGHTS, INC.
SUMTOTAL SYSTEMS LLC
THE NPD GROUP INC
WESTAT, INC.

HISTORICAL FINANCIALS

Company Type: Public

Income Statement — FYE: December 31

	NET REVENUE ($mil)	NET INCOME ($mil)	NET PROFIT MARGIN	EMPLOYEES
12/20	448.9	9.9	2.2%	1,798
12/19	461.6	(9.5)	—	1,795
12/18	357.5	15.3	4.3%	1,432
12/17	337.6	15.1	4.5%	1,392
12/16	326.0	17.6	5.4%	1,378
Annual Growth	8.3%	(13.3%)	—	6.9%

2020 Year-End Financials

Debt ratio: 16.7%   No. of shares ($ mil.): 19.0
Return on equity: 5.7%   Dividends
Cash ($ mil.): 90.2   Yield: —
Current Ratio: 0.81   Payout: —
Long-term debt ($ mil.): 95.2   Market value ($ mil.): 797.0

	STOCK PRICE ($) FY Close	P/E High/Low		PER SHARE ($) Earnings	Dividends	Book Value
12/20	41.90	87	43	0.53	0.00	9.77
12/19	41.70	—	—	(0.52)	0.00	8.48
12/18	44.70	58	44	0.84	0.80	8.28
12/17	44.20	56	42	0.83	0.76	7.83
12/16	42.95	45	28	0.97	0.72	8.17
Annual Growth	(0.6%)	—	—	(14.0%)	—	4.6%

Fortinet Inc

ortinet is a global leader in cybersecurity solutions provided to a wide variety of organizations, including enterprises, communication service providers, government organizations and small businesses. The company makes network security appliances (sold under its FortiGate line) and software that integrate antivirus, firewall, content filtering, intrusion prevention systems (IPS), and anti-spam functions to protect against computer viruses, worms, and inappropriate web content. The company also offers complementary products that include its FortiManager security management and FortiAnalyzer event analysis systems. To support its broadly dispersed global channel and end-customer base, it has sales professionals in over 100 countries around the world. About 30% of the revenue comes from the Americas.

Operations

Fortinet's area of businesses are Security-Driven Networking, which sells the FortiGate line of network security appliances; the Zero-Trust Access which enables customers to know and control who and what is on their network; Adaptive Cloud Security who enables customers to connect securely to and across their individual, hybrid cloud, multi-cloud and virtualized data center environments by offering security through the company's virtual firewall and other software products; AI-Driven Security Operations that provide a range of products and services for security operations ("SOC") teams; and Security as a Services which offers its services through FortiGuard security subscriptions as an add-on to the company's Fortinet Security Fabric.

The company's products account for about 40% of the company's revenues, followed by security subscriptions at about 35%, and technical support at 30%.

The company's Fortinet outsources the manufacturing of its appliance products to contract manufacturers and original design manufacturers. The company's manufacturers include Micro-Star International Co. Ltd., IBASE Technology, Adlink Technology Inc., Wistron, and several Taiwan-based manufacturers.

Geographic Reach

California-based Fortinet's sales are well spread geographically. The Americas accounts for over 30% of revenue, followed by the Europe, Middle East, and Africa region, about 40%, and the Asia/Pacific region, about 20%.

Sales and Marketing

Fortinet typically sells its security solutions to distributors that sell to resellers, service providers and managed security service providers (MSSPs), who, in turn, sell to end-customers that range from small businesses to large enterprises and industries that include government, telecommunications, technology, government, financial services, education, retail, manufacturing, and health care. Customers may also access its products via the cloud through certain cloud providers such as Amazon Web Services, Microsoft Azure, Google Cloud, Oracle Cloud, Alibaba Cloud and IBM Cloud. The company gets 40% of revenue from just two customers, Exclusive Networks Group, some 30% of revenue, and Ingram Micro Inc., approximately 10%.

Financial Performance

For the past five years, the company's revenues have grown year-over-year ending with 2021 as its highest performing year over the period.

Total revenue was $3.34 billion in 2021, an increase of 29% compared to $2.59 billion in 2020. Product revenue was $1.26 billion in 2021, an increase of 37% compared to $916.4 million in 2020. Service revenue was $2.09 billion in 2021, an increase of 24% compared to $1.68 billion in 2020.

The company's net income also had an increase of $118.3 million to $606.8 million compared to the prior year's $488.5 million.

The company's cash and cash equivalents for 2021 were $1.3 billion. Operating activities provided $1.5 billion. Investing activities used $1.3 billion, while financing activities provided $82.8 million. Main cash uses were for purchases of investments and purchases of property and equipment.

Strategy

Fortinet's marketing strategy is focused on building its brand and driving end-customer demand for security solutions. The company uses a combination of internal marketing professionals and a network of regional and global channel partners. The company also focuses its resources on campaigns, programs and activities that can be leveraged by partners worldwide to extend its marketing reaches, such as sales tools and collateral, product awards and technical certifications, media engagement, training, regional seminars and conferences, webinars and various other demand generation activities.

Another important part of its growth strategy is to increase sales of its products to large and medium-sized businesses, service providers and government organizations.

Mergers and Acquisitions

In 2021, Fortinet closed an acquisition of certain assets and liabilities of ShieldX Networks Inc. ("ShieldX"), a provider of a security platform focusing on protecting multi-cloud data centers from the risk of lateral movement that can lead to attacks such as ransomware, data loss and service disruption, for $10.8 million in cash.

EXECUTIVES

Chairman, Chief Executive Officer, Director, Ken Xie, $625,000 total compensation

Engineering President, Engineering Chief Technology Officer, Director, Michael Xie, $427,000 total compensation

Corporate Development Executive Vice President, Corporate Development General Counsel, Corporate Development Corporate Secretary, John Whittle, $395,000 total compensation

Chief Financial Officer, Chief Accounting Officer, Keith Jensen

Lead Independent Director, Director, William H. Neukom

Director, Ming Hsieh

Director, Kelly Ducourty

Director, Judith Sim

Director, Jean X. Hu

Director, James G. Stavridis

Director, Kenneth A. Goldman, $278,756 total compensation

Auditors : DELOITTE & TOUCHE LLP

LOCATIONS

HQ: Fortinet Inc
899 Kifer Road, Sunnyvale, CA 94086
Phone: 408 235-7700   **Fax:** 408 235-7737
Web: www.fortinet.com

2018 Sales

	$ mil.	% of total
United States	577.2	32
Latin America	120.8	7
Canada	64.9	38
Europe, Middle East & Africa	678	7
Asia/Pacific and Japan	360.3	20
Total	1,801.2	100

PRODUCTS/OPERATIONS

2018 Sales

	$ mil.	% of total
Security Subscription	606.1	34
Technical Support and Other	520.7	29
Products	674.4	37
Total	1,801.2	100

Selected Products

Database security appliance (FortiDB)
E-mail antispam (FortiMail)
Endpoint security software (FortiClient)
Endpoint vulnerability management appliance (FortiScan)
Network event correlation and content archiving (FortiAnalyzer)
Network security appliances (FortiGate)
Secure wireless access product (FortiAP)
Security management (FortiManager)
Spam and virus control subscription (FortiGuard)
Support (FortiCare)
Web application firewall appliance (FortiWeb)

COMPETITORS

ARISTA NETWORKS, INC.

ARUBA NETWORKS, INC.
CISCO SYSTEMS, INC.
F5 NETWORKS, INC.
JUNIPER NETWORKS, INC.
LANTRONIX, INC.
PALO ALTO NETWORKS, INC.
QUALYS, INC.
SILICON GRAPHICS INTERNATIONAL CORP.
SOPHOS LIMITED

HISTORICAL FINANCIALS
Company Type: Public

Income Statement — FYE: December 31

	REVENUE ($mil)	NET INCOME ($mil)	NET PROFIT MARGIN	EMPLOYEES
12/20	2,594.4	488.5	18.8%	8,238
12/19	2,156.2	326.5	15.1%	7,082
12/18	1,801.2	332.2	18.4%	5,845
12/17	1,494.9	31.3	2.1%	5,066
12/16	1,275.4	32.1	2.5%	4,665
Annual Growth	19.4%	97.4%	—	15.3%

2020 Year-End Financials
Debt ratio: —
Return on equity: 44.7%
Cash ($ mil.): 1,061.8
Current Ratio: 1.50
Long-term debt ($ mil.): —
No. of shares ($ mil.): 162.5
Dividends
 Yield: —
 Payout: —
Market value ($ mil.): 24,136.0

	STOCK PRICE ($) FY Close	P/E High	P/E Low	Earnings	Dividends	Book Value
12/20	148.53	51	25	2.91	0.00	5.27
12/19	106.76	57	35	1.87	0.00	7.70
12/18	70.43	47	22	1.91	0.00	5.95
12/17	43.69	251	167	0.18	0.00	3.51
12/16	30.12	196	125	0.18	0.00	4.84
Annual Growth	49.0%	—	—	100.5%	—	2.1%

Founders Bay Holdings

EXECUTIVES
President, Michael Thomas
Auditors : S.R. Chourasiya & Co.

LOCATIONS
HQ: Founders Bay Holdings
913 Market Street, Suite 200, Wilmington, DE 19801
Phone: 302 416-4816
Web: www.fbaytech.com

HISTORICAL FINANCIALS
Company Type: Public

Income Statement — FYE: December 31

	REVENUE ($mil)	NET INCOME ($mil)	NET PROFIT MARGIN	EMPLOYEES
12/20	15.6	7.1	45.4%	0
12/19	12.5	3.7	30.1%	0
12/18	10.1	3.2	32.3%	0
12/17	8.7	3.0	34.8%	0
12/16	7.0	1.7	25.1%	0
Annual Growth	22.3%	41.7%	—	—

2020 Year-End Financials
Debt ratio: —
Return on equity: 32.3%
Cash ($ mil.): 0.6
Current Ratio: 230.83
Long-term debt ($ mil.): —
No. of shares ($ mil.): 49.9
Dividends
 Yield: —
 Payout: —
Market value ($ mil.): 487.0

	STOCK PRICE ($) FY Close	P/E High	P/E Low	Earnings	Dividends	Book Value
12/20	9.75	—	—	0.00	0.00	0.51
12/19	9.28	160	61	0.07	0.00	0.37
12/18	8.47	—	—	0.00	0.00	0.29
12/17	6.25	—	—	0.00	0.00	0.23
12/16	0.01	—	—	0.00	0.00	0.00
Annual Growth	416.5%	—	—	—	—	—

Four Corners Property Trust Inc

EXECUTIVES
Chairman, Director, John S. Moody
President, Chief Executive Officer, Director, William H. Lenehan, $525,000 total compensation
Chief Financial Officer, Gerald R. Morgan, $357,000 total compensation
Chief Accounting Officer, Principal Accounting Officer, Controller, Niccole Stewart
Chief Transaction Officer, General Counsel, James L. Brat, $300,000 total compensation
Director, Toni S. Steele
Director, Liz Tennican
Director, Douglas B. Hansen
Director, Marran H. Ogilvie
Director, Paul E. Szurek
Director, Charles L. Jemley
Director, Eric S. Hirschhorn
Auditors : KPMG LLP

LOCATIONS
HQ: Four Corners Property Trust Inc
591 Redwood Highway, Suite 3215, Mill Valley, CA 94941
Phone: 415 965-8030
Web: www.fcpt.com

HISTORICAL FINANCIALS
Company Type: Public

Income Statement — FYE: December 31

	REVENUE ($mil)	NET INCOME ($mil)	NET PROFIT MARGIN	EMPLOYEES
12/20	170.9	77.3	45.2%	349
12/19	160.2	72.6	45.3%	361
12/18	143.6	82.3	57.4%	361
12/17	133.2	71.3	53.6%	342
12/16	124.0	156.8	126.4%	324
Annual Growth	8.4%	(16.2%)	—	1.9%

2020 Year-End Financials
Debt ratio: 45.2%
Return on equity: 9.8%
Cash ($ mil.): 11.0
Current Ratio: 0.75
Long-term debt ($ mil.): 753.8
No. of shares ($ mil.): 75.8
Dividends
 Yield: 4.1%
 Payout: 114.1%
Market value ($ mil.): 2,259.0

	STOCK PRICE ($) FY Close	P/E High	P/E Low	Earnings	Dividends	Book Value
12/20	29.77	30	13	1.08	1.23	11.09
12/19	28.19	28	24	1.06	1.15	10.30
12/18	26.20	22	17	1.28	1.10	10.13
12/17	25.70	23	17	1.18	1.00	8.39
12/16	20.52	9	5	2.63	9.29	7.76
Annual Growth	9.7%	—	—	(19.9%)	(39.6%)	9.3%

Fox Factory Holding Corp

Fox Factory Holding Corp., designs, engineers, manufactures and markets performance-defining products and systems for customers worldwide. The company's premium brand, performance-defining products and systems are used primarily on bicycles, side-by-side vehicles, on-road vehicles with and without off-road capabilities, off-road vehicles and trucks, all-terrain vehicles (ATVs), snowmobiles, specialty vehicles and applications, motorcycles and commercial trucks. Fox generates most of its sales from North America region.

Operations
Fox operates in one reportable segments: manufacturing, sale and service of performance-defining products. The company's products fall into two product categories: powered vehicles (around 55% of totals sales), which include Side-by-Sides, certain on-road vehicles with off-road capabilities, off-road vehicles and trucks, ATVs, snowmobiles, specialty vehicles and applications, motorcycles, and commercial trucks; and specialty sports products (some 45%), which consist primarily of bike suspension and component products.

Geographic Reach
Headquartered in Braselton, Georgia, Fox generates more than 60% of total revenue from North America, followed by Asia and Europe with almost 20% each. The remainder is from the rest of the world. Some of the company's administrative, research and development and manufacturing operations are located in California and Georgia. It also manufactures in the US States of Michigan, Colorado, Oregon, Alabama, and Indiana, and internationally in Taiwan and Canada, and maintain sales and service offices in the US and Europe.

Sales and Marketing
Fox sells its suspension products to approximately 150 OEMs and distributes its products to more than 5,000 retail dealers and distributors worldwide. Some 55% of total sales were to OEM customers and approximately 45% were to dealers and distributors for resale in the aftermarket channel. Some of the company's OEM

customers are Giant, Merida, Orbea, Kenstone Metal, Canyon Bicycles, Santa Cruz Bicycles, and Yeti Cycles in Specialty Sports and BRP, Ford, Polaris, Toyota, 4 Wheel Parts, Kawasaki, Yamaha, and Honda in Powered Vehicles.

Fox's advertising costs were $2.7 billion, $2.2 billion, and $1.4 billion for the years ended December 31, 2021, January 1, 2021 and January 3, 2020, respectively.

Financial Performance

The company's revenue has been rising in the last five years with an overall increase of 173% between 2017 and 2021. Net income follows a similar trend but dipped in 2020.

Sales for the year ended December 31, 2021 increased approximately $408.5 million, or 46% to $1.3 billion, compared to the year ended January 1, 2021. The increase in Specialty Sports product sales reflects higher demand primarily in the OEM channel.

In 2021, the company had a net income of $163.8 million, a 79% increase from the previous year's net income of $91.7 million.

The company's cash at the end of 2021 was $179.7 million. Operating activities generated $65.3 million, while investing activities used $106.7 million, mainly for purchases of property and equipment, as well as acquisition of businesses. Financing activities used another $24.1 million, primarily for payments on line of credit.

Strategy

Fox's goal is to expand its leadership position as a designer, manufacturer and marketer of performance-defining products designed to enhance ride dynamics and performance. The company intends to focus on the following key strategies in pursuit of this goal: continue to develop new and innovative products in current end-markets; leverage technology and brand to expand into new categories and end-markets; opportunistically expand the company's business platform through acquisitions; increase the company's aftermarket penetration; accelerate international growth; and improve operating and supply chain efficiencies.

Company Background

Fox Factory was founded in 1974 by Robert Fox, who built a racing suspension shock in his friend's garage. The company was bought by Compass Diversified Holdings in 2008. In 2013 Fox Factory went public and Compass held onto a majority share; Compass subsequently divested shares in Fox Factory but still maintains a minority ownership stake.

EXECUTIVES

Executive Chairman, Director, Larry L. Enterline, $750,000 total compensation
Chairman, Lead Independent Director, Director, Dudley W. Mendenhall
Chief Executive Officer, Director, Michael C. Dennison, $175,833 total compensation
Chief Financial Officer, Treasurer, Scott R. Humphrey
Finance Senior Vice President, Finance Interim Treasurer, John Blocher
Global Operations Operations Consultant, William H. Katherman, $307,092 total compensation
Chief Strategy Officer, Thomas Wittenschlaeger, $296,230 total compensation
Division Officer, Richard Winters
Division Officer, Christopher J. Tutton, $287,611 total compensation
Division Officer, Wesley E. Allinger, $275,846 total compensation
Director, Thomas Ellis Duncan
Director, Elizabeth A. Fetter
Director, Jean Hlay
Director, Sidney Johnson
Director, Ted Waitman
Auditors: Grant Thornton LLP

LOCATIONS

HQ: Fox Factory Holding Corp
2055 Sugarloaf Circle, Suite 300, Duluth, GA 30097
Phone: 831 274-6500
Web: www.ridefox.com

2015 Sales

	$ mil.	% of total
United States	163.1	44
Asia	101.9	28
Europe	72	20
Rest of the World	29.8	8
Total	366.8	100

PRODUCTS/OPERATIONS

2015 Sales

	$ mil.	% of total
Bikes	211.7	58
Power vehicles	155.1	42
Total	366.8	100

COMPETITORS

ARCTIC CAT INC.
COOPER TIRE & RUBBER COMPANY
CYCLING SPORTS GROUP, INC.
EDELBROCK, LLC
Giant Manufacturing Co.,Ltd.
HARLEY-DAVIDSON, INC.
HERO MOTOCORP LIMITED
HUFFY CORPORATION
SRAM, LLC
YAMAHA MOTOR CO., LTD.

HISTORICAL FINANCIALS

Company Type: Public

Income Statement
FYE: January 1

	REVENUE ($mil)	NET INCOME ($mil)	NET PROFIT MARGIN	EMPLOYEES
01/21	890.5	90.6	10.2%	3,000
01/20*	751.0	93.0	12.4%	2,600
12/18	619.2	84.0	13.6%	2,240
12/17	475.6	43.1	9.1%	1,800
12/16	403.0	35.6	8.9%	1,700
Annual Growth	21.9%	26.3%	—	15.3%

*Fiscal year change

2021 Year-End Financials

Debt ratio: 30.3%
Return on equity: 15.9%
Cash ($ mil.): 245.7
Current Ratio: 3.52
Long-term debt ($ mil.): 377
No. of shares ($ mil.): 41.8
Dividends
Yield: —
Payout: —
Market value ($ mil.): 4,419.0

Stock History

	STOCK PRICE ($) FY Close	P/E High/Low		PER SHARE ($)		
		High	Low	Earnings	Dividends	Book Value
01/21	105.71	49	16	2.22	0.00	17.20
01/20*	69.78	36	23	2.38	0.00	10.95
12/18	59.93	34	15	2.16	0.00	8.45
12/17	38.85	38	22	1.11	0.00	6.24
12/16	27.75	29	15	0.94	0.00	5.01
Annual Growth	39.7%	—	—	24.0%	—	36.1%

*Fiscal year change

Franchise Group Inc

Franchise Group, Inc., formerly known as Liberty Tax is an owner and operator of franchised and franchisable businesses that continually looks to grow its portfolio of brands while utilizing its operating and capital allocation philosophies to generate strong cash flows. Its business lines include American Freight, The Vitamin Shoppe, Badcock, Buddy's Home Furnishings, Sylvan, and Pet Supplies Plus, which was acquired in 2021 for $700 million. Franchise Group operates about 2,950 locations predominantly located in the US and Canada, consisting of around 1,220 franchised locations and some 1,410 company run locations.

Operations

The company's operations are conducted in six reporting business segments: Vitamin Shoppe (around 35% of sales), American Freight (around 30%), Pet Supplies Plus (about 30%), Badcock (about 5%), Buddy's (less than 5%), and Sylvan.

The Vitamin Shoppe segment is an omnichannel specialty retailer of vitamins, minerals, herbs, specialty supplements, sports nutrition, and other health and wellness products. The Vitamin Shoppe segment markets approximately 700 nationally recognized brands as well as its own brands, which include The Vitamin Shoppe, BodyTech, True Athlete, plnt, ProBioCare, Fitfactor Weight Management System and Vthrive The Vitamin Shoppe.

The American Freight segment is a retail chain offering in-store and online access to furniture, mattresses, new and out-of-box home appliances and home accessories and seasonal items in a showroom format. The American Freight segment consists of its operations under the American Freight banner.

The Pet Supplies Plus segment is a leading omnichannel retail chain and franchisor and retailer of pet supplies and services. Pet Supplies Plus has a diversified revenue model comprised of company-owned store revenue, franchise royalties and revenue generated from wholesale distribution to franchisees. The Pet Supplies Plus segment consists of the company's operations under the Pet Supplies Plus brand.

The Badcock segment is a specialty

retailer of furniture, appliances, bedding, electronics, home office equipment, accessories and seasonal items in a showroom format. Additionally, Badcock offers multiple and flexible payment solutions and credit options through its consumer financing services. The Badcock segment operates under the brand Badcock Home Furniture & More.

The Buddy's segment is a specialty retailer of high quality, name brand consumer electronics, residential furniture, appliances and household accessories through rent-to-own agreements. The Buddy's segment consists of the company's operations under the Buddy's brand.

The Sylvan segment is an established and growing franchisor of supplemental education for Pre-K-12 students and families in the US and Canada. The Sylvan segment consists of the company's operations under the Sylvan brand.

In all, about 95% of sales were generated from its products, while the rest were generated from service and other, and rental.

Geographic Reach

Headquartered in Delaware, Ohio, Franchise Group operates some 1,410 company-owned stores, operates more than 315 dealer-owned stores, and franchises of some 1,220 stores for a total of about 2,950 stores.

The Vitamin Shoppe segment is headquartered in Secaucus, New Jersey; Pet Supplies Plus is in Livonia, Michigan; Badcock in Mulberry, Florida; American Freight in Delaware, Ohio; Buddy's in Orlando, Florida; and Sylvan in Hunt Valley, Maryland.

Sales and Marketing

The company relies on a variety of marketing techniques, including telemarketing, email and social media marketing and postal mailings.

Financial Performance

The company's total revenue increased by $1.2 billion, or 60% to $3.3 billion, in 2021 compared to 2020. This increase was primarily due to the Pet Supplies Plus Acquisition in March 2021, which increased revenue by $917.4 million, the Badcock Acquisition in November 2021, which increased revenue by $102.1 million, and the Sylvan Acquisition in September 2021, which increased revenue by $9.7 million.

In 2021, the company had a net income of $363.8 million, a 1351% increase from the previous year's net income of $25.1 million.

The company's cash at the end of 2021 was $293.1 million. Operating activities generated $106 million, while investing activities used $914.2 million, primarily for acquisitions of businesses. Financing activities provided another $949.7 million.

Strategy

The company's strategy is to focus on the operation and acquisition of franchise and franchisable businesses.

The company's acquisition strategy typically targets businesses that are highly cash flow generative with compelling unit economics that can be scaled by adding franchise and company owned units, or that can be restructured to enhance performance and value to Franchise Group.

It has established a corporate platform that enables it to deploy capital to acquire assets that may have few natural buyers but become more valuable as part of the company.

Mergers and Acquisitions

In late 2021, Franchise Group completed the acquisition of W.S. Badcock Corporation (Badcock), a leading home furnishings company in the Southeast US, in an all cash transaction valued at approximately $580 million. W.S. Badcock Corporation operates about 385 stores in eight southeastern states comprised of about 70 corporate locations and some 315 independent dealer owned stores that offers a complete line of furniture, appliances, bedding, electronics, home office equipment, accessories and seasonal items. The addition of Badcock adds scale to, and anticipated synergies with its existing home furnishings franchise concepts.

Also in late 2021, Franchise Group completed the acquisition of Sylvan Learning (Sylva"), a leading tutoring franchisor for Pre-K-12 students and families in the US, in an all cash transaction valued at approximately $81 million. Sylvan is an established and growing franchisor of tutoring services. Sylvan addresses the full range of student needs with a broad variety of academic curriculums delivered in an omnichannel format. The addition of Sylvan provides Franchise Group another growing franchise concept and further diversification into consumer services.

In early 2021, Franchise Group announced the completion of its previously announced acquisition of Pet Supplies Plus (PSP), a leading omnichannel retail chain and franchisor of pet supplies and services. In conjunction with the closing of its acquisition of PSP, Franchise Group obtained $1.3 billion in new debt financing, which, together with cash on hand, funded the $700 million acquisition of PSP. PSP adds another franchise concept with strong unit economics, diversification into an economically resilient and secularly growing pet industry, and a brand that has and will continue to experience robust unit expansion from its franchise system. The additional scale and diversification that PSP will afford Franchise Group is expected to immediately lead to lower costs of capital and expanded free cash flow generation.

EXECUTIVES

Chief Executive Officer, Brian R. Kahn
Executive Vice President, Chief Administrative Officer, Andrew F. Kaminsky
Interim President, Chief Executive Officer, Brent Turner
Financial Products Chief Financial Officer, Michael S. Piper, $222,769 total compensation
Chief Information Officer, Scott Terrell
Chief Operating Officer, Shaun York
Chief Strategy Officer, Ryan Dodson
Executive Vice President, Andrew M. Laurence
Director, Matthew E. Avril
Director, Patrick A. Cozza
Director, Thomas Herskovits
Director, Lawrence Miller
Director, G. William Minner
Director, Bryant R. Riley
Director, Kenneth M. (Kenny) Young
Auditors : DELOITTE & TOUCHE LLP

LOCATIONS

HQ: Franchise Group Inc
109 Innovation Court, Suite J, Delaware, OH 43015
Phone: 740 363-2222
Web: www.franchisegrp.com

PRODUCTS/OPERATIONS

2016 sales

	$ mil.	% of total
Royalties & advertising fees	80.3	46
Financial products	45.3	26
Interest income	13.6	8
Tax preparation fees, net of discounts	19.3	11
Franchise Fee	5.0	3
AD fees	6.0	4
Other	3.9	2
Total	173.4	100

COMPETITORS

AMSCOT FINANCIAL, INC.
EDWARD D. JONES & CO., L.P.
EXACTAX, INC.
H&R BLOCK, INC.
JACKSON HEWITT TAX SERVICE INC.
NICHOLAS FINANCIAL, INC.
RUBINBROWN LLP
SKODA MINOTTI HOLDINGS LLC
SMALLBIZPROS, INC
WORLD ACCEPTANCE CORPORATION

HISTORICAL FINANCIALS

Company Type: Public

Income Statement — FYE: December 26

	REVENUE ($mil)	NET INCOME ($mil)	NET PROFIT MARGIN	EMPLOYEES
12/20	2,152.5	25.0	1.2%	8,083
12/19*	149.5	(68.4)	—	8,038
04/19	132.5	(2.1)	—	795
04/18	174.8	0.1	0.1%	1,514
04/17	173.9	13.0	7.5%	1,498
Annual Growth	87.5%	17.8%	—	52.4%

*Fiscal year change

2020 Year-End Financials

Debt ratio: 31.2%
Return on equity: 9.7%
Cash ($ mil.): 151.5
Current Ratio: 1.05
Long-term debt ($ mil.): 468.6
No. of shares ($ mil.): 40.0
Dividends
  Yield: —
  Payout: 160.7%
Market value ($ mil.): 1,148.0

	STOCK PRICE ($)	P/E		PER SHARE ($)		
	FY Close	High	Low	Earnings	Dividends	Book Value
12/20	28.64	42	9	0.70	1.13	9.61
12/19*	24.13	—	—	(4.11)	0.25	6.87
04/19	9.00	—	—	(0.16)	0.16	7.38
04/18	10.30	1490	780	0.01	0.64	8.56
04/17	14.05	17	11	0.94	0.64	9.04
Annual Growth	19.5%	—	—	(7.1%)	15.1%	1.5%

*Fiscal year change

Franklin Wireless Corp

Franklin Wireless hopes lightning strikes with its wireless data products. The company makes high speed connectivity products for wireless devices. Its products include USB, embedded, and standalone modems, as well as modules, PC cards, and Wi-Fi hotspot routers. Customers use its products to connect their mobile computers to wireless broadband networks. Franklin Wireless primarily sells directly to wireless operators, but also through partners and distributors. The US is its largest market, but the Caribbean and South America have collectively grown to nearly 25% of sales. The company uses contract manufacturers such as South Korea-based shareholder (about 13%) C-Motech and Samsung Electro-Mechanics.

EXECUTIVES

Chairman, Director, Gary Wendel Nelson
President, Secretary, Director, O.C. Kim, $200,000 total compensation
Chief Operating Officer, Yun J. Lee, $205,000 total compensation
Strategic Planning Interim Chief Financial Officer, Strategic Planning General Counsel, Strategic Planning Director, Bill Bauer
Director, Johnathan Chee
Director, Heidy Chow
Director, Kristina S. Kim
Auditors : Benjamin & Ko

LOCATIONS

HQ: Franklin Wireless Corp
9707 Waples Street, Suite 150, San Diego, CA 92121
Phone: 858 623-0000   Fax: 858 623-0050
Web: www.franklinwireless.com

COMPETITORS

FINISAR CORPORATION
INFINERA CORPORATION
MULTI-TECH SYSTEMS, INC.
NETGEAR, INC.
ZOOM TELEPHONICS, INC.

HISTORICAL FINANCIALS

Company Type: Public

Income Statement   FYE: June 30

	REVENUE ($mil)	NET INCOME ($mil)	NET PROFIT MARGIN	EMPLOYEES
06/21	184.1	17.6	9.6%	74
06/20	75.0	5.5	7.4%	71
06/19	36.4	(1.2)	—	71
06/18	30.0	(2.0)	—	67
06/17	48.5	0.8	1.8%	76
Annual Growth	39.5%	112.1%	—	(0.7%)

2021 Year-End Financials

Debt ratio: —   No. of shares ($ mil.): 11.5
Return on equity: 54.4%   Dividends
Cash ($ mil.): 51.1   Yield: —
Current Ratio: 4.92   Payout: —
Long-term debt ($ mil.): —   Market value ($ mil.): 106.0

	STOCK PRICE ($)	P/E		PER SHARE ($)		
	FY Close	High	Low	Earnings	Dividends	Book Value
06/21	9.17	16	3	1.53	0.00	3.86
06/20	5.52	11	4	0.52	0.00	1.92
06/19	2.45	—	—	(0.12)	0.00	1.40
06/18	1.85	—	—	(0.20)	0.00	1.52
06/17	2.25	38	24	0.08	0.00	1.72
Annual Growth	42.1%	—	—	109.1%	—	22.3%

Friedman Industries, Inc.

Steel processor Friedman Industries operates in two business segments: coil products and tubular products. The company's Texas Tubular Products unit, the larger of Friedman Industries' segments, buys pipe and coil material and processes it for use in pipelines, oil and gas drilling, and piling and structural applications. Friedman Industries' coil products unit purchases hot-rolled steel coils and processes them into sheet and plate products. The company's XSCP unit sells surplus prime, secondary, and transition steel coils. Friedman Industries' processing facilities are located near mills operated by U.S. Steel and Nucor Corp. and work closely with both facilities.

Operations

Friedman Industries operates two business segments: coil, and tubular. The coil business segment engages in the processing and distribution of hot-rolled steel coils at its locations in Hickman, Arkansas and Decatur, Alabama. Its XSCP division markets surplus prime and secondary hot-rolled steel coils.

The tubular business segment of Friedman Industries operates as Texas Tubular Products (TTP) division. TTP is located in Lone Star, Texas and engages in the manufacturing, processing, and distribution of steel pipe.

Geographic Reach

The company has locations in Humble, Lone Star, and Longview (all in Texas); Decatur, Alabama; and Hickman, Arkansas.

Sales and Marketing

U.S. Steel (USS)'s Tubular Products subsidiary is both a supplier to and a customer of Friedman Industries.

The company sells coil products and processing services to 150 customers primarily in the midwestern, southwestern, and southeastern areas of the US. Its principal customers include steel distributors and customers fabricating steel products such as storage tanks, steel buildings, farm machinery and equipment, construction equipment, transportation equipment, conveyors and other similar products. It sells most of its coil products through its own sales force.

Tubular products are sold across the US to 170 customers (steel and pipe distributors, piling contractors and USS. Sales of pipe to USS accounted for 14% of company's total sales in 2013, and 24% in 2012. Tubular products are sold through Friedman Industries' own sales team.

Financial Performance

The company's revenues declined by 16% in 2013. Tubular sales dropped by 25% as the result of lower volumes sold (111,500 tons in 2012 compared to 92,000 tons in 2013) and lower prices ($828 per ton in 2012 compared to $754 per ton in 2013).

Coil sales decreased by 3% due to lower prices (from $807 per ton in 2012 compared to $727 in 2013), partially offset by higher coil tons sold.

Friedman Industries' net income decreased by 25% in 2013 due to a decrease in revenues.

Strategy

The company's financial health is heavily affected by steel commodity and product pricing in the market as well as its dependency on one of two major suppliers.

HISTORY

In 1939 Mendel Friedman founded a steel business in El Dorado, Arkansas. His sons Jack and Harold joined him, and in 1965 the family consolidated its businesses to form Friedman Industries. The company had a steel service center in Houston and a steel service center and a structural pipe manufacturing plant in Fort Worth, Texas.

Faced with strong competition, the firm diversified in 1969 by building a steel coil-processing plant near the Lone Star Steel plant in Lone Star, Texas. In 1970 Friedman closed its Fort Worth facilities and sold its pipe manufacturing equipment. The company went public in 1972 and used the proceeds to expand the Lone Star plant.

Friedman performed well in the mid-1980s and returned to the pipe business. In the early 1990s steel producer Nucor asked the company to set up shop near its Hickman, Arkansas, minimill. Friedman agreed and construction was completed in early 1994.

Rising oil prices in 2000 led to sales increases in Friedman's tubular products, but softness in steel coil sales more than offset the gains and the company saw its profits decline about 7%. Again in 2001 Friedman prospered in its tubular sector with the increase in domestic oil drilling; however, the coil-processing sector took a hit with the influx of cheap imported steel.

In late 2002 the company announced that it would boost its higher-producing operations by closing its marginally productive coil-processing unit in Houston. In 2004 Friedman Industries opened a second pipe mill at its Lone Star facility.

In past years, it has generally purchased enough pipe from USS to account for about 30% of Friedman Industries' overall sales. In 2009, when its orders dried up, USS idled its Texas plant adjacent to the Friedman facility, significantly affecting sales. In response, Friedman cut its workforce and lowered its output. A weak economy also affected Friedman Industries' other operations.

By early 2010 the USS plant was operating again, but only at about half-capacity. By then, the financial damage was done: Friedman Industries' revenues for 2010 dropped almost 70% to $65 million from $208 million the previous year; net income dropped even further (some 95%) to about $650,000, down from almost $14 million in 2009.

EXECUTIVES

Chairman, President, Chief Executive Officer, Director, Michael J. Taylor, $31,949 total compensation
Chief Financial Officer, Treasurer, Secretary, Alex LaRue, $110,000 total compensation
Director, Durga D. Agrawal
Director, Max Alan Reichanthal
Director, Sandra K. Scott
Director, Joel Spira
Director, Tim Stevenson
Director, Sharon L. Taylor
Director, Joe L. Williams
Auditors : Moss Adams LLP

LOCATIONS

HQ: Friedman Industries, Inc.
  1121 Judson Road, Suite 124, Longview, TX 75601
Phone: 903 758-3431

PRODUCTS/OPERATIONS

2015 Segment Sales

	$ in mils	% of total
Coil	72.9	67
Tubular	35.4	33
Total	108.3	100

COMPETITORS

ACINDAR INDUSTRIA ARGENTINA DE ACEROS S.A.
AK STEEL HOLDING CORPORATION
HEIDTMAN STEEL PRODUCTS, INC.
HYDER CONSULTING GROUP HOLDINGS LIMITED
NUCOR CORPORATION
STEEL DYNAMICS, INC.
TOKYO STEEL MANUFACTURING CO.,LTD.
ULBRICH STAINLESS STEELS & SPECIAL METALS, INC.
WEBCO INDUSTRIES, INC.
WORTHINGTON INDUSTRIES, INC.

HISTORICAL FINANCIALS

Company Type: Public

Income Statement — FYE: March 31

	REVENUE ($mil)	NET INCOME ($mil)	NET PROFIT MARGIN	EMPLOYEES
03/21	126.1	11.4	9.1%	94
03/20	142.1	(5.2)	—	103
03/19	187.1	5.0	2.7%	104
03/18	121.1	2.7	2.3%	91
03/17	77.7	(2.6)	—	82
Annual Growth	12.8%	—	—	3.5%

2021 Year-End Financials

Debt ratio: 1.8%
Return on equity: 17.2%
Cash ($ mil.): 8.1
Current Ratio: 2.67
Long-term debt ($ mil.): 0.1
No. of shares ($ mil.): 6.9
Dividends
  Yield: 0.9%
  Payout: 4.9%
Market value ($ mil.): 56.0

	STOCK PRICE ($) FY Close	P/E High/Low		PER SHARE ($) Earnings	Dividends	Book Value
03/21	8.09	6	3	1.63	0.08	9.47
03/20	4.41	—	—	(0.75)	0.12	9.46
03/19	7.67	15	8	0.73	0.17	10.39
03/18	5.87	17	13	0.39	0.04	9.00
03/17	6.45	—	—	(0.39)	0.04	8.61
Annual Growth	5.8%	—	—	—	18.9%	2.4%

FRMO Corp.

EXECUTIVES

Chief Executive Officer, Chairman, Murray Stahl
President, Chief Financial Officer, Director, Steven M. Bregman
Vice President, Director, Peter Brendan Doyle
Corporate Secretary, Therese Byars
General Counsel, Jay Kesslen
Director, John C. Meditz
Director, Lawrence J. Goldstein
Director, Allan Kornfeld
Director, Jay P. Hirschson
Auditors : Baker Tilly US, LLP

LOCATIONS

HQ: FRMO Corp.
  1 North Lexington Avenue, Suite 12C, White Plains, NY 10601
Phone: 914 632-6730
Web: www.frmocorp.com

HISTORICAL FINANCIALS

Company Type: Public

Income Statement — FYE: May 31

	REVENUE ($mil)	NET INCOME ($mil)	NET PROFIT MARGIN	EMPLOYEES
05/21	150.5	60.1	40.0%	0
05/20	(22.1)	(14.5)	65.8%	5
05/19	19.5	4.7	24.1%	0
05/18	16.4	14.0	85.6%	0
05/17	7.6	3.4	45.9%	0
Annual Growth	110.8%	103.7%	—	—

2021 Year-End Financials

Debt ratio: 0.2%
Return on equity: 41.0%
Cash ($ mil.): 34.9
Current Ratio: 24.96
Long-term debt ($ mil.): 0.7
No. of shares ($ mil.): 44.0
Dividends
  Yield: —
  Payout: —
Market value ($ mil.): 513.0

	STOCK PRICE ($) FY Close	P/E High/Low		PER SHARE ($) Earnings	Dividends	Book Value
05/21	11.65	11	3	1.37	0.00	4.04
05/20	4.80	—	—	(0.33)	0.00	2.61
05/19	7.25	75	45	0.11	0.00	2.87
05/18	8.25	41	13	0.32	0.00	2.72
05/17	4.40	71	49	0.08	0.00	2.35
Annual Growth	27.6%	—	—	103.4%	—	14.5%

Frontdoor Inc

EXECUTIVES

Chairman, Chief Executive Officer, William C. Cobb
Senior Vice President, Chief Financial Officer, Jessica P. Ross
Vice President, Brian K. Turcotte, $384,836 total compensation
Senior Vice President, General Counsel, Corporate Secretary, Jeffrey A. Fiarman, $143,333 total compensation
Director, D. Steve Boland
Director, Anna Cheng Catalano
Director, Peter L. Cella
Director, Richard P. Fox
Director, Brian P. McAndrews
Director, Liane J. Pelletier
Director, Christopher L. Clipper
Auditors : DELOITTE & TOUCHE LLP

LOCATIONS

HQ: Frontdoor Inc
  150 Peabody Place, Memphis, TN 38103
Phone: 901 701-5000
Web: www.frontdoorhome.com

HISTORICAL FINANCIALS
Company Type: Public

Income Statement   FYE: December 31

	REVENUE ($mil)	NET INCOME ($mil)	NET PROFIT MARGIN	EMPLOYEES
12/20	1,474.0	112.0	7.6%	2,190
12/19	1,365.0	153.0	11.2%	2,300
12/18	1,258.0	125.0	9.9%	2,200
12/17	1,157.0	160.0	13.8%	2,700
12/16	1,020.0	124.0	12.2%	0
Annual Growth	9.6%	(2.5%)	—	

2020 Year-End Financials
Debt ratio: 69.4%
Return on equity: —
Cash ($ mil.): 597.0
Current Ratio: 1.55
Long-term debt ($ mil.): 968
No. of shares ($ mil.): 85.4
Dividends
Yield: —
Payout: —
Market value ($ mil.): 4,292.0

	STOCK PRICE ($) FY Close	P/E High/Low		PER SHARE ($) Earnings	Dividends	Book Value
12/20	50.21	39	23	1.31	0.00	(0.73)
12/19	47.42	29	14	1.80	0.00	(2.10)
12/18	26.61	33	14	1.47	0.00	(4.07)
Annual Growth	37.4%	—	—	(5.6%)	—	—

FRP Holdings Inc

Patriot Transportation Holding has plenty of tanks but hasn't fired a shot. The company's Transportation segment, comprising Florida Rock & Tank Lines subsidiary, transports liquid and dry bulk commodities, mainly petroleum (including ethanol) and chemicals, in tank trucks. Patriot Transportation's combined fleet of about 435 trucks and 530 trailers operates primarily in the southeastern and mid-Atlantic US. The company's Real Estate unit, comprising Florida Rock Properties and FRP Development, owns office and warehouse properties, as well as sand and gravel deposits on the East Coast that are leased to Vulcan Materials Company.

Operations
The company operates in three segments: transportation (67% of net sales), mining royalty (4%), and land and developed property rentals (16%). In addition fuel surcharges account for 13% of the remaining revenue.

Geographic Reach
Florida Rock & Tank Lines has 20 terminal locations spanning Florida, Georgia, North Carolina, South Carolina, Alabama, and Tennessee. In addition, the company has 13 locations used by its mining operations. Out of these, seven locations are being mined in Grandin, Keuka, and Newberry, Florida; Columbus, Macon, and Tyrone, Georgia; and Manassas, Virginia.

Sales and Marketing
Patriot's 10 largest customers accounted for 54% of its total transportation segment revenue for 2013. Murphy Oil alone accounts for roughly 20% of this segment's revenues each year. The loss of one of these customers could have a detrimental effect on its revenue and income.

Financial Performance
Patriot has enjoyed significant revenue growth over the years. Revenues jumped 10% from $128 million in 2012 to roughly $140 million in 2013. Profits skyrocketed by 97% from $7.8 million to $15 million. (Both represented the company's highest totals since the Great Recession.)

The growth for 2013 was fueled by a 18% spike in mining royalty revenues due to new royalties from property purchased in mid-2012. Patriot experienced a 14% jump in land property rentals due to higher occupancy rates and the purchase of a park it made in 2013. The transportation segment's revenue climbed due to increased revenue miles as a result of a slightly longer average haul length and increased revenue per mile due to rate increases throughout 2013. Fuel surcharge revenue also jumped in 2013 due to higher fuel costs.

The profit surge for 2013 was driven by the higher revenue coupled with a sizable gain on investment lands and properties it sold in 2013.

Strategy
Patriot's strategy for growth involves acquiring related businesses and increasing it fleet size so it can carry more loads and attract additional customers. In 2013 it purchased 96 new tractors and 33 trailers; for 2014 its capital budget includes 90 new tractors. and 30 new trailers.

It is also focused on growing its mining and property segments. In late 2013 its transportation subsidiary, Florida Rock and Tank Lines, acquired the assets of Florida-based Pipeline Transportation. Also that year, Patriot snatched up Transit Business Park in Baltimore, Maryland, which consists of 5 buildings on 14.5 acres totaling 232,318 sq. ft.

EXECUTIVES

Chief Executive Officer, Executive Chairman, John D. Baker, $222,500 total compensation
President, David H. Devilliers, $345,914 total compensation
Executive Vice President, Secretary, General Counsel, John D. Milton, $95,625 total compensation
Leasing, Acquisition & Development Vice President, David H. deVilliers, $221,055 total compensation
Chief Accounting Officer, Controller, John D. Klopfenstein, $98,258 total compensation
Subsidiary Officer, Robert E. Sandlin, $89,153 total compensation
Subsidiary Officer, Terry S. Phipps, $136,343 total compensation
Chairman Emeritus, Director, Edward L. Baker
Director, Charles E. Commander
Director, Harold William Shad
Director, Martin E. Stein
Director, William H. Walton
Director, Margaret Wetherbee
Auditors: Hancock Askew & Co., LLP

LOCATIONS

HQ: FRP Holdings Inc
200 West Forsyth Street, 7th Floor, Jacksonville, FL 32202
Phone: 904 396-5733
Web: www.frpholdings.com

PRODUCTS/OPERATIONS

2013 Sales

	$ mil.	% of total
Transportation	93.2	67
Property rentals	22.4	16
Fuel surcharges	18.9	13
Mining royalty land	5.3	4
Total	139.8	100

COMPETITORS

HEARTLAND EXPRESS, INC.
KNIGHT TRANSPORTATION, INC.
MARTEN TRANSPORT, LTD.
SEACO GLOBAL LIMITED
USA TRUCK, INC.

HISTORICAL FINANCIALS
Company Type: Public

Income Statement   FYE: December 31

	REVENUE ($mil)	NET INCOME ($mil)	NET PROFIT MARGIN	EMPLOYEES
12/20	23.5	12.7	53.9%	13
12/19	23.7	16.1	68.1%	12
12/18	22.0	124.4	565.2%	10
12/17	43.1	41.7	96.7%	19
12/16	9.5	1.6	17.7%	0
Annual Growth	25.5%	65.8%	—	—

2020 Year-End Financials
Debt ratio: 16.8%
Return on equity: 3.4%
Cash ($ mil.): 73.9
Current Ratio: 39.14
Long-term debt ($ mil.): 89.9
No. of shares ($ mil.): 9.3
Dividends
Yield: —
Payout: —
Market value ($ mil.): 427.0

	STOCK PRICE ($) FY Close	P/E High/Low		PER SHARE ($) Earnings	Dividends	Book Value
12/20	45.55	39	23	1.32	0.00	39.26
12/19	49.81	34	28	1.63	0.00	38.19
12/18	46.01	5	3	12.32	0.00	36.57
12/17	44.25	11	9	4.16	0.00	24.32
12/16	37.70	235	183	0.17	0.00	20.05
Annual Growth	4.8%	—	—	66.9%	—	18.3%

FS Bancorp (Indiana)

EXECUTIVES

Chairman, Subsidiary Officer, Director, Roger A. Bird
President, Chief Executive Officer, Subsidiary Officer, Director, Joseph Urbanski
Executive Vice President, Chief Financial Officer, Stacy Merrifield

Executive Vice President, Chief Loan Officer, T. J. Kempf
Executive Vice President, Chief Administration Officer, Renea Boots
Executive Vice President, Chief Operating Officer, Lori White
Executive Vice President, Chief Business Development Officer, Mark Cowen
Honorary Director, Frederic J. Brown
Honorary Director, Miles S. Perkins
Honorary Director, Gordon T. Anderson
Director, Jordi Disler
Director, Winford Jones
Director, Rodney Perkins
Director, Freeman D. Schlabach
Director, Kerry Sprunger
Director, Kevin Lambright
Honorary Director, Jerry O. Grogg
Honorary Director, Thomas L. Miller
Honorary Director, James W. Perkins
Honorary Director, Ruth R. Perry
Honorary Director, Joseph G. (Joe) Pierce
Honorary Director, C. Lynn Tracey
Auditors : Crowe LLP

LOCATIONS

HQ: FS Bancorp (Indiana)
220 South Detroit Street, La Grange, IN 46761
Phone: 260 463-7111   **Fax:** 260 463-7341
Web: www.farmersstatebank.com

HISTORICAL FINANCIALS
Company Type: Public

Income Statement — FYE: December 31

	ASSETS ($mil)	NET INCOME ($mil)	INCOME AS % OF ASSETS	EMPLOYEES
12/20	993.5	14.3	1.4%	0
12/19	837.9	13.2	1.6%	0
12/18	760.5	9.3	1.2%	0
12/17	734.0	7.5	1.0%	0
12/16	680.4	7.4	1.1%	0
Annual Growth	9.9%	17.6%	—	—

2020 Year-End Financials
Return on assets: 1.5%
Return on equity: 16.1%
Long-term debt ($ mil.): —
No. of shares ($ mil.): 4.3
Sales ($ mil.): 41
Dividends Yield: —
Payout: 51.9%
Market value ($ mil.): 217.0

	STOCK PRICE ($) FY Close	P/E High/Low		PER SHARE ($) Earnings	Dividends	Book Value
12/20	50.00	19	14	3.26	1.69	21.77
12/19	61.00	23	19	2.99	1.59	18.88
12/18	79.90	56	26	2.11	1.44	16.27
12/17	92.00	54	40	1.68	1.23	15.05
12/16	68.25	48	36	1.67	1.17	14.04
Annual Growth	(7.5%)	—	—	18.2%	9.6%	11.6%

FS Bancorp Inc (Washington)

FS Bancorp is the holding company for 1st Security Bank of Washington, which operates six branches in the Puget Sound region. The bank provides standard deposit products such as checking and savings accounts, CDs, and IRAs to area businesses and consumers. Its lending activities are focused on consumer loans (more than half of its portfolio), including home improvement, boat, and automobile loans. The bank also writes business and construction loans, and commercial and residential mortgages. FS Bancorp went public via in initial public offering in 2012.

EXECUTIVES

Chairman, Subsidiary Officer, Ted A. Leech
Chief Executive Officer, Subsidiary Officer, Director, Joseph C. Adams, $350,000 total compensation
Chief Financial Officer, Treasurer, Secretary, Matthew D. Mullet, $300,000 total compensation
Home Lending Executive Vice President, Debra Lynn Steck, $258,249 total compensation
Home Lending Executive Vice President, Donn C. Costa, $300,000 total compensation
Subsidiary Officer, Steven L. Haynes
Subsidiary Officer, Dennis V. O'Leary, $293,269 total compensation
Director, Marina Cofer-Wildsmith
Director, Mark H. Tueffers
Director, Michael J. Mansfield
Director, Margaret R. Piesik
Director, Joseph P. Zavaglia
Auditors : Moss Adams LLP

LOCATIONS

HQ: FS Bancorp Inc (Washington)
6920 220th Street SW, Mountlake Terrace, WA 98043
Phone: 425 771-5299
Web: www.fsbwa.com

COMPETITORS

CAMBRIDGE FINANCIAL GROUP INC
FIRST BANCTRUST CORPORATION
FIRSTRUST SAVINGS BANK
HOME CITY FINANCIAL CORPORATION
ISN BANK INC

HISTORICAL FINANCIALS
Company Type: Public

Income Statement — FYE: December 31

	ASSETS ($mil)	NET INCOME ($mil)	INCOME AS % OF ASSETS	EMPLOYEES
12/20	2,113.2	39.2	1.9%	506
12/19	1,713.0	22.7	1.3%	452
12/18	1,621.6	24.3	1.5%	424
12/17	981.7	14.0	1.4%	326
12/16	827.9	10.4	1.3%	306
Annual Growth	26.4%	39.1%	—	13.4%

2020 Year-End Financials
Return on assets: 2.0%
Return on equity: 18.2%
Long-term debt ($ mil.): —
No. of shares ($ mil.): 8.4
Sales ($ mil.): 144.1
Dividends Yield: 3.0%
Payout: 18.7%
Market value ($ mil.): 464.0

	STOCK PRICE ($) FY Close	P/E High/Low		PER SHARE ($) Earnings	Dividends	Book Value
12/20	54.80	14	6	4.49	0.84	27.14
12/19	63.79	25	17	2.51	0.65	22.45
12/18	42.88	20	13	3.15	0.53	20.04
12/17	54.57	25	15	2.14	0.22	16.58
12/16	35.95	21	13	1.76	0.19	13.24
Annual Growth	11.1%	—	—	26.4%	46.0%	19.6%

FTI Consulting Inc.

FTI Consulting, Inc. is a global business advisory firm dedicated to helping organizations manage change, mitigate risk and resolve disputes: financial, legal, operational, political & regulatory, reputational and transactional. With more than 6,800 employees located in roughly 30 countries, FTI Consulting professionals work closely with clients to anticipate, illuminate and overcome complex business challenges and make the most of opportunities. FTI was founded in 1982. FTI Consulting generates most of its revenue in the US.

Operations
FTI Consulting divides its operations into five segments: Corporate Finance & Restructuring, Economic Consulting, Forensic and Litigation Consulting, Strategic Communications, and Technology.

The Corporate Finance & Restructuring segment brings in around 35% of total sales. The segment focuses on the strategic, operational, financial, transactional and capital needs of its clients around the world. It offers: Finance & Office of the CFO Solutions; People & Transformation; Revenue & Operations; Strategy; and Technology Transformation.

The Economic Consulting segment brings in about 25% of sales. It is active in the fields of economic, finance, and accounting, and it provides expert insight and testimony in legal proceedings and public policy debates.

The Forensic and Litigation Consulting segment brings in another 20% of sales; it has risk advisory, investigation, and disputes operations.

The smaller segment, Strategic Communications and Technology, account for about 10% of sales each. The Strategic Communications segment creates and executes communication campaigns. The Technology segment provides information governance, e-discovery, and data analytics products and services.

Geographic Reach
The Washington, DC-based FTI

Consulting has office in: Americas, consisting of its 50 US offices located in about 25 states, and four offices located in Canada; Latin America, consisting of six offices located in Argentina, Brazil, Colombia, Mexico, the Cayman Islands and the Virgin Islands (British); Asia and the Pacific, consisting of about 20 offices located in Australia, China (including Hong Kong), India, Indonesia, Japan, Malaysia, Singapore and South Korea; and Europe, Middle East and Africa, consisting of about 35 offices located in Belgium, Denmark, Finland, France, Germany, Ireland, Israel, Italy, Qatar, South Africa, Spain, United Arab Emirates and the United Kingdom.

US-based clients account for the vast majority (more than 60%) of sales. Clients in the UK account for more than 15%.

Sales and Marketing

It serves a diverse group of clients, including global FORTUNE 500 companies, FTSE 100 companies, global banks, major law firms, and government agencies throughout the world.

The company's advertising costs totaled $13.0 million for 2021, $15.2 million for 2020, and $18.6 million for 2019.

Financial Performance

The company's revenue for fiscal 2021 increased to $2.8 billion compared from the prior year with $2.5 billion. Revenues increased $28.8 million, or 3.2%, from 2020 to 2021, which included a 2.0% estimated positive impact from FX.

Net income for fiscal 2021 increased to $235.0 million compared from the prior year with $210.7 million.

Cash held by the company at the end of fiscal 2021 increased to $494.5 million. Cash provided by operations was $355.5 million while cash used for investing and financing activities were $79.1 million and $61.7 million, respectively. Main uses of cash were purchases of property and equipment and other; and repayments under revolving line of credit.

Strategy

The company build client relationships based on the quality of its services, its brand and the reputation of its professionals. FTI provide diverse complementary services to meet its clients' needs around the world. The company emphasize client service and satisfaction. FTI aim to build strong brand recognition. The following are key elements of its business strategy: leverage its practitioners' and businesses' expertise, geographic reach, diverse service offerings and client relationships; grow organically; strategic acquisitions; enhance profitability; enhance value through capital allocation; marketing; and ESG & sustainability.

Company Background

FTI Consulting was established in 1982 as Forensic Technologies International by Dan Luczak and Joseph Reynolds. The two founders developed computer models to present technical courtroom evidence, helping courtroom staff and juries better understand technical details during trials. The company went public in 1996 to become one of the first public providers of litigation-support services.

The firm provided trial graphics and courtroom presentation technology in the Bush vs Gore case to resolve the disputed presidential election results in 2000.

EXECUTIVES

Chairman, Director, Gerard E. Holthaus
President, Chief Executive Officer, Director, Steven Henry Gunby, $1,000,000 total compensation
Vice President, Chief Risk Officer, Chief Compliance Officer, Matthew Pachman
Chief Financial Officer, Treasurer, Ajay Sabherwal, $536,539 total compensation
Chief Strategy and Transformation Officer, Paul Linton, $536,539 total compensation
Chief Human Resources Officer, Holly Paul, $536,539 total compensation
Chief Accounting Officer, Controller, Brendan J. Keating, $400,000 total compensation
General Counsel, Curtis P. Lu, $536,539 total compensation
Associate General Counsel, Corporate Secretary, Joanne F. Catanese
Director, Stephen C. Robinson
Director, Brenda J. Bacon
Director, Mark S. Bartlett
Director, Claudio Costamagna
Director, Vernon James Ellis
Director, Nicholas C. Fanandakis
Director, Laureen E. Seeger
Auditors : KPMG LLP

LOCATIONS

HQ: FTI Consulting Inc.
555 12th Street NW, Washington, DC 20004
Phone: 202 312-9100
Web: www.fticonsulting.com

2017 Sales

	$ mil.	% of total
US	1,262.7	70
UK	251.8	14
Rest of world	293.2	16
Total	1,807.7	100

PRODUCTS/OPERATIONS

2017 Sales by Segment

	$ mil.	% of total
Economic Consulting	496.0	27
Corporate Finance/Restructuring	482.0	27
Forensic and Litigation Consulting	462.3	26
Strategic Communications	192.5	10
Technology	174.9	10
Total	1,807.7	100

Selected Services and Operating Units

Corporate Finance
    Creditor and Lender Services
    Equity Sponsor Services
    FTI Capital Advisors, LLC
    FTI Palladium Partners (Interim Management)
    Transaction Advisory Services
Forensic and Litigation Consulting
    Construction Solutions
    Dispute Advisory Services
    Healthcare
    Insurance
    Intellectual Property
    Investigations and Forensic Accounting
    Trial Services
Economic Consulting
    FTI Helios
    Lexecon
    Network Industries Strategies
Strategic Communications
    FD
Technology
    Application Solutions
    Technology Consulting
    Technology Services

COMPETITORS

CEB INC.
CRA INTERNATIONAL, INC.
EDELMAN FINANCIAL ENGINES, LLC
EXAMWORKS GROUP, INC.
GARTNER, INC.
GUIDEHOUSE INC.
HURON CONSULTING GROUP INC.
KORN FERRY
MANPOWERGROUP INC.
RESOURCES CONNECTION, INC.

HISTORICAL FINANCIALS

Company Type: Public

Income Statement

FYE: December 31

	REVENUE ($mil)	NET INCOME ($mil)	NET PROFIT MARGIN	EMPLOYEES
12/20	2,461.2	210.6	8.6%	6,321
12/19	2,352.7	216.7	9.2%	5,567
12/18	2,027.8	150.6	7.4%	4,768
12/17	1,807.7	107.9	6.0%	4,609
12/16	1,810.3	85.5	4.7%	4,718
Annual Growth	8.0%	25.3%	—	7.6%

2020 Year-End Financials

Debt ratio: 10.3%
Return on equity: 14.5%
Cash ($ mil.): 294.9
Current Ratio: 1.69
Long-term debt ($ mil.): 286.1
No. of shares ($ mil.): 34.4
Dividends
    Yield: —
    Payout: —
Market value ($ mil.): 3,852.0

	STOCK PRICE ($) FY Close	P/E High/Low		PER SHARE ($) Earnings	Dividends	Book Value
12/20	111.72	24	16	5.67	0.00	40.61
12/19	110.66	20	11	5.69	0.00	39.83
12/18	66.64	20	10	3.93	0.00	35.36
12/17	42.96	16	11	2.75	0.00	31.59
12/16	45.08	22	15	2.05	0.00	28.72
Annual Growth	25.5%	—	—	29.0%	—	9.0%

Fulgent Genetics Inc

EXECUTIVES

Chairman, President, Chief Executive Officer, Director, Ming Hsieh, $240,000 total compensation
Chief Financial Officer, Paul Kim, $210,000 total compensation
Chief Scientific Officer, Lab Director, Han Lin Gao, $210,000 total compensation
Director, John C. Bolger
Director, Yun Yen

Director, Linda Marsh
Auditors : DELOITTE & TOUCHE LLP

LOCATIONS

HQ: Fulgent Genetics Inc
4978 Santa Anita Avenue, Temple City, CA 91780
Phone: 626 350-0537
Web: www.fulgentgenetics.com

HISTORICAL FINANCIALS
Company Type: Public

Income Statement				FYE: December 31
	REVENUE ($mil)	NET INCOME ($mil)	NET PROFIT MARGIN	EMPLOYEES
12/20	421.7	214.3	50.8%	429
12/19	32.5	(0.4)	—	139
12/18	21.3	(5.6)	—	123
12/17	18.7	(2.5)	—	98
12/16	18.2	(5.3)	—	70
Annual Growth	119.2%	—	—	57.3%

2020 Year-End Financials
Debt ratio: 2.1%
Return on equity: 65.5%
Cash ($ mil.): 87.4
Current Ratio: 4.02
Long-term debt ($ mil.): —
No. of shares ($ mil.): 28.1
Dividends
 Yield: —
 Payout: —
Market value ($ mil.): 1,468.0

	STOCK PRICE ($) FY Close	P/E High/Low		PER SHARE ($) Earnings	Dividends	Book Value
12/20	52.10	5	1	8.91	0.00	20.21
12/19	12.90	—	—	(0.02)	0.00	3.85
12/18	3.17	—	—	(0.31)	0.00	2.81
12/17	4.38	—	—	(0.14)	0.00	3.04
12/16	11.57	—	—	(1.00)	0.00	3.08
Annual Growth	45.7%	—	—	—	—	60.0%

Fuller (HB) Company

H.B. Fuller is one of the world's top adhesive, sealant, and specialty chemical manufacturers with sales in about 35 countries across the world. The company's core product, industrial adhesives, is used in the manufacturing process of a wide range of consumer and industrial goods like food and beverage containers, doors and windows, electronic appliances, textiles, marine products, and automobiles among others. With some 20 independently operating regional sales offices and manufacturing plants outside of the US, H.B. Fuller enjoys a wide market reach matched by only a few other global firms. The company's brands include Advantra, Clarity, Rakoll, Silaprene, and Eternabond among others. H.B. Fuller generates about 45% of sales from US.

Operations

H.B. Fuller makes products like resins, polymers, synthetic rubbers, vinyl acetate monomer and plasticizer. The company has three reportable segment: Hygiene, Health and Consumable Adhesives, Engineering Adhesives and Construction Adhesives.

The Hygiene, Health and Consumable Adhesives operating segment manufactures and supplies adhesives products in the assembly, packaging, converting, nonwoven and hygiene, health and beauty, flexible packaging, graphic arts and envelope markets and accounts for about 45% of total revenue.

The Engineering Adhesives segment (accounts for over 40% of revenue) provides high-performance adhesives to the transportation, electronics, medical, clean energy, aerospace and defense, performance wood, insulating glass, textile, appliance and heavy machinery markets.

The Construction Adhesives (accounts for over 10%) segment provides floor preparation, grouts and mortars for tile setting, and adhesives for soft flooring, and pressure-sensitive adhesives, tapes and sealants for the commercial roofing industry as well as sealants and related products for heating, ventilation and air conditioning installations.

Geographic Reach

H.B. Fuller has headquarters in St. Paul, Minnesota. The company has about 35 manufacturing plants in the US and more than 35 plants in some 20 other countries. Approximately 55% of the company's annual sales originate outside the US, of which China accounts for over 10%.

Sales and Marketing

H.B. Fuller's diverse customer base come from the food and beverages, hygiene products, clothing, major appliances, electronics, automobiles, aerospace and defense products, solar energy systems, filters, construction materials, wood flooring, furniture, cabinetry, windows, doors, tissue and towel, corrugation, tube winding, packaging, labels and tapes. Its products are delivered directly to customers primarily from its manufacturing plants, with additional deliveries made through distributors and retailers.

Financial Performance

Revenue grew by over 17% to $3.3 billion in 2021 from $2.8 billion in 2020. Growth is driven by a 22% increase in Engineering Adhesives, a 16% increase in Construction Adhesives and a 9% increase in Hygiene, Health and Consumable Adhesives. The positive 2% currency impact was primarily driven by a stronger Euro and Chinese renminbi partially offset by a weaker Brazilian real, Turkish lira and Argentinian peso compared to the US dollar.

In 2021, the company's net income increased by 30% to $161.4 million compared to $123.7 million in 2020.

H.B. Fuller's cash and cash equivalents dipped further by $38.7 million, ending 2021 with $61.8 million on hand. Cash from operations generated $231.3 million, while cash from investing used $94.7 million ($96 million spent on property, plant, and equipment). Financing activities used another $154.1 million, mainly for repayment of long-term debt.

Strategy

H.B. Fuller continues to invest in research and development for creating new and innovative adhesive technology platforms, enhancing product performance, ensuring a competitive cost structure as well as leveraging available raw materials. New product development provides higher-value solutions to existing customers or meeting new customers' needs. Its products are often developed in regional laboratories to serve the specific needs of the local customer base.

Mergers and Acquisitions

In 2022, H.B. Fuller acquired Apollo, the United Kingdom's largest independent manufacturer of liquid adhesives, coatings and primers for the roofing, industrial and construction markets. Apollo will operate within H.B. Fuller's existing Construction Adhesives and Engineering Adhesives business units, and is expected to enhance H.B. Fuller's position in key high-value, high-margin markets in the UK and Europe. Total purchase price for the acquisitions was $211 million.

Company Background

In 1887, armed with a wood stove and an iron kettle, Harvey Benjamin Fuller Sr. began making wet paste to sell to paperhangers in St. Paul, Minnesota. The company became incorporated as the Fuller Manufacturing Company with $600 in capital from three Minneapolis lawyers. It began marketing glue to shoe companies, bookbinders, and other customers and producing ink for the city's schools.

After the 1892 acquisition of competitor Minnesota Paste Company, Fuller grew largely through sales spurred by a series of inventions. Fuller's two cold-water products, a dry wall cleaner and dry paste, proved wildly successful. In 1905 the company was shipping adhesives to Australia, Germany, and the UK.

In 1915 Fuller reincorporated as the H.B. Fuller Company.

HISTORY

In 1887, armed with a wood stove and an iron kettle, Harvey Benjamin Fuller Sr. began making wet paste to sell to paperhangers in St. Paul, Minnesota. The company became incorporated as the Fuller Manufacturing Company with $600 in capital from three Minneapolis lawyers. It began marketing glue to shoe companies, bookbinders, and other customers and producing ink for the city's schools. In 1888 Fuller's son Albert joined his father, instantly doubling the firm's workforce.

After the 1892 acquisition of competitor Minnesota Paste Company, Fuller grew largely through sales spurred by a series of inventions. Fuller's two cold-water products, a dry wall cleaner and dry paste, proved wildly successful. In 1905 the company was shipping to Australia, Germany, and the UK. Fuller's son Harvey Jr. joined the company in 1909.

In 1915 Fuller reincorporated as the H.B. Fuller Company. During WWI it supplied adhesives for canned goods shipped to the troops, but business fell off after the war. Harvey Sr. died in 1921. Despite facing possible bankruptcy, Harvey Jr. made a fateful decision to hire a full-time chemist. With Ray Burgess' inventions, the company achieved record sales by the end of the 1920s.

After the stock market crashed, Fuller acquired the Selvasize Company, makers of a combination wallpaper- and plaster-adhesive. Fuller rode out the Depression with the success of new products such as Ice Proof (a glue resistant to cold water) and Nu-Type Hot Pick-Up (used in automated labeling). However, in 1937 the company learned that three salespeople had been undercutting orders through a phantom firm, which they then claimed to represent. Fuller's sales dropped almost $50,000 the following year. In 1939 Harvey Jr. suffered a stroke.

In 1941 competitor Paisley Products of Chicago offered to buy the company for $50,000. Instead, Elmer Andersen (a business whiz who had joined the company as a salesman in the mid-1930s) persuaded Harvey to turn the reins over to him and give him a majority stake. WWII began, bringing numerous government contracts to the company. During and after the war, H.B. Fuller decentralized operations by opening branch plants beginning with Kansas City in 1943. By 1950 H.B. Fuller was the fourth-largest adhesives company in the US.

Andersen went on to become a state senator and eventually governor of Minnesota. Under the leadership of Al Vigard in the 1950s and 1960s, the company expanded into Canada, Costa Rica, Panama, and other countries. H.B. Fuller went public in 1968. In 1971 Tony Andersen (Elmer's son) took over and further pushed international sales. From 1971 to 1980, the company made some two dozen acquisitions -- about half in foreign countries -- and increased sales fivefold. In 1980 Andersen began revamping the company, which had become inefficient because of its geographic expansion. By 1985 earnings were solid again.

In 1991 the company suffered adverse publicity after social activists accused it of marketing its Resistol glue in Latin America while knowing that street kids were sniffing the glue. In 1997 H.B. Fuller entered a joint venture with Switzerland's EMS-Chemie Holding AG to combine their automotive coatings, sealants, and adhesives businesses. CEO Walter Kissing, whose efforts to reduce costs in the 1990s failed to improve margins, retired in 1998.

The next year Andersen retired as chairman and Al Stroucken, a former Bayer executive, took the helm. Stroucken quickly announced a restructuring that would reduce the company's plant operations and lay off 10% of its workforce. From 2001-2003, the company eliminated 20% of its manufacturing plants and cut more than 550 employees. It restructured its adhesives business, which was run through four geographic regions, into one global unit. The company also reduced its product offerings by half, allowing it to deliver products on time more consistently.

While H.B. Fuller did increase sales in 2003 over the previous year, that improvement was due mainly to the weakened dollar (against the Euro and other foreign currencies) and the resulting exchange differences. Sales volume decreased, as did prices. Revenues increased again in 2004, partly due to the same trend; however, the company also benefited from the increased sales volume of global adhesives and specialty products and from its February 2004 acquisition of the adhesives business of Portugese chemical firm Probos.

Due to accounting irregularities during 1999 through 2004, H.B. Fuller conducted an internal investigation into the finances of its Chilean operations in 2005. As a result, the company made minor adjustments in its 2004 financial statements.

Also in 2005 the firm combined its Chinese and Japanese adhesives businesses with those of Sekisui Chemical through joint ventures. Three years later H.B. Fuller acquired a business in Egypt, called Egymelt, to establish a presence in North Africa.

The company reorganized its business segments in 2007. H.B. Fuller rearranged its operations along geographic lines, merging the former Global Adhesives and Full Valu/Specialty segments into regional operations. The new segments are Asia/Pacific, Europe, Latin America, and North America. The move followed a gradual coming-together of the company's product groups. Fuller had worked to make its adhesive products more specialized and less of a commodity.

Jim Owens was named president and CEO of H.B. Fuller in 2010. He replaced Michele Volpi, who resigned from the company. Owens was previously SVP of H.B. Fullers' Americas operations.

In 2011 the company bought a 20% stake that Sekisui Chemical had held in its Chinese operations for $8.6 million.

The company acquired the global industrial adhesives business of Forbo in 2012. The $394 million cash deal expanded H.B. Fuller's position in the international adhesives industry, increasing H.B. Fuller's business in China by as much as 50% and strengthening its position in such markets as packaging and durable assembly.

In 2012 the firm bought Engent, Inc., a provider of manufacturing, research and development services to the electronics industry, based in Norcross, Georgia. The deal added development capabilities, testing resources, and technical support infrastructure, increasing H.B. Fuller's capabilities in a wide range of microelectronic assembly technologies.

In 2012 the company sold its Central American paints business to Colombia-based paints company Compania Global de Pinturas (Pintuco), part of Grupo Mundial, for $120 million. Pintuco has a strong market position in Central America and H.B. Fuller wanted to focus on its core adhesives operations.

Solidifying its position in the South American adhesives industry, in 2013 the company bought Plexbond Quãmica S/A, a provider of chemical polyurethane specialties and polyester resins based in Curitiba, Brazil.

EXECUTIVES

Chairman, Director, Lee R. Mitau
President, Chief Executive Officer, Director, Celeste Beeks Mastin
Executive Vice President, Chief Financial Officer, John J. Corkrean, $497,223 total compensation
Vice President, General Counsel, Corporate Secretary, Timothy J. Keenan, $257,801 total compensation
Division Officer, Zhiwei Cai, $356,421 total compensation
Division Officer, Muhammad Shahbaz Malik
Director, Charles T. Lauber
Director, Michael J. Happe
Director, Daniel L. Florness
Director, Teresa J. Rasmussen
Director, Thomas W. Handley
Director, Ruth S. Kimmelshue
Director, Srilata Zaheer
Auditors : Ernst & Young LLP

LOCATIONS

HQ: Fuller (HB) Company
1200 Willow Lake Boulevard, St. Paul, MN 55110-5101
Phone: 651 236-5900   **Fax:** 651 236-5161
Web: www.hbfuller.com

2018 Sales

	$ mil	% of total
US	1,374.1	45
China	344	11
Other countries	1,322.9	44
Total	3041.0	100

PRODUCTS/OPERATIONS

2018 Sales

	$ mil	% of total
Americas Adhesives	1,099.9	36
EIMEA	738.6	24
Asia Pacific	278.1	9
Construction Products	446.1	15
Engineering Adhesives	478.3	16
Total	3,041	100

Selected Brands
Adecol
Advantra
Bacon
CILBOND
Chapco
Childers
Clarity
Clean Melt
Close Sesame
Conforma
Cyberbond
Flexel

Flextra
Full-Care
Prospec
ODOGard
Open Sesame
Rakoll
Rapidex
Royal
Sesame
Swiftbond
Swiftlock
Swiftmelt
Swifttak
Swifttherm
TEC
Tile Perfect
Thermonex
TONSAN
Weld Mount
Wisdom

COMPETITORS

BOSTIK SA
DIVERSIFIED CHEMICAL TECHNOLOGIES, INC.
ILLINOIS TOOL WORKS INC.
LYONDELLBASELL ADVANCED POLYMERS INC.
PRC - DESOTO INTERNATIONAL, INC.
RPM INTERNATIONAL INC.
SAINT-GOBAIN CORPORATION
SCAPA GROUP PUBLIC LIMITED COMPANY
TREMCO INCORPORATED
W. R. GRACE & CO.

HISTORICAL FINANCIALS

Company Type: Public

Income Statement — FYE: November 27

	REVENUE ($mil)	NET INCOME ($mil)	NET PROFIT MARGIN	EMPLOYEES
11/21	3,278.0	161.3	4.9%	6,500
11/20	2,790.2	123.7	4.4%	6,428
11/19*	2,897.0	130.8	4.5%	6,400
12/18	3,041.0	171.2	5.6%	6,500
12/17	2,306.0	58.2	2.5%	6,000
Annual Growth	9.2%	29.0%	—	2.0%

*Fiscal year change

2021 Year-End Financials

Debt ratio: 37.8%
Return on equity: 10.8%
Cash ($ mil.): 61.7
Current Ratio: 1.66
Long-term debt ($ mil.): 1,591.4
No. of shares ($ mil.): 52.7
Dividends
  Yield: —
  Payout: 22.3%
Market value ($ mil.): 3,900.0

	STOCK PRICE ($) FY Close	P/E High/Low		PER SHARE ($) Earnings	Dividends	Book Value
11/21	73.90	26	17	2.97	0.67	30.25
11/20	53.73	23	11	2.36	0.65	26.61
11/19*	49.88	20	15	2.52	0.64	23.85
12/18	48.24	17	12	3.29	0.62	22.70
12/17	55.65	51	41	1.13	0.59	20.71
Annual Growth	7.3%	—	—	27.3%	3.0%	9.9%

*Fiscal year change

FVCBankcorp Inc

EXECUTIVES

Chief Executive Officer, Chairman, David W. Pijor, $577,500 total compensation
Vice-Chairman, Lead Director, L. Burwell Gunn

President, Subsidiary Officer, Director, Patricia A. Ferrick, $336,667 total compensation
Executive Vice President, Chief Lending Officer, Subsidiary Officer, William G. Byers
Executive Vice President, Chief Financial Officer, Subsidiary Officer, Jennifer L. Deacon
Executive Vice President, Chief Operating Officer, Subsidiary Officer, B. Todd Dempsey, $270,899 total compensation
Executive Vice President, Chief Banking Officer, Subsidiary Officer, Sharon L. Jackson
Executive Vice President, Chief Credit Officer, Subsidiary Officer, Michael G. Nassy
Director, Marc N. Duber
Director, Morton A. Bender
Director, Meena Krishnan
Director, Scott Laughlin
Director, Thomas L. Patterson
Director, Devin Satz
Director, Lawrence W. Schwartz
Director, Sidney G. Simmonds
Director, Daniel M. Testa
Director, Phillip R. Wills
Director, Steven M. Wiltse
Auditors : Yount, Hyde & Barbour, P.C.

LOCATIONS

HQ: FVCBankcorp Inc
11325 Random Hills Road, Suite 240, Fairfax, VA 22030
Phone: 703 436-3800
Web: www.fvcbank.com

HISTORICAL FINANCIALS

Company Type: Public

Income Statement — FYE: December 31

	ASSETS ($mil)	NET INCOME ($mil)	INCOME AS % OF ASSETS	EMPLOYEES
12/20	1,821.4	15.5	0.9%	121
12/19	1,537.2	15.8	1.0%	124
12/18	1,351.5	10.8	0.8%	128
12/17	1,053.2	7.6	0.7%	0
12/16	909.3	6.9	0.8%	0
Annual Growth	19.0%	22.3%	—	—

2020 Year-End Financials

Return on assets: 0.9%
Return on equity: 8.3%
Long-term debt ($ mil.): —
No. of shares ($ mil.): 13.5
Sales ($ mil.): 69.9
Dividends
  Yield: —
  Payout: —
Market value ($ mil.): 199.0

	STOCK PRICE ($) FY Close	P/E High/Low		PER SHARE ($) Earnings	Dividends	Book Value
12/20	14.70	15	8	1.10	0.00	14.03
12/19	17.47	17	14	1.07	0.00	12.88
12/18	17.61	22	17	0.85	0.00	11.55
12/17	17.52	28	23	0.67	0.00	9.04
12/16	16.80	29	23	0.63	0.00	7.84
Annual Growth	(3.3%)	—	—	14.9%	—	15.6%

Gaming & Leisure Properties, Inc

EXECUTIVES

Chairman, Chief Executive Officer, Director, Peter M. Carlino, $1,808,468 total compensation
Executive Vice President, Chief Operating Officer, General Counsel, Secretary, Brandon John Moore, $425,000 total compensation
Senior Vice President, Chief Investment Officer, Matthew Demchyk
Chief Financial Officer, Treasurer, Desiree A. Burke, $400,000 total compensation
Director, Joseph W. Marshall
Director, E. Scott Urdang
Director, Earl C. Shanks
Director, James B. Perry
Director, Barry F. Schwartz
Director, JoAnne A. Epps
Director, Carol ("Lili") Lynton
Auditors : Deloitte & Touche

LOCATIONS

HQ: Gaming & Leisure Properties, Inc
845 Berkshire Blvd., Suite 200, Wyomissing, PA 19610
Phone: 610 401-2900
Web: www.glpropinc.com

HISTORICAL FINANCIALS

Company Type: Public

Income Statement — FYE: December 31

	REVENUE ($mil)	NET INCOME ($mil)	NET PROFIT MARGIN	EMPLOYEES
12/20	1,153.1	505.7	43.9%	560
12/19	1,153.4	390.8	33.9%	648
12/18	1,055.7	339.5	32.2%	644
12/17	971.3	380.5	39.2%	714
12/16	828.2	289.3	34.9%	751
Annual Growth	8.6%	15.0%	—	(7.1%)

2020 Year-End Financials

Debt ratio: 63.7%
Return on equity: 21.2%
Cash ($ mil.): 486.4
Current Ratio: 6.18
Long-term debt ($ mil.): 5,754.6
No. of shares ($ mil.): 232.4
Dividends
  Yield: 7.5%
  Payout: 154.5%
Market value ($ mil.): 9,856.0

	STOCK PRICE ($) FY Close	P/E High/Low		PER SHARE ($) Earnings	Dividends	Book Value
12/20	42.40	22	7	2.30	3.20	11.51
12/19	43.05	24	18	1.81	2.74	9.66
12/18	32.31	23	20	1.58	2.57	10.58
12/17	37.00	22	17	1.79	2.50	11.56
12/16	30.62	22	15	1.60	2.32	11.72
Annual Growth	8.5%	—	—	9.5%	8.4%	(0.5%)

Generac Holdings Inc

Generac Holdings is a leading global designer and manufacturer of a wide range of energy technology solutions. The company provides power generation equipment, energy storage systems, grid service solutions, and other power products serving the residential, light commercial and industrial markets. Generac's residential generator products provide emergency standby power for homes. The company's commercial and industrial backup generators provide standby power for everything from restaurants and gas stations to hospitals and manufacturing facilities. Other products include light towers, mobile generators, and heaters used in construction, mining, energy, and other industries. Generac sells its products through retailers and wholesale distributors. The US accounts for some 85% of the company's sales.

Operations
Generac's key focus is in power generation and offers one of the widest ranges of products in the market place. The company is a leading energy technology solutions company that provides backup and prime power generation systems for residential and commercial & industrial (C&I) applications, solar + battery storage solutions, energy management devices and controls, advanced power grid software platforms & services, and engine- & battery-powered tools and equipment. Its principal component parts are engines, alternators, batteries, electronic controls, and steel enclosures. It designs and manufactures air-cooled engines for certain of its generators up to 26kW, along with certain liquid-cooled, natural gas engines. It sources engines for certain of its smaller products and all of its diesel products.

Overall, the company generates around 65% of total sales from residential products, followed by over 25% from commercial & industrial products.

Geographic Reach
Generac is headquartered in Waukesha, Wisconsin and has other operations, manufacturing, and sales offices in Mexico, Italy, Spain, China, Brazil, Australia, India, the United Arab Emirates, France, Canada and the Dominican Republic, as well as several other countries throughout Europe.

Generac's Domestic segment generates some 85% of total sales and includes the legacy Generac business (excluding its traditional Latin American export operations) and the acquisitions that are based in the US and Canada.

The International segment, which accounts for around 15% of total sales, includes the Latin American export operations and the acquisitions from outside the US and Canada.

Sales and Marketing
Generac's power products and solutions are available globally through a broad network of independent dealers, distributors, retailers, e-commerce partners, wholesalers, and equipment rental companies, as well as sold direct to certain end user customers. The company's advertising expenses were $66,660 in 2021, $53,678 in 2020; and $44,153 in 2019.

Financial Performance
The company's net revenue increased by 50% from $2.5 billion in 2020 to $3.7 billion in 2021. The increase in Domestic segment sales for the year ended December 31, 2021 was primarily driven by strong growth in shipments of residential products highlighted by home standby generators. In addition, PWRcellTM energy storage systems experienced very robust growth as the company continues to expand in the clean energy market. This was supplemented by a return to growth for C&I products which was led by a substantial increase in shipments for telecom national account customers and C&I mobile products compared to the prior year.

In 2021, the company had a net income of $556.6 million, a 60% increase from the previous year's net income of $347.2 million.

The company's cash at the end of 2021 totaled $147.3 million. Operating activities generated $411.2 million, while investing activities used $817.3 million, primarily for acquisition of businesses. Financing activities used another $103 million, mainly for repayments of short-term borrowings.

Mergers and Acquisitions
In late 2021, Generac Holdings Inc. has closed on the strategic acquisition of ecobee Inc., a leader in sustainable smart home solutions. A pioneer in the smart thermostat market, ecobee was founded in 2007 and is headquartered in Toronto, Canada. Generac will pay $200 million in cash along with $450 million in GNRC common stock to the current equity holders of ecobee. With the addition of ecobee and its energy management products focused on conservation, convenience, peace of mind and comfort, it will be able to further build out Generac's suite of offerings around an intelligent home energy ecosystem.

In late 2021 also, Generac Holdings Inc. announced the signing of a purchase agreement to acquire the shares of Tank Utility, Inc., a provider of IoT propane tank monitoring that enables the optimization of propane fuel logistics. The deal further expands Generac's connectivity functionality and services with sophisticated remote monitoring capabilities for propane. Their solution has been able to help propane suppliers increase efficiency and reduce their emissions, and Generac believes that the Tank Utility monitoring platform can provide even further value to our dealers and peace of mind to its home standby generator owners. Terms were not disclosed.

In mid-2021, Generac Holdings Inc. announced the acquisition of Deep Sea Electronics Limited, an advanced controls designer and manufacturer based in the UK. With the addition of Deep Sea Electronics, Generac has bolstered its engineering and control capabilities which will advance and support innovation of its products to meet the dynamic needs of the evolving energy technology market and its customers. Terms were not disclosed.

EXECUTIVES

Chairman, President, Chief Executive Officer, Director, Aaron P. Jagdfeld, $862,986 total compensation
Executive Vice President, General Counsel, Secretary, Raj Kanuru
Chief Financial Officer, York A. Ragen, $422,370 total compensation
Chief Technical Officer, Patrick Forsythe, $375,484 total compensation
Division Officer, Erik Wilde, $355,721 total compensation
Lead Independent Director, Director, Bennett J. Morgan
Director, John D. Bowlin
Director, Andrew G. Lampereur
Director, Nam Tran Nguyen
Director, Marcia J. Avedon
Director, Dominick P. Zarcone
Director, Robert D. Dixon
Director, David A. Ramon
Director, William D. Jenkins
Director, Kathryn (Kathy) V. Roedel
Auditors : DELOITTE & TOUCHE LLP

LOCATIONS
HQ: Generac Holdings Inc
S45 W29290 Hwy 59, Waukesha, WI 53189
Phone: 262 544-4811
Web: www.generac.com

PRODUCTS/OPERATIONS
2015 Sales

	$ mil.	% of total
Residential power products	673.8	51
Commercial & Industrial products	548.4	42
Other	95.1	7
Total	1,317.3	100

Selected Products and Brands
Generators
    Commercial (QuietSource)
    Industrial (gaseous, diesel, bi-fuel, modular power systems (MPS), Gemini)
    Portable (GP, XG, XP, iX)
    Recreational vehicle (gasoline, propane, diesel)
    Residential (QuietSource, Guardian)

Selected Markets
Agricultural/mining
Business office
Commercial/retail
Data center
Education
Healthcare
Manufacturing
Municipal
Research
Residential
Telecom

COMPETITORS
ABB MOTORS AND MECHANICAL INC.
ALLIED MOTION TECHNOLOGIES INC.
BWX TECHNOLOGIES, INC.
FRANKLIN ELECTRIC CO., INC.

MITSUBISHI ELECTRIC CORPORATION
NIDEC CORPORATION
P10 HOLDINGS, INC.
REGAL BELOIT CORPORATION
THERMON GROUP HOLDINGS, INC.
WATSCO, INC.

HISTORICAL FINANCIALS
Company Type: Public

Income Statement — FYE: December 31

	REVENUE ($mil)	NET INCOME ($mil)	NET PROFIT MARGIN	EMPLOYEES
12/21	3,737.1	550.4	14.7%	9,540
12/20	2,485.2	350.5	14.1%	6,797
12/19	2,204.3	252.0	11.4%	5,689
12/18	2,023.4	238.2	11.8%	5,664
12/17	1,672.4	159.3	9.5%	4,556
Annual Growth	22.3%	36.3%	—	20.3%

2021 Year-End Financials
Debt ratio: 20.1%
Return on equity: 30.5%
Cash ($ mil.): 147.3
Current Ratio: 1.60
Long-term debt ($ mil.): 902
No. of shares ($ mil.): 63.7
Dividends
  Yield: —
  Payout: —
Market value ($ mil.): 22,424.0

	STOCK PRICE ($) FY Close	P/E High/Low		PER SHARE ($) Earnings	Dividends	Book Value
12/21	351.92	59	26	8.30	0.00	34.74
12/20	227.41	42	14	5.48	0.00	22.12
12/19	100.59	25	12	4.03	0.00	16.50
12/18	49.70	17	12	3.54	0.00	12.24
12/17	49.52	20	13	2.56	0.00	8.97
Annual Growth	63.3%	—	—	34.2%	—	40.3%

Genie Energy Ltd

Genie Energy is a global provider of residential and commercial energy services. The company operates through three subsidiaries ? Genie Retail Energy (GRE), Genie Solar Energy and Genie Retail Energy International (GREI). GRE resells electricity and natural gas bought from the wholesale commodities markets, reselling those commodities to residential and small to large commercial customers throughout the US. Genie Solar Energy offers a variety of products and configurations to meet efficiency and ROI goals, while GREI holds interests in a portfolio of innovative, growing companies that supply energy to retail customers in deregulated markets outside of the US. Headquartered in Newark, New Jersey, Genie Energy is controlled by CEO Michael Stein.

EXECUTIVES
Chairman, Subsidiary Officer, Howard S. Jonas, $50,000 total compensation
Vice-Chairman, Subsidiary Officer, James A. Courter
Chief Executive Officer, Subsidiary Officer, Michael M. Stein, $350,000 total compensation
Chief Financial Officer, Subsidiary Officer, Avi Goldin, $350,000 total compensation
Corporate Secretary, Director, Joyce J. Mason

Subsidiary Officer, Director, William Wesley Perry
Director, Alan B. Rosenthal
Director, Allan Sass
Auditors : BDO USA, LLP

LOCATIONS
HQ: Genie Energy Ltd
520 Broad Street, Newark, NJ 07102
Phone: 973 438-3500
Web: www.genie.com

PRODUCTS/OPERATIONS
2015 sales

	in mil.	% of total
Electricity	167.3	80
Natural gas	40.8	19
Other	2.0	1
Total	210.1	100

COMPETITORS
ATMOS ENERGY CORPORATION
BERKSHIRE HATHAWAY ENERGY COMPANY
CENTERPOINT ENERGY, INC.
NATIONAL FUEL GAS COMPANY
NEW JERSEY RESOURCES CORPORATION
ONEOK, INC.
REPSOL SA.
SEMPRA ENERGY
SOUTHERN COMPANY GAS
VECTREN CORPORATION

HISTORICAL FINANCIALS
Company Type: Public

Income Statement — FYE: December 31

	REVENUE ($mil)	NET INCOME ($mil)	NET PROFIT MARGIN	EMPLOYEES
12/20	379.3	13.1	3.5%	125
12/19	315.2	4.1	1.3%	163
12/18	280.3	22.7	8.1%	183
12/17	264.2	(6.9)	—	178
12/16	212.1	(24.5)	—	180
Annual Growth	15.6%	—	—	(8.7%)

2020 Year-End Financials
Debt ratio: 0.8%
Return on equity: 13.6%
Cash ($ mil.): 36.9
Current Ratio: 1.37
Long-term debt ($ mil.): —
No. of shares ($ mil.): 26.2
Dividends
  Yield: 4.5%
  Payout: 75.0%
Market value ($ mil.): 189.0

	STOCK PRICE ($) FY Close	P/E High/Low		PER SHARE ($) Earnings	Dividends	Book Value
12/20	7.21	21	12	0.44	0.33	3.74
12/19	7.73	119	64	0.10	0.30	3.60
12/18	6.03	9	5	0.83	0.30	3.86
12/17	4.36	—	—	(0.36)	0.30	3.38
12/16	5.75	—	—	(1.14)	0.24	3.92
Annual Growth	5.8%	—	—	—	8.3%	(1.1%)

German American Bancorp Inc

German American Bancorp is the holding company for German American Bank, which operates some 65 branches in southern Indiana and Kentucky. Founded in 1910, the bank offers such standard retail products as checking and savings accounts, certificates of deposit, and IRAs. It also provides trust services, while sister company German American Investment Services provides trust, investment advisory, and brokerage services. German American Bancorp also owns German American Insurance, which offers corporate and personal insurance products. The group's core banking operations provide more than 90% of its total sales.

Geographic Reach
German American is headquartered in Jasper, Indiana. Its subsidiaries operate from more than 60 locations in southern Indiana and Kentucky.

Sales and Marketing
German American Bancorp spent $3.5 million on advertising in 2017. Advertising expenses totaled $2.7 million in 2016 and $3.7 million in 2015.

Financial Performance
German American's revenue has been climbing steadily for the past five years, thanks to the company's acquisitions of other area banks. Similarly, net income has also been on the rise. In 2017, the company marked its eighth consecutive year of record earnings.

In 2017 revenue increased 4% to $131.8 million. That increase was partially due to the addition of River Valley Financial Bank, which German American acquired in 2016. Growth in the company's loan portfolio also boosted net interest income. This was slightly offset by a 1% decline in non-interest income. Although trust and insurance operations rose, other operating income declined $1.1 million (29%).

Net income rose 16% to $35.2 million in 2017; in addition to having higher revenue, the company recognized a benefit related to the reduced corporate tax rate that year.

German American ended 2017 with $70.4 million in net cash, $5.5 million more than it had at the end of 2016. Operating activities provided $54.9 million in cash and financing activities provided $139.9 million. Investing activities used $189.3 million.

Strategy
German American Bancorp has grown recently through a number of acquisitions, including bank branches, an insurance office, and other bank holding companies. These acquisitions have also helped the company grow into new geographic markets, including locations in Kentucky.

Growth by acquisition can be somewhat risky, though. The company could unknowingly acquire problem assets or have difficulties integrating other banks it purchases. These issues could bring down its financial performance.

German American operates in a relatively small region, which leaves it vulnerable to economic downturns in that area. If economic conditions in its market decline, German American faces the risk of increased delinquencies and charge-offs. The company's larger, more widespread competitors would be less impacted in such a case.

Mergers and Acquisitions

German American Bancorp agreed to acquire Citizens First in early 2019 in a cash-and-stock transaction valued at about $70 million. German American will gain Citizens' branch offices in the Barren, Hart, Simpson, and Warren counties of Kentucky. Citizens has about $475 million in assets, loans of some $375 million, and deposits of around $390 million.

In October 2018 German American Bancorp acquired Kentucky's First Security Bank for $101 million. With that deal, the company expanded into Kentucky's Owensboro, Bowling Green, and Lexington markets.

EXECUTIVES

Chairman, Chief Executive Officer, Subsidiary Officer, Director, Mark A. Schroeder, $390,000 total compensation

President, Secretary, Subsidiary Officer, Clay W. Ewing, $285,000 total compensation

Executive Vice President, Chief Financial Officer, Subsidiary Officer, Bradley M. Rust, $250,000 total compensation

Executive Vice President, Chief Commercial Banking Officer, Subsidiary Officer, D. Neil Dauby, $220,000 total compensation

Executive Vice President, Chief Development Officer, Chief Retail Banking Officer, Subsidiary Officer, Randall L. Braun, $220,000 total compensation

Executive Vice President, Chief Credit Officer, Subsidiary Officer, Keith A. Leinenbach, $225,000 total compensation

Lead Independent Director, Director, U. Butch Klem

Director, Zachary W. Bawel
Director, Christina M. Ernst
Director, Marc D. Fine
Director, Jason M Kelly
Director, J. David Lett
Director, Lee A. Mitchell
Director, Chris A. Ramsey
Director, M. Darren Root
Director, Christina M Ryan
Director, Thomas W. Seger
Director, Jack W Sheidler
Director, Raymond Ward Snowden
Director, Tyson J Wagler
Auditors : Crowe LLP

LOCATIONS

HQ: German American Bancorp Inc
711 Main Street, Jasper, IN 47546
Phone: 812 482-1314
Web: www.germanamerican.com

PRODUCTS/OPERATIONS

2017 Sales

	$ mil.	% of total
Interest		
Loans, including fees	91.7	64
Securities, including dividends	19.2	13
Short-term investments	0.1	-
Non-interest		
Insurance	8.0	6
Service charges on deposit accounts	6.2	4
Trust & investment product fees	5.3	4
Other	12.4	9
Adjustments	(11.1)	-
Total	131.8	100

COMPETITORS

AMERICAN NATIONAL BANKSHARES INC.
BANKUNITED, INC.
COLUMBIA BANKING SYSTEM, INC.
EAGLE BANCORP, INC.
F.N.B. CORPORATION
FIRST MIDWEST BANCORP, INC.
GLACIER BANCORP, INC.
HILLTOP HOLDINGS INC.
OLD LINE BANCSHARES, INC.
WINTRUST FINANCIAL CORPORATION

HISTORICAL FINANCIALS

Company Type: Public

Income Statement   FYE: December 31

	ASSETS ($mil)	NET INCOME ($mil)	INCOME AS % OF ASSETS	EMPLOYEES
12/20	4,977.5	62.2	1.2%	770
12/19	4,397.6	59.2	1.3%	817
12/18	3,929.0	46.5	1.2%	738
12/17	3,144.3	40.6	1.3%	614
12/16	2,955.9	35.1	1.2%	597
Annual Growth	13.9%	15.3%	—	6.6%

2020 Year-End Financials

Return on assets: 1.3%
Return on equity: 10.3%
Long-term debt ($ mil.): —
No. of shares ($ mil.): 26.5
Sales ($ mil.): 228.8
Dividends
Yield: 2.2%
Payout: 35.3%
Market value ($ mil.): 877.0

	STOCK PRICE ($) FY Close	P/E High	P/E Low	PER SHARE ($) Earnings	Dividends	Book Value
12/20	33.09	15	10	2.34	0.76	23.57
12/19	35.62	16	12	2.29	0.68	21.51
12/18	27.77	19	13	1.99	0.60	18.37
12/17	35.33	30	17	1.77	0.52	15.90
12/16	52.61	34	19	1.57	0.48	14.43
Annual Growth	(10.9%)	—	—	10.4%	12.2%	13.1%

Glacier Bancorp, Inc.

Glacier Bancorp provide a full range of banking services to both individuals and businesses to about 200 locations in Montana, Idaho, Utah, Washington, Arizona, Colorado, and Wyoming. The bank offers retail banking, business banking, real estate, commercial, agriculture and consumer loans, as well as mortgage originating and loan servicing.

Geographic Reach

The bank operates in roughly 200 locations, including more than 170 branches and more than 20 loan or administrative offices in about 70 counties within Montana, Idaho, Utah, Washington, Wyoming, Colorado, Arizona, and Nevada. The state of Montana accounts for the largest percent of deposits of the bank to more than 20%.

Financial Performance

Glacier's financial performance is seeing growth year-by-year for the span of five years with net income being the highest for 2020 and assets seeing an increase as well.

For 2020, the company generated an interest income and non-interest income of $627 million and $172 million, respectively. Net income for the year increased $55.8 million to $266 million, or 24% higher as compared to the prior year's net income of about $211 million.

Glacier Bancorp ended 2020 with $633 million in cash, an increase of more than $300 million over the previous year. Operating activities provided about $190 million. Financing activities provided $633 million while investing activities used $3.6 billion.

Strategy

Glacier Bancorp focuses its growth as a business through internal growth and selective acquisitions. The company continues to look for profitable expansion opportunities in existing and new markets in the Rocky Mountain and Western states.

Mergers and Acquisitions

On February 2020, Glacier Bancorp Inc. completed its acquisition of State Bank Corp., which is the bank holding company for the State Bank of Arizona. The company acquired the State Bank of Arizona for $125.8 million.

EXECUTIVES

Chairman, Director, Craig A. Langel

President, Chief Executive Officer, Subsidiary Officer, Director, Randall M. Chesler, $720,425 total compensation

Executive Vice President, Chief Administrative Officer, Don J. Chery, $336,730 total compensation

Executive Vice President, Chief Financial Officer, Treasurer, Assistant Secretary, Ron J. Copher, $406,867 total compensation

Director, David C. Boyles
Director, Robert A. Cashell
Director, Sherry L. Cladouhos
Director, Annie M. Goodwin
Director, Kristen Heck
Director, Michael B. Hormaechea
Director, Douglas J. McBride
Director, Jesus Thomas Espinoza
Auditors : BKD, LLP

LOCATIONS

HQ: Glacier Bancorp, Inc.
49 Commons Loop, Kalispell, MT 59901
Phone: 406 756-4200
Web: www.glacierbank.com

PRODUCTS/OPERATIONS

2016 Sales

	$ mil	% of total
Interest income		
Commercial loans	227.4	47
Investment securities	81.9	17
Residential real estate loans	33.1	7
Consumer and other loans	32.6	7
Non-interest income		
Service charges and other fees	67.7	14
Gain on sale of loans	30.4	6
Miscellaneous loan fees and charges	4.4	1
(Loss) gain on sale of investments	(0.6)	-
Other income	10.4	2
Total	487.2	100

Selected Services
Commercial loan
Consumer loan
Deposits
Mortgage origination services
Real estate loan
Retail brokerage services
Transaction and savings

Selected Bank Divisions
1st Bank (Wyoming)
Bank of the San Juans (Colorado)
Big Sky Western Bank (Montana)
Citizens Community Bank (Idaho)
Collegiate Peaks Bank
First Bank of Montana
First Bank of Wyoming
First Security Bank (Montana)
First State Bank (Wyoming)
Foothills Bank
Glacier Bank (Montana)
Mountain West Bank (Idaho)
North Cascades Bank (Washington)
Valley Bank of Helena (Montana)
Western Security Bank (Montana)

COMPETITORS

BYLINE BANCORP, INC.
CASCADE BANCORP
CNB FINANCIAL CORPORATION
EAGLE BANCORP, INC.
FIRST MIDWEST BANCORP, INC.
HANCOCK WHITNEY CORPORATION
HEARTLAND FINANCIAL USA, INC.
NATIONAL BANK HOLDINGS CORPORATION
REPUBLIC BANCORP, INC.
UNITED COMMUNITY BANKS, INC.

HISTORICAL FINANCIALS

Company Type: Public

Income Statement — FYE: December 31

	ASSETS ($mil)	NET INCOME ($mil)	INCOME AS % OF ASSETS	EMPLOYEES
12/20	18,504.2	266.4	1.4%	3,032
12/19	13,683.9	210.5	1.5%	3,046
12/18	12,115.4	181.8	1.5%	2,723
12/17	9,706.3	116.3	1.2%	2,354
12/16	9,450.6	121.1	1.3%	2,291
Annual Growth	18.3%	21.8%	—	7.3%

2020 Year-End Financials
Return on assets: 1.6%
Return on equity: 12.4%
Long-term debt ($ mil.): —
No. of shares ($ mil.): 95.4
Sales ($ mil.): 799.9
Dividends
  Yield: 2.9%
  Payout: 49.1%
Market value ($ mil.): 4,391.0

	STOCK PRICE ($) FY Close	P/E High/Low		PER SHARE ($) Earnings	Dividends	Book Value
12/20	46.01	17	10	2.81	1.38	24.18
12/19	45.99	19	16	2.38	1.41	21.25
12/18	39.62	22	17	2.17	1.01	17.93
12/17	39.39	27	21	1.50	1.44	15.37
12/16	36.23	24	14	1.59	1.10	14.59
Annual Growth	6.2%	—	—	15.3%	5.8%	13.4%

Gladstone Commercial Corp

Gladstone Commercial, a real estate investment trust (REIT), invests in and owns office and industrial real estate properties. The company owns more than 120 properties in more than 25 states with assets that include office buildings, medical office buildings, warehouses, retail stores, and manufacturing facilities. Gladstone generally provides net leases with terms between seven and 15 years for small to very large private and public companies. The business is managed by its external adviser, Gladstone Management, which is also headed by chairman and CEO David Gladstone. The company's largest revenue generating states are Texas and Florida.

Operations
Gladstone Commercial owns about 120 properties totaling nearly 15 million sq. ft. -- including office buildings, medical office buildings, warehouses, retail stores, and manufacturing facilities ? across the US states. Virtually all of the REIT's revenue comes from rental income from tenants, most of whom sign net leases which require them to pay most or all of a property's operating, maintenance, repair and insurance costs and real estate taxes.

Geographic Reach
Headquartered in McLean, Virginia, Gladstone Commercial owns properties in more than 25 states . Texas and Florida account for the most rental revenue with about 15% each, followed by Pennsylvania (more than 10%) and Ohio (about 10%). Other large markets include Utah, North Carolina, Georgia, and South Carolina.

Sales and Marketing
Gladstone's largest industry served is telecommunications with more than 15% of the company's total revenue. It also derives at least 10% of its rental revenue from tenants in each of the automobile, healthcare, and diversified/conglomerate services industries. Its five largest tenants account for approximately 15% of rental revenue.

Financial Performance
Since 2015, Gladstone Commercial's revenue reported yearly increases. Overall, revenue growth for that five-year period was 37%.

In 2019, the company reported a revenue of $114.4 million, up by 7% from the prior year as lease revenues increased by 7%.

The company net income decreased by 23% to $9.5 million in 2019, owing to increased operating expenses and higher interest expense.

Cash at the end of fiscal 2019 was $11.5 million, an increase of 26% from the prior year. Cash contributed from operations was $60.2 million and financing activities added another $74.2 million. Investing activities used $132 million mainly for acquisition of real estate.

Strategy
The company strategy is to invest in and own a diversified portfolio of leased properties (primarily office and industrial) that it believes will produce stable cash flow and increase in value. It may sell some of its real estate assets when its adviser determines that doing so would be advantageous to the company and its stockholders. It also expects to occasionally make mortgage loans secured by the income-producing office or industrial real estate, which loans may have some form of equity participation. In addition to cash on hand and cash from operations, it uses funds from various other sources to finance its acquisitions and operations, including equity, Credit Facility, mortgage financing, and other sources that may become available from time to time. It believes that moderate leverage is prudent and it aspires to become an investment grade borrower over time. It also intends to primarily use non-recourse mortgage financing that will allow it to limit its loss exposure on any property to the amount of equity invested in such property.

On the other hand, the company has formed relationships with nationally recognized strategic partners to assist it with the management of its properties in each of its markets. These relationships provide local expertise to ensure that its properties are properly maintained and that its tenants have local points of contact to address property issues. This strategy improves its operating efficiencies, increases local market intelligence for the adviser, and generally does not increase costs as the local property managers are reimbursed by the tenants in accordance with the lease agreements.

Mergers and Acquisitions
In late 2020, Gladstone Commercial announced that it acquired a 153,600 square foot distribution building in Terre Haute, Indiana for $10.6 million. The initial capitalization rate for the acquisition was 7.3%, with an average capitalization rate of 8.0%. The property is 100% leased by Clabber Girl Corporation with a full guaranty from Clabber Girl's publicly traded parent company, B&G Foods. The acquisition of the industrial property is consistent with Gladstone Commercial's strategy of acquiring high-

quality industrial assets with credit-worthy tenants located in its targeted growth markets.

In early 2020, Gladstone Commercial announced that it acquired a 504,400 square foot industrial distribution center in Crandall, GA for $30.3 million. The property is 100% leased to Haier US Appliance Solutions, Inc., a wholly-owned subsidiary of worldwide appliance leader Haier Smart Home. The acquisition of the Haier facility continues Gladstone Commercial's strategic expansion into its targeted growth locations and a great addition to the company's portfolio.

Company Background

The REIT Gladstone Commercial is part of the Gladstone Companies, which include the three affiliated public entities Gladstone Capital, Gladstone Investment, and Gladstone Land. Gladstone Capital and Gladstone Investment invest in small and medium sized private businesses, while Gladstone Land invests in farmland.

EXECUTIVES

Chairman, Chief Executive Officer, Associate/Affiliate Company Officer, Director, David Gladstone, $68,833 total compensation

Vice-Chairman, Chief Operating Officer, Associate/Affiliate Company Officer, Director, Terry Lee Brubaker, $71,838 total compensation

Co-President, Robert G. Cutlip

Co-President, Arthur S. Cooper

Chief Financial Officer, Gary Gerson, $109,469 total compensation

Treasurer, Associate/Affiliate Company Officer, Jay Beckhorn

General Counsel, Secretary, Associate/Affiliate Company Officer, Michael LiCalsi

Lead Independent Director, Director, Paul W. Adelgren

Director, Paula Novara

Director, John H. Outland

Director, Michela A. English

Director, Anthony W. Parker

Director, Walter H. Wilkinson

Auditors : PricewaterhouseCoopers LLP

LOCATIONS

HQ: Gladstone Commercial Corp
1521 Westbranch Drive, Suite 100, McLean, VA 22102
Phone: 703 287-5800   **Fax:** 703 287-5801
Web: www.gladstonecommercial.com

PRODUCTS/OPERATIONS

2017 Sales

	$ mil.	% of total
Rental	92.8	98
Tenant recovery	2.0	2
Total	94.8	100

COMPETITORS

EQUITY ONE, INC.
FIRST INDUSTRIAL REALTY TRUST, INC.
KITE REALTY GROUP TRUST
LIBERTY PROPERTY TRUST

WEINGARTEN REALTY INVESTORS

HISTORICAL FINANCIALS
Company Type: Public

Income Statement   FYE: December 31

	REVENUE ($mil)	NET INCOME ($mil)	NET PROFIT MARGIN	EMPLOYEES
12/21	137.6	9.7	7.1%	0
12/20	133.1	14.9	11.2%	0
12/19	114.3	9.6	8.4%	0
12/18	106.7	12.3	11.5%	0
12/17	94.7	5.9	6.3%	0
Annual Growth	9.8%	13.3%	—	—

2021 Year-End Financials
Debt ratio: 61.9%   No. of shares ($ mil.): 38.0
Return on equity: 2.6%   Dividends
Cash ($ mil.): 7.9   Yield: 5.8%
Current Ratio: 2.01   Payout: 3004.3%
Long-term debt ($ mil.): 707.5   Market value ($ mil.): 981.0

	STOCK PRICE ($) FY Close	P/E High/Low		PER SHARE ($) Earnings	Dividends	Book Value
12/21	25.77	—	—	(0.12)	1.50	9.76
12/20	18.00	251	87	0.09	1.50	10.32
12/19	21.86	—	—	(0.16)	1.50	10.79
12/18	17.92	694	561	0.03	1.50	11.13
12/17	21.06	—	—	(0.19)	1.50	11.96
Annual Growth	5.2%	—	—	—	0.0%	(5.0%)

Global Net Lease Inc

EXECUTIVES

President, Chief Executive Officer, Director, James L. Nelson

Chief Financial Officer, Treasurer, Secretary, Associate/Affiliate Company Officer, Christopher J. Masterson

Non-Executive Chairman, Independent Director, P. Sue Perrotty

Director, Therese M. Antone

Director, Edward M. Weil

Director, Lee M. Elman

Director, Edward G. Rendell

Director, Abby M. Wenzel

Auditors : PricewaterhouseCoopers LLP

LOCATIONS

HQ: Global Net Lease Inc
650 Fifth Ave., 30th Floor, New York, NY 10019
Phone: 212 415-6500
Web: www.globalnetlease.com

HISTORICAL FINANCIALS
Company Type: Public

Income Statement   FYE: December 31

	REVENUE ($mil)	NET INCOME ($mil)	NET PROFIT MARGIN	EMPLOYEES
12/20	330.1	10.7	3.3%	1
12/19	306.2	46.4	15.2%	1
12/18	282.2	10.8	3.9%	1
12/17	259.2	23.5	9.1%	1
12/16	214.1	47.1	22.0%	1
Annual Growth	11.4%	(30.9%)	—	0.0%

2020 Year-End Financials
Debt ratio: 57.1%   No. of shares ($ mil.): 89.6
Return on equity: 0.6%   Dividends
Cash ($ mil.): 124.2   Yield: 10.1%
Current Ratio: 0.36   Payout: —
Long-term debt ($ mil.): 1,774.9   Market value ($ mil.): 1,536.0

	STOCK PRICE ($) FY Close	P/E High/Low		PER SHARE ($) Earnings	Dividends	Book Value
12/20	17.14	—	—	(0.09)	1.73	17.10
12/19	20.28	51	44	0.39	2.13	18.98
12/18	17.62	2222	1564	0.01	2.13	18.74
12/17	20.58	83	25	0.30	1.78	21.00
12/16	7.83	11	8	0.81	0.00	20.34
Annual Growth	21.6%	—	—	—	—	(4.2%)

Globus Medical Inc

Globus Medical makes procedural and therapeutic medical devices used during spinal surgery. Offerings range from screws and plates to disc replacement systems and bone void fillers. The company has two product segments: Musculoskeletal Solutions (implantable devices, biologics, surgical instruments, and accessories) and Enabling Technologies (imaging, navigation, and robotic-assisted surgery systems). Globus Medical has more than 220 spinal devices on the market in the US, where it earns most of its revenue; its products are also sold in about 50 countries worldwide. Globus Medical was founded in 2003.

Operations

The company manages two product categories: Musculoskeletal Solutions and Enabling Technologies.

Musculoskeletal Solutions (more than 90% of total revenue) consist primarily of implantable devices, biologics, accessories, and unique surgical instruments used in an expansive range of spinal, orthopedic and neurosurgical procedures. Its broad spectrum of spine products addresses the vast majority of conditions affecting the spine including degenerative conditions, deformity, tumors, and trauma. It includes traditional fusion implants such as pedicle screw and rod systems, plating systems, intervertebral spacers and corpectomy devices.

Enabling Technologies (about 10%) are comprised of imaging, navigation and robotics (INR) solutions for assisted surgery which are advanced computer-assisted intelligent systems designed to enhance a surgeon's capabilities, and ultimately improve patient care and reduce radiation exposure for all involved, by streamlining surgical procedures to be safer, less invasive, and more accurate. It includes the ExcelsiusGPS platform, a robotic guidance and navigation system that supports minimally invasive and open procedures by improving visualization of patient anatomy using patient images and by guiding instruments and implants to the specified trajectory using a robotic arm, to ultimately enhance the surgeon's decision making process.

Geographic Reach

Headquartered in Audubon, Pennsylvania, Globus Medical has research and manufacturing facilities in Massachusetts, Pennsylvania and Texas, and distribution center in Heerlen, Netherlands for its international operations. The company maintains a distribution warehouse, along with sales and administrative offices in about 15 additional countries.

The US is the largest single market, accounting for about 85% of total revenue.

Sales and Marketing

Globus Medical serves hospitals, ambulatory surgery centers and physicians as wells as patients with musculoskeletal disorders. It sell products through a combination of direct sales representatives and distributor sales representatives by exclusive independent distributors, who distribute products for a commission that is generally based on a percentage of sales.

Financial Performance

The company's revenue for fiscal 2021 increased by 26% to $718.9 million compared from the prior year with $571.6 million.

Net income for fiscal 2021 increased to $149.2 million compared from the prior year with $102.3 million.

The company's cash at the end of 2021 totaled $193.1 million, a 19% decrease from the previous year's cash of $239.4 million. Operating activities generated $276.3 million, while investing activities used $375.9 million, mainly for purchases of marketable securities. Financing activities generated another $54.1 million.

Strategy

The company's goal is to become the market leader in providing innovative Musculoskeletal Solutions and Enabling Technologies to promote healing in patients with musculoskeletal disorders. To achieve this goal, it employs the following business strategies:

Leverage its integrated product development engine by developing new Musculoskeletal Solutions products and Enabling Technologies products, using its product development engine. The company believes its team-oriented approach, active surgeon input, and demonstrated capabilities position it to maintain a rapid rate of new product launches. It launched 10 new products in 20, have potential new products in various stages of development, and expect to regularly launch new products;

Increase the size, scope and productivity of its exclusive US sales force by increasing the number of its direct and distributor sales representatives in the United States to expand into new geographic territories and to deepen its penetration in existing territories. It will also continue to provide its sales representatives with specialized development programs designed to improve their productivity;

Continue to expand into international markets by increasing its international presence through the commercialization of additional Musculoskeletal Solutions and Enabling Technologies products and the expansion of its international sales force; and

Pursue strategic acquisitions and alliances that complement its strategic plan and provide innovative technologies, personnel with significant relevant experience, or increased market penetration. It is currently evaluating possible acquisitions and strategic relationships and believes that its resources and experience make it an attractive acquirer or partner.

Company Background

Globus Medical was founded in 2003 by CEO David Paul, a former product development director at medical device maker Synthes. Globus Medical relied on venture capital funding prior to its 2012 IPO.

In 2016 Globus Medical acquired the international business of medical device firm Alphatec for $80 million. The deal included international distribution operations in Japan, Brazil, the UK, Italy, and other nations.

In 2017 Globus Medical acquired KB Medical, a Swiss robotics developer. That transaction underscored the firm's commitment to producing robotic technology for surgeries.

EXECUTIVES

Chairman, David C. Paul, $380,158 total compensation
President, Chief Executive Officer, David M. Demski, $456,190 total compensation
Executive Vice President, Chief Commercial Officer, Daniel T. Scavilla, $355,136 total compensation
Senior Vice President, General Counsel, Corporate Secretary, Kelly G. Huller
Senior Vice President, Chief Financial Officer, Principal Financial Officer, Principal Accounting Officer, Keith W. Pfeil, $330,000 total compensation
Vice President, Controller, Steven M. Payne
Director, Daniel T. Lemaitre
Director, Ann D. Rhoads
Director, James R. Tobin
Director, David D. Davidar, $247,717 total compensation
Director, Stephen T. Zarrilli
Director, Robert A. Douglas
Auditors : DELOITTE & TOUCHE LLP

LOCATIONS

HQ: Globus Medical Inc
2560 General Armistead Avenue, Audubon, PA 19403
Phone: 610 930-1800   **Fax:** 302 636-5454
Web: www.globusmedical.com

2015 Sales

	$ mil.	% of total
US	498.2	91
International	46.6	9
Total	544.8	100

PRODUCTS/OPERATIONS

2015 Sales

	$ mil.	% of total
Innovative fusion	288.1	53
Disruptive technologies	256.7	47
Total	544.8	100

Selected Products

Innovative Fusion Products:
  Cervical
    ASSURE (anterior cervical plate system)
    ELLIPSE (posterior occipital cervical thoracic stabilization system)
    PROVIDENCE (anterior cervical plate system)
    VIP (anterior cervical plate system)
    XTEND (anterior cervical plate system)
Thoracolumbar:
    BEACON Posted Screw (posted pedicle screw system)
    REVERE Degen (comprehensive pedicle screw and rod system)
    SI-LOK (sacroiliac joint fixation system)
  Interbody/Corpectomy
    COALITION (anterior cervical stand-alone fusion device)
    COLONIAL (anterior cervical interbody fusion device)
    FORTIFY (self-locking expandable corpectomy device)
    INDEPENDENCE (anterior lumbar stand-alone fusion device)
    SUSTAIN (spacers for partial or complete vertebrectomy)
    XPAND (expandable corpectomy spacer)
  Deformity, Tumor, and Trauma
    REVERE Anterior (pedicle screw and rod deformity system)
    REVERE Deformity (comprehensive pedicle screw, hook, and rod deformity system)
    TRUSS (lateral compressible thoracolumbar plate system)
Minimally Invasive Surgery Products:
    CALIBER (expandable posterior lumbar interbody fusion device)
    CALIBER-L (expandable lateral lumbar interbody fusion device)
    INTERCONTINENTAL (lateral lumbar interbody fusion device)
    MARS 3V (three-blade retractor system)
    REVOLVE (minimally invasive pedicle screw and rod system)
    SIGNATURE (articulating transforaminal interbody fusion device)
    TRANSCONTINENTAL (lateral lumbar interbody fusion device)
Motion Preservation:
    FLEXUS (minimally invasive unilateral PEEK interspinous process spacer)
    ORBIT-R (anterior lumbar disc replacement)
    SECURE-CR (articulating cervical disc replacement device)
    SP-FIX (interspinous process fusion device)
    TRANSITION (stabilization system)
    TRIUMPH (transforaminal lumbar disc replacement device)
    ZYFLEX (stabilization system)

COMPETITORS

ACELITY L.P. INC.
ALLSCRIPTS HEALTHCARE SOLUTIONS, INC.
BOSTON SCIENTIFIC CORPORATION
CONMED CORPORATION

ENDOLOGIX, INC.
ESCALON MEDICAL CORP.
LANDAUER, INC.
MERIT MEDICAL SYSTEMS, INC.
STRYKER CORPORATION
TELEFLEX INCORPORATED

HISTORICAL FINANCIALS
Company Type: Public

Income Statement — FYE: December 31

	REVENUE ($mil)	NET INCOME ($mil)	NET PROFIT MARGIN	EMPLOYEES
12/21	958.1	149.1	15.6%	2,400
12/20	789.0	102.2	13.0%	2,200
12/19	785.3	155.2	19.8%	2,000
12/18	712.9	156.4	21.9%	1,800
12/17	635.9	107.3	16.9%	1,500
Annual Growth	10.8%	8.6%	—	12.5%

2021 Year-End Financials
Debt ratio: —
Return on equity: 9.1%
Cash ($ mil.): 193.0
Current Ratio: 6.17
Long-term debt ($ mil.): —
No. of shares ($ mil.): 101.5
Dividends
Yield: —
Payout: —
Market value ($ mil.): 7,331.0

	STOCK PRICE ($) FY Close	P/E High/Low		PER SHARE ($) Earnings	Dividends	Book Value
12/21	72.20	57	41	1.44	0.00	17.15
12/20	65.22	63	34	1.01	0.00	15.11
12/19	58.88	38	24	1.52	0.00	14.05
12/18	43.28	36	26	1.54	0.00	12.03
12/17	41.10	37	22	1.10	0.00	10.01
Annual Growth	15.1%	—	—	7.0%	—	14.4%

GMS Inc

EXECUTIVES

Chairman, Lead Independent Director, Director, John J. Gavin
President, Chief Executive Officer, Director, John C. Turner, $750,000 total compensation
Vice President, Chief Financial Officer, Principal Accounting Officer, Scott M. Deakin
Vice President, General Counsel, Corporate Secretary, Craig D. Apolinsky, $386,256 total compensation
Director, Randolph W. Melville
Director, J. David Smith
Director, Peter C. Browning
Director, Theron I. Gilliam
Director, Mitchell B. Lewis
Director, Lisa M. Bachmann
Director, Teri Plummer McClure
Auditors : Ernst & Young LLP

LOCATIONS

HQ: GMS Inc
  100 Crescent Centre Parkway, Suite 800, Tucker, GA 30084
Phone: 800 392-4619
Web: www.gms.com

HISTORICAL FINANCIALS
Company Type: Public

Income Statement — FYE: April 30

	REVENUE ($mil)	NET INCOME ($mil)	NET PROFIT MARGIN	EMPLOYEES
04/21	3,298.8	105.5	3.2%	5,843
04/20	3,241.3	23.3	0.7%	5,308
04/19	3,116.0	56.0	1.8%	5,800
04/18	2,511.4	62.9	2.5%	4,600
04/17	2,319.1	48.8	2.1%	4,400
Annual Growth	9.2%	21.2%	—	7.3%

2021 Year-End Financials
Debt ratio: 39.4%
Return on equity: 14.4%
Cash ($ mil.): 167.0
Current Ratio: 1.96
Long-term debt ($ mil.): 932.4
No. of shares ($ mil.): 43.0
Dividends
Yield: —
Payout: —
Market value ($ mil.): 1,883.0

	STOCK PRICE ($) FY Close	P/E High/Low		PER SHARE ($) Earnings	Dividends	Book Value
04/21	43.71	19	7	2.44	0.00	19.09
04/20	18.38	57	19	0.55	0.00	14.90
04/19	17.62	24	10	1.31	0.00	15.58
04/18	31.16	25	18	1.49	0.00	14.11
04/17	36.16	30	17	1.19	0.00	12.56
Annual Growth	4.9%	—	—	19.7%	—	11.0%

GoDaddy Inc

EXECUTIVES

Chairman, Director, Brian H. Sharples
Chief Executive Officer, Director, Amanpal S. Bhutani
Chief Financial Officer, Principal Financial Officer, Mark McCaffrey
Chief Operating Officer, Roger Chen
Chief Accounting Officer, Nick Daddario
Chief Legal Officer, Corporate Secretary, Michele Lau
Director, Charles J. Robel
Director, Caroline F. Donahue
Director, Herald Y. Chen
Director, Mark Garrett
Director, Leah Sweet
Director, Srinivas Tallapragada
Director, Sigal Zarmi
Auditors : Ernst & Young LLP

LOCATIONS

HQ: GoDaddy Inc
  2155 E. GoDaddy Way, Tempe, AZ 85284
Phone: 480 505-8800
Web: www.godaddy.com

HISTORICAL FINANCIALS
Company Type: Public

Income Statement — FYE: December 31

	REVENUE ($mil)	NET INCOME ($mil)	NET PROFIT MARGIN	EMPLOYEES
12/21	3,815.7	242.3	6.4%	6,611
12/20	3,316.7	(495.1)	—	6,621
12/19	2,988.1	137.0	4.6%	7,024
12/18	2,660.1	77.1	2.9%	6,821
12/17	2,231.9	136.4	6.1%	5,990
Annual Growth	14.3%	15.4%	—	2.5%

2021 Year-End Financials
Debt ratio: 52.3%
Return on equity: —
Cash ($ mil.): 1,255.7
Current Ratio: 0.78
Long-term debt ($ mil.): 3,858.2
No. of shares ($ mil.): 167.2
Dividends
Yield: —
Payout: —
Market value ($ mil.): 14,190.0

	STOCK PRICE ($) FY Close	P/E High/Low		PER SHARE ($) Earnings	Dividends	Book Value
12/21	84.86	64	46	1.42	0.00	0.49
12/20	82.95	—	—	(2.94)	0.00	(0.08)
12/19	67.92	103	76	0.76	0.00	4.43
12/18	65.62	168	98	0.45	0.00	4.53
12/17	50.28	41	28	0.79	0.00	2.90
Annual Growth	14.0%	—	—	15.8%	—	(35.9%)

Goldman Sachs BDC Inc

EXECUTIVES

Chairman, Director, Jaime Ardila
Co-President, Co-Chief Executive Officer, Co-Principal Executive Officer, Alex Chi
Co-President, Co-Chief Executive Officer, Co-Principal Executive Officer, David Miller
Executive Vice President, Subsidiary Officer, Michael Mastropaolo
Executive Vice President, Jordan Walter
Research Executive Vice President, Research Head, David Yu
Chief Financial Officer, Treasurer, Principal Accounting Officer, Subsidiary Officer, David Pessah
Chief Operating Officer, Subsidiary Officer, Gabriella N. Skirnick
Chief Compliance Officer, Julien Yoo
Director, Timothy J. Leach
Director, Susan B. McGee
Director, Ross J. Kari
Director, Richard A. Mark
Director, Kaysie Uniacke
Director, Carlos E. Evans
Auditors : PricewaterhouseCoopers LLP

LOCATIONS

HQ: Goldman Sachs BDC Inc
  200 West Street, New York, NY 10282
Phone: 212 902-0300
Web: www.goldmansachsbdc.com

HISTORICAL FINANCIALS
Company Type: Public

Income Statement — FYE: December 31

	REVENUE ($mil)	NET INCOME ($mil)	NET PROFIT MARGIN	EMPLOYEES
12/20	172.9	109.8	63.5%	0
12/19	147.2	79.7	54.1%	0
12/18	146.7	82.8	56.5%	0
12/17	136.7	79.9	58.5%	0
12/16	125.1	76.2	60.9%	0
Annual Growth	8.4%	9.6%	—	—

2020 Year-End Financials
Debt ratio: 49.1%
Return on equity: 9.5%
Cash ($ mil.): 32.1
Current Ratio: 0.87
Long-term debt ($ mil.): 1,627
No. of shares ($ mil.): 101.5
Dividends
Yield: 9.4%
Payout: 88.2%
Market value ($ mil.): 1,941.0

	STOCK PRICE ($) FY Close	P/E High/Low		PER SHARE ($) Earnings	Dividends	Book Value
12/20	19.12	11	4	2.04	1.80	15.91
12/19	21.28	11	9	1.98	1.80	16.75
12/18	18.38	11	9	2.06	1.80	17.65
12/17	22.18	20	17	1.28	1.80	18.09
12/16	23.52	21	16	1.12	1.80	18.31
Annual Growth	(5.0%)	—	—	16.2%	0.0%	(3.5%)

Good Times Restaurants Inc.

Good Times Restaurants operates and franchises more than 50 Good Times Drive Thru fast-food eateries located primarily in the Denver area. The hamburger chain is made up mostly of double drive-through and walk-up eateries that feature a menu of burgers, fries, and frozen custard. A limited number of Good Times outlets also offer dine-in seating. More than 20 of the locations are operated by franchisees, while the rest are co-owned and co-operated under joint venture agreements. The family of director Geoffrey Bailey owns almost 30% of the company.

EXECUTIVES

Chairman, Director, Geoffrey R. Bailey
President, Chief Executive Officer, Interim Chief Financial Officer, Principal Accounting Officer, Interim Principal Financial Officer, Director, Ryan M. Zink, $200,000 total compensation
Finance Senior Vice President, Matthew Karnes
Operations Vice President, Donald L. Stack
Director, Charles E. Jobson
Director, Jason S. Maceda
Director, Jennifer C. Stetson
Auditors : Moss Adams LLP

LOCATIONS

HQ: Good Times Restaurants Inc.
651 Corporate Circle, Golden, CO 80401
Phone: 303 384-1400
Web: www.goodtimesburgers.com

COMPETITORS
GODFATHER'S PIZZA, INC
MCDONALD'S RESTAURANTS LIMITED
PIZZA HUT, INC.
PORT OF SUBS INC.
TEXAS ROADHOUSE, INC.

HISTORICAL FINANCIALS
Company Type: Public

Income Statement — FYE: September 28

	REVENUE ($mil)	NET INCOME ($mil)	NET PROFIT MARGIN	EMPLOYEES
09/21	123.9	16.7	13.5%	2,230
09/20	109.8	(13.9)	—	2,318
09/19	110.7	(5.1)	—	2,535
09/18	99.2	(1.0)	—	2,368
09/17	79.0	(2.2)	—	1,970
Annual Growth	11.9%	—	—	3.1%

2021 Year-End Financials
Debt ratio: —
Return on equity: 77.5%
Cash ($ mil.): 8.8
Current Ratio: 0.89
Long-term debt ($ mil.): —
No. of shares ($ mil.): 12.1
Dividends
Yield: —
Payout: —
Market value ($ mil.): 62.0

	STOCK PRICE ($) FY Close	P/E High/Low		PER SHARE ($) Earnings	Dividends	Book Value
09/21	5.15	4	1	1.31	0.00	2.45
09/20	1.42	—	—	(1.10)	0.00	1.09
09/19	1.68	—	—	(0.41)	0.00	2.18
09/18	4.88	—	—	(0.08)	0.00	2.72
09/17	2.85	—	—	(0.18)	0.00	2.78
Annual Growth	15.9%	—	—	—	—	(3.1%)

Goosehead Insurance Inc

EXECUTIVES

Chief Executive Officer, Chairman, Mark E. Jones, $1,350,000 total compensation
Vice-Chairman, Director, Robyn Jones
President, Chief Operating Officer, Michael C. Colby, $360,209 total compensation
Vice President, General Counsel, P. Ryan Langston, $230,000 total compensation
Service Delivery Vice President, Michael Moxley
Chief Financial Officer, Mark S. Colby, $225,000 total compensation
Director, James Reid
Director, Peter R. Lane
Director, Mark K. Miller
Auditors : DELOITTE & TOUCHE LLP

LOCATIONS

HQ: Goosehead Insurance Inc
1500 Solana Blvd., Building 4, Suite 4500, Westlake, TX 76262
Phone: 469 480-3669
Web: www.goosehead.com

HISTORICAL FINANCIALS
Company Type: Public

Income Statement — FYE: December 31

	ASSETS ($mil)	NET INCOME ($mil)	INCOME AS % OF ASSETS	EMPLOYEES
12/20	185.8	9.2	5.0%	949
12/19	64.6	3.5	5.5%	595
12/18	34.7	(8.9)	—	403
12/17	16.7	8.6	51.9%	282
12/16	8.6	4.7	54.3%	0
Annual Growth	115.0%	18.4%	—	—

2020 Year-End Financials
Return on assets: 7.3%
Return on equity: 987650000000000.0%
Long-term debt ($ mil.): —
No. of shares ($ mil.): 36.7
Sales ($ mil.): 117
Dividends
Yield: 0.9%
Payout: 383.1%
Market value ($ mil.): 4,585.0

	STOCK PRICE ($) FY Close	P/E High/Low		PER SHARE ($) Earnings	Dividends	Book Value
12/20	124.76	238	71	0.51	1.15	(0.13)
12/19	42.40	213	103	0.22	0.41	(0.25)
12/18	26.29	—	—	(0.66)	0.00	0.00
Annual Growth	117.8%	—	—	—	—	—

GrafTech International Ltd

GrafTech International is a leading maker of high-quality graphite electrodes in the US, which are essential to the production of electric arc furnaces, steel, and various other ferrous and nonferrous metals. GrafTech has the most competitive portfolio of low-cost ultra-high power (UHP) graphite electrode manufacturing facilities in the industry, including three of the highest capacity facilities in the world. It is the only large scale graphite electrode producer that is substantially vertically integrated into petroleum needle coke. Customers have included major steel producers and other ferrous and non-ferrous metal producers, which sell their products into the automotive, construction, appliance, machinery, equipment and transportation industries. The majority of its sales were generated outside the US. The company traces its roots back to 1886.

Operations

GrafTech's only reportable segment, Industrial Materials, is comprised of its two major product categories: graphite electrodes and needle coke products. Petroleum needle coke is the key raw material to producing graphite electrodes. The Industrial Materials segment manufactures high-quality graphite electrodes essential to the production of EAF steel and other ferrous and non-ferrous metals.

Overall, its graphite electrodes generates

about 95% of sales, of which over 75% comes from long-term agreements. The remaining less than 5% comes from by-products and other.

Geographic Reach

Headquartered in Ohio, the company has sales offices and manufacturing facilities in Mexico, Pennsylvania, Texas, Brazil, France, Spain, and Switzerland. It currently has the capacity to manufacture approximately 200,000 metric tons of graphite electrodes annually. GrafTech gets about 80% of its total sales from outside the US with the EMEA region accounting to about 50%.

Sales and Marketing

The company sells its products primarily through a direct sales force, independent sales representatives, and distributors. Its customers include major steel producers and other ferrous and non-ferrous metal producers in Europe, Russia and other Commonwealth of Independent States countries, the Middle East and Africa (collectively, EMEA), the Americas and Asia-Pacific (APAC), which sell their products into the automotive, construction, appliance, machinery, equipment and transportation industries.

Financial Performance

Net sales increased $121.4 million, or 10%, from $1.2 billion in 2020 to $1.3 billion in 2021. Stronger demand for the company's products in 2021 resulted in a 24% increase in sales volume compared to 2020.

In 2021, the company had a net income of $388.3 million, an 11% decrease from the previous year's net income of $434.4 million. The decrease was primarily due to significantly higher selling and administrative expenses for the year.

The company's cash at the end of 2021 was $57.5 million. Operating activities generated $443 million, while financing activities used $471.8 million, primarily for principal payments on long-term debt. Investing activities used another $57.8 million, mainly for capital expenditures.

EXECUTIVES

Chairman, Director, Denis A. Turcotte
President, Chief Executive Officer, Director, Marcel Kessler
Operations Executive Vice President, Development Executive Vice President, Operations Chief Operating Officer, Development Chief Operating Officer, Jeremy S Halford
Commercial Senior Vice President, Inigo Perez Ortiz
Finance Vice President, Finance Chief Financial Officer, Finance Treasurer, Timothy K. Flanagan
Chief Legal Officer, Corporate Secretary, Gina K Gunning
Director, Michel J. Dumas
Director, Jean-Marc Germain
Director, David Gregory
Director, Henry R. Keizer
Director, Catherine L Clegg
Director, Debra Fine
Director, Anthony R. Taccone
Auditors : DELOITTE & TOUCHE LLP

LOCATIONS

HQ: GrafTech International Ltd
   982 Keynote Circle, Brooklyn Heights, OH 44131
Phone: 216 676-2000
Web: www.graftech.com

PRODUCTS/OPERATIONS

Selected Products

Carbon and graphite cathodes (conductors of electricity in aluminum smelters)
Carbon electrodes (used to produce silicon metal, ferronickel, and thermal phosphorus)
Flexible graphite (used in gaskets and other sealing applications)
Graphite electrodes (used to generate heat for melting steel in steel minimills)
Refractory products (carbon and graphite used to protect walls of blast furnaces)

COMPETITORS

3M TECHNICAL CERAMICS, INC.
ASBURY LOUISIANA, INC.
MERSEN
MINTEQ INTERNATIONAL INC.
NIPPON CARBON CO.,LTD.
SCHUNK CARBON TECHNOLOGY, LLC
SGL COMPOSITES INC.
SHOWA DENKO CARBON, INC.
SPECIAL METALS CORPORATION
ZOLTEK COMPANIES, INC.

HISTORICAL FINANCIALS

Company Type: Public

Income Statement				FYE: December 31
	REVENUE ($mil)	NET INCOME ($mil)	NET PROFIT MARGIN	EMPLOYEES
12/20	1,224.3	434.3	35.5%	1,285
12/19	1,790.7	744.6	41.6%	1,346
12/18	1,895.9	854.2	45.1%	1,387
12/17	550.7	7.9	1.4%	1,310
12/16	437.9	(235.8)	—	1,244
Annual Growth	29.3%	—	—	0.8%

2020 Year-End Financials

Debt ratio: 99.1%
Return on equity: —
Cash ($ mil.): 145.4
Current Ratio: 3.18
Long-term debt ($ mil.): 1,420
No. of shares ($ mil.): 267.1
Dividends
   Yield: 1.0%
   Payout: 7.0%
Market value ($ mil.): 2,848.0

	STOCK PRICE ($) FY Close	P/E High/Low		PER SHARE ($) Earnings	Dividends	Book Value
12/20	10.66	8	4	1.62	0.12	(1.23)
12/19	11.62	6	4	2.58	0.34	(2.55)
12/18	11.44	8	4	2.87	0.93	(3.71)
Annual Growth	(3.5%)	—	—	(24.9%)	(64.9%)	—

Granite Falls Energy LLC

EXECUTIVES

Chairman, Director, Paul Gerald Enstad
Vice-Chairman, Director, Rodney R. Wilkison
Chief Executive Officer, General Manager, Subsidiary Officer, Jeffrey Oestmann
Chief Financial Officer, Controller, Subsidiary Officer, Stacie Schuler, $159,387 total compensation
Risk Manager, Subsidiary Officer, Erik Baukol, $96,363 total compensation
Plant Manager, Cory Heinrich
Director, David Forkrud
Director, Dean Jerome Buesing
Director, Sherry Jean Larson
Director, Robin Spaude
Director, Kenton Johnson
Director, Bruce G. LaVigne
Director, Martin Frank Seifert
Director, Leslie Kenneth Bergquist
Auditors : Boulay PLLP

LOCATIONS

HQ: Granite Falls Energy LLC
   15045 Highway 23 S.E., Granite Falls, MN 56241-0216
Phone: 320 564-3100
Web: www.granitefallsenergy.com

HISTORICAL FINANCIALS

Company Type: Public

Income Statement				FYE: October 31
	REVENUE ($mil)	NET INCOME ($mil)	NET PROFIT MARGIN	EMPLOYEES
10/21	309.6	23.6	7.6%	82
10/20	164.9	(13.2)	—	82
10/19	208.7	(8.3)	—	82
10/18	210.3	2.8	1.4%	82
10/17	215.7	11.4	5.3%	82
Annual Growth	9.4%	19.8%	—	0.0%

2021 Year-End Financials

Debt ratio: 22.5%
Return on equity: 37.5%
Cash ($ mil.): 29.3
Current Ratio: 2.16
Long-term debt ($ mil.): 27.6
No. of shares ($ mil.): 0.0
Dividends
   Yield: —
   Payout: —
Market value ($ mil.): 0.0

Gray Television Inc

Gray Television is the nation's largest independent operator of TV stations in the US. It owns and operates local TV stations in nearly 115 markets, including ABC, NBC, CBS, and FOX. Its station portfolio reaches about 35% of total US TV households. The company also owns video production, marketing, and digital businesses including Raycom Sports, Tupelo Honey, PowerNation Studios and Third Rail Studios. Revenue comes primarily from broadcast and internet ads and retransmission consent fees. Gray Television's roots begin in January 1891 with the creation of the Albany Herald in Albany, Georgia.

Operations
The company operates in two business segments: Broadcasting and Production companies.

The broadcasting segment operates television stations in local markets in the United States. It generates for more than 95% of company's revenue.

The production companies segment, which accounts for less than 5% of revenue, includes the production of television and event content.

Among the company's type of revenues, retransmission consent generates most of the sales accounting to about 45%.

Geographic Reach
The company principal executive offices are located in Atlanta, Georgia. The company's largest market by revenue were Charlotte, North Carolina and Cleveland-Akron, Ohio which each contributed approximately 5% of total revenue.

Sales and Marketing
Gray Television is diversified across its markets and network affiliations. Its CBS-affiliated channels accounted for about 35% of the company's revenue; NBC-affiliated channels accounted for more than 30%; ABC-affiliated channels accounted for nearly 15%; and FOX-affiliated channels accounted for over 10%.

The company refers to CBS, NBC, ABC and FOX collectively as the "Big Four". Its top 10 markets by revenue contributed nearly 25% of sales.

Financial Performance
Total revenue increased approximately $32 million, or 1%, to $2.4 billion for 2021 compared to 2020, primarily as a result of the television stations acquired in the company's 2021 Acquisitions and increases in combined local and national advertising revenue and retransmission consent revenue at its legacy television stations.

In 2021, the company had a net income of $90 million, a 78% decrease from the previous year's net income of $410 million, driven by the increase in operating expenses.

The company's cash at the end of 2021 totaled $189 million. Operating activities generated $300 million, while investing activities used $3.5 billion, primarily for acquisitions of television businesses and licenses. Financing activities provided another 2.7 million.

Strategy
The company's success is based on the following strategies: Grow by leveraging its diverse national footprint; Maintain and grow its market leadership position; Continue to monetize digital spectrum; Continue to maintain prudent cost management; Further strengthen its balance sheet; and Continue to pursue strategic growth and accretive acquisition opportunities.

Gray Television intends to maintain its market leadership position through continued prudent investment in its news and syndicated programs, as well as continued technological advances and workflow improvements. Gray Television expects to continue to invest in technological upgrades in the future. The company believes the foregoing will help it maintain and grow its market leadership; thereby enhancing its ability to grow and further diversify its revenues and cash flows.

In addition to each of Gray Television stations' primary channels, the company also broadcasts a number of secondary channels. Certain of its secondary channels are affiliated with more than one network simultaneously. The company's strategy includes expanding upon its digital offerings and sales. Gay Television also evaluate opportunities to use spectrum for future delivery of data to mobile devices using a new transmission standard.

Mergers and Acquisitions
In 2021, Gray Television closed its previously announced acquisition of Meredith Corp. to acquire 17 TV stations for about 2.8 billion. Gray's acquisition of Meredith's television stations will transform Gray into the nation's second largest television broadcaster. Gray's portfolio of television stations, including all announced transactions and less divestitures, will serve 113 local markets reaching approximately 36 percent of US television households. Meredith plans to focus on magazine publishing and digital assets and to spin off its National Media Group unit to existing shareholders involved in the transaction with the company.

In mid-2021, Gray Television has completed the acquisition of all of the outstanding shares of capital stock of Illinois-based Quincy for $925 million in cash. Upon closing the transaction, Gray will own television stations serving 102 television markets that collectively reach 25.4 percent of US television households, including the number-one ranked television station in 77 markets and the first and/or second highest ranked television station in 93 markets according to Comscore's average all-day ratings for calendar year 2020. With the addition of these professionals and their stations, Gray will become a stronger company with an even larger platform of high quality television stations to better serve the public interest first.

EXECUTIVES

Executive Chairman, Chief Executive Officer, Director, Hilton H. Howell, $1,113,600 total compensation

President, Co-Chief Executive Officer, Director, Donald P. LaPlatney

Executive Vice President, Chief Financial Officer, James C. Ryan, $684,834 total compensation

Law and Development Executive Vice President, Law and Development Chief Legal Officer, Law and Development Chief Development Officer, Law and Development Secretary, Kevin Paul Latek, $720,565 total compensation

Local Media Executive Vice President, Local Media Chief Operating Officer, Bob L. Smith, $609,500 total compensation

Lead Independent Director, Director, Howell W. Newton

Director, Richard L. Boger

Director, T. L. Elder

Director, Luis A. Garcia

Director, Richard B. Hare

Director, Robin Robinson Howell

Director, Paul H. McTear

Director, Sterling A. Spainhour

Auditors : RSM US LLP

LOCATIONS

HQ: Gray Television Inc
4370 Peachtree Road N.E., Atlanta, GA 30319
Phone: 404 504-9828
Web: www.gray.tv

PRODUCTS/OPERATIONS

2016 sales

	$ in mil.	% of total
Local	403.3	50
National	98.3	12
Political	90.0	11
Retransmission consent	200.8	25
Other	19.8	2
Total	812.4	100

Selected Television Stations
KAKE (ABC; Wichita-Hutchinson, KS)
KBTX (CBS; Bryan, TX)
KCRG (ABC, MY, ANT; Cedar Rapids, IA)
KCWY (NBC; Casper, WY)
KGIN (CBS; Grand Island, NE)
KGWN (CBS, NBC, CW; Cheyenne, WY)
KKCO (NBC; Grand Junction, CO)
KKTV (CBS; Colorado Springs, CO)
KLBY (ABC; Colby, KS)
KMVT (CBS, CWTwin Falls, ID)
KNOE (CBS, CW, ABC; Monroe-El Dorado, LA)
KOLN (CBS; Lincoln-Hastings-Kearney, NE)
KOLO (ABC; Reno, NV)
KOSA(CBS, MY; Odessa - Midland, TX)
KSNB (NBC, MY; Lincoln - Hastings - Kearney, NE)
KSTB (CBS, CW; Scottsbluff, NE)
KSVT (FOX, MY; Twin Falls, ID)
KUPK (ABC; Garden City, KS)
KWTX (CBS; Waco-Temple-Bryan, TX)
KXII (CBS; Sherman,TX)
WAGM (FOX, CBS; Presque Isle, ME)
WAHU (FOX; Charlottesville, VA)
WBKO (ABC; Bowling Green, KY)
WCAV (CBS; Charlottesville, VA)
WCTV (CBS; Tallahassee, FL)
WEAU (NBC La Crosse-Eau Claire, WI)
WHSV (ABC; Harrisonburg, VA)
WIBW (CBS; Topeka, KS)
WIFR (CBS; Rockford, IL)
WILX (NBC; Lansing, MI)
WITN (NBC; Greenville, NC)
WJHG (NBC; Panama City, FL)
WKYT (CBS; Lexington, KY)
WMTV (NBC; Madison, WI)
WNDU (NBC; South Bend, IN)
WOWT (NBC; Omaha, NE)
WRDW (CBS; Augusta, GA)
WSAW (CBS; Wausau-Rhinelander, WI)
WSAZ (NBC; Charleston, WV)

WSWG (CBS; Albany, GA)
WTAP (NBC; Parkersburg, WV)
WTOK (ABC; Meridian, MS)
WTVY (CBS; Dothan, AL)
WVAW (ABC; Charlottesville, VA)
WLT (CBS; Knoxville, TN)
WYMT (CBS; Hazard, KY)

COMPETITORS

CM WIND DOWN TOPCO INC.
FOX CORPORATION
LIN MEDIA LLC
NEXSTAR MEDIA GROUP, INC.
QUINSTREET, INC.
SINCLAIR BROADCAST GROUP, INC.
TEGNA INC.
TRIBUNE MEDIA COMPANY
URBAN ONE, INC.
YOUNG BROADCASTING, LLC

HISTORICAL FINANCIALS
Company Type: Public

Income Statement — FYE: December 31

	REVENUE ($mil)	NET INCOME ($mil)	NET PROFIT MARGIN	EMPLOYEES
12/20	2,381.0	410.0	17.2%	7,262
12/19	2,122.0	179.0	8.4%	8,018
12/18	1,084.1	210.8	19.4%	8,523
12/17	882.7	261.9	29.7%	3,938
12/16	812.4	62.2	7.7%	3,996
Annual Growth	30.8%	60.2%	—	16.1%

2020 Year-End Financials
Debt ratio: 52.0%
Return on equity: 18.1%
Cash ($ mil.): 773.0
Current Ratio: 5.11
Long-term debt ($ mil.): 3,974
No. of shares ($ mil.): 95.1
Dividends
  Yield: —
  Payout: —
Market value ($ mil.): 1,703.0

	STOCK PRICE ($) FY Close	P/E High	P/E Low	Earnings	Dividends	Book Value
12/20	17.89	6	2	3.69	0.00	25.24
12/19	21.44	19	11	1.27	0.00	21.24
12/18	14.74	8	4	2.37	0.00	13.38
12/17	16.75	5	3	3.55	0.00	11.05
12/16	10.85	19	8	0.86	0.00	6.80
Annual Growth	13.3%			43.9%	—	38.8%

Green Brick Partners Inc

Green Brick Partners acquires and develops land and provides land and construction financing to its wholly owned and controlled builders. Also known as Green Brick, it is engaged in all aspects of the homebuilding process, including land acquisition and development, entitlements, design, construction, title and mortgage services, marketing and sales, and the creation of brand images at its residential neighborhoods and master planned communities. Based in Dallas, the company owns or controls over 12,000 prime home sites in high-growth sub-markets throughout the Dallas and Atlanta metropolitan areas, and the Vero Beach, Florida market.

EXECUTIVES

Chairman, Director, David Einhorn
Chief Executive Officer, Director, James R. Brickman, $233,333 total compensation
Development Executive Vice President, Land Acquisition Executive Vice President, Development Chief Operating Officer, Land Acquisition Chief Operating Officer, Jed Dolson, $550,000 total compensation
Finance Chief Financial Officer, Richard A. Costello, $400,000 total compensation
Lead Independent Director, Director, Richard S. Press
Director, Elizabeth K. Blake
Director, Harry Brandler
Director, Kathleen Olsen
Director, Lila A. Manassa Murphy
Auditors: RSM US LLP

LOCATIONS

HQ: Green Brick Partners Inc
2805 Dallas Parkway, Suite 400, Plano, TX 75093
Phone: 469 573-6755
Web: www.greenbrickpartners.com

COMPETITORS

CALATLANTIC GROUP, INC.
D.R. HORTON, INC.
GEVO, INC.
HASEKO CORPORATION
INTREPID POTASH, INC.
KB HOME
M/I HOMES, INC.
MASCOMA LLC
THE NEW HOME COMPANY INC
WILLIAM LYON HOMES

HISTORICAL FINANCIALS
Company Type: Public

Income Statement — FYE: December 31

	REVENUE ($mil)	NET INCOME ($mil)	NET PROFIT MARGIN	EMPLOYEES
12/20	976.0	113.6	11.6%	440
12/19	791.6	58.6	7.4%	460
12/18	623.6	51.6	8.3%	390
12/17	454.3	14.9	3.3%	260
12/16	380.3	23.7	6.2%	220
Annual Growth	26.6%	47.9%	—	18.9%

2020 Year-End Financials
Debt ratio: 22.2%
Return on equity: 19.0%
Cash ($ mil.): 19.4
Current Ratio: 8.36
Long-term debt ($ mil.): 219.8
No. of shares ($ mil.): 50.6
Dividends
  Yield: —
  Payout: —
Market value ($ mil.): 1,163.0

	STOCK PRICE ($) FY Close	P/E High	P/E Low	Earnings	Dividends	Book Value
12/20	22.96	11	3	2.24	0.00	12.90
12/19	11.48	10	6	1.16	0.00	10.63
12/18	7.24	12	7	1.02	0.00	9.43
12/17	11.30	40	30	0.30	0.00	8.23
12/16	10.05	21	10	0.49	0.00	7.86
Annual Growth	22.9%			46.2%	—	13.2%

Green Dot Corp

Bank holding company Green Dot offers prepaid debit cards through more than 90,000 retail locations in the US under brand names including Green Dot, Go2Bank, MoneyPak, and TPG. Through its retail and direct bank, Green Dot offers a broad set of financial products to consumers and businesses including debit, prepaid, checking, credit and payroll cards, as well as robust money processing services, tax refunds, cash deposits and disbursements. Founded in 1999, Green Dot has served more than 33 million customers directly.

Operations

Green Dot divide its operations into three reportable segments: Consumer Services, Business to Business (B2B) Services, and Money Movement Services.

The Consumer Services segment accounts for about 50% of total revenue and consists of revenues and expenses derived from deposit account programs, such as consumer checking accounts, prepaid cards, secured credit cards, and gift cards that it offer to consumers through distribution arrangements with more than 90,000 retail locations and thousands of neighborhood Financial Service Center locations, and directly through various marketing channels, such as online search engine optimization, online displays, direct mail campaigns, mobile advertising, and affiliate referral programs.

The B2B Services segment (more than 30% of revenue) consists of revenues and expenses derived from its partnerships with some of the US most prominent consumer and technology companies that make its banking products and services available to their consumers, partners and workforce through integration with banking platform, and a comprehensive payroll platform that it offer to corporate enterprises to facilitate payments for today's workforce. Its products and services include deposit account programs, such as consumer and small business checking accounts and prepaid cards, as well as its Simply Paid Disbursements services utilized by its partners.

The Money Movement Services segment (more than 15%) consists of revenues and expenses generated on a per transaction basis from its services that specialize in facilitating the movement of cash on behalf of consumers and businesses, such as money processing services and tax refund processing services. Its money processing services, such as cash deposit and disbursements, are marketed to third-party banks, program managers, and other companies seeking cash deposit and disbursement capabilities for their customers. Those customers, including its own cardholders, can access its cash deposit and disbursement services at any of the locations within its network of retail distributors and neighborhood Financial Service Centers. The company markets its tax-related financial services through a network of tax preparation franchises, independent tax professionals and online tax preparation providers.

The company also generates its revenue from cards and other fees (about 55% of revenue), interchange revenues (more than 25%), processing and settlement service (more than 15%), and interest income.

Geographic Reach
Green Dot is based in Austin, Texas and has more than 90,000 retail distribution location nationwide.

Sales and Marketing
Green Dot offers its products and services to a broad group of consumers, ranging from never-banked to fully-banked consumers. It focuses its sales and marketing efforts on acquisition of long-term users of its products, enhancing brands and image, building market adoption and awareness of products, improving customer retention, and increasing card usage.

The company's advertising and marketing expenses were $42.6 million, $37.5 million, and $51.1 million for the years 2021, 2020, and 2019, respectively.

Financial Performance
Green Dot's total operating revenues for the year ended December 31, 2021 increased $179.4 million, or 14% to $1.4 billion, over the prior year comparable period, generating revenue growth across its Consumer Services and B2B Services segments, partially offset by lower revenues earned from its Money Movement Services.

Net income for fiscal 2021 increased to $47.5 million compared from the prior year with $23.1 million.

Cash held by the company at the end of fiscal 2021 decreased to $1.3 billion. Cash provided by operations and financing activities were $162.5 million and $1.0 billion, respectively. Cash used for investing activities was $1.4 billion, mainly for purchases of available-for-sale investment securities.

Mergers and Acquisitions
In 2021, Green Dot and Republic Bank, a subsidiary of Republic Bancorp, announced they have entered into a definitive agreement pursuant to which Green Dot will purchase the assets and operations of Republic Bank's Tax Refund Solutions (TRS) business segment, for $165 million in cash. The acquisition of TRS presents unique opportunities for near- and long-term growth of its tax processing business, as it works to deliver more accessible and beneficial tax products and services to customers nationwide.

Company Background
The company's July 2010 initial public offering exceeded its own expectations, raising nearly $165 million. Although the IPO of secondary shares raised a significant amount, Green Dot did not keep any of the money for itself. Instead, the money was distributed to existing shareholders, the most prominent being Wal-Mart. Prior to the IPO, the retail giant took a minority stake in Green Dot -- a move that cemented the pair's partnership.

EXECUTIVES

Chairperson, Director, William I. Jacobs
President, Chief Executive Officer, Director, George W. Gresham
Chief Operating Officer, Teresa Watkins
Chief Financial Officer, Chief Accounting Officer, Jess Unruh
Chief Revenue Officer, Chris Ruppel
Chief Human Resources Officer, Jason Bibelheimer
General Counsel, Secretary, Kristina Lockwood
Division Officer, Amit Parikh
Director, George T. Shaheen
Director, Rajeev V. Date
Director, Saturnino Fanlo
Director, Peter Alexander Feld
Director, Jeffrey B. Osher
Director, Ellen Richey
Director, J. Chris Brewster
Auditors : Ernst & Young LLP

LOCATIONS

HQ: Green Dot Corp
3465 E. Foothill Blvd., Pasadena, CA 91107
Phone: 626 765-2000
Web: www.greendot.com

PRODUCTS/OPERATIONS

2018 Revenue

	$ mil.	% of total
Card revenues and other fees	482.9	46
Processing and settlement service revenues	248	24
Interchange revenues	310.9	30
Total	1,041.8	100

COMPETITORS

ALLIANCE DATA SYSTEMS CORPORATION
AMERICAN EXPRESS COMPANY
ATLANTICUS HOLDINGS CORPORATION
BLACKHAWK NETWORK HOLDINGS, INC.
CLAYTON, DUBILIER & RICE, INC.
CONSUMER PORTFOLIO SERVICES, INC.
CREDIT ACCEPTANCE CORPORATION
FLEETCOR TECHNOLOGIES, INC.
GENERAL MOTORS FINANCIAL COMPANY, INC.
WORLD ACCEPTANCE CORPORATION

HISTORICAL FINANCIALS
Company Type: Public

Income Statement — FYE: December 31

	REVENUE ($mil)	NET INCOME ($mil)	NET PROFIT MARGIN	EMPLOYEES
12/20	1,253.7	23.1	1.8%	1,200
12/19	1,108.5	99.8	9.0%	1,200
12/18	1,041.7	118.7	11.4%	1,100
12/17	890.1	85.8	9.6%	1,152
12/16	718.7	41.6	5.8%	974
Annual Growth	14.9%	(13.6%)	—	5.4%

2020 Year-End Financials
Debt ratio: —
Return on equity: 2.3%
Cash ($ mil.): 1,491.8
Current Ratio: 0.78
Long-term debt ($ mil.): —
No. of shares ($ mil.): 54.0
Dividends
Yield: —
Payout: —
Market value ($ mil.): 3,015.0

	STOCK PRICE ($) FY Close	P/E High/Low		PER SHARE ($) Earnings	Dividends	Book Value
12/20	55.80	150	39	0.42	0.00	18.69
12/19	23.30	44	12	1.88	0.00	17.90
12/18	79.52	41	25	2.18	0.00	17.19
12/17	60.26	38	14	1.61	0.00	14.95
12/16	23.55	31	19	0.80	0.00	13.54
Annual Growth	24.1%	—	—	(14.9%)	—	8.4%

Green Thumb Industries Inc

EXECUTIVES

Chief Executive Officer, Chairman, Benjamin Kovler
Chief Financial Officer, Director, Anthony Georgiadis
Director, Wendy Berger
Director, William R. Gruver
Director, Wes Moore
Director, Dorri McWhorter
Director, Swati Mylavarapu
Director, Glen T. Senk
Auditors : Macias Gini & O'Connell LLP

LOCATIONS

HQ: Green Thumb Industries Inc
325 West Huron Street, Suite 700, Chicago, IL 60654
Phone: 312 471-6720
Web: www.gtigrows.com

HISTORICAL FINANCIALS
Company Type: Public

Income Statement — FYE: December 31

	REVENUE ($mil)	NET INCOME ($mil)	NET PROFIT MARGIN	EMPLOYEES
12/20	556.5	14.9	2.7%	2,200
12/19	216.4	(59.1)	—	1,700
12/18	62.4	(5.2)	—	0
12/17	16.5	(4.2)	—	0
Annual Growth	222.9%	—	—	—

2020 Year-End Financials
Debt ratio: 7.3%
Return on equity: 1.7%
Cash ($ mil.): 83.7
Current Ratio: 1.54
Long-term debt ($ mil.): 98.7
No. of shares ($ mil.): 178.4
Dividends
Yield: —
Payout: —
Market value ($ mil.): 4,372.0

	STOCK PRICE ($)	P/E		PER SHARE ($)		
	FY Close	High/Low		Earnings	Dividends	Book Value
12/20	24.50	361	58	0.07	0.00	5.10
12/19	9.75	—	—	(0.31)	0.00	6.48
12/18	8.03	—	—	(0.04)	0.00	7.52
12/17	0.02	—	—	(0.07)	0.00	0.00
Annual Growth	970.0%	—		—	—	—

Greene County Bancorp Inc

This company helps put the "green" in upstate New York. Greene County Bancorp is the holding company for The Bank of Greene County, serving New York's Catskill Mountains region from about a dozen branches. Founded in 1889 as a building and loan association, the bank offers traditional retail products such as savings, NOW, checking, and money market accounts; IRAs; and CDs. Real estate loans make up about 85% of the bank's lending activities; it also writes business and consumer loans. Through affiliations with Fenimore Asset Management and Essex Corp., Greene County Bancorp offers investment products. Subsidiary Greene County Commercial Bank is a state-chartered limited purpose commercial bank.

EXECUTIVES

President, Chief Executive Officer, Subsidiary Officer, Donald E. Gibson, $443,000 total compensation
Executive Vice President, Chief Operating Officer, Chief Financial Officer, Subsidiary Officer, Michelle M. Plummer, $256,400 total compensation
Executive Vice President, Chief Lending Officer, Subsidiary Officer, Stephen E. Nelson, $227,200 total compensation
Director, Peter Hogan
Director, Jay P. Cahalan
Director, Charles H. Schaefer
Director, David H. Jenkins
Director, Paul Slutzky
Auditors : Bonadio & Co., LLP

LOCATIONS

HQ: Greene County Bancorp Inc
302 Main Street, Catskill, NY 12414
Phone: 518 943-2600
Web: www.tbogc.com

COMPETITORS

CHICOPEE BANCORP, INC.
HOME CITY FINANCIAL CORPORATION
JACKSONVILLE BANCORP, INC.
PRUDENTIAL BANCORP, INC. OF PENNSYLVANIA
RIDGEWOOD SAVINGS BANK

HISTORICAL FINANCIALS
Company Type: Public

Income Statement   FYE: June 30

	ASSETS ($mil)	NET INCOME ($mil)	INCOME AS % OF ASSETS	EMPLOYEES
06/21	2,200.3	23.9	1.1%	193
06/20	1,676.8	18.7	1.1%	186
06/19	1,269.4	17.4	1.4%	172
06/18	1,151.4	14.4	1.3%	164
06/17	982.2	11.1	1.1%	146
Annual Growth	22.3%	21.0%	—	7.2%

2021 Year-End Financials
Return on assets: 1.2%   Dividends
Return on equity: 17.2%   Yield: 1.7%
Long-term debt ($ mil.): —   Payout: 19.3%
No. of shares ($ mil.): 8.5   Market value ($ mil.): 239.0
Sales ($ mil.): 67.9

	STOCK PRICE ($) FY Close	P/E High/Low		PER SHARE ($) Earnings	Dividends	Book Value
06/21	28.12	11	7	2.81	0.48	17.57
06/20	22.30	13	8	2.20	0.44	15.13
06/19	29.42	17	14	2.05	0.40	13.16
06/18	33.90	22	13	1.69	0.39	11.27
06/17	27.20	21	12	1.31	0.38	9.82
Annual Growth	0.8%	—	—	21.0%	6.0%	15.6%

GreenSky Inc

EXECUTIVES

Chief Executive Officer, Chairman, Director, David Zalik, $500,000 total compensation
Vice-Chairman, Chief Administrative Officer, Gerald R. Benjamin, $450,000 total compensation
President, Chief Risk Officer, Timothy Kaliban, $339,615 total compensation
Executive Vice President, Chief Operating Officer, Ritesh Gupta
Executive Vice President, Chief Financial Officer, Andrew Kang
Executive Vice President, Chief Legal Officer, Corporate Secretary, Steven E. Fox
Division Officer, Robert Partlow
Division Officer, Dennis I. Kelly
Director, Arthur Bacci
Director, Joel M. Babbit
Director, Gregg Freishtat
Director, Robert Sheft
Auditors : PricewaterhouseCoopers LLP

LOCATIONS

HQ: GreenSky Inc
5565 Glenridge Connector, Suite 700, Atlanta, GA 30342
Phone: 678 264-6105
Web: www.greensky.com

HISTORICAL FINANCIALS
Company Type: Public

Income Statement   FYE: December 31

	REVENUE ($mil)	NET INCOME ($mil)	NET PROFIT MARGIN	EMPLOYEES
12/20	525.6	9.9	1.9%	1,164
12/19	529.6	31.9	6.0%	1,174
12/18	414.6	24.2	5.8%	1,088
12/17	325.8	103.2	31.7%	949
12/16	263.8	99.2	37.6%	0
Annual Growth	18.8%	(43.7%)	—	—

2020 Year-End Financials
Debt ratio: 62.7%   No. of shares ($ mil.): 182.9
Return on equity: —   Dividends
Cash ($ mil.): 147.7   Yield: —
Current Ratio: 4.84   Payout: —
Long-term debt ($ mil.): 955.6   Market value ($ mil.): 847.0

	STOCK PRICE ($) FY Close	P/E High/Low		PER SHARE ($) Earnings	Dividends	Book Value
12/20	4.63	64	21	0.14	0.00	(0.03)
12/19	8.90	31	12	0.49	0.00	0.14
12/18	9.57	62	20	0.41	0.00	0.14
Annual Growth	(30.4%)	—	—	(41.6%)	—	—

Griffon Corp.

Griffon Corporation is a diversified management and holding company that conducts business through wholly-owned subsidiaries. The company operates in two segments ? consumer and professional products, and home and building products. AMES, and ClosetMaid, Griffon's consumer and professional products subsidiaries, make wood and wire closet organizations, yard tools, cleaning and storage products. The home and building segment operates through Clopay, which has become the largest manufacturer and marketer of garage doors and rolling steel doors in North America. The US accounts for about 75% of Griffon's total revenue.

Operations

Griffon has two reportable segments: Consumer and Professional Products (CPP) and Home & Building Products (HBP).

CPP segment operates through AMES, a manufacturer of home storage and organizations, landscaping and outdoor lifestyle. CCP sells its product globally through its brands including True Temper, AMES, and ClosetMaid. The segment account for about 55% of total revenue.

HBP segment conducts its operation through Clopay, the largest manufacturer and marketer of garage doors and rolling steel doors in North America. Residential and commercial sectional garage doors are sold under the brands Clopay, Ideal, and Holmes. Rolling steel door and grille products designed are sold under the CornellCookson brand. The segment brings in about 45% of Griffon's total revenue.

Geographic Reach

Headquartered in New York, Griffon's various businesses sell products primarily in North America (the US accounts for about 75% of sales), but also in Canada, Australia, New Zealand, and Europe. The company has facilities (offices, factories, and warehouses) throughout the US, Canada, Mexico, Australia, the UK, and China.

Sales and Marketing

AMES, and ClosetMaid sell products through small retailers, hardware stores, garden centers, and mass merchandisers. Major customers include The Home Depot, Lowe's, Walmart, Bunnings, and Menards.

Telephonics sells to the US Department of Defense and other defense industry businesses like Lockheed Martin, Boeing, Northrop Grumman Corporation, Oshkosh, Airbus Helicopters, Leonardo Helicopters, SAAB, and Airbus Military.

The Home Depot accounts for about 20% of company's revenue.

Financial Performance

Revenue for the year ended September 30, 2021 was $2.3 million compared to $2.1 million in the year ended September 30, 2020, an increase of 10% resulting from increased revenue at HBP and CPP of 12% and 8%, respectively.

In 2021, the company had a net income of $79.2 million, a 48% increase from the previous year's net income of $53.4 million. This was mainly due to a higher sales volume coupled with a lower interest expense for the year.

The company's cash at the end of 2021 was $248.7 million. Operating activities generated $71 million, while investing activities used $56.2 million, primarily for acquisition of property, plant and equipment. Financing activities used another $28.2 million, mainly for payments of long-term debt.

Strategy

Griffon plans to seek and acquire businesses in multiple industries and geographic markets. The objective is to maintain leading positions in the markets it serves by providing innovative, branded products with superior quality and industry-leading service. It emphasizes its iconic and well-respected brands, which helps to differentiate the company's offerings from its competitors and strengthens the relationship with customers and those who ultimately use its products.

Through operating a diverse portfolio of businesses, the company expects to reduce variability caused by external factors such as market cyclicality, seasonality, and weather. It achieves diversity by providing various product offerings and brands through multiple sales and distribution channels and conducting business across multiple countries.

Griffon oversees the operations of its subsidiaries, allocates resources among them, and manages its capital structures. Griffon provides direction and assistance to its subsidiaries in connection with acquisition and growth opportunities as well as in connection with divestitures. As long-term investors, having substantial experience in a variety of industries, the intent of the company is to continue the growth and strengthening of its existing businesses and to diversify further through investments in its businesses and through acquisitions.

Mergers and Acquisitions

In late 2021, Griffon through its subsidiary The AMES Companies, Inc., has entered into a definitive agreement to acquire Hunter Fan Company, a market leader in residential ceiling, commercial, and industrial fans, from MidOcean Partners for $845 million. The acquisition of Hunter, along with the expected sale of Griffon's Defense Electronics business, marks a repositioning and strengthening of the Griffon portfolio which will further accelerate Griffon's growth, increase shareholder value, and is an effective use of its capital.

In 2021, Griffon announced that its subsidiary, The AMES Companies, Inc., acquired Quatro Design Pty Ltd, a leading Australian manufacturer and supplier of glass fiber reinforced concrete landscaping products for residential, commercial, and public sector projects. This acquisition further expands AMES's product portfolio and sales channels in the Australian market. Quatro is expected to contribute approximately $5 million in annualized revenue and be accretive to Griffon's earnings in the fiscal year ending September 30, 2021. Financial terms of the transaction were not disclosed.

Company Background

Griffon was founded in 1959 by Helmuth W. Waldorf as Waldorf Controls Corporation, but soon assumed the name Instrument System Corporation (ISC). In 1986, the company went public. ISC became Griffon in 1995, after the mythical creature that is part lion, part eagle. In 2010, Griffon relocates its headquarters from Jericho, NY to New York City.

HISTORY

Founded in 1959 as Waldorf Controls, the company changed its name to Instrument Systems that year. Under chairman Edward Garrett, the business acquired 80 companies in the 1960s and 1970s, including Telephonics (1962) and Concord Electronics (1971). In 1983 Harvey Blau assumed management, replacing Garrett, his father-in-law, as CEO. The company bought Clopay for $40 million in 1986.

Telephonics expanded Instrument Systems' market focus in the 1990s to include commercial and nondefense governmental clients. The company built its Clopay unit, adding garage door makers Ideal Door (1992) and Atlas Roll-lite (1995). The name Griffon Corporation was adapted in 1995.

In 1997 Telephonics won its largest contract ever -- a $114 million contract to supply British Aerospace (now BAE SYSTEMS) with communications systems. That year Griffon bought garage-door maker and installer Holmes-Hally Industries ($80 million in annual sales). The next year it picked up Bohme Verpackungsfolien (plastic packaging and specialty films, Germany).

Griffon faced restructuring charges and capacity restraints in 1999. To boost profits, it exited the self-storage warehouse-door business and closed or consolidated other operations.

Griffon bought the search and weather radar products business of Honeywell International for $16 million in 2000. In late 2001 Telephonics Corporation received a $13.5 million contract from the US Air Force to upgrade its Airborne Warning and Control System (AWACS) aircraft with new "friend or foe" identification technology.

In fiscal 2002 the company, citing unprofitability of the unit, adopted a plan to divest its peripheral operation selling slatted steel coiling doors for commercial users. That year, through its Clopay subsidiary, Griffon acquired majority ownership in Isofilme (plastic hygienic and specialty films, Brazil) and renamed the company Clopay do Brasil. Also that year its Telephonics subsidiary was awarded a $15 million contract from Boeing Defense, Space & Security (BDS; formerly Boeing Integrated Defense Systems) for the first production of Telephonics' Communications Open Systems Architecture (COSA) Integrated Radio Management System (IRMS) for use by the US Air Force on its C-17A Globemaster III transport aircraft.

In 2004 Telephonics was awarded a multi-year contract valued at more than $40 million from Lockheed Martin Systems Integration-Owego to produce cockpit communications management systems for the US Navy's MH-60R and MH-60S helicopters. The next year Telephonics purchased The Systems Engineering Group (SEG), based in Columbia, Maryland, to operate as a subsidiary. SEG provides electronic systems and subsystems analysis, simulation, and support.

Also in 2005 Telephonics was awarded a $20 million contract by the US Navy for a digital audio intercommunication system for its P-C3 Orion aircraft.

In 2013 its Telephonics subsidiary and Mahindra & Mahindra, one of India's leading business houses, formed a joint venture that provides the Indian Ministry of Defence and the Indian Civil sector with radar and surveillance systems, identification devices, and communication systems. In addition it will provide systems for air traffic management services, homeland security, and other emerging surveillance requirements.

As its profits fell in 2013, the company is also keeping a close lid on costs. It announced in 2013 it was closing manufacturing facilities in two Pennsylvania locations in order to improve its production efficiencies. Clopay Building Products also in 2013 closed an Auburn, Washington, facility and consolidated it into its Russia, Ohio, location in order to streamline its manufacturing processes.

EXECUTIVES

Chief Executive Officer, Chairman, Director, Ronald J. Kramer, $1,046,013 total compensation
President, Chief Operating Officer, Director, Robert F. Mehmel, $920,399 total compensation
Senior Vice President, Chief Financial Officer, Brian G. Harris, $401,042 total compensation
Senior Vice President, Secretary, General Counsel, Seth L. Kaplan, $384,375 total compensation
Director, Henry A. Alpert
Director, Jerome L. Coben
Director, Thomas J. Brosig
Director, H. C. Charles Diao
Director, Louis J. Grabowsky
Director, Lacy M. Johnson
Director, Victor Eugene Renuart
Director, James W. Sight
Director, Kevin F. Sullivan
Director, Samanta Hegedus Stewart
Director, Michelle Taylor
Director, Cheryl L. Turnbull
Director, Travis W. Cocke
Auditors : Grant Thornton LLP

LOCATIONS

HQ: Griffon Corp.
712 Fifth Avenue, 18th Floor, New York, NY 10019
Phone: 212 957-5000
Web: www.griffon.com

2018 Sales

	$ mil.	% of total
US	1,521.2	77
Australia	167.0	9
Canada	123.3	6
Europe	102.8	5
Other countries	63.6	3
Total	1,977.9	100

PRODUCTS/OPERATIONS

2018 Sales

	$ mil.	% of total
Home & Building Products		
CBP	698.0	35
AMES	953.6	48
Telephonics	326.3	17
Total	1,977.9	100

Selected Products

Home and building products
    Ames True Temper (non-powered lawn and garden tools)
        Garden hoses and hose reels
        Long-handle tools
        Planters and lawn accessories
        Pruning
        Snow tools
        Striking tools
        Wheelbarrows
    Clopay Building Products (residential, commercial, and industrial garage doors)

    ClosetMaid
    Containers
    Shelving
    Storage cabinets
Telephonics (high-technology integrated information, communication, and sensor systems)
    Airborne maritime surveillance radar
    Aircraft intercommunication management systems
    Air traffic management
    Identification friend or foe equipment
    Integrated circuits
    Integrated homeland security systems
    Logistical support for aircraft intercommunication systems
    Radar

COMPETITORS

CORNELLCOOKSON, LLC
Celestica Inc
ESTERLINE TECHNOLOGIES CORPORATION
FLEX LTD.
HORMANN LLC
JELD-WEN, INC.
KAWNEER COMPANY, INC.
OVERHEAD DOOR CORPORATION
PGT INNOVATIONS, INC.
RYTEC CORPORATION

HISTORICAL FINANCIALS

Company Type: Public

Income Statement   **FYE:** September 30

	REVENUE ($mil)	NET INCOME ($mil)	NET PROFIT MARGIN	EMPLOYEES
09/21	2,270.6	79.2	3.5%	6,700
09/20	2,407.5	53.4	2.2%	7,400
09/19	2,209.2	37.2	1.7%	7,300
09/18	1,977.9	125.6	6.4%	7,200
09/17	1,524.9	14.9	1.0%	4,700
Annual Growth	10.5%	51.8%	—	9.3%

2021 Year-End Financials

Debt ratio: 40.1%   No. of shares ($ mil.): 56.6
Return on equity: 10.5%   Dividends
Cash ($ mil.): 248.6   Yield: 1.3%
Current Ratio: 2.57   Payout: 21.6%
Long-term debt ($ mil.): 1,033.1   Market value ($ mil.): 1,393.0

	STOCK PRICE ($) FY Close	P/E High	P/E Low	PER SHARE ($) Earnings	PER SHARE ($) Dividends	PER SHARE ($) Book Value
09/21	24.60	18	12	1.48	0.32	14.26
09/20	19.54	20	8	1.19	0.30	12.47
09/19	20.97	23	11	0.87	0.29	10.21
09/18	16.15	8	5	2.96	1.28	10.39
09/17	22.20	75	45	0.35	0.24	8.47
Annual Growth	2.6%	—	—	43.4%	7.5%	13.9%

Grocery Outlet Holding Corp

EXECUTIVES

Chairman, Director, Erik D. Ragatz
Vice-Chairman, Director, S. MacGregor Read, $567,279 total compensation
President, Robert Joseph Sheedy, $475,000 total compensation
Executive Vice President, Division Officer, Heather L. Mayo

Executive Vice President, Chief Human Resources Officer, Andrea R. Bortner
Executive Vice President, Chief Administrative Officer, Chief Stores Officer, General Counsel, Secretary, Pamela B. Burke
Executive Vice President, Chief Financial Officer, Charles C. Bracher, $507,473 total compensation
Chief Executive Officer, Director, Eric J. Lindberg, $567,279 total compensation
Executive Vice President, Division Officer, Thomas H. McMahon, $347,783 total compensation
Senior Vice President, Chief New Store Development Office, Brian T. McAndrews
Senior Vice President, Chief Purchasing Officer, Steven K. Wilson, $314,150 total compensation
Director, Gail Moody-Byrd
Director, Carey F. Jaros
Director, John E. Bachman
Director, Mary Kay Haben
Director, Jeffrey York
Director, Norman S. Matthews
Director, Kenneth W. Alterman
Director, Thomas F. Herman
Auditors : DELOITTE & TOUCHE LLP

LOCATIONS

HQ: Grocery Outlet Holding Corp
5650 Hollis Street, Emeryville, CA 94608
Phone: 510 845-1999
Web: www.groceryoutlet.com

HISTORICAL FINANCIALS

Company Type: Public

Income Statement   **FYE:** January 2

	REVENUE ($mil)	NET INCOME ($mil)	NET PROFIT MARGIN	EMPLOYEES
01/21*	3,134.6	106.7	3.4%	946
12/19	2,559.6	15.4	0.6%	847
12/18	2,287.6	15.8	0.7%	906
12/17	2,075.4	20.6	1.0%	0
12/16	1,831.5	10.1	0.6%	0
Annual Growth	14.4%	79.9%	—	—

*Fiscal year change

2021 Year-End Financials

Debt ratio: 55.5%   No. of shares ($ mil.): 94.8
Return on equity: 12.5%   Dividends
Cash ($ mil.): 105.3   Yield: —
Current Ratio: 1.64   Payout: —
Long-term debt ($ mil.): 1,330.6   Market value ($ mil.): 3,723.0

	STOCK PRICE ($) FY Close	P/E High	P/E Low	PER SHARE ($) Earnings	PER SHARE ($) Dividends	PER SHARE ($) Book Value
01/21*	39.25	40	25	1.08	0.00	9.72
12/19	33.47	233	143	0.19	0.00	8.37
Annual Growth	17.3%	—	—	468.4%	—	16.1%

*Fiscal year change

Guaranty Bancshares Inc

Guaranty Bancshares is the holding company for Guaranty Bond Bank, which operates about a dozen branches in northeast Texas and another in West Texas. Guaranty Bond Bank's deposit products and services include CDs and savings, checking, NOW, and money market accounts. Its lending activities include one- to four-family residential mortgages (more than a third of the company's loan portfolio) in addition to commercial mortgage, construction, business, agriculture, and personal loans. The company's GB Financial division provides wealth management, retirement planning, and trust services.

EXECUTIVES

Chairman, Chief Executive Officer, Subsidiary Officer, Director, Tyson T. Abston, $363,000 total compensation
President, Subsidiary Officer, Director, Kirk L. Lee, $251,300 total compensation
Senior Executive Vice President, Chief Financial Officer, Subsidiary Officer, Director, Clifton A. Payne, $241,800 total compensation
Subsidiary Officer, Lisa Gallerano
Subsidiary Officer, A. Craig Roberts
Subsidiary Officer, Martin C. Bell, $100,200 total compensation
Subsidiary Officer, Charles A. Cowell
Subsidiary Officer, Shalene A. Jacobson
Subsidiary Officer, Harold E. Lower
Subsidiary Officer, Robert P. Sharp
Director, Richard W. Baker
Director, James S. Bunch
Director, Jeffrey W Brown
Director, Carl Johnson
Director, Bradley K. Drake
Director, James M Nolan
Director, Christopher B. Elliott
Director, Molly Curl
Director, Sondra Cunningham
Auditors: Whitley Penn LLP

LOCATIONS

HQ: Guaranty Bancshares Inc
16475 Dallas Parkway, Suite 600, Addison, TX 75001
Phone: 888 572-9881
Web: www.gnty.com

PRODUCTS/OPERATIONS

2008 Sales

	$ mil.	% of total
Interest		
Loans, including fees	31.2	70
Securities	6.3	13
Other	1.1	2
Noninterest		
Service charges	4.2	8
Other	3.3	7
Total	46.1	100

COMPETITORS

CHOICEONE FINANCIAL SERVICES, INC.
COMMUNITY SHORES BANK CORPORATION
DCB FINANCIAL CORP
EASTERN VIRGINIA BANKSHARES, INC.
EMCLAIRE FINANCIAL CORP.

HISTORICAL FINANCIALS
Company Type: Public

Income Statement				FYE: December 31
	ASSETS ($mil)	NET INCOME ($mil)	INCOME AS % OF ASSETS	EMPLOYEES
12/20	2,740.8	27.4	1.0%	467
12/19	2,318.4	26.2	1.1%	467
12/18	2,266.9	20.5	0.9%	454
12/17	1,962.6	14.4	0.7%	407
12/16	1,828.3	12.1	0.7%	397
Annual Growth	10.7%	22.6%	—	4.1%

2020 Year-End Financials
Return on assets: 1.0%
Return on equity: 10.2%
Long-term debt ($ mil.): —
No. of shares ($ mil.): 10.9
Sales ($ mil.): 119.2
Dividends
Yield: 2.6%
Payout: 35.4%
Market value ($ mil.): 328.0

	STOCK PRICE ($) FY Close	P/E High/Low		PER SHARE ($) Earnings	Dividends	Book Value
12/20	29.95	13	8	2.46	0.71	24.93
12/19	32.88	17	13	2.05	0.64	20.59
12/18	29.82	22	18	1.61	0.55	18.80
12/17	30.65	27	22	1.27	0.36	17.04
12/16	26.50	—	—	1.23	0.47	14.74
Annual Growth	3.1%	—	—	19.0%	10.7%	14.0%

Guaranty Federal Bancshares Inc (Springfield, MO)

EXECUTIVES

Chairman, Director, James R. Batten, $6,515 total compensation
President, Chief Executive Officer, Subsidiary Officer, Director, Shaun A. Burke, $314,167 total compensation
Executive Vice President, Chief Commercial Banking Officer, Craig E. Dunn
Executive Vice President, Chief Financial Officer, Subsidiary Officer, Carter M. Peters, $208,333 total compensation
Executive Vice President, Chief Credit Officer, Subsidiary Officer, Sheri D. Biser, $181,833 total compensation
Executive Vice President, Chief Operating Officer, Subsidiary Officer, Robin E. Robeson, $226,667 total compensation
Director, John F. Griesemer, $7,700 total compensation
Director, Kurt D. Hellweg, $8,125 total compensation
Director, Tim Rosenbury, $10,750 total compensation
Director, James L. Sivils, $8,675 total compensation
Director, David T. Moore
Director, Greg A. Horton
Director, Tony Scavuzzo
Auditors: BKD, LLP

LOCATIONS

HQ: Guaranty Federal Bancshares Inc (Springfield, MO)
2144 E. Republic Rd., Suite F200, Springfield, MO 65804
Phone: 833 875-2492
Web: www.gbankmo.com

HISTORICAL FINANCIALS
Company Type: Public

Income Statement				FYE: December 31
	ASSETS ($mil)	NET INCOME ($mil)	INCOME AS % OF ASSETS	EMPLOYEES
12/20	1,146.2	6.8	0.6%	234
12/19	1,012.0	9.4	0.9%	229
12/18	965.1	7.3	0.8%	226
12/17	794.4	5.1	0.6%	173
12/16	687.9	5.5	0.8%	172
Annual Growth	13.6%	5.1%	—	8.0%

2020 Year-End Financials
Return on assets: 0.6%
Return on equity: 7.8%
Long-term debt ($ mil.): —
No. of shares ($ mil.): 4.3
Sales ($ mil.): 50.9
Dividends
Yield: 3.4%
Payout: 31.7%
Market value ($ mil.): 76.0

	STOCK PRICE ($) FY Close	P/E High/Low		PER SHARE ($) Earnings	Dividends	Book Value
12/20	17.46	16	8	1.57	0.60	20.38
12/19	25.20	12	10	2.11	0.52	19.51
12/18	21.84	15	12	1.64	0.48	18.05
12/17	22.45	19	16	1.16	0.30	16.93
12/16	21.18	17	12	1.27	0.34	15.87
Annual Growth	(4.7%)	—	—	5.4%	15.3%	6.5%

Halozyme Therapeutics Inc

Halozyme Therapeutics is a biopharma technology platform company. Its Hylenex recombinant is used as an adjuvant for drug and fluid infusions. Most of Halozyme's products and candidates (including Hylenex) are based on rHuPH20, its patented recombinant human hyaluronidase enzyme, while its lead cancer program is PEGPH20, which targets solid tumors. Halozyme partners with such pharmaceuticals as Roche, Pfizer, Janssen, Baxalta, and AbbVie for its ENHANZE drug delivery platform, which enables biologics and small molecule compounds to be delivered subcutaneously. The US generates the majority of revenue which accounts for about 65%.

Operations

Halozyme operates its business in one

segment, which includes all activities related to the research, development and commercialization of proprietary enzymes. This segment also includes revenues and expenses related to royalties (about 45% of revenue), research and development and bulk rHuPH20 manufacturing activities conducted under collaborative agreements (about 30%), with third parties and product sales (about 25%) of Hylenex recombinant.

Geographic Reach

Halozyme is headquartered in and has research facilities in San Diego, California.

The US accounts for about 65% of the company's revenue, while Switzerland accounts for around 30%, and Japan some 5%.

Sales and Marketing

Integrated Commercialization Solutions, a division of AmerisourceBergen, is the exclusive distributor for Hylenex recombinant in the US.

The company employs outside vendors such as advertising agencies, market research firms, and marketing firms to help support its commercial activities.

Financial Performance

The company's revenue for fiscal 2021 increased to $443.3 million compared from the prior year with $267.6 million.

Net income for fiscal 2021 increased to $402.7 million compared from the prior year with $129.1 million.

Cash held by the company at the end of fiscal 2021 decreased to $119.2 million. Cash provided by operations and financing activities were $299.4 million and $77.9 million, respectively. Cash used for investing activities was $406.3 million, mainly for purchases of marketable securities.

Strategy

Halozyme are a leader in converting IV biologics to subcutaneous delivery using its commercially-validated ENHANZE technology. The company's ENHANZE technology also has the potential for subcutaneous delivery of small molecules, including those developed as long-acting injectables and other therapies that might benefit from larger dose/larger volume subcutaneous delivery. The company collaborate with leading pharmaceutical and biotechnology companies to help them develop products that combine our ENHANZE technology with their proprietary compounds. Halozyme target large, attractive markets, where ENHANZE-enabled subcutaneous delivery has the potential to deliver competitive differentiation and other important benefits to its partners, such as larger injection volumes administered rapidly, extended dosing intervals, and reduced treatment burden and healthcare costs. In addition, ENHANZE has been demonstrated to enable the combination of two therapeutic antibodies in a single injection, as well as the development of new co-formulation intellectual property. The company leverage its strategic, technical, regulatory and alliance management skills in support of its partners' efforts to develop new subcutaneously delivered products. Halozyme currently have eleven collaborations with five current approved products and additional product candidates in development using its ENHANZE technology. The company intend to work with its existing collaborators to expand our collaborations to add new targets and develop targets and product candidates under the terms of the operative collaboration agreements. Halozyme will also continue our efforts to enter into new collaborations to further derive additional value from its proprietary technology.

EXECUTIVES

Chairman, Director, Connie L. Matsui
President, Chief Executive Officer, Director, Helen I. Torley, $725,000 total compensation
Product Development Senior Vice President, Product Development Chief Technical Officer, Michael J. LaBarre, $248,606 total compensation
Senior Vice President, Chief Compliance Officer, General Counsel, Secretary, Mark Snyder
Accounting Senior Vice President, Finance Senior Vice President, Accounting Vice President, Finance Vice President, Accounting Chief Financial Officer, Finance Chief Financial Officer, Nicole LaBrosse
Director, Jeffrey W. Henderson
Director, Bernadette M. Connaughton
Director, Matthew L. Posard
Director, Moni Miyashita
Director, Jean-Pierre Bizzari
Director, James M. Daly
Director, Barbara G. Duncan
Auditors : Ernst & Young LLP

LOCATIONS

HQ: Halozyme Therapeutics Inc
11388 Sorrento Valley Road, San Diego, CA 92121
Phone: 858 794-8889
Web: www.halozyme.com

2014 Sales

	$ mil.	% of total
Switzerland	42.8	57
US	31.4	42
Other countries	1.1	1
Total	75.3	100

PRODUCTS/OPERATIONS

2014 Revenues

	$ mil.	% of total
Product sales	37.8	50
Collaborative agreements	28.1	37
Royalties	9.4	13
Total	75.3	100

COMPETITORS

AGENUS INC.
ARIAD PHARMACEUTICALS, INC.
CERUS CORPORATION
CURIS, INC.
CYTRX CORPORATION
DYAX CORP.
IDERA PHARMACEUTICALS, INC.
INCYTE CORPORATION
PROGENICS PHARMACEUTICALS, INC.
REPLIGEN CORPORATION

HISTORICAL FINANCIALS

Company Type: Public

Income Statement — FYE: December 31

	REVENUE ($mil)	NET INCOME ($mil)	NET PROFIT MARGIN	EMPLOYEES
12/20	267.5	129.0	48.2%	136
12/19	195.9	(72.2)	—	132
12/18	151.8	(80.3)	—	281
12/17	316.6	62.9	19.9%	255
12/16	146.6	(103.0)	—	259
Annual Growth	16.2%	—	—	(14.9%)

2020 Year-End Financials

Debt ratio: 68.5%
Return on equity: —
Cash ($ mil.): 147.7
Current Ratio: 1.32
Long-term debt ($ mil.): —
No. of shares ($ mil.): 135.0
Dividends
Yield: —
Payout: —
Market value ($ mil.): 5,767.0

	STOCK PRICE ($) FY Close	P/E High/Low		PER SHARE ($) Earnings	Dividends	Book Value
12/20	42.71	46	15	0.91	0.00	1.12
12/19	17.73	—	—	(0.50)	0.00	0.67
12/18	14.63	—	—	(0.56)	0.00	1.72
12/17	20.26	45	22	0.45	0.00	1.46
12/16	9.88	—	—	(0.81)	0.00	(0.25)
Annual Growth	44.2%	—	—	—	—	—

Hamilton Lane Inc

EXECUTIVES

Chairman, Director, Hartley R. Rogers, $302,500 total compensation
Vice-Chairman, Director, Erik R. Hirsch, $312,500 total compensation
Vice-Chairman, Division Officer, Juan Delgado-Moreira, $318,795 total compensation
Chief Financial Officer, Treasurer, Atul Varma
Chief Executive Officer, Director, Mario L. Giannini, $350,000 total compensation
Controller, Managing Director, Michael Donohue
General Counsel, Secretary, Lydia A. Gavalis
Director, David J. Berkman
Director, O. Griffith Sexton
Director, R. Vann Graves
Director, Leslie F. Varon
Auditors : Ernst & Young LLP

LOCATIONS

HQ: Hamilton Lane Inc
110 Washington Street, Suite 1300, Consholocken, PA 19428
Phone: 610 934-2222
Web: www.hamiltonlane.com

HISTORICAL FINANCIALS
Company Type: Public

Income Statement — FYE: March 31

	REVENUE ($mil)	NET INCOME ($mil)	NET PROFIT MARGIN	EMPLOYEES
03/21	341.6	98.0	28.7%	450
03/20	274.0	60.8	22.2%	400
03/19	252.1	33.5	13.3%	370
03/18	244.0	17.3	7.1%	340
03/17	179.8	0.6	0.3%	290
Annual Growth	17.4%	255.7%	—	11.6%

2021 Year-End Financials
Debt ratio: 14.4%
Return on equity: 49.8%
Cash ($ mil.): 87.3
Current Ratio: 0.50
Long-term debt ($ mil.): 163.1
No. of shares ($ mil.): 53.0
Dividends
Yield: 1.4%
Payout: 51.2%
Market value ($ mil.): 4,696.0

	STOCK PRICE ($) FY Close	P/E High	P/E Low	PER SHARE ($) Earnings	PER SHARE ($) Dividends	PER SHARE ($) Book Value
03/21	88.56	34	17	2.81	1.25	4.49
03/20	55.31	34	19	2.15	1.10	2.98
03/19	43.58	37	23	1.40	0.85	2.17
03/18	37.23	42	19	0.93	0.70	1.61
03/17	18.67	642	601	0.03	0.00	1.28
Annual Growth	47.6%	—	—	211.1%	—	36.9%

Hannon Armstrong Sustainable Infrastructure Capital Inc

Hannon Armstrong Sustainable Infrastructure Capital has its hands in both kinds of green. The REIT provides securitized funding for environmentally friendly infrastructure projects. It is a key provider of financing for the US government's energy efficiency projects. Hannon Armstrong focuses on energy efficiency, renewable energy, and other sustainable projects, including water and communications that improve energy consumption and the use of natural resources. The company manages approximately $6.2 billion in assets and operates mostly in the US.

IPO

Operations
Hannon Armstrong manages about $6.2 billion in assets across more than 200 investments in projects to improve energy efficiency and develop renewable energy sources and sustainable infrastructure. About 80% of the REIT's projects are focused on solar energy; wind or BTM; energy efficiency, some 10%; and sustainable infrastructure (which includes water and seismic retrofit projects), about 10%.

Nearly 55% of the company's revenue is derived from interest income on receivables. Almost 20% each comes from rental income and gain on sale of receivables and investments.

When making investment decisions, Hannon Armstrong calculates the estimated metric tons of carbon emissions or equivalent avoided, a calculation it calls CarbonCount. The company's 2019 CarbonCount calculation estimates its investments will reduce carbon emissions by about 385,000 metric tons.

Geographic Reach
Based in Annapolis, Maryland, Hannon Armstrong operates primarily in the US.

Sales and Marketing
Hannon Armstrong provides securitized funding for environmentally friendly infrastructure projects by US federal, state, and local governments and high credit quality institutions.

Financial Performance
Thanks to growing popularity and falling costs of efficient and renewable energy, Hannon Armstrong has seen more than a 141% expansion of revenue in the last five years, accompanying a jump in net income to more than $30 million in 2017 compared with $8 million in 2015.

In 2019 the REIT reported revenue of $142 million, up 1% from the prior year. Hannon Armstrong's fee income accounted for the majority of the slight increase, as fee income increased by 167%.

Hannon Armstrong's net income in 2019 ballooned 95% to $82 million as a result of a $2 million increase in total revenue, a $2 million decrease in total expenses, a $42 million increase in income from equity and method investments, and a $6 million increase in income tax expense.

Cash at the end of fiscal 2019 was $106.6 million, double that of the prior year. Cash from operations provided $29.5 million while investing activities used $201.1 million due mostly to equity method investments and purchases of and investments in receivables. Financing activities added another $218.9 million, primarily from proceeds from credit facilities.

Strategy
Hannon Armstrong intends to continue investing in clean energy technologies that it believes benefit society and that generally are tied to long-term utility contracts.

The company's investments are focused on three areas: Behind-the-Meter; Grid-Connected; and Sustainable Infrastructure. Hannon Armstrong prefers investments where the assets have a long-term, investment-grade rated off-taker or counterparties. As of 2019, the company's portfolio consisted of over 180 investments and Hannon Armstrong seeks to manage the diversity of its portfolio by, among other factors, project type, project operator, type of investment, type of technology, transaction size, geography, obligor and maturity.

In mid-2020, Hannon Armstrong formed a partnership with a subsidiary of ENGIE S.A. that owned a 2.3 gigawatt portfolio of wind and utility-scale solar assets. The partnership combined Hannon Armstrong's extensive experience in providing long-term investment for climate solutions with the best-in-class development and operations experience of ENGIE.

In 2019, Hannon Armstrong and Empower Energies to jointly invest in renewable energy products in the commercial & industrial (C&I) and municipal, university, school and hospital (MUSH) markets across the United States. Hannon Armstrong also partnered with Summit Ridge Energy in 2019 to jointly invest in community solar projects across several US markets, including Maryland, where the initial solar power plants will come online in Prince George's and Baltimore counties that summer.

Mergers and Acquisitions
In 2019, Hannon Armstrong and Morgan Properties announced a new joint venture that will acquire the B-Piece from Virginia-based, Freddie Mac's previously settled KG series focused on environmental and social impact, and part of Freddie Mac's flagship K-Deal program. The issuance, K-G02, is exclusively comprised of securitized workforce housing loans made through Freddie Mac's Green AdvantageÂ® program which requires borrowers to make energy and/or water efficiency improvements to their properties. Expansion into this new asset class will further diversify the company's portfolio and bolster its efforts to decarbonize buildings, including multi-family properties. Terms were not disclosed.

Company Background
Formed in 2012 to be a REIT, the company went public in 2013, though it traces its roots to the 1980s and Hannon Armstrong Capital, LLC.

EXECUTIVES

Chairman, President, Chief Executive Officer, Jeffrey W. Eckel, $632,833 total compensation

Executive Vice President, Chief Financial Officer, Chief Operating Officer, Treasurer, Jeffrey A. Lipson

Executive Vice President, Chief Client Officer, Susan D. Nickey

Executive Vice President, Chief Investment Officer, Nathaniel J. Rose, $357,208 total compensation

Executive Vice President, General Counsel, Chief Legal Officer, Steven L. Chuslo, $358,333 total compensation

Portfolio Management Executive Vice President, Portfolio Management Head, Daniel K. McMahon, $335,333 total compensation

Executive Vice President, Co-Chief Investment Officer, Marc Pangburn

Lead Independent Director, Director, Teresa M. Brenner

Director, Richard J. Osborne

Director, Clarence D. Armbrister
Director, Nancy C. Floyd
Director, Michael Eckhart
Director, Simone F. Lagomarsino
Director, Charles M. O'Neil
Director, Steven G. Osgood
Auditors : Ernst & Young LLP

LOCATIONS

HQ: Hannon Armstrong Sustainable Infrastructure Capital Inc
  1906 Towne Centre Blvd., Suite 370, Annapolis, MD 21401
Phone: 410 571-9860
Web: www.hannonarmstrong.com

PRODUCTS/OPERATIONS

2017 Sales

	$ mil.	% of total
Interest income, financing receivables	56.7	53
Rental income	19.8	19
Gain on sale of receivables and investments	21.0	20
Interest income, investments	5.1	5
Fee income	3.0	3
Total	105.6	100

Selected Project Types
Clean Energy
Energy Efficiency
Other Sustainable Infrastructure

COMPETITORS

HEALTHPEAK PROPERTIES, INC.
IMPAX ASSET MANAGEMENT GROUP PLC
INFRAREIT, INC.
ISTAR INC.
KITE REALTY GROUP TRUST
NEXTERA ENERGY PARTNERS, LP
PROLOGIS, INC.
SUNRUN INC.
TPG RE FINANCE TRUST, INC.
VENTAS, INC.

HISTORICAL FINANCIALS

Company Type: Public

Income Statement FYE: December 31

	REVENUE ($mil)	NET INCOME ($mil)	NET PROFIT MARGIN	EMPLOYEES
12/20	186.9	82.4	44.1%	73
12/19	141.5	81.5	57.6%	60
12/18	137.8	41.5	30.2%	49
12/17	105.5	30.8	29.2%	47
12/16	81.1	14.6	18.0%	40
Annual Growth	23.2%	54.0%	—	16.2%

2020 Year-End Financials
Debt ratio: 63.3%
Return on equity: 7.6%
Cash ($ mil.): 286.2
Current Ratio: 20.17
Long-term debt ($ mil.): 2,166.3
No. of shares ($ mil.): 76.4
Dividends
  Yield: 2.1%
  Payout: 123.6%
Market value ($ mil.): 4,850.0

	STOCK PRICE ($) FY Close	P/E High/Low		PER SHARE ($) Earnings	Dividends	Book Value
12/20	63.43	58	15	1.10	1.36	15.74
12/19	32.18	26	16	1.24	1.34	14.12
12/18	19.05	32	23	0.75	1.32	13.24
12/17	24.06	44	32	0.57	1.32	12.37
12/16	18.99	78	52	0.32	1.23	12.27
Annual Growth	35.2%	—	—	36.2%	2.5%	6.4%

HarborOne Bancorp Inc (New)

EXECUTIVES

Chairman, Subsidiary Officer, Director, Michael J. Sullivan
President, Chief Executive Officer, Subsidiary Officer, Director, Joseph F. Casey, $501,231 total compensation
Senior Vice President, General Counsel, Corporate Secretary, Subsidiary Officer, Inez H. Friedman-Boyce
Subsidiary Officer, Kevin Hamel
Subsidiary Officer, Brenda C. Kerr
Subsidiary Officer, Joseph E. McQuade
Subsidiary Officer, David B. Reilly
Subsidiary Officer, H. Scott Sanborn, $237,542 total compensation
Executive Vice President, Chief Financial Officer, Subsidiary Officer, Linda H. Simmons
Subsidiary Officer, David E. Tryder
Subsidiary Officer, Patricia M. Williams
Director, Joseph F. Barry
Director, Mandy Lee Berman
Director, James W. Blake, $739,815 total compensation
Director, David P. Frenette
Director, Gordon Jezard
Director, Barry R. Koretz
Director, Timothy R. Lynch
Director, William A. Payne
Director, Andreana Santangelo
Director, Damian W. Wilmot
Auditors : Crowe LLP

LOCATIONS

HQ: HarborOne Bancorp Inc (New)
  770 Oak Street, Brockton, MA 02301
Phone: 508 895-1000
Web: www.harborone.com

HISTORICAL FINANCIALS

Company Type: Public

Income Statement FYE: December 31

	ASSETS ($mil)	NET INCOME ($mil)	INCOME AS % OF ASSETS	EMPLOYEES
12/20	4,483.6	44.7	1.0%	633
12/19	4,058.9	18.2	0.5%	675
12/18	3,653.1	11.3	0.3%	658
12/17	2,684.9	10.3	0.4%	581
12/16	2,448.3	5.9	0.2%	614
Annual Growth	16.3%	65.8%	—	0.8%

2020 Year-End Financials
Return on assets: 1.0%
Return on equity: 6.5%
Long-term debt ($ mil.): —
No. of shares ($ mil.): 57.2
Sales ($ mil.): 287.7
Dividends
  Yield: 0.8%
  Payout: 15.5%
Market value ($ mil.): 621.0

	STOCK PRICE ($) FY Close	P/E High/Low		PER SHARE ($) Earnings	Dividends	Book Value
12/20	10.86	14	8	0.82	0.09	12.17
12/19	10.99	60	30	0.33	0.00	11.40
12/18	15.89	56	42	0.36	0.00	10.98
12/17	19.16	67	49	0.33	0.00	10.52
12/16	19.34	—	—	0.00	0.00	10.25
Annual Growth	(13.4%)	—	—	—	—	4.4%

Hawthorn Bancshares Inc

EXECUTIVES

President, Chief Executive Officer, Subsidiary Officer, Chairman, Director, David T. Turner, $476,019 total compensation
Senior Vice President, Chief Financial Officer, Subsidiary Officer, W. Bruce Phelps, $205,925 total compensation
Senior Vice President, Secretary, Kathleen L. Bruegenhemke, $195,700 total compensation
Director, Frank E. Burkhead
Director, Philip D. Freeman
Director, Jonathan D. Holtaway
Director, Kevin L. Riley
Director, Gus S. Wetzel
Auditors : KPMG LLP

LOCATIONS

HQ: Hawthorn Bancshares Inc
  132 East High Street, Box 688, Jefferson City, MO 65102
Phone: 573 761-6100
Web: www.hawthornbancshares.com

HISTORICAL FINANCIALS

Company Type: Public

Income Statement FYE: December 31

	ASSETS ($mil)	NET INCOME ($mil)	INCOME AS % OF ASSETS	EMPLOYEES
12/20	1,733.7	14.2	0.8%	306
12/19	1,492.9	16.1	1.1%	294
12/18	1,481.6	10.7	0.7%	301
12/17	1,429.2	3.4	0.2%	349
12/16	1,287.0	7.2	0.6%	343
Annual Growth	7.7%	18.4%	—	(2.8%)

2020 Year-End Financials
Return on assets: 0.8%
Return on equity: 11.6%
Long-term debt ($ mil.): —
No. of shares ($ mil.): 6.7
Sales ($ mil.): 77.6
Dividends
  Yield: 2.2%
  Payout: 22.7%
Market value ($ mil.): 148.0

	STOCK PRICE ($) FY Close	P/E High/Low		PER SHARE ($) Earnings	Dividends	Book Value
12/20	21.90	12	6	2.12	0.48	19.38
12/19	25.50	12	9	2.38	0.43	16.95
12/18	21.03	15	13	1.58	0.34	14.64
12/17	20.75	46	34	0.50	0.23	13.47
12/16	17.70	17	13	1.06	0.17	13.32
Annual Growth	5.5%	—	—	18.8%	29.8%	9.8%

Healthcare Trust Of America Inc

EXECUTIVES

Chairman, Director, John Knox Singleton
Vice-Chairman, Director, W. Bradley Blair
President, Chief Executive Officer, Director, Todd J. Meredith
Executive Vice President, Chief Financial Officer, J. Christopher Douglas
Senior Vice President, Secretary, Corporate Counsel, Andrew E. Loope
Senior Vice President, Chief Accounting Officer, Amanda L. Callaway
Director, Constance B. Moore
Director, Vicki U. Booth
Director, Jay Paul Leupp
Director, John V. Abbott
Director, Nancy Howell Agee
Director, Peter F. Lyle
Director, Christann M. Vasquez
Director, James J. Kilroy
Director, Edward H. Braman
Director, Ajay Gupta
Auditors : Deloitte & Touche LLP

LOCATIONS

HQ: Healthcare Trust Of America Inc
16435 N. Scottsdale Road, Suite 320, Scottsdale, AZ 85254
Phone: 480 998-3478   **Fax:** 480 991-0755
Web: www.htareit.com

HISTORICAL FINANCIALS

Company Type: Public

Income Statement — FYE: December 31

	REVENUE ($mil)	NET INCOME ($mil)	NET PROFIT MARGIN	EMPLOYEES
12/20	738.9	52.6	7.1%	333
12/19	692.0	30.1	4.4%	303
12/18	696.4	213.4	30.7%	282
12/17	613.9	63.9	10.4%	270
12/16	460.9	45.9	10.0%	214
Annual Growth	12.5%	3.5%	—	11.7%

2020 Year-End Financials

Debt ratio: 44.6%   No. of shares ($ mil.): 218.5
Return on equity: 1.6%   Dividends
Cash ($ mil.): 118.7   Yield: 4.5%
Current Ratio: 0.59   Payout: 527.0%
Long-term debt ($ mil.): 3,026.9   Market value ($ mil.): 6,020.0

	STOCK PRICE ($) FY Close	P/E High	P/E Low	Earnings	Dividends	Book Value
12/20	27.54	142	87	0.24	1.27	14.52
12/19	30.28	208	165	0.14	1.25	15.51
12/18	25.31	29	23	1.02	1.23	15.86
12/17	30.04	94	82	0.34	1.21	16.00
12/16	29.11	102	77	0.33	1.19	11.91
Annual Growth	(1.4%)	—	—	(7.7%)	1.5%	5.1%

HealthEquity Inc

EXECUTIVES

Chairman, Director, Robert W. Selander
Vice-Chairman, Director, Stephen D. Neeleman, $383,334 total compensation
President, Chief Executive Officer, Director, Jon Kessler, $483,334 total compensation
Executive Vice President, General Counsel, Corporate Secretary, Delano Ladd
Executive Vice President, Chief Financial Officer, Tyson Murdock
Executive Vice President, Chief Technology Officer, Elimelech Rosner
Executive Vice President, Chief Security Officer, Larry Trittschuh
Director, Frank A. Corvino
Director, Adrian T. Dillon
Director, Evelyn Dilsaver
Director, Debra McCowan
Director, Rajesh Natarajan
Director, Stuart B. Parker
Director, Ian Sacks
Director, Gayle Wellborn
Director, Paul M. Black
Auditors : PricewaterhouseCoopers LLP

LOCATIONS

HQ: HealthEquity Inc
15 West Scenic Pointe Drive, Suite 100, Draper, UT 84020
Phone: 801 727-1000
Web: www.healthequity.com

HISTORICAL FINANCIALS

Company Type: Public

Income Statement — FYE: January 31

	REVENUE ($mil)	NET INCOME ($mil)	NET PROFIT MARGIN	EMPLOYEES
01/21	733.5	8.8	1.2%	3,039
01/20	531.9	39.6	7.5%	2,931
01/19	287.2	73.8	25.7%	1,141
01/18	229.5	47.3	20.6%	1,027
01/17	178.3	26.3	14.8%	875
Annual Growth	42.4%	(23.9%)	—	36.5%

2021 Year-End Financials

Debt ratio: 36.4%   No. of shares ($ mil.): 77.1
Return on equity: 0.7%   Dividends
Cash ($ mil.): 328.8   Yield: —
Current Ratio: 2.25   Payout: —
Long-term debt ($ mil.): 924.2   Market value ($ mil.): 6,447.0

	STOCK PRICE ($) FY Close	P/E High	P/E Low	Earnings	Dividends	Book Value
01/21	83.55	758	338	0.12	0.00	17.87
01/20	66.06	143	88	0.58	0.00	14.50
01/19	62.34	84	42	1.17	0.00	7.64
01/18	50.62	69	50	0.77	0.00	5.69
01/17	46.25	108	35	0.44	0.00	4.40
Annual Growth	15.9%	—	—	(27.7%)	—	42.0%

Heartland BancCorp

EXECUTIVES

President, Chief Executive Officer, Subsidiary Officer, Chairman, G. Scott McComb
Vice-Chairman, Jay B. Eggspuehler
Treasurer, Carrie L. Almendinger
Secretary, Director, Jodi Garrison
Director Emeritus, Director, Arthur G.H. Bing
Director Emeritus, Director, John R. Haines
Director, Director Emeritus, Gerald K. McClain
Director Emeritus, Cheryl Poulton
Director Emeritus, Jack J. Eggspuehler
Director, David C. Kotary
Director, Robert C. Overs
Director, Gary D. Paine
Director, George R. Smith
Director, Richard A. Vincent
Director, William A. Dodson
Director Emeritus, I. Robert Amerine
Auditors : BKD, LLP

LOCATIONS

HQ: Heartland BancCorp
430 North Hamilton Road, Whitehall, OH 43213
Phone: 614 337-4600
Web: www.heartlandbank.com

HISTORICAL FINANCIALS

Company Type: Public

Income Statement — FYE: December 31

	ASSETS ($mil)	NET INCOME ($mil)	INCOME AS % OF ASSETS	EMPLOYEES
12/20	1,547.0	14.7	1.0%	279
12/19	1,114.8	13.1	1.2%	0
12/18	1,047.0	11.4	1.1%	0
12/17	900.9	8.8	1.0%	0
12/16	781.3	7.9	1.0%	0
Annual Growth	18.6%	16.6%	—	—

2020 Year-End Financials

Return on assets: 1.1%   Dividends
Return on equity: 10.9%   Yield: —
Long-term debt ($ mil.): —   Payout: 31.1%
No. of shares ($ mil.): 1.9   Market value ($ mil.): 165.0
Sales ($ mil.): 70.1

	STOCK PRICE ($) FY Close	P/E High	P/E Low	Earnings	Dividends	Book Value
12/20	82.99	13	7	7.33	2.28	70.70
12/19	95.15	15	12	6.45	2.08	63.55
12/18	81.00	15	12	6.68	1.89	57.08
12/17	82.60	15	12	5.40	1.72	48.77
12/16	64.01	14	9	4.97	1.55	45.10
Annual Growth	6.7%	—	—	10.2%	10.2%	11.9%

Heartland Financial USA, Inc. (Dubuque, IA)

Founded in 1981, Heartland Financial USA (HTLF) is a $19.3 billion multi-bank holding company that owns flagship subsidiary Dubuque Bank and Trust (Iowa) and ten other banks that together operates about 130 branches in about a dozen states, primarily in the West and Midwest. In addition to standard deposit, loan, and mortgage services, the banks also offer retirement, wealth management, insurance, and investment services. HTFL's principal services are FDIC-insured deposit accounts and related services, and loans to businesses and consumers.

Operations
Heartland Financial USA is engaged in the business of community banking. Its Banks provide a wide range of commercial, small business and consumer banking services to businesses, including public sector and non-profit entities, and to individuals. It has a broad customer base and are not dependent upon a single or a few customers. It provides a contemporary menu of traditional and non-traditional service channels including online banking, mobile banking and telephone banking. Its Banks provide a comprehensive suite of banking services comprised of competitively priced deposit and credit offerings, along with treasury management and retirement plan services.

Heartland's subsidiaries include: Citywide Banks (approximately $2.3 billion total deposits), New Mexico Bank & Trust ($2.3 billion), Dubuque Bank and Trust Company ($1.8 billion), Wisconsin Bank & Trust ($1.1 billion), First Bank & Trust ($2.4 billion) Premier Valley Bank ($1.1 billion), Illinois Bank & Trust ($1.5 billion), Arizona Bank & Trust ($1.8 billion), Rocky Mountain Bank ($640 million), Bank of Blue Valley ($1.2 billion), and Minnesota Bank & Trust ($719 million).

Geographic Reach
Dubuque, Iowa-based Heartland Financial USA operates through about 130 locations (including branches and loan production offices) in local communities in Iowa, Illinois, Wisconsin, New Mexico, Arizona, Montana, Colorado, Minnesota, Kansas, Missouri, Texas, and California. The company's three largest bank subsidiaries by number of locations are First Bank & Trust with over 20, Colorado's Citywide Banks with some 20, and New Mexico Bank & Trust with about 25 locations.

Sales and Marketing
Heartland Financial USA offers its banking services to businesses, public sector and non-profit entities, and individuals. The company provides a contemporary menu of traditional and non-traditional service channels including online banking, mobile banking and telephone banking. Its Banks provide a comprehensive suite of banking services comprised of competitively priced deposit and credit offerings, along with treasury management and retirement plan services.

Advertising expenses were $0.2 million, $0.1 million, and $0.2 million in 2021, 2020, and 2019, respectively.

Financial Performance
Total interest income increased $52.1 million or 10% to $588.8 million from $536.6 million due to an increase in average earning assets, which was partially offset by a decrease in the average rate on earning assets.

In 2021, the company had a net income of $211.9 million, a 59% increase from the previous year's net income of $133.5 million.

The company's cash at the end of 2021 was $435.6 million. Operating activities generated $326 million, while investing activities used $1.5 billion, mainly for purchase of securities available for sale. Financing activities provided another $1.3 billion.

Strategy
Heartland Financial USA's primary objectives are to increase profitability and diversify its deposits, assets and overall customer base through organic growth and acquisitions in the Bank Markets it serves. The company continues to seek opportunities for growth through acquisitions, capitalizing on an established record of successful transactions. HTLF's acquisition strategy is to augment organic growth by focusing on acquisition targets that compliment or supplement its current banking strategy. This includes transactions that increase penetration in existing geographic Bank Markets and expansion into adjacent markets.

In recent years, it has focused on markets with growth potential in the Midwestern, Southwestern and Western regions of the US. Its strategy is to balance the growth in its Southwestern and Western markets with the stability of its Midwestern markets.

Company Background
Heartland Financial USA was founded in 1981, although it traces its roots back to the 1935 establishment of Dubuque Bank and Trust. It made its first bank acquisition in in 1989 – Key City Bank – and has continued acquiring community banks since.

EXECUTIVES

Chairman, Director, John K. Schmidt, $197,072 total compensation
Vice-Chairman, Director, Thomas L. Flynn, $11,500 total compensation
President, Chief Executive Officer, Director, Bruce K. Lee, $576,000 total compensation
Executive Vice President, Chief Banking Officer, Kevin G. Quinn
Executive Vice President, Chief Operating Officer, Mark A. Frank
Executive Vice President, Deputy Chief Financial Officer, Principal Accounting Officer, Janet Quick
Executive Vice President, David A Prince
Executive Vice President, Chief Financial Officer, Bryan R. McKeag, $343,500 total compensation
Executive Vice President, Chief Administrative Officer, General Counsel, Corporate Secretary, Jay L. Kim
Director, Lynn B. Fuller, $512,963 total compensation
Director, Duane E. White
Director, Barry H. Orr
Director, Robert B Engel
Director, Jennifer K. Hopkins
Director, Christopher S. Hylen
Director, Susan G. Murphy
Director, Martin J. Schmitz
Director, Kathryn Graves Unger
Auditors : KPMG LLP

LOCATIONS

HQ: Heartland Financial USA, Inc. (Dubuque, IA)
1398 Central Avenue, Dubuque, IA 52001
Phone: 563 589-2100   **Fax:** 563 589-2011
Web: www.htlf.com

PRODUCTS/OPERATIONS

2017 Sales

	$ mil.	% of total
Interest		
Loans & leases, including fees	304.0	65
Securities	58.1	13
Other	1.6	-
Interest expense	(33.3)	-
Noninterest		
Gains on sales of loans	22.2	5
Service charges and fees	39.2	8
Trust fees	15.8	3
Loan serving income	5.6	1
Brokerage & insurance commissions	4.0	1
Security gains	7.0	2
Other	8.1	2
Total	432.3	100

Selected Subsidiaries
Arizona Bank & Trust
Citywide Banks (Colorado)
Dubuque Bank and Trust Company (Iowa)
   DB&T Community Development Corp.
   DB&T Insurance
Illinois Bank & Trust
Minnesota Bank & Trust
Morrill & Janes Bank and Trust Company (Kansas)
New Mexico Bank & Trust
Premier Valley Bank (California)
Rocky Mountain Bank (Montana)
Wisconsin Bank & Trust

COMPETITORS

COLUMBIA BANKING SYSTEM, INC.
F.N.B. CORPORATION
FIRST MERCHANTS CORPORATION
GLACIER BANCORP, INC.
IBERIABANK CORPORATION
PACWEST BANCORP
STATE BANK FINANCIAL CORPORATION

UNITED BANKSHARES, INC.
UNITED COMMUNITY BANKS, INC.
WINTRUST FINANCIAL CORPORATION

HISTORICAL FINANCIALS
Company Type: Public

Income Statement FYE: December 31

	ASSETS ($mil)	NET INCOME ($mil)	INCOME AS % OF ASSETS	EMPLOYEES
12/20	17,908.3	137.9	0.8%	2,013
12/19	13,209.5	149.1	1.1%	1,908
12/18	11,408.0	116.9	1.0%	2,045
12/17	9,810.7	75.2	0.8%	2,008
12/16	8,247.0	80.3	1.0%	1,864
Annual Growth	21.4%	14.5%	—	1.9%

2020 Year-End Financials
Return on assets: 0.8%
Return on equity: 7.5%
Long-term debt ($ mil.): —
No. of shares ($ mil.): 42.0
Sales ($ mil.): 656.9
Dividends
 Yield: 1.9%
 Payout: 22.0%
Market value ($ mil.): 1,699.0

	STOCK PRICE ($) FY Close	P/E High/Low		PER SHARE ($) Earnings	Dividends	Book Value
12/20	40.37	14	7	3.57	0.80	49.40
12/19	49.74	12	10	4.14	0.73	43.00
12/18	43.95	17	12	3.52	0.59	38.44
12/17	53.65	20	16	2.65	0.51	33.10
12/16	48.00	15	8	3.22	0.50	28.37
Annual Growth	(4.2%)	—	—	2.6%	12.5%	14.9%

Helios Technologies Inc

Helios Technologies Inc. (formerly known as Sun Hydraulics) develops and manufactures solutions for both the hydraulics and electronics markets. The Hydraulics segment includes products sold under the Sun Hydraulics, Faster and Custom Fluidpower brands. The Electronics segment includes products sold under the Enovation Controls, Balboa, and Murphy brands. Products are sold through value-add distributors and directly to OEMs. The Americas represents almost half of its sales. It was originally founded in 1970 as Sun Hydraulics Corporation, which designed and manufactured cartridge valves for hydraulics systems.

Operations
Helios operates in two business segments, Hydraulics (nearly 60% of the total sales) and Electronics (around 40%).

The Hydraulics segment markets and sells products globally under the brands of Sun Hydraulics for its cartridge valve technology, Custom Fluid Power for its hydraulic system design, and Faster which provides quick release coupling solutions.

Electronics segment offers custom-tailored solutions for many industrial and commercial applications, including engines, engine-driven equipment and specialty vehicles with a broad range of rugged and reliable instruments such as displays, controls and instrumentation products through its Enovation Controls, Zero Off, Murphy and HCT brands.

Geographic Reach
Headquartered in Sarasota, Florida, about 50% of Helios' sales are from the Americas, followed by APAC and EMEA accounts for around 25%, each.

Sales and Marketing
Helios' products are sold globally through a combination independent and authorized distributors. In addition to distributors, the company sells directly to other companies within the hydraulics industry, it markets and sells hydraulic products through value-add distributors and directly to OEMs. Globally, more than 55% of sales are attributed to its channel partners who generally combine its products with other hydraulic components to design a complete hydraulic system. Sales direct to OEMs for integration in their machines make up the remaining some 45%.

Furthermore, Helios provides end users with technical information through the websites of its operating companies and catalogs in multiple languages, including all information necessary to specify and obtain its products.

Financial Performance
Consolidated net sales for the 2021 year totaled $869.2 million, an increase of 66% over the prior year. Acquisitive growth accounted for a large portion of the increase, $206.6 million, and it also experienced significant organic growth of $139.6 million, 27%.

Net income for fiscal 2021 increased to $104.6 million compared with $14.2 million in the prior year.

Cash held by the company at the end of fiscal 2021 increased to $28.6 million. Operating activities provided $113.2 million while investing and financing activities used $90.3 million and $22.6 million, respectively. Main cash uses were acquisitions of businesses and repayment of borrowings on revolving credit facilities.

Strategy
One of the key drivers of future growth for both the Electronics and Hydraulics segments is its system sale approach to specific key OEMs who utilize both electronics and hydraulics. While always protecting its existing business, Helios will approach strategic partners with the ability to have Helios provide a "system solution" comprising components from its four primary world class brands to simplify supply chains and make doing business with Helios easier.

In 2021, Helios augmented its strategy and accelerated its growth plans to achieve the milestone of over $1 billion in sales with a top-tier adjusted EBITDA margin of approximately 25% in 2023.

Mergers and Acquisitions
In 2021, Helios completed the acquisition of assets related to the electronic control systems and parts business of Shenzhen Joyonway Electronics & Technology Co., Ltd and its related entities (collectively "Joyonway"). Joyonway is a fast-growing developer of control panels, software, systems and accessories for the health and wellness industry. Joyonway operates from two locations in China, Shenzhen and Dongguan, both of which are in the hub of electronics and software development in China.

EXECUTIVES

Executive Chairman, Director, Phillippe Lemaitre
President, Chief Executive Officer, Director, Josef Matosevic
Chief Financial Officer, Tricia L. Fulton, $322,817 total compensation
Subsidiary Officer, Matteo Arduini
General Counsel, Secretary, Marc Greenberg
Global Operations & Systems Sales Senior Vice President, Global Operations & Systems Sales Division Officer, Rick Martich
Division Officer, Lee Wichlacz
Director, Douglas M. Britt
Director, Laura D. Brown
Director, Cariappa (Cary) M. Chenanda
Director, Alexander Schuetz
Director, Diana Sacchi
Auditors : Grant Thornton LLP

LOCATIONS

HQ: Helios Technologies Inc
  7456 16th St. E., Sarasota, FL 34243
Phone: 941 362-1200
Web: www.sunhydraulics.com

2015 Sales

	$ mil.	% of total
Americas	97.7	49
Europe	61.3	30
Asia/Pacific	41.7	21
Total	200.7	100

PRODUCTS/OPERATIONS

Selected Products
Integrated packages (using custom designed manifolds)
Screw-in hydraulic cartridge valves (electrically actuated and non-electrically actuated)
Standard manifolds

COMPETITORS

BARNES GROUP INC.
COLUMBUS MCKINNON CORPORATION
CRANE CO.
DIXON VALVE & COUPLING COMPANY, LLC
GENTHERM INCORPORATED
HUSCO INTERNATIONAL, INC.
JET RESEARCH DEVELOPMENT, INC.
REGAL BELOIT CORPORATION
VALCOR ENGINEERING CORPORATION
VALLOUREC

HISTORICAL FINANCIALS

Company Type: Public

Income Statement — FYE: January 2

	REVENUE ($mil)	NET INCOME ($mil)	NET PROFIT MARGIN	EMPLOYEES
01/21*	523.0	14.2	2.7%	2,000
12/19	554.6	60.2	10.9%	1,960
12/18	508.0	46.7	9.2%	2,065
12/17	342.8	31.5	9.2%	1,150
12/16	196.9	23.3	11.8%	1,100
Annual Growth	27.7%	(11.6%)	—	16.1%

*Fiscal year change

2021 Year-End Financials

Debt ratio: 35.6%
Return on equity: 2.3%
Cash ($ mil.): 25.2
Current Ratio: 1.98
Long-term debt ($ mil.): 445.8
No. of shares ($ mil.): 32.1
Dividends
Yield: —
Payout: 81.8%
Market value ($ mil.): 1,712.0

	STOCK PRICE ($) FY Close	P/E High/Low		PER SHARE ($)		
				Earnings	Dividends	Book Value
01/21*	53.29	122	68	0.44	0.36	18.92
12/19	45.50	28	17	1.88	0.36	18.02
12/18	33.36	47	21	1.49	0.36	16.60
12/17	64.69	56	29	1.17	0.29	10.07
12/16	39.97	48	28	0.87	0.40	8.78
Annual Growth	7.5%	—	—	(15.7%)	(2.6%)	21.2%

*Fiscal year change

Helix Energy Solutions Group Inc

Helix Energy Solutions Group, Inc. is an international offshore energy company that provides specialty services to the offshore energy industry, with a focus on its growing well intervention and robotics operations. Its Contracting Services seek to provide services and methodologies which the company believes are critical to developing offshore reservoirs and maximizing production economics. Its well intervention unit primarily works in water depths ranging from 100 to 10,000 feet, using dynamically positioned and remotely operated vehicles (ROVs) that offer a range of engineering, repair, maintenance, and pipe and cable burial services in global offshore markets. About 35% of the company's total revenue comes from the US.

Operations

The company operates in three major segments: Well Intervention (generates more than 70% of total revenue), Robotics (roughly 20% of revenue), and Production Facilities (some 10%).

Well Intervention segment provides services enabling its customers to safely access offshore wells for the purpose of performing production enhancement or decommissioning operations primarily in the Gulf of Mexico, Brazil, the North Sea and West Africa. Its well intervention vessels include the Q4000, the Q5000, the Q7000, the Seawell, the Well Enhancer, and the Siem Helix 1 and Siem Helix 2 chartered vessels. Its well intervention equipment includes intervention systems, some of which the company provides on a stand-alone basis.

The Robotics segment provides offshore construction, trenching, seabed clearance and IRM services to both the oil and gas and the renewable energy markets globally. Additionally, the company's Robotics services are used in and complement its well intervention services. Its Robotics segment includes ROVs, trenchers and robotics support vessels under long-term charter as well as spot vessels as needed.

Its Production Facilities segment includes HP I, the HFRS and its ownership of oil and gas properties.

Geographic Reach

Texas-based, Helix operates in the Gulf of Mexico, Brazil, North Sea, Asia Pacific, and West Africa. In addition, it is currently leasing all of its facilities, which are primarily located in Texas, Scotland, Singapore and Brazil.

The US is the largest market in terms of revenue which generates for about 35%, followed by Brazil accounting for some 25%, while West Africa for about 20% and the UK accounts for about 15% of revenue.

Sales and Marketing

The company's more than 60 customers include major and independent oil and gas producers and suppliers, pipeline transmission companies, alternative (renewable) energy companies and offshore engineering and construction firms. In 2021, Petrobras and Shell (Helix Energy Solutions' major customers) accounted for about 25% and some 15%, a of the company's total revenues, respectively.

Customers from long-term contract generate almost 60% of the company's total sales, while the remainder comes from short-term contract.

Financial Performance

Consolidated net revenues decreased by 8% in 2021 to $674.7 million as compared to 2020, reflecting lower revenues from its Well Intervention and Robotics segments and higher intercompany eliminations, offset in part by higher revenues in its Production Facilities segment.

The company had a net loss of $61.7 million, a 407% decrease from the previous year's net income of $20.1 million.

The company's cash at the end of 2021 was $327.1 million. Operating activities generated $140.1 million, while investing activities used $8.3 million, mainly for capital expenditures. Financing activities used another $96 million, primarily for the repayment of Nordea Q5000 Loan.

Mergers and Acquisitions

In 2022, Helix announced that it has entered into a definitive agreement to acquire 100% of the equity interests of the Alliance group of companies (Alliance) for $120 million cash at closing, plus the potential for post-closing earnout consideration. Alliance is a Louisiana-based privately held company that provides services in support of the upstream and midstream industries in the Gulf of Mexico shelf, including offshore oil field decommissioning and reclamation, project management, engineered solutions, intervention, maintenance, repair, heavy lift and commercial diving services. The acquisition aligns with Helix's Energy Transition business model, by expanding its decommissioning presence in the Gulf of Mexico shelf and advancing Helix's ESG initiatives by responsibly supporting end-of-life requirements of oil and gas projects

Company Background

Helix Energy Solutions Group, Inc. was incorporated in 1979 and in 1983 was re-incorporated in the state of Minnesota.

EXECUTIVES

Chairman, Director, William L. Transier
President, Chief Executive Officer, Director, Owen E. Kratz, $700,000 total compensation
Operations Executive Vice President, Operations Chief Operating Officer, Scotty Andrew Sparks, $375,000 total compensation
Accounting Executive Vice President, Finance Executive Vice President, Accounting Chief Financial Officer, Finance Chief Financial Officer, Erik Staffeldt, $375,000 total compensation
Senior Vice President, General Counsel, Corporate Secretary, Kenneth E. Neikirk
Chief Accounting Officer, Corporate Controller, Brent Arriaga
Director, Paula M. Harris
Director, Diana Glassman
Director, T. Mitch Little
Director, John V. Lovoi
Director, Amy H. Nelson
Director, Amerino Gatti
Auditors: KPMG LLP

LOCATIONS

HQ: Helix Energy Solutions Group Inc
3505 West Sam Houston Parkway North, Suite 400, Houston, TX 77043
Phone: 281 618-0400 **Fax:** 281 618-0500
Web: www.helixesg.com

2013 Sales

	$ mil.	% of total
UK	403.8	46
US	345.5	39
Other countries	127.3	15
Total	876.6	100

PRODUCTS/OPERATIONS

2013 Sales

	$mil.	% of total
Well Intervention	452.5	48
Robotics	333.2	35
Production Facility	88.1	9
Subsea Construction	71.2	8
Adjustments	(68.6)	-
Total	876.6	100

COMPETITORS

BAM NUTTALL LIMITED
CHIYODA CORPORATION
FMC TECHNOLOGIES, INC.
FUELCELL ENERGY, INC.
GREAT LAKES DREDGE & DOCK CORPORATION
KBR, INC.
KEY ENERGY SERVICES, INC.
OCEANEERING INTERNATIONAL, INC.
ORION GROUP HOLDINGS, INC.
S & B ENGINEERS AND CONSTRUCTORS, LTD.

HISTORICAL FINANCIALS

Company Type: Public

Income Statement — FYE: December 31

	REVENUE ($mil)	NET INCOME ($mil)	NET PROFIT MARGIN	EMPLOYEES
12/20	733.5	22.1	3.0%	1,536
12/19	751.9	57.9	7.7%	1,650
12/18	739.8	28.5	3.9%	1,546
12/17	581.3	30.0	5.2%	1,600
12/16	487.5	(81.4)	—	1,474
Annual Growth	10.8%	—	—	1.0%

2020 Year-End Financials

Debt ratio: 14.0%
Return on equity: 1.2%
Cash ($ mil.): 291.3
Current Ratio: 1.88
Long-term debt ($ mil.): 258.9
No. of shares ($ mil.): 150.3
Dividends
 Yield: —
 Payout: —
Market value ($ mil.): 631.0

	STOCK PRICE ($) FY Close	P/E High/Low		PER SHARE ($) Earnings	Dividends	Book Value
12/20	4.20	74	8	0.13	0.00	11.58
12/19	9.63	25	15	0.38	0.00	11.42
12/18	5.41	57	27	0.19	0.00	10.92
12/17	7.54	48	25	0.20	0.00	10.61
12/16	8.82	—	—	(0.73)	0.00	10.63
Annual Growth	(16.9%)	—	—	—	—	2.2%

Heritage Commerce Corp

Heritage Commerce is the holding company for Heritage Bank of Commerce, which operates about 15 branches in the southern and eastern regions of the San Francisco Bay area. Serving consumers and small to midsized businesses and their owners and managers, the bank offers savings and checking accounts, money market accounts, and CDs, as well as cash management services and loans. Commercial and commercial real estate loans make up most of the company's loan portfolio, which is rounded out by land, construction, and home equity loans.

Operations

Heritage Commerce's two operating segments are banking and factoring (buying accounts receivables from clients at a discount); the divisions account for about 90% and 10% of the holding company's revenue, respectively.

Heritage offers savings and checking accounts, money market accounts, and CDs, as well as cash management services and loans to small to midsized businesses and their owners and managers. Loans account for about 75% of total revenue, with commercial real estate accounting for about half of its loan portfolio; commercial loans account for about a third. Home equity loans and land and construction loans each comprise about five percent of the portfolio.

The company's Bay View Funding subsidiary provides working capital factoring financing to industrial clients across the US.

Geographic Reach

San Jose-based Heritage Commerce serves banking customers in the Santa Clara, Alameda, Contra Costa, San Benito, and San Mateo counties of California through about 15 Heritage Bank of Commerce branches. The company's Santa Clara-based Bay View Funding subsidiary provides industry clients with working capital factoring financing across the US.

Sales and Marketing

Despite a focus on personalized banking with in-branch officers and staff, Heritage Commerce offers its customers internet banking services that do not include origination of deposit accounts or loan applications.

Financial Performance

Heritage Commerce has seen strong growth since 2013, doubling revenue and income and nearly tripling its cash as the company grew its loan portfolio through acquisitions. The company had about $40 million in long-term debt at the end of 2017, all of which it accrued that year.

Heritage's ? revenue trended up 8% to $111.1 million owing to increased interest income from loans, including fees, taxable securities, and other investments and interest-bearing deposits in other financial institutions.

Heritage's net income decreased 13% to $23.8 million due to increased income tax expense associated with the passage of the Tax Cuts and Jobs Act.

The company grew its cash stores by 19% to $316.2 million. Operations contributed $41.4 million, and financing activities provided $246.1 million primarily because of a net change in deposits. Investments used $237.3 million related to purchases of securities.

Strategy

Heritage Commerce's strategy is to grow through expanding its geographic footprint, primarily through acquisitions in the San Francisco Bay Area. The company also seeks to use acquisitions to inhibit competitors from expanding into local markets. The company is third in deposit market share among Bay Area independent community banks.

Mergers and Acquisitions

Heritage Commerce acquired Presidio Bank in 2019 for $200.3 million. The deal gave Heritage $4 billion in additional assets and 17 new branches in the San Francisco Bay Area.

In April 2018, Heritage purchased Tri-Valley Bank for $33.2 million. The bank had $150.3 million in assets, $134.1 million in deposits, and $125.2 million in net loans.

Heritage acquired United American Bank in May 2018 for $46.9 million. United had $319.7 million in assets, $286.6 million in deposits, and $218.3 million in net loans.

United American had three branches in San Mateo, Redwood City and Half Moon Bay. Tri-Valley had two branches in San Ramon and Livermore. Heritage closed the Half Moon Bay and San Ramon branches following the acquisitions.

Company Background

Heritage Commerce was founded in 1984.

EXECUTIVES

Chairman, Director, Jack W. Conner
President, Chief Executive Officer, Director, Walter T. Kaczmarek, $495,000 total compensation
Executive Vice President, Chief Financial Officer, Subsidiary Officer, Lawrence D. McGovern, $305,471 total compensation
Executive Vice President, Subsidiary Officer, Robertson C. Jones
Executive Vice President, Subsidiary Officer, Dustin Warford
Subsidiary Officer, Margo G. Butsch, $250,000 total compensation
Director, Julianne M. Biagini-Komas
Director, Bruce H. Cabral
Director, Jason P. DiNapoli
Director, Stephen G. Heitel
Director, Robert T. Moles
Director, Laura Roden
Director, Marina Park Sutton
Director, Ranson W. Webster
Director, Kamran F. Husain
Auditors : Crowe LLP

LOCATIONS

HQ: Heritage Commerce Corp
224 Airport Parkway, San Jose, CA 95110
Phone: 408 947-6900
Web: www.heritagecommercecorp.com

PRODUCTS/OPERATIONS

2017 Sales

	$ mil.	% of total
Interest		
Loans, including fees	86.4	74
Taxable securities	13.7	12
Other	6.8	6
Interest expense	(5.4)	-
Noninterest		
Service charges & fees on deposit accounts	3.2	3
Increase in cash surrender value of life insurance	1.7	1
Gain on sales of SBA loans	1.1	1
Servicing income	1.0	1
Other	2.6	2
Total	111.1	100

COMPETITORS

CENTRAL PACIFIC FINANCIAL CORP.
CITY HOLDING COMPANY
COLUMBIA BANKING SYSTEM, INC.
CVB FINANCIAL CORP.
HANCOCK WHITNEY CORPORATION
HERITAGE FINANCIAL CORPORATION
PACIFIC CONTINENTAL CORPORATION
PACWEST BANCORP
SOUTHSIDE BANCSHARES, INC.
WILSHIRE BANCORP, INC.

HISTORICAL FINANCIALS

Company Type: Public

Income Statement — FYE: December 31

	ASSETS ($mil)	NET INCOME ($mil)	INCOME AS % OF ASSETS	EMPLOYEES
12/20	4,634.1	35.2	0.8%	335
12/19	4,109.4	40.4	1.0%	357
12/18	3,096.5	35.3	1.1%	302
12/17	2,843.4	23.8	0.8%	278
12/16	2,570.8	27.3	1.1%	263
Annual Growth	15.9%	6.6%	—	6.2%

2020 Year-End Financials

Return on assets: 0.8%
Return on equity: 6.0%
Long-term debt ($ mil.): —
No. of shares ($ mil.): 59.9
Sales ($ mil.): 160.3
Dividends
Yield: 5.8%
Payout: 118.1%
Market value ($ mil.): 531.0

	STOCK PRICE ($) FY Close	P/E High/Low		PER SHARE ($) Earnings	Dividends	Book Value
12/20	8.87	22	11	0.59	0.52	9.64
12/19	12.83	17	13	0.84	0.48	9.71
12/18	11.34	21	13	0.84	0.44	8.49
12/17	15.32	26	21	0.62	0.40	7.10
12/16	14.43	20	13	0.72	0.36	6.85
Annual Growth	(11.5%)	—	—	(4.9%)	9.6%	8.9%

Heritage Financial Corp (WA)

Heritage Financial is ready to answer the call of Pacific Northwesterners seeking to preserve their heritage. Heritage Financial is the holding company for Heritage Bank, which operates more than 65 branches throughout Washington and Oregon. Boasting nearly $4 billion in assets, the bank offers a range of deposit products to consumers and businesses, such as CDs, IRAs, and checking, savings, NOW, and money market accounts. Commercial and industrial loans account for over 50% of Heritage Financial's loan portfolio, while mortgages secured by multi-family real estate comprise about 5%. The bank also originates single-family mortgages, land development, construction loans, and consumer loans.

Operations

The bank also does business under the Central Valley Bank name in the Yakima and Kittitas counties of Washington, and under the Whidbey Island Bank name on Whidbey Island.

About 79% of Heritage Financial's total revenue came from loan interest (including fees) in 2014, while another 7% came from interest on its investment securities. The rest of its revenue came from service charges and other fees (8%), Merchant Visa income (1%), and other miscellaneous fees. The company had a staff of 748 employees at the end of that year.

Geographic Reach

The Olympia-based bank operates more than 65 branches across Washington and the greater Portland area. It has additional offices in eastern Washington, mostly in Yakima county.

Sales and Marketing

Heritage targets small and medium-sized businesses along with their owners, as well as individuals.

Financial Performance

Fueled by loan and deposit growth from a series of bank acquisitions, Heritage Financial's revenues and profits have been on the rise in recent years.

The company's revenue jumped 70% to a record $137.6 million in 2014 mostly thanks to new loan business stemming from its acquisition of Washington Banking Company. Deposit service charge income also increased thanks to new deposit business from the acquisition.

Higher revenue in 2014 allowed Heritage Financial's net income to more than double to a record $21 million, while its operating cash levels rose 66% to $51.3 million on higher cash earnings and net proceeds from the sale of its loans.

Strategy

The bank reiterated in 2015 that it would continue to pursue strategic acquisitions of community banks to grow market share across the Pacific Northwest (its region of expertise), expand its business lines, and grow its loan and deposit business.

With its focus on business and commercial lending, the bank also in 2015 emphasized the importance of seeking high asset quality loans, lending to familiar markets that have a historical record of success. Recruiting and retaining "highly competent personnel" to execute its strategies was also key to its long-term agenda.

Mergers and Acquisitions

In May 2014, Heritage acquired Washington Banking Company and its Whidbey Island Bank subsidiary for $265 million, which "significantly expanded and enhanced" its product offerings across its core geographic market.

In July 2013, the bank acquired Puyallup, Washington-based Valley Community Bancshares and its eight Valley Bank branches for $44 million.

In January 2013, the company purchased Lakewood, Washington-based Northwest Commercial Bank, along with its two branch locations in Washington state, for $5 million.

EXECUTIVES

Chairman, Director, Brian L. Vance, $586,307 total compensation
President, Chief Executive Officer, Director, Jeffrey J. Deuel, $429,000 total compensation
Executive Vice President, Chief Operating Officer, Subsidiary Officer, Bryan D. McDonald, $333,250 total compensation
Executive Vice President, Chief Financial Officer, Subsidiary Officer, Donald J. Hinson, $302,302 total compensation
Executive Vice President, Chief Banking Officer, Subsidiary Officer, Cindy M. Huntley
Executive Vice President, Chief Credit Officer, Subsidiary Officer, Tony W. Chalfant
Subsidiary Officer, Steve Gahler
Subsidiary Officer, David A. Spurling, $290,786 total compensation
Director, Lead Independent Director, Brian S. Charneski
Director, John A. Clees
Director, Stephen A. Dennis
Director, Kimberly T. Ellwanger
Director, Deborah J. Gavin
Director, Jeffrey S. Lyon
Director, Gragg E. Miller
Director, Anthony B. Pickering
Director, Frederick B. Rivera
Director, Ann Watson
Auditors: Crowe LLP

LOCATIONS

HQ: Heritage Financial Corp (WA)
201 Fifth Avenue SW, Olympia, WA 98501
Phone: 360 943-1500
Web: www.hf-wa.com

PRODUCTS/OPERATIONS

2014 Sales

	$ mil.	% of total
Interest income		
Interest and fees on loans	110.4	79
Investment securities	10.2	7
Others	0.5	-
Non-interest income		
Service charges and others	11.1	8
Merchant Visa income	1.1	1
Others	4.3	5
Total	137.6	100

COMPETITORS

BANK OF THE WEST
CITY HOLDING COMPANY
EAGLE BANCORP, INC.
FIRST COMMUNITY BANCSHARES, INC.
FIRST HORIZON CORPORATION
NORTHWEST BANCORP, INC.
OLD LINE BANCSHARES, INC.
PEOPLES FINANCIAL SERVICES CORP.
WASHINGTON TRUST BANCORP, INC.
WILSHIRE BANCORP, INC.

HISTORICAL FINANCIALS
Company Type: Public

Income Statement				FYE: December 31
	ASSETS ($mil)	NET INCOME ($mil)	INCOME AS % OF ASSETS	EMPLOYEES
12/20	6,615.3	46.5	0.7%	856
12/19	5,552.9	67.5	1.2%	884
12/18	5,316.9	53.0	1.0%	859
12/17	4,113.2	41.7	1.0%	735
12/16	3,878.9	38.9	1.0%	760
Annual Growth	14.3%	4.6%	—	3.0%

2020 Year-End Financials
Return on assets: 0.7%
Return on equity: 5.6%
Long-term debt ($ mil.): —
No. of shares ($ mil.): 35.9
Sales ($ mil.): 251.5
Dividends
Yield: 3.4%
Payout: 73.3%
Market value ($ mil.): 840.0

	STOCK PRICE ($) FY Close	P/E High/Low		PER SHARE ($) Earnings	Dividends	Book Value
12/20	23.39	22	12	1.29	0.80	22.85
12/19	28.30	18	14	1.83	0.84	22.10
12/18	29.72	25	19	1.49	0.72	20.63
12/17	30.80	23	16	1.39	0.61	16.98
12/16	25.75	20	13	1.30	0.72	16.08
Annual Growth	(2.4%)	—	—	(0.2%)	2.7%	9.2%

HISTORICAL FINANCIALS
Company Type: Public

Income Statement				FYE: December 31
	REVENUE ($mil)	NET INCOME ($mil)	NET PROFIT MARGIN	EMPLOYEES
12/20	1,091.9	24.0	2.2%	196
12/19	848.3	15.1	1.8%	176
12/18	662.4	70.8	10.7%	0
12/17	565.8	41.2	7.3%	176
12/16	509.8	206.3	40.5%	0
Annual Growth	21.0%	(41.6%)	—	—

2020 Year-End Financials
Debt ratio: 56.6%
Return on equity: 18.6%
Cash ($ mil.): 2.6
Current Ratio: 0.81
Long-term debt ($ mil.): 1,900.1
No. of shares ($ mil.): 284.4
Dividends
Yield: 8.8%
Payout: 132.4%
Market value ($ mil.): 5,567.0

	STOCK PRICE ($) FY Close	P/E High/Low		PER SHARE ($) Earnings	Dividends	Book Value
12/20	19.57	19	5	1.31	1.73	0.44
12/19	22.68	19	15	1.20	1.62	0.46
12/18	16.98	19	13	1.27	1.41	61.13
12/17	19.81	35	25	0.75	0.90	57.84
Annual Growth	(0.4%)	—	—	20.4%	24.3%	(80.3%)

Hess Midstream LP

EXECUTIVES
Chairman, Chief Executive Officer, Holding/Parent Company Officer, Director, John B. Hess
President, Chief Operating Officer, Holding/Parent Company Officer, John A. Gatling
Vice President, Holding/Parent Company Officer, Director, John P. Rielly
Chief Financial Officer, Holding/Parent Company Officer, Jonathan C. Stein
General Counsel, Secretary, Holding/Parent Company Officer, Timothy B. Goodell
Director, Gregory P. Hill
Director, Gerbert G. Schoonman
Director, William J. Brilliant
Director, Scott E. Telesz
Director, James K. Lee
Director, David W. Niemiec
Director, John P. Reddy
Director, Stephen J. J. Letwin
Auditors : Ernst & Young LLP

LOCATIONS
HQ: Hess Midstream LP
1501 McKinney Street, Houston, TX 77010
Phone: 713 496-4200
Web: www.hessmidstream.com

Hibbett Inc

Hibbett is a leading athletic-inspired fashion retailer primarily located in underserved communities. The company sells brand-name sports equipment, athletic apparel, and footwear in small to midsized markets in some 35 states, mainly in the South and Midwest. Its flagship Hibbett chain boasts approximately 900 locations; stores are primarily found in malls and strip centers. Hibbett also operates nearly 180 of City Gear stores, which stock urban streewear, and more than 15 mall-based Sports Additions shoe shops, most of which are situated near Hibbett stores. The company also trades online. The company was founded in 1945.

Operations
Hibbett offers personalized customer service and access to coveted footwear (more than 60% of the total sales), apparel (about 30%) and equipment (approximately 10%) from top brands like Nike, Jordan Brand, Adidas, Puma, Crocs, The North Face, and Under Armour, among others.

Geographic Reach
Hibbett, headquartered in Birmingham, Alabama, most of its stores are located in Georgia, Texas, Alabama and Mississippi. It has presence in approximately 35 states and has about 1,095 stores in total. About 230 are in enclosed malls, more than 30 are free-standing and nearly 835 are in strip-shopping centers, which are frequently near a major chain retailer.

Sales and Marketing
In terms of sales, its mobile apps, buy online pickup in store (BOPIS) and reserve online pickup in store (ROPIS) complements its e-commerce site and provides its customers with customized advanced features and shopping experiences.

Financial Performance
Net sales increased $271.5 million, or 19%, to $1.69 billion for Fiscal 2022 from $1.42 billion for Fiscal 2021. Comparable store net sales for Fiscal 2022 increased 17% compared to Fiscal 2021 primarily driven by continued strength in footwear, with notable growth in the women's and kids' categories, and sneaker-connected apparel and accessories. For Fiscal 2022, 1,034 stores were included in the comparable store sales comparison.

In Fiscal 2022, the company had a net income of $174.3 million, a 135% increase from the previous year's net income of $74.3 million.

The company's cash at the end of Fiscal 2022 was $17.1 million. Operating activities generated $159.5 million, while investing activities used $70.2 million, mainly for capital expenditures. Financing activities used another $281.6 million, primarily for stock repurchases.

Strategy
Hibbett targets underserved markets with branded products and provide a high level of customer service. This market strategy establishes greater customer, vendor and landlord recognition as a leading specialty retailer in these communities. The company believes its ability to align its merchandising mix to local preferences and trends differentiates the company from its national competitors and delivers incremental sales opportunities for vendor partners. The company uses information systems to maintain tight controls over inventory and operating costs and continually search for ways to improve efficiencies and the customer experience through information system upgrades.

Hibbett uses information systems to maintain tight controls over inventory and operating costs and continually searches for ways to improve efficiencies and the customer experience through information system upgrades. In addition, it establishes greater customer, vendor and landlord recognition as a leading specialty retailer in these communities. The company believes its ability to align its merchandising mix to local preferences and trends differentiates it from its national competitors.

HISTORY
Rufus Hibbett, a high school coach and educator in Florence, Alabama, founded single-store Dixie Supply, which sold athletic, marine, and small aircraft equipment, in 1945. Rufus' boys Ike and George got involved in the business and in 1952 the company took the name Hibbett & Sons and began to focus on

team sports sales. It changed its name and emphasis again in the mid-1960s when, as Hibbett Sporting Goods, it became primarily a retailer.

The Anderson family, owners of the Alabama-based retailer now known as Books-A-Million, bought Hibbett in 1980 and continued its gradual expansion. With just over 10 stores, Hibbett promoted company veteran Mickey Newsome to president two years later.

Starting in 1993 the chain began opening about 10 new stores each year. Hibbett opened its first Sports & Co. store in 1995. That year the Anderson family sold control of the company to Saunders Karp & Megrue Partners, which took it public in 1996. Also in 1996 the chain doubled its store-opening pace.

Hibbett opened 33 stores in fiscal 1998 and 53 stores in fiscal 1999. Newsome was appointed CEO in 1999. By 2000 the company had weathered a shake-out of sporting goods retailers and expanded its store base more than 270% over five years, opening 50 stores in fiscal 2000. The company opened more than 60 stores the following year.

In March 2004, chairman John Megrue Jr. retired and Newsome was given the position. Overall, the company added 53 Hibbett Sports stores and a single Sports Additions store in 2004.

In August 2005 Brian Priddy joined Hibbett from Bombay Company as president. Newsome retained the titles of chairman and CEO.

In early 2007 the company created its holding company, Hibbett Sports, to separate itself from its existing operating entity. Priddy resigned in 2007 to pursue other interests. That fiscal year, the company opened 64 stores.

In fiscal 2008 it opened 75 retail stores, bringing its total count to 688. The following year it added 60 retail stores, which boosted its network to 748 locations.

In fiscal 2009 the company opened about 20 stores.

EXECUTIVES

Chairman, Director, Anthony F. Crudele
President, Chief Executive Officer, Director, Michael E. Longo
Finance Senior Vice President, Accounting Senior Vice President, Finance Chief Financial Officer, Accounting Chief Financial Officer, Robert J. Volke
Merchandising Executive Vice President, Jared S. Briskin, $325,000 total compensation
Division Officer, William G. Quinn
Senior Vice President, Chief Information Officer, Ronald P. Blahnik
Senior Vice President, General Counsel, David M. Benck
Store Operations Senior Vice President, Benjamin Knighten

Director, Karen S. Etzkorn
Director, Linda Hubbard
Director, Terrance G. Finley
Director, Dorlisa K. Flur
Director, James ("Jim") A. Hilt
Director, Jamere Jackson
Director, Lorna E. Nagler
Auditors: Ernst & Young LLP

LOCATIONS

HQ: Hibbett Inc
2700 Milan Court, Birmingham, AL 35211
Phone: 205 942-4292
Web: www.hibbett.com

2019 stores

	No.
Texas	123
Georgia	122
Alabama	105
Tennessee	78
Mississippi	74
Louisiana	67
Florida	64
North Carolina	60
Kentucky	58
Other	412
Total	1,163

PRODUCTS/OPERATIONS

2019 Stores

	No.
Hibbett Sports Stores	1,007
City Gear	138
Sports Additions	18
Total	1,163

2019 Sales

	$mil	% of total
Footwear	579.8	49
Apparel	276.7	29
Equipment	152.2	22
Total	1008.7	100

COMPETITORS

CALERES, INC.
DEBENHAMS PLC
FOOT LOCKER, INC.
GENESCO INC.
SHOE CARNIVAL, INC.
SPARTANNASH COMPANY
TARGET CORPORATION
THE BUCKLE INC
THE CATO CORPORATION
THE FINISH LINE INC

HISTORICAL FINANCIALS

Company Type: Public

Income Statement				FYE: January 30
	REVENUE ($mil)	NET INCOME ($mil)	NET PROFIT MARGIN	EMPLOYEES
01/21*	1,419.6	74.2	5.2%	10,700
02/20	1,184.2	27.3	2.3%	10,200
02/19	1,008.6	28.4	2.8%	10,600
02/18	968.2	35.0	3.6%	9,200
01/17	972.9	61.0	6.3%	9,300
Annual Growth	9.9%	5.0%	—	3.6%

*Fiscal year change

2021 Year-End Financials

Debt ratio: 0.4%
Return on equity: 20.6%
Cash ($ mil.): 209.2
Current Ratio: 1.95
Long-term debt ($ mil.): 2.5
No. of shares ($ mil.): 16.4
Dividends
Yield: —
Payout: —
Market value ($ mil.): 930.0

	STOCK PRICE ($) FY Close	P/E High/Low		PER SHARE ($) Earnings	Dividends	Book Value
01/21*	56.45	13	2	4.36	0.00	23.73
02/20	24.78	19	10	1.52	0.00	19.51
02/19	16.31	19	9	1.51	0.00	18.37
02/18	22.15	20	6	1.71	0.00	16.86
01/17	32.70	17	11	2.72	0.00	15.41
Annual Growth	14.6%	—	—	12.5%	—	11.4%

*Fiscal year change

Hillenbrand Inc

Hillenbrand is a global diversified industrial company with multiple leading brands that serve a wide variety of industries worldwide. It has three very distinct businesses: Advanced Process Solutions designs, develops, manufactures, and services highly engineered industrial equipment throughout the world; Molding Technology Solutions, a global leader in highly engineered and customized systems and service in plastic technology and processing; and Batesville, a recognized leader in the death care industry in North America. Founded by John A. Hillenbrand in 1906, Hillenbrand generates just more than 50% of its sales in the US.

Operations

Hillenbrand's Advanced Process Solutions generates about 45% of the overall revenue. The segment is a leading global provider of compounding, extrusion, and material handling; screening and separating; flow control; and size reduction products and services for a wide variety of manufacturing and other industrial processes. Its products include material handling equipment (under the Coperion and K-Tron names) and screening and separating equipment (Rotex and BM&M). Aftermarket parts and service account for about 30% of Advanced Process Solutions's revenue.

Molding Technology Solutions accounts for approximately 35% of the company's total revenue. The segment has a full-line product portfolio that includes injection molding and extrusion equipment, hot runner systems, process control systems, mold bases and components, and maintenance, repair, and operating (MRO) supplies. Aftermarket parts and services represents about 25% of Molding Technology Solutions' total net revenue.

Hillenbrand's Advanced Process Solutions generates about 45% of the overall revenue. The segment is a leading global provider of compounding, extrusion, and material handling; screening and separating; flow control; and size reduction products and services for a wide variety of manufacturing and other industrial processes. Its products include material handling equipment (under the Coperion and K-Tron names) and screening and separating equipment (Rotex and BM&M). Aftermarket parts and service account for about 30% of Advanced Process Solutions's revenue.

Molding Technology Solutions accounts for approximately 35% of the company's total revenue. The segment has a full-line product portfolio that includes injection molding and extrusion equipment, hot runner systems, process control systems, mold bases and components, and maintenance, repair, and operating (MRO) supplies. Aftermarket parts and services represents about 25% of Molding Technology Solutions' total net revenue.

By products and services, equipment provides about 55% of the company's total sales, parts and services account for nearly 25%, death care brings in more than 20% of total sales, while others generate the remaining. By timing of transfer, point in time provides about 80% of the company's total sales. Over time generates the remaining more than 20%.

Geographic Reach

Indiana-based Hillenbrand operates worldwide but generates more than 50% of its revenue from the US. Geographically, about 25% of Advanced Process Solutions' net revenue came from the Americas, nearly 45% from Asia, and about 30% from EMEA (Europe, the Middle East, and Africa). In addition, about 55% of Molding Technology Solutions' net revenue came from the Americas, some 30% from Asia, and more than 15% from EMEA (Europe, the Middle East, and Africa). The Batesville segment operates primarily in North America.

Advanced Process Solutions has about 15 significant manufacturing facilities in the US (New Jersey, Kansas, Ohio, Illinois, North Carolina, and Virginia), Germany, Switzerland, China, India, and the UK. It also has sales office in the US, Europe, Asia, Canada, and South America.

Molding Technology Solutions operates more than 10 significant manufacturing facilities located in the US (in Ohio, Kansas, Georgia, and Michigan), Germany, China, India, Canada, and the US, as well as warehouse distribution centers, service centers, and sales offices located in the US, Mexico, Canada, Europe, Asia, and South America.

Batesville has manufacturing facilities in Indiana, Tennessee, Mississippi, and Mexico, as well as warehouse distribution centers and other facilities in the US, Mexico, Canada, and Australia.

Sales and Marketing

Hillenbrand employs a direct sales team to market both its industrial equipment and funeral products. The company also uses a network of independent sales reps who work on commission for its industrial equipment.

Customers include local, regional, national, and global businesses in a variety of industries (plastics, pharmaceuticals, chemicals, fertilizers, wastewater treatment) for its industrial equipment, automotive, consumer goods, packaging, construction and electronics for Molding Technology Solutions and funeral directors and funeral homes for its funeral products.

By end market, plastics provide approximately 30% of the company's revenue. Automotive, chemicals, consumer goods, food and pharmaceuticals, custom molders, packaging, construction, minerals and mining, electronics, medical, death care and other industrial markets account for the rest.

Financial Performance

The company's revenue for fiscal 2021 increased by 14% to $2.9 billion compared with $2.5 billion.

Net income for fiscal 2021 was $249.9 million compared with a net loss of $60.1 million.

Cash held by the company at the end of fiscal 2021 increased to $450.9 million. Cash provided by operations and investing activities were $528.4 million and $126.0 million, respectively. Cash used for financing activities was $523.3 million, mainly for repayments of long-term debt.

Strategy

Hillenbrand's strategy is to leverage its historically strong financial foundation and the implementation of the HOM to deliver sustainable profit growth, revenue expansion and substantial free cash flow and then reinvest available cash in new growth initiatives focused on building platforms with leadership positions in its core markets and near adjacencies, both organically and inorganically, in order to create shareholder value.

In fiscal 2021, the company began aligning sustainability with the HOM. Hillenbrand believes sustainability to be a source of value creation that must be aligned with the core strategy of the company. The company expects to continue developing this part of its strategy as it grows in its sustainability practice. Among other things, the company believes climate change will require meaningful action on a global scale, and Hillenbrand expects that further developing its understanding of its energy consumption and emissions will be an important part of examining the challenges posed by climate change, as well as continuing to develop its sustainability strategy. To date, the company's costs relating to addressing climate change have not been material.

Company Background

Batesville Coffin Company was founded in 1884. In 1906 it was purchased by John A. Hillenbrand and renamed Batesville Casket Company. It became part of the larger family-owned Hillenbrand Industries, which went public in 1971.

In 2008 Hillenbrand Industries spun off its funeral business, with Hillenbrand, Inc. created as the parent company for Batesville Casket.

From 2010 to 2016 Hillenbrand, Inc. made multiple strategic acquisitions to add a second line of business, industrial equipment. It purchased diversified industrial manufacturer K-Tron in 2010, screening machine developer Rotex in 2011, bulk materials handling equipment seller Coperion in 2012, displacement pumps business ABEL Pumps in 2015, and flow control firm Red Valve in 2016.

EXECUTIVES

Chairperson, Director, Helen W. Cornell
President, Chief Executive Officer, Director, Kimberly K. Ryan, $485,892 total compensation
Senior Vice President, Chief Financial Officer, Robert M. VanHimbergen
Senior Vice President, Chief Human Resources Officer, Aneesha Arora
Senior Vice President, Chief Compliance Officer, Secretary, General Counsel, Subsidiary Officer, Nicholas R. Farrell
Senior Vice President, Subsidiary Officer, Christopher H. Trainor, $434,746 total compensation
Financial Reporting Vice President, Financial Reporting Chief Accounting Officer, Megan A. Walke
Director, Daniel C. Hillenbrand
Director, Neil S. Novich
Director, Inderpreet Sawhney
Director, Jennifer W. Rumsey
Director, Stuart A. Taylor
Director, Gary L. Collar
Director, Joy M. Greenway
Director, Dennis W. Pullin
Auditors : Ernst & Young LLP

LOCATIONS

HQ: Hillenbrand Inc
One Batesville Boulevard, Batesville, IN 47006
Phone: 812 934-7500
Web: www.hillenbrand.com

2018 Sales

	$ mil.	% of total
US	926.4	52
Germany	512.5	29
Other regions	331.2	19
Total	1,770.1	100

PRODUCTS/OPERATIONS

2018 Sales

	$ mil.	% of total
Process Equipment Group	1,219.5	69
Batesville	550.6	31
Total	1,770.1	100

COMPETITORS

ALLIANCE LAUNDRY HOLDINGS LLC
BATESVILLE CASKET COMPANY, INC.
CARPENTER TECHNOLOGY CORPORATION
ENERPAC TOOL GROUP CORP.
FASTENAL COMPANY

GOLIATH CASKET INC
HARDINGE INC.
HARSCO CORPORATION
UNIFIRST CORPORATION
WESFARMERS LIMITED

HISTORICAL FINANCIALS
Company Type: Public

Income Statement — FYE: September 30

	REVENUE ($mil)	NET INCOME ($mil)	NET PROFIT MARGIN	EMPLOYEES
09/21	2,864.8	249.9	8.7%	10,500
09/20	2,517.0	(60.1)	—	11,000
09/19	1,807.3	121.4	6.7%	6,500
09/18	1,770.1	76.6	4.3%	6,500
09/17	1,590.2	126.2	7.9%	6,000
Annual Growth	15.9%	18.6%	—	15.0%

2021 Year-End Financials
Debt ratio: 30.2%
Return on equity: 22.0%
Cash ($ mil.): 446.1
Current Ratio: 1.39
Long-term debt ($ mil.): 1,212.9
No. of shares ($ mil.): 72.7
Dividends
Yield: 2.0%
Payout: 34.6%
Market value ($ mil.): 3,101.0

	STOCK PRICE ($) FY Close	P/E High	P/E Low	PER SHARE ($) Earnings	Dividends	Book Value
09/21	42.65	15	9	3.31	0.86	16.64
09/20	28.36	—	—	(0.82)	0.85	14.16
09/19	30.88	27	14	1.92	0.84	12.03
09/18	52.30	44	32	1.20	0.83	11.74
09/17	38.85	20	15	1.97	0.82	11.91
Annual Growth	2.4%	—	—	13.9%	1.2%	8.7%

Hingham Institution for Savings

The Hingham Institution for Savings serves businesses and retail customers in Boston's south shore communities, operating more than 10 branches in Massachusetts in Boston, Cohasset, Hingham, Hull, Norwell, Scituate, South Hingham, and South Weymouth. Founded in 1834, the bank offers traditional deposit products, such as checking and savings accounts, IRAs, and certificates of deposit. More than 90% of its loan portfolio is split between commercial mortgages and residential mortgages (including home equity loans), though the bank also originates construction, business, and consumer loans. More than 95% of the company's revenue comes from loan interest.

Operations
The Hingham Institution for Savings made 96% of its total revenue from loan interest during 2015, while about 2% came from interest in equities, CODs, and other investments. The rest of its revenue mostly came from service fees on deposit accounts.

Of its $1.4 billion loan portfolio (at the end of 2015), about 48% was made up of commercial real estate mortgages (including multi-family housing), while 45% was tied to residential mortgages (including home equity). The remainder of the portfolio was made up of residential and commercial construction loans (7% of loan assets), and commercial business loans and consumer loans (1%).

Subsidiary Hingham Unpledged Securities Corporation holds title to certain securities available for sale.

Geographic Reach
The company mostly serves clients in Boston, the South Shore, and the island of Nantucket. Its branches are in Boston, Cohasset, Hingham, Hull, Nantucket, Norwell, Scituate, South Hingham, and South Weymouth, Massachusetts.

Sales and Marketing
The Hingham Institution for Savings serves both individuals and small businesses in its three target markets in Massachusetts. Some of its clients (as of mid-2016) include Lyons Associates, The Hub, TCR Development, SYA+FH Steven Young Architect + Fine Home Builder, and Park Drive Inc.

The bank spent $489,000 on marketing expenses during 2015, down from $557,000 in each of 2014 and 2013.

Financial Performance
The bank's annual revenues have slowly trended higher over the past several years as the promising Boston real estate market has fueled its commercial real estate and residential loan business growth.

Hingham's revenue dipped 1% to $64.34 million during 2015 despite 13% mortgage loan growth, mostly because in 2014 it earned a gains on life insurance distributions. The bank also continued to lose fee income as it has eliminated many fees on its deposit products to simplify offerings and attract customer deposits.

Revenue declines and higher income tax provisions in 2015 (in 2014 it earned non-taxed death benefit proceeds) caused the bank's net income to fall 13% to $19.34 million. Hingham's operating cash levels rose 11% to $20.2 million for the year thanks to a jump in cash-based earnings.

Strategy
The Hingham Institution for Savings continued in 2016 to focus on originating commercial, multi-family, and single-family mortgage loans in its target markets of Boston, the South Shore, and the island of Nantucket in Massachusetts, especially as the healthy real estate market in and around Boston has provided a tailwind for its lending business.

EXECUTIVES

President, Chief Executive Officer, Director, Robert H. Gaughen
Executive Vice President, Director, Patrick R. Gaughen
Vice President, Chief Financial Officer, Cristian A. Melej
Vice President, Chief Retail Lending Officer, Michael J. Sinclair
Commercial Lending Vice President, Shawn T. Sullivan
Director, Jacqueline M. Youngworth
Director, Howard M. Berger
Director, Michael J. Desmond
Director, Ronald D. Falcione
Director, Kevin W. Gaughen
Director, Kara Gaughen Smith
Director, Julio R. Hernando
Director, Brian T. Kenner
Director, Robert A. Lane
Director, Scott L. Moser
Director, Stacey M. Page
Director, Robert K. Sheridan
Director, Edward L. Sparda
Director, Geoffrey C. Wilkinson
Auditors: Wolf & Company, P.C.

LOCATIONS

HQ: Hingham Institution for Savings
55 Main Street, Hingham, MA 02043
Phone: 781 749-2200 **Fax:** 781 740-4889
Web: www.hinghamsavings.com

COMPETITORS

BROOKLINE BANCORP, INC.
FIRST CONNECTICUT BANCORP, INC.
FIRSTRUST SAVINGS BANK
HOMESTREET, INC.
NORTHWEST BANCORP, INC.

HISTORICAL FINANCIALS
Company Type: Public

Income Statement — FYE: December 31

	ASSETS ($mil)	NET INCOME ($mil)	INCOME AS % OF ASSETS	EMPLOYEES
12/20	2,857.0	50.7	1.8%	87
12/19	2,590.3	38.9	1.5%	90
12/18	2,408.5	30.3	1.3%	96
12/17	2,284.5	25.7	1.1%	101
12/16	2,014.5	23.4	1.2%	103
Annual Growth	9.1%	21.3%	—	(4.1%)

2020 Year-End Financials
Return on assets: 1.8%
Return on equity: 18.7%
Long-term debt ($ mil.): —
No. of shares ($ mil.): 2.1
Sales ($ mil.): 115.5
Dividends
Yield: 1.1%
Payout: 11.9%
Market value ($ mil.): 462.0

	STOCK PRICE ($) FY Close	P/E High	P/E Low	PER SHARE ($) Earnings	Dividends	Book Value
12/20	216.00	10	5	23.25	2.47	137.02
12/19	210.20	12	9	17.83	2.04	115.75
12/18	197.74	16	14	13.90	1.73	99.67
12/17	207.00	19	14	11.81	1.62	87.29
12/16	196.78	18	11	10.89	1.52	75.50
Annual Growth	2.4%	—	—	20.9%	12.9%	16.1%

Home Bancorp Inc

Making its home in Cajun Country, Home Bancorp is the holding company for Home Bank, a community bank which offers deposit and loan services to consumers and small to midsized businesses in southern Louisiana. Through about two dozen branches, the bank offers standard savings and checking accounts, as well as lending services such as mortgages, consumer loans, and credit cards. Its loan portfolio includes commercial real estate, commercial, and industrial loans, as well as construction and land loans. Home Bancorp also operates about half a dozen bank branches in west Mississippi, which were formerly part of Britton & Koontz Bank.

Geographic Reach

Home Bancorp serves the Louisiana areas of Greater Lafayette, Baton Rouge, Greater New Orleans, and Northshore (of Lake Pontchartrain). Its markets in Mississippi include Vicksburg and Natchez.

Financial Performance

Although the company saw assets and loans grow in 2013, net income fell 20% that year to $7.3 million on lower operating income.

Mergers and Acquisitions

In early 2014 Home Bancorp spent about $35 million on Britton & Koontz Capital Corporation, the holding company of Britton & Koontz Bank; the deal added five branches in west Mississippi to Home Bancorp's operations.

EXECUTIVES

President, Chief Executive Officer, Subsidiary Officer, Chairman, Director, John W. Bordelon, $357,500 total compensation
Executive Vice President, Chief Operations Officer, Subsidiary Officer, Jason P. Freyou, $230,792 total compensation
Executive Vice President, Chief Credit Officer, Subsidiary Officer, Darren E. Guidry, $177,871 total compensation
Executive Vice President, Chief Financial Officer, Subsidiary Officer, David T. Kirkley
Director, John A. Hendry
Director, Ann Forte Trappey
Director, Mark M. Cole
Director, Paul J. Blanchet
Director, Daniel G. Guidry
Director, Chris P. Rader
Director, J. Scott Ballard
Director, Donald W. Washington
Auditors : Wipfli LLP

LOCATIONS

HQ: Home Bancorp Inc
 503 Kaliste Saloom Road, Lafayette, LA 70508
Phone: 337 237-1960   **Fax:** 337 264-9280
Web: www.home24bank.com

COMPETITORS

BNCCORP, INC.
SOUTHERN CONNECTICUT BANCORP, INC.
SOUTHWEST BANCORP, INC.
THE FIRST BANCSHARES INC
ZIONS BANCORPORATION, NATIONAL ASSOCIATION

HISTORICAL FINANCIALS

Company Type: Public

Income Statement — FYE: December 31

	ASSETS ($mil)	NET INCOME ($mil)	INCOME AS % OF ASSETS	EMPLOYEES
12/20	2,591.8	24.7	1.0%	0
12/19	2,200.4	27.9	1.3%	0
12/18	2,153.6	31.5	1.5%	0
12/17	2,228.1	16.8	0.8%	0
12/16	1,556.7	16.0	1.0%	0
Annual Growth	13.6%	11.5%	—	—

2020 Year-End Financials

Return on assets: 1.0%
Return on equity: 7.7%
Long-term debt ($ mil.): —
No. of shares ($ mil.): 8.7
Sales ($ mil.): 118.4
Dividends
 Yield: 3.1%
 Payout: 39.2%
Market value ($ mil.): 245.0

	STOCK PRICE ($) FY Close	P/E High	P/E Low	PER SHARE ($) Earnings	Dividends	Book Value
12/20	27.99	14	7	2.85	0.88	36.82
12/19	39.19	13	11	3.05	0.84	34.19
12/18	35.40	14	10	3.40	0.71	32.14
12/17	43.22	19	14	2.28	0.55	29.57
12/16	38.61	17	10	2.25	0.41	24.47
Annual Growth	(7.7%)	—	—	6.1%	21.0%	10.8%

Home BancShares Inc

Home BancShares is the holding company for Centennial Bank (the bank), which operates about 160 branches in Arkansas, Alabama, New York and Florida. The bank offers traditional services such as checking, savings, and money market accounts; IRAs; and CDs. It focuses on commercial real estate lending, including construction, land development, and agricultural loans, which make up about 60% of its lending portfolio. The bank also writes residential mortgage, business, and consumer loans. Nonbank subsidiaries offer trust and insurance services. The company has a total assets of $18.1 billion. Home BancShares was formed by an investor group led by John W. Allison, its Chairman, and Robert H. "Bunny" Adcock, Jr., its Vice Chairman in 1998.

Operations

Broadly speaking, the bank makes roughly 85% of its revenue from interest income. The remainder of its revenue comes from mortgage lending income, service charges on deposit accounts and other miscellaneous and non-recurring sources.

Geographic Reach

The Arkansas-based bank holding company's Centennial Bank operates about 160 branches in Arkansas, Florida, Alabama and New York. It also operate loan production offices in Los Angeles, California; Miami, Florida and Dallas, Texas through its Centennial CFG division and in Chesapeake, Virginia and Baltimore, Maryland through its SPF division.

Financial Performance

The company reported a net interest income of $573 million in 2021, a 2% decline from the previous year's net interest income of $582.6 million. This was primarily due to a lower volume of loans for the year.

In 2021, the company had a net income of $319 million, a 49% increase from the previous year's net income of $214.4 million.

The company's cash at the end of 2021 was $3.7 billion. Operating activities generated $389.4 million, while investing activities provided $624.7 million. Financing activities provided another $1.4 billion.

Strategy

The company's growth strategy entails the following:

Strategic acquisitions ? Strategic acquisitions (both FDIC-assisted and non-FDIC-assisted) have been a significant component of the company's historical growth strategy, and it believes properly priced bank acquisitions can continue to be a large part of its growth strategy.

Organic growth ? Through its Centennial CFG franchise, the company is continuing to build out a national lending platform that focuses on commercial real estate plus commercial and industrial loans. Additionally, through its SPF division, the company is continuing to build a lending platform focusing on commercial and consumer marine loans. As opportunities arise, it will evaluate new (commonly referred to as de novo) branches in its current markets and in other attractive market areas. The company did not open any de novo branch locations during 2021. It will continue to evaluate de novo opportunities during 2022 and make decisions on a case-by-case basis in the best interest of the shareholders.

Mergers and Acquisitions

In 2022, Home BancShares, the parent company of Centennial Bank, announced that it has completed its previously announced acquisition of Happy Bancshares, Inc. (Happy), parent company of Happy State Bank (HSB). "The completion of the acquisition of Happy State Bank is a pivotal moment for Home and is another example of our ability to make smart, strategic deals that are immediately accretive," said John Allison, Chairman, President and CEO of Home.

In early 2022, Home BancShares, the parent company of Centennial Bank, announced that it has completed the purchase of the performing marine loan portfolio of Utah-based LendingClub Bank. Under the terms of the purchase agreement with LendingClub, Centennial acquired yacht loans totaling approximately $238 million. This portfolio of loans will be housed within Centennial's Shore Premier Finance ("SPF") division, which will be responsible for servicing the acquired loan portfolio and originating new loan production. SPF is a specialized marine lending division of Centennial with a national platform for dealership floor plan and retail consumer marine loans.

Company Background

Home Bancshares formed in 1998 as First State Bank.

EXECUTIVES

President, Chief Executive Officer, Subsidiary Officer, Chairman, Director, John W. Allison, $399,039 total compensation
Chief Financial Officer, Treasurer, Subsidiary Officer, Director, Brian S. Davis, $324,990 total compensation
Vice-Chairman, Director, Jack E. Engelkes
Chief Accounting Officer, Subsidiary Officer, Jennifer C. Floyd
Chief Lending Officer, Subsidiary Officer, Kevin D. Hester, $374,038 total compensation
Chief Operating Officer, Subsidiary Officer, J. Stephen Tipton
Investor Relations Senior Executive Vice President, Investor Relations Director, Investor Relations Subsidiary Officer, Director, Donna J. Townsell
Executive Officer, Subsidiary Officer, Russell D. Carter
Subsidiary Officer, Director, Robert H. Adcock
Subsidiary Officer, Director, Tracy M. French, $448,461 total compensation
Director, J. Pat Hickman
Director, Richard H. Ashley
Director, Milburn Adams
Director, Michael D. Beebe
Director, Karen Garrett
Director, James G. Hinkle
Director, Alex R. Lieblong
Director, Thomas J. Longe
Director, James Rankin
Director, Larry W. Ross
Auditors: BKD, LLP

LOCATIONS

HQ: Home BancShares Inc
719 Harkrider, Suite 100, Conway, AR 72032
Phone: 501 339-2929
Web: www.homebancshares.com

COMPETITORS

BEAR STATE FINANCIAL, INC.
BSB BANCORP, INC.
HANCOCK WHITNEY CORPORATION
HERITAGE FINANCIAL GROUP, INC.
IBERIABANK CORPORATION
LAKELAND BANCORP, INC.
LAKELAND FINANCIAL CORPORATION
REPUBLIC BANCORP, INC.
SOUTHSIDE BANCSHARES, INC.
UNITED COMMUNITY BANKS, INC.

HISTORICAL FINANCIALS

Company Type: Public

Income Statement — FYE: December 31

	ASSETS ($mil)	NET INCOME ($mil)	INCOME AS % OF ASSETS	EMPLOYEES
12/20	16,398.8	214.4	1.3%	2,018
12/19	15,032.0	289.5	1.9%	1,920
12/18	15,302.4	300.4	2.0%	1,815
12/17	14,449.7	135.0	0.9%	1,744
12/16	9,808.4	177.1	1.8%	1,503
Annual Growth	13.7%	4.9%	—	7.6%

2020 Year-End Financials
Return on assets: 1.3%
Return on equity: 8.3%
Long-term debt ($ mil.): —
No. of shares ($ mil.): 165.1
Sales ($ mil.): 787.7
Dividends
Yield: 2.7%
Payout: 40.7%
Market value ($ mil.): 3,216.0

	STOCK PRICE ($) FY Close	P/E High	P/E Low	PER SHARE ($) Earnings	Dividends	Book Value
12/20	19.48	16	8	1.30	0.53	15.78
12/19	19.66	12	10	1.73	0.51	15.10
12/18	16.34	15	9	1.73	0.46	13.76
12/17	23.25	33	24	0.89	0.40	12.70
12/16	27.77	35	15	1.26	0.34	9.45
Annual Growth	(8.5%)	—	—	0.8%	11.5%	13.7%

HomeTrust Bancshares Inc.

EXECUTIVES

Executive Chairman, Subsidiary Officer, Director, Dana L. Stonestreet, $505,000 total compensation
President, Chief Executive Officer, Chief Operating Officer, Subsidiary Officer, Director, C. Hunter Westbrook, $327,813 total compensation
Customer Executive Vice President, Customer Business Banking Group Executive, Customer Subsidiary Officer, Kristin Y. Powell
Executive Vice President, Chief Financial Officer, Treasurer, Corporate Secretary, Subsidiary Officer, Tony J. VunCannon, $238,692 total compensation
Executive Vice President, Chief Information Officer, Subsidiary Officer, Marty T. Caywood
Executive Vice President, Chief Credit Officer, Subsidiary Officer, Keith J. Houghton, $222,854 total compensation
Executive Vice President, Chief Risk Officer, Subsidiary Officer, R. Parrish Little
Executive Vice President, Chief People Officer, Subsidiary Officer, Megan Pelletier
Interim Executive Vice President, Subsidiary Officer, John Sprink
Director, Laura C. Kendall
Director, Rebekah M. Lowe
Director, Robert E. James
Director, Craig C. Koontz
Director, F.K. McFarland
Director, Sidney A. Biesecker
Director, John A. Switzer
Director, Richard T. Williams
Auditors: Dixon Hughes Goodman LLP

LOCATIONS

HQ: HomeTrust Bancshares Inc.
10 Woodfin Street, Asheville, NC 28801
Phone: 828 259-3939
Web: www.htb.com

HISTORICAL FINANCIALS

Company Type: Public

Income Statement — FYE: June 30

	ASSETS ($mil)	NET INCOME ($mil)	INCOME AS % OF ASSETS	EMPLOYEES
06/21	3,524.7	15.6	0.4%	575
06/20	3,722.8	22.7	0.6%	590
06/19	3,476.1	27.1	0.8%	582
06/18	3,304.1	8.2	0.2%	520
06/17	3,206.5	11.8	0.4%	486
Annual Growth	2.4%	7.3%	—	4.3%

2021 Year-End Financials
Return on assets: 0.4%
Return on equity: 3.8%
Long-term debt ($ mil.): —
No. of shares ($ mil.): 16.6
Sales ($ mil.): 158.5
Dividends
Yield: 1.1%
Payout: 19.1%
Market value ($ mil.): 464.0

	STOCK PRICE ($) FY Close	P/E High	P/E Low	PER SHARE ($) Earnings	Dividends	Book Value
06/21	27.90	31	14	0.94	0.31	23.83
06/20	16.00	20	9	1.30	0.27	23.99
06/19	25.14	20	16	1.46	0.18	22.74
06/18	28.15	65	50	0.44	0.00	21.49
06/17	24.40	41	27	0.65	0.00	20.96
Annual Growth	3.4%	—	—	9.7%	—	3.3%

Hope Bancorp Inc

EXECUTIVES

Honorary Chairman, Director, Steven S. Koh
Chairman, President, Chief Executive Officer, Subsidiary Officer, Director, Kevin Sung Kim, $916,154 total compensation
Chief Financial Officer, Director, David P. Malone, $462,462 total compensation
Senior Executive Vice President, Subsidiary Officer, Jason K. Kim, $231,577 total compensation
Senior Executive Vice President, Subsidiary Officer, Kyu S. Kim, $365,721 total compensation
Senior Executive Vice President, Chief Operating Officer, Subsidiary Officer, Peter Koh
Subsidiary Officer, Thomas P. Stenger
Lead Independent Director, Director, Scott Yoon-Suk Whang
Director, Donald D. Byun
Director, Jinho Doo
Director, Daisy Y. Ha

Director, Joon Kyung Kim
Director, William J. Lewis
Director, Lisa Kim Pai
Director, Mary ("Mimi") E. Thigpen
Director, Dale S. Zuehls
Auditors : Crowe LLP

LOCATIONS

HQ: Hope Bancorp Inc
3200 Wilshire Boulevard, Suite 1400, Los Angeles, CA 90010
Phone: 213 639-1700   Fax: 213 235-3033
Web: www.bankofhope.com

HISTORICAL FINANCIALS
Company Type: Public

Income Statement   FYE: December 31

	ASSETS ($mil)	NET INCOME ($mil)	INCOME AS % OF ASSETS	EMPLOYEES
12/20	17,106.6	111.5	0.7%	1,408
12/19	15,667.4	171.0	1.1%	1,441
12/18	15,305.9	189.5	1.2%	1,494
12/17	14,206.7	139.4	1.0%	1,470
12/16	13,441.4	113.7	0.8%	1,372
Annual Growth	6.2%	(0.5%)	—	0.6%

2020 Year-End Financials
Return on assets: 0.6%   Dividends
Return on equity: 5.4%   Yield: 5.1%
Long-term debt ($ mil.): —   Payout: 54.9%
No. of shares ($ mil.): 123.2 Market value ($ mil.): 1,345.0
Sales ($ mil.): 652.3

	STOCK PRICE ($) FY Close	P/E High/Low		PER SHARE ($) Earnings	Dividends	Book Value
12/20	10.91	17	8	0.90	0.56	16.66
12/19	14.86	11	9	1.35	0.56	16.19
12/18	11.86	13	8	1.44	0.54	15.03
12/17	18.25	22	15	1.03	0.50	14.23
12/16	21.89	20	13	1.10	0.45	13.72
Annual Growth	(16.0%)	—	—	(4.9%)	5.6%	5.0%

Horizon Bancorp Inc

For those in Indiana and Michigan, Horizon Bancorp stretches as far as the eye can see. The company is the holding company for Horizon Bank (and its Heartland Community Bank division), which provides checking and savings accounts, IRAs, CDs, and credit cards to customers through more than 50 branches in north and central Indiana and southwest and central Michigan. Commercial, financial, and agricultural loans make up the largest segment of its loan portfolio, which also includes mortgage warehouse loans (loans earmarked for sale into the secondary market), consumer loans, and residential mortgages. Through subsidiaries, the bank offers trust and investment management services; life, health, and property/casualty insurance; and annuities.

Operations
Horizon boasted more than $2.08 billion in total assets and $1.48 billion in deposits in 2014. Commercial loans made up 49% of the bank's total loan portfolio. The bank employed nearly 450 full and part time employees that year.

Horizon's subsidiaries include: Horizon Investments, which manages the bank's investment portfolio; Horizon Properties, which manages the real estate investment trust; Horizon Insurance Services, which sells through the company's Wealth Management; and Horizon Grantor Trust, which holds title to certain company-owned life insurance policies.

The bank generated 61% of its revenue from interest income on loans in 2014, while another 13% came from interest on its taxable and tax-exempt investments. About 8% of revenues came from gains on its mortgage sales, while the remainder of revenues were mostly generated by a mix of service charges on deposit accounts, interchange fees, and fiduciary activities fees.

Geographic Reach
The bank's more than 30 branches serve customers in north and central Indiana and southwest and central Michigan. Its mortgage-banking services are offered across the Midwest.

Financial Performance
Horizon Bancorp's revenues and profits have been trending higher over the past few years, mostly as it's continued to grow its loan business and deposit customer base through acquisitions.

The bank's revenue rose by 2% to $102.5 million in 2014 mostly as the bank increased its interest-earning assets during the year. Its non-interest income also increased thanks to higher service charges on deposits and interchange fee income resulting from the growth in transactional deposit accounts and volume.

Despite higher revenue in 2014, the company's net income fell by 9% to $18.1 million for the year on higher provisions for loan losses due to loan growth and a write off of a commercial account, coupled with an increase in transaction costs related to its Summit acquisition and an increase in salaries and employee benefits due to growth. Horizon's operating cash levels fell by 62% to $17.7 million after adjusting its earnings for non-cash items related to its net proceeds on the sale of its held-for-sale loans.

Strategy
Horizon Bancorp continues to expand its geographic reach and loan business through acquisitions and new branches. It acquired several banks and opened new branches throughout 2016 and 2017.

Mergers and Acquisitions
In 2017, Horizon Bancorp agreed to buy Wolverine Bancorp for $92 million and Lafayette Community Bancorp for $32 million

In 2016, Horizon Bancorp bought LaPorte Bancorp for $98.9 million, boosting its total assets by 20% to more than $3.24 billion while expanding its branch reach into the LaPorte area of Indiana. It also agreed to buy CNB Bancorp, which operates Central National Bank & Trust in Attica, Indiana.

In 2015, Horizon Bancorp agreed to buy Peoples Bancorp and subsidiary Peoples Federal Savings Bank of DeKalb County.

In April 2014, the company purchased SCP Bancorp, including subsidiary Summit Community Bank and its two branches.

EXECUTIVES

President, Chief Executive Officer, Subsidiary Officer, Thomas M. Prame
Executive Vice President, Noe S. Najera
Executive Vice President, Subsidiary Officer, Kathie A. DeRuiter, $250,000 total compensation
Executive Vice President, Chief Financial Officer, Subsidiary Officer, Mark E. Secor, $282,880 total compensation
Chief Commercial Banking Officer, Lynn M. Kerber
Region Officer, Dennis J. Kuhn, $250,000 total compensation
Lead Director, Director, Michele M. Magnuson
Director, Lawrence E. Burnell
Director, Julie Scheck Freigang
Director, Peter L. Pairitz
Director, Spero W. Valavanis
Director, James B. Dworkin
Director, Steven William Reed
Director, Susan D. Aaron
Director, Eric P. Blackhurst
Director, Vanessa P. Williams
Auditors : BKD, LLP

LOCATIONS

HQ: Horizon Bancorp Inc
515 Franklin Street, Michigan City, IN 46360
Phone: 219 879-0211
Web: www.horizonbank.com

PRODUCTS/OPERATIONS

Selected Subsidiaries
Horizon Bank National Association
    Horizon Insurance Services, Inc.
    Horizon Investments, Inc.
    Horizon Trust & Investment Management, N.A.

COMPETITORS

CASCADE BANCORP
CENTERSTATE BANK CORPORATION
FIRST FINANCIAL BANCORP.
S&T BANCORP, INC.
STATE BANK FINANCIAL CORPORATION

HISTORICAL FINANCIALS
Company Type: Public

Income Statement — FYE: December 31

	ASSETS ($mil)	NET INCOME ($mil)	INCOME AS % OF ASSETS	EMPLOYEES
12/20	5,886.6	68.4	1.2%	815
12/19	5,246.8	66.5	1.3%	839
12/18	4,246.6	53.1	1.3%	716
12/17	3,964.3	33.1	0.8%	701
12/16	3,141.1	23.9	0.8%	665
Annual Growth	17.0%	30.1%	—	5.2%

2020 Year-End Financials
Return on assets: 1.2%
Return on equity: 10.1%
Long-term debt ($ mil.): —
No. of shares ($ mil.): 43.8
Sales ($ mil.): 264.9
Dividends
Yield: 3.0%
Payout: 32.6%
Market value ($ mil.): 696.0

	STOCK PRICE ($) FY Close	P/E High	P/E Low	PER SHARE ($) Earnings	Dividends	Book Value
12/20	15.86	12	5	1.55	0.48	15.78
12/19	19.00	13	10	1.53	0.44	14.59
12/18	15.78	24	11	1.38	0.39	12.82
12/17	27.80	30	26	0.95	0.32	11.94
12/16	28.00	40	26	0.79	0.27	10.25
Annual Growth	(13.2%)	—	—	18.2%	15.8%	11.4%

Hostess Brands Inc

EXECUTIVES

Chairman, Director, Jerry D. Kaminski
President, Chief Executive Officer, Director, Andrew P. Callahan, $507,692 total compensation
Executive Vice President, Chief Customer Officer, Subsidiary Officer, Arist R. Mastorides
Executive Vice President, Chief Growth Officer, Subsidiary Officer, Daniel J. O'Leary
Executive Vice President, Chief Financial Officer, Chief Accounting Officer, Travis E. Leonard
Senior Vice President, General Counsel, Corporate Secretary, Jolyn J. Sebree, $346,345 total compensation
Senior Vice President, Chief People Officer, Subsidiary Officer, Robert C. Weber
Subsidiary Officer, Michael J. Gernigin
Division Officer, Subsidiary Officer, Darryl P. Riley
Director, Craig D. Steeneck
Director, Hugh G. Dineen
Director, Olufunlayo Olurinde Fajemirokun-Beck
Director, Laurence E. Bodner
Director, Gretchen R. Crist
Director, Rachel P. Cullen
Director, Ioannis Skoufalos
Auditors : KPMG LLP

LOCATIONS

HQ: Hostess Brands Inc
7905 Quivira Road, Lenexa, KS 66215
Phone: 816 701-4600

Web: www.hostessbrands.com

HISTORICAL FINANCIALS
Company Type: Public

Income Statement — FYE: December 31

	REVENUE ($mil)	NET INCOME ($mil)	NET PROFIT MARGIN	EMPLOYEES
12/20	1,016.6	64.7	6.4%	3,000
12/19	907.6	63.1	7.0%	2,000
12/18	850.3	62.8	7.4%	2,000
12/17	776.1	223.8	28.8%	1,340
12/16	111.9	(4.4)	—	1,350
Annual Growth	73.6%	—	—	22.1%

2020 Year-End Financials
Debt ratio: 33.5%
Return on equity: 4.1%
Cash ($ mil.): 173.0
Current Ratio: 1.95
Long-term debt ($ mil.): 1,113
No. of shares ($ mil.): 130.3
Dividends
Yield: —
Payout: —
Market value ($ mil.): 1,908.0

	STOCK PRICE ($) FY Close	P/E High	P/E Low	PER SHARE ($) Earnings	Dividends	Book Value
12/20	14.64	28	18	0.51	0.00	12.44
12/19	14.54	26	19	0.55	0.00	11.38
12/18	10.94	24	16	0.61	0.00	9.21
12/17	14.81	8	5	2.13	0.00	8.69
12/16	13.00	—	—	(0.05)	0.00	6.90
Annual Growth	3.0%	—	—	—	—	15.9%

Houlihan Lokey Inc

EXECUTIVES

Executive Chairman, Director, Irwin N. Gold, $400,000 total compensation
Co-President, Director, David A. Preiser, $400,000 total compensation
Chief Executive Officer, Director, Scott L. Beiser, $400,000 total compensation
Co-President, Director, Scott J. Adelson, $400,000 total compensation
Chief Financial Officer, J. Lindsey Alley, $375,000 total compensation
General Counsel, Secretary, Christopher M. Crain
Director, Ekpedeme M. Bassey
Director, Robert A. Schriesheim
Director, Jacqueline B. Kosecoff
Director, Paul A. Zuber
Director, Gillian B. Zucker
Director, Cyrus D. Walker
Director, Todd J. Carter
Auditors : KPMG LLP

LOCATIONS

HQ: Houlihan Lokey Inc
10250 Constellation Blvd., 5th Floor, Los Angeles, CA 90067
Phone: 310 788-5200
Web: www.hl.com

HISTORICAL FINANCIALS
Company Type: Public

Income Statement — FYE: March 31

	REVENUE ($mil)	NET INCOME ($mil)	NET PROFIT MARGIN	EMPLOYEES
03/21	1,525.4	312.7	20.5%	1,574
03/20	1,159.3	183.7	15.9%	1,491
03/19	1,084.3	159.1	14.7%	1,354
03/18	963.3	172.2	17.9%	1,228
03/17	872.0	108.3	12.4%	1,171
Annual Growth	15.0%	30.3%	—	7.7%

2021 Year-End Financials
Debt ratio: —
Return on equity: 26.4%
Cash ($ mil.): 1,055.4
Current Ratio: 1.61
Long-term debt ($ mil.): 0.8
No. of shares ($ mil.): 68.2
Dividends
Yield: 1.9%
Payout: 32.5%
Market value ($ mil.): 4,536.0

	STOCK PRICE ($) FY Close	P/E High	P/E Low	PER SHARE ($) Earnings	Dividends	Book Value
03/21	66.51	15	11	4.55	1.30	20.29
03/20	52.12	20	14	2.80	1.24	15.02
03/19	45.85	21	14	2.42	1.08	13.63
03/18	44.60	19	12	2.60	0.80	12.96
03/17	34.45	19	12	1.63	0.71	11.01
Annual Growth	17.9%	—	—	29.3%	16.3%	16.5%

HV Bancorp Inc

EXECUTIVES

Chairman, Chief Executive Officer, Subsidiary Officer, Director, Travis J. Thompson, $200,000 total compensation
President, Subsidiary Officer, Vice-Chairman, Director, Robert J. Marino
Executive Vice President, Chief Operating Officer, Subsidiary Officer, J. Chris Jacobsen
Executive Vice President, Division Officer, Subsidiary Officer, Charles S. Hutt, $175,000 total compensation
Executive Vice President, Division Officer, Hugh W. Connelly
Executive Vice President, Chief Credit Officer, Subsidiary Officer, Derek P.B. Warden
Executive Vice President, Division Officer, Subsidiary Officer, Barton Skurbe
Director, John D. Behm
Director, Joseph F. Kelly
Director, Scott W. Froggatt
Director, Carl Hj. Asplundh
Director, Michael L. Hammer
Auditors : S.R. Snodgrass, P.C.

LOCATIONS

HQ: HV Bancorp Inc
2005 South Easton Road, Suite 304, Doylestown, PA 18901
Phone: 267 280-4000
Web: www.myhvb.com

HISTORICAL FINANCIALS
Company Type: Public

Income Statement   FYE: December 31

	ASSETS ($mil)	NET INCOME ($mil)	INCOME AS % OF ASSETS	EMPLOYEES
12/20	861.6	5.7	0.7%	126
12/19*	354.5	0.5	0.2%	97
06/19	344.1	0.8	0.3%	92
06/18	297.7	0.7	0.3%	71
06/17	216.7	0.5	0.3%	74
Annual Growth	41.2%	78.4%	—	14.2%

*Fiscal year change

2020 Year-End Financials
Return on assets: 0.9%
Return on equity: 15.8%
Long-term debt ($ mil.): —
No. of shares ($ mil.): 2.1
Sales ($ mil.): 30.6
Dividends
Yield: —
Payout: —
Market value ($ mil.): 38.0

	STOCK PRICE ($) FY Close	P/E High/Low		PER SHARE ($) Earnings	Dividends	Book Value
12/20	17.17	6	3	2.84	0.00	17.78
12/19*	17.00	65	55	0.26	0.00	14.81
06/19	15.08	41	34	0.43	0.00	14.40
06/18	14.82	43	36	0.38	0.50	13.60
06/17	14.48	26	24	0.56	0.00	14.41
Annual Growth	4.4%	—	—	50.1%	—	5.4%

*Fiscal year change

IAC/InterActiveCorp (New)

EXECUTIVES

Chairman, Senior Executive, Director, Barry Diller
Vice-Chairman, Director, Victor A. Kaufman
Chief Executive Officer, Director, Joseph Levin
Executive Vice President, Chief Financial Officer, Chief Operating Officer, Christopher Halpin
Executive Vice President, Chief Legal Officer, Kendall Fox Handler
Director, Chelsea Clinton
Director, Michael D. Eisner
Director, Bonnie S. Hammer
Director, Bryan Lourd
Director, David S. Rosenblatt
Director, Alan G. Spoon
Director, Alexander von Furstenberg
Director, Richard F. Zannino

LOCATIONS

HQ: IAC/InterActiveCorp (New)
555 West 18th Street, New York, NY 10011
Phone: 212 314-7300
Web: www.iac.com

HISTORICAL FINANCIALS
Company Type: Public

Income Statement   FYE: December 31

	REVENUE ($mil)	NET INCOME ($mil)	NET PROFIT MARGIN	EMPLOYEES
12/20	3,047.6	269.7	8.9%	8,200
12/19	2,705.8	22.8	0.8%	6,400
12/18	2,533.0	246.7	9.7%	0
12/17	1,952.6	37.0	1.9%	0
Annual Growth	16.0%	93.9%	—	—

2020 Year-End Financials
Debt ratio: 7.8%
Return on equity: 5.8%
Cash ($ mil.): 3,701.1
Current Ratio: 5.49
Long-term debt ($ mil.): 712.2
No. of shares ($ mil.): 88.7
Dividends
Yield: —
Payout: —
Market value ($ mil.): 16,808.0

	STOCK PRICE ($) FY Close	P/E High/Low		PER SHARE ($) Earnings	Dividends	Book Value
12/20	189.35	102	34	2.97	0.00	74.33
12/19	249.11	—	—	0.00	0.00	29.78
12/18	183.04	—	—	0.00	0.00	0.00
12/17	122.28	—	—	0.00	0.00	0.00
Annual Growth	15.7%	—	—	—	—	—

Ichor Holdings Ltd

EXECUTIVES

Executive Chairman, Director, Thomas M. Rohrs, $519,231 total compensation
Chief Executive Officer, Director, Jeffrey S. Andreson, $373,846 total compensation
Chief Financial Officer, Larry J. Sparks
Chief Operating Officer, Bruce Ragsdale
Chief Commercial Officer, Christopher Smith
Chief Technology Officer, Philip Barros, $373,846 total compensation
Division Officer, Kevin M. Canty
Lead Independent Director, Director, Iain MacKenzie
Director, Wendy Arienzo
Director, Marc Haugen
Director, John Kispert
Director, Sarah O'Dowd
Director, Yuval Wasserman
Director, Jorge Luis Titinger
Director, Laura A. Black
Auditors: KPMG LLP

LOCATIONS

HQ: Ichor Holdings Ltd
3185 Laurelview Ct., Fremont, CA 94538
Phone: 510 897-5200
Web: www.ichorsystems.com

HISTORICAL FINANCIALS
Company Type: Public

Income Statement   FYE: December 25

	REVENUE ($mil)	NET INCOME ($mil)	NET PROFIT MARGIN	EMPLOYEES
12/20	914.2	33.2	3.6%	2,030
12/19	620.8	10.7	1.7%	1,715
12/18	823.6	57.8	7.0%	1,490
12/17	655.8	56.4	8.6%	1,760
12/16	405.7	16.6	4.1%	787
Annual Growth	22.5%	18.9%	—	26.7%

2020 Year-End Financials
Debt ratio: 25.9%
Return on equity: 10.5%
Cash ($ mil.): 252.9
Current Ratio: 3.06
Long-term debt ($ mil.): 191.5
No. of shares ($ mil.): 27.9
Dividends
Yield: —
Payout: —
Market value ($ mil.): 0.0

ICU Medical Inc

ICU is one of the world's leading pure-play infusion therapy companies with global operations and a wide-ranging product portfolio that includes IV solutions, IV smart pumps with pain management and safety software technology, dedicated and non-dedicated IV sets and needle-free connectors designed to help meet clinical, safety and workflow goals. In addition, ICU manufactures automated pharmacy IV compounding systems with workflow technology, closed system transfer devices for preparing and administering hazardous IV drugs and cardiac monitoring systems for critically ill patients. ICU Medical, which sells its products to other equipment makers and distributors, gets most of its revenue from US customers.

Operations

ICU Medical operates in four product lines: Infusion Consumables, IV Solutions, Infusion Systems, and Critical Care.

Infusion Consumables accounts for more than 40% of revenue, provides infusion therapy sets used in hospitals and ambulatory clinics, consist of a tube running from a bottle or plastic bag containing a solution to a catheter inserted in a patient's vein that may or may not be used with an IV pump.

The IV Solutions segment accounts for more than 25% of revenue, provides intravenous systems, irrigation, and nutritionals to help provide safe and effective patient care.

The Infusion Systems segment accounts for more than 25% of revenue, offers infusion pumps, dedicated IV sets and software, IV mediation safety software, and professional services.

Critical Care products segment accounts for about 5% of revenue, offers a portfolio of monitoring systems and advanced sensors and catheters that help clinicians get access to patients' hemodynamic and cardiac status.

Geographic Reach

ICU Medical, based in San Clemente,

California, sells its products in more than 90 countries around the world.

The company maintains manufacturing facilities in Salt Lake City, Utah; Austin, Texas; Baja California, Mexico; and La Aurora, Costa Rica. ICU Medical has distribution warehouses in Texas, Pennsylvania, and California. It has device service center in Sligo, Ireland.

ICU relies on the US for more than 70% of its revenue, while the Europe, the Middle East, and Africa region and other countries combining for about 30% of revenue.

Sales and Marketing

ICU sell its product through direct sales force and distributors to acute care hospitals, wholesalers, ambulatory clinics, and alternate site facilities, such as clinics, home health care providers, and long-term care facilities.

Advertising expenses were $0.2 million in 2021, $0.2 million in 2020, and $0.1 million in 2019.

Financial Performance

The company's revenue for fiscal 2021 increased to $1.32 billion compared from the prior year with $1.27 billion.

Net income for fiscal 2021 increased to $103.1 million compared from the prior year with $86.9 million.

Cash held by the company at the end of fiscal 2021 increased to $552.8 million. Cash provided by operations was $267.5 million while cash used for investing and financing activities were $90.7 million and $16.9 million, respectively. Main uses of cash were purchases of property, plant and equipment; and payments on finance leases.

Mergers and Acquisitions

In 2022, ICU completed its acquisition of Smiths Medical from Smiths Group plc. The Smiths Medical business includes syringe and ambulatory infusion devices, vascular access, and vital care products. When combined with ICU Medical's existing businesses, the combined companies create a leading infusion therapy company with estimated pro forma combined revenues of approximately $2.5 billion. The acquisition leverages significant investment into integration and infrastructure developed to support the Hospira Infusion Systems acquisition in 2017. It will allow ICU Medical to build on a corporate culture that creates value through accountability, acting with transparency, making quick and informed decisions, and staying focused on meeting customer needs. The acquisition closed for a purchase price of $1.9 billion in cash, 2.5 million of fully paid and non-assessable shares of its common stock.

Company Background

ICU released is signature product, the Clave needlefree intravenous connection device, in 1993. Subsequent products include the MicroClave Clear connector, the Tego needlefree connector for use in hemodialysis, and products for handling hazardous drugs including the ChemoClave and ChemoLock CSTDs (closed-system transfer devices), and the Diana hazardous drug compounding system.

EXECUTIVES

Chairman, Chief Executive Officer, Director, Vivek Jain, $650,000 total compensation
Business Development Chief Operating Officer, Christian B. Voigtlander, $420,000 total compensation
Finance Chief Financial Officer, Finance Treasurer, Brian Bonnell
Corporate Vice-President, Division Officer, Dan Woolson
Corporate Vice-President, General Counsel, Secretary, Compliance Officer, Virginia Sanzone, $300,000 total compensation
Director, George A. Lopez, $350,000 total compensation
Lead Independent Director, Director, David C. Greenberg
Director, Elisha W. Finney
Director, David F. Hoffmeister
Director, Donald M. Abbey
Director, Laurie Hernandez
Director, Kolleen T. Kennedy
Director, William Seeger
Auditors : DELOITTE & TOUCHE LLP

LOCATIONS

HQ: ICU Medical Inc
  951 Calle Amanecer, San Clemente, CA 92673
Phone: 949 366-2183
Web: www.icumed.com

2018 Sales

	$ mil.	% of total
US	1,054.7	75
EMEA	134.4	10
Other	211	15
Total	1,400.1	100

PRODUCTS/OPERATIONS

2018 Sales

	$ mil	% of total
IV Solutions	508	36
Infusion Consumables	483.1	35
Infusion Systems	355.5	25
Critical Care	53.5	4
Total	1,400.1	100

COMPETITORS

AVANOS MEDICAL, INC.
BAXTER INTERNATIONAL INC.
BOSTON SCIENTIFIC CORPORATION
CANTEL MEDICAL CORP.
FRESENIUS MEDICAL CARE HOLDINGS, INC.
INTEGER HOLDINGS CORPORATION
MERIT MEDICAL SYSTEMS, INC.
OMNICELL, INC.
STRYKER CORPORATION
TELEFLEX INCORPORATED

HISTORICAL FINANCIALS

Company Type: Public

Income Statement — FYE: December 31

	NET REVENUE ($mil)	NET INCOME ($mil)	NET PROFIT MARGIN	EMPLOYEES
12/20	1,271.0	86.8	6.8%	7,900
12/19	1,266.2	101.0	8.0%	8,000
12/18	1,400.0	28.7	2.1%	8,100
12/17	1,292.6	68.6	5.3%	6,802
12/16	379.3	63.0	16.6%	2,803
Annual Growth	35.3%	8.3%	—	29.6%

2020 Year-End Financials

Debt ratio: — | No. of shares ($ mil.): 21.0
Return on equity: 6.0% | Dividends
Cash ($ mil.): 410.7 | Yield: —
Current Ratio: 4.71 | Payout: —
Long-term debt ($ mil.): — | Market value ($ mil.): 4,517.0

	STOCK PRICE ($) FY Close	P/E High/Low		PER SHARE ($) Earnings	Dividends	Book Value
12/20	214.49	56	38	4.02	0.00	71.34
12/19	187.12	53	31	4.69	0.00	66.40
12/18	229.63	220	151	1.33	0.00	61.67
12/17	216.00	63	38	3.29	0.00	59.29
12/16	147.35	39	22	3.66	0.00	40.41
Annual Growth	9.8%	—	—	2.4%	—	15.3%

Idexx Laboratories, Inc.

A leading animal health care company, IDEXX develops, manufactures, and distributes products for pets, livestock, dairy, and poultry markets. Veterinarians use the company's VetTest analyzers for blood and urine chemistry and its SNAP in-office test kits to detect heartworms, feline leukemia, and other diseases. The company also provides lab testing services and practice management software. In addition, IDEXX makes products to test for contaminants in water. The company sells its products worldwide, but the US account for more than 60% of its total revenue.

Operations

IDEXX operates through three primary segments: Companion Animal Group (CAG), Water Quality Products (Water), and Livestock, Poultry, and Dairy (LPD).

CAG segment account for about 90% of IDEXX's revenue. Most of that revenue comes from diagnostic products and services, including chemistry analyzers, rapid test kits, and laboratory services. The company operates a network of laboratories, to which vets can send patient samples for analysis.

The Water segment (about 5% of sales) makes tests which detect coliforms and E. coli in water. Water utilities and government laboratories are the primary customers for these products.

The LPD segment (horses, cows, pigs, and

chickens) brings in about 5% of total revenue. The segment sells diagnostic tests, services, and related instrumentation. Its products can test for Bovine Viral Diarrhea Virus (BVDV) as well as porcine illnesses and poultry diseases.

The company also makes and distributes diagnostics for the human market, but those are not a substantial part of its business.

Majority of revenue is generated from its products which accounts for about 60% of company' sales and service revenue accounts for the remaining.

Geographic Reach

Approximately 60% of IDEXX's sales are made in the US, but it also maintains sales offices in Africa, the Asia/Pacific region, Europe, the Middle East, North America, and Latin America.

Based in Westbrook, Maine, IDEXX has more than 50 reference laboratories throughout the US and over 25 reference laboratories internationally, including locations in Europe, Canada, Australia, New Zealand, Brazil, Asia, and South Africa.

Sales and Marketing

IDEXX distributes its products through its own marketing, customer service, sales, and technical service groups, as well as through independent distributors and other resellers.

Advertising costs were $3.3 million, $1.4 million, and $1.5 million for 2021, 2020, and 2019 respectively.

Financial Performance

The company had a total revenue of $3.2 billion in 2021, a 19% increase from the previous year's total revenue of $2.7 billion. The increase was primarily due to a higher volume of sales in both the company's product and service revenue.

In 2021, the company had a net income of $744.8 million, a 28% increase from the previous year's net income of $582.1 million. The company's net income increased despite the higher volumes of expenses, due to the higher sales volume for the year.

The company's cash at the end of 2021 was $144.5 million. Operating activities generated $755.5 million, while investing activities used $293 million, primarily for acquisitions of businesses, as well as purchases of property and equipment. Financing activities used another $697.4 million, mainly for repurchases of common stock.

Strategy

IDEXX' strategy consists of:

Developing, manufacturing, and marketing innovative new or improved and cost competitive in-clinic laboratory analyzers that drive sales of IDEXX VetLab instruments, grow its installed base of instruments, and increase demand for related recurring sales of consumable products, services, and accessories;

Developing and introducing new innovative diagnostic tests and services for both its reference laboratories and in-clinic applications that provide valuable medical information to customers and effectively differentiate products and services from those of its competitors;

Developing and introducing innovative, data-insightful software solutions that increase the value to customers of the company's companion animal products and services by enhancing the integration of the information and transactions of these products and the management of diagnostic information derived from its products;

Maintaining premium pricing, including by effectively implementing price increases, for its differentiated products and services through, among other things, effective communication and promotion of the value of products and services in an environment where many competitors promote, market, and sell lesser offerings at prices lower than the company's; as well as

Providing its veterinary customers with the medical and business tools, information, and resources that enable them to grow their practices and the utilization of the company's diagnostic products and services, through increased pet visits, use of preventive care protocols, enhanced practice of real-time care, and improved practice efficiency.

Mergers and Acquisitions

In 2021, IDEXX acquired New Zealand-based ezyVet, a fast-growing, innovative practice information management system (PIMS). With the acquisition, IDEXX further expands its world-class cloud software offerings that support customers with technology solutions that raise the standard of care for patients, improve practice efficiency, and enable more effective communication with pet owners.

HISTORY

David Shaw founded IDEXX in 1984 as AgriTech Systems. An MBA who had specialized in agribusiness consulting, Shaw wanted to cut the costs and time involved in lab testing for diseases by producing kits that could be used on-site; an initial line of poultry disease tests proved successful. The company changed its name to IDEXX in 1988 and went public in 1991.

In 1994 IDEXX acquired AMIS International, a leading Japanese test lab for veterinarians. The next year the company opened offices in Spain and the Netherlands and introduced the SNAP test, which detects allergies in dogs.

In 1997 IDEXX acquired two software companies, Advanced Veterinary Systems and Professionals Software, and merged them to create IDEXX Informatics. That year the firm also bought Acumedia Manufacturers, a producer of more than 300 varieties of dehydrated culture media. Looking to expand into animal drug development, the company bought animal health firm Blue Ridge Pharmaceuticals in 1998. In 2000, IDEXX sold Acumedia, as well as its food microbiology operations. It also launched VetConnect.com, which provides veterinary information and support and product sales.

In 2008 the company sold its veterinary pharmaceutical operations, which were miniscule, to focus on its core test kit and consumable business.

EXECUTIVES

President, Chief Executive Officer, Director, Jonathan J. Mazelsky, $555,385 total compensation

Executive Vice President, Chief Financial Officer, Treasurer, Brian P. McKeon, $570,577 total compensation

Executive Vice President, Division Officer, Tina Hunt

Executive Vice President, Division Officer, Michael J. Lane, $365,385 total compensation

Executive Vice President, Chief Commercial Officer, James F. Polewaczyk

Corporate Vice-President, Corporate Secretary, General Counsel, Sharon E. Underberg

Corporate Vice-President, Chief Human Resources Officer, Giovani Twigge, $379,308 total compensation

Corporate Vice-President, Chief Marketing Officer, Kathy V. Turner, $387,500 total compensation

Independent Non-Executive Chairman, Director, Lawrence D. Kingsley

Director, Sophie V. Vandebroek

Director, Stuart M. Essig

Director, Asha S. Collins

Director, M. Anne Szostak

Director, Bruce L. Claflin

Director, Daniel M. Junius

Director, Sam A. Samad

Auditors : PricewaterhouseCoopers LLP

LOCATIONS

HQ: Idexx Laboratories, Inc.
One IDEXX Drive, Westbrook, ME 04092
Phone: 207 556-0300 **Fax:** 207 856-0346
Web: www.idexx.com

2016 Sales

	$ mil.	% of total
Americas	1,203.4	68
Europe, the Middle East and Africa	375.8	21
Asia Pacific	196.2	11
Total	1,775.4	100

PRODUCTS/OPERATIONS

2016 Sales

	$ mil.	% of total
CAG	1,522.7	86
Water	103.6	6
LPD	126.5	7
Other	22.6	1
Total	1,775.4	100

2016 Sales

	$ mil.	% of total
Product	1,071.0	60
Service	704.4	40
Total	1,775.4	100

COMPETITORS

ABAXIS, INC.
AFFYMETRIX, INC.
FLUIDIGM CORPORATION
Fabrinet
HESKA CORPORATION
NEOGEN CORPORATION
PACIFIC BIOSCIENCES OF CALIFORNIA, INC.
SHIMADZU SCIENTIFIC INSTRUMENTS, INC.
STRATEC SE
THERMO FISHER SCIENTIFIC INC.

HISTORICAL FINANCIALS
Company Type: Public

Income Statement — FYE: December 31

	REVENUE ($mil)	NET INCOME ($mil)	NET PROFIT MARGIN	EMPLOYEES
12/21	3,215.3	744.8	23.2%	10,350
12/20	2,706.6	581.7	21.5%	9,300
12/19	2,406.9	427.7	17.8%	9,200
12/18	2,213.2	377.0	17.0%	8,377
12/17	1,969.0	263.1	13.4%	7,600
Annual Growth	13.0%	29.7%	—	8.0%

2021 Year-End Financials
Debt ratio: 37.9%
Return on equity: —
Cash ($ mil.): 144.4
Current Ratio: 1.25
Long-term debt ($ mil.): 775.2
No. of shares ($ mil.): 84.5
Dividends
 Yield: —
 Payout: —
Market value ($ mil.): 55,681.0

	STOCK PRICE ($) FY Close	P/E High	P/E Low	Earnings	Dividends	Book Value
12/21	658.46	81	53	8.60	0.00	8.16
12/20	499.87	73	27	6.71	0.00	7.40
12/19	261.13	58	36	4.89	0.00	2.08
12/18	186.02	59	36	4.26	0.00	(0.11)
12/17	156.38	57	39	2.94	0.00	(0.62)
Annual Growth	43.2%	—	—	30.8%	—	—

IES Holdings Inc

IES installs and maintains electrical and communications systems for residential, commercial, and industrial customers. Work on commercial buildings and homes includes custom design, construction, and maintenance on electrical and mechanical systems, such as intrusion and fire alarms, audio/video, and data network systems. IES performs electrical and mechanical systems construction and installation for industrial properties including office buildings, manufacturing facilities, data centers, chemical plants, municipal infrastructure, and health care facilities. Banking investor Jeffrey Gendell, through Tontine Capital Partners, owns 56% of IES.

Operations
IES operates its business through four segments -- Residential, Communications, Commercial and Industrial, and Infrastructure Solutions.

The residential segment provides electrical installation services to single-family housing and multi-family apartment complexes, as well as HVAC and plumbing installation services in certain markets, and cable television installations for residential and light commercial applications. The segment accounts for about 45% of total sales.

Its communications segment provides infrastructure for corporate data centers, as well as design, building, and maintenance of data network systems for audio/visual, telephone, fire, and alarm systems. The segment accounts for nearly 30% of total sales.

IES's commercial and industrial segment provides electrical and mechanical design, construction, and maintenance services for projects including power plants, data centers, chemical plants, wind farms, solar facilities, and office buildings. The segment accounts for more than 15% of total sales.

The company's infrastructure solutions segment provides electro-mechanical solutions for industrial operations to domestic and international customers. Its Custom Power Solutions business includes the manufacture of custom commercial and industrial generator enclosures and the manufacture of custom-engineered power distribution equipment, including metal enclosed bus duct solutions used in power distribution. Its Industrial Services business includes the maintenance and repair of alternating current (AC) and direct current (DC) electric motors and generators, as well as power generating and distribution equipment; the manufacture, re-manufacture, and repair of industrial lifting magnets; and maintenance and repair of railroad main and auxiliary generators, main alternators, and traction motors. The segment accounts for some 10% of total sales.

Geographic Reach
Houston, Texas-based IES maintains about 100 locations in the US. The company has about 50 locations that house its residential business activities (Texas, Sunbelt, Western, Northeastern, and Mid-Atlantic regions), about 20 locations for its commercial and industrial unit (in Texas, Nebraska, Oregon, Wisconsin, and the Southeast and Mid-Atlantic regions), about 15 locations for its Tempe, Arizona-based communications division, and ten locations for its infrastructure operations (covering Alabama, Georgia, Illinois, Indiana, Ohio, West Virginia, and is headquartered in Massillon, Ohio).

Sales and Marketing
IES' commercial and industrial and communications segments rely significantly on long-term, repeat business, which the company continues to cultivate. The majority of its customers for infrastructure services are located within a 200-mile radius of its facilities, allowing the company to quickly respond to repair requests. For the company's residential services, most of its single-family sales come from Texas, while most of its multifamily sales come from the Mid-Atlantic and Western states.

Financial Performance
IES' revenue has been rising in the last few years, with a 90% overall increase between 2017 and 2021. The company's net income follows a similar trend with the exception of the drop in 2018. Still, it has an overall growth of 398% between 2017 and 2021.

Consolidated revenues for the year ended September 30, 2021 were $345.6 million higher at $1.5 billion, compared to the year ended September 30, 2020, an increase of 29% with increases across all segments, driven by strong demand and the contribution of acquired businesses.

In 2021, the company had a net income of $68.7 million, a 69% increase from the previous year's net income of $40.1 million. This was mainly due to the higher sales volume in 2021.

The company's cash at the end of 2021 was $23.1 million. Operating activities generated $37.9 million, while investing activities used $100 million, primarily for cash paid in conjunction with business combinations or dispositions. Financing activities provided another $31.2 million.

Strategy
IES seeks to create shareholder value through improving operating margins and generating free cash flow by investing in its existing businesses and completing acquisitions. The company seeks to acquire businesses that strategically complement its existing business segments or to acquire or invest in stand-alone platform companies based in North America.

Company Background
Between its 1997 IPO and its 2011 transition to a holding company model, IES comprised a group of electrical contractors. Member companies included South Texas-based Bexar Electric, (which became a founding subsidiary of IES), South Carolina-based Davis Electrical Constructors, Virginia-based ARC Electric, Texas-based Houston-Stafford Electric, Nebraska-based Kayton Electric, and Arizona-based Federal Communication Group.

EXECUTIVES

Chief Executive Officer, Chairman, Director, Jeffrey L. Gendell

Senior Vice President, Chief Financial Officer, Treasurer, Tracy A. McLauchlin, $345,250 total compensation

Director, Todd M. Cleveland
Director, Joseph L. Dowling
Director, David B. Gendell
Director, Joe D. Koshkin
Director, Donald L. Luke
Auditors : Ernst & Young LLP

LOCATIONS

HQ: IES Holdings Inc
5433 Westheimer Road, Suite 500, Houston, TX 77056
Phone: 713 860-1500
Web: www.ies-corporate.com

PRODUCTS/OPERATIONS

2018 Sales

	$ mil.	% of total
Residential	285.7	33
Commercial & Industrial	274.3	31
Communications	219.6	25
Infrastructure Solutions	97.2	11
Total	876.8	100

Selected Services
Alarm & safety systems
Construction services
Design/build
Engineering services
Home standby generators
Solar installation
Structured cabling
Support services
Training resources

COMPETITORS
ABM INDUSTRIES INCORPORATED
AMERESCO, INC.
COMFORT SYSTEMS USA, INC.
EMCOR GROUP, INC.
FERGUSON ENTERPRISES, LLC
LARSEN AND TOUBRO LIMITED
PRIMORIS SERVICES CORPORATION
QUANTA SERVICES, INC.
SSE CONTRACTING LIMITED
SUNRUN INC.

HISTORICAL FINANCIALS
Company Type: Public

Income Statement — FYE: September 30

	REVENUE ($mil)	NET INCOME ($mil)	NET PROFIT MARGIN	EMPLOYEES
09/21	1,536.4	66.6	4.3%	6,845
09/20	1,190.8	41.5	3.5%	5,243
09/19	1,076.9	33.2	3.1%	5,389
09/18	876.8	(14.1)	—	4,564
09/17	810.7	13.4	1.7%	3,532
Annual Growth	17.3%	49.3%	—	18.0%

2021 Year-End Financials
Debt ratio: 5.2%
Return on equity: 21.1%
Cash ($ mil.): 23.1
Current Ratio: 1.55
Long-term debt ($ mil.): 39.7
No. of shares ($ mil.): 20.7
Dividends
  Yield: —
  Payout: —
Market value ($ mil.): 947.0

	STOCK PRICE ($) FY Close	P/E High/Low		PER SHARE ($) Earnings	Dividends	Book Value
09/21	45.69	17	10	3.15	0.00	16.69
09/20	31.77	18	7	1.94	0.00	13.65
09/19	20.59	13	10	1.55	0.00	11.63
09/18	19.50	—	—	(0.67)	0.00	10.39
09/17	17.30	36	23	0.62	0.00	11.09
Annual Growth	27.5%	—	—	50.1%	—	10.7%

II-VI Inc

II-VI develops, manufactures, and markets engineered materials, optoelectronic components, and devices for use in optical communications, industrial, aerospace and defense, consumer electronics, semiconductor capital equipment, life sciences, and automotive applications and markets. The company products are deployed in a variety of applications, including optical, data, and wireless communications products; laser cutting, welding, and marking operations; 3D sensing consumer applications; aerospace and defense applications including intelligence, surveillance, and reconnaissance; semiconductor processing tools; and thermoelectric cooling and power-generation solutions. Customers have included Coherent Inc., Nikon Corporation, Aurubis AG, and Apple Inc., among others. The North America is its largest market accounting for about 55% of sales.

Operations
The company operates two reporting segments: Photonic Solutions (over 65% of sales) and Compound Semiconductors (nearly 35%).

The Photonic Solutions Segment leverages II-VI's compound semiconductor technology platforms and deep knowledge of end-user applications for its key end markets to deliver differentiated components and subsystems. Its segment ncludes ROADM, transceivers, and advanced optics.

The Compound Semiconductors Segment is a market leader in engineered materials and optoelectronic devices such as those based on GaAs, InP, GaN, and SiC. Its segment include engineered materials and laser optics, laser devices and systems, new ventures & wide-bandgap electronics, and optoelectronic & RF devices.

Geographic Reach
Headquartered in Saxonburg, Pennsylvania, the North America is II-VI's largest market, accounting for about 55% of its sales. China and Europe generated about 20% each, Japan with around 5%, and the remaining were generated from the rest of the world.

The company has RD&E, manufacturing, and sales facilities located in about 15 US states, including Arizona, California, Colorado, Connecticut, and Texas, and its non-US production and RD&E operations are based in Australia, China, Germany, India, Malaysia, the Philippines, Singapore, Sweden, Switzerland, Thailand, the UK, and Vietnam. In addition to sales offices co-located at most of its manufacturing sites, it has sales and marketing subsidiaries in Belgium, Canada, China, Germany, Hong Kong, Italy, Japan, South Korea, Switzerland, Taiwan, and the UK, and, following the Coherent acquisition, in France, Israel, the Netherlands, and Spain.

Sales and Marketing
The company market its products through a direct sales force and through representatives and distributors around the world. Its customers in communications industry account for approximately two-thirds of its sales, while the industrial, consumer, aerospace and defense, and other industries account for the rest. Its photonic solutions customers include Ciena Corp., Alibaba Group, and Coherent Inc., among others, while compound semiconductor customers include Bystronic Laser AG, ASML Holding NV, Aurubis AG, Lockheed Martin Corporation, and more.

Financial Performance
The company reported a revenue of $3.3 billion, a 7% increase from the previous year's revenue of $3.1 billion. The biggest driver of increased revenue was strength in the communications market, which grew by 7% year-over-year, contributing an incremental $151 million in sales. The strength in the communications market was due to strong demand in datacom and transceivers, specifically for transceivers with data rates greater than 100G. In addition, semiconductor capital equipment sales grew 29% and industrial sales grew 26% compared to the same period last year, with an additional $34 million and $85 million in incremental revenue, respectively. This growth was partially offset by decreased revenue in the consumer market, which fell 20%, or $56 million, year-over-year due to lower sales in 3D sensing.

In 2021, the company had a net income of $166.5 million, a 36% decrease from the previous year's net income of $260.3 million. This was primarily due to the higher volume of total costs, expenses and other expenses for the year.

The company's cash at the end of 2022 was $2.6 billion. Operating activities generated $413.3 million, while investing activities used $320.1 million, mainly for additions to property, plant & equipment. Financing activities provided another $863 million.

Strategy
II-VI's strategy is to grow businesses with world-class engineered materials capabilities to advance its current customers' strategies, reach new markets through innovative technologies and platforms, and enable new applications in large and growing markets. A key strategy of the company is to develop and manufacture high-performance materials and, in certain cases, components incorporating those materials, that are differentiated from those produced by its competitors.

The company continues to grow the number and size of its key accounts. A significant portion of its business is based on sales orders with market leaders, which enables its forward planning and production efficiencies. The company intends to continue capitalizing and executing on this proven model, participating effectively in the growth of the markets discussed above, and continuing its focus on operational excellence as the company executes its primary business strategies.

Company Background

Electrical engineer Carl Johnson, who had worked at Bell Labs (now part of Alcatel-Lucent), among other companies, founded II-VI in 1971 to produce infrared optical materials for the emerging laser market. These materials -- including cadmium zinc telluride, zinc selenide, and zinc sulfide -- gave the company its name; they are from the "two-six" family of materials. (Cadmium and zinc are from column two on the periodic table; tellurium and selenium are from column six.)

By the 1980s II-VI was the leading maker of optical components for carbon dioxide lasers. The company went public in 1987 and the next year added a factory in Singapore.

HISTORY

Electrical engineer Carl Johnson, who had worked at Bell Labs (now part of Alcatel-Lucent), among other companies, founded II-VI in 1971 to produce infrared optical materials for the emerging laser market. These materials -- including cadmium zinc telluride, zinc selenide, and zinc sulfide -- gave the company its name; they are from the "two-six" family of materials. (Cadmium and zinc are from column two on the periodic table; tellurium and selenium are from column six.)

By the 1980s II-VI was the leading maker of optical components for carbon dioxide lasers. The company went public in 1987 and the next year added a factory in Singapore.

EXECUTIVES

Chairman Emeritus, Director, Francis J. Kramer, $142,120 total compensation

Chief Executive Officer, Chairman, Director, Vincent D. Mattera, $686,200 total compensation

President, Walter R. Bashaw

Business Development Chief Legal Officer, Business Development Chief Compliance Officer, Business Development Corporate Secretary, Ronald Basso

Chief Financial Officer, Treasurer, Mary Jane Raymond, $399,300 total compensation

Chief Strategy Officer, Division Officer, Giovanni Barbarossa, $412,000 total compensation

Chief Technology Officer, Christopher Koeppen

Director, Stephen A. Skaggs

Director, Sandeep S. Vij

Director, Lisa Neal-Graves

Director, Stephen G. Pagliuca

Director, David L. Motley

Director, Michael L. Dreyer

Director, Howard H. Xia

Director, Enrico Digirolamo

Director, Shaker Sadasivam

Director, Joseph J. Corasanti

Director, Patricia Hatter

Auditors: Ernst & Young LLP

LOCATIONS

HQ: II-VI Inc
375 Saxonburg Boulevard, Saxonburg, PA 16056
Phone: 724 352-4455
Web: www.ii-vi.com

2015 Sales Chart

	$ in mils	% of total
Domestic	274.1	37
International	467.8	63
Total	741.9	100

2015 Sales Chart

	$ in mils	% of total
United States	242	32
China	140.6	19
Hong Kong	109.5	15
Germany	77.6	10
Switzerland	56.9	8
Japan	52.9	7
Vietnam	24.3	3
Philippines	11.4	2
Italy	9.3	1
United Kingdom	7.8	1
Belgium	5.7	1
Singapore	3.9	1
Total	741.9	100

Selected Production Operations

US
- California
- Connecticut
- Delaware
- Florida
- Massachusetts
- Mississippi
- New Jersey
- Pennsylvania
- Texas

International
- Australia
- China
- Germany
- Philippines
- Singapore
- Vietnam

PRODUCTS/OPERATIONS

2015 Sales Chart

	$ in mils	% of total
II-VI Laser Solutions	287.9	39
II-VI Photonics	260.8	35
II-VI Performance Products	193.2	26
Total	741.9	100

Selected Business Segments

dvanced Materials Development Center (AMDC)
AOFR
Aegis Lightwave
HIGHYAG Lasertechnologie
LightWorks Optical Systems
M Cubed
Marlow Industries
Max Levy Autograph
Photop Technologies
Pacific Rare Specialty Metals & Chemicals (PRM)
Wide Bandgap Materials Group

Selected Products

Beam expanders
Beam splitters
Detectors
Etalons
Infrared and near-infrared optics
Laser crystals
    Clear yttrium aluminum garnet (YAG) laser crystals
    Custom crystals and fluorides
    Machined and polished laser rods
    Monolithic crystal assemblies (MCA)
    Neodymium doped YAG
Non-linear crystals
Oxide laser crystal products
Ruby laser crystals
Laser gain materials
Lenses
Military infrared optics
Mirrors
Modulators
One micron laser
Optical assemblies
Optical coatings
Output windows
Partial reflectors
Phase retarders
Polarization devices
Prisms
Rhombs
Selenium metal (material processing and refinement)
Silicon carbide substrates (SiC)
Solid-state laser optics and optical cavities
Substrates
Tellurium metal (material processing and refinement)
Thermo-electric coolers
Wave plates

COMPETITORS

APPLIED MATERIALS, INC.
CYBEROPTICS CORPORATION
EXFO Inc
GOOCH & HOUSEGO PLC
KLA CORPORATION
LUMIBIRD
PORVAIR PLC
TEXAS INSTRUMENTS INCORPORATED
VEECO INSTRUMENTS INC.
ZYGO CORPORATION

HISTORICAL FINANCIALS

Company Type: Public

Income Statement — FYE: June 30

	REVENUE ($mil)	NET INCOME ($mil)	NET PROFIT MARGIN	EMPLOYEES
06/21	3,105.8	297.5	9.6%	23,000
06/20	2,380.0	(67.0)	—	22,969
06/19	1,362.4	107.5	7.9%	12,487
06/18	1,158.7	88.0	7.6%	11,443
06/17	972.0	95.2	9.8%	10,349
Annual Growth	33.7%	32.9%	—	22.1%

2021 Year-End Financials

Debt ratio: 21.1%
Return on equity: 9.5%
Cash ($ mil.): 1,591.8
Current Ratio: 4.15
Long-term debt ($ mil.): 1,313
No. of shares ($ mil.): 105.4
Dividends
  Yield: —
  Payout: —
Market value ($ mil.): 7,657.0

	STOCK PRICE ($) FY Close	P/E High/Low		PER SHARE ($) Earnings	Dividends	Book Value
06/21	72.59	40	15	2.37	0.00	39.17
06/20	47.22	—	—	(0.79)	0.00	22.44
06/19	36.56	30	18	1.63	0.00	17.79
06/18	43.45	38	24	1.35	0.00	16.18
06/17	34.30	26	12	1.48	0.00	14.26
Annual Growth	20.6%	—		12.5%	—	28.7%

Incyte Corporation

Incyte is a biopharmaceutical company focused on the discovery, development and commercialization of proprietary therapeutics. It is focused on developing and selling drugs that inhibit specific enzymes associated with cancer and other diseases. The company's lead program is its JAK (Janus associated kinase) inhibitor program. Its first commercial product, JAKAFI, is approved for treatment of polycythemia vera and myelofibrosis (two rare blood cancers) and graft-versus-host-disease in the US; partner Novartis markets the drug internationally. Another inhibitor drug, Iclusig, is marketed for certain forms of leukemia in Europe.

Operations

Incyte operates in two therapeutic areas that are defined by the indications of its approved medicines and the diseases for which its clinical candidates are being developed. One therapeutic area is Hematology/Oncology, which is comprised of Myeloproliferative Neoplasms (MPNs), Graft-Versus-Host Disease (GVHD), as well as solid tumors and hematologic malignancies. The other therapeutic area is Inflammation and Autoimmunity (IAI), which includes its newly established Dermatology commercial franchise. It is also eligible to receive milestones and royalties on molecules discovered by us and licensed to third parties.

The hematology and oncology franchise is comprised of four approved products, which are JAKAFI (ruxolitinib), MONJUVI (tafasitamab-cxix)/MINJUVI (tafasitamab), PEMAZYRE (pemigatinib) and ICLUSIG (ponatinib), as well as numerous clinical development programs.

Incyte Dermatology launched its first approved product, OPZELURA (ruxolitinib) cream, in October 2021, following FDA approval in September 2021. Incyte's IAI efforts also include numerous clinical development programs.

Its products accounts for less than 80% of total revenue, royalties for about 20%, and milestone and contract revenue accounts for the remainder.

Geographic Reach

Incyte's global headquarters is in Wilmington, Delaware, where it conducts its global clinical development and commercial operations. It leases approximately 112,000 square feet of office space in Chadds Ford, Pennsylvania and approximately 84,000 square feet of additional laboratory and office space in Wilmington, Delaware.

The company also conducts its clinical development and commercial operations from its European headquarters in Morges, Switzerland and its Japanese office in Tokyo. Its Canadian office is in Montreal.

Sales and Marketing

JAKAFI is marketed in the US through its own specialty sales force and commercial team. It distributed primarily through a network of specialty pharmacy providers and wholesalers which allows to deliver the medication by mail directly to patients or directly deliver to the patient's pharmacy. The distribution process uses a model that is well-established and familiar to physicians who practice within the oncology field.

Financial Performance

The company's revenue for fiscal 2021 increased to $3.0 billion compared from the prior year with $2.7 billion.

Incyte recorded net income for the year ended December 31, 2021 of $948.6 million and net loss for the year ended December 31, 2020 of $295.7 million.

Cash held by the company at the end of fiscal 2021 increased to $2.1 billion. Cash provided by operations and financing activities were $749.5 million and $6.2 million, respectively. Cash used for investing activities was $207.7 million, mainly for purchases of marketable securities.

Strategy

The company's strategy is to develop and commercialize compounds that the company have internally discovered or have acquired rights to in the markets where it believe that a company of its size can successfully compete. Incyte currently commercialize four compounds in the United States, three in Europe and one in Japan.

HISTORY

British entrepreneur Roy Whitfield and researcher Randal Scott met in 1989 while working for Invitron, a biotech company that soon went under. They founded Incyte Pharmaceuticals in 1991 to design, develop, and market genomic database products, software tools, and related services.

The company went public in 1993, and in 1994 Pfizer became its first gene expression database subscriber. Two years later Incyte bought gene-mapping firms Genome Systems and Combion. The firm opened an office in Cambridge, UK, and formed joint venture diaDexus with SmithKline Beecham (now GlaxoSmithKline) to create and market diagnostic tests that use genetic data to develop effective drug reagents and services.

In 1998 the firm bought microarray maker Synteni. It made its own attempt to map the human genome using LifeSeq, buying British firm Hexagen for the mapping unit. Two years later, diaDexus filed an IPO, and the company changed its name to Incyte Genomics to reflect its focus. The name change, however, seemed shortsighted when, in 2001, the firm announced plans to become a drug developer. It even teamed with one-time rival Agilent to share DNA microarray technologies.

In 2003 the company made another name change -- this time simply to "Incyte Corporation" -- to represent its growing focus on drug development. As part of that focus, that year Incyte acquired the rights to Reverset in 2003 through a licensing agreement with Pharmasset. It launched its janus associated kinase (JAK) research program that year.

In 2004, the company transitioned away from its former business -- providing access to its genomic database and set of patents. In that year Incyte closed its Palo Alto, California, research facilities and headquarters. It also terminated further development of its information products, including LifeSeq -- a library of information and expressed sequences that links biological information analysis with proprietary genetic information to aid drug discovery. In addition to closing the Palo Alto office, the company reduced its workforce by more than 50%.

Following the transition, a leading product candidate for the company was dexelvucitabine (also known as Reverset) to treat patients with HIV, but clinical trials were discontinued in 2006. In 2008 it also halted development on a CCR5 antagonist designed to prevent the entry of HIV into target cells.

Incyte gained FDA approval to market Jakafi for several types of myelofibrosis in the US market in November 2011, and the company launched the drug shortly after. The drug also gained approval for myelofibrosis treatment in the European Union in 2012 (through a partnership with Novartis). Jakafi gained approval in December 2014 for the treatment of certain forms of polycythemia vera.

EXECUTIVES

Chairman, President, Chief Executive Officer, Director, Herve Hoppenot, $995,575 total compensation

Executive Vice President, Region Officer, Barry P. Flannelly

Corporate Development Executive Vice President, Global Strategy Executive Vice President, Vijay K. Iyengar

Executive Vice President, Chief Financial Officer, Christiana Stamoulis

Executive Vice President, Chief Medical Officer, Steven H. Stein, $522,123 total compensation

Finance Vice President, Finance Chief Accounting Officer, Finance Principal Accounting Officer, Thomas Tray

Lead Independent Director, Director, Julian C. Baker, $37,000 total compensation

Director, Jean-Jacques Bienaime

Director, Paul J. Clancy

Director, Wendy L. Dixon

Director, Jacqualyn A. Fouse

Director, Edmund P. Harrigan

Director, Katherine A. High

Director, Otis W. Brawley

Auditors : Ernst & Young LLP

LOCATIONS

HQ: Incyte Corporation
1801 Augustine Cut-Off, Wilmington, DE 19803
Phone: 302 498-6700
Web: www.incyte.com

PRODUCTS/OPERATIONS

2016 Sales

	$ mil.	% of total
Product revenues, net	882.4	80
Product royalty revenues	110.7	10
Contract revenues	112.6	10
Other revenues	0.092	-
Total	1,105.7	100

COMPETITORS

ALNYLAM PHARMACEUTICALS, INC.
CELLDEX THERAPEUTICS, INC.
DYAX CORP.
EXELIXIS, INC.
LEXICON PHARMACEUTICALS, INC.
LIGAND PHARMACEUTICALS INCORPORATED
MEDIVATION, INC.
ONYX PHARMACEUTICALS, INC.
PROGENICS PHARMACEUTICALS, INC.
VERTEX PHARMACEUTICALS INCORPORATED

HISTORICAL FINANCIALS
Company Type: Public

Income Statement				FYE: December 31
	REVENUE ($mil)	NET INCOME ($mil)	NET PROFIT MARGIN	EMPLOYEES
12/21	2,986.2	948.5	31.8%	2,094
12/20	2,666.7	(295.6)	—	1,773
12/19	2,158.7	446.9	20.7%	1,456
12/18	1,881.8	109.4	5.8%	1,367
12/17	1,536.2	(313.1)	—	1,208
Annual Growth	18.1%	—	—	14.7%

2021 Year-End Financials
Debt ratio: 0.7%
Return on equity: 29.7%
Cash ($ mil.): 2,057.4
Current Ratio: 3.65
Long-term debt ($ mil.): 31.6
No. of shares ($ mil.): 221.0
Dividends
 Yield: —
 Payout: —
Market value ($ mil.): 16,228.0

	STOCK PRICE ($) FY Close	P/E High/Low		PER SHARE ($)		
				Earnings	Dividends	Book Value
12/21	73.40	23	15	4.27	0.00	17.05
12/20	86.98	—	—	(1.36)	0.00	11.90
12/19	87.32	46	31	2.05	0.00	12.02
12/18	63.59	194	113	0.51	0.00	9.03
12/17	94.71	—	—	(1.53)	0.00	7.72
Annual Growth	(6.2%)	—	—	—	—	21.9%

Independence Realty Trust Inc

EXECUTIVES

Chief Executive Officer, Chairman, Director, Scott F. Schaeffer, $700,000 total compensation
President, Farrell M. Ender, $400,000 total compensation
Executive Vice President, Chief Legal Officer, General Counsel, Secretary, Jessica K. Norman
Chief Financial Officer, Treasurer, James J. Sebra, $400,000 total compensation
Chief Accounting Officer, Controller, Jason R. Delozier
Director, Melinda H. McClure
Director, Richard D. Gebert
Director, DeForest Blake Soaries
Director, Lisa Washington
Director, Stephen R. Bowie
Director, Ned W. Brines
Director, Ana Marie del Rio
Director, Thomas H. Purcell
Auditors : KPMG LLP

LOCATIONS
HQ: Independence Realty Trust Inc
  1835 Market Street, Suite 2601, Philadelphia, PA 19103
Phone: 267 270-4800
Web: www.irtliving.com

HISTORICAL FINANCIALS
Company Type: Public

Income Statement				FYE: December 31
	REVENUE ($mil)	NET INCOME ($mil)	NET PROFIT MARGIN	EMPLOYEES
12/20	211.9	14.7	7.0%	444
12/19	203.2	45.8	22.6%	444
12/18	191.2	26.2	13.7%	455
12/17	161.2	30.2	18.7%	421
12/16	153.3	(9.8)	—	395
Annual Growth	8.4%	—	—	3.0%

2020 Year-End Financials
Debt ratio: 54.5%
Return on equity: 2.2%
Cash ($ mil.): 8.7
Current Ratio: 0.34
Long-term debt ($ mil.): 945.6
No. of shares ($ mil.): 101.8
Dividends
 Yield: 4.0%
 Payout: 192.8%
Market value ($ mil.): 1,367.0

	STOCK PRICE ($) FY Close	P/E High/Low		PER SHARE ($)		
				Earnings	Dividends	Book Value
12/20	13.43	103	44	0.16	0.54	6.96
12/19	14.08	30	18	0.51	0.72	6.73
12/18	9.18	35	28	0.30	0.72	6.99
12/17	10.09	26	21	0.41	0.72	7.37
12/16	8.92	—	—	(0.19)	0.72	7.35
Annual Growth	10.8%	—	—	—	(6.9%)	(1.4%)

Independent Bank Corp (MA)

Independent Bank is a state chartered, federally registered bank holding company. The company is the sole stockholder of Rockland Trust Company ("Rockland Trust"or the "Bank"). Its banking subsidiary, Rockland Trust, operates almost 95 retail branches as well two limited service branches located in Barnstable, Bristol, Dukes, and more in Eastern Massachusetts.Serving area consumers and small to midsized businesses, the bank offers standard services such as checking and savings accounts, CDs, and credit cards, in addition to insurance products, financial planning, trust services. Commercial loans, including industrial, construction, and small business loans. Incorporated in 1985, the bank boasts total assets of some $13.2 billion.

EXECUTIVES

Chairman, Subsidiary Officer, Director, Donna L. Abelli
President, Chief Executive Officer, Director, Jeffrey (Jeff) J. Tengel
Subsidiary Officer, Director, Gerard (Gerry) F. Nadeau, $419,231 total compensation
Executive Vice President, Chief Operating Officer, Subsidiary Officer, Robert D. Cozzone, $400,866 total compensation
Executive Vice President, Chief Technology Officer, Chief Operations Officer, Subsidiary Officer, Barry H. Jensen, $304,538 total compensation
Senior Vice President, Chief Financial Officer, Controller, Principal Accounting Officer, Subsidiary Officer, Mark J. Ruggiero
Senior Vice President, Controller, Principal Accounting Officer, Subsidiary Officer, Maureen A. Gaffney
General Counsel, Subsidiary Officer, Edward H. Seksay, $327,231 total compensation
Deputy General Counsel, Corporate Secretary, Patricia M. Natale
Subsidiary Officer, Maria Harris
Director, Michael P. Hogan
Director, Eileen C. Miskell
Director, Susan Perry O'Day
Director, Thomas R. Venables
Director, James O'Shanna Morton
Director, Daniel F. O'Brien
Director, Christopher Oddleifson, $739,231 total compensation
Director, Scott K. Smith
Director, Mary L. Lentz
Director, John J. Morrissey
Auditors : Ernst & Young LLP

LOCATIONS
HQ: Independent Bank Corp (MA)
  2036 Washington Street, Hanover, MA 02339
Phone: 781 878-6100
Web: www.rocklandtrust.com

PRODUCTS/OPERATIONS

2012 Sales

	$ mil.	% of total
Interest		
Loans	178.3	69
Taxable securities, including dividends	16.7	6
Other	1.0	-
Noninterest		
Service charges on deposit accounts	16.	6
Wealth management	14.8	6
Interchange & ATM fees	9.8	4
Other	21.7	9
Adjustments	(0.1)	-
Total	258.2	100

COMPETITORS

ASSOCIATED BANC-CORP
BANCFIRST CORPORATION
BOKF MERGER CORPORATION NUMBER SIXTEEN
CAMBRIDGE BANCORP
CENTRAL PACIFIC FINANCIAL CORP.
CENTURY BANCORP, INC.
CITY HOLDING COMPANY

FIRSTMERIT CORPORATION
STOCK YARDS BANCORP, INC.
UNIVEST FINANCIAL CORPORATION

HISTORICAL FINANCIALS
Company Type: Public

Income Statement — FYE: December 31

	ASSETS ($mil)	NET INCOME ($mil)	INCOME AS % OF ASSETS	EMPLOYEES
12/20	13,204.3	121.1	0.9%	1,375
12/19	11,395.1	165.1	1.4%	1,348
12/18	8,851.5	121.6	1.4%	1,188
12/17	8,082.0	87.2	1.1%	1,108
12/16	7,709.3	76.6	1.0%	1,103
Annual Growth	14.4%	12.1%	—	5.7%

2020 Year-End Financials
Return on assets: 0.9%
Return on equity: 7.0%
Long-term debt ($ mil.): —
No. of shares ($ mil.): 32.9
Sales ($ mil.): 512.8
Dividends
Yield: 2.5%
Payout: 50.5%
Market value ($ mil.): 2,408.0

	STOCK PRICE ($) FY Close	P/E High/Low		PER SHARE ($) Earnings	Dividends	Book Value
12/20	73.04	23	14	3.64	1.84	51.65
12/19	83.25	17	13	5.03	1.76	49.69
12/18	70.31	21	15	4.40	1.52	38.23
12/17	69.85	24	19	3.19	1.28	34.38
12/16	70.45	24	14	2.90	1.16	32.02
Annual Growth	0.9%	—	—	5.8%	12.2%	12.7%

Independent Bank Corporation (Ionia, MI)

Independent Bank Corporation is the holding company for Independent Bank, which serves rural and suburban communities of Michigan's Lower Peninsula from more than 100 branches. The bank offers traditional deposit products, including checking and savings accounts and CDs. Loans to businesses account for about 40% of the bank's portfolio; real estate mortgages are more than a third. Independent Bank also offers additional products and services like title insurance through subsidiary Independent Title Services, and investments through agreement with third-party provider PrimeVest.

Operations
The company also owns Mepco Finance, which acquires and services payment plans for extended automobile warranties.

Financial Performance
The company's revenue has been trending down year-over-year. However, its net income and cash on hand have both been spiking up across recent fiscal years.

Strategy
As Michigan's economy has exhibited signs of stabilizing, and the company's results have relatively improved, as well. Independent Bank has reduced its number of high-risk loans, non-performing loans, and delinquency rates.

EXECUTIVES

Executive Chairman, Subsidiary Officer, Director, Michael M. Magee, $582,000 total compensation
President, Chief Executive Officer, Chief Operating Officer, Subsidiary Officer, Director, William B. (Brad) Kessel, $480,000 total compensation
Executive Vice President, General Counsel, Mark L. Collins, $246,500 total compensation
Executive Vice President, Chief Financial Officer, Gavin A. Mohr
Mortgage Banking Executive Vice President, Patrick J. Ervin, $232,500 total compensation
Executive Vice President, Chief Risk Officer, Stefani M. Kimball, $258,700 total compensation
Executive Vice President, Chief Lending Officer, Dennis J. Mack, $258,700 total compensation
Executive Vice President, Subsidiary Officer, David C. Reglin, $243,600 total compensation
Human Resources Senior Vice President, Laurinda M. Neve
Internal Auditor Senior Vice President, Charles F. Schadler
Controller Senior Vice President, James J. Twarozynski
Operations Senior Vice President, Richard E. Butler
Commercial Loans Independent Senior Vice President, Peter R. Graves
Director, Charles C. Van Loan, $23,500 total compensation
Director, Dennis W. Archer
Director, Joan A. Budden
Director, Ronia F. Kruse
Director, Michael J. Cok
Director, Terance L. Beia
Director, Christina L. Keller
Director, William J. Boer
Director, Stephen L. Gulis, $22,000 total compensation
Director, Matthew J. Missad
Auditors: Crowe LLP

LOCATIONS

HQ: Independent Bank Corporation (Ionia, MI)
4200 East Beltline, Grand Rapids, MI 49525
Phone: 616 527-5820
Web: www.independentbank.com

COMPETITORS

BANCFIRST CORPORATION
EAGLE BANCORP, INC.
GUARANTY BANCORP
SIGNATURE BANK
WASHINGTON FEDERAL, INC.

HISTORICAL FINANCIALS
Company Type: Public

Income Statement — FYE: December 31

	ASSETS ($mil)	NET INCOME ($mil)	INCOME AS % OF ASSETS	EMPLOYEES
12/20	4,204.0	56.1	1.3%	983
12/19	3,564.6	46.4	1.3%	994
12/18	3,353.2	39.8	1.2%	976
12/17	2,789.3	20.4	0.7%	911
12/16	2,548.9	22.7	0.9%	885
Annual Growth	13.3%	25.3%	—	2.7%

2020 Year-End Financials
Return on assets: 1.4%
Return on equity: 15.1%
Long-term debt ($ mil.): —
No. of shares ($ mil.): 21.8
Sales ($ mil.): 220.5
Dividends
Yield: 4.3%
Payout: 33.7%
Market value ($ mil.): 404.0

	STOCK PRICE ($) FY Close	P/E High/Low		PER SHARE ($) Earnings	Dividends	Book Value
12/20	18.47	9	4	2.53	0.80	17.82
12/19	22.65	12	9	2.00	0.72	15.58
12/18	21.02	16	12	1.68	0.60	14.38
12/17	22.35	24	20	0.95	0.42	12.42
12/16	21.70	21	13	1.05	0.34	11.71
Annual Growth	(3.9%)	—	—	24.6%	23.9%	11.1%

Independent Bank Group Inc.

The bank holding company, Independent Bank Group does business through subsidiary Independent Bank, which operates about 95 full-services branches, which more than 70 of these branches are company-owned. The company operates in the Dallas/North Texas area, Austin/Central Texas Area, and the Houston Texas metropolitan area. The banks offer standard personal and business accounts and services including some focused on small business owners. IBG has total assets of more than $18.7 billion and loans of about $12.3 billion. The company traces its roots back 100 years but took its current shape in 2002.

IPO

Operations
The company's community banking services includes lending operations which offers a broad range of commercial and retail lending products to businesses, professionals and individuals. Commercial lending products include owner-occupied commercial real estate loans, interim construction loans, commercial loans to a diversified mix of small and midsized businesses, and loans to professionals, including medical practices. Retail lending products include residential first and second mortgage loans and consumer installment loans, such as loans to purchase cars, boats and other recreational vehicles. It also provides a full range of deposit products and services, including a variety of

checking and savings accounts, debit cards, online banking, including online account opening, mobile banking, eStatements and bank-by-mail and direct deposit services. Other services include residential mortgages through the mortgage brokerage division, as well as wealth management services to its customers through Private Capital Management, LLC, a registered investment advisory firm, which is a wholly owned subsidiary of the bank.

The company's portfolio is segmented into categories which includes: commercial real estate loans (about 55%), commercial loans (some 15% of company's loan portfolio), residential real estate loans (around 10%), construction, land & land development (about 10%), mortgage warehouse purchase loans (some 5%), consumer loans, and agricultural loans.

It generates about 85% of sales from interest and fees on loans.

Geographic Reach
Based in McKinney, Texas, Independent Bank has branches in the Dallas/North Texas area, including McKinney, Dallas, Fort Worth, and Sherman/Denison, the Austin/Central Texas area, including Austin and Waco, the Houston Texas metropolitan area and along the Colorado Front Range area, including Denver, Colorado Springs and Fort Collins.

Financial Performance
The company earned net interest income of $520.3 million for the year ended December 31, 2021, an increase of $3.9 million, or 0.8%, from $516.4 million for the year ended December 31, 2020. The slight increase in net interest income from the previous year was driven by overall decreased funding costs for the year.

The company's net income available to common shareholders increased by $23.5 million, or 12%, to $224.8 million for the year ended December 31, 2021, from $201.2 million for the year ended December 31, 2020. The increase in net income for 2021 over 2020 was primarily due to the $52 million decrease in provision for credit losses, as well as the $3.9 million increase in net interest income.

The company's cash at the end of 2021 was $10.7 million. Operating activities generated $123.8 million, while financing activities used $118.5 million, mainly for repayments of borrowings.

Strategy
Independent Bank operates based upon the following core strategies, which the company designed to enhance shareholder value by growing strategically while preserving asset quality, improving efficiency and increasing profitability:

Grow organically. The company focuses on continued organic growth through its existing footprint and business lines. The company utilizes a community-focused, relationship-driven customer strategy to increase loans and deposits through its existing locations. Preserving the safety and soundness of its loan portfolio is a fundamental element of the company's organic growth strategy.

Grow through acquisitions. The company plans to continue to take advantage of opportunities to acquire or strategically partner with other banking franchises both within and outside its current footprint. Since mid-2010, the company has completed twelve acquisitions that it believes has enhanced shareholder value and the company's market presence.

EXECUTIVES

Chairman, Chief Executive Officer, Director, David R. Brooks, $725,000 total compensation
Vice-Chairman, Director, Daniel W. Brooks, $425,000 total compensation
President, Chief Operating Officer, Subsidiary Officer, Michael B. Hobbs
Executive Vice President, Chief Risk Officer, John G. Turpen
Corporate Responsibility Executive Vice President, Corporate Responsibility Subsidiary Officer, James P. Tippit
Executive Vice President, Chief Operations Officer, Subsidiary Officer, James C. White, $310,000 total compensation
Executive Vice President, General Counsel, Subsidiary Officer, Mark S. Haynie
Executive Vice President, Chief Financial Officer, Subsidiary Officer, Paul B. Langdale
Corporate Secretary, Subsidiary Officer, Nicole Metcalf
Director, Alicia K Harrison
Director, John Webb Jennings
Director, Paul E. Washington
Director, William E. Fair
Director, Craig E. Holmes
Director, Donald L. Poarch
Director, G. Stacy Smith
Director, Michael T. Viola
Auditors: RSM US LLP

LOCATIONS

HQ: Independent Bank Group Inc.
7777 Henneman Way, McKinney, TX 75070-1711
Phone: 972 562-9004
Web: www.ibtx.com

PRODUCTS/OPERATIONS

2012 Loan Portfolio

	% of total
Real estate	
Commercial	47
Residential	23
Construction, land & land development	7
Single-family interim construction	5
Commercial	12
Agricultural	3
Consumer	3
Total	100

Selected Acquisition
Town Center Bank (2010, North Texas)
Farmersville Bancshares, Inc. (2010, North Texas)
I Bank Holding Company, Inc. (2012, Austin/Central Texas)
The Community Group, Inc. (2012, Dallas/North Texas)

COMPETITORS

BANK OF THE WEST
BANKUNITED, INC.
CIT GROUP INC.
CITIZENS FINANCIAL GROUP, INC.
HERITAGE FINANCIAL CORPORATION
HILLTOP HOLDINGS INC.
M&T BANK CORPORATION
PEOPLE'S UNITED FINANCIAL, INC.
REGIONS FINANCIAL CORPORATION
SUNTRUST BANKS, INC.

HISTORICAL FINANCIALS
Company Type: Public

Income Statement				FYE: December 31
	ASSETS ($mil)	NET INCOME ($mil)	INCOME AS % OF ASSETS	EMPLOYEES
12/20	17,753.4	201.2	1.1%	1,513
12/19	14,958.2	192.7	1.3%	1,469
12/18	9,849.9	128.2	1.3%	1,087
12/17	8,684.4	76.5	0.9%	924
12/16	5,852.8	53.5	0.9%	577
Annual Growth	32.0%	39.2%	—	27.3%

2020 Year-End Financials
Return on assets: 1.2%
Return on equity: 8.2%
Long-term debt ($ mil.): —
No. of shares ($ mil.): 43.1
Sales ($ mil.): 696.5
Dividends
Yield: 1.6%
Payout: 23.3%
Market value ($ mil.): 2,697.0

	STOCK PRICE ($) FY Close	P/E High/Low		PER SHARE ($)		
				Earnings	Dividends	Book Value
12/20	62.52	13	4	4.67	1.05	58.31
12/19	55.44	14	11	4.46	1.00	54.48
12/18	45.77	18	10	4.33	0.54	52.50
12/17	67.60	24	18	2.97	0.40	47.28
12/16	62.40	22	9	2.88	0.34	35.63
Annual Growth	0.0%	—	—	12.8%	32.6%	13.1%

Industrial Logistics Properties Trust

EXECUTIVES

President, Chief Financial Officer, Managing Trustee, John G. Murray
Vice President, Yael Duffy
Chief Financial Officer, Treasurer, Richard W. Siedel
Managing Trustee, Adam D. Portnoy
Trustee, Lisa Harris Jones
Trustee, Bruce M. Gans
Trustee, Joseph L. Morea
Director, Kevin C. Phelan
Director, Laura Wilkin
Auditors: DELOITTE & TOUCHE LLP

LOCATIONS

HQ: Industrial Logistics Properties Trust
Two Newton Place, 255 Washington Street, Suite 300, Newton, MA 02458-1634

Phone: 617 219-1460

HISTORICAL FINANCIALS
Company Type: Public

Income Statement   FYE: December 31

	REVENUE ($mil)	NET INCOME ($mil)	NET PROFIT MARGIN	EMPLOYEES
12/21	219.8	119.6	54.4%	0
12/20	254.5	82.0	32.2%	0
12/19	229.2	52.4	22.9%	0
12/18	162.5	74.3	45.8%	0
12/17	156.5	80.1	51.2%	0
Annual Growth	8.9%	10.6%	—	—

2021 Year-End Financials
Debt ratio: 43.4%
Return on equity: 11.7%
Cash ($ mil.): 29.4
Current Ratio: 3.51
Long-term debt ($ mil.): 828.1
No. of shares ($ mil.): 65.4
Dividends
 Yield: 5.2%
 Payout: 88.5%
Market value ($ mil.): 1,638.0

	STOCK PRICE ($) FY Close	P/E High	P/E Low	Earnings	Dividends	Book Value
12/21	25.05	16	12	1.83	1.32	15.87
12/20	23.29	19	11	1.26	1.32	15.36
12/19	22.42	28	23	0.81	1.32	15.28
12/18	19.67	21	16	1.16	0.93	15.80
Annual Growth	8.4%	—	—	16.4%	12.4%	0.1%

HISTORICAL FINANCIALS
Company Type: Public

Income Statement   FYE: December 31

	REVENUE ($mil)	NET INCOME ($mil)	NET PROFIT MARGIN	EMPLOYEES
12/20	97.3	17.3	17.8%	292
12/19	81.1	1.3	1.7%	269
12/18	67.1	(1.0)	—	251
12/17	71.0	(20.7)	—	245
12/16	70.4	(0.2)	—	250
Annual Growth	8.4%	—	—	4.0%

2020 Year-End Financials
Debt ratio: 40.0%
Return on equity: 54.7%
Cash ($ mil.): 9.6
Current Ratio: 1.29
Long-term debt ($ mil.): 29.3
No. of shares ($ mil.): 20.3
Dividends
 Yield: —
 Payout: —
Market value ($ mil.): 381.0

	STOCK PRICE ($) FY Close	P/E High	P/E Low	Earnings	Dividends	Book Value
12/20	18.78	23	7	0.80	0.00	2.01
12/19	8.53	123	49	0.07	0.00	1.12
12/18	3.44	—	—	(0.05)	0.00	1.04
12/17	2.30	—	—	(0.91)	0.00	1.36
12/16	2.55	—	—	(0.01)	0.00	2.24
Annual Growth	64.7%	—	—	—	—	(2.7%)

HISTORICAL FINANCIALS
Company Type: Public

Income Statement   FYE: December 31

	REVENUE ($mil)	NET INCOME ($mil)	NET PROFIT MARGIN	EMPLOYEES
12/20	116.8	65.7	56.2%	15
12/19	44.6	23.4	52.6%	13
12/18	14.7	6.9	47.2%	6
12/17	6.4	(0.0)	—	6
12/16	0.3	(4.3)	—	5
Annual Growth	336.8%	—	—	31.6%

2020 Year-End Financials
Debt ratio: 7.7%
Return on equity: 6.3%
Cash ($ mil.): 126.0
Current Ratio: 1.77
Long-term debt ($ mil.): 136.6
No. of shares ($ mil.): 23.9
Dividends
 Yield: 2.4%
 Payout: 136.6%
Market value ($ mil.): 4,384.0

	STOCK PRICE ($) FY Close	P/E High	P/E Low	Earnings	Dividends	Book Value
12/20	183.13	60	14	3.27	4.47	63.71
12/19	75.87	67	22	2.03	2.83	43.37
12/18	45.39	72	32	0.75	1.20	27.04
12/17	32.31	—	—	(0.13)	0.55	21.01
12/16	18.19	—	—	(4.56)	0.00	17.69
Annual Growth	78.1%	—	—	—	—	37.8%

InfuSystem Holdings Inc

EXECUTIVES

Chairman, Director, Scott A. Shuda
Vice-Chairman, Director, Gregg Owen Lehman
Oncology Sales Chief Executive Officer, Director, Richard Dilorio, $312,000 total compensation
President, Chief Operating Officer, Director, Carrie A. Lachance
Sales Executive Vice President, Marketing Executive Vice President, Sales Chief Commercial Officer, Marketing Chief Commercial Officer, Thomas Ruiz, $220,850 total compensation
Executive Vice President, Chief Administrative Officer, Jeannine Sheehan
Executive Vice President, Chief Financial Officer, Barry G. Steele
Director, Paul A Gendron
Director, Darrell B. Montgomery
Director, Christopher R. Sansone
Auditors : BDO USA, LLP

LOCATIONS

HQ: InfuSystem Holdings Inc
3851 West Hamlin Road, Rochester Hills, MI 48309
Phone: 248 291-1210
Web: www.infusystem.com

Innovative Industrial Properties Inc

EXECUTIVES

Executive Chairman, Alan D. Gold, $650,000 total compensation
Vice-Chairman, Director, Gary A. Kreitzer
President, Chief Executive Officer, Director, Paul E. Smithers, $400,000 total compensation
Vice President, General Counsel, Secretary, Brian J. Wolfe, $230,000 total compensation
Vice President, Chief Accounting Officer, Principal Accounting Officer, Andy Bui
Chief Financial Officer, Treasurer, Catherine Hastings, $235,000 total compensation
Director, Mary Allis Curran
Director, Scott Shoemaker
Director, David Stecher
Auditors : BDO USA, LLP

LOCATIONS

HQ: Innovative Industrial Properties Inc
1389 Center Drive, Suite 200, Park City, UT 84098
Phone: 858 997-3332
Web: www.innovativeindustrialproperties.com

Innoviva Inc

Innoviva (formerly Theravance) is a company with a portfolio of royalties that include respiratory assets partnered with Glaxo Group Limited (GSK). The company collaborates with GSK to develop and commercialize once-daily products for the treatment of chronic obstructive pulmonary disease (COPD) and asthma. The collaboration has developed three combination products, Relvar, once-daily combination medicine consisting of a LABA, vilanterol, and an inhaled corticosteroid, fluticasone furoate; Anoro Ellipta, once-daily medicine combining a long-acting muscarinic antagonist; and Trelegy Ellipta, once-daily combination medicine consisting of an inhaled corticosteroid, long-acting muscarinic antagonist, and LABA. Founded in 1996.

Operations
The company has LABA collaboration agreement with GSK to develop and commercialize once-daily products for the treatment of chronic obstructive pulmonary disease (COPD) and asthma. The collaboration has developed three combination products: Relvar/Breo that accounts for around 70% of total revenue, Trelegy and Anoro for about 15% each.

Geographic Reach
Headquartered in Burlingame, California, Innoviva sells its products in the US, Japan, and Canada, Germany, and Europe, among others.

Sales and Marketing
The company entered into a collaboration

agreement with GSK to develop and commercialize its product.

Financial Performance

The company's revenues grew by a whopping 384% to $261 million from 2015 to 2019. Over that span, net income had increased after a loss in 2015.

Total net revenue increased slightly in 2019 to $261 million. Royalties for RELVAR/BREO ELLIPTA decreased primarily due to increased pricing pressure in the US offset by volume growth in both the US and non-US markets. The decrease was offset by continued growth in prescriptions and market share for TRELEGY ELLIPTA. Royalties for ANORO ELLIPTA increased slightly year over year.

Innoviva has reported a net income of $157.3 million, lower by $237.8 million from 2018. An interest expense of $18.7 million, income tax expense of $41.9 million, and $33.7 million income from non-controlling interest contributed to the decrease in net income.

Cash and cash equivalents at the end of the period were $278.1 million. Net cash provided by operating activities was $257.5 million while investing and financing activities each used $18 million and $23.8 million, respectively. Main cash uses for the year were for purchases of marketable securities and payments of loans.

Strategy

The company strategy is currently focused on the goal of maximizing stockholder value by, among other things, maximizing the potential value of its respiratory assets partnered with GSK and optimizing its operations and capital allocation.

Company Background

Innoviva began operating in 1997 under the name Advanced Medicine.

EXECUTIVES

Chairman, Director, George W. Bickerstaff
Chief Executive Officer, Pavel Raifeld
Chief Accounting Officer, Secretary, Marianne Zhen, $239,602 total compensation
Director, Odysseas Kostas
Director, Deborah L. Birx
Director, Jules Haimovitz
Director, Mark A. Dipaolo
Director, Sarah J. Schlesinger
Director, Sapna Srivastava
Auditors : Grant Thornton LLP

LOCATIONS

HQ: Innoviva Inc
1350 Old Bayshore Highway Suite 400, Burlingame, CA 94010
Phone: 650 238-9600
Web: www.inva.com

PRODUCTS/OPERATIONS

2014 Sales

	$ mil	% of total
Royalty revenue	7.3	87
MABA program license	1.1	13
Total	8.4	100

Selected Development Products
Bacterial Infections
  TD-1792 (antibiotic for staph infections)
  VIBATIV (telavancin for complicated skin and skin structure infections, or cSSSI, including staph infections)
Central Nervous System/Pain
  TD-1211 (opioid-induced constipation)
  TD-9855 (chronic pain)
Cognitive Disorders
  TD-5108 (Alzheimer's disease)
Gastrointestinal
  TD-5108 (for severe constipation and irritable bowel syndrome)
  TD-8954 (motility)
Respiratory
  LAMA/LABA (or GSK573719/Vilanterol, for chronic obstructive pulmonary disease, or COPD, with GlaxoSmithKline)
  MABA (or GSK961081, for COPD, with GlaxoSmithKline)
  RELOVAIR (for asthma, with GlaxoSmithKline)

COMPETITORS

ACORDA THERAPEUTICS, INC.
AGENUS INC.
ALEXION PHARMACEUTICALS, INC.
CELLDEX THERAPEUTICS, INC.
CHIESI USA, INC.
IMMUNOMEDICS, INC.
INCYTE CORPORATION
NAVIDEA BIOPHARMACEUTICALS, INC.
SALIX PHARMACEUTICALS, LTD.
VECTURA GROUP PLC

HISTORICAL FINANCIALS

Company Type: Public

Income Statement   FYE: December 31

	REVENUE ($mil)	NET INCOME ($mil)	NET PROFIT MARGIN	EMPLOYEES
12/20	336.7	224.4	66.6%	5
12/19	261.0	157.2	60.3%	6
12/18	261.0	395.0	151.4%	6
12/17	217.2	134.1	61.8%	12
12/16	133.5	59.5	44.6%	14
Annual Growth	26.0%	39.3%	—	(22.7%)

2020 Year-End Financials

Debt ratio: 38.6%   No. of shares ($ mil.): 101.3
Return on equity: 52.4%   Dividends
Cash ($ mil.): 246.4   Yield: —
Current Ratio: 55.98   Payout: —
Long-term debt ($ mil.): 385.5   Market value ($ mil.): 1,256.0

	STOCK PRICE ($) FY Close	P/E High	P/E Low	PER SHARE ($) Earnings	PER SHARE ($) Dividends	PER SHARE ($) Book Value
12/20	12.39	7	4	2.02	0.00	5.32
12/19	14.16	13	6	1.43	0.00	3.10
12/18	17.45	5	3	3.53	0.00	1.52
12/17	14.19	12	8	1.17	0.00	(2.38)
12/16	10.70	26	15	0.53	0.00	(3.26)
Annual Growth	3.7%	—	—	39.7%	—	—

Inotiv Inc

Bioanalytical Systems, Inc. (BASi), now operating under the trade name "Inotiv", provides contract research and development services for the pharmaceutical, chemical, and medical device industries. The company also sells analytical instruments to these customers, which include pharmaceutical, biotechnology, biomedical device, academic and government organizations. Some of its services include analytical method development and validation, stability testing, archiving services, among others. Vast majority of its total revenue accounted in the US. The company has been providing services involving the research of products and treatment of diseases through products since 1974.

Operations

The company operates in two primary segments -- contract research services and research products. Contract research services offers screening and formulation development, as well as testing for quality control, regulatory compliance, and preclinical safety. Research products design, develop, manufacture in vivo sampling systems and accessories (including disposables, training and systems qualification), physiology monitoring tools, and liquid chromatography and electrochemistry instruments platforms. Services' revenue accounts for more than 90% of total revenue while products account the remainder.

BASi's blood sampling instrument lines are marketed under the Culex brand.

Geographic Reach

Headquarters in West Lafayette, the company has a network of about 20 distributors from Japan, South Korea, China, India, Central America, South America, South Africa, the Middle East, and Europe. Majority of the company's revenue is from its operations in the US.

Sales and Marketing

BASi's customers include pharmaceutical firms, biotechnology companies, biomedical device, academic institutions, and government organizations.

To promote its offerings, the company communicates directly with scientists and carries out centralized corporate marketing initiatives, concentrated business development efforts. In addition, the company uses social media to pharmaceutical and medical device companies, as well as academic and government research institutions.

Financial Performance

The company's performance for the span of five years have seen an upward trend with 2020 as its highest performing year.

BASi's 2020 revenue increased by 39%, or, $16.8 million to $60.4 million compared to $43.6 million. Internal growth from existing operations contributed approximately 33% or $5.6 million of the increase in revenue. While approximately $11.3 million, or 67%, of the growth was attributable to additional revenues from the Smithers Avanza Acquisition and the PCRS Acquisition of $6.5 million and $4.8 million, respectively.

Net loss in 2020 increased to about $4.7 million compared to net loss of about $790,000 in 2019.

Cash and cash equivalents at the end of the year were $1.4 million. Cash provided by operating activities was $1.3 million. Investing activities used $10.1 million, while financing activities provided $9.6 million. Main cash uses were for capital expenditures and cash paid in acquisitions.

Strategy

The company's strategy is to provide services that generates high-quality and timely data supporting new drug and product approval or expansion of their use.

EXECUTIVES

Chairman, Director, Gregory C. Davis

President, Chief Executive Officer, Director, Robert W. Leasure

Corporate Development Executive Vice President, Adrian Hardy

Finance Vice President, Finance Corporate Controller, Finance Principal Accounting Officer, Brennan Freeman

Finance Chief Financial Officer, Finance Principal Financial Officer, Beth A. Taylor

Chief Strategy Officer, Director, John E. Sagartz

Director, Richard Allen Johnson

Director, Nigel Brown

Director, David Landman

Director, R. Matthew Neff

Auditors : RSM US LLP

LOCATIONS

HQ: Inotiv Inc
2701 Kent Avenue, West Lafayette, IN 47906
Phone: 765 463-4527
Web: www.inotivco.com

2015 Sales

	$ mil	% of total
US	19.7	87
Other North America	1.1	5
Europe	0.9	4
Pacific Rim	0.7	3
Other	0.3	1
Total	22.7	100

PRODUCTS/OPERATIONS

2015 Sales

	$ mil	% of total
Services	17.8	78
Product	4.9	22
Total	22.7	100

COMPETITORS

CHARLES RIVER LABORATORIES INTERNATIONAL, INC.
COVANCE INC.
INTERTEK GROUP PLC
LANDAUER, INC.
OPKO HEALTH, INC.
PAREXEL INTERNATIONAL CORPORATION
PPD DEVELOPMENT, L.P.
PRA HEALTH SCIENCES, INC.
SYNEOS HEALTH, INC.
SYNEOS HEALTH, LLC

HISTORICAL FINANCIALS

Company Type: Public

Income Statement — FYE: September 30

	REVENUE ($mil)	NET INCOME ($mil)	NET PROFIT MARGIN	EMPLOYEES
09/21	89.6	10.8	12.2%	567
09/20	60.4	(4.6)	—	421
09/19	43.6	(0.7)	—	322
09/18	26.3	(0.1)	—	235
09/17	24.2	0.8	3.6%	155
Annual Growth	38.7%	87.4%	—	38.3%

2021 Year-End Financials

Debt ratio: 51.5%
Return on equity: 19.3%
Cash ($ mil.): 156.9
Current Ratio: 3.43
Long-term debt ($ mil.): 154.2
No. of shares ($ mil.): 15.9
Dividends
Yield: —
Payout: —
Market value ($ mil.): 466.0

	STOCK PRICE ($) FY Close	P/E High/Low		PER SHARE ($) Earnings	Dividends	Book Value
09/21	29.24	60	6	0.19	0.00	6.60
09/20	4.78	—	—	(0.43)	0.00	0.69
09/19	3.59	—	—	(0.08)	0.00	1.02
09/18	1.61	—	—	(0.02)	0.00	1.06
09/17	1.76	17	6	0.10	0.00	1.03
Annual Growth	101.9%	—	—	17.4%	—	59.2%

Installed Building Products Inc

Installed Building Products, Inc. (IBP) is one of the nation's largest insulation installers for the residential new construction market and is also a diversified installer of complementary building products, including waterproofing, fire-stopping and fireproofing, garage doors, rain gutters, shower doors, closet shelving and mirrors, throughout the US. The company manages all aspects of the installation process for its customers, including direct purchases of materials from national manufacturers, supply of materials to job sites and quality installation. It offers its portfolio of services for new and existing single-family and multi-family residential and commercial building projects from its national network of branch locations.

IPO

Operations

IBP operates through a single reporting segment. Residential new construction comprises about 75% of its revenue, while commercial construction accounts for more than 15%, and repair and remodel accounts for more than 5%.

About 65% of its sales are from insulation, of which fiberglass and cellulose insulation accounts for about 85% and spray foam insulation generates the remaining 15% of insulation revenue. Waterproofing; shower doors, shelving, and mirrors; garage doors; rain gutters; and other building products each contribute anywhere from about 5% of revenue.

Geographic Reach

Columbus, Ohio-based IBP has more than 210 branches serving almost all 50 continental US states the District of Columbia.

It also has warehouse and office space in about 40 states, with Ohio, Texas, and Indiana, representing the squarest footage. In addition, IBP also owns its cellulose manufacturing facility in Bucyrus, Ohio.

Sales and Marketing

IBP sales force is made up of about 700 employees who, on average, have been with the company for approximately ten years. The company focuses on cross-selling services to existing customers and identifying customers who may need multiple services. In addition to the efforts of its sales staff, IBP markets its product and service offerings on the internet, in the local yellow pages, on the radio and through advertisements in trade journals. It primarily conducts its marketing using local trademarks and trade names.

IBP serves a broad group of national, regional and local homebuilders, multi-family and commercial construction firms, individual homeowners and repair and remodeling contractors. The top 10 customers, which includes both national and regional builders, accounted for about 15% of revenue.

IBP's advertising expense were approximately $4.6 million in 2021 and $3.9 million, $3.9 million for both 2020 and 2019, respectively.

Financial Performance

The company's revenue for fiscal 2021 increased by 19% to $2.0 billion compared from the prior year with $1.7 billion.

Net income for fiscal 2021 increased to $118.8 million compared from the prior year with $97.2 million.

Cash held by the company at the end of fiscal 2021 increased to $333.5 million. Cash provided by operations and financing activities were $138.3 million and $242.1 million, respectively. Cash used for investing activities were $278.4 million, mainly for acquisitions.

Strategy

IBP believe its geographic footprint, long-standing relationships with national insulation manufacturers, streamlined value chain and proven track record of successful acquisitions provides the company with opportunities for continued growth in its existing markets and expansion into new markets. IBP believe its continued emphasis on expanding our product offering, further expansion into the commercial construction market and other lines of business, and targeting geographies where it look to grow market share will reduce potential future cyclicality of its operations. IBP's current strategic objectives include: capitalize on the new residential and large commercial construction markets; continue to strengthen our market share position by working with the best customers. The company seek to work with the most profitable and efficient builders and commercial general contractors in its markets; recruit, develop and retain an exceptional workforce by investing in its employees and its communities and promoting a family-oriented culture; capitalize on our ability to cross-sell products through existing markets as well as new markets entered as a result of organic expansion and acquisitions. In addition to insulation and air infiltration products, the company install garage doors, rain gutters, mirrors and shower doors, waterproofing, fireproofing and fire-stopping, window blinds and various other products; enhance profitability from its operating leverage and national scale; continue expansion in the multibillion-dollar commercial end market. This strategy includes acquiring more locations to serve the large commercial market and increasing overall commercial sales at its existing new residential locations; pursue value enhancing acquisitions in markets the company currently serve as well as markets that are new to IBP by continuing our disciplined approach to valuations and pricing; and the company integrate new acquisitions quickly and seamlessly into its corporate infrastructure, including its accounting and employee systems.

Mergers and Acquisitions

In 2022, IBP acquired Central Aluminum Supply Corporation and Central Aluminum Supply of North Jersey, LLC (CAS). Established in 2004, CAS is headquartered in Trenton, New Jersey and is a distributor of gutter supplies and accessories to residential, multifamily and commercial markets, primarily in existing or retrofit construction projects across the US Northeast and Mid-Atlantic. Stated Jeff Edwards, Chairman and Chief Executive Officer. "To date in 2022, we have acquired approximately $54 million of annual revenue. Acquisitions remain a key component of our growth strategy and we continue to have a robust pipeline of opportunities across multiple geographies, products, and end markets."

In early 2022, IBP acquired North Carolina-based Pisgah Insulation and Fireplaces (Pisgah), installs spray foam insulation, fiberglass insulation, and fireplaces into new residential homes in the Asheville, NC market. The acquisitions expands IBP's presences in North Carolina.

In late 2021, IBP acquired AMD Distribution, Inc. (AMD) headquartered in Spring Valley, Minnesota. AMD distributes of accessories and equipment used throughout the insulation installation process. Jeff Edwards, Chairman and Chief Executive Officer, stated, "I am excited to announce the acquisition of AMD Distribution, Inc. AMD's scale and experience serving our core insulation markets provides IBP with a distribution platform, which further diversifies our revenue mix, end-markets, and geographic footprint. Over the long-term, we expect AMD will improve the flexibility of both our supply chain and cost structure for insulation accessories.

Also in late 2021, IBP acquired Tennessee-based CFI Insulation (CFI), primarily installs fiberglass and spray foam insulation into new residential, multifamily and commercial construction projects. CFI expands its presence to residential, multifamily and commercial customers throughout Tennessee.

In mid-2021, IBP announced the acquisition of General Ceiling & Partitions, Inc. (GCP). Founded in 1986, GCP is headquartered in Colorado Springs, Colorado and primarily installs drywall, framing, ceiling tiles, and fire-stopping/insulation for commercial customers. IBP also announced the acquisition of Reliable Glass & Mirror, LLC, a Louisiana based provider of glass and mirror installation services to residential and commercial customers. GCP and Reliable Glass & Mirror further expands its commercial installation services to the compelling Colorado Springs market and increases its presence within Louisiana.

Company Background

Installed Building Products (IBP) was founded as Edwards Insulation in 1977. It had one location in Columbus, Ohio. In the late 1990s it established a national presence with an aggressive acquisition strategy.

EXECUTIVES

Chairman, President, Chief Executive Officer, Jeffrey W. Edwards, $660,000 total compensation
Finance Executive Vice President, Finance Chief Financial Officer, Director, Michael T. Miller, $336,346 total compensation
Chief Operating Officer, Jay P. Elliott, $385,000 total compensation
Chief Accounting Officer, Treasurer, Todd R. Fry, $241,346 total compensation
Division Officer, W. Jeffrey Hire, $299,152 total compensation
Division Officer, Director, Vikas Verma
Finance Chief Administrative Officer, Investor Relations Chief Administrative Officer, Finance Chief Sustainability Officer, Investor Relations Chief Sustainability Officer, Jason R. Niswonger, $271,346 total compensation
Subsidiary Officer, Randy Hall
Purchasing Senior Vice President, Supply Chain Senior Vice President, Internal Audit Senior Vice President, William W. Jenkins
Region Officer, R. Scott Jenkins
General Counsel, Secretary, Shelley A. McBride
Region Officer, Matthew J. Momper
Region Officer, Warren W. Pearce
Subsidiary Officer, Henry T. Schmueckle
Region Officer, Brad A. Wheeler
Region Officer, Randall S. Williamson
Presiding Independent Director, Director, Margot L. Carter
Director, Lawrence A. Hilsheimer
Director, Janet E. Jackson
Director, David R. Meuse
Director, Michael H. Thomas
Director, Robert H. Schottenstein
Auditors : Deloitte & Touche LLP

LOCATIONS

HQ: Installed Building Products Inc
495 South High Street, Suite 50, Columbus, OH 43215
Phone: 614 221-3399
Web: www.installedbuildingproducts.com

PRODUCTS/OPERATIONS

2017 Sales

	% of total
Residential new construction and repair and remodel	83
Commercial construction	17
Total	100

2017 Sales

	% of total
Insulation	67
Waterproofing	8
Shower doors, shelving & mirrors	7
Garage doors	5
Rain gutters	4
Other	9
Total	100

COMPETITORS

ASSOCIATED MATERIALS, LLC
BOWMER AND KIRKLAND LIMITED
BUILDERS FIRSTSOURCE, INC.
DAIWA HOUSE INDUSTRY CO., LTD.
LENDLEASE CORPORATION LIMITED
LINDUM GROUP LIMITED
RENEW HOLDINGS PLC.
RUSSELL ARMER LIMITED
SHIMIZU CORPORATION
TOPBUILD CORP.

HISTORICAL FINANCIALS

Company Type: Public

Income Statement — FYE: December 31

	REVENUE ($mil)	NET INCOME ($mil)	NET PROFIT MARGIN	EMPLOYEES
12/20	1,653.2	97.2	5.9%	8,950
12/19	1,511.6	68.1	4.5%	8,500
12/18	1,336.4	54.7	4.1%	7,700
12/17	1,132.9	41.1	3.6%	6,900
12/16	862.9	38.4	4.5%	5,292
Annual Growth	17.6%	26.1%	—	14.0%

2020 Year-End Financials

Debt ratio: 47.6%
Return on equity: 34.0%
Cash ($ mil.): 231.5
Current Ratio: 2.64
Long-term debt ($ mil.): 541.9
No. of shares ($ mil.): 29.6
Dividends
  Yield: —
  Payout: —
Market value ($ mil.): 3,020.0

	STOCK PRICE ($) FY Close	P/E High/Low		PER SHARE ($) Earnings	Dividends	Book Value
12/20	101.93	36	9	3.27	0.00	10.77
12/19	68.87	33	15	2.28	0.00	8.33
12/18	33.69	44	17	1.75	0.00	6.10
12/17	75.95	60	31	1.30	0.00	6.61
12/16	41.30	36	15	1.23	0.00	4.89
Annual Growth	25.3%	—	—	27.7%	—	21.8%

Insteel Industries, Inc.

Insteel Industries manufactures steel welded wire reinforcement (WWR), which is used primarily in concrete construction materials; pre-stressed concrete strand (PC strand); engineered structural mesh (ESM); concrete pipe reinforcement (CPR); and standard welded wire reinforcement (SWWR). Its PC strand products are the spine for concrete structures, from bridges to parking garages. Insteel's customers include manufacturers of concrete products, distributors, and rebar fabricators and contractors. A majority of its sales come from manufacturers of non-residential concrete construction products. The US is responsible for almost all of its total sales. The company was founded in 1953 by Howard O. Woltz, Jr.

Operations
Insteel's major products consist of WWR and PC strand. WWR product sales accounted for more than 60% of the company's total sales, while PC strand accounted for some 40%.

WWR is produced as either a standard or a specially engineered reinforcing product. It also produces a full range of WWR products, including ESM, CPR and SWWR. ESM is an engineered made-to-order product that is used as the primary reinforcement for concrete elements or structures. PC strand is a high strength, seven-wire strand that is used to impart compression forces into precast concrete elements and structures.

Geographic Reach
Headquartered in North Carolina, Insteel operates ten manufacturing facilities located in Dayton, Texas; Gallatin, Tennessee; Hazleton, Pennsylvania; Hickman, Kentucky; Houston, Texas; Jacksonville, Florida; Kingman, Arizona; Mount Airy, North Carolina; Sanderson, Florida; and St. Joseph, Missouri. Additionally, it is currently pursuing the sale of an idle facility located in Summerville, South Carolina.

The US operation accounts for the vast majority of the company's total revenue.

Sales and Marketing
Insteel sells its products nationwide as well as into Canada, Mexico, and Central and South America, delivering its products primarily by truck, using common or contract carriers. Products are sold primarily to manufacturers of concrete products that are used in nonresidential construction; and to a lesser extent, distributors, rebar fabricators and contractors.

About 85% of the company's net sales were to manufacturers of concrete products and 15% were to residential construction.

Financial Performance
Net sales increased 25% to $590.6 million in 2021 from $472.6 million in 2020, reflecting a 26% increase in selling prices partially offset by a 1% decrease in shipments. The increase in average selling prices was driven by price increases implemented in the current year primarily to recover the escalation in raw material costs together with strong demand for its products.

The company had net earnings of $66.6 million in 2020, a 250% increase from the previous year. The increase is primarily due to a higher sales volume for the year.

The company's cash for the year ended 2021 was $89.9 million. Operating activities generated $69.9 million, while investing activities used $17.8 million, mainly for capital expenditures. Financing activities used another $30.9 million, mainly for payment for dividends.

Strategy
The company's business strategy is focused on: Achieving leadership positions in its markets; Operating as the lowest cost producer in its industry; and pursuing growth opportunities within its core businesses that further the company's penetration of the markets it currently serves or expands its footprint.

Its growth strategy is focused on organic opportunities as well as strategic acquisitions in existing or related markets that leverage the company's infrastructure and core competencies in the manufacture and marketing of concrete reinforcing products.

Mergers and Acquisitions
In early 2020, Insteel Industries announced that its wholly-owned subsidiary, Insteel Wire Products Company, has acquired substantially all of the assets of Strand-Tech Manufacturing, Inc. (STM) for $19.4 million. STM is a leading manufacturer of PC strand for concrete construction applications based in South Carolina. The STM acquisition represents a significant milestone for the company's PC strand business and strengthens its competitive position by leveraging its operating costs and optimizing its manufacturing footprint.

Company Background
Howard Woltz Sr. bought a premixed concrete and concrete-block plant and formed Exposaic Industries, Inc. in 1953. Son Howard Woltz Jr. took over as chairman and president in 1958, adding welded-wire production equipment to the plant in 1975 during a shortage of wire reinforcing for its precast-concrete operations. Exposaic diversified again into industrial wire products in 1981 and went public in 1985. The company sold its precast concrete unit in 1988.

EXECUTIVES

President, Chief Executive Officer, Subsidiary Officer, Chairman, Director, H. O. Woltz, $606,731 total compensation
Senior Vice President, Chief Operating Officer, Richard T. Wagner, $305,769 total compensation
Senior Vice President, Chief Financial Officer, Treasurer, Mark A. Carano
Administration Vice President, Administration Secretary, James F. Petelle, $211,268 total compensation
Division Officer, James R. York
Lead Director, Director, W. Allen Rogers
Director, Abney S. Boxley
Director, Jon M. Ruth
Director, Joseph A. Rutkowski
Director, G. Kennedy Thompson
Director, Anne H. Lloyd
Auditors : Grant Thornton LLP

LOCATIONS

HQ: Insteel Industries, Inc.
1373 Boggs Drive, Mount Airy, NC 27030
Phone: 336 786-2141
Web: www.insteel.com

2015 Sales

	$ mil.	% of total
US	444.5	99
Other countries	3.0	1
Total	447.5	100

PRODUCTS/OPERATIONS

2015 Sales

	$ mil.	% of total
Welded wire reinforcement	225.2	57
Prestressed concrete strand	192.3	43
Total	447.5	100

Selected Products: Drawn wire: Continuous length (ASTM A1064) smooth or deformed Straightened and cut (ASTM A1064) smooth or deformed Prestressing single wire PC strand: Welded wire reinforcement Engineered structural mesh Standard welded wire reinforcement Concrete pipe reinforcement Formed wire **Selected Subsidiaries**
Insteel Wire Products Company
Intercontinental Metals Corporation (an inactive subsidiary)

COMPETITORS

BEKAERT CORPORATION
CAPARO STEEL PRODUCTS LIMITED
CENTRAL STEEL AND WIRE COMPANY
COMMERCIAL METALS COMPANY
DAYTON SUPERIOR CORPORATION
NORTHWEST PIPE COMPANY
STEEL DYNAMICS, INC.
SUNCOAST POST-TENSION, LTD.
THE HEICO COMPANIES L L C
voestalpine Wire Rod Austria GmbH

Insulet Corp

HISTORICAL FINANCIALS
Company Type: Public

Income Statement
FYE: October 2

	REVENUE ($mil)	NET INCOME ($mil)	NET PROFIT MARGIN	EMPLOYEES
10/21	590.6	66.6	11.3%	913
10/20*	472.6	19.0	4.0%	881
09/19	455.7	5.5	1.2%	834
09/18	453.2	36.2	8.0%	810
09/17	388.8	22.5	5.8%	803
Annual Growth	11.0%	31.1%	—	3.3%

*Fiscal year change

2021 Year-End Financials

Debt ratio: —
Return on equity: 23.5%
Cash ($ mil.): 89.8
Current Ratio: 3.59
Long-term debt ($ mil.): —
No. of shares ($ mil.): 19.4
Dividends
  Yield: —
  Payout: 47.5%
Market value ($ mil.): 757.0

	STOCK PRICE ($) FY Close	P/E High	P/E Low	PER SHARE ($) Earnings	PER SHARE ($) Dividends	PER SHARE ($) Book Value
10/21	39.00	13	6	3.41	1.62	15.56
10/20*	18.95	26	11	0.98	0.12	13.72
09/19	20.71	122	61	0.29	0.12	12.77
09/18	35.88	23	13	1.88	1.12	12.57
09/17	26.11	36	20	1.17	1.37	11.73
Annual Growth	10.6%	—	—	30.7%	4.3%	7.3%

*Fiscal year change

Insulet Corporation is primarily engaged in the development, manufacture and sale of its proprietary Omnipod System, a continuous insulin delivery system for people with insulin-dependent diabetes. The Omnipod System includes the Omnipod Insulin Management System (Omnipod), the Omnipod DASH Insulin Management System (Omnipod DASH), its digital mobile Omnipod platform and the Omnipod 5 Automated Insulin Delivery System (Omnipod 5). Most of its drug delivery revenue consists of sales of pods to Amgen for use in the Neulasta Onpro kit, a delivery system for Amgen's Neulasta to help reduce the risk of infection after intense chemotherapy. The US is the company's largest market which accounts for more than 65% of total revenue.

Operations

The Omnipod System includes the Omnipod Insulin Management System (Omnipod), the Omnipod DASHInsulin Management System (Omnipod DASH), its digital mobile Omnipod platform and the Omnipod 5 Automated Insulin Delivery System (Omnipod 5).

The Omnipod System features two discreet devices and easy-to-use devices that eliminates the need for the external tubing required with conventional pumps, a small, lightweight, self-adhesive disposable tubeless Omnipod device (Pod) that the user fills with insulin and wears directly on the body. It can be worn in multiple locations, including the abdomen, hip, back of upper arm, upper thigh, or lower back. The Pod delivers precise, personalized doses of insulin into the body through a small flexible tube (called a cannula); and the Personal Diabetes Manager (PDM) or Controller, a wireless, handheld device that programs the Pod with the user's personalized insulin-delivery instructions and, wirelessly monitors the Pod's operation.

Overall, sales of Omnipod in the US accounts about 60% of total revenue, while nearly 35% for international, and about 10% for drug delivery.

Geographic Reach

Headquartered in Massachusetts, Insulet leases more than 15 facilities in eight countries consisting of approximately 320,000 square feet of office, research and development, and warehousing space and other related facilities, primarily in North America, Asia and Europe.

The US accounts more than 65% of Insulet's total revenue while about 35% comes from International operations.

Sales and Marketing

The company markets its products directly to wholesalers, private healthcare organizations, healthcare facilities, mail order pharmacies and independent retailers. The Omnipod System is also marketed and sold through distributors, as well as marketed to physicians and consumers (generally have commercial insurance, Medicare or Medicaid coverage that pays for the product). It also sells directly to consumers, through distribution partners and most recently in the US through the pharmacy channel.

In addition, sales and marketing efforts are focused on customer retention and growing user, clinician and payor demand for the Omnipod System. It has a uniform sales and marketing approach, aligned across users, physicians and providers, to capitalize on the benefits of Omnipod System technology.

Financial Performance

Total revenue for 2021 increased $194.4 million, or 22%, to $1.1 billion, compared with $904.4 million in 2020. Constant currency revenue growth of 20% was primarily driven by higher volume and, to a lesser extent, favorable sales channel mix. This increase was partially offset by the normalization of inventory levels at distributors, which were elevated in the prior year due to the launch of Omnipod DASH.

In 2021, the company had a net income of $16.8 million, a 147% increase from the previous year's net income of $6.8 million.

The company's cash at the end of 2021 was $806.4 million. Financing activities generated $40.7 million, while investing activities used $82.7 million, mainly for capital expenditures. Operating activities used another $68.1 million, primarily for inventories.

Strategy

Insulet's mission is to improve the lives of people with diabetes. To assist in achieving this mission, the company is focused on the following key strategic imperatives: expanding access and awareness; delivering consumer-focused innovation; growing its global addressable market; and driving operational excellence.

The company's long-term financial objective is to sustain profitable growth. To achieve this goal, its efforts have been focused on the launch of Omnipod 5, which recently received FDA clearance for individuals aged six years and older with type 1 diabetes. Insulet's limited market release of Omnipod 5 is underway. Additionally, it has completed its FDA submission to expand Omnipod 5's indication down to age two, and are planning for an expanded indication in 2022. The company has also recently completed its type 2 feasibility study and plan to conduct additional studies with the goal to further expand Omnipod 5's indication to type 2 users. In its efforts to bring Omnipod 5 to international markets, Insulet has submitted for CE Marking in Europe under MDR.

In order to support Insulet's continued growth and the full commercial launch of Omnipod 5, the company continues to focus on adding capacity to its US manufacturing plant. During 2021, the company began producing salable product on its third highly automated manufacturing line. It haS also taken steps to strengthen its global manufacturing capabilities. Insulet has optimized its operations in China by consolidating the company's production in that region into one location and it plans to invest in a new manufacturing plant in another international location to further diversify globally and increase efficiency to drive higher gross margins over time.

Company Background

Insulet was founded in 2000 and went public through an IPO in 2007.

EXECUTIVES

Chairman, Director, Timothy J. Scannell

President, Chief Executive Officer, Director, Shacey Petrovic, $571,154 total compensation

Executive Vice President, Chief Financial Officer, Treasurer, Wayde D. McMillan

Global Manufacturing Executive Vice President, Operations Executive Vice President, Global Manufacturing Chief Operating Officer, Operations Chief Operating Officer, Charles Alpuche, $442,308 total compensation

Executive Vice President, Chief Commercial Officer, Bret Christensen, $415,000 total compensation

Senior Vice President, General Counsel, Secretary, John W. Kapples

Innovation Senior Vice President, Strategy Senior Vice President, Eric Benjamin

Quality, Regulatory, and Clinical Affairs Senior Vice President, Regulatory Affairs Senior Vice President, Compliance Senior Vice President, Michael P. Spears, $137,500 total compensation

Director, Sally W. Crawford
Director, John A. Fallon
Director, Jessica Hopfield
Director, Wayne A.I. Frederick
Director, James R. Hollingshead
Director, Corinne H. Nevinny
Director, David A. Lemoine
Director, Michael R. Minogue
Auditors : Grant Thornton LLP

LOCATIONS

HQ: Insulet Corp
100 Nagog Park, Acton, MA 01720
Phone: 978 600-7000
Web: www.insulet.com

COMPETITORS

CERUS CORPORATION
CRYOLIFE, INC.
DELTEX MEDICAL GROUP PLC
DEXCOM, INC.
GENMARK DIAGNOSTICS, INC.
MANNKIND CORPORATION
MGC DIAGNOSTICS CORPORATION
SURMODICS, INC.
TANDEM DIABETES CARE, INC.
ZELTIQ AESTHETICS, INC.

HISTORICAL FINANCIALS

Company Type: Public

Income Statement — FYE: December 31

	REVENUE ($mil)	NET INCOME ($mil)	NET PROFIT MARGIN	EMPLOYEES
12/20	904.4	6.8	0.8%	1,900
12/19	738.2	11.6	1.6%	1,350
12/18	563.8	3.2	0.6%	1,169
12/17	463.7	(26.8)	—	857
12/16	366.9	(28.8)	—	640
Annual Growth	25.3%	—	—	31.3%

2020 Year-End Financials

Debt ratio: 56.6%
Return on equity: 1.9%
Cash ($ mil.): 907.2
Current Ratio: 6.01
Long-term debt ($ mil.): 1,043.7
No. of shares ($ mil.): 66.0
Dividends
Yield: —
Payout: —
Market value ($ mil.): 16,876.0

	STOCK PRICE ($) FY Close	P/E High/Low		PER SHARE ($) Earnings	Dividends	Book Value
12/20	255.63	2417	1182	0.10	0.00	9.14
12/19	171.20	979	381	0.19	0.00	1.21
12/18	79.32	1802	1142	0.05	0.00	3.58
12/17	69.00	—	—	(0.46)	0.00	2.72
12/16	37.68	—	—	(0.51)	0.00	1.10
Annual Growth	61.4%	—	—	—	—	69.8%

Integra LifeSciences Holdings Corp

Integra LifeSciences is a world leader in medical technology.. The company develops medical equipment used in cranial procedures, small bone and joint reconstruction, and the repair and reconstruction of soft tissue, nerves, and tendons. Integra's products include tissue ablation equipment, drainage catheters, bone fixation devices, regenerative technologies, and basic surgical instruments. Its offerings are marketed in more than 130 countries through direct sales and distributors. The US market accounts for a majority of sales. Integra was founded in 1989 by Richard Caruso and the company acquired collagen technology.

Operations

Integra operates in two segments: Codman Specialty Surgical (CSS) and Tissue Technologies (TT).

The CSS segment, bringing in 65% of revenue, includes the Neurosurgery business, which sells a full line of products for neurosurgery and neuro critical care such as tissue ablation equipment, dural repair products, cerebral spinal fluid management devices, intracranial monitoring equipment, and cranial stabilization equipment and the Instruments business, which sells more than 40,000 instrument patterns and surgical and lighting products to hospitals, surgery centers, dental, podiatry, and veterinary offices.

The TT segment (35% of revenue) includes such offerings as skin and wound repair, plastics & surgical reconstruction products, bone grafts, and nerve and tendon repair products.

Geographic Reach

Headquartered in Princeton, New Jersey, Integra's main manufacturing and research centers are located in the US (California, Indiana, Maryland, Massachusetts, New Jersey, Ohio, Tennessee, and Utah), Canada, China, Switzerland, France, Germany, Ireland, and Puerto Rico. Its distribution centers are in the US (Nevada, Ohio, and Kentucky), Australia, Belgium, Canada, Japan and France. Integra also has repair centers in the US (and Ohio), Australia, Japan and Germany and field service presence in Canada, Dubai, India, Italy, Netherlands, Singapore, Thailand and United Kingdom.

In addition, Integra owns facilities in Biot, France, Saint Aubin Le Monial, France, Rietheim-Weilheim, Germany and Ohio while its third parties own and operate the facilities in US (Nevada and Kentucky), Japan and Belgium.

The US accounts for more than 70% of total revenue, while Europe accounts for more than 10% and Asia brings in about 10%.

Sales and Marketing

Integra sells its products worldwide through a direct sales force and via distributors, wholesalers, and strategic partnerships that serve hospitals, integrated health networks, group purchasing organizations, clinicians, surgery centers and health care providers.

Financial Performance

For the year ended December 31, 2021, total revenues increased by $170.6 million, or 12%, to $1.5 billion from $1.4 billion during the prior year.

Net income for fiscal 2021 increased to $169.1 million compared from the prior year with $133.9 million.

Cash held by the company at the end of fiscal 2021 increased to $513.4 million. Cash provided by operations was $312.4 million while cash used for investing and financing activities were $161.4 million and $98.2 million, respectively. Main uses of cash were cash paid for business acquisitions and payments on debt.

Strategy

Integra is committed to delivering high quality products that positively impact the lives of millions of patients and their families. The company focuses on four key pillars of its strategy: enabling an execution-focused culture, optimizing relevant scale, advancing innovation and agility, and leading in customer experience. Integra believes that by sharpening its focus on these areas through improved planning and communication, optimization of its infrastructure, and strategically aligned acquisitions, the company can build scale, increase competitiveness and achieve its long-term goals.

Mergers and Acquisitions

In 2021, Integra completed the previously-disclosed acquisition of ACell, Inc., for an upfront cash payment of $300 million. ACell is an innovative regenerative medicine company with a product portfolio based on a proprietary porcine urinary bladder matrix platform technology, MatriStem UBM. The acquisition of ACell is the next step in the expansion of Integra's Orthopedics and Tissue Technologies (OTT) segment. The porcine UBM technology is a strong strategic fit with its human amniotic tissue and bovine-derived engineered collagen and acellular dermal matrices. The acquisition also supports Integra's long-term growth and profitability strategy with a financial profile similar to Integra's tissue products.

Company Background

Integra LifeSciences was founded by Richard Caruso in 1989 to explore an acquired collagen technology. It developed a dermal regeneration template in 1995; the template was approved for use on third-degree burns in 1996. The Integra DuraGen graft matrix was approved by the FDA in 1999.

Acquisitions have included Jarit Surgical

(2003), Mayfield (2004), Miltex (2006), Ascension Orthopedics (2011), DuraSeal (2014), TEI (2015), Derma Sciences (2017), and Codman NeuroSurgery (2017).

To focus on core offerings, Integra separated its orthobiologics and spinal fusion hardware business into SeaSpine Holdings, which became a public company, in 2015.

EXECUTIVES

Chairman, Director, Stuart M. Essig, $343,269 total compensation

President, Chief Executive Officer, Director, Jan D. De Witte

Executive Vice President, Division Officer, Robert T. Davis, $458,350 total compensation

Executive Vice President, Chief Human Resources Officer, Lisa Evoli

Executive Vice President, Division Officer, Michael F. McBreen

Executive Vice President, Chief Legal Officer, Secretary, Eric I. Schwartz, $57,212 total compensation

Senior Vice President, Principal Accounting Officer, Jeffrey Mosebrook, $281,000 total compensation

Director, Keith Bradley

Director, Shaundra Clay

Director, Barbara B. Hill

Director, Donald Eugene Morel

Director, Raymond G. Murphy

Director, Christian S. Schade

Director, Renee Wonlai Lo

Auditors : PricewaterhouseCoopers LLP

LOCATIONS

HQ: Integra LifeSciences Holdings Corp
 1100 Campus Road, Princeton, NJ 08540
Phone: 609 275-0500
Web: www.integralife.com

2015 Sales

	$ mil.	% of total
United States	680.8	77
Europe	103.0	12
Rest of the World	98.9	11
Total	882.7	100

PRODUCTS/OPERATIONS

2015 Sales

	$ mil.	% of total
Specialty Surgical Solutions	586.9	66
Orthopedics and Tissue Technologies	295.8	34
Total	882.7	100

Selected Acquisitions

2009
Athrodax Healthcare ($3.3 million, UK, direct marketing network)
Innovative Spinal Technologies, Inc. (IST, $9.5 million, spinal implant products used in minimally invasive surgery)
2010
Select assets from Culley Investments ($1.6 million, Australia, direct distribution operations and extremity reconstruction product lines)
Surgical headlight business of Welch Allyn ($2.6 million, medical equipment maker)
2011
Ascension Orthopedics ($66.5 million; Austin, Texas; extremity implants)

SeaSpine ($89 million; Vista, California; spinal fixation products)

Selected Products

Orthopedics
 Extremity Reconstruction
 Bone and joint fixation devices and instruments
 Bone graft substitutes
 Dermal regeneration
 Foot and hand (nerve and tendon repair)
 Lower extremity solutions (foot and ankle implants)
 Matrix wound dressings
 Mid and hindfoot solutions
 Upper extremity solutions (wrist implants)
 Orthobiologics (scaffolds, grafts, chips; bone, collagen and synthetic)
 Spine (plate, rod, screws)
 Deformity correction system
 Interbody fusion devices
 Minimally invasive fixation devices
NeuroSciences
 NeuroCritical Care
 External CSF drainage
 Neuromonitoring
 Neurosurgery
 Brain mapping
 Brain retraction systems
 Cerbral spinal fluid management
 Cranial closure (with DuraGen dural graft matrix)
 Cranial stabilization
 Duraplasty
 Hydrocephalus management
 Monitoring systems (cranial pressure and oxygenation)
 Neurosurgical instruments
 Radiosurgery
 Stereotaxy
 Tissue ablation
Medical Instruments
 Miltex (surgical instruments including scissors, forceps, scopes)
 Surgical (Jarit instruments, Luxtec lights, Omni-Tract retractors)

COMPETITORS

ARTHROCARE CORPORATION
BOSTON SCIENTIFIC CORPORATION
CANTEL MEDICAL CORP.
CONMED CORPORATION
INTEGER HOLDINGS CORPORATION
MERIT MEDICAL SYSTEMS, INC.
STRYKER CORPORATION
TELEFLEX INCORPORATED
TERUMO CORPORATION
ZIMMER BIOMET HOLDINGS, INC.

HISTORICAL FINANCIALS

Company Type: Public

Income Statement

FYE: December 31

	REVENUE ($mil)	NET INCOME ($mil)	NET PROFIT MARGIN	EMPLOYEES
12/20	1,371.8	133.8	9.8%	3,700
12/19	1,517.5	50.2	3.3%	4,000
12/18	1,472.4	60.8	4.1%	4,500
12/17	1,188.2	64.7	5.4%	4,400
12/16	992.0	74.5	7.5%	3,700
Annual Growth	8.4%	15.8%	—	0.0%

2020 Year-End Financials

Debt ratio: 43.0%
Return on equity: 9.1%
Cash ($ mil.): 470.1
Current Ratio: 3.09
Long-term debt ($ mil.): 1,408.2
No. of shares ($ mil.): 84.3
Dividends
 Yield: —
 Payout: —
Market value ($ mil.): 5,475.0

	STOCK PRICE ($) FY Close	P/E High/Low		PER SHARE ($) Earnings	Dividends	Book Value
12/20	64.92	42	23	1.57	0.00	17.96
12/19	58.28	109	73	0.58	0.00	16.50
12/18	45.10	92	58	0.72	0.00	16.15
12/17	47.86	101	49	0.82	0.00	12.28
12/16	85.79	87	55	0.94	0.00	11.24
Annual Growth	(6.7%)	—	—	13.7%	—	12.4%

Interactive Brokers Group Inc

Interactive Brokers Group is an automated global electronic broker that custody and service accounts for hedge and mutual funds, exchange-traded funds (ETFs), registered investment advisors, proprietary trading groups, introducing brokers and individual investor. Catering to institutional and experienced individual investors, the company offers access to more than 150 electronic exchanges and trading centers worldwide, processing trades in stocks, options, futures, foreign exchange instruments, bonds, and mutual funds. The company also licenses its trading interface to large banks and brokerages through white branding agreements. Interactive Brokers operates worldwide, but generates about 70% of its revenue in the US.

Operations

Interactive Brokers offers IBKR Pro, IBKR Lite and IBKR Integrated Investment Account.

IBKR Pro is the traditional IBKR service designed for sophisticated investors. IBKR Pro offers the lowest cost access to stocks, options, futures, forex, bonds, mutual funds and ETFs on over 135 electronic exchanges and market centers in about 35 countries.

IBKR Lite provides unlimited commission-free trades on US exchange-listed stocks and ETFs as well as low cost access to global markets without required account minimums or inactivity fees to participating US customers.

IBKR Lite was designed to meet the needs of investors who are seeking a simple, commission-free way to trade US exchange-listed stocks and ETFs and do not wish to consider its efforts to obtain greater price improvement through its IB SmartRouting system.

BKR Integrated Investment Account include Interactive Brokers Debit Mastercard, Bill Pay, Direct Deposit and Mobile Check Deposit, Insured Bank Deposit Sweep Program, Investors' Marketplace, Mutual Fund Marketplace, Bonds Marketplace, Fractional Trading.

Interactive Brokers garners more than 45% of its revenue from net interest income, while around 45% comes from commissions.

Geographic Reach
Greenwich, Connecticut-based, Interactive Brokers' customers span in more than 200 countries and territories. It has US offices in cities including Chicago, Illinois and other nine locations. The company's overseas offices are in Canada, the United Kingdom, Ireland, Luxembourg, Switzerland, Hungary, India, China (Hong Kong and Shanghai), Japan, Singapore, and Australia. The US generates about 70% the company's revenue while international countries generates for about 30%.

Sales and Marketing
Interactive Brokers categorizes its clients into the two groups of cleared customers and non-cleared customers (or trade execution customers). Cleared customers include small group and individual market makers, institutional and individual traders, introducing brokers, financial advisors, and hedge funds. Non-cleared customers who clear with another prime broker or custodian bank encompass online brokers and commercial bank customer trading units.

Financial Performance
Total net revenue in 2021 increased $496 million, or 22%, compared to the prior year, to $2.7 billion. The increase in net revenues was primarily due to higher net interest income, commissions, and other fees and services, partially offset by lower other income.

Net income in 2021 increased to $1.6 billion compared with $1.2 billion in the prior year.

Cash held by the company at the end of 2021 increased to $25.3 billion. Cash provided by operations was $5.9 billion while cash investing and financing activities used $188 million and $523 million, respectively. Main cash uses were purchases of other investments and redemptions of senior notes.

Strategy
Interactive Brokers regularly evaluate potential strategic investments and acquisitions. The company holds strategic investments in certain electronic trading exchanges, including BOX Options Exchange, LLC. Interactive Brokers also hold strategic investments in certain businesses, including Tiger Brokers, an online stock brokerage established for Chinese retail and institutional customers, in which it has a beneficial ownership interest of 8%.

Company Background
Founder, chairman, and CEO Thomas Peterffy controls Interactive Brokers Group. Peterffy started the company in 1978 as T.P. & Co. It was the first market making firm to use daily-printed computer-generated fair value sheets.

EXECUTIVES

Chairman, Director, Thomas Peterffy, $800,000 total compensation

Vice-Chairman, Director, Earl H. Nemser, $580,000 total compensation

President, Chief Executive Officer, Subsidiary Officer, Director, Milan Galik, $455,000 total compensation

Executive Vice President, Chief Information Officer, Subsidiary Officer, Thomas A. Frank, $455,000 total compensation

Chief Financial Officer, Treasurer, Secretary, Subsidiary Officer, Director, Paul J. Brody, $455,000 total compensation

Director, Lawrence E. Harris

Director, Philip Uhde

Director, William Peterffy

Director, Nicole Yuen

Director, Jill Bright

Auditors : DELOITTE & TOUCHE LLP

LOCATIONS

HQ: Interactive Brokers Group Inc
One Pickwick Plaza, Greenwich, CT 06830
Phone: 203 618-5800
Web: www.interactivebrokers.com

2018 Revenue

	$ mil.	% of total
United States	1,501	79
International	402	21
Total	1,903	100

PRODUCTS/OPERATIONS

Trading Services
Account Management
Employee Track Management
Funding Reference
Investors' Marketplace
IRA Information
New Features Poll
Securities Financing

2018 Revenue

	$ mil.	% of total
Commissions	777	32
Interest income	1,392	59
Trading gains	39	2
Other	158	7
Interest expense	(463)	-
Total	1,903	100

2018 Revenue

	$ mil.	% of total
Electronic brokerage	1,842	96
Market making	76	4
Corporate	(15)	-
Total	1,903	100

COMPETITORS

CBOE GLOBAL MARKETS, INC.
E TRADE FINANCIAL CORPORATION
MARKETAXESS HOLDINGS INC.
NASDAQ, INC.
NUMIS CORPORATION PLC
S&P GLOBAL INC.
STONEX GROUP INC.
TD AMERITRADE HOLDING CORPORATION
VIRTU ITG HOLDINGS LLC
VIRTU KNIGHT CAPITAL GROUP LLC

HISTORICAL FINANCIALS
Company Type: Public

Income Statement — FYE: December 31

	REVENUE ($mil)	NET INCOME ($mil)	NET PROFIT MARGIN	EMPLOYEES
12/20	2,218.0	195.0	8.8%	2,033
12/19	1,937.0	161.0	8.3%	1,643
12/18	1,903.0	169.0	8.9%	1,413
12/17	1,702.0	76.0	4.5%	1,228
12/16	1,396.0	84.0	6.0%	1,204
Annual Growth	12.3%	23.4%	—	14.0%

2020 Year-End Financials
Debt ratio: 10.4%
Return on equity: 11.4%
Cash ($ mil.): 20,987.0
Current Ratio: 1.04
Long-term debt ($ mil.): —
No. of shares ($ mil.): 90.7
Dividends
Yield: 0.6%
Payout: 18.5%
Market value ($ mil.): 5,530.0

	STOCK PRICE ($) FY Close	P/E High/Low		PER SHARE ($)		
		High	Low	Earnings	Dividends	Book Value
12/20	60.92	26	14	2.42	0.40	21.49
12/19	46.62	23	21	2.10	0.40	18.92
12/18	55.78	35	24	2.28	0.40	17.07
12/17	59.21	57	31	1.07	0.40	15.25
12/16	36.51	34	24	1.25	0.40	14.33
Annual Growth	13.7%	—	—	18.0%	0.0%	10.7%

Investar Holding Corp

EXECUTIVES

Chairman, Director, William H. Hidalgo

President, Chief Executive Officer, Interim Chief Financial Officer, Principal Financial Officer, Subsidiary Officer, Director, John J. D'Angelo, $438,422 total compensation

Executive Vice President, Chief Financial Officer, Subsidiary Officer, John R. Campbell

Executive Vice President, Chief Operations Officer, Subsidiary Officer, Linda M. Crochet

Senior Vice President, Senior Financial Officer, Chief Accounting Officer, Subsidiary Officer, Corey E. Moore

Chief Credit Officer, Subsidiary Officer, Jeffrey Wayne Martin

Subsidiary Officer, Director, Suzanne O. Middleton

Director, Rose J. Hudson

Director, James H. Boyce

Director, Gordon H. Joffrion

Director, Robert Chris Jordan

Director, David J. Lukinovich

Director, Andrew C. Nelson

Director, Frank L. Walker

Auditors : HORNE LLP

LOCATIONS

HQ: Investar Holding Corp
10500 Coursey Boulevard, Baton Rouge, LA 70816
Phone: 225 227-2222

HISTORICAL FINANCIALS

Company Type: Public

Income Statement — FYE: December 31

	ASSETS ($mil)	NET INCOME ($mil)	INCOME AS % OF ASSETS	EMPLOYEES
12/20	2,321.1	13.8	0.6%	326
12/19	2,148.9	16.8	0.8%	324
12/18	1,786.4	13.6	0.8%	255
12/17	1,622.7	8.2	0.5%	258
12/16	1,158.9	7.8	0.7%	152
Annual Growth	19.0%	15.2%	—	21.0%

2020 Year-End Financials

Return on assets: 0.6%
Return on equity: 5.7%
Long-term debt ($ mil.): —
No. of shares ($ mil.): 10.6
Sales ($ mil.): 105.8
Dividends
Yield: 1.5%
Payout: 21.3%
Market value ($ mil.): 175.0

	STOCK PRICE ($) FY Close	P/E High/Low		PER SHARE ($) Earnings	Dividends	Book Value
12/20	16.54	19	7	1.27	0.25	22.93
12/19	24.00	15	13	1.66	0.23	21.55
12/18	24.80	21	15	1.39	0.17	19.22
12/17	24.10	26	20	0.96	0.07	18.15
12/16	18.65	18	12	1.10	0.04	15.88
Annual Growth	(3.0%)	—	—	3.7%	56.1%	9.6%

Investors Title Co.

Investors Title insures you in case your land is, well, not completely yours. It's the holding company for Investors Title Insurance and Northeast Investors Title Insurance, which underwrite land title insurance and sell reinsurance to other title companies. (Title insurance protects those who invest in real property against loss resulting from defective titles.) Investors Title Insurance serves customers from about 30 offices in North Carolina, South Carolina, Michigan, and Nebraska, and through branches or agents in 20 additional states. Northeast Investors Title operates through an agency office in New York. Founder and CEO J. Allen Fine and his family own more than 20% of Investors Title.

EXECUTIVES

Chairman, Chief Executive Officer, Subsidiary Officer, Director, J. Allen Fine, $422,900 total compensation
President, Chief Financial Officer, Treasurer, Subsidiary Officer, Director, James A. Fine, $360,000 total compensation
Executive Vice President, Secretary, Subsidiary Officer, Director, W. Morris Fine, $360,000 total compensation
Director, David L. Francis
Director, James Herbert Speed
Director, Tammy F. Coley
Director, Richard M. Hutson
Director, James E. Scott
Director, Elton C. Parker

Auditors : Dixon Hughes Goodman LLP

LOCATIONS

HQ: Investors Title Co.
121 North Columbia Street, Chapel Hill, NC 27514
Phone: 919 968-2200
Web: www.invtitle.com

PRODUCTS/OPERATIONS

Selected Subsidiaries
Investors Title Accommodation Corporation
Investors Title Exchange Corporation
Investors Title Insurance Company
Investors Title Management Services, Inc.
Northeast Investors Title Insurance Company

COMPETITORS

AMERICAN COAST TITLE COMPANY, INC.
CALATLANTIC TITLE GROUP, LLC
FIRST AMERICAN FINANCIAL CORPORATION
FIRST AMERICAN TITLE INSURANCE COMPANY
STEWART TITLE COMPANY

HISTORICAL FINANCIALS

Company Type: Public

Income Statement — FYE: December 31

	ASSETS ($mil)	NET INCOME ($mil)	INCOME AS % OF ASSETS	EMPLOYEES
12/20	282.9	39.4	13.9%	456
12/19	263.8	31.4	11.9%	402
12/18	244.2	21.8	9.0%	385
12/17	248.9	25.7	10.3%	383
12/16	228.9	19.5	8.5%	320
Annual Growth	5.4%	19.2%	—	9.3%

2020 Year-End Financials

Return on assets: 14.3%
Return on equity: 20.0%
Long-term debt ($ mil.): —
No. of shares ($ mil.): 1.8
Sales ($ mil.): 236.4
Dividends
Yield: 10.9%
Payout: 93.0%
Market value ($ mil.): 289.0

	STOCK PRICE ($) FY Close	P/E High/Low		PER SHARE ($) Earnings	Dividends	Book Value
12/20	153.00	9	5	20.80	16.76	105.93
12/19	159.20	11	8	16.59	9.60	101.30
12/18	176.68	18	14	11.54	12.20	93.08
12/17	198.35	15	9	13.56	3.75	94.29
12/16	158.18	17	8	10.19	0.72	82.28
Annual Growth	(0.8%)	—	—	19.5%	119.7%	6.5%

Invitation Homes Inc

EXECUTIVES

Chairman, Director, Michael D. Fascitelli
President, Chief Operating Officer, Charles D. Young, $525,000 total compensation
Chief Executive Officer, Director, Dallas B. Tanner, $525,000 total compensation
Executive Vice President, Chief Legal Officer, Secretary, Mark A. Solls, $425,000 total compensation
Corporate Strategy Executive Vice President, Finance Executive Vice President, Corporate Strategy Chief Financial Officer, Finance Chief Financial Officer, Corporate Strategy Treasurer, Finance Treasurer, Jonathan S. Olsen
Director, Jana Cohen Barbe
Director, Richard D. Bronson
Director, Jeffrey E. Kelter
Director, Joseph D. (Joe) Margolis
Director, John B. Rhea
Director, J. Heidi Roizen
Director, Janice L. Sears

Auditors : DELOITTE & TOUCHE LLP

LOCATIONS

HQ: Invitation Homes Inc
1717 Main Street, Suite 2000, Dallas, TX 75201
Phone: 972 421-3600
Web: www.invitationhomes.com

HISTORICAL FINANCIALS

Company Type: Public

Income Statement — FYE: December 31

	REVENUE ($mil)	NET INCOME ($mil)	NET PROFIT MARGIN	EMPLOYEES
12/21	1,996.6	261.4	13.1%	1,240
12/20	1,822.8	196.2	10.8%	1,149
12/19	1,764.6	145.4	8.2%	1,140
12/18	1,722.9	(4.9)	—	1,231
12/17	1,054.4	(105.3)	—	1,445
Annual Growth	17.3%	—	—	(3.8%)

2021 Year-End Financials

Debt ratio: 43.1%
Return on equity: 2.8%
Cash ($ mil.): 610.1
Current Ratio: 2.28
Long-term debt ($ mil.): 7,998.6
No. of shares ($ mil.): 601.0
Dividends
Yield: 1.4%
Payout: 151.1%
Market value ($ mil.): 27,251.0

	STOCK PRICE ($) FY Close	P/E High/Low		PER SHARE ($) Earnings	Dividends	Book Value
12/21	45.34	100	63	0.45	0.68	16.30
12/20	29.70	93	46	0.35	0.60	15.00
12/19	29.97	115	73	0.27	0.52	15.17
12/18	20.08	—	—	(0.01)	0.44	15.81
12/17	23.57	—	—	(0.26)	0.22	16.37
Annual Growth	17.8%	—	—	—	32.6%	(0.1%)

iRobot Corp

iRobot is a leading consumer robot company that designs and builds robots that empower people to do more around the globe. The company's portfolio of home robots and smart home devices features proprietary technologies for the connected home and advanced concepts in cleaning, mapping and navigation, human-robot interaction and physical solutions. With approximately 14 million connected customers, iRobot sells its robotic floor care products through distributor and retail sales channels, as well as the online store on its website and through its Home App. It operates worldwide but generates about 50% of its revenue in the US. Since its founding, iRobot has sold more than 40 million consumer robots around the world.

Operations
iRobot sells consumer products that are designed for both indoor and outdoor cleaning applications. It offers Roomba floor vacuuming robots at prices ranging from approximately $275 to $1,099. The company also offers the Braava family of mopping robots at price points ranging from $199 to $450. It also offers robots designed to help children learn how to code. The Root coding robots, priced at $129 and $199, are designed to make coding easy and natural to learn.

The company holds more than 565 US patents, more than 1,000 foreign patents, additional design registrations, and has more than 1450 patent applications pending worldwide.

Geographic Reach
Bedford, Massachusetts-based iRobot has offices and subsidiaries in the US, the UK, China, Austria, Belgium, France, Germany, Netherlands, Portugal, Spain, Switzerland, Japan, and Hong Kong. Its research and development facilities are in Bedford, Massachusetts and Pasadena, California. Sales to customers in the US account for nearly 50% of the company's revenue.

The company contracts manufacturing to third parties in China.

Sales and Marketing
iRobot sells products directly to consumers through online stores and indirectly through resellers and distributors.

The company markets its products through national advertising, consumer and industry trade shows, and direct marketing.

During the years ended 2021, 2020, and 2019 advertising expense totaled $147.2 million, $145.2 million, and $125.0 million, respectively.

Financial Performance
Revenue increased 9% to $1.6 billion in fiscal 2021 from $1.4 billion in fiscal 2020. Despite ongoing semiconductor chip constraints and shipping delays that impacted its ability to fulfill orders in fiscal 2021 during the holiday season, revenue increased $134.6 million, which was primarily attributable to a 4% increase in average gross selling price and a 2% increase in units shipped in fiscal 2021, as compared to fiscal 2020.

In 2021, the company had a net income of $30.4 million, a 79% decrease from the previous year's net income of $147.1 million.

The company's cash at the end of 2021 was $201.5 million. Operating activities used $32 million. Investing and financing activities used $48.1 million, and $148.4 million, respectively. Main cash uses for the year were for cash paid for business acquisition, as well as stock repurchases.

Strategy
iRobot's strategy to drive sustainable, profitable growth over the long term is focused on four concepts: innovate, get, keep and grow ? all of which is enabled by the company's talent, operational excellence and an expansive range of data and insights about products and the consumers who purchase them.

Innovate: The company is focused on maintaining RVC category leadership and further diversifying its product portfolio into adjacent categories by continuing to fund innovation. The company's investments in research and development support ongoing advances in its Genius platform by leveraging the company's extensive AI, home understanding and machine vision capabilities as well as developments that further enhance the design and performance of the company's hardware;

Get: iRobot ended 2021 with approximately 14 million connected customers who have opted into communications with the company either through its Home App, email or both;

Keep: It is important that customers are happy with the performance of products and use them consistently. The company believes that a highly satisfied iRobot customer is more likely to recommend products to others and purchase more products and accessories directly from the company over the course of their ownership. Accordingly, iRobot plans to invest in features and functionality aimed at elevating the iRobot experience as well as in customer care organization; and

Grow: An important element in iRobot's plan to drive profitable growth over the long term is increasing revenue from existing customers. To motivate more customers to purchase the company's products and services more frequently directly, the company continues to invest in enhancing the online buying experience on its website and through its Home App as well as by implementing marketing systems and tools designed to enable iRobot to target the right customers at the right time with the right promotions.

Mergers and Acquisitions
In late 2021, iRobot acquired privately-held Aeris Cleantec AG, a fast-growing provider of premium air purifiers headquartered in Cham, Zug Switzerland. The acquisition supports iRobot's vision of building the world's most thoughtful robotics and developing intelligent home innovations that make life better.

Company Background
iRobot Corporation was founded in 1990 by engineers from the Massachusetts Institute of Technology.

EXECUTIVES

Chief Executive Officer, Chairman, Director, Colin M. Angle, $742,308 total compensation
Executive Vice President, Chief Products Officer, Keith Hartsfield
Executive Vice President, Chief Financial Officer, Julie Zeiler
Executive Vice President, Chief Legal Officer, Secretary, Glen D. Weinstein, $380,000 total compensation
Corporate Communications Executive Vice President, Human Resources Executive Vice President, Russell J. Campanello, $350,000 total compensation
Executive Vice President, Chief Development Officer, Chief Research Officer, Faris Habbaba
Executive Vice President, Chief commercial Officer, Jean Jacques Blanc
Lead Director, Director, Mohamad S. Ali
Director, Deborah G. Ellinger
Director, Ruey-Bin Kao
Director, Karen M. Golz
Director, Eva Manolis
Director, Andrew Miller
Director, Michelle V. Stacy
Auditors : PricewaterhouseCoopers LLP

LOCATIONS
HQ: iRobot Corp
8 Crosby Drive, Bedford, MA 01730
Phone: 781 430-3000
Web: www.irobot.com

2018 Sales

	$ mil.	% of total
Americas	610.3	56
EMEA	311.7	28
APAC	170.6	16
Total	1,092.6	100

COMPETITORS
ATS Automation Tooling Systems Inc
Brita GmbH
EDGEWELL PERSONAL CARE COMPANY
ELECTROCOMPONENTS PUBLIC LIMITED COMPANY
FANUC CORPORATION
HIROTEC AMERICA INC.
Ovivo Inc
PMFG, INC.
WAYFAIR INC.
YASKAWA AMERICA, INC.

HISTORICAL FINANCIALS
Company Type: Public

Income Statement				FYE: January 1
	REVENUE ($mil)	NET INCOME ($mil)	NET PROFIT MARGIN	EMPLOYEES
01/22	1,564.9	30.3	1.9%	1,372
01/21*	1,430.3	147.0	10.3%	1,209
12/19	1,214.0	85.3	7.0%	1,128
12/18	1,092.5	87.9	8.1%	1,032
12/17	883.9	50.9	5.8%	920
Annual Growth	15.4%	(12.1%)	—	10.5%

*Fiscal year change

2022 Year-End Financials
Debt ratio: — No. of shares ($ mil.): 27.0
Return on equity: 4.0% Dividends
Cash ($ mil.): 201.4 Yield: —
Current Ratio: 2.00 Payout: —
Long-term debt ($ mil.): — Market value ($ mil.): 1,779.0

	STOCK PRICE ($) FY Close	P/E High/Low		PER SHARE ($) Earnings	Dividends	Book Value
01/22	65.88	147	58	1.08	0.00	26.54
01/21*	80.29	18	6	5.14	0.00	28.54
12/19	52.20	43	14	2.97	0.00	23.00
12/18	81.32	37	18	3.07	0.00	19.26
12/17	76.70	58	29	1.77	0.00	16.83
Annual Growth	(3.7%)	—		(11.6%)	—	12.1%

*Fiscal year change

Ironwood Pharmaceuticals Inc

Ironwood Pharmaceuticals develops internally discovered gastrointestinal drugs; its first commercial product, LINZESS (or linaclotide), a treatment for irritable bowel syndrome (IBS) and chronic constipation, is sold in the US and in Canada under the brand name Constella. To support the development and commercialization of linaclotide worldwide, it partnered with pharmaceutical companies including with AbbVie in the US and all countries worldwide other than China (including Hong Kong and Macau) with AstraZeneca and Japan with Astellas Pharma. Through collaboration with COUR Pharmaceutical, Ironwood has an option to acquire an exclusive license from COUR to research, develop, manufacture and commercialize, in the US, products containing CNP-104 for the potential treatment of PBC.

Operations

Ironwood is focused on creating first-in-class medicines, primarily for the treatment of gastrointestinal disorders. Manufacturing of its candidates is conducted through third parties and partners.

Ironwood's first FDA-approved drug, LINZESS, a treatment for adult patients suffering from irritable bowel syndrome with constipation or chronic idiopathic constipation. The company is also developing IW-3300, a GC-C agonist, for the potential treatment of visceral pain conditions, including interstitial cystitis/bladder pain syndrome and endometriosis.

The majority of Ironwood's revenue accounts from collaborative agreements.

Geographic Reach

Ironwood's headquarters and operations are located in Boston, Massachusetts. Its products are sold through its partnership in US and Europe, as well as in Mexico, Canada, Japan, and China (including Hong Kong and Macau).

Sales and Marketing

The company's partnership with AbbVie execute its commercialization plan that includes an agreed upon marketing campaign that targets the physicians who see patients who could benefit from LINZESS treatment. Its marketing campaign also targets the adult men and women who suffer from IBS-C or CIC.

Financial Performance

The company recognized $413.8 million in total revenues during the year ended December 31 2021, compared to $389.5 million during the year ended December 31, 2020. The increase of 6% was primarily driven by an increase of $31.8 million in collaborative arrangements revenue related to sales of LINZESS in the US.

In 2021, the company had a net income of $528.4 million, a 398% increase from the previous year's net income of $106.2 million.

The company's cash at the end of 2021 was $621.9 million. Operating activities generated $261.9 million, while investing activities used $0.3 million, mainly for purchases of property and equipment. Financing activities used another $4.6 million, mainly for repurchases of common stock.

Strategy

In 2021, Ironwood evolved its GI-focused strategy, building on the company's commercial success and GI development capabilities to focus on three core priorities: maximize LINZESS, strengthen its innovative GI pipeline, and deliver sustained profits and generate cash flow.

As part of its GI-focused strategy, the company has established development and commercial capabilities that it plans to leverage as the company seeks to bring multiple medicines to patients. Ironwood intends to play an active role in the development and commercialization of products in the US, either independently or with partners that have strong capabilities. Ironwood also intends to establish strong global brands by out-licensing development and commercialization rights to its products in other key territories to high-performing partners. The company plans to seek collaborations that increase the value of its products by providing meaningful economics and incentives for it and any potential partner. Ironwood intends to continue to expand its expertise in GI by accessing innovative externally developed products and to leverage its existing capabilities to develop and commercialize these products in the US.

Ironwood has pursued a partnering strategy for commercializing linaclotide that has allowed it to focus its commercialization efforts in the US and enabled partners with strong global capabilities to commercialize linaclotide in territories outside of the US.

Mergers and Acquisitions

In late 2021, Ironwood announced that it is expanding its pipeline by entering into a collaboration and license option agreement with COUR Pharmaceutical Development Company, Inc. (COUR), a biotechnology company developing novel immune-modifying nanoparticles to treat autoimmune diseases. This agreement gives Ironwood an option to acquire an exclusive license to develop and commercialize, in the US, COUR's investigational therapy CNP-104, which if successful, could transform the treatment of Primary Biliary Cholangitis ? otherwise known as PBC - a rare autoimmune disease targeting the liver that affects an estimated 133,000 people in the US. Currently there is no cure, and medical care is focused on disease management. PBC can lead to irreversible damage and scarring of the liver tissue, ultimately requiring liver transplant.

Company Background

Ironwood Pharmaceuticals conducted an IPO in 2010. The company's decision to go public helped it generate additional funds to push the development and commercialization of Linzess forward.

Founded in 1998 by CEO Peter Hecht and director Gina Borino Miller, the company changed its name from Microbia to Ironwood Pharmaceuticals in 2008 to reflect its focus on the development of human therapeutics. To further focus on its core operations, in 2010 Ironwood Pharmaceuticals sold its Microbia subsidiary, which was involved in the development of fermentation technologies used to produce specialty ingredients and biomaterials, to Royal DSM.

EXECUTIVES

Chairman, Director, Julie H. McHugh
Sales President, Marketing President, Thomas A. McCourt, $465,000 total compensation
Senior Vice President, Chief Financial Officer, Gina Consylman, $415,000 total compensation
Chief Executive Officer, Director, Mark Mallon
Senior Vice President, Chief Operating Officer, Jason Rickard
Chief Medical Officer, Division Officer, Michael Shetzline
Director, Mark G. Currie, $485,000 total compensation
Director, Jon R. Duane
Director, Marla L. Kessler
Director, Catherine Moukheibir
Director, Lawrence S. Olanoff
Director, Andrew Dreyfus
Director, Edward P. Owens
Director, Alexander J. Denner
Auditors : Ernst & Young LLP

LOCATIONS

HQ: Ironwood Pharmaceuticals Inc
100 Summer Street, Suite 2300, Boston, MA 02110
Phone: 617 621-7722
Web: www.ironwoodpharma.com

PRODUCTS/OPERATIONS

2014 Sales

	$ mil	% of total
Actavis plc	47.7	63
Astellas Pharma Inc.	17.7	23
Almirall S.A	7.6	10
AstraZeneca AB	3.4	4
Total	76.4	100

COMPETITORS

ADARE PHARMACEUTICALS, INC.
Boehringer Ingelheim International GmbH
EISAI CO., LTD.
MILLENNIUM PHARMACEUTICALS, INC.
NOVEN PHARMACEUTICALS, INC.
SCICLONE PHARMACEUTICALS, INC.
SUNOVION PHARMACEUTICALS INC.
U C B
VECTURA GROUP SERVICES LIMITED
XENOPORT, INC.

HISTORICAL FINANCIALS
Company Type: Public

Income Statement — FYE: December 31

	REVENUE ($mil)	NET INCOME ($mil)	NET PROFIT MARGIN	EMPLOYEES
12/21	413.7	528.4	127.7%	219
12/20	389.5	106.1	27.3%	232
12/19	428.4	21.5	5.0%	317
12/18	346.6	(282.3)	—	515
12/17	298.2	(116.9)	—	730
Annual Growth	8.5%	—	—	(26.0%)

2021 Year-End Financials
Debt ratio: 40.3%
Return on equity: —
Cash ($ mil.): 620.1
Current Ratio: 4.61
Long-term debt ($ mil.): 337.3
No. of shares ($ mil.): 162.0
Dividends
 Yield: —
 Payout: —
Market value ($ mil.): 1,889.0

	STOCK PRICE ($) FY Close	P/E High/Low		PER SHARE ($) Earnings	Dividends	Book Value
12/21	11.66	4	3	3.21	0.00	3.74
12/20	11.39	21	13	0.66	0.00	0.39
12/19	13.31	109	59	0.14	0.00	(0.59)
12/18	10.36	—	—	(1.85)	0.00	(1.27)
12/17	14.99	—	—	(0.78)	0.00	0.07
Annual Growth	(6.1%)	—	—	—	—	174.9%

Janus International Group Inc

EXECUTIVES

Chairman, José E. Feliciano
Chief Financial Officer, Executive Vice President, Anselm Wong
Executive Vice President, Morgan Hodges
Estimating Vice President, Sales Vice President, Peter Frayser
Manufacturing Vice President, Norman V. Nettie
Chief Executive Officer, Director, Ramey Pierce Jackson
Director, Colin M. Leonard
Director, Roger B. Fradin
Director, Brian Scott Cook
Director, David F. Doll
Director, Xavier A. Gutierrez
Director, Thomas A. Szlosek
Director, Heather Harding

LOCATIONS

HQ: Janus International Group Inc
 135 Janus International Blvd., , GA, Temple, GA 30179
Phone: 866 562-2580
Web: www.janusintl.com

HISTORICAL FINANCIALS
Company Type: Public

Income Statement — FYE: December 26

	REVENUE ($mil)	NET INCOME ($mil)	NET PROFIT MARGIN	EMPLOYEES
12/20	548.9	56.8	10.4%	1,603
12/19	565.2	39.3	7.0%	0
12/18*	438.9	5.4	1.3%	0
02/18	45.7	6.7	14.7%	0
Annual Growth	128.9%	103.8%		

*Fiscal year change

2020 Year-End Financials
Debt ratio: 71.5%
Return on equity: 41.9%
Cash ($ mil.): 45.2
Current Ratio: 1.77
Long-term debt ($ mil.): 617.6
No. of shares ($ mil.): 0.0
Dividends
 Yield: —
 Payout: —
Market value ($ mil.): 0.0

John Marshall Bancorp Inc

EXECUTIVES

President, Chief Executive Officer, Subsidiary Officer, Christopher W. Bergstrom
Executive Vice President, Chief Financial Officer, Subsidiary Officer, Kent D. Carstater
Auditors : Yount, Hyde & Barbour, P.C.

LOCATIONS

HQ: John Marshall Bancorp Inc
 1943 Isaac Newton Square E., Suite 100, Reston, VA 20190
Phone: 703 584-0840 **Fax:** 703 584-0859

HISTORICAL FINANCIALS
Company Type: Public

Income Statement — FYE: December 31

	REVENUE ($mil)	NET INCOME ($mil)	NET PROFIT MARGIN	EMPLOYEES
12/20	74.0	18.5	25.0%	0
12/19	70.3	15.9	22.6%	0
12/18	59.1	12.1	20.6%	0
12/17	50.5	8.9	17.8%	0
12/16	43.3	8.3	19.1%	0
Annual Growth	14.3%	22.2%	—	—

2020 Year-End Financials
Debt ratio: 2.5%
Return on equity: 10.6%
Cash ($ mil.): 138.4
Current Ratio: 0.18
Long-term debt ($ mil.): 46.6
No. of shares ($ mil.): 13.5
Dividends
 Yield: —
 Payout: —
Market value ($ mil.): 194.0

	STOCK PRICE ($) FY Close	P/E High/Low		PER SHARE ($) Earnings	Dividends	Book Value
12/20	14.30	13	7	1.35	0.00	13.75
12/19	16.50	14	12	1.17	0.00	12.39
12/18	14.95	20	16	0.89	0.00	11.08
12/17	17.80	33	25	0.66	0.00	10.12
12/16	20.75	32	24	0.63	0.00	9.38
Annual Growth	(8.9%)	—	—	20.9%	—	10.0%

Johnson Outdoors Inc

Founded in 1987, Johnson Outdoors keeps sports buffs from staying indoors. The company makes, markets, and sells camping and outdoor equipment (such as Jetboil cooking systems and Eureka! tents and backpacks). It also focuses on supplying equipment for water activities with its diving gear (Scubapro and Uwatec masks, fins, snorkels, and tanks), trolling motors (Minn Kota), fish finders (Humminbird), and watercraft (Old Town canoes). With GPS technologies and electric boat motors, The Johnson family, including CEO Helen Johnson-Leipold, controls the company. Most of the company's sales come from the US.

Operations

Johnson Outdoors operates under four reportable business segments; Fishing, Diving, Camping, and Watercraft recreation.

The fishing segment generate about 75% of net sales. It offers electric motors, marine battery chargers, shallow water anchors, sonar and GPS equipment. Through its key brands Minn Kota, Humminbird, and Cannon.

The Diving segment generate about 10% of net sales. It manufactures and markets underwater diving products for recreational divers, which it sells and distributes under the SCUBAPRO brand name.

Camping segment (more than 5% of net sales) offers portable outdoor cooking systems, tent, camping furniture, camping stoves and other recreational camping products.

Watercraft recreation gives in nearly 10% of net sales. designs and markets canoes and kayaks under the Ocean Kayaks and Old Town brand names for family recreation, touring, angling and tripping.

Geographic Reach

Wisconsin-based, Johnson Outdoors has domestic manufacturing facilities in Georgia, New York, Alabama, California, Minnesota, New Hampshire, and Maine. Some of its international manufacturing facilities are located in Spain, Indonesia, France, Belgium, Canada, Australia, and Mexico. The US is Johnson Outdoors' largest market, representing more than 85% of its sales. Other markets include Canada, Europe, and the Pacific Basin.

Sales and Marketing

Johnson Outdoors sells its products to major retailers, outdoor specialty stores (Cabela's, Bass Pro Shops), and catalog and online merchants. It also provides boat motors and other products for original equipment manufacturers of boat brands, such as Tracker, Skeeter, and Ranger.

The company's consumer marketing and promotion activities include: product placements on fishing-related TV shows; print advertising and editorial coverage in outdoor, general interest, and sport magazines; professional angler and tournament sponsorships; packaging and point-of-purchase materials, and offers to increase consumer appeal and sales; branded websites; social media networks; and online promotions.

Advertising and promotions expense in fiscal year 2021, 2020, and 2019 totaled $30,882, $26,727 and $28,397, respectively.

Financial Performance

Johnson Outdoors has reported steady revenue growth over the past five years, with sales increasing by about 53% between 2017 and 2021. Net income followed the same growth trend for the same period.

Net sales in fiscal 2021 increased by 26% to $751.7 million compared to $594.2 million in 2020, driven primarily by strong performance in the Fishing, Camping and Watercraft Recreation segments where the company saw strong demand for its outdoor recreation products as a result of consumers recreating outdoors in light of COVID-19.

The company reported net income of $83.4 million in fiscal 2021, an increase of 34% from $55.2 million in fiscal 2020.

Cash at the end of fiscal 2021 was $240.4 million. Cash provided by operating activities was $53.3 million, while cash used for investing activities was $21.4 million. Financing activities used $9.0 million for dividends paid.

Strategy

Through a combination of innovative products, strong marketing, a talented and passionate workforce and efficient distribution, the company seeks to set itself apart from the competition in its markets. Its subsidiaries operate as a network that promotes innovation and leverages best practices and synergies, following the strategic vision set by executive management.

Because the company expects that the same supply chain disruptions will continue into fiscal 2022, the company remains focused on evaluating and pursuing additional options (beyond building inventory) to manage its supply chain to meet the continued strong consumer demand for its products. Nonetheless, these supply chain disruptions remain fluid and will likely impact the cost of goods sold for future sales of product or the company's ability to fill all customer demand for its products, especially given the volatility and changing circumstances brought on by the COVID-19 pandemic.

HISTORY

Cleaning products maker S.C. Johnson & Son (Johnson Wax) set up subsidiary Johnson Diversified in 1970, which then began acquiring and developing a number of leisure products companies worldwide. Renamed Johnson Worldwide Associates (JWA), the unit was taken public in 1987. By decade's end JWA had emerged as the #1 maker of electric fishing-boat motors. The company went on a 19-company buying spree between 1989 and 1991, a growth strategy that led to declining earnings.

As sporting goods retailers consolidated in the mid-1990s, with fewer companies accumulating more buying power, manufacturers were forced to keep prices competitive. Ronald Whitaker became president and CEO in 1996 and reorganized the company, expanding product classifications from three (fishing/marine, camping, and diving) to five and assigning a manager to each. JWA also reduced inventory, taking an $11 million charge. It bought small manufacturers to expand its product offerings.

JWA dumped Plastimo, its unprofitable European marine division, in 1997. It also expanded its watercraft division, buying Ocean Kayak (1997), Plastiques (1997, Dimension kayaks), Leisure Life Limited (1998, recreational boats), and Necky Kayaks and Escape Sailboat (1999). Whitaker resigned in 1999, and Samuel Johnson's daughter Helen Johnson-Leipold, a former JWA executive, rejoined the company from S.C. Johnson as chairman and CEO.

In 2000 JWA changed its name to Johnson Outdoors to better reflect its core business. Johnson Outdoors also sold its fishing business to Berkley (Pure Fishing) for $34.5 million that year.

In 2001 the company acquired Fibrekraft Manufacturers, a New Zealand-based maker of paddles and other watercraft accessories, to accelerate growth in international markets. Also that year Johnson Outdoors won a hefty government contract to make extreme weather tents. Samuel Johnson was named the 2001 National Ernst & Young Master Entrepreneur Of The Year.

In September 2002 Johnson Outdoors sold its Jack Wolfskin subsidiary for $62.9 million to Bain Capital, a global private investment firm.

The company acquired sonar and video viewing equipment maker Techsonic Industries from Teleflex in May 2004. The purchase added the Humminbird brand to Johnson's marine electronics line. A significant decline in military tent sales in early 2005 led the company to eliminate more than 70 positions (5% of Johnson Outdoors' workforce) at its plant in Binghamton, New York.

Refocused on growth, Johnson Outdoors in late 2006 added Scotland-based Lendal Paddles to its paddle sports portfolio. In April 2007 the company acquired the German diving equipment company Seemann Sub from owners Robert and Ella Stoss for about $9 million. Also that year Johnson Outdoors purchased Italy's Geonav, which makes chart plotters, marine autopilots, VHF radios, and fish finders, for nearly $6 million.

EXECUTIVES

Chairman, Chief Executive Officer, Holding/Parent Company Officer, Helen P. Johnson-Leipold, $729,457 total compensation
Vice-Chairman, Thomas F. Pyle
Vice President, Chief Financial Officer, David W. Johnson, $384,043 total compensation
Director, Terry E. London
Director, John M. Fahey
Director, William D. Perez
Director, Katherine Button Bell
Director, Edward Stevens
Director, Edward F. Lang
Director, Richard Casey Sheahan
Auditors : RSM US LLP

LOCATIONS

HQ: Johnson Outdoors Inc
555 Main Street, Racine, WI 53403
Phone: 262 631-6600
Web: www.johnsonoutdoors.com

2016 Sales

	$ mil.	% of total
US	372.3	81
Europe	41.9	9
Canada	28.3	6
Other	15.8	4
Eliminations	(24.6)	-
Total	433.7	100

PRODUCTS/OPERATIONS

2016 Sales

	$ mil.	% of total
Marine electronics	274.9	63
Diving	69.1	16
Watercraft	50.4	12
Outdoor equipment	40.0	9
Adjustments	(0.7)	-
Total	433.7	100

Selected Brands

Diving
    SCUBAPRO
    Seemann
    UWATEC
Marine Electronics
    Cannon
    Humminbird
    Minn Kota
    Navicontrol
Outdoor Equipment
    Eureka!
    Jetboil
    Silva
    Tech40
Watercraft
    Carlisle

Extrasport
Lendal
Necky
Ocean Kayak
Old Town

COMPETITORS

ACUSHNET HOLDINGS CORP.
BRUNSWICK CORPORATION
CALLAWAY GOLF COMPANY
CAMELBAK PRODUCTS, LLC
COLUMBIA SPORTSWEAR COMPANY
CYBEX INTERNATIONAL, INC.
POLARIS INC.
THE BURTON CORPORATION
THE COLEMAN COMPANY INC
THE INTERTECH GROUP INC

HISTORICAL FINANCIALS

Company Type: Public

Income Statement — FYE: October 1

	REVENUE ($mil)	NET INCOME ($mil)	NET PROFIT MARGIN	EMPLOYEES
10/21	751.6	83.3	11.1%	1,400
10/20*	594.2	55.2	9.3%	1,200
09/19	562.4	51.4	9.1%	1,200
09/18	544.2	40.6	7.5%	1,200
09/17	490.5	35.1	7.2%	1,100
Annual Growth	11.3%	24.1%	—	6.2%

*Fiscal year change

2021 Year-End Financials

Debt ratio: —
Return on equity: 19.9%
Cash ($ mil.): 240.4
Current Ratio: 3.57
Long-term debt ($ mil.): —
No. of shares ($ mil.): 10.1
Dividends
 Yield: 0.7%
 Payout: 9.2%
Market value ($ mil.): 1,111.0

	STOCK PRICE ($) FY Close	P/E High/Low		PER SHARE ($) Earnings	Dividends	Book Value
10/21	109.67	18	10	16.42	0.84	45.27
10/20*	86.18	17	9	5.47	0.68	37.49
09/19	58.63	18	11	5.11	0.56	32.31
09/18	92.99	26	15	4.05	0.44	27.92
09/17	73.28	19	9	3.51	0.36	24.31
Annual Growth	10.6%	—	—	47.1%	23.6%	16.8%

*Fiscal year change

Joint Corp (New)

EXECUTIVES

President, Chief Executive Officer, Director,
Peter D. Holt, $409,084 total compensation
Chief Financial Officer, Jake Singleton, $183,013 total compensation
Secretary, Craig P. Colmar
Lead Director, Director, Matthew E. Rubel
Director, James H. Amos
Director, Ronald V. DaVella
Director, Suzanne M. Decker
Director, Abe Hong
Director, Glenn J. Krevlin
Auditors : BDO USA, LLP

LOCATIONS

HQ: Joint Corp (New)
16767 North Perimeter Drive, Suite 110, Scottsdale, AZ 85260

Phone: 480 245-5960
Web: www.thejoint.com

HISTORICAL FINANCIALS

Company Type: Public

Income Statement — FYE: December 31

	REVENUE ($mil)	NET INCOME ($mil)	NET PROFIT MARGIN	EMPLOYEES
12/20	58.6	13.1	22.4%	425
12/19	48.4	3.3	6.9%	150
12/18	31.7	0.2	0.8%	138
12/17	25.1	(3.2)	—	148
12/16	20.5	(15.1)	—	94
Annual Growth	30.0%	—	—	45.8%

2020 Year-End Financials

Debt ratio: 7.5%
Return on equity: 99.2%
Cash ($ mil.): 20.5
Current Ratio: 1.35
Long-term debt ($ mil.): 2.1
No. of shares ($ mil.): 14.1
Dividends
 Yield: —
 Payout: —
Market value ($ mil.): 372.0

	STOCK PRICE ($) FY Close	P/E High/Low		PER SHARE ($) Earnings	Dividends	Book Value
12/20	26.26	29	9	0.90	0.00	1.47
12/19	16.14	87	33	0.23	0.00	0.41
12/18	8.32	460	235	0.02	0.00	0.17
12/17	4.96	—	—	(0.25)	0.00	0.36
12/16	2.65	—	—	(1.20)	0.00	0.53
Annual Growth	77.4%	—	—	—	—	28.8%

Kadant Inc

Kadant is a global supplier of technologies and engineered systems that drive sustainable industrial processing. Its products and services play an integral role in enhancing efficiency, optimizing energy utilization, and maximizing productivity in process industries while helping its customers advance their sustainability initiatives with products that reduce waste or generate more yield with fewer inputs, particularly fiber, energy, and water. It develops and manufactures a range of products and equipment used in process industries such as paper, packaging, and tissue; wood products; mining; metals; food processing; and recycling and waste management, among others. Kadant's diverse customer base includes global and regional industrial manufacturers and distributors who participate in the broader resource transformation sector. Most of Kadant's revenues are generated outside the US.

Operations

Kadant operates three reportable operating segments: Flow Control, Industrial Processing, and Material Handling.

Its Industrial Processing segment (over 40%) provides equipment, machinery, and technologies used to recycle paper and paperboard and process timber for use in the packaging, tissue, wood products and alternative fuel industries, among others. In addition, it provides industrial automation and digitization solutions to process industries. The Industrial Processing segment consists of its wood processing and stock-preparation product lines.

Kadant's Flow Control segment (more than 35% of revenue) provides custom-engineered products, systems, and technologies that control the flow of fluids used in industrial and commercial applications to keep critical processes running efficiently in the packaging, tissue, food, metals, and other industrial sectors. The Flow Control segment consists of its fluid-handling and doctoring, cleaning, & filtration product lines.

The Material Handling segment (around 20%) provides products and engineered systems used to handle bulk and discrete materials for secondary processing or transport in the aggregates, mining, food, and waste management industries, among others. In addition, it manufactures and sells biodegradable, absorbent granules used as carriers in agricultural applications and for oil and grease absorption. The Material Handling segment consists of our conveying and screening, baling, and fiber-based product lines.

In all, parts and consumables generated around two-thirds i=of sales, while capital generated the remaining sales.

Geographic Reach

Based in Westford, Massachusetts, Kadant sell its products globally, including sales to customers in China, South America, Russia and India, and operate multiple manufacturing operations worldwide, including operations in Canada, China, Europe, Mexico, India, and Brazil.

About 60% of its sales are to customers outside the US, principally in Canada, Germany, and China.

Sales and Marketing

Kadant sells its products, services, and systems using a combination of direct sales, independent sales agents, and distributors. Technical service personnel, product specialists, and independent sales agents and distributors are utilized in certain markets and for certain product lines.

No single customer accounted for 10% or more of its consolidated revenues.

Financial Performance

Consolidated revenue in 2021 increased 24% to $786.6 million, driven by higher demand for both parts and consumables products and capital equipment principally at its Industrial Processing and Flow Control segments.

In 2021, the company had a net income of $84 million, a 52% increase from the previous year's net income of $55.2 million.

The company's cash at the end of 2021 was $94.2 million. Operating activities generated $162.4 million, while investing activities used $154.5 million, primarily for acquisitions. Financing activities provided another $22.8 million.

Strategy

The company develops a broad range of products for all facets of the markets it serve. Kadant operates research and development facilities in the United States, Europe, and Canada, and focuses its product innovations on process industry challenges and the need for improved fiber processing, heat transfer, roll and fabric cleaning, fluid handling, timber harvesting, wood processing, and secondary material handling. In addition to internal product development activities, its research centers allow customers to simulate their own operating conditions and applications to identify and quantify opportunities for improvement.

The company's research and development expenses were $11.4 million in 2021, $11.3 million in 2020, and $10.9 million in 2019.

EXECUTIVES

Executive Chairman, Director, Jonathan W. Painter, $675,000 total compensation
President, Chief Executive Officer, Director, Jeffrey L. Powell, $425,000 total compensation
Finance Executive Vice President, Finance Chief Financial Officer, Michael J. McKenney, $370,000 total compensation
Executive Vice President, Chief Operating Officer, Eric T. Langevin, $415,000 total compensation
Vice President, General Counsel, Secretary, Stacy D. Krause, $282,500 total compensation
Vice President, Subsidiary Officer, Peter J. Flynn
Vice President, Subsidiary Officer, Michael Colwel
Director, John M. Albertine
Director, Thomas C. Leonard
Director, Erin L. Russell
Director, William P. Tully
Auditors : KPMG LLP

LOCATIONS

HQ: Kadant Inc
One Technology Park Drive, Westford, MA 01886
Phone: 978 776-2000
Web: www.kadant.com

2015 Sales

	$ mil.	% of total
US	193.4	50
China	50.8	13
Other	145.9	37
Total	390.1	100

PRODUCTS/OPERATIONS

2017 Sales

	$ mil.	% of total
Papermaking Systems		
Stock Preparation	193.8	38
Doctoring, Cleaning & Filtration	109.6	21
Fluid Handling	104.1	20
Wood Processing Systems	95.1	19
Fiber-based Products	12.4	2
Total	515.0	100

Selected Products

Doctoring, Cleaning and Filtration
  Doctoring
  Cleaning
  Filtration
  Forming
Fluid Handling
  Rotary joints and unions
  Expansion joints and flexible connectors
  Jet devices
  Condensate pumps
  Steam systems
  Accessories
Fiber Processing
  OCC, recycled stock and pulp preparation
  Chemical pulping
Recycling Machinery
  Balers for recyclable materials
  Balers for waste, RDF, alfalfa
  Conveyors
Wood Processing
  Engineered wood (OSB)
  Chipping/screening
  Debarking
  Granules

COMPETITORS

ANDRITZ INC.
CHART INDUSTRIES, INC.
GLATFELTER CORPORATION
GRAHAM CORPORATION
HAYNES INTERNATIONAL, INC.
MAXCESS INTERNATIONAL CORPORATION
NORDSON CORPORATION
PAPER CONVERTING MACHINE COMPANY
QUIPP, INC.
TECNAU, INC

HISTORICAL FINANCIALS

Company Type: Public

Income Statement				FYE: January 2
	REVENUE ($mil)	NET INCOME ($mil)	NET PROFIT MARGIN	EMPLOYEES
01/21*	635.0	55.1	8.7%	2,600
12/19	704.6	52.0	7.4%	2,800
12/18	633.7	60.4	9.5%	2,500
12/17	515.0	31.0	6.0%	2,400
12/16	414.1	32.0	7.7%	2,000
Annual Growth	11.3%	14.5%	—	6.8%

*Fiscal year change

2021 Year-End Financials

Debt ratio: 25.2%
Return on equity: 11.7%
Cash ($ mil.): 65.6
Current Ratio: 2.15
Long-term debt ($ mil.): 232
No. of shares ($ mil.): 11.5
Dividends
  Yield: —
  Payout: 19.9%
Market value ($ mil.): 1,627.0

	STOCK PRICE ($) FY Close	P/E High/Low		PER SHARE ($)		
		High	Low	Earnings	Dividends	Book Value
01/21*	140.98	29	11	4.77	0.95	42.92
12/19	105.76	23	17	4.54	0.91	37.31
12/18	81.12	20	14	5.30	0.87	33.57
12/17	100.40	40	20	2.75	0.82	30.06
12/16	61.20	22	12	2.88	0.74	25.84
Annual Growth	23.2%	—	—	13.4%	6.4%	13.5%

*Fiscal year change

Kearny Financial Corp (MD)

EXECUTIVES

Chairman, Subsidiary Officer, Director, John J. Mazur
President, Chief Executive Officer, Subsidiary Officer, Craig L. Montanaro, $450,000 total compensation
Executive Vice President, Thomas D. DeMedici
Executive Vice President, Chief Financial Officer, Keith Suchodolski
Senior Executive Vice President, Chief Operating Officer, Subsidiary Officer, William C. Ledgerwood, $300,600 total compensation
Executive Vice President, Chief Financial Officer, Subsidiary Officer, Eric B. Heyer, $271,160 total compensation
Executive Vice President, Corporate Secretary, Subsidiary Officer, Sharon Jones
Subsidiary Officer, Patrick M. Joyce, $282,063 total compensation
Subsidiary Officer, Erika K. Parisi, $268,730 total compensation
Executive Vice President, Anthony V. Bilotta
Director, Leopold W. Montanaro
Director, Matthew T. McClane
Director, Joseph P. Mazza
Director, John N. Hopkins
Director, Paul M. Aguggia
Director, Charles J. Pivirotto
Director, Theodore J. Aanensen
Director, John F. McGovern
Director, John F. Regan
Director, Raymond E. Chandonnet
Director, Christopher D. Petermann
Director, Catherine A. Lawton
Director, Cynthia Sisco
Auditors : Crowe LLP

LOCATIONS

HQ: Kearny Financial Corp (MD)
120 Passaic Avenue, Fairfield, NJ 07004
Phone: 973 244-4500
Web: www.kearnybank.com

HISTORICAL FINANCIALS

Company Type: Public

Income Statement				FYE: June 30
	ASSETS ($mil)	NET INCOME ($mil)	INCOME AS % OF ASSETS	EMPLOYEES
06/21	7,283.7	63.2	0.9%	584
06/20	6,758.1	44.9	0.7%	552
06/19	6,634.8	42.1	0.6%	565
06/18	6,579.8	19.5	0.3%	565
06/17	4,818.1	18.6	0.4%	466
Annual Growth	10.9%	35.8%	—	5.8%

2021 Year-End Financials

Return on assets: 0.9%
Return on equity: 5.9%
Long-term debt ($ mil.): —
No. of shares ($ mil.): 78.9
Sales ($ mil.): 259.1
Dividends
  Yield: 2.9%
  Payout: 50.0%
Market value ($ mil.): 944.0

	STOCK PRICE ($) FY Close	P/E High/Low		PER SHARE ($) Earnings	Dividends	Book Value
06/21	11.95	18	9	0.77	0.35	13.21
06/20	8.18	26	14	0.55	0.29	12.96
06/19	13.29	31	26	0.46	0.37	12.65
06/18	13.45	65	54	0.24	0.25	12.74
06/17	14.85	73	57	0.22	0.10	12.53
Annual Growth	(5.3%)	—	—	36.8%	36.8%	1.3%

Kilroy Realty L.P.

EXECUTIVES

Chairman, Chief Executive Officer, Associate/Affiliate Company Officer, Director, John B. Kilroy, $1,225,000 total compensation
President, Executive Vice President, Secretary, Associate/Affiliate Company Officer, Tyler H. Rose
Executive Vice President, Chief Financial Officer, Chief Investment Officer, Treasurer, Eliott Trencher
Executive Vice President, Chief Administrative Officer, Heidi Rena Roth
Senior Vice President, Chief Accounting Officer, Controller, Associate/Affiliate Company Officer, Merryl E. Werber
Director, Lead Independent Director, Edward F. Brennan
Director, Jolie A. Hunt
Director, Scott S. Ingraham
Director, Louisa G. Ritter
Director, Gary R. Stevenson
Director, Peter B. Stoneberg
Auditors : DELOITTE & TOUCHE LLP

LOCATIONS

HQ: Kilroy Realty L.P.
 12200 W. Olympic Boulevard, Suite 200, Los Angeles, CA 90064
Phone: 310 481-8400
Web: www.kilroyrealty.com

HISTORICAL FINANCIALS
Company Type: Public

Income Statement				FYE: December 31
	REVENUE ($mil)	NET INCOME ($mil)	NET PROFIT MARGIN	EMPLOYEES
12/20	898.3	189.6	21.1%	252
12/19	837.4	198.7	23.7%	267
12/18	747.2	263.2	35.2%	276
12/17	719.0	167.4	23.3%	251
12/16	642.5	300.0	46.7%	245
Annual Growth	8.7%	(10.8%)	—	0.7%

2020 Year-End Financials
Debt ratio: 39.2%   No. of shares ($ mil.): 117.1
Return on equity: —   Dividends
Cash ($ mil.): 731.9   Yield: —
Current Ratio: 1.50   Payout: 121.6%
Long-term debt ($ mil.): 3,923.6   Market value ($ mil.): 0.0

Kimball Electronics Inc

EXECUTIVES

Chairman, Chief Executive Officer, Director, Donald D. Charron, $678,800 total compensation
Vice President, Chief Financial Officer, Jana T. Croom
Corporate Development Vice President, Mergers and Acquisitions Vice President, Corporate Development Chief Strategy Officer, Mergers and Acquisitions Chief Strategy Officer, Desiree L. Castillejos
Human Resources Vice President, Jessica L. DeLorenzo
Industrial Technology Vice President, Sandy A. Smith
Division Officer, LeRoy (Lee) W. Kemper
Chief Legal Officer, Chief Compliance Officer, Secretary, Douglas A. Hass
Division Officer, Steven T. Korn, $309,234 total compensation
Division Officer, Kathy R. Thomson
Business Development Division Officer, Christopher J. Thyen, $289,228 total compensation
Director, Colleen C. Repplier
Director, Gregory J. Lampert
Director, Holly A. Van Deursen
Director, Michele A. M. Holcomb
Director, Robert J. Phillippy
Director, Gregory A. Thaxton
Auditors : DELOITTE & TOUCHE LLP

LOCATIONS

HQ: Kimball Electronics Inc
 1205 Kimball Boulevard, Jasper, IN 47546
Phone: 812 634-4000
Web: www.kimballelectronics.com

HISTORICAL FINANCIALS
Company Type: Public

Income Statement				FYE: June 30
	REVENUE ($mil)	NET INCOME ($mil)	NET PROFIT MARGIN	EMPLOYEES
06/21	1,291.8	56.7	4.4%	6,400
06/20	1,200.5	18.1	1.5%	6,400
06/19	1,181.8	31.5	2.7%	6,300
06/18	1,072.0	16.7	1.6%	5,700
06/17	930.9	34.1	3.7%	5,400
Annual Growth	8.5%	13.5%	—	4.3%

2021 Year-End Financials
Debt ratio: 8.1%   No. of shares ($ mil.): 24.9
Return on equity: 13.8%   Dividends
Cash ($ mil.): 106.4   Yield: —
Current Ratio: 1.94   Payout: —
Long-term debt ($ mil.): 40   Market value ($ mil.): 543.0

	STOCK PRICE ($) FY Close	P/E High/Low		PER SHARE ($) Earnings	Dividends	Book Value
06/21	21.74	13	5	2.24	0.00	17.71
06/20	13.54	25	14	0.71	0.00	15.18
06/19	16.24	17	12	1.21	0.00	14.55
06/18	18.30	35	25	0.62	0.00	13.40
06/17	18.05	15	10	1.24	0.00	12.75
Annual Growth	4.8%	—	—	15.9%	—	8.6%

Kinsale Capital Group Inc

EXECUTIVES

Chairman, Director, Robert Lippincott
Senior Vice President, Chief Information Officer, Diane D. Schnupp
President, Chief Executive Officer, Director, Michael P. Kehoe, $500,000 total compensation
Senior Vice President, Chief Operating Officer, Brian D. Haney, $267,500 total compensation
Senior Vice President, Chief Information Officer, William J. Kenney, $258,317 total compensation
Senior Vice President, Chief Claims Officer, Ann Marie Marson, $258,317 total compensation
Senior Vice President, Chief Financial Officer, Treasurer, Bryan P. Petrucelli, $267,500 total compensation
Director, Anne C. Kronenberg
Director, Gregory M. Share
Director, Steven J. Bensinger
Director, James Joseph Ritchie
Director, Frederick L. Russell
Auditors : KPMG LLP

LOCATIONS

HQ: Kinsale Capital Group Inc
 2035 Maywill Street, Suite 100, Richmond, VA 23230
Phone: 804 289-1300   **Fax:** 804 673-5697
Web: www.kinsalecapitalgroup.com

HISTORICAL FINANCIALS
Company Type: Public

Income Statement				FYE: December 31
	ASSETS ($mil)	NET INCOME ($mil)	INCOME AS % OF ASSETS	EMPLOYEES
12/20	1,546.8	88.4	5.7%	335
12/19	1,090.5	63.3	5.8%	275
12/18	773.0	33.7	4.4%	190
12/17	667.8	24.9	3.7%	164
12/16	614.3	26.1	4.3%	145
Annual Growth	26.0%	35.6%	—	23.3%

2020 Year-End Financials
Return on assets: 6.6%   Dividends
Return on equity: 17.9%   Yield: —
Long-term debt ($ mil.): —   Payout: 9.3%
No. of shares ($ mil.): 22.7   Market value ($ mil.): 4,554.0
Sales ($ mil.): 459.8

	STOCK PRICE ($) FY Close	P/E High/Low		PER SHARE ($) Earnings	Dividends	Book Value
12/20	200.13	63	21	3.87	0.36	25.32
12/19	101.66	37	19	2.86	0.32	18.28
12/18	55.56	40	27	1.56	0.28	12.43
12/17	45.00	38	24	1.16	0.24	11.32
12/16	34.01	61	32	0.56	0.10	10.03
Annual Growth	55.7%	—	—	62.1%	37.7%	26.1%

	STOCK PRICE ($) FY Close	P/E High/Low		PER SHARE ($) Earnings	Dividends	Book Value
12/20	28.50	10	8	3.12	0.81	26.88
12/19	30.75	12	10	2.70	1.00	24.91
12/18	32.00	28	13	2.37	1.63	23.27
12/17	58.00	17	14	3.33	0.92	45.08
12/16	46.00	12	11	3.77	0.86	43.14
Annual Growth	(11.3%)	—	—	(4.6%)	(1.5%)	(11.2%)

	STOCK PRICE ($) FY Close	P/E High/Low		PER SHARE ($) Earnings	Dividends	Book Value
12/21	20.83	10	8	2.21	1.72	22.18
12/20	17.92	23	10	0.96	1.72	18.80
12/19	20.42	13	12	1.57	1.72	19.55
12/18	19.15	13	12	1.58	1.69	19.71
12/17	20.01	18	15	1.30	0.99	19.75
Annual Growth	1.0%	—	—	14.2%	14.8%	3.0%

Kish Bancorp Inc.

Get your banking needs sealed with a Kish. Kish Bancorp is the holding company for Kishacoquillas Valley National Bank, commonly referred to as Kish Bank. The bank serves individual and business customers through about 10 offices in Centre, Huntingdon, and Mifflin counties in central Pennsylvania. It offers checking and savings accounts, IRAs, CDs, and other retail products, and uses funds from deposits to write primarily real estate loans (commercial and residential mortgages each account for about one-third of its loan portfolio). Other subsidiaries of Kish Bancorp provide insurance, investment management, financial planning, and travel services.

Auditors : S.R. Snodgrass, P.C.

LOCATIONS

HQ: Kish Bancorp Inc.
  4255 East Main Street, Belleville, PA 17004
Phone: 844 554-4748
Web: www.kishbank.com

COMPETITORS

FIDELITY D & D BANCORP, INC.
LYONS NATIONAL BANK
NEFFS BANCORP, INC.
QNB CORP.
WCF FINANCIAL BANK

HISTORICAL FINANCIALS
Company Type: Public

Income Statement				FYE: December 31
	ASSETS ($mil)	NET INCOME ($mil)	INCOME AS % OF ASSETS	EMPLOYEES
12/20	1,106.6	8.0	0.7%	0
12/19	918.3	7.0	0.8%	0
12/18	850.5	6.0	0.7%	0
12/17	811.1	4.1	0.5%	0
12/16	725.0	4.6	0.6%	0
Annual Growth	11.1%	14.9%	—	—

2020 Year-End Financials
Return on assets: 0.7%
Return on equity: 11.9%
Long-term debt ($ mil.): —
No. of shares ($ mil.): 2.6
Sales ($ mil.): 49.5
Dividends
  Yield: 2.8%
  Payout: 25.9%
Market value ($ mil.): 74.0

KKR Real Estate Finance Trust Inc

EXECUTIVES

Chairman, Director, Ralph F. Rosenberg
Vice-Chairman, Director, Christen E.J. Lee, $0 total compensation
President, Chief Operating Officer, W. Patrick Mattson, $0 total compensation
Chief Executive Officer, Director, Matthew A. Salem, $0 total compensation
Chief Financial Officer, Treasurer, Kendra Decious
General Counsel, Secretary, Vincent J. Napolitano
Director, Terrance R. Ahern
Director, Irene M. Esteves
Director, Jonathan A. Langer
Director, Paula Madoff
Director, Deborah H. McAneny
Auditors : DELOITTE & TOUCHE LLP

LOCATIONS

HQ: KKR Real Estate Finance Trust Inc
  30 Hudson Yards, Suite 7500, New York, NY 10001
Phone: 212 750-8300
Web: www.kkrreit.com

HISTORICAL FINANCIALS
Company Type: Public

Income Statement				FYE: December 31
	REVENUE ($mil)	NET INCOME ($mil)	NET PROFIT MARGIN	EMPLOYEES
12/21	292.1	137.1	47.0%	0
12/20	270.4	54.3	20.1%	0
12/19	280.3	89.9	32.1%	0
12/18	203.6	89.7	44.1%	0
12/17	100.8	59.0	58.6%	0
Annual Growth	30.5%	23.5%	—	—

2021 Year-End Financials
Debt ratio: 79.1%
Return on equity: 11.3%
Cash ($ mil.): 271.4
Current Ratio: 7.32
Long-term debt ($ mil.): 5,302.4
No. of shares ($ mil.): 61.3
Dividends
  Yield: 8.2%
  Payout: 80.7%
Market value ($ mil.): 1,278.0

Lakeland Bancorp, Inc.

Lakeland Bancorp is the holding company for Lakeland Bank, which serves northern and central New Jersey from around 50 branch offices. Targeting individuals and small to midsized businesses, the bank offers standard retail products, such as checking and savings accounts, money market and NOW accounts, and CDs. It also offers financial planning and advisory services for consumers. The bank's lending activities primarily consist of commercial loans and mortgages (around three-quarters of the company's loan portfolio) and residential mortgages. Lakeland also offers commercial lease financing for commercial equipment.

Operations

Lakeland Bancorp operates through a single business segment. Around 70% of its $4.3 billion loan portfolio is made up of commercial mortgages. Industrial commercial loans, residential mortgages, real estate construction loans, and home equity and consumer loans each represent between 5%-10% of the company's lending activity. The company holds $5.5 billion in assets and $4.4 billion in deposits.

Geographic Reach

Headquartered in Oak Ridge, New Jersey, Lakeland Bancorp boasts about 50 banking offices across the New Jersey counties of Bergen, Essex, Morris, Ocean, Passaic, Somerset, Sussex, Union, and Warren. The company also has a branch in Highland Mills, New York; six New Jersey regional commercial lending centers in Bernardsville, Jackson, Montville, Newton, Teaneck and Waldwick; and two commercial loan production offices serving Middlesex and Monmouth counties in New Jersey and the Hudson Valley region of New York.

Sales and Marketing

Lakeland Bancorp serves a variety of customers, from individuals to businesses to municipalities.

One-fifth of Lakeland's commercial loan segment – the largest in its portfolio – is made up of owner-occupied real estate loans. Multifamily and retail loans make up about 15% each, and industrial and office loans each comprise around 10%.

Financial Performance

Lakeland Bancorp has seen major five-year growth, expanding revenue by 53% to $190.7 million, net income by 111% to $52.6 million, and cash by 39% to $142.9 million between 2013 and 2017. However, the company's debt has risen 85% to $296.9 million in that time.

The holding company's revenue increased 14% in 2017, owing primarily to increased net interest income from growing average earning assets. Net income added 27% on the strength of those gains.

Lakeland's cash dipped $32.9 million in 2017. Operations and financings contributed $67.5 million, and investments used $355.1 million. Financings provided $254.8 million, down nearly $200 million from the previous year following an increase in net deposits, federal funds purchased, and securities sold under repurchase agreements.

Strategy

Lakeland Bancorp is focused on growth through acquisitions. The company has acquired at least eight community banks since its inception, including Highlands Bancorp., which operates in northern New Jersey. The company also offers internet banking, mobile banking, and cash management services.

Mergers and Acquisitions

In January 2019 Lakeland Bancorp acquired Vernon, New Jersey-based Highlands Bancorp in a deal valued at $56.7 million. The holding company – which operated branches in the New Jersey municipalities of Sparta, Totowa, and Denville – had consolidated total assets of $5.53 billion.

Company Background

Lakeland Bancorp was founded in 1969. It organized into a bank holding company in 1989.

EXECUTIVES

Chairman, Subsidiary Officer, Director, Mary Ann Deacon

President, Chief Executive Officer, Subsidiary Officer, Director, Thomas J. Shara, $797,000 total compensation

Senior Executive Vice President, Chief Operating Officer, Subsidiary Officer, Ronald E. Schwarz, $361,154 total compensation

Executive Vice President, Chief Financial Officer, Subsidiary Officer, Thomas F. Splaine, $326,923 total compensation

Executive Vice President, Chief Administrative Officer, General Counsel, Corporate Secretary, Timothy J. Matteson, $291,923 total compensation

Executive Vice President, Chief Risk Officer, James M. Nigro

Executive Vice President, Chief Information Officer, Subsidiary Officer, Paul Ho Sing Loy

Executive Vice President, Chief Banking Officer, Subsidiary Officer, Ellen Lalwani

Executive Vice President, Chief Lending Officer, Subsidiary Officer, John F. Rath

Director, Bruce D. Bohuny

Director, Brian Flynn
Director, Brian A. Gragnolati
Director, Mark J. Fredericks
Director, James E. Hanson
Director, Lawrence R. Inserra
Director, Robert E. McCracken
Director, Robert B. Nicholson
Director, Janeth C. Hendershot
Director, Robert F. Mangano
Auditors: KPMG LLP

LOCATIONS

HQ: Lakeland Bancorp, Inc.
250 Oak Ridge Road, Oak Ridge, NJ 07438
Phone: 973 697-2000
Web: www.lakelandbank.com

PRODUCTS/OPERATIONS

2017 Sales

	$ mil.	% of total
Interest		
Loans & fees	172.3	80
Investment securities and other	17.9	8
Interest expense	(25.0)	-
Non-interest		
Service charges on deposit accounts	10.7	5
Commissions & fees	4.9	2
Income on bank owned life insurance	2.4	1
Other	7.5	4
Total	190.7	100

Selected Services

401K and IRA Rollovers
Certificates of deposit & individual retirement accounts
Checking accounts
Consumer loans
Home loans
Insurance
Investment management
Online services
Retirement income planning
Savings and money market accounts

COMPETITORS

FULTON FINANCIAL CORPORATION
HANCOCK WHITNEY CORPORATION
HEARTLAND FINANCIAL USA, INC.
HOME BANCSHARES, INC.
IBERIABANK CORPORATION
MERIDIAN INTERSTATE BANCORP, INC.
S&T BANCORP, INC.
UNITED BANKSHARES, INC.
UNITED COMMUNITY BANKS, INC.
WINTRUST FINANCIAL CORPORATION

HISTORICAL FINANCIALS

Company Type: Public

Income Statement — FYE: December 31

	ASSETS ($mil)	NET INCOME ($mil)	INCOME AS % OF ASSETS	EMPLOYEES
12/20	7,664.2	57.5	0.8%	711
12/19	6,711.2	70.6	1.1%	692
12/18	5,806.0	63.4	1.1%	652
12/17	5,405.6	52.5	1.0%	621
12/16	5,093.1	41.5	0.8%	592
Annual Growth	10.8%	8.5%	—	4.7%

2020 Year-End Financials

Return on assets: 0.7%
Return on equity: 7.7%
Long-term debt ($ mil.): —
No. of shares ($ mil.): 50.4
Sales ($ mil.): 275.9
Dividends
Yield: 3.9%
Payout: 44.2%
Market value ($ mil.): 641.0

	STOCK PRICE ($) FY Close	P/E High/Low		PER SHARE ($) Earnings	Dividends	Book Value
12/20	12.70	15	8	1.13	0.50	15.13
12/19	17.38	13	10	1.38	0.49	14.36
12/18	14.81	16	11	1.32	0.45	13.14
12/17	19.25	20	16	1.09	0.40	12.31
12/16	19.50	21	10	0.95	0.37	11.65
Annual Growth	(10.2%)	—	—	4.4%	7.8%	6.8%

Lakeland Financial Corp

Lakeland Financial is the holding company for Lake City Bank, which serves area business customers and individuals through around 50 branches scattered across about 15 northern and central Indiana counties. With $4.8 billion in assets, the community bank offers such standard retail services as checking and savings accounts, money market accounts, and CDs. Commercial loans, including agricultural loans and mortgages, make up about 90% of the bank's loan portfolio. Lake City Bank also offers investment products and services such as corporate and personal trust, brokerage, and estate planning.

Operations

Lakeland Financial operates through a single business segment. About 80% of the holding company's revenue is derived from net interest income, mostly from interest and fees on loans.

Commercial and industrial loans comprise about 40% of its loan portfolio, as does commercial real estate and multifamily residential loans. Consumer family mortgages make up about 10%, and agribusiness, and agricultural loans represent more than 5%.

Lakeland holds around $4 billion in deposits; retail, public funds, and commercial deposits make up about 40%, 30%, and 25% of that total, respectively.

Geographic Reach

Warsaw, Indiana-based Lakeland Financial serves customers at about 50 bank branches in around 15 northern and central Indiana counties, including some half a dozen in and around Indianapolis.

Sales and Marketing

Lakeland Financial targets larger Indiana cities it believes have better-than-average growth potential.

The company is focused on commercial banking and has a team of more than 40 commercial bankers. Lakeland offers internet business banking and online treasury management services to its commercial customers.

Financial Performance

Lakeland Financial has undergone moderate five-year revenue and net income growth of 42% and 48%, respectively, in conjunction with a 216% ballooning in its in cash. The company's long-term debt has remained flat in that time.

The holding company's revenue trended up 14% to $171.9 million in 2017 owing to improved net interest income driven by increased average earning assets and its average commercial loan portfolio. That growth also spurred the company's 10% rise in net income to $57.3 million.

Lakeland had cash of $176.2 million at the end of 2017, up $8.9 million from the previous year. Financings provided $327.7 million, while operations provided $19.9 million. Investments used $396 million, down $46.4 million from 2016 thanks mostly to a net increase in total loans with increased proceeds from sale of securities available for sale also contributing.

Lakeland had $40 million in long-term debt at the end of 2017.

Strategy

Lakeland Financial is focused on increasing the percentage of its portfolio made up of commercial loans and steadily growing its branch locations without making acquisitions.

In 2017 Lakeland's commercial loans comprised about 90% of its portfolio, with an average increase of 12.5% that year compared to the year prior.

The company opened five branches from 2013-2017.

Company Background

Lakeland Financial was founded in 1872.

EXECUTIVES

President, Chief Executive Officer, Chief Financial Officer, Subsidiary Officer, Director, David M. Findlay, $566,527 total compensation

Executive Vice President, Chief Financial Officer, Principal Accounting Officer, Subsidiary Officer, Lisa M. O'Neill, $238,769 total compensation

Commercial Executive Vice President, Eric H. Ottinger, $288,923 total compensation

Executive Vice President, Chief Administrative Officer, General Counsel, Kristin L. Pruitt, $258,923 total compensation

Retail Banking Administration Senior Vice President, Retail Banking Administration Subsidiary Officer, Stephanie R. Leniski

Finance Senior Vice President, Finance Chief Accounting Officer, Brok A. Lahrman

Director, Michael L. Kubacki, $326,328 total compensation

Director, Blake W. Augsburger

Director, Darrianne P. Christian

Director, Robert E. Bartels

Director, Daniel F. Evans

Director, Thomas A. Hiatt

Director, Emily E. Pichon

Director, Steven D. Ross

Director, Brian J. Smith

Director, Bradley J. Toothaker

Director, Ronald D. Truex

Director, M. Scott Welch

Director, A. Faraz Abbasi

Auditors : Crowe LLP

LOCATIONS

HQ: Lakeland Financial Corp
202 East Center Street, Warsaw, IN 46580
Phone: 574 267-6144
Web: www.lakecitybank.com

PRODUCTS/OPERATIONS

2017 Sales

	$ mil.	% of total
Interest		
Loans	151.0	75
Securities	14.3	7
Other	0.3	-
Interest expense	(29.8)	.
Noninteresst		
Service charges on deposit accounts	13.7	7
Loan and service fees	7.9	4
Wealth advisory fees	5.5	3
Investment brokerage fees	1.3	-
Other	7.7	4
Total	171.9	100

COMPETITORS

AMERICAN NATIONAL BANKSHARES INC.
AMERIS BANCORP
BSB BANCORP, INC.
CLIFTON BANCORP INC.
ENTERPRISE BANCORP, INC.
FIRSTMERIT CORPORATION
HANCOCK WHITNEY CORPORATION
HOME BANCSHARES, INC.
INDEPENDENT BANK CORP.
SOUTHSIDE BANCSHARES, INC.

HISTORICAL FINANCIALS

Company Type: Public

Income Statement				FYE: December 31
	ASSETS ($mil)	NET INCOME ($mil)	INCOME AS % OF ASSETS	EMPLOYEES
12/20	5,830.4	84.3	1.4%	585
12/19	4,946.7	87.0	1.8%	568
12/18	4,875.2	80.4	1.6%	553
12/17	4,682.9	57.3	1.2%	539
12/16	4,290.0	52.0	1.2%	524
Annual Growth	8.0%	12.8%	—	2.8%

2020 Year-End Financials

Return on assets: 1.5%
Return on equity: 13.4%
Long-term debt ($ mil.): —
No. of shares ($ mil.): 25.2
Sales ($ mil.): 239.9
Dividends
Yield: 2.2%
Payout: 37.6%
Market value ($ mil.): 1,352.0

	STOCK PRICE ($) FY Close	P/E High/Low		PER SHARE ($) Earnings	Dividends	Book Value
12/20	53.58	17	10	3.30	1.20	26.03
12/19	48.93	15	12	3.38	1.16	23.50
12/18	40.16	16	12	3.13	1.00	20.76
12/17	48.49	23	18	2.23	0.63	18.72
12/16	47.36	26	16	2.05	0.73	17.12
Annual Growth	3.1%	—	—	12.6%	13.4%	11.0%

Lakeland Industries, Inc.

The wrong clothing can be hazardous to your health -- not based on style, but by OSHA and EPA standards. Lakeland makes protective clothing for on-the-job hazards. It uses DuPont specialty fabrics, such as Kevlar, TyChem, and Tyvek, as well as its own fabrics, to make industrial disposable garments, toxic-waste cleanup suits, fire- and heat-resistant apparel (including Fyrepel gear for firefighters), industrial work gloves, high-visibility garments, and industrial/medical garments. Lakeland manufactures its products in Brazil, China, India, Mexico, and the US. Customers -- nearly 65% are outside of the US -- include high tech electronics manufacturers, construction companies, hospitals, and laboratories.

Operations

The company also supplies federal, state, and local government agencies such as the Department of Defense, the Department of Homeland Security, and the Centers for Disease Control. All total, Lakeland distributes to a network of more than 1,200 North American safety and mill supply distributors and end users, as well as to international clients. It has also developed a number of patented production machinery and fabrics, including Micromax, ChemMax, Despro, and Thermbar.

The company's business is fueled by crises. Its products are useful in situations involving fire and chemical/biological threats, such as the anthrax scare, SARs epidemic, ricin letters, and Avian flu -- all of which have occurred in the last decade. Many Asian and South American countries have since adopted legislation akin to the US Occupational Safety and Health Act, in order to be a part of the World Trade Organization. To meet the stricter WTO standards, these countries need to use appropriate gear, causing orders for protective clothing and equipment to increase.

Geographic Reach

Lakeland sells its products to more than 40 countries, primarily in Argentina, Australia, Brazil, Canada, Chile, China, Europe, and Southeast Asia. The US accounts for roughly 35% of total sales; China, 30%.

Sales and Marketing

Lakeland products are sold by an in-house customer service group, regional sales managers, and independent sales representatives selling to a network of over 1,200 North American safety and mill supply distributors.

The company spent $263 million on advertising in 2013 and $310 million in 2012. The Department for Homeland Security is one of its biggest clients.

Financial Performance

Lakeland's balance sheet is heading in the wrong direction; it has suffered revenue declines and net losses over the last two years. Revenues fell 2% from $96.3 million in 2012 to $95.1 million in 2013 as it posted a net loss of $26 million for 2013.

The decrease was driven by a 19% drop in US disposables sales resulting from the loss of its Tyvek license from DuPont. This offset international gains in Brazil, Chile, and Argentina. China sales also jumped 26% from 2012 to 2013.

Its net loss for 2013 increased primarily due to an arbitration settlement and goodwill impairment charge from its operations in Brazil.

Strategy

To be closer to customers and to take advantage of the lower production and workforce costs, the company has moved some of its manufacturing to international facilities in Brazil, China, India, and Mexico. It is also sourcing more raw materials from China than from the US or Europe. In 2011 it opened new sales offices in India, Kazakhstan, and Russia.

Lakeland has altered its product mix in an attempt to combat competition. Domestic sales of Tyvek, once a major staple in the company's line of products, have fallen off in recent years. Increased sales in the company's line of Hi-Visibility products have partially offset the decline in Tyvek's sales.

Lakeland's expansion strategy takes advantage of smaller companies that are experiencing their own crises -- economically. The protective gear industry is fragmented and made up of many smaller companies, unlike mega-competitors Kimberly Clark and DuPont, which, along with Lakeland, have jumped at the chance to pick up smaller companies that have hit on hard times. Lakeland has made acquisitions to build on its product portfolio, increase its ability to cross-sell, and give it a geographic foothold in emerging markets.

EXECUTIVES

Executive Chairman, Director, Christopher James Ryan, $400,000 total compensation
International Sales President, International Sales Chief Executive Officer, International Sales Secretary, Director, Charles D. Roberson, $245,460 total compensation
Marketing Executive Vice President, Sales Executive Vice President, Steven L. Harvey
Chief Financial Officer, Roger D. Shannon
Chief Operating Officer, Allen E. Dillard
Lead Independent Director, Director, Alfred John Kreft
Director, Thomas J. McAteer
Director, James M. Jenkins
Director, Nikki Hamblin
Director, Jeffrey T. Schlarbaum

Auditors : Friedman LLP

LOCATIONS

HQ: Lakeland Industries, Inc.
1525 Perimeter Parkway, Suite 325, Huntsville, AL 35806
Phone: 256 350-3873   **Fax:** 256 350-0773
Web: www.lakeland.com

PRODUCTS/OPERATIONS

Selected Products
Fire fighting and heat protective apparel
Gloves and arm guards
High-end chemical protective suits
High visibility clothing
Limited use/disposable protective clothing
Raingear
Reflective vests and other high visibility clothing
Reusable woven garments

COMPETITORS

ALLIANCE LAUNDRY HOLDINGS LLC
AVANOS MEDICAL, INC.
EXACTECH, INC.
GRAHAM PACKAGING COMPANY, L.P.
KINETIC CONCEPTS, INC.
MEDICAL ACTION INDUSTRIES INC.
TSO3 Inc
UNIFIRST CORPORATION
VCP MOBILITY, INC.
ZIMMER BIOMET HOLDINGS, INC.

HISTORICAL FINANCIALS
Company Type: Public

Income Statement				FYE: January 31
	REVENUE ($mil)	NET INCOME ($mil)	NET PROFIT MARGIN	EMPLOYEES
01/21	159.0	35.1	22.1%	2,000
01/20	107.8	3.2	3.0%	1,829
01/19	99.0	1.4	1.5%	1,632
01/18	95.9	0.4	0.5%	1,072
01/17	86.1	3.8	4.5%	993
Annual Growth	16.5%	73.3%	—	19.1%

2021 Year-End Financials

Debt ratio: —
Return on equity: 33.6%
Cash ($ mil.): 52.6
Current Ratio: 8.03
Long-term debt ($ mil.): —
No. of shares ($ mil.): 7.9
Dividends
 Yield: —
 Payout: —
Market value ($ mil.): 222.0

	STOCK PRICE ($) FY Close	P/E High/Low		PER SHARE ($) Earnings	Dividends	Book Value
01/21	27.80	7	3	4.31	0.00	15.39
01/20	13.94	39	24	0.41	0.00	10.67
01/19	11.12	89	56	0.18	0.00	10.39
01/18	14.10	274	166	0.06	0.00	10.21
01/17	10.85	25	15	0.53	0.00	9.84
Annual Growth	26.5%	—	—	68.9%	—	11.8%

Landmark Bancorp Inc

Landmark Bancorp is a tourist attraction for Kansas money. It is the holding company for Landmark National Bank, which has about 15 branches in communities in central, eastern, and southwestern Kansas. The bank provides standard commercial banking products including checking, savings, and money market accounts, as well as CDs and credit and debit cards. It primarily uses funds from deposits to write residential and commercial mortgages and business loans. Landmark National Bank offers non-deposit investment services through its affiliation with Investment Planners.

EXECUTIVES

Executive Chairman, Subsidiary Officer, Chairman, Director, Patrick L. Alexander, $195,000 total compensation
President, Chief Executive Officer, Subsidiary Officer, Director, Michael E. Scheopner, $350,000 total compensation
Vice President, Chief Financial Officer, Treasurer, Secretary, Subsidiary Officer, Mark A. Herpich, $223,250 total compensation
Subsidiary Officer, Dean R. Thibault
Subsidiary Officer, Larry R. Heyka, $115,000 total compensation
Subsidiary Officer, Mark J. Oliphant, $179,000 total compensation
Subsidiary Officer, Bradly L. Chindamo
Director, Sarah Hill-Nelson
Director, Wayne R. Sloan
Director, Brent A. Bowman
Director, Joseph L. Downey
Director, David H. Snapp
Director, Richard A. Ball
Director, Susan E. Roepke
Director, C. Duane Ross
Director, Jim W. Lewis
Director, Sandra J. Moll

Auditors : Crowe LLP

LOCATIONS

HQ: Landmark Bancorp Inc
701 Poyntz Avenue, Manhattan, KS 66502
Phone: 785 565-2000
Web: www.landmarkbancorpinc.com

COMPETITORS

FIRST NATIONAL BANKSHARES CORPORATION
NEFFS BANCORP, INC.
PRINCETON NATIONAL BANCORP, INC.
QNB CORP.
WCF FINANCIAL BANK

HISTORICAL FINANCIALS
Company Type: Public

Income Statement				FYE: December 31
	ASSETS ($mil)	NET INCOME ($mil)	INCOME AS % OF ASSETS	EMPLOYEES
12/20	1,188.0	19.4	1.6%	292
12/19	998.4	10.6	1.1%	289
12/18	985.7	10.4	1.1%	291
12/17	929.4	4.3	0.5%	286
12/16	911.3	8.9	1.0%	292
Annual Growth	6.9%	21.4%	—	0.0%

Lazydays Holdings Inc

EXECUTIVES

Chairman, Director, Christopher S. Shackelton
Chief Executive Officer, John F. North
Vice President, Division Officer, Ronald W. Fleming, $275,000 total compensation
Chief Financial Officer, Kelly Porter
Director, Jordan Gnat
Director, Erika Serow
Director, Jerry M. Comstock
Director, Robert T. DeVincenzi
Director, James F. Fredlake
Auditors : RSM US LLP

LOCATIONS

HQ: Lazydays Holdings Inc
6130 Lazy Days Blvd., Seffner, FL 33584
Phone: 813 246-4999
Web: www.lazydays.com

HISTORICAL FINANCIALS
Company Type: Public

Income Statement FYE: December 31

	REVENUE ($mil)	NET INCOME ($mil)	NET PROFIT MARGIN	EMPLOYEES
12/20	817.1	29.1	3.6%	1,000
12/19	644.9	0.7	0.1%	935
12/18*	474.2	(2.6)	—	880
03/18	133.9	2.3	1.7%	0
12/17	614.8	8.3	1.4%	775
Annual Growth	9.9%	51.9%	—	8.9%

*Fiscal year change

2020 Year-End Financials
Debt ratio: 49.1%
Return on equity: 19.8%
Cash ($ mil.): 63.5
Current Ratio: 1.17
Long-term debt ($ mil.): 87
No. of shares ($ mil.): 9.5
Dividends
 Yield: —
 Payout: —
Market value ($ mil.): 155.0

STOCK PRICE ($) FY Close	P/E High/Low		PER SHARE ($) Earnings	Dividends	Book Value
12/20	22.85	7	5	3.90	0.76	25.39
12/19	25.05	12	10	2.10	0.73	21.43
12/18	23.20	14	11	2.06	0.69	18.16
12/17	28.99	36	31	0.87	0.66	17.66
12/16	28.03	15	13	1.81	0.63	17.21
Annual Growth	(5.0%)	—	—	21.2%	5.0%	10.2%

2020 Year-End Financials
Return on assets: 1.7%
Return on equity: 16.5%
Long-term debt ($ mil.): —
No. of shares ($ mil.): 4.9
Sales ($ mil.): 64.1
Dividends
 Yield: 3.5%
 Payout: 19.5%
Market value ($ mil.): 114.0

STOCK PRICE ($) FY Close	P/E High/Low		PER SHARE ($) Earnings	Dividends	Book Value
12/20	16.25	11	1	1.56	0.00	16.35
12/19	4.10	—	—	(0.53)	0.00	16.17
12/18*	5.40	—	—	(1.02)	0.00	15.51
Annual Growth	73.5%	—	—	—	—	2.7%

*Fiscal year change

LCI Industries

LCI Industries makes components for recreational vehicle (RVs) and other original equipment manufacturers. Through its primary operating subsidiary, Lippert Components, the company makes windows and doors, chassis, furniture, and slide-out walls for travel trailers and fifth-wheel RVs. The company also serves adjacent markets including manufactured home, buses, trailers used to haul boats, livestock, equipment and other cargo, trucks, modular housing, and trains. LCI's aftermarket segment sells to RV and trailer dealers, distributors, and service centers. Over 90% of the company's sales came from its customers from its US customers.

Operations

LCI Industries operates through two segments: the original equipment manufacturers (OEM) segment and the aftermarket segment.

The OEM segment (around 80% of total sales) manufactures recreational vehicle components including windows and doors, slide-out mechanisms, axles, chassis, furniture, and awnings for travel trailers and fifth wheels (approximately 50% of segment sales) and motorhomes (around 5% of segment revenue). Customers in adjacent OEM markets account for some 25% of segment sales.

The company's aftermarket segment (about 20% of total sales) sells RV parts and accessories to RV dealers and service centers, warehouse distributors, and direct to consumers.

When it comes to its products' sales, chassis, chassis parts and slide-out mechanism accounts for about 30% of sales, followed by windows and doors with about 25%, and aftermarket product with about 20%. Other products include furniture and mattresses (about 15%), axles and suspensions (some 5%), and other (accounts for the rest).

Geographic Reach

Based in Indiana, LCI Industries has about 145 manufacturing and warehousing locations in the North America and Europe.

Over 90% of its total sales comes from domestic operations.

Sales and Marketing

LCI Industries' OEM products are sold primarily to major manufacturers of RVs such as Thor Industries, Forest River, and Winnebago as well as to manufacturers in other adjacent industries, including buses; trailers used to haul boats, livestock, equipment and other cargo; trucks; boats; trains; manufactured homes; and modular housing. The company's aftermarket products are sold to wholesale distributors, dealerships, service centers, and direct to customers. Aftermarket customers are supported by multiple call centers staffed by marketing and product training teams that provide quick response for product orders and technical support to limit customer downtime.

The company's marketing and advertising expenditures were $17.4 million, $10.4 million, and $6.4 million in 2021, 2020, and 2019, respectively.

Financial Performance

Consolidated net sales for the full-year 2021 were $4.5 billion, 60% higher than consolidated net sales for the full-year 2020 of $2.8 billion. The increase in year-over-year net sales was primarily driven by record RV retail demand and strong Aftermarket Segment sales growth.

Net income for the full-year 2021 increased 82% to $287.7 million, compared to net income of $158.4 million, for full-year 2020.

Cash held by the company at the end of fiscal 2021 increased to $62.9 million. Cash provided by financing activities was $404.6 million while cash used for operations and investing activities were $111.6 million and $281.2 million, respectively.

Company Background

In 1956 Larry Lippert and Don Baldwin founded B&L Industries in Indiana to manufacture galvanized roofing for mobile homes. Two years later, the company expanded into mobile home chassis and other components with the purchase of Riverdale Steel Works.

Throughout the 1960s the company expanded to additional locations in Indiana, Michigan, North Carolina, Texas, and Alabama. The company was incorporated in 1964 and became Drew National Corporation. The company's primary operating subsidiary was Lippert Components.

Demand for manufactured housing took off in the early 1970s and the company's North Carolina facility served the growing needs of Clayton Homes and Oxford Homes. Drew National managed to stay afloat when tighter monetary policy reversed the fortunes of the mobile home industry in the early 1980s. The company changed its name to Drew Industries in 1984.

In 1992 disaster brought opportunity for the company when Hurricane Andrew devastated Florida and Drew Industries received an order for 10,000 FEMA trailer chassis. The company expanded into travel trailer chassis in 1997. In 2000, the company opened a facility in Ontario, Canada.

Over the next dozen years, the company continued to expand its product offerings and manufacturing footprint in the US. By the end of 2012 Drew Industries operated 30 manufacturing facilities in 11 states. In 2014 the company changed its name to LCI Industries.

EXECUTIVES

Chairman, Director, James F. Gero
President, Chief Executive Officer, Subsidiary Officer, Jason D. Lippert, $975,000 total compensation
Group President, Ryan R. Smith
Vice President, Chief Legal Officer, Secretary, Andrew J. Namenye, $368,269 total compensation
Chief Financial Officer, Brian M. Hall, $386,539 total compensation
Chief Human Resources Officer, Nick C. Fletcher, $358,517 total compensation
Corporate Controller, Principal Accounting Officer, Kip A. Emenhiser
Division Officer, Jamie M. Schnur, $401,066 total compensation
Director, Frank J. Crespo
Director, Brendan J. Deely
Director, Ronald Fenech
Director, Tracy D. Graham
Director, Virginia L. Henkels
Director, Kieran M. O'Sullivan
Director, David A. Reed
Director, John A. Sirpilla
Auditors : KPMG LLP

LOCATIONS

HQ: LCI Industries
3501 County Road 6 East, Elkhart, IN 46514
Phone: 574 535-1125
Web: www.lci1.com

PRODUCTS/OPERATIONS

2013 Sales

	$ mil.	% of total
Recreational vehicles	893.7	88
Manufactured housing	121.9	12
Total	1,015.6	100

Selected Products
Manufactured housing (MH) products
    Aluminum and vinyl patio doors
    Axles
    Entry doors
    Steel and fiberglass entry doors
    Steel chassis
    Steel chassis parts
    Replacement windows, doors, thermoformed bath products
    Thermoformed bath and kitchen products
    Vinyl and aluminum windows and screens
Recreational vehicle (RV) products (travel trailers and fifth-wheel RVs)
    Aluminum windows and screens
    Chassis components
    Entry and baggage doors
    Entry steps
    Furniture and mattresses
    Manual, electric and hydraulic stabilizer and lifting systems
    Patio doors
    Slide-out mechanisms
    Specialty trailers for hauling boats, personal watercraft, snowmobiles and equipment
    Thermoformed bath, kitchen and other products
    Towable axles and suspensions
    Towable steel chassis
    Toy hauler ramp doors

COMPETITORS

CARLISLE COMPANIES INCORPORATED
GENERAL MOTORS COMPANY
NAVISTAR INTERNATIONAL CORPORATION
NFI Group Inc
OSHKOSH CORPORATION
PACCAR INC
REV GROUP, INC.
TOYOTA INDUSTRIES CORPORATION
WABASH NATIONAL CORPORATION
WINNEBAGO INDUSTRIES, INC.

HISTORICAL FINANCIALS
Company Type: Public

Income Statement — FYE: December 31

	REVENUE ($mil)	NET INCOME ($mil)	NET PROFIT MARGIN	EMPLOYEES
12/20	2,796.1	158.4	5.7%	12,400
12/19	2,371.4	146.5	6.2%	10,500
12/18	2,475.8	148.5	6.0%	10,260
12/17	2,147.7	132.8	6.2%	9,852
12/16	1,678.8	129.6	7.7%	7,654
Annual Growth	13.6%	5.1%	—	12.8%

2020 Year-End Financials

Debt ratio: 32.1%
Return on equity: 18.4%
Cash ($ mil.): 51.8
Current Ratio: 2.09
Long-term debt ($ mil.): 720.4
No. of shares ($ mil.): 25.1
Dividends
  Yield: 2.1%
  Payout: 51.0%
Market value ($ mil.): 3,262.0

	STOCK PRICE ($) FY Close	P/E High	P/E Low	Earnings	Dividends	Book Value
12/20	129.68	21	9	6.27	2.80	36.11
12/19	107.13	19	11	5.84	2.55	31.97
12/18	66.80	22	10	5.83	2.35	28.41
12/17	130.00	25	17	5.24	2.05	26.12
12/16	107.75	21	10	5.20	1.40	22.23
Annual Growth	4.7%	—	—	4.8%	18.9%	12.9%

LCNB Corp

It just makes cents that LCNB counts bucks in the Buckeye State. The firm is the holding company for LCNB National Bank, which operates some 36 offices across southwestern Ohio. The bank serves about 10 Ohio counties, offering personal and commercial banking services, such as checking and savings accounts, money markets, IRAs, and CDs. Residential mortgages account for nearly half of the company's loan book. Other offerings include commercial mortgages, consumer loans including credit cards, and business loans. It also provides trust services. LCNB's subsidiary Dakin Insurance Agency sells commercial and personal property/casualty insurance.

Geographic Reach
Headquartered in Ohio, LCNB Corp. serves several of the state's counties, including Butler, Clermont, Clinton, Fayette, Hamilton, Montgomery, Preble, Ross, and Warren.

Strategy
The financial institution has been growing through acquisitions.

The company expanded into Preble County in 2014, when it acquired Eaton National Bank & Trust Co. from Colonial Banc Corp. Eaton was folded into the company's LCNB National Bank network.

LCNB also bought First Capital Bancshares (FCB), a bank holding company, in a stock-and-cash deal valued at about $19.6 million. FCB is the parent of six-branch Citizens National Bank of Chillicothe. The purchase of FCB allowed LCNB to expand into the Ross and Fayette Country markets.

EXECUTIVES

Chairman, Subsidiary Officer, Director, Spencer S. Cropper
President, Chief Executive Officer, Subsidiary Officer, Director, Eric J. Meilstrup, $170,000 total compensation
Executive Vice President, Chief Financial Officer, Robert C. Haines, $170,000 total compensation
Executive Vice President, Chief Lending Officer, Matthew P. Layer, $170,000 total compensation
Executive Vice President, Chief Investment Officer, Subsidiary Officer, Bradley A. Ruppert
Executive Vice President, Chief Operating Officer, Subsidiary Officer, Lawrence P. Mulligan
Executive Vice President, Trust Officer, Michael R. Miller
Director, Steve P. Foster, $271,000 total compensation
Director, Stephen P. Wilson, $271,000 total compensation
Director, Mary Bradford
Director, William G. Huddle
Director, Craig M. Johnson
Director, Michael J. Johrendt
Director, William H. Kaufman
Director, Anne E. Krehbiel
Director, John H. Kochensparger
Auditors : BKD, LLP

LOCATIONS

HQ: LCNB Corp
2 North Broadway, Lebanon, OH 45036
Phone: 513 932-1414
Web: www.lcnb.com

COMPETITORS

NATIONAL BANCSHARES CORPORATION
NEFFS BANCORP, INC.
PENDLETON COMMUNITY BANK, INC.
TRI-STATE 1ST BANC, INC.
TRUIST FINANCIAL CORPORATION

HISTORICAL FINANCIALS
Company Type: Public

Income Statement   FYE: December 31

	ASSETS ($mil)	NET INCOME ($mil)	INCOME AS % OF ASSETS	EMPLOYEES
12/20	1,745.8	20.0	1.1%	331
12/19	1,639.3	18.9	1.2%	332
12/18	1,636.9	14.8	0.9%	325
12/17	1,295.6	12.9	1.0%	310
12/16	1,306.7	12.4	1.0%	282
Annual Growth	7.5%	12.6%	—	4.1%

2020 Year-End Financials
Return on assets: 1.1%
Return on equity: 8.5%
Long-term debt ($ mil.): —
No. of shares ($ mil.): 12.8
Sales ($ mil.): 79.5
Dividends
 Yield: 4.9%
 Payout: 49.3%
Market value ($ mil.): 189.0

	STOCK PRICE ($) FY Close	P/E High	P/E Low	Earnings	Dividends	Book Value
12/20	14.69	12	7	1.55	0.73	18.73
12/19	19.30	14	11	1.44	0.69	17.63
12/18	15.15	17	12	1.24	0.65	16.47
12/17	20.45	19	14	1.29	0.64	14.99
12/16	23.25	20	12	1.25	0.64	14.30
Annual Growth	(10.8%)	—	—	5.5%	3.3%	7.0%

Ledyard Financial Group Inc

EXECUTIVES
Client Services Senior Vice President, Client Services Director, Donna Batchelder
Auditors: Berry Dunn McNeil & Parker, LLC

LOCATIONS
HQ: Ledyard Financial Group Inc
38 South Main Street, P.O. Box 799, Hanover, NH 03755
Phone: 603 643-2244   **Fax:** 603 643-7464
Web: www.ledyardbank.com

HISTORICAL FINANCIALS
Company Type: Public

Income Statement   FYE: December 31

	ASSETS ($mil)	NET INCOME ($mil)	INCOME AS % OF ASSETS	EMPLOYEES
12/20	684.7	6.7	1.0%	0
12/19	500.3	5.8	1.2%	0
12/18	488.0	5.1	1.1%	0
12/17	476.6	3.8	0.8%	0
12/16	476.3	4.1	0.9%	0
Annual Growth	9.5%	13.0%	—	—

2020 Year-End Financials
Return on assets: 1.1%
Return on equity: 10.9%
Long-term debt ($ mil.): —
No. of shares ($ mil.): 3.3
Sales ($ mil.): 33.4
Dividends
 Yield: —
 Payout: 36.0%
Market value ($ mil.): 63.0

	STOCK PRICE ($) FY Close	P/E High	P/E Low	Earnings	Dividends	Book Value
12/20	18.99	12	7	2.11	0.76	20.13
12/19	24.90	14	11	1.83	0.74	17.19
12/18	22.25	14	13	1.64	0.70	15.02
12/17	21.60	56	16	1.23	0.65	14.05
12/16	54.20	41	35	1.29	0.64	14.03
Annual Growth	(23.1%)	—	—	13.1%	4.4%	9.4%

Lee Enterprises, Inc.

Lee Enterprises is a trusted local news provider and an innovative, digitally focused marketing solutions company operating in more than 75 mid-sized markets across some 25 states. Its local media operations range from large daily newspapers and the associated digital products, such as the St. Louis Post-Dispatch and The Buffalo News, to non-daily newspapers with news websites and digital platforms serving smaller communities. Lee also offers services including a full service digital marketing agency in Amplified Digital Agency as well as one of the largest web-hosting and content management services providers in North America through their majority-owned subsidiary, TownNews. The company's printed newspapers reach almost 1.2 million households daily.

Operations
The company's local media operations generate revenue through advertising (print and digital), digital marketing services, subscriptions, and digital services primarily through TownNews.

Advertising and Marketing Services accounts nearly 50% of revenue that was derived from advertising and marketing services: Local retail (top local accounts and Small to Medium Businesses); Classified (major categories of employment, real estate, automotive, obituaries and legal notices); National (print or digital display advertising space, preprinted advertising, and national accounts); Niche publications (specialty publications, such as lifestyle, business, health or home improvement); and Marketing services (events, contests and digital promotions).

Subscription Revenue produces over 40% of total sales that was derived from full access subscription model, whereby subscribers receive complete access to its content in all platforms, including print and digital, and from digital-only subscriptions. Lee also generates revenue from the sale of single copy editions.

Digital Services generates less than 5% of the company's revenue, most of which is revenue from TownNews that operates through owned subsidiary (INN Partners).

Lee operations also provide commercial printing, distribution of third party publications, and management services to other local media operations.

Geographic Reach
Iowa-based, Lee has a property leased for Madison, Wisconsin (which is owned by MNI) and Tucson, Arizona (which is jointly owned by Star Publishing and Citizen).

Sales and Marketing
The company's sales force uses a multi-platform sales approach that maximizes audience reach for their advertisers by tailoring advertising and marketing services packages based on the size and scale of the advertiser. Through Amplified, Lee creates sophisticated digital campaigns on their owned and operated sites and on third party inventory that give advertisers the ability to target their message. The company partners with Google to provide key metrics and analytics to measure campaign effectiveness.

Financial Performance
Total operating revenue totaled $618 million in 2020, or 21%, compared to 2019. Total operating revenue increased primarily due to acquired revenue of $203 million.

Net loss was $1.3 million in 2020 compared to net income of $15.9 million in 2019. The decrease in net income is predominately due to a reduction in operating income.

Cash held by the company at the end of 2020 was $33.7 million, higher by $25.1 million compared to the prior year. Cash provided by operations was $49.9 million, while investing activities used $118.2 million, primarily for acquisitions. Cash generated by financing activities was $93.4 million.

Strategy
Lee's focus is on the local market - including local news and information, local advertising and marketing services to top local accounts and SMBs, and digital services to local content curators. To align with the core strength of their company, their post-pandemic operating strategy is locally focused around three pillars.

To align with customer expectations, the company will transform the way they present local news and information and provide perspective, both in digital and print. The company seeks to maintain its position as the leading provider of news and information by providing best-in-class digital experiences to improve consumer engagement and grow its audiences. Lee aims to achieve this by delivering relevant, useful, and engaging content to the consumer using a multi-media approach with heavy emphases on video and audio.

Lee Enterprises will transform their print-centric audience model into a robust digital subscription model. In 2021, the company expects to use data and analytics combined with metering technology to drive its acquisition and retention tactics. This allows them to maximize meter stop rates and paid subscription conversion rates in order to drive consumers down the conversion funnel. Their primary acquisition tactics include sophisticated data-mining techniques leveraging both online and offline consumer behaviors to target full access and digital-only subscription offers.

The company will diversify and transform the services and products they offer advertisers, especially for top local accounts and SMB's.

Mergers and Acquisitions

In 2020, Lee Enterprises completed the acquisition of BH Media Group, Inc. (BH Media) and The Buffalo News, Inc. (Buffalo News) The acquisition nearly doubled Lee's audience size and added 30 daily newspapers, more than 49 paid weekly publications with digital sites, and 32 other print products from BHMG, as well as The Buffalo News, to Lee's portfolio of high-quality local publications. Lee's portfolio is now comprised of 77 publications in 77 communities.

Company Background

Lee was founded in 1890 in Iowa, by A.W. Lee. Most of thier papers trace their beginnings to the mid-1800s. Among thier alumni, teenage Sam Clemens wrote for the Muscatine Journal in Iowa before becoming world-renowned as Mark Twain. A reporter from the company's newspaper in Bismarck, North Dakota, died with George Custer at the Battle of the Little Big Horn. In 1973, their newspaper in Davenport, Iowa, became the first in the world to be produced totally by computer.

HISTORY

Alfred Lee began buying up newspapers in the Midwest in 1890, beginning with the Ottumwa Daily Courier (Iowa). His strategy was simple: Find a newspaper with potential and let a good manager run it without interference. Lee died in 1907, leaving one of those managers, E. P. Adler, to run the company. Adler continued building the company and in 1937 bought a radio station in Iowa (later sold). The company formed Madison Newspapers, a jointly owned venture with The Capital Times Co., in 1948. Adler died in 1949, and Lee Loomis, a nephew of Alfred Lee, took over.

Loomis expanded the company into TV broadcasting in 1953 and bought six Montana newspapers in 1960. That year the company was consolidated as Lee Enterprises, Incorporated. Loomis later retired and Philip Adler (son of E. P.) took charge. He brought Lee public in 1969, raising money for acquisitions. When Adler retired the next year, David Gottlieb (a distant relative) took control. The company had newspapers and radio and TV stations in 10 states.

In 1972 Lee began to produce advanced printing plates through a joint venture, NAPP Systems. (It bought out its partner in 1990 and sold the business in 1997.) Gottlieb died of a heart attack in 1973, and Lloyd Schermer (related to Gottlieb by marriage) became president. Under his leadership, the company acquired TV stations in western states during the 1980s. Schermer was elevated to chairman in 1986. By 1990 Lee had 19 newspapers and six stations in 13 states. Schermer stepped down as CEO in 1991, and was replaced by Richard Gottlieb, son of David Gottlieb. (Richard Gottlieb took the chairman title in 2000.)

In 1997 Lee acquired Pacific Northwest Publishing Group from Walt Disney, which gave it 24 publications mainly in the Northwest. In 1999 the company bought the Ravalli Republic, a daily in Montana. It also traded the Daily Sun in Nebraska and some cash for two dailies and two weeklies.

In 2000 it bought three more dailies -- Columbus Telegram and Fremont Tribune in Nebraska and Chippewa Herald in Wisconsin -- as well as 15 other publications. To focus on its core operations, the company sold its TV stations to Emmis Communications for about $560 million. Gottlieb stepped down as CEO in 2001 and was replaced by Mary Junck. She added chairman to her title in 2002, when Gottlieb retired. Also in 2002, the company sold off five specialty publications in the western US.

Lee purchased 16 daily newspaper titles from Howard Publications for $694 million in 2002. Its 50%-owned Madison Newspapers unit bought several publications in 2002, including a daily newspaper in Beaver Dam, Wisconsin. The company picked up Iowa's Sioux City Journal daily newspaper later that year. It also sold two publications to Ottaway Newspapers (later Dow Jones Local Media Group), a subsidiary of Dow Jones & Company.

In 2004, the company exchanged its daily newspapers in Freeport, Illinois and Corning, New York and about $2 million in cash for Liberty Group Publishing's two daily newspapers in Burley, Idaho and Elko, Nevada and eight weekly and specialty publications.

Lee took a major step to expand its business the following year when it acquired newspaper rival Pulitzer for about $1.4 billion. The deal included such papers as the St. Louis Post Dispatch and boosted the company's overall circulation by more than 50%.

Lee agreed to sell its Wisconsin daily, The Daily News, in Rhinelander as well as jointly-owned paper Shawano Leader to BlueLine Media Holdings for $2.2 million in 2006. That same year, it inked a pact with Yahoo! to sell job listings on the online giant's HotJobs employment portal. (HotJobs was eventually sold to industry leader Monster.com in 2010.)

As readership and advertising revenue continued to decline, the company began reducing staff at many of its papers in an effort to cut costs. It also shuttered the print edition of The Capital Times, owned by Madison Newspapers, during 2008 due to increasing losses.

Lee also worked to boost revenue through new technologies and investments in its online operations. The company launched a system of targeting online ads based on audience behavior during 2009 in an effort to attract new advertisers to its Internet properties.

The company filed for bankruptcy in 2011.

EXECUTIVES

Chairman, Director, Mary E. Junck, $575,000 total compensation
President, Chief Executive Officer, Director, Kevin D. Mowbray, $737,500 total compensation
Vice President, Chief Financial Officer, Treasurer, Timothy R. Millage
Business Development Vice President, Market Strategy Vice President, Jolene Sherman
Consumer Sales Vice President, Marketing Vice President, Nathan E. Bekke, $326,250 total compensation
Legal Vice President, Human Resources Vice President, Astrid J. Garcia
Marketing Vice President, Sales Vice President, Joseph J. Battistoni
Lead Director, Director, Herbert W. Moloney
Director, Shaun E. McAlmont
Director, Gregory P. Schermer, $220,000 total compensation
Director, Steven C. Fletcher
Director, Brent M. Magid
Director, Margaret R. Liberman
Director, David T. Pearson
Auditors : BDO USA LLP

LOCATIONS

HQ: Lee Enterprises, Inc.
4600 E. 53rd Street, Davenport, IA 52807
Phone: 563 383-2100

PRODUCTS/OPERATIONS

2016 Sales

	$ mil.	% of total
Advertising and marketing services revenue		
Retail	239.1	39
Classified	100.6	16
National	22.1	4
Niche publications and other	11.6	2
Subscription	194.0	32
Digital services	14.2	2
Commercial printing	12.3	2
Other	20.4	3
Total	614.3	100

Selected Operations
Daily newspapers
    Arizona Daily Star (Tucson)
    Billings Gazette (Montana)
    The Bismarck Tribune (North Dakota)
    Casper Star-Tribune (Wyoming)
    The Courier (Waterloo, IA)
    The Daily Herald (Provo, UT)
    Herald & Review (Decatur, IL)
    The Journal Times (Racine, WI)
    La Crosse Tribune (Wisconsin)
    Lincoln Journal Star (Nebraska)
    Missoulian (Missoula, MT)
    The Pantagraph (Bloomington, IL)
    The Post-Star (Glens Falls, NY)
    Quad-City Times (Davenport, IA)
    Rapid City Journal (South Dakota)

Sioux City Journal (Iowa)
St. Louis Post Dispatch
The Times (Munster, IN)
Wisconsin State Journal (50%, Madison)
Commercial printing
Farcountry Press (Helena, MT)
Hawkeye Printing and Trico Communications (Davenport, IA)
Journal Star Commercial Printing (Lincoln, NE)
Plaindealer Publishing (Tekamah, NE)
Platen Press (Butte, MT)
Selma Enterprises (Selma, CA)
William Street Press (Decatur, IL)
Wingra Printing (50%; Madison, WI)

COMPETITORS

ADVANCE PUBLICATIONS, INC.
DOW JONES & COMPANY, INC.
FREEDOM COMMUNICATIONS, INC.
JCK LEGACY COMPANY
MEDIANEWS GROUP, INC.
MEREDITH CORPORATION
REACH PLC
RENTPATH, LLC
THE NEW YORK TIMES COMPANY
WORLDWIDE MEDIA SERVICES GROUP INC.

HISTORICAL FINANCIALS
Company Type: Public

Income Statement — FYE: September 26

	REVENUE ($mil)	NET INCOME ($mil)	NET PROFIT MARGIN	EMPLOYEES
09/21	794.6	22.7	2.9%	5,130
09/20	618.0	(3.1)	—	5,613
09/19	509.8	14.2	2.8%	2,954
09/18	543.9	45.7	8.4%	3,241
09/17	566.9	27.4	4.8%	3,555
Annual Growth	8.8%	(4.6%)	—	9.6%

2021 Year-End Financials
Debt ratio: 57.2%
Return on equity: —
Cash ($ mil.): 26.1
Current Ratio: 0.77
Long-term debt ($ mil.): 476.5
No. of shares ($ mil.): 5.8
Dividends
 Yield: —
 Payout: —
Market value ($ mil.): 140.0

	STOCK PRICE ($) FY Close	P/E High/Low		PER SHARE ($) Earnings	Dividends	Book Value
09/21	23.74	9	0	3.91	0.00	9.27
09/20	0.82	—	—	(0.50)	0.00	(5.41)
09/19	2.01	1	1	2.50	0.00	(6.68)
09/18	2.65	0	0	8.20	0.00	(6.54)
09/17	2.10	1	0	5.00	0.00	(16.26)
Annual Growth	83.4%	—	—	(6.0%)	—	—

Legacy Housing Corp

EXECUTIVES

Executive Chairman, Director, Curtis D. Hodgson, $50,000 total compensation
Executive Vice President, Director, Kenneth E. Shipley, $50,000 total compensation
President, Chief Executive Officer, Robert D. Bates
Chief Financial Officer, Ronald Arrington
Chief Accounting Officer, Jeffrey V. Burt
Director, Jeffrey K. Stouder
Director, Joseph Lane
Director, Francisco J. Coll
Auditors: Weaver and Tidwell, LLP

LOCATIONS

HQ: Legacy Housing Corp
1600 Airport Freeway, #100, Bedford, TX 76022
Phone: 817 799-4900
Web: www.legacyhousingcorp.com

HISTORICAL FINANCIALS
Company Type: Public

Income Statement — FYE: December 31

	REVENUE ($mil)	NET INCOME ($mil)	NET PROFIT MARGIN	EMPLOYEES
12/20	176.7	37.9	21.5%	870
12/19	168.9	28.8	17.1%	800
12/18	161.8	21.5	13.3%	800
12/17	128.7	26.3	20.5%	800
12/16	110.5	17.3	15.7%	0
Annual Growth	12.4%	21.7%	—	—

2020 Year-End Financials
Debt ratio: 10.7%
Return on equity: 15.7%
Cash ($ mil.): 0.7
Current Ratio: 1.51
Long-term debt ($ mil.): 36.1
No. of shares ($ mil.): 24.1
Dividends
 Yield: —
 Payout: —
Market value ($ mil.): 366.0

	STOCK PRICE ($) FY Close	P/E High/Low		PER SHARE ($) Earnings	Dividends	Book Value
12/20	15.11	11	5	1.57	0.00	10.71
12/19	16.64	15	8	1.18	0.00	9.14
12/18	11.93	11	10	1.07	0.00	7.89
Annual Growth	12.5%	—	—	21.1%	—	16.5%

LeMaitre Vascular Inc

LeMaitre Vascular makes both disposable and implanted surgical vascular devices, including catheters and stents, under such brands as AnastoClip, and Pruitt-Inahara. Originally founded by a vascular surgeon to develop a valvulotome to prepare veins for arterial bypass surgery, the company has since expanded its offerings to include a device to create dialysis access sites and another to treat aortic aneurysms. Le Maitre sells about 15 product lines, most of which are used in open vascular surgery and some of which are used in endovascular procedures. Its US operation accounts for the highest geographic market.

Operations

LeMaitre has about 15 product offerings include seven that are biologic implants, and one that is a service of processing and cryopreserving human tissue for implantation. These offerings include the XenoSure patch (bovine pericardium), CardioCel and VascuCel patches (bovine pericardium), ProCol graft (bovine mesenteric vein), Artegraft (bovine carotid artery), Omniflow II biosynthetic graft (ovine tissue and synthetic mesh), surgical glue (porcine gelatin) and the RestoreFlow Allograft cryopreserved graft (human cadaver tissue). These biologic product lines represented some 45% of its sales.

Geographic Reach

LeMaitre's worldwide headquarters is located in Burlington, Massachusetts, and it also has North American sales offices in Chandler, Arizona and Vaughan, Canada. It European headquarters is located in Sulzbach, Germany, with additional European sales offices in Milan, Italy; Madrid, Spain; and Hereford, England. The Asia/Pacific Rim headquarters is located in Singapore, with additional Asia/Pacific Rim sales offices in Tokyo, Japan; Shanghai, China; and Kensington, Australia.

Americas region accounts for nearly 65% of sales, followed by EMEA region which accounts for about 30%, and the remaining accounts for Asia and Pacific region.

Sales and Marketing

LeMaitre sells its products and services through a direct sales force, comprising of about 80 sales representatives in North America, and Europe/ Asia Pacific, including two export managers. Outside its direct markets, it generally sells its products through country-specific distributors, such as South Korea, Russia and Brazil.

In addition, the company engage in direct marketing efforts, including direct mail and exhibitions at medical congresses, which were believe are important to its brand development.

Approximately 95% of its net sales were generated through its direct-to-hospital sales force.

The company advertising cost for the years ended 2020, 2019 and 2018 were approximately $0.2 million, $0.3 million and 0.3 million, respectively.

Financial Performance

Net sales increased 10% or $12.1 million to $129.4 million for the year ended December 31, 2020, compared to $117.2 million for the year ended December 31, 2019. The increase was largely from recently acquired products including Artegraft bovine grafts of $10.8 million and CardioCel bovine cardiac patches of $5.3 million.

Net income for fiscal 2020 increased to $21.2 million compared from the prior year with $17.9 million.

Cash held by the company at the end of fiscal 2020 increased to $26.8 million. Cash provided by operations and financing activities were $34.8 million and $32.2 million, respectively. Cash used for investing was $52.9 million, mainly for payments related to acquisitions.

Strategy

LeMaitre has grown its business by using a three-pronged strategy: focusing on the vascular surgeon call point, competing for sales in low rivalry niche markets, and expanding its growth platform through its worldwide direct sales force as well as acquiring and developing complementary vascular devices.

Focused call point. The company have historically directed its product offering and selling efforts towards the vascular surgeon, and estimate that in 2020 approximately 80% of the company's sales were to hospitals for use by vascular surgeons. As vascular surgeons are typically positioned to perform both open vascular surgeries and endovascular procedures, the company sells devices in both the open and endovascular markets to the same end user. More recently LeMaitre have begun to explore adjacent market customers, or non-vascular surgeon customers, who can be served by its vascular device technologies, such as cardiac surgeons and neurosurgeons.

Low rivalry niche segments. The company seeks to build and maintain leading positions in niche product and services segments, which LeMaitre defines as under $200 million in annual worldwide revenue. The company believes that the relative lack of competitive focus on these segments by larger competitors, as well as the differentiated features and consistent quality of its products, enable higher selling prices and market share gains.

Direct sales force expansion, and the addition of complementary products through acquisitions and to a lesser extent research and development. The company sells its products primarily through a direct sales force in North America, Europe and Asia/Pacific Rim. Since 1998, the company has built its sales force from zero to 80 direct sales representatives, including two export managers.

Mergers and Acquisitions

In 2020, LeMaitre has acquired the business and assets of Artegraft, Inc. for approximately $90.0 million as well as potential earnout payments of $17.5 million payable based upon future sales of the acquired business. Under the terms of the deal, LeMaitre will continue to operate Artegraft's manufacturing facility in North Brunswick, NJ for at least three and a half years and will retain most of Artegraft's employees, including seven sales & marketing personnel.

Company Background

LeMaitre was founded in 1983 by vascular surgeon George D. LeMaitre, to develop a valvulotome to prepare veins for arterial bypass surgery.

In 2006 LeMaitre Vascular raised more than $30 million from its initial public offering. The company spent part of the proceeds to pay off debt; it also used proceeds toward its goals of increasing research and development efforts, hiring new sales representatives, and acquiring complementary products or businesses.

EXECUTIVES

Chairman, Chief Executive Officer, Director, George W. LeMaitre, $437,750 total compensation

Operations Senior Vice President, Trent G. Kamke, $234,346 total compensation

Senior Vice President, General Counsel, Laurie A. Churchill

President, Director, David B. Roberts, $326,304 total compensation

Clinical, Regulatory and Quality Affairs Senior Vice President, Clinical Affairs Senior Vice President, Andrew Hodgkinson

Marketing Vice President, Kimberly L. Cieslak

Research & Development Vice President, Ryan H. Connelly

Regulatory Affairs Vice President, Xiang Zhang

Information Technology Vice President, Jonathan W. Ngau

Chief Financial Officer, Director, Joseph P. Pelligrino, $296,640 total compensation

Quality Assurance Director, Roli Kumar-Choudhury

Operations Director, James Russell

Region Officer, Stéphane Maier

Region Officer, Nobuhiro Okabe

Region Officer, Jacob Petersen

Region Officer, Giovannella Deiure

Region Officer, Chance Kriesel

Division Officer, Maik D. Helmers

Director, Lawrence J. Jasinski

Director, John J. O'Connor

Director, John A. Roush

Auditors : Grant Thornton LLP

LOCATIONS

HQ: LeMaitre Vascular Inc
63 Second Avenue, Burlington, MA 01803
Phone: 781 221-2266
Web: www.lemaitre.com

PRODUCTS/OPERATIONS

Selected Products

Vascular
  Balloon catheters (for removing blood clots; occlusion and facilitation of blood flow)
  Carotid shunts (facilitation of blood flow to brain during carotid plaque removal)
  Remote endarterectomy devices (for removing blockages in major arteries in the leg)
  Valvulotomes (destroys vein valves to create vein bypass grafts)
  Vascular grafts (synthetic vessels used in bypass and replacement procedures)
  Vascular patches (synthetic and biological patches used in closing incisions in a blood vessel)
  Vein strippers (single-incision removal of varicose veins)
  Vessel closure systems (attachment of blood vessels, mainly for dialysis access)
Endovascular
  Aortic stent grafts (endovascular repair of abdominal and thoracic aortic aneurysms and thoracic dissections; in clinical studies)
  Manual contrast injectors (contrast media injection into blood vessels)
  Modeling catheters (for improved sealing of aortic stent grafts; application submitted)
  Radiopaque tape (for improved precision of vascular and endovascular procedures)
General surgery
  Laparoscopic cholecystectomy devices (for introducing dye into the cystic duct and related uses)

COMPETITORS

ANGIODYNAMICS, INC.
ATRICURE, INC.
CARDIOVASCULAR SYSTEMS, INC.
CRYOLIFE, INC.
MEDTRONIC PUBLIC LIMITED COMPANY
NUVASIVE, INC.
SPECTRANETICS LLC
STRYKER CORPORATION
SURGICAL INNOVATIONS LIMITED
VASCULAR SOLUTIONS LLC

HISTORICAL FINANCIALS

Company Type: Public

Income Statement — FYE: December 31

	REVENUE ($mil)	NET INCOME ($mil)	NET PROFIT MARGIN	EMPLOYEES
12/20	129.3	21.2	16.4%	403
12/19	117.2	17.9	15.3%	479
12/18	105.5	22.9	21.7%	483
12/17	100.8	17.1	17.0%	423
12/16	89.1	10.5	11.9%	397
Annual Growth	9.8%	19.0%	—	0.4%

2020 Year-End Financials

Debt ratio: 15.0%
Return on equity: 13.1%
Cash ($ mil.): 26.7
Current Ratio: 3.75
Long-term debt ($ mil.): 35.5
No. of shares ($ mil.): 20.5
Dividends
  Yield: 0.9%
  Payout: 41.3%
Market value ($ mil.): 831.0

	STOCK PRICE ($) FY Close	P/E High/Low		PER SHARE ($) Earnings	Dividends	Book Value
12/20	40.50	39	20	1.04	0.38	8.41
12/19	35.95	40	25	0.88	0.34	7.35
12/18	23.64	35	19	1.13	0.28	6.64
12/17	31.84	43	24	0.86	0.22	5.70
12/16	25.34	45	22	0.55	0.18	4.71
Annual Growth	12.4%	—	—	17.3%	20.5%	15.6%

Leslie's Inc

EXECUTIVES

Chairman, Director, Steven L. Ortega

Chief Executive Officer, Director, Michael R. Egeck

Executive Vice President, Chief Financial Officer, Treasurer, Secretary, Principal Accounting Officer, Steven M. Weddell

Chief Revenue Officer, Paula F. Baker

Director, Eric J. Kufel

Director, Yolanda Daniel

Director, Susan C. O'Farrell

Lead Independent Director, Director, James R. Ray

Director, John Strain

Director, Claire Spofford

LOCATIONS

HQ: Leslie's Inc
2005 East Indian School Road, Phoenix, AZ 85016
Phone: 602 366-3999
Web: www.lesliespool.com

HISTORICAL FINANCIALS
Company Type: Public

Income Statement — FYE: October 2

	REVENUE ($mil)	NET INCOME ($mil)	NET PROFIT MARGIN	EMPLOYEES
10/21	1,342.9	126.6	9.4%	3,700
10/20*	1,112.2	58.5	5.3%	3,700
09/19	928.2	0.7	0.1%	5,081
09/18	892.6	17.1	1.9%	0
Annual Growth	14.6%	94.8%	—	—

*Fiscal year change

2021 Year-End Financials
Debt ratio: 76.1%
Return on equity: —
Cash ($ mil.): 345.0
Current Ratio: 1.94
Long-term debt ($ mil.): 786.1
No. of shares ($ mil.): 189.8
Dividends
Yield: —
Payout: —
Market value ($ mil.): 3,908.0

	STOCK PRICE ($) FY Close	P/E High/Low		PER SHARE ($) Earnings	Dividends	Book Value
10/21	20.59	46	29	0.67	0.00	(1.15)
10/20*	0.00	—	—	0.37	0.00	(5.28)
Annual Growth	—	—	—	81.1%	—	—

*Fiscal year change

Level One Bancorp Inc

EXECUTIVES

President, Chief Executive Officer, Subsidiary Officer, Chairman, Director, Patrick J. Fehring, $364,808 total compensation

Executive Vice President, Chief Lending Officer, Corporate Secretary, Subsidiary Officer, Gregory A. Wernette, $249,474 total compensation

Executive Vice President, Chief Financial Officer, Subsidiary Officer, Interim Principal Accounting Officer, David C. Walker, $219,415 total compensation

Assistant Corporate Secretary, Subsidiary Officer, Timothy R. Mackay

Assistant Corporate Secretary, Subsidiary Officer, Eva D. Scurlock

Executive Vice President, Chief Human Resources Officer, Subsidiary Officer, Melanie C. Barrett

Director, Barbara E. Allushuski
Director, Victor L. Ansara
Director, James L. Bellinson
Director, Michael A. Brillati
Director, Shukri W. David
Director, Thomas A. Fabbri
Director, Jacob W. Haas
Director, Mark J. Herman
Director, Steven H. Rivera
Director, Stefan Wanczyk

Auditors : Plante & Moran, PLLC

LOCATIONS

HQ: Level One Bancorp Inc
32991 Hamilton Court, Farmington Hills, MI 48334
Phone: 248 737-0300
Web: www.levelonebank.com

HISTORICAL FINANCIALS
Company Type: Public

Income Statement — FYE: December 31

	ASSETS ($mil)	NET INCOME ($mil)	INCOME AS % OF ASSETS	EMPLOYEES
12/20	2,442.9	20.4	0.8%	282
12/19	1,584.8	16.1	1.0%	253
12/18	1,416.2	14.3	1.0%	251
12/17	1,301.2	9.8	0.8%	235
12/16	1,127.5	11.0	1.0%	0
Annual Growth	21.3%	16.6%	—	—

2020 Year-End Financials
Return on assets: 1.0%
Return on equity: 10.5%
Long-term debt ($ mil.): —
No. of shares ($ mil.): 7.6
Sales ($ mil.): 112.3
Dividends
Yield: 0.9%
Payout: 9.3%
Market value ($ mil.): 154.0

	STOCK PRICE ($) FY Close	P/E High/Low		PER SHARE ($) Earnings	Dividends	Book Value
12/20	20.23	10	6	2.57	0.20	28.21
12/19	25.16	13	11	2.05	0.16	22.12
12/18	22.43	15	11	1.91	0.09	19.58
Annual Growth	(5.0%)	—	—	16.0%	49.1%	20.0%

LGI Homes, Inc.

LGI Homes is engaged in the design, construction, and sale of new homes in markets in West, Northwest, Central, Midwest, Florida, Southeast and Mid-Atlantic. Its product offerings include entry-level homes, including both detached and attached homes, and move-up homes, which are sold under its LGI Homes brand, and its luxury series homes, which are sold under its Terrata Homes brand. Its homes has an average price of $482,410 and ranged from 1,000 to 4,100 sq. ft. The builder's higher-quality Terrata Homes started at average sales price of $482,410 home. LGI Homes has constructed and closed over 50,000 homes since its founding in 2003.

Operations

The company operates in one principal homebuilding business that is organized and reports by division. It has seven operating segments (Central, Midwest, Southeast, Mid-Atlantic, Northwest, West and Florida divisions) that it aggregates into five qualifying reportable segments: Central (around 40% of sales), Southeast (nearly 20%), Northwest (more than 15%), West (over 10%) and Florida divisions (around 10%).

The company generated revenues primarily by delivering move-in ready entry-level and move-up spec homes sold under LGI Homes brand and luxury series spec homes sold under Terrata Homes brand.

Retail homes sold under both LGI Homes brand and Terrata Homes brand focus on providing move-in ready homes with standardized features within favorable markets that meet certain demographic and economic conditions. LGI Homes brand primarily markets to entry-level or first-time homebuyers, while Terrata Homes brand primarily markets to move-up homebuyers.

Wholesale homes are primarily sold under a bulk sales agreement and focus on providing move-in ready homes with standardized features to real estate investors that will ultimately use the single-family homes as rental properties.

Retail homes generated about 90% of sales while wholesale home generated the rest.

Geographic Reach

Headquartered in The Woodlands, Texas, the company also has offices in Arizona, Nevada, California, Washington, Colorado, Florida, Georgia, Minnesota, North Carolina, Tennessee, Texas, Utah and West Virginia.

Sales and Marketing

The company's well-defined sales and marketing approach is primarily focused on converting renters of apartments and single-family homes into homeowners. It uses extensive digital and print advertising to attract potential homebuyers and employs various marketing methods such as interactive online media, social media, direct mail and directional signage and billboards.

The company's advertising costs were $7.7 million, $10.7 million and $20.2 million for the years 2021, 2020, and 2019, respectively.

Financial Performance

Home sales revenues in 2021 were $3.1 billion, an increase of $682.2 million, or 29%, from $2.4 billion in 2020. The increase in home sales revenues is primarily due to a 12% increase in homes closed and an increase in the average sales price per home closed in 2021 as compared to 2020.

In 2021, the company had a net income of $429.6 million, a 33% increase from the previous year's net income of $323.9 million. The increase in net income is primarily attributed to operating leverage realized from the increase in home sales revenues and higher average sales price per home closed, partially offset by tax benefits relating to the federal energy efficient homes tax credits it recognized in 2020.

The company's cash at the end of 2021 was $50.5 million. Operating activities generated $21.7 million, while investing activities used $70.4 million, primarily for payment for business acquisitions. Financing activities provided another $63.3 million.

Strategy

The company's business strategy is focused on the acquisition of suitable land and the design, construction and sale of primarily single-family homes in residential subdivisions, including planned communities, in Texas, Arizona, Florida, Georgia, New Mexico, Colorado, North Carolina, South Carolina, Washington, Tennessee, Minnesota, Oklahoma, Alabama, California, Oregon, Nevada, West Virginia, Virginia, Pennsylvania, and Maryland.

Mergers and Acquisitions

In mid-2022, LGI Homes acquired the real estate assets of Buffington Homebuilding Group, Ltd. ("Buffington"), one of the largest privately held homebuilders in Austin, Texas, for approximately $40 million in cash. This acquisition further expands LGI Homes' land position in the highly attractive Central Texas market and marks another important step forward in LGI Homes' goal to become a top five national homebuilder.

Also in 2021, LGI Homes, Inc., has acquired the real estate assets of Minneapolis, Minnesota-based KenRoe, Inc., a privately held homebuilder and land development company, for approximately $27 million at closing. Additionally, LGI is acquiring control of approximately 2,500 raw, undeveloped lots that will be available for future sales as the Company continues to expand its operations throughout the Minneapolis market. Its combined operational excellence will allow for continued growth in the Minneapolis market.

EXECUTIVES

Chairman, Chief Executive Officer, Director, Eric Lipar, $825,000 total compensation

President, Chief Operating Officer, Michael Snider, $550,000 total compensation

Acquisitions Executive Vice President, Jack Lipar, $300,000 total compensation

Chief Financial Officer, Treasurer, Charles Merdian, $430,000 total compensation

Chief Marketing Officer, Rachel Eaton, $300,000 total compensation

General Counsel, Corporate Secretary, Scott H. Garber

Lead Independent Director, Bryan Sansbury

Director, Ryan Edone

Director, Shailee Parikh

Director, Maria Renna Sharpe

Director, Steven Smith

Director, Robert Vahradian

Auditors: Ernst & Young LLP

LOCATIONS

HQ: LGI Homes, Inc.
1450 Lake Robbins Drive, Suite 430, The Woodlands, TX 77380
Phone: 281 362-8998
Web: www.lgihomes.com

2015 Sales

	$ mil	% of total
Texas	350.7	56
Southwest	109.9	17
Southeast	95.9	15
Florida	73.7	12
Total	630.2	100

Selected Locations

Albuquerque
Atlanta
Athens
Austin
Colorado
Charlotte
Dallas/Fort Worth
Denver
Fort Myers
Houston
Jacksonville
Orlando
Phoenix
San Antonio
Seattle
Tampa
Tucson

COMPETITORS

ARMADA/HOFFLER PROPERTIES, L.L.C.
BELLWAY P L C
CALATLANTIC GROUP, INC.
COUNTRYSIDE PROPERTIES (UK) LIMITED
KEEPMOAT HOMES LIMITED
MCCARTHY & STONE LIMITED
MERITAGE HOMES CORPORATION
SHAFTESBURY PLC
THE NEW HOME COMPANY INC
VISTRY GROUP PLC

HISTORICAL FINANCIALS

Company Type: Public

Income Statement — FYE: December 31

	REVENUE ($mil)	NET INCOME ($mil)	NET PROFIT MARGIN	EMPLOYEES
12/21	3,050.1	429.6	14.1%	952
12/20	2,367.9	323.8	13.7%	938
12/19	1,838.1	178.6	9.7%	953
12/18	1,504.4	155.2	10.3%	857
12/17	1,257.9	113.3	9.0%	726
Annual Growth	24.8%	39.5%	—	7.0%

2021 Year-End Financials

Debt ratio: 34.2%
Return on equity: 33.8%
Cash ($ mil.): 50.5
Current Ratio: 15.37
Long-term debt ($ mil.): 805.2
No. of shares ($ mil.): 23.9
Dividends
Yield: —
Payout: —
Market value ($ mil.): 3,695.0

	STOCK PRICE ($) FY Close	P/E High/Low		PER SHARE ($) Earnings	Dividends	Book Value
12/21	154.48	11	6	17.25	0.00	58.36
12/20	105.85	10	3	12.76	0.00	45.59
12/19	70.65	11	6	7.02	0.00	33.33
12/18	45.22	11	5	6.24	0.00	28.89
12/17	75.03	15	5	4.73	0.00	22.42
Annual Growth	19.8%	—	—	38.2%	—	27.0%

LHC Group Inc

LHC Group administers post-acute health care services through some 970 home nursing agencies, hospices, and long-term acute care hospitals (LTACH) in about 35 US states and the District of Columbia ? reaching 60% of the US population aged 65 and older. LHC's home health nursing agencies provide care to Medicare beneficiaries, offering such services as private duty nursing, physical therapy, and medically-oriented social services. Its hospices provide palliative care for terminal patients, while its LTACHs serve patients who no longer need intensive care but still require complex care in a hospital setting.

Operations

LHC Group services are classified into five segments: home health services, hospice services, home and community-based services (HCBS), facility-based services, primarily offered through its long-term acute care hospitals (LTACHs), and healthcare innovations (HCI).

Home health service (about 70% of revenue) offers a wide range of services, including skilled nursing, medically-oriented social services and physical, occupational, and speech therapy.

Hospices (roughly 15%) provide end-of-life care to patients with terminal illnesses through interdisciplinary teams of physicians, nurses, home health aides, counselors, and volunteers. It offers a wide range of services, including pain and symptom management, emotional and spiritual support, inpatient and respite care, homemaker services, and counseling.

Home and Community-Based segment (about 10%) offer assistance with activities of daily living to elderly, chronically ill, and disabled patients, performed by skilled nursing and paraprofessional personnel.

LTACH (about 5%) provide services primarily to patients with complex medical conditions who have transitioned out of a hospital intensive care unit but whose conditions remain too severe for treatment in a non-acute setting.

HCI segment reports on developmental activities outside its other business segments. The HCI segment includes Imperium Health Management, LLC, an Accountable Care Organization (ACO) enablement and management company; Long Term Solutions, Inc., an in-home assessment company serving the long-term care insurance industry, and certain assets operated by Advance Care House Calls, which provides primary medical care for patients with chronic and acute illnesses who have difficulty traveling to a doctor's office.

Geographic Reach

Louisiana-based, LHC Group has some 970 service provider locations in about 35 states in the US and the District of Columbia.

Financial Performance

Net service revenue for 2021 was $2.2 billion, an 8% increase from the previous year's net service revenue of $2.1 billion.

In 2021, the company had a net income of $143.6 million, a 4% increase from the previous year's net income of $137.9 million.

The company's cash at the end of 2021 was $9.8 billion. Financing activities provided $431.4 million, while operating activities used $100.3 million. Investing activities used another $607.8 million, primarily for cash paid for acquisitions.

Strategy

LHC Group's objective is to become the

leading provider of in-home healthcare services in the United States, while also providing a complementary suite of other post-acute healthcare service offerings through its facility-based and HCI segments. To achieve this objective, the company intends to: drive internal growth in existing markets; achieve margin improvement through the active management of costs; expand into new markets; and pursue strategic acquisitions and develop joint ventures.

The company intends to drive internal growth in its current markets by increasing the number of (health care) providers from whom it receives referrals and by expanding the breadth of its services in each market. LHC intends to achieve this growth by continuing to educate health care providers about the benefits of its services, reinforcing the position of the company's agencies and facilities as community assets, maintaining its emphasis on high-quality medical care for its patients, identifying related products and services needed by its patients and their communities, and providing a superior work environment for the company's employees.

Company Background

LHC Group was founded in 1994 as a single home health agency in small-town America, with a mission to serve the neediest and most vulnerable members of the community.

EXECUTIVES

Chief Executive Officer, Chairman, Director, Keith G. Myers, $750,000 total compensation
President, Chief Operating Officer, Donald D. Stelly, $595,000 total compensation
Executive Vice President, Chief Financial Officer, Treasurer, Joshua L. Proffitt, $500,000 total compensation
Executive Vice President, Chief Strategy & Innovation Officer, Bruce Greenstein, $250,000 total compensation
Executive Vice President, Chief Strategy Officer, C. Steven Guenthner
Senior Vice President, Chief Accounting Officer, Jeffrey T. Reibel
Director, Monica F. Azare
Director, Teri G. Fontenot
Director, Jonathan D. Goldberg
Director, Clifford S. Holtz
Director, John L. Indest, $326,120 total compensation
Director, Ronald T. Nixon
Director, W. Earl Reed
Lead Director, Director, W. J. Tauzin
Director, Brent Turner
Director, Tyree G. Wilburn
Auditors : KPMG LLP

LOCATIONS

HQ: LHC Group Inc
901 Hugh Wallis Road South, Lafayette, LA 70508
Phone: 337 233-1307 **Fax:** 337 235-8037

Web: www.lhcgroup.com

PRODUCTS/OPERATIONS

2018 Sales

	$ mil.	% of total
Home health	1,291.5	71
Hospice	199.1	11
Home and community-based	172.5	10
Facility-based	113.8	6
Healthcare innovations	33.1	2
Total	1,810.0	100

COMPETITORS

ALMOST FAMILY, INC.
AMEDISYS, INC.
GENTIVA HEALTH SERVICES, INC.
IASIS HEALTHCARE LLC
LEGACY LIFEPOINT HEALTH, INC.
OPTION CARE HEALTH, INC.
ST. JOSEPH HEALTH SYSTEM
STEWARD HEALTH CARE SYSTEM LLC
THE ENSIGN GROUP INC
TIVITY HEALTH, INC.

HISTORICAL FINANCIALS

Company Type: Public

Income Statement				FYE: December 31
	REVENUE ($mil)	NET INCOME ($mil)	NET PROFIT MARGIN	EMPLOYEES
12/20	2,063.2	111.5	5.4%	27,959
12/19	2,080.2	95.7	4.6%	30,399
12/18	1,809.9	63.5	3.5%	30,985
12/17	1,072.0	50.1	4.7%	14,554
12/16	914.8	36.5	4.0%	11,598
Annual Growth	22.5%	32.2%	—	24.6%

2020 Year-End Financials
Debt ratio: 4.6%
Return on equity: 7.5%
Cash ($ mil.): 286.5
Current Ratio: 0.95
Long-term debt ($ mil.): 20
No. of shares ($ mil.): 31.1
Dividends
Yield: —
Payout: —
Market value ($ mil.): 6,643.0

	STOCK PRICE ($) FY Close	P/E High/Low		PER SHARE ($)	
			Earnings	Dividends	Book Value
12/20	213.32	64 29	3.56	0.00	49.09
12/19	137.76	44 29	3.07	0.00	45.60
12/18	93.88	45 26	2.29	0.00	42.93
12/17	61.25	25 16	2.79	0.00	25.29
12/16	45.70	22 16	2.07	0.00	22.45
Annual Growth	47.0%	— —	14.5%	—	21.6%

Liberty Broadband Corp

EXECUTIVES

Chairman, Director, John C. Malone
President, Chief Executive Officer, Director, Gregory B. Maffei, $0 total compensation
Senior Vice President, Principal Financial Officer, Controller, Chief Accounting Officer, Brian J. Wendling
Chief Corporate Development Officer, Albert E. Rosenthaler, $0 total compensation
Chief Legal Officer, Renee L. Wilm

Director, Richard R. Green
Director, John E. Welsh
Director, Julie D. Frist
Director, J. David Wargo
Director, Sue Ann Hamilton
Director, Gregg L. Engles
Auditors : KPMG LLP

LOCATIONS

HQ: Liberty Broadband Corp
12300 Liberty Boulevard, Englewood, CO 80112
Phone: 720 875-5700
Web: www.libertybroadband.com

HISTORICAL FINANCIALS

Company Type: Public

Income Statement				FYE: December 31
	REVENUE ($mil)	NET INCOME ($mil)	NET PROFIT MARGIN	EMPLOYEES
12/20	50.7	397.6	784.2%	0
12/19	14.8	117.2	788.9%	0
12/18	22.2	69.9	314.3%	0
12/17	13.0	2,033.6	15533.7%	0
12/16	30.5	917.3	2999.1%	0
Annual Growth	13.5%	(18.9%)	—	—

2020 Year-End Financials
Debt ratio: 23.0%
Return on equity: 3.2%
Cash ($ mil.): 1,417.8
Current Ratio: 3.02
Long-term debt ($ mil.): 4,878
No. of shares ($ mil.): 196.5
Dividends
Yield: —
Payout: —
Market value ($ mil.): 31,124.0

	STOCK PRICE ($) FY Close	P/E High/Low		PER SHARE ($)	
			Earnings	Dividends	Book Value
12/20	158.37	76 42	2.17	0.00	68.71
12/19	125.75	193 112	0.64	0.00	58.65
12/18	72.03	248 176	0.38	0.00	58.44
12/17	85.16	9 7	11.10	0.00	57.84
12/16	74.07	12 7	6.00	0.00	46.62
Annual Growth	20.9%	—	(22.5%)	—	10.2%

LICT Corp

LICT (formerly Lynch Interactive) is a holding company that operates through 12 small (mostly rural) local-exchange phone companies located primarily in the Midwestern and Western US; it also has a limited presence in the Northeast. The company provides local telephone service over nearly 60,000 access lines while dial-up and broadband Internet service lines number about 50,000. Subsidiaries include JBN Telephone, Haviland Telephone, and Giant Communications in Kansas; CentraCom Interactive in Utah; and Bretton Woods Telephone in New Hampshire. Chairman Mario Gabelli owns 24% of LICT.

EXECUTIVES

Chairman, President, Chief Executive Officer, Director, Mario J. Gabelli, $350,000 total compensation

Executive Vice President, Chief Financial Officer, Director, Robert E. Dolan, $285,146 total compensation
Regulatory Dynamics Senior Vice President, Evelyn C. Jerden, $244,467 total compensation
Finance Vice President, Stephen J. Moore
Chief Operating Officer, James DaBramo
Secretary, Thomas Hearity
Controller, John Aoki
Director, Salvatore Muoio
Director, Gary L. Sugarman
Auditors : BDO USA, LLP

LOCATIONS

HQ: LICT Corp
401 Theodore Fremd Avenue, Rye, NY 10580-1430
Phone: 914 921-8821   **Fax:** 914 921-6410
Web: www.lictcorp.com

COMPETITORS

ALTEVA, INC.
BREDA TELEPHONE CORP.
FARMERS TELECOMMUNICATIONS COOPERATIVE, INC.
FARMERS TELEPHONE COOPERATIVE, INC.
HARGRAY TELEPHONE COMPANY, INC.
HECTOR COMMUNICATIONS CORP
LEXCOM, INC.
OTELCO INC.
PIONEER TELEPHONE COOPERATIVE, INC.
TDS METROCOM, INC.

HISTORICAL FINANCIALS
Company Type: Public

Income Statement — FYE: December 31

	REVENUE ($mil)	NET INCOME ($mil)	NET PROFIT MARGIN	EMPLOYEES
12/20	124.1	37.2	30.0%	343
12/19	117.9	26.1	22.2%	338
12/18	115.8	25.7	22.3%	315
12/17	106.7	22.3	21.0%	206
12/16	90.7	7.2	8.0%	293
Annual Growth	8.2%	50.5%	—	4.0%

2020 Year-End Financials
Debt ratio: 22.3%
Return on equity: 22.1%
Cash ($ mil.): 67.3
Current Ratio: 1.89
Long-term debt ($ mil.): 20.8
No. of shares ($ mil.): 0.0
Dividends
 Yield: —
 Payout: —
Market value ($ mil.): 330.0

	STOCK PRICE ($) FY Close	P/E High/Low		Earnings	Dividends	Book Value
12/20	7,800.00	9		61,982.00	0.00	9,745
12/19	8,000.00	15		111,342.00	0.00	8,044
12/18	4,450.00	12		91,271.97	0.00	7,043
12/17	1,650.00	12		51,063.80	0.00	5,960
12/16	5,950.00	17	14	338.32	0.00	5,097
Annual Growth	31.5%	—	—	55.6%	—	17.6%

Limbach Holdings Inc

EXECUTIVES

Chairman, Director, Gordon G. Pratt
President, Chief Executive Officer, Director, Michael M. McCann
Executive Vice President, Chief Financial Officer, Jayme L. Brooks
Director, Laurel J. Krzeminski
Director, Charles A. Bacon, $618,000 total compensation
Director, Joshua S. Horowitz
Director, Linda G. Alvarado
Director, Norbert W. Young
Director, Michael F. McNally
Auditors : Crowe LLP

LOCATIONS

HQ: Limbach Holdings Inc
1251 Waterfront Place, Suite 201, Pittsburgh, PA 15222
Phone: 412 359-2100
Web: www.limbachinc.com

HISTORICAL FINANCIALS
Company Type: Public

Income Statement — FYE: December 31

	REVENUE ($mil)	NET INCOME ($mil)	NET PROFIT MARGIN	EMPLOYEES
12/20	568.2	5.8	1.0%	1,700
12/19	553.3	(1.7)	—	1,900
12/18	546.5	(1.8)	—	1,700
12/17	485.7	0.7	0.1%	1,580
12/16	225.6	(0.6)	—	1,420
Annual Growth	26.0%	—	—	4.6%

2020 Year-End Financials
Debt ratio: 16.4%
Return on equity: 11.5%
Cash ($ mil.): 42.1
Current Ratio: 1.33
Long-term debt ($ mil.): 36.5
No. of shares ($ mil.): 7.9
Dividends
 Yield: —
 Payout: —
Market value ($ mil.): 98.0

	STOCK PRICE ($) FY Close	P/E High/Low		Earnings	Dividends	Book Value
12/20	12.33	18	3	0.72	0.00	6.78
12/19	3.78	—	—	(0.23)	0.00	6.10
12/18	3.68	—	—	(0.52)	0.00	6.11
12/17	13.83	—	—	(0.13)	0.00	7.48
12/16	14.10	—	—	(0.19)	0.00	7.76
Annual Growth	(3.3%)	—	—	—	—	(3.3%)

Limestone Bancorp Inc

Porter Bancorp could be a stout evaluator of what "ales" your finances. It is the holding company for PBI Bank, which serves local residents and businesses through about 20 offices in Louisville and other portions of central Kentucky. The company also operates Ascencia, a nationwide online banking platform. PBI Bank offers standard financial services such as checking, savings, and money market accounts, certificates of deposit, and trust services. Loans collateralized by real estate, such as commercial mortgages (more than 35% of the company's loan portfolio), residential mortgages (more than 25%), and construction loans (approximately 20%), comprise the lion's share of the company's loan portfolio.

EXECUTIVES

Chairman Emeritus, General Counsel, Subsidiary Officer, J. Chester Porter, $193,750 total compensation
Chairman, Director, W. Glenn Hogan
President, Chief Executive Officer, Subsidiary Officer, Director, John T. Taylor, $425,000 total compensation
Executive Vice President, Chief Financial Officer, Subsidiary Officer, Phillip W. Barnhouse, $244,800 total compensation
Chief Accounting Officer, Corporate Secretary, John Michael Koehler
Subsidiary Officer, Joseph C. Seiler, $244,800 total compensation
Subsidiary Officer, John R. Davis, $255,000 total compensation
Director, Kevin J. Kooman
Director, Michael T. Levy
Director, James M. Parsons
Director, Bradford T. Ray
Director, Edmond J. Seifried
Director, Celia Catlett
Auditors : Crowe LLP

LOCATIONS

HQ: Limestone Bancorp Inc
2500 Eastpoint Parkway, Louisville, KY 40223
Phone: 502 499-4800
Web: www.limestonebank.com

COMPETITORS

ANNAPOLIS BANCORP, INC.
CLOVER COMMUNITY BANK
DNB FINANCIAL CORPORATION
NATIONAL BANK OF ARIZONA
NB&T FINANCIAL GROUP, INC.

HISTORICAL FINANCIALS
Company Type: Public

Income Statement — FYE: December 31

	ASSETS ($mil)	NET INCOME ($mil)	INCOME AS % OF ASSETS	EMPLOYEES
12/20	1,312.3	9.0	0.7%	226
12/19	1,245.7	10.5	0.8%	251
12/18	1,069.6	8.7	0.8%	214
12/17	970.8	38.4	4.0%	217
12/16	945.1	(2.7)	—	238
Annual Growth	8.6%	—	—	(1.3%)

2020 Year-End Financials
Return on assets: 0.7%
Return on equity: 8.0%
Long-term debt ($ mil.): —
No. of shares ($ mil.): 7.5
Sales ($ mil.): 57.5
Dividends
 Yield: —
 Payout: —
Market value ($ mil.): 94.0

	STOCK PRICE ($) FY Close	P/E High/Low		PER SHARE ($) Earnings	Dividends	Book Value
12/20	12.56	15	6	1.20	0.00	15.47
12/19	18.00	13	10	1.41	0.00	14.15
12/18	13.76	14	10	1.23	0.00	12.34
12/17	14.32	3	1	6.15	0.00	12.03
12/16	12.32	—	—	(0.46)	0.00	7.07
Annual Growth	0.5%	—	—	—	—	21.6%

Lincoln Educational Services Corp

Lincoln hopes its graduates are better " Abe -l" to get a career. Lincoln Educational Services provides vocational programs from schools including Lincoln Technical Institute and Nashville Auto-Diesel College. It offers programs in automotive technology and skilled trades (including HVAC and electronics). Some 14,000 students are enrolled at more than 30 campuses and five training sites more than 15 states throughout the US. Lincoln tends to grow by buying smaller schools and by opening campuses in new markets. It also expands its campus facilities to accommodate higher enrollment numbers. The company announced plans to divest its health care and other professions business in 2015.

Operations
All of Lincoln Educational Services schools offer diploma and certificate programs, 22 of its schools are approved to offer associate's degree programs, and three schools are approved to offer bachelor's degrees. The majority of its students pay for their educations with financial aid provided by the federal government. Indeed, in 2011 Title IV loans represented 84% of the company's revenue.

Geographic Reach
Lincoln Educational Services operates 31 campuses in 15 states. Of those schools, 16 are located in New Jersey, Connecticut, and Pennsylvania.

Financial Performance
Changes to regulations affecting for-profit schools like Lincoln have lead to declining enrollment in the last couple of years. In 2013 the company's revenue fell 14% as a result even though some fees were higher. Net loss also increased, by $14 million to $51 million, due to declining revenue and higher taxes. Cash from operations also decreased with $13 million going out, leaving Lincoln with about $3 million in cash from operations.

Strategy
Expanding areas of study, its facilities (including online options), and geographic presence are all part of Lincoln's growth strategy. For example in 2014 the company introduced a new Advanced Manufacturing diploma at campuses in Texas and Indiana with support from local manufacturing businesses. It also began partnering with high schools in New Jersey to offer introductory automotive technologies courses in conjunction with Chrysler and BMW.

Lincoln Educational Services' most popular areas of study are health sciences, automotive, and the skilled trades, which combined account for more than 80% of total enrollment. Business and information technology and hospitality services also see their fair share of student interest. Keeping student interest up (and with it, enrollment) is germane to Lincoln Educational Services' financial success. If enrollment drops, income drops, and the company suffers. In order to keep its curriculum fresh, the company assesses future job trends and adds degrees and classes accordingly. But the company missed in its forecasting and stricter government rules about transparency around financial aid - both factors lead to sagging enrollment. Between 2011 and 2014 the number of Lincoln campuses fell from 46 to 31 after the company decided to close four locations in Ohio and one in Kentucky; overall enrollment went from 20,000 to 13,700.

EXECUTIVES

President, Chief Executive Officer, Director, Scott M. Shaw, $500,000 total compensation
Finance Executive Vice President, Finance Chief Financial Officer, Finance Treasurer, Brian K. Meyers, $340,000 total compensation
Division Officer, Stephen M. Buchenot, $277,494 total compensation
Executive Vice President, Chief Innovation Officer, Chad D. Nyce
Senior Vice President, General Counsel, Corporate Secretary, Alexandra M. Luster
Non-Executive Chairman, Director, J. Barry Morrow
Director, John A. Bartholdson
Director, James J. Burke
Director, Kevin M. Carney
Director, Ronald Edward Harbour
Director, Michael A. Plater
Director, Felecia J. Pryor
Director, Carlton E. Rose
Auditors : DELOITTE & TOUCHE LLP

LOCATIONS

HQ: Lincoln Educational Services Corp
14 Sylvan Way, Suite A, Parsippany, NJ 07054
Phone: 973 736-9340
Web: www.lincolnedu.com

COMPETITORS

MT SAN ANTONIO COMMUNITY COLLEGE DISTRICT
NORTHEAST IOWA COMMUNITY COLLEGE FOUNDATION
PASADENA AREA COMMUNITY COLLEGE DISTRICT
RIVERSIDE COMMUNITY COLLEGE DISTRICT FOUNDATION
SALT LAKE COMMUNITY COLLEGE

HISTORICAL FINANCIALS
Company Type: Public

Income Statement — FYE: December 31

	REVENUE ($mil)	NET INCOME ($mil)	NET PROFIT MARGIN	EMPLOYEES
12/20	293.0	48.5	16.6%	1,933
12/19	273.3	2.0	0.7%	1,922
12/18	263.2	(6.5)	—	1,884
12/17	261.8	(11.4)	—	1,980
12/16	196.9	(28.3)	—	2,197
Annual Growth	10.5%	—	—	(3.1%)

2020 Year-End Financials
Debt ratio: 7.0%
Return on equity: 61.2%
Cash ($ mil.): 38.0
Current Ratio: 1.11
Long-term debt ($ mil.): 15.2
No. of shares ($ mil.): 26.4
Dividends
Yield: —
Payout: —
Market value ($ mil.): 172.0

	STOCK PRICE ($) FY Close	P/E High/Low		PER SHARE ($) Earnings	Dividends	Book Value
12/20	6.50	5	1	1.49	0.00	3.89
12/19	2.70	41	21	0.08	0.00	2.18
12/18	3.20	—	—	(0.27)	0.00	1.62
12/17	2.02	—	—	(0.48)	0.00	1.85
12/16	1.92	—	—	(1.21)	0.00	2.22
Annual Growth	35.6%	—	—	—	—	15.1%

Littelfuse Inc

Littelfuse is one of the world's largest fuse makers. In addition to its fuses, Littelfuse's other circuit protection devices include positive temperature coefficient devices that limit current when too much is being supplied and electrostatic discharge suppressors that redirect transient high voltage. The company's thyristors protect telecommunications circuits from transient voltage caused by lightning strikes. It also supplies fuses for HVAC systems, elevators, and machine tools. Littelfuse's over 6,900 customers include distributors, electronics manufacturers, automakers, and the automotive aftermarket.

Operations
Littelfuse operates through three business segments: Electronics, Transportation, and Industrial.

The Electronics segment offers fuses and fuse accessories, semiconductor and power semiconductor products, and insulated gate bipolar transistors technologies. It covers a broad range of end markets, including industrial and automotive electronics, electric vehicle infrastructure, data and telecommunications, medical devices, LED lighting, consumer electronics and appliances. Electronics account for more than 60% of sales.

The Transportation segment produces circuit protection, power control, and sensing products for Tier 1 auto manufacturers, suppliers, and parts distributors. Products include fuses and fuse accessories for combustion and electric engines, such as blade fuses, battery cable protectors, resettable fuses, and high current- and high-voltage fuses. Automotive sales account for around 25% of total revenue.

The Industrial segment makes power fuses, protection relays and controls, and other circuit protection products for use in various industrial applications such as oil, gas, mining, solar and wind energy, electric vehicle infrastructure, construction, HVAC systems, elevator and other industrial equipment. The segment accounts for more than 10% of sales.

Geographic Reach

Illinois-based Littelfuse operates in three geographic territories -- the Americas, Europe, and Asia/Pacific -- and has more than 75 manufacturing and distribution facilities in China, Germany, Italy, Japan, Lithuania, Mexico, Philippines, Portugal, the UK, and the US.

The company's largest market were the US and China with around 30% each.

Sales and Marketing

Littelfuse's customer base comprises over 6,900 customers and distributors worldwide. Sales to Arrow Electronics, Inc., an electronics distributor, account for around 10% of the Littelfuse's revenue.

Products from the Electronics segment are mainly sold through distribution partners, including Arrow as well as Future Electronics and TTI, Inc, and regional and high service distributors. The Transportation segment sells directly to all the major automotive and commercial vehicle OEMs (original equipment manufacturers), system suppliers, and Tier One automotive and aftermarket customers globally.

Financial Performance

The company's revenue in 2021 increased by 44% to $2.1 billion compared with $1.4 billion. The increase was due to volume growth across all segments and businesses while 2020 had temporary closures of manufacturing facilities resulting from government directives due to the impact of COVID-19.

Net income in 2021 increased to $283.8 million compared with $130.0 million in the prior year. The increase in net income reflects higher operating income of $223.3 million driven by a $156.9 million increase in operating income in the Electronics segment, the 2020 goodwill impairment charge of $33.8 million, a $24.3 million increase in operating income in the Transportation segment partially offset by higher foreign exchange losses of $32.0 million and a $19.9 million non-cash pension settlement charge associated with the completion of the buy-out of one of its UK pension plans.

Cash held by the company at the end of fiscal 2021 decreased to $482.4 million. Cash provided by operations was $373.3 million while investing and financing activities used $499.2 million and $69.0 million, respectively. Main cash uses were acquisitions of businesses and payments of revolving credit facility.

Strategy

In 2021, Littelfuse announced its new five-year strategic plan which builds upon its strengths from its previous strategy. The company is well-positioned within the center of the global structural growth themes of sustainability, connectivity, and safety, which will continue to drive increased demand for the company's products across the transportation, industrial and electronics end markets that it serves. It is targeting average annual organic sales growth of 5-7% and average annual sales growth from strategic acquisitions of 5-7% and expects to achieve this through content and share gains, expanded presence in high-growth markets and geographies, and targeting high-growth and niche applications. Littelfuse will continue to invest in its people, as well as customer-driven innovation, eMobility, and its digital infrastructure to improve customer experience, and its operating systems. It plans to capitalize on growth opportunities where technologies and applications are converging across its product segments, while continuing to acquire and integrate businesses that fit its strategic focus areas.

Mergers and Acquisitions

In late 2021, Littelfuse acquired Carling Technologies for $315 million in cash. Carling has a leading position in switching and circuit protection technologies with a strong global presence in commercial transportation, communications and marine markets. The combination of its companies significantly expands its technologies and capabilities. The addition of Carling more than doubles the sizes of its commercial vehicle business, and its complementary customers, channels, and products will accelerate its growth in strategic markets.

Company Background

Littelfuse was formed in 1927 to make the first small, fast-acting fuse able to protect test meters. In 1968 military electronics firm Tracor (later part of the UK's General Electric Company, now telent) bought the company. Littelfuse entered the power (industrial) fuse market in 1983. Tracor ran into financial troubles with the end of the Cold War and filed for bankruptcy protection in 1991. As a result of Tracor's reorganization, Littelfuse became an independent company in 1992.

EXECUTIVES

Chairman, Director, Gordon Hunter, $600,000 total compensation
Corporate Strategy Senior Vice President, Matthew J. Cole
Global Operations President, Global Operations Chief Executive Officer, Director, David W. Heinzmann, $763,000 total compensation
Executive Vice President, Chief Financial Officer, Meenal A. Sethna, $487,834 total compensation
Human Resources Executive Vice President, Human Resources Chief Legal Officer, Human Resources Chief Human Resources Officer, Human Resources Corporate Secretary, Ryan K. Stafford, $462,375 total compensation
Global Business Operations Senior Vice President, Global Business Operations Division Officer, Michael P. Rutz, $391,032 total compensation
Senior Vice President, Division Officer, Deepak Nayar, $366,428 total compensation
Director, Maria C. Green
Director, Kristina A. Cerniglia
Director, Tzau-Jin Chung
Director, Cary T. Fu
Director, Anthony Grillo
Director, John E. Major
Director, William P. Noglows
Director, Nathan Zommer
Auditors : Grant Thornton LLP

LOCATIONS

HQ: Littelfuse Inc
8755 West Higgins Road, Suite 500, Chicago, IL 60631
Phone: 773 628-1000
Web: www.littelfuse.com

2018 Sales

	$ mil.	% of total
Asia/Pacific	753.3	44
Americas	578.6	34
Europe	386.6	22
Total	1,718.5	100

PRODUCTS/OPERATIONS

2018 Sales

	$ mil.	% of total
Electronics		
Semiconductor	649	38
Passive Products and Sensors	475.3	28
Automotive		
Passenger Car	240.5	14
Commercial Vehicle	121.6	7
Automotive Sensor	117.7	7
Industrial	114.4	6
Total	1,718.5	100

Selected Brands
ATO
JCASE Fuse
MAXI
MEGA
MIDI
MINI
NANO2
OMNI-BLOK
PICO II
POWR-GARD
PulseGuard

Selected Products
Automotive Sensors
Battery Management
Custom-Engineered Electrical Equipment
DC Power Distribution Modules
DC Solenoids and Relays
Fuse Blocks, Fuse Holders and Fuse Accessories
Fuses
Fusible Switches and Panels
Gas Discharge Tubes
Magnetic Sensors and Reed Switches
Other Products and Accessories
Power Semiconductors
Protection Relays and Controls

Polymer ESD Suppressors
Resettable PTC Fuses
Semiconductors
Shock-Block GFCI
Surge Protection Module
Switches
Varistors

Selected Services
Custom Circuit Protection Solutions
Custom Power Centers and Electrical Equipment
Electrical Safety Services
MROplus Industrial Fuse Consolidation
Testing Services

COMPETITORS

ALPS ALPINE CO., LTD.
ELECTRIUM SALES LIMITED
GENTHERM INCORPORATED
HUBBELL INCORPORATED
LEVITON MANUFACTURING CO., INC.
MEIDENSHA CORPORATION
ON SEMICONDUCTOR CORPORATION
S & C ELECTRIC COMPANY
SWITCHCRAFT, INC.
TECHNOLOGY RESEARCH, LLC

HISTORICAL FINANCIALS
Company Type: Public

Income Statement — FYE: January 1

	REVENUE ($mil)	NET INCOME ($mil)	NET PROFIT MARGIN	EMPLOYEES
01/22*	2,079.9	283.8	13.6%	17,000
12/20	1,445.6	129.9	9.0%	12,200
12/19	1,503.8	139.0	9.2%	11,300
12/18	1,718.4	164.5	9.6%	12,300
12/17	1,221.5	119.5	9.8%	10,700
Annual Growth	14.2%	24.1%	—	12.3%

*Fiscal year change

2022 Year-End Financials
Debt ratio: 20.2%
Return on equity: 15.9%
Cash ($ mil.): 478.4
Current Ratio: 2.92
Long-term debt ($ mil.): 611.8
No. of shares ($ mil.): 24.6
Dividends
  Yield: —
  Payout: 17.7%
Market value ($ mil.): 7,768.0

	STOCK PRICE ($) FY Close	P/E High/Low		PER SHARE ($) Earnings	Dividends	Book Value
01/22*	314.68	29	21	11.38	2.02	76.70
12/20	251.66	47	20	5.29	1.92	65.69
12/19	192.02	36	27	5.60	1.82	61.35
12/18	168.03	35	23	6.52	1.60	59.67
12/17	197.82	40	28	5.21	1.40	41.64
Annual Growth	12.3%	—	—	21.6%	9.6%	16.5%

*Fiscal year change

Live Oak Bancshares Inc

EXECUTIVES

Chairman, Chief Executive Officer, Subsidiary Officer, James S. Mahan, $510,600 total compensation
Executive Vice President, Subsidiary Officer, Vice-Chairman, Director, William L. Williams
Chief Financial Officer, Subsidiary Officer, William C. Losch
Chief Credit Officer, Subsidiary Officer, Steven J. Smits, $400,008 total compensation
Chief Accounting Officer, Subsidiary Officer, John Wesley Sutherland
President, Director, Neil L. Underwood, $700,174 total compensation
General Counsel, Subsidiary Officer, Gregory W. Seward, $300,000 total compensation
Subsidiary Officer, Renato Derraik
Subsidiary Officer, M. Huntley Garriott
Subsidiary Officer, Susan N. Janson, $194,971 total compensation
Director, Casey Stuart Crawford
Director, Tonya Williams Bradford
Director, William H. Cameron
Director, Diane B. Glossman
Director, Glen F. Hoffsis
Director, Miltom E. Petty
Director, Yousef A. Valine
Director, David G. Lucht, $390,000 total compensation
Auditors: Dixon Hughes Goodman LLP

LOCATIONS

HQ: Live Oak Bancshares Inc
1741 Tiburon Drive, Wilmington, NC 28403
Phone: 910 790-5867
Web: www.liveoakbank.com

HISTORICAL FINANCIALS
Company Type: Public

Income Statement — FYE: December 31

	ASSETS ($mil)	NET INCOME ($mil)	INCOME AS % OF ASSETS	EMPLOYEES
12/20	7,872.3	59.5	0.8%	647
12/19	4,814.9	18.0	0.4%	635
12/18	3,670.4	51.4	1.4%	506
12/17	2,758.4	100.4	3.6%	528
12/16	1,755.2	13.7	0.8%	425
Annual Growth	45.5%	44.2%	—	11.1%

2020 Year-End Financials
Return on assets: 0.9%
Return on equity: 10.7%
Long-term debt ($ mil.): —
No. of shares ($ mil.): 42.4
Sales ($ mil.): 374.4
Dividends
  Yield: 0.2%
  Payout: 13.6%
Market value ($ mil.): 2,015.0

	STOCK PRICE ($) FY Close	P/E High/Low		PER SHARE ($) Earnings	Dividends	Book Value
12/20	47.46	34	6	1.43	0.12	13.38
12/19	19.01	45	29	0.44	0.12	13.21
12/18	14.81	25	11	1.24	0.12	12.29
12/17	23.85	9	7	2.65	0.10	10.95
12/16	18.50	50	30	0.39	0.07	6.51
Annual Growth	26.6%	—	—	38.4%	14.4%	19.7%

Live Ventures Inc

LiveDeal (formerly YP Corp.) is an Internet yellow pages and local online classifieds provider. The company offers goods and services listed for sale through its online classified marketplace at classifieds.livedeal.com; LiveDeal also publishes about 17 million business listings via its business directory at yellowpages.livedeal.com. Sources of revenue include advertising sales, a pay-per-lead program with major auto dealers, and optional listing upgrade and e-commerce/fraud prevention fees. The company changed its name from YP Corp. after its 2007 purchase of online local classifieds marketplace LiveDeal.

EXECUTIVES

Chairman, President, Chief Executive Officer, Director, John Isaac, $200,000 total compensation
Finance Chief Operating Officer, Finance Managing Director, Eric Althofer
Chief Financial Officer, Chief Accounting Officer, David E. Verret
Chief Legal Officer, Corporate Secretary, Wayne R. Ipsen
Subsidiary Officer, Weston A. Godfrey
Subsidiary Officer, Rodney Spriggs, $270,000 total compensation
Subsidiary Officer, Thomas Sedlak
Director, Tony Isaac, $98,615 total compensation
Director, Richard D. Butler
Director, Dennis Gao
Director, Tyler Sickmeyer
Auditors: Frazier & Deeter LLC

LOCATIONS

HQ: Live Ventures Inc
325 E. Warm Springs Road, Suite 102, Las Vegas, NV 89119
Phone: 702 997-5968
Web: www.liveventures.com

COMPETITORS

CITYSEARCH
EDMUNDS.COM, INC.
MARCHEX, INC.
VERIZON MEDIA UK LIMITED
YPM, INC.

HISTORICAL FINANCIALS
Company Type: Public

Income Statement — FYE: September 30

	REVENUE ($mil)	NET INCOME ($mil)	NET PROFIT MARGIN	EMPLOYEES
09/21	272.9	31.1	11.4%	1,253
09/20	191.7	10.9	5.7%	1,150
09/19	193.2	(4.0)	—	1,000
09/18	199.6	5.9	3.0%	1,155
09/17	152.0	6.5	4.3%	1,211
Annual Growth	15.8%	48.0%	—	0.9%

2021 Year-End Financials
Debt ratio: 26.3%
Return on equity: 52.2%
Cash ($ mil.): 4.6
Current Ratio: 1.52
Long-term debt ($ mil.): 39.5
No. of shares ($ mil.): 1.5
Dividends
  Yield: —
  Payout: —
Market value ($ mil.): 59.0

	STOCK PRICE ($) FY Close	P/E High/Low		PER SHARE ($) Earnings	Dividends	Book Value
09/21	37.00	4	0	9.80	0.00	47.73
09/20	8.94	2	1	3.09	0.00	27.65
09/19	8.57	—	—	(2.11)	0.00	18.69
09/18	9.00	7	3	1.58	0.00	20.28
09/17	12.40	9	1	1.61	0.00	16.86
Annual Growth	31.4%	—	—	57.1%	—	29.7%

Lovesac Co

EXECUTIVES

Chairman, Director, Andrew R. Heyer
Chief Executive Officer, Director, Shawn Nelson, $350,000 total compensation
President, Chief Operating Officer, Mary Fox
Chief Strategy Officer, Director, Jack Krause, $350,000 total compensation
Executive Vice President, Chief Financial Officer, Treasurer, Secretary, Donna L. Dellomo, $325,000 total compensation
Director, John Grafer
Director, Sharon M. Leite
Director, Walter F. McLallen
Director, Shirley Romig
Director, Vineet Mehra
Auditors : Marcum LLP

LOCATIONS

HQ: Lovesac Co
Two Landmark Square, Suite 300, Stamford, CT 06901
Phone: 888 636-1223
Web: www.lovesac.com

HISTORICAL FINANCIALS
Company Type: Public

Income Statement				FYE: January 31
	REVENUE ($mil)	NET INCOME ($mil)	NET PROFIT MARGIN	EMPLOYEES
01/21*	320.7	14.7	4.6%	778
02/20	233.3	(15.2)	—	781
02/19	165.8	(6.7)	—	590
02/18	101.8	(5.5)	—	441
01/17	76.3	(6.8)	—	0
Annual Growth	43.2%	—	—	—

*Fiscal year change

2021 Year-End Financials
Debt ratio: —
Return on equity: 14.9%
Cash ($ mil.): 78.3
Current Ratio: 2.55
Long-term debt ($ mil.): —
No. of shares ($ mil.): 15.0
Dividends
  Yield: —
  Payout: —
Market value ($ mil.): 849.0

	STOCK PRICE ($) FY Close	P/E High/Low		PER SHARE ($) Earnings	Dividends	Book Value
01/21*	56.54	57	4	0.96	0.00	7.19
02/20	11.35	—	—	(1.07)	0.00	6.23
02/19	23.74	—	—	(3.28)	0.00	5.80
Annual Growth	54.3%	—	—	—	—	11.4%

*Fiscal year change

Lumentum Holdings Inc

EXECUTIVES

President, Chief Executive Officer, Director, Alan S. Lowe, $734,615 total compensation
Executive Vice President, Chief Financial Officer, Wajid Ali
Global Sales Executive Vice President, Sales Executive Vice President, Global Sales Chief Transformation Officer, Sales Chief Transformation Officer, Jason Reinhardt, $423,846 total compensation
Development Executive Vice President, Research Executive Vice President, Development Chief Operating Officer, Research Chief Operating Officer, Vincent Retort, $454,231 total compensation
Senior Vice President, General Counsel, Secretary, Judy G. Hamel, $317,692 total compensation
Director, Harold L. Covert
Director, Isaac H. Harris
Director, Penelope A. Herscher
Director, Julie S. Johnson
Director, Brian J. Lillie
Director, Ian S. Small
Director, Pamela Fletcher
Director, Janet S. Wong
Auditors : DELOITTE & TOUCHE LLP

LOCATIONS

HQ: Lumentum Holdings Inc
1001 Ridder Park Drive, San Jose, CA 95131
Phone: 408 546-5483
Web: www.lumentum.com

HISTORICAL FINANCIALS
Company Type: Public

Income Statement				FYE: July 3
	REVENUE ($mil)	NET INCOME ($mil)	NET PROFIT MARGIN	EMPLOYEES
07/21*	1,742.8	397.3	22.8%	5,618
06/20	1,678.6	135.5	8.1%	5,473
06/19	1,565.3	(36.4)	—	5,161
06/18	1,247.7	248.1	19.9%	2,930
07/17	1,001.6	(102.5)	—	2,057
Annual Growth	14.9%	—	—	28.6%

*Fiscal year change

2021 Year-End Financials
Debt ratio: 33.2%
Return on equity: 21.0%
Cash ($ mil.): 774.3
Current Ratio: 3.67
Long-term debt ($ mil.): 789.8
No. of shares ($ mil.): 73.0
Dividends
  Yield: —
  Payout: —
Market value ($ mil.): 6,093.0

	STOCK PRICE ($) FY Close	P/E High/Low		PER SHARE ($) Earnings	Dividends	Book Value
07/21*	83.47	21	13	5.07	0.00	27.02
06/20	76.13	52	27	1.75	0.00	23.29
06/19	53.41	—	—	(0.54)	0.00	19.53
06/18	57.90	19	11	3.82	0.00	14.75
07/17	57.05	—	—	(1.71)	0.00	10.07
Annual Growth	10.0%	—	—	—	—	28.0%

*Fiscal year change

Luther Burbank Corp

EXECUTIVES

Chairman, Subsidiary Officer, Director, Victor S. Trione
President, Chief Executive Officer, Subsidiary Officer, Director, Simone Lagomarsino
Executive Vice President, Division Officer, William Fanter
Executive Vice President, Chief Risk Officer, Tammy Mahoney
Executive Vice President, Chief Operating Officer, Chief Technology Officer, Parham Medhat
Executive Vice President, Chief Credit Officer, Alexander Stefani
Executive Vice President, Chief Financial Officer, Subsidiary Officer, Laura Tarantino, $357,500 total compensation
Senior Vice President, Division Officer, Lisa Kepler
Lead Independent Director, Director, Thomas C. Wajnert
Director, John C. Erickson
Director, Anita Gentle Newcomb
Director, Bradley M. Shuster
Director, M. Max Yzaguirre
Director, Renu Agrawal
Auditors : Crowe LLP

LOCATIONS

HQ: Luther Burbank Corp
520 Third Street, Fourth Floor, Santa Rosa, CA 95401
Phone: 844 446-8201
Web: www.lutherbanksavings.com

HISTORICAL FINANCIALS
Company Type: Public

Income Statement				FYE: December 31
	ASSETS ($mil)	NET INCOME ($mil)	INCOME AS % OF ASSETS	EMPLOYEES
12/20	6,906.1	39.9	0.6%	277
12/19	7,045.8	48.8	0.7%	277
12/18	6,937.2	45.0	0.6%	278
12/17	5,704.3	69.3	1.2%	266
12/16	5,064.5	52.1	1.0%	274
Annual Growth	8.1%	(6.5%)		0.3%

2020 Year-End Financials
Return on assets: 0.5%
Return on equity: 6.4%
Long-term debt ($ mil.): —
No. of shares ($ mil.): 52.2
Sales ($ mil.): 243.9
Dividends
  Yield: 2.3%
  Payout: 28.3%
Market value ($ mil.): 512.0

	STOCK PRICE ($)		P/E		PER SHARE ($)		
	FY Close		High/Low		Earnings	Dividends	Book Value
12/20	9.80		16	10	0.75	0.23	11.75
12/19	11.53		14	11	0.87	0.23	10.97
12/18	9.02		17	10	0.79	0.19	10.31
12/17	12.04		8	7	1.62	1.58	9.74
Annual Growth	(6.6%)		—	—	(22.6%)	(47.4%)	6.4%

Lyons Bancorp Inc.

Auditors: Bonadio & Co., LLP

LOCATIONS

HQ: Lyons Bancorp Inc.
 399 Exchange Street, Geneva, NY 14456
Phone: 315 946-4871
Web: www.bankwithlnb.com

HISTORICAL FINANCIALS
Company Type: Public

Income Statement — FYE: December 31

	ASSETS ($mil)	NET INCOME ($mil)	INCOME AS % OF ASSETS	EMPLOYEES
12/20	1,423.1	10.2	0.7%	0
12/19	1,163.6	11.0	0.9%	0
12/18	1,081.6	9.9	0.9%	0
12/17	1,031.8	8.0	0.8%	0
Annual Growth	11.3%	8.6%	—	—

2020 Year-End Financials
Return on assets: 0.7%
Return on equity: 11.2%
Long-term debt ($ mil.): —
No. of shares ($ mil.): 3.1
Sales ($ mil.): 62.9
Dividends
 Yield: —
 Payout: 39.7%
Market value ($ mil.): 127.0

	STOCK PRICE ($)		P/E		PER SHARE ($)		
	FY Close		High/Low		Earnings	Dividends	Book Value
12/20	40.00		13	10	3.12	1.24	30.06
12/19	39.75		14	11	3.33	1.22	27.36
12/18	41.10		15	11	3.03	1.14	24.48
12/17	35.50		19	13	2.42	1.05	23.13
Annual Growth	4.1%		—	—	8.8%	5.7%	9.1%

M/I Homes Inc

M/I Homes is one of the nation's leading builders of single-family homes, having sold over 136,700 homes since commencing homebuilding activities in 1976. The company's homes are marketed and sold primarily under the M/I Homes brand. It delivers homes to first-time, move-up, empty-nest, and luxury buyers at prices ranging from about $210,000 to $788,000 and sizes ranging from 1,000 to 5,500 sq. ft. M/I Homes also builds attached townhomes in select markets. It caters to about 15 markets located in eleven states. Its M/I Financial mortgage banking subsidiary provides title and mortgage services. M/I Homes is founded by cousins Melvin and Irving Schottenstein in 1976.

Operations

M/I Homes' homebuilding operations comprise the Southern (some 55%) and Northern regions (over 40%), generating over 95% of total revenue.

Its homebuilding operations design, market, construct and sell single-family homes and attached townhomes to first-time, move-up, empty-nester, and luxury buyers. In addition to home sales, its homebuilding operations generate revenue from the sale of land and lots.

Other plans include Smart Series (entry-level and move-down buyers) and City Collection (upscale urban lifestyle). The company also currently develops new floor plans and communities specifically for the growing empty-nester market. It currently offers over 450 different floor plans across all of its divisions.

Complementing its homebuilding activities, the company provides mortgage banking and title services through its wholly owned subsidiary M/I Financial Corp. It accounts for less than 5% of total revenue.

In addition, over 95% of sales were generated from housing.

Geographic Reach

M/I Homes is based in Columbus, Ohio. The Northern region includes Ohio, Indiana, Illinois, Minnesota, and Michigan. M/I Homes' Southern region includes Florida, North Carolina, Tennessee, and Texas.

Sales and Marketing

The company markets its homes using traditional media such as newspapers, direct mail, billboards, radio and television. It also uses enhanced search engine optimization, search engine optimization, paid search, and display advertising to increase the reach of its website. It maintains a presence on referral sites, such as Zillow.com and NewHomeSource.com, to drive sales leads to online sales associates.

M/I Homes also uses email marketing to maintain communication with existing prospects and customers. It uses its social media presence to communicate to potential homebuyers the experiences of customers who have purchased its homes and to provide content about its homes and design features.

Financial Performance

The company's revenue has been rising in the last five years with an overall increase of 80% between 2017 and 2021. Its net income has been following a similar pattern.

In 2021, the company recorded a total revenue of $3.8 billion, of which $3.6 billion was from homes delivered, $13.4 million was from land sales, and $102 million was from its financial services operations. Revenue from homes delivered increased 23% from 2020 driven primarily by the 929 additional homes delivered in 2021 (a 12% increase) and a 10% increase in the average sales price of homes delivered ($39,000 per home delivered), which was primarily the result of the mix of homes delivered and higher demand.

In the same year, the company achieved a net income of $396.9 million, a 65% increase from the previous year's net income of $239.9 million. This was primarily due to a higher sales volume for the year.

Cash at the end of fiscal 2021 was $236.4 million, a decrease of $24.4 million over the previous year. Financing activities provided $44.1 million to the company coffers. Investing and operating activities used $51.7 million for purchases of property and equipment and Investment in and advances to joint venture arrangements, and mortgage loans originations, respectively.

Strategy

The company remains focused on increasing its profitability by generating additional revenue, continuing to expand its market share, shifting its product mix to include more affordable designs, and investing in attractive land opportunities to increase its number of active communities.

Consistent with its focus on improving long-term financial results, it expects to emphasize the following strategic business objectives in 2022: managing its land spend and inventory levels; accelerating the opening of new communities wherever possible; maintaining a strong balance sheet and liquidity levels; expanding the availability of its more affordable Smart Series homes; and emphasizing customer service, product quality and design, and premier locations.

Company Background

M/I Homes was founded in 1976 in Ohio by Melvin and Irving Schottenstein. The company expanded into new markets in the 1980s, including Florida, Indiana, and North Carolina. The company established M/I Financial in 1983.

EXECUTIVES

Chairman, President, Chief Executive Officer, Director, Robert H. Schottenstein, $900,000 total compensation

Executive Vice President, Chief Financial Officer, Subsidiary Officer, Director, Phillip G. Creek, $600,000 total compensation

Executive Vice President, Secretary, Chief Legal Officer, Director, J. Thomas Mason, $500,000 total compensation

Vice President, Chief Accounting Officer, Controller, Ann Marie W. Hunker

Subsidiary Officer, Derek J. Klutch

Division Officer, Fred J. Sikorski

Division Officer, Thomas W. Jacobs

Lead Independent Director, Director, Friedrich K.M. Bohm

Director, Kumi D. Walker

Director, Michael P. Glimcher

Director, Elizabeth (Lisa) K. Ingram

Director, William H. Carter

Director, Norman L. Traeger

Director, Nancy Jean Kramer

Auditors: Deloitte & Touche LLP

LOCATIONS

HQ: M/I Homes Inc
4131 Worth Avenue, Suite 500, Columbus, OH 43219
Phone: 614 418-8000 **Fax:** 614 418-8080
Web: www.mihomes.com

PRODUCTS/OPERATIONS

2015 Sales

	$ mil.	% of total
Southern Homebuilding	514.7	36
Midwest homebuilding	500.9	35
Mid-Atlantic homebuilding	366.8	26
Financial services	36.0	3
Total	1,418.4	100

Selected Markets

Charlotte, NC
Chicago, IL
Cincinnati, OH
Columbus, OH
Dayton, OH
Houston, TX
Indianapolis, IN
Maryland
Orlando, FL
Raleigh, NC
San Antonio, TX
Tampa, FL
Virginia

COMPETITORS

AV HOMES, INC.
CALATLANTIC GROUP, INC.
D.R. HORTON, INC.
HOVNANIAN ENTERPRISES, INC.
KB HOME
M.D.C. HOLDINGS, INC.
NVR, INC.
THE NEW HOME COMPANY INC
TRI POINTE GROUP, INC.
WILLIAM LYON HOMES

HISTORICAL FINANCIALS

Company Type: Public

Income Statement — FYE: December 31

	REVENUE ($mil)	NET INCOME ($mil)	NET PROFIT MARGIN	EMPLOYEES
12/21	3,745.8	396.8	10.6%	1,657
12/20	3,046.1	239.8	7.9%	1,515
12/19	2,500.2	127.5	5.1%	1,401
12/18	2,286.2	107.6	4.7%	1,359
12/17	1,961.9	72.0	3.7%	1,238
Annual Growth	17.5%	53.2%	—	7.6%

2021 Year-End Financials

Debt ratio: 29.7%
Return on equity: 27.5%
Cash ($ mil.): 236.3
Current Ratio: 7.63
Long-term debt ($ mil.): 961.8
No. of shares ($ mil.): 28.5
Dividends
  Yield: —
  Payout: —
Market value ($ mil.): 1,772.0

	STOCK PRICE ($) FY Close	P/E High/Low		PER SHARE ($) Earnings	Dividends	Book Value
12/21	62.18	5	3	13.28	0.00	56.99
12/20	44.29	6	1	8.23	0.00	43.68
12/19	39.35	10	5	4.48	0.00	35.35
12/18	21.02	10	5	3.70	0.00	31.08
12/17	34.40	14	9	2.26	0.00	26.83
Annual Growth	16.0%	—	—	55.7%	—	20.7%

Magnolia Oil & Gas Corp

EXECUTIVES

Chairman, Director, Dan F. Smith
President, Chief Executive Officer, Chief Financial Officer, Director, Christopher G. Stavros, $208,333 total compensation
Executive Vice President, General Counsel, Corporate Secretary, Timothy D. Yang, $120,462 total compensation
Operations Senior Vice President, Steve F. Millican, $48,333 total compensation
Director, Arcilia C. Acosta
Director, Angela M. Busch
Director, Edward P. Djerejian
Director, John B. Walker
Director, James R. Larson
Auditors: KPMG LLP

LOCATIONS

HQ: Magnolia Oil & Gas Corp
Nine Greenway Plaza, Suite 1300, Houston, TX 77046
Phone: 713 842-9050
Web: www.magnoliaoilgas.com

HISTORICAL FINANCIALS

Company Type: Public

Income Statement — FYE: December 31

	REVENUE ($mil)	NET INCOME ($mil)	NET PROFIT MARGIN	EMPLOYEES
12/21	1,078.3	417.2	38.7%	192
12/20	534.5	(1,208.3)	—	136
12/19	936.1	50.1	5.4%	45
12/18*	433.2	39.0	9.0%	27
07/18	449.1	218.5	48.7%	0
Annual Growth	33.9%	24.1%	—	—

*Fiscal year change

2021 Year-End Financials

Debt ratio: 22.2%
Return on equity: 61.1%
Cash ($ mil.): 366.8
Current Ratio: 2.37
Long-term debt ($ mil.): 388
No. of shares ($ mil.): 228.5
Dividends
  Yield: 0.4%
  Payout: 4.8%
Market value ($ mil.): 4,313.0

	STOCK PRICE ($) FY Close	P/E High/Low		PER SHARE ($) Earnings	Dividends	Book Value
12/21	18.87	9	3	2.36	0.08	3.57
12/20	7.06	—	—	(7.27)	0.00	2.20
12/19	12.58	48	34	0.28	0.00	7.02
12/18*	11.21	61	40	0.25	0.00	6.72
07/18	12.26	—	—	0.00	0.00	0.00
Annual Growth	15.5%	—	—	—	—	—

*Fiscal year change

MainStreet Bancshares Inc

EXECUTIVES

Chairman, President, Chief Executive Officer, Director, Jeff W. Dick, $342,500 total compensation
Division Officer, Bruce Gemmill
Executive Vice President, Chief Financial Officer, Director, Thomas J. Chmelik, $246,278 total compensation
Loans Executive Vice President, Michael Rudolph
Credit Senior Vice President, Credit Chief Risk Officer, Chris Johnston
Retail Senior Vice President, Retail Chief Compliance Officer, Thomas Lackey
Operations Senior Vice President, Jacob Hutchinson
Chief Lending Officer, Jimmy Olevson
Director, Elizabeth S. Bennett
Director, William E. Cox
Director, Darrell Green
Director, Paul Thomas Haddock
Director, Patsy I. Rust
Director, Terry M. Saeger
Auditors: Yount, Hyde & Barbour, P.C.

LOCATIONS

HQ: MainStreet Bancshares Inc
10089 Fairfax Boulevard, Fairfax, VA 22030
Phone: 703 481-4567
Web: www.mstreetbank.com

HISTORICAL FINANCIALS

Company Type: Public

Income Statement — FYE: December 31

	ASSETS ($mil)	NET INCOME ($mil)	INCOME AS % OF ASSETS	EMPLOYEES
12/20	1,643.1	15.7	1.0%	126
12/19	1,277.3	13.9	1.1%	126
12/18	1,100.6	9.2	0.8%	110
12/17	807.9	3.8	0.5%	0
12/16	575.7	3.8	0.7%	0
Annual Growth	30.0%	41.9%	—	—

2020 Year-End Financials

Return on assets: 1.0%
Return on equity: 10.2%
Long-term debt ($ mil.): —
No. of shares ($ mil.): 7.4
Sales ($ mil.): 69.5
Dividends
  Yield: —
  Payout: —
Market value ($ mil.): 126.0

	STOCK PRICE ($) FY Close	P/E High/Low		PER SHARE ($) Earnings	Dividends	Book Value
12/20	16.91	13	6	1.85	0.00	22.52
12/19	23.00	15	10	1.69	0.00	16.59
12/18	17.06	17	13	1.38	0.00	14.83
12/17	17.52	21	17	0.85	0.00	12.57
12/16	14.20	16	13	0.87	0.00	10.34
Annual Growth	4.5%	—	—	20.9%	—	21.5%

Malibu Boats Inc

EXECUTIVES

Chairman, Director, Michael K. Hooks
Chief Executive Officer, Jack D. Springer, $535,769 total compensation
Operations Vice President, Operations Chief Operating Officer, Ritchie L. Anderson, $277,500 total compensation
Product Design Vice President, Dan L. Gasper, $99,423 total compensation
Human Resources Vice President, Human Resources Director, Deborah S. Kent, $95,926 total compensation
Chief Financial Officer, Wayne R. Wilson, $287,019 total compensation
Subsidiary Officer, Director, William Paxson St. Clair
Director, James R. Buch
Director, Ivar S. Chhina
Director, Michael J. Connolly
Director, Mark W. Lanigan
Director, Joan M. Lewis
Director, Peter E. Murphy
Director, John E. Stokely
Auditors : KPMG LLP

LOCATIONS

HQ: Malibu Boats Inc
5075 Kimberly Way, Loudon, TN 37774
Phone: 865 458-5478
Web: www.malibuboats.com

HISTORICAL FINANCIALS

Company Type: Public

Income Statement — FYE: June 30

	REVENUE ($mil)	NET INCOME ($mil)	NET PROFIT MARGIN	EMPLOYEES
06/21	926.5	109.8	11.9%	2,645
06/20	653.1	61.5	9.4%	1,795
06/19	684.0	66.0	9.7%	1,835
06/18	497.0	27.6	5.6%	1,345
06/17	281.9	28.3	10.1%	586
Annual Growth	34.6%	40.3%	—	45.8%

2021 Year-End Financials

Debt ratio: 19.3%
Return on equity: 34.9%
Cash ($ mil.): 41.4
Current Ratio: 1.58
Long-term debt ($ mil.): 139
No. of shares ($ mil.): 20.8
Dividends
Yield: —
Payout: —
Market value ($ mil.): 1,529.0

	STOCK PRICE ($) FY Close	P/E High/Low		PER SHARE ($) Earnings	Dividends	Book Value
06/21	73.33	17	9	5.23	0.00	17.91
06/20	51.95	18	6	2.95	0.00	12.36
06/19	38.85	18	10	3.15	0.00	9.79
06/18	41.94	33	18	1.36	0.00	6.54
06/17	25.87	16	8	1.58	0.00	2.74
Annual Growth	29.8%	—	—	34.9%	—	59.9%

ManTech International Corp

ManTech International provides security-focused IT services to agencies, primarily US government intelligence entities, such as the Department of Defense (DoD), homeland security, and the military. Its national security offerings include intelligence, communications, computer forensics, and security systems development and support. Its solution sets, which include full-spectrum cyber; secure mission and enterprise IT; advanced data analytics; software and systems development; intelligent systems engineering; intelligence mission support; and mission operations, are aligned with the long-term needs of the company's customers. ManTech is active in other countries, but makes essentially all of its sales to US customers.

Operations

ManTech provides services in cyber security; enterprise information technology (IT); software application and systems development; multi-disciplined intelligence; intelligence, command, control, communications, computers, combat systems, intelligence surveillance, and reconnaissance (C5ISR); program protection and mission assurance; systems engineering; training; and supply chain management and logistics.

The company provides its services and solutions under three types of contracts: cost-reimbursable (about 70% of the total revenue); fixed-price (nearly 20%); and time-and-materials (account for the rest).

Geographic Reach

The company is headquartered in Virginia.

Sales and Marketing

ManTech's customers include intelligence community, the Department of Defense (DoD) and federal civilian agencies including the diplomatic, homeland security, healthcare and space communities. ManTech derives vast majority of its revenues from US government customers.

Financial Performance

The company's revenue for 2021 was $2.6 billion, a 1% increase from the previous year's revenue of $2.5 billion. The primary drivers of the increase in the company's revenues are revenues from new contract awards, growth on existing contracts and the acquisitions we completed in the prior year. These increases were offset by contracts and tasks that ended during the year and reduced scope of work on some contracts including contracts with variable material purchase requirements.

In 2021, the company had a net income of $137 million, a 14% increase from the previous year's net income of $120.5 million.

The company's cash at the end of 2021 was $53.4 million. Operating activities generated $212.2 million, while investing activities used $425.2 million, mainly for acquisition of businesses. Financing activities provided another $225.2 million.

Strategy

The company generates revenues under different types of government contracts, including cost-reimbursable, time-and-materials and fixed-price contracts. Its earnings and profitability may vary depending on changes in the amount of revenues it derives from each type of contract, the nature of services or solutions provided, or the level of achievement of performance objectives required to receive award fees.

Mergers and Acquisitions

In early 2022, ManTech acquired Maryland-based Technical and Management Assistance Corporation (TMAC), a leading provider of advanced data engineering services and solutions to the U.S. Intelligence Community. It offers a full range of data centric solutions and expertise with proven experience in systems engineering, data collection and governance, analytics and mission management systems.

In late 2021, ManTech acquired Gryphon Technologies, an industry-leading systems engineering firm, from AE Industrial Partners for $350 million in cash. Headquartered in Washington, DC, Gryphon Technologies provides advanced capabilities including model-based systems engineering, predictive analytics, data/computational science and cloud engineering solutions that drive mission success for an array of Department of Defense agencies. This acquisition expands ManTech's capabilities in the Defense Sector with new customers and programs ? and some 1,500 skilled professionals who will add momentum to ManTech's success at Bringing Digital to the Mission in innovative ways that support national and homeland security.

Company Background

ManTech was founded in 1968 to provide advanced technological services to the US government. Co-founder George J. Pedersen controls about 85% of the company's voting power.

EXECUTIVES

Chairman, President, Chief Executive Officer, Director, Kevin M. Phillips, $900,016 total compensation
Executive Vice President, Chief Financial Officer, Judith L. Bjornaas, $568,752 total compensation
Chief Operating Officer, Matthew A. Tait, $483,750 total compensation
Business Services Executive Vice President, Bonnie Cook
Corporate Affairs Senior Vice President, Regulatory Affairs Senior Vice President, Corporate Affairs Corporate Secretary, Regulatory Affairs Corporate Secretary, Michael R. Putnam
Director, Richard L. Armitage

Director, Mary K. Bush
Director, Barry G. Campbell
Director, Richard J. Kerr
Director, Peter B. LaMontagne
Director, Kenneth A. Minihan
Auditors : DELOITTE & TOUCHE LLP

LOCATIONS

HQ: ManTech International Corp
2251 Corporate Park Drive, Herndon, VA 20171
Phone: 703 218-6000
Web: www.mantech.com

PRODUCTS/OPERATIONS

2018 Sales

	% of total
Department of Defense and intelligence agencies	74
Federal civilian agencies	24
State agencies, international agencies and commercial entities	2
Total	100

2018 Sales

	$ in mil.	% of total
Cost-reimbursable	1,325	68
Fixed-price	435.6	22
Time-and-material	198	10
Total	1,958.6	100

Selected Services

C4ISR
  Ground, airborne, and space systems
  New technology development, testing, and infusion
  Telecommunications systems and elevated sensors
Cyber Security
  Computer forensics and exploitation
  Counter-intrusion support
  Insider threat protection
  Program protection and security
Health Care
  Behavioral health
  Health care research
  Imaging
  Informatics
Information Technology Services
  Biometrics and identity management
  Embedded software engineering
  Network and database administration
  Real-time software applications
  Social media and collaboration environments
Systems Engineering Services
  Border security
  Enterprise architecture
  Risk management
  Tactical systems development and integration

COMPETITORS

CACI INTERNATIONAL INC.
CSRA INC.
KRATOS DEFENSE & SECURITY SOLUTIONS, INC.
LEIDOS HOLDINGS, INC.
NCI, INC.
PRESIDIO, INC.
SCIENCE APPLICATIONS INTERNATIONAL CORPORATION
SERCO INC.
THE KEYW HOLDING CORPORATION
VALINAR, LLC

HISTORICAL FINANCIALS
Company Type: Public

Income Statement
FYE: December 31

	REVENUE ($mil)	NET INCOME ($mil)	NET PROFIT MARGIN	EMPLOYEES
12/20	2,518.3	120.5	4.8%	9,400
12/19	2,222.5	113.8	5.1%	8,900
12/18	1,958.5	82.0	4.2%	7,800
12/17	1,717.0	114.1	6.6%	7,600
12/16	1,601.5	56.3	3.5%	7,000
Annual Growth	12.0%	20.9%	—	7.6%

2020 Year-End Financials

Debt ratio: 0.7%
Return on equity: 7.8%
Cash ($ mil.): 41.1
Current Ratio: 1.42
Long-term debt ($ mil.): 15
No. of shares ($ mil.): 40.4
Dividends
  Yield: 1.4%
  Payout: 43.0%
Market value ($ mil.): 3,599.0

	STOCK PRICE ($) FY Close	P/E High/Low		PER SHARE ($) Earnings	Dividends	Book Value
12/20	88.94	29	19	2.97	1.28	39.03
12/19	79.88	28	18	2.83	1.08	37.10
12/18	52.30	32	23	2.06	1.00	35.24
12/17	50.19	18	11	2.91	0.84	34.23
12/16	42.25	31	18	1.47	0.84	32.05
Annual Growth	20.5%	—	—	19.2%	11.1%	5.0%

MarineMax Inc

MarineMax is the largest recreational boat and yacht retailer and superyacht services company in the world. It has nearly 80 locations in around 20 states. The company sells new and used recreational boats and related marine products, including engines, trailers, parts, and accessories. The company also arranges related boat financing, insurance, and extended service contracts; provides boat repair and maintenance services; offers yacht and boat brokerage sales; and, where available, offers slip and storage accommodations. MarineMax is the largest retailer of Sea Ray and Boston Whaler.

Operations
In 2021, MarineMax changed its reportable segments as a result of its acquisition of Cruisers Yachts. The company now operates through two new reportable segments: Retail Operations and Product Manufacturing.

Retail Operations segment accounting for nearly 100% of the total revenue, includes the sale of new and used recreational boats, including pleasure and fishing boats, with a focus on premium brands in each segment. The segment also includes selling related marine products, including engines, trailers, parts, and accessories. In addition, they provide repair, maintenance, and slip and storage services; arrange related boat financing, insurance, and extended service contracts; offer boat and yacht brokerage sales; yacht charter services.

Product Manufacturing segment includes activity of Cruisers Yachts, a wholly-owned MarineMax subsidiary, manufacturing sport yacht and yachts with sales through the company's select retail dealership locations and through independent dealers.

Geographic Reach
MarineMax is based in Florida (Clearwater) and the state accounts for more than half of its sales. The other 20 states in which it has retail locations are Alabama, California, Connecticut, Florida, Georgia, Illinois, Maryland, Massachusetts, Michigan, Minnesota, Missouri, New Jersey, New York, North Carolina, Ohio, Oklahoma, Rhode Island, South Carolina, Texas, Washington and Wisconsin. The company is also in the British Virgin Islands.

Sales and Marketing
MarineMax sells used boats at their retail locations, online, and at various third-party marinas and other offsite locations; Marine engines and propellers are sold primarily to its retail customers as replacements for its existing engines and propellers; a broad variety of parts and accessories are sold at its retail locations and at various offsite locations, and through its print catalog; the company offers maintenance, repair, and slip and storage services at most of its retail locations; finance and insurance products are offered at most of their retail locations and at various offsite locations and to its customers and independent boat dealers and brokers; MarineMax offers boat and yacht brokerage sales at most of its retail locations and at various offsite locations; and it conducts a charter business, which is based in the British Virgin Islands, in which the company offer customers the opportunity to charter third-party and company owned power catamarans.

MarineMax's advertising and promotional expenses approximated $18.8 million, $14.0 million and $14.8 million for 2019, 2020 and 2021, respectively.

Financial Performance
In fiscal 2021, MarineMax reported a revenue of $2 billion, or an increase of $554 million from the prior year. Of the revenue increase, $202.9 million was attributable to a 13.4% increase in comparable-store sales and an approximate $350.6 million net increase was related to stores opened, including acquired, or closed that were not eligible for inclusion in the comparable-store base. The increase in their comparable-store sales was primarily due to demand driven increases in new and used boat revenue and their higher margin finance and insurance products, brokerage, parts, service, and storage services.

In fiscal 2021, net income was $154.9 million, an increase of $80.3 million from $74.6 million in the prior year.

The company had about $222.2 million in cash in 2021, up from about $155.5 million in 2020. Cash provided by operating activities was $373.9 million. Cash used in investing activities was $56.3 million, primarily for acquisitions. Cash used in financing activities was approximately $45.71 million, primarily for net payments on short-term borrowings.

Strategy

MarineMax's primary goal remains to enhance its position as the nation's leading recreational boat and yacht retailer. In addition, it has broadened its strategy, including through recent acquisitions of Fraser Yachts Group, Northrop & Johnson and SkipperBud's, to increase the business' superyacht brokerage and luxury yacht services and marina/storage services. Expansion of strategy is aimed to potentially increase margins.

The company also continues to broaden and strengthen its digital initiatives which are always available and offer full selection of boats, yachts and charters, as well as expert team to answer customers' questions and help them find a boat virtually. Additionally, its Boatyard digital platform allows marine businesses effective and customized digital solutions delivering great customer experiences by enabling customers to interact through a personalized experience tailored to their needs.

Apart from acquisitions, the company opened 35 new retail locations in existing territories, excluding those opened on a temporary basis for a specific purpose.

Mergers and Acquisitions

In late 2021, MarineMax acquired Intrepid Powerboats, a premier manufacturer of powerboats, and Texas MasterCraft, a premier watersports dealer in Northern Texas. Intrepid is recognized as a world class producer of customized boats, carefully reflecting the unique desires of each individual owner. Texas Mastercraft specializes in ski and wakeboard boats. The activity of Intrepid will be included in their Product Manufacturing segment. The activity of Texas MasterCraft will be included in their Retail Operations segment.

In 2021, MarineMax acquired KCS International, Inc., better known as Cruisers Yachts, headquartered in Oconto, Wisconsin. Cruisers Yachts (Cruisers) is recognized as one of the world's premier manufacturers of premium yachts, producing models from 33' to 60' feet. The strategic acquisition of Cruisers Yachts benefits MarineMax's customers by filling a meaningful void in its product portfolio which was created in 2018 by the loss of Sea Ray sport yacht and yacht models. The acquisition also aligns with MarineMax's long-term strategy of expanding its gross margins by adding a higher margin business. Cruisers has a seasoned, passionate and successful team.

EXECUTIVES

Executive Chairman, Director, William H. McGill, $750,000 total compensation

West Operations President, West Operations Chief Executive Officer, Director, William Brett McGill, $396,000 total compensation

East Operations Executive Vice President, East Operations Chief Revenue Officer, Charles (Chuck) A. Cashman, $320,000 total compensation

Executive Vice President, Chief Financial Officer, Secretary, Director, Michael H. McLamb, $350,000 total compensation

Accounting & Shared Services Vice President, Accounting & Shared Services Chief Accounting Officer, Anthony E. Cassella, $220,000 total compensation

Lead Independent Director, Director, Clint Moore

Director, Hilliard M. Eure

Director, George E. Borst

Director, Evelyn V. Follit

Director, Charles R. Oglesby

Director, Joseph (Joe) A. Watters

Director, Rebecca White

Auditors : KPMG LLP

LOCATIONS

HQ: MarineMax Inc
2600 McCormick Drive, Suite 200, Clearwater, FL 33759
Phone: 727 531-1700
Web: www.marinemax.com

PRODUCTS/OPERATIONS

2017 Sales

	$ mil.	% of total
New boat sales	747	70
Used boat sales	157	15
Maintenance, repair & storage services	60	6
Marine Engines, Related Marine Equipment, and Boating Parts and Accessories	38	2
F&I Products	25	4
Brokerage Sales	20	2
Total	1,052.0	100

Selected Products & Trade Names

Motor Yachts
   Azimut
   Hatteras Motor Yachts
Convertibles
   Cabo
   Hatteras Convertibles
Pleasure Boats
   Meridian
   Sea Ray
Fishing Boats
   Boston Whaler
   Grady White
Ski Boats
   Axis
   Malibu

COMPETITORS

BRUNSWICK CORPORATION
CAMPING WORLD HOLDINGS, INC.
CAVCO INDUSTRIES, INC.
COPART, INC.
DEFENDER INDUSTRIES, INC.
FREEDOMROADS, LLC
MALIBU BOATS, LLC
PIER 1 IMPORTS, INC.
POLARIS INC.
WEST MARINE, INC.

HISTORICAL FINANCIALS

Company Type: Public

Income Statement
FYE: September 30

	REVENUE ($mil)	NET INCOME ($mil)	NET PROFIT MARGIN	EMPLOYEES
09/21	2,063.2	154.9	7.5%	2,666
09/20	1,509.7	74.6	4.9%	1,736
09/19	1,237.1	35.9	2.9%	1,754
09/18	1,177.3	39.3	3.3%	1,573
09/17	1,052.3	23.5	2.2%	1,516
Annual Growth	18.3%	60.2%	—	15.2%

2021 Year-End Financials

Debt ratio: 7.4%   No. of shares ($ mil.): 21.8
Return on equity: 29.5%   Dividends
Cash ($ mil.): 222.1   Yield: —
Current Ratio: 2.06   Payout: —
Long-term debt ($ mil.): 47.4   Market value ($ mil.): 1,059.0

	STOCK PRICE ($) FY Close	P/E High/Low		PER SHARE ($) Earnings	Dividends	Book Value
09/21	48.52	9	4	6.78	0.00	27.26
09/20	25.67	10	2	3.37	0.00	20.83
09/19	15.48	16	9	1.57	0.00	17.30
09/18	21.25	14	9	1.71	0.00	15.57
09/17	16.55	24	14	0.95	0.00	13.81
Annual Growth	30.9%	—	—	63.4%	—	18.5%

MarketAxess Holdings Inc.

MarketAxess operates leading electronic trading platforms delivering greater trading efficiency, a diversified pool of liquidity and significant cost savings to its clients across the global fixed-income markets. Almost 1,900 institutional investor and broker-dealer firms are active users of the company patent trading technology. The company also provides real-time the ability to view indicative prices from its broker-dealer clients' inventory available on its platform, access to real-time pricing information and analytical tools available through its Corporate BondTicker service. The majority of its revenue accounts in US. The company was incorporated in the year 2000.

Operations

Nearly 90% of the company's revenue comes from commissions for transactions executed on its platform between institutional investor and broker-dealer clients. About 5% of its revenue comes from its information services. Less than 5% of its revenue comes from its post-trade services. Other revenue includes revenue generated from telecommunications line charges to broker-dealer clients.

Geographic Reach

New York - based, MarketAxess generates about 80% of its revenue from the US, while around 15% comes from Europe and the remaining some 5% comes from Asia. The company has office locations in the US, UK,

Brazil, Netherlands, Hong Kong, and Singapore.

Sales and Marketing

To boost awareness of its brand and electronic trading platform, MarketAxess uses advertising, direct marketing, digital and social media, promotional mailings, and participates in industry conferences and media engagement. As an example, it worked with The Wall Street Journal to make its Corporate BondTicker service the source of WSJ's information for its daily corporate bond and high-yield tables.

MarketAxess has approximately 960 post-trade reporting and transparency clients, including broker-dealers, hedge funds and investment banks.

Financial Performance

The company's revenue for fiscal 2021 increased to $699.0 million compared from the prior year with $689.1 million.

Net income for fiscal 2021 decreased by 14% to $257.9 million compared from the prior year with $299.4 million.

Cash held by the company at the end of fiscal 2021 increased to $625.6 million. Cash provided by operations was $282.1 million while cash used for investing and financing activities were $67.7 million and $189.8 million, respectively. Main uses of cash were capitalization of software development costs and cash dividend on common stock.

Strategy

The company's objective is to be the leading global electronic trading platforms for fixed-income securities, connecting broker-dealers and institutional investors more easily and efficiently, while offering a broad array of information, trading and technology services to market participants across the trading cycle. The key elements of its strategy are: increase penetration in credit markets; continue expansion into new product areas; expand trading protocols and leverage the open trading network; and pursue select acquisitions and strategic alliances.

Mergers and Acquisitions

In 2021, MarketAxess announced the acquisition of MuniBrokers, a central electronic venue serving municipal bond inter-dealer brokers and dealers, for $17 million. The acquisition connects its leading trading technology with the liquidity of one of the industry's largest electronic inter-dealer marketplaces, creating a compelling and diverse liquidity solution that the company believes will ultimately deliver an improved execution experience.

EXECUTIVES

Chief Executive Officer, Chairman, Director, Richard M. McVey, $500,000 total compensation
President, Chief Operating Officer, Director, Christopher R. Concannon
Chief Financial Officer, Christopher N. Gerosa
Chief Information Officer, Nicholas Themelis, $300,000 total compensation
General Counsel, Corporate Secretary, Scott Pintoff
Global Head of Sales, Kevin M. McPherson, $300,000 total compensation
Region Officer, Christophe Roupie, $399,000 total compensation
Lead Independent Director, Director, Stephen P. Casper
Director, Nancy Altobello
Director, Richard L. Prager
Director, Justin G. Gmelich
Director, Kourtney Gibson
Director, Xiaojia Li
Director, Steven L. Begleiter
Director, Jane P. Chwick
Director, William F. Cruger
Director, Richard G. Ketchum
Director, Emily H. Portney
Auditors: PricewaterhouseCoopers LLP

LOCATIONS

HQ: MarketAxess Holdings Inc.
55 Hudson Yards, 15th Floor, New York, NY 10001
Phone: 212 813-6000 **Fax:** 212 813-6390
Web: www.marketaxess.com

2014 Sales

	$mil.	% of total
United States	223.8	85
United Kingdom	38.2	15
Others	0.8	-
Total	262.8	100

PRODUCTS/OPERATIONS

2014 Sales

	$ mil.	% of total
Commissions	221.1	84
Information and post-trade services	31.5	12
Technology products and services	6.9	3
Investment income	0.5	-
Others	2.8	1
Total	262.8	100

Selected Mergers and Acquisitions
FY2012
Xtrakter Limited (undisclosed price; London, UK; provider of regulatory transaction reporting)

COMPETITORS

CBOE GLOBAL MARKETS, INC.
EDWARD D. JONES & CO., L.P.
FIDESSA GROUP HOLDINGS LIMITED
INTERACTIVE BROKERS GROUP, INC.
NUMIS CORPORATION PLC
S&P GLOBAL INC.
STONEX GROUP INC.
VIRTU FINANCIAL, INC.
VIRTU ITG HOLDINGS LLC
VIRTU KNIGHT CAPITAL GROUP LLC

HISTORICAL FINANCIALS

Company Type: Public

Income Statement				FYE: December 31
	REVENUE ($mil)	NET INCOME ($mil)	NET PROFIT MARGIN	EMPLOYEES
12/21	698.9	257.8	36.9%	676
12/20	689.1	299.3	43.4%	606
12/19	511.3	204.9	40.1%	527
12/18	435.5	172.8	39.7%	454
12/17	397.4	148.0	37.3%	429
Annual Growth	15.2%	14.9%	—	12.0%

2021 Year-End Financials

Debt ratio: — No. of shares ($ mil.): 37.9
Return on equity: 25.8% Dividends
Cash ($ mil.): 506.7 Yield: 0.6%
Current Ratio: 2.66 Payout: 36.1%
Long-term debt ($ mil.): — Market value ($ mil.): 15,595.0

	STOCK PRICE ($) FY Close	P/E High/Low		PER SHARE ($) Earnings	Dividends	Book Value
12/21	411.27	84	50	6.77	2.64	27.46
12/20	570.56	74	35	7.85	2.40	25.13
12/19	379.11	76	38	5.40	2.04	20.30
12/18	211.31	49	37	4.57	1.68	16.15
12/17	201.75	52	37	3.89	1.32	13.68
Annual Growth	19.5%	—	—	14.9%	18.9%	19.0%

Marquette National Corp (IL)

EXECUTIVES

Chairman, Chief Executive Officer, Subsidiary Officer, Paul M. Mccarthy
Vice-Chairman, Subsidiary Officer, Barry M. Sabloff
President, Subsidiary Officer, Director, George S. Moncada
Director, Mary Acker Klingenberger
Director, Terese M. Best
Director, John G. Byrnes
Director, Michael D. Devlin
Director, James P. Mccarthy
Director, Anne M. Sabloff
Director, William G. Sullivan
Director, Malacky Walsh
Auditors: Wipfli LLP

LOCATIONS

HQ: Marquette National Corp (IL)
6316 South Western Ave, Chicago, IL 60636
Phone: 708 364-9011 **Fax:** 708 226-6933
Web: www.emarquettebank.com

HISTORICAL FINANCIALS

Company Type: Public

Income Statement				FYE: December 31
	ASSETS ($mil)	NET INCOME ($mil)	INCOME AS % OF ASSETS	EMPLOYEES
12/20	1,921.3	23.7	1.2%	0
12/19	1,670.0	15.7	0.9%	0
12/18	1,569.3	10.4	0.7%	0
12/17	1,580.7	7.4	0.5%	0
12/16	1,584.0	6.0	0.4%	0
Annual Growth	4.9%	40.7%	—	—

2020 Year-End Financials

Return on assets: 1.3% Dividends
Return on equity: 13.6% Yield: —
Long-term debt ($ mil.): — Payout: 19.2%
No. of shares ($ mil.): 4.3 Market value ($ mil.): 117.0
Sales ($ mil.): 96.8

	STOCK PRICE ($) FY Close	P/E High/Low		PER SHARE ($) Earnings	Dividends	Book Value
12/20	27.00	6	4	5.41	1.04	42.33
12/19	32.25	10	9	3.56	1.00	37.35
12/18	32.98	15	13	2.34	0.64	34.10
12/17	29.50	66	16	1.65	0.42	32.50
12/16	96.00	81	66	1.35	0.38	30.34
Annual Growth	(27.2%)	—	—	41.4%	29.0%	8.7%

Masimo Corp.

Masimo is a global medical technology company that develops, manufactures, and markets a variety of noninvasive monitoring technologies and hospital automation solutions. Its patient monitoring solutions generally incorporate a monitor or circuit board, proprietary single-patient use or reusable sensors, software and/or cables. The company provide its products to hospitals, emergency medical service (EMS) providers, home care providers, long-term care facilities, physician offices, veterinarians and consumers through our direct sales force, distributors and original equipment manufacturers (OEM) partners. Its US market generates the majority of sales. Joe Kiani founded Masimo in 1989 as a private "garage start-up" company.

Operations

Masimo's core business is Measure-through Motion and Low Perfusion pulse oximetry, known as Masimo Signal Extraction Technology (SET) pulse oximetry. Its product offerings have include noninvasive monitoring of blood constituents with an optical signature, optical regional oximetry monitoring, electrical brain function monitoring, acoustic respiration monitoring, exhaled gas monitoring, nasal high flow ventilation, minimally invasive neuromodulation technology for pain and addiction reduction, hospital automation and connectivity solutions and home wellness and monitoring.

All of the company's revenue came from product sales.

Geographic Reach

While the US accounts for more than 65% of its sales, Masimo is working to grow its operations in Africa, Asia, Australia, Europe, and the Middle East and accounting for the remaining sales.

Based in Irvine, California, Masimo has international headquarters in Neuchatel, Switzerland and two manufacturing facilities in Mexico. It also owns property in Hudson, New Hampshire, which is used to develop and manufacture advanced light emitting diodes and other component-level technologies, as well as warehousing and administrative operations.

Sales and Marketing

Masimo provide its products to hospitals, emergency medical service (EMS) providers, home care providers, long-term care facilities, physician offices, veterinarians and consumers through its direct sales force, distributors and original equipment manufacturers (OEM) partners. Two distributors, Medline Industries and Cardinal Health, account for some 15% and 10% of sales, respectively.

Advertising costs for the years 2022 (ended January), 2021 (ended January), and 2019 (ended December) were $9.0 million, $30.8 million, and $14.0 million, respectively.

Financial Performance

The company's revenue increased 8% from $1.1 billion in 2020 to $1.2 billion in 2021.

In 2021, the company had a net income of $229.6 million, a 4% decrease from the previous year's net income of $240.3 million.

The company's cash at the end of 2021 was $748.4 million. Operating activities generated $264.8 million, while investing activities used $37.5 million, mainly for purchases of property and equipment. Financing activities used another $122.4 million, primarily for repurchases of common stock.

Strategy

Masimo's mission is to develop technologies that improve patient outcomes and reduce the cost of patient care. The company intends to continue to grow its impact on patient care by not only providing patient-centered solutions to healthcare providers, but by also expanding outside of the hospital arena with its technologies that are improving lives in the hospitals.

The company's strategy consists of: Continuing to expand its market share in Pulse Oximetry; Expanding the Pulse Oximetry market to other patient care settings; Expanding the use of rainbow technology in hospital settings; Expanding the use of rainbow technology in non-hospital settings; as well as Expanding the use of root in hospital settings.

Mergers and Acquisitions

In 2022, Masimo has successfully completed the previously announced acquisition of Sound United, a leading consumer technology company and owner of multiple premium audio and home entertainment brands. Sound United will operate as a division of Masimo, under its existing leadership, from its headquarters in Carlsbad, California. The addition of Sound United's premium technology, established consumer channels, and well-known brands to Masimo's broad portfolio of hospital and home medical technology solutions.

In early 2021, Masimo completed the acquisition of the LiDCO Group Plc, a leading provider of advanced hemodynamic monitoring solutions (LiDCO). With the completion of this acquisition, Masimo will be able to provide clinicians with access to patients' cardiac output (CO), stroke volume (SV), systemic vascular resistance (SVR), oxygen delivery (DO2), stroke volume variation (SVV) and pulse pressure variation (PPV), which are used to assess preload and afterload, to help determine the current state of a patient's hemodynamic stability and whether any interventions are needed to optimize the delivery of oxygen to the tissues. Hemodynamic monitoring solutions are also used to monitor the response to therapies such as vasopressors, inotropes and fluids.

EXECUTIVES

Chief Executive Officer, Chairman, Director, Joe E. Kiani, $1,139,855 total compensation
Executive Vice President, Chief Financial Officer, Micah Young, $383,250 total compensation
Engineering, Marketing & Regulatory Affairs Chief Operating Officer, Bilal Muhsin, $432,360 total compensation
Business Development Executive Vice President, Tao Levy, $324,917 total compensation
Executive Vice President, General Counsel, Corporate Secretary, Tom McClenahan, $397,271 total compensation
Senior Vice President, Chief Accounting Officer, Principal Accounting Officer, Paul Hataishi
Division Officer, Blair Tripodi
Director, Julie A. Shimer
Director, H Michael Cohen
Director, Adam P. Mikkelson
Director, Craig B. Reynolds
Auditors : Grant Thornton LLP

LOCATIONS

HQ: Masimo Corp.
52 Discovery, Irvine, CA 92618
Phone: 949 297-7000
Web: www.masimo.com

2017 Sales

	$ mil.	% of total
US	506.8	64
Americas (excluding US)	24.0	3
Europe, Middle East & Africa	138.0	17
Asia & Australia	72.5	9
Royalties	56.8	7
Total	798.1	100

PRODUCTS/OPERATIONS

2017 Sales

	$ mil.	% of total
Products	741.3	93
Royalties	56.8	7
Total	798.1	100

COMPETITORS

CUTERA, INC.
ESCALON MEDICAL CORP.
LUMENIS LTD.
MESA LABORATORIES, INC.
NATUS MEDICAL INCORPORATED
NXSTAGE MEDICAL, INC.
OLYMPUS CORPORATION
PERKINELMER, INC.
SURMODICS, INC.
VOLCANO CORPORATION

HISTORICAL FINANCIALS
Company Type: Public

Income Statement — FYE: January 1

	REVENUE ($mil)	NET INCOME ($mil)	NET PROFIT MARGIN	EMPLOYEES
01/22	1,239.1	229.6	18.5%	6,200
01/21*	1,143.7	240.3	21.0%	6,200
12/19	937.8	196.2	20.9%	5,300
12/18	858.2	193.5	22.5%	4,500
12/17	798.1	131.6	16.5%	4,600
Annual Growth	11.6%	14.9%	—	7.7%

*Fiscal year change

2022 Year-End Financials
Debt ratio: —
Return on equity: 15.5%
Cash ($ mil.): 745.2
Current Ratio: 4.63
Long-term debt ($ mil.): —
No. of shares ($ mil.): 55.3
Dividends
Yield: —
Payout: —
Market value ($ mil.): 16,201.0

	STOCK PRICE ($) FY Close	P/E High/Low		PER SHARE ($) Earnings	Dividends	Book Value
01/22	292.78	73	50	3.98	0.00	28.02
01/21*	268.38	62	34	4.14	0.00	25.48
12/19	159.49	44	28	3.44	0.00	21.75
12/18	105.56	34	22	3.45	0.00	18.25
12/17	84.80	41	26	2.36	0.00	13.69
Annual Growth	36.3%	—	—	14.0%	—	19.6%

*Fiscal year change

Mastech Digital Inc

Mastech provides outsourced staffing services primarily for businesses in need of contract information technology (IT) personnel. The company provides systems integrators and other IT staffing companies with temporary technical staff on a wholesale basis. It also serves companies in other industries directly. The company mainly serves customers in the US, but it has international recruiting operations in India. Apart from finance, clients come from such industries as consumer products, health care, retail, technology, and telecom. Formerly a subsidiary of IGATE Corporation, Mastech was spun off to its parent company's shareholders in 2008.

EXECUTIVES

Co-Chairman, Sunil Wadhwani
Co-Chairman, Ashok Trivedi
President, Chief Executive Officer, Director, Vivek Gupta, $398,125 total compensation
Chief Financial Officer, Treasurer, Secretary, John J. Cronin, $291,250 total compensation
Vice President, Chief Operating Officer, Edward Meindl, $158,602 total compensation
Corporate Development Vice President, Steven C. Wolfe
Vice President, Risher G. Dumpit, $102,115 total compensation
Director, John Ausura
Director, Brenda Galilee
Director, Gerhard Watzinger
Auditors: UHY LLP

LOCATIONS

HQ: Mastech Digital Inc
1305 Cherrington Parkway, Building 210, Suite 400, Moon Township, PA 15108
Phone: 412 787-2100
Web: www.mastechdigital.com

COMPETITORS

ALLEGIS GROUP, INC.
COLLABERA INC.
Cobragon Limited
FIDELITY TALENTSOURCE LLC
GENESIS HR SOLUTIONS, INC.
HINDUJA GLOBAL SOLUTIONS LIMITED
MANAGEMENT AND CAPITAL PARTNERS LLC
Neusoft Corporation
PAULA ALLEN HOLDINGS, INC.
SALES CONSULTANTS OF SPARTA, NJ INC

HISTORICAL FINANCIALS
Company Type: Public

Income Statement — FYE: December 31

	REVENUE ($mil)	NET INCOME ($mil)	NET PROFIT MARGIN	EMPLOYEES
12/20	194.1	9.8	5.1%	1,671
12/19	193.5	11.1	5.8%	1,745
12/18	177.1	6.6	3.8%	1,680
12/17	147.8	1.6	1.1%	1,530
12/16	132.0	2.5	1.9%	1,125
Annual Growth	10.1%	40.6%	—	10.4%

2020 Year-End Financials
Debt ratio: 16.9%
Return on equity: 18.5%
Cash ($ mil.): 7.6
Current Ratio: 1.87
Long-term debt ($ mil.): 12.8
No. of shares ($ mil.): 11.3
Dividends
Yield: —
Payout: —
Market value ($ mil.): 181.0

	STOCK PRICE ($) FY Close	P/E High/Low		PER SHARE ($) Earnings	Dividends	Book Value
12/20	15.90	33	9	0.83	0.00	5.23
12/19	11.07	11	5	0.99	0.00	4.19
12/18	6.30	35	10	0.60	0.00	3.12
12/17	10.06	80	37	0.17	0.00	2.49
12/16	6.81	29	22	0.28	0.00	2.12
Annual Growth	23.6%	—	—	31.2%	—	25.3%

MasterCraft Boat Holdings Inc

EXECUTIVES

Chief Executive Officer, Chairman, Director, Frederick A. Brightbill
Chief Financial Officer, Treasurer, Secretary, Timothy M. Oxley, $267,200 total compensation
Chief Revenue Officer, George Steinbarger
Division Officer, Patrick May
Lead Independent Director, Director, Roch Lambert
Director, Jaclyn Baumgarten
Director, Donald C. Campion
Director, Jennifer Deason
Director, Peter G. Leemputte
Director, W. Patrick Battle
Director, Kamilah Mitchell-Thomas
Auditors: DELOITTE & TOUCHE LLP

LOCATIONS

HQ: MasterCraft Boat Holdings Inc
100 Cherokee Cove Drive, Vonore, TN 37885
Phone: 423 884-2221
Web: www.mastercraft.com

HISTORICAL FINANCIALS
Company Type: Public

Income Statement — FYE: June 30

	REVENUE ($mil)	NET INCOME ($mil)	NET PROFIT MARGIN	EMPLOYEES
06/21	525.8	56.1	10.7%	1,500
06/20	363.0	(24.0)	—	884
06/19	466.3	21.3	4.6%	1,195
06/18	332.7	39.6	11.9%	882
06/17	228.6	19.5	8.6%	490
Annual Growth	23.1%	30.2%	—	32.3%

2021 Year-End Financials
Debt ratio: 33.7%
Return on equity: 71.7%
Cash ($ mil.): 39.2
Current Ratio: 1.48
Long-term debt ($ mil.): 90.2
No. of shares ($ mil.): 18.9
Dividends
Yield: —
Payout: —
Market value ($ mil.): 498.0

	STOCK PRICE ($) FY Close	P/E High/Low		PER SHARE ($) Earnings	Dividends	Book Value
06/21	26.29	11	5	2.96	0.00	5.69
06/20	19.05	—	—	(1.28)	0.00	2.59
06/19	19.59	33	16	1.14	0.00	3.85
06/18	28.95	15	8	2.12	0.00	2.81
06/17	19.55	19	10	1.05	0.00	0.63
Annual Growth	7.7%	—	—	29.6%	—	73.3%

MaxLinear Inc

MaxLinear is a provider of communications systems-on-chip (SoC) solutions used in broadband, mobile and wireline infrastructure, data center, and industrial and multi-market applications. It is a fabless integrated circuit design company whose products integrate all or substantial portions of a high-speed communication system, including integrated radio-frequency (RF), high-performance analog, mixed-signal, digital signal processing, security engines, data compression and networking layers, and power management. Its products are used in cable TV, set-top boxes, cable modems, automobiles, and personal computers. The company sells to module makers, OEMs, distributors, and original design manufacturers (ODMs). Majority of its sales were generated from Asian customers.

Operations

MaxLinear operates in one segment as it has developed, marketed and sold primarily only one class of similar products, radio-frequency, high-performance analog and mixed-signal communications system-on-chip solutions for the connected home, wired and wireless infrastructure markets and industrial and multi-market applications. It provides communications systems-on-chip (SoC) solutions used in broadband, mobile and wireline infrastructure, data center, and industrial and multi-market applications.

The development of broadband (some 55% of sales), low power, integrated communication systems-on-chip solutions is at the heart of competitiveness across a range of different businesses spanning broadband wireline access, mobile data services, hyperscale cloud data centers, and cloud computation and storage markets.

In the Industrial & Multi-Market (some 15%), manufacturing equipment and appliances are connected to each other and to the cloud to better optimize utilization, improve power consumption, and plant management. Legacy equipment and new installations need to communicate with each other via newer and older connectivity protocol standards. Other end markets such as infrastructure and connected some accounts for around 15%, each.

Geographic Reach

Based in Carlsbad, California, MaxLinear has operations in Irvine, California; San Jose, California; Boston, Massachusetts; Burnaby, Canada; Bangalore and Chennai, India; Singapore; Taipei and Hsinchu, Taiwan; Shenzhen, Shanghai, and Hong Kong, China; Seoul, South Korea; Tokyo, Japan; Paterna, Spain; Villach, Austria; Munich, Germany; and in Petah Tikva, Israel.

MaxLinear has heavy customer concentration in Asia where it generates about 85% of revenue. US customers supply less than 5% of sales with the rest split among other markets.

Sales and Marketing

MaxLinear uses a direct sales force in the US and certain markets in Asia and Europe. In other areas it uses third-party sales representatives and a network of distributors. Distributors account for over 45% of sales. The company sells its products, directly and indirectly, to original equipment manufacturers, or OEMs, module makers and original design manufacturers, or ODMs.

The top ten customers account for about 70% of MaxLinear's sales with two of its direct customers represented around 25% of net revenue.

Financial Performance

The company's revenue for fiscal 2021 increased by 86% to $892.4 million compared from the prior year with $478.6 million.

Net income for fiscal 2021 was $42.0 million compared from the prior year with a net loss of $98.6 million.

Cash held by the company at the end of fiscal 2021 decreased to $131.7 million. Cash provided by operations was $168.2 million while cash used for investing and financing activities were $91.8 million and $91.9 million, respectively. Main uses of cash were acquisitions and repayment of debt.

Strategy

MaxLinear's objective is to be the leading provider of communications SoCs for the connected home, wired and wireless infrastructure, and industrial and multi-market applications. The company aim to continue to leverage its core analog and digital signal co-processing competencies to expand into other communications markets with similar performance requirements. The key elements of the company's strategy are: extend technology leadership in RF transceivers and RF transceiver + digital signal processing + embedded processor SoCs; leverage and expand the company's existing customer base; target additional high-growth markets; expand global presence; and attract and retain top talent.

EXECUTIVES

Chairman, President, Chief Executive Officer, Director, Kishore Seendripu, $538,189 total compensation
Chief Financial Officer, Chief Corporate Strategy Officer, Steven G. Litchfield, $142,806 total compensation
Corporate Controller, Principal Accounting Officer, Connie Kwong
Operations Vice President, Michael J. LaChance, $285,828 total compensation
Chief Technical Officer, Curtis Ling, $258,653 total compensation
Sales Vice President, Michael Bollesen, $109,795 total compensation
Worldwide Sales Vice President, Worldwide Sales Division Officer, William G. Torgerson, $297,989 total compensation
Division Officer, James Lougheed, $169,027 total compensation
IC and RF Systems Engineering Division Officer, Madhukar Reddy, $307,609 total compensation
Business Development Division Officer, Brendan Walsh, $170,000 total compensation
Lead Director, Director, Thomas E. Pardun
Director, Theodore L. Tewksbury
Director, Albert J. Moyer
Director, Carolyn D. Beaver
Director, Gregory P. Dougherty
Director, Donald E. Schrock
Director, Daniel A. Artusi
Auditors : Grant Thornton LLP

LOCATIONS

HQ: MaxLinear Inc
  5966 La Place Court, Suite 100, Carlsbad, CA 92008
Phone: 760 692-0711
Web: www.maxlinear.com

2017 Geographic Sales
	$ mil.	% of total
Asia	372.1	89
United States	10.8	2
Rest of the world	37.4	9
Total	420.3	100

PRODUCTS/OPERATIONS

2017 Sales by Product
	$ mil.	% of total
Connected Home	288.6	69
Infrastructure	71.8	17
Industrial and multi-market	59.9	14
Total	420.3	100

COMPETITORS

BROADCOM INC.
COMMSCOPE HOLDING COMPANY, INC.
CYPRESS SEMICONDUCTOR CORPORATION
DIGI INTERNATIONAL INC.
EXAR CORPORATION
LANTRONIX, INC.
OCLARO, INC.
RENESAS ELECTRONICS AMERICA INC.
SEMTECH CORPORATION
SIGMA DESIGNS, INC.

HISTORICAL FINANCIALS

Company Type: Public

Income Statement — FYE: December 31

	REVENUE ($mil)	NET INCOME ($mil)	NET PROFIT MARGIN	EMPLOYEES
12/21	892.3	41.9	4.7%	1,503
12/20	478.5	(98.5)	—	1,420
12/19	317.1	(19.8)	—	697
12/18	384.9	(26.1)	—	739
12/17	420.3	(9.1)	—	753
Annual Growth	20.7%	—	—	18.9%

2021 Year-End Financials

Debt ratio: 29.1%
Return on equity: 9.5%
Cash ($ mil.): 130.6
Current Ratio: 1.95
Long-term debt ($ mil.): 306.1
No. of shares ($ mil.): 76.7
Dividends
  Yield: —
  Payout: —
Market value ($ mil.): 5,788.0

	STOCK PRICE ($) FY Close	P/E High/Low		PER SHARE ($) Earnings	Dividends	Book Value
12/21	75.39	140	56	0.53	0.00	6.37
12/20	38.19	—	—	(1.35)	0.00	5.25
12/19	21.22	—	—	(0.28)	0.00	5.77
12/18	17.60	—	—	(0.38)	0.00	5.75
12/17	26.42	—	—	(0.14)	0.00	5.75
Annual Growth	30.0%			—	—	2.6%

Maxus Realty Trust Inc

Maxus Realty Trust believes in the value of maximizing housing space. The real estate investment trust (REIT) invests in income-producing properties, primarily multifamily residential properties. It owns a portfolio of approximately 10 apartment communities in the Midwest US. Maxus Realty Trust was originally established to invest in office and light industrial facilities, but switched gears and began focusing on residential real estate in 2000. The REIT de-registered with the SEC and stopped trading on the NASDAQ in 2008.

EXECUTIVES

Chairman, President, Chief Executive Officer, Trustee, David L. Johnson
Vice President, Chief Financial Officer, Principal Accounting Officer, Associate/Affiliate Company Officer, Ryan Snyder
Vice President, Chief Operating Officer, Associate/Affiliate Company Officer, Trustee, Michael P. McRobert
Vice President, Treasurer, Associate/Affiliate Company Officer, John W. Alvey
Reporting Vice President, Reporting Corporate Secretary, Reporting Associate/Affiliate Company Officer, DeAnn M. Totta
Trustee, Jose L. Evans
Trustee, Christopher J. Garlich
Trustee, Gregory J. Orman
Trustee, David M. Brain
Trustee, Monte McDowell
Auditors : Mayer Hoffman McCann P.C.

LOCATIONS

HQ: Maxus Realty Trust Inc
104 Armour Road, P.O. Box 34729, North Kansas City, MO 64116
Phone: 816 303-4500   **Fax:** 816 221-1829
Web: www.mrti.com

COMPETITORS

ACRE REALTY INVESTORS INC.
EQUITY RESIDENTIAL
PACIFIC OFFICE PROPERTIES TRUST, INC.
SILVER BAY REALTY TRUST CORP.
STEADFAST INCOME REIT, INC.

HISTORICAL FINANCIALS
Company Type: Public

Income Statement   FYE: December 31

	REVENUE ($mil)	NET INCOME ($mil)	NET PROFIT MARGIN	EMPLOYEES
12/19	118.7	13.1	11.1%	0
12/18	113.6	6.4	5.6%	0
12/17	89.1	13.9	15.7%	0
12/16	74.2	14.6	19.7%	0
12/15	60.5	4.5	7.5%	0
Annual Growth	18.3%	30.5%	—	—

2019 Year-End Financials

Debt ratio: 75.5%   No. of shares ($ mil.): 1.1
Return on equity: 29.7%   Dividends
Cash ($ mil.): 12.0   Yield: 5.9%
Current Ratio: 0.61   Payout: 84.3%
Long-term debt ($ mil.): 690.5   Market value ($ mil.): 142.0

	STOCK PRICE ($) FY Close	P/E High/Low		PER SHARE ($) Earnings	Dividends	Book Value
12/19	120.90	13	10	7.83	7.20	39.23
12/18	112.00	26	17	4.63	6.70	35.88
12/17	100.00	10	5	10.44	5.00	38.31
12/16	75.00	7	4	11.34	3.55	30.51
12/15	49.00	15	7	3.33	1.50	20.83
Annual Growth	25.3%	—	—	23.8%	48.0%	17.1%

Medical Properties Trust Inc

Hospitals trust Medical Properties is a self-advised real estate investment trust (REIT) formed in 2003 to acquire and develop net-leased healthcare facilities. It has investments in approximately 430 facilities and approximately 43,000 licensed beds in about 35 states in the US, in six countries in Europe, across Australia, and in Colombia in South America. Its facilities consist of more than 200 general acute care hospitals, 110 inpatient rehabilitation hospitals (IRFs), 20 long-term acute care hospitals (LTACHs), some 50 freestanding ER/urgent care facilities (FSERs), and 45 behavioral health facilities.

EXECUTIVES

Chairman, President, Chief Executive Officer, Director, Edward K. Aldag, $1,000,000 total compensation
Executive Vice President, Chief Operating Officer, Treasurer, Secretary, Emmett E. McLean, $550,000 total compensation
Executive Vice President, Chief Financial Officer, Director, R. Steven Hamner, $600,000 total compensation
Vice President, Chief Accounting Officer, Controller, James Kevin Hanna
Director, G. Steven Dawson
Director, Caterina Ardon Mozingo
Director, Emily W. Murphy
Director, Elizabeth N. Pitman
Director, Daniel Paul Sparks
Director, Michael G. Stewart, $141,665 total compensation
Director, C. Reynolds Thompson
Auditors : PricewaterhouseCoopers LLP

LOCATIONS

HQ: Medical Properties Trust Inc
1000 Urban Center Drive, Suite 501, Birmingham, AL 35242
Phone: 205 969-3755   **Fax:** 205 969-3756
Web: www.medicalpropertiestrust.com

2015 Sales

	mil $	% of total
Texas	87.5	20
California	66.1	15
New Jersey	27.7	6
Arizona	21.2	5
Missouri	17.7	4
Idaho	12.5	3
Louisiana	12.4	3
South Carolina	12.3	3
Kansas	11.1	2
Colorado	10.2	2
Nevada	9.8	2
Utah	9.8	2
Oregon	9.5	2
Oklahoma	9.4	2
Arkansas	9.3	2
New Mexico	5.9	1
Indiana	4.8	1
Pennsylvania	4.6	1
Wisconsin	2.9	1
Wyoming	2.7	1
West Virginia	2.6	1
Montana	2.5	1
Michigan	2.3	1
Florida	2.2	—
Virginia	1.1	—
Alabama	0.5	—
Connecticut	0.2	—
Massachusetts	0.07	—
Rhode Island	0.06	—
International		
Germany	78.5	18
United Kingdom	4.4	1
Spain	0.1	—
Total	441.9	100

PRODUCTS/OPERATIONS

2015 Sales by Property Type
$ mil / % of total
General acute care hospitals 254.7 / 58
Rehabilitation hospitals 134.2 / 30
Long-term acute care hospitals 52.7 / 12
Wellness centers 0.3 / —
Total 441.9 / 100

COMPETITORS

CARE CAPITAL PROPERTIES, INC.
DIVERSIFIED HEALTHCARE TRUST
Extendicare Real Estate Investment Trust
HEALTHCARE REALTY TRUST INCORPORATED
HEALTHPEAK PROPERTIES, INC.
NATIONAL HEALTH INVESTORS, INC.
OMEGA HEALTHCARE INVESTORS, INC.
SABRA HEALTH CARE REIT, INC.
VENTAS, INC.
WELLTOWER INC.

HISTORICAL FINANCIALS
Company Type: Public

Income Statement   FYE: December 31

	REVENUE ($mil)	NET INCOME ($mil)	NET PROFIT MARGIN	EMPLOYEES
12/20	1,249.2	431.4	34.5%	106
12/19	854.1	374.6	43.9%	86
12/18	784.5	1,016.6	129.6%	77
12/17	704.7	289.7	41.1%	66
12/16	541.1	225.0	41.6%	54
Annual Growth	23.3%	17.7%	—	18.4%

2020 Year-End Financials

Debt ratio: 52.7%   No. of shares ($ mil.): 541.4
Return on equity: 5.9%   Dividends
Cash ($ mil.): 549.8   Yield: 4.9%
Current Ratio: 2.29   Payout: 133.3%
Long-term debt ($ mil.): 8,865.4   Market value ($ mil.): 11,798.0

	STOCK PRICE ($) FY Close	P/E High/Low		PER SHARE ($) Earnings	Dividends	Book Value
12/20	21.79	30	16	0.81	1.08	13.55
12/19	21.11	25	18	0.87	1.02	13.58
12/18	16.08	6	4	2.76	1.00	12.27
12/17	13.78	17	15	0.82	0.96	10.48
12/16	12.30	18	11	0.86	0.91	10.13
Annual Growth	15.4%	—	—	(1.5%)	4.4%	7.5%

Medifast Inc

Medifast is the global company behind one of the fastest-growing health and wellness communities called OPTAVIA, which offers Lifelong Transformation, One Healthy Habit at a Time. Medifast help clients to achieve their health goals through a network of more than 59,800 independent OPTAVIA Coaches, approximately 90% of whom were clients first, and have impacted almost 2.0 million lives to date. OPTAVIA Coaches introduce clients to a set of healthy habits, in most cases starting with the habit of healthy eating, and offer exclusive OPTAVIA-branded nutritional products, or Fuelings. Fuelings are nutrient-dense, portion-controlled, nutritionally interchangeable and simple to use.

Operations

Medifast's OPTAVIA covers almost 100% of company's total sales. OPTAVIA brand offers a highly competitive and effective lifestyle solution centered on developing new healthy habits through smaller, foundational changes called micro-habits. The program is built around four key components: Independent OPTAVIA Coaches, the OPTAVIA Community, the Habits of Health Transformational System, and Products & Plans.

Medifast sells a variety of weight loss, weight management and healthy living products all based on its proprietary formulas under the OPTAVIA, Optimal Health by Take Shape for Life, and Flavors of Home brands. The company's product line includes more than 95 consumable options, including, but not limited to, bars, bites, pretzels, puffs, cereal crunch, drinks, hearty choices, oatmeal, pancakes, pudding, soft serve, shakes, smoothies, soft bakes, and soups. Medifast's nutritional products are formulated with high-quality ingredients. Its operations are conducted through the its wholly owned subsidiaries, Jason Pharmaceuticals, Inc., OPTAVIA, LLC, Jason Enterprises, Inc., Jason Properties, LLC, Medifast Franchise Systems, Inc., Seven Crondall Associates, LLC, Corporate Events, Inc., OPTAVIA (Hong Kong) Limited, OPTAVIA (Singapore) PTE. LTD and OPTAVIA Health Consultation (Shanghai) Co., Ltd.

Geographic Reach

Medifast operates a manufacturing plant in Owings Mills, Maryland and in Baltimore, Maryland, which serves as the company headquarters. It has distribution facilities in Ridgley, Maryland and outsources a domestic distribution center in Reno, Nevada, and Haltom City, Texas, and an international distribution center in Hong Kong. The company also has distribution center in Havre De Grace, Maryland.

Sales and Marketing

Medifast uses multiple marketing strategies to reach its target audiences. It uses word-of-mouth communications, digital marketing, public relations, events, direct mail and social media channels. Advertising costs totaled $ $1.6 million, $4.4 million and $5.3 million in 2021, 2020, and 2019, respectively.

Financial Performance

Company revenue increased $591.2 million, or 63%, to $1.5 billion in 2021 from $934.8 million in 2020.

Net income for fiscal 2021 increased by 60% to $164.0 million compared from the prior year with $102.9 million.

Cash held by the company at the end of fiscal 2021 decreased to $104.2 million. Cash provided by operations was $94.5 million while cash used for investing and financing activities were $29.1 million and $125.1 million, respectively. Main uses of cash were purchase of property and equipment; and cash dividends paid to stockholders.

Strategy

Consistent with business and brand strategy, the Company has completed the sunset of the Medifast Direct channel and Medifast-branded product line during the second quarter of 2021. By maintaining its commitment to building capabilities in the areas that matter most to its OPTAVIA Coaches and clients within the OPTAVIA channel, Medifast believe that the company will enhance its ability to further grow our business over the next several years, enabling robust revenue growth while also maintaining its profitability in the long-term.

Company Background

Medifast's promotion and distribution model has changed over time. When it was founded in 1993, the company primarily sold its products through doctor's offices. Customers received supervision from their family physician, who, in turn, received commissions on any products sold. However, as physicians had increasingly less time to spend with patients, the method grew less effective. At the beginning of 2018, the company discontinued the sales of products through physicians, thus reducing the complexity of its product distribution.

The company also exited the corporate support center model in 2014. It sold 41 centers to franchise partners and closed its remaining 34 corporate centers.

EXECUTIVES

Executive Chairman, Chief Executive Officer, Director, Daniel R. Chard, $675,000 total compensation
Human Resources Executive Vice President, Claudia Greninger
Executive Vice President, General Counsel, Corporate Secretary, Jason L. Groves, $200,000 total compensation
Supply Chain Operations Executive Vice President, Lauren Walker
Finance Vice President, Finance Chief Accounting Officer, Jonathan B. MacKenzie
Chief Financial Officer, James P. Maloney
Chief Marketing Officer, Anthony E. Tyree
Subsidiary Officer, Nicholas M. Johnson, $198,692 total compensation
Lead Independent Director, Director, Jeffrey J. Brown
Director, Constance J. Hallquist
Director, Michael A. Hoer
Director, Scott D. Schlackman
Director, Andrea B. Thomas
Director, Ming Xian
Auditors : RSM US LLP

LOCATIONS

HQ: Medifast Inc
100 International Drive, Baltimore, MD 21202
Phone: 410 581-8042
Web: www.medifastnow.com

PRODUCTS/OPERATIONS

2017 Sales

	$ mil.	% of total
OPTAVIA	256.6	85
Medifast Direct	31.9	11
MWCC	12.2	4
Medifast Wholesale	1.0	-
Total	301.7	100

Selected Subsidiaries

Jason Enterprises, Inc.
Jason Pharmaceuticals, Inc.
Jason Properties, LLC
Medifast Franchise Systems, Inc.
Medifast Nutrition, Inc.
OPTAVIA, LLC
Seven Crondall Associates, LLC

COMPETITORS

AJINOMOTO CO., INC.
AMERICAN ITALIAN PASTA COMPANY
CALAVO GROWERS, INC.
GENERAL MILLS, INC.
Herbalife Nutrition Ltd.
MCCORMICK & COMPANY, INCORPORATED
OVERSTOCK.COM, INC.
SAMWORTH BROTHERS (HOLDINGS) LIMITED
TERRAVIA HOLDINGS, INC.
USANA HEALTH SCIENCES, INC.

HISTORICAL FINANCIALS

Company Type: Public

Income Statement — FYE: December 31

	REVENUE ($mil)	NET INCOME ($mil)	NET PROFIT MARGIN	EMPLOYEES
12/20	934.8	102.8	11.0%	713
12/19	713.6	77.9	10.9%	550
12/18	501.0	55.7	11.1%	420
12/17	301.5	27.7	9.2%	399
12/16	274.5	17.8	6.5%	422
Annual Growth	35.8%	55.0%	—	14.0%

2020 Year-End Financials

Debt ratio: — No. of shares ($ mil.): 11.7
Return on equity: 78.2% Dividends
Cash ($ mil.): 163.7 Yield: 2.3%
Current Ratio: 2.10 Payout: 56.5%
Long-term debt ($ mil.): — Market value ($ mil.): 2,311.0

	STOCK PRICE ($) FY Close	P/E High/Low		PER SHARE ($) Earnings	Dividends	Book Value
12/20	196.34	24	6	8.68	4.52	13.36
12/19	109.58	24	11	6.43	3.38	8.91
12/18	125.02	55	14	4.62	2.19	9.19
12/17	69.81	32	17	2.29	1.44	9.07
12/16	41.63	28	18	1.49	1.07	8.09
Annual Growth	47.4%	—	—	55.4%	43.4%	13.4%

Medpace Holdings Inc

EXECUTIVES

Chief Executive Officer, Chairman, Director, August J. Troendle, $410,000 total compensation
Laboratory Operations President, Jesse J. Geiger, $400,267 total compensation
Operations Executive Vice President, Susan E. Burwig, $407,099 total compensation
Chief Financial Officer, Treasurer, Kevin M. Brady
General Counsel, Corporate Secretary, Stephen P. Ewald
Lead Director, Director, Fred B. Davenport
Director, Cornelius P. McCarthy
Director, Ashley M. Keating
Director, Brian T. Carley
Director, Robert O. Kraft
Director, Femida H. Gwadry-Sridhar
Auditors : DELOITTE & TOUCHE LLP

LOCATIONS

HQ: Medpace Holdings Inc
5375 Medpace Way, Cincinnati, OH 45227
Phone: 513 579-9911
Web: www.medpace.com

HISTORICAL FINANCIALS

Company Type: Public

Income Statement — FYE: December 31

	REVENUE ($mil)	NET INCOME ($mil)	NET PROFIT MARGIN	EMPLOYEES
12/21	1,142.3	181.8	15.9%	4,500
12/20	925.9	145.3	15.7%	3,600
12/19	860.9	100.4	11.7%	3,500
12/18	704.5	73.1	10.4%	2,900
12/17	436.1	39.1	9.0%	2,500
Annual Growth	27.2%	46.8%	—	15.8%

2021 Year-End Financials

Debt ratio: — No. of shares ($ mil.): 36.0
Return on equity: 20.6% Dividends
Cash ($ mil.): 461.3 Yield: —
Current Ratio: 1.24 Payout: —
Long-term debt ($ mil.): — Market value ($ mil.): 7,837.0

	STOCK PRICE ($) FY Close	P/E High/Low		PER SHARE ($) Earnings	Dividends	Book Value
12/21	217.64	45	26	4.81	0.00	26.47
12/20	139.20	37	15	3.84	0.00	22.69
12/19	84.06	31	18	2.67	0.00	20.14
12/18	52.93	31	16	1.97	0.00	16.53
12/17	36.26	38	22	0.98	0.00	14.20
Annual Growth	56.5%	—	—	48.8%	—	16.8%

Mercantile Bank Corp.

Mercantile Bank Corporation is a state banking company that provides banking services to businesses, individuals, and governmental units. It has assets of approximately $5.26 billion and operates about 45 branches in central and western and central Michigan. The bank's primary deposit products are checking, savings, and term certificate accounts, and its primary lending products are commercial loans, residential mortgage loans, and instalment loans. It owns more than 20 automated teller machines and about 20 video banking machines. Commercial loans make up about 55% of the bank's loan portfolio. Outside of banking, subsidiary Mercantile Insurance Center sells insurance products. Mercantile was founded in 1997 by directors and bankers.

Operations

Mercantile generates about 70% of its total revenue from loan interest (including fees) with securities interest contributing nearly 5% of total revenue. Mortgage banking activities provide approximately 15%, credit and debit card fees, service charges on deposit and sweep accounts, interest rate swap program fees, payroll processing, earnings on bank owned life insurance, and other income account for the rest.

Geographic Reach

Headquartered in Grand Rapids, Michigan, the bank operates nearly 45 banking offices primarily concentrated throughout western and central Michigan, most of which are full-service facilities. It also has a banking office in Troy, Michigan, and residential mortgage loan production offices in Petoskey, Michigan and the Cincinnati, Ohio metropolitan area. The company has larger banking facilities in Kalamazoo, Lansing, Mt. Pleasant, and West Branch.

Sales and Marketing

Mercantile provides its banking services to businesses, individuals, and government organizations. Its commercial banking services mostly cater to small- to medium-sized businesses.

The company spent approximately $1.2 million, $1.3 million, and $1.4 million on advertising in 2021, 2020, and 2019, respectively.

Financial Performance

Net interest income increased $1.8 million in 2021 compared to 2020. Both interest income and interest expense were impacted during 2021 by the Federal Open Market Committee's (FOMC) federal funds rate cuts totaling 150 basis points in March 2020 and a historically low interest rate environment since that time; however, growth in earning assets, especially core commercial loans, and income associated with the PPP, has provided for the increase in net interest income.

Mercantile Bank recorded net income of $59.0 million for 2021, compared to net income of $44.1 million for 2020. Costs and a charitable contribution related to the formation and initial funding of The Mercantile Bank Foundation decreased net income during 2021 by approximately $3.2 million. The increase in net income for 2021 resulted from a lower provision for loan losses and increased noninterest income and net interest income, which more than offset higher noninterest expense.

Cash and cash equivalents at the end of 2021 were $975.2 billion, a $349.2 billion increase from the year prior. Operations provided $64.6 billion, while financing activities contributed another $780.1 billion from deposits and notes proceeds. Investing activities used $495.5 billion, mainly for securities purchases, loan payments, and branch sales.

EXECUTIVES

Chairman, Subsidiary Officer, Director, Michael H. Price, $84,663 total compensation
President, Chief Executive Officer, Subsidiary Officer, Director, Robert B. Kaminski, $478,500 total compensation
Executive Vice President, Chief Financial Officer, Treasurer, Subsidiary Officer, Charles E. Christmas, $364,000 total compensation
Executive Vice President, Subsidiary Officer, Raymond E. Reitsma, $346,526 total compensation
Senior Vice President, Human Resources Director, Subsidiary Officer, Lonna L. Wiersma, $262,895 total compensation

Senior Vice President, Chief Operating Officer, General Counsel, Secretary, Subsidiary Officer, Robert T. Worthington, $245,000 total compensation

Director, David B. Ramaker
Director, Michael S. Davenport
Director, David M. Cassard
Director, Michelle L. Eldridge
Director, Jeff A. Gardner
Auditors : BDO USA, LLP

LOCATIONS

HQ: Mercantile Bank Corp.
 310 Leonard Street N.W., Grand Rapids, MI 49504
Phone: 616 406-3000
Web: www.mercbank.com

PRODUCTS/OPERATIONS

2014 Sales

	$ Mil.	% of Total
Interest income		
Loans and leases, including fees	80.8	82
Securities, taxable	6.4	6
Securities, tax-exempt	1.6	2
Other	0.2	-
Noninterest income		
Service charges on accounts	2.6	3
Credit and debit card fees	2.5	2
Mortgage banking activities	1.7	2
Other	3.3	3
Total	99.1	100

COMPETITORS

CASCADE BANCORP
CENTERSTATE BANK CORPORATION
CENTURY BANCORP, INC.
COLUMBIA BANKING SYSTEM, INC.
FIRST COMMONWEALTH FINANCIAL CORPORATION
FIRSTMERIT CORPORATION
OLD LINE BANCSHARES, INC.
STATE BANK FINANCIAL CORPORATION
TCF FINANCIAL CORPORATION
TRUSTCO BANK CORP N Y

HISTORICAL FINANCIALS

Company Type: Public

Income Statement — FYE: December 31

	ASSETS ($mil)	NET INCOME ($mil)	INCOME AS % OF ASSETS	EMPLOYEES
12/20	4,437.3	44.1	1.0%	665
12/19	3,632.9	49.4	1.4%	683
12/18	3,363.9	42.0	1.2%	693
12/17	3,286.7	31.2	1.0%	701
12/16	3,082.5	31.9	1.0%	682
Annual Growth	9.5%	8.4%	—	(0.6%)

2020 Year-End Financials

Return on assets: 1.0%
Return on equity: 10.2%
Long-term debt ($ mil.): —
No. of shares ($ mil.): 16.3
Sales ($ mil.): 193.4

Dividends
 Yield: 4.1%
 Payout: 42.1%
Market value ($ mil.): 444.0

	STOCK PRICE ($) FY Close	P/E High/Low		PER SHARE ($) Earnings	Dividends	Book Value
12/20	27.17	13	6	2.71	1.12	27.04
12/19	36.47	12	10	3.01	1.06	25.36
12/18	28.26	15	11	2.53	1.68	22.70
12/17	35.37	20	15	1.90	0.74	22.05
12/16	37.70	19	11	1.96	1.16	20.76
Annual Growth	(7.9%)	—	—	8.4%	(0.9%)	6.8%

Merchants Bancorp (Indiana)

EXECUTIVES

Chairman, Chief Executive Officer, Subsidiary Officer, Michael J. Petrie, $630,000 total compensation
President, Chief Operating Officer, Subsidiary Officer, Director, Michael J. Dunlap, $500,000 total compensation
Senior Vice President, Chief Accounting Officer, Subsidiary Officer, Bill D. Buchanan
Chief Financial Officer, Subsidiary Officer, John F. Macke
Subsidiary Officer, Director, Scott A. Evans
Subsidiary Officer, Michael R. Dury, $110,000 total compensation
Subsidiary Officer, Susan D. Kucer
Subsidiary Officer, Richard L. Belser
Subsidiary Officer, Kevin T. Langford
Division Officer, Jerry F. Koors
Director, Sue Anne Gilroy
Director, Andrew J. Juster
Director, Patrick D. O'Brien
Director, Anne E. Sellers
Director, David N. Shane
Auditors : BKD, LLP

LOCATIONS

HQ: Merchants Bancorp (Indiana)
 410 Monon Blvd., Carmel, IN 46032
Phone: 317 569-7420
Web: www.merchantsbankofindiana.com

HISTORICAL FINANCIALS

Company Type: Public

Income Statement — FYE: December 31

	ASSETS ($mil)	NET INCOME ($mil)	INCOME AS % OF ASSETS	EMPLOYEES
12/20	9,645.3	180.5	1.9%	404
12/19	6,371.9	77.3	1.2%	329
12/18	3,884.1	62.8	1.6%	259
12/17	3,393.1	54.6	1.6%	194
12/16	2,718.5	33.1	1.2%	157
Annual Growth	37.2%	52.8%	—	26.7%

2020 Year-End Financials

Return on assets: 2.2%
Return on equity: 24.5%
Long-term debt ($ mil.): —
No. of shares ($ mil.): 43.1
Sales ($ mil.): 410.2

Dividends
 Yield: 1.7%
 Payout: 8.3%
Market value ($ mil.): 1,191.0

	STOCK PRICE ($) FY Close	P/E High/Low		PER SHARE ($) Earnings	Dividends	Book Value
12/20	27.63	8	3	3.85	0.32	18.80
12/19	19.71	16	10	1.58	0.28	15.18
12/18	19.96	21	14	1.38	0.24	9.79
12/17	19.68	14	11	1.52	0.05	8.54
Annual Growth	12.0%	—	—	36.3%	85.7%	30.1%

Mercury Systems Inc

Mercury Systems is a technology company that delivers innovative technology solutions for the homeland security, military and aerospace, and telecommunications markets. As a leading manufacturer of essential components, products, modules and subsystems, it sells to defense prime contractors, the US government and original equipment manufacturers (OEM) commercial aerospace companies. Its products and solutions are deployed in more than 300 programs with over 25 different defense prime contractors and commercial aviation customers. The US accounts for the vast majority of revenue. The company was founded in 1981.

Operations

Mercury Systems group its products into the following categories: Integrated Subsystems (about 65% of revenue), Modules and Subassemblies (some 20%) and Components (around 15% of revenue).

Integrated Subsystems bring components, modules and sub-assemblies into one system, enabled with software. Subsystems are typically, but not always, integrated within an open standards-based chassis and often feature interconnect technologies to enable communication between disparate systems. Spares and replacement modules and sub-assemblies are provided for use with subsystems sold by the company. Its subsystems are deployed in sensor processing, aviation and mission computing and C4I applications.

Modules and Sub-assemblies combine multiple components to serve a range of complex functions, including processing, networking and graphics display. Typically delivered as computer boards or other packaging, modules and sub-assemblies are usually designed using open standards to provide interoperability when integrated in a subsystem. Examples of modules and sub-assemblies include embedded processing boards, switched fabrics and boards for high-speed input/output, digital receivers, graphics and video, along with multi-chip modules, integrated radio frequency and microwave multi-function assemblies and radio frequency tuners and transceivers.

Components represent the basic building blocks of an electronic system. They generally perform a single function such as switching, storing or converting electronic signals. Some examples include power amplifiers and limiters, switches, oscillators, filters, equalizers, digital and analog converters, chips, MMICs (monolithic microwave integrated circuits) and memory and storage devices.

Its mission critical solutions are deployed by its customers for a variety of applications including command, control, communications, computers, intelligence, surveillance and reconnaissance (C4ISR), electronic intelligence, mission computing avionics, electro-optical/infrared (EO/IR), electronic warfare, weapons and missile defense, hypersonics and radar.

Geographic Reach

Headquartered in Andover, Massachusetts, Mercury Systems has sales offices and subsidiaries in the UK, Japan and France and it has manufacturing and engineering facilities and subsidiaries in Switzerland, Spain and Canada.

It generates more than 95% of sales from the US; Europe and the Asia-Pacific region accounts for less than 5%.

Sales and Marketing

The company sells to defense prime contractors, the US government and original equipment manufacturers ("OEM") commercial aerospace companies.

Its top three customers are Raytheon Technologies, US Navy and Lockheed Martin Corporation. These three account for around 40% of the total sales. Other customers are customers include Airbus, BAE Systems, Boeing, General Atomics, General Dynamics, L3Harris Technologies, Leonardo and Northrop Grumman.

Financial Performance

The company's revenue for fiscal 2021 increased to $988.2 million compared from the prior year with $924.0 million.

Net income for fiscal 2021 decreased to $11.3 million compared from the prior year with $62.0 million.

Cash held by the company at the end of fiscal 2021 decreased to $65.7 million. Cash provided by financing activities was $245.8 million while cash used for operations and investing activities were $18.9 million and $274.3 million, respectively.

Strategy

Mercury's business strategy is based on a differentiated market position: the company make trusted, secure, mission critical technologies profoundly more accessible to the aerospace and defense industry. The Mercury Processing Platform serves customers with cutting-edge commercial technology innovations, purpose built and mission-ready for aerospace and defense applications, through above average industry investment on a percentage basis in R&D. Mercury's strategy is built to meet the aerospace and defense market's need for speed and affordability.

Mercury's strategies for growth are as follows: invest to grow organically; expand capabilities, market access and penetration through mergers & acquisitions; expand capabilities, market access and penetration through mergers & acquisitions; invest in trusted, secure Innovation that Matters; continuously improve operational capability and scalability; and attract and retain top talent.

Mergers and Acquisitions

In late 2021, Mercury Systems acquired Georgia-based Atlanta Micro, Inc., a leading designer and manufacturer of high-performance RF modules and components, including advanced monolithic microwave integrated circuits (MMICs) which are critical for high-speed data acquisition applications including electronic warfare, radar and weapons. Said Mark Aslett, Mercury's president and chief executive officer, "The acquisition directly supports our stated goal to provide next-generation trusted microelectronics capabilities for critical aerospace and defense applications. Atlanta Micro's state-of-the-art MMIC capabilities expand our prior investments in the RF and microwave domain, enabling us to both provide best-in-class solutions for our customers and to address new markets through our combined expertise".

Also in late 2021, Mercury Systems announced the completion of its acquisition of Avalex Technologies (Avalex). Said Mark Aslett, Mercury's president and chief executive officer, "The acquisition is directly aligned with our strategy and will enable us to address and enable the growing demand for digitally converged solutions in the C4I and platform/mission management markets. We welcome the Avalex team to the Mercury family."

In 2021, Mercury Systems acquired New Jersey-based Pentek Technologies, LLC and Pentek Systems, Inc. (collectively, "Pentek"), a leading designer and manufacturer of ruggedized, high-performance, commercial off-the-shelf ("COTS") software-defined radio and data acquisition boards, recording systems and subsystems for high-end commercial and defense applications, for $85 million. The acquisition of Pentek is an excellent fit for Mercury Systems' market and low-risk content expansion strategy.

Company Background

The company was founded in 1981. In 2011, Mercury acquired LNX Corporation of Salem, N.H.

EXECUTIVES

Chairman, Director, William K. O'Brien
President, Chief Executive Officer, Director, Mark Aslett, $546,133 total compensation
Senior Vice President, Interim Chief Financial Officer, Chief Accounting Officer, Treasurer, Michelle M. McCarthy
Executive Vice President, Division Officer, Charles R. Wells
Executive Vice President, Chief Growth Officer, James M. Stevison
Executive Vice President, General Counsel, Secretary, Christopher C. Cambria
Executive Vice President, Chief Transformation Officer, Thomas Huber
Executive Vice President, Division Officer, Brian E. Perry
Director, Orlando P. Carvalho
Director, Howard L. Lance
Director, Debora A. Plunkett
Director, Mary Louise Krakauer
Director, William L. Ballhaus
Director, Lisa S. Disbrow
Director, Barry R. Nearhos
Auditors: KPMG LLP

LOCATIONS

HQ: Mercury Systems Inc
50 Minuteman Road, Andover, MA 01810
Phone: 978 256-1300
Web: www.mrcy.com

2015 Sales

	$ mil.	% of total
US	232.7	98
Asia/Pacific	2.8	1
Europe	2.6	1
Adjustments	(3.3)	-
Total	234.8	100

PRODUCTS/OPERATIONS

2015 Sales

	$ mil.	% of total
Mercury Commercial Electronics	207.1	88
Mercury Defense Systems	27.4	12
Eliminations	0.3	-
Total	234.8	100

COMPETITORS

ADVANCED CIRCUITS, INC.
ASTRONICS CORPORATION
DUCOMMUN LABARGE TECHNOLOGIES, INC.
JABIL INC.
ORBOTECH LTD.
RAYTHEON COMPANY
SANMINA CORPORATION
SYPRIS ELECTRONICS, LLC
SYPRIS SOLUTIONS, INC.
XILINX, INC.

HISTORICAL FINANCIALS

Company Type: Public

Income Statement — FYE: July 2

	REVENUE ($mil)	NET INCOME ($mil)	NET PROFIT MARGIN	EMPLOYEES
07/21	923.9	62.0	6.7%	2,384
07/20*	796.6	85.7	10.8%	1,947
06/19	654.7	46.7	7.1%	1,661
06/18	493.1	40.8	8.3%	1,320
06/17	408.5	24.8	6.1%	1,159
Annual Growth	22.6%	25.7%	—	19.8%

*Fiscal year change

2021 Year-End Financials

Debt ratio: 10.2%
Return on equity: 4.3%
Cash ($ mil.): 113.8
Current Ratio: 4.26
Long-term debt ($ mil.): 200
No. of shares ($ mil.): 55.2
Dividends
Yield: —
Payout: —
Market value ($ mil.): 3,646.0

	STOCK PRICE ($) FY Close	P/E High/Low		PER SHARE ($) Earnings	Dividends	Book Value
07/21	66.00	78	51	1.12	0.00	26.87
07/20*	80.27	59	36	1.56	0.00	25.31
06/19	70.35	77	39	0.96	0.00	23.68
06/18	38.06	61	36	0.86	0.00	16.45
06/17	42.09	71	37	0.58	0.00	15.67
Annual Growth	11.9%	—	—	17.9%	—	14.4%

*Fiscal year change

Meridian Bioscience Inc.

Meridian is a fully-integrated life science company with principal businesses in the development, manufacture, sale and distribution of diagnostic testing systems and kits, primarily for certain gastrointestinal and respiratory infectious diseases, and elevated blood lead levels; and the manufacture and distribution of bulk antigens, antibodies, immunoassay blocking reagents, specialized Polymerase Chain Reaction (PCR) master mixes, and bioresearch reagents used by other diagnostic test manufacturers and researchers in immunological and molecular tests for human, animal, plant and environmental applications. Founded in 1977, majority of its sales were generated in Americas.

Operations
The company's reportable segments are Life Science (about 60% of revenue) and Diagnostics (about 40%).

The Life Science segment develops, manufactures, sells and distributes bulk antigens, antibodies, immunoassay blocking reagents, specialized PCR master mixes, isothermal reagents, enzymes, nucleotides, and bioresearch reagents used predominantly by in vitro device (IVD) manufacturing companies, and to a lesser degree, by researchers and non-human clinical customers such as veterinary, food and environmental.

The Diagnostic segment product portfolio includes approximately 200 diagnostic tests and transport media. Its testing platforms include: Real-time PCR Amplification (Revogene brand); Isothermal DNA Amplification (Alethia brand); Lateral Flow Immunoassay using fluorescent chemistry (Curian brand); Rapid Immunoassay (ImmunoCard and ImmunoCard STAT! brands); Enzyme-linked Immunoassay (PREMIER brand); Anodic Stripping Voltammetry (LeadCare and Pediastat brands); and urea breath testing for H. pylori (BreathID and BreathTek brand).

Non-molecular assay accounts for about 55% of revenue, and Molecular assays at more than 45%.

Geographic Reach
Headquartered in Cincinnati, Ohio, Meridian Bioscience sells its products and services into approximately 70 countries. The Life Science segment has manufacturing operations in Memphis, Tennessee; Boca Raton, Florida; London, England; and Luckenwalde, Germany, while Diagnostic segment has sales and distribution center near Milan, Italy and rents office space in Paris, France and Braine-l'Alleud, Belgium for sales and administrative functions, and space in Manasquan, New Jersey and Changzhou, China to house BreathID technical service and repair functions.

About 45% of sales were generated in the Americas, EMEA with over 35%, and the rest of the world with some 15%.

Sales and Marketing
Its Diagnostics Segment relies on a direct sales force in four countries, and distribution networks. It also uses independent distributors either in a complementary manner with its direct sales force or solely to supply its products to end-users. It has two independent distribution customers and a reference laboratory customer that together comprised roughly 35% of Diagnostics segment net revenues in fiscal 2021, with each contributing 10% or greater of the Diagnostics segment's net revenues.

Financial Performance
Consolidated revenues for fiscal 2021 totaled $317.9 million, an increase of 25% compared to fiscal 2020 (22% increase on a constant-currency basis). With a 66% increase in revenues from molecular reagents products and a 10% increase in revenues from immunological reagents products, revenues for the company's Life Science segment increased 43% to $190.1 million during fiscal 2021 compared to fiscal 2020.

In 2021, the company had a net income of $71.4 million, a 55% increase from the previous year's net income of $46.2 million.

The company's cash at the end of 2021 was $49.8 million. Operating activities generated $66.9 million, while investing activities used $40.4 million, primarily for acquisitions and purchase of property, plant and equipment. Financing activities used another $31.1 million, mainly for payment of acquisition consideration.

Strategy
Meridian Bioscience, Inc. announced in December 2020 that it has launched an Air-Dryable RT-qPCR Mix, driving innovation in the development of molecular tests with ambient temperature stability. This specialized master mix is designed for air-drying, a cost-effective and easier alternative to lyophilization. With this new product addition, Meridian has the most comprehensive offering of master mixes for developing both DNA and RNA based molecular diagnostic assays at ambient temperature, removing the need for cold chain shipping and storage.

Meridian's Air-Dryable RT-qPCR Mix has been designed to simplify development, manufacturing and storage of molecular assays while delivering fast detection of RNA targets, an ideal solution for COVID-19 assay development. Its one-tube format chemistry containing all reagents necessary for a RT-qPCR, including magnesium, dNTP and reverse transcriptase, not only shortens assay optimization but is also compatible with air-drying protocols. This new mix shows exceptionally high performance in both singleplex and multiplex reactions following rehydration, making it ideally suited for a wide range of instruments from automated high-throughput platforms to point-of-care devices.

Mergers and Acquisitions
In 2021, Meridian Bioscience has completed previously announced acquisition of the North American BreathTek business from Otsuka America Pharmaceutical, Inc for $20 million in cash. With this acquisition, Meridian will assume the customer relationships in North America to supply BreathTek, a urea breath test for the detection of Helicobacter pylori. The acquisition is expected to add more than $20 million of annual revenue, strengthening Meridian's position as a leading provider of gastrointestinal diagnostic solutions, and is expected to be accretive to earnings and cash immediately.

In early 2020, Meridian Bioscience has completed its previously announced acquisition of Exalenz Bioscience Ltd., the Modiin, Israel based provider of the BreathID Breath Test Systems, a urea breath test platform for the detection of Helicobacter pylori. The combination of Meridian's leading stool antigen tests with the Exalenz BreathID urea breath test positions Meridian as the only company in the U.S. with a complete offering of non-invasive diagnostic assays for a H. pylori active infection. The purchase price of the acquisition amounted to approximately $56.3 million.

HISTORY

Microbiology and diagnostics specialists William Motto and Jerry Ruyan launched Meridian Diagnostics in 1977, naming it for their desire to reach the highest point in diagnostic technology. The company began as a research and development lab, but soon developed a variety of commercial products, including test kits for pneumocystis carinii pneumonia (a leading cause of death in AIDS patients) and mycoplasmal (or "walking") pneumonia.

In the 1990s Meridian made key acquisitions to further its offerings, including the ImmunoCard rapid-response systems from Disease Detection International and the MonoSpot and Monolert mononucleosis diagnostics technologies from Johnson & Johnson. Other acquisitions include tests for Lyme disease and the viruses that cause pediatric diarrhea.

As a result of its entry into the life sciences market (spurred by its acquisitions of antibody reagent maker BIODESIGN in 1999 and antigens and test kits maker Viral Antigens in 2000), Meridian Diagnostics changed its name to Meridian Bioscience in 2001.

In 2005 the company expanded its life sciences division once again by purchasing OEM Concepts, a manufacturer of antibody products. The following year Meridian Bioscience combined BIODESIGN, Viral

Antigens, Meridian Biologics, and OEM Concepts into a new Life Sciences business segment, with the former businesses becoming four distinct brands within that unit.

The Life Sciences division expanded its operations in 2007 when it won a five-year contract with the National Institute for Allergies and Infectious Diseases (part of the NIH) to manufacture experimental vaccines; the contract was worth up to $12.2 million.

In 2008 the company broadened the Life Science division by acquiring technologies and products, including proteins and antigens for applications in infectious disease and cardiac research, from private life sciences firm Vybion.

EXECUTIVES

Chairman, Director, David C. Phillips
Executive Vice President, Chief Financial Officer, Chief Accounting Officer, Secretary, Bryan T. Baldasare
Division Officer, Lourdes G. Weltzien
Division Officer, Tony Serafini-Lamanna
Chief Executive Officer, Director, Jack P. Kenny
Director, James M. Anderson, $66,250 total compensation
Director, Anthony P. Bihl
Director, Dwight E. Ellingwood
Director, John C McIlwraith
Director, John McCune Rice
Director, Catherine A. Sazdanoff
Director, Felicia Williams
Auditors : Ernst & Young LLP

LOCATIONS

HQ: Meridian Bioscience Inc.
 3471 River Hills Drive, Cincinnati, OH 45244
Phone: 513 271-3700
Web: www.meridianbioscience.com

PRODUCTS/OPERATIONS

2016 Sales

	$ mil.	% of total
Diagnostics	145,1	74
Life Science	50.9	26
Total	196.0	100

Selected Products and Brands
Diagnostics
 Enzyme Immunoassay (EIA)/Rapid tests
 ImmunoCard
 MONOLERT
 Premier
 Immunofluorescence
 MERIFLUOR
 Molecular Amplification
 illumigene
 Particle Agglutination
 Meritec
 MonoSpot
 Other
 Macro-CON
 Para-Pak
 SpinCon
Life Science
 BIODESIGN (monoclonal and polyclongal antibodies and assay reagents)
 Bioline (biological reagents)
 Biologics (contract biologics development and manufacturing)
 OEM Concepts (custom antibody production)
 Viral Antigens (custom infectious disease antigens)

COMPETITORS

BIO-TECHNE CORPORATION
CEPHEID
LIFE TECHNOLOGIES CORPORATION
MYRIAD GENETICS, INC.
ORASURE TECHNOLOGIES, INC.
PRECIPIO, INC.
QUIDEL CORPORATION
ROCHE DIAGNOSTICS CORPORATION
SERACARE LIFE SCIENCES, INC.
VENTANA MEDICAL SYSTEMS, INC.

HISTORICAL FINANCIALS

Company Type: Public

Income Statement				FYE: September 30
	REVENUE ($mil)	NET INCOME ($mil)	NET PROFIT MARGIN	EMPLOYEES
09/21	317.8	71.4	22.5%	560
09/20	253.6	46.1	18.2%	750
09/19	201.0	24.3	12.1%	660
09/18	213.5	23.8	11.2%	585
09/17	200.7	21.5	10.7%	640
Annual Growth	12.2%	34.9%	—	(3.3%)

2021 Year-End Financials
Debt ratio: 13.3% No. of shares ($ mil.): 43.3
Return on equity: 24.7% Dividends
Cash ($ mil.): 49.7   Yield: —
Current Ratio: 4.09   Payout: —
Long-term debt ($ mil.): 60 Market value ($ mil.): 834.0

	STOCK PRICE ($) FY Close	P/E High/Low		PER SHARE ($) Earnings	Dividends	Book Value
09/21	19.24	18	10	1.62	0.00	7.57
09/20	16.98	24	5	1.07	0.00	5.75
09/19	9.49	35	16	0.57	0.38	4.47
09/18	14.90	30	24	0.56	0.50	4.14
09/17	14.30	38	24	0.51	0.58	4.02
Annual Growth	7.7%	—	—	33.5%	—	17.2%

Meridian Corp

EXECUTIVES

Chairman, President, Chief Executive Officer, Christopher J. Annas, $431,904 total compensation
Executive Vice President, Chief Financial Officer, Director, Denise Lindsay, $235,997 total compensation
Executive Vice President, Chief Credit Officer, Joseph L. Cafarchio, $200,473 total compensation
Executive Vice President, Chief Lending Officer, Charles D. Kochka, $186,683 total compensation
Lead Director, Director, Robert T. Holland
Director, Robert M. Casciato
Director, Christine M. Helmig
Director, George C. Collier, $0 total compensation
Director, Edward J. Hollin
Director, Anthony M. Imbesi
Auditors : Crowe LLP

LOCATIONS

HQ: Meridian Corp
 9 Old Lincoln Highway, Malvern, PA 19355
Phone: 484 568-5000
Web: www.meridianbanker.com

HISTORICAL FINANCIALS

Company Type: Public

Income Statement				FYE: December 31
	ASSETS ($mil)	NET INCOME ($mil)	INCOME AS % OF ASSETS	EMPLOYEES
12/20	1,720.1	26.4	1.5%	381
12/19	1,150.0	10.4	0.9%	0
12/18	997.3	8.1	0.8%	0
12/17	856.0	3.0	0.4%	0
12/16	733.6	4.9	0.7%	0
Annual Growth	23.7%	52.2%	—	—

2020 Year-End Financials
Return on assets: 1.8%   Dividends
Return on equity: 20.1%   Yield: 1.2%
Long-term debt ($ mil.): —   Payout: 7.5%
No. of shares ($ mil.): 6.1 Market value ($ mil.): 128.0
Sales ($ mil.): 149.5

	STOCK PRICE ($) FY Close	P/E High/Low		PER SHARE ($) Earnings	Dividends	Book Value
12/20	20.80	6	3	4.27	0.25	23.08
12/19	20.19	12	10	1.63	0.00	18.84
12/18	17.17	16	13	1.27	0.00	17.15
12/17	19.98	42	35	0.49	0.00	15.86
Annual Growth	1.3%	—	—	105.8%	—	13.3%

Meritage Hospitality Group Inc

This company is really big on the beef in Michigan. Meritage Hospitality Group is a leading franchisee of Wendy's fast food hamburger restaurants, with about 70 locations operating mostly in western and southern Michigan. The units, franchised from Wendy's/Arby's Group, offer a menu of burgers and other sandwiches, fries, and other items. In addition to its quick-service operations, Meritage runs four franchised O'Charley's casual dining restaurants in Michigan near Grand Rapids and Detroit. The company was founded in 1986 as Thomas Edison Inns. The family of chairman Robert Schermer, Sr., including CEO Robert Schermer, Jr., controls Meritage.

EXECUTIVES

Chairman, Robert E. Schermer
President, Chief Operating Officer, Gary A. Rose
Chief Executive Officer, Director, Robert E. Schermer, $185,000 total compensation
Vice President, Chief Financial Officer, Treasurer, Corporate Secretary, Tracey A. Smith
Director, Duane F. Kluting
Director, Joseph L. Maggini

Director, Peter D. Wierenga
Director, Dirk J. Pruis
Director, Chris A. Armbruster
Auditors : BDO USA LLP

LOCATIONS

HQ: Meritage Hospitality Group Inc
45 Ottawa Ave. S.W., Suite 600, Grand Rapids, MI 49503
Phone: 616 776-2600   Fax: 616 776-2776
Web: www.meritagehospitality.com

COMPETITORS

BISTRO MANAGEMENT, INC.
BRIAD CORP.
FILI ENTERPRISES, INC.
GREEN MILL RESTAURANTS, LLC
KITCHEN INVESTMENT GROUP, INC.
LEGAL SEA FOODS, LLC
MARY'S LONG BEACH INC
ROSE MANAGEMENT SERVICES
SERVUS!
THOMAS AND KING, INC.

HISTORICAL FINANCIALS

Company Type: Public

Income Statement — FYE: January 3

	REVENUE ($mil)	NET INCOME ($mil)	NET PROFIT MARGIN	EMPLOYEES
01/21*	516.1	14.9	2.9%	11,000
12/19	467.5	12.0	2.6%	11,000
12/18	435.2	13.0	3.0%	10,000
12/17	312.5	8.9	2.9%	6,800
01/17	235.7	6.4	2.7%	5,700
Annual Growth	21.6%	23.3%	—	17.9%

*Fiscal year change

2021 Year-End Financials

Debt ratio: 25.9%
Return on equity: 16.1%
Cash ($ mil.): 32.3
Current Ratio: 0.49
Long-term debt ($ mil.): 148.8
No. of shares ($ mil.): 6.6
Dividends
  Yield: —
  Payout: 8.8%
Market value ($ mil.): 128.0

	STOCK PRICE ($) FY Close	P/E High/Low		PER SHARE ($) Earnings	Dividends	Book Value
01/21*	19.20	10	5	1.58	0.14	14.81
12/19	19.80	12	10	1.27	0.24	13.09
12/18	17.50	—	—	0.00	0.15	9.17
12/17	20.00	—	—	0.00	0.10	6.25
01/17	11.15	—	—	0.00	0.07	4.37
Annual Growth	14.6%			—	18.9%	35.7%

*Fiscal year change

Mesabi Trust

In the Iron Range of Mesabi the stockholders trust. Mesabi Trust collects royalties and bonuses from the sale of minerals that are shipped from Northshore Mining's Silver Bay, Minnesota, facility. The mining company is a wholly owned subsidiary of Cliffs, a supplier of iron ore products to the steel industry. Northshore Mining pays royalties to Mesabi Trust based on production and sales of crude ore pulled from the trust's property; it has curtailed its extraction efforts, citing lack of demand. Independent consultants track production and sales for Mesabi Trust. Deutsche Bank Trust Company Americas is the corporate trustee of Mesabi Trust.

EXECUTIVES

Vice President, Trustee, Jeffrey Schoenfeld
Trustee, Robert C. Berglund
Trustee, James A. Ehrenberg
Trustee, Michael P. Mlinar
Trustee, Robin M. Radke
Auditors : Baker Tilly US, LLP

LOCATIONS

HQ: Mesabi Trust
c/o Deutsche Bank Trust Company Americas, Trust & Agency Services, 60 Wall Street, 24th Floor, New York, NY 10005
Phone: 904 271-2520
Web: www.mesabi-trust.com

COMPETITORS

Antarchile S.A.
CANDOVER INVESTMENTS PLC
CITY CAPITAL CORPORATION
Clairvest Group Inc.
THE FIDELITY GLOBAL GROUP LTD

HISTORICAL FINANCIALS

Company Type: Public

Income Statement — FYE: January 31

	REVENUE ($mil)	NET INCOME ($mil)	NET PROFIT MARGIN	EMPLOYEES
01/21	25.9	23.4	90.2%	0
01/20	31.9	30.0	94.0%	0
01/19	47.2	45.5	96.3%	0
01/18	34.5	33.4	96.9%	0
01/17	10.7	9.6	89.5%	0
Annual Growth	24.7%	24.9%	—	—

2021 Year-End Financials

Debt ratio: —
Return on equity: —
Cash ($ mil.): 12.5
Current Ratio: 3.55
Long-term debt ($ mil.): —
No. of shares ($ mil.): 13.1
Dividends
  Yield: —
  Payout: 80.1%
Market value ($ mil.): 327.0

	STOCK PRICE ($) FY Close	P/E High/Low		PER SHARE ($) Earnings	Dividends	Book Value
01/21	24.89	17	5	1.78	1.43	1.26
01/20	20.41	14	9	2.29	2.67	0.90
01/19	27.44	9	6	3.47	3.00	1.28
01/18	24.80	12	5	2.55	2.53	0.80
01/17	13.70	19	5	0.73	0.64	0.78
Annual Growth	16.1%			—	24.9%	22.3%	12.7%

Meta Financial Group Inc

Delivering financial products and services to Iowa and South Dakota is the calling of Meta Financial Group. The company's full-services banking subsidiary, MetaBank, primarily consists of attracting deposits and investing those funds in its loan and lease portfolios, along with providing prepaid cards and other financial products and solutions to business and consumer customers. In addition to originating loans and leases, the MetaBank also occasionally contracts to sell loans, such as tax refund advance loans, consumer credit product loans, and government guaranteed loans, to third party buyers. It holds $3.3 billion in loan portfolio and $4.98 billion deposit portfolio.

Operations

Meta Financial operates through three reportable segments Consumer (nearly 55% of total sales), Commercial (more than 40%), and Corporate Services/Other (less than 5% of sales).

The consumer segment includes Meta Payment Systems, consumer credit products, Tax Services and Warehouse finance, while commercial segment includes Crestmark division and AFS/IBEX division, and corporate services/other includes certain shared services, retained community bank portfolio, treasury and student loan lending portfolio.

Overall, net interest income accounts for about 55% of total sales.

Geographic Reach

Sioux Falls, SD-based Meta Financial has about 15 non-branch facilities from which its divisions of payments, commercial finance, tax services, and consumer lending operate.

The payments division operates out of the company's home office along with one additional office in Sioux Falls. The commercial finance division operates out of offices in Troy, Michigan; Dallas, Texas; Newport Beach, California; Boynton Beach, Florida; Baton Rouge, Louisiana; Franklin, Tennessee; and Toronto, Ontario, Canada.

The tax services division has offices located in Louisville, Kentucky, and Easton, Pennsylvania. The company has corporate and shared services offices located in Scottsdale, Arizona and Washington, D.C. The company also has an office located in Hurst, Texas.

Financial Performance

Total revenue for the fiscal year 2020 (ended September), was $498.8 million, an increase of 2% from the fiscal year 2019.

The company recorded net income of $104.7 million for the fiscal year 2020, compared to $97.0 million for the fiscal year ended 2019, an increase of $7.7 million. Total revenue for fiscal 2020 was $498.8 million, compared to $486.8 million for fiscal 2019, an increase of 2%. The increase in net income and revenue was primarily due to an increase in noninterest income and a decrease in noninterest expense, partially offset by a slight decrease in net interest income.

Cash held by the company at the end of fiscal 2020 decreased to $4.8 million compared to $8.1 million in the prior year. Cash provided by operations was $119.8 million while cash used for investing and financing activities were $0.8 million and $122.4

million, respectively. Main uses of cash were alternative Investments and shares repurchased for tax withholdings on stock compensation.

EXECUTIVES

Chairman, Subsidiary Officer, Director, Douglas J. Hajek
Subsidiary Officer, Vice-Chairman, Director, Becky S. Shulman
President, Subsidiary Officer, Anthony M. Sharett
Governance, Risk & Compliance Chief Executive Officer, Governance, Risk & Compliance Subsidiary Officer, Director, Brett L. Pharr
Finance and Investment Management Executive Vice President, Finance and Investment Management Chief Financial Officer, Finance and Investment Management Subsidiary Officer, Glen W. Herrick, $400,000 total compensation
Executive Vice President, Chief Governance, Risk, & Compliance Officer, Subsidiary Officer, Sonja Anne Theisen
Executive Vice President, Chief Technology and Product Officer, Subsidiary Officer, Charles C. Ingram
Executive Vice President, Chief Legal Officer, Subsidiary Officer, Nadia A. Dombrowski
Director, Frederick V. Moore
Director, Lizebeth H. Zlatkus
Director, Elizabeth G. Hoople
Director, Ronald D. McCray
Director, Michael R. Kramer
Director, Kendall E. Stork
Auditors: Crowe LLP

LOCATIONS

HQ: Meta Financial Group Inc
5501 South Broadband Lane, Sioux Falls, SD 57108
Phone: 877 497-7497
Web: www.metabank.com

COMPETITORS

AXOS FINANCIAL, INC.
BANKFINANCIAL CORPORATION
BOKF MERGER CORPORATION NUMBER SIXTEEN
COMMERCE BANCSHARES, INC.
DIME COMMUNITY BANCSHARES, INC.
EAGLE BANCORP, INC.
FLAGSTAR BANCORP, INC.
KEARNY FINANCIAL CORP.
PROVIDENT FINANCIAL SERVICES, INC.
THE SOUTHERN BANC COMPANY INC

HISTORICAL FINANCIALS

Company Type: Public

Income Statement — FYE: September 30

	ASSETS ($mil)	NET INCOME ($mil)	INCOME AS % OF ASSETS	EMPLOYEES
09/21	6,690.6	141.7	2.1%	1,134
09/20	6,092.0	104.7	1.7%	1,015
09/19	6,182.8	97.0	1.6%	1,186
09/18	5,835.0	51.6	0.9%	1,219
09/17	5,228.3	44.9	0.9%	827
Annual Growth	6.4%	33.3%	—	8.2%

2021 Year-End Financials
Return on assets: 2.2%
Return on equity: 16.5%
Long-term debt ($ mil.): —
No. of shares ($ mil.): 31.6
Sales ($ mil.): 556.7
Dividends Yield: 0.3%
Payout: 4.6%
Market value ($ mil.): 1,662.0

	STOCK PRICE ($) FY Close	P/E High/Low		PER SHARE ($) Earnings	Dividends	Book Value
09/21	52.48	12	5	4.38	0.20	27.49
09/20	19.22	14	5	2.94	0.20	24.55
09/19	32.61	33	7	2.49	0.20	22.22
09/18	82.65	70	46	1.67	0.18	19.00
09/17	78.40	66	39	1.61	0.17	15.05
Annual Growth	(9.5%)	—	—	28.4%	3.6%	16.3%

MetroCity Bankshares Inc

EXECUTIVES

Chairman, Chief Executive Officer, Subsidiary Officer, Director, Nack Y. Paek
Vice-Chairman, Director, Don T.P. Leung
President, Chief Executive Officer, Subsidiary Officer, Director, Farid Tan
Executive Vice President, Chief Financial Officer, Lucas Stewart
Executive Vice President, Chief Lending Officer, Subsidiary Officer, Director, Howard Hwasaeng Kim
Director, Frank Glover
Director, Sam Sang-Koo Shim
Director, William J. Hungeling
Director, Francis Lai
Director, Feiying Lu
Director, Young Park
Director, Aiit A. Patel
Director, Frank S. Rhee
Auditors: Crowe LLP

LOCATIONS

HQ: MetroCity Bankshares Inc
5114 Buford Highway, Doraville, GA 30340
Phone: 770 455-4989
Web: www.metrocitybank.bank

HISTORICAL FINANCIALS

Company Type: Public

Income Statement — FYE: December 31

	ASSETS ($mil)	NET INCOME ($mil)	INCOME AS % OF ASSETS	EMPLOYEES
12/20	1,897.4	36.3	1.9%	211
12/19	1,631.8	44.7	2.7%	208
12/18	1,432.6	41.3	2.9%	0
12/17	1,288.9	31.8	2.5%	0
12/16	1,100.0	20.2	1.8%	0
Annual Growth	14.6%	15.8%	—	—

2020 Year-End Financials
Return on assets: 2.0%
Return on equity: 15.7%
Long-term debt ($ mil.): —
No. of shares ($ mil.): 25.6
Sales ($ mil.): 104.8
Dividends Yield: 2.7%
Payout: 27.3%
Market value ($ mil.): 370.0

	STOCK PRICE ($) FY Close	P/E High/Low		PER SHARE ($) Earnings	Dividends	Book Value
12/20	14.42	13	6	1.41	0.40	9.54
12/19	17.51	16	7	1.81	0.42	8.49
12/18	33.00	19	11	1.69	0.38	6.95
12/17	19.90	—	—	0.00	0.23	5.61
Annual Growth	(10.2%)	—	—	—	21.1%	19.3%

Metropolitan Bank Holding Corp

EXECUTIVES

Chairman, Director, David M. Gavrin
President, Chief Executive Officer, Subsidiary Officer, Mark R. DeFazio, $700,000 total compensation
Executive Vice President, Chief Financial Officer, Subsidiary Officer, Sangeeta Kishore
Executive Vice President, Subsidiary Officer, Nick Rosenberg, $346,000 total compensation
Senior Vice President, Chief Credit Risk Officer, Subsidiary Officer, Karen Rojeski, $238,493 total compensation
Senior Vice President, Legal Counsel, Subsidiary Officer, Michael Guarino
Executive Vice President, Chief Lending Officer, Subsidiary Officer, Scott Lublin, $270,952 total compensation
Director, Dale C. Fredston
Director, David J. Gold
Director, Harvey M. Gutman
Director, Terence J. Mitchell
Director, Robert C. Patent
Director, Maria Fiorini Ramirez
Director, William Reinhardt
Director, Robert I. Usdan
Director, George J. Wolf
Auditors: Crowe LLP

LOCATIONS

HQ: Metropolitan Bank Holding Corp
99 Park Avenue, New York, NY 10016
Phone: 212 659-0600
Web: www.mcbankny.com

HISTORICAL FINANCIALS

Company Type: Public

Income Statement
FYE: December 31

	ASSETS ($mil)	NET INCOME ($mil)	INCOME AS % OF ASSETS	EMPLOYEES
12/20	4,330.8	39.4	0.9%	189
12/19	3,357.5	30.1	0.9%	167
12/18	2,182.6	25.5	1.2%	153
12/17	1,759.8	12.3	0.7%	129
12/16	1,220.3	5.0	0.4%	118
Annual Growth	37.3%	67.5%	—	12.5%

2020 Year-End Financials

Return on assets: 1.0%
Return on equity: 12.3%
Long-term debt ($ mil.): —
No. of shares ($ mil.): 8.3
Sales ($ mil.): 160.1
Dividends
Yield: —
Payout: —
Market value ($ mil.): 301.0

	STOCK PRICE ($) FY Close	P/E High	P/E Low	PER SHARE ($) Earnings	PER SHARE ($) Dividends	PER SHARE ($) Book Value
12/20	36.27	11	4	4.66	0.00	41.08
12/19	48.23	13	8	3.56	0.00	35.98
12/18	30.85	18	10	3.06	0.00	32.19
12/17	42.10	21	15	2.34	0.00	28.90
Annual Growth	(4.8%)	—	—	25.8%	—	12.4%

Mettler-Toledo International, Inc.

Mettler-Toledo International measures up as one of the top suppliers of precision instruments and services in the world. The company is recognized as an innovation leader and its solutions are critical in research and development, quality control, and manufacturing processes for its customers. The company makes a range of bench and floor scales that precisely weigh materials as little as one ten-millionth of a gram to more than 60 kilograms. The company's main markets are laboratory, industrial, and food retail, among others. Mettler-Toledo also makes analytical instruments and software for life science, engineering, and drug and chemical compound development. The US accounts for about a third of the company's revenue.

Operations

Mettler-Toledo has five reportable segments: U.S. Operations (about 35% of revenue), Chinese Operations (more than 20%), Western European Operations (more than 20%), Swiss Operations (some 5%), and Other.

Sales of Mettler-Toledo's laboratory products account for more than half of the company's revenue. Its lab product categories are laboratory balances, pipettes, analytical instruments, laboratory software (called LabX), automated chemistry tools, and process analytics.

Industrial products bring in nearly 40% of the company's revenue. Industrial product categories are weighing instruments, industrial terminals, transportation and logistics equipment, vehicle scale systems, industrial software, and product inspection (includes metal detectors and x-ray and camera-based systems).

Retail systems account for the remaining revenue. For retailers, the company offers networked scales and software, which can integrate information collected from throughout the store into an inventory management system. It also offers stand-alone scales for counter weighing and pricing, price finding, and label printing. In North America and select other markets, it offers automated packaging and labeling equipment for the meat backroom.

Mettler-Toledo also offers services, such as calibration, certification, repairs, and spare parts supply. The company makes proprietary components in its own plants and it contracts with other manufacturers to produce some non-proprietary components.

Geographic Reach

Mettler-Toledo's products are sold in more than 140 countries and has a direct presence in approximately 40 countries. The Americas accounts for about 40% of revenue and Europe and Asia (and other countries) each for about 30% each.

Mettler-Toledo makes components in plants in China, Switzerland, the UK, Germany, the UK, and Mexico. The company maintains executive offices in Columbus, Ohio and Greifensee, Switzerland.

Sales and Marketing

Mettler-Toledo sells through a variety of channels. Its direct sales force focuses on technically sophisticated products while less complicated products are handled by the company's indirect sales group. In the Americas, a significant portion of sales, including Ohaus-branded products, is made through indirect channels. Ohaus products target markets such as education in which customers pay less and get fewer features and less support and service.

Mettler-Toledo's customers are spread across the electronics, food retailing, laboratory, pharmaceutical, precious metals, and transportation markets, among others.

Financial Performance

Mettler-Toledo's performance for the past five years has continued to increase with 2021 as its highest performing year.

In 2021, net sales increased by $632 million or 18% to $3.7 billion in 2021 compared to $3.1 billion in 2020. The PendoTECH acquisition contributed 1% to its net sales in 2021. In 2021, Mettler-Toledo experienced broad-based growth with robust customer demand in most businesses and regions, with particularly strong growth in China.

The company's net income in 2021 increased by $167.2 million to $769 million compared to the prior year's $603 million, due to higher revenue in 2021.

Mettler-Toledo had cash and equivalents of $98.5 million at the end of the year. The company's operations generated $908.8 million in 2021. Investing activities and financing activities used $314.1 million and $590.5 million, respectively. Main cash uses were for acquisitions and repayments of borrowings.

Strategy

In 2022, Mettler-Toledo expects to continue to pursue the overall business growth strategies which they have followed in recent years:

Gaining Market Share - The company's global sales and marketing initiative, "Spinnaker," continues to be an important growth strategy. It aims to gain market share by implementing sophisticated sales and marketing programs, leveraging its extensive customer databases, and leveraging its product offering to larger customers through key account management.

Expanding Emerging Markets - Emerging markets, comprising Asia (excluding Japan), Eastern Europe, Latin America, Middle East, and Africa account for approximately 35% of its total net sales. The company has a two-pronged strategy in emerging markets: first, to capitalize on long-term growth opportunities in these markets, and second, to leverage its low-cost manufacturing operations in China.

Extending Its Technology Lead - Mettler-Toledo continues to focus on product innovation. In the last three years, the company spent approximately 5% of net sales on research and development. It seeks to accelerate product replacement cycles, as well as improve its product offerings and its capabilities with additional integrated technologies and software which also support its pricing differentiation. In addition, it aims to create value for its customers by having an intimate knowledge of its processes via the company's significant installed product base.

Expanding Its Margins - Mettler-Toledo continues to strive to improve its margins by more effectively pricing its products and services and optimizing its cost structure.

Pursuing Strategic Acquisitions - The company seeks to pursue "bolt-on" acquisitions that may leverage its global sales and service network, respected brand, extensive distribution channels, and technological leadership. It has identified life sciences, product inspection, and process analytics as three key areas for acquisitions.

Mergers and Acquisitions

In early 2021, Mettler-Toledo International acquired PendoTECH for an initial $185 million initial payment with a contingent consideration of up to $20 million and other post-closing amounts. PendoTECH is a manufacturer of single-use sensors, transmitters, control systems and software for measuring, monitoring and data collection primarily in bioprocess applications. The acquisition enables the company to expand its offering to include various sensors, including pressure, which is an important and common control parameter in downstream and upstream bioprocess applications.

HISTORY

Engineer Erhard Mettler weighed in to the precision scale industry in 1945 when he started Mettler Instrumente AG in Kusnacht, Switzerland. Mettler invented a single-pan analytical balance that proved to be more accurate than the then-standard two-pan weighing equipment. By the mid-1950s the company expanded into the US, and its equipment's popularity had the industry using "Mettler balance" to refer to nearly any high-precision laboratory scale.

In the early 1960s the company made its first acquisition and began expanding into analytical measuring instruments. Mettler moved its headquarters to Greifensee, Switzerland, near the decade's end. During the 1970s the company diversified into food retailing products and converted its product offerings from mechanical to electronic systems.

Swiss conglomerate Ciba-Geigy (now part of Novartis) bought Mettler in 1980; Erhard Mettler retired. In 1989 Ciba bought US industrial scale manufacturer Toledo Scale Corporation (founded 1901) and merged it with Mettler, renaming the unit Mettler-Toledo.

EXECUTIVES

Chairman, Director, Robert F. Spoerry, $368,121 total compensation

President, Chief Executive Officer, Patrick K. Kaltenbach

Chief Financial Officer, Shawn P. Vadala, $362,500 total compensation

General Counsel, Secretary, Michelle M. Roe

Region Officer, Marc de la Guéronnière, $282,442 total compensation

Division Officer, Peter Aggersbjerg, $322,218 total compensation

Division Officer, Gerhard Keller

Division Officer, Stefan Heiniger

Director, Wah-Hui Chu

Director, Domitille Doat-Le Bigot

Director, Olivier A. Filliol, $857,827 total compensation

Director, Elisha W. Finney

Director, Richard D. Francis

Director, Michael A. Kelly

Director, Thomas P. Salice

Director, Roland Diggelmann

Auditors : PricewaterhouseCoopers LLP

LOCATIONS

HQ: Mettler-Toledo International, Inc.
 1900 Polaris Parkway, Columbus, OH 43210

Phone: 614 438-4511   **Fax:** 614 438-4646
Web: www.mt.com

2018 Sales

	$ in mils	% of total
Americas		
United States	933.4	32
Other Americas	172.5	6
Europe		
Germany	205.3	7
France	141.5	5
United Kingdom	70.4	2
Switzerland	65.4	2
Other Europe	426.2	15
China	506.4	17
Rest of World	414.5	14
Total	2,935.6	100

PRODUCTS/OPERATIONS

2018 Sales by Sector

	% of total
Laboratory	51
Industrial	41
Retail	8
Total	100

2018 Sales

	$ mil.	% of total
Products	2,300.1	78
Service	635.5	22
Total	2,935.6	100

2018 Sales

	$ in mil.	% of total
U.S. Operations	1,112.2	27
Swiss Operations	895.8	22
Chinese Operations	767.6	19
Western European Operations	762.6	19
Other	556.4	13
Eliminations and Corporate	(1,159)	-
Total	2,935.6	100

Selected Products: Laboratory Instruments: Laboratory balances Liquid pipetting solutions Titrators Physical value analyzers Thermal analysis systems Other analytical instruments Moisture analyzers Density refractometers Food Retail Industrial Instruments: Industrial Weighing Instruments Industrial Terminals Transportation and Logistics Vehicle Scale Systems Industrial Software Product Inspection Selected Services: Value-added services Regulatory compliance Performance enhancements Application expertise Training Remote services

COMPETITORS

3M COMPANY
AVERY WEIGH-TRONIX, LLC
COGNEX CORPORATION
CROWN HOLDINGS, INC.
DIEBOLD NIXDORF, INCORPORATED
ELECTROCOMPONENTS PUBLIC LIMITED COMPANY
FASTENAL COMPANY
LAWSON PRODUCTS, INC.
MESA LABORATORIES, INC.
MSC INDUSTRIAL DIRECT CO., INC.

HISTORICAL FINANCIALS

Company Type: Public

Income Statement   FYE: December 31

	REVENUE ($mil)	NET INCOME ($mil)	NET PROFIT MARGIN	EMPLOYEES
12/21	3,717.9	768.9	20.7%	17,800
12/20	3,085.1	602.7	19.5%	16,500
12/19	3,008.6	561.1	18.6%	16,200
12/18	2,935.5	512.6	17.5%	16,000
12/17	2,725.0	375.9	13.8%	15,400
Annual Growth	8.1%	19.6%	—	3.7%

2021 Year-End Financials

Debt ratio: 50.6%   No. of shares ($ mil.): 22.8
Return on equity: —   Dividends
Cash ($ mil.): 98.5   Yield: —
Current Ratio: 1.11   Payout: —
Long-term debt ($ mil.): 1,580.8   Market value ($ mil.): 38,770.0

	STOCK PRICE ($) FY Close	P/E High/Low		PER SHARE ($) Earnings	Dividends	Book Value
12/21	1,697.21	51	31	32.78	0.00	7.50
12/20	1,139.68	47	23	24.91	0.00	12.04
12/19	793.28	38	22	22.47	0.00	17.44
12/18	565.58	34	26	19.88	0.00	23.68
12/17	619.52	47	28	14.24	0.00	21.43
Annual Growth	28.7%	—	—	23.2%	—	(23.1%)

Mid Penn Bancorp Inc

Mid Penn Bancorp is the holding company for Mid Penn Bank, which operates more than a dozen branches in central Pennsylvania's Cumberland, Dauphin, Northumberland, and Schuylkill counties. The bank offers full-service commercial banking, insurance, and trust services. Its deposit products include checking, savings, money market, and NOW accounts. Commercial real estate, construction, and land development loans account for nearly 80% of the company's loan portfolio; the bank also writes residential mortgages and business, agricultural, and consumer loans. Mid Penn is a descendant of Millersburg Bank, founded in 1868. Trust company CEDE & Co. owns about a third of Mid Penn Bancorp.

EXECUTIVES

President, Chief Executive Officer, Subsidiary Officer, Chairman, Director, Rory G. Ritrievi, $450,000 total compensation

Senior Executive Vice President, Chief Operating Officer, Subsidiary Officer, Justin T. Webb, $240,154 total compensation

Senior Executive Vice President, Chief Revenue Officer, Subsidiary Officer, Scott W. Micklewright, $240,154 total compensation

Senior Executive Vice President, Chief Financial Officer, Subsidiary Officer, Allison Johnson

Executive Vice President, Chief Retail Officer, Subsidiary Officer, Joan E. Dickinson
Subsidiary Officer, Joseph L. Paese, $188,731 total compensation
Director, Robert C. Grubic
Director, William A. Specht
Director, Howard R. Greenawalt
Director, Brian Arden Hudson
Director, John E. Noone
Director, Noble C. Quandel
Director, Kimberly J. Brumbaugh
Director, Maureen Gathagan
Director, Gregory M. Kerwin
Director, David E. Sparks
Director, Robert A. Abel
Director, Matthew G. DeSoto
Director, Theodore W. Mowery
Auditors : RSM US LLP

LOCATIONS

HQ: Mid Penn Bancorp Inc
349 Union Street, Millersburg, PA 17061
Phone: 866 642-7736
Web: www.midpennbank.com

COMPETITORS

COUNTY BANK CORP.
KS BANCORP, INC.
NORWAY BANCORP, INC.
POTOMAC BANCSHARES, INC.
SALISBURY BANCORP, INC.

HISTORICAL FINANCIALS
Company Type: Public

Income Statement — FYE: December 31

	ASSETS ($mil)	NET INCOME ($mil)	INCOME AS % OF ASSETS	EMPLOYEES
12/20	2,998.9	26.2	0.9%	466
12/19	2,231.1	17.7	0.8%	444
12/18	2,077.9	10.5	0.5%	406
12/17	1,170.3	7.0	0.6%	277
12/16	1,032.5	7.8	0.8%	257
Annual Growth	30.5%	35.4%	—	16.0%

2020 Year-End Financials
Return on assets: 0.9%
Return on equity: 10.5%
Long-term debt ($ mil.): —
No. of shares ($ mil.): 8.4
Sales ($ mil.): 125.8
Dividends Yield: 3.5%
Payout: 24.8%
Market value ($ mil.): 184.0

	STOCK PRICE ($) FY Close	P/E High	P/E Low	PER SHARE ($) Earnings	PER SHARE ($) Dividends	PER SHARE ($) Book Value
12/20	21.90	9	5	3.10	0.77	30.37
12/19	28.80	14	10	2.09	0.79	28.05
12/18	23.02	25	15	1.48	0.70	26.38
12/17	33.10	21	14	1.67	0.77	17.85
12/16	23.83	13	8	1.85	0.68	16.65
Annual Growth	(2.1%)	—	—	13.8%	3.2%	16.2%

Middlefield Banc Corp.

Here's your cash, stuck in the Middlefield Banc with you. The firm is the holding company for Middlefield Bank, which has about 10 offices in northeast and central Ohio. The community bank offers standard deposit services such as checking and savings accounts, CDs, and IRAs. Investments, insurance, and brokerage services are offered through an agreement with UVEST, a division of LPL Financial. Residential mortgage loans comprise more than 60% of the company's loan portfolio; commercial and industrial loans make up about 20%. The bank also offers commercial mortgages, construction loans, and consumer installment loans. Middlefield Banc is buying Liberty Bank, which operates three branches in northeast Ohio.

EXECUTIVES

Chairman, Director, William J. Skidmore
Vice-Chairman, Director, James J. McCaskey
President, Director, Ronald L. Zimmerly
Chief Executive Officer, Subsidiary Officer, Director, James R. Heslop, $233,135 total compensation
Finance Senior Vice President, Finance Chief Financial Officer, Finance Treasurer, Finance Subsidiary Officer, Michael C. Ranttila
Subsidiary Officer, Michael L. Allen
Subsidiary Officer, Courtney M. Erminio
Subsidiary Officer, Charles O. Moore
Subsidiary Officer, Alfred F. Thompson
Director, Carolyn J. Turk
Director, Thomas W. Bevan
Director, Spencer T. Cohn
Director, Mark R. Watkins
Director, Darryl E. Mast
Director, Kevin A. DiGeronimo
Director, Kenneth E. Jones
Director, Michael C. Voinovich
Auditors : S.R. Snodgrass, P.C.

LOCATIONS

HQ: Middlefield Banc Corp.
15985 East High Street, Middlefield, OH 44062-0035
Phone: 440 632-1666

COMPETITORS

COMMERCIAL BANCSHARES, INC.
EMCLAIRE FINANCIAL CORP.
FIRST KEYSTONE CORPORATION
GUARANTY BANCSHARES, INC.
PARKE BANCORP, INC.

HISTORICAL FINANCIALS
Company Type: Public

Income Statement — FYE: December 31

	ASSETS ($mil)	NET INCOME ($mil)	INCOME AS % OF ASSETS	EMPLOYEES
12/20	1,391.9	8.3	0.6%	0
12/19	1,182.4	12.7	1.1%	194
12/18	1,248.3	12.4	1.0%	200
12/17	1,106.3	9.4	0.9%	190
12/16	787.8	6.4	0.8%	139
Annual Growth	15.3%	6.8%	—	—

2020 Year-End Financials
Return on assets: 0.6%
Return on equity: 5.9%
Long-term debt ($ mil.): —
No. of shares ($ mil.): 6.3
Sales ($ mil.): 58.6
Dividends Yield: 2.6%
Payout: 43.1%
Market value ($ mil.): 144.0

	STOCK PRICE ($) FY Close	P/E High	P/E Low	PER SHARE ($) Earnings	PER SHARE ($) Dividends	PER SHARE ($) Book Value
12/20	22.50	20	10	1.30	0.60	22.54
12/19	26.09	25	12	1.95	0.57	21.45
12/18	42.43	28	21	1.92	0.59	19.77
12/17	48.20	35	25	1.55	0.54	18.63
12/16	38.70	26	21	1.52	0.54	17.00
Annual Growth	(12.7%)	—	—	(3.8%)	2.7%	7.3%

Midland States Bancorp Inc

Born in rural Illinois, Midland States Bancorp is now discovering banking life in new states. It is the $3 billion-asset holding company for Midland States Bank, a community bank that operates more than 35 branches in central and northern Illinois and around 15 branches in the St. Louis metropolitan area. The bank offers traditional consumer and commercial banking products and services, as well as merchant card services, insurance, and financial planning. Subsidiary Midland Wealth Management, which boasts $1.2 billion-plus in assets under administration, provides wealth management services, while Heartland Business Credit offers commercial equipment leasing services. Midland States Bancorp went public in 2016.

IPO

The bank holding company raised $80.1 million in its initial public offering. It plans to contribute some $25 million to Midland States Bank and use the rest for general corporate purposes including possible acquisitions.

Operations

About 57% of Midland States Bancorp's total revenue came from loan interest during 2014, while another 17% came from interest income from investment securities. The rest came from wealth management fees (8% of revenue), deposit account service charges (3%), ATM and interchange revenue (3%), mortgage banking revenue (3%), merchant services revenue (1%) and nonrecurring gains on the sales of assets (around 8%).

Subsidiary Love Funding provides multifamily and healthcare facility FHA financing.

Geographic Reach

Midland has more than 80 branches and offices across the US, with around 50 in Illinois and around the St. Louis metro area, and the rest in California, Colorado, Florida, Massachusetts, North Carolina, Ohio, Tennessee, and Texas.

Financial Performance

Midland States Bancorp's revenue climbed 3% to $93 million despite a decline in loan interest income during 2014, mostly thanks to profitable asset sales and other income.

Despite modest revenue growth in 2014, the bank's net income dove 67% to $3.2 billion as acquisition and integration expenses stemming from its late 2014 acquisition of Heartland ate up any revenue gains it had made. Excluding these nonrecurring items, the bank's net income grew modestly.

Strategy

Midland States Bancorp has been pursuing an acquisition and branch expansion growth strategy since 2007, after it replaced its executive management and laid out a plan to expand Midland States Bank's presence in Illinois. Midland States Bank continues to focus on moving into suburban areas and other markets in Illinois and Missouri that have growing populations. During 2015 it opened a new branches in the St. Louis region (in Jennings), downtown Joliet, and downtown Effingham areas, as well as a wealth management office in downtown Decatur.

The company also planned in 2016 to continue building its fast-growing wealth management business, which now makes up nearly 10% of its total revenue. Thanks to Midland's efforts, the business' wealth management assets under administration have skyrocketed twelve-fold since 2008, growing from $95 million then to $1.19 billion at the end of 2014.

Mergers and Acquisitions

Midland States Bancorp agreed to acquire HomeStar Financial Group in 2019 in a transaction valued at about $10 million. HomeStar's Manteno, Illinois-based HomeStar Bank and Financial Services has about $375 million in assets, $220 million in loans, and $330 million in deposits. HomeStar has five locations in northern Illinois. The deal expands Midland's presence in the Kankakee, Illinois metropolitan area.

In 2017 CEO Leon Holschbach signed a $175 million deal with rival Centrue Bank to merge. The two banks had been treading on each others' toes in Princeton, Illinois.

Company Background

Between 2008 and 2010, the bank's branch locations grew from just a half-dozen in central Illinois and St. Louis to nearly 30 around the state and in the St. Louis metropolitan area. During that time the bank acquired the assets of Waterloo Bancshares and WestBridge in St. Louis, AMCORE in northern Illinois, and Strategic Capital in central Illinois. It also opened new locations in some of its faster-growing markets. As a result of its efforts, Midland States Bancorp has watched its revenue and profits trend upward significantly from 2007 levels.

EXECUTIVES

Chairman, Director, Jeffrey C. Smith
President, Chief Executive Officer, Subsidiary Officer, Director, Jeffrey G. Ludwig, $472,000 total compensation
Executive Vice President, Subsidiary Officer, Jeffrey S. Mefford, $344,000 total compensation
Senior Vice President, Corporate Counsel, Subsidiary Officer, Douglas J. Tucker, $344,000 total compensation
Chief Financial Officer, Subsidiary Officer, Eric T. Lemke
Chief Accounting Officer, Principal Accounting Officer, Principal Financial Officer, Corporate Secretary, Donald J. Spring
Subsidiary Officer, Jeffrey A. Brunoehler
Subsidiary Officer, Sharon A. Schaubert
Subsidiary Officer, James R. Stewart, $315,000 total compensation
Director, R. Dean Bingham
Director, Jennifer L. DiMotta
Director, Deborah A. Golden
Director, Jerry L. McDaniel
Director, Jeffrey M. McDonnell
Director, Dwight A. Miller
Director, Richard T. Ramos
Director, Robert F. Schultz
Auditors: Crowe LLP

LOCATIONS

HQ: Midland States Bancorp Inc
1201 Network Centre Drive, Effingham, IL 62401
Phone: 217 342-7321
Web: www.midlandsb.com

PRODUCTS/OPERATIONS

2014 Sales

	$ in mil.	% of total
Interest income		
Loans	56.3	57
Investment Securities & others	16.8	17
Noninterest income		
Wealth management revenue	7.1	8
Service charges on deposit accounts	3.0	3
Mortgage banking revenue	3.0	3
Gain on sale of other assets	3.2	3
ATM and interchange revenue	2.6	3
Impairments	(2.6)	-
Other	4.1	6
Total	93.5	100

Selected Services
Bank By Phone
Bill Paying
Checking
Debit Card
Online Banking
Savings & CDs

COMPETITORS

F.N.B. CORPORATION
FIRST CITIZENS BANCSHARES, INC.
MAINSOURCE FINANCIAL GROUP, INC.
OLD NATIONAL BANCORP
PARK STERLING CORPORATION
PROSPERITY BANCSHARES, INC.
S&T BANCORP, INC.
UNITED BANKSHARES, INC.
UNITED COMMUNITY BANKS, INC.
WINTRUST FINANCIAL CORPORATION

HISTORICAL FINANCIALS

Company Type: Public

Income Statement				FYE: December 31
	ASSETS ($mil)	NET INCOME ($mil)	INCOME AS % OF ASSETS	EMPLOYEES
12/20	6,868.5	22.5	0.3%	904
12/19	6,087.0	55.7	0.9%	1,100
12/18	5,637.6	39.4	0.7%	1,100
12/17	4,412.7	16.0	0.4%	840
12/16	3,233.7	31.5	1.0%	715
Annual Growth	20.7%	(8.1%)	—	6.0%

2020 Year-End Financials
Return on assets: 0.3%
Return on equity: 3.5%
Long-term debt ($ mil.): —
No. of shares ($ mil.): 22.3
Sales ($ mil.): 306.1
Dividends
Yield: 5.9%
Payout: 97.2%
Market value ($ mil.): 399.0

	STOCK PRICE ($) FY Close	P/E High/Low		PER SHARE ($) Earnings	Dividends	Book Value
12/20	17.87	30	13	0.95	1.07	27.83
12/19	28.96	13	10	2.26	0.97	27.10
12/18	22.34	21	12	1.66	0.88	25.62
12/17	32.48	40	33	0.87	0.80	23.51
12/16	36.18	17	9	2.17	0.36	20.78
Annual Growth	(16.2%)	—	—	(18.7%)	31.3%	7.6%

MidWestOne Financial Group, Inc.

MidWestOne Financial Group is the holding company for MidWestOne Bank, which operates about 35 branches throughout central and east-central Iowa. The bank offers standard deposit products such as checking and savings accounts, CDs, and IRAs, in addition to trust services, private banking, home loans and investment services. More than two-thirds of MidWestOne Financial's loan portfolio consists of commercial real estate loans, and commercial mortgages and industrial loans. Founded in 1983, MidWestOne has total assets of $4.65 billion.

Operations

MidWestOne Financial Group provides a wide range of commercial and retail lending services to businesses, individuals and government agencies. The company's credit activities include commercial and residential real estate loans (approximately 70% of total loan portfolio), commercial and industrial loans (almost 25%), agricultural loans (nearly 5%), and consumer loans (less than 5%).

Overall, MidWestOne Financial Group generates roughly 85% of its revenue from interest income, more than 75% comes from interest and fees on loans, the remaining 10% comes from investment securities, the rest of its revenue comes from non-interest income.

Geographic Reach

Headquartered in Iowa City, MidWestOne Financial Group's MidWestOne Bank has branch offices and operating facilities in Minnesota, Wisconsin, Florida, and Colorado.

Sales and Marketing

MidWestOne Financial Group market its services to qualified lending customers. Lending officers actively solicit the business of new companies entering their market areas as well as long-standing members of the business communities in which the company operate.

Financial Performance

The company's revenue in 2019 increased by 36% to $174.9 million compared to $128.5 million in the prior year.

MidWestOne's consolidated net income for 2019 was $43.6 million, an increase of $13.3 million, or 44%, compared to $30.4 million for 2018. The increase in net income was due primarily to an increase in net interest income of $38.4 million, which was primarily attributable to the increased volume of interest-earning assets as a consequence of the ATBancorp merger.

Cash held by the company at the end of 2019 increased to $73.5 million. Cash provided by operations and investing activities were $47.3 million and $72.7 million, respectively. Cash used for financing activities was $92.1 million, mainly for short-term borrowings.

Strategy

MidWestOne's operating strategy is based upon a community banking model of delivering a comprehensive suite of financial products and services while following five operating principles: take care of its customers; hire and retain excellent employees; conduct business with the utmost integrity; work as one team; and learn constantly so the company can continually improve. Management believes the depth and breadth of the Company's products and services coupled with the personal and professional delivery of the same provides an appealing alternative to competitors.

Mergers and Acquisitions

In early 2019, MidWestOne Financial Group acquired ATBancorp, a bank holding company whose wholly-owned banking subsidiaries were ATSB and ABTW, for paid cash in the amount of $34.8 million. The acquisition helps to expand the company's business into new markets and grow the size of the company's business.

EXECUTIVES

Chairman, Subsidiary Officer, Director, Kevin W. Monson
President, Chief Operating Officer, Subsidiary Officer, Len D. Davaisher
Chief Executive Officer, Subsidiary Officer, Director, Charles N. Reeves
Senior Executive Vice President, Chief Financial Officer, Subsidiary Officer, Barry S. Ray, $162,256 total compensation
Senior Executive Vice President, Chief Investment Officer, Treasurer, Subsidiary Officer, James M. Cantrell, $222,200 total compensation
Senior Vice President, Chief Credit Officer, Subsidiary Officer, Gary L. Sims
Chief Accounting Officer, Subsidiary Officer, John J. Ruppel
Subsidiary Officer, David E. Lindstrom, $515,769 total compensation
Director, Janet E. Godwin
Director, Matthew J. Hayek
Director, Tracy S. McCormick
Director, Larry D. Albert
Director, Charles N. Funk, $437,000 total compensation
Director, Douglas H. Greeff
Director, Jennifer L. Hauschildt
Director, Richard R. Donohue
Director, Richard J. Hartig
Director, Nathaniel J. Kaeding
Director, Ruth E. Stanoch
Auditors : RSM US LLP

LOCATIONS

HQ: MidWestOne Financial Group, Inc.
 102 South Clinton Street, Iowa City, IA 52240
Phone: 319 356-5600
Web: www.midwestone.com

PRODUCTS/OPERATIONS

2015 Sales

	in mil.	% of total
Interest Income		
Interest and fees on loans	86.5	71
Interest on investment securities	13.3	11
Other	0.9	1
Non-Interest Income		
Trust, investment, and insurance fees	6.0	5
Other service charges, commissions and fees	5.7	5
Service charges and fees on deposit accounts	4.4	3
Mortgage origination and loan servicing fees	2.8	2
Other	2.3	2
Total	**121.9**	**100**

Selected Subsidiaries

MidWestOne Bank
MidWestOne Insurance Services, Inc.
MidWestOne Statutory Trust II

COMPETITORS

ASSOCIATED BANC-CORP
CNB FINANCIAL CORPORATION
FIRST FINANCIAL BANCORP.
INDEPENDENT BANK CORP.
UNIVEST FINANCIAL CORPORATION

HISTORICAL FINANCIALS

Company Type: Public

Income Statement — FYE: December 31

	ASSETS ($mil)	NET INCOME ($mil)	INCOME AS % OF ASSETS	EMPLOYEES
12/20	5,556.6	6.6	0.1%	780
12/19	4,653.5	43.6	0.9%	771
12/18	3,291.4	30.3	0.9%	597
12/17	3,212.2	18.6	0.6%	610
12/16	3,079.5	20.3	0.7%	587
Annual Growth	15.9%	(24.5%)	—	7.4%

2020 Year-End Financials

Return on assets: 0.1%
Return on equity: 1.2%
Long-term debt ($ mil.): —
No. of shares ($ mil.): 16.0
Sales ($ mil.): 223.4
Dividends
 Yield: 3.5%
 Payout: 400.0%
Market value ($ mil.): 392.0

	STOCK PRICE ($) FY Close	P/E High/Low		PER SHARE ($) Earnings	Dividends	Book Value
12/20	24.50	88	40	0.41	0.88	32.17
12/19	36.23	13	9	2.93	0.81	31.49
12/18	24.83	14	10	2.48	0.78	29.32
12/17	33.53	25	21	1.55	0.67	27.85
12/16	37.60	22	14	1.78	0.64	26.71
Annual Growth	(10.2%)	—	—	(30.7%)	8.3%	4.8%

Mitek Systems, Inc.

Mitek Systems is a company with character A software development company with expertise in computer vision, artificial intelligence, and machine learning. Serving more than 6,500 financial services organizations and leading marketplace and financial technology brands across the globe, its solutions are used by more than 80 million consumers. Using camera-equipped smartphone or tablet, Mobile Deposit allows its individuals and businesses to deposit checks remotely. Mobile Verify is an identity verification solution designed for the world's leading marketplace and sharing platforms, and financial services organizations. In addition, the company's other services include Mobile Fill and Mobile Docs.

EXECUTIVES

Chairman, Director, Bruce D. Hansen, $110,080 total compensation
Chief Executive Officer, Director, Scipio Maxaximus Carnecchia
Senior Vice President, Division Officer, Michael E. Diamond, $280,160 total compensation
Interim Chief Financial Officer, Principal Financial Officer, Principal Accounting Officer, Fuad Ahmad
Chief Technology Officer, Stephen J. Ritter, $283,920 total compensation
Director, Susan Repo
Director, William K. Aulet
Director, James C. Hale
Director, Alex W. Hart

Director, Kimberly S. Stevenson

Director, Donna C. Wells

Director, Scott R. Carter, $255,423 total compensation

Director, Rahul Gupta

Auditors : Mayer Hoffman McCann P.C.

LOCATIONS

HQ: Mitek Systems, Inc.
600 B Street, Suite 100, San Diego, CA 92101
Phone: 619 269-6800
Web: www.miteksystems.com

PRODUCTS/OPERATIONS

Selected Products and Services
ImageNet (financial document processing, payment processing, photo & video processing)
FraudProtect (image-based fraud detection, signature comparison)

COMPETITORS

DATACAP INC.
DOCUMENT SECURITY SYSTEMS, INC.
ECOPY, INC.
HEROIX LLC
INQUISITE, INC.
LATTICE TECHNOLOGY USA INC
MAVEN TECHNOLOGIES LLC
QUARK SOFTWARE INC.
RNA Productions, Inc
SECURITY FIRST CORP.

HISTORICAL FINANCIALS

Company Type: Public

Income Statement — FYE: September 30

	REVENUE ($mil)	NET INCOME ($mil)	NET PROFIT MARGIN	EMPLOYEES
09/21	119.7	7.9	6.7%	448
09/20	101.3	7.8	7.7%	360
09/19	84.5	(0.7)	—	284
09/18	63.5	(11.8)	—	308
09/17	45.3	14.0	31.0%	141
Annual Growth	27.5%	(13.3%)	—	33.5%

2021 Year-End Financials
Debt ratio: 28.8%
Return on equity: 4.9%
Cash ($ mil.): 30.3
Current Ratio: 5.20
Long-term debt ($ mil.): 120.9
No. of shares ($ mil.): 44.1
Dividends
  Yield: —
  Payout: —
Market value ($ mil.): 817.0

	STOCK PRICE ($) FY Close	P/E High/Low		PER SHARE ($) Earnings	Dividends	Book Value
09/21	18.50	128	63	0.18	0.00	4.37
09/20	12.74	69	29	0.18	0.00	3.17
09/19	9.65	—	—	(0.02)	0.00	2.66
09/18	7.05	—	—	(0.33)	0.00	2.51
09/17	9.50	25	13	0.40	0.00	1.82
Annual Growth	18.1%	—	—	(18.1%)	—	24.4%

MKS Instruments Inc

MKS Instruments makes systems that analyze and control gases during semiconductor manufacturing and other thin film industrial processes such as those used to make flat panel displays, LEDs, solar cells, and data storage media. Top customers include chip equipment heavyweights Applied Materials and Lam Research. Other applications include flexible and rigid printed circuit board (PCB) processing/fabrication, glass coating, laser marking, measurement and scribing, natural gas and oil production, electronic thin films, and environmental monitoring. MKS Instruments generates some 45% of its revenue from customers in the US. The company was founded in 1961.

Operations

The company groups its product offering by three segments: Vacuum & Analysis (some 60% of sales), Light & Motion (approximately 30%) and Equipment & Solutions (around 10%).

The Vacuum & Analysis segment provides a broad range of instruments, components and subsystems which are derived from our core competencies in pressure measurement and control, flow measurement and control, gas and vapor delivery, gas composition analysis, electronic control technology, reactive gas generation and delivery, power generation and delivery and vacuum technology.

The Light & Motion segment provides a broad range of instruments, components and subsystems which are derived from its core competencies in lasers, photonics, optics, precision motion control and vibration control.

The Equipment & Solutions segment provides a range of laser-based system and test products.

Overall, its products account for around 85% of sales, while its services account for the rest.

Geographic Reach

Headquartered in Andover, Massachusetts, the company has offices, manufacturing facilities, sales, research and development, and warehouses in Beaverton and Portland (Oregon), Broomfield (Colorado), Irvine and Milpitas (California), Rochester (New York), and Wilmington (Massachusetts). It also has international operations in China, France, Israel, Mexico, and Singapore.

The US market accounts for some 45% of sales, followed by South Korea, and China with over 10% of sales each. Sales Europe accounts for nearly 10%, and the rest were generated from other Asian countries.

Sales and Marketing

The company markets and sells its products and services through its global direct sales organization, an international network of independent distributors and sales representatives, its websites and product catalogs. It primary serves markets including semiconductor, industrial technologies, life and health sciences, research and defense.

Its top ten customers accounted for more than 45% of sales in 2021. Its two largest customers, Lam Research Corporation and Applied Materials, Inc., accounted for about 25% of sales combined.

Financial Performance

MKS Instrument's performance for the past five years have fluctuated but has had an upward trend for the latter part of the period with 2021 as its highest performing year.

The company's revenue increased by $619 million to $2.9 billion for 2021 as compared to 2020's revenue of $2.3 billion.

Net income for fiscal year end 2021 increased by $201 million to $551 million as compared to the prior year's net income of $350 million.

Cash held by the company at the end of fiscal 2021 increased to $966 million. Cash provided by operations was $639.5 million. Investing activities and financing activities used $204.6 million and $65.1 million, respectively. Main cash uses were for purchases of investments and dividend payments.

Strategy

MKS' products incorporate sophisticated technologies to measure, monitor, deliver, analyze, power, control and improve complex semiconductor and advanced manufacturing processes, thereby enhancing uptime, yield and throughput for its customers. The company's products have continuously advanced as it strives to meet its customers' evolving needs.

The company involves its marketing, engineering, manufacturing and sales personnel in the development of new products in order to reduce the time to market for new products. The company's employees also work closely with its customers' development personnel, helping MKS to identify and define future technical needs on which to focus research and development efforts. The company supports research at academic institutions targeted at advances in materials science, semiconductor process development and photonics.

EXECUTIVES

Chairman, Director, Gerald G. Colella, $993,269 total compensation

President, Chief Executive Officer, Director, John T.C. Lee, $542,431 total compensation

Corporate Marketing, Project Management Office & Global Service Senior Vice President, David P. Henry

Senior Vice President, Division Officer, Eric R. Taranto

Senior Vice President, Chief Financial Officer, Treasurer, Seth H. Bagshaw, $509,231 total compensation

Senior Vice President, Division Officer, Mark M. Gitin

Senior Vice President, General Counsel, Secretary, Kathleen F. Burke

Division Officer, James A. Schreiner

Lead Director, Director, Jacqueline F. Moloney

Director, Geoffrey Wild

Director, Peter J. Cannone

Director, Rajeev Batra
Director, Joseph B. Donahue
Director, Elizabeth A. Mora
Director, Michelle M. Warner
Auditors : PricewaterhouseCoopers LLP

LOCATIONS

HQ: MKS Instruments Inc
2 Tech Drive, Suite 201, Andover, MA 01810
Phone: 978 645-5500
Web: www.mksinst.com

2018 Sales

	$ mil	% of total
United States	1,022.6	49
Asia		
South Korea	203.6	10
Japan	193.3	9
Asia	411.6	20
Europe	244	12
Total	2,075.1	100

PRODUCTS/OPERATIONS

2018 Sales by Products

	$ mil	% of total
Vacuum Solutions Products	534.6	26
Power, Plasma, and Reactive Gas Solutions Products	610.1	29
Analytical and Control Solutions Products	116.1	6
Laser Products	274.8	13
Optics Products	227.6	11
Photonics Products	311.9	15
Total	2,075.1	100

2018 Sales

	$ mil	% of total
Vacuum and Analysis	1,260.8	61
Light and Motion	814.3	39
Total	2,075.1	100

Selected Products

Instruments and Control Systems
    Pressure Measurement and Control Products
    Baratron® Pressure Measurement Products
    Automatic Pressure and Vacuum Control Products
    Materials Delivery Products
    Flow Measurement and Control Products
    Gas Composition Analysis Products
    Mass Spectrometry-Based Gas Composition
Analysis Instruments
    Fourier Transform Infra-Red (FTIR) Based Gas Composition Analysis Products
    Control and Information Technology Products
    Control Products
    Information Technology Products
Power and Reactive Gas Products
    Power Delivery Products
    Reactive Gas Generation Products
    Processing Thin Films
    Equipment Cleaning
Vacuum Products
    Vacuum Gauging Products
    Vacuum Valves, Stainless Steel Components,
Process Solutions and Custom Stainless Steel Hardware
    Custom Manufactured Components

COMPETITORS

AMETEK, INC.
COGNEX CORPORATION
ENTEGRIS, INC.
FORTIVE CORPORATION
HURCO COMPANIES, INC.
KEYSIGHT TECHNOLOGIES, INC.
OMRON CO.,LTD.
ONTO INNOVATION INC.
Siemens AG

WATERS CORPORATION

HISTORICAL FINANCIALS
Company Type: Public

Income Statement   FYE: December 31

	REVENUE ($mil)	NET INCOME ($mil)	NET PROFIT MARGIN	EMPLOYEES
12/20	2,330.0	350.1	15.0%	5,800
12/19	1,899.7	140.3	7.4%	5,500
12/18	2,075.1	392.8	18.9%	4,851
12/17	1,915.9	339.1	17.7%	4,923
12/16	1,295.3	104.8	8.1%	4,667
Annual Growth	15.8%	35.2%	—	5.6%

2020 Year-End Financials
Debt ratio: 21.2%   No. of shares ($ mil.): 55.2
Return on equity: 15.9%   Dividends
Cash ($ mil.): 608.3   Yield: 0.5%
Current Ratio: 4.83   Payout: 12.6%
Long-term debt ($ mil.): 815   Market value ($ mil.): 8,304.0

	STOCK PRICE ($) FY Close	P/E High/Low		PER SHARE ($) Earnings	Dividends	Book Value
12/20	150.45	25	11	6.33	0.80	42.77
12/19	110.01	45	25	2.55	0.80	37.06
12/18	64.61	17	8	7.14	0.78	34.66
12/17	94.50	17	10	6.16	0.71	29.23
12/16	59.40	31	16	1.94	0.68	23.14
Annual Growth	26.2%	—	—	34.4%	4.1%	16.6%

Moelis & Co

EXECUTIVES

Chairman, Chief Executive Officer, Kenneth D. Moelis, $400,000 total compensation
Vice-Chairman, Managing Director, Director, Eric Cantor
Co-President, Managing Director, Navid Mahmoodzadegan, $400,000 total compensation
Co-President, Managing Director, Jeffrey Raich, $400,000 total compensation
Chief Financial Officer, Joseph W. Simon, $400,000 total compensation
Chief Operating Officer, Elizabeth Crain, $400,000 total compensation
Chief Compliance Officer, General Counsel, Secretary, Osamu R. Watanabe
Lead Independent Director, Director, Kenneth L. Shropshire
Director, John A. Allison
Director, Yolonda C. Richardson
Auditors : DELOITTE & TOUCHE LLP

LOCATIONS

HQ: Moelis & Co
399 Park Avenue, 5th Floor, New York, NY 10022
Phone: 212 883-3800
Web: www.moelis.com

HISTORICAL FINANCIALS
Company Type: Public

Income Statement   FYE: December 31

	REVENUE ($mil)	NET INCOME ($mil)	NET PROFIT MARGIN	EMPLOYEES
12/20	943.2	178.8	19.0%	903
12/19	746.5	105.0	14.1%	879
12/18	885.8	140.6	15.9%	845
12/17	684.6	29.4	4.3%	749
12/16	613.3	38.3	6.3%	645
Annual Growth	11.4%	46.9%	—	8.8%

2020 Year-End Financials
Debt ratio: —   No. of shares ($ mil.): 63.9
Return on equity: 38.6%   Dividends
Cash ($ mil.): 202.4   Yield: 8.8%
Current Ratio: 0.58   Payout: 332.2%
Long-term debt ($ mil.): —   Market value ($ mil.): 2,992.0

	STOCK PRICE ($) FY Close	P/E High/Low		PER SHARE ($) Earnings	Dividends	Book Value
12/20	46.76	15	8	2.95	4.15	7.50
12/19	31.92	23	14	1.89	3.25	7.33
12/18	34.38	21	10	2.78	4.88	7.21
12/17	48.50	52	35	0.78	2.48	6.09
12/16	33.90	19	12	1.58	3.29	4.10
Annual Growth	8.4%	—	—	16.9%	6.0%	16.3%

Monolithic Power Systems Inc

Monolithic Power Systems (MPS) is a global company that provides high-performance, semiconductor-based power electronics solutions. The fabless semiconductor company offers digital, mixed-signal and analog microchips ? especially DC-to-DC converters for powering networking and telecommunication infrastructure, wireless access points, notebook computers, and other consumer electronic devices. Its core strengths include deep system-level and applications knowledge, strong analog design expertise and innovative proprietary process technologies. The company was founded in 1997. It generates the majority of its sales outside the US.

Operations

MPS operates in one reportable segment that includes the design, development, marketing and sale of high-performance analog solutions. The company divides its revenue into two major product families. Its DC-to-DC products convert and control voltages within a broad range of electronic systems, such as portable electronic devices, wireless LAN access points, computers and notebooks, monitors, infotainment applications and medical equipment. The DC-to-DC chips are monolithic in which it accounts for some 95% of the company's total sales. MPS's lighting control products are used in backlighting and general illumination products. Lighting control ICs for backlighting are used in systems that provide the light source for LCD panels typically found in computers and notebooks, monitors, car navigation systems and televisions. Backlighting solutions are typically either white light emitting diode lighting sources or cold cathode fluorescent lamps. The segment generates approximately 5% of total sales.

Geographic Reach

MPS is headquartered in Kirkland, Washington, but generates most of its revenue in Asia. Its semiconductor products are assembled and packaged by independent subcontractors in China and Malaysia, while its wafers are manufactured in foundries located in China, Taiwan and Korea. The finished products don't have far to go since about 60% of sales are in China; followed by about 15% from Taiwan. MPS has sales offices in the US, Europe, Singapore, India, China, Korea, and Japan.

Sales and Marketing

MPS sells through distributors, value-added resellers, and directly to original equipment manufacturers (OEMs), original design manufacturers (ODMs), and electronic manufacturing service (EMS) companies. Sales to its largest distributor accounted for about 25% of revenue in 2021. In addition, MPS generates around 30% of total sales from Computing and Storage end market, followed by Consumers with about 25%. The remaining sales are from Industrial, Communications, and Automotive, which brings in around 45% of total sales combined.

Financial Performance

Revenue in 2021 was $1.2 billion, an increase of $363.3 million, or 43%, from $844.5 million in 2020. Overall unit shipments increased by 31% and average sales prices increased by approximately 8% compared to the same period in 2020. The increase in average sales prices was primarily driven by favorable changes in product mix with more sales coming from products with higher unit prices.

In 2021, the company had a net income of $242 million, a 47% increase from the previous year.

The company's cash at the end of 2021 was $189.4 million. Operating activities generated $320 million, while investing activities used $378.9 million, mainly for purchases of short-term investments. Financing activities used another $90.2 million, primarily for dividends and dividend equivalents paid.

EXECUTIVES

Chairman, President, Chief Executive Officer, Director, Michael R. Hsing, $643,846 total compensation

Sales Senior Vice President, Worldwide Sales Senior Vice President, Tactical Marketing Senior Vice President, Marketing Senior Vice President, Maurice Sciammas, $340,000 total compensation

Strategic Corporate Development Vice President, Strategic Corporate Development General Counsel, Strategic Corporate Development Corporate Secretary, Saria Tseng, $340,000 total compensation

Chief Financial Officer, Corporate Controller, Bernie Blegen, $295,308 total compensation

Region Officer, Deming Xiao, $340,000 total compensation

Director, Herbert Chang

Director, Victor K. Lee

Director, Carintia Martinez

Director, James C. Moyer, $175,385 total compensation

Director, Jeff Zhou

Director, Eileen Wynne

Auditors : Ernst & Young LLP

LOCATIONS

HQ: Monolithic Power Systems Inc
5808 Lake Washington Blvd. NE, Kirkland, WA 98033
Phone: 425 296-9956
Web: www.monolithicpower.com

2011 Sales

	$ mil.	% of total
China	113.5	58
Taiwan	23.6	12
Europe	14.4	7
South Korea	14.2	7
Japan	10.7	6
US	4.4	2
Other regions	15.7	8
Total	196.5	100

PRODUCTS/OPERATIONS

2011 Sales

	$ mil.	% of total
DC-to-DC converters	165.6	85
LCD backlight inverters	26.5	13
Audio amplifiers	4.4	2
Total	196.5	100

Selected Products

AC/DC Offline
  Bridge rectifier
  Controllers and regulators
  Synchronous rectifiers
Audio amplifiers
Backlighting solutions
  EL drivers
  White LED drivers (inductors and charge pumps)
Automotive
Battery chargers
  Cradle chargers
  Linear chargers
  Protection
  Switching chargers
Full-bridge and half-bridge power drivers
Isolated and transformer-based power supplies
Lighting and illumination
Low dropout (LDO) linear regulators
Motor drivers
  Brushless DC motor drivers
  Stepper DC motor drivers
Photo-flash chargers and drivers
Power Over Ethernet powered device (PD) solutions
  PD controllers
  PD identity
Precision analog
  Analog switches
  High-side current sense amplifiers
  Operational amplifiers
  Voltage reference
Supervisory circuits and voltage supervisors
Switching power supply regulators
  DC-DC (step-down)
  Controller
  Intelli-Phase (monolithic driver + MOSFET)
  Non-synchronous switcher
  Synchronous switcher
  DC-DC (step-up)
  Controller
  Energy storage and release management
  LNB power supply
  Non-synchronous switcher
  Synchronous switcher
USB and current-limit load switches

COMPETITORS

AVX CORPORATION
BEL FUSE INC.
CYPRESS SEMICONDUCTOR CORPORATION
DIODES INCORPORATED
MACOM TECHNOLOGY SOLUTIONS HOLDINGS, INC.
MULTI-FINELINE ELECTRONIX, INC.
OMNIVISION TECHNOLOGIES, INC.
SILICON IMAGE, INC.
SILICON LABORATORIES INC.
SKYWORKS SOLUTIONS, INC.

HISTORICAL FINANCIALS

Company Type: Public

Income Statement — FYE: December 31

	NET REVENUE ($mil)	NET INCOME ($mil)	NET PROFIT MARGIN	EMPLOYEES
12/20	844.4	164.3	19.5%	2,209
12/19	627.9	108.8	17.3%	2,002
12/18	582.3	105.2	18.1%	1,737
12/17	470.9	65.2	13.8%	1,534
12/16	388.6	52.7	13.6%	1,417
Annual Growth	21.4%	32.9%	—	11.7%

2020 Year-End Financials

Debt ratio: —   No. of shares ($ mil.): 45.2
Return on equity: 18.8%   Dividends
Cash ($ mil.): 334.9   Yield: 0.5%
Current Ratio: 5.73   Payout: 60.7%
Long-term debt ($ mil.): —   Market value ($ mil.): 16,578.0

	STOCK PRICE ($) FY Close	P/E High/Low		PER SHARE ($) Earnings	Dividends	Book Value
12/20	366.23	98	37	3.50	2.00	21.35
12/19	178.02	73	43	2.38	1.60	17.73
12/18	116.25	61	42	2.36	1.20	15.06
12/17	112.36	80	52	1.50	0.80	12.54
12/16	81.93	66	43	1.26	0.80	10.57
Annual Growth	45.4%	—	—	29.1%	25.7%	19.2%

Morningstar Inc

Morningstar offers investment management services and research to individuals, financial advisors, asset managers, retirement-plan providers and sponsors, and institutional investors in the private capital markets. The company supports asset managers, individual and institutional investors, and financial advisors with an extensive product line of web-based tools, investment data, and research. The company also provides investment-management services, investment analysis platforms, and portfolio management and accounting software tools to advisors and financial institutions. The US is the company's largest market; it provides around 70% of its revenue.

Operations
Morningstar operates through a single reporting segment and categorizes its revenue streams as license-, asset-, and transaction-based. License-based revenue derives from subscription services grant access to the company's technology and data on either a per-user or enterprise basis for a specified period of time. Its products include Morningstar Data, Morningstar Direct, Morningstar Advisor Workstation, Morningstar Office Cloud, PitchBook, Premium Memberships on Morningstar.com, and other similar products. License sales represent almost two-thirds of the company's revenue.

Morningstar garners asset-based revenue from fees for assets that it manages or on which it advises. Products in the category include Morningstar Investment Management, Workplace Solutions, and Morningstar Indexes. Ad sales on the company's website and credit rating products make up the company's transaction-based revenue. Asset-based and transaction-based sales account for around 15% of Morningstar's revenue each.

Geographic Reach
Chicago-based Morningstar has operations in about 30 countries, including Australia, Brazil, Switzerland, Taiwan, Thailand, the UK, the US, India, Japan, China, South Africa, the United Arab Emirates, and Singapore.

About 70% of its sales come from the US. The UK and Continent Europe provide nearly 10% each, while Canada accounts for over 5% of revenue.

Sales and Marketing
Its largest customer accounts for less than 5% of its revenue. The company focuses on six primary customer groups: advisor; asset management; fixed-income security issuers and arrangers; private market/venture capital investors; workplace/retirement; and individual investors.

Morningstar's sales and marketing expenses were $273.8 million, $206.4 million, and $177.9 million for the years 2021, 2020, and 2019, respectively.

Financial Performance
The company's revenue in 2021 increased by 22% to $1.7 billion compared to $1.4 billion in the prior year.

Net income in 2021 decreased to $193.3 million compared to $223.6 million in the prior year.

Cash held by the company at the end of 2021 increased to $483.8 million. Operating activities $449.9 million while investing and financing activities used $167.7 million and $211.8 million, respectively. Main cash uses were capital expenditures and repayment of term facility.

Strategy
Morningstar's strategy is to deliver insights and experiences essential to investing. Proprietary data sets, meaningful analytics, independent research, and effective investment strategies are at the core of the powerful digital solutions that investors across its client segments rely on. The company has a keen focus on innovation across data, research, product, and delivery so that it can effectively cater to the evolving needs and expectations of investors globally.

The company focused on these four strategic priorities: deliver differentiated insights across asset classes to public and private market investors; establish a leading ESG position across each business; drive operational excellence and scalability to support growth targets, and build an inclusive culture that drives exceptional talent engagement and development.

Mergers and Acquisitions
In 2022, Morningstar acquired Leveraged Commentary & Data (LCD), a market leader in news, research, data, insights, and indexes for the leveraged finance market from S&P Global, for $650 million in cash. The acquisition of LCD complements PitchBook's robust product and research capabilities and provide coverage of every metric of the leveraged loan market, including structure, pricing, yield, volume, along with secondary market performance and LBO/private equity activity.

In 2021, Morningstar agreed to acquire 100% of Praemium's operations in the UK, Jersey, Hong Kong, and Dubai. The consideration for the transaction will comprise cash of Â£35 million, subject to completion adjustments. The end-to-end solution from Praemium will add to Morningstar's existing data, fund profiles, portfolio analytics, and investment management capabilities available to advisers, creating a complete experience designed to empower investor success at scale. Praemium and Morningstar will work together to ensure a smooth transition for customers and employees.

Also in 2021, Morningstar announced the acquisition of Moorgate Benchmarks, a privately held European-based global provider of index design, calculation, and administration. ETFS Capital provided seed funding to Moorgate Benchmarks in 2019 and had been its sole external investor. With this transaction, Moorgate Benchmarks becomes a wholly owned subsidiary of Morningstar. Financial terms were not disclosed.

Company Background
In 1984, Joe Mansueto establishes Morningstar in his Chicago apartment. In 1999, Morningstar establishes presence in Australia and New Zealand and expands operations into Canada and launches online retirement advice service in 2000.

HISTORY
Joseph Mansueto founded Morningstar in 1984, using a line borrowed from Thoreau's Walden ("The sun is but a morning star"). Armed with an MBA and experience culled from a stint as a securities analyst for Harris Associates, Mansueto published Mutual Fund Sourcebook, a tome outlining performance histories and other information on 400 stock mutual funds. The boom in mutual funds during the early 1980s spurred interest in Morningstar's product and prompted the company to add a second publication, Morningstar Mutual Funds, two years later.

The company's 1994 acquisition of MarketBase helped the firm add stock information to its coverage. A 5% staff cut in 1996 and the cessation of some of its publications helped reverse Morningstar's sagging fortunes. It took to cyberspace the following year when it launched Morningstar.net (now Morningstar.com). That year the company partnered with Japanese digital dynamo SOFTBANK to create Morningstar Japan and present financial information to investors in that country.

Don Phillips, who had joined Morningstar as its first analyst in 1986, was appointed CEO in 1998. The company began offering a subscription-based premium service feature for its website to provide users with expanded financial coverage. In 1999 Morningstar extended its reach, partnering with FPG Research to offer financial information to residents of Australia and New Zealand. Later that year SOFTBANK invested $91 million in Morningstar.

In 2000 Morningstar established website MorningstarAdvisor.com, relaunched its flagship site with additional information and tools, and opened offices in Hong Kong, South Korea, and the UK. Founder and chairman Joe Mansueto also assumed the role of CEO in 2000 and made Phillips a managing director of the company.

The following year the company launched its website in Germany, Italy, the Netherlands, Spain, and the UK. Morningstar added Australian financial publisher Aspect Huntley to its stable in 2006. It paid nearly $23 million for the provider of equity information, research, and financial trade publishing in order to expand outside the US. In 2007 Morningstar paid some $58 million for the mutual fund data business from Standard & Poor's.

A significant acquisition for Morningstar was the 2008 purchase of 10-K Wizard, an electronic provider of SEC filing documents, for $12.5 million. The purchase bolstered Morningstar's research capabilities and aids in the company's goal of providing greater transparency to equity investments.

Other 2008 purchases included London market data firm Tenfore Systems for Â£13.5 million ($20.9 million). Tenfore provides information on stocks, commodities, derivatives, and other investments, and the deal allows Morningstar to bundle real-time data such as stock prices with its research. The company purchased Fundamental Data Limited, a provider of data on closed-end funds in the UK, for some Â£11 million (approximately $19 million), as well as the Hemscott data, media, and investor relations website businesses from Ipreo for about $52 million.

The acquisitive Morningstar entered a new distribution channel in 2009 with the nearly $52 million buy of Logical Information Machines, a provider of market pricing data and data management services to the agricultural, energy, and financial sectors. The Logical Information Machines acquisition complements and expands many of the services already provided by Morningstar, including data and software management.

Also in 2009 the company grew its investment management business with the acquisition of Intech Pty Ltd. Now doing business as Ibbotson Associates, the subsidiary provides multi-manager and investment portfolio solutions in Sydney, Australia.

In 2010 Morningstar acquired Realpoint, a statistical ratings organization that specializes in structured finance, for some $52 million in cash and stock. Morningstar made the deal to build on its recent entry into corporate credit ratings. (In 2011 it rebranded Realpoint under the Morningstar name.)

International acquisitions in 2010 included Old Broad Street Research, a provider of fund research, ratings, and investment consulting services in the UK, for about Â£12 million (or approximately $18 million). Also in 2010 it purchased Seeds Group, a provider of investment consulting services and fund research in France. The company launched local language versions of Morningstar Direct in Spain, France, and Germany in 2010, adding to existing versions in China and Italy.

EXECUTIVES

Executive Chairman, Joe Mansueto, $100,000 total compensation
Chief Executive Officer, Director, Kunal Kapoor, $387,500 total compensation
Chief Financial Officer, Jason M. Dubinsky, $400,000 total compensation
Chief Revenue Officer, Danny Dunn, $300,000 total compensation
General Counsel, Patrick J. Maloney
Division Officer, Bevin Desmond, $256,818 total compensation
Division Officer, Haywood Kelly, $300,000 total compensation
Division Officer, Daniel Needham, $300,000 total compensation
Director, Robin Diamonte
Director, Cheryl Francis
Director, Steve Kaplan
Director, Gail Landis
Director, Bill Lyons
Director, Jack Noonan
Director, Caroline J. Tsay
Director, Hugh J. Zentmyer
Auditors : KPMG LLP

LOCATIONS

HQ: Morningstar Inc
22 West Washington Street, Chicago, IL 60602
Phone: 312 696-6000
Web: www.morningstar.com

PRODUCTS/OPERATIONS

Selected Products and Services
Morningstar Advisor Workstation (Web-based investment planning software)
Morningstar FundInvestor (monthly mutual fund newsletter)
Morningstar Licensed Data (electronic investment data feeds)
Morningstar Mutual Funds (semimonthly information on 1,600 mutual funds)
Morningstar Principia (CD-ROM-based investment planning software)
Morningstar StockInvestor (monthly stock newsletter)
MorningstarAdvisor.com (market analysis, stock and fund information, portfolio tools, and investment research for advisors)
Morningstar.com (market analysis, stock and fund information, portfolio tools, and investment research for individuals)

COMPETITORS

ALLIANCEBERNSTEIN HOLDING L.P.
EATON VANCE CORP.
FRANKLIN RESOURCES, INC.
GAMCO INVESTORS, INC.
INVESCO LTD.
S&P GLOBAL INC.
SEI INVESTMENTS COMPANY
SS&C TECHNOLOGIES HOLDINGS, INC.
STONEX GROUP INC.
T. ROWE PRICE GROUP, INC.

HISTORICAL FINANCIALS
Company Type: Public

Income Statement				FYE: December 31
	REVENUE ($mil)	NET INCOME ($mil)	NET PROFIT MARGIN	EMPLOYEES
12/20	1,389.5	223.6	16.1%	7,979
12/19	1,179.0	152.0	12.9%	6,737
12/18	1,019.9	183.0	17.9%	5,416
12/17	911.7	136.9	15.0%	4,920
12/16	798.6	161.0	20.2%	4,595
Annual Growth	14.9%	8.6%	—	14.8%

2020 Year-End Financials
Debt ratio: 16.7%
Return on equity: 18.9%
Cash ($ mil.): 422.5
Current Ratio: 1.17
Long-term debt ($ mil.): 449.1
No. of shares ($ mil.): 42.9
Dividends
Yield: 0.5%
Payout: 29.9%
Market value ($ mil.): 9,934.0

	STOCK PRICE ($) FY Close	P/E High/Low		PER SHARE ($)		
				Earnings	Dividends	Book Value
12/20	231.57	44	21	5.18	1.22	29.64
12/19	151.31	46	30	3.52	1.12	25.29
12/18	109.84	33	21	4.25	1.00	21.93
12/17	96.97	30	23	3.18	0.92	18.92
12/16	73.56	24	18	3.72	0.88	16.22
Annual Growth	33.2%	—	—	8.6%	8.4%	16.3%

Morris St Bancshares Inc

LOCATIONS

HQ: Morris St Bancshares Inc
301 Bellevue Avenue, Dublin, GA 31021
Phone: 478 272-5202
Web: www.morris.bank

HISTORICAL FINANCIALS
Company Type: Public

Income Statement				FYE: December 31
	REVENUE ($mil)	NET INCOME ($mil)	NET PROFIT MARGIN	EMPLOYEES
12/20	59.1	17.4	29.4%	0
12/19	51.6	13.6	26.4%	0
12/18	41.1	15.2	37.0%	0
12/17	35.9	13.3	37.2%	0
12/16	32.0	11.0	34.5%	0
Annual Growth	16.5%	11.9%	—	—

2020 Year-End Financials
Debt ratio: 2.3%
Return on equity: 14.4%
Cash ($ mil.): 149.8
Current Ratio: 0.34
Long-term debt ($ mil.): 28.6
No. of shares ($ mil.): 2.0
Dividends
Yield: —
Payout: 21.0%
Market value ($ mil.): 127.0

	STOCK PRICE ($) FY Close	P/E High/Low		PER SHARE ($)		
				Earnings	Dividends	Book Value
12/20	60.50	8	6	8.31	1.75	61.81
12/19	65.00	11	9	6.87	0.00	53.10
Annual Growth	(6.9%)	—	—	21.0%	—	16.4%

Mountain Commerce Bancorp Inc

Auditors : Dixon Hughes Goodman LLP

LOCATIONS

HQ: Mountain Commerce Bancorp Inc
6101 Kingston Pike, P.O. Box 52942, Knoxville, TN 37919
Phone: —
Web: www.mcb.com

HISTORICAL FINANCIALS
Company Type: Public

Income Statement				FYE: December 31
	REVENUE ($mil)	NET INCOME ($mil)	NET PROFIT MARGIN	EMPLOYEES
12/20	46.1	10.1	22.0%	0
12/19	43.8	12.3	28.2%	0
12/18	37.5	10.1	27.1%	0
12/17	30.2	5.4	18.1%	0
12/16	25.1	4.2	16.8%	0
Annual Growth	16.3%	24.5%	—	—

MP Materials Corp

2020 Year-End Financials
Debt ratio: 6.6%
Return on equity: 10.4%
Cash ($ mil.): 72.3
Current Ratio: 0.17
Long-term debt ($ mil.): 63.9
No. of shares ($ mil.): 6.2
Dividends
  Yield: —
  Payout: —
Market value ($ mil.): 129.0

	STOCK PRICE ($) FY Close	P/E High/Low		PER SHARE ($) Earnings	Dividends	Book Value
12/20	20.50	14	8	1.62	0.00	16.52
12/19	22.10	—	—	0.00	0.00	14.57
12/18	17.72	13	11	1.63	0.00	12.45
12/17	17.50	21	14	0.89	0.00	11.04
Annual Growth	5.4%	—	—	22.1%	—	14.4%

MP Materials Corp

EXECUTIVES

Chief Executive Officer, Chairman, Director, James H. Litinsky
Chief Financial Officer, Ryan Corbett
Chief Operating Officer, Michael Rosenthal
General Counsel, Secretary, Elliot D. Hoops
Director, Andrew A. McKnight
Director, Maryanne R. Lavan
Director, Richard B. Myers
Director, Connie K. Duckworth
Director, Randall Weisenburger
Director, Daniel Gold

LOCATIONS

HQ: MP Materials Corp
1700 S. Pavilion Center Drive, 8th Floor, Las Vegas, NV 89135
Phone: 702 844-6111
Web: www.mpmaterials.com

HISTORICAL FINANCIALS
Company Type: Public

Income Statement — FYE: December 31

	REVENUE ($mil)	NET INCOME ($mil)	NET PROFIT MARGIN	EMPLOYEES
12/22	527.5	289.0	54.8%	486
12/21	331.9	135.0	40.7%	365
12/20*	134.3	(21.8)	—	277
01/20	0.0	(0.0)	—	4
12/19	73.4	(6.7)	—	0
Annual Growth	93.0%	—	—	—

*Fiscal year change

2022 Year-End Financials
Debt ratio: 30.3%
Return on equity: 24.8%
Cash ($ mil.): 1,182.3
Current Ratio: 13.27
Long-term debt ($ mil.): 678.4
No. of shares ($ mil.): 177.7
Dividends
  Yield: —
  Payout: —
Market value ($ mil.): 4,315.0

	STOCK PRICE ($) FY Close	P/E High/Low		PER SHARE ($) Earnings	Dividends	Book Value
12/22	24.28	36	14	1.52	0.00	7.39
12/21	45.42	63	32	0.73	0.00	5.67
12/20*	32.17	—	—	(0.27)	0.00	5.00
Annual Growth	(13.1%)	—	—	—	—	21.5%

*Fiscal year change

Mr Cooper Group Inc

Mr. Cooper Group Inc. is a leading servicer and originator of residential mortgage loans. Company's purpose is to keep the dream of homeownership alive, and Mr. Cooper do this by helping mortgage borrowers manage what is typically their largest financial asset, and by helping its investors maximize the returns from their portfolios of residential mortgages. The company performs operational activities behalf of investors and originates residential mortgages.

Operations

Company's operations are conducted through two segments: Servicing and Originations.

The Servicing segment performs operational activities on behalf of investors or owners of the underlying mortgages, including collecting and disbursing borrower payments, investor reporting, customer service, modifying loans where appropriate to help borrowers stay current, and, when necessary, performing collections, foreclosures, and the sale of REO. The segment accounts for approximate 40% of revenue.

The Originations segment originates residential mortgage loans through its direct-to-consumer channel, which provides refinance options for its existing customers, and through its correspondent channel, which purchases or originates loans from mortgage bankers. The segment accounts for around 55% of revenue.

The remaining 5% of revenue came from its corporate and other operations.

Geographic Reach

The company is headquartered at Coppell, Texas. Mr. Cooper have locations which operates in Texas, Arizona, Oregon, Colorado, California, and internationally in India.

Sales and Marketing

Company's customers are government sponsored enterprises such as the Federal National Mortgage Association and the Federal Home Loan Mortgage Corp, investors in private-label securitizations, the Government National Mortgage Association, as well as organizations owning mortgage servicing rights.

The company incurred advertising costs of $40 million, $38 million and $33 million for the years ended December 31, 2021, 2020 and 2019, respectively.

Financial Performance

Company's revenue for fiscal 2021 increased by $629 million to $3.3 billion compared from the prior year with $2.7 billion. The decrease was primarily due to the 48% fall on its net gain on loans originated and sold.

Net income for fiscal 2021 increased to $1.5 billion compared from the prior year with $307 million.

Cash held by the company at the end of fiscal 2021 increased to $1.0 billion. Cash provided by operations and investing activities were $2.6 billion and $1.2 billion, respectively. Cash used for financing activities was $3.7 billion, mainly for net cash attributable to financing activities from discontinued operations.

Strategy

Mr. Cooper's strategy to position the company for continued, sustainable long-term growth includes initiatives to improve profitability and generate a return on tangible equity of 12% or higher. Key strategic initiatives include the following: strengthen its balance sheet by building capital and liquidity, and managing interest rate and other forms of risk; improve efficiency by driving continuous improvement in unit costs for Servicing and Originations segments, as well as by taking corporate actions to eliminate costs throughout the organization; grow its servicing portfolio to $1 trillion in UPB by acquiring new customers and retaining existing customers; achieve a refinance recapture rate of 60%; delight its customers and keep Mr. Cooper a great place for its team members to work; reinvent the customer experience by acting as the customer's advocate and by harnessing technology to deliver user-friendly digital solutions; sustain the talent of its people and the culture of its organization; and maintain strong relationships with agencies, investors, regulators, and other counterparties and a strong reputation for compliance and customer service.

Mergers and Acquisitions

In 2022, Mr. Cooper Group has signed an agreement with Community Loan Servicing (CLS) a subsidiary of Bayview Asset Management where Mr. Cooper will assume the servicing of approximately 140,000 residential mortgage loans. In addition, more than 500 CLS employees will join the Mr. Cooper Group team, with the transaction expected to close in Q2 of 2022. At that time, Mr. Cooper will welcome CLS's customers and team to the Mr. Cooper Group family. Terms of the transaction were not disclosed.

EXECUTIVES

Chairman, Chief Executive Officer, Jesse "Jay" K. Bray, $672,116 total compensation

President, Chief Financial Officer, Vice-Chairman, Christopher Marshall
Executive Vice President, Chief Financial Officer, Kurt G. Johnson
Executive Vice President, Chief Financial Officer, Jaime Gow
Executive Vice President, Chief Risk Officer, Chief Compliance Officer, Christine Poland Paxton
Subsidiary Officer, Michael R. Rawls, $400,000 total compensation
Director, Busy Burr
Director, Roy A. Guthrie
Director, Daniela Jorge
Lead Independent Director, Director, Michael D. Malone
Director, Shveta Mujumdar
Director, Tagar C. Olson
Director, Steven D. Scheiwe
Auditors : Ernst & Young LLP

LOCATIONS
HQ: Mr Cooper Group Inc
  8950 Cypress Waters Blvd., Coppell, TX 75019
Phone: 469 549-2000
Web: www.mrcoopergroup.com

HISTORICAL FINANCIALS
Company Type: Public

Income Statement — FYE: December 31

	ASSETS ($mil)	NET INCOME ($mil)	INCOME AS % OF ASSETS	EMPLOYEES
12/21	14,204.0	1,454.0	10.2%	8,200
12/20	24,165.0	305.0	1.3%	9,800
12/19	18,305.0	274.0	1.5%	9,100
12/18	16,973.0	884.0	5.2%	8,500
07/18	0.0	154.0	—	0
Annual Growth	—	111.4%	—	—

2021 Year-End Financials
Return on assets: 7.5%
Return on equity: 49.5%
Long-term debt ($ mil.): —
No. of shares ($ mil.): 73.7
Sales ($ mil.): 3,318
Dividends
  Yield: —
  Payout: —
Market value ($ mil.): 3,070.0

	STOCK PRICE ($) FY Close	P/E High/Low		PER SHARE ($) Earnings	Dividends	Book Value
12/21	41.61	3	2	16.53	0.00	45.62
12/20	31.03	9	2	3.20	0.00	27.98
12/19	12.51	5	2	2.95	0.00	24.50
12/18*	11.67	2	0	9.54	0.00	21.39
07/18	1.36	1	0	1.55	0.00	0.00
Annual Growth	212.8%	—	—	120.1%	—	—

*Fiscal year change

MSCI Inc

MSCI, formerly Morgan Stanley Capital International, manages more than 267,000 daily equity, fixed income, and hedge fund indices use by large asset management firms. Its leading, research-enhanced products, and services include indexes; portfolio construction and risk management analytics; environmental, social, and governance (ESG) and climate solutions; and real estate benchmarks, return analytics, and market insights. MSCI has over 6,300 clients across more than 95 countries. The Americas accounts for about half of the company's total sales.

Operations
The company operates through five operating segments - Index, Analytics, ESG and Climate, Real Estate and Burgiss.

Clients use its indexes in many areas of the investment process, including for indexed product creation (e.g., ETFs, mutual funds, annuities, futures, options, structured products, over-the-counter derivatives), performance benchmarking, portfolio construction and rebalancing, and asset allocation.

The company's Analytics segment offers risk management, performance attribution and portfolio management content, applications and services that provide clients with an integrated view of risk and return and tools for analyzing market, credit, liquidity and counterparty risk across all major asset classes, spanning short-, medium- and long-term time horizons.

The ESG and Climate segment offers products and services that help institutional investors understand how ESG and climate considerations can impact the long-term risk and return of their portfolio and individual security-level investments. MSCI provide data, ratings, research and tools to help investors navigate increasing regulation, meet new client demands and better integrate ESG and climate elements into their investment processes.

Real Estate offerings include real estate market and transaction data, benchmarks, return-analytics, climate assessments and market insights for funds, investors, managers and other real estate market participants.

Real Estate and Burgiss operating segments are combined and presented as All Other ? Private Assets.

Geographic Reach
Headquartered at New York, MSCI has additional offices spaces in India, New York, Hungary, Mexico, Philippines, England, and California.

About 45% of the company's revenues come from outside the Americas.

Sales and Marketing
Clients receive index data directly from the company or from third-party vendors worldwide, while clients access the Analytics content through its proprietary applications and APIs (application programming interfaces), third-party applications or directly through the own platforms.

MSCI served over 9,800 clients which include Asset owners, Asset managers, Financial intermediaries, and Wealth managers. The company's largest client organization, BlackRock, accounted for over 10% of the company's total sales.

Financial Performance
The company's revenue in 2021 increased by 21% to $2.0 billion compared to $1.7 billion in the prior year.

Net income in 2021 increased to $726.0 million compared to $601.8 million in the prior year.

Cash held by the company at the end of 2021 increased to $1.4 billion. Operating and financing activities provided $936.1 million and $229.5 million, respectively. Investing activities used $1.0 billion, mainly for acquisitions.

Strategy
The company provides critical tools and solutions that enable investors to manage the transformations taking place in the investment industry, better understand performance and risk, and build portfolios more effectively and efficiently to achieve their investment objectives. MSCI is focused on the following key initiatives to deliver actionable and integrated client solutions: extend leadership in research-enhanced content across asset classes; lead the enablement of ESG and climate investment integration; enhance distribution and content-enabling technology; expand solutions that empower client customization; strengthen client relationships and grow into strategic partnerships with clients; and execute strategic relationships and acquisitions with complementary content and technology companies.

Mergers and Acquisitions
In 2021, MSCI announced it has completed its acquisition of global real estate data and analytics provider, Real Capital Analytics (RCA). This acquisition expands MSCI's robust suite of real estate solutions, providing the real estate industry with data, analytics and support tools to manage investments and understand performance and risk, including climate risk, within their portfolios. MSCI leverages Real Capital Analytics' database of more than $20 trillion of commercial property transactions linked to over 200,000 investor and lender profiles, enhancing MSCI's commercial real estate capabilities.

EXECUTIVES

Chief Executive Officer, Chairman, Director, Henry A. Fernandez, $1,000,000 total compensation
Index Business Unit President, Index Business Unit Chief Operating Officer, Director, C.D. Baer Pettit, $834,666 total compensation
Corporate Development Chief Financial Officer, Strategy Chief Financial Officer, Corporate Development Treasurer, Strategy Treasurer, Andrew C. Wiechmann
Chief Human Resources Officer, Scott A. Crum, $525,000 total compensation
General Counsel, Robert J. Gutowski
Lead Director, Director, Robert G. Ashe

Director, Wayne Edmunds
Director, Catherine R. Kinney
Director, Jacques P. Perold
Director, Sandy C. Rattray
Director, Linda H. Riefler
Director, Marcus L. Smith
Director, Rajat Taneja
Director, Paula J. Volent
Director, Robin L. Matlock
Auditors : PricewaterhouseCoopers LLP

LOCATIONS
HQ: MSCI Inc
7 World Trade Center, 250 Greenwich Street, 49th Floor, New York, NY 10007
Phone: 212 804-3900
Web: www.msci.com

2014 Sales

	$ mil.	% of total
Americas	508.3	51
Europe, Middle East & Africa	364.2	37
Asia & Australia	124.2	12
Total	996.7	100

PRODUCTS/OPERATIONS
2014 Sales

	$ mil.	% of total
Index, real estate and ESG	582.6	59
Risk management analytics	309.7	31
Portfolio management analytics	104.4	10
Total	996.7	100

Selected Offerings
Barra (equity and multi-asset class portfolio analytics product)
CFRA (forensic accounting risk research, legal/regulatory risk assessment, due-diligence and educational services)
FEA (entergy and commodity asset valuation analytics)
ISS (governance research and outsourced proxy voting and reporting services)
MSCI Indices (flagship global equity indices)
RiskMetrics (risk and wealth management products)

COMPETITORS
ACTIS CAPITAL LIMITED
AMERIPRISE FINANCIAL, INC.
Canaccord Genuity Group Inc
ECI PARTNERS LLP
ENVESTNET, INC.
EVERCORE INC.
EXLSERVICE HOLDINGS, INC.
S&P GLOBAL INC.
THE DEPOSITORY TRUST & CLEARING CORPORATION
W.H. IRELAND GROUP PLC

HISTORICAL FINANCIALS
Company Type: Public

Income Statement — FYE: December 31

	REVENUE ($mil)	NET INCOME ($mil)	NET PROFIT MARGIN	EMPLOYEES
12/21	2,043.5	725.9	35.5%	4,303
12/20	1,695.3	601.8	35.5%	3,633
12/19	1,557.7	563.6	36.2%	3,396
12/18	1,433.9	507.8	35.4%	3,112
12/17	1,274.1	303.9	23.9%	3,038
Annual Growth	12.5%	24.3%	—	9.1%

2021 Year-End Financials
Debt ratio: 75.6%
Return on equity: —
Cash ($ mil.): 1,421.4
Current Ratio: 1.71
Long-term debt ($ mil.): 4,161.4
No. of shares ($ mil.): 82.4
Dividends
Yield: 0.5%
Payout: 44.1%
Market value ($ mil.): 50,510.0

	STOCK PRICE ($) FY Close	P/E High	P/E Low	Earnings	Dividends	Book Value
12/21	612.69	77	45	8.70	3.64	(1.98)
12/20	446.53	62	31	7.12	2.92	(5.37)
12/19	258.18	40	21	6.59	2.52	(0.90)
12/18	147.43	31	22	5.66	1.92	(1.98)
12/17	126.54	38	23	3.31	1.32	4.45
Annual Growth	48.3%	—	—	27.3%	28.9%	—

Muncy Bank Financial, Inc. (Muncy, PA)

EXECUTIVES
Chairman, Chief Executive Officer, Subsidiary Officer, Daniel C. Berninger
Assistant Secretary, Beth A. Benson
President, Subsidiary Officer, Director, Robert J. Glunk
Senior Vice President, Subsidiary Officer, Craig W. Kremser
Senior Vice President, Subsidiary Officer, David Mayer
Treasurer, Subsidiary Officer, Rhonda L. Gingery
Secretary, Subsidiary Officer, Karen Brandis
Director, Todd M. Arthur
Director, J. Howard Langdon
Director, Richard H. Lloyd
Director, Harold E. Lowe
Director, Gary M. Peck
Director, Robert M. Rabb
Director, Bonnie M. Tompkins
Director, David E. Wallis
Honorary Director, Arlene R. Opp
Honorary Director, James L. Muffly
Auditors : S.R. Snodgrass, P.C.

LOCATIONS
HQ: Muncy Bank Financial, Inc. (Muncy, PA)
2 North Main Street, Muncy, PA 17756
Phone: 570 546-2211
Web: www.muncybank.com

HISTORICAL FINANCIALS
Company Type: Public

Income Statement — FYE: December 31

	ASSETS ($mil)	NET INCOME ($mil)	INCOME AS % OF ASSETS	EMPLOYEES
12/20	531.5	5.7	1.1%	0
12/19	489.4	5.2	1.1%	0
12/18	459.6	4.6	1.0%	0
12/17	427.4	2.8	0.7%	0
12/16	393.3	3.9	1.0%	62
Annual Growth	7.8%	10.0%	—	—

2020 Year-End Financials
Return on assets: 1.1%
Return on equity: 10.9%
Long-term debt ($ mil.): —
No. of shares ($ mil.): 1.5
Sales ($ mil.): 24.4
Dividends
Yield: 4.0%
Payout: 35.8%
Market value ($ mil.): 57.0

	STOCK PRICE ($) FY Close	P/E High	P/E Low	Earnings	Dividends	Book Value
12/20	37.00	11	7	3.75	1.41	35.55
12/19	41.00	13	10	3.26	1.32	31.03
12/18	34.75	12	11	2.89	1.24	28.28
12/17	34.55	22	20	1.72	1.11	26.83
12/16	34.90	17	12	2.39	1.03	26.05
Annual Growth	1.5%	—	—	12.0%	8.1%	8.1%

MVB Financial Corp

EXECUTIVES
Chairman, Subsidiary Officer, Director, W. Marston Becker
President, Chief Financial Officer, Subsidiary Officer, Donald T. Robinson, $381,370 total compensation
Chief Executive Officer, Subsidiary Officer, Director, Larry F. Mazza, $694,404 total compensation
Subsidiary Officer, Director, Gary A. LeDonne
Executive Vice President, Chief Administrative Officer, Subsidiary Officer, Craig B. Greathouse
Executive Vice President, Chief Operating Officer, Subsidiary Officer, John C. Marion
Subsidiary Officer, John T. Schirripa, $272,308 total compensation
Chief Financial Officer, Steven E. Crouse
Director, Jan L. Owen
Director, Lindsay A. Slader
Director, John W. Ebert
Director, Kelly R. Nelson
Director, Cheryl D Spielman
Director, Daniel W. Holt
Auditors : Dixon Hughes Goodman LLP

LOCATIONS
HQ: MVB Financial Corp
301 Virginia Avenue, Fairmont, WV 26554
Phone: 304 363-4800
Web: www.mvbbanking.com

HISTORICAL FINANCIALS

Company Type: Public

Income Statement — FYE: December 31

	ASSETS ($mil)	NET INCOME ($mil)	INCOME AS % OF ASSETS	EMPLOYEES
12/20	2,331.4	37.4	1.6%	344
12/19	1,944.1	26.9	1.4%	443
12/18	1,750.9	12.0	0.7%	0
12/17	1,534.3	7.5	0.5%	0
12/16	1,418.8	12.9	0.9%	382
Annual Growth	13.2%	30.5%	—	(2.6%)

2020 Year-End Financials

Return on assets: 1.7%
Return on equity: 16.5%
Long-term debt ($ mil.): —
No. of shares ($ mil.): 11.5
Sales ($ mil.): 172.2
Dividends
Yield: 1.5%
Payout: 14.8%
Market value ($ mil.): 261.0

	STOCK PRICE ($) FY Close	P/E High/Low		PER SHARE ($) Earnings	Dividends	Book Value
12/20	22.68	8	3	3.06	0.36	20.78
12/19	24.92	11	7	2.20	0.20	17.74
12/18	18.04	19	16	1.00	0.11	15.23
12/17	20.10	29	18	0.68	0.10	14.38
12/16	12.80	10	7	1.31	0.08	14.57
Annual Growth	15.4%	—	—	23.6%	45.6%	9.3%

MYR Group Inc

MYR Group is a holding company of specialty electrical construction service providers that was established in 1995 through the merger of long-standing specialty contractors and constructs transmission and distribution lines for the electric utility infrastructure, commercial, and industrial construction markets. The company also installs and maintains electrical wiring in commercial and industrial facilities and traffic and rail systems. The company operates nationwide through subsidiaries, including The L.E. Myers Co., Harlan Electric, Sturgeon Electric, MYR Transmission Services, and Great Southwestern Construction.

Operations

MYR Group's Transmission & Distribution (T&D) segment generated over 50% of revenue while Commercial & Industrial (C&I) segment brought in nearly 50%.

The T&D segment provides a broad range of services on electric transmission and distribution networks and substation facilities, which include design, engineering, procurement, construction, upgrade, and maintenance and repair services, with a focus on construction, maintenance and repair. T&D services also include the construction and maintenance of high voltage transmission lines, substations, lower voltage underground and overhead distribution systems, renewable power facilities, and limited gas construction services. It also provides emergency restoration services in response to hurricane, ice or other storm-related damage.

Its C&I segment provides services such as the design, installation, maintenance and repair of commercial and industrial wiring, the installation of traffic networks and the installation of bridge, roadway and tunnel lighting.

MYR Group provides services to customers through contracts. Its fixed price contracts accounted for roughly 60% of total revenue. The remaining sales are from unit price, T&E, and others.

Geographic Reach

MYR Group is based in Henderson, Colorado, it owns nearly 20 operating facilities. It serves markets in the US and western Canada.

Sales and Marketing

T&D customers include investor-owned utilities, cooperatives, private developers, government-funded utilities, independent power producers, independent transmission companies, industrial facility owners and other contractors. Its C&I segment provides electrical contracting services to property owners and general contractors, commercial and industrial facility owners, governmental agencies, and developers. Overall, its market from electric construction accounted for about 50% of total revenue followed by the transmission for over 30%, and distribution for some 20%.

Its top 10 customers accounted for about 35% of revenues, with no single customer accounting for more than 10% of revenue.

MYR Group's advertising costs were $0.8 million, $0.7 million, and $0.8 million in 2021, 2020, and 2019, respectively.

Financial Performance

MYR's revenue increased $250.9 million, or 11.2%, to $2.50 billion in 2021 from $2.25 billion in 2020. The increase was primarily due to an increase in revenue on various-sized C&I projects in certain geographic areas and an increase in revenue on distribution projects and large-sized T&D projects.

Net income increased to $85.0 million in 2021 from $58.8 million in 2020. The increase was primarily due to an increase in various revenues.

The company ended the fiscal year with $82.1 million in cash and cash equivalents. Net cash flows provided by operating activities amounted to $137.2 million, while investing and operating activities each used $49.3 million and $28.1 million, respectively. Main cash uses were for purchases of property and equipment, and payment of principal obligations under equipment notes.

Strategy

In an effort to support its growth strategy and maximize stockholder returns, MYR Group sought to efficiently manage its capital. Through 2021, it continued to implement strategies that further expanded its capabilities and effectively allocate capital.

It continues to manage its increasing costs for supporting its operations, including increasing insurance, equipment, labor and material costs. The company continued to invest in developing key management and craft personnel in both its T&D and C&I markets and in procuring the specific specialty equipment and tooling needed to win and execute projects of all sizes and complexity. In 2021 and 2020, it invested in capital expenditures of approximately $52.4 million and $44.4 million, respectively. Most of its capital expenditures supported opportunities in its T&D business. It plans to continue to evaluate its needs for additional equipment and tooling.

Mergers and Acquisitions

In early 2022, MYR Group announced that its Canadian subsidiary, MYR Group Construction Canada, Ltd. has acquired all issued and outstanding shares of capital stock of Powerline Plus Ltd. and its affiliate. The Powerline Plus Companies together comprise a leading full-service electrical distribution construction company headquartered in Toronto, Ontario. The addition of the Powerline Plus Companies to MYR Group continues to strengthen its Transmission & Distribution segment service offerings and geographic reach, while expanding its market position as the company continues to provide additional services to both new and existing customers. Terms were not disclosed.

Company Background

MYR was founded in 1891 by Lewis Edward Myers, who briefly worked as a salesman with Thomas Edison.

EXECUTIVES

Chairman, Director, Kenneth Michael Hartwick
President, Chief Executive Officer, Director, Richard S. Swartz, $591,250 total compensation
Senior Vice President, Division Officer, Tod M. Cooper, $384,750 total compensation
Senior Vice President, Division Officer, Subsidiary Officer, Jeffrey J. Waneka, $325,000 total compensation
Senior Vice President, Chief Financial Officer, Principal Financial Officer, Principal Accounting Officer, Kelly Michelle Huntington
Vice President, Chief Legal Officer, Secretary, William F. Fry
Director, Jennifer E. Lowry
Director, Donald C.I. Lucky
Director, Maurice E. Moore
Director, Shirin O'Connor
Director, Bradley T. Favreau
Director, Ajoy Hari Karna
Director, William D. Patterson
Auditors: Crowe LLP

LOCATIONS

HQ: MYR Group Inc
12150 East 112th Avenue, Henderson, CO 80640
Phone: 303 286-8000
Web: www.myrgroup.com

PRODUCTS/OPERATIONS

2014 Sales by Segment

	$ in mil.	% of total
Transmission & Distribution	699.6	74
Commercial & Industrial	244.3	26
Total	943.9	100

Selected Services
Electrical
    Commercial/Industrial
    Construction
    Design-build services
    Directional boring
    Emergency storm response
    Fiber optics
    Foundations & caissons
    Gas distribution
    Highway lighting
    Overhead distribution
    PCS/Cellular towers
    Preconstruction services
    Substation
    Telecommunications
    Traffic signals
    Transmission
    Underground distribution
Mechanical
    Boiler construction and maintenance
    Erection of piping systems
    General contracting
    In-house fabrication
    Instrumentation
    Maintenance
    Preconstruction services
    Retrofit to existing systems

Selected Subsidiaries
ComTel Technology, Inc.
Great Southwestern Construction, Inc.
Harlan Electric Company
Hawkeye Construction, Inc.
Meyers International, Inc.
MYR Transmission Services, Inc.
MYRpower, Inc.
The L.E. Myers Co.
Sturgeon Electric Company, Inc.

COMPETITORS
AEGION CORPORATION
DYCOM INDUSTRIES, INC.
INSITUFORM TECHNOLOGIES, LLC
JGC HOLDINGS CORPORATION
LAYNE CHRISTENSEN COMPANY
MASTEC, INC.
MUNICIPAL ELECTRIC AUTHORITY OF GEORGIA
PIKE CORPORATION
PRIMORIS SERVICES CORPORATION
WILLBROS GROUP, INC.

HISTORICAL FINANCIALS
Company Type: Public

Income Statement — FYE: December 31

	REVENUE ($mil)	NET INCOME ($mil)	NET PROFIT MARGIN	EMPLOYEES
12/20	2,247.3	58.7	2.6%	7,200
12/19	2,071.1	37.6	1.8%	7,100
12/18	1,531.1	31.0	2.0%	5,500
12/17	1,403.3	21.1	1.5%	5,275
12/16	1,142.4	21.4	1.9%	4,600
Annual Growth	18.4%	28.7%	—	11.9%

2020 Year-End Financials
Debt ratio: 3.0%
Return on equity: 14.7%
Cash ($ mil.): 22.6
Current Ratio: 1.44
Long-term debt ($ mil.): 25
No. of shares ($ mil.): 16.7
Dividends
  Yield: —
  Payout: —
Market value ($ mil.): 1,006.0

	STOCK PRICE ($) FY Close	P/E High/Low		PER SHARE ($) Earnings	Dividends	Book Value
12/20	60.10	17	5	3.48	0.00	25.65
12/19	32.59	17	12	2.26	0.00	21.89
12/18	28.17	21	14	1.87	0.00	19.50
12/17	35.73	33	18	1.28	0.00	17.43
12/16	37.68	32	15	1.23	0.00	16.11
Annual Growth	12.4%	—	—	29.7%	—	12.3%

NASB Financial Inc

NASB Financial is the holding company for North American Savings Bank, which operates about 15 branches and loan offices in the Kansas City and Springfield, Missouri areas. Established in 1927, the bank offers standard deposit products to retail and commercial customers, including checking and savings accounts and CDs. Mortgages secured by residential or commercial properties make up most of the bank's lending activities; it also originates business, consumer, and construction loans. Subsidiary Nor-Am sells annuities, mutual funds, and credit life and disability insurance. Chairman David Hancock and his wife Linda, who is also a member of the company's board of directors, own about 45% of NASB Financial.

Operations
In 2012 North American Savings Bank entered into a consent order with the Office of the Comptroller of the Currency to improve its asset quality and maintain adequate provisions for loan losses, among other measures. The order is a continuance of a similar one agreed to with the bank's former regulator, the Office of Thrift Supervision.

Financial Performance
The company's revenue decreased slightly in fiscal 2013 compared to the previous fiscal period. It reported revenue of $113.3 million in fiscal 2013 after bringing in $114.9 million in revenue for fiscal 2012.

However, even with the slight decline in annual revenue, the company's net income increased in fiscal 2013 compared to fiscal 2012. It cleared more than $27 million in net profit for fiscal 2013 after netting about $18 million in fiscal 2012.

Cash flow increased from negative levels during fiscal 2012 up to a positive $124 million in fiscal 2013.

EXECUTIVES

Chairman, Subsidiary Officer, Director, David H. Hancock, $323,958 total compensation
Chief Executive Officer, Subsidiary Officer, Director, Paul L. Thomas, $336,458 total compensation
Senior Vice President, Chief Financial Officer, Subsidiary Officer, Rhonda G. Nyhus, $195,042 total compensation
Vice President, Bruce J. Thielen, $182,292 total compensation
Vice President, Mike Anderson
Vice President, Matt Dayton
Vice President, John M. Nesselrode
Vice President, Dena Sanders
Vice President, Ron Stafford
Vice President, J. Enrique Venegas
Vice President, Subsidiary Officer, Director, Thomas B. Wagers
Corporate Secretary, Brian Zoellner
Director, E. Alexander Hancock
Director, Frederick V. Arbanas
Director, Barrett Brady
Director, Laura Brady
Director, W. Russell Welsh
Director, Linda S. Hancock
Auditors: BKD, LLP

LOCATIONS
HQ: NASB Financial Inc
  12498 South 71 Highway, Grandview, MO 64030
Phone: 816 765-2200
Web: www.nasb.com

COMPETITORS
ASTORIA FINANCIAL CORPORATION
BENEFICIAL MUTUAL BANCORP, INC.
FIRST FEDERAL SAVINGS AND LOAN ASSOCIATION OF LAKEWOOD
THE SOUTHERN BANC COMPANY INC
TIAA FSB HOLDINGS, INC.

HISTORICAL FINANCIALS
Company Type: Public

Income Statement — FYE: September 30

	ASSETS ($mil)	NET INCOME ($mil)	INCOME AS % OF ASSETS	EMPLOYEES
09/21	2,359.3	73.7	3.1%	0
09/20	2,552.1	103.5	4.1%	0
09/19	2,605.2	43.1	1.7%	0
09/18	2,060.3	29.1	1.4%	0
09/17	2,062.3	29.3	1.4%	0
Annual Growth	3.4%	25.8%	—	—

2021 Year-End Financials
Return on assets: 3.0%
Return on equity: 19.8%
Long-term debt ($ mil.): —
No. of shares ($ mil.): 7.4
Sales ($ mil.): 259
Dividends
  Yield: 6.4%
  Payout: 40.7%
Market value ($ mil.): 466.0

	STOCK PRICE ($) FY Close	P/E High/Low		PER SHARE ($) Earnings	Dividends	Book Value
09/21	63.00	8	6	9.94	4.05	53.13
09/20	60.00	4	2	14.01	2.15	47.42
09/19	44.20	8	6	5.85	2.00	35.56
09/18	40.60	11	9	3.94	3.82	31.37
09/17	36.11	10	8	3.98	1.22	31.55
Annual Growth	14.9%	—	—	25.7%	35.0%	13.9%

National Bank Holdings Corp

National Bank Holdings is the holding company for NBH Bank, which operates around 80 branches in located primarily in Colorado and the greater Kansas City region under various brands, including: Bank Midwest in Kansas and Missouri, Community Banks of Colorado in Colorado, and Hillcrest Bank in Texas, Utah, and New Mexico. Targeting small to medium-sized businesses and consumers, the banks offer traditional checking and savings accounts, as well as commercial and residential mortgages, agricultural loans, and commercial loans. The bank boasted some $7.2 billion in assets at the end of 2021, including some $4.5 billion in loans and $6.2 billion in deposits. About 65% of its total revenue is made up of interest income.

Operations

Through the bank, the company's primary business is to offer a full range of banking products and financial services to its commercial, business and consumer clients. It conducts its banking business through around 80 banking centers and offers a high level of personalized service to our clients through our relationship managers and banking center associates.

About 60% of the bank's total revenue came from loan interest (including fees) during 2021, while some 5% came from interest on its investment securities. The rest of its revenue came from mortgage banking (some 20%), service charges (roughly 5%), bank card fees (nearly 5%), and other miscellaneous income sources.

In addition, its loan portfolio comprises commercial loans with approximately 70%, commercial real estate non-owner occupied and residential real estate with nearly 15% each, and consumer loans, which generates the rest of sales.

Geographic Reach

Denver, Colorado-based, National Bank Holdings had a network of some 80 banking centers, with operations space in Kansas City, Missouri. It also operated some 40 banking centers in Colorado, about 35 in Kansas and Missouri, two in Texas, one in Utah and four in New Mexico. Of these banking centers, around 60 were owned and some 20 locations were leased.

Sales and Marketing

The bank serves small- to medium-sized businesses, and consumers via its network of banking locations and through online and mobile banking products.

Financial Performance

The company's revenue for fiscal 2021 decreased to $297.5 million compared form the prior year with $333.2 million.

Net income for fiscal 2021 increased to $93.6 million compared from the prior year with $88.6 million.

Cash held by the company at the end of fiscal 2021 increased to $850.2 million. Cash provided by operations and financing activities were $179.5 million and $529.0 million, respectively. Cash used for investing activities was $473.8 million, mainly for purchase of investment securities held-to-maturity.

Strategy

As part of the company's goal of becoming a leading regional community bank holding company, it seeks to continue to generate strong organic growth, as well as pursue selective acquisitions of financial institutions and other complementary businesses. Its focus is on building organic growth through strong banking relationships with small- and medium-sized businesses and consumers in its primary markets, while maintaining a low-risk profile designed to generate reliable income streams and attractive returns.

The key components of its strategic plan are: focus on client-centered, relationship-driven banking strategy; expansion of commercial banking, business banking and specialty businesses; expansion through organic growth, competitive product and digital offerings; expansion through its digital solution 2UniFi; continue to strengthen profitability through organic growth and operating efficiencies; maintain conservative risk profile and sound risk management practices; and pursue disciplined acquisitions or other expansionary opportunities.

Mergers and Acquisitions

In early 2022, National Bank Holdings Corporation announced the signing of a definitive merger agreement to acquire Bancshares of Jackson Hole Incorporated (BOJH), the holding company for Bank of Jackson Hole with operations in Jackson Hole, Wyoming and Boise, Idaho. Upon completion of the transaction, NBHC will have approximately $8.8 billion in pro forma assets and $7.7 billion in total deposits, and becomes the #2 ranked bank by deposits in Teton County, Wyoming. BOJH is a full service community bank with a Wyoming-domiciled trust business. Terms were not disclosed.

Company Background

Formed in 2009, National Bank Holdings went public in 2012. Prior to its filing, National Bank Holdings was minority-owned by a number of private shareholders and corporate entities, including Taconic Capital Advisors, Wellington Management, and Paulson & Co.

EXECUTIVES

Chairman, President, Chief Executive Officer, Subsidiary Officer, Director, G. Timothy Laney, $750,000 total compensation

Executive Vice President, Chief Financial Officer, Subsidiary Officer, Aldis Birkans, $255,072 total compensation

Executive Vice President, Chief Administrative Officer, General Counsel, Subsidiary Officer, Angela N. Petrucci

Chief Risk Management Officer, Subsidiary Officer, Richard U. Newfield, $325,000 total compensation

Chief Client Executive and Deposit Operations Executive, Subsidiary Officer, Ruth Stevenson

Subsidiary Officer, Christopher S. Randall

Subsidiary Officer, Brendan W. Zahl, $275,000 total compensation

Lead Independent Director, Director, Ralph W. Clermont

Director, Patrick G. Sobers, $260,673 total compensation

Director, Robert E. Dean

Director, Fred J. Joseph

Director, Maria F. Spring

Director, Burney S. Warren

Director, Art Zeile

Director, Alka Gupta

Auditors : KPMG LLP

LOCATIONS

HQ: National Bank Holdings Corp
7800 East Orchard Road, Suite 300, Greenwood Village, CO 80111
Phone: 303 892-8715
Web: www.nationalbankholdings.com

PRODUCTS/OPERATIONS

2015 Sales

	$ in mil	% of total
Interest and dividend income:		
Interest and fees on loans	131.2	63
Interest and dividends on investment securities	38.2	18
Dividends on non-marketable securities	1.2	1
Interest on interest-bearing bank deposits	0.8	-
Total interest and dividend income	171.4	82
Non-interest income:		
Service charges	14.8	7
Bank card fees	10.9	5
Gain on sales of mortgages, net	2	1
Bank-owned life insurance income	1.6	1
Other non-interest income	3.7	2
Bargain purchase gain	1	1
Gain on previously charged-off acquired loans	0.6	-
OREO related write-ups and other income	2.4	1
FDIC indemnification asset amortization, net of gain on termination	(15.9)	-
FDIC loss sharing income (expense)	0.3	-
Total non-interest income	21.4	18
Total	192.8	100

COMPETITORS

AMERICAN NATIONAL BANKSHARES INC.
AMERIS BANCORP
BEAR STATE FINANCIAL, INC.
CAPITAL BANK FINANCIAL CORP.
CITY HOLDING COMPANY
COLUMBIA BANKING SYSTEM, INC.
FIRST HORIZON CORPORATION
FIRST MIDWEST BANCORP, INC.
FIRSTMERIT CORPORATION
OLD NATIONAL BANCORP

HISTORICAL FINANCIALS
Company Type: Public

Income Statement   FYE: December 31

	ASSETS ($mil)	NET INCOME ($mil)	INCOME AS % OF ASSETS	EMPLOYEES
12/20	6,659.9	88.5	1.3%	1,224
12/19	5,895.5	80.3	1.4%	1,298
12/18	5,676.6	61.4	1.1%	1,332
12/17	4,843.4	14.5	0.3%	926
12/16	4,573.0	23.0	0.5%	1,004
Annual Growth	9.9%	40.0%	—	5.1%

2020 Year-End Financials
Return on assets: 1.4%
Return on equity: 11.1%
Long-term debt ($ mil.): —
No. of shares ($ mil.): 30.6
Sales ($ mil.): 358.2
Dividends
Yield: 2.4%
Payout: 30.8%
Market value ($ mil.): 1,004.0

	STOCK PRICE ($) FY Close	P/E High/Low		PER SHARE ($) Earnings	Dividends	Book Value
12/20	32.76	13	7	2.85	0.80	26.79
12/19	35.22	15	12	2.55	0.75	24.60
12/18	30.87	21	15	1.95	0.54	22.59
12/17	32.43	68	56	0.53	0.34	19.81
12/16	31.89	40	23	0.79	0.22	20.32
Annual Growth	0.7%	—	—	37.8%	38.1%	7.2%

National Rural Utilities Cooperative Finance Corp

Cooperation may work wonders on Sesame Street, but in the real world it takes money to pay the power bill. The National Rural Utilities Cooperative Finance Corporation provides financing and investment services for rural electrical and telephone projects throughout the US. The group is owned by some 1,500 member electric utility and telecommunications systems. National Rural supplements the government loans that traditionally have fueled rural electric utilities by selling commercial paper, medium-term notes, and collateral trust bonds to fund its loan programs. National Rural was formed in 1969 by the National Rural Electric Cooperative Association, a lobby representing the nation's electric co-ops.

EXECUTIVES

President, Director, Bruce A. Vitosh
Chief Executive Officer, J. Andrew Don, $455,000 total compensation
Senior Vice President, Chief Financial Officer, Interim Principal Accounting Officer, Yu Ling Wang
Senior Vice President, General Counsel, Nathan Howard
Corporate Relations Senior Vice President, Corporate Relations Chief Corporate Affairs Officer, Brad L. Captain
Senior Vice President, Chief Risk Officer, Gholam M. Saleh
Corporate Services Senior Vice President, Corporate Services Chief Operating Officer, Gary Bradbury
Strategic Services Senior Vice President, Mark D Snowden
Secretary, Treasurer, Director, David E. Felkel
Secretary, Treasurer, Director, G. Anthony Norton
Division Officer, Joel Allen
Director, Charles A. Abel
Director, Anthony A. Anderson
Director, Thomas A. Bailey
Director, Kevin M. Bender
Director, Robert J. Brockman
Director, Chris D. Christensen
Director, Jared Echternach
Director, Timothy Eldridge
Director, Dennis Fulk
Director, Barbara E. Hampton
Director, William Keith Hayward
Director, Michael J. Heinen
Director, Bradley P. Janorschke
Director, Anthony Larson
Director, Shane Larson
Director, Brent McRae
Director, John Metcalf
Director, Kendall Montgomery
Director, Jeffrey Allen Rehder
Director, Mark A. Suggs
Director, Marsha L. Thompson
Auditors : KPMG LLP

LOCATIONS

HQ: National Rural Utilities Cooperative Finance Corp
20701 Cooperative Way, Dulles, VA 20166
Phone: 703 467-1800   **Fax:** 703 709-6779
Web: www.nrucfc.coop

PRODUCTS/OPERATIONS

Selected Subsidiaries and Affiliates
National Cooperative Services Corporation (financing for members and affiliated not-for-profit entities)
Rural Telephone Finance Cooperative (rural telecommunications lending)

COMPETITORS

AMERICAN EXPRESS COMPANY
CLAYTON, DUBILIER & RICE, INC.
INTERNATIONAL PERSONAL FINANCE PLC
SOCIAL INVESTMENT SCOTLAND
WORLD ACCEPTANCE CORPORATION

HISTORICAL FINANCIALS
Company Type: Public

Income Statement   FYE: May 31

	REVENUE ($mil)	NET INCOME ($mil)	NET PROFIT MARGIN	EMPLOYEES
05/21	1,641.8	811.6	49.4%	248
05/20	384.0	(585.2)	—	253
05/19	787.6	(149.2)	—	257
05/18	1,326.6	455.1	34.3%	254
05/17	1,149.5	309.9	27.0%	248
Annual Growth	9.3%	27.2%	—	0.0%

2021 Year-End Financials
Debt ratio: 92.5%
Return on equity: 81.1%
Cash ($ mil.): 295.0
Current Ratio: 0.10
Long-term debt ($ mil.): 22,844
No. of shares ($ mil.): 0.0
Dividends
Yield: —
Payout: —
Market value ($ mil.): 0.0

National Storage Affiliates Trust

EXECUTIVES

Executive Chairman, Trustee, Tamara D. Fischer, $340,000 total compensation
Operations Executive Vice President, Operations Chief Operating Officer, Derek Bergeon
Vice-Chairman, Arlen D. Nordhagen, $495,000 total compensation
President, Chief Executive Officer, David Cramer
Executive Vice President, Chief Financial Officer, Treasurer, Chief Accounting Officer, Brandon Togashi, $235,000 total compensation
Lead Independent Trustee, Trustee, Paul W. Hylbert
Trustee, Charles F. Wu
Trustee, George L. Chapman
Trustee, Chad L. Meisinger
Trustee, Steven G. Osgood
Trustee, Dominic M. Palazzo
Trustee, Rebecca Lee Steinfort
Trustee, Mark Van Mourick
Auditors : KPMG LLP

LOCATIONS

HQ: National Storage Affiliates Trust
8400 East Prentice Avenue, 9th Floor, Greenwood Village, CO 80111
Phone: 720 630-2600
Web: www.nationalstorageaffiliates.com

HISTORICAL FINANCIALS
Company Type: Public

Income Statement   FYE: December 31

	REVENUE ($mil)	NET INCOME ($mil)	NET PROFIT MARGIN	EMPLOYEES
12/20	432.2	48.6	11.2%	1,684
12/19	387.8	3.9	1.0%	1,559
12/18	330.8	14.1	4.3%	1,561
12/17	268.1	2.9	1.1%	1,211
12/16	199.0	17.9	9.0%	995
Annual Growth	21.4%	28.3%	—	14.1%

2020 Year-End Financials
Debt ratio: 54.6%
Return on equity: 5.1%
Cash ($ mil.): 18.7
Current Ratio: 0.88
Long-term debt ($ mil.): 1,916.9
No. of shares ($ mil.): 71.2
Dividends
Yield: 3.7%
Payout: 281.2%
Market value ($ mil.): 2,569.0

	STOCK PRICE ($) FY Close	P/E High/Low		PER SHARE ($) Earnings	Dividends	Book Value
12/20	36.03	72	43	0.53	1.35	13.59
12/19	33.62	—	—	(0.15)	1.27	15.41
12/18	26.46	457	331	0.07	1.16	16.18
12/17	27.26	2759	2124	0.01	1.04	16.73
12/16	22.07	38	27	0.31	0.88	13.39
Annual Growth	13.0%	—	—	14.3%	11.3%	0.4%

National Vision Holdings Inc

EXECUTIVES

Chairman, Director, D. Randolph Peeler
Chief Executive Officer, Subsidiary Officer, Director, L. Reade Fahs, $900,000 total compensation
Senior Vice President, Chief Accounting Officer, Melissa Rasmussen
Senior Vice President, Chief Financial Officer, Subsidiary Officer, Patrick R. Moore, $421,923 total compensation
Senior Vice President, Chief People Officer, Bill Clark
Distribution Senior Vice President, Manufacturing Senior Vice President, Distribution Subsidiary Officer, Manufacturing Subsidiary Officer, Charlie Foell
Senior Vice President, General Counsel, Secretary, Jared Brandman
Senior Vice President, Chief Human Resources Officer, Subsidiary Officer, Jeff Busbee
Director, Susan Somersille Johnson
Director, Heather Cianfrocco
Director, Naomi Kelman
Director, Virginia A. Hepner
Director, Thomas V. Taylor
Director, David M. Tehle
Director, Jose Armario
Auditors : DELOITTE & TOUCHE LLP

LOCATIONS

HQ: National Vision Holdings Inc
2435 Commerce Avenue, Building 2200, Duluth, GA 30096
Phone: 770 822-3600
Web: www.nationalvision.com

HISTORICAL FINANCIALS
Company Type: Public

Income Statement — FYE: January 2

	REVENUE ($mil)	NET INCOME ($mil)	NET PROFIT MARGIN	EMPLOYEES
01/21*	1,711.7	36.2	2.1%	12,792
12/19	1,724.3	32.7	1.9%	11,781
12/18	1,536.8	23.6	1.5%	10,668
12/17	1,375.3	45.8	3.3%	10,902
12/16	1,196.1	14.7	1.2%	10,360
Annual Growth	9.4%	25.2%	—	5.4%

*Fiscal year change

2021 Year-End Financials
Debt ratio: 28.1%
Return on equity: 4.2%
Cash ($ mil.): 373.9
Current Ratio: 1.72
Long-term debt ($ mil.): 651.7
No. of shares ($ mil.): 81.2
Dividends
Yield: —
Payout: —
Market value ($ mil.): 3,679.0

	STOCK PRICE ($) FY Close	P/E High/Low		PER SHARE ($) Earnings	Dividends	Book Value
01/21*	45.29	107	30	0.44	0.00	11.16
12/19	33.10	84	54	0.40	0.00	9.74
12/18	28.98	147	85	0.30	0.00	9.51
12/17	40.61	53	36	0.74	0.00	8.84
Annual Growth	3.7%	—	—	(15.9%)	—	8.1%

*Fiscal year change

Natural Alternatives International, Inc.

Natural Alternatives International (NAI) is a natural alternative for nutritional supplement marketers who want to outsource manufacturing. The company provides private-label manufacturing of vitamins, minerals, herbs, and other customized nutritional supplements. Its main customers are direct sellers such as Mannatech and NSA International, for whom it makes JuicePlus+ chewables, capsules, and powdered products. NAI also makes some branded products for sale in the US: the Pathway to Healing brand of nutritional supplements, promoted by doctor and evangelist Reginald B. Cherry.

Operations

Natural Alternatives International (NAI) operates through three business segments. Private-label contract manufacturing is by far the largest, representing more than 85% of sales. Its Branded Products business (just 2% of sales) markets and distributes branded nutritional supplements through direct-to-consumer marketing programs. NAI's Patent and Trademark licensing business segment is engaged in the sale and licensing of beta-alanine (an amino acid used by bodybuilders) under the CarnoSyn trade name.

NSA International and Mannatech are the company's biggest clients, accounting for about 45% and 20%, respectively, of the company's sales. In addition to manufacturing products for its private-label clients, NAI offers a range of complementary services, such as regulatory assistance and packaging design.

Geographic Reach

The company has manufacturing and distribution facilities in California and in Switzerland. It also has sales support operations in Japan in order to assist clients operating in the Pacific Rim. The US accounts for 60% of NAI's sales. Outside the US, NAI's primary market is Europe.

Financial Performance

The company's net sales grew a robust 30% in fiscal 2012 (ends June) vs. the prior year, while net income fell by about 18% over the same period. Revenue from NAI's patent and trademark licensing business surged more than 350% in fiscal 2012 vs. 2011, driven by the increase in popularity of CarnoSyn as a sports nutrition supplement and expanded distribution of the product. The Private-label contract manufacturing segment saw its sales rise more than 20% due to increased sales to its two largest customers, NSA International and Mannatech. Branded products was the laggard, posting a 14% drop off in sales for the year, which NAI blamed on soft sales of the Pathway to Healing product line.

Strategy

A key element of NAI's growth strategy is the commercialization of its beta-alanine patent through contract manufacturing, royalty and licensing agreements, and the protection of its proprietary rights (by legal means where necessary). Indeed, the 350% surge in fiscal 2012 sales in the company's licensing business was credited to the CarnoSyn brand. To that end, NAI in 2011 expanded its beta-alanine licensing programs through a supply agreement with Nestle Nutrition and a license and supply agreement with Abbott Laboratories. While the Nestle agreement expired in mid-2012 and was not renewed, the agreement granting Abbott exclusive license for the use of beta-alanine in certain medical foods and medical nutritionals continues. Also, NAI is looking to growth the CarnoSyn beta-alanine business through accretive acquisitions.

The company is also focusing on developing and growing its own line of branded products primarily through direct-to-consumer sales and distribution channels. To bolster is faltering Pathway to Healing line of branded products, NAI relaunched the product line and increased its marketing and advertising activities to support future sales.

HISTORY

Marie Le Doux and her son Mark founded Natural Alternatives International (NAI) with $25,000 in 1980. Mark, a lawyer and former premed student, had previously worked for a small, California-based vitamin company and was a firm believer in the virtues of vitamins. He studied the beneficial properties of nutrients and began making vitamins for health food retailers and drugstores.

Finding the retail market too competitive for a small company, the Le Doux duo refocused on specialty direct markets. Mark ramped up their production facility, bringing in automated equipment from Italy. The company went public in 1986 and created private-label lines for several new customers.

Trouble struck in 1989 when NAI was forced to recall its products containing L-tryptophan (an amino acid often marketed as a sleep aid) after the FDA linked it to the potentially fatal eosinophilia-myalgia syndrome.

To help boost overseas sales, NAI in 1997 bought a tablet and chewables manufacturing plant, doubling its manufacturing capacity. In 1998 the firm acquired the rights to manufacture Glucotrol, a fat- and cholesterol-binding diet supplement used in Japan. The next year it established subsidiary Natural Alternatives International Europe in Switzerland and began manufacturing operations there.

Faced with increased competition and decreased demand in 2000 (the company lost the business of Nu Skin Enterprises, which had accounted for some 20% of its revenues), NAI cut jobs to reduce operating costs.

NAI expanded its branded products segment considerably with its 2005 Real Health Laboratories. The purchase brought in a line of products sold via mass retail outlets, as well as a mail-order catalog business (As We Change) that sold proprietary and third-party nutritional and personal care products aimed at women over 40. However, the lines did not meet the company's expectations and NAI first sold the catalog business to Miles Kimball Company in 2008 and then sold the remaining assets to PharmaCare in 2009.

EXECUTIVES

Chairman, Chief Executive Officer, Subsidiary Officer, Director, Mark A. LeDoux, $400,000 total compensation
President, Chief Operating Officer, Secretary, Kenneth E. Wolf, $375,000 total compensation
Chief Financial Officer, Michael E. Fortin, $200,000 total compensation
Director, Guru Ramanathan
Director, Alan G. Dunn, $27,000 total compensation
Director, Laura Kay Matherly
Auditors : Haskell & White LLP

LOCATIONS

HQ: Natural Alternatives International, Inc.
1535 Faraday Ave, Carlsbad, CA 92008
Phone: 760 736-7700
Web: www.nai-online.com

COMPETITORS

AKORN, INC.
Herbalife Nutrition Ltd.
MANNATECH, INCORPORATED
NATURE'S SUNSHINE PRODUCTS, INC.
PATHEON, INC.
PERRIGO COMPANY
PRESTIGE CONSUMER HEALTHCARE INC.
RELIV' INTERNATIONAL, INC.
SAGENT PHARMACEUTICALS, INC.
VIVUS, INC.

HISTORICAL FINANCIALS
Company Type: Public

Income Statement — FYE: June 30

	REVENUE ($mil)	NET INCOME ($mil)	NET PROFIT MARGIN	EMPLOYEES
06/21	178.5	10.7	6.0%	342
06/20	118.8	(1.6)	—	316
06/19	138.2	6.5	4.7%	312
06/18	132.4	5.0	3.8%	266
06/17	121.9	7.2	5.9%	227
Annual Growth	10.0%	10.5%	—	10.8%

2021 Year-End Financials
Debt ratio: —
Return on equity: 14.2%
Cash ($ mil.): 32.1
Current Ratio: 3.64
Long-term debt ($ mil.): —
No. of shares ($ mil.): 6.4
Dividends
Yield: —
Payout: —
Market value ($ mil.): 108.0

	STOCK PRICE ($) FY Close	P/E High/Low		PER SHARE ($) Earnings	Dividends	Book Value
06/21	16.83	11	4	1.69	0.00	12.44
06/20	6.84	—	—	(0.25)	0.00	10.57
06/19	11.66	15	10	0.92	0.00	10.53
06/18	10.15	16	12	0.73	0.00	9.03
06/17	9.95	13	8	1.09	0.00	8.81
Annual Growth	14.0%	—	—	11.6%	—	9.0%

Natural Grocers By Vitamin Cottage Inc

Natural Grocers by Vitamin Cottage (Natural Grocer) is an expanding specialty retailer of natural and organic groceries and dietary supplements. The fast-growing company (both in sales and store count) operates more than 160 stores in some 20 US states that sell natural and organic food, including fresh produce, meat, frozen food, and non-perishable bulk food; vitamins and dietary supplements; personal care products; pet care products; and books. The company sources from approximately 1,100 suppliers and offer approximately 3,200 brands that range from small independent businesses to multi-national conglomerates. Founded by Margaret and Philip Isely in 1958, Natural Grocers is run by members of the Isely family.

IPO

Operations

The company's stores range in size from 5,000 sq. ft. to 16,000 sq. ft. (A typical new store averages 11,000 sq. ft.) Each store offers about 21,000 different natural and organic products and 6,900 different dietary supplements.

Natural Grocers generates about 70% of its revenue from groceries, with dietary supplements accounting for around 20%, and the remainder coming from body care, pet care, books, and general merchandise.

Geographic Reach

Colorado is the company's home state and also its largest market with about a quarter of its stores. Other major markets for the company include Texas (home to about 15% of stores), as well as Oregon, Arizona, Utah, and Kansas. It operates a bulk food repackaging facility and distribution center in Colorado.

Sales and Marketing

The company seeks to attract new customers by enhancing their nutrition knowledge through the distribution of printed and digital versions of its broad range of educational resources, including the Health Hotline magazine. The chain devotes considerable marketing resources to educating customers on the benefits of natural and organic grocery products and dietary supplements. The company maintains www.naturalgrocers.com as its official company website to host store information, sale and discount offers, educational materials, product and standards information, policies and contact forms, advocacy and news items and e-commerce capabilities. Its website is interlinked with other online and social media outlets, including Facebook, Instagram, Twitter, Pinterest and YouTube.

Natural Grocers reported total advertising and marketing expenses for years ended 2021, 2020 and 2019 were $6.3 million, $6.6 million and $8.2 million, respectively.

Financial Performance

Net sales increased $18.7 million to $1.1 billion in fiscal 2021 (ended September) compared to $1 billion in fiscal 2020, primarily due to a $4.2 million increase in comparable store sales, and a $14.5 million increase in new store sales.

Net income in fiscal 2021 (ended September) was $20.6 million compared to $20 million fiscal 2020.

Cash held by the company at the end of 2021 decreased to $23.7 million compared to 2020 with $28.5 million. Cash provided by operations was $53.9 million, while cash used for investing and financing activities were $27.7 million and $30.9 million, respectively. Main uses of cash were acquisition of property and equipment; and repayments under credit facility.

Strategy

Natural Grocers is pursuing several strategies to continue its profitable growth, including expanding its store base; increasing sales from an existing customer; growing its customer base; and improving operating margins.

In order to increase its average ticket and the number of customer transactions, the company plan to continue offering an engaging customer experience by providing science-based nutrition education and a differentiated merchandising strategy that delivers affordable, high-quality natural and organic grocery products and dietary supplements. The company also plan to continue to utilize targeted marketing efforts to reach its existing customers, including through the {N}power customer loyalty program ({N}power), which it anticipates will drive customer transactions, increase the average ticket and convert occasional, single-category customers into a core, multi-category customers.

EXECUTIVES

Chairman, Co-President, Director, Kemper Isely, $607,800 total compensation

Co-President, Director, Zephyr Isely, $576,000 total compensation

Executive Vice President, Corporate Secretary, Director, Heather Isely, $528,000 total compensation

Executive Vice President, Director, Elizabeth Isely, $528,000 total compensation

Chief Financial Officer, Todd Dissinger, $329,970 total compensation

Director, Edward Cerkovnik

Director, Richard Halle

Director, David C. Rooney

Auditors : KPMG LLP

LOCATIONS

HQ: Natural Grocers By Vitamin Cottage Inc
12612 West Alameda Parkway, Lakewood, CO 80228
Phone: 303 986-4600
Web: www.naturalgrocers.com

2017 Stores

	No.
Colorado	37
Texas	21
Arizona	12
Kansas	8
Oregon	9
Oklahoma	7
New Mexico	5
Utah	7
Idaho	4
Montana	4
Missouri	4
Nebraska	3
Nevada	3
Arkansas	3
North Dakota	2
Washington	3
Wyoming	2
Iowa	5
Minnesota	1
Total	**140**

PRODUCTS/OPERATIONS

2017 Sales

	% of total
Grocery	67
Dietary supplements	22
Body care, pet care, and other	11
Total	**100**

COMPETITORS

BLUE BUFFALO PET PRODUCTS, INC.
CORE-MARK HOLDING COMPANY, INC.
GNC HOLDINGS, INC.
NATURE'S SUNSHINE PRODUCTS, INC.
SPROUTS FARMERS MARKET, INC.
TEAVANA CORPORATION
THE NATURE'S BOUNTY CO
VALOR ACQUISITION, LLC
VITACOST.COM INC.
VITAMIN WORLD, INC.

HISTORICAL FINANCIALS
Company Type: Public

Income Statement — FYE: September 30

	REVENUE ($mil)	NET INCOME ($mil)	NET PROFIT MARGIN	EMPLOYEES
09/21	1,055.5	20.5	1.9%	4,192
09/20	1,036.8	20.0	1.9%	4,272
09/19	903.5	9.4	1.0%	3,681
09/18	849.0	12.6	1.5%	3,598
09/17	769.0	6.8	0.9%	3,270
Annual Growth	8.2%	31.5%	—	6.4%

2021 Year-End Financials

Debt ratio: 10.1% No. of shares ($ mil.): 22.6
Return on equity: 13.0% Dividends
Cash ($ mil.): 23.6 Yield: 20.3%
Current Ratio: 1.01 Payout: 300.0%
Long-term debt ($ mil.): 61.3 Market value ($ mil.): 254.0

	STOCK PRICE ($) FY Close	P/E High/Low		PER SHARE ($) Earnings	Dividends	Book Value
09/21	11.22	20	11	0.91	2.28	6.31
09/20	9.86	19	7	0.89	0.28	7.68
09/19	9.99	54	20	0.42	0.00	6.99
09/18	16.89	34	8	0.56	0.00	6.56
09/17	5.58	44	18	0.31	0.00	5.96
Annual Growth	19.1%	—	—	30.9%	—	1.4%

Nautilus Inc

Nautilus makes and markets cardio and strength-building fitness equipment for home use. Its products include home gyms, free weights and benches, treadmills, exercise bikes, and elliptical machines that are sold under the popular brand names Bowflex, Nautilus, Schwinn, and JRNY. Nautilus sells its fitness equipment directly to consumers through its variety of brand websites and catalogs, as well as through TV commercials. The company also markets its gear through specialty retailers in the US, Europe, and Canada. The company generates the majority of its sales in the US. Nautilus was founded in 1986 and went public in 1999.

Operations

The company operates its fitness equipment business through a pair of reportable segments. As part of its Retail segment (more than 60%), Nautilus sells products through a network of retail companies, via brick and mortar locations and those retailers' websites. Its Direct segment (almost 40% of revenue) sells products directly to consumers through TV advertising, the Internet, and catalogs.

Nautilus also derives a portion of its revenue from the licensing of its brands and intellectual property.

Geographic Reach

Washington-based, Nautilus operates in the US, Europe, Asia and Canada with warehouse and distribution facilities located in California, Oregon, and Ohio in the US. Its quality assurance and software engineering office is located in China.

The US accounts for about 80% of revenue. The remaining revenues are from Canada, EMEA and other countries.

Sales and Marketing

Nautilus sells its products directly to consumers via its websites bowflex.com, bowflex.ca, schwinnfitness.com and nautilus.com. In addition to television advertising, its marketing mix includes a combination of digital, search, shopping and social media, as well as email and direct mail campaigns. The company's products are marketed through a network of retail companies, via brick and mortar locations and those retailers' websites. Retail partners include online-only retailers, sporting goods stores, electronics stores, furniture stores, large-format and warehouse stores, smaller specialty retailers, and independent bike dealers.

Advertising and promotion costs totaled $61.5 million, $12.3 million, and $36.3 million for fiscal years 2022, 2021, and 2020, respectively.

Financial Performance

Net sales were $589.5 million for 2022, reflecting an 11% decrease as compared to net sales of $664.9 million for 2021. Direct segment's net sales were $221.7 million for 2022, compared to $295.3 million, a decline of 24.9%, versus the same period in 2021. The net sales decrease was primarily driven by lower cardio sales. Retail Segment decrease in sales was primarily driven by lower demand for its bikes and higher sales discounting, partially offset by strong sales of SelectTech weights and benches. Royalty income increased by $0.01 million, or 0.2%, to $3.7 million for 2022, compared to 2021, primarily due to royalty settlements.

In 2022, the company had a net loss of $22.2 million, a 73% improvement from the previous year's net loss of $81.5 million.

The company's cash at the end of 2022 was $18.1 million. Operating activities used $66.6 million. Financing and investing activities generated $12.7 million and $34.4 million, respectively.

Strategy

Nautilus empowers healthier living through individualized connected fitness experiences. The company develops and markets home fitness equipment and related products to meet the needs of a broad range of consumers. It has diversified its business by expanding its portfolio of high quality fitness equipment into multiple product lines utilizing the company's well-recognized brand names. The company views the continual innovation of its product offerings as a key aspect of its business strategy. The company regularly refreshes its existing product lines with new technologies and finishes, and focuses significant effort and resources on the development or acquisition of innovative new fitness products and technologies for introduction to the marketplace at periodic intervals.

The company's long-term strategy involves: enhancing its product lines by designing personalized connected-fitness equipment that meets or exceeds the high expectations of its existing and new customers; continuing its investment in innovation, with a particular focus on expanding the reach of its digital platform, JRNY; creatively marketing its equipment, both directly to consumers and through its retail customers, while leveraging its well-known brand names; increasing its international retail sales and distribution; and maximizing available royalty revenues from the licensing of the company's brands and intellectual property.

Mergers and Acquisitions

In late 2021, Nautilus entered into a definitive agreement to acquire VAY (pronounced "way"), a leader in motion technology. Through a combination of machine learning expertise and a deep knowledge of human biomechanics, VAY's proprietary technology enables computers to understand human motion using cameras. The acquisition will allow Nautilus to scale its JRNY digital platform by providing foundational technologies to power the company's vision and motion tracking capabilities that enable real-time data analysis during workouts. Nautilus will integrate these capabilities into its JRNY platform to further advance and accelerate highly personalized one-on-one workout experiences. Financial terms of the transaction were not disclosed.

Company Background

Nautilus, Inc. was founded in 1986 and incorporated in the State of Washington in 1993. Their headquarters are located in Vancouver, Washington.

EXECUTIVES

Chairman, Director, M. Carl Johnson
Chief Executive Officer, Director, James "Jim" Barr IV, $550,000 total compensation
Senior Vice President, Chief Digital Officer, Garry R. Wiseman
Product Development Senior Vice President, Christopher K. Quatrochi, $254,808 total compensation
Senior Vice President, Region Officer, Jay E. McGregor

Marketing Chief Marketing Officer, Direct Chief Marketing Officer, Becky L. Alseth
Vice President, Division Officer, Jeffery L. Collins
Chief Financial Officer, Aina E. Konold
Chief People Officer, Ellen Raim
Chief Supply Chain Officer, John R. Goelz
Chief Legal Officer, Secretary, Alan L. Chan
Director, Anne G. Saunders
Director, Patricia "Patty" M. Ross
Director, Kelley K. Hall
Director, Shailesh Prakash
Director, Ruby Sharma
Auditors : Grant Thornton LLP

LOCATIONS

HQ: Nautilus Inc
17750 S.E. 6th Way, Vancouver, WA 98683
Phone: 360 859-2900
Web: www.nautilusinc.com

2014 Sales

	$ mil	% of total
US	231.2	84
Canada	35.4	13
Other countries	7.8	3
Total	274.4	100

PRODUCTS/OPERATIONS

2014 Sales

	$ mil	% of total
Direct	175.6	64
Retail	93.2	34
Royalty income	5.6	2
Total	274.4	100

Selected Brands
Bowflex
Nautilus
Schwinn Fitness
Universal

COMPETITORS

24 HOUR FITNESS WORLDWIDE, INC.
BODY CENTRAL CORP.
CURVES INTERNATIONAL, INC.
CYBEX INTERNATIONAL, INC.
GOLD'S GYM INTERNATIONAL, INC.
HAMILTON BEACH BRANDS HOLDING COMPANY
JAZZERCISE, INC.
NORTH CASTLE PARTNERS, L.L.C.
PFIP, LLC
PLANET FITNESS, INC.

HISTORICAL FINANCIALS

Company Type: Public

Income Statement — FYE: December 31

	REVENUE ($mil)	NET INCOME ($mil)	NET PROFIT MARGIN	EMPLOYEES
12/20	552.5	59.8	10.8%	412
12/19	309.2	(92.8)	—	434
12/18	396.7	14.6	3.7%	460
12/17	406.1	26.2	6.5%	491
12/16	406.0	34.1	8.4%	469
Annual Growth	8.0%	15.0%	—	(3.2%)

2020 Year-End Financials
Debt ratio: 4.2%
Return on equity: 48.9%
Cash ($ mil.): 92.7
Current Ratio: 2.00
Long-term debt ($ mil.): 10.7
No. of shares ($ mil.): 30.3
Dividends
 Yield: —
 Payout: —
Market value ($ mil.): 550.0

	STOCK PRICE ($) FY Close	P/E High/Low		PER SHARE ($) Earnings	Dividends	Book Value
12/20	18.14	14	1	1.86	0.00	5.05
12/19	1.75	—	—	(3.13)	0.00	3.04
12/18	10.90	34	21	0.48	0.00	6.18
12/17	13.35	23	14	0.85	0.00	5.91
12/16	18.50	23	14	1.09	0.00	5.22
Annual Growth	(0.5%)	—	—	14.3%	—	(0.8%)

Nelnet Inc

Nelnet is a publicly-traded diversified financial services and technology company focused on offering educational services, technology solutions, professional services, telecommunications and asset management. Nelnet has nearly $18 billion in assets and services over $530 billion in loan assets. Nelnet helps students and families plan and pay for their education and makes the administrative processes for schools more efficient with student loan servicing, tuition payment processing, school administration software, and college planning resources. Nelnet also offers fiber-optic services directly to homes and businesses for ultra-fast fiber internet, television, and telephone services. Substantially all of its revenue comes from US customers.

Operations

The company's operates through five reportable operating segments: Loan Servicing and Systems (LSS), Education Technology, Services, and Payment Processing (ETS&PP), Communications, Asset Generation and Management (AGM) and Nelnet Bank.

LSS focuses on student and consumer loan origination services and servicing, loan origination and servicing-related technology solutions, and outsourcing business services. Brands include Nelnet Diversified Solutions, Nelnet Loan Servicing, Nelnet Servicing, Great Lakes Educational Loan Services, Inc. (Great Lakes), Firstmark Services, GreatNet, Nelnet Renewable Energy and Nelnet Renewable Energy.

ETS&PP provide services such as tuition payment plans and billing, financial needs assessment services, online payment and refund processing, school information system software, payment technologies, and professional development and educational instruction services. Brands include FACTS, Nelnet Campus Commerce, PaymentSpring, Nelnet Engagement, and Nelnet International.

Communications focuses on providing fiber optic service directly to homes and businesses for internet, telephone, and television services. Includes the operations of ALLO prior to the deconsolidation of ALLO in late 2020.

AGM includes the acquisition and management of student and other loan assets.

AGM also referred to as Nelnet Financial Services.

Nelnet Bank is an internet Utah-chartered industrial bank focused on the private education loan marketplace.

Geographic Reach

Headquartered in Lincoln, Nebraska, Nelnet has facilities in Colorado, Idaho, Texas, New York, Minnesota, Connecticut, Rhode Island, Utah, Nebraska, South Dakota, Texas, Wisconsin, and Washington DC. Substantially all of its revenue comes from US customers.

Nelnet International provides services and technology in Australia, New Zealand, and Southeast Asia.

Sales and Marketing

The company's customers include students and families, colleges and universities, specifically financial aid, business, and admissions offices, K-12 schools, lenders, state agencies, and government entities.

Financial Performance

Net interest income for 2021 was $360 million, a 20% increase from the previous year's net interest income of $289.6 million.

In 2021, the company had a net income of $386.3 million, a 10% increase from the previous year's net income of $349.6 million.

The company's cash at the end of 2021 was $1.2 billion. Operating activities generated $544.9 million, while financing activities used $1.5 billion, mainly for payments on bonds and notes payable.

Strategy

The company's talent strategy is focused on attracting the best talent from a diverse range of sources, recognizing and rewarding their performance, and continually developing, engaging, and retaining them.

The company is committed to the continued development of its people. Strategic talent reviews and succession planning occur on a planned cadence annually across all business areas. The executive team convenes meetings with senior leadership and the board of directors to review top enterprise talent. The company continues to provide opportunities for associates to grow their careers internally, with over half of open management positions filled internally during 2021.

Mergers and Acquisitions

In 2021, Nelnet Business Services, a division of Nelnet, Inc., is expanding its church technology offerings with the recent acquisition of Catholic Faith Technologies (CFT), an online learning and formation platform company located in Overland Park, KS. This acquisition will enable the company to expand services to its faith community partners, as well as enter into and support new markets.

Company Background

Nelnet has been through a turbulent few years as student loan reform and the financial crisis disrupted business and sent revenues down. The company's ability to adapt to the economic pressures and policy changes have helped it land face-up following the recession. Measures taken, including laying off staff and tightening lending practices, helped boost profits despite lower revenues. Although non-FFELP servicing income and payment processing revenues grew in 2011, FFELP servicing revenues declined as the portfolio further shrunk, and school marketing sales decreased as schools cut back on spending. As a result, revenues fell that year by 8% to $979 million. Net income increased 8% (to $204 million) in 2011 compared to 2010, when the company had expenses related to restructuring. Also in 2010 Nelnet paid the US government $55 million to settle a lawsuit claiming it had made false statements to receive extra subsidies.

In a blow to the student lending industry, President Barack Obama eliminated the FFELP and prohibited private lenders from making federal student loans in 2010. All new federal student loans began going directly through the Department of Education's Direct Loan Program. As a result, Nelnet no longer originates new FFELP loans.

But the change didn't put an end to Nelnet. The company was awarded a five-year servicing contract for federally owned student loans, including existing FFELP loans. Nelnet also began servicing new loans generated directly under the Federal Direct Loan Program. The contract was a major win for the company. Nelnet expects that its fee-based revenue will increase as the servicing volume for these loans increases (while the FFELP portfolio declines). The company is also focusing on improving its customer service to increase the allotted percentage of new government loans it services.

CEO Michael Dunlap controls the company, holding 68% of the voting power for Nelnet. Dunlap and his family also own Farmers & Merchants Investment.

EXECUTIVES

Executive Chairman, Director, Michael S. Dunlap, $530,450 total compensation
President, Timothy A. Tewes, $550,000 total compensation
Chief Executive Officer, Jeffrey R. Noordhoek, $716,107 total compensation
Chief Business Development Officer, Division Officer, Director, Matthew W. Dunlap
Chief Financial Officer, James D. Kruger, $550,000 total compensation
Chief Operating Officer, Terry J. Heimes, $716,107 total compensation
Chief Governance Officer, General Counsel, Corporate Secretary, William J. Munn, $245,850 total compensation
Lead Director, Director, Thomas E. Henning, $20,000 total compensation
Director, Adam K. Peterson
Director, Jona M. Van Deun
Director, Preeta D. Bansal
Director, William R. Cintani
Director, Kimberly K. Rath
Director, Kathleen A. Farrell
Director, David S. Graff
Auditors : KPMG LLP

LOCATIONS

HQ: Nelnet Inc
121 South 13th Street, Suite 100, Lincoln, NE 68508
Phone: 402 458-2370
Web: www.nelnetinvestors.com

PRODUCTS/OPERATIONS

2015 Sales

	$ mil.	% of total
Interest		
Loans	726.3	60
Investments	7.8	1
Noninterest		
Loan & guaranty servicing	239.9	20
Enrollment services	70.7	6
Tuition payment processing & campus commerce revenue	120.4	10
Gains on sale of loans & debt repurchases, net	5.1	1
Other	32.0	2
Total	1,202.2	100

COMPETITORS

ATLANTICUS HOLDINGS CORPORATION
CLAYTON, DUBILIER & RICE, INC.
COGNITION FINANCIAL CORPORATION
CREDIT ACCEPTANCE CORPORATION
GENERAL MOTORS FINANCIAL COMPANY, INC.
HIGHER ONE HOLDINGS, INC.
IMPACT HOLDINGS (UK) PLC
NAVIENT CORPORATION
PENNSYLVANIA HIGHER EDUCATION ASSISTANCE AGENCY
WORLD ACCEPTANCE CORPORATION

HISTORICAL FINANCIALS

Company Type: Public

Income Statement			FYE: December 31	
	ASSETS ($mil)	NET INCOME ($mil)	INCOME AS % OF ASSETS	EMPLOYEES
12/20	22,646.1	352.4	1.6%	6,199
12/19	23,708.9	141.8	0.6%	6,600
12/18	25,220.9	227.9	0.9%	6,200
12/17	23,964.4	173.1	0.7%	4,300
12/16	27,180.1	256.7	0.9%	3,700
Annual Growth	(4.5%)	8.2%	—	13.8%

2020 Year-End Financials

Return on assets: 1.5%
Return on equity: 14.0%
Long-term debt ($ mil.): —
No. of shares ($ mil.): 38.3
Sales ($ mil.): 1,730
Dividends
Yield: 1.1%
Payout: 19.9%
Market value ($ mil.): 2,732.0

	STOCK PRICE ($) FY Close	P/E High/Low		PER SHARE ($) Earnings	Dividends	Book Value
12/20	71.24	8	4	9.02	0.82	68.63
12/19	58.24	20	15	3.54	0.74	60.07
12/18	52.34	11	9	5.57	0.66	57.24
12/17	54.78	14	9	4.14	0.58	52.67
12/16	50.75	9	5	6.02	0.50	48.96
Annual Growth	8.8%	—	—	10.6%	13.2%	8.8%

Neurocrine Biosciences, Inc.

For Neurocrine Biosciences, drug development is all about body chemistry. The development-stage biotech develops treatments for neurological and endocrine hormone-related diseases, such as insomnia, depression, and menstrual pain. Lead drug candidate Elagolix is designed to treat endometriosis which causes pain and irregular menstrual bleeding in women. Second in line is NBI-98854, a treatment for movement disorders. Neurocrine Biosciences works in additional therapeutic areas including anxiety, cancer, epilepsy, and diabetes. The company has about a dozen drug candidates in various stages of research and clinical development, through both internal programs and collaborative agreements with partners.

EXECUTIVES

Chairman, Director, William H. Rastetter
Chief Executive Officer, Director, Kevin Charles Gorman, $640,000 total compensation
Chief Financial Officer, Matthew C. Abernethy, $420,000 total compensation
Chief Commercial Officer, Eric Benevich, $432,600 total compensation
Chief Corporate Affairs Officer, David W. Boyer
Chief Human Resources Officer, Julie S. Cooke
Chief Business Development Officer, Chief Strategy Officer, Kyle Gano, $403,100 total compensation
Chief Legal Officer, Corporate Secretary, Darin M. Lippoldt
Chief Regulatory Officer, Malcolm Lloyd-Smith
Chief Scientific Officer, Jude Onyia
Chief Medical Officer, Eiry W. Roberts, $490,700 total compensation
Director, Richard F. Pops
Director, Shalini Sharp
Director, Stephen A. Sherwin
Director, George J. Morrow
Director, Leslie V. Norwalk
Director, Gary A. Lyons, $125,000 total compensation
Director, Johanna Mercier
Auditors : Ernst & Young LLP

LOCATIONS

HQ: Neurocrine Biosciences, Inc.
  12780 El Camino Real, San Diego, CA 92130
Phone: 858 617-7600
Web: www.neurocrine.com

PRODUCTS/OPERATIONS

Selected Drug Candidates
Aptiepileptic drug (epileptic seizures)
CRF 1 Antagonist (stree-related disorder)
Elagolix (endometriosis)
Elagolix (uterine fibroids, with AbbVie)
GPR 119 (type II diabetes, with Boehringer Ingelheim)
GnRH Antagonist (oncology and men and women's health, with AbbVie)
Indiplon (insomnia, with Dainippon Sumitomo Pharma)
VMAT2 Inhibitor (movement disorders, central nervous system)
VMAT2 (NBI-98854) (movement disorder, with AbbVie)

COMPETITORS

EMD SERONO, INC.
FIBROGEN, INC.
Helix BioPharma Corp
MEDICINOVA, INC.
NURX PHARMACEUTICALS, INC.
SAGE THERAPEUTICS, INC.
SEELOS THERAPEUTICS, INC.
SYNTHETIC BIOLOGICS, INC.
Transition Therapeutics Inc
UCB Pharma GmbH

HISTORICAL FINANCIALS
Company Type: Public

Income Statement — FYE: December 31

	REVENUE ($mil)	NET INCOME ($mil)	NET PROFIT MARGIN	EMPLOYEES
12/21	1,133.5	89.6	7.9%	900
12/20	1,045.9	407.3	38.9%	845
12/19	788.0	37.0	4.7%	700
12/18	451.2	21.1	4.7%	585
12/17	161.6	(142.5)	—	400
Annual Growth	62.7%	—	—	22.5%

2021 Year-End Financials
Debt ratio: 16.2%
Return on equity: 7.1%
Cash ($ mil.): 340.8
Current Ratio: 3.96
Long-term debt ($ mil.): 335.1
No. of shares ($ mil.): 94.9
Dividends
  Yield: —
  Payout: —
Market value ($ mil.): 8,083.0

	STOCK PRICE ($) FY Close	P/E High/Low		PER SHARE ($) Earnings	Dividends	Book Value
12/21	85.17	126	84	0.92	0.00	14.48
12/20	95.85	31	17	4.16	0.00	12.04
12/19	107.49	296	173	0.39	0.00	6.90
12/18	71.41	547	297	0.22	0.00	5.29
12/17	77.59	—	—	(1.62)	0.00	4.19
Annual Growth	2.4%	—	—	—	—	36.3%

New Residential Investment Corp

Rithm Capital Corp. (formerly known as New Residential Investment Corp.) is an investment manager with a vertically integrated mortgage platform. It is structured as a real estate investment trust (REIT) for US federal income tax purposes. Its diversified portfolio includes mortgage origination subsidiary NewRez; entities that provide mortgage servicing rights (MSRs), a leading mortgage origination and servicing company, related ancillary mortgage services businesses, residential mortgage-backed securities and loans, consumer loans, and other opportunistic investments. Other subsidiaries and affiliates include Shellpoint (mortgage services), Avenue 365 (title insurance), eStreet (appraisal management), Covius (diversified mortgage services), and Guardian Asset Management (field services and property management). Rithm Capital has more than $39.7 billion in total assets.

Operations
Rithm Capital conducts its business through six segments: Origination, Servicing, MSR Related Investments, Residential Securities, Properties and Loans, Consumer Loans, and Mortgage Loans Receivable.

Servicing and originations, which accounts for about 85% of total revenue, includes originations, servicing and MSR related investments segments. The residential securities and loans includes real estate securities, or RMBS, and residential mortgage loans; it accounts for roughly 15% of total revenue. The remainder of the company's revenue is generated from consumer loans.

Geographic Reach
Rithm Capital is headquartered in New York.

Sales and Marketing
As a lender, Rithm Capital provides refinance opportunities to eligible existing servicing customers, primarily through its direct-to-consumer channel and also originates or purchases loans from brokers or originators through retail, wholesale, and correspondent channels.

Financial Performance
The company's revenue for fiscal 2021 increased by 117% to $3.6 billion compared from the prior year with $1.7 billion.

Net income for fiscal 2021 was $805.6 million compared from the prior year with a net loss of $1.4 billion. This was primarily due to the higher volume of sales for the year.

Cash held by the company at the end of fiscal 2021 increased to $1.5 billion. Cash provided by operations and investing activities were $2.9 billion and $2.3 billion, respectively. Cash used for financing activities was $4.7 billion, mainly for repayments of warehouse credit facilities.

Strategy
The company's investment strategy also involves opportunistically pursuing acquisitions and seeking to establish strategic partnerships that enables the company to maximize the value of the mortgage loans it originates and/or services by offering products and services to customers, servicers, and other parties through the lifecycle of transactions that affect each mortgage loan and underlying residential property or collateral.

Rithm Capital's investment strategy may evolve in light of existing market conditions and investment opportunities, and this evolution may involve additional risks depending upon the nature of the assets in which the company invest and its ability to finance such assets on a short or long-term basis. Investment opportunities that present unattractive risk-return profiles relative to other available investment opportunities under particular market conditions may become relatively attractive under changed market conditions, and changes in market conditions may therefore result in changes in the investments it targets.

Mergers and Acquisitions

In late 2021, Rithm Capital acquired Genesis Capital LLC (Genesis), a leading business purpose lender that provides innovative solutions to developers of new construction, fix and flip and rental hold projects, and acquire a related portfolio of loans. The acquisition of Genesis adds a new complementary business line to its company and advances its ability to create and retain additional strong housing assets for its balance sheet.

In mid-2021, Rithm Capital completed the acquisition of Caliber Home Loans, Inc., a proven leader in the US mortgage market with a diversified, customer-centric, purchase-focused platform with headquarters in Coppell, Texas. With this acquisition, Rithm Capital intends to bring together the platforms of Caliber and NewRez LLC, New Residential's wholly owned mortgage originator and servicer. Terms were not disclosed.

Company Background

New Residential was spun off from real estate investment firm Newcastle Investment Corp. in mid-2013.

EXECUTIVES

Chairman, President, Chief Executive Officer, Director, Michael Nierenberg
Chief Financial Officer, Chief Accounting Officer, Treasurer, Nicholas Santoro
Director, Pamela F. Lenehan
Director, David Saltzman
Director, Kevin J. Finnerty
Director, Patrice M. Le Melle
Director, Andrew Sloves
Independent Director, Peggy Hwan Hebard
Auditors : Ernst & Young LLP

LOCATIONS

HQ: New Residential Investment Corp
1345 Avenue of the Americas, New York, NY 10105
Phone: 212 798-3150
Web: www.newresi.com

COMPETITORS

ACRES COMMERCIAL REALTY CORP.
ANNALY CAPITAL MANAGEMENT, INC.
APOLLO COMMERCIAL REAL ESTATE FINANCE, INC.
CAPSTEAD MORTGAGE CORPORATION
FIRST EAGLE PRIVATE CREDIT, LLC
IMPAC MORTGAGE HOLDINGS, INC.
OCWEN FINANCIAL CORPORATION
RAIT FINANCIAL TRUST
TPG RE FINANCE TRUST, INC.
TPG REAL ESTATE FINANCE TRUST

HISTORICAL FINANCIALS

Company Type: Public

Income Statement — FYE: December 31

	REVENUE ($mil)	NET INCOME ($mil)	NET PROFIT MARGIN	EMPLOYEES
12/21	3,521.4	772.2	21.9%	12,296
12/20	1,013.6	(1,410.3)	—	5,471
12/19	2,585.6	563.2	21.8%	3,387
12/18	2,237.5	963.9	43.1%	0
12/17	2,151.8	957.5	44.5%	0
Annual Growth	13.1%	(5.2%)	—	—

2021 Year-End Financials

Debt ratio: 74.9%
Return on equity: 12.9%
Cash ($ mil.): 1,332.5
Current Ratio: 1.40
Long-term debt ($ mil.): 29,780.9
No. of shares ($ mil.): 466.7
Dividends
  Yield: 8.4%
  Payout: 65.2%
Market value ($ mil.): 4,999.0

	STOCK PRICE ($) FY Close	P/E High/Low		PER SHARE ($) Earnings	Dividends	Book Value
12/21	10.71	7	6	1.51	0.90	14.15
12/20	9.94	—	—	(3.52)	0.50	12.83
12/19	16.11	13	10	1.34	2.00	17.23
12/18	14.21	7	5	2.81	2.00	16.25
12/17	17.88	6	5	3.15	1.98	15.26
Annual Growth	(12.0%)	—	—	(16.8%)	(17.9%)	(1.9%)

Newmark Group Inc

EXECUTIVES

Chairman, Principal Executive Officer, Director, Howard W. Lutnick, $500,000 total compensation
Chief Executive Officer, Barry M. Gosin, $1,000,000 total compensation
Executive Vice President, Chief Legal Officer, Assistant Secretary, Stephen M. Merkel
Chief Financial Officer, Michael J. Rispoli, $415,000 total compensation
Director, Jay Itzkowitz
Director, Kenneth A. McIntyre
Director, Michael Snow
Director, Virginia S. Bauer
Auditors : Ernst & Young LLP

LOCATIONS

HQ: Newmark Group Inc
125 Park Avenue, New York, NY 10017
Phone: 212 372-2000
Web: www.ngkf.com

HISTORICAL FINANCIALS

Company Type: Public

Income Statement — FYE: December 31

	REVENUE ($mil)	NET INCOME ($mil)	NET PROFIT MARGIN	EMPLOYEES
12/20	1,904.9	80.0	4.2%	5,800
12/19	2,218.1	117.3	5.3%	5,600
12/18	2,047.5	106.7	5.2%	5,200
12/17	1,596.4	144.4	9.1%	4,800
12/16	1,349.9	168.4	12.5%	4,600
Annual Growth	9.0%	(17.0%)	—	6.0%

2020 Year-End Financials

Debt ratio: 44.6%
Return on equity: 12.3%
Cash ($ mil.): 191.4
Current Ratio: 1.07
Long-term debt ($ mil.): 680.3
No. of shares ($ mil.): 182.4
Dividends
  Yield: 1.7%
  Payout: 39.3%
Market value ($ mil.): 1,330.0

	STOCK PRICE ($) FY Close	P/E High/Low		PER SHARE ($) Earnings	Dividends	Book Value
12/20	7.29	33	6	0.39	0.13	3.70
12/19	13.46	23	13	0.59	0.39	3.50
12/18	8.02	26	12	0.65	0.27	3.33
12/17	15.90	15	13	1.08	0.00	1.82
Annual Growth	(22.9%)	—	—	(28.8%)	—	26.6%

Newtek Business Services Corp

Newtek Business Services provides a suite of business and financial services to small to midsized businesses, including electronic merchant payment processing, website hosting, Small Business Administration (SBA) loans, data storage, insurance, accounts receivable financing, and payroll management. The company serves more than 100,000 business accounts throughout the US. Newtek also has investments in certified capital companies (Capcos), which are authorized in eight states and Washington, DC. It has stakes in about a dozen Capcos that traditionally have issued debt and equity securities to insurance firms, then used the funds to mainly invest in small and midsized financial and business services firms.

Operations

The company's largest business segment is electronic payment processing, which brings in about two-thirds of all sales. Web hosting services is comprised of its CrystalTech Web Hosting subsidiary and accounts for about 15% of revenues. Another segment, Small Business Finance, provides loans so small businesses.

Geographic Reach

Stationed in New York, Newtek has additional sales and support offices in Milwaukee and Brownsville, Texas. Although the majority of its revenue is generated from the US, the company provides pre-paid website hosting services to customers in 120 countries.

Sales and Marketing

Newtek markets its array of services under agreements with alliance partners, which are principally financial institutions, including banks, credit unions, and other related businesses that are able to refer potential customers through Newtek's NewTracker referral system. In addition, the company enters into agreements with independent sales agents throughout the country.

The company targets select markets such as restaurants, financial institutions, medical practices, law firms, accountants, retail, and technology service providers for channel business and reselling.

Financial Performance

Newtek's revenues have been growing slowly but steadily for years. Revenues were up 5% from $125 million in 2011 to $131 million in 2012, a historic milestone for the company. Profits also skyrocketed by 62% from $3.5 million in 2011 to nearly $5.6 million in 2012. (This marks the continuation of a major turnaround as the company lost money every year between 2006 and 2009.)

The revenue growth for 2012 was led by a 4% bump in electronic payment processing, a 30% surge in interest income, and a jump in servicing fee income. It also attributes the growth to its efforts to attract more business customers -- the company has been on a bit of a marketing blitz -- and increase its small business lending.

Newtek has been focused on cutting expenses and has even cut some staff positions that no longer fit in with its long-term growth strategy. Its rise in profits for 2012 was attributed to lower technology expenses driven by a decline in deprecation and amortization costs.

Strategy

Newtek plans to concentrate on organically growing its business services activities, which also includes bookkeeping and website design and development. It also grows through selective merchant portfolio acquisitions.

EXECUTIVES

Chairman, President, Chief Executive Officer, Director, Barry Sloane, $600,000 total compensation
Financial Reporting Executive Vice President, Finance Executive Vice President, Elise Chamberlain
Senior Vice President, Chief Administrative Officer, Director, Halli Razon-Feingold
Chief Lending Officer, Subsidiary Officer, Director, Peter Downs, $319,167 total compensation
Chief Accounting Officer, Subsidiary Officer, Nicholas J. Leger
Chief Compliance Officer, Chief Legal Officer, Secretary, Michael A. Schwartz, $329,167 total compensation
Chief Risk Officer, Nicolas Young
Director, Richard J. Salute
Director, Salvatore F. Mulia
Director, Gregory L. Zink
Director, Fernando Perez-Hickman
Auditors : RSM US LLP

LOCATIONS

HQ: Newtek Business Services Corp
  4800 T Rex Avenue, Suite 120, Boca Raton, FL 33431
Phone: 212 356-9500
Web: www.newtekone.com

PRODUCTS/OPERATIONS

Selected Subsidiaries
Automated Merchant Services, Inc.
Business Connect, LLC
CCC Real Estate Holdings Co., LLC
CDS Business Services, Inc. (dba Newtek Business Credit)
CrystalTech Web Hosting, Inc. (dba Newtek Technology Services)
Exponential Business Development Co., Inc.
First Bankcard Alliance of Alabama, LLC
Fortress Data Management, LLC
Newtek Insurance Agency, LLC
Newtek Small Business Finance, Inc.
Small Business Lending, Inc.
Solar Processing Solutions, LLC
Summit Systems and Design, LLC
The Texas Whitestone Group, LLC
Universal Processing Services of Wisconsin, LLC
The Whitestone Group, LLC
Wilshire Alabama Partners, LLC
Wilshire Colorado Partners, LLC
Wilshire DC Partners, LLC
Wilshire Holdings I, Inc.
Wilshire Holdings II, Inc.
Wilshire Louisiana Bidco, LLC
Wilshire Louisiana Capital Management Fund, LLC
Wilshire Louisiana Partners II, LLC
Wilshire Louisiana Partners III, LLC
Wilshire Louisiana Partners IV, LLC
Wilshire New York Advisers II, LLC
Wilshire New York Partners III, LLC
Wilshire New York Partners IV, LLC
Wilshire New York Partners V, LLC
Wilshire Partners, LLC
Wilshire Texas Partners I, LLC

COMPETITORS

CAPITAL ON DECK INC
CREDIT SAISON CO., LTD.
HITACHI CAPITAL (UK) PLC
NATIONAL FUNDING, INC.
NICHOLAS FINANCIAL, INC.

HISTORICAL FINANCIALS

Company Type: Public

Income Statement				FYE: December 31
	REVENUE ($mil)	NET INCOME ($mil)	NET PROFIT MARGIN	EMPLOYEES
12/20	92.2	31.9	34.7%	110
12/19	59.2	(5.6)	—	109
12/18	49.5	(7.4)	—	175
12/17	38.9	(7.8)	—	162
12/16	30.9	(9.2)	—	137
Annual Growth	31.4%	—	—	(5.3%)

2020 Year-End Financials

Debt ratio: 53.7%   No. of shares ($ mil.): 21.9
Return on equity: 9.6%   Dividends
Cash ($ mil.): 2.0   Yield: 10.4%
Current Ratio: 0.92   Payout: 152.9%
Long-term debt ($ mil.): 365.4   Market value ($ mil.): 433.0

	STOCK PRICE ($) FY Close	P/E High/Low		PER SHARE ($) Earnings	Dividends	Book Value
12/20	19.69	15	6	1.51	2.05	15.45
12/19	22.65	—	—	(0.29)	2.15	15.70
12/18	17.44	—	—	(0.40)	1.80	15.19
12/17	18.49	—	—	(0.45)	3.39	15.08
12/16	15.90	—	—	(0.64)	3.14	14.30
Annual Growth	5.5%	—	—	—	(10.1%)	1.9%

NexPoint Residential Trust Inc

EXECUTIVES

Chairman, President, Director, James D. Dondero
Finance Executive Vice President, Finance Chief Financial Officer, Finance Secretary, Finance Treasurer, Director, Brian Mitts
Executive Vice President, Chief Investment Officer, Matt McGraner
Asset Management Senior Vice President, Investments Senior Vice President, Matthew Goetz
General Counsel, Dennis Charles Sauter
Lead Independent Director, Director, Scott F. Kavanaugh
Director, Carol Swain
Director, Edward N. Constantino
Director, Arthur B. Laffer
Director, Catherine Wood
Auditors : KPMG LLP

LOCATIONS

HQ: NexPoint Residential Trust Inc
  300 Crescent Court, Suite 700, Dallas, TX 75201
Phone: 214 276-6300
Web: www.nexpointliving.com

HISTORICAL FINANCIALS

Company Type: Public

Income Statement				FYE: December 31
	REVENUE ($mil)	NET INCOME ($mil)	NET PROFIT MARGIN	EMPLOYEES
12/21	219.2	23.0	10.5%	3
12/20	204.8	44.0	21.5%	3
12/19	181.0	99.1	54.8%	3
12/18	146.5	(1.6)	—	2
12/17	144.2	53.3	37.0%	2
Annual Growth	11.0%	(18.9%)	—	10.7%

2021 Year-End Financials

Debt ratio: 75.3%   No. of shares ($ mil.): 25.5
Return on equity: 5.2%   Dividends
Cash ($ mil.): 49.4   Yield: 1.6%
Current Ratio: 3.00   Payout: 157.7%
Long-term debt ($ mil.): 1,554.5 Market value ($ mil.): 2,138.0

	STOCK PRICE ($) FY Close	P/E High/Low		PER SHARE ($) Earnings	Dividends	Book Value
12/21	83.83	90	43	0.89	1.40	18.42
12/20	42.31	29	12	1.74	1.28	16.31
12/19	45.00	12	8	4.03	1.14	16.88
12/18	35.05	—	—	(0.08)	1.03	12.60
12/17	27.94	12	9	2.49	0.91	11.38
Annual Growth	31.6%	—	—	(22.7%)	11.4%	12.8%

NI Holdings Inc

EXECUTIVES

Chairman, Director, Eric K. Aasmundstad

President, Chief Executive Officer, Director, Michael J. Alexander, $750,000 total compensation
Strategy Executive Vice President, Strategy Chief Financial Officer, Strategy Treasurer, Seth C. Daggett
Operations Senior Vice President, Patrick W. Duncan, $260,000 total compensation
Director, Prakash Mathew
Director, Cindy L. Launer
Director, Stephen V. Marlow
Director, Jeffrey R. Missling
Director, William R. Devlin
Director, Duaine C. Espegard
Auditors : Mazars USA LLP

LOCATIONS
HQ: NI Holdings Inc
1101 First Avenue North, Fargo, ND 58102
Phone: 701 298-4200
Web: www.niholdingsinc.com

HISTORICAL FINANCIALS
Company Type: Public

Income Statement — FYE: December 31

	ASSETS ($mil)	NET INCOME ($mil)	INCOME AS % OF ASSETS	EMPLOYEES
12/20	617.6	40.3	6.5%	205
12/19	508.1	26.4	5.2%	186
12/18	458.4	31.0	6.8%	178
12/17	376.9	15.9	4.2%	136
12/16	278.7	4.5	1.6%	129
Annual Growth	22.0%	72.6%	—	12.3%

2020 Year-End Financials
Return on assets: 7.1%
Return on equity: 12.3%
Long-term debt ($ mil.): —
No. of shares ($ mil.): 21.3
Sales ($ mil.): 306.3
Dividends
Yield: —
Payout: —
Market value ($ mil.): 350.0

	STOCK PRICE ($) FY Close	P/E High/Low		PER SHARE ($) Earnings	Dividends	Book Value
12/20	16.42	10	6	1.84	0.00	16.15
12/19	17.20	16	12	1.19	0.00	13.85
12/18	15.73	13	11	1.39	0.00	12.28
12/17	16.98	26	20	0.71	0.00	11.30
Annual Growth	(1.1%)	—	—	37.4%	—	12.6%

Nicolet Bankshares Inc

EXECUTIVES
Subsidiary Officer, Executive Chairman, Director, Robert B. Atwell, $495,000 total compensation
President, Chief Executive Officer, Subsidiary Officer, Director, Michael E. Daniels, $495,000 total compensation
Executive Vice President, Secretary, Eric J. Witczak, $270,000 total compensation
Chief Financial Officer, Subsidiary Officer, H. Phillip Moore
Subsidiary Officer, Brad V. Hutjens, $250,000 total compensation
Subsidiary Officer, Patrick J. Madson, $267,692 total compensation
Director, Marcia M. Anderson
Director, Hector Colon
Director, Lynn D. Davis
Director, John N. Dykema
Director, Christopher J. Ghidorzi
Director, Andrew F. Hetzel
Director, Brenda L. Johnson
Director, Ann K. Lawson, $275,000 total compensation
Director, Donald J. Long
Director, Dustin J. McClone
Director, Susan L. Merkatoris
Director, Oliver Pierce Smith
Director, Paul D. Tobias
Director, Robert J. Weyers
Auditors : BKD, LLP

LOCATIONS
HQ: Nicolet Bankshares Inc
111 North Washington Street, Green Bay, WI 54301
Phone: 920 430-1400
Web: www.nicoletbank.com

HISTORICAL FINANCIALS
Company Type: Public

Income Statement — FYE: December 31

	ASSETS ($mil)	NET INCOME ($mil)	INCOME AS % OF ASSETS	EMPLOYEES
12/20	4,551.7	60.1	1.3%	573
12/19	3,577.2	54.6	1.5%	575
12/18	3,096.5	41.0	1.3%	550
12/17	2,932.4	33.1	1.1%	535
12/16	2,300.8	18.4	0.8%	480
Annual Growth	18.6%	34.3%	—	4.5%

2020 Year-End Financials
Return on assets: 1.4%
Return on equity: 11.3%
Long-term debt ($ mil.): —
No. of shares ($ mil.): 10.0
Sales ($ mil.): 211.8
Dividends
Yield: —
Payout: —
Market value ($ mil.): 664.0

	STOCK PRICE ($) FY Close	P/E High/Low		PER SHARE ($) Earnings	Dividends	Book Value
12/20	66.35	13	8	5.70	0.00	53.86
12/19	73.85	13	9	5.52	0.00	48.76
12/18	48.80	14	11	4.12	0.00	40.72
12/17	54.74	17	13	3.33	0.00	37.09
12/16	47.69	19	12	2.37	0.00	32.26
Annual Growth	8.6%	—	—	24.5%	—	13.7%

NMI Holdings Inc

NMI Holdings provides mortgage insurance through two primary subsids ? National Mortgage Insurance Corp (NMIC) and National Mortgage Reinsurance Inc. One (Re One). NMIC is its primary insurance subsidiary, approved to write coverage in all 50 states and Washington, DC. Re One provides reinsurance to NMIC on insured loans with coverage levels in excess of about 25%. The company also provides outsourced loan review services to mortgage loan originators through NMI Services. Mortgage insurance protects lenders and investors from default-related losses.

Operations
NMI Holdings offers primary mortgage insurance, which provides protection on individual mortgage loans. Mortgages are insured on a loan-by-loan basis at the time of origination. The company previously offered pool insurance, which covers the excess of loss on defaulted mortgages not covered under primary mortgage insurance.

Net Premiums accounts for more than 90% of revenues, and the net investment income and net realized investment gains account for the rest.

Geographic Reach
NMI Holdings gets all of its revenue in the US. Ten states account for more than half of its total risk-in-force (RIF), or the total dollar amount of claims it expects to receive during the year. California, Texas, and Virginia account for more than 10%, nearly 10%, and less than 5% of RIF, respectively.

Its corporate office is located in Emeryville, California.

Sales and Marketing
NMI structure its sales force into National Accounts that focus on relationships with national or large regional lenders, and Regional Accounts that focus on relationships with small or regional lenders, such as community banks, credit unions, mortgage bankers and branches of National Accounts. It also maintains a dedicated customer service team, which is refer to as the Solution Center and which offers support in loan submission and underwriting service, risk management and technology to support our sales efforts. The company has Master Policies in around 1,475 customers.

Financial Performance
NIH's revenues have been climbing rapidly over the past five years, but net income has only been rising after a dip in 2017.

Revenue increased 38% to $378.8 million in 2019. Net premiums earned increased $93.8 million in 2019, primarily due to the growth of its IIF.

Net income rose 59% to $172 million in 2019, which were driven by growth in total revenues, partially offset by increases in total expenses.

The company ended 2019 with $41.1 million in cash and cash equivalents, 62% more than it had at the beginning of the year. Although operating cash flow provided $208.2 million and financing activities another $2 million, cash used for investments was $194.4 million, mainly for purchases of investments and software and equipment.

Strategy
The company strategy is to continue to

build on its position in the private MI market, expand its customer base and grow its insured portfolio of high-quality residential loans by focusing on long-term customer relationships, disciplined and proactive risk selection and pricing, fair and transparent claims payment practices, responsive customer service, financial strength and profitability.

National Mortgage Insurance Corporation (National MI), a subsidiary of NMI Holdings, Inc., announced in September 2020 that it is fully integrated with Lender Price, a leading cloud-based product, pricing and eligibility (PPE) engine provider for the mortgage finance industry. Loan officers now have instant access to National MI's risk-based Rate GPS through the Lender Price PPE platform. According to the company, this integration reinforces its commitment to streamlining and automating the process of ordering private mortgage insurance while mitigating the chance for errors. It also reduces the time from application to closing for loan originators and consumers.

EXECUTIVES

Executive Chairman, Bradley M. Shuster, $839,583 total compensation
President, Chief Executive Officer, Director, Adam S. Pollitzer, $466,250 total compensation
Executive Vice President, Chief Financial Officer, Ravi Mallela
Executive Vice President, Chief Legal Officer, General Counsel, Secretary, William J. Leatherberry, $428,167 total compensation
Field Sales Executive Vice President, Field Sales Chief Sales Officer, Norman P. Fitzgerald
Executive Vice President, Chief Risk Officer, Robert Smith
Business Development Executive Vice President, Operations Executive Vice President, Technology Partnerships Executive Vice President, Industrial Technology Executive Vice President, Mohammad Yousaf
Lead Director, Director, Steven L. Scheid
Director, Michael Embler
Director, Priya Cherian Huskins
Director, James G. Jones
Director, Lynn S. McCreary
Director, Michael Montgomery
Director, Regina Muehlhauser
Auditors : BDO USA, LLP

LOCATIONS

HQ: NMI Holdings Inc
27 2100 Powell Street, Emeryville, CA 94608
Phone: 855 530-6642
Web: www.nationalmi.com

PRODUCTS/OPERATIONS

2017 Sales

	% of total
Net premiums earned	91
Net investment income	9
Net realized investment gains	
Other	-
Total	**100**

COMPETITORS

ASSOCIATED BANC-CORP
EMC INSURANCE GROUP INC.
HILLTOP HOLDINGS INC.
LIBERTY MUTUAL HOLDING COMPANY INC.
MBIA INC.
MGIC INVESTMENT CORPORATION
ONEMAIN HOLDINGS, INC.
PROASSURANCE CORPORATION
RADIAN GROUP INC.
REPUBLIC MORTGAGE INSURANCE COMPANY

HISTORICAL FINANCIALS

Company Type: Public

Income Statement   FYE: December 31

	ASSETS ($mil)	NET INCOME ($mil)	INCOME AS % OF ASSETS	EMPLOYEES
12/21	2,450.5	231.1	9.4%	247
12/20	2,166.6	171.5	7.9%	262
12/19	1,364.8	171.9	12.6%	321
12/18	1,092.0	107.9	9.9%	304
12/17	894.8	22.0	2.5%	299
Annual Growth	28.6%	79.9%	—	(4.7%)

2021 Year-End Financials

Return on assets: 10.0%   Dividends
Return on equity: 15.7%   Yield: —
Long-term debt ($ mil.): —   Payout: —
No. of shares ($ mil.): 85.7   Market value ($ mil.): 1,875.0
Sales ($ mil.): 485

	STOCK PRICE ($) FY Close	P/E High	P/E Low	PER SHARE ($) Earnings	PER SHARE ($) Dividends	PER SHARE ($) Book Value
12/21	21.85	10	7	2.65	0.00	18.25
12/20	22.65	16	4	2.13	0.00	16.08
12/19	33.18	14	7	2.47	0.00	13.61
12/18	17.85	14	8	1.60	0.00	10.58
12/17	17.00	48	27	0.35	0.00	8.41
Annual Growth	6.5%	—	—	65.9%	—	21.4%

Northeast Bank (ME)

Northeast Bancorp is the holding company for Northeast Bank, which operates about a dozen branches in western and southern Maine. Founded in 1872, the bank offers standard retail services such asÂ checking and savings accounts, NOW and money market accounts, CDs, and trust services, as well as financial planning and brokerage. Residential mortgages account for about a third of all loans; commercial mortgages and consumer loans each make up about 25%. The bank also writes business and construction loans. Newly created investment entity FHB Formation acquired a 60% stake in Northeast Bancorp inÂ 2010. The deal brought in $16 million in capital. The 2011 sale of insurance agency Varney added another $8.4 million.

EXECUTIVES

Chairman, Director, Robert R. Glauber, $67,500 total compensation
President, Chief Executive Officer, Subsidiary Officer, Richard Wayne, $600,000 total compensation
Chief Risk Officer, Brian Pinheiro, $231,750 total compensation
Executive Vice President, Subsidiary Officer, Patrick D. Dignan, $400,000 total compensation
Senior Vice President, Julie Jenkins, $217,485 total compensation
Chief Financial Officer, Treasurer, Jean-Pierre L. (J.P.) Lapointe
Director, Matthew B. Botein, $41,250 total compensation
Director, Cheryl Lynn Dorsey, $40,000 total compensation
Director, John C. Orestis, $47,500 total compensation
Director, David A. Tanner, $40,000 total compensation
Director, Judith E. Wallingford, $48,750 total compensation
Auditors : RSM US LLP

LOCATIONS

HQ: Northeast Bank (ME)
27 Pearl Street, Portland, ME 04101
Phone: 207 786-3245
Web: www.northeastbank.com

COMPETITORS

BANCFIRST CORPORATION
EAGLE BANCORP, INC.
F.N.B. CORPORATION
OCEANFIRST FINANCIAL CORP.
S&T BANCORP, INC.

HISTORICAL FINANCIALS

Company Type: Public

Income Statement   FYE: June 30

	ASSETS ($mil)	NET INCOME ($mil)	INCOME AS % OF ASSETS	EMPLOYEES
06/21	2,174.4	71.5	3.3%	178
06/20	1,257.6	22.7	1.8%	182
06/19	1,153.8	13.8	1.2%	183
06/18	1,157.7	16.1	1.4%	185
06/17	1,076.8	12.3	1.1%	195
Annual Growth	19.2%	55.2%	—	(2.3%)

2021 Year-End Financials

Return on assets: 4.1%   Dividends
Return on equity: 36.0%   Yield: 0.1%
Long-term debt ($ mil.): —   Payout: 0.5%
No. of shares ($ mil.): 8.1   Market value ($ mil.): 243.0
Sales ($ mil.): 150.1

	STOCK PRICE ($) FY Close	P/E High	P/E Low	PER SHARE ($) Earnings	PER SHARE ($) Dividends	PER SHARE ($) Book Value
06/21	29.87	4	2	8.55	0.04	28.51
06/20	17.55	9	3	2.53	0.04	20.09
06/19	27.58	18	10	1.52	0.04	16.98
06/18	21.80	16	11	1.77	0.04	15.49
06/17	20.35	15	8	1.38	0.04	13.90
Annual Growth	10.1%	—	—	57.8%	0.0%	19.7%

NorthEast Community Bancorp Inc (MD)

Northeast Community Bancorp is the holding company for Northeast Community Bank, which serves consumers and businesses in the New York metropolitan area and Massachusetts. ThroughÂ about a half-dozen branches,Â the thrift offers traditional deposit services like checking and savings accounts, as well as a variety of lending products such as commercial and multi-family real estate loans, home equity, construction, and secured loans. While its deposit services are confined to New York and Massachusetts, it marketsÂ its loan products throughout the northeastern US. The bank offers investment and financial planning services through Hayden Wealth Management.Â Northeast Community Bank's roots date back to 1934.

EXECUTIVES

Chairman, Chief Executive Officer, Subsidiary Officer, Director, Kenneth A. Martinek, $275,750 total compensation

President, Chief Operating Officer, Subsidiary Officer, Director, Jose M. Callazo, $181,250 total compensation

Executive Vice President, Chief Financial Officer, Subsidiary Officer, Donald S. Hom, $150,000 total compensation

Subsidiary Officer, Director, Charles A. Martinek

Director, Diane B. Cavanaugh

Director, Charles M. Cirillo

Director, Eugene M. Magier

Director, John F. McKenzie

Director, Kenneth H. Thomas

Director, Kevin Patrick O'Malley

Auditors : S.R. Snodgrass, P.C.

LOCATIONS

HQ: NorthEast Community Bancorp Inc (MD)
325 Hamilton Avenue, White Plains, NY 10601
Phone: 914 684-2500
Web: www.necommunitybank.com

COMPETITORS

ASB FINANCIAL CORP
CITIZENS COMMUNITY BANCORP, INC.
FEDFIRST FINANCIAL CORPORATION
NORTHWEST INDIANA BANCORP
PEOPLES BANCORP

HISTORICAL FINANCIALS
Company Type: Public

Income Statement — FYE: December 31

	ASSETS ($mil)	NET INCOME ($mil)	INCOME AS % OF ASSETS	EMPLOYEES
12/20	968.2	12.3	1.3%	125
12/19	955.1	12.9	1.4%	0
12/18	870.3	13.0	1.5%	0
12/17	814.8	8.0	1.0%	0
12/16	734.5	5.0	0.7%	0
Annual Growth	7.2%	25.1%	—	—

2020 Year-End Financials
Return on assets: 1.2%
Return on equity: 8.3%
Long-term debt ($ mil.): —
No. of shares ($ mil.): 12.1
Sales ($ mil.): 51.4
Dividends Yield: —
Payout: 11.7%
Market value ($ mil.): 168.0

	STOCK PRICE ($) FY Close	P/E High	P/E Low	PER SHARE ($) Earnings	Dividends	Book Value
12/20	13.80	14	7	1.02	0.12	12.61
12/19	12.05	11	10	1.08	0.12	11.65
12/18	11.10	12	9	1.09	0.12	10.63
12/17	10.10	15	11	0.67	0.12	9.59
12/16	7.90	19	15	0.42	0.12	8.96
Annual Growth	15.0%	—	—	24.8%	0.0%	8.9%

Northern Technologies International Corp.

Northern Technologies International (NTIC) keeps rust away with its proprietary corrosion-inhibiting packaging. Its ZERUST product line features special packaging that emits corrosion-inhibiting molecules and compounds; the packaging comes in films and bags, liquids and coatings, rust removers and cleaners, vapor capsules, and pipe strips for residue-free protection of pipes, thermal spray coatings, and cathodic protection technologies. NTIC's customers include automotive, electronics, power generation, and metal processing firms. The company makes approximately 45% of its sales in United States.

Operations

Most of the company's sales come from ZERUST, but the company has expanded its product mix. Its new product development focus is on biodegradable polymer resins, which it sells under its Natur-Tec brand. The company is hoping to tap into a growing market emerging as a result of lower petroleum prices and increased interest in environmentally friendly alternatives to traditional plastics.

Its Natur-Tec resins are manufactured out of combination of biodegradable polymers and organic materials. Specific products include compost and trash bags, agricultural films, and various consumer goods packaging.

Geographic Reach

Based in Minnesota, the company sells its products in over about countries, including countries in North America, South America, Europe, Asia, and the Middle East. It generates approximately 45% of sales from United States, followed by around 5% from Brazil and about 35% each from India and China.

NTIC also maintains a manufacturing, laboratory, and warehouse space located in Beachwood, Ohio. It also has warehousing agreements in place in California and Indiana.

Sales and Marketing

NTIC's marketing activities include advertising and direct mail campaigns and also trade shows and technical forums. Customers include universities and school districts and film extruders and injection molders that produce bio-based and compostable end products such as film, bags and cutlery.

Financial Performance

NTIC's consolidated net sales increased 8% to $55.8 million during fiscal 2019 compared to $51.4 million during fiscal 2018. NTIC's consolidated net sales to unaffiliated customers excluding NTIC's joint ventures increased 10% to $53.1 million during fiscal 2019 compared to $48.5 million during fiscal 2018. These increases were primarily a result of an increase in sales of Natur-Tec products.

Net income attributable to NTIC decreased to $5.2 million for fiscal 2019 compared to $6.7 for fiscal 2018, a decrease of $1.5 million. This decrease was primarily the result of the increase in operating expenses and decrease in joint venture operations during fiscal 2019 compared to fiscal 2018, partially offset by the increase in gross profit.

Cash held by the company at the end of 2019 increased by $1.7 million to $5.9 million compared from the prior year with $4.2 million. Cash provided by operations was $5.5 million while cash provided by investing and financing activities were $1.3 million and $2.4 million, respectively. Main use for cash was proceeds from the sale of available for sale securities and dividends paid on NTIC common stock.

Strategy

One of NTIC's strategic initiatives is to expand into and penetrate other markets for its ZERUST corrosion prevention technologies. Accordingly, for the past several years, NTIC has focused significant sales and marketing efforts on the oil and gas industry, as the infrastructure that supports the industry is typically constructed using metals that are highly susceptible to corrosion.

NTIC's strategy of expanding its corrosion prevention solutions into the oil and gas industry and continuing the expansion of its Natur-Tec bioplastics resin compounds and finished products, either directly or indirectly through joint ventures and independent distributors and agents.

EXECUTIVES

Chairman, Director, Richard J. Nigon
President, Chief Executive Officer, Director, G. Patrick Lynch, $389,962 total compensation
Chief Financial Officer, Corporate Secretary, Matthew C. Wolsfeld, $288,233 total compensation
Director, Nancy E. Calderon
Director, Sarah E. Kemp
Director, Sunggyu Lee
Director, Ramani Narayan
Director, Konstantin von Falkenhausen
Auditors : Baker Tilly US, LLP

LOCATIONS

HQ: Northern Technologies International Corp.
4201 Woodland Road, P.O. Box 69, Circle Pines, MN 55014
Phone: 763 225-6600
Web: www.ntic.com

2015 Sales

	$ mil.	% of total
North America	25.7	85
Brazil	2.6	9
India	1.1	3
China	0.9	3
Total	30.3	100

PRODUCTS/OPERATIONS

2015 Sales

	$ mil.	% of total
ZERUST	26.0	86
Natur-Tec	4.3	14
Total	30.3	100

Selected Products
Corrosion Products Division (ZERUST products)
  Bags
  Bubble cushioning
  Can Liners
  Corrugated plastic and profile board
  Corrugated, solid fiber, and chipboard
  Cutlery
  Dunnage trays and bins
  Foam sheeting
  Lawn and leaf bags
  Pet waste collection bags
Pipe strips
  Shrink film
  Tube strips
  Vapor capsules

Selected Solutions
Diffusers
Liquids and Coatings
Plastic and Paper Packaging
Rust Removers and Cleaners
Z-CIS Technical Services
ZERUST Corrosion Prevention Solutions
ZERUST Corrosion Prevention Solutions
ZERUST Flange Savers
ZERUST ReCAST-R VCI Dispensers
ZERUST ReCAST-SSB Solutions
ZERUST Zerion

COMPETITORS

CLEARWATER PAPER CORPORATION
EVONIK CORPORATION
GRAPHIC PACKAGING HOLDING COMPANY
GREEN BAY PACKAGING INC.
HEXION INC.
INTERSTATE RESOURCES, INC.
KANEKA CORPORATION
PACKAGING CORPORATION OF AMERICA
SONOCO PRODUCTS COMPANY
WESTROCK COMPANY

HISTORICAL FINANCIALS
Company Type: Public

Income Statement — FYE: August 31

	REVENUE ($mil)	NET INCOME ($mil)	NET PROFIT MARGIN	EMPLOYEES
08/21	56.4	6.2	11.1%	171
08/20	47.6	(1.3)	—	142
08/19	55.7	5.2	9.3%	137
08/18	51.4	6.7	13.0%	136
08/17	39.5	3.4	8.6%	71
Annual Growth	9.3%	16.4%	—	24.6%

2021 Year-End Financials
Debt ratio: —
Return on equity: 10.5%
Cash ($ mil.): 7.6
Current Ratio: 3.96
Long-term debt ($ mil.): —
No. of shares ($ mil.): 9.1
Dividends
  Yield: 1.1%
  Payout: 72.2%
Market value ($ mil.): 153.0

	STOCK PRICE ($) FY Close	P/E High/Low		PER SHARE ($) Earnings	Dividends	Book Value
08/21	16.67	30	12	0.64	0.20	6.79
08/20	8.31	—	—	(0.15)	0.19	6.23
08/19	10.95	64	18	0.55	0.24	6.23
08/18	36.40	54	22	0.72	0.20	5.84
08/17	17.60	51	33	0.38	0.00	5.39
Annual Growth	(1.3%)	—	—	14.3%	—	6.0%

Northrim BanCorp Inc

Can you get banking services at the north rim of the world? Of course! Northrim BanCorp, formed in 2001 to be the holding company for Northrim Bank, provides a full range of commercial and retail banking services and products through some 10 banking offices in Alaska's Anchorage, Fairbanks North Star, and Matanuska Susitna counties. Division offices that provide short-term capital to customersÂ also are located in Washington and Oregon. The bank offers standard deposit products including checking, savings, and money market accounts; CDs; and IRAs. It uses funds from deposits to write commercial loans (40% of loan portfolio) andÂ real estate term loans (nearly 35%),Â as well asÂ construction and consumer loans.

EXECUTIVES

President, Chief Executive Officer, Chief Operating Officer, Subsidiary Officer, Chairman, Director, Joseph M. Schierhorn, $388,533 total compensation
Executive Vice President, Chief Financial Officer, Subsidiary Officer, Jed W. Ballard, $215,869 total compensation
Executive Vice President, General Counsel, Corporate Secretary, Subsidiary Officer, Michael A. Martin, $235,427 total compensation
Subsidiary Officer, Benjamin D. Craig, $225,361 total compensation
Subsidiary Officer, Michael G. Huston, $144,688 total compensation
Director, Larry S. Cash
Director, Anthony Drabek
Director, Karl L. Hanneman
Director, David W. Karp
Director, David J. McCambridge
Director, Krystal M. Nelson
Director, Aaron M. Schutt
Director, John C. Swalling
Director, Linda C. Thomas
Director, Joseph (Joe) Marushack
Director, David G. Wight
Auditors : Moss Adams LLP

LOCATIONS

HQ: Northrim BanCorp Inc
3111 C Street, Anchorage, AK 99503
Phone: 907 562-0062
Web: www.northrim.com

PRODUCTS/OPERATIONS

2007 Sales

	$ mil.	% of total
Interest		
Loans, including fees	66.5	80
Securities	4.6	6
Other	2.0	2
Noninterest		
Service charges on deposit accounts	3.1	4
Purchased receivable income	2.5	3
Other	4.2	5
Total	82.9	100

COMPETITORS

CAPITAL FINANCE AUSTRALIA LIMITED
FMR LLC
JAMES BREARLEY & SONS LIMITED
MOUND CITY BANK
PINNACLE SUMMER INVESTMENTS, INC.

HISTORICAL FINANCIALS
Company Type: Public

Income Statement — FYE: December 31

	ASSETS ($mil)	NET INCOME ($mil)	INCOME AS % OF ASSETS	EMPLOYEES
12/20	2,121.7	32.8	1.6%	438
12/19	1,643.9	20.6	1.3%	431
12/18	1,502.9	20.0	1.3%	430
12/17	1,519.1	13.1	0.9%	429
12/16	1,526.5	14.4	0.9%	451
Annual Growth	8.6%	22.9%	—	(0.7%)

2020 Year-End Financials
Return on assets: 1.7%
Return on equity: 15.3%
Long-term debt ($ mil.): —
No. of shares ($ mil.): 6.2
Sales ($ mil.): 140.2
Dividends
  Yield: 4.0%
  Payout: 32.7%
Market value ($ mil.): 212.0

	STOCK PRICE ($) FY Close	P/E High/Low		PER SHARE ($) Earnings	Dividends	Book Value
12/20	33.95	8	4	5.11	1.38	35.45
12/19	38.30	14	11	3.04	1.26	31.58
12/18	32.87	16	11	2.86	1.02	29.92
12/17	33.85	20	14	1.88	0.86	28.06
12/16	31.60	16	10	2.06	0.78	27.05
Annual Growth	1.8%	—	—	25.5%	15.3%	7.0%

Northwest Pipe Co.

Northwest Pipe is the largest manufacturer of engineered steel water pipeline systems in North America. In addition to being the largest manufacturer of engineered steel water pipeline systems in North America, the company manufactures high-quality precast and reinforced concrete products; water, wastewater, and storm water equipment; steel casing pipe, bar-wrapped concrete cylinder pipe, and one of the largest offerings of pipeline system joints, fittings, and specialized components. The company provides solution-based products for a wide range of markets under the ParkUSA, Geneva Pipe and Precast, Permalok, and Northwest Pipe Company lines. Northwest Pipe has around 15 manufacturing sites across North America. The US generates some 95% of the company's total revenue.

Operations

Effective in the fourth quarter of 2021, as a result of the acquisition of ParkUSA, Northwest Pipe revised its historical one segment position and identified the new operating segments, Engineered Steel Pressure Pipe (SPP) and Precast Infrastructure and Engineered Systems (Precast).

The SPP segment accounts for roughly 80% of total revenue, manufactures large-diameter, high-pressure steel pipeline systems for use in water infrastructure applications, which are primarily related to drinking water systems. These products are also used for hydroelectric power systems, wastewater systems, and other applications. In addition, SPP makes products for industrial plant piping systems and certain structural applications.

The Precast manufactures (more than 20%) high-quality precast and reinforced concrete products, including manholes, box culverts, vaults, catch basins, oil water separators, pump lift stations, biofiltration, and other environmental and engineered solutions.

Geographic Reach

Headquartered in Vancouver, Washington, Northwest Pipe generates about 95% of revenue in the US and some 5% in Canada.

Its SPP segment has manufacturing facilities located in Portland, Oregon; Adelanto, California; Saginaw, Texas; Tracy, California; Parkersburg, West Virginia; St. Louis, Missouri; and San Luis RÃo Colorado, Mexico. Precast segment has manufacturing facilities located in Houston, Texas; Orem, Utah; Dallas, Texas; Salt Lake City, Utah; San Antonio, Texas; and St. George, Utah.

Sales and Marketing

SPP's primary customers for its water infrastructure steel pipe products are installation contractors for projects funded by public water agencies. Its in-house sales force is comprised of sales representatives, engineers, and support personnel who work closely with public water agencies, contractors, and engineering firms, often years in advance of a project bid date.

Precast's primary customers for our water infrastructure precast and reinforced concrete products are installation contractors for various government, residential, and industrial projects. Its in-house sales force is comprised of sales representatives, engineers, and support personnel who work closely with the customers to find the right product or solution for their specific need.

One SPP customer accounts for more than 10% of total revenue and no Precast customer accounts for more than 10% of total revenue.

Financial Performance

Net sales increased 16.6% to $333.3 million in 2021 compared to $285.9 million in 2020. SPP net sales increased in 2021 driven by an increase in selling price per ton due to increased materials costs and changes in product mix, partially offset by a decrease in tons produced resulting from changes in project timing. Bidding activity, backlog, and production levels may vary significantly from period to period affecting sales volumes.

In 2021, the company had a net income of $11.5 million, a 40% decrease from the previous year's net income of $19.1 million.

The company's cash at the end of 2021 was $3 million. Financing activities generated $71 million, while operating activities used $5.8 million. Investing activities used another $100.2 million, mainly for acquisition of business.

Mergers and Acquisitions

In late 2021, Northwest Pipe completed the acquisition of 100% of Park Environmental Equipment, LLC for a purchase price of approximately $88.4 million in cash. ParkUSA is a precast concrete and steel fabrication-based company that develops and manufactures water, wastewater, and environmental solutions. This strategic acquisition provides a foothold into the water infrastructure technology market. Operations employ similar capabilities to Northwest Pipe's existing facilities and, looking forward, the company intends to expand production of ParkUSA's products to its other facilities.

Company Background

In 2012 Northwest Pipe announced plans to expand its Saginaw, Texas manufacturing facility. The expansion enables the company to better serve the needs of anticipated large water projects in the area. Completion of the Saginaw expansion will allow the company to leverage its proximity to Tarrant Regional Water District's planned Integrated Pipeline Project and give it expanded capabilities to serve additional water projects in the region.

Northwest Pipe was founded in 1966.

EXECUTIVES

Chairman, Director, Richard A. Roman, $505,000 total compensation

President, Chief Executive Officer, Director, Scott J. Montross, $530,001 total compensation

Operations Executive Vice President, Miles Brittain, $260,000 total compensation

Finance Senior Vice President, Finance Chief Financial Officer, Finance Corporate Secretary, Aaron Wilkins, $200,000 total compensation

Division Officer, Eric Stokes

Lead Director, Director, Michael C. Franson

Director, Amanda Kulesa

Director, Keith R. Larson

Director, John Paschal

Auditors : Moss Adams LLP

LOCATIONS

HQ: Northwest Pipe Co.
201 NE Park Plaza Drive, Suite 100, Vancouver, WA 98684
Phone: 360 397-6250   **Fax:** 360 397-6257
Web: www.nwpipe.com

COMPETITORS

AMERON INTERNATIONAL CORPORATION
AMSTED INDUSTRIES INCORPORATED
AMTROL INC.
CHART INDUSTRIES, INC.
ENERFAB, INC.
HILL & SMITH INFRASTRUCTURE PRODUCTS GROUP LIMITED
MODINE MANUFACTURING COMPANY
MUELLER WATER PRODUCTS, INC.
PERMA-PIPE INTERNATIONAL HOLDINGS, INC.
SPX CORPORATION

HISTORICAL FINANCIALS

Company Type: Public

Income Statement — FYE: December 31

	REVENUE ($mil)	NET INCOME ($mil)	NET PROFIT MARGIN	EMPLOYEES
12/20	285.9	19.0	6.7%	956
12/19	279.3	27.9	10.0%	765
12/18	172.1	20.3	11.8%	691
12/17	132.7	(10.1)	—	0
12/16	156.2	(9.2)	—	583
Annual Growth	16.3%	—	—	13.2%

2020 Year-End Financials

Debt ratio: 3.6%
Return on equity: 7.3%
Cash ($ mil.): 37.9
Current Ratio: 4.18
Long-term debt ($ mil.): 5.8
No. of shares ($ mil.): 9.8
Dividends
Yield: —
Payout: —
Market value ($ mil.): 277.0

	STOCK PRICE ($) FY Close	P/E High/Low		PER SHARE ($) Earnings	Dividends	Book Value
12/20	28.30	19	10	1.93	0.00	27.50
12/19	33.31	12	8	2.85	0.00	25.46
12/18	23.29	12	8	2.09	0.00	22.45
12/17	19.14	—	—	(1.06)	0.00	20.82
12/16	17.22	—	—	(0.97)	0.00	21.79
Annual Growth	13.2%	—	—	—	—	6.0%

Norwood Financial Corp.

Norwood Financial, not Batman, owns Wayne Bank. The bank serves individuals and local businesses through about 30 branches in northeastern Pennsylvania. It offers standard deposit products and services including checking and savings accounts, money market savings accounts, CDs, and IRAs. Mortgages account for about 80% of Wayne Bank's loan portfolio. The bank also runs a trust and wealth management division; subsidiary Norwood Investment provides annuities and mutual funds; Norwood Settlement (70%-owned) offers title and settlement services. Norwood Financial bought Delaware Bancshares and its National Bank of Delaware County subsidiary in mid-2016; the purchase nearly doubled its branch network.

EXECUTIVES

Vice-Chairman, Director, Andrew A. Forte
Chairman, Director, William W. Davis, $256,584 total compensation
President, Chief Executive Officer, Subsidiary Officer, Lewis J. Critelli, $325,000 total compensation
Executive Vice President, Chief Information Officer, Subsidiary Officer, Robert J. Mancuso, $136,500 total compensation
Executive Vice President, Chief Credit Officer, John F. Carmody, $135,000 total compensation
Executive Vice President, Chief Financial Officer, Secretary, William S. Lance, $191,000 total compensation
Executive Vice President, Chief Lending Officer, Subsidiary Officer, James F. Burke, $190,000 total compensation
Senior Vice President, Subsidiary Officer, John H. Sanders, $111,227 total compensation
Director, Susan Campfield
Director, Meg L. Hungerford
Director, Kevin M. Lamont
Director, Ralph A. Matergia
Director, Kenneth A. Phillips
Director, Joseph W. Adams
Auditors: S.R. Snodgrass, P.C.

LOCATIONS

HQ: Norwood Financial Corp.
717 Main Street, Honesdale, PA 18431

Phone: 570 253-1455
Web: www.waynebank.com

COMPETITORS

BAY BANCORP, INC.
CCFNB BANCORP, INC.
DCB FINANCIAL CORP
FIRST KEYSTONE CORPORATION
SOUTHWEST GEORGIA FINANCIAL CORPORATION

HISTORICAL FINANCIALS

Company Type: Public

Income Statement — FYE: December 31

	ASSETS ($mil)	NET INCOME ($mil)	INCOME AS % OF ASSETS	EMPLOYEES
12/20	1,851.8	15.0	0.8%	265
12/19	1,230.6	14.2	1.2%	220
12/18	1,184.5	13.6	1.2%	210
12/17	1,132.9	8.1	0.7%	214
12/16	1,111.1	6.7	0.6%	215
Annual Growth	13.6%	22.4%	—	5.4%

2020 Year-End Financials

Return on assets: 0.9%
Return on equity: 9.0%
Long-term debt ($ mil.): —
No. of shares ($ mil.): 8.2
Sales ($ mil.): 66.2
Dividends
Yield: 3.8%
Payout: 52.0%
Market value ($ mil.): 215.0

	STOCK PRICE ($) FY Close	P/E High/Low		PER SHARE ($) Earnings	Dividends	Book Value
12/20	26.17	19	10	2.09	1.00	23.68
12/19	38.90	17	12	2.25	0.96	21.72
12/18	33.00	18	13	2.17	0.88	19.43
12/17	33.00	34	21	1.31	0.86	18.51
12/16	33.14	30	23	1.15	0.83	17.80
Annual Growth	(5.7%)	—	—	16.0%	4.9%	7.4%

Novanta Inc

Novanta is a leading supplier of core technology solutions that uses its expertise in laser and motion control technologies to design and manufacture sets of products that are geared to the medical and healthcare and advanced industrial markets. Sealed CO2 lasers, ultrafast lasers, and optical light engines are sold primarily to the industrial and scientific markets. Novanta supplies lasers, optics, encoders, and air bearing spindles to the healthcare and medical markets, as well as OEM customers for high-precision cutting, trimming, marking, and measuring. The company changed its name to Novanta from GSI Group in 2016. International customers account for more than 60% of sales.

Operations

Novanta conducts business through three primary segments: Vision (more than 35%), Photonics (nearly 35% of net sales), and Precision Motion (approximately 30%).

The Vision segment makes and sells a range of medical technologies, including medical insufflators (tools for pumping powder or gas into a body cavity), pumps and related disposables; surgical displays and operating room integration technologies; optical data collection and machine vision technologies; radio frequency identification (RFID) technologies; thermal printers; spectrometry technologies; and embedded touch screens.

Photonics designs, makes and sells photonics-based tools that include laser scanning and laser beam delivery instruments, CO2 lasers, continuous wave and ultrafast lasers, and optical light engine products.

The Precision Motion segment's products include optical encoders, precision motor and motion control technology, air bearing spindles, and precision machines components.

Novanta operates through several trade names that include Cambridge Technology, Synrad, Laser Quantum, WOM, Reach Technology, JADAK, ThingMagic, Photo Research, Celera Motion, Applimotion, and Westwind.

Geographic Reach

Novanta, based in Bedford, Massachusetts, operates manufacturing and administration facilities in the US, Germany, and China. The US generates Novanta's largest amount of sales (about 40%), followed by Europe (nearly 35%), and China and other countries in the Asia/Pacific region (more than 25%).

Additional manufacturing, research and development, sales, service and logistics sites are located in California, Connecticut, Florida, Michigan, New York, and Oregon within the US, and in Germany, the UK, Czech Republic, Japan, China, Mexico, Spain and Italy.

Sales and Marketing

Novanta sells its products worldwide through a direct sales force and through resellers or distributors who in turn sell to OEMs. Novanta primarily customers are in the medical and advanced industrial markets.

Financial Performance

Novanta's revenue has been rising in the last five years with an exception in 2020, when it dipped. Still, it has an overall increase of 36% between 2017 and 2021. Net income has risen a couple of years after the trend of decline from 2017 to 2019. It still has an overall decline of 16% between 2017 and 2021.

The company's revenue increased 20% from $590.6 million in 2020 to $706.8 million in 2021. Precision Motion segment revenue in 2021 increased by $82.9 million, or 64%, versus 2020, primarily due to an increase in demand in advanced industrial market and certain medical robotic applications as well as an aggregate of $43.2 million revenue contributions from the ATI and SEM acquisitions.

In 2021, the company had a net income of $50.3 million, a 13% increase from the previous year's net income of $44.5 million. The higher volume of revenue offset the higher volume of operating expenses for the year.

The company's cash at the end of 2021

was $117.4 million. Operating activities generated $94.6 million, while investing activities used $306.7 million, mainly for the acquisition of businesses. Financing activities provided another $204.8 million.

Strategy

The company strategy is to drive sustainable, profitable growth through short-term and long-term initiatives, including: disciplined focus on its diversified business model of providing components and sub-systems to long life-cycle OEM customer platforms in attractive medical and advanced industrial niche markets; improving its business mix to increase medical sales as a percentage of total revenue; increasing its penetration of high growth advanced industrial applications, such as laser materials processing, robotics, laser additive manufacturing, automation and metrology, by working closely with OEM customers to launch application specific products that closely match the requirements of each application; broadening its portfolio of enabling proprietary technologies and capabilities through increased investment in new product development, and investments in application development to further penetrate existing customers, while expanding the applicability of its solutions to new markets; broadening its product and service offerings through the acquisition of innovative and complementary technologies and solutions in medical and advanced industrial technology applications, including increasing its recurring revenue streams such as services, spare parts and consumables; expanding sales and marketing channels to reach new target customers; improving its existing operations to expand profit margins and improve customer satisfaction by implementing lean manufacturing principles, strategic sourcing across its major production sites, and optimizing and limiting the growth of its fixed cost base; and attracting, retaining, and developing world-class talented and motivated employees.

Mergers and Acquisitions

In mid-2021, Novanta agreed to acquire Schneider Electric Motion USA (SEM, IMS, or Intelligent Motion Systems), a leader in innovative motion control solutions, specifically around brushless motor technology, integrated motor drives and electronic controls, for approximately $115 million in cash. The addition of SEM's technology expands the company's precision motion control portfolio, furthering its ability to serve customers with unique, high performance solutions.

Also in mid-2021, Novanta agreed to acquire privately held ATI Industrial Automation (ATI), a leading supplier of intelligent end-of-arm technology solutions to original equipment manufacturers (OEMs) for advanced industrial and surgical robots, for approximately $172 million upfront in cash. The business adds intelligent technology solutions and expands the company's position in mission critical robotic applications, such as electric vehicle production, medical robotics, and collaborative robotics.

Company Background

The Company was founded and in Massachusetts in 1968 as General Scanning, Inc. In 1999, General Scanning merged with Lumonics Inc. The post-merger entity, GSI Lumonics Inc., continued its operation in Canada. In 2005, the Company changed its name to GSI Group Inc. Through a series of strategic divestitures and acquisitions, the Company transformed from one that was more focused on the semiconductor industry to one that primarily sells components and sub-systems to OEMs in the medical and advanced industrial markets. The Company changed its name to Novanta Inc. in May 2016.

EXECUTIVES

Chief Executive Officer, Chairman, Director, Matthijs Glastra, $581,069 total compensation
Chief Financial Officer, Robert J. Buckley, $418,518 total compensation
Human Resources Chief Human Resources Officer, Brian S. Young, $280,440 total compensation
Lead Director, Director, Lonny J. Carpenter
Director, Ira J. Lamel
Director, Maxine L. Mauricio
Director, Katherine Ann Owen
Director, Thomas N. Secor
Director, Darlene J. S. Solomon
Director, Frank Anders (Andy) Wilson
Auditors : PricewaterhouseCoopers LLP

LOCATIONS

HQ: Novanta Inc
125 Middlesex Turnpike, Bedford, MA 01730
Phone: 781 266-5700   **Fax:** 781 266-5114
Web: www.gsig.com

2017 sales

	$ mil.	% of total
United States	220.6	42
Germany	68	13
Rest of Europe	81	16
China	56.1	11
Rest of Asia/Pacific	84.7	16
Other	10.8	2
Total	521.2	100

PRODUCTS/OPERATIONS

2017 sales

	$ mil.	% of total
Photonics	232.4	45
Vision	183	35
Precision Motion	105.8	20
Total	521.2	100

Selected Products and Brands

Laser products
    Lasers and laser-based systems (Synrad)
    Light and color measurement systems (Photo Research, Inc.)
    Optics (The Optical Corporation)
    Scanners (Cambridge Technology)
Precision motion
    Encoders (MicroE Systems)
    Lasers (eCO2 Lasers, Spectron Lasers)
    Optics (ExoTec Precision)
    Printed circuit board spindles (Westwind Air Bearings)
Medical technologies
Visualizations solutions
Imaging Informatics

COMPETITORS

AMETEK, INC.
APC TECHNOLOGY GROUP PLC
CHECKPOINT SYSTEMS, INC.
CYMER, INC.
Fabrinet
HUBBELL INCORPORATED
IPG PHOTONICS CORPORATION
MORGAN ADVANCED MATERIALS PLC
NEWPORT CORPORATION
ROFIN-SINAR TECHNOLOGIES LLC

HISTORICAL FINANCIALS

Company Type: Public

Income Statement — FYE: December 31

	REVENUE ($mil)	NET INCOME ($mil)	NET PROFIT MARGIN	EMPLOYEES
12/20	590.6	44.5	7.5%	2,200
12/19	626.0	40.7	6.5%	2,290
12/18	614.3	49.1	8.0%	2,133
12/17	521.2	60.0	11.5%	2,034
12/16	384.7	22.0	5.7%	1,269
Annual Growth	11.3%	19.3%	—	14.7%

2020 Year-End Financials

Debt ratio: 25.0%	No. of shares ($ mil.): 35.1
Return on equity: 9.9%	Dividends
Cash ($ mil.): 125.0	Yield: —
Current Ratio: 2.66	Payout: —
Long-term debt ($ mil.): 200.8	Market value ($ mil.): 4,157.0

	STOCK PRICE ($) FY Close	P/E High/Low		PER SHARE ($) Earnings	Dividends	Book Value
12/20	118.22	100	53	1.25	0.00	13.56
12/19	88.44	81	52	1.15	0.00	11.90
12/18	63.00	54	33	1.43	0.00	10.56
12/17	50.00	48	18	1.13	0.00	9.01
12/16	21.00	34	19	0.63	0.00	7.51
Annual Growth	54.0%	—	—	18.7%	—	15.9%

Nuvera Communications Inc

New Ulm Telecom operates three incumbent local-exchange carriers (ILECs) serving southern Minnesota and northern Iowa:Â an ILEC serving New Ulm, Minnesota, and surrounding communities; subsidiary Western Telephone, operatingÂ in the Springfield, Minnesota, area; and Peoples Telephone, serving portions of Cherokee and Buena Vista counties in Iowa. Operating under the common NU-Telecom brand, they make up New Ulm's Telecom Segment and provide traditional phone services, such as local exchange access and long-distance, as well as cable TV and Internet access. The company's Phonery division provides customer premise equipment (CPE), offers transport services, and resells long distance toll services.

EXECUTIVES

President, Chief Executive Officer, Glenn H Zerbe
Vice President, Chief Operating Officer, Secretary, Barbara A.J. Bornhoft, $180,400 total compensation
Chief Financial Officer, Treasurer, Nancy Blankenhagen, $102,038 total compensation
Chief Financial Officer, Curtis Owen Kawlewski, $165,000 total compensation
Chief Business Development, Craig Steven Anderson
Director, Perry L. Meyer
Director, Dennis E. Miller
Director, Wesley E. Schultz
Director, Colleen R. Skillings
Director, Suzanne M. Spellacy
Director, James J. Seifert
Auditors : Olsen Thielen & Co., Ltd.

LOCATIONS

HQ: Nuvera Communications Inc
27 North Minnesota Street, New Ulm, MN 56073
Phone: 507 354-4111
Web: www.nuvera.net

COMPETITORS

COMPORIUM, INC.
FARMERS TELEPHONE COOPERATIVE, INC.
SRT COMMUNICATIONS, INC.
TDS METROCOM, INC.
TRUCONNECT COMMUNICATIONS, INC.

HISTORICAL FINANCIALS

Company Type: Public

Income Statement — FYE: December 31

	REVENUE ($mil)	NET INCOME ($mil)	NET PROFIT MARGIN	EMPLOYEES
12/20	64.9	9.8	15.2%	204
12/19	64.9	8.3	12.8%	187
12/18	56.6	7.7	13.7%	172
12/17	46.8	9.9	21.2%	134
12/16	42.3	2.8	6.7%	145
Annual Growth	11.3%	36.2%	—	8.9%

2020 Year-End Financials

Debt ratio: 32.0%
Return on equity: 11.6%
Cash ($ mil.): 8.6
Current Ratio: 1.25
Long-term debt ($ mil.): 47.1
No. of shares ($ mil.): 5.2
Dividends
Yield: 1.3%
Payout: 15.1%
Market value ($ mil.): 100.0

	STOCK PRICE ($) FY Close	P/E High/Low		PER SHARE ($) Earnings	Dividends	Book Value
12/20	19.30	10	7	1.89	0.26	16.85
12/19	19.00	13	11	1.60	0.51	15.56
12/18	18.29	13	11	1.50	0.44	14.41
12/17	17.72	9	5	1.93	0.40	13.27
12/16	9.69	17	12	0.56	0.36	11.72
Annual Growth	18.8%	—	—	35.5%	(7.7%)	9.5%

NV5 Global Inc

NV5 Global is a provider of professional and technical engineering and consulting solutions to public and private sector clients in the infrastructure, utility services, construction, real estate, and environmental markets, operating nationwide and abroad. The company's clients include the US federal, state and local governments, and the private sector. NV5's projects include Boston Logan Airport, Bronx Zoo Astor Court Reconstruction, Dallas Fort Worth International Airport, Manhattan Waterfront Greenway Improvement and Atrium Health, among others. NV5 originally operated as Nolte Associates, Inc. in California prior to its acquisition in 2010. NV5 went public in 2013. Its US operations generate the majority of gross revenue of the company.

Operations

NV5 is now organized into three operating and reportable segments:

Infrastructure (INF) includes its engineering, civil program management, utility services, and construction quality assurance, testing and inspection practices; Building, Technology & Sciences (BTS) includes its environmental health sciences, buildings and program management, and MEP & technology engineering practices; and Geospatial Solutions (GEO) includes its geospatial technology services practice.

INF accounts for about 55% of gross revenue, while BTS for around 25% and GEO for some 20% of gross revenue.

Geographic Reach

Headquartered in Hollywood, Florida, NV5 operates its business from more than 110 locations in the US and abroad. All of the company's offices utilize its shared services platform, which consists of human resources, marketing, finance, information technology, legal, corporate development, and other resources.

Majority of the revenues came from the US. The state of California has historically been and is considered to be a key geographic region for the business, as approximately 25% of gross revenues.

Sales and Marketing

NV5 primary clients include US federal, state, municipal, and local government agencies, and military and defense clients. It also serves quasi-public (about 65% of gross revenue) and private sector (around 35%) clients from the education, healthcare, energy, and public utility industries, including schools, universities, hospitals, health care providers, insurance providers, large utility service providers, and large to small energy producers. Some 90% of gross revenue were generated from the cost-reimbursable contracts, while the rest were generated from fixed-unit contracts.

The company's advertising costs were $895, $940, and $939 for the years 2021, 2020, and 2019, respectively.

Financial Performance

The company's revenue for fiscal 2021 increased by 7% to $706.7 million compared from the prior year with $659.3 million. The increase in gross revenues was primarily due to incremental gross revenues of $31.1 million from acquisitions completed since the beginning of 2020 and increases in power delivery and utility services of $27.5 million and real estate transactional services of $17.1 million.

Net income for fiscal 2021 increased to $47.1 million compared from the prior year with $21.0 million.

Cash held by the company at the end of fiscal 2021 decreased to $48.0 million. Cash provided by operation was $101.4 million while cash used for investing and financing activities were $80.3 million and $38.1 million, respectively. Main uses of cash were for acquisitions and payments of borrowings from Senior Credit Facility.

Strategy

NV5 intends to pursue the following growth strategies as it seeks to expand its market share and position itself as a preferred, single-source provider of professional, engineering and technical consulting services to clients:

Seeking strategic acquisitions to enhance or expand the company's services offerings. NV5 seeks acquisitions that allow it to expand or enhance its capabilities in existing service offerings, or to supplement existing service offerings with new, closely related service offerings.

Continuing to focus on public sector clients while building private sector client capabilities. The company has historically derived the majority of its revenue from public and quasi-public sector clients. NV5 is also positioned to address the challenges presented by the aging infrastructure system of the United States, and the need to provide solutions for transportation, energy, water, and wastewater requirements.

Strengthening and supporting its human capital. The company's experienced employees and management team are its most valuable resources. Attracting, training, and retaining key personnel has been and will remain critical to the company's success. To achieve its human capital goals, NV5 intends to remain focused on providing its personnel with entrepreneurial opportunities to expand its business within their areas of expertise. The company will also continue to provide its personnel with personal and professional growth opportunities, including additional training, performance-based incentives such as opportunities for stock ownership, and other competitive benefits.

Mergers and Acquisitions

In late 2021, NV5 acquired Optimal Energy, Inc. (Optimal), an energy efficiency firm providing a full range of consulting services to government agencies, utilities, regulatory bodies, and state energy advisory councils. "NV5's energy efficiency and clean energy business has driven strong organic growth, and Optimal is the fourth acquisition we have made in the sector," said Dickerson Wright, PE, Chairman and CEO of NV5. "As energy efficiency continues to grow in importance in the government and utility markets, Optimal provides us with another specialized, high barrier to entry capability to differentiate NV5 and deliver value to our clients."

In 2021, NV5 acquired Sage Renewable Energy Consulting, Inc. (Sage), a leader in comprehensive sustainable energy planning and project management services. Sage operates nationwide and expands NV5's growing environmental, social, and governance (ESG) service portfolio. Sage's expertise in the renewables, battery storage, microgrid, and electric vehicle planning space enhances its ESG capabilities and presents opportunities for cross-selling with its existing ESG services.

Also in 2021, NV5 acquired PES Environmental, an environmental engineering and consulting company providing environmental site assessment, water resources and stormwater management, permitting and compliance, industrial hygiene, and litigation support services. PES Environmental's strong management team, regulatory expertise, and robust client portfolio make it a good fit for the continued expansion of NV5's environmental platform. PES Environmental's strong management team, regulatory expertise, and robust client portfolio make it a good fit for the continued expansion of its environmental platform.

EXECUTIVES

Chairman, Chief Executive Officer, Dickerson Wright, $543,186 total compensation
President, Chief Operating Officer, Director, Alexander A. Hockman, $378,846 total compensation
Executive Vice President, Chief Administrative Officer, Secretary, Director, MaryJo O'Brien
Executive Vice President, General Counsel, Richard Tong, $282,633 total compensation
Executive Vice President, Donald C. Alford, $295,385 total compensation
Chief Financial Officer, Edward H. Codispoti
Director, William D. Pruitt
Director, Francois Tardan
Director, Denise E. Dickins
Director, Laurie Conner
Auditors : DELOITTE & TOUCHE LLP

LOCATIONS

HQ: NV5 Global Inc
200 South Park Road, Suite 350, Hollywood, FL 33021
Phone: 954 495-2112
Web: www.nv5.com

COMPETITORS

ASGN INCORPORATED
CAPITA PLC
ENGLOBAL CORPORATION
JACOBS ENGINEERING GROUP INC.
JACOBS ONE LIMITED
MICHAEL BAKER INTERNATIONAL HOLDCO CORPORATION
R C M TECHNOLOGIES, INC.
Stantec Inc
TETRA TECH, INC.
TRC COMPANIES, INC.

HISTORICAL FINANCIALS
Company Type: Public

Income Statement — FYE: January 2

	REVENUE ($mil)	NET INCOME ($mil)	NET PROFIT MARGIN	EMPLOYEES
01/21*	659.2	21.0	3.2%	3,197
12/19	508.9	23.7	4.7%	3,362
12/18	418.0	26.8	6.4%	2,384
12/17	333.0	24.0	7.2%	2,023
12/16	223.9	11.6	5.2%	1,532
Annual Growth	31.0%	16.0%	—	20.2%

*Fiscal year change

2021 Year-End Financials
Debt ratio: 34.9%
Return on equity: 5.5%
Cash ($ mil.): 64.9
Current Ratio: 2.12
Long-term debt ($ mil.): 283.3
No. of shares ($ mil.): 13.2
Dividends
Yield: —
Payout: —
Market value ($ mil.): 1,045.0

	STOCK PRICE ($) FY Close	P/E High/Low		PER SHARE ($) Earnings	Dividends	Book Value
01/21*	78.78	47	17	1.65	0.00	29.70
12/19	48.31	44	23	1.90	0.00	27.70
12/18	58.24	37	17	2.33	0.00	25.30
12/17	54.15	25	14	2.23	0.00	16.62
12/16	33.40	29	12	1.22	0.00	14.02
Annual Growth	23.9%	—	—	7.8%	—	20.6%

*Fiscal year change

Oak Valley Bancorp (Oakdale, CA)

Oak Valley Bancorp was formed in 2008 to be the holding company for Oak Valley Community Bank, which serves individuals and local businesses through about 10 branches in California's Central Valley. Eastern Sierra Community Bank, a division of Oak Valley, has three locations. The banks provide standard deposit products such as savings, checking, and retirement accounts and CDs. Their lending activities consist of commercial real estate loans (more than half of their combined loan portfolio) and business, real estate construction, agricultural, residential mortgage, and consumer loans. Investment products and services are offered through an agreement with PrimeVest Financial Services.

EXECUTIVES

President, Subsidiary Officer, Chief Executive Officer, Christopher M. Courtney, $319,300 total compensation
Executive Vice President, Gary W. Stephens
Senior Executive Vice President, Chief Administrative Officer, Chief Operating Officer, Secretary, Subsidiary Officer, Richard A. McCarty, $221,450 total compensation
Commercial Banking Group Executive Vice President, David S. Harvey, $183,855 total compensation
Executive Vice President, Chief Credit Officer, Michael J. Rodrigues, $189,263 total compensation
Senior Vice President, Chief Financial Officer, Subsidiary Officer, Jeffrey A. Gall, $138,000 total compensation
Director, Donald L. Barton
Director, James L. Gilbert
Director, Thomas A. Haidlen
Director, H. Randolph Holder
Director, Michael Q. Jones
Director, Allison C. Lafferty
Director, David J. Leonard
Director, Ronald C. Martin, $267,714 total compensation
Director, Janet S. Pelton
Director, Danny L. Titus
Director, Terrance P. Withrow
Auditors : RSM US LLP

LOCATIONS

HQ: Oak Valley Bancorp (Oakdale, CA)
125 N. Third Ave., Oakdale, CA 95361
Phone: 209 848-2265
Web: www.ovcb.com

COMPETITORS

BANK OF OAK RIDGE
COMMUNITY SHORES BANK CORPORATION
FIRST WEST VIRGINIA BANCORP, INC.
SOUTHERN COMMUNITY FINANCIAL CORPORATION
TENNESSEE VALLEY FINANCIAL HOLDINGS, INC.

HISTORICAL FINANCIALS
Company Type: Public

Income Statement — FYE: December 31

	ASSETS ($mil)	NET INCOME ($mil)	INCOME AS % OF ASSETS	EMPLOYEES
12/20	1,511.4	13.6	0.9%	191
12/19	1,147.7	12.4	1.1%	192
12/18	1,094.8	11.5	1.1%	186
12/17	1,034.8	9.0	0.9%	175
12/16	1,002.1	7.6	0.8%	169
Annual Growth	10.8%	15.6%	—	3.1%

2020 Year-End Financials
Return on assets: 1.0%
Return on equity: 11.2%
Long-term debt ($ mil.): —
No. of shares ($ mil.): 8.2
Sales ($ mil.): 50.9
Dividends
Yield: 1.6%
Payout: 18.6%
Market value ($ mil.): 137.0

	STOCK PRICE ($) FY Close	P/E High/Low		PER SHARE ($) Earnings	Dividends	Book Value
12/20	16.62	11	7	1.68	0.28	15.78
12/19	19.46	13	10	1.54	0.27	13.71
12/18	18.30	17	12	1.42	0.26	12.09
12/17	19.54	18	11	1.13	0.25	11.21
12/16	12.55	13	10	0.95	0.24	10.19
Annual Growth	7.3%	—	—	15.3%	3.9%	11.5%

Oakworth Capital Inc

LOCATIONS
HQ: Oakworth Capital Inc
850 Shades Creek Pkwy, Suite 200, Mountain Brook, AL 35209
Phone: 205 263-4700

HISTORICAL FINANCIALS
Company Type: Public

Income Statement — FYE: December 31

	REVENUE ($mil)	NET INCOME ($mil)	NET PROFIT MARGIN	EMPLOYEES
12/21	43.1	10.7	24.9%	0
12/20	36.6	7.3	20.1%	0
12/19	37.4	7.9	21.2%	0
12/18	32.5	6.9	21.4%	0
Annual Growth	9.9%	15.4%	—	—

2021 Year-End Financials
Debt ratio: —
Return on equity: 10.8%
Cash ($ mil.): 332.9
Current Ratio: 0.31
Long-term debt ($ mil.): —
No. of shares ($ mil.): 4.8
Dividends
　Yield: —
　Payout: —
Market value ($ mil.): 0.0

Ocean Bio-Chem, Inc.

Ocean Bio-Chem provides everything but the elbow grease to scrub down boats, planes, RVs, and automobiles. The company makes and distributes Star Brite and StarTron brand maintenance and appearance products. Its marine and automotive lines include waxes, lubricants, and coolants, and its recreational vehicle and power sports equipment offerings primarily consist of polishes andÂ cleaners. Ocean Bio-Chem'sÂ products are soldÂ by bothÂ national retailers and specialty stores, including Wal-Mart, West Marine, and Bass Pro Shops.Â The company handles its manufacturing in-house through its Alabama-based Kinpak subsidiary, which also provides contract services. President and CEO Peter Dornau owns about 70% of the company.

EXECUTIVES
Chairman, President, Chief Executive Officer, Peter G. Dornau, $194,506 total compensation
Finance Vice President, Finance Chief Financial Officer, Director, Jeffrey S. Baracos, $197,077 total compensation
Sales Executive Vice President, Marketing Executive Vice President, Director, Gregor M. Dornau, $216,568 total compensation
Operations Chief Operating Officer, Director, William W. Dudman, $194,649 total compensation
Advertising Vice President, Marketing Vice President, George W. Lindsey
Director, Kim Krause
Director, Diana Mazuelos Conard
Director, James M. Kolisch
Director, John B. Turner
Auditors: Accell Audit & Compliance, PA

LOCATIONS
HQ: Ocean Bio-Chem, Inc.
4041 SW 47 Avenue, Fort Lauderdale, FL 33314
Phone: 954 587-6280
Web: www.oceanbiochem.com

COMPETITORS
Cantol Corp
GOJO INDUSTRIES, INC.
MEGUIAR'S, INC.
NCH CORPORATION
THE TRANZONIC COMPANIES

HISTORICAL FINANCIALS
Company Type: Public

Income Statement — FYE: December 31

	REVENUE ($mil)	NET INCOME ($mil)	NET PROFIT MARGIN	EMPLOYEES
12/20	55.5	9.6	17.3%	200
12/19	42.2	3.4	8.3%	154
12/18	41.7	2.7	6.7%	152
12/17	38.9	2.6	6.7%	142
12/16	36.2	2.0	5.8%	128
Annual Growth	11.3%	46.4%	—	11.8%

2020 Year-End Financials
Debt ratio: 8.8%
Return on equity: 27.1%
Cash ($ mil.): 11.1
Current Ratio: 9.70
Long-term debt ($ mil.): 3.7
No. of shares ($ mil.): 9.4
Dividends
　Yield: 0.5%
　Payout: 8.0%
Market value ($ mil.): 127.0

	STOCK PRICE ($) FY Close	P/E High/Low		PER SHARE ($) Earnings	Dividends	Book Value
12/20	13.36	19	3	1.02	0.08	4.21
12/19	3.31	11	8	0.37	0.05	3.25
12/18	3.28	15	10	0.30	0.12	2.94
12/17	4.34	19	13	0.28	0.06	2.69
12/16	3.76	19	8	0.23	0.06	2.46
Annual Growth	37.3%	—	—	45.1%	7.5%	14.4%

OceanFirst Financial Corp

OceanFirst Financial operates as the holding company for OceanFirst Bank, a regional bank operating throughout New Jersey, greater Philadelphia and metropolitan New York. The bank caters to individuals and small to midsized businesses, offering standard products such as checking and savings accounts, CDs, and IRAs. It uses funds from deposits mainly to invest in mortgages, loans, and securities. It has total loans outstanding of $8.62 billion, of which $5.43 billion, or about 65% of total loans, were commercial real estate, multi-family, and land loans.

Operations
The bank's principal business is attracting deposits from the general public in the communities surrounding its branch offices and investing those deposits primarily in single-family owner-occupied residential mortgage loans and commercial real estate loans. It active subsidiaries include OceanFirst REIT Holdings, Casaba Real Estate Holding Corporation, CBNJ Investment Corp, Country Property Holdings and TRCB Investment Corp.

Broadly speaking, the bank makes roughly 80% of its revenue from interest income. The remainder of its revenue comes from bankcard services, fees and services and other miscellaneous and non-recurring sources.

Geographic Reach
The bank conducts its business through its branch office and headquarters located in Toms River, New Jersey, its administrative office located in Red Bank, New Jersey, an administrative office located in Mount Laurel, New Jersey, about 45 additional branch offices, and four deposit production facilities located throughout central and southern New Jersey and the greater metropolitan area of New York City and Philadelphia. The bank also operates commercial loan production offices in New Jersey, New York City, the greater Philadelphia area, Baltimore, and Boston.

Financial Performance
Company's revenue for fiscal 2021 decreased to $357.3 million compared from the prior year with $386.9 million.

Net income available to common stockholders for the year ended December 31, 2021 was $106.1 million, as compared to $61.2 million for the prior year. These included merger-related expenses, branch consolidation expenses, and a net gain on equity investments of $1.5 million, $12.3 million, and $7.1 million, respectively.

The company's cash and due from banks and restricted cash at end of year was $224.8 million. Net cash provided by operating and financing activities were $160 million and $224 million, respectively. Net cash used in investing activities amounted to $1.5 billion, mainly for purchases of loans receivable, purchase of debt securities held-to-maturity, and purchase of debt securities available-for-sale.

Strategy
OceanFirst Financial's strategy has been to grow profitability while limiting exposure to credit, interest rate, and operational risks. To accomplish these objectives, the Bank has sought to: (1) grow commercial loans through

the offering of commercial lending services to local businesses and through strategic expansions to adjacent markets; (2) grow core deposits (defined as all deposits excluding time deposits) through product offerings appealing to a broadened customer base; and (3) increase non-interest income by expanding the menu of fee-based products and services and investing additional resources in these product lines. The growth in these areas has occurred both organically and through acquisitions.

The company focuses on prudent growth to create value for stockholders, which may include opportunistic acquisitions. The company will also continue to build additional operational infrastructure and invest in key personnel in response to growth and changing business conditions.

Mergers and Acquisitions

In 2022, OceanFirst acquired Tridaent, a family owned and operated business located in Wall Township, New Jersey. Chairman and Chief Executive Officer, Christopher D. Maher, commented on the Company's announcement, "The acquisition of Trident is a natural step for OceanFirst that provides our clients an opportunity for a substantially improved borrowing experience."

In late 2021, OceanFirst announced that they have entered into a definitive agreement and plan of merger pursuant to which Partners will merge into OceanFirst, with OceanFirst surviving. Upon completion of the Partners merger, The Bank of Delmarva and Virginia Partners Bank will each successively merge into OceanFirst Bank, with OceanFirst Bank surviving each bank merger. The transaction is valued at approximately $186 million in the aggregate. The acquisition accelerates OceanFirst's strategic expansion into attractive Baltimore/Washington D.C. region and adds high-growth, commercial-oriented franchise with stable deposit base.

Company Background

OceanFirst Bank's employee stock option plan owns more than 10% of OceanFirst Financial's shares. The company's charitable foundation, OceanFirst Foundation, owns 7%.

The Bank was founded as a state-chartered building and loan association in 1902. It converted to a Federal savings and loan association in 1945, and became a Federally-chartered mutual savings bank in 1989.

EXECUTIVES

President, Chief Executive Officer, Subsidiary Officer, Chairman, Director, Christopher D. Maher, $846,154 total compensation
Executive Vice President, Chief Operating Officer, Subsidiary Officer, Director, Joseph J. Lebel, $349,039 total compensation
Executive Vice President, Chief Risk Officer, Subsidiary Officer, Grace M. Vallacchi
Executive Vice President, General Counsel, Corporate Secretary, Subsidiary Officer, Steven James Tsimbinos, $299,039 total compensation
Executive Vice President, Chief Financial Officer, Subsidiary Officer, Patrick S. Barrett
Senior Vice President, Chief Accounting Officer, Corporate Controller, Patrick Chong
Chief Compliance Officer, Subsidiary Officer, Angela K. Ho
Subsidiary Officer, Michele B. Estep
Subsidiary Officer, Karthik Sridharan
Subsidiary Officer, Anthony Giordano III
Director, Anthony R. Coscia, $68,750 total compensation
Director, Michael D. Devlin
Director, Jack M. Farris
Director, Kimberly M. Guadagno
Director, Nicos Katsoulis
Director, Joseph M. Murphy
Director, Steven M. Scopellite
Director, Grace C. Torres
Director, Patricia L. Turner
Director, John E. Walsh
Auditors : DELOITTE & TOUCHE LLP

LOCATIONS

HQ: OceanFirst Financial Corp
110 West Front Street, Red Bank, NJ 07701
Phone: 732 240-4500
Web: www.oceanfirst.com

PRODUCTS/OPERATIONS

2016 sales

	$ mil	% of total
Interest Income		
Loans	123.0	80
Mortgage-backed securities	6.7	4
Investment securities & other	3.8	2
Non-interest		
Bankcard services revenue	4.8	3
Wealth management revenue	2.3	2
Fees & service charges	10.4	7
Loan Servicing income	0.3	-
Net gains on sales of loans	1.0	1
Net loss from other real estate operations	(0.9)	-
Income from Bank owned Life Insurance	2.2	1
Other	0.2	-
Total	153.8	100

COMPETITORS

BANCFIRST CORPORATION
CITIZENS & NORTHERN CORPORATION
CITY HOLDING COMPANY
EAGLE BANCORP, INC.
FINANCIAL INSTITUTIONS, INC.
FIRST HORIZON CORPORATION
GUARANTY BANCORP
MACATAWA BANK CORPORATION
PRIVATEBANCORP, INC.
SIGNATURE BANK

HISTORICAL FINANCIALS

Company Type: Public

Income Statement — FYE: December 31

	ASSETS ($mil)	NET INCOME ($mil)	INCOME AS % OF ASSETS	EMPLOYEES
12/20	11,448.3	63.3	0.6%	1,008
12/19	8,246.1	88.5	1.1%	924
12/18	7,516.1	71.9	1.0%	892
12/17	5,416.0	42.4	0.8%	684
12/16	5,167.0	23.0	0.4%	797
Annual Growth	22.0%	28.7%	—	6.0%

2020 Year-End Financials

Return on assets: 0.6%
Return on equity: 4.7%
Long-term debt ($ mil.): —
No. of shares ($ mil.): 60.3
Sales ($ mil.): 445.4
Dividends
Yield: 3.6%
Payout: 71.5%
Market value ($ mil.): 1,125.0

	STOCK PRICE ($) FY Close	P/E High	P/E Low	Earnings	Dividends	Book Value
12/20	18.63	25	12	1.02	0.68	24.57
12/19	25.54	15	12	1.75	0.68	22.88
12/18	22.51	20	14	1.51	0.62	21.68
12/17	26.25	23	18	1.28	0.60	18.47
12/16	30.03	30	16	0.98	0.54	17.80
Annual Growth	(11.3%)	—	—	1.0%	5.9%	8.4%

Old Second Bancorp., Inc. (Aurora, Ill.)

Old Second won't settle for a silver finish when it comes to community banking around Chicago. Old Second Bancorp is the holding company for Old Second National Bank, which serves the Chicago metropolitan area through 25 branches in Kane, Kendall, DeKalb, DuPage, LaSalle, Will, and Cook counties. The bank provides standard services such as checking and savings accounts, credit and debit cards, CDs, mortgages, loans, and trust services to consumers and business clients. Subsidiary River Street Advisors offers investment management and advisory services. Another unit, Old Second Affordable Housing Fund, provides home-buying assistance to lower-income customers.

Operations

Commercial real estate loans accounted for 53% of Old Second's loan portfolio at the end of 2015, while residential mortgages made up another 31%. The rest was made up of general commercial loans (12% of loan assets), and construction lending (2%).

Roughtly 70% of the bank's revenue comes from interest income. About 54% of its revenue came from loan interest (including fees) during 2015, with another 15% coming from interest on investment securities. The remainder of Old Second's revenue came from deposit account service charges (7%), trust income (6%), mortgage loan sale gains (6%), secondary mortgage fees (1%), and other sources.

Geographic Reach

The bank mostly serves customers in Aurora, Illinois (which is 40 miles west of Chicago) and surrounding communities. Its 24 branches are located in the Kane, Kendall, DeKalb, DuPage, LaSalle, Will, and Cook counties of Illinois.

Sales and Marketing

Old Second has been ramping up its advertising spend in recent years. It spent $1.34 million on advertising in 2015, up from $1.28 million and $1.23 million in 2014 and 2013, respectively.

Financial Performance

Old Second's annual revenues have fallen 20% since 2011 as it's had to sell of many of its non-performing loan assets to de-risk its loan portfolio. The company's profits, however, have been on the mend as its de-risking measures have led to declining loan loss provisions.

The bank's revenue rebounded by less than 1% to $97.46 million during 2015 as its average loans, including loans held for sale, grew by 2% for the year.

Revenue growth in 2015 combined with lower interest and amortization costs on deposits drove Old Second Bancorp's net income up by over 50% to $15.39 million. The bank's operating cash levels jumped sharply to $21.14 million (operations had used $6.3 million in 2014) partially thanks to earnings growth but mostly thanks to positive working capital changes related to sales proceeds from loans held for sale and changes in accrued interest payable and other liabilities.

Strategy

Old Second Bancorp continued in 2016 to focus on shedding riskier loan assets that led it to deep losses in 2011, while focusing on securing high-quality loans with more creditworthiness. Its efforts began to pay off in 2015 as its average loan balances and revenues began to grow again after years of being in decline.

EXECUTIVES

Chairman, Subsidiary Officer, Director, William B. Skoglund, $530,000 total compensation
Vice-Chairman, Director, Gary S. Collins, $306,875 total compensation
President, Chief Executive Officer, Chief Operating Officer, Subsidiary Officer, Director, James L. Eccher, $501,042 total compensation
Executive Vice President, Chief Financial Officer, Subsidiary Officer, Bradley S. Adams, $306,875 total compensation
Executive Vice President, Chief Lending Officer, Subsidiary Officer, Donald Pilmer, $267,909 total compensation
Executive Vice President, Division Officer, Richard A. Gartelmann

Lead Director, Director, Barry Finn
Director, John Williams
Director, Keith Kotche
Director, Billy J. Lyons
Director, William Kane
Director, John Ladowicz
Director, Patti Temple Rocks
Director, James F. Tapscott
Director, Hugh H. McLean
Director, Edward Bonifas
Director, Jill E. York
Director, Dennis L. Klaeser
Auditors : Plante & Moran PLLC

LOCATIONS

HQ: Old Second Bancorp., Inc. (Aurora, Ill.)
37 South River Street, Aurora, IL 60507
Phone: 630 892-0202
Web: www.oldsecond.com

PRODUCTS/OPERATIONS

2015 sales

	% of total
Interest and dividend income	
Loans, including fees	54
Taxable	14
Tax exempt	1
Non-interest income	
Service charges on deposits	7
Trust income	6
Net gain on sales of mortgage loans	6
Debit card interchange income	4
Secondary mortgage fees	1
Increase in cash surrender value of bank-owned life insurance	1
Other income	6
Total	100

Products/Services
Personal Banking
Card Services
Checking
Loans
Money Services
Online and Mobile Banking
Prime Time Club
Retirement Services
Savings
Loans
Auto and Personal Loans
Home Equity Loans
Home Loans
Mortgage Lenders
Required Documents
SAFE Act
Business Banking
Commercial Banking
Online and Mobile Banking
Small Business Banking
Wealth Management
Business Plan Options
Real Estate Services
Retirement Services

COMPETITORS

BANKFINANCIAL CORPORATION
BEAR STATE FINANCIAL, INC.
BSB BANCORP, INC.
CASCADE BANCORP
CNB FINANCIAL CORPORATION
FIRST FINANCIAL CORPORATION
FLAGSTAR BANCORP, INC.
GREAT SOUTHERN BANCORP, INC.
REPUBLIC FIRST BANCORP, INC.
TRUSTCO BANK CORP N Y

HISTORICAL FINANCIALS

Company Type: Public

Income Statement
FYE: December 31

	ASSETS ($mil)	NET INCOME ($mil)	INCOME AS % OF ASSETS	EMPLOYEES
12/20	3,040.8	27.8	0.9%	533
12/19	2,635.5	39.4	1.5%	535
12/18	2,676.0	34.0	1.3%	518
12/17	2,383.4	15.1	0.6%	450
12/16	2,251.1	15.6	0.7%	467
Annual Growth	7.8%	15.4%	—	3.4%

2020 Year-End Financials
Return on assets: 0.9%
Return on equity: 9.4%
Long-term debt ($ mil.): —
No. of shares ($ mil.): 29.3
Sales ($ mil.): 141.7
Dividends
Yield: 0.3%
Payout: 4.0%
Market value ($ mil.): 296.0

	STOCK PRICE ($) FY Close	P/E High/Low		PER SHARE ($) Earnings	Dividends	Book Value
12/20	10.10	14	7	0.92	0.04	10.47
12/19	13.47	11	9	1.30	0.04	9.28
12/18	13.00	14	11	1.12	0.04	7.70
12/17	13.65	28	20	0.50	0.04	6.76
12/16	11.05	22	12	0.53	0.03	5.93
Annual Growth	(2.2%)	—	—	14.8%	7.5%	15.3%

Ollie's Bargain Outlet Holdings Inc

EXECUTIVES

President, Chief executive Officer, Interim Chief Financial Officer, Director, John W. Swygert, $500,000 total compensation
Executive Vice President, Chief Operating Officer, Eric van der Valk
Senior Vice President, General Merchandise Manager, Kevin McLain, $246,058 total compensation
Senior Vice President, General Counsel, James J. Comitale
Vice President, Chief Information Officer, Larry Kraus
Senior Vice President, Chief Financial Officer, Robert F. Helm
Director, Alissa M. Ahlman
Director, Robert N. Fisch
Director, Stanley Fleishman
Director, Thomas Hendrickson
Director, Stephen W. White
Director, Richard F. Zannino
Director, Abid Rizvi
Auditors : KPMG LLP

LOCATIONS

HQ: Ollie's Bargain Outlet Holdings Inc
6295 Allentown Boulevard, Suite 1, Harrisburg, PA 17112
Phone: 717 657-2300
Web: www.ollies.us

HISTORICAL FINANCIALS
Company Type: Public

Income Statement — FYE: January 30

	REVENUE ($mil)	NET INCOME ($mil)	NET PROFIT MARGIN	EMPLOYEES
01/21*	1,808.8	242.6	13.4%	9,800
02/20	1,408.1	141.1	10.0%	8,300
02/19	1,241.3	135.0	10.9%	7,700
02/18	1,077.0	127.5	11.8%	6,700
01/17	890.3	59.7	6.7%	5,500
Annual Growth	19.4%	42.0%	—	15.5%

*Fiscal year change

2021 Year-End Financials
Debt ratio: —
Return on equity: 20.3%
Cash ($ mil.): 447.1
Current Ratio: 2.85
Long-term debt ($ mil.): 0.6
No. of shares ($ mil.): 65.4
Dividends
Yield: —
Payout: —
Market value ($ mil.): 6,201.0

	STOCK PRICE ($) FY Close	P/E High/Low		PER SHARE ($) Earnings	Dividends	Book Value
01/21*	94.73	30	9	3.68	0.00	20.39
02/20	53.04	45	24	2.14	0.00	16.80
02/19	79.35	45	24	2.05	0.00	14.96
02/18	53.75	28	14	1.96	0.00	12.85
01/17	29.35	33	19	0.96	0.00	10.72
Annual Growth	34.0%	—	—	39.9%	—	17.4%

*Fiscal year change

OneMain Finance Corp

EXECUTIVES

President, Chief Executive Officer, Director, Richard N. Tambor
Executive Vice President, Director, Jeannette Osterhout
Executive Vice President, Chief Financial Officer, Holding/Parent Company Officer, Director, Micah R. Conrad
Senior Vice President, Principal Accounting Officer, Group Controller, Holding/Parent Company Officer, Michael A. Hedlund

LOCATIONS

HQ: OneMain Finance Corp
601 Northwest Second Street, Evansville, IN 47708
Phone: 812 424-8031
Web: www.omf.com

HISTORICAL FINANCIALS
Company Type: Public

Income Statement — FYE: December 31

	REVENUE ($mil)	NET INCOME ($mil)	NET PROFIT MARGIN	EMPLOYEES
12/21	3,958.0	1,314.0	33.2%	8,800
12/20	3,867.0	730.0	18.9%	8,300
12/19	3,777.0	858.0	22.7%	9,700
12/18	3,314.0	461.0	13.9%	10,200
12/17	876.0	94.0	10.7%	2,500
Annual Growth	45.8%	93.4%	—	37.0%

2021 Year-End Financials
Debt ratio: 80.5%
Return on equity: 40.4%
Cash ($ mil.): 510.0
Current Ratio: 986.00
Long-term debt ($ mil.): 17,750
No. of shares ($ mil.): 10.1
Dividends
Yield: —
Payout: 127.7%
Market value ($ mil.): 0.0

OneWater Marine Inc

EXECUTIVES

Chairman, Director, John F. Schraudenbach
President, Chief Operating Officer, Subsidiary Officer, Director, Anthony M. Aisquith
Chief Executive Officer, Subsidiary Officer, Director, Philip Austin Singleton
Chief Financial Officer, Secretary, Subsidiary Officer, Jack P. Ezzell
Director, Christopher W. Bodine
Director, Bari A. Harlam
Director, Jeffrey B. Lamkin
Director, J. Steven Roy
Director, John G. Troiano

LOCATIONS

HQ: OneWater Marine Inc
6275 Lanier Islands Parkway, Buford, GA 30518
Phone: 678 541-6300
Web: www.onewatermarine.com

HISTORICAL FINANCIALS
Company Type: Public

Income Statement — FYE: September 30

	REVENUE ($mil)	NET INCOME ($mil)	NET PROFIT MARGIN	EMPLOYEES
09/21	1,228.2	79.0	6.4%	1,785
09/20	1,022.9	17.4	1.7%	1,169
09/19	767.6	35.6	4.6%	1,102
09/18	602.8	1.1	0.2%	0
09/17	391.4	(4.2)	—	0
Annual Growth	33.1%	—	—	—

2021 Year-End Financials
Debt ratio: 31.7%
Return on equity: 45.3%
Cash ($ mil.): 62.6
Current Ratio: 1.23
Long-term debt ($ mil.): 103
No. of shares ($ mil.): 15.1
Dividends
Yield: 4.4%
Payout: 25.8%
Market value ($ mil.): 607.0

	STOCK PRICE ($) FY Close	P/E High/Low		PER SHARE ($) Earnings	Dividends	Book Value
09/21	40.21	8	3	6.96	1.80	14.97
09/20	20.49	11	1	2.77	0.00	8.20
Annual Growth	96.2%	—	—	151.3%	—	82.4%

Onto Innovation Inc

Onto Innovation (formerly Nanometrics) is a worldwide leader in the design, development, manufacture and support of process control tools that perform macro defect inspection and 2D/3D optical metrology, lithography systems, and process control analytical software used by bare silicon wafer manufacturers, semiconductor wafer fabricators, and advanced packaging device manufacturers. Its products are also used in a number of other high technology industries including: light emitting diode (LED); vertical-cavity surface-emitting laser (VCSEL); micro-electromechanical system (MEMS); CMOS image sensor (CIS); power device; RF filter; data storage; and certain industrial and scientific applications. Top customers include Samsung Electronics, Taiwan Semiconductor Manufacturing Company, and SK Hynix. Onto innovation generates most of its sales in Asia. The company, Nanometrics, was founded in 1975.

Operations
Onto Innovation engaged in the design, development, manufacture and support of high-performance control metrology, defect inspection, lithography and data analysis systems used by microelectronics device manufacturers. It gets some 85% of sales from its systems and software, about 10% from parts, and the rest were generated from its services.

Its products have included the Automated Metrology Systems which are primarily consist of fully automated metrology systems that are employed in semiconductor production environments. The Atlas family of products represent our line of high-performance metrology systems providing OCD and thin film metrology and wafer stress metrology for transistor and interconnect metrology applications. It also offers Integrated Metrology Systems (installed directly onto wafer processing equipment to provide near real-time measurements for improved process control and maximum throughput); Silicon Wafer All-surface Inspection/Characterization (refers to inspection of the wafer frontside, edge, and backside as well as wafer's locator notch); and Macro Defect Inspection (deploy advanced macro defect inspection throughout the production line to monitor key process steps, gather process-enhancing information and ultimately, lower manufacturing costs). Other products include Automated Defect Classification and Pattern Analysis; Yield Analysis; Opaque Film Metrology; Probe Card Test and Analysis; Industrial, Scientific, and Research Markets- 4D Technology; and Advanced Packaging Lithography.

Geographic Reach
Onto Innovation is based in Wilmington, Massachusetts. It owns its facilities in Milpitas and Richardson, and lease facilities for corporate, engineering, manufacturing, sales and service-related purposes in the United States and seven other countries- China, France, Germany, Japan, South Korea, Singapore, and Taiwan.

The company's sales are concentrated in Asia with Taiwan with some 25% and China with about 20%, followed by South Korea with some 20%, and Japan with about 10%. The US accounts for roughly 10% of the company's revenue, while Europe and Southeast Asia accounts for the rest.

It has a manufacturing operations in Milpitas, California; Tucson, Arizona; Wilmington, Massachusetts; Bloomington, Minnesota; and at various contract manufacturers around the world.

Sales and Marketing

The company provides local direct sales, service and application support through its worldwide offices and work with selected dealers and sales representatives. Its top three customers include Samsung Electronics, Taiwan Semiconductor Manufacturing Co., and SK Hynix.

Financial Performance

Company's revenue for fiscal 2021 increased to $788.9 million compared from the prior year with $556.5 million.

Net income for fiscal 2021 increased to $142.4 million compared from the prior year with $31.0 million.

Cash held by the company at the end of fiscal 2021 increased to $169.6 million. Cash provided by operations and financing activities were $175.3 million and $2.7 million, respectively. Cash used for investing activities was $141.8 million, mainly for purchases of marketable securities.

Mergers and Acquisitions

In early 2021, Onto Innovation Inc. acquired Inspectrology, LLC. Headquartered in Sudbury, Massachusetts, USA, Inspectrology is a leading supplier of overlay metrology for controlling lithography and etch processes in the compound semiconductor market. The acquisition expands the company's position in the high growth compound semiconductor market driven by higher content in 5G RF and electric vehicles and its Onto Innovation's Advanced Process Control (APC) software and Dragonfly System are expected to provide revenue synergies when combined with Inspectrology products. Terms were not disclosed.

HISTORY

Nanometrics was incorporated in 1975 and has been publicly traded since 1984. In 2006 the company acquired Accent Optical Technologies, a supplier of semiconductor process control and metrology equipment, for around $81 million in stock and assumed debt. Following the merger, previous Nanometrics shareholders owned approximately 73% of the combined company and Accent Optical shareholders owned about 27%. Also that year the company acquired Soluris, a supplier of overlay and critical-dimension measurement equipment, for $7 million in cash.

Expanding its portfolio of metrology products in 2008, the company acquired the assets of Tevet Process Control Technologies, a supplier of integrated metrology systems for manufacturing semiconductors and solar cells, for about $3.5 million.

In 2011 Nanometrics bought Germany-based Nanda Technologies, a maker of fully automated wafer inspection systems, for $23 million in cash. With the acquisition, Nanometrics added a differentiated macro defect inspection technology to its portfolio of metrology products.

EXECUTIVES

Chief Executive Officer, Director, Michael P. Plisinski
Chairman, Director, Christopher A. Seams
Senior Vice President, Division Officer, Jun Jin
Senior Vice President, Division Officer, Robert Fiordalice
Vice President, General Counsel, Yoon Ah E. Oh
Chief Operating Officer, James Harlow
Chief Financial Officer, Mark Slicer
Director, Leo Berlinghieri
Director, David B. Miller
Director, Karen M. Rogge
Director, May Su
Director, Christine A. Tsingos
Director, Stephen Douglas Kelley
Auditors : Ernst & Young LLP

LOCATIONS

HQ: Onto Innovation Inc
  16 Jonspin Road, Wilmington, MA 01887
Phone: 978 253-6200
Web: www.ontoinnovation.com

2017 Sales

	$ mil.	% of total
South Korea	94.1	36
Japan	42	16
United States	34	13
China	29.8	12
Singapore	21.8	8
Taiwan	20.1	8
Other	16.8	7
Total	258.6	100

PRODUCTS/OPERATIONS

2017 Sales

	$ mil.	% of total
Products		
Automated systems	151.4	59
Integrated System	42.2	16
Material characterization systems	21.3	17
Service	43.7	17
Total	258.6	100

COMPETITORS

APPLIED MATERIALS, INC.
DANAHER CORPORATION
ELECTRO SCIENTIFIC INDUSTRIES, INC.
ENTEGRIS, INC.
ITRON, INC.
MEASUREMENT SPECIALTIES, INC.
MOCON, INC.
MTS SYSTEMS CORPORATION
RUDOLPH TECHNOLOGIES, INC.
TELEDYNE E2V LIMITED

HISTORICAL FINANCIALS

Company Type: Public

Income Statement FYE: December 26

	REVENUE ($mil)	NET INCOME ($mil)	NET PROFIT MARGIN	EMPLOYEES
12/20	556.4	31.0	5.6%	1,247
12/19	305.8	1.9	0.6%	1,340
12/18	324.5	57.6	17.8%	701
12/17	258.6	30.2	11.7%	592
12/16	221.1	44.0	19.9%	532
Annual Growth	26.0%	(8.4%)	—	23.7%

2020 Year-End Financials

Debt ratio: —
Return on equity: 2.4%
Cash ($ mil.): 373.7
Current Ratio: 6.09
Long-term debt ($ mil.): —
No. of shares ($ mil.): 48.7
Dividends
  Yield: —
  Payout: —
Market value ($ mil.): 2,341.0

	STOCK PRICE ($) FY Close	P/E High/Low		PER SHARE ($) Earnings	Dividends	Book Value
12/20	48.02	76	33	0.63	0.00	25.94
12/19	36.54	613	442	0.06	0.00	25.19
12/18	27.65	19	10	2.34	0.00	12.84
12/17	24.92	27	20	1.17	0.00	10.65
12/16	25.06	14	7	1.75	0.00	9.72
Annual Growth	17.7%	—	—	(22.5%)	—	27.8%

OP Bancorp

EXECUTIVES

Chairman, Director, Brian Choi
President, Chief Executive Officer, Subsidiary Officer, Director, Min J. Kim, $452,500 total compensation
Executive Vice President, Chief Financial Officer, Subsidiary Officer, Christine Y. Oh, $255,526 total compensation
Executive Vice President, Chief Credit Officer, Subsidiary Officer, Steve K. Park, $255,526 total compensation
Executive Vice President, Chief Lending Officer, Subsidiary Officer, Ki Won Yoon
Director, Ernest E. Dow
Director, Jason Hwang
Director, Soo Hun S. Jung
Director, Ock Hee Kim
Director, Myung Ja Park
Director, Yong Sin Shin
Auditors : Crowe LLP

LOCATIONS

HQ: OP Bancorp
  1000 Wilshire Blvd., Suite 500, Los Angeles, CA 90017
Phone: 213 892-9999
Web: www.myopenbank.com

HISTORICAL FINANCIALS
Company Type: Public

Income Statement   FYE: December 31

	ASSETS ($mil)	NET INCOME ($mil)	INCOME AS % OF ASSETS	EMPLOYEES
12/20	1,366.8	13.1	1.0%	173
12/19	1,179.5	16.7	1.4%	138
12/18	1,044.1	14.2	1.4%	154
12/17	900.9	9.2	1.0%	129
12/16	761.2	7.4	1.0%	0
Annual Growth	15.8%	15.3%	—	—

2020 Year-End Financials
Return on assets: 1.0%
Return on equity: 9.2%
Long-term debt ($ mil.): —
No. of shares ($ mil.): 15.0
Sales ($ mil.): 64.4
Dividends
Yield: 3.6%
Payout: 32.5%
Market value ($ mil.): 116.0

	STOCK PRICE ($) FY Close	P/E High	P/E Low	PER SHARE ($) Earnings	Dividends	Book Value
12/20	7.70	12	7	0.85	0.28	9.55
12/19	10.37	11	8	1.03	0.20	8.95
12/18	8.87	15	9	0.89	0.00	8.18
12/17	9.80	15	10	0.66	0.00	6.94
12/16	7.70	14	10	0.53	0.00	6.30
Annual Growth	0.0%	—	—	12.5%	—	10.9%

Oppenheimer Holdings Inc

Oppenheimer Holdings is a leading middle-market investment bank and full service broker-dealer. Through its subsidiaries, Oppenheimer & Co., Oppenheimer Asset Management and Oppenheimer Trust, it provides a range of financial services including brokerage, investment banking, asset management, lending, and research. The company's Private Client segment, which offers service brokerage, wealth planning, and margin lending to affluent and business clients in the Americas, makes up the bulk of sales. It held client assets under administration of approximately $122.1 billion. Oppenheimer employs more than 150 investment banking professionals in the US, the UK, Germany and Israel. The Americas accounts for about 95% of the company's revenues.

Operations
Oppenheimer operates three main business segments. Its Private Client segment, which brought in about 50% of its total revenue, has approximately 1,000 financial advisors at more than 90 offices throughout the US. The segment, which held some $122.1 billion in client assets under administration.

Oppenheimer's Capital Markets segment (around 45% of revenue) includes investment banking, institutional equities sales, trading, research, taxable fixed income sales, public finance and municipal trading.

The Asset Management segment (more than 5% of revenue) responsible for the company advisory programs and alternative investment business. It has approximately $46.2 billion of client assets under management in fee-based programs.

Geographic Reach
The New York-based the company generates about 95% of its revenue from customers in the Americas, while the rest came from Europe/Middle East (about 5%) and Asia. Oppenheimer has satellite US offices in Troy, Michigan; and Edison, New Jersey. Its international offices are in London, England, St. Helier, Isle of Jersey, Geneva, Switzerland, Frankfurt, Germany, Tel Aviv, Israel and Hong Kong, China.

Sales and Marketing
Oppenheimer serves high-net-worth individuals and families, corporate executives, and public and private businesses operating in a variety of sectors, including: consumer and retail, energy, financial institutions, healthcare, rental services, technology and transportation and logistics.

Financial Performance
The company's revenue in 2021 increased by 16% to $1.4 billion compared to $1.2 billion in the prior year.

Net income in 2021 increased by 29% to $159.0 million compared to $123.0 million in the prior year.

Cash held by the company at the end of 2021 increased by $341.5 million. Operating and financing activities were $227.8 million and $84.6 million, respectively. Cash used for investing activities was $6.3 million, mainly for purchase of furniture, equipment and leasehold improvements.

Strategy
Oppenheimer takes a pragmatic approach to human capital strategy and continuously makes investments in its people, processes and technology. This approach allows the company to adapt quickly to evolving business needs and maintain a competitive position, with the ability to readily implement change and employ best practices to meet or exceed industry standards. Its methods have proven to motivate and empower its employees, to cultivate an entrepreneurial mindset while fostering a culture of compliance.

The company continuously invests in and improves its technology platform to support client service and to remain competitive while continuously managing expenses. The company's long-term growth plan is to continue to expand existing offices by hiring experienced professionals as well as expand through the purchase of operating branch offices from other broker-dealers or the opening of new branch offices in attractive locations, and to continue to grow and develop the existing trading, investment banking, investment advisory and other divisions.

EXECUTIVES

Chairman, Chief Executive Officer, Subsidiary Officer, Director, Albert G. Lowenthal, $500,000 total compensation
Chief Financial Officer, Jeffrey J. Alfano
Director, Evan Behrens
Director, Timothy Martin Dwyer
Director, William J. Ehrhardt
Director, Paul M. Friedman
Director, R. Lawrence Roth
Director, Robert S. Lowenthal, $200,000 total compensation
Director, A. Winn Oughtred
Director, Teresa A. Glasser
Auditors: DELOITTE & TOUCHE LLP

LOCATIONS

HQ: Oppenheimer Holdings Inc
85 Broad Street, New York, NY 10004
Phone: 212 668-8000
Web: www.oppenheimer.com

2014 Sales

	$ mil.	% of total
United States	955.4	95
Europe/Middle East	43.1	4
Asia	6.0	1
Total	1,004.5	100

PRODUCTS/OPERATIONS

2014 Sales

	$ mil.	% of total
Commissions	469.8	47
Advisory fees	281.7	28
Investment banking	125.6	12
Interest	49.2	5
Principal transactions, net	29.7	3
Other	48.4	5
Total	1,004.5	100

2014 Sales by Segment

	$ mil.	% of total
Private Client	582.4	58
Capital Markets	298.6	30
Asset Management	100.0	10
Commercial Mortgage banking	23.3	2
Others	0.2	-
Total	1,004.5	100

COMPETITORS

Canaccord Genuity Group Inc
EVERCORE INC.
FRANKLIN RESOURCES, INC.
GREENHILL & CO., INC.
INVESTEC PLC
JEFFERIES FINANCIAL GROUP INC.
NUMIS CORPORATION PLC
PRIVATEBANCORP, INC.
STIFEL FINANCIAL CORP.
THE ZIEGLER COMPANIES INC

HISTORICAL FINANCIALS
Company Type: Public

Income Statement   FYE: December 31

	REVENUE ($mil)	NET INCOME ($mil)	NET PROFIT MARGIN	EMPLOYEES
12/20	1,198.6	122.9	10.3%	2,908
12/19	1,033.3	52.9	5.1%	2,971
12/18	958.1	28.8	3.0%	2,976
12/17	920.3	22.8	2.5%	2,992
12/16	857.7	(1.1)	—	3,098
Annual Growth	8.7%	—	—	(1.6%)

2020 Year-End Financials
Debt ratio: 7.6%
Return on equity: 19.1%
Cash ($ mil.): 35.4
Current Ratio: 1.25
Long-term debt ($ mil.): 123.8
No. of shares ($ mil.): 12.4
Dividends
  Yield: 4.7%
  Payout: 29.9%
Market value ($ mil.): 392.0

	STOCK PRICE ($) FY Close	P/E High	P/E Low	PER SHARE ($) Earnings	PER SHARE ($) Dividends	PER SHARE ($) Book Value
12/20	31.43	3	2	9.30	1.48	54.93
12/19	27.48	8	6	3.82	0.46	46.31
12/18	25.55	16	11	2.05	0.44	41.81
12/17	26.80	17	9	1.67	0.44	39.55
12/16	18.60	—	—	(0.09)	0.44	38.22
Annual Growth	14.0%	—	—	—	35.4%	9.5%

Orange County Bancorp Inc

EXECUTIVES

Chairman, Director, Louis Heimbach
President, Chief Executive Officer, Subsidiary Officer, Director, Michael J. Gilfeather
Senior Vice President, Chief Financial Officer, Chief Accounting Officer, Controller, Subsidiary Officer, Michael Lesler
Subsidiary Officer, Gregory Sousa
Subsidiary Officer, Michael Listner
Subsidiary Officer, Michael J. Coulter
Subsidiary Officer, Joseph A. Ruhl
Subsidiary Officer, Elizabeth Jones
Subsidiary Officer, Frank J. Skuthan
Subsidiary Officer, David Dineen
Director, Terry R. Saturno
Director, Richard B. Rowley
Director, William D. Morrison
Director, Gustave "Gus" . J. Scacco
Director, Jonathan F. Rouis
Director, Kevin J. Keane
Director, Marianna R. Kennedy
Director, Gregory F. Holcombe
Auditors : Crowe LLP

LOCATIONS
HQ: Orange County Bancorp Inc
212 Dolson Ave, Middletown, NY 10940
Phone: 845 341-5000
Web: www.orangebanktrust.com

HISTORICAL FINANCIALS
Company Type: Public

Income Statement   FYE: December 31

	ASSETS ($mil)	NET INCOME ($mil)	INCOME AS % OF ASSETS	EMPLOYEES
12/20	1,664.9	11.6	0.7%	0
12/19	1,228.4	11.0	0.9%	0
12/18	1,064.8	7.5	0.7%	0
12/17	960.7	2.3	0.2%	150
12/16	909.7	3.6	0.4%	0
Annual Growth	16.3%	33.9%	—	—

2020 Year-End Financials
Return on assets: 0.8%
Return on equity: 9.0%
Long-term debt ($ mil.): —
No. of shares ($ mil.): 4.4
Sales ($ mil.): 64.8
Dividends
  Yield: 2.9%
  Payout: 32.1%
Market value ($ mil.): 122.0

	STOCK PRICE ($) FY Close	P/E High	P/E Low	PER SHARE ($) Earnings	PER SHARE ($) Dividends	PER SHARE ($) Book Value
12/20	27.25	12	8	2.59	0.80	30.21
12/19	29.40	12	11	2.47	0.80	26.85
12/18	27.00	30	13	1.87	0.80	24.11
12/17	56.05	93	77	0.60	0.82	23.32
12/16	46.52	52	49	0.93	0.82	23.61
Annual Growth	(12.5%)	—	—	29.2%	(0.6%)	6.4%

Origin Bancorp Inc

EXECUTIVES

Chairman, President, Chief Executive Officer, Subsidiary Officer, Director, Drake Mills, $835,800 total compensation
Senior Executive Officer, Chief Financial Officer, William "Wally" Wallace
Chief Accounting Officer, Subsidiary Officer, Stephen H. Brolly, $436,442 total compensation
Senior Executive Officer, Chief Operating Officer, Subsidiary Officer, M. Lance Hall
Senior Executive Vice President, Chief Risk Officer, Jim Crotwell
Senior Executive Officer, Chief Credit Officer, Chief Banking Officer, Preston Moore
Lead Independent Director, Director, James Samuel D'Agostino
Director, James E. Davison
Director, Steven Taylor
Director, Gary Luffey
Director, Elizabeth Solender
Director, Michael A. Jones
Director, Farrell J. Malone
Director, Richard Gallot
Director, A. La'Verne Edney
Director, Meryl Kennedy Farr
Director, Stacey W. Goff
Director, Daniel Chu
Director, Lori Sirman
Director, Jay Dyer
Auditors : BKD, LLP

LOCATIONS
HQ: Origin Bancorp Inc
500 South Service Road East, Ruston, LA 71270
Phone: 318 255-2222
Web: www.origin.bank

HISTORICAL FINANCIALS
Company Type: Public

Income Statement   FYE: December 31

	ASSETS ($mil)	NET INCOME ($mil)	INCOME AS % OF ASSETS	EMPLOYEES
12/20	7,628.2	36.3	0.5%	749
12/19	5,324.6	53.8	1.0%	751
12/18	4,821.5	51.6	1.1%	761
12/17	4,153.9	14.6	0.4%	686
12/16	4,071.4	12.8	0.3%	0
Annual Growth	17.0%	29.7%	—	—

2020 Year-End Financials
Return on assets: 0.5%
Return on equity: 5.8%
Long-term debt ($ mil.): —
No. of shares ($ mil.): 23.5
Sales ($ mil.): 293.3
Dividends
  Yield: 1.3%
  Payout: 27.9%
Market value ($ mil.): 653.0

	STOCK PRICE ($) FY Close	P/E High	P/E Low	PER SHARE ($) Earnings	PER SHARE ($) Dividends	PER SHARE ($) Book Value
12/20	27.77	24	11	1.55	0.38	27.53
12/19	37.84	17	14	2.28	0.28	25.52
12/18	34.08	19	15	2.20	0.10	23.17
Annual Growth	(9.7%)	—	—	(16.1%)	96.8%	9.0%

Orion Energy Systems Inc

Orion Energy Systems wants customers to see the light ... high intensity fluorescent (HIF) lighting systems, that is. Orion designs, manufactures, and installs energy management systems that include HIF lighting and intelligent lighting controls. Its Apollo Light Pipe product collects and focuses daylight, without consuming electricity. The firm estimates its HIF lineup can help cut customers' lighting-related electricity costs by up to 50%, boost quantity and quality of light, and reduce related carbon-dioxide emissions. In addition, its engineered systems division makes solar photovoltaic products that allow customers to convert sunlight into electricity.

Operations

Orion divides its operations across several segments. Energy management (almost 75% of total sales) supplies its HIF lighting systems, while the engineered systems division makes solar and wind alternative renewable energy systems (primarily solar photovoltaic systems). In mid-2014, the company restructured its business and added a new division -- US markets -- which includes the US operations of its Orion engineered systems and Orion distribution services.

Geographic Reach

Operating majorly in North America, the company has its manufacturing unit and a technology center located in Manitowoc, Wisconsin, and office properties in Green Cove Springs, Florida; and Jacksonville, Florida.

Sales and Marketing

The company sells its products and services indirectly to customers through electrical contractors or distributors. Orion also sells its products on a wholesale basis to electrical contractors and value-added resellers. (About 60% of its total lighting revenue comes from its reseller network.) As such, its sales strategy involves building upon these customer relationships with these electrical contractors and value-added resellers to widen the geographic scope of its sales reach.

Financial Performance

In fiscal 2014 Orion's revenues climbed by 3% to $89 million. The growth was due to an increase in service revenues fueled by high installations from a previous acquisition and a single landfill solar project installed during the year.

Orion has posted two straight years of net losses, mostly due to a bump in expenses related to acquisitions. In 2014 the company's operating cash flow increased to $10 million, due to an increase in accounts receivable attributed to decreased inventories and increased cash collections.

Strategy

Orion largely targets commercial and industrial customers who are kept awake at night trying to choose the right technology to reduce their business expenses. These customers call Orion for an energy "retrofit," or replacement of high-intensity discharge products with the company's HIF lighting system. The company is specifically targeting utilities and electrical grid operators for this type of need. It has been growing its LED offerings to customers to capitalize on the fast-growing LED trend in the lighting manufacturing industry. While still predominantly a HIF and solar lighting company, Orion has joined Cree, Revolution Lighting, and several other lighting manufacturers offering LED lighting and systems to customers.

Orion capitalizes on its customers' existing electrical contractor to deliver installation and monitoring services, as well as sells its products wholesale to electrical contractors and resellers. Wholesale channels are a promising route to market and have grown to about 60% of the company's revenue.

Mergers and Acquisitions

Expanding its product portfolio, in 2013 Orion acquired Florida-based Harris Manufacturing, Inc. and Harris LED, LLC. for $10 million. Harris engineers, designs, sources, and makes energy-efficient lighting systems, including fluorescent and LED lighting, and day-lighting products.

EXECUTIVES

Chairman, Director, Anthony L. Otten
Executive Vice President, Subsidiary Officer, Scott A. Green, $275,000 total compensation
Executive Vice President, Chief Executive Officer, Director, Michael H. Jenkins
Executive Vice President, Chief Financial Officer, Chief Accounting Officer, Treasurer, J. Per Brodin
Director, Michael W. Altschaefl, $325,000 total compensation
Director, Ellen B. Richstone
Director, Sally A. Washlow
Auditors : BDO USA, LLP

LOCATIONS

HQ: Orion Energy Systems Inc
2210 Woodland Drive, Manitowoc, WI 54220
Phone: 920 892-9340
Web: www.orionlighting.com

PRODUCTS/OPERATIONS

2014 Sales

	$ mil.	% of total
Energy management	66.8	75
Engineered systems	21.8	22
Total	88.6	100

Selected Products
Apollo Solar Light Pipe (lens-based device that collects & focuses renewable daylight)
Compact Modular product line (high intensity fluorescent (HIF) lighting systems)
    Agribusiness fixtures
    LED freezer applications
    Outdoor application fixtures
    Parking lot fixtures
    Private label resale
    Roadway fixtures
InteLite Wireless Controls (remote control of fixtures via web-based software)
Renewable Energy Projects (test solar photovoltaic electricity generating projects)

COMPETITORS

ACUITY BRANDS, INC.
ADB SAFEGATE AMERICAS LLC
B&Q LIMITED
Carmanah Technologies Corporation
DIALIGHT PLC
ENPHASE ENERGY, INC.
LIME ENERGY CO.
PELICAN PRODUCTS, INC.
SOLAREDGE TECHNOLOGIES, INC.
XENONICS HOLDINGS, INC.

HISTORICAL FINANCIALS

Company Type: Public

Income Statement — FYE: March 31

	REVENUE ($mil)	NET INCOME ($mil)	NET PROFIT MARGIN	EMPLOYEES
03/21	116.8	26.1	22.4%	213
03/20	150.8	12.4	8.3%	181
03/19	65.7	(6.6)	—	321
03/18	60.3	(13.1)	—	214
03/17	70.2	(12.2)	—	264
Annual Growth	13.6%	—	—	(5.2%)

2021 Year-End Financials

Debt ratio: 0.1%
Return on equity: 58.6%
Cash ($ mil.): 19.3
Current Ratio: 1.86
Long-term debt ($ mil.): —
No. of shares ($ mil.): 30.8
Dividends
  Yield: —
  Payout: —
Market value ($ mil.): 214.0

	STOCK PRICE ($) FY Close	P/E High/Low		PER SHARE ($) Earnings	Dividends	Book Value
03/21	6.96	14	4	0.83	0.00	1.89
03/20	3.70	15	2	0.40	0.00	1.03
03/19	0.89	—	—	(0.23)	0.00	0.61
03/18	0.85	—	—	(0.46)	0.00	0.81
03/17	1.98	—	—	(0.44)	0.00	1.25
Annual Growth	36.9%	—	—	—	—	10.8%

Orrstown Financial Services, Inc.

Orrstown Financial Services keeps both paddles in the money pool. The institution is the holding company for Orrstown Bank, which operates some 20 branches in Pennsylvania's Cumberland, Perry, and Franklin counties as well as in Maryland's Washington County. In addition to traditional retail deposit offerings, Orrstown also provides investment management services including retirement planning and investment analysis. Real estate mortgages account for about 40% of the bank's lending portfolio, followed by commercial, construction, and consumer loans. Orrstown is growing its mortgage lending capabilities. It launched an online application system in order to increase mortgage origination sales.

EXECUTIVES

Chairman, Subsidiary Officer, Joel R. Zullinger
President, Chief Executive Officer, Subsidiary Officer, Director, Thomas R. Quinn, $514,723 total compensation
Executive Vice President, Chief Financial Officer, Subsidiary Officer, Thomas R. Brugger
Executive Vice President, Chief Risk Officer, Secretary, Subsidiary Officer, Robert G. Coradi, $221,731 total compensation
Executive Vice President, Assistant Secretary, Subsidiary Officer, Philip E. Fague, $236,480 total compensation
Chief Accounting Officer, Neil Kalani
Subsidiary Officer, Jeffrey S. Gayman, $180,281 total compensation
Subsidiary Officer, Robert J. Fignar
Subsidiary Officer, David Hornberger
Subsidiary Officer, Christopher Holt
Subsidiary Officer, Zachary Khuri
Subsidiary Officer, Barbara E. Brobst, $154,274 total compensation
Subsidiary Officer, Luke Bernstein
Subsidiary Officer, Adam L. Metz, $265,502 total compensation

Director, Cindy Jeannette Joiner
Director, Eric Andrew Segal
Director, Thomas D. Longenecker
Director, Andrea Pugh
Director, Floyd E. Stoner
Director, Mark K. Keller
Director, Michael J. Rice
Director, Glenn W. Snoke
Director, Linford Weaver
Auditors : Crowe LLP

LOCATIONS

HQ: Orrstown Financial Services, Inc.
77 East King Street, P.O. Box 250, Shippensburg, PA 17257
Phone: 717 532-6114
Web: www.orrstown.com

COMPETITORS

COMMUNITY SHORES BANK CORPORATION
EMCLAIRE FINANCIAL CORP.
GUARANTY BANCSHARES, INC.
LIBERTY BANCORP, INC.
OCEANFIRST FINANCIAL CORP.

HISTORICAL FINANCIALS
Company Type: Public

Income Statement — FYE: December 31

	ASSETS ($mil)	NET INCOME ($mil)	INCOME AS % OF ASSETS	EMPLOYEES
12/20	2,750.5	26.4	1.0%	418
12/19	2,383.2	16.9	0.7%	460
12/18	1,934.3	12.8	0.7%	386
12/17	1,558.8	8.0	0.5%	338
12/16	1,414.5	6.6	0.5%	327
Annual Growth	18.1%	41.4%	—	6.3%

2020 Year-End Financials
Return on assets: 1.0%
Return on equity: 11.2%
Long-term debt ($ mil.): —
No. of shares ($ mil.): 11.2
Sales ($ mil.): 127.9
Dividends
Yield: 4.1%
Payout: 36.3%
Market value ($ mil.): 185.0

	STOCK PRICE ($) FY Close	P/E High/Low		PER SHARE ($) Earnings	Dividends	Book Value
12/20	16.55	9	5	2.40	0.68	21.98
12/19	22.62	14	11	1.61	0.60	19.93
12/18	18.21	18	12	1.50	0.51	18.39
12/17	25.25	27	20	0.98	0.42	17.34
12/16	22.40	29	20	0.81	0.35	16.28
Annual Growth	(7.3%)	—	—	31.2%	18.1%	7.8%

OTC Markets Group Inc

EXECUTIVES

Chairman, Neal L. Wolkoff, $77,512 total compensation
President, Chief Executive Officer, Director, R. Cromwell Coulson, $564,940 total compensation
Market Data Licensing Executive Vice President, Matthew Fuchs, $277,500 total compensation
Issuer Executive Vice President, Corporate Services Executive Vice President, Information Services Executive Vice President, Lisabeth Heese, $275,000 total compensation
Chief Financial Officer, Antonia Georgieva
Chief Technology Officer, Bruce Ostrover, $247,500 total compensation
General Counsel, Corporate Secretary, Chief of Staff, Daniel Zinn, $290,000 total compensation
Subsidiary Officer, Michael Modeski, $430,000 total compensation
Division Officer, Jason L. Paltrowitz, $308,000 total compensation
Director, Gary Baddeley, $9,000 total compensation
Director, Louisa Serene Schneider
Director, Andrew T. Wimpfheimer, $9,000 total compensation
Auditors : DELOITTE & TOUCHE LLP

LOCATIONS

HQ: OTC Markets Group Inc
300 Vesey Street, 12th Floor, New York, NY 10282
Phone: 212 896-4400 **Fax:** 212 868-3848
Web: www.otcmarkets.com

HISTORICAL FINANCIALS
Company Type: Public

Income Statement — FYE: December 31

	REVENUE ($mil)	NET INCOME ($mil)	NET PROFIT MARGIN	EMPLOYEES
12/20	71.2	18.2	25.7%	102
12/19	62.8	14.9	23.8%	99
12/18	59.2	16.2	27.4%	93
12/17	54.6	12.5	23.0%	90
12/16	50.8	10.5	20.7%	88
Annual Growth	8.8%	14.8%	—	3.8%

2020 Year-End Financials
Debt ratio: —
Return on equity: 97.9%
Cash ($ mil.): 33.7
Current Ratio: 1.40
Long-term debt ($ mil.): —
No. of shares ($ mil.): 11.7
Dividends
Yield: 3.6%
Payout: 91.2%
Market value ($ mil.): 398.0

	STOCK PRICE ($) FY Close	P/E High/Low		PER SHARE ($) Earnings	Dividends	Book Value
12/20	34.00	23	15	1.53	1.25	1.67
12/19	35.00	31	23	1.25	1.25	1.52
12/18	29.04	23	17	1.36	1.23	1.42
12/17	29.05	29	17	1.06	1.16	1.21
12/16	23.00	25	16	0.90	1.16	1.36
Annual Growth	10.3%	—	—	14.2%	1.9%	5.2%

Otter Tail Corp.

Otter Tail covers a swath of businesses, from electric services and construction to manufacturing equipment and plastic pipe businesses. The electric utility (Otter Tail Power Company (OTP)) is the company's core business; it keeps the lights on for more than 133,000 customers in more than 400 communities across a predominantly rural and agricultural service territory in Minnesota and the Dakotas. The company also makes PVC pipes (Northern Pipe Products and Vinyltech Corporation), primarily sold in the western half of the US and Canada, and manufactures parts and trays (BTD Manufacturing and T.O. Plastics), primarily sold in the US.

Operations

The Otter Tail's businesses are divided into three major segments: Electric, Plastics and Manufacturing. Electric accounts for approximately 40% of the company's revenues; Plastics brings in more than 30% and Manufacturing generates about 30%.

The Electric segment includes the production, purchase, transmission, distribution and sale of electric energy in Minnesota, North Dakota and South Dakota by OTP. In addition, OTP is a participant in the Midcontinent Independent System Operator, Inc. (MISO) markets.

The Plastics segment consists of businesses producing polyvinyl chloride (PVC) pipe at plants in North Dakota and Arizona.

Manufacturing segment consists of businesses in the following manufacturing activities: contract machining, metal parts stamping, fabrication and painting, and production of plastic thermoformed horticultural containers, life science and industrial packaging, material handling components and extruded raw material stock.

Overall, product sales bring in approximately 60% of the company's revenue while electric provides some 40%.

Geographic Reach

Headquartered in Fergus Falls, Minnesota, and Fargo, North Dakota, Otter Tail has manufacturing facilities in Georgia, Illinois, and Minnesota. Minnesota has the largest retail electric revenue with over 50%.

Sales and Marketing

The OTP provides electricity to more than 133,000 customers. Its commercial and industrial customers account for about 65% of revenue while residential customers generate the remaining nearly 35%.

Primarily serves Midwestern and Southeastern US manufacturers in the recreational vehicle, lawn and garden, agricultural, construction, and industrial and energy equipment end markets, the company's plastic products business serves primarily US customers in the horticulture, medical and life sciences, industrial, recreational and electronics industries. The principal method for distribution of the manufacturing companies' products is by direct shipment to the customer through direct customer pick-up or common carrier ground transportation. The manufacturing segment's top two customers combined account for about 45% of its Manufacturing segment operating revenue.

PVC pipe products are marketed through

a combination of independent sales representatives, company salespersons, and customer service representatives to serve wholesalers and distributors. Its top two customers combined account for approximately 50% of the company's Plastics segment operating revenue.

Financial Performance

The company had total operating revenues of $480.3 million, an 8% increase from the previous year's total operating revenue of $446.1 million. This was primarily due to a higher sales volume across all of the company's segments.

Collectively in 2021, the company's businesses generated net income of $176.8 million, or $4.23 per diluted share, an increase of 84% from $95.9 million, or $2.34 per diluted share, in 2020. In 2021, the company paid an annual dividend of $1.56 per share, or $64.9 million, completing its 83rd consecutive year of dividend payments to its shareholders. The company's cash at the end of 2021 was $1.5 billion. Operating activities generated $231.2 million, while investing activities used $171.5 million, mainly for capital expenditures. Financing activities used another $59.4 million, primarily for payments for retirement of long-term debt.

Strategy

The company maintains a moderate risk profile by investing in rate base growth opportunities in its Electric segment and organic growth opportunities in its Manufacturing and Plastics segments. This strategy and risk profile are designed to provide a more predictable earnings stream, maintain the company's credit quality and preserve its ability to fund its dividend payments. The company's goal is to deliver annual growth in earnings per share between five and seven percent over the next several years, using 2020 diluted earnings per share as the base for measurement. The company expects its earnings growth to come from rate base investments in its Electric segment and from existing capacities and planned investments within its Manufacturing and Plastics segments.

Company Background

Otter Tail was founded in 1907.

EXECUTIVES

Chairman, Director, Nathan I. Partain, $74,000 total compensation

President, Chief Executive Officer, Subsidiary Officer, Director, Charles S. MacFarlane, $650,000 total compensation

Senior Vice President, Chief Financial Officer, Kevin G. Moug, $444,000 total compensation

Vice President, General Counsel, Corporate Secretary, Subsidiary Officer, Jennifer O. Smestad, $315,000 total compensation

Division Officer, Subsidiary Officer, John S. Abbott, $350,000 total compensation

Division Officer, Subsidiary Officer, Timothy J. Rogelstad, $370,000 total compensation

Director, Michael E. LeBeau

Director, Karen M. Bohn, $67,000 total compensation

Director, Thomas J. Webb

Director, Steven L. Fritze

Director, Kathryn O. Johnson

Director, John D. Erickson, $469,583 total compensation

Director, James B. Stake, $60,000 total compensation

Auditors : DELOITTE & TOUCHE LLP

LOCATIONS

HQ: Otter Tail Corp.
215 South Cascade Street, P.O. Box 496, Fergus Falls, MN 56538-0496
Phone: 866 410-8780
Web: www.ottertail.com

COMPETITORS

BROADWIND ENERGY, INC.
DYNEGY INC.
FIRSTENERGY CORP.
HARSCO CORPORATION
KANEMATSU CORPORATION
PACIFICORP
PINNACLE WEST CAPITAL CORPORATION
PPL CORPORATION
PROGRESS ENERGY, INC.
Vattenfall AB

HISTORICAL FINANCIALS
Company Type: Public

Income Statement				FYE: December 31
	REVENUE ($mil)	NET INCOME ($mil)	NET PROFIT MARGIN	EMPLOYEES
12/21	1,196.8	176.7	14.8%	2,487
12/20	890.1	95.8	10.8%	2,074
12/19	919.5	86.8	9.4%	2,208
12/18	916.4	82.3	9.0%	2,321
12/17	849.3	72.4	8.5%	2,097
Annual Growth	9.0%	25.0%	—	4.4%

2021 Year-End Financials
Debt ratio: 31.0%
Return on equity: 18.9%
Cash ($ mil.): 1.5
Current Ratio: 0.95
Long-term debt ($ mil.): 734
No. of shares ($ mil.): 41.5
Dividends
  Yield: 2.1%
  Payout: 45.2%
Market value ($ mil.): 2,968.0

	STOCK PRICE ($) FY Close	P/E High/Low		PER SHARE ($) Earnings	Dividends	Book Value
12/21	71.42	17	9	4.23	1.56	23.84
12/20	42.61	24	14	2.34	1.48	21.00
12/19	51.29	26	21	2.17	1.40	19.46
12/18	49.64	25	19	2.06	1.34	18.38
12/17	44.45	26	20	1.82	1.28	17.62
Annual Growth	12.6%	—	—	23.5%	5.1%	7.9%

Overstock.com Inc (DE)

Overstock.com offers a broad range of price-competitive products, including furniture, dÃ©cor, area rugs, bedding and bath, home improvement, outdoor, and kitchen and dining items, among others. The company sells its products and services through its Internet websites located at www.overstock.com, www.o.co, www.overstock.ca, and www.overstockgovernment.com and through its mobile app. It offers millions of products which about 100% are in-line products (products in active production). In addition to Overstock's more than 1,240 facilities, the company's supply chain allows it to ship directly to customers from its suppliers or from its warehouses. Started in 1999, Dr. Patrick M. Byrne acquired the company Discounts Direct and rebranded it as Overstock.com.

Operations

Overstock is consists of one reportable segment, Retail, which primarily consists of amounts earned through e-commerce product sales through the company's website.

Nearly all of the company's retail sales through its website are from transactions in which it fulfilled orders through the company's network of approximately 3,000 third-party manufacturers, distributors and other suppliers (partners) selling on the company's website.

In addition, the company offers additional products or services that may complement its primary retail offerings but are not significant to its revenues, including: businesses advertising products or services on the company's website; Market Partner, a service it provides to partners where they can sell their products through third party sites; international business where the company offers products to customers outside the US using third party logistics providers; and Supplier Oasis, a single integration point through which its partners can manage their products, inventory and sales channels, and obtain multi-channel fulfillment services through the company's distribution network.

Geographic Reach

Based in Salt Lake City, Utah, Overstock has over 1,240 facilities, mostly in the US, used for corporate office space, data centers, warehouse, fulfillment and customer service space.

Sales and Marketing

Overstock uses a variety of methods to target its retail consumer audience, including online campaigns, such as advertising through keywords, product listing ads, display ads, search engines, affiliate marketing, social coupon websites, portals, banners, email, direct mail, viral and social media. It also advertises on TV, video on demand, radio, print, and event sponsorship.

Overstock's advertising expense totaled $302.4 million and $261.0 million during the years ended 2021 and 2020, respectively.

Financial Performance

The company had a revenue of $2.8 billion, an 11% increase from the previous year's revenue of $2.5 billion. The increase in revenue was primarily due to increased product sales resulting from a 23% increase in average order value driven by a continued product mix shift into home furniture categories, partially offset by a 10% decrease in customer orders.

In 2021 the company had a net income of $389 million, a 743% increase from the previous year's net income of $46.2 million.

The company's cash at the end of 2021 was $503.3 million. Operating activities generated $80.9 million, while investing activities used $86.1 million, mainly for contributions for capital calls. Financing activities used another $10.6 million, primarily for payments of taxes withheld upon vesting of restricted stock.

Strategy

Overstock.com's business initiatives enable our long-term focus on its three brand pillars, "Product Findability," "Smart Value," and "Easy Delivery and Support." 2021 initiatives for the business included:

Improve Product Findability ? Directly supporting its "Product Findability" brand pillar by improving customer search and navigation through refinement of the company's search taxonomy and product attribute infrastructure with the goal of enhanced search relevancy and recommendations.

Grow Canada Market Share ? Expanding geographical engagement to grow its Canadian customer base by providing a wholesale change in the company's Canadian "Smart Value" and "Easy Delivery and Support" customer shopping experience.

Grow Government Market Share ? Improving its Government website with more competitive market features and products that offer an intuitive procurement experience, and provide the flexibility to expand the platform to additional government customers.

Improve Enterprise Platform ? Improving the company's data strategy to connect high-quality, intuitive data with its business users to enable faster insights. Additionally, embracing the public cloud in order to promote greater resilience for the business in the event of unforeseen circumstances.

Company Background

EXECUTIVES

Chairwoman, Director, Allison H. Abraham
Chief Executive Officer, Subsidiary Officer, Director, Jonathan E. Johnson, $350,000 total compensation
Software Engineering Senior Vice President, Amit Goyal, $338,079 total compensation
People Care Senior Vice President, Technology Senior Vice President, People Care Chief Administrative Officer, Technology Chief Administrative Officer, Carter P. Lee
Finance Vice President, Finance Controller, Anthony D. Strong
Strategy Senior Vice President, Seth A. Moore
Chief Financial Officer, Adrianne Lee
Chief Legal Officer, E. Glen Nickle
Chief Technology Officer, Joel Weight
Division Officer, David J. Nielsen, $300,000 total compensation
Risk Management Subsidiary Officer, Finance Subsidiary Officer, Robert P. Hughes, $254,232 total compensation
Marketing Subsidiary Officer, Saum Noursalehi, $828,846 total compensation
Director, Barclay F. Corbus
Director, Joseph J. Tabacco
Director, Robert Shapiro
Director, William E. Nettles
Director, Barbara H. Messing
Auditors : KPMG LLP

LOCATIONS

HQ: Overstock.com Inc (DE)
799 West Coliseum Way, Midvale, UT 84047
Phone: 801 947-3100
Web: www.overstock.com

PRODUCTS/OPERATIONS

Selected Product Categories
Bed & Bath
Décor
Furniture
Home Improvement
Jewelry
Kids & Baby
Kitchen
Men
Outdoor
Rugs
Watches
Women

COMPETITORS

AMAZON.COM, INC.
BAZAARVOICE, INC.
DICK'S SPORTING GOODS, INC.
ETSY, INC.
KIRKLAND'S, INC.
PC CONNECTION, INC.
PCM, INC.
QVC, INC.
WAYFAIR INC.
ZULILY, INC.

HISTORICAL FINANCIALS

Company Type: Public

Income Statement — FYE: December 31

	REVENUE ($mil)	NET INCOME ($mil)	NET PROFIT MARGIN	EMPLOYEES
12/20	2,549.7	56.0	2.2%	1,750
12/19	1,459.4	(121.8)	—	1,613
12/18	1,821.5	(206.0)	—	2,060
12/17	1,744.7	(109.8)	—	1,800
12/16	1,799.9	12.5	0.7%	1,800
Annual Growth	9.1%	45.4%	—	(0.7%)

2020 Year-End Financials

Debt ratio: 5.0%
Return on equity: 22.8%
Cash ($ mil.): 519.1
Current Ratio: 1.78
Long-term debt ($ mil.): 41.3
No. of shares ($ mil.): 42.7
Dividends
  Yield: —
  Payout: —
Market value ($ mil.): 2,052.0

	STOCK PRICE ($) FY Close	P/E High/Low		PER SHARE ($) Earnings	Dividends	Book Value
12/20	47.97	98	2	1.24	0.00	8.74
12/19	7.05	—	—	(3.46)	0.00	2.92
12/18	13.58	—	—	(6.83)	0.00	4.10
12/17	63.90	—	—	(4.28)	0.00	6.39
12/16	17.50	39	21	0.49	0.00	6.89
Annual Growth	28.7%	—	—	26.1%	—	6.1%

Pacific Premier Bancorp Inc

EXECUTIVES

President, Chief Executive Officer, Subsidiary Officer, Chairman, Director, Steven R. Gardner, $750,800 total compensation
Subsidiary Officer, Edward Earl Wilcox, $464,100 total compensation
Senior Executive Vice President, Chief Financial Officer, Subsidiary Officer, Ronald J. Nicolas, $409,000 total compensation
Subsidiary Officer, Michael S. Karr, $315,600 total compensation
Subsidiary Officer, Thomas Rice, $364,700 total compensation
Corporate Secretary, Subsidiary Officer, Steven R. Arnold
Subsidiary Officer, Daniel C. Borland
Subsidiary Officer, Teresa M. Dawson
Subsidiary Officer, Ernest Hwang
Subsidiary Officer, Donn B. Jakosky
Senior Executive Vice President, Chief Human Resources Officer, Peggy Ohlhaver
Subsidiary Officer, James A. Robinson
Principal Accounting Officer, Subsidiary Officer, Lori A. Wright
Lead Independent Director, Director, Jeff C. Jones
Director, M. Christian Mitchell
Director, Barbara S. Polsky
Director, Zareh H. Sarrafian
Director, Jaynie M. Studenmund
Director, Ayad A. Fargo
Director, Joseph L. Garrett
Director, Cora M. Tellez
Director, Richard C. Thomas
Director, George M. Pereira
Auditors : Crowe LLP

LOCATIONS

HQ: Pacific Premier Bancorp Inc
17901 Von Karman Avenue, Suite 1200, Irvine, CA 92614
Phone: 949 864-8000
Web: www.ppbi.com

HISTORICAL FINANCIALS

Company Type: Public

Income Statement — FYE: December 31

	ASSETS ($mil)	NET INCOME ($mil)	INCOME AS % OF ASSETS	EMPLOYEES
12/20	19,736.5	60.3	0.3%	1,478
12/19	11,776.0	159.7	1.4%	1,006
12/18	11,487.3	123.3	1.1%	1,030
12/17	8,024.5	60.1	0.7%	846
12/16	4,036.3	40.1	1.0%	448
Annual Growth	48.7%	10.8%	—	34.8%

2020 Year-End Financials

Return on assets: 0.3%
Return on equity: 2.5%
Long-term debt ($ mil.): —
No. of shares ($ mil.): 94.4
Sales ($ mil.): 702
Dividends
Yield: 3.2%
Payout: 257.5%
Market value ($ mil.): 2,960.0

	STOCK PRICE ($) FY Close	P/E High/Low		PER SHARE ($) Earnings	Dividends	Book Value
12/20	31.33	44	20	0.75	1.03	29.07
12/19	32.61	13	10	2.60	0.88	33.82
12/18	25.52	20	10	2.26	0.00	31.52
12/17	40.00	26	20	1.56	0.00	26.86
12/16	35.35	24	13	1.46	0.00	16.54
Annual Growth	(3.0%)	—	—	(15.3%)	—	15.1%

Pacira BioSciences Inc

Pacira BioSciences (formerly Pacira Pharmaceuticals) is the industry leader in its commitment to non-opioid pain management and providing a non-opioid option to as many patients as possible to redefine the role of opioids as a rescue therapy only. It is advancing a pipeline of unique, safe, best-in-class products across a variety of therapeutic areas that include acute postsurgical pain; acute and chronic osteoarthritis, or OA, pain of the knee; low back and other areas; spasticity and stellate ganglion block of the sympathetic nerves.

Operations

It has three commercialized non-opioid treatments: EXPAREL (bupivacaine liposome injectable suspension), a long-acting, local analgesic currently approved for postsurgical pain management; ZILRETTA (triamcinolone acetonide extended-release injectable suspension), an extended-release, intra-articular, corticosteroid injection indicated for the management of OA knee pain; and iovera, a novel, handheld device for delivering immediate, long-acting, drug-free pain control using precise, controlled doses of cold temperature to a targeted nerve.

EXPAREL generates some 95% of total revenue, while ZILRETTA, iovera Bupivacaine liposome injectable suspension account for the remaining 5%.

Geographic Reach

Pacira has manufacturing and research facilities in Fremont and San Diego, California. It also has administration and commercialization offices in Parsippany, New Jersey.

Sales and Marketing

Pacira has marketing and sales organization to commercialize its products. Its primary target markets are healthcare practitioners who influence pain management decisions including anesthesiologists, surgeons, pharmacists and nurses.

Financial Performance

Total revenues in 2021 increased 26% to $541.5 million. The increase was due to a higher sales volume in the company's net product sales.

In 2021, the company had a net income of $42 million, a 71% decrease from the previous year's net income of $145.5 million.

The company's cash at the end of 2021 was $585.6 million. Operating activities generated $125.7 million, while investing activities used $20.8 million, mainly for purchases of available-for-sale investments. Financing activities provided another $380.7 million.

Strategy

To achieve its goal of global leadership in non-opioid pain management and regenerative health solutions, Pacira is advancing a three-pronged strategy:

Expanding the use of the company's opioid-free commercial assets. For EXPAREL, Pacira is advancing two Phase 3 studies in lower extremity nerve block procedures, as well as a development program for pediatric patients under six years of age. For ZILRETTA, the company plans to initiate a Phase 3 study in shoulder OA and it is defining label expansion studies to include safety superiority in patients with Type 2 diabetes and repeat dosing for OA knee pain. For iovera, Pacira is developing new iovera Smart Tips for chronic lower back pain and spine procedures. It is also advancing plans to develop iovera as a treatment for spasticity;

Advancing Pacira's clinical-stage pipeline within multiple areas of unmet need. The company is advancing its pipeline of clinical-stage assets that utilize the company's proprietary multivesicular liposome (pMVL) technology; and

Accessing complementary innovative assets using a combination of strategic investment, in-licensing, or acquisition. The company believes EXPAREL, ZILRETTA, iovera and its pMVL drug delivery technology offer a strong foundation to address the opioid epidemic. Building on these proprietary assets, the company has also made investments in the musculoskeletal and chronic pain spaces. It plans to continue to advance these two key areas with a focus on the knee and spine continuums of care and chronic pain.

Mergers and Acquisitions

In 2021, Pacira acquired Flexion Therapeutics, Inc., a commercial-stage biopharmaceutical company focused on the development and commercialization of novel, local non-opioid therapies for the treatment of patients with musculoskeletal conditions, including osteoarthritis (OA), postsurgical pain and low back pain, for $578.8 million. The acquisition expands its industry leadership and marks a major milestone in its strategy to build a robust offering of novel, non-opioid treatments to improve patient care along the neural pain pathway.

Company Background

Once the injectables subsidiary of drug-delivery company SkyePharma PLC, Pacira Pharmaceuticals was bought out in 2007 by an investor group led by MPM Capital, OrbiMed, HBM Bioventures, and Sanderling Ventures. Pacira went public in early 2011 through an IPO valued at about $42 million.

In 2019, the company acquired MyoScience and its iovera pain management system. Upon the closing of that transaction, Pacira Pharmaceuticals changed its name to Pacira BioSciences.

EXECUTIVES

Chairman, Chief Executive Officer, Director, David M. Stack, $807,695 total compensation
Division Officer, Max Reinhardt
Technical Operations Chief Technical Officer, Charles Laranjeira
Chief Administrative Officer, Secretary, Kristen Williams Williams, $458,962 total compensation
Chief Financial Officer, Charles A. Reinhart, $420,827 total compensation
Chief Customer Officer, Dennis McLoughlin, $319,231 total compensation
Chief Clinical Officer, Roy Winston
Director, Lead Director, Paul J. Hastings
Director, Laura A. Brege
Director, Christopher Christie
Director, Mark Froimson
Director, Yvonne L. Greenstreet
Director, Mark A. Kronenfeld
Director, John P. Longenecker
Director, Gary W. Pace
Director, Andreas Wicki
Auditors: KPMG LLP

LOCATIONS

HQ: Pacira BioSciences Inc
5401 West Kennedy Boulevard, Suite 890, Tampa, FL 33609
Phone: 813 553-6680
Web: www.pacira.com

PRODUCTS/OPERATIONS

2015 Sales

	$ mil.	% of total
Exparel	239.9	96
DepoCyt	4.6	2
Royalties	3.1	1
Collaborative licensing & development	1.4	1
Total	249.0	100

COMPETITORS

ACORDA THERAPEUTICS, INC.
ARENA PHARMACEUTICALS, INC.
ASSERTIO THERAPEUTICS, INC.
DYAX CORP.
INCYTE CORPORATION
LIGAND PHARMACEUTICALS INCORPORATED
MEDIVATION, INC.
OPKO HEALTH, INC.
PLUS THERAPEUTICS, INC.
SHIRE-NPS PHARMACEUTICALS, INC.

HISTORICAL FINANCIALS
Company Type: Public

Income Statement — FYE: December 31

	REVENUE ($mil)	NET INCOME ($mil)	NET PROFIT MARGIN	EMPLOYEES
12/20	429.6	145.5	33.9%	624
12/19	421.0	(11.0)	—	606
12/18	337.2	(0.4)	—	518
12/17	286.6	(42.6)	—	489
12/16	276.3	(37.9)	—	503
Annual Growth	11.7%	—	—	5.5%

2020 Year-End Financials
Debt ratio: 38.5%
Return on equity: 29.7%
Cash ($ mil.): 99.9
Current Ratio: 2.57
Long-term debt ($ mil.): 326.6
No. of shares ($ mil.): 43.6
Dividends
 Yield: —
 Payout: —
Market value ($ mil.): 2,611.0

	STOCK PRICE ($) FY Close	P/E High/Low		PER SHARE ($) Earnings	Dividends	Book Value
12/20	59.84	19	8	3.33	0.00	14.20
12/19	45.30	—	—	(0.27)	0.00	8.47
12/18	43.02	—	—	(0.01)	0.00	7.79
12/17	45.65	—	—	(1.07)	0.00	6.87
12/16	32.30	—	—	(1.02)	0.00	5.84
Annual Growth	16.7%			—	—	24.9%

Palomar Holdings Inc

EXECUTIVES

Chairman, Chief Executive Officer, Director, Mac Armstrong, $500,000 total compensation
President, Heath A. Fisher, $410,000 total compensation
Chief Financial Officer, Corporate Secretary, Principal Accounting Officer, T. Christopher Uchida
Chief Underwriting Officer, Jon Christianson
Chief Risk Officer, Jon Knutzen
Chief Strategy Officer, Bill Bold
Chief Legal Officer, Corporate Secretary, Angela Grant
Chief Talent & Diversity Officer, Michelle Johnson
Lead Independent Director, Director, Richard H. Taketa
Director, Daryl Bradley
Director, Robert (Bob) E. Dowdell
Director, Daina Middleton
Director, Martha Notaras
Director, Catriona M. Fallon
Auditors : Ernst & Young LLP

LOCATIONS

HQ: Palomar Holdings Inc
7979 Ivanhoe Avenue, Suite 500, La Jolla, CA 92037
Phone: 619 567-5290
Web: www.palomarspecialty.com

HISTORICAL FINANCIALS
Company Type: Public

Income Statement — FYE: December 31

	ASSETS ($mil)	NET INCOME ($mil)	INCOME AS % OF ASSETS	EMPLOYEES
12/20	729.0	6.2	0.9%	122
12/19	395.4	10.6	2.7%	77
12/18	231.1	18.2	7.9%	63
12/17	188.3	3.7	2.0%	0
12/16	0.0	6.6	—	0
Annual Growth	—	(1.4%)	—	—

2020 Year-End Financials
Return on assets: 1.1%
Return on equity: 2.1%
Long-term debt ($ mil.): —
No. of shares ($ mil.): 25.5
Sales ($ mil.): 168.4
Dividends
 Yield: —
 Payout: —
Market value ($ mil.): 2,268.0

	STOCK PRICE ($) FY Close	P/E High/Low		PER SHARE ($) Earnings	Dividends	Book Value
12/20	88.84	477	168	0.24	0.00	14.25
12/19	50.49	113	38	0.49	0.00	9.31
Annual Growth	76.0%			(51.0%)	—	53.0%

Pangaea Logistics Solutions Ltd.

EXECUTIVES

Interim Chairman, Director, Richard T. du Moulin
Interim Chief Executive Officer, Chief Operating Officer, Director, Mark L. Filanowski
Chief Financial Officer, Gianni Del Signore
Chief Operating Officer, Mads Boye Petersen
Director, Eric S. Rosenfeld
Director, Carl Claus Boggild
Director, Anthony Laura
Director, David D. Sgro
Auditors : Grant Thornton LLP

LOCATIONS

HQ: Pangaea Logistics Solutions Ltd.
c/o Phoenix Bulk Carriers (US) LLC, 109 Long Wharf, Newport, RI 02840
Phone: 401 846-7790
Web: www.pangaeals.com

HISTORICAL FINANCIALS
Company Type: Public

Income Statement — FYE: December 31

	REVENUE ($mil)	NET INCOME ($mil)	NET PROFIT MARGIN	EMPLOYEES
12/20	382.8	11.3	3.0%	445
12/19	412.1	11.6	2.8%	500
12/18	372.9	17.7	4.8%	504
12/17	385.0	7.8	2.0%	504
12/16	238.0	7.4	3.1%	446
Annual Growth	12.6%	11.1%	—	(0.1%)

2020 Year-End Financials
Debt ratio: 35.9%
Return on equity: 6.4%
Cash ($ mil.): 46.9
Current Ratio: 1.02
Long-term debt ($ mil.): 95
No. of shares ($ mil.): 45.4
Dividends
 Yield: 3.7%
 Payout: 7.6%
Market value ($ mil.): 0.0

Parade Technologies Ltd.

EXECUTIVES

Chief Executive Officer, Chairman, Ji Zhao
President, Vice-Chairman, Ming Qu
Finance Senior Vice President, Judy Wang
Marketing Executive Vice President, Jimmy Jingwu Chiu
Product Development Executive Vice President, Ding Lu
Worldwide Sales Senior Vice President, Stephen M. Donovan
Sales Vice President, Jing-Ming Kung
Operations Associate Vice President, KP Yang
Director, Jackie Yang
Director, Hao Chen
Director, Darren Huang
Director, Cyrus Tsui
Independent Director, Dennis Segers
Independent Director, Norman Jen-Lin Shen
Independent Director, Charlie Xiaoli Huang
Auditors : PricewaterhouseCoopers, Taiwan

LOCATIONS

HQ: Parade Technologies Ltd.
2720 Orchard Parkway, San Jose, CA 95134
Phone: 408 329-5540   **Fax:** 408 329-5541
Web: www.paradetech.com

HISTORICAL FINANCIALS
Company Type: Public

Income Statement — FYE: December 31

	REVENUE ($mil)	NET INCOME ($mil)	NET PROFIT MARGIN	EMPLOYEES
12/20	543.7	124.7	22.9%	0
12/19	394.4	81.2	20.6%	0
12/18	338.8	64.3	19.0%	0
12/17	349.1	65.1	18.7%	0
12/16	281.4	41.9	14.9%	0
Annual Growth	17.9%	31.3%	—	—

Park National Corp (Newark, OH)

2020 Year-End Financials

Debt ratio: —
Return on equity: 29.2%
Cash ($ mil.): 303.1
Current Ratio: 3.29
Long-term debt ($ mil.): —
No. of shares ($ mil.): 80.6
Dividends
  Yield: —
  Payout: 49.8%
Market value ($ mil.): 0.0

Park National Bank is a financial holding company with the principal business of owning and supervising its subsidiaries. The holding company owns Park National Bank, which operates more than 100 branches in Ohio and northern Kentucky and Carolina. The bank engages in commercial banking and trust business in small and medium population areas such Ohio, North Carolina, and South Carolina. Park National Bank delivers financial services through more than 95 financial services offices and a network of more than 115 automated teller machines. Park National's nonbank units include consumer finance outfit Guardian Finance, SE Property Holdings, Scope Leasing, and Vision Bancshares Trust.

EXECUTIVES

Chairman, Chief Executive Officer, Subsidiary Officer, Director, David L. Trautman, $785,000 total compensation
President, Subsidiary Officer, Director, Matthew R. Miller
Chief Financial Officer, Secretary, Treasurer, Subsidiary Officer, Brady T. Burt, $350,000 total compensation
Subsidiary Officer, Director, C. Daniel DeLawder, $575,000 total compensation
Division Officer, Director, Mark Russell Ramser
Director, Frederic Bertley
Director, Donna M. Alvarado
Director, F. William Englefield
Director, Jason Nathaniel Judd
Director, Stephen J. Kambeitz
Director, Timothy S. McLain
Director, Robert E. O'Neill
Director, Leon Zazworsky
Director, D. Byrd Miller
Auditors : Crowe LLP

LOCATIONS

HQ: Park National Corp (Newark, OH)
  50 North Third Street, P.O. Box 3500, Newark, OH 43058-3500
Phone: 740 349-8251
Web: www.parknationalcorp.com

PRODUCTS/OPERATIONS

2015 Sales

	$ mil.	% of total
Interest and fees on loans	228.0	66
Interest and dividends	37.1	10
Income from fiduciary activities	20.2	7
Service charges on deposit accounts	14.7	4
Checkcard fee income	14.6	4
Other service income	11.4	3
Other	16.6	6
Total	342.6	100

Selected Affiliates
Century National Bank
Fairfield National Bank
Farmers Bank
First-Knox National Bank
Guardian Finance Company
Park National Bank
Richland Bank
Scope Aircraft Finance
Second National Bank
Security National Bank
United bank
Unity National Bank

COMPETITORS

AMES NATIONAL CORPORATION
CAMDEN NATIONAL CORPORATION
CITY HOLDING COMPANY
COLUMBIA BANKING SYSTEM, INC.
FIRST COMMONWEALTH FINANCIAL CORPORATION
HEARTLAND FINANCIAL USA, INC.
NATIONAL BANK HOLDINGS CORPORATION
NATIONAL BANKSHARES, INC.
OLD NATIONAL BANCORP
STATE BANK FINANCIAL CORPORATION

HISTORICAL FINANCIALS

Company Type: Public

Income Statement — FYE: December 31

	ASSETS ($mil)	NET INCOME ($mil)	INCOME AS % OF ASSETS	EMPLOYEES
12/20	9,279.0	127.9	1.4%	1,778
12/19	8,558.3	102.7	1.2%	1,907
12/18	7,804.3	110.3	1.4%	1,782
12/17	7,537.6	84.2	1.1%	1,746
12/16	7,467.5	86.1	1.2%	1,726
Annual Growth	5.6%	10.4%	—	0.7%

2020 Year-End Financials

Return on assets: 1.4%
Return on equity: 12.6%
Long-term debt ($ mil.): —
No. of shares ($ mil.): 16.3
Sales ($ mil.): 483.3
Dividends
  Yield: 4.0%
  Payout: 54.8%
Market value ($ mil.): 1,713.0

	STOCK PRICE ($) FY Close	P/E High/Low		PER SHARE ($) Earnings	Dividends	Book Value
12/20	105.01	14	8	7.80	4.28	63.76
12/19	102.38	17	14	6.29	4.24	59.28
12/18	84.95	17	11	7.07	4.07	53.03
12/17	104.00	22	17	5.47	3.76	49.46
12/16	119.66	22	14	5.59	3.76	48.38
Annual Growth	(3.2%)	—	—	8.7%	3.3%	7.1%

Parke Bancorp Inc

Community banking is a walk in the park for Parke Bancorp, holding company for Parke Bank, which has three branches in the New Jersey communities of Sewell and Northfield, as well as two loan production offices in the Philadelphia area. The bank provides such traditional products as checking and savings accounts, money market and individual retirement accounts, and certificates of deposit. Parke Bank has a strong focus on business lending -- including operating loans, commercial mortgages, and construction loans -- which accounts for about 90% of the company's loan portfolio. The bank also writes residential real estate and consumer loans.

EXECUTIVES

Chairman, Director, Daniel J. Dalton
Chairman Emeritus, Director Emeritus, Celestino R. Pennoni
Vice-Chairman, Director, Arret F. Dobson
President, Chief Executive Officer, Subsidiary Officer, Director, Vito S. Pantilione, $738,700 total compensation
Executive Vice President, Chief Operating Officer, Ralph Gallo
Senior Vice President, Chief Lending Officer, Nicholas J. Pantilione
Senior Vice President, Chief Financial Officer, John S. Kaufman
Subsidiary Officer, Paul E. Palmieri, $125,000 total compensation
Director, Fred G. Choate
Director, Jeffrey H. Kripitz
Director, Jack C. Sheppard
Director, Edward Infantolino
Director, Elizabeth A. Milavsky, $286,500 total compensation
Director, Anthony J. Jannetti
Auditors : RSM US LLP

LOCATIONS

HQ: Parke Bancorp Inc
  601 Delsea Drive, Washington Township, NJ 08080
Phone: 856 256-2500
Web: www.parkebank.com

COMPETITORS

COMMUNITY SHORES BANK CORPORATION
EMCLAIRE FINANCIAL CORP.
FIDELITY BANCORP, INC.
SVB & T CORPORATION
VOLUNTEER BANCORP, INC

HISTORICAL FINANCIALS

Company Type: Public

Income Statement — FYE: December 31

	ASSETS ($mil)	NET INCOME ($mil)	INCOME AS % OF ASSETS	EMPLOYEES
12/20	2,078.3	28.4	1.4%	97
12/19	1,681.1	29.8	1.8%	101
12/18	1,467.3	24.8	1.7%	98
12/17	1,137.4	11.8	1.0%	91
12/16	1,016.1	18.5	1.8%	86
Annual Growth	19.6%	11.3%	—	3.1%

Parkway Acquisition Corp

2020 Year-End Financials
Return on assets: 1.5%
Return on equity: 14.9%
Long-term debt ($ mil.): —
No. of shares ($ mil.): 11.8
Sales ($ mil.): 88.7
Dividends
Yield: 4.0%
Payout: 26.9%
Market value ($ mil.): 185.0

	STOCK PRICE ($) FY Close	P/E High	P/E Low	PER SHARE ($) Earnings	PER SHARE ($) Dividends	PER SHARE ($) Book Value
12/20	15.60	10	4	2.37	0.63	16.95
12/19	25.39	10	7	2.48	0.60	14.99
12/18	18.72	11	7	2.07	0.50	13.08
12/17	20.55	21	16	1.02	0.35	13.89
12/16	20.15	11	6	1.55	0.22	13.92
Annual Growth	(6.2%)	—	—	11.2%	29.5%	5.1%

EXECUTIVES

Chairman, Thomas M. Jackson
Vice-Chairman, Director, James W. Shortt
President, Chief Executive Officer, Subsidiary Officer, Director, Blake M. Edwards, $190,000 total compensation
Executive Vice President, Chief Financial Officer, Subsidiary Officer, Lori Vaught
Secretary, Suzanne S. Yearout
Subsidiary Officer, Beth R. Worrell
Subsidiary Officer, Rodney H. Halsey
Subsidiary Officer, C. Greg Edwards
Subsidiary Officer, Jonathan L. Kruckow
Subsidiary Officer, Milo L. Cockerham
Director, Jacky K. Anderson
Director, Joseph Howard Conduff
Director, Bryan L. Edwards
Director, T. Mauyer Gallimore
Director, A. Melissa Gentry
Director, R. Devereux Jarratt
Director, Theresa S. Lazo
Director, W. David McNeill
Director, Frank A. Stewart
Director, John Michael Turman
Director, J. David Vaughan
Auditors: Elliott Davis, PLLC

LOCATIONS

HQ: Parkway Acquisition Corp
101 Jacksonville Circle, Floyd, VA 24091
Phone: 540 745-4191

Pathfinder Bancorp Inc. (MD)

HISTORICAL FINANCIALS
Company Type: Public

Income Statement				FYE: December 31
	ASSETS ($mil)	NET INCOME ($mil)	INCOME AS % OF ASSETS	EMPLOYEES
12/20	855.3	5.8	0.7%	230
12/19	706.2	7.1	1.0%	216
12/18	680.2	4.5	0.7%	211
12/17	547.9	2.4	0.4%	177
12/16	558.8	2.4	0.4%	176
Annual Growth	11.2%	24.8%	—	6.9%

2020 Year-End Financials
Return on assets: 0.7%
Return on equity: 7.0%
Long-term debt ($ mil.): —
No. of shares ($ mil.): 6.0
Sales ($ mil.): 37
Dividends
Yield: 2.6%
Payout: 27.0%
Market value ($ mil.): 59.0

	STOCK PRICE ($) FY Close	P/E High	P/E Low	PER SHARE ($) Earnings	PER SHARE ($) Dividends	PER SHARE ($) Book Value
12/20	9.80	13	8	0.97	0.26	14.08
12/19	12.65	11	9	1.16	0.24	13.27
12/18	10.90	16	14	0.81	0.20	12.17
12/17	12.25	27	18	0.48	0.16	11.39
12/16	8.65	15	13	0.60	0.06	11.05
Annual Growth	3.2%	—	—	12.8%	44.3%	6.2%

EXECUTIVES

Chairman, Subsidiary Officer, Director, Chris R. Burritt
President, Chief Executive Officer, Subsidiary Officer, Thomas W. Schneider, $360,000 total compensation
Executive Vice President, Chief Operating Officer, Subsidiary Officer, James A. Dowd, $205,000 total compensation
Senior Vice President, General Counsel, Corporate Secretary, Subsidiary Officer, Edward A. Mervine, $178,000 total compensation
Executive Vice President, Chief Banking Officer, Subsidiary Officer, Ronald A. Tascarella, $205,000 total compensation
Controller, Lisa A. Kimball
Subsidiary Officer, Daniel R. Phillips
Director, David A. Ayoub
Director, William A. Barclay
Director, John P. Funiciello
Director, Adam C. Gagas
Director, George P. Joyce
Director, Melanie Littlejohn
Director, John F. Sharkey
Director, Lloyd Stemple
Auditors: Bonadio & Co., LLP

LOCATIONS

HQ: Pathfinder Bancorp Inc. (MD)
214 West First Street, Oswego, NY 13126

Phone: 315 343-0057
Web: www.pathfinderbank.com

Patrick Industries Inc

HISTORICAL FINANCIALS
Company Type: Public

Income Statement				FYE: December 31
	ASSETS ($mil)	NET INCOME ($mil)	INCOME AS % OF ASSETS	EMPLOYEES
12/20	1,227.4	6.9	0.6%	183
12/19	1,093.8	4.2	0.4%	163
12/18	933.1	4.0	0.4%	163
12/17	881.2	3.4	0.4%	144
12/16	749.0	3.2	0.4%	139
Annual Growth	13.1%	20.7%	—	7.1%

2020 Year-End Financials
Return on assets: 0.5%
Return on equity: 7.3%
Long-term debt ($ mil.): —
No. of shares ($ mil.): 4.5
Sales ($ mil.): 48.9
Dividends
Yield: 2.0%
Payout: 20.3%
Market value ($ mil.): 52.0

	STOCK PRICE ($) FY Close	P/E High	P/E Low	PER SHARE ($) Earnings	PER SHARE ($) Dividends	PER SHARE ($) Book Value
12/20	11.48	12	8	1.17	0.24	21.51
12/19	13.90	20	16	0.80	0.24	19.20
12/18	15.66	17	14	0.94	0.24	14.72
12/17	15.40	19	15	0.83	0.21	14.44
12/16	13.49	17	14	0.78	0.20	13.67
Annual Growth	(4.0%)	—	—	10.7%	4.7%	12.0%

Patrick Industries is a leading manufacturer and distributor of building materials and prefinished products, primarily for the manufactured home (MH), recreational vehicle (RV), and marine industries. Patrick Industries manufactures decorative paper and vinyl panels, moldings, countertops, doors, and cabinet and slotwall components. In addition to these, the firm distributes roofing, siding, flooring, drywall, ceiling and wall panels, household electronics, electrical and plumbing supplies, and adhesives. Founded in 1959, the company operates roughly 175 manufacturing plants and about 65 distribution centers and warehouses in about two dozen US states, with a small presence in China and Canada.

Operations

Patrick Industries operates roughly 175 manufacturing plants where it makes furniture, shelving, wall, counter, and cabinet products, mouldings, interior passage doors, and slotwall panels and components, among other products. Its manufacturing segment contributes more than 70% of annual revenue.

The company also distributes prefinished wall and ceiling panels, drywall and drywall finishing products, electronics, wiring, electrical and plumbing products, shower doors, fireplaces, and other miscellaneous products from about 65 warehouse and distribution facilities. Distribution accounts for the remaining revenue (about 30%).

Geographic Reach

Patrick Industries is based in Elkhart, Indiana, where a number of RV makers are clustered. The company operates facilities in nearly two dozen US states as well as internationally in Canada and China.

Sales and Marketing

Patrick Industries counts most of the major manufactured housing (MH), and recreational vehicle (RV) manufacturers among its clientele, but it also serves customers in the kitchen cabinet, office and household furniture, fixtures and commercial furnishings markets. The company has over 3,700 active customers, of which two (Forest River and Thor) account for more than 40% of its sales.

The RV industry represents roughly 60% of the company's sales, while marine, manufactured housing and industrial account for the rest.

Financial Performance

The company had revenues of $4.1 billion in 2021, a 64% increase from the previous year's revenue of $2.5 billion. The increase was attributable to a 73% increase in sales to our RV end market, a 96% increase in sales to its marine end market, a 26% increase in sales to its MH end market, and a 43% increase in sales to its industrial end market.

In 2021, the company had a net income of $224.9 million, a 132% increase from the previous year's net income of $97.1 million.

The company's cash at the end of 2021 was $122.8 million. Operating activities generated $252.1 million, while investing activities used $574.7 million, mainly for business acquisitions. Financing activities provided another $400.7 million.

Strategy

The company's strategic and capital allocation strategy is to optimally manage and utilize its resources and leverage its platform of operating brands to continue to grow and reinvest in its business. Through strategic acquisitions, geographic expansion, expansion into new product lines, and investment in infrastructure and capital expenditures, Patrick seek to ensure that its operating network contains capacity, technology, and innovative thought processes to support anticipated growth needs, effectively respond to changes in market conditions, inventory and sales levels, and successfully integrate manufacturing, distribution, and administrative functions.

Over the last three years, we have executed several new product initiatives and invested approximately $880 million in acquisitions that directly complement the company's core competencies and existing product lines as well as expand its presence in our primary end markets.

Mergers and Acquisitions

In early 2022, Patrick Industries completed its previously announced acquisition by merger of Arizona-based Rockford Corporation (Rockford) and the Rockford Fosgate brand. Rockford is a global leader in the design and distribution of premier, high-performance audio systems and components, primarily serving the powersports, marine, and automotive markets and aftermarkets.

In late 2021, Patrick Industries completed the acquisitions of Indiana-based Williamsburg Marine LLC and Williamsburg Furniture, Inc. (collectively Williamsburg), a manufacturer of marine and motorized RV seating. These acquisitions are an excellent fit with the company's entrepreneurial philosophy, while providing the company the opportunity to continue to better serve its customers.

In mid-2021, Patrick Industries acquired Elkhart, Indiana-based Alpha Systems (Alpha), a leading manufacturer and distributor of component products and accessories, primarily serving the recreational vehicle (RV) industry, in addition to the manufactured housing, commercial building and marine markets. Alpha's major product categories include adhesives and sealants, roofing membranes for RVs, roto/blow and injection molded products, butyl tape, shutters and various other parts and accessories.

In early 2021, Patrick Industries acquired Hyperform, a leading manufacturer of high-quality, non-slip foam flooring, operating under the SeaDek brand name, for the marine OEM market and aftermarket. Hyperform also serves the pool and spa, powersports and utility markets under the highly complementary brands of SwimDek and EndeavorDek (collectively, SeaDek). SeaDek operates out of two manufacturing facilities located in Rockledge, Florida and in Cocoa, Florida, which possess full marketing, laboratory, prototyping, and research and development capabilities.

In a separate transaction in 2021, Patrick Industries acquired Everett, Washington-based Sea-Dog Corporation, a leading distributor of a comprehensive suite of marine and powersports hardware and accessories to distributors, wholesalers, retailers, on-line providers and manufacturers, and its sister company, Sea-Lect Plastics, which provides plastic injection molding, design, product development and expert tooling to companies and government entities (collectively, Sea-Dog).

Company Background

Patrick Industries, Inc. was founded in 1959 and is a major manufacturer and distributor of component and building products for the Recreational Vehicle, Marine, Manufactured Housing and industries.

EXECUTIVES

Chairman, Director, Todd M. Cleveland, $690,383 total compensation

Sales President, Jeffrey M. Rodino, $396,058 total compensation

Finance Chief Executive Officer, Director, Andy L. Nemeth, $472,596 total compensation

Finance Executive Vice President, Finance Chief Financial Officer, Finance Treasurer, Finance Principal Accounting Officer, Jacob R. Petkovich

Executive Vice President, Chief Operating Officer, Kip B. Ellis, $391,250 total compensation

Interim Chief Financial Officer, Director, John A. Forbes

Lead Independent Director, Director, M. Scott Welch

Director, Joseph M. Cerulli

Director, Michael A. Kitson

Director, Pamela Klyn

Director, Derrick B. Mayes

Director, Denis Suggs

Auditors : DELOITTE & TOUCHE LLP

LOCATIONS

HQ: Patrick Industries Inc
107 West Franklin Street, P.O. Box 638, Elkhart, IN 46515
Phone: 574 294-7511
Web: www.patrickind.com

PRODUCTS/OPERATIONS

Selected Products: AdornAIA CountertopsBetter Way ProductsCarrera Custom PaintingCharlestonCreative Wood DesignsCustom VinylsDécor ManufacturingForemost FabricatorsFrontline ManufacturingGravure Ink, Praxis GroupGustafson LightingInfinity GraphicsInterior Components PlusMiddlebury Hardwood ProductsMillennium PaintPatrick DistributionPolyDyn3Precision PaintingPremier ConceptsQuest Audio VideoSCI and North AmericanWest Side Furniture2015 Sales

	$ mil.	% of total
Manufacturing	720.4	78
Distribution	199.9	22
Total	920.3	100

2015 Sales by Customer Type

	% of total
RV industry	75
Manufactured housing	14
Industrial market	11
Total	100

COMPETITORS

AMERICAN GYPSUM COMPANY
BRITISH GYPSUM LIMITED
CERTAINTEED GYPSUM PRODUCTS, INC.
FERGUSON ENTERPRISES, LLC
FORTUNE BRANDS HOME & SECURITY, INC.
FOUNDATION BUILDING MATERIALS, INC.
Knauf Gips KG
OLYMPIC STEEL, INC.
PACIFIC COAST BUILDING PRODUCTS, INC.
STANDEX INTERNATIONAL CORPORATION

HISTORICAL FINANCIALS
Company Type: Public

Income Statement — FYE: December 31

	REVENUE ($mil)	NET INCOME ($mil)	NET PROFIT MARGIN	EMPLOYEES
12/20	2,486.5	97.0	3.9%	8,700
12/19	2,337.0	89.5	3.8%	7,500
12/18	2,263.0	119.8	5.3%	8,113
12/17	1,635.6	85.7	5.2%	6,721
12/16	1,221.8	55.5	4.5%	4,497
Annual Growth	19.4%	15.0%	—	17.9%

2020 Year-End Financials
Debt ratio: 46.7%
Return on equity: 18.3%
Cash ($ mil.): 44.7
Current Ratio: 2.32
Long-term debt ($ mil.): 810.9
No. of shares ($ mil.): 23.3
Dividends
  Yield: 1.5%
  Payout: 30.1%
Market value ($ mil.): 1,597.0

	STOCK PRICE ($) FY Close	P/E High/Low		PER SHARE ($) Earnings	Dividends	Book Value
12/20	68.35	17	5	4.20	1.03	23.95
12/19	52.43	14	8	3.85	0.25	20.94
12/18	29.61	14	6	4.93	0.00	17.37
12/17	69.45	29	17	3.48	0.00	14.63
12/16	76.30	32	12	2.43	0.00	8.07
Annual Growth	(2.7%)	—	—	14.7%	—	31.3%

HISTORICAL FINANCIALS
Company Type: Public

Income Statement — FYE: December 31

	REVENUE ($mil)	NET INCOME ($mil)	NET PROFIT MARGIN	EMPLOYEES
12/21	1,055.5	195.9	18.6%	5,385
12/20	841.4	143.4	17.0%	4,218
12/19	737.6	180.5	24.5%	3,765
12/18	566.3	137.0	24.2%	3,050
12/17	433.0	66.8	15.4%	2,548
Annual Growth	24.9%	30.9%	—	20.6%

2021 Year-End Financials
Debt ratio: 0.9%
Return on equity: 25.2%
Cash ($ mil.): 277.9
Current Ratio: 1.13
Long-term debt ($ mil.): 27.3
No. of shares ($ mil.): 58.0
Dividends
  Yield: —
  Payout: —
Market value ($ mil.): 24,086.0

	STOCK PRICE ($) FY Close	P/E High/Low		PER SHARE ($) Earnings	Dividends	Book Value
12/21	415.19	163	90	3.37	0.00	15.41
12/20	452.25	187	66	2.46	0.00	11.36
12/19	264.76	89	37	3.09	0.00	9.13
12/18	122.45	69	34	2.34	0.00	5.84
12/17	80.33	74	38	1.13	0.00	2.34
Annual Growth	50.8%	—	—	31.4%	—	60.1%

HISTORICAL FINANCIALS
Company Type: Public

Income Statement — FYE: June 30

	REVENUE ($mil)	NET INCOME ($mil)	NET PROFIT MARGIN	EMPLOYEES
06/21	635.6	70.8	11.1%	4,150
06/20	561.3	64.4	11.5%	3,600
06/19	467.6	53.8	11.5%	3,050
06/18	377.5	38.5	10.2%	2,600
06/17	300.0	6.7	2.2%	2,115
Annual Growth	20.6%	80.2%	—	18.4%

2021 Year-End Financials
Debt ratio: —
Return on equity: 16.2%
Cash ($ mil.): 202.2
Current Ratio: 1.09
Long-term debt ($ mil.): —
No. of shares ($ mil.): 54.5
Dividends
  Yield: —
  Payout: —
Market value ($ mil.): 10,417.0

	STOCK PRICE ($) FY Close	P/E High/Low		PER SHARE ($) Earnings	Dividends	Book Value
06/21	190.80	165	98	1.26	0.00	8.74
06/20	145.89	125	62	1.15	0.00	7.30
06/19	93.82	101	53	0.97	0.00	5.80
06/18	58.86	86	58	0.70	0.00	4.03
06/17	45.18	378	230	0.12	0.00	2.85
Annual Growth	43.4%	—	—	80.0%	—	32.3%

Paycom Software Inc

EXECUTIVES

Chairman, President, Chief Executive Officer, Director, Chad Richison, $667,133 total compensation
Chief Financial Officer, Treasurer, Secretary, Craig E. Boelte, $350,391 total compensation
Chief Sales Officer, Holly Faurot
Software Development Chief Information Officer, Bradley Scott (Brad) Smith, $305,769 total compensation
Operations Chief Operating Officer, Jon D. Evans, $294,303 total compensation
Director, Robert J. Levenson
Director, Frederick C. (Ted) Peters
Director, Jason D. Clark
Director, Henry C. (Ric) Duques
Director, J. C. Watts
Director, Sharen J. Turney
Auditors : Grant Thornton LLP

LOCATIONS

HQ: Paycom Software Inc
  7501 W. Memorial Road, Oklahoma City, OK 73142
Phone: 405 722-6900
Web: www.paycom.com

Paylocity Holding Corp

EXECUTIVES

Chairman, Director, Steven I. Sarowitz, $275,000 total compensation
President, Co-Chief Executive Officer, Director, Toby J. Williams, $285,000 total compensation
Co-Chief Executive Officer, Director, Steven R. Beauchamp, $516,667 total compensation
Vice President, Chief Accounting Officer, Nicholas Rost
Chief Financial Officer, Treasurer, Ryan Glenn
Chief Technology Officer, Rachit Lohani
Lead Independent Director, Director, Ronald V. Waters
Director, Virginia G. Breen
Director, Robin Pederson
Director, Andres D. Reiner
Director, Kenneth B. Robinson
Director, Ellen Carnahan
Director, Jeffrey T. Diehl
Auditors : KPMG LLP

LOCATIONS

HQ: Paylocity Holding Corp
  1400 American Lane, Schaumburg, IL 60173
Phone: 847 463-3200
Web: www.paylocity.com

PBF Logistics LP

EXECUTIVES

Chairman, Chief Executive Officer, Holding/Parent Company Officer, Thomas J. Nimbley
Executive Vice President, Holding/Parent Company Officer, Director, Matthew C. Lucey
Senior Vice President, Secretary, General Counsel, Trecia M. Canty
Chief Accounting Officer, Holding/Parent Company Officer, Associate/Affiliate Company Officer, John Barone
Auditors : Deloitte & Touche LLP

LOCATIONS

HQ: PBF Logistics LP
  One Sylvan Way, Second Floor, Parsippany, NJ 07054
Phone: 973 455-7500
Web: www.pbflogistics.com

HISTORICAL FINANCIALS
Company Type: Public

Income Statement — FYE: December 31

	REVENUE ($mil)	NET INCOME ($mil)	NET PROFIT MARGIN	EMPLOYEES
12/21	355.5	153.2	43.1%	89
12/20	360.2	147.4	40.9%	91
12/19	340.2	100.2	29.5%	92
12/18	283.4	85.4	30.2%	82
12/17	254.8	100.2	39.4%	39
Annual Growth	8.7%	11.2%	—	22.9%

PCB Bancorp

2021 Year-End Financials

Debt ratio: 69.1%
Return on equity: 73.7%
Cash ($ mil.): 33.9
Current Ratio: 3.65
Long-term debt ($ mil.): 622.5
No. of shares ($ mil.): 62.5
Dividends
 Yield: 10.6%
 Payout: 53.3%
Market value ($ mil.): 707.0

	STOCK PRICE ($) FY Close	P/E High	P/E Low	PER SHARE ($) Earnings	Dividends	Book Value
12/21	11.30	7	4	2.44	1.20	3.97
12/20	9.15	9	1	2.36	1.42	2.68
12/19	20.25	14	11	1.71	2.05	1.69
12/18	20.10	13	11	1.73	1.97	0.52
12/17	20.95	10	9	2.17	1.86	(0.35)
Annual Growth	(14.3%)	—	—	3.0%	(10.4%)	—

EXECUTIVES

Chairman, Subsidiary Officer, Director, Sang Young Lee

President, Chief Executive Officer, Subsidiary Officer, Director, Henry Kim, $348,221 total compensation

Executive Vice President, Chief Financial Officer, Subsidiary Officer, Timothy Chang, $217,703 total compensation

Executive Vice President, Chief Risk Officer, Corporate Secretary, Subsidiary Officer, Andrew Chung, $141,923 total compensation

Subsidiary Officer, Brian Bang, $149,423 total compensation

Director, Janice Chung

Director, Kijun Ahn

Director, Daniel Cho

Director, Haeyoung Cho, $338,596 total compensation

Director, Sarah Jun

Director, Hong Kyun Park

Director, Don Rhee

Auditors : Crowe LLP

LOCATIONS

HQ: PCB Bancorp
3701 Wilshire Boulevard, Suite 900, Los Angeles, CA 90010
Phone: 213 210-2000
Web: www.paccitybank.com

HISTORICAL FINANCIALS

Company Type: Public

Income Statement — FYE: December 31

	ASSETS ($mil)	NET INCOME ($mil)	INCOME AS % OF ASSETS	EMPLOYEES
12/20	1,922.8	16.1	0.8%	248
12/19	1,746.3	24.1	1.4%	256
12/18	1,697.0	24.3	1.4%	248
12/17	1,441.9	16.4	1.1%	228
12/16	1,226.6	14.0	1.1%	0
Annual Growth	11.9%	3.7%	—	—

Peapack-Gladstone Financial Corp.

Peapack-Gladstone Financial is the $3.4 billion-asset holding company for the near-century-old Peapack-Gladstone Bank, which operates more than 20 branches in New Jersey's Hunterdon, Morris, Somerset, Middlesex, and Union counties. Founded in 1921, the bank provides traditional deposit accounts, credit cards, and loans to individuals and small businesses, as well as trust and investment management services through its PGB Trust and Investments unit. Multifamily residential mortgages represent nearly 50% of the company's loan portfolio, while commercial mortgages make up around 15%. The bank also originates construction, consumer, and business loans.

Operations

Peapack-Gladstone Financial operates two main divisions: Banking, which offers traditional deposit and loan services, merchant card services; and Wealth Management, which boasts more than $3.3 billion in assets under administration (as of early 2016) and operates through PGB Trust and Investments, which offers asset management services for individuals and institutions as well as personal trust services. More than 80% of the bank's total revenue came from interest income (mostly on its loans) during 2015, while 14% came from its wealth management fee income, and 3% came from service charges and fees.

Multifamily residential mortgages represented nearly 50% of the company's loan portfolio at the end of 2015, while commercial mortgages made up another 15%. The rest of its portfolio was made up of construction, consumer, and business loans.

Geographic Reach

The bank's branches are located across New Jersey in Somerset, Morris, Hunterdon, Middlesex, and Union counties, Its private banking and wealth management locations are located in Bedminster, Morristown, Princeton, and Teaneck.

2020 Year-End Financials

Return on assets: 0.8%
Return on equity: 7.0%
Long-term debt ($ mil.): —
No. of shares ($ mil.): 15.3
Sales ($ mil.): 91.5
Dividends
 Yield: 4.7%
 Payout: 51.6%
Market value ($ mil.): 156.0

	STOCK PRICE ($) FY Close	P/E High	P/E Low	PER SHARE ($) Earnings	Dividends	Book Value
12/20	10.11	16	8	1.04	0.48	15.19
12/19	17.28	12	9	1.49	0.25	14.44
12/18	15.65	12	8	1.65	0.12	13.16
12/17	15.50	13	10	1.21	0.12	10.60
12/16	13.00	12	9	1.11	0.11	9.48
Annual Growth	(6.1%)	—	—	(1.6%)	44.8%	12.5%

Sales and Marketing

The bank's commercial banking business serves business owners, professionals, retailers, contractors, and real estate investors. Its wealth management division serves individuals, families, foundations, endowments, trusts, and estates.

Peapack-Gladstone has been ramping up its advertising spend in recent years. It spent $637,000 on advertising during 2015, up from $594,000 and $519,000 in 2014 and 2013, respectively.

Financial Performance

Peapack-Gladstone's annual revenues and profits have swelled more than 60% since 2011 as its nearly tripled its loan assets to over $2.9 billion.

The bank's revenue jumped 27% to $122.86 million during 2015 mostly thanks to higher interest income as its loan assets grew by 30%, with exceptional increases in its multifamily mortgage and commercial loan volumes. Peapack-Gladstone's wealth management division income grew 20% with increases in securities gains, service charges, and other non-interest income.

Strong revenue growth in 2015 drove Peapack-Gladstone's net income up 34% to $19.97 million. The bank's operating cash levels climbed 11% to $30.31 million thanks to a rise in cash-based earnings.

Strategy

Peapack-Gladstone Financial continued in 2016 to focus on: enhancing its risk management to keep its loan provisions at a minimum and its profits up; expanding its multi-family loans as well as its commercial real estate loans (to a lesser extent); growing its commercial and industrial (C&I) lending business through its private banking divisions; and expanding its wealth management business, which now accounts for 15% of its annual revenue.

Mergers and Acquisitions

In May 2015, Peapack-Gladstone bolstered its wealth management division after buying Morristown-based Wealth Management Consultants, LLC for $2.8 million. The deal boosted the bank's assets under advisement and administration to $3.5 billion.

EXECUTIVES

Chairman, Subsidiary Officer, Director, F. Duffield Meyercord

President, Chief Executive Officer, Subsidiary Officer, Director, Douglas L. Kennedy, $669,423 total compensation

Senior Executive Vice President, Chief Financial Officer, Subsidiary Officer, Jeffrey J. Carfora, $359,846 total compensation

Executive Vice President, Chief Operating Officer, Subsidiary Officer, Robert A. Plante, $347,500 total compensation

Senior Vice President, Chief Accounting Officer, Subsidiary Officer, Francesco S. (Frank) Rossi
Subsidiary Officer, John P. Babcock, $532,884 total compensation
Division Officer, Gregory M. Smith
Director, Carmen M. Bowser
Director, Susan A. Cole
Director, Anthony J. Consi
Director, Richard Daingerfield
Director, Edward A. Gramigna
Director, Peter D. Horst
Director, Steven A. Kass
Director, Patrick J. Mullen
Director, Philip W. Smith
Director, Tony Spinelli
Director, Beth Welsh
Auditors : Crowe LLP

LOCATIONS

HQ: Peapack-Gladstone Financial Corp.
500 Hills Drive, Suite 300, Bedminster, NJ 07921-0700
Phone: 908 234-0700
Web: www.pgbank.com

PRODUCTS/OPERATIONS

2015 Sales

	$ mil.	% of total
Interest Income		
Loans, including fees	94.3	77
Securities available for sale	4.6	4
Other	0.3	-
Other Income		
Wealth management fee income	17.0	14
Service charges and fees	3.3	3
Bank owned life insurance	1.3	1
Other Income	1.0	1
Other	1.1	-
Total	122.9	100

COMPETITORS

BOKF MERGER CORPORATION NUMBER SIXTEEN
FIRST REPUBLIC BANK
FULTON FINANCIAL CORPORATION
HSBC USA, INC.
PROVIDENT FINANCIAL SERVICES, INC.
SHINSEI BANK, LIMITED
Shanghai Pudong Development Bank Co., Ltd.
TURKIYE GARANTI BANKASI ANONIM SIRKETI
TURKIYE IS BANKASI ANONIM SIRKETI
UNIVEST FINANCIAL CORPORATION

HISTORICAL FINANCIALS

Company Type: Public

Income Statement — FYE: December 31

	ASSETS ($mil)	NET INCOME ($mil)	INCOME AS % OF ASSETS	EMPLOYEES
12/20	5,890.4	26.1	0.4%	501
12/19	5,182.8	47.4	0.9%	446
12/18	4,617.8	44.1	1.0%	409
12/17	4,260.5	36.4	0.9%	384
12/16	3,878.6	26.4	0.7%	338
Annual Growth	11.0%	(0.3%)	—	10.3%

2020 Year-End Financials

Return on assets: 0.4%
Return on equity: 5.0%
Long-term debt ($ mil.): —
No. of shares ($ mil.): 18.9
Sales ($ mil.): 227.5
Dividends
Yield: 0.8%
Payout: 10.8%
Market value ($ mil.): 432.0

	STOCK PRICE ($) FY Close	P/E High/Low		PER SHARE ($) Earnings	Dividends	Book Value
12/20	22.76	23	9	1.37	0.20	27.78
12/19	30.90	13	10	2.44	0.20	26.61
12/18	25.18	16	10	2.31	0.20	24.25
12/17	35.02	18	14	2.03	0.20	21.68
12/16	30.88	20	10	1.60	0.20	18.79
Annual Growth	(7.3%)	—	—	(3.8%)	0.0%	10.3%

Pennant Group Inc

EXECUTIVES

Chairman, Daniel H. Walker, $325,000 total compensation
President, John J. Gochnour, $255,000 total compensation
Chief Executive Officer, Brent Guerisoli
Chief Financial Officer, Interim Chief Financial Officer, Jennifer L. Freeman, $250,000 total compensation
Holding/Parent Company Officer, Director, Christopher R. Christensen
Director, Gregory K. Morris
Director, John G. Nackel
Director, Stephen M. R. Covey
Director, JoAnne Stringfield
Director, Scott E. Lamb
Director, Barry M. Smith
Auditors : DELOITTE & TOUCHE LLP

LOCATIONS

HQ: Pennant Group Inc
1675 East Riverside Drive, Suite 150, Eagle, ID 83616
Phone: 208 506-6100
Web: www.pennantgroup.com

HISTORICAL FINANCIALS

Company Type: Public

Income Statement — FYE: December 31

	REVENUE ($mil)	NET INCOME ($mil)	NET PROFIT MARGIN	EMPLOYEES
12/20	390.9	15.7	4.0%	5,223
12/19	338.5	2.5	0.8%	4,700
12/18	286.0	15.6	5.5%	0
12/17	250.9	9.8	3.9%	0
12/16	217.2	7.8	3.6%	0
Annual Growth	15.8%	18.8%	—	—

2020 Year-End Financials

Debt ratio: 1.6%
Return on equity: 18.7%
Cash ($ mil.): —
Current Ratio: 0.67
Long-term debt ($ mil.): 8.2
No. of shares ($ mil.): 28.2
Dividends
Yield: —
Payout: —
Market value ($ mil.): 1,640.0

	STOCK PRICE ($) FY Close	P/E High/Low		PER SHARE ($) Earnings	Dividends	Book Value
12/20	58.06	112	18	0.52	0.00	3.42
12/19	33.07	317	137	0.11	0.00	2.55
Annual Growth	75.6%	—	—	372.7%	—	33.9%

PennyMac Financial Services Inc (New)

The parent of investment management, loan services, and investment trust companies, PennyMac Financial Services (PennyMac) focuses on the US residential mortgage market offering loans and investment management services. Through its Private National Mortgage Acceptance Company, the company's PennyMac Loan Services (PLS) originates service loans in all 50 states, the District of Columbia, Guam and the US Virgin Island, and loans in 49 states, and District of Columbia. The PennyMac Correspondent Group (PCG), also known as PennyMac Corp., specializes in the acquisition of newly originated US residential home loans from small and mid-sized banks, credit unions, and other mortgage lenders. PennyMac went public in 2013.

Operations

PennyMac conducts its business in three segments: production, servicing (together, production and servicing comprise its mortgage banking activities) and investment management.

The production segment performs loan sources new prime credit quality first-lien residential conventional and government-insured or guaranteed mortgage loans through three channels: correspondent production, consumer direct lending and broker direct lending. The segment accounts for about three-fourths of total revenue.

The servicing segment (some 25%) performs loan administration, collection, and default management activities, including the collection and remittance of loan payments; response to customer inquiries; accounting for principal and interest; holding custodial (impounded) funds for the payment of property taxes and insurance premiums; counseling delinquent borrowers; and supervising foreclosures and property dispositions.

The investment management segment represents its investment management activities, which include the activities associated with investment asset acquisitions and dispositions such as sourcing, due diligence, negotiation and settlement. It operates as an investment manager through PNMAC Capital Management (PCM). PCM manages PennyMac Mortgage Investment Trust (PMT), a mortgage real estate investment trust.

Geographic Reach

While PennyMac serves nearly the entire US, its portfolio is heavily weighted toward California, Florida, Texas, Virginia and Maryland.

Based in California, PennyMac has three loan production centers location in Roseville, CA, Honolulu, HI, Edina, MN, and one collocated in its Summerlin, NV office. Its loan servicing operations are primarily housed in Moorpark, CA, Fort Worth, TX and Summerlin, NV. The consumer direct lending business occupies a 36,000 square foot leased facility in Pasadena, CA. Additionally, it has facilities in Plano, TX, Tampa, FL, Phoenix AZ, and St. Louis, MO, primarily for its correspondent production activities.

Financial Performance

Revenue for fiscal 2020 increased to $2.7 billion compared to $1.5 billion from the prior year.

The company's net income for fiscal 2020 increased to $1.6 billion compared to $393.0 million from the prior year.

Cash held by the company at the end of fiscal 2020 increased to $532.8 million. Cash provided by investing and financing activities were $783.0 million and $5.8 billion, respectively. Operating activities used $6.2 billion, mainly for the purchase of loans from Ginnie Mae securities and early buyout investors for modification and subsequent sale.

Strategy

The company's growth strategies include: Growing consumer direct lending through portfolio recapture and non-portfolio originations; Growing broker direct lending; Growing correspondent production through expanding seller relationships and adding products and services; Growing its mortgage loan servicing portfolio; and Expansion into new markets and products.

PennyMac expects to grow its correspondent production business by expanding the number and types of sellers from which it purchases loans and increasing the volume of loans that it purchases from its sellers as it continues to expand to the loan products and services it offers. Over the past several years, a number of large banks have exited or reduced the size of their correspondent production businesses, creating an opportunity for non-bank entities to gain market share.

EXECUTIVES

Chairman, President, Chief Executive Officer, Subsidiary Officer, Director, David A. Spector, $750,000 total compensation
President, Chief Mortgage Banking Officer, Director, Douglas Jones, $500,000 total compensation
Chief Servicing Officer, Senior Managing Director, Steven Richard Bailey
Chief Investment Officer, Senior Managing Director, Vandad Fartaj, $325,000 total compensation
Chief Mortgage Fulfillment Officer, Senior Managing Director, James Follette
Chief Financial Officer, Senior Managing Director, Daniel S. Perotti
Chief Legal Officer, Senior Managing Director, Secretary, Derek W. Stark
Chief Risk Officer, Senior Managing Director, Don White
Lead Independent Director, Director, Jeffrey A. Perlowitz
Director, James K. Hunt
Director, Jonathon S. Jacobson
Director, Patrick Kinsella
Director, Joseph Mazzella
Director, Anne D. McCallion, $325,000 total compensation
Director, Farhad Nanji
Director, Lisa M. Shalett
Director, Theodore W. Tozer
Director, Emily Ann Youssouf
Auditors : DELOITTE & TOUCHE LLP

LOCATIONS

HQ: PennyMac Financial Services Inc (New)
3043 Townsgate Road, Westlake Village, CA 91361
Phone: 818 224-7442
Web: www.pennymacfinancial.com

2016 Sales

	$ mil.	% of total
Net gains on mortgage loans held for sale	531.8	56
Net mortgage loan servicing fees	185.5	19
Loan origination fees	125.5	13
Fulfillment fees from PennyMac Mortgage Investment Trust	86.5	9
Management fees and Carried Interest	23.7	2
Other	4.0	1
Net interest expense	-25.1	-
Total	931.9	

COMPETITORS

ACCESS NATIONAL CORPORATION
BOKF MERGER CORPORATION NUMBER SIXTEEN
DITECH HOLDING CORPORATION
FIRST EAGLE PRIVATE CREDIT, LLC
NATIONSTAR MORTGAGE HOLDINGS INC.
NAVIENT CORPORATION
OCWEN FINANCIAL CORPORATION
PENNYMAC MORTGAGE INVESTMENT TRUST
READY CAPITAL CORPORATION
THE SOUTHERN BANC COMPANY INC

HISTORICAL FINANCIALS

Company Type: Public

Income Statement — FYE: December 31

	ASSETS ($mil)	NET INCOME ($mil)	INCOME AS % OF ASSETS	EMPLOYEES
12/20	31,597.7	1,646.8	5.2%	6,000
12/19	10,204.0	392.9	3.9%	4,215
12/18	7,478.5	87.6	1.2%	3,460
12/17	7,368.0	100.7	1.4%	3,189
12/16	5,133.9	66.0	1.3%	3,038
Annual Growth	57.5%	123.4%	—	18.5%

2020 Year-End Financials

Return on assets: 7.8%
Return on equity: 60.2%
Long-term debt ($ mil.): —
No. of shares ($ mil.): 70.9
Sales ($ mil.): 3,977.1
Dividends
Yield: 0.8%
Payout: 3.1%
Market value ($ mil.): 4,653.0

	STOCK PRICE ($) FY Close	P/E High/Low		PER SHARE ($) Earnings	Dividends	Book Value
12/20	65.62	3	1	20.92	0.54	47.80
12/19	34.04	7	4	4.89	0.12	26.26
12/18	21.26	9	7	2.59	0.40	21.34
12/17	22.35	5	4	4.03	0.00	19.95
12/16	16.65	6	4	2.94	0.00	15.49
Annual Growth	40.9%	—	—	63.3%	—	32.5%

Pennymac Mortgage Investment Trust

PennyMac Mortgage Investment Trust trusts in its ability to acquire distressed US residential mortgage loans. The company seeks to acquire primarily troubled home mortgage loans and mortgage-backed securities, mortgage servicing right and credit risk transfer including CRT agreements and CRT securities. PennyMac is managed by investment adviser PNMAC Capital Management and offers primary and special loan servicing through PennyMac Loan Services. The company is held by Private National Mortgage Acceptance Company (PNMAC).

Operations

The Company operates in four segments: credit sensitive strategies, interest rate sensitive strategies, correspondent production, and corporate.

The credit sensitive strategies segment represents the Company's investments in credit risk transfer (CRT) arrangements, including CRT Agreements and CRT strips (together, CRT arrangements), distressed loans, real estate and non-Agency subordinated bonds. The segment accounts for about 40% of revenues.

The correspondent production segment (about 50%) represents the Company's operations aimed at serving as an intermediary between lenders and the capital markets by purchasing, pooling and reselling newly originated prime credit quality loans either directly or in the form of MBS.

The interest rate sensitive strategies segment (about 10%) represents the Company's investments in mortgage servicing rights (MSRs), excess servicing spread (ESS) purchased from PennyMac Financial Services, Inc. (PFSI), Agency and senior non-Agency mortgage-backed securities (MBS) and the related interest rate hedging activities.

The corporate segment includes management fees, corporate expense amounts and certain interest income.

Geographic Reach

Its corporate headquarters is located in Westlake Village, California.

Financial Performance

The company had a net investment

income of $488.8 million in 2019, a 39% growth from the previous year. This was primarily due to net gain on investments more than tripling in the year.

Net income for 2019 totaled $226.4 million, a 48% growth from the previous year.

The company's cash at the end of 2019 was $104.1 million, a 74% growth from the previous year. Operating activities used $3.0 billion, mainly for purchase of loans acquired for sale at fair value from non-affiliates. Investing activities used another $704.7 million, mainly for purchases of mortgage-backed securities at fair value. Financing activities generated $3.7 billion.

Strategy

The company's investment focus is on residential mortgage-backed securities (MBS) and mortgage-related assets that it creates through its correspondent production activities, including mortgage servicing rights (MSRs) and credit risk transfer (CRT) investments, including CRT agreements (CRT Agreements) and CRT securities (together, CRT arrangements).

EXECUTIVES

Chairman, Chief Executive Officer, Subsidiary Officer, Trustee, David A. Spector, $750,000 total compensation

President, Chief Mortgage Banking Officer, Trustee, Doug Jones, $500,000 total compensation

Chief Financial Officer, Senior Managing Director, Daniel S. Perotti

Chief Legal Officer, Secretary, Senior Managing Director, Derek W. Stark

Chief Investment Officer, Senior Managing Director, William Chang

Chief Mortgage Fulfillment Officer, Senior Managing Director, James Follette

Independent Lead Trustee, Trustee, Preston Paul DuFauchard

Trustee, Randall D. Hadley

Trustee, Scott W. Carnahan

Trustee, Marianne Sullivan

Trustee, Renee R. Schultz

Trustee, Nancy McAllister

Trustee, Stacey D. Stewart

Trustee, Catherine A. Lynch

Auditors : DELOITTE & TOUCHE LLP

LOCATIONS

HQ: Pennymac Mortgage Investment Trust
3043 Townsgate Road, Westlake Village, CA 91361
Phone: 818 224-7442
Web: www.pennymacmortgageinvestmenttrust.com

PRODUCTS/OPERATIONS

2015 Sales

	$ mil.	% of total
Interest income	201.3	51
Net gain on investments	54.0	14
Net gain on mortgage loans acquired for sale	51.0	13
Net mortgage loan servicing fee	49.3	13
Mortgage Loan origination fees	28.7	7
Other	8.3	2
Results of real estate acquired in settlement of loans	(19.2)	-
Total	373.4	100

COMPETITORS

ANNALY CAPITAL MANAGEMENT, INC.
ARLINGTON ASSET INVESTMENT CORP.
DITECH HOLDING CORPORATION
FIRST EAGLE PRIVATE CREDIT, LLC
GUILD MORTGAGE COMPANY
IMPAC MORTGAGE HOLDINGS, INC.
NATIONSTAR MORTGAGE HOLDINGS INC.
OCWEN FINANCIAL CORPORATION
PNMAC HOLDINGS, INC.
TIAA FSB HOLDINGS, INC.

HISTORICAL FINANCIALS

Company Type: Public

Income Statement — FYE: December 31

	REVENUE ($mil)	NET INCOME ($mil)	NET PROFIT MARGIN	EMPLOYEES
12/20	740.1	52.3	7.1%	1
12/19	786.2	226.3	28.8%	1
12/18	526.2	152.7	29.0%	3
12/17	469.3	117.7	25.1%	3
12/16	421.8	75.8	18.0%	3
Annual Growth	15.1%	(8.8%)	—	(24.0%)

2020 Year-End Financials

Debt ratio: 19.8%
Return on equity: 2.2%
Cash ($ mil.): 57.7
Current Ratio: 0.02
Long-term debt ($ mil.): 331.5
No. of shares ($ mil.): 97.8
Dividends
Yield: 8.6%
Payout: 562.9%
Market value ($ mil.): 1,721.0

	STOCK PRICE ($) FY Close	P/E High/Low		PER SHARE ($) Earnings	Dividends	Book Value
12/20	17.59	87	21	0.27	1.52	23.47
12/19	22.29	9	7	2.42	1.88	24.46
12/18	18.62	10	7	1.99	1.88	25.69
12/17	16.07	12	10	1.48	1.88	25.18
12/16	16.37	16	10	1.08	1.88	20.26
Annual Growth	1.8%	—	—	(29.3%)	(5.2%)	3.7%

People's United Financial Inc

People's United Financial is the holding company for People's United Bank (formerly People's Bank), which boasts about 390 traditional branches, supermarket branches, commercial banking offices, investment and brokerage offices, and equipment leasing offices across New England and eastern New York. In addition to retail and commercial banking services, the bank offers trust, wealth management, brokerage, and insurance services. Its lending activities consist mainly of commercial real estate (more than a third of its loan portfolio), commercial and industrial loans (about a quarter), residential mortgages, equipment financing, and home equity loans. Founded in 1842, the bank has $64.5 billion in assets. In early 2021, M&T Bank Corporation and People's United Financial, Inc. have entered into a definitive agreement under which M&T will acquire People's United in an all-stock transaction.

Operations

People's United operates two core business segments, Commercial Banking (over 75% of net income) and Retail Banking (some 20%), which both share duties of the bank's now-defunct Wealth Management division. The bank also has a non-core Treasury division that manages the company's securities portfolio and other investments.

Commercial Banking provides business loans, equipment financing (through People's Capital and Leasing Corp., or PCLC, and People's United Equipment Finance Corp, or PUEFC), and municipal banking, as well as trust services for corporations and institutions and private banking services for wealthy individuals.

Retail Banking provides deposit services, residential mortgages and home equity loans, financial advisory and investment management services.

Overall, the bank generated some 70% of its total revenue from loan interest, and approximately 10% from interest on securities. About 5% of total revenues came from bank service charges, while investment management fees, commercial banking lending fees, and insurance revenue, each made up less than 5% of overall revenue.

Geographic Reach

Connecticut is its largest lending market, with nearly 25% of the bank's loan portfolio being extended to consumers and businesses in the region in 2021. Massachusetts and New York are the bank's next largest markets, with about 20% each share of its loan portfolio.

People's United's corporate headquarters is located in Bridgeport, Connecticut. The headquarters building had a net book value of $38 million and People's United occupies about 90% of the building. People's United delivers its financial services through a network of about 390 branches located throughout Connecticut, southeastern New York, Massachusetts, Vermont, New Hampshire and Maine. People's United's branch network is primarily concentrated in Connecticut, where it has more than 170 offices (including nearly 85 located in Stop & Shop supermarkets). People's United also has over 70 branches in southeastern New York (including nearly 25 located in Stop & Shop supermarkets), some 65 branches in Massachusetts, nearly 40 branches in Vermont, 25 branches in New Hampshire and more than 15 branches in Maine. People's United owns roughly 140 of its branches, which had an aggregate net book value of

$110 million.

Sales and Marketing

The bank sells its products and services through investment and brokerage offices, commercial branches, online banking and investment trading, and through its 24-hour telephone banking service. The company's PCLC, PUEFC, and LEAF affiliates have a sales presence in more than 15 states to support equipment financing operations throughout the US. The Bank maintains a mortgage warehouse lending group located in Kentucky and a national credits group that has participations in commercial loans and commercial real estate loans to borrowers in various industries on a national scale.

People's United spent $12.1 million on advertising in 2021, $13.3 million in 2020, and $16.4 million in 2019, respectively.

Financial Performance

The company's revenue for fiscal 2021 decreased to $1.9 billion compared from the prior year with $2.1 billion.

Net income for fiscal 2021 increased to $604.9 million compared from the prior year with $219.6 million.

Cash held by the company at the end of fiscal 2021 increased to $10.6 billion. Cash provided by operations, investing and financing activities were $1.2 billion, $4.0 billion, and $1.1 billion, respectively.

Mergers and Acquisitions

In early 2021, M&T Bank Corporation and People's United Financial, Inc. have entered into a definitive agreement under which M&T will acquire People's United in an all-stock transaction. The combined company will create a diversified, community-focused banking franchise with approximately $200 billion in assets and a network of more than 1,100 branches and over 2,000 ATMs that spans 12 states from Maine to Virginia and the District of Columbia. The implied total transaction value based on closing prices is approximately $7.6 billion. M&T Bank Corporation is a financial holding company headquartered in Buffalo, New York.

Company Background

One of the main goals of People's United has been to build its presence in the two largest metropolitan areas in its market, New York City and Boston. One of the largest in the Boston area, Danvers Bancorp, added some 30 branches and carried a price tag of approximately $493 million. People's United also acquired LSB Corporation and Butler Bank, the latter in an FDIC-assisted transaction that included a loss-sharing agreement with the regulator covering all acquired loans and foreclosed real estate of the failed bank, bringing in another 10 branches in the Boston area. In 2010, People's United bought Bank of Smithtown, which had about 30 branches, primarily on Long Island in New York.

People's United Financial acquired commercial lender Financial Federal Corporation in 2010 (now People's United Equipment Finance), which provides financing and leasing to small and midsized business nationwide.

People's United Financial underwent significant transformation in past years. The company demutualized and converted to a stock holding company in 2007, and early the following year acquired multibank holding company Chittenden Corporation. The deal added some 140 branches, doubling People's United Bank's branch network and expanding its reach beyond Connecticut and New York and into the rest of New England.

EXECUTIVES

Chief Executive Officer, Chairman, Director, John P. Barnes, $1,073,471 total compensation
Commercial Banking Group President, Commercial Banking Group Subsidiary Officer, Jeffrey (Jeff) J. Tengel, $500,958 total compensation
Executive Vice President, Chief Credit Officer, Richard Barry
Executive Vice President, General Counsel, Corporate Secretary, Subsidiary Officer, Kristy Berner
Wealth Management Executive Vice President, Wealth Management Head, Michael Boardman
Executive Vice President, Chief Marketing Officer, Mark Herron
Senior Executive Vice President, Chief Human Resources Officer, David K. Norton, $411,231 total compensation
Senior Executive Vice President, Chief Administrative Officer, Lee C. Powlus, $489,613 total compensation
Executive Vice President, Chief Risk Officer, Daniel G. Roberts
Senior Executive Vice President, Chief Financial Officer, Subsidiary Officer, R. David Rosato, $485,602 total compensation
Senior Executive Vice President, Director, Kirk W. Walters, $495,280 total compensation
Division Officer, Sara M. Longobardi
Lead Director, Director, George P. Carter
Director, Collin P. Baron
Director, Jane P. Chwick
Director, William F. Cruger
Director, John K. Dwight
Director, Jerry Franklin
Director, Janet M. Hansen
Director, Nancy McAllister
Director, Mark W. Richards
Auditors : KPMG LLP

LOCATIONS

HQ: People's United Financial Inc
850 Main Street, Bridgeport, CT 06604
Phone: 203 338-7171   Fax: 203 338-2545
Web: www.peoples.com

PRODUCTS/OPERATIONS

2014 Sales

	$ mil.	% of total
Interest & dividends		
Loans		
Commercial real estate	354.2	26
Commercial	351.0	26
Residential mortgage	153.5	12
Consumer	73.9	5
Securities	96.8	7
Other	1.2	-
Noninterest		
Bank service charges	128.6	10
Investment management fees	41.6	3
Operating lease income	41.6	3
Commercial banking lending fees	33.4	2
Insurance revenue	29.9	2
Other	76.6	4
Adjustment	(0.9)	-
Total	1,381.4	100

COMPETITORS

AXOS FINANCIAL, INC.
BANKUNITED, INC.
CITIZENS FINANCIAL GROUP, INC.
FIRST FEDERAL SAVINGS AND LOAN ASSOCIATION OF LAKEWOOD
FLAGSTAR BANCORP, INC.
INVESTORS BANCORP, INC.
KEYCORP
MUFG AMERICAS HOLDINGS CORPORATION
PROVIDENT FINANCIAL SERVICES, INC.
UMPQUA HOLDINGS CORPORATION

HISTORICAL FINANCIALS

Company Type: Public

Income Statement   FYE: December 31

	ASSETS ($mil)	NET INCOME ($mil)	INCOME AS % OF ASSETS	EMPLOYEES
12/20	63,091.8	219.6	0.3%	5,987
12/19	58,589.8	520.4	0.9%	6,499
12/18	47,877.3	468.1	1.0%	5,920
12/17	44,453.4	337.2	0.8%	5,584
12/16	40,609.8	281.0	0.7%	5,173
Annual Growth	11.6%	(6.0%)	—	3.7%

2020 Year-End Financials

Return on assets: 0.3%
Return on equity: 2.8%
Long-term debt ($ mil.): —
No. of shares ($ mil.): 424.6
Sales ($ mil.): 2,256.8
Dividends
Yield: 5.5%
Payout: 61.8%
Market value ($ mil.): 5,491.0

	STOCK PRICE ($) FY Close	P/E High/Low		PER SHARE ($) Earnings	Dividends	Book Value
12/20	12.93	34	19	0.49	0.72	17.90
12/19	16.90	14	11	1.27	0.71	17.91
12/18	14.43	16	11	1.29	0.70	17.32
12/17	18.70	20	16	0.97	0.69	16.79
12/16	19.36	22	15	0.92	0.68	16.28
Annual Growth	(9.6%)	—	—	(14.6%)	1.4%	2.4%

PerkinElmer, Inc.

PerkinElmer is a leading provider of products, services, and solutions for the diagnostics, life sciences, and applied markets. It develops and sells equipment such as instruments, tests, and software used by scientists, researchers, and clinicians to address the most critical challenges across science and healthcare. More than 2 million scientists are using PerkinElmer's laboratory software to store and analyze research data and collaborate on experiments. To date, over 735 million babies have been tested for life-threatening diseases using PerkinElmer's newborn screening tools. The company, which distributes its offerings in more than 190 countries, generates most of its sales outside the US. Richard Perkin and Charles Elmer came together to form the Perkin-Elmer brand in 1937.

Operations

PerkinElmer sells its products in two segments: Diagnostics and Discovery & Analytical Solutions.

Diagnostics, about 60% of revenue, sells tools and applications for clinical customers in the reproductive health, emerging market diagnostics, and applied genomics markets. Among its brands are Vanadis (prenatal and maternal health screening), NeoBase (detection of metabolic disorders in newborns), and ViaCord (stem cell banking).

Discovery & Analytical Solutions, which offers products and services for the environmental, industrial, food, life sciences research, and laboratory services markets, generates more than 40% of sales. The unit's brands include Radiometric (detection instruments), Opera Phenix (high content screening systems), Clarus (gas chromatography and mass spectrometery equipment), and Flexar (liquid chromatography systems).

Among its brands are Vanadis (prenatal and maternal health screening), NeoBase (detection of metabolic disorders in newborns), and ViaCord (stem cell banking).

Overall, product sales bring in about 65% while services account for the rest.

Geographic Reach

Based in Waltham, Massachusetts, PerkinElmer market its products and services in more than 190 countries. About 40% of PerkinElmer's sales are to customers in the US. China is the next biggest market with about 15% of sales. Customers in the UK and other countries account for the rest.

Sales and Marketing

PerkinElmer's customers include pharmaceutical and biotechnology companies, laboratories, academic and research institutions, public health authorities, private healthcare organizations, doctors, and government agencies.

PerkinElmer tries to reach many of those customers through its direct sales unit of approximately 6,500 sales and service representatives in some 40 countries. The company operates through distributors in areas where it does not have staff on the ground.

The diagnostics generates the largest share with nearly 60% of the company's total sales. The life sciences products account for about 25%, and nearly 15% came from applied markets products.

Financial Performance

The company had a total revenue of $5.1 billion, a 34% increase from the previous year's revenue of $3.8 billion. The increase was primarily due to a higher volume of product and service revenue for the year.

In 2021, the company had a net income of $943.2 million, a 30% increase from the previous year's net income of $727.9 million.

The company's cash at the end of 2021 was $619.3 million. Operating activities generated $1.4 billion, while investing activities used $4.1 billion, mainly for acquisitions. Financing activities provided another $2.9 billion.

Strategy

The company's strategy is to develop and deliver innovative products, services and solutions in high-growth markets that utilizes its knowledge and expertise to address customers' critical needs and drive scientific breakthroughs. To execute on this strategy and accelerate revenue growth, it focuses on broadening its offerings through both the acquisition of innovative technology and investment in research and development and the acquisition of innovative technology.

The strategy includes: Strengthening its position within key markets by expanding its global product and service offerings, maintaining superior product quality and driving an enhanced customer experience; Attracting, retaining and developing talented and engaged employees; Accelerating transformational innovation through both internal research and development and third-party collaborations and alliances; Augmenting growth in both of the company's core business segments, Discovery & Analytical Solutions and Diagnostics, through strategic acquisitions and licensing; Engraining focused operational excellence to improve organizational efficiency and agility; and Opportunistically utilizing its share repurchase programs to help drive shareholder value.

Mergers and Acquisitions

In late 2021, PerkinElmer acquired BioLegend, a leading, worldwide provider of life science antibodies and reagents for a total consideration of approximately $5.25 billion. The acquisition further expands the company's life science franchise into high-growth areas such as cytometry, proteogenomics, multiplex assays, recombinant proteins, magnetic cell separation and bioprocessing.

In early 2021, PerkinElmer completed the acquisition of UK-based Oxford Immunotec Global PLC, a global leader of proprietary test kits for latent tuberculosis. Through this acquisition, PerkinElmer will grow its portfolio of advanced infectious disease testing solutions to include tuberculosis detection to better serve customers around the world. Moreover, the deal will enable PerkinElmer to combine its channel expertise and leading workflow and testing capabilities with Oxford Immunotec's leading proficiencies in T cell immunology with its proprietary test kits for latent tuberculosis.

Company Background

PerkinElmer traces its roots back to the invention of the strobe light in 1931. MIT professor Harold Edgerton, who invented the strobe light while doing research on electric motors, formed a consulting business with former student Kenneth Germeshausen that used strobe lights and high-speed photography to solve manufacturing problems.

PerkinElmer was founded by Richard Perkin and Charles Elmer in 1937 to design optical products. The company moved into the analytical instruments business in the 1940s.

The companies merged in 1999 and took the PerkinElmer name.

HISTORY

PerkinElmer traces its roots back to the invention of the strobe light in 1931. MIT professor Harold Edgerton, who invented the strobe light while doing research on electric motors, formed a consulting business with former student Kenneth Germeshausen that used strobe lights and high-speed photography to solve manufacturing problems. As business picked up, they brought in another former student, Herbert Grier, and in 1947 formed Edgerton, Germeshausen and Grier. Their first contract job was to photograph nuclear weapons tests for the US government. The company went public in 1959 and changed its name to EG&G in 1966.

Over the next 30 years, EG&G bought scores of companies involved in electronic instruments and components, biomedical services, energy and nuclear weapons R&D, seal and gasket manufacturing, automotive testing, and the aerospace industry. Key acquisitions included Reynolds Electrical & Engineering (1967), which provided support services for the Department of Defense (including the nuclear weapons testing program); Sealol (1968), a maker of seals for industrial applications; and Automotive Research Associates (1973).

EXECUTIVES

President, Chief Executive Officer, Prahlad R. Singh, $875,000 total compensation
Senior Vice President, Chief Financial Officer, James M. Mock, $331,154 total compensation
Administration Senior Vice President, Administration General Counsel, Administration Secretary, Joel S. Goldberg, $486,639 total compensation
Senior Vice President, Chief Human Resources Officer, Deborah Butters
Non-Executive Chairman, Alexis P. Michas
Director, Peter Barrett
Director, Samuel R. Chapin

Director, Sylvie L. Gregoire
Director, Michel Vounatsos
Director, Frank R. Witney
Director, Pascale Witz
Auditors : DELOITTE & TOUCHE LLP

LOCATIONS

HQ: PerkinElmer, Inc.
   940 Winter Street, Waltham, MA 02451
Phone: 781 663-6900   **Fax:** 781 663-6052
Web: www.perkinelmer.com

2018 Sales

	$ mil.	% of total
US	906.4	33
China	559.9	20
Germany	142.4	5
France	98	4
Italy	95.9	3
India	92.3	3
Japan	79.3	3
UK	72.1	3
Other countries	731.7	26
Total	2,778	100

PRODUCTS/OPERATIONS

2018 Sales

	$ mil.	% of total
Discovery & Analytical Solutions		
Product	1,010.9	36
Service	682.3	25
Diagnostics		
Product	924.6	33
Service	160.2	6
Total	2,778	100

Selected Products

Human health
  Diagnostics
    BACs-on-Beads (chromosomal abnormality detection)
    DELFIA Xpress (prenatal screening)
    GSP Neonatal (congenital screening from a drop of blood)
    NeoGram (metabolic disorder detection)
  Research
    AlphaLISA (research assays)
    Columbus (image data storage and analysis)
    EnVision (label reader)
    JANUS Automated Workstation (liquid handling)
    Opera/Operetta (cell-based assay high content screening/imaging)
    TSA Plus (biotin kits for increasing sensitivity of histochemistry and cytochemistry)
    Volocity (3D image analysis software)
Environmental health
    Atomax (cathode lamps)
    Clarus (gas sample handling)
    Flexar (liquid chromatography)
    NexION (mass spectrometer)
    Spectrum (infrared analysis)

COMPETITORS

AGILENT TECHNOLOGIES, INC.
BIO-RAD LABORATORIES, INC.
CONMED CORPORATION
FUJIFILM SONOSITE, INC.
GRIFOLS SA
HOLOGIC, INC.
LUMENIS LTD.
MASIMO CORPORATION
OLYMPUS CORPORATION
THERMO FISHER SCIENTIFIC INC.

HISTORICAL FINANCIALS

Company Type: Public

Income Statement   FYE: January 3

	REVENUE ($mil)	NET INCOME ($mil)	NET PROFIT MARGIN	EMPLOYEES
01/21*	3,782.7	727.8	19.2%	14,000
12/19	2,883.6	227.5	7.9%	13,000
12/18	2,777.9	237.9	8.6%	12,500
12/17	2,256.9	292.6	13.0%	11,000
01/17	2,115.5	234.2	11.1%	8,000
Annual Growth	15.6%	32.8%	—	15.0%

*Fiscal year change

2021 Year-End Financials

Debt ratio: 25.0%   No. of shares ($ mil.): 112.0
Return on equity: 21.8%   Dividends
Cash ($ mil.): 402.0   Yield: —
Current Ratio: 1.36   Payout: 4.3%
Long-term debt ($ mil.): 1,609.7   Market value ($ mil.): 16,085.0

	STOCK PRICE ($) FY Close	P/E High	P/E Low	PER SHARE ($) Earnings	PER SHARE ($) Dividends	PER SHARE ($) Book Value
01/21*	143.50	23	10	6.49	0.28	33.33
12/19	97.05	49	35	2.04	0.28	25.32
12/18	77.29	45	33	2.13	0.28	23.37
12/17	73.12	28	19	2.64	0.28	22.68
01/17	52.15	27	19	2.12	0.28	19.65
Annual Growth	28.8%	—	—	32.3%	0.0%	14.1%

*Fiscal year change

PGT Innovations Inc

PGT makes and sells WinGuard impact-resistant doors and windows for the residential market. The energy-efficient, customizable doors and windows are made of aluminum or vinyl with laminated glass and are designed to withstand hurricane-strength winds. PGT also makes Eze-Breeze porch enclosure panels and garage door screens, NewSouth Window replacement windows and doors, and Estate Collection windows and doors for high-end homes, resorts, hotels and in schools and office buildings. The company has various manufacturing facilities in California, Florida and Arizona. PGT sells its products through some 2,300 window distributors, dealers, and contractors in the Southeastern US, Canada, Central America, and the Caribbean.

Operations

PGT have two reportable segments: the Southeast segment (about 85%), and the Western segment (over 15%).

The Southeast reporting segment, which is also an operating segment, is composed of sales from its facilities in Florida. The Western reporting segment, also an operating segment, is composed of sales from its facilities in Arizona and California.

Geographic Reach

Florida-based PGT currently conducts business in the Southeastern US, Western US, Gulf Coast, Coastal mid-Atlantic, the Caribbean, Central America, and Canada.

Sales and Marketing

The home repair and remodeling end markets represented over 55% each of PGT's sales while new construction markets account for the rest. The company's advertising expenses were $15.8 million, $11.6 million, and $5.2 million for the years 2021, 2020, and 2019, respectively.

PGT markets its products through print and web-based advertising, consumer, dealer, and builder promotions, and selling and collateral materials. It markets its products based on quality, building code compliance, outstanding service, shorter lead times, and on-time delivery utilizing its fleet of trucks and trailers. Its top ten customers account for approximately 20% of sales.

Financial Performance

Net sales for 2021 were $1.2 billion, a $278.9 million, or 32%, increase in sales, from $882.6 million in the prior year. The increase in net sales in 2021 of $278.9 million was primarily driven by organic sales growth at both its Southeast and Western segments and the effects of the recovery from the Pandemic, as well as revenues added through acquisitions, which included $107.1 million from its Eco and Anlin Acquisitions.

Net income for fiscal 2021 decreased to $35.2 million compared from the prior year with $45.1 million.

Cash held by the company at the end of fiscal 2021 decreased to $96.1 million. Cash provided by operations and financing activities were $63.7 million and $186.1 million, respectively. Cash used for investing activities was $253.9 million, mainly for business acquisitions.

EXECUTIVES

Chairman, Director, Rodney Hershberger, $524,326 total compensation

President, Chief Executive Officer, Director, Jeffrey T. Jackson, $597,633 total compensation

Corporate Development Senior Vice President, Corporate Development Treasurer, Bradley R. West, $284,712 total compensation

Senior Vice President, Division Officer, Mike Wothe

General Counsel, Corporate Secretary, Ryan S. Quinn

Corporate Sales and Innovation Subsidiary Officer, Sales Subsidiary Officer, Brent Boydston, $264,615 total compensation

Division Officer, Robert Andrew Keller, $299,615 total compensation

Director, Floyd F. Sherman
Director, Sheree L. Bargabos
Director, Xavier F. Boza
Director, Alexander R. Castaldi
Director, William J. Morgan
Director, Brett N. Milgrim
Director, Richard D. Feintuch
Director, Frances Powell Hawes
Auditors : Ernst & Young LLP

LOCATIONS

HQ: PGT Innovations Inc
1070 Technology Drive, North Venice, FL 34275
Phone: 941 480-1600
Web: www.pgtinnovations.com

2013 Sales by Region

	$ mil.	% of total
US	232.7	97
Other	6.6	3
Total	239.3	100

PRODUCTS/OPERATIONS

2013 Sales

	$ mil.	% of total
Impact window and door products	183.4	77
Other window & door products	56.9	23
Total	239.3	100

COMPETITORS

ASSOCIATED MATERIALS, LLC
CORNELLCOOKSON, LLC
GRIFFON CORPORATION
HORMANN LLC
JELD-WEN, INC.
KAWNEER COMPANY, INC.
LIXIL CORPORATION
OVERHEAD DOOR CORPORATION
PLY GEM HOLDINGS, INC.
RYTEC CORPORATION

HISTORICAL FINANCIALS

Company Type: Public

Income Statement FYE: January 2

	REVENUE ($mil)	NET INCOME ($mil)	NET PROFIT MARGIN	EMPLOYEES
01/21*	882.6	45.1	5.1%	3,500
12/19	744.9	43.6	5.9%	3,000
12/18	698.4	53.9	7.7%	3,000
12/17	511.0	39.8	7.8%	2,700
12/16	458.5	23.7	5.2%	2,600
Annual Growth	17.8%	17.4%	—	7.7%

*Fiscal year change

2021 Year-End Financials

Debt ratio: 38.8%
Return on equity: 9.6%
Cash ($ mil.): 100.3
Current Ratio: 3.33
Long-term debt ($ mil.): 412
No. of shares ($ mil.): 59.0
Dividends
 Yield: —
 Payout: —
Market value ($ mil.): 1,200.0

	STOCK PRICE ($) FY Close	P/E High/Low		PER SHARE ($) Earnings	Dividends	Book Value
01/21*	20.34	27	9	0.76	0.00	8.22
12/19	14.80	24	18	0.74	0.00	7.38
12/18	15.72	25	14	1.00	0.00	6.64
12/17	16.85	21	13	0.77	0.00	3.52
12/16	11.45	25	18	0.47	0.00	2.69
Annual Growth	15.4%	—	—	12.8%	—	32.2%

*Fiscal year change

Phillips 66 Partners LP

How many ways can you break up an oil and gas company? The ConocoPhillips and Phillips 66 family of companies may be trying to find out. Phillips 66 Partners is the midstream component, owning and acquiring crude oil, refined petroleum, and natural gas liquids pipelines, terminals, and storage facilities in the US. The company has capacity for about 650 million barrels a day and its assets include 135 miles of pipeline, terminals, and docks connected to Phillips 66 refineries in Texas, Louisiana, and Illinois. Phillips 66 Partners earns revenue from fees it charges for transportation and storage of petroleum. In 2017, it bought mid-stream assets from its general partner, Phillips 66, for a total transaction value of $2.4 billion.

IPO

The company plans to use its $378 million in IPO proceeds to repay debt and for general corporate purposes including possible future acquisitions.

Strategy

Going forward, Phillips 66 Partners plans to provide its transportation and storage services to Phillips 66 and third parties. It also intends to pursue acquisitions through a right-of-first-refusal deal with Phillips 66 and through third parties.

EXECUTIVES

Chairman, Chief Executive Officer, Holding/Parent Company Officer, Greg C. Garland, $0 total compensation
Vice President, Chief Financial Officer, Holding/Parent Company Officer, Director, Kevin J. Mitchell
Operations Vice President, Operations Chief Operating Officer, Operations Holding/Parent Company Officer, Director, Timothy D. Roberts
Vice President, Controller, J. Scott Pruitt
Vice President, Holding/Parent Company Officer, Director, Robert A. Herman
Operations General Manager, Operations Holding/Parent Company Officer, Casey B. Gorder
Auditors : Ernst & Young LLP

LOCATIONS

HQ: Phillips 66 Partners LP
2331 CityWest Blvd., Houston, TX 77042
Phone: 855 283-9237
Web: www.phillips66partners.com

COMPETITORS

ANDEAVOR LLC
CHESAPEAKE ENERGY CORPORATION
ENLINK MIDSTREAM, INC.
PAR PACIFIC HOLDINGS, INC.
PHILLIPS 66

HISTORICAL FINANCIALS

Company Type: Public

Income Statement FYE: December 31

	REVENUE ($mil)	NET INCOME ($mil)	NET PROFIT MARGIN	EMPLOYEES
12/20	1,618.0	791.0	48.9%	0
12/19	1,667.0	923.0	55.4%	0
12/18	1,486.0	796.0	53.6%	0
12/17	1,169.0	524.0	44.8%	0
12/16	873.0	408.0	46.7%	0
Annual Growth	16.7%	18.0%	—	—

2020 Year-End Financials

Debt ratio: 53.9%
Return on equity: —
Cash ($ mil.): 7.0
Current Ratio: 0.22
Long-term debt ($ mil.): 3,444
No. of shares ($ mil.): 228.3
Dividends
 Yield: 13.2%
 Payout: 107.0%
Market value ($ mil.): 6,030.0

	STOCK PRICE ($) FY Close	P/E High/Low		PER SHARE ($) Earnings	Dividends	Book Value
12/20	26.41	20	7	3.27	3.50	12.25
12/19	61.64	14	10	4.29	3.40	12.41
12/18	42.11	13	10	4.00	2.94	19.82
12/17	52.35	22	17	2.59	2.41	17.42
12/16	48.64	29	20	2.20	1.98	14.32
Annual Growth	(14.2%)	—	—	10.4%	15.4%	(3.8%)

Phillips Edison & Co Inc

EXECUTIVES

Chairman, Chief Executive Officer, Director, Jeffrey S. Edison, $725,385 total compensation
President, Devin Ignatius Murphy, $464,827 total compensation
Senior Vice President, Chief Financial Officer, Treasurer, John R Caulfield
Senior Vice President, Chief Operating Officer, Robert F. Myers, $474,731 total compensation
Senior Vice President, General Counsel, Secretary, Tanya E. Brady
Senior Vice President, Chief Accounting Officer, Associate/Affiliate Company Officer, Jennifer L. Robison
Director, Leslie T. Chao
Director, Elizabeth Fischer
Director, David W. Garrison
Director, Paul J. Massey
Director, Stephen R. Quazzo
Director, Jane Silfen
Director, John A. Strong
Director, Gregory S. Wood
Auditors : DELOITTE & TOUCHE LLP

LOCATIONS

HQ: Phillips Edison & Co Inc
11501 Northlake Drive, Cincinnati, OH 45249
Phone: 513 554-1110
Web: www.phillipsedison.com

Photronics, Inc.

Photronics is the world's leading manufacturer of photomasks, which are high precision photographic quartz or glass plates containing microscopic images of electronic circuits. Photomasks is a key tool in the process for manufacturing integrated circuits (ICs) and flat-panel displays (FPDs) and are used as masters to transfer circuit patterns onto semiconductor wafers and FPD substrates during the fabrication of ICs, a variety of FPDs and, to a lesser extent, other types of electrical and optical components. About 80% of the company's sales are from customers in Asia. The company was founded in 1969.

Operations
Photronics operates as a single operating segment as a manufacturer of photomasks, which are high precision quartz or glass plates containing microscopic images of electronic circuits for use in the fabrication of IC's and FPDs.

It gets about 70% of its revenue from making photomasks for integrated circuits and the rest from photomasks for flat panel displays.

Geographic Reach
Photronics' products are made at some 10 manufacturing plants - one in South Korea, two in China, two in Europe (Germany and Wales), three in Taiwan, and three in the US (Connecticut, Idaho, and Texas). It primarily conducts research and development activities for IC photomasks at Boise, Idaho, facility, as well as at Photronics, Cheonan, Ltd. (formerly PK, Ltd.), its subsidiary in Korea and Photronics DNP Mask Corporation (PDMC), one of its joint venture subsidiaries in Taiwan.

Research and development for FPD photomasks is primarily conducted at Photronics Cheonan, Ltd.

Over 35% of Photronics' revenue comes from customers in Taiwan and about 25% from Korean manufacturers. China customers generate over 15% of sales. The company gets around 15% of sales from US, while Europe generated some 5%.

Sales and Marketing
The market for photomasks primarily consists of domestic and non-US semiconductor and FPD manufacturers and designers. Photronics conducts its sales and marketing activities primarily through a staff of full-time sales personnel and customer service representatives who work closely with the company's management and technical personnel.

Photronics has about 530 customers with its five biggest customers accounting for about 45% of its company's sales. The company's sales might become even more concentrated because of consolidation in the semiconductor manufacturing business. Customers include United Microelectronics Corp. Co., Ltd. (more than 15% of sales), and Samsung Electronics (over 10% of sales).

Financial Performance
Revenue increased 9% in 2021, compared with 2020, to $663.8 million. IC revenue increased 10%, due to both improved pricing for mainstream photomasks, and improved pricing and increased demand for high-end masks at the largest node levels.

In the fiscal year 2021, net income has increased about 95% to $78.8 million from the prior year.

Photronics had cash and cash equivalents of $276.7 million at the end of 2021, compared with $278.6 million at the end of fiscal 2020. Net cash provided by operating activities was $150.8 million. Net cash used in investing activities was $103.5 million, mostly for purchases of property, plant and equipment. Net cash used in financing activities was $53.9 million for purchases of treasury stock.

Strategy
As part of Photronics' business growth strategy, it has acquired businesses and entered into joint ventures in the past, and it may pursue acquisitions and joint venture opportunities in the future. Future efforts to grow the company may include expanding into new or related markets or industries.

HISTORY

Constantine (Deno) Macricostas, who came to the US from Greece in 1954 as an exchange student, and four partners started Photronic Labs in a garage in 1969. Weary of infighting, Macricostas left the firm in 1972 but bought it two years later with the help of banker (and later long-time board member) Michael Yomazzo and a loan from the Small Business Administration. The company went public in 1987 and changed its name to Photronics in 1990.

A string of acquisitions, starting with Beta Squared in 1990, increased the company's customer base. In 1993 it became the #1 independent photomask maker in the US with the purchase of Toppan Printronics, the US operations of Toppan Printing. The deal gave Toppan Printing a stake in Photronics, which Photronics bought back five years later.

EXECUTIVES

Chairman, Director, Constantine S. Macricostas, $365,792 total compensation
President, Chief Executive Officer, Director, Franki Lee, $419,027 total compensation
Executive Vice President, Chief Administrative Officer, General Counsel, Secretary, Richelle E. Burr, $266,102 total compensation
Executive Vice President, Chief Financial Officer, John P. Jordan, $345,000 total compensation
Strategic Planning Executive Vice President, Strategic Planning Chief Technology Officer, Christopher J. Progler, $345,933 total compensation
Lead Independent Director, Director, Walter M. Fiederowicz
Director, Adam M. Lewis
Director, Daniel Liao
Director, George Macricostas
Director, Mary Paladino
Director, Mitchell G. Tyson
Auditors: Deloitte & Touche LLP

LOCATIONS

HQ: Photronics, Inc.
15 Secor Road, Brookfield, CT 06804
Phone: 203 775-9000
Web: www.photronics.com

2016 Sales

	$ mil.	% of total
Taiwan	193.2	40
Korea	141.0	29
United States	113.7	24
Europe	33.4	7
All other Asia	2.2	0
Total	483.5	100

PRODUCTS/OPERATIONS

2016 Sales

	$ mil.	% of total
Integrated Circuits	364.6	75
Flat Panel Displays	118.9	25
Total	483.5	100

COMPETITORS

AMKOR TECHNOLOGY, INC.
APPLIED MATERIALS, INC.
ELECTRO SCIENTIFIC INDUSTRIES, INC.
KOPIN CORPORATION
LATTICE SEMICONDUCTOR CORPORATION
MICRON TECHNOLOGY, INC.
OCLARO, INC.
SUNEDISON SEMICONDUCTOR LIMITED
ULTRATECH, INC.
VISHAY INTERTECHNOLOGY, INC.

HISTORICAL FINANCIALS
Company Type: Public

Income Statement
FYE: December 31

	REVENUE ($mil)	NET INCOME ($mil)	NET PROFIT MARGIN	EMPLOYEES
12/21	532.8	15.1	2.8%	290
12/20	498.0	4.7	1.0%	300
12/19	536.7	(63.5)	—	300
12/18	430.3	39.1	9.1%	300
12/17	311.5	(38.3)	—	304
Annual Growth	14.4%	—	—	(1.2%)

2021 Year-End Financials
Debt ratio: 40.5%
Return on equity: 0.7%
Cash ($ mil.): 92.5
Current Ratio: 0.74
Long-term debt ($ mil.): 1,891.7
No. of shares ($ mil.): 113.2
Dividends
Yield: 1.3%
Payout: 293.3%
Market value ($ mil.): 3,741.0

	STOCK PRICE ($) FY Close	P/E High/Low		PER SHARE ($) Earnings	Dividends	Book Value
12/21	33.04	228	181	0.15	0.44	18.99
Annual Growth	—	—	—	—	—	—

HISTORICAL FINANCIALS
Company Type: Public

Income Statement — FYE: October 31

	REVENUE ($mil)	NET INCOME ($mil)	NET PROFIT MARGIN	EMPLOYEES
10/21	663.7	55.4	8.4%	1,728
10/20	609.6	33.8	5.5%	1,728
10/19	550.6	29.7	5.4%	1,775
10/18	535.2	42.0	7.9%	1,575
10/17	450.6	13.1	2.9%	1,475
Annual Growth	10.2%	43.4%	—	4.0%

2021 Year-End Financials
Debt ratio: 8.6%
Return on equity: 6.8%
Cash ($ mil.): 276.6
Current Ratio: 3.13
Long-term debt ($ mil.): 89.4
No. of shares ($ mil.): 60.0
Dividends
 Yield: —
 Payout: —
Market value ($ mil.): 780.0

	STOCK PRICE ($) FY Close	P/E High/Low		PER SHARE ($) Earnings	Dividends	Book Value
10/21	12.99	17	11	0.89	0.00	13.72
10/20	9.75	31	16	0.52	0.00	12.75
10/19	11.80	28	18	0.44	0.00	11.74
10/18	9.74	18	12	0.59	0.00	11.31
10/17	9.55	62	40	0.19	0.00	10.84
Annual Growth	8.0%	—	—	47.1%	—	6.1%

Physicians Realty Trust

Physicians Realty Trust doesn't make house calls. The real estate investment trust (REIT) owns and manages healthcare properties that are leased to physicians, hospitals and healthcare delivery systems. A self-managed REIT, its portfolio consists of more than 250 medical office buildings in about 30 states. Tenants include Hackley Hospital, and Valley West Hospital. Physicians Realty Trust was formed in 2013. As a REIT, it is exempt from paying federal income tax as long as it distributes about 90% of profits back to shareholders. Physicians Realty Trust went public in 2013, raising $120 million.

Operations
The company receive a cash rental stream from healthcare providers under our leases. Approximately 95% of the annualized base rent payments from properties as of 2019 are from absolute and triple-net leases, pursuant to which the tenants are responsible for all operating expenses relating to the property, including but not limited to real estate taxes, utilities, property insurance, routine maintenance and repairs, and property management.

The company's rental revenues account for nearly 75% of sales, while expense recoveries and interest income on real estate loans and other accounts for the rest.

Geographic Reach
Based in Milwaukee, Physicians Realty Trust has properties in about 30 states, including Georgia, Texas, and Michigan.

Sales and Marketing
The company's five largest tenants based upon rental revenue represents approximately $57.6 million, or about 20%, of the annualized base rent from its consolidated properties. No single tenant accounted for more than 5% of total annualized base rent or about 5% of total base revenue as of December 31, 2019; however, more than 15% of total annualized base rent as of December 31, 2019 were from tenants affiliated with CommonSpirit.

Financial Performance
The revenue of the company is on an upward trend in the last five years despite a slight dip in 2019. Net income is also going on the same path over the same period.

In 2019, the revenue of the company had a slight drop of 2% to $415.3 million. Rental revenue had a 3% drop, Interest income on real estate loans and others had a 6% decrease, offset by a 3% increase in expense recoveries.

Net income for 2019 was $74.5 million, up 32% from the prior year. The increase was due to lower operating expenses and a gain of $31.3 million from sale of investment properties.

Cash at the end of the year for the company was $2.4 million. Net cash provided by operating activities was $201.2 million and cash provided by financing activities was $37.3 million. Investing activities used $255.3 million for acquisitions and issuance of real estate loans receivables.

Strategy
The company intends to grow its portfolio of high-quality healthcare properties leased to physicians, hospitals, healthcare delivery systems, and other healthcare providers primarily through acquisitions of existing healthcare facilities that provide stable revenue growth and predictable long-term cash flows. It may also selectively finance the development of new healthcare facilities through a joint venture or fee arrangements with premier healthcare real estate developers. Generally, it expects to make investments in new development properties when approximately 80% or more of the development property has been pre-leased before construction commences.

The company also seeks to invest in properties where it can develop strategic alliances with financially sound healthcare providers and healthcare delivery systems that offer need-based healthcare services in sustainable healthcare markets. It focuses its investment activity on the following types of healthcare properties: medical office buildings; outpatient treatment and diagnostic facilities; physician group practice clinics; ambulatory surgery centers; and specialty hospitals and treatment centers.

EXECUTIVES

President, Chief Executive Officer, Trustee, John T. Thomas, $834,330 total compensation
Executive Vice President, Chief Financial Officer, Jeffrey N. Theiler, $504,896 total compensation
Executive Vice President, Chief Investment Officer, Del Mar Deeni Taylor, $521,569 total compensation
Asset and Investment Management Executive Vice President, Mark D. Theine, $352,306 total compensation
Senior Vice President, Controller, Laurie P. Becker
Chief Accounting Officer, Chief Administrative Officer, John W. Lucey, $315,000 total compensation
Senior Vice President, Deputy Chief Investment Officer, Daniel M. Klein, $293,615 total compensation
Senior Vice President, General Counsel, Bradley D. Page, $331,000 total compensation
Non-Executive Chairman, Trustee, Tommy G. Thompson
Trustee, Mark A. Baumgartner
Trustee, Stanton D. Anderson
Trustee, Albert C. Black
Trustee, Richard A. Weiss
Trustee, William A. Ebinger
Trustee, Pamela J. Kessler
Auditors: Ernst & Young LLP

LOCATIONS

HQ: Physicians Realty Trust
309 N. Water Street, Suite 500, Milwaukee, WI 53202
Phone: 414 367-5600
Web: www.docreit.com

COMPETITORS

DIVERSIFIED HEALTHCARE TRUST
HEALTHCARE REALTY TRUST INCORPORATED
MEDICAL PROPERTIES TRUST, INC.
NATIONAL HEALTH INVESTORS, INC.
OMEGA HEALTHCARE INVESTORS, INC.

HISTORICAL FINANCIALS
Company Type: Public

Income Statement — FYE: December 31

	REVENUE ($mil)	NET INCOME ($mil)	NET PROFIT MARGIN	EMPLOYEES
12/20	437.5	66.1	15.1%	81
12/19	415.2	74.4	17.9%	77
12/18	422.5	56.2	13.3%	70
12/17	343.5	38.1	11.1%	63
12/16	241.0	29.9	12.4%	41
Annual Growth	16.1%	21.9%	—	18.6%

2020 Year-End Financials
Debt ratio: 32.6%
Return on equity: 2.6%
Cash ($ mil.): 2.5
Current Ratio: 0.12
Long-term debt ($ mil.): 1,438.8
No. of shares ($ mil.): 209.5
Dividends
 Yield: 5.1%
 Payout: 287.5%
Market value ($ mil.): 3,730.0

	STOCK PRICE ($) FY Close	P/E High/Low	PER SHARE ($) Earnings	Dividends	Book Value
12/20	17.80	65 36	0.32	0.92	12.60
12/19	18.94	49 40	0.39	0.92	12.68
12/18	16.03	60 48	0.30	0.92	13.04
12/17	17.99	95 75	0.23	0.91	13.63
12/16	18.96	100 72	0.22	0.90	12.79
Annual Growth	(1.6%)	— —	9.8%	0.6%	(0.4%)

Pinnacle Financial Partners Inc

Pinnacle Financial Partners is the holding company for Tennessee-based Pinnacle Bank, which has grown to about 120 offices in Tennessee, North Carolina, South Carolina, Virginia, Georgia, and Alabama since its founding in 2000. Serving consumers and small- to mid-sized business, the $38.5 billion financial institution provides standard services such as checking and savings accounts, CDs, credit cards, and loans and mortgages. The company also offers investment and trust services through Pinnacle Asset Management, while its insurance brokerage subsidiary, Miller Loughry Beach, specializes in property/casualty policies.

Operations
Pinnacle Financial Partners' commercial and industrial loans and commercial real estate loans (owner and non-owner occupied) account for 35% each, of its total portfolio of loans.

As part of its primary services to both individual and commercial clients, Tennessee-based subsidiary Pinnacle Bank provides core deposits, including savings, checking, interest-bearing checking, money market, and certificate of deposit accounts.

The bank's lending products include commercial, real estate, and consumer loans to individuals and small- to medium-sized businesses and professional entities. Additionally, it offers Pinnacle-branded consumer credit cards to select clients.

Pinnacle Bank contracts with Raymond James Financial Services, Inc. (RJFS), a registered broker-dealer and investment adviser, to offer and sell various securities and other financial products to the public through associates who are employed by both Pinnacle Bank and RJFS. RJFS is a subsidiary of Raymond James Financial, Inc.

Overall, approximately two-thirds of its sales were generated from loans, including fees.

Geographic Reach
Based in Tennessee, Pinnacle Financial Partners has about 120 offices, including nearly 50 offices in Tennessee, over 35 in North Carolina, some 20 in South Carolina, nine offices in Virginia, two in Georgia, and one in Alabama. It boasts locations in Nashville, Knoxville, Davidson, Murfreesboro, Chattanooga, Memphis, Greensboro, Highpoint, Charlotte, Concord, Gastonia, Roanoke, Winston, and Salem.

Sales and Marketing
Pinnacle Bank traditionally has obtained its deposits through personal solicitation by its officers and directors, although it has used media advertising more in recent years due to its advertising and banking sponsorship with the Tennessee Titans NFL Football team and the Memphis Grizzlies NBA basketball team.

Its convenience-centered products and services include 24-hour telephone and Internet banking, debit and credit cards, direct deposit, and cash management services.

Its marketing and other business development costs have risen in recent years: $12.9 million, $10.7 million, and $13.3 million in 2021, 2020, and 2019, respectively.

Financial Performance
The company's revenue has been rising in the last five years with an overall increase of 83% between 2017 and 2021. Net income follows a similar pattern but declined in 2020. Still it has an overall increase of 203% in the same period.

For the year ended December 31, 2021, it recorded net interest income of approximately $932.4 million, which resulted in a net interest margin of 3%. The increase in net interest income in 2021 as compared to 2020 was largely the result of lower cost of funds as short-term interest rates remain low and organic loan growth.

In 2021, the company had a net income of $527.3 million, a 69% increase from the previous year's net income of $312.3 million.

The company's cash at the end of 2021 was $4.1 billion. Operating activities generated $657.4 million, while investing activities used $3.6 billion, mainly for purchases of activities in securities available-for-sale. Financing activities provided another $3.1 billion.

Strategy
A substantial focus of Pinnacle's marketing and business strategy is to serve small to medium-sized businesses in its market areas. As a result, a relatively high percentage of its loan portfolio consists of commercial loans primarily to small to medium-sized businesses. The bank expects to seek to expand the amount of commercial and industrial loans and commercial real-estate loans in its portfolio during 2022. During periods of lower economic growth or challenging economic periods like those resulting from the COVID-19 pandemic, small to medium-sized businesses may be impacted more severely and more quickly than larger businesses.

Much of Pinnacle's organic loan growth that it experienced in recent years (and a key part of its loan growth strategy in 2022 and beyond) was the result not of strong loan demand but rather of its ability to attract experienced financial services professionals who have been able to attract customers from other financial institutions. Pinnacle's growth strategy necessarily entails growth in overhead expenses as it adds new offices and staff.

EXECUTIVES

Chairman, Subsidiary Officer, Director, Robert A. McCabe, $862,000 total compensation
President, Chief Executive Officer, Subsidiary Officer, Director, M. Terry Turner, $908,000 total compensation
Division Officer, Subsidiary Officer, Director, Richard D. Callicutt
Executive Vice President, Chief Financial Officer, Principal Accounting Officer, Harold R. Carpenter, $518,000 total compensation
Chief Credit Officer, Timothy H. Huestis
Director, Abney S. Boxley
Director, Charles E. Brock
Director, Renda J Burkhart
Director, Gregory L. Burns
Director, Marty G. Dickens
Director, Thomas C. Farnsworth
Director, Joseph C. Galante
Director, Glenda Baskin Glover
Director, David B. Ingram
Director, Decosta E. Jenkins
Director, G. Kennedy Thompson
Director, Reese L. Smith
Auditors : Crowe LLP

LOCATIONS

HQ: Pinnacle Financial Partners Inc
150 Third Avenue South, Suite 900, Nashville, TN 37201
Phone: 615 744-3700
Web: www.pnfp.com

PRODUCTS/OPERATIONS

2014 Revenue

	% of total
Interest Income	80
Non-interest Income	20
Total	100

Selected Subsidiaries
Pinnacle Advisory Services, Inc.
Pinnacle Credit Enhancement Holdings, Inc.
Pinnacle National Bank
    Miller & Loughry, Inc. (dba Miller Loughry Beach)
    PFP Title Company
    Pinnacle Community Development Corporation
    Pinnacle Nashville Real Estate, Inc.
    Pinnacle Rutherford Real Estate, Inc.
    Pinnacle Rutherford Towers, Inc.
    Pinnacle Service Company, Inc.
PNFP Insurance, Inc.

COMPETITORS

CITY HOLDING COMPANY
F.N.B. CORPORATION
FINANCIAL INSTITUTIONS, INC.
FIRST HORIZON CORPORATION
FIRST MIDWEST BANCORP, INC.
HERITAGE FINANCIAL CORPORATION
MUFG AMERICAS HOLDINGS CORPORATION
OLD NATIONAL BANCORP

PRIVATEBANCORP, INC.
TRUIST FINANCIAL CORPORATION

HISTORICAL FINANCIALS
Company Type: Public

Income Statement — FYE: December 31

	ASSETS ($mil)	NET INCOME ($mil)	INCOME AS % OF ASSETS	EMPLOYEES
12/20	34,932.8	312.3	0.9%	2,634
12/19	27,805.4	400.8	1.4%	2,487
12/18	25,031.0	359.4	1.4%	2,297
12/17	22,205.6	173.9	0.8%	2,132
12/16	11,194.6	127.2	1.1%	1,180
Annual Growth	32.9%	25.2%	—	22.2%

2020 Year-End Financials
Return on assets: 0.9%
Return on equity: 6.7%
Long-term debt ($ mil.): —
No. of shares ($ mil.): 75.8
Sales ($ mil.): 1,338.8
Dividends
 Yield: 0.9%
 Payout: 16.5%
Market value ($ mil.): 4,885.0

	STOCK PRICE ($) FY Close	P/E High/Low		PER SHARE ($) Earnings	Dividends	Book Value
12/20	64.40	16	8	4.03	0.64	64.66
12/19	64.00	12	9	5.22	0.64	56.89
12/18	46.10	15	9	4.64	0.58	51.18
12/17	66.30	26	21	2.70	0.56	47.70
12/16	69.30	24	15	2.91	0.56	32.28
Annual Growth	(1.8%)	—	—	8.5%	3.4%	19.0%

Pinterest Inc

EXECUTIVES

Chairman, President, Director, Benjamin Silbermann, $197,100 total compensation
Chief Executive Officer, Director, William J. Ready
Products Senior Vice President, Products Head, Naveen Gavini
Chief Accounting Officer, Andrea Acosta
Lead Independent Director, Director, Andrea Wishom
Director, Marc S. Steinberg
Director, Jeffrey D. Jordan
Director, Leslie J. Kilgore
Director, Jeremy S. Levine
Director, Gokul Rajaram
Director, Fredric G. Reynolds
Director, Evan Sharp
Director, Salaam Coleman Smith
Auditors : Ernst & Young LLP

LOCATIONS

HQ: Pinterest Inc
 505 Brannan Street, San Francisco, CA 94107
Phone: 415 762-7100
Web: www.pinterest.com

HISTORICAL FINANCIALS
Company Type: Public

Income Statement — FYE: December 31

	REVENUE ($mil)	NET INCOME ($mil)	NET PROFIT MARGIN	EMPLOYEES
12/21	2,578.0	316.4	12.3%	3,225
12/20	1,692.6	(128.3)	—	2,545
12/19	1,142.7	(1,361.3)	—	2,217
12/18	755.9	(62.9)	—	1,797
12/17	472.8	(130.0)	—	0
Annual Growth	52.8%	—	—	—

2021 Year-End Financials
Debt ratio: —
Return on equity: 11.9%
Cash ($ mil.): 1,419.6
Current Ratio: 12.25
Long-term debt ($ mil.): —
No. of shares ($ mil.): 656.8
Dividends
 Yield: —
 Payout: —
Market value ($ mil.): 23,877.0

	STOCK PRICE ($) FY Close	P/E High/Low		PER SHARE ($) Earnings	Dividends	Book Value
12/21	36.35	182	71	0.46	0.00	4.63
12/20	65.90	—	—	(0.22)	0.00	3.58
12/19	18.64	—	—	(3.24)	0.00	3.55
Annual Growth	39.6%	—	—	—	—	14.1%

Piper Sandler Companies

Investment bank Piper Sandler Companies specializes in supplying clients with mergers and acquisitions advice, financing, and industry research. Founded in 1895, Piper Sandler provides a broad set of products and services, including financial advisory services; equity and debt capital markets products; public finance services; equity research and institutional brokerage; fixed income services; and private equity strategies. Piper Sandler targets a variety of clients including corporations, government entities, not-for-profits, and middle-market companies across the consumer, financial services, healthcare, technology, and industrial sectors. Majority of its revenue comes from US customers.

Operations
Piper Sandler operates in one reportable segment providing investment banking and institutional sales, trading and research services for various equity and fixed income products.

Investment Banking provides advisory services, which includes mergers and acquisitions; equity and debt private placements; and debt and restructuring advisory for its corporate clients. For its government and non-profit clients, it underwrite municipal issuances, provide municipal financial advisory and loan placement services, and offer various over-the-counter derivative products. Its public finance investment banking capabilities focus on state and local governments, cultural and social service non-profit entities, special districts, project financings, and the education, healthcare, hospitality, senior living and transportation sectors.

Through Equity and Fixed Income Institutional Brokerage, Piper Sandler offers equity and fixed income advisory and trade execution services for institutional investors and government and non-profit entities. Fixed income services provides advice on balance sheet management, investment strategy and customized portfolio solutions.

Alternative Asset Management Funds involve alternative asset management funds in merchant banking and healthcare in order to invest firm capital and to manage capital from outside investors.

Overall, its investment banking accounts for about 75% total revenue, while some 20% comes from institutional brokerage, and investment income accounts for the remaining revenue.

Geographic Reach
Headquartered in Minneapolis, Minnesota Piper Sandler conduct its operations through some 65 principal offices in about 30 US states, and the District of Columbia, and in London, Aberdeen and Hong Kong.

The majority of its revenue comes from US.

Sales and Marketing
Piper Sandler serves corporations, private equity groups, public entities, non-profit entities and institutional investors.

Financial Performance
Net revenues from continuing operations for the year ended December 31, 2021 increased 64% to $2 billion, compared with $1.2 billion in the year-ago period. In 2021, investment banking revenues increased 81% to $1.6 billion, compared with $858.5 million in 2020, driven by a significant increase in advisory services revenues, as well as higher corporate and municipal financing revenues.

In 2021, the company had a net income of $330.4 million, a 569% increase from the previous year's net income of $49.4 million.

The company's cash at the end of 2021 was $971 million. Operating activities generated $707.1 million, while investing activities used $20.6 million, mainly for purchases of fixed assets. Financing activities used another $223.1 million, primarily for payment of cash dividend.

Strategy
The company's long-term strategic objectives are to drive revenue growth, build a stronger and more durable platform, continue to gain market share, and maximize shareholder value. In order to meet these objectives, we are focused on the following: continuing to transform its business through strategic investments and selectively adding partners who share its client-centric culture and who can leverage the company's platform to better serve clients; growing its investment

banking platform through market share gains, accretive combinations, developing internal talent, and continued sector and geographic expansion. The company also believes there is an opportunity to capitalize on the strength of its US franchises by expanding in Europe; leveraging the scale within the equity brokerage and fixed income services platforms, driven by its recently expanded client base and product offerings, to grow market share; and prudently managing capital to maintain its balance sheet strength with ample liquidity and flexibility through all market conditions.

Mergers and Acquisitions

In 2022, Piper Sandler completes the acquisition of Cornerstone Macro, an independent research firm that offers best-in-class macro research and equity derivatives trading to institutional investors. The acquisition further strengthens Piper Sandler's position as a top institutional equities research, sales, and trading platform.

In early 2022, Piper Sandler agreed to acquire Stamford Partners, a London-based entrepreneurial, specialist M&A boutique offering high quality investment banking services to European food & beverage as well as related consumer sectors. "Stamford Partners offers differentiated, best-in-class M&A advisory services tailored to the unique needs of clients in the European consumer industry. The addition is complementary to our existing consumer practice and creates significant opportunities to further expand our reach in partnership with them," said James Baker, global co-head of investment banking at Piper Sandler.

HISTORY

In 1913 Harry Piper and Palmer Jaffray founded a commercial paper brokerage that helped finance companies like Pillsbury and Archer-Daniels-Midland. It soon moved into public finance and underwriting. It gained a seat on the NYSE with its purchase of Hopwood & Co., which was hard hit by the 1929 crash. Piper Jaffray & Hopwood grew over the next 40 years, going public in 1971. Three years later it became Piper Jaffray.

During the 1980s boom Piper Jaffray, still managed by the Piper family, expanded into asset management and mutual funds. It was relatively unscathed by the 1987 crash.

Real trouble hit in 1994 when a derivatives-heavy bond mutual fund foundered. Investors, claiming they were uninformed of the risk, brought a class-action suit against the firm, which paid out more than $100 million in settlements beginning in 1995.

In 1997 Piper Jaffray began offering new classes of shares of its mutual funds to provide more fee options for investors. The SEC sued the company for fraud related to the 1994 mutual fund debacle in 1998.

That year U. S. Bancorp, looking to expand its securities business, bought the company and bundled its own investment operations into U. S. Bancorp Piper Jaffray. In 1999 the unit expanded with the purchase of investment banker Libra Investments. The firm also entered an alliance with Tel Aviv-based investment bank Nessuah Zannex to back technology and health care ventures in Israel.

Piper Jaffray traditionally has taken pride in its investment research, yet it was one of several investment banks scrutinized for alleged conflicts-of-interest between research and I-banking operations. In 2003 the firm was fined $25 million, and required to pay an additional $7.5 million to provide independent research for investors. As part of the settlement, the company combined its research functions into a single group, and implemented firewalls between its analysts and investment bankers. Losing money, Piper Jaffray was spun off from U.S. Bancorp and returned to the publicly traded arena that same year.

Piper Jaffray sold its Private Client business, which offered mutual funds, securities, and annuities to individual investors, to UBS Financial Services in 2006. Piper Jaffray used proceeds from the sale of the unit, which included some 90 branches mainly west of the Mississippi, to expand its industry focus. It built its asset management business with the 2007 purchases of St. Louis-based Fiduciary Asset Management (FAMCO), which brought in some $6 billion of assets under management, and Hong Kong-based Goldbond Capital.

EXECUTIVES

Chairman, Chief Executive Officer, Director, Chad R. Abraham, $550,000 total compensation
Division Officer, Vice-Chairman, Director, Jonathan J. Doyle
President, Debbra L. Schoneman, $500,000 total compensation
Chief Financial Officer, Timothy L. Carter, $425,000 total compensation
General Counsel, Secretary, John W. Geelan, $300,000 total compensation
Division Officer, James P. Baker
Lead Director, Director, Philip E. Soran
Director, Brian R. Sterling
Director, Robbin Mitchell
Director, William R. Fitzgerald
Director, Victoria M. Holt
Director, Thomas S. Schreier
Director, Sherry M. Smith
Director, Scott C. Taylor
Auditors : Ernst & Young LLP

LOCATIONS

HQ: Piper Sandler Companies
800 Nicollet Mall, Suite 900, Minneapolis, MN 55402
Phone: 612 303-6000
Web: www.piperjaffray.com

PRODUCTS/OPERATIONS

2018 Revenue

	$ mil.	% of total
Investment banking	589	74
Institutional brokerage	124.5	15
Asset management	49.8	6
Interest	32.7	4
Other	4.9	1
Adjustments	(16.5)	-
Total	784.4	100

Selected Services
Investment Banking
    Services
    Mergers & Acquisitions
    Capital Markets
    Private Placements
    Restructuring
    Debt Advisory
    Corporate & Venture Services
Public Finance
    Government Expertise
    Local Municipalities
    States & State Agencies

COMPETITORS

ARES CAPITAL CORPORATION
BLACKROCK, INC.
COWEN INC.
E TRADE FINANCIAL CORPORATION
EVERCORE INC.
OPPENHEIMER HOLDINGS INC.
RAYMOND JAMES FINANCIAL, INC.
SCHRODERS PLC
STIFEL FINANCIAL CORP.
THE ZIEGLER COMPANIES INC

HISTORICAL FINANCIALS

Company Type: Public

Income Statement   FYE: December 31

	REVENUE ($mil)	NET INCOME ($mil)	NET PROFIT MARGIN	EMPLOYEES
12/20	1,252.6	40.5	3.2%	1,511
12/19	846.2	111.7	13.2%	1,565
12/18	800.9	57.0	7.1%	1,262
12/17	895.1	(61.9)	—	1,301
12/16	769.8	(21.9)	—	1,315
Annual Growth	12.9%	—	—	3.5%

2020 Year-End Financials

Debt ratio: 17.3%
Return on equity: 5.1%
Cash ($ mil.): 507.9
Current Ratio: 1.29
Long-term debt ($ mil.): 195
No. of shares ($ mil.): 13.7
Dividends
  Yield: 1.9%
  Payout: 73.5%
Market value ($ mil.): 1,390.0

	STOCK PRICE ($) FY Close	P/E High/Low		PER SHARE ($) Earnings	Dividends	Book Value
12/20	100.90	36	12	2.72	2.00	60.21
12/19	79.94	10	8	7.69	2.51	53.31
12/18	65.84	26	16	3.72	3.12	52.13
12/17	86.25	—	—	(5.07)	1.25	53.70
12/16	72.50	—	—	(1.73)	0.00	61.27
Annual Growth	8.6%	—	—	—	—	(0.4%)

PJT Partners Inc

EXECUTIVES

Chairman, Chief Executive Officer, Director, Paul J. Taubman, $1,000,000 total compensation
Chief Financial Officer, Helen T. Meates, $500,000 total compensation
General Counsel, James W. Cuminale, $500,000 total compensation
Managing Partner, Ji-Yeun Lee, $1,000,000 total compensation
Managing Director, Corporate Secretary, General Counsel, Salvatore Rappa
Lead Director, Director, Dennis S. Hersch
Director, James Costos
Director, Emily K. Rafferty
Director, Thomas M. Ryan
Director, Grace Reksten Skaugen
Director, Kenneth C. Whitney
Auditors : DELOITTE & TOUCHE LLP

LOCATIONS

HQ: PJT Partners Inc
  280 Park Avenue, New York, NY 10017
Phone: 212 364-7800
Web: www.pjtpartners.com

HISTORICAL FINANCIALS
Company Type: Public

Income Statement — FYE: December 31

	REVENUE ($mil)	NET INCOME ($mil)	NET PROFIT MARGIN	EMPLOYEES
12/20	1,052.3	117.5	11.2%	749
12/19	717.6	29.5	4.1%	678
12/18	580.2	27.1	4.7%	590
12/17	499.2	(32.5)	—	473
12/16	499.4	(3.0)	—	419
Annual Growth	20.5%	—	—	15.6%

2020 Year-End Financials
Debt ratio: —
Return on equity: —
Cash ($ mil.): 299.5
Current Ratio: 2.22
Long-term debt ($ mil.): —
No. of shares ($ mil.): 23.8
Dividends
 Yield: 0.2%
 Payout: 4.5%
Market value ($ mil.): 1,792.0

	STOCK PRICE ($) FY Close	P/E High/Low		PER SHARE ($) Earnings	Dividends	Book Value
12/20	75.25	16	5	4.40	0.20	6.48
12/19	45.13	38	29	1.21	0.20	1.36
12/18	38.76	49	29	1.16	0.20	(3.83)
12/17	45.60	—	—	(1.73)	0.20	(8.48)
12/16	30.88	—	—	(0.17)	0.20	(0.48)
Annual Growth	24.9%	—	—	—	0.0%	—

Plumas Bancorp Inc

Plumas Bancorp is the holding company for Plumas Bank, which serves individuals and businesses in the northeastern corner of California, from Lake Tahoe to the Oregon border. Through more than a dozen branches, the bank offers deposit products such as checking, savings, and retirement accounts and certificates of deposit. Loans secured by real estate account for more than half of Plumas Bank's loan portfolio; combined, commercial and agricultural loans make up about a quarter. The bank writes consumer loans, as well. It also provides access to investment products and services such as financial planning, mutual funds, and annuities.

EXECUTIVES

Chairman, Daniel E. West
Vice-Chairman, Director, Robert J. McClintock
President, Chief Executive Officer, Subsidiary Officer, Andrew J. Ryback, $300,009 total compensation
Executive Vice President, Chief Financial Officer, Controller, Subsidiary Officer, Richard L. Belstock, $190,100 total compensation
Subsidiary Officer, B. J. North, $182,450 total compensation
Subsidiary Officer, Dennis C. Irvine, $129,966 total compensation
Subsidiary Officer, Kerry Dale Wilson, $135,000 total compensation
Director, Gerald W. Fletcher
Director, Michonne R Ascuaga
Director, Steven M. Coldani
Director, William E. Elliott, $171,142 total compensation
Director, Heidei S Gansert
Director, Richard F. Kenny
Director, Terrance J. Reeson
Auditors : Eide Bailly LLP

LOCATIONS

HQ: Plumas Bancorp Inc
  5525 Kietzke Lane, Suite 100, Reno, NV 89511
Phone: 775 786-0907
Web: www.plumasbank.com

COMPETITORS

CITIZENS BANK INC
COMMUNITY SHORES BANK CORPORATION
DENMARK BANCSHARES, INC.
EMCLAIRE FINANCIAL CORP.
FIRST NORTHERN COMMUNITY BANCORP

HISTORICAL FINANCIALS
Company Type: Public

Income Statement — FYE: December 31

	ASSETS ($mil)	NET INCOME ($mil)	INCOME AS % OF ASSETS	EMPLOYEES
12/20	1,111.5	14.4	1.3%	177
12/19	865.1	15.5	1.8%	183
12/18	824.3	13.9	1.7%	174
12/17	745.4	8.1	1.1%	161
12/16	657.9	7.4	1.1%	155
Annual Growth	14.0%	18.0%	—	3.4%

2020 Year-End Financials
Return on assets: 1.4%
Return on equity: 15.6%
Long-term debt ($ mil.): —
No. of shares ($ mil.): 5.1
Sales ($ mil.): 48
Dividends
 Yield: 1.5%
 Payout: 13.3%
Market value ($ mil.): 122.0

	STOCK PRICE ($) FY Close	P/E High/Low		PER SHARE ($) Earnings	Dividends	Book Value
12/20	23.50	10	5	2.77	0.36	19.33
12/19	26.38	9	7	2.97	0.46	16.36
12/18	22.71	11	8	2.68	0.36	13.03
12/17	23.20	14	10	1.58	0.28	11.00
12/16	19.00	12	5	1.47	0.10	9.80
Annual Growth	5.5%	—	—	17.2%	37.7%	18.5%

Pool Corp

Pool Corporation is the world's largest wholesale distributor of swimming pool supplies, equipment and related leisure products and is one of the leading distributors of irrigation and landscape products in the US. It operates some 410 service centers throughout the North America, Europe, and Australia, serving some wholesale customers such as pool builders and remodelers, retail pool stores, and pool repair and service companies. Pool Corporation's more than 200,000 products include private-label and name-brand pool maintenance items (chemicals, cleaners), equipment (pumps, filters), accessories (heaters, lights), and packaged pool kits. Founded in 1993 as SCP Holding, Pool Corporation generates most of its sales in the US.

Operations

Pool Corporation operates through five distribution networks: SCP Distributors, Superior Pool Products, Horizon Distributors, National Pool Tile, and Sun Wholesale Supply.

The SCP Distribution and Superior Pool Products networks offer pool supplies, equipment, and related leisure products. Horizon Distributors locations sell supply irrigation and related products and National Pool Tile stores feature tile, decking materials, and interior pool finishes, as well as hardscape and natural stone products, pool supplies, and equipment.

Pool Corporation has some 600 product lines and more than 50 product categories. Its largest product category is pool and hot tub chemicals, which account for some 10% of total sales.

The company's largest suppliers include Pentair plc (approximately 20%), Hayward Pool Products (some 10%), and Zodiac Pool Systems (about 10%).

Geographic Reach

The US accounts for some 90% of Pool Corporation's sales. The company's largest markets -- with the highest concentration of swimming pools -- are California, Florida, Texas, and Arizona, representing about 55% of total sales.

Beyond the US, Covington, Louisiana-based Pool Corporation has operations in Australia, Canada, Mexico, and more than half a dozen countries in Europe (Belgium, Croatia, France, Germany, Italy, Portugal,

Spain, and the UK).

The company's network of about 400 sales centers spans the Americas, Europe, and Australia.

Sales and Marketing

Pool Corporation sells its products primarily to swimming pool remodelers and builders; specialty retailers that sell swimming pool supplies; swimming pool repair and service businesses; irrigation construction and landscape maintenance contractors; and commercial customers who service large commercial installations such as hotels, universities and community recreational facilities. Most customers are small, family-owned businesses with relatively limited capital resources.

The company's advertising costs were $9.4 million, $6.8 million, and $7.8 million for the years 2021, 2020, and 2019, respectively.

Financial Performance

Net sales increased 35% to $5.3 billion for the year ended December 31, 2021 compared to $3.9 billion in 2020, while base business sales increased 29%. Sales were driven by strong customer demand for outdoor living products throughout the year and benefited from inflation and warmer weather trends across most of the United States.

In 2021, the company had a net income of $650.6 million, a 77% increase from the previous year's net income of $366.7 million.

The company's cash at the end of 2021 was $24.3 million. Operating activities generated $313.5 million, while investing activities used $849.6 million, mainly for acquisition of businesses. Financing activities provided another $526.1 million.

Strategy

The company's mission is to provide exceptional value to its customers and suppliers, creating exceptional return to its shareholders, while providing exceptional opportunities to its employees. Pool Corporation's core strategies are as follows: to promote the growth of its industry; to promote the growth of its customers' businesses; and to continuously strive to operate more effectively.

Mergers and Acquisitions

In late 2021, Pool Corporation has completed its previously announced acquisition of Largo, Florida-based Porpoise Pool & Patio, Inc. (Porpoise). Porpoise's primary operations consist of Sun Wholesale Supply, Inc., a wholesale distributor of swimming pool and outdoor-living products, including a specialty chemical packaging operation. The acquisition strengthens both companies' distribution networks, broadens POOLCORP's sales channels and expansion opportunities in key pool markets, and provides Porpoise Pool & Patio with access to a convenient and expanded range of products through POOLCORP's sales center network. Terms were not disclosed.

Company Background

Pool Corporation traces its history to Frank St. Romain, who began his career in the pool distribution industry as a warehouse manager. Romain and partner Richard Smith established their own company, South Central Pool Supply, in 1981. It grew, opening sales centers across the southeastern US.

Industry veteran Wilson B. "Rusty" Sexton joined the company as a consultant in 1990 and became CEO of the entity created when the company partnered with investment firm Code Hennessy & Simmons in 1993 -- SCP Pool Corporation.

SCP Pool went public in 1995. It took the Pool Corporation name in 2006.

EXECUTIVES

Chairman, Lead Independent Director, Director, John E. Stokely

Vice-Chairman, Director, Manuel J. Perez de la Mesa, $500,000 total compensation

President, Chief Executive Officer, Director, Peter D. Arvan, $440,000 total compensation

Group Vice President, Kenneth G. St. Romain, $310,000 total compensation

Chief Accounting Officer, Corporate Controller, Principal Accounting Officer, Walker F. Saik

Vice President, Corporate Secretary, Chief Legal Officer, Jennifer M. Neil, $190,000 total compensation

Vice President, Chief Financial Officer, Treasurer, Melanie M. Housey Hart

Director, Martha Gervasi

Director, Debra S. Oler

Director, Robert C. Sledd

Director, David G. Whalen

Director, Carlos A. Sabater

Director, James D. Hope

Auditors : Ernst & Young LLP

LOCATIONS

HQ: Pool Corp
  109 Northpark Boulevard, Covington, LA 70433-5001
Phone: 985 892-5521   **Fax:** 985 892-2438
Web: www.poolcorp.com

2018 Sales

	$ mil.	% of total
US	2,720.1	91
International	278.0	9
Total	2,998.1	100

PRODUCTS/OPERATIONS

Selected Products
ASME heaters
Building materials
Chemicals
Cleaners
Commercial pumps
Decking materials
Electrical supplies
Filters
Grills
Hardscapes
Heaters
irrigation and landscape products
Lights
Liners
Natural stone
Packaged pools
Parts and supplies
Pumps
Recreational products
Replacement parts
Repair parts
Spas and spa accessories
Swimming pool equipment and accessories
Tiles
Walls

COMPETITORS

ALLIANCE LAUNDRY HOLDINGS LLC
ATLANTIC DIVING SUPPLY, INC.
BERETTA U.S.A. CORP.
FERGUSON ENTERPRISES, LLC
HD SUPPLY HOLDINGS, INC.
KING PAR, LLC
LESLIE'S POOLMART, INC.
MAURICE SPORTING GOODS OF DELAWARE, INC.
RAWLINGS SPORTING GOODS COMPANY, INC.
WILSON SPORTING GOODS CO.

HISTORICAL FINANCIALS

Company Type: Public

Income Statement
FYE: December 31

	REVENUE ($mil)	NET INCOME ($mil)	NET PROFIT MARGIN	EMPLOYEES
12/20	3,936.6	366.7	9.3%	4,500
12/19	3,199.5	261.5	8.2%	4,500
12/18	2,998.0	234.4	7.8%	4,000
12/17	2,788.1	191.6	6.9%	4,000
12/16	2,570.8	148.9	5.8%	3,900
Annual Growth	11.2%	25.3%	—	3.6%

2020 Year-End Financials

Debt ratio: 23.9%
Return on equity: 69.6%
Cash ($ mil.): 34.1
Current Ratio: 2.32
Long-term debt ($ mil.): 404.1
No. of shares ($ mil.): 40.2
Dividends
  Yield: 0.6%
  Payout: 28.7%
Market value ($ mil.): 14,986.0

	STOCK PRICE ($) FY Close	P/E High/Low		PER SHARE ($) Earnings	Dividends	Book Value
12/20	372.50	42	18	8.97	2.29	15.89
12/19	212.38	33	22	6.40	2.10	10.24
12/18	148.65	30	22	5.62	1.72	5.66
12/17	129.65	28	21	4.51	1.42	5.55
12/16	104.34	30	21	3.47	1.19	4.99
Annual Growth	37.5%	—	—	26.8%	17.8%	33.6%

PotlatchDeltic Corp

PotlatchDeltic Corporation (formerly Potlatch Corporation) is a real estate investment trust (REIT) harvests timber from some 1.8 million acres of hardwood and softwood forestland in Alabama, Arkansas, Idaho, Mississippi, Louisiana, and Minnesota; it claims to be the largest private landowner in Idaho. PotlatchDeltic operates six sawmills and an industrial grade plywood mill, a residential and commercial real estate development business and a rural timberland sales program. Beyond wood product sales, the company generates revenue by leasing its land for hunting, recreation, mineral rights, and carbon sequestration. It also sells real estate through PotlatchDeltic TRS.

Operations

PotlatchDeltic operates three main business segments: Wood Products, Timberlands and Real Estates.

Its Wood Products segment, which made up of about 65% of its revenue, makes and sells lumber, plywood, and residual products. Its Timberlands segment (some 30% of revenue) manages timberland leases it for hunting, recreation, mineral rights, biomass production, and carbon sequestration. The real estate segment (about 5% of revenue) sells non-strategic or low-revenue generating land holdings through PotlatchDeltic TRS.

Geographic Reach

Washington-based PotlatchDeltic harvested almost all of its revenue from sales in the US. The company have sawmills in Alabama, Arkansas, Idaho, Louisiana, Mississippi, and Minnesota.

Sales and Marketing

The company sells its products directly through its sales offices to end users, retailers, or national wholesalers. Its products are mostly used in home building, industrial products, or other construction. Timberlands' customers range in size from small operators to multinational corporations.

Financial Performance

Revenues were approximately $1.3 billion, an increase of $296.5 million compared to 2020, primarily due to historically high lumber and Idaho sawlog prices in 2021. These increases were partially offset by lower lumber shipments which were impacted by the loss of production at its Ola, Arkansas sawmill following a fire in June 2021.

Net income for fiscal 2021 increased to $423.9 million compared from the prior year with $166.8 million.

Cash held by the company at the end of fiscal 2021 increased to $296.8 million. Cash provided by operations was $504.9 million while cash used for investing activities were $59.1 million and $401.3 million, respectively. Main uses of cash were property, plant and equipment additions; and dividends to common stockholders.

Strategy

The company's business strategy encompasses the following key elements: timberlands provide stability; leverage to lumber prices; integrated timberlands and wood products operating model; efficient and productive wood products facilities; capturing incremental value of its real estate holdings; pursuing attractive acquisitions; committed to responsible environmental, social and governance values.

Internal log sales to the company's mills comprised 37% of its Timberlands revenues in 2021. This represented 51% of its mill needs on a volume basis. This strategy enables the company to maximize the value of its assets, and, because Potlatchdeltic are a net log buyer in the South, its integrated model provides a natural hedge against southern sawlog prices that remain below long-term levels.

Company Background

Founded in 1903 by Frederick Weyerhaeuser, Potlatch have a rich history in timberland management and forest products. The Potlatch Lumber Company was founded along the banks of the Palouse River in North Central Idaho. The rugged and colorful lumberjacks and lumber mill workers from its early founding years transitioned into modern day forestry professionals and wood products experts. Both were and continue to be admirers of the trees and of the forests where they grow.

HISTORY

Lumber magnate Frederick Weyerhaeuser led a swarm of midwestern lumber companies into virgin northern Idaho forests at the turn of the 20th century. Two primary rivals -- William Deary of Northland Pine Company (a firm helped by Weyerhaeuser) and Henry Turrish of Wisconsin Log & Lumber -- bought thousands of acres of white pine around the state's Palouse, Potlatch, and Elk river basins. They kept land prices down by purchasing it together. In 1903 they merged more than 100,000 acres and created Potlatch Lumber. Weyerhaeuser's son Charles served as president.

Potlatch struggled for three decades in the high-risk lumber business. Maintaining a mill and a company town (Potlatch, Idaho) was expensive, and the company's policy of harvesting all tree varieties instead of those in demand didn't help. With the opening of the Panama Canal in 1914, Pacific Coast companies were able to undercut Potlatch in eastern markets by using the cheap transportation alternative. Before his death in 1914, Weyerhaeuser reportedly referred to Potlatch as an appropriate name for a company that spent piles of money with miniscule returns. To survive the Depression, the company merged with two major competitors, Clearwater and Edward Rutledge, in 1931. The new company, Potlatch Forests, was headed by Weyerhaeuser's descendants.

The WWII boom helped Potlatch raise badly needed profits from lumber orders. Afterwards, the company introduced new products, including paperboard used in milk cartons, plywood, and laminated decking. It expanded its timber reserves through acquisitions in Arkansas and Minnesota. In the 1960s Potlatch bought Clearwater Tissue Mills. The company moved its headquarters to San Francisco in 1965 and changed its name in 1973 to Potlatch Corporation.

Richard Madden became chairman and CEO in 1971 and reduced operations from 20 product lines to four -- wood, printed papers, pulp and paperboard, and tissue. The company emphasized capital expenditures, such as its 1981 construction of the first US plant to make plywood-alternative oriented strand board.

In 1994 Madden retired and COO Pendleton Siegel succeeded him. In 1997 the company moved its headquarters to Spokane, Washington; the following year it announced plans to spend more than $200 million to modernize and expand its Cloquet, Minnesota, pulp mill.

Potlatch and Anderson-Tully Company hatched a plan in 1998 to combine their Arkansas timber holdings into the Timberland Growth Corporation, the first public real estate investment trust (REIT) to focus on timber ownership. The plan fell apart in 1999, however, because of a weak timber market in Asia and weakened confidence in US markets after declines in the autumn of 1998.

The company's upgrade of its Cloquet pulp mill (including a new pulp machine) was completed in late 1999. Poor performance by the company's Minnesota pulp and paper division in 2000 led the company to trim about 300 jobs. It eliminated an additional 124 positions early in 2001.

In 2002 Potlatch sold its Cloquet, Minnesota, coated fine pulp and printing papers facilities to a subsidiary of Sappi Limited for $480 million in cash. Early the next year the company sold its Brainerd, Minnesota, paper mill and related assets to Missota Paper Company for $4.44 million in cash.

The company reorganized itself as a REIT in 2006. Under this arrangement, Potlatch was able to derive tax benefits from its timberland holdings without having to divest its non-real estate operations. It handled those operations through taxable subsidiary Potlatch Forest Products. As a result, much of the company's activities became geared toward shifting around its forestland holdings.

Pendleton Siegel stepped down as chairman and CEO in 2006. He was succeeded by Michael Covey, a 23-year veteran of competitor Plum Creek Timber.

In 2007, Potlatch acquired more than 75,000 acres of Wisconsin forestland in a deal worth about $65 million. It picked up more forestland the following year, when it acquired about 180,000 acres in central Idaho from Western Pacific Timber.

Soon after the 2008 financial crisis, softened demand in the US brought on by the weak housing market compelled the company to curtail some of its plywood and lumber production operations. It cut or halted production at many of its facilities in 2009 (but did not do so in 2010). It closed down an Arkansas lumber mill in 2008 and sold the property two years later. The company also sold its particleboard plant and a railroad in Idaho in 2010.

In 2012 the REIT completed two timberland purchases -- totaling 9,285 acres -- in and around land it owns in Arkansas for a total consideration of $11.8 million.

EXECUTIVES

Chairperson, Director, Michael J. Covey, $863,154 total compensation
Finance President, Finance Chief Executive Officer, Eric J. Cremers, $577,046 total compensation
Vice President, Chief Financial Officer, Jerald W. Richards, $375,076 total compensation
Real Estate Vice President, Lake States Resource Vice President, William R. DeReu, $215,129 total compensation
Vice President, Corporate Secretary, General Counsel, Lorrie D. Scott, $308,242 total compensation
Timberlands Vice President, Darin R. Ball, $276,000 total compensation
Vice President, General Counsel, Corporate Secretary, Michele L. Tyler
Controller, Principal Accounting Officer, Wayne Wasechek
Division Officer, Ashlee Townsend Cribb
Director, Linda M. Breard
Director, Anne L. Alonzo
Director, William L. Driscoll
Director, Lawrence S. Peiros
Director, D. Mark Leland
Director, R. Hunter Pierson
Director, James M. DeCosmo
Director, Lenore M. Sullivan
Auditors : KPMG LLP

LOCATIONS

HQ: PotlatchDeltic Corp
601 West First Avenue, Suite 1600, Spokane, WA 99201
Phone: 509 835-1500
Web: www.potlatch.com

PRODUCTS/OPERATIONS

2015 Sales

	$ mil.	% of total
Wood Products	336.3	53
Resource	263.9	42
Real estate	29.0	5
Intersegment eliminations	(53.7)	-
Total	575.3	100

COMPETITORS

BOISE CASCADE COMPANY
COLVILLE TRIBAL ENTERPRISE CORPORATION
DELTIC TIMBER CORPORATION
INCH KENNETH KAJANG RUBBER PUBLIC LTD CO.
Imperial Ginseng Products Ltd
LOUISIANA-PACIFIC CORPORATION
RAYONIER INC.
Resolute Forest Products Inc
WEYERHAEUSER COMPANY
West Fraser Timber Co. Ltd

HISTORICAL FINANCIALS
Company Type: Public

Income Statement FYE: December 31

	REVENUE ($mil)	NET INCOME ($mil)	NET PROFIT MARGIN	EMPLOYEES
12/21	1,337.4	423.8	31.7%	1,299
12/20	1,040.9	166.8	16.0%	1,316
12/19	827.0	55.6	6.7%	1,307
12/18	974.5	122.8	12.6%	1,471
12/17	678.5	86.4	12.7%	963
Annual Growth	18.5%	48.8%	—	7.8%

2021 Year-End Financials

Debt ratio: 29.9%
Return on equity: 29.9%
Cash ($ mil.): 296.1
Current Ratio: 3.34
Long-term debt ($ mil.): 715.2
No. of shares ($ mil.): 69.0
Dividends
Yield: 9.4%
Payout: 79.1%
Market value ($ mil.): 4,159.0

	STOCK PRICE ($) FY Close	P/E High	P/E Low	PER SHARE ($) Earnings	Dividends	Book Value
12/21	60.22	10	8	6.26	5.67	22.10
12/20	50.02	21	9	2.47	1.61	19.51
12/19	43.27	54	38	0.82	1.60	18.25
12/18	31.64	27	14	1.99	5.14	19.46
12/17	49.90	25	19	2.10	1.53	4.94
Annual Growth	4.8%	—	—	31.4%	38.9%	45.4%

Power Integrations Inc.

Power Integrations designs, develops and markets analog and mixed-signal integrated circuits (ICs) and other electronic components and circuitry used in high-voltage power conversion. A large percentage of its products are ICs used in AC-DC power supplies, which convert the high-voltage AC from a wall outlet to the low-voltage DC required by most electronic devices. It also offers high-voltage gate drivers?either standalone ICs or circuit boards containing ICs, electrical isolation components and other circuitry?used to operate high-voltage switches such as insulated-gate bipolar transistors (IGBTs) and silicon-carbide (SiC) MOSFETs. Power Integrations sells its chips to electronics manufacturers and distributors such Avnet. The company makes nearly all of its sales overseas.

Operations

The company is organized and operates as one reportable segment, the design, development, manufacture and marketing of integrated circuits and related components for use primarily in the high-voltage power conversion markets.

The fabless manufacturing model allows Power Integrations to focus on engineering and design and still have access to high-volume manufacturing capacity. Power Integrations relies on manufacturers to fabricate its chips: Lapis Semiconductor, Seiko Epson, and X-FAB. These contractors manufacture wafers using its proprietary high-voltage process technologies at fabrication facilities located in Japan, Germany and the United States.

Geographic Reach

Asia is Power Integrations' largest market, representing majority of sales (China and Hong Kong, the company's fastest-growing market, contribute nearly 65% of overall revenue). Europe and Americas account for over 5% and less than 5% of sales, respectively.

Power Integrations has principal executive, administrative, manufacturing and technical offices located in San Jose, California (headquarters). The company has research and development (R&D) facility in New Jersey and a test facility in Biel, Switzerland. The company also have administrative office space in Singapore and Switzerland, and R&D facilities in Canada, United Kingdom, the Philippines, and Malaysia.

Sales and Marketing

The company sell their products to original equipment manufacturers (OEMs), and merchant power-supply manufacturers through its direct sales staff and a worldwide network of independent sales representatives and distributors. Some 75% of the company's sales are made to distributors such as Avnet (which accounted for about 30% of revenue) and Honestar Technologies (around 15%), while the rest come from original equipment manufacturers and merchant power supply manufacturers.

In 2021, advertising costs amounted to $1.3 million and $1.2 million, and $1.4 million in 2020 and 2019, respectively.

Financial Performance

The company's revenue for fiscal 2021 increased to $703.3 million compared from the prior year with $488.3 million.

Net income for fiscal 2021 increased to $164.4 million compared from the prior year with $71.2 million.

Cash held by the company at the end of fiscal 2021 decreased to $158.1 million. Cash provided by operations was $230.9 million while cash used for investing and financing activities were $232.8 million and $98.8 million, respectively. Main uses of cash were purchases of marketable securities; and repurchase of common stock.

Strategy

Power Integrations' growth strategy includes the following elements: increase its penetration of the markets it serves; and increase the size of its addressable market.

Through its research and development efforts, Power Integrations seek to introduce more advanced products for these markets offering higher levels of integration and performance compared to earlier products. The company also continue to expand its sales and application-engineering staff and its network of distributors, as well as its offerings of technical documentation and design-support tools and services to help customers use its products. These tools and services include its PI Expert design software, which Power Integration offer free of charge, and its transformer-sample service.

Company Background

In 1988, Power Integrations founded by Klas Eklund, Art Fury and Steve Sharp. TOPSwitch family debuted as company's first commercial product in 1994. In 1997, Initial public offering on NASDAQ at $4/share (split-adjusted).

HISTORY

At the end of 2007 Power Integrations acquired Potentia Semiconductor, a Canadian developer of controller chips for high-power AC-DC power supplies. The company paid about $5.5 million in cash for Potentia.

In another example of the widening corporate scandals on options backdating, where executives and board members have skirted US regulations on the timing and purchasing of stock-option grants, Power Integrations reported in 2006 that its board of directors formed a special committee of independent directors to investigate company practices related to stock-option grants to executives and board members. Chairman Howard Earhart, a former CEO of Power Integrations, and CFO John Cobb resigned. The board soon after named Steven Sharp as non-executive chairman to succeed Earhart. Power Integrations later restated financial results for 2001 through 2004, and for the first three quarters of 2005.

The SEC's staff notified the company in 2007 that the commission's investigation into its past practices in granting stock options ended, without any enforcement action recommended against Power Integrations. The company still faces a probe by the US Department of Justice regarding stock options. In addition, Power Integrations is being audited by the Internal Revenue Service.

EXECUTIVES

Chairman, Director, William L. George
President, Chief Executive Officer, Director, Balu Balakrishnan, $592,673 total compensation
Finance Vice President, Finance Chief Financial Officer, Sandeep Nayyar, $362,942 total compensation
Technology Vice President, Radu Barsan, $337,846 total compensation
Product Development Vice President, David Matthews, $308,884 total compensation
Worldwide Sales Vice President, Yang Chiah Yee
Director, Nancy L. Gioia
Director, Wendy Arienzo
Director, Nicholas E. Brathwaite
Director, Anita Ganti
Director, Balakrishnan S. Iyer
Director, Necip Sayiner

Auditors: DELOITTE & TOUCHE LLP

LOCATIONS

HQ: Power Integrations Inc.
5245 Hellyer Avenue, San Jose, CA 95138
Phone: 408 414-9200 **Fax:** 408 414-9201
Web: www.power.com

2014 Sales

	% of total
Asia/Pacific	
China & Hong Kong	47
Taiwan	15
South Korea	11
Japan	5
Singapore	1
Europe	
Germany	2
Other countries	11
Americas	5
Other regions	3
Total	100

PRODUCTS/OPERATIONS

2014 Sales by Market

	% of total
Consumer	37
Industrial electronics	35
Communications	18
Computer	10
Total	100

Selected Products

AC-to-DC power conversion products (LinkSwitch)
DC-to-DC power conversion products (DPA-Switch)
Capacitor discharge ICs (CAPZero)
High-voltage analog ICs for power conversion (TOPSwitch, TinySwitch, Hiper, SENZero)
Off-line switcher ICs (PeakSwitch)

COMPETITORS

AMKOR TECHNOLOGY, INC.
BEL FUSE INC.
EXAR CORPORATION
INFINEON TECHNOLOGIES AMERICAS CORP.
IXYS, LLC
LINEAR TECHNOLOGY LLC
ON SEMICONDUCTOR CORPORATION
RENESAS ELECTRONICS AMERICA INC.
SEMTECH CORPORATION
VICOR CORPORATION

HISTORICAL FINANCIALS

Company Type: Public

Income Statement — FYE: December 31

	REVENUE ($mil)	NET INCOME ($mil)	NET PROFIT MARGIN	EMPLOYEES
12/21	703.2	164.4	23.4%	773
12/20	488.3	71.1	14.6%	725
12/19	420.6	193.4	46.0%	699
12/18	415.9	69.9	16.8%	662
12/17	431.7	27.6	6.4%	646
Annual Growth	13.0%	56.2%	—	4.6%

2021 Year-End Financials

Debt ratio: —
Return on equity: 19.0%
Cash ($ mil.): 158.1
Current Ratio: 9.50
Long-term debt ($ mil.): —
No. of shares ($ mil.): 59.9
Dividends
  Yield: 0.5%
  Payout: 21.8%
Market value ($ mil.): 5,565.0

	STOCK PRICE ($) FY Close	P/E High/Low		PER SHARE ($) Earnings	Dividends	Book Value
12/21	92.89	40	27	2.67	0.54	15.22
12/20	81.86	106	43	1.17	0.42	13.53
12/19	98.91	30	17	3.25	0.70	12.31
12/18	60.98	67	42	1.16	0.64	9.12
12/17	73.55	181	134	0.45	0.28	9.19
Annual Growth	6.0%	—	—	56.1%	17.8%	13.4%

Preferred Bank (Los Angeles, CA)

Preferred Bank wants to be the bank of choice of Chinese-Americans in Southern California. Employing a multilingual staff, the bank provides international banking services to companies doing business in the Asia/Pacific region. It targets middle-market businesses, typically manufacturing, service, distribution, and real estate firms, as well as entrepreneurs, professionals, and high-net-worth individuals, through about a dozen branches in Los Angeles, Orange, and San Francisco Counties. Preferred Bank offers standard deposit products such as checking accounts, savings, money market, and NOW accounts. Specialized services include private banking and international trade finance.

Geographic Reach

Preferred Bank markets its services in half a dozen Southern Californian counties: Los Angeles, Orange, Riverside, San Bernardino, San Francisco, and Ventura.

Financial Performance

In 2013 Preferred Bank reported about $72 million in revenue, up just more than 10% from the prior year. The increase was solely from interest income as non-interest income (a very small part of overall revenue anyway) fell more than 40%. The company saw growth in its loan portfolio that year, as well as overall deposit growth. Net income fell 20% to $19 million; the decline was primarily related to a boost in net income for 2012 because of a $20 million income tax benefit (compared to income tax expense of $12 million in 2013).

Strategy

Historically the company was focused on the Chinese-American market and although it continues to cater to that clientele, most of its current customer base is from the diversified mainstream market.

EXECUTIVES

Chairman, Chief Executive Officer, Li Yu
President, Chief Operating Officer, Wellington Chen
Executive Vice President, Senior Vice President, Chief Financial Officer, Edward J. Czajka
Executive Vice President, Chief Credit Officer, Nick Pi

Director, J. Richard Belliston
Director, William C. Y. Cheng
Director, Clark Hsu
Director, Gary S. Nunnelly
Director, Ching-Hsing Kao
Director, Chih-Wei Wu
Director, Wayne Wu
Auditors: Crowe LLP

LOCATIONS

HQ: Preferred Bank (Los Angeles, CA)
 601 S. Figueroa Street, 48th Floor, Los Angeles, CA 90017
Phone: 213 891-1188
Web: www.preferredbank.com

PRODUCTS/OPERATIONS

2015 Sales

	mil $	% of total
Interest income		
Loans and leases	88.2	90
Investment securities, available for sale	6.3	6
Federal funds sold	0.2	-
Non-interest income		
Fees and service charges on deposit accounts	1.2	1
Trade finance income	1.6	2
BOLI income	0.4	-
Other income	0.7	1
Total	98.6	100

COMPETITORS

BANCFIRST CORPORATION
CITIZENS & NORTHERN CORPORATION
EAGLE BANCORP, INC.
FIRST REPUBLIC BANK
HSBC USA, INC.
PRIVATEBANCORP, INC.
TEXAS CAPITAL BANCSHARES, INC.
TURKIYE GARANTI BANKASI ANONIM SIRKETI
WESTERN ALLIANCE BANCORPORATION
WILSHIRE BANCORP, INC.

HISTORICAL FINANCIALS

Company Type: Public

Income Statement — FYE: December 31

	ASSETS ($mil)	NET INCOME ($mil)	INCOME AS % OF ASSETS	EMPLOYEES
12/20	5,143.6	69.4	1.4%	266
12/19	4,628.4	78.3	1.7%	279
12/18	4,216.4	70.9	1.7%	263
12/17	3,769.8	43.3	1.2%	238
12/16	3,221.5	36.3	1.1%	218
Annual Growth	12.4%	17.6%	—	5.1%

2020 Year-End Financials

Return on assets: 1.4%
Return on equity: 13.9%
Long-term debt ($ mil.): —
No. of shares ($ mil.): 14.9
Sales ($ mil.): 220.3
Dividends
 Yield: 2.3%
 Payout: 26.2%
Market value ($ mil.): 754.0

	STOCK PRICE ($) FY Close	P/E High/Low		PER SHARE ($) Earnings	Dividends	Book Value
12/20	50.47	14	6	4.65	1.20	35.19
12/19	60.09	12	8	5.16	1.20	31.47
12/18	43.35	15	9	4.64	0.94	27.22
12/17	58.78	22	16	2.96	0.76	23.48
12/16	52.42	20	10	2.56	0.60	20.94
Annual Growth	(0.9%)	—	—	16.1%	18.9%	13.9%

Preformed Line Products Co.

Preformed Line Products (PLP) is an international designer and manufacturer of products and systems employed in the construction and maintenance of overhead, and underground networks for the energy, telecommunication, cable operators, information (data communication) and other similar industries. It provides formed wire products, protective fiber-optic closures, solar hardware systems and mounting hardware for a variety of solar power applications, and data communication cabinets for data communications networks. PLP-USA is responsible for some 50% of the total sales. The company was founded in 1947.

Operations

PLP's operations are divided into four operating segments along geographic lines: PLP-USA (some 50% of total sales), The Americas (around 15%), EMEA (around 20%; Europe, Middle East, & Africa), and Asia/Pacific (roughly 20%). US operations adhere specifically to domestic energy and telecommunications products, while the other three segments work across geographic regions.

The company's products include energy (around 60% of sales), communications (some 30%), and special industries (roughly 10%) products.

Energy Products are used to support, protect, terminate and secure both power conductor and fiber communication cables and to control cable dynamics (such as vibration). Formed wire products are based on the principle of forming a variety of stiff wire materials into a helical (spiral) shape.

Communications Products, including protective closures, are used to protect fixed line communication networks, such as copper cable or fiber optic cable, from moisture, environmental hazards and other potential contaminants.

Special Industries Products include hardware assemblies, pole line hardware, resale products, underground connectors, solar hardware systems, guy markers, tree guards, fiber optic cable markers, pedestal markers and urethane products.

Geographic Reach

Headquartered in Mayfield Village, Ohio, PLP serves worldwide markets through international operations in Argentina, Australia, Austria, Brazil, Czech Republic, Canada, China, Indonesia, Malaysia, Mexico, New Zealand, Poland, South Africa, Spain, Great Britain, and Thailand.

Sales and Marketing

Domestically and internationally, the company markets its products through a direct sales force and manufacturing representatives. The direct sales force is employed by the company and works with manufacturers' representatives, as well as key direct accounts and distributors who also buy and resell the company's products. The manufacturer's representatives are independent organizations that represent the company as well as other complimentary product lines. These organizations are paid a commission based on the sales amount they generate. Additionally, the company markets its products to the energy, telecommunication, cable, data communication and special industries.

Advertising costs are expensed as incurred and totaled $1.5 million in 2021, $0.3 million in 2020, and $1.9 million in 2019.

Financial Performance

The company's revenue for fiscal 2021 increased by 11% to $517.4 million compared from the prior year with $466.4 million.

Net income for fiscal 2021 increased to $35.7 million compared from the prior year with $29.8 million.

Cash held by the company at the end of fiscal 2021 decreased to $36.4 million. Cash provided by operations was $33.6 million while cash used for investing and financing activities were $18.2 million and $23.2 million, respectively.

EXECUTIVES

Chairman, President, Chief Executive Officer, Director, Robert G. Ruhlman, $866,700 total compensation

Business Development Chief Operating Officer, Marketing Chief Operating Officer, Global Business Development Chief Operating Officer, Dennis F. McKenna, $400,008 total compensation

Finance Vice President, Finance Treasurer, Michael A. Weisbarth, $250,008 total compensation

Human Resources Vice President, Tim J. O'Shaughnessy

Manufacturing Vice President, Research Vice President, Engineering Vice President, David C. Sunkle, $320,004 total compensation

Global Communications Markets Vice President, Sales Vice President, Business Development Vice President, John M. Hofstetter

Marketing Vice President, Business Development Vice President, Director, Jon Ryan Ruhlman

Corporate Secretary, General Counsel, Caroline Saylor Vaccariello

Region Officer, William H. Haag, $307,200 total compensation

Director, Glenn E. Corlett
Director, Maegan A.R. Cross
Director, Matthew D. Frymier
Director, Richard R. Gascoigne
Director, Michael E. Gibbons
Director, R. Steven Kestner
Auditors: Ernst & Young LLP

LOCATIONS

HQ: Preformed Line Products Co.
 660 Beta Drive, Mayfield Village, OH 44143

Phone: 440 461-5200 Fax: 440 442-8816
Web: www.preformed.com

2015 Sales

	$ mil.	% of total
Americas		
US	142.5	40
Other countries	59.3	17
Asia/Pacific	99.1	28
Europe, Middle East & Africa (EMEA)	53.8	15
Total	354.7	100

PRODUCTS/OPERATIONS

2015 sales

	% of total
Formed wire	61
Protective closures	17
Plastic products	4
Other products	18
Total	100

Selected Products
Copper splice closures
Data communication cabinets
Fiber optic products (COYOTE brand)
Formed wire and related hardware products
High-speed cross-connect devices
Plastic products
Power transmission products (THERMOLIGN)
Protective closures (ARMADILLO stainless vault closures)
RAPTOR PROTECTOR (protects birds from power lines)

Selected Markets
Communication and cable
Data communication
Electric utilities and distribution
Electric utilities and transmission
Energy
Solar

COMPETITORS

CHASE CORPORATION
EDGEN GROUP INC.
ENTEGRIS PROFESSIONAL SOLUTIONS, INC.
FLUIDRA, SA
LEONI AG
LINEAR TECHNOLOGY LLC
REXEL
STEEL CONNECT, INC.
THE DURHAM CO
VON ROLL USA, INC.

HISTORICAL FINANCIALS
Company Type: Public

Income Statement   FYE: December 31

	REVENUE ($mil)	NET INCOME ($mil)	NET PROFIT MARGIN	EMPLOYEES
12/20	466.4	29.8	6.4%	2,969
12/19	444.8	23.3	5.2%	2,983
12/18	420.8	26.5	6.3%	2,650
12/17	378.2	12.6	3.3%	2,762
12/16	336.6	15.2	4.5%	2,579
Annual Growth	8.5%	18.2%	—	3.6%

2020 Year-End Financials

Debt ratio: 12.1%
Return on equity: 10.6%
Cash ($ mil.): 45.1
Current Ratio: 2.47
Long-term debt ($ mil.): 33.3
No. of shares ($ mil.): 4.9
Dividends
 Yield: 1.1%
 Payout: 12.2%
Market value ($ mil.): 336.0

	STOCK PRICE ($) FY Close	P/E High/Low		PER SHARE ($) Earnings	Dividends	Book Value
12/20	68.44	11	6	5.98	0.80	59.58
12/19	60.35	16	10	4.58	0.80	53.78
12/18	54.25	17	9	5.21	0.80	49.67
12/17	71.05	34	18	2.47	0.80	47.35
12/16	58.12	20	11	2.95	0.80	43.68
Annual Growth	4.2%	—	—	19.3%	0.0%	8.1%

Premier Financial Corp

Named for its hometown, not its attitude, First Defiance Financial is the holding company for First Federal Bank of the Midwest, which operates more than 30 branches serving northwestern Ohio, western Indiana, and southern Michigan. The thrift offers standard deposit products including checking, savings, and money market accounts and CDs. Commercial real estate loans account for more than half of the bank's loan portfolio; commercial loans make up another quarter of all loans. The company's insurance agency subsidiary, First Insurance Group of the Midwest, which accounts for some 7% of the company's revenues, provides life insurance, property/casualty coverage, and investments. In 2019 First Defiance Financial agreed to merge with Ohio-based United Community Financial (the holding company for Home Savings Bank and HSB Insurance) in a deal valued at $473 million.

Strategy

First Defiance Financial has boosted its non-banking product lines via acquisitions. It bought the employee benefits insurance business of another local agency, Andres O'Neil & Lowe, in 2010; and property/casualty agency Payak-Dubbs Insurance Agency in 2011. Both additions became part of First Insurance Group of the Midwest (formerly named First Insurance & Investments).

In 2016 the company agreed to buy another bank serving northwest Ohio, Commercial Bancshares. The deal is valued at some $63 million and adds seven branches and $342 million in assets.

Mergers and Acquisitions

In 2019 First Defiance Financial agreed to merge with Ohio-based United Community Financial (the holding company for Home Savings Bank and HSB Insurance) in a deal valued at $473 million. United Community's Home Savings Bank subsidiary will merge into First Federal to create a bank with more than $6 billion in assets. First Defiance shareholders will have a 52.5% stake in the new company.

EXECUTIVES

Subsidiary Officer, Executive Chairman, Director, Donald P. Hileman, $472,500 total compensation
President, Chief Executive Officer, Subsidiary Officer, Director, Gary M. Small
Executive Vice President, Chief Information Officer, Chief Operations Officer, Varun Chandhok
Executive Vice President, Chief Risk Officer, Subsidiary Officer, Tina M. Shaver
Executive Vice President, Chief Legal Officer, Subsidiary Officer, Shannon M. Kuhl
Executive Vice President, Chief Human Resources Officer, Subsidiary Officer, Sharon L. Davis
Executive Vice President, Chief Lending Officer, Matthew T. Garrity
Finance Executive Vice President, Accounting Executive Vice President, Finance Chief Financial Officer, Accounting Chief Financial Officer, Finance Subsidiary Officer, Accounting Subsidiary Officer, Paul D. Nungester
Executive Vice President, Chief Strategy Officer, Subsidiary Officer, Dennis E. Rose, $173,806 total compensation
Senior Vice President, Chief Marketing Officer, Kathy Bushway
Wealth Management Senior Vice President, Wealth Management Director, Wealth Management Subsidiary Officer, Jennifer Scroggs
Subsidiary Officer, Jason L. Gendics
Director, John L. Bookmyer, $34,750 total compensation
Director, Nikki R. Lanier
Director, Louis Michael Altman
Director, Zahid Afzal
Director, Terri A. Bettinger
Director, Lee J. Burdman
Director, Jean A. Hubbard
Director, Charles D. Niehaus
Director, Mark Andrew Robison
Director, Richard J. Schiraldi
Director, Marty E. Adams
Director, Samuel S. Strausbaugh, $40,600 total compensation
Auditors : Crowe LLP

LOCATIONS

HQ: Premier Financial Corp
601 Clinton Street, Defiance, OH 43512
Phone: 419 782-5015
Web: www.fdef.com

PRODUCTS/OPERATIONS

2016 Sales

	$ mil.	% of total
Interest		
Loans	80.2	66
Investment securities		
Taxable	3.2	3
Tax-exempt	3.0	2
Interest-bearing deposits	0.4	-
FHLB stock dividends	0.6	1
Non-interest		
Service fees & other charges	10.9	9
Insurance commissions	10.4	9
Mortgage banking income	7.3	6
Trust income	1.7	1
Gain on sale of non-mortgage loans	0.8	1
Income from bank owned life insurance	0.9	1
Gain on sale or call of securities	0.5	-
Other	1.5	1
Total	121.4	100

COMPETITORS

BANKUNITED, INC.
CHARTER FINANCIAL CORPORATION
FIRST FEDERAL SAVINGS AND LOAN ASSOCIATION OF LAKEWOOD
INVESTORS BANCORP, INC.
MIDLAND FINANCIAL CO.
NORTHWEST BANCORP, INC.
OLD NATIONAL BANCORP
PEOPLE'S UNITED FINANCIAL, INC.
TRUIST FINANCIAL CORPORATION
UNITED FINANCIAL BANCORP, INC.

HISTORICAL FINANCIALS
Company Type: Public

Income Statement — FYE: December 31

	ASSETS ($mil)	NET INCOME ($mil)	INCOME AS % OF ASSETS	EMPLOYEES
12/20	7,211.7	63.0	0.9%	1,195
12/19	3,468.9	49.3	1.4%	699
12/18	3,181.7	46.2	1.5%	696
12/17	2,993.4	32.2	1.1%	674
12/16	2,477.5	28.8	1.2%	581
Annual Growth	30.6%	21.6%	—	19.8%

2020 Year-End Financials

Return on assets: 1.1%
Return on equity: 8.9%
Long-term debt ($ mil.): —
No. of shares ($ mil.): 37.2
Sales ($ mil.): 318.6
Dividends
Yield: 3.8%
Payout: 63.3%
Market value ($ mil.): 858.0

	STOCK PRICE ($) FY Close	P/E High/Low		PER SHARE ($) Earnings	Dividends	Book Value
12/20	23.00	18	7	1.75	0.88	26.34
12/19	31.49	13	10	2.48	0.79	21.60
12/18	24.51	30	10	2.26	0.64	19.81
12/17	51.97	35	29	1.61	0.50	18.38
12/16	50.74	32	22	1.60	0.44	16.31
Annual Growth	(17.9%)	—	—	2.3%	18.9%	12.7%

Primerica Inc

EXECUTIVES

President, Peter W. Schneider, $550,000 total compensation
Distribution Executive Vice President, Distribution Chief Marketing Officer, Robert H. Peterman
Executive Vice President, Chief Financial Officer, Alison S. Rand, $500,000 total compensation
Executive Vice President, Chief Operating Officer, Gregory C. Pitts, $500,000 total compensation
Executive Vice President, Chief Business Technology Officer, Michael C. Adams
Executive Vice President, Chief Compliance Officer, Chief Risk Officer, Jeffrey S. Fendler
Chief Executive Officer, Director, Glenn J. Williams, $750,000 total compensation
Executive Vice President, General Counsel, Alexis P. Ginn
Executive Vice President, Chief Reputation Officer, Kathryn E. Kieser
Executive Vice President, Chief Governance Officer, Deputy General Counsel, Corporate Secretary, Stacey K. Geer
Subsidiary Officer, William A. Kelly, $475,088 total compensation
Subsidiary Officer, John A. Adams
Subsidiary Officer, Julie A. Seman
Non-Executive Chairman, Donald Richard Williams, $190,341 total compensation
Distribution Non-Executive Chairman, Distribution Director, John A. Addison, $190,341 total compensation
Lead Director, Director, P. George Benson
Director, Joel M. Babbit
Director, C. Saxby Chambliss
Director, Gary L. Crittenden
Director, Cynthia N. Day
Director, Sanjeev Dheer
Director, Beatriz R. Perez
Director, Barbara A. Yastine
Auditors : KPMG LLP

LOCATIONS

HQ: Primerica Inc
1 Primerica Parkway, Duluth, GA 30099
Phone: 770 381-1000
Web: www.primerica.com

HISTORICAL FINANCIALS
Company Type: Public

Income Statement — FYE: December 31

	ASSETS ($mil)	NET INCOME ($mil)	INCOME AS % OF ASSETS	EMPLOYEES
12/20	14,905.2	386.1	2.6%	2,824
12/19	13,688.5	366.3	2.7%	2,803
12/18	12,595.0	324.0	2.6%	2,699
12/17	12,460.7	350.2	2.8%	2,718
12/16	11,438.9	219.4	1.9%	2,662
Annual Growth	6.8%	15.2%	—	1.5%

2020 Year-End Financials

Return on assets: 2.6%
Return on equity: 22.0%
Long-term debt ($ mil.): —
No. of shares ($ mil.): 39.3
Sales ($ mil.): 2,217.5
Dividends
Yield: 1.1%
Payout: 16.7%
Market value ($ mil.): 5,264.0

	STOCK PRICE ($) FY Close	P/E High/Low		PER SHARE ($) Earnings	Dividends	Book Value
12/20	133.93	15	6	9.57	1.60	46.71
12/19	130.56	16	11	8.62	1.36	40.10
12/18	97.71	17	12	7.33	1.00	34.23
12/17	101.55	14	9	7.61	0.78	32.07
12/16	69.15	16	9	4.59	0.70	26.71
Annual Growth	18.0%	—	—	20.2%	23.0%	15.0%

Primis Financial Corp

Southern National Bancorp of Virginia is the holding company for Sonabank, which has some 20 locations in central and northern Virginia and southern Maryland. Founded in 2005, the bank serves small and midsized businesses, their owners, and retail consumers. It offers standard deposit products, including checking, savings, and money market accounts, and CDs. The bank's lending is focused on commercial real estate, single-family residential construction, and single-family homes, as well as other types of consumer and commercial loans. In 2009 Southern National Bancorp acquired the failed Greater Atlantic Bank in an FDIC-assisted transaction; in 2012 it acquired the loans and deposits of HarVest Bank of Maryland.

EXECUTIVES

Chairman, Subsidiary Officer, Director, W. Rand Cook
President, Chief Executive Officer, Subsidiary Officer, Director, Dennis J. Zember
Executive Vice President, Chief Financial Officer, Subsidiary Officer, Matthew A. Switzer
Executive Vice President, Chief Credit Officer, Subsidiary Officer, Marie T. Leibson
Executive Vice President, Chief Operating Officer, Chief Information Officer, Subsidiary Officer, George Cody Sheflett
Executive Vice President, Chief Strategy Officer, Subsidiary Officer, Stephen B. Weber
Secretary, Subsidiary Officer, Cheryl B. Wood
Director, John Fitzgerald Biagas
Director, John M. Eggemeyer
Director, F. L. Garrett
Director, Allen R. Jones
Director, Eric A. Johnson
Director, Robert Y. Clagett
Director, Deborah B. Diaz
Director, Charles A. Kabbash
Auditors : Dixon Hughes Goodman LLP

LOCATIONS

HQ: Primis Financial Corp
6830 Old Dominion Drive, McLean, VA 22101
Phone: 703 893-7400
Web: www.sonabank.com

COMPETITORS

BCSB BANCORP, INC.
FIRST WEST VIRGINIA BANCORP, INC.
HERITAGE BANKSHARES, INC.
KS BANCORP, INC.
PACIFIC FINANCIAL CORPORATION

HISTORICAL FINANCIALS

Company Type: Public

Income Statement — FYE: December 31

	ASSETS ($mil)	NET INCOME ($mil)	INCOME AS % OF ASSETS	EMPLOYEES
12/20	3,088.6	23.2	0.8%	382
12/19	2,722.1	33.1	1.2%	350
12/18	2,701.2	33.6	1.2%	348
12/17	2,614.2	2.4	0.1%	393
12/16	1,142.4	10.3	0.9%	162
Annual Growth	28.2%	22.6%	—	23.9%

2020 Year-End Financials

Return on assets: 0.7%
Return on equity: 6.0%
Long-term debt ($ mil.): —
No. of shares ($ mil.): 24.3
Sales ($ mil.): 143.2
Dividends
Yield: 3.3%
Payout: 41.6%
Market value ($ mil.): 295.0

	STOCK PRICE ($) FY Close	P/E High/Low		PER SHARE ($) Earnings	Dividends	Book Value
12/20	12.11	17	8	0.96	0.40	16.03
12/19	16.35	12	10	1.36	0.36	15.60
12/18	13.22	13	9	1.39	0.32	14.48
12/17	16.03	142	118	0.13	0.32	13.48
12/16	16.34	20	14	0.83	0.32	10.30
Annual Growth	(7.2%)	—	—	3.7%	5.7%	11.7%

Primoris Services Corp

Primoris Services is one of the leading providers of specialty contracting services operating mainly in the US and Canada. The company provide a wide range of specialty construction services, maintenance, replacement, fabrication, and engineering services to a diversified base of customers through its three segments: Utilities, Energy/Renewables and Pipeline Services (Pipeline). Primoris Services' clients are public and private gas and electric utilities, state departments of transportation, pipeline operators, and chemical and energy producers such as Xcel Energy, Pacific Gas & Electric, Southern California Gas, and Oncor Electric, among other. Primoris Services traces its roots back to 1960 as ARB, Inc.

Operations

Primoris Services is well diversified across five primary segments: Utilities segment, Energy/Renewables segment and Pipeline segment.

The Utilities segment generates nearly half of revenue and specializes in a range of services, including the installation and maintenance of new and existing natural gas and electric utility distribution and transmission systems, and communications systems.

The Energy/Renewables segment (about 40% of total revenue) specializes in a range of services that include engineering, procurement, and construction, retrofits, highway and bridge construction, demolition, site work, soil stabilization, mass excavation, flood control, upgrades, repairs, outages, and maintenance services for entities in the renewable energy and energy storage, renewable fuels, and petroleum, refining, and petrochemical industries, as well as state departments of transportation.

The Pipeline segment generates more than 10% of total revenue and specializes in a range of services, including pipeline construction and maintenance, pipeline facility and integrity services, installation of compressor and pump stations, and metering facilities for entities in the petroleum and petrochemical industries, as well as gas, water, and sewer utilities.

By contract type, Primoris Services generates more than 40% of revenue from unit-price, while about 35% from fixed-price and more than 20% from cost reimbursable.

Geographic Reach

Dallas, Texas-based Primoris Services garners almost all its revenue in the US, although its operations extend to Canada. The company has regional offices in Louisiana, California, Colorado, Texas, Florida, Minnesota, and Canada.

Sales and Marketing

Primoris Services' customers include major utility, refining, petrochemical, power, renewable energy, communications, midstream, and engineering companies and state departments of transportation. Its customers have included the Texas and Louisiana Departments of Transportation, Chevron, Sempra, Kinder Morgan, and among others. The company's top ten customers generate some 45% of its total revenue.

Revenue derived from projects performed under MSAs was about 45% and non-MSAs generate the remaining 55% of revenue.

Financial Performance

Net sales increased $6.1 million to $3.5 billion in 2021. This was primarily due to a higher sales volume in the company's utilities segment.

The company's net income grew 10% from $105 million in 2020 to $115.7 million in 2021.

The company ended fiscal year 2021 with $205.6 million in cash. Operating activities provided $79.7 million. Investing activities used $691.3 million, mainly for cash paid for acquisitions. Financing activities provided another $485.7 million.

Strategy

The company's strategy has remained consistent from year to year and continues to emphasize the following key elements:

Diversification through controlled expansion - Primoris continues to emphasize the expansion of its scope of services beyond its current focus by increasing the scope of services offered to current customers and by adding new customers.

Emphasis on MSA revenue growth and retention of existing customers - In order to fully leverage relationships with existing customer base, the company believes it is important to maintain strong customer relationships. The company is also focused on expanding its base of services provided under MSAs, which are generally multi-year agreements that provide visible recurring revenue.

Ownership of equipment. Many of its services are equipment intensive - The company believes that its ownership of a large and varied construction fleet and maintenance facilities enhances its access to reliable equipment at a favorable cost.

Stable work force - Primoris' business model emphasizes self-performance of a significant portion of its work. In each of its segments, the company maintains a stable work force of skilled, experienced craft professionals, many of whom are cross-trained on projects such as pipeline and facility construction, refinery maintenance, gas and electrical distribution, and piping systems.

Selective bidding - The company selectively bids on projects that it believes offer an opportunity to meet profitability objectives or that offer the opportunity to enter promising new markets.

Maintain a strong balance sheet and a conservative capital structure - The company has maintained a capital structure that provides access to debt financing as needed while relying on strong operating cash flows to provide the primary support for its operations.

Mergers and Acquisitions

In 2021, Primoris acquired Future Infrastructure in an all-cash transaction valued at $620 million. The transaction directly aligns with Primoris' strategy to grow in large, higher growth, higher margin markets, and expands the company's utility services capabilities. Future Infrastructure is a provider of non-discretionary maintenance, repair, upgrade, and installation services to the telecommunication, regulated gas utility, and infrastructure markets. As a result of the acquisition, Future Infrastructure will be integrated into the company's Utilities Segment, furthering Primoris' strategic plan to expand its service lines, enter new markets, and grow the company's MSA revenue base.

Company Background

Traces its roots to 1960 with the founding of ARB, Inc. of Bakersfield, CA a pipeline construction company. ARB met the growing demand for energy infrastructure that accompanied the mid-century oil boom in the west and quickly established the reputation for great quality and reliability. ARB's work and reputation fueled significant growth and laid the foundation for Primoris which is today one of the largest specialty contractors in the country.

Primoris was formed in 2004 as the parent company and is traded on NASDAQ under the symbol PRIM.

EXECUTIVES

Chairman, Director, David L. King, $712,743 total compensation
President, Chief Executive Officer, Director, Thomas E. McCormick, $559,834 total compensation
Executive Vice President, Chief Financial Officer, Kenneth M. Dodgen, $320,193 total compensation
Executive Vice President, Chief Operating Officer, John F. Moreno
Executive Vice President, Chief Legal Officer, Secretary, John M. Perisich, $447,869 total compensation
Lead Director, Director, Stephen C. Cook
Director, Carla S. Mashinski
Director, Terry D. McCallister
Director, Jose R. Rodriguez
Director, John P. Schauerman, $231,441 total compensation
Director, Michael E. Ching
Director, Patricia K. Wagner
Auditors: Moss Adams LLP

LOCATIONS

HQ: Primoris Services Corp
2300 N. Field Street, Suite 1900, Dallas, TX 75201
Phone: 214 740-5600
Web: www.prim.com

PRODUCTS/OPERATIONS

2018 Sales

	$ mil.	% of total
Utilities	902.8	31
Power	694.1	23
Pipeline	590.9	20
Civil	465	16
Transmission	286.7	10
Total	2,939.5	100

2018 Sales

	$ mil.	% of total
MSA	1,128.6	38
Non-MSA	1,810.9	62
Total	2,939.5	100

2018 Sales

	$ mil.	% of total
Unit-Price	1,139.7	39
Cost Reimbursable	996	34
Fixed-Price	803.8	37
Total	2,939.5	100

Selected Subsidiaries
ARB, Inc.
Stellaris, LLC
ARB Structures, Inc.
BW Primoris, LLC
Cardinal Contractors, Inc.
James Construction Group, LLC
JCG Heavy Civil DivisionJCG Industrial DivisionJCG Infrastructure and Maintenance Division
OnQuest, Canada, ULC
OnQuest, Inc.
Primoris Energy Services Corporation
Q3 Contracting, Inc.
Rockford Corporation
Silva Group

COMPETITORS
AEGION CORPORATION
CH2M HILL COMPANIES, LTD.
DYCOM INDUSTRIES, INC.
INSITUFORM TECHNOLOGIES, LLC
JGC HOLDINGS CORPORATION
LAYNE CHRISTENSEN COMPANY
MUNICIPAL ELECTRIC AUTHORITY OF GEORGIA
MYR GROUP INC.
QUANTA SERVICES, INC.
WILLBROS GROUP, INC.

HISTORICAL FINANCIALS
Company Type: Public

Income Statement — FYE: December 31

	REVENUE ($mil)	NET INCOME ($mil)	NET PROFIT MARGIN	EMPLOYEES
12/20	3,491.4	104.9	3.0%	10,414
12/19	3,106.3	82.3	2.7%	9,700
12/18	2,939.4	77.4	2.6%	10,600
12/17	2,379.9	72.3	3.0%	7,102
12/16	1,996.9	26.7	1.3%	7,926
Annual Growth	15.0%	40.8%	—	7.1%

2020 Year-End Financials
Debt ratio: 16.1%
Return on equity: 15.5%
Cash ($ mil.): 326.7
Current Ratio: 1.46
Long-term debt ($ mil.): 268.8
No. of shares ($ mil.): 48.1
Dividends
 Yield: 0.8%
 Payout: 11.8%
Market value ($ mil.): 1,328.0

	STOCK PRICE ($) FY Close	P/E High/Low		PER SHARE ($) Earnings	Dividends	Book Value
12/20	27.61	13	5	2.16	0.24	14.86
12/19	22.24	15	11	1.61	0.24	12.91
12/18	19.13	19	12	1.50	0.24	11.91
12/17	27.19	21	16	1.40	0.23	10.82
12/16	22.78	48	33	0.51	0.22	9.64
Annual Growth	4.9%	—	—	43.5%	2.2%	11.4%

Private Bancorp Of America Inc

EXECUTIVES

Chairman, Subsidiary Officer, Selwyn Isakow
Chief Credit Officer, Subsidiary Officer, Director, Stephen N. Rippe
President, Chief Executive Officer, Subsidiary Officer, Director, Thomas V. Wornham
Director, David S. Engelman
Director, Ernest S. Rady
Director, Leon Kassel
Director, David Ellman
Director, Keith B. Jones
Director, Marjory Kaplan
Director, Jerry Suppa
Auditors: Eide Bailly LLP

LOCATIONS

HQ: Private Bancorp Of America Inc
9404 Genesee Avenue, Suite 100, La Jolla, CA 90237
Phone: 858 875-6900
Web: www.calprivate.bank

HISTORICAL FINANCIALS
Company Type: Public

Income Statement — FYE: December 31

	REVENUE ($mil)	NET INCOME ($mil)	NET PROFIT MARGIN	EMPLOYEES
12/20	55.3	10.8	19.7%	0
12/19	44.5	(0.4)	—	0
12/18	31.6	4.1	13.1%	0
12/17	23.4	3.4	14.6%	0
12/16	20.1	4.3	21.4%	0
Annual Growth	28.7%	26.0%	—	—

2020 Year-End Financials
Debt ratio: 7.0%
Return on equity: 10.6%
Cash ($ mil.): 276.2
Current Ratio: 0.25
Long-term debt ($ mil.): 92.9
No. of shares ($ mil.): 5.6
Dividends
 Yield: —
 Payout: —
Market value ($ mil.): 104.0

	STOCK PRICE ($) FY Close	P/E High/Low		PER SHARE ($) Earnings	Dividends	Book Value
12/20	18.50	12	6	1.94	0.00	19.24
12/19	22.25	—	—	(0.08)	0.00	17.15
12/18	22.95	33	28	0.80	0.00	16.41
12/17	25.45	35	27	0.71	0.00	15.88
12/16	19.38	18	14	1.06	0.00	14.20
Annual Growth	(1.2%)	—	—	16.3%	—	7.9%

Professional Holding Corp

EXECUTIVES

Chief Executive Officer, Subsidiary Officer, Director, Abel L. Iglesias
Chief Accounting Officer, Chief Financial Officer, Subsidiary Officer, Mary Usategui
Corporate Secretary, Michael C. Sontag
Subsidiary Officer, Ryan L. Gorney
Director, Norman Edelcup
Director, Joseph Timothy Willett
Director, Jon L. Gorney
Non-Executive Chairman, Director, Herbert R. Martens
Director, Margaret S. Blakey
Director, Carlos M. Garcia
Director, Lawrence Schimmel
Director, Ava L. Parker

LOCATIONS

HQ: Professional Holding Corp
396 Alhambra Circle, Suite 255, Coral Gables, FL 33134
Phone: 786 483-1757
Web: www.proholdco.com

HISTORICAL FINANCIALS
Company Type: Public

Income Statement — FYE: December 31

	ASSETS ($mil)	NET INCOME ($mil)	INCOME AS % OF ASSETS	EMPLOYEES
12/20	2,057.2	8.3	0.4%	0
12/19	1,053.1	2.3	0.2%	0
12/18	662.3	6.8	1.0%	135
12/17	539.1	3.9	0.7%	0
Annual Growth	56.3%	28.0%	—	—

2020 Year-End Financials
Return on assets: 0.5%
Return on equity: 5.6%
Long-term debt ($ mil.): —
No. of shares ($ mil.): 13.5
Sales ($ mil.): 73.4
Dividends
  Yield: —
  Payout: —
Market value ($ mil.): 209.0

	STOCK PRICE ($) FY Close	P/E High	P/E Low	Earnings	Dividends	Book Value
12/20	15.43	29	15	0.67	0.00	15.93
12/19	19.00	48	38	0.40	0.00	13.52
12/18	15.20	9	8	1.91	0.00	14.89
12/17	15.51	13	11	1.14	0.00	12.71
Annual Growth	(0.2%)	—	—	(16.2%)	—	7.8%

Progyny Inc

EXECUTIVES

Chairman, Director, Beth C. Seidenberg
President, Chief Financial Officer, Chief Operating Officer, Peter Anevski
Chief Executive Officer, Director, David J. Schlanger
Executive Vice President, Chief Client Officer, Lisa Greenbaum
Executive Vice President, General Counsel, Jennifer Bealer
Finance Executive Vice President, Finance Chief Accounting Officer, Mark Livingston
Director, Kevin K. Gordon
Director, Cheryl Scott
Director, Jeff Park
Director, Fred E. Cohen
Director, Norman C. Payson
Auditors : Ernst & Young LLP

LOCATIONS

HQ: Progyny Inc
1359 Broadway, New York, NY 10018
Phone: 212 888-3124
Web: www.progyny.com

HISTORICAL FINANCIALS
Company Type: Public

Income Statement — FYE: December 31

	REVENUE ($mil)	NET INCOME ($mil)	NET PROFIT MARGIN	EMPLOYEES
12/20	344.8	46.4	13.5%	210
12/19	229.6	(8.5)	—	167
12/18	105.4	0.6	0.6%	163
12/17	48.5	(12.4)	—	0
Annual Growth	92.2%	—	—	—

2020 Year-End Financials
Debt ratio: —
Return on equity: 32.9%
Cash ($ mil.): 70.3
Current Ratio: 2.45
Long-term debt ($ mil.): —
No. of shares ($ mil.): 87.0
Dividends
  Yield: —
  Payout: —
Market value ($ mil.): 3,690.0

	STOCK PRICE ($) FY Close	P/E High	P/E Low	Earnings	Dividends	Book Value
12/20	42.39	80	31	0.47	0.00	1.92
12/19	27.45	—	—	(0.41)	0.00	1.36
Annual Growth	54.4%	—	—	—	—	41.3%

Prosperity Bancshares Inc.

Prosperity Bancshares reaches banking customers across the Lone Star State. The holding company for Prosperity Bank operates about 230 branches across Texas and about 15 more in Oklahoma. Serving consumers and small to midsized businesses, the bank offers traditional deposit and loan services, in addition to wealth management, retail brokerage, and mortgage banking investment services. Prosperity Bank focuses on real estate lending: Commercial mortgages make up the largest segment of the company's loan portfolio (33%), followed by residential mortgages (24%). Credit cards, business, auto, consumer, home equity loans round out its lending activities.

Operations
About 63% of Prosperity's total revenue came from loan interest (including fees) in 2014, while another 22% came from interest on its investment securities. The rest of its revenue came from non-sufficient fund fees (4%), credit and debit card income (3%), deposit account service charges (2%), trust income (1%), mortgage income (1%), and brokerage income (1%).

Geographic Reach
Prosperity Bancshares operates 230 Texas banking locations across Houston, South Texas, the Dallas/Fort Worth metroplex, East Texas, Bryan/College Station, Central Texas, and West Texas. It also has 15 branch locations in Oklahoma (including Tulsa).

Sales and Marketing
The bank mainly targets consumers and small and medium-sized businesses, and tailors its products to the specific needs of a given market.

Financial Performance
Prosperity's revenues and profits have been prospering thanks to loan and deposit business growth from acquisitions, and declining loan loss provisions as its loan portfolio's credit quality has improved with higher property valuations in a strengthened economy.

The company's revenue jumped by 32% to $837.7 million in 2014 mostly as its loan interest income swelled by 40% on loan asset growth from its F&M acquisition. The bank's non-interest income rose by 29% as well from new deposit account service fees from the acquisition and additional income from its newly added brokerage and trust business.

Higher revenue and strong operating cost controls in 2014 drove Prosperity's net income higher by 34% to $297.4 million, while its operating cash levels rose by 13% to $348.3 million on higher cash earnings.

Strategy
Prosperity Bancshares bases its growth strategy on three key elements: Internal loan and deposit business growth through "individualized customer service" and service line expansion opportunities; cost controls to maximize profitability; and acquisitions.

Toward its internal business growth initiatives, Prosperity spent 2012 and 2013 launching its new trust, brokerage, mortgage lending, and credit card products and services to customers for the first time.

With cost-controls in mind, the bank tracks its branches "as separate profit centers," noting each branch's interest income, efficiency ratio, deposit growth, loan growth, and overall profitability. That way it can reward individual branch managers and presidents accordingly by merit, rather than giving higher compensation across the board.

The acquisitive Prosperity Bancshares has been buying up small banks in Texas -- and now Oklahoma -- as it hopes to hit a sweet spot in the market between the national giants that dominate the Texas banking scene and smaller community banks.

Mergers and Acquisitions
In January 2016, furthering its presence in the Houston market, Prosperity Bancshares purchased Tradition Bancshares along with its seven branches in the Houston Area (Bellaire, Katy, and the Woodlands), $540 million in assets, $239 million in loans, and $483.8 million in deposits.

In April 2014, toward expansion in the Oklahoma and Dallas markets, Prosperity purchased Tulsa-based F&M Bancorporation and its subsidiary, The F&M Bank & Trust Company. The deal added 13 branches, including nine in Tulsa and surrounding areas, three in Dallas, and a loan production office in Oklahoma City.

In April 2013, it acquired Coppermark Bank, one of Oklahoma City's largest banks with six branches in Oklahoma City and three locations in North Dallas for $194 million. The deal also added the credit card and agent bank merchant processing business from its subsidiary, Bankers Credit Card Services.

In January 2013, the company boosted its market share in East Texas after buying East Texas Financial Services and its four First Federal Bank Texas branch locations, including three branches in Tyler and one in Gilmer.

Company Background

In early 2012 Prosperity acquired Texas Bankers, a three-branch Austin bank with some $72 million in assets. The merger increased Prosperity's number of Central Texas branches to 34 banking locations. It followed that deal with the purchase of The Bank Arlington, a single-branch bank operating in the Dallas/Ft. Worth area. It acquired single-branch Community National Bank of Bellaire, Texas, in late 2012.

Also in 2012, Prosperity expanded into West Texas after it merged American State Financial Corporation and its American State Bank subsidiary into its operations. The deal added $3 billion in assets and 37 West Texas banking offices in Lubbock, Midland/Odessa, and Abilene.

EXECUTIVES

Senior Chairman, Chief Executive Officer, Subsidiary Officer, Director, David Zalman, $973,372 total compensation

Chairman, Subsidiary Officer, Director, H. E. Timanus, $512,372 total compensation

Vice-Chairman, Subsidiary Officer, Edward Z. Safady, $499,556 total compensation

President, Chief Operating Officer, Subsidiary Officer, Kevin J. Hanigan, $970,806 total compensation

Corporate Strategy Executive Vice President, Corporate Strategy Director, Corporate Strategy Subsidiary Officer, J. Mays Davenport, $415,000 total compensation

Executive Vice President, Subsidiary Officer, Robert J. Dowdell

Executive Vice President, Subsidiary Officer, Randy Hester, $366,579 total compensation

Executive Vice President, General Counsel, Subsidiary Officer, Charlotte M. Rasche, $366,579 total compensation

Chief Financial Officer, Subsidiary Officer, Asylbek Osmonov, $300,000 total compensation

Director, James A. Bouligny
Director, W. R. Collier
Director, George A. Fisk
Director, Leah Henderson
Director, Ned S. Holmes
Director, Bruce W. Hunt
Director, L. Jack Lord
Director, William T. Luedke
Director, Perry Mueller
Director, Harrison Stafford
Director, Robert Steelhammer
Auditors: DELOITTE & TOUCHE LLP

LOCATIONS

HQ: Prosperity Bancshares Inc.
Prosperity Bank Plaza, 4295 San Felipe, Houston, TX 77027
Phone: 281 269-7199
Web: www.prosperitybankusa.com

PRODUCTS/OPERATIONS

2014 Sales

	$ mil.	% of total
Interest		
Loans, including fees	525.7	63
Securities	188.7	22
Federal funds sold	0.3	—
Noninterest		
Non-sufficient funds fees	37.0	4
Debit card and ATM card income	22.9	3
Service charges on deposit accounts	16.5	2
Trust income	8.1	1
Brokerage income	5.9	1
Mortgage income	4.4	1
Other	28.2	3
Total	837.7	100

COMPETITORS

CITY HOLDING COMPANY
CVB FINANCIAL CORP.
F.N.B. CORPORATION
FIRST CITIZENS BANCSHARES, INC.
FIRST HORIZON CORPORATION
S&T BANCORP, INC.
SOUTHWEST BANCORP, INC.
WASHINGTON TRUST BANCORP, INC.
WESTERN ALLIANCE BANCORPORATION
WILSHIRE BANCORP, INC.

HISTORICAL FINANCIALS

Company Type: Public

Income Statement — FYE: December 31

	ASSETS ($mil)	NET INCOME ($mil)	INCOME AS % OF ASSETS	EMPLOYEES
12/20	34,059.2	528.9	1.6%	3,756
12/19	32,185.7	332.5	1.0%	3,901
12/18	22,693.4	321.8	1.4%	3,036
12/17	22,587.2	272.1	1.2%	3,035
12/16	22,331.0	274.4	1.2%	3,035
Annual Growth	11.1%	17.8%	—	5.5%

2020 Year-End Financials

Return on assets: 1.5%
Return on equity: 8.7%
Long-term debt ($ mil.): —
No. of shares ($ mil.): 92.5
Sales ($ mil.): 1,275.4
Dividends
Yield: 2.6%
Payout: 36.1%
Market value ($ mil.): 6,421.0

	STOCK PRICE ($) FY Close	P/E High/Low		PER SHARE ($) Earnings	Dividends	Book Value
12/20	69.36	13	8	5.68	1.87	66.23
12/19	71.89	17	14	4.52	1.69	63.02
12/18	62.30	17	12	4.61	1.49	58.02
12/17	70.07	20	14	3.92	1.38	55.03
12/16	71.78	19	9	3.94	1.24	52.41
Annual Growth	(0.9%)	—	—	9.6%	10.8%	6.0%

Proto Labs Inc

Proto Labs is the world's largest and fastest digital manufacturer of custom prototypes and on-demand production parts. The company targets its products to the millions of product developers and engineers who use three-dimensional computer-aided design (3D CAD) software to design products across a diverse range of end-markets. It manufactures prototype and low volume production parts for companies worldwide, who are under increasing pressure to bring their finished products to market faster than their competition. It utilizes injection molding, computer numerical control (CNC) machining, 3D printing and sheet metal fabrication to manufacture custom parts for its customers. The US accounts for around 80% of Proto Labs' sales. The company was founded in 1999 by Larry Lukis.

Operations

The company derived its revenue from its Injection Molding, CNC Machining, 3D Printing and Sheet Metal product lines.

The Injection Molded division (about 45% of sales) product line uses its 3D CAD-to-CNC machining technology for the automated design and manufacture of molds, which are then used to produce custom plastic and liquid silicone rubber injection-molded parts and over-molded and insert-molded injection-molded parts on commercially available equipment.

Proto Labs' CNC Machining segment (nearly 35% of sales) uses commercially available CNC machines to offer milling and turning. CNC milling is a manufacturing process that cuts plastic and metal blocks into one or more custom parts based on the 3D CAD model uploaded by the product developer or engineer.

The 3D Printing division (approximately 15% of sales) product line includes SL, SLS, DMLS, MJF, PolyJet and Carbon DLS processes, which offers customers a wide-variety of high-quality, precision rapid prototyping and low volume production.

The company's Sheet Metal segment (around 5% of sales) product line includes quick-turn and e-commerce-enabled custom sheet metal parts, providing customers with prototype and low-volume production parts.

Geographic Reach

Proto Labs' headquarters are located in Maple Plain, Minnesota. Its operations are comprised of three geographic operating segments in the US (about 80% of sales), Europe (nearly 20%), and Japan (accounts for the rest). It also manufacture all of its products in over 10 manufacturing facilities, located in Rosemount, Minnesota; Plymouth, Minnesota; Brooklyn Park, Minnesota; Cary, North Carolina; Nashua, New Hampshire (two facilities); Telford, UK; Putzbrunn, Germany; Eschenlohe, Germany; and Zama, Kanagawa,

Japan.

Sales and Marketing

The company maintains an internal sales team trained in the basics of part design and the capabilities of its manufacturing product lines, as well as the key advantages of its processes over alternate methods of custom parts manufacturing.

Proto Labs' advertising expenses were approximately $11.6 million, $11.5 million, and $13.0 million for the years ended December 31, 2021, 2020, and 2019, respectively.

Financial Performance

Proto Labs' revenue increased $53.7 million, or 12% to $488.1 million, for 2021 compared with 2020. By product line, the company's revenue increase was driven by a 27% increase in CNC Machining revenue, a 16% increase in 3D Printing revenue, a 4% increase in Injection Molding revenue, and an 8% increase in Sheet Metal revenue, which was partially offset by a 41% decrease in Other Revenue, in each case for 2021 compared with 2020.

Net income for fiscal 2021 decreased by 34% to $33.4 million compared from the prior year with $50.9 million. This was primarily due to a higher volume of total operating expenses for the year.

The company's cash at the end of 2021 was $65.9 million. Operating activities generated $55.2 million, while investing activities used $94.7 million, mainly for cash of acquisitions. Financing activities used another $22.2 million, primarily for repurchases of common stock.

Strategy

Proto Labs currently operates in a global custom contract manufacturing market which is a form of outsourcing where companies enter into an arrangement or formal agreement with another company or individual for the manufacture of complete parts, products, or components. Since the company's inception, it has focused on areas where it could automate the manufacturing process via digital model. Proto Labs' initial focus was on prototypes and simple parts and have added complexity over time. The company has added product lines and expanded those product lines to meet the needs of customers, which has ultimately driven its growth. Historically, the company focused on speed, reliability and quality as key components of its differentiation, and customers used the company for production where there was a good fit.

Proto Labs has further expanded its offering through the acquisition of Hubs to be able to serve customers more holistically, augmenting its in-house manufacturing capabilities with a network of premium manufacturing partners to serve customer needs that currently reside outside of its internal manufacturing capabilities.

Mergers and Acquisitions

In early 2021, Proto Labs completed its acquisition of 3D Hubs, Inc., a leading online manufacturing platform that provides customers with on-demand access to a global network of approximately 240 premium manufacturing partners based in Amsterdam. The completion of this transaction creates the world's most comprehensive digital manufacturing offer for custom parts. It also brings two great benefits to Protolabs' customers: a complementary network of manufacturing partners to fulfill a breadth of capabilities outside of its current envelope, and a broader selection of pricing and lead time options. Protolabs acquired 3D Hubs for aggregate closing consideration of $280 million, consisting of $130 million in cash and $150 million in Protolabs stock.

Company Background

Proto Labs began as The Protomold Company (molded plastic parts) but added CNC metal part machining, its Firstcut business, in 2007. In 2009 both branches began operating under the Proto Labs banner. It all started when founder and computer geek Lawrence Lukis started a desktop printer design business and was astounded at the long turnaround (weeks) and cost (thousands) for prototype parts. He turned his computer skills to solving the problem and found a way to completely automate the entire process and produce a part in a day for prices starting at $1,500.

EXECUTIVES

Chairman, Lead Director, Director, Sven A. Wehrwein

President, Chief Executive Officer, Director, Robert Bodor, $300,456 total compensation

Development Executive Vice President, Development Chief Financial Officer, John A. Way, $351,880 total compensation

Chief Technology Officer, Arthur R. Baker III., $300,300 total compensation

Region Officer, Bjoern Klaas

Director, Victoria M. Holt, $550,000 total compensation

Director, Archie C. Black

Director, Sujeet Chand

Director, Moonhie Chin

Director, Rainer Gawlick

Director, John B. Goodman

Director, Donald G. Krantz, $286,083 total compensation

Auditors : Ernst & Young LLP

LOCATIONS

HQ: Proto Labs Inc
 5540 Pioneer Creek Drive, Maple Plain, MN 55359
Phone: 763 479-3680
Web: www.protolabs.com

2013 Sales

	% of total
US	73
International	27
Total	100

PRODUCTS/OPERATIONS

2013 Sales

	$ mil.	% of total
Protomold	115.1	71
Firstcut	48.0	29
Total	163.1	100

COMPETITORS

APTARGROUP, INC.
ASSOCIATED MATERIALS, LLC
BERRY GLOBAL GROUP, INC.
COGNEX CORPORATION
ELECTRO SCIENTIFIC INDUSTRIES, INC.
ENTEGRIS, INC.
ILLINOIS TOOL WORKS INC.
MYERS INDUSTRIES, INC.
PHILLIPS MEDISIZE
STRATASYS LTD

HISTORICAL FINANCIALS

Company Type: Public

Income Statement — FYE: December 31

	REVENUE ($mil)	NET INCOME ($mil)	NET PROFIT MARGIN	EMPLOYEES
12/21	488.0	33.3	6.8%	2,663
12/20	434.3	50.8	11.7%	2,408
12/19	458.7	63.6	13.9%	2,535
12/18	445.5	76.5	17.2%	2,487
12/17	344.4	51.7	15.0%	2,266
Annual Growth	9.1%	(10.4%)	—	4.1%

2021 Year-End Financials

Debt ratio: 0.2%
Return on equity: 4.5%
Cash ($ mil.): 65.9
Current Ratio: 3.34
Long-term debt ($ mil.): 1.3
No. of shares ($ mil.): 27.4
Dividends
 Yield: —
 Payout: —
Market value ($ mil.): 1,410.0

	STOCK PRICE ($) FY Close	P/E High/Low		PER SHARE ($) Earnings	Dividends	Book Value
12/21	51.35	208	40	1.21	0.00	30.16
12/20	153.40	99	34	1.89	0.00	24.06
12/19	101.55	55	38	2.35	0.00	21.87
12/18	112.79	58	36	2.81	0.00	20.07
12/17	103.00	55	25	1.93	0.00	17.19
Annual Growth	(16.0%)	—	—	(11.0%)	—	15.1%

Provident Bancorp Inc (MD)

EXECUTIVES

Chairperson, Director, Laurie H. Knapp

Co-President, Co-Chief Executive Officer, Subsidiary Officer, Director, Joseph B. Reilly

Co-President, Co-Chief Executive Officer, Chief Financial Officer, Subsidiary Officer, Carol L. Houle, $270,000 total compensation

Executive Vice President, Chief Operating Officer, Subsidiary Officer, Joseph Mancini

Director, Lisa DeStefano

Director, Jay E. Gould

Director, Kathleen Chase Curran

Director, Mohammad Shaikh

Director, James A. DeLeo
Director, Barbara A. Piette
Director, Frank G. Cousins
Director, Arthur Sullivan
Auditors : Crowe LLP

LOCATIONS

HQ: Provident Bancorp Inc (MD)
  5 Market Street, Amesbury, MA 01913
Phone: 978 834-8555
Web: www.theprovidentbank.com

HISTORICAL FINANCIALS
Company Type: Public

Income Statement — FYE: December 31

	ASSETS ($mil)	NET INCOME ($mil)	INCOME AS % OF ASSETS	EMPLOYEES
12/20	1,505.7	11.9	0.8%	158
12/19	1,121.7	10.8	1.0%	144
12/18	974.0	9.3	1.0%	132
12/17	902.2	7.9	0.9%	135
12/16	795.5	6.3	0.8%	128
Annual Growth	17.3%	17.3%	—	5.4%

2020 Year-End Financials
Return on assets: 0.9%
Return on equity: 5.1%
Long-term debt ($ mil.): —
No. of shares ($ mil.): 19.0
Sales ($ mil.): 63.9
Dividends
  Yield: 0.7%
  Payout: 60.0%
Market value ($ mil.): 229.0

	STOCK PRICE ($) FY Close	P/E High/Low		PER SHARE ($) Earnings	Dividends	Book Value
12/20	12.00	19	11	0.66	0.09	12.38
12/19	12.45	47	18	0.60	0.00	11.86
12/18	21.68	30	20	1.00	0.00	13.05
12/17	26.45	31	20	0.86	0.00	12.02
12/16	17.90	28	19	0.69	0.00	11.31
Annual Growth	(9.5%)	—	—	(1.1%)	—	2.3%

Prudential Bancorp Inc (New)

EXECUTIVES

Chairman, Director, Bruce E. Miller
President, Chief Executive Officer, Subsidiary Officer, Director, Dennis Pollack, $398,375 total compensation
Executive Vice President, Chief Operating Officer, Subsidiary Officer, Anthony V. Migliorino, $281,538 total compensation
Senior Vice President, Chief Financial Officer, Treasurer, Subsidiary Officer, Jack E. Rothkopf, $177,874 total compensation
Vice President, Controller, Subsidiary Officer, Robert E. Pollard
Director, John C. Hosier
Director, A. J. Fanelli
Director, Raymond J. Vanaria
Auditors : S.R. Snodgrass, P.C.

LOCATIONS

HQ: Prudential Bancorp Inc (New)
  1834 West Oregon Avenue, Philadelphia, PA 19145
Phone: 215 755-1500
Web: www.prudentialsavingsbank.com

HISTORICAL FINANCIALS
Company Type: Public

Income Statement — FYE: September 30

	ASSETS ($mil)	NET INCOME ($mil)	INCOME AS % OF ASSETS	EMPLOYEES
09/21	1,100.4	7.7	0.7%	90
09/20	1,223.3	9.5	0.8%	93
09/19	1,289.4	9.5	0.7%	88
09/18	1,081.1	7.0	0.7%	83
09/17	899.5	2.7	0.3%	87
Annual Growth	5.2%	29.4%	—	0.9%

2021 Year-End Financials
Return on assets: 0.6%
Return on equity: 5.9%
Long-term debt ($ mil.): —
No. of shares ($ mil.): 7.7
Sales ($ mil.): 41.6
Dividends
  Yield: 1.8%
  Payout: 34.5%
Market value ($ mil.): 119.0

	STOCK PRICE ($) FY Close	P/E High/Low		PER SHARE ($) Earnings	Dividends	Book Value
09/21	15.26	16	11	0.98	0.28	16.79
09/20	10.54	17	9	1.12	0.71	15.86
09/19	17.01	17	14	1.07	0.65	15.71
09/18	17.31	25	21	0.78	0.70	14.29
09/17	18.53	57	44	0.32	0.12	15.12
Annual Growth	(4.7%)	—	—	32.3%	23.6%	2.7%

PTC Inc

PTC is a global software and services company that serves industrial companies through its offerings in CAD, PLM, the IoT, and AR that help customers digitize operations and collaborate. In computer aided design (CAD), its Creo offering is used to create 3D computer models for products ranging from engines to phones. PTC's Windchill software suite for product lifecycle management (PLM) enables collaborative content and process management over the internet. With ThingWorx, PTC provides a platform for developing applications for the Internet of Things (IoT). The augmented reality (AR) product, Vuforia Studio, overlays digital information such as repair instructions onto the view of physical objects and processes. The Americas account for more than 40% of PTC's revenue.

Operations

PTC has two operating and reportable segments: Software Products (90% of sales) and Professional Services (about 10% of sales).

Software Products, which includes license, subscription and related support revenue (including updates and technical support) for all its products; and Professional Services, which includes consulting, implementation and training services.

Geographic Reach

Boston-based PTC has nearly 90 office locations used in operations in the United States and internationally, predominately as sales and/or support offices and for research and development work. Most of its research and development activities are conducted in India. Operations in Americas accounts for more than 40% of PTC's revenue.

Sales and Marketing

PTC devices most of its sales from products and services sold directly by its sales force to end-user customers. Approximately 30% to 35% of its sales of products and services are through third-party resellers. Its sales force focuses on large accounts, while its reseller channel provides a cost-effective means of covering the small-and-medium-size business market.

Total advertising expenses incurred were $7.1 million, $3.8 million, and $3.6 million in 2021, 2020, and 2019, respectively.

Financial Performance

PTC's revenue has consistently increased in the last five years, ending it with 2021 as its highest performing year.

The company's revenue for fiscal 2021 increased by $346 million to $1.8 billion compared to $1.5 billion in the prior year. Professional services revenue grew in fiscal 2021 by 10%; where fiscal 2020 revenue was negatively impacted by the COVID-19 pandemic, fiscal 2021 benefited from increased delivery activity associated with PLM deployments.

PTC's net income also increased by $345 thousand to $476.9 million as compared to the prior year's net income of about $130.7 million.

The company held about $327 million by the end of the year. Operations of the company provided about $368.8 million. Investing activities used about $688 million, while financing activities used about $370.3 million. Main cash uses were for acquisition of businesses, additions to property and equipment and repayments of borrowings under credit facility.

Strategy

The three key elements to the company's strategy to deliver long-term shareholder value include aligning with market demand to build a strong pipeline; optimizing new and renewal sales and customer success to power top line ARR growth; and creating an efficient business model and operation that enables the company to drive free cash flow growth. Further, the company aims to shift the company's organizational structure to align better with a traditional SaaS model and create an improved customer experience.

Mergers and Acquisitions

In 2021, PTC completed the acquisition of Arena Solutions, the industry's leading software as a services (SaaS) product lifecycle management (PLM) solution, for $715 million. The combination of Arena Solutions and Onshape, which PTC acquired in 2019, establishes PTC as the leading provider of pure SaaS solutions for the product development market and broadly extends PTC's presence in the attractive mid-market, where SaaS solutions are becoming the standards.

HISTORY

Geometry professor Samuel Geisberg fled the USSR in 1974 and worked for computer-aided design (CAD) software development firms Computervision and Applicon. At the urging of his brother Vladimir (who had emigrated in 1980 and started his own software firm) he founded Parametric Technology in 1985 to remedy flaws in mechanical design software.

With financial backing from Charles River Ventures and other investors, Geisberg developed his CAD/CAM (computer-aided manufacturing) product. Charles River also brought in Steven Walske as CEO in 1986. The first Pro/ENGINEER product was shipped in 1988, and Parametric went public the next year, building market strength by marketing to engineers and keeping prices at half those of competitors' products.

In 1994 Walske became chairman when Geisberg retired and took up the position of senior scientist. The next year Parametric purchased Evans & Sutherland Computer's conceptual design and rendering software business and model simulation firm Rasna, which offered tools that let users simulate the operation of products in real-life settings. In 1996 Parametric acquired project modeling and management software from Greenshire License Company.

EXECUTIVES

Chairman, Director, Robert P. Schechter
Software Solutions President, Software Solutions Chief Executive Officer, Director, James E. Heppelmann, $800,000 total compensation
Executive Vice President, Chief Financial Officer, Kristian Talvitie
Executive Vice President, General Counsel, Secretary, Aaron C. von Staats
Corporate & Securities Counsel Senior Vice President, Corporate & Securities Counsel Assistant Secretary, Catherine Kniker
Sales Division Officer, Michael DiTullio
Director, Amarpreet Hanspal
Director, Michal Katz
Director, Mark D. Benjamin
Director, Janice D. Chaffin
Director, Klaus Hoehn
Director, Paul A. Lacy
Director, Corinna Lathan
Director, Blake D. Moret
Auditors : PricewaterhouseCoopers LLP

LOCATIONS

HQ: PTC Inc
121 Seaport Boulevard, Boston, MA 02210
Phone: 781 370-5000
Web: www.ptc.com

2014 Sales

	$ mil.	% of total
Americas	558.7	41
Europe	528.1	39
Pacific Rim	148.2	11
Japan	122.0	9
Total	1,357	100

PRODUCTS/OPERATIONS

2018 Sales

	$ mil.	% of total
Software	1,088.5	88
Services	153.5	12
Total	1,241.8	100

2018 Sales by Product

	$ mil.	% of total
CAD	499.8	40
PLM	483.3	39
IoT	139.3	11
IoT	119.4	10
Total	1,241.8	100

Selected Software

2-D and 3-D visualization and virtual reality mockup (Division)
Collaborative product development (Windchill)
Entry-level product development (Pro/DESKTOP)
Product design automation and management (Pro/ENGINEER)
Simulation (Pro/MECHANICA)

COMPETITORS

AEROHIVE NETWORKS, INC.
ALTERYX, INC.
CIENA CORPORATION
CMTSU LIQUIDATION, INC
MENTOR GRAPHICS CORPORATION
N MODEL INC
NANTHEALTH, INC.
NETSCOUT SYSTEMS, INC.
PEGASYSTEMS INC.
UNISYS CORPORATION

HISTORICAL FINANCIALS

Company Type: Public

Income Statement   FYE: September 30

	REVENUE ($mil)	NET INCOME ($mil)	NET PROFIT MARGIN	EMPLOYEES
09/21	1,807.1	476.9	26.4%	6,709
09/20	1,458.4	130.6	9.0%	6,243
09/19	1,255.6	(27.4)	—	6,055
09/18	1,241.8	51.9	4.2%	6,110
09/17	1,164.0	6.2	0.5%	6,041
Annual Growth	11.6%	195.7%	—	2.7%

2021 Year-End Financials

Debt ratio: 31.9%   No. of shares ($ mil.): 117.1
Return on equity: 27.4%   Dividends
Cash ($ mil.): 326.5   Yield: —
Current Ratio: 1.38   Payout: —
Long-term debt ($ mil.): 1,439.4   Market value ($ mil.): 14,035.0

	STOCK PRICE ($) FY Close	P/E High/Low		PER SHARE ($) Earnings	Dividends	Book Value
09/21	119.79	37	20	4.03	0.00	17.40
09/20	82.72	86	43	1.12	0.00	12.39
09/19	68.18	—	—	(0.23)	0.00	10.46
09/18	106.19	236	125	0.44	0.00	7.41
09/17	56.28	1194	865	0.05	0.00	7.68
Annual Growth	20.8%	—	—	199.6%	—	22.7%

Pure Cycle Corp.

Struggling to survive in the barren waste without a trace of water is no longer the fate of inhabitants of the Lowry Range, thanks to Pure Cycle. The water utility has the exclusive right to provide water and wastewater services to about 24,000 acres of the Lowry Range, near Denver. Pure Cycle generates revenues from three sources: water and wastewater fees; construction fees; and monthly service fees. In 2009 it served 247 single-family water connections and 157 wastewater connections in the southeastern Denver area. It also has 60,000 acre-feet of water rights in the Arkansas River basin in Southern Colorado. In 2010Â Pure CycleÂ acquired the 931-acre Sky Ranch Property near DenverÂ for $7 million.

EXECUTIVES

Chairperson, Director, Patrick J. Beirne
President, Chief Executive Officer, Corporate Secretary, Director, Mark W. Harding, $400,000 total compensation
Vice President, Chief Financial Officer, Principal Accounting Officer, Kevin B. McNeill
Director, Jeffrey Sheets
Director, Daniel R. Kozlowski
Director, Fredrick A. Fendel
Director, Arthur G. Epker
Director, Peter C. Howell
Auditors : Plante & Moran PLLC

LOCATIONS

HQ: Pure Cycle Corp.
34501 E. Quincy Avenue, Building 34, Watkins, CO 80137
Phone: 303 292-3456
Web: www.purecyclewater.com

COMPETITORS

DENVER BOARD OF WATER COMMISSIONERS
LAS VEGAS VALLEY WATER DISTRICT
SAN ANTONIO WATER SYSTEM
SAN DIEGO COUNTY WATER AUTHORITY
SJW GROUP

HISTORICAL FINANCIALS

Company Type: Public

Income Statement   FYE: August 31

	REVENUE ($mil)	NET INCOME ($mil)	NET PROFIT MARGIN	EMPLOYEES
08/21	17.1	20.1	117.4%	31
08/20	25.8	6.7	26.1%	31
08/19	20.3	4.8	23.6%	29
08/18	6.9	0.4	6.0%	19
08/17	1.2	(1.7)	—	11
Annual Growth	93.3%	—	—	29.6%

2021 Year-End Financials

Debt ratio: —   No. of shares ($ mil.): 23.9
Return on equity: 21.7%   Dividends
Cash ($ mil.): 20.1   Yield: —
Current Ratio: 3.11   Payout: —
Long-term debt ($ mil.): —   Market value ($ mil.): 358.0

	STOCK PRICE ($) FY Close	P/E High/Low		PER SHARE ($) Earnings	Dividends	Book Value
08/21	14.95	20	10	0.83	0.00	4.30
08/20	9.76	49	28	0.28	0.00	3.44
08/19	10.85	59	46	0.20	0.00	3.14
08/18	11.25	560	333	0.02	0.00	2.92
08/17	7.25	—	—	(0.07)	0.00	2.84
Annual Growth	19.8%	—	—	—	—	10.9%

QCR Holdings Inc

QCR Holdings is the holding company for Quad City Bank & Trust, Cedar Rapids Bank & Trust, Springfield First Community Bank, and Community State Bank. Together, the banks have about 40 offices serving the Quad Cities, Cedar Rapids, Cedar Valley, Des Moines/Ankeny and Springfield communities. The banks provide full-service commercial and consumer banking and trust and wealth management services. Its other operating subsidiaries include m2 which is based in Brookfield, Wisconsin, is engaged in the business of lending and leasing machinery and equipment to C&I businesses under direct financing lease contracts and equipment financing agreements. The company has approximately $7.7 billion in assets, $6.0 billion in loans and $5.9 billion in deposits.

Operations

The company's Commercial Banking business is geographically divided by markets into the operating segments corresponding to the four subsidiary banks wholly owned by the company: Cedar Rapids Bank & Trust (accounts for about 30% of revenue), Quad City Bank & Trust (more than 20%), Community State Bank (about 10%) and Springfield First Community Bank (some 10%).

Geographic Reach

QCR Holdings, headquartered in Moline, Illinois, serves the Quad Cities, Cedar Rapids, Waterloo/Cedar Valley, Des Moines/Ankeny, and Springfield communities.

Financial Performance

Net interest income grew $11.3 million, or 7% to $178.2 million in 2021 compared to the prior year. The increase in 2021 was primarily due to strong loan/lease growth funded by core deposit growth while maintaining modest excess liquidity.

In 2021, the company had a net income of $98.9 million, a 62% increase from the previous year's net income of $60.6 million.

The company's cash at the end of 2021 was $37.5 million. Operating activities generated $88.2 million, while investing activities used $411.8 million, mainly for net increase in loans/leases originated and held for investment. Financing activities provided another $299.7 million.

Strategy

The company took the following actions in 2021 to support its corporate strategy:

The company grew loans and leases organically in 2021 by 16.9%, excluding PPP loans (non-GAAP), driven by both its specialty finance group and the company's traditional lending and leasing business.

Correspondent banking continues to be a core line of business for the company. The company is competitively positioned with experienced staff, software systems and processes to continue growing in the four states it currently serves ? Iowa, Wisconsin, Missouri and Illinois. The company acts as the correspondent bank for 187 downstream banks with total average noninterest bearing deposits of $349.0 million and total average interest bearing deposits of $305.3 million for 2021. This line of business provides a strong source of noninterest bearing and interest bearing deposits, fee income, high-quality loan participations and bank stock loans.

The company is focused on executing interest rate swaps on select commercial loans, including LIHTC permanent loans. The interest rate swaps allow the commercial borrowers to pay a fixed interest rate while the company receives a variable interest rate as well as an upfront nonrefundable fee dependent on the pricing. Management believes that these swaps help position the company more favorably for rising rate environments. The company will continue to review opportunities to execute these swaps at all of its subsidiary banks, as the circumstances are appropriate for the borrower and the company. Future levels of swap fees are somewhat dependent upon prevailing interest rates. Swap fee income/capital markets revenue totaled $61.0 million in 2021 as compared to $74.8 million in 2020. Swap fee income relative to the increase in notional amount of the non-hedging interest rate swap contracts was 11.5% in 2021 and 10.6% in 2020.

Mergers and Acquisitions

In 2022, QCR Holdings announced the successful completion of the acquisition of Guaranty Federal Bancshares, Inc. (Guaranty). Guaranty's banking subsidiary, Guaranty Bank, merged into QCR Holdings' Springfield-based charter, Springfield First Community (SFC) Bank. The new combined bank retain the Guaranty Bank name and operate under the leadership of CEO Monte McNew and President Shaun Burke. "This combination brings together two organizations that share core values and business strategies, and we look forward to further building upon our market share in the region," said Larry Helling, QCR Holdings Chief Executive Officer. The transaction is valued at approximately $151.6 million.

EXECUTIVES

Chairman, Director, Marie Z. Ziegler
President, Chief Financial Officer, Chief Operating Officer, Director, Todd A. Gipple, $270,000 total compensation
Chief Executive Officer, Subsidiary Officer, Director, Larry J. Helling, $270,000 total compensation
Subsidiary Officer, Director, Elizabeth S. Jacobs
Subsidiary Officer, Director, Mark C. Kilmer
Human Resources Director, Human Resources Senior Vice President, Anne E. Howard
Subsidiary Officer, Kurt Gibson
Subsidiary Officer, James D. Klein
Subsidiary Officer, John H. Anderson, $212,500 total compensation
Subsidiary Officer, Director, Donna J. Sorensen
Subsidiary Officer, Director, Brent R. Cobb
Director, Patrick S. Baird
Director, Mary Kay Bates
Director, John-Paul E. Besong
Director, James M. Field
Director, John F. Griesemer
Auditors : RSM US LLP

LOCATIONS

HQ: QCR Holdings Inc
3551 7th Street, Moline, IL 61265
Phone: 309 736-3580
Web: www.qcrh.com

PRODUCTS/OPERATIONS

2015 Sales

	$ mil.	% of total
Quad City Bank & Trust	52.8	46
Cedar Rapids Bank & Trust	37.5	32
Rockford Bank & Trust	14.8	13
Wealth Management	9.1	8
All other	0.7	1
Inter-company Eliminations	(0.4)	-
Total	114.5	100

COMPETITORS

AMERICAN RIVER BANKSHARES
APOLLO BANCORP, INC.
ARVEST BANK GROUP, INC.
BLUE VALLEY BAN CORP.
BREMER FINANCIAL CORPORATION
COMMUNITY SHORES BANK CORPORATION
FIRSTBANK CORPORATION
MIDLAND FINANCIAL CO.
NORTHEAST COMMUNITY BANCORP, INC.
OAK VALLEY BANCORP.

HISTORICAL FINANCIALS

Company Type: Public

Income Statement				FYE: December 31
	ASSETS ($mil)	NET INCOME ($mil)	INCOME AS % OF ASSETS	EMPLOYEES
12/20	5,682.7	60.5	1.1%	739
12/19	4,909.0	57.4	1.2%	697
12/18	4,949.7	43.1	0.9%	755
12/17	3,982.6	35.7	0.9%	641
12/16	3,301.9	27.6	0.8%	572
Annual Growth	14.5%	21.6%	—	6.6%

2020 Year-End Financials

Return on assets: 1.1%   Dividends
Return on equity: 10.7%   Yield: 0.6%
Long-term debt ($ mil.): —   Payout: 6.5%
No. of shares ($ mil.): 15.8   Market value ($ mil.): 626.0
Sales ($ mil.): 312.1

	STOCK PRICE ($) FY Close	P/E High/Low		PER SHARE ($) Earnings	Dividends	Book Value
12/20	39.59	11	6	3.80	0.24	37.57
12/19	43.86	12	9	3.60	0.24	33.82
12/18	32.09	17	10	2.86	0.24	30.10
12/17	42.85	18	15	2.61	0.20	25.38
12/16	43.30	20	10	2.17	0.16	21.82
Annual Growth	(2.2%)	—	—	15.0%	10.7%	14.5%

	STOCK PRICE ($) FY Close	P/E High/Low		PER SHARE ($) Earnings	Dividends	Book Value
12/20	253.39	116	50	2.22	1.55	73.97
12/19	164.52	108	69	2.08	1.51	69.96
12/18	177.71	47	32	4.45	1.45	32.62
12/17	150.79	108	82	1.52	1.40	30.63
12/16	127.94	29	15	4.63	1.33	30.33
Annual Growth	18.6%	—	—	(16.8%)	3.9%	25.0%

Quaker Houghton

EXECUTIVES

Chairman, Director, Michael F. Barry, $845,192 total compensation
President, Chief Executive Officer, Director, Andrew E. Tometich
Finance Senior Vice President, Finance Chief Financial Officer, Shane W. Hostetter
Global Operations, Environmental, Health & Safety and Procurement Senior Vice President, Wilbert L. Platzer, $338,253 total compensation
Senior Vice President, General Counsel, Corporate Secretary, Robert T. Traub
Chief Commercial Officer, Joseph A. Berquist, $343,939 total compensation
Chief Strategy Officer, Jeewat Bijlani
Lead Director, Director, Donald R. Caldwell
Director, Mark A. Douglas
Director, Sanjay Hinduja
Director, William H. Osborne
Director, Fay West
Director, Robert H. Rock
Director, Ramaswami Seshasayee
Director, Charlotte C. Decker
Director, Jeffry D. Frisby
Director, Michael J. Shannon
Auditors : PricewaterhouseCoopers LLP

LOCATIONS

HQ: Quaker Houghton
  901 E. Hector Street, Conshohocken, PA 19428-2380
Phone: 610 832-4000   Fax: 610 832-8682
Web: www.quakerchem.com

HISTORICAL FINANCIALS

Company Type: Public

Income Statement   FYE: December 31

	REVENUE ($mil)	NET INCOME ($mil)	NET PROFIT MARGIN	EMPLOYEES
12/20	1,417.6	39.6	2.8%	4,200
12/19	1,133.5	31.6	2.8%	4,500
12/18	867.5	59.4	6.9%	2,160
12/17	820.0	20.2	2.5%	2,110
12/16	746.6	61.4	8.2%	2,020
Annual Growth	17.4%	(10.4%)	—	20.1%

2020 Year-End Financials

Debt ratio: 30.7%
Return on equity: 3.0%
Cash ($ mil.): 181.8
Current Ratio: 2.07
Long-term debt ($ mil.): 849
No. of shares ($ mil.): 17.8
Dividends
  Yield: 0.6%
  Payout: 69.8%
Market value ($ mil.): 4,523.0

Qualys, Inc.

Qualys is a pioneer and leading provider of a cloud-based platform delivering information technology (IT), security and compliance solutions. The Qualys Cloud Platform offers an integrated suite of solutions that automates the lifecycle of asset discovery and management, security assessments, and compliance management for an organization's IT infrastructure and assets, whether such infrastructure and assets reside inside the organization, on their network perimeter, on endpoints or in the cloud. Its biggest product, Vulnerability Management, includes continuous monitoring, threat protection, and IT asset tracking through a cloud agent. The company counts more than 10,000 customers in over 130 countries. Qualys reaches many customers through partnerships with managed service providers, consultants, and resellers, including IBM, Fujitsu, Optiv, and Verizon Communications.

Operations

Qualys designed its qualys cloud platform to transform the way organizations secure and protect their IT infrastructures and applications. The company's cloud platform offers an integrated suite of solutions that automates the lifecycle of asset discovery and management, security assessments, and compliance management for an organization's IT infrastructure and assets, whether such infrastructure and assets reside inside the organization, on their network perimeter, on endpoints or in the cloud. Since inception, Qualys' solutions have been designed to be delivered through the cloud and to be easily and rapidly deployed on a global scale, enabling faster implementation and lower total cost of ownership than traditional on-premises enterprise software products. Its customers, ranging from some of the largest global organizations to small businesses, are served from the company's globally-distributed cloud platform, enabling Qualys to rapidly deliver new solutions, enhancements and security updates.

The company's direct sales generates almost 60% of the company's revenue, while the rest is provided by its partner sales.

Geographic Reach

Qualys is based in Foster, California and has additional US offices in North Carolina and Washington and other offices in France, Germany, Italy, Japan, the Netherlands, Russia, United Arab Emirates and United Kingdom.

It operates principal data centers at third-party facilities in Santa Clara, California; Las Vegas, Nevada; Ontario, Canada; Geneva, Switzerland; Pune, India; and Amsterdam, the Netherlands.

Over 65% of its revenue comes from the US operations.

Sales and Marketing

Qualys markets its products through customers directly through the company sales teams as well in indirectly through network channel partners. In addition, the company markets and sell through enterprise, government entities, small and medium sized businesses across a broad range of industries, including education, financial services, government, healthcare, insurance, manufacturing, media, retail, technology and utilities.

Advertising costs were $2.1 million, $1.6 million and $1.5 million for the years 2021, 2020 and 2019, respectively.

Financial Performance

Revenues increased by $48.2 million to $411.2 million in 2021 compared to 2020, due to an increase in IT Security, Compliance, Web Application Security, Asset Management and Cloud and Container Security subscriptions. The revenue growth was primarily from an increase in renewal and expansion business in 2021 compared to 2020.

In 2021, Qualys had a net income of $71 million, a 23% decrease from the previous year.

The company's cash at the end of 2021 was $138.5 million. Operating activities provided $200.6 million, while investing activities used $29.5 million, mainly for purchases of marketable securities. Financing activities used another $107.9 million, mainly for repurchases of common stock.

Strategy

Qualys intends to strengthen its leadership position as a trusted provider of cloud-based IT, security and compliance solutions. The key elements of its growth strategy are:

Continuing to innovate and enhance its cloud platform and suite of solutions. Qualys intends to continue to make significant investments in research and development to extend its cloud platform's functionality by developing new security solutions and capabilities and further enhancing the company's existing suite of solutions;

Expanding the use of the company's suite of solutions by its large and diverse customer base. With more than 19,000 customers, including active subscribers of the company's free services, across many industries and geographies, Qualys believes it has a significant opportunity to sell additional solutions to customers and expand their use of its suite of solutions;

Driving new customer growth and broadening its global reach. The company is pursuing new customers by targeting key accounts, releasing free IT, security and compliance services and expanding both sales and marketing organization and network of channel partners; and

Selectively pursuing technology acquisitions to bolster its capabilities and leadership position. Qualys may explore acquisitions that are complementary to and can expand the functionality of its cloud platform. The company may also seek to acquire development teams to supplement its own personnel and acquire technology to increase the breadth of the company's cloud-based IT, security and compliance solutions.

Mergers and Acquisitions

In 2021, Qualys has entered into an agreement to acquire TotalCloud, a cloud workflow management and no-code automation platform. Upon closing, this acquisition will further strengthen Qualys' Cloud Security solution allowing customers to build user-defined workflows for custom policies and execute them on-demand for simplified security and compliance. To implement a workflow in a multi-cloud environment, users simply drag and drop componentized blocks to build any flow of actions to achieve a particular output, such as a compliance check or remediation.

EXECUTIVES

Chairman, Director, Jeffrey P. Hank
Engineering President, Engineering Chief Executive Officer, Director, Sumedh S. Thakar, $325,000 total compensation
Chief Legal Officer, Corporate Secretary, Bruce K. Posey, $275,000 total compensation
Chief Financial Officer, Principal Financial Officer, Principal Accounting Officer, Joo Mi Kim
Chief Revenue Officer, Allan Peters
Director, Kristi Marie Rogers
Director, William Berutti
Director, Peter Pace
Director, Wendy M. Pfeiffer
Director, John A. Zangardi
Auditors: Grant Thornton LLP

LOCATIONS

HQ: Qualys, Inc.
919 E. Hillsdale Boulevard, 4th Floor, Foster City, CA 94404
Phone: 650 801-6100
Web: www.qualys.com

2018 Sales

	$ mil.	% of total
US	185.9	67
Foreign	93	33
Total	278.9	100

PRODUCTS/OPERATIONS

2018 Sales

	$ in mil.	% of total
Direct	164.1	59
Partner	114.8	41
Total	278.9	100

COMPETITORS

BLACKLINE, INC.
COGNIZANT TECHNOLOGY SOLUTIONS CORPORATION
IMPERVA, INC.
INFOBLOX INC.
INFOR, INC.
JUNIPER NETWORKS, INC.
MICROSTRATEGY INCORPORATED
PERFICIENT, INC.
SERVICENOW, INC.
VERINT SYSTEMS INC.

HISTORICAL FINANCIALS
Company Type: Public

Income Statement — FYE: December 31

	REVENUE ($mil)	NET INCOME ($mil)	NET PROFIT MARGIN	EMPLOYEES
12/20	362.9	91.5	25.2%	1,498
12/19	321.6	69.3	21.6%	1,289
12/18	278.8	57.3	20.5%	1,194
12/17	230.8	40.4	17.5%	869
12/16	197.9	19.2	9.7%	684
Annual Growth	16.4%	47.7%	—	21.7%

2020 Year-End Financials
Debt ratio: —
Return on equity: 23.0%
Cash ($ mil.): 74.1
Current Ratio: 1.86
Long-term debt ($ mil.): —
No. of shares ($ mil.): 39.2
Dividends
Yield: —
Payout: —
Market value ($ mil.): 4,784.0

	STOCK PRICE ($) FY Close	P/E High/Low		PER SHARE ($) Earnings	Dividends	Book Value
12/20	121.87	54	29	2.24	0.00	10.30
12/19	83.37	54	39	1.68	0.00	9.88
12/18	74.74	66	40	1.37	0.00	9.18
12/17	59.35	57	30	1.01	0.00	8.90
12/16	31.65	71	32	0.50	0.00	7.21
Annual Growth	40.1%	—	—	45.5%	—	9.3%

Quidel Corp.

Quidel Corporation makes rapid diagnostic in vitro test products used at the point-of-care (POC), usually at a doctor's office or other outpatient setting. The diagnostic solutions aid in the detection and diagnosis of many critical diseases and other medical conditions, including infectious diseases, cardiovascular diseases and conditions, women's health, gastrointestinal diseases, autoimmune diseases, bone health and thyroid diseases. Its cardiac immunoassay tests are used in physician offices, hospital laboratories and emergency departments, and other urgent care or alternative site settings. Majority of its revenue comes from its domestic operation.

Operations

The company's diagnostic testing solutions are divided in four product categories: rapid immunoassay, cardiac immunoassay, specialized diagnostic solutions and molecular diagnostic solutions.

Rapid Immunoassay offers the easy-to-use Sofia and Sofia 2 analyzers combined with unique software and Sofia FIA tests to yield an automatic, objective result that is readily available on the instrument's screen, in a hard-copy printout, and in a transmissible electronic form that can network via a lab information system to hospital and medical center databases. QuickVue is the brand name for its rapid, visually-read, lateral flow immunoassay products and InflammaDry and AdenoPlus products for lateral-flow based. It accounts for around 70% of total revenue.

Cardiac Immunoassay offers Triage MeterPro, a portable testing platform that runs a comprehensive menu of tests that enable physicians to promote improved health outcomes through the rapid diagnosis of critical diseases and health conditions, as well as the detection of certain drugs of abuse. It also offers a version of the Triage BNP Test for use on Beckman Coulter lab analyzers. It accounts for about 15% of total revenue.

Specialized Diagnostic Solutions (more than 15%) provide a wide variety of traditional cell lines, specimen collection devices, media and controls for use in laboratories and also provide a variety of biomarkers for bone health and produce both clinical and research products for the assessment of osteoporosis.

Molecular Diagnostic Solutions (less than 5%) offers Solana an easy to run amplification and detection system that has the ability to concurrently run up to 12 assays at a time, Lyra (open system molecular assays run on several thermocyclers), and developing the Savanna system as a low-cost, fully-integrated system with sample in/result out simplicity.

Geographic Reach

Headquartered in San Diego, California, Quidel has five manufacturing sites. Two are in San Diego, California, one in Carlsbad, California, one in Athens, Ohio and one in Europe. It also has operations in China and Ireland.

Domestic operation accounts for roughly 85%, while international operations account for more than 15% of revenue.

Sales and Marketing

Quidel currently sells its products directly to end users and distributors, in each case, for professional use in physician offices, hospitals, clinical laboratories, reference laboratories, urgent care clinics, leading universities, retail clinics, pharmacies and wellness screening centers, as well as for individual, non-professional, OTC use. The company markets its products through a network of distributors and a direct sales force.

The company's advertising costs were $13.7 million, $1.1 million, and $1.3 million for the years 2021, 2020, and 2019, respectively.

Financial Performance

For the year ended December 31, 2021, total revenue increased 2% to $1.7 billion as compared to the year ended December 31, 2020, and currency exchange rates had a minimal impact on the growth rate. The company's revenues can be highly concentrated over a small number of products.

In 2021, the company had a net income of $704.2 million, a 13% decrease from the previous year's net income of $810.3 million.

The company's cash at the end of 2021 was $802.8 million. Operating activities generated $805.9 million, while investing activities used $319.5 million, primarily for acquisitions of property, equipment, investments and intangibles. Financing activities used another $173.2 million, primarily for repurchases of common stock.

Strategy

The company's primary strategy is to target market segments that represent significant total market opportunities, and in which it can be successful by applying its expertise and know-how to develop differentiated technologies and products.

In order to achieve this strategy, the company must focus on innovative products and markets and leverage its core competency in new product development for its QuickVue, Sofia and Triage immunoassay brands and next-generation products; leveraging its manufacturing expertise to address increasing demand for products, including through expanded manufacturing capacity; utilizing the company's molecular assay development competencies to further develop its molecular diagnostics franchise that includes distinct testing platforms, such as Lyra, Solana and Savanna; as well as strengthening its position with distribution partners and its end-user customers to gain more emphasis on the company's products and enter new markets.

The company is also focusing its research and development efforts on three areas: new proprietary product platform development, the creation of new and improved products for use on its established platforms to address unmet clinical needs, and pursuit of collaborations with, or acquisitions of, other companies for new and existing products and markets that advance its differentiated strategy.

Company Background

Originally incorporated as Monoclonal Antibodies, Inc. in California in 1979 and re-incorporated as Quidel Corporation in the State of Delaware in 1987.

EXECUTIVES

Chairman, Director, Kenneth F. Buechler
President, Chief Executive Officer, Director,
Douglas C. Bryant, $589,438 total compensation
Chief Financial Officer, Joseph M. Busky
Director, Evelyn S. Dilsaver
Director, Edward L. Michael
Director, Mary Lake Polan
Director, Ann D. Rhoads
Director, Robert R. Schmidt
Director, Christopher M. Smith
Director, Matthew W. Strobeck
Director, Kenneth J. Widder
Director, Joseph D. Wilkins
Director, Stephen H. Wise
Auditors : Ernst & Young LLP

LOCATIONS

HQ: Quidel Corp.
9975 Summers Ridge Road, San Diego, CA 92121
Phone: 858 552-1100
Web: www.quidel.com

2013 Sales

	$ in mil.	% of total
US	152.7	87
Other countries	22.7	13
Total	175.4	100

2015 Sales

	$ in mil.	% of total
US	168.8	86
Other countries	27.3	14
Total	196.1	100

PRODUCTS/OPERATIONS

2015 Sales

	$ mil.	% of total
Infectious disease products	141.8	72
Women's health products	37.2	19
Gastrointestinal disease products	7.2	4
Royalty, license fees and grants	6.2	3
Other products	3.7	2
Total	196.1	100

Selected Subsidiaries

BioHelix Corporation
Diagnostic Hybrids, Inc.
Litmus Concepts, Inc.
Metra Biosystems, Inc.
Osteo Sciences Corporation
Pacific Biotech, Inc.
Quidel China, Ltd.
Quidel Germany, GmbH
Quidel International, LLC

Selected Brands

AmpliVue
Copan
D3 Direct Detection
ELVIS
Lyra brands
QuickVue
Sofia
Thyretain

COMPETITORS

AKERS BIOSCIENCES, INC.
ALEXION PHARMACEUTICALS, INC.
BIO-TECHNE CORPORATION
GENMARK DIAGNOSTICS, INC.
IDEXX LABORATORIES, INC.
IMMUCOR, INC.
MERIDIAN BIOSCIENCE, INC.
MYRIAD GENETICS, INC.
ORASURE TECHNOLOGIES, INC.
SERACARE LIFE SCIENCES, INC.

HISTORICAL FINANCIALS

Company Type: Public

Income Statement
FYE: December 31

	REVENUE ($mil)	NET INCOME ($mil)	NET PROFIT MARGIN	EMPLOYEES
12/21	1,698.5	704.2	41.5%	1,600
12/20	1,661.6	810.2	48.8%	1,370
12/19	534.8	72.9	13.6%	1,250
12/18	522.2	74.1	14.2%	1,224
12/17	277.7	(8.1)	—	1,193
Annual Growth	57.3%	—	—	7.6%

2021 Year-End Financials

Debt ratio: —
Return on equity: 43.1%
Cash ($ mil.): 802.7
Current Ratio: 4.45
Long-term debt ($ mil.): —
No. of shares ($ mil.): 41.6
Dividends
Yield: —
Payout: —
Market value ($ mil.): 5,627.0

	STOCK PRICE ($) FY Close	P/E High/Low		PER SHARE ($) Earnings	Dividends	Book Value
12/21	134.99	15	6	16.43	0.00	46.28
12/20	179.65	16	4	18.60	0.00	31.51
12/19	75.03	42	27	1.73	0.00	13.37
12/18	48.82	39	21	1.86	0.00	10.81
12/17	43.35	—	—	(0.24)	0.00	6.58
Annual Growth	32.8%	—	—	—	—	62.9%

QuinStreet, Inc.

QuinStreet is a pioneer in delivering online marketplace solutions to match searchers with brands in digital media, and is committed to providing consumers with the information and tools they need to research, find and select the products and brands that meet their needs. The company specializes in customer acquisition for clients in high value, information-intensive markets or "verticals," including financial services and home services. Its clients include some of the world's largest companies and brands in those markets. The company was founded in 1999 and generates vast majority of sales domestically.

Operations

QuinStreet's two largest client verticals are financial services and home services. Its financial services segment represented roughly 75% of revenue. QuinStreet's home services client vertical represented about 25% of revenue.

Geographic Reach

QuinStreet's corporate headquarters is located in Foster City, California, with additional offices in the US and India. Nearly all of the company's revenues come from the US.

Sales and Marketing

QuinStreet generates revenue from fees earned through the delivery of qualified leads, clicks, inquiries, calls, customers, and display advertisements.

QuinStreet's sales and marketing expenses were $11.0 million in 2021, $8.9

million in 2020 and $8.8 million in 2019.

Financial Performance

Net revenue increased by $88.1 million, or 18% to $578.5 million in fiscal year 2021 compared to fiscal year 2020. Revenue from home services client vertical increased by $84.6 million, or 169%, primarily as a result of inorganic and organic (synergy) revenue effects from the acquisition of Modernize completed in fiscal year 2021.

In 2021, the company had a net income of $23.6 million, a 30% increase from the previous year's net income of $18.1 million.

QuinStreet's cash at the end of fiscal 2021 was $110.3 million. Operations generated $50.6 million in cash, while investing activities used $36.5 million, mainly for business acquisitions. Financing activities used another $11.3 million for payment of withholding taxes and contingent considerations related to acquisitions.

Strategy

QuinStreet's goal is to continue to be one of the largest and most successful performance marketing companies on the Internet and eventually in other digitized media forms. It believes that it is in the early stages of a very large and long-term market opportunity. The strategy for pursuing this opportunity includes the following key components: focus on generating sustainable revenues by providing measurable value to its clients; build QuinStreet and its industry sustainably by behaving ethically in all it does and by providing quality content and website experiences to Internet visitors; remain vertically focused, choosing to grow through depth, expertise and coverage in its current client verticals; enter new client verticals selectively over time, organically and through acquisitions; build a world class organization, with best-in-class capabilities for delivering measurable marketing results to clients and high yields or returns on media costs; develop and evolve the best products, technologies and platform for managing successful performance marketing campaigns on the Internet; focus on technologies that enhance media yield, improve client results and achieve scale efficiencies; build and apply unique data advantages from running some of the largest campaigns over long periods of time in its client verticals, including the steep learning curves of what campaigns work best to optimize each media type and each client's results; build and partner with vertical content websites that attract high intent visitors in the client and media verticals it serves; and be a client-driven organization and develop a broad set of media sources and capabilities to reliably meet client needs.

Mergers and Acquisitions

In mid-2020, QuinStreet acquired Texas-based Modernize, a leader in home improvement performance marketing services. Modernize Home Services will serve as QuinStreet's flagship brand in home services going forward, advancing its mission to set the standard for transparency and trust in the home improvement and home services selection process, enabling millions of homeowners to make good and confident decisions. The consideration paid for the acquisition totaled $67.5 million in cash.

EXECUTIVES

Chairman, Chief Executive Officer, Director, Douglas Valenti, $540,750 total compensation
Product and Technology President, Product and Technology Chief Technology Officer, Nina Bhanap, $377,000 total compensation
Executive Vice President, Tim Stevens
Corporate Development Chief Legal Officer, Corporate Development Chief Privacy Officer, Martin J. Collins, $312,000 total compensation
Senior Vice President, Division Officer, Alan Godfrey
Senior Vice President, Division Officer, Andreja Stevanovic
Chief Financial Officer, Gregory Wong, $307,000 total compensation
Director, Andrew T. Sheehan
Director, David J. Pauldine
Director, James R. Simons
Director, Matthew Glickman
Director, Anna Fieler
Director, Stuart M. Huizinga
Director, Hillary B. Smith
Director, Asmau Ahmed
Auditors : PricewaterhouseCoopers LLP

LOCATIONS

HQ: QuinStreet, Inc.
950 Tower Lane, 6th Floor, Foster City, CA 94404
Phone: 650 578-7700
Web: www.quinstreet.com

2017 Sales

	$ mil.	% of total
United States	292.4	98
International	7.4	2
Total	299.8	100

PRODUCTS/OPERATIONS

Selected Industries Served
Financial services
Education
Business-to-business technology
Home services
Medical

COMPETITORS

AMERIPRISE FINANCIAL, INC.
CBIZ, INC.
CITY OF LONDON GROUP PLC.
COTIVITI HOLDINGS, INC.
CRITEO
ENVESTNET, INC.
FIDELITY NATIONAL INFORMATION SERVICES, INC.
INNERWORKINGS, INC.
MARCHEX, INC.
STARTEK, INC.

HISTORICAL FINANCIALS

Company Type: Public

Income Statement — FYE: June 30

	REVENUE ($mil)	NET INCOME ($mil)	NET PROFIT MARGIN	EMPLOYEES
06/21	578.4	23.5	4.1%	614
06/20	490.3	18.1	3.7%	592
06/19	455.1	62.4	13.7%	637
06/18	404.3	15.9	3.9%	506
06/17	299.7	(12.2)	—	469
Annual Growth	17.9%	—	—	7.0%

2021 Year-End Financials

Debt ratio: —
Return on equity: 8.5%
Cash ($ mil.): 110.3
Current Ratio: 1.78
Long-term debt ($ mil.): —
No. of shares ($ mil.): 53.7
Dividends
  Yield: —
  Payout: —
Market value ($ mil.): 999.0

	STOCK PRICE ($) FY Close	P/E High/Low		PER SHARE ($) Earnings	Dividends	Book Value
06/21	18.58	56	23	0.43	0.00	5.49
06/20	10.46	48	17	0.34	0.00	4.90
06/19	15.85	16	10	1.18	0.00	4.41
06/18	12.70	43	10	0.32	0.00	3.08
06/17	4.17	—	—	(0.27)	0.00	2.60
Annual Growth	45.3%	—	—	—	—	20.5%

R1 RCM Inc

R1 RCM (formerly known as Accretive Health) is a leading provider of technology-driven solutions that transform the patient experience and financial performance of healthcare providers. It handles patient registration, benefits verification, medical treatment documentation and coding, billing, and other tasks for clients. The company specializes in enhancing efficiencies and quality while reducing costs. It provides technology solutions and process workflows. Typical customers are not-for-profit and for-profit hospital systems, such as Ascension Health and Intermountain Health, as well as independent medical centers, physician groups, and EMS organizations. The company operates about 15 offices in the US and six offices overseas. In mid-2022, R1 RCM acquired Cloudmed for approximately $4.1 billion.

Operations

R1 RCM's significant operations are organized around the single business of providing revenue cycle management operations for healthcare providers. The company views its operations and manages its business as one operating and reporting segment. All of the net services revenue and trade accounts receivable are derived from healthcare providers domiciled in the US. R1 RCM's significant operations are organized around the single business of providing revenue cycle management operations for healthcare providers. All of the net services revenue and trade accounts receivable are derived from healthcare providers domiciled in the US.

The company's primary service offering consists of end-to-end RCM services for health systems, hospitals, and physician groups, which it deploys through an operating partner relationship or a co-managed relationship. Under an operating partner relationship, the company provides comprehensive revenue cycle infrastructure to providers, including all revenue cycle personnel, technology solutions, and process workflow. It also offers modular services, allowing customers to engage it for specific components of the company's end-to-end RCM service offering, such as patient experience, physician advisory services (PAS), clinical documentation integrity (CDI), coding management, revenue integrity solutions (RIS), business office services, and practice management (PM).

Most of the company's sales were generated from net operating fees accounting for more than 80% of total sales, while incentive fees and other services account for the rest.

Geographic Reach

R1 RCM's headquarters is located in Murray, Utah. The company has about 15 offices domestically, and approximately 420,000 square feet of office space throughout six offices internationally.

Sales and Marketing

R1 RCM has more than 900 clients nationwide. New business opportunities are generated by the company's sales and marketing team and other members of its senior management team. The company's customer acquisition process utilizes traditional and non-traditional techniques to inform the marketplace of R1's solutions. R1 RCM has more than 900 clients nationwide. New business opportunities are generated by the company's sales and marketing team and other members of its senior management team. The company's customer acquisition process utilizes traditional and non-traditional techniques to inform the marketplace of R1's solutions.

The company's customers typically are healthcare providers, including health systems and hospitals, physician groups, and municipal and private EMS providers. Hospital systems affiliated with Ascension have accounted for about 60% of the company's net services revenue.

Financial Performance

The company had total net services revenue of $1.5 billion, a 16% increase from the previous year's $1.3 billion. The increase was driven by improvement in net operating and incentive fees aided by a recovery in patient volumes, new customers onboarded in the last twelve months, and the RevWorks and VisitPay acquisitions, partially offset by the disposition of the emergency medical services (EMS) business. The company had total net services revenue of $1.5 billion, a 16% increase from the previous year's $1.3 billion. The increase was driven by improvement in net operating and incentive fees aided by a recovery in patient volumes, new customers onboarded in the last twelve months, and the RevWorks and VisitPay acquisitions, partially offset by the disposition of the emergency medical services (EMS) business.

In 2021, the company had a net income of $97.2 million, a 17% decrease from the previous year's net income of $117.1 million.

The company's cash at the end of 2021 was $130.1 million. Operating activities generated $264.8 million, while investing activities used $340.4 million, mainly for payment for business acquisitions. Financing activities provided another $31.4 million.

Strategy

R1 RCM continues to invest capital to achieve its strategic initiatives. In addition, the company plans to continue to enhance customer service by continuing its investment in technology to enable its systems to more effectively integrate with customers' existing technologies in connection with its strategic initiatives. The company plans to continue to deploy resources to strengthen its information technology infrastructure, including automation, to drive additional value for customers. R1 RCM also expects to continue to invest in its global business services infrastructure and capabilities, and selectively pursue acquisitions and/or strategic relationships that will enable it to broaden or further enhance its offerings.

Mergers and Acquisitions

In mid-2021, R1 RCM completed the acquisition of VisitPay, the leading digital payment solution provider for approximately $300 million in cash. The acquisition will combine VisitPay's best-in-class consumer payments platform with R1's leading patient access technology to enable providers to deliver a seamless financial journey for their patients.

Company Background

The company was formed in 2003 as Healthcare Services. It changed its name to Accretive Health in 2009 and went public in 2010. Accretive Health changed its name to R1 RCM in 2017.

R1 has had a relationship with Ascension Health since its founding; the companies expanded their agreement to encompass a larger number of Ascension-affiliated hospitals in 2016.

EXECUTIVES

Chairman, Director, Anthony J. Speranzo
Chief Executive Officer, Director, Lee Rivas
Senior Vice President, Chief Accounting Officer, Corporate Controller, Richard B. Evans
Chief Financial Officer, Treasurer, Jennifer D. Williams
Lead Independent Director, Director, John B. Henneman
Director, Bradford Kyle Armbrester
Director, Agnes Bundy Scanlan
Director, Brian K. Dean
Director, Jeremy Delinsky
Director, David M. Dill
Director, Michael C. Feiner
Director, Joseph Gerard Flanagan, $895,000 total compensation
Director, Matthew S. Holt
Director, Neal Moszkowski
Director, Ian Sacks
Director, Jill D. Smith
Director, Anthony R. Tersigni
Director, Janie Wade
Auditors : Ernst & Young LLP

LOCATIONS

HQ: R1 RCM Inc
434 W. Ascension Way, 6th Floor, Murray, UT 84123
Phone: 312 324-7820
Web: www.r1rcm.com

PRODUCTS/OPERATIONS

2013 Sales

	$ mil.	% of total
RCM services, net operating fee	225.0	44
RCM services, incentive fees	210.3	42
Other services	69.5	14
Total	504.8	100

Selected Customers

Ascension Health
Catholic Health East
Fairview Health Services
Intermountain Healthcare

COMPETITORS

ATOS DIGITAL HEALTH SOLUTIONS, INC.
CHARTERHOUSE GROUP, INC.
CONDUENT INCORPORATED
CORVEL CORPORATION
ENVISION HEALTHCARE HOLDINGS, INC.
LEE MEMORIAL HEALTH SYSTEM
LIFETIME BENEFIT SOLUTIONS, INC.
MEDASSETS, INC.
NORTON HEALTHCARE, INC.
TEAM HEALTH HOLDINGS, INC.

HISTORICAL FINANCIALS

Company Type: Public

Income Statement				FYE: December 31
	REVENUE ($mil)	NET INCOME ($mil)	NET PROFIT MARGIN	EMPLOYEES
12/21	1,474.6	97.2	6.6%	22,000
12/20	1,270.8	117.1	9.2%	20,200
12/19	1,186.1	12.0	1.0%	22,500
12/18	868.5	(45.3)	—	18,600
12/17	449.8	(58.8)	—	9,965
Annual Growth	34.6%	—	—	21.9%

2021 Year-End Financials

Debt ratio: 53.3%
Return on equity: 28.3%
Cash ($ mil.): 130.1
Current Ratio: 1.43
Long-term debt ($ mil.): 754.9
No. of shares ($ mil.): 278.2
Dividends
  Yield: —
  Payout: —
Market value ($ mil.): 7,092.0

	STOCK PRICE ($) FY Close	P/E High/Low		PER SHARE ($) Earnings	Dividends	Book Value
12/21	25.49	—	—	(1.86)	0.00	1.25
12/20	24.02	59	18	0.33	0.00	2.80
12/19	12.98	—	—	(0.08)	0.00	2.17
12/18	7.95	—	—	(0.60)	0.00	1.94
12/17	4.41	—	—	(0.75)	0.00	2.13
Annual Growth	55.1%	—	—	—	—	(12.6%)

	STOCK PRICE ($) FY Close	P/E High/Low		PER SHARE ($) Earnings	Dividends	Book Value
06/21	15.10	27	18	0.62	1.75	0.18
06/20	11.50	16	9	0.71	0.25	1.61
06/19	6.70	—	—	0.00	0.00	1.17
06/18	3.14	—	—	0.00	0.00	0.79
06/17	2.70	—	—	0.00	0.00	0.71
Annual Growth	53.8%	—	—	—	—	(28.8%)

Executive Vice President, Secretary, General Counsel, Holding/Parent Company Officer, P. Matt Zmigrosky
Auditors: Grant Thornton LLP

LOCATIONS

HQ: Rattler Midstream LP
500 West Texas, Suite 1200, Midland, TX 79701
Phone: 432 221-7400
Web: www.rattlermidstream.com

HISTORICAL FINANCIALS
Company Type: Public

Income Statement   FYE: December 31

	REVENUE ($mil)	NET INCOME ($mil)	NET PROFIT MARGIN	EMPLOYEES
12/20	423.9	34.6	8.2%	0
12/19	447.6	185.7	41.5%	0
12/18	184.4	62.9	34.1%	0
12/17	39.2	20.6	52.6%	0
Annual Growth	121.0%	18.8%	—	—

2020 Year-End Financials
Debt ratio: 31.5%
Return on equity: —
Cash ($ mil.): 23.9
Current Ratio: 2.26
Long-term debt ($ mil.): 569.9
No. of shares ($ mil.): 150.1
Dividends
 Yield: 11.2%
 Payout: 133.7%
Market value ($ mil.): 1,424.0

	STOCK PRICE ($) FY Close	P/E High/Low		PER SHARE ($) Earnings	Dividends	Book Value
12/20	9.48	24	4	0.74	1.07	2.58
12/19	17.79	31	22	0.64	0.34	4.88
Annual Growth	(46.7%)	—	—	15.6%	214.7%	(47.2%)

Rand Worldwide Inc.

EXECUTIVES

Chairman, Director, Peter H. Kamin
President, Chief Executive Officer, Director, Lawrence Rychlak, $260,068 total compensation
Corporate Information Systems Vice President, Corporate Information Systems Chief Information Officer, Nedim Celik
Business Development Vice President, Scott Hale
Human Resources Vice President, Kathy Herold
Vice President, Chief Financial Officer, Treasurer, Secretary, John Kuta, $149,667 total compensation
Vice President, Chantale Marchand
Division Officer, Bill Zavadil
Division Officer, Timothy Johnson
Director, Philip B. Livingston
Director, David Schneider
Auditors: Dixon Hughes Goodman LLP

LOCATIONS

HQ: Rand Worldwide Inc.
11201 Dolfield Boulevard, Suite 112, Owings Mills, MD 21117
Phone: 410 581-8080
Web: www.rand.com

HISTORICAL FINANCIALS
Company Type: Public

Income Statement   FYE: June 30

	REVENUE ($mil)	NET INCOME ($mil)	NET PROFIT MARGIN	EMPLOYEES
06/21	257.3	20.8	8.1%	0
06/20	281.0	23.3	8.3%	0
06/19	222.4	12.0	5.4%	0
06/18	116.4	2.6	2.2%	0
06/17	81.0	3.6	4.5%	0
Annual Growth	33.5%	54.2%	—	—

2021 Year-End Financials
Debt ratio: 44.7%
Return on equity: 71.8%
Cash ($ mil.): 1.6
Current Ratio: 0.75
Long-term debt ($ mil.): 30.2
No. of shares ($ mil.): 33.5
Dividends
 Yield: 11.5%
 Payout: 282.2%
Market value ($ mil.): 507.0

Randolph Bancorp Inc

Auditors: Crowe LLP

LOCATIONS

HQ: Randolph Bancorp Inc
2 Batterymarch Park, Suite 301, Quincy, MA 02169
Phone: 781 963-2100
Web: www.randolphsavings.com

HISTORICAL FINANCIALS
Company Type: Public

Income Statement   FYE: December 31

	ASSETS ($mil)	NET INCOME ($mil)	INCOME AS % OF ASSETS	EMPLOYEES
12/20	721.0	19.9	2.8%	208
12/19	631.0	3.4	0.5%	217
12/18	614.3	(2.0)	—	199
12/17	531.8	(2.1)	—	187
12/16	481.2	0.4	0.1%	220
Annual Growth	10.6%	156.1%	—	(1.4%)

2020 Year-End Financials
Return on assets: 2.9%
Return on equity: 22.2%
Long-term debt ($ mil.): —
No. of shares ($ mil.): 5.5
Sales ($ mil.): 78.9
Dividends
 Yield: —
 Payout: —
Market value ($ mil.): 121.0

	STOCK PRICE ($) FY Close	P/E High/Low		PER SHARE ($) Earnings	Dividends	Book Value
12/20	22.06	6	2	3.86	0.00	18.16
12/19	17.65	27	21	0.64	0.00	14.07
12/18	14.15	—	—	(0.37)	0.00	13.21
12/17	15.35	—	—	(0.39)	0.00	13.50
12/16	16.12	—	—	0.00	0.00	14.19
Annual Growth	8.2%	—	—	—	—	6.4%

Rattler Midstream LP

EXECUTIVES

President, Holding/Parent Company Officer, Director, Matthew Kaes Van't Hof
Chief Executive Officer, Holding/Parent Company Officer, Director, Travis D. Stice
Executive Vice President, Holding/Parent Company Officer, Chief Financial Officer, Assistant Secretary, Teresa L. Dick

RBB Bancorp

EXECUTIVES

Chairman, Subsidiary Officer, Director, James W. Kao
President, Chief Executive Officer, Chief Financial Officer, Subsidiary Officer, Director, David R. Morris, $290,694 total compensation
Executive Vice President, Chief Strategy Officer, Subsidiary Officer, Simon Pang, $238,500 total compensation
Executive Vice President, Chief Risk Officer, Subsidiary Officer, I-Ming (Vincent) Liu
Executive Vice President, Chief Credit Officer, Subsidiary Officer, Jeffrey Yeh
Secretary, Subsidiary Officer, Director, Feng (Richard) Lin
Subsidiary Officer, Gary Fan
Subsidiary Officer, Tsu Te Huang
Subsidiary Officer, Ashley Chang
Director, Geraldine Pannu
Director, Joyce Wong Lee
Director, Wendell Chen
Director, Christina Kao
Director, Chie Min (Christopher) Koo
Director, Chuang-I (Christopher) Lin
Director, Paul Lin

Director, Fui Ming (Catherine) Thian
Auditors : Eide Bailly LLP

LOCATIONS
HQ: RBB Bancorp
1055 Wilshire Blvd., Suite 1200, Los Angeles, CA 90017
Phone: 213 627-9888
Web: www.royalbusinessbankusa.com

HISTORICAL FINANCIALS
Company Type: Public

Income Statement   FYE: December 31

	ASSETS ($mil)	NET INCOME ($mil)	INCOME AS % OF ASSETS	EMPLOYEES
12/20	3,350.0	32.9	1.0%	371
12/19	2,788.5	39.2	1.4%	355
12/18	2,974.0	36.1	1.2%	365
12/17	1,691.0	25.5	1.5%	203
12/16	1,395.5	19.0	1.4%	177
Annual Growth	24.5%	14.6%	—	20.3%

2020 Year-End Financials
Return on assets: 1.0%   Dividends
Return on equity: 7.8%   Yield: 2.1%
Long-term debt ($ mil.): —   Payout: 20.4%
No. of shares ($ mil.): 19.5   Market value ($ mil.): 301.0
Sales ($ mil.): 153.1

	STOCK PRICE ($) FY Close	P/E High/Low		PER SHARE ($) Earnings	Dividends	Book Value
12/20	15.38	13	6	1.65	0.33	21.90
12/19	21.17	11	9	1.92	0.40	20.35
12/18	17.57	16	8	2.01	0.43	18.73
12/17	27.37	15	12	1.68	0.08	16.67
Annual Growth	(17.5%)	—	—	(0.6%)	60.4%	9.5%

Re/Max Holdings Inc

EXECUTIVES
Chairman, Non-Executive Chairman, Director, David L. (Dave) Liniger, $0 total compensation
Vice-Chairman, Director, Gail A. Liniger
President, Subsidiary Officer, Nicholas R. Bailey
Chief Executive Officer, Director, Stephen P. Joyce
Chief Financial Officer, Karri R. Callahan, $320,000 total compensation
Vice President, Chief Accounting Officer, Principal Accounting Officer, Adam Grosshans
Vice President, General Counsel, Secretary, Adam Lindquist Scoville
Chief Operating Officer, Chief of Staff, Serene M. Smith, $316,667 total compensation
Division Officer, Ward M. Morrison
Director, Teresa S. Van De Bogart
Director, Roger J. Dow
Director, Ronald E. Harrison
Director, Kathleen J. Cunningham
Director, Christine M. Riordan
Director, Laura G. Kelly
Auditors : KPMG LLP

LOCATIONS
HQ: Re/Max Holdings Inc
5075 South Syracuse Street, Denver, CO 80237
Phone: 303 770-5531   **Fax:** 303 796-3599
Web: www.remax.com

HISTORICAL FINANCIALS
Company Type: Public

Income Statement   FYE: December 31

	REVENUE ($mil)	NET INCOME ($mil)	NET PROFIT MARGIN	EMPLOYEES
12/20	266.0	10.9	4.1%	545
12/19	282.2	25.0	8.9%	500
12/18	212.6	27.0	12.7%	500
12/17	195.9	12.8	6.5%	350
12/16	176.3	22.7	12.9%	344
Annual Growth	10.8%	(16.7%)	—	12.2%

2020 Year-End Financials
Debt ratio: 40.1%   No. of shares ($ mil.): 18.3
Return on equity: 2.1%   Dividends
Cash ($ mil.): 101.3   Yield: 2.4%
Current Ratio: 1.42   Payout: 146.6%
Long-term debt ($ mil.): 221.1 Market value ($ mil.): 668.0

	STOCK PRICE ($) FY Close	P/E High/Low		PER SHARE ($) Earnings	Dividends	Book Value
12/20	36.33	68	24	0.60	0.88	28.12
12/19	38.49	31	18	1.40	0.84	27.91
12/18	30.75	40	19	1.52	0.80	0.00
12/17	48.50	93	64	0.72	0.72	0.00
12/16	56.00	44	24	1.29	0.60	0.00
Annual Growth	(10.3%)	—	—	(17.4%)	10.0%	

Ready Capital Corp

Ready Capital is a multi-strategy real estate finance company that originates, acquires, finances, and services SBC loans, SBA loans, residential mortgage loans, and to a lesser extent, MBS collateralized primarily by SBC loans, or other real estate-related investments. Its loans range in original principal amounts generally up to approximately $35 million and are used by businesses to purchase real estate used in their operations or by investors seeking to acquire small multi-family, office, retail, mixed use or warehouse properties. In addition to its loan portfolio which concentrates across California, Texas, New York, Florida, and Illinois, the company also invests in countries outside the US.

Operations
Ready Capital's origination and acquisition platforms consist of four operating segments: SBC Originations, Acquisitions, SBA Originations, Acquisitions, and Servicing and Residential Mortgage Banking.

Under the Residential Mortgage Banking segment (generates more than 40% of total revenue), the company operates its residential mortgage loan origination segment through its wholly-owned subsidiary, GMFS. GMFS originates residential mortgage loans eligible to be purchased, guaranteed or insured by the Federal National Mortgage Association (Fannie Mae), Freddie Mac, Federal Housing Administration (FHA), U.S. Department of Agriculture (USDA) and U.S. Department of Veterans Affairs (VA) through retail, correspondent and broker channels. These originated loans are then sold to third parties, primarily agency lending programs.

SBC Originations segment, generates about 30% of the company's total revenue, originates SBC loans secured by stabilized or transitional investor properties using multiple loan origination channels through its wholly-owned subsidiary, ReadyCap Commercial (ReadyCap Commercial). These originated loans are generally held-for-investment or placed into securitization structures. Additionally, as part of this segment, the company originates and services multi-family loan products under the Federal Home Loan Mortgage Corporation's Small Balance Loan Program (Freddie Mac and the Freddie Mac program). These originated loans are held for sale, then sold to Freddie Mac.

SBA Originations, Acquisitions and Servicing segment represents approximately 15% of the company's total revenue. It acquires, originates and services owner-occupied loans guaranteed by the SBA under its Section 7(a) loan program (the SBA Section 7(a) Program) through its wholly-owned subsidiary, ReadyCap Lending. It holds an SBA license as one of only 14 non-bank Small Business Lending Companies (SBLCs) and has been granted preferred lender status by the SBA. These originated loans are either held-for-investment, placed into securitization structures, or sold.

Accounts for nearly 15% of the company's total revenue, Acquisitions segment holds performing SBC loans to term, and it seeks to maximize the value of the non-performing SBC loans acquired by the company through borrower-based resolution strategies. It typically acquires non-performing loans at a discount to their unpaid principal balance (UPB). Ready Capital also acquires purchased future receivables through Knight Capital LLC (Knight Capital) platfor

Geographic Reach
New York-based, Ready Capital has office locations in New Jersey, Texas, Florida, and Louisiana, among other.

Sales and Marketing
The company has extensive relationships with commercial real estate brokers, bank loan officers and mortgage brokers.

Financial Performance
The company's revenue in 2020 increased by 65% to $417.9 million compared with $252.7 million in the prior year.

Consolidated net income of $46.1 million for 2020 represented a decrease of $29.0 million from the prior year, primarily due to an increase of reserves on loans due to the uncertainty of loan performance and recovery related to COVID-19 as well as an increase in unrealized losses on residential mortgage servicing rights, partially offset by net income on PPP activities.

Cash held by the company at the end of fiscal 2020 increased to $200.5 million. Cash provided by operations and financing activities were $68.9 million and $63.1 million, respectively. Investing activities used $59.4 million, mainly for origination of loans.

Strategy

The company's investment strategy is to opportunistically expand its market presence in its acquisition and origination segments and to further grow its SBC securitization capabilities which serve as a source of attractively priced, match-term financing. Capitalizing on its experience in underwriting and managing commercial real estate loans, Ready Capital has grown its SBC and SBA origination and acquisition capabilities and selectively complimented its SBC strategy with residential agency mortgage originations.

The company acquisition strategy complements its origination strategy by increasing its market intelligence in potential origination geographies, providing additional data to support its underwriting criteria and offering securitization market insight for various product offerings.

Mergers and Acquisitions

In late 2021, Ready Capital entered into a definitive merger agreement pursuant to which Ready Capital has agreed to acquire a series of privately held, real estate structured finance opportunities funds, with a focus on construction lending, managed by MREC Management (the Mosaic Manager). The acquisition is expected to further expand Ready Capital's investment portfolio to include a diverse portfolio of construction assets with attractive portfolio yields resulting in expected earnings accretion and a reduced leverage profile. Under the terms of the merger agreement, Ready Capital will acquire all of the outstanding equity interests in Mosaic Real Estate Credit (MREC Onshore), Mosaic Real Estate Credit TE (MREC TE) and MREC International Incentive Split (MREC IIS and together with MREC Onshore and MREC TE, the Mosaic Merger Entities). Expected value of deal at closing is approximately $471 million and could surpass $550 million with earn-out provisions.

EXECUTIVES

Chairman, Chief Executive Officer, Chief Investment Officer, Director, Thomas E. Capasse
President, Director, Jack J. Ross
Chief Financial Officer, Andrew Ahlborn
Chief Operating Officer, Gary Taylor, $250,000 total compensation
Chief Credit Officer, Adam Zausmer
Director, Frank P. Filipps
Director, Dominique Mielle
Director, Gilbert E. Nathan
Director, Andrea Petro
Director, J. Mitchell Reese
Director, Todd M. Sinai
Auditors : Deloitte & Touche LLP

LOCATIONS

HQ: Ready Capital Corp
1251 Avenue of the Americas, 50th Floor, New York, NY 10020
Phone: 212 257-4600
Web: www.readycapital.com

COMPETITORS

ARLINGTON ASSET INVESTMENT CORP.
DITECH HOLDING CORPORATION
NATIONSTAR MORTGAGE HOLDINGS INC.
PENNYMAC MORTGAGE INVESTMENT TRUST
PNMAC HOLDINGS, INC.

HISTORICAL FINANCIALS

Company Type: Public

Income Statement				FYE: December 31
	REVENUE ($mil)	NET INCOME ($mil)	NET PROFIT MARGIN	EMPLOYEES
12/20	478.8	44.8	9.4%	0
12/19	352.7	72.9	20.7%	0
12/18	295.1	59.2	20.1%	4
12/17	211.4	43.2	20.5%	0
12/16	171.4	49.1	28.7%	0
Annual Growth	29.3%	(2.3%)	—	—

2020 Year-End Financials

Debt ratio: 76.7%
Return on equity: 5.4%
Cash ($ mil.): 138.9
Current Ratio: 2.24
Long-term debt ($ mil.): 4,120.7
No. of shares ($ mil.): 54.3
Dividends
Yield: 10.4%
Payout: 160.4%
Market value ($ mil.): 677.0

	STOCK PRICE ($) FY Close	P/E High/Low		PER SHARE ($)		
				Earnings	Dividends	Book Value
12/20	12.45	21	5	0.81	1.30	15.00
12/19	15.42	10	8	1.72	1.60	16.14
12/18	13.83	9	7	1.84	1.57	16.97
12/17	15.15	12	9	1.38	1.48	16.75
12/16	13.45	8	7	1.85	1.55	16.80
Annual Growth	(1.9%)	—	—	(18.7%)	(4.3%)	(2.8%)

Realty Income Corp

Realty Income Corporation is an S&P 500 company and member of the S&P 500 Dividend Aristocrats index. The self-administered real estate investment trust (REIT) acquires, owns, and manages primarily free-standing commercial properties that generate rental revenue under long-term net lease agreements with its commercial clients. Realty Income owns around 11,135 (mostly retail) properties spanning approximately 210.1 million sq. ft. of leasable space across every US state except Hawaii, though over 35% of the REIT's rental revenue comes from its properties in Texas, Florida, Ohio, Georgia, Illinois, and Tennessee. Realty Income's top five tenants include Walgreens, FedEx, 7 Eleven, Dollar General, FedEx, and Dollar Tree/Family Dollar.

Operations

Realty Income owns around 11,135 properties during 2021, more than 95% of which were retail, and the rest being industrial, and other.

About 95% of its revenues came from rentals and about 5% came from reimbursements and others.

Geographic Reach

San Diego, California-based Realty Income's largest markets include Texas, Florida, Ohio, Georgia, Illinois and Tennessee. Nearly 15% of its properties are in Texas in 2021, while properties in Florida contributed another more than 5%.

Sales and Marketing

Realty Income's occupancy rate for the year is almost a hundred percent; with an average remaining lease term of approximately 9.0 years.

Its tenants have included owners of restaurants, convenience stores, theaters, child care providers, automotive care centers, health and fitness facilities, grocery stores, and drug stores. Realty Income's top five tenants ? Walgreens, 7 Eleven, Dollar General, FedEx, and Dollar Tree/Family Dollar ? combined generated about 20% of its total revenue in 2021.

Financial Performance

The company's total revenue for 2021 was $2.1 billion, a 26% increase from the previous year's revenue of $1.6 billion.

In 2021, the company had a net income of $360.7 million, a 9% decrease from the previous year's net income of $396.5 million.

The company's cash at the end of 2021 was $332.4 million. Operating activities generated $1.3 billion, while investing activities used $6.4 billion, mainly for investment in real estate. Financing activities provided another $4.6 billion.

Strategy

The company seeks to invest in high-quality real estate that clients consider important to the successful operation of their businesses. It generally seeks to acquire commercial real estate that has some or all of the following characteristics: Properties in markets or locations important to clients; Properties that the company deems to be profitable for clients (e.g., retail stores or revenue generating sites); Properties with strong demographic attributes relative to the specific business drivers of clients; Properties with real estate valuations that approximate replacement costs; as well as Properties with rental or lease payments that approximate market rents for similar properties.

The company also seeks to invest in properties owned or leased by clients that are already or could become leaders in their respective businesses supported by mechanisms including (but not limited to) occupancy of prime real estate locations, pricing, merchandise assortment, service, quality, economies of scale, consumer branding, e-commerce, and advertising. In addition, it frequently acquires large portfolios of single-client properties net leased to different clients operating in a variety of industries.

Mergers and Acquisitions

In late 2021, Realty Income, The Monthly Dividend Company, and VEREIT announced the completion of their previously announced merger. The common stock of the combined company will trade under the symbol "O" on the NYSE. The closing follows the satisfaction of all conditions to the closing of the merger, including receipt of approval of the transaction by Realty Income and VEREIT stockholders, which stockholder approvals were obtained in mid-2021. Realty Income acquired VEREIT in an all-stock transaction, creating a combined company with an enterprise value of approximately $50 billion. Under the terms of the agreement, VEREIT shareholders will receive 0.705 shares of Realty Income stock for every share of VEREIT stock they own. "We are pleased to announce the completion of our merger with VEREIT, strengthening our position as the leading net lease REIT and global consolidator of the net lease space," said Sumit Roy, Realty Income's President and Chief Executive Officer.

EXECUTIVES

President, Chief Executive Officer, Director, Sumit Roy, $613,288 total compensation
Executive Vice President, Chief Financial Officer, Treasurer, Christie B. Kelly
Executive Vice President, Chief Strategy Officer, Division Officer, Neil M. Abraham, $385,000 total compensation
Executive Vice President, Chief Investment Officer, Mark E. Hagan, $237,910 total compensation
Executive Vice President, Chief Legal Officer, General Counsel, Secretary, Michelle Bushore
Executive Vice President, Chief People Officer, Shannon Kehle
Executive Vice President, Chief Operating Officer, Gregory J. Whyte
Senior Vice President, Controller, Principal Accounting Officer, Sean P. Nugent
Non-Executive Chairman, Director, Michael D. McKee
Director, Priscilla Almodovar
Director, Jacqueline Brady
Director, A. Larry Chapman
Director, Reginald (Reggie) Harold Gilyard
Director, Mary Hogan Preusse
Director, Priya Cherian Huskins
Director, Gerardo I. Lopez
Director, Gregory T. McLaughlin
Director, Ronald L. Merriman
Auditors : KPMG LLP

LOCATIONS

HQ: Realty Income Corp
11995 El Camino Real, San Diego, CA 92130
Phone: 858 284-5000
Web: www.realtyincome.com

PRODUCTS/OPERATIONS

2014 Properties

	% of rental revenue
Retail	79
Industrial and distribution	10
Office	7
Manufacturing	2
Agriculture	2
Total	100

2014 Sales

	$ mil	% of total
Rental	893.5	96
Tenant reimbursement	37.1	4
Others	2.9	—
Total	933.5	100

COMPETITORS

ACADIA REALTY TRUST
AGREE REALTY CORPORATION
AMERICAN ASSETS TRUST, INC.
HIGHWOODS PROPERTIES, INC.
KENNEDY-WILSON HOLDINGS, INC.
LEXINGTON REALTY TRUST
NATIONAL RETAIL PROPERTIES, INC.
ONE LIBERTY PROPERTIES, INC.
Pure Industrial Real Estate Trust
RAIT FINANCIAL TRUST

HISTORICAL FINANCIALS

Company Type: Public

Income Statement   FYE: December 31

	REVENUE ($mil)	NET INCOME ($mil)	NET PROFIT MARGIN	EMPLOYEES
12/21	2,080.4	359.4	17.3%	371
12/20	1,651.6	395.4	23.9%	210
12/19	1,491.5	436.4	29.3%	194
12/18	1,327.8	363.6	27.4%	165
12/17	1,215.7	318.7	26.2%	152
Annual Growth	14.4%	3.0%	—	25.0%

2021 Year-End Financials

Debt ratio: 35.8%
Return on equity: 1.9%
Cash ($ mil.): 258.5
Current Ratio: 0.66
Long-term debt ($ mil.): 15,442.6
No. of shares ($ mil.): 591.2
Dividends
  Yield: 3.9%
  Payout: 233.1%
Market value ($ mil.): 42,328.0

	STOCK PRICE ($) FY Close	P/E High/Low		PER SHARE ($) Earnings	Dividends	Book Value
12/21	71.59	85	66	0.87	2.85	42.37
12/20	62.17	72	37	1.14	2.80	30.41
12/19	73.63	59	45	1.38	2.72	29.30
12/18	63.04	53	38	1.26	2.64	26.63
12/17	57.02	57	48	1.10	2.54	25.94
Annual Growth	5.9%	—	—	(5.7%)	2.9%	13.1%

Red River Bancshares Inc

EXECUTIVES

President, Chief Executive Officer, Subsidiary Officer, R. Blake Chatelain, $389,053 total compensation
Executive Vice President, Chief Financial Officer, Treasurer, Assistant Secretary, Subsidiary Officer, Isabel V. Carriere
Senior Vice President, General Counsel, Corporate Secretary, Subsidiary Officer, Amanda Wood Barnett
Senior Vice President, Subsidiary Officer, Andrew B. Cutrer
Subsidiary Officer, Debbie B. Triche
Subsidiary Officer, Gary A. Merrifield
Subsidiary Officer, Jeffrey R. Theiler
Subsidiary Officer, Bryon C. Salazar, $223,344 total compensation
Subsidiary Officer, David K. Thompson
Subsidiary Officer, G. Bridges Hall
Subsidiary Officer, Harold W. Turner
Subsidiary Officer, Tammi R. Salazar, $241,318 total compensation
Non-Executive Chairman, John C. Simpson
Director, M. Scott Ashbrook
Director, Kirk D. Cooper
Director, F. William Hackmeyer
Director, Barry D. Hines
Director, Robert A. Nichols
Director, Willie P. Obey
Director, Teddy R. Price
Director, Don L. Thompson
Director, H. Lindsey Torbett
Auditors : Postlethwaite & Netterville

LOCATIONS

HQ: Red River Bancshares Inc
1412 Centre Court Drive, Suite 501, Alexandria, LA 71301
Phone: 318 561-5028
Web: www.redriverbank.net

HISTORICAL FINANCIALS

Company Type: Public

Income Statement   FYE: December 31

	ASSETS ($mil)	NET INCOME ($mil)	INCOME AS % OF ASSETS	EMPLOYEES
12/20	2,642.6	28.1	1.1%	336
12/19	1,988.2	24.8	1.2%	325
12/18	1,860.5	23.0	1.2%	321
12/17	1,724.2	13.9	0.8%	309
Annual Growth	15.3%	26.3%	—	2.8%

2020 Year-End Financials

Return on assets: 1.2%
Return on equity: 10.4%
Long-term debt ($ mil.): —
No. of shares ($ mil.): 7.3
Sales ($ mil.): 100.5
Dividends
  Yield: 0.4%
  Payout: 6.3%
Market value ($ mil.): 363.0

	STOCK PRICE ($) FY Close	P/E High/Low		PER SHARE ($) Earnings	Dividends	Book Value
12/20	49.55	15	8	3.83	0.24	38.97
12/19	56.06	16	12	3.49	0.00	34.48
Annual Growth	(11.6%)	—	—	9.7%	—	13.0%

Regional Management Corp

Regional Management Corp. is a diversified consumer finance company that provides attractive, easy-to-understand installment loan products primarily to customers with limited access to consumer credit from banks, thrifts, credit card companies, and other lenders. Regional Management operates under the name "Regional Finance" in about 365 branch locations across a dozen states in the Southeastern, Southwestern, Mid-Atlantic, and Midwestern US. Regional Management sources loans through its multiple channel platform, which includes branches, centrally-managed direct mail campaigns, digital partners, retailers, and its consumer website. The company offers loan products that are structured on a fixed rate, fixed term basis with fully amortizing equal monthly installment payments, repayable at any time without penalty.

EXECUTIVES

Chairman, Director, Carlos Palomares
President, Chief Executive Officer, Director, Robert W. Beck
Executive Vice President, Chief Financial Officer, Harpreet Rana
Executive Vice President, Chief Operating Officer, John D. Schachtel, $360,000 total compensation
Executive Vice President, Chief Strategy Officer, Chief Development Officer, Brian J. Fisher, $300,000 total compensation
Executive Vice President, Chief Credit Officer, Manish Parmar
Senior Vice President, General Counsel, Secretary, Catherine R. Atwood
Director, Michael R. Dunn, $802,623 total compensation
Director, Jonathan David Brown
Director, Roel C. Campos
Director, Maria Contreras-Sweet
Director, Steven Jay Freiberg
Director, Philip V. Bancroft
Director, Sandra K. Johnson
Auditors : RSM US LLP

LOCATIONS

HQ: Regional Management Corp
979 Batesville Road, Suite B, Greer, SC 29651
Phone: 864 448-7000
Web: www.regionalmanagement.com

PRODUCTS/OPERATIONS

2015 Sales

	$ in mil.	% of total
Interest and fee income	195.8	90
Insurance income, net	11.7	5
Other	9.8	5
Total	217.3	100

COMPETITORS

EAGLE BANCORP, INC.
EQUIFAX INC.
FIRST DATA CORPORATION
Hanley Economic Building Society
MARLIN BUSINESS SERVICES CORP.
MASTERCARD INCORPORATED
MUFG AMERICAS HOLDINGS CORPORATION
WALKER & DUNLOP, INC.
WORLD ACCEPTANCE CORPORATION
WORLDPAY, INC.

HISTORICAL FINANCIALS

Company Type: Public

Income Statement — FYE: December 31

	ASSETS ($mil)	NET INCOME ($mil)	INCOME AS % OF ASSETS	EMPLOYEES
12/20	1,103.8	26.7	2.4%	1,542
12/19	1,158.5	44.7	3.9%	1,638
12/18	956.3	35.3	3.7%	1,535
12/17	829.4	29.9	3.6%	1,448
12/16	712.2	24.0	3.4%	1,363
Annual Growth	11.6%	2.7%	—	3.1%

2020 Year-End Financials

Return on assets: 2.3%
Return on equity: 9.2%
Long-term debt ($ mil.): —
No. of shares ($ mil.): 10.9
Sales ($ mil.): 373.9
Dividends
Yield: 0.6%
Payout: 8.3%
Market value ($ mil.): 326.0

	STOCK PRICE ($) FY Close	P/E High/Low		PER SHARE ($) Earnings	Dividends	Book Value
12/20	29.86	12	4	2.40	0.20	24.89
12/19	30.03	9	6	3.80	0.00	27.49
12/18	24.05	12	8	2.93	0.00	23.70
12/17	26.31	10	7	2.54	0.00	20.53
12/16	26.28	13	6	1.99	0.00	18.12
Annual Growth	3.2%	—	—	4.8%	—	8.3%

Renasant Corp

Renasant Corporation is the holding company owns Renasant Bank, which serves consumers and local business through about 195 locations in Mississippi, Tennessee, Alabama, Florida, Georgia, North Carolina and South Carolina.. The bank offers standard products such as checking and savings accounts, CDs, credit cards, and loans and mortgages, as well as trust, retail brokerage, and retirement plan services. Its loan portfolio is dominated by residential and commercial real estate loans. The bank also offers agricultural, business, construction, and consumer loans, and lease financing. Subsidiary Renasant Insurance sells personal and business coverage. Renasant has assets of approximately $16.5 billion.

Operations

The company has three reportable segments: Community Banks segment, Insurance segment and Wealth Management segment.

The Community Banks segment accounts for about 95% of total revenue, delivers a complete range of banking and financial services to individuals and small to medium-size businesses including checking and savings accounts, business and personal loans, asset-based lending and equipment leasing, as well as safe deposit and night depository facilities.

The Wealth Management segment (less than 5%), through the Trust division, offers a broad range of fiduciary services including the administration (as trustee or in other fiduciary or representative capacities) of benefit plans, management of trust accounts, inclusive of personal and corporate benefit accounts and custodial accounts, as well as accounting and money management for trust accounts. In addition, the Wealth Management segment, through the Financial Services division, provides specialized products and services to customers, which include fixed and variable annuities, mutual funds and other investment services through a third party broker-dealer.

The Insurance segment includes a full service insurance agency offering all major lines of commercial and personal insurance through major carriers.

Broadly speaking, Renasant gets about 70% of its revenue from interest income. The rest of its revenue comes from mortgage banking, insurance commissions, fees and commissions, trust fee income, deposit account service charges, wealth management and other miscellaneous income sources.

Geographic Reach

Based in Mississippi, Renasant operates some 150 full-services branches, about 10 limited-service branches, nearly 175 ATMs and roughly 40 Interactive Teller Machine (ITM). The bank also operates about 20 locations used exclusively for mortgage banking and seven locations used exclusively for loan production. The Wealth Management segment operates two locations used exclusively for investment services. Renasant Insurance, a wholly-owned subsidiary of the bank, operates out of eight stand-alone offices throughout Mississippi.

Financial Performance

The company reported a revenue of $424 million in 2021, a 1% decrease from the previous year's net interest income of $498.1 million.

In 2021, the company had a net income of $175.9 million, a 110% increase from the previous year's net income of $83.7 million.

The company's cash at the end of 2021 was $1.9 billion. Operating activities generated $142.7 million, while investing activities used $660 million, primarily for purchases of securities available for sale. Financing activities provided another $1.8 billion.

EXECUTIVES

Executive Chairman, Subsidiary Officer, Chairman, Director, E. Robinson McGraw, $617,077 total compensation

President, Chief Executive Officer, Subsidiary Officer, Director, C. Mitchell Waycaster, $630,000 total compensation
Executive Vice President, Bartow Morgan
Principal Financial Officer, James C. Mabry
Executive Vice President, Chief Financial Officer, Chief Operating Officer, Subsidiary Officer, Kevin D. Chapman, $475,000 total compensation
Executive Vice President, Subsidiary Officer, Tracey Morant Adams
Executive Vice President, Region Officer, James Scott Cochran, $400,000 total compensation
Executive Vice President, General Counsel, Subsidiary Officer, Stephen M. Corban, $156,000 total compensation
Executive Vice President, Curtis J. Perry
Executive Vice President, Subsidiary Officer, James W. Gray, $230,000 total compensation
Executive Vice President, Subsidiary Officer, Mark W. Jeanfreau
Executive Vice President, Subsidiary Officer, Stuart R. Johnson, $254,519 total compensation
Executive Vice President, Subsidiary Officer, David L. Meredith
Executive Vice President, Subsidiary Officer, Barlow Morgan, $147,115 total compensation
Executive Vice President, Subsidiary Officer, William Mark Williams
Executive Vice President, Subsidiary Officer, Mary John Witt
Division Officer, Director, R. Rick Hart, $445,477 total compensation
Lead Director, Director, John M. Creekmore
Director, Gary D. Bulter
Director, Donald Clark
Director, Albert J. Dale
Director, Jill V. Deer
Director, Marshall H. Dickerson
Director, Connie L. Engel
Director, John T. Foy
Director, Richard L. Heyer
Director, Neal A. Holland
Director, Michael D. Shmerling
Director, Sean M. Suggs
Auditors : HORNE LLP

LOCATIONS
HQ: Renasant Corp
209 Troy Street, Tupelo, MS 38804-4827
Phone: 662 680-1001
Web: www.renasant.com

PRODUCTS/OPERATIONS

2015 Sales

	$ mil.	% of total
Interest income		
Loans	236.3	64
Securities	26.5	7
Other	0.2	-
Non-interest income		
Mortgage banking income	35.8	10
Service charges on deposit accounts	29.3	8
Fees and commissions	16.1	4
Wealth management	9.8	3
Other	17.3	4
Total	371.3	100

COMPETITORS
COMMUNITY BANK OF THE BAY
FIDELITY SOUTHERN CORPORATION
FIRST INTERSTATE BANCSYSTEM, INC.
FULTON FINANCIAL CORPORATION
PEAPACK-GLADSTONE FINANCIAL CORPORATION
PT. BANK MANDIRI (PERSERO) TBK
SHINSEI BANK, LIMITED
WESBANCO, INC.
WEST BANCORPORATION, INC.
YAPI VE KREDI BANKASI ANONIM SIRKETI

HISTORICAL FINANCIALS
Company Type: Public

Income Statement
FYE: December 31

	ASSETS ($mil)	NET INCOME ($mil)	INCOME AS % OF ASSETS	EMPLOYEES
12/20	14,929.6	83.6	0.6%	2,524
12/19	13,400.6	167.5	1.3%	2,527
12/18	12,934.8	146.9	1.1%	2,359
12/17	9,829.9	92.1	0.9%	2,102
12/16	8,699.8	90.9	1.0%	1,965
Annual Growth	14.5%	(2.1%)	—	6.5%

2020 Year-End Financials
Return on assets: 0.5%
Return on equity: 3.9%
Long-term debt ($ mil.): —
No. of shares ($ mil.): 56.2
Sales ($ mil.): 733.6
Dividends
Yield: 2.6%
Payout: 59.4%
Market value ($ mil.): 1,893.0

	STOCK PRICE ($) FY Close	P/E High/Low		PER SHARE ($) Earnings	Dividends	Book Value
12/20	33.68	24	13	1.48	0.88	37.95
12/19	35.42	13	11	2.88	0.87	37.39
12/18	30.18	18	10	2.79	0.80	34.91
12/17	40.89	23	19	1.96	0.73	30.72
12/16	42.22	20	14	2.17	0.71	27.81
Annual Growth	(5.5%)	—	—	(9.1%)	5.5%	8.1%

Repligen Corp.

Repligen supplies bio-engineered drug ingredients to the pharmaceutical industry. The company's bioprocessing business develops and commercializes proteins and other agents used in the production of biopharmaceuticals. Repligen is a major supplier of Protein A, a recombinant protein used in the production of monoclonal antibodies and other biopharmaceutical manufacturing applications. Its product portfolio also includes filtration products and chromatography devices. North America accounts for about 40% of the company's total revenue.

Operations
Revenue from its filtration products (about 60%) includes the sale of its XCell ATF systems and consumables, KrosFlo filtration products and SIUS filtration products. Revenue from chromatography products (around 10%) includes the sale of its OPUS chromatography columns, chromatography resins and ELISA test kits. Revenue from protein products (about 20%) includes the sale of its Protein A ligands and cell culture growth factors. Revenue from its Process Analytics products (more than 5%) includes the sale of its SoloVPE and FlowVPE systems and consumables. Other revenue primarily consists of revenue from the sale of its operating room products to hospitals as well as freight revenue.

Geographic Reach
Headquartered in Massachusetts, Repligen has manufacturing facilities in the US (Massachusetts, California, New York and New Jersey), Estonia, France, Germany, Ireland, the Netherlands and Sweden.

The company's largest market is the North America, which accounts for about 40% of revenue, followed by Europe, for another roughly 40%. APAC and other countries account for the remaining 20%.

Sales and Marketing
Customers for its bioprocessing products include major life sciences companies, contract manufacturing organizations, biopharmaceutical companies, diagnostics companies and laboratory researchers. The company's largest customers, MilliporeSigma and Cytiva (formerly GE Healthcare), account for around 10% each of revenue.

Advertising expenses for the years 2021, 2020, and 2019 was approximately $0.6 million, $0.3 million, and $0.1 million, respectively.

Financial Performance
The company had a revenue of $670.5 million in 2021, an 83% increase from the previous year's revenue of $366.3 million. This was primarily due to a higher sales volume in the company's product segment.

In 2021, the company had a net income of $128.3 million, a 114% increase from the previous year's net income of $59.9 million.

The company's cash at the end of 2021 was $603.8 million. Operating activities generated $119 million, while investing activities used $221.2 million, mainly for acquisitions. Financing activities provided another $961 million.

Strategy
Repligen is focused on the development, production and commercialization of differentiated, technology-leading solutions or products that address specific pressure points in the biologics manufacturing process and delivers substantial value to its customers. The company's products are designed to increase customers' product yield, and Repligen is committed to supporting its customers with strong customer service and applications expertise.

The company intends to build on its recent history of developing market-leading solutions and delivering strong financial performance through the following strategies:

Continued innovation. The company plans to capitalize on its internal technological expertise to develop products that address unmet needs in upstream and downstream bioprocessing. Repligen intends to invest further in its Proteins franchise while developing platform and derivative products to support its Filtration, Chromatography and Process Analytics franchises.

Platforming its products. A key strategy for accelerating market adoption of its products is delivery of enabling technologies that become the standard, or "platform," technology in markets where it compete. Repligen focuses its efforts on winning early-stage technology evaluations through direct interaction with the key biomanufacturing decision makers in process development labs.

Targeted acquisitions. The company intends to continue to selectively pursue acquisitions of innovative technologies and products. Repligen intends to leverage its balance sheet to acquire technologies and products that improve its overall financial performance by improving its competitiveness in filtration, chromatography or process analytics or by moving the company into adjacent markets with common commercial call points.

Geographical expansion. The company intends to expand its global commercial presence by continuing to selectively build out its global sales, marketing, field applications and services infrastructure.

Operational efficiency. Repligen seeks to expand operating margins through capacity utilization and process optimization strategies designed to increase its manufacturing yields. The company plans to invest in systems to support its global operations, optimizing resources across its global footprint to maximize productivity.

Mergers and Acquisitions

In 2021, Repligen acquired BioFlex Solutions (and manufacturing arm Newton T & M) of Newton, New Jersey, for $31.8 million. The acquisition complements and expands on Repligen's single-use fluid management product offering and simplifies its supply chain. The addition of BioFlex Solutions further integrates components and assemblies, supporting our systems offering.

In late 2021, Repligen agreed to acquire privately-held Avitide Inc., for approximately $150 million, comprised of $75 million in cash plus $75 million in Repligen common stock in addition to performance-based earnout payments over the next three years. Avitide is a leading chromatography developer with diverse affinity ligand libraries and best-in-class ligand-to-resin development timelines. The acquisition gives the company a new platform for affinity resin development, including C&GT, and advances and expands the company's proteins and chromatography franchise to address the unique purification needs of gene therapies and other emerging modalities.

Also in 2021, Repligen agreed to acquire Toulouse, France based Polymem S.A. (Polymem), a leading industrial expert in the development and manufacture of hollow fiber membranes and modules, for $47 million in cash. This acquisition substantially also increases the company's membrane and module manufacturing capacity and establishes a world-class center of excellence in Europe to address the accelerating global demand for these innovative products.

Company Background

Repligen was founded in 1981 by two distinguished scientists who pioneered breakthrough advances in science and technology.

EXECUTIVES

Chairwoman, Director, Karen A. Dawes
President, Chief Executive Officer, Director, Anthony J. Hunt, $600,000 total compensation
development Senior Vice President, Research Senior Vice President, Ralf Kuriyel, $320,000 total compensation
Chief Financial Officer, Jon K. Snodgres, $360,500 total compensation
Chief Operating Officer, Principal Operating Officer, James R. Bylund
Division Officer, Christine Gebski
Director, Nicolas M. Barthelemy
Director, Carrie Eglinton Manner
Director, Rohin Mhatre
Director, Glenn P. Muir
Auditors : Ernst & Young LLP

LOCATIONS

HQ: Repligen Corp.
41 Seyon Street, Bldg. 1, Suite 100, Waltham, MA 02453
Phone: 781 250-0111   **Fax:** 781 250-0115
Web: www.repligen.com

2017 Sales

	% of total
US	43
Sweden	20
UK	4
Other countries	33
Total	100

PRODUCTS/OPERATIONS

2017 Sales

	$ mil.	% of total
Product revenue		
Protein products	54.0	38
Filtration products	49.0	35
Chromatography products	36.3	26
Other	1.8	1
Royalties & other	0.1	-
Total	141.2	100

COMPETITORS

AGENUS INC.
ALBANY MOLECULAR RESEARCH, INC.
APTARGROUP, INC.
ARIAD PHARMACEUTICALS, INC.
CATALENT, INC.
CERUS CORPORATION
GRIFOLS SA
HALOZYME THERAPEUTICS, INC.
LUNDBECK SEATTLE BIOPHARMACEUTICALS, INC.
OSIRIS THERAPEUTICS, INC.

HISTORICAL FINANCIALS

Company Type: Public

Income Statement — FYE: December 31

	REVENUE ($mil)	NET INCOME ($mil)	NET PROFIT MARGIN	EMPLOYEES
12/21	670.5	128.2	19.1%	309
12/20	366.2	59.9	16.4%	1,100
12/19	270.2	21.4	7.9%	761
12/18	194.0	16.6	8.6%	548
12/17	141.2	28.3	20.1%	476
Annual Growth	47.6%	45.8%	—	(10.2%)

2021 Year-End Financials

Debt ratio: 10.8%   No. of shares ($ mil.): 55.3
Return on equity: 7.8%   Dividends
Cash ($ mil.): 603.8   Yield: —
Current Ratio: 2.48   Payout: —
Long-term debt ($ mil.): —   Market value ($ mil.): 14,651.0

	STOCK PRICE ($) FY Close	P/E High/Low		PER SHARE ($) Earnings	Dividends	Book Value
12/21	264.84	139	71	2.24	0.00	31.63
12/20	191.63	181	75	1.11	0.00	27.92
12/19	92.50	217	112	0.44	0.00	20.35
12/18	52.74	181	81	0.37	0.00	14.02
12/17	36.28	62	39	0.72	0.00	13.57
Annual Growth	64.4%	—	—	32.8%	—	23.6%

Republic Bancorp, Inc. (KY)

As one of the top five bank holding companies based in Kentucky, $4 billion-asset Republic Bancorp is the parent of Republic Bank & Trust (formerly First Commercial Bank), which offers deposit accounts, loans and mortgages, credit cards, private banking, and trust services through more than 30 branches in across Kentucky and around 10 more in southern Indiana, Nashville, Tampa, and Cincinnati, Ohio. About one-third of the bank's $3 billion-loan portfolio is tied to residential real estate, while another 25% is made up of commercial real estate loans. Warehouse lines of credit, home equity loans, and commercial and industrial loans make up most of the rest. The company also offers short-term consumer loans and tax refund loans.

Operations

Republic Bancorp operates three "core banking" segments: Traditional Banking, which generated more than 80% of the company's total profit during 2015; Warehouse (almost 20% of profit), and Mortgage Banking (less than 1%). Its Warehouse lending business offers short-term credit facilities secured by single-family residences to mortgage bankers nationwide. Its Republic Processing Group segment offers short-term consumer loans, prepaid debit cards, and tax refund loans.

The bank made 75% of its total revenue

from interest income almost entirely from loans during 2015, though a small percentage came from taxed investments and Federal Home Loan Bank stock. The rest of its revenue came from net refund transfer fees from its Republic Processing Group segment (9% of revenue), deposit account service charges (7%), interchange fee income (4%), mortgage banking income (2%), and other miscellaneous income sources.

Subsidiary Republic Insurance Services (also known as the Captive) provides property and casualty insurance coverage to the company and eight other third-party insurance captives for which insurance may not be available or cost effective.

Geographic Reach

The company had 40 RB&T branches at the end of 2015, including 32 in Kentucky mostly in the Louisville Metro area and others in the Central, Western, and Northern parts of the state. It had 3 branches in southern Indiana (in Floyds Knobs, Jeffersonville, and New Albany); two branches in the Tampa, Florida metro area; two branches in the Nashville, Tennessee metro area; and one more in the Cincinnati, Ohio metro area.

Sales and Marketing

Republic spent $3.16 million on marketing and development expenses during 2015, compared to $3.26 million and $3.11 million in 2014 and 2013, respectively.

Financial Performance

Republic Bancorp's revenues and profits have been trending higher since 2013 as its loan assets have risen more than 30% over the period.

The company's revenue climbed 9% to $190 million during 2015 mostly thanks to higher interest income as its loan assets grew by 9% to $3.33 billion, with commercial loans (real estate and business loans) and residential mortgage loans and lines of credit driving most of the growth.

Strong revenue growth in 2015 drove Republic's net income up 22% to $35 million for the year. The company's operating cash levels nearly doubled to $50 million after adjusting its earnings for non-cash items related to mortgage loan sales and thanks to favorable working capital changes related to changes in other liabilities.

Strategy

Republic Bancorp is moving toward building its commercial loans business, launching a Corporate Banking division in 2015 to originate commercial loans with amounts ranging from $2.5 million to $25 million to borrowers with the highest credit ratings in its existing geographic markets. It also acquires smaller community banks to expand into new geographic markets while building its loan and deposit business.

Additionally, Republic Bancorp has been moving into other revolving credit lines while also looking to take advantage of the rapidly growing prepaid card market. During 2015, for example, it partnered with netSpend to become a pilot issuer of netSpend-branded prepaid cards; and partnered with ClearBalance to originate revolving lines of credit nationally for hospital receivables.

Mergers and Acquisitions

In October 2015, Republic Bancorp expanded its presence in Florida and grew its loan business after agreeing to buy $250 million-asset Cornerstone Bancorp, along its four Cornerstone Community Bank branches in the Tampa, Florida metro area, $190 million in loans and $200 million in deposits. The deal was expected to be completed in the first half of 2016.

Company Background

In 2012 Republic Bancorp entered the Nashville and Minneapolis market through the FDIC-assisted acquisitions of the failed Tennessee Commerce Bank and First Commercial Bank, respectively.

EXECUTIVES

Chief Executive Officer, Subsidiary Officer, Executive Chairman, Director, Steven E. Trager, $382,502 total compensation

Vice-Chairman, President, Subsidiary Officer, Director, A. Scott Trager, $372,000 total compensation

Executive Vice President, Chief Financial Officer, Treasurer, Subsidiary Officer, Kevin D. Sipes, $333,731 total compensation

Subsidiary Officer, Director, Kusman Andrew Trager

Mortgage Lending Executive Vice President, Mortgage Lending Chief Mortgage Banking Officer, Juan M. Montano, $285,000 total compensation

Subsidiary Officer, Director, Logan M. Pichel

Subsidiary Officer, William R. Nelson, $292,013 total compensation

Director, Jennifer N. Green

Director, David P. Feaster

Director, Heather V. Howell

Director, Ernest W. Marshall

Director, William Patrick Mulloy

Director, George Nichols

Director, W. Kenneth Oyler

Director, Michael T. Rust

Director, Susan Stout Tamme

Director, Mark A. Vogt

Director, Timothy S. Huval

Auditors : Crowe LLP

LOCATIONS

HQ: Republic Bancorp, Inc. (KY)
  601 West Market Street, Louisville, KY 40202
Phone: 502 584-3600
Web: www.republicbank.com

PRODUCTS/OPERATIONS

2015 Sales

	$ mil.	% of total
Interest		
Loans, including fees	134.0	70
Taxable investment securities	7.0	4
Other	1.4	1
Noninterest		
Net refund transfer fees	17.4	9
Service charges on deposit accounts	13.0	7
Interchange fee income	8.4	4
Mortgage banking	4.4	2
Other	5.1	3
Adjustments	(0.3)	-
Total	**190.4**	**100**

Selected Services

Checking
Credit & Debit Cards
Internet & Mobile Banking
Lending
Private Banking & Wealth Management
Savings & Investing

COMPETITORS

BEAR STATE FINANCIAL, INC.
CENTURY BANCORP, INC.
CITY HOLDING COMPANY
CUSTOMERS BANCORP, INC.
F.N.B. CORPORATION
FIRST FINANCIAL CORPORATION
FLAGSTAR BANCORP, INC.
REPUBLIC FIRST BANCORP, INC.
STATE BANK FINANCIAL CORPORATION
WILSHIRE BANCORP, INC.

HISTORICAL FINANCIALS

Company Type: Public

Income Statement — FYE: December 31

	ASSETS ($mil)	NET INCOME ($mil)	INCOME AS % OF ASSETS	EMPLOYEES
12/20	6,168.3	83.2	1.3%	1,104
12/19	5,620.3	91.6	1.6%	1,092
12/18	5,240.4	77.8	1.5%	1,064
12/17	5,085.3	45.6	0.9%	1,009
12/16	4,816.3	45.9	1.0%	954
Annual Growth	6.4%	16.0%	—	3.7%

2020 Year-End Financials

Return on assets: 1.4%
Return on equity: 10.4%
Long-term debt ($ mil.): —
No. of shares ($ mil.): 20.9
Sales ($ mil.): 339.3
Dividends
  Yield: 3.1%
  Payout: 12.5%
Market value ($ mil.): 754.0

	STOCK PRICE ($) FY Close	P/E High/Low		PER SHARE ($) Earnings	Dividends	Book Value
12/20	36.07	6	4	7.62	1.14	39.40
12/19	46.80	6	5	8.38	1.06	36.49
12/18	38.72	7	5	7.14	0.97	33.03
12/17	38.02	19	15	2.20	0.87	30.33
12/16	39.54	18	11	2.22	0.83	28.97
Annual Growth	(2.3%)	—	—	36.1%	8.5%	8.0%

ResMed Inc.

ResMed a global leader in the development, manufacturing, distribution and marketing of medical devices and cloud-based software applications that diagnose, treat and manage respiratory disorders, including SDB, COPD, neuromuscular disease and other chronic diseases. Its cloud-based digital health applications, along with its devices, are designed to provide connected care to improve patient outcomes and efficiencies for its customers. ResMed was founded in Australia in 1989 by Dr. Peter Farrell, who remains chairman. The US generates about 65% of total sales.

Operations

ResMed operates in two operating segments: Sleep and Respiratory Care and Software as a Service (SaaS).

Sleep and Respiratory Care generates about 90% of total sales, supports clinical trials in many countries to develop new clinical applications for its technology. SaaS accounts roughly 10% of total sales, relates primarily to the provision of software access with maintenance and support over an agreed term and material rights associated with future discounts upon renewal of some SaaS contracts.

The company also produces cloud-connected CPAP, APAP, bi-level, and ASV devices that deliver positive airway pressure through a patient interface, either a mask or cannula. Its APAP devices, known as AutoSet, are based on a proprietary technology to monitor breathing and can also be used in the diagnosis, treatment and management of OSA.

Geographic Reach

Headquartered in San Diego, California, ResMed has primary research and development facilities, as well as office and manufacturing facilities at its owned site in Sydney, Australia. Other facilities are in Atlanta, Georgia, Moreno Valley, California, Chatsworth, California, and Bloomington, Minnesota; Singapore; Munich, Germany; Lyon, France; Suzhou, China; Halifax, Canada; and Johor Bahru, Malaysia.

The US accounts for nearly 65% of sales.

Sales and Marketing

ResMed's products are sold through its own subsidiaries (mainly in the US, Europe, and the Asia Pacific region) and through its direct sales forces and independent distributors. Marketing efforts target consumers and health care professionals, sleep clinics, hospitals, home health care systems, and third-party payors.

Financial Performance

Net revenue for the year ended June 30, 2022 increased to $3.6 billion from $3.2 billion for the year ended June 30, 2021, an increase of $381.3 million or 12%.

Net income for fiscal 2021 increased to $779.4 million compared from the prior year with $474.5 million.

Cash held by the company at the end of fiscal 2021 decreased to $273.7 million. Cash provided by operations was $351.1 million while cash used for investing and financing activities were $229.9 million and $128.4 million, respectively.

Strategy

ResMed believe that the sleep apnea and respiratory care markets will continue to grow in the future due to a number of factors, including increasing awareness of OSA, CSA and COPD, improved understanding of the role of sleep apnea treatment in the management of cardiac, neurologic, metabolic and related disorders, improved understanding of the role of non-invasive ventilation in the management of COPD, and an increase in the use of digital and product technology to improve patient outcomes and create efficiencies for customers and providers.

The company's strategy for expanding its business operations and capitalizing on the growth of the sleep apnea and respiratory care markets, as well as growth in out-of-hospital care settings, consists of the following key elements: continue product development and innovation in sleep apnea and respiratory care products; broaden its digital health technology foundation; expand SaaS solutions in Out-of-Hospital care settings; expand geographic presence; increase public and clinical awareness; expand into new clinical applications; and leverage the experience of its management team.

Mergers and Acquisitions

In 2022, ResMed announced the acquisition of Leipzig-based company mementor, a developer of digital medical products for various indications. With this acquisition, ResMed strengthens its overall sleep portfolio in Germany with a digital solution for insomnia. The financial terms of the transaction were not disclosed.

In mid-2022, ResMed nnounced a definitive agreement to acquire privately-held MEDIFOX DAN, a German leader in out-of-hospital software solutions for providers in major settings across the care continuum, from Hg, a leading software and services investor. MEDIFOX DAN's German customer base is complementary to the customers of ResMed's US-based SaaS business. In addition, the acquisition of MEDIFOX DAN builds on ResMed's existing business in Germany as a leading provider of innovative cloud-connected medical devices that transform care for patients with sleep apnea and other respiratory conditions. Under the agreement terms, ResMed will acquire MEDIFOX DAN for approximately $1.0 billion (EUR950 million).

HISTORY

ResMed was founded as ResCare in 1989 after Peter Farrell led a management buyout of Baxter Healthcare's respiratory technology unit. ResCare initially developed the SULLIVAN nasal CPAP systems (named after inventor Colin Sullivan) in Australia. In 1991 it introduced the Bubble Mask and the APD2 portable CPAP device. Three years later ResCare began marketing its first VPAP, which applied different air pressures for inhalation and exhalation, in the US.

In 1995 the company went public, changing its name to ResMed (its former name was already taken by another medical company). Over the next two years, ResMed expended a lot of oxygen in court suing rival Respironics for patent infringements; judgments in 1997 and 1998 found in favor of Respironics, but ResMed made plans to appeal. In 1998 the firm received FDA approval to market its VPAP device as a critical-care treatment for lung diseases.

The firm's listing was switched from Nasdaq to the NYSE in 1999 to stabilize stock prices after court losses against Respironics; it also listed on the Australian Stock Exchange.

EXECUTIVES

Chairman, Director, Peter C. Farrell, $788,654 total compensation
President, Chief Operating Officer, Division Officer, Robert Andrew Douglas, $833,720 total compensation
Chief Executive Officer, Director, Michael J. Farrell, $967,490 total compensation
Organizational Development Chief Administrative Officer, Organizational Development Global General Counsel, Organizational Development Secretary, David B. Pendarvis, $533,710 total compensation
Chief Technology Officer, Division Officer, Kaushik Ghoshal
Chief Financial Officer, Brett Sandercock, $445,943 total compensation
Division Officer, Lucile Blaise
Region Officer, Justin Leong
Lead Independent Director, Director, Ronald R. Taylor
Director, Karen Drexler
Director, Harjit Gill
Director, John Hernandez
Director, Desney Tan
Director, Carol J. Burt
Director, Jan De Witte
Director, Richard Sulpizio
Auditors : KPMG LLP

LOCATIONS

HQ: ResMed Inc.
 9001 Spectrum Center Blvd., San Diego, CA 92123
Phone: 858 836-5000
Web: www.resmed.com

2018 Sales

	$ mil.	% of total
US	1,345.2	57
Rest of world	995.0	43
Total	2,340.2	100

PRODUCTS/OPERATIONS

Selected Products
Accessories
 Astral external battery
 Chin restraint
 ClimateLineAir heated tube
 Gecko nasal pad
 SlimLine tubing
 Standard Trolley
Devices
 AirMini

AirStart 10 CPAP
Astral 100
Astral 150
Lumis 100 VPAP S
Stellar 100
Stellar 150
Humidifiers
  H4i
Masks
  AirFit N20 Classic
  AirFit P10
  AirTouch F20
  Mirage FX
  Pixi
  Quattro Air
Swift FX

COMPETITORS

ACORDA THERAPEUTICS, INC.
BAXTER INTERNATIONAL INC.
BOSTON SCIENTIFIC CORPORATION
CONVATEC INC.
CRYOLIFE, INC.
DEXCOM, INC.
NATUS MEDICAL INCORPORATED
THE MEDICINES COMPANY
TRIVASCULAR TECHNOLOGIES, INC.
UTAH MEDICAL PRODUCTS, INC.

HISTORICAL FINANCIALS
Company Type: Public

Income Statement — FYE: June 30

	REVENUE ($mil)	NET INCOME ($mil)	NET PROFIT MARGIN	EMPLOYEES
06/21	3,196.8	474.5	14.8%	7,970
06/20	2,957.0	621.6	21.0%	7,770
06/19	2,606.5	404.5	15.5%	740
06/18	2,340.1	315.5	13.5%	5,940
06/17	2,066.7	342.2	16.6%	6,080
Annual Growth	11.5%	8.5%	—	7.0%

2021 Year-End Financials
Debt ratio: 13.9%
Return on equity: 17.6%
Cash ($ mil.): 295.2
Current Ratio: 1.73
Long-term debt ($ mil.): 643.2
No. of shares ($ mil.): 145.6
Dividends
  Yield: 0.6%
  Payout: 49.8%
Market value ($ mil.): 35,905.0

	STOCK PRICE ($) FY Close	P/E High/Low		PER SHARE ($) Earnings	Dividends	Book Value
06/21	246.52	76	51	3.24	1.56	19.81
06/20	192.00	44	27	4.27	1.56	17.23
06/19	122.03	44	32	2.80	1.48	14.42
06/18	103.58	49	33	2.19	1.40	14.43
06/17	77.87	33	24	2.40	1.32	13.79
Annual Growth	33.4%	—	—	7.8%	4.3%	9.5%

Retractable Technologies Inc

Retractable Technologies knows you can't be too safe when you work around needles all day. The company develops, makes, and markets safety syringes and other injection technologies for the health care industry. Its flagship VanishPoint syringe retracts after injection, reducing the risk of both syringe reuse and accidental needlesticks (both are means of transmitting HIV and other infectious diseases). Retractable also makes blood collection needles and IV catheters using the VanishPoint technology, which was invented by Thomas Shaw, the company's founder, CEO, and majority owner. The firm sells to hospitals and other care providers in the US and abroad, both directly and through distributors.

EXECUTIVES

Chairman, President, Chief Executive Officer, Director, Thomas J. Shaw, $490,247 total compensation
Vice President, Chief Financial Officer, Principal Accounting Officer, Treasurer, Douglas W. Cowan, $290,000 total compensation
Vice President, Secretary, General Counsel, Michele M. Larios, $350,000 total compensation
Sales Development Vice President, Russell B. Kuhlman, $148,728 total compensation
Global Health Executive Director, Kathryn M. Duesman, $174,999 total compensation
Operations Director, Lawrence G. Salerno
Marketing Logistics Director, Sales Director, Shayne Blythe
Accounting Director, John W. Fort
Quality Assurance Director, James A. Hoover
National Accounts Director, Patti S. King
Director, Marco Laterza
Director, Amy Mack
Director, Walter O. Bigby
Director, Darren E. Findley
Auditors: Moss Adams LLP

LOCATIONS

HQ: Retractable Technologies Inc
511 Lobo Lane, Little Elm, TX 75068-5295
Phone: 972 294-1010
Web: www.retractable.com

PRODUCTS/OPERATIONS

Selected Products and Brands
Syringes
  Patient Safe® syringes
  Tuberculin; insulin; allergy antigen VanishPoint® syringes (1mL)
  VanishPoint® syringes (2mL, 3mL, 5mL, and 10mL)
Other
  Patient Safe® Luer Caps
  Small-diameter tube adapters
  VanishPoint® blood collection tube holders
  VanishPoint® IV safety catheters

COMPETITORS

Beijing Dehaier Medical Technology Co., Ltd.
DEROYAL INDUSTRIES, INC.
OWEN MUMFORD LIMITED
SPACELABS HEALTHCARE, INC.
UTAH MEDICAL PRODUCTS, INC.

HISTORICAL FINANCIALS
Company Type: Public

Income Statement — FYE: December 31

	REVENUE ($mil)	NET INCOME ($mil)	NET PROFIT MARGIN	EMPLOYEES
12/20	81.8	24.2	29.6%	182
12/19	41.7	3.1	7.5%	140
12/18	33.2	(1.3)	—	125
12/17	34.4	(3.7)	—	150
12/16	29.8	(3.6)	—	135
Annual Growth	28.7%	—	—	7.8%

2020 Year-End Financials
Debt ratio: 3.6%
Return on equity: 61.6%
Cash ($ mil.): 17.5
Current Ratio: 2.49
Long-term debt ($ mil.): 2.7
No. of shares ($ mil.): 33.9
Dividends
  Yield: —
  Payout: —
Market value ($ mil.): 365.0

	STOCK PRICE ($) FY Close	P/E High/Low		PER SHARE ($) Earnings	Dividends	Book Value
12/20	10.74	19	1	0.80	0.00	1.47
12/19	1.50	22	8	0.07	0.00	0.87
12/18	0.60	—	—	(0.06)	0.00	0.78
12/17	0.68	—	—	(0.14)	0.00	0.83
12/16	0.93	—	—	(0.15)	0.00	0.95
Annual Growth	84.3%	—	—	—	—	11.6%

Revolve Group Inc

EXECUTIVES

Co-Chief Executive Officer, Director, Michael Karanikolas, $328,846 total compensation
Co-Chief Executive Officer, Director, Michael Mente, $328,846 total compensation
Chief Financial Officer, Jesse Timmermans, $296,154 total compensation
Director, Hadley Mullin
Director, Marc D. Stolzman
Director, Melanie Cox
Director, Oana Ruxandra
Auditors: KPMG LLP

LOCATIONS

HQ: Revolve Group Inc
12889 Moore Street, Cerritos, CA 90703
Phone: 562 677-9480
Web: www.revolve.com

HISTORICAL FINANCIALS
Company Type: Public

Income Statement — FYE: December 31

	REVENUE ($mil)	NET INCOME ($mil)	NET PROFIT MARGIN	EMPLOYEES
12/20	580.6	56.7	9.8%	843
12/19	600.9	35.6	5.9%	1,008
12/18	498.7	30.6	6.2%	1,055
12/17	399.5	5.3	1.3%	0
Annual Growth	13.3%	119.8%	—	—

2020 Year-End Financials

Debt ratio: —
Return on equity: 34.2%
Cash ($ mil.): 146.0
Current Ratio: 2.62
Long-term debt ($ mil.): —
No. of shares ($ mil.): 71.4
Dividends
Yield: —
Payout: —
Market value ($ mil.): 2,225.0

	STOCK PRICE ($) FY Close	P/E High/Low		PER SHARE ($) Earnings	Dividends	Book Value
12/20	31.17	40	9	0.79	0.00	2.80
12/19	18.36	—	—	(0.09)	0.00	1.89
Annual Growth	69.8%	—	—	—	—	48.0%

Rexford Industrial Realty Inc

Rexford Industrial Realty knows that there's more to business in Southern California than moviemaking and fashion. A real estate investment trust, or REIT, Rexford Industrial owns and manages a portfolio of nearly 215 industrial properties in Southern California and surrounding areas. Its portfolio comprises about 26.6 million sq. ft. of warehouse, distribution, and light manufacturing space that's leased to small and midsized businesses. It manages about 20 more properties -- altogether comprising about 1.0 million sq. ft. of rentable space. A self-administered and self-managed REIT, Rexford Industrial was formed in 2013 from the assets of its predecessor.

Operations
Rexford Industrial's portfolio spans several California counties, including Los Angeles, Orange, Ventura, San Bernardino, and San Diego.

Geographic Reach
The company portfolio is geographically diversified within the Southern California market across the following submarkets: Los Angeles (53%); San Bernardino (14%); Orange County (13%); San Diego (11%); and Ventura (9%).

Its corporate headquarters is located in Los Angeles, California.

Sales and Marketing
No single tenant accounts for more than 5% of total annualized base rent. By industry, Rexford Industrial top tenants hail from the wholesale trade; warehousing; manufacturing; retail; and transportation.

Financial Performance
Revenue rose for Rexford Industrial by 185% in the last five years, buoyed by rising rental rates.

In 2019, revenue increased by 26% to $267.2 million. The increase in revenue was due to a 26% increase in rental income and an 85% increase in interest income, offset by a 14% decrease in management, leasing and development services.

Net income increased by 36% to $64 million in 2019, which was mostly due to higher revenue for that year.

Cash and cash equivalents at the end of the period were $78.9 million. Net cash provided by operating activities was $139.5 million and another $731.5 million was added by financing activities. Investing activities used $972.7 million for acquisitions of investments and capital expenditures.

Strategy
The company's primary business objective is to generate attractive risk-adjusted returns for its stockholders through dividends and capital appreciation. Rexford believes that pursuing the following strategies will enable the company to achieve this objective.

Internal growth through intensive, value-add asset management through a proactive renewal of existing tenants, re-tenanting to achieve higher rents, and repositioning industrial property by renovating, modernizing, or increasing functionality to increase cash flow and value.

External growth through disciplined acquisitions in prime Southern California infill markets. The company seeks to acquire assets with value-add opportunities to increase its cash flow and asset values, often targeting off-market or lightly marketed transactions where its execution abilities and market credibility encourage owners to sell assets to Rexford at what it considers pricing that is more favorable than heavily marketed transactions. It also seeks to source transactions from owners with generational ownership shift, fund divestment, sale-leaseback/corporate surplus, maturing loans, some facing liquidity needs or financial stress, including loans that lack economical refinancing options. The company believes its deep market presence and relationships may enable it to selectively acquire assets in marketed transactions that may be difficult to access for less focused buyers.

Mergers and Acquisitions
In 2020, Rexford Industrial Realty announced the acquisition of five industrial properties for about $73.2 million. The acquisitions were funded using cash on hand. The Company acquired a three-property industrial portfolio located in Sun Valley, within the LA ? San Fernando Valley submarket, for $35.1 million, or $169 per square foot. It also acquired 15650-15700 S. Avalon Boulevard, located in Los Angeles within the LA ? South Bay submarket, for $28.1 million, or $169 per square foot and acquired 15850 Slover Avenue, located in Fontana within the Inland Empire ? West submarket, for $10.0 million, or $166 per square foot.

EXECUTIVES

Chairman, Director, Richard S. Ziman
Co-Chief Executive Officer, Director, Michael S. Frankel, $550,000 total compensation
Chief Financial Officer, Laura E. Clark
General Counsel, Secretary, David E. Lanzer, $325,000 total compensation
Co-Chief Executive Officer, Director, Howard Schwimmer, $550,000 total compensation
Director, Robert L. Antin
Director, Diana J. Ingram
Director, Angela L. Kleiman
Director, Debra L. Morris
Director, Tyler H. Rose
Auditors : Ernst & Young LLP

LOCATIONS

HQ: Rexford Industrial Realty Inc
11620 Wilshire Boulevard, Suite 1000, Los Angeles, CA 90025
Phone: 310 966-1680
Web: www.rexfordindustrial.com

PRODUCTS/OPERATIONS

2015 Revenue

	$ mil.	% of total
Rental		
Rental Revenues	81.1	86
Tenant Reimbursements	10.5	11
Management, Leasing & Development Services	0.6	1
Other Income	1.0	1
Interest Income	0.7	1
Total	93.9	100

Selected Property Categories
Core
Core Plus
First Mortgages Tied to Target Industrial Property
Value Add

COMPETITORS

DCT INDUSTRIAL TRUST INC.
EQUITY ONE, INC.
FIRST INDUSTRIAL REALTY TRUST, INC.
LIBERTY PROPERTY TRUST
TERRENO REALTY CORPORATION

HISTORICAL FINANCIALS

Company Type: Public

Income Statement — FYE: December 31

	REVENUE ($mil)	NET INCOME ($mil)	NET PROFIT MARGIN	EMPLOYEES
12/21	452.2	128.2	28.4%	186
12/20	330.1	76.4	23.1%	147
12/19	267.2	61.9	23.2%	123
12/18	212.4	46.2	21.7%	108
12/17	161.3	40.7	25.2%	98
Annual Growth	29.4%	33.2%	—	17.4%

2021 Year-End Financials

Debt ratio: 20.6%
Return on equity: 3.1%
Cash ($ mil.): 43.9
Current Ratio: 0.18
Long-term debt ($ mil.): 1,399.5
No. of shares ($ mil.): 160.5
Dividends
Yield: 1.1%
Payout: 141.1%
Market value ($ mil.): 13,019.0

	STOCK PRICE ($)	P/E		PER SHARE ($)		
	FY Close	High	Low	Earnings	Dividends	Book Value
12/21	81.11	101	58	0.80	0.96	29.81
12/20	49.11	105	67	0.51	0.86	24.69
12/19	45.67	103	61	0.47	0.74	22.46
12/18	29.47	79	63	0.41	0.64	19.38
12/17	29.16	66	45	0.48	0.58	17.07
Annual Growth	29.1%	—	—	13.6%	13.4%	15.0%

RF Industries Ltd.

RF Industries (RFI) helps keep the world connected. The company's core business is conducted by its RF Connector division, which makes coaxial connectors used in radio-frequency (RF) communications and computer networking equipment. Its Neulink Division makes wireless digital transmission devices, such as modems and antennas used to link wide-area computer networks and global positioning systems. Through its Bioconnect division, RF Industries also makes cable assemblies, including electric cabling and interconnect products used in medical monitoring applications. Customers in the US account for more than 80% of sales. In 2019, RF Industries bought C Enterprises, a maker of connectivity tools sold to telecommunications and data communications distributors.

EXECUTIVES

Chairman, Director, Mark K. Holdsworth
President, Chief Executive Officer, Director, Robert D. Dawson, $400,000 total compensation
Chief Operating Officer, Ray Michael Bibisi
Chief Financial Officer, Corporate Secretary, Peter Yin
Director, Sheryl Lynn Cefali
Director, Gerald T. Garland
Director, Jason W. Cohenour
Director, Kay L. Tidwell
Auditors : CohnReznick LLP

LOCATIONS

HQ: RF Industries Ltd.
7610 Miramar Road, Building 6000, San Diego, CA 92126-4202
Phone: 858 549-6340
Web: www.rfindustries.com

PRODUCTS/OPERATIONS

Selected Products
Adapters
Antennas
Coaxial cable assemblies
Coaxial connectors
Disposable ECG cables
Electromechanical wiring harnesses
Hand tools
Radio-frequency (RF) data links
Receivers
Safety and snap leads
Wireless modems

COMPETITORS

AMPHENOL CORPORATION
MEGAPHASE, L.L.C.
METHODE ELECTRONICS, INC.
PPC BROADBAND, INC.
WOODHEAD INDUSTRIES, LLC

HISTORICAL FINANCIALS
Company Type: Public

Income Statement			FYE: October 31	
	REVENUE ($mil)	NET INCOME ($mil)	NET PROFIT MARGIN	EMPLOYEES
10/21	57.4	6.1	10.8%	300
10/20	43.0	(0.0)	—	271
10/19	55.3	3.5	6.4%	281
10/18	50.1	5.8	11.6%	186
10/17	30.9	0.3	1.2%	195
Annual Growth	16.7%	100.6%	—	11.4%

2021 Year-End Financials
Debt ratio: —
Return on equity: 17.2%
Cash ($ mil.): 13.0
Current Ratio: 4.34
Long-term debt ($ mil.): —
No. of shares ($ mil.): 10.0
Dividends
Yield: —
Payout: —
Market value ($ mil.): 77.0

	STOCK PRICE ($)	P/E		PER SHARE ($)		
	FY Close	High	Low	Earnings	Dividends	Book Value
10/21	7.61	15	7	0.61	0.00	3.94
10/20	4.28	—	—	(0.01)	0.04	3.27
10/19	5.94	23	16	0.36	0.08	3.33
10/18	7.76	19	4	0.61	0.08	2.99
10/17	2.45	68	35	0.04	0.08	2.41
Annual Growth	32.8%	—	—	97.6%	—	13.1%

Rhinebeck Bancorp Inc

EXECUTIVES

Chairman, Louis Tumolo
President, Chief Executive Officer, Michael J. Quinn, $418,000 total compensation
Chief Operating Officer, Senior Vice President, Jamie J. Bloom, $245,000 total compensation
Chief Financial Officer, Senior Vice President, Michael J. McDermott, $212,850 total compensation
Chief Credit Officer, James T. McCardle.III, $212,500 total compensation
General Counsel, Chief Risk Officer, Corporate Secretary, Karen E. Morgan-D'Amelio
Division Officer, Francis X. Dwyer
Director, Frederick L. Battenfeld
Director, Christopher W. Chestney
Director, Freddimir Garcia
Director, William C. Irwin R.Ph.
Director, Shannon Martin LaFrance
Director, Suzanne Loughlin
Auditors : Wolf & Company, P.C.

LOCATIONS

HQ: Rhinebeck Bancorp Inc
2 Jefferson Plaza, Poughkeepsie, NY 12601

Phone: 845 454-8555
Web: www.rhinebeckbank.com

HISTORICAL FINANCIALS
Company Type: Public

Income Statement				FYE: December 31
	ASSETS ($mil)	NET INCOME ($mil)	INCOME AS % OF ASSETS	EMPLOYEES
12/20	1,128.8	5.9	0.5%	176
12/19	973.9	5.9	0.6%	173
12/18	882.4	4.3	0.5%	166
12/17	742.1	3.0	0.4%	153
12/16	722.5	2.6	0.4%	152
Annual Growth	11.8%	21.8%	—	3.7%

2020 Year-End Financials
Return on assets: 0.5%
Return on equity: 5.2%
Long-term debt ($ mil.): —
No. of shares ($ mil.): 11.1
Sales ($ mil.): 52.6
Dividends
Yield: —
Payout: —
Market value ($ mil.): 95.0

	STOCK PRICE ($)	P/E		PER SHARE ($)		
	FY Close	High	Low	Earnings	Dividends	Book Value
12/20	8.55	21	11	0.55	0.00	10.46
12/19	11.31	22	18	0.56	0.00	9.87
Annual Growth	(24.4%)	—	—	(1.8%)	—	6.0%

Ribbon Communications Inc

EXECUTIVES

Chairman, Director, Shaul Shani
President, Chief Executive Officer, Director, Bruce William McClelland
Executive Vice President, Chief Financial Officer, Miguel A. Lopez
Executive Vice President, Division Officer, Sam Bucci
Executive Vice President, Chief Legal Officer, Corporate Secretary, Patrick W. Macken
Research & Development Executive Vice President, Products Executive Vice President, Research & Development Division Officer, Products Division Officer, Anthony Scarfo, $331,154 total compensation
Global Sales & Services Region Officer, Steven M. Bruny, $341,667 total compensation
Division Officer, Region Officer, Dan Redington
Lead Independent Director, Director, Bruns H. Grayson
Director, Scott Mair
Director, Mariano S. de Beer
Director, Beatriz V. Infante
Director, Richard W. Smith
Director, Tanya Tamone
Director, R. Stewart Ewing
Auditors : DELOITTE & TOUCHE LLP

LOCATIONS

HQ: Ribbon Communications Inc
6500 Chase Oaks Boulevard, Suite 100, Plano, TX 75023
Phone: 978 614-8100
Web: www.ribboncommunications.com

HISTORICAL FINANCIALS
Company Type: Public

Income Statement				FYE: December 31
	REVENUE ($mil)	NET INCOME ($mil)	NET PROFIT MARGIN	EMPLOYEES
12/20	843.7	88.5	10.5%	3,784
12/19	563.1	(130.0)	—	2,209
12/18	577.9	(76.8)	—	2,245
12/17	329.9	(35.2)	—	2,457
12/16	252.5	(13.9)	—	0
Annual Growth	35.2%	—	—	—

2020 Year-End Financials
Debt ratio: 24.9%
Return on equity: 15.1%
Cash ($ mil.): 128.4
Current Ratio: 1.37
Long-term debt ($ mil.): 370.5
No. of shares ($ mil.): 145.4
Dividends
Yield: —
Payout: —
Market value ($ mil.): 954.0

	STOCK PRICE ($) FY Close	P/E High	P/E Low	PER SHARE ($) Earnings	Dividends	Book Value
12/20	6.56	12	3	0.61	0.00	4.72
12/19	3.10	—	—	(1.19)	0.00	4.37
12/18	4.82	—	—	(0.74)	0.00	5.53
12/17	7.73	—	—	(0.60)	0.00	6.05
Annual Growth	(5.3%)	—	—	—	—	(7.9%)

Richmond Mutual Bancorporation Inc

EXECUTIVES

Chairman, President, Chief Executive Officer, Holding/Parent Company Officer, Subsidiary Officer, Garry D. Kleer, $394,615 total compensation
Executive Vice President, Chief Financial Officer, Subsidiary Officer, Donald A. Benziger, $207,692 total compensation
Human Resources Senior Vice President, Human Resources Corporate Secretary, Human Resources Director, Human Resources Subsidiary Officer, Human Resources Holding/Parent Company Officer, Beth A. Brittenham
Senior Vice President, Chief Information Officer, Chief Information Security Officer, Subsidiary Officer, Albert E. Fullerton
Senior Vice President, Chief Audit Examiner and Training Director, Cathy J. Hays
Senior Vice President, Senior Trust Officer, Subsidiary Officer, Alan M. Spears
Retail Lending Senior Vice President, Retail Lending Manager, Retail Lending Subsidiary Officer, Pamela S. Stoops
Retail Banking Senior Vice President, Operations Senior Vice President, Retail Banking Subsidiary Officer, Operations Subsidiary Officer, Robin S. Weinert
Subsidiary Officer, Paul J. Witte
Subsidiary Officer, Dean W. Weinert, $195,154 total compensation
Director, E. Michael Blum
Director, Harold T. Hanley
Director, Jeffrey A. Jackson
Director, Lindley S. Mann
Director, Kathryn Griten
Director, M. Lynn Wetzel
Auditors: BKD, LLP

LOCATIONS

HQ: Richmond Mutual Bancorporation Inc
31 North 9th Street, Richmond, IN 47374
Phone: 765 962-2581
Web: www.mutualbancorp.com

HISTORICAL FINANCIALS
Company Type: Public

Income Statement				FYE: December 31
	REVENUE ($mil)	NET INCOME ($mil)	NET PROFIT MARGIN	EMPLOYEES
12/20	49.6	10.0	20.2%	170
12/19	45.4	(14.0)	—	166
12/18	39.4	5.6	14.4%	172
12/17	33.6	2.7	8.1%	174
Annual Growth	13.9%	54.5%	—	(0.8%)

2020 Year-End Financials
Debt ratio: 15.7%
Return on equity: 5.2%
Cash ($ mil.): 48.7
Current Ratio: 0.08
Long-term debt ($ mil.): 170
No. of shares ($ mil.): 13.1
Dividends
Yield: 1.0%
Payout: 18.2%
Market value ($ mil.): 180.0

	STOCK PRICE ($) FY Close	P/E High	P/E Low	PER SHARE ($) Earnings	Dividends	Book Value
12/20	13.66	19	11	0.82	0.15	14.61
12/19	15.96	—	—	0.00	0.00	13.88
Annual Growth	(14.4%)	—	—	—	—	5.2%

Risk George Industries Inc

George Risk Industries (GRI) wants customers to be able to manage risks. The company makes burglar alarm components and systems, including panic buttons (for direct access to alarm monitoring centers). In addition to security products, GRI manufactures pool alarms, which are designed to sound alerts when a pool or spa area has been entered. The company also makes thermostats, specialty computer keyboards and keypads, custom-engraved key caps, and push-button switches. Chairman, President, and CEO Stephanie Risk-McElroy, granddaughter of founder George Risk, and daughter of former CEO Ken Risk, controls the company.

EXECUTIVES

Chairman, President, Chief Executive Officer, Chief Financial Officer, Director, Stephanie M. Risk-McElroy, $87,000 total compensation
Secretary, Treasurer, Division Officer, Director, Sharon Alberta Westby
Sales Director, Scott McMurray, $25,000 total compensation
Director, Donna Dean Debowey
Director, Joel H. Wiens
Director, Bonita Pauline Risk, $38,000 total compensation
Director, Jerry Knutsen
Auditors: Haynie & Company

LOCATIONS

HQ: Risk George Industries Inc
802 South Elm St., Kimball, NE 69145
Phone: 308 235-4645
Web: www.grisk.com

George Risk Industries operates manufacturing plants in Gering and Kimball, Nebraska.

COMPETITORS

BOSCH SECURITY SYSTEMS, INC.
ECONOLITE CONTROL PRODUCTS, INC.
NAPCO SECURITY TECHNOLOGIES, INC.
SYSTEM SENSOR, LTD.
UNIVERSAL SECURITY INSTRUMENTS, INC.

HISTORICAL FINANCIALS
Company Type: Public

Income Statement				FYE: April 30
	REVENUE ($mil)	NET INCOME ($mil)	NET PROFIT MARGIN	EMPLOYEES
04/21	18.5	10.8	58.5%	195
04/20	14.8	2.1	14.2%	175
04/19	14.1	3.2	23.2%	175
04/18	11.9	2.5	21.3%	175
04/17	10.9	2.4	22.0%	130
Annual Growth	14.1%	45.7%	—	10.7%

2021 Year-End Financials
Debt ratio: —
Return on equity: 24.5%
Cash ($ mil.): 7.3
Current Ratio: 16.86
Long-term debt ($ mil.): —
No. of shares ($ mil.): 4.9
Dividends
Yield: 3.3%
Payout: 31.8%
Market value ($ mil.): 62.0

	STOCK PRICE ($) FY Close	P/E High	P/E Low	PER SHARE ($) Earnings	Dividends	Book Value
04/21	12.52	6	3	2.18	0.42	9.79
04/20	8.40	25	17	0.42	0.40	8.00
04/19	8.25	13	12	0.66	0.38	7.98
04/18	8.55	17	15	0.51	0.36	7.59
04/17	8.49	18	15	0.48	0.35	7.23
Annual Growth	10.2%	—	—	46.0%	4.7%	7.9%

River City Bank

LOCATIONS

HQ: River City Bank
2485 Natomas Park Drive, Suite 100, Sacramento, CA 95833

Phone: 916 567-2600
Web: www.rivercitybank.com

HISTORICAL FINANCIALS
Company Type: Public

Income Statement   FYE: December 31

	REVENUE ($mil)	NET INCOME ($mil)	NET PROFIT MARGIN	EMPLOYEES
12/21	115.8	44.4	38.4%	0
12/20	105.9	31.6	29.9%	0
12/19	91.9	25.3	27.5%	0
12/18	77.6	24.0	30.9%	0
Annual Growth	14.3%	22.8%	—	—

2021 Year-End Financials
Debt ratio: 0.2%
Return on equity: 15.3%
Cash ($ mil.): 161.0
Current Ratio: 0.28
Long-term debt ($ mil.): 8
No. of shares ($ mil.): 1.4
Dividends
  Yield: —
  Payout: 4.1%
Market value ($ mil.): 0.0

River Financial Corp

Auditors: Mauldin & Jenkins, LLC

LOCATIONS
HQ: River Financial Corp
2611 Legends Drive, Prattville, AL 36066
Phone: 334 290-1012
Web: www.riverbankandtrust.com

HISTORICAL FINANCIALS
Company Type: Public

Income Statement   FYE: December 31

	REVENUE ($mil)	NET INCOME ($mil)	NET PROFIT MARGIN	EMPLOYEES
12/20	75.2	17.0	22.7%	231
12/19	58.8	11.1	18.9%	232
12/18	43.5	8.5	19.5%	195
12/17	38.4	8.2	21.6%	151
12/16	35.1	7.9	22.5%	134
Annual Growth	20.9%	21.3%	—	14.6%

2020 Year-End Financials
Debt ratio: 1.1%
Return on equity: 10.8%
Cash ($ mil.): 60.2
Current Ratio: 0.35
Long-term debt ($ mil.): 20.3
No. of shares ($ mil.): 6.5
Dividends
  Yield: —
  Payout: 13.8%
Market value ($ mil.): 137.0

	STOCK PRICE ($) FY Close	P/E High/Low		PER SHARE ($) Earnings	Dividends	Book Value
12/20	21.00	11	6	2.60	0.36	25.87
12/19	28.00	15	15	1.88	0.33	22.66
12/18	30.00	18	13	1.60	0.27	19.60
Annual Growth	(16.3%)	—	—	27.5%	15.5%	14.9%

RLI Corp

RLI Corp. underwrites select property and casualty insurance through major subsidiaries collectively known as RLI Insurance Group. Through its subsidiaries, the company mainly offers coverage for US niche markets -- risks that are hard to place in the standard market and are otherwise underserved. It focuses on public and private companies. RLI's commercial property/casualty lines include products liability, property damage, marine cargo, directors and officers liability, medical malpractice, and general liability. It also writes commercial surety bonds and a smattering of specialty personal insurance.

Operations
RLI operates into three segments; Casualty, Property, and Surety. Casualty segment accounts for about 55% of revenue, followed by property (some 20%), and surety (about 10%).

RLI's specialty commercial property/casualty operations are conducted through its RLI Insurance, Mt. Hawley Insurance, and Contractors Bonding and Insurance Company. Personal offerings account for small portion of RLI's revenues and include homeowners insurance in Hawaii, home business coverage, and personal umbrella (supplemental property/casualty) policies.

The company's net premium earns generated nearly 85% of sales, while net investment income, net realized gains, and net unrealized gains on equity securities account for the rest.

Geographic Reach
While the company operates in all 50 US states, the District of Columbia, the Virgin Islands, Guam, and Puerto Rico, California is RLI's largest market, accounting for more than 15% of the company's premiums.

Its corporate headquarters is located in Peoria, Illinois.

Sales and Marketing
RLI markets its products to brokers, independent agents, and carrier partners through branch offices scattered across the US.

Financial Performance
The company's revenue in 2021 increased to $1.2 billion compared with $983.6 million in the prior year.

Net earnings for 2021 totaled $279.4 million, up from $157.1 million in 2020. Improved underwriting income was bolstered by an increase in unrealized gains on equity securities.

Cash held by the company at the end of 2021 increased to $88.8 million. Operating activities provided $384.9 million while investing and financing activities used $274.8 million and $83.5 million, respectively. Main cash uses were purchase of fixed income securities and cash dividends paid.

Strategy
RLI's investment portfolio serves as the primary resource for loss payments and secondly as a source of income to support operations. Its investment strategy is based on the preservation of capital as the priority, with a secondary focus on growing book value through total return. Investments of the highest quality and marketability are critical for preserving its claims-paying ability.

Company Background
Gerald Stephens founded the company in 1961 and served as its chairman from 2001 until his retirement in 2011.

EXECUTIVES
Chairman, Director, Jonathan E. Michael, $775,000 total compensation
President, Chief Executive Officer, Director, Craig W. Kliethermes, $490,385 total compensation
Human Resources Senior Vice President, Human Resources Chief Legal Officer, Human Resources Corporate Secretary, Human Resources Subsidiary Officer, Jeffrey D. Fick, $326,154 total compensation
Finance Vice President, Finance Chief Financial Officer, Todd W. Bryant, $330,000 total compensation
Vice President, Controller, Seth A. Davis
Vice President, Chief Investment Officer, Treasurer, Aaron P. Diefenthaler
Chief Operating Officer, Jennifer L. Klobnak, $334,231 total compensation
Director, Kaj Ahlmann
Director, Michael E. Angelina
Director, Calvin G. Butler
Director, David B. Duclos
Director, Susan S. Fleming
Director, Jordan W. Graham
Director, Robert P. Restrepo
Director, Debbie S. Roberts
Director, Michael J. Stone, $525,000 total compensation
Auditors: DELOITTE & TOUCHE LLP

LOCATIONS
HQ: RLI Corp
9025 North Lindbergh Drive, Peoria, IL 61615
Phone: 309 692-1000   Fax: 309 692-1068
Web: www.rlicorp.com

PRODUCTS/OPERATIONS
2016 Revenues

	$ mil.	% of total
Net premiums earned		
Casualty	454.8	56
Property	152.2	19
Surety	121.6	15
Net investment income	53.1	6
Net realized gains	34.6	4
Total	816.3	100

Selected Products
Commercial
  Casualty
  Contractors bonding and insurance
  Executive products liability
  Marine
  Professional services
  Property
  Reinsurance
  Specialty programs
  Transportation
Personal
  Homeowners (Hawaii)
  Home business owners
  Personal umbrella
Surety Bonds

COMPETITORS

AMERITRUST GROUP, INC.
AUTO-OWNERS INSURANCE COMPANY
CINCINNATI FINANCIAL CORPORATION
CNA FINANCIAL CORPORATION
FEDNAT HOLDING COMPANY
GUARDIA LLC
HCI GROUP, INC.
MARKEL CORPORATION
NATIONAL GENERAL HOLDINGS CORP.
UNIVERSAL INSURANCE HOLDINGS, INC.

HISTORICAL FINANCIALS

Company Type: Public

Income Statement — FYE: December 31

	ASSETS ($mil)	NET INCOME ($mil)	INCOME AS % OF ASSETS	EMPLOYEES
12/21	4,508.3	279.3	6.2%	913
12/20	3,938.4	157.0	4.0%	875
12/19	3,545.7	191.6	5.4%	905
12/18	3,105.0	64.1	2.1%	912
12/17	2,947.2	105.0	3.6%	902
Annual Growth	11.2%	27.7%	—	0.3%

2021 Year-End Financials

Return on assets: 6.6%
Return on equity: 23.6%
Long-term debt ($ mil.): —
No. of shares ($ mil.): 45.2
Sales ($ mil.): 1,179.2
Dividends
Yield: 2.6%
Payout: 50.9%
Market value ($ mil.): 5,077.0

	STOCK PRICE ($) FY Close	P/E High	P/E Low	Earnings	Dividends	Book Value
12/21	112.10	19	16	6.11	2.99	27.14
12/20	104.15	31	20	3.46	1.95	25.16
12/19	90.02	23	15	4.23	1.91	22.18
12/18	68.99	55	40	1.43	1.87	18.13
12/17	60.66	26	21	2.36	2.58	19.33
Annual Growth	16.6%	—	—	26.8%	3.8%	8.9%

RMR Group Inc (The)

EXECUTIVES

President, Chief Executive Officer, Subsidiary Officer, Chairman, Managing Director, Adam D. Portnoy, $300,000 total compensation

Executive Vice President, General Counsel, Secretary, Subsidiary Officer, Managing Director, Jennifer B. Clark, $300,000 total compensation

Executive Vice President, Chief Financial Officer, Treasurer, Subsidiary Officer, Matthew P. Jordan

Executive Vice President, Subsidiary Officer, Jennifer Francis Mintzer

Executive Vice President, Subsidiary Officer, John G. Murray

Executive Vice President, Subsidiary Officer, Jonathan M. Pertchik

Lead Independent Director, Independent Director, Rosen Plevneliev

Independent Director, Ann Logan

Independent Director, Jonathan Veitch

Independent Director, Walter C. Watkins

Auditors: Deloitte & Touche LLP

LOCATIONS

HQ: RMR Group Inc (The)
Two Newton Place, 255 Washington Street, Suite 300, Newton, MA 02458-1634
Phone: 617 796-8230
Web: www.rmrgroup.com

HISTORICAL FINANCIALS

Company Type: Public

Income Statement — FYE: September 30

	REVENUE ($mil)	NET INCOME ($mil)	NET PROFIT MARGIN	EMPLOYEES
09/21	607.2	35.6	5.9%	600
09/20	589.5	28.7	4.9%	600
09/19	713.3	74.5	10.5%	50,600
09/18	404.9	96.0	23.7%	52,600
09/17	271.7	42.2	15.6%	53,475
Annual Growth	22.3%	(4.2%)	—	(67.5%)

2021 Year-End Financials

Debt ratio: —
Return on equity: 14.5%
Cash ($ mil.): 159.8
Current Ratio: 3.14
Long-term debt ($ mil.): —
No. of shares ($ mil.): 31.4
Dividends
Yield: 25.4%
Payout: 504.1%
Market value ($ mil.): 1,053.0

	STOCK PRICE ($) FY Close	P/E High	P/E Low	Earnings	Dividends	Book Value
09/21	33.45	21	12	2.15	8.52	6.20
09/20	27.47	28	13	1.75	1.52	9.43
09/19	45.48	20	9	4.59	1.40	9.22
09/18	92.80	16	9	5.92	1.00	7.45
09/17	51.35	21	13	2.63	1.00	4.80
Annual Growth	(10.2%)	—	—	(4.9%)	70.8%	6.6%

Roku Inc

EXECUTIVES

Chairman, President, Chief Executive Officer, Director, Anthony Wood, $1,084,615 total compensation

Senior Vice President, General Counsel, Secretary, Stephen H. Kay, $500,000 total compensation

Senior Vice President, Division Officer, Mustafa A. Ozgen

Senior Vice President, Division Officer, Scott Rosenberg, $641,346 total compensation

Corporate Controller Vice President, Corporate Controller Chief Accounting Officer, Matthew C. Banks

Chief Financial Officer, Steve Louden, $627,885 total compensation

Director, Laurie Simon Hodrick

Director, Gina A. Luna

Director, Ray A. Rothrock

Director, Jeffrey Hastings

Director, Neil Hunt

Director, Ravi Ahuja

Director, Mai Fyfield

Auditors: DELOITTE & TOUCHE LLP

LOCATIONS

HQ: Roku Inc
1155 Coleman Avenue, San Jose, CA 95110
Phone: 408 556-9040
Web: www.roku.com

HISTORICAL FINANCIALS

Company Type: Public

Income Statement — FYE: December 31

	REVENUE ($mil)	NET INCOME ($mil)	NET PROFIT MARGIN	EMPLOYEES
12/21	2,764.5	242.3	8.8%	3,000
12/20	1,778.3	(17.5)	—	1,925
12/19	1,128.9	(59.9)	—	1,650
12/18	742.5	(8.8)	—	1,111
12/17	512.7	(63.5)	—	817
Annual Growth	52.4%	—	—	38.4%

2021 Year-End Financials

Debt ratio: 2.2%
Return on equity: 11.8%
Cash ($ mil.): 2,146.0
Current Ratio: 4.19
Long-term debt ($ mil.): 79.9
No. of shares ($ mil.): 135.1
Dividends
Yield: —
Payout: —
Market value ($ mil.): 30,838.0

	STOCK PRICE ($) FY Close	P/E High	P/E Low	Earnings	Dividends	Book Value
12/21	228.20	262	111	1.71	0.00	20.47
12/20	332.02	—	—	(0.14)	0.00	10.37
12/19	133.90	—	—	(0.52)	0.00	5.83
12/18	30.64	—	—	(0.08)	0.00	2.23
12/17	51.78	—	—	(2.24)	0.00	1.54
Annual Growth	44.9%	—	—	—	—	91.1%

Rollins, Inc.

Rollins is an international services company that provides provide essential pest and wildlife control services and protection against termite damage, rodents and insects. Rollins also provides recurring maintenance, monitoring or inspection services to help protect consumer's property for any future sign of termite activities after the original treatment. The company serves more than 2 million customers in some 70 countries globally. The US operations account for more than 90% of revenue. Other Rollins brands include and HomeTeam Pest Defense Clark Pest Control, Western Pest Services, Critter Control Wildlife, and Northwest Pest Control, among others.

Operations

The company has only one reportable segment, its pest and termite control business.

Rollins provides pest control services to protect residential and commercial properties from common pests, including rodents and insects. Pest control generally consists of assessing a customer's property for conditions that invite pests, tackling current infestations, and stopping the life cycle to prevent future invaders. It also provides both traditional and baiting termite protection services. Traditional termite protection uses "Termidor" liquid treatment and/or dry foam and Orkin foam to treat voids and spaces around the property, while baiting termite protection uses baits to disrupt the molting process termites require for growth and offers ongoing protection.

In connection with the initial service offerings, Rollins may offer other miscellaneous services, such as cleaning, and equipment rentals.

Geographic Reach

Atlanta, Georgia-based, Rollins owns or leases over 600- branch offices and operating facilities used in its business as well as the Rollins Training Center located in Atlanta, Georgia; and the Pacific Division Administration and Training Center in Riverside, California. The company has operations in the US, Canada, Australia, Europe, and Asia with international franchises in Mexico, Canada, Central and South America, the Caribbean, Europe, the Middle East, Asia, Africa, and Australia.

The US accounts for more than 90% of the company's total sale.

Sales and Marketing

The company serves over 2 million customers. The residential customers generate around 45% of sales, while the commercial customers bring in some 35%.

The advertising cost for the years 2021, 2020, and 2019 were $91.9 million, $86.3 million, and $81.2 million, respectively.

Financial Performance

Rollins' revenue has been steadily increasing for the last five years with an overall growth of 45% between 2017 and 2021.

Revenue in 2021 was $2.4 billion, an increase of $263.1 million, or 12%, from 2020 revenues of $2.2 billion. Comparing 2021 to 2020, residential pest control revenue increased 13%, commercial pest control revenue increased 10% and termite and ancillary services grew 14%.

In 2021, the company had a net income of $350.7 million, a 34% increase from the previous year's net income of $260.8 million. The increase was primarily due to the higher volume of sales that the company generated for the year.

The company's cash at the end of 2021 was $105.3 million. Operating activities generated $401.8 million, while investing activities used $99 million, mainly for acquisitions. Financing activities used another $290.2 million, primarily for payment of dividends.

Strategy

The company has relationships with a national pest control product distributor and other suppliers for pest and termite control treatment products. The company maintains a sufficient level of chemicals, materials and other supplies to fulfill its immediate servicing needs and to alleviate any potential short-term shortage in availability from its national network of suppliers.

Expenditures by the company on research activities relating to the development of new products or services are not significant. The company utilizes the relationships with its manufacturer and materials suppliers to provide new and innovative products and services, coupled with in-depth reviews by Rollins' tenured Technical Services department to ensure they meet its strict requirements. The company also conducts tests of new products with the specific manufacturers of such products and it relies on research performed by leading universities.

Rollins maintains a close relationship with several universities for research and validation of treatment procedures and material selection.

Mergers and Acquisitions

In early 2022, Orkin, a subsidiary of Rollins, finalized the acquisition of NBC Environment headquartered at Banham, Norfolk, UK. The company centered on bird control using falcons, but it has since grown into a nationwide, full-range pest control servicing business. Terms were not disclosed.

In late 2021, Rollins completed the purchase of seven branches in Southeast and Southwest Florida from Hulett Environmental Services, Inc. Based in West Palm Beach, Hulett retained its core operations and will continue to serve communities from Palm Beach County to Vero Beach. This expansion into South Florida will be an acquisition under Northwest Exterminating. Terms were not disclosed.

Company Background

Rollins has taken on several education initiatives. The company partners with the Centers for Disease Control in efforts to teach the public about pest-related illnesses, and its O. Orkin Insect Zoo at the Smithsonian Museum of Natural History in Washington, DC, remains a popular exhibit. The Orkin name for the pest control business came from Atlanta businessman Otto Orkin who founded the company in 1901.

HISTORY

Brothers O. Wayne and John Rollins founded the company in 1948 as Rollins Broadcasting. John's auto leasing company, which later became Rollins Truck Leasing, was an early advertiser on Wayne's radio station. The company went public in 1961 and soon extended its reach to include cosmetics and citrus-fruit growing.

Rollins engineered one of the first leveraged buyouts in history when it purchased the much larger Orkin in 1964. (Orkin was founded in 1901 by Otto Orkin, who launched his extermination empire by selling rat killer door-to-door; his efforts earned him the nickname "Orkin the Rat Catcher.") Adopting the Rollins, Inc. name in 1965, the company diversified further in the 1970s and 1980s, making purchases that included oil and gas, textiles, and burglar alarms systems. In 1984 Rollins spun off Rollins Communications and RPC Energy Services and retained its consumer services, which included pest control, lawn care (Orkin Lawncare), and security services (Rollins Protective Services).

The company was forced to modify its termite services when the Environmental Protection Agency banned the use of Chlordane in 1988 (the insecticide had caused cancer in laboratory animals). Chlordane had been the most widely used termite insecticide prior to the ban; its prohibition prompted confusion among consumers, which translated into a downturn in consumer demand for termite services. In 1998 a jury found Orkin liable for treating a Florida family's home with Chlordane in 1993. The family was awarded a $2 million judgment.

Wayne Rollins died in 1991, leaving his sons Randall and Gary in charge. Recognizing heightened demand for commercial services, the company formed a commercial division in 1996. The following year, Rollins sold its security and lawn care businesses, allowing the company to focus exclusively on pest control.

Orkin expanded its pest control empire that year with acquisitions of 10 pest control businesses in the US and Canada. In 1999 Orkin bought the pest control business of S.C. Johnson Professional (a division of S.C. Johnson & Son). The two companies also teamed to market pest elimination services to retailers. In 2001 the company launched Acurid, a customized approach to pest control that helps businesses meet industry regulations.

In 2003 the company began limited offerings of mosquito control programs in response to fears of West Nile virus, which is carried by the insect. The company strengthened its presence in the northeastern US through the 2004 acquisition of New Jersey-based Western Pest Services, the pest control operation of Western Industries.

Rollins obtained pest management business Crane Pest Control in 2009 after buying the assets of rival HomeTeam Pest Defense from homebuilder Centex for about $137 million in 2008. In 2010 Rollins acquired pest control firm Waltham Services and the company also expanded its international presence, opening several foreign locations.

EXECUTIVES

Chief Executive Officer, Chairman, Director, Gary W. Rollins, $1,000,000 total compensation

Vice-Chairman, Director, John F. Wilson, $775,000 total compensation

President, Chief Operating Officer, Director, Jerry E. Gahlhoff

Vice President, General Counsel, Corporate Secretary, Elizabeth Brannen Chandler, $355,000 total compensation

Finance Vice President, Investor Relations Vice President, Finance Interim Chief Financial Officer, Investor Relations Interim Chief Financial Officer, Finance Treasurer, Investor Relations Treasurer, Finance Principal Financial Officer, Investor Relations Principal Financial Officer, Finance Principal Accounting Officer, Investor Relations Principal Accounting Officer, Julie K. Bimmerman
Chief Accounting Officer, Principal Accounting Officer, Traci Hornfeck
Lead Independent Director, Director, Jerry W. Nix
Director, Susan R. Bell
Director, Donald P. Carson
Director, Louise S. Sams
Director, Patrick J. Gunning
Director, Gregory B. Morrison
Director, Pamela R. Rollins
Auditors : Grant Thornton LLP

LOCATIONS

HQ: Rollins, Inc.
 2170 Piedmont Road, N.E., Atlanta, GA 30324
Phone: 404 888-2000
Web: www.rollins.com

2016 Sales

	% of total
US	93
Other countries	7
Total	100

PRODUCTS/OPERATIONS

Selected Subsidiaries
Crane Acquisitions, Inc.
  PCO Holdings, Inc.
    Orkin Canada Limited Partnership
HomeTeam Pest Defense, Inc.
IFC Company Holdings, Inc.
  IFC Properties LLC
    The Industrial Fumigant Company
International Food Consultants LLC
Orkin
  Orkin International, Inc.
  Orkin Systems, Inc
Orkin-IFC Properties LLC
Rollins Continental, Inc.
  Rollins—Western Real Estate Holding LLC
Trutech LLC
Waltham Services LLC
Western Industries North, Inc.
Western Industries South, Inc

Selected Pest Control Products and Services
Baits
Crack and crevice treatment
Direct contact services
Dusting treatment
Inspections
Mosquito control
Perimeter defense system
Traps
Void treatment

COMPETITORS
AGGREKO PLC
AIRE-MASTER OF AMERICA, INC.
ASHTEAD GROUP PUBLIC LIMITED COMPANY
CARTER & ASSOCIATES ENTERPRISES, INC.
COPESAN SERVICES, INC.
ORKIN, LLC
RENTOKIL INITIAL PLC
SPAM ARREST LLC
TERMINIX GLOBAL HOLDINGS, INC.

THE TERMINIX INTERNATIONAL COMPANY LIMITED PARTNERSHIP

HISTORICAL FINANCIALS
Company Type: Public

Income Statement				FYE: December 31
	REVENUE ($mil)	NET INCOME ($mil)	NET PROFIT MARGIN	EMPLOYEES
12/20	2,161.2	260.8	12.1%	15,616
12/19	2,015.4	203.3	10.1%	14,952
12/18	1,821.5	231.6	12.7%	13,734
12/17	1,673.9	179.1	10.7%	13,126
12/16	1,573.4	167.3	10.6%	12,153
Annual Growth	8.3%	11.7%	—	6.5%

2020 Year-End Financials
Debt ratio: 11.0%
Return on equity: 29.6%
Cash ($ mil.): 98.4
Current Ratio: 0.67
Long-term debt ($ mil.): 185.8
No. of shares ($ mil.): 491.6
Dividends
  Yield: 0.6%
  Payout: 61.6%
Market value ($ mil.): 19,207.0

	STOCK PRICE ($) FY Close	P/E High/Low		PER SHARE ($)		
				Earnings	Dividends	Book Value
12/20	39.07	119	60	0.53	0.33	1.91
12/19	33.16	106	76	0.41	0.31	1.66
12/18	36.10	136	71	0.47	0.31	1.45
12/17	46.53	131	90	0.36	0.25	1.33
12/16	33.78	100	70	0.34	0.22	1.16
Annual Growth	3.7%	—	—	11.6%	10.1%	13.3%

Royalty Pharma plc

EXECUTIVES

Chief Executive Officer, Chairman, Director, Pablo Legorreta
Executive Vice President, Chief Financial Officer, Terrance Coyne
Investments Executive Vice President, Investments General Counsel, George Lloyd
Research Executive Vice President, Investments Executive Vice President, James Reddoch
Executive Vice President, Vice-Chairman, Christopher Hite
Director, Errol De Souza
Director, William Ford
Director, Catherine M. Engelbert
Director, M. Germano Giuliani
Director, Gregory Norden
Director, Bonnie L. Bassler
Director, Rory B. Riggs

LOCATIONS

HQ: Royalty Pharma plc
 110 East 59th Street, New York, NY 10022
Phone: 212 883-0200
Web: www.royaltypharma.com

HISTORICAL FINANCIALS
Company Type: Public

Income Statement				FYE: December 31
	REVENUE ($mil)	NET INCOME ($mil)	NET PROFIT MARGIN	EMPLOYEES
12/21	2,289.4	619.7	27.1%	66
12/20	2,122.3	975.0	45.9%	51
12/19	1,814.2	2,348.5	129.4%	35
12/18	1,794.8	1,377.7	76.8%	0
12/17	1,597.9	1,210.0	75.7%	0
Annual Growth	9.4%	(15.4%)	—	—

2021 Year-End Financials
Debt ratio: 40.5%
Return on equity: 11.6%
Cash ($ mil.): 1,541.0
Current Ratio: 16.81
Long-term debt ($ mil.): 7,096
No. of shares ($ mil.): 968.4
Dividends
  Yield: 1.7%
  Payout: 35.0%
Market value ($ mil.): 0.0

Sachem Capital Corp

EXECUTIVES

President, Chief Executive Officer, Treasurer, Chairman, John L. Villano
Executive Vice President, Chief Financial Officer, John E. Warch
Director, Leslie Bernhard
Director, Arthur L. Goldberg
Director, Brian Prinz
Auditors : Hoberman & Lesser, CPA's, LLP

LOCATIONS

HQ: Sachem Capital Corp
 698 Main Street, Branford, CT 06405
Phone: 203 433-4736
Web: www.sachemcapitalcorp.com

HISTORICAL FINANCIALS
Company Type: Public

Income Statement				FYE: December 31
	REVENUE ($mil)	NET INCOME ($mil)	NET PROFIT MARGIN	EMPLOYEES
12/20	18.6	8.9	48.3%	17
12/19	12.6	6.1	48.9%	10
12/18	11.7	7.7	66.3%	11
12/17	6.9	4.8	69.5%	7
12/16	4.1	3.0	73.8%	0
Annual Growth	45.7%	31.0%	—	—

2020 Year-End Financials
Debt ratio: 61.2%
Return on equity: 10.9%
Cash ($ mil.): 19.4
Current Ratio: 29.68
Long-term debt ($ mil.): 138.4
No. of shares ($ mil.): 22.1
Dividends
  Yield: 8.6%
  Payout: 87.8%
Market value ($ mil.): 92.0

	STOCK PRICE ($) FY Close	P/E High/Low		PER SHARE ($)		
				Earnings	Dividends	Book Value
12/20	4.16	11	3	0.41	0.36	3.66
12/19	4.34	18	12	0.32	0.53	3.73
12/18	3.91	9	7	0.50	0.61	3.42
12/17	3.94	14	10	0.38	0.26	3.54
Annual Growth	1.8%	—	—	2.6%	11.5%	1.1%

Safehold Inc

EXECUTIVES

Chairman, Chief Executive Officer, Holding/Parent Company Officer, Jay Sugarman
Vice-Chairman, Chief Legal Officer, Holding/Parent Company Officer, Nina B. Matis
Interim Chief Financial Officer, Holding/Parent Company Officer, Andrew C. Richardson
Chief Investment Officer, Holding/Parent Company Officer, Marcos Alvarado
Director, Dean S. Adler
Director, Robin J. Josephs
Director, Jay S. Nydick
Director, Stefan M. Selig
Auditors : Deloitte & Touche LLP

LOCATIONS

HQ: Safehold Inc
1114 Avenue of the Americas, 39th Floor, New York, NY 10036
Phone: 212 930-9400
Web: www.safeholdinc.com

HISTORICAL FINANCIALS

Company Type: Public

Income Statement — FYE: December 31

	REVENUE ($mil)	NET INCOME ($mil)	NET PROFIT MARGIN	EMPLOYEES
12/21	187.0	73.1	39.1%	0
12/20	155.4	59.2	38.1%	0
12/19	93.3	27.6	29.7%	0
12/18	49.7	11.7	23.6%	0
12/17	17.2	(3.6)	—	0
Annual Growth	81.6%	—	—	—

2021 Year-End Financials

Debt ratio: 59.7%
Return on equity: 4.7%
Cash ($ mil.): 29.6
Current Ratio: 3.32
Long-term debt ($ mil.): 2,697.5
No. of shares ($ mil.): 56.6
Dividends
 Yield: 0.8%
 Payout: 52.9%
Market value ($ mil.): 4,521.0

	STOCK PRICE ($) FY Close	P/E High/Low		PER SHARE ($) Earnings	Dividends	Book Value
12/21	79.85	70	50	1.35	0.67	29.71
12/20	72.49	63	34	1.17	0.64	25.92
12/19	40.30	48	19	0.89	0.61	22.85
12/18	18.81	31	24	0.64	0.60	19.44
12/17	17.60	—	—	(0.25)	0.31	19.57
Annual Growth	45.9%	—	—	—	21.7%	11.0%

Saia Inc

Saia is a holding company for less-than-truckload (LTL) carrier Saia Motor Freight Line, a leading LTL carrier that serves about 45 states and provides LTL services to Canada and Mexico through relationships with third-party interline carriers. Saia Motor Freight specializes in offering its customers a range of LTL services, including time-definite and expedited options. The carrier operates a fleet of some 5,600 tractors and approximately 19,300 trailers from a network of about 175 terminals. Saia's service territory spans throughout the South, Southwest, Midwest, as well as Pacific Northwest, West, and portions of the Northeast US. The company was founded in 1924.

Operations

Saia provides less-than-truckload (LTL) services through a single integrated organization. While more than 95% of its revenue is derived from transporting LTL shipments, it also offers customers a wide range of other value-added services, including non-asset truckload, expedited and logistics services across North America through its wholly-owned subsidiaries: Saia Motor Freight Line. The trucking industry consists of three segments: private fleets and two "for-hire" carrier groups. The private carrier segment consists of fleets owned and operated by shippers who move their own goods. The two "for-hire" carrier groups, truckload and LTL, are defined by the typical shipment sizes handled by the transportation service companies.

Saia Motor Freight provides its customers with solutions for shipments between 100 and 10,000 pounds.

Geographic Reach

The company operates through about 175 terminals in nearly 45 US states, in the South, Southwest, Midwest, Pacific Northwest, West, and portions of Northeast. It also provides LTL services to Canada and Mexico through relationships with third-party interline carriers.

Sales and Marketing

Saia's advertising costs were $5.7 million, $4.6 million, and $6.1 million in 2021, 2020, and 2019, respectively.

Financial Performance

The company's revenue in 2021 increased by 26% to $2.3 billion compared with $1.8 billion in the prior year. The increase resulted primarily from pricing actions, including a 6% general rate increase taken in early 2021, for customers subject to general rate increases, in addition to increased volumes, terminal expansion and improvements in mix of business.

Net income in 2021 increased to $253.2 million compared with $138.3 million in the prior year.

Cash held by the company at the end of 2021 increased to $106.6 million. Cash provided by operations was $382.6 million while investing and financing activities used $277.8 million and $23.5 million, respectively. Main cash uses were acquisition of property and equipment; and repayment of revolving credit agreement.

Strategy

Saia has grown historically through a combination of organic growth and geographic integration or "tuck-in" acquisitions of smaller trucking and logistics companies. More recently, Saia has grown largely through organic growth.

Key elements of its business strategy include: Continuing to focus on operating safely; Managing yields and business mix; Increasing density in existing geographies; Continuing to focus on delivering best-in-class service; Continuing to focus on improving operating efficiencies; Preparing the organization for growth and enhanced geographic footprint; and Continuing to address environmental and social issues.

EXECUTIVES

Chairman, Director, Richard D. O'Dell, $749,196 total compensation
Finance President, Finance Chief Executive Officer, Director, Frederick J. Holzgrefe, $550,000 total compensation
Finance Executive Vice President, Finance Vice President, Finance Chief Financial Officer, Finance Secretary, Douglas L. Col
Executive Vice President, Chief Customer Officer, Raymond R. Ramu, $415,648 total compensation
Operations Executive Vice President, Patrick D. Sugar
Executive Vice President, Chief Information Officer, Rohit Lal
Executive Vice President, Chief Human Resources Officer, Anthony Norwood
Vice President, Controller, Principal Accounting Officer, Kelly W. Benton
Director, Kevin A. Henry
Director, Donald R. James
Director, Donna E. Epps
Director, John P. Gainor
Lead Independent Director, Director, Randolph W. Melville
Director, Di-Ann Eisnor
Director, Jeffrey C. Ward
Director, Susan F. Ward
Auditors : KPMG LLP

LOCATIONS

HQ: Saia Inc
11465 Johns Creek Parkway, Suite 400, Johns Creek, GA 30097
Phone: 770 232-5067
Web: www.saia.com

PRODUCTS/OPERATIONS

Selected Coverage Area
Alabama
Arizona
Arkansas
California
Colorado
Florida
Georgia
Idaho
Illinois
Indiana
Iowa
Kansas
Kentucky
Louisiana
Michigan

Minnesota
Mississippi
Missouri
Nebraska
Nevada
New Mexico
North Carolina
North Dakota
Ohio
Oklahoma
Oregon
South Carolina
South Dakota
Tennessee
Texas
Utah
Virginia
Washington
Wisconsin

COMPETITORS

COVENANT LOGISTICS GROUP, INC.
FORWARD AIR CORPORATION
FROZEN FOOD EXPRESS INDUSTRIES, INC.
KNIGHT TRANSPORTATION, INC.
MARTEN TRANSPORT, LTD.
OLD DOMINION FREIGHT LINE, INC.
P.A.M. TRANSPORTATION SERVICES, INC.
UNIVERSAL LOGISTICS HOLDINGS, INC.
USA TRUCK, INC.
WERNER ENTERPRISES, INC.

HISTORICAL FINANCIALS

Company Type: Public

Income Statement — FYE: December 31

	REVENUE ($mil)	NET INCOME ($mil)	NET PROFIT MARGIN	EMPLOYEES
12/20	1,822.3	138.3	7.6%	10,600
12/19	1,786.7	113.7	6.4%	10,400
12/18	1,653.8	104.9	6.3%	10,300
12/17	1,378.5	91.1	6.6%	9,800
12/16	1,218.4	48.0	3.9%	8,900
Annual Growth	10.6%	30.3%	—	4.5%

2020 Year-End Financials

Debt ratio: 4.6%
Return on equity: 15.5%
Cash ($ mil.): 25.3
Current Ratio: 0.99
Long-term debt ($ mil.): 50.3
No. of shares ($ mil.): 26.2
Dividends
  Yield: —
  Payout: —
Market value ($ mil.): 4,744.0

	STOCK PRICE ($) FY Close	P/E High/Low		PER SHARE ($) Earnings	Dividends	Book Value
12/20	180.80	36	12	5.20	0.00	36.64
12/19	93.12	24	12	4.30	0.00	31.43
12/18	55.82	21	13	3.99	0.00	27.08
12/17	70.75	20	12	3.49	0.00	22.80
12/16	44.15	25	10	1.87	0.00	19.08
Annual Growth	42.3%	—	—	29.1%	—	17.7%

Sandy Spring Bancorp Inc

Sandy Spring Bancorp is the holding company for Sandy Spring Bank, which operates around 50 branches in the Baltimore and Washington, DC, metropolitan areas. Founded in 1868, the bank is one of the largest and oldest headquartered in Maryland. It provides standard deposit services, including checking and savings accounts, money market accounts, and CDs. Commercial and residential real estate loans account for nearly three-quarters of the company's loan portfolio; the remainder is a mix of consumer loans, business loans, and equipment leases. The company also offers personal investing services, wealth management, trust services, insurance, and retirement planning.

Operations

Sandy Spring Bancorp's nonbank subsidiaries include money manager West Financial Services and Sandy Spring Insurance, which sells annuities and operates insurance agencies Chesapeake Insurance Group and Neff & Associates.

Financial Performance

The company's revenue increased in fiscal 2013 compared to the previous year. It reported $196.9 million in revenue for fiscal 2013 after bringing in revenue of $190.8 million in fiscal 2012.

The company's net income also went up in fiscal 2013 compared to the prior period. It claimed a profit of about $44 million in fiscal 2013 after netting a little more than $36 million in fiscal 2012.

Sandy Spring Bancorp's cash on hand increased by about $43 million in fiscal 2013 compared to fiscal 2012 levels.

Mergers and Acquisitions

In 2012 Sandy Spring Bancorp acquired CommerceFirst Bancorp, a small Maryland bank with a strong Small Business Administration lending practice. The $25.4 million transaction added five branches to Sandy Spring Bank's network.

EXECUTIVES

Chairman, Director, Robert L. Orndorff
President, Chief Executive Officer, Subsidiary Officer, Daniel J. Schrider, $694,254 total compensation
Executive Vice President, Secretary, General Counsel, Subsidiary Officer, Ronald E. Kuykendall, $285,846 total compensation
Executive Vice President, Chief Financial Officer, Subsidiary Officer, Philip J. Mantua, $380,038 total compensation
Executive Vice President, Chief Risk Officer, Kevin Slane, $220,769 total compensation
Executive Vice President, Aaron M. Kaslow
Subsidiary Officer, Joseph J. O'Brien, $412,885 total compensation
Subsidiary Officer, Ronda M. McDowell
Subsidiary Officer, R. Louis Caceres, $371,577 total compensation
Subsidiary Officer, John D. Sadowski
Director, Ralph F. Boyd
Director, Mark E. Friis
Director, Robert E. Henel
Director, Brian J. Lemek
Director, Pamela A. Little
Director, James J. Maiwurm
Director, Walter C. Martz
Director, Mark C. Michael
Director, Mark C. Micklem
Director, Gary G. Nakamoto
Director, Christina B. O'Meara
Director, Joe R. Reeder
Director, Craig A. Ruppert
Director, Mona Abutaleb Stephenson
Auditors: Ernst & Young

LOCATIONS

HQ: Sandy Spring Bancorp Inc
17801 Georgia Avenue, Olney, MD 20832
Phone: 301 774-6400
Web: www.sandyspringbank.com

PRODUCTS/OPERATIONS

2015 Sales

	$ mil.	% of total
Interest Income:		
Interest and fees on loans and leases	135.2	65
Interest and dividends on investment securities	22.5	11
Other	0.6	-
Non-interest Income:		
Wealth management income	19.9	10
Service charges on deposit accounts	7.6	4
Insurance agency commissions	5.2	2
Bank card fees	4.7	2
Mortgage banking activities	3.1	2
Other Income	9.4	4
Total	208.2	100

COMPETITORS

BERKSHIRE HILLS BANCORP, INC.
CARDINAL FINANCIAL CORPORATION
CITY HOLDING COMPANY
FIRST COMMONWEALTH FINANCIAL CORPORATION
FIRST MIDWEST BANCORP, INC.
OLD NATIONAL BANCORP
S&T BANCORP, INC.
SUFFOLK BANCORP.
WESBANCO, INC.
WEST BANCORPORATION, INC.

HISTORICAL FINANCIALS

Company Type: Public

Income Statement — FYE: December 31

	ASSETS ($mil)	NET INCOME ($mil)	INCOME AS % OF ASSETS	EMPLOYEES
12/21	12,590.7	235.1	1.9%	1,116
12/20	12,798.4	96.9	0.8%	1,152
12/19	8,629.0	116.4	1.3%	932
12/18	8,243.2	100.8	1.2%	932
12/17	5,446.6	53.2	1.0%	754
Annual Growth	23.3%	45.0%	—	10.3%

2021 Year-End Financials

Return on assets: 1.8%
Return on equity: 15.7%
Long-term debt ($ mil.): —
No. of shares ($ mil.): 45.1
Sales ($ mil.): 552.3
Dividends
  Yield: 2.6%
  Payout: 24.5%
Market value ($ mil.): 2,169.0

	STOCK PRICE ($) FY Close	P/E High/Low		PER SHARE ($) Earnings	Dividends	Book Value
12/21	48.08	10	6	4.98	1.28	33.68
12/20	32.19	17	9	2.18	1.20	31.24
12/19	37.88	12	9	3.25	1.18	32.40
12/18	31.34	15	11	2.82	1.10	30.06
12/17	39.02	21	17	2.20	1.04	23.50
Annual Growth	5.4%	—	—	22.7%	5.3%	9.4%

Santa Cruz County Bank (CA)

EXECUTIVES

Vice-Chairman, William J. Hansen
President, Chief Executive Officer, Director, David V. Heald
Senior Vice President, Chief Administrative Officer, Heather La Fontaine
Senior Vice President, Chief Credit Officer, George T. Harrison
Senior Vice President, Chief Credit Officer, Angelo DeBernardo
Senior Vice President, Chief Financial Officer, Cashier, Victor F. Davis
Senior Vice President, Chief Information Security Officer, Chief Information Officer, Jaime Manriquez
Senior Vice President, Corporate Secretary, Janice Zappa
Senior Vice President, Controller, Tracy Ruelas-Hashimoto
Director, Thomas N. Griffin
Director, Harvey J. Nickelson
Director, Kenneth R. Chappell
Auditors : Crowe LLP

LOCATIONS

HQ: Santa Cruz County Bank (CA)
  740 Front Street Ste 220, Santa Cruz, CA 95060
Phone: 831 457-5003
Web: www.sccountybank.com

HISTORICAL FINANCIALS

Company Type: Public

Income Statement				FYE: December 31
	ASSETS ($mil)	NET INCOME ($mil)	INCOME AS % OF ASSETS	EMPLOYEES
12/20	1,422.8	17.5	1.2%	0
12/19	1,070.9	12.2	1.1%	0
12/18	662.4	11.3	1.7%	0
12/17	629.9	6.7	1.1%	0
12/16	588.2	6.4	1.1%	0
Annual Growth	24.7%	28.2%	—	—

2020 Year-End Financials

Return on assets: 1.4%
Return on equity: 10.9%
Long-term debt ($ mil.): —
No. of shares ($ mil.): 4.2
Sales ($ mil.): 55.9
Dividends
  Yield: 0.8%
  Payout: 7.8%
  Market value ($ mil.): 172.0

	STOCK PRICE ($) FY Close	P/E High/Low		PER SHARE ($) Earnings	Dividends	Book Value
12/20	40.51	14	7	4.13	0.30	39.76
12/19	52.50	13	11	4.06	0.27	35.68
12/18	45.60	13	11	4.19	0.28	25.44
12/17	48.95	20	15	2.51	0.17	21.49
12/16	39.50	16	11	2.43	0.17	19.13
Annual Growth	0.6%	—	—	14.2%	16.1%	20.1%

SB Financial Group Inc

SB Financial Group (formerly Rurban Financial) is the holding company The State Bank and Trust Company (dba State Bank), which has more than 20 branches in northwestern Ohio and another in northeastern Indiana. The banks offer products, including checking and savings accounts, money market accounts, credit cards, IRAs, and CDs. Commercial and agricultural loans account for approximately two-thirds of the company's loan portfolio; the bank also writes mortgage and consumer loans. State Bank Wealth Management (formerly Reliance Financial Services), a unit of State Bank, offers trust and investment management services, as well as brokerage services through an alliance with Raymond James.

Strategy

The company changed its name to SB Financial Group in April 2013. Concurrently, it changed the name of its bank to State Bank to more closely identify the holding company with its primary revenue generator, State Bank. The firm also changed its trading symbol from RBNF to SBFG.

The company spun off its technology subsidiary, RDSI Banking Systems, as a separate entity in 2010.

EXECUTIVES

President, Chief Executive Officer, Subsidiary Officer, Chairman, Director, Mark A. Klein, $361,789 total compensation
Executive Vice President, Chief Financial Officer, Subsidiary Officer, Anthony Van Cosentino, $207,129 total compensation
Executive Vice President, Chief Risk Officer, Corporate Secretary, Subsidiary Officer, Keeta J. Diller
Chief Lending Officer, Steven A. Walz
Subsidiary Officer, Ernesto Gaytan, $186,609 total compensation
Subsidiary Officer, David A. Homoelle
Lead Independent Director, Director, Richard L. Hardgrove, $29,575 total compensation
Director, Timothy L. Claxton
Director, Gaylyn J. Finn
Director, Rita A. Kissner, $28,675 total compensation
Director, George W. Carter
Director, Tom R. Helberg
Director, William G. Martin
Director, Timothy J. Stolly
Auditors : BKD, LLP

LOCATIONS

HQ: SB Financial Group Inc
  401 Clinton Street, Defiance, OH 43512
Phone: 419 783-8950
Web: www.yoursbfinancial.com

PRODUCTS/OPERATIONS

Selected Subsidiaries and Divisions
The State Bank and Trust Company
Reliance Financial Services
RDSI Banking Systems

COMPETITORS

CITIZENS HOLDING COMPANY
CIVISTA BANCSHARES, INC.
FB CORPORATION
FIFTH THIRD BANCORP
UNITED BANCSHARES, INC.

HISTORICAL FINANCIALS

Company Type: Public

Income Statement				FYE: December 31
	ASSETS ($mil)	NET INCOME ($mil)	INCOME AS % OF ASSETS	EMPLOYEES
12/20	1,257.8	14.9	1.2%	244
12/19	1,038.5	11.9	1.2%	252
12/18	986.8	11.6	1.2%	250
12/17	876.6	11.0	1.3%	234
12/16	816.0	8.7	1.1%	227
Annual Growth	11.4%	14.2%	—	1.8%

2020 Year-End Financials

Return on assets: 1.2%
Return on equity: 10.6%
Long-term debt ($ mil.): —
No. of shares ($ mil.): 7.7
Sales ($ mil.): 72.7
Dividends
  Yield: 2.2%
  Payout: 21.4%
  Market value ($ mil.): 142.0

	STOCK PRICE ($) FY Close	P/E High/Low		PER SHARE ($) Earnings	Dividends	Book Value
12/20	18.28	11	5	1.87	0.40	18.46
12/19	19.69	12	10	1.44	0.36	16.70
12/18	16.45	13	10	1.44	0.32	19.10
12/17	18.49	9	7	1.66	0.27	18.68
12/16	16.05	11	7	1.31	0.23	17.02
Annual Growth	3.3%	—	—	9.2%	15.0%	2.1%

Schnitzer Steel Industries Inc

Schnitzer Steel Industries is one of North America's largest recyclers of ferrous and nonferrous metal, including end-of-life vehicles, and a manufacturer of finished steel products. The company scrap to steelmakers primarily in the Western US and Western Canada. Schnitzer offers a range of products and services to meet global demand through its network that includes approximately 50 retail self-service auto parts stores, more than 50 metals recycling facilities and an electric arc furnace (EAF) steel mill. Its Pick-n-Pull unit procures the significant majority of the company's salvaged vehicles and sell serviceable used auto parts from these vehicles. The US accounts for more than 40% of the total sales.

Operations

Schnitzer acquires, processes, and recycles end-of-life (salvaged) vehicles, rail cars, home appliances, industrial machinery, manufacturing scrap, and construction and demolition scrap through its facilities.

The company invests in nonferrous metal extraction and separation technologies in order to maximize the recoverability of valuable nonferrous metal and to meet the metal purity requirements of customers. In addition to the sale of recycled metal processed at the company's facilities, it also provides a variety of recycling and related services including brokering the sale of ferrous and nonferrous scrap metal generated by industrial entities and demolition projects to customers in the domestic market, among other services.

Its steel mill melt shop includes an EAF, a ladle refining furnace with enhanced steel chemistry refining capabilities, and a five-strand continuous billet caster. The rolling mill has an effective annual production capacity under current conditions of approximately 580 thousand tons of finished steel products.

Recycled ferrous metal is a key feedstock used in the production of finished steel and is largely categorized into heavy melting steel (HMS), plate and structural (bonus), and shredded scrap (shred). Selling catalytic converters to specialty processors that extract the nonferrous precious metals including platinum, palladium and rhodium, nonferrous products include mixed metal joint products recovered from the shredding process, as well as aluminum, copper, stainless steel, nickel, brass, titanium, lead, and high temperature alloys.

Overall, ferrous products account for about 55%, nonferrous provides approximately 25%, steel products generates nearly 15% and retail and other represent the remaining sales.

Geographic Reach

Headquartered in Portland, Oregon, Schnitzer has about 45 operating facilities and administrative offices in some two dozen US states, Puerto Rico, and Western Canada. It has seven deep water export facilities located on both the East and West Coasts of the US and in Hawaii and Puerto Rico. The company's auto parts business sells used auto parts through its nearly 50 self-service facilities located in North America. Schnitzer serves customers in nearly 25 countries. About more than 40% of the company's revenue is generated from the US.

Sales and Marketing

The company sells steel directly from its mini-mill in McMinnville, Oregon, and its owned distribution center in California (near Los Angeles).

Specialty steelmakers, foundries, refineries, smelters, wholesalers, and other recycled metal processors globally are the primary end markets for its recycled nonferrous metal products. It delivers recycled ferrous and nonferrous scrap metal to customers outside of the US by ship and to US-based customers by barge, rail, and truck.

The company spends $6 million annually on advertising.

Financial Performance

The company's revenue, for 2021 was $2.8 billion, a 61% growth compared to the previous year's revenue of $1.7 billion. The increase is primarily due to a higher sales volume in the company's ferrous and nonferrous business.

In 2021, the company had a net income of $170 million, a $172.2 million increase from the previous year's net loss of $2.2 million.

The company's cash at the end of 2021 was $27.8 million. Operating activities generated $190.1 million, while investing activities used $117.6 million, mainly for capital expenditures. Financing activities used another $62.8 million, primarily for repayments of long-term debt.

Strategy

Schnitzer invests in nonferrous metal extraction and separation technologies in order to maximize the recoverability of valuable nonferrous metal and to meet the metal purity requirements of customers. It has a major strategic initiative currently underway and partially complete to replace, upgrade and add to its existing nonferrous metal recovery technologies that is expected to increase metal recovery yields, provide for additional product optionality, create higher quality furnace-ready products, and reduce the metallic portion of shredder residue disposed in landfills. The rollout of these new technologies is anticipated to be completed in fiscal 2022, with total capital expenditures estimated to be $115 million, of which $77 million has been incurred, including $36 million during fiscal 2021.

Mergers and Acquisitions

In mid-2021, Schnitzer entered into a definitive agreement with the US-based Columbus Recycling, a leading provider of ferrous and non-ferrous metal recycling products and services, to acquire eight operating facilities across several states in the Southeast, including Mississippi, Tennessee, and Kentucky.

HISTORY

Sam Schnitzer, a draftee into the Russian army, found his way to Austria, then to the US in 1904. The next year he moved to Portland, where he and partner Henry Wolf formed Alaska Junk in 1908. The enterprise grew, buying sawmills, logging camps, and shipyards. Sam's son, Morris, formed Schnitzer Steel Products on his own in 1936. After WWII the patriarch turned Alaska Junk over to sons Gilbert, Leonard, Manuel, and Morris.

The brothers changed the company's name to Alaska Steel and acquired Woodbury, a local steel distributor, in 1956. The Schnitzers formed Lasco Shipping in 1963. Morris' Schnitzer Steel Products returned to family control, and in 1978 Alaska Steel and Woodbury combined to make Metra Steel. The company boosted its vertical integration by acquiring the Cascade Steel minimill in 1984.

Leonard Schnitzer's son-in-law Robert Philip became president in 1991. Two years later the family's steel businesses went public as Schnitzer Steel Industries. In 1994 the company launched a $42 million expansion program. It bought Manufacturing Management (then Washington's #1 scrap processor, 1995) and Proler International (scrap-related environmental services, 1996), adding 17 scrap-collecting and -processing facilities, primarily on the East Coast.

Schnitzer Steel Industries began producing wire rod and coiled rebar at its Oregon facility in 1997.The next year Schnitzer Steel Industries and joint venture partner Hugo Neu added facilities in Maine, Massachusetts, and New Hampshire.

In 2002 the company's Portland, Oregon, metals recycling facility went through a $4.4 million renovation to increase efficiency in loading recycled metal cargoes. The next year, Schnitzer Steel Industries purchased Pick-N-Pull, a major operator of auto salvage yards, for about $71 million.

Schnitzer Steel Industries unwound its joint ventures with Hugo Neu in 2005.

In 2009 the company divested its full-service auto parts operations, selling the business to LKQ Corporation in exchange for that company's self-service auto parts business. Schnitzer then rebranded the former LKQ businesses with the Pick-N-Pull name.

In fiscal 2013 the company spent $26 million to buy four used auto parts facilities in Richmond and Surrey, British Columbia; two used auto parts facilities in Kansas and Missouri; two used auto parts facilities in Massachusetts; and one used auto parts facility in Rhode Island.

In 2013 Schnitzer acquired all of the equity interests of Pick A Part, Inc., a used auto parts business with one store in the Olympia metropolitan area in Washington, which expanded its presence in the Pacific Northwest.

EXECUTIVES

**Chairman, President, Chief Executive Officer,
Director,** Tamara L. Lundgren, $1,104,231 total compensation
**Corporate Operations Senior Vice President,
Corporate Operations Chief Financial Officer,
Corporate Operations Chief,** Richard D. Peach, $663,904 total compensation
Senior Vice President, Division Officer, Michael Henderson, $564,404 total compensation
Senior Vice President, Division Officer, Steven G. Heiskell, $482,305 total compensation
Lead Director, Director, Wayland R. Hicks
Director, Judith A. Johansen
Director, Michael W. Sutherlin
Director, Rhonda D. Hunter
Director, David L. Jahnke
Director, Glenda J. Minor
Auditors : PricewaterhouseCoopers LLP

LOCATIONS

HQ: Schnitzer Steel Industries Inc
  299 SW Clay Street, Suite 350, Portland, OR 97201
Phone: 503 224-9900
Web: www.schnitzersteel.com

2016 sales

	$ mil.	% of total
US	668.9	49
Other countries	683.6	51
Total	1,352.5	100

PRODUCTS/OPERATIONS

2016 sales

	$ mil.	% of total
Ferrous scrap metal	619.1	46
Nonferrous scrap metal	340.0	25
Finished steel products	269.4	20
Retail & Other	123.5	9
Semi-finished steel products	0.5	-
Total	1,352.5	100

2016 sales

	$ mil.	% of total
Auto & Metal Recycling Business	1,173.0	87
Steel Manufacturing Business	269.9	20
Eliminations	(90.2)	(7)
Total	1,352.5	100

COMPETITORS

AK STEEL HOLDING CORPORATION
ERAMET
LKQ CORPORATION
METALICO, INC.
OMNISOURCE, LLC
RENEWI PLC
RYERSON HOLDING CORPORATION
SGK VENTURES, LLC
THE DAVID J JOSEPH COMPANY
WORTHINGTON INDUSTRIES, INC.

HISTORICAL FINANCIALS

Company Type: Public

Income Statement   FYE: August 31

	REVENUE ($mil)	NET INCOME ($mil)	NET PROFIT MARGIN	EMPLOYEES
08/21	2,758.5	165.1	6.0%	3,167
08/20	1,712.3	(4.1)	—	3,032
08/19	2,132.7	56.3	2.6%	3,363
08/18	2,364.7	156.4	6.6%	3,575
08/17	1,687.5	44.5	2.6%	3,183
Annual Growth	13.1%	38.8%	—	(0.1%)

2021 Year-End Financials

Debt ratio: 5.0%
Return on equity: 21.8%
Cash ($ mil.): 27.8
Current Ratio: 1.54
Long-term debt ($ mil.): 71.2
No. of shares ($ mil.): 27.5
Dividends
  Yield: 1.9%
  Payout: 21.6%
Market value ($ mil.): 1,303.0

	STOCK PRICE ($) FY Close	P/E High/Low		PER SHARE ($) Earnings	Dividends	Book Value
08/21	47.31	10	3	5.66	0.94	30.36
08/20	19.74	—	—	(0.15)	0.75	24.97
08/19	22.14	14	10	2.00	0.75	26.14
08/18	26.35	7	4	5.47	0.75	24.94
08/17	26.90	19	11	1.58	0.75	19.72
Annual Growth	15.2%	—	—	37.6%	5.7%	11.4%

SciPlay Corp

EXECUTIVES

Chairman, Director, Antonia Korsanos
Chief Executive Officer, Director, Joshua J. Wilson, $492,138 total compensation
Finance Vice President, Finance Interim Chief Financial Officer, Finance Principal Accounting Officer, Finance Secretary, Daniel O'Quinn
Director, Gerald D. Cohen
Director, Michael Marchetti
Director, William C. Thompson
Director, Nick Earle
Director, Charles Prober
Director, Constance P. James
Director, April Henry
Auditors : DELOITTE & TOUCHE LLP

LOCATIONS

HQ: SciPlay Corp
  6601 Bermuda Road, Las Vegas, NV 89119
Phone: 702 897-7150
Web: www.sciplay.com

HISTORICAL FINANCIALS

Company Type: Public

Income Statement   FYE: December 31

	REVENUE ($mil)	NET INCOME ($mil)	NET PROFIT MARGIN	EMPLOYEES
12/20	582.2	20.9	3.6%	602
12/19	465.8	32.4	7.0%	501
12/18	416.2	39.0	9.4%	390
12/17	361.4	23.1	6.4%	0
Annual Growth	17.2%	(3.3%)	—	—

2020 Year-End Financials

Debt ratio: —
Return on equity: 31.0%
Cash ($ mil.): 268.9
Current Ratio: 6.03
Long-term debt ($ mil.): —
No. of shares ($ mil.): 126.3
Dividends
  Yield: —
  Payout: —
Market value ($ mil.): 1,749.0

	STOCK PRICE ($) FY Close	P/E High/Low		PER SHARE ($) Earnings	Dividends	Book Value
12/20	13.85	20	7	0.86	0.00	0.63
12/19	12.29	11	6	1.43	0.00	0.43
Annual Growth	12.7%	—	—	(39.9%)	—	47.8%

Scripps (EW) Company (The)

The E. W. Scripps Company (Scripps) is a diverse media enterprise, serving audiences and businesses through a portfolio of local television stations and national media brands, including next-generation national news network Newsy; and five national multicast networks ? Bounce, Grit, Laff, Court TV and Court TV Mystery. Scripps also owns about 60 local TV stations in nearly 40 markets that reach about 25% of US television households. The company has affiliations with all of the "Big Four" television networks as well as the CW network. The Scripps family controls the company through various trusts. The company was founded in 1878 by entrepreneurial journalist E.W. Scripps.

Operations

The company operates in two business segments: Local Media (over 55% of sales), and Scripps Networks (more than 40%).

The Local Media segment includes some 60 local broadcast stations and its related digital operations. It is comprised of roughly 20 ABC affiliates, some 10 NBC affiliates, nine CBS affiliates, and four FOX affiliates. It also has more than 10 CW affiliates ? four on full power stations and eight on multicast; five independent stations and ten additional low power stations. It primarily earns revenue from the sale of advertising to local, national and political advertisers and retransmission fees received from cable operators, telecommunication companies and satellite carriers, and over-the-top virtual MVPDs.

The Scripps Networks segment, which includes the recently acquired ION business, is comprised of nine national television networks that reach nearly every US television home through free over-the-air broadcast, cable/satellite, connected TV and digital distribution. These operations earn revenue primarily through the sale of advertising.

Scripps' portfolio of content holdings includes Newsy, a next-generation national news network; as well as Bounce, Grit, Laff, Court TV and Court TV Mystery.

The company also runs an investigative reporting newsroom in Washington, DC and is the steward of the Scripps National Spelling Bee.

Overall, over 55% of the company's revenue came from advertising, while retransmission and carriage, and other account for the rest.

Geographic Reach
The Cincinnati, Ohio-based Scripps has some 60 stations in about 40 markets.

Sales and Marketing
The company's core advertising is comprised of sales to local and national customers. The advertising includes a combination of broadcast spots, as well as digital and OTT advertising. Its core advertising revenues accounted for some 50% of Local Media segment's revenues in 2021. National advertising time is generally sold through national sales representative firms that call upon advertising agencies, whose clients typically include automobile manufacturers and dealer groups, telecommunications companies and insurance providers. Through its sales offices in Washington DC, Political advertising is sold to presidential, gubernatorial, Senate and House of Representative candidates, as well as for state races and local issues. It is also sold to political action groups (PACs) or other advocacy groups. Political advertising revenues were less than 5% of its Local Media segment's revenues in 2021.

The company also has consent agreements with multi-channel video programming distributors (MVPD). The MVPDs are cable operators, telecommunication companies and satellite carriers who pays the company to offer its programming to the customers.

Financial Performance
The company's revenue for fiscal 2021 increased by 23% to $2.3 billion compared with $1.9 billion, due to the acquisition of ION as well as of the WPIX television station that was sold in the fourth quarter of 2020.

Net income for fiscal 2021 decreased to $122.7 million compared with $269.3 million.

Cash held by the company at the end of fiscal 2021 decreased to $100.5 million. Operating and financing activities provided $237.0 million and $693.5 million, respectively. Investing activities used $2.5 billion, mainly for acquisitions.

Strategy
In addition to news programming, the company's television stations run network programming, syndicated programming, and original programming. Scripps' strategy is to balance syndicated programming with original programming that we control. The company believes this strategy improves its Local Media division's financial performance. Original shows it produces itself or in partnership with others.

Mergers and Acquisitions
In early 2021, Scripps acquired the Florida-based ION Media from Black Diamond, a national broadcast television network that delivers popular crime and justice procedural programming to more than 100 million US homes through its over-the-air broadcast and pay TV platforms for approximately $2.65 billion. The acquisition strengthens the Scripps' leadership position in broadcasting and accelerates its multiplatform strategy to serve diverse audiences everywhere they seek to be informed and entertained.

Company Background
Founded in 1878 by entrepreneurial journalist E.W. Scripps, the company has a long and proud legacy of innovation and an unwavering commitment to journalism.

HISTORY

Edward Willis "E. W." Scripps launched a newspaper empire in 1878 with his creation of The Penny Press in Cleveland. While adding to his string of inexpensive newspapers, Scripps demonstrated his fondness for economy by shunning "extras" such as toilet paper and pencils for his employees.

In 1907 Scripps gave the Associated Press a new rival, combining three wire services to form United Press. E. W. Scripps' health began deteriorating in the 1920s, and Roy Howard was named chairman. Howard's contribution to the burgeoning media enterprise soon was acknowledged when the company's name was changed to the Scripps Howard League. E. W. Scripps died in 1926, leaving a newspaper chain second in size only to Hearst.

In the 1930s Scripps made a foray into radio, buying WCPO (Cincinnati) and KNOX (Knoxville, Tennessee). Roy Howard placed his son Jack in charge of Scripps' radio holdings; under Jack's leadership, Scripps branched into TV. Its first TV station, Cleveland's WEWS, began broadcasting in 1947. Scripps also made Charlie Brown a household name when it launched the Peanuts comic strip in 1950. By the time Charles Scripps (E. W.'s grandson) became chairman and Jack Howard was appointed president in 1953, the company had amassed 19 newspapers and a handful of radio and TV stations.

United Press merged with Hearst's International News Service in 1958 to become United Press International (UPI). In 1963 Scripps took its broadcasting holdings public as Scripps Howard Broadcasting Company (Scripps retained controlling interest). Scripps Howard Broadcasting expanded its TV station portfolio in the 1970s and 1980s, buying KJRH (Tulsa, Oklahoma; 1971), KSHB (Kansas City; 1977), KNXV (Phoenix; 1985), WFTS (Tampa; 1986), and WXYZ (Detroit; 1986).

With UPI facing mounting losses, Scripps sold the news service in 1982. Under leadership of chief executive Lawrence Leser, Scripps began streamlining, jettisoning extraneous investments and refocusing on its core business lines. In 1988 after decades of family ownership, the company went public as The E. W. Scripps Company (the Scripps family retained a controlling interest).

In 1994 Scripps Howard Broadcasting merged back into E. W. Scripps Company. That year Scripps branched into cable TV when its Home & Garden Television network went on the air. Former newspaper editor William Burleigh became CEO in 1996. Scripps' 1997 purchase of the newspaper and broadcast operations of Harte-Hanks marked the largest acquisition in its history. Scripps promptly traded Harte-Hanks' broadcasting operations for a controlling interest in the Food Network.

Scripps sold television production unit Scripps Howard Productions in 1998. The company sold its Dallas Community Newspaper Group in 1999 and launched the Do It Yourself cable network and affiliated Web site later that year. In 2000 Scripps' financially struggling Rocky Mountain News entered into a joint operating agreement with rival The Denver Post (owned by MediaNews). The Justice Department approved the agreement in 2001. Scripps launched cable channel Fine Living in 2002 aimed at affluent households. (Fine Living was rebranded as the Cooking Channel in 2010.) That year the company shuttered its Scripps Ventures fund, which invested in Internet and online commerce businesses.

In late 2002 the company bought a 70% stake in home shopping network company Summit America Television (owner of the Shop At Home cable network) for $49 million. It bought the remaining 30% of the company in 2004.

The Shop At Home network came to an end in 2006 when Scripps shut down the network after several years of nothing but losses at the channel. Scripps later sold its five Shop At Home affiliate television stations to Multicultural Television Broadcasting for $170 million.

Former chairman Charles Scripps died in 2007. At the end of that year, the company shuttered the Cincinnati Post , and the following year it ceased publication of The Albuquerque Tribune . E. W. Scripps spun off its cable TV operations as Scripps Networks Interactive later in 2008. It shuttered the Rocky Mountain News early in 2009 after attempts to sell the money-losing paper failed.

EXECUTIVES

Chairman, Director, Kim Williams
President, Chief Executive Officer, Director, Adam P. Symson, $950,000 total compensation
Human Resources Chief Operating Officer, Lisa A. Knutson, $564,000 total compensation
Executive Vice President, Chief Financial Officer, Jason P. Combs
Executive Vice President, General Counsel, William Appleton, $475,000 total compensation
Executive Vice President, Chief Administrative Officer, Laura M. Tomlin
Vice President, Secretary, Julie McGehee
Vice President, Controller, Daniel W. Perschke
Chief Marketing Officer, Keisha Taylor

Division Officer, Brian G. Lawlor, $615,000 total compensation
Division Officer, Kate O'Brian
Director, Lauren Rich Fine
Director, Marcellus W. Alexander
Director, Charles L. Barmonde
Director, Kelly P. Conlin
Director, John W. Hayden
Auditors : Deloitte & Touche LLP

LOCATIONS

HQ: Scripps (EW) Company (The)
312 Walnut Street, Cincinnati, OH 45202
Phone: 513 977-3000
Web: www.scripps.com

PRODUCTS/OPERATIONS

Selected Operations
Newspapers
    Abilene Reporter-News (Texas)
    Anderson Independent-Mail (South Carolina)
    Corpus Christi Caller-Times (Texas)
    Evansville Courier & Press (Indiana)
    Ft. Pierce Tribune (Florida)
    Henderson Gleaner (Kentucky)
    Kitsap Sun (Washington)
    Knoxville News Sentinel (Tennessee)
    Memphis Commercial Appeal (Tennessee)
    Naples Daily News (Florida)
    Redding Record-Searchlight (California)
    San Angelo Standard-Times (Texas)
    Stuart News (Florida)
    Ventura County Star (California)
    Wichita Falls Times Record News (Texas)
Television stations
    KJRH (NBC; Tulsa, OK)
    KMCI (Ind; Lawrence, KS)
    KNXV (ABC, Phoenix)
    KSHB (NBC, Kansas City)
    WCPO (ABC, Cincinnati)
    WEWS (ABC, Cleveland)
    WFTS (ABC, Tampa)
    WMAR (ABC, Baltimore)
    WPTV (NBC; West Palm Beach, FL)
    WXYZ (ABC, Detroit)

COMPETITORS

A&E TELEVISION NETWORKS, LLC
COMCAST CORPORATION
COX COMMUNICATIONS, INC.
COX ENTERPRISES, INC.
DIRECTV GROUP HOLDINGS, LLC
MEDIANEWS GROUP, INC.
QURATE RETAIL, INC.
RCN TELECOM SERVICES, LLC
THE HEARST CORPORATION
WARNER MEDIA, LLC

HISTORICAL FINANCIALS

Company Type: Public

Income Statement — FYE: December 31

	REVENUE ($mil)	NET INCOME ($mil)	NET PROFIT MARGIN	EMPLOYEES
12/20	1,857.4	269.3	14.5%	5,400
12/19	1,423.8	(18.3)	—	5,900
12/18	1,208.4	20.3	1.7%	3,950
12/17	864.8	(13.1)	—	4,100
12/16	943.0	67.2	7.1%	4,100
Annual Growth	18.5%	41.5%	—	7.1%

2020 Year-End Financials
Debt ratio: 60.4%
Return on equity: 26.0%
Cash ($ mil.): 576.0
Current Ratio: 5.84
Long-term debt ($ mil.): 2,923.3
No. of shares ($ mil.): 81.7
Dividends
Yield: 1.3%
Payout: 50.0%
Market value ($ mil.): 1,250.0

	STOCK PRICE ($) FY Close	P/E High/Low		PER SHARE ($) Earnings	Dividends	Book Value
12/20	15.29	5	2	3.21	0.20	14.23
12/19	15.71	—	—	(0.23)	0.20	11.09
12/18	15.73	71	43	0.24	0.20	11.48
12/17	15.63	—	—	(0.16)	0.00	11.48
12/16	19.33	24	16	0.79	0.00	11.54
Annual Growth	(5.7%)	—	—	42.0%	—	5.4%

Seacoast Banking Corp. of Florida

Seacoast Banking Corporation is the holding company for Seacoast National Bank, a wholly-owned national banking association (Seacoast Bank), which has about 55 branches in Florida, with a concentration on the state's southeastern coast. Serving individuals and areas businesses, the bank offers a range of financial products and services, including deposit accounts, credit cards, trust services, and private banking. Commercial and residential real estate loans account for most of the bank's lending activities; to a lesser extent, it also originates business and consumer loans. The bank also provides financial planning services, as well as mutual funds and other investments. Seacoast has total consolidated assets of $9.7 billion and total deposits of $8.1 billion.

Operations

The company provides integrated financial services including commercial and retail banking, wealth management and mortgage services to customers through advanced online and mobile banking solutions, and through Seacoast Bank's network of about 55 traditional branches. Seacoast Bank also provides brokerage and annuity services. Seacoast Bank personnel managing the sale of these services are dual employees with LPL Financial, the company through which Seacoast Bank presently conducts brokerage and annuity services. Seacoast Insurance Services, Inc., a wholly owned subsidiary of Seacoast, facilitates access for the company to provide customers with a range of insurance products.

Broadly speaking, the bank makes roughly 80% of its revenue from interest income. The remainder of its revenue comes from interchange income, wealth management income, mortgage banking fee, marine finance fees, service charges on deposit accounts and other miscellaneous income.

Geographic Reach

Seacoast Bank has about 55 branch offices, stand-alone commercial lending offices, and its main office, all located in Florida. Seacoast maintains its corporate headquarters in Stuart, Florida.

Financial Performance

Net interest income for the year ended December 31, 2021 totaled $276 million, increasing $13.3 million, or 5%, compared to the year ended December 31, 2020.

In 2021, the company had a net income of $124.4 million, a 60% increase from the previous year's net income of $77.8 million.

The company's cash at the end of 2021 was $737.7 million. Operating activities generated $154.6 million, while investing activities used $412.5 million, mainly for purchases of available-for-sale debt securities. Financing activities provided another $591.6 million.

Strategy

Seacoast has in recent years sought to complement organic growth with the acquisition of financial institutions that support the company's strategy and expand its ability to serve customers in Florida's key markets. Since 2014, Seacoast has acquired 13 institutions that have enhanced the company's presence in the strongest and fastest growing markets in Florida, including Orlando, Tampa, and South Florida.

In 2021, the company grew organically as well, adding 20 new commercial bankers across the state and key personnel across departments including treasury management, mortgage banking, credit operations, and loan operations as the company seeks to complement its current and future growth. The company has also invested in its branch network, opening two new branches in South Florida, with additional new branches planned for 2022. The company continues to benefit from previous investments in technology to improve banker productivity and to enhance the banking experience for customers.

Mergers and Acquisitions

In 2022, Seacoast announced the completion of its acquisitions of Apollo Bancshares, Inc. (Apollo), parent company of Apollo Bank and of Drummond Banking Company (Drummond), parent company of Drummond Community Bank, for approximately $146 million and $158 million, respectively. The acquisition strengthen Seacoast's presence and expand its acquisition in South Florida by complementing Apollo's strengths with Seacoast's innovation and breadth of offerings. The combined franchise will continue to provide exceptional service with expanded products and services for this dynamic market.

In mid-2022, Seacoast agreed to acquire Professional Holding Corp. (Professional), the parent company of Professional Bank. The proposed transaction will expand Seacoast's footprint in the dynamic tri-county South Florida market, which includes Miami-Dade,

Broward, and Palm Beach Counties, the largest MSA in Florida and the eighth largest in the nation. In addition, the proposed transaction is a natural continuation of Seacoast's M&A strategy, adding a premier franchise in one of Florida's fastest-growing markets. The transaction is valued at approximately $488.6 million.

Also in 2022, Seacoast announced the completion of its acquisitions of Florida-based Sabal Palm Bancorp, Inc. (Sabal Palm), parent company of Sabal Palm Bank, and of Business Bank of Florida, Corp. (BBFC), parent company of Florida Business Bank. "We're excited to enter the highly attractive and dynamic Sarasota market and to continue to grow our presence in Brevard County. We are delighted to welcome Sabal Palm Bank and Florida Business Bank customers and employees into the Seacoast family," said Charles Shaffer, Seacoast's president and chief executive officer.

In 2021, Seacoast announced the completion of its acquisition of Legacy Bank of Florida (Legacy Bank), for about $102.2 million. Headquartered in Boca Raton, Legacy Bank had deposits of approximately $485 million and loans of approximately $476 million as of June 30, 2021. The acquisition increases Seacoast's presence in South Florida, one of the strongest and fastest growing markets in the country, and complements Seacoast's prior acquisitions in the market.

EXECUTIVES

Executive Chairman, Director, Dennis S. Hudson, $600,000 total compensation
President, Chief Executive Officer, Director, Charles M. Shaffer, $331,250 total compensation
Executive Vice President, Chief Financial Officer, Subsidiary Officer, Tracey Dexter
Executive Vice President, Chief Banking Officer, Juliette P. Kleffel, $285,000 total compensation
Executive Vice President, Chief Risk Officer, Joseph Forlenza
Director, Alvaro J. Monserrat
Director, Dennis J. Arczynski
Director, Jacqueline L. Bradley
Director, H. Gilbert Culbreth
Director, Christopher E. Fogal
Director, Maryann B. Goebel
Director, Robert J. Lipstein
Director, Thomas E. Rossin
Auditors: Crowe LLP

LOCATIONS

HQ: Seacoast Banking Corp. of Florida
815 Colorado Avenue, Stuart, FL 34994
Phone: 772 287-4000
Web: www.seacoastbanking.com

PRODUCTS/OPERATIONS

Selected Services
Commercial and retail banking
Mortgage services
Wealth management

COMPETITORS

AMERIS BANCORP
BANKUNITED, INC.
BYLINE BANCORP, INC.
CENTERSTATE BANK CORPORATION
CITIZENS FINANCIAL GROUP, INC.
CUSTOMERS BANCORP, INC.
FIRSTMERIT CORPORATION
M&T BANK CORPORATION
OLD LINE BANCSHARES, INC.
TRUSTCO BANK CORP N Y

HISTORICAL FINANCIALS
Company Type: Public

Income Statement				FYE: December 31
	ASSETS ($mil)	NET INCOME ($mil)	INCOME AS % OF ASSETS	EMPLOYEES
12/20	8,342.3	77.7	0.9%	965
12/19	7,108.5	98.7	1.4%	867
12/18	6,747.6	67.2	1.0%	902
12/17	5,810.1	42.8	0.7%	805
12/16	4,680.9	29.2	0.6%	725
Annual Growth	15.5%	27.7%	—	7.4%

2020 Year-End Financials
Return on assets: 1.0%
Return on equity: 7.3%
Long-term debt ($ mil.): —
No. of shares ($ mil.): 55.2
Sales ($ mil.): 348.6
Dividends
Yield: —
Payout: —
Market value ($ mil.): 1,627.0

	STOCK PRICE ($) FY Close	P/E High/Low		PER SHARE ($)		
				Earnings	Dividends	Book Value
12/20	29.45	21	10	1.44	0.00	20.46
12/19	30.57	16	12	1.90	0.00	19.13
12/18	26.02	24	17	1.38	0.00	16.83
12/17	25.21	26	21	0.99	0.00	14.70
12/16	22.06	29	17	0.78	0.00	11.45
Annual Growth	7.5%	—	—	16.6%	—	15.6%

Security Federal Corp (SC)

Security Federal is the holding company for Security Federal Bank, which has about a dozen offices in southwestern South Carolina's Aiken and Lexington counties. It expanded into Columbia, South Carolina and eastern Georgia in 2007. The bank offers checking and savings accounts, credit cards, CDs, IRAs, and other retail products and services. Commercial business and mortgage loans make up more than 60% of the company's lending portfolio, which also includes residential mortgages (about 25%), and consumer loans. Security Federal also offers trust services, investments, and life, home, and auto insurance.

EXECUTIVES

Chairman, Timothy W. Simmons, $93,615 total compensation
Vice-Chairman, Gasper L. Toole
Chief Executive Officer, Subsidiary Officer, Director, J. Chris Verenes, $315,000 total compensation
Chief Financial Officer, Subsidiary Officer, Director, Jessica T. Cummins
Secretary, Subsidiary Officer, Director, Robert E. Alexander
President, Director, Roy G. Lindburg, $245,000 total compensation
Subsidiary Officer, Director, Richard T. Harmon, $215,000 total compensation
Director, Frampton W. Toole, III
Director, Thomas L. Moore
Director, William Clyburn
Director, Harry Odell Weeks
Director, Francis M. Thomas, $181,000 total compensation
Auditors: Elliott Davis, LLC

LOCATIONS

HQ: Security Federal Corp (SC)
238 Richland Avenue Northwest, Aiken, SC 29801
Phone: 803 641-3000
Web: www.securityfederalbank.com

PRODUCTS/OPERATIONS

Selected Subsidiaries
Federal Trust
Security Federal Bank
  Security Federal Insurance, Inc.
  Security Federal Investments, Inc.
  Security Federal Services Corporation
  Security Federal Trust, Inc.

COMPETITORS

FIRST UNITED CORPORATION
FIRST US BANCSHARES, INC.
KS BANCORP, INC.
SB ONE BANCORP
THE COMMUNITY FINANCIAL CORPORATION

HISTORICAL FINANCIALS
Company Type: Public

Income Statement				FYE: December 31
	ASSETS ($mil)	NET INCOME ($mil)	INCOME AS % OF ASSETS	EMPLOYEES
12/20	1,171.7	7.0	0.6%	0
12/19	963.2	7.7	0.8%	250
12/18	912.6	7.2	0.8%	233
12/17	868.8	5.9	0.7%	223
12/16	812.6	5.9	0.7%	219
Annual Growth	9.6%	4.4%	—	—

2020 Year-End Financials
Return on assets: 0.6%
Return on equity: 6.9%
Long-term debt ($ mil.): —
No. of shares ($ mil.): 3.2
Sales ($ mil.): 48.5
Dividends
Yield: —
Payout: 18.2%
Market value ($ mil.): 84.0

	STOCK PRICE ($) FY Close	P/E High/Low		PER SHARE ($)		
				Earnings	Dividends	Book Value
12/20	25.75	16	10	2.19	0.40	34.40
12/19	35.00	13	11	2.50	0.38	31.03
12/18	28.30	13	12	2.32	0.36	27.26
12/17	31.30	16	12	1.91	0.36	26.39
12/16	35.00	17	10	1.99	0.32	22.60
Annual Growth	(7.4%)	—	—	2.4%	5.7%	11.1%

Security National Financial Corp

There are three certainties -- life, death, and mortgage payments -- and Security National Financial has you covered on all fronts. Its largest unit, SecurityNational Mortgage, makes residential and commercial mortgage loans through some 70 offices in more than a dozen states. Its Security National Life, Memorial Insurance Company, and Southern Security Life subsidiaries sell life and diving or related sports accident insurance, annuities, and funeral plans in about 40 states. Security National Financial also owns about 15 mortuaries and cemeteries in Utah, Arizona, and California. The family of chairman and CEO George Quist controls more than half of Security National Financial.

EXECUTIVES

Chairman, President, Chief Executive Officer, Director, Scott M. Quist, $489,174 total compensation
Internal Operations Senior Vice President, Christie Q. Overbaugh, $111,655 total compensation
Memorial Services Vice President, Memorial Services Assistant Secretary, Memorial Services General Counsel, Adam George Quist
Vice President, Assistant Secretary, Subsidiary Officer, Jason G. Overbaugh
Vice President, General Counsel, Subsidiary Officer, S. Andrew Quist, $221,228 total compensation
Chief Financial Officer, Treasurer, Garrett S. Sill, $214,165 total compensation
Senior General Counsel, Corporate Secretary, Jeffrey R. Stephens, $190,250 total compensation
Division Officer, Subsidiary Officer, Stephen C. Johnson, $361,284 total compensation
Director, John L. Cook
Director, Gilbert A. Fuller
Director, Robert G. Hunter
Director, H. Craig Moody
Director, Norman G. Wilbur
Auditors : DELOITTE & TOUCHE LLP

LOCATIONS

HQ: Security National Financial Corp
  433 West Ascension Way, Salt Lake City, UT 84123
Phone: 801 264-1060   **Fax:** 801 265-9882
Web: www.securitynational.com

PRODUCTS/OPERATIONS

Selected Subsidiaries
California Memorial Estates, Inc.
Cottonwood Mortuary, Inc.
Crystal Rose Funeral Home, Inc.
Deseret Memorial, Inc.
Greer-Wilson Funeral Home, Inc.
Holladay Memorial Park, Inc.
Insuradyne Corporation
Memorial Estates, Inc.
Memorial Insurance Company of America
Memorial Mortuary
Paradise Chapel Funeral Home, Inc.
Security National Capital, Inc.
Security National Life Insurance Company

COMPETITORS

AMERICAN GENERAL LIFE INSURANCE COMPANY
DIRECT GENERAL CORPORATION
THE NATIONAL SECURITY GROUP INC
TRANSAMERICA PREMIER LIFE INSURANCE COMPANY
WEST COAST LIFE INSURANCE COMPANY

HISTORICAL FINANCIALS
Company Type: Public

Income Statement   FYE: December 31

	ASSETS ($mil)	NET INCOME ($mil)	INCOME AS % OF ASSETS	EMPLOYEES
12/20	1,548.9	55.5	3.6%	1,708
12/19	1,334.4	10.8	0.8%	1,293
12/18	1,050.8	21.6	2.1%	1,433
12/17	982.1	14.1	1.4%	1,453
12/16	854.0	14.2	1.7%	1,657
Annual Growth	16.0%	40.5%	—	0.8%

2020 Year-End Financials
Return on assets: 3.8%
Return on equity: 24.0%
Long-term debt ($ mil.): —
No. of shares ($ mil.): 19.9
Sales ($ mil.): 481.4
Dividends
  Yield: —
  Payout: 5.6%
Market value ($ mil.): 167.0

	STOCK PRICE ($) FY Close	P/E High	P/E Low	Earnings	Dividends	Book Value
12/20	8.35	3	1	2.74	0.00	13.21
12/19	5.85	11	8	0.56	0.00	10.09
12/18	5.16	5	4	1.11	0.00	8.84
12/17	5.25	10	7	0.73	0.00	7.78
12/16	6.50	10	6	0.75	0.00	6.85
Annual Growth	6.5%	—	—	38.1%	—	17.8%

Selective Insurance Group Inc

Property/casualty insurance holding company Selective Insurance Group's reach primarily covers the US. Various state departments of insurance license nine of its subsidiaries as admitted carriers to write specific lines of property and casualty insurance in the standard marketplace and authorize the tenth subsidiary as a non-admitted carrier to write property and casualty insurance in the excess and surplus (E&S) lines market. Commercial policies include workers' compensation and commercial automobile, property, and liability insurance. Personal lines include homeowners and automobile insurance. Selective Insurance Group operates through four reportable segments: Standard Commercial Lines, Standard Personal Lines, E&S Lines, and Investments.

Operations

Selective operates in four segments: Standard Commercial Lines; Investments; Standard Personal Lines; and E&S Lines.

Investments (some 10% of total revenue), which invests the premiums collected by its insurance operations and amounts generated through its capital management strategies, which include the issuance of debt and equity securities.

Selective's Standard Commercial Lines segment is comprised of property and casualty insurance products and services provided in the standard marketplace to commercial enterprises; typically businesses, non-profit organizations, and local government agencies and accounts for about three-fourths of Selective's total revenue.

Standard Personal Lines is comprised of property and casualty insurance products and services provided primarily to individuals acquiring coverage in the standard marketplace. It generates about 10% of total revenue.

The E&S Lines segment is comprised of property and casualty insurance products and services provided to customers who are unable to obtain coverage in the standard marketplace. The company is currently only write commercial lines E&S coverages. The segment accounts for nearly 10% of total revenue.

The company's flood insurance is sold to businesses and individuals through the National Flood Insurance Program.

In all, net premiums earned generated nearly 90% of sales.

Geographic Reach

Selective primarily writes commercial policies in more than 25 Eastern, Midwestern, and Southwestern states and the Washington, DC. Personal policies are primarily sold in some 15 states in the Eastern, Southwestern, and Midwest. The company also offers flood and E&S insurance policies in all 50 states and the District of Columbia.

It maintains its headquarters in New Jersey and regional branch offices in New Jersey, Indiana, Maryland, North Carolina, and Arizona.

Sales and Marketing

Some 1,430 independent retail agents sell Selective's Standard Commercial Lines products, and the all of these distribution partners also sells its Standard Personal Lines business, with a focus on providing policies to small and mid-sized businesses and government entities. The company's nationwide flood protection products are sold by a network of some 6,200 retail agents, while E&S policies are sold through some 80 wholesale agencies and brokers.

Target clients include manufacturing and wholesale, contractor, community and public services, and mercantile and services customers.

Financial Performance

The company's revenue in 2021 increased by 16% to $3.4 billion compared with $2.9

billion in 2020.

Net income in 2021 increased by 64% to $403.8 million compared from $246.4 million in the prior year.

Cash held by the company at the end of fiscal 2021 increased to $45.1 million. Cash provided by operations was $771.4 million while cash used for investing and financing activities were $618.8 million and $122.8 million, respectively. Main cash uses were purchase of fixed income securities; and dividends to common stockholders.

Strategy

The company has three key sustainable competitive advantages:

A distribution model that emphasizes franchise value, meaning the company focus on appointing high-quality independent distribution partners, with whom Selective has meaningful and close business relationships;

A unique field model, in which the company locate its Standard Commercial Lines underwriting and safety management personnel in the geographic territories they serve, organize its claims operation regionally by specialty, with local personnel managing its customer, claimant, and agency relationships, and provide its teams with sophisticated tools and technologies to inform underwriting, pricing, safety management, and claims decisions; and

A superior omnichannel customer experience provided by best-in-class employees, enhanced by digital platforms and value-added services to increase customer engagement and retention.

Company Background

In the 1920s, Daniel L.B. Smith was a general store operator in Sussex County, New Jersey. Almost by accident, he began selling insurance out of one of his store locations, and he decided that the area needed a local insurance company. With an initial investment of $20,000, Smith and several partners opened Selected Risks Insurance Company. The company expanded beyond its New Jersey origins over the next several decades.

EXECUTIVES

Executive Chairman, Director, Gregory E. Murphy, $950,000 total compensation
President, Chief Executive Officer, Director, John J. Marchioni, $800,000 total compensation
Executive Vice President, Chief Compliance Officer, General Counsel, Michael H. Lanza, $540,000 total compensation
Executive Vice President, Chief Financial Officer, Mark A. Wilcox, $600,002 total compensation
Insurance Strategy Executive Vice President, Business Development Executive Vice President, Insurance Strategy Subsidiary Officer, Business Development Subsidiary Officer, Shadi Albert
Executive Vice President, Chief Information Officer, Subsidiary Officer, John Bresney
Executive Vice President, Chief Innovation Officer, Subsidiary Officer, Gordon Gaudet
Commercial Lines Executive Vice President, Commercial Lines Chief Operating Officer, Commercial Lines Subsidiary Officer, Brenda Hall
Operations Senior Vice President, IT Infrastructure Senior Vice President, Fadi Elsaid
Actuarial Reserving Senior Vice President, Actuarial Reserving Subsidiary Officer, Nathan Rugge
Director of Safety Management Vice President, Scott Smith
Brokerage Underwriting Vice President, William Becker
Bond Strategic Business Unit Underwriting Assistant Vice President, Hans Buvary
Management Liability Assistant Vice President, Jeff Weaver
Strategy Assistant Vice President, Innovation Assistant Vice President, Strategy Subsidiary Officer, Innovation Subsidiary Officer, Amy Cusack
Enterprise Development Services Assistant Vice President, Enterprise Development Services Subsidiary Officer, Robert England
Underwriting Quality Assurance Assistant Vice President, Underwriting Quality Assurance Subsidiary Officer, Linda Link
Line of Business Manager Assistant Vice President, Line of Business Manager Subsidiary Officer, Steven Neal
Claims Operations and Automation Assistant Vice President, Claims Operations and Automation Subsidiary Officer, George Melvin
Assistant Vice President, Assistant Controller, Subsidiary Officer, Ernest Williams
Division Officer, Eva Gonzalez
Lead Independent Director, Director, J. Brian Thebault
Director, John C. Burville
Director, Terrence W. Cavanaugh
Director, Robert Kelly Doherty
Director, Thomas A. McCarthy
Director, H. Elizabeth Mitchell
Director, Michael J. Morrissey
Director, Cynthia S. Nicholson
Director, William M. Rue
Director, John Stephen Scheid
Director, Philip H. Urban
Director, Wole C. Coaxum
Director, Ainar D. Aijala
Director, Stephen C. Mills
Director, Lisa R. Bacus
Auditors: KPMG LLP

LOCATIONS

HQ: Selective Insurance Group Inc
40 Wantage Avenue, Branchville, NJ 07890
Phone: 973 948-3000 **Fax:** 973 948-0282
Web: www.selective.com

PRODUCTS/OPERATIONS

2017 Sales by Segment

	$ mil.	% of total
Standard Commercial Lines	1,798	73
Standard Personal Lines	290.9	12
E&S Lines	212.8	8
Investments	168.2	7
Total	2,470	100

2017 Sales

	$ mil.	% of total
Net premiums earned	2,291	93
Net investment income earned	161.8	7
Other	10.7	-
Net realized gains	6.4	-
Total	2,470	100

COMPETITORS

A ACUITY MUTUAL INSURANCE COMPANY
AMERITRUST GROUP, INC.
CNA FINANCIAL CORPORATION
GAINSCO, INC.
HALLMARK FINANCIAL SERVICES, INC.
INFINITY PROPERTY AND CASUALTY CORPORATION
LIVERPOOL VICTORIA FRIENDLY SOCIETY LTD
MAIN STREET AMERICA GROUP, INC.
PROTECTIVE INSURANCE CORPORATION
THE HANOVER INSURANCE GROUP INC

HISTORICAL FINANCIALS

Company Type: Public

Income Statement — FYE: December 31

	ASSETS ($mil)	NET INCOME ($mil)	INCOME AS % OF ASSETS	EMPLOYEES
12/21	10,461.3	403.8	3.9%	2,440
12/20	9,687.9	246.3	2.5%	2,400
12/19	8,797.1	271.6	3.1%	2,400
12/18	7,952.7	178.9	2.3%	2,290
12/17	7,686.4	168.8	2.2%	2,260
Annual Growth	8.0%	24.4%	—	1.9%

2021 Year-End Financials

Return on assets: 4.0%
Return on equity: 14.1%
Long-term debt ($ mil.): —
No. of shares ($ mil.): 60.1
Sales ($ mil.): 3,379.1
Dividends Yield: 1.2%
Payout: 14.6%
Market value ($ mil.): 4,932.0

	STOCK PRICE ($) FY Close	P/E High/Low		PER SHARE ($) Earnings	Dividends	Book Value
12/21	81.94	13	10	6.50	1.03	49.56
12/20	66.98	17	10	4.09	0.94	45.72
12/19	65.19	18	13	4.53	0.83	36.91
12/18	60.94	22	18	3.00	0.74	30.40
12/17	58.70	21	14	2.84	0.66	29.28
Annual Growth	8.7%	—	—	23.0%	11.8%	14.1%

SelectQuote Inc

EXECUTIVES

Chairman, Director, Donald L. Hawks
Vice-Chairman, Director, William T. Grant
President, Robert Grant
Chief Executive Officer, Director, Timothy Robert Danker
Financial Planning Chief Financial Officer, Ryan M. Clement

Chief Operating Officer, William Thomas Grant
Chief Accounting Officer, Principal Accounting Officer, Stephanie D. Fisher
Chief Information Officer, Floyd O'Lander May
Chief Customer Experience Officer, Matthew Gunter
General Counsel, Secretary, Daniel Al Boulware
Division Officer, Ryan Souan
Director, Earl H. Devanny
Director, Raymond F. Weldon
Director, Kavita K. Patel
Director, Denise L. Devine

LOCATIONS

HQ: SelectQuote Inc
6800 West 115th Street, Suite 2511, Overland Park, KS 66211
Phone: 913 599-9225
Web: www.selectquote.com

HISTORICAL FINANCIALS
Company Type: Public

Income Statement — FYE: June 30

	REVENUE ($mil)	NET INCOME ($mil)	NET PROFIT MARGIN	EMPLOYEES
06/21	937.8	131.0	14.0%	1,944
06/20	531.5	81.1	15.3%	1,900
06/19	337.4	72.5	21.5%	1,800
06/18	233.6	34.8	14.9%	0
Annual Growth	58.9%	55.4%	—	—

2021 Year-End Financials
Debt ratio: 32.2%
Return on equity: 21.4%
Cash ($ mil.): 286.4
Current Ratio: 4.53
Long-term debt ($ mil.): 459
No. of shares ($ mil.): 163.5
Dividends
 Yield: —
 Payout: —
Market value ($ mil.): 3,149.0

	STOCK PRICE ($) FY Close	P/E High/Low		PER SHARE ($) Earnings	Dividends	Book Value
06/21	19.26	40	21	0.79	0.00	4.13
06/20	25.33	—	—	(0.16)	0.00	3.36
Annual Growth	(24.0%)	—	—	—	—	22.7%

Semler Scientific Inc

Semler Scientific is an emerging medical device maker with a single product. The company markets the FloChec, a medical device that measures arterial blood flow to the extremities (fingers and toes) quickly and easily in the doctor's office, to diagnose peripheral artery disease. FloChec received FDA clearance in early 2010 and the company began commercially leasing the product in 2011. Founded in 2007 by Dr. Herbert Semler, who invented the technology used in FloChec, the Portland-based company went public in 2014 with an offering valued at $10 million.

IPO
Semler Scientific went public in February 2014 with an offering of 1.4 million shares of stock priced at $7 each. The IPO raised about $10 million, well below the initial expectations of nearly $16 million.

Financial Performance
In 2012 Semler reported total revenue of $1.2 million and a net loss of $2.7 million, compared with revenue of $316,000 and a loss of nearly $1.9 million in 2011.

EXECUTIVES

Chairman, Herbert J. Semler
Senior Vice President, Andrew B. Weinstein
President, Chief Executive Officer, Douglas Murphy-Chutorian, $350,000 total compensation
Chief Technical Officer, Robert G. McRae, $195,479 total compensation
Finance Vice President, Finance Principal Accounting Officer, Daniel E. Conger, $157,500 total compensation
Director, Arthur N. (Abbie) Leibowitz
Director, Wayne T. Pan
Auditors : BDO USA, LLP

LOCATIONS

HQ: Semler Scientific Inc
2340-2348 Walsh Avenue, Suite 2344, Santa Clara, CA 95051
Phone: 877 774-4211
Web: www.semlerscientific.com

COMPETITORS

HEARTWARE INTERNATIONAL, INC.
INTERSECT ENT, INC.
LIVANOVA PLC
SURMODICS, INC.
UNILIFE CORPORATION

HISTORICAL FINANCIALS
Company Type: Public

Income Statement — FYE: December 31

	REVENUE ($mil)	NET INCOME ($mil)	NET PROFIT MARGIN	EMPLOYEES
12/20	38.6	14.0	36.3%	86
12/19	32.7	15.0	46.0%	67
12/18	21.4	5.0	23.3%	46
12/17	12.4	(1.5)	—	37
12/16	7.4	(2.5)	—	29
Annual Growth	51.0%	—	—	31.2%

2020 Year-End Financials
Debt ratio: —
Return on equity: 65.1%
Cash ($ mil.): 22.0
Current Ratio: 5.82
Long-term debt ($ mil.): —
No. of shares ($ mil.): 6.7
Dividends
 Yield: —
 Payout: —
Market value ($ mil.): 630.0

	STOCK PRICE ($) FY Close	P/E High/Low		PER SHARE ($) Earnings	Dividends	Book Value
12/20	94.00	43	14	1.74	0.00	4.45
12/19	48.00	22	15	1.88	0.00	2.00
12/18	34.40	48	9	0.66	0.00	0.66
12/17	8.00	—	—	(0.28)	0.00	(0.44)
12/16	1.45	—	—	(0.50)	0.00	(0.57)
Annual Growth	183.8%	—	—	—	—	—

ServisFirst Bancshares Inc

ServisFirst Bancshares is a bank holding company for ServisFirst Bank, a regional commercial bank with about a dozen branches located in Alabama and the Florida panhandle. The bank also has a loan office in Nashville. ServisFirst Bank targets privately-held businesses with $2 million to $250 million in annual sales, as well as professionals and affluent customers. The bank focuses on traditional commercial banking services, including loan origination, deposits, and electronic banking services, such as online and mobile banking. Founded in 2005 by its chairman and CEO Thomas Broughton III, the bank went public in 2014 with an offering valued at nearly $57 million.

IPO
ServisFirst Bancshares sold 625,000 shares priced at $91 per share. Proceeds from the May 2014 IPO will be used to support the bank's growth plans, both in Alabama and in other states.

Geographic Reach
Birmingham-based ServisFirst Bank has branches in Birmingham, Huntsville, Montgomery, Mobile, Dothan, Pensacola, and Nashville.

Financial Performance
The bank reported net income of $41.2 million in 2013, compared with $34 million in 2012. The increase was primarily due to an increase in net interest income, which rose nearly 20% to $112.5 million. Noninterest income increased 4% to $10 million in 2013.

As of March 2014, the bank had total assets of approximately $3.6 billion, total loans of $2.9 billion, and total deposits of about $3.0 billion.

EXECUTIVES

President, Chief Executive Officer, Subsidiary Officer, Chairman, Director, Thomas A. Broughton, $475,000 total compensation
Executive Vice President, Chief Operating Officer, Subsidiary Officer, Rodney E. Rushing, $297,000 total compensation
Executive Vice President, Chief Financial Officer, Subsidiary Officer, William M. Foshee, $280,000 total compensation
Senior Vice President, Chief Credit Officer, Subsidiary Officer, Henry F. Abbott, $175,000 total compensation
Lead Independent Director, Director, James J. Filler
Director, J. Richard Cashio
Director, Christopher J. Mettler
Director, Hatton C. V. Smith
Director, Irma L. Tuder
Auditors : Dixon Hughes Goodman LLP

LOCATIONS

HQ: ServisFirst Bancshares Inc
2500 Woodcrest Place, Birmingham, AL 35209
Phone: 205 949-0302
Web: www.servisfirstbank.com

2013 Branches

	No.
Alabama	10
Florida	2
Total	12

COMPETITORS

BANK OF THE OZARKS, INC.
COMMUNITY BANK OF THE BAY
DIME COMMUNITY BANCSHARES, INC.
FIDELITY SOUTHERN CORPORATION
FULTON FINANCIAL CORPORATION
HERITAGE FINANCIAL GROUP, INC.
NATIONAL BANK HOLDINGS CORPORATION
PEAPACK-GLADSTONE FINANCIAL CORPORATION
PT. BANK MANDIRI (PERSERO) TBK
RENASANT CORPORATION

HISTORICAL FINANCIALS

Company Type: Public

Income Statement — FYE: December 31

	ASSETS ($mil)	NET INCOME ($mil)	INCOME AS % OF ASSETS	EMPLOYEES
12/20	11,932.6	169.5	1.4%	493
12/19	8,947.6	149.2	1.7%	505
12/18	8,007.3	136.9	1.7%	473
12/17	7,082.3	93.0	1.3%	434
12/16	6,370.4	81.4	1.3%	420
Annual Growth	17.0%	20.1%	—	4.1%

2020 Year-End Financials

Return on assets: 1.6%
Return on equity: 18.4%
Long-term debt ($ mil.): —
No. of shares ($ mil.): 53.9
Sales ($ mil.): 419.1
Dividends
 Yield: 1.7%
 Payout: 23.1%
Market value ($ mil.): 2,173.0

	STOCK PRICE ($) FY Close	P/E High	P/E Low	PER SHARE ($) Earnings	PER SHARE ($) Dividends	PER SHARE ($) Book Value
12/20	40.29	13	8	3.13	0.73	18.40
12/19	37.68	14	10	2.76	0.63	15.71
12/18	31.87	17	12	2.53	0.48	13.39
12/17	41.50	25	19	1.72	0.20	11.46
12/16	37.44	48	23	1.52	0.19	9.93
Annual Growth	1.9%	—	—	19.8%	39.8%	16.7%

Sharps Compliance Corp.

Sharps Compliance is on the cutting edge of the medical waste disposal business -- and wants to make sure people don't get hurt. The company offers services to health care providers to make the disposal of medical waste safer and more efficient. It also serves customers in the pharmaceutical, agricultural, hospitality, industrial, and retail industries. Products include medical sharps (needles and other sharp objects) disposal systems, disposable IV poles, waste and equipment return boxes, linen recovery systems, and biohazardous spill clean-up kits. Sharps Compliance also provides regulatory compliant waste tracking, incineration, and disposal verification services, as well as consulting services.

EXECUTIVES

Chairman, Director, Sharon R. Gabrielson
President, Chief Executive Officer, Director, David P. Tusa, $333,866 total compensation
Vice President, Chief Financial Officer, Diana P. Diaz, $206,406 total compensation
Operations Vice President, Gregory C. Davis, $186,984 total compensation
Marketing Vice President, Dennis P. Halligan, $131,654 total compensation
Director, John W. Dalton
Director, Jack A. Holmes
Director, Parris H. Holmes
Director, Susan L.N. Vogt
Director, William Patrick Mulloy II
Auditors : BDO USA, LLP

LOCATIONS

HQ: Sharps Compliance Corp.
9220 Kirby Drive, Suite 500, Houston, TX 77054
Phone: 713 432-0300
Web: www.sharpsinc.com

COMPETITORS

BIOMEDICAL TECHNOLOGY SOLUTIONS HOLDINGS, INC.
PSC, LLC
Promotora Ambiental, S.A.B. de C.V.
US ECOLOGY HOLDINGS, INC.
VEOLIA ENVIRONMENTAL SERVICES NORTH AMERICA CORP.

HISTORICAL FINANCIALS

Company Type: Public

Income Statement — FYE: June 30

	REVENUE ($mil)	NET INCOME ($mil)	NET PROFIT MARGIN	EMPLOYEES
06/21	76.4	12.8	16.8%	192
06/20	51.1	2.2	4.4%	184
06/19	44.3	0.2	0.5%	164
06/18	40.1	(0.6)	—	152
06/17	38.1	(1.2)	—	130
Annual Growth	18.9%	—	—	10.2%

2021 Year-End Financials

Debt ratio: 6.6%
Return on equity: 33.7%
Cash ($ mil.): 27.7
Current Ratio: 2.63
Long-term debt ($ mil.): 4
No. of shares ($ mil.): 17.1
Dividends
 Yield: —
 Payout: —
Market value ($ mil.): 177.0

	STOCK PRICE ($) FY Close	P/E High	P/E Low	PER SHARE ($) Earnings	PER SHARE ($) Dividends	PER SHARE ($) Book Value
06/21	10.30	24	7	0.76	0.00	2.71
06/20	7.03	57	25	0.14	0.00	1.81
06/19	3.56	402	307	0.01	0.00	1.62
06/18	3.69	—	—	(0.04)	0.00	1.57
06/17	4.23	—	—	(0.08)	0.00	1.58
Annual Growth	24.9%	—	—	—	—	14.5%

Shell Midstream Partners LP

EXECUTIVES

Chairman, Director, Paul R.A. Goodfellow
Commercial President, Commercial Chief Executive Officer, Commercial Associate/ Affiliate Company Officer, Director, Steve C. Ledbetter
Vice President, Chief Financial Officer, Director, Shawn J. Carsten
Vice President, General Counsel, Secretary, Lori M. Muratta
Operations Vice President, Gregory T. Mouras
Commercial Vice President, Commercial Associate/Affiliate Company Officer, Sean Guillory
Director, Cynthia V. Hablinski
Auditors : Ernst & Young LLP

LOCATIONS

HQ: Shell Midstream Partners LP
150 N. Dairy Ashford, Houston, TX 77079
Phone: 832 337-2034
Web: www.shellmidstreampartners.com

HISTORICAL FINANCIALS

Company Type: Public

Income Statement — FYE: December 31

	REVENUE ($mil)	NET INCOME ($mil)	NET PROFIT MARGIN	EMPLOYEES
12/20	481.0	543.0	112.9%	0
12/19	503.0	528.0	105.0%	0
12/18	524.7	464.1	88.5%	0
12/17	470.1	295.3	62.8%	0
12/16	291.3	244.9	84.1%	0
Annual Growth	13.4%	22.0%	—	—

2020 Year-End Financials

Debt ratio: 115.7%
Return on equity: —
Cash ($ mil.): 320.0
Current Ratio: 4.80
Long-term debt ($ mil.): 2,716
No. of shares ($ mil.): 393.2
Dividends
 Yield: 18.2%
 Payout: 147.2%
Market value ($ mil.): 3,964.0

	STOCK PRICE ($) FY Close	P/E High	P/E Low	PER SHARE ($) Earnings	PER SHARE ($) Dividends	PER SHARE ($) Book Value
12/20	10.08	18	6	1.25	1.84	(1.22)
12/19	20.21	13	10	1.66	1.69	(3.26)
12/18	16.41	20	11	1.50	1.43	(1.24)
12/17	29.82	27	20	1.28	1.19	(3.07)
12/16	29.09	32	20	1.32	0.97	0.54
Annual Growth	(23.3%)	—	—	(1.4%)	17.4%	—

Shutterstock Inc

Shutterstock brings the online marketplace mentality to the world of digital images, illustrations, and videos. It is a global technology company offering a creative platform, which provides high-quality content, tools, and services to creative professionals. The company's primary customers include marketing professionals and organization, media and broadcast companies, and small- and medium-sizes businesses. Shutterstock's marketplace is available in more than 20 languages and some 150 countries where its images are used for corporate communications, websites, ads, books, and other published materials. The company was formed in 2003.

Operations
The company's high-quality products and services and the experience it provides to the customers, combined with its focus on continuous innovation, have allowed Shutterstock to establish premium brands, including: Shutterstock, Bigstock, Offset, PremiumBeat and TurboSquid.

The Shutterstock is the company's flagship brand that includes various content types and offerings such as image, footage, editorial, music and studios. The Bigstock maintains a separate, extensive library of images, vectors, illustrations, and footage that is specifically curated to meet the needs of independent creators and others seeking to incorporate cost-effective imagery into their projects. The Offset brand provides authentic and exceptional content, featuring work from top assignment photographers and illustrators from around the world. PremiumBeat's library of exclusive high-quality music tracks provides producers, filmmakers and marketers. TurboSquid operates a marketplace that offers more than one million 3D models and a 2 dimensional (2D) marketplace derived from 3D objects.

Geographic Reach
Headquartered in New York, Shutterstock has office facilities in the US and abroad. The North America generates about 40% of the company's total revenues, Europe with nearly 35% of sales, and the rest of the world accounts for the remaining.

Sales and Marketing
Customer sales are made through E-commerce (around 65% of sales) and Enterprise (more than 35% of sales).

Marketing and communications professionals incorporate licensed content in the work they produce for their organization or clients' business communications. Whether providing graphic design, web design, interactive design, advertising, public relations, communications or marketing materials, these professional users and teams support organizations of various sizes including the largest global agencies, large not-for-profit organizations and Fortune 500 companies.

Media organizations and professionals incorporate licensed content into their work, which includes digital publications, newspapers, books, magazines, television and film, as well as to market their products effectively.

Organizations of all sizes utilize creative content for a wide range of internal- and external-use communications such as websites, print and digital advertisements, merchandise, brochures, employee communications, newsletters, social media, email marketing campaigns and other presentations.

The company's advertising costs totaled approximately $112.9 million, $81.2 million and $102.3 million for the years ended 2021, 2020 and 2019, respectively.

Financial Performance
Revenue increased by $106.7 million, or 16%, to $773.4 million in 2021 compared to 2020. The company's revenue growth in 2021 is primarily driven by revenue generated from its 2021 acquisitions and the increase in its subscription business.

Net income for fiscal 2021 increased to $91.9 million compared to the prior year's $71.8 million.

Cash held by the company at the end of fiscal 2021 decreased to $314.0 million. Cash provided by operations was $216.4 million, while cash used for investing and financing activities were $250.4 million and $77.7 million, respectively. Main cash uses were business combination and payment of cash dividends.

Mergers and Acquisitions
In late 2021, Shutterstock acquired PicMonkey, a leading online graphic design and image editing platform that enables creators of any skill level to design high-quality visual assets ? from presentations, advertisements and logos, to business cards and banners ? for an array of use cases, including digital marketing, advertising, and social media posts. The acquisition of the Seattle, Washington-based company will further empower the company's customers, regardless of their skill level or expertise, to create beautiful, best-in-class content with efficiency and ease in just a few clicks. Consideration for the transaction consists of approximately $110 million of cash paid at closing.

Company Background
Shutterstock launched its platform in 2003, and in 2012, it reorganized as Shutterstock, Inc., a Delaware corporation, from Shutterstock Images LLC, a New York limited liability company and completed its initial public offering. Its common stock is listed on the New York Stock Exchange under the symbol "SSTK".

EXECUTIVES
Executive Chairman, Director, Jonathan (Jon) Oringer, $1 total compensation
Chief Executive Officer, Director, Paul J. Hennessy
Chief Financial Officer, Jarrod Yahes
E-Commerce Global Head, John Caine
Director, Rachna Bhasin
Director, Deirdre M. Bigley
Director, Thomas R. Evans
Director, Alfonse L. Upshaw
Auditors : PricewaterhouseCoopers LLP

LOCATIONS
HQ: Shutterstock Inc
350 Fifth Avenue, 21st Floor, New York, NY 10118
Phone: 646 710-3417
Web: www.shutterstock.com

2011 Sales
	$ mil.	% of total
Europe	48.0	40
North America	40.5	33
Other regions	31.8	25
Total	120.3	100

COMPETITORS
ALPHABET INC.
BLACKBIRD PLC
CASTLIGHT HEALTH, INC.
COVISINT CORPORATION
FACEBOOK, INC.
INNODATA INC.
MINDBODY, INC.
QLIK TECHNOLOGIES INC.
SENDGRID, INC.
YEXT, INC.

HISTORICAL FINANCIALS
Company Type: Public

Income Statement — FYE: December 31

	REVENUE ($mil)	NET INCOME ($mil)	NET PROFIT MARGIN	EMPLOYEES
12/21	773.4	91.8	11.9%	1,148
12/20	666.6	71.7	10.8%	967
12/19	650.5	20.1	3.1%	1,116
12/18	623.2	54.6	8.8%	1,029
12/17	557.1	16.7	3.0%	1,130
Annual Growth	8.5%	53.1%	—	0.4%

2021 Year-End Financials
Debt ratio: —
Return on equity: 20.6%
Cash ($ mil.): 314.0
Current Ratio: 1.16
Long-term debt ($ mil.): —
No. of shares ($ mil.): 36.4
Dividends
  Yield: 0.7%
  Payout: 30.9%
Market value ($ mil.): 4,038.0

	STOCK PRICE ($) FY Close	P/E High/Low		PER SHARE ($) Earnings	Dividends	Book Value
12/21	110.88	50	26	2.46	0.84	12.86
12/20	71.70	37	15	1.97	0.68	11.64
12/19	42.88	85	59	0.57	0.00	9.24
12/18	36.01	35	21	1.54	3.00	8.18
12/17	43.03	114	66	0.47	0.00	9.06
Annual Growth	26.7%	—	—	51.3%	—	9.2%

Sierra Bancorp

Sierra Bancorp is the holding company for the nearly $2 billion-asset Bank of the Sierra, which operates approximately 30 branches in Central California's San Joaquin Valley between (and including) Bakersfield and Fresno. The bank offers traditional deposit products and loans to individuals and small and mid-size businesses. About 70% of its loan portfolio is made up of real estate loans, while another 15% is made up of mortgage warehouse loans and a further 10% is tied to commercial and industrial loans (including SBA loans and direct finance leases). The bank also issues agricultural loans, and consumer loans.

Operations
Bank of the Sierra makes almost 80% of its revenue from interest income. About 64% of its total revenue came from interest income on loans and leases (including fees) during 2015, while another 14% came from interest income on taxed and tax-exempt securities. The rest of its revenue came from deposit account service charges (12% of revenue), checkcard fees (5%), and other non-interest income sources.

Geographic Reach
The Porterville, California-based bank operates branches and offices mostly in the San Joaquin Valley, in Porterville, Arroyo Grande, Atascadero, Bakersfield, California City, Clovis, Delano, Dinuba, Exeter, Farmersville, Fillmore, Fresno, Hanford, Lindsay, Oxnard, Paso Robles, Reedley, San Luis Obispo, Santa Clarita, Santa Paula, Selma, Tehachapi, Three Rivers, Visalia, and Tulare.

Sales and Marketing
Bank of the Sierra has been gradually increasing its advertising spend in recent years. It spent $2.3 million on advertising and promotion in 2015, up from $2.2 million and $1.9 million in 2014 and 2013, respectively.

Financial Performance
The bank's revenue has been steadily rising over the past few years mostly as bank acquisitions and organic loan business growth has spurred higher interest income. Meanwhile, its profits have more than doubled since 2011 thanks to declining loan loss provisions as its loan portfolio's credit quality has improved with higher property valuations in the strengthened economy.

Sierra Bancorp's revenue jumped 13% to $80.4 million during 2015 thanks to higher interest income from continued double-digit loan asset growth, led by a jump in mortgage warehouse lines from increased line utilization, a first-quarter purchase of residential mortgage loans, and strong organic growth in non-farm real estate and agricultural production loans. Deposit account service fees also grew thanks to organic deposit client growth.

Strong revenue growth and lower acquisition costs in 2015 drove the bank's net income up 19% to $18 million. Sierra's operating cash levels rose 4% to $29.78 million during the year as its cash-based earnings increased.

Strategy
While the Bank of Sierra has traditionally grown organically by opening around one new branch per year in the Central Valley, it has more recently acquired small area banks and individual branches to bolster its deposit and loan business while expanding into untapped markets, such as further south into the Santa Clara Valley.

Mergers and Acquisitions
In July 2016, the bank bought $145 million-asset Coast Bancorp and its Coast National Bank branches in San Luis Obispo, Paso Robles, Arroyo Grande, and Atascadero, California.

In November 2014, Sierra Bancorp bought $129 million-asset Santa Clara Valley Bank N.A. and its branches in Santa Paula, Santa Clarita, and Fillmore in California for $15 million. the deal expanded Sierra's reach outside of its traditional market for the first time more south into the Santa Clara Valley of California.

EXECUTIVES

Chairman, Subsidiary Officer, Morris A. Tharp
Vice-Chairman, Director, James C. Holly, $163,901 total compensation
President, Chief Executive Officer, Subsidiary Officer, Director, Kevin J. McPhaill, $475,000 total compensation
Executive Vice President, Chief Administrative Officer, Subsidiary Officer, Jennifer A. Johnson
Executive Vice President, Chief Credit Officer, Chief Risk Officer, Subsidiary Officer, Hugh F. Boyle
Executive Vice President, Chief Banking Officer, Subsidiary Officer, Michael W. Olague, $300,000 total compensation
Executive Vice President, Chief Financial Officer, Christopher G. Treece
Director, Susan M. Abundis
Director, Albert L. Berra
Director, Vonn R. Christenson
Director, Laurence S. Dutto
Director, Lynda B. Scearcy
Director, Gordon T. Woods
Director, Julie G. Castle
Auditors : Eide Bailly LLP

LOCATIONS

HQ: Sierra Bancorp
86 North Main Street, Porterville, CA 93257
Phone: 559 782-4900
Web: www.bankofthesierra.com

COMPETITORS

CVB FINANCIAL CORP.
PARK STERLING CORPORATION
UNITED BANKSHARES, INC.
UNITED COMMUNITY BANKS, INC.
WESTERN ALLIANCE BANCORPORATION

HISTORICAL FINANCIALS
Company Type: Public

Income Statement — FYE: December 31

	ASSETS ($mil)	NET INCOME ($mil)	INCOME AS % OF ASSETS	EMPLOYEES
12/20	3,220.7	35.4	1.1%	512
12/19	2,593.8	35.9	1.4%	513
12/18	2,522.5	29.6	1.2%	556
12/17	2,340.2	19.5	0.8%	576
12/16	2,032.8	17.5	0.9%	497
Annual Growth	12.2%	19.2%	—	0.7%

2020 Year-End Financials
Return on assets: 1.2% Dividends
Return on equity: 10.8% Yield: 3.3%
Long-term debt ($ mil.): — Payout: 34.3%
No. of shares ($ mil.): 15.3 Market value ($ mil.): 368.0
Sales ($ mil.): 136.3

	STOCK PRICE ($) FY Close	P/E High/Low		PER SHARE ($) Earnings	Dividends	Book Value
12/20	23.92	13	6	2.32	0.80	22.35
12/19	29.12	13	10	2.33	0.74	20.24
12/18	24.03	16	12	1.92	0.64	17.84
12/17	26.56	21	17	1.36	0.56	16.81
12/16	26.59	20	12	1.29	0.48	14.94
Annual Growth	(2.6%)	—	—	15.8%	13.6%	10.6%

SIGA Technologies Inc

SIGA Technologies is trying to put itself on the front lines of US biodefense efforts. The drug company has a number of development programs for vaccines, antivirals, and antibiotics for drug resistant infections; however, its main focus is on vaccines for biodefense. Its lead product TPOXX (aka tecovirimat) was the first treatment to be approved for the treatment of smallpox in case of a bioterrorist attack; it was given approval in mid-2018. SIGA is also developing vaccines for use against hemorrhagic fevers and other infectious diseases and biothreats. Much of its work is done through funding from the NIH and the HHS. SIGA emerged from a short stint under Chapter 11 bankruptcy protection in 2016.

Bankruptcy
The company filed for bankruptcy protection after it was given a court ruling to pay $232 million in damages to competitor PharmAthene. SIGA plans to continue operating as usual, as well as pursuing a lowering of the penalty. Because of its status as the country's only maker of smallpox treatment, the company enjoys a certain level of government protection.

PharmAthene sued SIGA in 2006, claiming it should share in the potential $5 billion in sales, primarily from the manufacture of Arestvyr (the development of which it helped fund).

Operations
SIGA's lead candidate is Arestvyr, which is still going through trials despite being fast-tracked by the FDA. Other candidates in testing include treatments and preventions for dengue fever, Lassa fever, Junin, Ebola, Marburg, and bunyaviruses. All told, the company has about $420 million in grant money available if it can deliver on various projects.

Geographic Reach
SIGA has its headquarters in New York and R&D facilities in Oregon. Its treatments

have the potential to be used worldwide.

Sales and Marketing
The company uses a small force of its own personnel to sell Arestvyr to the US government. As it expands its products, and customer base, it may expand its sales force or use third-parties.

Financial Performance
SIGA reported a 30% drop in revenue as some contracts concluded and others got restructured. It also saw related net loss and drop in cash flow as it used operating cash for the manufacture and marketing of Arestvyr.

Strategy
The company's key strategy is to expand its customer base beyond the US government.

EXECUTIVES

Executive Vice President, Chief Financial Officer, Secretary, Daniel J. Luckshire, $600,000 total compensation

Vice President, Chief Scientific Officer, Dennis E. Hruby, $597,027 total compensation

Lead Independent Director, Director, Michael C. Plansky

Director, Jaymie A. Durnan

Director, Julie M. Kane

Director, Joseph W. Marshall

Director, Gary J. Nabel

Director, Julian Nemirovsky

Director, Holly L. Phillips

Director, Harold Eugene Ford

Director, Jay Varma

Auditors : PricewaterhouseCoopers LLP

LOCATIONS

HQ: SIGA Technologies Inc
31 East 62nd Street, New York, NY 10065
Phone: 212 672-9100
Web: www.siga.com

COMPETITORS

ACHAOGEN, INC.
ADAMAS PHARMACEUTICALS, INC.
MANNKIND CORPORATION
OMTHERA PHARMACEUTICALS, INC.
PARATEK PHARMACEUTICALS, INC.

HISTORICAL FINANCIALS

Company Type: Public

Income Statement — FYE: December 31

	REVENUE ($mil)	NET INCOME ($mil)	NET PROFIT MARGIN	EMPLOYEES
12/20	124.9	56.3	45.1%	42
12/19	26.7	(7.2)	—	41
12/18	477.0	421.8	88.4%	41
12/17	12.2	(36.2)	—	37
12/16	14.9	(39.6)	—	36
Annual Growth	69.9%	—	—	3.9%

2020 Year-End Financials

Debt ratio: —
Return on equity: 49.3%
Cash ($ mil.): 117.8
Current Ratio: 13.70
Long-term debt ($ mil.): —
No. of shares ($ mil.): 77.2
Dividends
  Yield: —
  Payout: —
Market value ($ mil.): 561.0

	STOCK PRICE ($) FY Close	P/E High/Low		PER SHARE ($) Earnings	Dividends	Book Value
12/20	7.27	11	6	0.71	0.00	1.68
12/19	4.77	—	—	(0.15)	0.00	1.20
12/18	7.90	2	1	5.18	0.00	1.27
12/17	4.85	—	—	(0.46)	0.00	(4.09)
12/16	2.88	—	—	(0.69)	0.00	(3.65)
Annual Growth	26.0%	—	—	—	—	—

Signature Bank (New York, NY)

Signature Bank is a full-service commercial bank that provides customized banking and financial services to smaller private businesses, their owners, and their top executives through some 35 branches across the New York metropolitan area, including those in Connecticut, as well as in California and North Carolina. The bank's lending activities mainly entail real estate and business loans. Subsidiary Signature Securities offers wealth management, brokerage services, asset management, and insurance, while its Signature Financial subsidiary offers equipment financing and leasing. Founded in 2001, the bank now boasts assets of approximately $118.45 billion.

Operations
Signature Bank's operations are organized into two reportable segments representing its core businesses ? Commercial Banking and Specialty Finance.

Commercial Banking accounts for more than 90% of revenue and principally consists of commercial real estate lending, fund banking, venture banking, and other commercial and industrial lending, and commercial deposit gathering activities, while Specialty Finance (nearly 10%) principally consists of financing and leasing products, including equipment, transportation, taxi medallion, commercial marine, municipal and national franchise financing or leasing.

Mortgage loans, including commercial real estate loans, multifamily residential mortgages, home loans and lines of credit, and construction and land loans, comprise the bulk of Signature Bank's loan portfolio (and much of its asset base as well).

The bank generated over 80% of its revenue from interest on loans and leases that year, while nearly 10% came from interest on its securities available-for-sale, and less than 5% came from securities held-to-maturity.

In addition, the bank has approximately $118.45 billion in assets, $106.13 billion in deposits, $64.86 billion in loans, $7.84 billion in equity capital, and $5.01 billion in other assets under management.

Geographic Reach
Based in New York, Signature Bank operates more than 35 private client offices throughout New York metropolitan area, including those in Connecticut, as well as in California and North Carolina.

Sales and Marketing
Signature Bank mostly serves privately-owned businesses, their owners, and senior managers.

Financial Performance
In 2021, the company had a net income of $918.4 million, a 74% increase from the previous year's net income of $528.4 million. The increase in net income was primarily due to an increase of $361.4 million in net interest income, fueled by growth in average interest-earning assets and a decrease of $198.1 million in the provision for credit losses predominantly attributable to improved macroeconomic conditions.

The company's cash at the end of 2021 was $29.6 billion. Operating activities generated $879.6 million, while investing activities used $27.1 billion, mainly for net increase in loans and leases. Financing activities provided another $43.5 billion.

Strategy
The company intends to increase its presence as a premier relationship-based financial services organization serving the needs of privately owned business clients, their owners and their senior managers in major metropolitan areas by continuing to:

Focus on its niche market of privately owned businesses, their owners and their senior managers; Provide clients a wide array of high quality banking, brokerage and insurance products and services through its private client group structure and a seamless financial services solution; as well as Recruit experienced, talented and motivated private client group directors who are top producers and who believe in its banking model.

Company Background
The bank's emphasis on personal service helped it to grow its deposit base and loan portfolio in 2011. During a time when many other banks struggled under the weight of bad loans in a bad economy, Signature Bank achieved record earnings for the fourth consecutive year.

Founded in 2001 as an alternative to mega-banks, Signature Bank was spun off from Bank Hapoalim in 2004.

EXECUTIVES

Chairman, Subsidiary Officer, Director, Scott A. Shay, $501,750 total compensation

Vice-Chairman, Director, John Tamberlane, $375,750 total compensation

President, Chief Executive Officer, Director, Joseph J. Depaolo, $606,500 total compensation

Executive Vice President, Chief Financial Officer, Vito Susca

Director, Derrick D. Cephas

Director, Barney Frank

Director, Kathryn A. Byrne

Director, Alfonse M. D'Amato
Director, Judith Huntington
Director, Jeffrey Wayne Meshel
Auditors : KPMG LLP

LOCATIONS

HQ: Signature Bank (New York, NY)
565 Fifth Avenue, New York, NY 10017
Phone: 646 822-1500
Web: www.signatureny.com

PRODUCTS/OPERATIONS

2014 Sales

	$ mil.	% of total
Interest		
Loans, net	655.6	68
Securities available for sale	193.6	20
Securities held to maturity	69.8	7
Other	5.3	1
Noninterest		
Fees & service charges	19.3	2
Commissions	10.6	1
Net gains on sales of loans	5.4	1
Net gains on sales of securities	5.3	-
Other	2.2	-
Adjustments	(7.8)	-
Total	959.3	100

COMPETITORS

BANCFIRST CORPORATION
BOKF MERGER CORPORATION NUMBER SIXTEEN
CITY HOLDING COMPANY
CVB FINANCIAL CORP.
EAGLE BANCORP, INC.
GUARANTY BANCORP
M&T BANK CORPORATION
OCEANFIRST FINANCIAL CORP.
PRIVATEBANCORP, INC.
THE SOUTHERN BANC COMPANY INC

HISTORICAL FINANCIALS
Company Type: Public

Income Statement				FYE: December 31
	ASSETS ($mil)	NET INCOME ($mil)	INCOME AS % OF ASSETS	EMPLOYEES
12/20	73,888.3	528.3	0.7%	1,652
12/19	50,616.4	588.9	1.2%	1,472
12/18	47,364.8	505.3	1.1%	1,393
12/17	43,117.7	387.2	0.9%	1,305
12/16	39,047.6	396.3	1.0%	1,218
Annual Growth	17.3%	7.5%	—	7.9%

2020 Year-End Financials
Return on assets: 0.8%   Dividends
Return on equity: 9.9%   Yield: 1.6%
Long-term debt ($ mil.): —   Payout: 23.6%
No. of shares ($ mil.): 53.5   Market value ($ mil.): 7,247.0
Sales ($ mil.): 2,006.8

	STOCK PRICE ($) FY Close	P/E High/Low		PER SHARE ($) Earnings	Dividends	Book Value
12/20	135.29	15	7	9.96	2.24	108.78
12/19	136.61	13	10	10.87	2.24	89.12
12/18	102.81	17	11	9.23	1.12	80.07
12/17	137.26	23	17	7.12	0.00	73.33
12/16	150.20	21	15	7.37	0.00	66.15
Annual Growth	(2.6%)	—	—	7.8%	—	13.2%

Sila Realty Trust Inc

EXECUTIVES

Chairman, Independent Director, Jonathan Kuchin
President, Chief Executive Officer, Independent Director, Michael A. Seton
Executive Vice President, Chief Financial Officer, Treasurer, Secretary, Kay C. Neely
Data Centers Chief Administrative Officer, Jason C. Reed
Chief Investment Officer, Jon C. Sajeski
Independent Director, Z. Jamie Behar
Independent Director, Verett Mims
Independent Director, Adrienne Kirby
Independent Director, Roger Pratt

LOCATIONS

HQ: Sila Realty Trust Inc
4890 West Kennedy Blvd., Suite 650, Tampa, FL 33609
Phone: 813 287-0101
Web: www.silarealtytrust.com

HISTORICAL FINANCIALS
Company Type: Public

Income Statement				FYE: December 31
	REVENUE ($mil)	NET INCOME ($mil)	NET PROFIT MARGIN	EMPLOYEES
12/20	276.5	36.7	13.3%	74
12/19	210.9	2.7	1.3%	0
12/18	177.3	28.8	16.3%	0
12/17	125.0	21.2	17.0%	0
Annual Growth	30.3%	20.0%	—	—

2020 Year-End Financials
Debt ratio: 43.3%   No. of shares ($ mil.): 222.0
Return on equity: 2.1%   Dividends
Cash ($ mil.): 53.1   Yield: —
Current Ratio: 0.66   Payout: 282.3%
Long-term debt ($ mil.): 1,386.5   Market value ($ mil.): 0.0

Silvergate Capital Corp

EXECUTIVES

Chairman, Director, Michael T. Lempres
Chief Executive Officer, Subsidiary Officer, Director, Alan J. Lane
Chief Operating Officer, Chief Risk Officer, Subsidiary Officer, Kathleen M. Fraher
Chief Financial Officer, Subsidiary Officer, Antonio Martino
Chief Legal Officer, Subsidiary Officer, John M. Bonino
Director, Aanchal Gupta
Director, Karen F. Brassfield
Director, Scott A. Reed
Director, Paul D. Colucci
Director, Thomas C. Dircks
Auditors : Crowe LLP

LOCATIONS

HQ: Silvergate Capital Corp
4250 Executive Square, Suite 300, La Jolla, CA 92037
Phone: 858 362-6300
Web: www.silvergatebank.com

HISTORICAL FINANCIALS
Company Type: Public

Income Statement				FYE: December 31
	ASSETS ($mil)	NET INCOME ($mil)	INCOME AS % OF ASSETS	EMPLOYEES
12/20	5,586.2	26.0	0.5%	218
12/19	2,128.1	24.8	1.2%	215
12/18	2,004.3	22.3	1.1%	209
12/17	1,891.9	7.6	0.4%	0
Annual Growth	43.5%	50.5%	—	—

2020 Year-End Financials
Return on assets: 0.6%   Dividends
Return on equity: 9.8%   Yield: —
Long-term debt ($ mil.): —   Payout: —
No. of shares ($ mil.): 18.8   Market value ($ mil.): 1,400.0
Sales ($ mil.): 98.7

	STOCK PRICE ($) FY Close	P/E High/Low		PER SHARE ($) Earnings	Dividends	Book Value
12/20	74.31	53	5	1.36	0.00	15.63
12/19	15.91	12	9	1.35	0.00	12.38
Annual Growth	367.1%	—	—	0.7%	—	26.3%

Simmons First National Corp

Simmons First National is a financial holding company of Simmons Bank, an Arkansas state-chartered bank that has been operating since 1903. Simmons Bank provides banking and other financial products and services to individuals and businesses using a network of about 200 financial centers in Arkansas, Kansas, Missouri, Oklahoma, Tennessee and Texas. The company offers commercial banking products and services to business and other corporate customers; it extends loans for a broad range of corporate purposes, including financing commercial real estate, construction of particular properties, commercial and industrial uses, acquisition and equipment financings, and other general corporate needs.

Operations

Aside from banking products and services offered to corporate customers, as well as loans and financing, Simmons Bank also engages in small business administration (SBA) and agricultural finance lending, and it offers corporate credit card products, as well as corporate deposit products and treasury management services. The bank also offers a variety of consumer banking products and services, including savings, time, and checking deposit products; ATM services; internet and mobile banking platforms;

overdraft facilities; real estate, home equity, and other consumer loans and lines of credit; consumer credit card products; and safe deposit boxes.

Like other retail banks, Simmons makes the bulk of its money from interest income (over 75% of sales). The majority of the company's revenue comes from loans (about 65%) and investment securities (nearly 15). Its loan portfolio averaged $12.0 billion, wherein the most significant components of the loan portfolio were real estate loans with around 75%, commercial loans with nearly 20%, and consumer and other with around 5% combined.

Simmons First Insurance Services, Inc. and Simmons First Insurance Services of TN, LLC are wholly-owned subsidiaries of Simmons Bank and are insurance agencies that offer various lines of personal and corporate insurance coverage to individual and commercial customers.

Geographic Reach

Headquartered in Pine Bluff, Arkansas, Simmons First Financial and its subsidiaries own or lease additional offices in the states of Arkansas, Kansas, Missouri, Oklahoma, Tennessee and Texas. They conduct financial operations from about 200 financial centers located in communities throughout Arkansas, Kansas, Missouri, Oklahoma, Tennessee and Texas.

Sales and Marketing

Simmons Bank also maintains a networking arrangement with a third-party broker-dealer that offers brokerage services to Simmons Bank customers, as well as a trust department that provides a variety of trust, investment, agency, and custodial services for individual and corporate clients (including, among other things, administration of estates and personal trusts, and management of investment accounts).

The company's marketing expenses were $22.2 million, $19.4 million, and $16.5 million in 2021, 2020, and 2019, respectively.

Financial Performance

For the year ended December 31, 2021, net interest income on a fully taxable equivalent basis was $610.8 million, a decrease of $40 million, or 6%, over the same period in 2020. The decrease in net interest income was primarily the result of an $80.4 million decrease in interest income, partially offset by a $40.5 million decrease in interest expense.

In 2021, the company had a net income of $271.1 million, a 6% increase from the previous year's net income of $254.9 million.

The company's cash at the end of 2021 was $1.7 billion. Operating activities generated $277.8 million, while investing activities used $2.5 billion, mainly for purchases of available-for-sale securities. Financing activities provided another $438.5 million.

Strategy

Over the past 32 years, Simmons First National has expanded its markets and services, the company's growth strategy has evolved and diversified. It has used varying acquisition and internal branching methods to enter key growth markets and increase the size of its footprint.

Merger and acquisition activities are an important part of the company's growth strategy. The company intends to focus its near-term merger and acquisition strategy on traditional mergers and acquisitions. The company continues to believe that the current economic conditions combined with the possibility of a more restrictive bank regulatory environment will cause many financial institutions to seek merger partners in the near-to-intermediate future. It also believes it community banking philosophy, access to capital and successful merger and acquisition history positions the company as a purchaser of choice for community and regional banks seeking a strong partner.

Mergers and Acquisitions

In early 2022, Simmons First National Corp. has completed the acquisition of Spirit of Texas Bancshares, Inc. (Spirit), the parent company of Spirit of Texas Bank SSB, based in Conroe, Texas in a transaction consisting of a mixture of cash and Simmons' common stock with an aggregate value of approximately $581 million. As a result of the acquisition, Spirit of Texas Bank SSB was merged into Simmons Bank (the subsidiary bank of Simmons), with Simmons Bank as the surviving institution. Conversion of technology systems and customer accounts for Spirit of Texas Bank SSB were completed over the weekend, with former Spirit of Texas Bank SSB branches opening under the Simmons Bank. It also further enhances the size and scale of our Texas franchise and positions us to increase shareholder value over time by bringing our broad array of products, services and leading-edge digital capabilities to new markets and clients.

In 2021, Simmons First National Corp has completed the acquisitions of Landmark Community Bank (Landmark) based in Collierville, Tenn., and Triumph Bancshares, Inc. (Triumph), the parent company of Triumph Bank, based in Memphis, Tenn. Landmark and Triumph are two successful, local community banks who share its philosophy of a strong credit culture, significant community involvement and a passion for delivering excellent customer service. The opportunity to combine forces with these two institutions also highly complements its existing footprint in Tennessee and enhances scale in two of its key growth markets ? Memphis and Nashville. Terms were not disclosed.

EXECUTIVES

Executive Chairman, Chairman, Chief Executive Officer, Director, George A. Makris, $745,000 total compensation

President, Chief Executive Officer, Chief Operating Officer, Subsidiary Officer, Robert A. Fehlman, $392,500 total compensation

President, Executive Vice President, Chief Financial Officer, Treasurer, Subsidiary Officer, James (Jay) M. Brogdon

Executive Vice President, Chief Administrative Officer, Chief Investor Relations Officer, Subsidiary Officer, Stephen C. Massanelli, $304,500 total compensation

Executive Vice President, General Counsel, Secretary, Subsidiary Officer, George A. Makris

Executive Vice President, Chief People Officer, Chief Strategy Officer, Subsidiary Officer, Jennifer B. Compton

Accounting Executive Vice President, Finance Executive Vice President, Accounting Chief Accounting Officer, Finance Chief Accounting Officer, Accounting Director, Finance Director, Accounting Subsidiary Officer, Finance Subsidiary Officer, David W. Garner, $170,030 total compensation

Executive Vice President, Chief Information Officer, Subsidiary Officer, Ann Madea

Subsidiary Officer, Matthew S. Reddin

Subsidiary Officer, Chad Rawls

Subsidiary Officer, Brad Yaney

Director, Jay D. Burchfield

Director, Marty D. Casteel, $392,500 total compensation

Director, William E. Clark

Director, Steven A. Cosse

Director, Mark C. Doramus

Director, Edward Drilling

Director, Eugene Hunt

Director, Jerry Hunter

Director, Susan S. Lanigan

Director, W. Scott McGeorge

Director, Tom Purvis

Director, Robert L. Shoptaw

Director, Julie L. Stackhouse

Director, Russell W. Teubner

Director, Mindy K. West

Director, Dean O. Bass

Auditors : BKD, LLP

LOCATIONS

HQ: Simmons First National Corp
501 Main Street, Pine Bluff, AR 71601
Phone: 870 541-1000
Web: www.simmonsbank.com

PRODUCTS/OPERATIONS

2015 Sales	in mil.	% of total
Interest Income		
Loans	268.4	65
Investment securities	30.6	8
Others	2.0	-
Non-interest income		
Service charges on deposit accounts	31.0	8
Debit and credit card fees	26.7	6
Mortgage lending income	11.4	3
Trust income	9.2	2
Other service charges and fees	9.9	2
others	22.4	6
Net (loss) gain on assets covered by FDIC loss share agreements	(14.8)	-
Total	396.8	100

COMPETITORS

AMES NATIONAL CORPORATION
CAMDEN NATIONAL CORPORATION
CAPITAL BANK FINANCIAL CORP.
CITY HOLDING COMPANY
F.N.B. CORPORATION
FIRST COMMONWEALTH FINANCIAL CORPORATION
FIRST MERCHANTS CORPORATION
FIRST MIDWEST BANCORP, INC.
OLD NATIONAL BANCORP
PROSPERITY BANCSHARES, INC.

HISTORICAL FINANCIALS
Company Type: Public

Income Statement — FYE: December 31

	ASSETS ($mil)	NET INCOME ($mil)	INCOME AS % OF ASSETS	EMPLOYEES
12/20	22,359.7	254.9	1.1%	2,923
12/19	21,259.1	238.1	1.1%	3,270
12/18	16,543.3	215.7	1.3%	2,654
12/17	15,055.8	92.9	0.6%	2,640
12/16	8,400.0	96.8	1.2%	1,875
Annual Growth	27.7%	27.4%	—	11.7%

2020 Year-End Financials

Return on assets: 1.1%
Return on equity: 8.5%
Long-term debt ($ mil.): —
No. of shares ($ mil.): 108.0
Sales ($ mil.): 1,008.2
Dividends
  Yield: 3.1%
  Payout: 29.6%
Market value ($ mil.): 2,333.0

	STOCK PRICE ($) FY Close	P/E High/Low		PER SHARE ($) Earnings	Dividends	Book Value
12/20	21.59	12	6	2.31	0.68	27.54
12/19	26.79	11	9	2.41	0.64	26.30
12/18	24.13	26	10	2.32	0.60	24.33
12/17	57.10	47	37	1.33	0.50	22.65
12/16	62.15	42	25	1.57	0.48	18.40
Annual Growth	(23.2%)	—	—	10.2%	9.1%	10.6%

Simply Good Foods Company (The)

EXECUTIVES

Chairman, Director, James M. Kilts
Vice-Chairman, Director, David J. West
President, Chief Executive Officer, Subsidiary Officer, Director, Joseph E. Scalzo, $715,000 total compensation
Operations Senior Vice President, David Wallis
Senior Vice President, Chief Human Resources Officer, Susan K. Hunsberger
Vice President, Chief Accounting Officer, Controller, Subsidiary Officer, Timothy A. Matthews
Business Development Senior Vice President, Strategy Senior Vice President, Business Development Chief Financial Officer, Strategy Chief Financial Officer, Shaun P. Mara, $456,666 total compensation
Chief Marketing Officer, C. Scott Parker, $451,675 total compensation
Chief Customer Officer, Jill Short Clark
Chief Legal Officer, Chief Compliance Officer, Secretary, Timothy Richard Kraft
Subsidiary Officer, Linda M. Zink
Director, Robert G. Montgomery
Director, James D. White
Director, Clayton C. Daley
Director, Nomi P. Ghez
Director, David W. Ritterbush
Director, Michelle P. Goolsby
Director, Joseph J. Schena
Director, Brian K. Ratzan
Auditors : DELOITTE & TOUCHE LLP

LOCATIONS

HQ: Simply Good Foods Company (The)
1225 17th Street, Suite 1000, Denver, CO 80202
Phone: 303 633-2840
Web: www.thesimplygoodfoodscompany.com

HISTORICAL FINANCIALS
Company Type: Public

Income Statement — FYE: August 28

	REVENUE ($mil)	NET INCOME ($mil)	NET PROFIT MARGIN	EMPLOYEES
08/21	1,005.6	40.8	4.1%	263
08/20	816.6	34.7	4.2%	300
08/19	523.3	47.5	9.1%	150
08/18	431.4	70.4	16.3%	141
08/17	56.3	0.4	0.8%	145
Annual Growth	105.5%	208.7%	—	16.1%

2021 Year-End Financials

Debt ratio: 22.0%
Return on equity: 3.3%
Cash ($ mil.): 75.3
Current Ratio: 2.63
Long-term debt ($ mil.): 450.5
No. of shares ($ mil.): 95.7
Dividends
  Yield: —
  Payout: —
Market value ($ mil.): 3,386.0

	STOCK PRICE ($) FY Close	P/E High/Low		PER SHARE ($) Earnings	Dividends	Book Value
08/21	35.35	88	44	0.42	0.00	12.41
08/20	25.39	82	40	0.35	0.00	12.89
08/19	29.63	51	29	0.56	0.00	10.23
08/18	17.98	18	11	0.96	0.00	9.53
08/17	11.88	122	31175	0.01	0.00	8.48
Annual Growth	31.3%	—	—	154.6%	—	10.0%

Simpson Manufacturing Co., Inc. (DE)

Through its subsidiaries, Simpson Manufacturing designs, engineers and is a leading manufacturer of high quality wood and concrete building construction products designed to make structures safer and more secure, and that perform at high levels. Subsidiary Simpson Strong-Tie (SST) makes more than 14,000 types of standard and custom products that are used to connect and reinforce joints between wood, concrete, and masonry building components, which the company markets globally and distributes through home centers and a network of contractor and dealer distributors. The company's products are sold primarily in Canada, Europe, Asia, the US, and the Pacific. More than 85% of sales were generated from the US.

Operations

The company is organized into three reporting segments: North America (over 85% of sales), Europe (over 10%), and the Asia/Pacific.

The North America segment is comprised primarily of the company's operations in the US and Canada, the Europe segment and the Asia/Pacific segment is comprised of the company's operations in Asia, the South Pacific, and the Middle East.

Simpson divides its product lines across two main categories: wood construction (more than 85% of sales) and concrete construction (about 15%).

Geographic Reach

Headquartered in Pleasanton, California, Simpson has manufacturing facilities in Stockton and San Bernardino County, California, McKinney, Texas, West Chicago, Illinois, Columbus, Ohio, and Gallatin, Tennessee. The principal manufacturing facilities located outside the US, are in France, Denmark, Germany, Poland, Switzerland, Sweden, Portugal and China. It also owns and leases smaller manufacturing facilities, warehouses, research and development facilities and sales offices in the US, Canada, the UK, Europe, Asia, Australia, New Zealand, and Chile. The US accounted for more than 85% of its revenue, the company's largest market.

Sales and Marketing

Simpson sells its products through multiple channels including contractor distributors, home centers and co-ops, lumber dealers and OEMs. SST markets its products to the residential construction, light industrial, and commercial construction, remodeling, and do-it-yourself (DIY) markets.

Advertising costs were $8.4 million, $8.2

million, and 8.2 million in 2021, 2020, and 2019 respectively.

Financial Performance

Net Sales increased 24% to $1.6 billion from $1.3 billion primarily due to product price increases that took effect throughout 2021 in an effort to offset rising material costs as well as higher sales volumes.

Net income for fiscal 2021 was $266.4 million compared to the prior year with $187.0 million.

Cash held by the company at the end of fiscal 2021 increased to $301.2 million. Cash provided by operations was $151.3 million while cash used for investing and financing activities were $58.8 million and $71.6 million, respectively. Main uses of cash were capital expenditures and dividends paid.

Strategy

The company intends to continue efforts to increase market share in both the wood construction and concrete construction product groups by: maintaining frequent customer contacts and service levels; continuing to sponsor seminars to inform architects, engineers, contractors and building officials on appropriate use, proper installation and identification of the company's products; continuing to invest in mobile, web and software applications for customers to both help them do their jobs more efficiently and allow us to connect with them utilizing social media, blog posts and videos; continuing to invest in Building Information Modeling ("BIM") software services and solutions for home builders and lumber-building material suppliers; and continuing to innovate, advance and diversify its product offerings.

Mergers and Acquisitions

In 2022, Simpson completes the acquisition of the ETANCO Group (ETANCO), a leading designer and manufacturer of fixing and fastening solutions for the European building construction market, for 725 million euros (approximately $800 million), net of cash. The acquisition of Etanco fortifies its footprint and expands its geographical reach in Europe, deepens Simpson's portfolio of solutions with new and existing customers, and allows Simpson to enter into new commercial building markets and grow its direct sales activity across the region. Further, Simpson expects the acquisition to drive significant net sales growth with operating income synergies of approximately $30 million on an annual run rate basis.

EXECUTIVES

Chairman, Director, James S. Andrasick
President, Chief Executive Officer, Director, Michael Olosky
Finance Senior Vice President, Kevin Swartzendruber, $270,000 total compensation
Chief Financial Officer, Treasurer, Brian J. Magstadt, $500,000 total compensation
Subsidiary Officer, Roger Dankel, $460,000 total compensation
Director, Kenneth D. Knight
Director, Karen W. Colonias, $740,000 total compensation
Director, Jennifer A. Chatman
Director, Gary M. Cusumano
Director, Philip E. Donaldson
Director, Celeste Volz Ford
Director, Robin Greenway MacGillivray
Auditors: Grant Thornton LLP

LOCATIONS

HQ: Simpson Manufacturing Co., Inc. (DE)
5956 W. Las Positas Blvd., Pleasanton, CA 94588
Phone: 925 560-9000   **Fax:** 925 833-1496
Web: www.simpsonmfg.com

2015 Sales

	$ mil.	% of total
North America	676.6	85
Europe	108.1	14
Asia/Pacific	9.4	1
Total	794.1	100

PRODUCTS/OPERATIONS

2015 Sales

	$ in mil	% of total
Wood construction	674.3	85
Concrete construction	119.5	15
Other	0.3	-
Total	794.1	100

Selected Products

Simpson Strong-Tie
   Adhesives
   Mechanical anchors
   Powder-actuated tools
   Screw fastening systems
   Shearwalls
   Wood-to-concrete connectors
   Wood-to-masonry connectors
   Wood-to-wood connectors

Selected Subsidiaries

Simpson Strong-Tie Australia, Inc.
Simpson Strong-Tie Canada, Limited
Simpson Strong-Tie Company Inc.
Simpson Strong-Tie Europe EURL
Simpson Strong-Tie International, Inc.
Simpson Strong-Tie Japan, Inc.

COMPETITORS

BEACON ROOFING SUPPLY, INC.
DMC GLOBAL INC.
GEORGIA TN INC
GIBRALTAR INDUSTRIES, INC.
GOULD ELECTRONICS INC.
NV Bekaert SA
Q.E.P. CO., INC.
RMI TITANIUM COMPANY, LLC
Raymor Industries Inc
Rio Tinto Fer et Titane Inc

HISTORICAL FINANCIALS

Company Type: Public

Income Statement

FYE: December 31

	NET REVENUE ($mil)	NET INCOME ($mil)	NET PROFIT MARGIN	EMPLOYEES
12/20	1,267.9	187.0	14.7%	3,562
12/19	1,136.5	133.9	11.8%	3,337
12/18	1,078.8	126.6	11.7%	3,135
12/17	977.0	92.6	9.5%	2,902
12/16	860.6	89.7	10.4%	2,647
Annual Growth	10.2%	20.1%	—	7.7%

2020 Year-End Financials

Debt ratio: —   No. of shares ($ mil.): 43.3
Return on equity: 19.9%   Dividends
Cash ($ mil.): 274.6   Yield: 0.9%
Current Ratio: 3.88   Payout: 21.5%
Long-term debt ($ mil.): —   Market value ($ mil.): 4,049.0

	STOCK PRICE ($) FY Close	P/E High/Low		PER SHARE ($) Earnings	Dividends	Book Value
12/20	93.45	24	11	4.27	0.92	22.64
12/19	80.23	28	18	2.98	0.91	20.18
12/18	54.13	28	18	2.72	0.86	19.01
12/17	57.41	31	21	1.94	0.78	18.93
12/16	43.75	26	16	1.86	0.68	18.25
Annual Growth	20.9%	—	—	23.1%	7.8%	5.5%

Simulations Plus Inc

Molecular modeling software plus applications to help individuals with disabilities equals Simulations Plus. The company is a leading provider of applications used by pharmaceutical researchers to model absorption rates for orally dosed drug compounds. Its Words+ subsidiary provides augmentative communication software and input devices that help people with disabilities use computers. Simulations Plus also provides educational software targeted to high school and college students through its FutureLab unit. Pharmaceutical giants GlaxoSmithKline and Roche are among its clients. CEO Walter Woltosz and his wife, Virginia (a director), together own about 40% of the company.

EXECUTIVES

Chairman, Director, Walter S. Woltosz, $199,010 total compensation
Chief Executive Officer, Shawn O'Connor, $54,167 total compensation
Chief Financial Officer, Secretary, William W. Frederick
Marketing Division Officer, Sales Division Officer, John Anthony DiBella, $229,657 total compensation
Division Officer, Jill Fiedler-Kelly
Division Officer, Brett Howell
Lead Independent Director, Director, Daniel Weiner
Director, Sharlene Evans
Director, John Kenneth Paglia
Director, Lisa LaVange

Auditors : Rose, Snyder & Jacobs LLP

LOCATIONS

HQ: Simulations Plus Inc
42505 10th Street West, Lancaster, CA 93534-7059
Phone: 661 723-7723   **Fax:** 661 723-5524
Web: www.simulations-plus.com

PRODUCTS/OPERATIONS

Selected Products
Augmentative Communication Products
  Cyberlink
  E Z Keys for Windows
  Freedom 2000
  HeadMouse
  MessageMate
  SoftSwitch
  Talking Screen for Windows
  Tracker One
  TuffTalker
Educational Software
  Circuits for Physical Science
  Gravity for Physical Science
  Ideal Gas for Chemistry
  Optics for Physical Science
  Universal Gravitation for Physical Science
Pharmaceutical Applications
  GastroPlus
  QMPRchitect
  QMPRPlus

COMPETITORS

CDW TECHNOLOGIES LLC
CERNER CORPORATION
INFORMATION BUILDERS, INC.
SOFT COMPUTER CONSULTANTS INC.
SUNQUEST INFORMATION SYSTEMS, INC.

HISTORICAL FINANCIALS

Company Type: Public

Income Statement — FYE: August 31

	REVENUE ($mil)	NET INCOME ($mil)	NET PROFIT MARGIN	EMPLOYEES
08/21	46.4	9.7	21.1%	146
08/20	41.5	9.3	22.4%	137
08/19	33.9	8.5	25.3%	111
08/18	29.6	8.9	30.1%	95
08/17	24.1	5.7	24.0%	86
Annual Growth	17.8%	14.0%	—	14.1%

2021 Year-End Financials

Debt ratio: —   No. of shares ($ mil.): 20.1
Return on equity: 6.0%   Dividends
Cash ($ mil.): 36.9   Yield: 0.5%
Current Ratio: 12.04   Payout: 42.8%
Long-term debt ($ mil.): —   Market value ($ mil.): 892.0

	STOCK PRICE ($) FY Close	P/E High/Low		PER SHARE ($) Earnings	Dividends	Book Value
08/21	44.30	183	86	0.47	0.24	8.23
08/20	59.58	139	52	0.50	0.24	7.83
08/19	36.11	85	36	0.48	0.24	2.14
08/18	20.85	46	28	0.50	0.24	1.83
08/17	14.50	47	25	0.33	0.20	1.49
Annual Growth	32.2%	—	—	9.2%	4.7%	53.2%

SiteOne Landscape Supply Inc

EXECUTIVES

Chairman, Chief Executive Officer, Director, Doug Black, $750,000 total compensation
Executive Vice President, Chief Financial Officer, Assistant Secretary, John T. Guthrie, $336,538 total compensation
Executive Vice President, General Counsel, Secretary, L. Briley Brisendine, $378,269 total compensation
Development Executive Vice President, Strategy Executive Vice President, Scott Salmon
Human Resources Executive Vice President, Joseph Ketter, $114,231 total compensation
Operations Division Officer, Greg Weller
Lead Director, Director, William W. Douglas
Director, Fred M. Diaz
Director, W. Roy Dunbar
Director, Larisa J. Drake
Director, Jeri L. Isbell
Director, Jack L. Wyszomierski
Auditors : DELOITTE & TOUCHE LLP

LOCATIONS

HQ: SiteOne Landscape Supply Inc
300 Colonial Center Parkway, Suite 600, Roswell, GA 30076
Phone: 470 277-7000
Web: www.siteone.com

HISTORICAL FINANCIALS

Company Type: Public

Income Statement — FYE: January 3

	REVENUE ($mil)	NET INCOME ($mil)	NET PROFIT MARGIN	EMPLOYEES
01/21*	2,704.5	121.3	4.5%	4,900
12/19	2,357.5	77.7	3.3%	4,600
12/18	2,112.3	73.9	3.5%	4,300
12/17	1,861.7	54.6	2.9%	3,800
01/17	1,648.2	30.6	1.9%	3,300
Annual Growth	13.2%	41.1%	—	10.4%

*Fiscal year change

2021 Year-End Financials

Debt ratio: 18.0%   No. of shares ($ mil.): 44.2
Return on equity: 20.0%   Dividends
Cash ($ mil.): 55.2   Yield: —
Current Ratio: 2.31   Payout: —
Long-term debt ($ mil.): 293.1   Market value ($ mil.): 7,024.0

	STOCK PRICE ($) FY Close	P/E High/Low		PER SHARE ($) Earnings	Dividends	Book Value
01/21*	158.63	56	20	2.75	0.00	17.95
12/19	90.46	49	25	1.82	0.00	9.46
12/18	55.59	52	28	1.73	0.00	7.38
12/17	76.70	56	26	1.29	0.00	5.33
01/17	34.73	—	—	(3.01)	0.00	3.76
Annual Growth	46.2%	—	—	—	—	47.8%

*Fiscal year change

SJW Group

It is hard to water down SJW Group's contribution in quenching America's thirst. A holding company, it owns public utility services that engage in the production, storage, purification, distribution, and retail sale of water. Its two main subsidiaries, the San Jose Water Company and Canyon Lake Water Service Company (CLWSC), serves nearly 1.5 million residents in California and Texas through nearly 250,000 water connections. The SJW Land Company is a holder of some undeveloped land in Tennessee. In October 2019, the SJW Group announced the close of their merger with the public utility Connecticut Water Service.

Operations

SJW Group owns four subsidiaries.

Public utility San Jose Water serves about one million Californians through approximately 231,000 connections in the San Jose county. It also provides non-tariffed services (water system operations, maintenance, antenna site leases) under agreements with municipalities and other utilities. The utility's water supply comprises groundwater from wells, surface water from watershed run-off and diversion, reclaimed water, and water purchased from third parties.

CLWSC, the second subsidiary supplies water to 54,000 Texans through 18,000 connections in the growing region between the cities of San Antonio and Austin. Its water supply consists of groundwater from wells and purchased treated and raw water from a third party.

SJWNE LLC, is a special purpose entity established to hold SJW Group's investment in Connecticut Water Service, Inc. The business provides water service to approximately 137,000 connections that serve a population of approximately 480,000 people in 80 municipalities throughout Connecticut and Maine and more than 3,000 wastewater connections in Southbury, Connecticut.

SJW Land Company, owns undeveloped real estate property, commercial and warehouse properties in Tennessee.

Overall, SJW Group generates its revenue from Water Utility Services.

Geographic Reach

San Jose Water Company's water production system is in Santa Clara, California. It owns 7,000 acres of land, a storage capacity of 2.3 billion-gallon reservoirs and 248 million gallons of distribution, as well as about 2,500 miles of transmission and distribution mains.

The CLWSC subsidiary has more than 245 sq. mile service area located in the southern region of the Texas hill country in Comal and Blanco counties with 8,200 surface acre reservoir (Canyon Lake). It also holds a contract for 2 billion gallons of untreated surface water and 235 million gallons of treated surface water from annually. Additionally, the subsidiary owns and operates three surface water treatment plants (9 million gallons/d), about 645 miles of transmission and distribution mains, and maintains 63 storage tanks.

SJW Land Company owns approximately 55 acres of property in the state of Tennessee.

Sales and Marketing
SJW Group serves residential, business, Industrial, and Public customers.

Financial Performance
SJW Group revenue has shown an upward trajectory in the last five years. Net income peaked in 2017 but declined the next two years.

Revenue increased 6% to $420.5 million in 2019 primarily due to revenue increase of $22.9 million in Water Utility Services offset by a decrease of $0.08 million from Real Estate Services.

SJW Group's consolidated net income in 2019 was $23,403, compared to $38,767 for the same period in 2018. The decrease in net income was primarily due to costs incurred related to integration with the new operations in CTWS, an increase in production expenses due to higher usage and higher per unit costs for purchased water, ground water extraction and energy charges, and higher depreciation expenses due to assets placed in service in 2018, partially offset by an increase in operating revenue and decrease in costs due to the increased use of surface water.

SJW Group had only around $18 million in cash holdings at the end of 2019. Operations provided $130 million, and financing activities added another $485 million. Investment activities used $1 billion for business payments and acquisitions.

Strategy
The company's business strategy focuses on Regional regulated water utility operations, Regional non-tariffed water utility - related services provided following the guidelines established by the Regulators, and Out-of-region water and utility - related services. As part of our pursuit of the above three strategic areas, we consider from time to time opportunities to acquire businesses and assets, for example, the merger with CTWS.

SJW Group plans and applies a diligent and disciplined approach to maintaining and improving its water system infrastructures and also seeks to acquire regulated water systems adjacent to or near its existing service territory. CTWS also provides regulated wastewater services through HVWC. It also seeks appropriate non-tariffed business opportunities that complement its existing operations or that allow it to extend its core competencies beyond existing operations.

Mergers and Acquisitions
In late 2019, SJW Group and Connecticut Water Service, Inc. closed their merger. "As a leading national water and wastewater utility, we are well positioned to deliver significant benefits to all of our stakeholders, including shareholders, customers, employees and the local communities we serve," said Eric W. Thornburg, Chairman, President and Chief Executive Officer of SJW Group.

Company Background
The company has geographically diversified its regulated water operations, moving into Central Texas (through the acquisition of Canyon Lake Water Service) in 2006. SJW acquired four water systems in Comal County (Texas) in 2011.

EXECUTIVES

Chairman, President, Chief Executive Officer, Subsidiary Officer, Director, Eric W. Thornburg, $700,000 total compensation
Chief Financial Officer, Principal Accounting Officer, Treasurer, Subsidiary Officer, Andrew F. Walters, $357,000 total compensation
Chief Operating Officer, Subsidiary Officer, Bruce A. Hauk
Finance Senior Vice President, Finance Principal Accounting Officer, Finance Subsidiary Officer, Mohammed (Rally) G. Zerhouni
Subsidiary Officer, Andrew R. Gere, $461,000 total compensation
Director, Carl Guardino
Director, Mary Ann Hanley
Director, Heather Hunt
Director, Rebecca A. Klein
Director, Gregory P. Landis
Director, Daniel B. More
Director, Carol P. Wallace
Director, Katharine Armstrong
Auditors: Deloitte & Touche LLP

LOCATIONS
HQ: SJW Group
110 West Taylor Street, San Jose, CA 95110
Phone: 408 279-7800
Web: www.sjwater.com

PRODUCTS/OPERATIONS

2016 Sales

	$ mil.	% of total
Water utility services		
Regulated	326.6	96
Non-regulated	6.4	2
Real estate services	6.7	2
Total	339.7	100

Selected Subsidiaries and Affiliates
California Water Service Group (minority stake, water utility)
San Jose Water Company (water utility)
SJW Land Company (parking facilities and commercial real estate)
SJWTX, Inc. (Canyon Lake Water Service Company -- water utility)
Texas Water Alliance Limited (water supply development)

COMPETITORS

AMERICAN STATES WATER COMPANY
AMERICAN WATER WORKS COMPANY, INC.
ARTESIAN RESOURCES CORPORATION
COLORADO SPRINGS UTILITIES
CONNECTICUT WATER SERVICE, INC.
DEE VALLEY GROUP LIMITED
LOS ANGELES DEPARTMENT OF WATER AND POWER
NORTHWEST NATURAL GAS COMPANY
SAN ANTONIO WATER SYSTEM
THE YORK WATER COMPANY

HISTORICAL FINANCIALS
Company Type: Public

Income Statement — FYE: December 31

	REVENUE ($mil)	NET INCOME ($mil)	NET PROFIT MARGIN	EMPLOYEES
12/20	564.5	61.5	10.9%	748
12/19	420.4	23.4	5.6%	732
12/18	397.6	38.7	9.7%	416
12/17	389.2	59.2	15.2%	411
12/16	339.7	52.8	15.6%	406
Annual Growth	13.5%	3.9%	—	16.5%

2020 Year-End Financials
Debt ratio: 46.5%
Return on equity: 6.7%
Cash ($ mil.): 5.2
Current Ratio: 0.36
Long-term debt ($ mil.): 1,287.5
No. of shares ($ mil.): 28.5
Dividends
  Yield: 1.8%
  Payout: 59.8%
Market value ($ mil.): 1,981.0

	STOCK PRICE ($) FY Close	P/E High/Low		PER SHARE ($) Earnings	Dividends	Book Value
12/20	69.36	35	23	2.14	1.28	32.12
12/19	71.06	91	67	0.82	1.20	31.28
12/18	55.62	37	28	1.82	1.29	31.31
12/17	63.83	24	16	2.86	1.04	22.57
12/16	55.98	22	11	2.57	0.81	20.61
Annual Growth	5.5%	—	—	(4.5%)	12.1%	11.7%

Skyline Champion Corp

Skyline's idea of a beautiful skyline would probably include several rows of double-wides. The company and its subsidiaries design and make manufactured homes. It distributes them to independent dealers and manufactured housing communities throughout the US and Canada. About half of Skyline's revenues come from selling HUD-code manufactured homes (products built according to US Housing and Urban Development standards); the rest of its typically two- to four-bedroom homes are modular in design.

HISTORY

Julius Decio started Skyline Coach in 1951 in a friend's welding garage. At first the company made mobile homes, but by 1959 it was also producing travel trailers and recreational vehicles (RVs). Skyline went public in 1960. Two years later it acquired Homette and Layton Homes, and in 1963 it bought Buddy Mobile Homes. The company changed its name to Skyline Corporation and acquired Academy Mobile Homes in 1966. It purchased Country Vans Conversion in 1978.

Skyline's manufactured home sales

increased during the 1990s, but they failed to keep pace with industrywide growth. The company's market share faded. Blaming the loss of market share on a lack of dealers in high-growth regions, in 1995 Skyline made plans to increase production, expand its product line, and boost market penetration. Product lines in 1997 stressed luxury features such as solid-oak cabinets and cedar-lined wardrobes. Harsh winter weather lowered sales that year. A long-reaching industrywide recession, which continued into 2004, began during that time.

Although RV sales -- especially fifth-wheel and truck camper sales -- dropped in fiscal 1998, sales of higher-priced multi-section homes increased. By 2000 rising interest rates and inventories were contributing to industrywide declines: That year Skyline's RV sales fell nearly 25% and its manufactured homes sales were off by more than 15%. Sales of manufactured homes dropped again in fiscal 2001 by 20%. The company's sales continued to drop in 2002 although its operating income increased by about 10%, due in part to increased RV sales and containment of operating costs. The next year saw more declines for Skyline. By 2004 the manufactured housing industry hit its lowest level in more than a dozen years. Restrictive retail financing, global tensions, and uncertain economic conditions were primary factors that contributed to the recession.

In 2004 Skyline moved to expand its product offerings by gaining approval to produce modular homes at 12 of its manufactured housing facilities. The company also began to reposition its RV segment to accommodate a shift in consumer demand for towable RVs.

EXECUTIVES

Chairman, Director, Timothy J. Bernlohr
President, Chief Executive Officer, Director, Mark H. Yost, $395,833 total compensation
Executive Vice President, Chief Financial Officer, Secretary, Laurie Hough, $312,500 total compensation
Operations Executive Vice President, Joseph Kimmell, $208,333 total compensation
Business Development Executive Vice President, Sales Executive Vice President, J. Wade Lyall
Senior Vice President, Secretary, General Counsel, Robert Spence
Vice President, Controller, Timothy A. Burkhardt, $250,000 total compensation
Chief Growth Officer, Tim Larson
Director, Keith Anderson, $520,833 total compensation
Director, Michael Berman
Director, Eddie Capel
Director, Michael Kaufman
Director, Erin Mulligan Nelson
Director, Gary E. Robinette

Director, Nikul Patel
Auditors : Ernst & Young LLP

LOCATIONS

HQ: Skyline Champion Corp
755 West Big Beaver Road, Suite 1000, Troy, MI 48084
Phone: 248 614-8211
Web: www.skylinechampion.com

COMPETITORS

APEX HOMES, INC.
CAVCO INDUSTRIES, INC.
CHAMPION ENTERPRISES HOLDINGS, LLC
DANDI SYSTEMS, INC
DYNAMIC HOMES, LLC
GLOBAL DIVERSIFIED INDUSTRIES, INC.
HOVNANIAN ENTERPRISES, INC.
LOG CABIN HOMES LTD.
PLAYCORE HOLDINGS, L.L.C.
Viceroy Homes Limited

HISTORICAL FINANCIALS
Company Type: Public

Income Statement — FYE: April 3

	REVENUE ($mil)	NET INCOME ($mil)	NET PROFIT MARGIN	EMPLOYEES
04/21*	1,420.8	84.8	6.0%	7,700
03/20	1,369.7	58.1	4.2%	6,600
03/19	1,360.0	(58.2)	—	7,000
03/18	1,064.7	15.8	1.5%	0
05/17	236.5	0.0	0.0%	1,300
Annual Growth	56.6%	1041.5%	—	56.0%

*Fiscal year change

2021 Year-End Financials
Debt ratio: 4.3%
Return on equity: 16.0%
Cash ($ mil.): 262.5
Current Ratio: 1.90
Long-term debt ($ mil.): 39.3
No. of shares ($ mil.): 56.6
Dividends
  Yield: —
  Payout: —
Market value ($ mil.): 2,686.0

	STOCK PRICE ($) FY Close	P/E High/Low		PER SHARE ($) Earnings	Dividends	Book Value
04/21*	47.42	32	8	1.49	0.00	10.04
03/20	15.42	35	13	1.02	0.00	8.37
03/19	19.00	—	—	(1.09)	0.62	7.27
03/18	22.00	74	16	0.33	0.00	0.00
05/17	5.26	—	—	0.00	0.00	3.01
Annual Growth	73.3%	—	—	—	—	35.1%

*Fiscal year change

Sleep Number Corp

Sleep Number Corporation (formerly Select Comfort Corporation) is at the forefront of delivering this life-changing benefit with its revolutionary Sleep Number 360 smart beds and SleepIQ technology, which improved nearly 14 million lives. A leading bedding retailer in the US, the company operates about 650 company-owned stores in the US. The air-bed maker also sells through a company-operated call center, its own website, phone and chat. Sleep Number was founded in 1987 and has grown to become one of the nation's leading bed makers and retailers.

Operations

Sleep Number's vertically integrated business model and role as the exclusive designer, manufacturer, marketer, retailer and servicer of Sleep Number beds offers high-quality, individualized sleep solutions and services.

Sleep Number 360 smart beds effortlessly deliver proven quality sleep by allowing each sleeper to set their ideal firmness, support and pressure-relieving comfort ? their Sleep Number setting. SleepIQ technology optimizes the smart benefits of the bed, continually improving a sleeper's restful time asleep ? their SleepIQ score ? to deliver a life-changing difference to their overall health and wellness.

The company unveils the next generation of 360 smart beds with technology to advance its health and wellness platform and made several new sleep innovations available through SleepIQ technology platform that include Sleep Circadian Analytics, Sleep Wellness Reports, Heart Rate Variability, My Daytime Alertness and My Sleep Health.

In addition, Sleep Number offers a full line of exclusive FlexFit smart adjustable bases that allow customers to raise the head or foot of the bed. These industry-leading bases seamlessly integrate with the 360 smart bed to deliver features like the company's Partner Snore technology, which allows a sleeping partner to temporarily relieve mild snoring by raising the companion's head at the touch of a button.

The company's retail accounts for more than 85% of the revenue, while online, phone and chat sales generate about 15%.

Geographic Reach

Headquartered in Minneapolis, Minnesota, Sleep Number has nearly 650 retail stores in about 50 US states. The company leases two manufacturing, assembly, and distribution centers in Irmo, South Carolina and Salt Lake City, Utah.

Sales and Marketing

Sleep Number markets and sells its products through customer service staff, brochures, videos, websites, customer mailings, and in-store signage. The company's customer touchpoints include Stores, online, phone and chat. Online, phone, chat and other sales account for nearly 15% of the company's net sales.

The company's advertising expenses were approximately $323 million, $253 million and $242 million in 2021, 2020 and 2019, respectively.

Financial Performance

Adjusting to exclude the estimated impact from this additional week in 2020, it increased annual 2021 net sales by 20% to $2.2 billion, grew 2021 earnings per diluted share (EPS) by 34% to $6.16 and generated cash from operations of $300 million.

In 2021, the company had a net income of $153.7 million, a 10% increase from the previous year's net income of $139.2 million.

The company's cash at the end of 2021 was $2.4 million. Operating activities generated $300 million, while investing activities used $66.6 million, mainly for purchases of property and equipment. Financing activities used another $235.2 million, mainly for repurchases of common stock.

Strategy

In 2022, Select Comfort formed a landmark partnership with the American Cancer Society to study the connection between cancer and quality sleep, with the goal of developing the first-ever sleep strategies and guidance for cancer patients and survivors. Over six years, American Cancer Society will conduct research with contributions from Sleep Number's proprietary sleep data, leading to improved sleep outcomes for cancer patients and survivors. The company's partnership will advance not only the fundamental understanding of the science of sleep but also the translation of that knowledge into practical actions that provide meaningful outcomes.

Mergers and Acquisitions

In 2015, Select Comfort acquired BAM Labs Inc., a provider of biometric sensor and sleep monitoring for data-driven health and wellness. The acquisition broadens and deepens Select Comfort's electrical, biomedical, software, and backend capabilities in providing sleep-related information to mattress customers.

Company Background

Sleep Number was incorporated in 1987 and became publicly traded in 1998, listed on the Nasdaq Stock Market LLC (Nasdaq Global Select Market) under the symbol "SNBR".

EXECUTIVES

President, Chief Executive Officer, Director,
Shelly R. Ibach, $926,923 total compensation

Executive Vice President, 2021, Joseph H. Saklad

Executive Vice President, Interim Chief Financial Officer, Chief Human Resources Officer, Chris Krusmark

Executive Vice President, Chief Innovation Officer, Andrea L. Bloomquist, $429,484 total compensation

Executive Vice President, Chief Sales and Services Officer, Melissa Barra

Vice President, Treasurer, Chief Accounting Officer, Joel Laing

Director, Michael J. Harrison
Director, Deborah L. Kilpatrick
Director, Barbara R. Matas
Director, Julie M. Howard
Director, Angel L. Mendez
Director, Daniel Alegre
Director, Phillip M. Eyler
Director, Stephen L. Gulis
Director, Brenda J. Lauderback
Auditors: DELOITTE & TOUCHE LLP

LOCATIONS

HQ: Sleep Number Corp
1001 Third Avenue South, Minneapolis, MN 55404
Phone: 763 551-7000
Web: www.sleepnumber.com

2015 Company-Owned Stores

	No.
Alabama	7
Arizona	8
Arkansas	4
California	59
Colorado	11
Connecticut	5
Delaware	2
Florida	30
Georgia	17
Idaho	2
Illinois	18
Indiana	11
Iowa	8
Kansas	6
Kentucky	7
Louisiana	7
Maine	2
Maryland	11
Massachusetts	9
Michigan	13
Minnesota	13
Mississippi	5
Missouri	14
Montana	2
Nebraska	3
Nevada	5
New Hampshire	4
New Jersey	15
New Mexico	3
New York	14
North Carolina	13
North Dakota	3
Ohio	18
Oklahoma	4
Oregon	6
Pennsylvania	18
Rhode Island	1
South Carolina	7
South Dakota	2
Tennessee	10
Texas	45
Utah	4
Vermont	1
Virginia	17
Washington	11
Wisconsin	11
West Virginia	1
Wyoming	1
Total	**488**

PRODUCTS/OPERATIONS

2015 Sales

	% of total
Retail	92
Online and call center	6
Wholesale	2
Total	**100**

Selected Products

Bed frames
Foundations
Mattress pads
Mattresses
Pillows
Pillowtops
Sleep Number SofaBed

COMPETITORS

BAZAARVOICE, INC.
BF REALISATIONS LIMITED
FLEXSTEEL INDUSTRIES, INC.
HAVERTY FURNITURE COMPANIES, INC.
KOZEE SLEEP PRODUCTS LTD
LEGGETT & PLATT, INCORPORATED
SEALY CORPORATION
SSB MANUFACTURING COMPANY
TEMPUR SEALY INTERNATIONAL, INC.
WAYFAIR INC.

HISTORICAL FINANCIALS

Company Type: Public

Income Statement			FYE: January 2	
	REVENUE ($mil)	NET INCOME ($mil)	NET PROFIT MARGIN	EMPLOYEES
01/21*	1,856.5	139.1	7.5%	4,679
12/19	1,698.3	81.8	4.8%	4,476
12/18	1,531.5	69.5	4.5%	4,220
12/17	1,444.4	65.0	4.5%	4,099
12/16	1,311.2	51.4	3.9%	3,768
Annual Growth	9.1%	28.3%	—	5.6%

*Fiscal year change

2021 Year-End Financials

Debt ratio: 30.5%
Return on equity: —
Cash ($ mil.): 4.2
Current Ratio: 0.28
Long-term debt ($ mil.): —
No. of shares ($ mil.): 25.3
Dividends
  Yield: —
  Payout: —
Market value ($ mil.): 2,078.0

	STOCK PRICE ($) FY Close	P/E High/Low		PER SHARE ($) Earnings	Dividends	Book Value
01/21*	81.86	18	3	4.90	0.00	(8.82)
12/19	49.59	19	11	2.70	0.00	(5.70)
12/18	32.13	20	14	1.92	0.00	(3.55)
12/17	37.59	24	12	1.55	0.00	2.30
12/16	22.62	25	14	1.10	0.00	3.68
Annual Growth	37.9%	—	—	45.3%	—	—

*Fiscal year change

SLM Corp.

SLM Corporation, more commonly known as Sallie Mae, holds some $19.6 billion in private education loans and originates some $5.4 billion of loans. Its Private Education Loans include important protections for the family, including loan forgiveness in case of death or permanent disability of the student borrower, a free, quarterly FICO score benefit to students and cosigners and, for borrowers with a Smart Option Student Loan, on-line tutoring services to help students succeed in school. SLM's main subsidiary Sallie Mae Bank is one of the nation's largest education loan providers, and specializes in originating, acquiring, financing, and servicing private student loans, which are not guaranteed by the government.

Operations

SLM's primary business is to originate and service high-quality private education loans. It helps students and families to funds their education through financial aid, federal loans and student and families' resources. Its main subsidiary, Sallie Mae Bank, offers traditional savings products, such as high-yield savings accounts, money market accounts, and certificates of deposit, originates private education loans, and manages a loan portfolio that also includes personal loans, loans insured or guaranteed under the previously existing Federal Family Education program, (FFELP Loans) and credit card loans.

Sallie Mae offers three types of credit cards, each uniquely designed to promote and reward financial responsibility, including a card that offers a cash back bonus that cardholders can apply to pay down a student loan.

SmartyPig product is a free, FDIC-insured, online, goal-based savings account that helps consumers save for long- and short-term goals. Its tiered interest rates reward consumers for growing their savings.

It also offers six loan products for specific graduate programs of study. These include the Sallie Mae Law School Loan, the Sallie Mae MBA Loan, the Sallie Mae Health Professions Graduate Loan, the Sallie Mae Medical School Loan, the Sallie Mae Dental School Loan, and the Sallie Mae Graduate School Loan. These products were designed to address the specific needs of graduate students, such as extended grace periods for medical students.

About 75% of sales were generated through loans. Its loan portfolio consists of private education loans with over 95%, and FFELP loans with less than 5%.

Geographic Reach
Newark, Delaware-based Sallie Mae serves students attending schools and universities in the US and has operations in Indiana, Virginia, Massachusetts, and Utah.

Sales and Marketing
The core of Sallie Mae's marketing strategy is to promote its loan products through financial aid offices at universities, colleges, and other centers of higher education. Its on-campus operations are led by sales force who work with some 2,300 higher education institutions are led by its relationship management team, the largest in the industry, which has become a trusted resource for financial aid offices.

Financial Performance
For the last five years, SLM's revenue increased by 80% and net income jumped by 302%.

Total revenue for the year increased to $2.0 billion on the back of a $301 million increase in non-interest income, partially offset by an $85 million increase in net interest income.

In 2021, the company had a net income of $1.2 billion, a 32% increase from the previous year. The year-over-year increase was primarily attributable to increases in gains on sales of loans, net, other income, lower provisions for credit losses, and lower operating expenses, which were offset by a decline in total net interest income.

The company's cash at the end of 2021 was $4.5 billion. Investing activities generated $2.6 billion, while operating and financing activities each used $49.5 million and $2.6 billion, respectively. Main cash uses were for repaid borrowings and decrease in certificates of deposit.

Strategy
SLM's focus remains on maximizing the profitability and growth of its core private student loan business, while harnessing and optimizing the power of its brand and attractive client base. In addition, it continues to seek to better inform the external narrative about student lending and Sallie Mae's role in helping students and families responsibly plan and pay for college. It also strives to maintain a rigorous and predictable capital allocation and return program to create shareholder value. Its internal focus is to drive a mission-led culture that continues to make Sallie Mae a great place to work. Finally, SLM continue to strengthen its risk and compliance efforts, to enhance and build upon its risk management framework, and to keep focused and aligned on assessing and monitoring enterprise-wide risk.

Mergers and Acquisitions
In early 2022, Sallie Mae, formally SLM Corporation has entered into a definitive agreement with Epic Research LLC to acquire Delaware-based Nitro College (Nitro), a digital marketing and education solutions company. The deal will bring innovative products, tools, and resources to help students and families confidently navigate their higher education journey and enhance future strategic growth opportunities for Sallie Mae. Terms of the acquisition are not being disclosed.

Company Background
Founded in 1974 as a government-sponsored enterprise, SLM borrowed money at near-government rates to purchase government-guaranteed loans. In the 1990s, though, Congress took away SLM's funding edge, making privatization attractive. The company completed the separation in late 2004, but more changes followed.

HISTORY
The Student Loan Marketing Association was chartered in 1972 as a response to problems in the Guaranteed Student Loan Program of 1965. For years the GSL program had tinkered with rates to induce banks to make loans, but servicing the small loans was expensive and troublesome. Sallie Mae began operations in 1973, buying loans from their originators; its size provided economies of scale in loan servicing.

Originally, only institutions making educational or student loans were allowed to own stock in Sallie Mae. This was later changed so that anyone could buy nonvoting stock. In 1993 voting stock was listed on the NYSE.

Sallie Mae was always a political football, altered again and again to reflect the education policies of the party in power. When it was founded during the Nixon administration, its loans were restricted by a needs test, which was repealed during the Carter years. The Reagan administration reimposed the needs test and at the same time sped up the schedule under which the company was to become self-supporting, which it did by late 1981.

Forced to rely on its own resources, Sallie Mae turned to creative financing. One of its traditional advantages was that its loan interest rates were linked to Treasury bills, traditionally about 3% above the T-bill rate. The company became a master at riding the spread between its cost of funds and the interest rates it charged.

Between 1983 and 1992 Sallie Mae's assets swelled by more than 400% and its income rose by almost 500%. As the firm grew, management became more visible, with high pay and extravagant perks. Although salaries were not inconsistent with those of executives at comparable private corporations, the remuneration level and perks irked Congress. But Sallie Mae kept growing -- in 1992 it expanded its facilities and added 900 new staff members.

The 1993 Omnibus Budget Reconciliation Act, with its transfer of the student loan program directly to the government and its surcharge on Sallie Mae, began to adversely affect earnings in 1994. While awaiting permission to alter its charter, the company stepped up its marketing efforts, especially to school loan officers who advised students on loan options.

In 1995 then-COO Albert Lord led a group of stockholders in a push to cut operating expenses and repackage student loans as securities, Ã la Freddie Mac and Fannie Mae. Lord and some of his supporters won seats on the board (as well as the enmity of Lawrence Hough, who resigned as CEO in the midst of the melee). That year Sallie Mae bought HICA Holding, one of two private insurers of education loans. In 1996 Congress passed legislation forcing Sallie Mae's privatization.

Despite SLM's rising stock, shareholders were unhappy with chairman William Arceneaux's status quo business plan. Lord gained control in 1997.

In 1998 the organization became SLM Holding. Assets and earnings were muted that year when unfavorable market conditions prevented Sallie Mae from securitizing its loans.

The firm the next year expanded its lending operations by buying Nellie Mae. Also in 1999 Sallie Mae teamed with Answer Financial to sell insurance. Growth continued in 2000 when the company bought loan servicer Student Loan Funding Resources, as well as the marketing, student loan servicing, and administrative operations of USA Group; the company changed its name to USA Education following the acquisition. The company also cut some 1,700 jobs, approximately 25% of its workforce.

The following year Sallie Mae teamed with

Intuit, allowing the financial software company access to Sallie Mae's 7 million customers. It also launched online recruiting service TrueCareers that year.

In 2002 it bought Pioneer Credit Recovery and General Revenue Corporation, two of the nation's largest student loan collection agencies. It also reverted to the SLM moniker to reconnect with the name by which it has so long been known.

The privatization plan put into place in the mid-'90s (orchestrated in large part by then-CEO Lord) came to fruition nearly four years ahead of schedule when SLM transitioned to a private organization in December 2004.

In 2007 SLM saw its stock values plummet to their lowest levels in about a decade. A number of industry-wide factors figured into the losses, not the least of which was the downturn in the credit market. Also affecting the company was the signing into law of the College Cost Reduction and Access Act (CCRAA). Intended to reform student lending and cut costs for borrowers, the act slashed subsidies for lenders participating in the Federal Family Education Loan Program (FFELP). The reform cut into the company's interest-earning operations. As a result, SLM increased its focus on higher-yielding private education loans, which carry a lower risk.

Additionally, SLM that year became ensnared in a student-lending industry probe led by New York attorney general Andrew Cuomo. The company agreed to a $2 million settlement and to abide by a code of conduct regarding its dealings with college employees.

One of the most dramatic results of the troubles was the collapse of a planned acquisition by a consortium of investment firms. The planned $8.8 billion deal included buyers J.C. Flowers (which was to own about a half of SLM), Bank of America, and JPMorgan Chase. In the midst of the industry probe, J.C. Flowers sought a change in SLM's leadership in an effort to secure regulatory approval for the acquisition; Thomas J. (Tim) Fitzpatrick was ousted as CEO. Ultimately, the buyers canceled the deal, citing the reduced potential value of SLM. The student lender filed a lawsuit to challenge the termination but eventually dropped the suit. It later cut more than 10% of its workforce.

EXECUTIVES

Chairman, Director, Mary Carter Warren Franke
Executive Vice President, Chief Financial Officer, Steven J. McGarry, $476,155 total compensation
Executive Vice President, Chief Operational Officer, Subsidiary Officer, Kerri A. Palmer
Executive Vice President, Chief Commercial Officer, Donna F. Vieira
Chief Executive Officer, Director, Jonathan W. Witter
Senior Vice President, Controller, Jonathan R. Boyles
Senior Vice President, Chief Communications Officer, Chief Legal Officer, Chief Government Affairs Officer, Nicolas Jafarieh, $377,058 total compensation
Director, Paul G. Child, $115,000 total compensation
Director, Marianne M. Keler, $350,000 total compensation
Director, Mark L. Lavelle
Director, Ted Manvitz
Director, James D. Matheson
Director, Samuel T. Ramsey
Director, Vivian C. Schneck-Last
Director, Robert S. Strong
Director, Kirsten O. Wolberg
Director, Richard Scott Blackley
Auditors : KPMG LLP

LOCATIONS

HQ: SLM Corp.
  300 Continental Drive, Newark, DE 19713
Phone: 302 451-0200
Web: www.salliemakessense.com

PRODUCTS/OPERATIONS

2016 Sales

	$ mil.	% of total
Interest		
Loans	1,060.5	79
Investments	9.2	1
Cash & cash equivalents	7.6	1
Non-Interest income		
Gain on sale of loans	0.2	14
(Losses) gains on derivatives and hedging activities, net	(0.9)	5
Other income	69.5	-
Total	1,146.1	100

Selected Subsidiaries

HICA Holding
Sallie Mae Bank
Sallie Mae, Inc.
SLM Education Credit Finance Corporation
  Bull Run I LLC
    SLM Education Credit Funding LLC
SLM Investment Corporation
Southwest Student Services Corporation

COMPETITORS

AGFIRST FARM CREDIT BANK
AMBAC FINANCIAL GROUP, INC.
BANKIA SA
CREDIT ACCEPTANCE CORPORATION
FEDERAL HOME LOAN BANK OF BOSTON
FEDERAL HOME LOAN BANK OF PITTSBURGH
FEDERAL HOME LOAN MORTGAGE CORPORATION
FEDERAL NATIONAL MORTGAGE ASSOCIATION
NAVIENT CORPORATION
NORINCHUKIN BANK, THE

HISTORICAL FINANCIALS

Company Type: Public

Income Statement				FYE: December 31
	ASSETS ($mil)	NET INCOME ($mil)	INCOME AS % OF ASSETS	EMPLOYEES
12/20	30,770.4	880.6	2.9%	1,600
12/19	32,686.4	578.2	1.8%	1,900
12/18	26,638.1	487.4	1.8%	1,700
12/17	21,779.5	288.9	1.3%	1,500
12/16	18,533.0	250.3	1.4%	1,300
Annual Growth	13.5%	37.0%	—	5.3%

2020 Year-End Financials

Return on assets: 2.7%
Return on equity: 29.9%
Long-term debt ($ mil.): —
No. of shares ($ mil.): 375.2
Sales ($ mil.): 2,353.1
Dividends
  Yield: 0.9%
  Payout: 8.5%
Market value ($ mil.): 4,650.0

	STOCK PRICE ($) FY Close	P/E High/Low		PER SHARE ($) Earnings	Dividends	Book Value
12/20	12.39	5	3	2.25	0.12	6.83
12/19	8.91	9	6	1.30	0.12	7.86
12/18	8.31	11	8	1.07	0.00	6.82
12/17	11.30	20	16	0.62	0.00	5.72
12/16	11.02	21	10	0.53	0.00	5.47
Annual Growth	3.0%	—	—	43.5%	—	5.7%

Smart Sand Inc

EXECUTIVES

Co-Chairman, José E. Feliciano
Co-Chairman, Director, Andrew R. Speaker
Chief Executive Officer, Director, Charles E. Young, $512,308 total compensation
Executive Vice President, General Counsel, Secretary, James Douglas Young
Operations Executive Vice President, Robert Kiszka, $375,000 total compensation
Business Development Executive Vice President, Sales Executive Vice President, Ronald P. Whelan
Sales Chief Operating Officer, Logistics Chief Operating Officer, William John Young, $310,154 total compensation
Chief Financial Officer, Principal Accounting Officer, Lee E. Beckelman, $388,269 total compensation
Director, Frank Porcelli
Director, Sharon Spurlin
Director, Timothy J. Pawlenty
Auditors : Grant Thornton LLP

LOCATIONS

HQ: Smart Sand Inc
  1725 Hughes Landing Blvd., Suite 800, The Woodlands, TX 77380
Phone: 281 231-2660
Web: www.smartsand.com

HISTORICAL FINANCIALS

Company Type: Public

Income Statement				FYE: December 31
	REVENUE ($mil)	NET INCOME ($mil)	NET PROFIT MARGIN	EMPLOYEES
12/20	122.3	37.9	31.0%	228
12/19	233.0	31.6	13.6%	285
12/18	212.4	18.6	8.8%	323
12/17	137.2	21.5	15.7%	198
12/16	59.2	10.3	17.5%	103
Annual Growth	19.9%	38.3%	—	22.0%

2020 Year-End Financials

Debt ratio: 6.9%
Return on equity: 14.2%
Cash ($ mil.): 11.7
Current Ratio: 3.01
Long-term debt ($ mil.): 22.4
No. of shares ($ mil.): 41.5
Dividends
  Yield: —
  Payout: —
Market value ($ mil.): 72.0

	STOCK PRICE ($) FY Close	P/E High/Low		PER SHARE ($) Earnings	Dividends	Book Value
12/20	1.72	3	1	0.94	0.00	6.95
12/19	2.52	6	3	0.78	0.00	6.07
12/18	2.22	24	4	0.46	0.00	5.24
12/17	8.66	39	9	0.53	0.00	4.70
12/16	16.55	38	25	0.42	0.00	3.67
Annual Growth	(43.2%)	—	—	22.3%	—	17.3%

SmartFinancial Inc

Cornerstone Bancshares is the holding company for Cornerstone Community Bank, which operates about five locations in Chattanooga, Tennessee, and surrounding communities, in addition to two loan production offices in Knoxville, Tennessee, and Dalton, Georgia. The bank offers standard retail and commercial services, including checking and savings accounts, money market accounts, and CDs. Its lending activities primarily consist of commercial real estate loans, residential mortgages, real estate construction loans, and business and agricultural loans. Another subsidiary of Cornerstone Bancshares, Eagle Financial, purchases accounts receivable and acts as a conduit lender.

EXECUTIVES

Chairman, Subsidiary Officer, Director, Wesley Miller Welborn, $248,978 total compensation
Vice-Chairman, Subsidiary Officer, Director, William Young Carroll, $248,978 total compensation
President, Chief Executive Officer, Subsidiary Officer, Director, William Y. Carroll, $379,920 total compensation
Executive Vice President, Chief Lending Officer, Subsidiary Officer, Gregory L. Davis, $178,258 total compensation
Executive Vice President, Chief Risk Officer, Subsidiary Officer, Gary Wayne Petty, $125,000 total compensation
Executive Vice President, Chief Credit Officer, Rhett D. Jordan, $188,522 total compensation
Executive Vice President, Chief Financial Officer, Subsidiary Officer, Ronald J. Gorczynski
Subsidiary Officer, Daniel Hereford
Subsidiary Officer, Rebecca C. Boyd
Subsidiary Officer, Cynthia A. Cain
Lead Independent Director, Director, David A. Ogle
Director, Victor L. Barrett
Director, Monique P. Berke
Director, Ted C. Miller
Director, Ottis H. Phillips
Director, Steven B. Tucker
Director, Keith E. Whaley
Director, Geoffrey A. Wolpert
Director, Cathy G. Ackermann
Director, John Presley
Auditors : Dixon Hughes Goodman LLP

LOCATIONS

HQ: SmartFinancial Inc
5401 Kingston Pike, Suite 600, Knoxville, TN 37919
Phone: 865 437-5700
Web: www.smartfinancialinc.com

COMPETITORS

CORNERSTONE BANCORP
FIRST CHEROKEE BANCSHARES INC
FIRST PULASKI NATIONAL CORPORATION
FIRST VICTORIA NATIONAL BANK
NEFFS BANCORP, INC.

HISTORICAL FINANCIALS

Company Type: Public

Income Statement				FYE: December 31
	ASSETS ($mil)	NET INCOME ($mil)	INCOME AS % OF ASSETS	EMPLOYEES
12/20	3,304.9	24.3	0.7%	475
12/19	2,449.1	26.5	1.1%	399
12/18	2,274.4	18.1	0.8%	387
12/17	1,720.7	5.0	0.3%	343
12/16	1,062.4	5.7	0.5%	222
Annual Growth	32.8%	43.1%	—	20.9%

2020 Year-End Financials

Return on assets: 0.8%
Return on equity: 7.2%
Long-term debt ($ mil.): —
No. of shares ($ mil.): 15.1
Sales ($ mil.): 133
Dividends
  Yield: 1.1%
  Payout: 13.3%
Market value ($ mil.): 274.0

	STOCK PRICE ($) FY Close	P/E High/Low		PER SHARE ($) Earnings	Dividends	Book Value
12/20	18.14	14	7	1.62	0.20	23.64
12/19	23.65	13	9	1.89	0.05	22.33
12/18	18.27	19	12	1.45	0.00	20.31
12/17	21.70	47	33	0.55	0.00	18.46
12/16	18.56	24	18	0.78	0.00	17.85
Annual Growth	(0.6%)	—	—	20.0%	—	7.3%

SolarWinds Corp

EXECUTIVES

Chairman, Director, William G. Bock
President, Chief Executive Officer, Director, Sudhakar Ramakrishna
Executive Vice President, Chief Financial Officer, Chief Accounting Officer, Treasurer, James Barton Kalsu, $380,000 total compensation
Corporate Development Executive Vice President, Corporate Development Chief Administrative Officer, Corporate Development Secretary, Jason W. Bliss
Director, Michael K. Hoffmann
Director, Dennis Howard
Director, Seth Boro
Director, Kenneth Y. Hao
Director, Catherine R. Kinney
Director, James K. Lines
Director, Easwaran Sundaram
Director, Michael Widmann
Director, Cathleen A. Benko

Auditors : PricewaterhouseCoopers LLP

LOCATIONS

HQ: SolarWinds Corp
7171 Southwest Parkway, Building 400, Austin, TX 78735
Phone: 512 682-9300
Web: www.solarwinds.com

HISTORICAL FINANCIALS

Company Type: Public

Income Statement				FYE: December 31
	REVENUE ($mil)	NET INCOME ($mil)	NET PROFIT MARGIN	EMPLOYEES
12/20	1,019.2	158.4	15.5%	3,340
12/19	932.5	18.6	2.0%	3,251
12/18	833.0	(102.0)	—	2,738
12/17	728.0	(83.8)	—	2,540
12/16	422.0	(262.5)	—	0
Annual Growth	24.7%	—	—	—

2020 Year-End Financials

Debt ratio: 33.3%
Return on equity: 5.5%
Cash ($ mil.): 370.5
Current Ratio: 1.04
Long-term debt ($ mil.): 1,882.6
No. of shares ($ mil.): 156.5
Dividends
  Yield: —
  Payout: —
Market value ($ mil.): 2,340.0

	STOCK PRICE ($) FY Close	P/E High/Low		PER SHARE ($) Earnings	Dividends	Book Value
12/20	14.95	23	12	1.00	0.00	19.24
12/19	18.55	171	109	0.12	0.00	17.19
12/18	13.83	4	2	5.12	0.00	17.16
Annual Growth	4.0%	—	—	(55.8%)	—	5.9%

Solera National Bancorp Inc

EXECUTIVES

President, Chief Executive Officer, Subsidiary Officer, Director, Martin P. May
Commercial Lending Senior Vice President, Scott Hovey
Chairman, Director, Michael Quagliano
Senior Vice President, Chief Financial Officer, Secretary, Subsidiary Officer, Melissa Larkin
Director, Robert J. Fenton, $175,000 total compensation
Director, Eric Liebman
Director, Rene Morin
Auditors : Eide Bailly, LLP

LOCATIONS

HQ: Solera National Bancorp Inc
319 S. Sheridan Blvd, Lakewood, CO 80226
Phone: 303 209-8600
Web: www.solerabank.com

HISTORICAL FINANCIALS
Company Type: Public

Income Statement   FYE: December 31

	ASSETS ($mil)	NET INCOME ($mil)	INCOME AS % OF ASSETS	EMPLOYEES
12/20	435.7	5.9	1.4%	0
12/19	282.1	3.5	1.3%	0
12/18	220.6	2.2	1.0%	0
12/17	173.8	0.5	0.3%	0
12/16	156.0	3.1	2.0%	0
Annual Growth	29.3%	17.4%	—	—

2020 Year-End Financials
Return on assets: 1.6%
Return on equity: 13.3%
Long-term debt ($ mil.): —
No. of shares ($ mil.): 4.2
Sales ($ mil.): 16.6
Dividends
  Yield: —
  Payout: —
Market value ($ mil.): 47.0

	STOCK PRICE ($) FY Close	P/E High	P/E Low	PER SHARE ($) Earnings	Dividends	Book Value
12/20	11.00	8	6	1.41	0.00	11.23
12/19	11.55	14	10	0.86	0.00	9.78
12/18	8.90	17	13	0.62	0.00	8.68
12/17	8.25	45	38	0.19	0.00	8.64
12/16	7.40	7	4	1.15	0.00	8.38
Annual Growth	10.4%	—	—	5.2%	—	7.6%

Sonos Inc

EXECUTIVES

Chairperson, Director, Michelangelo A. Volpi
President, Chief Executive Officer, Director, Patrick Spence, $350,000 total compensation
Chief People Officer, Anna Fraser
Chief Legal Officer, Interim Chief Financial Officer, Corporate Secretary, Edward Lazarus
Chief Products Officer, Nicholas Millington, $350,000 total compensation
Chief Commercial Officer, Matthew Siegel, $362,500 total compensation
Director, Karen Boone
Director, Joanna Coles
Director, Panos Panay
Director, Thomas Conrad
Director, Julius Genachowski
Director, Deirdre Findlay
Auditors : PricewaterhouseCoopers LLP

LOCATIONS

HQ: Sonos Inc
  614 Chapala Street, Santa Barbara, CA 93101
Phone: 805 965-3001
Web: www.sonos.com

HISTORICAL FINANCIALS
Company Type: Public

Income Statement   FYE: October 2

	REVENUE ($mil)	NET INCOME ($mil)	NET PROFIT MARGIN	EMPLOYEES
10/21	1,716.7	158.5	9.2%	1,525
10/20*	1,326.3	(20.1)	—	1,427
09/19	1,260.8	(4.7)	—	1,446
09/18	1,137.0	(15.6)	—	1,352
09/17	992.5	(14.2)	—	1,478
Annual Growth	14.7%	—	—	0.8%

*Fiscal year change

2021 Year-End Financials
Debt ratio: —
Return on equity: 36.6%
Cash ($ mil.): 640.1
Current Ratio: 2.01
Long-term debt ($ mil.): —
No. of shares ($ mil.): 126.9
Dividends
  Yield: —
  Payout: —
Market value ($ mil.): 4,097.0

	STOCK PRICE ($) FY Close	P/E High	P/E Low	PER SHARE ($) Earnings	Dividends	Book Value
10/21	32.26	34	11	1.13	0.00	4.48
10/20*	15.50	—	—	(0.18)	0.00	2.65
09/19	13.51	—	—	(0.05)	0.00	2.59
09/18	16.04	—	—	(0.24)	0.00	2.08
Annual Growth	26.2%	—	—	—	—	29.1%

*Fiscal year change

Sound Financial Bancorp Inc

EXECUTIVES

Chairman, Director, Tyler K. Myers
Subsidiary Officer, Vice-Chairman, Director, David S. Haddad
President, Chief Executive Officer, Subsidiary Officer, Director, Laura Lee Stewart, $395,437 total compensation
Executive Vice President, Chief Operating Officer, Subsidiary Officer, Heidi J. Sexton
Senior Vice President, Chief Accounting Officer, Subsidiary Officer, Jennifer L. Mallon
Senior Vice President, Chief Credit Officer, Subsidiary Officer, Charles L. Turner
Executive Vice President, Chief Financial Officer, Chief Strategy Officer, Subsidiary Officer, Wes Ochs
Director, Debra A. Jones
Director, Rogelio Riojas
Director, Robert F. Carney
Director, James E. Sweeney
Auditors : Moss Adams LLP

LOCATIONS

HQ: Sound Financial Bancorp Inc
  2400 3rd Avenue, Suite 150, Seattle, WA 98121
Phone: 206 448-0884
Web: www.soundcb.com

HISTORICAL FINANCIALS
Company Type: Public

Income Statement   FYE: December 31

	ASSETS ($mil)	NET INCOME ($mil)	INCOME AS % OF ASSETS	EMPLOYEES
12/20	861.4	8.9	1.0%	120
12/19	719.8	6.6	0.9%	132
12/18	716.7	7.0	1.0%	119
12/17	645.2	5.1	0.8%	121
12/16	588.3	5.3	0.9%	106
Annual Growth	10.0%	13.5%	—	3.1%

2020 Year-End Financials
Return on assets: 1.1%
Return on equity: 10.9%
Long-term debt ($ mil.): —
No. of shares ($ mil.): 2.5
Sales ($ mil.): 42.3
Dividends
  Yield: 2.5%
  Payout: 28.5%
Market value ($ mil.): 82.0

	STOCK PRICE ($) FY Close	P/E High	P/E Low	PER SHARE ($) Earnings	Dividends	Book Value
12/20	31.75	11	5	3.42	0.80	32.97
12/19	36.00	14	13	2.57	0.56	30.27
12/18	32.55	14	12	2.74	0.54	28.15
12/17	34.02	17	13	2.00	0.60	25.95
12/16	28.00	14	10	2.09	0.30	24.12
Annual Growth	3.2%	—	—	13.1%	27.8%	8.1%

South Atlantic Bancshares Inc

EXECUTIVES

Chairman, Chief Executive Officer, Subsidiary Officer, K. Wayne Wicker
President, Subsidiary Officer, Director, R. Scott Plyler
Executive Vice President, Chief Financial Officer, Chief Operating Officer, ISO, Director, Richard N. Burch
Executive Vice President, Chief Credit Officer, C. Alec Elmore
Mortgage Loans Executive Vice President, Mortgage Loans Director, Travis A. Minter
Executive Vice President, Charleston Regional Executive, Kenneth M. Pickens
Executive Vice President, Grand Strand Regional Executive, Mary Jo Rogers
Director, Michael C. Tawes
Director, James Carson Benton
Director, Thomas C. Brittain
Director, Tony K. Cox
Director, Miles M. Herring
Director, Albert A. Springs
Director, Martha S. Lewis
Director, Jack L. Springs
Director, Edgar L. Woods
Auditors : Elliot Davis LLC

LOCATIONS

HQ: South Atlantic Bancshares Inc
  630 29th Avenue North, Myrtle Beach, SC 29577

Phone: 843 839-4412
Web: www.southatlantic.bank

HISTORICAL FINANCIALS
Company Type: Public

Income Statement   FYE: December 31

	ASSETS ($mil)	NET INCOME ($mil)	INCOME AS % OF ASSETS	EMPLOYEES
12/20	946.5	7.1	0.8%	146
12/19	718.4	6.0	0.8%	0
12/18	630.2	3.4	0.5%	0
12/17	519.1	3.4	0.7%	97
12/16	444.5	2.6	0.6%	0
Annual Growth	20.8%	28.9%	—	—

2020 Year-End Financials
Return on assets: 0.8%
Return on equity: 7.7%
Long-term debt ($ mil.): —
No. of shares ($ mil.): 7.5
Sales ($ mil.): 41.5
Dividends
 Yield: —
 Payout: —
Market value ($ mil.): 92.0

	STOCK PRICE ($) FY Close	P/E High	P/E Low	Earnings	Dividends	Book Value
12/20	12.25	13	8	0.96	0.00	13.03
12/19	12.60	16	13	0.80	0.00	11.78
12/18	11.03	34	23	0.47	0.00	10.57
12/17	16.35	31	22	0.57	0.00	9.44
12/16	16.00	26	16	0.60	0.00	8.88
Annual Growth	(6.5%)	—	—	12.5%	—	10.0%

South Jersey Industries Inc

South Jersey Industries (SJI) is Atlantic City's answer to cold casino nights. Its main subsidiary, South Jersey Gas (SJG), provided natural gas to nearly 411,300 residential, commercial and industrial customers in southern New Jersey, including Atlantic City. The utility has more than 6,800 miles of transmission and distribution mains; it also sells and transports wholesale gas. The company was founded in 1969. In 2022, South Jersey Industries Inc. agreed to be purchased by Infrastructure Investment Fund, a private vehicle focused on investing critical infrastructure assets, for $ 8.1 billion.

Operations
SJI operates in several different reportable operating segments. These segments are as follows:

SJG utility operations account for about 30% of revenue and consist primarily of natural gas distribution to residential, commercial and industrial customers in southern New Jersey.

ETG utility operations (around 15% of revenue) consist primarily of natural gas distribution to residential, commercial and industrial customers in northern and central New Jersey.

Prior to its divestiture, ELK utility operations consist of natural gas distribution to residential, commercial and industrial customers in Maryland.Wholesale energy operations include the activities of SJRG and SJEX.

Retail electric operations at SJE consist of electricity acquisition and transportation to commercial, industrial and residential customers.

Appliance service operations includes SJESP, which receives commissions on appliance service contracts from a third party.

Midstream was formed to invest in infrastructure and other midstream projects, including an investment in PennEast.

Corporate & Services segment includes costs related to acquisitions and divestitures, along with other unallocated costs.

Geographic Reach
Headquartered in Folsom, New Jersey, SJI's South Jersey Gas service territory covers approximately 2,500 square miles in southern New Jersey, including about 115 towns and cities in Atlantic, Cape May, Cumberland, and Salem counties and portions of Burlington, Camden, and Gloucester counties. SJI also markets natural gas storage, commodity, and transportation assets on a wholesale basis in the mid-Atlantic, Appalachia, and the southern US.

Sales and Marketing
SJG served approximately 411,300 residential, commercial and industrial customers in southern New Jersey. SJG served around 384,100 residential customers, 26,825 commercial customers and 415 industrial customers.

Financial Performance
The company's revenue in 2021 increased to $2.0 billion compared to $1.5 billion in the prior year.

Net income in 2021 decreased to $88.1 million compared to $157.1 million in the prior year.

Cash held by the company at the end of fiscal 2021 decreased to $29.4 million. Operating and financing activities were $273.1 million and $360.0 million, respectively. Investing activities used $645.5 million, mainly for capital expenditures.

Strategy
In developing SJI's current business model, SJI's focus has been on its core Utilities and natural extensions of those businesses, as well as strategic opportunities in its nonutility business that align with the goals of the EMP. That focus enables the company to concentrate on business activities that match its core competencies. Going forward, the company expects to pursue business opportunities that fit and complement this model.

EXECUTIVES
Chairman, Director, Joseph M. Rigby
President, Chief Executive Officer, Director, Michael J. Renna, $748,077 total compensation
Senior Vice President, Chief Financial Officer, Steven R. Cocchi
Director, Melissa J. Orsen, $277,731 total compensation
Director, Sarah M. Barpoulis
Director, Victor A. Fortkiewicz
Director, Sheila Hartnett-Devlin
Director, G. Edison Holland
Director, Sunita Holzer
Director, Kevin M. O'Dowd
Director, Christopher J. Paladino
Director, Frank L. Sims
Auditors : DELOITTE & TOUCHE LLP

LOCATIONS
HQ: South Jersey Industries Inc
1 South Jersey Plaza, Folsom, NJ 08037
Phone: 609 561-9000
Web: www.sjiindustries.com

PRODUCTS/OPERATIONS
2014 Sales

	$ mil.	% of total
Gas utility	501.9	57
Energy Group:		
Retail Gas and other operations	127.0	14
Retail electricity operation	123.8	14
Wholesale energy operation	77.0	9
Energy Services:		
On-Site energy production	56.1	6
Corporate & services	30.2	3
Appliance service operations	10.5	1
Adjustment (intersegment sales)	(39.5)	(4)
Total	887	100

Selected Subsidiaries
Marina Energy LLC (energy project development)
South Jersey Energy Company (retail energy marketer, energy management services)
South Jersey Energy Service Plus, LLC (HVAC systems installation and appliance servicing)
South Jersey Exploration, LLC (oil and gas assets)
South Jersey Gas Company (natural gas utility)
South Jersey Resources Group, LLC (wholesale natural gas marketing, trading, transportation, and management services)

COMPETITORS
ALLIANT ENERGY CORPORATION
CH ENERGY GROUP, INC.
Enmax Corporation
INTERSTATE POWER AND LIGHT COMPANY
MDU RESOURCES GROUP, INC.
NEW JERSEY RESOURCES CORPORATION
PECO ENERGY COMPANY
SOUTHERN COMPANY GAS
UNITIL CORPORATION
VECTREN CORPORATION

HISTORICAL FINANCIALS
Company Type: Public

Income Statement   FYE: December 31

	REVENUE ($mil)	NET INCOME ($mil)	NET PROFIT MARGIN	EMPLOYEES
12/20	1,541.3	157.0	10.2%	1,130
12/19	1,628.6	76.9	4.7%	1,100
12/18	1,641.3	17.6	1.1%	1,100
12/17	1,243.0	(3.4)	—	760
12/16	1,036.5	118.8	11.5%	750
Annual Growth	10.4%	7.2%	—	10.8%

South Plains Financial Inc

2020 Year-End Financials
Debt ratio: 43.6%
Return on equity: 10.1%
Cash ($ mil.): 34.0
Current Ratio: 0.44
Long-term debt ($ mil.): 2,776.4
No. of shares ($ mil.): 100.5
Dividends
  Yield: 5.5%
  Payout: 73.3%
Market value ($ mil.): 2,168.0

	STOCK PRICE ($) FY Close	P/E High	P/E Low	PER SHARE ($) Earnings	PER SHARE ($) Dividends	PER SHARE ($) Book Value
12/20	21.55	21	11	1.62	1.19	16.51
12/19	32.98	41	32	0.84	1.16	15.41
12/18	27.80	172	124	0.21	1.13	14.82
12/17	31.23	—	—	(0.04)	1.10	14.99
12/16	33.69	22	15	1.56	1.06	16.22
Annual Growth	(10.6%)	—	—	0.9%	2.8%	0.4%

EXECUTIVES

Chairman, Chief Executive Officer, Subsidiary Officer, Curtis C. Griffith, $402,796 total compensation
President, Subsidiary Officer, Director, Cory T. Newsom, $766,956 total compensation
Chief Financial Officer, Treasurer, Subsidiary Officer, Steven B. Crockett
Chief Risk Officer, Secretary, Subsidiary Officer, Mikella D. Newsom
Subsidiary Officer, Kelly L. Deterding, $110,893 total compensation
Lead Independent Director, Director, Richard D. Campbell
Director, Cynthia B. Keith
Director, Allison S. Navitskas
Director, Noe G. Valles
Director, Kyle R. Wargo
Auditors : Weaver and Tidwell, LLP

LOCATIONS

HQ: South Plains Financial Inc
  5219 City Bank Parkway, Lubbock, TX 79407
Phone: 806 792-7101
Web: www.spfi.bank

HISTORICAL FINANCIALS
Company Type: Public

Income Statement — FYE: December 31

	ASSETS ($mil)	NET INCOME ($mil)	INCOME AS % OF ASSETS	EMPLOYEES
12/20	3,599.1	45.3	1.3%	682
12/19	3,237.1	29.2	0.9%	679
12/18	2,712.7	29.2	1.1%	684
12/17	2,573.3	23.6	0.9%	0
Annual Growth	11.8%	24.3%	—	—

2020 Year-End Financials
Return on assets: 1.3%
Return on equity: 13.3%
Long-term debt ($ mil.): —
No. of shares ($ mil.): 18.0
Sales ($ mil.): 239.8
Dividends
  Yield: 0.7%
  Payout: 5.6%
Market value ($ mil.): 343.0

	STOCK PRICE ($) FY Close	P/E High	P/E Low	PER SHARE ($) Earnings	PER SHARE ($) Dividends	PER SHARE ($) Book Value
12/20	18.95	9	5	2.47	0.14	20.47
12/19	20.87	12	9	1.71	0.06	16.98
Annual Growth	(9.2%)	—	—	44.4%	133.3%	20.6%

Southern First Bancshares, Inc.

Southern First Bancshares operates in two markets: Greenville, South Carolina, where it operates under the Greenville First BankÂ moniker, and in Columbia, South CarolinaÂ as Southern First Bank.Â Selling itself as a local alternative to larger institutions, theÂ company, which has more than fiveÂ bank branches,Â targets individuals and small to midsized businesses. It offers traditional deposit services and products, including checking accounts, savings accounts, and CDs. The banks use funds from deposits mainlyÂ to write commercial mortgages, residential mortgages, andÂ commercial business loans.

EXECUTIVES

Chairman, James B. Orders
Chief Executive Officer, Subsidiary Officer, R. Arthur Seaver, $475,000 total compensation
Executive Vice President, Chief Financial Officer, Chief Operating Officer, Subsidiary Officer, Michael D. Dowling, $275,000 total compensation
Director, Andrew B. Cajka
Director, Mark A. Cothran
Director, Leighton M. Cubbage
Director, Anne S. Ellefson
Director, David G. Ellison
Director, Frederick Gilmer
Director, Tecumseh Hooper
Director, Rudolph G. Johnstone
Director, Anna T. Locke
Auditors : Elliott Davis, LLC

LOCATIONS

HQ: Southern First Bancshares, Inc.
  100 Verdae Boulevard, Suite 100, Greenville, SC 29607
Phone: 864 679-9000
Web: www.southernfirst.com

COMPETITORS

BCSB BANCORP, INC.
FREMONT BANCORPORATION
PACIFIC FINANCIAL CORPORATION
SOUTHERN BANCSHARES (N.C.), INC.
UNION BANKSHARES, INC.

HISTORICAL FINANCIALS
Company Type: Public

Income Statement — FYE: December 31

	ASSETS ($mil)	NET INCOME ($mil)	INCOME AS % OF ASSETS	EMPLOYEES
12/20	2,482.5	18.3	0.7%	254
12/19	2,267.1	27.8	1.2%	242
12/18	1,900.6	22.2	1.2%	229
12/17	1,624.6	13.0	0.8%	198
12/16	1,340.9	13.0	1.0%	179
Annual Growth	16.6%	8.9%	—	9.1%

2020 Year-End Financials
Return on assets: 0.7%
Return on equity: 8.4%
Long-term debt ($ mil.): —
No. of shares ($ mil.): 7.7
Sales ($ mil.): 122.1
Dividends
  Yield: —
  Payout: —
Market value ($ mil.): 275.0

	STOCK PRICE ($) FY Close	P/E High	P/E Low	PER SHARE ($) Earnings	PER SHARE ($) Dividends	PER SHARE ($) Book Value
12/20	35.35	18	9	2.34	0.00	29.37
12/19	42.49	12	9	3.58	0.00	26.83
12/18	32.07	16	10	2.88	0.00	23.29
12/17	41.25	23	17	1.76	0.00	20.37
12/16	36.00	18	11	1.94	0.00	17.00
Annual Growth	(0.5%)	—	—	4.8%	—	14.7%

Southern Michigan Bancorp Inc (United States)

Southern Michigan Bancorp is the holding company for Southern Michigan Bank & Trust, which operates about 20Â branches in a primarily rural area near Michigan's border with Indiana and Ohio. The bankÂ provides standard deposit services, such as checking and savings accounts, money market and heath savings accounts, CDs, and IRAs. ItÂ originates commercial, financial, agricultural, consumer, and mortgage loans. TheÂ banks also offers trust and investment services. Southern Michigan Bank & Trust got its start in the room of a hotel named Southern Michigan HotelÂ in 1872.

EXECUTIVES

Chairman, Chief Executive Officer, Subsidiary Officer, Director, John H. Castle, $232,188 total compensation
President, Subsidiary Officer, Director, Kurt G. Miller, $185,961 total compensation
Lending Executive Vice President, Lending Head, Lending Subsidiary Officer, Nicholas M. Grabowski
Business Development Executive Vice President, Business Development Chief Strategy Officer, Business Development Head, Business Development Subsidiary Officer, Eric M. Anglin

Senior Vice President, Chief Financial Officer, Subsidiary Officer, Danice L. Chartrand, $127,152 total compensation
Subsidiary Officer, Aaron Lewis
Subsidiary Officer, Sarah Headley
Subsidiary Officer, Douglas W. Kiessling
Subsidiary Officer, Tom Swoish
Subsidiary Officer, Gabriel Alvez
Subsidiary Officer, Deborah Davis
Subsidiary Officer, Corey Donner
Subsidiary Officer, Rachel Doty
Subsidiary Officer, Adam Losinski
Subsidiary Officer, Greg Miller
Subsidiary Officer, Jim Sobeske
Subsidiary Officer, Samantha Gripman
Subsidiary Officer, Justin Horn
Subsidiary Officer, G. Trent Pierre
Subsidiary Officer, Tom Schlueter
Subsidiary Officer, Joseph Spoerl
Subsidiary Officer, Derek Naylor
Subsidiary Officer, DeAnne Hawley
Subsidiary Officer, Connie Caudill
Subsidiary Officer, Jodie Johnson
Subsidiary Officer, Shari Kline
Subsidiary Officer, Diane Krimmel
Subsidiary Officer, Stephanie Minniear
Subsidiary Officer, Kristen Niedzwiecki
Subsidiary Officer, LeAndra Otis
Subsidiary Officer, Tina Mack
Subsidiary Officer, Phyllis Ellen Wingate
Subsidiary Officer, Lori Neill
Subsidiary Officer, Tina Cronkhite
Subsidiary Officer, Lisa Walker
Subsidiary Officer, Jenny Haydon
Subsidiary Officer, Felicia Landis
Director, Melissa J. Bauer
Director, Charles James Scott Clark
Director, Patrick H. Flannery
Director, Stacey Hamlin
Director, Nolan E. Hooker
Director, Brian P. McConnell
Director Emeritus, Dean Calhoun
Director Emeritus, John S. Carton
Director Emeritus, H. Kenneth Cole
Director Emeritus, James T. Grohalski
Director Emeritus, Gregory J. Hull
Director Emeritus, Thomas E. Kolassa
Director Emeritus, Thomas D. Meyer
Director Emeritus, Jane L. Randall
Auditors : CliftonLarsonAllen LLP

LOCATIONS

HQ: Southern Michigan Bancorp Inc (United States)
51 West Pearl Street, Coldwater, MI 49036
Phone: 517 279-5500   **Fax:** 517 279-5578
Web: www.smb-t.com

COMPETITORS

COUNTY BANK CORP.
HERITAGE BANKSHARES, INC.
POTOMAC BANCSHARES, INC.

SOUTHEASTERN BANK FINANCIAL CORPORATION
SOUTHERN BANCSHARES (N.C.), INC.

HISTORICAL FINANCIALS
Company Type: Public

Income Statement — FYE: December 31

	ASSETS ($mil)	NET INCOME ($mil)	INCOME AS % OF ASSETS	EMPLOYEES
12/20	997.5	7.3	0.7%	0
12/19	809.7	8.6	1.1%	208
12/18	738.8	8.1	1.1%	0
12/17	712.3	5.4	0.8%	0
12/16	641.5	6.0	1.0%	0
Annual Growth	11.7%	4.9%	—	—

2020 Year-End Financials
Return on assets: 0.8%
Return on equity: 8.3%
Long-term debt ($ mil.): —
No. of shares ($ mil.): 2.3
Sales ($ mil.): 40.1
Dividends
  Yield: —
  Payout: 14.3%
Market value ($ mil.): 78.0

	STOCK PRICE ($) FY Close	P/E High/Low		PER SHARE ($) Earnings	Dividends	Book Value
12/20	34.00	12	8	3.21	0.46	40.40
12/19	37.60	11	10	3.74	0.45	36.00
12/18	38.10	13	10	3.51	0.43	32.62
12/17	37.10	17	13	2.30	0.41	30.23
12/16	29.90	12	10	2.54	0.36	29.14
Annual Growth	3.3%	—	—	6.0%	6.3%	8.5%

Southern Missouri Bancorp, Inc.

Southern Missouri Bancorp is the holding company for Southern Bank (formerly Southern Missouri Bank and Trust), which serves local residents and businesses in southeastern Missouri and northeastern Arkansas through more than 10 branches. Residential mortgages account for the largest percentage of the bank's loan portfolio, followed by commercial mortgages and business loans. Construction and consumer loans round out its lending activities. Deposit products include checking, savings and money market accounts, CDs, and IRAs. The bank also offers financial planning and investment services. Originally chartered in 1887, Southern Bank acquired Arkansas-based Southern Bank of Commerce in 2009.

EXECUTIVES

Chairman, Director, L. Douglas Bagby
President, Chief Executive Officer, Subsidiary Officer, Greg A. Steffens, $372,077 total compensation
Executive Vice President, Region Officer, Justin G. Cox, $213,231 total compensation
Executive Vice President, Chief Credit Officer, Mark E. Hecker, $234,231 total compensation
Secretary, Director, Charles R. Love

Executive Vice President, Chief Financial Officer, Matthew T. Funke, $213,231 total compensation
Executive Vice President, Chief Lending Officer, Rick A. Windes, $228,231 total compensation
Chief Operating Officer, Kimberly A. Capps, $166,769 total compensation
Chief Risk Officer, Lora Lee Daves, $149,615 total compensation
Chief Strategy Officer, Brett A. Dorton
Subsidiary Officer, Director, Sammy A. Schalk
Director, Todd E. Hensley
Director, Rebecca M. Brooks
Director, Dennis C. Robison
Director, David J. Tooley
Director, Daniel L. Jones
Auditors : BKD, LLP

LOCATIONS

HQ: Southern Missouri Bancorp, Inc.
2991 Oak Grove Road, Poplar Bluff, MO 63901
Phone: 573 778-1800
Web: www.bankwithsouthern.com

COMPETITORS

EMIGRANT SAVINGS BANK
HOME CITY FINANCIAL CORPORATION
JACKSONVILLE BANCORP, INC.
TIMBERLAND BANCORP, INC.
WVS FINANCIAL CORP.

HISTORICAL FINANCIALS
Company Type: Public

Income Statement — FYE: June 30

	ASSETS ($mil)	NET INCOME ($mil)	INCOME AS % OF ASSETS	EMPLOYEES
06/21	2,700.5	47.1	1.7%	488
06/20	2,542.1	27.5	1.1%	492
06/19	2,214.4	28.9	1.3%	470
06/18	1,886.1	20.9	1.1%	415
06/17	1,707.7	15.5	0.9%	390
Annual Growth	12.1%	32.0%	—	5.8%

2021 Year-End Financials
Return on assets: 1.7%
Return on equity: 17.4%
Long-term debt ($ mil.): —
No. of shares ($ mil.): 8.9
Sales ($ mil.): 129.5
Dividends
  Yield: 1.3%
  Payout: 13.9%
Market value ($ mil.): 400.0

	STOCK PRICE ($) FY Close	P/E High/Low		PER SHARE ($) Earnings	Dividends	Book Value
06/21	44.96	9	4	5.22	0.62	31.83
06/20	24.30	13	7	2.99	0.60	28.30
06/19	34.83	13	10	3.14	0.52	25.66
06/18	39.02	17	13	2.39	0.44	22.31
06/17	32.26	18	11	2.07	0.40	20.15
Annual Growth	8.7%	—	—	26.0%	11.6%	12.1%

SouthState Corp

South State Corporation (formerly First Financial Holdings) is the holding company for South State Bank. The bank operates through correspondent banking and capital markets service division for over 700 small and medium sized community banks through United States. The bank has 285 network branches located in Florida, South Carolina, Alabama, Georgia, and more. The company provides commercial real estate, residential real estate loans, commercial and industrial loans and consumer loans. , the banks provide deposit accounts, loans, and mortgages, as well as trust and investment planning services. .In 2020, the company acquired all the outstanding common stock of CFSL of Winter Haven. CFSL merged with the company and South State Bank.

EXECUTIVES

Chairman, Director, Robert R. Horger
Executive Chairman, Director, Robert R. Hill, $782,134 total compensation
Chief Executive Officer, Subsidiary Officer, Director, John C. Corbett
Chief Financial Officer, William E. Matthews
Senior Executive Vice President, Chief Credit Officer, Subsidiary Officer, Joseph E. Burns, $349,094 total compensation
Senior Executive Vice President, John C. Pollok, $558,667 total compensation
Senior Executive Vice President, Chief Administrative Officer, Subsidiary Officer, Renee R. Brooks, $249,094 total compensation
Chief Risk Officer, Subsidiary Officer, L. Andrew Westbrook
Subsidiary Officer, John F. Windley, $374,307 total compensation
Subsidiary Officer, Greg A. Lapointe
Subsidiary Officer, John S. Goettee
Director, Martin B. Davis
Director, Robert H. Demere
Director, Cynthia A. Hartley
Director, John H. Holcomb
Director, Charles W. McPherson
Director, G. Ruffner Page
Director, Ernest S. Pinner
Director, William Know Pou
Director, David G. Salyers
Director, Joshua A. Snively
Director, Kevin P. Walker
Auditors : Dixon Hughes Goodman LLP

LOCATIONS

HQ: SouthState Corp
1101 First Street South, Suite 202, Winter Haven, FL 33880
Phone: 863 293-4710
Web: www.southstatebank.com

PRODUCTS/OPERATIONS

2011 Sales

	$ mil.	% of total
Interest		
Loans, including fees	319.9	70
Investment securities	20.3	4
Other	1.8	-
Noninterest		
Service charges on deposit accounts	36.2	10
Bankcard services income	29.6	6
Trust and investment services income	18.3	4
Mortgage banking	16.2	4
Securities gains, net	-	0
Amortization of FDIC indemnification asset	(21.9)	0
Other	16.2	4
Total	**436.7**	**100**

COMPETITORS

ALDERMORE GROUP PLC
BYLINE BANCORP, INC.
CENTRAL COMMUNITY CORPORATION
F.N.B. CORPORATION
FIRST CITIZENS BANCSHARES, INC.
LLOYDS BANKING GROUP PLC
METROPOLITAN BANK HOLDING CORP.
NORTHWEST BANCORP, INC.
Shinhan Financial Group Co., Ltd.
Woori Finance Holdings Co., Ltd.

HISTORICAL FINANCIALS

Company Type: Public

Income Statement — FYE: December 31

	ASSETS ($mil)	NET INCOME ($mil)	INCOME AS % OF ASSETS	EMPLOYEES
12/20	37,789.8	120.6	0.3%	5,311
12/19	15,921.0	186.4	1.2%	2,547
12/18	14,676.3	178.8	1.2%	2,602
12/17	14,466.5	87.5	0.6%	2,719
12/16	8,900.5	101.2	1.1%	2,055
Annual Growth	43.5%	4.5%	—	26.8%

2020 Year-End Financials

Return on assets: 0.4%
Return on equity: 3.4%
Long-term debt ($ mil.): —
No. of shares ($ mil.): 70.9
Sales ($ mil.): 1,221.1
Dividends
Yield: 2.6%
Payout: 122.8%
Market value ($ mil.): 5,131.0

	STOCK PRICE ($) FY Close	P/E High/Low		PER SHARE ($) Earnings	Dividends	Book Value
12/20	72.30	40	20	2.19	1.88	65.49
12/19	86.75	16	11	5.36	1.67	70.32
12/18	59.95	19	12	4.86	1.38	66.04
12/17	87.15	32	27	2.93	1.32	62.81
12/16	87.40	22	14	4.18	1.21	46.82
Annual Growth	(4.6%)	—	—	(14.9%)	11.6%	8.7%

Spirit of Texas Bancshares Inc

EXECUTIVES

Chairman, Chief Executive Officer, Subsidiary Officer, Dean O. Bass, $491,740 total compensation
President, Subsidiary Officer, Director, David M. McGuire, $476,771 total compensation
Executive Vice President, Chief Financial Officer, Chief Accounting Officer, Subsidiary Officer, Allison Johnson
Executive Vice President, Chief Operating Officer, Subsidiary Officer, Jerry D. Golemon, $268,394 total compensation
Senior Vice President, Chief Accounting Officer, Edward Poole
Director, Allen C. Jones
Director, Akash J. Patel
Director, H. D. Patel
Director, Thomas C Sooy
Director, Robert S. Beall
Director, Steven Gregory ("Greg") Kidd
Director, Steven M. Morris
Director, William K. Nix
Director, Thomas Jones
Director, Leo T. Metcalf
Director, Nelda Luce Blair
Auditors : BDO USA, LLP

LOCATIONS

HQ: Spirit of Texas Bancshares Inc
1836 Spirit of Texas Way, Conroe, TX 77301
Phone: 936 521-1836
Web: www.sotb.com

HISTORICAL FINANCIALS

Company Type: Public

Income Statement — FYE: December 31

	ASSETS ($mil)	NET INCOME ($mil)	INCOME AS % OF ASSETS	EMPLOYEES
12/20	3,084.7	31.3	1.0%	383
12/19	2,384.6	21.1	0.9%	409
12/18	1,466.7	9.9	0.7%	289
12/17	1,030.2	4.7	0.5%	195
12/16	980.4	3.7	0.4%	0
Annual Growth	33.2%	70.4%	—	—

2020 Year-End Financials

Return on assets: 1.1%
Return on equity: 8.8%
Long-term debt ($ mil.): —
No. of shares ($ mil.): 17.0
Sales ($ mil.): 142.4
Dividends
Yield: 0.4%
Payout: 4.9%
Market value ($ mil.): 287.0

	STOCK PRICE ($) FY Close	P/E High/Low		PER SHARE ($) Earnings	Dividends	Book Value
12/20	16.80	13	5	1.77	0.07	21.12
12/19	23.00	16	14	1.40	0.00	18.93
12/18	22.78	21	17	1.03	0.00	16.42
Annual Growth	(14.1%)	—	—	31.1%	—	13.4%

Sportsman's Warehouse Holdings Inc

EXECUTIVES

Chairman, Director, Joseph P. Schneider

President, Chief Executive Officer, Director, Jon Barker, $609,628 total compensation
Finance Chief Financial Officer, Finance Secretary, Jeffrey R. White
Director, Martha H. Bejar
Director, Richard McBee
Director, Gregory P. Hickey
Director, Philip C. Williamson
Director, Nancy A. Walsh
Auditors : Grant Thornton LLP

LOCATIONS

HQ: Sportsman's Warehouse Holdings Inc
1475 West 9000 South Suite A, West Jordan, UT 84088
Phone: 801 566-6681   **Fax:** 801 304-4388
Web: www.sportsmans.com

HISTORICAL FINANCIALS
Company Type: Public

Income Statement — FYE: January 30

	REVENUE ($mil)	NET INCOME ($mil)	NET PROFIT MARGIN	EMPLOYEES
01/21*	1,451.7	91.3	6.3%	7,000
02/20	886.4	20.2	2.3%	5,400
02/19	849.1	23.7	2.8%	5,100
02/18	809.6	17.7	2.2%	5,000
01/17	779.9	29.6	3.8%	4,800
Annual Growth	16.8%	32.5%	—	9.9%

*Fiscal year change

2021 Year-End Financials

Debt ratio: —
Return on equity: 58.1%
Cash ($ mil.): 65.5
Current Ratio: 1.43
Long-term debt ($ mil.): —
No. of shares ($ mil.): 43.6
Dividends
  Yield: —
  Payout: —
Market value ($ mil.): 764.0

	STOCK PRICE ($) FY Close	P/E High/Low		PER SHARE ($) Earnings	Dividends	Book Value
01/21*	17.52	9	2	2.06	0.00	4.69
02/20	6.48	18	7	0.46	0.00	2.55
02/19	5.12	11	7	0.55	0.00	1.83
02/18	4.91	18	8	0.42	0.00	1.17
01/17	7.89	20	11	0.70	0.00	0.71
Annual Growth	22.1%	—	—	31.0%	—	60.3%

*Fiscal year change

SPS Commerce, Inc.

Founded in 1987 as St. Paul Software, SPS Commerce is a leading provider of cloud-based supply chain management services that make it easier for suppliers, retailers, distributors, and logistics companies to orchestrate the management of item data, order fulfillment, inventory control, and sales analytics across all channels. The services offered by SPS Commerce eliminate the need for on-premise software and support staff by taking on that capability on the customer's behalf. Its business model fundamentally changes how organizations use electronic communication to manage their omnichannel, supply chain, and other business requirements by replacing the collection of traditional, custom-built, point-to-point integrations with a model that facilitates a single automated connection to the entire SPS Commerce network of trading partners. The company has approximately 105,000 customers across approximately 80 countries.

Operations

SPS has only one segment, which is supply chain management products.

Supply chain management products for critical business processes, any defect in its solutions, any disruption to its solutions or any error in execution could cause recurring revenue customers to cancel their contracts with them, cause potential customers to not join its network and harm its reputation.

The company's recurring revenues consist of recurring subscriptions from customers that utilize the company's fulfillment (some 80% of sales), analytics (about 10%), and other cloud-based supply chain management solutions. The one-time revenues, which account for the remaining sales, consist of set-up fees from customers and miscellaneous one-time fees.

Geographic Reach

Headquartered in Minnesota, the company operates in New Jersey, Ukraine, Canada, Australia, China, and Netherlands.

Sales and Marketing

SPS boasts approximately 105,000 customers. It also generated revenues from other members of the supply chain ecosystem, including retailers, distributors, third-party logistics providers, and other trading partners.

Financial Performance

The company had a 23% increase in revenue to $385.3 million. The increase in revenues resulted from two primary factors: the increase in recurring revenue customers, which is driven by continued business growth and by business acquisitions, and the increase in average recurring revenues per recurring revenue customer, which we also refer to as wallet share.

In 2021, the company had a net income of $44.6 million, a 2% decrease from the previous year's net income of $45.6 million.

The company's cash at the end of 2021 was $207.6 million. Operating activities generated $112.9 million, while investing activities used $46.7 million, mainly for purchases of investments. Financing activities used another $8.4 million, primarily for repurchases of common stock.

Strategy

The company's objective is to be the leading global provider of supply chain management solutions. Key elements of its strategy include:

Further, penetrate its current market by continue leveraging its relationships with customers and their trading partners to obtain new sales leads;

Increase revenues from its customer base by introducing new solutions to sell to its customers;

Expand its distribution channels to gain new customers. The company believes there are valuable opportunities to promote and sell its solutions through collaboration with other providers;

Expand its international presence by increasing its global sales efforts to obtain new customers around the world. It intends to leverage its current global presence to increase the number of integrations it has with retailers in foreign markets to make its solutions more valuable to its trading partners based overseas;

Enhance and expand its services by improving and developing the functionality and features of its cloud-based Platform, including, from time to time, developing new solutions and applications; and

Selectively pursue strategic acquisitions by evaluating potential acquisitions based on the number of new customers, revenue, functionality, or geographic reach the acquisition would provide relative to the purchase price and its ability to integrate and operate the acquired business.

Mergers and Acquisitions

In late 2021, SPS Commerce acquired Genius Central, a leader in in-aisle ordering for natural and specialty food grocer, for approximately $17 million in cash. The acquisition strengthens company's leadership in the food retail, food distribution, and health and wellness categories.

EXECUTIVES

Chairwoman, Director, Tami L. Reller
President, Chief Executive Officer, Director, Archie C. Black, $495,000 total compensation
Executive Vice President, Chief Operating Officer, James J. Frome, $360,000 total compensation
Executive Vice President, Chief Financial Officer, Kimberly K. Nelson, $345,000 total compensation
Director, Martin J. Leestma
Director, James B. Ramsey
Director, Marty M. Reaume
Director, Philip E. Soran
Director, Sven A. Wehrwein
Auditors : KPMG LLP

LOCATIONS

HQ: SPS Commerce, Inc.
333 South Seventh Street, Suite 1000, Minneapolis, MN 55402
Phone: 612 435-9400
Web: www.spscommerce.com

COMPETITORS

COVISINT CORPORATION
CSG SYSTEMS INTERNATIONAL, INC.
DEMANDWARE, INC.
PROS HOLDINGS, INC.
QLIK TECHNOLOGIES INC.
SENDGRID, INC.
STARTEK, INC.

SUPPORT.COM, INC.
SYNNEX CORPORATION
TOTAL SYSTEM SERVICES, INC.

HISTORICAL FINANCIALS
Company Type: Public

Income Statement   FYE: December 31

	REVENUE ($mil)	NET INCOME ($mil)	NET PROFIT MARGIN	EMPLOYEES
12/20	312.6	45.5	14.6%	1,572
12/19	279.1	33.7	12.1%	1,363
12/18	248.2	23.8	9.6%	1,231
12/17	220.5	(2.4)	—	1,336
12/16	193.2	5.7	3.0%	1,217
Annual Growth	12.8%	68.1%	—	6.6%

2020 Year-End Financials
Debt ratio: —
Return on equity: 11.7%
Cash ($ mil.): 149.6
Current Ratio: 3.39
Long-term debt ($ mil.): —
No. of shares ($ mil.): 35.4
Dividends
  Yield: —
  Payout: —
Market value ($ mil.): 3,854.0

	STOCK PRICE ($) FY Close	P/E High/Low		PER SHARE ($) Earnings	Dividends	Book Value
12/20	108.59	86	25	1.26	0.00	11.86
12/19	55.42	118	48	0.94	0.00	10.18
12/18	82.38	144	70	0.68	0.00	9.19
12/17	48.59	—	—	(0.07)	0.00	8.08
12/16	69.89	436	231	0.17	0.00	7.30
Annual Growth	11.6%	—	—	66.2%	—	12.9%

SStarTrade Tech Inc

EXECUTIVES

President, Chief Executive Officer, Director, Mustafa Laz
Vice President, Chief Technology Officer, Director, Ismail Uslu
Chief Financial Officer, Director, Besim Diril
Chief Operating Officer, Director, Huseyin Etem Laz
Auditors: Robert L. White & Associates, Inc.

LOCATIONS

HQ: SStarTrade Tech Inc
3773 Howard Hughes Parkway, South Tower, Suite 500, Las Vegas, NV 89169
Phone: 212 371-7799
Web: www.sstartradetech.com

HISTORICAL FINANCIALS
Company Type: Public

Income Statement   FYE: December 31

	REVENUE ($mil)	NET INCOME ($mil)	NET PROFIT MARGIN	EMPLOYEES
12/20	298.4	45.3	15.2%	0
12/19	195.6	9.7	5.0%	0
12/18	188.4	1.7	0.9%	0
12/17	142.2	5.1	3.7%	0
12/16	0.1	(0.0)	—	0
Annual Growth	522.2%	—	—	0

2020 Year-End Financials
Debt ratio: 12.0%
Return on equity: 86.4%
Cash ($ mil.): 56.2
Current Ratio: 0.84
Long-term debt ($ mil.): 9.6
No. of shares ($ mil.): 99.6
Dividends
  Yield: —
  Payout: —
Market value ($ mil.): 4.0

	STOCK PRICE ($) FY Close	P/E High/Low		PER SHARE ($) Earnings	Dividends	Book Value
12/20	0.04	—	—	0.00	0.00	0.63
12/19	0.05	—	—	0.00	0.00	0.42
12/18	0.02	—	—	0.00	0.00	0.00
12/17	0.06	—	—	0.00	0.00	0.00
Annual Growth	99.5%	—	—	—	—	25.3%

St. Joe Co. (The)

Wanna buy some swampland in Florida? Perhaps something a bit more upscale? St. Joe has it, along with timberland and beaches. Formerly operating in paper, sugar, timber, telephone systems, and railroads, St. Joe is a Florida real estate developer and one of the state's largest private landowners. It holds some 175,000 acres of land, entitled for future development located mostly in northwest Florida. Approximately 90% of its land holdings are within 15 miles of the Gulf of Mexico, including beach frontage and other waterfront properties. The company is primarily engaged in developing residential resorts and towns, commerce parks, and rural property sales. St. Joe also operates a forestry segment, which grows, harvests, and sells timber and wood fiber.

Operations

The company operates its business in four reportable operating segments: hospitality, residential real estate, commercial leasing and sales and forestry.

The hospitality segment (accounts more than 35% of total revenue) features a private membership club (The Clubs by JOE), hotel operations, food and beverage operations, golf courses, beach clubs, retail outlets, gulf-front vacation rentals, management services, marinas and other entertainment assets.

The residential real estate segment (nearly 35% of total revenue) typically plans and develops residential communities of various sizes across a wide range of price points and sells homesites to builders or retail consumers. Residential real estate segment also evaluates opportunities to enter into JV agreements for specific communities such as Latitude Margaritaville Watersound. Some of its major residential development communities includes the WaterColor, Camp Creek, Watersound Origins, and Breakfast Point community.

The commercial leasing and sales segment (more than 15%) includes construction and leasing of multi-family, retail, office and commercial property, cell towers and other assets, an assisted living community, as well as planning, development, entitlement, management and sale of the company's commercial land holdings for a variety of uses.

Forestry segment (nearly 15%) which holds approximately 113,000 acres of lands focuses on the timber holdings in Northwest Florida and generates revenue primarily from open market sales of timber on site. It grow and sell pulpwood, sawtimber and other forest products.

Geographic Reach

St. Joe is based in Watersound, Florida, and owns approximately 175,000 acres of land located in Northwest Florida.

Sales and Marketing

The company's customers includes builders and to consumers in communities. In addition, one of its joint ventures has initiated more than 55 active adult community in Bay County, Florida.

Financial Performance

After a slight dip in 2016, the company posted consecutive years of increase in revenue. Overall revenue growth since 2015 was 21%.

Revenue in 2019 was $127.1 million, an increase of 15% from the prior year. Real estate, Hospitality, and Leasing segments all have increased revenue, partially offset by a $1.7 million decrease in the Timber segment.

Net income attributable to the company in 2019 was $26.8 million. Higher revenue and a $5.3 million increase from Other income contributed to the increase in net income.

Cash and cash equivalents at the end of the period were $188.7 million. Net cash provided by operating activities was $30.4 million while investing and financing activities each used $29.3 million and $10.5 million, respectively. Main cash uses were for capital expenditures and repurchases of common shares.

Strategy

The company believes that its present liquidity position and its land holdings can provide it with numerous opportunities to continue to increase recurring revenue and create long-term value for its shareholders by allowing it to focus on its core business activity of real estate development and asset management near the Gulf of Mexico, Gulf Intracoastal Waterway, Northwest Florida Beaches International Airport, the Pier Park area and the Scenic Highway 30A corridor.

In 2018, it began the development or construction of 9 new residential, hospitality, multi-family, or commercial projects or phases. By contrast, in 2019, it began the development or construction of 27 new residential, hospitality, multi-family, or commercial projects or phases. Several of these projects were completed as of December 31, 2019. In addition, it continued to develop residential homesites in several communities to deliver on the 930 homesites it has under contract to builders or retail consumers.

As of the end of 2019, it has a total of 468 apartment or assisted living units, 597 hotel rooms, and 130,785 square feet of commercial and hospitality space under development or construction. It anticipates the completion of the construction and placement of these new assets into operations at various times in 2020 and 2021.

In addition to the projects the company began in 2018 and 2019, it also began planning, designing, and permitting other projects that are expected to move into construction or development in 2020 and beyond. Some of the projects will be constructed through third party joint venture partners. While it expects to commence development and construction of a number of projects in 2020 and beyond, timing of some projects may be delayed due to factors beyond its control.

It presently owns and/or operates a wide range of hospitality assets, which already generate significant recurring revenue for them. It is expanding the scope and scale of its hospitality assets and services to enable it to enhance the value and revenue those assets provide. It presently owns a wide range of income producing commercial assets. It intends to explore opportunities to increase the size and scope of its assets in ways that can increase recurring revenue while supporting the growth of its residential and hospitality assets.

The company plan to continue to maintain a high degree of liquidity while seeking opportunities to invest its cash in ways that it believes can increase shareholder value, including share repurchases, real estate, and other strategic investments.

Company Background

Formerly engaged in the residential construction and related industries, the company saw its sales plummet when Florida was among the hardest-hit markets of the housing bust and economic downturn. The 2010 explosion of the Deepwater Horizon drilling platform off the coast of Louisiana also impacted St. Joe as a result of widespread environmental damage. To combat the economic challenges, the company exited several lines of business in order to focus on real estate development and managing its timberland holdings.

HISTORY

After Alfred I. du Pont scandalized society by divorcing his first wife to marry his cousin in 1907, he began investing in Florida land.

Du Pont, who lived in Florida for nine years, wanted to help revitalize Florida's Depression-era economy. Du Pont died in 1935 and the family's legendary success was passed in part to the Alfred I. du Pont Testamentary Trust, formed the year after du Pont's death to unify his holdings and to benefit a charitable foundation.

Edward Ball, du Pont's brother-in-law and executor of his estate, opened St. Joe Paper in 1936. With his shrewd business sense, Ball also invested in transportation infrastructure and banks. St. Joe Paper made scattershot investments over the next several decades, including telephone companies, railroad and highway improvements, and real estate development. Ball made a point of keeping good relations with his employees.

When Ball died in 1981, chairmanship of Alfred du Pont's trust passed to Ball's friend and St. Joe Paper chairman, Jacob Belin.

St. Joe Paper sold a 17% stake in itself to the public in 1990. Galvanized by stockholder complaints, the company sold its paper mills and telecommunications operations and changed its name to St. Joe Corp. (1996). Income spiked that year with the $98 million condemnation sale of land to the State of Florida for Everglades restoration.

In 1997 St. Joe tapped Disney veteran Peter Rummell as chairman and CEO; he refocused the company on real estate, buying into planned-community company Arvida.

St. Joe Corp. changed its name to The St. Joe Company in 1998 and bought Prudential Florida Realty, the state's largest residential real estate company.

St. Joe announced in 1999 that it would sell off most of its raw land. In 2000 regulators approved the company's spinoff to investors of its 54% stake in Florida East Coast Industries, a member of the company's transportation segment. The company also formed an alliance with a London-based real estate brokerage to promote real estate business between the UK and Florida that year.

The following year, St. Joe sold 26 acres of land to the Port Authority of Port St. Joe, a city on the Gulf Coast in northwestern Florida, for the renovation of a deepwater port. In 2002 the company sold Arvida Realty (the former Prudential Florida Realty) to Cendant, now Avis Budget Group, Inc. Cendant spun off its real estate operations in 2006 as Realogy.

In 2003 the company opened the first of its RiverCamps series of homesites within rustic developments in northwestern Florida (as part of its New Ruralism product portfolio, which also includes farm and ranch developments).

The company sold its property management subsidiary Advantis/GVA in 2005 to that company's management, although Advantis/GVA retained management responsibilities for much of its portfolio. The sale was described as a step in strengthening St. Joe's core geographic focus (Advantis/GVA is active in a broader geographic area).

The company undertook a significant restructuring in 2007, at which time it exited the homebuilding market, cut its workforce, and sold its office holdings in Florida, Tennessee, and Virginia to Eola Capital. St. Joe's decision to shut down its homebuilding operations didn't mean the company quit the residential market. Instead, it concentrated on the land development side, actively seeking business partners interested in purchasing entitled land and investing capital into projects. The restructuring also meant giving up the property management side of business. St. Joe began outsourcing property management of its resorts, golf courses, and marinas.

St. Joe saw its sales plummet when Florida was among the hardest-hit markets of the housing bust and economic downturn. To free up some liquidity, St. Joe in 2009 sold property developments including communities and golf courses in central Florida and homes in North and South Carolina. It also renegotiated its credit terms and utilized a tax strategy to help its earnings, but the books ultimately reflected a loss of $130 million that year.

EXECUTIVES

Chairman, Bruce R. Berkowitz
President, Chief Executive Officer, Director, Jorge Luis Gonzalez, $400,000 total compensation
Executive Vice President, Chief Financial Officer, Chief Accounting Officer, Marek Bakun, $350,000 total compensation
Senior Vice President, General Counsel, Corporate Secretary, Elizabeth J. (Lisa) Walters, $90,000 total compensation
Senior Vice President, Chief Administrative Officer, Rhea Goff
Director, Cesar L. Alvarez
Director, Howard S. Frank
Director, Thomas P. Murphy
Auditors : Grant Thornton LLP

LOCATIONS

HQ: St. Joe Co. (The)
130 Richard Jackson Boulevard, Suite 200, Panama City Beach, FL 32407
Phone: 850 231-6400
Web: www.joe.com

PRODUCTS/OPERATIONS

2015 Sales

	$ mil.	% of total
Resorts and leisure revenues	54.5	53
Real estate sales	33.7	32
Leasing revenues	9.0	9
Timber sales	6.7	6
Total	103.9	100

2015 sales

	$ mil	% of total
Resorts and leisure	54.5	52
Residential real estate	21.2	20
Forestry	12.0	12
Leasing operations	9.0	9
Commercial real estate	7.2	7
Total	103.9	100

Selected Subsidiaries

Artisan Park, L.L.C.
Crooked Creek Utility Company
East San Marco, LLC
Florida Timber Finance I, LLC
Georgia Timber Finance I, LLC

Panama City Beach Venture, LLC
Paradise Pointe, L.L.C.
Park Point Land, LLC
Paseos, LLC
Plume Street, LLC
Plume Street Manager, LLC
Residential Community Title Company
Rivercrest, LLC
St. James Island Utility Company
SweetTea Publishing, L.L.C.
Talisman Sugar Corporation

COMPETITORS

HAMMERSON PLC
JONES LANG LASALLE INCORPORATED
MAXXAM INC.
REDROW PLC
THE HOWARD HUGHES CORPORATION
THE IRVINE COMPANY LLC
THE TRUMP ORGANIZATION INC
TISHMAN CONSTRUCTION CORPORATION
TISHMAN SPEYER PROPERTIES, L.P.
WYNDHAM VACATION OWNERSHIP, INC.

HISTORICAL FINANCIALS
Company Type: Public

Income Statement — FYE: December 31

	REVENUE ($mil)	NET INCOME ($mil)	NET PROFIT MARGIN	EMPLOYEES
12/20	160.5	45.2	28.2%	48
12/19	127.0	26.7	21.1%	55
12/18	110.2	32.3	29.4%	53
12/17	98.7	59.5	60.3%	47
12/16	95.7	15.8	16.6%	47
Annual Growth	13.8%	29.9%	—	0.5%

2020 Year-End Financials

Debt ratio: 32.4%
Return on equity: 8.4%
Cash ($ mil.): 106.7
Current Ratio: 1.48
Long-term debt ($ mil.): 336.2
No. of shares ($ mil.): 58.8
Dividends
Yield: 0.1%
Payout: 9.0%
Market value ($ mil.): 2,500.0

	STOCK PRICE ($) FY Close	P/E High/Low		PER SHARE ($) Earnings	Dividends	Book Value
12/20	42.45	64	21	0.77	0.07	9.35
12/19	19.83	45	29	0.45	0.00	8.74
12/18	13.17	38	25	0.52	0.00	8.54
12/17	18.05	23	19	0.84	0.00	8.76
12/16	19.00	102	69	0.21	0.00	9.00
Annual Growth	22.3%	—	—	38.4%	—	1.0%

Staar Surgical Co.

STAAR Surgical Company designs, develops, manufactures, and sells implantable lenses for the eye and delivery systems used to deliver the lenses into the eye. STAAR is the leading manufacturer of lenses used worldwide in corrective or "refractive" surgery. The company also makes lenses for use in surgery that treats cataracts. Its primary products include Visian-branded implantable lenses (ICLs) for correcting such refractive conditions as near- and far-sightedness and astigmatism. The company sells its products in about 75 countries. China is STAAR's largest single market.

Operations

STAAR manufactures the proprietary collagen-containing raw material used in its ICLs internally. The company's principal products are ICLs (accounting for nearly 90% of total sales) used in refractive surgery and IOLs used in cataract surgery (more than 10% of total sales).

The company had about 80 domestic and foreign patents and some 25 patent applications pending.

Geographic Reach

California-based, STAAR operates from leased facilities around the world. It has corporate offices, manufacturing operations, and warehousing and distribution operations in Monrovia, California, and in Nidau, and Brugg Switzerland. The company also has additional R&D facilities and a raw material production facility in California. In Japan, the company has corporate offices and an inspection, packaging, and distribution site.

China brings in about 45% of STAAR's revenue, followed by Japan which gives in more than 20% of revenue. The US generate roughly 5% and the rest comes from other countries combined.

Sales and Marketing

STARR sells its products in more than 75 countries around the world. It has direct distribution channels in the US, Canada, Singapore, Japan, Spain, Germany, and the UK; it sells through independent distributors elsewhere.

Products are marketed to a variety of health care providers, including hospitals, ophthalmic surgeons, surgical centers, vision centers, and government agencies.

The company spent $9.2 million, $11 million, and $9 million for advertising in fiscal years 2020, 2019, and 2018 respectively.

Financial Performance

STAAR has seen rising revenue in the past five years, especially due to higher sales of ICL products, and in 2019 the company started to post profits after several years of losses.

Revenue increased by 9% to $163.5 million in 2020. The increase in net sales was due to an increase in ICL sales of $12.1 million.

Net income decreased by 58% to $5.9 million in 2020.

The company ended 2020 with $150 million in net cash, $32 million more than it had at the end of 2019. Operating activities provided $20.9 million, and financing activities provided $19.6 million. Investing activities used $8.4 million in cash for the acquisition of property and equipment.

Strategy

The strategic priority of the company for 2021 is to continue achieving and strengthening its 2020 strategic priorities which are to position EVO implantable lenses as a special and transformational pathway to Visual Freedom; execute a go-to-market strategy to significantly expand market share globally; innovate and develop a pipeline of next generation premium Collamer-based intraocular lenses; support the transformation of the refractive surgery paradigm to lens-based through clinical validation and medical affairs excellence; continue our focus on and commitment to STAAR's Culture of Quality; and deliver shareholder value.

To realize these priorities, it is planning to continue to invest in manufacturing and facilities expansion that includes, among other things: (i) increasing manufacturing capacity at the Monrovia, California facility for its myopia ICLs; (ii) reopening and expanding its manufacturing and distribution facilities in Switzerland; (iii) preparing for the validation of its Lake Forest, California facility for the manufacturing of its ICL with EDOF for presbyopia lenses, which it expects to be approved for sale initially in CE Mark countries; Continue market share gains in all global markets, including China; Continue to increase investment in Direct-to-Consumer marketing and patient education in targeted markets; and Continue to strengthen existing and finalize new strategic agreements and alliances with global partners.

EXECUTIVES

President, Chief Executive Officer, Director, Caren L. Mason, $585,312 total compensation
Vice President, Chief Medical Officer, Scott Barnes
Research & Development Vice President, Research & Development Chief Technology Officer, Keith Holliday, $363,569 total compensation
Business Development Vice President, Business Development Chief Legal Officer, Business Development Chief Compliance Officer, Business Development Secretary, Samuel J. Gesten, $357,590 total compensation
Chief Financial Officer, Patrick F. Williams
Global Marketing Region Officer, James E. Francese, $274,185 total compensation
Director, Lin Elizabeth Yeu
Director, K. Peony Yu
Director, Gilbert H. Kliman
Director, Thomas G. Frinzi
Director, Stephen C. Farrell
Director, Aimee S. Weisner
Director, Louis E. Silverman
Auditors: BDO USA, LLP

LOCATIONS

HQ: Staar Surgical Co.
25651 Atlantic Ocean Drive, Lake Forest, CA 92630
Phone: 626 303-7902
Web: www.staar.com

2016 Sales

	$ mil.	% of total
Japan	17,329	21
China	16,019	19
U.S.	9,859	12
Korea	7,455	9
Other	31,770	39
Total	82,432	100

PRODUCTS/OPERATIONS

2017 Sales

	$ mil.	% of total
ICL	68.3	75
IOL	17.3	19
Other	5.0	6
Total	90.6	100

Selected Products
ICL
    EVO Visian ICL
    EVO+ Visian ICL
    Visian ICL
IOL
    Collamer IOL
    Pre-loaded IOL

COMPETITORS

1-800 CONTACTS, INC.
ASENSUS SURGICAL, INC.
BAUSCH & LOMB INCORPORATED
COOPERVISION, INC.
ENDOLOGIX, INC.
ESSILOR OF AMERICA, INC.
ESSILORLUXOTTICA
NATIONAL VISION HOLDINGS, INC.
SURMODICS, INC.
THE COOPER COMPANIES INC

HISTORICAL FINANCIALS

Company Type: Public

Income Statement   FYE: January 1

	REVENUE ($mil)	NET INCOME ($mil)	NET PROFIT MARGIN	EMPLOYEES
01/21	163.4	5.9	3.6%	575
01/20*	150.1	14.0	9.4%	550
12/18	123.9	4.9	4.0%	475
12/17	90.6	(2.1)	—	353
12/16	82.4	(12.1)	—	336
Annual Growth	18.7%	—	—	14.4%

*Fiscal year change

2021 Year-End Financials

Debt ratio: 0.7%
Return on equity: 3.3%
Cash ($ mil.): 152.4
Current Ratio: 5.25
Long-term debt ($ mil.): —
No. of shares ($ mil.): 46.4
Dividends
  Yield: —
  Payout: —
Market value ($ mil.): 3,680.0

	STOCK PRICE ($) FY Close	P/E High/Low		PER SHARE ($) Earnings	Dividends	Book Value
01/21	79.22	637	192	0.12	0.00	4.25
01/20*	34.38	127	72	0.30	0.00	3.57
12/18	31.26	422	116	0.11	0.00	3.00
12/17	15.50	—	—	(0.05)	0.00	1.04
12/16	10.85	—	—	(0.30)	0.00	0.93
Annual Growth	64.4%	—	—	—	—	46.2%

*Fiscal year change

STAG Industrial Inc

If STAG Industrial were to show up alone at a party, it would likely be on the hunt for single tenants looking to lease industrial space. The self-managed and self-administered real estate investment trust (REIT) has built a business acquiring and managing single-tenant industrial properties located across more than 35 states. The company's portfolio consists primarily of about 91.4 million sq. ft. of leasable warehouse, distribution, manufacturing, and office space located in secondary markets. STAG conducts most of its business through its operating partner, STAG Industrial Operating Partnership. Pennsylvania accounts for the highest annual base rental revenue.

Operations

STAG's property portfolio consists of 450 buildings spanning about 91.4 million sq. ft. across more than 35 states. Approximately 75% of its rental income comes from its fixed lease payments, while about 20% comes from its variable lease payments. The rest of its rental revenue comes from its straight-line rental. Its properties are about 95% leased to a collective nearly 415 tenants.

Key subsidiaries include STAG Industrial Operating Partnership, STAG Industrial GP, STAG Industrial Management, STAG Industrial TRS, and STAG Investments Holdings III, among others.

Geographic Reach

Based in Massachusetts, STAG owns and manages single-tenant industrial properties across 35-plus states. More than 35% of its rental income came from its properties in the states of North Carolina, Ohio, Illinois, Pennsylvania, and Texas.

Sales and Marketing

STAG made about 40% of its rental income from tenants out of five industries, including: Automotive; Commercial Services & Supplies; Containers & Packaging; Air Freight and Logistics; and Machinery. While none of its tenants accounted for more than 2% of its total rental income, its top five customers in 2019 included Amazon, General Service Administration, XPO Logistics, Inc., DHL Supply Chain, and Solo Cup.

Financial Performance

STAG Industrial's revenues have nearly doubled since 2015 as it has expanded its property portfolio through acquisitions and has charged higher rental rates as the economy has strengthened. The REIT has also experienced a fluctuation in recent years, mostly as its interest expenses on its long-term debt have been higher than its operating profits.

The REIT's revenue jumped 16% to a new record of $406 million in 2019, thanks to a $55.7 million increase in rental income.

Net income in 2019 decreased by $45.6 million to $49.3 million. The decrease in net income was due to a $30 million increase in operating expenses and higher Other expenses.

Cash at the end of the period was $11.9 million. Net cash provided by operating activities was $233.4 million and cash provided by financing activities was $978.5 million. Investing activities used $1.2 billion for acquisition and building improvements.

Strategy

The company's primary business objectives are to own and operate a balanced and diversified portfolio of binary risk investments (individual single-tenant industrial properties) that maximize cash flows available for distribution to its stockholders and to enhance stockholder value over time by achieving sustainable long-term growth in distributable cash flow from operations.

Stag Industrial believes that its focus on owning and operating a portfolio of individually-acquired, single-tenant industrial properties throughout the United States will when compared to other real estate portfolios, generate returns for its stockholders that are attractive to them.

It seeks to identify properties for acquisition that offer relative value across all locations, industrial property types, and tenants through the principled application of its proprietary risk assessment model; operate its properties in an efficient, cost-effective manner; and capitalize its business appropriately given the characteristics of its assets.

Company Background

The company's CEO and founder, Benjamin S. Butcher, founded STAG Industrial's predecessor companies in 2003. Butcher and other investors formed STAG Industrial to consolidate the companies' assets under a REIT umbrella for tax purposes and to raise public funds.

EXECUTIVES

Chairman, President, Chief Executive Officer, Benjamin S. Butcher, $650,000 total compensation

Executive Vice President, Chief Financial Officer, Treasurer, William R. Crooker, $360,000 total compensation

Executive Vice President, Chief Operating Officer, Stephen C. Mecke, $375,000 total compensation

Executive Vice President, Secretary, General Counsel, Jeffrey M. Sullivan, $300,000 total compensation

Lead Independent Director, Director, Larry T. Guillemette

Director, Virgis W. Colbert

Director, Jit Kee Chin

Director, Michelle Dilley

Director, Jeffrey D. Furber

Director, Francis X. Jacoby

Director, Christopher P. Marr

Director, Hans S. Weger

Auditors : PricewaterhouseCoopers LLP

LOCATIONS

HQ: STAG Industrial Inc
  One Federal Street, 23rd Floor, Boston, MA 02110
Phone: 617 574-4777   **Fax:** 617 574-0052
Web: www.stagindustrial.com

Selected States
Florida
Indiana
Iowa

Kansas
Kentucky
Maine
Massachusetts
Michigan
New York
North Carolina
Ohio
Pennsylvania
South Dakota
Texas
Virginia
Wisconsin

PRODUCTS/OPERATIONS

2014 Sales

	$ mil.	% of total
Rental income	149.5	86
Tenant recoveries	23.6	14
Others	0.7	-
Total	173.8	100

COMPETITORS

A & J MUCKLOW GROUP LIMITED
ARMADA/HOFFLER PROPERTIES, L.L.C.
CAPITACOMMERCIAL TRUST
DCT INDUSTRIAL TRUST INC.
FIRST INDUSTRIAL REALTY TRUST, INC.
GLADSTONE COMMERCIAL CORPORATION
Granite REIT Inc
INVESTORS REAL ESTATE TRUST
KITE REALTY GROUP TRUST
LIBERTY PROPERTY TRUST

HISTORICAL FINANCIALS
Company Type: Public

Income Statement — FYE: December 31

	REVENUE ($mil)	NET INCOME ($mil)	NET PROFIT MARGIN	EMPLOYEES
12/21	562.1	192.3	34.2%	86
12/20	483.4	202.1	41.8%	78
12/19	405.9	49.2	12.1%	72
12/18	350.9	92.9	26.5%	73
12/17	301.0	31.2	10.4%	72
Annual Growth	16.9%	57.5%	—	4.5%

2021 Year-End Financials

Debt ratio: 38.0%
Return on equity: 6.3%
Cash ($ mil.): 18.9
Current Ratio: 0.77
Long-term debt ($ mil.): 2,218.2
No. of shares ($ mil.): 177.7
Dividends
Yield: 3.0%
Payout: 115.0%
Market value ($ mil.): 8,526.0

	STOCK PRICE ($) FY Close	P/E High/Low		PER SHARE ($) Earnings	Dividends	Book Value
12/21	47.96	42	26	1.15	1.45	18.72
12/20	31.32	26	14	1.32	1.44	17.17
12/19	31.57	90	69	0.35	1.43	16.14
12/18	24.88	36	28	0.79	1.42	14.39
12/17	27.33	120	95	0.23	1.41	14.01
Annual Growth	15.1%	—	—	49.5%	0.8%	7.5%

Starwood Property Trust Inc.

Starwood Property Trust hopes to shine brightly in the world of mortgages. A real estate investment trust (REIT), the company originates, finances, and manages US commercial and residential mortgage loans, commercial mortgage-backed securities, and other commercial real estate debt investments. It acquires discounted loans from failed banks and financial institutions, some through the FDIC, which typically auctions off large pools of loan portfolios. Starwood Property Trust is externally managed by SPT Management, LLC, an affiliate of Starwood Capital Group. As a REIT, the trust is exempt from paying federal income tax so long as it distributes quarterly dividends to shareholders.

Financial Performance

Overall revenues grew 63% in 2012 to $327 million, up from $201 million in 2011. The trust primarily earns money on interest income from mortgage-backed securities and loans.

Mergers and Acquisitions

In 2013 Starwood Property Trust bought LNR Property LLC, a real estate investment, finance, management and development firm. The trust paid $862 million for LNR's US special servicer, the US investment securities portfolio, Archetype Mortgage Capital (now Starwood Mortgage Capital), Archetype Financial Institution Services, LNR Europe, and 50% of LNR's interest in Auction.com.

Later that year it moved to spin off its single-family residential business as a new REIT named Starwood Waypoint Residential Trust. The trust, which will be affiliated with Waypoint Homes, will invest, own, and operate single-family rental homes and non-performing residential mortgage loans in the US.

EXECUTIVES

Chairman, Chief Executive Officer, Director, Barry S. Sternlicht, $0 total compensation
President, Jeffrey F. DiModica, $450,000 total compensation
Executive Vice President, Chief Operating Officer, Chief Compliance Officer, General Counsel, Secretary, Andrew Jay Sossen, $400,000 total compensation
Chief Financial Officer, Treasurer, Principal Financial Officer, Chief Accounting Officer, Rina Paniry, $600,000 total compensation
Lead Director, Director, Richard D. Bronson
Director, Jeffrey G. Dishner
Director, Camille J. Douglas
Director, Solomon J. Kumin
Director, Frederick Perpall
Director, Fred S. Ridley
Director, Strauss Zelnick
Auditors : DELOITTE & TOUCHE LLP

LOCATIONS

HQ: Starwood Property Trust Inc.
591 West Putnam Avenue, Greenwich, CT 06830
Phone: 203 422-7700
Web: www.starwoodpropertytrust.com

COMPETITORS

ANWORTH MORTGAGE ASSET CORPORATION
BLACKSTONE MORTGAGE TRUST, INC.
CHERRY HILL MORTGAGE INVESTMENT CORPORATION
HUNT COMPANIES FINANCE TRUST, INC.
LNR PROPERTY LLC
NEW YORK MORTGAGE TRUST, INC.
PETRA REAL ESTATE OPPORTUNITY TRUST
RAIT FINANCIAL TRUST
REDWOOD TRUST, INC.
WESTERN ASSET MORTGAGE CAPITAL CORPORATION

HISTORICAL FINANCIALS
Company Type: Public

Income Statement — FYE: December 31

	ASSETS ($mil)	NET INCOME ($mil)	INCOME AS % OF ASSETS	EMPLOYEES
12/20	80,873.5	331.6	0.4%	282
12/19	78,042.3	509.6	0.7%	296
12/18	68,262.4	385.8	0.6%	290
12/17	62,941.2	400.7	0.6%	312
12/16	77,256.2	365.1	0.5%	340
Annual Growth	1.2%	(2.4%)	—	(4.6%)

2020 Year-End Financials

Return on assets: 0.4%
Return on equity: 7.1%
Long-term debt ($ mil.): —
No. of shares ($ mil.): 284.6
Sales ($ mil.): 1,136.1
Dividends
Yield: 9.9%
Payout: 165.5%
Market value ($ mil.): 5,494.0

	STOCK PRICE ($) FY Close	P/E High/Low		PER SHARE ($) Earnings	Dividends	Book Value
12/20	19.30	23	8	1.16	1.92	15.77
12/19	24.86	14	11	1.79	1.92	16.66
12/18	19.71	16	13	1.42	1.92	16.70
12/17	21.35	15	14	1.52	1.92	17.13
12/16	21.95	15	11	1.50	1.92	17.44
Annual Growth	(3.2%)	—	—	(6.2%)	0.0%	(2.5%)

StepStone Group Inc

EXECUTIVES

Chairman, Co-Chief Executive Officer, Director, Monte M. Brem
Co-Chief Executive Officer, Director, Scott W. Hart
Chief Financial Officer, Johnny D. Randel
Co-Chief Operating Officer, Director, Jose A. Fernandez
Chief Accounting Officer, David Y. Park
Strategy Head, Director, Michael I. McCabe
Director, Valerie G. Brown
Director, David F. Hoffmeister
Director, Thomas Keck
Director, Mark Maruszewski
Director, Steven R. Mitchell
Director, Anne L. Raymond
Director, Robert A. Waldo

LOCATIONS

HQ: StepStone Group Inc
450 Lexington Avenue, 31st Floor, New York, NY 10017

Phone: 212 351-6100
Web: www.stepstonegroup.com

HISTORICAL FINANCIALS
Company Type: Public

Income Statement — FYE: March 31

	REVENUE ($mil)	NET INCOME ($mil)	NET PROFIT MARGIN	EMPLOYEES
03/21	787.7	62.6	8.0%	570
03/20	446.6	131.9	29.5%	526
03/19	256.2	54.1	21.1%	0
03/18	264.2	81.4	30.8%	0
Annual Growth	43.9%	(8.4%)	—	—

2021 Year-End Financials
Debt ratio: —
Return on equity: 26.9%
Cash ($ mil.): 179.8
Current Ratio: 0.33
Long-term debt ($ mil.): —
No. of shares ($ mil.): 94.8
Dividends
Yield: 0.1%
Payout: 3.3%
Market value ($ mil.): 3,344.0

	STOCK PRICE ($) FY Close	P/E High/Low		PER SHARE ($) Earnings	Dividends	Book Value
03/21	35.27	19	12	2.06	0.07	2.63
Annual Growth	—	—	—	—	—	—

Sterling Construction Co Inc

Sterling Construction company specializes in the building, reconstruction, and repair of transportation and water infrastructure. It also works on specialty projects such as excavation, shoring, and drilling. The heavy civil construction company and its subsidiaries (Texas Sterling Construction, Ralph L. Wadsworth Contractors, RDI Foundation Drilling, Myers and Sons, Banicki Construction, and Road and Highway Builders) primarily serve public sector clients throughout the Southwest and West. Transportation projects include excavation and asphalt paving, as well as construction of bridges and rail systems. Water projects include work on sewers and storm drainage systems.

Geographic Reach
Houston-based Sterling Construction and its subsidiaries operate from offices in Texas, California, Arizona, Utah, and Nevada. The firm's major markets include Texas, Utah, and Nevada.

Financial Performance
The economic recession and prolonged recovery has taken its toll on Sterling Construction. The company reported a net loss of $297 million in 2012, following a loss of $36 million in 2011. The company attributed the losses, which continued in 2013, primarily to additional write-downs on three large projects booked prior to 2012 in Texas that continue to have a negative impact on profitability. Sterling says it expects the projects to be substantially complete by mid-2014.

Revenue is improving however. In 2012, sales increased 26% compared with 2011, to $630.5 million, driven by projects in in Arizona and California. Indeed 2012 marked the third consecutive year of rising sales for the firm. While the revenue picture is brighter, profits are still expected to suffer as Sterling faces increased competitive pressure to bid low for construction projects.

Strategy
Sterling Construction and other companies that rely heavily on government highway work have been hurt buy Congress' inability to pass the Federal Highway Bill. Without new legislation, new projects and funding for the work is uncertain. In response to the uncertain outlook Sterling refocused on project execution and conservative bidding. The company also sold some equipment in order to raise cash to upgrade its fleet.

Sterling Construction's long-term strategy is to expand its geographic footprint to attractive markets. The company also seeks to add to its construction capabilities. It has mostly used acquisitions to achieve those goals.

Increased competition has sent Sterling looking for work in new markets. As a result it has landed contracts in places such as Hawaii, Montana, Idaho, and Louisiana. Sterling also expanded its operations in Texas to include El Paso and Corpus Christi. The company continues to seek opportunities in new markets in western, southwestern, and southeastern states. Sterling also is seeking to work on larger, higher-margin design/build projects by entering joint ventures. One example is Ralph L. Wadsworth Contractors' joint venture with Fluor and two other companies to build a $1.2 billion project on I-15 in Utah.

Mergers and Acquisitions
In January 2013, the firm acquired the remaining 20% interest in Ralph L. Wadsworth Construction Co. from its management for $23.1 million. In 2011 Sterling expanded into Arizona and California with the acquisition of J. Banicki Construction. Also that year Sterling bought a 50% stake in California-based Myer & Sons Construction.

EXECUTIVES
Chairman, Director, Thomas M. White
Chief Executive Officer, Director, Joseph A. Cutillo, $631,731 total compensation
Executive Vice President, Chief Financial Officer, Chief Accounting Officer, Treasurer, Ronald A. Ballschmiede, $464,517 total compensation
Chief Compliance Officer, General Counsel, Corporate Secretary, Mark D. Wolf
Division Officer, Con L. Wadsworth, $425,000 total compensation
Director, Julie A. Dill
Director, Roger A. Cregg
Director, Raymond F. Messer
Director, Dana C. O'Brien
Director, Charles R. Patton
Director, Dwayne A. Wilson
Auditors: Grant Thornton LLP

LOCATIONS
HQ: Sterling Construction Co Inc
1800 Hughes Landing Blvd., The Woodlands, TX 77380
Phone: 281 214-0777
Web: www.strlco.com

PRODUCTS/OPERATIONS
Selected Subsidiaries
J. Banicki Construction, Inc. (Banicki)
Myers and Sons Construction
Ralph L. Wadsworth Contractors, LLC (RLW)
RDI Foundation Drilling (RDI)
Road and Highway Builders, LLC (RHB)
Road and Highway Builders of California (RHBCa)
Texas Sterling Construction Co. (TSC)

COMPETITORS
BALFOUR BEATTY INFRASTRUCTURE, INC.
COLAS SA
GRANITE CONSTRUCTION INCORPORATED
KELLER GROUP PLC
OBAYASHI CORPORATION
PETER KIEWIT SONS', INC.
SKANSKA USA CIVIL INC.
SUMMIT MATERIALS, INC.
TAKENAKA CORPORATION
THE SUNDT COMPANIES INC

HISTORICAL FINANCIALS
Company Type: Public

Income Statement — FYE: December 31

	REVENUE ($mil)	NET INCOME ($mil)	NET PROFIT MARGIN	EMPLOYEES
12/20	1,427.4	42.3	3.0%	2,600
12/19	1,126.2	39.9	3.5%	2,800
12/18	1,037.6	25.1	2.4%	1,935
12/17	957.9	11.6	1.2%	1,740
12/16	690.1	(9.2)	—	1,684
Annual Growth	19.9%	—	—	11.5%

2020 Year-End Financials
Debt ratio: 38.7%
Return on equity: 17.3%
Cash ($ mil.): 66.1
Current Ratio: 1.12
Long-term debt ($ mil.): 291.2
No. of shares ($ mil.): 28.1
Dividends
Yield: —
Payout: —
Market value ($ mil.): 525.0

	STOCK PRICE ($) FY Close	P/E High/Low		PER SHARE ($) Earnings	Dividends	Book Value
12/20	18.61	13	5	1.50	0.00	9.48
12/19	14.08	11	7	1.47	0.00	7.92
12/18	10.89	17	11	0.93	0.00	6.18
12/17	16.28	41	18	0.43	0.00	5.22
12/16	8.46	—	—	(0.40)	0.00	4.30
Annual Growth	21.8%	—	—	—	—	21.9%

Stifel Financial Corp

Stifel Financial, through its wholly owned subsidiaries, is principally engaged in retail brokerage; securities trading; investment banking; investment advisory; retail, consumer, and commercial banking; and related financial services. Some of its subsidiaries include Stifel Independent Advisors (SIA), an independent contractor broker-dealer firm; Keefe, Bruyette & Woods, Inc. (KBW), Miller Buckfire & Co, and Vining Sparks IBG, broker-dealer firms; and 1919 Investment Counsel, LLC, an asset management firm The company's major geographic area of concentration is throughout the US (about 90% of total revenue), with a growing presence in the UK, Europe, and Canada.

Operations

Stifel Financial operates three business segments: Global Wealth Management, Institutional Group, and Other.

The Global Wealth Management segment, which generates around 55% of the company's total revenue, the Private Client Group and Stifel Bancorp. The Private Client Group includes branch offices and independent contractor offices of its broker-dealer subsidiaries located throughout the US. These branches provide securities brokerage services, including the sale of equities, mutual funds, fixed income products, and insurance, as well as offering banking products to their private clients through its bank subsidiaries, which provide residential, consumer, and commercial lending, as well as FDIC-insured deposit accounts to customers of our broker-dealer subsidiaries and to the general public.

The Institutional Group segment (about 45% of revenue) includes research, equity and fixed income institutional sales and trading, investment banking, public finance, and syndicate.

The Other segment includes interest income from stock borrow activities, unallocated interest expense, interest income and gains and losses from investments held, amortization of stock-based awards, and all unallocated overhead cost.

Investment banking accounts for about one-third of revenue, followed by asset management for around 25%, while commissions (more than 15%), principal transactions (more than 10%) and interest (about 10%).

Geographic Reach

Headquartered in St. Louis, Missouri, Stifel Financial maintains its operations in more than 465 leased in various locations throughout the US and in certain foreign countries.

The US accounts for about 90% of total revenue, followed by the UK for about 5%, Canada and other countries for less than 5%.

Sales and Marketing

With more than 2,200 financial advisors and about 90 independent contractors, Stifel serves individuals, corporations, municipalities, and institutions.

Financial Performance

The company's revenue for fiscal 2021 increased by 6% to $809.5 million compared from the prior year with $760.6 million.

Net income for fiscal 2021 increased to $824.9 million compared from the prior year with $503.5 million.

Cash held by the company at the end of fiscal 2021 increased to $2.1 billion. Cash provided by operations and financing activities were $872.1 million and $5.8 billion, respectively. Cash used for investing activities was $7.0 billion, mainly for increase in loans held for investment.

Strategy

Stifel believe its strategy for growth will allow the company to increase its revenues and to expand its role with clients as a valued partner. In executing its growth strategy, Stifel take advantage of the consolidation among mid-tier firms, which the company believe provides it opportunities in its global wealth and institutional group segments. The company do not create specific growth or business plans for any particular type of acquisition, focus on specific firms, or geographic expansion, nor do Stifel establish quantitative goals, such as intended numbers of new hires or new office openings; however, its corporate philosophy has always been to be in a position to take advantage of opportunities as they arise, while maintaining sufficient levels of capital. The company intends to pursue the following strategies with discipline: further expand its private client footprint in the US; further expand its institutional business both domestically and internationally; grow its investment banking business; focus on asset generation within Stifel Bancorp by offering banking services to its clients; and approach acquisition opportunities with discipline.

EXECUTIVES

Chairman, Chief Executive Officer, Subsidiary Officer, Director, Ronald J. Kruszewski, $200,000 total compensation
Senior Managing Director, Co-Chairman, Director, Thomas W. Weisel, $200,000 total compensation
Co-President, Subsidiary Officer, James M. Zemlyak, $250,000 total compensation
Institutional Group Co-President, Institutional Group Director, Victor J. Nesi, $250,000 total compensation
Senior Vice President, Subsidiary Officer, Richard J. Himelfarb, $250,000 total compensation
Senior Vice President, Subsidiary Officer, Thomas B. Michaud, $250,000 total compensation
Vice-Chairman, Senior Vice President, Subsidiary Officer, Ben A. Plotkin, $250,000 total compensation
Senior Vice President, General Counsel, Mark P. Fisher
Chief Financial Officer, Subsidiary Officer, James M. (Jim) Marischen, $200,000 total compensation
Technology Senior Vice President, Strategic Planning Senior Vice President, Operations Senior Vice President, Strategic Planning Chief Operating Officer, Operations Chief Operating Officer, Technology Chief Operating Officer, Strategic Planning Subsidiary Officer, Operations Subsidiary Officer, Technology Subsidiary Officer, David D. Sliney, $15,000 total compensation
Division Officer, David Kelman
Division Officer, Alain Dobkin
Lead Director, Director, Robert E. Grady
Director, Adam T. Berlew
Director, Kathleen L. Brown
Director, Michael W. Brown
Director, Daniel Ludeman
Director, Maura A. Markus
Director, James M. Oates
Director, David A. Peacock
Director, Michael J. Zimmerman
Auditors: Ernst & Young LLP

LOCATIONS

HQ: Stifel Financial Corp
501 North Broadway, St. Louis, MO 63102-2188
Phone: 314 342-2000
Web: www.stifel.com

2016 Sales

	% of total
US	94
UK	5
Other European countries	1
Total	100

PRODUCTS/OPERATIONS

2016 Sales

	$ mil.	% of total
Commissions	730.1	28
Asset management and service fees	582.8	22
Investment banking	513.0	19
Principal transactions	475.4	18
Interest	294.3	11
Others	46.8	2
Total	2,642.4	100

Selected Services

Individual
Bonds
Corporate Executive Services
Estate Planning
Exchange Traded Funds
Financial And Wealth Planning
Insurance
Investment Advisory Services
Market News
Mutual Funds
Options
Portfolio Tracker
Prospectus
Retirement Plans
Stifel Bank & Trust
Stifel Cash Management Accounts
Stifel Mobile Announcement
Stifel Trust
Institutions
Asset Management
Conferences & Events
Equity Capital Markets
Equity Sales & Trading
Fixed Income Sales & Trading
Investment Banking
Public Finance

Research
Senior Management

Selected Subsidiaries
Broadway Air Corp.
    CSA Insurance Agency, Incorporated
Choice Financial Partners, Inc.
    Stifel Bank & Trust
Stifel Nicolaus Limited (UK)
Stifel, Nicolaus & Company, Incorporated
    Ryan Beck Holdings, LLC
Thomas Weisel Partners Group, Inc.

COMPETITORS

ALLIANCEBERNSTEIN HOLDING L.P.
Canaccord Genuity Group Inc
ENVESTNET, INC.
EVERCORE INC.
HOULIHAN LOKEY, INC.
INVESTEC PLC
JANNEY MONTGOMERY SCOTT LLC
NUMIS CORPORATION PLC
OPPENHEIMER HOLDINGS INC.
THE ZIEGLER COMPANIES INC

HISTORICAL FINANCIALS

Company Type: Public

Income Statement — FYE: December 31

	ASSETS ($mil)	NET INCOME ($mil)	INCOME AS % OF ASSETS	EMPLOYEES
12/21	34,049.7	824.8	2.4%	8,600
12/20	26,604.2	503.4	1.9%	8,500
12/19	24,610.2	448.3	1.8%	8,300
12/18	24,519.5	393.9	1.6%	7,500
12/17	21,383.9	182.8	0.9%	7,100
Annual Growth	12.3%	45.7%	—	4.9%

2021 Year-End Financials
Return on assets: 2.7%
Return on equity: 17.7%
Long-term debt ($ mil.): —
No. of shares ($ mil.): 104.5
Sales ($ mil.): 4,783
Dividends
Yield: 0.8%
Payout: 9.8%
Market value ($ mil.): 7,359.0

	STOCK PRICE ($) FY Close	P/E High/Low		PER SHARE ($) Earnings	Dividends	Book Value
12/21	70.42	11	7	6.66	0.60	48.18
12/20	50.46	17	7	4.16	0.45	41.09
12/19	60.65	16	10	3.66	0.40	35.27
12/18	41.42	19	11	3.15	0.32	29.83
12/17	59.56	36	25	1.43	0.13	26.92
Annual Growth	4.3%	—	—	47.0%	45.6%	15.7%

Stock Yards Bancorp Inc

Stock Yards Bancorp is the holding company of Stock Yards Bank & Trust, which operates about 35 branches mostly in Louisville, Kentucky, but also in Indianapolis and Cincinnati. Founded in 1904, the $3 billion-asset bank targets individuals and regional business customers, offering standard retail services, such as checking and savings accounts, credit cards, certificates of deposit, and IRAs. It also provides trust services, while brokerage and credit card services are offered through agreements with other banks. Commercial real estate mortgages make up 40% of the bank's loan portfolio, which also includes commercial and industrial loans (30%), residential mortgages (15%), construction loans, and consumer loans.

Operations

Stock Yards Bank & Trust operates two main business lines: Commercial Banking, which provides loans and deposits to individual consumers and businesses as well as mortgage origination and company brokerage activity; and Investment Management and Trust, which provides wealth management services such as investment management, trust, estate administration, and retirement plan services.

About 63% of the company's total revenue came from loan interest during 2015, while another 7% came from interest income on its securities. The rest came from its investment management and trust services (13% of revenue), deposit account service charges (7%), bankcard transaction revenue (4%), mortgage banking revenue (3%), brokerage commissions and fees (1%), and other non-interest sources.

Geographic Reach

Kentucky-based Stock Yards Bancorp had 37 branches at the end of 2015, including 28 branches in the Louisville, Kentucky metro area and the rest in the Indianapolis, Indiana and Cincinnati, Ohio metro areas.

Financial Performance

Stock Yards' annual revenues have risen 11% since 2011 thanks to a combination of mostly organic loan growth and investment management and trust services fee growth. Meanwhile, its annual profits have grown more than 55% on declining loan loss provisions as its loan portfolio's credit quality has improved with higher property valuations in the strengthened economy.

The bank's revenue climbed 4% to a record $133.12 million during 2015 on higher interest income mostly as its loan assets grew 9% to $2 billion with record loan production.

Revenue growth and a decline in interest expense on deposits in 2015 drove Stock Yard's net income up 7% to a record $34.82 million. The bank's operating cash levels jumped 8% to $43.17 million mostly thanks to the increase in cash-based earnings.

Strategy

Stock Yards outlined its plans for 2016 and beyond to maintain stable net interest margins, achieve near-double digit loan growth, manage credit quality to keep loan loss provisions down, and increasing its regulatory readiness.

Mergers and Acquisitions

In 2013, the bank extended the reach of its operations into Oldham County through its purchase of $146 million-asset The BANcorp, Inc. and its five THE BANK branches in the region for $19.9 million.

EXECUTIVES

Chairman, Subsidiary Officer, Director, David P. Heintzman, $479,000 total compensation
President, Subsidiary Officer, Philip S. Poindexter, $328,000 total compensation
Chief Executive Officer, Subsidiary Officer, Director, James A. Hillebrand, $444,000 total compensation
Senior Executive Vice President, Subsidiary Officer, Director, Kathy C. Thompson, $364,000 total compensation
Executive Vice President, Chief risk Officer, Subsidiary Officer, William M. Dishman, $275,000 total compensation
Executive Vice President, Chief Financial Officer, Chief Strategy Officer, Subsidiary Officer, Thomas Clay Stinnett
Subsidiary Officer, Michael J. Croce
Director, Paul J. Bickel
Director, J. McCauley Brown
Director, Donna L. Heitzman
Director, Carl G. Herde
Director, Richard A. Lechleiter
Director, Stephen M. Priebe
Director, John L. Schutte
Director, Norman Tasman
Auditors: BKD, LLP

LOCATIONS

HQ: Stock Yards Bancorp Inc
1040 East Main Street, Louisville, KY 40206
Phone: 502 582-2571
Web: www.syb.com

PRODUCTS/OPERATIONS

2015 Revenues by Category

	$ mil.	% of total
Interest income	93.1	70
Non-interest income	40.0	30
Total	133.1	100

Selected Products & Services
Personal Banking
    Banking
    Personal Lending
    Personal Investing & Wealth Management Services
Business Banking
    Credit, Loans & Leasing
    Deposit Services
    Treasury Management
    Business Retirement Plans
Wealth Management Services
    Investment Management
    Financial Planning
    Trust & Estate Services
    Brokerage Service

COMPETITORS

ASSOCIATED BANC-CORP
CAMBRIDGE BANCORP
FIRST BUSEY CORPORATION
INDEPENDENT BANK CORP.
UNIVEST FINANCIAL CORPORATION

HISTORICAL FINANCIALS

Company Type: Public

Income Statement   FYE: December 31

	ASSETS ($mil)	NET INCOME ($mil)	INCOME AS % OF ASSETS	EMPLOYEES
12/20	4,608.6	58.8	1.3%	641
12/19	3,724.1	66.0	1.8%	615
12/18	3,302.9	55.5	1.7%	591
12/17	3,239.6	38.0	1.2%	580
12/16	3,039.4	41.0	1.3%	578
Annual Growth	11.0%	9.4%	—	2.6%

2020 Year-End Financials

Return on assets: 1.4%
Return on equity: 13.8%
Long-term debt ($ mil.): —
No. of shares ($ mil.): 22.6
Sales ($ mil.): 199.7
Dividends
  Yield: 2.6%
  Payout: 42.5%
Market value ($ mil.): 919.0

	STOCK PRICE ($) FY Close	P/E High/Low		PER SHARE ($) Earnings	Dividends	Book Value
12/20	40.48	17	9	2.59	1.08	19.42
12/19	41.06	15	11	2.89	1.04	17.97
12/18	32.80	17	12	2.42	0.96	16.11
12/17	37.70	28	19	1.66	0.80	14.71
12/16	46.95	26	15	1.80	0.72	13.88
Annual Growth	(3.6%)	—	—	9.5%	10.8%	8.8%

STORE Capital Corp

Auditors: Ernst & Young LLP

LOCATIONS

HQ: STORE Capital Corp
8377 East Hartford Drive, Suite 100, Scottsdale, AZ 85255
Phone: 480 256-1100
Web: www.storecapital.com

HISTORICAL FINANCIALS

Company Type: Public

Income Statement   FYE: December 31

	REVENUE ($mil)	NET INCOME ($mil)	NET PROFIT MARGIN	EMPLOYEES
12/20	694.2	212.6	30.6%	106
12/19	665.7	284.9	42.8%	97
12/18	540.7	216.9	40.1%	90
12/17	452.8	162.0	35.8%	80
12/16	376.3	123.3	32.8%	68
Annual Growth	16.5%	14.6%	—	11.7%

2020 Year-End Financials

Debt ratio: 41.3%
Return on equity: 4.4%
Cash ($ mil.): 166.3
Current Ratio: 1.74
Long-term debt ($ mil.): 3,722.2
No. of shares ($ mil.): 266.1
Dividends
  Yield: 4.1%
  Payout: 169.0%
Market value ($ mil.): 9,043.0

	STOCK PRICE ($) FY Close	P/E High/Low		PER SHARE ($) Earnings	Dividends	Book Value
12/20	33.98	48	17	0.84	1.42	18.85
12/19	37.24	33	22	1.24	1.36	18.70
12/18	28.31	29	21	1.06	1.28	17.48
12/17	26.04	29	22	0.90	1.20	16.36
12/16	24.71	38	27	0.82	1.12	15.58
Annual Growth	8.3%	—	—	0.6%	6.1%	4.9%

Strategic Education Inc

Strategic Education is an education services company that provides access to high-quality education through campus-based and online post-secondary education offerings, as well as through programs to develop job-ready skills for high-demand markets. It operates primarily through our wholly-owned subsidiaries Strayer University and Capella University, both accredited post-secondary institutions of higher education located in the United States, as well as Torrens University, an accredited post-secondary institution of higher education located in Australia. Its operations emphasize relationships through its Education Technology Services segment (formerly called the Alternative Learning segment) with employers to build employee education benefits programs that provide employees with access to affordable and industry relevant training, certificate, and degree programs.

Operations

Strategic Education has three segments: US Higher Education (USHE), Australia/New Zealand and Education Technology Services.

The USHE segment provides flexible and affordable certificate and degree programs to working adults primarily through Strayer University and Capella University (the "USHE Universities"), including the Jack Welch Management Institute MBA, which is a unit of Strayer University. USHE also offers non-degree web and mobile application development courses through Hackbright Academy and Devmountain, which are units of Strayer University. The segment accounts for about 75% of total revenue.

The Australia/New Zealand segment is comprised of Torrens University, Think Education, and Media Design School that together offer undergraduate, graduate, higher degree by research, and specialized degree courses as well as vocational programs in Australia and New Zealand. The segment generates more than 20% of total revenue.

Education Technology Services (some 5%), a new segment that is primarily focused on developing and maintaining relationships with employers to build employee education benefits programs that provide employees with access to affordable and industry relevant training, certificate, and degree programs.

Geographic Reach

Virginia-based Strategic Education operates about 80 campus and administrative facilities in the US. Other primary locations are in Minneapolis, also the headquarters for Capella University and Washington, DC, serves as the headquarters and main campus of Strayer University. The headquarters of ANZ is located in New South Wales, Australia.

Sales and Marketing

Strayer University engages in a broad range of activities to identify its potential students, as well as to inform working adults and their employers about the programs offered. These activities include direct, digital, and social media marketing, marketing to existing students and graduates, print and broadcast advertising, student referrals, and corporate and government outreach activities. All information relevant to prospective students is published on the website, www.strayer.edu. Strayer University maintains booths and information tables at appropriate conferences and expos, as well as at transfer days at community colleges.

Advertising costs were $149.8 million, $161.5 million and $165.1 million for the years ended 2019, 2020, and 2021, respectively.

Financial Performance

In 2021, Strayer Education generated $1.1 billion in revenue compared to $1 billion in 2020. The company's income from operations decreased to $73.9 million in 2021 compared to $109.4 million in 2020, primarily due to lower earnings in the USHE segment and higher restructuring costs, partially offset by the inclusion of ANZ's income from operations and lower amortization expense related to intangible assets.

In 2021, the company had a net income of $55.1 million, a 34% decrease from the previous year's net income of $86.3 million.

The company's cash at the end of 2021 was $279.2 million. Operating activities generated $180.5 million, while investing activities used $33.1 million, mainly for purchases of property and equipment. Financing activities used another $67.9 million, primarily for common dividends paid.

Strategy

Strategic Education's goal is to be the leading innovator and provider of career-relevant and meaningful education programs that prepare students for advancement in their careers and professional lives, and promote economic mobility. Its strategic priorities are as follows: improve student success; enhance the student experience; address affordability; establish new platforms for growth; and build a high performing culture.

As the company's success depends on the success of its students, it continues to hire outstanding faculty, produce high quality academic content, and employ cutting edge technology that enables it to deploy faculty and content in increasingly efficient and effective ways.

The company's Strayer University and Capella University have also instituted various other tuition reductions and scholarships. It continues to monitor and assess the impact of its affordability initiatives and explore other ways to make its offerings as affordable as possible. Strategic Education has also begun to deploy more aggressive technology innovations, including artificial intelligence and automation, which enables it to lower its operating costs and thus improve its ability to support lower tuition.

Company Background

Then-named Strayer Education moved to add "name brand" education to its offerings through its 2011 acquisition of the Jack Welch Management Institute. Its online executive MBA program and certification programs are based on the management lessons of the former General Electric chairman and CEO, and are geared for both individual students and corporations seeking continuing education for their executives.

EXECUTIVES

Executive Chairman, Director, Robert S. Silberman, $702,000 total compensation
Subsidiary Officer, Director, Charlotte F. Beason
Executive Vice President, Chief Financial Officer, Daniel W. Jackson, $425,000 total compensation
Senior Vice President, Chief Accounting Officer, Corporate Controller, Thomas J. Aprahamian, $310,000 total compensation
Chief Executive Officer, Director, Karl McDonnell, $702,000 total compensation
Chief Operating Officer, Division Officer, Andrew E. Watt
Senior Vice President, General Counsel, Lizette B. Herraiz, $319,791 total compensation
Subsidiary Officer, Brian W. Jones, $415,000 total compensation
Subsidiary Officer, Chad D. Nyce
Subsidiary Officer, Andrea S. Backman
Director, J. Kevin Gilligan
Director, Robert R. Grusky
Director, Rita D. Brogley
Director, John T. Casteen
Director, H. James Dallas
Director, Nathaniel C. Fick
Director, Todd A. Milano
Director, Thomas G. Waite
Auditors : PricewaterhouseCoopers LLP

LOCATIONS

HQ: Strategic Education Inc
2303 Dulles Station Boulevard, Herndon, VA 20171
Phone: 703 247-2500
Web: www.strategiceducation.com

Selected Campus Locations
Alabama
Arkansas
Delaware
Florida
Georgia
Louisiana
Maryland
Mississippi
New Jersey
North Carolina
Pennsylvania
South Carolina
Tennessee
Texas
Virginia
Washington, DC
West Virginia

PRODUCTS/OPERATIONS

2016 Students by Program Level
% of total
Bachelor's degree 67
Master's degree 27
Associate degree 5
Non-degree 1
Total 100

Selected Degrees and Programs
Master of Business Administration (M.B.A.) Degree
Master of Education (M.Ed.) Degree
Master of Health Services Administration (M.H.S.A.) Degree
Master of Public Administration (M.P.A.) Degree
Master of Science (M.S.) Degree
   Information Systems (with multiple concentrations)
   Professional Accounting
Executive Graduate Certificate Programs
   Business Administration
   Information Systems
   Professional Accounting
Bachelor of Science (B.S.) Degree
   Accounting
   Information Systems
   Economics
   International Business
   Criminal Justice
Bachelor of Business Administration (B.B.A.) Degree
Associate in Arts (A.A.) Degree
   Accounting
   Acquisition and Contract Management
   Business Administration
   Criminal Justice
   Information Systems
   Economics
   General Studies
   Marketing
Diploma Programs
   Accounting
   Acquisition and Contract Management
   Information Systems
Undergraduate Certificate Programs
   Accounting
   Business Administration
   Information Systems

COMPETITORS

AMERICAN PUBLIC EDUCATION, INC.
ARIZONA STATE UNIVERSITY
BOISE STATE UNIVERSITY
CAPELLA EDUCATION COMPANY
DELAWARE STATE UNIVERSITY
GRAND CANYON EDUCATION, INC.
PURDUE UNIVERSITY
ROCHESTER INSTITUTE OF TECHNOLOGY (INC)
UNIVERSITY OF THE PACIFIC
ZOVIO INC

HISTORICAL FINANCIALS

Company Type: Public

Income Statement   FYE: December 31

	REVENUE ($mil)	NET INCOME ($mil)	NET PROFIT MARGIN	EMPLOYEES
12/20	1,027.6	86.2	8.4%	3,679
12/19	997.1	81.1	8.1%	3,229
12/18	634.1	(15.6)	—	3,158
12/17	454.8	20.6	4.5%	1,544
12/16	441.0	34.8	7.9%	1,869
Annual Growth	23.5%	25.5%	—	18.4%

2020 Year-End Financials
Debt ratio: 7.7%
Return on equity: 5.3%
Cash ($ mil.): 187.5
Current Ratio: 1.43
Long-term debt ($ mil.): 141.8
No. of shares ($ mil.): 24.4
Dividends
   Yield: 2.5%
   Payout: 48.8%
Market value ($ mil.): 2,328.0

	STOCK PRICE ($) FY Close	P/E High	P/E Low	PER SHARE ($) Earnings	Dividends	Book Value
12/20	95.33	48	22	3.77	2.40	71.60
12/19	158.90	50	29	3.67	2.10	66.59
12/18	113.42	—	—	(1.03)	1.50	65.55
12/17	89.58	52	39	1.84	1.00	18.73
12/16	80.63	25	13	3.21	0.00	16.98
Annual Growth	4.3%	—	—	4.1%	—	43.3%

Stride Inc

Stride, formerly known as K12, is an education services company providing virtual and blended company. The company's technology-based products and services enable its clients to attract, enroll, educate, track progress, and support students. These products and services, spanning curriculum, systems, instruction, and support services are designed to help learners of all ages reach their full potential through inspired teaching and personalized learning. The company's clients are primarily public and private schools, school districts, and charter boards. Additionally, it offers solutions to employers, government agencies and consumers. More than three million students have attended schools powered by Stride curriculum and services since 2000.

Operations

Stride's solutions address two growing markets: General Education (about 75% of total revenue) and Career Learning (around 25% of revenue).

General Education market are predominantly focused on core subjects, including math, English, science and history, for kindergarten through twelfth grade students to help build a common foundation of knowledge.

Career Learning products and services are focused on developing skills to enter and succeed in careers in high-growth, in-demand industries?including information technology, health care and general business. The company provides middle and high school students with Career Learning programs that complement their core general education coursework in math, English, science and history. Stride offers multiple career pathways supported by a diverse catalog of Career Learning courses. The middle school program exposes students to a variety of career options and introduces career skill development. In high school, students may engage in industry content pathway courses, project-based learning in virtual teams, and career development services.

Geographic Reach

Stride provides its school-as-a-service offering to some 80 schools in about 30 states and the District of Columbia in the General Education market, and more than 40 schools in roughly 25 states in the Career Learning market. It also serve schools in about 50 states and the District of Columbia through its Learning Solutions sales channel. Its headquarters is located in Reston, Virginia.

Sales and Marketing

Stride's customers include public and private schools, school districts, and charter boards. Additionally, it offer solutions to employers, government agencies and consumers. Additionally, the company sells online courses and supplemental educational materials directly to families.

The company's advertising costs totaled $86.5 million, $60.3 million and $63.1 million for the years ended June 30, 2022, 2021 and 2020, respectively.

Financial Performance

Stride's revenues for the year ended June 30, 2022 were $1.7 billion, representing an increase of $149.9 million, or 10%, from $1.6 billion for the year ended June 30, 2021. Career Learning revenues increased $156.3 million, or 61%, primarily due to a 42% increase in enrollments, school mix, as well as from the acquisition of MedCerts and Tech Elevator.

In 2022, the company had a net income of $107.1 million, a 50% increase from the previous year's net income of $71.5 million.

The company's cash at the end of 2022 was $389.4 million. Operating activities generated $206.9 million, while investing activities used $110.8 million, mainly for purchases of marketable securities. Financing activities used another $93.3 million, primarily for repurchase of restricted stock for income tax withholding.

Strategy

Stride is committed to maximizing every child's potential by personalizing their educational experience, delivering quality education to schools and their students, and supporting its customers in their quest to improve academic outcomes and prepare them for college and career readiness. In furtherance of those objectives, the company plan to continue investing in its curriculum and learning systems. These investments include initiatives to create and deploy a next generation curriculum and learning platform, improve the effectiveness of its school workforce, develop new instructional approaches to increase student and parental engagement, and improve the company's systems and security architecture. This strategy consists of the following key elements: affect better student outcomes; improve student retention in the company's virtual schools; grow DCA enrollments and expand career training market; introduce new and improved products and services; increase enrollments at existing virtual and blended public schools; expand virtual and blended public school presence into additional states and cities; grow the company's institutional business; add enrollments in its private schools; pursue international opportunities to offer its learning systems; develop additional channels through which to deliver the company's learning systems; and pursue strategic partnerships and acquisitions.

EXECUTIVES

Chairman, Lead Independent Director, Director, Craig R. Barrett

Strategy President, Marketing President, Technology President, Technology Chief Executive Officer, Strategy Chief Executive Officer, Marketing Chief Executive Officer, Director, James Jeaho Rhyu, $500,000 total compensation

Executive Vice President, General Counsel, Secretary, Vincent W. Mathis

Chief Financial Officer, Donna Blackman

Chief Information Officer, Chief Technology Officer, Les Ottolenghi

Director, Aida M. Alvarez

Director, Robert L. Cohen

Director, Steven B. Fink

Director, Robert E. Knowling

Director, Eliza McFadden

Director, Joseph A. Verbrugge

Director, Victoria D. Harker

Auditors : BDO USA, LLP

LOCATIONS

HQ: Stride Inc
 2300 Corporate Park Drive, Herndon, VA 20171
Phone: 703 483-7000
Web: www.k12.com

PRODUCTS/OPERATIONS

2016 Sales

Revenue	$ mil.	% of total
Managed Public School Programs Institutional	717.1	82
Non-managed Public School Programs	55.6	6
Institutional Software & Services	53	6
Private Pay Schools and Other	47	6
Total	872.7	100

Selected Schools and Programs

Early Learning Programs
High School Program
K-8 Program
Online Privatre Schools
Online Public Schools

Selected Students Served/Services

Advanced and Enrichable Learners
Athletes and Performers
Credit Recovery (for missed classes, make-up credits)
Expat, Foreign Service, Overseas
Homebound
Homeschoolers
Military Families
Reading Program
Struggling Students
Summer School
Supplemental Education
World Languages

COMPETITORS

BPP HOLDINGS LIMITED
IMAGINE SCHOOLS, INC.
JUNIOR ACHIEVEMENT USA
LINCOLN EDUCATIONAL SERVICES CORPORATION
NOBEL LEARNING COMMUNITIES, INC.
NORTH ATL REGIONAL SCHOOLS
SAN DIEGO COUNTY OFFICE OF EDUCATION
THE GIRLS' DAY SCHOOL TRUST
UNIVERSITY OF OREGON
ZOVIO INC

HISTORICAL FINANCIALS

Company Type: Public

Income Statement — FYE: June 30

	NET REVENUE ($mil)	NET INCOME ($mil)	NET PROFIT MARGIN	EMPLOYEES
06/21	1,536.7	71.4	4.6%	7,100
06/20	1,040.7	24.5	2.4%	4,950
06/19	1,015.7	37.2	3.7%	4,550
06/18	917.7	27.6	3.0%	4,700
06/17	888.5	0.4	0.1%	4,750
Annual Growth	14.7%	254.8%	—	10.6%

2021 Year-End Financials

Debt ratio: 23.3%
Return on equity: 9.6%
Cash ($ mil.): 386.0
Current Ratio: 2.80
Long-term debt ($ mil.): 340.8
No. of shares ($ mil.): 41.5
Dividends
 Yield: —
 Payout: —
Market value ($ mil.): 1,336.0

	STOCK PRICE ($) FY Close	P/E High/Low		PER SHARE ($) Earnings	Dividends	Book Value
06/21	32.13	29	12	1.71	0.00	19.35
06/20	27.24	51	26	0.60	0.00	16.47
06/19	30.41	39	17	0.91	0.00	15.74
06/18	16.37	26	19	0.68	0.00	14.84
06/17	17.92	209	1060	0.01	0.00	14.07
Annual Growth	15.7%	—	—	261.6%	—	8.3%

Sturgis Bancorp Inc

Sturgis Bancorp is the holding company for Sturgis Bank & Trust, which has about 10 branches in south-central Michigan. Founded in 1905, the bank offers checking and savings accounts, CDs, trust services, and other standard banking fare. Real estate loans comprise the bulk of its lending activities: one- to four-family residential mortgages make up more than half of the company's loan portfolio. Subsidiary Oak Leaf Financial Services provides insurance and investment products and services from third-party provider Linsco/Private Ledger.

EXECUTIVES

Chairman, Director, Donald L. Frost
President, Chief Executive Officer, Subsidiary Officer, Director, Eric L. Eishen, $175,983 total compensation
Vice President, Chief Operating Officer, Subsidiary Officer, Ronald W. Scheske, $105,988 total compensation
Chief Financial Officer, Treasurer, Secretary, Subsidiary Officer, Brian P. Hoggatt, $117,292 total compensation
Director, Michael R. Frost
Director, Jeffrey M. Mohney
Director, John T. Wiedlea
Director, David L. Franks
Director, Kimberlee Bontrager
Auditors : Crowe LLP

LOCATIONS

HQ: Sturgis Bancorp Inc
  113-125 East Chicago Road, Sturgis, MI 49091
Phone: 269 651-9345
Web: www.sturgisbank.com

COMPETITORS

COLONIAL FINANCIAL SERVICES, INC.
FEDFIRST FINANCIAL CORPORATION
LIBERTY CAPITAL, INC.
LIFESTORE BANK
NORTHEAST COMMUNITY BANCORP, INC.

HISTORICAL FINANCIALS

Company Type: Public

Income Statement — FYE: December 31

	ASSETS ($mil)	NET INCOME ($mil)	INCOME AS % OF ASSETS	EMPLOYEES
12/20	643.6	6.0	0.9%	0
12/19	473.3	4.9	1.0%	0
12/18	431.5	4.3	1.0%	0
12/17	414.4	3.1	0.8%	0
12/16	398.6	2.6	0.7%	0
Annual Growth	12.7%	22.6%	—	—

2020 Year-End Financials

Return on assets: 1.0%
Return on equity: 13.2%
Long-term debt ($ mil.): —
No. of shares ($ mil.): 2.1
Sales ($ mil.): 30.7
Dividends
  Yield: 3.4%
  Payout: 24.8%
Market value ($ mil.): 39.0

	STOCK PRICE ($) FY Close	P/E High/Low		PER SHARE ($) Earnings	Dividends	Book Value
12/20	18.45	8	5	2.84	0.64	22.19
12/19	21.50	14	9	2.34	0.60	20.61
12/18	19.80	11	9	2.08	0.57	19.11
12/17	18.80	13	9	1.52	0.48	17.78
12/16	13.75	11	8	1.28	0.42	16.65
Annual Growth	7.6%	—	—	22.0%	11.1%	7.4%

Summit Financial Group Inc

Summit Financial Group is at the peak of community banking in West Virginia and northern Virginia. The company owns Summit Community Bank, which operates about 20 branches that offer standard retail banking fare such as deposit accounts, loans, and cash management services. Commercial real estate loans, including land development and construction loans, account for about 40% of Summit Financial Group's loan portfolio, which also includes residential mortgages and a smaller percentage of business and consumer loans. The bank's Summit Insurance Services unit sells both commercial and personal coverage.

EXECUTIVES

Chairman, Director, Oscar M. Bean
President, Chief Executive Officer, Subsidiary Officer, Director, H. Charles Maddy, $467,500 total compensation
Executive Vice President, Chief Banking Officer, Subsidiary Officer, Patricia L. Owens
Executive Vice President, Chief Financial Officer, Subsidiary Officer, Robert S. Tissue, $251,250 total compensation
Executive Vice President, Chief of Credit Administration, Patrick N. Frye, $242,250 total compensation
Executive Vice President, Chief Operating Officer, Scott C. Jennings, $251,250 total compensation
Executive Vice President, Subsidiary Officer, Bradford E. Ritchie, $237,250 total compensation
Senior Vice President, Chief Accounting Officer, Julie R. Markwood
Director, Jill S. Upson
Director, Ronald B. Spencer
Director, Ronald L. Bowling
Director, Jason A. Kitzmiller
Director, James M. Cookman
Director, Gary L. Hinkle
Director, Dewey F. Bensenhaver
Director, J. Scott Bridgeforth
Director, John W. Crites
Director, James P. Geary
Director, Georgette R. George
Director, John B. Gianola
Director, Charles S. Piccirillo
Director, John H. Schott
Auditors : Yount, Hyde & Barbour, P.C.

LOCATIONS

HQ: Summit Financial Group Inc
  300 North Main Street, Moorefield, WV 26836
Phone: 304 530-1000
Web: www.summitfgi.com

COMPETITORS

CODORUS VALLEY BANCORP, INC.
COMMUNITY SHORES BANK CORPORATION
EMCLAIRE FINANCIAL CORP.
PINNACLE BANCSHARES, INC.
SOUTHERN COMMUNITY FINANCIAL CORPORATION

HISTORICAL FINANCIALS

Company Type: Public

Income Statement — FYE: December 31

	ASSETS ($mil)	NET INCOME ($mil)	INCOME AS % OF ASSETS	EMPLOYEES
12/20	3,106.3	31.3	1.0%	415
12/19	2,403.4	31.8	1.3%	383
12/18	2,200.5	28.0	1.3%	371
12/17	2,134.2	11.9	0.6%	349
12/16	1,758.6	17.2	1.0%	251
Annual Growth	15.3%	16.0%	—	13.4%

2020 Year-End Financials

Return on assets: 1.1%
Return on equity: 11.8%
Long-term debt ($ mil.): —
No. of shares ($ mil.): 12.9
Sales ($ mil.): 135
Dividends
  Yield: 3.0%
  Payout: 29.8%
Market value ($ mil.): 286.0

	STOCK PRICE ($) FY Close	P/E High/Low		PER SHARE ($) Earnings	Dividends	Book Value
12/20	22.08	11	6	2.41	0.68	21.76
12/19	27.09	11	8	2.53	0.59	19.97
12/18	19.31	12	8	2.26	0.53	17.85
12/17	26.32	28	19	1.00	0.44	16.30
12/16	27.53	18	7	1.61	0.40	14.47
Annual Growth	(5.4%)	—	—	10.6%	14.2%	10.7%

Summit Materials Inc

EXECUTIVES

Chairman, Director, Howard L. Lance
President, Chief Executive Officer, Director, Anne P. Noonan
Executive Vice President, Chief Financial Officer, Scott Anderson
Executive Vice President, Chief Legal Officer, Secretary, Christopher Gaskill
Communications Executive Vice President, Communications Chief People Officer and Chief ESG Officer, Communications Head, Karli S. Anderson
Director, Joseph S. Cantie
Director, Anne M. Cooney
Director, Tamla D. Oates-Forney
Director, John Raymond Murphy
Director, Steven H. Wunning
Director, Susan A. Ellerbusch
Director, Anne K. Wade
Auditors : KPMG LLP

LOCATIONS

HQ: Summit Materials Inc
  1550 Wynkoop Street, 3rd Floor, Denver, CO 80202
Phone: 303 893-0012
Web: www.summit-materials.com

HISTORICAL FINANCIALS
Company Type: Public

Income Statement　　　　　　　　　　　　　FYE: January 2

	REVENUE ($mil)	NET INCOME ($mil)	NET PROFIT MARGIN	EMPLOYEES
01/21*	2,332.4	137.9	5.9%	6,000
12/19	2,222.1	61.1	2.8%	6,000
12/18	2,101.0	36.3	1.7%	6,000
12/17	1,932.5	125.8	6.5%	6,000
12/16	1,626.0	46.1	2.8%	5,000
Annual Growth	9.4%	31.5%	—	4.7%

*Fiscal year change

2021 Year-End Financials
Debt ratio: 44.1%　　　　　　　No. of shares ($ mil.): 114.3
Return on equity: 8.9%　　　　Dividends
Cash ($ mil.): 418.1　　　　　　 Yield: —
Current Ratio: 2.77　　　　　　 Payout: —
Long-term debt ($ mil.): 1,892.3　Market value ($ mil.): 2,297.0

	STOCK PRICE ($) FY Close	P/E High/Low		PER SHARE ($) Earnings	Dividends	Book Value
01/21*	20.08	20	7	1.20	0.00	13.97
12/19	23.84	47	23	0.52	0.00	12.60
12/18	12.30	112	38	0.30	0.00	11.89
12/17	31.44	29	21	1.11	0.00	11.40
12/16	23.79	47	26	0.52	0.00	8.65
Annual Growth	(4.1%)	—	—	23.1%	—	12.7%

*Fiscal year change

Summit State Bank (Santa Rosa, CA)

Contrary to its name, Summit State Bank does business in both the hills and the valleys of Sonoma County in western California. Serving consumers and small to midsized businesses, the bank offers standard deposit services like checking, savings, and retirement accounts, as well as lending services such as real estate and commercial loans. Commercial real estate loans account for about 40% of the bank's loan portfolio, while commercial and agriculture loans make up about 20%. Its other lending products include single-family and multifamily mortgages, construction loans, and consumer loans. Summit State Bank operates about half a dozen branches in Petaluma, Rohnert Park, Santa Rosa, and Windsor.

EXECUTIVES
Chairman, Allan J. Hemphill
President, Chief Executive Officer, Director, James E. Brush
Executive Vice President, Chief Financial Officer, Dennis E. Kelley
Executive Vice President, Chief Operating Officer, Linda Bertauche
Executive Vice President, Chief Credit Officer, Brandy A. Seppi
Director, Jeffery B. Allen
Director, Josh C. Cox
Director, Todd R. Fry
Director, Ronald A. Metcalfe
Director, Richard E. Pope
Director, Nicholas J. Rado
Director, Marshall T. Reynolds
Director, Bridget M. Doherty
Director, John W. Wright
Auditors : Moss Adams LLP

LOCATIONS
HQ: Summit State Bank (Santa Rosa, CA)
500 Bicentennial Way, Santa Rosa, CA 95403
Phone: 707 568-6000
Web: www.summitstatebank.com

COMPETITORS
ASB FINANCIAL CORP
FIRST CAPITAL, INC.
HERITAGE SOUTHEAST BANCORPORATION, INC.
HIGH COUNTRY BANCORP, INC.
PEOPLES BANCORP

HISTORICAL FINANCIALS
Company Type: Public

Income Statement　　　　　　　　　　　FYE: December 31

	ASSETS ($mil)	NET INCOME ($mil)	INCOME AS % OF ASSETS	EMPLOYEES
12/20	865.8	10.5	1.2%	99
12/19	695.9	6.4	0.9%	93
12/18	622.1	5.8	0.9%	89
12/17	610.8	3.2	0.5%	78
12/16	513.7	4.9	1.0%	74
Annual Growth	13.9%	20.6%	—	7.5%

2020 Year-End Financials
Return on assets: 1.3%　　　　Dividends
Return on equity: 14.6%　　　 Yield: 3.5%
Long-term debt ($ mil.): —　　Payout: 27.7%
No. of shares ($ mil.): 5.5　　 Market value ($ mil.): 74.0
Sales ($ mil.): 40.8

	STOCK PRICE ($) FY Close	P/E High/Low		PER SHARE ($) Earnings	Dividends	Book Value
12/20	13.48	7	3	1.90	0.44	13.71
12/19	12.97	11	9	1.18	0.44	12.20
12/18	11.77	15	10	1.06	0.44	11.16
12/17	12.60	30	20	0.59	0.41	10.87
12/16	15.00	16	14	0.90	0.35	10.71
Annual Growth	(2.6%)	—	—	20.5%	5.7%	6.4%

Sun Communities Inc

Sun Communities is a self-managed real estate investment trust (REIT) that owns, develops, and operates manufactured housing communities (trailer and recreation vehicle parks) in nearly 40 states, Ontario, Canada, and Puerto Rico. Its portfolio includes more than 600 properties with nearly 11,000 additional MH and RV sites suitable for development. Through its taxable REIT subsidiary, Sun Home Services, the company is engaged in the marketing, selling, and leasing of new and pre-owned homes to current and future residents in its communities. The company has been in the business of acquiring, operating, developing, and expanding manufactured home and RV communities since 1975.

Operations
Sun Communities' three reportable segments are: Manufactured Home (MH) communities, Recreational Vehicle (RV) resorts, and Marina.

The MH segment, generates about 50% of the company's revenue, owns, operates, develops, or has an interest in, a portfolio of MH communities and is in the business of acquiring, operating and developing ground up MH communities to provide affordable housing solutions to residents. The segment also provides manufactured home sales and leasing services to tenants and prospective tenants of its communities. Modern MH communities contain improvements similar to other garden-style residential developments, including centralized entrances, paved streets, curbs, gutters and parkways. In addition, these communities also often provide a number of amenities, such as a clubhouse, a swimming pool, basketball courts, shuffleboard courts, tennis courts, and laundry facilities.

The RV segment (more than 25%) owns, operates, develops, or has an interest in, a portfolio of RV resorts and is in the business of acquiring, operating, and developing ground up RV resorts throughout the US and in Ontario, Canada. It also provides leasing services for vacation rentals within the RV resorts. RV resorts may also provide vacation rental homes and may include a number of amenities such as restaurants, golf courses, swimming pools, water parks, tennis courts, fitness centers, planned activities, and spacious social facilities.

The Marina segment owns, operates, and develops marinas, and is in the business of acquiring, and operating marinas throughout the US with the majority of such marinas concentrated in coastal regions, others located in various inland regions, and Puerto Rico. The segment provides approximately 25% of the company's revenue. A marina is a specially-designed harbor that can be located on oceans, lakes, bays or rivers and typically includes dry storage systems that provide storage solutions for the placement of vessels ranging in size from small boats to super yachts for varied lengths of time. It also provides ancillary services, such as fuel stations, ship stores, restaurants, swimming pools, cabin and lodging rentals, boat rentals, tennis courts, fitness centers, shower and laundry facilities, planned activities and other services to create a robust member experience.

In addition, Sun Home Services had approximately 9,870 occupied leased homes in its portfolio. Overall, real property accounts for nearly 70% of the company's revenue, service, retail, dining, and entertainment bring in approximately 15%, home sales provide more than 10%, interest and brokerage commissions and others account for the rest.

Geographic Reach

Sun Communities has more than 600 properties across about 40 states. The properties contained an aggregate of nearly 204,165 developed sites comprised of about 98,620 developed MH sites, some 30,540 annual RV sites (inclusive of both annual and seasonal usage rights), over 29,845 transient RV sites, and some 45,155 wet slips and dry storage spaces.

Its properties are located throughout the US, and in Ontario, Canada, and Puerto Rico and consists of about 285 MH communities, some 160 RV resorts, nearly 35 properties containing both MH and RV sites, and approximately 125 marinas.

Sales and Marketing

Sun Communities spent approximately $9.9 million, $8.3 million, and $6.7 million on advertising in 2021, 2020, and 2019, respectively.

Financial Performance

Sun Communities' revenue has been rising in the last five years, most notably in 2021. It has an overall increase of 135% between 2017 and 2021.

The company reported a total revenue of $2.3 billion in 2021. The 63% increase was primarily due to the higher volume of sales in the company's real property segment.

In 2021, the company had a net income of $380.2 million, a 189% increase from the previous year's net income of $131.6 million. The increase is primarily attributable to the higher volume of sales for the year.

The company's cash at the end of 2021 was $78.2 million. Operating activities generated $753.6 million, while investing activities used $2.3 billion, mainly for acquisitions of properties. Financing activities provided another $1.6 billion.

Mergers and Acquisitions

In early 2022, Sun Communities announced the closing of its previously announced acquisition of Park Holidays UK (Park Holidays). The company acquired 40 owned and two managed communities in the UK primarily located in irreplaceable, seaside locations in the south of England. The aggregate purchase price for Park Holidays is approximately £950 million, or approximately $1.3 billion. This acquisition provides the company with the opportunity to establish a strong presence within the highly fragmented UK market.

EXECUTIVES

President, Chief Executive Officer, Subsidiary Officer, Chairman, Director, Gary A. Shiffman, $691,837 total compensation
Division Officer, John B. McLaren, $525,000 total compensation
Executive Vice President, Chief Financial Officer, Secretary, Treasurer, Fernando Castro-Caratini
Corporate Strategy Executive Vice President, Business Development Executive Vice President, Aaron Weiss
Special Project Executive Vice President, Karen J. Dearing, $425,000 total compensation
Sales Executive Vice President, Operations Executive Vice President, Sales Chief Operating Officer, Operations Chief Operating Officer, Bruce Thelen
Subsidiary Officer, Baxter R. Underwood
Lead Independent Director, Director, Clunet R. Lewis
Director, Tonya Allen
Director, Meghan G. Baivier
Director, Stephanie W. Bergeron
Director, Brian M. Hermelin
Director, Ronald A. Klein
Director, Arthur A. Weiss
Director, Jeff T. Blau
Auditors : Grant Thornton LLP

LOCATIONS

HQ: Sun Communities Inc
27777 Franklin Rd., Suite 200, Southfield, MI 48034
Phone: 248 208-2500
Web: www.suncommunities.com

2014 Properties

	% of total
Michigan	70
Florida	29
Northest	26
Southwest	18
Texas	18
Indiana	17
Ohio	11
Other states	28
Total	217

PRODUCTS/OPERATIONS

2014 Sales

	$ mil.	% of total
Real property income	357.7	77
Home sales	54.0	11
Home rentals	39.2	8
Interest and other	19.8	4
Brokerage commission and other income	1.0	-
Total	471.7	100

Selected Mergers and Acquisitions

2013
Gwynns Island RV Resort LLC, Indian Creek RV Resort LLC, Lake Laurie RV Resort LLC, Newpoint RV Resort LLC, Peters Pond RV Resort Inc., Seaport LLC, Virginia Tent LLC, Wagon Wheel Maine LLC, Westward Ho RV Resort LLC and Wild Acres LLC (Connecticut, Maine, Massachusetts, New Jersey, Ohio, Virginia, and Wisconsin; $112.8 million)
2012
Three Lakes RV Resort, Blueberry Hill RV Resort and Grand Lake Estates; Florida
Blazing Star RV Resort; San Antonio, Texas
Northville Crossing Manufactured Home Community; Michigan

COMPETITORS

AV HOMES, INC.
AVALONBAY COMMUNITIES, INC.
EQUITY ONE, INC.
ESSEX PROPERTY TRUST, INC.
GOV NEW OPPTY REIT
LIBERTY PROPERTY TRUST
LSREF4 LIGHTHOUSE CORPORATE ACQUISITIONS, LLC
MERITAGE HOMES CORPORATION
POST PROPERTIES, INC.
UDR, INC.

HISTORICAL FINANCIALS

Company Type: Public

Income Statement — FYE: December 31

	REVENUE ($mil)	NET INCOME ($mil)	NET PROFIT MARGIN	EMPLOYEES
12/21	2,272.6	392.2	17.3%	5,961
12/20	1,398.3	138.5	9.9%	4,872
12/19	1,264.0	167.6	13.3%	3,146
12/18	1,126.8	111.7	9.9%	2,784
12/17	982.5	76.7	7.8%	2,727
Annual Growth	23.3%	50.3%	—	21.6%

2021 Year-End Financials

Debt ratio: 42.0%
Return on equity: 6.1%
Cash ($ mil.): 78.2
Current Ratio: 1.12
Long-term debt ($ mil.): 5,671.8
No. of shares ($ mil.): 115.9
Dividends
Yield: 1.5%
Payout: 101.8%
Market value ($ mil.): 24,351.0

	STOCK PRICE ($) FY Close	P/E High/Low		PER SHARE ($) Earnings	Dividends	Book Value
12/21	209.97	63	41	3.36	3.32	59.61
12/20	151.95	129	76	1.34	3.16	53.79
12/19	150.10	92	54	1.80	3.00	41.83
12/18	101.71	84	65	1.29	2.84	36.71
12/17	92.78	112	90	0.85	2.68	33.15
Annual Growth	22.7%	—	—	41.0%	5.5%	15.8%

Sun Country Airlines Holdings Inc

EXECUTIVES

Chairman, Director, David N. Siegel
President, Chief Financial Officer, Director, Dave Davis
Chief Executive Officer, Director, Jude I. Bricker
Executive Vice President, Chief Operating Officer, Gregory Mays
Legal Executive Vice President, Legal Chief Administrative Officer, Legal General Counsel, Legal Secretary, Eric Levenhagen
Executive Vice President, Chief Information Officer, Jeffrey Mader
Senior Vice President, Chief Marketing Officer, Brian Davis
Executive Vice President, Chief Revenue Officer, Grant Whitney
Finance Vice President, Finance Chief Accounting Officer, John Gyurci
Financial Planning Vice President, Analysis Vice President, Financial Planning Treasurer, Analysis Treasurer, Bill Trousdale
Director, Marion C. Blakey
Director, Patrick Kearney

Director, Thomas C. Kennedy
Director, Antoine G. Munfakh
Director, Kerry Philipovitch
Director, Patrick O'Keeffe

LOCATIONS

HQ: Sun Country Airlines Holdings Inc
2005 Cargo Road, Minneapolis, MN 55450
Phone: 651 681-3900
Web: www.suncountry.com

HISTORICAL FINANCIALS

Company Type: Public

Income Statement — FYE: December 31

	REVENUE ($mil)	NET INCOME ($mil)	NET PROFIT MARGIN	EMPLOYEES
12/21	623.0	77.4	12.4%	2,181
12/20	401.4	(3.9)	—	1,699
12/19	701.3	46.0	6.6%	0
12/18*	384.9	(0.3)	—	0
04/18	197.4	25.9	13.1%	0
Annual Growth	33.3%	31.5%	—	—

*Fiscal year change

2021 Year-End Financials

Debt ratio: 34.1%
Return on equity: 20.1%
Cash ($ mil.): 309.3
Current Ratio: 1.33
Long-term debt ($ mil.): 428.4
No. of shares ($ mil.): 57.8
Dividends
 Yield: —
 Payout: —
Market value ($ mil.): 1,577.0

	STOCK PRICE ($) FY Close	P/E High/Low		PER SHARE ($)	
			Earnings	Dividends	Book Value
12/21	27.25	31 17	1.31	0.00	8.41
Annual Growth	—	— —	—	—	—

Super Micro Computer Inc

Super Micro Computer is a provider of accelerated compute platforms that are application-optimized high-performance and high-efficiency server and storage systems for various markets, including enterprise data centers, cloud computing, artificial intelligence, 5G and edge computing. In addition to its complete server and storage systems business, the company offers a large array of modular server subsystems and accessories, such as server boards, chassis, power supplies and other accessories. The company also sells a host of subsystems and accessories. Super Micro markets its products, sold directly and through distributors and resellers, to customers in over 100 countries; less than 60% of its sales are generated in the US.

Operations

Super Micro offer a broad range of application-optimized server solutions, including storage, rackmount and blade server and storage systems and subsystems and accessories. The company's server and storage systems account for around 85% of the total revenue.

The company's server subsystems and accessories products, about 15% of revenue, range from the entry-level single and dual processor server segment to the high-end multiprocessor market.

Geographic Reach

Super Micro is based in San Jose, California and has an office in Jersey City, New Jersey. Its European operations are centered in the Netherlands while it maintains a research and development operation in Taiwan with sales and service facilities in China.

The company generates nearly 60% of its sales from the US, with Asia contributing over 20%, and Europe with around 15%.

Sales and Marketing

Super Micro Computer sells to indirect sales channels, directly to OEMs and end-users, and through distributors, resellers, and systems integrators. In 2021, the company sold to over 1,000 direct customers in over 100 countries.

The company's total advertising and promotional expenses were $0.1 million, $4.1 million and $3.0 million for the fiscal years 2022, 2021 and 2020, respectively.

Financial Performance

Net sales increased by 46% to $5.2 billion in fiscal year 2022 as compared to fiscal year 2021. The year-over-year increase in net sales of server and storage systems was primarily due to an increase of average selling prices per compute node by approximately 32% as well as an increase of approximately 23% in the number of units of compute nodes sold.

In 2022, the company had a net income of $285.2 million, a 155% increase from the previous year's net income of $111.9 million, which was primarily due to the higher net sales and lower operating expenses as a percentage of revenues in fiscal year 2022 as compared to fiscal year 2021.

The company's cash at the end of 2022 was $268.6 million. Financing activities generated $522.9 million, while operating activities generated $440.8 million. Investing activities used another $46.3 million, mainly for purchases of property, plant and equipment.

Strategy

Super Micro's objective is to be the world's leading provider of application-optimized, high-performance server, storage and networking solutions. Achieving this objective requires continuous development and innovation of its solutions with better price-performance and architectural advantages compared with its prior generation of solutions and with solutions offered by its competitors. Through its strategy, the company seeks to maintain or improve its relative competitive position in many product areas and pursue markets that provide the company with additional long-term growth opportunities.

Key elements of Super Micro's strategy include executing upon the following: a strong internal research and development and internal manufacturing capability; introducing more innovative products, faster; capitalizing on new applications and technologies; driving software and services sales to the company's global enterprise customers; and leveraging its global operating structure.

EXECUTIVES

Chairman, President, Chief Executive Officer, Charles Liang, $363,776 total compensation
Operations Senior Vice President, George Kao
Senior Vice President, Director, Sara Liu
Senior Vice President, Chief Financial Officer, Corporate Secretary, David Weigand
Worldwide Sales Senior Vice President, Don Clegg
Division Officer, Region Officer, Alex Hsu, $171,683 total compensation
Director, Tally C. Liu
Director, Sherman Tuan
Director, Michael S. McAndrews
Director, Daniel W. Fairfax
Director, Shiu Leung (Fred) Chan
Director, Judy Lin
Director, Robert L. Blair
Auditors : DELOITTE & TOUCHE LLP

LOCATIONS

HQ: Super Micro Computer Inc
980 Rock Avenue, San Jose, CA 95131
Phone: 408 503-8000
Web: www.supermicro.com

2016 Sales

	$ mil.	% of total
US	1,398.4	63
Europe	385.8	17
Asia	324.2	15
Other regions	107.2	5
Total	2,215.6	100

PRODUCTS/OPERATIONS

2016 Sales

	$ mil.	% of total
Server systems	1,525.6	69
Subsystems & accessories	690	31
Total	2,215.6	100

Selected Products

Chassis enclosures (pedestal, rack-mount, tower)
Motherboards (desktop, server, workstation)
Power supplies
Serverboards
Servers (rack-mount, tower)

COMPETITORS

CIENA CORPORATION
CONCURRENT TECHNOLOGIES PLC
CRAY INC.
DELL TECHNOLOGIES INC.
Diebold Nixdorf AG
HP INC.
MOSYS, INC.
ONTO INNOVATION INC.
PEGATRON CORPORATION

Quanta Computer Inc.

HISTORICAL FINANCIALS
Company Type: Public

Income Statement   FYE: June 30

	REVENUE ($mil)	NET INCOME ($mil)	NET PROFIT MARGIN	EMPLOYEES
06/21	3,557.4	111.8	3.1%	4,155
06/20	3,339.2	84.3	2.5%	3,987
06/19	3,500.3	71.9	2.1%	3,670
06/18	3,360.4	46.1	1.4%	3,266
06/17	2,484.9	66.8	2.7%	2,996
Annual Growth	9.4%	13.7%	—	8.5%

2021 Year-End Financials
Debt ratio: 4.4%
Return on equity: 10.3%
Cash ($ mil.): 232.2
Current Ratio: 1.93
Long-term debt ($ mil.): 34.7
No. of shares ($ mil.): 50.5
Dividends
Yield: —
Payout: —
Market value ($ mil.): 1,779.0

	STOCK PRICE ($) FY Close	P/E High/Low		PER SHARE ($) Earnings	Dividends	Book Value
06/21	35.18	18	10	2.09	0.00	21.67
06/20	28.39	20	10	1.60	0.00	20.33
06/19	19.35	17	8	1.39	0.00	18.84
06/18	23.65	29	17	0.89	0.00	17.01
06/17	24.65	21	14	1.29	0.00	15.81
Annual Growth	9.3%	—	—	12.8%	—	8.2%

Superior Group of Companies Inc

Superior Group of Companies (formerly Superior Uniform Group) manufactures (through third parties or its own facilities) and sells a wide range of uniforms, corporate identity apparel, career apparel and accessories for the medical and health fields, as well as those who work in hotels, fast food joints and other restaurants, and public safety, industrial, and commercial markets. The company also makes and distributes specialty labels, such as BAMKO, Tangerine, and Public Identity. Chairman Gerald Benstock and his son, CEO Michael, run the company, which began as Superior Surgical Mfg. Co. in 1920.

Operations
The company operates its business through three reportable segments: Uniforms and Related Products (about 50% of sales), Promotional Products (some 40% of sales) and Remote Staffing Solutions (over 10%).

Uniforms and Related Products segment, its signature marketing brands Fashion Seal Healthcare, HPI, and WonderWink, manufactures and sells a wide range of uniforms, corporate identity apparel, career apparel and accessories for the hospital and healthcare fields; hotels; fast food and other restaurants; transportation; and the private security, industrial and commercial markets.

The Promotional Products segment, sells wide range of apparel through its brands BAMKO, Tangerine and Public Identity.

Remote Staffing Solutions segment services the Office Gurus entities, including its subsidiaries in El Salvador, Belize, Jamaica, and the US. TOG is a near-shore premium provider of cost effective multilingual telemarketing and business process outsourced solutions.

Geographic Reach
From its headquarters in Florida, Superior Uniform serves to outfit companies and customers nationwide, boasting manufacturing operations overseas. It operates in El Salvador, Belize, Jamaica, and the US through its The Office Gurus businesses. It has domestic facilities in Georgia, Arkansas, Mississippi, Arkansas, Louisiana, and California, international facilities are located in El Salvador, Haiti, Jamaica, and BeliZe.

Sales and Marketing
The Uniform and Related Products segment has a substantial number of customers, but none of its customers accounted for more than 10% of net sales. The Promotional Products segment's largest customer represented about 15% of net sales. No customer accounted for more than 10% of the Remote Staffing Solutions segment's net sales.

Financial Performance
Net sales for the company increased 2% from $526.7 million in 2020 to $537.0 million in 2021.The increase in net sales were due to a decrease in net sales for its Uniforms and Related Products segment (contributing (4%)); an increase in net sales for its Remote Staffing Solutions segment after intersegment eliminations (contributing 4%) and an increase in net sales for its Promotional Products segment (contributing 3%).

Net income in 2021 decreased to $29.4 million compared with $41.0 million in the prior year.

Cash held by the company at the end of 2021 increased to $8.9 million. Cash provided by operations and financing activities were $17.1 million and $21.0 million, respectively. Cash used for investing activities was $34.1 million, mainly for additions to property, plant and equipment.

Company Background
Superior Group of Companies was founded in 1920 began as Superior Surgical Manufacturing Co. Inc. In 1968, the company went public and issued it initial public offering in AMEX.

EXECUTIVES

Chairman Emeritus, Honorary Director, Gerald M. Benstock, $156,000 total compensation

Chairperson, Director, Sidney Kirschner

Chief Executive Officer, Director, Michael Benstock, $541,702 total compensation

Chief Operating Officer, Chief Financial Officer, Treasurer, Director, Andrew D. Demott, $400,400 total compensation

Senior Vice President, General Counsel, Secretary, Jordan M. Alpert, $166,670 total compensation

Subsidiary Officer, Jake Himelstein

Customer Support Subsidiary Officer, Administration Subsidiary Officer, Dominic Leide, $229,845 total compensation

Chief Strategy Officer, Philip Koosed, $150,000 total compensation

Director, Robin M. Hensley

Director, Paul V. Mellini

Director, Todd E. Siegel

Director, Venita Fields

Auditors: Mayer Hoffman McCann P.C.

LOCATIONS
HQ: Superior Group of Companies Inc
10055 Seminole Boulevard, Seminole, FL 33772-2539
Phone: 727 397-9611
Web: www.superiorgroupofcompanies.com

PRODUCTS/OPERATIONS
2016 sales

	in mil.	% of total
Uniforms and related products	210.4	82
Promotional Products	27.8	11
Remote staffing solutions	17.9	7
Inter-segment elimination	(3.5)	-
Total	252.6	100

Selected Brands
Blade
Fashion Seal
Fashion Seal Healthcare
Martin's
Worklon
UniVogue

COMPETITORS
APP WINDDOWN, LLC
COHEN & WILKS INTERNATIONAL LIMITED
CROWN CRAFTS, INC.
DECKERS OUTDOOR CORPORATION
LIXIL CORPORATION
LightInTheBox Holding Co., Ltd.
SCHUH LIMITED
SELFRIDGES RETAIL LIMITED
SWANK, INC.
UNIFIRST CORPORATION

HISTORICAL FINANCIALS
Company Type: Public

Income Statement   FYE: December 31

	REVENUE ($mil)	NET INCOME ($mil)	NET PROFIT MARGIN	EMPLOYEES
12/20	526.6	41.0	7.8%	4,600
12/19	376.7	12.0	3.2%	3,400
12/18	346.3	16.9	4.9%	2,906
12/17	266.8	15.0	5.6%	2,280
12/16	252.5	14.6	5.8%	1,632
Annual Growth	20.2%	29.4%	—	29.6%

2020 Year-End Financials
Debt ratio: 22.3%
Return on equity: 23.4%
Cash ($ mil.): 5.1
Current Ratio: 2.37
Long-term debt ($ mil.): 72.3
No. of shares ($ mil.): 15.3
Dividends
Yield: 1.7%
Payout: 19.5%
Market value ($ mil.): 358.0

	STOCK PRICE ($)	P/E		PER SHARE ($)		
	FY Close	High	/Low	Earnings	Dividends	Book Value
12/20	23.24	10	2	2.65	0.40	12.45
12/19	13.54	23	16	0.79	0.40	10.35
12/18	17.65	25	14	1.10	0.39	9.93
12/17	26.71	27	16	0.99	0.37	8.29
12/16	19.62	20	14	0.98	0.34	7.62
Annual Growth	4.3%	—	—	28.2%	4.1%	13.1%

Supernus Pharmaceuticals Inc

Supernus Pharmaceuticals is a biopharmaceutical company focused on developing and commercializing products for the treatment of central nervous system (CNS) diseases. Its diverse neuroscience portfolio includes approved treatments for epilepsy, migraine, hypomobility in Parkinson's Disease (PD), cervical dystonia, and chronic sialorrhea. It is developing a broad range of novel CNS product candidates, including new potential treatments for attention-deficit hyperactivity disorder (ADHD), hypomobility in PD, epilepsy, depression, and other CNS disorders. The company utilizes third-party commercial manufacturing organizations (CMOs) for all of its manufacturing. Its products are sold through pharmacies, hospitals, as well as federal and state entities.

Operations
The company's two products are Trokendi XR (accounts for more than 50% of total revenue) and Oxtellar XR (nearly 20%). These two products are the first once-daily extended release oxcarbazepine and topiramate products indicated for the treatment of epilepsy in the US market. Trokendi XR is for the prophylaxis of migraine headaches in adults and adolescents, while Oxtellar XR for monotherapy treatment of partial onset epilepsy seizures in adults and children 6 to 17 years of age.

Other product candidates include SPN-812 (viloxazine hydrochloride) as a novel, non-stimulant product candidate to treat children 6 to 17 years of age who have ADHD; SPN-830 (apomorphine infusion device) is a late-stage drug/device combination product candidate for the treatment of continuous prevention of "off" episodes in PD patients; and SPN-817 for the treatment of severe pediatric epilepsy disorders through its acquisition with Biscayne Neurotherapeutics.

Its key proprietary technology platforms include Microtrol, Solutrol and EnSoTrol. These technologies create novel, customized product profiles, designed to enhance efficacy, reduce the frequency of dosing so as to improve patient compliance and improve tolerability. It has employed the technologies in the development of a total of ten products that are currently on the market, including its products Trokendi XR and Oxtellar XR, along with eight products being marketed by the company's partners.

Geographic Reach
Supernus has its corporate office and laboratory space in Rockville, Maryland. It markets its product throughout the US.

Sales and Marketing
Supernus markets its products through its own sales representatives in the US and seek strategic collaborations with other pharmaceutical companies to commercialize our products, and those of our subsidiaries, outside of the US. .

The majority of its product sales are to pharmaceutical wholesalers, specialty pharmacies, and distributors who, in turn, sell its products to pharmacies, hospitals, and other customers, including federal and state entities. The majority of sales of Oxtellar XR, Trokendi XR, Qelbree, and XADAGO are made to wholesalers and distributors. In addition, MYOBLOC is available for direct purchase by physicians and hospitals. The majority of sales of APOKYN and GOCOVRI are made to specialty pharmacies. Its three customers, AmerisourceBergen, Cardinal Health, and McKesson, accounted for more than 25% of total product revenue.

The company incurred approximately $86.0 million, $54.5 million, and $40.8 million in advertising expenses in 2021, 2020, and 2019, respectively.

Financial Performance
Net product sales increased by $58.2 million from $509.4 million in 2020 to $567.5 million in 2021. The increase in net product sales was primarily due to a $51.1 million increase in net product sales of the acquired commercial products from both the USWM Acquisition in June 2020 and Adamas Acquisition in November 2021, as well as a $12.0 million increase in net product sales of Oxtellar XR and $9.9 million net product sales from Qelbree, which was launched in May 2021.

Net income for fiscal 2021 decreased to $53.4 million compared from the prior year with $127.0 million.

Cash held by the company at the end of fiscal 2021 decreased to $203.4 million. Cash provided by operations was $127.1 million while cash used for investing and financing activities were $81.9 million and $130.4 million, respectively. Main uses for cash were purchases of marketable securities and repayment of acquired Adamas loan.

Strategy
Supernus mission is to improve the lives of patients suffering from CNS diseases. Company's vision is to be a leader in the CNS industry by developing and commercializing new medicines for the treatment of CNS diseases. Key elements of its strategy to achieve this vision include:

Drive growth and profitability. Using dedicated sales and marketing resources in the U., the company will continue to drive the revenue growth of its market products.

Advance its current pipeline toward commercialization. The company have a portfolio of early to late-stage product candidates. Supernus continue to advance its late-stage product candidate, Qelbree (viloxazine hydrochloride) for treatment of ADHD in adults and SPN-830 (apomorphine infusion device) for treatment of hypomobility in PD, to regulatory approval and commercialization.

Continue to grow its pipeline. Supernus will continue to evaluate and develop additional CNS product candidates that the company believe have significant commercial potential through our internal research and development efforts.

Target strategic business development opportunities. Supernus are actively exploring a broad range of strategic opportunities. This includes in-licensing products and entering into co-promotion and co-development partnerships for its commercial products and product candidates.

Mergers and Acquisitions
In late 2021, Supernus acquired Adams Pharmaceuticals, Inc., for an aggregate of approximately $400 million. The acquisition strengthens Parkinson's disease portfolio with GOCOVRI (amantadine) extended release capsules, the first and only FDA-approved medicine indicated for the treatment of both OFF and dyskinesia in patients with Parkinson's disease receiving levodopa-based therapy and Osmolex ER (amantadine) extended release tablets, approved for the treatment of Parkinson's disease and drug-induced extrapyramidal reactions in adult patients. It also Diversifies and increases revenue base and cash flow, and combined with the acquisition of US WorldMeds CNS products in 2020, significantly reduces the reliance on net sales of Trokendi XR.

EXECUTIVES

Chairman, Director, Charles W. Newhall
President, Chief Executive Officer, Secretary, Director, Jack A. Khattar, $719,417 total compensation
Senior Vice President, Chief Financial Officer, Timothy C. Dec
Intellectual Property Senior Vice President, Intellectual Property Chief Scientific Officer, Padmanabh P. Bhatt, $368,542 total compensation
Research & Development Senior Vice President, Research & Development Chief Medical Officer, Jonathan Rubin
Regulatory Affairs Senior Vice President, Tami T. Martin, $240,000 total compensation
Quality, GMP Operations Senior Vice President, Information Technology Senior Vice President, Frank Mottola
Director, Carrolee Barlow

Director, Frederick M. Hudson
Director, Georges Gemayel
Director, John M. Siebert
Auditors : KPMG LLP

LOCATIONS

HQ: Supernus Pharmaceuticals Inc
9715 Key West Avenue, Rockville, MD 20850
Phone: 301 838-2500
Web: www.supernus.com

PRODUCTS/OPERATIONS

2015 Sales

	$ mil.	% of total
Net product sales	143.5	99
Revenue from royalty agreement	-	-
Licensing revenue	0.9	1
Total	144.4	100

Selected Products
Oxtellar XR (marketed)
SPN-809 (under trail)
SPN-810 (under trail)
SPN-812 (under trail)
Trokendi XR (marketed)

COMPETITORS
BIODELIVERY SCIENCES INTERNATIONAL, INC.
CELGENE CORPORATION
CHEMOCENTRYX, INC.
DURECT CORPORATION
LEXICON PHARMACEUTICALS, INC.
REGENERON PHARMACEUTICALS, INC.
SPECTRUM PHARMACEUTICALS, INC.
SUCAMPO PHARMACEUTICALS, INC.
TESARO, INC.
VANDA PHARMACEUTICALS INC.

HISTORICAL FINANCIALS
Company Type: Public

Income Statement — FYE: December 31

	REVENUE ($mil)	NET INCOME ($mil)	NET PROFIT MARGIN	EMPLOYEES
12/20	520.3	126.9	24.4%	563
12/19	392.7	113.0	28.8%	464
12/18	408.8	110.9	27.1%	448
12/17	302.2	57.2	19.0%	422
12/16	215.0	91.2	42.4%	363
Annual Growth	24.7%	8.6%	—	11.6%

2020 Year-End Financials
Debt ratio: 24.1%
Return on equity: 18.8%
Cash ($ mil.): 288.6
Current Ratio: 2.57
Long-term debt ($ mil.): 361.7
No. of shares ($ mil.): 52.8
Dividends
Yield: —
Payout: —
Market value ($ mil.): 1,330.0

	STOCK PRICE ($) FY Close	P/E High/Low		PER SHARE ($) Earnings	Dividends	Book Value
12/20	25.16	11	6	2.36	0.00	14.09
12/19	23.72	19	9	2.10	0.00	11.33
12/18	33.22	28	14	2.05	0.00	8.66
12/17	39.85	44	21	1.08	0.00	5.21
12/16	25.25	15	6	1.76	0.00	3.84
Annual Growth	(0.1%)	—	—	7.6%	—	38.4%

Surface Oncology Inc

EXECUTIVES

Chair, Director, Denice M. Torres
Chief Executive Officer, President, Director, Robert W. Ross, $361,000 total compensation
Legal Senior Vice President, Legal Secretary, Legal General Counsel, Theresa R. Boni
Clinical Development Chief Medical Officer, Alison O'Neill
Business Operations Chief Financial Officer, Finance Chief Financial Officer, Business Operations Principal Accounting Officer, Finance Principal Accounting Officer, Business Operations Principal Financial Officer, Finance Principal Financial Officer, Business Operations Treasurer, Finance Treasurer, Jessica Fees
Chief Scientific Officer, Vito J. Palombella, $371,000 total compensation
Chief Business Officer, Henry Rath
Director, J. Jeffrey Goater, $429,000 total compensation
Director, David S. Grayzel
Director, Ramy Ibrahim
Director, Benjamin J. Hickey
Director, Armen B. Shanafelt
Director, Charles Elliott Sigal
Director, Laurie D. Stelzer
Director, Carsten Brunn
Auditors : PricewaterhouseCoopers LLP

LOCATIONS

HQ: Surface Oncology Inc
50 Hampshire Street, 8th Floor, Cambridge, MA 02139
Phone: 617 714-4096
Web: www.surfaceoncology.com

HISTORICAL FINANCIALS
Company Type: Public

Income Statement — FYE: December 31

	REVENUE ($mil)	NET INCOME ($mil)	NET PROFIT MARGIN	EMPLOYEES
12/20	126.1	59.3	47.0%	51
12/19	15.3	(54.7)	—	49
12/18	59.4	(6.5)	—	76
12/17	12.8	(45.3)	—	56
12/16	6.6	(17.4)	—	0
Annual Growth	108.8%	—	—	—

2020 Year-End Financials
Debt ratio: 6.8%
Return on equity: 55.7%
Cash ($ mil.): 175.1
Current Ratio: 10.23
Long-term debt ($ mil.): 14.7
No. of shares ($ mil.): 40.7
Dividends
Yield: —
Payout: —
Market value ($ mil.): 376.0

	STOCK PRICE ($) FY Close	P/E High/Low		PER SHARE ($) Earnings	Dividends	Book Value
12/20	9.24	6	1	1.57	0.00	3.83
12/19	1.88	—	—	(1.97)	0.00	2.03
12/18	4.24	—	—	(0.33)	0.00	3.70
Annual Growth	47.6%	—	—	—	—	1.6%

SVB Financial Group

SVB Financial Group is the holding company for Silicon Valley Bank, which serves emerging and established companies involved in technology, life sciences/healthcare, and private equity/venture capital, and provides customized financing to entrepreneurs, executives, and investors in those industries. It also offers deposit accounts products and services, including checking, money market, certificates of deposit accounts, online banking, credit cards and other personalized banking services. SVB also provides asset management services private wealth management and other investment services. SVB has $211.5 billion in assets and holds $189.2 billion in deposits.

Operations
SVB Financial Group has four reporting segments: Global Commercial Bank (nearly 65% of sales), SVB Securities (over 10%), SVB Capital (some 10%), and SVB Private Bank (around 5%).

SVB's comprises three subunits: Commercial Bank, Global Fund Banking Division, and SVB Wine.

SVB Securities is an investment bank focused on the innovation economy and operates as a wholly-owned subsidiary of SVB Financial Group. SVB Securities provides investment banking services across all major sub-sectors of Healthcare and Technology. Healthcare sub-sectors include Biopharma, Digital Health and HealthTech, Healthcare Services, Medical Devices and Tools and Diagnostics.

SVB Capital is the venture capital and credit investment arm of SVB Financial Group, which focuses primarily on funds management. SVB Private Bank is the private banking and wealth management division of the Bank and provides a broad array of personal financial solutions for consumers.

Geographic Reach
Santa Clara, California-based SVB Financial has around 55 regional offices in the US as well as international offices in Canada, the UK, Israel, Germany, Denmark, India, Hong Kong, and China.

Sales and Marketing
Clients to SVB Financial Group's Global Commercial Bank primarily encompass technology, life science, healthcare, private equity, and venture capital entities. The company serve a variety of clients in the technology and life science/healthcare industries. Our technology clients tend to be in the industries of frontier tech and hardware (such as semiconductors, communications, data, storage and electronics); enterprise and consumer software/internet (such as infrastructure software, applications, software services, digital content and advertising technology); fintech; and climate technology and sustainability. SVB Securities customers

include biotechs, pharmas, medical device and diagnostic makers, healthcare services and digital health firms, and life science tool companies.

Financial Performance

Company's revenue for fiscal 2021 increased to $5.9 billion compared from the prior year with $4.0 billion.

Net income for fiscal 2021 increased to $1.8 billion compared from the prior year with $1.2 billion.

Cash held by the company at the end of fiscal 2021 increased to $2.3 billion. Cash provided by financing activities was $7.3 billion while cash used for investing and financing activities were $271 million and $5.3 billion, respectively.

Strategy

A key component of SVB's technology and life science/healthcare business strategy is to develop relationships with clients at an early stage and offer them banking services that will continue to meet their needs as they mature and expand.

Mergers and Acquisitions

In late 2021, SVB Financial announced its continued expansion into technology investment banking with the acquisition of MoffettNathanson LLC, a New York-based independent sell-side research firm known for its coverage of high-growth, disruptive companies in the Media, Communications and Technology sectors. The acquisition enables SVB's investment banking business, SVB Leerink, to expand its research coverage to include companies in both the healthcare and technology industries. Terms were not disclosed.

In mid-2021, SVB Financial has completed the acquisition of Boston Private Financial Holdings, Inc., the parent company of Boston Private Bank & Trust Company, a leading provider of integrated wealth management, trust and banking services to individuals, families, businesses and nonprofits for a total consideration value of approximately $900 million. With the acquisition of Boston Private, SVB Private Banking & Wealth Management provides the guidance and solutions that fuel its clients to build wealth and expand opportunities for today and tomorrow.

Company Background

Established in 1983, SVB Financial Group went public on Nasdaq five years later. By 1996 it had expanded to 15 US states.

HISTORY

Silicon Valley Bank was founded in 1983 by Roger Smith to provide banking services to tech startups in San Jose. The bank boomed along with tech companies during the 1980s, lending to the likes of Cisco Systems.

In 1990 the bank spread east to Boston's burgeoning technology alley. It also expanded into residential and commercial real estate lending. The recession of 1989 to 1991 found Silicon Valley Bancshares with an overextended loan portfolio, and in 1992 the bank booked a loss due to nonperforming loans; the next year it was put under federal supervision.

To rally stockholder confidence, the company brought in new management and demoted Smith from chairman to vice chairman; he left the in 1995. The bank reduced its real estate lending and diversified into factoring, foreign exchange, and executive banking for venture capitalists and clients' upper management.

The 1995 IPO frenzy aided the company's turnaround. Silicon Valley cashed in on warrants it had taken as collateral from young companies. Regulatory supervision was lifted in 1996, and the bank soon opened offices in the Atlanta; Austin, Texas; Boulder, Colorado; Phoenix; and Seattle areas.

In 1999 Silicon Valley Bancshares created a website targeted at technology firms in need of financing, employees, office space, and equipment. However, nonperforming loans began to dog the bank once again, affecting profits and bringing a regulatory request to boost capital reserves.

In 2000, despite being hammered by the high-tech stock selloff, the company continued to expand, opening offices in West Palm Beach, Florida, and North Carolina's Research Triangle and successfully capitalizing its first venture fund. The following year it bought tech-focused investment bank Alliant Partners (later renamed SVB Alliant) to broaden its service offerings.

Still licking its wounds from the tech bust, the company ceased lending to the entertainment industry and to churches in 2002. Silicon Valley Bancshares changed its name to SVB Financial Services in 2005.

SVB Alliant struggled with losses for years and SVB Financial explored its options, including spinning the unit off to management. It ultimately decided to shut down the division, which ceased operations in 2008.

EXECUTIVES

Chairman, Director, Beveryly Kay Matthews
President, Chief Executive Officer, Director, Gregory W. Becker, $953,654 total compensation
Chief Financial Officer, Daniel J. Beck, $547,789 total compensation
Chief Human Resources Officer, Christopher D. Edmonds-Waters
Chief Operations Officer, Philip C. Cox, $328,013 total compensation
Chief Marketing Officer, Chief Strategy Officer, Michelle A. Draper
Chief Credit Officer, Marc C. Cadieux, $447,308 total compensation
Chief Risk Officer, Laura H. Izurieta
Chief Restructuring Officer, William Kosturos
General Counsel, Michael S. Zuckert
Subsidiary Officer, Michael Descheneaux, $723,462 total compensation
Division Officer, John D. China, $5,566,096 total compensation
Director, Elizabeth Burr
Director, Eric A. Benhamou
Director, Richard Daniels
Director, Alison Davis
Director, Joel P. Friedman
Director, Jeffrey Nacey Maggioncalda
Director, Mary John Miller
Director, Kate D. Mitchell
Director, Garen K. Staglin
Director, Thomas C. King
Auditors : KPMG LLP

LOCATIONS

HQ: SVB Financial Group
  3003 Tasman Drive, Santa Clara, CA 95054-1191
Phone: 408 654-7400
Web: www.svb.com

Selected Offices
US
  Atlanta
  Austin, TX
  Broomfield, CO
  Chicago
  Dallas
  Irvine, CA
  Menlo Park, CA
  Minnetonka, MN
  New York
  Newton, MA
  Palo Alto, CA
  Philadelphia
  Phoenix
  Pleasanton, CA
  Portland, OR
  Raleigh, NC
  Salt Lake City
  San Diego
  San Francisco
  Santa Rosa, CA
  Seattle
  St. Helena, CA
  Tysons Corner, VA
International
  Bangalore, India
  Beijing
  Herzliya Pituach, Israel
  London
  Mumbai, India
  Shanghai

PRODUCTS/OPERATIONS

2016 Sales

	$ mil.	% of total
Interest		
Loans	834.2	51
Investment securities	359.3	22
Noninterest		
Net gains on investment securities	51.7	3
Net gains on derivative instruments	48.6	3
Foreign exchange fees	104.2	6
Credit card fees	68.2	4
Deposit service charges	52.5	3
Lending related fees	33.4	2
Letters of credit	25.6	2
Client investment fees	32.2	2
Other	40.0	2
Total	1,649.9	100

Selected Subsidiaries and Affiliates
Silicon Valley Bank

SVB Analytics, Inc.
SVB Asset Management
SVB Business Partners (Beijing) Co. Ltd.
SVB Business Partners (Shanghai) Co. Ltd.
SVB Global Financial, Inc.
SVB Global Investors, LLC
SVB Growth Investors, LLC
SVB India Advisors, Pvt. Ltd.
SVB Israel Advisors, Ltd.
SVB Qualified Investors Fund, LLC
SVB Real Estate Investment Trust
SVB Securities
SVB Strategic Investors, LLC
SVB Strategic Investors Fund, L.P.
Venture Investment Managers, L.P.

COMPETITORS

BOSTON PRIVATE FINANCIAL HOLDINGS, INC.
M&T BANK CORPORATION
NORTHERN TRUST CORPORATION
PIPER SANDLER COMPANIES
PRIVATEBANCORP, INC.
RAYMOND JAMES FINANCIAL, INC.
REGIONS FINANCIAL CORPORATION
STATE STREET CORPORATION
STIFEL FINANCIAL CORP.
THE BANK OF NEW YORK MELLON CORPORATION

HISTORICAL FINANCIALS
Company Type: Public

Income Statement — FYE: December 31

	ASSETS ($mil)	NET INCOME ($mil)	INCOME AS % OF ASSETS	EMPLOYEES
12/20	115,511.0	1,208.3	1.0%	4,461
12/19	71,004.9	1,136.8	1.6%	3,564
12/18	56,927.9	973.8	1.7%	2,900
12/17	51,214.4	490.5	1.0%	2,438
12/16	44,683.6	382.6	0.9%	2,311
Annual Growth	26.8%	33.3%	—	17.9%

2020 Year-End Financials
Return on assets: 1.2%
Return on equity: 16.4%
Long-term debt ($ mil.): —
No. of shares ($ mil.): 51.8
Sales ($ mil.): 4,081.7
Dividends
 Yield: —
 Payout: —
Market value ($ mil.): 20,124.0

	STOCK PRICE ($) FY Close	P/E High/Low		PER SHARE ($) Earnings	Dividends	Book Value
12/20	387.83	17	6	22.87	0.00	158.41
12/19	251.04	12	8	21.73	0.00	125.26
12/18	189.92	18	10	18.11	0.00	97.29
12/17	233.77	26	17	9.20	0.00	79.11
12/16	171.66	24	11	7.31	0.00	69.71
Annual Growth	22.6%	—	—	33.0%	—	22.8%

Switch Inc

EXECUTIVES

Chairman, Chief Executive Officer, Subsidiary Officer, Rob Roy, $1,025,000 total compensation
President, Chief Legal Officer, General Counsel, Secretary, Subsidiary Officer, Thomas Morton, $792,325 total compensation
Digital Solutions Executive Vice President, Bill Kleyman
Chief Financial Officer, Subsidiary Officer, Gabe Nacht, $400,000 total compensation
Global Sales Vice President, Jocelyn McCaslin
Director, Zareh H. Sarrafian
Director, Kim Sheehy
Director, Donald D. Snyder
Director, Tom Thomas
Director, Bryan Wolf
Auditors: PricewaterhouseCoopers LLP

LOCATIONS

HQ: Switch Inc
7135 S. Decatur Boulevard, Las Vegas, NV 89118
Phone: 702 444-4111
Web: www.switch.com

HISTORICAL FINANCIALS
Company Type: Public

Income Statement — FYE: December 31

	REVENUE ($mil)	NET INCOME ($mil)	NET PROFIT MARGIN	EMPLOYEES
12/20	511.5	15.5	3.0%	759
12/19	462.3	8.9	1.9%	789
12/18	405.8	4.0	1.0%	731
12/17	378.2	(15.2)	—	723
12/16	318.3	31.3	9.9%	689
Annual Growth	12.6%	(16.1%)	—	2.4%

2020 Year-End Financials
Debt ratio: 49.6%
Return on equity: 6.5%
Cash ($ mil.): 90.7
Current Ratio: 1.19
Long-term debt ($ mil.): 1,048.7
No. of shares ($ mil.): 240.6
Dividends
 Yield: 0.9%
 Payout: 113.4%
Market value ($ mil.): 3,939.0

	STOCK PRICE ($) FY Close	P/E High/Low		PER SHARE ($) Earnings	Dividends	Book Value
12/20	16.37	127	75	0.14	0.16	1.11
12/19	14.82	140	57	0.11	0.12	0.86
12/18	7.00	200	71	0.09	0.07	0.58
12/17	18.19	—	—	(1.88)	0.01	0.43
Annual Growth	(3.5%)	—	—	—	124.7%	36.9%

Synovus Financial Corp

Synovus Financial Corp. is a financial services company and a registered bank holding company that provides commercial and consumer banking, as well as private banking, treasury management, wealth management, mortgage services, premium finance, asset-based lending, structured lending, and international banking through Synovus Bank. The company operates nearly 280 branches and approximately 370 ATMs throughout Alabama, Florida, Georgia, South Carolina, and Tennessee. It also provides other financial services through direct and indirect wholly-owned non-bank subsidiaries such as Synovus Securities and Synovus Trust. The company has total consolidated assets of $57.32 billion and total consolidated deposits of $49.43 billion.

Operations

Synovus Financial has three major reportable business segments: Community Banking, Wholesale Banking, and Financial Management Services (FMS), with functional activities such as treasury, technology, operations, marketing, finance, enterprise risk, legal, human resources, corporate communications, executive management, among others, included in Treasury and Corporate Other.

The Community Banking business segment (accounts for more than 45% of total revenue) serves customers using a relationship-based approach through its branch, ATM, commercial, and private wealth network in addition to mobile, Internet, and telephone banking. This segment primarily provides individual, small business, and corporate clients with an array of comprehensive banking products and services including commercial, home equity, and other consumer loans, credit and debit cards, and deposit accounts.

The Wholesale Banking business segment (some 30% of total sales) provides commercial lending and deposit services through specialty teams including middle market, CRE, senior housing, national accounts, premium finance, structured lending, healthcare, asset-based lending, and community investment capital.

The FMS business segment (approximately 15% of total sales) serves its customers by providing mortgage and trust services and also specializing in professional portfolio management for fixed-income securities, investment banking, the execution of securities transactions as a broker/dealer, asset management, financial planning, and family office services, as well as the provision of individual investment advice on equity and other securities. Treasury and Corporate Other segment accounts for the rest.

The company's non-bank subsidiaries, such as Synovus Securities and Synovus Trust, offer other financial services including professional portfolio management for fixed-income securities, investment banking, the execution of securities transactions as a broker/dealer, asset management and financial planning services, among others.

Overall, interest income brings in about 80% of the company's revenue. Service charges on deposit accounts, fiduciary and asset management fees, card fees, brokerage revenue, mortgage banking income, capital markets income, income from bank-owned life insurance, and other non-interest income account for the rest.

Geographic Reach

Georgia-based Synovus Financial has about 280 branches and some 370 ATMS in Alabama, Florida, Georgia, South Carolina, and Tennessee.

Sales and Marketing

Synovus Financial serves individual, small business, and corporate customers with an array of comprehensive banking products and services including commercial, home equity, and other consumer loans, credit and debit cards, and deposit accounts through its Community Banking segment. The company's Wholesale Banking segment serves primarily larger corporate customers.

Financial Performance

The company reported a revenue of $2 billion in 2021, a 2% decrease from the previous year's revenue. This was primarily due to a lower non-interest revenue for 2021.

In 2021, the company had a net income of $760.5 million, a 103% increase from the previous year's net income of $373.7 million.

The company's cash at the end of 2021 was $3 billion. Operating activities generated $794 million, while investing activities used $4.4 billion, mainly for purchases of investment securities available for sale. Financing activities generated another $2.3 billion.

Strategy

Throughout 2021, Synovus' strategic focus remained on expanding and diversifying the franchise in terms of revenue, profitability and asset size while maintaining a community banking, relationship-based approach to banking. In addition, the company navigated through a CEO transition beginning in April 2021 with Kevin S. Blair succeeding Kessel Stelling as President and Chief Executive Officer and Mr. Stelling stepping into the role of Executive Chairman of the Board, all while remaining focused on execution of key strategic priorities, including Synovus Forward. As previously announced in the first quarter of 2020 and executed throughout 2021, the cost savings and revenue-generating initiatives underpinning Synovus Forward include expense reductions around Synovus' third party spend program, branch optimization, back-office staff optimization, an early retirement program, market-based repricing of certain product offerings, deposit repricing, commercial analytics and digital enhancements. As of December 31, 2021, Synovus had realized approximately $110 million in pre-tax benefits from Synovus Forward and remains on track to achieve a cumulative pre-tax run rate benefit of $175 million by the end of 2022.

In December 2021, Synovus introduced a streamlined strategic plan focused on growth and performance through four core pillars. The four core pillars are reposition for advantage, simplify and streamline, adopt high-tech meets high touch, and enhance talent and culture. Each of these pillars is supported by various strategic initiatives designed to drive growth and improve performance, with a prioritization on such matters as investing in commercial growth, fortifying consumer banking, optimizing wealth, refreshing the brand, re-imagining the client journey, automating systems and processes, using advanced analytics, enhancing modern core enabled banking products, developing diverse leaders and establishing a growth based culture. We believe disciplined execution of these core pillars will position us for long-term top quartile performance.

Company Background

Synovus history can be traced back in 1888 when G. Gunby Jordan established two banks namely, Third National Bank and The Columbus Savings Bank. In 1930, the two banks merged and became Columbus Bank and Trust. In 1972, CB&T Bancshares, Inc. was created and became the holding company for Columbus Bank and Trust. Two years later, the holding company started offering third-party credit card transaction processing to banks in Georgia and other states through The Total System, its bankcard processing software. CB&T expanded into other states through acquisitions in Florida and Alabama in the late 80s. In 1989, CB&T Bancshares, Inc. became Synovus Financial Corp. and started trading under the symbol SNV on the New York Stock Exchange.

HISTORY

In 1885 W. C. Bradley founded his eponymous company (today a manufacturing and development concern). Three years later he invested in a new bank that would eventually bear the name of its Georgia hometown: Columbus Bank and Trust. (Bradley's investment in Atlanta-based Coca-Cola today accounts for the lion's share of his family's wealth.) When Bradley died, his son-in-law Abbott Turner joined the bank's board of directors, followed by Turner's son William.

In 1958 the bank hired James Blanchard as president. The next year Columbus Bank and Trust became one of the first banks to issue credit cards. The company's credit processing business grew, leading it to computerize the process in 1966 and train its own employees to operate the equipment. (It decided to go it alone after a failed joint-venture attempt with corporate cousin W.C. Bradley Co.)

In a little more than a decade, Blanchard led the bank to triple its assets. When he died in 1969, the search for a new leader took the bank's directors in a surprising direction: They offered the position to Blanchard's son Jimmy, a young attorney with no banking experience. The board pressed him to take the job, which he did in 1971 after a brief apprenticeship.

From the start, the younger Blanchard emphasized the company's financial services operations, such as credit card processing. Taking advantage of new laws opening up the banking and financial services industry in the early 1970s, the bank reorganized in 1972, incorporating CB&T Bancshares to serve as a holding company for Columbus Bank and Trust. In 1973 CB&T's financial services division finished a new software product called the Total System, which allowed electronic access to account information. CB&T used the groundbreaking software to start processing other banks' paperwork, including an ever-growing number of credit card accounts. In 1983 CB&T spun off financial services division Total System Services (TSYS), but retained a majority stake in the company.

Blanchard helped win passage of Georgia's multibank holding law, and further deregulation in the early 1980s allowed the company to operate across state lines. It bought four banks in Florida and Georgia in 1983 and 1984, and snapped up six more (including an Alabama bank) in 1985. Meanwhile, TSYS benefited from the trend to outsource credit card processing.

In 1989 CB&T changed its name to Synovus, a combination of the words "synergy" and "novus," the latter word meaning (according to the company) "of superior quality and different from the others listed in the same category."

During the early 1990s Synovus swept up 20 banks in its market area after the bank bust. After 1993, acquisitions dropped off until 1998, when Synovus announced three acquisitions in two weeks. That year it also said it was planning to move further into Internet and investment banking, as well as auto and life insurance. In 1999 the company bought banks in Georgia and Florida; it also moved into debt collection with its purchase of Wallace & de Mayo, which was renamed Total System Services (TSYS). In 2007 Synovus spun off TSYS.

The company grew its retail investment operations with the acquisitions of Atlanta-area asset managers Creative Financial Group in 2001 and GLOBALT in 2002. Jimmy Blanchard, who had ultimately become Synovus Financial's chairman, retired as an executive in 2005, but remained on the board. The long-time executive stepped down from the board in 2012.

Fred Green abruptly stepped down as president of Synovus in 2009. CEO Richard Anthony assumed his responsibilities until early 2010 when Kessel Stelling was named president and COO of the company. Stelling was named CEO later that year after Anthony, who remained chairman, took a medical leave of absence. Anthony retired from the board in 2012. Stelling then took on the additional roll of chairman.

In May 2013 the bank acquired three branches of a failed Valdosta-based bank.

EXECUTIVES

Executive Chairman, Director, Kessel D. Stelling, $1,125,000 total compensation

President, Chief Executive Officer, Chief Operating Officer, Director, Kevin S. Blair, $695,250 total compensation

Executive Vice President, General Counsel, Corporate Secretary, Allan E. Kamensky, $440,789 total compensation

Executive Vice President, Chief Financial Officer, Andrew J. Gregory, $475,000 total compensation
Executive Vice President, Chief Credit Officer, Robert W. Derrick
Chief Accounting Officer, Controller, Jill Hurley
Secretary, Mary Maurice Young
Lead Director, Director, Elizabeth W. Camp
Director, Tim E. Bentsen
Director, Frederick Dixon Brooke
Director, Stephen T. Butler
Director, Pedro P. Cherry
Director, Diana M. Murphy
Director, Harris Pastides
Director, Joseph J. Prochaska
Director, John L. Stallworth
Director, Barry L. Storey
Director, Teresa White
Auditors : KPMG LLP

LOCATIONS

HQ: Synovus Financial Corp
1111 Bay Avenue, Suite 500, Columbus, GA 31901
Phone: 706 641-6500
Web: www.synovus.com

Bank Branch Locations

	No.
Georgia	114
Florida	48
South Carolina	38
Alabama	37
Tennessee	11
Total	**248**

PRODUCTS/OPERATIONS

2016 Sales

	$ mil.	% of total
Interest income:		
Loans, including fees	944.2	73
Investment securities available for sale	67.5	5
Trading account assets	0.1	-
Mortgage loans held for sale	2.6	-
Federal Reserve Bank balances	4.4	-
Other earning assets	4.0	-
Non-interest income:		
Service charges on deposit accounts	81.4	6
Fiduciary and asset management fees	46.6	4
Bankcard fees	33.3	3
Other non-interest income	34.3	3
Brokerage revenue	27.0	2
Mortgage banking income	24.3	2
Other fee income	20.2	2
Investment securities gains, net	6.0	-
Total	**1,296**	**100**

COMPETITORS

CIT GROUP INC.
CLOSE BROTHERS GROUP PLC
FB CORPORATION
FIFTH THIRD BANCORP
INVESTAR HOLDING CORPORATION
KEYCORP
NORTHERN TRUST CORPORATION
REGIONS FINANCIAL CORPORATION
STATE STREET CORPORATION
THE JONES FINANCIAL COMPANIES L L L P

HISTORICAL FINANCIALS
Company Type: Public

Income Statement — FYE: December 31

	ASSETS ($mil)	NET INCOME ($mil)	INCOME AS % OF ASSETS	EMPLOYEES
12/20	54,394.1	373.6	0.7%	5,247
12/19	48,203.2	563.7	1.2%	5,389
12/18	32,669.1	428.4	1.3%	4,651
12/17	31,221.8	275.4	0.9%	4,541
12/16	30,104.0	246.7	0.8%	4,436
Annual Growth	15.9%	10.9%	—	4.3%

2020 Year-End Financials
Return on assets: 0.7%
Return on equity: 7.3%
Long-term debt ($ mil.): —
No. of shares ($ mil.): 148.0
Sales ($ mil.): 2,311
Dividends Yield: 4.0%
Payout: 57.3%
Market value ($ mil.): 4,792.0

	STOCK PRICE ($) FY Close	P/E High	P/E Low	PER SHARE ($) Earnings	Dividends	Book Value
12/20	32.37	17	6	2.30	1.32	34.86
12/19	39.20	11	9	3.47	1.20	33.58
12/18	31.99	16	9	3.47	1.00	27.05
12/17	47.94	23	18	2.17	0.60	24.91
12/16	41.08	22	14	1.89	0.48	23.95
Annual Growth	(5.8%)	—	—	5.0%	28.8%	9.8%

Take-Two Interactive Software, Inc.

Take-Two is a leading developer, publisher and marketer of interactive entertainment for consumers around the globe. The company's popular mature-rated Grand Theft Auto series and other games are developed by subsidiary Rockstar Games. Its 2K Games subsidiary publishes franchises such as BioShock, Borderlands, and Sid Meier's Civilization; the 2K Sports unit carries titles such as Major League Baseball 2K and NBA 2K. Take-Two's games are played on Microsoft, Sony, and Nintendo game consoles, but also on PCs and handheld devices. Its products are sold through outlets including retail chains, such as GameStop and Steam, and as digital downloads. Approximately 60% of its sales comes from the US.

Operations

Take-Two's Rockstar Games subsidiary established a uniquely original, popular cultural phenomenon with its Grand Theft Auto series, which is the interactive entertainment industry's most iconic and critically acclaimed brand and has sold-in over 375 million units worldwide. Focused on hardcore action games, its other titles alongside golden child GTA include open-world racing game Midnight Club, the Wild West-themed Red Dead Redemption series, 1940s-era action-detective game L.A. Noire, and gritty action shooter Max Payne.

Its 2K label has published a variety of popular entertainment properties across all key platforms and across a range of genres including shooter, action, role-playing, strategy, sports and family/casual entertainment. The NBA 2K series is one of the company's top sellers. As part of that push Take-Two established the 2K Play label for its casual gaming and family-oriented efforts, offering titles such as BioShock, Mafia, and Sid Meier's Civilization.

Over 70% of the company's revenue comes from console games. Games for PCs and other devices account for the remaining revenue.

Geographic Reach

Take-Two is based in New York City and gets some 60% of its sales from customers in the US with international customers supplying the rest. The company's subsidiaries Rockstar North is located in Edinburgh while 2K's corporate office is in Novato, California.

The company operates development studios in Australia, Canada, China, Czech Republic, Hungary, India, Serbia, South Korea, Spain, the UK, and the US.

Sales and Marketing

The company sells software titles both physically and digitally through direct relationships with large retail customers, including digital storefronts and platform partners, and third-party distributors. The company's top customers include Sony, Microsoft, Steam, GameStop, Apple, Google, and Epic globally. Sales to its five largest customers accounted for about 80%, with Sony and Microsoft each accounting for more than 10%.

The company's products delivered through digital online services (digital download, online platforms, and cloud streaming) accounts for some 90% of sales and physical retail and other account for some 10%.

Advertising, marketing, and other promotional expenses for the fiscal years 2022, 2021, and 2020 amounted to $297,299, $241,068 and $285,607, respectively.

Financial Performance

The company had revenues of $3.5 billion, a 4% increase from the previous year's revenue of $3.4 billion.

In 2021, the company had a net income of $418 million, a 29% decrease from the previous year's net income of $588.9 million.

The company's cash at the end of 2021 was $2.2 billion. Operating activities generated $258 million, while financing activities used $256.8 million, mainly for repurchase of common stock. Investing activities generated $139.2 million.

Strategy

The company's core strategy is to capitalize on the popularity of video games by developing and publishing high-quality interactive entertainment experiences across a range of genres. It focuses on building compelling entertainment franchises by publishing a select number of titles for which it can create sequels and incremental revenue opportunities through virtual currency, add-on content, and in-game purchases. Most of its intellectual property is internally owned and developed, which the company believes best positions its financially and competitively. It has established a portfolio of proprietary software content for the major hardware platforms in a wide range of genres, including action, adventure, family/casual, role-playing, shooter, sports and strategy, which the company distributes worldwide.

Mergers and Acquisitions

In mid-2021, Take-Two Interactive Software has acquired privately-held Dynamixyz, a world-class leader in video-based facial animation services. Cesson-SÃ©vignÃ©, France-based, Dynamixyz owns and operates a suite of leading-edge, proprietary motion capture, facial-analysis, and full 3D processing tools and technology that combines computer graphics, computer vision, and machine learning. Take-Two's acquisition of Dynamixyz is the company's latest strategic initiative to invest further in its internal development capabilities and to continue its goal to be the most creative, innovative, and efficient entertainment company. Terms were not disclosed.

Also in mid-2021, Take-Two Interactive Software has acquired privately-held Nordeus for up to $378 million. Nordeus is a mobile games company based in Belgrade, Serbia, best known for Top Eleven, the world's most successful mobile soccer management game with over 240 million registered users. The acquisition of Nordeus strengthens further Take-Two's mobile game business and is highly complementary to Social Point and Playdots. It also broadens its sports portfolio with its first-ever soccer offerings.

Company Background

Take-Two exited the third-party distribution business in 2010.

EXECUTIVES

Executive Chairman, Chief Executive Officer, Director, Strauss Zelnick, $1 total compensation
President, Karl Slatoff, $1 total compensation
Executive Vice President, Chief Legal Officer, General Counsel, Daniel P. Emerson, $540,000 total compensation
Senior Vice President, General Counsel Americas, Corporate Secretary, Matthew K. Breitman
Chief Financial Officer, Lainie Goldstein, $850,000 total compensation
Lead Independent Director, Director, Michael Dornemann
Director, Ellen F. Siminoff
Director, William B. Gordon
Director, Roland A. Hernandez
Director, Jon J. Moses
Director, Michael James Sheresky
Director, LaVerne Evans Srinivasan
Director, Susan M. Tolson
Director, Paul E. Viera
Auditors: Ernst & Young LLP

LOCATIONS

HQ: Take-Two Interactive Software, Inc.
110 West 44th Street, New York, NY 10036
Phone: 646 536-2842
Web: www.take2games.com

2019 Sales

	$ mil.	% of total
US	1,426.9	53
International	1,241.5	47
Total	1,779.7	100

PRODUCTS/OPERATIONS

2019 Sales

	$ in mil.	% of total
Consoles	2,233.9	84
PCs and other	434.5	16
Total	2,668.4	100

2019 Sales

	$ mil.	% of total
Product	1,349.4	51
Physical retail and other	1,319	49
Total	2,668.4	100

2017 Sales

	$ mil.	% of total
Full game and other	1,597.5	60
Recurrent consumer spending	1,070.9	40
Total	2,668.4	100

Selected Titles

Rockstar Games
    Beaterator
    Bully
    Grand Theft Auto
    L.A. Noire
    Manhunt
    Max Payne
    Midnight Club
    Red Dead Redemption
2K Games
    The Bigs
    Bioshock
    Borderlands
    The Darkness
    Duke Nukem Forever
    Mafia
    Sid Meier's Civilization
    Sid Meier's Pirates!
2K Play
    Carnival Games
    Deal or No Deal
    Dora the Explorer
    Family Feud
    Go, Diego, Go!
2K Sports
    Major League Baseball 2K
    NBA 2K
    NHL 2K
    Top Spin

Selected Customers

GameStop
Wal-Mart
Best Buy
Microsoft
Sony
Steam

COMPETITORS

3517667 Canada Inc
ACTIVISION BLIZZARD, INC.
ALPHABET INC.
ELECTRONIC ARTS INC.
FORESCOUT TECHNOLOGIES, INC.
GLU MOBILE INC.
INTRALOT S.A.
LIVEPERSON, INC.
PROS HOLDINGS, INC.
ZYNGA INC.

HISTORICAL FINANCIALS

Company Type: Public

Income Statement   FYE: March 31

	REVENUE ($mil)	NET INCOME ($mil)	NET PROFIT MARGIN	EMPLOYEES
03/21	3,372.7	588.8	17.5%	6,495
03/20	3,088.9	404.4	13.1%	5,800
03/19	2,668.3	333.8	12.5%	4,896
03/18	1,792.8	173.5	9.7%	4,492
03/17	1,779.7	67.3	3.8%	3,707
Annual Growth	17.3%	72.0%	—	15.1%

2021 Year-End Financials

Debt ratio: —   No. of shares ($ mil.): 115.1
Return on equity: 20.0%   Dividends
Cash ($ mil.): 1,422.8   Yield: —
Current Ratio: 1.89   Payout: —
Long-term debt ($ mil.): —   Market value ($ mil.): 20,349.0

	STOCK PRICE ($) FY Close	P/E High/Low		PER SHARE ($) Earnings	Dividends	Book Value
03/21	176.70	42	23	5.09	0.00	28.93
03/20	118.61	37	25	3.54	0.00	22.37
03/19	94.37	47	29	2.90	0.00	18.19
03/18	97.78	81	37	1.54	0.00	13.06
03/17	59.27	82	46	0.72	0.00	9.78
Annual Growth	31.4%	—	—	63.1%	—	31.1%

Teb Bancorp Inc

EXECUTIVES

Chairman, Subsidiary Officer, Director, John P. Matter
President, Chief Executive Officer, Subsidiary Officer, Director, Jennifer L. Provancher
Marketing Executive Vice President, Sales Executive Vice President, Marketing Subsidiary Officer, Sales Subsidiary Officer, Director, Thomas Sattler
Chief Credit Officer, Subsidiary Officer, Willim A. Behm
Chief Financial Officer, Subsidiary Officer, Lauren Poppen
Corporate Secretary, Subsidiary Officer, Erin K. Arneson
Subsidiary Officer, Director, Charles R. Pittelkow
Director, Rachelle Marquardt
Director, Julia A. Taylor
Director, Joseph J. Becker
Director, Christopher C. Conlon
Auditors: Baker Tilly US, LLP

LOCATIONS

HQ: Teb Bancorp Inc
2290 North Mayfair Road, Wauwatosa, WI 53226
Phone: 414 476-6434
Web: www.tebbancorp.com

HISTORICAL FINANCIALS

Company Type: Public

Income Statement — FYE: June 30

	REVENUE ($mil)	NET INCOME ($mil)	NET PROFIT MARGIN	EMPLOYEES
06/21	23.7	6.3	26.9%	115
06/20	18.1	1.0	6.0%	116
06/19	15.1	(0.3)	—	116
06/18	10.7	(0.6)	—	0
Annual Growth	30.3%	—	—	—

2021 Year-End Financials

Debt ratio: 1.6%
Return on equity: 22.5%
Cash ($ mil.): 49.7
Current Ratio: 0.31
Long-term debt ($ mil.): 5
No. of shares ($ mil.): 2.6
Dividends
Yield: —
Payout: —
Market value ($ mil.): 24.0

	STOCK PRICE ($) FY Close	P/E High/Low		PER SHARE ($) Earnings	Dividends	Book Value
06/21	9.31	4	2	2.43	0.00	12.62
06/20	6.61	23	14	0.42	0.00	8.96
06/19	8.95	—	—	(0.15)	0.00	9.30
Annual Growth	2.0%	—	—	—	—	16.5%

Techpoint Inc

LOCATIONS

HQ: Techpoint Inc
2550 N. First Street, #550, San Jose, CA 95131
Phone: 408 324-0588
Web: www.techpoint.co.jp.

HISTORICAL FINANCIALS

Company Type: Public

Income Statement — FYE: December 31

	REVENUE ($mil)	NET INCOME ($mil)	NET PROFIT MARGIN	EMPLOYEES
12/21	64.7	17.2	26.7%	78
12/20	34.3	3.3	9.7%	78
12/19	32.0	2.1	6.9%	0
12/18	31.0	1.8	6.1%	0
Annual Growth	27.7%	109.3%	—	—

2021 Year-End Financials

Debt ratio: —
Return on equity: 38.7%
Cash ($ mil.): 27.3
Current Ratio: 5.98
Long-term debt ($ mil.): —
No. of shares ($ mil.): 17.9
Dividends
Yield: —
Payout: 26.8%
Market value ($ mil.): 0.0

TechTarget Inc

TechTarget can help you hit the IT professional's bull's-eye. The company operates a network of over 140 websites that focus on information technology topics such as storage, security, and networking. TechTarget offers original, vendor-generated, and user-generated content to approximately 20 million registered members, many of whom are technology buyers. Websites include Whatis.com, Computerweekly.de, SearchCIO.com and LemagIT.fr. TechTarget additionally produces digital media offerings (e-mail newsletters, online white papers, webcasts, and podcasts) aimed at IT professionals. The company generates most of its revenue through lead-generation advertising campaigns. Roughly two-thirds of revenue comes from North America.

Operations

Techtarget offers different products and services to B2B technology companies.

IT Deal Alert. IT Deal Alert is a suite of products and services for B2B technology companies that leverages the detailed purchase intent data that Techtarget collected to end-user enterprise technology organizations.

Demand Solutions. Enable its customers to reach and influence prospective buyers through content marketing programs designed to generate demand for their solutions, and through display advertising and other brand programs that influence consideration by prospective buyers.

Brand Solutions. Its suite of brand solutions provides B2B Technology Companies exposure to targeted audiences of enterprise technology and business professionals actively researching information related to their products and services.

Geographic Reach

Headquartered in Massachusetts, TechTarget operates through offices in the U.S., U.K., France, Germany, Australia and Singapore. Two-thirds of the company's revenue comes from North America.

Sales and Marketing

The company maintains an internal direct sales department that works closely with existing and potential customers to develop customized marketing programs. TechTarget's sales and marketing staff consists of approximately 330 people. The majority of the company's sales staff is located at its Newton, Massachusetts headquarters and its office in San Francisco.

Financial Performance

Revenues in 2019, increased 10% to $134.0 million, over the year 2018. The increase in revenues was due to its successful efforts in obtaining new Priority Engine customers and existing customers increasing its spending on data-driven marketing products.

The company's net income in 2019 increased by 12% to $16.9 million compared to $13.0 million in the prior year. The change was primarily due to higher revenue and provision for income taxes while having almost the same operating expense in the prior year.

Cash held by the company at the end of 2019 increased by $17.8 million to $52.5 million compared to $34.7 million in the prior year. Cash provided by operations was $39.4 million and cash used for investing activities was $10.8 million, mainly for purchases of investments. Cash used for financing activities was $10.7 million.

Strategy

The company's goal is to deliver superior performance by continuously enhancing its position as a global leader in purchase intent-driven marketing and sales services that deliver business impact for B2B technology companies by strengthening Techtarget's offerings in its three core capability areas ? its specialized content that connects enterprise technology and business professionals with B2B technology companies in the sectors and sub-sectors that it serves, the purchasing intent insight analytics and data services its content and member traffic enables, and the marketing services it provides to clients to help meet their business growth objectives.

In order to achieve this goal, the company intends to continue to innovate in the area of data-enabled marketing services; expand long-term contractual relationships with customers; expand into complementary sectors; continue to expand the company's international presence; and selectively acquire or partner with complementary businesses.

Mergers and Acquisitions

In early 2020, TechTarget Acquired California-based, Data Science Central an independent digital publishing and media company focused on data science and business analytics for an undisclosed amount. "The data science function is a true catalyst for driving data transformation and competitive edge for modern organizations and we are committed to serving these organizations by further enhancing our extensive coverage in this market," said Eileen Corrigan, VP and Publisher, Information Management Markets, TechTarget.

EXECUTIVES

Executive Chairman, Gregory Strakosch, $600,000 total compensation

Chief Executive Officer, Director, Michael Cotoia, $600,000 total compensation

Vice President, General Counsel, Corporate Secretary, Charles D. Rennick

Chief Financial Officer, Treasurer, Daniel T. Noreck, $225,000 total compensation

Product Innovation Executive Director, Don Hawk, $480,000 total compensation

Lead Independent Director, Director, Bruce Levenson

Director, Perfecto Sanchez

Director, Christina G. Van Houten

Director, Robert D. Burke

Director, Roger M. Marino

Auditors : Stowe & Degon, LLC

LOCATIONS

HQ: TechTarget Inc
275 Grove Street, Newton, MA 02466
Phone: 617 431-9200
Web: www.techtarget.com

2015 Sales

	$ mil.	% total
United States	85.3	76
International	26.5	24
Total	111.8	100

PRODUCTS/OPERATIONS

2015 Sales

	$ mil.	% of total
Online	105.6	94
Events	6.2	6
Total	111.8	100

Selected Products and Operations
Conferences
    The CIO Decisions Conference
    IT Knowledge Exchange
    The ServerSide Java Symposium
Websites
    UK
        SearchSecurity.co.uk
        SearchStorage.co.uk
    US
        Ajaxian.com
        Bitpipe.com
        Brighthand.com
        DigitalCameraReview.com
        KnowledgeStorm.com
        NotebookReview.com
        SearchCIO.com
        SearchCRM.com
        SearchDataCenter.com
        SearchDomino.com
        SearchEnterpriseLinux.com
        SearchExchange.com
        SearchMobileComputing.com
        SearchNetworking.com
        SearchOracle.com
        SearchSAP.com
        SearchSecurity.com
        SearchSMB.com
        SearchSQLServer.com
        SearchStorage.com
        SearchVMware.com
        SearchWindowsServer.com
        TheServerSide.com
        TheServerSide.NET
        Whatis.com

Online Offerings:
IT Deal Alert: Qualified Sales Opportunities
IT Deal Alert: Priority Engine
IT Deal Alert: Deal Data
IT Deal Alert: TechTarget Research
White Papers
Webcasts, Podcasts, Videocasts and Virtual Trade Shows
Content Sponsorships
On-Network Branding
Off-Network Branding
Microsites

COMPETITORS

ACXIOM LLC
BAZAARVOICE, INC.
BOOKING HOLDINGS INC.
FACEBOOK, INC.
INTRALINKS HOLDINGS, INC.
LANYON SOLUTIONS, INC.
LINKEDIN CORPORATION
NAVER Corporation
YELP INC.
YEXT, INC.

HISTORICAL FINANCIALS
Company Type: Public

Income Statement   FYE: December 31

	REVENUE ($mil)	NET INCOME ($mil)	NET PROFIT MARGIN	EMPLOYEES
12/20	148.3	17.0	11.5%	940
12/19	133.9	16.8	12.6%	649
12/18	121.3	12.9	10.7%	647
12/17	108.5	6.8	6.3%	622
12/16	106.6	2.4	2.3%	659
Annual Growth	8.6%	63.0%	—	9.3%

2020 Year-End Financials
Debt ratio: 33.7%   No. of shares ($ mil.): 28.1
Return on equity: 9.5%   Dividends
Cash ($ mil.): 82.6   Yield: —
Current Ratio: 2.75   Payout: —
Long-term debt ($ mil.): 153.8   Market value ($ mil.): 1,662.0

	STOCK PRICE ($) FY Close	P/E High/Low		PER SHARE ($) Earnings	Dividends	Book Value
12/20	59.11	101	28	0.61	0.00	7.20
12/19	26.10	48	19	0.60	0.00	5.43
12/18	12.21	72	24	0.45	0.00	4.77
12/17	13.92	56	34	0.24	0.00	4.39
12/16	8.53	115	75	0.08	0.00	4.28
Annual Growth	62.2%	—	—	66.2%	—	13.9%

Teledyne Technologies Inc

Teledyne Technologies provides enabling technologies for industrial growth markets that require advanced technology and high reliability. The company's products include digital imaging sensors, cameras and systems within the visible, infrared and X-ray spectra, monitoring and control instrumentation for marine and environmental applications, harsh environment interconnects, electronic test and measurement equipment, aircraft information management systems, and defense electronics and satellite communication subsystems. It also supplies engineered systems for defense, space, environmental and energy applications. Teledyne gets most of its sales from customers in the US.

Operations
Teledyne's four operational segments provide balanced streams of revenue with the biggest, Digital Imaging, accounting for more than 50%, followed by Instrumentation (approximately 25%), Aerospace and Defense Electronics (about 15%), and Engineered Systems (nearly 10%).

Digital Imaging provides high-performance sensors, cameras and systems, within the visible, infrared, ultraviolet, and X-ray spectra for use in industrial, scientific, government, defense and security, and medical applications, as well as micro electro-mechanical systems (MEMS) and high-performance, high-reliability semiconductors including analog-to-digital and digital-to-analog converters.

Instrumentation provides monitoring and control instruments for marine, environmental, industrial and other applications, as well as electronic test and measurement equipment. Its main product lines are Environmental Instrumentation, Marine Instrumentation, and Test and Measurement Instrumentation.

The Aerospace and Defense Electronics segment makes electronic components and subsystems, data acquisition and communications components and equipment, harsh environment interconnects, general aviation batteries and other components for a variety of commercial and defense applications that require high performance and high reliability. Such applications include aircraft, radar, electronic countermeasures, weapon systems, space, wireless and satellite communications and terminals and test equipment.

Engineered Systems offers systems engineering and integration and advanced technology development as well as complex manufacturing equipment for defense, space, environmental, and energy applications.

Geographic Reach
California-based Teledyne operates through more than 75 principal facilities across some 20 states and 10 international countries.

Teledyne relies in the US for about 65% of its revenue, while Canada supplies approximately 10%, the UK, Belgium, and the Netherlands, provides nearly 5% each, and all other countries account for the rest.

Sales and Marketing
A significant portion of Teledyne's sales are to the US government, directly or through prime contractors. The biggest customer is the US Department of Defense, which accounts for about 25% of the company's revenue.

Other customers include aerospace and defense, factory automation, air and water quality environmental monitoring, medical imaging equipment makers, pharmaceutical firms, electronics design and development, oceanographic research and deep-water oil and gas exploration and production companies. The company sells its products through an internal sales force, third-party distributors, and third-party representatives and distributors.

Financial Performance
The company reported net sales of $4.6 billion in 2021, compared with net sales of $3.1 million for 2020, an increase of 50%. Net income increased 11% to $445.3 million in 2021, compared with net income of $401.9 million in 2020.

In 2021, the company had a net income of $445.3 million, an 11% increase from the previous year's net income of $401.9 million.

The company's cash at the end of 2021 was $474.7 million. Operating activities generated $824.6 million, while investing activities used $3.8 billion, mainly for purchase of businesses and other investments. Financing activities generated another $2.8 billion.

Strategy

Teledyne's strategy continues to emphasize growth in its core markets of instrumentation, digital imaging, aerospace and defense electronics and engineered systems. Teledyne intends to strengthen and expand its core businesses with targeted acquisitions and through product development. It continues to focus on balanced and disciplined capital deployment among capital expenditures, product development, acquisitions and share repurchases. Teledyne also pursues operational excellence to continually improve its margins and earnings by emphasizing cost containment and cost reductions in all aspects of its business. The company seeks to create new products to grow the company and expand its addressable markets. Teledyne continues to evaluate its businesses to ensure that these are aligned with the company's strategy.

Mergers and Acquisitions

In 2021, Teledyne Technologies announced the successful completion of the acquisition of US-based, FLIR Systems, Inc., a world-leading industrial technology company focused on intelligent sensing solutions for defense and industrial applications. The aggregate consideration for the transaction was approximately $8.2 billion. FLIR will now be included in Teledyne's Digital Imaging segment and operate under the name Teledyne FLIR. Teledyne expects the acquisition to be immediately accretive to earnings, excluding transaction costs and purchase price accounting, and accretive to GAAP earnings in the first full calendar year following the acquisition.

EXECUTIVES

Executive Chairman, Director, Robert Mehrabian, $995,000 total compensation
President, Chief Executive Officer, Aldo (Al) Pichelli, $576,581 total compensation
Investor Relations Executive Vice President, Corporate Development Executive Vice President, Jason VanWees, $397,800 total compensation
Senior Vice President, Treasurer, Stephen F. Blackwood
Senior Vice President, Chief Compliance Officer, General Counsel, Secretary, Melanie Susan Cibik, $416,441 total compensation
Senior Vice President, Chief Financial Officer, Susan L. Main, $456,164 total compensation
Vice President, Controller, Cynthia Y. Belak
Litigation Vice President, Contracts Vice President, Litigation Division Officer, Contracts Division Officer, George C. Bobb

Vice President, Division Officer, Edwin Roks, $402,697 total compensation
Lead Director, Director, Michael T. Smith
Director, Michelle A. Kumbier
Director, Denise R. Cade
Director, Simon M. Lorne
Director, Wesley W. von Schack
Director, Charles Crocker
Director, Jane C. Sherburne
Director, Kenneth C. Dahlberg
Director, Robert A. Malone
Auditors : DELOITTE & TOUCHE LLP

LOCATIONS

HQ: Teledyne Technologies Inc
  1049 Camino Dos Rios, Thousand Oaks, CA 91360-2362
Phone: 805 373-4545

2018 Sales

	$ mil.	% of total
United States	2,044.90	71
Canada	294.80	10
United Kingdom	178.80	6
France	40.10	1
All Other Countries	343.20	12
Total	2,901.80	100

PRODUCTS/OPERATIONS

2018 Sales

	$ mil.	% of total
Instrumentation	1,021.20	35
Aerospace and Defense Electronics	885.20	31
Digital Imaging	696.50	24
Engineered Systems	298..90	10
Total	2,901.80	100

COMPETITORS

ADVANCED ENERGY INDUSTRIES, INC.
AMETEK, INC.
ANAREN, INC.
FORTIVE CORPORATION
PEBBLE BEACH SYSTEMS GROUP PLC
PULSE ELECTRONICS CORPORATION
RENESAS ELECTRONICS AMERICA INC.
ROPER TECHNOLOGIES, INC.
SOLID STATE PLC
ULTRALIFE CORPORATION

HISTORICAL FINANCIALS

Company Type: Public

Income Statement				FYE: January 3
	REVENUE ($mil)	NET INCOME ($mil)	NET PROFIT MARGIN	EMPLOYEES
01/21*	3,086.2	401.9	13.0%	10,670
12/19	3,163.6	402.3	12.7%	11,790
12/18	2,901.8	333.8	11.5%	10,850
12/17	2,603.8	227.2	8.7%	10,340
01/17	2,149.9	190.9	8.9%	8,970
Annual Growth	9.5%	20.5%	—	4.4%

*Fiscal year change

2021 Year-End Financials

Debt ratio: 15.3%
Return on equity: 13.3%
Cash ($ mil.): 673.1
Current Ratio: 2.26
Long-term debt ($ mil.): 680.9
No. of shares ($ mil.): 36.9
Dividends
  Yield: —
  Payout: —
Market value ($ mil.): 14,484.0

	STOCK PRICE ($) FY Close	P/E High/Low		PER SHARE ($) Earnings	Dividends	Book Value
01/21*	391.98	36	18	10.62	0.00	87.37
12/19	347.82	32	18	10.73	0.00	74.28
12/18	202.77	27	19	9.01	0.00	61.79
12/17	181.15	29	19	6.26	0.00	54.79
01/17	123.00	23	14	5.37	0.00	44.27
Annual Growth	33.6%	—	—	18.6%	—	18.5%

*Fiscal year change

Teleflex Incorporated

Teleflex is a global provider of medical technology products that enhance clinical benefits, improve patient and provider safety and reduce total procedural costs. The company designs, develops, manufactures and supplies single-use medical devices used by hospitals and healthcare providers for common diagnostic and therapeutic procedures in critical care and surgical applications. Although the company primarily distributes its products to hospitals and health care providers worldwide, the US accounts for roughly 65% of revenue. Teleflex manufactures its products in the US, the Czech Republic, Germany, Malaysia, and Mexico.

Operations

Teleflex is now operating into four segments: Americas (around 60% of revenue), EMEA (Europe, the Middle East and Africa; more than 20% of total revenue), Asia (Asia Pacific; about 10% of revenue) and OEM (Original Equipment Manufacturer and Development Services).

Each of its three geographic segments provides a comprehensive portfolio of medical technology products used by hospitals and healthcare providers. Its product categories within its geographic segments include vascular access (about 25% of revenue), anesthesia (some 15%), interventional (about 15% of revenue), surgical (nearly 15%), interventional urology (more than 10%), respiratory and urology.

The OEM segment (nearly 10% of revenue) designs, manufactures and supplies devices and instruments for other medical device manufacturers. Its OEM division, which includes the TFX Medical OEM, TFX OEM, Deknatel and HPC Medical brands, provides custom extrusions, micro-diameter film-cast tubing, diagnostic and interventional catheters, balloons and balloon catheters, film-insulated fine wire, coated mandrel wire, conductors, sheath/dilator introducers, specialized sutures and performance fibers, bioabsorbable sutures, yarns and resins.

Geographic Reach

Headquartered in Wayne, PA, Teleflex has about 90 properties consisting of manufacturing plants, engineering and research centers, distribution warehouses, offices and other facilities located in Czech Republic, Malaysia, Mexico, and the US.

The US generates nearly 65% of the company's revenue while Europe accounts for approximately 25% of sales, Asia Pacific and other region together accounts for about 15%.

Sales and Marketing

Teleflex distributes its medical products directly to hospitals, healthcare providers, distributors and to original equipment manufacturers of medical devices through its own sales forces, independent representatives and independent distributor networks. Customers include hospitals and health care providers (about 90% of sales), medical device manufacturers (around 10% of sales), and home care providers (less than 5% of sales).

Financial Performance

Net revenues for the year ended December 31, 2021 increased by $272.4 million, or 11%, to $2.8 billion compared to the prior year, which was primarily attributable to a $94.4 million increase in sales volume of existing products, largely stemming from the impact that the COVID-19 pandemic had on the prior year, net revenues of $70.4 million generated by acquired businesses, primarily Z-Medica, a $50.0 million increase in new product sales and $44.9 million of favorable fluctuations in foreign currency exchange rates.

In 2021, the company had a net income of $485.4 million, a 45% increase from the previous year's net income of $335.3 million.

The company's cash at the end of 2021 was $445.1 million. Operating activities generated $652.1 million, while financing activities used $715.8 million, mainly for reduction in borrowings. Investing activities provided another $156.7 million.

Strategy

Teleflex is engaged in both internal and external research and development. The company's research and development efforts support its strategic objectives to provide innovative new, safe and effective products that enhance clinical value by reducing infections, improving patient and clinician safety, enhancing patient outcomes and enabling less invasive procedures.

Teleflex is focused on achieving consistent, sustainable and profitable growth and improving its financial performance by increasing the company's market share and improving its operating efficiencies through: development of new products and product line extensions; investment in new technologies and broadening the application of its existing technologies; expansion of the use of its products in existing markets and introduction of the company's products into new geographic markets; achievement of economies of scale as the company continue to expand by utilizing its direct sales force and distribution network to sell new products, as well as by increasing efficiencies in its sales and marketing organizations, research and development activities and manufacturing and distribution facilities; and expansion of the company's product portfolio through select acquisitions, licensing arrangements and business partnerships that enhance, expand or expedite its development initiatives or its ability to increase its market share.

EXECUTIVES

Chairman, President, Chief Executive Officer, Director, Liam J. Kelly, $845,669 total compensation
Executive Vice President, Chief Financial Officer, Thomas E. Powell, $535,387 total compensation
Corporate Vice-President, Chief Human Resources Officer, Cameron P. Hicks, $317,803 total compensation
Manufacturing Corporate Vice-President, Supply Chain Corporate Vice-President, James Winters
Corporate Vice-President, General Counsel, Secretary, Daniel V. Logue
Lead Director, Director, George Babich, $44,917 total compensation
Director, Candace H. Duncan
Director, Stephen K. Klasko
Director, Stuart A. Randle
Director, John C. Heinmiller
Director, Andrew A. Krakauer
Director, Gretchen R. Haggerty
Auditors : PricewaterhouseCoopers LLP

LOCATIONS

HQ: Teleflex Incorporated
550 East Swedesford Road, Suite 400, Wayne, PA 19087
Phone: 610 225-6800
Web: www.teleflex.com

2017 Sales

	$ mil.	% of total
US	1,254.8	58
Europe	591.4	28
Asia & Asia/Pacific	220.1	10
Other	80	4
Total	2,146.3	100

Selected Facilities

US
    Arlington Heights, IL
    Asheboro, NC
    Jaffrey, NH
    Reading, PA
International
    Bad Liebenzell, Germany
    Chihuahua, Mexico
    Hradec Kralove, Czech Republic
    Kamunting, Malaysia
    Kernen, Germany
    Nuevo Laredo, Mexico

PRODUCTS/OPERATIONS

2017 Sales by Segment

	$ mil.	% of total
EMEA	552.7	26
Vascular North America	313.6	15
Asia	269.2	13
Interventional North America	220.6	10
Anesthesia North America	198	9
Surgical North America	175.2	8
OEM	183.0	8
Other	234.0	11
Total	2,146.3	100

2017 Sales

	% of total
Hospitals & health care providers	85
Medical device manufacturers	10
Home care	5
Total	100

Selected Brands

Arrow
Deknatel
Hudson RCI
LMA
Pilling
Rusch
Urolift
Wreck

COMPETITORS

ATRICURE, INC.
ATRION CORPORATION
BOSTON SCIENTIFIC CORPORATION
CONMED CORPORATION
EDWARDS LIFESCIENCES CORPORATION
ICU MEDICAL, INC.
MERIT MEDICAL SYSTEMS, INC.
SPECTRANETICS LLC
STRYKER CORPORATION
TERUMO CORPORATION

HISTORICAL FINANCIALS

Company Type: Public

Income Statement — FYE: December 31

	REVENUE ($mil)	NET INCOME ($mil)	NET PROFIT MARGIN	EMPLOYEES
12/20	2,537.1	335.3	13.2%	14,000
12/19	2,595.3	461.4	17.8%	14,400
12/18	2,448.3	200.8	8.2%	15,200
12/17	2,146.3	152.5	7.1%	14,400
12/16	1,868.0	237.3	12.7%	12,600
Annual Growth	8.0%	9.0%	—	2.7%

2020 Year-End Financials

Debt ratio: 34.7%
Return on equity: 10.5%
Cash ($ mil.): 375.8
Current Ratio: 2.63
Long-term debt ($ mil.): 2,377.8
No. of shares ($ mil.): 46.6
Dividends
  Yield: 0.3%
  Payout: 19.1%
Market value ($ mil.): 19,212.0

	STOCK PRICE ($) FY Close	P/E High/Low		PER SHARE ($) Earnings	Dividends	Book Value
12/20	411.57	57	31	7.09	1.36	71.48
12/19	376.44	37	25	9.80	1.36	64.27
12/18	258.48	66	52	4.29	1.36	55.20
12/17	248.82	80	47	3.27	1.36	53.81
12/16	161.15	34	23	4.98	1.36	48.54
Annual Growth	26.4%	—	—	9.2%	0.0%	10.2%

Teradyne, Inc.

Teradyne designs, develops, manufactures and sells automated test equipment, systems for testing semiconductors, wireless products, data storage and complex electronics systems in many industries including consumer electronics, wireless, automotive, industrial, computing, communications, and aerospace and defense industries. Teradyne's customers are integrated device manufacturers, fables, foundries, and semiconductor assembly and test providers (OSAT). Teradyne developed its industrial robot business mainly through acquisitions. The company has operations in Asia, Europe, and the Americas, but it generates most of its sales from customers in Asia. The company was founded in 1960.

Operations
Teradyne operates through four reportable segments: the Semiconductor Test, Systems Test, Industrial Automation segments, and Wireless Test.

The Semiconductor Test group, which accounts for more than 70% of sales, includes the design, manufacturing, and marketing of semiconductor test products and services used both for wafer level and device package testing.

The Systems Test segment, roughly 10% of revenue, makes testing products and services for military and aerospace instruments, hard disk drive storage, and circuit boards.

The Industrial Automation segment, more than 10% of revenue, is composed of Universal Robots, Mobile Industrial Robots (MIR), and Energid. The unit produces collaborative robotic arms, autonomous mobile robots, and advanced robotic control software.

The Wireless segment (10% of revenue) provides testing tools used in developing and manufacturing wireless devices.

The company relies on subcontractors and outsourced contract manufacturers to make its FLEX and J750 products.

Geographic Reach
Headquartered in Massachusetts, Teradyne has operations in Costa Rica, Denmark, China, Japan, the Philippines, South Korea, Singapore, Taiwan, and the US.

Its two biggest markets are Taiwan, about 30% of sales, and China, some 15%, with other Asian countries accounting for another nearly 40% of revenue. US customers account for some 10% of sales.

Sales and Marketing
Teradyne primarily uses a direct sales force to sell most of its products, but its robotics are sold through distributors. The company relies on its five largest customers for around 35% of revenue.

The company's advertising costs were $13.4 million, $12.8 million, and $16.6 million in 2021, 2020, and 2019, respectively.

Financial Performance
The company's performance for the past five years has seen an overall growth, although having a slight fluctuation in the first part of the period, they still ended the period with 2021 as its highest performing year.

The company's revenue in 2021 increased by $581 million to $3.7 billion compared to $3.1 billion in the prior year. This was due to increase in all segments.

Net income in 2021 also increased by $230 million to $1 billion compared to the prior year's $784.1 million.

Cash held by the company at the end of fiscal 2021 increased to $1.1 billion. Operating activities provided about $1.1 billion. Investing activities used $120.3 million, while financing activities used $1 billion. Main cash uses were payments of b and repurchase of common stock.

Strategy
The company's strategy is to focus on profitably growing market share in its test businesses through the introduction of differentiated products that target growth segments and accelerating growth through continued investment in its Industrial Automation businesses. Teradyne plans to execute its strategy while balancing capital allocations between returning capital to its shareholders through dividends and stock repurchases and using capital for opportunistic acquisitions.

HISTORY
College pals Nicholas DeWolf and Alexander d'Arbeloff (who met in an alphabetical ROTC lineup at MIT) founded Teradyne in 1960 to develop industrial-grade electronic test equipment. The name combines "tera" (10 to the 12 th power) and "dyne" (a unit of force); to the founding duo, it meant "rolling a 15,000-ton boulder uphill." The company's first headquarters was a loft over Joe & Nemo's hot dog stand in downtown Boston. In 1961 the company sold its first product -- an automatic tester for semiconductor diodes called a go/no-go diode tester -- to Raytheon for $5,000.

Teradyne grew rapidly during the 1960s as it introduced new products, including testers for integrated circuits, resistors, transistors, and diodes. In the latter part of the decade, the company began using computers to speed up the testing process, helping create the automatic test equipment (ATE) industry. It formed Teradyne Components (later Teradyne Connection Systems) in 1968 to produce electronics connection assemblies.

Teradyne went public in 1970. That year, with the first slump in the semiconductor industry, the company laid off 15% of its workforce and began diversifying its customer base. DeWolf departed Teradyne in 1971, leaving d'Arbeloff to run operations. The market quickly recovered, and the company grew and prospered again. In 1972 it began working on a telephone system testing device, the 4Tel. However, the market slumped again, and in 1975 Teradyne cut its staff by 15% a second time.

EXECUTIVES
Chairman, Director, Paul J. Tufano
President, Chief Executive Officer, Director, Gregory S. Smith, $396,067 total compensation
Vice President, Chief Financial Officer, Treasurer, Sanjay Mehta, $500,000 total compensation
Vice President, Secretary, General Counsel, Charles J. Gray, $375,000 total compensation
Vice President, Division Officer, Bradford B. Robbins, $339,000 total compensation
Business Development Vice President, Walter G. Vahey, $319,300 total compensation
Division Officer, Richard Burns
Director, Michael A. Bradley, $126,654 total compensation
Director, Edwin J. Gillis
Director, Timothy E. Guertin
Director, Peter Herweck
Director, Mercedes Johnson
Director, Marilyn Matz
Director, Ford G. Tamer
Director, Ernest E. Maddock
Auditors: PricewaterhouseCoopers LLP

LOCATIONS
HQ: Teradyne, Inc.
600 Riverpark Drive, North Reading, MA 01864
Phone: 978 370-2700
Web: www.teradyne.com

2014 Sales
	% of total
Taiwan	30
China	18
US	13
Korea	9
Singapore	7
Europe	6
Malaysia	5
Philippines	4
Japan	4
Thailand	3
Rest of world	1
Total	100

PRODUCTS/OPERATIONS
2018 Sales
	$ mil.	% of total
Semiconductor Test	1,492.4	71
Industrial Automation	261.5	13
System Test	216.1	10
Wireless Test	132	6
Corporate and Other	(1.2)	-
Total	2,100.8	100

2018 Sales
	$ mil.	% of total
Product	1,729.6	82
Service	371.2	18
Total	2,100.8	100

Selected Products
Semiconductor test systems
    Memory test
    Microcontroller test
    Mixed-signal test (A5 line)
    System-on-a-chip test
    Very large scale integration (VLSI) chip test
Circuit board test and inspection systems
    Automated optical inspection
    In-circuit and functional board test
    Software
Military and aerospace
    Spectrum CTS (avionics systems)
    VICTORY (boundary scan and fault diagnostic software)
Wireless test
    IQfact (chipset)
    IQflex (WLAN)
    IQxstream (multi-device tester for devices)

COMPETITORS

AMKOR TECHNOLOGY, INC.
ANALOGIC CORPORATION
APPLIED MATERIALS, INC.
COHU, INC.
IXIA
QORVO, INC.
RADISYS CORPORATION
SANMINA CORPORATION
TRANSCAT, INC.
XCERRA CORPORATION

HISTORICAL FINANCIALS

Company Type: Public

Income Statement — FYE: December 31

	REVENUE ($mil)	NET INCOME ($mil)	NET PROFIT MARGIN	EMPLOYEES
12/21	3,702.8	1,014.5	27.4%	5,900
12/20	3,121.4	784.1	25.1%	5,500
12/19	2,294.9	467.4	20.4%	5,400
12/18	2,100.8	451.7	21.5%	4,900
12/17	2,136.6	257.6	12.1%	4,500
Annual Growth	14.7%	40.9%	—	7.0%

2021 Year-End Financials

Debt ratio: 2.8%
Return on equity: 42.4%
Cash ($ mil.): 1,122.2
Current Ratio: 3.20
Long-term debt ($ mil.): 89.2
No. of shares ($ mil.): 162.2
Dividends
  Yield: 0.2%
  Payout: 7.5%
Market value ($ mil.): 26,533.0

	STOCK PRICE ($) FY Close	P/E High	P/E Low	PER SHARE ($) Earnings	Dividends	Book Value
12/21	163.53	27	17	5.53	0.40	15.80
12/20	119.89	26	9	4.28	0.40	13.31
12/19	68.19	25	11	2.60	0.36	8.89
12/18	31.38	21	12	2.35	0.36	8.67
12/17	41.87	34	20	1.28	0.28	9.99
Annual Growth	40.6%	—	—	44.2%	9.3%	12.1%

Terreno Realty Corp

Terreno Realty has its eyes set on acquiring industrial real estate. The real estate investment trust (REIT) invests in and operates industrial properties in major US coastal markets, including Los Angeles, San Francisco Bay Area, Seattle, Miami, Northern New Jersey/New York City, and Washington, DC. The REIT typically invests in warehouse and distribution facilities, flex buildings for light manufacturing and research and development, and transshipment and improved land. The company owns about 220 buildings spanning about 13.3 million square feet and about 20 improved land parcels totaling about 77.6 acres.

Operations

About 80% of Terreno Realty's property portfolio consisted of warehouse/distribution properties, while flex buildings (including light industrial and R&D facilities) made up another nearly 10%. Trans-shipment properties and improved land made up the rest.

Geographic Reach

San Francisco, California- based, Terreno Realty operates in six major US markets; Los Angeles, Northern New Jersey/New York City, San Francisco Bay Area, Seattle, Miami, and Washington, D.C.

Sales and Marketing

Some of Terreno Realty's tenants include FedEx, Amazon, Northrop Grumman, Danaher, AmerisourceBergen, and the US government. No tenant accounts for more than 5% of annual base rent.

Financial Performance

Total revenues increased approximately $19.4 million for 2019 compared to the prior year, primarily due to property acquisitions during 2018 and 2019 and increased revenue on new and renewed leases.

Net income for the year 2019 decreased by 12% to $55.5 million compared to the prior year with $63.3 million.

Cash held by the company at the end of 2019 increased by $78.3 million to $112.7 million. Cash provided by operations and financing activities were $94.7 million and $235.1 million, respectively. Cash used for investing activities was $251.5 million mainly for proceeds from sales of real estate investments.

Strategy

The primary objective of Terreno Realty's financing strategy is to maintain financial flexibility with a conservative capital structure using retained cash flows, proceeds from dispositions of properties, long-term debt and the issuance of common and perpetual preferred stock to finance its growth. Over the long term, the company intends to: limit the sum of the outstanding principal amount of its consolidated indebtedness and the liquidation preference of any outstanding perpetual preferred stock to less than 35% of the company's total enterprise value; maintain a fixed charge coverage ratio in excess of 2.0x; have staggered debt maturities that are aligned to its expected average lease term (5-7 years), positioning the company to re-price parts of its capital structure as its rental rates change with market conditions.

Mergers and Acquisitions

In 2020, Terreno Realty acquired an industrial property located in South San Francisco, California for a purchase price of approximately $6.3 million. The property consists of one industrial building containing approximately 22,000 square feet on 0.7 acres. The property is at 179 Starlite Street, adjacent to Highway 101 between San Francisco International.

Also, in 2020, Terreno Realty acquired an industrial property located in Seattle, Washington for a purchase price of approximately $5.6 million. The property consists of one industrial building containing approximately 13,000 square feet on 1.1 acres.

In 2019, Terreno Realty acquired an industrial property located in Puyallup, Washington for a purchase price of approximately $6.7 million. The property consists of one industrial distribution building containing approximately 41,000 square feet on approximately 2.3 acres less than four miles from the Port of Tacoma. The property, at 917 Valley Avenue NW, provides ten dock-high and four grade-level loading positions, parking for 50 cars and is 100% leased to two tenants.

Company Background

The company took itself public in February 2010 in an effort to capitalize on a distressed market ripe with foreclosures and troubled loans. Portions of the net proceeds from its public offering were used to invest in interest-bearing, short-term securities to help it gain REIT status.

EXECUTIVES

Chief Executive Officer, Chairman, W. Blake Baird, $791,250 total compensation

President, Director, Michael A. Coke, $791,250 total compensation

Executive Vice President, Andrew T. Burke, $322,875 total compensation

Executive Vice President, John T. Meyer, $322,875 total compensation

Executive Vice President, Chief Financial Officer, Secretary, Jaime J. Cannon, $322,875 total compensation

Lead Director, Director, Douglas M. Pasquale

Director, Linda Assante

Director, LeRoy T. Carlson

Director, David M. Lee

Director, Gabriela Franco Parcella

Director, Dennis J. Polk

Auditors : Ernst & Young LLP

LOCATIONS

HQ: Terreno Realty Corp
  10500 NE 8th Street, Suite 301, Bellevue, WA 98004
Phone: 415 655-4580
Web: www.terreno.com

PRODUCTS/OPERATIONS

2012 Sales

	$ mil.	% of total
Rental	24.5	78
Tenant expense reimbursements	6.7	22
Total	31.2	100

COMPETITORS

AMERICAN ASSETS TRUST, INC.
DCT INDUSTRIAL TRUST INC.
EQUITY ONE, INC.
FIRST INDUSTRIAL REALTY TRUST, INC.
GOV NEW OPPTY REIT

HISTORICAL FINANCIALS
Company Type: Public

Income Statement — FYE: December 31

	REVENUE ($mil)	NET INCOME ($mil)	NET PROFIT MARGIN	EMPLOYEES
12/21	221.9	87.2	39.3%	34
12/20	186.8	79.7	42.7%	26
12/19	171.0	55.5	32.5%	24
12/18	151.6	63.2	41.7%	23
12/17	132.4	53.0	40.1%	22
Annual Growth	13.8%	13.2%	—	11.5%

2021 Year-End Financials

Debt ratio: 24.6%
Return on equity: 4.7%
Cash ($ mil.): 204.4
Current Ratio: 2.17
Long-term debt ($ mil.): 720.6
No. of shares ($ mil.): 75.0
Dividends
  Yield: 1.4%
  Payout: 128.5%
Market value ($ mil.): 6,403.0

	STOCK PRICE ($) FY Close	P/E High	P/E Low	PER SHARE ($) Earnings	PER SHARE ($) Dividends	PER SHARE ($) Book Value
12/21	85.29	69	44	1.23	1.26	27.41
12/20	58.51	53	37	1.16	1.12	23.23
12/19	54.14	67	40	0.85	1.02	22.56
12/18	35.17	36	29	1.09	0.92	20.45
12/17	35.06	40	28	0.95	0.84	18.56
Annual Growth	24.9%	—	—	6.7%	10.7%	10.2%

Texas Pacific Land Corp

Texas Pacific Land Trust was created to sell the Texas & Pacific Railway's land after its 1888 bankruptcy, and yup, they're still workin' on it. The trust began with the railroad of about 3.5 million acres; today it is one of the largest private landowners in Texas, with more than 901,000 acres in about 20 counties. Texas Pacific Land Trust's sales come from oil and gas royalties (about 85% of sales), easements, and land sales. It has a perpetual oil and gas royalty interest under some 900,000 acres in West Texas.

Operations

The company has two segments: Land and Resource Management, and Water Services and Operations. The Land and Resource Management segment encompasses the business of managing approximately 900,000 acres of land and related resources in West Texas owned by the Trust. The revenue streams of this segment consist primarily of royalties from oil and gas, revenues from easements and commercial leases and land and material sales. The segment accounts for about 75% of revenues. The Water Services and Operations segment encompasses the business of providing full-service water offerings to operators in the Permian Basin. The revenue streams of this segment consist of revenue generated from sales of sourced and treated water as well as revenue from royalties on water service-related activity and accounts for about 25% of total revenues.

Geographic Reach

Texas Pacific owned the surface estate in more than 901,000 acres of land, comprised of numerous separate tracts, located in about 20 counties in the western part of Texas. The trust lease office space in Dallas, Texas for its corporate headquarters.

Sales and Marketing

Its top customers include WPX Energy Permian, LLC and Anadarko E&P Onshore, LLC which accounts for approximately 25% of total revenue.

Financial Performance

In the last five years, the revenue performance of the company was outstanding. In such a short span, revenue grew by 529%.

Revenues increased $190.3 million, or 63%, to $490.5 million in 2019 compared to $300.2 million in 2018. Land and Resource Management segment revenues increased $151.9 million and Water Services and Operations segment revenues increased $38.4 million.

Net income increased $109.0 million, or 52.0%, to $318.7 million in 2019, compared to $209.7 million in 2018. The increase in net income was mainly due to higher revenue.

Cash and cash equivalents at the end of the period were $303.6 million. Cash provided by operating activities was $342.8 million while investing and financing activities was $111.7 million and $50.9 million, respectively. Main cash uses were for acquisition of real estate and payments of dividends.

Strategy

In early 2020, the Trust acquired approximately 671 surface acres of land and approximately 755 net royalty acres in Culberson County for a combined purchase price of approximately $14.9 million.

EXECUTIVES

Co-Chair, Director, David E. Barry
Co-Chair, Director, John R. Norris
President, Chief Executive Officer, Subsidiary Officer, Director, Tyler Glover, $112,083 total compensation
Senior Vice President, General Counsel, Secretary, Micheal W. Dobbs
Chief Financial Officer, Chris Steddum
Chief Accounting Officer, Stephanie Buffington
Subsidiary Officer, Robert A. Crain
Director, Karl F. Kurz
Director, Rhys J. Best
Director, Donald G. Cook
Director, Barbara J. Duganier
Director, Donna E. Epps
Director, Eric Lee Oliver
Director, Murray Stahl
Auditors: DELOITTE & TOUCHE LLP

LOCATIONS

HQ: Texas Pacific Land Corp
1700 Pacific Avenue, Suite 2900, Dallas, TX 75201

Phone: 214 969-5530 **Fax:** 214 871-7139
Web: www.texaspacific.com

PRODUCTS/OPERATIONS

2015 sales

	$ mil	% of total
Easements and sundry income	31.4	40
Oil and gas royalties	24.9	31
Land sales	22.6	28
Grazing lease rentals	0.5	1
Interest income from notes receivable	0	-
Total	79.4	100

COMPETITORS

CATCHMARK TIMBER TRUST, INC.
GETTY REALTY CORP.
RAYONIER INC.
SELECT INCOME REIT
THE HOWARD HUGHES CORPORATION

HISTORICAL FINANCIALS
Company Type: Public

Income Statement — FYE: December 31

	REVENUE ($mil)	NET INCOME ($mil)	NET PROFIT MARGIN	EMPLOYEES
12/20	302.5	176.0	58.2%	102
12/19	490.4	318.7	65.0%	94
12/18	300.2	209.7	69.9%	71
12/17	132.3	76.3	57.7%	32
12/16	59.9	37.2	62.2%	10
Annual Growth	49.9%	47.5%	—	78.7%

2020 Year-End Financials

Debt ratio: —
Return on equity: 35.2%
Cash ($ mil.): 281.0
Current Ratio: 6.90
Long-term debt ($ mil.): —
No. of shares ($ mil.): 7.7
Dividends
  Yield: —
  Payout: 114.5%
Market value ($ mil.): 5,639.0

	STOCK PRICE ($) FY Close	P/E High	P/E Low	PER SHARE ($) Earnings	PER SHARE ($) Dividends	PER SHARE ($) Book Value
12/20	727.00	36	14	22.70	26.00	62.55
12/19	781.22	22	14	41.09	6.00	66.03
12/18	541.63	32	16	26.93	4.05	31.52
12/17	446.63	46	27	9.72	1.35	10.12
12/16	296.77	65	24	4.66	0.31	6.01
Annual Growth	25.1%	—	—	48.6%	202.6%	79.6%

The Bancorp Inc

The Bancorp, Inc. is a financial holding company of The Bancorp Bank, its primary subsidiary. They have four primary lines of specialty lending: securities-backed lines of credit (SBLOC) and insurance policy cash value-backed lines of credit (IBLOC), vehicle fleet and other equipment leasing (direct lease financing), small business administration (SBA) and loans and non-SBA commercial real estate (CRE) loans. The company generated for sale into capital markets through commercial loan securitizations and other sales (CMBS). The company offers deposit products and services through its payments business line, lending activities through specialty finance, as well as affinity group banking products and services.

Operations

The Bancorp operates in four business segments: Specialty Finance (around 65% of the company's revenue) which consists of SBLOC, IBLOC and advisor financing; lease financing for commercial and government vehicle fleets; SBL loans for small businesses; and commercial real estate loans. Payments (around 35%) which include checking accounts, savings accounts, money market accounts, commercial accounts, and various types of prepaid and debit cards, as well as ACH bill payment and other bill payment services. Corporate includes the company's investment portfolio, corporate overhead and non-allocated expenses.

About 60% of its total revenue came from loan interest (including fees), while nearly 10% came from interest income on investment securities. The rest of its revenue came from fees from prepaid and debit cards (about 25%) and service fees on deposit accounts, among others.

In terms of loans, SBLOC / IBLOC accounts for over 50%, real estate bridge lending with over 15%, small business and loans and direct lease financing with about 15% each, and advisor financing with less than 5%.

Geographic Reach

Wilmington, Delaware-based The Bancorp maintains business development and administrative offices for SBL in Morrisville, North Carolina, and Westmont, Illinois (suburban Chicago), primarily for SBA lending. Leasing offices are located in Crofton, Maryland, Kent, Washington, Logan, Utah, Orlando, Florida, Raritan, New Jersey, and Norristown and Warminster, Pennsylvania. The company also maintains a loan operations office in New York, New York. Prepaid and debit card offices and other executive offices are located in Sioux Falls, South Dakota.

Sales and Marketing

The company offers deposit products and services to their affinity group clients and their customer bases through direct or private label banking strategies. Specialty Finance services, such as SBLOC, IBLOC and advisor financing services, are offered to individuals, trusts and entities which are secured by a pledge of marketable securities maintained in one or more accounts with respect to which it obtain a securities account control agreement.

The Bancorp's card issuing services are offered to end users through their relationships with benefits administrators, third-party administrators, insurers, corporate incentive companies, rebate fulfillment organizations, payroll administrators, large retail chains, consumer service organizations and FinTech disruptors. The majority of fees it earns result from contractual fees paid by third-party sponsors, computed on a per transaction basis, and monthly service fees. The company also acts as the bank sponsor and depository institution for independent service organizations that process such payments and for other companies, such as bill payment companies for which they process ACH payments.

The company has a national scope for its affinity group banking operations, and it uses a personal sales/targeted media advertising approach to market to existing and potential commercial affinity group organizations. The affinity group organizations with which it has relationships perform marketing functions to the ultimate individual customers. Its marketing program to affinity group organizations consists of print advertising, attending and making presentations at trade shows and other events for targeted affinity organizations; and direct contact with potential affinity organizations by their marketing staff, with relationship managers focusing on particular regional markets.

Advertising and marketing costs amounted to $1.6 million, $1.3 million, and $0.8 million for 2021, 2020, and 2019, respectively.

Financial Performance

Company's revenue for fiscal 2021 increased to $315.6 million compared from the prior year with $279.5 million. The increase in net interest income reflected the impact of loan growth, which more than offset the impact of loan prepayments and reductions in securities interest, which reflected balance and yield reductions.

In 2021, the company had a net income of $110.4 million, a 37% increase from the previous year's net income of $80.6 million.

The company's cash and cash equivalents at the end of 2021 was $601.8 million. Operations generated $83.9 million, while investing activities used another $305.9 million, mainly for net increase in loans. Financing activities provided $509 million in 2020.

Strategy

The company's principal strategies are to fund their loan and investment portfolio growth with stable deposits and generate non-interest income from prepaid and debit card accounts and other payment processing; develop relationships with Affinity Groups to gain sponsored access to their membership, client or customer bases to market their services; and use their existing infrastructure as a platform for growth.

Company Background

The Bancorp was founded by Betsy Z. Cohen in 1999. The company has gained industry recognition as the top issuer of prepaid cards in the US, leading merchant servicer, and a top ACH originator.

EXECUTIVES

Chairman, Subsidiary Officer, Director, James J. McEntee

Chief Executive Officer, Subsidiary Officer, Director, Damian M. Kozlowski, $900,000 total compensation

Executive Vice President, Chief Operating Officer, Subsidiary Officer, Gregor Garry

Executive Vice President, Chief Credit Officer, Division Officer, Subsidiary Officer, Mark Leo Connolly, $300,000 total compensation

Strategy Executive Vice President, Strategy Chief Financial Officer, Strategy Principal Accounting Officer, Strategy Secretary, Strategy Subsidiary Officer, Paul Frenkiel, $310,660 total compensation

Senior Vice President, General Counsel, Subsidiary Officer, Thomas G. Pareigat, $355,192 total compensation

Lead Independent Director, Director, Michael J. Bradley

Director, Cheryl Creuzot

Director, Daniela A. Mielke

Director, Stephanie B. Mudick

Director, Walter T. Beach

Director, Matthew N. Cohn

Director, John M. Eggemeyer

Director, Hersh Kozlov

Director, William H. Lamb

Director, Mei-Mei H. Tuan

Auditors : Grant Thornton LLP

LOCATIONS

HQ: The Bancorp Inc
409 Silverside Road, Wilmington, DE 19809
Phone: 302 385-5000
Web: www.thebancorp.com

PRODUCTS/OPERATIONS

2015 sales

	$ mil.	% of total
Payments	98.0	45
Specialty finance	67.6	31
Corporate	51.0	24
Total	216.6	100

2015 Sales

	$ mil.	% of total
Interest income		
Loans, including fees	49.9	23
Interest on investment securities:	30.7	14
Federal funds sold/securities purchased under agreements to resell	0.6	-
Interest earning deposits	2.3	1
Non-interest income		
Prepaid card fees	47.5	22
Gain on sale of health savings portfolio	33.6	15
Gain on sale of investment securities	14.4	7
Gain on sale of loans	10.1	5
Service fees on deposit accounts	7.5	3
Card payment and ACH processing fees	5.7	3
Affinity fees	3.4	2
Other	5.3	2
Change in value of investment in unconsolidated entity	1.7	1
Leasing income	2.3	1
Debit card income	1.6	1
Total	216.6	100

COMPETITORS

BOKF MERGER CORPORATION NUMBER SIXTEEN
CAPITAL BANK FINANCIAL CORP.
CITY HOLDING COMPANY

FIRSTMERIT CORPORATION
NATIONAL BANK HOLDINGS CORPORATION
NBT BANCORP INC.
REPUBLIC BANCORP, INC.
STOCK YARDS BANCORP, INC.
TCF FINANCIAL CORPORATION
UNIVEST FINANCIAL CORPORATION

HISTORICAL FINANCIALS
Company Type: Public

Income Statement				FYE: December 31
	ASSETS ($mil)	NET INCOME ($mil)	INCOME AS % OF ASSETS	EMPLOYEES
12/20	6,276.8	80.0	1.3%	635
12/19	5,656.9	51.5	0.9%	612
12/18	4,437.9	88.6	2.0%	589
12/17	4,708.1	21.6	0.5%	538
12/16	4,858.1	(96.4)	—	589
Annual Growth	6.6%	—	—	1.9%

2020 Year-End Financials
Return on assets: 1.3%
Return on equity: 14.9%
Long-term debt ($ mil.): —
No. of shares ($ mil.): 57.6
Sales ($ mil.): 295.3
Dividends
  Yield: —
  Payout: —
Market value ($ mil.): 787.0

	STOCK PRICE ($) FY Close	P/E High/Low		PER SHARE ($) Earnings	Dividends	Book Value
12/20	13.65	10	3	1.37	0.00	10.08
12/19	12.97	15	9	0.90	0.00	8.51
12/18	7.96	7	5	1.55	0.00	7.22
12/17	9.88	26	12	0.39	0.00	5.81
12/16	7.86	—	—	(2.17)	0.00	5.40
Annual Growth	14.8%	—	—	—	—	16.9%

The Trade Desk Inc

EXECUTIVES

President, Chief Executive Officer, Director, Jeff T. Green, $800,000 total compensation
Chief Financial Officer, Principal Accounting Officer, Blake Grayson
Chief Operating Officer, Michelle Hulst
Chief Technology Officer, Director, David R. Pickles, $450,000 total compensation
Chief Marketing Officer, Susan Vobejda, $450,000 total compensation
Chief Legal Officer, Vivian W. Yang, $450,000 total compensation
Lead Independent Director, Director, Lise J. Buyer
Director, Thomas Falk
Director, Kathryn E. Falberg
Director, Eric B. Paley
Director, Gokul Rajaram
Director, David B. Wells
Auditors : PricewaterhouseCoopers LLP

LOCATIONS
HQ: The Trade Desk Inc
  42 N. Chestnut Street, Ventura, CA 93001
Phone: 805 585-3434
Web: www.thetradedesk.com

HISTORICAL FINANCIALS
Company Type: Public

Income Statement				FYE: December 31
	REVENUE ($mil)	NET INCOME ($mil)	NET PROFIT MARGIN	EMPLOYEES
12/21	1,196.4	137.7	11.5%	1,967
12/20	836.0	242.3	29.0%	1,545
12/19	661.0	108.3	16.4%	1,310
12/18	477.2	176.2	36.9%	944
12/17	308.2	101.5	33.0%	713
Annual Growth	40.4%	7.9%	—	28.9%

2021 Year-End Financials
Debt ratio: —
Return on equity: 10.8%
Cash ($ mil.): 754.1
Current Ratio: 1.71
Long-term debt ($ mil.): —
No. of shares ($ mil.): 483.4
Dividends
  Yield: —
  Payout: —
Market value ($ mil.): 44,303.0

	STOCK PRICE ($) FY Close	P/E High/Low		PER SHARE ($) Earnings	Dividends	Book Value
12/21	91.64	3115	210	0.28	0.00	3.16
12/20	801.00	1853	276	0.50	0.00	2.14
12/19	259.78	1146	451	0.23	0.00	1.35
12/18	116.06	749	206	0.19	0.00	0.90
12/17	45.73	528	214	0.12	0.00	0.59
Annual Growth	19.0%	—	—	24.9%	—	52.1%

Thomasville Bancshares, Inc.

This Thomasville is more about the money under your bed than the bed itself. Thomasville Bancshares is the holding company for Thomasville National Bank, which serves area consumersÂ and businesses from two offices in Thomasville, Georgia. Established in 1995, the bank offers standard services such as deposit accounts and credit cards. Real estate mortgagesÂ compriseÂ most of the company's loan portfolio, followed byÂ commercial, financial, and agricultural loans. The company provides trust, asset management, and brokerage services through its TNB Financial Services unit. Executive officers and directors of Thomasville Bancshares collectively own more than a quarter of the company.

EXECUTIVES

President, Chief Executive Officer, Director, Stephen H. Cheney
Executive Vice President, Charles H. Hodges
Director, Randall L. Moore
Director, Charles A. Balfour
Director, Joel W. Barrett
Director, David A. Cone
Director, Charles E. Hancock
Director, Harold L. Jackson
Director, Diane W. Parker
Director, Cochran A. Scott
Director, Richard L. Singletary
Auditors : Mauldin & Jenkins, LLC

LOCATIONS
HQ: Thomasville Bancshares, Inc.
  301 North Broad Street, Thomasville, GA 31792
Phone: 229 226-3300
Web: www.tnbank.com

COMPETITORS
EXTRACO CORPORATION
LYONS NATIONAL BANK
OLD POINT FINANCIAL CORPORATION
PINNACLE BANKSHARES CORPORATION
PRINCETON NATIONAL BANCORP, INC.

HISTORICAL FINANCIALS
Company Type: Public

Income Statement				FYE: December 31
	ASSETS ($mil)	NET INCOME ($mil)	INCOME AS % OF ASSETS	EMPLOYEES
12/20	1,227.4	19.3	1.6%	0
12/19	956.6	18.7	2.0%	0
12/18	880.5	16.8	1.9%	0
12/17	806.4	12.0	1.5%	0
12/16	780.2	11.8	1.5%	0
Annual Growth	12.0%	13.0%	—	—

2020 Year-End Financials
Return on assets: 1.7%
Return on equity: 19.8%
Long-term debt ($ mil.): —
No. of shares ($ mil.): 6.0
Sales ($ mil.): 60.3
Dividends
  Yield: 2.9%
  Payout: 51.3%
Market value ($ mil.): 307.0

	STOCK PRICE ($) FY Close	P/E High/Low		PER SHARE ($) Earnings	Dividends	Book Value
12/20	51.00	17	13	2.92	1.50	17.06
12/19	46.00	15	13	2.84	1.40	15.31
12/18	40.99	15	14	2.56	1.30	13.60
12/17	40.00	20	17	1.83	1.00	12.05
12/16	35.00	18	14	1.81	0.85	11.10
Annual Growth	9.9%	—	—	12.7%	15.3%	11.3%

Timberland Bancorp, Inc.

Located among the tall trees of the Pacific Northwest, Timberland Bancorp is the holding company for Timberland Savings Bank, which operates more than 20 branches in western Washington. The bank targets individuals and regional businesses, offering checking, savings, and money market accounts, and CDs. Timberland Savings Bank, concentrates on real estate lending, including commercial and residential mortgages, multifamily residential loans, and land develoment loans; it also writes business loans and other types of loans. Timberland Savings Bank was founded in 1915 as a savings and loan.

EXECUTIVES

Chairman, Director, Jon C. Parker

Chief Lending Officer, Subsidiary Officer, Matthew DeBord
President, Chief Financial Officer, Subsidiary Officer, Dean J. Brydon, $193,194 total compensation
Chief Executive Officer, Subsidiary Officer, Director, Michael R. Sand, $322,125 total compensation
Senior Vice President, Chief Operating Officer, Chief Risk Officer, Subsidiary Officer, Corporate Secretary, Jonathan A. Fischer, $170,100 total compensation
Chief Financial Officer, Treasurer, Subsidiary Officer, Marci A. Basich
Director, Michael John Stoney
Director, Kelly A. Suter
Director, Andrea M. Clinton
Director, Kathy D. Leodler
Director, Parul Bhandari
Director, David A. Smith
Auditors : Delap LLP

LOCATIONS

HQ: Timberland Bancorp, Inc.
624 Simpson Avenue, Hoquiam, WA 98550
Phone: 360 533-4747
Web: www.timberlandbank.com

COMPETITORS

CAMBRIDGE FINANCIAL GROUP INC
EMIGRANT SAVINGS BANK
PRUDENTIAL BANCORP, INC. OF PENNSYLVANIA
SOUTHERN MISSOURI BANCORP, INC.
WVS FINANCIAL CORP.

HISTORICAL FINANCIALS

Company Type: Public

Income Statement — FYE: September 30

	ASSETS ($mil)	NET INCOME ($mil)	INCOME AS % OF ASSETS	EMPLOYEES
09/21	1,792.1	27.5	1.5%	288
09/20	1,565.9	24.2	1.5%	286
09/19	1,247.1	24.0	1.9%	298
09/18	1,018.2	16.7	1.6%	268
09/17	952.0	14.1	1.5%	274
Annual Growth	17.1%	18.1%	—	1.3%

2021 Year-End Financials
Return on assets: 1.6%
Return on equity: 13.9%
Long-term debt ($ mil.): —
No. of shares ($ mil.): 8.3
Sales ($ mil.): 72.1
Dividends
Yield: 3.5%
Payout: 31.0%
Market value ($ mil.): 241.0

	STOCK PRICE ($) FY Close	P/E High/Low		PER SHARE ($) Earnings	Dividends	Book Value
09/21	28.90	9	5	3.27	1.03	24.76
09/20	18.00	11	5	2.88	0.85	22.58
09/19	27.50	11	8	2.84	0.78	20.54
09/18	31.24	17	12	2.22	0.60	16.84
09/17	31.34	16	8	1.92	0.50	15.08
Annual Growth	(2.0%)	—	—	14.2%	19.8%	13.2%

TopBuild Corp

EXECUTIVES

President, Chief Executive Officer, Director, Robert M. Buck, $546,667 total compensation
Operations Division Officer, Steven P. Raia, $372,500 total compensation
Vice President, Chief Financial Officer, Robert M. Kuhns
Vice President, General Counsel, Corporate Secretary, Luis Francisco Machado
Vice President, Chief Accounting Officer, Carrie Wood
Vice President, Chief Operating Officer, Joseph Viselli
Division Officer, Robert J. Franklin
Director, Alec C. Covington
Director, Ernesto Bautista
Director, Joseph S. Cantie
Director, Tina M. Donikowski
Director, Mark A. Petrarca
Director, Nancy M. Taylor
Director, Deirdre C. Drake
Auditors : PricewaterhouseCoopers LLP

LOCATIONS

HQ: TopBuild Corp
475 North Williamson Boulevard, Daytona Beach, FL 32114
Phone: 386 304-2200
Web: www.topbuild.com

HISTORICAL FINANCIALS

Company Type: Public

Income Statement — FYE: December 31

	REVENUE ($mil)	NET INCOME ($mil)	NET PROFIT MARGIN	EMPLOYEES
12/20	2,718.0	247.0	9.1%	10,540
12/19	2,624.1	190.9	7.3%	10,400
12/18	2,384.2	134.7	5.7%	10,300
12/17	1,906.2	158.1	8.3%	8,400
12/16	1,742.8	72.6	4.2%	7,900
Annual Growth	11.8%	35.8%	—	7.5%

2020 Year-End Financials
Debt ratio: 25.1%
Return on equity: 19.6%
Cash ($ mil.): 330.0
Current Ratio: 1.89
Long-term debt ($ mil.): 683.3
No. of shares ($ mil.): 33.0
Dividends
Yield: —
Payout: —
Market value ($ mil.): 6,078.0

	STOCK PRICE ($) FY Close	P/E High/Low		PER SHARE ($) Earnings	Dividends	Book Value
12/20	184.08	27	8	7.42	0.00	40.85
12/19	103.08	20	8	5.56	0.00	34.43
12/18	45.00	23	11	3.78	0.00	31.01
12/17	75.74	17	8	4.32	0.00	28.00
12/16	35.60	20	12	1.92	0.00	25.72
Annual Growth	50.8%	—	—	40.2%	—	12.3%

Toro Company (The)

The Toro Company is a worldwide provider of turf maintenance equipment and precision irrigation systems. It manufactures lawn mowers, snow throwers, and other such tools for professional and residential landscaping. Its lineup of products helps create, illuminate, and irrigate lawns and landscapes; install, repair and replace underground utilities; and manage ice and snow. Toro's products are typically used in golf courses, sports fields, municipal, residential, and commercial properties. About 80% of its revenue derives from US customers. Toro traces its roots back to 1914 as The Toro Motor Company.

Operations

Toro has two primary business segments: Professional and Residential.

The Professional segment (about 75% of total sales) designs turf, landscape, construction, and agricultural products and markets them worldwide. It also includes professional snow and ice removal equipment. This segment serves the landscape contractor equipment market through the Toro, Ventrac and Exmark brands, with products such as zero-turn radius mowers, heavy- and mid-duty mowers, and tree care equipment. Products for the golf course include specialty mowers, sprayers and sprinklers, and controls and sensors that measure soil moisture and salinity. Snow and ice management products are sold under the BOSS brand and include snow plows, salt and sand spreaders, and ATVs. The Professional segment also includes rental and specialty products as well as underground construction products such as directional drills and riding trenchers.

Toro's Residential segment (approximately 25% of sales) offers products similar to those of the Professional segment, but for use on a smaller scale. Brands include Toro, Lawn-Boy, and Pope ? and Hayter in the UK. Yard tools include walking and riding mowers, trimmers and blowers, and snow throwers.

Overall, sales to its equipment accounts for nearly 80% of sales and the rest comes from irrigation.

Geographic Reach

Bloomington, Minnesota-based Toro rings up about 80% of its sales in the US. The remainder comes from more than 125 other countries including Australia, Canada, and several in Europe. The company manufactures its products at in the US, as well as sites in Mexico, Australia, and China, and five facilities in Europe. It also maintain sales offices in Belgium, UK, Australia, Japan, China, Italy, Poland, Germany, Spain, France, and the US.

Sales and Marketing

Toro markets and sells the majority of its products through more than 150 distributors worldwide, as well as a large number of equipment dealers, irrigation dealers and distributors, mass retailers, hardware retailers, equipment rental centers, home centers, and online (direct to end-users).

The company's Professional segment sells to clients who manage facilities such as golf courses and sports fields, as well as municipal properties and private landscapes. It also sells directly to property owners such as governmental entities and retailers. Its BOSS snow and ice management products are sold through distributors and dealers.

Residential segment products, such as walk power mowers, zero-turn riding mowers, and snow throwers, are generally sold to home centers, mass retailers, dealers, hardware retailers, as well as online (direct to end-users). In certain markets, these same products are sold to distributors for resale to hardware retailers and dealers. Home solutions products are primarily sold to home centers, mass retailers, and hardware retailers.

Marketing channels include television, radio, print, direct mail, email, and online channels like social media. Toro's spends approximately $50.5 million, $50.3 million, and $43.5 million for the fiscal years ended 2021, 2020, and 2019, respectively.

Financial Performance

Consolidated net sales in fiscal 2021 were $4.0 billion compared to $3.4 billion in fiscal 2020, an increase of 17%. The increase was primarily driven by increased sales of Professional landscape contractor zero-turn riding mowers due to strong retail demand and low field inventory levels; price increases across its Professional and Residential segment product lines; and strong demand for rental and specialty construction equipment due to favorable construction industry trends.

Net earnings for fiscal 2021 increased to $409.9 million compared from $329.7 million in the prior year. The net earnings increase for fiscal 2021 was primarily driven by the higher sales volumes, which were further benefited from improved net price realization as a result of price increases across its Professional and Residential segment product line and favorable product mix; productivity improvements; and acquisition-related costs for its acquisitions of Venture Products and CMW recorded in fiscal 2020 that did not repeat in fiscal 2021.

Cash held by the company at the end of fiscal 2021 decreased to $405.6 million. Cash provided by operations was $555.5 billion while cash used for investing and financing activities were $128.5 million and $503.7 million, respectively. Main uses of cash were purchases of property, plant and equipment; and repayments under debt arrangements

Strategy

Toro has continued to complement its brands, enhance its product portfolios, and improve its technologies through innovation and strategic acquisitions over the more than 100 years it has been in business. The company plan to continue to leverage a strategic and disciplined approach to pursue targeted acquisitions that add value to TTC by complementing its existing brands, enhancing its product portfolio, and/or improving its technologies.

Toro believes that its longstanding commitment to quality and innovation in its products has been a key driver of its history of market success. The company is committed to an ongoing engineering program dedicated to developing innovative new products and improvements in the quality and performance of existing products and when applicable, it may pursue targeted and strategic acquisitions to acquire innovative technologies that the company believe uphold and bolster its longstanding commitment to quality and innovation in its products. For example, during the first quarter of fiscal 2021, Toro completed the asset acquisition of Turflynx, Lda, a developer of innovative autonomous solutions for turf management, and during the second quarter of fiscal 2021, the company completed the asset acquisition of Left Hand Robotics, Inc., a developer of innovative autonomous solutions for turf and snow management. These strategic asset acquisitions complement and support the development of alternative power, smart-connected, and autonomous products within its Professional and Residential segments.

Mergers and Acquisitions

In early 2021, Toro acquired Colorado-based Left Hand Robotics, a recognized for developing innovative autonomous solutions for turf and snow management. Its patent-pending software and advanced technologies for autonomous navigation are designed to provide professional contractors and grounds managers with future solutions to improve their operational efficiency and tackle outdoor tasks with precision. The acquisition supports the company's strategy of leadership in next generation technologies, including alternative power, smart connected, and autonomous products. Terms of the transaction were not disclosed.

Company Background

Toro, Spanish for "bull," was founded in 1914 as The Toro Motor Company to make engines for The Bull Tractor Company. In 1921 Toro provided a tractor fitted with 30-inch lawn mower blades to replace a horse-drawn grass-cutting machine at a Minneapolis country club, and the modern power mower industry was born. By 1925 Toro turf maintenance machines were used on many of the US's major golf courses and parks, and by 1928 its products were used in Europe.

The company went public in 1935. Toro introduced its first walk-behind power mower for consumers four years later. In 1948 the company entered the rotary mower market when it bought Whirlwind. Toro started making snow removal equipment in 1951. With its 1962 purchase of Moist O' Matic, the company's offerings included automatic irrigation for golf courses.

It was renamed The Toro Company in 1971.

HISTORY

Toro -- Spanish for "bull" -- was founded in 1914 as The Toro Motor Company to make engines for The Bull Tractor Company. In 1921 Toro provided a tractor fitted with 30-inch lawn mower blades to replace a horse-drawn grass-cutting machine at a Minneapolis country club, and the modern power mower industry was born. By 1925 Toro turf maintenance machines were used on many of the US's major golf courses and parks, and by 1928 its products were used in Europe.

The company went public in 1935. Toro introduced its first walk-behind power mower for consumers four years later. In 1948 the company entered the rotary mower market when it bought Whirlwind. Toro started making snow removal equipment in 1951. With its 1962 purchase of Moist O' Matic, the company's offerings included automatic irrigation for golf courses.

It was renamed The Toro Company in 1971.

EXECUTIVES

International Business Chairman, International Business President, International Business Chief Executive Officer, Chairman, Director, Richard M. Olson, $875,000 total compensation
Vice President, General Counsel, Corporate Secretary, Amy E. Dahl
Vice President, Chief Financial Officer, Angela C. Drake
Division Officer, Kevin N. Carpenter
Director, Jeffrey M. Ettinger
Director, Eric P. Hansotia
Director, D. Christian Koch
Director, Janet K. Cooper
Director, Gary Lee Ellis
Director, Jill M. Pemberton
Director, Michael G. Vale
Director, Jeffrey L. Harmening
Director, Joyce A. Mullen
Director, James Calvin O'Rourke
Auditors : KPMG LLP

LOCATIONS

HQ: Toro Company (The)
8111 Lyndale Avenue South, Bloomington, MN 55420-1196
Phone: 952 888-8801
Web: www.thetorocompany.com

2018 Sales

	$ mil.	% of total
US	1,975.5	75
Other countries	643.1	25
Total	2,618.6	100

PRODUCTS/OPERATIONS

2018 Sales

	$ mil.	% of total
Equipment	2,210.0	84
Irrigation & lighting	408.6	16
Total	2,618.6	100

2018 Sales

	$ mil.	% of total
Professional	1,947.0	74
Residential	654.4	25
Other	17.2	1
Total	2,618.6	100

BRANDS
Boss
Exmark
Hayter
Irritrol
Lawn-Boy
Pope
Toro
Unique Lighting Systems

Selected Products
Professional
    Agricultural irrigation
    Aqua-TraXX PBX drip tape
    Blue Stripe polyethylene tubing
    BlueLine drip line
    NGE emittters
    Evolution Ag controller
    Golf course
    Bunker maintenance equipment
    Greens rollers
    Turf sprayers
    Walking and riding mowers
    Landscape contractor
    Heavy-duty walk-behind mowers
    Mid-sized walk-behind mowers
    Stand-on movers
    Turf renovation and tree care equipment
    Zero-turning-radius riding mowers
    Sports fields and grounds
    Aerators
    Blowers
    Multipurpose vehicles
    Sweepers
    Vacuums
Residential
    Home solutions
    Electric blower-vacuums
    Grass trimmers
    Lighting
    Riding products
    Garden tractor models
    Lawn tractor models
    Zero-turning-radius mowers
    Snow removal
    Single-stage snow throwers
    Two-stage snow throwers
    Walk power mowers
    Bagging mowers
    Mulching mowers
    Side discharging mowers
Snow and Ice Management
    Snowplows
    Salt and sand spreaders
    Rental and specialty construction
    Compact utility loaders
    Walk-behind trenchers
    Stump grinders

COMPETITORS
AGCO CORPORATION
ALAMO GROUP INC.
BLOUNT INTERNATIONAL, INC.
BRIGGS & STRATTON CORPORATION
Buhler Industries Inc
CNH INDUSTRIAL N.V.
DEERE & COMPANY
KUBOTA CORPORATION

LINDSAY CORPORATION
OXBO INTERNATIONAL CORPORATION

HISTORICAL FINANCIALS
Company Type: Public

Income Statement   FYE: October 31

	REVENUE ($mil)	NET INCOME ($mil)	NET PROFIT MARGIN	EMPLOYEES
10/21	3,959.5	409.8	10.4%	10,982
10/20	3,378.8	329.7	9.8%	10,385
10/19	3,138.0	273.9	8.7%	9,329
10/18	2,618.6	271.9	10.4%	6,715
10/17	2,505.1	267.7	10.7%	6,779
Annual Growth	12.1%	11.2%	—	12.8%

2021 Year-End Financials
Debt ratio: 23.5%   No. of shares ($ mil.): 105.2
Return on equity: 36.1%   Dividends
Cash ($ mil.): 405.6   Yield: —
Current Ratio: 1.59   Payout: 27.7%
Long-term debt ($ mil.): 691.2   Market value ($ mil.): 10,044.0

	STOCK PRICE ($) FY Close	P/E High	P/E Low	PER SHARE ($) Earnings	PER SHARE ($) Dividends	PER SHARE ($) Book Value
10/21	95.47	31	22	3.78	1.05	10.94
10/20	82.10	29	18	3.03	1.00	10.36
10/19	77.13	30	21	2.53	0.90	8.05
10/18	56.33	26	21	2.50	0.80	6.33
10/17	62.85	30	19	2.41	0.70	5.77
Annual Growth	11.0%	—	—	11.9%	10.7%	17.3%

Touchmark Bancshares Inc

EXECUTIVES

Chairman, Director, Jayendrakumar J. Shah
Vice-Chairwoman, Director, Vivian A. Wong
President, Chief Executive Officer, Subsidiary Officer, Director, Jorge L. Forment, $154,000 total compensation
Chief Financial Officer, Subsidiary Officer, Kellie Pressnall
Director, William D. Crosby
Director, Sudhirkumar C. Patel
Director, Mukund C. Raja
Director, Hasmukh P. Rama
Director, Mahendra R. Shah
Director, Meena J. Shah

LOCATIONS

HQ: Touchmark Bancshares Inc
   3651 Old Milton Parkway, Alpharetta, GA 30005
Phone: 770 407-6700
Web: www.touchmarknb.com

HISTORICAL FINANCIALS
Company Type: Public

Income Statement   FYE: December 31

	ASSETS ($mil)	NET INCOME ($mil)	INCOME AS % OF ASSETS	EMPLOYEES
12/21	421.7	8.3	2.0%	0
12/20	427.7	4.7	1.1%	0
12/15	196.9	1.7	0.9%	0
12/14	162.2	0.7	0.5%	0
12/13	132.9	0.5	0.4%	0
Annual Growth	15.5%	40.8%	—	—

2021 Year-End Financials
Return on assets: 1.9%   Dividends
Return on equity: 13.8%   Yield: —
Long-term debt ($ mil.): —   Payout: 26.8%
No. of shares ($ mil.): 4.4   Market value ($ mil.): 49.0
Sales ($ mil.): 21.2

	STOCK PRICE ($) FY Close	P/E High	P/E Low	PER SHARE ($) Earnings	PER SHARE ($) Dividends	PER SHARE ($) Book Value
12/21	11.00	—	—	0.00	0.50	14.12
12/20	7.30	—	—	0.00	0.35	12.81
12/15	6.00	14	12	0.51	0.00	9.32
12/14	6.00	27	17	0.22	0.00	8.83
12/13	3.75	29	20	0.16	0.00	8.48
Annual Growth	14.4%	—	—	—	—	6.6%

TowneBank

EXECUTIVES

Chairman, Chief Executive Officer, G. Robert Aston, $696,843 total compensation
Vice-Chairman, Thomas C. Broyles
Vice-Chairman, Jeffrey F. Benson
Vice-Chairman, John W. Failes
Vice-Chairman, W. Ashton Lewis
President, Chief Banking Officer, Director, J. Morgan Davis
Senior Executive Vice President, Chief Financial Officer, Clyde E. McFarland, $216,810 total compensation
Senior Executive Vice President, Chief Legal Officer, George P. Whitley
Senior Executive Vice President, Chief Operating Officer, Director, Brad E. Schwartz
Senior Executive Vice President, Chief Administrative Officer, Keith D. Horton
Finance Senior Executive Vice President, Finance Chief Strategy Officer, William B. Littreal
Retail Banking Senior Vice President, Marketing Senior Vice President, Retail Banking Chief Marketing Officer, Marketing Chief Marketing Officer, Retail Banking Chief Human Resources Officer, Marketing Chief Human Resources Officer, U. Starr Oliver
Corporate Administration Senior Vice President, Corporate Administration Chief Credit Officer, Philip M. Rudisill
Senior Executive Vice President, Thomas V. Rueger
Executive Vice President, Chief Accounting Officer, David A. Patterson

Division Officer, Director, Gordon L. Gentry
Region Officer, Director, William I. Foster
Subsidiary Officer, Director, William T. Morrison
Director, Jacqueline B. Amato, $44,760 total compensation
Director, E. Lee Baynor
Director, Richard S. Bray
Director, Bradford L. Cherry
Director, Douglas E. Ellis
Director, Paul J. Farrell
Director, Andrew S. Fine
Director, John R. Lawson
Director, Harry T. Lester
Director, Stephanie J. Marioneaux
Director, R. Scott Morgan, $406,400 total compensation
Director, Thomas K. Norment
Director, Juan M. Montero
Director, R.V. Owens
Director, Richard B. Thurmond
Director, Alan S. Witt
Director, F. Lewis Wood
Director, Richard T. Wheeler
Director, Dwight C. Schaubach
Director, Elizabeth T. Patterson
Director, Elizabeth W. Robertson
Director, Robert M. Oman
Auditors : Dixon Hughes Goodman LLP

LOCATIONS

HQ: TowneBank
5716 High Street, Portsmouth, VA 23703
Phone: 757 638-7500
Web: www.townebank.com

HISTORICAL FINANCIALS
Company Type: Public

Income Statement			FYE: December 31
	ASSETS ($mil)	**NET INCOME ($mil)**	**INCOME AS % OF ASSETS**	**EMPLOYEES**
12/20	14,626.4	145.5	1.0%	2,897
12/19	11,947.6	138.7	1.2%	2,853
12/18	11,163.0	133.7	1.2%	2,897
12/17	8,522.1	87.6	1.0%	2,727
12/16	7,973.9	67.2	0.8%	2,529
Annual Growth	16.4%	21.3%	—	3.5%

2020 Year-End Financials
Return on assets: 1.0%
Return on equity: 8.5%
Long-term debt ($ mil.): —
No. of shares ($ mil.): 72.6
Sales ($ mil.): 744.3
Dividends
Yield: 3.0%
Payout: 40.0%
Market value ($ mil.): 1,706.0

	STOCK PRICE ($) FY Close	P/E High/Low	PER SHARE ($) Earnings	Dividends	Book Value
12/20	23.48	14 8	2.01	0.72	24.31
12/19	27.82	15 12	1.92	0.70	22.58
12/18	23.95	18 12	1.88	0.62	21.05
12/17	30.75	25 21	1.41	0.55	18.06
12/16	33.25	29 14	1.18	0.51	17.20
Annual Growth	(8.3%)	— —	14.2%	9.0%	9.0%

Tradeweb Markets Inc

EXECUTIVES

Chairperson, Director, Lee Olesky, $770,000 total compensation
President, Director, Thomas Pluta
Chief Financial Officer, Sara Furber
Chief Executive Officer, Director, William Hult, $660,000 total compensation
Chief Administrative Officer, Chief Risk Officer, Scott Zucker
Chief Technology Officer, Justin Peterson
General Counsel, Secretary, Douglas Friedman
Business Development Managing Director, Business Development Global Head, Simon Maisey
Managing Director, Region Officer, Enrico Bruni
Lead Independent Director, Director, Paula Madoff
Director, Steven Berns
Director, John G. Finley
Director, Scott Ganeles
Director, Von Hughes
Director, Murray Roos
Director, Balbir Bakhshi
Director, Jacques Aigrain
Director, Rana Yared
Auditors : DELOITTE & TOUCHE LLP

LOCATIONS

HQ: Tradeweb Markets Inc
1177 Avenue of the Americas, New York, NY 10036
Phone: 646 430-6000
Web: www.tradeweb.com

HISTORICAL FINANCIALS
Company Type: Public

Income Statement			FYE: December 31
	REVENUE ($mil)	**NET INCOME ($mil)**	**NET PROFIT MARGIN**	**EMPLOYEES**
12/20	892.6	166.2	18.6%	961
12/19	775.5	83.7	10.8%	919
12/18*	178.6	29.3	16.4%	919
09/18	478.9	130.1	27.2%	0
12/17	504.4	83.6	16.6%	0
Annual Growth	21.0%	25.7%	—	—

*Fiscal year change

2020 Year-End Financials
Debt ratio: —
Return on equity: 4.3%
Cash ($ mil.): 791.2
Current Ratio: 4.49
Long-term debt ($ mil.): —
No. of shares ($ mil.): 229.0
Dividends
Yield: 0.5%
Payout: 36.3%
Market value ($ mil.): 14,302.0

	STOCK PRICE ($) FY Close	P/E High/Low	PER SHARE ($) Earnings	Dividends	Book Value
12/20	62.45	74 39	0.88	0.32	18.79
12/19	46.35	88 63	0.54	0.24	15.18
Annual Growth	34.7%	— —	63.0%	33.3%	23.8%

TransUnion

EXECUTIVES

Chairperson, Director, Pamela A. Joseph
International President, Todd C. Skinner
President, Chief Executive Officer, Director, Christopher A. Cartwright, $700,000 total compensation
Executive Vice President, Chief Financial Officer, Todd M. Cello, $496,811 total compensation
Executive Vice President, Chief Legal Officer, Corporate Secretary, Heather J. Russell
Executive Vice President, Chief Information Officer, Chief Technology Officer, Abhinav Dhar
Senior Vice President, Corporate Secretary, Mick Forde
Region Officer, Steven M. Chaouki
Director, George M. Awad
Director, Suzanne P. Clark
Director, Russell P. Fradin
Director, Thomas L. Monahan
Director, Andrew Prozes
Director, William (Billy) Bosworth
Auditors : PricewaterhouseCoopers LLP

LOCATIONS

HQ: TransUnion
555 West Adams, Chicago, IL 60661
Phone: 312 985-2000
Web: www.transunion.com

HISTORICAL FINANCIALS
Company Type: Public

Income Statement			FYE: December 31
	REVENUE ($mil)	**NET INCOME ($mil)**	**NET PROFIT MARGIN**	**EMPLOYEES**
12/21	2,960.2	1,387.1	46.9%	10,200
12/20	2,716.6	343.2	12.6%	8,200
12/19	2,656.1	346.9	13.1%	8,000
12/18	2,317.2	276.6	11.9%	7,100
12/17	1,933.8	441.2	22.8%	5,100
Annual Growth	11.2%	33.2%	—	18.9%

2021 Year-End Financials
Debt ratio: 50.4%
Return on equity: 43.0%
Cash ($ mil.): 1,842.4
Current Ratio: 1.94
Long-term debt ($ mil.): 6,251.3
No. of shares ($ mil.): 191.8
Dividends
Yield: 0.3%
Payout: 14.7%
Market value ($ mil.): 22,744.0

	STOCK PRICE ($) FY Close	P/E High/Low	PER SHARE ($) Earnings	Dividends	Book Value
12/21	118.58	17 12	7.19	0.36	20.38
12/20	99.22	56 30	1.79	0.30	13.33
12/19	85.61	47 29	1.81	0.30	11.90
12/18	56.80	51 35	1.45	0.23	10.18
12/17	54.96	23 13	2.32	0.00	9.44
Annual Growth	21.2%	— —	32.7%	—	21.2%

Trex Co Inc

HOOVER'S HANDBOOK OF EMERGING COMPANIES 2023

Trex Company is one of the world's largest maker of wood-alternative decking and railing products, which are used in the construction of residential and commercial decks and rails. Marketed under the Trex name, products resemble wood and have the workability of wood, but require less long-term maintenance. The Trex Residential composite is made of waste wood fibers and reclaimed plastic. Trex serves professional installation contractors and do-it-yourselfers through the company's more than 50 distributors and two national merchandisers, which in turn sell to retailers including Home Depot and Lowe's. Trex products are available in more than 40 countries worldwide.

Operations
Trex operates in two reportable segments: Trex Residential Products (Trex Residential) and Trex Commercial Products (Trex Commercial).

Trex Residential, which generates approximately 95% of the company's total sales, offers a comprehensive set of aesthetically appealing and durable, low-maintenance product offerings in the decking, railing, fencing, steel deck framing, and outdoor lighting categories. Stocked in more than 6,700 retail locations around the world, Trex outdoor living products are marketed under the brand name Trex and manufactured in the US.

Trex Commercial (some 5% of total sales) is a leading national provider of custom-engineered railing and staging systems. The segment designs and engineers custom railing solutions which target commercial and high-rise applications, and portable staging equipment for the performing arts, sports, and event production and rental market.

Trex produces decking and accessories that include Trex Transcend, Trex Enhance, Trex Select, Trex Hideaway and Trex DeckLighting. Its railing products include Trex Transcend Railing, Trex Select Railing, Trex Enhance Railing and Trex Signature aluminum railing. The company's collection also includes Trex Seclusions (a fencing product), Trex DeckLighting (a deck lighting system), and Trex Hideaway (a hidden fastening system for specially grooved boards). The company also has polyethylene pellets made from recycled plastic that it sells to plastic bag, and film makers.

Overall, products transferred at a point in time and variable consideration contracts generate approximately 95% of the company's total revenue, while products transferred over time and fixed price contracts account for some 5%.

Geographic Reach
Based in Virginia, Trex has its Trex Residential manufacturing facilities in Arkansas, Virginia and Nevada while its Trex Commercial has a manufacturing facility in Minnesota. It operates globally through international dealers and retailers.

Sales and Marketing
The company's Trex Residential products are sold to distributors and home centers for final resale primarily to the residential market, while its Trex Commercial products are marketed to architects, specifiers, contractors, and building owners. Its wood is also the only composite lumber to be code-listed by the nation's building code agencies.

For the years ended in 2021, 2020, and 2019, the company's branding expenses, including advertising expenses, were approximately $30.7 million, $31.7 million, and $35.7 million, respectively.

Financial Performance
The company had $1.2 billion in net sales for the year 2021. The 36% increase in total net sales in 2021 compared to 2020 was substantially due to volume growth at Trex Residential across all product lines. The company's capacity expansion program and the additional lines installed at its new Virginia facility were fully operational in 2021 enabling the company's ability to capture additional growth.

In 2021, the company had a net income of $208.7 million, a 19% increase from the previous year's net income of $175.6 million.

The company's cash at the end of 2021 was $141.1 million. Operating activities generated $258.1 million, while investing activities used $158 million, mainly for expenditures for property, plant and equipment and intangibles. Financing activities used another $80.7 million, primarily for principal payments under line of credit.

Strategy
Trex's long-term goals are to continue leading the category with beautiful, high-performance, low-maintenance Trex products, including outdoor living products, such as composite decking and railing for the residential market and custom-engineered railing systems for the commercial market. To do this, the company will increase market share and expand into new product categories and geographic markets through the design, creation and marketing of outdoor living products that offer superior aesthetics and quality and by expanding sales to the commercial market. Trex Residential will expand its offering of eco-friendly decking and railing products for a breadth of audiences, whether by converting wood buyers who have not previously considered composite decking or appealing to the most discriminating high-end homeowners seeking superior aesthetics and quality. Trex Commercial will extend its position as a leading national provider of custom-engineered railing for the commercial and multi-family market, including sports stadiums. Additionally, Trex will continue to explore opportunities that leverage its manufacturing and extrusion expertise and recycling heritage.

It intends to employ long-term strategies to achieve its goals through innovation, brand, channels, quality, cost, and customer service.

Company Background
Trex was formed in 1996 through a buyout of a division of Mobil Corporation. It went public in 1999.

EXECUTIVES

Chairman, James E. Cline, $545,000 total compensation

Vice-Chairman, Director, Ronald W. Kaplan, $554,630 total compensation

President, Chief Executive Officer, Bryan H. Fairbanks, $322,870 total compensation

Senior Vice President, General Counsel, Secretary, William R. Gupp, $337,700 total compensation

Sales Vice President, Christopher P. Gerhard, $262,500 total compensation

Vice President, Chief Financial Officer, Principal Financial Officer, Principal Accounting Officer, Dennis Charles Schemm

Marketing Division Officer, Adam Dante Zambanini, $302,737 total compensation

Director, Michael F. Golden

Director, Jay M. Gratz

Director, Kristine L. Juster

Director, Richard E. Posey

Director, Patricia B. Robinson, $39,750 total compensation

Director, Gerald (Jerry) Volas

Auditors: Ernst & Young LLP

LOCATIONS

HQ: Trex Co Inc
160 Exeter Drive, Winchester, VA 22603-8605
Phone: 540 542-6300
Web: www.trex.com

PRODUCTS/OPERATIONS

Selected Brands
Decking
    Trex Accents
    Trex Enhance
    Trex Escapes
    Trex Select
    Trex Transcend
Deck Lighting System
    Trex DeckLighting
Fencing
    Trex Seclusions
Hidden Fastening System
    Trex Hideaway
Porch
    Trex Transcend Porch Flooring & Railing System
PVC Outdoor Trim
    TrexTrim
Railing
    Trex Designer Series
    Trex Transcend
Steel Deck Framing System
    Trex Elevations

Selected Products
Decking
Fencing
Railing
Trim

COMPETITORS

ARMSTRONG WORLD INDUSTRIES, INC.
BOISE CASCADE COMPANY
BUILDERS FIRSTSOURCE, INC.
Canfor Corporation
ENVIVA PARTNERS, LP
LUMBER LIQUIDATORS HOLDINGS, INC.
PLY GEM HOLDINGS, INC.
SIERRA PACIFIC INDUSTRIES
STIMSON LUMBER COMPANY
UFP INDUSTRIES, INC.

HISTORICAL FINANCIALS

Company Type: Public

Income Statement — FYE: December 31

	REVENUE ($mil)	NET INCOME ($mil)	NET PROFIT MARGIN	EMPLOYEES
12/20	880.8	175.6	19.9%	1,719
12/19	745.3	144.7	19.4%	1,173
12/18	684.2	134.5	19.7%	1,214
12/17	565.1	95.1	16.8%	815
12/16	479.6	67.8	14.1%	830
Annual Growth	16.4%	26.8%	—	20.0%

2020 Year-End Financials

Debt ratio: —
Return on equity: 33.7%
Cash ($ mil.): 121.7
Current Ratio: 3.03
Long-term debt ($ mil.): —
No. of shares ($ mil.): 115.8
Dividends
 Yield: —
 Payout: —
Market value ($ mil.): 9,695.0

	STOCK PRICE ($) FY Close	P/E High/Low		PER SHARE ($) Earnings	Dividends	Book Value
12/20	83.72	102	41	1.51	0.00	5.08
12/19	89.88	74	47	1.24	0.00	3.86
12/18	59.36	113	47	1.14	0.00	2.93
12/17	108.39	145	77	0.81	0.00	1.96
12/16	64.40	123	56	0.57	0.00	1.14
Annual Growth	6.8%	—	—	27.4%	—	45.3%

Tri Pointe Homes Inc

EXECUTIVES

Chairman, Director, Steven J. Gilbert
Chief Executive Officer, Director, Douglas F. Bauer, $793,269 total compensation
President, Chief Operating Officer, Thomas J. Mitchell, $763,269 total compensation
Vice President, General Counsel, Secretary, David C. Lee, $471,154 total compensation
Chief Financial Officer, Chief Accounting Officer, Treasurer, Glenn J. Keeler, $287,308 total compensation
Director, Lawrence B. Burrows
Director, R. Kent Grahl
Director, Vicki D. McWilliams
Director, Constance B. Moore
Auditors: Ernst & Young LLP

LOCATIONS

HQ: Tri Pointe Homes Inc
940 Southwood Blvd., Suite 200, Incline Village, NV 89451
Phone: 775 413-1030
Web: www.tripointehomes.com

HISTORICAL FINANCIALS

Company Type: Public

Income Statement — FYE: December 31

	REVENUE ($mil)	NET INCOME ($mil)	NET PROFIT MARGIN	EMPLOYEES
12/21	3,970.7	469.2	11.8%	1,390
12/20	3,251.3	282.2	8.7%	1,163
12/19	3,079.0	207.1	6.7%	1,386
12/18	3,261.0	269.9	8.3%	1,435
12/17	2,808.9	187.1	6.7%	1,251
Annual Growth	9.0%	25.8%	—	2.7%

2021 Year-End Financials

Debt ratio: 30.8%
Return on equity: 20.0%
Cash ($ mil.): 681.5
Current Ratio: 21.07
Long-term debt ($ mil.): 1,337.7
No. of shares ($ mil.): 109.6
Dividends
 Yield: —
 Payout: —
Market value ($ mil.): 3,058.0

	STOCK PRICE ($) FY Close	P/E High/Low		PER SHARE ($) Earnings	Dividends	Book Value
12/21	27.89	7	4	4.12	0.00	22.32
12/20	17.25	9	3	2.17	0.00	18.32
12/19	15.58	11	8	1.47	0.00	16.06
12/18	10.93	11	6	1.81	0.00	14.52
12/17	17.92	15	9	1.21	0.00	12.77
Annual Growth	11.7%	—	—	35.8%	—	15.0%

TriCo Bancshares (Chico, CA)

People looking for a community bank in California's Sacramento Valley can try TriCo. TriCo Bancshares is the holding company for Tri Counties Bank, which serves customers through some 65 traditional and in-store branches in 23 counties in Northern and Central California. Founded in 1974, Tri Counties Bank provides a variety of deposit services, including checking and savings accounts, money market accounts, and CDs. Most patrons are retail customers and small to midsized businesses. The bank primarily originates real estate mortgages, which account for about 65% of its loan portfolio; consumer loans contribute about 25%. TriCo has agreed to acquire rival North Valley Bancorp.

Operations

In addition to its retail banking products and services, the company provides wholesale banking and investment services; TriCo offers brokerage services through an arrangement with Raymond James Financial. The company does not provide trust or international banking services.

Geographic Reach

Based in Chico, California, Tri Counties Bank operates 66 branches (41 traditional branches and 25 in-store branches) in 23 counties in Northern and central California, including Fresno, Kern, Mendocino, Napa, Sacramento, and Yuba counties.

Financial Performance

In 2013 net interest income, the company's primary source of revenue, rose 0.6% compared with 2012 to $102.2 million. The slight increase in net interest income was mainly due to a decrease in average balance of other borrowings, a shift in deposit balances from relatively high interest rate earning time deposits to noninterest-earning, demand, and savings deposits, an increase in the average balance of investments securities, and an increase in the average balance of loans; all of which were substantially offset by a decrease in the average yield on loans.

Strategy

The bank's growth has been fueled by acquisitions and the opening of new branches; it frequently opens branches within grocery stores or other retailers, including Wal-Mart. TriCo in 2010 acquired the three branches of Granite Community Bank, which had been seized by regulators. The transaction, which also included most of the failed bank's assets and deposits, was facilitated by the FDIC and includes a loss-sharing agreement with the agency. The following year TriCo acquired Citizens Bank of Northern California. The FDIC-assisted deal included seven branches. The acquisitions are part of TriCo's strategy of adding new customers.

Mergers and Acquisitions

TriCo in January 2014 announced plans to buy its rival in Northern California North Valley Bancorp (NVB) for about $178.4 million. NVB is the parent company of North Valley Bank, which had about $918 million in assets and 22 commercial banking offices across eight Northern California counties at the end of 2013. At closing, which is expected in the second or third quarter of 2014, NVB will be merged into Tri Counties Bank. The combined bank would have about $3.6 billion in assets.

EXECUTIVES

Chairman, President, Chief Executive Officer, Subsidiary Officer, Director, Richard P. Smith, $715,000 total compensation
Subsidiary Officer, Vice-Chairman, Director, Michael W. Koehnen
Executive Vice President, Chief Banking Officer, Subsidiary Officer, Daniel K. Bailey, $279,769 total compensation
Executive Vice President, Chief Credit Officer, Subsidiary Officer, Craig B. Carney, $319,829 total compensation
Executive Vice President, Chief Operating Officer, Subsidiary Officer, John S. Fleshood, $409,000 total compensation
Executive Vice President, Chief Financial Officer, Subsidiary Officer, Peter G. Wiese, $480,000 total compensation
Senior Vice President, Chief Human Resources Officer, Subsidiary Officer, Judi A. Giem
Senior Vice President, General Counsel, Subsidiary Officer, Gregory A. Gehlmann

Lead Independent Director, Director, Cory W. Giese

Director, John S. A. Hasbrook
Director, Margaret L. Kane
Director, Martin A. Mariani
Director, Thomas C. McGraw
Director, Kimberley H. Vogel
Director, Anthony L. Leggio
Director, Kirsten E. Garen
Director, Jon Nakamura
Director, Donald J. Amaral
Auditors : Moss Adams LLP

LOCATIONS

HQ: TriCo Bancshares (Chico, CA)
63 Constitution Drive, Chico, CA 95973
Phone: 530 898-0300
Web: www.tcbk.com

PRODUCTS/OPERATIONS

2015 Sales

	$ mil.	% of total
Interest		
Loans, including fees	131.8	64
Debt securities	26.8	13
Dividends	2.1	1
Other	0.7	—
Noninterest		
Service charges & fees	31.8	16
Commissions	3.4	2
Gain on sale of loans	3.1	1
Other	7.1	3
Total	**206.8**	**100**

Selected Services
Business debit cards
Business online banking
Business workshops
Cash management
Education savings and CDs
Loans and credits
Merchant services
Order checks
Overdraft services
Pension and retirement
Personal certificates of deposit
Personal checking
Personal savings and money market
Retirement savings and CDs

COMPETITORS

F.N.B. CORPORATION
FB CORPORATION
FIRST COMMUNITY BANCSHARES, INC.
FIRST HORIZON CORPORATION
FIRST MIDWEST BANCORP, INC.
HERITAGE FINANCIAL CORPORATION
MAINSOURCE FINANCIAL GROUP, INC.
NEVADA STATE BANK
OLD NATIONAL BANCORP
WILSHIRE BANCORP, INC.

HISTORICAL FINANCIALS

Company Type: Public

Income Statement — FYE: December 31

	ASSETS ($mil)	NET INCOME ($mil)	INCOME AS % OF ASSETS	EMPLOYEES
12/20	7,639.5	64.8	0.8%	1,068
12/19	6,471.1	92.0	1.4%	1,184
12/18	6,352.4	68.3	1.1%	1,174
12/17	4,761.3	40.5	0.9%	1,023
12/16	4,517.9	44.8	1.0%	1,063
Annual Growth	14.0%	9.7%	—	0.1%

2020 Year-End Financials
Return on assets: 0.9%
Return on equity: 7.0%
Long-term debt ($ mil.): —
No. of shares ($ mil.): 29.7
Sales ($ mil.): 322.3
Dividends Yield: 2.4%
Payout: 41.5%
Market value ($ mil.): 1,049.0

	STOCK PRICE ($) FY Close	P/E High	P/E Low	PER SHARE ($) Earnings	Dividends	Book Value
12/20	35.28	19	11	2.16	0.88	31.12
12/19	40.81	14	11	3.00	0.82	29.70
12/18	33.79	16	12	2.54	0.70	27.20
12/17	37.86	25	19	1.74	0.66	22.03
12/16	34.18	18	12	1.94	0.60	20.87
Annual Growth	0.8%	—	—	2.7%	10.0%	10.5%

Trimble Inc

Trimble Inc. is a leading provider of technology solutions that enable professionals and field mobile workers to improve or transform their work processes. The company makes GPS, Global Navigation Satellite System, laser, and optical technologies, inertial, or other technologies to establish real-time position. The company's products target areas such as agriculture, architecture, civil engineering, survey, construction, geospatial, government, natural resources, transportation, and utilities. Trimble sells to end users, such as government entities, farmers, engineering and construction firms as well as equipment manufacturers. More than half of the company's sales were generated in the North America.

Operations

Trimble's operating segments are Buildings and Infrastructure, Geospatial, Resources and Utilities, and Transportation.

The Buildings and Infrastructure segment (about 40% of revenue) focuses on civil engineering and construction and building construction. The Trimble building construction portfolio of solutions for the residential, commercial and industrial building industry spans the entire life cycle of a building and is used by owners, architects, designers, general contractors, sub-contractors, engineers, and facility owners or lessees.

The Geospatial segment (around 20% of revenue) is composed of the company's surveying and geospatial offerings and geographic information systems.

The Transportation segment (approximately 20% of revenue) provides capabilities for the long-haul trucking and freight shipper markets to create a connected supply chain and integrate all forms of transportation, drivers, back office management, shippers and freight. It provides enterprise and mobility solutions focused on business intelligence and data analytics, safety and regulatory compliance, navigation and routing, freight brokerage, supply chain visibility and final mile, and transportation management and fleet maintenance.

The Resources and Utilities segment (some 20% of revenue) digs into agriculture, forestry, and utilities.

Trimble makes its own laser and optics-based products as well as some GPS products. The company sends the rest of its hardware manufacturing work to Flex Limited, Benchmark Electronics Inc., and Jabil.

Overall, the company generates almost 60% of its revenue from products, while the remainder is evenly split between services and subscriptions.

Geographic Reach

Besides its US operations, California-based Trimble Inc.'s global operations include major development, manufacturing, or logistics operations in the United States, the Netherlands, India, China, Germany, the United Kingdom, Finland, Canada, and New Zealand. Domestically, the company has locations in Dayton, Ohio and Westminster, Colorado.

The company currently has a physical presence in over 40 countries and distribution channels over 85 countries.

Sales and Marketing

Trimble Inc. sells through dealers, representatives, joint ventures, and other channels throughout the world, as well as direct sales to end-users. Its solutions are used across a range of industries including architecture, building construction, civil engineering, geospatial, survey and mapping, agriculture, natural resources, utilities, transportation, and government. Its key distribution partners include CNH Global, Caterpillar, and Nikon.

The company's advertising and promotional expense were approximately $31.6 million, $28.6 million, and $42.7 million in fiscal 2021, 2020, and, respectively.

Financial Performance

Trimble's performance for the past five years has continued to grow year-over year with 2021 as its highest performing year.

The company's revenue in fiscal 2021 increased by $512 million to $3.7 billion as compared to 2020's revenue of $3.1 billion.

Net income for 2021 also increased by $102 million to $561 million as compared to the prior year's net income of $419 million.

Cash held by the company at the end of 2021 amounted to $325.7 million. Cash provided by operations was $750.5 million. Investing activities and financing activities used $203.5 million and $447.7 million, respectively. Main cash uses were for acquisitions of businesses and payments on debt and revolving credit lines.

Strategy

Trimble's growth strategy is centered on multiple elements: Executing on its Connect & Scale 2025 strategy; Focus on attractive markets with significant growth and profitability potential; Domain knowledge and technological innovation that benefit a diverse customer base; Increasing focus on software and services; Geographic expansion with localization strategy; Optimized go-to-market strategies to best access its markets; and Strategic acquisitions.

Trimble's focus on these growth drivers has led over time to growth in revenue and profitability as well as an increasingly diversified business model. Software and subscription growth is driving increased recurring revenue and is leading to improved visibility in some of its businesses. As the company's solutions have expanded, its go-to-market model has also evolved, with a balanced mix between direct, distribution, and OEM customers, and an increasing number of enterprise level customer relationships.

HISTORY

Charles Trimble founded Trimble Navigation in 1978 to design navigation products for recreational boating. In 1982 the company began developing devices using the Global Positioning System (GPS) satellite network; in 1984 Trimble introduced its first GPS product. The company went public in 1990, 10 days before Saddam Hussein invaded Kuwait. Trimble gained worldwide recognition when allied troops used its GPS devices during the Persian Gulf War.

The war left Trimble expanding too quickly and overproducing. In 1992 Trimble rebounded after reorganizing to focus on nonmilitary products. Two years later it introduced a low-cost, handheld unit that helped with utilities fieldwork. In 1998 Trimble ceased manufacturing products for general aviation and allied with Siemens to develop GPS products. That year Charles Trimble was named vice chairman after he stepped down as the company's CEO. The company in 1998 also launched a cost reduction plan that cut its workforce by 8%.

The next year Trimble sold its Sunnyvale, California, manufacturing operations to contract manufacturer Solectron, which agreed to make Trimble's GPS and radio-frequency products for three years. Also in 1999 Steven Berglund, a former president of a Spectra-Physics subsidiary, was named CEO of Trimble.

In 2000 Trimble acquired the Spectra Precision businesses of Thermo Electron (which later became Thermo Fisher Scientific) for about $294 million. That year the US government stopped scrambling GPS signals, opening the door for more precise devices. In 2001 the company formed a subsidiary, Trimble Information Services, to expand the company's wireless location-based services, including fleet management.

The next year Trimble and Caterpillar formed a joint venture, Caterpillar Trimble Control Technologies, to develop advanced electronic guidance and control technologies for earth-moving construction and mining machines.

The company acquired Eleven Technology, a mobile application software developer focused on the consumer packaged goods market, in 2006. The company also expanded its laser scanning business by acquiring the assets -- including software for engineering and construction plant design -- of BitWyse Solutions. Later in 2006 it purchased Visual Statement, a developer of crime and collision incident investigation software, and XYZ Solutions, a 3-D intelligence software provider. It also acquired Meridian Systems, a provider of enterprise project management and lifecycle software. Still later in 2006 Trimble bought Spacient Technologies, a privately held provider of field service management and mobile mapping software used by municipalities and utilities.

Trimble's buying spree continued in 2007, when it purchased @Road, a developer of mobile resource management systems, for about $493 million.

The company expanded its ability to serve the farming industry when it acquired NTech Industries in 2009. NTech developed optical crop-sensing technology that helps farmers reduce costs by managing the application of nitrogen, herbicides, and other crop inputs. Also that year Trimble purchased Accutest Engineering Solutions, a UK-based maker of mobile resource management applications for trucking fleets.

In 2010 Trimble acquired Punch Telematix from majority shareholder Punch International for nearly ?14 million ($18 million) in cash and rebranded it as Trimble Transport and Logistics. Punch Telematix made onboard computers for trucks. That year the company also bought ThingMagic, a developer of radio frequency identification (RFID) products and RFID integration services for commercial clients in the construction and transportation industries, and Cengea, a provider of operations and supply chain management software for the forestry, agriculture, and natural resource industries.

Additionally, Trimble bought Mumbai-based Tata AutoComp Mobility Telematics (TMT) in a move to expand its mobile resource management services business in India. TMT provided vehicle tracking and other telematics services to such customers as Bharat Petroleum and Tata Motors. Also that year, expanding its engineering and construction portfolio for electrical and mechanical contractors, Trimble bought the assets of Accubid, a provider of estimating, project management and service management software.

Trimble bought 3D modeling software maker Tekla in 2011 in a deal valued at nearly ? 340 million ($485 million) to better equip building contractors and engineers to manage construction projects. The follow-up investment came in 2012 when Trimble completed the acquisition of the StruCad and StruEngineer business from AceCad Software. StruCad offers 3D structural detailing, while StruEngineer provides engineering companies with 3D steelwork modeling and construction management.

The company acquired a line of software products in 2011 from Norway-based Mesta EntreprenÃ¸r, a subsidiary of road and highway construction contractor Mesta Konsern. The deal added office and field data collection applications and improved the company's ability to provide customized systems to construction clients, particularly in the area of managing local application requirements compliance. Also in 2011 Trimble strengthened its portfolio and Asia presence with the purchase of China-based Yamei Electronics, a manufacturer of electronic automotive products, including anti-theft GPS monitoring and tracking systems, RFID smart keys, and diagnostics systems.

Also that year, Trimble acquired the OmniSTAR satellite system assets of Dutch geological engineering company Fugro. The company was interested in OmniSTAR's GPS signal correction technology (used to improve the accuracy of satellite navigation devices), which it is using to expand the functionality of its mapping systems for agricultural and construction purposes, among others. It also acquired France-based Ashtech to expand Garmin's selection of survey products, including the flagship application Spectra Precision, for construction clients. Ashtech became part of Trimble's engineering and construction division.

EXECUTIVES

Executive Chairman, Director, Steven W. Berglund, $961,400 total compensation
President, Chief Executive Officer, Director, Robert Painter, $482,437 total compensation
Senior Vice President, Division Officer, Darryl Matthews, $422,073 total compensation
Senior Vice President, James Langley
Senior Vice President, Bryn A. Fosburgh, $451,000 total compensation
Senior Vice President, General Counsel, Secretary, James A. Kirkland, $413,000 total compensation
Chief Financial Officer, David G. Barnes
Lead Independent Director, Director, Mark S. Peek
Director, James C. Dalton
Director, Börje Ekholm
Director, Kaigham (Ken) Gabriel
Director, Meaghan Lloyd
Director, Sandra MacQuillan
Director, Johan Wibergh
Director, Ann Fandozzi
Auditors : Ernst & Young LLP

LOCATIONS

HQ: Trimble Inc
935 Stewart Drive, Sunnyvale, CA 94085

Phone: 408 481-8000
Web: www.trimble.com

2018

	$ mil.	% of total
North America	1,670	53
Europe	873.5	28
Asia/Pacific	418.3	14
Other	170.2	5
Total	3,132	100

PRODUCTS/OPERATIONS

2018 Sales

	$ in mil.	% of total
Buildings and Infrastructure	1,087.7	35
Geospatial	723.1	23
Resources and Utilities	568.1	18
Transportation	753.1	24
Total	3,132	100

COMPETITORS

ASPEN TECHNOLOGY, INC.
FARO TECHNOLOGIES, INC.
ITRON, INC.
MEGGITT PLC
MTS SYSTEMS CORPORATION
ONTO INNOVATION INC.
ROCKWELL AUTOMATION, INC.
ROPER TECHNOLOGIES, INC.
RUDOLPH TECHNOLOGIES, INC.
SPECTRIS PLC

HISTORICAL FINANCIALS

Company Type: Public

Income Statement — FYE: December 31

	REVENUE ($mil)	NET INCOME ($mil)	NET PROFIT MARGIN	EMPLOYEES
12/21*	3,659.1	492.7	13.5%	11,931
01/21	3,147.7	389.9	12.4%	11,402
01/20	3,264.3	514.3	15.8%	11,484
12/18	3,108.4	282.8	9.1%	11,287
12/17	2,654.2	121.1	4.6%	9,523
Annual Growth	8.4%	42.0%	—	5.8%

*Fiscal year change

2021 Year-End Financials

Debt ratio: 18.2%
Return on equity: 13.1%
Cash ($ mil.): 325.7
Current Ratio: 1.22
Long-term debt ($ mil.): 1,293.2
No. of shares ($ mil.): 250.9
Dividends
  Yield: —
  Payout: —
Market value ($ mil.): 21,876.0

	STOCK PRICE ($) FY Close	P/E High/Low		PER SHARE ($) Earnings	Dividends	Book Value
12/21*	87.19	49	34	1.94	0.00	15.72
01/21	66.77	43	14	1.55	0.00	14.34
01/20	41.51	22	15	2.03	0.00	12.48
12/18	31.94	40	27	1.12	0.00	10.66
12/17	40.64	89	61	0.47	0.00	9.51
Annual Growth	21.0%	—	—	42.5%	—	13.4%

*Fiscal year change

TriState Capital Holdings Inc

TriState Capital Holdings has found its niche right in the middle of the banking industry. The holding company owns TriState Capital Bank, a regional business bank that caters to middle-market businesses, executives and high-net-worth individuals. TriState Capital has three wholly owned subsidiaries: TriState Capital Bank, Chartwell Investment Partners, LLC and Chartwell TSC Securities Corp. Its loan portfolio consists of less than 50% for middle-market banking loans, less than 30% commercial real estate loans, and more than 50% for private banking loans. The bank serves clients from branches in Cleveland; New Jersey; New York City, Philadelphia, and Pittsburgh. Altogether, it has $7.6 billion in assets.

Operations

The company operates two reportable segments: Bank and Investment Management.

The Bank segment provides commercial banking products and services to middle-market businesses and private banking products and services to high-net-worth individuals through the Bank. The Investment Management segment provides investment management services primarily to institutional investors, mutual funds and individual investors through Chartwell and also supports marketing efforts for Chartwell's proprietary investment products through CTSC Securities.

Geographic Reach

Headquartered in Pittsburgh, Pennsylvania, the company also leases office space for each of the four representative bank offices in the metropolitan areas of Philadelphia, Pennsylvania; Cleveland, Ohio; Edison, New Jersey; and New York, New York; and it leases office space for Chartwell Investment Partners, LLC in Berwyn, Pennsylvania.

Sales and Marketing

The company caters to middle-market businesses. Its primary markets and private banking business also serve high-net-worth individuals on a national basis. It primarily sources this business through referral relationships with independent broker/dealers, wealth managers, family offices, trust companies and other financial intermediaries. In addition, its distribution channels pursue and create deposit relationships, including treasury management relationships, with customers in its primary markets and throughout the US.

Financial Performance

In 2019, total revenue increased $18.0 million, or 11%, to $179.4 million from $161.4 million in 2018, driven largely by higher net interest income and swap fees for the Bank.

In 2019, the company's net was $54.4 million compared to $52.3 million in 2018, an increase of $2.1 million, or 4%. This increase was primarily due to the net impact of a $13.7 million, or 12%, increase in its net interest income; an increase in the credit to provision for loan and lease losses of $0.8 million; an increase of $4.9 million, or 10%, in non-interest income; offset by an increase of $11.0 million, or 11%, in our non-interest expense; a $2.5 million increase in income taxes; and an increase in preferred stock dividends of $3.6 million.

Cash held by the company at the end of 2019 increased to $403.9 million compared to the prior year with $213.9 million. Cash provided by operations and financing activities were $68.2 million and $1.6 billion, respectively. Cash used for investing activities was $1.5 billion, mainly for net increase in loans and leases.

Strategy

Tristate Capital's success has been built upon the vision and focus of its executive management team to combine the sophisticated products, services and risk management efforts of a large financial institution with the personalized service of a community bank. The company believe that a results-based culture, combined with a well-managed middle-market and private banking business, and its targeted investment management business, will continue to grow and generate attractive returns for shareholders. The following are the key components of the company's business strategies: Sales and Distribution Culture; Disciplined Risk Management; Experienced Professionals; Lending Strategy; Deposit Funding Strategy; and Investment Management Strategy.

Company Background

TriState Capital was founded in 2007 by two banking industry executives -- chairman and CEO James Getz, who spent 20 years at Federated Investors, and vice chairman William Schenck, the former secretary of banking for Pennsylvania.

EXECUTIVES

Executive Chairman, Chairman, Subsidiary Officer, Director, James F. Getz, $945,000 total compensation

Vice-Chairman, Subsidiary Officer, Director, A. William Schenck, $425,000 total compensation

President, Chief Executive Officer, Subsidiary Officer, Director, Brian S. Fetterolf, $495,833 total compensation

Executive Vice President, Chief Financial Officer, Subsidiary Officer, David J. Demas, $450,000 total compensation

Executive Officer, Subsidiary Officer, Timothy J. Riddle

Director, E. H. "Gene" Dewhurst

Director, Audrey Palombo Dunning

Director, John B. Yasinsky

Director, Anthony J. Buzzelli

Director, Helen Hanna Casey

Director, David L. Bonvenuto

Director, James J. Dolan

Director, Kim A. Ruth

Director, Michael Harris

Director, Christopher M. Doody
Auditors : KPMG LLP

LOCATIONS

HQ: TriState Capital Holdings Inc
One Oxford Centre, 301 Grant Street, Suite 2700,
Pittsburgh, PA 15219
Phone: 412 304-0304   **Fax:** 412 304-0391
Web: www.tristatecapitalbank.com

PRODUCTS/OPERATIONS

2015 Sales

	$ mil	% of total
Interest income		
Loans	79.2	67
Investments	3.6	3
Interest-earning deposits	0.4	-
Noninterest income		
Investment management fees	29.6	25
Commitment and other fees	2.0	2
Other income	4.3	3
Total	119.1	100

COMPETITORS

BANK OF THE WEST
BANKERS TRUST COMPANY
BOSTON PRIVATE FINANCIAL HOLDINGS, INC.
CITY NATIONAL CORPORATION
KEYCORP
PEOPLE'S UNITED FINANCIAL, INC.
PRIVATEBANCORP, INC.
REGIONS FINANCIAL CORPORATION
SIGNATURE BANK
THE BANK OF NEW YORK MELLON CORPORATION

HISTORICAL FINANCIALS

Company Type: Public

Income Statement — FYE: December 31

	ASSETS ($mil)	NET INCOME ($mil)	INCOME AS % OF ASSETS	EMPLOYEES
12/20	9,896.8	45.2	0.5%	308
12/19	7,765.8	60.1	0.8%	276
12/18	6,035.6	54.4	0.9%	257
12/17	4,777.8	37.9	0.8%	230
12/16	3,930.4	28.6	0.7%	224
Annual Growth	26.0%	12.1%	—	8.3%

2020 Year-End Financials

Return on assets: 0.5%   Dividends
Return on equity: 6.5%   Yield: —
Long-term debt ($ mil.): —   Payout: —
No. of shares ($ mil.): 32.6   Market value ($ mil.): 568.0
Sales ($ mil.): 274.3

	STOCK PRICE ($) FY Close	P/E High/Low		PER SHARE ($) Earnings	Dividends	Book Value
12/20	17.40	20	6	1.30	0.00	23.21
12/19	26.12	13	10	1.89	0.00	21.16
12/18	19.46	16	10	1.81	0.00	16.60
12/17	23.00	18	15	1.32	0.00	13.61
12/16	22.10	22	11	1.01	0.00	12.38
Annual Growth	(5.8%)	—	—	6.5%	—	17.0%

Triumph Bancorp Inc

EXECUTIVES

Chairman, Subsidiary Officer, Director, Carlos M. Sepulveda
Vice-Chairman, President, Chief Executive Officer, Subsidiary Officer, Director, Aaron P. Graft, $515,000 total compensation
Executive Vice President, Chief Operating Officer, Subsidiary Officer, Edward J. Schreyer
Executive Vice President, Chief Financial Officer, Subsidiary Officer, William Bradley Voss
Executive Vice President, Chief Regulatory and Governance Officer, Secretary, Subsidiary Officer, Gail Lehmann, $275,000 total compensation
Executive Vice President, General Counsel, Assistant Secretary, Subsidiary Officer, Adam D. Nelson, $265,000 total compensation
Subsidiary Officer, Melissa Forman-Barenblit
Subsidiary Officer, Todd Ritterbusch
Director, Davis R. Deadman
Director, Harrison B. Barnes
Director, Charles A. Anderson
Director, Debra A. Bradford
Director, Richard L. Davis
Director, Laura K. Easley
Director, Maribess L. Miller
Director, Michael P. Rafferty
Director, C. Todd Sparks
Auditors : Crowe LLP

LOCATIONS

HQ: Triumph Bancorp Inc
12700 Park Central Drive, Suite 1700, Dallas, TX 75251
Phone: 214 365-6900
Web: www.triumphbancorp.com

HISTORICAL FINANCIALS

Company Type: Public

Income Statement — FYE: December 31

	ASSETS ($mil)	NET INCOME ($mil)	INCOME AS % OF ASSETS	EMPLOYEES
12/21	5,956.2	112.9	1.9%	1,250
12/20	5,935.7	64.0	1.1%	1,126
12/19	5,060.2	58.5	1.2%	1,107
12/18	4,559.7	51.7	1.1%	1,122
12/17	3,499.0	36.2	1.0%	821
Annual Growth	14.2%	32.9%	—	11.1%

2021 Year-End Financials

Return on assets: 1.8%   Dividends
Return on equity: 14.2%   Yield: —
Long-term debt ($ mil.): —   Payout: —
No. of shares ($ mil.): 25.1   Market value ($ mil.): 2,996.0
Sales ($ mil.): 442

	STOCK PRICE ($) FY Close	P/E High/Low		PER SHARE ($) Earnings	Dividends	Book Value
12/21	119.08	30	11	4.35	0.00	34.14
12/20	48.55	20	8	2.53	0.00	29.23
12/19	38.02	17	12	2.25	0.00	25.50
12/18	29.70	22	13	2.03	0.00	23.62
12/17	31.50	19	11	1.81	0.00	18.81
Annual Growth	39.4%	—	—	24.5%	—	16.1%

TTEC Holdings Inc

TTEC Holdings (formerly known as TeleTech Holdings) is leading global customer experience as a service (CXaaS) provider for a number of brands. The company provides a range of business process outsourcing (BPO) services including customer acquisition, customer care, tech support, and order fulfillment services, as well as digitally enabled back office and specialty services. The company delivered its inshore, nearshore and offshore services to about 20 countries on six continents. Customers are mainly major global enterprises such as automotive, communications, financial services, government, health care, logistics, media and entertainment retail, technology and travel and transportation industries. TTEC also offers management consulting services. Most of the company's sales are generated in the US accounting to around 70% of total sales.

Operations

The segment information was reported consistent with these updated reportable segments comprised of TTEC Engage and TTEC Digital.

TTEC Engage segment accounts for more than 80% of revenue and provides the essential technologies, human resources, infrastructure and processes to operate customer care, acquisition, and fraud detection and prevention services. It operated under three services: Customer Acquisition; Customer Care and, Digitally enabled back office and specialty services.

TTEC Digital segment (generates about 20% of company's total revenue) designs, builds and delivers tech-enabled, insight-based and outcome-driven customer experience solutions through its professional services and suite of technology offerings. It also provides Technology Services and Professional Services.

Geographic Reach

Headquartered in Englewood, Colorado, TTEC has almost more than 70 customer engagement centers across North America (US, Mexico, Canada), Europe (Bulgaria, the UK, Ireland, Germany, Poland, Greece), and Asia (Thailand, India) and the Pacific Rim (China, the Philippines, Australia). The company also has centers in South Africa and Brazil.

The US accounts for around 70% of the company's revenue. Other major markets include the Philippines (nearly 25%) and Latin America (some 5%).

Sales and Marketing

TTEC has expertise in several major industries, including automotive, communications, government, healthcare, logistics, financial services, media and entertainment, retail, technology, travel and transportation industries. It targets Fortune 1000 clients and serves about 750 clients around the world.

In 2021, the company's top five and ten clients represented about 40% and 50% of total revenue, respectively. Certain of their communications clients provide them with telecommunication services through arm's length negotiated transactions. These clients currently represent over 5% of the total annual revenue.

Financial Performance

TTEC Holdings' performance for the past five years have continued to increase year-over-year with 2021 as its highest performing year over the period, in terms of revenue.

In 2021, TTEC's revenue increased by almost 17% to $2,273 million over 2020, including an increase of 1.0% or $18.7 million due to foreign currency fluctuations. The increase in revenue was comprised of a $107.1 million, or some 35%, increase for TTEC Digital and a $216.7 million, or 13%, increase for TTEC Engage.

In 2021, profits rose by $22.3 billion to $141.0 billion compared to $118.6 billion in 2020, primarily due to increase in revenue.

Cash on hand at the end of 2021 amounted to $180 billion. Operating activities provided $251.3 million. Investing activities used $541.9 million while financing activities used $319 million. Main cash uses were acquisitions and purchase of property, plant, and equipment.

Strategy

TTEC Holdings aim to grow its revenue and profitability by focusing on its core customer engagement operational capabilities, linking them to higher - margin, insights, and technology-enabled platforms and managed services to drive a superior experience for their clients' customers. To that end the company continually strive to build deeper, more strategic relationships with existing global clients to drive enduring, transformational change within its organizations; Pursue new clients who lead its respective industries and who are committed to customer engagement as a differentiator; Invest in its sales leadership team at both the segment level to improve collaboration and speed-to-market and consultative sales level to deliver more integrated, strategic, and transformational solutions; Execute strategic acquisitions that further complement and expands its integrated solutions; Invest in technology-enabled platforms and innovation through technology advancements, broader and globally protected intellectual property, and process optimization; and Work within the company's technology partner ecosystem to deliver best in class solutions with expanding intellectual property through value-add applications, integrations, services, and solutions.

Mergers and Acquisitions

In 2022, TTEC acquired certain public sector citizen experience and smart city assets of Faneuil, Inc. a wholly owned subsidiary of ALJ Regional Holdings, Inc. The combination of TTEC and the newly acquired business enables TTEC to holistically address fast-growing public sector demand in mobility, fleet management, congestion management, health and wellness, healthcare exchanges, labor and social benefits delivery, tolling and transportation, and emergent infrastructure citizen response systems. The addition of back office capabilities including image review and data annotation processes will build a broader foundation for growth. The acquired business is now part of the TTEC Engage business segment.

In early 2021, TTEC agreed to acquire Avtex, an award-winning full-service CX technology and solutions leader. The acquisition, once completed, will be immediately accretive and highly complementary to TTEC's well-established CX-as-a-Service (CXaaS) customer experience technology and services platform. With this acquisition, TTEC will further expand its position as one of the leading global CX technology innovators and largest providers of end-to-end digital customer experience solutions worldwide.

Company Background

In 1982 Tuchman founded TeleTech. The company m went public in 1996 and continues to expand its operations to Scotland, Canada, Argentina, and Brazil, among other countries. The company shortened its name to TTEC in 2018.

EXECUTIVES

Chief Executive Officer, Chairman, Director, Kenneth D. Tuchman, $1 total compensation
President, Division Officer, Michelle Swanback
Chief Risk Officer, General Counsel, Margaret B. McLean, $354,846 total compensation
Chief Revenue Officer, Judi A. Hand, $400,000 total compensation
Division Officer, David J. Seybold
Senior Vice President, Global Controller, Interim Chief Financial Officer, Francois Bourret
Division Officer, Richard Sean Erickson
Division Officer, George S. Demou
Director, Steven J. Anenen
Director, Tracy L. Bahl
Director, Gregory A. Conley
Director, Robert N. Frerichs
Director, Marc L. Holtzman
Director, Gina L. Loften
Director, Ekta Singh-Bushell
Auditors : PricewaterhouseCoopers LLP

LOCATIONS

HQ: TTEC Holdings Inc
9197 South Peoria Street, Englewood, CO 80112
Phone: 303 397-8100
Web: www.ttec.com

2018 Sales

	$ mil.	% of total
US	862.0	57
Philippines	351.8	23
Latin America	109.1	7
Europe, Middle East & Africa	67.2	5
Canada	61.1	4
Asia/Pacific	58.0	4
Total	1,509.2	100

PRODUCTS/OPERATIONS

2018 Sales

	$ mil.	% of total
Customer Management Services	1,129.1	75
Customer Technology Services	170.2	11
Customer Growth Services	141.3	9
Customer Strategy Services	68.6	5
Total	1,509.2	100

Selected Operations & Services

Account collections
Benefits and claims administration
Complex customer management
Customer acquisition
Customer retention
Customer support
Data collection
Direct sales and marketing
Loan processing
Outbound calling
Payroll administration
Recruiting, staffing, and workforce management
Service provisioning
Training development and delivery
Vendor management
Consulting
Technology
Care services
Growth services

COMPETITORS

EPLUS INC.
FIRCROFT ENGINEERING SERVICES LIMITED
HUDSON GLOBAL, INC.
KELLY SERVICES, INC.
KFORCE INC.
MANPOWERGROUP INC.
ROBERT HALF INTERNATIONAL INC.
SYNNEX CORPORATION
TRUEBLUE, INC.
VIRTUSA CORPORATION

HISTORICAL FINANCIALS

Company Type: Public

Income Statement FYE: December 31

	REVENUE ($mil)	NET INCOME ($mil)	NET PROFIT MARGIN	EMPLOYEES
12/20	1,949.2	118.6	6.1%	61,000
12/19	1,643.7	77.1	4.7%	49,500
12/18	1,509.1	35.8	2.4%	52,400
12/17	1,477.3	7.2	0.5%	56,000
12/16	1,275.2	33.6	2.6%	48,000
Annual Growth	11.2%	37.0%	—	6.2%

2020 Year-End Financials

Debt ratio: 25.4% No. of shares ($ mil.): 46.7
Return on equity: 27.4% Dividends
Cash ($ mil.): 132.9 Yield: 3.9%
Current Ratio: 1.66 Payout: 132.1%
Long-term debt ($ mil.): 385 Market value ($ mil.): 3,409.0

	STOCK PRICE ($) FY Close	P/E High/Low		PER SHARE ($) Earnings	Dividends	Book Value
12/20	72.93	31	11	2.52	2.88	9.51
12/19	39.62	30	17	1.65	0.62	9.00
12/18	28.57	54	31	0.77	0.55	7.47
12/17	40.25	271	180	0.16	0.47	7.76
12/16	30.50	45	34	0.71	0.39	7.70
Annual Growth	24.4%	—	—	37.3%	65.4%	5.4%

Turning Point Brands Inc

EXECUTIVES

Chairman, Director, David E. Glazek
President, Chief Executive Officer, Subsidiary Officer, Director, Lawrence S. Wexler, $749,995 total compensation
Senior Vice President, General Counsel, Secretary, James W. Dobbins, $379,875 total compensation
Chief Financial Officer, Senior Vice President, Robert M. Lavan, $274,615 total compensation
Chief Operating Officer, Graham A. Purdy
Director, Gregory H.A. Baxter
Director, H. C. Charles Diao
Director, Ashley Davis Frushone
Director, Peggy Hwan Hebard
Director, Arnold Zimmerman
Auditors : RSM US LLP

LOCATIONS

HQ: Turning Point Brands Inc
5201 Interchange Way, Louisville, KY 40229
Phone: 502 778-4421
Web: www.turningpointbrands.com

HISTORICAL FINANCIALS
Company Type: Public

Income Statement — FYE: December 31

	REVENUE ($mil)	NET INCOME ($mil)	NET PROFIT MARGIN	EMPLOYEES
12/20	405.1	33.0	8.2%	408
12/19	361.9	13.7	3.8%	466
12/18	332.6	25.2	7.6%	520
12/17	285.7	20.2	7.1%	289
12/16	206.2	26.9	13.1%	286
Annual Growth	18.4%	5.3%	—	9.3%

2020 Year-End Financials
Debt ratio: 62.6%
Return on equity: 28.2%
Cash ($ mil.): 41.7
Current Ratio: 2.78
Long-term debt ($ mil.): 294
No. of shares ($ mil.): 19.1
Dividends
  Yield: 0.4%
  Payout: 11.9%
Market value ($ mil.): 853.0

	STOCK PRICE ($) FY Close	P/E High/Low		PER SHARE ($) Earnings	Dividends	Book Value
12/20	44.56	28	9	1.67	0.20	6.63
12/19	28.60	78	29	0.69	0.18	5.42
12/18	27.22	34	15	1.28	0.17	4.23
12/17	21.13	20	12	1.04	0.04	2.78
12/16	12.25	10	4	1.49	0.00	1.85
Annual Growth	38.1%	—	—	2.9%	—	37.6%

Turtle Beach Corp

Using proprietary technology, Turtle Beach (formerly Parametric Sound) makes speakers that offer focused and directional sound for an immersive experience. Its current product is the HS-3000 line of speakers for the commercial market including digital kiosks and slot machines. The company is developing its Hypersonic line for the consumer market where it hopes its thin, two-speaker system will rival traditional multi-speaker setups used for surround sound and be used in computers, video games, and mobile devices. Turtle Beach sells its products in North America, Asia, and Europe to OEMs for inclusion in new and existing products.

EXECUTIVES

President, Chief Executive Officer, Subsidiary Officer, Chairman, Director, Juergen M. Stark, $550,000 total compensation
Chief Financial Officer, Treasurer, Secretary, John T. Hanson, $360,500 total compensation
Lead Independent Director, Director, William E. Keitel
Director, Andrew L. Wolfe
Director, L. Gregory Ballard
Director, Katherine Lee Scherping
Director, Michelle D. Wilson
Director, Brian Stech
Director, Terry Jimenez
Director, Julia W. Sze
Auditors : BDO USA, LLP

LOCATIONS

HQ: Turtle Beach Corp
44 South Broadway, 4th Floor, White Plains, NY 10601
Phone: 888 496-8001
Web: www.parametricsound.com

COMPETITORS

CAMBRIDGE MECHATRONICS LIMITED
CONTROL4 CORPORATION
FKA DISTRIBUTING CO., LLC
FRONTIER SMART TECHNOLOGIES LIMITED
HIWAVE TECHNOLOGIES PLC
MICROVISION, INC.
QSC, LLC
SARANTEL LIMITED
SKULLCANDY, INC.
VENTURE CORPORATION LIMITED

HISTORICAL FINANCIALS
Company Type: Public

Income Statement — FYE: December 31

	REVENUE ($mil)	NET INCOME ($mil)	NET PROFIT MARGIN	EMPLOYEES
12/20	360.0	38.7	10.8%	300
12/19	234.6	17.9	7.6%	245
12/18	287.4	39.1	13.6%	154
12/17	149.1	(3.2)	—	135
12/16	173.9	(87.1)	—	172
Annual Growth	19.9%	—	—	14.9%

2020 Year-End Financials
Debt ratio: —
Return on equity: 42.9%
Cash ($ mil.): 46.6
Current Ratio: 2.16
Long-term debt ($ mil.): —
No. of shares ($ mil.): 15.4
Dividends
  Yield: —
  Payout: —
Market value ($ mil.): 333.0

	STOCK PRICE ($) FY Close	P/E High/Low		PER SHARE ($) Earnings	Dividends	Book Value
12/20	21.55	10	2	2.37	0.00	7.52
12/19	9.45	14	7	1.04	0.00	4.38
12/18	14.27	11	0	2.74	0.00	2.63
12/17	0.45	—	—	(0.28)	0.00	(1.79)
12/16	1.31	—	—	(7.16)	0.00	(1.68)
Annual Growth	101.4%	—	—	—	—	—

Tyler Technologies, Inc.

Tyler Technologies is a major provider of integrated information management solutions and services for the public sector, with a focus on local governments. Tyler's products include software for accounting and financial management, filing court documents electronically, tracking and managing court cases, and automating appraisals and assessments. In addition to its electronic document filing (e-filing) solutions, the company also provides digital government services and payment solutions. The company counts approximately 3,000 counties, some 36,000 cities and towns and approximately 12,900 school districts customers in all 50 states, Canada, the Caribbean, Australia, the UK, and other international locations.

Operations

The company divides its operations into three segments ? Enterprise software, NIC, and Appraisal and tax.

Enterprise software, which accounts for some 70% of sales, provides public sector entities with software systems and services to meet their information technology and automation needs for mission-critical "back-office" functions such as: financial management; courts and justice processes; public safety; planning, regulatory and maintenance; data analytics; and platform technologies. NIC segment generates about 25% of sales. Appraisal and tax segment, which makes up the other more than 5% of sales, provides systems and software that automate the appraisal and assessment of real and personal property, land and vital records management as well as property appraisal outsourcing services for local governments and taxing authorities.

Property appraisal outsourcing services include: the physical inspection of commercial and residential properties; data collection and processing; computer analysis for property valuation; preparation of tax rolls; community education; and arbitration between taxpayers and the assessing jurisdiction.

Overall, around 50% of sales comes from subscription, maintenance accounts for approximately 30%, software services account for over 15%, and software licenses and royalties with some 5%. Appraisal services and hardware and other account for the rest.

Geographic Reach

Headquartered in Texas, Tyler owns or leases offices for its major operations in the states of Arizona, Arkansas, California, Colorado, Connecticut, Georgia, Illinois, Iowa, Maine, Massachusetts, Michigan, Missouri, Montana, New Hampshire, New York, North Carolina, Ohio, Tennessee, Texas, Virginia, Washington, Washington D.C., Wisconsin, Ontario and British Columbia, Canada, Bahamas, and the Philippines.

Sales and Marketing

The company uses a direct sales force and marketing personnel. It participates in government associations and attends annual meetings, trade shows, and educational events to attract new customers. Its customers are primarily county and municipal agencies, school districts, and other local government offices.

Financial Performance

The company's revenue has been climbing consistently in the last few years. It has an overall increase of 89% between 2017 and 2021. Its net income has been declining in the same period with the exception of 2020. It has an overall decline of 5% between 2017 and 2021.

Tyler's revenue increased 43% from $1.1 billion in 2020 to $1.6 billion in 2021. Subscription-based revenue increased 124% compared to 2020, primarily due to the inclusion of NIC's revenues from the date of acquisition.

In 2021, the company had a net income of $161.5 million, a 17% decrease from the previous year's net income of $194.8 million. The decrease was primarily due to a higher volume of subscriptions, software services and maintenance cost.

The company's cash at the end of 2021 was $309.2 million. Operating activities generated $371.8 million, while investing activities used $2.1 billion, mainly for cost of acquisitions. Financing activities generated another $1.4 billion.

Strategy

The company's objective is to grow its revenue and earnings organically, supplemented by focused strategic acquisitions.

The key components of its business strategy are to: Provide high quality, value-added products and services to its clients; Continue to expand its product and service offerings; Expand its client base; Expand its existing client relationships; Grow recurring revenues; Maximize economies of scale and take advantage of financial leverage in its business; Attract and retain highly qualified employees; Pursue selected strategic acquisitions; and Establish strategic alliances.

Mergers and Acquisitions

In mid- 2022, Tyler Technologies acquired Quatred, a systems integrator and solution provider that assists clients with implementing advanced touchless technologies, including barcoding. The acquisition allows Tyler to leverage its current ERP client base, as well as drive growth opportunities in public safety and public administration. The acquisition will provide a single barcoding solution for all Tyler platforms.

In early 2022, Tyler Technologies acquired US eDirect, a market-leading provider of technology solutions for campground and outdoor recreation management. Through this acquisition, Tyler will add US eDirect's Recreation Dynamics product to its digital government and payment services. Recreation Dynamics is a large-scale, enterprise-grade cloud transaction management system focused on the government recreation and tourism industry.

In late 2021, Tyler Technologies acquired Arx, a cloud-based software platform which creates accessible technology to enable a modern-day police force that is fully transparent, accountable, and a trusted resource to the community it serves. "The acquisition of Arx allows Tyler to offer a full suite of public safety solutions designed to maximize efficiency and safety for law enforcement officers while increasing transparency and trust-building with the communities they serve," said Bryan Proctor, president of Tyler's Public Safety Division.

Also in late 2021, Tyler Technologies completed the previously announced acquisition of VendEngine, a privately-held cloud-based software provider focused on financial technology for the corrections market, for approximately $84 million in cash. Tyler's acquisition of VendEngine enables both companies to better respond to the evolving needs of local and state government agencies, and the residents they serve.

In mid-2021, Tyler Technologies completed the previously announced acquisition of Kansas-based, NIC, a leading digital government solutions and payments company that serves more than 7,100 federal, state, and local government agencies across the nation for approximately $2.3 billion. With the addition of NIC's highly complementary, industry-leading digital government solutions and payment services to Tyler's broad client base and multiple sales channels, the combined company will be well equipped to address the tremendous demand at the federal, state, and local levels for innovative platform solutions.

Also in mid-2021, Tyler Technologies, Inc. acquired ReadySub, a cloud-based platform, based in Washington, which assists school districts with absence tracking, filling substitute teacher assignments, and automating essential payroll processes. The acquisition of ReadySub strengthens Tyler's school portfolio and brings more comprehensive solutions to the school districts that it serves. Additionally, ReadySub can integrate with districts' payroll processes, eliminating duplicate work and streamlining related payroll tasks. Terms were not disclosed.

In early 2021, Tyler Technologies, Inc. acquired DataSpec, a market leader dedicated to providing better electronic management of veterans' claims, based in Michigan. DataSpec was developed by sisters Tina Roff and Ann Graham. The acquisition offers existing DataSpec clients the strength and stability of Tyler, as well as a simple path forward to a next generation of technology. This acquisition will position Tyler as the new market leader in veterans' benefits management solutions. Tyler also has the opportunity to expand its veteran-focused software offerings to VA departments in additional states. Terms were not disclosed.

Company Background

Formerly an auto parts and supplies company established in 1966, Tyler sold its chain of auto parts stores in 1999 and used acquisitions to transform itself into a provider of software for the local government and education markets

EXECUTIVES

Executive Chairman, Director, John S. Marr, $300,000 total compensation

President, Chief Executive Officer, H. Lynn Moore, $500,000 total compensation

Executive Vice President, Chief Financial Officer, Treasurer, Brian K. Miller, $383,000 total compensation

Chief Legal Officer, Corporate Secretary, Abigail (Abby) Diaz

Director, Donald R. Brattain

Director, Glenn A. Carter

Director, Brenda A. Cline

Director, J. Luther King

Director, Mary L. Landrieu

Director, Daniel M. Pope

Auditors : Ernst & Young LLP

LOCATIONS

HQ: Tyler Technologies, Inc.
  5101 Tennyson Parkway, Plano, TX 75024
Phone: 972 713-3700
Web: www.tylertech.com

Mergers and Acquisitions
FY2012
Akanda Innovation (geographic information system software)
Computer Software Associates (financial management systems)
EnerGov Solutions (land management software)
UniFund (enterprise resource planning)
FY2011
Windsor Management Group (education software)
  Yotta MVS (field property data verification and collection software)
FY2010
Cole-Layer-Trumble (government appraisal software)
Wiznet (electronic document filing software)
FY2009
PulseMark (data warehousing software)

PRODUCTS/OPERATIONS

2014 Sales

	$ mil	% of total
Enterprise software	438.6	89
Appraisal & tax software	54.8	11
Corporate	(0.3)	-
Total	493.1	100

2014 Sales

	$ mil	% of total
Maintenance	212.7	43
Software services	113.8	23
Subscriptions	87.8	18
Software licenses and royalties	49.1	10
Appraisal services	21.8	4
Hardware & other	7.9	2
Total	493.1	100

Selected Products
Appraisal and assessment software (property appraisal and assessment)
Criminal justice software (court case tracking and management)
Document management and recording software (image storage and retrieval)
Education software
Finance and accounting software
Law enforcement and corrections software (police dispatch, records, and jail management)
Municipal court software (case management)
Odyssey (case and court management)
Public Records and content management
Tax collections software (tax collections office operations)
Utility billing software (billing and collections)

Selected Services
Information technology and professional services
Maintenance
Outsourced property appraisals for tax jurisdictions

COMPETITORS

ACI WORLDWIDE, INC.
BLACK KNIGHT, INC.
CA, INC.
CONDUENT INCORPORATED
CORNERSTONE ONDEMAND, INC.
DST SYSTEMS, INC.
EGAIN CORPORATION
IDOX PLC
JAGGAER, LLC
SS&C TECHNOLOGIES HOLDINGS, INC.

HISTORICAL FINANCIALS
Company Type: Public

Income Statement — FYE: December 31

	REVENUE ($mil)	NET INCOME ($mil)	NET PROFIT MARGIN	EMPLOYEES
12/21	1,592.2	161.4	10.1%	6,800
12/20	1,116.6	194.8	17.4%	5,536
12/19	1,086.4	146.5	13.5%	5,368
12/18	935.2	147.4	15.8%	4,525
12/17	840.6	163.9	19.5%	4,069
Annual Growth	17.3%	(0.4%)	—	13.7%

2021 Year-End Financials
Debt ratio: 28.3%
Return on equity: 7.4%
Cash ($ mil.): 309.1
Current Ratio: 1.16
Long-term debt ($ mil.): 1,311.2
No. of shares ($ mil.): 41.3
Dividends
  Yield: —
  Payout: —
Market value ($ mil.): 22,226.0

	STOCK PRICE ($) FY Close	P/E High	P/E Low	PER SHARE ($) Earnings	Dividends	Book Value
12/21	537.95	140	96	3.82	0.00	56.25
12/20	436.52	95	54	4.69	0.00	48.99
12/19	300.02	79	47	3.65	0.00	41.14
12/18	185.82	65	45	3.68	0.00	34.61
12/17	177.05	42	33	4.18	0.00	30.81
Annual Growth	32.0%	—	—	(2.2%)	—	16.2%

U&I Financial Corp

Auditors: Moss Adams LLP

LOCATIONS

HQ: U&I Financial Corp
  19315 Highway 99, Lynnwood, WA 98036
Phone: 425 275-9700
Web: www.unibankusa.com

HISTORICAL FINANCIALS
Company Type: Public

Income Statement — FYE: December 31

	REVENUE ($mil)	NET INCOME ($mil)	NET PROFIT MARGIN	EMPLOYEES
12/20	21.3	6.2	29.1%	0
12/19	20.1	5.6	27.9%	0
12/18	16.0	4.5	28.1%	0
12/17	12.6	3.1	25.3%	0
12/16	14.1	3.5	25.2%	0
Annual Growth	10.8%	14.8%	—	—

2020 Year-End Financials
Debt ratio: 1.2%
Return on equity: 11.3%
Cash ($ mil.): 24.9
Current Ratio: 0.08
Long-term debt ($ mil.): 5
No. of shares ($ mil.): 5.5
Dividends
  Yield: —
  Payout: —
Market value ($ mil.): 50.0

	STOCK PRICE ($) FY Close	P/E High	P/E Low	PER SHARE ($) Earnings	Dividends	Book Value
12/20	8.90	9	6	1.12	0.00	10.59
12/19	9.25	9	8	1.02	0.00	9.05
12/18	9.00	12	10	0.82	0.34	7.72
12/17	9.00	16	14	0.58	0.24	7.23
12/16	8.50	13	10	0.71	0.00	7.41
Annual Growth	1.2%	—	—	12.1%	—	9.4%

Ubiquiti Inc

EXECUTIVES

Chief Executive Officer, Chairman, Director, Robert J. Pera, $0 total compensation
Chief Accounting Officer, Chief Financial Officer, Kevin Radigan, $367,500 total compensation
Director, Ronald A. Sege
Director, Brandon Arrindell
Director, Rafael Torres
Auditors : KPMG LLP

LOCATIONS

HQ: Ubiquiti Inc
  685 Third Avenue, 27th Floor, New York, NY 10017
Phone: 646 780-7958
Web: www.ubnt.com

HISTORICAL FINANCIALS
Company Type: Public

Income Statement — FYE: June 30

	REVENUE ($mil)	NET INCOME ($mil)	NET PROFIT MARGIN	EMPLOYEES
06/21	1,898.0	616.5	32.5%	1,223
06/20	1,284.5	380.2	29.6%	1,021
06/19	1,161.7	322.6	27.8%	955
06/18	1,016.8	196.2	19.3%	843
06/17	865.2	257.5	29.8%	725
Annual Growth	21.7%	24.4%	—	14.0%

2021 Year-End Financials
Debt ratio: 55.1%
Return on equity: —
Cash ($ mil.): 249.4
Current Ratio: 2.51
Long-term debt ($ mil.): 467
No. of shares ($ mil.): 62.5
Dividends
  Yield: 0.5%
  Payout: 18.2%
Market value ($ mil.): 19,538.0

	STOCK PRICE ($) FY Close	P/E High	P/E Low	PER SHARE ($) Earnings	Dividends	Book Value
06/21	312.19	40	16	9.78	1.60	0.04
06/20	174.56	34	19	5.80	1.20	(4.64)
06/19	131.50	38	18	4.51	1.00	1.43
06/18	84.72	35	20	2.51	0.00	4.26
06/17	51.97	20	12	3.09	0.00	7.50
Annual Growth	56.6%	—	—	33.4%	—	(72.5%)

Ultra Clean Holdings Inc

Ultra Clean Holdings is a leading developer and supplier of critical subsystems, components, parts, and ultra-high purity cleaning and analytical services primarily for the semiconductor industry. The company, which does business as Ultra Clean Technology (UCT), designs, engineers, and manufactures production tools, modules and subsystems for the semiconductor and display capital equipment markets. UCT has extended its know-how in the semiconductor industry to move into display, consumer, medical, industrial, research, and energy markets.

Majority of the company's sales were generated outside the US. UCT was founded as a unit of Mitsubishi Metals in 1991.

Operations

The company operates and reports results for two operating segments: Products (around 85% of sales) and Services (nearly 15%).

Its Products business primarily designs, engineers and manufactures production tools, modules and subsystems for the semiconductor and display capital equipment markets. Products include chemical delivery modules, frame assemblies, gas delivery systems, fluid delivery systems, precision robotics, process modules as well as other high-level assemblies.

Its Services business provides ultra-high purity parts cleaning, process tool part recoating, surface encapsulation and high sensitivity micro contamination analysis primarily for the semiconductor device makers and wafer fabrication equipment (WFE) markets.

Geographic Reach

Headquartered in Hayward, California, Ultra Clean Technology has manufacturing and engineering facilities in California, Texas, Arizona, China, Malaysia, Singapore, South Korea, United Kingdom, Philippines and Czech Republic. The company has parts cleaning, analytics and engineering facilities in Colorado, Arizona, California, Oregon, Maine, Texas, Israel, Taiwan, South Korea, Singapore and China. It also owns buildings and land that are located in South Korea, China and the UK.

Approximately 35% of sales were generated in the US, followed by Singapore with over 35%, while Korea, Taiwan, China, and Austria generated around 5% each.

Sales and Marketing

Ultra Clean Technology sells its products and services primarily to customers in the semiconductor capital equipment and semiconductor integrated device manufacturing industries, and it also sells to the display, consumer, medical, energy, industrial, and research equipment industries. The majority of its total revenues comes from the semiconductor capital equipment industry (OEM customers), which is highly concentrated. After several round of consolidation in the semiconductor industry, just two customers account for about 65% of UCT's revenue. They are LAM Research, and Applied Materials, which accounted for more than 10% each.

Financial Performance

The company had a total revenue of $2.1 billion in 2021, a 50% increase from the previous year's total revenue of $1.4 billion in 2020. This was primarily due to an increase in customer demand in the semiconductor industry, in particular, the wafer fabrication equipment industry and in part to the inclusion of Ham-Let which contributed $187.5 million of revenues for fiscal year 2021.

In 2021, the company had a net income of $119.5 million, a 54% increase from the previous year's net income of $77.6 million.

The company's cash at the end of 2021 was $466.5 million. Operating activities generated $211.6 million, while investing activities used $404.8 million, mainly for acquisition of businesses. Financing activities provided another $460.8 million.

Strategy

Ultra Clean Holdings' strategy is to grow its position and enhance its value to its customers as a leading solution and service provider in the semiconductor markets it serves, while supporting other technologically similar markets in the display, consumer, medical, energy, industrial, and research industries.

The company's strategy is comprised of the following key elements: expanding its solutions and service market share with semiconductor OEMs and IDMs; developing or acquiring solutions that allow its customers to succeed at the leading edge of the semiconductor processing nodes; leveraging its geographic presence in lower cost manufacturing regions; providing production flexibility to respond rapidly to demand changes; driving profitable growth with its flexible cost structure; continuing to selectively pursue strategic acquisitions; and strengthening vertical integration.

Mergers and Acquisitions

In early 2021, Ultra Clean has completed the acquisition of Ham-Let (Israel-Canada) Ltd. (Ham-Let) for approximately $351 million. Ham-Let Group is one of the world's leading companies in development, manufacturing, and distribution of industrial flow control systems ? connectors, fittings and valves for high pressure and high temperatures transmission systems (gases and liquids). The acquisition expands UCT's addressable market in semiconductors and increases UCT's vertical capabilities and adds high value, high gross margin product offerings.

EXECUTIVES

Chairman, Director, Clarence L. Granger, $51,783 total compensation
Chief Executive Officer, Director, James P. (Jim) Scholhamer, $494,620 total compensation
Finance Senior Vice President, Finance Chief Financial Officer, Finance Chief Accounting Officer, Sheri L. Savage, $441,694 total compensation
Chief Operating Officer, Vijayan S. Chinnasami
Chief Accounting Officer, Brian E. Harding
Division Officer, Amir Widmann
Division Officer, Christopher S. Cook
Division Officer, William C. Bentinck
Director, David T. ibnAle
Director, Emily M. Liggett
Director, Thomas T. Edman
Director, Barbara V. Scherer
Director, Ernest E. Maddock
Director, Jacqueline A. Seto
Auditors: Moss Adams LLP

LOCATIONS

HQ: Ultra Clean Holdings Inc
26462 Corporate Avenue, Hayward, CA 94545
Phone: 510 576-4400
Web: www.uct.com

2016 Sales

	$ mil.	% of total
US	308.1	55
China	13.2	2
Singapore	175.8	31
Austria	35.7	6
Others	29.9	5
Total	562.7	100

Product & Services
Engineering
NPI
Supply Chain Management
Chemical & Gas Delivery
Metal Fabrication
Precision Machining
System Integration
Thermal Control
3D Printing

COMPETITORS

AMKOR TECHNOLOGY, INC.
APPLIED MATERIALS, INC.
APPLIED OPTOELECTRONICS, INC.
ELECTRO SCIENTIFIC INDUSTRIES, INC.
ENTEGRIS, INC.
Fabrinet
MACOM TECHNOLOGY SOLUTIONS HOLDINGS, INC.
MATTSON TECHNOLOGY, INC.
NORTECH SYSTEMS INCORPORATED
RENESAS ELECTRONICS CORPORATION

HISTORICAL FINANCIALS

Company Type: Public

Income Statement — FYE: December 25

	REVENUE ($mil)	NET INCOME ($mil)	NET PROFIT MARGIN	EMPLOYEES
12/20	1,398.6	77.6	5.5%	4,996
12/19	1,066.2	(9.4)	—	4,400
12/18	1,096.5	36.5	3.3%	4,280
12/17	924.3	75.0	8.1%	2,747
12/16	562.7	10.0	1.8%	2,183
Annual Growth	25.6%	66.7%	—	23.0%

2020 Year-End Financials

Debt ratio: 24.4%
Return on equity: 16.0%
Cash ($ mil.): 200.3
Current Ratio: 2.71
Long-term debt ($ mil.): 261.6
No. of shares ($ mil.): 40.6
Dividends
 Yield: —
 Payout: —
Market value ($ mil.): 1,285.0

	STOCK PRICE ($) FY Close	P/E High/Low		PER SHARE ($) Earnings	Dividends	Book Value
12/20	31.65	19	6	1.89	0.00	13.12
12/19	23.40	—	—	(0.24)	0.00	10.94
12/18	8.21	28	8	0.94	0.00	11.17
12/17	23.09	15	4	2.19	0.00	8.92
12/16	9.70	34	15	0.30	0.00	6.56
Annual Growth	34.4%	—	—	58.4%	—	18.9%

UMB Financial Corp

UMB Financial is a financial holding company that provides banking services and asset servicing to its customer in the US and around the globe. The company's national bank, UMB Bank offers a full complement of banking products and other services to commercial, retail, government, and correspondent-bank customers, including a wide range of asset-management, trust, bankcard, and cash-management services. The bank operates about 90 banking centers. Loans represent the company's largest source of interest income, with commercial loans having the largest percent of total loans. Beyond its banking business, it offers insurance, brokerage services, leasing, treasury management, health savings accounts, and proprietary mutual funds.

Operations

The company's products and services are grouped into three segments: Commercial Banking, Institutional Banking, and Personal Banking.

Commercial Banking serves the commercial banking and treasury management needs of the company's small to mid-market businesses through a variety of products and services. Such services include commercial loans, commercial real estate financing, commercial credit cards, letters of credit, loan syndication services, consultative services. Its specialty lending group offers solutions such as asset-based lending, accounts receivable financing, mezzanine debt and minority equity investments. It also offers treasury management services including depository services, account reconciliation and cash management tools. The segment accounts for approximately 50% of total revenue.

Institutional Banking is a combination of banking services, fund services, asset management services, and healthcare services provided to institutional clients. This segment also provides fixed income sales, trading and underwriting, corporate trust and escrow services, as well as institutional custody. It includes UMBFS, which provides fund administration and accounting, investor services and transfer agency, marketing and distribution, custody, and alternative investment services. Healthcare services provides healthcare payment solutions including custodial services for health savings accounts (HSAs) and private label, multipurpose debit cards to insurance carriers, third-party administrators, software companies, employers, and financial institutions. The segment accounts for nearly 30% of total revenue.

Personal Banking combines consumer banking and wealth management services offered to clients and delivered through personal relationships and the company's bank branches, ATM network and internet banking. Products offered include deposit accounts, retail credit cards, private banking, installment loans, home equity lines of credit, residential mortgages, and small business loans. The segment accounts for more than 20% of total revenue.

Overall, net interest income generates approximately 65% of total revenue.

Geographic Reach

UMB Financial is headquartered in Kansas City, Missouri and has branches in Arizona, Colorado, Illinois, Kansas, Nebraska, Oklahoma, and Texas.

Sales and Marketing

UMB Financial serves small to mid-market businesses, institutional clients, insurance carriers, third-party administrators, employers, and financial institutions, among others, through its branches, ATM network, and internet banking.

The company's marketing and business development expenses were approximately $18.5 million, $14.7 million, and $26.3 million in 2021, 2020, and 2019, respectively.

Financial Performance

Company's revenue for fiscal 2021 decreased to $1.28 billion compared from the prior year with $1.29 billion.

Net income for fiscal 2021 increased to $353.0 million compared from the prior year with $286.5 million.

Cash held by the company at the end of fiscal 2021 increased to $9.2 billion. Cash provided by operations and financing activities were $534.1 million and $9.4 billion, respectively. Cash used for investing activities was $4.2 billion, mainly for purchases of securities.

Company Background

To grow its fee-based business and diversify its business model, UMB has made several acquisitions in its past. The company built up its investment advisory and corporate trust business through several 2009 purchases. In 2010, UMB made 10 acquisitions, including Prairie Capital Management and Indiana-based Reams Asset Management. The deals more than doubled UMB's Scout Investment Advisors' assets under management to more than $27 billion.

EXECUTIVES

Chairman, President, Chief Executive Officer, Subsidiary Officer, Region Officer, J. Mariner Kemper, $905,216 total compensation
Operations Executive Vice President, Operations Subsidiary Officer, Kevin M. Macke, $324,077 total compensation
Chief Accounting Officer, David Odgers
Chief Financial Officer, Ramakrishna Shankar, $374,615 total compensation
Chief Lending Officer, Thomas S. Terry, $318,269 total compensation
Executive Vice President, Chief Administrative Officer, Shannon A. Johnson
Secretary, John C. Pauls
Subsidiary Officer, James D. Rine, $396,154 total compensation
Subsidiary Officer, James Cornelius, $364,615 total compensation
Director, Robin C. Beery
Director, Janine A. Davidson
Director, Kevin Charles Gallagher
Director, Greg M. Graves
Director, Alexander C. Kemper
Director, Gordon E. Lansford
Director, Timothy R. Murphy
Director, Tamara M. Peterman
Director, Kris A. Robbins
Director, L. Joshua Sosland
Director, Paul Uhlmann
Director, Leroy J. Williams
Auditors : KPMG LLP

LOCATIONS

HQ: UMB Financial Corp
1010 Grand Boulevard, Kansas City, MO 64106
Phone: 816 860-7000   Fax: 816 860-7143
Web: www.umb.com

PRODUCTS/OPERATIONS

2016 Sales

	$ mil.	% of total
Interest income		
Loans	386.3	29
Securities	131.0	13
Federal funds and resell agreements	2.7	-
Interest-bearing due from banks		2.4
Trading securities		0.6
Non-interest income		
Trust and securities processing	239.9	24
Trading and investment banking	21.5	2
Service charges on deposit accounts	86.7	9
Insurance fees and commissions	4.1	-
Brokerage fees	17.8	2
Bankcard fees	68.8	7
Gains on sales of securities available for sale, net	8.5	1
Equity earnings (losses) on alternative investments	2.7	-
Other	26.1	3
Total	999.1	100

Selected Subsidiaries & Affiliates

Grand Distribution Services, LLC
J.D. Clark & Company
Kansas City Financial Corporation
Kansas City Realty Company
Prairie Capital Management, LLC
Scout Distributors, LLC
Scout Investment Advisors, Inc.
UMB Banc Leasing Corp.
UMB Bank and Trust, n.a.
UMB Bank Arizona, n.a.
UMB Bank Colorado, n.a.
UMB Capital Corporation
UMB Community Development Corporation
UMB Distribution Services, LLC
UMB Financial Services, Inc.
UMB Fund Services, Inc.
UMB Insurance, Inc.
UMB National Bank of America
UMB Realty Company, LLC
UMB Redevelopment Corporation
UMB Trust Company of South Dakota
United Missouri Insurance Company

COMPETITORS

BOKF MERGER CORPORATION NUMBER SIXTEEN

CITY HOLDING COMPANY
COMMERCE BANCSHARES, INC.
FINANCIAL INSTITUTIONS, INC.
FIRST BUSINESS FINANCIAL SERVICES, INC.
FIRST MIDWEST BANCORP, INC.
Laurentian Bank of Canada
PRIVATEBANCORP, INC.
TCF FINANCIAL CORPORATION
WSFS FINANCIAL CORPORATION

HISTORICAL FINANCIALS
Company Type: Public

Income Statement — FYE: December 31

	ASSETS ($mil)	NET INCOME ($mil)	INCOME AS % OF ASSETS	EMPLOYEES
12/20	33,127.5	286.5	0.9%	3,591
12/19	26,561.3	243.6	0.9%	3,670
12/18	23,351.1	195.5	0.8%	3,573
12/17	21,771.5	247.1	1.1%	3,570
12/16	20,682.5	158.8	0.8%	3,688
Annual Growth	12.5%	15.9%	—	(0.7%)

2020 Year-End Financials
Return on assets: 0.9% Dividends
Return on equity: 10.1% Yield: 1.8%
Long-term debt ($ mil.): — Payout: 30.7%
No. of shares ($ mil.): 48.0 Market value ($ mil.): 3,312.0
Sales ($ mil.): 1,368.6

	STOCK PRICE ($) FY Close	P/E High	P/E Low	Earnings	Dividends	Book Value
12/20	68.99	12	7	5.93	1.25	62.84
12/19	68.64	14	12	4.96	1.21	53.09
12/18	60.97	20	15	3.93	1.17	45.37
12/17	71.92	16	13	4.96	1.04	43.72
12/16	77.12	25	13	3.22	0.99	39.51
Annual Growth	(2.7%)	—	—	16.5%	6.0%	12.3%

Union Bankshares, Inc. (Morrisville, VT)

Union Bankshares is the holding company for Union Bank, which serves individuals and small to mid-sized businesses in northern Vermont and Northwestern New Hampshire through 17 branches; it opened its first office in New Hampshire in 2006. Founded in 1891, the bank offers standard deposit products such as savings, checking, money market, and NOW accounts, as well as certificates of deposit, retirement savings programs, investment management, and trust services. It uses fund from deposits primarily to originate commercial real estate loans and residential real estate loans. Other loan products include business, consumer, construction, and municipal loans.

EXECUTIVES
Chairman, Subsidiary Officer, Kenneth D. Gibbons, $141,625 total compensation
Vice-Chairman, Director, Cornelius J. Van Dyke
President, Chief Executive Officer, Subsidiary Officer, Director, David S. Silverman, $350,000 total compensation
Vice President, Chief Financial Officer, Treasurer, Subsidiary Officer, Karyn J. Hale, $151,600 total compensation
Vice President, Subsidiary Officer, Jeffrey G. Coslett, $139,500 total compensation
Secretary, Director, John H. Steel, $29,425 total compensation
Director, Joel S. Bourassa
Director, Steven J. Bourgeois
Director, Dawn D. Bugbee
Director, John M. Goodrich
Director, Nancy C. Putnam
Director, Timothy Willis Sargent
Director, Schuyler Wallace Sweet
Director, Richard C. Sargent, $30,175 total compensation
Auditors: Berry Dunn McNeil & Parker, LLC

LOCATIONS
HQ: Union Bankshares, Inc. (Morrisville, VT)
20 Lower Main Street, P.O. Box 667, Morrisville, VT 05661
Phone: 802 888-6600
Web: www.ublocal.com

COMPETITORS
BCSB BANCORP, INC.
COMMERCIAL NATIONAL FINANCIAL CORPORATION
EASTERN VIRGINIA BANKSHARES, INC.
FREMONT BANCORPORATION
LIBERTY BANCORP, INC.

HISTORICAL FINANCIALS
Company Type: Public

Income Statement — FYE: December 31

	ASSETS ($mil)	NET INCOME ($mil)	INCOME AS % OF ASSETS	EMPLOYEES
12/20	1,093.5	12.8	1.2%	193
12/19	872.9	10.6	1.2%	201
12/18	805.3	7.0	0.9%	195
12/17	745.8	8.4	1.1%	194
12/16	691.3	8.5	1.2%	191
Annual Growth	12.1%	10.8%	—	0.3%

2020 Year-End Financials
Return on assets: 1.2% Dividends
Return on equity: 16.7% Yield: 4.9%
Long-term debt ($ mil.): — Payout: 48.8%
No. of shares ($ mil.): 4.4 Market value ($ mil.): 115.0
Sales ($ mil.): 52.7

	STOCK PRICE ($) FY Close	P/E High	P/E Low	Earnings	Dividends	Book Value
12/20	25.71	13	6	2.85	1.28	18.05
12/19	36.26	21	11	2.38	1.24	16.07
12/18	47.75	34	28	1.58	1.20	14.44
12/17	52.95	29	21	1.89	1.16	13.14
12/16	45.45	26	14	1.91	1.11	12.61
Annual Growth	(13.3%)	—	—	10.5%	3.6%	9.4%

United Bancorp, Inc. (Martins Ferry, OH)

United Bancorp is the holding company of Ohio's Citizens Savings Bank, which operates as Citizens Savings Bank and The Community Bank. The bank divisions together operate some 20 branches, offering deposit and lending products including savings and checking accounts, commercial and residential mortgages, and consumer installment loans. Commercial loans and mortgages combined account for about 60% of the company's loan portfolio. In 2008 Citizens Savings Bank acquired the deposits of three failed banking offices from the FDIC.

EXECUTIVES
Chairman, Director, Richard L. Riesbeck
President, Chief Executive Officer, Chief Operating Officer, Subsidiary Officer, Scott A. Everson, $355,040 total compensation
Senior Vice President, Chief Operating Officer, Subsidiary Officer, Matthew Fredrick Branstetter, $201,016 total compensation
Chief Financial Officer, Senior Vice President, Treasurer, Secretary, Randall M. Greenwood, $190,021 total compensation
Vice President, Chief Retail Banking Offier, Elmer K. Leeper
Vice President, Chief Information Officer, Michael A. Lloyd
Director, Gary W. Glessner
Director, John M. Hoopingarner
Auditors: BKD, LLP

LOCATIONS
HQ: United Bancorp, Inc. (Martins Ferry, OH)
201 South Fourth Street, Martins Ferry, OH 43935-0010
Phone: 740 633-0445 **Fax:** 740 633-1448
Web: www.unitedbancorp.com

COMPETITORS
CIVISTA BANCSHARES, INC.
COMMERCIAL BANCSHARES, INC.
EMCLAIRE FINANCIAL CORP.
FIRST KEYSTONE CORPORATION
UNITED BANCSHARES, INC.

HISTORICAL FINANCIALS
Company Type: Public

Income Statement — FYE: December 31

	ASSETS ($mil)	NET INCOME ($mil)	INCOME AS % OF ASSETS	EMPLOYEES
12/20	693.4	7.9	1.1%	132
12/19	685.7	6.8	1.0%	132
12/18	593.2	4.2	0.7%	132
12/17	459.3	3.5	0.8%	126
12/16	438.0	3.5	0.8%	138
Annual Growth	12.2%	22.1%	—	(1.1%)

2020 Year-End Financials
Return on assets: 1.1% Dividends
Return on equity: 12.3% Yield: 4.3%
Long-term debt ($ mil.): — Payout: 45.9%
No. of shares ($ mil.): 5.7 Market value ($ mil.): 76.0
Sales ($ mil.): 34.5

	STOCK PRICE ($) FY Close	P/E High/Low		PER SHARE ($) Earnings	Dividends	Book Value
12/20	13.18	11	7	1.39	0.57	11.80
12/19	14.30	13	9	1.19	0.55	10.86
12/18	11.43	17	13	0.82	0.57	8.82
12/17	13.25	19	16	0.71	0.51	8.37
12/16	13.50	19	12	0.71	0.47	8.19
Annual Growth	(0.6%)	—	—	18.3%	4.9%	9.6%

United Bancshares Inc. (OH)

United Bancshares is a blend of checks and (account) balances.Â The institution is the holding company for The Union Bank Company, a community bank serving northwestern Ohio through about a dozen branches. The commercial bank offers such retail services and products as checking and savings accounts, NOW and money market accounts, IRAs, and CDs. It uses funds from deposits to write commercial loans (about half of its lending portfolio), residential mortgages, agriculture loans, and consumer loans. The Union Bank Company was originally established in 1904.

EXECUTIVES

Chairman, Director, Daniel W. Schutt, $171,593 total compensation
President, Chief Executive Officer, Interim Chief Financial Officer, Subsidiary Officer, Director, Brian D. Young, $299,260 total compensation
Chief Financial Officer, Subsidiary Officer, Klint D. Manz
Secretary, Heather Marie Oatman, $128,750 total compensation
Director, Robert L. Benroth
Director, Herbert H. Huffman
Director, David P. Roach
Director, R. Steven Unverferth
Director, H. Edward Rigel
Auditors : Clifton Gunderson LLP

LOCATIONS

HQ: United Bancshares Inc. (OH)
105 Progressive Drive, Columbus Grove, OH 45830
Phone: 419 659-2141
Web: www.theubank.com

COMPETITORS

CITIZENS BANK INC
COMMERCIAL BANCSHARES, INC.
FIRST KEYSTONE CORPORATION
FIRST US BANCSHARES, INC.
GUARANTY BANK AND TRUST COMPANY

HISTORICAL FINANCIALS

Company Type: Public

Income Statement — FYE: December 31

	ASSETS ($mil)	NET INCOME ($mil)	INCOME AS % OF ASSETS	EMPLOYEES
12/20	978.5	13.7	1.4%	222
12/19	880.0	10.6	1.2%	217
12/18	830.3	8.2	1.0%	179
12/17	780.4	3.8	0.5%	177
12/16	633.1	5.5	0.9%	155
Annual Growth	11.5%	25.6%	—	9.4%

2020 Year-End Financials

Return on assets: 1.4%
Return on equity: 13.2%
Long-term debt ($ mil.): —
No. of shares ($ mil.): 3.2
Sales ($ mil.): 67
Dividends
Yield: 2.0%
Payout: 10.3%
Market value ($ mil.): 83.0

	STOCK PRICE ($) FY Close	P/E High/Low		PER SHARE ($) Earnings	Dividends	Book Value
12/20	25.44	6	3	4.16	0.51	34.11
12/19	22.71	7	6	3.25	0.52	29.00
12/18	20.02	9	7	2.51	0.48	24.76
12/17	22.20	20	17	1.18	0.48	23.17
12/16	21.42	13	10	1.68	0.44	22.21
Annual Growth	4.4%	—	—	25.4%	3.8%	11.3%

United Bankshares Inc

United Bankshares offers a full range commercial and consumer banking services and products. Its subsidiary, the Union Bank is an Ohio state-chartered bank supervised by the State of Ohio, Division of Financial Institutions (the ODFI), and the Federal Deposit Insurance Corporation (the FDIC). The bank operates about 20 full-service branches and three loan production offices. The bank provides deposit, treasury management, wealth management, and other traditional banking products through its full-service branch office network and its electronic banking services. The company was founded in 1839.

Operations

The bank's deposit services include checking accounts, savings and money market accounts; certificates of deposit and individual retirement accounts. Additional supportive services include online banking, bill pay, mobile banking, Zelle payment service, ATM's and safe deposit box rentals. Treasury management and remote deposit capture products are also available to commercial deposit customers. Loan products offered include commercial and residential real estate loans, agricultural loans, commercial and industrial loans, home equity loans, various types of consumer loans and small business administration loans. Wealth management services are offered by Union Bank through an arrangement with LPL Financial LLC, a registered broker/dealer. Licensed representatives offer a full range of investment services and products, including financial needs analysis, mutual funds, securities trading, annuities and life insurance.

About 70% of sales were generated from interest income, of which some 60% came from loans. Its loan portfolio comprises commercial and multi-family real estate (over 65% of loans), residential 1-4 family (about 20%), commercial (nearly 15%), and consumer.

Geographic Reach

Headquartered in Columbus Grove, Ohio, the bank has 18 full service banking centers and three loan production offices in northwest and central Ohio.

Sales and Marketing

Customers are predominately small and middle-market businesses and individuals.

Financial Performance

Net interest income for 2021 was $35.7 million, an increase of $2.7 million (8.2%) from 2020 due to a decrease in interest expense of $3.9 million, offset by a decrease in interest income of $1.2 million. The $3.9 million decline in interest expense is due to the prepayment of $50.0 million of Federal Home Loan Bank advances in the second, third, and fourth quarters of 2020 as well as a declining cost of funds.

In 2021, the company had a net income of $13.6 million, a 1% decrease from the previous year's net income of $13.8 million.

The company's cash at the end of 2021 was $75.2 million. Operating activities generated $26.4 million, while investing activities used $96.5 million, mainly for purchases of available-for-sale securities. Financing activities provided another $88.2 million.

Mergers and Acquisitions

In late 2021, United Bankshares announced the completion of its acquisition of Community Bankers Trust Corporation, the parent company of Essex Bank with $1.7 billion in assets, headquartered in the greater Richmond region. The merger brings together two high-performing banking companies and strengthens United's position as one of the largest and best performing regional banking companies in the Mid-Atlantic and Southeast. The exchange ratio will be fixed at 0.3173 of United's shares for each share of Community Bankers Trust, resulting in an aggregate transaction value of approximately $303.3 million.

EXECUTIVES

Chairman, Chief Executive Officer, Subsidiary Officer, Director, Richard M. Adams, $1,076,250 total compensation
President, Subsidiary Officer, Richard M. Adams, $492,308 total compensation

Executive Vice President, Chief Operating Officer, Subsidiary Officer, James J. Consagra, $492,308 total compensation

Executive Vice President, Chief Financial Officer, Subsidiary Officer, William Mark Tatterson, $392,308 total compensation

Executive Vice President, Subsidiary Officer, Douglas Bryon Ernest

Executive Vice President, Chief Information Officer, Chief Administrative Officer, Subsidiary Officer, Craige L. Smith, $334,231 total compensation

Executive Vice President, Chief Risk Officer, Darren K. Williams

Director, Robert G. Astorg
Director, Peter A. Converse
Director, Michael P. Fitzgerald
Director, Theodore J. Georgelas
Director, J. Paul McNamara
Director, Mark R. Nesselroad
Director, Albert H. Small
Director, Mary K. Weddle
Director, Gary G. White
Director, P. Clinton Winter

Auditors: Ernst & Young LLP

LOCATIONS

HQ: United Bankshares Inc
300 United Center, 500 Virginia Street, East, Charleston, WV 25301
Phone: 304 424-8716
Web: www.ubsi-inc.com

PRODUCTS/OPERATIONS

2014 Sales

	$ mil.	% of total
Interest		
Loans, including fees	383.7	75
Interest and dividends on securities	33.9	7
Other	0.9	-
Noninterest		
Fees from deposit services	42.4	9
Fees from trust & brokerage services	18.1	4
Other	28.9	5
Adjustment (losses)	(8.4)	—
Total	499.5	100

COMPETITORS

AMERICAN NATIONAL BANKSHARES INC.
F.N.B. CORPORATION
MAINSOURCE FINANCIAL GROUP, INC.
OLD NATIONAL BANCORP
PACIFIC CONTINENTAL CORPORATION
S&T BANCORP, INC.
UNITED COMMUNITY BANKS, INC.
WASHINGTON TRUST BANCORP, INC.
WESTERN ALLIANCE BANCORPORATION
WINTRUST FINANCIAL CORPORATION

HISTORICAL FINANCIALS

Company Type: Public

Income Statement — FYE: December 31

	ASSETS ($mil)	NET INCOME ($mil)	INCOME AS % OF ASSETS	EMPLOYEES
12/20	26,184.2	289.0	1.1%	3,051
12/19	19,662.3	260.0	1.3%	2,204
12/18	19,250.4	256.3	1.3%	2,230
12/17	19,058.9	150.5	0.8%	2,381
12/16	14,508.8	147.0	1.0%	1,701
Annual Growth	15.9%	18.4%	—	15.7%

2020 Year-End Financials

Return on assets: 1.2%
Return on equity: 7.5%
Long-term debt ($ mil.): —
No. of shares ($ mil.): 129.1
Sales ($ mil.): 1,153.1
Dividends
Yield: 4.3%
Payout: 58.3%
Market value ($ mil.): 4,186.0

	STOCK PRICE ($) FY Close	P/E High/Low		PER SHARE ($) Earnings	Dividends	Book Value
12/20	32.40	16	9	2.40	1.40	33.27
12/19	38.66	16	12	2.55	1.37	33.12
12/18	31.11	16	12	2.45	1.36	31.78
12/17	34.75	30	21	1.54	1.33	30.85
12/16	46.25	25	16	1.99	1.32	27.59
Annual Growth	(8.5%)	—	—	4.8%	1.5%	4.8%

United Community Banks Inc (Blairsville, GA)

United Community Banks is the holding company for United Community Bank (UCB). UCB provides consumer and business banking products and services through some 195 branches across Florida, Georgia, North Carolina, Tennessee, and South Carolina. Approximately 75% of its loan portfolio consisted of commercial loans, including commercial and industrial, equipment financing, commercial construction and commercial real estate mortgage loans. The company also has a mortgage lending division, and provides insurance through its United Community Insurance Services subsidiary. The company has some $24.2 billion in assets.

Operations

UCB provide a wide range of financial products and services, including deposit products, secured and unsecured loans, mortgage loans, payment and commerce solutions, equipment finance services, wealth management, trust services, private banking, investment advisory services, insurance services, and other related financial services. The company's retail mortgage lending division United Community Mortgage Services (UCMS), sells and services mortgages for Fannie Mae and Freddie Mac, and provides fixed and adjustable-rate home mortgages. It also offers retail brokerage services through an affiliation with a third-party broker/dealer.

About 70% of UCB's total revenue came from loan interest (including fees), while some 10% from investments securities. The rest of its revenue come from service charges and fees (about 5%), mortgage loan fees (around 10%), and brokerage fees, among other sources.

Geographic Reach

UCB has about 195 offices in Florida, Georgia, North Carolina, South Carolina, and Tennessee. The company's executive offices are located in Georgia and South Carolina.

Sales and Marketing

The company provides a wide range of financial products and services to the commercial, retail, governmental, educational, energy, health care and real estate sectors through a variety of channels including its branches, other offices, the internet, and mobile applications.

Financial Performance

The company reported a total revenue of $744.4 million in 2021, a 29% increase from the previous year's total revenue of $577.4 million.

In 2021, the company had a net income of $269.8 million, a 64% increase from the previous year's net income of $164.1 million.

The company's cash at the end of 2021 was $2.2 billion. Operating activities generated $359.3 million, while investing activities used $1.8 billion, mainly for purchases of debt securities available-for-sale and equity securities with readily determinable fair values.

Strategy

In 2022, the company's strategy is to continue to invest resources in its banking businesses and operations as it integrates the businesses and operations of FinTrust, Aquesta and Reliant and seek to exploit opportunities for cost and revenue synergies. Organic growth, including exploitation of revenue synergies, is expected to be coordinated with a focus on strong and stable returns on capital. Organically, the company has enhanced its market share in the company's traditional banking markets with targeted hires and marketing, expanded into other southern US markets with similar characteristics, and expanded with specialty commercial lending and private client banking. In the future, it expects to continue to nurture profitable organic growth. The company may pursue acquisitions or strategic transactions if appropriate opportunities, within or outside of its current markets, present themselves.

Mergers and Acquisitions

In late 2021, UCB acquired Aquesta, a bank headquartered in Cornelius, North Carolina. Aquesta's high-touch customer service is delivered to retail and business customers through a network of branches primarily located in the Charlotte metropolitan area. The company acquired total assets of $756 million, including $498 million in loans, and it assumed $658 million in deposits as of the acquisition date.

In 2021, UCB acquired FinTrust, an investment advisory firm headquartered in Greenville, South Carolina, with additional locations in Anderson, South Carolina, and Athens and Macon, Georgia. The firm provides wealth and investment management services to individuals and institutions within its markets, which expands our Wealth

Management division. The addition of FinTrust, a strong and growing Registered Investment Adviser, continues the expansion of UCB's product offerings and gives additional opportunities to provide a full range of financial services to its customers.

EXECUTIVES

President, Chief Executive Officer, Subsidiary Officer, Chairman, Director, H. Lynn Harton, $725,000 total compensation

Executive Vice President, General Counsel, Corporate Secretary, Subsidiary Officer, Melinda Davis Lux

Executive Vice President, Chief Financial Officer, Subsidiary Officer, Jefferson L. Harralson, $400,000 total compensation

Executive Vice President, Chief Banking Officer, Subsidiary Officer, Richard W. Bradshaw, $315,625 total compensation

Executive Vice President, Chief Credit Officer, Subsidiary Officer, Robert A. Edwards, $343,750 total compensation

Chief Information Officer, Subsidiary Officer, Mark Aaron Terry

Lead Director, Director, Thomas A. Richlovsky

Director, James P. Clements

Director, George B. Bell

Director, Jennifer Mumby Bazante

Director, Robert H. Blalock

Director, Kenneth L. Daniels

Director, Lance F. Drummond

Director, Jeffifer K. Mann

Director, David C. Shaver

Director, Tim R. Wallis

Director, David H. Wilkins

Auditors : PricewaterhouseCoopers LLP

LOCATIONS

HQ: United Community Banks Inc (Blairsville, GA)
125 Highway 515 East, Blairsville, GA 30512
Phone: 706 781-2265
Web: www.ucbi.com

PRODUCTS/OPERATIONS

2011 Sales

	$ mil.	% of total
Interest		
Loans, including fees	239.1	69
Taxable investment securities	55.2	16
Other	3.3	1
Noninterest		
Service charges & fees	29.1	8
Mortgage loans & related fees	5.4	2
Brokerage fees	3.0	1
Net securities gains	0.8	-
Other	12.3	3
Adjustment	(0.7)	
Total	347.5	100

COMPETITORS

AMERICAN NATIONAL BANKSHARES INC.
CENTERSTATE BANK CORPORATION
CITY HOLDING COMPANY
F.N.B. CORPORATION
PACWEST BANCORP
REPUBLIC BANCORP, INC.
SOUTHSIDE BANCSHARES, INC.
STATE BANK FINANCIAL CORPORATION
UNITED BANKSHARES, INC.
WILSHIRE BANCORP, INC.

HISTORICAL FINANCIALS

Company Type: Public

Income Statement — FYE: December 31

	ASSETS ($mil)	NET INCOME ($mil)	INCOME AS % OF ASSETS	EMPLOYEES
12/20	17,794.3	164.0	0.9%	2,406
12/19	12,916.0	185.7	1.4%	2,309
12/18	12,573.1	166.1	1.3%	2,312
12/17	11,915.4	67.8	0.6%	2,137
12/16	10,708.6	100.6	0.9%	1,916
Annual Growth	13.5%	13.0%	—	5.9%

2020 Year-End Financials

Return on assets: 1.0%
Return on equity: 8.9%
Long-term debt ($ mil.): —
No. of shares ($ mil.): 86.6
Sales ($ mil.): 714.1
Dividends
Yield: 2.5%
Payout: 38.9%
Market value ($ mil.): 2,465.0

	STOCK PRICE ($) FY Close	P/E High/Low		PER SHARE ($) Earnings	Dividends	Book Value
12/20	28.44	16	8	1.91	0.72	23.16
12/19	30.88	14	9	2.31	0.68	20.70
12/18	21.46	16	10	2.07	0.58	18.40
12/17	28.14	33	27	0.92	0.38	16.80
12/16	29.62	21	11	1.40	0.30	15.17
Annual Growth	(1.0%)	—	—	8.1%	24.5%	11.2%

United States 12 Month Oil Fund LP

EXECUTIVES

Chairman, President, Chief Executive Officer, Management Director, Associate/Affiliate Company Officer, John P. Love

Vice President, Management Director, Associate/Affiliate Company Officer, Nicholas D. Gerber, $0 total compensation

Chief Financial Officer, Secretary, Treasurer, Associate/Affiliate Company Officer, Stuart P. Crumbaugh

Chief Operating Officer, Management Director and Portfolio Manager, Associate/Affiliate Company Officer, Andrew F. Ngim

Chief Compliance Officer, Associate/Affiliate Company Officer, Carolyn M. Yu

Chief Investment Officer, Portfolio Manager, Associate/Affiliate Company Officer, Kevin A. Baum

Management Director, Associate/Affiliate Company Officer, Robert Long Nguyen, $0 total compensation

Portfolio Manager, Ray W. Allen

Director, Gordon Lloyd Ellis

Director, Malcolm R. Fobes

Director, Peter M. Robinson

Auditors : Spicer Jeffries LLP

LOCATIONS

HQ: United States 12 Month Oil Fund LP
1850 Mt. Diablo Boulevard, Suite 640, Walnut Creek, CA 94596
Phone: 510 522-9600
Web: www.uscfinvestments.com

HISTORICAL FINANCIALS

Company Type: Public

Income Statement — FYE: December 31

	REVENUE ($mil)	NET INCOME ($mil)	NET PROFIT MARGIN	EMPLOYEES
12/20	110.3	108.7	98.6%	0
12/19	14.9	14.4	96.7%	0
12/18	(4.8)	(5.5)	113.4%	0
12/17	2.6	1.7	64.9%	0
12/16	30.1	29.3	97.3%	0
Annual Growth	38.3%	38.7%	—	—

2020 Year-End Financials

Debt ratio: —
Return on equity: —
Cash ($ mil.): 181.5
Current Ratio: 7.88
Long-term debt ($ mil.): —
No. of shares ($ mil.): 11.4
Dividends
Yield: —
Payout: —
Market value ($ mil.): 196.0

	STOCK PRICE ($) FY Close	P/E High/Low		PER SHARE ($) Earnings	Dividends	Book Value
12/20	17.19	—	—	(5.72)	0.00	17.23
12/19	22.99	4	3	5.52	0.00	22.95
12/18	17.96	—	—	(1.62)	0.00	17.82
12/17	20.92	72	54	0.29	0.00	21.05
12/16	20.40	4	3	4.69	0.00	20.39
Annual Growth	(4.2%)	—	—	—	—	(4.1%)

United States Brent Oil Fund L.P.

EXECUTIVES

Chairman, President, Chief Executive Officer, Management Directo, Associate/Affiliate Company Officer, John P. Love

Vice President, Management Director, Associate/Affiliate Company Officer, Director, Nicholas D. Gerber

Chief Operating Officer, Management Director and Portfolio Manager, Associate/Affiliate Company Officer, Andrew F. Ngim

Chief Financial Officer, Secretary, Treasurer, Associate/Affiliate Company Officer, Stuart P. Crumbaugh

Chief Compliance Officer, Associate/Affiliate Company Officer, Carolyn M. Yu

Chief Investment Officer, Portfolio Manager, Associate/Affiliate Company Officer, Kevin A. Baum

Portfolio Manager, Associate/Affiliate Company Officer, Ray W. Allen

Management Director, Robert Long Nguyen

Director, Peter M. Robinson

Director, Gordon Lloyd Ellis

Director, Malcolm R. Fobes
Auditors : Spicer Jeffries LLP

LOCATIONS

HQ: United States Brent Oil Fund L.P.
1850 Mt. Diablo Boulevard, Suite 640, Walnut Creek, CA 94596
Phone: 510 522-9600
Web: www.uscfinvestments.com

HISTORICAL FINANCIALS
Company Type: Public

Income Statement — FYE: December 31

	REVENUE ($mil)	NET INCOME ($mil)	NET PROFIT MARGIN	EMPLOYEES
12/20	121.6	119.0	97.9%	0
12/19	27.5	26.7	97.1%	0
12/18	(14.3)	(15.1)	106.0%	0
12/17	16.3	15.4	94.5%	0
12/16	38.0	37.0	97.4%	0
Annual Growth	33.8%	33.9%	—	—

2020 Year-End Financials
Debt ratio: —
Return on equity: —
Cash ($ mil.): 311.5
Current Ratio: 857.31
Long-term debt ($ mil.): —
No. of shares ($ mil.): 27.1
Dividends
Yield: —
Payout: —
Market value ($ mil.): 349.0

	STOCK PRICE ($) FY Close	P/E High/Low		PER SHARE ($) Earnings	Dividends	Book Value
12/20	12.88	5	1	4.45	0.00	12.91
12/19	20.85	4	3	5.76	0.00	20.91
12/18	15.33	—	—	(3.14)	0.00	15.18
12/17	18.10	8	5	2.24	0.00	18.18
12/16	15.68	4	2	4.49	0.00	15.70
Annual Growth	(4.8%)	—	—	(0.2%)	—	(4.8%)

United States Gasoline Fund LP

EXECUTIVES

Chairman, President, Chief Executive Officer, Associate/Affiliate Company Officer, Director, John P. Love
Vice President, Management Director, Associate/Affiliate Company Officer, Nicholas D. Gerber
Chief Financial Officer, Secretary, Treasurer, Associate/Affiliate Company Officer, Stuart P. Crumbaugh
Portfolio Manager, Ray W. Allen
Associate/Affiliate Company Officer, Director, Andrew F. Ngim
Associate/Affiliate Company Officer, Carolyn M. Yu
Associate/Affiliate Company Officer, Kevin A. Baum
Director, Robert Long Nguyen
Director, Gordon Lloyd Ellis
Director, Malcolm R. Fobes
Director, Peter M. Robinson
Auditors : Spicer Jeffries LLP

LOCATIONS

HQ: United States Gasoline Fund LP
1850 Mt. Diablo Boulevard, Suite 640, Walnut Creek, CA 94596
Phone: 510 522-9600
Web: www.uscfinvestments.com

HISTORICAL FINANCIALS
Company Type: Public

Income Statement — FYE: December 31

	REVENUE ($mil)	NET INCOME ($mil)	NET PROFIT MARGIN	EMPLOYEES
12/20	43.0	42.5	98.7%	0
12/19	13.6	13.3	98.0%	0
12/18	(11.1)	(11.4)	102.9%	0
12/17	0.6	0.2	34.1%	0
12/16	5.6	5.1	90.3%	0
Annual Growth	66.0%	69.7%	—	—

2020 Year-End Financials
Debt ratio: —
Return on equity: —
Cash ($ mil.): 72.5
Current Ratio: 59.20
Long-term debt ($ mil.): —
No. of shares ($ mil.): 3.3
Dividends
Yield: —
Payout: —
Market value ($ mil.): 80.0

	STOCK PRICE ($) FY Close	P/E High/Low		PER SHARE ($) Earnings	Dividends	Book Value
12/20	24.31	3	1	11.14	0.00	24.29
12/19	32.36	3	2	10.69	0.00	32.31
12/18	22.91	—	—	(8.43)	0.00	22.74
12/17	31.85	299	204	0.11	0.00	32.03
12/16	31.32	17	11	1.81	0.00	31.37
Annual Growth	(6.1%)	—	—	57.5%	—	(6.2%)

Unity Bancorp, Inc.

Unity Bancorp wants to keep you and your money united. The institution is the holding company for Unity Bank, a commercial bank that serves small and midsized businesses, as well as individual consumers, through nearly 20 offices in north-central New Jersey and eastern Pennsylvania. Unity Bank's deposit products include checking, savings, money market, and NOW accounts, and CDs. Lending to businesses is the company's life blood: Commercial loans, including Small Business Administration (SBA) and real estate loans, account for about 60% of its loan portfolio, which is rounded out by residential mortgage and consumer loans.

EXECUTIVES

Chairman, Subsidiary Officer, Director, David D. Dallas
President, Chief Executive Officer, Subsidiary Officer, Director, James A. Hughes, $470,002 total compensation
Executive Vice President, Chief Financial Officer, George Boyan
Executive Vice President, Chief Administrative Officer, Subsidiary Officer, Janice Bolomey, $200,000 total compensation
Executive Vice President, Chief Operating Officer, Subsidiary Officer, John J. Kauchak, $202,501 total compensation
Mortgage Lending First Senior Vice President, Mortgage Lending Director, Vincent Geraci
Senior Vice President, Chief Lending Officer, James Donovan
Director, Mark S. Brody
Director, Wayne Courtright
Director, Robert H. Dallas, $15,500 total compensation
Director, Mary E. Gross
Director, Peter E. Maricondo
Director, Raj Patel
Director, Donald E. Souders
Director, Aaron Tucker
Auditors : RSM US LLP

LOCATIONS

HQ: Unity Bancorp, Inc.
64 Old Highway 22, Clinton, NJ 08809
Phone: 908 730-7630
Web: www.unitybank.com

PRODUCTS/OPERATIONS

Selected Subsidiaries
Unity Bank
  Unity Financial Services, Inc.
  Unity Investment Company, Inc.

COMPETITORS

BCSB BANCORP, INC.
CF BANKSHARES INC.
FIRST US BANCSHARES, INC.
LIBERTY BANCORP, INC.
SOUTHCOAST FINANCIAL CORPORATION

HISTORICAL FINANCIALS
Company Type: Public

Income Statement — FYE: December 31

	ASSETS ($mil)	NET INCOME ($mil)	INCOME AS % OF ASSETS	EMPLOYEES
12/20	1,958.9	23.6	1.2%	210
12/19	1,718.9	23.6	1.4%	209
12/18	1,579.1	21.9	1.4%	207
12/17	1,455.4	12.8	0.9%	208
12/16	1,189.9	13.2	1.1%	194
Annual Growth	13.3%	15.7%	—	2.0%

2020 Year-End Financials
Return on assets: 1.2%
Return on equity: 14.0%
Long-term debt ($ mil.): —
No. of shares ($ mil.): 10.4
Sales ($ mil.): 91.8
Dividends
Yield: 1.8%
Payout: 15.6%
Market value ($ mil.): 184.0

	STOCK PRICE ($) FY Close	P/E High/Low		PER SHARE ($) Earnings	Dividends	Book Value
12/20	17.55	10	4	2.19	0.32	16.63
12/19	22.57	11	8	2.14	0.31	14.77
12/18	20.76	12	9	2.01	0.27	12.85
12/17	19.75	17	13	1.20	0.23	11.13
12/16	15.70	12	7	1.38	0.17	10.15
Annual Growth	2.8%	—	—	12.2%	17.4%	13.2%

Universal Display Corp

Universal Display thinks the world should be flat and lit with its organic light-emitting diode (OLED) technologies and materials. With its own research and through sponsored research agreements with PPG Industries and several universities, the company develops OLED technologies and materials, which use less energy than other lighting technologies including new and next-generation red, green, yellow and blue emitters and hosts, for screens from cell phones to large flat panel displays and solid-state lighting. Based in the US, it has facilities in Europe and the Asia/Pacific region. Universal Display was founded by Sherwin Seligsohn in 1994.

EXECUTIVES

Chairman, Director, Sherwin I. Seligsohn, $424,703 total compensation

Vice President, Janice K. Mahon

President, Chief Executive Officer, Steven V. Abramson, $701,989 total compensation

Executive Vice President, Chief Financial Officer, Treasurer, Secretary, Sidney D. Rosenblatt, $701,989 total compensation

Senior Vice President, Chief Technical Officer, Julia J. Brown, $501,838 total compensation

Legal Vice President, Legal Division Officer, Mauro Premutico, $423,383 total compensation

Director, Cynthia J. Comparin

Director, Richard C. Elias

Lead Independent Director, Director, Elizabeth H. Gemmill

Director, C. Keith Hartley

Director, Celia M. Joseph

Director, Lawrence Lacerte

Auditors: KPMG LLP

LOCATIONS

HQ: Universal Display Corp
375 Phillips Boulevard, Ewing, NJ 08618
Phone: 609 671-0980
Web: www.oled.com

2017 Sales

	$ mil.	% of total
South Korea	289.5	86
China	24.9	7
United States	10.3	3
Japan	8.5	3
Other non-U.S. locations	2.4	1
Total	335.6	100

PRODUCTS/OPERATIONS

2017 Sales

	$ mil.	% of total
Material sales	200.3	60
Royalty and license fees	126.5	38
Contract research services	8.8	2
Total	335.6	100

COMPETITORS

AMKOR TECHNOLOGY, INC.
APPLIED MATERIALS, INC.
COGNEX CORPORATION
KOPIN CORPORATION
OCLARO, INC.
ONTO INNOVATION INC.
PHOTRONICS, INC.
SIGMA DESIGNS, INC.
SKYWORKS SOLUTIONS, INC.
Samsung Electronics Co., Ltd.

HISTORICAL FINANCIALS

Company Type: Public

Income Statement — FYE: December 31

	REVENUE ($mil)	NET INCOME ($mil)	NET PROFIT MARGIN	EMPLOYEES
12/20	428.8	133.3	31.1%	350
12/19	405.1	138.3	34.1%	311
12/18	247.4	58.8	23.8%	267
12/17	335.6	103.8	31.0%	224
12/16	198.8	48.0	24.2%	203
Annual Growth	21.2%	29.1%	—	14.6%

2020 Year-End Financials

Debt ratio: —
Return on equity: 15.4%
Cash ($ mil.): 630.0
Current Ratio: 5.61
Long-term debt ($ mil.): —
No. of shares ($ mil.): 47.6
Dividends
Yield: 0.2%
Payout: 26.9%
Market value ($ mil.): 10,949.0

	STOCK PRICE ($) FY Close	P/E High/Low		PER SHARE ($) Earnings	Dividends	Book Value
12/20	229.80	86	38	2.80	0.60	19.16
12/19	206.07	77	27	2.92	0.40	17.09
12/18	93.57	166	65	1.24	0.24	14.59
12/17	172.65	87	19	2.18	0.12	13.99
12/16	56.30	72	41	1.02	0.00	11.26
Annual Growth	42.1%	—	—	28.7%	—	14.2%

Universal Insurance Holdings Inc

Universal Insurance Holdings is a holding company offering property and casualty insurance and value-added insurance services. The company develops, markets and underwrites insurance products for consumers predominantly in the personal residential homeowners lines of business and perform substantially all other insurance-related services for our primary insurance entities, including risk management, claims management, and distribution. Our primary insurance entities, Universal Property & Casualty Insurance Company (UPCIC) and American Platinum Property and Casualty Insurance Company (APPCIC), offer insurance products through both its appointed independent agent network and its online distribution channels across some 20 states (primarily in Florida), with licenses to write insurance in two additional states. Florida generates some 85% of its total direct premiums written.

Operations

Universal Property & Casualty Insurance Company (UPCIC; which accounts for the majority of its insurance entities' business) currently offers the following types of personal residential insurance: homeowners, renters/tenants, condo unit owners, and dwelling/fire. UPCIC also offers allied lines, coverage for other structures, and personal property, liability and personal articles coverages. American Platinum Property and Casualty Insurance Company (APPCIC) currently writes similar lines of insurance as UPCIC, but historically for properties valued in excess of $1 million. More recently, APPCIC has commenced a standard market homeowners insurance program in Florida in conjunction with its digital platforms.

Other subsidiaries include Evolution Risk Advisors (managing general agent for UPCIC and APPCIC); Universal Inspection (conducts inspection for Evolution Risk, UPCIC and APPCIC); and Universal Adjusting (manages its claims processing and adjusting functions). In addition, The Grand Palm Development Group (Grand Palm) is UVE's real estate development entity. Grand Palm develops and either operates or sells residential properties. Grand Palm also evaluates undeveloped parcels of land for investment opportunities on an ongoing basis.

About 90% of sales were generated from net premiums earned.

Geographic Reach

The company is headquartered in Fort Lauderdale, Florida. While Florida remains its largest market, it also operates in nearly 20 other states: Alabama, Delaware, Florida, Georgia, Hawaii, Illinois, Indiana, Iowa, Maryland, Massachusetts, Michigan, Minnesota, New Hampshire, New Jersey, New York, North Carolina, Pennsylvania, South Carolina, and Virginia. It has additional licenses to write in Tennessee and Wisconsin.

Sales and Marketing

Universal Insurance distributes its products through a network of some 10,200 independent agents. It also sells its policies through its online platform Universal Direct.

Financial Performance

Total revenues increased by $49.1 million, or 5%, to $1.1 billion. This growth was driven by premium growth within the company's Florida business and premium growth in its other states business.

In 2021, the company had a net income of $20.4 million, a 7% increase from the previous year's net income of $19.1 million. This was primarily due to the higher volume of revenue for the year.

The company's cash at the end of 2021 was $253.1 million. Operating activities generated $234.4 million, while investing activities used $229.4 million, mainly for purchases of available-for-sale debt securities. Financing activities provided another $68.3 million.

Strategy

Universal Insurance's strategic focus is on creating a best-in-class experience for its customers. It has more than 20 years of experience providing protection solutions. It continues to focus on disciplined underwriting in opportune markets and maintaining a resilient balance sheet enhanced by its strengthening reserve position, the company's reinsurance programs, and the completion of a private placement for general corporate purposes and growth capital to optimize its capital position.

EXECUTIVES

Executive Chairman, Director, Sean P. Downes, $1,000,000 total compensation
Chief Executive Officer, Director, Stephen J. Donaghy, $804,375 total compensation
Finance Chief Financial Officer, Finance Principal Accounting Officer, Finance Subsidiary Officer, Frank C. Wilcox, $412,500 total compensation
Chief Administrative Officer, Chief Information Officer, Director, Kimberly D. Campos, $298,077 total compensation
Principal Accounting Officer, Corporate Secretary, Gary L. Ropiecki
Subsidiary Officer, Ryan Donaghy
Subsidiary Officer, Matthew J. Palmieri
Lead Independent Director, Director, Michael A. Pietrangelo
Director, Scott P. Callahan
Director, Marlene M. Gordon
Director, Richard D. Peterson
Director, Ozzie A. Schindler
Director, Jon W. Springer, $1,000,000 total compensation
Director, Joel M. Wilentz
Director, Francis X. McCahill
Auditors : Plante & Moran, PLLC

LOCATIONS

HQ: Universal Insurance Holdings Inc
1110 West Commercial Blvd., Fort Lauderdale, FL 33309
Phone: 954 958-1200
Web: www.universalinsuranceholdings.com

PRODUCTS/OPERATIONS

2017 Sales

	$ mil.	% of total
Net premiums earned	688.8	92
Commissions	21.2	3
Policy fees	18.8	2
Net investment income	13.5	2
Net realized gains on investments	2.6	-
Other	7.0	1
Total	751.9	100

Selected Products and Services
Condominium policy
Dwelling coverage
Dwelling fire policy
Homeowners policy
Other structures coverage
Personal liability coverage
Personal property coverage
Renter's policy

COMPETITORS

AUTO-OWNERS INSURANCE COMPANY
CENTRAL MUTUAL INSURANCE COMPANY
ERIE INDEMNITY COMPANY
FEDNAT HOLDING COMPANY
GREATER NEW YORK MUTUAL INSURANCE CO
MAIN STREET AMERICA GROUP, INC.
MUTUAL OF ENUMCLAW INSURANCE COMPANY
NATIONAL GENERAL HOLDINGS CORP.
RLI CORP.
STATE FARM MUTUAL AUTOMOBILE INSURANCE COMPANY

HISTORICAL FINANCIALS

Company Type: Public

Income Statement — FYE: December 31

	ASSETS ($mil)	NET INCOME ($mil)	INCOME AS % OF ASSETS	EMPLOYEES
12/20	1,758.7	19.1	1.1%	909
12/19	1,719.8	46.5	2.7%	805
12/18	1,858.3	117.0	6.3%	734
12/17	1,454.9	106.9	7.3%	558
12/16	1,060.0	99.4	9.4%	483
Annual Growth	13.5%	(33.8%)	—	17.1%

2020 Year-End Financials
Return on assets: 1.0%
Return on equity: 4.0%
Long-term debt ($ mil.): —
No. of shares ($ mil.): 31.1
Sales ($ mil.): 1,072.7
Dividends
Yield: 4.2%
Payout: 128.3%
Market value ($ mil.): 470.0

	STOCK PRICE ($) FY Close	P/E High	P/E Low	Earnings	Dividends	Book Value
12/20	15.11	46	18	0.60	0.77	14.43
12/19	27.99	30	18	1.36	0.77	15.13
12/18	37.92	15	8	3.27	0.73	14.42
12/17	27.35	9	5	2.99	0.69	12.67
12/16	28.40	10	6	2.79	0.69	10.59
Annual Growth	(14.6%)	—	—	(31.9%)	2.8%	8.0%

University Bancorp Inc. (MI)

University Bancorp is the holding company for University Bank. From one branch in Ann Arbor (the home of The University of Michigan), the bank offers standard services such as deposit accounts and loans. It mainly originates residential mortgages, with commercial mortgages, business loans, and consumer loans rounding out its lending activities. Shariah-compliant banking services (banking consistent with Islamic law) are offered through University Islamic Financial, which operates within University Bank's office. University Bancorp also owns University Insurance and Investments Services, and a majority of Midwest Loan Services, which provides mortgage origination and subservicing to credit unions.

EXECUTIVES

Chairman, Subsidiary Officer, Alma Wheeler Smith
Vice-Chairman, Subsidiary Officer, Willie Powell
President, Chief Executive Officer, Subsidiary Officer, Director, Stephen Lange Ranzini, $100,000 total compensation
Subsidiary Officer, Edie Jackson
Subsidiary Officer, Edward Burger, $130,000 total compensation
Subsidiary Officer, John N. Sickler, $97,391 total compensation
Lead Independent Director, Michael A. Talley
Auditors : UHY LLP

LOCATIONS

HQ: University Bancorp Inc. (MI)
959 Maiden Lane, Ann Arbor, MI 48105
Phone: 734 741-5858   **Fax:** 734 741-5859
Web: www.university-bank.com

COMPETITORS

CCFNB BANCORP, INC.
CENTRAL VIRGINIA BANKSHARES, INC.
FIRST KEYSTONE CORPORATION
MICHIGAN COMMUNITY BANCORP LIMITED
UNITED BANCSHARES, INC.

HISTORICAL FINANCIALS

Company Type: Public

Income Statement — FYE: December 31

	ASSETS ($mil)	NET INCOME ($mil)	INCOME AS % OF ASSETS	EMPLOYEES
12/20	557.6	28.0	5.0%	0
12/19	361.9	3.6	1.0%	0
12/18	247.0	2.2	0.9%	0
12/17	245.9	5.1	2.1%	0
12/16	190.9	3.8	2.0%	0
Annual Growth	30.7%	64.7%	—	—

2020 Year-End Financials
Return on assets: 6.0%
Return on equity: 61.9%
Long-term debt ($ mil.): —
No. of shares ($ mil.): 5.2
Sales ($ mil.): 136.9
Dividends
Yield: 1.1%
Payout: 2.8%
Market value ($ mil.): 65.0

	STOCK PRICE ($) FY Close	P/E High	P/E Low	Earnings	Dividends	Book Value
12/20	12.56	2	1	5.31	0.15	10.87
12/19	8.06	15	12	0.63	0.00	6.45
12/18	9.00	28	19	0.42	0.00	5.80
12/17	9.10	—	—	0.00	0.00	4.49
12/16	7.20	—	—	0.00	0.11	3.54
Annual Growth	14.9%	—	—	—	8.8%	32.3%

Univest Financial Corp

Univest Financial, including its wholly-owned subsidiary Univest Bank and Trust, has approximately $6.9 billion in assets and $4.0 billion in assets under management and supervision through its wealth management lines of business. Founded in 1876, Univest and its subsidiaries provide a full-range of financial solutions for individuals, businesses, municipalities and nonprofit organizations primarily in the Mid-Atlantic Region. The company delivers these services through a network of more than 50 offices and through online at www.univest.net.

Operations

Univest operates three main business segments: Banking, Wealth Management and Insurance.

The Banking segment accounts for about 85% of revenue and provides financial services to individuals, businesses, municipalities and non-profit organizations. These services include a full range of banking services such as deposit taking, loan origination and servicing, mortgage banking, other general banking services and equipment lease financing.

The Wealth Management segment (some 10% of total revenue) offers investment advisory, financial planning, trust and brokerage services. The Wealth Management segment serves a diverse client base of private families and individuals, municipal pension plans, retirement plans, trusts and guardianships.

The Insurance segment (more than 5% of total revenue) includes a full-service insurance brokerage agency offering commercial property and casualty insurance, employee benefit solutions, personal insurance lines and human resources consulting.

Broadly speaking, Univest gets about 70% of its revenue from interest income. The rest of its revenue comes from insurance commissions and fees, investment advisory commission and fee income, trust fee income, deposit account service charges, and other miscellaneous income sources.

Geographic Reach

Souderton, Pennsylvania-based Univest provides banking and financial services to customers primarily in Bucks, Berks, Chester, Cumberland, Dauphin, Delaware, Lancaster, Lehigh, Montgomery, Northampton, Philadelphia and York counties in Pennsylvania and Atlantic, Burlington and Cape May counties in New Jersey. The highest concentration of its deposits and loans are in Montgomery and Bucks counties where 20 out of its more than 35 financial centers are located.

Sales and Marketing

Univest serves individuals, businesses, municipalities, and non-profit organizations.

Financial Performance

The company reported a net interest income of $188.4 million in 2021, an 8% increase from the previous year's net interest income of $174.4 million. This was primarily due to a higher interest income for the year.

In 2021, the company had a net income of $91.8 million, a 96% increase from the previous year's net income of $46.9 million.

The company's cash at the end of 2021 was $890.2 million. Operating activities generated $102.3 million, while investing activities used $126.8 million mainly for purchases of investment securities available-for-sale. Financing activities provided another $890.2 million.

EXECUTIVES

Chairman, Subsidiary Officer, Director, William S. Aichele, $475,000 total compensation
President, Chief Executive Officer, Chief Operating Officer, Subsidiary Officer, Director, Jeffrey M. Schweitzer, $600,000 total compensation
Senior Executive Vice President, Subsidiary Officer, Michael S. Keim, $390,000 total compensation
Senior Executive Vice President, Chief Risk Officer, Subsidiary Officer, Duane J. Brobst, $252,000 total compensation
Executive Vice President, General Counsel, Chief Risk Officer, Subsidiary Officer, Megan D. Santana, $268,846 total compensation
Finance Executive Vice President, Finance Chief Financial Officer, Finance Subsidiary Officer, Brian J. Richardson
Director, Roger H. Ballou
Director, Todd S. Benning
Director, Suzanne Keenan
Director, Glenn E. Moyer
Director, K. Leon Moyer, $335,000 total compensation
Director, Natalye Paquin
Director, Thomas M. Petro
Director, Michael L. Turner
Director, Robert C. Wonderling
Director, Charles H. Zimmerman
Auditors: KPMG LLP

LOCATIONS

HQ: Univest Financial Corp
14 North Main Street, Souderton, PA 18964
Phone: 215 721-2400
Web: www.univest.net

PRODUCTS/OPERATIONS

2015 sales

	$ mil.	% of total
Banking	120.9	79
Wealth Management	18.9	12
Insurance	14.4	9
Other	0.3	-
Total	154.5	100

COMPETITORS

AMERICAN NATIONAL BANKSHARES INC.
ASSOCIATED BANC-CORP
CITIZENS & NORTHERN CORPORATION
CNB FINANCIAL CORPORATION
FIRSTMERIT CORPORATION
HANCOCK WHITNEY CORPORATION
INDEPENDENT BANK CORP.
PEAPACK-GLADSTONE FINANCIAL CORPORATION
STOCK YARDS BANCORP, INC.
WINTRUST FINANCIAL CORPORATION

HISTORICAL FINANCIALS

Company Type: Public

Income Statement
FYE: December 31

	ASSETS ($mil)	NET INCOME ($mil)	INCOME AS % OF ASSETS	EMPLOYEES
12/20	6,336.4	46.9	0.7%	896
12/19	5,380.9	65.7	1.2%	873
12/18	4,984.3	50.5	1.0%	841
12/17	4,554.8	44.0	1.0%	855
12/16	4,230.5	19.5	0.5%	840
Annual Growth	10.6%	24.5%	—	1.6%

2020 Year-End Financials

Return on assets: 0.7% Dividends
Return on equity: 6.8% Yield: 3.8%
Long-term debt ($ mil.): — Payout: 64.0%
No. of shares ($ mil.): 29.3 Market value ($ mil.): 603.0
Sales ($ mil.): 282.2

	STOCK PRICE ($) FY Close	P/E High/Low		PER SHARE ($) Earnings	Dividends	Book Value
12/20	20.58	17	9	1.60	0.80	23.64
12/19	26.78	12	10	2.24	0.80	23.01
12/18	21.57	17	12	1.72	0.80	21.32
12/17	28.05	20	16	1.64	0.80	20.57
12/16	30.90	37	22	0.84	0.80	19.00
Annual Growth	(9.7%)	—	—	17.5%	0.0%	5.6%

Upstart Holdings Inc

EXECUTIVES

Chairperson, Chief Executive Officer, Director, Dave Girouard
Product and Data Science Senior Vice President, Product and Data Science Chief Technology Officer, Director, Paul Gu
Operations Senior Vice President, People Senior Vice President, Business Operations Senior Vice President, Anna M. Counselman
Chief Financial Officer, Sanjay Datta
Chief Legal Officer, Corporate Secretary, Scott Darling
Director, Lead Independent Director, Sukhinder Singh Cassidy
Director, Ciaran O'Kelly
Director, Mary Hentges
Director, Jeffrey T. Huber
Director, Hilliard C. Terry
Director, Kerry Whorton Cooper

LOCATIONS

HQ: Upstart Holdings Inc
2950 S. Delaware Street, Suite 300, San Mateo, CA 94403
Phone: 650 204-1000
Web: www.upstart.com

HISTORICAL FINANCIALS
Company Type: Public

Income Statement — FYE: December 31

	REVENUE ($mil)	NET INCOME ($mil)	NET PROFIT MARGIN	EMPLOYEES
12/21	848.5	135.4	16.0%	1,497
12/20	233.4	5.9	2.6%	554
12/19	164.1	(0.4)	—	429
12/18	99.3	(12.3)	—	0
12/17	57.2	(7.7)	—	0
Annual Growth	96.2%	—	—	—

2021 Year-End Financials
Debt ratio: 38.2%
Return on equity: 24.4%
Cash ($ mil.): 1,191.2
Current Ratio: 6.39
Long-term debt ($ mil.): 695.4
No. of shares ($ mil.): 83.6
Dividends
Yield: —
Payout: —
Market value ($ mil.): 12,658.0

	STOCK PRICE ($) FY Close	P/E High/Low		PER SHARE ($) Earnings	Dividends	Book Value
12/21	151.30	225	25	1.43	0.00	9.65
12/20	40.75	—	—	0.00	0.00	4.10
Annual Growth	271.3%	—	—	—	—	135.6%

US Global Investors Inc

While it may be a small world, financial investment company U.S. Global Investors wants to make it a little greener, after all. Primarily serving the U.S. Global Investors Funds and the U.S. Global Accolade Funds, the company is a mutual fund manager providing investment advisory, transfer agency, broker-dealer, and mailing services. It offers a family of no-load mutual funds generally geared toward long-term investing. The company also engages in corporate investment activities. U.S. Global Investors had about $724 million in assets under management in 2015.

EXECUTIVES

Chairman, Director, Jerold H. Rubinstein
Vice-Chairman, Director, Roy D. Terracina
Chief Executive Officer, Chief Investment Officer, Director, Frank E. Holmes, $422,000 total compensation
Chief Financial Officer, Lisa C. Callicotte, $135,000 total compensation
Director, Thomas F. Lydon
Auditors: BDO USA, LLP

LOCATIONS

HQ: US Global Investors Inc
7900 Callaghan Road, San Antonio, TX 78229
Phone: 210 308-1234
Web: www.usfunds.com

COMPETITORS

EPOCH HOLDING CORPORATION
FORESTERS FINANCIAL SERVICES, INC.
NUVEEN INVESTMENTS, INC.
OPPENHEIMERFUNDS, INC.
THE CAPITAL GROUP COMPANIES INC

HISTORICAL FINANCIALS
Company Type: Public

Income Statement — FYE: June 30

	REVENUE ($mil)	NET INCOME ($mil)	NET PROFIT MARGIN	EMPLOYEES
06/21	21.6	31.9	147.6%	23
06/20	4.4	(4.6)	—	23
06/19	4.9	(3.3)	—	24
06/18	6.2	0.6	10.3%	25
06/17	6.7	(0.5)	—	26
Annual Growth	33.8%	—	—	(3.0%)

2021 Year-End Financials
Debt ratio: —
Return on equity: 89.9%
Cash ($ mil.): 15.4
Current Ratio: 5.20
Long-term debt ($ mil.): —
No. of shares ($ mil.): 15.0
Dividends
Yield: 0.6%
Payout: 1.8%
Market value ($ mil.): 93.0

	STOCK PRICE ($) FY Close	P/E High/Low		PER SHARE ($) Earnings	Dividends	Book Value
06/21	6.19	6	1	2.12	0.04	3.61
06/20	1.90	—	—	(0.31)	0.03	1.11
06/19	1.81	—	—	(0.22)	0.03	1.43
06/18	1.61	171	32	0.04	0.03	1.69
06/17	1.52	—	—	(0.03)	0.03	1.57
Annual Growth	42.1%	—	—	—	9.1%	23.1%

USA Compression Partners LP

EXECUTIVES

President, Chief Executive Officer, Associate/Affiliate Company Officer, Director, Eric D. Long, $625,233 total compensation
Vice President, Chief Operating Officer, Associate/Affiliate Company Officer, Eric A. Scheller
Vice President, Secretary, General Counsel, Associate/Affiliate Company Officer, Christopher W. Porter
Human Resources Vice President, Human Resources Associate/Affiliate Company Officer, Sean T. Kimble
Finance Vice President, Finance Chief Accounting Officer, George Tracy Owens
Vice President, Chief Financial Officer, Treasurer, Associate/Affiliate Company Officer, Michael C. Pearl
Director, Christopher R. Curia
Director, Matthew Stephen Hartman
Director, Glenn E. Joyce
Director, Thomas E. Long
Director, Thomas P. Mason
Director, W. Brett Smith
Director, William S. Waldheim
Director, Bradford D. Whitehurst
Auditors: Grant Thornton LLP

LOCATIONS

HQ: USA Compression Partners LP
111 Congress Avenue, Suite 2400, Austin, TX 78701
Phone: 512 473-2662
Web: www.usacompression.com

HISTORICAL FINANCIALS
Company Type: Public

Income Statement — FYE: December 31

	REVENUE ($mil)	NET INCOME ($mil)	NET PROFIT MARGIN	EMPLOYEES
12/21	632.6	10.2	1.6%	697
12/20	667.6	(594.7)	—	742
12/19	698.3	39.1	5.6%	879
12/18	584.3	(10.5)	—	864
12/17	280.2	11.4	4.1%	426
Annual Growth	22.6%	(2.6%)	—	13.1%

2021 Year-End Financials
Debt ratio: 71.3%
Return on equity: 2.1%
Cash ($ mil.): —
Current Ratio: 1.09
Long-term debt ($ mil.): 1,973.2
No. of shares ($ mil.): 97.3
Dividends
Yield: 12.0%
Payout: —
Market value ($ mil.): 1,699.0

	STOCK PRICE ($) FY Close	P/E High/Low		PER SHARE ($) Earnings	Dividends	Book Value
12/21	17.45	—	—	(0.40)	2.10	5.94
12/20	13.60	—	—	(6.65)	2.10	8.40
12/19	18.14	—	—	(0.02)	2.10	17.16
12/18	12.98	—	—	(0.43)	2.10	19.26
12/17	16.54	123	92	0.16	2.10	10.19
Annual Growth	1.3%	—	—	—	0.0%	(12.6%)

USA Truck, Inc.

Truckload carrier USA Truck moves freight not only in the US, but also in Canada, and, through partners, into Mexico. USA Truck has a fleet of over 2,155 tractors and nearly 6,550 trailers. The company provides both medium-haul and regional truckload services, along with dedicated contract carriage. USA Truck team members have cultivated a thorough understanding of the needs of shippers in key industries, which the company believes helps with the development of long-term, service-oriented relationships with its customers.

Operations

The company has two reportable segments: Trucking, consisting of the company's truckload and dedicated freight service offerings, and USAT Logistics, consisting of the company's freight brokerage and rail intermodal service offerings.

The company's trucking segment provides motor carrier services as a medium-haul common and contract carrier, utilizing equipment owned or leased by the company or independent contractors. Its dedicated freight service offering provides truckload motor carrier services to specific customers for movement of freight over particular routes at specified times. The segment accounts for about 60% of revenue.

USAT Logistics (over 40% of sales) provides freight brokerage, logistics, and intermodal rail service to its customers by utilizing third party capacity.

Geographic Reach

Headquartered in Van Buren, Arkansas, USA Truck offers its services throughout the continental US and in portions of Mexico and Canada.

The company's network consists of about 20 facilities, including USAT Logistics offices. USAT's facilities were located in or near the following cities: Arkansas, Florida, Georgia, Illinois, Ohio, Pennsylvania, Texas, and Washington.

Sales and Marketing

One customer accounted for more than 10% of the company's consolidated operating revenues. The company's largest 10 customers comprised over 45% of the company's consolidated operating revenue. The company provided services to more than 600 customers across all USA Truck service offerings.

Financial Performance

The company had a total operating revenue of $710.4 million in 2021, a 29% increase from the previous year's total operating revenue of $551.1 million.

In 2021, the company had a net income of $24.8 million, a 422% increase from the previous year's net income of $4.7 million.

The company's cash at the end of 2021 was $1.3 million. Operating activities generated $31.2 million, while investing activities used $1.1 million, mainly for capital expenditures. Financing activities used another $29.1 million, mainly for payments on long-term debt.

Company Background

The company got its start in 1983 as Crawford Produce, Inc. (with fewer than 10 tractors in operation). It was incorporated under the name USA Truck in 1986 and was purchased by its management in 1989. USA Truck's IPO was completed in 1992.

EXECUTIVES

Chairman, Director, Robert A. Peiser
President, Chief Executive Officer, James D. Reed, $456,250 total compensation
Executive Vice President, Chief Commercial Officer, Timothy W. Guin
Executive Vice President, Chief Financial Officer, Jason R. Bates, $315,000 total compensation
Vice President, Chief Technology Officer, Kimberly K. Littlejohn, $138,173 total compensation
Division Officer, George T. Henry
Director, Robert E. Creager
Director, Alexander David Greene
Director, Gary R. Enzor
Director, Thomas M. Glaser, $38,417 total compensation
Director, Barbara J. Faulkenberry
Director, M. Susan Chambers

Auditors : Grant Thornton LLP

LOCATIONS

HQ: USA Truck, Inc.
3200 Industrial Park Road, Van Buren, AR 72956
Phone: 479 471-2500
Web: www.usa-truck.com

PRODUCTS/OPERATIONS

2014 Sales

	$ mil.	% of total
Trucking	423.5	70
Strategic capacity Solutions	179.0	30
Total	602.5	100

COMPETITORS

COVENANT LOGISTICS GROUP, INC.
GATX CORPORATION
KNIGHT TRANSPORTATION, INC.
KNIGHT-SWIFT TRANSPORTATION HOLDINGS INC.
MARTEN TRANSPORT, LTD.
NAVISTAR INTERNATIONAL CORPORATION
P.A.M. TRANSPORTATION SERVICES, INC.
SCHNEIDER NATIONAL, INC.
UNIVERSAL LOGISTICS HOLDINGS, INC.
WERNER ENTERPRISES, INC.

HISTORICAL FINANCIALS

Company Type: Public

Income Statement — FYE: December 31

	REVENUE ($mil)	NET INCOME ($mil)	NET PROFIT MARGIN	EMPLOYEES
12/21	710.3	24.7	3.5%	2,100
12/20	551.1	4.7	0.9%	2,000
12/19	522.6	(4.6)	—	2,050
12/18	534.0	12.2	2.3%	2,500
12/17	446.5	7.4	1.7%	2,000
Annual Growth	12.3%	34.8%	—	1.2%

2021 Year-End Financials

Debt ratio: 39.8%
Return on equity: 25.2%
Cash ($ mil.): 1.3
Current Ratio: 1.30
Long-term debt ($ mil.): 119.6
No. of shares ($ mil.): 8.9
Dividends
Yield: —
Payout: —
Market value ($ mil.): 177.0

	STOCK PRICE ($) FY Close	P/E High/Low		PER SHARE ($) Earnings	Dividends	Book Value
12/21	19.88	8	3	2.76	0.00	12.53
12/20	8.93	23	5	0.53	0.00	9.69
12/19	7.45	—	—	(0.55)	0.00	9.14
12/18	14.97	19	10	1.49	0.00	9.62
12/17	18.13	20	6	0.93	0.00	8.02
Annual Growth	2.3%	—	—	31.3%	—	11.8%

Uwharrie Capital Corp.

Uwharrie Capital is the multibank holding company for Anson Bank & Trust, Bank of Stanly, and Cabarrus Bank & Trust, which operate a total of about ten branches in west-central North Carolina. Serving consumers and local business customers, the banks offer a variety of deposit accounts and credit cards, as well as investments, insurance, asset management, and brokerage services offered by other Uwharrie subsidiaries such as insurance agency BOS Agency, securities broker-dealer Strategic Alliance, mortgage brokerage Gateway Mortgage, and Strategic Investment Advisors. The banks mainly write residential and commercial mortgages, but also construction, business, and consumer loans.

EXECUTIVES

President, Chief Executive Officer, Subsidiary Officer, Roger L. Dick, $258,455 total compensation
Chief Risk Officer, Subsidiary Officer, Roy David Beaver, $200,000 total compensation
Subsidiary Officer, Christy D. Stoner, $153,493 total compensation
Executive Vice President, Controller, Barbara S. Williams, $99,585 total compensation
Chief Financial Officer, Subsidiary Officer, Heather H. Almond
Subsidiary Officer, W. D. "Bill" Lawhon, $139,337 total compensation
Director, Dean M. Bowers
Director, James O. Campbell
Director, Tara G. Eudy
Director, Deidre B. Foster
Director, Allen K. Furr
Director, S. Todd Swaringen
Director, Thomas M. Hearne
Director, Matthew R. Hudson
Director, Harvey H. Leavitt
Director, Cynthia L. Mynatt
Director, James E. Nance
Director, Chris M. Poplin
Director, Vernon A. Russell
Director, Merlin Amirtharaj
Director, Joe S. Brooks
Director, W. Chester Lowder
Director, Wesley A. Morgan
Director, Frank A. Rankin
Director, Randy T. Russell
Director, Matthew A. Shaver
Auditors : Dixon Hughes Goodman LLP

LOCATIONS

HQ: Uwharrie Capital Corp.
132 North First Street, Albemarle, NC 28001
Phone: 704 983-6181
Web: www.uwharrie.com

COMPETITORS

CAPITAL BANK CORPORATION
COMMERCIAL NATIONAL FINANCIAL CORPORATION
DCB FINANCIAL CORP
FAUQUIER BANKSHARES, INC.
SOUTHWEST GEORGIA FINANCIAL CORPORATION

Valley National Bancorp (NJ)

Valley National Bancorp owns Valley National Bank, which serves commercial and retail clients through more than 230 branches in northern and central New Jersey and in the New York City boroughs of Manhattan, Brooklyn, and Queens, as well as on Long Island. The bank provides standard services like checking and savings accounts, loans and mortgages, credit cards, and trust services. Subsidiaries offer asset management, mortgage and auto loan servicing, title insurance, and property/casualty, life, and health insurance. The company was founded in 1927 as the Passaic Park Trust Company.

Operations

The company operates in four business segments: Commercial Lending (over 70% of sales), Consumer Lending (around 20%), Investment Management (some 5%), and Corporate and other.

Commercial Lending segment includes Commercial and industrial loans which represented around 17% of the total loan portfolio. It makes commercial loans to small and middle market businesses most often located in New Jersey, New York, Florida and Alabama. It also offers commercial real estate loans (around 60% of loan portfolio). Property types in this portfolio range from multi-family residential properties to non-owner occupied commercial, industrial/warehouse and retail.

The Consumer Lending segment includes residential mortgage loans (about 15%), and other consumer loans (about 10%). The residential mortgage loans include fixed and variable interest rate loans, while other consumer loan portfolio is primarily comprised of direct and indirect automobile loans, loans secured by the cash surrender value of life insurance, home equity loans and lines of credit, and to a lesser extent, secured and unsecured other consumer loans (including credit card loans).

The Investment Management segment primarily focused on its lending and wealth management services, a large portion of our income is generated through investments in various types of securities, and depending on our liquid cash position, interest-bearing deposits with banks (primarily the Federal Reserve Bank of New York), as part of our asset/liability management strategies.

Geographic Reach

Based in Manhattan, New York, Valley National Bancorp conducts business at over 230 retail banking centers locations in northern and central New Jersey, the New York City boroughs of Manhattan, Brooklyn and Queens, Long Island, Florida, and Alabama.

Financial Performance

The company's revenue for fiscal 2021 increased to $1.4 billion compared from the prior year with $1.3 billion.

Net income for fiscal 2021 increased to $473.8 million compared from the prior year with $390.6 million.

Cash held by the company at the end of fiscal 2021 increased to $2.0 billion. Cash provided by operations and financing activities were $837.1 million and $964.4 million, respectively. Cash used for investing activities was $1.1 billion, mainly for net loan originations and purchases.

EXECUTIVES

Chairman, President, Chief Executive Officer, Subsidiary Officer, Director, Ira D. Robbins, $850,000 total compensation
President, Chief Banking Officer, Thomas A. Iadanza, $600,000 total compensation
Senior Executive Vice President, Chief Financial Officer, Subsidiary Officer, Michael D. Hagedorn, $590,000 total compensation
Senior Executive Vice President, General Counsel, Subsidiary Officer, Ronald H. Janis, $515,000 total compensation
Commercial Banking Senior Vice President, Joseph V. Chillura
Director, Andrew B. Abramson
Director, Peter J. Baum
Director, Eric P. Edelstein
Director, Marc J. Lenner
Director, Peter V. Maio
Director, Avner Mendelson
Director, Suresh L. Sani
Director, Lisa J. Schultz
Director, Jennifer W. Steans
Director, Jeffrey S. Wilks
Director, Sidney S. Williams
Auditors: KPMG LLP

LOCATIONS

HQ: Valley National Bancorp (NJ)
One Penn Plaza, New York, NY 10119
Phone: 973 305-8800
Web: www.valleynationalbank.com

PRODUCTS/OPERATIONS

2016 Sales

	$ mil.	% of total
Interest Income		
Interest and fees on loans	685.9	79
Interest and dividends on investment securities	79.9	9
Interest on federal funds sold and other short-term investments	1.1	0
Non-Interest Income		
Gains on sales of loans, net	22.0	3
Service charges on deposit accounts	20.9	2
Insurance commissions	19.1	2
Trust and investment services	10.3	1
Bank owned life insurance	6.7	1
Fees from loan servicing	6.4	1
Gains on sales of assets, net	1.4	0
Gains on securities transactions, net	0.8	0
Change in FDIC loss-share receivable	(1.3)	0
Other	16.9	2
Total	870.1	100

COMPETITORS

CITY HOLDING COMPANY
CITY NATIONAL CORPORATION
FIRST HORIZON CORPORATION
HOMESTREET, INC.
MIDLAND FINANCIAL CO.
MUFG AMERICAS HOLDINGS CORPORATION
OLD NATIONAL BANCORP
PEOPLE'S UNITED FINANCIAL, INC.
SOUTHWEST BANCORP, INC.
TRUIST FINANCIAL CORPORATION

HISTORICAL FINANCIALS

Company Type: Public

Income Statement — Valley National Bancorp (first table)

FYE: December 31

	ASSETS ($mil)	NET INCOME ($mil)	INCOME AS % OF ASSETS	EMPLOYEES
12/20	827.7	7.5	0.9%	315
12/19	656.7	2.5	0.4%	191
12/18	632.3	1.9	0.3%	189
12/17	576.3	1.0	0.2%	184
12/16	548.2	1.6	0.3%	181
Annual Growth	10.9%	46.9%	—	14.9%

2020 Year-End Financials

Return on assets: 1.0%
Return on equity: 17.3%
Long-term debt ($ mil.): —
No. of shares ($ mil.): 7.2
Sales ($ mil.): 44.9
Dividends Yield: —
Payout: 10.0%
Market value ($ mil.): 38.0

	STOCK PRICE ($) FY Close	P/E High	P/E Low	PER SHARE ($) Earnings	PER SHARE ($) Dividends	PER SHARE ($) Book Value
12/20	5.25	6	4	1.03	0.00	6.69
12/19	5.74	18	14	0.33	0.00	5.12
12/18	5.25	24	18	0.25	0.00	4.52
12/17	5.68	45	41	0.13	0.00	4.36
12/16	5.45	29	19	0.21	0.00	4.19
Annual Growth	(0.9%)	—	—	49.4%	—	12.4%

Income Statement — (second table)

FYE: December 31

	ASSETS ($mil)	NET INCOME ($mil)	INCOME AS % OF ASSETS	EMPLOYEES
12/20	40,686.0	390.6	1.0%	3,155
12/19	37,436.0	309.7	0.8%	3,174
12/18	31,863.0	261.4	0.8%	3,192
12/17	24,002.3	161.9	0.7%	2,842
12/16	22,864.4	168.1	0.7%	2,828
Annual Growth	15.5%	23.5%	—	2.8%

2020 Year-End Financials

Return on assets: 0.9%
Return on equity: 8.6%
Long-term debt ($ mil.): —
No. of shares ($ mil.): 403.8
Sales ($ mil.): 1,566.7
Dividends Yield: 4.5%
Payout: 57.1%
Market value ($ mil.): 3,938.0

	STOCK PRICE ($) FY Close	P/E High	P/E Low	PER SHARE ($) Earnings	PER SHARE ($) Dividends	PER SHARE ($) Book Value
12/20	9.75	12	7	0.93	0.44	11.37
12/19	11.45	14	10	0.87	0.44	10.87
12/18	8.88	18	11	0.75	0.44	10.11
12/17	11.22	22	18	0.58	0.44	9.58
12/16	11.64	19	13	0.63	0.44	9.02
Annual Growth	(4.3%)	—	—	10.2%	0.0%	6.0%

Valley Republic Bancorp

EXECUTIVES

Chairman, Eugene Voiland
President, Chief Executive Officer, Subsidiary Officer, Director, Geraud Smith
Executive Vice President, Chief Financial Officer, Subsidiary Officer, Stephen M. Annis
Executive Vice President, Chief Credit Officer, Subsidiary Officer, Jack Smith
Executive Vice President, Subsidiary Officer, Philip McLaughlin
Loans Vice President, Loans Subsidiary Officer, Brian Sabin
Senior Credit Analyst Assistant Vice President, Senior Credit Analyst Subsidiary Officer, Davin Jensen
Relationship Manager Assistant Vice President, Peri Jonas
Human Resources Senior Vice President, Administration Senior Vice President, Human Resources Subsidiary Officer, Administration Subsidiary Officer, Marcy Unruh
Agribusiness Senior Vice President, Agribusiness Subsidiary Officer, John Etchison
Assistant Loan Servicing Manager Assistant Vice President, Assistant Loan Servicing Manager Subsidiary Officer, Milagros Rodriguez
Branch Manager Vice President, Branch Manager Subsidiary Officer, Pritesh Patel
Branch Manager Vice President, Branch Manager Subsidiary Officer, Stan Newman
Compliance Manager Vice President, Compliance Manager Subsidiary Officer, Margie Schwartz
Credit Administration Specialist Vice President, Karen Elizabeth Campbell
Loan Servicing Manager Vice President, Loan Servicing Manager Subsidiary Officer, Roxana Chavez
IT Manager Vice President, IT Manager subsidiary Officer, Daniel Cardenas
Loans Vice President, Tracie Gregorio
Loans Vice President, Loans Subsidiary Officer, Janet Hepp
Operations Vice President, Operations Subsidiary Officer, Cathy Davies
BSA Officer Assistant Vice President, BSA Officer Subsidiary Officer, Marjie Hanlin
Electronic Banking Manager Assistant Vice President, Julie Cheeseman
Operations Manager Assistant Vice President, Bock Soutchay
Operations Support Manager Assistant Vice President, Melissa McDermott
Training Officer Assistant Vice President, Chasity Briese
Vice President, Controller, Subsidiary Officer, Garth Corrigan
Director, Greg Bynum
Director, Annette Davis
Director, Michael Hair
Director, Bruce Jay
Director, Anthony L. Leggio
Director, Angelo Mazzei
Director, Willy Reyneveld
Director, Carlos Sanchez
Director, Shawn C. Shambaugh
Director, James Shuler
Director, Warner Williams
Auditors: Eide Bailly, LLP

LOCATIONS

HQ: Valley Republic Bancorp
5000 California Avenue, Suite 110, Bakersfield, CA 93309
Phone: 661 371-2000 **Fax:** 661 371-2010
Web: www.valleyrepublicbank.com

HISTORICAL FINANCIALS
Company Type: Public

Income Statement				FYE: December 31
	REVENUE ($mil)	NET INCOME ($mil)	NET PROFIT MARGIN	EMPLOYEES
12/20	40.4	12.5	31.0%	0
12/19	36.5	9.7	26.6%	0
12/18	28.7	8.9	31.1%	0
12/17	23.2	5.2	22.6%	0
12/16	18.7	4.4	23.8%	0
Annual Growth	21.2%	29.4%	—	—

2020 Year-End Financials
Debt ratio: 3.6%
Return on equity: 14.4%
Cash ($ mil.): 140.7
Current Ratio: 0.13
Long-term debt ($ mil.): 39.3
No. of shares ($ mil.): 4.2
Dividends
Yield: —
Payout: —
Market value ($ mil.): 92.0

	STOCK PRICE ($) FY Close	P/E High/Low		PER SHARE ($) Earnings	Dividends	Book Value
12/20	21.75	9	5	2.97	0.00	22.55
12/19	26.01	14	11	2.33	0.00	18.59
12/18	31.50	15	12	2.14	0.00	16.87
12/17	29.00	21	12	1.29	0.00	14.94
12/16	16.80	14	11	1.16	0.00	13.60
Annual Growth	6.7%	—	—	26.4%	—	13.5%

Valvoline Inc

EXECUTIVES

Chairman, Director, Richard J. Freeland
Chief Executive Officer, Director, Samuel J. Mitchell, $950,000 total compensation
Senior Vice President, Division Officer, Lori A. Flees
Senior Vice President, Chief Legal Officer, Corporate Secretary, Julie M. O'Daniel, $390,000 total compensation
Senior Vice President, Chief Marketing Officer, Chief Transformation Officer, Heidi J. Matheys, $270,220 total compensation
Chief Financial Officer, Principal Accounting Officer, Mary E. Meixelsperger, $543,000 total compensation
Chief Accounting Officer, Controller, Dione R. Sturgeon
Director, Gerald W. Evans
Director, Carol H. Kruse
Director, Vada O. Manager
Director, Charles (Chuck) M. Sonsteby
Director, Mary J. Twinem
Director, Jennifer Slater
Auditors: Ernst & Young LLP

LOCATIONS

HQ: Valvoline Inc
100 Valvoline Way, Lexington, KY 40509
Phone: 859 357-7777
Web: www.valvoline.com

HISTORICAL FINANCIALS
Company Type: Public

Income Statement				FYE: September 30
	REVENUE ($mil)	NET INCOME ($mil)	NET PROFIT MARGIN	EMPLOYEES
09/21	2,981.0	420.0	14.1%	9,800
09/20	2,353.0	317.0	13.5%	8,800
09/19	2,390.0	208.0	8.7%	7,900
09/18	2,285.0	166.0	7.3%	6,700
09/17	2,084.0	304.0	14.6%	5,600
Annual Growth	9.4%	8.4%	—	15.0%

2021 Year-End Financials
Debt ratio: 53.1%
Return on equity: —
Cash ($ mil.): 230.0
Current Ratio: 1.82
Long-term debt ($ mil.): 1,677
No. of shares ($ mil.): 180.0
Dividends
Yield: 1.6%
Payout: 24.7%
Market value ($ mil.): 5,612.0

	STOCK PRICE ($) FY Close	P/E High/Low		PER SHARE ($) Earnings	Dividends	Book Value
09/21	31.18	15	8	2.29	0.50	0.75
09/20	19.04	14	5	1.69	0.45	(0.41)
09/19	22.03	21	16	1.10	0.42	(1.37)
09/18	21.51	30	24	0.84	0.30	(1.90)
09/17	23.45	17	13	1.49	0.20	(0.58)
Annual Growth	7.4%	—	—	11.3%	26.4%	—

Vanda Pharmaceuticals Inc

Vanda Pharmaceuticals is a leading biopharmaceutical company focused on the development and commercialization of innovative therapies to address high unmet medical needs and improve the lives of patients. The company's first commercial drug was schizophrenia treatment Fanapt (iloperidone). It continues to commercialize another drug, Hetlioz (tasimelteon) for the treatment of non-24-hour sleep-wake disorder. Other drug candidates are for the treatments of atopic dermatitis, gastroparesis and motion sickness, as well as a portfolio of Cystic Fibrosis Transmembrane Conductance Regulator (CFTR) activators and inhibitors for the treatment of dry eye and ocular inflammation. Vanda typically licenses development and commercialization rights for its compounds from (and to) companies including Bristol-Myers Squibb, Eli Lilly, and Novartis.

Operations

Vanda's product pipeline includes Tradipitant, a small molecule neurokinin-1 receptor (NK-1R) receptor antagonist, for the treatment of gastroparesis, motion sickness, atopic dermatitis, and COVID-19 pneumonia; VTR-297, a small molecule histone deacetylase (HDAC) inhibitor for the treatment of hematologic malignancies and with potential use as a treatment for several oncology indications; VQW-765, a small molecule nicotinic acetylcholine receptor partial agonist, with potential use for the treatment of psychiatric disorders; VHX-896 (formerly P88), the active metabolite of iloperidone, and a portfolio of Cystic Fibrosis Transmembrane Conductance Regulator (CFTR) activators and inhibitors for the treatment of dry eye and ocular inflammation and for the treatment of secretory diarrhea disorders, including cholera.

Hetlioz accounts for some 65% of the company's revenue, while Fanapt brings in approximately 35%.

Geographic Reach

Headquartered in Washington, DC, Vanda commercializes its products in the US and Canada. Its distribution partners launched Fanapt in Israel and Mexico. Vanda began rolling out Hetlioz in some countries in Europe.

Sales and Marketing

HETLIOZ capsules were approved in the US for the treatment of Non-24 in 2014 and HETLIOZ capsules and oral suspension were approved for the treatment of nighttime sleep disturbances in SMS in 2020. It commercially launched HETLIOZ capsules in the US in 2014 and the oral suspension in 2021. Additionally, HETLIOZ capsules were approved in the EU for the treatment of Non-24 in totally blind adults in 2015 and, in 2016, it commercially launched HETLIOZ in Germany. Given the range of potential indications for HETLIOZ, the company may pursue one or more partnerships for the development and commercialization of HETLIOZ worldwide.

Fanapt oral tablets were approved in the US for the treatment of schizophrenia in 2009 and commercially launched in the US in 2010. It continues to explore the regulatory path and commercial opportunity for Fanapt oral formulation in other regions.

Its revenues are generated from product sales and are concentrated with specialty pharmacies, including OptumRx (a subsidiary of UnitedHealth Group) and Accredo (a subsidiary of Express Scripts), and wholesalers, including Cardinal Health, Inc., AmerisourceBergen Drug Corporation, and McKesson Corporation. These five major customers each accounted for more than 10% of total revenues and, as a group, represented some 90% of total revenues.

Its advertising expenses were $6.7 million, $12.6 million, and $3.2 million for the years 2021, 2020, and 2019, respectively.

Financial Performance

Total revenues increased by $20.5 million, or 8%, to $268.7 million for the year ended December 31, 2021 compared to $248.2 million for the year ended December 31, 2020. HETLIOZÂ® net product sales increased by $12.9 million, or 8%, to $173.5 million for the year ended December 31, 2021 compared to $160.7 million for the year ended December 31, 2020. The increase to net product sales was attributable to an increase in price net of deductions partially offset by a decrease in volume.

Net income for fiscal 2021 increased to $33.2 million compared from the prior year with $23.3 million.

Cash held by the company at the end of fiscal 2021 decreased to $52.6 million. Cash provided by operations and financing activities were $64.2 million and $3.6 million, respectively. Cash used for investing activities was $76.7 million, mainly for purchases of marketable securities.

Strategy

Vanda's goal is to further solidify its position as a leading global biopharmaceutical company focused on developing and commercializing innovative therapies addressing high unmet medical needs through the application of its drug development expertise and its pharmacogenetics and pharmacogenomics expertise. The key elements of Vanda's strategy to accomplish this goal are to: Maximize the commercial success of HETLIOZ and Fanapt; Enter into strategic partnerships to supplement our capabilities and to extend its commercial reach; Pursue the clinical development and regulatory approval of its products, including tradipitant; Apply its pharmacogenetics and pharmacogenomics expertise to differentiate its products; Expand its product portfolio through the identification and acquisition of additional products; and Utilize novel and innovative approaches in pursuit of each of these strategies.

Company Background

The company was established in 2003 by Dr. Mihael Polymeropoulos, Vanda's CEO and a former researcher for Novartis.

EXECUTIVES

President, Chief Executive Officer, Director,
Mihael H. Polymeropoulos, $700,000 total compensation

Senior Vice President, Chief Financial Officer, Treasurer, Kevin Patrick Moran

Business Development Senior Vice President, Gunther Birznieks, $375,000 total compensation

Senior Vice President, Chief Marketing Officer, Joakim Wijkstrom

Senior Vice President, General Counsel, Secretary, Timothy Williams, $144,886 total compensation

Director, Richard W. Dugan
Director, Anne Sempowski Ward
Director, Phaedra S. Chrousos
Director, Stephen Ray Mitchell
Auditors : PricewaterhouseCoopers LLP

LOCATIONS

HQ: Vanda Pharmaceuticals Inc
2200 Pennsylvania Avenue N.W., Suite 300 E, Washington, DC 20037
Phone: 202 734-3400
Web: www.vandapharma.com

PRODUCTS/OPERATIONS

2015 Sales

	$ mil	% of total
Fanapt	65.6	60
Hetlioz	44.3	40
Total	109.9	100

COMPETITORS

ARIAD PHARMACEUTICALS, INC.
BIOCRYST PHARMACEUTICALS, INC.
BIODELIVERY SCIENCES INTERNATIONAL, INC.
CELGENE CORPORATION
EAGLE PHARMACEUTICALS, INC.
INCYTE CORPORATION
LEXICON PHARMACEUTICALS, INC.
SUCAMPO PHARMACEUTICALS, INC.
SUPERNUS PHARMACEUTICALS, INC.
VIVUS, INC.

HISTORICAL FINANCIALS

Company Type: Public

Income Statement — FYE: December 31

	REVENUE ($mil)	NET INCOME ($mil)	NET PROFIT MARGIN	EMPLOYEES
12/20	248.1	23.3	9.4%	292
12/19	227.1	115.5	50.9%	284
12/18	193.1	25.2	13.1%	270
12/17	165.0	(15.5)	—	273
12/16	146.0	(18.0)	—	142
Annual Growth	14.2%	—	—	19.7%

2020 Year-End Financials

Debt ratio: — No. of shares ($ mil.): 54.8
Return on equity: 5.3% Dividends
Cash ($ mil.): 61.0 Yield: —
Current Ratio: 6.21 Payout: —
Long-term debt ($ mil.): — Market value ($ mil.): 721.0

	STOCK PRICE ($) FY Close	P/E High/Low		PER SHARE ($) Earnings	Dividends	Book Value
12/20	13.14	39	17	0.42	0.00	8.26
12/19	16.41	14	6	2.11	0.00	7.67
12/18	26.13	63	28	0.48	0.00	5.25
12/17	15.20	—	—	(0.35)	0.00	2.92
12/16	15.95	—	—	(0.41)	0.00	2.98
Annual Growth	(4.7%)	—	—	—	—	29.0%

Veeva Systems Inc

Veeva Systems is breathing new life into software for the health care industry. Its cloud-based software and mobile apps are used by pharmaceutical and biotechnology companies to manage critical business functions. Veeva Systems' customer relationship management software uses Salesforce's platform to manage sales and marketing functions. Its Veeva Vault provides content management and collaboration software for quality management in clinical trials and regulatory compliance for new drug submissions. Its software is used in 75 countries and available in more than 25 languages, but North America is its largest market. Founded in 2007, Veeva Systems went public in 2013.

Operations
Veeva sells its products through subscriptions and they account for about three-quarters of its business. The rest comes from professional services it provides for installing and training on its software.

Geographic Reach
Veeva Systems operates from three offices in the US and one in Canada. It also has locations in China, Japan, and Spain. North America is its largest market, accounting for 55% of sales. Europe makes up another 26%, while customers in Asia account for about 20% of sales. Sales outside North American increased about 64% in 2015 (ended January).

The company runs its software on data centers in California, Illinois, and Virginia and Germany, Japan, and the UK.

Sales and Marketing
The company uses a direct sales force with representatives in more than a dozen countries. Veeva Systems counts about 275 customers, including global pharmaceutical companies such as Bayer, Boehringer Ingelheim, Eli Lilly, Gilead Sciences, Merck, and Novartis.

Financial Performance
Veeva Systems has posted big gains in revenue since 2011. Sales zoomed from $30 million in fiscal 2011 (year-end January) to $313 million in 2015. In addition, it has been consistently profitable, which is uncommon for a relatively new and growing company. Profit increased almost 50% in 2015. While the company has increased spending on research and development and sales and marketing, revenue growth covered the higher spending and then some.

Strategy
The company makes 95% of sales from its Veeva CRM customer relationship management software, but new products are also being developed. Its latest software offering is Veeva Network, a customer master solution that creates and maintains healthcare provider and organization master data. Veeva Network also contains a proprietary database of people and companies in China and the US using data gathered from state, federal, and industry sources.

While Veeva Systems currently focuses on the life sciences industry, specifically pharmaceutical and biotechnology companies, it would like to expand to other specialized companies, such as contract research organizations (CROs) and contract manufacturing organizations (CMOs).

Mergers and Acquisitions
In 2015 Veeva acquired Qforma CrowdLink, a developer of key opinion leader (KOL) data and services for life sciences' brand, medical, and market access teams. Veeva introduced a product based on Qforma technology to help its customers get more sophisticated information for introducing products.

EXECUTIVES

Chairman, Director, Gordon Ritter
President, Chief Operating Officer, Thomas D. Schwenger
Chief Executive Officer, Director, Peter P. Gassner, $322,917 total compensation
Global Sales Executive Vice President, Alan V. Mateo, $322,917 total compensation
Senior Vice President, General Counsel, Corporate Secretary, Jonathan (Josh) Faddis, $322,917 total compensation
Chief Financial Officer, Brent Bowman
Chief Marketing Officer, Eleni Nitsa Zuppas, $322,917 total compensation
Division Officer, Howard Hsueh
Division Officer, Frederic Lequient, $322,917 total compensation
Director, Timothy S. Cabral, $322,917 total compensation
Director, Mark T. Carges
Director, Mary Lynne Hedley
Director, Priscilla Hung
Director, Tina Hunt
Director, Marshall L. Mohr
Director, Paul J. Sekhri
Director, Matthew J. Wallach, $322,917 total compensation
Auditors : KPMG LLP

LOCATIONS

HQ: Veeva Systems Inc
4280 Hacienda Drive, Pleasanton, CA 94588
Phone: 925 452-6500   **Fax:** 925 452-6504
Web: www.veeva.com

2015 Sales

	$mil.	% of total
North America	173.2	55
Europe	81.8	26
Asia/Pacific	58.2	19
Total	313.2	100

PRODUCTS/OPERATIONS

2015 Sales

	% of total
Subscription fees	74
Professional services	26
Total	100

Selected Products
Veeva CRM (customer relationship management)
　Veeva CLM (closed-loop marketing)
　Veeva iRep (mobile app for Apple products)
　Veeva CRM Approved Email (tracks regulatory compliant emails between sales reps and physicians)
Veeva Vault (content management and collaboration software)
　Veeva Vault eTMF (document management for clinical trials)
　Veeva Vault Investigator Portal (secure file exchange for clinical trials)
　Veeva Vault MedComms (medical content management)
　Veeva Vault PromoMats (promotional materials management)
　Veeva Vault QualityDocs (quality management)
　Veeva Vault Submissions (document management for regulatory submissions)
Veeva Network (master software and data stewardship)
　Veeva Network Provider Database (proprietary database of people and companies in China and the US)
　Veeva Network Customer Master (cleanse and match people and company data)
　Veeva Network Data Stewardship Services (data management)

COMPETITORS

CA, INC.
DATAWATCH CORPORATION
E2OPEN, LLC
INFOR (US), LLC
INFOR, INC.
MEDIDATA SOLUTIONS, INC.
PEGASYSTEMS INC.
STILO INTERNATIONAL LIMITED
VERSANT CORPORATION
WELLSKY CORPORATION

HISTORICAL FINANCIALS

Company Type: Public

Income Statement
FYE: January 31

	REVENUE ($mil)	NET INCOME ($mil)	NET PROFIT MARGIN	EMPLOYEES
01/21	1,465.0	379.9	25.9%	4,506
01/20	1,104.0	301.1	27.3%	3,501
01/19	862.2	229.8	26.7%	2,553
01/18	685.5	141.9	20.7%	2,171
01/17	544.0	68.8	12.6%	1,794
Annual Growth	28.1%	53.3%	—	25.9%

2021 Year-End Financials

Debt ratio: —
Return on equity: 19.2%
Cash ($ mil.): 730.5
Current Ratio: 3.23
Long-term debt ($ mil.): —
No. of shares ($ mil.): 152.0
Dividends
　Yield: —
　Payout: —
Market value ($ mil.): 42,035.0

	STOCK PRICE ($) FY Close	P/E High/Low		PER SHARE ($) Earnings	Dividends	Book Value
01/21	276.44	122	48	2.36	0.00	14.90
01/20	146.61	86	55	1.90	0.00	11.17
01/19	109.06	69	34	1.47	0.00	8.47
01/18	62.86	66	42	0.92	0.00	6.13
01/17	42.33	93	40	0.47	0.00	4.74
Annual Growth	59.9%	—	—	49.7%	—	33.2%

Verisk Analytics Inc

Verisk Analytics is a leading data analytics provider serving customers in insurance, energy and specialized markets, and financial services. Verisk's customers include the top property/casualty insurers in the US; leading credit card issuers in North America, the UK, and Australia; and the world's largest energy companies, as well as chemicals, metals, and mining, power utilities, and renewables companies; financial institutions; and governments, among others. Verisk was created by subsidiary Insurance Services Office (ISO) as a means of going public. More than 75% of the company's revenue is generated from the US.

Operations

Verisk operates through three segments: Insurance, Energy and Specialized Markets, and Financial Services.

The Insurance business, which brings in roughly 75% of revenue, primarily serves its P&C insurance customers and focuses on the prediction of loss, the selection and pricing of risk, and compliance with their reporting requirements in each US state in which they operate. It also develops and utilize machine learned and artificially intelligent models to forecast scenarios and produce both standard and customized analytics that help its customers better manage their businesses, including detecting fraud before and after a loss event and quantifying losses.

Energy and Specialized Markets, account more than 20% of revenue, provide analytics for customers in the global energy, chemicals, power, renewables, and mining and metals industries.

Financial Services, generate about 5% of revenue, provide financial institutions, regulators, payment processors, lenders, and merchants with competitive benchmarking, decision-making algorithms, business intelligence, and customized analytics.

Geographic Reach

Based in New Jersey, Verisk has offices in over 20 US states and international operations in Australia, Bahrain, Brazil, Bulgaria, Canada, China, Czech Republic, Denmark, France, Germany, India, Indonesia, Ireland, Israel, Italy, Japan, Malaysia, Mexico, Nepal, Netherlands, New Zealand, Nigeria, Poland, Russia, Singapore, South Africa, South Korea, Spain, the United Arab Emirates, and the UK.

The company's revenue is concentrated in the US, which provides more than 75% of revenue. The UK supplies over 5% and other countries account for more than 15%.

Sales and Marketing

A majority of Verisk's revenue is generated through annual subscriptions and long-term agreements. The company sells its products and services through salespeople, sales support, and technical consultants. Verisk serves clients in the insurance, energy, financial services, and risk management industries.

The company's advertising costs were $12.0 million, $8.5 million, and $10.7 million for the years 2021, 2020, and 2019, respectively.

Financial Performance

For the year ended December 31, 2021, Verisk had revenues of $3 billion and net income of $666.3 million. For the five-year period ended December 31, 2021, the company's consolidated revenues grew at a compound annual growth rate ("CAGR") of 9% and its net income grew at 4.7%.

In 2021, the company had a net income of $666.3 million, a 7% decrease from the previous year's net income of $712.7 million.

The company's cash at the end of 2021 was $280.3 million. Operating activities generated $1.2 billion, while investing activities used $592 million, mainly for acquisitions and purchases of controlling interests. Financing activities used another $498.9 million primarily for repurchases of common stock.

Strategy

Over the past five years, Verisk has grown its revenues at a CAGR of 9% through the successful execution of its business plan. Those results reflect strong organic revenue growth, new product development, and acquisitions. The company has made and continues to make, investments in people, data sets, analytic solutions, technology, and complementary businesses. The key components of its strategy include the following: increase solution penetration with customers; develop new proprietary data sets and predictive analytics; leverage the company's intellectual capital to expand into adjacent markets and new customer sectors; and pursue strategic acquisitions that complement its leadership positions.

Mergers and Acquisitions

In 2022, Verisk acquired Opta, Canada's leading provider of property intelligence and innovative technology solutions. The acquisition further expands Verisk's footprint in the Canadian market and supports Opta in reshaping risk management with valuable business intelligence.

In late 2021, Verisk acquired Driven Safety, a leading public record data aggregation firm that specializes in driver risk assessment in the US. The acquisition will expand Verisk's robust auto insurance analytics, providing insurers with information to further refine underwriting, improve the customer experience and promote public safety.

In 2021, Wood Mackenzie, a Verisk business, acquired Roskill, a privately-owned company and leader in metals and materials supply chain intelligence. Combining Roskill's capabilities with Wood Mackenzie reinforces its ability to provide comprehensive, integrated analysis across the energy, and metals and mining value chain. In particular, Roskill adds market-leading analysis, data, and insight on battery raw materials metals, which are an integral component of the energy transition.

In early 2021, FAST, a Verisk business, is a leading software provider in individual life insurance, is acquiring assets and capabilities of Norway-based 4C Solutions, a software advisory firm in group life insurance, to help insurers meet the rapidly changing coverage needs of companies and their employees. 4C's experienced staff, proven methodology and proprietary data architecture will help FAST serve the unmet needs of group life insurers and institutional annuity providers. Terms were not disclosed.

Company Background

Verisk traces its roots back to 1971, when ISO was created by an association of insurance companies. Verisk went public in 2009 in one of the largest offerings of the year, raising almost $2 billion.

EXECUTIVES

President, Chief Executive Officer, Director, Lee M. Shavel, $550,000 total compensation
Executive Vice President, Chief Financial Officer, Elizabeth Mann
Executive Vice President, Chief Information Officer, Nick Daffan
Executive Vice President, General Counsel, Corporate Secretary, Kathy Card Beckles
Chief Human Resources Officer, Sunita Holzer
Lead Independent Director, Director, Christopher M. Foskett
Director, Olumide Soroye
Director, Constantine P. Iordanou
Director, Jeffrey J. Dailey
Director, Wendy E. Lane
Director, Kimberly S. Stevenson
Director, Annell R. Bay
Director, David B. Wright
Director, Vincent K. Brooks
Director, Samuel G. Liss
Director, Bruce Hansen
Director, Therese M. Vaughan
Director, Kathleen A. Hogenson
Auditors : DELOITTE & TOUCHE LLP

LOCATIONS

HQ: Verisk Analytics Inc
545 Washington Boulevard, Jersey City, NJ 07310-1686
Phone: 201 469-3000
Web: www.verisk.com

PRODUCTS/OPERATIONS

2018 Sales by Segment

	$ mil.	% of total
Insurance	1,705.9	71
Energy & Specialized Markets	513.3	22
Financial Services	175.9	7
Total	2,395.1	100

Selected Markets:
P/C Insurance

Energy, Metals, and Mining
Financial Services
Supply Chain
HR Departments
Retail
Commercial Real Estate
Community Hazard Mitigation

COMPETITORS

ACXIOM LLC
CORESITE REALTY CORPORATION
COSTAR GROUP, INC.
EXLSERVICE HOLDINGS, INC.
INFOR, INC.
PERFORMANT FINANCIAL CORPORATION
S&P GLOBAL INC.
TECHTARGET, INC.
YELP INC.
YEXT, INC.

HISTORICAL FINANCIALS
Company Type: Public

Income Statement — FYE: December 31

	REVENUE ($mil)	NET INCOME ($mil)	NET PROFIT MARGIN	EMPLOYEES
12/21	2,998.6	666.2	22.2%	9,367
12/20	2,784.6	712.7	25.6%	8,960
12/19	2,607.1	449.9	17.3%	9,300
12/18	2,395.1	598.7	25.0%	8,184
12/17	2,145.2	555.1	25.9%	7,304
Annual Growth	8.7%	4.7%	—	6.4%

2021 Year-End Financials
Debt ratio: 42.4%
Return on equity: 24.1%
Cash ($ mil.): 280.3
Current Ratio: 0.49
Long-term debt ($ mil.): 2,342.8
No. of shares ($ mil.): 161.6
Dividends
  Yield: 0.5%
  Payout: 27.1%
Market value ($ mil.): 36,975.0

	STOCK PRICE ($) FY Close	P/E High/Low		PER SHARE ($) Earnings	Dividends	Book Value
12/21	228.73	56	39	4.08	1.16	17.42
12/20	207.59	47	28	4.31	1.08	16.57
12/19	149.34	60	38	2.70	1.00	13.86
12/18	109.04	34	25	3.56	0.00	12.63
12/17	96.00	29	23	3.29	0.00	11.68
Annual Growth	24.2%	—	—	5.5%	—	10.5%

Veritex Holdings Inc

EXECUTIVES

President, Chief Executive Officer, Subsidiary Officer, Chairman, Director, C. Malcolm Holland, $460,000 total compensation

Senior Executive Vice President, Chief financial Officer, Subsidiary Officer, Terry S. Earley

Senior Executive Vice President, Chief Credit Officer, Subsidiary Officer, Clay Riebe, $285,000 total compensation

Senior Executive Vice President, Subsidiary Officer, James Recer

Senior Executive Vice President, Subsidiary Officer, LaVonda Renfro, $225,000 total compensation

Senior Executive Vice President, Subsidiary Officer, Angela Harper

Senior Executive Vice President, Subsidiary Officer, Cara McDaniel

Director, Arcilia C. Acosta
Director, Pat S. Bolin
Director, William D. Ellis
Director, William E. Fallon
Director, Mark C. Griege
Director, Steven J. Lerner
Director, Manuel J. Mehos
Director, Gregory B. Morrison
Director, John T. Sughrue
Director, April Box
Director, Blake Bozman
Director, Gordon Huddleston
Auditors : Grant Thornton LLP

LOCATIONS

HQ: Veritex Holdings Inc
  8214 Westchester Drive, Suite 800, Dallas, TX 75225
Phone: 972 349-6200
Web: www.veritexbank.com

HISTORICAL FINANCIALS
Company Type: Public

Income Statement — FYE: December 31

	ASSETS ($mil)	NET INCOME ($mil)	INCOME AS % OF ASSETS	EMPLOYEES
12/20	8,820.8	73.8	0.8%	643
12/19	7,954.9	90.7	1.1%	679
12/18	3,208.5	39.3	1.2%	330
12/17	2,945.5	15.1	0.5%	324
12/16	1,408.5	12.5	0.9%	171
Annual Growth	58.2%	55.8%	—	39.3%

2020 Year-End Financials
Return on assets: 0.8%
Return on equity: 6.1%
Long-term debt ($ mil.): —
No. of shares ($ mil.): 49.3
Sales ($ mil.): 369.1
Dividends
  Yield: 2.6%
  Payout: 43.3%
Market value ($ mil.): 1,266.0

	STOCK PRICE ($) FY Close	P/E High/Low		PER SHARE ($) Earnings	Dividends	Book Value
12/20	25.66	20	7	1.48	0.68	24.39
12/19	29.13	17	13	1.68	0.50	23.32
12/18	21.38	20	13	1.60	0.00	21.88
12/17	27.59	36	30	0.80	0.00	20.28
12/16	26.71	23	11	1.13	0.00	15.73
Annual Growth	(1.0%)	—	—	7.0%	—	11.6%

Veru Inc

Move over, Trojan Man! Business at The Female Health Company (FHC), maker of condoms for women, is gaining momentum. The female condom is the only female contraceptive that is FDA-approved for preventing both pregnancy and sexually transmitted diseases, including HIV/AIDS. The firm's condoms are sold in 140-plus countries worldwide (under the FC2 name), mostly in South Africa, Brazil, and Uganda. Outside the US, many of its products bear the Femidom name, among others. FHC also provides low-cost female condoms in Africa through an agreement with the Joint United Nations Programme on HIV/AIDS (UNAIDS). It sponsors the Female Health Foundation, which provides women with health education.

Operations
Focused on developing, manufacturing, and marketing consumer health care products, FHC operates its business in one industry segment. The company's FC2 Female Condom, which is available in the US and in more than 140 countries, offers women dual protection against sexually transmitted diseases, such as HIV/AIDS, as well as unintended pregnancy.

It owns certain worldwide rights to the FC2 Female Condom, including patents that have been issued in several countries. Patents cover the key aspects of FC2, such as its overall design and manufacturing process.

Geographic Reach
Headquartered in Chicago, FHC generated a third of its fiscal 2013 revenue from South Africa and Brazil. The balance of its customers is located in Uganda, Nigeria, the US, Congo, Zimbabwe, India, the UK, and Malaysia.

The company boasts manufacturing locations in the UK, Malaysia, and India.

Sales and Marketing
The FC2 Female Condom is the only currently available female-controlled product that's approved by the FDA. Additionally, the World Health Organization (WHO) has cleared FC2 for purchase in United Nations agencies.

Among the company's relatively small customer base are large global agencies, such as its three largest customers: the United Nations Population Fund (62% of unit sales), the United States Agency for International Development (less than 10% of unit sales), and South Africa's distributor Sekunjalo Investments Corporation (PTY) Ltd. (less than 10% of unit sales). Other customers include ministries of health or other governmental agencies, which either purchase directly from FHC or through in-country distributors or non-governmental organizations (NGOs).

The personal health care products company significantly boosted advertising costs in fiscal 2013. It spent $221,718 in 2013, up from $52,949 in 1012 and $32,858 in 2011.

Financial Performance
Thanks to its increased advertising expenses paired with revenue losses, FHC's profits decreased some 6% in fiscal 2013 vs. 2012. The company's revenue dropped by 10% during the reporting period. Unit sales dropped 11% as compared to 2012 due to the Brazil and South Africa shipping large orders. To its benefit, the average FC2 sales price rose 1% in 2013.

Strategy
FHC has pledged to significantly boost

its global education and training investment through 2018.

The company has built a strong foundation for its current FC2 Female Condom from its first generation product, FC1. It's further supported by representatives in global locales who provide technical support and assist with customers' prevention and family planning programs.

FHC generates most of its revenue from the sale of its FC2 Female Condom, recognized upon shipment of the product to customers. The company also earns revenue by licensing its intellectual property to Hindustan Lifecare Limited, an exclusive distributor that makes and sells the FC2 Female Condom in India.

The FC2 Female Condom is made of a nitrile polymer, which allows for a faster, cheaper manufacturing process. The primary difference between the first-generation FC1 condom and the FC2 condom is that the FC1 condom can be cleaned and reused several times (a benefit the company doesn't necessarily recommend).

EXECUTIVES

Chairman, President, Chief Executive Officer, Director, Mitchell S. Steiner, $383,250 total compensation
Vice-Chairman, Chief Corporate Officer, Director, Harry Fisch
Finance Chief Financial Officer, Finance Chief Administrative Officer, Michele Greco, $269,208 total compensation
Chief Scientific Officer, K. Gary Barnette, $26,125 total compensation
Secretary, Michael J. Purvis
Director, Mario Eisenberger
Director, Michael L. Rankowitz
Director, Grace Hyun
Director, Lucy Lu
Auditors : RSM US LLP

LOCATIONS

HQ: Veru Inc
   48 N.W. 25th Street, Suite 102, Miami, FL 33127
Phone: 305 509-6897
Web: www.veruhealthcare.com

2013 Sales

	$ mil.	% of total
South Africa	5.4	17
Brazil	4.5	14
Uganda	3.0	10
Nigeria	2.9	9
US	2.6	8
Congo	2.5	8
Other	10.6	34
Total	31.5	100

COMPETITORS

BIOVERATIV INC.
DYAX CORP.
NATURAL ALTERNATIVES INTERNATIONAL, INC.
RELIV' INTERNATIONAL, INC.
THE MEDICINES COMPANY

HISTORICAL FINANCIALS

Company Type: Public

Income Statement FYE: September 30

	REVENUE ($mil)	NET INCOME ($mil)	NET PROFIT MARGIN	EMPLOYEES
09/21	61.2	7.3	12.1%	252
09/20	42.5	(18.9)	—	339
09/19	31.8	(12.0)	—	386
09/18	15.8	(23.9)	—	171
09/17	13.6	(6.6)	—	175
Annual Growth	45.5%	—	—	9.5%

2021 Year-End Financials

Debt ratio: —
Return on equity: 8.1%
Cash ($ mil.): 122.3
Current Ratio: 9.62
Long-term debt ($ mil.): —
No. of shares ($ mil.): 79.9
Dividends
   Yield: —
   Payout: —
Market value ($ mil.): 682.0

	STOCK PRICE ($) FY Close	P/E High/Low		PER SHARE ($) Earnings	Dividends	Book Value
09/21	8.53	208	24	0.09	0.00	1.90
09/20	2.62	—	—	(0.28)	0.00	0.43
09/19	2.16	—	—	(0.19)	0.00	0.50
09/18	1.42	—	—	(0.44)	0.00	0.53
09/17	2.65	—	—	(0.25)	0.00	0.91
Annual Growth	33.9%	—	—	—	—	20.3%

Viavi Solutions Inc

Viavi Solutions is a leading provider of test and measurement instruments and test tools that are used to build and improve communications equipment and broadband networks. Viavi's AvComm products are a global leader in test and measurement (T&M) instrumentation for communication and safety in the government, aerospace and military markets.? It also provides test products and services for private enterprise networks. Another Viavi offering is optical technology, which includes tools for detecting counterfeit currency as well as optical filters for sensor applications. About a third of Viavi's sales are to customers in the US. Viavi was created in 2015 when JDS Uniphase split into two companies.

Operations

Viavi operates in three segments: Network Enablement (NE), Service Enablement (SE), and Optical Security and Performance products (OSP).

The NE segment, about 65% of revenue, provides testing tools for network build-out and maintenance tasks. The tools include instruments, software, and services to design, build, activate, certify, troubleshoot, and optimize networks.

The OSP segment, about a quarter of revenue, offers optics for anti-counterfeit efforts, guidance systems, laser-eye protection, smartphone security, and night vision systems.

The SE segment, about 10% of revenue, provides embedded systems and enterprise performance management that provide information about network, service, and application data. The segment's instruments, microprobes, and software monitor, collect, and analyze network data to show customer experience and identify revenue and network optimization opportunities.

Viavi operates its own manufacturing facilities and uses contract manufacturers as well.

Geographic Reach

Viavi's sales are spread among major geographic regions. The US accounts for about 30% of revenue, China supplies about 20% of revenue, and the Europe, the Middle East, and Africa region provides more than 25% of revenue.

Based in Arizona, Viavi has manufacturing facilities in China, France, Germany, Mexico, the UK, and the US, while its most significant contract manufacturers are in China and Mexico.

Sales and Marketing

Viavi's customers include major telecommunications providers, government agencies, and corporations. Among its customers are América Móvil, AT&T Inc., Lumen Technologies, Cisco Systems, Comcast, British Telecom Openreach, Deutsche Telekom, Nokia, and Verizon Communications as well as SICPA, STMicroelectronics, Lockheed Martin and Seiko Epson Inc.

Financial Performance

The company reported a net revenue of $1.3 billion for the year ended June 2022. The 8% increase from the previous year was primarily due to the higher volume of product sales for the year.

In 2022, the company had a net income of $15.5 million, a 77% decrease from the previous year's net income of $67.5 million.

The company's cash at the end of 2022 was $572.8 million. Operating activities generated $178.1 million, while investing activities used $71 million, mainly for capital expenditures. Financing activities used another $210.4 million, primarily for cash paid to note holders in convertible note settlement.

Strategy

Viavi's objective is to continue to be a leading provider in the markets and industries it serves. In support of its business segments, the company is pursuing a corporate strategy that it believes will best position it for future opportunities as follows:

Market leadership in physical and virtualized test and measurement instruments and assurance systems with opportunity to grow market share;

Market leadership in anti-counterfeiting pigments, 3D sensing optical filters and other light management technologies;

Market leadership in 5G wireless, public safety radio and navigation/communication transponder test instruments as well as passive optical components for 3D sensing and other optical sensors;

Increase benefit from the use of its net operating loss carryforwards (NOL) by improving its profitability organically and inorganically; and

Greater flexibility in capital structure in support of its strategic plans.

Its near-term strategy, and next transformation phase, will be more focused on growth, both organic and inorganic. The company plans to leverage major secular growth trends in 5G wireless, fiber and 3D sensing to achieve higher levels of revenue and profitability.

HISTORY

Engineer Dale Crane was already making helium neon lasers in his garage when he left laser developer Spectra-Physics in 1979 to start Uniphase. Initially the company developed and marketed gas laser subsystems to manufacturers of biomedical, industrial process control, and printing equipment. In 1992 Demax Software executive Kevin Kalkhoven became CEO, and Uniphase formed Ultrapointe, introducing the Ultrapointe laser imaging system for semiconductor production the following year. Expenses related to a gas laser subsystem patent-infringement suit filed by Spectra-Physics caused losses in 1993, the year Uniphase went public.

In the mid-1990s Uniphase began to use acquisitions to expand its market share and consolidate product lines. In 1995 the company bought optical components supplier United Technologies Photonics from United Technologies, entering the telecom market.

In 1997 it bought IBM's laser business and Australia-based Indx, a maker of reflection filters used to increase the carrying capacity of a fiber-optic strand. Uniphase's 1998 acquisitions included Philips Optoelectronics (semiconductor lasers) and Broadband Communications Products (fiber-optic transmitters and receivers). The company sold its Ultrapointe unit to chip equipment maker KLA-Tencor late that year. The acquisition spree contributed to losses for fiscal 1997 and 1998.

In 1999 Uniphase merged with JDS FITEL, a Canada-based maker of fiber-optic communications gear, in a $7 billion deal. JDS FITEL, founded in 1981 by four Nortel engineers, focused on making so-called "passive" fiber-optic components that route and manipulate optical signals. It was a complementary fit to Uniphase's "active" gear that generates and transmits signals. The combined company named itself JDS Uniphase. Both JDS FITEL and Uniphase aggressively pursued acquisitions prior to the merger, and JDS Uniphase continued shopping.

In fiscal 2000, following a huge run-up in its share price, JDS Uniphase made 10 acquisitions, including EPITAXX (optical detectors and receivers) and Optical Coating Laboratory. Its largest acquisition was of rival E-Tek Dynamics (for $20.4 billion), which JDSU used to further increase its capacity to produce passive components such as amplifiers and better equip itself to offer customers complete optical systems. That year Kalkhoven retired, and co-chairman Jozef Straus (former CEO of JDS FITEL) was named as his replacement.

After making a series of acquisitions in the early 2000s, JDSU announced that it would split into two companies.

EXECUTIVES

Chairman, Director, Richard nn Belluzzo, $410,501 total compensation
President, Chief Executive Officer, Director, Oleg Khaykin, $282,692 total compensation
Executive Vice President, Chief Financial Officer, Henk Derksen
Executive Vice President, Chief Marketing Officer, Chief Strategy Officer, Paul McNab
Senior Vice President, Division Officer, Luke M. Scrivanich, $353,769 total compensation
Senior Vice President, General Counsel, Secretary, Kevin Christopher Siebert
Division Officer, Ralph Rondinone
Division Officer, Gary Staley
Director, Masood A. Jabbar
Director, Keith L. Barnes
Director, Douglas Gilstrap
Director, Laura A. Black
Director, Tor R. Braham
Director, Donald A. Colvin
Director, Joanne Solomon
Auditors : PricewaterhouseCoopers LLP

LOCATIONS

HQ: Viavi Solutions Inc
7047 E Greenway Pkwy Suite 250, Scottsdale, AZ 85254
Phone: 408 404-3600
Web: www.viavisolutions.com

2019 Sales

	$ mil.	% of total
United States	342.1	30
Other Americas	84.2	7
Greater China	216.6	19
Other Asia/Pacific	155.6	14
Switzerland	97	9
Other EMEA	234.8	21
Total	1,130.3	100

PRODUCTS/OPERATIONS

2019 Sales

	$ mil.	% of total
Network Enablement	737.8	65
Service Enablement	103.4	9
Optical Security & Performance Products	289.1	26
Total	1,130.3	100

Selected Products

Communications test & measurement (CommTest)
  Service Assurance Systems
  Services
  Software
  Test instruments
Communications & commercial optical products (CCOP)
  Lasers
  Optical Communications
  Amplifiers
  Couplers/Splitters
  Lasers
  Optical communications
  Detectors/receivers
  Lasers
  Modulators
  Multiplexers
  Switches
  Transceivers
  Transmitter modules
  Transponders
  Photovoltaics
Advanced optical technologies (AOT)
  Custom colors for product finishes and decorative packaging
  Optical thin-film coatings

Selected Customers

Communications test & measurement
  AT&T
  Bell Canada
  Bharti Airtel
  British Telecom
  Brocade
  China Mobile
  China Telecom
  Comcast
  Deutsche Telecom
  EMC
  France Telecom
  Hewlett-Packard
  IBM
  TalkTalk
  Telefónica
  TimeWarner Cable
  Verizon
Communications and commercial optical
  Optical communications equipment manufacturers
  Alcatel-Lucent
  Cisco Systems
  Ericsson
  Fujitsu
  Huawei
  Nokia Siemens Networks
  Tellabs
  Commercial lasers
  ASML
  Beckman Coulter
  Becton Dickinson
  Electro Scientific
  KLA-Tencor
  Solar cell
  Amplifier Research
  Beijing Bosin Industrial Technology
  ETS-Lindgren
  Siemens
Advanced Optical Technologies
  3M
  American Express
  DuPont
  Kingston
  Lockheed Martin
  MasterCard
  Northrop Grumman
  Seiko Epson

COMPETITORS

COHERENT, INC.
EXAR CORPORATION
FEI COMPANY
FLIR SYSTEMS, INC.
Fabrinet
KEYSIGHT TECHNOLOGIES, INC.
MSA SAFETY INCORPORATED
PACIFIC BIOSCIENCES OF CALIFORNIA, INC.
SEMTECH CORPORATION
THERMO FISHER SCIENTIFIC INC.

HISTORICAL FINANCIALS

Company Type: Public

Income Statement FYE: July 3

	REVENUE ($mil)	NET INCOME ($mil)	NET PROFIT MARGIN	EMPLOYEES
07/21*	1,198.9	46.1	3.8%	3,600
06/20	1,136.3	28.7	2.5%	3,600
06/19	1,130.3	5.4	0.5%	3,600
06/18	880.4	(46.0)	—	3,500
07/17	811.4	166.9	20.6%	2,700
Annual Growth	10.3%	(27.5%)	—	7.5%

*Fiscal year change

2021 Year-End Financials

Debt ratio: 31.8% No. of shares ($ mil.): 228.3
Return on equity: 6.1% Dividends
Cash ($ mil.): 697.8 Yield: —
Current Ratio: 1.58 Payout: —
Long-term debt ($ mil.): 209.8 Market value ($ mil.): 3,988.0

	STOCK PRICE ($) FY Close	P/E High/Low		PER SHARE ($) Earnings	Dividends	Book Value
07/21*	17.47	90	57	0.20	0.00	3.39
06/20	12.50	124	69	0.12	0.00	3.12
06/19	13.29	688	468	0.02	0.00	3.17
06/18	10.24	—	—	(0.20)	0.00	3.17
07/17	10.53	16	9	0.71	0.00	3.45
Annual Growth	13.5%	—	—	(27.1%)	—	(0.4%)

*Fiscal year change

VICI Properties Inc

EXECUTIVES

Chairman, James R. Abrahamson
President, Chief Operating Officer, John W.R. Payne, $1,200,000 total compensation
Executive Vice President, Chief Financial Officer, Treasurer, David A. Kieske, $450,000 total compensation
Executive Vice President, General Counsel, Secretary, Samantha Sacks Gallagher, $245,540 total compensation
Chief Executive Officer, Director, Edward Baltazar Pitoniak, $725,000 total compensation
Director, Diana F. Cantor
Director, Monica Howard Douglas
Director, Elizabeth I. Holland
Director, Craig Macnab
Director, Michael D. Rumbolz
Auditors : Deloitte & Touche LLP

LOCATIONS

HQ: VICI Properties Inc
535 Madison Avenue, 20th Floor, New York, NY 10022
Phone: 646 949-4631
Web: www.viciproperties.com

HISTORICAL FINANCIALS

Company Type: Public

Income Statement FYE: December 31

	REVENUE ($mil)	NET INCOME ($mil)	NET PROFIT MARGIN	EMPLOYEES
12/20	1,225.5	891.6	72.8%	147
12/19	894.7	545.9	61.0%	140
12/18	897.9	523.6	58.3%	140
12/17	187.6	42.6	22.7%	140
12/16	18.7	0.0	0.0%	140
Annual Growth	184.2%	—	—	1.2%

2020 Year-End Financials

Debt ratio: 39.6% No. of shares ($ mil.): 536.6
Return on equity: 10.2% Dividends
Cash ($ mil.): 315.9 Yield: 4.9%
Current Ratio: 1.03 Payout: 71.7%
Long-term debt ($ mil.): 6,765.5 Market value ($ mil.): 13,685.0

	STOCK PRICE ($) FY Close	P/E High/Low		PER SHARE ($) Earnings	Dividends	Book Value
12/20	25.50	16	6	1.75	1.26	17.54
12/19	25.55	20	15	1.24	1.17	17.28
12/18	18.78	16	12	1.43	1.00	16.84
12/17	20.50	111	95	0.19	0.00	15.62
Annual Growth	7.5%	—	—	109.6%	—	3.9%

Vicor Corp

Vicor designs, develops, manufactures, and markets modular power components and power systems for converting electrical power. In electrically-powered devices utilizing alternating current (AC) voltage from a primary AC source, a power system converts AC voltage into the stable direct current (DC) voltage necessary to power subsystems and/or individual applications and devices (loads). Customers includes global OEMs and small manufacturers of specialized electronics devices. Vicor power component design methodology offers a comprehensive range of modular building blocks enabling rapid design of a power system. The company also sell a range of electrical and mechanical accessories for use with their products. Vicor derives about 35% of its sales from customers in the US.

Operations

The company categorize their product portfolios as Brick Products and Advanced Products.

The Brick Products generates about 55% of company's total revenue, it provides integrated transformation, rectification, isolation, regulation, filtering, and/or input protection necessary to power and protect loads, across a range of conventional power architectures. This product also offers a wide range of brick-format DC-DC converters, as well as complementary components providing AC line rectification, input filtering, power factor correction, and transient protection.

The Advanced Products consist of the remaining revenue. This portfolio consists of the company's most innovative products, which are used to implement its proprietary distribution architecture, Factorized Power Architecture (FPA), a highly differentiated approach to power distribution that enables flexible, rapid power system design using individual components optimized to perform a specific function.

Geographic Reach

Andover, Massachusetts-based, Vicor has domestic locations in California, Illinois, Oregon, Rhode Island, Texas and Massachusetts. International locations reside in China, Germany, India, Italy, Korea, Japan, Taiwan and the UK. The Asia Pacific generated around 55% of sales, followed by the US with nearly 35%, and Europe with some 10%.

Sales and Marketing

The company's products are sold worldwide to customers ranging from smaller, independent manufacturers of highly specialized electronic devices to larger original equipment manufacturers (OEMs), ODMs, and their contract manufacturers.

Vicor reach and serve customers through several channels: a direct sales force; a network of independent sales representative organizations in North America; independent, authorized non-stocking distributors in Europe and Asia; and four authorized stocking distributors world-wide, Arrow Electronics, Inc., Digi-Key Corporation, Future Electronics Incorporated, and Mouser Electronics, Inc. In fiscal 2021, direct customers, contract manufacturers and non-stocking distributors generates about 80% of company's total sales. Followed by stocking distributors that produces about 20% of revenue and the remaining is from non-recurring engineering.

The company incurred approximately $3.0 million, $2.6 million, and $2.7 million in advertising costs during 2021, 2020, and 2019, respectively.

Financial Performance

Net revenues increased 21% to $359.4 million for 2021, from $296.6 million for 2020. The increase was primarily in sales of Advanced Products, due to an increase in new orders in 2021, compared to 2020.

Net income in 2021 increased to $56.6 million compared with $17.9 million in the prior year.

Cash held by the company at the end of fiscal 2021 increased to $182.4 million. Cash provided by operations and financing activities were $54.4 million and $10.1 million, respectively. Cash used for investing activities was $43.7 million, mainly for purchases of short-term investments.

Strategy

Vicor's strategy emphasizes demonstrable product differentiation and a value proposition based on competitively superior solution performance, advantageous design flexibility, and a compelling total cost of ownership ("TCO"). Since the company was founded, its competitive position has been maintained by continuous innovations in product design and achievements in product performance, largely enabled by its focus on the research and development of advanced technologies and processes, often implemented in proprietary semiconductor circuitry, materials, and packaging. Many of its products incorporate patented or proprietary implementations of high-frequency switching topologies, which enable the design of power system solutions more efficient and much smaller than conventional alternatives. This efficiency and small size is enabled by its proprietary switching circuitry and magnetic structures, as well as its use of highly differentiated packaging.

Given the growth profiles and performance requirements of the market segments served with Advanced Products and Brick Products, its strategy involves a transition in organizational focus, emphasizing investment in Advanced Products design and manufacturing, targeting high growth market segments with a low-mix, high-volume operational model, while maintaining a profitable business in mature market segments it serves with Brick Products with a high-mix, low-volume operational model.

HISTORY

Inspired by an incident in the 1970s -- his hi-fi system blew up -- Italian physicist Patrizio Vinciarelli left his Princeton fellowship in 1980 to experiment with power-supply technology. Borrowing $500,000 from friends and their families, he founded Vicor in 1981. By 1982 he developed the basic technology that the company's products are based on. Vicor shipped its first product in 1985 and was profitable by 1987. Early customers included Xcerra and Telco Systems. Vicor went public in 1990.

EXECUTIVES

Chairman, President, Chief Executive Officer, Director, Patrizio Vinciarelli, $390,142 total compensation
Division Officer, Alex Gusinov
Division Officer, Robert Gendron
Division Officer, Director, Philip D. Davies, $338,452 total compensation
Human Resources Corporate Vice-President, Nancy L. Grava
Division Officer, Sean Crilly
Corporate Vice-President, Chief Information Officer, Joseph A. Jeffery
Operations Corporate Vice-President, Operations General Manager, Director, Michael S. McNamara, $308,947 total compensation
General Counsel, Director, Andrew D'Amico
Corporate Vice-President, Chief Financial Officer, Treasurer, Corporate Secretary, Director, James F. Schmidt
Vice President, Chief Accounting Officer, Interim Principal Financial Officer, Interim Corporate Secretary, Richard J. Nagel, $0 total compensation
Corporate Vice-President, Division Officer, Director, Claudio Tuozzolo, $374,893 total compensation
Director, Samuel J. Anderson
Director, Jason L. Carlson
Director, Estia J. Eichten
Director, James A. Simms, $360,307 total compensation
Auditors : KPMG LLP

LOCATIONS

HQ: Vicor Corp
25 Frontage Road, Andover, MA 01810
Phone: 978 470-2900
Web: www.vicorpower.com

2016 Sales

	% of total
US	41
International	59
Total	100

PRODUCTS/OPERATIONS

2016 Sales

	$ mil.	% of total
Brick Business Unit	151.4	76
VI Chip	38.4	19
Picor	10.5	5
Total	200.3	100

Selected Products
AC-DC power systems
AC-DC filters
Accessory power-system components
Bus converters
DC-DC filters
DC-DC modular power converters (for mounting on printed circuit boards)
DC-DC power systems
Configurable products
Customer-specific power converters and supplies
EMI filters
Regulators

COMPETITORS

ADVANCED ENERGY INDUSTRIES, INC.
BEL FUSE INC.
CONTROL4 CORPORATION
ELECTROCOMPONENTS PUBLIC LIMITED COMPANY
MAXIM INTEGRATED PRODUCTS, INC.
PULSE ELECTRONICS CORPORATION
RENESAS ELECTRONICS AMERICA INC.
SANMINA CORPORATION
SOITEC
ULTRALIFE CORPORATION

HISTORICAL FINANCIALS

Company Type: Public

Income Statement   FYE: December 31

	REVENUE ($mil)	NET INCOME ($mil)	NET PROFIT MARGIN	EMPLOYEES
12/20	296.5	17.9	6.0%	1,049
12/19	262.9	14.0	5.4%	1,014
12/18	291.2	31.7	10.9%	1,007
12/17	227.8	0.1	0.1%	980
12/16	200.2	(6.2)	—	971
Annual Growth	10.3%	—	—	2.0%

2020 Year-End Financials
Debt ratio: —   No. of shares ($ mil.): 43.3
Return on equity: 6.4%   Dividends
Cash ($ mil.): 161.7   Yield: —
Current Ratio: 7.82   Payout: —
Long-term debt ($ mil.): —   Market value ($ mil.): 3,996.0

	STOCK PRICE ($) FY Close	P/E High	P/E Low	PER SHARE ($) Earnings	PER SHARE ($) Dividends	Book Value
12/20	92.22	227	78	0.41	0.00	8.10
12/19	46.72	137	77	0.34	0.00	5.07
12/18	37.79	80	21	0.78	0.00	4.57
12/17	20.90	—	—	0.00	0.00	3.45
12/16	15.10	—	—	(0.16)	0.00	3.35
Annual Growth	57.2%	—	—	—	—	24.7%

Victory Capital Holdings Inc (DE)

EXECUTIVES

Chairman, Chief Executive Officer, Subsidiary Officer, David C. Brown, $600,000 total compensation
President, Chief Financial Officer, Chief Administrative Officer, Michael D. Policarpo, $425,000 total compensation
Chief Legal Officer, Nina Gupta
Division Officer, Kelly S. Cliff, $425,000 total compensation
Director, Milton R. Berlinski
Director, Alex Binderow
Director, Lawrence Davanzo
Director, Richard M. Demartini
Director, James B. Hawkes
Director, Karin Hirtler-Garvey
Director, Robert J. Hurst
Director, Alan H. Rappaport
Auditors : Ernst & Young LLP

LOCATIONS

HQ: Victory Capital Holdings Inc (DE)
15935 La Cantera Parkway, San Antonio, TX 78256
Phone: 216 898-2400

HISTORICAL FINANCIALS

Company Type: Public

Income Statement   FYE: December 31

	REVENUE ($mil)	NET INCOME ($mil)	NET PROFIT MARGIN	EMPLOYEES
12/20	775.3	212.5	27.4%	429
12/19	612.3	92.4	15.1%	358
12/18	413.4	63.7	15.4%	263
12/17	409.6	25.8	6.3%	267
12/16	297.8	(6.0)	—	276
Annual Growth	27.0%	—	—	11.7%

2020 Year-End Financials
Debt ratio: 44.4%   No. of shares ($ mil.): 67.5
Return on equity: 34.0%   Dividends
Cash ($ mil.): 22.7   Yield: 0.9%
Current Ratio: 0.64   Payout: 8.6%
Long-term debt ($ mil.): 769   Market value ($ mil.): 1,676.0

	STOCK PRICE ($) FY Close	P/E High/Low		PER SHARE ($) Earnings	Dividends	Book Value
12/20	24.81	8	4	2.88	0.23	10.48
12/19	20.97	16	8	1.26	0.10	7.95
12/18	10.22	14	8	0.90	0.00	6.74
Annual Growth	55.8%	—	—	78.9%	—	24.6%

Viemed Healthcare Inc

EXECUTIVES

Director, Casey Hoyt
Director, Nitin Kaushal
Auditors : Ernst & Young LLP

LOCATIONS

HQ: Viemed Healthcare Inc
625 E. Kaliste Saloom Rd., Lafayette, LA 70508
Phone: 337 504-3802
Web: www.viemed.com

HISTORICAL FINANCIALS

Company Type: Public

Income Statement   FYE: December 31

	REVENUE ($mil)	NET INCOME ($mil)	NET PROFIT MARGIN	EMPLOYEES
12/20	131.3	31.5	24.0%	511
12/19	80.2	8.5	10.6%	418
12/18	64.4	9.5	14.7%	293
12/17	46.9	8.1	17.4%	0
Annual Growth	40.9%	56.8%	—	—

2020 Year-End Financials

Debt ratio: 6.8%
Return on equity: 50.1%
Cash ($ mil.): 30.9
Current Ratio: 2.05
Long-term debt ($ mil.): 5.7
No. of shares ($ mil.): 39.1
Dividends
  Yield: —
  Payout: —
Market value ($ mil.): 304.0

	STOCK PRICE ($) FY Close	P/E High/Low		PER SHARE ($) Earnings	Dividends	Book Value
12/20	7.76	14	3	0.78	0.00	2.08
12/19	6.20	37	14	0.21	0.00	1.15
12/18	3.80	25	7	0.24	0.00	0.87
Annual Growth	42.9%	—	—	80.3%	—	54.9%

Village Bank & Trust Financial Corp

Does it take a village to raise a bank? Village Bank & Trust is the holding company for Village Bank, which has about a dozen branches in the suburbs of Richmond, Virginia. It offers standard services, including deposit accounts, loans, and credit cards. Deposit funds are used to write loans for consumers and businesses in the area; commercial real estate loans, mainly secured by owner-occupied businesses, account for about half of the bank's lending portfolio, which also includes business, construction, residential mortgage, and consumer loans. In 2008 Village Bank & Trust acquired the three-branch River City Bank in a transaction worth more than $20 million.

EXECUTIVES

Chairman, Director, Craig D. Bell
President, Chief Executive Officer, Subsidiary Officer, Director, James E. (Jay) Hendricks, $210,728 total compensation
Executive Vice President, Chief Financial Officer, Subsidiary Officer, Donald M. Kaloski
Subsidiary Officer, Rebecca L. (Joy) Kline
Subsidiary Officer, Max C. Morehead, $186,224 total compensation
Subsidiary Officer, James C. Winn
Subsidiary Officer, Christy F. Quesenbery
Subsidiary Officer, Roy I. Barzel
Director, R. T. Avery
Director, Frank E. Jenkins
Director, Michael A. Katzen
Director, Michael L. Toalson
Director, Devon M. Henry
Director, George R. Whittemore
Director, Mary Margaret Kastelberg
Auditors : Yount, Hyde & Barbour, P.C.

LOCATIONS

HQ: Village Bank & Trust Financial Corp
13319 Midlothian Turnpike, Midlothian, VA 23113
Phone: 804 897-3900
Web: www.villagebank.com

COMPETITORS

FULTON FINANCIAL CORPORATION
HERALD NATIONAL BANK
MECHANICS BANK
MUTUALFIRST FINANCIAL, INC.
SURUGA BANK LTD.

HISTORICAL FINANCIALS

Company Type: Public

Income Statement   FYE: December 31

	ASSETS ($mil)	NET INCOME ($mil)	INCOME AS % OF ASSETS	EMPLOYEES
12/20	706.2	8.5	1.2%	152
12/19	540.3	4.4	0.8%	146
12/18	514.8	3.0	0.6%	150
12/17	476.9	(3.0)	—	161
12/16	444.8	13.5	3.0%	178
Annual Growth	12.3%	(10.8%)	—	(3.9%)

2020 Year-End Financials

Return on assets: 1.3%
Return on equity: 17.9%
Long-term debt ($ mil.): —
No. of shares ($ mil.): 1.4
Sales ($ mil.): 38
Dividends
  Yield: —
  Payout: —
Market value ($ mil.): 50.0

	STOCK PRICE ($) FY Close	P/E High/Low		PER SHARE ($) Earnings	Dividends	Book Value
12/20	34.39	8	4	5.86	0.00	35.46
12/19	37.11	12	10	3.10	0.00	29.53
12/18	30.45	17	14	2.04	0.00	25.87
12/17	30.65	—	—	(2.55)	0.00	27.49
12/16	26.70	3	2	8.99	0.00	30.54
Annual Growth	6.5%	—	—	(10.1%)	—	3.8%

Virginia National Bankshares Corp

EXECUTIVES

Chairman, Subsidiary Officer, Director, William D. Dittmar
Vice-Chairman, Subsidiary Officer, Director, John B. Adams
President, Chief Executive Officer, Subsidiary Officer, Director, Glenn W. Rust, $375,000 total compensation
Executive Vice President, Chief Financial Officer, Subsidiary Officer, Tara Y. Harrison
Executive Vice President, General Counsel, Secretary, Subsidiary Officer, Donna G. Shewmake, $232,875 total compensation
Subsidiary Officer, Virginia R. Bayes, $239,456 total compensation
Director, Steven W. Blaine
Director, Kevin T. Carter
Director, Hunter E. Craig
Director, Randolph D. Frostick
Director, James T. Holland
Director, Linda M. Houston
Director, Jay B. Keyser
Director, Sterling T. Strange
Director, Gregory L. Wells
Auditors : Yount, Hyde & Barbour, P.C.

LOCATIONS

HQ: Virginia National Bankshares Corp
404 People Place, Charlottesville, VA 22911
Phone: 434 817-8621
Web: www.vnbcorp.com

HISTORICAL FINANCIALS

Company Type: Public

Income Statement   FYE: December 31

	ASSETS ($mil)	NET INCOME ($mil)	INCOME AS % OF ASSETS	EMPLOYEES
12/20	848.4	7.9	0.9%	86
12/19	702.6	6.6	1.0%	97
12/18	644.8	8.4	1.3%	86
12/17	643.8	6.5	1.0%	81
12/16	605.0	5.7	1.0%	85
Annual Growth	8.8%	8.5%	—	0.3%

2020 Year-End Financials

Return on assets: 1.0%
Return on equity: 10.0%
Long-term debt ($ mil.): —
No. of shares ($ mil.): 2.7
Sales ($ mil.): 33.7
Dividends
  Yield: —
  Payout: 40.8%
Market value ($ mil.): 74.0

	STOCK PRICE ($) FY Close	P/E High/Low		PER SHARE ($) Earnings	Dividends	Book Value
12/20	27.15	13	8	2.94	1.20	30.43
12/19	37.70	16	14	2.49	1.20	28.27
12/18	34.51	17	11	3.15	1.09	26.49
12/17	39.00	16	11	2.46	0.61	24.50
12/16	28.50	13	10	2.19	0.47	22.61
Annual Growth	(1.2%)	—	—	7.7%	26.6%	7.7%

VirnetX Holding Corp

VirnetX is involved in a net of legal battles. The company owns more than 70 US technology patents for establishing secure mobile internet communications over the 4G LTE network, but it claims several major tech firms including Apple and Cisco Systems are giving away its patented internet security software for free. VirnetX bought the core patents from federal IT contractor Leidos in 2006, and has been working to commercialize its mobile communications software, branded as GABRIEL Connection Technology, as well as a secure domain name registry service. Before the company can convince customers to license its software, it must resolve about 10 patent infringement lawsuits against Apple and Cisco.

Operations

VirnetX owns some 185 patents and pending applications. About 40% are in the US and the rest have been granted or filed overseas. The company's patents focus on securing real-time communications over the internet, as well as related services such as establishing and maintaining a secure domain name registry.

The company's Gabriel Security Platform allows application developers to automatically perform user authentication, cryptographic peer device authentication, domain and user policy enforcement, and zero click VPN access.

The Gabriel Collaboration Suite includes applications that allow businesses and individuals to communicate and collaborate in a secure, end-to-end encrypted invisible network. These applications include Secure Mail, Secure Messaging, Secure Voice Call, Secure Share & Sync, and Secure Gateway Service.

Sales and Marketing

VirnetX works with partners to sell its technology has agreements with resellers and managed service providers that target specific markets. They include Asgard MSP (healthcare), Above PAR Advisors (financial), and Max Cybersecurity (government). The company sells its Gabriel line directly to small and medium-sized businesses using online marketing programs and tools.

Financial Performance

VirnetX's revenue of about $1.5 million a year since 2014 comes from a lawsuit settled in 2013. For the record, its 2017 revenue was $1.5 million compared to $1.6 million in 2016.

The company's net loss dropped to about $17 million in 2017 from about $28 million in 2016. Its selling, general, and administrative expenses were $10,000 lower in 2017 than 2016 because of a decrease in legal costs.

VirnetX had about $3 million in cash on hand at the end of 2017 compared to about $6.6 million in 2016.

Strategy

VirnetX planned to develop sales and marketing promotions in the US and Japan to recruit more resellers and partners to increase international sales. It also plans to develop direct sales programs. Along those lines, the company planned direct marketing of its Gabriel Secure Communication Platform and Gabriel Collaboration Suite products and domain name registry services to service providers and system integrators.

In 2017, the company ended two revenue-sharing marketing programs to develop sales in Japan because of what it termed lack of results.

EXECUTIVES

Chairman, President, Chief Executive Officer, Subsidiary Officer, Kendall Larsen, $696,775 total compensation
Chief Financial Officer, Richard H. Nance, $167,076 total compensation
Chief Technology Officer, Chief Scientist, Director, Robert D. Short, $413,062 total compensation
Director, Gary W. Feiner
Director, Thomas M. O'Brien
Director, Michael F. Angelo
Auditors : Farber Hass Hurley LLP

LOCATIONS

HQ: VirnetX Holding Corp
308 Dorla Court, Suite 206, Zephyr Cove, NV 89448
Phone: 775 548-1785
Web: www.virnetx.com

PRODUCTS/OPERATIONS

Selected Services
Connection server software
GABRIEL Connection Technology Software Development Kit
Registrar server software
Relay server software
Secure domain name master registry and connection service
Secure domain name registrar service
Technical support service
VirnetX technology licensing

COMPETITORS

ACACIA RESEARCH CORPORATION
CEVA, INC.
CROSSROADS SYSTEMS, INC.
PENDRELL CORPORATION
TIVO CORPORATION

HISTORICAL FINANCIALS

Company Type: Public

Income Statement — FYE: December 31

	REVENUE ($mil)	NET INCOME ($mil)	NET PROFIT MARGIN	EMPLOYEES
12/20	302.6	280.4	92.7%	21
12/19	0.0	(19.1)	—	20
12/18	0.0	(25.4)	—	21
12/17	1.5	(17.2)	—	21
12/16	1.5	(28.5)	—	20
Annual Growth	273.8%	—	—	1.2%

2020 Year-End Financials
Debt ratio: —
Return on equity: —
Cash ($ mil.): 192.9
Current Ratio: 21.67
Long-term debt ($ mil.): —
No. of shares ($ mil.): 71.0
Dividends
  Yield: 19.8%
  Payout: 25.5%
Market value ($ mil.): 358.0

	STOCK PRICE ($) FY Close	P/E High/Low		PER SHARE ($) Earnings	Dividends	Book Value
12/20	5.04	2	1	3.92	1.00	3.16
12/19	3.80	—	—	(0.28)	0.00	0.08
12/18	2.40	—	—	(0.40)	0.00	0.15
12/17	3.70	—	—	(0.30)	0.00	0.03
12/16	2.20	—	—	(0.51)	0.00	0.19
Annual Growth	23.0%	—	—	—	—	101.5%

Virtu Financial Inc

EXECUTIVES

Chairman Emeritus, Director, Vincent J. Viola, $0 total compensation
Chairman, Director, Robert Greifeld
Business Development Co-President, Business Development Co-Chief Operating Officer, Brett Fairclough
Co-President, Co-Chief Operating Officer, Joseph Molluso, $500,000 total compensation
Chief Executive Officer, Director, Douglas A. Cifu, $1,000,000 total compensation
Executive Vice President, Chief Financial Officer, Sean P. Galvin
Markets Executive Vice President, Stephen Cavoli, $400,000 total compensation
Director, William F. Cruger
Director, Christopher C. Quick
Director, Joseph J. Grano
Director, Joanne M. Minieri
Director, Virginia Gambale
Director, John D. Nixon
Director, David J. Urban
Director, Michael T. Viola
Auditors : PricewaterhouseCoopers LLP

LOCATIONS

HQ: Virtu Financial Inc
1633 Broadway, New York, NY 10019
Phone: 212 418-0100
Web: www.virtu.com

Virtus Investment Partners Inc

HISTORICAL FINANCIALS

Company Type: Public

Income Statement

FYE: December 31

	REVENUE ($mil)	NET INCOME ($mil)	NET PROFIT MARGIN	EMPLOYEES
12/21	2,811.4	476.8	17.0%	973
12/20	3,239.3	649.1	20.0%	976
12/19	1,530.0	(58.5)	—	1,012
12/18	1,878.7	289.4	15.4%	483
12/17	1,027.9	2.9	0.3%	560
Annual Growth	28.6%	256.9%	—	14.8%

2021 Year-End Financials

Debt ratio: 27.2%
Return on equity: 31.6%
Cash ($ mil.): 1,071.4
Current Ratio: 0.57
Long-term debt ($ mil.): 1,605.1
No. of shares ($ mil.): 182.6
Dividends
Yield: 3.3%
Payout: 24.9%
Market value ($ mil.): 5,265.0

	STOCK PRICE ($) FY Close	P/E High/Low		PER SHARE ($) Earnings	Dividends	Book Value
12/21	28.83	8	6	3.91	0.96	8.48
12/20	25.17	5	3	5.16	0.96	7.64
12/19	15.99	—	—	(0.53)	0.96	4.87
12/18	25.76	13	7	2.78	0.96	5.55
12/17	18.30	630	445	0.03	0.96	4.43
Annual Growth	12.0%	—	—	237.9%	0.0%	17.6%

Virtus Investment Partners provides investment management services to individuals, and institutions. Boasting more than $187.2 billion in assets under management, it operates through affiliated advisors, including Duff & Phelps, Kayne Anderson Rudnick, and Newfleet Asset Management, as well as outside subadvisors. Virtus markets diverse investment products, such as open- and closed-end funds, and managed account services, to high-net-worth individuals. It also manages institutional accounts for corporations and other investors. The firm was formed in 1995 through a reverse merger with Duff & Phelps.

Operations

The asset manager operates through several boutique investment firms including: Duff & Phelps Investment Management, Ceredex Value Advisors, Kayne Anderson Rudnick Investment Management, Newfleet Asset Management, NFJ Investment Group, Seix Investment Advisors, Silvant Capital Management, Sustainable Growth Advisers, and Westchester Capital Management. Virtus offers investors a menu of investment products and services through its affiliates.

Virtus generates some 80% of its revenue from investment management fees. Some 40% of its total revenue from investment management fees were generated from open-end funds, while about 20% came from retail separate accounts. The rest of its revenue came from distribution and service fees (about 10% of revenue), and administration and transfer agent fees (some 10% of revenue).

Of the firm's $187.2 billion in assets under management, about 40% of the assets were invested in open-end mutual funds, while investments in closed-end funds, around 5% of the assets and retail separate managed accounts made up another nearly 25% of the portfolio. The rest of the portfolio was invested in institutional assets and exchange traded funds (ETFs), as well as structured products.

Geographic Reach

Hartford, Connecticut-based Virtus has offices in California, Connecticut, Florida, Georgia, Illinois, New Jersey, New York, and Texas.

Sales and Marketing

Like other mutual fund asset managers, Virtus distributes its open-end funds and ETFs through financial intermediaries such as national and regional broker-dealers and registered investment advisers, banks and insurance companies. Its retail separate accounts are distributed through financial intermediaries and directly to private clients by teams at an affiliated manager. Its institutional services are marketed through relationships with consultants as well as directly to clients. Its target key market segments, including foundations and endowments, corporate, public and private pension plans, and subadvisory relationships.

Its sales efforts are supported by regional sales professionals, a national account relationship group and separate teams for ETFs and the retirement and insurance channels.

Financial Performance

The company's revenue for fiscal 2021 increased by 62% to $979.2 million compared from the prior year with $603.9 million.

Net income for fiscal 2021 increased to $208.1 million compared from the prior year with $80.0 million.

Cash held by the company at the end of fiscal 2021 increased to $586.1 million. Cash provided by operations was $665.7 million while cash used for investing and financing activities were $175.0 million and $244.4 million, respectively. Main uses of cash were acquisition of business and payments on borrowings by CIP.

Mergers and Acquisitions

In early 2022, Virtus Investment Partners, Inc. completed the previously announced acquisition of New York-based, Stone Harbor Investment Partners, a premier manager of emerging markets debt, multi-asset credit, global corporates, and other strategies with $14.5 billion1 of assets under management. The addition of Stone Harbor as an affiliated manager enhances and diversifies the investment capabilities available through Virtus' multi-boutique model. Stone Harbor also increases the company's non-U.S. institutional client base, expands global distribution resources, and adds a proprietary operating and analytical platform that can be leveraged by other affiliates. Terms were not disclosed.

In late 2021, Virtus Investment Partners, Inc. completed its previously announced acquisition of New York-based, Westchester Capital Management, a recognized leader in global event-driven strategies for more than 30 years with $5.0 billion1 of assets under management.The transaction further diversifies Virtus' investment offerings with Westchester Capital's differentiated, non-correlated strategies that invest in publicly announced events such as mergers, acquisitions, takeovers, spin-offs, and other corporate reorganizations. Terms were not disclosed.

Company Background

Virtus in October 2012 acquired the business and assets of Boston-based Rampart Investment Management Co., a registered investment adviser specializing in customized options strategies for institutional and high-net-worth individuals, for $700,000 in cash. The Rampart purchase added $1.3 billion in assets under management and added another investment partner to Virtus' group of boutique investment managers.

EXECUTIVES

Chairman, Director, Timothy A. Holt
President, Chief Executive Officer, Director, George R. Aylward, $550,000 total compensation
Executive Vice President, Chief Operating Officer, Richard W. Smirl
Executive Vice President, Chief Financial Officer, Treasurer, Michael A. Angerthal, $375,000 total compensation
Distribution Executive Vice President, Distribution Head, Barry M. Mandinach, $415,000 total compensation
Human Resources Executive Vice President, Mardelle W. Pena
Executive Vice President, Chief Legal Officer, General Counsel, Secretary, Wendy J. Hills
Division Officer, W. Patrick Bradley, $275,000 total compensation
Director, Susan S. Fleming
Director, Melody L. Jones
Director, Stephen T. Zarrilli
Director, Paul G. Greig
Director, W. Howard Morris
Director, Peter L. Bain
Auditors : DELOITTE & TOUCHE LLP

LOCATIONS

HQ: Virtus Investment Partners Inc
One Financial Plaza, Hartford, CT 06103
Phone: 800 248-7971
Web: www.virtus.com

PRODUCTS/OPERATIONS

2015 Sales

	$ in mil.	% of total
Investment management fees	264.9	69
Distribution & service fees	67.1	18
Administration & transfer agent fees	48.2	13
Other	1.8	-
Total	382	100

Selected Subsidiaries & Affiliates

Duff & Phelps Investment Management (Chicago)
Kayne Anderson Rudnick Investment Management (Los Angeles)
Newfleet Asset Management (Hartford, Connecticut)
Rampart Investment Management Company, LLC (Boston)
Virtus Investment Advisers, Inc. (Massachusetts)
Zweig/Euclid Advisors, LLC (New York)

COMPETITORS

AFFILIATED MANAGERS GROUP, INC.
AGF Management Limited
ARES MANAGEMENT CORPORATION
BLACKROCK, INC.
CALAMOS ASSET MANAGEMENT, INC.
CIFC CORP.
COHEN & STEERS, INC.
SEI INVESTMENTS COMPANY
WESTWOOD HOLDINGS GROUP, INC.
WISDOMTREE INVESTMENTS, INC.

HISTORICAL FINANCIALS
Company Type: Public

Income Statement				FYE: December 31
	REVENUE ($mil)	NET INCOME ($mil)	NET PROFIT MARGIN	EMPLOYEES
12/20	603.8	79.9	13.2%	581
12/19	563.2	95.6	17.0%	578
12/18	552.2	75.5	13.7%	577
12/17	425.6	37.0	8.7%	543
12/16	322.5	48.5	15.0%	406
Annual Growth	17.0%	13.3%	—	9.4%

2020 Year-End Financials

Debt ratio: 69.0%
Return on equity: 11.4%
Cash ($ mil.): 339.8
Current Ratio: 17.58
Long-term debt ($ mil.): 2,391.6

No. of shares ($ mil.): 7.5
Dividends
Yield: 1.3%
Payout: 38.0%
Market value ($ mil.): 1,646.0

	STOCK PRICE ($) FY Close	P/E High/Low		PER SHARE ($) Earnings	Dividends	Book Value
12/20	217.00	21	5	10.02	2.83	93.78
12/19	121.72	10	6	11.74	2.32	99.23
12/18	79.43	15	8	8.86	1.90	90.02
12/17	115.05	31	24	3.96	1.80	82.20
12/16	118.05	20	11	6.20	1.80	54.62
Annual Growth	16.4%	—	—	12.8%	12.0%	14.5%

Vital Farms Inc

EXECUTIVES

Executive Chairman, Director, Matthew O'Hayer
President, Chief Executive Officer, Director, Russell Diez-Canseco
Finance Vice President, Daniel Jones
Chief Operating Officer, Chief Financial Officer, Jason Dale
Chief Marketing Officer, Scott Marcus
Director, Karl Khoury
Director, Gisel Ruiz
Director, Brent Drever
Director, Glenda J. Flanagan
Director, Kelly J. Kennedy
Director, Denny Marie Post

LOCATIONS

HQ: Vital Farms Inc
3601 South Congress Avenue, Suite C100, Austin, TX 78704
Phone: 877 455-3063
Web: www.vitalfarms.com

HISTORICAL FINANCIALS
Company Type: Public

Income Statement				FYE: December 27
	REVENUE ($mil)	NET INCOME ($mil)	NET PROFIT MARGIN	EMPLOYEES
12/20	214.2	8.8	4.1%	215
12/19	140.7	2.3	1.7%	161
12/18	106.7	5.7	5.4%	0
12/17	74.0	(1.9)	—	0
Annual Growth	42.5%	—	—	—

2020 Year-End Financials

Debt ratio: —
Return on equity: 10.1%
Cash ($ mil.): 29.5
Current Ratio: 5.30
Long-term debt ($ mil.): —

No. of shares ($ mil.): 39.4
Dividends
Yield: —
Payout: —
Market value ($ mil.): 1,052.0

	STOCK PRICE ($) FY Close	P/E High/Low		PER SHARE ($) Earnings	Dividends	Book Value
12/20	26.66	134	80	0.27	0.00	3.60
Annual Growth	—	—	—	—	—	—

Vitesse Energy Inc

EXECUTIVES

Chairman, Chief Executive Officer, Director, Robert W. Gerrity
President, Brian J. Cree
Chief Financial Officer, David R. Macosko
General Counsel, Secretary, Christopher I. Humber
Lead Independent Director, Director, Daniel O'Leary
Director, Linda L. Adamany
Director, Brian P. Friedman
Director, Cathleen M. Osborn
Director, Randy I. Stein
Director, Joseph S. Steinberg

LOCATIONS

HQ: Vitesse Energy Inc
9200 E. Mineral Avenue, Suite 200, Centennial, CO 80112
Phone: 720 361-2500
Web: www.vitesseoil.com

HISTORICAL FINANCIALS
Company Type: Public

Income Statement				FYE: December 31
	REVENUE ($mil)	NET INCOME ($mil)	NET PROFIT MARGIN	EMPLOYEES
12/22*	300.0	118.9	39.6%	40
11/21	185.1	18.1	9.8%	38
11/20	97.2	(8.8)	—	0
11/19	171.3	35.8	21.0%	0
Annual Growth	20.5%	49.1%	—	—

*Fiscal year change

2022 Year-End Financials

Debt ratio: 7.3%
Return on equity: 22.2%
Cash ($ mil.): 10.0
Current Ratio: 1.48
Long-term debt ($ mil.): 48

No. of shares ($ mil.): 450.0
Dividends
Yield: —
Payout: —
Market value ($ mil.): 0.0

Voyager Therapeutics Inc

EXECUTIVES

Chairman, Director, Michael Higgins
Interim Chief Scientific Officer, Director, Glenn F. Pierce
President, Chief Executive Officer, Director, Alfred W. Sandrock
Senior Vice President, General Counsel, Robert W. Hesslein
Finance Vice President, Finance Principal Accounting Officer, Finance Principal Financial Officer, Julie Burek
Chief Operating Officer, Robin Swartz
Director, Steven E. Hyman
Director, James A. Geraghty
Director, Nancy Vitale
Auditors: Ernst & Young LLP

LOCATIONS

HQ: Voyager Therapeutics Inc
75 Sidney Street, Cambridge, MA 02139
Phone: 857 259-5340
Web: www.voyagertherapeutics.com

HISTORICAL FINANCIALS
Company Type: Public

Income Statement				FYE: December 31
	REVENUE ($mil)	NET INCOME ($mil)	NET PROFIT MARGIN	EMPLOYEES
12/20	171.1	36.7	21.5%	179
12/19	104.3	(43.5)	—	186
12/18	7.6	(88.2)	—	124
12/17	10.1	(70.6)	—	89
12/16	14.2	(40.1)	—	78
Annual Growth	86.3%	—	—	23.1%

2020 Year-End Financials

Debt ratio: —
Return on equity: 28.8%
Cash ($ mil.): 104.4
Current Ratio: 7.39
Long-term debt ($ mil.): —

No. of shares ($ mil.): 37.3
Dividends
Yield: —
Payout: —
Market value ($ mil.): 267.0

	STOCK PRICE ($)	P/E		PER SHARE ($)		
	FY Close	High/Low		Earnings	Dividends	Book Value
12/20	7.15	15	7	0.98	0.00	4.13
12/19	13.95	—	—	(1.21)	0.00	2.70
12/18	9.40	—	—	(2.75)	0.00	1.44
12/17	16.60	—	—	(2.64)	0.00	4.25
12/16	12.74	—	—	(1.59)	0.00	5.31
Annual Growth	(13.4%)	—	—	—	—	(6.1%)

W.P. Carey Inc

Need help managing your property portfolio? Keep calm and Carey on. W. P. Carey invests in and manages commercial real estate, including office, distribution, retail, and industrial facilities. The company owns more than 1,000 properties mainly in the US and Europe, and manages properties for several non-traded real estate investment trusts (REITs). Its management portfolio totals some $15 billion. W. P. Carey typically acquires properties and then leases them back to the sellers/occupants on a long-term basis. It also provides build-to-suit financing for investors worldwide. W. P. Carey is converting to a REIT, a corporate structure that comes with tax benefits and more flexibilty in investing in real estate.

Geographic Reach

New York-based W. P. Carey owns some 1,020 properties in 21 countries. The firm has offices in Dallas, London, Amsterdam, Hong Kong, and Shanghai. International investments account for about 31% of the REIT's annual revenue.

Financial Performance

Carey's revenue increased 31% in 2013 versus 2012, to $489.9 million. Revenue growth was spurred by additions to the firm's real estate portfolio made in 2012, including 19 self-storage properties. Net income rose 59% over the same period to $98.9 million, due primarily to higher revenue and income from discontinued operations.

Strategy

Since 1979 the REIT has sponsored a series of 18 income-generating investment programs that invest primarily in commercial properties net leased to single tenants, under the Corporate Property Associates, or CPA, brand name. In 2013, the firm managed four global active funds: CPA 16, CPA 17, and CPA 18. W.P. Carey looks to diversify its managed funds and make investments in properties that provide consistent long-term sources of income. Property diversity helps shield W.P. from being reliant on any single industry. A few of its recent investments include a hypermarket in Germany operated by Metro AG, a newly-constructed office in Wales, the new Siemens AS headquarters in Oslo, Norway, and a 302-room Hampton Inn & Suites/Homewood Suites by Hilton hotel in Denver's central business district.

In addition to making property investments, the firm is focused on diversifying its asset management capabilities. W.P. Carey has launched a lodging-focused fund (Carey Watermark Investors). The new investment program is dedicated to investing in the lodging sector and made its first investments in 2011.

In late 2014, the firm made its first investment in Australia via a 20-year net-lease transaction with Inghams Enterprises Pty. Ltd. The $138 million deal included industrial and agricultural properties.

EXECUTIVES

President, John J. Park, $525,000 total compensation
Global Investments Chief Executive Officer, Director, Jason E. Fox, $700,000 total compensation
Chief Financial Officer, ToniAnn Sanzone, $425,000 total compensation
Chief Accounting Officer, Brian Zander
Managing Director, Chief Administrative Officer, Secretary, Susan C. Hyde
Managing Director, Division Officer, Gino M. Sabatini, $500,000 total compensation
Managing Director, Division Officer, Brooks G. Gordon, $300,000 total compensation
Non-Executive Chairman, Director, Christopher J. Niehaus
Director, Mark A. Alexander
Director, Constantin H. Beier
Director, Peter J. Farrell
Director, Robert J. Flanagan
Director, Axel K.A. Hansing
Director, Jean E. Hoysradt
Director, Margaret G. Lewis
Director, Nick J.M. van Ommen
Director, Tonit M. Calaway
Auditors : PricewaterhouseCoopers LLP

LOCATIONS

HQ: W.P. Carey Inc
One Manhattan West, 395 9th Avenue, 58th Floor, New York, NY 10001
Phone: 212 492-1100
Web: www.wpcarey.com

PRODUCTS/OPERATIONS

2015 sales

	in mil.	% of total
Real estate ownership	735.4	78
Investment management	203.0	22
Total	938.4	100

COMPETITORS

APARTMENT INVESTMENT AND MANAGEMENT COMPANY
CAPLEASE, INC.
DUKE REALTY CORPORATION
GGL GROUP NUMBER TWO LIMITED
GRAMERCY PROPERTY TRUST INC.
ISTAR INC.
KENNEDY-WILSON HOLDINGS, INC.
LENDLEASE CORPORATION LIMITED
RAIT FINANCIAL TRUST
SELECT INCOME REIT

HISTORICAL FINANCIALS

Company Type: Public

Income Statement
FYE: December 31

	REVENUE ($mil)	NET INCOME ($mil)	NET PROFIT MARGIN	EMPLOYEES
12/21	1,331.5	409.9	30.8%	183
12/20	1,209.3	455.3	37.7%	188
12/19	1,232.7	305.2	24.8%	204
12/18	885.7	411.5	46.5%	206
12/17	848.3	277.2	32.7%	207
Annual Growth	11.9%	10.3%	—	(3.0%)

2021 Year-End Financials

Debt ratio: 43.9%
Return on equity: 5.6%
Cash ($ mil.): 165.4
Current Ratio: 0.22
Long-term debt ($ mil.): 6,791.6
No. of shares ($ mil.): 190.0
Dividends
Yield: 5.1%
Payout: 170.9%
Market value ($ mil.): 15,591.0

	STOCK PRICE ($)	P/E		PER SHARE ($)		
	FY Close	High/Low		Earnings	Dividends	Book Value
12/21	82.05	37	29	2.24	4.21	39.90
12/20	70.58	34	17	2.60	4.17	39.21
12/19	80.04	53	36	1.78	4.14	40.29
12/18	65.34	20	17	3.49	4.09	41.29
12/17	68.90	28	23	2.56	4.01	29.86
Annual Growth	4.5%	—	—	(3.3%)	1.2%	7.5%

Walker & Dunlop Inc

Walker & Dunlop is one of the leading commercial real estate services and finance companies in the US, with a primary focus on multifamily lending and property sales, commercial real estate debt brokerage, and affordable housing investment management. It originates and sells its products (e.g. mortgages, supplemental financing, construction loans, and mezzanine loans) primarily through government-sponsored enterprises (GSEs) like Fannie Mae and Freddie Mac, as well as through HUD. To a lesser extent, the company originates loans for insurance companies, banks, and institutional investors.

Operations

The company offers a range of multifamily and other commercial real estate financing products, including Agency Lending, Debt Brokerage, Principal Lending and Investing, Property Sales, Appraisal Services, Housing Market Research, Real Estate Investment Banking Services, and Affordable Housing and other Commercial Real Estate-related Investment Management Services. It also offers a broad range of commercial real estate finance products to its customers, including first mortgage, second trust, supplemental, construction, mezzanine, preferred equity, small-balance, and bridge/interim loans. The company provide property sales services to owners and developers of multifamily properties and commercial real estate investment management services for various investors. Through a joint venture, it also provide multifamily property appraisals.

In all, loan origination and debt brokerage fees, net generated some 35%, fair value of expected net cash flows from servicing, net with about 25%, and servicing fees with over 20%.

Geographic Reach
Walker & Dunlop is headquartered at Bethesda, Maryland.

Sales and Marketing
Walker & Dunlop originates and sells loans through the programs of the Federal National Mortgage Association, the Federal Home Loan Mortgage Corporation, the Government National Mortgage Association, and the Federal Housing Administration, a division of the US Department of Housing and Urban Development.

Financial Performance
The company's revenue in 2021 was $1.3 billion, a 16% increase from the previous year's revenue of $1.1 billion. The increase in revenues was mainly driven by increases in loan origination and debt brokerage fees, net ("origination fees"), servicing fees, property sales broker fees, and other revenues, partially offset by decreases in the fair value of expected net cash flows from servicing, net ("MSR Income"), net warehouse interest income for both loans held for sale and held for investment, and escrow earnings and other interest income.

In 2021, the company had a net income of $265.6 million, an 8% increase from the previous year's net income of $246 million.

The company's cash at the end of 2021 was $393.2 million. Operating activities generated $870.5 million, while investing activities used $377.6 million, mainly for originations of loans held for investment as well as acquisitions. Financing activities used another $457.7 million, mainly for repayments of warehouse notes payable.

Strategy
Walker & Dunlop believe its success in achieving its 2020 goal of $1 billion in revenues positions the company to continue growing and diversifying its business by leveraging its people, brand and technology. In the fourth quarter of 2020, the company set new long-term goals to accomplish by the end of 2025 that include:

Grow debt financing volume to $65 billion annually, including $5 billion of annual small balance multifamily lending, with a servicing portfolio of $160 billion by continuing to hire and acquire the best mortgage bankers in the industry, leveraging its brand to continue growing its client base, and leveraging proprietary technology to be more insightful and relevant to its clients. Walker & Dunlop continues to increase its market share in the multifamily financing market, with a 9% share in 2020.

Grow property sales volume to $25 billion annually by leveraging the strengths of its current team, growing volumes within its current markets and continuing to build out its brand and footprint nationally by hiring brokers in new geographic markets and brokers who specialize in different multifamily product types.

Establish investment banking capabilities with a goal to reach $10 billion in assets under management by building on its existing capabilities and developing new capabilities to meet more of its client's needs. The company has routinely been asked by its clients to help them in providing market insights, raising more complex capital solutions, and undertaking platform valuations. Walker & Dunlop's market-leading position in debt financing and its national reach in its property sales platform gives the company access to substantial amounts of local and macro environmental data.

Remain a leader in environmental, social, and governance ("ESG") efforts by increasing the percentage of women and minorities within the ranks of its top earners and senior management, remaining carbon neutral while reducing its carbon emissions, and donating 1% of its annual income from operations to charitable organizations.

Mergers and Acquisitions
In early 2022, Walker & Dunlop has losed on the previously announced acquisition of GeoPhy, a leading commercial real estate technology company. GeoPhy's data analytics and development capabilities will dramatically accelerate the growth of Walker & Dunlop's lending, brokerage, and emerging businesses including Apprise, its tech-enabled appraisal business and its small balance lending (SBL) platform. Under the terms of the purchase agreement, Walker & Dunlop acquired GeoPhy for $85 million in cash.

In late 2021, Walker & Dunlop closed on the previously announced acquisition of Alliant Capital (Alliant), a privately held alternative investment manager focused on the affordable housing sector through low-income housing tax credit (LIHTC) syndication, joint venture development, and community preservation fund management. Alliant brings benefits to Walker & Dunlop such as market-leading affordable housing platform. Under the terms of the purchase agreement, Walker & Dunlop acquired Alliant at a total enterprise value of $696 million.

In mid-2021, Walker & Dunlop closed on the previously announced acquisition of Zelman & Associates (Zelman), the leading housing research and investment banking firm in the United States. The combination of Zelman's research and market insights with Walker & Dunlop's growing property sales platform, which continues to add top talent including a recent team in Denver, Colorado, will be a differentiator for that area of the business on its path to growing sales volume to $25 billion by 2025. Terms were not disclosed.

Company Background
Walker & Dunlop's relationship with government-related housing finance companies began in the late 1980s after it started originating, underwriting, and selling loans through Fannie Mae. In 2008 it began working with Freddie Mac and HUD after acquiring a loan servicing portfolio worth $5 billion from Column Guaranteed LLC. The acquisition served to widen Walker & Dunlop's revenue base and increase its sales volume.

EXECUTIVES

Chief Executive Officer, Chairman, Director, William M. Walker, $900,000 total compensation
President, Subsidiary Officer, Director, Howard W. Smith, $625,000 total compensation
Executive Vice President, Chief Financial Officer, Stephen P. Theobald, $500,000 total compensation
Executive Vice President, General Counsel, Secretary, Richard M. Lucas, $500,000 total compensation
Executive Vice President, Chief Human Resources Officer, Paula A. Pryor
Lead Director, Director, Alan J. Bowers
Director, Michael D. Malone
Director, John E. Rice
Director, Dana L. Schmaltz
Director, Michael J. Warren
Director, Ellen D. Levy
Auditors : KPMG LLP

LOCATIONS
HQ: Walker & Dunlop Inc
7501 Wisconsin Avenue, Suite 1200E, Bethesda, MD 20814
Phone: 301 215-5500
Web: www.walkerdunlop.com

PRODUCTS/OPERATIONS
2014 Sales

	% mil.	% of total
Gains from mortgage banking activities	222.0	62
Servicing fees	98.4	27
Net warehouse interest income	17.5	5
Escrow earnings & other interest income	4.5	1
Other	18.4	5
Total	360.8	100

Selected Products and Services
Capital Markets and Investment Services
Construction loans
Equity investments
FHA Finance
First mortgage loans
Healthcare Finance
Mezzanine loans
Multifamily Finance
Second trust loans
Supplemental financings
Underwriting

COMPETITORS
CARILLION PLC
CASS INFORMATION SYSTEMS, INC.
CELTIC INVESTMENT, INC.
Chubb Limited
EAGLE BANCORP, INC.
FIRST CONNECTICUT BANCORP, INC.
HOMESTREET, INC.

Hanley Economic Building Society
MARLIN BUSINESS SERVICES CORP.
REGIONAL MANAGEMENT CORP.

HISTORICAL FINANCIALS
Company Type: Public

Income Statement — FYE: December 31

	REVENUE ($mil)	NET INCOME ($mil)	NET PROFIT MARGIN	EMPLOYEES
12/20	1,083.7	246.1	22.7%	988
12/19	817.2	173.3	21.2%	823
12/18	725.2	161.4	22.3%	723
12/17	711.8	211.1	29.7%	623
12/16	575.2	113.8	19.8%	550
Annual Growth	17.2%	21.3%	—	15.8%

2020 Year-End Financials
Debt ratio: 60.4%
No. of shares ($ mil.): 30.6
Return on equity: 21.9%
Dividends
Cash ($ mil.): 321.1
Yield: 1.5%
Current Ratio: 23.54
Payout: 18.7%
Long-term debt ($ mil.): 2,808.7
Market value ($ mil.): 2,823.0

	STOCK PRICE ($) FY Close	P/E High	P/E Low	PER SHARE ($) Earnings	Dividends	Book Value
12/20	92.02	12	3	7.69	1.44	38.99
12/19	64.68	12	8	5.45	1.20	34.48
12/18	43.25	12	7	4.96	1.00	30.58
12/17	47.50	8	4	6.56	0.00	26.97
12/16	31.20	8	5	3.65	0.00	20.65
Annual Growth	31.0%	—	—	20.5%	—	17.2%

Waterstone Financial Inc (MD)

EXECUTIVES

Chairman, Subsidiary Officer, Director, Patrick S. Lawton
President, Subsidiary Officer, William F. Bruss, $308,654 total compensation
Chief Executive Officer, Subsidiary Officer, Director, Douglas S. Gordon, $850,000 total compensation
Executive Vice President, Subsidiary Officer, Ryan Gordon
Executive Vice President, Chief Financial Officer, Principal Accounting Officer, Subsidiary Officer, Mark Raymond Gerke, $197,308 total compensation
Executive Vice President, Subsidiary Officer, Julie A. Glynn, $132,192 total compensation
Subsidiary Officer, Jeffrey R. McGuiness
Director, Ellen S. Bartel
Director, Thomas E. Dalum
Director, Kristine A. Rappe
Director, Michael L. Hansen
Director, Stephen J. Schmidt
Director, Derek L. Tyus
Auditors: CliftonLarsonAllen LLP

LOCATIONS
HQ: Waterstone Financial Inc (MD)
11200 W. Plank Court, Wauwatosa, WI 53226

Phone: 414 761-1000
Web: www.wsbonline.com

HISTORICAL FINANCIALS
Company Type: Public

Income Statement — FYE: December 31

	ASSETS ($mil)	NET INCOME ($mil)	INCOME AS % OF ASSETS	EMPLOYEES
12/20	2,184.5	81.1	3.7%	812
12/19	1,996.3	35.9	1.8%	824
12/18	1,915.3	30.7	1.6%	888
12/17	1,806.4	25.9	1.4%	927
12/16	1,790.6	25.5	1.4%	895
Annual Growth	5.1%	33.5%	—	(2.4%)

2020 Year-End Financials
Return on assets: 3.8%
Dividends
Return on equity: 20.0%
Yield: 6.8%
Long-term debt ($ mil.): —
Payout: 50.9%
No. of shares ($ mil.): 25.0
Market value ($ mil.): 472.0
Sales ($ mil.): 322.5

	STOCK PRICE ($) FY Close	P/E High	P/E Low	PER SHARE ($) Earnings	Dividends	Book Value
12/20	18.82	6	4	3.30	1.28	16.47
12/19	19.03	14	11	1.37	0.98	14.50
12/18	16.76	16	14	1.11	0.98	14.04
12/17	17.05	21	18	0.93	0.98	13.97
12/16	18.40	20	14	0.93	0.26	13.95
Annual Growth	0.6%	—	—	37.2%	49.0%	4.2%

Weber Inc

EXECUTIVES

Chief Executive Officer, Alan D. Matula
Chief Marketing Officer, Mary A. Sagripanti
Chief Operating Officer, Chief Supply Chain Officer, Michael G. Jacobs
Finance Senior Vice President, Finance Interim Chief Financial Officer, Marla Mala Yvonne Kilpatrick
General Counsel, Erik W. Chalut
Global Controller, Chief Accounting Officer, Michael P. Bayer
Division Officer, Hans-Jurgen Herr
Non-Executive Chairman, Director, Kelly D. Rainko
Director, Susan T. Congalton
Director, Melinda R. Rich
Director, Magesvaran Suranjan
Director, James C. Stephen
Director, Elliott J. Hill
Director, Martin McCourt

LOCATIONS
HQ: Weber Inc
1415 S. Roselle Road, Palatine, IL 60067
Phone: 847 934-5700
Web: www.weber.com

HISTORICAL FINANCIALS
Company Type: Public

Income Statement — FYE: September 30

	REVENUE ($mil)	NET INCOME ($mil)	NET PROFIT MARGIN	EMPLOYEES
09/21	1,982.4	47.7	2.4%	2,534
09/20	1,525.2	88.8	5.8%	2,156
09/19	1,296.2	50.1	3.9%	0
09/18	1,340.0	113.2	8.5%	0
Annual Growth	13.9%	(25.0%)	—	—

2021 Year-End Financials
Debt ratio: 66.8%
No. of shares ($ mil.): 286.1
Return on equity: —
Dividends
Cash ($ mil.): 107.5
Yield: —
Current Ratio: 1.30
Payout: —
Long-term debt ($ mil.): 1,023.2
Market value ($ mil.): 5,033.0

	STOCK PRICE ($) FY Close	P/E High/Low	PER SHARE ($) Earnings	Dividends	Book Value
09/21	17.59	—	(0.13)	0.00	(0.04)
Annual Growth	—	—	—	—	—

WesBanco Inc

WesBanco offers a full range of financial services including retail banking, corporate trust services, personal and corporate trust services, brokerage services, mortgage banking, and insurance. WesBanco operates one commercial bank: WesBanco Bank which has more than 200 branches and ATM machines located in Indiana, Kentucky, Ohio, Pennsylvania, and West Virginia. WesBanco offers its services through its community banking and trust and investment services segments. WesBanco's non-banking operations include brokerage firm WesBanco Securities and multi-line insurance provider WesBanco Insurance Services. The company was founded in 1968.

Financial Performance

The company's revenue increased in fiscal 2013 compared to the prior fiscal period. WesBanco reported $287.2 million in revenue for fiscal 2013, up from $276.5 in fiscal 2012.

The company's net income also increased in fiscal 2013 compared to the previous year. It reported net income of $63.9 million in fiscal 2013, up from net income of $49.5 million for fiscal 2012.

As another sign of the company's health, WesBanco's cash on hand spiked by about $65 million during fiscal 2013 compared to fiscal 2012 levels.

EXECUTIVES

Chairman, Director, Christopher V. Criss
President, Chief Executive Officer, Subsidiary Officer, Director, Todd F. Clossin, $812,492 total compensation

Human Resources Senior Executive Vice President, Human Resources Division Officer, Anthony F. Pietranton, $216,940 total compensation
Senior Executive Vice President, Chief Banking Officer, Jayson M. Zatta, $353,097 total compensation
Senior Executive Vice President, Division Officer, Michael L. Perkins
Executive Vice President, Chief Internal Audit, Stephen J. Lawrence
Executive Vice President, Chief Credit Officer, Ivan L. Burdine
Wealth Management Executive Vice President, Jonathan D. Dargusch, $266,520 total compensation
Strategic Planning Executive Vice President, Treasury Executive Vice President, Brent E. Richmond
Executive Vice President, Chief Financial Officer, Daniel K. Weiss
Subsidiary Officer, Director, James W. Cornelsen
Director, Rosie Allen-Herring
Director, Michael J. Crawford
Director, Abigail M. Feinknopf
Director, Robert J. Fitzsimmons
Director, D. Bruce Knox
Director, Lisa A. Knutson
Director, Gary L. Libs
Director, Jay T. McCamic
Director, F. Eric Nelson
Director, Gregory S. Proctor
Director, Joseph R. Robinson
Director, Kerry M. Stemler
Director, Reed J. Tanner
Director, Denise Knouse-Snyder
Auditors : Ernst & Young LLP

LOCATIONS

HQ: WesBanco Inc
  1 Bank Plaza, Wheeling, WV 26003
Phone: 304 234-9000
Web: www.wesbanco.com

PRODUCTS/OPERATIONS

2016 Sales

	$ mil.	% of total
Interest and Dividend Income		
Loans, including fees	227.0	61
Interest and dividends on securities	56.9	15
Other interest income	2.2	1
Non-Interest Income		
Trust fees	21.6	6
Service charges on deposits	18.3	5
Electronic banking fees	15.6	4
Net securities brokerage	6.4	2
Bank-owned life insurance	4.1	1
Net gains on sales of mortgage loans	2.5	1
Net securities gains	2.4	1
Net gain / (loss) on other real estate owned and other assets	0.8	—
others	9.8	3
Total	367.6	100

Selected Products and Services
Personal Banking
Internet Banking
Checking
Savings
Time Deposits
Debit Cards
Credit Cards
Loans
Mortgage Lending
Other Services
Business
Internet Banking
Checking
Savings
Time Deposits
Credit Cards
Loans
Treasury Management
Insurance Services
Wealth Management

COMPETITORS

CARDINAL FINANCIAL CORPORATION
CITY HOLDING COMPANY
FIRST COMMONWEALTH FINANCIAL CORPORATION
FIRST MIDWEST BANCORP, INC.
LEGACYTEXAS FINANCIAL GROUP, INC.
NATIONAL BANK HOLDINGS CORPORATION
OLD LINE BANCSHARES, INC.
RENASANT CORPORATION
SUFFOLK BANCORP.
TCF FINANCIAL CORPORATION

HISTORICAL FINANCIALS
Company Type: Public

Income Statement — FYE: December 31

	ASSETS ($mil)	NET INCOME ($mil)	INCOME AS % OF ASSETS	EMPLOYEES
12/20	16,425.6	122.0	0.7%	2,612
12/19	15,720.1	158.8	1.0%	2,705
12/18	12,458.6	143.1	1.1%	2,383
12/17	9,816.1	94.4	1.0%	1,940
12/16	9,790.8	86.6	0.9%	1,928
Annual Growth	13.8%	8.9%	—	7.9%

2020 Year-End Financials

Return on assets: 0.7%
Return on equity: 4.5%
Long-term debt ($ mil.): —
No. of shares ($ mil.): 67.2
Sales ($ mil.): 669.4
Dividends Yield: 4.2%
Payout: 79.0%
Market value ($ mil.): 2,015.0

	STOCK PRICE ($) FY Close	P/E High	P/E Low	PER SHARE ($) Earnings	Dividends	Book Value
12/20	29.96	21	10	1.77	1.28	40.99
12/19	37.79	15	12	2.83	1.24	38.24
12/18	36.69	17	12	2.92	1.16	36.24
12/17	40.65	20	16	2.14	1.04	31.68
12/16	43.06	20	13	2.16	0.96	30.53
Annual Growth	(8.7%)	—	—	(4.9%)	7.5%	7.6%

West Bancorporation, Inc.

West Bancorporation is the holding company for West Bank, which serves individuals and small to midsized businesses through about a dozen branches, mainly in the Des Moines and Iowa City, Iowa areas. Founded in 1893, the bank offers checking, savings, and money market accounts, CDs, Visa credit cards, and trust services. The bank's lending activities primarily consist of commercial mortgages; construction, land, and land development loans; and business loans, such as revolving lines of credit, inventory and accounts receivable financing, equipment financing, and capital expenditure loans, to borrowers in Iowa.

Sales and Marketing
West Bank focuses on small to medium-sized businesses in its local markets. The thinking is that smaller, local firms want to develop an exclusive relationship with a single bank.

Financial Performance
The company's revenue has been remarkably consistent year-over-year. It reported $61.2 million in annual revenue for fiscal 2013 after claiming $61.7 million in fiscal 2012 and $64.1 million in fiscal 2011.

Net income has also remained very consistent in recent years. The bank reported net income of $16.8 million for fiscal 2013 after clearing $16 million in fiscal 2012 and $15.27 million in fiscal 2011.

The company's net cash on hand has decreased dramatically in recent fiscal years, however, mostly as a result of property investments.

Strategy
West Bank has slowly but surely been expanding its territory. The company is working on building a new headquarters building and expanding into Minnesota.

EXECUTIVES

Chairman, Director, James W. Noyce
President, Chief Executive Officer, Subsidiary Officer, Director, David D. Nelson, $436,000 total compensation
Executive Vice President, Subsidiary Officer, Bradley P. Peters
Executive Vice President, Chief Financial Officer, Treasurer, Subsidiary Officer, Jane M. Funk
Executive Vice President, Chief Risk Officer, Subsidiary Officer, Harlee N. Olafson, $300,000 total compensation
Executive Vice President, Subsidiary Officer, Brad L. Winterbottom, $300,000 total compensation
Vice President, Corporate Secretary, Assistant General Counsel, Melissa L. Gillespie
Director, Rosemary Parson
Director, Lisa J. Elming
Director, Douglas R. Gulling, $300,000 total compensation
Director, Patrick J. Donovan
Director, Steven K. Gaer
Director, Sean Patrick McMurray
Director, George D. Milligan, $179,000 total compensation
Director, Steven T. Schuler
Director, Therese M. Vaughan
Director, Philip Jason Worth
Auditors : RSM US LLP

LOCATIONS

HQ: West Bancorporation, Inc.
  1601 22nd Street, West Des Moines, IA 50266
Phone: 515 222-2300
Web: www.westbankstrong.com

PRODUCTS/OPERATIONS

2015 Sales

	$ mil.	% of total
Interest		
Loans, including fees	52.5	77
Taxable investment Securities	4.4	6
Tax-exempt investment Securities	3.2	5
Federal funds sold	0.08	-
Noninterest		
Service charges on deposit accounts	2.6	4
Debit card usage fees	1.8	3
Trust services	1.3	2
Revenue from residential mortgage banking	0.1	-
Increase in cash value of bank-owned life insurance	0.7	1
Realized investment securities gains, net	0.05	-
Other income	1.6	2
Total	**68.4**	**100**

COMPETITORS

AMERIS BANCORP
FIRST INTERSTATE BANCSYSTEM, INC.
NEWBRIDGE BANCORP
REPUBLIC FIRST BANCORP, INC.
TRUSTCO BANK CORP N Y

HISTORICAL FINANCIALS

Company Type: Public

Income Statement — FYE: December 31

	ASSETS ($mil)	NET INCOME ($mil)	INCOME AS % OF ASSETS	EMPLOYEES
12/20	3,185.7	32.7	1.0%	350
12/19	2,473.6	28.6	1.2%	171
12/18	2,296.5	28.5	1.2%	163
12/17	2,114.3	23.0	1.1%	162
12/16	1,854.2	23.0	1.2%	165
Annual Growth	14.5%	9.2%	—	20.7%

2020 Year-End Financials

Return on assets: 1.1%
Return on equity: 14.9%
Long-term debt ($ mil.): —
No. of shares ($ mil.): 16.4
Sales ($ mil.): 109.8
Dividends
  Yield: 4.3%
  Payout: 43.7%
Market value ($ mil.): 318.0

	STOCK PRICE ($) FY Close	P/E High	P/E Low	PER SHARE ($) Earnings	Dividends	Book Value
12/20	19.30	13	8	1.98	0.84	13.58
12/19	25.63	15	11	1.74	0.83	12.93
12/18	19.09	15	10	1.74	0.78	11.72
12/17	25.15	20	15	1.41	0.71	10.98
12/16	24.70	17	11	1.42	0.67	10.25
Annual Growth	(6.0%)	—	—	8.7%	5.8%	7.3%

West Pharmaceutical Services, Inc.

West Pharmaceutical Services is a leading global manufacturer in the design and production of technologically advanced, high-quality, integrated containment and delivery components for pharmaceutical and health care products. The company's proprietary drug and biologic packaging products include seals and stoppers for injectable medicine, syringe components, and injection systems. It also has vast expertise in product design and development, including in-house mold design, process design and validation and high-speed automated assemblies for pharmaceutical, diagnostic, and medical device customers. The US is West's largest single market, accounting for about 40% of total revenue.

Operations

West operates through two reportable segments: Proprietary Products and Contract-Manufactured Products.

The Proprietary Products segment, accounting for more than 80% of total revenue, makes containment, packaging, and drug delivery devices for injectable pharmaceuticals and biologic therapies. It also provides analytical lab services to its customers in the biologic and pharmaceutical sectors, along with other product development support services. Products include syringe and cartridge components, seals and stoppers, administration systems, films and coatings, polymer vials, and self-injection devices. This segment's product portfolio also includes drug containment solutions, including Crystal Zenith, a cyclic olefin polymer, in the form of vials, syringes and cartridges.

The Contract-Manufactured Products segment, bringing in some 20% of total revenue, serves as a fully integrated business, focused on the design, manufacture, and automated assembly of complex devices, primarily for pharmaceutical, diagnostic, and medical device customers. These products include a variety of custom contract-manufacturing and assembly solutions, which use such technologies as multi-component molding, in-mold labeling, ultrasonic welding, clean room molding and device assembly. It manufacture customer-owned components and devices used in surgical, diagnostic, ophthalmic, injectable, and other drug delivery systems, as well as consumer products.

Geographic Reach

Headquartered in Exton, Pennsylvania, West has manufacturing facilities throughout the world, including locations in Arizona, Florida, Michigan, Nebraska, North Carolina, and Pennsylvania in the US, and in Brazil, China, Germany, Denmark, France, India, Ireland, Puerto Rico, Serbia, Singapore, and the UK abroad. It also has affiliates in Mexico and Japan.

The US makes up more than 40% of revenue, followed by Germany (over 15%), Ireland, (about 10%) France (more than 5%) and other European countries (about 10%). Countries in other regions account for nearly 15% of revenue.

Sales and Marketing

West's products are distributed through its direct sales force and distribution facilities, as well as through select contracted sales agents and regional distributors.

The Proprietary Products segment's customers include major biologic, pharma, and generic drug companies. The Contract-Manufactured Products segment's customers include pharma, medical device, and diagnostic companies.

The company's ten largest customers account for more than 40% of revenue.

Financial Performance

The company's revenue for fiscal 2021 increased by 32% to $2.8 billion compared from the prior year with $2.1 billion.

Net income for fiscal 2021 increased to $661.8 million compared from the prior year with $346.2 million.

Cash held by the company at the end of fiscal 2021 increased to $762.6 million. Cash provided by operations was $584.0 million while cash used for investing and financing activities were $253.1 million and $168.1 million, respectively. Main uses of cash were capital expenditures and shares purchased under share repurchase programs.

Company Background

West Pharmaceutical was founded in Pennsylvania in 1923.

EXECUTIVES

Chairman, Lead Independent Director, Director, Patrick J. Zenner, $100,000 total compensation
President, Chief Executive Officer, Director, Eric M. Green, $879,615 total compensation
Senior Vice President, General Counsel, Corporate Secretary, Kimberly Banks MacKay
Senior Vice President, Chief Financial Officer, Treasurer, Bernard J. Birkett, $279,231 total compensation
Senior Vice President, Chief Operations and Supply Chain Officer, David A. Montecalvo, $401,461 total compensation
Senior Vice President, Chief Digital and Transformation Officer, Siliji Abraham, $339,038 total compensation
Vice President, Chief Accounting Officer, Corporate Controller, Principal Accounting Officer, Chad R. Winters
Director, Molly E. Joseph
Director, Mark A. Buthman
Director, William F. Feehery
Director, Robert F. Friel
Director, Thomas W. Hofmann
Director, Deborah L. V. Keller
Director, Myla P. Lai-Goldman
Director, Douglas A. Michels
Director, Paolo Pucci
Auditors: PricewaterhouseCoopers LLP

LOCATIONS

HQ: West Pharmaceutical Services, Inc.
  530 Herman O. West Drive, Exton, PA 19341-0645
Phone: 610 594-2900
Web: www.westpharma.com

2017 Sales

	$ mil.	% of total
US	734.6	46
Europe		
Germany	226.4	14
France	125.6	8
Other	318.5	20
Other	194.0	12
Total	1,599.1	100

PRODUCTS/OPERATIONS

2017 Sales by Segment

	$ mil.	% of total
Proprietary Products	1,236.9	77
Contract-Manufactured Products	362.5	23
Adjustments	(0.3)	-
Total	1,599.1	100

Product Categories
Vial containment solutions
Prefillable systems
Self-injection platforms
Cartridge systems and components
Reconstitution and transfer systems
Intradermal delivery solutions
Specialty components

COMPETITORS

AMERICAN BILTRITE INC.
APTARGROUP, INC.
AirBoss of America Corp
CATALENT, INC.
COOPER-STANDARD INDUSTRIAL AND SPECIALTY GROUP, LLC
Gerresheimer AG
KRAUSSMAFFEI GROUP UK LIMITED
PARK-OHIO HOLDINGS CORP.
TOYODA GOSEI NORTH AMERICA CORPORATION
VICTREX PLC

HISTORICAL FINANCIALS
Company Type: Public

Income Statement — FYE: December 31

	REVENUE ($mil)	NET INCOME ($mil)	NET PROFIT MARGIN	EMPLOYEES
12/21	2,831.6	661.8	23.4%	10,065
12/20	2,146.9	346.2	16.1%	9,200
12/19	1,839.9	241.7	13.1%	8,200
12/18	1,717.4	206.9	12.0%	7,700
12/17	1,599.1	150.7	9.4%	7,500
Annual Growth	15.4%	44.8%	—	7.6%

2021 Year-End Financials

Debt ratio: 7.6%
Return on equity: 31.5%
Cash ($ mil.): 762.6
Current Ratio: 2.93
Long-term debt ($ mil.): 208.8
No. of shares ($ mil.): 74.2
Dividends
Yield: 0.1%
Payout: 8.5%
Market value ($ mil.): 34,801.0

	STOCK PRICE ($) FY Close	P/E High	P/E Low	PER SHARE ($) Earnings	Dividends	Book Value
12/21	469.01	53	29	8.67	0.69	31.47
12/20	283.31	64	28	4.57	0.65	25.06
12/19	150.33	46	29	3.21	0.61	21.23
12/18	98.03	44	30	2.74	0.57	18.84
12/17	98.67	50	39	1.99	0.53	17.32
Annual Growth	47.7%	—	—	44.5%	6.8%	16.1%

Western Alliance Bancorporation

Western Alliance Bancorporation and its flagship Western Alliance Bank (WAB) have an alliance with several bank brands in the West, operating as the Alliance Bank of Arizona; Bank of Nevada; as well as Bridge Bank and Torrey Pines Bank. The bank provides an array of specialized financial services to business customers across the country, and has added to these capabilities with the acquisition of AmeriHome which provides mortgage banking services. More than 45% of the Western Alliance's loan portfolio is made up of commercial and industrial loans, while around 25% is made up of residential real estate loans. It also makes land development loans and consumer residential mortgages and other lines of credit.

Operations

Western Alliance focuses on three reportable segments: Commercial segment, which provides commercial banking and treasury management products and services to small and middle-market businesses, specialized banking services to sophisticated commercial institutions and investors within niche industries, as well as financial services to the real estate industry; Consumer Related segment, which offers consumer banking services, such as residential mortgage banking, and commercial banking services to enterprises in consumer-related sectors; and Corporate & Other segment, which consists of the company's investment portfolio, corporate borrowings and other related items, income and expense items not allocated to its other reportable segments, and inter-segment eliminations.

More than 45% of the bank's loan portfolio consisted of commercial and industrial loans at the end of 2021, while over 15% was made up of commercial real estate loans (non-owner and owner occupied). The bank also had residential mortgages (about 25%), construction and land development loans (over 5% of loan assets), and commercial real estate - owner occupied (some 5%).

In all, the company generated around 70% of sales from loans, including fees, while net gain on loan origination and sale activities generated some 15%.

Geographic Reach

Phoenix-based Western Alliance has around 35 branches, which includes six executive and administrative offices.

Financial Performance

The company's revenue for fiscal 2021 increased to $2.0 billion compared from the prior year with $1.2 billion.

Net income for fiscal 2021 increased to $899.2 million compared from the prior year with $506.6 million.

Cash held by the company at the end of fiscal 2021 decreased to $516.4 million. Cash provided by financing activities was $15.2 billion while cash used for operations and investing activities were $2.7 billion and $14.7 billion, respectively.

Mergers and Acquisitions

In early 2022, Western Alliance Bank has completed the acquisition of Digital Settlement Technologies, DBA Digital Disbursements, the leading digital payments platform for the class action legal industry. Joining forces with Digital Disbursements, which enables the seamless integration of a customizable pay menu into settlement claim forms and other payment selection websites, positions Western Alliance as the leading digital payments platform for the class action market and broader legal industry. Terms were not disclosed.

In 2021, Western Alliance Bancorporation acquired Aris Mortgage Holding Company, LLC (parent company of AmeriHome Mortgage Company, LLC) for a total consideration of approximately $1.22 billion. AmeriHome Mortgage offers a B2B approach to the mortgage ecosystem through relationships with more than 700 independent correspondent mortgage clients. The acquisition of AmeriHome enable the company to extend its national commercial business with a complementary low-risk national mortgage franchise.

EXECUTIVES

Chairman, Lead Independent Director, Director, Bruce Beach

Vice-Chairman, Chief Financial Officer, Dale Gibbons, $666,346 total compensation

President, Chief Executive Officer, Director, Kenneth A. Vecchione, $1,088,462 total compensation

Executive Vice President, Chief Credit Officer, Tim R. Bruckner

Executive Vice President, Chief Human Resources Officer, Barbara J. Kennedy, $238,942 total compensation

Executive Vice President, Secretary, General Counsel, Randall S. Theisen

Chief Operating Officer, Timothy W. Boothe

Director, Juan R. Figuereo
Director, Howard N. Gould
Director, Marianne Boyd Johnson
Director, Patricia L. Arvielo
Director, Robert P. Latta
Director, Adriane McFetridge
Director, Michael M. Patriarca
Director, Bryan Segedi
Director, Donald D. Snyder
Director, Sung Won Sohn
Director, Kevin M. Blakley
Director, Paul S. Galant

Auditors: RSM US LLP

LOCATIONS

HQ: Western Alliance Bancorporation
One E. Washington Street, Suite 1400, Phoenix, AZ 85004
Phone: 602-389-3500
Web: www.westernalliancebancorporation.com

PRODUCTS/OPERATIONS

2015 Sales

	$ in mil	% of total
Interest income		
Loans, including fees	476.4	86
Investment securities	37.9	7
Dividends	10.3	2
Other	0.5	-
Non-interest income		
Service charges and fees	14.6	2
Income from bank owned life insurance	3.9	1
Card income	3.8	1
Other	7.5	1
Total	554.9	100

Selected Services
Business Checking & Savings
Business Loans & Credit
Card Services
International Banking
Personal Banking
Treasury Management

COMPETITORS

BANCFIRST CORPORATION
CITIZENS & NORTHERN CORPORATION
CITY HOLDING COMPANY
EAGLE BANCORP, INC.
F.N.B. CORPORATION
FIRST CITIZENS BANCSHARES, INC.
FIRST HORIZON CORPORATION
PACWEST BANCORP
WILSHIRE BANCORP, INC.
WINTRUST FINANCIAL CORPORATION

HISTORICAL FINANCIALS

Company Type: Public

Income Statement
FYE: December 31

	ASSETS ($mil)	NET INCOME ($mil)	INCOME AS % OF ASSETS	EMPLOYEES
12/20	36,461.0	506.6	1.4%	1,915
12/19	26,821.9	499.1	1.9%	1,835
12/18	23,109.4	435.7	1.9%	1,787
12/17	20,329.0	325.4	1.6%	1,725
12/16	17,200.8	259.7	1.5%	1,557
Annual Growth	20.7%	18.2%	—	5.3%

2020 Year-End Financials
Return on assets: 1.5%
Return on equity: 15.7%
Long-term debt ($ mil.): —
No. of shares ($ mil.): 100.8
Sales ($ mil.): 1,332.6
Dividends
  Yield: 1.6%
  Payout: 22.8%
Market value ($ mil.): 6,046.0

	STOCK PRICE ($) FY Close	P/E High/Low		PER SHARE ($) Earnings	Dividends	Book Value
12/20	59.95	12	4	5.04	1.00	33.85
12/19	57.00	12	8	4.84	0.50	29.42
12/18	39.49	15	9	4.14	0.00	24.90
12/17	56.62	19	14	3.10	0.00	21.14
12/16	48.71	20	11	2.50	0.00	18.00
Annual Growth	5.3%	—	—	19.2%	—	17.1%

Western Midstream Partners LP

Western Midstream Partners, LP ("WES") is a Delaware master limited partnership formed to acquire, own, develop, and operate midstream assets. With midstream assets located in the Rocky Mountains, North-central Pennsylvania, Texas, and New Mexico, WES is engaged in the business of gathering, compressing, treating, processing, and transporting natural gas; gathering, stabilizing, and transporting condensate, NGLs, and crude oil; and gathering and disposing of produced water for its customers. In addition, in its capacity as a processor of natural gas, WES also buys and sells natural gas, NGLs, and condensate on behalf of itself and as an agent for its customers under certain of its contracts.

Operations
Its operations are organized into a single operating segment that engages in gathering, compressing, treating, processing, and transporting natural gas; gathering, stabilizing, and transporting condensate, NGLs, and crude oil; and gathering and disposing of produced water.

Overall, services account for about 90% of revenue and products account for the remaining 10% of revenue.

Geographic Reach
Western Midterms operates in Texas, New Mexico, Colorado, Utah, Wyoming, and North-central Pennsylvania, with a substantial portion of our business concentrated in West Texas and the Rocky Mountains.

Financial Performance
The company reported a revenue of $2.9 billion in 2021, a 4% increase from the previous year's total revenue of $2.8 billion. The increase is primarily attributable to a higher sales volume in the company's product-based service revenues and product sales.

In 2021, the company had a net income of $916.3 million, a 74% increase from the previous year's net income of $527 million.

The company's cash at the end of 2021 was $202 million. Operating activities generated $1.8 billion, while investing activities used $257.5 million, mainly for capital expenditures. Financing activities used another $1.8 billion, primarily for repayments of debt.

Strategy
The company's primary business objective is to create long-term value for unitholders through continued delivery of profitable operations and return of capital to stakeholders over time. Its foundational principles of operational excellence, superior customer service, and sustainable operations influence the company's decision making and long-term strategy. To accomplish its primary business objective, the company intends to execute the following strategy:

Capitalizing on organic growth opportunities. Western Midstream intends to grow certain of its systems organically over time by meeting customers' midstream service needs that arise from drilling activity in its areas of operation. The company continually pursues economically attractive organic business development and expansion opportunities in existing or new areas of operation that allow it to leverage its infrastructure, operating expertise, and customer relationships, to meet new or increased demand of the company's services.

Controlling the company's operating, capital, and administrative costs. The establishment of WES as a stand-alone midstream business has generated efficiencies between Western Midstream's commercial, engineering, and operations teams, and it continues to optimize and maximize the operability of existing assets to realize cost and capital savings.

Optimizing the return of cash to stakeholders. Western Midstream intends to operate its assets and make strategic capital decisions that optimize its leverage levels consistent with investment-grade metrics in its sector while returning additional excess cash flow to stakeholders that enhances overall return.

EXECUTIVES

Chairman, Holding/Parent Company Officer, Associate/Affiliate Company Officer, Director, Peter J. Bennett

President, Chief Executive Officer, Chief Financial Officer, Holding/Parent Company Officer, Associate/Affiliate Company Officer, Director, Michael P. Ure

Holding/Parent Company Officer, Director, Oscar K. Brown

Senior Vice President, Chief Financial Officer, Kristen S. Shults

Senior Vice President, Chief Commercial Officer, Robert W. Bourne

Senior Vice President, General Counsel, Corporate Secretary, Christopher B. Dial

Senior Vice President, Chief Accounting Officer, Associate/Affiliate Company Officer, Catherine A. Green

Division Officer, Holding/Parent Company Officer, Daniel P. Holderman

Division Officer, Michael S. Forsyth

Director, Nicole E. Clark

Director, Frederick A. Forthuber

Director, Kenneth F. Owen

Director, David J. Schulte

Director, Lisa A. Stewart

Auditors : KPMG LLP

LOCATIONS

HQ: Western Midstream Partners LP
9950 Woodloch Forest Drive, Suite 2800, The Woodlands, TX 77380

Phone: 346 786-5000
Web: www.westerngas.com

PRODUCTS/OPERATIONS

2011 Sales

	$ mil.	% of total
Natural gas, NGLs, and condensate sales	502.4	61
Gathering, processing, & transporation of natural gas & NGLs	301.3	36
Equity income & other	19.6	3
Total	823.3	100

COMPETITORS

AMERISUR RESOURCES LIMITED
ANADARKO PETROLEUM CORPORATION
BRAZOS VALLEY LONGHORN, L.L.C.
LINNCO, LLC
NEW SOURCE ENERGY PARTNERS L.P.

HISTORICAL FINANCIALS

Company Type: Public

Income Statement FYE: December 31

	REVENUE ($mil)	NET INCOME ($mil)	NET PROFIT MARGIN	EMPLOYEES
12/20	2,772.5	527.0	19.0%	1,045
12/19	2,746.1	697.2	25.4%	19
12/18	1,990.2	369.4	18.6%	0
12/17	2,248.3	376.6	16.8%	0
12/16	1,804.2	345.7	19.2%	0
Annual Growth	11.3%	11.1%	—	—

2020 Year-End Financials

Debt ratio: 66.4%
Return on equity: —
Cash ($ mil.): 444.9
Current Ratio: 0.98
Long-term debt ($ mil.): 7,415.8
No. of shares ($ mil.): 422.9
Dividends
Yield: 11.2%
Payout: 126.4%
Market value ($ mil.): 5,844.0

	STOCK PRICE ($) FY Close	P/E High/Low		PER SHARE ($) Earnings	Dividends	Book Value
12/20	13.82	18	3	1.18	1.56	6.53
12/19	19.69	22	11	1.59	2.45	7.05
12/18	27.73	25	16	1.69	2.30	4.35
12/17	37.16	28	20	1.72	2.02	4.85
12/16	42.35	30	13	1.53	1.71	4.79
Annual Growth	(24.4%)	—	—	(6.3%)	(2.3%)	8.1%

Western New England Bancorp Inc

Westfield Financial is the holding company for Westfield Bank, which serves western Massachusetts' Hampden County and surrounding areas from more than 20 branch locations. Founded in 1853, the bank has traditionally been a community-oriented provider of retail deposit accounts and loans, but it is placing more emphasis on serving commercial and industrial clients. Commercial real estate loans account for approximately 45% of the company's loan portfolio and business loans are more than 25%. The bank also makes a smaller number of consumer and home equity loans. In 2016, Westfield Financial merged with Chicopee Bancorp, the holding company of Chicopee Savings Bank (another bank serving Hampden County).

EXECUTIVES

Chairman, Subsidiary Officer, Director, Christos A. Tapases
President, Chief Executive Officer, Subsidiary Officer, Director, James C. Hagan, $467,213 total compensation
Chief Financial Officer, Treasurer, Subsidiary Officer, Leo R. Sagan, $197,123 total compensation
Executive Vice President, Subsidiary Officer, Allen J. Miles, $272,808 total compensation
Human Resources Vice President, Human Resources Secretary, Human Resources General Counsel, Human Resources Director, Human Resources Subsidiary Officer, Gerald P. Ciejka, $216,031 total compensation
Credit Administration Vice President, Credit Administration Chief Credit Officer, Louis O. Gorman, $172,299 total compensation
Vice President, Residential Loan Officer, Subsidiary Officer, Rebecca S. Kozaczka, $117,598 total compensation
Information Systems Vice President, Operations Vice President, Information Systems Manager, Operations Manager, Information Systems Subsidiary Officer, Operations Subsidiary Officer, Deborah J. McCarthy, $119,990 total compensation
Retail Banking Vice President, Kevin C. O'Connor
Chief Investment Officer, Michael J. Janosco, $218,894 total compensation
Chief Financial Officer, Treasurer, Subsidiary Officer, Guida R. Sajdak, $215,062 total compensation
Senior Vice President, Chief Business Development Officer, William J. Wagner, $350,000 total compensation
Director, William Wagner
Director, Gary G. Fitzgerald
Director, Lisa G. McMahon
Director, Laura Benoit
Director, Kevin M. Sweeney
Director, David C. Colton
Director, Philip R. Smith
Director, Victor J. Carra, $174,173 total compensation
Director, Robert T. Crowley
Director, Donna J. Damon
Director, Richard C. Placek
Director, Paul R. Pohl
Director, Steven G. Richter
Director, Charles E. Sullivan
Director, William D. Masse
Director, Paul C. Picknelly
Director, Gregg F. Orlen
Auditors : Wolf & Company, P.C.

LOCATIONS

HQ: Western New England Bancorp Inc
141 Elm Street, Westfield, MA 01086
Phone: 413 568-1911
Web: www.westfieldbank.com

COMPETITORS

ALLIANCE BANCORP, INC. OF PENNSYLVANIA
CMS BANCORP, INC.
COMMUNITY FINANCIAL CORPORATION
FIRST PLACE BANK
MIDLAND FINANCIAL CO.

HISTORICAL FINANCIALS

Company Type: Public

Income Statement FYE: December 31

	ASSETS ($mil)	NET INCOME ($mil)	INCOME AS % OF ASSETS	EMPLOYEES
12/20	2,365.8	11.2	0.5%	358
12/19	2,181.4	13.3	0.6%	340
12/18	2,118.8	16.4	0.8%	320
12/17	2,083.0	12.3	0.6%	317
12/16	2,076.0	4.8	0.2%	310
Annual Growth	3.3%	23.4%	—	3.7%

2020 Year-End Financials

Return on assets: 0.4%
Return on equity: 4.8%
Long-term debt ($ mil.): —
No. of shares ($ mil.): 25.2
Sales ($ mil.): 92.1
Dividends
Yield: 2.9%
Payout: 54.0%
Market value ($ mil.): 174.0

	STOCK PRICE ($) FY Close	P/E High/Low		PER SHARE ($) Earnings	Dividends	Book Value
12/20	6.89	21	10	0.45	0.20	8.97
12/19	9.63	20	17	0.51	0.20	8.74
12/18	10.04	20	16	0.57	0.16	8.35
12/17	10.90	27	22	0.41	0.12	8.11
12/16	9.35	38	30	0.24	0.03	7.85
Annual Growth	(7.3%)	—	—	17.0%	60.7%	3.4%

WidePoint Corp

WidePoint stretches to provide a variety of ITÂ services to government and enterprise customers.Â The companyÂ provides wireless telecom management and business process outsourcing (BPO) services.Â Its cybersecurity segment provides identity managementÂ services includingÂ identity proofing,Â credential issuing, and public key infrastructure. The company also providesÂ more traditionalÂ IT services such asÂ architecture and planning, integration services, andÂ vulnerability testing. WidePoint focuses its operations toward US federal government clients including the Department of Homeland Security (more than a quarter of sales), the TSA (nearly a quarter), the FBI, Customs and Border Protection,Â andÂ the Justice department.

EXECUTIVES

President, Chief Executive Officer, Subsidiary Officer, Director, Jin Kang, $300,000 total compensation
Executive Vice President, Chief Sales Officer, Chief Marketing Officer, Subsidiary Officer, Jason Holloway, $265,000 total compensation
Director, John J. Fitzgerald
Director, Julia A. Bowen

Director, J. Bernard Rice
Director, Philip N. Garfinkle
Auditors : Moss Adams LLP

LOCATIONS

HQ: WidePoint Corp
11250 Waples Mill Road, South Tower 210, Fairfax, VA 22030
Phone: 703 349-2577
Web: www.widepoint.com

PRODUCTS/OPERATIONS

Selected Services
Consulting
    Application development, integration, and management
        Business intelligence
        IT architecture and strategic planning
        Infrastructure management
        Project management
        Software selection
Forensic Informatics
Identity Management
Wireless Telecommunications Expense Management

COMPETITORS

CSRA INC.
MANTECH INTERNATIONAL CORPORATION
SMARTRONIX, LLC
TELOS CORPORATION
VISTRONIX, LLC

HISTORICAL FINANCIALS
Company Type: Public

Income Statement — FYE: December 31

	REVENUE ($mil)	NET INCOME ($mil)	NET PROFIT MARGIN	EMPLOYEES
12/20	180.3	10.3	5.7%	238
12/19	101.7	0.2	0.2%	249
12/18	83.6	(1.4)	—	227
12/17	75.8	(3.5)	—	247
12/16	78.4	(4.1)	—	279
Annual Growth	23.1%	—	—	(3.9%)

2020 Year-End Financials
Debt ratio: —
Return on equity: 31.4%
Cash ($ mil.): 16.0
Current Ratio: 1.24
Long-term debt ($ mil.): —
No. of shares ($ mil.): 9.0
Dividends
  Yield: —
  Payout: —
Market value ($ mil.): 91.0

	STOCK PRICE ($) FY Close	P/E High/Low		PER SHARE ($) Earnings	Dividends	Book Value
12/20	10.11	9	0	1.20	0.00	4.48
12/19	0.40	—	—	0.00	0.00	2.97
12/18	0.42	—	—	(0.20)	0.00	2.90
12/17	0.65	—	—	(0.40)	0.00	3.04
12/16	0.81	—	—	(0.50)	0.00	3.42
Annual Growth	88.0%	—	—	—	—	7.0%

Willis Lease Finance Corp.

Hey, buddy, got any spare Pratt & Whitneys? Willis Lease Finance buys and sells aircraft engines that it leases to commercial airlines, air cargo carriers, and maintenance/repair/overhaul organizations in some 30 countries. Its portfolio includes about 180 aircraft engines and related equipment made by Pratt & Whitney, Rolls-Royce, CFMI, GE Aviation, and International Aero. The engine models in the company's portfolio are used on popular Airbus and Boeing aircraft. The Willis Lease portfolio also includes four de Havilland DHC-8 commuter aircraft. Customers include Island Air, Alaska Airlines, American Airlines, and Southwest Airlines. Almost 80% of the company's engines are leased and operated outside the US.

Operations

The company divides its revenue streams across three segments. Lease rent accounted for 64% of its total sales in 2012, while maintenance reserve generated 28%. The gain of sale on leased equipment and other operations contribute the remainder of revenue.

Geographic Reach

Willis Lease has operations in Africa, Asia, Canada, Europe, Mexico, the Middle East, and the US. The majority of lease revenue comes from Europe (37% of total lease revenue in 2012), Asia (20%), the US (12%), and South America (10%).

Financial Performance

After experiencing revenue and profit increases in 2011, Willis Lease suffered a 6% drop in net revenue and a massive 90% nosedive in profits during 2012. From 2011 to 2012 its revenues dipped from $157 million to $148 million, while its profits slipped from $14.5 million to $1.5 million.

The decrease in revenues was attributed a 10% decline in lease rent revenues. This slump reflected lower portfolio utilization in 2012 and a decrease in the average size of the lease portfolio (which translated into a lower amount of equipment on lease). In addition, the lower revenue translated to a decrease on the sale of leased equipment, which was $5 million in 2012 compared with $11 million in 2011.

The plunge in profits was mainly due to a $15 million loss stemming from the extinguish of debt and derivative instruments.

Strategy

Growth in the spare engine leasing industry is contingent on the number of commercial aircraft in the market and the proportion of leased versus owned engines. Willis Lease is on the flip-side of most companies during economic downturns because it offers cash-strapped businesses a more affordable route -- to lease engines rather than buying or repairing them. The company explains that engine repairs can cost as much as $3 million, while leasing an engine may cost only $80,000.

With fluctuating fuel costs, an airline can spend the difference between maintenance and leasing on the cost of fuel. Additionally, industry experts estimate that approximately 36,000 aircraft will be in flight in less than 20 years. Growth is expected in both established markets, as well as emerging markets, especially Asia, which is showing extraordinary growth in both passenger and cargo traffic.

EXECUTIVES

Chief Executive Officer, Chairman, Charles F. Willis, $1,050,000 total compensation
President, Brian R. Hole, $435,750 total compensation
Senior Vice President, General Counsel, Secretary, Dean Michael Poulakidas, $391,125 total compensation
Senior Vice President, Secretary, General Counsel, Thomas C. Nord, $328,889 total compensation
Marketing Senior Vice President, Sales Senior Vice President, Paul David Johnson, $262,500 total compensation
Corporate Development Senior Vice President, Austin C. Willis, $262,500 total compensation
Chief Financial Officer, Senior Vice President, Scott B. Flaherty, $391,125 total compensation
Director, Robert J. Keady
Director, Robert T. Morris
Director, Hans Jorg Hunziker
Director, Austin Chandler Willis
Auditors : Grant Thornton LLP

LOCATIONS

HQ: Willis Lease Finance Corp.
4700 Lyons Technology Parkway, Coconut Creek, FL 33073
Phone: 561 349-9989
Web: www.willislease.com

COMPETITORS

AIR LEASE CORPORATION
AIRCASTLE LIMITED
CAI INTERNATIONAL, INC.
FLYBE GROUP LIMITED
H&E EQUIPMENT SERVICES, INC.
HARSCO CORPORATION
HERC HOLDINGS INC.
INTELSAT INFLIGHT LLC
PATRIOT TRANSPORTATION, INC.
TRITON CONTAINER INTERNATIONAL, INCORPORATED OF NORTH AMERICA

HISTORICAL FINANCIALS
Company Type: Public

Income Statement — FYE: December 31

	REVENUE ($mil)	NET INCOME ($mil)	NET PROFIT MARGIN	EMPLOYEES
12/20	288.6	9.7	3.4%	232
12/19	409.1	66.9	16.4%	232
12/18	348.3	43.2	12.4%	175
12/17	274.8	62.1	22.6%	155
12/16	207.2	14.0	6.8%	147
Annual Growth	8.6%	(8.8%)	—	12.1%

2020 Year-End Financials
Debt ratio: 71.6%
Return on equity: 2.3%
Cash ($ mil.): 42.5
Current Ratio: 1.02
Long-term debt ($ mil.): 1,693.7
No. of shares ($ mil.): 6.5
Dividends
  Yield: —
  Payout: —
Market value ($ mil.): 200.0

	STOCK PRICE ($) FY Close	P/E High/Low		PER SHARE ($) Earnings	Dividends	Book Value
12/20	30.46	58	14	1.05	0.00	62.97
12/19	58.91	7	3	10.50	0.00	62.93
12/18	34.60	6	4	6.60	0.00	54.46
12/17	24.97	3	2	9.69	0.00	48.04
12/16	25.58	13	8	2.05	0.00	33.74
Annual Growth	4.5%	—	—	(15.4%)		16.9%

Wilson Bank Holding Co.

EXECUTIVES

President, Chief Executive Officer, Subsidiary Officer, Director, John C. McDearman, $367,000 total compensation
Executive Vice President, Chief Operating Officer, Subsidiary Officer, Clark Oakley, $212,423 total compensation
Subsidiary Officer, Director, J. Randall Clemons, $510,260 total compensation
Executive Vice President, Subsidiary Officer, John Foster, $325,000 total compensation
Subsidiary Officer, Taylor Walker
Director, Deborah Varallo
Director, James F. Comer
Director, Michael G. Maynard
Director, Clinton M. Swain
Director, William P. Jordan
Director, James Anthony Patton
Director, Jack W. Bell
Director, H. Elmer Richerson, $351,426 total compensation
Auditors : Maggart & Associates, P.C.

LOCATIONS

HQ: Wilson Bank Holding Co.
623 West Main Street, Lebanon, TN 37087
Phone: 615 444-2265
Web: www.wilsonbank.com

HISTORICAL FINANCIALS
Company Type: Public

Income Statement — FYE: December 31

	ASSETS ($mil)	NET INCOME ($mil)	INCOME AS % OF ASSETS	EMPLOYEES
12/20	3,369.6	38.4	1.1%	522
12/19	2,794.2	36.0	1.3%	530
12/18	2,543.6	32.5	1.3%	487
12/17	2,317.0	23.5	1.0%	471
12/16	2,198.0	25.6	1.2%	444
Annual Growth	11.3%	10.7%	—	4.1%

2020 Year-End Financials
Return on assets: 1.2%
Return on equity: 10.7%
Long-term debt ($ mil.): —
No. of shares ($ mil.): 10.9
Sales ($ mil.): 156.1
Dividends
Yield: —
Payout: 34.1%
Market value ($ mil.): 0.0

Wingstop Inc

EXECUTIVES

Chairman, Director, Lynn Crump-Caine
President, Chief Executive Officer, Director, Michael J. Skipworth, $368,923 total compensation
Executive Vice President, Chief Digital and Technology Officer, Stacy Peterson, $379,231 total compensation
Strategy Senior Vice President, Strategy Chief Growth Officer, Marisa J. Carona
Senior Vice President, Chief Financial Officer, Principal Accounting Officer, Alex R. Kaleida
Senior Vice President, General Counsel, Secretary, Albert G. McGrath
Senior Vice President, Chief People Officer, Donnie S. Upshaw
Director, Ania Smith
Director, Krishnan Anand
Director, David L. Goebel
Director, Michael J. Hislop
Director, Kilandigalu M. Madati
Director, Wesley S. McDonald
Director, Kate S. Lavelle
Auditors : KPMG LLP

LOCATIONS

HQ: Wingstop Inc
15505 Wright Brothers Drive, Addison, TX 75001
Phone: 972 686-6500
Web: www.wingstop.com

HISTORICAL FINANCIALS
Company Type: Public

Income Statement — FYE: December 25

	REVENUE ($mil)	NET INCOME ($mil)	NET PROFIT MARGIN	EMPLOYEES
12/21	282.5	42.6	15.1%	890
12/20	248.8	23.3	9.4%	819
12/19	199.6	20.4	10.3%	784
12/18	153.1	21.7	14.2%	661
12/17	105.5	27.3	25.9%	530
Annual Growth	27.9%	11.8%	—	13.8%

2021 Year-End Financials
Debt ratio: 188.4%
Return on equity: —
Cash ($ mil.): 48.5
Current Ratio: 1.77
Long-term debt ($ mil.): 469.3
No. of shares ($ mil.): 29.8
Dividends
Yield: —
Payout: 43.6%
Market value ($ mil.): 5,161.0

	STOCK PRICE ($) FY Close	P/E High/Low		PER SHARE ($) Earnings	Dividends	Book Value
12/21	172.97	129	81	1.42	0.62	(10.37)
12/20	140.76	214	63	0.78	5.50	(11.50)
12/19	86.21	152	87	0.69	0.40	(7.11)
12/18	64.64	100	53	0.73	6.54	(7.67)
12/17	38.98	45	27	0.93	0.14	(1.66)
Annual Growth	45.1%	—	—	11.2%	45.1%	

Winnebago Industries, Inc.

Winnebago Industries is one of the leading North American manufacturers of recreation vehicles (RVs) and marine products with a diversified portfolio used primarily in leisure travel and outdoor recreational activities. Majority of the company's sales come from its motor homes and towables, which are sold via independent dealers throughout the US and Canada under the Winnebago, Grand Design RV, Chris-Craft, Newmar, Barletta, Adventurer, and Micro Minnie brands, among others. In addition, the company produces original equipment manufacturing (OEM) parts for other RV manufacturers and for use in commercial vehicles. The company traces its roots back in 1958. About 95% of the company's sales were generated from the US.

Operations

The company operates through three segments: Towable (over 50% of sales), Motorhome (roughly 40%), and Marine (about 10%).

The Towable is a non-motorized vehicle that is designed to be towed by automobiles, pickup trucks, SUVs, or vans and is used as temporary living quarters for recreational travel. The Recreation Vehicle Industry Association (RVIA) classifies towables into four types: conventional travel trailers, fifth wheels, folding camper trailers, and truck campers. It manufactures and sells conventional travel trailers and fifth wheels under the Winnebago and Grand Design brand names.

The Motorhome is a self-propelled mobile dwelling used primarily as temporary living quarters during vacation and camping trips, or to support active and mobile lifestyles. The RVIA classifies motorhomes into four types (Class, A, B, and C and Accessibility Enhanced), all of which are manufactured and sold under the Winnebago and Newmar brand names.

The Marine segment includes the manufacture and sale of premium quality boats under its Chris-Craft and Barletta brands in the recreational powerboat industry through an established network of independent authorized dealers.

Geographic Reach

Winnebago is based in Eden Prairie, Minnesota. It owns facilities in Forest City, Lake Mills, Waverly and Charles City, Iowa; Middlebury, Bristol, Elkhart, and Nappanee, Indiana; White Pigeon, Michigan; and Sarasota, Florida.

Roughly 95% of sales were generated from the US, while the rest were generated from international.

Sales and Marketing

The company markets its RVs on a wholesale basis to a diversified independent dealer network located throughout the US and, to a limited extent, in Canada. The RV dealer network in the US and Canada includes some 750 physical dealer locations, many of which carry more than one of our brands.

The company's advertising expenses were $23.3 million, $11.6 million, and $12.5 million in 2022, 2021, and 2020, respectively.

Financial Performance

The company's revenue for fiscal 2022 increased by 37% to $5.0 billion compared from the prior year with $3.6 billion. Net revenues increased primarily due to incremental sales from the acquisition of Barletta, price increases, and unit growth.

Net income for fiscal 2022 increased to $390.6 million compared to $281.9 million in the prior fiscal year. Net income and diluted earnings per share increased primarily due to leverage gained on higher revenues, partially offset by increased operating expenses and higher income tax expense.

Cash held by the company at the end of fiscal 2022 decreased to $282.2 million. Operating activities provided $400.6 million while investing and financing activities used $315.7 million and $237.3 million, respectively. Main cash uses were acquisition of business and repayments on long-term debt.

Mergers and Acquisitions

In mid-2021, Winnebago Industries has completed its acquisition of Indiana-based Barletta Pontoon Boats, the industry's fastest-growing, premium pontoon boat manufacturer. Consideration paid included $255 million in cash and Winnebago Industries shares. Winnebago Industries will pay an additional $15 million in Winnebago Industries shares This acquisition of Barletta extends Winnebago Industries' marine platform into one of the fastest-growing boating segments, advances its ongoing evolution into a premier outdoor lifestyle company, and is expected to drive significant financial accretion.

Company Background

During a mid-1950s economic downturn, furniture store owner John Hanson convinced Forest City officials to welcome a local subsidiary of California trailer maker Modernistic Industries. The company's first trailer rolled off the line in 1958. Hanson later bought the plant and in 1960 named the business Winnebago Industries after Forest City's home county. Winnebago Industries went public in 1966. Sales took off when the company offered less-expensive RVs than its competitors.

EXECUTIVES

Chairman, Director, David W. Miles
President, Chief Executive Officer, Michael J. Happe, $657,692 total compensation
Vice President, Subsidiary Officer, Donald Jeff Clark, $400,000 total compensation
Vice President, Division Officer, Steven Scott Degnan, $341,571 total compensation
Vice President, Division Officer, Brian Daniel Hazelton, $472,588 total compensation
Vice President, Chief Financial Officer, Bryan L. Hughes, $457,356 total compensation
Information Technology Vice President, Information Technology Chief Information Officer, Jeff D. Kubacki
Operations Vice President, Christopher D. West
Administration Vice President, Bret A. Woodson
Development Vice President, Strategic Planning Vice President, Ashis Nayan Bhattacharya
Vice President, General Counsel, Secretary, Stacy L. Bogart, $271,346 total compensation
Director, Maria F. Blase
Director, Christopher J. Braun
Director, Robert M. Chiusano
Director, William C. Fisher
Director, Richard D. Moss
Director, John M. Murabito
Auditors : DELOITTE & TOUCHE LLP

LOCATIONS

HQ: Winnebago Industries, Inc.
  13200 Pioneer Trail, Eden Prairie, MN 55347
Phone: 952 829-8600 **Fax:** 641 585-6966
Web: www.winnebagoind.com

2016

	$ mil.	% of total
United States	940.2	96
International	35.0	4
Total	975.2	100

PRODUCTS/OPERATIONS

2016 Sales

	$ mil.	% of total
Motorhomes, parts and service	875.0	90
Towables and parts	89.4	9
Other manufactured products	10.8	1
Total	975.2	100

Selected Products
ERA
  ERA
Itasca
  Cambria
  Ellipse
  Impulse
  Impulse Silver
  Meridian
  Meridian V Class
  Navion
  Navion IQ
  Reyo
  Suncruiser
  Sunova
  Sunstar
Winnebago
  Access
  Access Premier
  Adventurer
  Aspect
  Journey
  Journey Express
  Sightseer
  Tour
  Via
  View
  View Profile
  Vista

COMPETITORS

AIRSTREAM INC.
ALL AMERICAN GROUP, INC.
COPART, INC.
FEATHERLITE, INC.
GENERAL MOTORS COMPANY
NAVISTAR INTERNATIONAL CORPORATION
NEWMAR CORPORATION
REXHALL INDUSTRIES, INC.
THOR INDUSTRIES, INC.
TITAN MACHINERY INC.

HISTORICAL FINANCIALS

Company Type: Public

Income Statement — FYE: August 28

	REVENUE ($mil)	NET INCOME ($mil)	NET PROFIT MARGIN	EMPLOYEES
08/21	3,629.8	281.8	7.8%	6,532
08/20	2,355.5	61.4	2.6%	5,505
08/19	1,985.6	111.7	5.6%	4,500
08/18	2,016.8	102.3	5.1%	4,700
08/17	1,547.1	71.3	4.6%	4,060
Annual Growth	23.8%	41.0%	—	12.6%

2021 Year-End Financials

Debt ratio: 25.6%   No. of shares ($ mil.): 33.0
Return on equity: 29.9%   Dividends
Cash ($ mil.): 434.5   Yield: —
Current Ratio: 2.60   Payout: 5.7%
Long-term debt ($ mil.): 528.5   Market value ($ mil.): 2,417.0

	STOCK PRICE ($) FY Close	P/E High/Low		PER SHARE ($) Earnings	Dividends	Book Value
08/21	73.11	10	5	8.28	0.48	31.97
08/20	58.41	38	11	1.84	0.44	24.60
08/19	32.02	11	6	3.52	0.43	20.06
08/18	37.30	18	11	3.22	0.40	16.95
08/17	34.55	16	9	2.32	0.40	13.98
Annual Growth	20.6%	—	—	37.4%	4.7%	23.0%

Wintrust Financial Corp (IL)

Wintrust Financial is a holding company of about 15 subsidiary banks (mostly named after the individual communities it serves) with branches primarily located in metropolitan Chicago, southern Wisconsin, and northwest Indiana. Boasting assets of more than $50.1 billion, the banks offer personal and commercial banking, wealth management, and specialty finance services, with real estate accounting for about 35% of its loan portfolio, the majority of which is commercial real estate. Wintrust's banks target individuals, small to mid-sized businesses, local governmental units, and institutional clients, among others.

Operations

Wintrust operates three business segments: community banking, specialty finance, and wealth management.

Through its Community Banking segment, its banks provide community-oriented, personal and commercial banking services to customers located in its market area. It also engages in the retail origination and purchase of residential mortgages through Wintrust Mortgage as well as consumer direct lending primarily to veterans through its Veterans First brand. The segment accounts for about 75% of the bank's consolidated net revenues.

The Specialty Finance segment provides financing of insurance premiums for businesses and individuals; accounts receivable financing, value-added, out-sourced administrative services; and other specialty finance businesses. FIRST Insurance Funding and Wintrust Life Finance engage in the premium finance receivables business, the bank's most significant specialized lending niche, including commercial insurance premium finance and life insurance premium finance. In addition, the bank also engages in commercial insurance premium finance in Canada through its wholly-owned subsidiary FIFC Canada. The segment accounts for more than 15% of its consolidated net revenues.

Through its Wealth Management segment, the bank offers a full range of wealth management services through four separate subsidiaries (Wintrust Investments, CTC, Great Lakes Advisors and CDEC): trust and investment services, tax-deferred like-kind exchange services, asset management, securities brokerage services and 401(k) and retirement plan services. The segment brings in nearly 10%.

Wintrust makes almost 70% of its revenue from interest income.

Geographic Reach

Wintrust's community banking segment operates through nearly 175 banking facilities, the majority of which are owned. The bank owns nearly 230 automatic teller machines, the majority of which are housed at banking locations. Its wealth management offices are in Chicago; Appleton, Wisconsin; and Tampa, Florida. Its Wintrust Mortgage is headquartered in its corporate headquarters in Rosemont, Illinois and has some 40 locations in about ten states.

Wintrust Financial is based in Rosemont, Illinois.

Sales and Marketing

The bank's customers include individuals, small to mid-sized businesses, local governmental units and institutional clients residing primarily in the banks' local service areas.

Advertising and marketing expenses in 2021, 2020, and 2019 were $47.3 million, $36.6 million, and $48.6 million, respectively.

Financial Performance

The company's revenue for fiscal 2021 increased by 4% to $1.7 billion compared from the prior year with $1.6 billion.

Net income for fiscal 2021 increased to $466.2 million compared from the prior year with $293.0 million.

Cash held by the company at the end of fiscal 2021 increased to $411.2 million. Cash provided by operations and financing activities were $1.1 billion and $4.9 billion, respectively. Cash used for investing activities was $5.9 billion, mainly for purchases of held-to-maturity securities.

Strategy

The company has employed certain strategies since 2013 to achieve strong net income amid an environment characterized by low interest rates and increased competition. In general, the company has taken a steady and measured approach to grow strategically and manage expenses. Specifically, the company has: leveraged its internal loan pipeline and external growth opportunities to grow earnings assets to increase net interest income; continued efforts to reduce interest costs by improving its funding mix; written call option contracts on certain securities as an economic hedge to mitigate overall interest rate risk and enhance the securities' overall return by using fees generated from these options; entered into mirror-image swap transactions to both satisfy customer preferences and maintain variable rate exposure; completed strategic acquisitions to expand our presence in existing and complimentary markets; focused on cost control and leveraging its current infrastructure to grow without a commensurate increase in operating expenses; and expanded the Wintrust Asset Finance direct leasing niche.

Mergers and Acquisitions

In late 2021, Wintrust Financial Corporation and its wholly-owned subsidiary, Lake Forest Bank & Trust Company, N.A., announced they have agreed to purchase approximately $570 million of loans from The Allstate Corporation. The portfolio is comprised of approximately 1,800 loans to Allstate agents nationally, which agents use to establish and grow their businesses, as well as meet other working capital needs. The terms of the transaction were not disclosed.

Company Background

In 2012 Wintrust expanded its premium funding business into Canada with the acquisition of Macquarie Premium Funding Inc, which was a subsidiary of Macquarie Group. The deal marked Wintrust's first international venture.

EXECUTIVES

Vice-Chairman, Chief Operating Officer, Subsidiary Officer, David A. Dykstra, $799,115 total compensation
Chief Lending Officer, Subsidiary Officer, Vice-Chairman, Richard B. Murphy, $588,673 total compensation
Chief Executive Officer, Director, Edward J. Wehmer, $1,150,000 total compensation
President, Timothy S. Crane, $474,115 total compensation
Executive Vice President, Chief Financial Officer, David L. Stoehr, $474,115 total compensation
Risk Management Executive Vice President, Risk Management Subsidiary Officer, John S. Fleshood, $292,750 total compensation
Technology Executive Vice President, Technology Subsidiary Officer, Lloyd M. Bowden
Executive Vice President, Leona A. Gleason, $343,894 total compensation
Executive Vice President, Subsidiary Officer, John Albert Carstens
Executive Vice President, Region Officer, Subsidiary Officer, James H. Bishop
Executive Vice President, Corporate Secretary, General Counsel, Kathleen M. Boege
Director, Peter D. Crist
Director, Bruce K. Crowther
Director, William J. Doyle
Director, Marla F. Glabe
Director, H. Patrick Hackett
Director, Scott K. Heitmann
Director, Deborah L. Hall Leferve
Director, Christopher J. Perry
Director, Ingrid S. Stafford
Director, Gary D. Sweeney
Director, Karin Gustafson Teglia
Auditors: Ernst & Young LLP

LOCATIONS

HQ: Wintrust Financial Corp (IL)
9700 W. Higgins Road, Suite 800, Rosemont, IL 60018
Phone: 847 939-9000
Web: www.wintrust.com

PRODUCTS/OPERATIONS

2015 Sales

	$ mil.	% of total
Interest		
Loans, including fees	651.8	66
Securities	61.0	6
Other	5.6	-
Non-interest		
Mortgage banking	115.0	12
Wealth management	73.5	7
Service charges on deposit accounts	27.4	3
Fees from covered call options	15.4	2
Other	40.6	4
Trading (losses) gains, net	(0.2)	-
Total	990.1	100

Selected Subsidiaries and Affiliates

Banking
    Barrington Bank & Trust Company, N.A.
    Beverly Bank & Trust Company, N.A.
    Crystal Lake Bank & Trust Company, N.A.
    Hinsdale Bank & Trust Company
    Lake Forest Bank & Trust Company
    Libertyville Bank & Trust Company
    North Shore Community Bank & Trust Company
    Northbrook Bank & Trust Company
    Old Plank Trail Community Bank, N.A.
    Schaumburg Bank & Trust Company, N.A.
    St. Charles Bank & Trust
    State Bank of The Lakes
    Town Bank
    Village Bank & Trust
    Wheaton Bank and Trust Company
Non-banking
    Chicago Trust Company, N.A.
    First Insurance Funding Corporation

Great Lakes Advisors, LLC
Tricom, Inc. of Milwaukee
Wayne Hummer Asset Management Company
Wayne Hummer Investments, LLC
Wayne Hummer Trust Company, N.A.
Wintrust Information Technology Services Company
Wintrust Mortgage Corporation (formerly WestAmerica Mortgage Company)

COMPETITORS

BANCFIRST CORPORATION
CITIZENS & NORTHERN CORPORATION
CITIZENS FINANCIAL GROUP, INC.
COMMUNITY BANK SYSTEM, INC.
EAGLE BANCORP, INC.
F.N.B. CORPORATION
FIRSTMERIT CORPORATION
M&T BANK CORPORATION
OLD NATIONAL BANCORP
S&T BANCORP, INC.

HISTORICAL FINANCIALS

Company Type: Public

Income Statement — FYE: December 31

	ASSETS ($mil)	NET INCOME ($mil)	INCOME AS % OF ASSETS	EMPLOYEES
12/20	45,080.7	292.9	0.6%	5,364
12/19	36,620.5	355.6	1.0%	5,057
12/18	31,244.8	343.1	1.1%	4,727
12/17	27,915.9	257.6	0.9%	4,075
12/16	25,668.5	206.8	0.8%	3,878
Annual Growth	15.1%	9.1%	—	8.4%

2020 Year-End Financials

Return on assets: 0.7%
Return on equity: 7.4%
Long-term debt ($ mil.): —
No. of shares ($ mil.): 56.7
Sales ($ mil.): 1,897.2
Dividends
Yield: 1.8%
Payout: 25.0%
Market value ($ mil.): 3,468.0

	STOCK PRICE ($) FY Close	P/E High/Low		PER SHARE ($) Earnings	Dividends	Book Value
12/20	61.09	15	5	4.68	1.12	72.50
12/19	70.90	13	10	6.03	1.00	63.84
12/18	66.49	16	11	5.86	0.76	57.93
12/17	82.37	19	14	4.40	0.56	53.19
12/16	72.57	19	10	3.66	0.48	51.96
Annual Growth	(4.2%)	—	—	6.3%	23.6%	8.7%

World Wrestling Entertainment Inc

The action might be fake, but the business of World Wrestling Entertainment (WWE) is very real. The company is a leading producer and promoter of wrestling matches for TV and live audiences, exhibiting approximately 100 live events each year across the globe. Its WWE Network, available on a variety of digital streaming and mobile devices, has more than 85 million subscribers. Its most famous live pay-per-view event is its flagship program, WrestleMania. Other core content includes RAW and SmackDown Live. WWE also licenses characters for merchandise, and sells video games, toys, and apparel. Two-time WWE world champion Vince McMahon has the majority voting control of the company. WWE's largest market is North America, accounting for around 80% of revenues.

Operations

The company operates three segments: Media, Live Events, and Consumer Products.

Media, the largest segment, which accounts for about 85% of total revenue reflects the production and monetization of long-form and short-form video content across various platforms, including WWE Network, broadcast and pay television, digital and social media, as well as filmed entertainment.

Live Events (around 5%) provide ongoing content for the media platforms. The segment's revenues primarily consist of ticket sales, including primary and secondary distribution, revenues from events for which WWE receive a fixed fee, as well as the sale of travel packages associated with the company's global live events.

Lastly, its Consumer Products segment, which merchandise the WWE branded products, such as video games, toys and apparel, through licensing arrangements and direct-to-consumer sales, accounts for about 10% of total revenue. The segment's revenues principally consist of royalties and licensee fees related to WWE branded products, and sales of merchandise distributed at the live events and through eCommerce platforms.

Geographic Reach

Based in Stamford, Connecticut ? WWE has performance centers located in Orlando, Florida and the UK, which are also used for development and training activities.

WWE produces events throughout North America which is also the company's largest market accounting for around 80% of total revenue. Europe/Middle East/Africa produce nearly 15%, while Asia Pacific and Latin America account for the remaining revenue.

Sales and Marketing

WWE Network is available on select gaming consoles, computers, mobile devices, internet connected TVs, and popular digital media players and has around 85 million subscribers.

WWEShop is the direct-to-consumer e-commerce storefront. WWE merchandise is also distributed on other domestic and international e-commerce platforms, including Amazon. It also offers venue merchandise business which consists of the design, sourcing, marketing, and distribution of numerous WWE-branded products such as t-shirts, belts, caps, and other novelty items, all of which feature Superstars and/or logos.

Its customers include content distributors of WWE media content through its networks and platforms, fans who purchase tickets to live events, purchase merchandise at venues or online through eCommerce platforms and subscribers to WWE Network, advertisers and sponsors, consumer product licensees, and film distributors/buyers.

The company spent about $9.2 million, $13.5 million, and $21.2 million on advertising for FY 2021, 2020, and 2019, respectively.

Financial Performance

The company's revenue for fiscal 2021 increased by 12% to $1.1 billion compared from the prior year with $974.2 million.

Net income for fiscal 2021 increased to $180.4 million compared from the prior year with $131.8 million.

Cash held by the company at the end of fiscal 2021 decreased to $134.8 million. Cash provided by operations was $178.6 million while cash used for investing and financing activities were $188.8 million and $317.1 million, respectively. Main uses of cash were purchases of short-term investments and repayment of debt.

Strategy

The company's strategy of creating compelling original content for broadcast on WWE Network has contributed to the popularity of WWE Network, which premiered nearly 380 hours of original content during 2021.

HISTORY

Jesse McMahon made a name for himself as a boxing promoter in the 1940s before switching to wrestling. His son Vincent joined him in the business, and they founded the World Wide Wrestling Federation in 1963. The company operated in Northeastern cities such as New York, Philadelphia, and Washington, DC, remaining a regional operation until the early 1980s (it dropped Wide from its name in 1979).

Vince McMahon Jr. inherited control of the WWF from his sick father in 1982, changed its name to Titan Sports, and focused on gaining national exposure. McMahon made wrestling hugely popular but angered promoters, as well as some fans, with his nontraditional ideas. He embraced the idea of wrestling as show business instead of sport, involving celebrities such as Cyndi Lauper and Mr. T, and pursued a presence on cable TV. McMahon also purchased or put out of business many regional promoters as he spread the business across the US.

In the mid-1980s McMahon hit the jackpot with a former bodybuilder named Terry Gene Bollea. Christened Hulk Hogan, he quickly became lord of the ring, making the cover of Sports Illustrated and performing for sellout crowds across the US. His likeness spawned toys, clothing, and a Saturday morning cartoon. Titan set a record for attracting the largest indoor crowd (more than 93,000 fans packed Detroit's Pontiac Silverdome for Wrestlemania III) in 1987 and by the following year was selling $80 million in tickets annually.

Titan was body slammed in 1993 when

competitor World Championship Wrestling (WCW, formed in 1988 by Ted Turner to broadcast on his TBS network) lured away several major stars, including Hogan. Also that year the US government charged Titan with illegal distribution of steroids. The company was acquitted in 1994, but the bad press, along with the star defections, allowed WCW to take the ratings lead by 1996.

Titan's refashioning of the WWF with more violence and sexual innuendo unleashed a hailstorm of criticism, but returned it to the top spot by mid-1998; meanwhile former WWF star Jesse "The Body" Ventura was elected governor of Minnesota. Titan was named a defendant in a wrongful death suit in 1999 filed by the family of wrestler Owen Hart, who fell to his death during a pay-per-view event (the case was settled in 2000). The company also changed its name to World Wrestling Federation Entertainment (WWFE) and went public that year. The company later licensed the WWF name for a theme restaurant in New York City.

WWFE continued its bone-crunching ways in 2000 by launching XFL, a professional football league that played in the winter following the NFL season. Still smarting from the loss of the NFL broadcast rights to CBS, NBC bought half of the new league and broadcast the games on its network. The deal also gave NBC a 3% stake in WWF. The league was a disaster during its first season, and it quickly folded. (The company repurchased NBC's shares in 2002.)

Later that year the firm bought the WWF New York Times Square Entertainment Complex from its licensee for $24.5 million. (It closed the location in 2003.) It also abandoned its broadcasting contract with USA Networks (now IAC/InterActiveCorp) in favor of a more lucrative deal with Viacom, which also took a 3% stake in the company. (Viacom sold the stake back to the company in 2003.) In 2001 WWFE put a headlock on the wrestling world when it bought the WCW from Turner Broadcasting.

In 2002 WWE received the smackdown in a court battle with the World Wildlife Fund, which claimed the company (formerly WWF) lifted the animal preservation group's initials. The company had to change its name from World Wrestling Federation Entertainment to World Wrestling Entertainment as part of a settlement.

After ending its partnership with Viacom's Spike TV in 2005, the WWE cut a deal with NBCUniversal to air Monday Night Raw on the USA Network and on Spanish-language network Telemundo. The following year, after The WB and the UPN merged to form The CW Network, WWE inked a deal with the upstart broadcaster to air Friday Night SmackDown. (The show moved to MyNetworkTV, owned by News Corporation, in 2008.) It also created a new show, ECW: Extreme Championship Wrestling, for NBCUniversal's SCI FI Channel (now Syfy).

The company inked a lucrative toy licensing partnership with Mattel in 2010.

EXECUTIVES

Executive Chairman, Director, Vincent K. McMahon, $1,400,000 total compensation
President, Chief Financial Officer, Frank A. Riddick
Staff Executive Vice President, Operations Executive Vice President, Staff Chief, Operations Chief, Bradley M. Blum
Television Production Executive Producer & Chief Global Television Production, Kevin Dunn, $922,625 total compensation
Global Talent Strategy & Development Executive Vice President, Talent, Live Events and Creative Executive Vice President, Director, Paul Levesque, $678,875 total compensation
Chief Executive Officer, Director, Nick Khan
Director, Michelle McKenna
Director, Steven R. Koonin
Director, Steve Pamon
Director, George A. Barrios, $856,694 total compensation
Director, Michelle D. Wilson, $857,853 total compensation
Auditors: DELOITTE & TOUCHE LLP

LOCATIONS

HQ: World Wrestling Entertainment Inc
1241 East Main Street, Stamford, CT 06902
Phone: 203 352-8600
Web: www.wwe.com

PRODUCTS/OPERATIONS

Selected Operations
Live and televised entertainment
  Live wrestling events
  Pay-per-view programming
  Television programming
  A.M. RAW (USA Network)
  Friday Night SmackDown (Syfy)
  Monday Night Raw (USA Network)
  WWE NXT (WWE.com)
  WWE Superstars (WGN America)
  WWE Classics On Demand (video on demand service)
Consumer products
  Home video
  Magazines
  Product licensing
Digital media
  WWE.com
  WWEShop
WWE Studios (film production)

COMPETITORS

A&E TELEVISION NETWORKS, LLC
ITV PLC
LIONS GATE ENTERTAINMENT INC.
MATCH GROUP, INC.
METRO-GOLDWYN-MAYER, INC.
SESAME WORKSHOP
SONIFI SOLUTIONS, INC.
SONY PICTURES ENTERTAINMENT INC.
THE KUSHNER LOCKE COMPANY
WARNER MEDIA, LLC

HISTORICAL FINANCIALS

Company Type: Public

Income Statement — FYE: December 31

	REVENUE ($mil)	NET INCOME ($mil)	NET PROFIT MARGIN	EMPLOYEES
12/21	1,095.1	180.4	16.5%	870
12/20	974.2	131.7	13.5%	900
12/19	960.4	77.0	8.0%	960
12/18	930.1	99.5	10.7%	915
12/17	800.9	32.6	4.1%	850
Annual Growth	8.1%	53.3%	—	0.6%

2021 Year-End Financials

Debt ratio: 50.6%   No. of shares ($ mil.): 74.8
Return on equity: 46.8%   Dividends
Cash ($ mil.): 134.8   Yield: 0.9%
Current Ratio: 1.52   Payout: 31.3%
Long-term debt ($ mil.): 395.9   Market value ($ mil.): 3,692.0

	STOCK PRICE ($) FY Close	P/E High/Low		PER SHARE ($) Earnings	Dividends	Book Value
12/21	49.34	27	20	2.12	0.48	5.09
12/20	48.05	39	18	1.56	0.48	5.00
12/19	64.87	100	54	0.85	0.48	3.56
12/18	74.72	76	24	1.12	0.48	4.05
12/17	30.58	77	42	0.42	0.48	3.28
Annual Growth	12.7%	—	—	49.9%	0.0%	11.6%

WSFS Financial Corp

WSFS Financial Corporation (WSFS) is a multi-billion dollar financial services company. Its primary subsidiary, WSFS Bank, is the oldest and largest banks in the US. WSFS has $20.0 billion in assets and $61.4 billion in assets under management and administration. WSFS operates from about 120 offices, more than 90 of which are banking offices, located in Pennsylvania (about 60), Delaware (around 40), New Jersey (over 15), one in Virginia and one in Nevada and provides comprehensive financial services including commercial banking, retail banking, cash management and trust and wealth management. Other subsidiaries or divisions include Arrow Land Transfer, Bryn Mawr Trust, The Bryn Mawr Trust Company of Delaware, Cash Connect, Cypress Capital Management, LLC, NewLane Finance, Powdermill Financial Solutions, West Capital Management, WSFS Institutional Services, WSFS Mortgage, and WSFS Wealth Investments.

Operations

WSFS operates through three segments: WSFS Bank, Wealth Management, and Cash Connect.

The WSFS Bank segment, which accounts for more than 80% of revenue, provides loans and leases and other financial products to commercial and retail customers. It also offers a broad variety of consumer loan products, retail securities and insurance brokerage services through its retail branches, and mortgage and title services in collaboration with WSFS Mortgage. WSFS Mortgage is a mortgage banking company and abstract and title company specializing in a variety of residential mortgage and refinancing solutions.

The Wealth Management segment (about 10%) provides a broad array of planning and advisor services, investment management, personal and institutional trust services, and credit and deposit products to individuals, corporate, and institutional clients. WSFS Wealth Investments provides financial advisory services along with insurance and brokerage products. Cypress, a registered investment adviser, is a fee-only wealth management firm managing a "balanced" investment style portfolio focused on preservation of capital and generating current income. West Capital, a registered investment adviser, is a fee-only wealth management firm operating under a multi-family office philosophy to provide customized solutions to institutions and high-net-worth individuals. The trust division of WSFS, comprised of WSFS Institutional Services and Christiana Trust DE, provides trustee, agency, bankruptcy administration, custodial and commercial domicile services to institutional and corporate clients and special purpose vehicles.

Cash Connect provides (more than 5%) ATM vault cash, smart safe and other cash logistics services in the US through strategic partnerships with several of the largest networks, manufacturers and service providers in the cash logistics industry. Cash Connect manages approximately $1.7 billion in total cash and services approximately 27,400 non-bank ATMs and approximately 6,300 smart safes nationwide. Cash Connect also supports over 600 owned and branded ATMs for WSFS Bank, which has one of the largest branded ATM networks in its market.

Overall, WSFS generates roughly 60% of its total revenue from interest and fees on loans and leases, plus an additional 10% from interest on its mortgage-back and other investment securities. About 10% of its total revenue comes from investment management and fiduciary, while credit/debit card, mortgage banking activities and ATM income and deposit service charges account for 5% each.

Geographic Reach

Based in Wilmington, Delaware, WSFS conducts its business through some 90 banking offices located in Delaware, southeastern Pennsylvania and southern New Jersey. In addition to its branch network, the company leases office space for some 25 other loan production offices and facilities located in Delaware, southeastern Pennsylvania, southern New Jersey, Virginia and Nevada to house operational activities, Cash Connect and its Wealth Management businesses.

Financial Performance

Net interest income for the year ended December 31, 2021 was $433.6 million, a decrease of $32.3 million compared to 2020, primarily due to lower purchase accounting accretion, the lower interest rate environment and balance sheet mix, as well as the impact of PPP loans.

In 2021, the company had a net income of $271.6 million, a 140% increase from the previous year's net income of $113.3 million.

The company's cash and equivalents at the end of 2021 was $1.5 billion. Operating activities generated $125.6 million, while investing activities used $1.5 billion, mainly for purchases of investment securities available-for-sale. Financing activities provided another $1.2 billion.

Strategy

The company's strategy of "Engaged Associates, living its culture, making a better life for all it serves" focuses on exceeding customer expectations, delivering stellar experiences and building customer advocacy through highly-trained, relationship-oriented, friendly, knowledgeable and empowered Associates.

Mergers and Acquisitions

In early 2022, WSFS completed the acquisition of the Bryn Mawr Bank Corporation ("Bryn Mawr"), and its primary subsidiary, The Bryn Mawr Trust Company (Bryn Mawr Trust). With the acquisition finalized, WSFS strengthens its position as the premier, locally headquartered bank and wealth management franchise in the Greater Philadelphia and Delaware region with approximately $20 billion in assets, and approximately $49 billion in assets under administration and management.

EXECUTIVES

Chairman, President, Chief Executive Officer, Subsidiary Officer, Director, Rodger Levenson, $471,572 total compensation
Executive Vice President, Chief Risk Officer, Michael P. Reed
Executive Vice President, Chief Wealth Officer, Arthur J. Bacci
Executive Vice President, Chief Financial Officer, Dominic C. Canuso, $365,083 total compensation
Executive Vice President, Chief Commercial Banking Officer, Steve Clark, $358,583 total compensation
Executive Vice President, Chief Information Officer, Lisa Brubaker
Executive Vice President, Chief Customer Officer, Peggy H. Eddens, $366,575 total compensation
Division Officer, Paul S. Greenplate
Subsidiary Officer, Michael L. Conklin
Subsidiary Officer, Patrick J. Ward, $322,917 total compensation
Subsidiary Officer, Richard M. Wright, $357,350 total compensation
Director, Mark A. Turner, $756,209 total compensation
Director, Marvin N. (Skip) Schoenhals, $385,833 total compensation
Lead Independent Director, Director, Eleuthere I. Du Pont
Director, Anat M. Bird
Director, Francis B. Brake
Director, Jennifer W. Davis
Director, Christopher Gheysens
Director, Karen D. Buchholz
Director, David G. Turner
Director, Michael J. Donahue
Director, Nancy J. Foster
Director, Diego F. Calderin
Director, Lynn B. McKee
Director, Francis J. Leto
Auditors : KPMG LLP

LOCATIONS

HQ: WSFS Financial Corp
500 Delaware Avenue, Wilmington, DE 19801
Phone: 302 792-6000
Web: www.wsfsbank.com

2012 Branches

	No.
Delaware	42
Pennsylvania	7
Nevada	1
Virginia	1
Total	51

PRODUCTS/OPERATIONS

2014 Sales

	$ mil.	% of total
Interest		
Loans, including fees	137.0	57
Mortgage-backed securities	13.5	6
Investment securities	9.8	4
Noninterest		
Credit/debit card & ATM income	24.1	11
Deposit service charges	17.1	7
Wealth management income	17.4	7
Mortgage baning activities	4.0	2
Other	15.7	6
Total	238.6	100

COMPETITORS

BOKF MERGER CORPORATION NUMBER SIXTEEN
CAPITAL BANK FINANCIAL CORP.
CITY HOLDING COMPANY
COMMERCE BANCSHARES, INC.
FIRST COMMONWEALTH FINANCIAL CORPORATION
Laurentien Bank of Canada
M&T BANK CORPORATION
S&T BANCORP, INC.
TCF FINANCIAL CORPORATION
UMB FINANCIAL CORPORATION

HISTORICAL FINANCIALS

Company Type: Public

Income Statement — FYE: December 31

	ASSETS ($mil)	NET INCOME ($mil)	INCOME AS % OF ASSETS	EMPLOYEES
12/20	14,333.9	114.7	0.8%	1,838
12/19	12,256.3	148.8	1.2%	1,782
12/18	7,248.8	134.7	1.9%	1,177
12/17	6,999.5	50.2	0.7%	1,159
12/16	6,765.2	64.0	0.9%	1,116
Annual Growth	20.6%	15.7%	—	13.3%

2020 Year-End Financials

Return on assets: 0.8%
Return on equity: 6.2%
Long-term debt ($ mil.): —
No. of shares ($ mil.): 47.7
Sales ($ mil.): 713.1

Dividends
Yield: 1.0%
Payout: 21.1%
Market value ($ mil.): 2,143.0

	STOCK PRICE ($) FY Close	P/E High/Low		PER SHARE ($) Earnings	Dividends	Book Value
12/20	44.88	20	9	2.27	0.48	37.52
12/19	43.99	15	12	3.00	0.47	35.88
12/18	37.91	13	9	4.19	0.42	26.17
12/17	47.85	33	27	1.56	0.30	23.05
12/16	46.35	22	13	2.06	0.25	21.90
Annual Growth	(0.8%)	—	—	2.5%	17.7%	14.4%

XOMA Corp

XOMA Corporation doesn't want to toil in anonymity. Instead, the company pairs with larger drug firms to develop and market its products, primarily monoclonal antibodies (biotech drugs based on cloned proteins). It's developing lead candidate gevokizumab with Novartis. The firm partners on therapeutics for various clinical development stages, targeting the adenosine pathway with potential applications in solid tumors, non-Hodgkin's lymphoma, asthma/chronic obstructive pulmonary disease, inflammatory bowel disease, idiopathic pulmonary fibrosis, lung cancer, psoriasis and nonalcoholic steatohepatitis and other indications. XOMA has collaborative agreements with pharma companies Takeda Pharmaceutical and Merck; it also has metabolic and oncology candidates. The US generates about 95% of the company's revenue.

Operations

Xoma has a pipeline of unique monoclonal antibodies and technologies available to license to pharmaceutical and biotechnology companies to further their clinical development. Some of its proprietary product candidates include IL-2 program. Interleukin 2 has long been recognized as an effective therapy for metastatic melanoma and renal cell carcinoma; PTH1R program, generated an anti-parathyroid receptor pipeline that includes several functional antibody antagonists targeting PTH1R, a G-protein-coupled receptor involved in the regulation of calcium metabolism; XMetA is an insulin receptor-activating antibody designed to provide long-acting reduction of hyperglycemia in Type 2 diabetic patients, potentially reducing the advancement to a number of insulin injections needed to control their blood glucose levels; and X213 (formerly LFA 102) is an allosteric inhibitor of prolactin action. It is a humanized IgG1-Kappa monoclonal antibody that binds to the extracellular domain of the human prolactin receptor with high affinity at an allosteric site.

Geographic Reach

Based in Emeryville, California, the US market accounts the largest for about 95% of total sales while Europe and other countries account the remainder.

Financial Performance

Over the last five years, the revenue of the company reported a fluctuation. It's either increasing very high or going down very low. And only in 2017 that the company reported a net income.

In 2019, revenue increased by 247% to $18.4 million. The primary components of revenue from contracts with customers in 2019 was $14.0 million recognized under the license agreement and common stock purchase agreement with Rezolute and $2.5 million in revenue earned from a one-time payment under its license agreement with Janssen.

The company incurred a net loss of $2 million in 2019, $11.5 million lower from 2018. The decrease in net loss was due to higher revenue and $3.8 million from Other income.

Cash at the end of the period was $56.7 million. Operations and Investing activities each used $0.3 million and $19.3 million, respectively, while financing activities provided $30.5 million to the company.

Strategy

The company strategy is to expand its pipeline by acquiring additional potential milestone and royalty revenue streams on drug product candidates from third parties. Expanding its pipeline through these acquisitions can allow for further diversification across therapeutic areas and development stages. Its ideal target acquisitions are in pre-commercial stages of development, have an expected long duration of market exclusivity, high revenue potential, and are partnered with a large pharmaceutical or biopharmaceutical enterprise.

As part of its royalty aggregator strategy, it will purchase future milestone and royalty streams associated with drug products that are in clinical development and have not yet been commercialized. To the extent that any such drug products are not successfully developed and subsequently commercialized, the value of its acquired potential milestone and royalty streams will be negatively affected. The ultimate success of its royalty aggregator strategy will depend on its ability to properly identify and acquire high quality products and the ability of the applicable counterparty to innovate, develop and commercialize its products, in increasingly competitive and highly regulated markets. Its inability to do so would negatively affect its ability to receive royalty and/or milestone payments. In addition, the company is dependent, to a large extent, on third parties to enforce certain rights for its benefit, such as protection of a patent estate, adequate reporting and other protections, and its failure to do so would presumably negatively impact its financial condition and results of operations.

EXECUTIVES

Chairman, Director, Lead Independent Director, W. Denman Van Ness
Finance Senior Vice President, Finance Chief Financial Officer, Thomas M. Burns, $360,500 total compensation
Chief Executive Officer, Director, James R. Neal, $484,100 total compensation
Director, Jack L. Wyszomierski
Director, Joseph M. Limber
Director, Matthew D. Perry
Director, Natasha A. Hernday
Director, Barbara A. Kosacz
Director, Heather L. Franklin
Auditors : DELOITTE & TOUCHE LLP

LOCATIONS

HQ: XOMA Corp
2200 Powell Street, Suite 310, Emeryville, CA 94608
Phone: 510 204-7200
Web: www.xoma.com

2016 Sales

	$ mil.	% of total
US	3.8	69
Europe	1.7	29
Asia/Pacific	0.1	2
Total	5.6	100

PRODUCTS/OPERATIONS

2016 Sales

	$ mil.	% of total
License & collaborative fees & royalties	3.3	59
Contract and other	2.3	41
Total	5.6	100

2016 Contract & Other Revenue

	$ mil.	% of total
The National Institute of Allergy and Infectious Diseases (NIAID)	1.1	48
Servier	0.6	26
Other	0.6	26
Total	2.3	100

Selected Pipeline Products

XOMA 358 - Congenital hyperinsulinism & Post-bariatric surgery hyperinsulinism
XOMA 129 - Short-acting reversal of drug-induced hypoglycemia
XOMA 213 - Various hyperprolactinemias
Anti-PTH1R - Hyperparathyroidism, Malignancy induced hypercalcemia
Anti-IL-2 - Oncology, anti-tumor immunity

COMPETITORS

AGENUS INC.
ALNYLAM PHARMACEUTICALS, INC.
CELLDEX THERAPEUTICS, INC.
Clementia Pharmaceuticals Inc
DYAX CORP.
HALOZYME THERAPEUTICS, INC.
IMMUNOGEN, INC.
IMMUNOMEDICS, INC.
INCYTE CORPORATION
PROGENICS PHARMACEUTICALS, INC.

HISTORICAL FINANCIALS

Company Type: Public

Income Statement — FYE: December 31

	REVENUE ($mil)	NET INCOME ($mil)	NET PROFIT MARGIN	EMPLOYEES
12/20	29.3	13.2	45.3%	10
12/19	18.3	(1.9)	—	10
12/18	5.2	(13.3)	—	11
12/17	52.6	14.5	27.7%	12
12/16	5.5	(53.5)	—	18
Annual Growth	51.6%	—	—	(13.7%)

2020 Year-End Financials

Debt ratio: 16.6%
Return on equity: 20.3%
Cash ($ mil.): 84.2
Current Ratio: 7.16
Long-term debt ($ mil.): 12.7
No. of shares ($ mil.): 11.2
Dividends
Yield: —
Payout: —
Market value ($ mil.): 496.0

	STOCK PRICE ($) FY Close	P/E High/Low		PER SHARE ($) Earnings	Dividends	Book Value
12/20	44.13	56	18	0.78	0.00	7.70
12/19	27.30	—	—	(0.23)	0.00	4.51
12/18	12.65	—	—	(1.59)	0.00	2.16
12/17	35.60	49	5	0.73	0.00	0.70
12/16	4.22	—	—	(8.89)	0.00	(7.72)
Annual Growth	79.8%	—	—	—	—	—

XPEL Inc

Auditors: DELOITTE & TOUCHE LLP

LOCATIONS

HQ: XPEL Inc
618 W. Sunset Road, San Antonio, TX 78216
Phone: 210 678-3700 **Fax:** 210 678-3701
Web: www.xpel.com

HISTORICAL FINANCIALS

Company Type: Public

Income Statement — FYE: December 31

	REVENUE ($mil)	NET INCOME ($mil)	NET PROFIT MARGIN	EMPLOYEES
12/20	158.9	18.2	11.5%	330
12/19	129.9	13.9	10.8%	230
12/18	109.9	8.7	7.9%	0
12/17	67.7	1.1	1.8%	0
12/16	51.7	2.2	4.3%	0
Annual Growth	32.4%	69.5%	—	—

2020 Year-End Financials

Debt ratio: 7.3%
Return on equity: 41.2%
Cash ($ mil.): 29.0
Current Ratio: 2.96
Long-term debt ($ mil.): 3.5
No. of shares ($ mil.): 27.6
Dividends
Yield: —
Payout: —
Market value ($ mil.): 1,424.0

	STOCK PRICE ($) FY Close	P/E High/Low		PER SHARE ($) Earnings	Dividends	Book Value
12/20	51.56	81	13	0.66	0.00	1.93
12/19	14.65	31	9	0.51	0.00	1.27
12/18	6.10	22	4	0.32	0.00	0.75
12/17	1.40	57	32	0.04	0.00	0.51
12/16	1.40	17	8	0.08	0.00	0.40
Annual Growth	146.3%	—	—	67.4%	—	48.1%

Xperi Holding Corp

Tessera Technologies licenses its portfolio of patented technologies for semiconductor packaging, interconnects, and imaging in exchange for royalty payments. More than 100 companies, such as Intel, Sony, LG Electronics, and Samsung, use its designs to produce high-performance packages for mobile computing and communications, memory and data storage, and 3D integrated circuit technologies. Tessera has more than 4,000 US and foreign patents and patents applications. The US is Tessera's biggest geographic market.

Operations

Tessera licenses technologies through subsidiaries. The Invensas subsidiary handles semiconductor related technologies; The FotoNation unit licenses software and technologies for mobile imaging; and the Ziptronix licenses wafer bonding technologies.

While it typically heavily on R&D $32 million in 2015), Tessera also supports a sizable budget for litigation expenses, which cost around $14 million in 2015, down from $25 million in 2014. The reduced litigation spending was due to settlements reached in 2014 and early 2015.

Geographic Reach

Tessera has R&D and marketing support offices in Ireland, Japan, Romania, and the US. Its manufacturing plants are located in China and Taiwan. About 35% of the company's revenue comes from customers in the US followed, followed by 32% from South Korea, and 21% from Taiwan.

Sales and Marketing

The company is focused on developing direct product design relationships at the technical level with companies that manufacture camera modules and smartphones. Top customers in 2015 were Samsung (19% of sales), Micron Technology (15%), Amkor Technology (14%), and SK Hynix (13%).

Financial Performance

Overall sales fell 2% in 2015 to $273 million from a decline in episodic revenue. Tessera's profit fell 31% to $117 million in 2015 from $170 million in 2014. The main year-to-year difference was a lower tax benefit in 2015. Cash flow was $146 million in 2015, compared to $134 million in 2014.

Strategy

Tessera has gotten its business on a more stable footing with the settlement of several lawsuits, which should produce regularly recurring revenue, and the signing of new licensing deals.

In January 2015, Tessera reached a settlement with Amkor, in which Amkor agreed to pay a total of $155 million of 16 quarterly payments through the fourth quarter of 2018. The company signed new license agreements with Samsung and Micron that resulted in significant revenue.

In 2015 the company closed the last manufacturing operation of its DigitalOptics business. More than 300 workers were let go and facilities in California, New York, Taiwan, and Japan were closed.

Mergers and Acquisitions

The company's acquisition strategy is focused on buy companies that strengthen its position in various markets, largely focused on imaging. In 2015 Tessera bought Ziptronix. The $39 million deal expanded Tessera's advanced packaging capabilities by adding a low-temperature wafer bonding technology platform that help it get newer technologies to its semiconductor industry customers.

In 2014 the FotoNation subsidiary bought Smart Sensors Limited, which develops iris recognition biometric technology.

EXECUTIVES

Chairman, Director, Daniel M. Moloney
President, Chief Executive Officer, Director, Paul E. Davis, $340,008 total compensation
Chief Financial Officer, Keith A. Jones
Chief People Officer, Denise Morgan
Chief Legal Officer, Kevin Tanji
Chief Licensing Officer, Division Officer, Mark Kokes
Chief Licensing Officer, Division Officer, Dana Escobar
Director, V. Sue Molina
Director, Raghavendra Rau
Director, Tonia O'Connor
Auditors: PricewaterhouseCoopers LLP

LOCATIONS

HQ: Xperi Holding Corp
3025 Orchard Parkway, San Jose, CA 95134
Phone: 408 321-6000
Web: www.xperi.com

COMPETITORS

EMCORE CORPORATION
EXFO Inc
FORMFACTOR BEAVERTON, INC.
INPHI CORPORATION
MATTSON TECHNOLOGY, INC.
MULTI-FINELINE ELECTRONIX, INC.
OCLARO, INC.
OMNIVISION TECHNOLOGIES, INC.
ONTO INNOVATION INC.
XPERI CORPORATION

HISTORICAL FINANCIALS

Company Type: Public

Income Statement — FYE: December 31

	REVENUE ($mil)	NET INCOME ($mil)	NET PROFIT MARGIN	EMPLOYEES
12/20	892.0	146.7	16.5%	1,850
12/19	280.0	(62.5)	—	700
12/18	406.1	(0.2)	—	700
12/17	373.7	(56.5)	—	700
12/16	259.5	56.0	21.6%	700
Annual Growth	36.2%	27.2%	—	27.5%

2020 Year-End Financials

Debt ratio: 31.1%
Return on equity: 14.6%
Cash ($ mil.): 170.1
Current Ratio: 2.43
Long-term debt ($ mil.): 795.6
No. of shares ($ mil.): 104.7
Dividends
  Yield: 0.4%
  Payout: 5.7%
Market value ($ mil.): 2,190.0

	STOCK PRICE ($) FY Close	P/E High	P/E Low	PER SHARE ($) Earnings	Dividends	Book Value
12/20	20.90	12	6	1.75	0.10	13.90
12/19	18.50	—	—	(1.27)	0.00	11.04
12/18	18.39	—	—	(0.01)	0.80	12.80
12/17	24.40	—	—	(1.15)	0.80	8.87
12/16	44.20	40	23	1.12	0.80	10.39
Annual Growth	(17.1%)	—	—	11.8%	(40.5%)	7.5%

Zedge Inc

EXECUTIVES

Chairman, Executive Chairman, Director, Michael C. Jonas, $0 total compensation
Vice-Chairman, Director, Howard S. Jonas
President, Chief Executive Officer, Jonathan Reich, $327,500 total compensation
Chief Financial Officer, Treasurer, Yi Tsai
Director, Mark Ghermezian
Director, Elliot Gibber
Director, Paul Packer
Director, Gregory Suess
Auditors : Friedman LLP

LOCATIONS

HQ: Zedge Inc
  1178 Broadway, 3rd Floor, #1450, New York, NY 10001
Phone: 330 577-3424
Web: www.zedge.com

HISTORICAL FINANCIALS

Company Type: Public

Income Statement — FYE: July 31

	REVENUE ($mil)	NET INCOME ($mil)	NET PROFIT MARGIN	EMPLOYEES
07/21	19.5	8.2	42.1%	53
07/20	9.4	(0.5)	—	39
07/19	8.8	(3.3)	—	53
07/18	10.8	(1.5)	—	57
07/17	10.0	(0.6)	—	64
Annual Growth	18.2%	—	—	(4.6%)

2021 Year-End Financials

Debt ratio: —
Return on equity: 39.2%
Cash ($ mil.): 24.9
Current Ratio: 6.61
Long-term debt ($ mil.): —
No. of shares ($ mil.): 14.3
Dividends
  Yield: —
  Payout: —
Market value ($ mil.): 221.0

	STOCK PRICE ($) FY Close	P/E High	P/E Low	PER SHARE ($) Earnings	Dividends	Book Value
07/21	15.36	31	2	0.59	0.00	2.30
07/20	1.39	—	—	(0.05)	0.00	0.72
07/19	1.61	—	—	(0.33)	0.00	0.67
07/18	2.97	—	—	(0.16)	0.00	0.97
07/17	2.07	—	—	(0.06)	0.00	1.10
Annual Growth	65.0%	—	—	—	—	20.3%

Ziff Davis Inc

EXECUTIVES

Chairman, Lead Director, Director, Sarah Ann Fay
President, Chief Executive Officer, Director, Vivek Shah, $1,000,000 total compensation
Vice President, General Counsel, Secretary, Jeremy D. Rossen, $417,347 total compensation
Chief Financial Officer, Bret Richter
Chief Accounting Officer, Layth Taki
Subsidiary Officer, R. Scott Turicchi, $715,559 total compensation
Director, William Brian Kretzmer
Director, Jonathan Frank Miller
Director, Scott C. Taylor
Auditors : BDO USA, LLP

LOCATIONS

HQ: Ziff Davis Inc
  114 5th Avenue, New York, NY 10011
Phone: 212 503-3500
Web: www.j2.com

HISTORICAL FINANCIALS

Company Type: Public

Income Statement — FYE: December 31

	REVENUE ($mil)	NET INCOME ($mil)	NET PROFIT MARGIN	EMPLOYEES
12/20	1,489.5	150.6	10.1%	4,700
12/19	1,372.0	218.9	15.9%	3,090
12/18	1,207.2	128.6	10.7%	2,587
12/17	1,117.8	139.4	12.5%	2,487
12/16	874.2	152.4	17.4%	2,426
Annual Growth	14.3%	(0.3%)	—	18.0%

2020 Year-End Financials

Debt ratio: 43.1%
Return on equity: 11.9%
Cash ($ mil.): 242.6
Current Ratio: 0.71
Long-term debt ($ mil.): 1,182.6
No. of shares ($ mil.): 44.3
Dividends
  Yield: —
  Payout: —
Market value ($ mil.): 4,332.0

	STOCK PRICE ($) FY Close	P/E High	P/E Low	PER SHARE ($) Earnings	Dividends	Book Value
12/20	97.69	32	17	3.18	0.00	27.31
12/19	93.71	22	15	4.39	1.34	27.51
12/18	69.38	34	25	2.59	1.68	21.81
12/17	75.03	32	25	2.83	1.52	21.32
12/16	81.80	26	18	3.13	1.36	19.28
Annual Growth	4.5%	—	—	0.4%	—	9.1%

Zoom Video Communications Inc

EXECUTIVES

Chairman, Chief Executive Officer, Director, Eric S. Yuan, $300,000 total compensation
Product and Engineering President, Velchamy Sankarlingam
Chief Financial Officer, Kelly Steckelberg
Chief Revenue Officer, Ryan Azus
Chief Operating Officer, Interim Chief Legal Officer, Aparna Bawa, $102,083 total compensation
Chief Marketing Officer, Janine Pelosi, $224,167 total compensation
Lead Independent Director, Director, Daniel Scheinman
Director, Cindy L. Hoots
Director, William R. McDermott
Director, Herbert Raymond McMaster
Director, Janet Napolitano
Director, Santiago Subotovsky
Director, Peter P. Gassner
Director, Jonathan C. Chadwick
Director, Kimberly L. Hammonds
Auditors : KPMG LLP

LOCATIONS

HQ: Zoom Video Communications Inc
  55 Almaden Boulevard, 6th Floor, San Jose, CA 95113
Phone: 888 799-9666
Web: www.zoom.com

HISTORICAL FINANCIALS

Company Type: Public

Income Statement — FYE: January 31

	REVENUE ($mil)	NET INCOME ($mil)	NET PROFIT MARGIN	EMPLOYEES
01/21	2,651.3	672.3	25.4%	4,422
01/20	622.6	25.3	4.1%	2,532
01/19	330.5	7.5	2.3%	1,702
01/18	151.4	(3.8)	—	0
01/17	60.8	(0.0)	0.0%	0
Annual Growth	157.0%	—	—	—

2021 Year-End Financials

Debt ratio: —
Return on equity: 28.5%
Cash ($ mil.): 2,240.3
Current Ratio: 3.80
Long-term debt ($ mil.): —
No. of shares ($ mil.): 293.5
Dividends
  Yield: —
  Payout: —
Market value ($ mil.): 109,221.0

	STOCK PRICE ($) FY Close	P/E High	P/E Low	PER SHARE ($) Earnings	Dividends	Book Value
01/21	372.07	240	36	2.25	0.00	13.15
01/20	76.30	1142	689	0.09	0.00	2.99
Annual Growth	387.6%	—	—2400.0%	—	—339.6%

Zynex Inc

EXECUTIVES

Chairman, President, Chief Executive Officer, Thomas Sandgaard, $400,000 total compensation
Chief Financial Officer, Daniel J. Moorhead
Chief Operating Officer, Anna Lucsok
Director, Barry D. Michaels
Director, Michael Cress
Director, Joshua R. Disbrow
Auditors : Plante & Moran, PLLC

LOCATIONS

HQ: Zynex Inc
9655 Maroon Circle, Englewood, CO 80112
Phone: 303 703-4906
Web: www.zynex.com

HISTORICAL FINANCIALS
Company Type: Public

Income Statement   FYE: December 31

	REVENUE ($mil)	NET INCOME ($mil)	NET PROFIT MARGIN	EMPLOYEES
12/20	80.1	9.0	11.3%	768
12/19	45.4	9.4	20.9%	283
12/18	31.9	9.5	29.9%	182
12/17	23.4	7.3	31.4%	109
12/16	13.3	0.0	0.5%	106
Annual Growth	56.6%	238.6%	—	64.1%

2020 Year-End Financials

Debt ratio: 0.5%   No. of shares ($ mil.): 38.2
Return on equity: 23.6%   Dividends
Cash ($ mil.): 39.1   Yield: —
Current Ratio: 6.23   Payout: —
Long-term debt ($ mil.): 0.2   Market value ($ mil.): 515.0

	STOCK PRICE ($) FY Close	P/E High/Low		PER SHARE ($) Earnings	Dividends	Book Value
12/20	13.46	116	32	0.24	0.00	1.49
12/19	7.87	47	11	0.25	0.00	0.55
12/18	2.94	20	9	0.25	0.07	0.26
12/17	3.18	15	1	0.21	0.00	0.14
12/16	0.30	—	—	0.00	0.00	(0.11)
Annual Growth	158.8%	—	—	—	—	—

Hoover's Handbook of Emerging Companies

2023 Indexes

Index by Headquarters

ARE

Abu Dhabi
Abu Dhabi Islamic Bank W8
First Abu Dhabi Bank Pjsc W241
Abu Dhabi Commercial Bank W8

Dubai
Mashreqbank W387
Dubai Islamic Bank Ltd W205

AUS

Alexandria
Ampol Ltd W36

Sydney
Commonwealth Bank Of Australia W163
Macquarie Group Ltd W376
Westpac Banking Corp W646
Qbe Insurance Group Ltd. W487
Woolworths Group Ltd W650

Brisbane
Suncorp Group Ltd. W574

Newstead
Bank Of Queensland Ltd W85

Docklands
Australia & New Zealand Banking Group Ltd W63
Anz Bank W41

Hawthorn East
Coles Group Ltd (new) W162

Melbourne
Rio Tinto Ltd W497
Telstra Corp., Ltd. W595
National Australia Bank Ltd. W418

East Perth
Gold Corp Holdings W260
Fortescue Metals Group Ltd W245

Perth
Wesfarmers Ltd. W644

AUT

Linz
Voestalpine Ag W638
Oberbank Ag (austria) W453

Vienna
Uniqa Insurance Group Ag W627
Bawag Group Ag W93
Omv Ag (austria) W456
Vienna Insurance Group Ag W633
Erste Group Bank Ag W228

Villach
Strabag Se-br W562

BEL

Brussels
Umicore Sa W622
Dexia Sa W199
Kbc Group Nv W336
Ageas Nv W18
Solvay Sa W553

Leuven
Anheuser-busch Inbev Sa/nv W40

BHR

Manama
Ahli United Bank W18
Arab Banking Corporation (b.s.c.) (bahrain) W46

BMU

Hamilton
Brookfield Business Partners Lp W113
Everest Re Group Ltd W232

Pembroke
Renaissancere Holdings Ltd. W491
Arch Capital Group Ltd W50

BRA

Rio De Janeiro
Vale Sa W629
Petroleo Brasileiro Sa W467

Sao Paulo
Banco Btg Pactual S.a. W69
Banco Santander Brasil Sa W71
Marfrig Global Foods Sa W382
Itau Unibanco Holding S.a. W314
Ultrapar Participacoes Sa W621
Jbs Sa W323
Banco Bradesco Sa W69

CAN

Calgary
Imperial Oil Ltd W298
Enbridge Inc W217
Suncor Energy Inc W572
Cenovus Energy Inc W132
Canadian Natural Resources Ltd W119

Edmonton
Canadian Western Bank W122

Vancouver
Telus Corp W596
Hsbc Bank Canada W287

Winnipeg
Great-west Lifeco Inc W261

Halifax
Bank Of Nova Scotia Halifax W83

Stellarton
Empire Co Ltd W216

Aurora
Magna International Inc W377

Brampton
Loblaw Companies Ltd W371

Ottawa
Bank Of Canada (ottawa) W80

Toronto
Brookfield Asset Management Inc W112
Intact Financial Corp W307
Fairfax Financial Holdings Ltd W235
Royal Bank Of Canada (montreal, Quebec) W506
Sun Life Assurance Company Of Canada W570
Canadian Imperial Bank Of Commerce (toronto, Ontario) W117
Weston (george) Ltd W644
Canadian Tire Corp Ltd W120
Manulife Financial Corp W381
Sun Life Financial Inc W571
Toronto Dominion Bank W610

Laval
Alimentation Couche-tard Inc W30

Levis
Desjardins Group W193

Montreal
Metro Inc W398
Power Corp. Of Canada W479
Laurentian Bank Of Canada W358
National Bank Of Canada W419
Bank Of Montreal (quebec) W82

Quebec City
Ia Financial Corp Inc W294

Verdun
Bce Inc W98

Saskatoon
Nutrien Ltd W451

CHE

Baar
Glencore Plc W259

Basel
Novartis Ag Basel W449
Baloise Holding Ag W67
Roche Holding Ltd W501

Emmen
Also Holding Ag W34

Hergiswil
Schindler Holding Ag W522

Lausanne
Banque Cantonale Vaudoise W87

Liestal
Basellandschaftliche Kantonalbank (switzerland) W91

Lucerne
Valiant Holding Bern (switzerland) W631

Rapperswil-jona
Holcim Ltd (new) W281

Schaffhausen
Te Connectivity Ltd W589

Schindellegi
Kuehne & Nagel International Ag W354

Worblaufen
Swisscom Ag W581

Zurich
Ubs Group Ag W621
Abb Ltd W5
Adecco Group Ag W12
Credit Suisse Group Ag W175
Zurich Insurance Group Ag W665
Vontobel Holding Ag W642
Chubb Ltd W153
Swiss Life Holding Ag W580

INDEX BY HEADQUARTERS LOCATION

```
A = AMERICAN BUSINESS
E = EMERGING COMPANIES
P = PRIVATE COMPANIES
W = WORLD BUSINESSS
```

Dksh Holding Ltd W202
Swiss Life (uk) Plc (united Kingdom) W580
Swiss Re Ltd W580

Geneva
Compagnie Financiere Richemont Sa W166

Basel
Bank Sarasin & Co W86

Vevey
Nestle Sa W428

CHL

Santiago
Enel Americas Sa W220
Corporacion Nacional Del Cobre De Chile W172
Banco Santander Chile W73
Banco De Chile W70
Empresas Copec Sa W217
Antarchile S.a. (chile) W41
Itau Corpbanca W313
Cencosud Sa W131

CHN

Beijing
China Communications Constructions Group Ltd W138
Meituan W394
Beijing Shougang Co Ltd W100
China Telecom Corp Ltd W151
China Shenhua Energy Co., Ltd. W148
Bbmg Corp W98
Boe Technology Group Co Ltd W105
Longfor Group Holdings Ltd W372
Jd.com, Inc. W324
Gd Power Development Co, Ltd. W256
Aluminum Corp Of China Ltd. W34
Datang International Power Generation Co Ltd W189
China Construction Bank Corp W138
China Life Insurance Co Ltd W141
China Railway Construction Corp Ltd W146
China Coal Energy Co Ltd W137
Metallurgical Corp China Ltd W397
Baidu Inc W67
Crrc Corp Ltd W178
New China Life Insurance Co Ltd W431
Petrochina Co Ltd W466
China Railway Group Ltd W146
Industrial And Commercial Bank Of China Ltd W301
Huadian Power International Corp., Ltd. W290
China Petroleum & Chemical Corp W145
Huaneng Power International Inc W291

Chongqing
Jinke Property Group Co., Ltd. W327

Chong Qing Changan Automobile Co Ltd W153

Dalian
Zhongsheng Group Holdings Ltd. W663

Guangzhou
Vipshop Holdings Ltd W636

Shanghai
Saic Motor Corp Ltd W511
Shanghai Electric Group Co Ltd W529
China Pacific Insurance (group) Co., Ltd. W145
Shanghai Pharmaceuticals Holding Co Ltd W529
Future Land Development Holdings Ltd W254
Huayu Automotive Systems Company Ltd W292
Baoshan Iron & Steel Co Ltd W88
Shanghai Jinfeng Investment Co Ltd W529
China United Network Communications Ltd W152
Shanghai Construction Group Co., Ltd. W529

Tianjin
Sunac China Holdings Ltd W572
Tianjin Tianhai Investment Co Ltd W603
Cosco Shipping Holdings Co Ltd W172

Maanshan City
Maanshan Iron & Steel Co., Ltd. W375

Tongling
Tongling Nonferrous Metal Group Co Ltd W608

Wuhu City
Anhui Conch Cement Co Ltd W40

Fuzhou
Sunshine City Group Co., Ltd. W574

Longyan
Zijin Mining Group Co Ltd W663

Xiamen
Xiamen International Trade Group Corp Ltd W655
Xiamen C & D Inc W655
Xiamen Xiangyu Co Ltd W656

Guangzhou
Poly Developments And Holdings Group Co Ltd W477
China Southern Airlines Co Ltd W149

Shenzhen
China Vanke Co Ltd W152
China Evergrande Group W139
Shenzhen Shenxin Taifeng Group Co Ltd W533
Ping An Insurance (group) Co Of China Ltd. W471
China Merchants Shekou Industrial Zone Holdings Co Ltd W142
Zte Corp. W664
Shenzhen Overseas Chinese Town Co Ltd W533
Tencent Holdings Ltd. W596
China International Marine Containers Group Ltd. W141
Gemdale Corp W257

Zhuhai
Gree Electric Appliances Inc Of Zhuhai W263

Renhuai
Kweichow Moutai Co., Ltd. W355

Beijing
Xiaomi Corp W656
Didi Global Inc W202
Fih Mobile Ltd W240

Baoding
Great Wall Motor Co Ltd W261

Shijiazhuang
Hebei Iron & Steel Co Ltd W271

Luoyang City
China Molybdenum Co Ltd W144

Zhengzhou
Hengyi Petrochemical Co Ltd W275

Wuhan
China Gezhouba Group Co., Ltd. W140

Changsha
Sany Heavy Industry Co Ltd W515
Hunan Valin Steel Co Ltd W292
Zhejiang Materials Development Co., Ltd. W663

Hohhot
Inner Mongolia Yili Industrial Group Co., Ltd. W307

Changzhou
Changlin Co Ltd W136

Nanjing
Suning.com Co Ltd W574

Nanchang
Jiangxi Copper Co., Ltd. W326

Changchun
Faw Car Co., Ltd. W239

Anshan City
Angang Steel Co Ltd W37

Dalian
Hengli Petrochemical Co Ltd W274
China Grand Automotive Services Co Ltd W140
Jiangsu Zhongnan Construction Group Co., Ltd. W326

Xian
Shaanxi Yanchang Petroleum Chemical Engineering Co., Ltd. W528
China Hongqiao Group Ltd W141

Jinan
Shandong Iron & Steel Co Ltd W528

Qingdao
Haier Smart Home Co Ltd W268

Weifang
Weichai Power Co Ltd W644

Zoucheng
Yankuang Energy Group Co Ltd W659

Chengdu
New Hope Liuhe Co Ltd W431

Mianyang
Sichuan Chang Hong Electric Co Ltd W542

Urumqi
Xinjiang Zhongtai Chemical Co Ltd W656

Kunming
Yunnan Copper Co., Ltd. W662

Hangzhou
Zhejiang Material Industrial Zhongda Yuantong Group Co., Ltd. W662

Shangyu
China Fortune Land Development Co Ltd W140

COL

Bogota
Ecopetrol Sa W209

Medellin
Bancolombia Sa W76

CSK

Prague 1
Komercni Banka As (czech Republic) W347

DEU

Bad Homburg
Fresenius Medical Care Ag & Co Kgaa W248
Fresenius Se & Co Kgaa W250

Bonn
Deutsche Post Ag W197
Deutsche Telekom Ag W198

Darmstadt
Merck Kgaa (germany) W395

Duesseldorf
Henkel Ag & Co Kgaa W275
Metro Ag (new) W398
Ceconomy Ag W128

Erlangen
Siemens Healthineers Ag W545

Essen
Innogy Se W307
Thyssenkrupp Ag W601
Brenntag Se W109
Hochtief Ag W279
Rwe Ag W509
Evonik Industries Ag W233
E.on Se W206

Frankfurt
Deutsche Lufthansa Ag (germany, Fed. Rep.) W195
Dekabank Deutsche Girozentrale W191

Frankfurt Am Main
Commerzbank Ag W162
Deutsche Bank Ag W194

Hamburg
Hapag-lloyd Aktiengesellschaft W270
Aurubis Ag W61

Hannover
Hannover Rueckversicherung Se W268

INDEX BY HEADQUARTERS LOCATION

A = AMERICAN BUSINESS
E = EMERGING COMPANIES
P = PRIVATE COMPANIES
W = WORLD BUSINESSS

Talanx Ag W585
Hanover
Continental Ag (germany, Fed. Rep.) W170
Heidelberg
Heidelbergcement Ag W272
Herzogenaurach
Schaeffler Ag W521
Adidas Ag W13
Ingolstadt
Audi Ag W61
Leverkusen
Covestro Ag W174
Bayer Ag W94
Ludwigshafen
Basf Se W91
Munich
Muenchener Rueckversicherungs-gesellschaft Ag (germany) W414
Traton Se W618
Bayerische Motoren Werke Ag W95
Siemens Ag (germany) W542
Siemens Energy Ag W544
Baywa Bayerische Warenvermittlung Landwirtschaftlicher Genossenschaften Ag W97
Allianz Se W31
Neubiberg
Infineon Technologies Ag W302
Stuttgart
Mckesson Europe Ag W389
Mercedes-benz Ag W394
Walldorf
Sap Se W516
Wiesbaden
Aareal Bank Ag W2
Wolfsburg
Volkswagen Ag W639

DNK

Aarhus N.
Vestas Wind Systems A/s W632
Bagsvaerd
Novo-nordisk As W449
Copenhagen K
Kommunekredit (denmark) W348
Danske Bank A/s W187
A.p. Moller - Maersk A/s W1
Hedehusene
Dsv As W205
Silkeborg
Jyske Bank A/s W329

ESP

Alicante
Banco De Sabadell Sa W70

Bilbao
Iberdrola Sa W295
Banco Bilbao Vizcaya Argentaria Sa (bbva) W68
Madrid
Telefonica Sa W593
Endesa S.a. W218
Repsol S.a. W492
Naturgy Energy Group Sa W423
Acs Actividades De Construccion Y Servicios, S.a. W10
Bankinter, s.a. W87
La Coruna
Industria De Diseno Textil (inditex) Sa W299
Madrid
Banco Santander Sa (spain) W74
Compania De Distribucion Integral Logista Holdings Sa W169
Mapfre Sa W382
Vizcaya
Siemens Gamesa Renewable Energy Sa W544

FIN

Espoo
Kone Oyj W348
Neste Oyj W426
Fortum Oyj W246
Nokia Corp W442
Kesko
Kesko Oyj W339

FRA

Bezons
Atos Origin W61
Boulogne-billancourt
Carrefour S.a. W123
Charenton-le-pont
Essilorluxottica W230
Clermont-ferrand
Compagnie Generale Des Etablissements Michelin Sca W168
Courbevoie
Engie Sa W223
Compagnie De Saint-gobain W165
Totalenergies Se W612
Thales W599
Ergue-gaberic
Compagnie De L Odet W164
Nanterre
Faurecia Se (france) W237
Paris
Bnp Paribas (france) W102
Veolia Environnement Sa W631
Scor S.e. (france) W525
Danone W185
Orange W458
L'oreal S.a. (france) W358
Societe Generale W548
Schlumberger Ltd W523
Axa Sa W65
Air France-klm W21
Lvmh Moet Hennessy Louis Vuitton W372

Kering Sa W337
Rci Banque S.a. W489
Publicis Groupe S.a. W485
Bouygues S.a. W106
Sanofi W515
Rueil-malmaison
Ald Sa W26
Velizy-villacoublay
Eiffage Sa W212
Boulogne-billancourt
Renault S.a. (france) W492
Montrouge
Credit Agricole Sa W174
Paris
Colas Sa Boulogne W161
Paris La Defense
Suez Sa W564
Rueil-malmaison
Vinci Sa W634
Schneider Electric Se W523
Paris
L'air Liquide S.a. (france) W357
Vivendi Se W636
Electricite De France W214
Saint-etienne
Casino Guichard Perrachon S.a. W125
Paris
Safran Sa W511
Rexel S.a. W494
Valeo Se W630
Issy-les-moulineaux
Sodexo W549
Paris
Capgemini Se W123

GBR

Bradford
Yorkshire Building Society W661
Bristol
Imperial Brands Plc W297
Cambridge
Astrazeneca Plc W56
Edinburgh
Natwest Group Plc W423
Kent
Osb Group Plc W462
London
Bunzl Plc W114
Barclays Bank Plc W88
M&g Plc W374
Phoenix Group Holdings Plc W470
Hsbc Holdings Plc W288
Cnh Industrial Nv W157
Wpp Plc (new) W652
Barclays Plc W89
Lewis (john) Partnership Plc (united Kingdom) W364
Lloyds Banking Group Plc W371
Hsbc Bank Plc (united Kingdom) W288
Royal Mail Plc W508
Unilever Plc (united Kingdom) W625
Johnson Matthey Plc (united Kingdom) W327

Investec Plc W311
Lloyds Bank Plc W371
Bae Systems Plc W65
National Grid Plc W421
Rolls-royce Holdings Plc W503
National Westminster Bank Plc W422
J Sainsbury Plc W317
Aviva Plc (united Kingdom) W63
Lewis (john) Plc (united Kingdom) W364
Swire (john) & Sons Ltd. (united Kingdom) W579
Marks & Spencer Group Plc W383
Diageo Plc W200
Lyondellbasell Industries Nv W374
Associated British Foods Plc W54
British American Tobacco Plc (united Kingdom) W110
Currys Plc W179
Kingfisher Plc W340
Rio Tinto Plc W499
Bt Group Plc W113
Tsb Banking Group Plc W618
Anglo American Plc (united Kingdom) W38
Bp Plc W108
Legal & General Group Plc (united Kingdom) W359
Bupa Finance Plc W116
Bhp Group Ltd W100
Manchester
Co-operative Bank Plc W159
Co-operative Group (cws) Ltd. W159
Newcastle Upon Tyne
Technipfmc Plc W590
Uxbridge
Coca-cola Europacific Partners Plc W161
Welwyn Garden City
Tesco Plc (united Kingdom) W597
Wokingham
Ferguson Plc (new) W239
Newbury
Vodafone Group Plc W637
Slough
Reckitt Benckiser Group Plc W490
Windsor
Centrica Plc W134
Dublin 1
Aon Plc (ireland) W42
Brentford
Glaxosmithkline Plc W257
Glasgow
Clydesdale Bank Plc (united Kingdom) W157
Chertsey
Compass Group Plc (united Kingdom) W169

INDEX BY HEADQUARTERS LOCATION

```
A = AMERICAN BUSINESS
E = EMERGING COMPANIES
P = PRIVATE COMPANIES
W = WORLD BUSINESSS
```

Guildford
Linde Plc W367

GRC

Athens
Eurobank Ergasias Services & Holdings Sa W231
Piraeus Financial Holdings Sa W472
Alpha Services & Holdings Sa W33

HKG

China Mobile Limited W142
China Resources Land Ltd W147
Ck Hutchison Holdings Ltd W157
Cathay Pacific Airways Ltd. W128
Bank Of East Asia Ltd. W80
Citic Ltd W156
Alibaba Group Holding Ltd W29
Geely Automobile Holdings Ltd W256
China Unicom (hong Kong) Ltd W151
Hongkong & Shanghai Banking Corp Ltd W286
Kunlun Energy Co., Ltd. W355
Wh Group Ltd W648
Prudential Plc W480
Dah Sing Financial Holdings Ltd. W179
Far East Horizon Ltd. W236
Cnooc Ltd W158
Country Garden Holdings Co Ltd W173
China Resources Pharmaceutical Group Ltd W148
Standard Chartered Plc W559
Byd Co Ltd W116
Hang Seng Bank Ltd. W268
Shimao Group Holdings Ltd W534
Fosun International Ltd W248
Boc Hong Kong Holdings Ltd W104
Aia Group Ltd. W19
China Overseas Land & Investment Ltd W144
Lenovo Group Ltd W361
China Taiping Insurance Holding Co., Ltd. W150
Dah Sing Banking Group Ltd W179
Jardine Matheson Holdings Ltd. W322

HUN

Budapest
Mol Magyar Olaj Es Gazipari Reszvenytar W411

IDN

Jakarta
Pt Bank Negara (indonesia) W483
P.t. Astra International Tbk W464

IND

Fort Mumbai
Tata Steel Ltd W588

Mumbai
Larsen & Toubro Ltd W358
Icici Bank Ltd (india) W295
Reliance Industries Ltd W491
Hdfc Bank Ltd W271
State Bank Of India W561
Union Bank Of India W626

Bangalore
Infosys Ltd. W303

Mumbai
Tata Motors Ltd W586

IRL

Cork
Johnson Controls International Plc W327

Dublin
Dcc Plc W190
Accenture Plc W8
Aptiv Corp W45
Bank Of Ireland Group Plc W81
Aib Group Plc W20
Crh Plc W177
Aptiv Plc W45
Medtronic Plc W393

Dublin 1
Adient Plc W15

Dublin 4
Eaton Corp Plc W209

Swords
Trane Technologies Plc W617

ISR

Ramat Gan
Mizrahi Tefahot Bank Ltd W410

Tel Aviv
Teva Pharmaceutical Industries Ltd W597

Tel-aviv
Israel Discount Bank Ltd. W311
Bank Leumi Le-israel B.m. W78
Bank Hapoalim B.m. (israel) W77

ITA

Bologna
Unipol Gruppo Spa W627
Unipolsai Assicurazioni Spa W627

Milan
Mediobanca Banca Di Credito Finanziario Spa W390
Prysmian Spa W482
Telecom Italia Spa W591

Milano
Unicredito Spa W624

Reggio Emilia
Credito Emiliano Spa Credem Reggio Emilia W177

Rome
Leonardo Spa W362
Eni S.p.a. W226

Poste Italiane Spa W479
Enel Societa Per Azioni W221

Torino
Intesa Sanpaolo S.p.a. W309

Trieste
Assicurazioni Generali S.p.a. W53

JPN

Akita
Akita Bank Ltd (the) (japan) W26

Aomori
Aomori Bank, Ltd. (the) (japan) W41

Chiba
Aeon Co Ltd W17
Chiba Bank, Ltd W137
Keiyo Bank, Ltd. (the) (japan) W336

Fukui
Fukui Bank Ltd. W253

Fukuoka
Kyushu Electric Power Co Inc W356

Fukushima
Toho Bank, Ltd. (the) W603

Gifu
Juroku Financial Group Inc W329

Hiroshima
Hirogin Holdings Inc W278

Kochi
Shikoku Bank, Ltd. (japan) W534

Kyoto
Nidec Corp W431
Nintendo Co., Ltd. W433
Kyocera Corp W356
Bank Of Kyoto Ltd (japan) W82

Miyazaki
Miyazaki Bank, Ltd. (the) W409

Nagano
Hachijuni Bank, Ltd. (japan) W267

Nara
Nanto Bank, Ltd. W418

Oita
Oita Bank Ltd (japan) W454

Okayama
Chugoku Bank, Ltd. (the) W155

Osaka
Kansai Electric Power Co., Inc. (kansai Denryoku K. K.) (japan) W331
Daikin Industries Ltd W182
Daiwa House Industry Co Ltd W184
Osaka Gas Co Ltd (japan) W461
Kubota Corp. (japan) W353
Sumitomo Electric Industries, Ltd. (japan) W566
Sumitomo Life Insurance Co. (japan) W568
Nippon Life Insurance Co. (japan) W435
Itochu Corp (japan) W315
Sekisui House, Ltd. (japan) W526

Saitama
Musashino Bank, Ltd. W417

Shizuoka
Shizuoka Bank Ltd (japan) W539

Tokushima
Awa Bank, Ltd. W64

Tokyo
Alfresa Holdings Corp Tokyo W28
Sompo Holdings Inc W554
Nippon Telegraph & Telephone Corp (japan) W439
Canon Inc W123
Tokyo Gas Co Ltd W608
Nippon Express Holdings Inc W434
East Japan Railway Co. W208
T&d Holdings Inc W581
Mitsui & Co., Ltd. W408
Sony Group Corp W555
Softbank Corp (new) W550
Takeda Pharmaceutical Co Ltd W584
Isuzu Motors, Ltd. (japan) W312
Nippon Steel Corp (new) W436
Subaru Corporation W563
Sumitomo Mitsui Financial Group Inc Tokyo W569
Kirin Holdings Co Ltd W342
Agc Inc W18
Daito Trust Construction Co., Ltd. W183
Sumitomo Mitsui Trust Holdings Inc W570
Ms&ad Insurance Group Holdings W412
Rakuten Group Inc W487
Recruit Holdings Co Ltd W490
Tdk Corp W588
Shin-etsu Chemical Co., Ltd. W535
Mitsubishi Materials Corp. W404
Tokyo Electron, Ltd. W607
Toray Industries, Inc. W610
Medipal Holdings Corp W392
Tokyo Electric Power Company Holdings Inc W606
Fujitsu Ltd W253
Ntt Data Corp W451
Tokio Marine Holdings Inc W604
Dai Nippon Printing Co Ltd W180
Ricoh Co Ltd W496
Otsuka Holdings Co., Ltd. W462
Idemitsu Kosan Co Ltd W296
Mitsubishi Shokuhin Co., Ltd. W405
Hitachi, Ltd. W278
Toshiba Corp W612
Bridgestone Corp (japan) W110
Mitsui Fudosan Co Ltd W408
Asahi Kasei Corp W51
Pan Pacific International Holdings Corp W464
Mitsubishi Corp W400
Shoko Chukin Bank (the) (japan) W539
Eneos Holdings Inc W222
Resona Holdings Inc Osaka W493
Cosmo Energy Holdings Co Ltd W173
Yamato Holdings Co., Ltd. W659
Aozora Bank Ltd W44
Japan Tobacco Inc. W319
Mitsubishi Heavy Industries Ltd W403

INDEX BY HEADQUARTERS LOCATION

```
A = AMERICAN BUSINESS
E = EMERGING COMPANIES
P = PRIVATE COMPANIES
W = WORLD BUSINESSS
```

Oji Holdings Corp W454
Obayashi Corp W452
Taisei Corp W582
Shimizu Corp. W534
Toppan Inc W608
Kao Corp W332
Nippon Yusen Kabushiki Kaisha W439
Dai-ichi Life Holdings Inc W181
Nec Corp W425
Sumitomo Chemical Co., Ltd. W565
Komatsu Ltd W347
Jfe Holdings Inc W325
Meiji Yasuda Life Insurance Co. W393
Nomura Holdings Inc W443
Japan Post Bank Co Ltd W319
Shinsei Bank Ltd W538
Fujifilm Holdings Corp W252
Orix Corp W460
Japan Post Holdings Co Ltd W319
Mitsubishi Chemical Holdings Corp W399
Asahi Group Holdings Ltd. W50
Bank Of Japan W81
Japan Post Insurance Co Ltd W319
Hanwa Co Ltd (japan) W269
Marubeni Corp. W385
Mitsubishi Motors Corp. (japan) W405
Seven & I Holdings Co. Ltd. W527
Honda Motor Co Ltd W284
Mitsubishi Ufj Financial Group Inc W406
Fast Retailing Co., Ltd. W236
Kajima Corp. (japan) W330
Kddi Corp W336
Lixil Corp W369
Sojitz Corp W551
Mitsubishi Electric Corp W402
Sumitomo Corp. (japan) W566

Toyama
Hokuhoku Financial Group Inc W281

Kariya
Aisin Corporation W25
Denso Corp W192
Toyota Industries Corporation (japan) W613

Nagoya
Chubu Electric Power Co Inc W154
Bank Of Nagoya, Ltd. W83
Aichi Bank, Ltd. W21
Suzuken Co Ltd W576
Toyota Tsusho Corp W616

Toyota
Toyota Motor Corp W614

Matsuyama
Iyo Bank, Ltd. (japan) W316

Ogaki
Ogaki Kyoritsu Bank, Ltd. W454

Maebashi
Gunma Bank Ltd (the) W266

Takasaki
Yamada Holdings Co Ltd W657

Aki-gun
Mazda Motor Corp. (japan) W388

Sapporo
North Pacific Bank Ltd W449

Kobe
Kobe Steel Ltd W344
Kawasaki Heavy Industries Ltd W334

Kanazawa
Hokkoku Financial Holdings Inc W280

Morioka
Bank Of Iwate, Ltd. (the) (japan) W81

Takamatsu
Hyakujushi Bank, Ltd. W293

Yokohama
Nissan Motor Co., Ltd. W440

Nagaokakyo
Murata Manufacturing Co Ltd W416

Tsu
Hyakugo Bank Ltd. (japan) W292

Sendai
Tohoku Electric Power Co., Inc. (japan) W604
77 Bank, Ltd. (the) (japan) W1

Kadoma
Panasonic Corp W465

Sakai
Sharp Corp (japan) W530

Otsu
Shiga Bank, Ltd. W533

Matsue
San-in Godo Bank, Ltd. (the) (japan) W515

Hamamatsu
Suzuki Motor Corp. (japan) W576

Iwata
Yamaha Motor Co Ltd W657

Numazu
Suruga Bank, Ltd. W576

Tokyo
Nippon Steel Trading Corp W438

Hino
Hino Motors, Ltd. W277

Musashino
Iida Group Holdings Co., Ltd. W297

Kofu
Yamanashi Chuo Bank, Ltd. (japan) W659

KOR

Seoul
Shinhan Financial Group Co. Ltd. W536
Lg Electronics Inc W366
Samsung C&t Corp (new) W513
Lg Display Co Ltd W365
Kb Financial Group, Inc. W335
Woori Financial Group Inc W652
Sk Telecom Co Ltd (south Korea) W545
Lg Energy Solution Ltd W367
Hyundai Motor Co., Ltd. W293
Posco (south Korea) W477

Suwon-si
Samsung Electronics Co Ltd W513

Changwon-si
Doosan Heavy Industries & Construction Co Ltd W204

Naju-si
Korea Electric Power Corp W351

Seol
Kt Corp (korea) W352

LBN

Beirut
Bank Audi Sal W77
Blom Bank Sal W102

LUX

Luxembourg
Arcelormittal Sa W47

MEX

Mexico City
Grupo Financiero Banorte S.a. Bde C V W265
Grupo Bimbo Sab De Cv (mexico) W264
Banco Santander Mexico Sa, Institucion De Banca Multiple, Grupo Financiero Santander Mexico W73
Petroleos Mexicanos (pemex) (mexico) W469
Wal-mart De Mexico S.a.b. De C.v. W642
Grupo Financiero Citibanamex Sa De Cv W266
America Movil Sab De Cv W34

Monterrey
Fomento Economico Mexicano, S.a.b. De C.v. W243

San Pedro Garza Garcia
Cemex S.a.b. De C.v. W130
Alfa Sab De Cv W27

MYS

Kuala Lumpur
Public Bank Berhad (malaysia) W484
Rhb Bank Berhad W495
Cimb Group Holdings Bhd W155
Ammb Holdings Bhd W36
Hong Leong Bank Berhad W286
Malayan Banking Berhad W380

NLD

Amstelveen
Klm Royal Dutch Airlines W343

Amsterdam
X5 Retail Group Nv W655
Ing Groep Nv W305
Heineken Nv (netherlands) W274
Koninklijke Philips Nv W351
Heineken Holding Nv (netherlands) W274

Diemen
Randstad Nv W488

Leiden
Airbus Se W22

Lijnden
Stellantis Nv W562

The Hague
Shell Plc W531
Aegon Nv W15

The Hauge
Nn Group Nv (netherlands) W442

Veldhoven
Asml Holding Nv W52

Zaandam
Koninklijke Ahold Delhaize Nv W348

Amsterdam
Exor Nv W235

NOR

Fornebu
Telenor Asa W593

Lysaker
Storebrand Asa W562

Oslo
Dnb Bank Asa W203
Norsk Hydro Asa W447
Kommunalbanken A/s (norway) W347

Stavanger
Sparebank 1 Sr Bank Asa W558
Equinor Asa W227

NZL

Auckland
Fonterra Co-operative Group Ltd W244

OMN

Seeb
Bank Muscat S.a.o.g W79

PER

Lima
Credicorp Ltd. W174

PHL

Makati City
Bank Of The Philippine Islands W85
Bdo Unibank Inc. W99
Metropolitan Bank & Trust Co. (philippines) W399

Mandaluyong City
San Miguel Corp W513

POL

Warsaw
Bank Polska Kasa Opieki Sa W86

INDEX BY HEADQUARTERS LOCATION

```
A = AMERICAN BUSINESS
E = EMERGING COMPANIES
P = PRIVATE COMPANIES
W = WORLD BUSINESSS
```

Mbank Sa W389

PRT

Lisboa
Jeronimo Martins S.g.p.s. Sa W324
Lisbon
Galp Energia, Sgps, Sa W254
Porto
Banco Comercial Portugues Sa W70
Lisbon
Edp Energias De Portugal S.a. W210

QAT

Doha
Qatar National Bank W486
Qatar Islamic Bank W486
Commercial Bank Of Qatar W162

RUS

Krasnodar
Magnit Pjsc W379
Moscow
Inter Rao Ues Pjsc W308
Pjsc Gazprom W473
Mmc Norilsk Nickel Pjsc W410
Rosneft Oil Co Ojsc (moscow) W505
Transneft W617
Sberbank Of Russia W521
Pjsc Lukoil W475
Pjsc Rosseti W476
Saint-petersburg
Jsc Vtb Bank W329
St. Petersburg
Gazprom Neft Pjsc W255
Tyumenskaya Oblast
Surgutneftegas Pjsc W575

SAU

Riyadh
Riyad Bank (saudi Arabia) W501
Arab National Bank W47
Samba Financial Group W512
Saudi Electricity Co W520
Saudi Basic Industries Corp - Sabic (saudi Arabia) W519
Saudi British Bank (the) W520
Saudi Telecom Co W520

SGP

Great Eastern Holdings Ltd (singapore) W261
Flex Ltd W241
Oversea-chinese Banking Corp. Ltd. (singapore) W463
Olam International Ltd. W455
Jardine Cycle & Carriage Ltd W321
Dbs Group Holdings Ltd. W189
Wilmar International Ltd W648
United Overseas Bank Ltd. (singapore) W628

SWE

Goeteborg
Volvo Ab W640
Stockholm
Svenska Handelsbanken W578
Ericsson W228
Skandinaviska Enskilda Banken W546
Essity Aktiebolag (publ) W231
Hennes & Mauritz Ab W277
Nordea Bank Abp W445
Atlas Copco Ab (sweden) W58
Ab Electrolux (sweden) W3
Skanska Ab W548
Sundbyberg
Swedbank Ab W579

THA

Bangkok
Charoen Pokphand Foods Public Co., Ltd. (thailand) W136
Bank Of Ayudhya Public Co Ltd W79
Bangkok Bank Public Co., Ltd. (thailand) W77
Kasikornbank Public Co Ltd W333
Krung Thai Bank Public Co. Ltd. W352
Ptt Public Co Ltd W483
Siam Cement Public Co. Ltd. W539
Siam Commercial Bank Public Co Ltd (the) W541
C.p. All Public Co Ltd W117
Tmbthanachart Bank Public Co Ltd W603

TUR

Istanbul
Haci Omer Sabanci Holding As W267
Turkiye Garanti Bankasi As W618
Korfez
Turkiye Petrol Rafinerileri As W620
Istanbul
Koc Holdings As W345
Yapi Ve Kredi Bankasi As W660
Akbank W26
Turkiye Is Bankasi As W619

TWN

Hsinchu
Taiwan Semiconductor Manufacturing Co., Ltd. W582
Wistron Corp W649
Kaohsiung
Ase Technology Holding Co Ltd W51
New Taipei
Hon Hai Precision Industry Co Ltd W283
Taipei
Fubon Financial Holding Co Ltd W251
Compal Electronics Inc W168
Cathay Financial Holding Co W127
E Sun Financial Holdings Co Ltd W205

USA

ALABAMA

ALEXANDER CITY
Medco, L.l.c. P339
ANDALUSIA
Powersouth Energy Cooperative P439
AUBURN
Auburn University P54
BESSEMER
Piggly Wiggly Alabama Distributing Co., Inc. P432
BIRMINGHAM
Mayer Electric Supply Company, Inc. P335
B.l. Harbert Holdings, L.l.c. P57
City Of Birmingham P129
Navigate Affordable Housing Partners, Inc P379
The Southeastern Conference P606
Alabama Power Co A32
Regions Financial Corp (new) A883
Servisfirst Bancshares Inc A931
Hibbett Inc E253
Childrens Hospital Inc P122
Servisfirst Bancshares Inc E436
The Children's Hospital Of Alabama P572
Proassurance Corp A847
Consolidated Pipe & Supply Company, Inc. P159
University Of Alabama Health Services Foundation, P.c. P646
Protective Life Insurance Co A853
Medical Properties Trust Inc E315
DOTHAN
Construction Partners Inc E117
Aaa Cooper Transportation P1
HOOVER
Southern Nuclear Operating Company, Inc. P514
HUNTSVILLE
The Health Care Authority Of The City Of Huntsville P585
Lakeland Industries, Inc. E290
Huntsville Hospital Health System P272
Huntsville Utilities P272
MOBILE
Infirmary Health System, Inc. P276
University Of South Alabama P660
MONTGOMERY
State Of Alabama A966
State Of Alabama P532
MOUNTAIN BROOK
Oakworth Capital Inc E358
OPELIKA
Hl Mando America Corporation P264

PRATTVILLE
River Financial Corp E422
TUSCALOOSA
University Of Alabama P646
The Dch Health Care Authority P577

ALASKA

ANCHORAGE
Alaska Native Tribal Health Consortium P15
Arctic Slope Regional Corporation P42
Nana Development Corporation P375
Northrim Bancorp Inc E352
Petro Star Inc. P428
Chenega Corporation P116
Chugach Alaska Corporation P124
Anchorage, Municipality Of (inc) P38
First National Bank Alaska A428
Gci, Llc P235
Alaska Housing Finance Corp A34
Anchorage School District P38
JUNEAU
State Of Alaska A966
Sealaska Corporation P491
Alaska Permanent Fund Corporation, An Instrumentality Of The State Of Alaska A35
State Of Alaska P532
Alaska Permanent Fund Corporation, An Instrumentality Of The State Of Alaska P15
KOTZEBUE
Nana Regional Corporation, Inc., P375

ARIZONA

CHANDLER
Microchip Technology Inc A696
GLENDALE
Don Ford Sanderson Inc P201
MESA
City Of Mesa P134
Empire Southwest, Llc P214
Mesa Unified School District 4 P349
PEORIA
R. Directional Drilling & Underground Technology, Inc. P449
R. Directional Drilling & Underground Technology, Inc. A872
PHOENIX
Blue Cross And Blue Shield Of Arizona, Inc. P84
Southern Copper Corp A953
Arizona State Lottery P43
Banner Health A136
Republic Services Inc A891

INDEX BY HEADQUARTERS LOCATION

```
A = AMERICAN BUSINESS
E = EMERGING COMPANIES
P = PRIVATE COMPANIES
W = WORLD BUSINESSS
```

Cable One Inc E71
Shell Medical Plan P502
Western Alliance Bancorporation A1120
Phoenix Children's Hospital, Inc. P430
State Of Arizona P532
Sprouts Farmers Market Inc A959
Mercy Care P344
County Of Maricopa P172
Avnet Inc A116
City Of Phoenix P137
Western Alliance Bancorporation E535
Shamrock Foods Company P498
John C. Lincoln Health Network P287
Banner Health P59
On Semiconductor Corp A779
Leslie's Inc E297
State Of Arizona A966
Maricopa County Special Health Care District P327
Freeport-mcmoran Inc A450
Cavco Industries Inc (de) E84

SCOTTSDALE
Store Capital Corp E466
Resideo Technologies Inc A893
City Of Scottsdale P140
Viavi Solutions Inc E522
Meritage Homes Corp A686
Joint Corp (new) E285
Taylor Morrison Home Corp (holding Co) A997
Honorhealth P267
Healthcare Trust Of America Inc E247

TEMPE
Align Technology Inc E15
United Dairymen Of Arizona P641
Insight Enterprises Inc. A557
Drivetime Automotive Group, Inc. P202
Amkor Technology Inc. A77
Godaddy Inc E234
Salt River Project Agricultural Improvement And Power District P480
Sundt Construction, Inc. P546
Carvana Co A208
Opendoor Technologies Inc A784
Crexendo Inc E129
Arizona State University P43
Arizona State University P44

TUCSON
City Of Tucson P142
Banner-university Medical Center Tucson Campus Llc P60
The Sundt Companies Inc P607
Pima County P433

ARKANSAS

BENTONVILLE
Walmart Inc A1102
Walton Family Foundation Inc P680

CONWAY
Home Bancshares Inc E257
Home Bancshares Inc A523

EL DORADO
Murphy Usa Inc A718

LITTLE ROCK
Baptist Health P60
University Of Arkansas System P646
State Of Arkansas P532
Earthlink Holdings, Llc P206
Bank Ozk A133
Bank Ozk E53
Arkansas Electric Cooperatives, Inc. P45
Arkansas Electric Cooperative Corporation P44
State Of Arkansas A967
Vcc, Llc P673

LOWELL
Hunt (j.b.) Transport Services, Inc. A542

NORTH LITTLE ROCK
Comfort Systems Usa (arkansas), Inc. P151
Bruce Oakley, Inc. P96

PINE BLUFF
Simmons First National Corp A937
Simmons First National Corp E441

ROGERS
Ccf Brands Llc P108
America's Car-mart Inc E22

SPRINGDALE
Tyson Foods Inc A1048

VAN BUREN
Usa Truck, Inc. E514

CALIFORNIA

ALAMEDA
Exelixis Inc E177

ALHAMBRA
Apollo Medical Holdings Inc E33

ANAHEIM
City Of Anaheim P127
Eaco Corp E147

AUBURN
County Of Placer P175

BAKERSFIELD
Valley Republic Bancorp E517
Jaco Oil Company P285
City Of Bakersfield P128
Kern High School Dst P298
County Of Kern P171
Bakersfield Memorial Hospital P58

BEVERLY HILLS
Endeavor Group Holdings Inc A367
Cedars-sinai Medical Care Foundation P109
Live Nation Entertainment Inc A640
Pacwest Bancorp A799

BREA
Sun Mar Management Services P546

BRISBANE
Brisbane School District A176
Brisbane School District P93

BURBANK
Disney (walt) Co. (the) A334

BURLINGAME
Mills-peninsula Health Services P358

Innoviva Inc E271

CALEXICO
Coppel Corporation P163

CARLSBAD
Natural Alternatives International, Inc. E341
Bergelectric Corp. P75
Maxlinear Inc E313

CARMICHAEL
San Juan Unified School District P482

CERRITOS
Revolve Group Inc E418

CHICO
Trico Bancshares (chico, Ca) E495
Trico Bancshares (chico, Ca) A1038

CHINO HILLS
Victory International Group, Llc P674

CHULA VISTA
Chg Foundation P118
Sweetwater Union High School District P552

CITY OF INDUSTRY
America Chung Nam (group) Holdings Llc P31

CONCORD
Swinerton Builders P552
Ufcw & Employers Trust Llc P639
Ufcw & Employers Trust Llc P638

CORONA
Monster Beverage 1990 Corporation P365

CUPERTINO
Apple Inc A87

CYPRESS
United Food And Commercial Workers Unions And Food Employers Ben Fund P641

DAVIS
University Of California, Davis P647

DOWNEY
Los Angeles County Office Of Education P319

DUARTE
City Of Hope National Medical Center P132

DUBLIN
Ross Stores Inc A904

EL SEGUNDO
A-mark Precious Metals, Inc A4
The Aerospace Corporation P565

ELK GROVE
Grove Elk Unified School District P247

EMERYVILLE
Nmi Holdings Inc E349
Xoma Corp E545
Grocery Outlet Holding Corp E242

FAIRFIELD
County Of Solano P177

FONTANA
Fontana Unified School District P227
California Steel Industries, Inc. P100

FOSTER CITY
Gilead Sciences Inc A472

Qualys, Inc. E404
Quinstreet, Inc. E406

FOUNTAIN VALLEY
Memorial Health Services P341
Memorial Health Services Group Return P341

FREMONT
Enphase Energy Inc. E162
Asi Computer Technologies Inc P46
Concentrix Corp A287
Td Synnex Corp A998
Ichor Holdings Ltd E261
Acm Research Inc E3
Lam Research Corp A618

FRESNO
Dairyamerica, Inc. P186
City Of Fresno P132
Community Hospitals Of Central California P156
Valley Childrens Health Care P671
Communities First Financial Corp E111
California's Valued Trust P100
Central Valley Community Bancorp E90
Fresno Community Hospital And Medical Center P232
Saint Agnes Medical Center P476
Fresno Unified School District Educational Facilities Corporation P232
County Of Fresno P169

FULLERTON
St. Jude Hospital P527

GARDEN GROVE
Southland Industries P515
Garden Grove Unified School District P235

GLENDALE
Avery Dennison Corp A113

GOLETA
Deckers Outdoor Corp. E136
Community West Bancshares E114

HAYWARD
Ultra Clean Holdings Inc E503

HUNTINGTON BEACH
Boardriders, Inc. P87

IMPERIAL
Imperial Irrigation District P275

IRVINE
Irvine Unified School Distict P281
Edwards Lifesciences Corp A360
Pacific Premier Bank A797
Boot Barn Holdings Inc E64
Pacific Premier Bancorp Inc A796
Skyworks Solutions Inc A942
Pacific Premier Bancorp Inc E368
American Funds International Vantage Fund P33
Cw Bancorp E134
Masimo Corp. E312
Pacific Premier Bank P419
St. Joseph Health System P524
Newport Corporation P390
Vizio, Inc. P677

INDEX BY HEADQUARTERS LOCATION

```
A = AMERICAN BUSINESS
E = EMERGING COMPANIES
P = PRIVATE COMPANIES
W = WORLD BUSINESSS
```

IRWINDALE
Superior Communications, Inc. P548
LA CANADA FLINTRIDGE
Allen Lund Company, Llc P24
LA JOLLA
Palomar Holdings Inc E370
Silvergate Capital Corp E441
Private Bancorp Of America Inc E397
Silvergate Capital Corp A937
LA MESA
Grossmont Hospital Foundation P246
LA PUENTE
Public Health Foundation Enterprises Incorporated P447
LAKE FOREST
Staar Surgical Co. E460
LANCASTER
Simulations Plus Inc E444
LIVERMORE
Formfactor Inc E213
LODI
Farmers & Merchants Bancorp (lodi, Ca) E183
Farmers & Merchants Bancorp (lodi, Ca) A392
Pacific Coast Producers P418
LOMA LINDA
Loma Linda University Children's Hospital P317
Loma Linda University Medical Center P317
LONG BEACH
Long Beach Medical Center P318
Ta Chen International, Inc. P553
City Of Long Beach P133
Farmers & Merchants Bank Of Long Beach (ca) A393
Beauty Health Co (the) E57
Molina Healthcare Inc A707
LOS ALTOS
The David And Lucile Packard Foundation P576
LOS ANGELES
Preferred Bank (los Angeles, Ca) E392
Crescent Capital Bdc Inc E129
Rbb Bancorp A878
Hope Bancorp Inc E258
Preferred Bank (los Angeles, Ca) A843
Amcap Fund, Inc. P30
Cathay General Bancorp A211
Cathay General Bancorp E83
Rbb Bancorp E409
Los Angeles Unified School District A646
City Of Los Angeles A250
Aids Healthcare Foundation P12
The Bond Fund Of America Inc P569
County Of Los Angeles A300
American Business Bank (los Angeles, Ca) E24
The Ucla Foundation P610
American High Income Trust A64

Pcb Bancorp E375
Capital Income Builder A197
The Childrens Hospital Los Angeles P572
Rexford Industrial Realty Inc E419
Keck Hospital Of Usc E297
Kilroy Realty L.p. E287
Reliance Steel & Aluminum Co. A887
American Business Bank (los Angeles, Ca) A57
New World Fund P383
Los Angeles Department Of Water And Power P319
Kb Home A593
American Mutual Fund A66
Mercury General Corp. A684
Houlihan Lokey Inc E260
Los Angeles Lomod Corporation P319
Amcap Fund, Inc. A52
B Riley Financial Inc E49
Capital World Growth And Income Fund, Inc. P104
Los Angeles Unified School District P320
City Of Los Angeles P133
Hanmi Financial Corp. A497
The Ucla Foundation A1025
County Of Los Angeles P171
American High Income Trust P33
Capital Income Builder P103
University Of California, Los Angeles P647
Op Bancorp E362
American Funds Portfolio Series P33
Ares Management Corp E34
American Mutual Fund P36
Hope Bancorp Inc A530
Air Lease Corp E9
LOS GATOS
Netflix Inc A729
MADERA
Valley Children's Healthcare Foundation P671
Valley Children's Hospital P671
MARTINEZ
County Of Contra Costa P168
MENLO PARK
Robert Half International Inc. A897
Meta Platforms Inc A688
Novo Construction, Inc. P404
Corcept Therapeutics Inc E121
MERCED
County Of Merced P172
MILL VALLEY
Four Corners Property Trust Inc E217
Redwood Trust Inc A880
MILPITAS
Kla Corp A605
Devcon Construction Incorporated P195
Inspur Systems, Inc. P277
MISSION VIEJO
Mission Hospital Regional Medical Center Inc P360
MODESTO
Doctors Medical Center Of Modesto, Inc. P201
County Of Stanislaus P178
Stan Boyett & Son, Inc. P531

MONTEREY
Community Hospital Of The Monterey Peninsula P155
MORENO VALLEY
Moreno Valley Unified School District P367
MOUNTAIN VIEW
Intuit Inc A570
Alphabet Inc A44
El Camino Healthcare District P210
NEWARK
Logitech International Sa A645
NEWPORT BEACH
Chipotle Mexican Grill Inc A232
Hoag Memorial Hospital Presbyterian P266
California First Leasing Corp E75
American Vanguard Corp. E26
NORCO
Corona-norco Unified School District P165
NOVATO
Bank Of Marin Bancorp A130
OAKDALE
Oak Valley Bancorp (oakdale, Ca) E357
OAKLAND
City Of Oakland P136
East Bay Municipal Utility District, Water System P207
Kaiser Foundation Hospitals Inc P294
Children's Hospital & Research Center At Oakland P119
County Of Alameda P166
Kfhp Of The Mid-atlantic States Inc. P299
Clorox Co (the) A253
Kaiser Foundation Hospitals Inc A591
Kaiser Fdn Health Plan Of Colorado P293
Oakland Unified School District P406
ONTARIO
Cvb Financial Corp A308
Cvb Financial Corp E133
ORANGE
St. Joseph Hospital Of Orange P525
Children's Hospital Of Orange County P121
Orange County Health Authority, A Public Agency P412
Orange County Transportation Authority Scholarship Foundation, Inc. P412
PALO ALTO
Lucile Salter Packard Children's Hospital At Stanford P322
Vmware Inc A1097
Hp Inc A537
Sutter Bay Medical Foundation P549
Avidbank Holdings Inc E46
PASADENA
East West Bancorp, Inc E149
Schaumbond Group, Inc. P486
Pasadena Hospital Association, Ltd. P421
California Institute Of Technology P99
Huntington Hospital P271
East West Bancorp, Inc A350

Green Dot Corp E238
Alexandria Real Estate Equities Inc E14
Western Asset Mortgage Capital Corp A1121
PERRIS
Val Verde Unified Sch Dis P671
PETALUMA
Frontrow Calypso Llc P233
PITTSBURG
Uss-upi, Llc P669
PLEASANTON
Simpson Manufacturing Co., Inc. (de) E443
Veeva Systems Inc E519
PORTERVILLE
Sierra Bancorp E438
Sierra Bancorp A935
R. M. Parks, Inc. P450
POWAY
Cohu Inc E106
RANCHO CORDOVA
Dignity Health Medical Foundation P197
RCHO STA MARG
Applied Medical Resources Corporation P42
REDWOOD CITY
Dpr Construction, Inc. P201
Electronic Arts, Inc. A361
County Of San Mateo P176
Equinix Inc A376
Coherus Biosciences Inc E106
RIVERSIDE
Riverside Unified School District P465
County Of Riverside P175
ROCKLIN
Farm Credit West P221
Farm Credit West A392
ROSEMEAD
Southern California Edison Co. A951
Edison International A358
ROSEVILLE
Adventist Health System/west, Corporation P6
Sutter Roseville Medical Center P551
SACRAMENTO
Sutter Valley Hospitals P551
Sutter Health Plan P551
State Of California A967
Sutter Health P550
River City Bank E421
River City Petroleum, Inc. P463
Alston Construction Company, Inc. P28
Sacramento City Unified School District P474
Sutter Valley Medical Foundation P551

INDEX BY HEADQUARTERS LOCATION

A = AMERICAN BUSINESS
E = EMERGING COMPANIES
P = PRIVATE COMPANIES
W = WORLD BUSINESSS

Sutter Health Sacramento Sierra Region P551
State Of California P533
Sutter Health A982
County Of Sacramento P176
Sacramento Municipal Utility District P475
City Of Sacramento P139

SAN BERNARDINO
San Bernardino County Transportation Authority P482
San Bernardino County P482
Inland Counties Regional Center, Inc. P276
San Bernardino City Unified School District P482

SAN CARLOS
Rudolph And Sletten, Inc. P471

SAN CLEMENTE
Icu Medical Inc E261
Caretrust Reit Inc E81

SAN DIEGO
Mitek Systems, Inc. E328
Dexcom Inc E137
Franklin Wireless Corp E220
Axos Bank P57
Mercy Scripps Hospital P348
Southern Cal Schools Vol Emp Benefits Assoc P512
Sharp Healthcare P499
Resmed Inc. E416
Lpl Financial Holdings Inc. A648
Sharp Memorial Hospital P500
Scripps Health P488
Sempra A927
Halozyme Therapeutics Inc E243
Rady Children's Hospital And Health Center P452
Qualcomm Inc A866
Rady Children's Hospital-san Diego P452
Quidel Corp. E405
Encore Capital Group Inc E158
Rf Industries Ltd. E420
City Of San Diego P140
Axos Bank A119
San Diego Unified School District P482
Realty Income Corp E411
Neurocrine Biosciences, Inc. E346

SAN FRANCISCO
Chinese Hospital Association P123
Ilwu-pma Welfare Trust P275
Schwab Charitable Fund P487
Twitter Inc A1046
The Income Fund Of America Inc P586
University Of California P647
Swinerton Incorporated P553
Williams Sonoma Inc A1131
Levi Strauss & Co. P312
City & County Of San Francisco P126
Pg&e Corp (holding Co) A822
First Republic Bank (san Francisco, Ca) E205

Sutter Bay Hospitals P548
Dignity Health P196
American Balanced Fund, Inc. P31
Chinese Hospital Association A232
Wilbur-ellis Holdings Ii, Inc. P690
University Of California A1077
University Of California, San Francisco Foundation P648
Federal Reserve Bank Of San Francisco, Dist. No. 12 A402
Levi Strauss & Co. A629
Lendingclub Corp A627
Fundamental Investors, Inc. P234
The Gap Inc A1017
Visa Inc A1095
Block Inc A162
Glu Mobile Inc. P240
Dropbox Inc E145
Levi Strauss & Co. A631
Federal Home Loan Bank Of San Francisco A398
Uber Technologies Inc A1052
Pinterest Inc E386
City & County Of San Francisco A249
Wells Fargo & Co (new) A1115
First Republic Bank (san Francisco, Ca) A430
Ilwu-pma Benefit Plans P275
Dignity Health A327
American Balanced Fund, Inc. A57
Salesforce.com Inc A912
University Of San Francisco Inc P660

SAN JOSE
Heritage Commerce Corp A509
Mellanox Technologies, Inc. P340
Roku Inc E423
Mcafee Corp. P336
Paypal Holdings Inc A807
Sjw Group E445
Atmel Corporation P51
Xperi Holding Corp E546
Santa Clara Valley Transportation Authority P484
Western Digital Corp A1121
Cadence Design Systems Inc E73
County Of Santa Clara P176
Power Integrations Inc. E391
Ebay Inc. A355
Heritage Commerce Corp E251
Techpoint Inc E481
Parade Technologies Ltd. E370
Good Samaritan Hospital, L.p. P242
Super Micro Computer Inc E472
Sanmina Corp A913
Broadcom Inc (de) A179
City Of San Jose P140
Adobe Inc A14
Netapp, Inc. A728
Zoom Video Communications Inc E547
Lumentum Holdings Inc E305
Cisco Systems Inc A242

SAN JUAN CAPISTRANO
Capistrano Unified School District P102
Ensign Group Inc E163

SAN LEANDRO
Regional Center Of The East Bay, Inc. P460
Energy Recovery Inc E161

SAN MATEO
Franklin Resources Inc A447

Upstart Holdings Inc E513
Tesla Energy Operations, Inc. P560

SAN PEDRO
Port Of Los Angeles P438

SAN RAFAEL
County Of Marin P172
Biomarin Pharmaceutical Inc E61
Westamerica Bancorporation A1119
Autodesk Inc E43

SAN RAMON
Cooper Companies, Inc. (the) E117
Chevron Corporation A228

SANTA ANA
Allied Universal Holdco Llc P26
County Of Orange P174
Banc Of California Inc A123
Allied Universal Holdco Llc A40
County Of Orange A301
First American Financial Corp A412

SANTA BARBARA
Sonos Inc E452
American Riviera Bancorp E25
Appfolio Inc E33
Direct Relief Foundation P197
County Of Santa Barbara P176

SANTA CLARA
Nvidia Corp A760
Agilent Technologies, Inc. A27
Ehealth Inc E154
Semler Scientific Inc E436
Intel Corp A559
Svb Financial Group A983
Svb Financial Group E475
Servicenow Inc A930
Arista Networks Inc E35
Advanced Micro Devices Inc A17
Applied Materials, Inc. A89

SANTA CRUZ
Santa Cruz County Bank (ca) E428
County Of Santa Cruz P177

SANTA MONICA
Activision Blizzard, Inc. A13

SANTA ROSA
Redwood Credit Union A880
Luther Burbank Corp E305
Luther Burbank Corp A650
Summit State Bank (santa Rosa, Ca) E470
Exchange Bank (santa Rosa, Ca) A381
County Of Sonoma P177

STANFORD
Stanford Health Care A960
Leland Stanford Junior University A626
Stanford Health Services P531
Stanford Health Care P531
Leland Stanford Junior University P310

STOCKTON
Stockton Unified School District P542
Coastal Pacific Food Distributors, Inc. P146

STUDIO CITY
Motion Picture Industry Health Plan P368

SUNNYVALE
Intuitive Surgical Inc A572
Hcl America Inc. P255

Trimble Inc E496
Fortinet Inc E216

SYLMAR
Tutor Perini Corp A1045

TEMPLE CITY
Fulgent Genetics Inc E224

THOUSAND OAKS
Amgen Inc A75
Teledyne Technologies Inc E482

TORRANCE
Harbor-ucla Medical Center P253
American Honda Finance Corporation A65
Torrance Memorial Medical Center P624
Torrance Health Association, Inc. P624
American Honda Finance Corporation P34

TUSTIN
Avid Bioservices Inc E45

VALENCIA
Sunkist Growers, Inc. P546

VENTURA
The Trade Desk Inc E489

VISALIA
County Of Tulare P178
Kaweah Delta Health Care District Guild P297

WALNUT
Shea Homes Limited Partnership, A California Limited Partnership P502

WALNUT CREEK
United States Brent Oil Fund L.p. E509
United States 12 Month Oil Fund Lp E509
Central Garden & Pet Co E88
Baycom Corp E56
John Muir Health P288
United States Gasoline Fund Lp E510

WEST HOLLYWOOD
Cedars-sinai Medical Center P109

WEST SACRAMENTO
Raley's P453

WESTLAKE VILLAGE
Pennymac Mortgage Investment Trust E377
Pennymac Financial Services Inc (new) A810
Pennymac Financial Services Inc (new) E376

WHITTIER
County Sanitation District No. 2 Of Los Angeles County P180
Pih Health Whittier Hospital P432

INDEX BY HEADQUARTERS LOCATION

> A = AMERICAN BUSINESS
> E = EMERGING COMPANIES
> P = PRIVATE COMPANIES
> W = WORLD BUSINESSS

COLORADO

AURORA
Graebel Holdings, Inc. P244
University Of Colorado Health A1077
Poudre Valley Health Care, Inc. P438
University Of Colorado Health P649
Joint School District No. 28-j Of The Counties Of Adams And Arapahoe P292
Children's Hospital Colorado P120

BOULDER
The Regents Of The University Of Colorado P602

BRIGHTON
County Of Adams P166

BROOMFIELD
Mwh Global, Inc. P374
Danone Us, Inc. P189
Crocs Inc E129
Flatiron Constructors, Inc. P224
Sisters Of Charity Of Leavenworth Health System, Inc. P504

CASTLE ROCK
Douglas County School District P201

CENTENNIAL
Catholic Health Initiatives Colorado P107
Arrow Electronics, Inc. A96
Vitesse Energy Inc E529

COLORADO SPRINGS
Uch-mhs P638
Compassion International Inc P156

DENVER
Colorado State University System Foundation, Delinquent February 1, 2020 P150
Saint Joseph Hospital, Inc P477
Simply Good Foods Company (the) E443
St. Joseph Hospital, Inc. P525
Newmont Corp A735
University Of Denver P650
Vf Corp. A1090
Colorado Housing And Finance Authority A269
Civitas Resources Inc E100
University Of Colorado Hospital Authority P649
Pcl Construction Enterprises, Inc. P422
Dcp Midstream Lp A318
Denver Health And Hospitals Authority Inc P194
State Of Colorado P533
Farmland Partners Inc E185
School District 1 In The City And County Of Denver And The State Of Colorado P487
Summit Materials Inc E469
Scl Health - Front Range, Inc. P487
Antero Midstream Corp E33
First Western Financial Inc E206
Advanced Energy Industries Inc E5
M.d.c. Holdings, Inc. A652

Ovintiv Inc A791
University Of Colorado P649
Davita Inc A316
Modivcare Solutions, Llc P363
Re/max Holdings Inc E410
State Of Colorado A967

DURANGO
Saddle Butte Pipeline Llc P475

ENGLEWOOD
Zynex Inc E547
Ttec Holdings Inc E499
Dish Network Corp A332
Qurate Retail Inc A872
American Furniture Warehouse Co. P33
Liberty Media Corp (de) A633
Commonspirit Health Research Institute P152
Qurate Retail Inc A870
Liberty Broadband Corp E300

FORT COLLINS
Colorado State University P150

GLENWOOD SPRINGS
Alpine Banks Of Colorado E19

GOLDEN
Jefferson County School District No. R-1 P286
Good Times Restaurants Inc. E235

GREELEY
Hensel Phelps Construction Co. P261
Hensel Phelps Construction Co. A508
Pilgrims Pride Corp. A827

GREENWOOD VILLAGE
National Bank Holdings Corp A721
National Storage Affiliates Trust E340
Air Methods Corporation P12
National Bank Holdings Corp E339
Cobank, Acb P147
Cobank, Acb A261

HENDERSON
Myr Group Inc E337

LAKEWOOD
Solera National Bancorp Inc E451
Natural Grocers By Vitamin Cottage Inc E342

LITTLETON
Kiewit Building Group Inc. P300
Thompson Creek Metals Company Usa P621

LOVELAND
Medical Center Of The Rockies P339

WATKINS
Pure Cycle Corp. E402

WESTMINSTER
Ball Corp A122

CONNECTICUT

BLOOMFIELD
Cigna Corp (new) A237

BRANFORD
Sachem Capital Corp E425

BRIDGEPORT
Bridgeport Hospital P93
People's United Financial Inc E378
People's United Financial Inc A813

BROOKFIELD
Photronics, Inc. E383

CHESHIRE
Bozzuto's, Inc. P91
Lane Industries Incorporated P307
The Lane Construction Corporation P588

DANBURY
The Danbury Hospital P576

FAIRFIELD
Save The Children Federation, Inc. P485

FARMINGTON
Otis Worldwide Corp A790

GREENWICH
Xpo Logistics, Inc. A1142
Berkley (wr) Corp A149
Interactive Brokers Group Inc E278
Starwood Property Trust Inc. E462
Starwood Property Trust Inc. A965
Gxo Logistics Inc A493

HARTFORD
City Of Hartford P132
Hartford Financial Services Group Inc. A500
Eversource Energy Service Company P218
Virtus Investment Partners Inc E528
Hartford Healthcare Corporation P254

MASHANTUCKET
Mashantucket Pequot Gaming Enterprise Inc P331

MILFORD
Doctor's Associates Inc. P199

NEW BRITAIN
Stanley Black & Decker Inc A961

NEW HAVEN
Knights Of Columbus P302
City Of New Haven P134
Knights Of Columbus A607
Yale New Haven Hospital, Inc. P694
Yale University P695
Yale New Haven Health Services Corporation P694

NORWALK
Frontier Communications Parent Inc A452
Emcor Group, Inc. A363
Xerox Holdings Corp A1140
Booking Holdings Inc A168

OLD GREENWICH
Ellington Residential Mortgaging Real Estate Investment Trust E155

ORANGE
The United Illuminating Company P610
Avangrid Inc A112

SHELTON
Prudential Annuities Life Assurance Corp A855

SOUTH WINDSOR
Gerber Scientific Products Inc P239

STAMFORD
Dorian Lpg Ltd. E144
Lovesac Co E305
Synchrony Financial A985
Americares Foundation, Inc. P37
Equinor Natural Gas Llc P217
Tenerity, Inc. P559

World Wrestling Entertainment Inc E542
Equinor Marketing & Trading (us) Inc. P217
United Rentals Inc A1070
Cara Therapeutics Inc E80
Charter Communications Inc (new) A222
Tudor Investment Corporation P634
Lexa International Corporation P314
Equinor Marketing & Trading (us) Inc. A377
The Stamford Hospital P606
City Of Stamford P141

WALLINGFORD
Amphenol Corp. A78

WATERBURY
City Of Waterbury P142
Webster Financial Corp (waterbury, Conn) A1112

WESTPORT
Csc Sugar, Llc P184
Compass Diversified E114

WILTON
Blue Buffalo Pet Products, Inc. P82

WINDSOR
Trc Companies, Inc. P625

DELAWARE

DOVER
State Of Delaware A967
State Of Delaware P533
Bayhealth Medical Center, Inc. P68

LEWES
Beebe Medical Center, Inc. P73

NEWARK
University Of Delaware P649
Slm Corp. A943
Slm Corp. E448

WILMINGTON
Wsfs Financial Corp A1137
Wilmington Trust Company P691
Navient Corp A723
Alfred I.dupont Hospital For Children P21
Dupont De Nemours Inc A348
Founders Bay Holdings E217
Incyte Corporation E266
Barclays Bank Delaware A138
Balfour Beatty, Llc P59
Wilmington Trust Company A1132
The Bancorp Inc A1013
Chemours Co (the) A224
Wsfs Financial Corp E543
The Bancorp Inc E487
Barclays Bank Delaware P64

INDEX BY HEADQUARTERS LOCATION

A = AMERICAN BUSINESS
E = EMERGING COMPANIES
P = PRIVATE COMPANIES
W = WORLD BUSINESSS

DISTRICT OF COLUMBIA

WASHINGTON
Costar Group, Inc. E122
Financial Industry Regulatory Authority, Inc. P223
Easterly Government Properties Inc E150
Aarp P2
Medstar-georgetown Medical Center, Inc. P340
National Association Of Letter Carriers P376
Corporation For Public Broadcasting P165
Children's Hospital P119
U.s. General Services Administration P636
District Of Columbia Water & Sewer Authority P197
Fannie Mae A390
Population Services International P437
Federal Reserve System A402
American Chemical Society P31
Carlyle Group Inc (the) A201
National Railroad Passenger Corporation P377
Pti Consulting Inc. E223
Government Of District Of Columbia P243
Vanda Pharmaceuticals Inc E517
Pan American Health Organization Inc P419
Washington Hospital Center Corporation P681
Publishing Office, Us Government P449
Wgl Holdings, Inc. P687
Securities Investor Protection Corporation A924
U.s. General Services Administration A1050
Dc Water And Sewer Authority P192
Smithsonian Institution P507
Childrens Hospital P122
Danaher Corp A314
The George Washington University P583
Federal Agricultural Mortgage Corp A395
The Georgetown University P584
Federal Agricultural Mortgage Corp E186
Government Of District Of Columbia A483

FLORIDA

ALTAMONTE SPRINGS
Adventist Health System/sunbelt, Inc. P5
Adventist Health System/sunbelt, Inc. A19

BARTOW
Polk County P437
Polk County School District P437

BOCA RATON
Adt Inc (de) A16
Newtek Business Services Corp E347
Celsius Holdings Inc E88
Johnson Controls Fire Protection Lp P291
Odp Corp (the) A769
Dcr Workforce, Inc. P192

BRADENTON
Beall's, Inc. P71

CLEARWATER
Morton Plant Hospital Association, Inc. P367
Marinemax Inc E309
Baycare Health System, Inc. P68

COCOA
Southeast Petro Distributors, Inc. P512

COCONUT CREEK
Food For The Poor, Inc. P227
Willis Lease Finance Corp. E538

CORAL GABLES
Professional Holding Corp E397
Mastec Inc. (fl) A667
Amerant Bancorp Inc A52

DANIA BEACH
Chewy Inc A231

DAVIE
Nova Southeastern University, Inc. P403

DAYTONA BEACH
Alpine Income Property Trust Inc E19
Topbuild Corp E490
Brown & Brown Inc E67

DELAND
County Of Volusia P179

DELRAY BEACH
Morse Operations, Inc. P367

ESTERO
The Hertz Corporation A1019
Hertz Global Holdings Inc (new) A512
The Hertz Corporation P585

FORT LAUDERDALE
North Broward Hospital District P394
County Of Broward P167
Eyp Stockbridge, Llc P219
School Board Of Broward County, The (inc) P486
Universal Insurance Holdings Inc E511
Seacor Holdings Inc. P490
Autonation, Inc. A108
Ocean Bio-chem, Inc. E358
Avant Garde Academy Foundation, Inc. P55

FORT MYERS
21st Century Oncology Holdings, Inc P1
County Of Lee P171
Lee Memorial Hospital, Inc. P308
Finemark Holdings Inc E190
Lee Memorial Health System Foundation, Inc. P307

GAINESVILLE
University Of Florida P651

Florida Clinical Practice Association, Inc. P224
Shands Teaching Hospital And Clinics, Inc. P499

HOLLYWOOD
South Broward Hospital District P509
Nv5 Global Inc E356

JACKSONVILLE
Shands Jacksonville Medical Center, Inc. P498
Equity One, Inc. A378
Csx Corp A303
Fidelity National Financial Inc A406
Shands Jacksonville Healthcare, Inc. P498
Frp Holdings Inc E222
Southern Baptist Hospital Of Florida Inc. P512
Fidelity National Information Services Inc A407
City Of Jacksonville P132
Crowley Maritime Corporation P182
Duval County School Board (inc) P206
Jacksonville Electric Authority P284
Landstar System, Inc. A619
Baptist Health System, Inc. P62

JUNO BEACH
Nextera Energy Inc A738
Florida Power & Light Co. A436

KISSIMMEE
The School District Of Osceola County Florida P605

LAKELAND
Publix Super Markets, Inc. A859
Lakeland Regional Health Systems, Inc. P306
Lakeland Regional Medical Center, Inc. P306

MAITLAND
Florida Hospital Medical Group, Inc. P225

MELBOURNE
L3harris Technologies Inc A612

MIAMI
Ryder System, Inc. A908
The School Board Of Miami-dade County P605
Miami Children's Health System Management Services, Llc P354
The Public Health Trust Of Miami-dade County P602
Lennar Corp A627
City Of Miami P134
Evi Industries Inc E176
Watsco Inc. A1110
Baptist Hospital Of Miami, Inc. P63
Veru Inc E521
World Fuel Services Corp. A1134
Ladenburg Thalmann Financial Services Inc. P305
Aura Minerals Inc (british Virgin Islands) E43
Miami-dade Aviation Department P355

MIAMI BEACH
Mount Sinai Medical Center Of Florida, Inc. P369

MIAMI LAKES
Bankunited Inc. A134

MULBERRY
W.s. Badcock Corporation P677

NEW PORT RICHEY
County Of Pasco P175

NORTH VENICE
Pgt Innovations Inc E381

ORLANDO
County Of Orange P174
City Of Orlando P137
Florida Municipal Power Agency P225
The University Of Central Florida Board Of Trustees P610
The Orange County Public School District P598
Orlando Health, Inc. P414
School Board Of Orange County Florida P487
Campus Crusade For Christ Inc P101
Darden Restaurants, Inc. A315

PALM BEACH GARDENS
Carrier Global Corp A206

PANAMA CITY BEACH
St. Joe Co. (the) E458

PONTE VEDRA BEACH
Pga Tour, Inc. P429

ROCKLEDGE
Health First Shared Services, Inc. P256

SAINT PETERSBURG
Raymond James & Associates Inc A874
Johns Hopkins All Children's Hospital, Inc. P288
Pscu Incorporated P446
Raymond James & Associates Inc P454

SARASOTA
County Of Sarasota P177
Helios Technologies Inc E249
Roper Technologies Inc A902
Sarasota County Public Hospital District P484

SEFFNER
Lazydays Holdings Inc E292

SEMINOLE
Superior Group Of Companies Inc E473

SOUTH MIAMI
Baptist Health South Florida, Inc. P61

ST. PETERSBURG
Raymond James Financial, Inc. A874
Duke Energy Florida Llc A347
Jabil Inc A577
United Insurance Holdings Corp A1066

STUART
Seacoast Banking Corp. Of Florida E432
Seacoast Banking Corp. Of Florida A922

INDEX BY HEADQUARTERS LOCATION

```
A = AMERICAN BUSINESS
E = EMERGING COMPANIES
P = PRIVATE COMPANIES
W = WORLD BUSINESSS
```

Martin Memorial Medical Center, Inc. P329
SUNNY ISLES BEACH
Icahn Enterprises Lp A548
SUNRISE
Alliance Entertainment Holding Corporation P25
TALLAHASSEE
Florida Department Of Lottery P224
Florida State University P226
Capital City Bank Group, Inc. E79
Florida Department Of Lottery A435
Capital City Bank Group, Inc. A196
TAMPA
Shriners Hospitals For Children P503
Avi-spl Holdings, Inc. P57
County Of Hillsborough P170
City Of Tampa P142
Seminole Electric Cooperative, Inc. P493
H. Lee Moffitt Cancer Center And Research Institute, Inc. P251
Florida Health Sciences Center, Inc. P225
Helm Fertilizer Corporation (florida) P259
Mosaic Co (the) A714
Hillsborough County School District P264
Sila Realty Trust Inc E441
St. Joseph's Hospital, Inc. P527
University Community Hospital, Inc. P643
University Of South Florida P661
H. Lee Moffitt Cancer Center And Research Institute Hospital, Inc. P251
Pacira Biosciences Inc E369
VERO BEACH
Armour Residential Reit Inc. A96
Orchid Island Capital Inc A787
VIERA
School Board Of Brevard County P486
WEST PALM BEACH
The School District Of West Palm Beach County P605
County Of Palm Beach P174
South Florida Water Management District Leasing Corp. P511
School Board Of Palm Beach County P487
WINTER HAVEN
Southstate Corp E455
Southstate Corp A954
WINTER PARK
Anc Healthcare, Inc. P38

GEORGIA

ACWORTH
Cobb County Public Schools P148
ALPHARETTA
Touchmark Bancshares Inc E492
Evans General Contractors, Llc P218
National Christian Charitable Foundation, Inc. P376
Jackson Healthcare, Llc P284
ATHENS
University Of Georgia P651
Piedmont Athens Regional Medical Center, Inc. P431
ATLANTA
Georgia Caresource Co P238
Federal Reserve Bank Of Atlanta, Dist. No. 6 A398
Cooperative For Assistance And Relief Everywhere, Inc. (care) P162
Westrock Co A1124
Piedmont Hospital, Inc. P431
Board Of Regents Of The University System Of Georgia P87
Cousins Properties Inc E124
Ameris Bancorp A71
County Of Fulton P169
Rollins, Inc. E423
Floor & Decor Holdings Inc E210
Ncr Corp A724
Greensky Inc E240
Global Payments Inc A476
State Of Georgia P533
Ameris Bancorp E28
Northside Hospital, Inc. P400
Delta Air Lines Inc (de) A322
Atlanticus Holdings Corp E41
Newell Brands Inc A734
Intercontinental Exchange Inc A560
Georgia Power Co A470
Wells Real Estate Investment Trust Ii P683
Heartland Payment Systems, Llc P258
Invesco Mortgage Capital Inc A573
Fulton County Board Of Education P234
Norfolk Southern Corp A746
Pratt Industries, Inc. P440
Veritiv Corp A1086
Lettie Pate Evans Foundation, Inc. A629
Georgia Housing Finance Authority A470
Pultegroup Inc A860
Emory University Hospital Midtown P214
Municipal Electric Authority Of Georgia P371
Board Of Regents Of The University System Of Georgia A163
City Of Atlanta P128
Altisource Solutions, Inc. P30
Unipro Foodservice, Inc. P640
Gray Television Inc E236
Invesco Ltd A573
Dlh Holdings Corp E143
United Parcel Service Inc A1069
State Of Georgia A967
Coca-cola Co (the) A262
Georgia Tech Applied Research Corporation P239
Grady Memorial Hospital Corporation P244
Genuine Parts Co. A467
Graphic Packaging Holding Co A485
Southern Company (the) A952
Atlantic Capital Bancshares Inc A105
Home Depot Inc A524
AUGUSTA
Au Health System, Inc. P53

BALL GROUND
Chart Industries Inc E95
BLAIRSVILLE
United Community Banks Inc (blairsville, Ga) A1064
United Community Banks Inc (blairsville, Ga) E508
BRUNSWICK
Map International P327
BUFORD
Onewater Marine Inc E361
CALHOUN
Mohawk Industries, Inc. A705
COLUMBUS
Synovus Financial Corp A986
Synovus Financial Corp E477
Aflac Inc A23
CONYERS
Pratt Corrugated Holdings, Inc. P440
CUMMING
Forsyth County Board Of Education P228
DECATUR
Dekalb County Public Library P194
Global Health Solutions, Inc. P240
County Of Dekalb P168
DORAVILLE
Metrocity Bankshares Inc E323
DUBLIN
Morris St Bancshares Inc E333
DULUTH
Fox Factory Holding Corp E217
Primerica Inc E395
Agco Corp. A25
National Vision Holdings Inc E341
Asbury Automotive Group Inc A99
Primerica Inc A845
FITZGERALD
Colony Bankcorp, Inc. E108
GAINESVILLE
Northeast Georgia Medical Center, Inc. P398
Sun Valley Energy, Inc. P546
JEFFERSON
Jackson Electric Membership Corporation P283
JOHNS CREEK
Ebix Inc E152
Saia Inc E426
LAWRENCEVILLE
Gwinnett Hospital System, Inc. P250
MARIETTA
The Conlan Company P575
Cobb Electric Membership Corporation P148
Kennestone Hospital At Windy Hill, Inc. P297
Cobb County School District P148
Cobb County Medical Examiner's Office P148
Kennestone Hospital Inc P297
Cobb County Board Of Education P148
NORCROSS
The Salvation Army P604
Corecard Corp E122

PENDERGRASS
Toray Tcac Holding Usa Inc. P623
ROSWELL
Siteone Landscape Supply Inc E445
SAVANNAH
The Savannah College Of Art And Design Inc P604
Board Of Education For The City Of Savannah And The County Of Chatham (inc) P86
Savannah-chatham County Board Of Education P485
Memorial Health, Inc. P342
STONE MOUNTAIN
Dekalb County Board Of Education P193
SUWANEE
Gwinnett County Board Of Education P250
TEMPLE
Janus International Group Inc E283
THOMASVILLE
Thomasville Bancshares, Inc. E489
TUCKER
Gms Inc E234
WEST POINT
Hyundai Transys Georgia Powertrain, Inc. P273

HAWAII

HILO
County Of Hawaii P170
HONOLULU
University Of Hawaii System P652
Central Pacific Financial Corp A219
Barnwell Industries, Inc. E56
Hawai I Pacific Health P255
Suasin Cancer Care Inc. P543
Servco Pacific Inc. P495
State Of Hawaii P533
City & County Of Honolulu P126
Bank Of Hawaii Corp A128
First Hawaiian Inc A423
The Queen's Health Systems P602
University Of Hawai'i Of Manoa P652
Trustees Of The Estate Of Bernice Pauahi Bishop P632
State Of Hawaii A967
WAILUKU
County Of Maui P172

IDAHO

BOISE
St. Luke's Regional Medical Center, Ltd. P529

INDEX BY HEADQUARTERS LOCATION

```
A = AMERICAN BUSINESS
E = EMERGING COMPANIES
P = PRIVATE COMPANIES
W = WORLD BUSINESSS
```

Albertsons Companies, Inc. P18
Micron Technology Inc. A698
The Amalgamated Sugar Company Llc P566
Albertsons Companies Inc A35
Public Employee Retirement System, Idaho A857
Dbsi Inc P192
Saint Alphonsus Regional Medical Center, Inc. P476
State Of Idaho P533
Albertsons Companies, Inc. A35
St. Luke's Health System, Ltd. P528
Boise Cascade Co. (de) A165
Saint Alphonsus Regional Medical Center Inc. P476
Public Employee Retirement System, Idaho P447
Snake River Sugar Company P508
Winco Holdings, Inc. P691
State Of Idaho A967

COEUR D ALENE
Kootenai Hospital District P303

EAGLE
Pennant Group Inc E376

ILLINOIS

ABBOTT PARK
Abbott Laboratories A5

AURORA
Old Second Bancorp., Inc. (aurora, Ill.) E359
Old Second Bancorp., Inc. (aurora, Ill.) A774

BLOOMINGTON
Hbt Financial Inc A503
Growmark, Inc. P247
Growmark, Inc. A492

BOLINGBROOK
Ulta Beauty Inc A1055

BUFFALO GROVE
Produce Alliance, L.l.c. P444

CARBONDALE
Southern Illinois University Inc P513
Southern Illinois Healthcare Enterprises, Inc. P512

CARLINVILLE
Cnb Bank Shares Inc E102

CHAMPAIGN
First Busey Corp E193
First Busey Corp A415

CHICAGO
Hometown America Management Corp. A528
Kemper Corp (de) A598
Illinois Housing Development Authority (inc) P274
Ggp, Inc. P239
Chicago Community Trust P118
Motorola Solutions Inc A715
Regional Transportation Authority P460

Central Steel And Wire Company, Llc P112
Old Republic International Corp. A773
Crowe Llp P182
Newark Corporation P389
Commonspirit Health P152
Metropolitan Water Reclamation District Of Greater Chicago P352
Usg Corporation P669
Enova International Inc E162
Loyola University Of Chicago Inc P321
Pepper Construction Group, Llc P426
United Airlines Holdings Inc A1061
The Walsh Group Ltd P618
Mondelez International Inc A707
Federal Reserve Bank Of Chicago, Dist. No. 7 A399
Chicago Park District P118
De Paul University P192
Green Thumb Industries Inc E239
Board Of Education Of City Of Chicago A163
Littelfuse Inc E302
Ggp, Inc. A472
The University Of Chicago Medical Center P611
Rush University Medical Center P471
Mcdonald's Corp A673
Northwestern Memorial Hospital P402
University Of Chicago P648
Morningstar Inc P331
Northern Trust Corp A747
Brookfield Properties Retail Inc. P95
North Advocate Side Health Network P393
Cboe Global Markets Inc E86
Blue Cross & Blue Shield Association P83
Commonspirit Health A278
Exelon Corp A381
Byline Bancorp Inc A188
Jones Lang Lasalle Inc A587
Archer Daniels Midland Co. A93
Telephone & Data Systems Inc A1000
Ge Healthcare Technologies Inc A458
The Pepper Companies Inc P601
Transunion E493
Ann & Robert H. Lurie Children's Hospital Of Chicago P39
Boeing Co. (the) A163
Cna Financial Corp A257
Lkq Corp A642
Walsh Construction Company P680
Byline Bancorp Inc E71
Family Health Network, Inc. P220
Conagra Brands Inc A284
R. R. Donnelley & Sons Company P450
Pepper Construction Company P426
Marquette National Corp (il) E311
Board Of Education Of City Of Chicago P86
Azek Co Inc (the) E48

DEERFIELD
Baxter International Inc A140
Caterpillar Inc. A209
Walgreens Boots Alliance Inc A1100
Scai Holdings, Llc P486
Fortune Brands Home & Security, Inc. A446

DES PLAINES
Brg Sports, Inc. P92

DOWNERS GROVE
Univar Solutions Inc A1075
Advocate Health And Hospitals Corporation P7
Ftd Companies, Inc. P234
Advocate Health And Hospitals Corporation A19
Illinois State Of Toll Highway Authority P275
Dover Corp A340

EDWARDSVILLE
Prairie Farms Dairy, Inc. P439

EFFINGHAM
Midland States Bancorp Inc E326
Midland States Bancorp Inc A702

EVANSTON
Northwestern University P402
North Shore University Health System P397

FRANKLIN PARK
Hill Fire Protection, Llc P263
Hill Fire Protection, Llc A515

GLENVIEW
Illinois Tool Works, Inc. A551

HARVEY
Atkore Inc E39

HINSDALE
Adventist Midwest Health P7

JOLIET
Central Grocers, Inc. P111

LAKE FOREST
Grainger (w.w.) Inc. A484
Tenneco Inc A1003
Packaging Corp Of America A798

LINCOLNSHIRE
Cdw Corp A214
Camping World Holdings Inc A195
Zebra Technologies Corp. A1147
Wipro, Llc P691

MATTOON
Consolidated Communications Holdings Inc E116
First Mid Bancshares Inc A427
First Mid Bancshares Inc E204

MAYWOOD
Loyola University Medical Center P321

METTAWA
Brunswick Corp. A181

MILAN
Group O, Inc. P246

MOLINE
Qcr Holdings Inc E403
Qcr Holdings Inc A865
Deere & Co. A319

NAPERVILLE
Edward Hospital P210

NORTH CHICAGO
Abbvie Inc A7

NORTHBROOK
Allstate Corp A41

OAK BROOK
Ace Hardware Corporation A11
Federal Signal Corp. E187
Ace Hardware Corporation P4

OTTAWA
First Ottawa Bancshares Inc E204

PALATINE
Weber Inc E532

PARIS
North American Lighting, Inc. P393

PARK RIDGE
Advocate Health And Hospitals Corporation P7

PEORIA
Rli Corp A895
Rli Corp E422
Osf Healthcare System P415

RIVERWOODS
Discover Financial Services A329

ROCK ISLAND
Modern Woodmen Of America A704
Modern Woodmen Of America P362

ROCKFORD
Mercy Health Corporation P347

ROLLING MEADOWS
Kimball Hill Inc P301
Gallagher (arthur J.) & Co. A455
Cambium Networks Corp E77

ROSEMONT
Wintrust Financial Corp (il) A1133
The Big Ten Conference Inc P568
Wintrust Financial Corp (il) E540
Us Foods Holding Corp A1083

SCHAUMBURG
Paylocity Holding Corp E374

SPRINGFIELD
State Of Illinois A968
Memorial Medical Center P342
Horace Mann Educators Corp. A531
State Of Illinois P533
St. John's Hospital Of The Hospital Sisters Of The Third Order Of St. Francis P523

TINLEY PARK
Panduit Corp. P419

URBANA
Carle Foundation Hospital P105

VERNON HILLS
Graham Enterprise, Inc. P244

WARRENVILLE
Edward-elmhurst Healthcare P210

WESTCHESTER
Ingredion Inc A556

WOODSTOCK
Mercy Woodstock Medical Center P349

INDIANA

BATESVILLE
Hillenbrand Inc E254

BLOOMINGTON
Indiana University P276

INDEX BY HEADQUARTERS LOCATION

```
A = AMERICAN BUSINESS
E = EMERGING COMPANIES
P = PRIVATE COMPANIES
W = WORLD BUSINESSS
```

Hoosier Energy Rural Electric
  Cooperative Inc P267
Trustees Of Indiana University P632

BROOKVILLE
Fcn Banc Corp E185

CARMEL
Merchants Bancorp (indiana) E318
Cno Financial Group Inc A260
Merchants Bancorp (indiana) A681

COLUMBUS
Cummins, Inc. A305

CONVERSE
First Farmers Financial Corp E196

DANVILLE
Hendricks County Hospital P259

ELKHART
Thor Industries, Inc. A1027
Lci Industries E292
Patrick Industries Inc E372

EVANSVILLE
Deaconess Hospital Inc P193
Berry Global Group Inc A152
Southern Indiana Gas & Electric
  Company P513
Escalade, Inc. E172
Old National Bancorp (evansville, In)
  A772
Van Atlas Lines Inc P672
Onemain Finance Corp E361
St. Mary's Health, Inc. P529
Atlas World Group, Inc. P51
Onemain Holdings Inc A780

FISHERS
First Internet Bancorp E201
First Internet Bancorp A425

FORT WAYNE
Steel Dynamics Inc. A974
Petroleum Traders Corporation P429
Do It Best Corp. P199

HIGHLAND
Strack And Van Til Super Market Inc.
  P543

INDIANAPOLIS
State Of Indiana A968
Duke Realty Corp E146
The Finish Line Inc P580
Anthem Inc A83
Lilly (eli) & Co A634
State Of Indiana P533
Community Health Network, Inc.
  P154
National Collegiate Athletic
  Association P376
Countrymark Cooperative Holding
  Corporation P165
Citizens Energy Group P125
Corteva Inc A298

JASPER
German American Bancorp Inc E229
Kimball Electronics Inc E287
German American Bancorp Inc A471

JEFFERSONVILLE
First Savings Financial Group Inc
  E206

LA GRANGE
Fs Bancorp (indiana) E222

MERRILLVILLE
Northern Indiana Public Service
  Company Llc P399

MICHIGAN CITY
Horizon Bancorp Inc E259
Horizon Bancorp Inc A532

MISHAWAKA
Franciscan Alliance, Inc. P229

MUNCIE
First Merchants Corp E203
First Merchants Corp A426

MUNSTER
Community Foundation Of Northwest
  Indiana, Inc. P154
Finward Bancorp E191
Munster Medical Research
  Foundation, Inc P373

NOBLESVILLE
Riverview Hospital P465

RICHMOND
Richmond Mutual Bancorporation Inc
  E421

SOUTH BEND
1st Source Corp A1

TERRE HAUTE
First Financial Corp. (in) A422

UNION CITY
Cardinal Ethanol Llc E81

WARSAW
Lakeland Financial Corp A617
Lakeland Financial Corp E289
Zimmer Biomet Holdings Inc A1149

WEST LAFAYETTE
Inotiv Inc E272

IOWA

AMES
Danfoss Power Solutions Inc. P189
Ames National Corp. E29
Iowa State University Of Science And
  Technology P280

ANKENY
Casey's General Stores, Inc. A208
Perishable Distributors Of Iowa, Ltd.
  P426

CEDAR RAPIDS
Crst International, Inc. P183
United Fire Group, Inc. A1065

DAVENPORT
Lee Enterprises, Inc. E294
Genesis Health System P237

DES MOINES
Principal Financial Group Inc A845
Central Iowa Hospital Corp P112
State Of Iowa P534
Federal Home Loan Bank Of Des
  Moines A397
Catholic Health Initiatives - Iowa,
  Corp. P107
State Of Iowa A968

DUBUQUE
Heartland Financial Usa, Inc.
  (dubuque, Ia) A506
Heartland Financial Usa, Inc.
  (dubuque, Ia) E248

FARNHAMVILLE
Farmers Cooperative Company P221

HILLS
Hills Bancorporation A515

IOWA CITY
The University Of Iowa P612
Midwestone Financial Group, Inc.
  E327
Midwestone Financial Group, Inc.
  A703
University Of Iowa Hospitals And
  Clinics P653
The University Of Iowa P613

JOHNSTON
Iowa Physicians Clinic Medical
  Foundation P280

MASON CITY
Mercy Health Services-iowa, Corp.
  P347

MONTICELLO
Innovative Ag Services Co. P276

WEST BURLINGTON
Big River Resources, Llc. P79

WEST DES MOINES
American Equity Investment Life
  Holding Co A60
Hy-vee, Inc. P272
West Bancorporation, Inc. E533
Heartland Co-op P258
West Bancorporation, Inc. A1118
Hy-vee, Inc. A548
Iowa Health System P280

KANSAS

KANSAS CITY
Associated Wholesale Grocers, Inc.
  P48
The University Of Kansas Hospital
  Authority P613
Dairy Farmers Of America, Inc. P185
Associated Wholesale Grocers, Inc.
  A101
Dairy Farmers Of America, Inc. A311

LEAWOOD
The Sunderland Foundation P607
Tallgrass Energy, Lp P554
Crossfirst Bankshares Inc A301
Crossfirst Bankshares Inc E131
Amc Entertainment Inc. P30

LENEXA
Hostess Brands Inc E260

MANHATTAN
Landmark Bancorp Inc E291
Kansas State University P296

MCPHERSON
Chs Mcpherson Refinery Inc. P124

MERRIAM
Seaboard Corp. A921

OLATHE
Tsvc, Inc. P634
D. H. Pace Company, Inc. P185
County Of Johnson P171
Terracon Consultants, Inc. P560

OVERLAND PARK
Selectquote Inc E435

Servant Foundation P495
Npc Restaurant Holdings, Llc
  P404
Black & Veatch International
  Company P81
Black & Veatch Holding
  Company P81
Bvh, Inc. P98

SHAWNEE MISSION
Shawnee Mission Medical Center,
  Inc.
  P501

TOPEKA
State Of Kansas P534
Capitol Federal Financial Inc A199
Stormont-vail Healthcare, Inc.
  P543
Kansas Department Of
  Transportation
  P295
State Of Kansas A968

WICHITA
Equity Bancshares Inc A378
Ascension Via Christi Hospitals
  Wichita, Inc. P46
Wesley Medical Center, Llc P684
Unified School District 259 P639

KENTUCKY

ASHLAND
King's Daughters Health System,
  Inc.
  P301

BOWLING GREEN
Houchens Industries, Inc. P268
Commonwealth Health
  Corporation,
  Inc. P153

EDGEWOOD
Saint Elizabeth Medical Center,
  Inc.
  P477

FRANKFORT
Commonwealth Of Kentucky
  A278
Commonwealth Of Kentucky
  P153

FRANKLIN
Keystops, Llc P299

HENDERSON
Big Rivers Electric Corporation
  P79

LEXINGTON
Appalachian Regional Healthcare,
  Inc.
  P41
Valvoline Inc E517
The Board Of Education Of
  Fayette
  County P568

LOUISVILLE
Humana Inc. A540
Baptist Healthcare System, Inc.
  P62
Stock Yards Bancorp Inc A977
Yum! Brands Inc A1145
Republic Bancorp, Inc. (ky) E415

INDEX BY HEADQUARTERS LOCATION

```
A = AMERICAN BUSINESS
E = EMERGING COMPANIES
P = PRIVATE COMPANIES
W = WORLD BUSINESSS
```

Louisville-jefferson County Metro Government P320
Turning Point Brands Inc E501
Uofl Health, Inc. P667
Almost Family, Inc. P26
University Health Care, Inc. P643
University Of Louisville P653
Republic Bancorp, Inc. (ky) A889
Stock Yards Bancorp Inc E465
Limestone Bancorp Inc E301
University Medical Center Inc P645
Norton Hospitals, Inc P403

PIKEVILLE
Pikeville Medical Center, Inc. P432
Community Trust Bancorp, Inc. A282

LOUISIANA

ABBEVILLE
Coastal Chemical Co., L.l.c. P146

ALEXANDRIA
Red River Bancshares Inc A880
Red River Bancshares Inc E412

BATON ROUGE
Mmr Constructors, Inc. P362
State Of Louisiana A968
Mmr Group, Inc. P362
Franciscan Missionaries Of Our Lady Health System, Inc. P230
City Of Baton Rouge P129
Business First Bancshares Inc A188
Amedisys, Inc. E20
State Of Louisiana P534
University Of Louisiana System Foundation P653
Our Lady Of The Lake Hospital, Inc. P416
Investar Holding Corp E279
Business First Bancshares Inc E69

CHALMETTE
Chalmette Refining, L.l.c. A222
Chalmette Refining, L.l.c. P114

COVINGTON
Cgb Enterprises, Inc. P114
Pool Corp E388
Zen-noh Grain Corporation P696
St. Tammany Parish School Board P530
Cgb Enterprises, Inc. A221
Zen-noh Grain Corporation A1148

GRETNA
Parish Of Jefferson P420

HAMMOND
First Guaranty Bancshares, Inc. E199

JEFFERSON
Ochsner Clinic Foundation P407
Ochsner Clinic Foundation A769

LAFAYETTE
Home Bancorp Inc A523
Home Bancorp Inc E257
Viemed Healthcare Inc E526
Lhc Group Inc E299

LAKE CHARLES
Central Crude, Inc. P111

MONROE
Lumen Technologies Inc A649
Qwest Corp A872

NEW ORLEANS
Entergy Corp A369
Ochsner Health System P407
Entergy Services, Llc P215
Louisiana Childrens Medical Center, Inc P320
Orleans Parish School District P415
Walton Construction - A Core Company, Llc P680
University Medical Center Management Corporation P645
The Administrators Of The Tulane Educational Fund P565
City Of New Orleans P135

RUSTON
Origin Bancorp Inc A788
Origin Bancorp Inc E364

SCHRIEVER
Rouse's Enterprises, L.l.c. P470

MAINE

AUGUSTA
Mainegeneral Health P325
State Of Maine P534
Maine Municipal Bond Bank A654
State Of Maine A968

BANGOR
Eastern Maine Medical Center P209

BAR HARBOR
Bar Harbor Bankshares E55
Bar Harbor Bankshares A137

BREWER
Eastern Maine Healthcare Systems P208

CAMDEN
Camden National Corp. (me) A192

DAMARISCOTTA
Miles Health Care, Inc P357
First Bancorp Inc (me) E192

PORTLAND
Northeast Bank (me) E350
Martin's Point Health Care, Inc. P330
Mainehealth P325
Maine Medical Center P325

WESTBROOK
Idexx Laboratories, Inc. E262

MARYLAND

ADELPHI
University System Of Maryland P665

ANNAPOLIS
Hannon Armstrong Sustainable Infrastructure Capital Inc E245
State Of Maryland A968
County Of Anne Arundel P166
State Of Maryland P534
Luminis Health Anne Arundel Medical Center, Inc P322
Anne Arundel County Board Of Education P40

BALTIMORE
T Rowe Price Group Inc. A990
Johns Hopkins University A583
Franklin Square Hospital Center, Inc. P231
Mercy Health Services, Inc. P347
Catholic Relief Services - United States Conference Of Catholic Bishops P108
Under Armour Inc A1058
Johns Hopkins Hospital P290
Constellation Energy Corp A292
The Whiting-turner Contracting Company P619
Lifebridge Health, Inc. P316
University Of Maryland Medical System Corporation P654
City Of Baltimore P129
Sinai Hospital Of Baltimore, Inc. P504
The Johns Hopkins Health System Corporation P587
Maryland Transportation Authority P331
Gbmc Healthcare, Inc. P235
Johns Hopkins University P290
Johns Hopkins Bayview Medical Center, Inc. P289
The Whiting-turner Contracting Company A1025
Baltimore City Public Schools P59
Medifast Inc E316
The Johns Hopkins Health System Corporation A1019

BEL AIR
County Of Harford P170

BETHESDA
Marriott International, Inc. A659
Eagle Bancorp Inc (md) E148
Lockheed Martin Corp A643
Enviva Inc E169
Eagle Bancorp Inc (md) A349
Agnc Investment Corp A28
The Henry M Jackson Foundation For The Advancement Of Military Medicine Inc P585
Walker & Dunlop Inc E530

COLLEGE PARK
University Of Maryland, College Park P655

COLUMBIA
Medstar Health, Inc. A679
Medstar Health, Inc. P339
Maxim Healthcare Services, Inc. P334

EDGEMERE
Bv Financial Inc E69

ELLICOTT CITY
Howard County Of Maryland (inc) P271

FREDERICK
Frederick County, Maryland P231

GAITHERSBURG
Emergent Biosolutions Inc E156
Adventist Healthcare, Inc. P6

GLEN BURNIE
R. E. Michel Company, Llc P450

GREENBELT
Sgt, Llc P497

HANOVER
Maryland Department Of Transportation P331
Allegis Group, Inc. A40
Johns Hopkins Healthcare Llc P290

Aerotek Affiliated Services, Inc. P8
Maryland Department Of Transportation A664
Teksystems, Inc. P557
Allegis Group, Inc. P22
Aerotek Affiliated Services, Inc. A21

HUNT VALLEY
Sinclair Broadcast Group Inc A938
Mccormick & Co Inc A671

LARGO
Georges Prince County Government P238

LAUREL
Washington Suburban Sanitary Commission (inc) P681

OLNEY
Sandy Spring Bancorp Inc A913
Sandy Spring Bancorp Inc E427

OWINGS MILLS
Rand Worldwide Inc. E409

ROCKVILLE
Capital Bancorp Inc (md) E78
Bioqual Inc E61
Montgomery County, Md P366
Supernus Pharmaceuticals Inc E474

SILVER SPRING
Holy Cross Health, Inc. P267

UPPER MARLBORO
Prince George's County Public Schools P443

WALDORF
Community Financial Corp (the) E113

MASSACHUSETTS

ACTON
Insulet Corp E276

AMESBURY
Provident Bancorp Inc (md) E400

ANDOVER
Mks Instruments Inc E329
Vicor Corp E524
Mercury Systems Inc E318

AUBURNDALE
Atrius Health, Inc. P52
Parexel International Corporation P420

BEDFORD
Novanta Inc E354
Irobot Corp E280
Ice Data Services, Inc. A550
Aspen Technology Inc E38
The Mitre Corporation P594
Ice Data Services, Inc. P273

BEVERLY
Axcelis Technologies Inc E46

BILLERICA
Entegris Inc E165

BOSTON
Fidelity Inv Charitable Gift Fund P223
Boston Medical Center Corporation P90

INDEX BY HEADQUARTERS LOCATION

```
A = AMERICAN BUSINESS
E = EMERGING COMPANIES
P = PRIVATE COMPANIES
W = WORLD BUSINESSS
```

Brookline Bancorp Inc (de) A180
The Children's Hospital Corporation P571
Berkshire Hills Bancorp Inc A151
Tufts Medical Center, Inc. P634
Boston University P91
Massachusetts Port Authority P333
Santander Holdings Usa Inc. A915
The Massachusetts General Hospital P589
University Of Massachusetts Incorporated P655
Commonwealth Of Massachusetts P153
Mass General Brigham Incorporated A666
Massachusetts School Building Authority P334
Eastern Bankshares Inc A351
Massachusetts Housing Finance Agency A667
Harvard Management Private Equity Corporation P254
Cra International Inc E126
Dana-farber Cancer Institute, Inc. P188
Shawmut Woodworking & Supply, Inc. P500
Northeastern University P399
Commonwealth Care Alliance, Inc. P153
American Tower Corp (new) A68
Harvard Medical Faculty Physicians At Beth Israel Deaconess Medical Center, Inc. P255
General Electric Co A460
Massachusetts Water Resources Authority P334
Houghton Mifflin Harcourt Company P268
State Street Corp. A972
The Brigham And Women's Hospital Inc P569
Ptc Inc E401
Beth Israel Deaconess Medical Center, Inc. P77
Wayfair Inc A1112
The President And Fellows Of Harvard College P601
Commonwealth Of Massachusetts A279
Massachusetts Department Of Transportation P332
Ironwood Pharmaceuticals Inc E282
Suffolk Construction Company, Inc. P543
Boston Beer Co Inc (the) E65
Mass General Brigham Incorporated P332
Stag Industrial Inc E461
Vertex Pharmaceuticals, Inc. A1088
Massachusetts Housing Finance Agency P332

BROCKTON
Harborone Bancorp Inc (new) A499
Harborone Bancorp Inc (new) E246

BURLINGTON
Lahey Clinic Hospital, Inc. P306
Keurig Dr Pepper Inc A599
Lemaitre Vascular Inc E296
Cerence Inc E91

CAMBRIDGE
City Of Cambridge P129
Massachusetts Institute Of Technology P333
Cambridge Bancorp A191
Forrester Research Inc. E214
Biogen Inc A157
Voyager Therapeutics Inc E529
Akamai Technologies Inc E11
The Broad Institute Inc P569
Cargurus Inc E81
Cambridge Bancorp E77
The Charles Stark Draper Laboratory Inc P570
Surface Oncology Inc E475

CHESTNUT HILL
Trustees Of Boston College P631

CHICOPEE
Consumer Product Distributors, Llc P161

CONCORD
Welch Foods Inc., A Cooperative P681

DANVERS
Abiomed, Inc. E2

FALL RIVER
Southcoast Hospitals Group, Inc. P511

FRAMINGHAM
Tjx Companies, Inc. A1029
Ameresco Inc E21

HANOVER
Independent Bank Corp (ma) E268
Independent Bank Corp (ma) A554

HINGHAM
Hingham Institution For Savings E256
Hingham Institution For Savings A518

HYANNIS
Cape Cod Hospital P102
Cape Cod Healthcare, Inc. P101

LOWELL
Enterprise Bancorp, Inc. (ma) A371
Enterprise Bancorp, Inc. (ma) E166

LYNNFIELD
New England Petroleum Limited Partnership P382

MARLBOROUGH
Boston Scientific Corp. A173
Hologic Inc A521

MIDDLEBORO
Ocean Spray Cranberries, Inc. P406

MILFORD
Consigli Construction Co. Inc. P159

NATICK
Cognex Corp E104

NEWTON
Rmr Group Inc (the) E423
Industrial Logistics Properties Trust E270
Techtarget Inc E481

NORTH READING
Teradyne, Inc. E484

QUINCY
Randolph Bancorp Inc E409
Granite Telecommunications Llc P245

SOMERVILLE
Allways Health Partners, Inc. P26
Trustees Of Tufts College P633

SOUTH WEYMOUTH
South Shore Hospital, Inc. P511

SPRINGFIELD
Baystate Medical Center, Inc. P71
Eversource Energy A379
City Of Springfield P141
Baystate Health System Health Services, Inc. P70

STOUGHTON
Collegium Pharmaceuticals Inc E107

TAUNTON
Dennis K. Burke Inc. P194

TEWKSBURY
Covenant Health, Inc. P181

WALTHAM
Repligen Corp. E414
Global Partners Lp A475
Dynatrace Inc E147
Thermo Fisher Scientific Inc A1026
Raytheon Technologies Corp A876
Perkinelmer, Inc. E379

WESTBOROUGH
Bj's Wholesale Club Holdings Inc A158

WESTFIELD
Western New England Bancorp Inc E537

WESTFORD
Kadant Inc E285

WILMINGTON
Charles River Laboratories International Inc. E93
Analog Devices Inc A80
Onto Innovation Inc E361

WORCESTER
Umass Memorial Health Care Inc And Affiliates Group Return P639
City Of Worcester P143
Umass Memorial Medical Center, Inc. P639
Hanover Insurance Group Inc A498

MICHIGAN

ADA
Access Business Group Llc P3
Alticor Inc. A45
Solstice Holdings Inc. A947
Alticor Inc. P29
Solstice Holdings Inc. P509

ANN ARBOR
Tecumseh Products Company Llc P556
Regents Of The University Of Michigan P459
Truven Holding Corp. P633
University Bancorp Inc. (mi) E512
Regents Of The University Of Michigan A883

AUBURN HILLS
Old Dura, Inc. P410
Borgwarner Inc A172

BATTLE CREEK
Kellogg Co A596

BENTON HARBOR
Whirlpool Corp A1127

BIRMINGHAM
Atlas Oil Company P50

BLOOMFIELD HILLS
Penske Automotive Group Inc A811
Agree Realty Corp. E8

CENTER LINE
St. John Providence Physicians-cmg P523

COLDWATER
Southern Michigan Bancorp Inc (united States) E454

DEARBORN
Ford Motor Credit Company Llc A445
Ford Motor Co. (de) A443

DETROIT
Metaldyne Performance Group Inc. P350
American Axle & Manufacturing Holdings Inc A56
Dte Electric Company A342
Henry Ford Health System P260
Uaw Retiree Medical Benefits Trust A1052
General Motors Co A466
Rocket Companies Inc A900
Dte Energy Co A343
Henry Ford Health System A507
Uaw Retiree Medical Benefits Trust P637
Ally Financial Inc A43
Detroit Wayne Mental Health Authority P195

EAST LANSING
Greenstone Farm Credit Services Aca P246
Michigan State University P356
Greenstone Farm Credit Services Aca A489

FARMINGTON HILLS
Robert Bosch Llc A896
Level One Bancorp Inc E298
Robert Bosch Llc P465

FENTON
Fentura Financial Inc E189

FLINT
Mott, Charles Stewart Foundation Inc A717

GRAND RAPIDS
Corewell Health P163
Ufp Industries Inc A1052
Corewell Health A296

INDEX BY HEADQUARTERS LOCATION

```
A = AMERICAN BUSINESS
E = EMERGING COMPANIES
P = PRIVATE COMPANIES
W = WORLD BUSINESSS
```

Independent Bank Corporation (ionia, Mi) E269
Meritage Hospitality Group Inc E321
Mercantile Bank Corp. A680
Spartannash Co A956
Mercantile Bank Corp. E317
Independent Bank Corporation (ionia, Mi) A554

HILLSDALE
Cnb Community Bancorp Inc E102

HOLLAND
Macatawa Bank Corp. A653

JACKSON
Alro Steel Corporation P27
Cms Energy Corp A255
Consumers Energy Co. A293

KALAMAZOO
Bronson Methodist Hospital Inc P94
Stryker Corp A980

LANSING
Sparrow Health System P516
State Of Michigan A968
Housing Development Authority, Michigan State P270
State Of Michigan P534

LIVONIA
Trinity Health-michigan P629
Mercy Health Services-iowa, Corp. P347
Trinity Health Corporation P628
Masco Corp. A664

MADISON HEIGHTS
Mcnaughton-mckay Electric Co. P338

MASON
Dart Financial Corp E134

MIDDLEVILLE
Hps Llc P271

MIDLAND
Dow Inc A342
Midmichigan Medical Center-midland P357

MOUNT PLEASANT
American Mitsuba Corporation P35

MUSKEGON
Mercy Health Partners P347
Mercy General Health Partners P345

NOVI
Nhk International Corporation P392
Michigan Milk Producers Association P356

PONTIAC
County Of Oakland P174

PORT HURON
Semco Energy, Inc. P493

ROCHESTER HILLS
Infusystem Holdings Inc E271

ROCKFORD
Rockford Public Schools P469

ROYAL OAK
Beaumont Health P72

William Beaumont Hospital P691
Barrick Enterprises, Inc. P66

SAGINAW
Covenant Medical Center, Inc. P181

SOUTHFIELD
Ascension Providence Hospital P45
Veoneer, Inc. P673
Credit Acceptance Corp (mi) E127
Sun Communities Inc E470
Sterling Bancorp Inc (mi) A976
Federal-mogul Holdings Llc P222
Barton Malow Company P67
Barton Malow Enterprises, Inc. P67
Federal-mogul Holdings Llc A403
Lear Corp. A621

SPARTA
Choiceone Financial Services, Inc. E96

STURGIS
Sturgis Bancorp Inc E468

TRAVERSE CITY
Munson Healthcare P372
Munson Medical Center P373

TROY
Flagstar Bancorp, Inc. E209
Flagstar Bancorp, Inc. A434
Skyline Champion Corp E446

WARREN
St. John Hospital And Medical Center P523

MINNESOTA

ANOKA
Anoka-hennepin School Dist No 11 P40

AUSTIN
Hormel Foods Corp. A533

BLOOMINGTON
Lamex Foods Inc. P307
Bridgewater Bancshares Inc A175
Bridgewater Bancshares Inc E66
Toro Company (the) E490
Healthpartners, Inc. P258

BROOKLYN PARK
Clearfield Inc E101

BURNSVILLE
Ames Construction, Inc. P37

CIRCLE PINES
Northern Technologies International Corp. E351

DULUTH
Smdc Medical Center P506

EDEN PRAIRIE
Robinson (c.h.) Worldwide, Inc. A898
Winnebago Industries, Inc. E539

EDINA
Production Technologies, Inc. P444

FERGUS FALLS
Otter Tail Corp. E366

GRANITE FALLS
Granite Falls Energy Llc E236

HERMANTOWN
Miners Incorporated P359

HOPKINS
Digi International Inc E138

INVER GROVE HEIGHTS
Chs Inc A233

LITCHFIELD
The First District Association P580

MAPLE GROVE
Great River Energy P245

MAPLE PLAIN
Proto Labs Inc E399

MEDINA
Polaris Inc A834

MINNEAPOLIS
Riversource Life Insurance Co A895
Hennepin County P260
University Of Minnesota Physicians P656
Bio-techne Corp E58
Minneapolis Public School P359
Sleep Number Corp E447
Park Nicollet Clinic P421
Sps Commerce, Inc. E457
Ameriprise Financial Inc A70
Target Corp A995
Cliftonlarsonallen Llp P145
Us Bancorp (de) A1081
Children's Health Care P118
Sun Country Airlines Holdings Inc E471
Ecmc Group, Inc. A357
Xcel Energy Inc A1138
Hennepin Healthcare System, Inc. P260
City Of Minneapolis P134
Piper Sandler Companies E386
Datasite Global Corporation P191
General Mills Inc A462
Regions Hospital P460

MINNETONKA
Unitedhealth Group Inc A1073

MOORHEAD
American Crystal Sugar Company P32

NEW BRIGHTON
Api Group, Inc. P40

NEW ULM
Nuvera Communications Inc E355

RICHFIELD
Best Buy Inc A153

ROCHESTER
Saint Marys Hospital P479
Mayo Foundation For Medical Education And Research P336

SAINT CLOUD
Coborn's, Incorporated P149
The Saint Cloud Hospital P604

SAINT PAUL
United Hospital Incorporated P642
Fairview Health Services A389
State Of Minnesota A969
County Of Ramsey P175
Regions Hospital P460
Regions Hospital Foundation P460
Fairview Health Services P219
Saint Paul Public Schools, District 625 P480
Hmo Minnesota P265
City Of Saint Paul P139
Augustana Health Care Center Of Apple Valley P54

State Of Minnesota P534

ST. LOUIS PARK
Two Harbors Investment Corp A1048

ST. PAUL
Patterson Companies Inc A805
Ecolab Inc A357
Fuller (hb) Company E225
3m Co A2

WINONA
Fastenal Co. A394

MISSISSIPPI

COLUMBUS
Bankfirst Capital Corp. E54

GREENVILLE
Farmers Grain Terminal, Inc. P222

GREENWOOD
Staple Cotton Cooperative Association P532

GULFPORT
Hancock Whitney Corp A495

HATTIESBURG
Cooperative Energy, A Mississippi Electric Cooperative P162
First Bancshares Inc (ms) A414
First Bancshares Inc (ms) E193
Forrest County General Hospital P228

JACKSON
Trustmark Corp A1044
State Of Mississippi A969
University Of Mississippi Medical Center P656
Board Of Trustees Of State Institutions Of Higher Learning P87
State Of Mississippi P535

MISSISSIPPI STATE
Mississippi State University P360

RIDGELAND
Eastgroup Properties Inc E151

TUPELO
North Mississippi Medical Center, Inc. P396
Cadence Bank A190
Cadence Bank E72
Renasant Corp A888
Renasant Corp E413
North Mississippi Health Services, Inc. P396

MISSOURI

CAPE GIRARDEAU
Saint Francis Healthcare System P477

CARTHAGE
Leggett & Platt, Inc. A623

CHESTERFIELD
Mhm Support Services P354
Reinsurance Group Of America, Inc. A885

HOOVER'S HANDBOOK OF EMERGING COMPANIES 2023

INDEX BY HEADQUARTERS LOCATION

```
A = AMERICAN BUSINESS
E = EMERGING COMPANIES
P = PRIVATE COMPANIES
W = WORLD BUSINESSS
```

CLAYTON
Enterprise Financial Services Corp E167
Olin Corp. A775
Enterprise Financial Services Corp A372

COLUMBIA
Mfa Oil Company P353
American Outdoor Brands Inc E25
University Of Missouri Health Care P656
University Of Missouri System P656
Mfa Incorporated P353

DES PERES
Jones Financial Companies Lllp A586

FENTON
Cic Group, Inc. P125

GRANDVIEW
Nasb Financial Inc E338

JEFFERSON CITY
Missouri Department Of Transportation P361
State Of Missouri A969
State Of Missouri P535
Hawthorn Bancshares Inc E246

JOPLIN
The Empire District Electric Company P578
Freeman Health System P231

KANSAS CITY
Evergy Missouri West, Inc. P218
J.e. Dunn Construction Group, Inc. P282
Saint Luke's Health System, Inc. P479
Dst Systems, Inc. P203
Saint Luke's Hospital Of Kansas City P479
Commerce Bancshares Inc A275
Mercy Children's Hospital P344
Kansas City Life Insurance Co (kansas City, Mo) A592
Umb Financial Corp E505
Truman Medical Center, Incorporated P630
J.e. Dunn Construction Company P282
Missouri City Of Kansas City P361
St Luke's Hospital Of Kansas City P521
Umb Financial Corp A1056

NORTH KANSAS CITY
Maxus Realty Trust Inc E314
Cerner Corp. A220

POPLAR BLUFF
Southern Missouri Bancorp, Inc. E455
Southern Missouri Bancorp, Inc. A953

SAINT JOSEPH
Heartland Regional Medical Center P259
Mosaic Health System P367

SAINT LOUIS
Mercy Health A685
Mercy Hospitals East Communities P348
Ascension Health Alliance P45
Mccarthy Holdings, Inc. P337
Barry-wehmiller Group, Inc. P66
Alberici Group, Inc. P17
Alberici Constructors, Inc. P16
World Wide Technology, Llc P692
World Wide Technology Holding Co., Llc P692
Tom Lange Company, Inc. P623
Missouri Baptist Medical Center P361
Ssm Health Care Corporation P520
Mccarthy Building Companies, Inc. P336
Spire Missouri Inc. P518
Mercy Health P346
St. Louis Children's Hospital P528
Ascension Health Alliance A100
Saint Louis University P478
City Of St. Louis P141
World Wide Technology, Llc A1136
World Wide Technology Holding Co., Llc A1136
Barnes-jewish Hospital P66
The Washington University P618
County Of St Louis P178
Alberici Corporation P16
Ssm Health Care Corporation A960

SIKESTON
Food Giant Supermarkets, Inc. P227

SPRINGFIELD
O'reilly Automotive, Inc. A764
Mercy Hospital Springfield P348
New Prime, Inc. P382
Great Southern Bancorp, Inc. A488
Guaranty Federal Bancshares Inc (springfield, Mo) E243
Hiland Dairy Foods Company., Llc P263
Lester E. Cox Medical Centers P312

ST. LOUIS
Bellring Brands Inc E57
Bunge Ltd. A184
Graybar Electric Co., Inc. A487
Post Holdings Inc A837
Stifel Financial Corp E463
Stifel Financial Corp A976
Energizer Holdings Inc (new) E160
Ameren Corp A53
Centene Corp A216
Emerson Electric Co. A365

MONTANA

BILLINGS
Billings Clinic P80
First Interstate Bancsystem Inc E201
First Interstate Bancsystem Inc A425

BOZEMA
Fair Isaac Corp E181

COLUMBUS
Stillwater Mining Company P542

GREAT FALLS
Benefis Health System, Inc P75
Benefis Hospitals, Inc P75

HELENA
Eagle Bancorp Montana, Inc. E148
State Of Montana A969
State Of Montana P535

KALISPELL
Glacier Bancorp, Inc. E230
Glacier Bancorp, Inc. A474
Cityservicevalcon, Llc P143

LEWISTOWN
Sports, Inc. P518

NEBRASKA

COLUMBUS
Nebraska Public Power District P381

DORCHESTER
Farmers Cooperative P221

KIMBALL
Risk George Industries Inc E421

LINCOLN
Board Of Regents Of The University Of Nebraska P87
Bryan Medical Center P97
Crete Carrier Corporation P182
State Of Nebraska P535
Nelnet Inc A726
Nelnet Inc E344
Union Bank And Trust Company A1059
State Of Nebraska A969

NORFOLK
Affiliated Foods Midwest Cooperative, Inc. P9

OMAHA
Tmv Corp. A1031
Farm Credit Services Of America P221
The Scoular Company A1023
Kiewit Industrial Group Inc P300
Kiewit Corporation A603
Omaha Public Power District P410
Hdr Engineering, Inc. P255
Peter Kiewit Sons', Inc. P426
Sapp Bros., Inc. P484
The Nebraska Medical Center P595
First National Of Nebraska, Inc. A428
Creighton University P181
Northern Natural Gas Company P400
Kiewit Infrastructure Co. P300
Farm Credit Services Of America A392
Tmv Corp. P623
Omaha Public Schools P411
The Scoular Company P605
Hdr, Inc. P256
Kiewit Corporation P300
Peter Kiewit Sons', Inc. A818
Tenaska Energy, Inc. P559
Lozier Corporation P322
Berkshire Hathaway Inc A150
Ag Processing Inc A Cooperative P10
City Of Omaha P136
Union Pacific Corp A1060
Alegent Health - Bergan Mercy Health System P20
Alegent Creighton Health P20

NEVADA

CARSON CITY
State Of Nevada P535
State Of Nevada A969

INCLINE VILLAGE
Tri Pointe Homes Inc E495

LAS VEGAS
Mp Materials Corp E334
City Of Las Vegas P133
City Center Holdings, Llc P127
Axos Financial Inc A119
Axos Financial Inc E47
Clark County School District P145
Sstartrade Tech Inc E458
Switch Inc E477
Sciplay Corp E430
Mgm Resorts International A694
Live Ventures Inc E304
County Of Clark P168
Boomer Holdings Inc E64

RENO
Nevada System Of Higher Education P381
Washoe County School District P681
University Of Nevada, Reno P657
Employers Holdings Inc A366
Plumas Bancorp Inc E388
County Of Washoe P179

SPARKS
Sierra Nevada Corporation P503

ZEPHYR COVE
Virnetx Holding Corp E527

NEW HAMPSHIRE

CONCORD
University System Of New Hampshire P666
State Of New Hampshire P535
Concord Hospital, Inc. P158
State Of New Hampshire A969

HANOVER
Trustees Of Dartmouth College P631
Dartmouth College P190
Ledyard Financial Group Inc E294

LEBANON
Dartmouth-hitchcock Health P190
Dartmouth-hitchcock Clinic P190
Maxifacial Dental Surgery P334

MANCHESTER
Allegro Microsystems, Llc P23
Elliot Health System P212
Southern New Hampshire University P514
Elliot Hospital Of The City Of Manchester P213

NEW JERSEY

ATLANTIC CITY
Marina District Development Company, Llc P327

BAYONNE
Bcb Bancorp Inc E56
Bcb Bancorp Inc A143

BEDMINSTER
Peapack-gladstone Financial Corp. E375

INDEX BY HEADQUARTERS LOCATION

```
A = AMERICAN BUSINESS
E = EMERGING COMPANIES
P = PRIVATE COMPANIES
W = WORLD BUSINESSS
```

Peapack-gladstone Financial Corp. A809

BRANCHVILLE
Selective Insurance Group Inc E434
Selective Insurance Group Inc A926

BRIDGEWATER
Amneal Pharmaceuticals Inc E30
Brother International Corporation P95

BURLINGTON
Burlington Stores Inc A186

CAMDEN
The Cooper Health System A New Jersey Non-profit Corporation P575
Campbell Soup Co A193
Virtua-west Jersey Health System, Inc. P677
County Of Camden P167

CLINTON
Unity Bancorp, Inc. E510

EAST HANOVER
Novartis Pharmaceuticals Corporation A756
Novartis Pharmaceuticals Corporation P404

EDISON
Jfk Health System, Inc. P286
Hmh Hospitals Corporation P264
The Community Hospital Group Inc P575

ELIZABETH
County Of Union P179

ENGLEWOOD
Englewood Hospital And Medical Center Foundation Inc. P215

ENGLEWOOD CLIFFS
Connectone Bancorp Inc (new) A287
Avio Inc. P57
Connectone Bancorp Inc (new) E115

EWING
Antares Pharma Inc. E32
New Jersey Transportation Trust Fund Authority P382
Universal Display Corp E511
Church & Dwight Co Inc A235

FAIR LAWN
Columbia Financial Inc E109
Columbia Financial Inc A271

FAIRFIELD
Kearny Financial Corp (md) A596
Kearny Financial Corp (md) E286

FOLSOM
South Jersey Industries Inc E453

FRANKLIN LAKES
Becton, Dickinson & Co A145

FREEHOLD
County Of Monmouth P172

HACKENSACK
County Of Bergen P167

HAMILTON
First Bank (williamstown, Nj) E193

HOBOKEN
Jarden Llc A580
Jarden Llc P286

JERSEY CITY
Organon & Co A787
Verisk Analytics Inc E520
Provident Financial Services Inc A854

KEASBEY
Wakefern Food Corp. P678
Wakefern Food Corp. A1099

KENILWORTH
Merck & Co Inc A682

LINDEN
Turtle & Hughes, Inc P635

LIVINGSTON
St Barnabas Medical Center (inc) P520

LONG BRANCH
Monmouth Medical Center Inc. P364

MADISON
Realogy Holdings Corp A879
Realogy Group Llc A878

MATAWAN
Key Food Stores Co-operative, Inc. P299

MONTVALE
Berry Global Films, Llc P75

MORRISTOWN
Ahs Hospital Corp. P12
Atlantic Health System Inc. P50

NEPTUNE
Meridian Hospitals Corporation P349

NEW BRUNSWICK
Middlesex, County Of (inc) P357
Johnson & Johnson A584
Johnson & Johnson Patient Assistance Foundation Inc P291
Robert Wood Johnson University Hospital, Inc. P467

NEWARK
The New Jersey Transit Corporation P596
County Of Essex P169
Public Service Enterprise Group Inc A857
Port Newark Container Terminal Llc P437
University Hospital P644
Genie Energy Ltd E229
Prudential Financial Inc A855

OAK RIDGE
Lakeland Bancorp, Inc. E288
Lakeland Bancorp, Inc. A616

PARSIPPANY
Pbf Energy Inc A808
Zoetis Inc A1152
B&g Foods Inc E50
Pbf Logistics Lp E374
Avis Budget Group Inc A114
Lincoln Educational Services Corp E302

PATERSON
St. Joseph's University Medical Center Inc P527
St. Joseph's Health Partners Llc P525
Paterson Public School District P422

PISCATAWAY
The Institute Of Electrical And Electronics Engineers Incorporated P586

POMONA
Atlanticare Regional Medical Center P50

PRINCETON
The Trustees Of Princeton University P608
Integra Lifesciences Holdings Corp E277
Bank Of Princeton (the) E53
Educational Testing Service P209
Essential Properties Realty Trust Inc E173

RED BANK
Oceanfirst Financial Corp E358
Oceanfirst Financial Corp A767

RIDGEWOOD
The Valley Hospital Inc P616

ROSELAND
Automatic Data Processing Inc. A107

SECAUCUS
Unique Designs, Inc. P640
Quest Diagnostics, Inc. A869

SHORT HILLS
Investors Bancorp Inc (new) A574

SOMERSET
Shi International Corp. A934
Shi International Corp. P502
Catalent Inc E83

TEANECK
Cognizant Technology Solutions Corp. A266

TRENTON
New Jersey Housing And Mortgage Finance Agency A730

UNION
Bed, Bath & Beyond, Inc. A147

WASHINGTON TOWNSHIP
Parke Bancorp Inc E371

WEST ORANGE
A-1 Specialized Services & Supplies, Inc. P1
Barnabas Health, Inc. P64
Rwj Barnabas Health, Inc. P471

WHIPPANY
Stephen Gould Corporation P540

WOODBRIDGE
New Jersey Turnpike Authority Inc P382
Dhpc Technologies, Inc. A325
Northfield Bancorp Inc (de) A749
Dhpc Technologies, Inc. P195
Township Of Woodbridge P625

NEW MEXICO

ALBUQUERQUE
Albuquerque Public School District P19
University Of New Mexico P657
City Of Albuquerque P127
Albuquerque Municipal School District Number 12 P19

NEW YORK

ALBANY
St. Peter's Health Care Services P530
Capital District Physicians' Health Plan, Inc. P103
Albany Medical Center Hospital P16
The Research Foundation For The State University Of New York P603
Dormitory Authority - State Of New York P201
State University Of New York A974
County Of Albany P166
Thruway Authority Of New York State P622
New York State Energy Research And Development Authority P387
St. Peter's Health Partners P530
New York State Energy Research And Development Authority P388
Albany Med Health System P15
State University Of New York P538

AMHERST
Allied Motion Technologies Inc E17

ARMONK
International Business Machines Corp A563

BALLSTON SPA
Stewart's Shops Corp. P541

BINGHAMTON
Broome County P95
United Health Services Hospitals, Inc. P642

BRONX
Lincoln Medical And Mental Health Center P317
Bronxcare Health System P94
Montefiore Medical Center P366
Physician Affiliate Group Of New York Pc P430
Fordham University P227

BROOKLYN
Newyork-presbyterian/brooklyn Methodist P391
Etsy Inc E175
Maimonides Medical Center P323

BUFFALO
Kaleida Health P294
Erie County Medical Center Corp. P217
M & T Bank Corp A650
Buffalo City School District P97
Rich Products Corporation P462
County Of Erie P169

CAMDEN
International Wire Group, Inc. P279

INDEX BY HEADQUARTERS LOCATION

A = AMERICAN BUSINESS
E = EMERGING COMPANIES
P = PRIVATE COMPANIES
W = WORLD BUSINESSS

CANANDAIGUA
Canandaigua National Corp. E78
Canandaigua National Corp. A196
CATSKILL
Greene County Bancorp Inc E240
COOPERSTOWN
The Mary Imogene Bassett Hospital P589
CORNING
Corning Inc A297
DEWITT
Community Bank System Inc A279
Community Bank System Inc E111
EAST ELMHURST
Skanska Usa Civil Northeast Inc. P506
Skanska Usa Civil Inc. P505
EAST SYRACUSE
D/l Cooperative Inc. P185
FLUSHING
Newyork-presbyterian/queens P391
GENEVA
Lyons Bancorp Inc. E306
GLEN HEAD
First Of Long Island Corp A429
GLENS FALLS
Arrow Financial Corp. A98
Arrow Financial Corp. E36
GLENVILLE
Trustco Bank Corp. (n.y.) A1042
GOSHEN
County Of Orange P174
GOUVERNEUR
Kph Healthcare Services, Inc. P303
HAUPPAUGE
Dime Community Bancshares Inc (new) A328
County Of Suffolk P178
HEMPSTEAD
Town Of Hempstead P624
HICKSVILLE
New York Community Bancorp Inc. A732
ITHACA
Tompkins Financial Corp A1032
Cornell University P164
JAMAICA
St John's University, New York P521
JERICHO
Esquire Financial Holdings Inc E173
1-800 Flowers.com, Inc. E1
LANCASTER
Upstate Niagara Cooperative, Inc. P668
LIVERPOOL
Raymours Furniture Company, Inc. P454
LONG ISLAND CITY
Altice Usa Inc A45
New York City School Construction Authority P384
Jetblue Airways Corp A581
MANHASSET
North Shore University Hospital P397
Town Of North Hempstead P624
MELVILLE
Schein (henry) Inc A916
MENANDS
Health Research, Inc. P257
MIDDLETOWN
Orange County Bancorp Inc E364
MINEOLA
County Of Nassau P173
Nassua County Interim Finance Authority P376
NEW CITY
County Of Rockland P176
NEW HYDE PARK
Long Island Jewish Medical Center P318
NEW YORK
Goldman Sachs Group Inc A479
Virtu Financial Llc P677
Ubiquiti Inc E503
Pvh Corp A862
Memorial Hospital For Cancer And Allied Diseases P342
Ziff Davis Inc E547
Colgate-palmolive Co. A267
Nielsen Holdings Plc A742
1199 Seiu National Benefit Fund For Health And Human Service Employees P1
Vici Properties Inc E524
Metropolitan Transportation Authority P351
The Ford Foundation A1016
Blackrock Inc A159
New York University P389
Exxe Group Inc E181
Mesabi Trust E322
Newmark & Company Real Estate, Inc. P390
Vns Choice P677
Ares Commercial Real Estate Corp A95
Nielsen Holdings Plc P393
Newmark Group Inc E347
Blackstone Mortgage Trust Inc E62
Tapestry Inc A992
New York State Housing Finance Agency P388
New Residential Investment Corp E346
Macy's Inc A654
Guildnet, Inc. P249
Barnes & Noble, Inc. P65
Moody's Corp. A710
Turner Construction Company Inc A1045
News Corp (new) A737
Plan International, Inc. P436
Signature Financial Llc P504
Assurant Inc A102
Moelis & Co E330
New York Presbyterian Hospital Weill Cornell University Medical Center P386
The Trustees Of Columbia University In The City Of New York P608
International Rescue Committee, Inc. P279
The Simons Foundation Inc P606
Progyny Inc E398
The New York And Presbyterian Hospital P597
Nasdaq Inc A720
Goldman Sachs Bdc Inc E234
Brixmor Llc A179
Federal Reserve Bank Of New York, Dist. No. 2 A400
Iac/interactivecorp (new) E261
Federal Home Loan Bank New York A396
Exlservice Holdings Inc E178
Interpublic Group Of Companies Inc. A569
Metropolitan Bank Holding Corp A691
City Of New York P135
Enerkon Solar International Inc E162
Discovery Inc A330
Virtu Financial Inc E527
Stepstone Group Inc E462
State Of New York Mortgage Agency P536
Nfp Corp. P392
Msci Inc E335
Hsbc Usa, Inc. A538
The New School P596
Fox Corp A447
Federal Home Loan Bank New York E186
American Express Co. A61
Pace University P418
Blackstone Inc A160
Pjt Partners Inc E387
New York University A733
Alleghany Corp. A37
The Turner Corporation A1023
Lauder (estee) Cos., Inc. (the) A620
Reckson Operating Partnership, L.p. A880
Cowen Inc E125
S&p Global Inc A910
Brookfield Business Corp A180
Paramount Global A801
Memorial Sloan-kettering Cancer Center A680
Siga Technologies Inc E439
Axel Johnson Inc. P57
Bristol Myers Squibb Co. A176
New York City Health And Hospitals Corporation P383
Chimera Investment Corp A231
St Lukes-roosevelt Institute P521
Kkr Real Estate Finance Trust Inc E288
The St Luke's-roosevelt Hospital Center P606
New York Hotel Trades Council And Hotel Association Of New York City Health Center, Inc., P385
Mfa Financial, Inc. A693
Virtu Financial Llc A1095
Jewish Communal Fund P286
Pfizer Inc A820
Oppenheimer Holdings Inc E363
Foot Locker, Inc. A441
Lenox Hill Hospital P312
Jpmorgan Chase & Co A589
Apollo Commercial Real Estate Finance Inc. A86
Management-ila Managed Health Care Trust Fund P326
Metropolitan Transportation Authority A692
Shutterstock Inc E437
Travelers Companies Inc (the) A1036
Griffon Corp. E240
Catholic Medical Mission Board Inc P108
Consolidated Edison Inc A289
Consolidated Edison Co. Of New York, Inc. A288
Metropolitan Bank Holding Corp E323
The Ford Foundation P581
Metlife Inc A690
Genpact Limited P237
Ready Capital Corp E410
Jefferies Financial Group Inc A580
Mphasis Corporation P370
Ambac Financial Group, Inc. A51
Signature Bank (new York, Ny) E440
Omnicom Group, Inc. A777
The Associated Press P567
Voya Financial Inc A1098
New York City Transit Authority P384
Focus Financial Partners Inc E212
Valley National Bancorp (nj) E516
Signature Financial Llc A937
Bluerock Residential Growth Reit Inc E62
Valley National Bancorp (nj) A1085
The Trustees Of Columbia University In The City Of New York A1023
Morgan Stanley A712
Marketaxess Holdings Inc. E310
The Simons Foundation Inc A1023
Turner Construction Company Inc P634
Ladder Capital Corp A615
Tradeweb Markets Inc E493
The New York And Presbyterian Hospital A1021
Signature Bank (new York, Ny) A936
Stonex Group Inc A978
Evercore Inc E175
Hunter Roberts Construction Group Llc P271
International Flavors & Fragrances Inc. A565
Granite Point Mortgage Trust Inc A485
Royalty Pharma Plc E425
Warner Music Group Corp A1105
Henry Modell & Company, Inc. P260
Community Funds, Inc. A281
Verizon Communications Inc A1087
City Of New York A250
State Of New York Mortgage Agency A970

INDEX BY HEADQUARTERS LOCATION

A = AMERICAN BUSINESS
E = EMERGING COMPANIES
P = PRIVATE COMPANIES
W = WORLD BUSINESSS

Sirius Xm Holdings Inc A940
The Andrew W Mellon Foundation P567
Loews Corp. A644
Equitable Holdings Inc A377
Triborough Bridge & Tunnel Authority P627
Abm Industries, Inc. A8
Global Net Lease Inc E232
Trammo, Inc. P625
Otc Markets Group Inc E366
Marsh & Mclennan Companies Inc. A661
Lhh Corporation P315
Kyndryl Holdings Inc A612
Beth Israel Medical Center P77
Take-two Interactive Software, Inc. E479
American International Group Inc A65
New York City Health And Hospitals Corporation A730
Bank Of New York Mellon Corp A131
Blue Tee Corp. P85
Zedge Inc E547
New York University P388
The Turner Corporation P608
Annaly Capital Management Inc A82
Reckson Operating Partnership, L.p. P457
Amalgamated Financial Corp E19
Citigroup Inc A244
Memorial Sloan-kettering Cancer Center P342
W.p. Carey Inc E530
Rtw Retailwinds, Inc. P470
Philip Morris International Inc A824
The Bloomberg Family Foundation Inc P568
Safehold Inc E426

NORWICH
Nbt Bancorp. Inc. A723

OCEANSIDE
South Nassau Communities Hospital P511

OSWEGO
Pathfinder Bancorp Inc. (md) E372

PEARL RIVER
Orange And Rockland Utilities, Inc. P412

POUGHKEEPSIE
Health Quest Systems, Inc. P257
Rhinebeck Bancorp Inc E420
Dutchess, County Of (inc) P206
Central Hudson Gas & Electric Corporation P112

PURCHASE
Mastercard Inc A668
Mbia Inc. A670
Pepsico Inc A816

REGO PARK
New York State Catholic Health Plan, Inc. P387

RICHMOND HILL
The Jamaica Hospital P586

ROCHESTER
Rochester Institute Of Technology (inc) P468
Rochester City School District P467
Rochester Regional Health P468
Home Properties, Limited Partnership A527
City Of Rochester P139
County Of Monroe P173
Rochester Gas And Electric Corporation P467
Broadstone Net Lease Inc E67

ROSLYN
St. Francis Hospital, Roslyn, New York P522

RYE
Lict Corp E300

SCHENECTADY
The Golub Corporation P584
General Electric International, Inc. A462
Mvp Health Plan, Inc. P374
General Electric International, Inc. P237

SMITHTOWN
The Town Of Smithtown P607

STATEN ISLAND
Staten Island University Hospital P539

SYRACUSE
St. Joseph's Hospital Health Center P526
City Of Syracuse P141
County Of Onondaga P174
Srctec, Llc P519

TARRYTOWN
Regeneron Pharmaceuticals, Inc. A881

UNIONDALE
Arbor Realty Trust Inc E34
Long Island Power Authority P318
Flushing Financial Corp. A439

VALHALLA
Westchester County Health Care Corporation P686

VICTOR
Constellation Brands Inc A291

WARSAW
Financial Institutions Inc. A410

WEST ISLIP
Good Samaritan Hospital Medical Center P241

WEST NYACK
The Salvation Army P604

WESTBURY
North Shore-long Island Jewish Health Care P398

WESTFIELD
National Grape Co-operative Association, Inc. P377

WHITE PLAINS
Northeast Community Bancorp Inc (md) E351
New York Power Authority P385
Turtle Beach Corp E501
White Plains Hospital Medical Center P688
County Of Westchester P179
Frmo Corp. E221
Db Us Holding Corporation P192

WILLIAMSVILLE
Evans Bancorp, Inc. E175

NORTH CAROLINA

ALBEMARLE
Uwharrie Capital Corp. E515

ASHEVILLE
Mission Hospital, Inc. P360
Hometrust Bancshares Inc. E258
Hometrust Bancshares Inc. A528

BOONE
Samaritan's Purse P481

BURLINGTON
Laboratory Corporation Of America Holdings A614

CARY
Wake County Public School System P678
Cary Oil Co., Inc. P107
Coc Properties, Inc. P149
Ply Gem Holdings, Inc. P436

CHAPEL HILL
The University Of North Carolina P613
University Of North Carolina At Chapel Hill P657
The University Of North Carolina Health System P613
Investors Title Co. E280

CHARLOTTE
Snyder's-lance, Inc. P508
Extended Stay America, Inc. P218
Duke Energy Corp A345
Spx Flow, Inc. P519
City Of Charlotte P130
Bank Of America Corp A126
Parsons Environment & Infrastructure Group Inc. P421
Sealed Air Corp A923
County Of Mecklenburg P172
Brighthouse Life Insurance Co - Insurance Products A176
Brighthouse Financial Inc A176
The Charlotte-mecklenburg Hospital Authority P570
Premier Healthcare Alliance, L.p. P443
Presbyterian Hospital P443
Sonic Automotive, Inc. A947
Coca-cola Consolidated Inc A265
Nucor Corp. A758
Duke Energy Carolinas Llc A345
Truist Financial Corp A1040
The Charlotte-mecklenburg Hospital Authority A1014
Honeywell International Inc A528

CONCORD
Carolinas Medical Center Northeast P106
Cardinal Logistics Holdings, Llc P104

DURHAM
Family Health International Inc P220
The North Carolina Mutual Wholesale Drug Company P598
Duke University Health System, Inc. P205
Research Triangle Institute Inc P461
Iqvia Holdings Inc A575
Avaya Holdings Corp. P55
Duke University P204
Duke University Hospital P206

FAYETTEVILLE
Cape Fear Valley Medical Center P102
Cumberland County Hospital System, Inc. P184
Carolina Healthcare Center Of Cumberland Lp P106

GASTONIA
Mann+hummel Filtration Technology Intermediate Holdings Inc. P327

GREENSBORO
The Fresh Market Inc P582
Atlantic Coast Conference P49
County Of Guilford P170
Guilford County School System P249

GREENVILLE
Pitt County Memorial Hospital, Incorporated P434

HICKORY
Commscope Holding Co Inc A279
Alex Lee, Inc. P20

HUNTERSVILLE
American Tire Distributors Holdings, Inc. P36

LEXINGTON
Wake Forest University Health Sciences P678

MOORESVILLE
Lowe's Companies Inc A646

MORRISVILLE
Syneos Health Inc A986
Charles & Colvard Ltd E93
Channeladvisor Corp E92

MOUNT AIRY
Insteel Industries, Inc. E275

RALEIGH
Rex Healthcare, Inc. P462
Biodelivery Sciences International Inc E60
Martin Marietta Materials, Inc. A662
State Of North Carolina P536
Advance Auto Parts Inc A16
City Of Raleigh P138
Raleigh Duke Hospital Guild P453
First Citizens Bancshares Inc (de) A417
Wake, County Of North Carolina P678
North Carolina Electric Membership Corporation P395
Rex Hospital, Inc. P462
State Of North Carolina A970
Suntory International P548
Wakemed P679

SOUTHERN PINES
First Bancorp (nc) A414

INDEX BY HEADQUARTERS LOCATION

```
A = AMERICAN BUSINESS
E = EMERGING COMPANIES
P = PRIVATE COMPANIES
W = WORLD BUSINESSS
```

First Bancorp (nc) E191
THOMASVILLE
Old Dominion Freight Line, Inc. A771
WILMINGTON
Live Oak Bancshares Inc E304
Live Oak Banking Company A642
Live Oak Bancshares Inc A641
WINSTON SALEM
Quality Oil Company, Llc P449
North Carolina Baptist Hospital Fdn P395
North Carolina Baptist Hospital P394
Novant Medical Group, Inc. P403
WINSTON-SALEM
Hanesbrands Inc A496

NORTH DAKOTA

BISMARCK
State Of North Dakota P536
Bnccorp Inc E63
Sanford Bismarck P483
State Of North Dakota A970
Mdu Resources Group Inc A678
FARGO
Ni Holdings Inc E348
Sanford North P484
North Dakota University System P395
Rdo Construction Equipment Co. P455
Sanford P482
GRAND FORKS
Alerus Financial Corp E14
Alerus Financial Corp A37
Altru Health System P30
WEST FARGO
Clark Equipment Company P145

OHIO

AKRON
Metropolitan Edison Company P351
West Penn Power Company P684
American Transmission Systems, Incorporated P37
Akron General Medical Center Inc P14
Pennsylvania Electric Company P424
Childrens Hospital Medical Center Of Akron P122
The Cleveland Electric Illuminating Company P574
Goodyear Tire & Rubber Co. A481
Summa Health System P544
Jersey Central Power & Light Company P286
Firstenergy Corp A431
Ohio Edison Company P407
ARCHBOLD
Farmers & Merchants Bancorp Inc (oh) E184
BARBERTON
Christian Healthcare Ministries, Inc. P123

BATAVIA
Multi-color Corporation P370
BROOKLYN HEIGHTS
Graftech International Ltd E235
CANFIELD
Farmers National Banc Corp. (canfield,oh) A393
Farmers National Banc Corp. (canfield,oh) E184
CHAGRIN FALLS
Nicholas Properties & Developments, Inc. P392
CINCINNATI
Fifth Third Bancorp (cincinnati, Oh) A408
Medpace Holdings Inc E317
Federal Home Loan Bank Of Cincinnati A397
First Financial Bancorp (oh) A420
Bon Secours Mercy Health, Inc. A167
Bethesda, Inc. P79
University Of Cincinnati P648
Kroger Co (the) A610
Cincinnati Public Schools P125
Messer Construction Co. P349
The Christ Hospital P572
Bethesda Foundation Inc P78
Scripps (ew) Company (the) E430
Phillips Edison & Co Inc E382
Cintas Corporation A241
Bon Secours Mercy Health, Inc. P88
Bethesda Hospital, Inc. P78
First Financial Bancorp (oh) E196
Meridian Bioscience Inc. E320
Procter & Gamble Company (the) A848
Uc Health, Llc. P637
City Of Cincinnati P130
Good Samaritan Hospital Of Cincinnati P242
General Electric International Operations Company, Inc. P237
Kgbo Holdings, Inc P299
American Financial Group Inc A63
CLEVELAND
Cleveland-cliffs Inc (new) A251
Eaton Corporation A355
Parker Hannifin Corp A803
Metrohealth Medical Center P351
County Of Cuyahoga P168
Case Western Reserve University P107
Sherwin-williams Co (the) A932
Tfs Financial Corp A1012
The Metrohealth System P591
Keycorp A601
The Cleveland Clinic Foundation A1015
Crawford United Corp E127
Cleveland Municipal School District P145
Eaton Corporation P209
City Of Cleveland P130
The Cleveland Clinic Foundation P574
COLUMBUS
The Fishel Company P580
Mount Carmel Health Plan Medig P368
Columbus City School District P151
Ohiohealth Corporation P408

City Of Columbus P131
Hexion Inc. P262
Ohiohealth Riverside Methodist Hospital P408
American Electric Power Service Corporation P32
American Electric Power Co Inc A58
Installed Building Products Inc E273
Franklin County Board Of Commissioners P230
Columbia Gas Of Ohio, Inc. P150
The Ohio State University Wexner Medical Center P598
M/i Homes Inc E306
American Municipal Power, Inc. P35
Huntington Bancshares Inc A543
Mount Carmel Health System P368
Mettler-toledo International, Inc. E324
Big Lots, Inc. A156
Bath & Body Works Inc A139
Jobsohio Beverage System P287
Battelle Memorial Institute P67
Ohio State University Physicians, Inc. P407
State Auto Financial Corp. A965
Mount Carmel Health Plan, Inc. P368
Ohiohealth Corporation Group Return P408
COLUMBUS GROVE
United Bancshares Inc. (oh) E507
DAYTON
The University Of Dayton P612
Med America Health Systems Corporation P338
County Of Montgomery P173
Dayton Children's Hospital P191
Kettering Adventist Healthcare P298
Miami Valley Hospital P354
DEFIANCE
Sb Financial Group Inc E428
Premier Financial Corp A844
Premier Financial Corp E394
DELAWARE
Greif Inc A489
Franchise Group Inc E218
DOVER
Ffd Financial Corp E189
DUBLIN
Cardinal Health, Inc. A200
FAIRFIELD
Cincinnati Financial Corp. A239
FINDLAY
Mplx Lp A717
Marathon Petroleum Corp. A657
GROVE CITY
Mount Carmel Health System P368
HILLIARD
Advanced Drainage Systems Inc E5
HUDSON
The American Endowment Foundation P567
HURON
Huron Health Care Center, Inc P272
KENT
Carter-jones Companies, Inc. P107
Davey Tree Expert Co. (the) E135
KETTERING
Kettering Medical Center P299

LEBANON
Lcnb Corp E293
MARIETTA
Peoples Bancorp Inc (marietta, Oh) A814
MARTINS FERRY
United Bancorp, Inc. (martins Ferry, Oh) E506
MASON
Atricure Inc E42
MASSILLON
Fresh Mark, Inc. P232
MAUMEE
Andersons Inc A81
Dana Inc A312
MAYFIELD HEIGHTS
Vibrantz Corporation P674
MAYFIELD VILLAGE
Preformed Line Products Co. E393
Progressive Corp. (oh) A850
MEDINA
Rpm International Inc (de) A906
MIDDLEFIELD
Middlefield Banc Corp. E326
MILLERSBURG
Csb Bancorp Inc (oh) E132
MINERVA
Consumers Bancorp, Inc. (minerva, Oh) E117
NEWARK
Park National Corp (newark, Oh) E371
Park National Corp (newark, Oh) A803
NORTH RIDGEVILLE
Invacare Corporation (tw) P280
ORRVILLE
Smucker (j.m.) Co. A945
OXFORD
Miami University P354
PERRYSBURG
O-i Glass Inc A763
Mercy Health P345
REYNOLDSBURG
Victorias Secret & Co A1094
RICHFIELD
Element14 Us Holdings Inc P212
SANDUSKY
Civista Bancshares Inc A251
Civista Bancshares Inc E100
SHAKER HEIGHTS
University Hospitals Health System, Inc. P644
TOLEDO
Owens Corning A794
Pilkington North America, Inc. P433
The University Of Toledo P614
Toledo Promedica Hospital P623

INDEX BY HEADQUARTERS LOCATION

```
A = AMERICAN BUSINESS
E = EMERGING COMPANIES
P = PRIVATE COMPANIES
W = WORLD BUSINESSS
```

WALBRIDGE
The Rudolph/libbe Companies Inc P604
WHITEHALL
Heartland Banccorp E247
WILMINGTON
Air Transport Services Group, Inc. E10
WORTHINGTON
Cf Bankshares Inc E91

OKLAHOMA

ANADARKO
Western Farmers Electric Cooperative P686
CATOOSA
Cherokee Nation Businesses Llc P116
Cherokee Nation Entertainment, Llc P117
CHOUTEAU
Grand River Dam Authority P244
OKLAHOMA CITY
Candid Color Systems, Inc. P101
Ou Medicine, Inc. P416
State Of Oklahoma A970
Integris Baptist Medical Center, Inc. P277
Devon Energy Corp. A323
Bancfirst Corp. (oklahoma City, Okla) E51
Paycom Software Inc E374
Kirby - Smith Machinery, Inc. P302
Seventy Seven Energy Llc P496
Candid Color Systems, Inc. A196
Bancfirst Corp. (oklahoma City, Okla) A124
Chesapeake Energy Corp. A227
State Of Oklahoma P536
Continental Resources Inc. A294
Hobby Lobby Stores, Inc. P266
Mercy Hospital Oklahoma City, Inc. P348
City Of Oklahoma City P136
Bank7 Corp E54
Integris Health, Inc. P278
STILLWATER
Oklahoma State University P409
TAHLEQUAH
The Cherokee Nation P571
TULSA
St. John Health System, Inc. P522
Oneok Partners, L.p. P411
Williams Cos Inc (the) A1131
Bok Financial Corp A167
Ngl Energy Partners Lp A740
Saint Francis Hospital, Inc. P477
Magellan Pipeline Company, L.p. P323
Oneok Partners, L.p. A783
Oneok Inc A781
Continuum Energy Services, L.l.c. P161
Continuum Midstream, L.l.c. P162

Educational Development Corp. E153
Bok Financial Corp E63

OREGON

BEAVERTON
Nike Inc A742
Beaverton School District P73
BEND
St. Charles Health System, Inc. P521
CORBETT
County Of Multnomah P173
CORVALLIS
Samaritan Health Services, Inc. P481
ESTACADA
Portland General Electric Comp P438
EUGENE
Oregon University System P414
University Of Oregon P658
Bi-mart Acquisition Corp. P79
HEPPNER
Beo Bancorp, Heppner Or E57
HILLSBORO
County Of Washington P179
LAKE OSWEGO
Precision Castparts Corp. P441
Precision Castparts Corp. A841
MEDFORD
Lithia Motors Inc A638
MONMOUTH
Western Oregon University P687
PORTLAND
Legacy Health P309
Careoregon, Inc. P104
Bonneville Power Administration P89
Oregon Health & Science University P413
Shoestring Valley Holdings Inc. P503
Portland Public Schools P438
Fortis Construction, Inc. P229
County Of Multnomah P173
Uti, (u.s.) Holdings, Inc. P670
Pacificorp A797
Umpqua Holdings Corp A1057
Legacy Emanuel Hospital & Health Center P308
Blount International, Inc. P82
Schnitzer Steel Industries Inc E428
City Of Portland P138
Fctg Holdings, Inc. P222
SALEM
Oregon State Lottery P414
State Of Oregon P537
Salem Health P480
Oregon Department Of Transportation P413
State Of Oregon A970
WILSONVILLE
Mentor Graphics Corporation P343

PENNSYLVANIA

ABINGTON
Abington Memorial Hospital P3
ALLENTOWN
Lehigh Valley Hospital-coordinated Health Allentown P310

Air Products & Chemicals Inc A28
Computer Aid, Inc. P156
Lehigh Valley Health Network, Inc. P310
Lehigh Gas Corporation P309
Ppl Corp A840
American Bank Inc (pa) E23
AUDUBON
Globus Medical Inc E232
BALA CYNWYD
Philadelphia Consolidated Holding Corp. A823
Philadelphia Consolidated Holding Corp. P429
BELLEVILLE
Kish Bancorp Inc E288
BERWYN
Ametek Inc A74
BETHLEHEM
Saint Luke's Hospital Of Bethlehem, Pennsylvania P479
St. Luke's Hospital & Health Network P529
Embassy Bancorp Inc E156
St. Luke's Health Network, Inc. P528
St. Luke's University Health Network P529
BLAIRSVILLE
Excela Health P218
BLUE BELL
Brightview Holdings Inc E66
BRYN MAWR
Main Line Hospitals, Inc. P324
Essential Utilities Inc E174
CAMP HILL
Rite Aid Corp A893
CANONSBURG
Viatris Inc A1091
Ansys Inc. E31
Centimark Corporation P110
Equitrans Midstream Corp E171
CLEARFIELD
Cnb Financial Corp. (clearfield, Pa) E102
Cnb Financial Corp. (clearfield, Pa) A258
CLIFTON HEIGHTS
Harlee Manor, Inc. P253
COLMAR
Dorman Products Inc E144
CONSHOHOCKEN
Quaker Houghton E404
Amerisourcebergen Corp. A72
Allied Security Holdings Llc P25
CONSHOLOCKEN
Hamilton Lane Inc E244
CORAOPOLIS
Dick's Sporting Goods, Inc A325
DANVILLE
Geisinger Health P235
Geisinger Health Plan P236
The Geisinger Clinic P583
Geisinger Health A458
Geisinger Medical Center P236
DENVER
Ugi Utilities, Inc. P639

DOYLESTOWN
Hv Bancorp Inc E260
The County Of Bucks P576
DUNCANSVILLE
Value Drug Company P671
DUNMORE
Fidelity D&d Bancorp Inc E190
EMLENTON
Emclaire Financial Corp. E156
EPHRATA
Enb Financial Corp E158
ERIE
Erie Indemnity Co. E171
EXTON
West Pharmaceutical Services, Inc. E534
FORT WASHINGTON
Nutrisystem, Inc. P405
Ditech Holding Corporation P198
Toll Brothers Inc. A1031
GETTYSBURG
Acnb Corp A12
Acnb Corp E3
HARRISBURG
Pennsylvania Housing Finance Agency P425
Ollie's Bargain Outlet Holdings Inc E360
Psecu Services, Inc. A857
Upmc Pinnacle Hospitals P668
Pennsylvania Housing Finance Agency A810
United Concordia Life And Health Insurance Company P640
Pinnacle Health Hospital P434
Pennsylvania Higher Education Assistance Agency P425
HERSHEY
Hershey Company (the) A511
Milton Hershey School & School Trust P359
HONESDALE
Norwood Financial Corp. E354
INDIANA
First Commonwealth Financial Corp (indiana, Pa) A418
First Commonwealth Financial Corp (indiana, Pa) E195
S & T Bancorp Inc (indiana, Pa) A909
JENKINTOWN
Redeemer Health Holy System P458
KENNETT SQUARE
Constellation Energy Generation, Llc P160
Exelon Generation Co Llc A383
Constellation Energy Generation, Llc A292

HOOVER'S HANDBOOK OF EMERGING COMPANIES 2023

INDEX BY HEADQUARTERS LOCATION

A = AMERICAN BUSINESS
E = EMERGING COMPANIES
P = PRIVATE COMPANIES
W = WORLD BUSINESSS

KING OF PRUSSIA
Ugi Corp. A1053
Universal Health Services, Inc. A1076

LANCASTER
Fulton Financial Corp. (pa) A454
The Lancaster General Hospital P588

LANSDALE
Skf Usa Inc. P506

MALVERN
Meridian Corp E321

MANHEIM
Worley & Obetz, Inc. P693

MANSFIELD
Citizens Financial Services Inc E99

MECHANICSBURG
Pennsylvania - American Water Company P424
Select Medical Holdings Corp A925

MEDIA
County Of Delaware P169

MIDDLETOWN
Turnpike Commission, Pa P635

MILLERSBURG
Mid Penn Bancorp Inc A702
Mid Penn Bancorp Inc E325

MOON TOWNSHIP
Mastech Digital Inc E313
Calgon Carbon Corporation P98

MUNCY
Muncy Bank Financial, Inc. (muncy, Pa) E336

NEWTOWN
Epam Systems, Inc. E169

NEWTOWN SQUARE
Trinity Health Of The Mid-atlantic Region P629

NORRISTOWN
County Of Montgomery P173

PHILADELPHIA
Five Below Inc E208
The School District Of Philadelphia P605
City Of Philadelphia A251
Independence Realty Trust Inc E268
Hospital Of The University Of Pennsylvania P268
The Children's Hospital Of Philadelphia Foundation P572
Fs Kkr Capital Corp. Ii P234
Community Behavioral Health P154
Temple University Health System, Inc. P558
Trustees Of The Univ Of Penna Retiree Med And Death Benefits Trust P633
Republic First Bancorp, Inc. A890
Presbyterian Medical Center Of The University Of Pennsylvania Health System P443
Aramark A91
Health Partners Plans, Inc. P257
Pennsylvania Intergovernmental Cooperation Authority P425
Thomas Jefferson University P620
City Of Philadelphia P137
Prudential Bancorp Inc (new) E401
Fs Kkr Capital Corp. Ii A454
The Pennsylvania Hospital Of The University Of Pennsylvania Health System P600
Temple University-of The Commonwealth System Of Higher Education P558
Comcast Corp A271
Thomas Jefferson University Hospitals, Inc. P621
Cohen & Company Inc (new) E105
Trustees Of The Univ Of Penna Retiree Med And Death Benefits Trust A1043
Albert Einstein Medical Associates, Inc. P17

PITTSBURGH
County Of Allegheny P166
Kraft Heinz Co (the) A609
Tristate Capital Holdings Inc E498
Carnegie Mellon University P106
Fnb Corp E211
Wabtec Corp A1099
Upmc P667
City Of Pittsburgh P138
Tristate Capital Holdings Inc A1039
Upmc Presbyterian Shadyside A1081
University Of Pittsburgh-of The Commonwealth System Of Higher Education P659
Board Of Public Education School District Of Pittsburgh (inc) P86
Alcoa Corporation A37
Ppg Industries Inc A838
Arconic Corp A95
Smmh Practice Plan, Inc. P508
Wesco International, Inc. A1116
Allegheny General Hospital Inc P22
Pnc Financial Services Group (the) A833
Limbach Holdings Inc E301
Upmc A1080
Upmc Magee-womens Hospital P667
Pittsburgh School District P434
Fnb Corp A440
United States Steel Corp. A1072
Upmc Presbyterian Shadyside P668

PITTSTON
Benco Dental Supply Co. P74

RADNOR
Avantor Inc A112
Airgas, Inc. P13
Main Line Health System P324
Lincoln National Corp. A637
Airgas, Inc. A30

READING
Boscov's, Inc. P90
Reading Hospital P455
Redner's Markets, Inc. P458
Reading Hospital Services Inc P456
County Of Berks P167

SAXONBURG
Ii-vi Inc E265

SCRANTON
Peoples Financial Services Corp A815

SHIPPENSBURG
Orrstown Financial Services, Inc. A788

Orrstown Financial Services, Inc. E365

SOUDERTON
Univest Financial Corp A1078
Univest Financial Corp E512

TREVOSE
Broder Bros., Co. P93

TUNKHANNOCK
County Of Wyoming P179
County Of Wyoming A301

UNIVERSITY PARK
The Pennsylvania State University P601
The Pennsylvania State University A1022

UPPER CHICHESTER
Sunoco Pipeline L.p. P547

WARREN
Northwest Bancshares, Inc. (md) A752

WAYNE
Radian Group, Inc. A872
Teleflex Incorporated E483

WELLSBORO
Citizens & Northern Corp E97

WEST CHESTER
Accesslex Institute A10

WEST READING
Customers Bancorp Inc E132
Customers Bancorp Inc A307

WORCESTER
Allan Myers, Inc. P21

WYOMISSING
Gaming & Leisure Properties, Inc E227

YARDLEY
Crown Holdings Inc A302

YORK
Wellspan Medical Group P683
York Hospital P696
County Of York P179

PUERTO RICO

RIO GRANDE
Desarolladora Del Norte S E P194

SAN JUAN
Popular Inc. A835

TOA BAJA
Best Petroleum Corporation P76

RHODE ISLAND

LINCOLN
Narragansett Electric Comp P375

NEWPORT
Pangaea Logistics Solutions Ltd. E370

PAWTUCKET
Teknor Apex Company P556
Hasbro, Inc. A502

PROVIDENCE
State Of Rhode Island A971
City Of Providence P138
United Natural Foods Inc. A1067
Care New England Health System Inc P104
State Of Rhode Island P537
Rhode Island Hospital P462
Gilbane Building Company P239
Textron Inc A1011
Citizens Financial Group Inc (new) A247
Brown University P96

WARWICK
Vanguard Charitable Endowment Program P673
Plan International, Inc. P436

WESTERLY
Washington Trust Bancorp, Inc. A1107

WOONSOCKET
Cvs Health Corporation A309

SOUTH CAROLINA

AIKEN
Security Federal Corp (sc) E433

ANDERSON
Anmed Health P39

CHARLESTON
Roper St. Francis Healthcare P469
Medical University Hospital Authority P339
The Medical University Of South Carolina P590

COLUMBIA
Agfirst Farm Credit Bank A26
Central Electric Power Cooperative, Inc. P111
State Of South Carolina P537
Agfirst Farm Credit Bank P11
State Of South Carolina A971

CONWAY
Horry County School District P268

FLORENCE
First Reliance Bancshares Inc E205
Mcleod Regional Medical Center Of
The Pee Dee, Inc. P338

GREENVILLE
Prisma Health-upstate P443
Athene Annuity & Life Assurance Company A105
St. Francis Hospital, Inc. P521
Athene Annuity & Life Assurance Company P49
Southern First Bancshares, Inc. E454

GREER
Regional Management Corp E413

HARTSVILLE
Sonoco Products Co. A949

HILTON HEAD ISLAND
Coastalsouth Bancshares Inc E104

LEXINGTON
First Community Corp (sc) E195

INDEX BY HEADQUARTERS LOCATION

A = AMERICAN BUSINESS
E = EMERGING COMPANIES
P = PRIVATE COMPANIES
W = WORLD BUSINESSS

MONCKS CORNER
South Carolina Public Service Authority (inc) P510
MYRTLE BEACH
South Atlantic Bancshares Inc E452
SPARTANBURG
Security Finance Corporation Of Spartanburg P492
Spartanburg Regional Health Services District, Inc. P516
J M Smith Corporation P281
Security Group, Inc. P492
SUMMERVILLE
Advanced Technology International A19
Advanced Technology International P5
WEST COLUMBIA
Lexington Medical Center P314
Lexington County Health Services District, Inc. P314

SOUTH DAKOTA

ABERDEEN
Dacotah Banks Inc. A311
Agtegra Cooperative P11
PIERRE
State Of South Dakota P537
State Of South Dakota A971
RAPID CITY
Monument Health Rapid City Hospital, Inc. P367
SIOUX FALLS
Meta Financial Group Inc E322
Sanford Health P483
Meta Financial Group Inc A688
The Evangelical Lutheran Good Samaritan Society P579
Sanford Health P484

TENNESSEE

BRENTWOOD
Delek Us Holdings Inc (new) A321
Tractor Supply Co. A1035
CHATTANOOGA
Emj Corporation P213
Unum Group A1079
Memorial Health Care System, Inc. P341
Electric Power Board Of Chattanooga P211
Hamilton Chattanooga County Hospital Authority P252
COOKEVILLE
Averitt Incorporated P56
Averitt Express, Inc. P56
FRANKLIN
Community Healthcare Trust Inc E114
Community Health Systems, Inc. A281

Clarcor Inc. P144
GOODLETTSVILLE
Dollar General Corp A335
JACKSON
Jackson-madison County General Hospital District P284
JOHNSON CITY
Ballad Health P59
KINGSPORT
Eastman Chemical Co A352
Wellmont Health System P682
KNOXVILLE
Educational Funding Of The South, Inc. A360
Cfj Properties Llc A221
University Of Tennessee P661
Smartfinancial Inc E451
Mountain Commerce Bancorp Inc E333
Regal Entertainment Group P459
Scripps Networks Interactive, Inc. P489
Covenant Health P180
Cfj Properties Llc P113
Knoxville Utilities Board P303
Tennessee Valley Authority A1005
Smartfinancial Inc A945
LEBANON
Wilson Bank Holding Co. E539
Wilson Bank Holding Co. A1132
LOUDON
Malibu Boats Inc E308
MEMPHIS
First Horizon Corp A423
First Horizon Corp E200
American Lebanese Syrian Associated Charities, Inc. A35
County Of Shelby P177
International Paper Co A567
Baptist Memorial Hospital P64
Autozone, Inc. A110
Monogram Food Solutions, Llc P364
Methodist Healthcare- Memphis Hospitals P350
Fedex Corp A404
City Of Memphis P133
Frontdoor Inc E221
Baptist Memorial Health Care Corporation P63
Board Of Education-memphis City Schools P86
MURFREESBORO
The Middle Tennessee Electric Membership Corporation P594
NASHVILLE
Fb Financial Corp A395
Vanderbilt University Medical Center P672
Yellow Corp (new) A1143
Tri Star Energy, Llc P627
Electric Power Board Of The Metropolitan Government Of Nashville & Davidson County P212
State Of Tennessee P537
Metropolitan Government Of Nashville & Davidson County P351
Fb Financial Corp E185
The Vanderbilt University P617
Hca Healthcare Inc A504

Capstar Financial Holdings Inc A199
Alliancebernstein Holding Lp E17
Pinnacle Financial Partners Inc E385
Dialysis Clinic, Inc. P195
State Of Tennessee A971
Ryman Hospitality Properties, Inc. P472
Capstar Financial Holdings Inc E79
Pinnacle Financial Partners Inc A828
VONORE
Mastercraft Boat Holdings Inc E313

TEXAS

ABILENE
First Financial Bankshares, Inc. E197
First Financial Bankshares, Inc. A421
ADDISON
Xmed Oxygen & Medical Equipment, Lp P693
Guaranty Bancshares Inc A492
Guaranty Bancshares Inc E243
Wingstop Inc E539
AMARILLO
Affiliated Foods, Inc. P9
Bruckner Truck Sales, Inc. P97
ARLINGTON
Forestar Group Inc (new) E212
Horton (dr) Inc A535
Texas Health Resources P564
Arlington Independent School District (inc) P45
AUSTIN
Attorney General, Texas P53
Farm Credit Bank Of Texas A392
Whole Foods Market, Inc. A1129
Texas Department Of Transportation A1009
City Of Austin P128
American Campus Communities Operating Partnership Lp P31
Oracle Corp A785
Solarwinds Corp E451
Austin Independent School District (inc) P55
Higher Education Coordinating Board, Texas P263
State Of Texas P537
Digital Realty Trust Inc E140
Vital Farms Inc E529
County Of Travis P178
Texas County And District Retirement System P563
Texas State University System P565
Texas Workforce Commission P565
Usa Compression Partners Lp E514
Texas Department Of Housing & Community Affairs P563
Farm Credit Bank Of Texas P221
Whole Foods Market, Inc. P688
Texas Department Of Transportation P563
American Campus Communities Operating Partnership Lp A58
National Western Life Group Inc A722
State Of Texas A971
Digital Turbine Inc E141
Tesla Inc A1007
Texas County And District Retirement System A1009
BEAUMONT
Communitybank Of Texas, N.a. A283

BEDFORD
Legacy Housing Corp E296
BELLAIRE
Harris County Hospital District P253
CONROE
Spirit Of Texas Bancshares Inc A958
Conroe Independent School District P159
Spirit Of Texas Bancshares Inc E456
COPPELL
Mr Cooper Group Inc E334
Mr Cooper Group Inc A717
CORPUS CHRISTI
Driscoll Childrens Health Plan P202
Spohn Investment Corporation P518
DALLAS
Cyrusone Holdco Llc P184
Southwest Airlines Co A955
Sunoco Lp A982
Children's Medical Center Of Dallas P121
Hilltop Holdings, Inc. A515
Texas Instruments Inc. A1009
Cyrusone Inc E134
Spirit Realty Capital, Inc. A958
Stevens Transport, Inc. P540
First Foundation Inc A423
Dallas Independent School District P187
Copart Inc E119
Veritex Holdings Inc A1086
Placid Refining Company Llc P435
Builders Firstsource Inc. A183
At&t Inc A104
First Foundation Inc E199
Placid Holding Company P434
Baylor Scott & White Holdings A143
Jacobs Engineering Group, Inc. A578
Crossroads Systems Inc (new) E131
Aecom A20
Baylor Scott & White Health P68
Tenet Healthcare Corp. A1001
Truman Arnold Companies P630
Baylor University Medical Center P69
Primoris Services Corp E396
Texas Capital Bancshares Inc A1008
City Of Dallas P131
Invitation Homes Inc E280
Bearingpoint, Inc. P72
Mv Transportation, Inc. P373
Sixth Street Specialty Lending Inc A941
Steward Health Care System Llc P541
Southern Methodist University Inc P514

HOOVER'S HANDBOOK OF EMERGING COMPANIES 2023

INDEX BY HEADQUARTERS LOCATION

A = AMERICAN BUSINESS
E = EMERGING COMPANIES
P = PRIVATE COMPANIES
W = WORLD BUSINESSS

Spirit Realty Capital, Inc. P518
Dallas County Hospital District P186
Cbre Group Inc A212
Gwg Holdings Inc A493
Comerica, Inc. A273
County Of Dallas P168
Triumph Bancorp Inc A1040
Parkland Community Health Plan, Inc., A Program Of Dallas County Hospital P421
Energy Transfer Lp A368
Veritex Holdings Inc E521
Texas Pacific Land Corp E487
Hollyfrontier Corp A519
Baylor Scott & White Holdings P69
Triumph Bancorp Inc E499
Baylor Scott & White Health A143
Kimberly-clark Corp. A603
Nexpoint Residential Trust Inc E348
Balfour Beatty Construction, Llc P58
Balfour Beatty Construction Group, Inc. P58

DEER PARK
Deer Park Refining Limited Partnership P193

DENTON
University Of North Texas System P658

DFW AIRPORT
Dallas-fort Worth International Airport Facility Improvement Corporation P187

EDINBURG
Doctors Hospital At Renaissance, Ltd. P200

EL PASO
El Paso Independent School District Education Foundation P211
Socorro Independent School District P509
El Paso County Hospital District P211
City Of El Paso P131

FORT WORTH
Cook Children's Medical Center P162
Bnsf Railway Company P85
Fort Worth Independent School District P228
Tarrant County Texas (inc) P555
Cook Children's Health Plan P162
Texas Christian University Inc P562
Bnsf Railway Company A162
American Airlines Group Inc A55
Texas Health Harris Methodist Hospital Fort Worth P563
Wesco Aircraft Holdings, Inc. P683
Tarrant County Hospital District P554
County Of Tarrant P178
Firstcash Holdings Inc E207

FRISCO
Addus Homecare Corp E4
The Core Group Ltd P576

GAINESVILLE
Ses Holdings, Llc P496

GALVESTON
American National Group Inc A67

GARLAND
Garland Independent School District P235

GRAPEVINE
Gamestop Corp A456

HOUSTON
Baker Hughes Company A120
Centerpoint Energy, Inc A217
Tmh Physician Organization P622
Alief Independent School District P21
Memorial Hermann Health System P342
Anr Pipeline Company P40
Chemium International Corp. P116
Ep Energy Llc P217
Plains Gp Holdings Lp A832
Hess Midstream Lp E253
Geokinetics Inc. P238
Apa Corp A85
Nrg Energy Inc A756
Texas Aromatics, Lp P561
Mid-america Pipeline Company, Llc P357
Phillips 66 Partners Lp E382
Community Health Choice Texas, Inc. P154
County Of Harris P170
Harris County Fire Marshal P253
Plains Pipeline, L.p. P435
Westlake Corp A1122
Quanta Services, Inc. A867
Comfort Systems Usa Inc E110
Houston Methodist St. John Hospital A537
Tauber Oil Company P555
Community Health Choice, Inc. P154
Cima Energy, Lp P125
Halliburton Company A493
Kbr Inc A595
Shell Midstream Partners Lp E437
Tricon International, Ltd. P628
Aldine Independent School District P19
Spectra Energy, Llc P517
Hewlett Packard Enterprise Co A513
Crown Castle International Corp (new) A301
Eog Resources, Inc. A375
Cypress-fairbanks Independent School District P184
Technip Usa, Inc P555
Financial Trader Corporation P224
Natural Gas Pipeline Company Of America Llc P379
Plains All American Pipeline Lp A831
Enterprise Te Products Pipeline Company Llc P216
University Of Houston System P652
Targa Resources Corp A994
Waste Management, Inc. (de) A1108
The Methodist Hospital P590
Houston Independent School District P270
Kraton Polymers U.s. Llc P304
Conocophillips A288
Phillips 66 A825
Cheniere Energy Inc. A224
Allegiance Bancshares Inc E17
Cameron International Corporation P100
Memorial Hermann Health System A680
Cbtx Inc A213
Sysco Corp A988
Texas Children's Hospital P561
Sharps Compliance Corp. E437
Nov Inc A754
Magnolia Oil & Gas Corp E307
Enterprise Crude Pipeline Llc P215
Corebridge Financial Inc A295
Methodist Health Care System P350
Group 1 Automotive, Inc. A490
Cactus Inc E72
Helix Energy Solutions Group Inc E250
S & B Engineers And Constructors, Ltd. P474
Biourja Trading, Llc P81
Lukoil Pan Americas, Llc P322
United Space Alliance, Llc P642
Ies Holdings Inc E264
Houston Methodist St. John Hospital P271
Tricon International, Ltd. A1039
Midcoast Energy Partners, L.p. P357
Enterprise Products Partners L.p. A373
Prosperity Bancshares Inc. E398
Cheniere Energy Partners L P A226
Baker Hughes Holdings Llc A120
Spring Branch Independent School District (inc) P518
Sun Coast Resources, Inc. P545
Southern Natural Gas Company, L.l.c. P514
Allegiance Bancshares Inc A40
Prosperity Bancshares Inc. A852
El Paso Natural Gas Company, L.l.c. P211
Ep Energy Corporation P216
Centerpoint Energy Services Retail Llc P110
Occidental Petroleum Corp A765
Kinder Morgan Inc. A604
Marathon Oil Corp. A655
Cameron International Corporation A193
Chi St. Luke's Health Baylor College Of Medicine Medical Center Condominium Association P118
Texas Eastern Transmission, Lp P563

HUMBLE
Humble Independent School District P271

IRVING
Forterra, Inc. P229
Finance Of America Companies Inc E190
Nch Corporation P380
Mckesson Corp A675
Old Claimco, Llc P409
Pioneer Natural Resources Co A829
The Michaels Companies Inc A1020
Exxon Mobil Corp A387
Federal Home Loan Bank Of Dallas A397
Federal Home Loan Bank Of Dallas E187
Vistra Corp A1097
Commercial Metals Co. A276
The Michaels Companies Inc P592
Celanese Corp (de) A214
Gruma Corporation P248
Envela Corp E168

Hms Holdings Llc P265
Fluor Corp. A436

JOHNSON CITY
Pedernales Electric Cooperative, Inc. P424

KATY
Academy Sports & Outdoors Inc A10
Katy Independent School District P296

KELLER
Kiewit Infrastructure South Co. P301

KILGORE
Martin Product Sales Llc P329
Martin Resource Management Corporation P329

KILLEEN
Killeen Independent School District P301

LAREDO
International Bancshares Corp. A562

LEWISVILLE
Kmm Telecommunications P302

LITTLE ELM
Retractable Technologies Inc E418

LONGVIEW
Friedman Industries, Inc. E220

LUBBOCK
Covenant Health System P180
South Plains Financial Inc E454
Plains Cotton Cooperative Association P435
South Plains Financial Inc A950
Pro Petroleum Llc P444

MCKINNEY
Encore Wire Corp. E159
Globe Life Inc A477
Independent Bank Group Inc. A555
Independent Bank Group Inc. E269

MIDLAND
Wtg Gas Processing, L.p. P693
Rattler Midstream Lp E409

NORTH RICHLAND HILLS
Calloway's Nursery, Inc. E76

PASADENA
Floworks International Llc P226
Pasadena Independent School District P422
Floworks Usa Lp P227

PLANO
Plano Independent School District P436
Ribbon Communications Inc E420
Diodes, Inc. E142
Tyler Technologies, Inc. E501
North Texas Tollway Authority P398

INDEX BY HEADQUARTERS LOCATION

A = AMERICAN BUSINESS
E = EMERGING COMPANIES
P = PRIVATE COMPANIES
W = WORLD BUSINESSS

Toyota Motor Credit Corp. A1034
Yum China Holdings Inc A1145
Green Brick Partners Inc E238
RICHARDSON
Realpage, Inc. P456
Richardson Independent School
  District P463
RICHMOND
County Of Fort Bend P169
ROUND ROCK
Dell Technologies Inc A322
Round Rock Independent School
  District (inc) P469
SAN ANTONIO
San Antonio Independent School
  District Fac P482
Southwest Research Institute Inc
  P515
County Of Bexar P167
Cullen/frost Bankers, Inc. A304
Victory Capital Holdings Inc (de) E525
Us Global Investors Inc E514
Xpel Inc E546
Northside Independent School
  District P401
Bcfs Health And Human Services P71
City Public Services Of San Antonio
  P143
Valero Energy Corp A1083
City Of San Antonio P140
North East Independent School
  District P395
The University Of Texas Health
  Science Center At San Antonio P614
University Health System Services Of
  Texas, Inc. P643
Christus Santa Rosa Health Care
  Corporation P123
SEGUIN
Alamo Group, Inc. E12
SPRING
Klein Independent School District
  P302
SUGAR LAND
Meglobal Americas Inc. P340
Noble Holding (u.s.) Corporation
  P393
TEMPLE
Scott And White Health Plan P488
Mclane Company, Inc. P337
Scott & White Memorial Hospital
  P488
Mclane Company, Inc. A677
TEXARKANA
Yates Group, Inc. P695
THE WOODLANDS
Smart Sand Inc E450
Western Midstream Partners Lp E536
Chevron Phillips Chemical Company
  Llc A230
H. J. Baker Sulphur, Llc P250
Chevron Phillips Chemical Company
  Lp P117

Sterling Construction Co Inc E463
Huntsman Corp A547
Lgi Homes, Inc. E298
Talen Energy Supply, Llc P554
Championx Corp E91
Chevron Phillips Chemical Company
  Lp A231
Chevron Phillips Chemical Company
  Llc P117
TYLER
East Texas Medical Center Regional
  Healthcare System P207
Christus Northeast Texas Health
  System Corporation P123
Trinity Mother Frances Health System
  Foundation P629
Southside Bancshares, Inc. A953
VICTORIA
South Texas Electric Cooperative, Inc.
  P511
WACO
Brazos Electric Power Cooperative,
  Inc. P91
Baylor University P69
WESLACO
Idea Public Schools P274
WEST LAKE HILLS
The Drees Company P577
WESTLAKE
Goosehead Insurance Inc E235
Schwab (charles) Corp (the) A918
WICHITA FALLS
The Priddy Foundation A1022
The Priddy Foundation P602
WYLIE
North Texas Municipal Water District
  P398

UTAH
AMERICAN FORK
Alpine School District P27
CENTERVILLE
Management & Training Corporation
  P326
DRAPER
Comenity Bank A273
Healthequity Inc E247
Comenity Bank P151
FARMINGTON
Davis School District P191
HURRICANE
Dats Trucking, Inc. P191
LOGAN
Utah State University P670
MIDVALE
Overstock.com Inc (de) E367
Ally Bank P26
Ally Bank A42
MURRAY
R1 Rcm Inc E407
NORTH SALT LAKE
Big West Oil, Llc P79
OGDEN
Big West Of California, Llc P79
Afj, Llc P9

PARK CITY
Innovative Industrial Properties Inc
  E271
SALT LAKE CITY
Alsco Inc. P28
Zions Bancorporation, N.a. A1150
University Of Utah Health Hospitals
  And Clinics P662
State Of Utah A971
Big-d Construction Corp. P80
The University Of Utah P615
Intermountain Health Care Inc A562
Western Governors University P687
County Of Salt Lake P176
Associated Food Stores, Inc. P47
Security National Financial Corp
  E434
State Of Utah P538
Extra Space Storage Inc E180
C.r. England, Inc. P98
Intermountain Health Care Inc P278
Garff Enterprises, Inc. P235
SOUTH SALT LAKE
Granite School District P244
R.c. Willey Home Furnishings P451
ST GEORGE
Ihc Health Services, Inc. A550
Ihc Health Services, Inc. P274
WEST JORDAN
Jordan School District P292
Sportsman's Warehouse Holdings Inc
  E456

VERMONT
BURLINGTON
The University Of Vermont Medical
  Center Inc P616
University Of Vermont & State
  Agricultural College P662
MONTPELIER
State Of Vermont P538
State Of Vermont A971
MORRISVILLE
Union Bankshares, Inc. (morrisville,
  Vt) E506
RUTLAND
Casella Waste Systems, Inc. E82

VIRGIN ISLANDS
CHRISTIANSTED
Limetree Bay Terminals Llc P316
Limetree Bay Terminals Llc A636

VIRGINIA
ALEXANDRIA
Burke Herbert Financial Services
  Corp A185
City Of Alexandria P127
95 Express Lanes Llc P1
ARLINGTON
American Institutes For Research In
  The Behavioral Sciences P34
Aerovironment, Inc. E7
Aes Corp A21
The Nature Conservancy P595
Ceb Inc. P108

County Of Arlington P166
ASHBURN
Dxc Technology Co A349
BERRYVILLE
Eagle Financial Services, Inc.
  E149
BLACKSBURG
Virginia Polytechnic Institute &
  State
  University P676
BLUEFIELD
First Community Bankshares Inc
  (va)
  A419
BROADLANDS
Loudoun County Public School
  District P320
CENTREVILLE
The Parsons Corporation P598
CHANTILLY
Dyncorp International Llc P206
CHARLOTTESVILLE
The University Of Virginia P616
Rector & Visitors Of The
  University Of
  Virginia P457
Virginia National Bankshares
  Corp
  E526
Blue Ridge Bankshares Inc (luray,
  Va)
  E62
University Of Virginia P663
CHESAPEAKE
City Of Chesapeake P130
Dollar Tree Inc A337
CHESTERFIELD
County Of Chesterfield P167
CHRISTIANSBURG
Carilion New River Valley Medical
  Center P105
DANVILLE
American National Bankshares,
  Inc.
  (danville, Va) A66
American National Bankshares,
  Inc.
  (danville, Va) E24
DULLES
National Rural Utilities
  Cooperative
  Finance Corp E340
FAIRFAX
Fairfax County Virginia A389
Fvcbankcorp Inc E227
Fairfax County Virginia P219
Inova Health System Foundation
  P277
Mainstreet Bancshares Inc E307
Widepoint Corp E537
FALLS CHURCH
Inova Health Care Services P277
Northrop Grumman Corp A750
FLOYD
Parkway Acquisition Corp E372
FREDERICKSBURG
Washington Healthcare
  Physicians,
  Mary P680

HOOVER'S HANDBOOK OF EMERGING COMPANIES 2023   577

INDEX BY HEADQUARTERS LOCATION

```
A = AMERICAN BUSINESS
E = EMERGING COMPANIES
P = PRIVATE COMPANIES
W = WORLD BUSINESSS
```

GLEN ALLEN
Markel Corp (holding Co) A658
Asgn Inc E37

HENRICO
County Of Henrico P170

HERNDON
Beacon Roofing Supply Inc A144
Stride Inc E467
Strategic Education Inc E466
Mantech International Corp E308

LEESBURG
Loudoun County P320

LYNCHBURG
Bwx Technologies Inc E69
Centra Health, Inc. P110
Liberty University, Inc. P316

MANASSAS
Prince William County Public Schools P443

MARTINSVILLE
Carter Bankshares Inc A207

MCLEAN
Primis Financial Corp A845
Primis Financial Corp E395
Hilton Worldwide Holdings Inc A516
Capital One Financial Corp A197
Freddie Mac A449
Booz Allen Hamilton Holding Corp. A170
Gladstone Commercial Corp E231

MECHANICSVILLE
Owens & Minor, Inc. A792

MIDLOTHIAN
Village Bank & Trust Financial Corp E526

NEWPORT NEWS
Huntington Ingalls Industries, Inc. A546
Ferguson Enterprises, Llc A405
Riverside Healthcare Association, Inc. P463
Riverside Regional Medial Center P464
Ferguson Enterprises, Llc P222
City Of Newport News P135
Riverside Hospital, Inc. P464

NORFOLK
Virginia International Terminals, Llc P675
Sentara Healthcare P494
Sentara Healthcare A929
Sentara Hospitals - Norfolk P495
City Of Norfolk P136

PORTSMOUTH
Townebank A1033
Townebank E492

RESTON
Maryland And Virginia Milk Producers Cooperative Association, Incorporated P330
Caci International Inc A188

General Dynamics Corp A459
Idemia Identity & Security Usa Llc P274
Leidos Holdings Inc A624
John Marshall Bancorp Inc E283
Nvr Inc. A761
Science Applications International Corp (new) A920

RICHMOND
Atlantic Union Bankshares Corp E40
Vcu Health System Authority P673
Virginia Housing Development Authority A1094
Virginia Housing Development Authority P675
Arko Corp E35
Virginia Department Of Transportation P675
Virginia Commonwealth University P675
Virginia Premier Health Plan, Inc. P676
Gpm Investments, Llc P243
Carmax Inc. A204
Commonwealth Of Virginia P154
Genworth Financial, Inc. (holding Co) A469
Virginia College Building Authority P674
Altria Group Inc A46
Kinsale Capital Group Inc E287
Federal Reserve Bank Of Richmond, Dist. No. 5 A401
Apple Hospitality Reit, Inc. P42
Estes Express Lines P217
Performance Food Group Co A818
Atlantic Union Bankshares Corp A106
Commonwealth Of Virginia A279
Dominion Energy Inc (new) A338
City Of Richmond P139
Virginia Electric & Power Co. A1094

ROANOKE
Carilion Services, Inc. P105
Carilion Medical Center P105

TIMBERVILLE
F & M Bank Corp. E181

TYSONS
Alarm.com Holdings Inc E13
Computer Sciences Corporation P157
Computer Sciences Corporation A283

VIRGINIA BEACH
Armada Hoffler Properties Inc E35
Atlantic Diving Supply, Inc. P49
City Of Virginia Beach P142
Navy Exchange Service Command P379

WINCHESTER
Trex Co Inc E493
Valley Health System Group Return P671
American Woodmark Corp. E27

WOODBRIDGE
County Of Prince William P175

WASHINGTON

BELLEVUE
Paccar Inc. A795
Terreno Realty Corp E486
T-mobile Us Inc A991

Overlake Hospital Medical Center P417
Overlake Hospital Association P417

BELLINGHAM
Exp World Holdings Inc E179
Haggen, Inc. P252

BREMERTON
Harrison Medical Center P254

CASHMERE
Cashmere Valley Bank Washington (new) E83

EVERETT
Public Utility District 1 Of Snohomish County P448
County Of Snohomish P177
Coastal Financial Corp (wa) E103

HOQUIAM
Timberland Bancorp, Inc. E489

ISSAQUAH
Costco Wholesale Corp A299

KENT
Petrocard, Inc. P428

KIRKLAND
Monolithic Power Systems Inc E330
King County Public Hospital District 2 P301

LYNNWOOD
U&i Financial Corp E503

MOUNTLAKE TERRACE
Fs Bancorp Inc (washington) E223

OLYMPIA
State Of Washington A972
Heritage Financial Corp (wa) E252
State Of Washington P538
Heritage Financial Corp (wa) A510

PORT ANGELES
First Northwest Bancorp E204

REDMOND
Lake Washington School District P306
Microsoft Corporation A700

RENTON
First Financial Northwest Inc E198
Providence Health & Services P445
Providence Health & Services - Oregon P446
Providence Health & Services A853
Public Hospital District 1 Of King County P447

RICHLAND
Kadlec Regional Medical Center P293

SEATTLE
Seattle Schools District No. 1 Of King County Washington P492
Starbucks Corp. A962
University Of Washington Inc A1077
Amazon.com Inc A48
Expedia Group Inc A384
Homestreet Inc A527
City Of Seattle P141
Northwest Dairy Association P401
County Of King P171
Virginia Mason Medical Center P676
Alaska Air Group, Inc. A33
University Of Washington Inc P663
Swedish Health Services P551
Zillow Group Inc A1148

Nordstrom, Inc. A744
Sound Financial Bancorp Inc E452
Weyerhaeuser Co A1125
Broadmark Realty Capital Inc E67
Washington Federal Inc A1106
The City Of Seattle-city Light Department P573
Expeditors International Of Washington, Inc. A386

SPOKANE
Northwest Farm Credit Services P401
Potlatchdeltic Corp E389
W.t.b. Financial Corp. A1099
Northwest Farm Credit Services A753
Urm Stores, Inc. P668

TACOMA
Tacoma Public Schools P554
County Of Pierce P175
Columbia Banking System Inc E108
Franciscan Health System P230
Columbia Banking System Inc A270
Multicare Health System P371

VANCOUVER
Public Utility District 1 Of Clark County P447
Peacehealth P423
Kiewit Infrastructure West Co. P301
Nautilus Inc E343
Northwest Pipe Co. E353

WALLA WALLA
Banner Corp. A135

YAKIMA
Yakima Valley Memorial Hospital Association Inc P693

WEST VIRGINIA

CHARLESTON
State Of West Virginia A972
Charleston Area Medical Center, Inc. P114
United Bankshares Inc A1063
City Holding Co. A249
United Bankshares Inc E507
City Holding Co. E99
State Of West Virginia P538

FAIRMONT
Mvb Financial Corp E336
Monongahela Power Company P365

MOOREFIELD
Summit Financial Group Inc A981
Summit Financial Group Inc E469

MORGANTOWN
West Virginia University Hospitals, Inc. P684
West Virginia University P685
West Virginia United Health System, Inc. P684

INDEX BY HEADQUARTERS LOCATION

A = AMERICAN BUSINESS
E = EMERGING COMPANIES
P = PRIVATE COMPANIES
W = WORLD BUSINESSS

WHEELING
Wesbanco Inc E532
Wesbanco Inc A1115

WISCONSIN

APPLETON
U.s. Venture, Inc. A1051
U.s. Venture, Inc. P637
The Boldt Group Inc P568

BEAVER DAM
United Cooperative P640

BELOIT
Blackhawk Bancorp Inc E61

BROOKFIELD
Fiserv Inc A432
Cib Marine Bancshares Inc E97

EAU CLAIRE
Citizens Community Bancorp Inc (md) E98

FITCHBURG
Certco, Inc. P113
Promega Corporation P445

GLENDALE
Wheaton Franciscan Services, Inc. P688

GREEN BAY
Nicolet Bankshares Inc E349
Nicolet Bankshares Inc A741
St. Vincent Hospital Of The Hospital Sisters Of The Third Order Of St. Francis P531
Krueger International, Inc. P304
Schneider National Inc (wi) A917
Associated Banc-corp A100

JANESVILLE
Mercy Health System Corporation P347

LA CROSSE
Gundersen Lutheran Medical Center, Inc. P250
Gundersen Lutheran Administrative Services Inc. P249
Kwik Trip, Inc. P305

LA FARGE
Cooperative Regions Of Organic Producer Pools P163

MADISON
First Business Financial Services, Inc. A416
County Of Dane P168
State Of Wisconsin P538
University Of Wisconsin Hospitals And Clinics Authority P663
University Of Wisconsin System P664
Wisconsin Alumni Research Foundation A1134
Wisconsin Housing And Economic Development Authority A1134
State Of Wisconsin A972

MANITOWOC
Bank First Corp E52

Bank First Corp A125
Orion Energy Systems Inc E364

MARSHFIELD
Security Health Plan Of Wisconsin, Inc. P493
Mchs Hospitals Inc P337
Marshfield Clinic, Inc. P328

MENOMONEE FALLS
Kohl's Corp. A608

MEQUON
Charter Manufacturing Company, Inc. P115

MIDDLETON
University Of Wisconsin Medical Foundation, Inc. P664

MILWAUKEE
Rockwell Automation, Inc. A901
Marquette University P328
Wec Energy Group Inc A1113
The Medical College Of Wisconsin Inc P590
Manpowergroup Inc A654
Children's Hospital Of Wisconsin, Inc P121
Aurora Health Care, Inc. A107
Froedtert Memorial Lutheran Hospital, Inc. P233
Aurora Health Care Metro, Inc P54
Mgic Investment Corp. (wi) A693
Johnson Controls, Inc. P291
Physicians Realty Trust E384
Wisconsin Milwaukee County P692
Aurora Health Care, Inc. P54
Milwaukee Public Schools (inc) P359
Rite-hite Holding Corporation P463
Robert W Baird & Co Inc P466
Froedtert Health, Inc. P233
Johnson Controls, Inc. A585

MOUNT HOREB
Duluth Holdings Inc E146

NEENAH
Thedacare, Inc. P619

OSHKOSH
Oshkosh Corp (new) A789

RACINE
Johnson Outdoors Inc E283

RIPON
Alliance Laundry Holdings Llc P25

SUN PRAIRIE
Independent Pharmacy Cooperative P276

WAUKESHA
Generac Holdings Inc E227

WAUSAU
Aspirus Wausau Hospital, Inc. P46
Aspirus, Inc. P47

WAUWATOSA
Waterstone Financial Inc (md) E532
Teb Bancorp Inc E480

WYOMING

GILLETTE
Cloud Peak Energy Resources Llc P146

ZAF

Gauteng
Mtn Group Ltd (south Africa) W413

Johannesburg
Standard Bank Group Ltd W558
Absa Group Ltd (new) W7

Pretoria
South African Reserve Bank W558

Sandton
Investec Ltd W310
Bid Corp Ltd W102
Sasol Ltd. W517
Nedbank Group Ltd W425

Stellenbosch
Steinhoff International Holdings Nv W562

Index Of Executives

(

(Ret.), Ellen M. Pawlikowski A907
(Ret.), Ellen M. Pawlikowski A877

A

Aadland, Todd A399
Aagaard, Aleksander W348
Aaholm, Sherry A. A771
Aaholm, Sherry A. A306
Aamund, Marie-Louise W205
Aanensen, Theodore J. A596
Aanensen, Theodore J. E286
Aarnes, Robert B. A893
Aaron, Susan D. A532
Aaron, Susan D. E259
Aaron, Thomas J. A240
Aaronson, Daniel R. A399
Aarsheim, Rolf W558
Aasheim, Hilde Merete W448
Aasmundstad, Eric K. E348
Abacan, Antonio S. W399
Abaitua, Asis Canales W295
Abani, Priya A580
Abanumay, Mohammed S. W519
Abascal, Juan W493
Abate, Christopher J. A881
Abbal, Frederic W524
Abbasi, A. Faraz A618
Abbasi, A. Faraz E290
Abbate, Salvatore A. A1086
Abbey, Donald M. E138
Abbey, Donald M. E262
Abbey, Richard W. A381
Abbott, Henry F. A932
Abbott, Henry F. E436
Abbott, James R. A1151
Abbott, John W427
Abbott, John S. E367
Abbott, John V. E247
Abbruzzese, Marco A. A129
Abdalla, Zein A267
Abdelmaula, Yousef W47
Abdo, Michael N. A280
Abdo, Michael N. E113
Abdool-Samad, Tasneem W8
Abdul-Jawad, Ghazi M. W47
Abdullah, A. W8
Abe, Atsushi A780
Abe, Atsushi W253
Abe, Jun W279
Abe, Masanori W449
Abe, Noriaki W285
Abe, Shinichi W527
Abe, Toshinori W604
Abe, Yasuyuki W564
Abecasis, Teresa W254
Abel, Brian J. Van A1139
Abel, Charles A. E340
Abel, Gregory E. A151
Abel, Gregory E. A798
Abel, Gregory E. A610
Abel, Nir W312

Abel, Robert A. A702
Abel, Robert A. E326
Abelli, Donna L. A554
Abelli, Donna L. E268
Abelman, Jerome B. W111
Abernathy, Kathleen Quinn A333
Abernathy, Lawrence S. E136
Abernethy, Matthew C. E346
Abgrall-Teslyk, Karine W358
Ables, Dorothy M P517
Ables, Dorothy M. A663
Ablo, Awo A786
Abney, David P. A452
Abney, David P. A752
Abney, David P. A997
Aboaf, Eric W. A973
Aboumrad, Carlos Hajj W73
Aboumrad, Daniel Hajj W35
Abraham, Allison H. E368
Abraham, Brian A972
Abraham, Brian P538
Abraham, Chad R. E387
Abraham, E. Spencer A757
Abraham, E. Spencer A1048
Abraham, Joseph W162
Abraham, Neil M. E412
Abraham, Siliji E534
Abraham, Spencer A809
Abraham, Tara M. A815
Abraham, Thomas A188
Abraham, Thomas E71
Abrahams, Darrow A. A764
Abrahams, Gary C. E170
Abrahams, Sam E. W310
Abrahamson, James R. E524
Abrahamson, James R. E66
Abrahim, A. W8
Abramov, Nikolay W410
Abramovich, Aharon W312
Abramovitz, Aaron P. A471
Abrams, Mark A231
Abramson, Andrew B. A1086
Abramson, Andrew B. E516
Abramson, Steven V. E511
Absher, Jody K. A277
Abston, Tyson T. A492
Abston, Tyson T. E243
Abt, Roland W581
Abullhassan, Sawsan W18
Abundis, Susan M. A935
Abundis, Susan M. E439
Abuzaakouk, Anas W93
Acciari, Luciano W363
Ace, Brian R. A280
Ace, Brian R. E113
Ace, Heather A867
Acebedo, Eduardo Bernal E6
Acevedo, Sylvia A867
Achard, Aime W87
Achard, Stephane W420
Achary, Michael M. A496
Acheson, Eleanor D P378
Achi, Georges A. W77

Achleitner, Ann-Kristin W415
Achleitner, Ann-Kristin W369
Achleitner, Paul W95
Achten, Dominik von W273
Achurra, Emiliano Lopez W423
Acikalin, Faik W346
Ackarapolpanich, Nipaporn W117
Acker, Laurens van den W492
Acker, Tanya M. A800
Ackerman, Joel A317
Ackerman, Paul A317
Ackermann, Cathy G. A945
Ackermann, Cathy G. E451
Ackermann, Hilary E. A1097
Ackland, Michael W595
Acosta, Andrea E386
Acosta, Andrea E61
Acosta, Arcilia C. A1097
Acosta, Arcilia C. A1086
Acosta, Arcilia C. E307
Acosta, Arcilia C. E521
Acosta, Jose Humberto W76
Acut, Sabino E. W100
Adachi, Kazuyuki W610
Adachi, Seiji W82
Adachi, Tamaki W515
Adair, A. Jayson E120
Adair, Troy A393
Adair, Troy E184
Adam, Mark P437
Adamany, Linda L. A581
Adamany, Linda L. E529
Adamczyk, Darius A530
Adamczyk, Darius A585
Adame, David A398
Adamo, Emma W56
Adamo, Robert A854
Adams, Andy A964
Adams, Ann A. A747
Adams, Bradley S. A774
Adams, Bradley S. E360
Adams, Christopher D. E103
Adams, D. Scott A853
Adams, Edward B. A301
Adams, Gary Kramer A826
Adams, Holly B. A427
Adams, Holly B. E204
Adams, John A. A845
Adams, John A. E395
Adams, John B. E526
Adams, John K. A919
Adams, John. T. A732
Adams, Joseph C. E223
Adams, Joseph W. E354
Adams, Katherine L. A89
Adams, Ken W63
Adams, Mark W. E75
Adams, Martin E. E190
Adams, Marty E. A844
Adams, Marty E. E394
Adams, Mary P467
Adams, Michael E113
Adams, Michael C. A845
Adams, Michael C. E395

Adams, Milburn A524
Adams, Milburn E258
Adams, Natasha W597
Adams, Paul W504
Adams, Richard M. A1063
Adams, Richard M. E507
Adams, Robert J. E27
Adams, Sarah P. A471
Adams, Shirley A20
Adams, Stephen A195
Adams, Steven A. A413
Adams, Thomas E. A224
Adams, Tracey Morant A889
Adams, Tracey Morant E414
Adamsen, David A. A922
Adamson, Clive W157
Adamson, Clive W374
Adcock, Robert H. A524
Adcock, Robert H. E258
Addicott, Virginia C. A214
Addison, Ann M. A752
Addison, John A. A845
Addison, John A. E395
Addison, Linda L. A478
Adebowale, Victor W160
Adefioye, Elizabeth A557
Adelgren, Paul W. E232
Adelson, Scott J. E260
Adelt, Bruno W61
Adiba, Patrick W61
Adkerson, Richard C. A452
Adkins, Dave K. E61
Adkins, Kedrick D. A848
Adkins, Lewis W. A910
Adkins, Rodney C. A485
Adkins, Rodney C. A1069
Adkins, Rodney C. A118
Adkins, Rodney C. A807
Adler, Brooke A1066
Adler, Dean S. E426
Adler, Reuven W410
Adler, Reuven W312
Adofo-Wilson, Baye A152
Adolf, Ruediger E212
Adolph, Gerald S. A242
Adrian, Tobias A400
Adt, Katrin W129
Advaithi, Revathi A1052
Advaithi, Revathi W242
Adzema, Gregg D. E124
Adzema, Kurt A914
Adzick, Susan A678
Adzick, Susan P337
Aebischer, Patrick A645
Aebischer, Patrick W430
Aellig, Matthias W580
Aellig, Matthias W580
Affleck-Graves, John A1
Aftab, Dana T. E178
Afzal, Zahid A844
Afzal, Zahid E394
Agarwal, Achal A603
Agarwal, Jai A87

COMBINED HOOVER'S HANDBOOK INDEX OF EXECUTIVES

A = AMERICAN BUSINESS
E = EMERGING COMPANIES
P = PRIVATE COMPANIES
W = WORLD BUSINESSS

Agarwal, Naveen A856
Agarwal, Vikram W187
Agassi, Ronen W79
Agbaje, Segun A817
Ageborg, Katarina W57
Agee, Nancy Howell A66
Agee, Nancy Howell E25
Agee, Nancy Howell E247
Agerbo, Sussie Dvinge W632
Agg, Andy W422
Aggarwal, Rohit A547
Aggersbjerg, Peter E325
Aghi, Mukesh A349
Aghili, Aziz S. A313
Agnefjall, Peter W351
Agnelli, Andrea W562
Agnelli, Andrea W235
Agogue, Christophe W225
Agon, Jean-Paul W357
Agon, Jean-Paul W358
Agrawal, Ajay A207
Agrawal, Durga D. E221
Agrawal, Renu A650
Agrawal, Renu E305
Agrawal, Saurabh Mahesh W588
Agree, Joel (Joey) N. E9
Agree, Richard E9
Aguggia, Paul M. A596
Aguggia, Paul M. E286
Aguilar, Alvaro Gomez-Trenor W161
Aguirre, Fernando A985
Aguirre, Fernando A311
Agureev, Dmitry W655
Ahern, Terrance R. E288
Ahlborn, Andrew E411
Ahlman, Alissa M. E360
Ahlmann, Kaj A896
Ahlmann, Kaj E422
Ahluwalia, Narpal S. A446
Ahmad, Faiz A627
Ahmad, Fawad A874
Ahmad, Fuad E328
Ahmad, Zubaid A924
Ahmadjian, Christina W567
Ahmadjian, Christina W425
Ahmadjian, Christina L. W50
Ahmed, Asmau E407
Ahmed, B. W8
Ahmed, Fahim A231
Ahmed, Nadim A178
Ahmed, Sohail U. A619
Ahn, John J. A497
Ahn, Jun Sik W537
Ahn, Jung Ho W546
Ahn, Kijun E375
Ahn, Michael W366
Ahn, Nadine W507
Ahn, Phillip J. E49
Ahn, Skott W366
Aho, Esko W247
Aho, Esko Tapani W521
Ahola, Aaron S. E12
Ahola, Kari W446
Ahrendts, Angela J. W654

Ahuja, Amrita A162
Ahuja, Deepak A729
Ahuja, Ravi E423
Ahuja, Sanjiv W638
Ai, Angela A1145
Ai, Sachiko W455
Aichele, William S. A1078
Aichele, William S. E513
Aigrain, Jacques E493
Aigrain, Jacques W654
Aigrain, Jacques W374
Aihara, Risa W319
Aijala, Ainar D. A927
Aijala, Ainar D. E435
Aikawa, Yoshiro W582
Aiken, Jason W. A460
Aiken, Jason W. A1143
Aila, Minna W427
Aisquith, Anthony M. E361
Aitken, Stuart W. A611
Aizpiri, Arturo Gonzalo W493
Ajemyan, Arthur A887
Ajer, Jeffrey Robert E61
Akabayashi, Tomiji W436
Akahori, Kingo W565
Akalski, Frank J. A439
Akama, Tatsuya W434
Akamatsu, Tamame W432
Akar, Laszlo W412
Akashi, Mamoru W181
Akbari, Homaira A620
Akbari, Homaira W76
Akella-Mishra, Sadhana E104
Akella, Janaki A952
Akerson, Daniel F. A643
Akerson, Eileen G. A595
Akerstrom, Carina W579
Akhavan, Chris P241
Akhlaghi, Banafsheh A398
Akhtar, Muhammad Rizwan A878
Akhtar, Rizwan A879
Akimov, Andrey I. W474
Akins, Nicholas K. A410
Akins, Nicholas K. A59
Akishita, Soichi W515
Akita, Masaki W394
Akiya, Fumio W536
Akiyama, Katsusada W336
Akiyama, Sakie W460
Akiyama, Sakie W402
Akiyama, Sakie W557
Akiyama, Sakie W319
Akiyama, Satoru W336
Akiyama, Yasuji W357
Akkus, Senar W619
Akman, Matthew W218
Akoma, Latasha E27
Akrasanee, Narongchai W20
Akriche, Vivianne W495
Aksel, Murat W640
Aksyutin, Oleg E. W474
Akten, Mahmut W618
Akutagawa, Tomomi W44
Al-Dughaither, Riyal M. W47
Al-Essa, Tarek Sultan W205
Al-Ghanim, Mohammed W18
Al-Haffar, Maher W131
Al-Hail, Salah W486
Al-Hajri, Rashid Misfer W486
Al-Hakami, Ahmed Ibrahim W519

Al-homaizi, Suad Hamad W77
Al-Husseini, Saleh E. W519
Al-Issa, Abdullah M. W519
Al-Jarf, Mulham W412
Al-Khater, Turki Bin Mohammed W18
Al-Kindi, Khalifa Mohammed W47
Al-Mahmoud, Mansoor Ebrahim W486
Al-Mansouri, Mubarak Rashid W47
Al-Marzouk, Mohammed Jassim W19
Al-Meer, Rashid Ismail W18
Al-Mudhaf, Anwar Ali W47
Al-Mutairi, Hilal Mishari W47
Al-Raeesi, Abdulla W18
Al-Rajaan, Fahad W18
Al-Rumayyan, Yasir A1052
Al-sabbah, Mariam Nasser W77
Al-Saleh, Adel W199
Al-Saleh, Adel W114
Al-Sumait, Abdulla MH W19
Ala-Mello, Jukka W348
Alahuhta, Matti W641
Alahuhta, Matti W348
Alahuhta, Matti W7
Alameddine, A.R. A830
Alamina, Marcos Manuel Herreria W470
Alanis, David Penaloza W265
Albaisa, Alfonso W441
Albanese, Craig P386
Albanese, Robert C. A575
Albano, Ryan M. E67
Albaugh, James F. A56
Alber, Laura J. A1132
Alber, Laura J. A912
Albers, Oliver A721
Albert, Larry D. A704
Albert, Larry D. E328
Albert, Shadi A927
Albert, Shadi E435
Albertine, John M. E286
Albertoni, Walter Luis Bernardes W69
Alberts, Jim P218
Albertson, Tim W26
Albo, Pina A886
Albrecht, Michael W251
Albrecht, William E. A494
Albrechtsen, John P. E164
Albrectsen, Anne-Birgitte P436
Albright, John P. E19
Albright, Todd R P191
Albuquerque, Isabella Saboya de W630
Aldach, Rene W273
Aldag, Edward K. E315
Aldeborgh, John E. E47
Alderman, Heidi S. A776
Alderman, Heidi S. E91
Alderson, Christopher D. A991
Aldott, Zoltan W412
Alegre, Daniel E448
Alegria, Esther M. E45
Alejo, Francisco S W514
Alekperov, Vagit W476
Alemany, Ellen R. A408
Alemany, Ellen R. A417
Alessandrini, Evaline P638
Alessandro, Gianpaolo W625
Alexander, Bobby J. E54
Alexander, Bruce K. A1151
Alexander, Douglas A. A78
Alexander, James A599

Alexander, Joanne L. A792
Alexander, John E. A1033
Alexander, John M. A418
Alexander, Keith B. A50
Alexander, Lee A248
Alexander, Marcellus W. E432
Alexander, Marilyn A. A478
Alexander, Mark A616
Alexander, Mark A. A184
Alexander, Mark A. E530
Alexander, Mark R. A666
Alexander, Michael J. E349
Alexander, Patrick L. E291
Alexander, Ralph P554
Alexander, Ralph C. E169
Alexander, Robert E. E433
Alexander, Robert M. A198
Alexander, Susan H. A158
Alexander, Tim A954
Alexandra, Habeler-Drabek W229
Alexandre, Patrick W22
Alexos, Nicholas W. A1075
Alexy, Kimberly E. A1122
Alfano, Jeffrey J. E363
Alfieri, Romano W177
Alfonso, Humberto P. A354
Alford, Bradley A. A114
Alford, Donald C. E357
Alford, George F. O. W310
Alford, Peggy A689
Alford, Peggy A807
Alfred, Jim D. A954
Alger, Eugene K. A386
Alger, Glenn M. A386
Algiere, Dennis L. A1108
Ali, Backer A396
Ali, Backer E187
Ali, Kevin A787
Ali, Mohamad S. E281
Ali, Wajid E305
Alias, Patrick A. E105
Alicea, Michael A742
Alicea, Michael P393
Alisov, Vladimir Ivanovich W256
Alix, Gilles W637
Allain, Bernard W107
Allaire, Bella Loykhter A876
Allaire, Martin W398
Allak, Hasan W171
Allan, Donald A962
Allan, Graham W55
Allan, John W597
Allan, M. Elyse W112
Allanson, Joe A912
Allardice, Robert B. A502
Allardice, Robert B. E155
Allatt, Graham W462
Allaway, Patrick W85
Allcorn-Walker, Anita A32
Allen-Herring, Rosie A1115
Allen-Herring, Rosie E533
Allen, Analisa M. A694
Allen, Barbara K. A536
Allen, Bertrand-Marc A850
Allen, Bruno V. Di Leo A306
Allen, Damon v. A397
Allen, Edward Thomas A271
Allen, Edward Thomas E109
Allen, George F. E35
Allen, Herbert P226

COMBINED HOOVER'S HANDBOOK INDEX OF EXECUTIVES

A = AMERICAN BUSINESS
E = EMERGING COMPANIES
P = PRIVATE COMPANIES
W = WORLD BUSINESSS

Allen, Herbert A. A264
Allen, Hubert L. A6
Allen, James D. E213
Allen, Jeffery B. E470
Allen, Jennifer W235
Allen, Jerold W P464
Allen, Jimmy E. A395
Allen, Jimmy E. E185
Allen, Joel E340
Allen, Ken W198
Allen, Lee A968
Allen, Lee P534
Allen, Mark R. A404
Allen, Michael L. E326
Allen, Mike P12
Allen, Nicholas Charles W362
Allen, Quincy L. A770
Allen, Quincy L. A10
Allen, Quincy L. A649
Allen, Ray W. E509
Allen, Ray W. E510
Allen, Ray W. E509
Allen, Richard D P604
Allen, Richard E. A558
Allen, Samuel R. A1129
Allen, Samuel R. A342
Allen, Sharon L. A35
Allen, Sharon L. A128
Allen, Steve W500
Allen, Tonya E471
Allen, William Benton A580
Allerheiligen, Gary C. A378
Alley, J. Lindsey E260
Allinger, Wesley E. E218
Allison, Gordon Y. A1104
Allison, John A. E330
Allison, John W. A524
Allison, John W. E258
Allison, Michael R. A187
Allison, R. Dirk E5
Allison, Richard E. A964
Allman, Keith J. A666
Allman, Keith J. A790
Allnutt, Lauren E. A748
Allon, Andrea A307
Allon, Andrea E133
Allred, Mark P82
Allsop, Jeff W287
Allton, Nicholas W85
Allushuski, Barbara E. E298
Alm, Roger W641
Almaguer, Everardo Elizondo W131
Almaguer, Everardo Elizondo W265
Almaraz, Frank P143
Almeida, Andrea Marques de W468
Almeida, David W40
Almeida, Edmar de W254
Almeida, Flavia Buarque de W622
Almeida, Jose E. A128
Almeida, Jose E. A142
Almendinger, Carrie L. E247
Almodovar, Priscilla A391
Almodovar, Priscilla E412
Almond, Heather H. E515

Almquist, Jeff P177
Aloian, D. Pike E152
Aloma, Angel P227
Alonso, Joseph Anthony M. W85
Alonso, Mercedes W427
Alonzo, Anne L. E391
Alonzo, Annette M. A305
Alpart, Stephen A485
Alpen, Joachim W547
Alper, Cenk W267
Alperin, Barry J. A917
Alperin, Barry J. A581
Alpern, Robert J. A6
Alpern, Robert J. A8
Alpert, Henry A. E242
Alpert, Jordan M. E473
Alpert, Marc A. A645
Alpuche, Charles E276
Alqueres, Jose Luiz W622
Alsaad, Bader A160
Alseth, Becky L. E344
Alsfine, Joel A99
Alshehhi, A. Z. W8
Alsobrooks, Angela P238
Alstead, Troy M. A631
Alston, Cheryl D. A478
Alt, Aaron E. A989
Alt, Aaron E. A201
Alterman, Kenneth W. E242
Althann, Natica von A841
Althofer, Eric E304
Althoff, Sven W269
Althusmann, Bernd W640
Altig, David E. A399
Altman, Dara F. A941
Altman, Louis Michael A844
Altman, Louis Michael E394
Altman, Luci Staller A13
Altman, Randall S. A182
Altman, Roger C. E176
Altman, Samuel A385
Altman, Steven R. E138
Altmeyer, John W. A364
Alto, Palo A398
Altobello, Nancy E311
Altobello, Nancy A. A80
Alton, Gregg H. E121
Altozano, Angel Garcia W280
Altschaefl, Michael W. E365
Alva, Emily Peterson E31
Alvarado, Albert A400
Alvarado, Anna M. A1008
Alvarado, Donna M. A803
Alvarado, Donna M. A304
Alvarado, Donna M. E371
Alvarado, Joseph A. A834
Alvarado, Linda G. E301
Alvarado, Marcos E426
Alvarado, Paulina P366
Alvarez, Aida M. A538
Alvarez, Aida M. E468
Alvarez, Ana Isabel Fernandez W382
Alvarez, Carlos A305
Alvarez, Cesar L. A1111
Alvarez, Cesar L. E459
Alvarez, German Carmona A679
Alvarez, Ignacio A836
Alvarez, Jose Antonio Alvarez W75
Alvarez, Jose Antonio Alvarez W72
Alvarez, Jose B. A1030

Alvarez, Jose B. A1071
Alvarez, Manuel Fernandez W423
Alvarez, Manuel P. A351
Alvarez, Manuel P. E150
Alvarez, Oscar A. A982
Alvarez, Ralph A635
Alvarez, Raul A647
Alvera, Marco A911
Alvero, Gumer C. A895
Alves, Dave A608
Alves, Paget L. A1146
Alves, Paget L. A985
Alves, Paget L. A103
Alvey, John W. E315
Alvez, Gabriel E455
Alvez, Leo S. W514
Alving, Amy E. A349
Alving, Amy E. A391
Alviti, Paulette R. A710
Alwin, Martin P. E114
Alziari, Lucien A. A856
Amamiya, Masayoshi W82
Amamiya, Toshitake W336
Amano, Hiromasa W330
Amano, Reiko W209
Amara, Ana Sofia W358
Amaral, Donald J. A1038
Amaral, Donald J. E496
Amatayakul, Parnsiree W77
Amato, Elizabeth B. E174
Amato, Jacqueline B. A1033
Amato, Jacqueline B. E493
Amato, Joseph E. A398
Amato, Thomas A. A74
Ambani, Mukesh Dhirubhai W491
Ambani, Nita M. W491
Ambe, Kazushi W557
Amble, Joan C. Lordi A171
Amble, Joan Lordi W666
Ambrecht, Kenneth C. A64
Ambrose, Richard F. A1012
Ambrozie, Tony P61
Amdahl, Rachel R. E149
Amen, Darrell van A527
Amen, Robert E77
Amend, Michael R. W262
Amerine, I. Robert E247
Ames, Johanna R. A724
Amig, Eric P. A396
Amig, Eric P. E187
Amirtharaj, Merlin E515
Ammann, Christoph W86
Ammann, Daniel L. A514
Ammann, Erich W523
Ammerman, Douglas K. A407
Amon, Cristiano R. A867
Amon, Rogerio A867
Amore, John J. W233
Amorim, Marta W254
Amorim, Paula W254
Amos, Daniel P. A24
Amos, James H. E285
Ampornpong, Arasa W334
Amsbary, Joseph B. A1101
Amsden, Mark W509
Amunátegui, Domingo Cruzat W220
An, Cong Hui W257
An, Hyo-ryul W537
An, Qing Heng W257
Anada, Kazuhisa W293

Anagnost, Andrew E44
Anami, Masaya W82
Anand, Krishnan E539
Anand, Krishnan W111
Anand, Mala A27
Anasenes, Nicole A1098
Anasenes, Nicole E31
Anastasio, Curtis V. A224
Anbouba, Imad K. A982
Ancira, Carlos Eduardo Aldrete W244
Ancius, Michael J. A394
Anda, Javier de A563
Anderberg, Eric E61
Andersen, Connie P485
Andersen, Eric C. W44
Andersen, Jens Bjorn W205
Andersen, Kim Krogh W595
Andersen, Nils Smedegaard W300
Andersen, Nils Smedegaard W626
Andersen, Ole W188
Andersen, Paul P271
Andersen, Tonny Thierry W188
Andersen, Tove W227
Anderson, A. Scott A1151
Anderson, André A399
Anderson, Anthony A. E340
Anderson, Anthony K. A383
Anderson, Anthony K. A114
Anderson, Anthony K. A662
Anderson, Barbara J. A1013
Anderson, Beverly J. A385
Anderson, Brad E58
Anderson, Bradley S. A536
Anderson, Brian P. A862
Anderson, Carl D. A1143
Anderson, Carrie L. A195
Anderson, Charles A. A1040
Anderson, Charles A. E499
Anderson, Charlotte Jones A516
Anderson, Craig L. A378
Anderson, Craig Steven E356
Anderson, Darby E5
Anderson, Darcy G. E111
Anderson, David J. A59
Anderson, Doug P581
Anderson, Elizabeth McKee E61
Anderson, Elizabeth McKee W258
Anderson, Eric T. W122
Anderson, Gerard M. A343
Anderson, Gerard M. A82
Anderson, Gordon T. E223
Anderson, Harvey A538
Anderson, J. Lynn A397
Anderson, Jacky K. E372
Anderson, James M. A420
Anderson, James M. E197
Anderson, James M. E321
Anderson, James Robert E166
Anderson, Jeremy W481
Anderson, Jeremy W621
Anderson, Joel D. A959
Anderson, Joel D. E209
Anderson, John H. A865
Anderson, John H. E403
Anderson, John R. A816
Anderson, Karl V. A411
Anderson, Karli S. E469
Anderson, Katherine A296
Anderson, Keith E447
Anderson, Kerrii B. A934

HOOVER'S HANDBOOK OF EMERGING COMPANIES 2023

COMBINED HOOVER'S HANDBOOK INDEX OF EXECUTIVES

A = AMERICAN BUSINESS
E = EMERGING COMPANIES
P = PRIVATE COMPANIES
W = WORLD BUSINESSS

Anderson, Kerrii B. A615
Anderson, Lars C. A410
Anderson, Laurence Lazelle A954
Anderson, Magali W283
Anderson, Marcia M. A741
Anderson, Marcia M. E349
Anderson, Michael J. A82
Anderson, Michelle A880
Anderson, Mike E338
Anderson, Natalie U. A722
Anderson, Nick W66
Anderson, Nicolas C. A130
Anderson, R. Jamie W122
Anderson, Richard H. W393
Anderson, Ritchie L. E308
Anderson, Roderick Stuart W179
Anderson, S. Elaine A954
Anderson, Samuel J. E525
Anderson, Scott E146
Anderson, Scott E469
Anderson, Scott P. A900
Anderson, Selynto P308
Anderson, Sherilyn G. E204
Anderson, Stanton D. E384
Anderson, Steven R. A369
Anderson, Suzanne P676
Anderson, Terry A. E204
Anderson, William D. W572
Anderton, Niall W31
Ando, Hiromichi W155
Ando, Hisayoshi W387
Ando, Yoshiko W326
Andolina, Massimo A825
Andorfer, Ludwig W453
Andrada, Marissa A232
Andrade, Miguel Stilwell De W212
Andrasick, James S. E444
Andre, Axel A60
Andreessen, Marc L. A689
Andreotti, Lamberto A298
Andreotti, Lamberto W625
Andres, Carmen Garcia de W593
Andres, Juan A112
Andreski, Peter A1096
Anderson, Jeffrey S. E261
Andreu, Joan Llonch W71
Andreve, Vicente Ariztegui A953
Andrew, Ewan W201
Andrews, Brian G. E119
Andrews, Charles Elliott A763
Andrews, Claudia P90
Andrews, Giles W81
Andrews, Kirkland (Kirk) B. A907
Andrews, Michael G. E65
Andrews, Nancy C. E94
Andrews, Nancy C. W449
Andrews, R D P234
Andrews, Simon Patrick W603
Andrews, Susan Mc P464
Andrews, Thomas J. E15
Andrews, Todd K. E117
Andrich, Lyne B. A373
Andrich, Lyne B. E168
Andries, Olivier W511

Andrieux, Nathalie W127
Andronikakis, Spyridon A. W33
Androsov, Kirill Gennadievich W329
Anenen, Steven J. E500
Anevski, Peter E398
Ang, Lawrence Siu Lung W257
Ang, Ramon S. W514
Angagaw, Aster A794
Angel, David P176
Angel, Stephen F. A462
Angel, Stephen F. A840
Angel, Stephen F. W369
Angelakis, Michael J. A388
Angelastro, Philip J. A778
Angelina, Michael E. A896
Angelina, Michael E. E422
Angelo, Bernard J. A348
Angelo, Bernard J. A345
Angelo, Michael F. E527
Angeloro, Vincent P241
Angerthal, Michael A. E528
Angiolillo, Bruce D. A848
Angle, Colin M. E281
Anglin, Eric M. E454
Angove, Duncan B. A530
Angus, Derek A1080
Angus, Derek P667
Anjolras, Pierre W635
Anna, Gregory J. E99
Annas, Christopher J. E321
Annis, Stephen M. E517
Ansara, Victor L. E298
Ansari, Anousheh A578
Ansari, Shoeb E180
Ansay, Michael G. A125
Ansay, Michael G. E52
Anscheit, Heike W162
Anschutz, J Barron P109
Ansell, William C. A68
Ansin, Kenneth S. A372
Ansin, Kenneth S. E167
Anthony, April A421
Anthony, April E198
Anthony, F. Scott A266
Anthony, Nicholas C. E146
Antin, Robert L. E50
Antin, Robert L. E419
Antoine, Robert A196
Antoine, Robert E79
Antolik, David G. A910
Anton, Arthur F. A934
Antonakes, Steven L. A352
Antone, Therese M. E232
Antonelli, Cecille A971
Antonelli, Cecille P537
Antonelli, Giovanni W627
Antonelli, Leornado Pietro W468
Antonello, Katherine H. A367
Antonov, Igor W256
Antonovich, Michael D A301
Antonovich, Michael D P171
Anuchitanukul, Anuchit W352
Anwar, Shafqat W18
Anzalone, John M. A574
Ao, Hong W34
Aoki, John E301
Aoki, Masakazu W279
Aoki, Shigeki W455
Aoki, Shoichi W356
Aoki, Shuhei W418

Aoki, Yoshihisa W462
Aoyama, Atsushi W356
Aoyama, Yasuhiro W389
Apfalter, Guenther F. W379
Apichatabutra, Pannipa W352
Apolinsky, Craig D. E234
Apoliona, S. Haunani A129
Apostolides, Jim A121
Apotheker, Leo W524
Appel, David B. A207
Appel, Frank W198
Apperson, Eric E. E35
Apperson, Kevin P335
Appert, Olivier W215
Appert, Raphael W174
Apple, Robert E. A668
Apple, Robert F. E32
Appleton, Grady P. A397
Appleton, William E431
Aprahamian, Thomas J. E467
Aprigliano, William A430
April, Rand Scott A95
Apte, Shirish W164
Aqraou, Jacob W594
Aquilino, Brian A5
Aractingi, Farid W490
Aragane, Kumi W354
Arai, Yuko W183
Arakawa, Ryuji W28
Aramburuzabala, Maria Asuncion W40
Aramouni, Michel E. W77
Aran, Hakan W619
Aranguren-Trellez, Luis A557
Aratani, Masao W394
Araujo, Leandro de Miranda W69
Araumi, Jiro W570
Aravena, Marcos Lima W172
Araya, Akihiro W26
Arbanas, Frederick V. E338
Arbel, Shmulik W79
Arboe, Susanne W188
Arbola, Gérald W565
Arbour, Paola M. A1008
Arbour, Paola M. A1003
Arbuckle, Stuart A. A1089
Arce, Demetrio Carceller W423
Arce, Jose W266
Arcelli, Marco W398
Archambeau, Shellye L. A904
Archambeau, Shellye L. A1088
Archer, Dennis W. A555
Archer, Dennis W. E269
Archer, Timothy M. A619
Archer, William A223
Archibald, Nolan D. A548
Archibong, Ime A198
Archila, Jorge Arturo Calvache W210
Arczynski, Dennis J. A923
Arczynski, Dennis J. E433
Ardalan, Natalie Bani W269
Arden, Elaine W289
Ardenghy, Roberto Furian W468
Ardila, Jaime E234
Ardila, Jaime W10
Ardisana, Lizabeth A. A545
Arduini, Matteo E249
Arduini, Peter J. A178
Arduini, Peter J. A458
Arellano, Ian W84
Arenivas, Jesse A605

Arfert, MajBritt W228
Argalas, James S. A120
Argalas, James S. E48
Arias, Fernan Ignacio Bejarano W210
Arias, Rolando Sanchez W70
Arienzo, Wendy E392
Arienzo, Wendy E261
Arima, Akira W413
Arima, Akito W436
Arima, Koji W193
Ariqat, Ghassan A1046
Aris, Antoinette P. W52
Aristeguieta, Francisco A. A499
Ariyoshi, Yoshinori W185
Arizumi, Alan H. A423
Ark, Jon Vander A892
Arkley, Peter A1046
Arlin, Wendy C. A140
Arlt, Tim P381
Armada, Jose Sainz A112
Armada, Jose Sainz W295
Armani, Tara A389
Armani, Tara P219
Armario, Jose E341
Armbrester, Bradford Kyle E408
Armbrister, Clarence D. E246
Armbruster, Chris A. E322
Armes, Roy V. A1004
Armitage, Richard L. E308
Armock, Greg L. E96
Armour, Mark W597
Armour, Tim A197
Armour, Tim P103
Armstrong, Alan S. A167
Armstrong, Alan S. A1131
Armstrong, Alan S. E64
Armstrong, Annie A627
Armstrong, Bradley E204
Armstrong, Bruce W. A558
Armstrong, Christopher D. A400
Armstrong, David W419
Armstrong, Greg L. A755
Armstrong, Greg L. A832
Armstrong, Greg L. A833
Armstrong, Jason A272
Armstrong, Katharine E446
Armstrong, M. Brett E117
Armstrong, Mac E370
Armstrong, Robert M. E58
Armstrong, Timothy M. A170
Armstrong, Whit A32
Arnaboldi, Nicole S. A740
Arnall, Robert M. E190
Arnault, Antoine W373
Arnault, Bernard W373
Arnault, Bernard W125
Arnault, Delphine W373
Arneson, Erin K. E480
Arnett, David J. E102
Arney, Claudia I. W341
Arnold, Bradley C. A26
Arnold, Colleen F. A1125
Arnold, Craig W209
Arnold, Craig W393
Arnold, Dan H. A648
Arnold, Frances H. A45
Arnold, Frederick A723
Arnold, Helen W274
Arnold, Jonathan E83
Arnold, Ken E. A118

COMBINED HOOVER'S HANDBOOK INDEX OF EXECUTIVES

A = AMERICAN BUSINESS
E = EMERGING COMPANIES
P = PRIVATE COMPANIES
W = WORLD BUSINESSS

Arnold, Kirk E. W617
Arnold, Mark John W79
Arnold, Michael C. A26
Arnold, Steven R. A796
Arnold, Steven R. E368
Arnold, Susan E. A335
Arnold, T. L. A954
Arnold, Thomas G A389
Arnold, Thomas G P219
Arnoldi, Melissa M. A721
Arnst, Thomas A1003
Aronin, Jeffrey S. A330
Arooni, Amir S. A330
Arora, Aneesha E255
Arora, Anil A286
Arora, Nikesh W167
Arougheti, Michael J. A95
Arougheti, Michael J. E34
Arpey, Gerard J. A526
Arrechea, Juan Francisco Gallego W593
Arredondo, Fabiola R. A195
Arredondo, Fabiola R. E183
Arriaga, Brent E250
Arrigoni, Daniel A. A694
Arrindell, Brandon E503
Arrington, D. Burt A176
Arrington, Darren R. A513
Arrington, Ronald E296
Arriola, Dennis Victor A288
Arroliga, Alejandro A143
Arroliga, Alejandro P69
Arrowsmith, Carol W170
Arrowsmith, Carol W135
Arroyo, F. Thaddeus A477
Arroyo, Manolo W161
Arroyo, Manuel A264
Arroyo, Quemuel A692
Arroyo, Quemuel P352
Arsdell, Stephen C. Van A773
Arsel, Semahat Sevim W621
Arsel, Semahat Sevim W346
Arsenault, Dominique W193
Arseneault, Tom W66
Arsjad, Mohammad W483
Arsong, Blair P436
Arthur, Lavone A143
Arthur, Lavone P69
Arthur, Tanya P544
Arthur, Todd M. E336
Arthur, Vicki B. A950
Articus, Stephans W192
Arts, Frank W18
Artusi, Daniel A. E314
Artz, Eric F. A1068
Arunanondchai, Sunthorn W137
Arunkundrum, Prakash A645
Arustamov, Mikhail Mikhailovich W617
Arvan, Peter D. E389
Arvielo, Patricia L. A1120
Arvielo, Patricia L. E535
Arway, Pamela M. A317
Arway, Pamela M. A512

Asahi, Satoshi W436
Asahi, Toshiya W630
Asai, Keiichi W173
Asai, Takahiko W267
Asam, Dominik W24
Asami, Takao W441
Asano, Kikuo W329
Asano, Shigeru W576
Asano, Toshio W392
Asavanich, Bodin W541
Asbury, John C. A106
Asbury, John C. E40
Ascençao, Léonel Pereira W231
Asch, Andrew E159
Asche-Holstein, Manuela W517
Aschenbroich, Jacques W104
Aschenbroich, Jacques W613
Aschenbroich, Jacques W630
Aschenbroich, Jacques W631
Aschendorf, Antonia W586
Ascuaga, Michonne R E388
Ash, Thomas P. E91
Ash, W. Patrick E33
Ashaboglu, Ahmet F. W661
Ashaboglu, Ahmet F. W346
Ashar, Mayank (Mike) M. W218
Ashbrook, M. Scott A880
Ashbrook, M. Scott E412
Ashby, Crystal E. W66
Ashby, Ian R. W39
Ashe, Gena L. A493
Ashe, Robert G. E335
Asher, Andrew Lynn A216
Asher, Anique W84
Asher, Anthony J. A1013
Ashida, Akimitsu W180
Ashida, Kosuke W26
Ashkenazi, Anat A635
Ashley, Euan W57
Ashley, Mike W90
Ashley, Mike W89
Ashley, Richard H. A524
Ashley, Richard H. E258
Ashton, Tracy M. A432
Ashworth, Richard E20
Ask, Lars W641
Aske, Jennings P386
Aslam, Farsha A828
Aslett, Mark E319
Åslund, Anna Sävinger W231
Asmussen, Erick R. A95
Aso, Mitsuhiro W570
Aspillaga, Marea P61
Asplund, Dale A. A1071
Asplundh, Carl Hj. E260
Assante, Linda E486
Asscher-Vonk, Irene P. W344
Asshoff, Gregor W280
Assouad, Yannick W600
Assouad, Yannick W635
Aston, G. Robert A1033
Aston, G. Robert E492
Astorg, Robert G. A1063
Astorg, Robert G. E508
Asvanunt, Amorn W603
Atanasov, Atanas H. A521
Atay, Temel W346
Athanassopoulos, Andreas D. W231
Athreya, Kartik B. A401
Athreya, Ranganath W296

Atieh, Michael G. W154
Atikul, Jumlong W352
Atiya, Sami W6
Atkar, Neeta A. K. W662
Atkins, John L. E15
Atkins, Margaret Shan A958
Atkins, Margaret Shan A316
Atkinson, Matt W160
Atkinson, Robert A737
Atkinson, Tracy A. A877
Atkinson, Tracy A. A1073
Atlas, Ilana R. W63
Attal, Alain A457
Attal, Laurent W515
Attavipach, Pricha W540
Attaway, John A. A860
Attiyah, Abdullah Hamad Al W635
Attolini, Gerardo Estrada W244
Attor, Terry Goddard A966
Attor, Terry Goddard P532
Attwood, James A. A742
Atwell, Robert B. A741
Atwell, Robert B. E349
Atwell, William L. A1113
Atwood, Catherine R. E413
Aubert, Anne W511
Aubrey, William E. A816
Aubry, Marc W511
Auchincloss, Murray W109
Auchinleck, R. H. W596
Audette, Matthew J. A648
Audi, Georges W. W77
Audi, Marc J. W77
Audi, Patricia Souto W72
Audi, Raymond W. W77
Audia, Damon J. A26
Audier, Agnes W174
Auer, Alexander W458
Auer, Johann-Anton W628
Auerbach, Jonathan L. A846
Auerbach, Jonathan L. A807
Auerbacher, Petra W15
Aufreiter, Nora A. A611
Aufreiter, Nora A. W84
Augenstein, Mark J. A815
Augliera, Anthony R. A1115
Augostini, Christopher L. A150
Augsburger, Blake W. A618
Augsburger, Blake W. E290
August-deWilde, Katherine A431
August-deWilde, Katherine E205
Auguste, Laurent W631
Augustinos, Nicholas E138
Aujouannet, Arnaud P764
Aulagnon, Maryse W631
Aulagnon, Maryse W22
Auld, David V. A536
Aulet, William K. E328
Aumont, Dominique W373
Aurenz, Helmut W61
Auris, Jan-Dirk W276
Ausburn, Kevin R. A488
Auschel, Roland W14
Ausman, Sara A37
Ausman, Sara E14
Austen, William F. A97
Austen, William F. A95
Austin, Earl C. A868
Austin, J. Douglas A311

Austin, Pam P59
Austin, Roxanne S. A1088
Austin, Roxanne S. A8
Austin, Wanda M. A76
Austin, Wanda M. A230
Austreid, Arne W558
Ausura, John E313
Autenried, Paul von A178
Avedon, Marcia J. E228
Avedon, Marcia J. W617
Averill, Howard M. A195
Avery, Chris M. A305
Avery, R. T. E526
Avery, Susan K. A388
Avery, Thomas A. E126
Avila, Nancy A274
Avila, Sergio W73
Avitabile, Daniel M. A671
Avner, Iris W312
Avrane, Julie W631
Avrett, Shannon R. E90
Avril-Groves, Vicki L. A490
Avril-Groves, Vicki L. A277
Avril, Matthew E. E219
Awad, George M. E493
Awad, Karina W643
Awaji, Mutsumi W137
Awuah, Patrick G. A737
Ax, Peter L. A687
Axelrod, Norman H. E210
Ayada, Yujiro W293
Ayai, Yasuyuki W394
Ayala, Fernando Zobel de W85
Ayala, Jaime Augusto Zobel de W85
Ayala, John C. A108
Ayala, Orlando A216
Ayala, Raul W266
Aydt, Timothy J. A657
Aydt, Timothy J. A717
Ayer, William S. A530
Ayers, Andrea J. A962
Ayers, Andrea J. A1073
Ayers, Christopher L. A95
Ayers, J. Jonathan (Jon) A395
Ayers, J. Jonathan (Jon) E185
Ayla, Ahmet Fuat W26
Aylward, George R. E528
Aymerich, Philippe W548
Ayotte, Kelly A. A738
Ayotte, Kelly A. A161
Ayotte, Kelly A. A210
Ayoub, David A. E372
Ayub, Alfredo Elias W265
Ayub, Arturo Elias W35
Ayuthaya, Chirayu Isarangkul Na W541
Ayyappan, Ajay E179
Azar, Georges Y. W77
Azare, Monica F. E300
Azarian, Michael A. A439
Azcarraga, Laura Renee Diez Barroso de W73
Azevedo, Lucio W630
Azevedo, Sandra Maria Guerra de W630
Azinovic, Drago A825
Aziz, Ismat A599
Aznar, Jose Maria A738
Azuma, Seiichiro W437
Azus, Ryan E547

COMBINED HOOVER'S HANDBOOK INDEX OF EXECUTIVES

A = AMERICAN BUSINESS
E = EMERGING COMPANIES
P = PRIVATE COMPANIES
W = WORLD BUSINESSS

Azzone, Giovanni W479

B

Baack, Jerry J. A175
Baack, Jerry J. E66
Baack, Sara A377
Baade, Arve W448
Baalmann, Richard F. E173
Baba, Chiharu W494
Baba, Hiroyuki W345
Babatz, Guillermo E. W84
Babb, James G. E63
Babbit, Joel M. A845
Babbit, Joel M. E395
Babbit, Joel M. E240
Babcock, Beverley A. A776
Babcock, John P. A810
Babcock, John P. E376
Babeau, Emmanuel A825
Babeau, Emmanuel W524
Babej, Peter A246
Babiak, Janice M. A1102
Babiak, Janice M. W82
Babich, George E484
Babin, Sylvie St. pierre W193
Babineaux-Fontenot, Claire A6
Babule, Christophe W358
Bacardí, Joaquín E. A836
Bacci, Arthur E240
Bacci, Arthur J. A1138
Bacci, Arthur J. E544
Bachelder, Cheryl A. A1083
Bachke, Tone Hegland W594
Bachman, John E. E242
Bachmann, Lisa M. E234
Bachmann, Richard H. A374
Bachmann, Stephan A. J W88
Bacigalupo, George F. A152
Backman, Andrea S. E467
Backovsky, Bernhard W633
Bacon, Brenda J. E224
Bacon, Charles A. E301
Bacon, Graham W. A374
Bacon, Kenneth J. A272
Bacon, Kenneth J. A43
Bacon, Kenneth J. E34
Bacon, Marie-Claude W398
Bacon, Renee M. A719
Bacus, Lisa R. A927
Bacus, Lisa R. E435
Badcock, Henry C P678
Baddeley, Gary E366
Bade, Aasif M. A425
Bade, Aasif M. E201
Badenoch, Alexandra W595
Bader, Eric S. E173
Bader, Kathleen M. A1012
Bader, Nicole L. E46
Baderschneider, Jean W246
Badhorn, Dayna C. A118
Badia, Jose Maria Nus W72

Badias, Alfonso Rebuelta W382
Badinter, Elisabeth W486
Badinter, Simon W486
Badlani, Sameer A389
Badlani, Sameer P220
Badran, Souheil A1082
Bae, Hoon W537
Bae, Joseph Y. W235
Baena, Douglas W. A922
Baer, Jakob W580
Baer, Richard N. A633
Baez, Yeimy W210
Bagal, Vinod A349
Bagby, L. Douglas A953
Bagby, L. Douglas E455
Bagchi, Anup W296
Bagel-Trah, Simone W95
Bagel-Trah, Simone W277
Bagley, Christopher A. A190
Bagley, Christopher A. E73
Bagley, Shannon A216
Baglino, Andrew A1007
Bagnarol, Stephen W84
Bagshaw, Seth H. E329
Bagué, Hugo A588
Bagwell, Edward Lee E108
Bagwell, Norman P. A167
Bagwell, Norman P. E64
Bahadur, Sanjay W430
Bahk, Byong-Won W478
Bahl, Tracy L. E500
Bahl, William F. A240
Bahrawi, Fouad Abdulwahab W520
Bahri, Rajat A823
Bai, Fugui W189
Bai, Jieke W142
Bai, Jing W603
Bai, Li W307
Bai, Lizhong W326
Bai, Yanchun W88
Bai, Zhongen W149
Baicker, Katherine A635
Baier, Frank W. A287
Baier, Frank W. E115
Baier, Horst W95
Baier, Wolfgang W203
Baiera, Gavin R. A1097
Baijal, Sanjeev W18
Bailey, D. P. A539
Bailey, Daniel K. A1038
Bailey, Daniel K. E495
Bailey, David W. A421
Bailey, David W. E198
Bailey, Geoffrey R. E235
Bailey, H. C. E152
Bailey, Ian W644
Bailey, Jeff L. E57
Bailey, Jerome R. E79
Bailey, John E57
Bailey, Kathryn M. A815
Bailey, Kevin D. A1091
Bailey, Malcolm W245
Bailey, Nicholas R. E410
Bailey, Sallie B. A613
Bailey, Sallie B. A763
Bailey, Sallie B. E49
Bailey, Steven Richard A811
Bailey, Steven Richard E377
Bailey, Thomas A. E340
Bailey, Vicky A. A767

Bailey, Vicky A. A225
Bailey, Vicky A. E171
Baillie, James C. W571
Bailliencourt, Cedric de W637
Bailliencourt, Cédric de W165
Bailo, Carla J. A17
Bain, Adam A785
Bain, Peter L. E528
Bainbridge, Guy L. T. W662
Bainbridge, Guy L.T. W382
Baine, Edward H. A1094
Bains, Harrison M. E80
Baio, Richard Mark A149
Baiquni, Achmad W483
Bair, Michael D. A223
Bair, Sheila Colleen A185
Baird, Charles J. A283
Baird, Kevin W. A1004
Baird, Patrick S. A865
Baird, Patrick S. E403
Baird, Thomas A A883
Baird, Thomas A P459
Baird, W. Blake E486
Baitinger, Vicki A389
Baitinger, Vicki P219
Baivier, Meghan G. E471
Baivier, Meghan G. E150
Bakas, Michael T. E22
Baker, Adolphus B. A1044
Baker, Charles E. A123
Baker, Charles E. E97
Baker, Christine P596
Baker, Douglas M. A997
Baker, Edward L. E222
Baker, Emily A P127
Baker, G. Leonard E121
Baker, Holleigh E102
Baker, James P. E387
Baker, Jeffery C. E30
Baker, John D. E222
Baker, Julian C. E267
Baker, Kathy L. E30
Baker, Kevin L. A488
Baker, Laurie A. A305
Baker, LeighAnne G. A10
Baker, Paula F. E297
Baker, Raymond T. A652
Baker, Raymond T. E19
Baker, Richard W. A493
Baker, Richard W. E243
Baker, Robert E81
Baker, Robert E. A966
Baker, Robert K. E132
Baker, Ron P285
Baker, Tony E102
Bakhshi, Balbir E493
Bakhshi, Sandeep W296
Bakish, Robert M. A802
Bakker, Gerrit Jan A45
Baksaas, Jon Fredrik W579
Baksaas, Jon Fredrik W228
Bakshi, Ken A1136
Bakstad, Gro W204
Bakun, Marek E459
Balachandran, Madhavan E83
Balagour, Alexander E98
Balaguer, Susan P599
Balaji, Pathamadai Balachandran W587
Balakrishnan, Balu E392

Balbi, Arnaldo Gorziglia W217
Balbi, Arnaldo Gorziglia W41
Balbinot, Sergio W33
Baldacci, John E. A112
Baldanza, B. Ben A583
Baldasare, Bryan T. E321
Baldauf, Sari A443
Baldauf, Sari A395
Baldauf, Sari W247
Baldocchi, Albert S. A232
Baldock, Alex W179
Baldock, Henrietta W311
Baldock, Henrietta W360
Baldridge, Don A319
Baldwin, Christopher J. A158
Baldwin, Deborah G. A398
Baldwin, Dennis A193
Baldwin, Dennis P101
Baldwin, John T. A252
Baldwin, Lisa L. A888
Baldwin, Mark E. A595
Baldwin, Robert H.B. A477
Baldwin, Stacy P656
Baledge, Les R. A1050
Baler, Christian W398
Bales, Brian A. A892
Balfour, Charles A. E489
Bali, Adnan W619
Bali, Vinita A267
Balice-Gordon, Rita E107
Baliff, Jonathan E. A1008
Balkcom, Renee A742
Balkcom, Renee P393
Balkenende, Jan Peter (J.P.) W306
Ball, C. Fred A167
Ball, C. Fred E64
Ball, Calvin P271
Ball, Darin R. E391
Ball, Frederick A. E6
Ball, Gail S. A401
Ball, James Robert A226
Ball, Jeffrey K. A398
Ball, Richard A. E291
Ballance, Robert A143
Ballance, Robert E57
Ballard, C. Andrew E175
Ballard, J. Scott A523
Ballard, J. Scott E257
Ballard, Jashua E161
Ballard, Jed W. E352
Ballard, L. Gregory E501
Ballard, Shari L. A358
Ballbach, John M. A907
Ballester, Alejandro M. A836
Ballhaus, William L. E319
Ballinas, Carlos P345
Balling, Stephanie W251
Ballmer, Adrian W91
Ballou, Roger H. A1078
Ballou, Roger H. E513
Ballout, Benjamin E162
Ballschmiede, Ronald A. E463
Balmann, Yves C. de A292
Balmes, Christian W161
Balo, Andrew K. E138
Baltimore, Thomas J. A856
Baltins, Andris A. A195
Bambawale, Ajai K. W611
Bambeck, Douglas G. E189
Bammann, Linda B. A591

COMBINED HOOVER'S HANDBOOK INDEX OF EXECUTIVES

A = AMERICAN BUSINESS
E = EMERGING COMPANIES
P = PRIVATE COMPANIES
W = WORLD BUSINESSS

Banati, Amit A597
Banati, Amit A447
Bancroft, Charles W258
Bancroft, Natalie A738
Bancroft, Philip V. E413
Bando, Mariko W413
Bandrowczak, Steven (Steve) John A1141
Banducci, Brad L. W651
Bane, Richard C. A352
Banerjee, M. Moina A385
Banerji, Shumeet A538
Banerji, Shumeet W491
Banet, Virginie W391
Banez, Rene G. W85
Bang, Brian E375
Bang, Dong-kwon W537
Bang, Su-Ran W352
Bangert, Steven A167
Bangert, Steven E64
Banister, Gaurdie E. A342
Banister, Gaurdie E. W218
Banko, Frank E156
Banks, Bernard B. A307
Banks, Bernard B. E133
Banks, Lee C. A804
Banks, Lee C. A1099
Banks, M. Katherine A494
Banks, Matthew C. E423
Bannantine, James E43
Banner, Jennifer S. A1042
Bannister, David G. A620
Banno, Masato W110
Bansal, Arun W228
Bansal, Preeta D. A727
Bansal, Preeta D. E345
Bansal, Rishi A135
Banse, Amy L. A15
Banse, Amy L. A629
Banse, Amy L. A254
Bantegnie, Pascal W511
Bao, Shuowang W152
Baoshnakova, Sirma W33
Baquedano, Laura Abasolo Garcia de W593
Bar-Adon, Eshel A119
Bar-Adon, Eshel E48
Bar, Roselyn R. A663
Baracos, Jeffrey S. A358
Barajas, Rene P401
Baranco, Juanita Powell A952
Baratta, Giovanni Battista W627
Baratta, Joseph P. A161
Barba, Catherine W492
Barba, Glenn P. A294
Barba, Glenn P. A256
Barba, Ricardo Naya W131
Barbara, Antonio Jose da W69
Barbarossa, Giovanni E266
Barbas, Paul M. A1097
Barbashev, Sergey W410
Barbe, Jana Cohen E280
Barbeau, Patrick W308
Barbee, Angela A624

Barbeito, Horacio A1018
Barber, James J. (Jim) A1083
Barber, Samantha W295
Barbi, Leslie A886
Barbier, Francois P. W242
Barbizet, Patricia W65
Barbizet, Patricia W613
Barbo, William D. E94
Barbosa, Fabio Colletti W315
Barbosa, Vanessa de Souza Lobato W72
Barbour, Alastair W471
Barbour, D. Scott E5
Barbour, Sondra L. A26
Barcala, Cheryl P140
Barcelon, George T. W100
Barchi, Daniel P386
Barclay, Dan W82
Barclay, Kathleen S. E209
Barclay, William A. E372
Bard, Margot W231
Bardin, Romolo W54
Bardin, Romolo W231
Bardot, Anne W550
Bareford, Becky C. A401
Bareford, Steven T. A401
Barer, Sol J. W598
Barfield, John E. A256
Barfield, Jon E. A294
Barg, Steven K. A201
Bargabos, Sheree L. A975
Bargabos, Sheree L. E381
Baridwan, Zaki W483
Baril, Jacques W193
Baril, Thierry W24
Barilla, Guido W187
Bariquit, Teri J. A745
Barker, James A. A124
Barker, Jon E457
Barker, Peter K. A114
Barkidjija, John M. A188
Barkidjija, John M. E71
Barkin, Thomas I. A399
Barkley, Michael T. A796
Barkov, Mikhail Viktorovich W617
Barksdale, Harold G. W590
Barley, Hattie R. C. A401
Barlow, Carrolee E474
Barlow, Jeff D. A707
Barmonde, Charles L. E432
Barnaba, Mark W246
Barnard, Keith P226
Barner, Sharon R. A306
Barnes-Smith, Matthew E35
Barnes, David A. A349
Barnes, David Eugene A57
Barnes, David G. E497
Barnes, Francesca W423
Barnes, Harrison B. A1040
Barnes, Harrison B. E499
Barnes, John P. A651
Barnes, John P. A814
Barnes, John P. E379
Barnes, Keith L. E523
Barnes, Melissa Stapleton A635
Barnes, Melody C. A171
Barnes, Pamela A. A799
Barnes, Scott E460
Barnett, Amanda Wood A880
Barnett, Amanda Wood E412

Barnett, Hoyt R. A860
Barnette, K. Gary E522
Barnholt, Edward W. A607
Barnhouse, Phillip W. E301
Barns, Dwight M A742
Barns, Dwight M P393
Barnum, Jeremy A591
Baron, Collin P. A814
Baron, Collin P. E379
Baron, Mali W78
Barone, John E374
Baroni, Gino J. A372
Baroni, Gino J. E167
Baroni, Giuliano W177
Baroni, Paul W84
Barouski, William A. A399
Barpoulis, Sarah M. E453
Barpoulis, Sarah M. E171
Barquin, Alfredo A1071
Barr, George R. A415
Barr, George R. E194
Barr, John D. A812
Barr, Keith A1146
Barr, Kevin W157
Barra, Jose M. A594
Barra, Mary T. A335
Barra, Mary T. A466
Barra, Melissa E448
Barra, Ornella A1101
Barra, Ornella A73
Barrack, Thomas J. W125
Barragan, Alejandro M. Elizondo W27
Barral, Diego J. A254
Barranco, David A52
Barrat, Frederic W492
Barrat, Sherry S. A455
Barrat, Sherry S. A740
Barratt, Craig H. A572
Barreda, Hector de la A512
Barrena, Juan Muldoon W265
Barrenechea, Mark J. A326
Barrenechea, Mark J. A114
Barrera, Carlos Jimenez W27
Barrett, Craig R. E468
Barrett, Deborah J. W262
Barrett, George S. A997
Barrett, Joel W. E489
Barrett, John P692
Barrett, John E. E102
Barrett, John F. A242
Barrett, Katherine W40
Barrett, Melanie C. E298
Barrett, Patrick S. A768
Barrett, Patrick S. E359
Barrett, Peter E380
Barrett, Victor L. A945
Barrett, Victor L. E451
Barrie, Andrew J. A595
Barrington, Martin J. (Marty) W40
Barrington, William Edward James W128
Barrios, Alf W499
Barrios, Alf W500
Barrios, Erik E129
Barrios, George A. E543
Barrios, Raymond E129
Barron, Arnold S. A337
Barron, Hal V. W258
Barron, Kathleen A384
Barron, Kathleen A292

Barron, Thomas A. A196
Barron, Thomas A. E79
Barron, William G. A420
Barron, William G. E197
Barros, Marcel Juviniano W630
Barros, Philip E261
Barroso, Gina Diez W76
Barry, Anthony (Tony) A199
Barry, Chloe W341
Barry, Corie S. A155
Barry, David E. E487
Barry, David V. A447
Barry, Edward F. E79
Barry, Joseph F. A500
Barry, Joseph F. E246
Barry, Kevin M. A806
Barry, Michael F. E404
Barry, Richard A814
Barry, Richard E379
Barsan, Radu E392
Barsetti, Joshua J. E85
Barshefsky, Charlene A620
Barshefsky, Charlene A62
Barstad, Melanie W. A242
Barsz, Peter R. A910
Bartel, Ellen S. E532
Bartel, Ricardo W73
Bartels, Robert E. A618
Bartels, Robert E. E290
Barth, Carin M. A374
Barth, Carin M. A491
Barth, Kevin G. A592
Barth, Kevin G. A276
Barth, Stefan W93
Barth, Stephanie A. A679
Barth, Werner A825
Barthelemy, Nicolas M. E415
Bartholdson, John A. E302
Bartholomew, James R. E156
Bartholow, Peter B. A891
Bartlein, Robert H. E114
Bartlett, Mark S. A991
Bartlett, Mark S. E224
Bartlett, Rhian W318
Bartlett, Thomas (Tom) A. A69
Bartok, Daniel C. E213
Bartolo, Anthony F P56
Bartolo, P. Robert A301
Bartolome, Beatriz Angela Lara W625
Bartolomeo, Eduardo de Salles W630
Bartolotta, Peter W362
Barton, Denise A549
Barton, Dominic W500
Barton, Donald L. E357
Barton, Harry V. A242
Barton, Harry V. E200
Barton, Jeffrey P326
Barton, Kurt D. A1035
Barton, Lisa M. A59
Barton, Lisa M. A277
Barton, Richard N. A730
Barton, Richard N. A871
Barton, Richard N. A1148
Bartschat, Michael A586
Bartschat, Michael P292
Baruch, Philip W330
Baruffi, Kumi Y. A270
Baruffi, Kumi Y. E109
Barwood, Marlene A P286
Barzel, Roy I. E526

HOOVER'S HANDBOOK OF EMERGING COMPANIES 2023   587

COMBINED HOOVER'S HANDBOOK INDEX OF EXECUTIVES

A = AMERICAN BUSINESS
E = EMERGING COMPANIES
P = PRIVATE COMPANIES
W = WORLD BUSINESSS

Baschera, Pius W523
Baser, Didem Dincer W618
Bash, Jeffrey Parr E129
Bash, Ruth P520
Bashaw, Walter R. E266
Bashkirov, Alexey W410
Basho, Chan E33
Basich, Marci A. E490
Basile, Cinzia V. W231
Baskin, Dorsey L. A397
Baskin, Dorsey L. E187
Baskin, Scott D. E26
Basler, Bruno W642
Basol, Mehmet Mete W267
Basolis, Elbert G. E193
Bason, John W170
Bason, John G. W55
Bass, Dean O. A958
Bass, Dean O. A938
Bass, Dean O. E442
Bass, Dean O. E456
Bassa, Zarina BM W311
Bassell, Donald E35
Bassett, Lawton E. A71
Bassett, Lawton E. E29
Bassewitz, Christian Graf von W3
Bassey, Ekpedeme M. E260
Bassham, Terry D P218
Bassham, Terry D. A276
Bassi, Peter A. A1145
Bassil, Alain W22
Bassler, Bonnie L. A882
Bassler, Bonnie L. E425
Basso, Ronald E266
Basson, Shai W79
Bast, Christopher J. E136
Bastian, Edward H. A323
Bastioli, Catia W158
Basto, Edgar W101
Basto, Jose Guilherme Xavier de W70
Bastoni, Elizabeth Ann W325
Bastos-Licht, Valdirene A557
Bastos, Marcelo W39
Bastug, Recep W618
Basu, Arijit W561
Basu, Rajiv A103
Batato, Magdi W429
Batchelder, David H. A647
Batchelder, Donna E294
Batcheler, Colleen R. A286
Batcheler, Colleen R. A513
Batchelor, Steven R. A1110
Bate, Oliver W33
Batekhin, Sergey L. W410
Bateman, Leonard H. E108
Bateman, Steven J. A773
Bates, Ann Torre A1068
Bates, Anthony J. A1098
Bates, David J. A771
Bates, Ernest A. E33
Bates, Jason R. E515
Bates, John Christopher A397
Bates, Mary Kay A865
Bates, Mary Kay E403

Bates, Robert D. E296
Batey, Alan S. A942
Batista, Joesley Mendonca W323
Batista, Wesley W323
Batista, Wesley Mendonca W323
Batistoni, Peter E96
Batke, Andreas W563
Batkin, Roger N. A26
Batra, Nishant W443
Batra, Rajeev E330
Batra, Sandeep W296
Batsel, Roger B. A397
Battaglia, Concetta W338
Battaglia, Paul J. A1033
Battaglioli, Michael R. A221
Batten, James R. E243
Battenfeld, Frederick L. E420
Battenfield, Keith P110
Battifarano, Christopher T. E190
Battista, Valerio W482
Battistoni, Joseph J. E295
Battle, Michael A. E175
Battle, W. Patrick E313
Battles, Kelly E35
Battles, Michael Louis E82
Battley, Todd A20
Baty, Darren A548
Baty, Darren P272
Baty, Roderick R. E13
Baublies, Nicoley W196
Bauche, Douglas N. A373
Bauche, Douglas N. E168
Bauer, Bill E220
Bauer, Brett A. A1
Bauer, Daniel M A1026
Bauer, Daniel M P620
Bauer, Douglas F. E495
Bauer, Karl-Heinz W522
Bauer, Matthew N. A384
Bauer, Matthew N. A292
Bauer, Melissa J. E455
Bauer, Milissa S. E156
Bauer, Robert P. E13
Bauer, Scott T. E30
Bauer, Virginia S. E347
Baukol, Erik E236
Baum, Kevin A. E509
Baum, Kevin A. E509
Baum, Kevin A. E510
Baum, Peter J. A1086
Baum, Peter J. E516
Baumann, Barbara M. A325
Baumann, Maja W642
Baumann, Markus W621
Baumann, Urs W91
Baumann, Werner W95
Baumgarten, Jaclyn E313
Baumgartl, Wolf-Dieter W586
Baumgartner, Mark A. E384
Baumgartner, Robert V. E59
Baumscheiper, Michael W277
Baur, Wolfgang W129
Bautista, Ernesto E490
Bauza, Carmen W643
Bawa, Aparna E547
Bawel, Zachary W. A472
Bawel, Zachary W. E230
Bax, William L. A455
Baxby, David W644
Baxendale, Sonia W358

Baxter, Charles B. W487
Baxter, David E. A1059
Baxter, Gregory H.A. E501
Baxter, Scott H. A647
Baxter, Warner L. A1082
Baxter, Warner L. A54
Bay, Annell R. A86
Bay, Annell R. E520
Bay, Walter D. A455
Bayardo, Jose A. A754
Bayer, Michael P. E532
Bayes, Virginia R. E526
Bayh, B. Evan A410
Bayh, B. Evan A153
Bayh, Evan A657
Bayly, Walter W174
Baynor, E. Lee A1033
Baynor, E. Lee E493
Baz, Freddie C. W77
Bazante, Jennifer Mumby A1065
Bazante, Jennifer Mumby E509
Bazemore, Teresa Bryce A398
Bazin, Benoit W635
Bazin, Benoit W165
Bazin, Sebastien M. A462
Bazire, Nicolas W373
Bazire, Nicolas W125
Bazire, Nicolas W61
Bazire, Nicolas W565
Beach, Bruce A1120
Beach, Bruce E535
Beach, Walter T. A1014
Beach, Walter T. E488
Beachy, Matthew L. E189
Beacom, Joseph J. A620
Beal, Anne W258
Beale, Graham W423
Beale, Inga K. W442
Bealer, Jennifer E398
Beall, Robert S. A958
Beall, Robert S. E456
Beam, S. Craig A815
Beamish, Judith M. W570
Beams, Mary Elizabeth A846
Bean, John T. E97
Bean, Oscar M. A981
Bean, Oscar M. E469
Beard, Grant H. E6
Beard, Robert F. A1054
Beard, Robert P. A700
Beard, Simon M. E16
Beardall, Brent J. A1107
Beasley, Bill P437
Beasley, J. Barnie A59
Beasley, Scott C. A453
Beason, Charlotte F. E467
Beato, Paulina W618
Beattie, Arthur P. A841
Beattie, Richard I. E176
Beattie, W. Geoffrey A121
Beattie, W. Geoffrey A120
Beaty, Anne L. A494
Beauchamp, Steven R. E374
Beauchesne, Nina P510
Beaudoin, Pierre W480
Beaudoin, Thomas L. E91
Beaudry, France W295
Beaulieu, Valerie W13
Beautz, Janet K P177
Beaver, Carolyn D. E314

Beaver, David A. A302
Beaver, Paula A1015
Beaver, Paula P571
Beaver, Roy David E515
Beazer, Craig T. A602
Bebek, Ahmet W620
Beber, Justin B. W112
Beber, Shawn W119
Bebon, Marc W165
Bech, Jens W462
Bechat, Jean-Paul W61
Becher, Michael R. A427
Becher, Michael R. E203
Bechtolsheim, Andreas E35
Beck, Barbara J. A358
Beck, Barbara J. A818
Beck, Christophe A358
Beck, Daniel J. A984
Beck, Daniel J. E476
Beck, David E. A401
Beck, Mark A. A794
Beck, Marla Malcolm E57
Beck, Robert R. A332
Beck, Robert W. E413
Beck, Wendy A. A10
Beckelman, Lee E. E450
Becker, Burkhard W62
Becker, Christopher A430
Becker, David B. A425
Becker, David B. E201
Becker, David M. A922
Becker, Gregory W. A984
Becker, Gregory W. E476
Becker, Joseph J. E480
Becker, Laurie P. E384
Becker, Marc E. A16
Becker, Sonja De W336
Becker, W. Marston E336
Becker, Wendy A645
Becker, Wendy W557
Becker, William A927
Becker, William E435
Beckerle, Mary C. A548
Beckerle, Mary C. A585
Beckham, Brad W. A765
Beckham, Sophie A568
Beckhorn, Jay E232
Beckles, Kathy Card E520
Beckley, Thomas P. E75
Beckman, David J. A235
Beckman, Mitchell R P590
Beckman, Per W579
Beckmann, Barbara A. A439
Beckton, Dana A930
Beckton, Dana P494
Beckwitt, Richard A629
Bedard, Christina W398
Bedell, Jeffrey A. E14
Bedi, Christopher A931
Bedient, Patricia M. A34
Bedient, Patricia M. W573
Bédier, Jérôme W125
Bedingfield, Robert A. A920
Bednarz, Brian W31
Bedore, James M. A726
Beebe, Cheryl K. A799
Beebe, Cheryl K. A715
Beebe, Cheryl K. E497
Beebe, Kevin L. A942
Beebe, Kevin L. A453

588   HOOVER'S HANDBOOK OF EMERGING COMPANIES 2023

COMBINED HOOVER'S HANDBOOK INDEX OF EXECUTIVES

A = AMERICAN BUSINESS
E = EMERGING COMPANIES
P = PRIVATE COMPANIES
W = WORLD BUSINESSS

Beebe, Michael D. A1050
Beebe, Michael D. A524
Beebe, Michael D. E258
Beeck, Hans van W27
Beekhuizen, Mick J. A195
Beer, James A. A34
Beer, Mariano S. de E420
Beerli, Andreas W68
Beerman, Molly S. A37
Beery, Joseph C. A573
Beery, Robin C. A1056
Beery, Robin C. E505
Beesley, Bradley L. A427
Beesley, Bradley L. E204
Beeuwsaert, Dirk W565
Begemann, Brett D. A354
Begle, Curtis L. A153
Begleiter, Steven L. E311
Begley, Charlene T. A518
Begley, Charlene T. A721
Begley, Christopher B. A1150
Begley, Jody L. A47
Begor, Mark W. A726
Behan, Mark L. A98
Behan, Mark L. E36
Behar, Dana D. E204
Behar, Gregory W430
Behar, Z. Jamie A96
Behar, Z. Jamie E441
Beharel, Francois W489
Behbehani, Mohammed Saleh W19
Behle, Christine W196
Behlert, Bernd W251
Behm, John D. E260
Behm, Willim A. E480
Behr, Allen C. A759
Behrendt, Birgit A. W602
Behrendt, Jens Bloch W348
Behrendt, Michael W270
Behrens, David Alan A68
Behrens, Evan E363
Behrens, Manfred W3
Behrens, Oliver W191
Beia, Terance L. A555
Beia, Terance L. E269
Beier, Constantin H. E530
Beinecke, Candace K. A802
Beirne, Patrick J. E402
Beiser, Scott L. E260
Beitel, David A. A1149
Bejar, Martha H. A650
Bejar, Martha H. E457
Beke, Guy W623
Bekke, Nathan E. E295
Bekker, Jacobus Petrus W597
Belair, Diana H. A138
Belair, Diana H. E55
Belair, Sebastian W358
Belak, Cynthia Y. E483
Belanoff, Joseph K. E121
Belcher, Jason R. A419
Belcher, Samuel L. A432
Belec, Anne W295
Belingard, Jean-Luc A615

Belisle, Jeffrey A. A43
Belismelis, Luis Enrique Romero W174
Beliveau-Dunn, Jeanne A359
Beliveau-Dunn, Jeanne M. A951
Belk, William I. A948
Bell-Knight, Christopher A. W100
Bell, Aurelia J. E190
Bell, Bernice E. A28
Bell, Craig D. E526
Bell, Genevieve W164
Bell, George B. A1064
Bell, George B. E509
Bell, Hermann W453
Bell, Jack W. A1132
Bell, Jack W. E539
Bell, James A. A89
Bell, James A. A214
Bell, Karin A195
Bell, Katherine Button E284
Bell, Madeline S. A272
Bell, Marc H. A96
Bell, Martin C. A493
Bell, Martin C. E243
Bell, Ryan B. E159
Bell, Sandra A231
Bell, Susan R. E425
Bell, Thomas A. A625
Bell, Thomas D. A747
Bell, Thomas J. A188
Bell, Thomas J. E71
Bell, Victor E. A418
Bellemare, Alain M. A323
Bellemere, Gilles W26
Beller, Alan L. A1037
Bellezza, Alisha A224
Belling, Joseph A. E96
Bellinger, Patricia S. A140
Bellinger, Patricia S. W511
Bellini, Alessandra W597
Bellinson, James L. E298
Belliston, J. Richard A843
Belliston, J. Richard E393
Bello, Adam J P173
Bello, Ivanhoe Lo W363
Belloeil-Melkin, Marie-Veronique W373
Bellon-Szabo, Nathalie W550
Bellon, Francois-Xavier W550
Bellon, Sophie W550
Bellon, Sophie W358
Bellone, Steven P178
Belloni, Antonio W373
Bellos, Alex A1132
Belluzzo, Richard nn E523
Belousov, Andrey W506
Belser, Richard L. A681
Belser, Richard L. E318
Belske, Gary L. A306
Belsky, Scott A15
Belstock, Richard L. E388
Beltran, Francisco Camacho W244
Belur, Raghuveer R. E163
Ben-nun, Avihu W410
Ben-Zur, Liat W623
Ben-Zvi, Bosmat W79
Ben, Shenglin W662
Bena, Pamela A. A441
Bena, Pamela A. E212
Benacci, Nancy C. A240

Benacin, Philippe W637
Benck, David M. E254
Bender, James J. A1048
Bender, Joel E72
Bender, Kevin M. E340
Bender, M. Steven A1124
Bender, Michael J. A608
Bender, Morton A. E227
Bender, Scott E72
Bender, Shannon Lowry W491
Bender, Steven E72
Bendiek, Sabine W517
Bendotti, Charles A825
Bendush, William E. E107
Bene, Robert F. Del A565
Beneby, Doyle N. A868
Benedetti, Dante B. A381
Benedetto, Paolo Di W54
Benedict, Danielle A1068
Benedict, Rod P671
Benet, Lincoln E. A1106
Benet, Lincoln E. W374
Benevich, Eric E346
Benfield, James H P625
Benfield, Stephanie Stuckey P128
Bengtsson, Bo W579
Bengtsson, Goran W579
Benhamou, Eric A. W984
Benhamou, Eric A. E476
Benioff, Marc A912
Benitez, Jorge L. A1136
Benitez, Jorge L. A410
Benjamin, Eric E276
Benjamin, Gerald A. A917
Benjamin, Gerald R. E240
Benjamin, Jeffrey D. A56
Benjamin, Jeffrey D. A5
Benjamin, Mark D. E402
Benjamin, Valerie C. A411
Benjamin, William Stephen A95
Benjumea, Francisco Javier Garcia-Carranza W73
Benko, Brittany A547
Benko, Cathleen A. A743
Benko, Cathleen A. E451
Benner, Christiane W96
Benner, Christiane W171
Bennett-Martin, Pamela E206
Bennett, Adam W574
Bennett, Alan M. A438
Bennett, Alan M. A1030
Bennett, Alan M. A494
Bennett, David W157
Bennett, Elizabeth S. E307
Bennett, James A. A340
Bennett, James D. A439
Bennett, Jonathan S. A145
Bennett, Kelvin Eugene A26
Bennett, Peter J. E536
Bennett, Ricardo W132
Bennett, Robert R. A538
Bennett, Robert R. A872
Bennett, Robert R. A633
Bennett, Robert R. A633
Bennett, Rodney D. A414
Bennett, Rodney D. E193
Bennett, Ruth B. A398
Bennett, Walter J. A1131
Benning, Todd S. A1078
Benning, Todd S. E513

Bennink, Jan W161
Benoist, Gilles W565
Benoit, Laura E537
Benroth, Robert L. E507
Bens, Geert W623
Bensalah-Chaqroun, Miriem W492
Bensalah, Nocair E161
Bensema, David J P62
Bensen, Peter (Pete) J. A205
Bensenhaver, Dewey F. A981
Bensenhaver, Dewey F. E469
Bensinger, Steven J. E287
Benson, Beth A. E336
Benson, David C. A391
Benson, David W. E30
Benson, James M. E147
Benson, Jeffrey F. A1033
Benson, Jeffrey F. E492
Benson, Laurie S. A416
Benson, Marta H. A1132
Benson, Michael A305
Benson, Molly R. A657
Benson, Molly R. A717
Benson, P. George A845
Benson, P. George E395
Benstock, Gerald M. E473
Benstock, Michael E473
Bentinck, William C. E504
Bentley, Sarah W371
Benton, James Carson E452
Benton, Kelly W. E426
Benton, Patrick M. A1053
Bentsen, Tim E. A988
Bentsen, Tim E. E479
Bentz, L. Earl A200
Bentz, L. Earl E79
Benvenuto, Suzanne A400
Benz, Hanz U. E153
Benziger, Donald A. E421
Bepler, Stephen E P586
Beppu, Rikako W404
Berahas, Solomon A. W473
Beran, Josette A1015
Beran, Josette P574
Berard, Patrick A643
Berard, Patrick W495
Berardinelli-Krantz, Nancy L. A485
Berardini, Francesco W627
Berardini, Francesco W627
Beraud, Jill A631
Berba, Carlos Antonio M. W514
Berberian, Lance V. A615
Berce, Daniel E. E207
Berchtold, Joe A641
Berding, John B. A64
Beredo, Gina A. A795
Beressi, Joseph W311
Berg, Charles G. A318
Berg, Jeffrey S. A786
Berg, Mark S. A830
Berg, Sandra A. E23
Berg, Stephen M. Van De A722
Bergamaschi, Paola A65
Bergan, Chad D. A311
Bergeon, Derek E340
Berger, Genevieve B. W357
Berger, Howard M. A519
Berger, Howard M. E256
Berger, Michael L. E11
Berger, Pascale W174

COMBINED HOOVER'S HANDBOOK INDEX OF EXECUTIVES

```
A = AMERICAN BUSINESS
E = EMERGING COMPANIES
P = PRIVATE COMPANIES
W = WORLD BUSINESSS
```

Berger, Pierre W213
Berger, Wendy E239
Bergeron, Stephanie W. E471
Bergfors, Stina W579
Berggren, Arne W473
Bergh, Charles V. (Chip) A538
Berglund, James L. A378
Berglund, Robert C. E322
Berglund, Steven W. E497
Bergman, David E. A1059
Bergman, Jason W. A1144
Bergman, Rick A18
Bergman, Stanley M. A917
Bergman, William T P558
Bergmann, Theo W98
Bergonzi, Adam T. A671
Bergquist, Leslie Kenneth E236
Bergstedt, Mikael W60
Bergstein, Joseph P. A841
Bergstroem, Henrik W4
Bergstrom, Christopher W. E283
Bergstrom, John F. A17
Bergstrom, Pal W579
Bergstrom, Stephen W. A1131
Bergwall, Timothy L. A489
Bergy, Dean H. A981
Berke, Monique P. A945
Berke, Monique P. E451
Berkemeyer, Thomas G. A59
Berkenhagen, Ulf W61
Berkery, Rosemary T. A438
Berkery, Rosemary T. A1030
Berkley, W. Robert A149
Berkley, William R. A149
Berkman, David J. E244
Berkowitz, Bruce R. E459
Berksoy, Tugay W619
Berlew, Adam T. A977
Berlew, Adam T. E464
Berlinger, Stefanie W109
Berlinghieri, Leo E362
Berlinski, Milton R. E525
Berlinski, Philip A480
Berman, Ann E. A645
Berman, Bridget Ryan A735
Berman, Mandy Lee A500
Berman, Mandy Lee E246
Berman, Michael E447
Berman, Michael A. A652
Berman, Robert A. A305
Berman, Steven L. E145
Berman, Walter Stanley A70
Bermanzohn, Fran A513
Bermejo, Angel L. Davila W382
Bermudez, Jorge A. A711
Bernard, Alison M. E150
Bernard, Betsy J. A1150
Bernard, Daniel W123
Bernard, Edward C. A648
Bernardes, Ricardo P100
Bernardi, Carlo De W157
Bernardini, Roberto di W187
Bernardo, Romeo L. W85
Berne, April A. E185

Berner, Anne-Catherine W548
Berner, Kristy A814
Berner, Kristy E379
Bernhard, Leslie E425
Bernhard, Robert J. A306
Bernhard, Spalt W229
Bernicke, Jutta W277
Bernier, Jean W31
Bernier, Sam W398
Berninger, Daniel C. E336
Bernis, Valérie W565
Bernlohr, Timothy J. A1125
Bernlohr, Timothy J. E447
Berns, Steven E493
Bernstein, Jacob D. A171
Bernstein, Joshua B. E79
Bernstein, Luke A788
Bernstein, Luke E365
Bernstein, Seth P. A377
Bernstein, Seth P. E17
Berquist, Carl T. A145
Berquist, Joseph A. E404
Berra, Albert L. A935
Berra, Albert L. E439
Berro, Alan N P33
Berry, J. Wade A397
Berry, Mark S. A952
Berry, Michael J. A729
Berry, Robert W90
Berry, Ryan E34
Berry, Thomas W. A854
Berry, William B. A295
Berryman, Kevin C. A580
Berson, Jory A. A198
Berta, Vincent A. A420
Berta, Vincent A. E197
Bertauche, Linda E470
Berthelin, Michel W15
Bertiere, Francois W161
Bertley, Frederic A803
Bertley, Frederic E371
Bertolini, Mark T. A1088
Bertolini, Massimo W391
Bertolini, Robert J. E94
Bertozzi, Carolyn R. A635
Bertrand, Greg D. A989
Bertrand, Maryse W399
Bertrand, Maryse W420
Bertrandt, Rachael A. A558
Bertreau, François W631
Bertsch, Jan A. E70
Bertschi, Hans-Joerg W631
Bertucci, Frank E. A496
Berutti, William E405
Berzin, Ann C. W617
Bes, Xabier Anoveros Trias de W423
Besca, Mark M. A659
Besga, Francisco Borja Acha W220
Besga, Francisco Borja Acha W219
Beshar, Sarah E. A573
Besharat, Alex W84
Beskid, Tina M. A893
Besnier, Stephanie W225
Besombes, Beatrice W107
Besong, John-Paul E. A865
Besong, John-Paul E. A1065
Besong, John-Paul E. E403
Bessant, Catherine W666
Bessette, Diane J. A629
Bessho, Yoshiki W576

Besson, Philippe W550
Best, C. Munroe A145
Best, Catherine M. W120
Best, Craig W. A816
Best, Rhys J. E487
Best, Terese M. E311
Bester, Andrew W159
Bestic, Gregory C. A393
Bestic, Gregory C. E184
Betancourt, Joseph P589
Bethancourt, John E. A325
Bethell, Melissa W201
Bethell, Melissa W235
Bethell, Melissa W597
Betrus, Lisa P589
Bettag, Michael W395
Bettinelli, Gregory M. E64
Bettinger, Douglas R. A619
Bettinger, Terri A. A844
Bettinger, Terri A. E394
Bettinger, Walter W. A919
Beullier, Alain W225
Beurden, Ben Van W395
Beurden, Ben Van W532
Beuren, Archbold D. van A195
Beuret, Jean-Baptiste W631
Bevan, Thomas W. E326
Bexiga, Annabelle G. A979
Beyeler, Rolf W631
Beyer, Hans W548
Beyer, Richard M. A700
Beyer, Robert D. A581
Bezard, Bruno W631
Bezos, Jeffrey P. A50
Bezverhov, Anatoly Aleksandrovich W617
Bezzeccheri, Maurizio W220
Bhagat, Smita W271
Bhakta, Mansingh L. W491
Bhalla, Ajay A864
Bhalla, Ajay A670
Bhalla, Anant A60
Bhalla, Pavan E153
Bhalla, Vikas E179
Bhanap, Nina E407
Bhandari, Inderpal S. A1102
Bhandari, Parul E490
Bhandarkar, Vedika W587
Bhanji, Nabeel W612
Bharucha, Kaizad W271
Bhasin, Puneet A1079
Bhasin, Rachna E438
Bhasin, Sanjay A397
Bhasin, Sanjay E187
Bhat, Ashima W271
Bhathal, Alex E115
Bhatia, Kamal A846
Bhatia, Manish H. A700
Bhatia, Nina W364
Bhatia, Raveesh K. W271
Bhatia, Sangeeta N. A1089
Bhatia, Vaishali S. A521
Bhatia, Vanisha Mittal W49
Bhatnagar, Atul E77
Bhatt, Deepak L. A178
Bhatt, O. P. W588
Bhatt, Om Prakash W587
Bhatt, Padmanabh P. E474
Bhatt, Prama A534
Bhatt, Prat S. A244

Bhattacharya, Abhijit W351
Bhattacharya, Arundhati W491
Bhattacharya, Ashis Nayan E540
Bhela, Harvinder S. A729
Bhojwani, Gary C. A534
Bhojwani, Gary C. A261
Bhusri, Aneel A466
Bhutani, Amanpal S. E234
Bi, Mingjian W146
Biagas, John Fitzgerald A845
Biagas, John Fitzgerald E395
Biagini-Komas, Julianne M. A509
Biagini-Komas, Julianne M. E251
Biamonti, Jean-luc W231
Bian, Deyun W656
Bian, Jiajun W529
Bian, Xuemei E257
Bianchi, Mirko D. G. W661
Bianchi, Stephen M. E98
Bibby, Andrew J. W122
Bibelheimer, Jason E239
Bibic, Mirko W99
Bibic, Mirko W507
Bibisi, Ray Michael E420
Bible, Daryl N. A651
Bible, Hannah M. E131
Bice, Shawn A1107
Bich, Genevieve W398
Bichsel, Stefan W87
Bickel, Paul J. A978
Bickel, Paul J. E465
Bickerstaff, George W. E272
Bickerstaffe, Katie W385
Bickford, Natalie W515
Bickham, John R. A223
Bickham, W. Bradley E5
Bicking, Rachel P559
Bickley, Ian Martin E130
Biddle, James E. E175
Biderman, Mark C. A87
Bie, Ave M. A1114
Biedenkopf, Sebastian W251
Biegger, David B. A286
Biegler, David W. A956
Bielan, Judith Q. A143
Bielan, Judith Q. E57
Bielen, Richard J. A853
Bienaime, Jean-Jacques E267
Bienaime, Jean-Jacques E61
Bienfait, Robin A. W262
Bierman, James L. A1003
Biermann, Albert W294
Biesecker, Sidney A. A528
Biesecker, Sidney A. E258
Biesterfeld, Robert C. (Bob) A900
Bievre, Martine W65
Bigby, Walter O. E418
Biggam, Megan A188
Biggam, Megan E71
Biggar, Lynne A1099
Biggar, Lynne A1096
Biggins, J. Veronica A956
Biggs, Brett A15
Biggs, Brett W643
Biggs, M. Brett A1104
Bigham, Justin K. A411
Bigley, Deirdre M. E438
Bigne, Anne-Sophie De La W168
Bigot, Domitille Doat-Le E325
Biguet, Stephane W523

COMBINED HOOVER'S HANDBOOK INDEX OF EXECUTIVES

A = AMERICAN BUSINESS
E = EMERGING COMPANIES
P = PRIVATE COMPANIES
W = WORLD BUSINESSS

Bihan, Sandrine Le W637
Bihl, Anthony P. E321
Bijapurkar, Rama W296
Bijlani, Jeewat E404
Bilbrey, John P. A993
Bilbrey, John P. A195
Bilbrey, John P. A269
Bilbrey, Mary E. A588
Bilgic, Murat W619
Bilicic, George W. A835
Billes, Martha G. W122
Billes, Owen G. W122
Billhorn, Jill M. A214
Billings, Clyde A. A424
Billings, Clyde A. E200
Billingsley, Lori George A830
Billson, Margaret S. A95
Bilodeau, Steven J. E107
Bilotta, Anthony V. A596
Bilotta, Anthony V. E286
Bilunas, Matthew A155
Bimmerman, Julie K. E425
Binbasgil, Sabri Hakan W26
Binda, Marc E. E15
Binde, Alana M. E149
Binderow, Alex E525
Bindra, Jagjeet S. W374
Bing, Arthur G.H. E247
Bingham-Hall, Penny W246
Bingham, Gwendolyn M. A794
Bingham, Kim R. A211
Bingham, Kim R. E84
Bingham, R. Dean A703
Bingham, R. Dean E327
Bingold, Michael A439
Binnie, William H. E150
Binning, Paviter S. W371
Binning, Paviter S. W646
Binns, Justin T. A933
Bintz, William E47
Biorck, Hans W579
Biorn, Kristofer W. E46
Birch, Jean M. E215
Birch, Peter Gibbs W180
Bird, Anat M. A1138
Bird, Anat M. E544
Bird, Graham R. W262
Bird, Roger A. E222
Bird, Stefan A. A798
Birkans, Aldis A722
Birkans, Aldis E339
Birkett, Bernard J. E534
Birmingham-Byrd, Melody A1
Birmingham, Martin K. A411
Birmingham, Michael J. E69
Birnbaum, Leonhard W207
Birns, Ira M. A1135
Birrell, Gordon W109
Birtel, Thomas W562
Birx, Deborah L. E272
Birznieks, Gunther E518
Bisagni, Gianfranco W661
Bisaro, Paul M. A1153
Bisbee, Gerald E. A221

Biscardi, Joseph P1
Bischof, Harrington A773
Bischofberger, Norbert W. W95
Biser, Sheri D. E243
Bishar, John J. E34
Bishop, Hans Edgar A27
Bishop, James H. A1133
Bishop, James H. E541
Bisignano, Frank J. A434
Bisignano, Frank J. A541
Bismarck, Nilufer von W360
Bisson, Peter E. A108
Bitner, Rachel G. E158
Bito, Masaaki W552
Bitting, W. Coleman A787
Bitzer, Marc R. A1129
Bitzer, Marc R. W96
Bixby, Robert Philip A592
Bixby, Walter E. A592
Bixler, Steven K. A895
Bizzari, Jean-Pierre E244
Bizzocchi, Adolfo W177
Bjerke, Rune W448
Bjorck, Meredith W P265
Björklund, Joséphine Edwall W231
Bjorklund, K. Gunnar A905
Bjorknert, Mikael W579
Bjorlin, Alexis Black E141
Björling, Ewa W231
Bjornaas, Judith L. E308
Bjornaas, Judith L. E144
Bjornholt, James Eric A697
Bjorstedt, Marie W277
Blachford, Erik C. A1149
Black, Albert C. E384
Black, Archie C. E457
Black, Archie C. E400
Black, Barton E. E181
Black, David Lee A235
Black, Doug E445
Black, Jeffrey H. A791
Black, Jerome Thomas W612
Black, Lance A853
Black, Laura A. E261
Black, Laura A. E523
Black, Maria A108
Black, Paul M. E247
Black, Randall E. E99
Black, Steven D. A1115
Black, Steven D. A721
Black, Thomas E. A514
Black, William W80
Black, William J. A800
Blackburn, Katherine B. A410
Blackett, Karen W201
Blackett, Kelly S. W122
Blackford, David E. A652
Blackhurst, Eric P. A532
Blackhurst, Eric P. E259
Blackley, Richard Scott A945
Blackley, Richard Scott E450
Blackman, Donna E468
Blackwell, Jean S. A215
Blackwell, Jean S. W327
Blackwell, Thomas A. A722
Blackwood, Stephen F. E483
Blade, Mark J. A422
Blades, Alexander W473
Blaesing, Joanne M. P. E97
Blahnik, Ronald P. E254

Blaine, Steven W. E526
Blair, Bryce A862
Blair, Donald W. A298
Blair, Donald W. E145
Blair, Kevin S. A987
Blair, Kevin S. E478
Blair, Nelda Luce A958
Blair, Nelda Luce E456
Blair, Rainer M. A315
Blair, Robert L. E472
Blair, W. Bradley E247
Blais, John F. E190
Blais, Thomas W193
Blaise, Lucile E417
Blake, Christopher D. A800
Blake, Elizabeth K. E238
Blake, Francis S. A654
Blake, Francis S. A323
Blake, James W. A500
Blake, James W. E246
Blake, Joseph J P444
Blake, Katryn Shineman A43
Blake, Ryan A143
Blake, Ryan E56
Blakely, Caroline E. A95
Blakemore, Dominic W170
Blakeney, John M. A378
Blakey, Margaret S. E397
Blakey, Marion C. A34
Blakey, Marion C. E471
Blakley, Kevin M. A1120
Blakley, Kevin M. E535
Blalock, Robert H. A1065
Blalock, Robert H. E509
Blanc, Amanda W64
Blanc, Jean Jacques E281
Blanc, Jean-Sebastien W225
Blanca, Tere A135
Blance, Andrea W64
Blanch, Jodi A857
Blanchard, Cameron R. A223
Blanchet, Jean-Didier F.C. W344
Blanchet, Lucie W420
Blanchet, Paul J. A523
Blanchet, Paul J. E257
Blanco, Alex N. A806
Blanco, Juan Sebastian Moreno W72
Blanco, Maria Luisa Garcia W593
Blanco, Tomás García W493
Blank, Donna J. A28
Blank, Gregory R. A726
Blanka-Graff, Markus W355
Blankenhagen, Nancy E356
Blankstein, Leon I. A57
Blankstein, Leon I. E24
Blase, Maria F. E540
Blaser, Stefanie W398
Blasing, Karen E45
Blaske, Stephen P. A895
Blass, Gus J. A190
Blass, Gus J. E73
Blau, David A. A941
Blau, Jeff T. E471
Blauwhoff, Peter W588
Blavatnik, Alex A1106
Blavatnik, Len A1106
Blaylock, Ronald E. A205
Blaylock, Ronald E. A150
Blaylock, Ronald E. A821
Blazer, Randolph C. E38

Blazheev, Victor W476
Blazquez, Pedro Azagra A112
Blazquez, Pedro Azagra W295
Blears, Hazel W160
Blegen, Bernie E331
Bleser, Philip F. A851
Bless, Michael A. A258
Blessing, Cliff Donald E5
Blew, Clinton J. A235
Bley, Daniel H. A1113
Blickley, Matthew J. A266
Blidner, Jeffrey Miles A180
Blidner, Jeffrey Miles W113
Blidner, Jeffrey Miles W112
Bliesener, Kai W640
Blin, Bruno W641
Blinn, Mark A. A366
Blinn, Mark A. A624
Blinn, Mark A. A1010
Blinn, Mark A. A478
Bliss, Jason W. E451
Bliss, Timothy E34
Blix, Svein W347
Blixt, Dianne Neal A70
Blocher, John E218
Block, Philippe W283
Block, Stanley E76
Blok, Eelco W596
Blood, John W40
Bloodworth, Veronica A453
Bloom, Jamie J. E420
Bloom, Mark W16
Bloom, Mark H. A450
Bloom, William A. A502
Bloomquist, Andrea L. E448
Blottnitz, Andreas von E33
Blouin, Ann S. E164
Blouin, Pierre W420
Blount, Sally E. A6
Blount, Sally E. A1055
Blount, Susan L. E85
Bloxam, Richard A588
Blue, Daniel T. A414
Blue, Daniel T. E191
Blue, Robert M. A1094
Blue, Robert M. A340
Bluedorn, Todd M. A1010
Bluestone, Jeffrey A473
Bluhm, Christian W621
Blum, Bradley M. E543
Blum, E. Michael E421
Blum, Kristen E. A959
Blum, Olivier W524
Blum, Steven M. E45
Blume, Jessica L. A216
Blume, Jessica L. A860
Blume, Oliver W640
Blumofe, Robert E12
Blunck, Thomas W415
Blunt, Matt E120
Blyer, David E177
Blythe, Shayne E418
Bø, Frode W558
Bo, Shaochuan W663
Board, Bruce Leino P246
Board, George Cowden Iii P71
Boardman, Michael A814
Boardman, Michael E379
Boatright, Nancy Rinaldi A130
Boattini, Jennifer R. A543

COMBINED HOOVER'S HANDBOOK INDEX OF EXECUTIVES

A = AMERICAN BUSINESS
E = EMERGING COMPANIES
P = PRIVATE COMPANIES
W = WORLD BUSINESSS

Boatwright, Scott A232
Bobadilla, Luis Isasi Fernandez de W76
Bobb, George C. E483
Bobbitt, Rhodes R. A516
Bobo, Donald E. A361
Boccardelli, Paolo W592
Bochenek, David R. A939
Bochinsky, Michael W510
Bochner, Steven E. A402
Bochnowski, Benjamin J. E191
Bochnowski, David A. E191
Bock, Kurt Wilhelm W93
Bock, Kurt Wilhelm W96
Bock, William G. E451
Bodaken, Bruce G. A894
Bodart, Paul W200
Bodem, Barbara W. A986
Bodine, Bruce A714
Bodine, Christopher W. E361
Bodner, Jeff A90
Bodner, Laurence E. E260
Bodnyk, Sandra L. A816
Bodor, Robert E400
Boe, Veronica Pascual W593
Boeck, Karel De W199
Boeck, Karel De W473
Boeckmann, Alan L. A929
Boedeker, Kenneth W. A376
Boege, Kathleen M. A1133
Boege, Kathleen M. E541
Boehm, Doris W628
Boehmer, Mark D. A1144
Boehnlein, Glenn S. A981
Boel, Harold W565
Boel, Nicolas W554
Boel, Stefan W62
Boelte, Craig E. E374
Boer, Dick W430
Boer, Dick W532
Boer, William J. A555
Boer, William J. E269
Boerman, Manja E83
Boerner, Christopher (Chris) A. A178
Boersig, Clemens A. H. A366
Boersig, Clemens A. H. W395
Boesinger, Rolf W199
Boetger, Bruno D'Avila Melo W69
Boettcher, Charles C. A1110
Bogart, Karen A. Smith A706
Bogart, Stacy L. E540
Bogart, Teresa S. Van De E410
Bogart, Thomas A. W570
Bogdanov, Vladimir Leonidovich W575
Boger, Richard L. E237
Boggild, Carl Claus E370
Boggs, Scott M. A527
Bogliolo, Alessandro A140
Bogner, Hannes W627
Boguski, Michael L. A848
Boguslavskiy, Leonid W521
Boguslawski, Nadine W395
Bohigian, Catherine R. A223
Bohle, Birgit W199
Bohlig, Tamara N. A120

Bohlig, Tamara N. E48
Bohlin, Garen G. E107
Bohm, Friedrich K.M. E306
Bohman, Staffan W60
Bohn, Karen M. A37
Bohn, Karen M. E14
Bohn, Karen M. E367
Bohnen, Shane E59
Bohnert, Denise M. E20
Bohnet, Iris W176
Bohrson, Christopher G. E107
Bohuny, Bruce D. A617
Bohuny, Bruce D. E289
Bohuon, Oliver W585
Bohuon, Olivier W490
Bohutinsky, Amy C. A1149
Boigegrain, Barbara A. A772
Boillat, Pascal W164
Boinay, Vincent W358
Boise, A. Miller W209
Boise, April Miller W617
Boissard, Sophie W33
Boivin, Pierre W420
Boivin, Pierre W399
Boix, Angel Vila W593
Boizard, Christophe W18
Bok, Oscar de W198
Bokan, Michael W. A700
Boland, D. Steve E221
Bolash, Brian W. E172
Bold, Bill E370
Boldea, Lucian A530
Bolen, Dianne W. A397
Bolen, Dianne W. E187
Boleslawski, Alexandra W174
Bolger, Andrea W358
Bolger, John C. E224
Bolin, Pat S. A1086
Bolin, Pat S. E521
Bolland, Marc J. A264
Bolland, Marc J. W235
Bollesen, Michael E314
Bollingberg, Karl A. A37
Bollingberg, Karl A. A397
Bollingberg, Karl A. E14
Bollore, Cyrille W165
Bollore, Cyrille W637
Bollore, Marie W165
Bollore, Sebastien W165
Bollore, Thierry W587
Bolloré, Vincent W165
Bollore, Yannick W165
Bollore, Yannick W637
Bolomey, Janice E510
Bolster, Jennifer P527
Bolt, Tracy A. A516
Bolte, David Albert A979
Bolten, Joshua B. A366
Bolton, H. Eric E151
Boltz, William P. A647
Bolus, Mark J. A280
Bolus, Mark J. E113
Bom, Luis Todo W254
Boman, Par W579
Boman, Pär W231
Bomba, Jane Okun E66
Bombard, Tate P462
Bombick, Megan A. A1073
Bomboy, David W. A414
Bomboy, David W. E193

Bomhard, Nikolaus von W415
Bomhard, Nikolaus von W198
Bomhard, Stefan W297
Bomhard, Stefan W170
Bompard, Alexandre W459
Bond, Phillip J. A393
Bone, Dennis M. A575
Bonekamp, Berthold A. W234
Boneparth, Peter A583
Boneparth, Peter A608
Bonewell, Fred P143
Bonfield, Andrew R.J. A210
Bonfield, Andrew R.J. W490
Bonfield, Peter Leahy W584
Bonham, Scott B. W84
Bonham, Scott B. W371
Bonham, Scott B. W379
Boni, Theresa R. E475
Bonifas, Edward A774
Bonifas, Edward E360
Bonilla, Emily P174
Bonilla, Luis Miguel Palomino A953
Bonino, John M. A937
Bonino, John M. E441
Bonnafe, Jean-Laurent W103
Bonnafé, Jean-Laurent W125
Bonnard, Luc W523
Bonnechose, Benedicte De W168
Bonnell, Brian E262
Bonnell, William E. W420
Bonner, Joseph J. E180
Bonner, Suzanne M. A888
Bonnet, Henri W347
Bonnot, Vincent P. A568
Bono, Raquel C. A541
Bonomi, Marco Ambrogio Crespi W315
Bonomo, Paola W592
Bontrager, Kimberlee E469
Bontrager, Wendell L. A378
Bonvenuto, David L. A1040
Bonvenuto, David L. E498
Bonzani, Andrew A570
Booker, Niall W287
Bookmyer, John L. A844
Bookmyer, John L. E394
Boon, Yoon Chiang W322
Boondech, Prasobsook W117
Boone, Cornelius A357
Boone, David S. A722
Boone, Karen E452
Boone, Kevin S. A304
Boone, Torrence A654
Boonklum, Peangpanor W484
Boonpoapichart, Kriengchai W117
Boonyachai, Krishna W484
Boonyawat, Teerawat W484
Boonyoung, Pridi W117
Boor, Kathryn J. A567
Boor, William C. E85
Booth, Clement B. W415
Booth, Cynthia O. A420
Booth, Cynthia O. E197
Booth, Julie A900
Booth, Kenneth S. E128
Booth, Lewis W. K. A710
Booth, Lewis W. K. W504
Booth, Vicki U. E247
Boothe, Timothy W. A1120
Boothe, Timothy W. E535
Boots, Renea E223

Bootsma, Pieter W22
Booysen, Steve W562
Boparai, Nevin Singh E67
Boratto, Eva C. A1069
Borba, George A. A308
Borba, George A. E133
Borchert, Stephen W390
Bordelon, Ann G. E23
Bordelon, John W. A523
Bordelon, John W. E257
Borden, Ian F. A675
Bordin, Jose Sergio W69
Borg, Deborah A185
Borgen, Luis A. A352
Borges, Steven D. A578
Borgman, Charles L A269
Borgmann, Kevin S. A198
Borgne, Gilles Le W492
Borgonovi, Barbara A877
Bori, Carlos S. A942
Borisov, Sergei Renatovich W476
Borkar, Rani A90
Borland, Daniel C. A797
Borland, Daniel C. E368
Borneman, J. Ralph E172
Bornemann, Keith E. A516
Bornhoft, Barbara A.J. E356
Bornmann, David E. A860
Boro, Seth E147
Boro, Seth E451
Borowicz, Klaus W390
Borras, Maria Claudia A121
Borras, Maria Claudia A1050
Borras, Maria Claudia A120
Borrego, Miguel Angel Lopez W544
Borrelli, Jerry G. A39
Bors, Kimberly K. A342
Borst, George E. E310
Bort, M. Shawn A1054
Bortenlanger, Christine W174
Borthwick, Alastair A128
Bortner, Andrea R. E242
Bortoloto, Emerson Macedo W315
Borum, Jens W330
Borup, Jens A. W330
Bosch, Jose Manuel Lara W71
Boschelli, John M. A599
Boscia, Jon Andrew A952
Boshold, Steve A1148
Boskin, Michael J. A786
Boss, Jane P102
Bosse, Christine W33
Bossemeyer, Sandra W510
Bossidy, Paul T. E173
Bost, Hunter H. E62
Bostian, Elizabeth B. A414
Bostian, Elizabeth B. E191
Bostick, Thomas P. A304
Bostock, Ed W644
Bostoen, Alain W336
Boston, Oray A600
Bostrom, Brian E96
Bostrom, Susan L. A931
Boswell, Donald K. A411
Boswell, Gina R. A140
Boswell, Stephen T. A287
Boswell, Stephen T. E115
Bosworth, Andrew A689
Bosworth, Michael J. A954
Bosworth, William (Billy) E493

COMBINED HOOVER'S HANDBOOK INDEX OF EXECUTIVES

A = AMERICAN BUSINESS
E = EMERGING COMPANIES
P = PRIVATE COMPANIES
W = WORLD BUSINESSS

Bot, Bernard Ladislas W341
Bot, Bernard Ladislas W2
Botein, Matthew B. E350
Botha, Roelof Frederik A162
Botin, Ana A915
Botta, G. Andrea A225
Bottger, Miriam W174
Bouc, Hervé Le W161
Bouchard, Alain W30
Boucher, Richard W178
Bouchiat, Pascal W600
Bouda, Christopher M. A315
Boudreaux, Chad N. A546
Boudreaux, Gail K. A1150
Boudreaux, Gail K. A85
Boudreaux, Gail K. A997
Bouek, Kirill E129
Bouet, Vivan P143
Bouet, Vivian E. A489
Bouffard, Donald E. E19
Bough, Bonin A825
Bougrov, Andrey Evgenyevich W410
Bouillot, Isabelle W22
Boulanger, Serge W398
Boulden, Melanie A15
Boulet, Jean-Francois W294
Bouligny, James A. A852
Bouligny, James A. E399
Boulware, Daniel Al E436
Boundreault, Laurier W193
Bouquot, Geoffrey W631
Bourassa, Joel S. E506
Bourbulas, Mary-Kay H. A125
Bourbulas, Mary-Kay H. E52
Bourdeau, James O. A291
Bourdeau, Jocyanne W371
Bourgeois, Steven J. E506
Bourges, Olivier W562
Bourget, Kristina E98
Bourke, Evelyn W81
Bourla, Albert A821
Bourne, Robert W. E536
Bourqui, Elisabeth W642
Bourret, Francois E500
Boursanoff, Alexander W162
Boursier, Jean-Marc W565
Bousbib, Ari A526
Bousbib, Ari A576
Bousfield, Clare W374
Boushka, Julie H. A995
Boutain, Dana L. E114
Boutebba, Frederic W187
Boutinet, Martine W174
Bouton, Daniel W631
Boutte, Brian P515
Boutte, Gregory W338
Boutz, Richard W. A1099
Bouverot, Anne W123
Bouygues, Cyril W107
Bouygues, Edward W107
Bouygues, Martin W107
Bouygues, Olivier W107
Bouygues, Olivier W161
Bovich, Francine J. A83

Bowden, Lloyd M. A1133
Bowden, Lloyd M. E541
Bowe, Patrick E. A82
Bowen, John J. A1108
Bowen, Julia A. E537
Bowen, Sharon Y. A561
Bowen, Sharon Y. E12
Bowen, Terry J. W101
Bowen, William I. A72
Bowen, William I. E29
Bower, Huw S. A182
Bower, Joseph B. A259
Bower, Joseph B. E103
Bower, Joseph L. A645
Bower, Matthew L. E98
Bower, Vivienne W487
Bowers, Alan J. E531
Bowers, Dean M. E515
Bowers, J. Gregory (Greg) A395
Bowers, J. Gregory (Greg) E185
Bowers, Louis F. A588
Bowers, Reveta F. A14
Bowers, W. Paul A383
Bowers, W. Paul A952
Bowers, W. Paul A24
Bowie, Peter G. W379
Bowie, Stephen R. E268
Bowker, Michael E. E72
Bowler, E. Joseph A1119
Bowles, Jack Marie Henry David W111
Bowles, Wendy Y. A747
Bowlin, John D. E228
Bowling, Brian A399
Bowling, Ronald L. A981
Bowling, Ronald L. E469
Bowman, Beth A. A995
Bowman, Brent E519
Bowman, Brent A. E291
Bowman, C. Alvin A504
Bowman, Kara P654
Bowman, Stephen B. A426
Bowman, Stephen B. E202
Bowser, Carmen M. A810
Bowser, Carmen M. E376
Box, April A1086
Box, April E521
Boxer, Gene E123
Boxer, Mark A239
Boxer, Michael A. A1027
Boxley, Abney S. A829
Boxley, Abney S. E385
Boxley, Abney S. E275
Boxley, Tracee P449
Boxmeer, Jean-Francois M. L. van W274
Boxmeer, Jean-Francois van W637
Boyan, George E510
Boyce, David E215
Boyce, David S. A1033
Boyce, Gregory H. A736
Boyce, James H. E279
Boychuk, Jamie J. A304
Boychuk, Michael T. W358
Boyd, Jeffery H. A526
Boyd, Katherine M. E192
Boyd, Lyman E83
Boyd, Martin R. A408
Boyd, Peter M. A954
Boyd, Ralph F. A913
Boyd, Ralph F. E427

Boyd, Rebecca C. A945
Boyd, Rebecca C. E451
Boydston, Brent E381
Boydston, Cory J. A184
Boye, Anker W348
Boyer, Andrew E31
Boyer, David W. A346
Boyer, Ellen R.M. A136
Boyer, Geoffrey F. E156
Boyer, K. David A1042
Boyington, Sheila P253
Boykin, Jennifer R. A546
Boyko, Eric W31
Boyland, Gloria R. A1068
Boyle, Bryan P436
Boyle, David P. A186
Boyle, Dein A1094
Boyle, Edward F. A747
Boyle, Hugh F. A935
Boyle, Hugh F. E439
Boyle, Robert E. A855
Boyles, David C. A474
Boyles, David C. E230
Boyles, Jonathan R. A944
Boyles, Jonathan R. E450
Boynton, Charles D. A645
Boynton, Timothy J P306
Boza, Xavier F. E381
Boze, Brandon B. A213
Bozer, Kamil Omer W620
Bozgedik, Ertugrul W619
Bozman, Blake A1086
Bozman, Blake E521
Bozotti, Carlo A118
Braams, Conny W626
Braathen, Kjerstin R. W204
Braca, Joan A. A1075
Braca, Joan A. W328
Bracey, Esi Eggleston A1132
Bracher, Candido Botelho A670
Bracher, Candido Botelho W315
Bracher, Charles C. E242
Bracher, Paul H. A305
Brachlianoff, Estelle W631
Brack, Dennis L. A395
Brack, Dennis L. E186
Bracken, Franklin R. A443
Bracy, Kevin A543
Bradbury, Gary E340
Bradford, Dana C. A687
Bradford, Debra A. A1040
Bradford, Debra A. E499
Bradford, Gregory R. A189
Bradford, Mary E293
Bradford, Neil E215
Bradford, Tonya Williams A642
Bradford, Tonya Williams E304
Bradicich, Kevin J. A499
Bradicich, Thomas Michael E39
Bradie, Stuart J.B. A595
Bradley, Bryan C. W120
Bradley, Catherine W341
Bradley, Daryl E370
Bradley, Graham John W286
Bradley, Jacqueline L. A923
Bradley, Jacqueline L. E433
Bradley, Keith E278
Bradley, Michael A. E485
Bradley, Michael A. E166
Bradley, Michael J. A1014

Bradley, Michael J. E488
Bradley, Noralee W451
Bradley, Thomas A. A531
Bradley, W. Patrick E528
Bradshaw, Jami L. A427
Bradshaw, Jami L. E203
Bradshaw, Richard W. A1064
Bradshaw, Richard W. E509
Bradshaw, Stanley J. A415
Bradshaw, Stanley J. E194
Bradway, Robert A. A164
Bradway, Robert A. A76
Brady, Amy G. A602
Brady, Amy G. A349
Brady, Barrett E338
Brady, Deanna T. A534
Brady, Elizabeth A. A42
Brady, Jacqueline E412
Brady, Kevin M. E317
Brady, Laura E338
Brady, Lucy A140
Brady, Robert T. A651
Brady, Tanya E. E382
Brady, Vicki W595
Braemer, Richard J. A1032
Brafman, Lester Raymond E105
Braford, Lee A. E96
Braga, Rogerio Carvalho W314
Brager, David A. A308
Brager, David A. E133
Braham, Tor R. E523
Brahim, John W123
Brain, David M. E315
Brainard, Lael A403
Brainerd, Mary K. A981
Brake, Francis B. A1138
Brake, Francis B. E544
Braly, Angela F. A850
Braly, Angela F. A388
Braly, Angela F. W112
Braman, Edward H. E247
Bramble, Frank P. A128
Bramble, James H. E180
Bramhall, Dylan A. A369
Bramhall, Dylan A. A982
Bramlage, Stephen P. A209
Bramman, Anne L. A673
Branagan, Ian D. W491
Branch, Gregory C. A1066
Branch, Scott J. A979
Branco, Roberto da Cunha Castello W468
Brand, Dennis L. A125
Brand, Dennis L. E52
Brand, H. C. W518
Brand, Rachel A1104
Branderiz, Eric A267
Branderiz, Eric E163
Brandis, Karen E336
Brandler, Harry E238
Brandman, Jared E341
Brandon, David A. A345
Brandon, David A. A343
Brandon, Joseph P. A39
Brandon, Rajna Gibson W580
Brandstetter, Andreas W627
Brandt, Christopher W. A232
Brandt, Eric K. A619
Brandt, Tim A40
Brandt, Tim P26

COMBINED HOOVER'S HANDBOOK INDEX OF EXECUTIVES

A = AMERICAN BUSINESS
E = EMERGING COMPANIES
P = PRIVATE COMPANIES
W = WORLD BUSINESSS

Brandt, Werner W510
Brandt, Werner W543
Brandtzæg, Svein Richard W204
Brannan, C. Scott E79
Brannan, Jamie A1153
Brannen, James P. A426
Brannen, James P. A478
Brannen, James P. E202
Brannon, Richard D. A369
Branstetter, Matthew Fredrick E506
Brant, Cherie L. W611
Brase, John P. A947
Brasher, Robert S. A620
Brasier, Barbara L. A707
Brassac, Philippe W174
Brasseux, Murray E. A374
Brassfield, Karen F. A937
Brassfield, Karen F. E441
Brast, Scott Frankie A68
Braswell, Bill P437
Brat, James L. E217
Brathwaite, Nicholas E. E392
Bratspies, Stephen B. A497
Brattain, Donald R. E502
Bratukhin, Sergey W410
Braude, Michael A592
Brauer, Blackford F. A276
Braun, Christopher J. E540
Braun, Joseph P. E145
Braun, Randall L. A472
Braun, Randall L. E230
Braun, Vianei Lopez A421
Braun, Vianei Lopez E198
Braunegg, George G. A685
Braunig, Guenther W199
Braunig, Gunther W198
Braunwalder, Peter F. W446
Braveman, Peter E P109
Bravo, Rose Marie A620
Brawley, Charles A. A195
Brawley, Otis W. E267
Bray, Dee L P542
Bray, Jesse "Jay" K. A718
Bray, Jesse "Jay" K. E334
Bray, Justin L. A940
Bray, Richard S. A1033
Bray, Richard S. E493
Brazeal, Mark David A180
Brazier, Allan J. W46
Brbovic, Brett A152
Bready, Cameron M. A477
Breakiron-Evans, Maureen A. A43
Breard, Linda M. A558
Breard, Linda M. E391
Breaux, Jason A. E129
Breaux, Paul A208
Breaux, Randall P. A468
Breber, Pierre R. A230
Brebisson, Fabienne de W631
Brecht, Michael W395
Bredow, Eugene J. A762
Breedon, Tim W89
Breedon, Tim J. W90
Breen, Edward D. A272

Breen, Edward D. A567
Breen, Edward D. A298
Breen, Edward D. A349
Breen, Virginia G. E374
Breeze, Diana W116
Brege, Laura A. E369
Bregier, Fabrice W225
Bregier, Fabrice W526
Bregman, Steven M. E221
Bréhier, Régine W22
Breidenbach, Fred A. A999
Breig, Geralyn R. A497
Breig, Geralyn R. E1
Breish, Abdulmagid W47
Breitbard, Mark A1018
Breithaupt, Chantelle E39
Breitman, Matthew K. E480
Brekelmans, Harry W532
Brekke, Sigve W594
Brekke, Stein-erling A377
Brekke, Stein-erling P217
Brem, Monte M. E462
Brendish, Clay W167
Breneol, Beatrice W213
Brenna, Nathan P. E63
Brennan, Daniel J. A175
Brennan, Edward F. E287
Brennan, Ita M. E75
Brennan, Ita M. E35
Brennan, Joe A438
Brennan, John J. (Jack) A62
Brennan, Karen A588
Brennan, Katherine J. A662
Brennan, Michelle M. A201
Brennan, Thomas P. A209
Brennan, Troyen A. A311
Brenneman, Gregory D. A121
Brenneman, Gregory D. A526
Brenneman, Gregory D. A120
Brenneman, Rodney K. A301
Brenneman, Rodney K. E131
Brenner, Kenneth D. E46
Brenner, Teresa M. E245
Brenner, Timothy L. A724
Bresingham, Daniel M. A16
Bresky, Ellen S. A922
Bresky, Jacob (Jack) A. A922
Breslawski, James P. A917
Breslin, Stephen E9
Bresnahan, Ann W. A192
Bresney, John A927
Bresney, John E435
Bretches, Clay D. A86
Breton, Thierry Jacques Lucien W125
Breton, Thierry Jacques Lucien W61
Brett, Anton A941
Breu, Raymund W580
Breuer, Kirsten Joachim W129
Breuer, Mark W191
Breuer, Michael W192
Breuninger, Barbara W273
Breves, Christine S. A717
Brewer, Allen M. A439
Brewer, Brady A964
Brewer, Kevin J. E47
Brewer, Nicola Mary W295
Brewer, Rosalind Gates A1101
Brewster, David W162
Brewster, J. Chris E239
Breyer, James W. A161

Brezonik, Lisa M. A175
Brezonik, Lisa M. E66
Brian, Brad D. E72
Briard, Carole W80
Briatta, Gilles W548
Bricker, Jude I. E471
Brickley, Peter W161
Brickman, James R. E238
Bricks, Maury E35
Bridgeford, Gregory M. A337
Bridgeforth, J. Scott A981
Bridgeforth, J. Scott E469
Bridges, David E. A860
Bridges, Dorothy J. A1082
Bridges, Wendy W. A274
Bridgewater, Diane C. A209
Briese, Chasity E517
Briesemeister, Nathan A99
Briggs, Andrew J. E184
Briggs, Andy W471
Briggs, Gary S. E175
Briggs, Max A423
Briggs, Max E199
Briggs, Stephen E19
Briggs, Teresa A931
Briggs, Vikki G. E132
Bright, Craig W90
Bright, Jill E279
Bright, W. Byron A595
Brightbill, Frederick A. E313
Brighton, W. Curtis A422
Brijs, Erik W623
Brill, James L. E38
Brillati, Michael A. E298
Brillet, René W125
Brilliant, William J. E253
Brimmer, Andrea C. E154
Brin, Sergey A45
Brinch, Brian M. A395
Brinch, Brian M. E186
Brindamour, Charles J. G. W119
Brindamour, Charles J. G. W308
Brines, Ned W. E268
Brink, Dolf van den W274
Brink, Martin A. Van den W52
Brinkley, Amy W. W611
Brinkley, Amy Woods A904
Brinkley, Cynthia J. A54
Brinkley, Cynthia J. E160
Brinkman, Joseph R. E96
Brinkman, Richard A. E189
Brinton, Elisabeth W39
Brinton, Jon D. E129
Brisac, Juliette W104
Brisch, Donald R. A125
Brisch, Donald R. E52
Briscoe-Tonic, Kimberly C. E113
Briscoe, Kathleen S. E129
Brisendine, L. Briley E445
Briskin, Jared S. E254
Bristow, Peter M. A417
Britenriker, Barbara J. E184
Brito, Carlos Alves de W40
Britt, Douglas M. E249
Britt, Irene Chang A176
Britt, Irene Chang A1094
Brittain, Alison W385
Brittain, Miles E353
Brittain, Thomas C. E452
Brittenham, Beth A. E421

Brlas, Laurie A292
Brlas, Mary Lauren A486
Broad, Matthew R. A316
Broadbent, Jillian Rosemary W651
Broadbent, Jillian Rosemary W377
Broadhurst, Vanessa A1153
Broadley, Philip W360
Broadley, Philip W57
Brobst, Barbara E. A788
Brobst, Barbara E. E365
Brobst, Duane J. A1078
Brobst, Duane J. E513
Brochick, George W. A812
Brochu, Sophie W82
Brock, Charles E. A829
Brock, Charles E. E385
Brock, Gunnar W7
Brockbank, Mark E. A150
Brockman, Dawn A70
Brockman, Dennis A964
Brockman, Robert J. E340
Brockmann, Jan W4
Brockwell, Mathew D A350
Brockwell, Mathew D E148
Broden, Max K. A24
Broderick, Craig W83
Brodeur, Pierre W295
Brodin, J. Per E365
Brodsky, James A. A693
Brodsky, Stephen P418
Brody, Hubert Rene W426
Brody, Mark S. E510
Brody, Paul J. E279
Broek, Harold van den W274
Broek, Jacques van den W489
Brogdon, James (Jay) M. A938
Brogdon, James (Jay) M. E442
Brogley, Rita D. E467
Broich, Andre Van W95
Brokaw, George R. A333
Brolick, Heather D. E96
Brolly, Stephen H. A788
Brolly, Stephen H. E364
Bromage, Kathleen M. A502
Bromagen, Ellen J. A399
Bronczek, David J. A1050
Bronder, Anette W357
Brondum, Helle W188
Bronner, Philip L. A781
Brons, Paul A917
Bronselaer, Bart W200
Bronson, Richard D. A965
Bronson, Richard D. E280
Bronson, Richard D. E462
Bronstein, Andrew E77
Brook, Bruce R. A737
Brooke, Beth A. E154
Brooke, Frederick Dixon A988
Brooke, Frederick Dixon E479
Brooks-Williams, Denise E67
Brooks, Alexandra D A1019
Brooks, Alexandra D P585
Brooks, Amy A162
Brooks, Charles T. A599
Brooks, Christopher T. A771
Brooks, Daniel W. A556
Brooks, Daniel W. E270
Brooks, David R. A555
Brooks, David R. E270
Brooks, Douglas H. A956

COMBINED HOOVER'S HANDBOOK INDEX OF EXECUTIVES

```
A = AMERICAN BUSINESS
E = EMERGING COMPANIES
P = PRIVATE COMPANIES
W = WORLD BUSINESSS
```

Brooks, Harley P415
Brooks, J. Ryan E117
Brooks, Janytra M. A181
Brooks, Jayme L. E301
Brooks, Jody P285
Brooks, Joe S. E515
Brooks, Martha Finn W641
Brooks, Michael A986
Brooks, Raymond L. A717
Brooks, Rebecca M. A953
Brooks, Rebecca M. E455
Brooks, Renee R. A955
Brooks, Renee R. E456
Brooks, Vincent K. A580
Brooks, Vincent K. E520
Brooks, William R. A948
Broomhead, Malcolm W101
Brophy, Gerard A112
Brophy, Keith D. E96
Brosig, Thomas J. E242
Brosnan, Sean G. W491
Brossoit, Jean-Francois A294
Brossoit, Jean-Francois A256
Brost, Mike P285
Brothers, Norman M. A1069
Brouaux, Marie-Noëlle W125
Broucek, James S. E98
Brough, Paul J. W612
Brougher, Francoise W550
Broughton, George W. A815
Broughton, Thomas A. A932
Broughton, Thomas A. E436
Brouillard, Rheo A. A152
Brouillette, Manon W420
Brous, David A917
Broussard, Bruce D. A538
Broussard, Bruce D. A541
Broussard, Bruce D. A602
Brouwer, Sybolt W623
Browdy, Michelle H. A565
Brower, Linda S. A1107
Brown-Philpot, Stacy A538
Brown-Philpot, Stacy A745
Brown, Adriane M. A357
Brown, Adriane M. A56
Brown, Andy W254
Brown, Archie M. A420
Brown, Archie M. E197
Brown, Bruce W443
Brown, C. David A311
Brown, Carlos M. A340
Brown, Celeste Mellet E176
Brown, Celia R. E1
Brown, Charles W. E54
Brown, Christopher A1143
Brown, Darrell R. A358
Brown, Darryl A159
Brown, David C. E525
Brown, David D. A419
Brown, Donald C. E136
Brown, Donald E. A42
Brown, Douglas V. E25
Brown, Frederic J. E223
Brown, Greg A399

Brown, Gregory Q. A716
Brown, Hugh M. E68
Brown, J. David A724
Brown, J. Frank A526
Brown, J. Hyatt E68
Brown, J. McCauley A978
Brown, J. McCauley E465
Brown, J. Powell A1125
Brown, J. Powell E68
Brown, James W. A512
Brown, Jay A. A301
Brown, Jeff A249
Brown, Jeff P126
Brown, Jeffrey J. A43
Brown, Jeffrey J. E316
Brown, Jeffrey W A493
Brown, Jeffrey W E243
Brown, Joachim J. E204
Brown, Jocelyn P365
Brown, Jonathan David E413
Brown, Joy A1035
Brown, Julia J. E511
Brown, Julie W502
Brown, Julie Turner A488
Brown, Kathleen L. A977
Brown, Kathleen L. E464
Brown, Kevin M. A611
Brown, Laura D. E249
Brown, Lori A. A367
Brown, Marcus V P215
Brown, Marcus V. A371
Brown, Marcy E102
Brown, Marianne C. A752
Brown, Marianne C. A919
Brown, Marianne C. A1098
Brown, Marianne C. E12
Brown, Melissa E8
Brown, Michael P176
Brown, Michael P366
Brown, Michael G P136
Brown, Michael S. A882
Brown, Michael W. A977
Brown, Michael W. A1098
Brown, Michael W. E464
Brown, Michael William Thomas W426
Brown, Mike A166
Brown, Nicholas A. A134
Brown, Nicholas A. E54
Brown, Nigel E273
Brown, Oscar K. E536
Brown, P. Barrett E68
Brown, Palmer W170
Brown, Peter A922
Brown, Peter C. A650
Brown, Priscilla Sims E19
Brown, Priscilla Sims W164
Brown, Randolph A400
Brown, Reginald J. A161
Brown, Robert A. A298
Brown, Robin D. E195
Brown, Ruth W415
Brown, Sam E19
Brown, Sébastien W231
Brown, Shannon A. A190
Brown, Shannon A. E73
Brown, Shona L. A817
Brown, Terry A504
Brown, Thomas C. E195
Brown, Thomas K. A286
Brown, Thomas K. A4

Brown, Thomas L. A772
Brown, Valerie G. E462
Brown, Vance R. A175
Brown, William A A1044
Brown, William E. E90
Brown, William M. A147
Brown, William M. A215
Brown, William P. A660
Browne, Colin A1059
Browne, Helen W65
Browne, Lori M P229
Browne, Robert P. A748
Browner, Carol M. A185
Browning, James H. A1008
Browning, Peter C. E234
Browning, Scott R. E79
Browning, William L. A95
Broyles, Rob P226
Broyles, Thomas C. A1033
Broyles, Thomas C. E492
Bruaene, Pierre Van De W623
Brubaker, Lisa A1138
Brubaker, Lisa E544
Brubaker, Scott E. A860
Brubaker, Terry Lee E232
Bruce, George A301
Bruce, George E131
Bruce, Karla A389
Bruce, Karla P219
Bruce, Kofi A. A363
Bruce, Kofi A. A465
Bruce, Maryann E19
Bruck, Jorge Bande W172
Bruckmann, Bruce C. A706
Bruckner, Tim R. A1120
Bruckner, Tim R. E535
Brudermuller, Martin W93
Brudermuller, Martin W395
Brueckner, Ronny W18
Bruegenhemke, Kathleen L. E246
Bruehlman, Ronald E. A576
Bruffett, Stephen L. A917
Brugarolas, Catalina Minarro W382
Brugarolas, Catalina Minarro W11
Brugger, Thomas R. A788
Brugger, Thomas R. E365
Bruhl, Elise A251
Bruhl, Elise P137
Brulard, Jean-Pierre A1098
Brumback, Emerson L. A410
Brumbaugh, Kimberly J. A702
Brumbaugh, Kimberly J. E326
Brummer, Christopher J. A391
Brummer, Derek V. A874
Brun, Leslie A. A298
Brune, Catherine S. A54
Brunelle, David M. A152
Bruner, Judy A90
Brunetti, Michelle P671
Brunfield, Brian P573
Brungger, Renata Jungo W415
Brungger, Renata Jungo W395
Bruni, Enrico E493
Brunila, Anne W247
Brunila, Anne W348
Brunk, James F. A706
Brunn, Carsten E475
Brunner, Robert E. A624
Bruno, Barry A. A567
Bruno, Barry A. A237

Bruno, James E. A1073
Bruno, John G. A477
Bruno, John G. A1141
Bruno, Marc A. A1071
Bruno, Marc A. A92
Brunoehler, Jeffrey A. A703
Brunoehler, Jeffrey A. E327
Bruns, Casey E81
Brunts, DeAnn L. E50
Bruny, Steven M. E420
Brusadelli, Maurizio A709
Brusgaard, Kurt W330
Brush, James E. E470
Bruss, William F. E532
Bruton, John G. W617
Brutto, Daniel J. A989
Brutto, Daniel J. A553
Bruxelles, Henri W187
Bruzzese, Maria A45
Bruzzo, Christopher A363
Bruzzo, Christopher E64
Bryan, Alex P6
Bryan, Glynis A. A558
Bryan, James S. A418
Bryan, Tracy W84
Bryant, Deric E91
Bryant, Diane M. A180
Bryant, Douglas C. E406
Bryant, Hope H. A417
Bryant, Jenny W644
Bryant, John W170
Bryant, John W161
Bryant, John A. A654
Bryant, John A. A123
Bryant, John J. A790
Bryant, Kevin E P218
Bryant, Todd W. A896
Bryant, Todd W. E422
Bryant, Warren W371
Bryant, Warren F. A336
Bryce, Kristin Jones P654
Brydon, Dean J. E490
Buberl, Thomas A565
Buberl, Thomas W65
Buc, Hernan Buchi W70
Buc, Marcos Buchi W172
Buc, Richard Buchi W132
Bucci, Sam E420
Buch, Anand E129
Buch, James R. E308
Buchan, Jane M. A478
Buchanan, Ashley A654
Buchanan, Bill D. A681
Buchanan, Bill D. E318
Buchanan, Edison C. A830
Buchanan, Ian W81
Buchanan, Joan A399
Buchanan, Michael R. A536
Buchanan, Robin W374
Buchband, Richard D. A655
Buchenot, Stephen M. E302
Buchert, Brian A237
Buchholz, Karen D. A1138
Buchholz, Karen D. E544
Buchleitner, Klaus W98
Buchner, Stefan E. W171
Buchner, Stefan Erwin W602
Buchwald, Herbert T. A652
Buck, John D. A806
Buck, Michele G. A512

COMBINED HOOVER'S HANDBOOK INDEX OF EXECUTIVES

A = AMERICAN BUSINESS
E = EMERGING COMPANIES
P = PRIVATE COMPANIES
W = WORLD BUSINESSS

Buck, Robert M. E490
Buck, Robert R. A145
Buckingham, Geraldine W289
Buckiso, Scott D. A1073
Buckley, Guy G P517
Buckley, Michael C. A898
Buckley, Robert J. E355
Buckley, Timothy J. E92
Buckminster, Douglas E. A62
Buckup, Jorge C. A1075
Budargin, Oleg Mikhailovich W476
Budd, Wayne A. A809
Budden, Joan A. A555
Budden, Joan A. A1053
Budden, Joan A. E269
Budenberg, Robin W371
Budiwiyono, Eko W483
Budnik, Marianne N. E91
Buechele, Wolfgang W397
Buechler, Kenneth F. E406
Buechner, Ton W449
Buehl, Todd E61
Buehler, Alexander Jon E161
Buenaventura, Jose F. W100
Buergler, William M. E54
Buergy, Dominik W355
Buescher, John P336
Buese, Nancy K. A121
Buese, Nancy K. A1131
Buese, Nancy K. A737
Buese, Nancy K. A120
Buesing, Dean Jerome E236
Buesinger, Robert F. A1124
Buess, Thomas W580
Buess, Thomas W580
Buffett, Howard G. A151
Buffett, Howard W. W157
Buffett, Susan A. A151
Buffett, Warren E. A151
Buffington, Stephanie E487
Buford, Robert J. A307
Buford, Robert J. E133
Buganim, Ilan W79
Bugbee, Dawn D. E506
Bugbee, Robert R. A106
Buggeln, Catherine Elizabeth E209
Bugh, John M. A488
Bugher, Mark D. A416
Bugnion, Edouard A645
Buhr, Gunnar de W162
Buhr, Jeffrey L. A1
Buhrandt, Jeff P665
Buhrkall, Sven W330
Buhrow, Jason A548
Buhrow, Jason P272
Bui, Andy E271
Buick, Craig A. E159
Buie, Herbert C. A954
Bukaev, Gennady Ivanovich W506
Bula, Patrice W523
Bula, Patrice W449
Bulach, Matthias W229
Bulanda, Mark J. A366
Bulanov, Alexander Nikolaevich W576

Bulatao, Brian A14
Bulcke, Paul W430
Bulcke, Paul W502
Bulcke, Paul W358
Bulgarino, Nicole A. E22
Bulgurlu, Bulent W346
Bull, Kenneth R. E209
Bullard, Geri E204
Bullard, Rodney D. A72
Bullard, Rodney D. E29
Bullock, Brian H. A372
Bullock, Brian H. E166
Bullock, William L. A288
Bulls, Herman E. E111
Bulmer, Donald S. A818
Bulnes, Juan Luis Ossa W172
Bulow, York-Detlef W3
Bulsook, Somchai W334
Bulter, Gary D. A889
Bulter, Gary D. E414
Bulut, Fazli W619
Bumann, Steven L. A398
Bumb, Duane A251
Bumb, Duane P137
Bumgarner, David L. A249
Bumgarner, David L. E99
Bumgarner, John C. E169
Bunce, John L. W50
Bunch, C. Robert A776
Bunch, Charles E. A710
Bunch, Charles E. A657
Bunch, James S. A493
Bunch, James S. E243
Bunder, Michael L. A738
Bunderla, Hubert W458
Bunger, Steven G. E85
Bunn, James E. A876
Bunn, Willard E97
Bunnell, Ron A137
Bunnell, Ron P59
Bunnenberg, Lutz W277
Bunston, Andrew W646
Bunsumpun, Prasert W352
Bunting, Hans Friedrich W510
Bunting, Theodore H. A1079
Bunting, Theodore H. A499
Bunyasaranand, Boonsong W77
Bunye, Ignacio R. W85
Buquet, James J. A188
Buquet, James J. E69
Burak, Mark A. A129
Buran, John R. A396
Buran, John R. A439
Buran, John R. E187
Buranamanit, Tanin W117
Burbach, Gerhard F. E70
Burbage, Charles Thomas E8
Burbank, John R. A371
Burbidge, Eileen W179
Burch, Richard N. E452
Burchfield, Jay D. A765
Burchfield, Jay D. A938
Burchfield, Jay D. A442
Burck, William A. A447
Burckhardt, Andreas W68
Burckhardt, Carsten W280
Burckhart, Camille A836
Burdick, Kenneth A. A216
Burdick, Kevin L. A783
Burdick, Rick L. A109

Burdine, Ivan L. A1115
Burdine, Ivan L. E533
Burdiss, Paul E. A1151
Burdman, Lee J. A844
Burdman, Lee J. E394
Burek, Julie E529
Buretta, Sheri P124
Burgdoerfer, Stuart B. A851
Burger, Armin W453
Burger, Edward E512
Burger, Ernst W627
Burger, Glynn R. W310
Burgess, Kevin A432
Burgess, Robert K. A761
Burgess, Shari L. A622
Burghardt, Stefan W162
Burk, Adam A296
Burk, Michael J. A400
Burk, Victor A832
Burk, Victor A833
Burke, Andrew T. E486
Burke, Catherine L. A726
Burke, Colleen A400
Burke, Courtney P16
Burke, Desiree A. E227
Burke, Edmund Hunt A186
Burke, James A. (Jim) A1097
Burke, James F. E354
Burke, James J. E302
Burke, James M. E113
Burke, Kate C. E17
Burke, Kathleen F. E329
Burke, Kenneth M. E171
Burke, Kevin G. A530
Burke, Michael J. E96
Burke, Michael K. E82
Burke, Michael S. A94
Burke, Pamela B. E242
Burke, Paul R. A800
Burke, Richard T. A1075
Burke, Robert D. E481
Burke, Sean A575
Burke, Shaun A. E243
Burke, Sheila P. W154
Burke, Simon W160
Burke, Stephen B. A151
Burke, Stephen B. A591
Burke, William J. A74
Burke, Yvonne Brathwaite A301
Burke, Yvonne Brathwaite P171
Burkey, Rick B. A307
Burkey, Rick B. E133
Burkhard, Oliver W602
Burkhardt-Berg, Gabriele W33
Burkhardt, Erika A1146
Burkhardt, Timothy A. E447
Burkhart, Megan D. A274
Burkhart, Renda J A829
Burkhart, Renda J E385
Burkhead, Frank E. E246
Burkholder, Edward Ray E181
Burkholder, Eugene N. E184
Burks, Derrick A347
Burlew, Dawn H. A411
Burley, Christopher M. W451
Burman, Darryl M. A491
Burmistrova, Elena V. W474
Burnell, Lawrence E. A532
Burnell, Lawrence E. E259
Burnett, Don P168

Burnette, Don P168
Burnette, Thomas L. A249
Burnette, Thomas L. E99
Burns, Annette L. A724
Burns, David W595
Burns, Gregory L. A829
Burns, Gregory L. E385
Burns, Harold J. E96
Burns, Jennifer J. A401
Burns, Joseph E. A955
Burns, Joseph E. E456
Burns, M. Anthony A548
Burns, M. Michele A244
Burns, M. Michele A480
Burns, M. Michele E175
Burns, M. Michele W40
Burns, Mark Lagrand A471
Burns, Mark Lagrand A460
Burns, Michael J. A1069
Burns, Michael R. A503
Burns, Richard E485
Burns, Stephanie A. A538
Burns, Stephanie A. A597
Burns, Stephanie A. A298
Burns, Thomas M. E545
Burns, Ursula M. A388
Burns, Ursula M. A1052
Burns, Ursula M. A367
Burns, William A1148
Burns, William S. A287
Burns, William S. E115
Burnside, William H.L. A8
Buros, Philippe W490
Burr, Busy A718
Burr, Busy E335
Burr, Elizabeth A894
Burr, Elizabeth A984
Burr, Elizabeth E476
Burr, Gwyn W398
Burr, Richelle E. E383
Burrell, Cheryl A971
Burrell, Cheryl P537
Burrill, Jeffrey A905
Burris, Jerry W. A706
Burritt, Chris R. E372
Burritt, David B. A1073
Burritt, David B. A643
Burrough, Eric E. E96
Burrowes, Astrid A439
Burrowes, Todd A. A316
Burrows, Lawrence B. E495
Burt, Brady T. A803
Burt, Brady T. A397
Burt, Brady T. E371
Burt, Carol J. A576
Burt, Carol J. E417
Burt, Gene Eddie E64
Burt, Jeffrey V. E296
Burt, Tye W49
Burton, Caroline A1149
Burton, Eve B. A571
Burton, John W260
Burton, Spencer W. E164
Buruspat, Jatuporn W484
Burville, John C. A927
Burville, John C. E435
Burwell, Dorothy M. A838
Burwell, Eric E. A504
Burwell, Sylvia M. A604
Burwick, David A. E65

596   HOOVER'S HANDBOOK OF EMERGING COMPANIES 2023

COMBINED HOOVER'S HANDBOOK INDEX OF EXECUTIVES

A = AMERICAN BUSINESS
E = EMERGING COMPANIES
P = PRIVATE COMPANIES
W = WORLD BUSINESSS

Burwick, David A. E137
Burwig, Susan E. E317
Burzer, Jorg W395
Burzik, Catherine M. A147
Burzo, Steven A16
Busbee, Jeff E341
Busch, Angela M. A358
Busch, Angela M. E307
Busch, Patrick F. A503
Busch, Roland W545
Busch, Roland W61
Busch, Roland W543
Buscone, Gregory P. A352
Buse, Elizabeth L. A1082
Buser, Curtis L. A203
Bush, Antoinette E34
Bush, Mary K. A330
Bush, Mary K. A991
Bush, Mary K. E309
Bush, Michael J. A905
Bush, Tim P183
Bush, Wesley G. A244
Bush, Wesley G. A466
Bush, Wesley G. A342
Bushman, Julie L. A826
Bushman, Julie L. E59
Bushman, Julie L. W15
Bushnell, David C. W491
Bushore, Michelle E412
Bushway, Kathy A844
Bushway, Kathy E394
Busk, Douglas W. E128
Busky, Joseph M. E406
Buss, Albert G. A1099
Buss, Brad W. A17
Buss, Brad W. A1007
Buss, Bradley W. A20
Busse, Keith E. A975
Bussells, Walter P285
Buster, Bob P175
Butcher, Arthur C. A175
Butcher, Benjamin S. E461
Butcher, Bruce E43
Butel, Jean-Luc D. W585
Buthman, Mark A. E534
Butier, Mitchell R. A114
Butler, Adrian M. A209
Butler, Anne B. E93
Butler, Calvin G. A383
Butler, Calvin G. A896
Butler, Calvin G. E422
Butler, Deborah H. A294
Butler, Deborah H. A256
Butler, Eric L. A354
Butler, Gregory B. A380
Butler, Mike P446
Butler, Monika W523
Butler, Richard D. E304
Butler, Richard E. A555
Butler, Richard E. E269
Butler, Ronald David A421
Butler, Ronald David E197
Butler, Stephen T. A988
Butler, Stephen T. E479

Butler, William F. A196
Butler, William F. E79
Butler, Yvette S. A1099
Butman, James W. A1001
Butner, Geoffrey E. E46
Butsch, Margo G. A509
Butsch, Margo G. E251
Butschek, Guenter W587
Butterfield, Cleon P. A398
Butters, Deborah E380
Button, Angie Chen E143
Butts, Tanya A. E195
Butz, Stefan P. W203
Buvary, Hans A927
Buvary, Hans E435
Buyer, Lise J. E489
Buys, Stefan W49
Buzy, Peter L. E83
Buzzelli, Anthony J. A1040
Buzzelli, Anthony J. E498
Byars, Therese E221
Bye, Stephen J. A333
Byeon, Yang-ho W537
Byers, Brittany P639
Byers, Deborah E101
Byers, William G. E227
Byerwalter, Mariann A448
Byington, Carrie L. A147
Byl, Alain W623
Bylund, James R. E415
Bynoe, Linda Walker A748
Bynum, Greg E517
Byoung, Ho Lee W365
Byrd, Heath R. A948
Byrd, Richard A147
Byrd, Thomas T. E149
Byrne, Barbara M. A802
Byrne, Bobbie P210
Byrne, Darragh W191
Byrne, Kathryn A. A936
Byrne, Kathryn A. E440
Byrne, Mark J. A1075
Byrnes, Doreen R. A575
Byrnes, John G. E311
Byun, Donald D. A530
Byun, Donald D. E258
Byun, Kyung-Hoon W366
Byung, Suk Chung W513

C

Cabanis, Cecile W187
Cabanis, Cecile W524
Cabiallavetta, Mathis W580
Cablik, Anna R. A1042
Cabral, Anna Escobedo A723
Cabral, Bruce H. A509
Cabral, Bruce H. E251
Cabral, Timothy S. E519
Cabrera, Ivonne M. A342
Cabrera, Phillip R. A188
Cabrera, Phillip R. E71
Cabrier, Patrice W490
Cacciamatta, Danilo E76
Caceres, R. Louis A913
Caceres, R. Louis E427
Cade, Denise R. A826
Cade, Denise R. E483

Cadieux, Chester A167
Cadieux, Chester E64
Cadieux, Marc C. A984
Cadieux, Marc C. E476
Cadoret, Frank W592
Caesar, Nerida W648
Cafarchio, Joseph L. E321
Cafaro, Debra A. A834
Caforio, Giovanni A981
Caforio, Giovanni A178
Cafritz, Diane L. A205
Cage, Christopher R. A625
Caggia, Andrew M. E107
Cagle, R Jack P170
Cagno, Mark L. A581
Cahalan, Jay P. E240
Cahill, John P. A1113
Cahill, John T. A56
Cahill, John T. A269
Cahill, John T. A610
Cahill, Kieran A444
Cahill, Patricia P165
Cahill, Peter J. E193
Cahillane, Steven A. (Steve) A597
Cahir, Dan E180
Cahuzac, Antoine W215
Cai, Chang W660
Cai, Cunqiang W236
Cai, Dunyi W169
Cai, Fangfang W472
Cai, Hongbin W146
Cai, Hongping W117
Cai, Jiangnan W530
Cai, Jianjiang W128
Cai, Jin-Yong W44
Cai, Jinyong W466
Cai, Manli W664
Cai, Manli W431
Cai, Tianyuan W168
Cai, Yuanming W307
Cai, Zhiwei E226
Caimi, Lara A931
Cain, Brian E101
Cain, Cynthia A. A945
Cain, Cynthia A. E451
Cain, James P. E15
Cain, Steven W162
Cain, Susan O. A639
Caine, John E438
Caine, Patrice W358
Caine, Patrice W600
Cairnie, Ruth W55
Cairns, Ann M. A670
Cairns, Gordon McKellar W651
Cajka, Andrew B. E454
Cakiroglu, Levent W661
Cakiroglu, Levent W346
Cakiroglu, Levent W621
Calabrese, Vincent J. A441
Calabrese, Vincent J. E211
Calantzopoulos, Andre A825
Calari, Cesare W222
Calavia, Philippe W344
Calaway, Tonit M. A30
Calaway, Tonit M. A173
Calaway, Tonit M. E530
Calbert, Michael M. A864
Calbert, Michael M. A336
Caldart, Gilberto A670
Caldera, Louis E. A687

Calderin, Diego F. A1138
Calderin, Diego F. E544
Calderon, Nancy E. E352
Calderone, Matthew A. A171
Calderoni, Frank A. A15
Calderoni, Robert M. A607
Calderoni, Robert M. E32
Caldwell, Christopher A. A287
Caldwell, Donald R. E404
Caldwell, Jeremy B. A401
Caldwell, Nanci E. A377
Caldwell, Nanci E. W119
Caldwell, Phyllis R. A781
Caldwell, Samantha A. A317
Caldwell, Troy M A1026
Caldwell, Troy M P620
Calhoun, David L. A164
Calhoun, David L. A210
Calhoun, Dean E455
Cali, Brian J. E190
Calio, Christopher T. A877
Calkins, Carol A188
Calkins, Carol E69
Call, Michael A. A600
Call, Michael A. A710
Call, Valerie Mc P130
Callaghan, Brian J. E38
Callahan, Andrew P. E260
Callahan, Daniel H. W84
Callahan, Emily P35
Callahan, Karri R. E410
Callahan, Patrick K. A851
Callahan, Scott P. E512
Callan, John D. E67
Callan, Patricia Ann A954
Callard, George D. A742
Callaway, Amanda L. E247
Callazo, Jose M. E351
calle, Javier De la W266
Callen, David A757
Callender, Robert G P387
Callewaert, Katelijn W336
Callicotte, Lisa C. E514
Callicutt, Richard D. A829
Callicutt, Richard D. E385
Callinicos, Brent A864
Callinicos, Brent W67
Callison, Edwin H. A838
Callister, James E81
Callol, Ana W161
Callon, Scott W253
Calmejane, Claire W548
Calmels, Régis W631
Caltagirone, Francesco Gaetano W54
Calvo, Domingo Armengol W68
Calvo, Miguel Klingenberg W493
Calvosa, Lucia W227
Cama, Domenick A. A575
Cama, Zarir J. W520
Camagni, Paola W592
Camara, Fiona W526
Camara, Rogerio Pedro W69
Camaren, James L. A740
Camargo, Jorge Marques de Toledo W622
Cambefort, Pierre W174
Cambiaso, Enrique Ostalé W643
Cambria, Christopher C. E319
Cameron, Dennis C. A325
Cameron, Jim A1117

COMBINED HOOVER'S HANDBOOK INDEX OF EXECUTIVES

A = AMERICAN BUSINESS
E = EMERGING COMPANIES
P = PRIVATE COMPANIES
W = WORLD BUSINESSS

Cameron, Susan M. A92
Cameron, William H. A642
Cameron, William H. E304
Camilleri, Kurt A121
Camino, Javier Cavada W254
Cammisecra, Antonio W219
Camp, Christine H. H. A219
Camp, Elizabeth W. A468
Camp, Elizabeth W. A988
Camp, Elizabeth W. E479
Camp, Garrett A1052
Camp, James S. E56
Camp, Lynne J. E107
Camp, Peter Van A377
Campana, Robert M. A753
Campanella, Edward J. A98
Campanella, Edward J. E36
Campanello, Russell J. E281
Campani, Angelo W177
Campbell, Alan A780
Campbell, Ann-Marie A526
Campbell, Barbara P331
Campbell, Barry G. E309
Campbell, Ben G. A900
Campbell, Brandi A130
Campbell, Bruce L. A332
Campbell, C R W116
Campbell, Carolyn M. A868
Campbell, Chad A. A282
Campbell, Cheryl F. A823
Campbell, David D. A486
Campbell, Douglas E23
Campbell, Elizabeth S. A73
Campbell, George A290
Campbell, James E. A190
Campbell, James E. E73
Campbell, James O. E515
Campbell, Jeffrey C. A62
Campbell, Jeffrey C. W44
Campbell, Jill A471
Campbell, Joanne T. A192
Campbell, John R. E279
Campbell, Justine W422
Campbell, Karen Elizabeth E517
Campbell, Kathleen M. E99
Campbell, Kristin A. A770
Campbell, Lisa F. E181
Campbell, Lisa M. E145
Campbell, Mary A624
Campbell, Michael Earl A377
Campbell, Michael P. A103
Campbell, Molly C. A351
Campbell, Molly C. E150
Campbell, Norie C. W611
Campbell, Patrick D. A735
Campbell, Patrick D. A962
Campbell, Paul A1093
Campbell, Phyllis J. E11
Campbell, Richard D. A950
Campbell, Richard D. E454
Campbell, Robert C. A668
Campbell, Ryan D. A320
Campbell, Steven F. A83
Campbell, Steven K. A82

Campbell, William B. A441
Campbell, William B. E212
Campelli, Fabrizio W195
Campfield, Susan E354
Campion, Andrew A743
Campion, Andrew A964
Campion, Donald C. E313
Campos, Didier Mena W73
Campos, Joselito D. W514
Campos, Kimberly D. E512
Campos, Melisza P467
Campos, Roel C. E413
Campos, Sandra Y. A157
Campos, Tony P177
Camunez, Michael C. A951
Camunez, Michael C. A359
Camuti, Paul A. W617
Canabal, Humberto Domingo Mayans W470
Canarick, Paul T. A430
Canas, Cristian Toro W314
Cancelmi, Daniel J. A1003
Caneman, Monica W562
Canestrari, Kenneth A1030
Canfield, Steven R. E111
Cang, Daqiang W272
Cangemi, Thomas R. A732
Canham, Rachel W114
Canida, Teresa Alvarez A599
Cannada, Charles T. E124
Cannady, David A168
Cannady, David P89
Cannavino, James A. E1
Canney, Jacqueline P. (Jacqui) A931
Canning, Charles W662
Cannizzaro, Edward G. A905
Cannizzaro, Edward G. A823
Cannon, Deborah M. A190
Cannon, Deborah M. E73
Cannon, Gillian M. E121
Cannon, Jaime J. E486
Cannon, Larry N. A747
Cannon, M. Elizabeth W120
Cannon, Marc K. A109
Cannon, Michael R. A619
Cannone, Peter J. E329
Cano, Andre Rodrigues W69
Canova, Walter Fabian W210
Canseco, Leslie Pierce Diez W174
Cantarella, Paolo W363
Cantera, Jose Antonio Garcia W75
Cantie, Joseph S. E469
Cantie, Joseph S. E490
Cantlin, John L. E204
Cantor, Diana F. E524
Cantor, Eric E330
Cantrell, James M. A704
Cantrell, James M. E328
Cantrell, Mike P168
Cantu, Javier Beltran W265
Canty, Kevin M. E261
Canty, Trecia M. A809
Canty, Trecia M. E374
Canuso, Dominic C. A1138
Canuso, Dominic C. E544
Cao, Liqun W301
Cao, Min W583
Cao, Qingyang W142
Cao, Sanxing W663
Cao, Xingquan W153

Cao, Xirui W146
Cao, Yitang W326
Cao, Yu W662
Cao, Zhiqiang W292
Cao, Zhiqiang W246
Capasse, Thomas E. E411
Capatides, Michael G. W119
Cape, Shavon R. E149
Capel, Eddie E447
Capel, Mary Clara A414
Capel, Mary Clara E191
Capellas, Michael D. A244
Capellas, Michael D. E57
Capellas, Michael D. W242
Capello, Ramona L. A685
Capener, John T P552
Capener, John T P553
Capitani, Todd L. E113
Caplan, Deborah H. A739
Caplan, Deborah H. A436
Caplan, Lindsey A213
Caple, Steven W. A301
Caple, Steven W. E131
Caplinger, Larry A. E181
Capo, Brian A641
Capo, Thomas P. A622
Capone, Michael L. E147
Caponi, Julie A. A418
Caponi, Julie A. E206
Caponi, Julie A. E195
Capozzi, Daniel Peter A330
Capozzi, Heidi B. A675
Capozzoli, Robert A854
Cappello, Maria Elena W482
Cappi, Luiz Carlos Trabuco W69
Capps, Allen C. W218
Capps, Kimberly A. A953
Capps, Kimberly A. E455
Capps, Stacey P176
Capps, Vickie L. E20
Capri, Daniel E64
Capriles, Alberto A52
Capron, Philippe W631
Captain, Brad L. E340
Capuano, Anthony G. A675
Capuano, Anthony G. A660
Caputo, Lisa M. A155
Caputo, Thomas E81
Carannante, Rocco W627
Carano, Mark A. E275
Caras, Matthew L. A138
Caras, Matthew L. E55
Carbajal, Francisco Javier Fernandez W244
Carbajal, Francisco Javier Fernandez W27
Carbajal, Francisco Javier Fernandez W131
Carbajal, Jose Antonio Fernandez W274
Carbajal, Jose Antonio Fernandez W244
Carbajal, Jose Antonio Fernandez W274
Carbonari, Bruce A. A907
Carbone, Kathleen A65
Card, Andrew H. A1061
Card, Robert G. A20
Cardenas, Alberto de A668
Cardenas, Alvaro W201

Cardenas, Daniel E517
Cardenas, Ricardo A1035
Cardenas, Ricardo A316
Cardew, Jason M. A622
Cardiff, Michele L. A1094
Cardona, Andres Felipe Mejia W76
Cardoso, Mariana Botelho Ramalho W69
Cardoso, Paulo W637
Cardy, Marc J. A395
Cardy, Marc J. E186
Carell, Thomas W93
Caret, Leanne G. A877
Carethers, John A112
Carey, Albert P. A526
Carey, Chase A447
Carey, James D. E212
Carey, Jennifer Craighead A454
Carey, Mathew A. A232
Carey, Matthew A. A526
Carfagna, Maurizio W391
Carfora, Jeffrey J. A810
Carfora, Jeffrey J. E375
Carges, Mark T. E519
Cargill, Jan W425
Cargill, Jan W423
Cariello, Vincenzo W625
Carillo, Brooke E. A881
Cariola, Gianfranco W227
Carlen, Joe P581
Carleone, Joseph E45
Carleton, Mark D. A633
Carletti, Elena W625
Carletti, Milva W627
Carley, Brian T. E317
Carley, Donald M. A531
Carli, Maurizio W592
Carlier, Didier W127
Carlile, Robert P. A386
Carlile, Thomas E. A166
Carlin, Jane D. A499
Carlin, Peter H. W15
Carlino, Peter M. E227
Carlisle, Stephen K. A466
Carls, Andre W389
Carlsen, Bent Erik W632
Carlson, Bruce A. A643
Carlson, Carl M. A118
Carlson, Craig A. A800
Carlson, J.D. A812
Carlson, Jan W228
Carlson, Jason L. E525
Carlson, John (Jack) R. A279
Carlson, John D. A812
Carlson, LeRoy T. A1001
Carlson, LeRoy T. E486
Carlson, Letitia G. A1001
Carlson, Nels A37
Carlson, Nels E14
Carlson, Prudence E. A1001
Carlson, Thomas J. A488
Carlson, W. Erik A333
Carlson, Walter C.D. A1001
Carlton, Pamela G. A87
Carlton, Pamela G. E176
Carlton, Scott L. A1065
Carlton, William F. A68
Carman, Stephen F. E193
Carmany, George W. W571
Carmody, Christine M. A380

COMBINED HOOVER'S HANDBOOK INDEX OF EXECUTIVES

A = AMERICAN BUSINESS
E = EMERGING COMPANIES
P = PRIVATE COMPANIES
W = WORLD BUSINESSS

Carmody, John F. E354
Carmona, Richard H. A677
Carnahan, Ellen E374
Carnahan, Ellen E162
Carnahan, Karen L. A242
Carnahan, Scott W. E378
Carnecchia, Scipio Maxaximus E328
Carnegie-Brown, Bruce W75
Carnegie, Maile W63
Carneiro, Vera de Morais Pinto Pereira W212
Carney, Craig B. A1038
Carney, Craig B. E495
Carney, Kevin M. E302
Carney, Lloyd A. A1089
Carney, Lloyd A. A1096
Carney, Mark J. W80
Carney, Robert F. E452
Carnwath, Alison W666
Carnwath, Dame Alison J. A796
Carnwath, Dame Alison J. W93
Caro, Jodi J. A1055
Carolin, Roger A. A78
Carolus, Cheryl A. W310
Carome, Kevin M. A573
Caron, Joseph P. W382
Carona, Marisa J. E539
Carotenuto, Michael F. A191
Carotenuto, Michael F. E77
Caroti, Stefano E137
Carpenter, Dan P280
Carpenter, Harold R. A829
Carpenter, Harold R. E385
Carpenter, Kevin N. E491
Carpenter, Lonny J. E355
Carpenter, Michael A. A418
Carpenter, Scott K. E49
Carpenter, Tod E. A74
Carpenter, William (Bill) F. A395
Carpenter, William (Bill) F. E185
Carpenter, Zachary N A395
Carpenter, Zachary N E186
Carpio, Mariano Marzo W493
Carr, Chris A518
Carr, Eric A858
Carr, J. McGregor A274
Carr, James Tomlinson A592
Carr, Jeff W341
Carr, Jeff W490
Carr, Jeffrey B. E99
Carr, Kerry A. A14
Carr, Roger W66
Carra, Victor J. E537
Carrady, Robert A836
Carranza, Jorge Sáenz-Azcúnaga W618
Carrara, Dario E32
Carrasco, Rafael E. A1110
Carraud, Lauren Burns W526
Carraway, Barbara O P130
Carre, Eric J. A494
Carrel, Michael H. E42
Carrico, Paul D. A486
Carriere, Isabel V. A880
Carriere, Isabel V. E412

Carriere, Jacques W294
Carrigan, Gerry P398
Carrillo, Antonio A757
carrillo, Ramon Renato W266
Carrion, Richard L. A836
Carrión, Richard L. A400
Carro, Lourdes Maiz W69
Carroll, Christopher F. A570
Carroll, Cynthia W279
Carroll, Cynthia Blum A121
Carroll, Cynthia Blum A120
Carroll, Cynthia Blum W260
Carroll, J. Martin E83
Carroll, James A. E35
Carroll, Kathleen S. A485
Carroll, Milton A494
Carroll, William C. A323
Carroll, William Y. A945
Carroll, William Y. E451
Carroll, William Young A945
Carroll, William Young E451
Carron, Michael J. E190
Carrothers, Douglas A. W294
Carrupt, Alain W581
Carruthers, Court D. A1083
Carruthers, Wendy A175
Carson, Benjamin S. A536
Carson, Crystal A279
Carson, Crystal P154
Carson, Donald P. E425
Carson, Keith P166
Carson, Neil W532
Carson, Russell L. A926
Carstater, Kent D. E283
Carsten, Shawn J. E437
Carstens, John Albert A1133
Carstens, John Albert E541
Carter-Miller, Jocelyn E. A846
Carter-Miller, Jocelyn E. A570
Carter, Alexandra P572
Carter, Ashton A462
Carter, Ashton B. A323
Carter, Brett C. A1139
Carter, Bruce W85
Carter, Charles J. A799
Carter, Dedric P618
Carter, George P. A814
Carter, George P. E379
Carter, George W. E428
Carter, Glenn A. E502
Carter, J. Braxton A103
Carter, J. Lance A503
Carter, John A134
Carter, John E54
Carter, Kevin T. E526
Carter, Kyle M. E25
Carter, Margot L. E274
Carter, Matthew A588
Carter, Matthew A757
Carter, Maverick A641
Carter, Monique W450
Carter, Pamela L. A514
Carter, Pamela L. W218
Carter, Peter W. A323
Carter, Robert A1034
Carter, Robert B. A405
Carter, Russell D. A524
Carter, Russell D. E258
Carter, Scott R. E329
Carter, Shawn A162

Carter, Stefani D. A120
Carter, Stefani D. E48
Carter, Susan K. A780
Carter, Tim H. A397
Carter, Tim H. E187
Carter, Timothy L. E387
Carter, Todd J. E260
Carter, William H. E306
Carter, William T. A747
Cartier, Guillaume W441
Carton, John S. E455
Cartwright, Christopher A. E493
Cartwright, Doctor Vickie L P486
Carty, Douglas A. A1144
Carty, Michael A. A422
Carucci, Richard T. A1091
Caruso, Dominic J. A677
Caruso, Dominic J. A612
Caruso, Michael B. E67
Carvalho-Heineken, Charlene Lucille de W274
Carvalho, A.A.C. de W274
Carvalho, Eduardo Navarro de W593
Carvalho, M. R. de W274
Carvalho, Michel R. de W274
Carvalho, Orlando P. E319
Carvalho, Renato da Silva W315
Cary, William H. A43
Casaccio, Tenee R. A98
Casaccio, Tenee R. E36
Casady, Mark S. A531
Casamento, Benedetta I. E93
Casas, Isidro Faine W593
Casati, Gianfranco W10
Casbon, John N. A424
Casbon, John N. E200
Casciato, Robert M. E321
Case, David G. A411
Case, Gregory C. A330
Case, Gregory C. W44
Case, John P. E146
Case, Lloyd G. A37
Case, Lloyd G. E14
Case, Thomas D. E190
Casella, Douglas R. E82
Casella, John W. E82
Casellas, Alberto A985
Casellas, Gilbert F. A856
Casely-Hayford, Margaret W160
Caser, Carlos Alberto W324
Casey, Chris P514
Casey, Donald J. A879
Casey, Donald J. A878
Casey, Donald P. E39
Casey, Geraldine W20
Casey, Helen Hanna A1040
Casey, Helen Hanna E498
Casey, Joseph F. A499
Casey, Joseph F. E246
Casey, Kathleen L. A450
Casey, Keith M. W133
Casey, Lynn A1139
Cash, Larry S. E352
Cashaw, Brad A237
Cashell, Robert A. A474
Cashell, Robert A. E230
Cashio, J. Richard A932
Cashio, J. Richard E436
Cashion, Tana K. A325
Cashman, Charles (Chuck) A. E310

Casiano, Kimberly A. A444
Casimir-Lambert, Charles W554
Caspari, Stefan A26
Casper, David B. W82
Casper, Marc N. A1027
Casper, Stephen P. E311
Caspi, Orit W311
Cassabaum, Michelle R. E30
Cassaday, John M. W382
Cassard, David M. A681
Cassard, David M. E318
Cassayre, Christian W213
Cassella, Anthony E. E310
Cassens, Michael D. A415
Cassens, Michael D. E194
Cassidy, Andrew W377
Cassidy, Brian P. A195
Cassidy, Meghan A298
Cassidy, Rick W583
Cassidy, Ronan W532
Cassidy, Sukhinder Singh E513
Cassin, Brian J. W318
Cassinadri, Giuliano W177
Casso, Katie A216
Cassotis, Christina A. A910
Cast, Carter A. A597
Castaigne, Robert W635
Castaldi, Alexander R. E381
Castaldo, Nicholas (Nick) A E88
Casteel, Marty D. A938
Casteel, Marty D. E442
Casteen, John T. E467
Castellano, Christine M. A82
Castellanos, Jesus Martinez W382
Castellví, Beatriz A836
Castillejos, Desiree L. E287
Castillo-Schulz, Jorg Oliveri del W162
Castillo, Jaime Gutierrez W172
Castle, John H. E454
Castle, Julie G. A935
Castle, Julie G. E439
Castries, Henri de W430
Castries, Henri de W562
Castro-Caratini, Fernando E471
Castro, Henrique de A434
Castro, Henrique de W76
Castro, Jones M. W100
Castro, Maria Luisa Jorda W265
Castro, Thomas H. A742
Catalano, Anna Cheng E221
Catalano, Filippo W490
Catalano, Giuseppe W54
Cataldo, Robert F. A1065
Catanese, George A876
Catanese, Joanne F. E224
Catanzaro, Giovanni W363
Catanzaro, Stephen E147
Catasta, Christine W458
Catena, Cornelio P153
Cathcart, R. Calvin A1099
Catino, Annette A749
Catlett, Celia E301
Catlett, Scott A. A1146
Catoggio, Nicolas A838
Catoir, Christophe W13
Catoire, Caroline W174
Cattabiani, Paolo W627
Catti, Joseph R. E190
Catz, Safra A. A786
Catz, Safra A. A335

COMBINED HOOVER'S HANDBOOK INDEX OF EXECUTIVES

A = AMERICAN BUSINESS
E = EMERGING COMPANIES
P = PRIVATE COMPANIES
W = WORLD BUSINESSS

Caubet, Maria Eugenia Bieto W219
Caudill, Connie E455
Caudill, Greg W. A397
Cauley, Robert E. A787
Caulfield, John E34
Caulfield, John R E382
Caulfield, Thomas A1122
Cavaliere, Joseph W. A497
Cavallo-miller, Linda P522
Cavanagh, Michael J. A272
Cavanah, Michael P548
Cavanaugh, Diane B. E351
Cavanaugh, Sandra A. A527
Cavanaugh, Terrence W. A927
Cavanaugh, Terrence W. E435
Cave, George H. A780
Cave, Melanie J. W260
Cave, Michael J. A123
Caveney, Brian J. A615
Cavens, Darrell A993
Cavoli, Stephen E527
Cawen, Klaus W348
Cawley, Timothy P. A290
Cawley, Timothy P. A288
Caylor, Mark A. A752
Caywood, Marty T. A528
Caywood, Marty T. E258
Cebulla, Jorg W196
Cecere, Andrew A1082
Cecilia, Manuel Manrique W493
Cederschiold, Carl W579
Cefali, Sheryl Lynn E420
Ceiley, Glen F. E147
Ceiley, Zachary E147
Celebican, Kutsan W346
Celebioglu, Levent W26
Celeste, Marguerite A639
Celik, Nedim E409
Celis, Arquimedes A. A828
Cella, Kenneth R. A587
Cella, Peter L. E221
Cello, Todd M. E493
Celorio, Victor Alberto Tiburcio W244
Centers, Melissa A. A966
Cento, Juan N. A103
Centoni, Liz W395
Cepero, Monica P167
Cephas, Derrick D. A936
Cephas, Derrick D. E440
Cerami, Carlo W479
Ceremony, Glen A1052
Cerepak, Brad M. A342
Cerezo, Adolfo W643
Cerezo, Rafael Mateu de Ros W87
Cerkovnik, Edward E343
Cerniglia, Kristina A. E303
Cernuda, Cesar A729
Ceroni, Steven A. E61
Cerrai, Francesco A251
Cerrai, Francesco P137
Cerulli, Joseph M. E373
Ceruti, Franco W310
Cerutti, Romeo W176
Cervantes, Victor Manuel Navarro W470

Cerveny, Miroslav W563
Cesar, Diana Ferreira W268
Cesaris, Ada Lucia De W227
Cesarone, Nando A1069
Cestare, Andre Balestrin W315
Cestero, Luis E. A836
Ceverha, Mary E. A397
Ceverha, Mary E. E187
Ch'ien, Raymond Kuo Fung W580
Ch'ien, Raymond Kuo Fung W286
Cha, Laura May Lung W286
Chabauty, Christine W215
Chabot, Rene W294
Chadha, Rajive A781
Chadsey, Deborah J. A753
Chadwick, Ana Maria A336
Chadwick, Jonathan C. A931
Chadwick, Jonathan C. E547
Chadwick, Suzanne M. E114
Chae, Michael S. A161
Chaffin, H. Douglas A427
Chaffin, H. Douglas E203
Chaffin, J. Brian E97
Chaffin, Janice D. E402
Chaffin, Patrick P473
Chai, Nelson J. A1027
Chai, Nelson J. A1052
Chai, Qiang W142
Chai, Qiaolin W137
Chai, Roland A721
Chai, Shouping W466
Chaibi, Anesa T. E5
Chaigneau, Alain W565
Chaillou, Herve W511
Chaipromprasith, Yongyutt W352
Chairasmisak, Korsak W117
Chakarun, Courtney E180
Chakraborty, Atanu W271
Chakravarthy, Anil A15
Chakravarthy, Anil E32
Chakrian, Vic A400
Chalendar, Pierre-Andre de W104
Chalendar, Pierre-Andre de W165
Chalendar, Pierre-André de W631
Chalfant, Thomas E81
Chalfant, Tony W. A510
Chalfant, Tony W. E252
Challon-Kemoun, Adeline W168
Chalmers, Derek T. E80
Chalmers, Sabine W40
Chalmers, William W371
Chalmers, William W371
Chalon, Marie-Laure Sauty de W373
Chaltraw, William P671
Chalut, Erik W. E532
Chamarthi, Mamatha E91
Chambas, Corey A. A416
Chamberlain, Elise E348
Chamberlain, Paul Edward A931
Chamberland, Serges W193
Chambers, Brian D. A795
Chambers, George T. A1044
Chambers, James R. A157
Chambers, M. Susan E515
Chambers, Matthew A143
Chambers, Matthew P69
Chambers, Stuart J. W39
Chambless, Robert G. A266
Chambliss, C. Saxby A845
Chambliss, C. Saxby E395

Chambliss, Kelly C. A69
Chambolle, Thomas P88
Chameau, Jean-Lou W511
Chammas, Emile Z. A924
Champagne, Alain W398
Champalimaud, Luis de Melo W70
Champy, James A. A81
Chan-o-cha, Prayut W603
Chan, Alan L. E344
Chan, Caleb Y.M. W287
Chan, Dennis W652
Chan, Derek Chi On W372
Chan, Ericson W666
Chan, John Cho Chak W268
Chan, Joseph A1145
Chan, Kelly L. A211
Chan, Kelly L. E84
Chan, Kok Seong W628
Chan, Leng Jin (Max) A118
Chan, Man Ko W150
Chan, Mary S. A279
Chan, Mary S. W379
Chan, Nelson C. E137
Chan, Raymond T. W596
Chan, Shiu Leung (Fred) E472
Chan, Wai Kin W254
Chancellor, Beth P656
Chancellor, James P285
Chancy, Mark A. A1115
Chand, Sujeet A902
Chand, Sujeet E400
Chandarasomboon, Amorn W77
Chandel, Lalit Kumar W296
Chandhok, Varun A844
Chandhok, Varun E394
Chandler, A. Russell E122
Chandler, Chris R. A832
Chandler, Chris R. A833
Chandler, Elizabeth Brannen E424
Chandler, Paul W160
Chandoha, Marie A. A973
Chandoha, Marie A. A654
Chandonnet, Raymond E. A596
Chandonnet, Raymond E. E286
Chandra, Subodh P130
Chandrakasan, Anantha P. A81
Chandrasekaran, N. W587
Chandrasekaran, Natarajan W588
Chandrasekaran, Sujatha A201
Chandrasen, Abhijai W334
Chandrashekar, Lavanya W201
Chandy, Ruby R. A1027
Chandy, Ruby R. A349
Chaney, Carla J. A486
Chaney, Kimberly S. A12
Chaney, Kimberly S. E4
Chaney, Michael W644
Chang, Amy L. A850
Chang, Amy L. A335
Chang, Ashley A878
Chang, Ashley E409
Chang, Chia-Sheng W128
Chang, David W252
Chang, Dong-Woo W652
Chang, Dongjuan W140
Chang, Guangshen W272
Chang, Herbert E331
Chang, Hong-Chang W252
Chang, In-Hwa W478
Chang, Jason C. S. W51

Chang, Jimmy Ban Ja W240
Chang, Joanne B. A181
Chang, Jonathan A. A1007
Chang, Kat Kiam W484
Chang, Leonard R. E212
Chang, Lisa V. A453
Chang, Michael A231
Chang, Michael M.Y. A211
Chang, Michael M.Y. E84
Chang, Richard H. P. W51
Chang, Rutherford W51
Chang, See Hiang W322
Chang, Seung-Wha W478
Chang, T.S. W583
Chang, Timothy E375
Chang, Vanessa C.L. A359
Chang, Vanessa C.L. A951
Chang, William E378
Chang, Yang Lee W365
Chang, Zheng W189
Chanrai, Narain Girdhar W456
Chant, Diana L. W122
Chao, Albert A1124
Chao, Chimin J. E195
Chao, David T. A1124
Chao, Elaine L. A611
Chao, James Y. A1124
Chao, John T. A1124
Chao, Leslie T. E382
Chaouki, Steven M. E493
Chapa, Ramon A. Leal W27
Chapek, Robert A. A335
Chapin, David C. A181
Chapin, Samuel R. A764
Chapin, Samuel R. E380
Chaplin, C. Edward A694
Chaplin, C. Edward A176
Chapman-Hughes, Susan E. A947
Chapman, A. Larry E412
Chapman, Brehan A397
Chapman, Brehan E187
Chapman, Frank W504
Chapman, George L. E340
Chapman, Gil A749
Chapman, James R. A1094
Chapman, Joyce A. A60
Chapman, Kevin D. A889
Chapman, Kevin D. E414
Chapman, Laurence A. E141
Chapman, Matthew W. A697
Chapman, Neil A. A388
Chapman, Robert M. E124
Chapman, W. Kyle A276
Chapot, Yves W168
Chapoulaud-Floque, Valerie W201
Chappell, Elizabeth A. A57
Chappell, Kathleen J. E149
Chappell, Kenneth R. A428
Chappell, Robert W. E99
Chappelle, John A. E113
Chappelow, Fred E185
Chapuy, Cyril W358
Char, Neill A423
Charbonneau, Louise W193
Charbonnier, Maryjo A612
Charbonniere, Eric Bourdais de W238
Chard, Daniel R. E316
Charest, Jean W486
Charest, Yvon W420
Charest, Yvon W294

COMBINED HOOVER'S HANDBOOK INDEX OF EXECUTIVES

A = AMERICAN BUSINESS
E = EMERGING COMPANIES
P = PRIVATE COMPANIES
W = WORLD BUSINESSS

Charette, Gary C P40
Charles, Anthony W. St. A283
Charles, Bernard W515
Charles, Carlton J. A651
Charles, Dirkson R. A184
Charletta, Diana M. E171
Charley, Ray T. A418
Charley, Ray T. E195
Charlton, Henry L. A573
Charman, Nikki P437
Charneski, Brian S. A510
Charneski, Brian S. E252
Charnley, Nina A. A152
Charoen-Rajapark, Chatchawin W77
Charoenkiatikul, Sompis W352
Charpentier, Abigail A92
Charreton, Didier W39
Charron, Donald D. E287
Chartbunchachai, Patchara W137
Chartier, Kirk E162
Chartrand, Danice L. E455
Chartsuthipol, Payungsak W352
Charvat, Peter P527
Charvier, Robert W631
Chase, Anthony R. A305
Chase, Debra Martin E50
Chase, Garrett L. A323
Chase, Paul E11
Chassat, Sophie W373
Chatelain, R. Blake A880
Chatelain, R. Blake E412
Chatfield, Clare A493
Chatillon, Jean-Baptiste Chasseloup de W550
Chatillon, Jean-Baptiste Chasseloup de W515
Chatman, Jennifer A. E444
Chatterjee, Koushik W588
Chattopadhyay, Sanat A684
Chaturvedi, Girish Chandra W296
Chatzidis, Odysseus D. W199
Chau, David Shing Yim W139
Chau, Ho W648
Chau, William Siu Cheong W128
Chaudhary, Harpreet S. E56
Chaudhry, Jawad A143
Chaudhry, Jawad E56
Chaumartin, Anik W21
Chaussade, Jean-Louis W565
Chausse, Melinda A. A274
Chavali, Radha R. E140
Chavalitcheewingul, Aree W540
Chavarria, Carla C. A416
Chavasse, Desmond P437
Chavers, Kevin G. A231
Chavez, Francisco Medina W35
Chavez, JoAnn A344
Chavez, Linda L. A10
Chavez, R. Martin A45
Chavez, Roxana E517
Chawla, Sona A214
Chawla, Sona A205
Chazen, Stephen I. A767
Chazen, Stephen I. A1131

Che, Shujian W150
Che, Xingyu W356
Cheah, Kim Teck W322
Cheah, Teik Seng W380
Chearavanont, Dhanin W137
Chearavanont, Narong W117
Chearavanont, Soopakij W117
Chearavanont, Suphachai W117
Cheatham, Tim A1021
Cheatham, Tim P593
Cheatman, Lora C P218
Cheav, Sotheara E3
Checa, Hector Blas Grisi A915
Checa, Hector Blas Grisi W73
Chee, Johnathan E220
Chee, Menes O. E155
Cheeks, George A864
Cheeseman, Julie E517
Cheesewright, David W162
Cheesewright, David W643
Cheesman, Chris H. A39
Cheetham, Kate W371
Cheetham, Kate W371
Cheever, Dan J. A37
Cheever, Dan J. E14
Chellew, Mark P. W37
Chemodurow, Tanya J. E149
Chen-Langenmayr, Nina A1076
Chen, Bian W257
Chen, Bin W291
Chen, Bin W144
Chen, Chun W37
Chen, Dayang W146
Chen, Devin A485
Chen, Donghua W136
Chen, Dongxu W655
Chen, Eddie W252
Chen, Eric Xun A90
Chen, Fang W656
Chen, Feng W136
Chen, Fufa E3
Chen, Fung Ming W240
Chen, Gang W327
Chen, Gang W142
Chen, Gloria A15
Chen, Grace W128
Chen, Guochuan W168
Chen, Hanwen W149
Chen, Hao E370
Chen, Heidi C. A1153
Chen, Heng W. A211
Chen, Heng W. E84
Chen, Hengliu W572
Chen, Herald Y. E234
Chen, Hong W148
Chen, Hong W292
Chen, Hong W512
Chen, Hua W529
Chen, Huajhao W169
Chen, Huakang W254
Chen, Huanchun W431
Chen, Jeffrey W51
Chen, Jianping W656
Chen, Jing W257
Chen, Jinghe W663
Chen, Jinming W656
Chen, Jinshi W326
Chen, Jinzhu W530
Chen, Jizhong W145
Chen, Jolene W481

Chen, Jun W529
Chen, Kaixian W248
Chen, Kexiang W472
Chen, Kok-Choo W584
Chen, Kuan W662
Chen, Lijie W34
Chen, Liming W93
Chen, Lixin W140
Chen, Mao-Cin W206
Chen, Mingyong W608
Chen, Ni W575
Chen, Peiyuan W168
Chen, Qi W140
Chen, Qing W142
Chen, Quanshi W153
Chen, Ran W145
Chen, Ray Jui-Tsung W168
Chen, Roger E234
Chen, Ron-Chu W206
Chen, Rong W148
Chen, Rosemarie A328
Chen, Sanlian W275
Chen, Sanlian W663
Chen, Shaopeng W362
Chen, Shengguang W151
Chen, Shengsyong W169
Chen, Shimin W140
Chen, Shoude W655
Chen, Shuai W172
Chen, Shuping W291
Chen, Siguan W169
Chen, Siqing W301
Chen, Steve T.H. W252
Chen, Suka W206
Chen, Tianming W168
Chen, Tien-Szu W51
Chen, Tom Hsu Tang W240
Chen, Tsu-Pei W128
Chen, Warren E143
Chen, Wei W291
Chen, Wellington A843
Chen, Wellington E392
Chen, Wendell A878
Chen, Wendell E409
Chen, Wenjian W147
Chen, Xiaobei W106
Chen, Xiaohong W528
Chen, Xiaohua W140
Chen, Xiaoman W529
Chen, Xiaoming W529
Chen, Xiaowei W100
Chen, Xiaoyi W179
Chen, Xingyao W431
Chen, Xinying W472
Chen, Yan W142
Chen, Yanshun W106
Chen, Yaohuan W145
Chen, Yi W100
Chen, Yifang W301
Chen, Yilun W575
Chen, Yinghai W141
Chen, Yuehua W533
Chen, Yuhan W326
Chen, Yumin W98
Chen, Yun W147
Chen, Yunian W326
Chen, Zhenhan W178
Chen, Zhenyu W574
Chen, Zhongyue W152
Chen, Zhongyue W151

Chenanda, Cariappa (Cary) M. E249
Chenault, Kenneth I. A151
Cheney, Andrew B. A72
Cheney, Andrew B. E29
Cheney, Stephen H. E489
Cheng, Cheng W355
Cheng, Christopher Wai Chee W286
Cheng, Courtney E62
Cheng, Dunson K. A211
Cheng, Dunson K. E84
Cheng, Eva W105
Cheng, Eva W430
Cheng, Genghong W88
Cheng, Heng W291
Cheng, Hong W148
Cheng, Hui-Ming W252
Cheng, Jian E180
Cheng, Lawrence A457
Cheng, Lehman W252
Cheng, Li W29
Cheng, Lie W431
Cheng, Longdi W274
Cheng, Mei-Wei A622
Cheng, Min W263
Cheng, Moses Mo Chi W143
Cheng, Pam P. W57
Cheng, Peng-Yuan W252
Cheng, Ping W542
Cheng, Ruey-Cherng W252
Cheng, Sophia W128
Cheng, Tony A886
Cheng, Victor C.J. W650
Cheng, Wen W146
Cheng, Will Wei W202
Cheng, William C. Y. A843
Cheng, William C. Y. E393
Cheng, Xiaoming W140
Cheng, Yiliang W656
Cheng, Yong W150
Cheng, Yuanguo W138
Cheng, Yunlei W144
Chennapragada, Aparna A357
Chenneveau, Didier W366
Cheong, Choong Kong W464
Cheong, Thomas A846
Cherecwich, Peter B. A748
Cherfan, Samir W562
Cherner, Anatoly W256
Chernin, Peter A62
Chernow, David S. A925
Cherofsky, Keriann A576
Cherry, Bradford L. A1033
Cherry, Bradford L. E493
Cherry, James C. E35
Cherry, Pedro P. A988
Cherry, Pedro P. E479
Cheruvatath, Nandakumar W209
Cherwoo, Sharda A1136
Chery, Don J. A474
Chery, Don J. E230
Cheshire, Ian W89
Cheshire, Ian W114
Cheshire, Marjorie Rodgers A383
Cheshire, Marjorie Rodgers A834
Chesler, Randall M. A474
Chesler, Randall M. E230
Chestney, Christopher W. E420
Chestnutt, Roy H. E142
Chestnutt, Roy H. W596
Cheung, Ava P548

COMBINED HOOVER'S HANDBOOK INDEX OF EXECUTIVES

A = AMERICAN BUSINESS
E = EMERGING COMPANIES
P = PRIVATE COMPANIES
W = WORLD BUSINESSS

Cheung, David Chung Yan W257
Cheung, Keith W144
Cheung, Kenny K. A513
Cheung, Linus Wing Lam W151
Cheung, Martina L. A911
Cheval, Jean L. W77
Cheval, Jean L. W33
Chevardiere, Patrick de La W523
Chevardiere, Patrick De La W168
Cheves, Brad P514
Chevre, Claude W269
Chew, Jeffrey W464
Chew, Lewis E75
Chew, Lewis E35
Chhina, Ivar S. E308
Chi, Alex E234
Chi, Hun Choi W513
Chi, Xun W572
Chia, Lee Kee W484
Chia, Tai Tee W628
Chiafullo, James D. A441
Chiafullo, James D. E212
Chiang, Daniel W252
Chiang, Hock Woo E107
Chiang, John E33
Chiang, Lai Yuen W268
Chiang, Wilfred (Willie) C.W. A832
Chiang, Wilfred (Willie) C.W. A832
Chiaravanont, Phongthep W137
Chiarelli, Peter W. A613
Chiarello, Guy A434
Chiarini, Andre Barreto W468
Chiasson, Keith A. W133
Chiba, Yuji W81
Chien, Kathleen W636
Chien, Mark W284
Chien, Wei-Chin W206
Chierchia, Giulia W109
Chiesa, Melanie Martella A1119
Chiew, Sin Cheok W322
Chih, Yu Yang W240
Child, Paul G. A945
Child, Paul G. E450
Child, Peter W17
Childears, Linda S. E19
Childers, Shelly M. E96
Childers, Steven L. E116
Childs, Jeffrey J. A1055
Chillura, Joseph V. A1086
Chillura, Joseph V. E516
Chilton, Kevin P. A650
Chilton, Linda M. E149
Chima, Fumbi E49
Chiminski, John R. E83
Chin, Bobby Yoke Choong W464
Chin, Jit Kee E461
Chin, Moonhie E400
Chin, Samuel Wai Leung W240
Chin, Y.P. W583
China, John D. A984
China, John D. E476
Chinavicharana, Krisada W352
Chinavicharana, Krisada W484
Chindamo, Bradly L. E291

Chinea, Manuel A836
Ching, David T. A1030
Ching, Donny W532
Ching, Glenn K.C. A219
Ching, Michael E. E397
Ching, Wei Hong W464
Chini, Marc A. A608
Chinn, Bruce A231
Chinn, Bruce P117
Chinn, Bruce E. A1110
Chinnasami, Vijayan S. E504
Chinniah, Nim P656
Chiplock, Mark A. E22
Chippendale, Ian Hugh A39
Chirachavala, Arun W77
Chirakitcharern, Paisan W136
Chirico, Emanuel A326
Chisholm, Andrew A. W507
Chisholm, John P692
Chisholm, Nancy E. E33
Chitale, Uday M. W296
Chiu, Adolph Yeung W257
Chiu, Jimmy Jingwu E370
Chiu, Lung-Man W179
Chiu, P. Diana A27
Chiu, Sung Hong W158
Chiu, Tzu-Yin E47
Chiu, Vivien Wai Man W268
Chiusano, Robert M. E540
Chivinski, Beth Ann L. A454
Chizen, Bruce R. A786
Chlebos, Uwe W635
Chmelik, Thomas J. E307
Chng, Kai Fong W190
Chng, Sok Hui W190
Cho, Alex A538
Cho, Alice S. A478
Cho, Alice S. A426
Cho, Alice S. E202
Cho, Bonghan W190
Cho, Dae-Sik W546
Cho, Daniel E375
Cho, Haeyoung E375
Cho, Kyung-Yup W335
Cho, Michael A1148
Cho, Nam-Hoon W335
Cho, Rose Mui W268
Cho, Yong-Byoung W537
Choate, Fred G. E371
Choate, William Millard A72
Choate, William Millard E29
Chocat, Noemie W165
Chodak, Paul A59
Choe, Michael W. A1112
Choi, Brian E362
Choi, Brian J. A116
Choi, Caroline A359
Choi, Caroline A951
Choi, Dong-Su W652
Choi, Eun Soo W294
Choi, Gee-Sung W513
Choi, Hyounghee W205
Choi, Jae Boong W537
Choi, Jeong-Woo W478
Choi, Justin C. A279
Choi, Koon Shum W105
Choi, Kyong-rok W537
Choi, Myung-Hee W335
Choi, Seok-Mun W335
Choi, Seung-Kook W352

Choi, Young-Ho W351
Choksi, Mary C. A778
Cholmondeley, Paula H. J. A134
Cholmondeley, Paula H. J. E54
Chombar, Françoise W623
Chon, Jung-Son W478
Chong, Mark C. A214
Chong, Patrick A768
Chong, Patrick E359
Chong, Quince Wai Yan W128
Choong, Yee How W286
Chopra, Daveen A361
Chopra, Deepak W572
Chopra, Jyoti A918
Chopra, Naveen K. A802
Chorin, Jacky W215
Chosy, James L. A1082
Chotikaprakai, Thanomsak W603
Chotsuparach, Praderm W136
Chou, John G. A73
Chou, Scott W206
Chou, Teh-Chien A287
Choudhry, Jeffer P659
Choufuku, Yasuhiro W392
Chouinard, Scott E215
Chow, Chung-Kong W19
Chow, Gonzaga J. A279
Chow, Heidy E220
Chow, Jacqueline W162
Chow, John Wai-Wai W180
Chow, Liz Tan Ling W268
Chow, Paul Man Yiu W143
Chowdary, Kosaraju Veerayya W587
Chowdhury, Badrul A. A825
Chretien, Benedicte W174
Chriss, J. Alexander A571
Christen, Marc-Alain W631
Christensen, Bret E276
Christensen, Chris D. E340
Christensen, Christopher R. E164
Christensen, Christopher R. E376
Christensen, Joergen W330
Christensen, Roy E. E164
Christenson, Vonn R. A935
Christenson, Vonn R. E439
Christian, Darrianne P. A618
Christian, Darrianne P. E290
Christian, Jeanine M. E144
Christian, Justin P. A425
Christian, Justin P. E201
Christiansen, Niels B. W188
Christianson, Jon E370
Christianson, Wei Sun A620
Christie, Christopher E369
Christie, James R. W122
Christino, Genuino M. W49
Christman, Albert C. A397
Christman, Albert C. E187
Christmann, John J. A86
Christmas, Charles E. A681
Christmas, Charles E. E317
Christodoro, Jonathan A807
Christophe, Cleveland A. A184
Christopherson, David V. E210
Christy, Cynthia K. A301
Christy, James A. A854
Chromik, Marcus W162
Chronican, Philip W419
Chronister, Thomas E81
Chrousos, Phaedra S. E518

Chryssikos, Georgios K. W231
Chu, Christie K. A498
Chu, Daniel A788
Chu, Daniel E364
Chu, Ivan Kwok Leung W128
Chu, Karen Man Yee W236
Chu, Victor W24
Chu, Victor W445
Chu, Wah-Hui E325
Chu, Yiyun W472
Chu, Zhiqi W397
Chua, Sock Koong W351
Chubachi, Mitsuo W1
Chubachi, Ryoji W319
Chubachi, Ryoji W439
Chubak, David A586
Chuenchom, Chansak W484
Chuengviroj, Vichien W117
Chugg, Juliana L. A316
Chugg, Juliana L. A1091
Chumley, Robert J. A719
Chumura, Thomas P655
Chun, Courtnee A. E90
Chun, Dong-Soo W513
Chung, Andrew E375
Chung, Chan-Hyoung W652
Chung, Eui Sun W294
Chung, Harry H. A498
Chung, Janice E375
Chung, Joseph T. A352
Chung, Kenneth Patrick W138
Chung, Moon-Ki W478
Chung, Nelson A211
Chung, Nelson E84
Chung, Paul W. A995
Chung, Seok-Young W652
Chung, Timpson Shui Ming W151
Chung, Tzau-Jin E303
Churchill, David J. E96
Churchill, Laurie A. E297
Churchill, Winston J. A78
Churchouse, Frederick Peter W372
Chuslo, Steven L. E245
Chutima, Sarunthorn W541
Chuvaev, Aleksander W247
Chwick, Jane P. A814
Chwick, Jane P. A651
Chwick, Jane P. A1099
Chwick, Jane P. E311
Chwick, Jane P. E379
Chybowski, Joseph M. A175
Chybowski, Joseph M. E66
Chytil, Kamila K. A985
Ciaffoni, Joseph E107
Ciaffoni, Joseph E60
Ciampa, Dominick A732
Ciampitti, Tony J. A74
Cianfrocco, Heather E341
Ciardella, Robert L. E107
Cibik, Melanie Susan E483
Cicconi, Fiona Clare W562
Cichocki, Paul A158
Ciejka, Gerald P. E537
Cieslak, Kimberly L. E297
Cifrian, Roberto Campa W244
Ciftciogiu, Ersin Onder W619
Cifu, Douglas A. E527
Cifuentes, Gilberto Perezalonso A953
Cima, Danielle M. A280
Cima, Danielle M. E113

COMBINED HOOVER'S HANDBOOK INDEX OF EXECUTIVES

A = AMERICAN BUSINESS
E = EMERGING COMPANIES
P = PRIVATE COMPANIES
W = WORLD BUSINESSS

Cimaglia, Amanda E49
Cimbri, Carlo W627
Cimbri, Carlo W627
Cimen, Cenk W346
Cimenoglu, Ahmet W661
Cimino, Anthony J. E193
Cinar, Cahit W619
Cintani, William R. A727
Cintani, William R. E345
Cioli, Laura W391
Ciongoli, Adam Grey A195
Ciou, Pinghe W169
Cirelli, Jean-Francois W165
Cirelli, Jean-François W565
Cirera, Carmina Ganyet i W493
Ciria, Antonio Gomez W382
Cirillo, Anthony O. A400
Cirillo, Charles M. E351
Cirillo, Mary A. W154
Cirina, Luciano W453
Ciroli, James K. A435
Ciroli, James K. E210
Ciruzzi, Vincent R. E15
Cisne, Richard A134
Cisne, Richard E54
Cissell, Rob W127
Citrino, Mary Anne A538
Citrino, Mary Anne A37
Citrino, Mary Anne W351
Ciulla, John R. A1113
Civil, Patricia T. A724
Cladouhos, Sherry L. A474
Cladouhos, Sherry L. E230
Claflin, Bruce L. E263
Clagett, Robert Y. A845
Clagett, Robert Y. E395
Clair, William Paxson St. E308
claire, Marisa St. E61
Clamadieu, Jean-Pierre W554
Clamadieu, Jean-Pierre W225
Clamadieu, Jean-Pierre W238
Clamadieu, Jean-Pierre W65
Clamadieu, Jean-Pierre W590
Clamadieu, Jean-Pierre W24
Clancy, Brenda Kay A1065
Clancy, John P. A372
Clancy, John P. E166
Clancy, Paul J. E267
Clappison, John H. W571
Clara, Daniel A99
Clare, Peter J. A203
Clariza, Ronnie J. E199
Clarizio, Lynda M. A214
Clark, Agenia W. A395
Clark, Agenia W. E185
Clark, Benjamin G. A386
Clark, Bill E341
Clark, Celeste A. A1115
Clark, Charles James Scott E455
Clark, Christie J. B. W371
Clark, Christina J. A291
Clark, David H. A50
Clark, David V. A764
Clark, Denise M. A1068

Clark, Donald A889
Clark, Donald E414
Clark, Donald Jeff E540
Clark, Gina K. A73
Clark, Henry A. (Hal) A952
Clark, Ian W585
Clark, Janet F. A1010
Clark, Janet F. A376
Clark, Jason D. E374
Clark, Jennifer B. E423
Clark, Jill Short E443
Clark, John B A974
Clark, John B P539
Clark, Jonathan C. E159
Clark, Kevin P. W45
Clark, Kevin P. W46
Clark, Laura E. E419
Clark, Laura F. E149
Clark, Lawrence S. E26
Clark, Mark T P575
Clark, Matthew A968
Clark, Matthew P534
Clark, Maura J. A737
Clark, Maura J. W451
Clark, Mayree C. A43
Clark, Megan W500
Clark, Megan W499
Clark, Morris R. E101
Clark, Nicole E. A767
Clark, Nicole E. E536
Clark, Paul N. A27
Clark, R. Kerry A85
Clark, R. Kerry A465
Clark, R. Kerry A1012
Clark, Richard T. A108
Clark, Richard T. A298
Clark, Rodney A586
Clark, Rodney E166
Clark, Rodney P292
Clark, Scott W168
Clark, Stanley L. A80
Clark, Steve A1138
Clark, Steve E544
Clark, Sue W298
Clark, Suzanne P. A26
Clark, Suzanne P. E493
Clark, Suzanne P. W662
Clark, Talisa R P168
Clark, William E. A938
Clark, William E. E442
Clark, Yvette Hollingsworth E10
Clarke, Alison W298
Clarke, Bruce R. W287
Clarke, Christopher E102
Clarke, Donald E. E14
Clarke, Emmanuel W308
Clarke, Jeffrey W. A322
Clarke, Michael B. A98
Clarke, Michael B. E36
Clarke, Peter W235
Clarke, Richard A460
Clarke, Sheilagh M. A443
Clarke, Teresa H. A69
Clarke, Teresa H. A455
Clarkson, Daniel J P49
Clarkson, Tom W481
Clarno, Bev A970
Clarno, Bev P537
Classon, Rolf A. E83
Classon, Rolf A. W249

Clatterbuck, Janice E. A401
Clatterbuck, Michelle M. A571
Claudia, Ontiveros P639
Claure, Marcelo A992
Claus, Gary R. A418
Claus, Gary R. E195
Claxton, Hazel W596
Claxton, Timothy L. E428
Clay, Shaundra E278
Clay, Shonda A399
Clayton, Annette K. A347
Clayton, Norma B. A760
Cleare, Christy R. A401
Cleary, Alan W462
Cleary, James Dominic W383
Cleary, James F. A73
Cleaver, Bruce W39
Clees, John A. A510
Clees, John A. E252
Clegg, Catherine L E236
Clegg, Don E472
Clegg, Nicholas A689
Cleland, Abigail Pip W162
Clem, Jackie E15
Clemens, Stacey E102
Clemensen, Hal R. A235
Clement-Holmes, Linda W. A240
Clement-Holmes, Linda W. A410
Clement, Dallas S. A1042
Clement, Luis Miguel Briola W265
Clement, Ryan M. E435
Clemente, Mario L. A574
Clemente, Rodney E161
Clementi, Enrich W207
Clementi, John R. A372
Clementi, John R. E167
Clements, James P. A1064
Clements, James P. E509
Clemeson, Marry A52
Clemeson, Marry P30
Clemmenson, Larry A64
Clemmenson, Larry P34
Clemmer, Richard L. A538
Clemmer, Richard L. W45
Clemmer, Richard L. W46
Clemons, J. Randall A1132
Clemons, J. Randall E539
Clemons, Jack W203
Clerc, Vincent W1
Clerico, John A. A282
Clerico, John A. E153
Clermont, Ralph W. A722
Clermont, Ralph W. E339
Cless, Gerhard A1148
Cleveland, Cotton Mather A380
Cleveland, Goll Shawn E63
Cleveland, Todd M. E373
Cleveland, Todd M. E264
Clever, Xiaoqun W101
Clever, Xiaoqun W303
Clevers, Hans W502
Click, Betty A337
Cliff, Kelly S. E525
Clifford, Deborah L. E44
Clifford, Peter G. E49
Clinck, Erik W336
Cline, Brenda A. E502
Cline, James E. E494
Clinton, Andrea M. E490
Clinton, Chelsea A385

Clinton, Chelsea E261
Clinton, Malissia R. A687
Clinton, Stephen G. E189
Clipper, Christopher L. E221
Cloninger, Kriss A477
Clontz, Steven T. A650
Cloonan, Wendy Montoya A218
Clossin, Todd F. A1115
Clossin, Todd F. E532
Clothier, Kevin Charles A302
Clough, Jeanette G. A191
Clough, Jeanette G. E77
Clouse, Benjamin R. A301
Clouse, Benjamin R. E131
Clouse, Mark A. A195
Cloutier, Jean W235
Clubb, Megan F. A402
Clulow, Christopher C. A306
Clulow, Thomas J. W570
Cluney, Bruce R. W379
Clyburn, Franklin K. A567
Clyburn, Franklin K. A349
Clyburn, William E433
Clyde, R. Andrew A719
Clymo, David W522
Co, Erin Niewinski P373
Co, Gary Richardson P373
Co, Nora K Carr P249
Coady, Shawn W. A741
Coallier, Robert W295
Coates, Peter W260
Coates, Ralph W618
Coatsworth, John H A1023
Coatsworth, John H P608
Coaxum, Wole C. A927
Coaxum, Wole C. E435
Cobaleda, Manuel Garcia W423
Cobb, Brent R. A865
Cobb, Brent R. E403
Cobb, Christopher G. A282
Cobb, Heather N. E153
Cobb, William C. E221
Coben, Jerome L. E242
Coben, Lawrence S. A757
Cobert, Beth F. A213
Cobian, Mauricio Doehner W131
Coblentz, Julian L. E132
Cobo, Santiago Cobo W423
Coburn, Fergal W20
Coby, Paul W157
Cocchi, Steven R. E453
Cochet, Philippe W513
Cochran, Edward W. E91
Cochran, George N. A599
Cochran, Hope F. A503
Cochran, James Scott A889
Cochran, James Scott E414
Cochran, Leeann M. E134
Cochran, Sandra B. A647
Cochran, Steven S. E72
Cochrane, Collin Lee A881
Cock, Paul De A706
Cocke, Travis W. E242
Cockerham, Gregory C. E113
Cockerham, Milo L. E372
Cockerill, Ian W101
Cocks, Chris A503
Cockwell, Jack L. W112
Code, Corey D. A792
Codispoti, Edward H. E357

COMBINED HOOVER'S HANDBOOK INDEX OF EXECUTIVES

A = AMERICAN BUSINESS
E = EMERGING COMPANIES
P = PRIVATE COMPANIES
W = WORLD BUSINESSS

Coe, Mary Ellen A684
Coe, Pamela L. A453
Coe, Pamela L. A633
Coe, Scott P90
Coe, Sebastian W246
Coelho, Anthony L. E173
Coelho, Jose Mauricio Pereira W622
Coelho, Jose Mauricio Pereira W630
Coen, William W138
Coetsee, Benita W310
Cofer-Wildsmith, Marina E223
Cofer, Timothy (Tim) P. E90
Coffey, John W. A167
Coffey, John W. E64
Coffey, Philip M. W377
Coffey, Robert A436
Cogan, Andrew B. E27
Cogen, Jeff P173
Cognetti, John T. E190
Cogut, Charles I. A30
Cogut, Charles I. A1131
Cohade, Pierre E. W327
Cohan, Steven D. E120
Cohen-Welgryn, Myriam W358
Cohen, Adam A638
Cohen, Andrew B. A891
Cohen, Ari A400
Cohen, Daniel G. E105
Cohen, David W164
Cohen, Evan P376
Cohen, Fred E. E398
Cohen, Gerald D. E430
Cohen, H Michael E312
Cohen, Jonathan Z. A657
Cohen, Lanny W123
Cohen, Martin J. A1013
Cohen, Martin M. A713
Cohen, Monique W104
Cohen, Monique W511
Cohen, Robert L. E468
Cohen, Ryan A457
Cohen, Stephen A160
Cohen, Tal A721
Cohenour, Jason W. E420
Cohn, Gary D. A565
Cohn, Jesse A. A1047
Cohn, Matthew N. A1014
Cohn, Matthew N. E488
Cohn, Spencer T. E326
Cohon, Jared L. W617
Coisne-Roquette, Marie-Christine W613
Coisne-Roquette, Marie-Christine W231
Cojuangco, Eduardo M. W514
Cok, Michael J. A555
Cok, Michael J. E269
Coke, Michael A. E486
Coke, Michael A. E67
Coker, Robert Howard A950
Col, Douglas L. E426
Colaco, Russ W323
Colanero, Stephen A P30
Colberg, Alan B. A1082

Colberg, Alan B. A296
Colberg, Wolfgang W602
Colbert, Enrique A1112
Colbert, Michael P173
Colbert, Michael B P173
Colbert, Theodore A94
Colbert, Theodore A164
Colbert, Virgis W. E461
Colby, Mark S. E235
Colby, Michael C. E235
Coldani, Steven M. E388
Coldman, David John A455
Cole, David W642
Cole, David A. W580
Cole, David A. W442
Cole, H. Kenneth E455
Cole, James A65
Cole, Kenneth G. A666
Cole, M. Ray A414
Cole, M. Ray E193
Cole, Mark M. A523
Cole, Mark M. E257
Cole, Martin I. A1122
Cole, Matthew J. E303
Cole, Michael R. A1053
Cole, Michel' Philipp A199
Cole, Rischa P207
Cole, Sue W. A663
Cole, Susan A. A810
Cole, Susan A. E376
Colella, Gerald G. E329
Coleman, Casey A1050
Coleman, Casey P636
Coleman, Denis P. A480
Coleman, J. Edward A54
Coleman, John F. E151
Coleman, Leonard S. A778
Coleman, Lisa E90
Coleman, Michael B. E5
Coleman, Michael J. W377
Coleman, Peter John W523
Coleman, Richard Kenneth E131
Coleman, Thomas J. E144
Coles, Joanna E452
Coles, N. Anthony A882
Coles, Pamela W504
Coletta, Edmond R. E82
Coletti, Julie E16
Coletti, Robert E. A242
Coley, Tammy F. E280
Colgan, N. W178
Colin, Didier W347
Colin, John E. E206
Coll, Francisco J. E296
Collar, Gary L. E255
Collar, Mark A. E43
Collary, Scott W648
Collawn, Patricia K. A225
Colleran, Donald F. A10
Colleran, Donald F. E152
Collier, George C. E321
Collier, Jeffrey S. E69
Collier, T. Harris A1044
Collier, W. R. A852
Collier, W. R. E399
Collina, Piero W627
Collingsworth, Connie R. A136
Collingsworth, J M P357
Collingsworth, James M. A741
Collins, Arthur Reginald A594

Collins, Asha S. E263
Collins, Augustus Leon A1044
Collins, Augustus Leon A546
Collins, Brian M. A372
Collins, Brian M. E166
Collins, Christine E142
Collins, Daniel J. E63
Collins, David A283
Collins, Gary S. A774
Collins, Gary S. E360
Collins, James C. A94
Collins, James C. A298
Collins, James E. A143
Collins, James E. E57
Collins, Jeffery L. E344
Collins, John M. W260
Collins, Kenneth J. A1151
Collins, Kevin M. A574
Collins, Mark L. A555
Collins, Mark L. E269
Collins, Martin J. E407
Collins, Michael E. A274
Collins, Michelle L. A1055
Collins, Michelle L. W119
Collins, Richard A. E138
Collins, Ryan M. E151
Collins, Susan E. A1006
Collins, Terrance L. A1148
Collins, Tomago A892
Collis, Steven H. A73
Collopy, Jenny P573
Colmar, Craig P. E285
Colombas, Juan W371
Colombas, Juan W306
Colombini, Jay J. A392
Colombini, Jay J. E183
Colombo, Marion A138
Colombo, Marion E55
Colombo, Paolo Andrea W310
Colombo, Russell A. A130
Colombo, William J. A326
Colon, Hector A741
Colon, Hector E349
Colonias, Karen W. A888
Colonias, Karen W. E444
Colony, George F. E215
Colorado, Lisa P639
Colpitts, Bernard R. A780
Colpo, Charles C. A794
Colpron, Françoise A924
Colson, Nathaniel H. A694
Colter, David M. A138
Colter, David M. E55
Coltharp, Douglas E. A1059
Colton, David C. E537
Colucci, Marlene A493
Colucci, Paul D. A937
Colucci, Paul D. E441
Columb, Barry K. W371
Colvin, Donald A. E523
Colvin, Paul A986
Colwel, Michael E286
Colwell, Keary L. E56
Comadran, Sol Daurella W76
Combes, Michel A825
Combs, Jason P. E431
Combs, Todd Anthony A591
Comer, Diane A591
Comer, Diane P294
Comer, James F. A1132

Comer, James F. E539
Comin, Luciano W111
Comitale, James J. E360
Commander, Charles E. E222
Comneno, Maurizia Angelo W391
Comolli, Jean-Dominiqe W22
Comparin, Cynthia J. A305
Comparin, Cynthia J. E511
Compton, Bob L. A311
Compton, Jennifer B. A938
Compton, Jennifer B. E442
Compton, John C. A424
Compton, John C. E200
Compton, Kris E. A37
Compton, Kris E. E14
Compton, Paul H. W89
Comstock, Elizabeth J. A743
Comstock, Jerry M. E292
Comyn, Matthew W164
Conard, Diana Mazuelos E358
Conaway, Mary Ann A259
Conaway, Mary Ann E103
Concannon, Christopher R. E311
Concannon, William F. E126
Concewitz, Robert Kunze W298
Concha, Raimundo Espinoza W172
Concolino, Doreen P598
Conde, Cesar A817
Conde, Cesar A1104
Condon, Patrick J. A371
Condrin, J. Paul A499
Conduff, Joseph Howard E372
Cone, David A. E489
Conerly, Tracy T. A1044
Cones, Robert W362
Conesa, Andres A929
Congalton, Susan T. E532
Congdon, David S. A771
Congdon, Earl E. A771
Congdon, John R. A771
Conger, Daniel E. E436
Conine, Steven A1112
Conine, Steven E81
Conix, Birgit W53
Conklin, Bret A. A531
Conklin, Michael L. A1138
Conklin, Michael L. E544
Conley, Fatimah P650
Conley, Gregory A. E500
Conley, Jason P. A904
Conley, Karen P437
Conlin, Kelly P. E432
Conlon, Christopher C. E480
Conlon, Gregory S. A595
Conn, Iain C. W114
Conn, W. Lance A224
Connally, Stanley W. A196
Connally, Stanley W. E79
Connaughton, Bernadette M. A986
Connaughton, Bernadette M. E244
Connaughton, John P. A576
Connell, Eugene C. E172
Connell, K. Bruce A659
Connelly, Deirdre P. A654
Connelly, Deirdre P. A638
Connelly, Elizabeth H. A214
Connelly, Hugh W. E260
Connelly, Marjorie Mary (Marge) A47
Connelly, Ryan H. E297
Connelly, Susan M. A316

COMBINED HOOVER'S HANDBOOK INDEX OF EXECUTIVES

```
A = AMERICAN BUSINESS
E = EMERGING COMPANIES
P = PRIVATE COMPANIES
W = WORLD BUSINESSS
```

Connelly, William W548
Connelly, William L. W16
Conner, Brad L. A874
Conner, David W463
Conner, David W261
Conner, David Philbrick W561
Conner, Jack W. A509
Conner, Jack W. E251
Conner, Judy E83
Conner, Laurie E357
Conner, Peter J. A136
Conner, Raymond L. A34
Conner, Raymond L. W15
Conner, Robert W. A207
Connerton, John B. E175
Connett, Brad A917
Connolly, Mark Leo A1014
Connolly, Mark Leo E488
Connolly, Michael Colin E124
Connolly, Michael J. E308
Connolly, Patrick J. W122
Connolly, Paul M. A352
Connolly, Sean M. A286
Connor, Christopher M. A568
Connor, Christopher M. A1146
Connor, Craig S. E102
Connor, Frank T. A1012
Connor, James B. E146
Connor, Martin P. A1032
Connors, John P. A749
Connors, Julie M. A570
Connors, Michael P. W154
Connors, Nelda J. A175
Connors, Nelda J. A121
Connors, Nelda J. A400
Connors, Nelda J. A120
Connors, Nelda J. A791
Connors, Robert R. A427
Connors, Robert R. E203
Conoscente, Jean-Paul W526
Conrad, Diana E258
Conrad, G. Kent A470
Conrad, Jared A857
Conrad, Melinda W37
Conrad, Micah R. A781
Conrad, Micah R. E361
Conrad, Thomas E452
Conrades, George H. A786
Conroy, James G. E64
Consagra, James J. A1063
Consagra, James J. E508
Consi, Anthony J. A810
Consi, Anthony J. E376
Consing, Cezar Peralta W85
Constable, David W7
Constable, David E. A438
Constantine, Dow P171
Constantine, Thomas M. A119
Constantine, Thomas M. E48
Constantine, Tom A119
Constantine, Tom P57
Constantini, Carlos Fernando Rossi W315
Constantino, Edward N. E348

Constantino, Ferdinand K. W514
Consylman, Gina E282
Contamine, Jerome W613
Contamine, Jerome W548
Conte, Tricia W419
Conti, Anthony James A74
Conti, Fulvio W44
Conto, Claudio De W482
Contreras-Sweet, Maria A929
Contreras-Sweet, Maria A1151
Contreras-Sweet, Maria E413
Contreras, Fernando A120
Contreras, Tiffany P401
Converse, Peter A. A1063
Converse, Peter A. E508
Conway, Craig A912
Conway, Heather E. W262
Conway, James F. A372
Conway, James F. E166
Conway, James T. A1012
Conway, John W. A302
Conway, Michael A964
Conway, Michael A. A673
Conway, William E. A203
Cook, Alasdair W227
Cook, Bonnie E308
Cook, Brian Scott E283
Cook, Christopher S. E504
Cook, Donald G. E487
Cook, Ian M. A817
Cook, Jill E. A306
Cook, John L. E434
Cook, Linda Zarda A132
Cook, Patricia L. E190
Cook, Paul R. W559
Cook, Robert S. A427
Cook, Robert S. E204
Cook, Scott D. A571
Cook, Sharon Lee W419
Cook, Stephen C. E397
Cook, Timothy D. A743
Cook, Timothy D. A89
Cook, W. Rand A845
Cook, W. Rand E395
Cook, Zerick D. E99
Cooke, Julie P49
Cooke, Julie S. E346
Cooke, Scott A1034
Cookman, James M. A981
Cookman, James M. E469
Cooksen, Lindsey M. A995
Cooley, Toni D. A1044
Coolidge, R. Lowell E99
Coolidge, Rhonda A1015
Coolidge, Rhonda P571
Coombe, Robert Neil W156
Coomber, John R. W580
Cooney, Anne M. A1118
Cooney, Anne M. E469
Cooper, Angus R. A32
Cooper, Arthur S. E232
Cooper, Brad A741
Cooper, Cathy E. A1107
Cooper, Diane L. A979
Cooper, Edith W. A50
Cooper, Ellen G. A638
Cooper, Janet K. E491
Cooper, John W. E19
Cooper, Kerry Whorton A823
Cooper, Kerry Whorton E513

Cooper, Kirk D. A880
Cooper, Kirk D. E412
Cooper, Kirstine W64
Cooper, Mark P110
Cooper, Matthew W. A198
Cooper, Nancy E. A182
Cooper, Nancy E. A715
Cooper, Nancy E. W46
Cooper, Nancy E. A45
Cooper, Nick W328
Cooper, Shantella E. A561
Cooper, Shantella E. A106
Cooper, Shantella E. A1086
Cooper, Shantella E. A471
Cooper, Simon W520
Cooper, Stephen F. A1106
Cooper, Stephen F. W374
Cooper, Steven C. A166
Cooper, Tod M. E337
Cooperman, Daniel A707
Coorigan, Micheal P201
Coosvp, Lisa Getzfrid P257
Cope, George A. W82
Copeland, David L. A421
Copeland, David L. E198
Copeland, John G. A190
Copeland, John G. E73
Copeland, Rex A. A488
Copeland, Roy Dallis E108
Copeland, Scott A125
Copeland, Scott E52
Copher, Ron J. A474
Copher, Ron J. E230
Coppey, Pierre W635
Corachan, Joaquin Folch-Rusinol W71
Coradi, Robert G. A788
Coradi, Robert G. E365
Corasanti, Joseph J. E266
Corbally, Kevin W63
Corban, Stephen M. A889
Corban, Stephen M. E414
Corbett, John C. A955
Corbett, John C. E456
Corbett, Ryan E334
Corbin, Patrick E. A106
Corbin, Patrick E. E40
Corbus, Barclay F. E368
Corby, Lindsay Y. A188
Corby, Lindsay Y. E71
Corcoles, Francisco Martinez W295
Corcoran, Thomas A. A613
Cordani, David M. A465
Cordani, David M. A239
Cordeiro, Eduardo E. A795
Cordero, Maribel Gomez P174
Cordes, Eckhard W641
Cordes, Rebecca H. A800
Cordes, Scott A. A235
Corio, Norma E190
Corker, Ricky W443
Corkrean, John J. E226
Corlett, Glenn E. E393
Corley, Christina M. A214
Corley, Donna M. A450
Corley, Elizabeth A713
Corley, Elizabeth W66
Cormack, Ian W423
Cormier, Rufus A397
Cormier, Rufus E187
Cornelius, James A1056

Cornelius, James E505
Cornell, Brian C. A1146
Cornell, Brian C. A996
Cornell, Helen W. E255
Cornelsen, James W. A1115
Cornelsen, James W. E533
Cornetta, Richard F. E92
Cornew, Kenneth W. A975
Cornhill, David W. W299
Cornil, Therese W213
Cornille, Douglas J. E57
Cornish, David L. A915
Cornish, Thomas M. A135
Cornog, William L. E66
Cornwell, W. Don A65
Cornwell, W. Don A1093
Coro, Ricardo S A620
Coronado, Julia L. A898
Corporate, Kiera Page P394
Corporate, Shane Thielman P489
Corradi, Enrico W73
Corrado, Richard Francis E11
Corrales, Edgard Aguilar A953
Correa, Alvaro W174
Correa, Christy E58
Correa, Marcelo Maia de Azevedo W383
Correnti, Salvatore E172
Corrigan, Garth E517
Corrigan, Scott W561
Corrsin, David J. E22
Corry, Carlos de la Isla W265
Corsini, Bryan M. A800
Corson, Bradley W. W299
Cortan, Ljiljana W306
Corte-Real, Ana Rita Pontífice Ferreira de Almeida W212
Cortes, Lydie W165
Corti, Robert J. A14
Cortina, Ignacio A. A789
Corum, Edward A392
Corum, Edward E183
Corvi, Carolyn A1062
Corvino, Frank A. E247
Coscia, Anthony R. A768
Coscia, Anthony R. E359
Cosentino, Anthony Van E428
Cosgel, Patricia A112
Cosgrove, William V. A575
Coslett, Jeffrey G. E506
Cosman, James M. A181
Coss, Stephen K. A948
Cosse, Steven A. A938
Cosse, Steven A. E442
Cosset, Yael A608
Cosset, Yael A611
Cossitt, Karen E58
Cosslett, Andrew W341
Costa, Donn C. E223
Costa, Francisco Manuel Seixas da W325
Costa, James M. A136
Costa, Maria Leticia de Freitas W382
Costa, Mark J. A354
Costa, Mark J. A567
Costa, Maurizio W391
Costa, Roland A401
Costalli, Sergio W627
Costamagna, Claudio E224
Costanzo, Brian J. A659
Costello, Beth A. A502

HOOVER'S HANDBOOK OF EMERGING COMPANIES 2023

COMBINED HOOVER'S HANDBOOK INDEX OF EXECUTIVES

A = AMERICAN BUSINESS
E = EMERGING COMPANIES
P = PRIVATE COMPANIES
W = WORLD BUSINESSS

Costello, Ellen M. A246
Costello, Joseph G P460
Costello, Richard A. E238
Costes, Yseulys W338
Costos, James E388
Cote, David M. A401
Cote, Diane W548
Cote, Jacynthe W507
Cote, Sonya W308
Cothran, Mark A. E454
Cotman, Cathrine E114
Cotnoir, Frederic W308
Cotoia, Michael E481
Cotter, Martin P. A81
Cottignoli, Lorenzo W627
Cotton, Alanna Y. A545
Cotton, Leonard W. E62
Cottrill, Scott A. E5
Couchara, Georgeann F. A315
Couchman, Glen A143
Couchman, Glen P69
Coughenou, Peter E9
Coughlin, Brendan A248
Coughlin, Christopher J. A216
Coughlin, Daniel E. A37
Coughlin, Daniel E. E14
Coughlin, Stephen A23
Coughlin, Thomas Michael A143
Coughlin, Thomas Michael E56
Coughlin, Zachary A864
Coull-Cicchini, Debbie W308
Coulombe, Stephen P88
Coulson, R. Cromwell E366
Coulter, James G. W362
Coulter, Linda M. W532
Coulter, Michael J. E364
Council, LaVerne H. A287
Counselman, Anna M. E513
Counts, Travis L. E101
Courage, Catherine A558
Courbe, Thomas W492
Coureil, Herve W524
Couret, Adrien W526
Courkamp, Julie A. E206
Court, David C. A180
Court, David C. W113
Court, David C. W122
Court, James John A120
Court, James John E48
Courter, James A. E229
Courtney, Christopher M. E357
Courtois, Jean-Philippe A655
Courtois, Jean-Philippe A701
Courtright, Wayne E510
Coury, Robert J. A1093
Cousin, Ertharin A710
Cousin, Ertharin W95
Cousins, Frank G. E401
Couto, Rodrigo Luis Rosa W314
Coutu, Francois J. W399
Coutu, Marcel R. W262
Coutu, Marcel R. W112
Coutu, Marcel R. W480
Coutu, Michel W399

Couvreur, Christophe E91
Covarrubias, Jonathan W73
Coventry, Elaine Bowers A266
Cover, Alexander L. A430
Covert, Harold L. E305
Covert, Stephanie E183
Covey, Michael J. E391
Covey, Patrick M. E135
Covey, Stephen M. R. E376
Covey, Susan A372
Covey, Susan E166
Coviello, Arthur W. A985
Covington, Alec C. E490
Cowan, Alister W573
Cowan, Carole A. A372
Cowan, Carole A. E167
Cowan, Douglas W. E418
Cowan, Joseph L. E92
Cowell, Charles A. A493
Cowell, Charles A. E243
Cowell, Janet R. E92
Cowen, Mark E223
Cowley, Samuel C. A558
Cox, Caroline W101
Cox, Carrie S. A201
Cox, Carrie S. A1010
Cox, Carrie S. A787
Cox, Chris A P30
Cox, Christopher K. A689
Cox, Colby P214
Cox, David L. E156
Cox, Heather A757
Cox, Jeremy K. A514
Cox, Josh C. E470
Cox, Julius A823
Cox, Julius A59
Cox, Justin G. A953
Cox, Justin G. E455
Cox, Melanie E418
Cox, Michael F. A747
Cox, Philip C. A984
Cox, Philip C. E476
Cox, Richard A468
Cox, Robert C. A659
Cox, Tony K. E452
Cox, William E. E307
Coxe, Tench A761
Coye, Molly J. E20
Coyle, Arlene A398
Coyle, Maurice A428
Coyles, Stephanie L. W572
Coyles, Stephanie L. W399
Coyne, Patrick A400
Coyne, Terrance E425
Cozad, John C. A592
Cozza, Patrick A. E219
Cozzone, Robert D. A554
Cozzone, Robert D. E268
Crabtree, Cary B. A401
Cracchiolo, James M. A70
Craft, Joseph W. A167
Craft, Joseph W. E64
Craig, Andronico Luksic W70
Craig, Benjamin D. E352
Craig, David P170
Craig, Gregory G. W121
Craig, Hunter E. E526
Craig, Mary A400
Craig, Pamela J A298
Craig, Pamela J A851

Craig, Pamela J A684
Craig, Pamela J A4
Craig, Sandra A1015
Craig, Sandra P571
Craighead, Martin S. A366
Craighead, Martin S. A1010
Craigie, James R. A735
Crain, Christopher M. E260
Crain, Elizabeth E330
Crain, Robert A. E487
Crain, Robert B. A26
Cramer, David E340
Cramm, Bettina W65
Crandall, J. Taylor A516
Crandall, Steven J. A1108
Crane-Oliver, Evelyn A898
Crane, Ann B. A545
Crane, Christopher A292
Crane, Jennifer Ray E131
Crane, Rosemary A. E83
Crane, Rosemary A. W598
Crane, Timothy S. A1133
Crane, Timothy S. E541
Cranston, Mary B. A1096
Cranston, Mary B. A224
Crapps, Michael C. E195
Crate, Darrell W. E150
Craven, Philip W616
Craver, Theodore F. A347
Craver, Theodore F. A1115
Crawford, Anne Frederick A393
Crawford, Anne Frederick E184
Crawford, Casey Stuart A642
Crawford, Casey Stuart E304
Crawford, Curtis J. A224
Crawford, Frederick John A24
Crawford, Gordon A52
Crawford, Gordon P30
Crawford, James C. A414
Crawford, James C. E191
Crawford, John P449
Crawford, Kermit R. A42
Crawford, Kermit R. A900
Crawford, Kermit R. A1096
Crawford, Linda M. E92
Crawford, Mark A381
Crawford, Matthew V. E127
Crawford, Michael J. A1115
Crawford, Michael J. E533
Crawford, Millar W600
Crawford, Nigel W209
Crawford, Peter B. A919
Crawford, Sally W. A522
Crawford, Sally W. E277
Crawford, Seth H. A26
Crawford, Stephen G. A354
Crawford, Victor L. A512
Creager, Robert E. E515
Creagh, Gerard A231
Credle, Eric P. A414
Credle, Eric P. E191
Cree, Brian J. E529
Creed, Greg A323
Creed, Greg A1129
Creed, Greg A92
Creedon, Michael C. A17
Creek, Phillip G. E306
Creekmore, John M. A889
Creekmore, John M. E414
Creel, Diane C. A20

Creel, Michael A. A1131
Creery, Thomas G. A521
Cregg, Daniel J. A858
Cregg, Roger A. A274
Cregg, Roger A. E463
Cremers, Eric J. E391
Cremin, Mary C A64
Cremin, Mary C P34
Crepin, Frederic W637
Crespi, Megan D. A274
Crespo, Frank J. E293
Cress, Michael E547
Cressey, Bryan C. A926
Creus, Jose Oliu W71
Creus, Josep Oliu W70
Creutzer, Annika W579
Creux, Antoine W548
Creuzot, Cheryl A1014
Creuzot, Cheryl E488
Crevoiserat, Joanne C. A993
Crew, Debra W201
Crew, Debra Ann A962
Crews, Terrell K. A94
Crews, Terrell K. A534
Crews, Terrell K. A1125
Crews, Terrell Kirk A436
Crews, Terrell Kirk A739
Cribb, Ashlee Townsend E391
Crilly, Sean E525
Crimmins, John D. A187
Crisci, Robert C. A904
Criser, Marshall M. A196
Criser, Marshall M. E79
Crisostomo, Michele W222
Crisp, Charles R. A376
Crisp, Charles R. A995
Crisp, Charles R. A561
Criss, Christopher V. A1115
Criss, Christopher V. E532
Crist, Gretchen R. E260
Crist, Peter D. A1133
Crist, Peter D. E541
Critelli, Lewis J. E354
Crites, John W. A981
Crites, John W. E469
Crittenden, Gary L. A845
Crittenden, Gary L. A1151
Crittenden, Gary L. E180
Crittenden, Gary L. E395
Croce, Michael J. A978
Croce, Michael J. E465
Crochet, Linda M. E279
Crocker, Charles E483
Crocker, Mary Jayne A175
Crocker, Mary Jayne E66
Crocker, Matthew R. W299
Crockett, John R. A841
Crockett, Kyle A207
Crockett, Steven B. A950
Crockett, Steven B. E454
Crofton, Meg G. A505
Crofts, Sharon M. A129
Croisetiere, Jacques M. A95
Croisset, Charles de W373
Cronin, Charles F. A499
Cronin, John J. E313
Cronin, Kathe P633
Cronin, Kathleen M. A599
Cronin, Patrick W82
Cronin, Patrick A. E96

COMBINED HOOVER'S HANDBOOK INDEX OF EXECUTIVES

A = AMERICAN BUSINESS
E = EMERGING COMPANIES
P = PRIVATE COMPANIES
W = WORLD BUSINESSS

Cronkhite, Tina E455
Crooker, William R. E461
Crooks, James M. E156
Croom, Jana T. E287
Cropper, Spencer S. E293
Cropper, Stephen L. A741
Cros, Christophe W565
Cros, Pierre-Yves W123
Crosbie, Debbie W618
Crosby, Gary M. A602
Crosby, Michael J. A1136
Crosby, Ralph D. A59
Crosby, Ralph D. W24
Crosby, William D. E492
Crosen, Kaley P. E149
Croson, Rachel P656
Cross, Anna W90
Cross, Christine W161
Cross, James W. A395
Cross, James W. E185
Cross, Jeffrey D P33
Cross, Maegan A.R. E393
Cross, Patricia W64
Cross, Susan Lee A1079
Crossen, Laura A148
Crosswhite, Mark A. A952
Crosswhite, Mark A. A32
Crosswhite, Mark A. A885
Crosthwaite, Perry K.O. W311
Croteau, Lise W613
Crotwell, Jim A788
Crotwell, Jim E364
Crouse, Steven E. E336
Crouzet, Philippe W215
Crowder, Andy A1014
Crowder, Andy P570
Crowder, Heather A319
Crowell, Kimberly A196
Crowell, Kimberly E79
Crowley, Andrew G. A659
Crowley, Robert T. E537
Crown, James S. A591
Crown, James S. A460
Crown, Susan A553
Crown, Susan A748
Crown, Timothy A. A558
Crowther, Bruce K. A1133
Crowther, Bruce K. E541
Crowther, Chip P79
Crowther, Elizabeth Hinton E62
Crudele, Anthony F. E254
Cruden, James David Ramsay W383
Cruger, William F. A651
Cruger, William F. A814
Cruger, William F. E311
Cruger, William F. E379
Cruger, William F. E527
Crum, Scott A. E335
Crumbaugh, Stuart P. E509
Crumbaugh, Stuart P. E510
Crumbaugh, Stuart P. E509
Crump-Caine, Lynn E539
Crusinberry, Dawn P. E90
Crutchfield, Lisa A454

Crutchfield, Lisa A1097
Cruz, Dimitri J P215
Cruz, Rosemarie B. W85
Csanyi, Sandor W412
Csiszar, Ernst N. A668
Cuambe, Manual J. W518
Cubbage, Leighton M. E454
Cubbin, Robert S. A545
Cubbon, M. W580
Cucchiani, Enrico Tommaso W473
Cudjoe, Bindu W122
Cueni, Othmar W91
Cueva, Adrian G. Sada W265
Cuevas, Diego Gaxiola W265
Cuffe, Michael S. A505
Cui, David W636
Cui, Shanshan W67
Culang, Howard B. A874
Culbreth, H. Gilbert A923
Culbreth, H. Gilbert E433
Culbreth, Michael Scott E27
Culhaci, Hayri W26
Culhaci, Hayri W267
Culham, Harry W119
Cullen, Rachel P. E260
Cullen, Susan K. A439
Cullen, Thomas A. A333
Culmer, George W504
Culmer, George W64
Culp, H. Lawrence A462
Culp, H. Lawrence A458
Culver, Chester J. A395
Culver, Chester J. E186
Culver, Curt S. A694
Culver, Curt S. A1114
Culver, John W. A604
Cuminale, James W. E388
Cumming, Christine M. A248
Cummings, Earl M. A218
Cummings, Earl M. A494
Cummings, John A1008
Cummings, Kevin A248
Cummings, Kevin A396
Cummings, Kevin A575
Cummings, Kevin E187
Cummings, Robert F. A298
Cummins, Hugh S. (Beau) A1042
Cummins, Jessica T. E433
Cummins, John J. W8
Cuneo, Andrew A1093
Cunha, Maria da W509
Cunha, Paulo Roberto Simoes da W69
Cunillera, Jose Permanyer W71
Cuningham, David P543
Cunningham, Daniel N. E90
Cunningham, Danny L. A1114
Cunningham, Diane M. E156
Cunningham, Jeffrey L. A200
Cunningham, Jeffrey L. E79
Cunningham, Jessica A696
Cunningham, John H. E15
Cunningham, Kathleen J. E410
Cunningham, Peter W500
Cunningham, Peter W499
Cunningham, Rebecca A883
Cunningham, Rebecca P459
Cunningham, Rose E38
Cunningham, Sondra A493
Cunningham, Sondra E243
Cunningham, Stacey A561

Cunningham, Steven E. E162
Cunningham, Susan M. W218
Cunningham, T. Jefferson A651
Cunningham, William H. A638
Cunningham, William H. A956
Cunnington, Kathleen K. W31
Cuny, Olivier W61
Curadeau-Grou, Patricia W420
Curado, Frederico Fleury W7
Curado, Frederico Pinheiro Fleury W622
Curatolo, Tom A528
Curci, Brian E. A757
Curet, Myriam J. A572
Curia, Christopher R. A982
Curia, Christopher R. E514
Curl, Gregory Lynn A838
Curl, Gregory Lynn W156
Curl, Molly A493
Curl, Molly E243
Curley, Kevin M. A1043
Curnow, Randy P345
Curran, Kathleen Chase E400
Curran, Laura P173
Curran, Mary Allis A124
Curran, Mary Allis E271
Curran, Teresa M. A402
Currarino, Giancarlo A764
Currault, Douglas N. A452
Currey, Robert J. E116
Currey, Russell M. A1125
Currie, Alistair W90
Currie, Gordon A. M. W646
Currie, Mark G. E282
Currie, William G. A1053
Currier, Rand P245
Curry, Ken P381
Curtin, Terrence R. A349
Curtin, Terrence R. W590
Curtis, Craig A. E204
Curtis, Roger A294
Curtis, Ross A. W491
Curtis, Scott A. A876
Cusack, Amy A927
Cusack, Amy E435
Cushing, Brenda J. A60
Cushing, Robert B. A17
Custer, J. Michael A1111
Cusumano, Gary M. E444
Cusumano, Michael W460
Cutifani, Mark W613
Cutifani, Mark W39
Cutillo, Joseph A. E463
Cutler, Alexander M. A602
Cutler, Alexander M. A349
Cutlip, Robert G. E232
Cutrer, Andrew B. A880
Cutrer, Andrew B. E412
Cutrignelli, Raffaele W220
Cuyper, Vincent De W554
Czajka, Edward J. A843
Czajka, Edward J. E392
Czerwinski, Frank A271
Czerwinski, Frank E110
Czeschin, Frank N. E206
Czichowski, Frank W162

D

D'agosta, Jeffrey P375
D'Agostino, James Samuel A788
D'Agostino, James Samuel E364
D'Agostino, Robert E50
D'Agostino, Thomas P. A438
D'Alimonte, Christa A. A802
D'Amarzit, Delphine W200
D'Amato, Alfonse M. A936
D'Amato, Alfonse M. E441
D'Ambrosio, Alexandre Silva W630
D'Amelio, Frank A. A1153
D'Amelio, Frank A. A514
D'Amelio, Frank A. A541
d'Amico, Cesare W482
D'Amico, Lance E. A79
D'Amours, Jacques W31
D'Angelo, John J. E279
d'Estaing, Henri Giscard W489
d'Estaing, Henri Giscard W127
D'Iorio, Steven J. A439
d'iribarne, Benoit W165
D'Amico, Andrew E525
D'Aniello, Daniel A. A203
d'Apice, Leon Royden Thomas E153
d'Eeckenbrugge, Herve Coppens W554
d'Este, Lorenz W565
D'Haene, Shelley L. E98
D'Souza, Francisco A462
Dabarno, Susan F. W382
Daberkow, Mario W198
Dabiri, John O. A761
Daboud, Juan Jose A825
DaBramo, James E301
Dacey, John R. W580
Dachbash, Eilon W79
Dacus, Shannon A954
Dacus, Stephen Hayes W528
Dada, Uzair A120
Dada, Uzair E48
Daddario, Nick E234
Dadlani, Sunil P50
Dadyburjor, Khush W646
Daehnke, Arno W559
Daffan, Nick E520
Dagach, Fernando Aguad W314
Daggett, Seth C. E349
Dahan, Rene W493
Dahl, Amy E. E491
Dahlberg, Annika W548
Dahlberg, Gregory R. A625
Dahlberg, Kenneth C. E483
Dahlin, P. Andrew W133
Dahlmann, David S. A418
Dahlmann, David S. E195
Dahlvig, Anders W277
Dahnke, Scott Arnold A1132
Dahut, Karen M. A171
Dahut, Karen M. E138
Dahya, Hanif W. (Wally) A732
Dai, Deming W477
Dai, Deming W268
Dai, Houliang W466
Dai, Kazuhiko W582
Dai, Trudy Shan W29
Dai, Weili E33
Dai, Yiyi W656
Dai, Yiyi W655

HOOVER'S HANDBOOK OF EMERGING COMPANIES 2023

COMBINED HOOVER'S HANDBOOK INDEX OF EXECUTIVES

```
A = AMERICAN BUSINESS
E = EMERGING COMPANIES
P = PRIVATE COMPANIES
W = WORLD BUSINESSS
```

Dailey, Grace E. A246
Dailey, Jeffrey J. E520
Daimler, Matt A1149
Daingerfield, Richard A810
Daingerfield, Richard E376
Daitch, Peggy A976
Dake, Gary C. A98
Dake, Gary C. E36
Dalbies, Eric W511
Dale, Albert J. A889
Dale, Albert J. E414
Dale, Andrew R. E104
Dale, Christopher P670
Dale, Jason E529
Dalen, Laila S. W562
Daley, Clayton C. E443
Daley, Michael John A301
Daley, Michael John E131
Daley, Pamela A160
Daley, Pamela W109
Dalibard, Barbara W168
Dallara, Que Thanh A530
Dallas, David D. E510
Dallas, H. James A602
Dallas, H. James A216
Dallas, H. James E467
Dallas, Kevin E16
Dallas, Robert H. E510
Dallenbach, Wally E19
Dalton, Daniel J. E371
Dalton, James C. E497
Dalton, John Merritt A581
Dalton, John W. E437
Dalton, Joshua R. A401
Dalton, Michael C. E164
Dalton, Travis A221
Dalum, Thomas E. E532
Daly, Fiona W85
Daly, James M. E244
Daly, Jay E127
Daly, Mary C. A402
Daly, Michelle Lynn A721
Dalzell, Richard (Rick) L. A571
Dam, Anders W330
Damas, Philippe G.J.E.O. W603
Dames, Brian A. W426
Damholt, Sandra A397
Damholt, Sandra E187
Damiano, Harold L. A1099
Damico, Jennifer B. A821
Damico, Lance P670
Damme, Alexandre Van W40
Damme, Niek Jan van W596
Damon, Donna J. E537
Dan, Michael T. A846
Dana, Pamella J. A52
Dandridge, Nicole A653
Daneau, Guy W294
Danella, Kate R. A885
Danforth, David J. A796
Dang, Kimberly Allen A605
Dangeard, Frank E. W425
Danhakl, John G. A576
Daniel, Kareem A675

Daniel, Karen L. A276
Daniel, Matthew L. E94
Daniel, Patrick D. W119
Daniel, William C P479
Daniel, Yolanda E297
Daniele, Philip B. A111
Daniell, Mark Haynes W456
Daniell, Richard W598
Daniels, C. Bryan A410
Daniels, James Todd A24
Daniels, Jennifer M. A291
Daniels, Jennifer M. A269
Daniels, Kenneth L. A1065
Daniels, Kenneth L. E509
Daniels, Lee A. E164
Daniels, Michael A. A189
Daniels, Michael E. A741
Daniels, Michael E. E349
Daniels, Michael E. W327
Daniels, Mitchell E. A747
Daniels, Mitchell E. A221
Daniels, Richard A984
Daniels, Richard E476
Daniels, Robert P. A376
Daniels, Vincent C P498
Danielsson, Anders W548
Danielsson, Lars-Erik W579
Dankel, Roger E444
Danker, Timothy Robert E435
Dannenfeldt, Thomas W443
Dannenfeldt, Thomas W129
Dannes, Matthias W192
Danon, Jacob W410
Dant, Joe P210
Dantas, Joao Marcello Leite W69
Danusasmita, Johnny D. W464
Daochai, Predee W334
Darby, Jason E19
Darby, Jeffrey L. E145
Darby, Kristin H. A397
Darcy, Stathy A258
Darden, J. Matthew A478
Dardis, David A384
Dardis, David A292
Dargusch, Jonathan D. A1115
Dargusch, Jonathan D. E533
Darko, Alex B. W8
Darling, Alistair M. A713
Darling, Richard W. A393
Darling, Scott E513
Darmaillac, Marie-Annick W492
Darmon, Marc W600
Darnall, Matthew S. A776
Darrah, Ryan D. E215
Darrell, Bracken P. A645
Darrow, Kurt L. A256
Darrow, Kurt L. A294
Dartt, William E81
Daruvala, Toos N. A781
Daruvala, Toos N. W507
Das, Maarten W274
Dascupta, Anindya W297
Dassault, Laurent W637
Dassen, Roger J. M. W52
Dasso, Raimundo Morales W174
Dastoor, Michael (Meheryar) K. A578
Datar, Srikant M. A981
Datar, Srikant M. A992
Date, Rajeev V. E239
Datesh, LuAnn E172

Datta, Sanjay E513
Dattilo, Thomas A. A613
Dauby, D. Neil A472
Dauby, D. Neil E230
Dauch, David C. A57
Daudin, Herve W127
Daulton, Howard A381
Daun, Claas W562
Daurella, Alfonso Libano W161
Daurella, Sol W161
Davaisher, Len D. A704
Davaisher, Len D. E328
davalos, Juan G. Mijares W266
Davanzo, Lawrence E525
DaVella, Ronald V. E285
Davenport, Bonnie A196
Davenport, Bonnie E79
Davenport, Darcy Horn E57
Davenport, Fred B. E317
Davenport, J. Mays A852
Davenport, J. Mays E399
Davenport, Leah A399
Davenport, Michael S. A681
Davenport, Michael S. E318
Daves, Lora Lee A953
Daves, Lora Lee E455
Daveu, Marie-Claire W338
Daveu, Marie-Claire W174
Davey, Bradley W49
David, Francois W495
David, Glenn C. A1153
David, Laurent W490
David, O'Mahony W229
David, Shukri W. E298
David, Stephen N. A261
Davidar, David D. E233
Davidson, Carol A. (John) W590
Davidson, Carol Anthony A567
Davidson, Charles D. A645
Davidson, Janet G. A23
Davidson, Janine A. A1056
Davidson, Janine A. E505
Davidson, Martin N. E169
Davidson, Richard H. A396
Davidson, Richard H. E186
Davidson, Wendy P. A424
Davidson, Wendy P. E200
Davies, Cathy E517
Davies, Christa W44
Davies, Howard W425
Davies, Howard W423
Davies, John B. A152
Davies, Mark W500
Davies, Pamela Lewis A950
Davies, Philip D. E525
Davies, Stuart Jeffrey W360
Davies, Todd E. A320
Davies, William A70
Davila, Alejandro Santo Domingo W40
Davila, Marco A. A796
Davis, Alicia Boler A591
Davis, Alicia J. A1073
Davis, Alison A434
Davis, Alison A984
Davis, Alison E476
Davis, Annette E517
Davis, Brian E471
Davis, Brian P210
Davis, Brian C. A657
Davis, Brian S. A524

Davis, Brian S. E258
Davis, C. William A419
Davis, Charles A. A851
Davis, Chris W159
Davis, Christopher C. A151
Davis, Christopher C. A264
Davis, Clarence A. A1001
Davis, Claude E. A420
Davis, Claude E. E197
Davis, Crispin H. W638
Davis, Cynthia L. E137
Davis, D. Scott A530
Davis, D. Scott A585
Davis, Darrell L. W31
Davis, Dave E471
Davis, Debbie P464
Davis, Deborah E455
Davis, Douglas E91
Davis, Erika T. A794
Davis, Erika T. A818
Davis, G. Eric E61
Davis, Glenn E19
Davis, Greg W162
Davis, Gregory C. E273
Davis, Gregory C. E437
Davis, Gregory L. A945
Davis, Gregory L. E451
Davis, Ian E. L. A585
Davis, Ian E. L. W504
Davis, J. Morgan A1033
Davis, J. Morgan E492
Davis, James E. A870
Davis, James G. E27
Davis, Jane Ann A207
Davis, Jeffrey A. A615
Davis, Jeffrey L. A280
Davis, Jeffrey L. E113
Davis, Jennifer W. A1138
Davis, Jennifer W. E544
Davis, John A. A200
Davis, John A. E79
Davis, John R. E301
Davis, Julia K. E23
Davis, Karen B. A809
Davis, Kelly A397
Davis, Kelly E187
Davis, Kern Michael A1066
Davis, Leigh A32
Davis, Leslie A1080
Davis, Leslie P667
Davis, Lisa A. A30
Davis, Lisa A. A812
Davis, Lisa A. A826
Davis, Lorna W4
Davis, Lynn D. A741
Davis, Lynn D. E349
Davis, Martin B. A955
Davis, Martin B. E456
Davis, Mike H. W426
Davis, Morris A. A28
Davis, Noopur A885
Davis, Paul E. E546
Davis, R. Matt A47
Davis, Reed P90
Davis, Reginald E. A638
Davis, Richard W462
Davis, Richard K. A1115
Davis, Richard K. A670
Davis, Richard K. A342
Davis, Richard L. A1040

COMBINED HOOVER'S HANDBOOK INDEX OF EXECUTIVES

A = AMERICAN BUSINESS
E = EMERGING COMPANIES
P = PRIVATE COMPANIES
W = WORLD BUSINESSS

Davis, Richard L. E499
Davis, Robert E81
Davis, Robert P179
Davis, Robert M. A684
Davis, Robert M. A347
Davis, Robert T. E278
Davis, Rocco E56
Davis, Sarah Ruth A1094
Davis, Scott Trevor W555
Davis, Scott Trevor W110
Davis, Seth A. A896
Davis, Seth A. E422
Davis, Sharon L. A844
Davis, Sharon L. E394
Davis, Smith W. A663
Davis, Steven A. A840
Davis, Steven A. A35
Davis, Stuart W84
Davis, Suni A954
Davis, Timothy Paul A809
Davis, Victor F. E428
Davis, Waters S. A995
Davis, Wilbur R. A753
Davis, William W. E354
Davis, Zach A226
Davis, Zach A225
Davison, James E. A788
Davison, James E. E364
Davisson, Katherine A926
Dawes, Karen A. E415
Dawidowsky, Tim W544
Dawson, Dame Sandra W618
Dawson, G. Steven E105
Dawson, G. Steven E315
Dawson, Jonathan W422
Dawson, Leah K. A1144
Dawson, Pat D. A776
Dawson, Robert D. E420
Dawson, Samuel G. A305
Dawson, Teresa M. A797
Dawson, Teresa M. E368
Dawson, William F. A818
Day, C. Sean E115
Day, Christine M. A608
Day, Cynthia N. A845
Day, Cynthia N. E395
Day, Edwin P176
Day, John S. A574
Day, Joseph E. E136
Day, Ricky D. A188
Day, Ricky D. E69
Day, Twila A547
Dayton, Matt E338
Dea, Joan T. A919
Dea, Peter A. A792
Dea, Peter A. E33
Deacon, Jennifer L. E227
Deacon, Mary Ann A616
Deacon, Mary Ann E289
Deadman, Davis R. A1040
Deadman, Davis R. E499
Deakin, Scott M. E234
Deal, Clifford M. A266
Deal, Stanley (Stan) A. A164

Dealy, Richard P. A830
Dean, Brian K. E408
Dean, Lia A198
Dean, Lloyd H. A675
Dean, Martha A. A352
Dean, Mensel D. E62
Dean, Robert E. A722
Dean, Robert E. E339
Deane, Timothy M. A90
Deardorff, Kevin G. E30
Dearing, Karen J. E471
Dearing, Karen J. E9
Deason, Jennifer A287
Deason, Jennifer E313
Deaton, Chadwick C. A656
Deaupre, Paul P242
Debackere, Koenraad W336
Debackere, Koenraad W623
Debbink, Dirk J. A240
DeBeer, Anne M. A399
Debel, Marlene A876
DeBenedictis, Nicholas E174
DeBernardo, Angelo E428
Debertin, Jay D. A235
DeBiase, Christine M. A176
DeBiase, Francesca A. A675
DeBoer, Bryan B. A639
DeBoer, Scott J. A700
DeBoer, Sidney B. A639
Debon, Marie-Ange W565
DeBord, Matthew E490
Debow, Daniel W371
Debowey, Donna Dean E421
Debroux, Laurence W235
Dec, Timothy C. E474
Dechant, Johann W303
Decherd, Robert W. A604
Decious, Kendra E288
Deck, Philip W80
Deckard, Jennifer D. A907
Deckelman, William L. A349
Decker, Charlotte C. E404
Decker, Edward P. A526
Decker, Mark O. E19
Decker, Sharon Allred A266
Decker, Susan L. A151
Decker, Susan L. A300
Decker, Suzanne M. E285
Decker, W Cody P646
Decoene, Ulrike W65
DeCola, Michael A. A373
DeCola, Michael A. E168
Decolli, Debbie A251
Decolli, Debbie P137
DeCosmo, James M. E391
Decoudreaux, Alecia A. A311
DeCrona, Bruce E. A381
Dedi, Liren W466
Dedrick, Tracey A. A976
Dedullen, Xavier W228
Dee, Ann Colussi A425
Dee, Ann Colussi E146
Dee, Ann Colussi E201
Deely, Brendan J. E293
Deer, Aaron J. A270
Deer, Aaron J. E109
Deer, Jill V. A889
Deer, Jill V. E414
Deere, Joshua P30
Deering, Christopher J. E134

Deering, Michael P319
Dees, Kimberly A110
Dees, Larry E62
Deese, Willie A. A858
Deevy, Brian M. A633
Deevy, Brian M. A633
DeFazio, Gary A147
DeFazio, Mark R. A691
DeFazio, Mark R. E323
DeFerie, Suzanne S. A414
DeFerie, Suzanne S. E191
Deffenbaugh, Danny P516
Deflesselle, Raphaelle W107
DeFrancesco, Salvatore R. E190
DeFranco, James A333
DeFrie, Douglas L. A398
Defurio, Anthony A1015
Defurio, Anthony P571
DeGenova, Cathleen A116
DeGiorgio, Kenneth D. A413
Degnan, Steven Scott E540
DeGrazio, Marygrace A738
DeHaas, Deborah L. A342
Dehaze, Alain W13
Dehecq, Jean-François W22
Dehelly, Charles W61
Dehl, Jaspreet A180
Dehl, Jaspreet W113
Dehne, Tanuja M. A485
Dehner, Torsten R.W. A26
Dehring, Timothy A P399
Deibel, Jeffrey B. A401
Deible, Henry H. E156
Deighton, Paul A162
Deily, Karl R. A924
Deines, Matthew P. E204
Deitrich, Thomas L. A780
Deiure, Giovannella E297
Dejaco, Lynn P253
Dejakaisaya, Voranuch W79
Dekker, Christopher F. A182
Dekker, Wout W489
Dekle, Christopher P219
Dekura, Kazuhito W185
Delabriere, Yann W123
Delabriere, Yann W238
Delage, Jacinthe W225
Delaney, Christopher R. A483
Delaney, Emma W109
Delaney, Eugene A. A914
Delaney, Mark E. A870
Delaney, Martin J. E144
Delaney, Timothy E. A724
DeLaney, William J. (Bill) A1061
DeLaney, William J. (Bill) A239
DeLawder, C. Daniel A803
DeLawder, C. Daniel E371
Delbos, Clotilde W492
Delbos, Clotilde W65
DeLeo, James A. E401
DeLeon, Rudy F. A460
Delfassy, Gilles A780
DelFrari, Rhona M. W133
Delgadillo, Joe P401
Delgado-Moreira, Juan E244
Delgado, Agustin A112
Delgado, Luz Maria Zarza W470
DelGhiaccio, Brian M. A892
Delhaye, Catherine W631
Deli, Efthymia P. W231

Delie, Vincent J. A441
Delie, Vincent J. E211
Delinsky, Jeremy E408
DeLio, Anthony P. A557
Delk, Christopher P. A288
Dell, Michael S. A1098
Dell, Michael S. A322
Dell'Amore, Christopher A226
Dell'Osso, Domenic J. A227
Dellaquila, Frank J. A888
Dellaquila, Frank J. A366
Dellaquila, Frank J. W46
Dellenback, Steve P516
DelliBovi, Alfred A. A439
Dellomo, Donna L. E305
Delly, Gayla J. A180
Delmas, Bernard W441
Delmoro, Scott R. A319
DeLoach, LaNell E62
Delong, Angela E189
DeLongchamps, Peter C. A491
DelOrefice, Christopher J. A147
DeLorenzo, Jessica L. E287
Delorme, Marie Y. W122
Delorme, Philippe W524
Delozier, Jason R. E268
Delpit, Bernard W492
Delport, Dominique W637
DelSanto, Anne T. E6
Deltenre, Ingrid W198
Deltort, Didier A1150
DeLucca, Joyce E173
Demaille, Frank W225
DeMaio, Donnalee A. A973
DeMarco, David S. A98
DeMarco, David S. E36
Demarco, Nick A251
Demarco, Nick P137
DeMare, James P. A128
Demare, Michel W638
Demare, Michel W57
DeMark, Eugene F. E1
Demartini, Richard M. E525
Demas, David J. A1039
Demas, David J. E498
Demchak, William S. A834
Demchenkov, Peter W655
Demchyk, Matthew E227
DeMedici, Thomas D. A596
DeMedici, Thomas D. E286
Demere, Robert H. A955
Demere, Robert H. E456
Demers, John C. A164
Demetriou, Steven J. A432
Demetriou, Steven J. A580
Deming, Claiborne P. A719
Demir, Feray W619
Demirag, Levent W267
Demiray, Aykut W26
Demmerle, Stefan A173
Demmings, Keith W. A103
Demott, Andrew D. E473
Demou, George S. E500
Dempsey, B. Todd E227
Dempsey, June P360
Dempsey, Michael P. A125
Dempsey, Michael P. E52
Dempsey, Patrick J. A760
Demsey, John D. A620
Demski, David M. E233

COMBINED HOOVER'S HANDBOOK INDEX OF EXECUTIVES

A = AMERICAN BUSINESS
E = EMERGING COMPANIES
P = PRIVATE COMPANIES
W = WORLD BUSINESSS

Demyashkevich, Svetlana W655
Denault, Leo P. A546
Denby, Nigel Christopher William W36
Dench, Robert G. W159
Denecour, Jessica L. A823
Denekas, Craig N. A192
Denenno, Leanne E61
Deng, Feng W431
Deng, Huangjun W172
Deng, Jianjun W272
Deng, Qidong W656
Deng, Weidong W141
Deng, Wenqiang W141
Deng, Xiaobo W263
Deng, Yinqi W140
Deng, Yunhua W158
Deng, Zhuming W663
Denham, Robert Edwin W244
Denholm, Robyn M. A1007
Denien, Mark A. E146
Deninger, Paul F. A893
DeNinno, David L. A1099
Denis, Jean-Pierre W338
Denison, David F. W99
Denison, David F. W507
Denison, John G. A956
Denker, Bud A812
Denman, Julia A254
Denman, Kenneth D. A716
Denman, Kenneth D. A300
Denman, Kenneth D. A1098
Dennen, Richard S. A420
Dennen, Richard S. E197
Denner, Alexander J. A158
Denner, Alexander J. E282
Dennis, Robert J. A505
Dennis, Stephen A. A510
Dennis, Stephen A. E252
Dennis, Thomas St. E47
Dennis, Thomas St. E214
Dennison, Ann M. A721
Dennison, Michael C. E218
Denny, Mike B. A421
Denny, Mike B. E198
Denny, Steven A. E210
Denomme, Yves W358
DeNooyer, Mary Beth A600
Denton, David M. A993
Denton, Todd A319
DeNunzio, Tony W179
Denzel, Nora M. A18
Denzel, Nora M. W228
DePaola, Rinaldo A. E99
Depaolo, Joseph J. A936
Depaolo, Joseph J. E440
DeParle, Nancy-Ann M. A505
DeParle, Nancy-Ann M. A311
DePasquale, Gregory R. E120
Depickere, Franky W336
Depies, Lori P231
DePinto, Joseph Michael W527
Depler, Thomas A. A251
Depler, Thomas A. E100
Deppe, Michael J. A870

DePree, Alexis A745
DePrey, Mary P. A918
Derbyshire, Mark E. W122
Dere, Willard H. E61
Derella, Matthew A1047
Derendinger, Peter W86
DeReu, William R. E391
Dergunova, Olga Konstantinovna W617
Deriso, Walter M. A106
DeRito, John A. A249
DeRito, John A. E99
Derksen, Brian L. A783
Derksen, Henk E523
Derman, Emre W26
DeRose, Kathleen Traynor A1099
DeRose, Nathaniel D. E171
Derraik, Renato A642
Derraik, Renato E304
Derrey, Herve W600
Derrick, Robert W. A988
Derrick, Robert W. E479
Derry, Lucas E61
Derryberry, Jim H. E169
Dersch, David E81
DeRuiter, Kathie A. A532
DeRuiter, Kathie A. E259
Derville, Vianney W358
Dery, William H. E189
Desai, Chirantan A1148
Desai, Chirantan A931
Desai, Jayshree S. A868
Desai, Jigisha A1046
Desai, Mihir A. A152
Desai, Sonali P569
DeSanctis, Ellen R. A832
DeSanctis, Ellen R. A288
DeSanctis, Ellen R. A833
DeSantis, Bob A572
DeSantis, Damon E88
Descalzi, Claudio W227
Deschamps, Ignacio W84
Deschamps, Isabelle W500
Deschamps, Yvan W358
Deschene, Normand E. A372
Deschene, Normand E. E167
Descheneaux, Michael A984
Descheneaux, Michael E476
DeShon, Larry Dean A1071
Desjacques, Yves W127
Desjardins, Kristi L. W299
Desjardins, Luc W119
Desjarlais, Roger P171
Deskus, Archana A267
Deskus, Archana A351
Deskus, Archana E150
Deslarzes, Jean-Christophe W13
Desmarais, Andre W479
Desmarais, Andre W263
Desmarais, Michael E123
Desmarais, Olivier W480
Desmarais, Paul W479
Desmarais, Paul W263
Desmond-Hellmann, Susan D. A821
Desmond, Bevin E333
Desmond, John J. A430
Desmond, Laura B. A15
Desmond, Michael J. A519
Desmond, Michael J. E256
Desoer, Barbara J. A246

Desoer, Barbara J. A318
DeSoto, Matthew G. A702
DeSoto, Matthew G. E326
deSouza, Francis A. A335
Desrochers, Mark R. A531
Desroches, Jeff A158
Desroches, Pascal A105
DeStefano, Allison M. E168
DeStefano, Lisa E400
Destrebohn, Karine W27
Desvaux, Georges W65
Deterding, Kelly L. A950
Deterding, Kelly L. E454
Dethlefs, Sven W598
Deuel, Jeffrey J. A510
Deuel, Jeffrey J. E252
Deun, Jona M. Van A727
Deun, Jona M. Van E345
Deursen, Holly A. Van E287
Deutsch, Esther W311
Deutsch, Todd E173
Deutschman, Robert M. E141
DeVane, Sam A200
DeVane, Sam E79
Devanny, Earl H. A276
Devanny, Earl H. E436
DeVard, Jerri L. A342
DeVard, Jerri L. A1059
deVeer, R. Kipp E34
Deveydt, Wayne S. A216
Devgan, Anirudh E75
Devgun, Shaleen A918
deVilliers, David H. E222
DeVincenzi, Robert T. E292
Devine, Caroline Maury A288
Devine, Caroline Maury W631
Devine, Cynthia J. W507
Devine, Cynthia J. W216
Devine, David Moore A270
Devine, David Moore E109
Devine, Denise L. A454
Devine, Denise L. E436
Devine, Michael F. E209
Devine, Michael F. E137
Devine, Michael P. A328
Devita, Betty K. A836
DeVito, Michael J. A450
Devlin, Michael D. A768
Devlin, Michael D. E311
Devlin, Michael D. E359
Devlin, William R. E349
DeVolder, Steven M. E96
DeVore, Kim R. A398
DeVore, Susan D. A85
DeVore, Susan D. A1079
DeVrie, Jamess David A10
DeVries, James D. A16
Dew, David W520
Dew, Jimmy A. A773
DeWalt, David G. A323
Dewan, Feroz A315
Dewbrey, Diane L. A671
Dewey, Duane A. A1044
Dewhurst, E. H. "Gene" A1039
Dewhurst, E. H. "Gene" E498
Dewitt, Daniel J. A1001
Dexter, Robert P. W99
Dexter, Tracey A923
Dexter, Tracey E433
Dezellem, Janet E57

Dhanda, Anuj A35
Dhandapani, Chandra A213
Dhanidina, Halim A407
Dhar, Abhinav E493
Dhawan, Neelam W296
Dhawan, Sumit A1098
Dheer, Sanjeev A845
Dheer, Sanjeev E395
Dhore, Prasanna G. A367
Dial, Christopher B. E536
Dial, Debra L. A342
Diamond, Lawrence J. E15
Diamond, Margae P487
Diamond, Michael E. E328
Diamond, Robert P295
Diamond, Susan M. A541
Diamonte, Robin E333
Diana, Edward A P174
Diao, H. C. Charles E242
Diao, H. C. Charles E501
Dias, Anne A447
Dias, Fiona P. A871
Dias, Fiona P. A878
Dias, Fiona P. A879
Diaz, Abigail (Abby) E502
Diaz, Deborah B. A845
Diaz, Deborah B. E395
Diaz, Diana P. E437
Diaz, Fred M. A1085
Diaz, Fred M. E445
Diaz, Jorge E P604
Diaz, Lewis A397
Diaz, Manuel Bartlett W470
Diaz, Maria Angeles Alcala W295
Diaz, Paul J. A318
Dibadj, Ali A989
Dibblee, Jennifer W294
DiBella, John Anthony E444
DiBenedetto, Joseph A860
Dibkey, Brett A. A182
DiCamillo, Gary T. A1129
Dicciani, Nance K. W374
DiChiaro, Steven J. A478
Dichter, Harold B. A92
Dick, Jeff W. E307
Dick, Michael W61
Dick, Roger L. E515
Dick, Teresa L. E409
Dickens, Marty G. A829
Dickens, Marty G. E385
Dickenson, James P285
Dicker, Karl E79
Dickerman, Jeffrey F. A386
Dickerson, Gary E. A90
Dickerson, Marshall H. A889
Dickerson, Marshall H. E414
Dickerson, Mary C. A874
Dickerson, Mike A1026
Dickerson, Mike P620
Dickins, Denise E. A1111
Dickins, Denise E. E357
Dickinson, Alan W371
Dickinson, Alan W371
Dickinson, Andrew D. A473
Dickinson, Daniel M. A210
Dickinson, Joan E. A702
Dickinson, Joan E. E326
Dickler, Louis A1106
Dickson, James M. W216
Dickson, John J. E104

COMBINED HOOVER'S HANDBOOK INDEX OF EXECUTIVES

A = AMERICAN BUSINESS
E = EMERGING COMPANIES
P = PRIVATE COMPANIES
W = WORLD BUSINESSS

Dickson, Julie E. W382
Dickson, Kristine A231
Dickson, R. Andrew A160
Dickson, Rebecca T P167
Dickson, Richard A1019
Dickson, Thomas W. A338
Dickson, Ward H. A54
Dicus, John B. A199
DiDomenico, Vincent A143
DiDomenico, Vincent E57
DiDonato, Thomas A. A622
Diefenthaler, Aaron P. A896
Diefenthaler, Aaron P. E422
Dieffenbacher, Timothy D. E67
Diehl, Jeffrey T. E374
Diehl, Scott R. A498
Diehm, Russell C P90
Diekmann, Michael W251
Diekmann, Michael W543
Diekmann, Michael W33
Diercksen, John W. A836
Dierker, David F. A815
Dierker, Richard A. A237
Diesel, R Wayne A974
Diesel, R Wayne P539
Diess, Herbert W640
Diethelm, Markus U. W621
Diether, Tatjana W93
Dietiker, Ueli W580
Dietiker, Ueli W580
Dietrich, Martin A. A724
Dietrich, Sabine U. W162
Dietz, Diane M. A1129
Dietz, Harry C. W258
Dietz, James A. A167
Dietz, James A. E64
Dietzler, Edward J. E53
Diez-Canseco, Russell E529
Diez, John J. A909
Diezhandino, Cristina W201
DiFranco, Michael E62
Diganci, Todd P224
DiGeronimo, Kevin A. E326
DiGeronimo, Richard J. A224
Digeso, Amy A70
Diggelmann, Roland E325
DiGiacomo, John N. A135
Digirolamo, Enrico E266
Dignam, Denise A224
Dignan, Patrick D. E350
DiGrande, Sebastian J. A157
Digrazia, G. Gino A860
Dijanosic, Michael W111
Diker, Charles M. A645
Diliberto, Matthew J A880
Diliberto, Matthew J P457
Dill, David M. E408
Dill, Julie P517
Dill, Julie A. E463
Dillard, Allen E. E291
Dillard, Rob A950
Diller, Barry A264
Diller, Barry A696
Diller, Barry A385

Diller, Barry E261
Diller, Keeta J. E428
Dilley, Michelle E461
Dillingham, Frederick P. E189
Dillon, Adrian T. E247
Dillon, David B. A1061
Dillon, David B. A4
Dillon, JoEllen Lyons A1093
Dillon, Kenneth A767
Dillon, Mary N. A443
Dillon, Mary N. A1055
Dillon, Tim P271
Dilorio, Richard E271
Dilsaver, Evelyn E247
Dilsaver, Evelyn S. E406
DiMaio, Jack J. E105
DiMarco, Kathryn A787
DiMarco, Paul A668
DiMartino, Michele B. A573
Dimauro, Vincent A P169
Dimick, Steven H. A138
Dimick, Steven H. E55
DiModica, Jeffrey F. A965
DiModica, Jeffrey F. E462
Dimon, James A591
Dimopoulos, Christos A185
DiMotta, Jennifer L. A703
DiMotta, Jennifer L. E327
DiMuccio, Robert A. A1108
DiNapoli, Jason P. A509
DiNapoli, Jason P. E251
Dincer, Haluk W267
Dincer, Suzan Sabanci W26
Dincer, Suzan Sabanci W267
Dineen, David E364
Dineen, Hugh G. E260
Dineen, John M. A267
Dineen, John M. A986
Dinello, Alessandro P. A435
Dinello, Alessandro P. E210
Ding, Feng W40
Ding, Guoqi W248
Ding, Huande W291
Ding, James W67
Ding, Jesse Y. W252
Ding, Jianguo W663
Ding, Jianzhong W664
Ding, Michael W252
Ding, Shiqi W608
Ding, Yi W375
Ding, Yongzhong W656
Dingee, Mark E102
Dingemans, Simon W654
Dingle, Frank W. E69
Dinh, Viet D. A447
Dinichenko, Ivan Kalistratovich W575
Dinkel, Thomas T. A422
Dinkins, Michael A282
Dinsmore, Deborah A214
Dion, Steven M. E128
Dionis, Javier Bernal W618
DiPalma, Sheila M. E105
Dipaolo, Mark A. E272
DiPietro, Kenneth W362
Dirac'h, Albert Le W347
Dircks, Thomas C. A937
Dircks, Thomas C. E441
Diril, Besim E458
Dirks, Thorsten W196
DiRomualdo, Robert F. A1055

DiSanto, Kristen L. A1108
DiSanzo, Deborah W57
Disbrow, Joshua R. E547
Disbrow, Lisa S. A189
Disbrow, Lisa S. E319
Dishman, William M. A978
Dishman, William M. E465
Dishner, Jeffrey G. A965
Dishner, Jeffrey G. E462
DiSimone, Harry F. A434
Diskul, Disnadda W541
Disler, Jordi E223
Dissinger, Todd E343
DiStasio, James S. A380
Distler, Stephen E53
Ditillo, David A296
Dittmar, William D. E526
Dittmeier, Carolyn G. W33
DiTullio, Michael E402
Dively, Joseph R. A427
Dively, Joseph R. E204
Dively, Mary Jo A441
Dively, Mary Jo E212
Divitto, Meg A. A643
Dixo, Gregory M. A259
Dixo, Gregory M. E103
Dixon, Heather Brianne E5
Dixon, John M. A773
Dixon, Kimberly D. A1001
Dixon, Robert D. A228
Dixon, Robert L. A85
Dixon, Robert W. A398
Dixon, Todd E. A401
Dixon, Wendy L. E267
Dixson-Decleve, Sandrine W212
Dixton, Grant M. A14
Diya, Fadi M. A54
Djerejian, Edward P. E307
Djou, Amy A423
Djou, Amy E199
Dmitriev, Andrey W256
Dmuchowski, Hope A424
Dmuchowski, Hope E200
Doane, W. Allen A423
Dobak, Miklos W412
Dobber, Ruud W57
Dobbins, James W. E501
Dobbs, Micheal W. E487
Dobbs, Stephen B. A306
Dobkin, Alain A977
Dobkin, Alain E464
Dobkin, Anthony K. E173
Dobkin, Arkadiy E170
Doboczky, Stefan W458
Dobrinski, Everett M. A396
Dobrinski, Everett M. E186
Dobrowski, Thomas E. E62
Dobry, Thomas (Tom) M. A639
Dobson, Arret F. E371
Dobyns, Tom L. E114
Docherty, Alan W164
Dockendorff, Charles J. A175
Dockendorff, Charles J. E522
Dockery, Kimberly C. E108
Dodderer, Arnold D. A982
Dodds, Christopher V. A919
Dodds, Scott E. E117
Doddy, Hurley A941
Dodge, Margaret Lauritzen A429
Dodgen, Kenneth M. E397

Dodig, Victor G. W119
Dods, Christopher L. A423
Dods, Sarah A912
Dodson-reed, Candace P271
Dodson, Ryan E219
Dodson, William A. E247
Doeden, Dan A37
Doeden, Dan E14
Doer, Gary A. W480
Doer, Gary A. W263
Doerfler, Mari A795
Doerr, David M P12
Doerr, L. John A45
Doheny, Daniel P. A1075
Doheny, Edward L. A924
Doheny, Edward L. A354
Doheny, Matthew A. (Matt) A1144
Doherty, Bridget M. E470
Doherty, Catherine T. A870
Doherty, Elizabeth W449
Doherty, Liz W351
Doherty, Matthew J. A503
Doherty, Robert Kelly A927
Doherty, Robert Kelly E435
Doherty, Sharon W371
Doherty, William J. A80
Dohm, Karin W129
Doi, Miwako W564
Doi, Nobuhiro W82
Doi, Tracey C. A870
Doig, David P118
Doig, John W84
Dolan, James J. A1040
Dolan, James J. E498
Dolan, Janet M. A1037
Dolan, John Joseph E154
Dolan, Lisa Marie A586
Dolan, Paul J. A947
Dolan, Paula D. A411
Dolan, Raymond P. A69
Dolan, Robert E. E301
Dolan, S K W116
Dolan, Terrance R. A1082
Dolan, Traci M. A975
Dole, Rodney P177
Doliveux, Roch A981
Doll, David F. E283
Dolloff, J. Mitchell A624
Dolson, Jed E238
Dolsten, Mikael A27
Dolsten, Mikael A821
Doluca, Tunc A1122
Domange, Didier W511
Dombrowski, Nadia A. A688
Dombrowski, Nadia A. E323
Domenech, Daniel A. A531
Domenici, Nella L. A267
Domenici, Nella L. E17
Domichi, Hideaki W577
Domier, Tanya L. A1146
Domingo, Marangal I. A398
Dominguez, Andres Tagle W172
Dominguez, Carlos A502
Dominguez, Christian Tauber W314
Dominguez, Dorene C. A594
Dominguez, Jaime Muguiro W131
dominguez, Jose Eladio Seco W11
Dominguez, Joseph A292
Dominguez, Joseph A384
Dominici, Peter W453

HOOVER'S HANDBOOK OF EMERGING COMPANIES 2023

COMBINED HOOVER'S HANDBOOK INDEX OF EXECUTIVES

A = AMERICAN BUSINESS
E = EMERGING COMPANIES
P = PRIVATE COMPANIES
W = WORLD BUSINESSS

Dominick, Jeffrey A. E11
Dominissini, Esther W79
Domit, Carlos Slim W35
Domit, Marco Antonio Slim A160
Domit, Patrick Slim W35
Dommel, Thomas W398
Don, J. Andrew E340
Donadio, Marcela E. A452
Donadio, Marcela E. A656
Donadio, Marcela E. A747
Donadio, Marcela E. A755
Donaghy, Ryan E512
Donaghy, Stephen J. E512
Donahoe, John J. A743
Donahoe, John J. A807
Donahue, Caroline F. E234
Donahue, James A. E107
Donahue, Joseph B. E330
Donahue, Michael A976
Donahue, Michael J. A1138
Donahue, Michael J. E544
Donahue, Paul D. A468
Donahue, Paul D. A1042
Donahue, Paul J. A809
Donahue, Timothy J. A302
Donald, Arnold W. A128
Donald, Arnold W. A912
Donald, James L. A35
Donald, James L. A745
Donald, Kirkland H. A371
Donald, Kirkland H. A546
Donaldson, Michael P. A375
Donaldson, Philip E. E444
Donato, Thomas A902
Donatsch, Reto W88
Donck, Frank W336
Dondero, James D. E348
Dong, Angela Wei A620
Dong, Daping W144
Dong, Junqing W117
Dong, Mingzhu W263
Dong, Weijun W272
Dong, Xin W143
Dong, Yang W301
Dong, Zhonglang W239
Donges, Jutta A. W162
Dongwana, Neo Phakama W426
Donheiser, Gail P241
Donikowski, Tina M. E490
Donikowski, Tina M. E6
Donikowski, Tina M. W60
Donis, Emi A843
Donis, Emi P442
Donkers, Wijnand P. W109
Donlan, Daniel P. E173
Donnelly, Abby A414
Donnelly, Abby E191
Donnelly, Michael J. A910
Donnelly, Michael J. A611
Donnelly, Patricia A864
Donnelly, Patrick L. A941
Donnelly, Roisin W425
Donnelly, Scott C. A1012
Donnelly, Scott C. W393

Donnelly, Thomas C. E66
Donnelly, Timothy J. E26
Donner, Corey E455
Donnet, Philippe W54
Donnley, Deneen L. A290
Donnley, Deneen L. A288
Donofrio, John W327
Donofrio, Nicholas M. W46
Donofrio, Nicholas M. W45
Donofrio, Paul M. A128
Donohoe, Brian A1119
Donohoe, Bryan P. A95
Donohue, Elisabeth B. A757
Donohue, Elisabeth B. A1019
Donohue, Michael E244
Donohue, Richard R. A704
Donohue, Richard R. E328
Donohue, Steve W651
Donovan, James E510
Donovan, John M. A643
Donovan, Michael S. A515
Donovan, Patrick J. A1118
Donovan, Patrick J. E533
Donovan, Stephen M. E370
Dontas, Periklis W473
Dontsop, Jean Felix Tematio A1054
Doo, Jinho A530
Doo, Jinho E258
Doo, William Junior Guiherme W80
Doody, Christopher M. A1040
Doody, Christopher M. E499
Doody, Joseph G. E82
Dooley, Charles P178
Dooley, Helen W20
Dooley, Shaun W419
Dopfner, Mathias A1106
Dopfner, Mathias A730
Doppstadt, Eric W. W50
Doramus, Mark C. A938
Doramus, Mark C. E442
Doran, Brian F. A575
Dorchak, Glenda M. E32
Dorchester, Wendy P318
Dorduncu, Ahmet C. A568
Dore, Stacey H. A1131
Dorer, Benno O. A1091
Dorig, Rolf W580
Dorig, Rolf W580
Dorjee, Frank W482
Dorlack, Jerome J. W15
Dorman, David W. A807
Dorman, David W. A322
Dorn, Andrew W. A411
Dornau, Gregor M. E358
Dornau, Peter G. E358
Dornemann, Michael E480
Dorner, Irene M. W504
Dornetto, Mary Anne A910
Dorr, Michael W192
Dorrance, Bennett A195
Dorrego, Ana W73
Dorris, Gregory W. E189
Dors, Laurence W174
Dors, Laurence W123
Dorsa, Caroline D. A347
Dorsa, Caroline D. A158
Dorsey, Cheryl Lynn E350
Dorsey, Jack A1047
Dorsey, Jack A162
Dorssers, Leon W441

Dort, Helene M. Vletter-van W442
Dorton, Brett A. A953
Dorton, Brett A. E455
Dorwart, Stephen M. E98
Dosch, Eric J. E199
Dosch, Theodore A. A1054
Dosky, Jorg von W198
Doss, Michael P. A924
Doss, Micheal P. A486
Dotan, Ido A124
Doti, James L. A413
Dottori-Attanasio, Laura W119
Doty, Elmer L. A95
Doty, Rachel E455
Dou, Jian W148
Doubles, Brian D. A985
Doucette, John P. W233
Doudna, Jennifer A. A585
Dougher, Brendan P. E90
Dougherty, Dawna E58
Dougherty, Gregory P. E314
Dougherty, Linda M. W572
Dougherty, Lucy Clark A835
Doughtie, Lynne M. A164
Douglas, Camille J. A965
Douglas, Camille J. E462
Douglas, Gary A. A82
Douglas, J. Alexander (Sandy) M A1068
Douglas, J. Christopher E247
Douglas, James H. A724
Douglas, Keith A A1026
Douglas, Keith A P620
Douglas, Laurie Z. A647
Douglas, Laurie Z. A860
Douglas, Mark A. E404
Douglas, Monica Howard E524
Douglas, Robert A. E233
Douglas, Robert Andrew E417
Douglas, Scott S. A624
Douglas, William W. E445
Dourado, Esmeralda da Silva Santos W212
Doustdar, Maziar Mike W450
Douvas, Maria W507
Dow, Ernest E. E362
Dow, Lisa K. A270
Dow, Lisa K. E109
Dow, Roger J. E410
Dowd, James A. E372
Dowdell, Robert (Bob) E. E370
Dowdell, Robert J. A852
Dowdell, Robert J. E399
Dowdie, George A964
Dowdle, Jeffrey A. A876
Dowdle, Stephen F. A82
Dowling, Ann W109
Dowling, Caroline W191
Dowling, Joseph L. E264
Dowling, Michael D. E454
Dowling, Michael J. A135
Dowling, Ruth A69
Down, Stephen G P498
Downe, William A. W371
Downe, William A. (Bill) A655
Downer, Michael P104
Downer, Michael J A64
Downer, Michael J P34
Downes, Sean P. E512
Downey, Bruce L. A201
Downey, Carolyn A96

Downey, Chris A. E185
Downey, David J. A415
Downey, David J. E194
Downey, Joseph L. E291
Downey, Roger Allan W630
Downing, John Matthew W298
Downing, John Matthew W169
Downing, Scott Lowell E108
Downs, Peter E348
Doyle, Amy A. A622
Doyle, Daniel J. E90
Doyle, Francis (Frank) A. A380
Doyle, J. Patrick A155
Doyle, James E. E136
Doyle, John E83
Doyle, John J. A181
Doyle, John Q. A662
Doyle, Jonathan J. E387
Doyle, Katie W351
Doyle, M. Christopher E101
Doyle, Peter Brendan E221
Doyle, Robert P585
Doyle, William J. A1133
Doyle, William J. E541
Dozier, C. Michael A796
Dozier, Michael J. E66
Drabek, Anthony E352
Drabik, John J. E160
Dragas, Helen E. A340
Dragash, Mickey R. E85
Drahi, David A45
Drahi, Patrick A45
Drahnak, Stephen A. A910
Drahozal, Christopher R. A1065
Drake, Allen C. A504
Drake, Angela C. E491
Drake, Bradley K. A493
Drake, Bradley K. E243
Drake, Deirdre C. E490
Drake, Fred L. A503
Drake, George E. A504
Drake, Larisa J. E445
Drake, Michael V. A76
Drake, Scott William E43
Drapé, Eric W598
Draper, Michelle A. A984
Draper, Michelle A. E476
Drath, Susan K. E160
Draughn, James B. A282
Drayson, Paul W24
Dreckmann, Johannes W234
Drees, Christopher A182
Drehobl, Stephen V. A697
Dreiling, Richard W. A647
Drell, Persis S. A761
Drendel, Frank M. A279
Drennan, Mark W. A954
Drescher, Stephanie A16
Dressel, Jeanne A129
Dressen, Michael W34
Dreuzy, Pascaline de W107
Drever, Brent E529
Dreves, Franz W61
Drew, J. Everitt A196
Drew, J. Everitt E79
Drew, Joel P102
Drew, Mark L. A853
Drew, Theresa J. A950
Drexler, Andrew S. A604
Drexler, Karen E417

COMBINED HOOVER'S HANDBOOK INDEX OF EXECUTIVES

```
A = AMERICAN BUSINESS
E = EMERGING COMPANIES
P = PRIVATE COMPANIES
W = WORLD BUSINESSS
```

Dreyer, Michael L. E266
Dreyer, Scott E107
Dreyfus, Andrew E282
Dreyfus, Maria S. Jelescu A830
Driesen, Maya vanden W644
Driggers, Timothy K. A375
Drilling, Edward A938
Drilling, Edward E442
Drimer, Adam M. A401
Drinkwater, Anne W228
Driot-Argentin, Veronique W637
Driscoll, Sharon W216
Driscoll, William L. E391
Drohan, Michael E. E190
Dronen, Bill E83
Dror, Nira W78
Drosos, Virginia (Gina) C. A64
Drosos, Virginia (Gina) C. A443
Drouven, Bernd W62
Drozdov, Anton V. W329
Druker, Brian J. A76
Drummond, F. Ford A125
Drummond, F. Ford E52
Drummond, Lance F. A1065
Drummond, Lance F. A450
Drummond, Lance F. E509
Drury, Mark J. E119
Drutman, Nadine R. W7
Dryburgh, Kerry W109
Du, Jian W137
Du, Michael A498
Du, Qingshan W663
Du, Trinh W252
Duan, Chenggang W158
Duan, Liangwei W466
Duan, Peilin W431
Duan, Rachel W65
Duan, Rachel W515
Duan, Rachel W13
Duan, Rachel W289
Duan, Wenwei W189
Duan, Xiannian W533
Duan, Xiufeng W263
Duan, Yinghui W239
Duane, Jon R. E282
Duarte, Pedro Maria Calainho Teixeira W70
Duato, Joaquin A585
Dube, Muriel Betty Nicolle W518
Duber, Marc N. E227
Dubey, Asmita W358
Dubinsky, Jason M. E333
Dublon, Dina A817
Dublon, Dina A991
DuBois, James M. A386
Dubois, Stephane W511
Dubourg, Saori W93
Dubovitsky, Sergey W410
Dubovoy, Hugo A485
Dubow, Adam A178
Dubrulle, Philippe W357
Dubuc, Nancy A1106
Dubugras, Henrique A385
Ducatman, Barbara P72

Duch, Linda P. E18
DuCharme, Stephan W655
Duckett, Thasunda Brown A743
Duckles, Kristen E67
Duckworth, Connie K. E334
Duclos, David B. A896
Duclos, David B. E422
Ducourty, Kelly E216
Duda, Kenneth E35
Dudkin, Gregory N. A841
Dudley-Williams, Carol A. A764
Dudley, Robert W506
Dudley, Robert W. A452
Dudley, William C. A400
Dudley, William C. W621
Dudman, Martha T. A138
Dudman, Martha T. E55
Dudman, William W. E358
Duenas, Luis Cabra W493
Dueser, F. Scott A421
Dueser, F. Scott E197
Duesman, Kathryn M. E418
Duesmann, Markus W640
DuFauchard, Preston Paul E378
Dufetel, Celine S. A991
Duffy, David W157
Duffy, Julie G. A1012
Duffy, Michael A. A892
Duffy, Robert A112
Duffy, Yael E270
Dufour, Gregory A. (Greg) A192
Dufour, Sandrine W654
Dufourcq, Nicolas W562
Dufresne, Daphne J. A1068
Dufresne, Richard W371
Dufresne, Richard W646
Dugan, John Cunningham A246
Dugan, Joseph L. A196
Dugan, Joseph L. A411
Dugan, Joseph L. E78
Dugan, Regina E. A514
Dugan, Richard W. E518
Dugan, Sean E172
Duganier, Barbara J. E487
Dugas, Jason P670
Dugenske, John E. A42
Duggins, J. Nathan A66
Duggins, J. Nathan E25
Dugle, Lynn A. A700
Dugle, Lynn A. A376
Dugle, Lynn A. A595
Dugle, Lynn A. W590
Duguay, Denis W193
Duh, Wu-Lin W206
Duhamel, Philippe W600
Duijl, Milko van W362
Dukeman, Van A. A415
Dukeman, Van A. E194
Dukes, L. Allison A573
Dulá, Sonia A548
Dulac, Fabienne W358
Dulac, Sophie W486
Dumais, Michael R. A121
Dumais, Michael R. A120
Dumas, Alain W193
Dumas, Claire W548
Dumas, Jacques W127
Dumas, Jose Tomas Guzman W217
Dumas, Jose Tomas Guzman W41
Dumas, Michel J. E236

Dumazy, Bertrand W357
Dumbleton, Sonia Marie A411
Dummer, Arthur Oleen A68
Dumont, Philippe W174
Dumont, Serge A351
Dumont, Serge E150
Dumpit, Risher G. E313
Dun, Haiping E3
Dunavan, Mark D. E204
Dunaway, William J. A979
Dunbar, R. Reid E151
Dunbar, W. Roy A347
Dunbar, W. Roy E445
Dunbar, Webster Roy W327
Duncan, Barbara G. E244
Duncan, Candace H. A330
Duncan, Candace H. E484
Duncan, David R. E206
Duncan, David S. A860
Duncan, Douglas G. A543
Duncan, George L. A372
Duncan, George L. E166
Duncan, Patrick W. E349
Duncan, Paul B. A747
Duncan, Thomas Ellis E218
Duncan, Timothy S. A228
Dunford, Joseph F. A643
Dunham, Kara P112
Dunigan, James P. A854
Dunigan, Joseph B. E102
Dunkel, Gunter W171
Dunkerley, Mark B. W24
Dunlap, Matthew W. A727
Dunlap, Matthew W. E345
Dunlap, Michael J. A681
Dunlap, Michael J. E318
Dunlap, Michael S. A727
Dunlap, Michael S. E345
Dunlap, Nancy A549
Dunlap, Terry L. A1073
Dunlop, Marcus B. A770
Dunley, Pamela P210
Dunn, Alan G. E342
Dunn, Craig E. E243
Dunn, Craig W. W596
Dunn, Danny E333
Dunn, Kenneth B. A740
Dunn, Kevin E543
Dunn, Leslie D. A732
Dunn, Lydia Selina W580
Dunn, Michael R. E413
Dunn, Micheal G. A1131
Dunn, Ryan C. A372
Dunn, Ryan C. E167
Dunn, Sarah A993
Dunne, Michael H. A436
Dunning, Audrey Palombo A1039
Dunning, Audrey Palombo E498
Dunning, J. G. W380
Dunnwald, Achim W509
Dunoyer, Marc W57
Dunphey, Rebecca A254
Dunsmore, Stan R. E98
Duplaix, Jean-Marc W338
DuPont, Bonnie W80
Dupont, Laurent W213
Dupont, Xavier W631
Duport, Valerie W338
Duprat, Pierre W635
DuPre, Daniel A. E188

Duprieu, Jean-Pierre W168
Dupui, Jean Pierre W72
Dupuy, David H. E114
Duque, Bruno Horta Nogueria W69
Duques, Henry C. (Ric) E374
Duran, Maria Juliana Alban W210
Durand, Patrice W225
Durand, Xavier W27
Durante, Nicandro W490
Durban, Egon P. A716
Durban, Egon P. A1047
Durban, Egon P. A322
Durban, Egon P. A367
Durban, Egon P. A1098
Durbaum, Matthias W510
Durbin, Jennifer J. A277
Durbin, Sean W369
Durburg, John E. A213
Durcan, D. Mark A73
Durcan, Mark D. M. A18
Durcan, Mark D. M. W52
Düren, Avi Aydin W618
Durette, Peter C. A1125
Durfey, Stephen M. A399
Durham, H. Lee A418
Durham, Jeffrey W. A887
Durham, Kari A. A942
Durham, Mikel A. A1050
Durheimer, Wolfgang A812
Durn, Daniel J. A15
Durnan, Jaymie A. E440
Durongkaveroj, Pichet W77
Durrfeld, Katja W171
Durst, Douglas A616
Dury, Michael R. A681
Dury, Michael R. E318
Duschmale, Jorg W502
Dusek, Richard A. A235
Dussault, Claude W399
Dussault, Claude W308
Duster, Benjamin C. A891
Duster, Benjamin C. A228
Dutey, James L. A441
Dutey, James L. E212
Dutkowsky, Robert M. A876
Dutkowsky, Robert M. A512
Dutkowsky, Robert M. A1083
Dutra, Felipe W40
Dutto, Laurence S. A935
Dutto, Laurence S. E439
Dutton, Richard J. A251
Dutton, Richard J. E100
Dutton, Steven G. A381
Duverne, Denis W65
Dvorak, Kelly M. A125
Dvorak, Kelly M. E52
Dvorin, Pnina W78
Dvorkin, Viktar E170
Dvorkovich, Arkady V. W329
Dwight, John K. A814
Dwight, John K. E379
Dworkin, James B. A532
Dworkin, James B. E259
Dwozan, Michael Frederick E108
Dwyer, Francis X. E420
Dwyer, Robert J. A668
Dwyer, Timothy Martin E363
Dy, Lucy C. W99
Dybal, Alexander W256
Dyck, Mark Van W170

COMBINED HOOVER'S HANDBOOK INDEX OF EXECUTIVES

A = AMERICAN BUSINESS
E = EMERGING COMPANIES
P = PRIVATE COMPANIES
W = WORLD BUSINESSS

Dyck, Robert G. A124
Dyckerhoff, Claudia Suessmuth W502
Dyer, Corey E141
Dyer, Jay A788
Dyer, Jay E364
Dyer, Joseph W. E38
Dyer, Karen P639
Dyk, Robert Van A271
Dyk, Robert Van E109
Dyke, Cornelius J. Van E506
Dyke, Jeff A948
Dyke, Kahina Van A851
Dyke, Litz H. Van A207
Dykema, John N. A741
Dykema, John N. E349
Dykes, Melissa P285
Dykhouse, Richard R. A223
Dykstra, David A. A1133
Dykstra, David A. E541
Dykstra, Karen E. A1098
Dynysiuk, Joanna W86
Dyson, Karen E. A470
Dyukov, Alexander Valerievich W256
Dziadzio, Richard S. A103
Dzielak, Robert J. A385

E

Eagleston, Brian J. E190
Eakle, Jason M. A815
Eamigh, Kevin J P519
Earle, Nick E430
Earley, Anthony F. A952
Earley, Anthony F. A444
Earley, Michael M. E5
Earley, Terry S. A1086
Earley, Terry S. E521
Earp, Pedro W40
Easi, Vincent G. E204
Easley, Laura K. A1040
Easley, Laura K. E499
Easley, Paul P516
Easley, Stephen T P218
East, Robert A134
East, Robert E54
East, Stephen A1032
East, Warren D. A. W53
East, Warren D. A. W504
Easter, William H. A323
Easter, William H. A366
Easterly, Joshua A941
Eastman, Stephen L. A394
Eastman, Stephen L. A835
Eastwood, Bill A1059
Eastwood, M. Glen W122
Eaton, Perry A428
Eaton, Rachel E299
Eaves, Hayden C. E152
Eazor, Joseph F. A330
Ebbe, Michael W205
Ebel, Gregory L. A714
Ebel, Gregory L. W218

Eberhart, H. Paulett A648
Eberhart, H. Paulett A438
Eberhart, H. Paulett A1085
Eberhart, Ralph E. A580
Eberl, Stephan W415
Eberly, Paul E. E181
Ebert, John W. E336
Eberwein, Elise R. A55
Ebinger, William A. E384
Ebner, Bernhard W96
Ebron, B. Scot E113
Eccher, James L. A774
Eccher, James L. E360
Ecclestone, Andrew A214
Ecclissato, Reginaldo W626
Echavarria, Luis Fernando Restrepo W76
Echavez, Luis Hernandez W131
Echevarria, Joseph J. A132
Echevarria, Joseph J. A821
Echevarria, Joseph J. A1079
Echeverri, Juan Emilio Posada W210
Echeverria, Jose Antonio W161
Echols, Matthew A1068
Echternach, Jared E340
Eck, Robert J. A909
Eckardt, Daniela W129
Eckart, Samuel E. E206
Eckel, Jeffrey W. E245
Eckersley, Debra W85
Eckerstrom, Hans W579
Eckert, Bret J. E160
Eckert, Jean-Blaise W167
Eckert, Neil D. E153
Eckert, R. Andrew A147
Eckert, Robert A. A76
Eckert, Robert A. A675
Eckert, Robert A. A631
Eckert, Thomas D. A763
Eckhardt, Sabine W129
Eckhart, Michael E246
Eda, Makiko W607
Eda, Makiko W253
Edahiro, Junko W608
Eddens, Peggy H. A1138
Eddens, Peggy H. E544
Eddington, Rod W343
Eddy, Jodi Euerle A175
Eddy, Robert W. A158
Edelcup, Norman E397
Edelman, Harriet A103
Edelman, Harriet A148
Edelman, Yitzhak W79
Edelson, David B. A110
Edelstein, Eric P. A1086
Edelstein, Eric P. E516
Edelstein, Gara P241
Edelstenne, Charles W601
Edelstenne, Charles W125
Eder, Noelle K. A54
Eder, Wolfgang W639
Eder, Wolfgang W453
Eder, Wolfgang W303
Ederington, L. Benjamin A1124
Edgar, Jason A138
Edgar, Jason E55
Edgell, Matthew M. A815
Ediboglu, Ayse Canan W620
Edin, Betul Ebru W618
Edison, Jeffrey S. E382

Edison, Sheri H. A1061
Edison, Sheri H. A201
Edman, Thomas T. E504
Edmiston, Sherman K. E35
Edmonds-Waters, Christopher D. A984
Edmonds-Waters, Christopher D. E476
Edmonds, Scott A. E190
Edmondson, Travis K. A395
Edmondson, Travis K. E185
Edmunds, C. Coleman A109
Edmunds, Cynthia P655
Edmunds, Wayne E336
Edney, A. La'Verne A788
Edney, A. La'Verne E364
Edone, Ryan E299
Edouard, SCHMID W431
Edozien, Ngozi W298
Eduardo, Marcelo A1044
Edwards, B. Joanne E40
Edwards, Blake M. E372
Edwards, Brian E. A225
Edwards, Bruce A. A489
Edwards, Bryan L. E372
Edwards, C. Greg E372
Edwards, Carladenise A508
Edwards, Carladenise P260
Edwards, Christine A. W83
Edwards, Crawford H. A305
Edwards, Debra F. E26
Edwards, Harold S. E115
Edwards, Jeffrey N. A876
Edwards, Jeffrey W. E274
Edwards, Joel G. E103
Edwards, Jon S. A71
Edwards, Jon S. E29
Edwards, Julie H. A783
Edwards, Lisa M. A269
Edwards, Murray A421
Edwards, Murray E198
Edwards, N. Murray W120
Edwards, Robert W410
Edwards, Robert A. A1064
Edwards, Robert A. E509
Edwards, Robert L. A997
Edwards, S. Eugene A809
Edwards, Susan C. A924
Edwardson, Francesca Maher A543
Edwardson, Francesca Maher E147
Eerkes, Craig D. A270
Eerkes, Craig D. E109
Effron, Caryn E34
Egami, Setsuko W494
Egan, Connie E79
Egan, Cynthia L. A547
Egan, Cynthia L. A499
Egan, Cynthia L. A1079
Egan, Joe P671
Egawa, Masako W606
Egawa, Masako W408
Egebjerg-Johansen, John W330
Egeck, Michael R. E297
Egerth-Stadlhuber, Henrietta W229
Eggemeyer, John M. A800
Eggemeyer, John M. A1014
Eggemeyer, John M. A845
Eggemeyer, John M. E488
Eggemeyer, John M. E395
Eggers, Daniel L. A384
Eggers, Daniel L. A292

Eggspuehler, Jack J. E247
Eggspuehler, Jay B. E247
Egidius, Nanna W347
Egler-Whytsell, Kerry E189
Egorov, Valery Nikolaevich W575
Eguia, Jose Antonio Chedraui W265
Egusa, Shun W577
Ehlers, Fredric M. A747
Ehrenberg, James A. E322
Ehrenpreis, Ira Matthew A1007
Ehrhardt, William J. E363
Ehrling, Marie W446
Ehrmann, Jacques W125
Ehrnrooth, Henrik W348
Eibensteiner, Herbert W639
Eichelmann, Thomas W280
Eichenbaum, Martin S. W83
Eicher, Carol S. A95
Eichiner, Friedrich W33
Eichiner, Friedrich W303
Eichmann, Matthew D. A489
Eichten, Estia J. E525
Eid, Eric J. A270
Eid, Eric J. E109
Eid, Joseph A178
Eid, Robert W47
Eidesvik, Kristian W558
Eilers, Peter E. E26
Eilertsen, Carsten W188
Einhorn, David E238
Eisen, David P682
Eisenberg, Glenn A. A615
Eisenberger, Mario E522
Eisenson, Michael R. A812
Eishen, Eric L. E469
Eisman, Robert B. A52
Eismann, Gabriele W397
Eisner, Michael D. E261
Eisnor, Di-Ann E426
Eissenstat, Eric S. A295
Eitrheim, Pal W227
Ekabut, Chaovalit W540
Ekdara, Farhat Omar W47
Ekedahl, Anders W579
Ekeren, Janice Rae Van W79
Ekholm, Börje E497
Ekholm, Borje E. W228
Eki, Yuji W278
Eklund, Andrea P280
Ekudden, Erik W228
El-Arbah, Saleh Lamin W47
El-Khoury, Hassane A780
El-Labban, Adel A. W18
Elbers, Pieter J.TH. W22
Elbers, Pieter J.TH. W344
Elcock, Peter Charles W462
Eldar, Assaf W311
Elder, Larry P79
Elder, Richard M. E192
Elder, T. L. E237
Eldert-Klep, Cindy van W306
Eldridge, Andrea E81
Eldridge, Michelle L. A681
Eldridge, Michelle L. E318
Eldridge, Timothy E340
Elenio, Paul E34
Elhedery, Georges W289
Elias, Richard C. E511
Eliasson, Tomas W4
Elicker, John E. A178

COMBINED HOOVER'S HANDBOOK INDEX OF EXECUTIVES

A = AMERICAN BUSINESS
E = EMERGING COMPANIES
P = PRIVATE COMPANIES
W = WORLD BUSINESSS

Elinson, Andrei W562
Elinson, Andrei W655
Eliopoulos, Elias J. A429
Elizalde, Raul A. Anaya W70
Elizondo, Carlos Jose Garcia Moreno W35
Elkann, Ginevra W235
Elkann, John W562
Elkann, John W235
Elkins, Claude E. A747
Elkins, David V. A178
Elkowitz, Robin S. A248
Ellefson, Anne S. E454
Ellen, David G. A223
Eller, Lars B. E184
Ellerbusch, Susan A. E469
Ellett, Frank Russell A106
Ellett, Frank Russell E40
Ellinger, Deborah G. E281
Ellingsen, Catharine D. A892
Ellingsen, Eric A1151
Ellington, Kimberly J. A427
Ellington, Kimberly J. E203
Ellingwood, Dwight E. E321
Elliot, Cynthia P467
Elliot, Douglas (Doug) G. A502
Elliot, John R. A249
Elliot, John R. E99
Elliott, Anita C. A336
Elliott, Brad S. A378
Elliott, Christopher B. A493
Elliott, Christopher B. E243
Elliott, Frank Tommy E90
Elliott, Geraldine T. A1129
Elliott, Jay P. E274
Elliott, Matt W81
Elliott, Shayne C. W63
Elliott, Shayne Cary W36
Elliott, Steven G. A841
Elliott, Steven G. A545
Elliott, William E. E388
Ellis, Brian W. A371
Ellis, Brian W. A315
Ellis, David P678
Ellis, Douglas E. A1033
Ellis, Douglas E. E493
Ellis, Earl R. A10
Ellis, Gary Lee E491
Ellis, Gordon Lloyd E509
Ellis, Gordon Lloyd E510
Ellis, Gordon Lloyd E509
Ellis, Ian W160
Ellis, James G. A685
Ellis, James O. A643
Ellis, James O. A340
Ellis, Juliet S. A86
Ellis, Kip B. E373
Ellis, Matthew D. A1088
Ellis, Stephen A. A919
Ellis, Vernon James E224
Ellis, William D. A1086
Ellis, William D. E521
Ellison-Taylor, Kimberly A1082
Ellison, David G. E454

Ellison, Lawrence J. A1007
Ellison, Lawrence J. A786
Ellison, Marvin R. A405
Ellison, Marvin R. A647
Ellison, Richard P90
Ellison, Seth A633
Ellison, Seth P314
Ellison, Seth M. A631
Ellman, David E397
Ellman, Mark A. W16
Ellwanger, Kimberly T. A510
Ellwanger, Kimberly T. E252
Elman, Lee M. E232
Elmer, Russell S. A931
Elmin, Henrik W60
Elming, Lisa J. A1118
Elming, Lisa J. E533
Elmore, C. Alec E452
Elmore, Leonard J. E2
Elmore, Samuel L. A419
Elmslie, Nick W427
Elosua, Federico Toussaint W27
Elphick, Jason W462
Elrich, Marc P366
Elsaesser, Ford A271
Elsaesser, Ford E109
Elsaid, Fadi A927
Elsaid, Fadi E435
Elsenhans, Lynn Laverty A121
Elsenhans, Lynn Laverty A120
Elsner, Adrienne (Deanie) A795
Elsner, Frank A12
Elsner, Frank E4
Elsner, Thomas W95
Elste, Mark A. E97
Elstein, Amir W598
Eltife, Kevin Paul A594
Elting, Lauren B. E188
Elton, Kristin P581
Elvira, Susana W1
Elwell, Daniel K. A34
Elwyn, Tashtego S. A876
Ely, James S. A282
Ely, James S. A926
Elzen, Ronald den W274
Elzvik, Eric W641
Elzvik, Eric A. W228
Emanuel, Ariel Z. A367
Embler, Michael E350
Embler, Michael J. A56
Embree, Tracy A. A306
Emenhiser, Kip A. E293
Emerson, Daniel P. E480
Emerson, Kenneth G. A143
Emerson, Kenneth G. E56
Emerson, Kevin W. A677
Emerson, Sarah A. A228
Emery, Karen P43
Emkes, Mark A. A490
Emmert, Mark A. A386
Emmert, Mark A. A1127
Emmet, James W288
Emoto, Yasutoshi W21
Empey, Rachel Claire W96
Empey, Rachel Claire W251
Empey, Rachel Claire W249
Emsley, Douglas W80
Emswiler, Melody E181
Emswiler, Shane R. E31
Enboy, Karla E102

Enden, Henchy R. A106
Ender, Farrell M. E268
Enders, Thomas W369
Endo, Isao W555
Endo, Junichi W441
Endo, Nobuhiro W606
Endo, Noriko W439
Endo, Yasuaki W357
Endo, Yoshinari W606
Endresen, William D. A527
Endrizzi, James A. A1107
Eng, Michael F. E33
Engebretsen, James R. A396
Engebretsen, James R. E186
Engel, Ashley P581
Engel, Connie L. A889
Engel, Connie L. E414
Engel, Ditlev W632
Engel, Hans-Ulrich W93
Engel, John J. A1073
Engel, John J. A1117
Engel, John J. A207
Engel, Klaus A. A298
Engel, Marc W2
Engel, Robert B A507
Engel, Robert B E248
Engel, Robert B. E18
Engelbert, Catherine M. A675
Engelbert, Catherine M. E425
Engelfried, Annette W303
Engelkes, Jack E. A524
Engelkes, Jack E. E258
Engelman, David S. E397
Engelstoft, Morten Henrick W1
Engfors, Tina Elvingsson W231
England, Evan A971
England, Evan P537
England, James A. A397
England, James Herb W218
England, Robert A927
England, Robert E435
Englander, Daniel J. E23
Englander, Daniel J. E120
Engle, Bridget E. A132
Engle, John B P489
Engleder, Birgitte W453
Englefield, F. William A803
Englefield, F. William E371
Englehart, Michael P369
Engles, Amanda L. E156
Engles, Gregg L. A232
Engles, Gregg L. E300
Englesson, John G. E156
English, Bill W644
English, Michela A. E232
English, Ted A187
Engquist, John M. A706
Enns, Peter W154
Enomoto, Koichi W405
Enqvist, Torbjorn ("Toby") J. A1062
Ensinger, George Steven A1119
Enstad, Paul Gerald E236
Enterline, Larry L. E218
Entler, Paul P516
Entwistle, Darren W596
Enzor, Gary R. E515
Epaillard, Hugues W104
Ephrat, Zvi W410
Epker, Arthur G. E402
Eppinger, Frederick H. A216

Epps, Donna E. E487
Epps, Donna E. E426
Epps, JoAnne A. E227
Epron, Daniel W174
Eran-Zick, Hilla W79
Eran, Oded W78
Erb, Thomas C. A838
Erceg, Mark J. A221
Erdem, Ahmet W267
Erdoes, Mary Callahan A591
Ergen, Cantey M. A333
Ergen, Charles W. A333
Erginbilgic, Tufan W191
Erichson, Richard S. A392
Erichson, Richard S. E183
Erickson, Andrew J. A973
Erickson, John C. A129
Erickson, John C. A650
Erickson, John C. E305
Erickson, John D. E367
Erickson, Kevin P683
Erickson, Larry Jon A235
Erickson, Randall J. A101
Erickson, Richard Sean E500
Erickson, Thomas P. E57
Ericson, Amy R. A840
Ericson, Magnus W579
Eriksen, Jan Otto W594
Eriksson, Hakan W632
Erkan, Hafize Gaye A662
Erkilla, Jack R. A781
Erkonen, Scott E. A426
Erkonen, Scott E. E202
Erlen, Hubertus W390
Erlich, Craig E9
Erlich, Morton D. E26
Erlinger, Joseph A675
Erlund, Jukka W340
Erminio, Courtney M. E326
Ernest, Douglas Bryon A1063
Ernest, Douglas Bryon E508
Ernst, Christina M. A472
Ernst, Christina M. E230
Ernst, Edgar W398
Ernst, Michael A1026
Ernst, Michael P620
Erokhin, Vladimir Petrovich W575
Erskine, Peter W593
Erün, Gökhan W661
Ervasti-Vaintola, Ilona W247
Ervin, Patrick J. A555
Ervin, Patrick J. E269
Erwin, Tamra A. A320
Escajadillo, Ricardo Ernesto Saldivar W244
Escalante, Augusto W266
Escandar, Pedro Samhan W314
Escobar, Dana E546
Escobar, Diana Hoyos W210
Esculier, Jacques R. A911
Eskew, Michael L. A635
Eskew, Michael L. A4
Eslinger, Lisa M. E30
Esparza, Ryan P284
Espe, Matthew J. A1118
Espe, Matthew J. A878
Espe, Matthew J. A879
Espegard, Duaine C. E349
Espeland, Curtis E. A548
Esper, Richard Eric A1068

COMBINED HOOVER'S HANDBOOK INDEX OF EXECUTIVES

A = AMERICAN BUSINESS
E = EMERGING COMPANIES
P = PRIVATE COMPANIES
W = WORLD BUSINESSS

Esperanza, Chrysty A162
Esperdy, Therese A711
Esperdy, Therese W422
Esperdy, Therese W298
Espinola, Javier de Pedro W265
Espinosa, Ivan W441
Espinoza, Jesus Thomas A474
Espinoza, Jesus Thomas E230
Espiritu, Octavio Victor R. W85
Esposito, Anthony V. A616
Esposito, Carl A. A622
Esposito, Jose W174
Esq, David J Felicio P583
Esq, Lynn Taylor P522
Esser, Frank W581
Esser, Frank V. W238
Esser, Isabelle W187
Esser, Juergen W187
Essex, Bruce J. E96
Essig, Stuart M. E263
Essig, Stuart M. E278
Essner, Robert A. A787
Estabrook, Anne Evans A396
Estabrook, Anne Evans E187
Estby, Rebecca P149
Estep, J. Seth A1035
Estep, Michele B. A768
Estep, Michele B. E359
Estep, Sandra J. A860
Esterhay, Carl A. E149
Estes, Jason E. E54
Estes, Scott A. E173
Esteves, Irene M. A904
Esteves, Irene M. E288
Estill, James C. E76
Estrada, Rudolph I. A351
Estrada, Rudolph I. E150
Estradas, J. Lorraine E33
Esty, Benjamin C. A876
Etchart, Eric P. E13
Etchison, John E517
Etheridge, Felicia P143
Etienne, Jean-Michel W486
Etlin, Holly Felder A148
Ettedgui, Edouard A1145
Etter, Steven S A454
Ettinger, Jeffrey M. A358
Ettinger, Jeffrey M. E491
Ettinger, Michael S. A917
Etzkorn, Karen S. E254
Eua-arporn, Bundhit W77
Euarchukiati, Yos W540
Eubanks, Richard M. W209
Eudy, Tara G. E515
Euenheim, Andrea W398
Eulen, Jan W62
Eulitz, Bernd Hugo W369
Eure, Hilliard M. E310
Eureyecko, John F. E23
Eurlings, Camiel M.P.S. W22
Eurlings, Camiel M.P.S. W344
Eusey, Shannon F. A124
Evanko, Brian C. A239
Evanko, Jillian C. A804

Evanko, Jillian C. E96
Evanoff, Douglas D. A399
Evans, Aicha W517
Evans, Alejandra E136
Evans, Andrew W. A952
Evans, Andrew W. A471
Evans, Bruce R. A81
Evans, Carl Thomas A599
Evans, Carlos E. E234
Evans, Charles L. A399
Evans, Daniel F. A618
Evans, Daniel F. E290
Evans, David C. A201
Evans, G M W116
Evans, Gay Huey A911
Evans, Gay Huey A288
Evans, Gay Huey W561
Evans, Gerald W. E517
Evans, Godfrey B. A527
Evans, H. Malloy A391
Evans, J. Michael W29
Evans, James E. A64
Evans, Javier A1144
Evans, Javier A1113
Evans, Jon D. E374
Evans, Jose L. E315
Evans, Mark W593
Evans, Michael E P270
Evans, Michele M. A391
Evans, Mike W374
Evans, Nicola M. Wakefield W377
Evans, Richard B. E408
Evans, Robert B. A995
Evans, Scott A. A681
Evans, Scott A. E318
Evans, Shad E. A595
Evans, Sharlene E444
Evans, Stephen A367
Evans, Stephen C. E14
Evans, Thomas R. E438
Evans, Timothy L. A493
Evans, Wilburn J. A395
Evans, Wilburn J. E185
Even, Shai S. E169
Evenson, Jeffrey W. A298
Everett, Junetta M. A378
Everett, Morgan H. A265
Everist, Thomas S. A679
Everitt, David C. A182
Evernham, Scott J. A772
Evers, Johannes W192
Evers, Sherri L. W299
Evers, Tami P671
Eversole, Robert M. E5
Everson, Carolyn N. A1059
Everson, Scott A. E506
Evesque, Wendy A853
Evlioglu, Isil Akdemir W618
Evoli, Lisa E278
Ewald, Stephen P. E317
Ewald, Thaddeaus B. A306
Ewens, Peter A. A992
Ewing, Christopher J. A287
Ewing, Christopher J. E115
Ewing, Clay W. A472
Ewing, Clay W. E230
Ewing, D. Eugene E115
Ewing, Gregg L. A895
Ewing, Justin A35
Ewing, R. Stewart E420

Ewing, Stephen E. A294
Exel, Audette E. W648
Exnicios, Joseph S. A496
Exum, James (Jimmy) L. A395
Exum, James (Jimmy) L. E185
Eyer, Heinz W61
Eyigun, Gokhan W267
Eyler, Phillip M. E448
Eyuboglu, Yagiz W620
Ezama, Sergio Maebe A730
Ezekiel, Laurent W654
Ezekowitz, R. Alan A787
Ezzat, Aiman W123
Ezzat, Aiman W357
Ezzell, Jack P. E361
Ezzell, Robert Dale A72
Ezzell, Robert Dale E29

F

Fa, Yuxiao W355
Faasen, William C. Van A380
Fabara, Paul A62
Fabara, Paul A1096
Fabbri, Luca E185
Fabbri, Thomas A. E298
Faber, Barry M. A940
Faber, Hanneke A993
Faber, Johanna W W95
Faber, Karsten W586
Faber, Tracy L. A677
Fabri, Eurico Ramos W69
Fabri, Hubert W165
Fabrication, John Higgins Pres P226
Fabrin, Erik W348
Facchin, Claudio W279
Facchini, Pier Francesco W482
Faddis, Jonathan (Josh) E519
Fadool, Joseph F. A173
Faerber, Craig P30
Fagan, Cathlyn P398
Fagg, Jenny W85
Fagg, Karen B. A679
Fagg, Kathryn W419
Fague, Philip E. A788
Fague, Philip E. E365
Fahey, John M. E284
Fahrenkopf, Frank J. A431
Fahrenkopf, Frank J. E205
Fahs, L. Reade E341
Failes, John W. A1033
Failes, John W. E492
Fails, Karl R. A982
Fair, William E. A556
Fair, William E. E270
Fairbairn, Carolyn W66
Fairbairn, Dame Carolyn W289
Fairbank, Richard D. A198
Fairbanks, Bryan H. E494
Fairchilds, Charles W. A249
Fairchilds, Charles W. E99
Faircloth, Michael E. A497
Fairclough, Brett E527
Fairey, Michael W188
Fairfax, Daniel W. E472
Fairhead, Rona Alison A786
Faivre, Sara L. A396
Faivre, Sara L. E186

Fajemirokun-Beck, Olufunlayo Olurinde E260
Fajerman, Sergio Guillinet W315
Fakude, Nolitha W39
Falberg, Kathryn E. E489
Falcione, Aaron A787
Falcione, Ronald D. A519
Falcione, Ronald D. E256
Falck, David P. A80
Falcon, Armando A881
Falcone, Cristiana W592
Falcone, Philip P526
Falconer, Brendon B. A772
Falero, Barbara W174
Falk, Kathleen P168
Falk, Thomas E489
Falk, Thomas J. A643
Falkenhausen, Konstantin von E352
Fall, Clinton P581
Fallon, Catriona M. E370
Fallon, John A. E107
Fallon, John A. E277
Fallon, Katherine Beirne A675
Fallon, Lynnette C. E47
Fallon, William C. (Bill) A671
Fallon, William E. A1086
Fallon, William E. E521
Fallowfield, Tim W318
Falotico, Joy A444
Falotico, Nancy Joy A446
Falzon, Robert M. A856
Falzon, Sylvia W574
Fan, Bo W542
Fan, Cheng W128
Fan, Chengyang W656
Fan, Dan W656
Fan, Gary A878
Fan, Gary E409
Fan, Hongwei W274
Fan, Rita Hsu Lai Tai W144
Fan, Wei W248
Fan, Wensheng W663
Fan, Wenye W136
Fan, Xiping W529
Fan, Yunjun W151
Fanandakis, Nicholas C. A347
Fanandakis, Nicholas C. E224
Fandozzi, Ann E497
Fandrey, Edward A648
Fanelli, A. J. E401
Fang, Ai Lian E261
Fang, Ai Lian W464
Fang, Ming W148
Fang, Rong W664
Fang, Sylvia W583
Fang, Xiangming W152
Fang, Xianming W574
Fang, Xianshui W275
Fanlo, Saturnino E239
Fannin, Timothy B. A753
Fanning, Thomas A. A952
Fanning, Thomas A. A399
Fansler, Janet P306
Fante, Matteo del W479
Fanter, William A650
Fanter, William E305
Fappani, Silvia Alessandra W222
Faraci, John V. A207
Faraci, John V. A1073
Farah, Pedro W643

COMBINED HOOVER'S HANDBOOK INDEX OF EXECUTIVES

> A = AMERICAN BUSINESS
> E = EMERGING COMPANIES
> P = PRIVATE COMPANIES
> W = WORLD BUSINESSS

Farah, Pedro W451
Farah, Roger N. A851
Farah, Roger N. A311
Farahat, Tarek W654
Farahat, Tarek Mohamed Noshy Nasr Mohamed W324
Farber, Jeffrey M. A499
Fargo, Ayad A. A797
Fargo, Ayad A. E368
Faria, Joao V. W209
Farias, Humberto Junqueira de W323
Farina, Maria Bianca W479
Farina, Terry E19
Farless, Leslie S. A747
Farley, Claire S. W374
Farley, Claire S. W590
Farley, James D. A444
Farmar, Richard A. E62
Farmer, Colin M. A513
Farmer, Curtis C. A1010
Farmer, Curtis C. A274
Farmer, Michael A. A184
Farmer, Richard T. A242
Farmer, Scott D. A242
Farner, Jay A900
Farnsworth, David F. A308
Farnsworth, David F. E133
Farnsworth, Ronald L. A1057
Farnsworth, Thomas C. A829
Farnsworth, Thomas C. E385
Farooqui, Duriya M. A561
Farooqui, Rafay A652
Farr, David N. A565
Farr, Kevin M. A835
Farr, Meryl Kennedy A788
Farr, Meryl Kennedy E364
Farr, Sue W111
Farrar, Jeffrey W. A66
Farrar, Jeffrey W. E25
Farrell, Dawn L. A224
Farrell, Dawn L. W120
Farrell, Edward J. E34
Farrell, Ellen L. A1034
Farrell, Kathleen A. A727
Farrell, Kathleen A. E345
Farrell, Mark L. A235
Farrell, Mary C. A150
Farrell, Matthew Thomas A237
Farrell, Michael J. A1150
Farrell, Michael J. A486
Farrell, Michael J. E417
Farrell, Nicholas R. E255
Farrell, Paul J. A1033
Farrell, Paul J. E493
Farrell, Peter C. E417
Farrell, Peter J. E530
Farrell, Stephen C. E460
Farrell, Thomas W495
Farrell, William J. A66
Farrell, William J. E25
Farrelly, Ian W245
Farrington, Deborah A. A726
Farrington, Duane C. A799
Farris, Franklin H. A283

Farris, Jack M. A768
Farris, Jack M. E359
Farrow, William M. A400
Farrow, William M. A1114
Farrow, William M. E87
Fartaj, Vandad A811
Fartaj, Vandad E377
Faruqui, Farhan W63
Farwick, Hermann W234
Fasanella, David V. A749
Fasano, Gerard A. A625
Fasano, James A. A576
Fasching, Steven J. E137
Fascitelli, Michael D. E280
Fasman, Steven L. E83
Fassbind, Renato W355
Fassbind, Renato W430
Fassbind, Renato W580
Fassin, Frank W415
Fast, Barbara G. A145
Fato, Lucy A296
Fato, Lucy A65
Fatovic, Robert D. A909
Faubel, Joachim W62
Fauber, Robert A711
Faubert, Richard J. E47
Fauerbach, William V. A860
Faujour, Veronique W174
Faulkenberry, Barbara J. E515
Faulkingham, Ryan J. E115
Faulkner, Caroline A856
Faulkner, Jennifer P386
Faulkner, Mikel D. E207
Faurot, Holly E374
Faury, Guillaume W65
Faury, Guillaume W24
Fausing, Kim W283
Faust, Erwin W62
Faust, Jon A538
Faust, Megan A78
Favre, Juliette W231
Favre, Michel W495
Favreau, Bradley T. E25
Favreau, Bradley T. E337
Fawcett, Amelia C. A973
Fawcett, Dave P683
Fawcett, Mark E33
Fay, Kristine P308
Fay, Sarah Ann E547
Fay, William D. A99
Fayard, Gary P. A468
Fayock, Daniel G. A95
Fazzolari, Salvatore D. A907
Fearon, Mark W240
Fearon, Richard H. A303
Fearon, Richard H. W178
Feaster, David P. A890
Feaster, David P. E416
Feder, Franklin L. A796
Federico, Peter J. A28
Federico, Richard D. E18
Fedor, Terry G. A252
Fedotov, Gennady W476
Fedun, Leonid W476
Feehan, Daniel R. E207
Feehan, Daniel R. E162
Feehery, William F. E534
Feeney, Caroline A855
Feeney, Caroline A856
Feeney, Siobhán Mc A608

Fees, Jessica E475
Fehlman, Robert A. A938
Fehlman, Robert A. E442
Fehrenbach, Franz W93
Fehring, Nicolas A. A565
Fehring, Patrick J. E298
Fehrman, William J. A798
Fehrmann, Andrea W543
Fei, Xinyi W98
Feiger, Mitchell S. A410
Feight, R. Preston A796
Feikin, Jennifer A513
Feinberg, David M. A59
Feinberg, David T. A221
Feinberg, Hill A. A516
Feinberg, Joshua H. A10
Feinberg, Melody A396
Feinberg, Melody E187
Feiner, Gary W. E527
Feiner, Michael C. E408
Feingold, Anton A95
Feinknopf, Abigail M. A1115
Feinknopf, Abigail M. E533
Feintuch, Richard D. E381
Fejes, Balazs E170
Fekete, Frank L. A854
Felber, Francis E. E98
Felcht, Utz-hellmuth W234
Feld, Peter Alexander E239
Feldbaum, Carl B. E178
Feldman, Alan D. A443
Feldman, Craig A. A760
Feldman, Joshua D. A129
Feldman, Martin J P525
Feldstein, Andrew T. A834
Felice, Laura L. A158
Feliciani, Joseph E212
Feliciano, Javier A687
Feliciano, José E. E450
Feliciano, José E. E283
Feliciano, Lynette P176
Felkel, David E. E340
Fellenberg, Ian von E107
Feller, Maya W410
Felli, Luis F.S. A26
Felsinger, Donald E. A94
Felsinger, Donald E. A752
Felt, Bruce C. E77
Feltenstein, Sidney J. A1046
Feltz, Lorianne E171
Fendel, Fredrick A. E402
Fendler, Jeffrey S. A845
Fendler, Jeffrey S. E395
Fenech, Ronald E293
Feng, Bo W140
Feng, Boming W173
Feng, Changli W37
Feng, Jinyi W372
Feng, Lisa E3
Feng, Rong W291
Feng, Weidong W301
Feng, Wenhong W533
Feng, Xiaodong W239
Feng, Xinglong W140
Feng, Zhenping W291
Fenimore, Christopher A882
Fennebresque, Kim W93
Fennebresque, Kim S. A43
Fennebresque, Kim S. A35
Fennell, Charles P527

Fennell, Kevin M. E67
Fennell, Laura A. A571
Fenstermaker, William H. A424
Fenstermaker, William H. E200
Fenton, Robert J. E451
Fenwick, Nicholas Adam Hodnett W580
Feragen, Jody H. A806
Ferdman, David H. E134
Ferebee, Galeel Maliek E144
Ferguson, Brian C. W611
Ferguson, Jeffrey W. A203
Ferguson, Keith D. A436
Ferguson, Mark E. A823
Ferguson, Rhonda S. A42
Ferguson, Roger E102
Ferguson, Roger W. A567
Ferguson, Roger W. A298
Ferguson, Roger W. A45
Ferguson, Roy C. A125
Ferguson, Roy C. E52
Ferguson, Scott D. A1083
Fergusson, Kevin W. A401
Ferland, Martine A662
Ferlazzo, Thomas A400
Fernald, Lauri E. A138
Fernald, Lauri E. E55
Fernandes, Andre Lopes Dias W69
Fernandes, Larry A557
Fernandes, Oswaldo Tadeu W69
Fernandes, Ruben W39
Fernandes, Vitor Manuel Lopes W70
Fernandez-Carbajal, Francisco Javier A1096
Fernandez, Carlos Javier Alvarez W423
Fernandez, Eliseo Santiago Perez W323
Fernandez, Felix S. A211
Fernandez, Felix S. E84
Fernandez, Henry A. E335
Fernandez, Jose A. E462
Fernandez, Jose Walfredo W295
Fernandez, Juan Ignacio Echeverria W73
Fernandez, Manuel A. (Manny) A182
Fernandez, Manuel A. (Manny) A624
Fernandez, Manuel A. (Manny) A818
Fernandez, Manuel J. A580
Fernandez, Ramon W65
Fernandez, Ramon W459
Fernandez, Raul J. A180
Fernandez, Raul J. A349
Fernández, Renato W132
Fernandez, Ricardo Alonso W73
Fernkorn, Thomas W129
Ferraby, Stephen W203
Ferraioli, Brian K. A1097
Ferran, Javier W201
Ferrara, Nancy A1098
Ferrari, Daniele A548
Ferrari, Gianfranco W174
Ferrari, Giorgio W177
Ferrari, Paolo W110
Ferraro, John F. A655
Ferraro, John F. A17
Ferraro, John F. A567
Ferraro, Joseph A. A116
Ferraro, Maria W544
Ferraz, Joao Carlos W324
Ferre, Maria Luisa A836

COMBINED HOOVER'S HANDBOOK INDEX OF EXECUTIVES

A = AMERICAN BUSINESS
E = EMERGING COMPANIES
P = PRIVATE COMPANIES
W = WORLD BUSINESSS

Ferre, Maria Luisa A150
Ferreira, Alfonso W643
Ferreira, Carlos Jorge Ramalho dos Santos W70
Ferreira, Diana A742
Ferreira, Diana P393
Ferreira, Eduardo Bacellar Leal W468
Ferreira, Jose de Paiva W72
Ferreira, Laurent W420
Ferreira, Piet W562
Ferrer, Antonio Garcia W11
Ferrer, Javier D. A836
Ferrero, Pablo A. A929
Ferretti, Joseph M. A816
Ferrezuelo, Isabel Torremocha W493
Ferrick, Patricia A. E227
Ferrier, Andrew W646
Ferrier, Susan W419
Ferris, Stephanie L. A408
Ferriss, Stephen A. A915
Ferro, Claudio Braz W40
Fesette, Neil E. A280
Fesette, Neil E. E113
Fesko, Donald P. E191
Fess, Darryl J. A181
Fessenden, Daniel J. A1033
Festa, Alfred E. A763
Festa, Alfred E. A795
Fetsko, Francis M. A1033
Fetter, Elizabeth A. E218
Fetter, Trevor A502
Fetterolf, Brian S. A1039
Fetterolf, Brian S. E498
Fettig, Jeff M. A342
Fettig, Jeff M. A934
Feuer, Bradley A P65
Feuerhake, Rainer W270
Few, Julius E57
Feygin, Anatol A225
Ffolkes, Marie A. A1085
Ffolkes, Marie A. A666
Fiala, Robert A. A1013
Fiarman, Jeffrey A. E221
Fibig, Andreas E179
Ficalora, Joseph R. A396
Ficalora, Joseph R. E187
Fick, Daniel A548
Fick, Daniel P272
Fick, Jeffrey D. A896
Fick, Jeffrey D. E422
Fick, Nathaniel C. E467
Fiddelke, Michael J. A997
Fiedelman, Cindy A. E141
Fiederowicz, Walter M. E383
Fiedler-Kelly, Jill E444
Fiedler, Susanne A787
Fiedler, Terri A296
Field, Callie R. A992
Field, Dale F. E149
Field, Darren A543
Field, James M. A865
Field, James M. E403
Fieldly, John E88
Fields, Janice L. W31

Fields, Kwame A398
Fields, Mark A867
Fields, Mark A513
Fields, Mark E. A438
Fields, Venita E473
Fieler, Anna E407
Fier, Walter J. A306
Fierro, Carlos A. E91
Figari, Alberta W54
Figliuolo, Stephen V. A435
Figliuolo, Stephen V. E210
Fignar, Robert J. A788
Fignar, Robert J. E365
Figueiredo, João (John) M. de A367
Figuereo, Juan R. A1120
Figuereo, Juan R. E137
Figuereo, Juan R. E535
Figueroa, Juan Jose Paullada W470
Figueroa, Julio Santiago W70
Filanowski, Mark L. E370
Filaretos, Spyros N. W33
File, William H. A250
File, William H. E99
Filho, Antonio Carlos Canto Porto W69
Filho, Eduardo de Oliveira Rodrigues W630
Filho, Eleazar de Carvalho W590
Filho, Lincoln da Cunha Pereira A491
Filho, Lucio de Castro Andrade W622
Filho, Marcelo Mesquita de Siqueira W468
Filho, Milton Maluhy W315
Filho, Milton Maluhy W314
Filho, Oscar Augusto de Camargo W630
Filho, Oswaldo de Assis W69
Fili-Krushel, Patricia D. A336
Fili-Krushel, Patricia D. A232
Filiberto, Ruth E. A439
Filipkowski, Greg A59
Filipovic, Damir W580
Filipovic, Damir W580
Filipowska, Joanna Karolina E181
Filippelli, Maria W122
Filippin, William F. E114
Filipps, Frank P. A787
Filipps, Frank P. E411
Filler, James J. A932
Filler, James J. E436
Filler, Linda P. Hefner A203
Filler, Linda P. Hefner A315
Filliol, Olivier A. E325
Filosa, Antonio W562
Filton, Steve G. A1076
Fimiani, Grazia W227
Finan, Irial A447
Finch, David C. E147
Finch, Mary E. A349
Finch, Shannon W648
Findlay, D. Cameron A94
Findlay, David M. A617
Findlay, David M. E290
Findlay, Deirdre E452
Findlay, Martha Hall W573
Findlay, Michael W509
Findley, Darren E. E418
Fine, Andrew S. A1033
Fine, Andrew S. E493
Fine, Debra E236
Fine, J. Allen E280

Fine, James A. E280
Fine, Lauren Rich E432
Fine, Marc D. A472
Fine, Marc D. E230
Fine, W. Morris E280
Finer, Timothy D. A515
Fines, Robert E. E188
Fink, Anne A326
Fink, Kristina V. A62
Fink, Laurence D. A160
Fink, Monika W162
Fink, Nicholas I. A291
Fink, Nicholas I. A447
Fink, Steven B. E468
Finke, Thomas M. A573
Finkelstein, David L. A83
Finkelstein, Mark A. A270
Finkelstein, Mark A. E109
Finlayson, Jock W80
Finley, John G. A161
Finley, John G. E493
Finley, Tammy M. A17
Finley, Tammy M. A66
Finley, Tammy M. E25
Finley, Terrance G. E254
Finley, Wayne P170
Finn, Barry A774
Finn, Barry E360
Finn, Gaylyn J. E428
Finn, L. Christian E215
Finnegan, Paul J. A214
Finnell, Scott C. E189
Finneran, John G. A198
Finnerty, Kevin J. E347
Finnerty, William J. A321
Finney, Elisha W. A1093
Finney, Elisha W. E325
Finney, Elisha W. E262
Finnie, Cindy H. E204
Finser, Mark A. E19
Finucane, Anne M. A311
Finucane, Anne M. A1132
Fiordalice, Robert E362
Fiore, Anthony C. A1046
Fiore, Pasquale (Pat) A37
Fiorile, Michael J. A966
Fipps, Paul A1059
Firek, Marcin W651
Firestone, James A. A483
Firouzbakht, Farid A279
First, Mark L. E5
Fisch, Harry E522
Fisch, Robert N. E360
Fischer, Alexander R. E5
Fischer, David B. A557
Fischer, Elizabeth E382
Fischer, Hans-Peter W640
Fischer, Jessica M. A223
Fischer, Jonathan A. E490
Fischer, Mark D. A864
Fischer, Rudolph W. W523
Fischer, Stanley A403
Fischer, Tamara D. E146
Fischer, Tamara D. E340
Fish, James C. A1110
Fish, Simon A. W82
Fisher, Andrew C. W385
Fisher, Brian J. E413
Fisher, Cynthia A. E150
Fisher, Cynthia A. E65

Fisher, Dan A357
Fisher, Daniel W. A123
Fisher, David A. E162
Fisher, Donne F. A872
Fisher, E. Beauregarde A266
Fisher, Gregory J. E160
Fisher, Heath A. E370
Fisher, Helene Loraine E144
Fisher, Joe A723
Fisher, Jonas D. M. A399
Fisher, Kenneth M. E91
Fisher, Mark P. A977
Fisher, Mark P. E464
Fisher, Martin W390
Fisher, Michael J. (Jud) A427
Fisher, Michael J. (Jud) E203
Fisher, Mike E175
Fisher, Richard W. A817
Fisher, Richard W. A1003
Fisher, Robert (Bob) J. A1018
Fisher, Robert D. A249
Fisher, Robert D. E99
Fisher, Robert P. A252
Fisher, Stephanie D. E436
Fisher, Stephen E120
Fisher, William (Bill) Sydney A1018
Fisher, William C. E540
Fishman, Alan H. A616
Fishman, Alan H. A915
Fishman, Michael A941
Fisk, George A. A852
Fisk, George A. E399
Fisk, John D. A28
Fister, Todd A795
Fitch, Laurie W212
Fite, Charles D. A130
Fitt, Lawton Wehle A851
Fitt, Lawton Wehle A203
Fitterling, James R. A342
Fitterling, James R. A4
Fitzer, Jan A37
Fitzer, Jan E14
Fitzgerald, Ari Q. A301
Fitzgerald, Emma A737
Fitzgerald, Gary G. E537
Fitzgerald, James B. A351
Fitzgerald, John J. E537
Fitzgerald, Joseph Michael A175
Fitzgerald, Larry A326
Fitzgerald, Margaret Boles A181
Fitzgerald, Meghan M. A1003
Fitzgerald, Michael P. A1063
Fitzgerald, Michael P. E508
Fitzgerald, Norman P. E350
Fitzgerald, Stephen W487
Fitzgerald, William R. E387
Fitzpatrick, Daniel B. A1
Fitzpatrick, Dawn W90
Fitzpatrick, Edward J. E87
Fitzpatrick, Eileen W81
FitzPatrick, Mark Thomas W481
Fitzpatrick, Nora A400
Fitzsimmons, Ellen M. A54
Fitzsimmons, Robert J. A1115
Fitzsimmons, Robert J. E533
Fitzwater, Matthew W90
Fjell, Olav E161
Flach, Gloria A. A366
Flaherty, Lauren Patricia A182
Flaherty, Mark A. A480

COMBINED HOOVER'S HANDBOOK INDEX OF EXECUTIVES

```
A = AMERICAN BUSINESS
E = EMERGING COMPANIES
P = PRIVATE COMPANIES
W = WORLD BUSINESSS
```

Flaherty, Scott B. E538
Flake, Jeffry (Jeff) L. A998
Flaminia, Alinka E75
Flanagan, David C. A192
Flanagan, Glenda J. E128
Flanagan, Glenda J. E529
Flanagan, Joseph Gerard E408
Flanagan, Laura J. A818
Flanagan, Martin L. A573
Flanagan, Robert J. E530
Flanagan, Timothy K. E236
Flanigan, Matthew C. A818
Flannelly, Barry P. E267
Flannery, Matthew (Matt) J. A1071
Flannery, Patrick H. E455
Flanzraich, Neil W. A232
Flato, Ilan W410
Flaton, Carol A148
Flatt, J. Bruce W112
Flaugher, Brett A. A776
Flautt, Robert J. E90
Fleche, Eric Richer La W83
Fleche, Eric Richer La W398
Flees, Lori A. E517
Fleischer, Egbert W93
Fleischer, Spencer C. A254
Fleischer, Spencer C. A631
Fleishman, Stanley E360
Fleming, Campbell W471
Fleming, Gary G. A106
Fleming, Graham A. E190
Fleming, Jean W61
Fleming, Ned N. E117
Fleming, Richard H. A166
Fleming, Ronald W. E292
Fleming, Susan S. A896
Fleming, Susan S. E422
Fleming, Susan S. E528
Fleming, William K. A541
Flesch, John G. A37
Flesch, John G. E14
Fleshood, John S. A1038
Fleshood, John S. A1133
Fleshood, John S. E495
Fleshood, John S. E541
Flessner, Kyle M. A1010
Fletcher, Gerald W. E388
Fletcher, Jeremy A. A765
Fletcher, Nick C. E293
Fletcher, Pamela E305
Fletcher, R. John E47
Fletcher, Robert A981
Fletcher, Steven C. E295
Fleurant, James W288
Fleuriot, Pierre W492
Fleuriot, Pierre W441
Fleury, Alison J P500
Flexon, Robert C. A823
Flichy, Bruno W213
Flieger, Erwin W3
Flint, Deborah A530
Flitman, David (Dave) E. A1087
Flitman, David E. A1083
Floel, Martina W518

Floel, Martina W427
Floerke, Gregory S. A717
Flood, Eugene A418
Florance, Andrew C. E123
Florence, Cristian W73
Florence, John M. A950
Flores, Ashlee A152
Flores, Hector Avila W265
Flores, Jeanne P109
Flores, Jose Antonio Gonzalez W131
Flores, Rafael A54
Flores, Rose P137
Florey, Reinhard W458
Florian, Gerard W63
Floriani, Kimberly A. A252
Florie, Walter M. A393
Florin, Daniel P. E43
Florness, Daniel L. A394
Florness, Daniel L. E226
Flournoy, Michele A. A171
Flowers, David A. A872
Flowers, M. L. A539
Flowers, Robert E. A848
Flowers, Robert P. E117
Floyd, H. Charles A608
Floyd, Jennifer C. A524
Floyd, Jennifer C. E258
Floyd, Johnny W. A72
Floyd, Johnny W. E29
Floyd, Nancy C. A246
Fløystøl, Kirsti Valborgland W562
Fluhler, Stephan H. A427
Fluhler, Stephan H. E203
Flur, Dorlisa K. E254
Flutter, Naomi W644
Flynn, Brian A617
Flynn, Brian E289
Flynn, Brian C. A1043
Flynn, Karen E83
Flynn, Michael T. A350
Flynn, Michael T. E148
Flynn, Patrick W64
Flynn, Patrick W425
Flynn, Patrick W423
Flynn, Paul E138
Flynn, Peter J. E286
Flynn, Rachel A389
Flynn, Rachel P219
Flynn, Thomas E. W82
Flynn, Thomas E. W596
Flynn, Thomas L. A507
Flynn, Thomas L. E248
Flynn, Thomas R. A200
Flynn, Thomas R. E79
Flynn, Timothy P. A1075
Flynn, Timothy Patrick A591
Flynn, Timothy Patrick A1104
Foad, Keiran W75
Fobes, Malcolm R. E510
Fobes, Malcolm R. E509
Fobes, Malcolm R. E510
Foda, Sherif E161
Foden, Ross Neil W36
Foell, Charlie E341
Fogal, Christopher E. A923
Fogal, Christopher E. E433
Fogarty, Elizabeth A493
Fogarty, James P. A316
Fogarty, Jane C. A287
Fogarty, Kevin P304

Fogel, Glenn D. A170
Fogelberg, Anders W548
Fok, Canning K. N. W133
Fok, Winnie W548
Folberth, William P104
Foletta, Mark G. E138
Foley, Brendan M. A673
Foley, Christopher D. A195
Foley, D Sue P604
Foley, John W374
Foley, Ursuline F. A854
Foley, William P. A406
Folland, Nick P385
Follen, Geert W60
Follette, James A811
Follette, James E378
Follette, James E377
Folliard, Thomas J. A205
Folliard, Thomas J. A862
Follit, Evelyn V. E310
Follmer, Cathy P345
Folse, Mark P. A188
Folse, Mark P. E69
Folsom, Suzanne R. A825
Fomperosa, Esteban Malpica W266
Fong, Christopher L. W120
Fong, Ivan K. A4
Fong, Ivan K. E87
Fong, Jimmy Kar Chun W139
Fonseca, Ana E. A398
Fonseca, Cristina W254
Fonseca, Dhiren R. A34
Fonseca, Lidia L. A821
Fonseca, Lidia L. W393
Fontaine, Heather La E428
Fontan, Kimberly A. A371
Fontana, Bernard W601
Fontanesi, Giorgia W177
Fontbona, Jean Paul Luksic W70
Fontenot, Teri G. E300
Fontes, Teresa Cristina Athayde Marcondes W315
Foo, Jixun W67
Fooks, Elik I. A902
Foos, John G. A39
Foote, William C. A1102
Foraker, Randy P. A125
Foraker, Randy P. E52
Foran, Margaret Madden A856
Foran, Matthew R. A1065
Forberg, Lars W7
Forbes, John A. E373
Ford, Beth E. A796
Ford, Beth E. A964
Ford, Celeste Volz E444
Ford, Darrell L. A553
Ford, Darrell L. A349
Ford, Edsel B. A444
Ford, Gary P350
Ford, Gerald J. A516
Ford, Harold Eugene E440
Ford, James W258
Ford, Jay M. A396
Ford, Jay M. E187
Ford, Jeremy B. A516
Ford, Joseph A125
Ford, Joseph E52
Ford, Monte E. A216
Ford, Monte E. A583
Ford, Monte E. E12

Ford, Robert B. A6
Ford, Scott T. A105
Ford, William E425
Ford, William (Bill) E. A160
Ford, William Clay A444
Ford, William R P687
Forde, Mick E493
Fordham, Scott W. E124
Fordyce, L. Chris E206
Forese, James A. W289
Forkrud, David E236
Forlenza, Joseph A923
Forlenza, Joseph E433
Forlenza, Vincent A. A711
Forman-Barenblit, Melissa A1040
Forman-Barenblit, Melissa E499
Forman, Alan N. E49
Forment, Jorge L. E492
Forneri, Jean-Marc A561
Fornés, Maite Ballester W493
Forney, Alan M. A1151
Forrest, Andrew W246
Forrest, Eric S. A271
Forrest, Eric S. E109
Forry, Linda Dorcena A380
Forsberg, Mattias W579
Forsee, Gary D. W617
Forssell, Johan W60
Forsyte, Carol H. E10
Forsyth, Michael S. E536
Forsythe, Gerald E81
Forsythe, Patrick E228
Fort, John W. E418
Forte, Andrew A. E354
Forth, Steven D. E30
Forthuber, Frederick A. E536
Fortin, Anne W308
Fortin, Michael E. E342
Fortin, Richard W31
Fortino, Carmine W398
Fortkiewicz, Victor A. E453
Fortunat, David E3
Fortunato, Joseph M. A959
Fosburgh, Bryn A. E497
Foschi, Marianella E101
Foshee, William M. A932
Foshee, William M. E436
Foskett, Christopher M. E520
Foss, David B. A261
Foss, Eric J. A239
Fossati, Giorgio W562
Fosse, Gaelle de la W13
Fossum, Erik W448
Foster, Byron S. A1099
Foster, Byron S. A313
Foster, Christopher A. A823
Foster, David A355
Foster, David P209
Foster, Deidre B. E515
Foster, James C. E94
Foster, John A1132
Foster, John E539
Foster, Jon M. A505
Foster, Jonathan F. A153
Foster, Jonathan F. A622
Foster, Kelly A125
Foster, Kelly E52
Foster, Lee B. A1099
Foster, Nancy J. A1138
Foster, Nancy J. E544

HOOVER'S HANDBOOK OF EMERGING COMPANIES 2023

COMBINED HOOVER'S HANDBOOK INDEX OF EXECUTIVES

A = AMERICAN BUSINESS
E = EMERGING COMPANIES
P = PRIVATE COMPANIES
W = WORLD BUSINESSS

Foster, Ronald C. E6
Foster, Steve P. E293
Foster, Vincent D. A868
Foster, William I. A1033
Foster, William I. E493
Fouberg, Rodney W. A311
Fouche, Lori Dickerson A610
Fougner, Else Bugge W347
Foulke, Ken P639
Foulkes, Anne M. A840
Foulkes, David M. A182
Foulon-Tonat, Martha A350
Foulon-Tonat, Martha E148
Foulon, Hugues W459
Fountain, David A1006
Fountain, T. Heath E108
Fouque, Jorge Andueza W217
Fournier, Michele P421
Fouse, Jacquelyn A. E267
Foust, Donald R. A1144
Fowden, Jeremy S.G. A292
Fowler, Cameron W82
Fowler, Christopher H. W122
Fowler, Fed J. A319
Fowler, Hardy B. A496
Fowler, John M. A979
Fowler, June McAllister A276
Fowler, Michael J. A200
Fowler, Michael J. E79
Fowler, Peggy Y. A1057
Fowler, W. Randall A374
Fowlkes, Steven H A392
Fowlkes, Steven H P221
Fox-Martin, Adaire A377
Fox, Ann G. A325
Fox, Carrie M. E101
Fox, Edward D. A1121
Fox, Jason E. E530
Fox, Jennifer E157
Fox, Jennifer J. A398
Fox, Lynne P. E19
Fox, Martha Lane A1047
Fox, Mary E305
Fox, Richard C. A196
Fox, Richard C. E78
Fox, Richard P. A1075
Fox, Richard P. E221
Fox, Richard Scott (Rick) E174
Fox, Stephen A. E72
Fox, Steven E. E240
Foxx, Anthony R. A663
Foxx, Anthony R. A214
Foy, John T. A889
Foy, John T. E414
Fraccaro, Michael A670
Frachet, Stephanie W631
Fradin, Roger B. A893
Fradin, Roger B. A613
Fradin, Roger B. E283
Fradin, Russell P. E493
Fradkin, Steven L. A748
Fraga, Vasco Esteves W70
Fraher, Kathleen M. A937
Fraher, Kathleen M. E441

Frailey, Alton L. A954
Frampton, Marcus A35
Frampton, Marcus P15
France, Gina D. A545
Franceschini, Luca W227
Francese, James E. E460
Franchini, Roberto W310
Francioli, Richard W635
Francioni, Reto W621
Francis, Cheryl E333
Francis, Cheryl A. W44
Francis, David L. E280
Francis, Julian G. A145
Francis, Mary W89
Francis, Mary W90
Francis, Mary A. A230
Francis, Richard D. E325
Francisco, Fama A850
Francisco, Fatima Ma. A787
Franck, John M. A505
Franco, Javier Augusto Gonzalez W265
Franco, Jorge Elman Osorio W210
Franco, Juan David Escobar W76
Francoeur, Bruno W573
Francois-Poncet, Andre W65
Francq, Thierry W199
Frandberg, Sofia W641
Frandsen, Freddy W632
Frank, Barney A936
Frank, Barney E440
Frank, Edward H. A81
Frank, Howard S. E459
Frank, John B. A230
Frank, Kenneth R. A69
Frank, Mark A. A507
Frank, Mark A. E248
Frank, Simon R. E184
Frank, Thomas A. E279
Franke, Mary Carter Warren A944
Franke, Mary Carter Warren E450
Franke, Norman E19
Frankel, Merrie S. E9
Frankel, Michael S. E419
Frankiewicz, Rebecca E160
Franklin, Christopher H. A218
Franklin, Christopher H. E174
Franklin, Heather L. E545
Franklin, Jerry A814
Franklin, Jerry E379
Franklin, Katherine F. E173
Franklin, Robert J. E490
Franklin, Robert R. A213
Frankola, Jim E32
Franks, David L. E469
Franks, Wendy A. E174
Franson, Michael C. E353
Frantz, Mark A. E38
Franz, Christoph W666
Franz, Christoph W502
Franz, Timothy J. E63
Franzi, Cristiano A142
Franzini, Caren S. A396
Franzini, Caren S. E187
Frappier, Marc W495
Frasch, Ronald L. E130
Fraser-Moleketi, Geraldine W559
Fraser, Anna E452
Fraser, Claire M. A147
Fraser, James C. W491
Fraser, Jane Nind A246

Fraser, Jason W. A1085
Fraser, Liz A993
Frasinetti, Ethel W627
Fratto, Tanya D. E5
Frauenberg, James H. E91
Frayser, Peter E283
Frazell, Chad M. A209
Frazer, Preston B. A111
Frazier, A. D. A1006
Frazier, John R. A860
Frazier, Kenneth C. A684
Frazier, Larry D. A488
Frazier, Steve W122
Frazis, George W85
Freda, Fabrizio A620
Freda, Fabrizio A160
Freda, William C. A973
Fredell, Thomas P191
Frederick, Eugene E180
Frederick, Wayne A.I. A541
Frederick, Wayne A.I. E277
Frederick, William W. E444
Fredericks, Mark J. A617
Fredericks, Mark J. E289
Frederickson, Philip L. A371
Frederiksen-england, Matt P656
Fredette, Eric Antoine W631
Fredlake, James F. E292
Fredman, Sheara J. A480
Fredo, Scot E81
Fredrickson, David W57
Fredrickson, Glenn H. W400
Fredston, Dale C. A691
Fredston, Dale C. E323
Freedberg, Catherine Blanton A134
Freedberg, Catherine Blanton E54
Freedman, Ian W371
Freedman, Paul L. A23
Freeland, Clint C. A714
Freeland, Richard J. E517
Freeman, Brenda L. A118
Freeman, Brennan E273
Freeman, Cathy S. A190
Freeman, Cathy S. E73
Freeman, Dena P341
Freeman, Jennifer L. E376
Freeman, Jody L. A288
Freeman, Karen P401
Freeman, Kevin M. A771
Freeman, Philip D. E246
Freeman, Robert W. E156
Freeman, Scott D. E150
Freeman, Thomas E. E99
Freemer, Mark A. E156
Frega, Lorraine W168
Frei, Barbara W581
Frei, Maye Head A848
Freiberg, Steven Jay A670
Freiberg, Steven Jay E413
Freier, Jonathan A. A992
Freigang, Julie Scheck A532
Freigang, Julie Scheck E259
Freire, Maria C. A158
Freire, Maria C. E15
Freire, Maria C. E178
Freishtat, Gregg E240
Freitas, Jorge Seabra de W254
French, Doug W596
French, R. Reid E45
French, Tara L. A749

French, Tracy M. A524
French, Tracy M. E258
Frenette, David P. A500
Frenette, David P. E246
Frenkiel, Paul A1014
Frenkiel, Paul E488
Frenzel, Michael W280
Frenzel, Michael W270
Frenzel, Robert C. A1139
Frenzel, Robert C. A806
Frerichs, Robert N. E500
Frérot, Antoine W631
Fretwell, Betsy P133
Fretz, Joseph H. A652
Freudenstein, Richard J. W162
Freund, John G. E107
Frew, Anita W371
Frew, Nicole W84
Frey, Andrew E116
Frey, Daniel S. A1037
Frey, Kirsten H. A515
Freydberg, Ronald A. A693
Freyman, Thomas C. A1004
Freyman, Thomas C. A8
Freyne, Colm J. W570
Freyne, Colm J. W572
Freyou, Jason P. A523
Freyou, Jason P. E257
Friar, Sarah J. A1104
Frias, Yanela A856
Fribourg, Paul J. A185
Fribourg, Paul J. A620
Fribourg, Paul J. A645
Frick, David P. W430
Fridman, Mikhail M. W655
Fridriksdottir, Hafrun W598
Fried, Bernard A868
Friedland, David W311
Friedman-Boyce, Inez H. A499
Friedman-Boyce, Inez H. E246
Friedman, Adena T. A721
Friedman, Alexander S. A448
Friedman, Brian P. A581
Friedman, Brian P. E529
Friedman, David A. A631
Friedman, Douglas E493
Friedman, Gregory R. A298
Friedman, Hanan W79
Friedman, Howard E. A940
Friedman, Joel P. A984
Friedman, Joel P. E476
Friedman, Joel S. E168
Friedman, Lester M. E50
Friedman, Paul M. E363
Friedrich, Matthew W. A1075
Friel, Robert F. E534
Friend, Matthew A743
Friend, Matthew A1062
Friese, Lard W16
Frieson, Donald E. A209
Frigerio, Dario W363
Friis, Mark E. A913
Friis, Mark E. E427
Friis, Morten N. W425
Friis, Morten N. W423
Friman, Maija-Liisa W231
Frink, Lloyd D. A1148
Frinzi, Thomas G. E460
Frisby, Jeffry D. E404
Friscia, Anthony J. E215

COMBINED HOOVER'S HANDBOOK INDEX OF EXECUTIVES

A = AMERICAN BUSINESS
E = EMERGING COMPANIES
P = PRIVATE COMPANIES
W = WORLD BUSINESSS

Frishman, Arik W312
Frisk, Mikael W247
Frist, Julie D. E300
Frist, Thomas F. A505
Frist, William Harrison A926
Frist, William R. A505
Fritel, Steven James A235
Fritz, Connie E83
Fritz, Lance M. A804
Fritz, Lance M. A1061
Fritz, Sandra W639
Fritze, Steven L. E367
Froedge, James P. A366
Froehlich, Fritz W. W489
Froehlich, Stephan P581
Froetscher, Janet P. E87
Froggatt, Scott W. E260
Fröhlich, Fritz Wilhelm W495
Fröhlich, Fritz Wilhelm W482
Frohlich, Klaus W207
Froimson, Mark E369
Froman, Michael B. A335
Froman, Michael B. A670
Frome, James J. E457
Frondorf, James C. A397
Frooman, Thomas E. A242
Frost, Donald L. E469
Frost, Jennifer L. A307
Frost, Jennifer L. E132
Frost, Joshua L. A400
Frost, Michael R. E469
Frost, Patrick W502
Frost, Patrick W580
Frost, Patrick W580
Frost, Patrick B. A305
Frost, Richard W. A145
Frostick, Randolph D. E526
Frotte, Gaetan A757
Frowsing, Sheila E111
Fruchterman, Todd M. W242
Frudden, Constance B. A401
Fruit, Molly Strader A94
Frushone, Ashley Davis E501
Frutos, Pilar Gonzalez de W219
Fry, Earl E. A219
Fry, James A. A1144
Fry, John A. A282
Fry, Stephen F. (Steve) A635
Fry, Todd R. E274
Fry, Todd R. E470
Fry, William F. E337
Frye, Andrew A142
Frye, Patrick N. A981
Frye, Patrick N. E469
Frymier, Matthew D. E393
Fu, Cary T. E303
Fu, David Yat Hung W128
Fu, Fan W145
Fu, Gangfeng W142
Fu, Jianguo W88
Fu, Jun W477
Fu, Junyuan W477
Fu, Ming W375
Fu, Ping A641

Fu, Rong W529
Fu, Suotang W466
Fu, Tingmei W148
Fu, Yuanlue W274
Fu, Zhigang W356
Fuangfu, Chansak W77
Fubini, David G. A625
Fuchs, Christine A191
Fuchs, Christine E77
Fuchs, Henry J. E61
Fuchs, Jaroslaw W86
Fuchs, Matthew E366
Fucinato, Mark A188
Fucinato, Mark E71
Fuda, Domenico W286
Fuder, Andrea W641
Fudge, Ann M. A752
Fudge, Ann M. W449
Fuentes, Jose Ernesto W266
Fuentes, Laura A518
Fugate, William Craig A823
Fuhr, Matthew D. A498
Fuhrmann, Heinz Joerg W62
Fujibayashi, Kiyotaka W409
Fujihara, Kazuhiko W550
Fujii, Hiroshi W65
Fujii, Ichirou W357
Fujii, Mariko W451
Fujii, Mariko W407
Fujii, Takashi W181
Fujikawa, Osamu W425
Fujikura, Katsuaki W604
Fujimori, Masayuki W313
Fujimori, Shun W313
Fujimori, Yoshiaki A175
Fujimori, Yoshiaki W585
Fujimoto, Jason R. A219
Fujimoto, Junichi W357
Fujimoto, Masayoshi W552
Fujimoto, Michael K. A423
Fujimoto, Nobuto W436
Fujimoto, Tomoko W293
Fujimura, Akihiko W293
Fujimura, Hiroshi W535
Fujisaki, Kazuo W336
Fujisaki, Kei W538
Fujisawa, Kumi W539
Fujisawa, Kumi W616
Fujita, Kazuko W357
Fujita, Motohiro W17
Fujito, Masahito W568
Fujiwara, Ichiro W83
Fujiwara, Ken W400
Fujiwara, Masataka W462
Fujiwara, Satoru W292
Fujiwara, Shuichi W81
Fujiwara, Toshi W451
Fujiyama, Ian A171
Fukai, Akihiko W266
Fukakusa, Janice W371
Fukakusa, Janice R. W112
Fukasawa, Yuji W208
Fukuchi, Junichi W321
Fukuda, Haruko W310
Fukuda, Masahito W413
Fukuda, Nobuo W400
Fukuda, Takaharu W330
Fukuda, Takayuki W657
Fukuda, Toshihiko W607
Fukui, Akira W657

Fukui, Toshihiko W536
Fukujin, Yusuke W28
Fukunaga, Takehisa W65
Fukushima, Sakie Tachibana W357
Fukushima, Yutaka W539
Fukutome, Akihiro W570
Fukuzawa, Toshihiko A24
Fulk, Dennis E340
Fuller, Daniel P. A196
Fuller, Daniel P. E78
Fuller, David G. E116
Fuller, David G. W262
Fuller, Gilbert A. E434
Fuller, Joseph B. A864
Fuller, Julie A. A864
Fuller, Lynn B. A507
Fuller, Lynn B. E248
Fuller, Rodger D. A950
Fuller, Samuel R. E213
Fuller, Vicki L. A1131
Fullerton, Albert E. E421
Fulmer, H. Andrew E25
Fulmer, James W. A1033
Fulmer, James W. A396
Fulmer, James W. E187
Fulton, Laura C. A995
Fulton, Tricia L. E249
Fumagalli, Adrienne Corboud W580
Fumagalli, Adrienne Corboud W580
Funaki, Ryuichiro W418
Funamoto, Kaoru W281
Funck, Florian W129
Funck, Florian W390
Funck, Robert E. A6
Fung, Anita Yuen Mei W105
Fung, Kwok King Victor W346
Funiciello, John P. E372
Funk, Andrea J. A303
Funk, Charles N. A704
Funk, Charles N. E328
Funk, Jane M. A1118
Funk, Jane M. E533
Funk, Michael S. A1068
Funke, Matthew T. A953
Funke, Matthew T. E455
Furber, Jeffrey D. E461
Furber, Sara E493
Furberg, Petter-Borre W594
Fure, Hiroshi W356
Furer, Guido W580
Furey, John P. E117
Furlong, Matthew A457
Furner, John R. A1104
Furr, Allen K. E515
Furr, William B. A516
Furse, Clara Hedwig Frances W638
Furstenberg, Alexander von A385
Furstenberg, Alexander von E261
Furuichi, Takeshi W436
Furukawa, Hironari W269
Furukawa, Koji W330
Furukawa, Shuntaro W433
Furumoto, Shozo W437
Furuta, Hidenori W253
Furuta, Katsuya W402
Furuya, Fumihiko W659
Furuya, Hiromichi W155
Furuya, Takayuki W387
Furuya, Yoshiaki W659
Furuyama, Hideaki W515

Fusco, G. Robert A396
Fusco, G. Robert E187
Fusco, Jack A. A225
Fusco, Jack A. A226
Fushitani, Kiyoshi W460
Futagawa, Kazuo W610
Futter, Ellen V. A289
Futter, Ellen V. A290
Futter, Ellen V. E176
Fyfield, Mai E423
Fyrwald, J. Erik A635
Fyrwald, J. Erik A185

G

Gaba, David L. E134
Gabanna, Louis W161
Gabas, Antonio Gallart W423
Gabbard, Dan W399
Gabbay, Mark A588
Gabbay, Yoram W79
Gabelli, Mario J. E300
Gabosch, Bradley R. A771
Gabriel, Jamie L. A372
Gabriel, Jamie L. E167
Gabriel, Kaigham (Ken) E497
Gabriel, Stuart A. A594
Gabriele, Judy R. E102
Gabrielson, Sharon R. E437
Gadbois, L. G. Serge W295
Gadde, Vijaya A1047
Gade, Michael J. E35
Gadhia, Jayne-Anne W625
Gadola, Marco W203
Gadomski, Marcin W86
Gadre, Ambika Kapur E147
Gaeddert, Gregory L. A378
Gaemperle, Chantal W373
Gaer, Steven K. A1118
Gaer, Steven K. E533
Gaffney, Maureen A. A554
Gaffney, Maureen A. E268
Gaffney, Sean E5
Gafner, Martin W631
Gagas, Adam C. E372
Gage, Cheryl D. E204
Gage, Michelle A. A68
Gage, Vanessa A785
Gagey, Frederic W22
Gagle, Suzanne A657
Gagle, Suzanne A717
Gagne, Andre W193
Gagnier, Hugh K. A1148
Gagnon, Martin W420
Gahler, Steve A510
Gahler, Steve E252
Gahlhoff, Jerry E. E424
Gaillard, Jean-Pierre W174
Gaines, Bennett L. A432
Gaines, Elizabeth Anne W246
Gainor, John P. E426
Gajaria, Rajan A298
Galan, Ignacio Sanchez A112
Galan, Jose Ignacio Sanchez W295
Galanda, Gabriel S. E204
Galant, Paul S. A1120
Galant, Paul S. E535
Galante, Ann M P624

HOOVER'S HANDBOOK OF EMERGING COMPANIES 2023

COMBINED HOOVER'S HANDBOOK INDEX OF EXECUTIVES

A = AMERICAN BUSINESS
E = EMERGING COMPANIES
P = PRIVATE COMPANIES
W = WORLD BUSINESSS

Galante, Edward G. A215
Galante, Edward G. A657
Galante, Edward G. W369
Galante, Joseph C. A829
Galante, Joseph C. E385
Galanti, Richard A. A300
Galanti, Richard A. A402
Galanti, Vanes W627
Galanti, Vanes W627
Galardi, Guido W627
Galbato, Chan W. A35
Galbo, Julie W204
Galbraith, Susan W57
Galbreath, Kristen P670
Gale, Keith W18
Galeazzi, Claudio Eugenio Stiller W69
Gales, Amy H. A396
Gales, Amy H. E186
Galford, Robert M. E215
Galhotra, Kumar A444
Galifi, Vincent J. W379
Galik, Milan E279
Galilee, Brenda E313
Galin, Amira W410
Galindo, Susan P395
Galioto, Frank A251
Galioto, Frank P137
Galipeau, Linda W489
Gall-Robinson, Claire Le W526
Gall, David W419
Gall, Gary D. E90
Gall, Jeffrey A. E357
Galla, Christopher T. A468
Gallagher, Daniel J. E69
Gallagher, Gerard M. E1
Gallagher, J. Patrick A455
Gallagher, James D. W382
Gallagher, Kevin Charles A1056
Gallagher, Kevin Charles E505
Gallagher, Marie T. A817
Gallagher, Mary E. E25
Gallagher, Matthew M. A228
Gallagher, Matthew M. A830
Gallagher, Michael J. A372
Gallagher, Michael J. E167
Gallagher, Philip R. A118
Gallagher, Samantha Sacks E524
Gallagher, Terence A854
Gallagher, Thomas J. A455
Gallahue, Kieran T. A361
Galle, Jean-Loic W600
Gallego, Emilio Garcia W11
Gallerano, Lisa A492
Gallerano, Lisa E243
Galli, Dario W363
Gallienne, Ian W14
Galligani, Siv F. W347
Galliker, Max W631
Gallimore, Alec D. E32
Gallimore, Chester A. A207
Gallimore, T. Mauyer E372
Gallina, John E. A85
Gallion, Brett A. E132
Gallo-Aquino, Cristina A. A909

Gallo, Jose W622
Gallo, Livio W220
Gallo, Ralph E371
Gallopoulos, Gregory S. A460
Gallot, Richard A788
Gallot, Richard E364
Gallotta, Steven E. A976
Galloway, Rick A643
Galloway, Tracey U. E190
Galtney, William F. W233
Galuccio, Miguel Matias W523
Galuchie, John W. E23
Galvagni, Agostino W580
Galvanoni, Matthew R. A828
Galvez, Jean-Marc A153
Galvez, Jose Damian Bogas W219
Galvin, Brandi L. A377
Galvin, Donal W20
Galvin, Sean P. E527
Gamal, Bassel W18
Gamba, Angela W391
Gamba, Philippe W490
Gambale, Virginia E527
Gambee, Stephen M. A1057
Gamble, John W. E134
Gamble, Sondra A168
Gamble, Sondra P89
Games, Gregory R. E134
Gamez, Jose P639
Gamgort, Robert James A600
Gammell, Damian P. W161
Gan, David Y. A20
Gan, Kathleen Chieh Huey W268
Gan, Larry Nyap Liou W36
Gan, Pin W529
Gandhi, Aditya J. A950
Ganeev, Oleg W521
Ganeles, Scott E493
Gannfors, John W. A770
Gano, Kyle E346
Ganong, David A. W571
Gans, Bruce M. E270
Gansberg, David E. W50
Gansert, Heidei S E388
Ganti, Anita E392
Ganzin, Michel W174
Gao, Bingxue W662
Gao, Chenxia W656
Gao, Debu W256
Gao, Debu W307
Gao, Dennis E304
Gao, Dongzhang W272
Gao, Fengjuan W528
Gao, Fenglong W663
Gao, Han Lin E224
Gao, Jianmin W326
Gao, Jie W257
Gao, Shaoyong W656
Gao, Shujun W528
Gao, Tongqing W143
Gao, W. Victor A97
Gao, Weidong W356
Gao, Wenbao W106
Gao, Xiang W141
Gao, Xingfang W662
Gao, Yunhu W152
Gaona, Amancio Ortega W300
Garber, Alan M. A1089
Garber, Alan M. E178
Garber, Scott H. E299

Garbiso, Sandra K. E101
Garceau, Mary L. A933
Garcia-Ansorena, Ramiro Mato W76
Garcia-Ivald, Romain W613
Garcia-Thomas, Cristina A. A1114
Garcia, Adrian P170
Garcia, Alberto Velazquez W470
Garcia, Antonio Botella W11
Garcia, Art A. A10
Garcia, Art A. A59
Garcia, Astrid J. E295
Garcia, Begoña Elices W493
Garcia, Belen Romana W64
Garcia, Belen Romana W76
Garcia, Carlos M. E397
Garcia, Claudio W40
Garcia, David Rogue A143
Garcia, David Rogue E56
Garcia, Elisa D. A654
Garcia, Ernest C. A208
Garcia, Fernando Perez-Serrabona W382
Garcia, Freddimir E420
Garcia, Gerard A P644
Garcia, Gloria Hernandez W544
Garcia, Juan Carlos W266
Garcia, Luis A. E237
Garcia, Norma Rocio Nahle W470
Garcia, Rosa Maria Garcia W382
Garcia, Thomas E137
Garcia, Winston F. W514
Garcin-Meunier, Delphine W27
Garden, Edward P. A462
Gardiner, Warren A561
Garding, Edward A. A398
Gardner, Alan E114
Gardner, Anthony W113
Gardner, Anthony L. W295
Gardner, Gerald A969
Gardner, Gerald P535
Gardner, James E57
Gardner, Jeff A. A681
Gardner, Jeff A. E318
Gardner, Kenny A794
Gardner, Kirt W621
Gardner, L. Kristine E19
Gardner, Lee W238
Gardner, Mark A. A870
Gardner, Mary W. A207
Gardner, Paul W573
Gardner, Steven R. A796
Gardner, Steven R. A402
Gardner, Steven R. E368
Gardner, Ted A. A605
Gardner, Tracy A1018
Gardshol, Annemarie W231
Garen, Kirsten E. A1038
Garen, Kirsten E. E496
Garfield, Mark S. A15
Garfinkle, Philip N. E538
Garg, Parag W157
Gargiulo, Mario E83
Garibaldi, James J. A575
Garijo, Belen W397
Garijo, Belen W358
Garland, Gerald T. E420
Garland, Greg C. A826
Garland, Greg C. A76
Garland, Greg C. E382
Garland, Kim Burton A966

Garlich, Christopher J. E315
Garner, Curtis E. (Curt) A232
Garner, David W. A938
Garner, David W. E442
Garner, Denise A. A254
Garnick, Murray R. A47
Garnier, Jean-Pierre A207
Garnier, Thierry W341
Garrabrants, Geogory A119
Garrabrants, Geogory E48
Garratt, John W. A541
Garrett, B J P651
Garrett, F. L. A845
Garrett, F. L. E395
Garrett, John Robert A954
Garrett, Joseph L. A797
Garrett, Joseph L. E368
Garrett, Karen A524
Garrett, Karen E258
Garrett, Kristine R. A410
Garrett, Mark E234
Garrett, Mark W623
Garrett, Mark W458
Garrett, Mark S. A244
Garrett, Paula K. E207
Garrett, Scott T. A522
Garrett, Sharon D. A905
Garrido, Santiago Martinez A112
Garrido, Santiago Martinez W295
Garriott, M. Huntley A642
Garriott, M. Huntley E304
Garrison, Barrett E142
Garrison, Christine M. E185
Garrison, David W. E382
Garrison, Jodi E247
Garrison, Michael J. A147
Garrison, Ty L. A277
Garrison, Wayne A543
Garrity, Matthew T. A844
Garrity, Matthew T. E394
Garrity, Thomas J. E32
Garros, Julio A185
Garry, Gregor A1014
Garry, Gregor E488
Garske, Steven R P572
Garsys, Lucia P170
Gart, Thomas A. E206
Gartelmann, Richard A. A774
Gartelmann, Richard A. E360
Garten, Yael A631
Garth, William E81
Gartland, Thomas M. A10
Gartner, James J. A282
Gartner, Mathias W283
Garton, Joan T. A401
Gartside, Nicholas W415
Garutti, Randy A162
Garvey, Christine N. A1032
Garvin, Robert M. A1114
Garza, Alfonso Garza W244
Garza, Alvaro Fernandez W27
Garza, Danette E191
Garza, Eugenio Garza y W244
Garza, Jose Manuel Madero A292
Garza, Jose Manuel Madero A737
Garza, Manuel Rivera W27
Garza, Rafael Arana de la W265
Gasaway, Sharilyn S. A543
Gascoigne, Richard R. E393
Gaskill, Christopher E469

A = AMERICAN BUSINESS
E = EMERGING COMPANIES
P = PRIVATE COMPANIES
W = WORLD BUSINESSS

Gasmen, Dino R. W85
Gaspar, Clay M. A325
Gasper, Dan L. E308
Gasperment, Sophie A. W341
Gass, John D. W573
Gass, Michelle D. A817
Gass, Michelle D. A631
Gasselsberger, Franz W453
Gasselsberger, Franz W639
Gassner, Peter P. E519
Gassner, Peter P. E547
Gasssel, Helmut W303
Gast, Alice P. A230
Gast, Kelly S. E5
Gates, Anne T. A993
Gates, Anne T. A876
Gates, Anne T. A611
Gates, Ellen P446
Gates, Greg A648
Gathagan, Maureen A702
Gathagan, Maureen E326
Gather, Ursula W602
Gather, Ursula W415
Gati, Toby W476
Gatling, John A. E253
Gattei, Francesco W227
Gatti, Amerino E250
Gatti, Anna W310
Gattoni, James B. A620
Gatz, Ronald F P579
Gaudet, Gordon A927
Gaudet, Gordon E435
Gaudette, Kevin P231
Gaudette, Robert J. A757
Gaudiosi, Monica M. A1054
Gaugg, Peter W453
Gaughen, Kevin W. A519
Gaughen, Kevin W. E256
Gaughen, Patrick R. A519
Gaughen, Patrick R. E256
Gaughen, Robert H. A519
Gaughen, Robert H. E256
Gaul, Scott A856
Gaumond, Mark E. A171
Gaunt, John W462
Gaus, Norbert W545
Gaut, C. Christopher A376
Gautam, Rajeev A530
Gauthier, John J. A886
Gautier, Todd W. A613
Gavalis, Lydia A. E244
Gavant, Judy C. E62
Gaveau, Nathalie W161
Gavelle, Jean-Luc A80
Gavezotti, Graziella W635
Gavgani, Bernard W104
Gavigan, John M. A420
Gavigan, John M. E197
Gavin, Deborah J. A510
Gavin, Deborah J. E252
Gavin, John J. E145
Gavin, John J. E234
Gavin, Lillian A423
Gavin, Lillian E199

Gavinet, Andres R. E15
Gavini, Naveen E386
Gavrielov, Moshe N. W584
Gavrin, David M. A691
Gavrin, David M. E323
Gawlick, Rainer E400
Gay, Caroline P306
Gay, Lori R. A398
Gayares, Marita Socorro D. W85
Gayle, Helene D. A264
Gayle, Helene D. A787
Gaylor, Doug E129
Gayman, Jeffrey S. A788
Gayman, Jeffrey S. E365
Gaymard, Clara W107
Gaymard, Clara W187
Gaymard, Clara W373
Gayner, Thomas S. A659
Gayner, Thomas S. E72
Gaytan, Ernesto E428
Gcabashe, Thulani S. W559
Gdański, Przemyslaw W389
Ge, Dawei W530
Ge, Yafei W144
Geale, Leanne W430
Gealogo, Noravir A. W85
Gear, Kelly A398
Geary, James P. A981
Geary, James P. E469
Geary, Sean T. A475
Geary, William Clayton A1117
Gebert, Richard D. E268
Gebo, Kate A1062
Gebski, Christine E415
Gecaj, Mirlanda A1142
Gecht, Guy A645
Geelan, John W. E387
Geenen, Charles A. A653
Geer, Charles E. A494
Geer, Stacey K. A845
Geer, Stacey K. E395
Geers, Alex E189
Geest, Alexandre De W200
Geheran, Tony W596
Gehl, Carey P664
Gehlmann, Gregory A. A1038
Gehlmann, Gregory A. E495
Geiger, Jesse J. E317
Geisel, Gary N. A651
Geisel, Thomas X. A891
Geisler, Heather A508
Geisler, Heather P260
Geissinger, Uwe W379
Geissler, Werner A483
Geissler, Werner A825
Geist, John C. E65
Geist, Ron A301
Geist, Ron E131
Geist, William Alexander E59
Gelard, Yves Le W225
Gelbmann, Kerstin W563
Geldmacher, Jay L. A893
Gelhorn, Ursel W234
Geller, Michal J. A735
Gellerstad, Christian W176
Gellerstedt, Lawrence L. A471
Gellerstedt, Lawrence L. E68
Gelsinger, Patrick P. A560
Gemayel, Georges E475
Gemkow, Stephan W390

Gemkow, Stephen W24
Gemmel, James H. A679
Gemmell, Constance D. W299
Gemmill, Bruce E307
Gemmill, Elizabeth H. E511
Gempeler, Stefan W631
Genachowski, Julius A670
Genachowski, Julius E452
Genc, Onur W68
Gendell, David B. E264
Gendell, Jeffrey L. E264
Gendics, Jason L. A844
Gendics, Jason L. E394
Gendron, Paul A E271
Gendron, Robert E525
Gendron, Teresa S. A581
Gendron, Teresa S. A659
Genereux, Claude W263
Genereux, Claude W480
Genereux, Nathalie W420
Genest, Paul C. W480
Genestar, Thierry W161
Geng, Jianxin W431
Geng, Jing W529
Geng, Jingyan W375
Geng, Litang W272
Geniusahardja, Gunawan W464
Gennadios, Aristippos E83
Gennaro, Dennis A. De A1043
Gennaro, Giovanni De W363
Gennette, Jeffrey (Jeff) A654
Genola, Gabriele Galateri di W54
Genova, Juan Maria Nin W548
Genova, Juan Maria Nin W423
Genovesi, John A902
Genschaw, Andrea A649
Genschaw, Andrea A872
Genster, Grit W251
Genter, Robert S. A920
Gentil, Richard W492
Gentilcore, James F. E166
Gentle, Meg A. A792
Gentoso, Jamie M. A858
Gentoso, Jamie M. W283
Gentry, A. Melissa E372
Gentry, Felicia J. E180
Gentry, Gordon L. A1033
Gentry, Gordon L. E493
Gentzkow, Paul F. A898
Geny-stephann, Delphine W601
Geoghegan, Basil W21
George, Arthur L. E47
George, Gary Charles A543
George, Georgette R. A981
George, Georgette R. E469
George, Jeffrey P. E31
George, Kimberly D P21
George, Mark R. A747
George, Mark R. W617
George, Mary J. A195
George, Michael A. A111
George, Norman C. A266
George, Roger E. E16
George, William E111
George, William L. E392
Georgelas, Theodore J. A1063
Georgelas, Theodore J. E508
Georgeoff, Robert E22
Georgiadis, Anthony E239
Georgiadis, Mary Margaret Hastings A675

Georgieva, Antonia E366
Gephardt, Richard A. A216
Geraci, Vincent E510
Geraghty, James A. E529
Geraghty, Joanna L. A583
Geraghty, Joanna L. A613
Geraghty, Sharon C. W262
Gerard, Steven L. A110
Gerbaulet, Ute W510
Gerber, Murry S. A494
Gerber, Murry S. A160
Gerber, Murry S. A1073
Gerber, Nicholas D. E509
Gerber, Nicholas D. E509
Gerber, Nicholas D. E510
Gerber, William K. A252
Gerberding, Julie L. A221
Gere, Andrew R. E446
Gerhard, Christopher P. E494
Gericke, Johan E190
Geringer, Steven I. E5
Gerke, Mark Raymond E532
Gerke, Thomas A. E116
Gerken, R. Jay A101
Gerlach, Jeffrey R. A401
Gerlach, Rachel E19
Gerlach, Rolf W192
Gerlin, Simon R. A191
Gerlin, Simon R. E77
Germain, Jean-Marc E236
Germain, Maurice W294
Germany, Rhonda A1075
Gernandt, Karl W355
Gernigin, Michael J. E260
Gero, James F. E293
Gerosa, Christopher N. E311
Gerrard, Ron W328
Gerrity, Robert W. E529
Gersh, Lisa A503
Gershenhorn, Alan A145
Gershman, Harold A. A37
Gershman, Harold A. E14
Gerskovich, Philip A1148
Gerson, Gary E232
Gerst, Carl W. E105
Gerst, Christopher E. A900
Gerstein, Mark D. A778
Gervais, Michel W295
Gervasi, Martha E389
Gesing, Jason E180
Gesten, Samuel J. E460
Getz, James F. A1039
Getz, James F. E498
Geus, Aart J. de A90
Geveden, Rex D. E70
Geyer, David L. A918
Geyer, Guenter W633
Ghai, Rahul A215
Ghaith, Ahmed Khalfan Al W205
Ghandour, Marwan M. W77
ghaoui, Ghaoui C. Al W77
Gharbi, Hinda W499
Ghartey-Tagoe, Kodwo A347
Ghartey-Tagoe, Kodwo A348
Ghasemi, Seifollah (Seifi) A30
Ghasripoor, Farshad E161
Gheorghe, Mariana W306
Ghermezian, Mark E547
Gherson, Diane J. A610
Gheysens, Christopher A1138

COMBINED HOOVER'S HANDBOOK INDEX OF EXECUTIVES

A = AMERICAN BUSINESS
E = EMERGING COMPANIES
P = PRIVATE COMPANIES
W = WORLD BUSINESSS

Gheysens, Christopher E544
Ghez, Nomi P. E443
Ghidorzi, Christopher J. A741
Ghidorzi, Christopher J. E349
Ghiglieno, Giorgio W627
Ghoshal, Kaushik E417
Ghotmeh, Lina W165
Ghurair, Abdul-Aziz Abdulla Al W387
Ghurair, Mohammed Abdulla Al W387
Ghylin, Gaylen E63
Giacin, Judith A. E53
Giacometti, Pierre W127
Giamartino, Emma E. A213
Giancarlo, Charles H. E35
Giancarlo, J. Christopher W445
Giangrave, Andrew A418
Giannelli, Andrew A400
Giannini, Mario L. E244
Giannola, Vito A854
Giannoni, Marc A400
Gianola, John B. A981
Gianola, John B. E469
Gianotti, Anthony W644
Giansante, Filippo W227
Giay, Roberto W627
Giay, Roberto W627
Gibara, Germaine W571
Gibb, Matthew P158
Gibber, David B. A939
Gibber, Elliot E547
Gibbons, Dale A1120
Gibbons, Dale E535
Gibbons, James L. W491
Gibbons, Kenneth D. E506
Gibbons, Michael E. E393
Gibbons, Thomas P. A573
Gibbs, Christopher Patrick W128
Gibbs, David W. A1146
Gibbs, David W. A1059
Gibbs, Lawrence S. A1076
Gibbs, Michael W304
Giblin, Mike V P591
Gibney, Dennis E. A271
Gibney, Dennis E. E109
Gibson-Brandon, Rajna W104
Gibson, Allen M. A35
Gibson, Donald E. E240
Gibson, Donald J. A188
Gibson, Donald J. E71
Gibson, E. Ricky A414
Gibson, E. Ricky E193
Gibson, Gregory L. A422
Gibson, Kourtney E311
Gibson, Kurt A865
Gibson, Kurt E403
Gibson, Lee R. A954
Gidumal, Shyam W491
Giem, Judi A. A1038
Giem, Judi A. E495
Giertz, James R. A918
Giese, Cory W. A1038
Giese, Cory W. E496
Giet, Pascale W495
Giffin, Gordon D. W120

Gifford, Angelika W602
Gifford, Gerard H. A302
Gifford, Russell M. E56
Gifford, William F. A47
Gifford, William F. W40
Giger, Peter W666
Gil, Ryan P341
Gilbert, Daniel A900
Gilbert, James L. E357
Gilbert, Jennifer A900
Gilbert, Martin J. W260
Gilbert, Richard B. A401
Gilbert, Steven J. A671
Gilbert, Steven J. E495
Gilbertson, H. John A342
Gilchrist, M. Ian G. A633
Gilchrist, Malcolm Ian Grant A871
Gilchrist, Malcolm Ian Grant A872
Gilchrist, Malcolm Ian Grant A633
Gildea, Richard R. W33
Gile, Elizabeth R. A602
Gileadi, Ido A408
Giles, William T. E210
Gilet, Jean-Yves W213
Gilfeather, Michael J. E364
Gilio, Teresa E90
Gilkie, Jennifer P190
Gill, Daniel A208
Gill, Harjit E417
Gill, Melissa M. A401
Gillan-Myer, Maureen A280
Gillan-Myer, Maureen E112
Gillani, Aleem A450
Gillespie, Melissa L. A1118
Gillespie, Melissa L. E533
Gillespie, Richard E53
Gillespie, Robert W423
Gillham, Simon W637
Gilliam, Theron I. A629
Gilliam, Theron I. E234
Gillian, Cheri A428
Gillies, Crawford W90
Gillies, Crawford W89
Gilligan, Brendan W371
Gilligan, J. Kevin E467
Gilligan, James E185
Gilligan, Thomas W. A956
Gilligan, Thomas W. A594
Gilliland, D. Gary A615
Gilliland, M. Amy A132
Gilliland, Stewart W597
Gillis, Edwin J. E485
Gillis, Michelle A. A64
Gillis, Ruth Ann M. A602
Gillis, Ruth Ann M. A1099
Gillis, Steven W585
Gillum, Roderick A597
Gilmartin, MaryAnne A581
Gilmer, Frederick E454
Gilmore, Dennis J. A413
Gilpin, Thomas T. E149
Gilroy, Sue Anne A681
Gilroy, Sue Anne E318
Gilson, Jean-Marc W400
Gilstrap, Douglas E523
Giltner, F Phillips P498
Giltner, F. Phillips A429
Gilvary, Brian W90
Gilyard, Reginald (Reggie) Harold A213

Gilyard, Reginald (Reggie) Harold A413
Gilyard, Reginald (Reggie) Harold E412
Gim, Mark K.W. A1108
Ginascol, John F. A6
Gingery, Rhonda L. E336
Gingrich, Christopher P304
Ginn, Alexis P. A845
Ginn, Alexis P. E395
Ginn, Scott G. E20
Ginn, William J. E136
Ginneken, Marnix van W351
Ginnetti, Michael P. E145
Gioia, Nancy L. E392
Giordano, Michael R E143
Giordano, Philip A1142
Giordano, Susie A560
Giornelli, Lillian C. E124
Giovinazzi, Brian A854
Gipple, Todd A. A865
Gipple, Todd A. E403
Gipson, William P. A902
Gipson, William P. A655
Girardot, Paul-Louis W631
Giraud, Hubert W123
Girgin, Sinan W620
Girling, Russell W573
Girouard, Dave E513
Girouard, Denis W420
Giroux, Marc W398
Girshick, Birgit E94
Girsky, Stephen J. A180
Girsky, Stephen J. W113
Girton, Tani A130
Git, Haim W410
Gitin, Mark M. E329
Gitlin, David L. A164
Gitlin, David L. A207
Gitlin, Mike A197
Gitlin, Mike P103
Gitzel, Timothy S. A715
Giuliani, M. Germano E425
Giuliano, Mark A573
Given, Mark W318
Givens, Gregory D. A792
Giza, Helen W249
Gjerdrum, Thor G. A5
Glabe, Marla F. A1133
Glabe, Marla F. E541
Gladstone, David E232
Gladu, Jean Paul W573
Gladwin, Alison C. A982
Glaize, Mary Bruce E149
Glandon, Gary M. A639
Glanzer, Edeltraud W397
Glaser, Daniel S. (Dan) A662
Glaser, Jurgen W397
Glaser, Rachel C. E175
Glaser, Robert M. A411
Glaser, Thomas A993
Glaser, Thomas M. E515
Glasgow, Stephen E. A722
Glashauser, Renate W98
Glass, Dennis R. A638
Glass, Johnston A. A418
Glass, Johnston A. E195
Glass, Robert W. A898
Glasscock, Larry C. A989
Glasscock, Larry C. A1150

Glasser, Teresa A. E363
Glassman, Diana E250
Glastra, Matthijs E355
Glauber, Joseph W. E185
Glauber, Robert R. E350
Glavey, Patrick P374
Glavin, William F. A573
Glavin, William F. A648
Glazek, David E. E501
Glazer, Rose Marie E. A65
Glazer, Walter P. E172
Gleason, George A134
Gleason, George E54
Gleason, Leona A. A1133
Gleason, Leona A. E541
Gleason, Linda A134
Gleason, Linda E54
Gleespen, Melissa M. A294
Gleespen, Melissa M. A256
Glendinning, Stewart T. A1050
Glenn, R. Alexander A348
Glenn, Ryan E374
Glenn, T. Michael A649
Glenn, Timothy R. A298
Glessner, Coleen E157
Glessner, Gary W. E506
Glessner, John A450
Glew, James P. E85
Glick, Barry P28
Glickman, Jason M. A823
Glickman, Matthew E407
Glidden, Craig B. A466
Glieberman, Bernard P270
Glimcher, Laurie H. A81
Glimcher, Michael P. E306
Glimstrom, Anna-Karin W548
Glocer, Thomas H. A713
Glocer, Thomas H. A684
Glocer, Thomas H. W486
Glockner, David A383
Gloeckler, Michelle J. A159
Glomnes, Einar W448
Glosser, April E61
Glosser, Ludwig W129
Glosserman, Michael J. E123
Glossman, Diane B. A642
Glossman, Diane B. E304
Glover, Frank E323
Glover, Glenda Baskin A829
Glover, Glenda Baskin E385
Glover, Renée Lewis A399
Glover, Renée Lewis A391
Glover, Tyler E487
Gluchowski, Gregory J. E25
Gluck, Michelle H. A401
Gluher, Alexandre da Silva W69
Glunk, Robert J. E336
Gluski, Andres R. A1110
Gluski, Andres R. A23
Gluskie, Kevin Gerard W273
Glynn, Julie A. E532
Glynn, Martin J. G. W572
Gmelich, Justin G. E311
Gnat, Jordan E292
Go, Alvin C. W100
Go, Timothy A521
Goaer, Jean-Clade Le W33
Goar, Michael P359
Goater, J. Jeffrey E475
Gobe, Phillip A. A830

A = AMERICAN BUSINESS
E = EMERGING COMPANIES
P = PRIVATE COMPANIES
W = WORLD BUSINESSS

Gobert, Wilfred A. W120
Gochnauer, Richard W. A73
Gochnour, John J. E376
Godal, Bjorn Tore W227
Godbehere, Ann W532
Godbehere, Ann Frances W562
Godbole, Seemantini A647
Godfrey, Adam P. A918
Godfrey, Alan E407
Godfrey, Darren W308
Godfrey, John W360
Godfrey, Patty P. E204
Godfrey, Ronald S P670
Godfrey, Weston A. E304
Godin, Ingrid W277
Godridge, Leslie V. A651
Godwin, Janet E. A704
Godwin, Janet E. E328
Goebel, David L. A719
Goebel, David L. E539
Goebel, Jeremy A832
Goebel, Jeremy L. A833
Goebel, Maryann B. A923
Goebel, Maryann B. E433
Goeckeler, David A108
Goeckeler, David A1122
Goei, Dexter A45
Goelz, John R. E344
Goepel, Patrick E101
Goergen, Todd A. E129
Goettee, John S. A955
Goettee, John S. E456
Goettler, Michael A821
Goettler, Michael A1093
Goetz, Fidelis M. W86
Goetz, James J. A560
Goetz, Matthew E348
Goff, Gregory J. A388
Goff, Rhea E459
Goff, Stacey W. A649
Goff, Stacey W. A788
Goff, Stacey W. A872
Goff, Stacey W. E364
Goggins, Colleen A. A576
Goggins, Colleen A. W95
Goggins, Colleen A. W611
Goggins, John J. A711
Goh, Choon Phong A670
Goh, Euleen W532
Goh, Linus Ti Liang W464
Goings, William C. E159
Goiricelaya, Sara de la Rica W295
Gokey, Timothy C. A900
Gold, Alan D. E271
Gold, Christina A. A567
Gold, Daniel E334
Gold, David J. A691
Gold, David J. E323
Gold, Irwin N. E260
Gold, Richard S. A651
Goldberg, Arthur L. E425
Goldberg, Gary J. W101
Goldberg, Joel S. E380
Goldberg, Jonathan D. E300

Goldberg, Michael P226
Goldberg, Rebecca A401
Goldberg, Scott L. A261
Golden, Arthur F. A366
Golden, Deborah A. A703
Golden, Deborah A. E327
Golden, Michael F. E494
Goldenberg, Scott A1030
Goldenstein, Ihno W390
Golder, Jill M. A989
Golder, Jill M. A10
Goldfarb, Mark A. A919
Goldfarb, Shlomo W79
Goldfine, Howard S. A401
Goldin, Avi E229
Golding, Andy John W462
Golding, Benjamin Kristoffer W204
Golding, John J. A753
Goldman, Jay C. A249
Goldman, Jay C. E99
Goldman, Kenneth A915
Goldman, Kenneth A. E216
Goldman, Nathan D. A304
Goldman, Neal I. E93
Goldmann, Volker W192
Goldrick, Michael P. A181
Goldsberry, John P. A914
Goldsmith, Andrea J. A560
Goldsmith, Andrea J. A301
Goldsmith, Andrea J. W393
Goldstein, Abner K P586
Goldstein, Adam D. A396
Goldstein, Adam D. E187
Goldstein, Jeffrey A. A408
Goldstein, Jeffrey A. A132
Goldstein, Jennifer Friel E15
Goldstein, Joseph L. A882
Goldstein, Lainie E480
Goldstein, Lawrence J. E221
Goldstein, Robert L. A160
Golemon, Jerry D. A958
Golemon, Jerry D. E456
Gollahalli, Anil P568
Golling, Stefan W415
Gollotto, Jamie C. E66
Golodryga, Zhanna A885
Golsby, Steve W597
Golston, Allan C. A981
Golub, Mona J P585
Golub, Todd P569
Golz, Karen M. A81
Golz, Karen M. E281
Golz, Karen M. E39
Gomes, Fernando Jorge Buso W630
Gomez, Ignacio Baeza W382
Gomez, Oscar W73
Gomez, Pablo Fernando Quesada W73
Gomez, Sylvia Escovar W76
Gomi, Hirofumi W538
Gomo, Steven J. A700
Gomo, Steven J. E163
Goncalves, Celso L. A252
Goncalves, Joana E80
Goncalves, Lourenco A252
Goncalves, Rui Paulo W254
Goncharov, Sergei W655
Gonda, Barbara Garza Laguera W73
Gonda, Barbara Garza Laguera W244
Gonda, Eva Maria Garza Laguera W244
Gonda, Mariana Garza Laguera W244

Gong, Huadong W608
Gong, Kevin A. A398
Gong, Shaozu W168
Gong, Tao W274
Gong, Wei W268
Gong, Xingfeng W431
Gong, Zhijie W660
Gong, Zuchun W140
Gonick, Lev P44
Gonzalez, Adrian Sada W27
Gonzalez, Alberto Baillères W244
Gonzalez, Alejandro Diego Cecchi W73
Gonzalez, Bertha Paula Michel W244
Gonzalez, Carlos Hank W265
Gonzalez, Cipriano Lopez W76
Gonzalez, Edward A. A922
Gonzalez, Eva A927
Gonzalez, Eva E435
Gonzalez, Isaias Velazquez W265
Gonzalez, Joe E58
Gonzalez, Jorge Luis E459
Gonzalez, Jose Ramon A377
González, José Ramón A396
González, José Ramón E187
Gonzalez, Juan Obach W217
Gonzalez, Lucy E58
González, Maria Christina A836
Gonzalez, Maria Luisa Albores W470
Gonzalez, Monica Jimenez W210
Gonzalez, Pablo de Carvajal W593
Gonzalez, Paola A6
Gonzalez, Rachel A. A313
Gonzalez, Rachel A. A363
Gonzalez, Richard A. A8
Gonzalo, José W231
Gonzalo, Steven M. E204
Gooch, Mark A. A282
Good, John A. E185
Good, Lynn J. A164
Good, Lynn J. A347
Good, Lynn J. A348
Good, M. Carson E19
Goodarzi, Sasan K. A571
Goodburn, Mark A. A900
Goode, Carol A920
Goodell, Timothy B. E253
Gooden, Linda R. A466
Gooden, Linda R. A526
Goodfellow, Paul R.A. E437
Goodhew, J. William E122
Goodin, Amy C. A200
Goodin, Amy C. E79
Goodin, David L. E679
Gooding, Marie A399
Gooding, Valerie W638
Goodman, Jesse E258
Goodman, Jill R. A470
Goodman, Jill R. E87
Goodman, John E166
Goodman, John B. E400
Goodman, Kim Crawford A224
Goodman, Laurie S. A693
Goodman, Laurie S. W50
Goodman, Leslie E. E193
Goodman, Nicholas W112
Goodman, Richard A. W15
Goodman, Russell W399
Goodman, Scott R. A373
Goodman, Scott R. E168
Goodman, Shira D. A213

Goodman, Shira D. A917
Goodman, Shira D. A205
Goodman, Vicki L. E177
Goodrich, John M. E506
Goodson, Stephen Mitford W558
Goodspeed, Linda A. A111
Goodspeed, Linda A. A59
Goodwin, Annie M. A474
Goodwin, Annie M. E230
Goodwin, C. Kim A836
Goodwin, C. Kim A465
Goodwin, C. Kim A1030
Goodwin, Keith R.G. A401
Goodwin, Michael A187
Goodyear, William M. E162
Goolsby, Michelle P. E443
Goon, Fay Sien E34
Goonan, Nathan W419
Goorevich, Charlie P497
Gopal, Ajei S. E31
Gopalan, Geeta W157
Gopalan, Srini W199
Gopalan, Srinivasan A992
Gorczynski, Ronald J. A945
Gorczynski, Ronald J. E451
Gorder, Casey B. E382
Gorder, Joseph W. A1085
Gordillo, Rodrigo Echenique W300
Gordillo, Rodrigo Echenique W73
Gordon, Brooks G. E530
Gordon, Darin J. E5
Gordon, Douglas S. E532
Gordon, Ilene S. A568
Gordon, Ilene S. A643
Gordon, J. Lindsay W287
Gordon, Jennifer A941
Gordon, Kevin K. E398
Gordon, Marc D. A62
Gordon, Marlene M. E512
Gordon, Murdo A76
Gordon, Riske W644
Gordon, Russell L. A907
Gordon, Ryan E532
Gordon, Steve P521
Gordon, Susan M. A189
Gordon, William B. E480
Gore, Albert A. A89
Goreglyad, Valery W521
Gorelick, Jamie S. A50
Gorelick, Joel E191
Goren, Isabella (Bella) D. A462
Goren, Isabella (Bella) D. A660
Gorevic, Jason N. A599
Gori, Roy W382
Gorin, Ariane W13
Goris, Bradley E117
Goris, Patrick P. A207
Gorman, Christopher M. A602
Gorman, James P. A713
Gorman, Kevin Charles E346
Gorman, Louis O. E537
Gorman, M. Ryan A878
Gorman, Michael Ryan A879
Gorman, Robert Michael A106
Gorman, Robert Michael E40
Gorman, Stephen E. A405
Gorman, Thomas J. A37
Gormley, Debra A. A1108
Gorney, Jon L. A418
Gorney, Jon L. E195

COMBINED HOOVER'S HANDBOOK INDEX OF EXECUTIVES

A = AMERICAN BUSINESS
E = EMERGING COMPANIES
P = PRIVATE COMPANIES
W = WORLD BUSINESSS

Gorney, Jon L. E397
Gorney, Ryan L. E397
Gorrie, M. James A848
Gorsky, Alex A591
Gorsky, Alex A89
Gorsky, Alex A565
Gosa, J. Jake A145
Gosa, N. P. W414
Gosch, Kennith L. A311
Gosin, Barry M. E347
Goss-Custard, Rakhi W341
Gosset-Grainville, Antoine W65
Gossett, Barry P P666
Gossweiler, Anne C. A401
Gostoli, Michel W213
Gotelli, Robert A130
Goto, Akihiro W266
Goto, Katsuhiro W527
Goto, Shigeki W336
Goto, Teiichi W253
Goto, Tomiichiro W454
Goto, Yasuhiro W515
Gottesfeld, Stephen P. A737
Gottlieb, Scott A821
Gottlieb, Tamar W79
Gottron, Joseph A. A167
Gottron, Joseph A. E64
Gottschalk, Helmut W162
Gottschalk, Marla C. A157
Gottschalk, Marla C. A1083
Gottschling, Andreas W176
Gottscho, Richard A. A619
Gottsegen, Jonathan M. E66
Gottstein, Thomas P. W176
Gotzl, Stephan W98
Gou, Hsiao Ling W240
Gou, Terry W284
Goudet, Olivier A600
Goudge, James D. A397
Goudge, James D. E187
Goughnour, Holly G. A568
Gouin, Suzanne W358
Goulart, Steven J. A691
Gould, Andrew F. J. A767
Gould, Dixon P191
Gould, Howard N. A1120
Gould, Howard N. E535
Gould, Jay E. E400
Gould, John B. (Chip) A414
Gould, John B. (Chip) E191
Gould, Mark A. A402
Gould, Paul A. A332
Goulden, David I. A170
Goulding, Richard W81
Gouldson, Conor W21
Goulet, Beverly K. W504
Gourmelon, Nicole W174
Gouvea, Alexandre W174
Gove, Sue E. A148
Govil, Sucheta W174
Gow, Jaime A718
Gow, Jaime E335
Gowdy, Franklin P234
Gowland, Glen W84

Gowland, Karen E. A166
Gowrappan, K. Guru A132
Goyal, Amit E368
Goyal, Kruti Patel E175
Goyal, Vijay W49
Goyne, Joe R. A125
Goyne, Joe R. E52
Graaf, Raymond de E77
Graaf, Sumona De A892
Graafland, D. Rene Hooft W351
Grabe, Wiliam O. W362
Grabowski, M. Tracey A850
Grabowski, Nicholas M. E454
Grabowsky, Louis J. E242
Grace, Adrian W157
Grace, Ted A1071
Gracias, Antonio J. A1007
Graddick-Weir, Mirian M. A170
Graddick-Weir, Mirian M. A1146
Grady, Edward C. E6
Grady, John T. A372
Grady, John T. E167
Grady, Robert E. A977
Grady, Robert E. E464
Graeber, Bram W22
Graf, Alan B. A743
Graf, John A. W233
Graf, Michael A941
Grafe, Karl J. A64
Grafer, John E305
Graff, David S. A727
Graff, David S. E345
Graff, Michael J. A1124
Graff, Michael J. W357
Graft, Aaron P. A1040
Graft, Aaron P. E499
Gragnolati, Brian A. A617
Gragnolati, Brian A. E289
Graham, Anthony R. W480
Graham, Carolyn J. W122
Graham, Garth N. A920
Graham, Ginger L. A1102
Graham, James W162
Graham, James D. A252
Graham, Jonathan P. A76
Graham, Jordan W. A896
Graham, Jordan W. E422
Graham, Kristiane C. A342
Graham, Michelle P421
Graham, Peter J. E32
Graham, Roger C. E99
Graham, Stephen M. A1107
Graham, Stuart E. W548
Graham, Terri Funk A959
Graham, Tracy D. A1
Graham, Tracy D. E293
Grahl, R. Kent E495
Grahmann, Kevin A605
Grain, David J. A322
Grain, David J. A952
Gramigna, Edward A. A810
Gramigna, Edward A. E376
Granat, Carolina W6
Granat, Sari Beth A103
Granata, Claudio W227
Granata, Matias W314
Granata, Matias W315
Grand, Jean-Claude Le W358
Grandin, Michael A. W287
Grandisson, Marc W50

Grandke, Gerhard W192
Grandstaff, Douglas S. A796
Graney, Patrick C. A1042
Grange, Ben la W562
Grange, Marjolaine W511
Grange, Pascal W107
Grangeon, Philippe W123
Granger, Alberto Consuegra W210
Granger, Clarence L. E504
Granger, Elder A239
Granger, Elder A221
Granger, Elder E144
Graniere, Rick P341
Grano, Joseph J. E527
Granoff, Jill A654
Grant, Angela E370
Grant, David K. A1107
Grant, Declan P683
Grant, Eric A196
Grant, Eric E79
Grant, Hugh A452
Grant, Hugh A840
Grant, Kimberly S. A818
Grant, Mirella E. W204
Grant, Norman W193
Grant, Robert E435
Grant, Shane W187
Grant, William T. E435
Grant, William Thomas E436
Grantham, Helen W160
Grapa, Enrique W266
Grapinet, Gilles W61
Grasby, Darren A18
Grassadonia, Brian A162
Grassi, Louis C. A439
Grasso, Maria A. A439
Gratz, Jay M. E494
Grau, Alberto W116
Grauer, Andreas E121
Grauer, Scott B. A167
Grauer, Scott B. E64
Grava, Nancy L. E525
Gravallese, Julie P595
Gravelle, Michael L. A407
Graves, Andrew E. A1028
Graves, Christopher A685
Graves, Earl G. A111
Graves, Greg M. A1056
Graves, Greg M. E505
Graves, James H. A106
Graves, James H. E207
Graves, John A. A188
Graves, John A. E69
Graves, Peter R. A555
Graves, Peter R. E269
Graves, R. Vann E244
Gray, Brian G.J. W491
Gray, Brian R. A679
Gray, Charles J. E485
Gray, DeEtte A189
Gray, Denise A1005
Gray, Diedre A. A838
Gray, James A. E162
Gray, James D. A557
Gray, James W. A889
Gray, James W. E414
Gray, Jonathan D. A518
Gray, Jonathan D. A296
Gray, Jonathan D. A161
Gray, Julie A. A765

Gray, Sean A. A152
Gray, Stephen C. A279
Gray, W. Todd A773
Gray, William E130
Grayfer, Valery W476
Grayless, Robert P169
Grayson, Blake E489
Grayson, Bruns H. E420
Grayzel, David S. E475
Graziano, Jessica T. A1073
Greathouse, Craig B. E336
Greathouse, Steven R. E19
Grebenc, Jane A418
Grebenc, Jane E195
Grecco, Tatiana W315
Greco, Mario W666
Greco, Michele E522
Greco, Thomas R. A993
Greco, Thomas R. A17
Greeff, Douglas H. A704
Greeff, Douglas H. E328
Green-cheatwood, Toni P81
Green, Anthony C. A83
Green, Catherine A. E536
Green, Darrell E307
Green, David L. A477
Green, Edgar A. A546
Green, Emily Nagle E82
Green, Eric M. A358
Green, Eric M. E534
Green, Frederec Charles A321
Green, Gary W170
Green, George R. A319
Green, J. Markham A516
Green, Jared A954
Green, Jeff T. E489
Green, Jeffrey A. A527
Green, Jennifer N. A890
Green, Jennifer N. E416
Green, John M. W487
Green, Karen W471
Green, Kirsten A. A745
Green, Kylenne P277
Green, Logan D. A357
Green, Louis A. A200
Green, Louis A. E79
Green, Maria C. A1114
Green, Maria C. E303
Green, Mark A. A1065
Green, Mike P366
Green, Nicholas Stewart E45
Green, Phillip D. (Phil) A305
Green, Richard R. E300
Green, S. D. W377
Green, Scott A. E365
Green, Stephenson K. A392
Green, Stephenson K. E183
Green, Susan M. A252
Green, William C. E34
Green, William D. A911
Green, William D. A322
Greenawalt, Howard R. A702
Greenawalt, Howard R. E326
Greenbaum, Lisa E398
Greenberg, David W358
Greenberg, David C. E262
Greenberg, Evan G. W154
Greenberg, Jordan E. E50
Greenberg, Lon R. A73
Greenberg, Marc E249

COMBINED HOOVER'S HANDBOOK INDEX OF EXECUTIVES

A = AMERICAN BUSINESS
E = EMERGING COMPANIES
P = PRIVATE COMPANIES
W = WORLD BUSINESSS

Greenberg, Mark W323
Greenberg, Mark Spencer W322
Greenberg, William A1048
Greenblatt, David A. E85
Greenblum, Irving A563
Greene, Alexander David A52
Greene, Alexander David E515
Greene, Chris E46
Greene, D. Christopher A330
Greene, James S. A1057
Greene, Jason K. A153
Greene, John T. A330
Greene, Kimberly S. A952
Greene, Kimberly S. A1085
Greene, Michele W81
Greene, Yoon Hi A400
Greenebaum, John de Zulueta W87
Greener, Fred P79
Greenfield, Andrew J. E3
Greenfield, David W. A418
Greenfield, David W. E195
Greenfield, Susan Wright A135
Greenland, Adom J. E96
Greenleaf, Peter S. E32
Greenlees, Sharon A178
Greenplate, Paul S. A1138
Greenplate, Paul S. E544
Greenstein, Bruce E300
Greenstein, Sara A. A173
Greenstein, Scott A. A941
Greenstreet, Yvonne L. E369
Greenthal, Jill A. E12
Greenway, Joy M. E255
Greenwood, Randall M. E506
Greer, Robert S. A188
Greer, Robert S. E69
Greer, Steven K. A478
Gref, Herman W521
Greffin, Judith P. A101
Grefstad, Odd Arild W562
Gregg, Steven W37
Gregg, Vicky B. A870
Gregoire, Michael P. A18
Gregoire, Sylvie L. E381
Gregor, Joie A. A286
Gregori, Nazzareno W177
Gregoriadi, Alice K. W231
Gregorio, Tracie E517
Gregorski, Robert D. A125
Gregorski, Robert D. E52
Gregory, Andrew J. A988
Gregory, Andrew J. E479
Gregory, David E236
Gregory, Paul Craig A868
Gregory, Regina L. A995
Gregory, Robert B. E192
Greifeld, Robert E527
Greifeneder, Bernd E147
Greig, Henry F. A985
Greig, Paul G. E528
Greiner, Doris W91
Greisch, John J. A207
Greisch, John J. A221
Greisch, John J. E83

Greninger, Claudia E316
Grensteiner, Ronald James A60
Grescovich, Mark J. A136
Grese, Frank A491
Gresham, George W. E239
Greslick, Richard Lee A259
Greslick, Richard Lee E103
Greubel, Steffen W398
Greulach, Scot A962
Greve, Brad W66
Greve, Constantin W199
Grevy, Brian W14
Grey, Michael G. E61
Grez, Kelly E. W. A684
Gri, Francoise W174
Gri, Francoise W495
Gridley, Maryanne P201
Grieb, Frances Pallas A426
Grieb, Frances Pallas E202
Griebenow, Jill E87
Grieco, Maria Patrizia W219
Grieg, Elisabeth W446
Griege, Mark C. A1086
Griege, Mark C. E521
Griego, Linda M. A802
Grier, Kelly J. A553
Grier, Mark B. A450
Grier, Stacey A254
Griesemer, John F. A865
Griesemer, John F. E403
Griesemer, John F. E243
Griffin, Alexandra C. E168
Griffin, B R P444
Griffin, Bobby J. A1071
Griffin, Bobby J. A1118
Griffin, Bobby J. A497
Griffin, Caroline P201
Griffin, David F. A167
Griffin, David F. E64
Griffin, J Timothy P378
Griffin, John M. A522
Griffin, Liam K. A942
Griffin, Patrick J. E173
Griffin, Phil A428
Griffin, R. Kent E124
Griffin, Rita W509
Griffin, Thomas N. E428
Griffin, Tracey R. A16
Griffith, B. V. W518
Griffith, Christopher A1066
Griffith, Curtis C. A950
Griffith, Curtis C. E454
Griffith, James W. A553
Griffith, John Alan A235
Griffith, John B. A1
Griffith, Martin T. A259
Griffith, Martin T. E103
Griffith, Michael J. E90
Griffith, Peter H. A76
Griffith, Susan Patricia A851
Griffith, Susan Patricia A405
Griffiths, Anthony F. W235
Griffiths, Ben A991
Griffiths, Jane W66
Griffiths, Jane W328
Grigg, Christopher M. W66
Griggs, Dan C. A647
Griggs, Malcolm D. A248
Griggs, P.C. Nelson A721
Grigsby, Jennifer M. A301

Grigsby, Jennifer M. E131
Grijalva, Laurie E64
Griling, Russell K. W451
Grill, Donald L. E189
Grillo, Anthony E303
Grillo, Ulrich W207
Grimes, Karen H. A1032
Grimm, Chris D. A398
Grimm, Michael K. A369
Grimm, Peter W633
Grimnell, David L. E65
Grimstone, Gerry W89
Grinberg, Paul J. A119
Grinberg, Paul J. E48
Grindal, Corey A226
Grindal, Corey A225
Grinnan, Richard R. A659
Grinnell, Bruce Edward A401
Grioli, Francesco W171
Gripman, Samantha E455
Grise, Cheryl W. A862
Grise, Cheryl W. A691
Grishanin, Maksim Sergeevich W617
Grison, Arnaud W635
Griten, Kathryn E421
Gritz, Josef W639
Grivet, Jerome W174
Grobler, Fleetwood Rawstorne W518
Grobler, Stehan W562
Groepe, Francois Engelbrecht W558
Grogg, Jerry O. E223
Groh, Kevin W371
Grohalski, James T. E455
Groom, Steve A199
Groom, Steve E79
Grooms, Nina C. E13
Groos, Holly Hess E142
Groot, Jan Ernst de W351
Gros-Pietro, Gian Maria W310
Gross, Daniel L P500
Gross, Joli L. A493
Gross, Joli L. A1071
Gross, Joseph B. A666
Gross, Mary E. E510
Grosshans, Adam E410
Grossman, Eric F. A713
Grossman, Kenneth S. E56
Grossman, Marc D. E179
Grosso, Douglas G. Del W15
Grote, Byron E. W39
Grote, Byron E. W561
Grote, Byron E. W597
Grote, Robert E. A838
Groth, Magnus W231
Grover, Michael David A411
Groves, Jason L. E316
Groves, Regina E. E43
Growbowsky, Donald R. A190
Growbowsky, Donald R. E73
Groysberg, Boris A431
Groysberg, Boris E205
Grubbs, Robert W. A918
Grube, James A457
Grube, Jeffrey D. A910
Gruber, Anna W628
Gruber, Desiree E57
Gruber, Julie A1018
Gruber, Mark R. A96
Gruber, Peter W303
Gruber, Scott L. A1033

Gruber, Vinzenz P. A709
Grubic, Robert C. A702
Grubic, Robert C. E326
Grubka, Robert L. A1099
Gruending, Colin K. W218
Grunau, Paul W P41
Grund, Burkhart W167
Grundler, Martina W33
Grundmann, Hans-Juergen W62
Gruner, Raymond E185
Grunst, Martin E. A167
Grunst, Martin E. E64
Grusky, Robert R. A110
Grusky, Robert R. E467
Gruttman, Judith A400
Gruver, William R. E239
Grynberg, Marc W623
Gu, Biquan W291
Gu, Chaoyang W530
Gu, Feng W257
Gu, Guoda W662
Gu, Huizhong W150
Gu, Jiadan W152
Gu, Jianguo W291
Gu, Junying W664
Gu, Liji W472
Gu, Meifeng W144
Gu, Paul E513
Gu, Qiang W145
Gu, Shisheng W660
Gu, Yuchun W256
Guadagno, Kimberly M. A768
Guadagno, Kimberly M. E359
Guajardo, Pablo Roberto Gonzalez W35
Gualtieri, Giuseppina W627
Guan, Bingchun W292
Guan, Shan W533
Guan, Xiaoguang W34
Guan, Xueqing W301
Guan, Xueqing W559
Guan, Yongmin W326
Guardino, Carl E446
Guarini, George J. E56
Guarino, Michael A691
Guarino, Michael E323
Guat, Janet Har Ang W85
Guay, Marc W399
Guba, Thomas K. A96
Guberman, Steven M. A1083
Gucht, Karel de W49
Gudduschat, Cordula W165
Guderian, Bryan K. A741
Guei, Tan Ching W261
Guénard, Jean W213
Guenthner, C. Steven E300
Guercio, Stephen A. Del A308
Guercio, Stephen A. Del E134
Guerin-Boutaud, Philippe W492
Guerin, Eric J. A942
Guerin, Jean-Christophe W168
Guerin, Nicolas W459
Guerisoli, Brent E376
Guéronnière, Marc de la E325
Guerra, Karen W111
Guerra, R. David A563
Guerra, Ricardo Ribeiro Mandacaru W315
Guerra, Rodrigo A308
Guerra, Rodrigo E134

COMBINED HOOVER'S HANDBOOK INDEX OF EXECUTIVES

A = AMERICAN BUSINESS
E = EMERGING COMPANIES
P = PRIVATE COMPANIES
W = WORLD BUSINESSS

Guerrero, Angel Alija W35
Guerrero, Juan O. A836
Guerrero, Pedro Guerrero W87
Guerrieri, Gary L. A441
Guerrieri, Gary L. E211
Guerriero, Ronald A377
Guerrini, Martino Scabbia A1091
Guertin, Shawn M. A311
Guertin, Timothy E. E485
Guest, Robert E. A373
Guest, Robert E. E168
Gueth, Anton G. E32
Guevarra, Lazaro Jerome C. W99
Guez, Gilbert W490
Guffey, Lawrence H. A992
Guge, Brett P100
Guggenheimer, Steven W289
Guglielmetti, Antonella W479
Gui, Sheng Yue W257
Guibert, Thierry W562
Guichard, Antoine W127
Guidry, Daniel G. A523
Guidry, Daniel G. E257
Guidry, Darren E. A523
Guidry, Darren E. E257
Guilarte, Juan Sanchez-Calero W219
Guiley, Thomas E P201
Guilfoile, Mary J. Steele A570
Guilfoile, Mary J. Steele A900
Guilherme, Carlos Alberto Rodrigues W69
Guill, Ben A. A755
Guillaume-Grabisch, Beatrice W429
Guillaume-Grabisch, Beatrice W358
Guillaume, Henri W344
Guillaume, Stephen J. E99
Guillemet, Bruno W631
Guillemette, Larry T. E461
Guillemin, Jean-Francois W161
Guillemot, Philippe A950
Guillen, Federico W443
Guillen, Jerome A1007
Guillory, Sean E437
Guillot, Laurent W511
Guillou, Marion W104
Guillou, Marion W631
Guillouard, Catherine W24
Guimaraes, Enderson A111
Guin, Timothy W. E515
Guindani, Pietro A. W227
Guinn, Patricia Lynn A886
Guiony, Jean-Jacques W373
Guirkinger, Bernard W565
Guitard, Juan A915
Guitard, Philippe W631
Guiu, Jose Antonio Colomer W382
Gujral, Raminder Singh W491
Gularte, Miguel W323
Guldu, Selahattin W618
Güler, Aydin W618
Gulich, Frank Ch. W203
Gulis, Stephen L. A555
Gulis, Stephen L. E269
Gulis, Stephen L. E448

Gulling, Douglas R. A1118
Gulling, Douglas R. E533
Gulliver, Kate A1112
Gulliver, Stuart W323
Gulliver, Stuart T W286
Gullo, Samuel M. A411
Gullons, Darla E181
Gulmi, Claire E114
Gultekin, Ege W26
Gultom, Maruli W464
Gulyas, Diane H. A386
Gulyayev, Valery Alexeyevich W476
Gulzau, Gabriele W198
Guma, Xolile W558
Guma, Xolile Pallo W558
Gumaer, Andrew E49
Gummadi, Surya A267
Gumpel, Damian A776
Gunby, Steven Henry A97
Gunby, Steven Henry E224
Gund, G. Zachary A597
Gundersen, Elin Rødder W558
Gunderson, Kelsey W358
Gunderson, Tricia E58
Gundlach, Robert W95
Gundy, Leonard L. E189
Guney, Turgut W26
Gunn, Brian M. A915
Gunn, David A. A587
Gunn, George C. A1044
Gunn, L. Burwell E227
Gunn, Robert J. W235
Gunning, Gina K E236
Gunning, Patrick J. E425
Gunsett, Daniel J. A490
Gunter, Aydin W26
Gunter, Bernhard W602
Gunter, Emer OBroin E26
Gunter, Matthew E436
Gunther, Conrad J. A328
Gunther, Scott E83
Guo, Guangchang W248
Guo, Guangwen W140
Guo, Hong W189
Guo, Hongjin W145
Guo, Huawei W172
Guo, Kaitian W596
Guo, Lijun W648
Guo, Liyan W100
Guo, Mengchao W477
Guo, Peng (Patrick) A1004
Guo, Ruixiang W431
Guo, Shihui W528
Guo, Shiqing W148
Guo, Shuzhan W263
Guo, Wei W533
Guo, Wei W150
Guo, Wenqing W397
Guo, Yimin W144
Guo, Yongqing W575
Guo, Yuming W100
Gupp, William R. E494
Gupta, Aanchal A937
Gupta, Aanchal E441
Gupta, Ajay E247
Gupta, Alka A722
Gupta, Alka E339
Gupta, Anuradha A148
Gupta, Ash E159
Gupta, Ashok K. W572

Gupta, Ashwani W441
Gupta, Jan W13
Gupta, Navdeep A326
Gupta, Nina E525
Gupta, P. K. W561
Gupta, Peeyush W419
Gupta, Piyush W190
Gupta, Purnima W561
Gupta, Rahul E329
Gupta, Rajiv L. A349
Gupta, Rajiv L. W45
Gupta, Rajiv L. W46
Gupta, Ritesh E240
Gupta, Rohit A470
Gupta, Sunil A1083
Gupta, Suren K. A42
Gupta, Suren K. A1151
Gupta, Vipin A1034
Gupta, Vivek E313
Gur, Kaan W26
Gur, Sharon W79
Gurander, Jan W641
Gurdal, Hakan W273
Gurganious, Valora A200
Gurganious, Valora E79
Gursahaney, Naren K. A740
Gusenbauer, Alfred W562
Gusinov, Alex E525
Gustafsson, Anders A568
Gustafsson, Anders A1148
Gustavson, Timothy B. A878
Gut, Alexander W13
Gutenberger, Hans-Juergen W192
Guthart, Gary S. A572
Guthertz, Patricia Lizarraga W174
Guthrie, John T. E445
Guthrie, Roy A. A718
Guthrie, Roy A. A781
Guthrie, Roy A. A985
Guthrie, Roy A. E335
Gutierrez, Alberto W24
Gutierrez, Arturo Herrera W470
Gutierrez, Carlos M. A691
Gutierrez, Carlos M. A767
Gutierrez, Jaime Alberto Villegas W76
Gutierrez, Jose M. W15
Gutierrez, Laline P341
Gutierrez, Mauricio A757
Gutierrez, Mauricio A232
Gutierrez, Pedro Fernando Manrique W210
Gutierrez, Xavier A. E283
Gutman, Harvey M. A691
Gutman, Harvey M. E323
Gutmann, Kathleen M. A1069
Gutovic, Miljan W283
Gutowski, Robert J. E335
Gutt, Jack A400
Guy, Peter N. E19
Guyer, C. Stephen E61
Guyman, Charlotte A151
Guyton, Jeffrey H. W389
Guziewicz, Andrew E34
Guzman, David Martinez W27
Guzman, David Martinez W131
Guzman, David Martinez W71
Guzman, Jorge Andres Saieh W314
Guzman, Melinda A398
Guzzi, Anthony J. A364
Guzzone, Brandon P437

Gwadry-Sridhar, Femida H. E317
Gwillim, Ryan M. A182
Gwin, Robert G. W590
Gyani, Mohan S. E142
Gygax, Markus W87
Gyulaine, Magdolna P. W563
Gyurci, John E471

H

Ha, Daisy Y. A530
Ha, Daisy Y. E258
Ha, Eon Tae W294
Haack, Calvin D. A798
Haag, Markus W229
Haag, Natalie G. A199
Haag, William H. E393
Haan, Ronald L. A653
Haas, Achim W602
Haas, G. Hunter A787
Haas, Herbert K. W269
Haas, Herbert K. W586
Haas, Jacob W. E298
Haas, John J P198
Haas, Kimberly J. W299
Haas, Lena A586
Haas, Marius A. A1124
Haase, Margarete W306
Haasis, Heinrich W192
Habayeb, Elias F. A295
Habbaba, Faris E281
Haben, Mary Kay A512
Haben, Mary Kay E242
Haber, Ron E102
Haberhauer, Regina W229
Haberle, Michael W395
Haberman, Michael A. E13
Hablinski, Cynthia V. E437
Habu, Yuki W17
Hachigian, Kirk S. A740
Hachigian, Kirk S. A796
Hachimura, Tsuyoshi W316
Hackel, Danielle Remis A191
Hackel, Danielle Remis E77
Hacker, Douglas A. A958
Hacker, Howard B. A1003
Hacker, Mark S. A716
Hackett, Ann Fritz A198
Hackett, Ann Fritz A447
Hackett, H. Patrick A1133
Hackett, H. Patrick E541
Hackett, James Patrick (Jim) A444
Hackett, James T. A374
Hackett, James T. A438
Hackett, James T. A755
Hackett, John A. A181
Hackett, Sylvia P462
Hackman, Gregory V. E64
Hackmeyer, F. William A880
Hackmeyer, F. William E412
Hackney, James R P399
Haddad, David S. E452
Haddad, Frederick S. W93
Haddad, Louis S. E35
Haddad, Mary Jo W596
Haddad, Michael J. A101
Hadders, Jan Zegering W18
Haddock, Gerald W. A687

COMBINED HOOVER'S HANDBOOK INDEX OF EXECUTIVES

A = AMERICAN BUSINESS
E = EMERGING COMPANIES
P = PRIVATE COMPANIES
W = WORLD BUSINESSS

Haddock, Paul Thomas E307
Hadjipateras, Alexander C. E144
Hadjipateras, John C. E144
Hadley, Randall D. E378
Haeberli, Gerard W87
Haemisegger, David J. A305
Haendiges, Brian K. A470
Haenggi, Jamie E. E163
Haeusermann, Markus W631
Hafetz, Abraham W410
Haft, Ian David A52
Hagan, Annmarie T. W154
Hagan, Clifford L. A223
Hagan, James C. E537
Hagan, Mark E. E412
Hagan, Patrick G. E30
Hageboeck, Charles R. A249
Hageboeck, Charles R. E99
Hagedorn, Michael D. A1086
Hagedorn, Michael D. E516
Hageman, Hilary A920
Hagemann, Reiner W234
Hagemann, Robert A. A909
Hagemann, Robert A. A1150
Hagemann, Robert A. A486
Hagen, Jonathan Hirt E172
Hagen, Per N. W347
Hagen, Peter W633
Hagen, Russell S. A1127
Hagen, Scott A900
Hagen, Thomas B. E171
Hagenauer, Florian W453
Hagens, Robert A295
Hagerman, Melissa A470
Hagerty, James M. A1108
Hagerty, Patrick T. A818
Hagerty, Thomas M. A407
Hagey, Alec A1034
Haggart, Dylan G. A434
Hagge, Stephen J. A303
Haggerty, Gretchen R. E484
Haggerty, Gretchen R. W327
Haggerty, Scott P166
Haggerty, Stephen G. E67
Haghighi, Farshad A78
Hagino, Yoshinori W319
Hagiwara, Satoru W610
Hagman, Martijn A864
Hagood, D. Maybank A340
Hague, John W. E39
Hague, William Jefferson A561
Hahn, Carl H. W61
Hai, Hillary P. E173
Hai, Yancey W252
Hai, Yancey W584
Haidar, Wael A168
Haidar, Wael P89
Haidlen, Thomas A. E357
Haigis, Kevin P188
Hailer, John T. A475
Hailey, V. Ann A878
Hailey, V. Ann A879
Hailey, V. Ann A485
Haim, Eyal Ben W79

Haimovitz, Jules E272
Hain, Robert C. A96
Hainer, Herbert W196
Hainer, Herbert W33
Haines, Douglas A. E54
Haines, John R. E247
Haines, Lisa K. E54
Haines, Robert C. E293
Haines, William B. E54
Hair, Michael E517
Hairston, John P90
Hairston, John M. A495
Hajek, Douglas J. A688
Hajek, Douglas J. E323
Hajeri, Omar W358
Hajjar, Karim W554
Hakamata, Naoto W313
Hakanson, Peter W495
Hakim, Anat A635
Hakim, Veronique A692
Hakim, Veronique P352
Hakimi, Miloud W635
Hakman, Joseph E15
Hakopian, John A423
Hakopian, John E199
Håland, Gunn-Jane W558
Halberstadt, Peter A191
Halberstadt, Peter E77
Halbherr, Michael W666
Halde, Jean-Rene W611
Halderman, F. Howard A427
Halderman, F. Howard E203
Hale, James C. E328
Hale, James C. (Jim) A130
Hale, Jordan A971
Hale, Jordan P537
Hale, Karen L. W449
Hale, Karyn J. E506
Hale, Leslie D. A323
Hale, Leslie D. A654
Hale, Scott E409
Haley, Jeffrey V. A66
Haley, Jeffrey V. E25
Haley, John R. A950
Haley, Michael P. A66
Haley, Michael P. E25
Haley, Patrick J. E177
Haley, Stephen W. A392
Haley, Stephen W. E183
Haley, Timothy M. A730
Halfon, Jean-Michel W598
Halford, Andy W385
Halford, Andy N. W561
Halford, Jeremy S E236
Halkyard, Jonathan S. A696
Hall, Anthony W. A605
Hall, Brenda A927
Hall, Brenda E435
Hall, Brian M. E293
Hall, Charles E. A207
Hall, Chaundra P646
Hall, Colin W283
Hall, Douglas K. E136
Hall, G. Bridges A880
Hall, G. Bridges E412
Hall, J. D. A830
Hall, Jeff W495
Hall, Jennifer J. A401
Hall, John J P580
Hall, John L. A181

Hall, Kathryn A. A1019
Hall, Kathryn W. A45
Hall, Kelley K. E344
Hall, Linda S. A860
Hall, M. Lance A788
Hall, M. Lance E364
Hall, Mary C A52
Hall, Mary C P31
Hall, Michael J. A1043
Hall, O. B. Grayson A32
Hall, Patricia (Pat) A. Hemingway A655
Hall, Patricia A. Hemingway A201
Hall, Randy E274
Hall, Richard John W128
Hall, Sheldon F. A198
Halle, Richard E343
Haller, Bettina W543
Haller, Julia A. A178
Halley, Chryssa C. A391
Halley, Robert W125
Hallgren, Wendy A. A1046
Hallian, Terence A249
Hallian, Terence P126
Halliday, Matthew W37
Halliday, Robert J. A90
Halligan, Catherine Ann A1055
Halligan, Dennis P. E437
Hallinan, Patrick D. A962
Hallquist, Constance J. E316
Halpin, Christopher E261
Halsey, Casey S P283
Halsey, Casey S P282
Halsey, Rodney H. E372
Halstead, Peter D. E193
Halter, Patrick G. (Pat) A846
Halterman, Craig E47
Halton, Jane W63
Halverson, Bradley M. A989
Halverson, Bradley M. A622
Halverson, Bradley M. A292
Halverson, Steven T. A304
Halvorson, Gary Justin A235
Hama, Naoki W253
Hamada, Hiroyuki W534
Hamada, Masahiro W534
Hamada, Masahiro W555
Hamada, Michiyo W267
Hamaguchi, Daisuke W370
Hamalainen-Lindfors, Sirkka W348
Hamalainen, James L. A60
Hamamoto, Wataru W409
Hamann, Jennifer A1061
Hamano, Miyako W267
Hamasaki, Hideaki W281
Hamberger, Scott M. E149
Hamblen, Brannon A134
Hamblen, Brannon E54
Hamblin, Nikki E291
Hamburg, Marc D. A151
Hamel, Judy G. E305
Hamel, Kevin A499
Hamel, Kevin E246
Hamers, Ralph A.J.G. W621
Hameseder, Erwin W562
Hameseder, Erwin W628
Hamic, William Thomas A568
Hamil, Steven M. E153
Hamill, David A180
Hamill, David W113

Hamill, Patrick H. E206
Hamilton, Aimee T. A395
Hamilton, Aimee T. E185
Hamilton, Dori E46
Hamilton, Gail E. A97
Hamilton, Sue Ann E300
Hamilton, Thomas A83
Hamilton, Tiffany P418
Hamlin, Frank H. A196
Hamlin, Frank H. E78
Hamlin, George W. A196
Hamlin, George W. E78
Hamlin, Pamela A. A191
Hamlin, Pamela A. E77
Hamlin, Stacey E455
Hamlin, Stephen D. A196
Hamlin, Stephen D. E78
Hamm, Harold G. A295
Hamm, Richard F. A364
Hammer, Bonnie S. E261
Hammer, Jutta W586
Hammer, Michael L. E260
Hammes, Eric D. A4
Hammond, Frederic G. E39
Hammond, Howard A410
Hammond, Ian W574
Hammond, John P166
Hammond, Karen A1048
Hammond, Maryclaire A493
Hammonds, Kimberly L. E547
Hammons, Kevin J. A282
Hamner, R. Steven E315
Hampel, Sylvia A1107
Hampton, Barbara E. E340
Hampton, Shelly R. E35
Hampton, Tonya Jackman P260
Hamrah, Craig A941
Hamre, John J. A920
Hamren, Elizabeth A503
Han, Amy W. E191
Han, Benwen W141
Han, Bing W142
Han, Chong W327
Han, Cyril A1145
Han, Dong-Whan W335
Han, Fangming W239
Han, Huihua W152
Han, Jerry W252
Han, Jingen W662
Han, Kun Tai W365
Han, Quanzhi W529
Han, Sam S. A439
Han, Sen W292
Han, Seung Soo W367
Han, Wensheng W150
Han, Xiaojing W236
Hance, James H. A203
Hancock, C. Wayne A282
Hancock, Charles E. E489
Hancock, David H. E338
Hancock, E. Alexander E338
Hancock, Linda S. E338
Hancock, Richard B. E45
Hancock, William S. A1083
Hand, Brian A. A982
Hand, Erik D. A527
Hand, Judi A. E500
Handa, Junichi W614
Handa, Kimio W535
Handel, Michael J. Van A655

HOOVER'S HANDBOOK OF EMERGING COMPANIES 2023

COMBINED HOOVER'S HANDBOOK INDEX OF EXECUTIVES

A = AMERICAN BUSINESS
E = EMERGING COMPANIES
P = PRIVATE COMPANIES
W = WORLD BUSINESSS

Handjinicolaou, George P. W473
Handler, Greg A1121
Handler, Kendall Fox E261
Handler, Richard B. A581
Handley, Thomas W. A892
Handley, Thomas W. E226
Handlon, Carolyn B. A920
Handlon, Carolyn B. A574
Handy, Edward O. A1108
Hanebeck, Jochen W303
Haneda, Takao W535
Hanemann, Kim C. A858
Hanerkson, David P148
Haney, Brian D. E287
Haney, Cecil D. A460
Haney, Cecil D. A1003
Haney, Mark A. E5
Hanft, Adam E2
Hanhinen, Reino W348
Hanigan, Kevin J. A852
Hanigan, Kevin J. E399
Hank, Jeffrey P. E405
Hanke, Troy D. E206
Hankin, Michael D. A962
Hankins, Anthony P. A547
Hankinson, Craig A. A653
Hankinson, Garth A291
Hankowsky, William P. A248
Hanks, W. Bruce A649
Hanley, Harold T. E421
Hanley, Jeneanne Michelle A607
Hanley, Joseph R. A1001
Hanley, Mary Ann E446
Hanley, Michael W374
Hanley, Michael S. A173
Hanley, Patrick D. A771
Hanley, Walter P. A643
Hanlin, Marjie E517
Hanna, David G. E41
Hanna, James Kevin E315
Hanna, Mark C. E181
Hanna, Randall W. A496
Hanna, Samir N. W77
Hannah, David H. A166
Hannam, Wendy G. E159
Hannan, Kathy Hopinkah A791
Hannan, Kathy Hopinkah A83
Hannasch, Brian P. A111
Hannasch, Brian P. W30
Hanneman, Karl L. A352
Hannequin, Jean-Marc W238
Hannigan, Deirdre W20
Hannon, Michael J. A834
Hannoraseth, Puntipa W79
Hanrahan, Kathleen A. A693
Hanrahan, Paul T. A557
Hanratty, P. B. W414
Hansell, Carol W80
Hansen, Bruce E520
Hansen, Bruce D. E328
Hansen, Cynthia L. W218
Hansen, Daniel I. A106
Hansen, Daniel I. E40
Hansen, Douglas B. A881

Hansen, Douglas B. E217
Hansen, George E. A301
Hansen, George E. E131
Hansen, Hakon W204
Hansen, J. Michael A242
Hansen, Janet M. A814
Hansen, Janet M. E379
Hansen, Jay J. A435
Hansen, Jay J. E210
Hansen, Michael L. E532
Hansen, Rick E. A466
Hansen, Sarah P612
Hansen, Signhild Arnegard W548
Hansen, Staffan W562
Hansen, Tim T. E144
Hansen, Wilhelm W91
Hansen, William J. E428
Hansing, Axel K.A. E530
Hanson, Bryan C A293
Hanson, Bryan C P161
Hanson, Bryan C. A1150
Hanson, Bryan C. A384
Hanson, Bryan C. A1102
Hanson, Bryan Craig A292
Hanson, Diana C. A124
Hanson, Gregory B. A475
Hanson, James E. A617
Hanson, James E. E289
Hanson, Jodee A970
Hanson, Jodee P536
Hanson, John E90
Hanson, John T. E501
Hanson, Robert Lee A291
Hanson, Theodore S. E38
Hansotia, Eric P. A26
Hansotia, Eric P. E491
Hanspal, Amarpreet E402
Hanspal, Amarpreet E39
Hanssen, Maria Moræus W523
Hanstveit, Arve E161
Hantson, Ludwig N. A522
Hanus, Jean-Claude W238
Hanway, H. Edward A662
Hanzawa, Junichi W407
Hao, Jian Min W144
Hao, Kenneth Y. E451
Happe, Carolina Dybeck A462
Happe, Carolina Dybeck W207
Happe, Michael J. E540
Happe, Michael J. E226
Hara, Hideo W110
Hara, Noriyuki W413
Hara, Shinichi W555
Hara, Takeshi W28
Haraburda, Jack E105
Harada, Hiroki W440
Harada, Ikuhide W155
Harada, Kazuyuki W319
Haraf, William S. A919
Haraguchi, Tetsuji W410
Haraguchi, Tsunekazu W25
Harapiak, Maurice D. A252
Harashima, Akira W606
Harbert, Patrick J. A378
Harbo, Ingrid W579
Harbour, Ronald Edward E302
Hardaker-Jones, Emma W360
Hardegg, Maximilian W229
Harder, V. Peter W379
Hardgrove, Richard L. E428

Hardie, Gordon J. A764
Hardie, Graeme W618
Hardin, Edward J. A574
Hardin, John Wesley A74
Hardin, P. Russell A468
Harding, Brian E. E504
Harding, Heather E283
Harding, Mark W. E402
Harding, Matthew K. A854
Harding, Roger G. E101
Hardis, Stephen R. E47
Hardman, Kevin C. A547
Hardwick, Elanor R. W33
Hardwick, Mark K. A427
Hardwick, Mark K. E203
Hardy, Adrian E273
Hardy, Anne W165
Hardy, Eva S. E35
Hare, Richard B. E237
Harel-Buchris, Yodfat W312
Harf, Peter A600
Harford, Barney A1062
Hargis, Jonathan A223
Hargis, V. Burns A167
Hargis, V. Burns E64
Hargrove, Robin S. A710
Hariharan, Anu A116
Harik, Mario A. A1143
Harings, Lothar A. W355
Haris, Clinton M. E166
Harkel-Rumford, Lynne Louise A218
Harker, Victoria D. A546
Harker, Victoria D. E468
Harkness, Austin B. A982
Harlam, Bari A. A352
Harlam, Bari A. A895
Harlam, Bari A. E361
Harlan, Joe W279
Harlan, Kristy T. A1127
Harlow, David R. A125
Harlow, David R. E52
Harlow, James E362
Harlow, Jo W318
Harman, Donna A. A799
Harman, Terry P176
Harmening, Andrew J. A101
Harmening, Jeffrey L. A465
Harmening, Jeffrey L. E491
Harmon, Eric A284
Harmon, Eric P158
Harmon, John E. A575
Harmon, Richard T. E433
Harmon, Sarah W. A419
Harnacke, Ulrich M. W109
Harness, Carl P170
Harnett, Samantha A645
Harper, Angela A1086
Harper, Angela E521
Harper, Craig A543
Harper, Ed P353
Harper, Gordon M. A96
Harper, Jack F. A288
Harper, John L. E117
Harper, Katherine C. W518
Harper, Meredith R. A153
Harper, Troy D. A527
Harquail, David W83
Harralson, Jefferson L. A1064
Harralson, Jefferson L. E509
Harreguy, Maite Aranzabal W174

Harrell, Joanne A528
Harrigan, Edmund P. E267
Harriman, Morril A967
Harriman, Morril P532
Harrington, Charles L. A292
Harrington, Lauren A. A92
Harrington, Michael ("Mike") W. A891
Harris-Lowe, Keith E43
Harris, Alan N. A1054
Harris, Andrea W654
Harris, Arno L. A823
Harris, Bernard A. A877
Harris, Brian A616
Harris, Brian G. E242
Harris, C. Martin A1027
Harris, C. Martin A269
Harris, Carla A. A306
Harris, Carla A. A691
Harris, Carla A. A1104
Harris, Charles S. A66
Harris, Charles S. E25
Harris, Darrel J. A1144
Harris, David G. A325
Harris, Donald J. E204
Harris, Gail B. E176
Harris, Greta J. A659
Harris, Isaac N. E305
Harris, Isaiah A239
Harris, Ivory M. A26
Harris, Jason W487
Harris, John D. A388
Harris, John D. A244
Harris, John D. A612
Harris, John D. W242
Harris, John J. A416
Harris, John W. A948
Harris, Joi M. A345
Harris, Jonathan C. A671
Harris, Kelly J. E54
Harris, Kimberley D. A481
Harris, Kimberly J. A1082
Harris, Lawrence E. E279
Harris, M. Marianne W572
Harris, M. Marianne W371
Harris, Maria A554
Harris, Maria E268
Harris, Marion B. A446
Harris, Mary W490
Harris, Mattison W. A401
Harris, Michael A1040
Harris, Michael E498
Harris, Parker A912
Harris, Paula M. E96
Harris, Paula M. E250
Harris, Robert A190
Harris, Robert E73
Harris, Roger P378
Harris, Stayce D. A164
Harris, Sue W159
Harris, Timothy P. A856
Harris, Toi B A680
Harris, Toi B P342
Harris, Walter L. A645
Harrison, Alicia K A556
Harrison, Alicia K E270
Harrison, Andrew R. A34
Harrison, Ann S. A401
Harrison, Brandon P98
Harrison, Dalen D. E199
Harrison, David D. A755

COMBINED HOOVER'S HANDBOOK INDEX OF EXECUTIVES

A = AMERICAN BUSINESS
E = EMERGING COMPANIES
P = PRIVATE COMPANIES
W = WORLD BUSINESSS

Harrison, Dean M. A749
Harrison, Deborah Marriott A660
Harrison, Elizabeth E63
Harrison, George T. E428
Harrison, J. Frank A265
Harrison, John W24
Harrison, John Barrie W19
Harrison, Lisa W574
Harrison, Marc W351
Harrison, Michael J. E448
Harrison, Robert S. A423
Harrison, Ronald E. E410
Harrison, Sam W487
Harrison, Suzan F. A1125
Harrison, Suzan F. A94
Harrison, Tara Y. E526
Harrison, Timothy C. A749
Harrison, Wade A853
Harrod, Tricia A979
Harsanyi, Zsolt E157
Harshman, Daniel J. E181
Harshman, Ellen F. A838
Harshman, Richard (Rich) J. A54
Harshman, Richard (Rich) J. A834
Harsono, Sudargo (Dan) W79
Hart, Alex W. E328
Hart, Brett J. A1062
Hart, Brett J. A8
Hart, Daniel P. E130
Hart, Daniel R. E45
Hart, Debra Mallonee (Shantz) A488
Hart, Eric H. E50
Hart, James R. A401
Hart, Jeffrey R. W133
Hart, John D. A295
Hart, Matthew J. A56
Hart, Matthew J. E10
Hart, Melanie M. A145
Hart, Melanie M. Housey E389
Hart, R. Rick A889
Hart, R. Rick E414
Hart, Scott W. E462
Hart, Timothy D. A429
Hartenstein, Eddy W. A941
Hartenstein, Eddy W. A180
Harter, Hans-Georg W238
Hartert, Brian E. A895
Hartfield, Nicholas P394
Hartig, Richard J. A704
Hartig, Richard J. E328
Hartin, Tim W648
Hartley, C. Keith E511
Hartley, Cynthia A. A955
Hartley, Cynthia A. E456
Hartley, Susan E. E98
Hartman, Matthew Stephen E514
Hartman, Peter F. W344
Hartman, Peter F. W22
Hartman, Todd G. A155
Hartmann, Christopher W495
Hartmann, Judith W626
Hartmann, Ronald A439
Hartnett-Devlin, Sheila E453
Hartnett, Thomas G. E1

Harton, H. Lynn A1064
Harton, H. Lynn E509
Hartsfield, Keith E281
Hartshorn, Michael J. A905
Hartung, John R. (Jack) A232
Hartung, Michael W242
Hartwick, Gary T. A381
Hartwick, Kenneth Michael E337
Harty, Harriet K. A16
Harty, Linda A. A986
Harty, Linda A. A1099
Harty, Linda A. A804
Harty, Linda A. E96
Hartz, C. Scott E172
Hartz, Scott S. W382
Hartzband, Meryl D. W233
Hartzell, Jay C. A694
Harvey, A. H. W377
Harvey, Anne A251
Harvey, Anne P137
Harvey, Darin S. E5
Harvey, David C. A308
Harvey, David C. E133
Harvey, David S. E357
Harvey, Jason A. A478
Harvey, Richard H. A487
Harvey, Robert B. A1044
Harvey, Roy C. A37
Harvey, Steven L. E291
Harvey, Thomas H. A410
Harvey, William D. A294
Harvey, William D. A256
Harvey, William W. A753
Harwell, Beth A1006
Harwerth, Noel W462
Haryanto, Agus W483
Hasan, Saifuddien W483
Hasan, Zafar A. A349
Hasbrook, John S. A. A1038
Hasbrook, John S. A. E496
Hasebe, Akio W455
Hasebe, Yoshihiro W333
Hasegawa, Eiichi W253
Hasegawa, Eiichi W297
Hasegawa, Hiroki W441
Hasegawa, Masahiko W279
Hasegawa, Nobuyoshi W83
Hasegawa, Yasuo W21
Hasegawa, Yasushi W436
Haselsteiner, Hans Peter W562
Hash, Steven R. E15
Hashimoto, Eiji W437
Hashimoto, Hirofumi W181
Hashimoto, Katsunori W612
Hashimoto, Kiyoshi W336
Hashimoto, Masahiro W568
Hashimoto, Masaru W570
Hashimoto, Takashi W418
Hashimoto, Takayuki W155
Hashimoto, Takayuki W400
Hashimoto, Yasuhiko W334
Hashitani, Masato W534
Hasimoglu, Tamer W346
Hass, A. John E154
Hass, Douglas A. E287
Hassanein, Ahmed P305
Hassell, Gerald L. A691
Hassell, Gerald L. A272
Hassett, Joseph John A81
Hassfurther, Thomas A. A799

Hassid, Michele A1119
Hastings, Annette D P644
Hastings, Catherine E271
Hastings, Jeffrey E423
Hastings, Joseph A. A282
Hastings, Paul J. E369
Hastings, Reed A730
Hastings, Trevor J. A679
Hasuwa, Kenji W453
Hata, Hiroyuki W82
Hata, Takashi W441
Hataishi, Paul E312
Hatanaka, Yasushi W270
Hatanaka, Yoshihiko W557
Hatano, Mutsuko W496
Hatao, Katsumi W538
Hatazawa, Mamoru W612
Hatcher, Patrick A818
Hatchoji, Takashi W387
Hatem, John P. E134
Hatfield, John S. A747
Hathaway, Richard Guy W169
Hato, Hideo W567
Hatsukawa, Koji W585
Hatter, Patricia E266
Hatto, Christopher T. A466
Hattori, Nobumichi W237
Hattori, Rikiya W533
Hattori, Satoru W83
Hattori, Shigehiko W394
Hattrem, Lillian W204
Hau, Robert W. A434
Haub, Christian W. E. W399
Hauber, Steve A723
Hauck, Andy A420
Hauck, Andy E197
Haudrich, John A. A764
Hauenstein, Glen W. A323
Hauer, Jerome M. E157
Haufschild, Wade D. A633
Haug, Knut Dyre W562
Haugel, Didier W27
Haugen, John M. E104
Haugen, Marc E261
Haught, Thomas A. E136
Haugland, Thor-Christian W558
Hauk, Amy A1094
Hauk, Bruce A. E446
Hauschildt, Jennifer L. A704
Hauschildt, Jennifer L. E328
Hauser, Anita W502
Hauser, Heijo J. G. W442
Hauser, Wolfhart W55
Hausfeld, Heike W95
Hausler, Gerd W415
Hausman, Rick P233
Havard, Michael A. A214
Havel, James M. A373
Havel, James M. E168
Havens, Tom A909
Haverinen, Merja W340
Haverkamp, Michael F P79
Havey, Adam R. E157
Haward-Laird, Sharon W82
Hawaux, Andre J. A862
Hawaux, Andre J. A1035
Hawel, Thomas W3
Hawes, Frances Powell E381
Hawk, Don E481
Hawke, Benjamin A588

Hawker, Michael J. W648
Hawkes, James B. E525
Hawkes, Laurie A. E67
Hawkins, Darren D. A1144
Hawkins, Keith W618
Hawkins, Ronald E P316
Hawkins, Ronnie S. A778
Hawkins, William A. A158
Hawks, Donald L. E435
Hawley, Christopher A742
Hawley, Christopher P393
Hawley, DeAnne E455
Hawley, George P. E129
Haworth, Jennifer A. A478
Hawthorne, Douglas D. A167
Hawthorne, Douglas D. E64
Hawthorne, Maria R. E38
Hawthorne, Nancy E126
Hay, Kurt W234
Hay, Lewis A85
Hay, Lewis A613
Hayakawa, Shigeru W616
Hayasaki, Yasuhiro W538
Hayashi, Keiji W454
Hayashi, Kingo W155
Hayashi, Masahiro W253
Hayashi, Naomi W407
Hayashi, Nobuhide W333
Hayashi, Toshiyasu W21
Hayata, Fumiaki W564
Haydar, Ziad R. A848
Hayden, Edmund M. A192
Hayden, John W. E432
Haydon, Jenny E455
Hayek, Matthew J. A704
Hayek, Matthew J. E328
Hayes, Gregory J. A877
Hayes, James K. A401
Hayes, Martha M. E27
Hayes, Rejji P. A256
Hayes, Rejji P. A294
Hayes, Richard G. W260
Hayes, Robin A583
Hayes, Robin N. A602
Hayes, William Bradley A184
Hayford, Michael D. A726
Hayles, E. Carol A357
Hayles, E. Carol A1113
Hayley, Kathryn J. A772
Hayley, Kathryn J. A287
Haylon, Michael E. A83
Haynes-Welsh, Kontessa S. A288
Haynes, Jean A168
Haynes, Jean P89
Haynes, Kenneth A1015
Haynes, Kenneth P571
Haynes, Steven L. E223
Haynesworth, Linnie M. A1042
Haynesworth, Linnie M. A700
Haynesworth, Linnie M. A108
Haynesworth, Linnie M. A354
Haynie, Mark S. A556
Haynie, Mark S. E270
Hays, Cathy J. E421
Hays, J. Clay A1044
Hays, James C. E68
Hays, Rick F. E149
Hays, Von E. A274
Hayslip, Ashley A426
Hayslip, Ashley E202

COMBINED HOOVER'S HANDBOOK INDEX OF EXECUTIVES

A = AMERICAN BUSINESS
E = EMERGING COMPANIES
P = PRIVATE COMPANIES
W = WORLD BUSINESSS

Haysom, Brenna A87
Hayssen, Charles N. E101
Haytaian, Peter D. A85
Hayter, William G. A393
Hayward, Donald R. E101
Hayward, Godfrey Robert W33
Hayward, Jeffery R. A391
Hayward, William Keith E340
Hazel, Mark D. A410
Hazelton, Brian Daniel E540
Hazen, John E64
Hazen, Samuel N. (Sam) A505
Hazleton, Christopher A. A323
Hazou, Kyra W548
He, Biao W151
He, Daopin W106
He, Fei W142
He, Fulong W663
He, Hongyun W375
He, Jiale W141
He, Jing W660
He, Jun W583
He, Mei W575
He, Miaoling W139
He, Ping W261
He, Qi W139
He, Qiju W529
He, Wen W147
He, Zhiqiang W362
Headley, Sarah E455
Heagarty, Chris P678
Heald, David V. E428
Healey, Melanie L. A840
Healey, Melanie L. A1088
Healey, Melanie L. A518
Healy, Douglas T. A60
Heaps, John R. W662
Hearity, Thomas E301
Hearn, Peter C. A662
Hearne, Thomas M. E515
Hearty, James O. A317
Heath, Ralph D. A1012
Heath, Tara L. E65
Heaton, Michael R. A659
Hebard, George W. E153
Hebard, Peggy Hwan E347
Hebard, Peggy Hwan E501
Hebert, Brigitte W420
Hebert, Maurice S. A707
Heck, Denny A972
Heck, Denny P538
Heck, Kristen A474
Heck, Kristen E230
Hecker, Mark E. A953
Hecker, Mark E. E455
Heckes, Howard C. E49
Heckman, Gregory A. A185
Heckmann, Fritz-Juergen W273
Hedberg, Jeffrey Alan W625
Hedberg, Tomas W579
Hedger, Sarah W462
Hedin, Maria W579
Hedley, David V. A914
Hedley, Mary Lynne E519

Hedlund, Michael A. E361
Heel, Joachim A1148
Hees, Bernardo Vieira A185
Hees, Bernardo Vieira A116
Heese, Lisabeth E366
Heeter, Jeffrey D. A37
Heffernan, Christine W597
Heffernan, Michael Thomas E107
Hefter, Marcia Z. A328
Hegarty, Sean P. E2
Hegde, Beth P446
Hegeman, John A689
Hegwood, Paul E83
Hehir, Brian P. A1099
Heid, Michael J. A391
Heiden, Cara K. A209
Heider, Michael W398
Heidtbrink, Scott P218
Heil, Scott E189
Heilbron, James P. A32
Heilbronn, Charles A1055
Heilbronner, Anne-Gabrielle W459
Heilbronner, Anne-Gabrielle W486
Heilbronner, Lawrence A. A196
Heilbronner, Lawrence A. E78
Heim, Christopher D. E140
Heim, Philippe W27
Heimbach, Louis E364
Heimes, Terry J. A727
Heimes, Terry J. E345
Heimlich, Ken A958
Heimlich, Ken P518
Heinberg, Marshall A. E92
Heinemann, Barbara A352
Heinen, Michael J. E340
Heiniger, Stefan E325
Heinmiller, John C. E484
Heinrich, Cory E236
Heinrich, Daniel J. A647
Heintz, Melanie L. A400
Heintzman, David P. A978
Heintzman, David P. E465
Heinz, Michael W93
Heinzel, Matthias A567
Heinzel, Matthias A349
Heinzl, Thomas W642
Heinzmann, David W. E303
Heise, Rita J. A394
Heiskell, Steven G. E430
Heiss, Xavier A1141
Heisz, Leslie Stone A361
Heitel, Stephen G. A509
Heitel, Stephen G. E251
Heitkamp, John R. A773
Heitmann, Scott K. A1133
Heitmann, Scott K. E541
Heitmuller, Frauke W269
Heitzman, Donna L. A978
Heitzman, Donna L. E465
Helander, Mikko W340
Helber, Andreas W98
Helber, Waldemar W93
Helberg, Tom R. E428
Held, Gerald A729
Held, Sascha W397
Held, Thomas W198
Helderman, Mark W. A783
Heldman, Susan P487
Heleen, Mark L. A723

Helfer, Friederike W602
Helfgott, Ludovic W450
Helfrick, Susan A231
Helgøy, Stian W558
Hellemondt-Gerdingh, Marjolien van W75
Heller, Bridgette P. A92
Heller, Bridgette P. E138
Heller, Bridgette P. W449
Heller, Paul G. A545
Heller, Robert A130
Helling, Larry J. A865
Helling, Larry J. E403
Hellmann, Elisabeth (Lisa) A. A522
Hellweg, Kurt D. E243
Helm, Larry L. A1008
Helm, Robert F. E360
Helm, Scott B. A1097
Helman, William W. A444
Helmer, Richard P412
Helmers, Maik D. E297
Helmes, Marion W274
Helmes, Marion W390
Helmes, Marion W545
Helmick, Kevin J. A393
Helmick, Kevin J. E184
Helmig, Christine M. E321
Helmkamp, Katrina L. A878
Helmrich, Klaus W543
Helms, Christopher A. A717
Helms, Lloyd W. A375
Helmsdoerfer, John W. E91
Helt, James P. A12
Helt, James P. E4
Helten-Kindlein, Birgit W277
Helton, Sandra L. A846
helu, Alfredo Harp W266
Helvey, James R. A266
Heminger, Gary R. A410
Heminger, Gary R. A840
Hemmer, Tara J. A1110
Hemphill, Allan J. E470
Hemsey, Rene M. A237
Hemsley, Stephen J. A1075
Hemstreet, Tim P320
Hemstrom, Helena W60
Henaff, Thierry Le W168
Henchoz, Jean-Jacques W269
Henchoz, Jean-Jacques W580
Hendershot, Janeth C. A617
Hendershot, Janeth C. E289
Henderson, Frederick A. A660
Henderson, Frederick A. A95
Henderson, Frederick A. W15
Henderson, George H. (Trey) A954
Henderson, George W. A638
Henderson, Jason W287
Henderson, Jay L. A553
Henderson, Jay L. A748
Henderson, Jay L. A947
Henderson, Jeffrey W. A867
Henderson, Jeffrey W. A147
Henderson, Jeffrey W. E244
Henderson, Leah A852
Henderson, Leah E399
Henderson, Mary E. A478
Henderson, Mary R. (Nina) A261
Henderson, Michael E430
Henderson, Michael A. A656
Henderson, Steven K. A624

Henderson, William H. (Hank) E23
Hendon, Jack G. E96
Hendrian, Catherine A. A256
Hendrian, Catherine A. A294
Hendricks, Dana S. A848
Hendricks, James E. (Jay) E526
Hendricksen, Matthew A398
Hendrickson, Gary E. A835
Hendrickson, Gary E. E49
Hendrickson, Lisa B. E46
Hendrickson, Tami L. A397
Hendrickson, Thomas E360
Hendrickson, Thomas T. A765
Hendrix, Anthony S. E26
Hendrix, Daniel T. E27
Hendry, John A. A523
Hendry, John A. E257
Hendry, Jon N. A37
Hendry, Jon N. E14
Heneghan, Steven P589
Heneghan, Thomas P. E185
Henel, Robert E. A913
Henel, Robert E. E427
Heng, Ho Ming W261
Henion, Bradley A. E96
Henkel, Herbert L. A4
Henkel, Robert J. A794
Henkels, Virginia L. E293
Henley, Brian W80
Henley, Jeffrey O. A786
Henn, Nicholas W371
Hennah, Adrian W626
Hennah, Adrian W318
Henneke, Hans-Guenter W192
Henneman, John B. E408
Hennes, Duncan P. A246
Hennes, Duncan P. W491
Hennessey, Logan A737
Hennessy, John L. A44
Hennessy, Paul J. E438
Henney, Jane E. A73
Hennigan, Michael J. A657
Hennigan, Michael J. A717
Henning, Mats W641
Henning, Thomas E. A727
Henning, Thomas E. E345
Henning, Thomas Edward A426
Henning, Thomas Edward E202
Henretta, Deborah A. A687
Henretta, Deborah A. A298
Henricks, Gwenne A. A835
Henrie, Michael Shane A478
Henrikson, C. Robert A573
Henrikson, C. Robert W580
Henriksson, Jens W579
Henry, Alyssa A560
Henry, Alyssa A162
Henry, April E430
Henry, Brent L A667
Henry, Brent L P332
Henry, Daniel T. A1087
Henry, David P. E329
Henry, Devon M. E526
Henry, Emil W. E150
Henry, George T. E515
Henry, J. William A429
Henry, Kathleen C. A351
Henry, Kevin A. A266
Henry, Kevin A. E426
Henry, Kimberley D. A167

COMBINED HOOVER'S HANDBOOK INDEX OF EXECUTIVES

A = AMERICAN BUSINESS
E = EMERGING COMPANIES
P = PRIVATE COMPANIES
W = WORLD BUSINESSS

Henry, Kimberley D. E64
Henry, Maria G. A465
Henry, Maria G. A604
Henry, Mary Anne P670
Henry, Mike W101
Henry, Peter Barr A743
Henry, Peter Blair A246
Henry, Simon W371
Henry, Simon W499
Henry, Simon W500
Henseler, Peter J. A773
Henseler, Reinhard W192
Hensing, John A137
Hensing, John P59
Henslee, Gregory L. A765
Hensley, Jennifer A288
Hensley, Robert E. A478
Hensley, Robert Z. E114
Hensley, Robin M. E473
Hensley, Todd E. A953
Hensley, Todd E. E455
Hentges, Mary E513
Heo, Young Taeg W537
Hepner, Virginia A. E341
Hepp, Janet E517
Heppelmann, James E. E402
Hepworth, Graeme W507
Herbert-Jones, Sian W357
Herbert, Christopher Edward A450
Herbert, Clifford Francis W36
Herbert, James H. A431
Herbert, James H. E205
Herbert, Teresa A. A112
Herbold, Chris A833
Herbold, Chris A832
Herde, Carl G. A978
Herde, Carl G. E465
Herdman, Robert K. A306
Hereford, Daniel A945
Hereford, Daniel E451
Herencia, Roberto R. A188
Herencia, Roberto R. A136
Herencia, Roberto R. E71
Herkes, Anne Ruth A180
Herlihy, John R. (J.R.) E155
Herlin, Antti W348
Herlin, Jussi W348
Herlofsen, Rebekka Glasser W227
Herlyn, Jeremey E81
Herman, Alexis M. A371
Herman, Alexis M. A264
Herman, Alexis M. A696
Herman, Benedikt-Richard Freiherr von W277
Herman, Cipora A785
Herman, Hugh S. W310
Herman, Linda P366
Herman, Mark J. E298
Herman, Robert A. E382
Herman, Russ M. E173
Herman, Sally W574
Herman, Thomas F. E242
Hermance, David F. A74
Hermance, Frank S. A1054

Hermann, Daniel S. A772
Hermann, Roswitha W15
Hermansson, Kerstin W579
Hermelin, Brian M. E471
Hermelin, Paul W123
Hernadi, Zsolt W412
Hernandez, Carlos A854
Hernandez, Carlos M. A823
Hernandez, Catherine A591
Hernandez, Catherine P294
Hernandez, Enrique A230
Hernandez, Enrique A675
Hernandez, Ernesto M. A292
Hernandez, Ernesto M. A313
Hernandez, Jacinto J. A830
Hernandez, Jacqueline A1094
Hernandez, John E417
Hernandez, Jose Eduardo Beltran W470
Hernandez, Laurie E262
Hernandez, Roland A. A447
Hernandez, Roland A. A1082
Hernandez, Roland A. E480
Hernández, Sandra R. A431
Hernández, Sandra R. E205
Hernandez, William H. A752
Hernando, Julio R. A519
Hernando, Julio R. E256
Hernday, Natasha A. E545
Herold, F. W377
Herold, Jeffery R. E66
Herold, Kathy E409
Heron, Elaine J. E61
Heroux, Paul B. A396
Heroux, Paul B. E187
Herpich, Mark A. E291
Herpich, Peter M P65
Herr, Hans-Jurgen E532
Herr, Robert L. A653
Herraiz, Lizette B. E467
Herren, R. Scott A244
Herrera, Dennis A249
Herrera, Dennis P126
Herrera, Jesus Vicente Gonzalez W131
Herrero, Fernando Maria Masaveu W212
Herrero, Fernando Masaveu W87
Herreros, Mariano Hernandez W11
Herrewyn, Jean-Michel W631
Herrick, Bea P176
Herrick, Glen W. A688
Herrick, Glen W. E323
Herring, Joseph L. A917
Herring, Miles M. E452
Herring, Todd L. A12
Herring, Todd L. E4
Herringer, Frank C. A919
Herrington, Matthew E180
Herrman, Ernie L. A1030
Herrmann, Gerald W586
Herrmann, Ronald A886
Herron, Dallas P144
Herron, Danny J. A397
Herron, John T. A347
Herron, Kevin E. A468
Herron, Mark A814
Herron, Mark E379
Herron, Stephen J. A184
Hersch, Dennis S. E388
Herscher, Penelope A. E305

Herscovici, Lucas W40
Herseth, Mary Jo S. A188
Herseth, Mary Jo S. E71
Hershberger, Pamela S. A82
Hershberger, Rodney E381
Herskovits, Thomas E219
Herter, Rolf E153
Hertz, Douglas J. A471
Hertz, Douglas J. A106
Hertz, Noreena A1106
Hertzman, Brian S. A64
Herweck, Peter E485
Herweijer, Celine W289
Herz, Irwin Max A68
Herz, Robert H. A391
Herz, Robert H. A713
Herzog, Angelika Judith W415
Herzog, Daniel R. E101
Herzog, David L. A52
Herzog, David L. A691
Herzog, David L. A349
Herzog, James J. A274
Heslop, James R. E326
Hess, Beat W. W283
Hess, David P. A956
Hess, Debra Ann A874
Hess, John B. E253
Hess, Jonathan S A1026
Hess, Jonathan S P620
Hess, Lisa W. A874
Hessan, Diane S. A352
Hesse, Daniel R. A834
Hesse, Daniel R. E12
Hessekiel, Jeffrey J. E177
Hessenthaler, Leader Brian P576
Hession, David E145
Hessius, Kerstin W579
Hesslein, Robert W. E529
Hessling, Rick D. A717
Hester, Kevin D. A524
Hester, Kevin D. E258
Hester, Randy A852
Hester, Randy E399
Hester, Stephen Alan Michael A612
Hester, Stephen Alan Michael W135
Hesterberg, Earl J. A491
Heston, Grant J P675
Hete, Joseph C. E11
Hetherington, Kim W116
Hetterich, F. Paul A291
Hetz, Rodrigo W132
Hetzel, Andrew F. A741
Hetzel, Andrew F. E349
Heuberger, Alan C. A320
Heuch, Cecile Blydt W594
Heun, Judy L. A125
Heun, Judy L. E52
Heuschel, Mary Alice A972
Heuschel, Mary Alice P538
Heuveldop, Niklas W228
Hewett, Wayne M. A1115
Hewett, Wayne M. A1069
Hewett, Wayne M. A526
Hewitt, Liz W422
Hewson, Marillyn A. A230
Hewson, Marillyn A. A585
Hexter, David W473
Heya, Toshio W278
Heydemann, Christel W459
Heyden, Henry van der W245

Heyden, Jim van der W245
Heydlauff, Dale E P33
Heyer, Andrew R. E35
Heyer, Andrew R. E305
Heyer, Eric B. A596
Heyer, Eric B. E286
Heyer, Richard L. A889
Heyer, Richard L. E414
Heyer, Steven J. E35
Heyka, Larry R. E291
Heyman, Francois W174
Heymann, Andres Ergas W70
Heyn, Markus A896
Heyn, Markus P465
Heyneman, John M. A426
Heyneman, John M. E202
Heynitz, Harald von W544
Heywood, Suzanne W157
Hianik, Mark W. A1086
Hiatt, Thomas A. A618
Hiatt, Thomas A. E290
Hibbard, Mike P345
Hibben, Thomas H. A747
Hibberd, Sally-Ann W159
Hibbs, Kelly E. A166
Hickel, Greg J. E46
Hickenlooper, Robin S. A232
Hickenlooper, Robin S. A941
Hickey, Benjamin J. E475
Hickey, David B. A147
Hickey, Gregory P. E457
Hickey, John P. E97
Hickman, J. Pat A524
Hickman, J. Pat E258
Hickman, Juliette A600
Hickok, Lori A. E81
Hickok, Steven G P90
Hickox, Michelle S. A421
Hickox, Michelle S. E197
Hicks, Bradley H. A543
Hicks, Cameron P. E484
Hicks, Greg W121
Hicks, Helen M. Mallovy W572
Hicks, Juanita A163
Hicks, Juanita P87
Hicks, Ken C. A114
Hicks, Ken C. A10
Hicks, Kennedy Jane E124
Hicks, Lisa Winston A432
Hicks, Randy D. E189
Hicks, Tim A134
Hicks, Tim E54
Hicks, Wayland R. E430
Hickson, Nina P128
Hickson, Richard G. E124
Hidai, Shohei W267
Hidaka, Yoshihiro W658
Hidalgo, William H. E279
Hidetaka, Makoto W453
Hieb, William J. A910
Hiebler, Jessica M. A991
Hieronimus, Nicolas W358
Hierro, Jorge W266
Hiesinger, Heinrich W198
Hiesinger, Heinrich W251
Hiesinger, Heinrich W96
Hietala, Kaisa H. A388
Hietala, Kaisa H. W500
Higaki, Seiji W581
Higashi, Emiko A607

COMBINED HOOVER'S HANDBOOK INDEX OF EXECUTIVES

A = AMERICAN BUSINESS
E = EMERGING COMPANIES
P = PRIVATE COMPANIES
W = WORLD BUSINESSS

Higashi, Emiko W585
Higashi, Kazuhiro W285
Higashi, Kazuhiro W555
Higashi, Masahiro W110
Higashi, Tetsuro W527
Higashihara, Toshiaki W278
Higashino, Hirokazu W566
Higginbotham, Richard A. A941
Higginbotham, Robert A443
Higgins, Arthur J. A358
Higgins, Arthur J. A1150
Higgins, Barbara A. A367
Higgins, Bren D. A607
Higgins, Brian S. A786
Higgins, Jimmy W574
Higgins, John L. E59
Higgins, Melina E. A1093
Higgins, Melina E. A470
Higgins, Michael E529
Higgins, Nigel W90
Higgins, Patricia L. A1037
Higgins, Stephen T. A452
High, Katherine A. E267
Highmark, David A. E190
Highsmith, Carlton L. A602
Hightower, Maia P611
Higo, Takashi W608
Higuchi, Kojiro W604
Higuchi, Masayuki W253
Higuchi, Tatsuo W462
Higuchi, Tetsuji W413
Higurashi, Yutaka W440
Hikita, Sakae W181
Hilado, Maria Teresa A195
Hilado, Maria Teresa A1150
Hilal, Nabil P42
Hilal, Paul C. A304
Hilal, Paul C. A92
Hildebrand, Arthur K. E185
Hileman, Donald P. A844
Hileman, Donald P. E394
Hilferty, Daniel J. E174
Hilfiger, Janie E99
Hill-Milbourne, Veronica E5
Hill-Nelson, Sarah E291
Hill, Anne A114
Hill, Barbara B. E278
Hill, Bonnie Guiton A124
Hill, Brice A90
Hill, Bryan A389
Hill, Bryan P219
Hill, Edward E149
Hill, Elliott J. E532
Hill, George S. E209
Hill, Grant H. A195
Hill, Gregory P. E253
Hill, J. Thomas A885
Hill, Janet M. E173
Hill, John P. E101
Hill, John W. E123
Hill, Jonathan D. A891
Hill, Kathryn M. A711
Hill, Kathryn M. A729
Hill, Kathryn M. A215

Hill, Leo J. A72
Hill, Leo J. E29
Hill, Michael E. A153
Hill, Patrick X. A580
Hill, Richard S. A97
Hill, Robert R. A955
Hill, Robert R. A950
Hill, Robert R. E456
Hill, Stephanie C. A643
Hill, Stephanie C. A911
Hill, Sylvia W6
Hill, Thad A543
Hill, Thomas W A392
Hill, Thomas W P221
Hill, Willard I. A181
Hill, William T. A516
Hillebrand, James A. A978
Hillebrand, James A. E465
Hillebrand, Lana L. A59
Hillenbrand, Daniel C. E255
Hiller, Michael A184
Hillery, Martin T. A97
Hillier, Scott A. A639
Hills, Wendy J. E528
Hilsheimer, Lawrence A. A489
Hilsheimer, Lawrence A. E274
Hilt, Angela A254
Hilt, James ("Jim") A. E254
Hilton, Christopher J. A430
Hilton, Michael F. A909
Hilton, Steven J. A687
Hilzinger, Jeffrey A. E159
Hilzinger, Kurt J. A541
Himawan, Tossin W464
Himeiwa, Yasuo W530
Himelfarb, Richard J. A977
Himelfarb, Richard J. E464
Himelstein, Jake E473
Himes, Vicki P429
Hinchli, Andrew W164
Hinchliffe, Michelle A. W377
Hinchliffe, Michelle A. W101
Hinde, David Richard W179
Hinderhofer, Kathryn M. A191
Hinderhofer, Kathryn M. E77
Hinduja, Anil D. A450
Hinduja, Sanjay E404
Hines, Barry D. A880
Hines, Barry D. E412
Hines, George N. A639
Hines, Michael F. A1030
Hines, Perry G. A531
Hingle, Donald A. A188
Hingle, Donald A. E69
Hingtgen, Tim L. A282
Hinkle, Gary L. A981
Hinkle, Gary L. E469
Hinkle, James G. A524
Hinkle, James G. E258
Hinman, Jacqueline C. A342
Hinman, Jacqueline C. A568
Hinojosa, Claudio Melandri W73
Hinojosa, Guillermo F. Vogel W27
Hinrichs, John W. H. A393
Hinrichs, Joseph R. A304
Hinrichs, Lars W199
Hinsch, Christian W586
Hinshaw, John M. A989
Hinshaw, John M. A289
Hinshelwood, Nigel W371

Hinson, Donald J. A510
Hinson, Donald J. E252
Hinson, Jeffrey T. A641
Hinton, Angela P128
Hinton, James H. A677
Hipp, C. Johnson A72
Hipp, C. Johnson E29
Hippe, Alan W502
Hippeau, Eric A660
Hippel, James T. E59
Hipple, Richard J. A602
Hirai, Ryutaro W552
Hirai, Toshihiro W441
Hirai, Yasuteru W402
Hirai, Yoshinori W18
Hiraizumi, Nobuyuki W330
Hirakawa, Hiroyuki W454
Hiraku, Tomofumi W405
Hiramoto, Tatsuo W155
Hirano, Atsuhiko W297
Hirano, Eiji W451
Hirano, Keiji W582
Hirano, Nobuya W410
Hirano, Nobuyuki A713
Hirano, Nobuyuki W403
Hirano, Shiro W316
Hirata, Masayoshi W612
Hirawat, Samit A178
Hire, W. Jeffrey E274
Hirji, Rahim W382
Hiroi, Takashi W439
Hironaka, Yasuaki W319
Hirono, Michiko W319
Hirose, Ichiro W389
Hirose, Michiaki W608
Hirose, Shinichi W606
Hirowatari, Kiyohide W321
Hirsch, Chuck A547
Hirsch, Daniel J. E67
Hirsch, Didier A645
Hirsch, Elizabeth T. A282
Hirsch, Erik R. E244
Hirsch, Jim P436
Hirsch, Marilyn V. A296
Hirschheimer, Ruy Roberto W4
Hirschhorn, Eric S. E217
Hirschmann, James W. A1121
Hirschson, Jay P. E221
Hirsty, Daniel E67
Hirtler-Garvey, Karin E525
Hisabayashi, Yoshinari W297
Hisada, Ichiro W278
Hishiyama, Reiko W550
Hislop, Michael J. E539
Hitch, Jordan A187
Hitchcock-Gear, Salene A856
Hite, Christopher E425
Hlay, Jean E218
Ho, Andy W351
Ho, Angela K. A768
Ho, Angela K. E359
Ho, Bosco Hin Ngai W148
Ho, David H. Y. W572
Ho, David Hing-Yuen A30
Ho, Lora W583
Ho, Maykin E61
Ho, Mei-Yueh W51
Ho, Peter S. A129
Ho, Peter S. A402
Ho, Tian Yee W190

Ho, Wing Yan W141
Hoag, Jay C. A730
Hoag, Jay C. A1149
Hoaglin, Thomas E. A59
Hoang, Giang Thi E64
Hobart, Lauren R. A326
Hobart, Lauren R. A1146
Hobbs, Franklin W. A43
Hobbs, Helen H. A821
Hobbs, Michael B. A556
Hobbs, Michael B. E270
Hobbs, Nicholas A543
Hobby, Jean M. A1010
Hobby, Jean M. A514
Hobby, Paul W. A757
Hobmeier, Michael W631
Hobson, David P210
Hobson, Mellody L. A591
Hobson, Mellody L. A964
Hochberg, Mitchell P686
Hochegger, Alois W633
Hochet, Xavier W123
Hochman, Rodney P446
Hochman, Rodney F. A458
Hochman, Shalom W312
Hochmuth, Shaina A168
Hochmuth, Shaina P89
Hochschild, Roger C. A846
Hochschild, Roger C. A330
Hochschwender, J. Michael A545
Hockaday, Irvine O. A620
Hocken, Natalie L. A798
Hockfield, Susan J. A821
Hockman, Alexander A. E357
Hockridge, Stuart A. E16
Hodge, Michael A948
Hodge, Michael E. A515
Hodges, Amanda A892
Hodges, Charles H. E489
Hodges, Ernest M A392
Hodges, Ernest M P221
Hodges, Georganne A809
Hodges, George W. A454
Hodges, Mark Blakeley A470
Hodges, Morgan E283
Hodgkinson, Andrew E297
Hodgson, Christine Mary W561
Hodgson, Curtis D. E296
Hodnesdal, Hege W562
Hodnett, David P58
Hodnett, David W. P. W559
Hodo, Chikatomo W460
Hodo, Chikatomo W400
Hodrick, Laurie Simon E423
Hodson, Beverley W489
Hoechtel, Elfiede W453
Hoedt, Robert J.W. Ten W393
Hoeg, Krystyna T. W299
Hoeg, Krystyna T. W571
Hoegenhaven, Soeren W348
Hoehn, Klaus E402
Hoekstra, Dave E63
Hoelter, Michael T. A82
Hoepner, Theodore J. E68
Hoer, Michael A. E316
Hoeven, Maria van der W613
Hoeweler, Robert E. E91
Hof, Matthew Kaes Van't E409
Hofer, Udo W398
Hoff, Olga A1151

COMBINED HOOVER'S HANDBOOK INDEX OF EXECUTIVES

A = AMERICAN BUSINESS
E = EMERGING COMPANIES
P = PRIVATE COMPANIES
W = WORLD BUSINESSS

Hoffler, Daniel A. E35
Hoffman, Bridget C. A397
Hoffman, Cindy L. E158
Hoffman, Edward J. A874
Hoffman, James D. A888
Hoffman, James E. A1144
Hoffman, Joshua E. E158
Hoffman, Reid G. A701
Hoffman, Tony A534
Hoffmann, Andre W502
Hoffmann, Andreas C. W545
Hoffmann, Charlotte W188
Hoffmann, Michael K. E451
Hoffmann, Reiner W95
Hoffmeister, David F. A215
Hoffmeister, David F. E462
Hoffmeister, David F. E262
Hoffmeister, James H. A1096
Hoffsis, Glen F. A642
Hoffsis, Glen F. E304
Hofheins, Todd P446
Hofilena, Hector L. W514
Hofing, Gary S. E193
Hofmann, Jorg W640
Hofmann, Thomas W. E534
Hofmeister, Brandon J. A256
Hofstetter, John M. E393
Hofstetter, Karl W34
Hofstetter, Sarah A195
Hogan, Howard Thomas A430
Hogan, Joseph (Joe) M. E16
Hogan, Kathleen T. A34
Hogan, Kevin T. A295
Hogan, Lee W. A301
Hogan, Mark D. A143
Hogan, Mark D. E56
Hogan, Michael P. A554
Hogan, Michael P. E268
Hogan, Michael R. A1066
Hogan, Peter E240
Hogan, Randall J. W393
Hogan, W. Glenn E301
Hogans, Mack L. A166
Hogenson, Kathleen A. E520
Hogg, Rupert Bruce Grantham Trower W128
Hogg, Sarah W509
Hoggatt, Brian P. E469
Hoggett, Tony W597
Hoglund, Robert N. A288
Hoglund, Robert N. A290
Hogna, Egil W448
Hoguet, Karen M. A611
Hoguet, Karen M. A742
Hohlmeier, Monika W98
Hohmeister, Harry W196
Hohol, Linda M. O. W122
Hoidahl, Hans-Olav W31
Hojland, Peter W188
Hokanson, Mark E. A175
Hokanson, Mark E. E66
Holaday, A. Bart A37
Holaday, A. Bart E14
Holbrook, Richard E. A352

Holcomb, James A1075
Holcomb, John H. A955
Holcomb, John H. E456
Holcomb, Michele A. M. E287
Holcombe, Gregory F. E364
Hold, Renate W62
Holden-Baker, Sue P90
Holden, James P. A941
Holdenried, Hans-Ulrich W303
Holder, Duane P678
Holder, H. Randolph E357
Holder, John R. A468
Holder, Julie Fasone A354
Holder, Thomas M. A471
Holder, Thomas M. A106
Holderman, Daniel P. E536
Holding, Frank B. A417
Holdsworth, Mark K. E420
Hole, Brian R. E538
Hole, Spencer Doran E22
Holguin, Maria Angela W325
Holiday, Edith E. A915
Hollan, Michael K. A311
Holland, C. Malcolm A1086
Holland, C. Malcolm E521
Holland, Christopher S. A578
Holland, Elizabeth I. E524
Holland, G. Edison E453
Holland, James E. A605
Holland, James T. E526
Holland, Karl-Heinz W655
Holland, Murray T. A493
Holland, Neal A. A889
Holland, Neal A. E414
Holland, Noel R. A271
Holland, Noel R. E109
Holland, Richard O. A311
Holland, Robert T. E321
Hollar, Jan H. E195
Hollar, Jason M. A201
Hollenbeck, Martin F. A240
Holley, Charles M. A76
Holley, Charles M. A207
Holley, Charles M. A826
Holley, Rick R. A1127
Holliday, Charles (Chad) O. A505
Holliday, Charles O. A320
Holliday, Charles O. W532
Holliday, Keith E460
Holliday, Steven Harold A422
Holliday, Susan Riedman A411
Holliger, Fred L. A719
Hollihan, John P. A96
Holliman, William G. "Skipper" A190
Holliman, William G. "Skipper" E73
Hollin, Edward J. E321
Hollinger, William R. A594
Hollingshead, James R. E277
Hollingsworth, Audrey E108
Hollingsworth, Chad A641
Hollis, M. Clayton A860
Hollister, Thomas J. A181
Hollman, Michael E9
Holloman, J. Phillip A862
Holloman, James Phillip A902
Holloway, Duane D. A1073
Holloway, Jason E537
Hollub, Vicki A. A643
Hollub, Vicki A. A767
Holly, James C. A935

Holly, James C. E439
Holm, Alan A235
Holm, George L. A818
Holman, Jonathan S. E38
Holmberg, James L. A391
Holmberg, Per W228
Holmes, Chad M. E126
Holmes, Christopher (Chris) T. A395
Holmes, Christopher (Chris) T. E185
Holmes, Craig E. A556
Holmes, Craig E. E270
Holmes, Frank E. E514
Holmes, Jack A. E437
Holmes, James W. A864
Holmes, John J. E125
Holmes, Joseph A1027
Holmes, Keith F. A16
Holmes, Michael R. A373
Holmes, Michael R. E168
Holmes, Ned S. A852
Holmes, Ned S. E399
Holmes, Parris H. E437
Holmes, Robert C. A1008
Holmes, Robert S. A276
Holmes, Robert W. A125
Holmes, Robert W. E52
Holmgren, Geir W562
Holmstrom, Mats W547
Holroyd, Samantha F. A52
Holsten, Joseph M. A643
Holston, Michael J. A462
Holt, Christopher A788
Holt, Christopher E365
Holt, Daniel W. E336
Holt, Jack E111
Holt, Kevin W351
Holt, Mark A. E196
Holt, Matthew S. A112
Holt, Matthew S. E408
Holt, Peter D. E285
Holt, Tim Oliver W544
Holt, Timothy A. A694
Holt, Timothy A. E528
Holt, Victoria M. A1110
Holt, Victoria M. E387
Holt, Victoria M. E400
Holtaway, Jonathan D. E246
Holthaus, Gerard E. E224
Holthaus, Michelle Johnston A560
Holthausen, Robert W. E126
Holtinger, Jens W641
Holtz, Clifford S. E300
Holtzman, Marc L. E500
Holz, Kelli J. A1107
Holzer, Sunita E520
Holzer, Sunita E453
Holzgrefe, Frederick J. E426
Holzrichter, Julie A292
Holzshu, Christopher (Chris) S. A639
Holzwarth, Andrew C. E62
Hom, Donald S. E351
Homan, Jan W229
Hombach, Robert J. E61
Homma, Tetsuro W465
Homma, Toshio W123
Homoelle, David A. E428
Homolka, David S. E147
Honda, Keiko W18
Honda, Keiko W407
Honda, Keiko W490

Honda, Osamu W577
Hondal, Francis A. A140
Hondal, Francis A. A377
Honeycutt, Jennifer L. A315
Hong, Abe E285
Hong, Arlene S. A148
Hong, Arthur Xiaobo W636
Hong, Changlong W139
Hong, Liang W530
Honickman, Jeffrey A. A272
Honig, Benjamin A16
Honjo, Takehiro W462
Honma, Yo W451
Honorable, Colette D. A952
Hood, Amy E. A701
Hood, Amy E. A4
Hood, Christopher M. A597
Hood, John Antony A161
Hood, Mark C. E131
Hood, Warren A. A190
Hood, Warren A. E73
Hood, William K. E199
Hood, William W. A1066
Hoody, Dan P260
Hoogeveen, Gary W. A798
Hooi, Ng Keng W261
Hook, Lisa A. A408
Hook, Lisa A. A825
Hook, Richard A. A812
Hooker, Nolan E. E455
Hooks, Michael K. E308
Hooley, Joseph L. A388
Hooley, Joseph L. W45
Hooley, Joseph L. W46
Hooley, Stephen C. A176
Hooper, Barbara W611
Hooper, Charles W. A86
Hooper, Michele J. A1062
Hooper, Michele J. A1075
Hooper, Tecumseh E454
Hoopingarner, John M. E506
Hoople, Elizabeth G. A688
Hoople, Elizabeth G. E323
Hoops, Elliot D. E334
Hoose, Harold F. E98
Hooston, David E. E83
Hoots, Cindy L. E547
Hoovel, Catherine A. A675
Hoover, Erik T. A349
Hoover, James A. E418
Hoover, Jan S. A106
Hoover, Jan S. E40
Hoover, Jewell D. A410
Hope, James D. E389
Hopeman, Wei A170
Hopfield, Jessica E277
Hopgood, Daniel Roy W209
Hopkin, Vince A780
Hopkins, Deborah (Debby) C. A662
Hopkins, Deborah (Debby) C. A1061
Hopkins, Denver P184
Hopkins, Herbert Derek A600
Hopkins, Jennifer K. A507
Hopkins, Jennifer K. E248
Hopkins, John N. A596
Hopkins, John N. E286
Hoplamazian, Mark S. A1091
Hopmans, John A641
Hoppe, Robert R. A418
Hoppenot, Herve E267

COMBINED HOOVER'S HANDBOOK INDEX OF EXECUTIVES

A = AMERICAN BUSINESS
E = EMERGING COMPANIES
P = PRIVATE COMPANIES
W = WORLD BUSINESSS

Horak, H. Lynn A209
Horan, Jeanette A. W443
Horen, Clive van W574
Horey, Annie E83
Horgan, Tanya W21
Horger, Robert R. A955
Horger, Robert R. E456
Hori, Kenichi W408
Hori, Ryuji W270
Horiba, Atsushi W567
Horiba, Atsushi W550
Horie, Nobuyuki W266
Horie, Toshiyasu W51
Horiguchi, Tadayoshi W297
Horikiri, Satoshi W434
Horikoshi, Takeshi W347
Horiuchi, Katsuyoshi W533
Horiuchi, Yosuke W527
Hormaechea, Michael B. A474
Hormaechea, Michael B. E230
Hormats, Robert D. A69
Hormell, Robert A. A441
Hormell, Robert A. E212
Horn, Johann W61
Horn, Johann W96
Horn, Justin E455
Horn, Michael M. A396
Horn, Michael M. E187
Horn, R. Lawrence Van E114
Horn, Zachary I. A427
Horn, Zachary I. E204
Hornaday, F. D. A66
Hornaday, F. D. E25
Hornbaker, Renee J. A354
Hornberger, David A788
Hornberger, David E365
Hornbuckle, William Joseph A696
Horne, James H. A496
Horne, Timothy A1050
Horne, Timothy P636
Hornfeck, Traci E425
Horning, Sandra J. A473
Horninger, Thomas D. E185
Hornish, Jo Ellen E184
Horodniceanu, Michael F. A1046
Horowitz, Beth S. W287
Horowitz, Joshua S. E56
Horowitz, Joshua S. E301
Horowitz, Sara A401
Horowitz, William N. E190
Horras, Betty A. Baudler E30
Horst, Peter D. A810
Horst, Peter D. E376
Horst, Toney C. E23
Horstedt, Richard W548
Horstmann, Anne W415
Horstmeier, Ilka W96
Horta-Osorio, Antonio W371
Horta-Osorio, António W235
Hortefeux, Valerie W392
Hortman, Edwin W. A72
Hortman, Edwin W. E29
Horton, Andrew W487
Horton, Anthony R. A493

Horton, Donald R. A536
Horton, Greg A. E243
Horton, Keith D. A1033
Horton, Keith D. E492
Horton, Thomas W. A462
Horton, Thomas W. A1104
Horton, William L. A1088
Horvat, Sinischa W93
Horvath, Debora D. A881
Horvath, Ferenc W412
Horvath, Gabor W412
Horvath, Lawrence J. A504
Horwedel, Gregory P170
Hosaka, Masayuki W487
Hosemann, Delbert A969
Hosemann, Delbert P535
Hoshi, Tomoko W451
Hoshihara, Kazuhiro W410
Hoshino, Asako W441
Hosier, John C. E401
Hoskins, Craig H. A818
Hoskins, W. Wesley A397
Hoskins, W. Wesley E187
Hosler, C. William A800
Hosoya, Kazuo W564
Hosseini, Abby A685
Host, Gerard R. A399
Host, Gerard R. A1044
Hoster, David H. E151
Hostetler, Cynthia L. A893
Hostetter, Shane W. E404
Hotchkiss, Herbert G. E96
Hotchkiss, Malcolm F. E56
Hotchkiss, Richard M. E190
Hotsuki, Keishi A713
Hottges, Timotheus A992
Hottges, Timotheus W395
Hottges, Timotheus W199
Hotz, Lauren D. A571
Hou, Angui W88
Hou, Cliff W583
Hou, Enlong W574
Hou, Jinglei W202
Hou, Qicai W326
Hou, Yung-Hsung W206
Houchens, Steve P133
Houde, Jean W420
Hough, David P260
Hough, G. Thomas A860
Hough, Laurie E447
Houghtaling, Kathleen R. A401
Houghton, Chris W228
Houghton, Keith J. A528
Houghton, Keith J. E258
Houghton, Sue W487
Houle, Carol L. E400
Houle, Leo W. W157
Hountalas, Jon W119
Hourican, Kevin P. A989
Hourquebie, Philip A W311
House, Andrew W441
House, Rebecca (Becky) W. A902
Householder, Joseph A. A18
Housel, Morgan E. A659
Housman, Diane P581
Houssaye, France W548
Houston, Andrew W. A689
Houston, Andrew W. E145
Houston, Daniel J. A846
Houston, Dennis M. W573

Houston, Helga S. A545
Houston, Linda M. E526
Houten, Christina G. Van E481
Houten, Frans van W449
Hovde, Steven D. E104
Hovell-Patrizi, Allegra van W16
Hovey, Scott E451
Hovsepian, Ronald W. E31
Howard, Anne E. A865
Howard, Anne E. E403
Howard, Ayanna A716
Howard, Ayanna E45
Howard, Christopher P500
Howard, David A993
Howard, Dennis E451
Howard, Jeffrey A. E41
Howard, John M. A1042
Howard, John W. A1068
Howard, Julie M. A655
Howard, Julie M. E448
Howard, Kevin D. A223
Howard, Lois E102
Howard, Michelle A565
Howard, Nathan E340
Howdyshell, Cathy I. A401
Howe, Geoffrey M. T. W310
Howe, Jerald S. A625
Howe, Robert L. A60
Howeg, Stephan W13
Howell, Andrew S. A397
Howell, Brett E444
Howell, Douglas K. A455
Howell, Heather V. A890
Howell, Heather V. E416
Howell, Hilton H. E237
Howell, Laura F. E111
Howell, Laura F. E12
Howell, Lloyd W. A711
Howell, Lloyd W. A458
Howell, Michael W.D. A1099
Howell, Peter C. E402
Howell, Robin Robinson E237
Howes, Constance A. A1108
Howes, Richard Allan W116
Howie, Craig W233
Howland, Douglas B. A563
Howle, Carol W109
Howorka, Johannes W280
Howorth, Derek P401
Howse, Curtis A985
Howson, David E87
Hoxsie, Katherine W. A1108
Hoy, Thomas L. A98
Hoy, Thomas L. A396
Hoy, Thomas L. E36
Hoy, Thomas L. E187
Hoy, William L. A427
Hoy, William L. E203
Hoyle, M. Eddie E108
Hoyos, Jaime Carvajal W169
Hoysradt, Jean E. E530
Hoyt, Bob W289
Hoyt, Bob W89
Hoyt, Casey E526
Hoyt, Kelcey E. W369
Hoyt, Marlene P. A372
Hoyt, Marlene P. E167
Hoyt, Rebecca A. A86
Hrabowski, Freeman A. A991
Hrabowski, Freeman A. E673

Hrabrov, Max A400
Hrabusa, John T. A860
Hrevus, Tina A587
Hromadko, Gary F. A377
Hruby, Dennis E. E440
Hsieh, Haydn W650
Hsieh, Louis T. A1145
Hsieh, Louis T. W324
Hsieh, Ming E216
Hsieh, Ming E224
Hsieh, Tsun-Yan W382
Hsing, Michael R. E331
Hsiung, Ming-ho W128
Hsu, Alex E472
Hsu, Clark A843
Hsu, Clark E393
Hsu, David W323
HSU, Hsenghung Sam A394
Hsu, Jonathan Chung Chang W240
Hsu, Judie W128
Hsu, Kevin P486
Hsu, Michael D. A603
Hsu, Michael D. A1010
Hsu, Rita Lai Tai Fan W80
Hsu, Rock Sheng-Hsiun W168
Hsu, Tai-Lin W51
Hsu, Ting-Chen W530
Hsu, Wen-Bin W168
Hsuan, John Min-Chih W650
Hsueh, Howard E519
Hu, Aimin W431
Hu, Anna M. A219
Hu, Changmiao W138
Hu, Chenming C. E3
Hu, Daoyi W98
Hu, Fred A1145
Hu, Fred W621
Hu, Fred Zuliu W301
Hu, Guangjie W158
Hu, Guobin W152
Hu, Hanjie W239
Hu, Hong W88
Hu, Hongwei W326
Hu, Jean X. A18
Hu, Jean X. E216
Hu, Jia W542
Hu, Jiabiao W145
Hu, Jianxin W142
Hu, Kang W529
Hu, Lisong W662
Hu, Shihai W34
Hu, Shujie W261
Hu, Xianfu W141
Hu, Xiangqun W257
Hu, Xiaolin W106
Hu, Xiaoling W572
Hu, Xin W529
Hu, Xinfu W608
Hu, Yebi W257
Hu, Yiming W529
Hu, Yong W142
Hu, Yuntong W327
Hu, Zhengliang W603
Hua, Jie Run W98
Hua, Li W142
Hua, Min W529
Hua, Zhisong W574
Huan, Jianchun W530
Huang, Baokui W472
Huang, Baoxin W472

COMBINED HOOVER'S HANDBOOK INDEX OF EXECUTIVES

A = AMERICAN BUSINESS
E = EMERGING COMPANIES
P = PRIVATE COMPANIES
W = WORLD BUSINESSS

Huang, Bin W98
Huang, Chaoquan W291
Huang, Charlie Xiaoli E370
Huang, Ching Lu W128
Huang, Claire A. A1151
Huang, Darren E370
Huang, Dawen W542
Huang, Dinan W145
Huang, Duoduo A1145
Huang, Feng W326
Huang, Hai W477
Huang, Hao W140
Huang, Hongyan W173
Huang, Jen-Hsun A761
Huang, Jian W291
Huang, Jiang W15
Huang, Jiangfeng W117
Huang, Jianlong W516
Huang, Joe W206
Huang, Johnson A1145
Huang, Joseph N.C. W206
Huang, Juncan W257
Huang, Junlong W142
Huang, Li W301
Huang, Liangbo W301
Huang, Lixin W291
Huang, Long W138
Huang, Ming W324
Huang, Ming W648
Huang, Ou W529
Huang, Qing W149
Huang, Roberto N. W514
Huang, Shaoming W292
Huang, Shuping W572
Huang, Tetsai W284
Huang, Tiao-Kuei W128
Huang, Tsu Te A878
Huang, Tsu Te E409
Huang, Wei W472
Huang, Wei W574
Huang, Wendell W583
Huang, Wensheng W145
Huang, Wenzhou W655
Huang, Xiao W173
Huang, Xiaowen W173
Huang, Xiumei W142
Huang, Yi W663
Huang, Yongzhang W466
Huang, Yung-Jen W206
Huang, Yunjing W662
Huat, Seek Ngee W112
Hubbard, Glenn W613
Hubbard, Jean A. A844
Hubbard, Jean A. E394
Hubbard, Kym Marie A966
Hubbard, Linda E254
Hubbard, R. Glenn A691
Hubble, Susan L. A816
Hubbs, Miranda C. W299
Hubbs, Miranda C. W451
Huber, Andreas W631
Huber, Berthold W61
Huber, Doreen W129
Huber, Jeffrey T. A363

Huber, Jeffrey T. E513
Huber, Julie A. A378
Huber, Linda S. W83
Huber, Lydia A. E184
Huber, Marie Oh A357
Huber, Thomas E319
Hucher, François W123
Hudak, Carrie L. E101
Huddle, William G. E293
Huddleston, Gordon A1086
Huddleston, Gordon E521
Hudson, Ann A381
Hudson, Bill P278
Hudson, Brian Arden A702
Hudson, Brian Arden E326
Hudson, Brian Arden E172
Hudson, Dawn E. A761
Hudson, Dawn E. A570
Hudson, Deal W. E42
Hudson, Dennis S. A923
Hudson, Dennis S. E433
Hudson, Floyd E. A747
Hudson, Frederick M. E475
Hudson, Ian A. E188
Hudson, Isabel W114
Hudson, Isabel W65
Hudson, Linda P. A128
Hudson, Linda P. W617
Hudson, Lydie W176
Hudson, Matthew R. E515
Hudson, Paul W515
Hudson, Rose J. E279
Hudson, Scott A. A1097
Hudson, Scott R. A455
Hudson, Sherrill W. A629
Hudson, Sherrill W. A1066
Huebert, Michael G. E5
Huebscher, Grace A. A450
Huef, Hermann W234
Huen, Po Wah W173
Huerta, Javier W297
Huerta, Michael P. A323
Huestis, Christine A. E199
Huestis, Timothy H. A829
Huestis, Timothy H. E385
Huet, Jean-Marc W274
Huey, Morris J. A199
Hufenbecher, Constanze W303
Huffard, John C. A747
Huffman, Herbert H. E507
Hufschmid, Hans W86
Hug, Paul W91
Huggins, Daniel W419
Huggins, James S. A815
Hughes-Hallett, James Edward W580
Hughes-Hallett, James Edward W128
Hughes-Hallett, James Wyndham John W128
Hughes, Amanda W487
Hughes, Bryan L. E540
Hughes, Catherine J. W532
Hughes, David P P295
Hughes, Emily A. A515
Hughes, James A. A37
Hughes, James A. E510
Hughes, Keith W. A408
Hughes, Lily Yan A97
Hughes, Mark W621
Hughes, Mark A. E98
Hughes, Martin P. A499

Hughes, Melanie A711
Hughes, Michael P P295
Hughes, Robert P. E368
Hughes, Von E493
Hughes, William H. A152
Hugin, ?Robert J. W154
Huh, Yong-hak W537
Hui, Jason Sai Tan W534
Hui, Julian W323
Hui, Ka Yan W139
Hui, Wing Mau W534
Huillard, Jacques W213
Huillard, Xavier W357
Huillard, Xavier W635
Huizinga, Stuart M. E407
Hulbert, Thomas M. A271
Hulbert, Thomas M. E109
Hulet, Steven P481
Hulgrave, Shelley A812
Hull, Gregory J. E455
Huller, Kelly G. E233
Hulligan, William P. E82
Hulse, Walter S. A783
Hulst, Herman W306
Hulst, Michelle A129
Hulst, Michelle E489
Hult, David W. A99
Hult, William E493
Hultquist, Gary L. A605
Humaidan, Saleh Helwan Al W47
Humaidhi, Abdallah Saud Al W47
Humber, Christopher I. E529
Hume, Jeffrey B. A295
Hume, Richard T. A999
Hume, Richard T. A42
Humphrey, John A764
Humphrey, Peter G. A411
Humphrey, Scott R. E218
Humphreys, Lance A301
Humphreys, Lance E131
Humphries, Stanley B. A1149
Humphries, T. Anthony A399
Humrichouse, Ximena G. A274
Hund-Mejean, Martina A269
Hund-Mejean, Martina A856
Hund-Mejean, Martina W532
Hundeshagen, Ilka W269
Hung, Priscilla E519
Hung, Su-Gin W252
Hungeling, William J. E323
Hungerford, Meg L. E354
Hunhoff, Darin Mark A235
Hunker, Ann Marie W. E306
Hunn, L. Neil A904
Hunn, Robert P341
Hunsberger, Susan K. E443
Hunsicker, Judith A. E156
Hunt, Anthony J. E415
Hunt, Bruce W. A852
Hunt, Bruce W. E399
Hunt, Bryan A543
Hunt, Colin W20
Hunt, David A856
Hunt, Donald C. A502
Hunt, Eugene A938
Hunt, Eugene E442
Hunt, Gary H. A998
Hunt, Heather E446
Hunt, James K. A811
Hunt, James K. E377

Hunt, James S. E68
Hunt, James W. A398
Hunt, James W. A380
Hunt, Jolie A. E287
Hunt, Kevin J. E160
Hunt, Neil E423
Hunt, Orlagh W662
Hunt, Tina E519
Hunt, Tina E263
Hunter, Christopher H. A400
Hunter, Constance A65
Hunter, Gordon E303
Hunter, Jeff D. A1097
Hunter, Jerry A938
Hunter, Jerry E442
Hunter, Rhonda D. E430
Hunter, Robert G. E434
Hunter, Robert L. E156
Hunter, Sarah W644
Hunter, Timothy M. A753
Huntington, Amelia A1028
Huntington, Judith A936
Huntington, Judith E441
Huntington, Kelly Michelle E337
Huntley, Cindy M. A510
Huntley, Cindy M. E252
Huntley, David S. A1008
Huntsman, Jon M. A230
Huntsman, Jon M. A444
Huntsman, Peter R. A547
Huntzicker, James P177
Hunziker, Hans Jorg E538
Huo, Wenxun W530
Hur, Yin W335
Hurd, Jeffrey J. A377
Hurd, Jeffrey J. E17
Hurley, Jill A988
Hurley, Jill E479
Hurley, Robert S. E154
Hurley, Ursula A583
Hurlston, Michael E. W242
Hurst, Robert J. E525
Hurtsellers, Christine A1099
Husain, Kamran F. A509
Husain, Kamran F. E251
Husain, M. W8
Huskins, Priya Cherian E412
Huskins, Priya Cherian E350
Hussain, Abbas W598
Hussain, Mahrukh A1068
Hussain, Turab A65
Huston, Benjamin A208
Huston, Danny E81
Huston, John J. A269
Huston, Michael G. E352
Huston, Peter Ernest W246
Hutcheson, E.M. Blake A213
Hutcheson, Jennifer P473
Hutchings, W. Preston W50
Hutchins, Curtis J. W209
Hutchins, Glenn H. A400
Hutchins, Glenn H. A105
Hutchins, Michael T. A450
Hutchinson, Alison E. W662
Hutchinson, Jacob E307
Hutchison, Sue W287
Hutchkin, Christine P90
Huth, Dana A893
Hutjens, Brad V. A741
Hutjens, Brad V. E349

HOOVER'S HANDBOOK OF EMERGING COMPANIES 2023
637

COMBINED HOOVER'S HANDBOOK INDEX OF EXECUTIVES

A = AMERICAN BUSINESS
E = EMERGING COMPANIES
P = PRIVATE COMPANIES
W = WORLD BUSINESSS

Hutman, Hannah W. E181
Hutsell, Michael C. A397
Hutsell, Michael C. E187
Hutsell, Roberta A1015
Hutsell, Roberta P571
Hutson, Denise W. A747
Hutson, Richard M. E280
Hutt, Charles S. E260
Huttenlocher, Daniel P. A50
Huttenlocher, Daniel P. A298
Huttle, Frank A287
Huttle, Frank E115
Hutton, Benjamen M. A378
Hutton, John R. A895
Hutton, William L. A886
Huval, Timothy S. A890
Huval, Timothy S. A541
Huval, Timothy S. E416
Huynh, Toan A435
Huynh, Toan E210
Hwang, Angela A821
Hwang, Angela A1069
Hwang, B.B. W366
Hwang, Cheol-Ho W352
Hwang, Ernest A797
Hwang, Ernest E368
Hwang, Jason E362
Hwang, Julian E154
Hwang, Kyu-Mok W652
Hwang, Po-Tuan W650
Hyakuno, Kentaro W487
Hyakutome, Yoshihiro W570
Hyde, James A. E185
Hyde, Susan C. E530
Hyland, Donna W. A468
Hyland, Donna W. E124
Hyland, M. Elise A371
Hyland, M. Elise A656
Hylander, Kenneth P378
Hylbert, Paul W. E340
Hyle, Charles S. A1008
Hyle, Kathleen W. A185
Hyle, Kathleen W. A73
Hylen, Christopher S. A507
Hylen, Christopher S. E248
Hylton, Tracy W. A250
Hylton, Tracy W. E99
Hyman, David A. A730
Hyman, Edward S. E176
Hyman, Jennifer Y. A620
Hyman, Steven E. E529
Hyodo, Masayuki W566
Hyun, Grace E522
Hyun, Soo Lee W513

I

Iacobucci, Andrew A1083
Iadanza, Thomas A. A1086
Iadanza, Thomas A. E516
Ianieri, Linda H. A1113
Iannaccone, Marco W661

Iannacone, Nicole M. A373
Iannacone, Nicole M. E168
Iannarelli, Rocco P386
Iannelli, Josephine A138
Iannelli, Josephine E55
Iannone, Jamie A356
Iannone, Malvina E34
Iannotti, Thomas J. A90
Ibach, Shelly R. E448
Ibanez, Jaime Tamayo W382
Ibarguen, Anthony A. A558
Ibarra, Inigo Victor de Oriol W295
Ibarra, Maximo W392
Ibe, Michael P. E150
ibnAle, David T. E504
Ibrahim, J. Jay A595
Ibrahim, Maha E137
Ibrahim, Ramy E475
Icahn, Brett C. A549
Icahn, Brett C. A735
Icahn, Carl C. A549
Ichikawa, Akira W565
Ichikawa, Miki W659
Ichikawa, Sachiko W607
Ichikawa, Takeshi W316
Ichikawa, Tatsushi W336
Ichikawa, Totaro W209
Ichiki, Nobuya W185
Ichikura, Noboru W319
Ida, Shuichi W515
Ide, Akiko W604
Ide, Akiko W566
Ideguchi, Yutaka W436
Idehen, Francis O. E174
Idekoba, Hisayuki W490
Idemitsu, Masakazu W297
Idrac, Anne-Marie W165
Idrac, Anne-Marie W613
Ifuku, Masahiro W394
Igarashi, Koji W404
Igarashi, Makoto W1
Iglesias, Abel L. E397
Iglesias, Henry A742
Iglesias, Lisa G. A1079
Iglhaut, Michael W171
Ignatiev, Sergey W521
Igoe, Paul G P204
Ihamuotila, Timo W6
Ihara, Ichiro W155
Ihara, Katsumi W279
Ihara, Keiko W441
Ihara, Michiyo W293
Ihara, Toru W441
Ihlenfeld, Jay V. A215
Ihori, Eishin W281
Ii, John Tavaglinoe P175
Ii, Joseph T Giglia P217
Ii, Masako W403
Ii, Odie Donald P128
II, William Patrick Mulloy E437
III, Andrew J. "Randy" Paine A602
III, Anthony Giordano A768
III, Anthony Giordano E359
Iii, Carlisle Ky C Lewis P500
III, Frampton W. Toole, E433
III, Francis J. Oelerich A693
III, George Raymond Zage W612
III, Harold (Hal) G. Cummings, A950
III, Harold W. Wyatt, E108
III, Harry A. Lawton A924

III, James A. Harrell A950
Iii, John B Jewell P627
Iii, Kenneth W Lott P511
Iii, Louis J Hutchinson P687
III, Paul Desmarais W480
III, Samuel A. Calagione, E65
III., Arthur R. Baker E400
Iijima, Masami W496
Iijima, Masami W585
Iiyama, Toshiyasu W445
Iizuka, Atsushi W319
Ikawa, Takashi W581
Ikdal, Adam W559
Ike, Fumihiko W451
Ike, Fumihiko W494
Ikebe, Kazuhiro W357
Ikeda, Kentaro W535
Ikeda, Koji W278
Ikeda, Naoki W329
Ikeda, Norito W319
Ikeda, Norito W319
Ikegawa, Yoshihiro W400
Ikemoto, Tetsuya W313
Ikeya, Koji W405
Iki, Noriko W425
Ikushima, Takahiko W405
Ilan, Haviv A1010
Illek, Christian P. A992
Illek, Christian P. W199
Illgen, John D. E114
Ilube, Tom W654
Ilyin, Alexander W655
Ilyukhina, Elena A. W256
Im, Pil-Kyu W335
Imaeda, Tetsuro W569
Imagawa, Kuniaki W392
Imai, Eijiro W612
Imai, Kazuo W436
Imai, Tadashi W437
Imai, Yasuyuki W550
Imaki, Toshiyuki W535
Imaoka, Shoichi W515
Imbert, Franck W238
Imbert, Vincent W511
Imbesi, Anthony M. E321
Imhoff, Scott E77
Imokawa, Hisato W321
Imperatore, Deborah Hanson E193
Imsang, Kris W484
In, Byeong Kang W365
Ina, Gregory M. E136
Ina, Koichi W354
Ina, Norihiko W356
Inada, Chieko W534
Inada, Hitoshi W405
Inada, Koji W331
Inagaki, Seiji W83
Inagaki, Seiji W181
Inamasu, Mitsuko W451
Inamochi, Hiromii W410
Inano, Kazutoshi W539
Indaravijaya, Kattiya W334
Indest, John L. E300
Indo, Mami W608
Indralak, Padungdej W540
Infante, Beatriz V. E420
Infantolino, Edward E371
Ingerø, Gyrid Skalleberg W562
Inglis, Mike W114
Ingo, Bleier W229

Ingraham, Scott S. E287
Ingram, Charles C. A688
Ingram, Charles C. E323
Ingram, David B. A829
Ingram, David B. E385
Ingram, Diana J. E419
Ingram, Donald Glynn A1044
Ingram, Elizabeth (Lisa) K. E306
Ingram, Orrin H. A395
Ingram, Orrin H. E185
Ingram, Robert W. A478
Ingram, Tamara A662
Ingram, Tamara W385
Ingulli, Alfred F. E26
Innes, Ross Mc W238
Innes, Tara S. E150
Inoue, Atsuhiko W570
Inoue, Haruo W552
Inoue, Kazuyuki W535
Inoue, Keitaro W223
Inoue, Makoto W462
Inoue, Makoto W460
Inoue, Noriyuki W182
Inoue, Osamu W567
Inoue, Ryuko W173
Inoue, Ryuko W439
Inoue, Satoru W181
Inoue, Yukari W616
Inoue, Yuriko W182
Inscho, Bill A428
Inserra, Lawrence R. A617
Inserra, Lawrence R. E289
Insley, John S. A401
Insuasty, Jorge A825
Insull, Jonathan R. E129
Int, Thomas Jeitschko P356
Intrieri, Vincent J. A513
Inzerillo, Joseph A941
Ioannou, Stavros E. W231
ior, Sister Bernice Coreil D.c. Sen A100
ior, Sister Bernice Coreil D.c. Sen P45
Iordanou, Constantine P. E520
Iordanou, Constantine P. W50
Ioroi, Seiichi W534
Iovine, Jimmy A641
Ippolito, Peter J. A933
Ipsen, Wayne R. E304
Iqbal, Javed W111
Irazoki, Enrique Alcantara-Garcia W423
Irby, Mark R. A860
Ireland, Gordon R. W662
Ireland, Susan Leslie A246
Irie, Shuji W460
Irisawa, Hiroyuki W266
Irish, Stephen J. A372
Irish, Stephen J. E167
Iritani, Atsushi W184
Irvine, Andrew W419
Irvine, Dennis C. E388
Irving, Blake J. E45
Irving, Paul H. A351
Irving, Paul H. E150
Irwin, Bradley C. A237
Irwin, Hale S. E191
Irwin, Scotty A168
Irwin, Scotty P89
Isaac, John E304
Isaac, Tony E304
Isaacs-Lowe, Arlene A377

COMBINED HOOVER'S HANDBOOK INDEX OF EXECUTIVES

A = AMERICAN BUSINESS
E = EMERGING COMPANIES
P = PRIVATE COMPANIES
W = WORLD BUSINESSS

Isaacs-Lowe, Arlene W170
Isaacson, Christopher A. E87
Isaacson, Kenneth S. A400
Isaacson, Mark J. A714
Isaacson, Walter A1062
Isagoda, satoshi W604
Isaka, Ryuichi W527
Isakow, Selwyn E397
Isaza, Sergio Restrepo W210
Isbell, Jeri L. E445
Isbell, Jeri L. E40
Ise, Katsumi W208
Isely, Elizabeth E343
Isely, Heather E343
Isely, Kemper E343
Isely, Zephyr E343
Iseman, Jay C. A527
Isfendiyaroglu, Ari W26
Isgro, Francesca W479
Ishibashi, Shuichi W110
Ishida, Koji W566
Ishida, Mie W42
Ishida, Norihisa W42
Ishida, Satoshi W418
Ishiguro, Akihide W329
Ishiguro, Shigenao W589
Ishiguro, Shigenao W451
Ishihara, Kunio W319
Ishihara, Takako W281
Ishii, Atsuko W334
Ishii, Keita W316
Ishii, Takayuki W603
Ishii, Toru W527
Ishii, Yuji W464
Ishikawa, Hiroshi W330
Ishikawa, Hiroshi W345
Ishikawa, Keitaro W42
Ishikawa, Kensei W81
Ishikawa, Takatoshi W253
Ishimaru, Fumio W515
Ishimizu, Koichi W535
Ishimoto, Hiroshi W65
Ishimura, Kazuhiko W445
Ishimura, Kazuhiko W496
Ishiwata, Akemi W413
Ishiyama, Kazuhiro W604
Ishizuka, Kunio W316
Ishizuka, Shigeki W387
Ishizuki, Mutsumi W387
Ishmael, Cheryl P201
Ishrak, Omar A560
Ishrak, S. Omar A76
Isla, Elena Sanz W382
Isla, Pablo W430
Isobe, Takeshi W253
Isom, Robert D. A55
Isono, Hiroyuki W455
Isozaki, Yoshinori W343
Israel, Ronen W78
Isshiki, Toshihiro W570
Istavridis, Eleni A950
Itakura, Kazumasa W576
Itambo, Eric A262
Itambo, Eric P147

Itani, Futoshi W570
Itani, Imad I. W77
Ito, Hisanori W155
Ito, Hitoshi W330
Ito, Junro W527
Ito, Kenichiro W193
Ito, Kumi W555
Ito, Kunio W527
Ito, Kunio W610
Ito, Masatoshi W425
Ito, Motoshige W539
Ito, Motoshige W209
Ito, Satoko W329
Ito, Shinichiro W409
Ito, Shintaro W25
Ito, Tomonori W44
Ito, Toshiyasu W292
Ito, Yujiro W185
Ito, Yukinori W21
Ito, Yumiko W345
Itoh, Atsuko W209
Itoh, Junichi W293
Itoh, Motoshige W565
Iturrate, Orlando Poblete W73
Itzkowitz, Jay E347
IV, Frank R Palmer A1026
IV, Frank R Palmer P620
IV, James "Jim" Barr E344
Ivanchenko, Anna E181
Ivanova, Nadezhda W521
Ives, Angela R. A804
Ives, Dune E. A123
Ives, Jeffrey L. E80
Ives, Louisa M. A430
Ivey, Craig S. A54
Ivie, Stanley R. A800
Iwahashi, Toshiro W82
Iwai, Mutsuo W589
Iwai, Mutsuo W321
Iwamoto, Hideyuki W616
Iwamoto, Hiroshi W392
Iwamoto, Tamotsu W535
Iwamoto, Toshio W209
Iwasa, Hiromichi W409
Iwasaki, Hirohiko W436
Iwasaki, Masato W585
Iwasaki, Takashi W253
Iwata, Keiichi W565
Iwata, Kimie W566
Iwata, Kimie W494
Iwatani, Toshiaki W576
Iwatsubo, Hiroshi W417
Iwayama, Toru W81
Iyengar, Vijay K. E267
Iyer, Balakrishnan S. E392
Izakson, Irit W78
Izawa, Yoshiyuki W527
Izumisawa, Seiji W403
Izumiya, Naoki W453
Izumiya, Naoki W490
Izurieta, Laura H. A984
Izurieta, Laura H. E476
Izzo, Ralph A132

J

Jaarsveld, Johan van W101
Jabal, Kimberly A. A405

Jabbar, Masood A. E523
Jabes, Aliza W637
Jabre, Wissam G. A1122
Jacinto, Jesus A. W99
Jacinto, Virgilio S. W514
Jackert, Timothy W. A393
Jacklin, Darren Lee E180
Jackman, Worthing F. A868
Jackow, Francois W357
Jacks, Tyler A76
Jacks, Tyler A1027
Jackson, Benjamin R. A561
Jackson, Christina A389
Jackson, Christina P219
Jackson, Claire P565
Jackson, Daniel W. E467
Jackson, Darrell E19
Jackson, Darryl R. A835
Jackson, David W245
Jackson, Deborah C. A352
Jackson, Denise L. A1035
Jackson, Donald G. A306
Jackson, Edie E512
Jackson, Harold L. E489
Jackson, J Brooks P612
Jackson, J. David A. W480
Jackson, Jamere A111
Jackson, Jamere A635
Jackson, Jamere E254
Jackson, Janet E. E274
Jackson, Jeanne P. A323
Jackson, Jeffrey A. E421
Jackson, Jeffrey T. E381
Jackson, Jimmy L P168
Jackson, Keith J. A190
Jackson, Keith J. E73
Jackson, Larry P345
Jackson, Lawrence Johnell A931
Jackson, Lawrence V. A103
Jackson, Martin F. A925
Jackson, Michael J. A399
Jackson, Peter M. A184
Jackson, Ramey Pierce E283
Jackson, Reginald T. A371
Jackson, Richard A. A767
Jackson, Rick C. A199
Jackson, Robert M. E134
Jackson, Rosa P P514
Jackson, Rosa P P211
Jackson, Rudy P664
Jackson, Sally W258
Jackson, Sharon L. E227
Jackson, Shirley Ann A612
Jackson, Thomas G. A918
Jackson, Thomas M. E372
Jacob, Leonard S. E32
Jacob, Renato Lulia W315
Jacob, Sony A960
Jacob, Sony P520
Jacobs, Ashley P678
Jacobs, Bradley S. A493
Jacobs, Bradley S. A1143
Jacobs, Charles R W311
Jacobs, David A. A337
Jacobs, Elizabeth S. A865
Jacobs, Elizabeth S. E403
Jacobs, James K P680
Jacobs, Julie A538
Jacobs, Kathleen E A734
Jacobs, Kathleen E P389

Jacobs, Kerry J. A39
Jacobs, Kevin J. A518
Jacobs, Lisa R. A891
Jacobs, Michael G. E532
Jacobs, Patricia A112
Jacobs, Paul E. E145
Jacobs, Terry S. A64
Jacobs, Thomas W. E306
Jacobs, William I. E239
Jacobs, William R. A749
Jacobsen, J. Chris E260
Jacobsen, Jon Arnt W562
Jacobsen, Kevin B. A254
Jacobsen, Lennart W446
Jacobsen, Rene A10
Jacobsen, Svein S. W446
Jacobson, Craig A. A224
Jacobson, Craig A. A385
Jacobson, Dan A37
Jacobson, Dan E14
Jacobson, Jonathon S. A811
Jacobson, Jonathon S. E377
Jacobson, Kenneth A. (Ken) A118
Jacobson, Paul A. A466
Jacobson, Richard P. E199
Jacobson, Shalene A. A493
Jacobson, Shalene A. E243
Jacobstein, David M. E67
Jacoby, Francis X. E461
Jacoby, Rebecca J. A911
Jacovatos, James P. A439
Jacquemin, Tanja W602
Jacubasch, Mario W198
Jaderberg, Tina W277
Jafarieh, Nicolas A944
Jafarieh, Nicolas E450
Jafarnia, Kamal E63
Jaffe, Jonathan M. A629
Jaffe, Jonathan M. A785
Jaffe, Seth R. A631
Jafry, Syed A. A1150
Jagdfeld, Aaron P. E228
Jagdishan, Sashidhar W271
Jager, Martine W85
Jaggers, Jeffrey W. A190
Jaggers, Jeffrey W. E73
Jaggers, Travis L. A214
Jahn, Greg A381
Jahn, Timothy P62
Jahnke, David L. A426
Jahnke, David L. E430
Jahnke, David L. E202
Jain, Ajit B. A151
Jain, Dipak C. A320
Jain, Dipak C. W491
Jain, Vivek E262
Jaindl, Mark W. E23
Jaindl, Zachary J. E24
Jakob, Ulrike W640
Jakobs, Roy W351
Jakobsen, Niels Erik W330
Jakoet, Fatima W558
Jakosky, Donn A797
Jakosky, Donn P419
Jakosky, Donn B. A797
Jakosky, Donn B. E368
Jakosuo-Jansson, Hannele W427
Jalkh, Jocelyne A. W77
Jallal, Bahija A85
Jamal, Arshil W262

COMBINED HOOVER'S HANDBOOK INDEX OF EXECUTIVES

A = AMERICAN BUSINESS
E = EMERGING COMPANIES
P = PRIVATE COMPANIES
W = WORLD BUSINESSS

James, Brooke W. A815
James, Catherine C. A605
James, Constance P. E430
James, Deborah Lee A1012
James, Dennis A134
James, Dennis E54
James, Donald M. A952
James, Donald R. E426
James, Donna A. A1094
James, Dwight E210
James, Erika H. A713
James, Hamilton E. A300
James, Juanita T. A99
James, Letitia A250
James, Letitia P135
James, Renee Jo A786
James, Renee Jo A246
James, Renee Jo W638
James, Robert E. A528
James, Robert E. E258
James, Thomas A. A876
James, Todd J. E61
James, Wilbert W. E40
Jamet, Marc-Antoine W373
Jamieson, Lisa H. E213
Jamieson, Roberta L. W507
Jamieson, VeraLinn E141
Jamil, Dhiaa M. A348
Jamil, Dhiaa M. A347
Jamison, Cynthia T. A157
Jamison, Cynthia T. A316
Jamison, Cynthia T. A770
Jammaron, Glen E19
Jammet, Mary Chris A696
Jamula, Robert M. E96
Jan, Rizwan P585
Jandzio, Bronislao W132
Janes, Maria N. A1108
Jang, Dong-ki W537
Jang, Simon W583
Jang, Won-Ki W513
Janiak, Claude W91
Janis, Ronald H. A1086
Janis, Ronald H. E516
Janjariyakun, Vichai W117
Janki, Daniel C. A323
Jannetti, Anthony J. E371
Janney, Robert S. E62
Janorschke, Bradley P. E340
Janosco, Michael J. E537
Janow, Merit E. A670
Janow, Merit E. W45
Jansen, Daniela W602
Jansen, Philip W114
Janson, Deborah K. A68
Janson, Julia S. A347
Janson, Julia S. A348
Janson, Susan N. A642
Janson, Susan N. E304
Janssen, Brigid W80
Janssen, Friedrich W234
Jansseune, Thomas W623
Jansson, Mats W188
Janthanakul, Voravit W136

Jany, Patrick W1
Janzaruk, Matthew W. A850
Jaramillo, Claudia A580
Jaramillo, Mauricio Galvis W210
Jared, David P147
Jaros, Carey F. E242
Jarratt, R. Devereux E372
Jarrett, Valerie B. A1102
Jarupanich, Prasert W117
Jarvis, Kasey A1059
Jarwaarde, Ewout van W109
Jasinski, Lawrence J. E297
Jaska, James M. E70
Jaskolka, Norman W122
Jasper, James Chris A989
Jaspon, Katherine (Kate) D. A485
Jassy, Andrew R. A50
Jastrzebski, Ted J. A1054
Javaid, Mohammad Arshed E113
Javitz, Joseph T. A287
Javitz, Joseph T. E115
Jawa, Kanwal Jeet W183
Jay, Bruce E517
Jay, Colleen E. E119
Jay, Sylvia W127
Jayant, Ayuth W603
Jayanthi, Aruna W168
Jayanthi, Aruna W123
jean, Emilio Azcarraga W266
Jeanfreau, Mark W. A889
Jeanfreau, Mark W. E414
Jearavisitkul, Pittaya W117
Jeavons, Mick W509
Jee, Sung-Ha W513
Jeffe, Robert A. A101
Jefferies, Suzanne W116
Jeffery, Joseph A. E525
Jeffery, Nick A453
Jeffery, Reuben W89
Jefford, Stephen W471
Jeffrey, William A. W590
Jeffries, Ross E. A128
Jego-Laveissiere, Mari-Noelle W631
Jego-Laveissiere, Mari-Noelle W225
Jehi, Lara A1015
Jehi, Lara P574
Jejdling, Fredrik W228
Jejurikar, Shailesh G. A850
Jejurikar, Shailesh G. A791
Jelenko, Jane H. A211
Jelenko, Jane H. E84
Jelinek, W. Craig A300
Jelito, Ernest W273
Jellison, Douglas J. A759
Jemison, Mae C. A604
Jemley, Charles L. E217
Jemmett-Page, Shonaid W64
Jenah, Susan Wolburgh W358
Jenisch, Jan W283
Jenkins, Charles H. A860
Jenkins, David H. E240
Jenkins, Decosta E. A829
Jenkins, Decosta E. E385
Jenkins, Frank E. E526
Jenkins, James M. E291
Jenkins, Jo Ann A465
Jenkins, Jo Ann C. A118
Jenkins, John Huw Gwili W69
Jenkins, John S. W590
Jenkins, Julie E350

Jenkins, Louis P. E113
Jenkins, Margaret L. A608
Jenkins, Mark W. A208
Jenkins, Michael H. E365
Jenkins, Norman K. A110
Jenkins, Norman K. E146
Jenkins, R. Scott E274
Jenkins, Robert W. W442
Jenkins, W. Paul W80
Jenkins, William D. E228
Jenkins, William W. E274
Jenks, Maria P218
Jennapar, Worapol W540
Jenne, Myra NanDora A200
Jenne, Myra NanDora E79
Jennes, Stefan W162
Jennings, Craig E117
Jennings, John Webb A556
Jennings, John Webb E270
Jennings, Kevin D. A619
Jennings, Scott C. A981
Jennings, Scott C. E469
Jennings, Toni E68
Jennings, William N. A282
Jenny, Christopher T. A213
Jensen-Marren, Joelyn R. A397
Jensen, Barry H. A554
Jensen, Barry H. E268
Jensen, Claus Torp A680
Jensen, Claus Torp P343
Jensen, Corey E149
Jensen, Davin E517
Jensen, Derrick A. A868
Jensen, Henning G. W348
Jensen, Karen M. A415
Jensen, Karen M. E194
Jensen, Keith E216
Jensen, Kirk D. A426
Jensen, Kirk D. E202
Jeong, James Ho-Young W365
Jeong, Kouwhan W335
Jeong, Mun-Cheol W335
Jeong, Tak W478
Jepsen, Edward G. A80
Jepsen, Mary Lou A622
Jerabek, Vladimir W347
Jerbich, Michael E50
Jerchel, Kerstin W162
Jerden, Evelyn C. E301
Jerding, Pat A1075
Jernberg, Melker W641
Jesselson, Michael G. A1143
Jessen, Polly B. A800
Jessup, Alan A134
Jessup, Alan E54
Jeter, Daniel B. A72
Jeter, Daniel B. E29
Jetha, Yasmin W425
Jetha, Yasmin W423
jetley, Vivek E179
Jew, Ken A905
Jewell, Sally A300
Jewett, Ellen A583
Jewett, Ellen A171
Jewett, Joshua R. A337
Jewett, S. Leslie E76
Jewkes, Roger S. A406
Jeworrek, Torsten W415
Jews, William L. A189
Jezard, Gordon A500

Jezard, Gordon E246
Jha, Rakesh W296
Jha, Sanjay K. E91
Jhang, Bosyong W168
Jhang, Fucyuan W169
Jhang, Jhaosian W168
Jhang, Mingjhih W168
Jhang, Ying W168
Jhang, Yongcing W168
Jhang, Yongnan W169
Jhangiani, Nik W161
Jheng, Jhihcyuan W168
Jhou, Tingjyun W168
Jhou, Zongkai W284
Ji, Shao W307
Ji, Zhengrong W145
Ji, Zhihong W138
Jia, Guosheng W272
Jia, Huiping W147
Jia, Jinzhong W149
Jia, Yimin W656
Jia, Yuzeng W142
Jian, Qin W143
Jiang, Aihua W152
Jiang, Baoxin W512
Jiang, Changliang W355
Jiang, Deyang W292
Jiang, Dongyue W292
Jiang, Guizhi W655
Jiang, Hairong W662
Jiang, Hongyuan W256
Jiang, Jiali W575
Jiang, Jianjun W662
Jiang, Kaixi W663
Jiang, Kui W644
Jiang, Lifu W466
Jiang, Peijin W608
Jiang, Sihai W327
Jiang, Tao W603
Jiang, Wenbo W326
Jiang, Xiaoming W466
Jiang, Xin W104
Jiang, Xuping W145
Jiang, Yan W644
Jiang, Yanbo W117
Jiang, Zhenying W145
Jiao, Fangzheng W466
Jiao, Shijing W136
Jiao, Shuge W648
Jibson, Ronald W. A340
Jimenez, Alejandro Cantu W35
Jimenez, Frank R. A458
Jimenez, Frank R. A546
Jimenez, Jorge Desormeaux W41
Jimenez, Joseph A466
Jimenez, Joseph A850
Jimenez, Luis E. E127
Jimenez, Menardo R. W514
Jimenez, Pedro J. Lopez W280
Jimenez, Pedro Lopez W11
Jimenez, Terry E501
Jin, Danwen W275
Jin, Hyun-duk W537
Jin, Jeoung A439
Jin, Jun E362
Jin, Keyu W167
Jin, Li W472
Jin, Lishan W528
Jin, Ok-dong W537
Jin, Panshi W138

COMBINED HOOVER'S HANDBOOK INDEX OF EXECUTIVES

A = AMERICAN BUSINESS
E = EMERGING COMPANIES
P = PRIVATE COMPANIES
W = WORLD BUSINESSS

Jin, Qingbin W660
Jin, Shaoliang W18
Jin, Song W148
Jin, Yongchuan W136
Jing, Hong W572
Jinks, Maria K. E193
Jiraadisawong, Thupthep W117
Jirapongphan, Siri W77
Jo, Kisan A219
Joachimczyk, Paul E27
Jobim, Nelson Azevedo W69
Jobin, Luc W111
Jobson, Charles E. E235
Jochens, Birgit W273
Jochims, Jeffrey T. A794
Jocson, Ramon L. W85
Joerres, Jeffrey A. A399
Joerres, Jeffrey A. A288
Joffrion, Gordon H. E279
Jofs, Kurt W228
Jofs, Kurt W641
Johanns, Michael O. A320
Johanns, Michael O. A298
Johannson, Ernie W82
Johansen, Judith A. E430
Johansson-Hedberg, Birgitta W247
Johansson, Camilla W641
Johansson, Hasse W4
Johansson, Inge W548
Johansson, Leif W57
John, Dacey Robert W145
John, Frank A. St. A643
John, Miriam E. A625
John, Steve W289
JohnBull, Kathryn M. E143
Johns, John D. A885
Johns, John D. A468
Johns, John D. A952
Johns, Raymond E. E11
Johnsen, John R. A279
Johnsen, Richard A1062
Johnson-Leipold, Helen P. E284
Johnson, Alan W298
Johnson, Allison A702
Johnson, Allison A958
Johnson, Allison E325
Johnson, Allison E456
Johnson, Amal M. A573
Johnson, Amy K. A398
Johnson, Andrew A. A28
Johnson, Arthur E. A171
Johnson, B. Kristine E43
Johnson, Bart E. A418
Johnson, Bart E. E195
Johnson, Belinda J. A807
Johnson, Betty R. E40
Johnson, Brenda L. A741
Johnson, Brenda L. E349
Johnson, Carl A493
Johnson, Carl E243
Johnson, Carol C A969
Johnson, Carol C P535
Johnson, Carrie E215
Johnson, Claire Hughes E22

Johnson, Clinton Bradley E101
Johnson, Craig M. E293
Johnson, Daniel W80
Johnson, Daniel L. A394
Johnson, David L. E315
Johnson, David P. E40
Johnson, David S. A455
Johnson, David T. E26
Johnson, David W. E284
Johnson, Denise C. A210
Johnson, Denise C. A715
Johnson, Dennis L. A426
Johnson, Dennis L. E202
Johnson, Dennis W. A679
Johnson, Devin A851
Johnson, Edwin D. E82
Johnson, Elizabeth S. A248
Johnson, Elizabeth S. A573
Johnson, Ellen Tobi A570
Johnson, Enda W81
Johnson, Eric A. A845
Johnson, Eric A. E395
Johnson, Eric G. A638
Johnson, Esther L. A697
Johnson, Frank P129
Johnson, Gary P42
Johnson, Gerald A210
Johnson, Gordon L. A876
Johnson, Gregory A. A401
Johnson, Gregory D. A765
Johnson, Gregory E. A448
Johnson, Gregory G. A189
Johnson, Gregory N. A867
Johnson, Helen K. A558
Johnson, J. Thomas E195
Johnson, Jack C. E184
Johnson, James C. A54
Johnson, James C. A497
Johnson, James C. E161
Johnson, James J. A242
Johnson, James S. A175
Johnson, James S. E66
Johnson, James W. A789
Johnson, Janilee A1080
Johnson, Janilee P667
Johnson, Jason K. A282
Johnson, Jay L. A735
Johnson, Jeffrey M. A199
Johnson, Jeh C. A643
Johnson, Jeh C. A691
Johnson, Jeh C. A1073
Johnson, Jennifer A. A935
Johnson, Jennifer A. A378
Johnson, Jennifer A. E439
Johnson, Jennifer Amy A567
Johnson, Jennifer M. A448
Johnson, Jodie E455
Johnson, Johnny David A67
Johnson, Joia M. A477
Johnson, Joia M. A885
Johnson, Jonathan E. A947
Johnson, Jonathan E. E368
Johnson, Julia L. A432
Johnson, Julia L. A668
Johnson, Julie S. E305
Johnson, Karlton A697
Johnson, Kathleen E. A649
Johnson, Kathleen E. A1069
Johnson, Kathleen E. A872
Johnson, Kathryn O. E367

Johnson, Kenton E236
Johnson, Kevin R. A481
Johnson, Kimberly A. A531
Johnson, Kimmerly D. E185
Johnson, Kristin M. A587
Johnson, Kristina M. A244
Johnson, Kurt G. A718
Johnson, Kurt G. E335
Johnson, Lacy M. A599
Johnson, Lacy M. E242
Johnson, Laura L. A196
Johnson, Laura L. E79
Johnson, M. Carl E344
Johnson, Margaret L. A160
Johnson, Margy A428
Johnson, Marianne Boyd A1120
Johnson, Marianne Boyd E535
Johnson, Mercedes E485
Johnson, Michael A399
Johnson, Michael P177
Johnson, Michael A. E169
Johnson, Michelle E370
Johnson, Michelle Lynn A188
Johnson, Michelle Lynn E71
Johnson, Mitchell A. A396
Johnson, Mitchell A. E186
Johnson, Netha N. A1139
Johnson, Nicholas M. E316
Johnson, Patricia A. A1033
Johnson, Paul David E538
Johnson, Paula A. A585
Johnson, Richard A. A443
Johnson, Richard Allen E273
Johnson, Richard Scott A419
Johnson, Rick W31
Johnson, Robbie P63
Johnson, Robert D. A904
Johnson, Robert E. E191
Johnson, Robert L. A332
Johnson, Rodney D P191
Johnson, Roger A600
Johnson, Ronald L. A364
Johnson, Rupert H. A448
Johnson, Samuel J. A10
Johnson, Sandra K. E413
Johnson, Sean O. A1121
Johnson, Shannon A. A1056
Johnson, Shannon A. E505
Johnson, Shaun M. A256
Johnson, Shaun M. A294
Johnson, Shelley P497
Johnson, Sidney E218
Johnson, Simon H R A391
Johnson, Starlette B. E35
Johnson, Stephen C. E434
Johnson, Stephen E. A125
Johnson, Stephen E. E52
Johnson, Stephen L. A56
Johnson, Steven P. A478
Johnson, Stuart R. A889
Johnson, Stuart R. E414
Johnson, Susan A. A914
Johnson, Susan Somersille A292
Johnson, Susan Somersille E341
Johnson, Suzanne M. Nora A571
Johnson, Suzanne M. Nora A821
Johnson, Thomas H. W161
Johnson, Thomas S. A915
Johnson, Timothy E409
Johnson, Timothy (Tim) A. A1094

Johnson, Timothy D. A184
Johnson, Tracy P224
Johnson, Vernon J. A188
Johnson, Vernon J. E69
Johnson, Wilbur E. A401
Johnson, William L. A319
Johnson, William P. W249
Johnson, William R. A1069
Johnson, Willis J. E120
Johnsrud, David Alan A235
Johnston, Chris E307
Johnston, Cristian Eyzaguirre W132
Johnston, David L. W235
Johnston, Hugh F. A701
Johnston, Hugh F. A817
Johnston, Hugh F. A505
Johnston, Lori A. A76
Johnston, Lori A. E184
Johnston, Michael F. A342
Johnston, Richard M. E42
Johnston, Steve W574
Johnston, Steven J. A240
Johnstone, Rudolph G. E454
Johnstone, William O. A125
Johnstone, William O. E52
Johrendt, Michael J. E293
Johri, Akhil A164
Johri, Akhil A201
Johri, Rajive A286
Joiner, Cindy Jeannette A788
Joiner, Cindy Jeannette E366
Jojo, Linda P. A383
Jojo, Linda P. A1062
Jokinen, Tracy C. E13
Joko, Keiji W316
Joliet, Mariel A. E38
Jolley, Burke P292
Jolly, Bruce A. W299
Jolly, Linda E. A298
Joly-Pottuz, Dominique Muller W635
Joly, Hubert A585
Jonas, Howard S. E547
Jonas, Howard S. E229
Jonas, M. H. W414
Jonas, Michael C. E547
Jonas, Peri E517
Jones, AJ A964
Jones, Allen C. A958
Jones, Allen C. E456
Jones, Allen R. A845
Jones, Allen R. E395
Jones, Andrew A283
Jones, Anne M. A679
Jones, Brian W. E467
Jones, Christopher Ian Montague A147
Jones, Christopher T. A747
Jones, Clayton M. A716
Jones, Clayton M. A320
Jones, Daniel E529
Jones, Daniel L. A953
Jones, Daniel L. E160
Jones, Daniel L. E455
Jones, Darrell R. W122
Jones, David A. A541
Jones, Debra A. E452
Jones, Doug E378
Jones, Douglas A811
Jones, Douglas E377
Jones, Eli A421
Jones, Eli E198

COMBINED HOOVER'S HANDBOOK INDEX OF EXECUTIVES

A = AMERICAN BUSINESS
E = EMERGING COMPANIES
P = PRIVATE COMPANIES
W = WORLD BUSINESSS

Jones, Elizabeth E364
Jones, Ellis Allen A95
Jones, Gregory M. A380
Jones, Hal Stanley A650
Jones, Hannah A1019
Jones, Hannah P587
Jones, Harvey C. A761
Jones, J. Thomas A249
Jones, J. Thomas E99
Jones, James G. E350
Jones, Jeanne M. A383
Jones, Jeff C. A797
Jones, Jeff C. E368
Jones, Jeffrey D. A415
Jones, Jeffrey D. E107
Jones, Jeffrey D. E194
Jones, Jeffrey J. A17
Jones, John Michael W169
Jones, John P. A108
Jones, Jon M. A398
Jones, Keith A. E546
Jones, Keith B. E397
Jones, Kenneth E. A326
Jones, Kim Harris A1071
Jones, Kristi A970
Jones, Kristi P536
Jones, Larry W. A282
Jones, Lisa Harris E270
Jones, Marc A16
Jones, Mark E. E235
Jones, Mary K.W. A320
Jones, Mautra Staley A125
Jones, Mautra Staley E52
Jones, Melody L. E528
Jones, Michael A175
Jones, Michael P121
Jones, Michael A. A788
Jones, Michael A. E364
Jones, Michael Q. E357
Jones, Mickey L. E99
Jones, Myrtle L. A494
Jones, Nicole S. A239
Jones, Randall T. A860
Jones, Ray E. E195
Jones, Regina Bynote A121
Jones, Rene F. A651
Jones, Richard A. A399
Jones, Robertson C. A509
Jones, Robertson C. E251
Jones, Robyn E235
Jones, Ross M. E5
Jones, Sharon A596
Jones, Sharon E286
Jones, Shaunna D. A1144
Jones, Stephen P64
Jones, Steven M. E128
Jones, Tammy K. A301
Jones, Thomas A958
Jones, Thomas E456
Jones, Thomas H. A752
Jones, Thomas W. A581
Jones, Todd Matthew W487
Jones, Tracy George A235
Jones, Walter E101

Jones, Wendy Elizabeth A856
Jones, William D. A158
Jones, William H. A266
Jones, Wilson R. A1028
Jones, Winford E223
Jonsson, Karin W399
Jonsson, Patrik A635
Joo, In-Ki W366
Joo, Jong-Nam W366
Joong, Chi-Wei W128
Joos, Astrid Simonsen W594
Joosen, Andrea Gisle W179
Joost, Gesche W517
Jope, Alan W626
Jorda, Daniel Lopez W423
Jordan, Alister W162
Jordan, Clark L. A354
Jordan, D. Bryan A424
Jordan, D. Bryan A111
Jordan, D. Bryan A200
Jordan, Donald Shawn E195
Jordan, Gregory B. A834
Jordan, Jeffrey D. E386
Jordan, John P. E383
Jordan, Lori A435
Jordan, Lori E210
Jordan, Mark W116
Jordan, Matthew P. E423
Jordan, Phil W318
Jordan, Philip A188
Jordan, Philip E69
Jordan, Rhett D. A945
Jordan, Rhett D. E451
Jordan, Rhonda L. A557
Jordan, Robert Chris E279
Jordan, Robert E. A956
Jordan, Tyrone Michael A790
Jordan, William P. A1132
Jordan, William P. E539
Jorg., Ingrid W639
Jorge, Daniela A718
Jorge, Daniela E335
Jorgenrud, Karl J. A934
Jorgensen, Blake J. A503
Jorgensen, Blake J. A363
Jorgensen, Lars Fruergaard W450
Jorgensen, Nate A166
Jorgensen, Steven C. A547
Jorgensen, Torsten Hagen W446
Jors, Bill E102
Jors, Mike E102
Josefowicz, Gregory W216
Joseph, Anthony A. A32
Joseph, Celia M. E511
Joseph, Fred J. A722
Joseph, Fred J. E339
Joseph, George A685
Joseph, Gregory G. A64
Joseph, Isaac H. A755
Joseph, Molly E. E534
Joseph, Pamela A. E493
Joseph, Paul C. E12
Joseph, Victor George A685
Joseph, Wetteny A1153
Joseph, Wetteny E83
Josephs, Glenn M. E193
Josephs, Robin J. A693
Josephs, Robin J. E426
Joseu, Alicia Koplowitz Romero de W219

Joshi, Mohit W64
Joshi, Mohit W304
Joshi, Rahul M. W382
Joslyn, Scott P318
Jotikasthira, Charamporn W77
Joubert, Paul G. E34
Joullian, E. Carey A167
Joullian, E. Carey E64
Joulwan, George A. E157
Joung, Chansoo A86
Journell, Jacqueline R. E206
Jouvenal, Joe P336
Joy, Dan A. E136
Joyce, David Leon A164
Joyce, George P. E372
Joyce, Glenn E. E514
Joyce, Meghan V. E65
Joyce, Patrick M. A596
Joyce, Patrick M. E286
Joyce, Rene R. A995
Joyce, Robert Joseph A599
Joyce, Stephen P. E410
Joyce, Thomas (Tom) Patrick A904
Joyce, William J. E190
Joyner, Pamela J. A431
Joyner, Pamela J. E205
Jozuka, Yumiko W535
Jr, John M Starcher A168
Jr, John M Starcher P89
Jr, John M Starcher P345
Jr, Lawrence C Franklin A971
Jr, Lawrence C Franklin P537
Jr, Leonard A Cannatelli A1026
Jr, Leonard A Cannatelli P620
Jr, Paul G Haaga A52
Jr, Paul G Haaga P31
Jr, Richard L Vogel A1026
Jr, Richard L Vogel P620
Jr, Roy Hawkins A1015
Jr, Roy Hawkins P571
Jr., Harry B. Harris A613
Jr., Joseph A. Kraft W557
Jr., Joseph P. Schmelzeis W193
Ju, Jennifer P548
Ju, Tina A588
Juarez, Jesus Santiago Martin W73
Jubran, Raja J. A395
Jubran, Raja J. E185
Juchelka, Jan W347
Jud, Waldemar W453
Judd, Jason Nathaniel A803
Judd, Jason Nathaniel E371
Jude, Justin L. A643
Juden, Alexander W523
Judge, Ann Powell A178
Judge, Julie P335
Judlowe, Michael E9
Judy, Vickie D. E23
Jueckstock, Rainer A1004
Jueger, Gerd W234
Juel, Carol A985
Juerss, Detlef W631
Juhnke, Klaus Juergen W270
Jukes, David C. A1075
Jukes, David C. W191
Jula, Margaret B. A410
Julian, Jerome E. A399
Julian, Kenneth D. A1028
Juliber, Lois D. A710
Juliber, Lois D. A298

Julius, Christian W602
Jullienne, J. Paul A1079
Juma, Hassan Ali W47
Jun, Sarah E375
Junck, Mary E. E295
Juneja, Girish A342
Jung, Alexandra A. A763
Jung, Andrea A89
Jung, Andrea A1112
Jung, Andrea W626
Jung, Do-Hyun W366
Jung, Helga W199
Jung, Keun Soo W537
Jung, Soo Hun S. E362
Jung, Suk Koh W513
Jung, Yeonin W205
Juniac, Alexandre de W22
Junior, Alan R Crain P216
Junior, Alfred W Young P198
Junior, Alphonso Jefferson P167
Junior, Jose Geraldo Franco Ortiz W315
Junior, Kenneth Bennett P516
Junior, Norman J Beauchamp P356
Junior, Robert Campbell P212
Junior, Robert E Swaney A717
Junior, Robert F Hull P519
Junior, Robert Hale P245
Junior, Samuel Monteiro dos Santos W69
Junior, William G Gisel P462
Junior, William J Gilbane P239
Junior, Woodrow Myers P84
Junius, Daniel M. E263
Junker, Jennifer A134
Junker, Jennifer E54
Junkins, Lowell L. A395
Junkins, Lowell L. E186
Junyent, Miquel Roca W11
Juran, David B. A175
Juran, David B. E66
Juras, Kristen A969
Juras, Kristen P535
Jurecka, Christoph W415
Jurgensen, William G. A65
Jurjevich, Karen L. W235
Jurvetson, Stephen T. A1007
Jussup, W. John W80
Juster, Andrew J. A681
Juster, Andrew J. E318
Juster, Kristine L. E494
Justice, Ronald L. E189
Juti, Blanca W358

K

K., Prof.Dr. Ferdinand W61
Kaback, Neil J. A393
Kaback, Neil J. E184
Kabat, Kevin T. A1079
Kabbash, Charles A. A845
Kabbash, Charles A. E395
Kacenga, Shannon A168
Kacenga, Shannon P89
Kaczmarek, Walter T. A509
Kaczmarek, Walter T. E251
Kaczynski, Thomas A717
Kadise, Nadia W266

A = AMERICAN BUSINESS
E = EMERGING COMPANIES
P = PRIVATE COMPANIES
W = WORLD BUSINESSS

Kado, Maki W297
Kadre, Manuel A892
Kadre, Manuel A526
Kadri, Ilham W358
Kadri, Ilham W554
Kaeding, Nathaniel J. A704
Kaeding, Nathaniel J. E328
Kaelin, William G. A635
Kaeser, Joe W543
Kaeser, Josef W369
Kaewrathtanapattama, Taweesak W117
Kafer, Ann A492
Kafer, Ann P248
Kaga, Atsuko W331
Kaga, Kunihiko W402
Kagami, Mitsuko W392
Kagata, Takeshi W582
Kagawa, Ryohei W293
Kaguchi, Hitoshi W403
Kahan, James S. A641
Kahan, Rony W490
Kahkonen, Matti W427
Kahla, Vuyo Dominic W518
Kahn, Barbara E. E138
Kahn, Brian R. E219
Kahn, Todd A993
Kahramanzade, Ozgur W620
Kahrs, Benjamin A37
Kaiami, Makoto W319
Kaihara, Noriya W285
Kail, Tiffany A. E189
Kain, Gary D. A28
Kaindl, Stefan W415
Kainersdorfer, Franz W639
Kainuma, Tsutomu W417
Kaiser, David D. A98
Kaiser, David D. E36
Kaiser, George B. A167
Kaiser, George B. E64
Kaiser, Keri A. A948
Kaiwa, Makoto W319
Kaji, Katsuhiko W539
Kajita, Naoki W453
Kakar, Rajeev K. L. W232
Kakei, Masaki W454
Kakigi, Koji W325
Kakinoki, Masumi W387
Kakiuchi, Eiji W356
Kakiuchi, Takehiko W402
Kakiuchi, Takehiko W405
Kakizaki, Tamaki W26
Kakizaki, Tamaki W405
Kakoullis, Panos W504
Kaku, Masatoshi W455
Kakuchi, Yuji W281
Kalamaras, Paul A575
Kalamarides, Jamie A856
Kalanda, Larisa Vyacheslavovna W617
Kalani, Neil A788
Kalani, Neil E365
Kalathur, Rajesh A320
Kalaus, Christy L. A302
Kalborg, Ted E144
Kaleida, Alex R. E539

Kaleta, Paul J. A432
Kaliban, Timothy E240
Kalif, Eli W598
Kalla, Christine K. A1037
Kallembach, Larry J. A503
Kallenius, Ola W395
Kallevik, Eivind W448
Kalmanson, Steven R. A902
Kalmbach, Thomas P. A478
Kalmin, Steven W260
Kalnitsky, Alexander W583
Kaloski, Donald M. E526
Kalscheur, Denis P. A124
Kalsu, James Barton E451
Kaltenbach, Patrick K. E325
Kam, Wendy Mei Ha W663
Kama, Kazuaki W568
Kamada, Kazuhiko W455
Kamanga, Deland W82
Kamaras, Miklos W412
Kamark, Robin W562
Kambayashi, Hyo W417
Kambe, Shiro W557
Kambeitz, Stephen J. A803
Kambeitz, Stephen J. E371
Kamenetzky, David W355
Kamensky, Allan E. A988
Kamensky, Allan E. E478
Kamerick, Eileen A. A101
Kamezawa, Hironori A713
Kamezawa, Hironori W407
Kamfar, R. Ramin E62
Kamieth, Markus W93
Kamigama, Takehiro W658
Kamigama, Takehiro W550
Kamijo, Tsutomu W604
Kamin, John A854
Kamin, Peter H. E76
Kamin, Peter H. E409
Kaminaga, Susumu W610
Kaminski, Jeff J. A594
Kaminski, Jerry D. E260
Kaminski, Mark V. A888
Kaminski, Robert B. A681
Kaminski, Robert B. E317
Kaminsky, Andrew F. E219
Kamke, Trent G. E297
Kamo, Masaharu W464
Kampf, Serge W123
Kampfer, Thomas D. E107
Kampling, Patricia L. A1139
Kamsickas, James K. A313
Kamsky, Virginia A. A313
Kan, Alice Lai Kuen W534
Kan, Anna A308
Kan, Anna E134
Kanaan, Mona Aboelnaga A1113
Kanagawa, Chihiro W536
Kanai, Takayuki W267
Kanamaru, Muneo W570
Kanamoto, Hideaki W293
Kanamoto, Yasushi W534
Kanan, A. W8
Kanary, Maryann P67
Kanasugi, Yasuzo W413
Kanazawa, Yugo W370
Kanchanachitra, Nontigorn W352
Kanchanadul, Veeravat W137
Kanchinadham, Parvatheesam W588
Kanda, Masaaki W454

Kandarian, Steven A. A388
Kandikonda, Ravi A1149
Kandpur, Ashish A292
Kane-williams, Edna P2
Kane, Erin N. A224
Kane, Jacqueline P. A274
Kane, John M. A723
Kane, Julie M. E440
Kane, Linda S. A860
Kane, Margaret L. A1038
Kane, Margaret L. E496
Kane, William A774
Kane, William E360
Kane, William J. A1037
Kanehana, Yoshinori W334
Kanei, Masashi W297
Kaneko, Shingo W609
Kanema, Yuji W281
Kang, Andrew E240
Kang, Chung-Gu W352
Kang, Dian W152
Kang, Fuxiang W146
Kang, Ho-Moon W513
Kang, Jin E537
Kang, Kook-Hyun W352
Kang, Lan A112
Kang, Shin Tae W537
Kang, Simon W366
Kang, Yu-Sig W366
Kang, Yulin W528
Kania, Don R. A573
Kano, Koichi W356
Kano, Riyo W659
Kano, Riyo W336
Kanouff, Yvette A920
Kanouff, Yvette E166
Kantor, Bernard W310
Kantor, Ian R. W310
Kantor, Ian R. W311
Kanuru, Raj E228
Kanzawa, Eiji W267
Kao, Chao-Yang W252
Kao, Ching-Hsing A843
Kao, Ching-Hsing E393
Kao, Christina A878
Kao, Christina E409
Kao, Daniel Tsun-Ming W636
Kao, George E472
Kao, James W. A878
Kao, James W. E409
Kao, Ruey-Bin E281
Kaocharern, Sukri W334
Kaperi, Ari W446
Kapil, Arvind W271
Kapil, Pawan Kumar W491
Kapilashrami, Tanuj W318
Kapito, Robert (Rob) S. A160
Kaplan, David B. E34
Kaplan, Gregg A. E162
Kaplan, Jeffrey A. W374
Kaplan, Laura Cox E123
Kaplan, Marjory E397
Kaplan, Michael L. A652
Kaplan, Ronald W. E494
Kaplan, Seth L. E242
Kaplan, Steve E333
Kapoor, Deepak W588
Kapoor, Gaurav A20
Kapoor, Kunal E333
Kapoor, Navneet W1

Kapoor, Rajan W462
Kapoor, Rohit E179
Kapoor, Sunir Kumar W69
Kapples, John W. E276
Kapur, Vimal A530
Kaput, Jim L. A1148
Karaboutis, Adriana E39
Karaivanov, Dimitar A. A280
Karaivanov, Dimitar A. E113
Karalis, Veronique W231
Karam, Celia A198
Karam, Thomas F. E171
Karanikolas, Michael E418
Karasawa, Yasuyoshi W413
Karavatakis, Phyllis Q. A207
Karavias, Fokion C. W231
Karawan, Gregory S. A470
Karayalcin, Murat W619
Karber, Michael J. A485
Karbowski, Jeffrey W. A730
Karchunas, Scott A853
Karczmer, Aaron A807
Kardis, Phillip J. A231
Kargar, Peyman W441
Kari, Ross J. E234
Karish, Jeffrey E142
Kariyada, Fumitsugu W278
Karley, James J. A37
Karley, James J. E14
Karlin, Bridget E. A313
Karlsson, Anders C. W579
Karlsson, Arne W2
Karlsson, Jan W228
Karlstrom, Johan W178
Karlstrom, Roger W548
Karna, Ajoy Hari E337
Karnad, Renu W271
Karnes, Matthew E235
Karoleski, Joanita Maria A828
Karon, Adam E12
Karow, Andrew E19
Karp, David A. E67
Karp, David W. E352
Karr, Michael A797
Karr, Michael P419
Karr, Michael S. A796
Karr, Michael S. E368
Karrip, Brian G. A418
Karrip, Brian G. E195
Karrmann, Sandi A604
Karsanbhai, Surendralal L. A365
Karsner, Alexander A. A90
Karsner, Alexander A. A388
Karttinen, Timo W247
Karuth-Zelle, Barbara W33
Karuturi, Monica A218
Kasai, Satoshi W555
Kasama, Takayuki W319
Kasarda, John D. A771
Kasbar, Michael J. A1135
Kasbekar, Umesh M. A266
Kaschke, Michael W199
Kaschke, Michael W277
Kasdin, Robert A. A87
Kashima, Kaoru W570
Kashitani, Ichiro W616
Kashiwada, Yoshinori W410
Kashiwagi, Yutaka W402
Kaskeala, Juhani W348
Kaslow-Ramos, Robert A999

COMBINED HOOVER'S HANDBOOK INDEX OF EXECUTIVES

A = AMERICAN BUSINESS
E = EMERGING COMPANIES
P = PRIVATE COMPANIES
W = WORLD BUSINESSS

Kaslow, Aaron M. A913
Kaslow, Aaron M. E427
Kasnet, Stephen G. A1048
Kasnet, Stephen G. E485
Kass-Hout, Taha A458
Kass, Steven A979
Kass, Steven A. A810
Kass, Steven A. E376
Kassab, Leanne D. A259
Kassab, Leanne D. E103
Kassai, Ali W492
Kassar, Richard A. A1136
Kassel, Leon E397
Kassimiotis, Tony W471
Kassis, Gaby G. W77
Kassling, William E. A1099
Kasson, Michelle E49
Kassow, Achim W415
Kassow, Achim W389
Kastanis, John N P653
Kastelberg, Mary Margaret E526
Kastner, Christopher D. A546
Kastner, Janeen B. A907
Kasutani, Seiichi W392
Kasutani, Toshihide W608
Katanozaka, Shinya W606
Katanyutanon, Prayoonsri W334
Kataoka, Goushi W82
Katayama, Hiroshi W400
Katayama, Masanori W313
Katayama, Toshiko W568
Katayama, Yoshihiro W440
Katayama, Yutaka W330
Katerbau, Karin W389
Katherman, William H. E218
Kathpal, Prateek E91
Katinakis, Nikos W596
Katkin, Keith A. E157
Kato, Hiromichi W155
Kato, Hiroyuki W453
Kato, Isao W604
Kato, Kaoru W343
Kato, Kaoru W407
Kato, Kazumaro W83
Kato, Kikuo W417
Kato, Kosuke W576
Kato, Masahiro W21
Kato, Nobuaki W570
Kato, Nobuhisa W334
Kato, Nobuya W321
Kato, Sadanori W155
Kato, Sotaro W445
Kato, Takao W405
Kato, Tetsuya W292
Kato, Wataru W405
Kato, Yasumichi W269
Katsoudas, Francine S. A108
Katsoulis, Nicos A768
Katsoulis, Nicos E359
Katsukawa, Yoshihiko W345
Katsuki, Atsushi W50
Katsuki, Hisashi W28
Katsumi, Takeshi W330
Katsuno, Satoru W155

Katsuragawa, Akira W21
Katz, David M. A265
Katz, Jacob M. A581
Katz, Karen W. A541
Katz, Karen W. A1059
Katz, Michael A1098
Katz, Michael J. A992
Katz, Michal E402
Katz, Miriam W312
Katz, Robert L. (Bobby) A578
Katzen, Michael A. E526
Katzin, Jackie W426
Katzman, James C. A512
Kau, Melanie W31
Kauchak, John J. E510
Kaufer, Stephen E81
Kauffmann, Herbert W14
Kaufman, David W. E189
Kaufman, Irvin A P452
Kaufman, Ivan E34
Kaufman, John S. E371
Kaufman, Michael E447
Kaufman, Victor A. E261
Kaufman, William H. E293
Kaufmann, Bernhard W442
Kaufmann, Marli P436
Kaul-Hottinger, Mary A235
Kaul, Priyanka E153
Kaur, Pam W135
Kaur, Pam W289
Kaushal, Nitin E526
Kausmeyer, Gary M. E79
Kauten, Ralph R. A416
Kavanagh, Michael Joseph A301
Kavanaugh, James J. A565
Kavanaugh, Scott F. A423
Kavanaugh, Scott F. E348
Kavanaugh, Scott F. E199
Kawa, Mark H. A399
Kawabata, Fumitoshi W51
Kawabe, Kentaro W550
Kawachi, Katsunori W410
Kawada, Junichi W535
Kawada, Tatsuo W183
Kawagoishi, Tadashi W402
Kawai, Eriko W409
Kawai, Shuji W184
Kawai, Toshiki W607
Kawakita, Hisashi W292
Kawamoto, Hiroaki W319
Kawamoto, Hiroko W209
Kawamoto, Hiroko W570
Kawamura, Akihiro W42
Kawamura, Hajime W387
Kawamura, Hiroshi W319
Kawamura, Kanji W313
Kawamura, Yoshihiko W279
Kawamura, Yusuke W123
Kawan, Khaled S. W47
Kawana, Masatoshi W316
Kawano, Ichiro W539
Kawano, Ichiro W603
Kawano, Mitsuo W454
Kawanobe, Osamu W604
Kawasaki, Yasuyuki W570
Kawashima, Katsuya W538
Kawazoe, Katsuhiko W439
Kawlewski, Curtis Owen E356
Kawwas, Charlie B. A179
Kay, Sabrina A351

Kay, Sabrina E150
Kay, Stephen H. E423
Kay, Valerie A627
Kayano, Masayasu W330
Kaye, Daniel G. A377
Kaye, Daniel G. E17
Kaye, Mark B. A711
Kayhan, Muharrem Hilmi W620
Kayser, C. Dallas A249
Kayser, C. Dallas E99
Kayser, David Robert A235
Kazama, Masaru W330
Kazarian, Kristina A. A657
Kazarian, Kristina A. A717
Kazim, Essa Abdulfattah A721
Kazmi, Hasan W462
Ke, Peng W139
Ke, Qiubi W40
Ke, Ruiwen W151
Ke, Yang W597
Keach, John K. A425
Keach, John K. E201
Keady, Robert J. E538
Kealey, Michael B. E145
Kean, Steven J. A605
Keane, James P. A902
Keane, Kevin J. E364
Keane, Loretta D. A380
Keane, Margaret M. A42
Keane, Margaret M. A985
Keaney, Timothy F. A1079
Keanly, Rose A. W8
Kearney, Christopher J. A760
Kearney, Christopher J. A791
Kearney, Patrick E471
Kearney, Terrence C. A1089
Kearns, Roger L. A1124
Keating, Ashley M. E317
Keating, Brendan J. E224
Keating, Catherine M. A915
Keating, Francis (Frank) A. A125
Keating, Francis (Frank) A. E52
Keating, Valerie Soranno A781
Keatley, Travis A. A1127
Keck, Sharon J P12
Keck, Thomas E462
Kedia, Gunjan A1082
Keefe, Michelle A986
Keegan, Joseph D. E59
Keegan, Teresa J. A398
Keegans, Karen L. A902
Keeler, Anne B E181
Keeler, Brian P366
Keeler, Glenn J. E495
Keeley, Brian E. A1111
Keels, Floyd L. A418
Keenan, David R. A885
Keenan, Katharine A. E62
Keenan, Suzanne A1078
Keenan, Suzanne E513
Keenan, Timothy J. E226
Keenan, W. Howard E33
Keene, Nazzic S. A108
Keene, Nazzic S. A920
Keene, Ruth Ann E44
Keener, Larry H. E85
Keens, David W318
Keesling, Rebecca D. A167
Keesling, Rebecca D. E64
Keetch, Chad A. E164

Keeth, Martha Frances (Fran) A97
Keeton, Ryan A208
Keeton, Simon A780
Keeve, Thinus W162
Kefeli, Hulya W26
Keffer, David F. A752
Keffer, Pueo A785
Kehl, George J. A1139
Kehl, Russell A. A235
Kehle, Shannon E412
Kehoe, James A1101
Kehoe, Michael P. E287
Keim, Mark Lowell A707
Keim, Michael S. A1078
Keim, Michael S. E513
Keinan, Elly A612
Keitel, Hans-Peter W510
Keitel, William E. E501
Keith, Cynthia B. A950
Keith, Cynthia B. E454
Keith, Daniel C. A940
Keith, R. Alexandra A850
Keith, R. Alexandra A1027
Keith, Stephen E43
Keithley, Joseph P. E47
Keithley, Russ A. E104
Keizer, Henry R. A924
Keizer, Henry R. E236
Kelderman, Kim E59
Keler, Marianne M. A945
Keler, Marianne M. E450
Kellaway, Racheal W85
Kelleher, Annette M. W328
Kelleher, Thomas C. A747
Kelleher, Thomas J. E49
Keller-Busse, Sabine W621
Keller-Busse, Sabine W666
Keller, Adrian T. W203
Keller, Andreas W. W203
Keller, Anne P408
Keller, Christina L. A555
Keller, Christina L. E269
Keller, Deborah L. V. E534
Keller, Gerhard E325
Keller, Hans Ueli E153
Keller, Kenneth C. ("Casey") E50
Keller, Mark K. A788
Keller, Mark K. E366
Keller, Robert Andrew E381
Keller, Ulrich E. A423
Keller, Ulrich E. E199
Kellerhals, Jurgen W129
Kellermann, Kimberly A. A489
Kelley, Angela M.W. A800
Kelley, Dennis E. E470
Kelley, Katharine M. A574
Kelley, Laurie A854
Kelley, Laurie P446
Kelley, Robert W. E76
Kelley, Scott L. A12
Kelley, Scott L. E4
Kelley, Stephen Douglas E362
Kelley, Stephen Douglas E6
Kelliher, Susan M. A224
Kellner, Lawrence W. A164
Kellner, Lawrence W. A388
Kellogg, Clark C. A427
Kellogg, Clark C. E203
Kelly-Bisla, Balbir W654
Kelly-Ennis, Debra J. A47

COMBINED HOOVER'S HANDBOOK INDEX OF EXECUTIVES

```
A = AMERICAN BUSINESS
E = EMERGING COMPANIES
P = PRIVATE COMPANIES
W = WORLD BUSINESSS
```

Kelly, Alfred F. A1096
Kelly, Alicia C. A1030
Kelly, Anastasia D. A546
Kelly, Ann P P639
Kelly, Braden R. E183
Kelly, Brian G. A13
Kelly, Christie B. E412
Kelly, Christopher W160
Kelly, Daniel S. E40
Kelly, Dennis I. E240
Kelly, Douglas N. A595
Kelly, Edward J. A248
Kelly, Edward J. A691
Kelly, Eric A363
Kelly, Francis J. E56
Kelly, Gary C. A956
Kelly, Gary C. A638
Kelly, Gennifer F. A325
Kelly, Geri M. A271
Kelly, Geri M. E109
Kelly, Haywood E333
Kelly, Ian W526
Kelly, Jason M A472
Kelly, Jason M E230
Kelly, Jeffrey D. A851
Kelly, Joseph F. E260
Kelly, Julie E19
Kelly, Katherine R. A178
Kelly, Katherine R. A689
Kelly, Kevin J. W119
Kelly, Laura G. E410
Kelly, Liam J. E484
Kelly, Mary E. A289
Kelly, Michael A. E325
Kelly, Michele J. E69
Kelly, Renee W. E192
Kelly, Robert P. A911
Kelly, Sara A964
Kelly, Shaun W178
Kelly, Stephen M. A893
Kelly, Terri L. A1071
Kelly, Terri L. W53
Kelly, Theresa A439
Kelly, Thomas F. A215
Kelly, Tim P498
Kelly, William A. A845
Kelly, William A. E395
Kelman, David A977
Kelman, David E464
Kelman, Naomi E341
Kelpy, Matthew B. A763
Kelroy, Jason J. A608
Kelsey, Margaret C. A1114
Kelter, Jeffrey E. E280
Kelton, Justin P336
Kemaloglu, I. Serdar W620
Kemenes, Erno W412
Kemler, Hans Dieter W389
Kemly, Thomas J. A271
Kemly, Thomas J. E109
Kemna, Angelien W65
Kemna, Horst Paulmann W132
Kemori, Nobumasa W326
Kemp, Harry A. A622

Kemp, J. Michael A424
Kemp, J. Michael E200
Kemp, Jon A349
Kemp, Sarah E. E352
Kempczinski, Christopher J. A675
Kempen, Wouter T. van E101
Kemper, Alexander C. A1056
Kemper, Alexander C. E505
Kemper, David W. A276
Kemper, David W. A838
Kemper, J. Mariner A1056
Kemper, J. Mariner E505
Kemper, John W. A276
Kemper, Jonathan M. A276
Kemper, LeRoy (Lee) W. E287
Kempf, T. J. E223
Kempner, Michael W. A287
Kempner, Michael W. E115
Kemppainen, Pekka W348
Kempston-Darkes, Maureen W112
Kempthorne, Dirk A. A898
Kendall, Laura C. A528
Kendall, Laura C. E258
Kendall, Lloyd W. E56
Kendall, Ronald E. E150
Kendle, Candace A366
Kendrick, Bradford M. A207
Kenefick, Jeffrey Patrick A411
Kenesey, Timothy A610
Kennard, Lydia H. A20
Kennard, Lydia H. A452
Kennard, William E. A691
Kennard, William E. A444
Kennard, William E. A105
Kennealy, G. M. Beatrix W518
Kennealy, Trix W559
Kennedy, Barbara J. A1120
Kennedy, Barbara J. E535
Kennedy, Douglas L. A810
Kennedy, Douglas L. E375
Kennedy, James A. C. A1062
Kennedy, John W201
Kennedy, Kelly J. E529
Kennedy, Kevin J. A607
Kennedy, Kevin J. E141
Kennedy, Kevin M. A439
Kennedy, Kevin R. A130
Kennedy, Kolleen T. E262
Kennedy, Marianna R. E364
Kennedy, Melina M. A306
Kennedy, Melissa J. W572
Kennedy, Michael D. A773
Kennedy, Michael N. E33
Kennedy, Parker S. A413
Kennedy, Patricia J. E43
Kennedy, Patrick W81
Kennedy, Stacey A825
Kennedy, Thomas A. A1012
Kennedy, Thomas C. E472
Kenner, Brian T. A519
Kenner, Brian T. E256
Kenney, Frederic L. A415
Kenney, Frederic L. E194
Kenney, Jim A251
Kenney, Jim P137
Kenney, William J. E287
Kenning, Thomas H. E19
Kenningham, Daryl A. A491
Kenny, David W. A155
Kenny, David W. A742

Kenny, Gregory B. A201
Kenny, Gregory B. A557
Kenny, Jack P. E321
Kenny, Richard F. E388
Kenny, Thomas J. A24
Kent, Ahmet Muhtar A4
Kent, Deborah S. E308
Kent, Geoff P279
Kent, Nevada A. A373
Kent, Nevada A. E168
Kent, Remi A851
Kent, Steven P. A188
Kent, Steven P. E71
Kent, Suzette K. A496
Keogh, Elizabeth M. A976
Keogh, John W. W154
Keohane, Sean D. A224
Keough, Joseph A687
Kepler, David E. W611
Kepler, Jody P363
Kepler, Lisa A650
Kepler, Lisa E305
Keptner, Erik A895
Kerber, Lynn M. A532
Kerber, Lynn M. E259
Kereere, Suzan A434
Kereere, Suzan A4
Keresty, Georgia E39
Kerin, Andrew Charles A97
Kerins, Sean J. A97
Kerley, Richard A. E85
Kermisch, Marc W157
Kern, Harald W543
Kern, Peter M. A385
Kern, Robert R. E69
Kerner, Juergen W543
Kerner, Jurgen W602
Kerr, Brenda C. A499
Kerr, Brenda C. E246
Kerr, David W. W571
Kerr, Deborah L. A729
Kerr, Derek J. A55
Kerr, Derek J. A274
Kerr, James Y. A952
Kerr, Janet E. E34
Kerr, Jason S. E70
Kerr, Michael T. A376
Kerr, Richard J. E309
Kerrey, J. Robert (Bob) A1003
Kerrick, Michelle C. E57
Kerrien, Jean-Paul W174
Kerrigan, Dennis F. A499
Kersey, Frances P136
Kersey, Melissa D. A1035
Kershaw, Justin A. E40
Kerwin, Gregory M. A702
Kerwin, Gregory M. E326
Keryer, Philippe W600
Kerzner, Daniel E14
Kesavan, Sudhakar A10
Keshavan, Santhosh A1098
Kesler, Joe R. A398
Kesner, Idalene F. A153
Kesner, Idalene F. A347
Kesner, Idalene F. W571
Kess, Avrohom J. A1037
Kessel, William B. (Brad) A554
Kessel, William B. (Brad) E269
Kesseler, Brian J. A1004
Kessiakoff, Peter W547

Kesslen, Jay E221
Kessler, Bernd F. A835
Kessler, Denis A573
Kessler, Denis W526
Kessler, Jon E247
Kessler, Karen J. A749
Kessler, Marcel E236
Kessler, Marla L. E282
Kessler, Pamela J. E384
Kessler, Scott A159
Kestner, R. Steven E393
Keswick, Adam W323
Keswick, Ben W323
Keswick, Benjamin William W322
Keswick, Chips W310
Ketchum, John W. A436
Ketchum, John W. A739
Ketchum, Richard G. E311
Ketschke, Matthew A290
Ketschke, Matthew A288
Ketter, Joseph E445
Keum, Yong Chung W513
Keuper, Frank W. W580
Keuper, Frank W. W580
Keverian, Kenneth M. A92
Kevin, Medica John W168
Kewalramani, Reshma A1089
Key, John P. W63
Key, Matthew W114
Keyes, James W. A719
Keysberg, Klaus W602
Keyser, Jay B. E526
Keyser, Richard L. A1148
Keyte, David H. E33
Kganyago, Lesetja W558
Khaili, Jawaan Awaidha Suhail Al W8
Khalaf, Michel A. A691
Khan, Ahmad A. A607
Khan, M. W8
Khan, Mehmood W490
Khan, Nick E543
Khan, Zafar W111
Khanani, A. Qadir W8
Khanna, Deeptha W351
Khanna, Tarun A23
Khanuja, Parvinderjit Singh A926
Khanuja, Satbir E140
Khara, Dinesh Kumar W561
Kharbash, Mohammad K. W205
Khasis, Lev W521
Khator, Renu A834
Khattar, Jack A. E474
Khatu, Satish W171
Khavkin, Evgeny W476
Khaykin, Oleg A118
Khaykin, Oleg E523
Khayyal, Abdulaziz Fahd Al A494
Khayyal, Abdulaziz Fahd Al A657
Khazraji, W. Al W8
Kheradpir, S. W414
Kheraj, Naguib W561
Khezrian, Amir A742
Khezrian, Amir P393
Khidir, Murtada W486
Khilnani, Vinod M. A1
Khiong, Kellee Kam Chee W495
Khoba, Lyubov W476
Khol, Florian W639
Khomyakov, Sergey F. W474
Khoo, Shulamite N. K. W156

COMBINED HOOVER'S HANDBOOK INDEX OF EXECUTIVES

A = AMERICAN BUSINESS
E = EMERGING COMPANIES
P = PRIVATE COMPANIES
W = WORLD BUSINESSS

Khosla, Sanjay A1153
Khosrowshahi, Dara A385
Khosrowshahi, Dara A1052
Khouri, Khaled Abdulla Neamat W8
Khoury, Karl E529
Khuny, Marion W229
Khurana, Akash A1117
Khurana, Vineet A612
Khuri, Zachary A788
Khuri, Zachary E365
Khvalin, Igor Vladimirovich W476
Kiani, Joe E. E312
Kiatkumjai, Patcharasiri W352
Kicinski, Stephen C. W570
Kidd, Steven Gregory ("Greg") A958
Kidd, Steven Gregory ("Greg") E456
Kiddoo, Bruce E. A780
Kidwai, Naina Lal W283
Kiefer, Kathleen S. A85
Kielholz, Walter B. W580
Kiely, John J. E31
Kiely, Sharon P606
Kiely, W. Leo A47
Kiener, Pascal W87
Kiernan, Daniel J. A316
Kiernan, Eileen A570
Kiers, Deborah W85
Kieser, Kathryn E. A845
Kieser, Kathryn E. E395
Kieske, David A. E524
Kiesling, Louise W640
Kiessling, Douglas W. E455
Kigawa, Makoto W347
Kiiskinen, Esa W340
Kijima, Tatsuo W462
Kikkawa, Takeo W297
Kiko, Richard T. E117
Kikuchi, Kiyomi W400
Kikuta, Tetsuya W181
Kilaas, Liselott W448
Kilani, O. W8
Kilar, Jason A785
Kilbane, Catherine M. A82
Kilbane, Catherine M. E136
Kilberg, James A. A1127
Kilbride, William B. A1006
Kilcoyne, Gerald (Jerry) L. A416
Kildahl, Jorgen W594
Kildemo, Pal W448
Kiley, Joseph W. E199
Kiley, Krystal P223
Kilgore, Gene E34
Kilgore, Leslie J. A730
Kilgore, Leslie J. E386
Kilgour, Peter Alan W128
Kilian, Gunnar W640
Killalea, Peter Thomas A198
Killalea, Peter Thomas E12
Killefer, Nancy A201
Killefer, Nancy A689
Killen, Tracey W364
Killen, Tracey W364
Killerlane, James J. A132
Killian, John F. A289

Killian, John F. A290
Killinger, Elizabeth R. A757
Killinger, Ollie W364
Killingsworth, Kelly T. E146
Killmer, John L. E26
Kilmer, Bobbi J. E98
Kilmer, Mark C. A865
Kilmer, Mark C. E403
Kilpatrick, Deborah L. E448
Kilpatrick, Marla Mala Yvonne E532
Kilroy, James J. E247
Kilroy, John B. E287
Kilsby, Susan W201
Kilsby, Susan Saltzbart A447
Kilsby, Susan Saltzbart W626
Kilts, James M. A1093
Kilts, James M. E443
Kim, Anthony I. A498
Kim, Bernard E209
Kim, Charles G. A276
Kim, Dae-You W352
Kim, Daeki W205
Kim, Denny A976
Kim, Dongsoo W205
Kim, Hae In W111
Kim, Hag-Dong W478
Kim, Henry E375
Kim, Hong-Tae W652
Kim, Howard Hwasaeng E323
Kim, Hye Joo W537
Kim, Hyun-Jong W513
Kim, James A231
Kim, James W366
Kim, James J. A78
Kim, James J. E90
Kim, Jason K. A530
Kim, Jason K. E258
Kim, Jay A37
Kim, Jay E14
Kim, Jay L. A507
Kim, Jay L. E248
Kim, John A267
Kim, John Y. A448
Kim, John Y. A380
Kim, JongKap W351
Kim, Joo Mi E405
Kim, Joo-Hyun W478
Kim, Joon Kyung A531
Kim, Joon Kyung E259
Kim, Joseph A982
Kim, Junmo W546
Kim, Kevin Sung A530
Kim, Kevin Sung E258
Kim, Ki-Hwan W335
Kim, Ki-Nam W513
Kim, Kristina S. E220
Kim, Kyu S. A530
Kim, Kyu S. E258
Kim, Kyung-Ho W335
Kim, Lisa L. A351
Kim, Lisa L. A211
Kim, Lisa L. E150
Kim, Lisa L. E84
Kim, Lorence H. A73
Kim, Min J. E362
Kim, O.C. E220
Kim, Ock Hee E362
Kim, Paul E224
Kim, Sang-Gyun W513
Kim, Sang-Hee W366

Kim, Sang-Hyun W294
Kim, Seok-Dong W546
Kim, Shin-Bae W478
Kim, Soon-Taek W513
Kim, Soung Jo W537
Kim, Sung-Jin W478
Kim, Susan Y. A78
Kim, Tae-Ok W351
Kim, Yong-Hak W546
Kim, Young-Kee W366
Kimata, Masatoshi W353
Kimball, Carly W625
Kimball, Lisa A. E372
Kimball, Stefani M. A555
Kimball, Stefani M. E269
Kimbell, David C. A1055
Kimble, Donald R. A602
Kimble, Sean T. E514
Kimble, William F. A319
Kimbrough, Bradly A678
Kimbrough, Bradly P338
Kimbrough, Karin J. A391
Kimijima, Shoko W370
Kimm, Nicola W273
Kimmel, Colleen A976
Kimmel, David Scott A592
Kimmell, Joseph E447
Kimmelshue, Ruth S. E226
Kimmerle, Derek R. A652
Kimmet, Pamela O. W382
Kimmitt, Robert M. A689
Kimoto, Kentaro W608
Kimura, Hiroshi W582
Kimura, Hiroto W353
Kimura, Kazuhiro W353
Kimura, Shunichi W348
Kimura, Yasushi W441
Kinast-Poetsch, Brigitta W633
Kinder, Richard D P379
Kinder, Richard D. A605
Kindi, Butti Saeed Al W205
Kindick, Kelt A325
Kindle, Becky E57
Kindle, Fred W524
Kindle, Manfred W495
Kindred, Jonathan B. A219
King, A. Brent A818
King, Andrew D. (Andy) A97
King, Brian W. E5
King, Christine A942
King, Christopher John W603
King, Darren J. A651
King, David L. E397
King, David Randolf A1132
King, Deeanne A992
King, Donnie D. A1050
King, Gale V. A543
King, Gale V. A1079
King, Gale V. A111
King, Geoff W655
King, J. Luther E502
King, Jamie Wade A721
King, Janet L. E56
King, Jeremy A1112
King, Justin M. W385
King, Karen M. A92
King, Karen M. A448
King, Marie A651
King, Mark James A1146
King, Mary Jane A372

King, Mary Jane E167
King, Mason A301
King, Mason E131
King, Michael P275
King, Patti S. E418
King, Peter W647
King, Richard H. A545
King, Robert J. A82
King, Sarah H. A316
King, Stephen V. A415
King, Stephen V. E194
King, Steven W486
King, Thomas C. A984
King, Thomas C. E476
Kingman, John Oliver Frank W360
Kingo, Lise W174
Kingo, Lise W515
Kingsbury, Thomas A608
Kingsbury, Thomas A. A608
Kingsley, Lawrence D. A835
Kingsley, Lawrence D. A902
Kingsley, Lawrence D. E263
Kingsley, Scott A. A724
Kington, Mark J. A340
Kini, Narasimha E179
Kinloch, Kathy W596
Kinnart, Peter W60
Kinney, Catherine R. A691
Kinney, Catherine R. E336
Kinney, Catherine R. E451
Kinney, Jane E. W308
Kinney, Jane E. W133
Kinoshita, Keishiro W439
Kinoshita, Manabu W28
Kinsella, Patrick A811
Kinsella, Patrick E377
Kinser, Timothy R. A907
Kinsey, Armond P50
Kinsley, Karen A. W420
Kinugawa, Kazuhide W319
Kinzler, Alexander C. E56
Kip, Jeffrey W. A152
Kirac, Inan W346
Kiranandana, Khunying Suchada W334
Kirby, Adrienne E441
Kirby, Brent G. A765
Kirby, Carrie Lee A1097
Kirby, J. Scott A1062
Kirby, Jefferson W. A39
Kirby, Pamela J. W490
Kirby, Pamela J. W191
Kirby, Robert F. A214
Kircher, Monika W510
Kirchgraber, Paul R. A615
Kirchoff, Bob P163
Kirgan, Danielle L. A654
Kiriwat, Ekamol W541
Kiriyama, Hiroshi W173
Kirk, A. Russell E35
Kirk, Ewan W66
Kirk, J. Christopher A213
Kirk, Jennifer M. A892
Kirk, Jennifer M. W393
Kirk, Larry G. A190
Kirk, Larry G. E73
Kirk, Matrice Ellis A581
Kirk, Ronald A1010
Kirk, Rose Stuckey E82
Kirk, Spencer F. E180

COMBINED HOOVER'S HANDBOOK INDEX OF EXECUTIVES

A = AMERICAN BUSINESS
E = EMERGING COMPANIES
P = PRIVATE COMPANIES
W = WORLD BUSINESSS

Kirkbride, Cheryl M. E132
Kirkby, Allison W114
Kirkham, Michael Ryan A815
Kirkhorn, Zachary A1007
Kirkland, James A. E497
Kirkland, Scott D. A358
Kirkley, David T. A523
Kirkley, David T. E257
Kirkpatrick, Linda A670
Kirloskar, Virendra A. A607
Kirsanova, Svetlana W521
Kirsch, Dieter W3
Kirsch, Eric M. A24
Kirsch, Frank W33
Kirsch, Harry W449
Kirsch, Wolfgang W251
Kirschner, Sidney E473
Kirsis, Karlis P. A493
Kirsner, James D. E183
Kirsten, Artur Stefan W325
Kirt, Christopher J. A325
Kirtley, Timothy H. A816
Kirwan, Jeffrey A. A148
Kiscaden, Bradley James A659
Kise, Teruo W394
Kise, Yoichi W208
Kiser, Carrie H. E192
Kiser, Georgette D. A726
Kiser, Georgette D. A24
Kiser, Georgette D. A580
Kish, Donald A450
Kishida, Seiichi W28
Kishigami, Keiko W557
Kishman, Thomas M. E117
Kishore, Sangeeta A691
Kishore, Sangeeta E323
Kispert, John E261
Kissam, Luther C. A349
Kissel, Joseph B. A71
Kissel, Joseph B. E29
Kissick, John H. E34
Kissire, Deborah J. A778
Kissire, Deborah J. A215
Kissire, Deborah J. E72
Kissling, Willy R. W524
Kissner, Rita A. E428
Kistner, William G. A188
Kistner, William G. E71
Kiszka, Robert E450
Kita, Norio W330
Kitachi, Tatsuaki W462
Kitagawa, Hirokuni W281
Kitagawa, Shinsuke W345
Kitagawa, Shinsuke W408
Kitahara, Mutsuro W581
Kitajima, Motoharu W181
Kitajima, Yoshinari W181
Kitajima, Yoshitoshi W181
Kitamura, Akira W389
Kitamura, Keiko W394
Kitamura, Kunitaro W253
Kitamura, Matazaemon W418
Kitamura, Takumi W445
Kitano, Hiroaki W557

Kitano, Shun W582
Kitano, Yoshihisa W325
Kitao, Yuichi W353
Kitayama, Mitchell W. E33
Kitazawa, Toshifumi W527
Kitchell, Ryan C. A772
Kitchen, Carol A492
Kitchen, Carol P248
Kitchens, W. James E195
Kitcher, Julie W24
Kitchin, James L. A747
Kitera, Masato W321
Kitera, Masato W387
Kitera, Masato W437
Kito, Shunichi W297
Kitsch, William J. E158
Kitson, Michael A. E373
Kittayarak, Kittipong W117
Kittisataporn, Karun W79
Kittrell, Marty R. E38
Kitzmiller, Jason A. A981
Kitzmiller, Jason A. E469
Kiuchi, Takahide W137
Kivisto, Nicole A. A679
Kivits, Patrick M. A1125
Kiyokawa, Koichi W539
Kiyomune, Kazuo W278
Kiyono, Yukiyo W155
Kizer, Diana L. E190
Klaas, Bjoern E400
Klaeser, Dennis L. A774
Klaeser, Dennis L. E360
Klane, Larry A. A723
Klane, Polly Nyquist A248
Klappa, Gale E. A1114
Klappa, Gale E. A101
Klapstein, Julie D. E20
Klasko, Stephen K. E484
Klass, Cheryl P295
Klatten, Susanne W96
Klaue, David A. A136
Klauke, Sabine W24
Klaus, Peter W234
Klausner, Rob A197
Klausner, Rob P103
Klayko, Michael A. E134
Klebba, John A. A398
Klee, Ann R. A1099
Klee, Stephan E104
Kleer, Garry D. E421
Kleffel, Juliette P. A923
Kleffel, Juliette P. E433
Klehm, Henry W491
Kleiman, Angela L. E419
Kleiman, Joel P174
Klein, Barbara A. A557
Klein, Christian W15
Klein, Christian W517
Klein, Christopher J. A1028
Klein, Dale E. A952
Klein, Daniel M. E384
Klein, James D. A865
Klein, James D. E403
Klein, Jonathan D. E175
Klein, Mark A. E428
Klein, Michael F. A1037
Klein, Michael R. A1046
Klein, Michael R. E123
Klein, Michael S. W176
Klein, Michel W495

Klein, Nicholas D. E158
Klein, Rebecca A. E446
Klein, Richard H. E15
Klein, Robert M. E5
Klein, Ronald A. E471
Klein, Roxanne B. E169
Klein, Steven M. A749
Kleine, Walter W192
Kleinemeier, Michael W397
Kleiner, Madeleine A. A752
Kleinman, Scott D. A545
Kleisterlee, Gerard J. W52
Klem, U. Butch A472
Klem, U. Butch E230
Klemash, Stephen W. A794
Klemm, Lynette M. E191
Klesse, William R. A767
Klestil, Guido W633
Klevorn, Marcy S. A541
Klevorn, Marcy S. A749
Kley, Karl Ludwig W207
Kley, Karl-Ludwig W196
Kleyboldt, Claas W270
Kleyman, Bill E477
Klieger, Robert N. A802
Kliethermes, Craig W. A896
Kliethermes, Craig W. E422
Kliman, Gilbert H. E460
Klimley, Brooks J. E33
Klimowich, John A271
Klimowich, John E109
Kline, David A223
Kline, Katherine M.A. (Allie) A545
Kline, Rebecca L. (Joy) E526
Kline, Shari E455
Kline, Teresa L. E20
Klingenberg, Bernard Ekhard W518
Klingenberger, Mary Acker E311
Klinger, John A1030
Klinken, Onno van W16
Kliphouse, Kirsten M. A615
Klisura, Dean A662
Klitgaard, William E. A986
Klobnak, Jennifer L. A896
Klobnak, Jennifer L. E422
Klockenga, Kevin P524
Kloet, Thomas A. A721
Klohs, Birgit M. A653
Klopfenstein, John D. E222
Klopfer, Jane A428
Klotzbach, Kevin B. A411
Klurfeld, Jason E176
Klutch, Derek J. E306
Kluting, Duane F. E321
Klyn, Pamela E373
Knabe, Don A301
Knabe, Don P171
Knapp, Diane R. A401
Knapp, Laurie H. E400
Knapp, Pamela W165
Knapp, Tracy W. A592
Knauf, Isabel Corinna W171
Knauss, Donald R. A597
Knauss, Donald R. A997
Knauss, Donald R. A677
Knauss, Jeffery J. A280
Knauss, Jeffery J. E113
Knavish, Timothy M. A840
Kneale, Jennifer R. A995
Knecht, Julie A1010

Kneeland, Michael (Mike) J. A1071
Kneller, Michael K. A620
Kng, Hwee Tin W464
Knibbe, David W442
Knieriem, Karlyn M. A426
Knieriem, Karlyn M. E202
Knight, Angela A. E159
Knight, Cecil W. A496
Knight, Chris W360
Knight, Erin D. A52
Knight, Jeffrey L. A772
Knight, Jessie J. A34
Knight, Kenneth D. E444
Knight, Lester B. W44
Knight, Malcom D. W580
Knight, Mark P602
Knight, Natalie W351
Knight, Reginald P589
Knight, Robert M. A918
Knight, Travis A. A743
Knighten, Benjamin E254
Knightly, Kevin C. A576
Kniker, Catherine E402
Knisely, Philip W. A145
Knobel, Carsten W276
Knobel, Carsten W196
Knoblauch, Michael W. E128
Knoche-Brouillon, Carinne W415
Knoche, Philippe W600
Knoess, Christoph W507
Knof, Manfred W162
Knoll, Linda I. W524
Knook, Pieter Cornelis W594
Knopek, Dagmar W3
Knopik, Stephen M. A860
Knospe, Elizabeth A. A399
Knott, Karen A976
Knouse-Snyder, Denise A1115
Knouse-Snyder, Denise E533
Knowles, Alana K. A230
Knowling, Robert E. A895
Knowling, Robert E. E468
Knox, D. Bruce A1115
Knox, D. Bruce E533
Knox, Judith Amanda Sourry A864
Knox, Judith Amanda Sourry A611
Knox, Lesley W360
Knox, Wendell J. A499
Knudsen, Jeannette L. A947
Knudsen, Karsten Munk W450
Knudstorp, Jorgen Vig A964
Knueven, Ronald J. E185
Knupling, Frieder W526
Knust, Susan L. A420
Knust, Susan L. E197
Knutson, Jerry E421
Knutson, Craig L. A693
Knutson, Lisa A. A1115
Knutson, Lisa A. E533
Knutson, Lisa A. E431
Knutson, Lottie W277
Knutzen, Jon E370
Knutzen, Tom W446
Ko, Albert J. A648
Ko, Chen-En W206
Ko, Elizabeth E. E129
Koa, Linda D. E67
Kobayakawa, Tomoaki W607
Kobayashi, Ayako W417
Kobayashi, Fumihiko W316

COMBINED HOOVER'S HANDBOOK INDEX OF EXECUTIVES

A = AMERICAN BUSINESS
E = EMERGING COMPANIES
P = PRIVATE COMPANIES
W = WORLD BUSINESSS

Kobayashi, Hidefumi W1
Kobayashi, Izumi W408
Kobayashi, Katsuma W184
Kobayashi, Kazuo W604
Kobayashi, Ken W403
Kobayashi, Kenichi W26
Kobayashi, Koji W25
Kobayashi, Makoto W407
Kobayashi, Masahiko W281
Kobayashi, Masayuki W462
Kobayashi, Michael A905
Kobayashi, Nagahisa W292
Kobayashi, Nobuyuki W567
Kobayashi, Tatsuji W534
Kobayashi, Tetsuya W331
Kobayashi, Toshifumi W325
Kobayashi, Yoichi W659
Kobayashi, Yoko W453
Kobayashi, Yoshimitsu W607
Kobbeman, Robert D. A199
Kobe, Hiroshi W432
Kobliha, Nikki L. A798
Kobori, Hideki W51
Kobori, Michael A185
Kobrinsky, Shaul W312
Koc, Ali Y. W661
Koc, Ali Y. W346
Koc, Ali Y. W621
Koc, Mustafa V. W346
Koc, Omer M. W346
Koc, Omer M. W620
Koc, Rahmi M. W621
Koc, Rahmi M. W346
Koch, C. James E65
Koch, D. Christian E491
Koch, David J. W260
Koch, J Robert A1021
Koch, J Robert P593
Koch, Jonathan A917
Koch, Lori D. A349
Koch, Nicole W199
Koch, Olaf G. W395
Koch, Stephen P. A887
Koch, Thorsten W602
Kochensparger, John H. E293
Kochevar, Deborah T. E94
Kochhar, Rakesh W441
Kochka, Charles D. E321
Kochvar, Mark A910
Koci, Keith A. A252
Kociancic, Mark W233
Kocsis, Andrea W198
Koczelnik, Thomas W198
Koder, Matthew M. A128
Kodera, Akira W155
Kodera, Kazuhiro W297
Kodialam, Rajini Sundar E212
Koefoed, William A. A134
Koefoed, William A. E54
Koegel, J. William A189
Koehler, Bryson R. A878
Koehler, Bryson R. A879
Koehler, John Michael E301
Koehler, Martin W196

Koehler, Michael R. A384
Koehler, Mike A292
Koehler, Renate W397
Koehnen, Michael W. A1038
Koehnen, Michael W. E495
Koellner, Laurette T. A483
Koellner, Laurette T. A760
Koenecke-grant, Carol P119
Koenig, Emery N. A715
Koenig, Michael A215
Koenigheit, Gerard W127
Koenigs, Margaret K. A399
Koepfer, Heike Paulmann W132
Koepfer, Peter Paulmann W132
Koeppel, Holly Keller A23
Koeppel, Holly Keller W111
Koeppen, Christopher E266
Koerber, Hans-Joachim A989
Koessler, Peter W61
Koezuka, Miharu W319
Koffler, E. George E57
Koga, Akira W389
Kogame, Kotaro W155
Koger, Randee R. A378
Kogure, Megumi W657
Koh, Beng Seng W105
Koh, Boon Hwee A27
Koh, Ching Ching W463
Koh, Peter A530
Koh, Peter E258
Koh, Steven S. A530
Koh, Steven S. E258
Koharik, Edward J. E11
Kohda, Main W405
Kohda, Main W321
Kohleisen, Sabine W395
Kohler, Annette G. W203
Kohler, Jens W96
Kohlhagen, Steven W. A74
Kohli, Vikram A213
Kohlpaintner, Christian W109
Kohnke, Gilbert W463
Kohno, Masaharu W570
Koid, Phaik Gunn W36
Koide, Hiroko W402
Koike, Masamichi W569
Koji, Akiyoshi W50
Kojima, Chikara W607
Kojima, Keiji W278
Kojo, Yoshiko W253
Kok, Michael W322
Koken, Mary Diane A512
Kokes, Mark E546
Kokke, Jorgen A557
Kokkila, Ilpo W340
Kokubu, Fumiya W582
Kokubu, Fumiya W285
Kokubu, Fumiya W387
Kokue, Haruko W553
Kolassa, Thomas E. E455
Kolbe, Martin W355
Kolbl, Konrad W251
Kolding, Eivind W188
Kolisch, James M. E358
Kolk, Wouter W351
Koll, Kathy Mitsuko W237
Koller, Dan W78
Koller, Franz Michael W628
Koller, Patrick W238
Kolli, Sreelakshmi E16

Kollmann, Dagmar P. W199
Kollmann, Dagmar P. W161
Kollorz, Fritz W234
Kolloway, Michael R P599
Kolmsee, Ines W623
Kolobkov, Pavel W256
Kolsky, Shifra A330
Komatsu, Yayoi W432
Kometani, Yoshio W408
Komiya, Satoru W605
Komiyama, Hiroshi W536
Komoda, Masanobu W409
Kon, Kenta W616
Kon, Kenta W278
Konar, Len W558
Konar, Len W562
Kondo, Fusakazu W182
Kondo, Jun W266
Kondo, Takao W83
Konen, Mark E. A531
Konezny, Ronald E. E140
Kong, Cheong Choong W261
Kong, Chiang Boon W261
Kong, Dejun W239
Kong, Dong W128
Kong, Dun W147
Kong, Fanxing W236
Kong, Garheng A615
Kong, Guoliang W141
Kong, Junfeng W477
Kong, Qingping W144
Kong, Qingwei W145
Konidaris, Anastasios G. E31
Konig, Michael L. E63
Konig, Peter W98
Konig, Thomas W207
König, Wolfgang W276
Konishi, Masako W603
Konishi, Toshiyuki W281
Konno, Shiho W370
Konno, Takayuki W612
Konnova, Elena W655
Kono, Haruhiro W316
Kono, Masaaki W345
Konold, Aina E. E344
Konow, Amy L. A397
Konrad, Christian W627
Kontogouris, Venetia W473
Kontselidze, Archil W329
Koo, Bon-Joon W366
Koo, Chie Min (Christopher) A878
Koo, Chie Min (Christopher) E409
Kooijman, Wim W22
Kooman, Kevin J. E301
Koong, Chua Sock W481
Koonin, Steven R. E543
Koontz, Craig C. A528
Koontz, Craig C. E258
Koors, Jerry F. A681
Koors, Jerry F. E318
Koosed, Philip E473
Kooyman, John W. A269
Kopcho, Darcy P586
Kopf, MaryKay W4
Kopischke, Leanne C. A415
Kopischke, Leanne C. E194
Koplin, Neal D. A816
Kopnisky, Jack L. A1113
Kopp, Rochelle W413
Kopra, Panu W427

Koraleski, John J. A663
Korbel, Sandy A37
Korbel, Sandy E14
Korde, Kishore E10
Kordestani, Omid R. A1047
Koren, Moshe W78
Koretz, Barry R. A500
Koretz, Barry R. E246
Korkiakoski, Anne W348
Korkmaz, Dogan W620
Korkmaz, Ozcal W619
Korman, Harry A. A1093
Korn, Jeffrey G. E129
Korn, Steven T. E287
Kornasiewicz, Stan E19
Kornfeld, Allan E221
Kornhaber, Ari P. E173
Kornitzer, Clive W462
Korol, Boris Mihaylovich W617
Korosue, Hiroyoshi A1034
Korsanos, Antonia E430
Korsch, Marija G. W3
Korsh, Les B. A806
Kortlang, Benjamin John E163
Kortman, Kelley A231
Korvenranta, Markku W427
Korzekwinski, Francis W. A439
Kosa, E. Gene E99
Kosacz, Barbara A. E545
Kosaka, Tatsuro W402
Kosasa, Paul J. A219
Kosecoff, Jacqueline B. A924
Kosecoff, Jacqueline B. E260
Koseff, Stephen W310
Koshi, Naomi W550
Koshiba, Mitsunobu W297
Koshiishi, Fusaki W345
Koshijima, Keisuke W330
Koshikawa, Kazuhiro W439
Koshkin, Joe D. E264
Koskull, Casper von W446
Koskull, Casper Wilhelm von A246
Kosokabe, Takeshi W185
Kosonen, Mikko W340
Kosowsky, J. Allen A1028
Koss, Kristen K P542
Kossover, Gregory H. A378
Kostalnick, Chuck A97
Kostas, Odysseas E272
Koster, Barbara G. A856
Koster, Christopher A. A216
Koster, John P446
Kostin, Andrey L. W329
Kosturos, William A984
Kosturos, William E476
Kosuge, Yasuharu W659
Kotagiri, Seetarama W379
Kotary, David C. E247
Kotche, Keith A774
Kotche, Keith E360
Kotchka, Claudia W371
Koten, Martijn van W458
Kotera, Yasuo W453
Kothandaraman, Badrinarayanan E163
Kotick, Robert A. A13
Kotler, Arie E35
Kotohda, Minoru W319
Kottman, Bill P210
Kotwal, Shailesh M. A1082
Kotz, Christian W171

COMBINED HOOVER'S HANDBOOK INDEX OF EXECUTIVES

```
A = AMERICAN BUSINESS
E = EMERGING COMPANIES
P = PRIVATE COMPANIES
W = WORLD BUSINESSS
```

Kotzbauer, Michael W162
Kou, Youmin W144
Koumoto, Kunihito W616
Koury, Jaime A. El W265
Koutsaftes, George A530
Koutsos, John A. A372
Koutsos, John A. E167
Kovachka-Dimitrova, Monika W517
Kovalchuk, Boris Yurievich W308
Kovaleski, Charles J. A774
Kovarik, Robert C. A625
Kovler, Benjamin E239
Kowalczyk, Andrew S. A724
Kowalski, Robert W449
Kowlzan, Mark W. A799
Koyanagi, Stan H. W460
Koyano, Akiko W356
Koza, Eric P56
Kozaczka, Rebecca S. E537
Kozanian, Hagop H. A1010
Kozel, Edward R. W443
Kozlak, Jodeen A. A900
Kozlak, Jodeen A. A694
Kozlak, Jodeen A. A594
Kozlov, Hersh A1014
Kozlov, Hersh E488
Kozlowski, Damian M. A1014
Kozlowski, Damian M. E488
Kozlowski, Daniel R. E402
Kozy, William A. E119
Kozyra, William L. A57
Kraats, Robert Jan van de W489
Krabill, Anthony J. A489
Kraemer, Harry M. Jansen A625
Kraemer, Peter W40
Kraft, Brian A37
Kraft, Brian E14
Kraft, Robert O. E317
Kraft, Stefan W98
Kraft, Timothy Richard E443
Krakauer, Andrew A. E484
Krakauer, Mary Louise A349
Krakauer, Mary Louise E75
Krakauer, Mary Louise E319
Krakowsky, Philippe A570
Kralingen, Bridget A. van A1037
Kralingen, Bridget A. van W507
Kralowetz, Donna A986
Kramer, Adam M. A595
Kramer, Christina W119
Kramer, Francis J. E266
Kramer, Holly S. W651
Kramer, Kelly A. A473
Kramer, Lewis A613
Kramer, Michael R. A688
Kramer, Michael R. E323
Kramer, Nancy Jean E306
Kramer, Richard J. A483
Kramer, Richard J. A934
Kramer, Robert G. E157
Kramer, Ronald J. E242
Kramer, William J. A420
Kramer, William J. E197
Krammer, Peter W562

Krammer, Rudolf W544
Krane, Hilary K. A743
Krane, Spencer D. A399
Krantz, Donald G. E400
Krantz, Theodor E105
Krapek, Karl J. A856
Krapf, Josef W98
Krarup, Lars W348
Krasna, Beth W88
Krasnoperova, Tatiana W655
Kratz, Owen E. E250
Krauel, Jose Maria Egea W423
Kraus, Larry E360
Kraus, Timothy R. A313
Krause, Douglas P. A351
Krause, Douglas P. E150
Krause, Jack E305
Krause, Kim E358
Krause, L. William A279
Krause, Stacy D. E286
Krause, Steven T. E189
Krause, Thomas H. W280
Krauss, George H. A693
Krauss, Seth D. A367
Krausz, Keira P405
Kravchenko, Kirill W256
Kravchenko, Vyacheslav Mikhailovich W476
Kravis, Marie-Josee W373
Kravis, Marie-Josee W486
Kravitz, Hal E88
Kravtsova, Yanina A. E169
Krebber, Markus W510
Krebber, Monika W207
Kreft, Alfred John E291
Kreger, David E102
Krehbiel, Anne E. E293
Krehbiel, Bruce W. A979
Kreienberg, William L. A411
Kreinbihl, Kristofer A. E189
Kreiner, Mordechai W410
Kreis, Melanie W198
Kreis, Wolfgang W563
Kreitzer, Gary A. E271
Kreiz, Ynon A1106
Kremer, Wesley D. A877
Kremser, Craig W. E336
Krenicki, John A325
Kress, Colette M. A761
Kretzmer, William Brian E547
Kreusel, Petra Steffi W199
Kreuzburg, Christa E83
Krevitt, Jennifer A573
Krevlin, Glenn J. E285
Krick, Gerd W249
Kridakon, Chayotid W484
Krieble, William Randolph A422
Krieg, Kenneth J. E70
Krieger, Alexandra W162
Kriegner, Martin W283
Kriesel, Chance E297
Krimbill, H. Michael A741
Krimmel, Diane E455
Kripalani, Ranjit M. A1121
Kripitz, Jeffrey H. E371
Krishna, Arvind A565
Krishna, Arvind A752
Krishna, Varun A571
Krishnan, K. Ranga A282
Krishnan, Meena E227

Krishnan, Ram R. A366
Krishnan, Ramkumar S. A1035
Krishoolndmangalam, Chandrashekar Subramanian W79
Kristiansen, Thore W254
Kristjansson, Gudmundur A693
Kristoffersen, Helle W613
Kristoffersen, Helle W459
Krivosheev, Viktor Mikhailovich W575
Kroeger, Barry F. A539
Kroeger, Shadrak W. W590
Kroes, Neelie A912
Krog, Sverre W204
Krogstad, Jon E46
Krominga, Lynn A116
Kron, Patrick W283
Kron, Patrick W515
Krone, Roger A. A622
Krone, Roger A. A625
Kronen, Petra W174
Kronenberg, Anne C. E287
Kronenfeld, Mark A. E369
Kroner, James R. A367
Krongard, Alvin Bernard A549
Krongard, Cheryl Gordon E10
Kronick, Susan D. A56
Kruckow, Jonathan L. E372
Kruczlnicki, David G. A98
Kruczlnicki, David G. E36
Krueger, Brendan E. E33
Krueger, Doris W196
Krueger, Harald W199
Krueger, William E. A82
Kruger-Steinhoff, Angela W562
Kruger, Errol M. W426
Kruger, Glen L177
Kruger, James D. A727
Kruger, James D. E345
Krukar, Mark S. A271
Krukar, Mark S. E109
Krump, Paul J. W154
Krupinski, Kenneth V. E191
Kruse, Carol H. E517
Kruse, Hans Jakob W270
Kruse, Ronia F. A555
Kruse, Ronia F. E269
Krusi, Alan P. E111
Krusmark, Chris E448
Kruszewski, Ronald J. A977
Kruszewski, Ronald J. E464
Krystopolski, Ruth P483
Krzeminski, Laurel J. A97
Krzeminski, Laurel J. E301
Ksenak, Stephen M. A52
Ku, Hyeon-Mo W352
Kuai, Jeff A1145
Kuang, Kuntang W644
Kubacki, Jeff D. E540
Kubacki, Michael L. A618
Kubacki, Michael L. E290
Kubasik, Christopher E. A613
Kubiak, Tomasz W86
Kubicek, Greg H. A881
Kubitschek, Maria W639
Kubler, Raphael A992
Kubo, Isao W464
Kubo, Robert G. E111
Kubohara, Kazunari W297
Kubota, Shinya W533
Kucer, Susan D. A681

Kucer, Susan D. E318
Kuchiishi, Takatoshi W270
Kuchin, Jonathan E441
Kuchment, Michael W655
Kuck, Brian T. E101
Kuczynski, Stephen E. A952
Kudelski, Andre W486
Kudo, Akiko W439
Kudo, Koshiro W51
Kudo, Teiko W570
Kudo, Teiko W616
Kudo, Yasumi W223
Kudo, Yoko W155
Kudryavtsev, Nikolay W521
Kudryavy, Viktor Vasilyevich W476
Kuehl, Christopher J. A28
Kuehl, Kevin A157
Kuehn, Christopher (Chris) J. W617
Kuehn, Kurt P. A917
Kuehn, Ronald L. A605
Kuehne, Klaus-Michael W355
Kufel, Eric J. E297
Kufen, Thomas W510
Kuffner, James W616
Kuffner, Michael W98
Kuga, Noriyuki W659
Kugel, Janina A612
Kuhl, Shannon M. A844
Kuhl, Shannon M. E394
Kuhlman, Russell B. E418
Kuhlmann, Shirley E107
Kuhlow, John A543
Kuhn, Christian W627
Kuhn, Dennis J. A532
Kuhn, Dennis J. E259
Kuhn, Rebecca A137
Kuhn, Rebecca P59
Kuhn, Susan J. A443
Kuhn, Thomas J. A140
Kuhn, Thorsten W198
Kuhn, Volker W490
Kuhnert, Marcus W397
Kuhnke, Frank W195
Kuhns, Robert M. E490
Kuhnt, Dietmar W270
Kuiken, James M. A271
Kuiken, James M. E109
Kujawa, Rebecca J. A436
Kujawa, Rebecca J. A740
Kukielski, Peter W448
Kukies, Jorg W198
Kukuchka, Ronald G. A816
Kulas, Jason A. A915
Kulaszewicz, Frank C. A902
Kulesa, Amanda E353
Kuleshov, Aleksandr W521
Kulevich, Frederick J. A214
Kulibaev, Timur A. W474
Kull, Matthew A1015
Kull, Matthew P574
Kullman, Ellen J. A481
Kullman, Ellen J. A76
Kullman, Ellen J. A322
Kullmann, Christian W234
Kulper, Michael P1
Kumagai, Toshiyuki W336
Kumar-Choudhury, Roli E297
Kumar, Gopa A402
Kumar, Jaya P552
Kumar, Rajnish W561

COMBINED HOOVER'S HANDBOOK INDEX OF EXECUTIVES

A = AMERICAN BUSINESS
E = EMERGING COMPANIES
P = PRIVATE COMPANIES
W = WORLD BUSINESSS

Kumar, Suresh A1104
Kumazawa, Shinichiro W534
Kumbier, Michelle A. A6
Kumbier, Michelle A. E483
Kume, Yuji W329
Kumihashi, Kazuhiro W293
Kumin, Michael Andrew A1112
Kumin, Solomon J. A965
Kumin, Solomon J. E462
Kummeth, Charles R. E59
Kunes, Christopher W. E99
Kung, Chih-Jung W128
Kung, Jing-Ming E370
Kung, Mimi W479
Kung, Ming-Hsin W583
Kung, Victor W252
Kung, Wan-Chong A398
Kunibe, Takeshi W347
Kunibe, Takeshi W570
Kunii, Hideko W607
Kunimasa, Kimiko W28
Kunisch, Haggai W330
Kuniya, Hiroko W440
Kunkel, William R. A60
Kunst, Michael A825
Kuntz, John F. A854
Kunz, Heidi A27
Kuo, Andrew Ming-Jian W128
Kuo, Tung-Long W206
Kuok, Khoon Chen W649
Kuok, Khoon Ean W649
Kuok, Khoon Hong W649
Kuperman, Jennifer A838
Kuperman, Jennifer E57
Kupper, Elmer Funke W574
Kuppusamy, Karthik A870
Kuraishi, Seiji W285
Kurali, Andreas A825
Kuras, Mary Tuuk A1053
Kurata, Hideyuki W18
Kurata, Yasuharu W270
Kuratomi, Nobuhiko W21
Kuratsu, Yasuyuki W515
Kurbatov, Vladislav W655
Kuri, Luis Alejandro Soberon W35
Kurian, George A729
Kuribrena, Jose Antonio Meade W289
Kurihara, Mitsue W155
Kurilin, Yuri Igorevich W506
Kurisu, Duane K. A219
Kurisu, Toshizo W659
Kurita, Takuya W173
Kuriyama, Yoshifumi W357
Kuriyel, Ralf E415
Kurnick, Robert H. A812
Kurobe, Takashi W609
Kuroda, Haruhiko W82
Kuroda, Yukiko W453
Kurokawa, Hiroyuki W293
Kurosawa, Toshihiko W353
Kuroyanagi, Masafumi W181
Kurren, Faye Watanabe A423
Kurtzweil, John T. E47
Kurumado, Joji W237

Kurunsaari, Minna W340
Kuruöz, Ilker W618
Kurz, Karl F. A325
Kurz, Karl F. E487
Kurzius, Lawrence E. A673
Kurzman, Ceci A1106
Kusakabe, Satoshi W402
Kusaki, Yoriyuki W576
Kuse, Kazushi W51
Kushel, J. Richard A160
Kushibiki, Toshisada W42
Kushida, Shigeki W193
Kushner, Brian A893
Kushwaha, Raj W451
Kusserow, Paul B. K. E20
Kustner, Irena W174
Kusumi, Yuki W465
Kuta, John E409
Kutaragi, Ken W487
Kutovoi, Gheorgy Petrovich W476
Kutz, Jeffrey A30
Kuula, Tapio W247
Kuwabara, Satoko W407
Kuwano, Yukinori W185
Kuwar, Ahmed A. Al W486
Kux, Barbara W277
Kuykendall, James W. A301
Kuykendall, James W. E131
Kuykendall, Ronald E. A913
Kuykendall, Ronald E. E427
Kuznets, Sergey I. W474
Kuznets, Sergey I. W256
Kuznetsov, Stanislav W521
Kvart, Sussi W277
Kvasnicka, Jay A. A1083
Kvisle, Harold N. W133
Kwah, Thiam Hock W649
Kwak, Su Keun W537
Kwan, Savio Ming Sang W111
Kwauk, Walter Teh-Ming W29
Kwek, Leng Hai W286
Kwek, Leng San W286
Kwist, C. M. W274
Kwok, Clement King Man W268
Kwok, Eva L. W133
Kwok, Kin Fun W148
Kwon, Bong Seok W367
Kwon, Oh-Hyun W513
Kwon, Seon-Joo W335
Kwon, Soon-Bum W335
Kwon, Young-Soo W365
Kwon, Young-Soo W367
Kwong, Connie E314
Kwong, Kwok-Leung W179
Kyle, Lanny A. A207
Kyle, Richard G. A950
Kymes, Stacy C. A167
Kymes, Stacy C. E64
Kyncl, Robert A1106
Kyoya, Yutaka W405
Kyoya, Yutaka W237

L

l., Maria Asuncion Aramburuzabala W266
L., Miguel A. Capriles A52
L., S. W558

L'Helias, Sophie W338
L'Estrange, Michael W499
Laaksonen, Juha W247
Laan, Remmert W344
LaBarre, Michael J. E244
Labat, Jerome A221
Laben, Nancy J. A171
LaBenne, Andrew E627
Laber, Gerald J. E18
Laberge, Alice D. W451
Labeyrie, Christian W635
Labozzetta, Anthony J. A854
Labrador, Rafael Matute W643
Labraten, Per Martin W228
Labrecque, Rachel S P42
Labriola, Pietro W592
LaBrosse, Nicole E244
Labruyere-Cuilleret, Diane W125
Lacapria, Michael E173
Lacaze, Claire W338
Lacerda, Francisco de W219
Lacerte, Lawrence E511
Lacey, John S. A180
Lacey, John S. W113
Lacey, William F. A804
Lachance, Carrie A. E271
LaChance, Michael J. E314
Lachapelle, Andre W193
Lachapelle, Lise W295
Lacharriere, Marc Ladreit de W127
Lachenmann, Susanne W303
Lacher, Joseph P. A599
Lachman, M. Leanne A638
Lachs, Andreas W229
Lackey, Thomas E307
LaClair, Jennifer A. A1129
LaClair, Jennifer A. A43
Lacob, Joseph S. E16
Lacorte, Jaime Felix Caruana W68
Lacoste, Patricia W526
Lacoste, Patricia W27
Lacroix, Franck W631
LaCroix, Larry E46
Lacy, Paul A. E402
Lacy, Stephen M. A426
Lacy, Stephen M. A534
Lacy, Stephen M. E202
Ladd, Amy L. A573
Ladd, Delano E247
Ladd, Malissa M. A401
Laderman, Gerald (Gerry) A1062
Laderman, Gerald (Gerry) A599
Ladhani, Holli C. A656
Ladhani, Holli C. A868
Ladowicz, John A774
Ladowicz, John E360
Laegreid, Stig W228
Laffer, Arthur B. E348
Lafferty, Allison C. E357
Lafon, Serge W168
Lafont, Bruno W215
Lafont, Bruno W49
Lafont, Jean-Jacques A468
Lafontaine, Daniel W193
Lafontaine, Henri W215
Lafortune, Andree W193
LaFrance, Shannon Martin E420
LaFreniere, Nora E. A791
Lagacy, Julie A. A1097
Lagacy, Julie A. A907

Lagarde, Michel A1027
Lagarrigue, Emmanuel W524
Lageweg, Paul W111
Lagomarsino, Simone A650
Lagomarsino, Simone E305
Lagomarsino, Simone F. A398
Lagomarsino, Simone F. E246
Lagomasino, Maria Elena A264
Lagomasino, Maria Elena A335
Laguarta, Ramon A817
Laguarta, Ramon A1096
Lagubeau, Julien W127
Laguiche, Bernard de W554
Lagunes, José Octavio Reyes A670
LaHaise, James A. A71
LaHaise, James A. E29
Lahanas, Nicholas (Niko) E90
Lahey, John L. A112
Lahrman, Brok A. A618
Lahrman, Brok A. E290
Lai-bitker, Ellis P166
Lai-Goldman, Myla P. E534
Lai, Francis E323
Lai, Joseph Ming W173
Lai, Lixin W139
Lai, Teck Poh W464
Lai, Yanda W655
Laidlaw, Sam W500
Laidlaw, Sam W499
Laidley, David W80
Laidley, David H. A364
Laigneau, Marianne W215
Laing, Diana M. E81
Laing, Ian R. W299
Laing, Joel E448
Laing, Ronald K. W120
Laird, David A. A592
Laitasalo, Riitta W340
Laixuthai, Adit W334
Lake, Charles Ditmars W319
Lake, David G. A423
Lake, David G. E199
Lake, Marianne A591
Lake, R. Alexander A1136
Lakshminarayanan, Ramesh W271
Lal, Punita W190
Lal, Rohit E426
Lalanne, Jean-Christophe W22
Lally, James Brian A373
Lally, James Brian E168
Lalonde, Kenn W611
Lalor, William P57
Lalwani, Ellen A617
Lalwani, Ellen E289
Lam, Barry W252
Lam, Ching Kam W534
Lam, Donald Yin Shing W268
Lam, Jocelyn Yin Shan W257
Lam, John Cheung-Wah W179
Lam, Katherine Yee Mei W534
Lam, Kun Kin W463
Lam, Kwong Siu W144
Lam, Thomas S. E33
LaMacchia, Timothy P. E177
Lamach, Michael W. A840
Lamade, Lars W517
Lamale, Ellen Z. A397
Lamarche, Gerard W623
Lamarche, Gerard W565
Lamartine, Sandra E49

COMBINED HOOVER'S HANDBOOK INDEX OF EXECUTIVES

A = AMERICAN BUSINESS
E = EMERGING COMPANIES
P = PRIVATE COMPANIES
W = WORLD BUSINESSS

Lamb, Peter E177
Lamb, Scott E. E376
Lamb, William H. A1014
Lamb, William H. E488
Lamba, Sanjiv W369
Lambert, Christiane W174
Lambert, H David P584
Lambert, Jean-Marie W631
Lambert, Jerome W167
Lambert, Leo F. E98
Lambert, Myles J. A176
Lambert, Myles J. A176
Lambert, Pippa W64
Lambert, Roch E313
Lambert, Ty A190
Lambert, Ty E73
Lambertz, Shelly A295
Lambright, Kevin E223
Lameier, Robert T. A397
Lamel, Ira J. E355
Lamkin, Jeffrey B. E361
Lamlieng, Chumpol Na W541
Lamm-Tennant, Joan M. A377
Lamm-Tennant, Joan M. E17
Lamneck, Kenneth T. A558
LaMonica, Susan A248
Lamont, David M. W101
Lamont, Kevin M. E354
Lamont, Robert B. A311
Lamont, William S. A311
LaMontagne, Peter B. E309
Lamothe, Marie-Josee W31
Lamouche, Didier R. W13
Lamoureux, Claude W295
Lampereur, Andrew G. E228
Lampert, Gregory J. E287
Lampman, Michael A. E160
Lampo, Craig A. A79
Lamps, Mark F. E40
Lamsam, Banthoon W334
Lamsam, Banyong W334
Lamsam, Krisada W334
Lamsam, Sujitpan W334
Lamuniere, Pierre W88
Lan, Fusheng W663
Lan, Jia W431
Lanaway, John B. W158
Lancaster, Ivan Tim A421
Lancaster, Ivan Tim E198
Lance, Bill G. A125
Lance, Bill G. E52
Lance, Howard L. E319
Lance, Howard L. E469
Lance, Jean Fitterer A137
Lance, Jean Fitterer P59
Lance, Rodrigo A597
Lance, Ryan M. A452
Lance, Ryan M. A288
Lance, William S. E354
Landau, Ellis A5
Landazuri, Pierre Perez Y. A557
Lande, Rashida La A610
Landel, Michel W187
Landen, Diane N. A719

Landen, Gordana W13
Landes, Jonathan W590
Landgraf, Kurt M. A298
Landiribar, Javier Echenique W11
Landiribar, Jose Javier Echenique W71
Landiribar, Jose Javier Echenique W593
Landis, Christopher S. E99
Landis, Felicia E455
Landis, Gail E333
Landis, Gregory P. E446
Landis, Melvin F. A266
Landman, David E273
Landon, Allan R. A627
Landon, John C. E61
Landrieu, Mary L. E502
Landry, Allison A1143
Landry, Robert E. A882
Landy, James J. A1113
Landy, Katherine A400
Landy, R. Joseph E99
Lane, Alan J. A937
Lane, Alan J. E441
Lane, Amy B. A740
Lane, Amy B. A405
Lane, Amy B. A1030
Lane, Brian E. E111
Lane, Daniel D. (Ron) A407
Lane, H. Merritt A496
Lane, Jeannine J. A893
Lane, Joseph E296
Lane, Kathleen S. A499
Lane, Kenneth W374
Lane, Michael J. E263
Lane, Nicholas E17
Lane, Nick A377
Lane, Peter R. A998
Lane, Peter R. E235
Lane, Raymond J. A514
Lane, Rita S. A914
Lane, Rita S. A80
Lane, Rita S. A613
Lane, Robert A. A519
Lane, Robert A. E256
Lane, Thomas D. E104
Lane, Thomas K. A1114
Lane, Wendy E. E520
Laney, G. Timothy A722
Laney, G. Timothy E339
Lanfear, Dennis M. E106
Lanfre, Melissa A393
Lang, Edward F. E284
Lang, James R. E98
Lang, Johann W98
Lang, Laura W. A1091
Lang, Trevor S. E210
Langa, Doug W450
Langdale, Paul B. A556
Langdale, Paul B. E270
Langdon, J. Howard E336
Lange, Anne W397
Lange, Bertrand W490
Lange, Bob De A26
Lange, Bob De A210
Lange, Martin Holst W450
Lange, Thorsten W427
Langel, Craig A. A474
Langel, Craig A. E230
Langelier, Simon W298
Langer, Jonathan A. E288

Langer, Per W247
Langevin, Eric T. E286
Langford, Kevin T. A681
Langford, Kevin T. E318
Langford, Stephen P73
Langhans, Jarrod E88
Langheim, Thorsten A992
Langheim, Thorsten W199
Langley-hawthorne, Timothy M A1019
Langley-hawthorne, Timothy M P585
Langley, Bryan E210
Langley, James E497
Langoni, Carlos Geraldo W383
Langston, P. Ryan E235
Lanier, Diane H. A504
Lanier, Nikki R. A844
Lanier, Nikki R. E394
Lanigan, Mark W. E308
Lanigan, Susan S. A938
Lanigan, Susan S. E442
Lankler, Douglas M. (Doug) A821
Lannie, P. Anthony A86
Lanning, Mark R. E43
Lansford, Gordon E. A1056
Lansford, Gordon E. E505
Lansing, Gerrit L. E169
Lansing, William J. E183
Lantis, Kelly E102
Lantow, Michelle M. A271
Lantow, Michelle M. E109
Lantrip, Mark S. A952
Lanza, Michael H. A927
Lanza, Michael H. E435
Lanzer, David E. E419
Lao, Marjorie A645
Laourde, Jean-Christophe W168
Lape, Rachael R. A106
Lape, Rachael R. E40
LaPerch, William G. E141
Lapeyre, Pierre F. E169
Lapidus, Sidney A629
LaPlaca, Theresa G A350
LaPlaca, Theresa G E148
LaPlante, Michael A891
LaPlatney, Donald P. E237
LaPlume, Joseph E94
LaPoint, Francene A308
LaPoint, Francene E133
Lapointe, Greg A. A955
Lapointe, Greg A. E456
Lapointe, Jean-Pierre L. (J.P.) E350
laporte, Claudio X. Gonzalez W266
Laporte, Claudio X. Gonzalez W27
LaPrade, Frank G. A198
LaQuinta, Francis A587
Lara, Rodrigo Brand de W73
Laranjeira, Charles E369
Lardy, Eric Michael E72
Larios, Michele M. E418
Larkin, C. Raymond E16
Larkin, D. Keith A401
Larkin, Jep A196
Larkin, Jep E79
Larkin, Kevin T. A398
Larkin, Melissa E451
Larkin, Michele L. E189
Larnach, Fiona W487
Larocca, Prue B. A28
LaRocco, Michael E. A966
Laroche, Michael J. A907

Larochelle, Steven R. A372
Larochelle, Steven R. E167
Larocque, Peter A999
LaRosa, Joseph J. A882
LaRossa, Ralph A. A858
LaRouche, Michael W. A920
Laroyia, Varun A1075
Laroyia, Varun A643
Larrabee, Steve A349
Larrain, Bernardo Matte W217
Larrain, Rodrigo W132
Larranaga, Arantza Estefania W493
Larre, Andres Bianchi W217
Larrimer, Karen L. A834
Larsen, Christine E. W119
Larsen, Kendall E527
Larsen, Kirk T. A726
Larsen, Leif F. W330
Larsen, Marshall O. A401
Larsen, Marshall O. A147
Larsen, Marshall O. E10
Larsen, Michael M. A553
Larsen, Sallie R. A648
Larson, Anthony E340
Larson, Betty D. A458
Larson, Bruce M. A203
Larson, Gloria C. A1079
Larson, Gregory M. A228
Larson, James R. E30
Larson, James R. E307
Larson, Joshua W247
Larson, Keith R. E353
Larson, Matthew (Matt) S. A581
Larson, Michael A358
Larson, Michael A892
Larson, Michael W244
Larson, Randall J. A783
Larson, Robert Bruce A35
Larson, Shane E340
Larson, Sherry Jean E236
Larson, Tim E447
Larson, Todd C. A886
Larson, Todd L. E61
Larsson, Benny W60
Larsson, Claes W548
Larsson, Mari W641
Larsson, Stefan A864
LaRue, Alex E221
Lasch-Weber, Beate W192
Laschinger, Mary A. A597
Laschinger, Mary A. A737
Laschinger, Mary A. A1086
Laschkar, Henri-Paul W495
Lashier, Mark E. A826
Lashley, Richard J. A124
Lashway, Heather A152
Laskawy, Phil W123
Laskawy, Philip A. A917
Laskey, Ryan W. A313
Lasota, Stephen A. E125
Lassiter, Wright L. A870
Lastortras, Juan Rosell W423
Lategan, Theunie W562
Latek, Kevin Paul E237
Latella, Robert N. A411
Laterza, Marco E418
Lathan, Corinna E402
Lathi, Dinesh S. E209
Lathion-Zweifel, Sandra W581
Latimer, Luke A. A418

HOOVER'S HANDBOOK OF EMERGING COMPANIES 2023

COMBINED HOOVER'S HANDBOOK INDEX OF EXECUTIVES

A = AMERICAN BUSINESS
E = EMERGING COMPANIES
P = PRIVATE COMPANIES
W = WORLD BUSINESSS

Latimer, Luke A. E206
Latimer, Luke A. E195
Latkovic, Christopher E49
LaTorre, Craig M. A663
Latreille, Stephen K. A557
Latta, David A37
Latta, David E14
Latta, Marcia Sloan E184
Latta, Robert P. A1120
Latta, Robert P. E535
Latypov, Ural Alfretovich W506
Lau, Don Jin Tin W648
Lau, Frederic Suet-Cjiu W179
Lau, Hak Woon W355
Lau, Lawrence J. W158
Lau, Lawrence Juen-Yee W20
Lau, Martin Chi Ping W636
Lau, Martin Chi Ping W324
Lau, Martin Chi Ping W596
Lau, Martin Chi Ping W202
Lau, Michele E234
Lau, Russell J. A398
Lau, Siu Ki W240
Lau, Wah Sum W355
Laub, Jeffrey A187
Laube, Lisa G. E64
Lauber, Charles T. E226
Lauber, Scott J. A1114
Lauder, Jane A620
Lauder, Leonard A. A620
Lauder, Ronald S. A620
Lauder, William P. A620
Lauderback, Brenda J. E448
Lauenroth-Mago, Joerg W390
Lauer, Gary L. A408
Lauer, Trevor F. A345
Lauer, Trevor F. A343
Laughlin, Scott E227
Laughter, John E. A323
Laughton, Kim P487
Laughton, Mary Beth A1018
Lauhon, Blaine C. E90
Lauk, Kurt J. W379
Laulis, Julia M. A23
Laulis, Julia M. E72
Launay, Romain W526
Launer, Cindy L. E349
Laura, Anthony E370
Laurence, Andrew M. E219
Laurin, Peter W228
Lauritzen, Bruce R. A429
Laursen, Thomas E. A1151
Laury, Veronique W111
Laury, Veronique W550
Laut, Steve W. W120
Lautenbach, Marc B. A195
Lauvergeon, Anne L. A62
Lauzon, Marcel W193
Lavallee, Heather H. A1098
Lavan, Maryanne R. A643
Lavan, Maryanne R. E334
Lavan, Robert M. E501
LaVange, Lisa E444
Lavelle, Kate S. E539

Lavelle, Mark L. A945
Lavelle, Mark L. E450
Lavender, Kevin P. A410
Laver, Sue W596
Laverne, Robert G. E56
Lavernos, Barbara W358
Lavey, Richard W. A499
LaVigne, Bruce G. E236
LaVigne, Mark S. E160
Lavin, Pablo Granito W70
LaViolette, Paul A. A361
Lavizzo-Mourey, Risa J. A560
Lavizzo-Mourey, Risa J. A684
Lavizzo-Mourey, Risa J. A458
Law, Alson Chun-tak W80
Law, David W481
Law, Fanny Fan Chiu Fun W151
Law, Melissa E72
Law, Quinn Yee Kwan W105
Law, Scott A. A1151
Lawal, Kikelomo W119
Lawal, Mohammed A175
Lawal, Mohammed E66
Lawande, Sachin S. E105
Lawer, Betsy A428
Lawer, David A428
Lawhon, W. D. "Bill" E515
Lawler, John T. A444
Lawler, Mary K. A553
Lawler, Robert Douglas (Doug) A295
Lawless, Robert J. A292
Lawley, Scott J. E206
Lawlis, V. Bryan E61
Lawlor, Brian G. E432
Lawlor, David A597
Lawrence, Jake W84
Lawrence, James A. A118
Lawrence, Kevin A125
Lawrence, Kevin E52
Lawrence, Norma J. E67
Lawrence, Paul J. A277
Lawrence, Stephen J. A1115
Lawrence, Stephen J. E533
Lawrence, Steven Paul A10
Lawrenz, Jurgen W33
Laws, Christopher W. A367
Lawson-Hall, Cathia W637
Lawson, Ann K. A741
Lawson, Ann K. E349
Lawson, Brian D. W112
Lawson, David C. A270
Lawson, David C. E109
Lawson, Erik A. E102
Lawson, John P. E206
Lawson, John R. A1033
Lawson, John R. E493
Lawson, John W P675
Lawson, Michael A. A723
Lawther, Robin W374
Lawton, Catherine A. A596
Lawton, Catherine A. E286
Lawton, Harry A. (Hal) A1035
Lawton, Patrick S. E532
Lax, Rosalinde W398
Laxton, Stephen D. A759
Layade, Nashira W. A879
Layade, Nashira W. A878
Layas, Mohammed Husain W47
Layden, Donald W. A726
Layden, Mickey E E195

Layer, Matthew P. E293
Layfield, Diana W57
Layman, John R. A136
Laytart, David P345
Layton, Brent D. A216
Laz, Huseyin Etem E458
Laz, Mustafa E458
Lazar, Jack R. A893
Lazar, Melvin F. E34
Lazar, Robert H. E177
Lazar, Victoria W590
Lazarev, Peter Ivanovich W506
Lazari, Octavio de W69
Lazarus, Anne A251
Lazarus, Anne P137
Lazarus, Edward E452
Lazarus, Rochelle B. A787
Lazarus, Rochelle B. A161
Lazat, Beatrice W338
Lazo, Theresa S. E372
Lazzari, Melanie A. A910
Lazzaris, Diane E. A1117
Le, Tan W487
Lea, Doretha F. A802
Leach, Michael R. E18
Leach, Timothy (Tim) A. A288
Leach, Timothy J. E234
Leader, Martin R. A940
Leahy, Christine A. A997
Leahy, Christine A. A214
Leal, Guilherme Muller W69
Leao, Mario Roberto Opice W72
Leap, Arnold P. (Arnie) E1
Leary, Robert G. A248
Leary, Robert G. W308
Leasure, Robert W. E273
Leatherberry, Antoinette R. A1153
Leatherberry, William J. E350
Leavell, Christopher M. A413
Leavitt, Harvey H. E515
Leavitt, Jesse A1119
Leavitt, Michael O. A62
Leavy, David A332
LeBeau, Michael E. E367
Lebel, Joseph J. A768
Lebel, Joseph J. E359
LeBlanc, Claude L. A52
LeBlanc, Glen W99
Leblanc, Pierre W193
Leblanc, Stephen P190
LeBon, Cherylyn Harley E120
Lebot, Diony W548
Leboucher, Nathalie W27
LeBoutillier, John W295
Lebowitz, Gavin A742
Lebowitz, Gavin P393
Lecea, Rafael Salinas Martínez De W618
Léchevin, Bruno W215
Lechleiter, John C. A444
Lechleiter, Richard A. A978
Lechleiter, Richard A. E465
Lechner, Eduard W628
Lecorvaisier, Fabienne W515
Lecorvaisier, Fabienne W357
Lecorvaisier, Fabienne W511
Ledbetter, Steve C. E437
Lede, Cornelis J. A. van W22
Lederer, James P. E166

Lederer, John A. A1102
Lederer, Paul R. E145
Lederman, Baruch W312
Ledgerwood, William C. A596
Ledgerwood, William C. E286
Ledgett, Richard H. A651
Ledohowski, Leo W80
LeDonne, Gary A. E336
LeDoux, Mark A. E342
Leduc, Michel R. W570
Leduc, Robert F. A583
Lee, Adrianne E368
Lee, Bonita I. A497
Lee, Brian J. A480
Lee, Bruce K. A507
Lee, Bruce K. E248
Lee, Byeong-cheol W537
Lee, Byung Kook W294
Lee, Carter P. E368
Lee, Chae-Woong W513
Lee, Chang Sil W367
Lee, Chang-Ken W128
Lee, Chang-Kwon W335
Lee, Chi-Jen W206
Lee, Christen E.J. E288
Lee, Conway Kong Wai W150
Lee, Conway Kong Wai W648
Lee, Cynthia S. A348
Lee, Cynthia S. A347
Lee, Cynthia S. A345
Lee, Danielle M. A140
Lee, Dannis Cheuk Yin W257
Lee, Daryl A570
Lee, David C. E495
Lee, David M. E486
Lee, Deborah W170
Lee, Debra L. A660
Lee, Debra L. A850
Lee, Delman W80
Lee, Dong Kyu W294
Lee, Een-kyoon W537
Lee, Erica A400
Lee, Esther A254
Lee, Eugene (Gene) I. A17
Lee, Eugene (Gene) I. A316
Lee, Felitia A660
Lee, Franki E383
Lee, Gang-Cheol W352
Lee, George Lap Wah W463
Lee, Gilbert Man Lung W268
Lee, Gyu-Min W366
Lee, Hau L. A999
Lee, Heyn-Bin W351
Lee, Hsien Yang W504
Lee, In-Ho W513
Lee, Irene Yun Lien W128
Lee, Irene Yun Lien W268
Lee, Irene Yun-lien W286
Lee, Jae-Yong W513
Lee, James E88
Lee, James J. E162
Lee, James K. E253
Lee, Janet E31
Lee, Janice W513
Lee, Jeannie E141
Lee, Ji-Yeun E388
Lee, Jin Ming W240
Lee, Jin-Yi W252
Lee, Joann E. E199
Lee, John Hin Hock W380

HOOVER'S HANDBOOK OF EMERGING COMPANIES 2023

A = AMERICAN BUSINESS
E = EMERGING COMPANIES
P = PRIVATE COMPANIES
W = WORLD BUSINESSS

Lee, John T.C. E329
Lee, John T.C. E105
Lee, Jong-Hwan W351
Lee, Joon A1080
Lee, Joon P667
Lee, Joonho J. A400
Lee, Joyce Wong A878
Lee, Joyce Wong E409
Lee, Judy W190
Lee, Junho W205
Lee, Katherine W99
Lee, Kee-Man W352
Lee, Kirk L. A492
Lee, Kirk L. E243
Lee, Kitty W299
Lee, Kok Kwan W156
Lee, Kong Lam W484
Lee, Kun-Hee W513
Lee, Lori A105
Lee, Lori M. A366
Lee, Margaret Singer A188
Lee, Margaret Singer E69
Lee, Marian Dicus A730
Lee, Mark H. A211
Lee, Mark H. E84
Lee, Melanie W515
Lee, Myles P. W617
Lee, Rannie Wah Lun W268
Lee, Rose A530
Lee, Rose A349
Lee, Rose Wai Mun W286
Lee, Sang Young E375
Lee, Sang-Hoon W513
Lee, Seng Wee W464
Lee, Seok-Tae W652
Lee, Sue W216
Lee, Sunggyu E352
Lee, Susan Yun E129
Lee, Tai-Chi W206
Lee, Ted A1145
Lee, Tih Shih W464
Lee, Victor K. E331
Lee, Vivian S. A1151
Lee, Wai Fai W628
Lee, William A249
Lee, William P126
Lee, Won Hee W294
Lee, Won-Duk W652
Lee, Woo-Yeul W335
Lee, Yong Guk W537
Lee, Yoon-jae W537
Lee, Yoon-Woo W513
Lee, Young-Ha W366
Lee, Yuan Siong W19
Lee, Yuchun A1089
Lee, Yun J. E220
Leech, Ted A. E223
Leeming, Rosemary P236
Leemputte, Peter G. E313
Leen, Steve E46
Leenaars, Eli A198
Leeper, Elmer K. E506
Leeper, Terry A770
Leer, Steven F. A747

Leestma, Martin J. E457
LeFebvre, Dale A638
Lefebvre, Dominique W174
Leferve, Deborah L. Hall A1133
Leferve, Deborah L. Hall E541
Lefever, Willis R. E158
LeFevre, Cyril E81
Lefevre, Deb Hall A964
Lefevre, Deborah Hall W30
Lefkowitz, Robin A749
Legault, Frederic W399
Leger, Jeff W371
Leger, Nicholas J. E348
Legg, Benson Everett A940
Legg, Michael P638
Legg, Sarah W371
Legg, Sarah Catherine W371
Legge, Jeffrey Dale A249
Legge, Jeffrey Dale E99
Leggett, Karen A. W382
Leggio, Anthony L. A1038
Leggio, Anthony L. E496
Leggio, Anthony L. E517
Lego, Catherine P. A619
Legorreta, Pablo E425
Legrand, Jeff P226
Legrand, Marc W213
Legros, Éric W125
Leh, Tan Hak W261
Lehman, Daniel L. A199
Lehman, Gary J. A427
Lehman, Gary J. E203
Lehman, Gregg Owen E271
Lehman, John I. Von A64
Lehman, Katherine A. A723
Lehman, Michael E. A694
Lehman, Robert W. A1121
Lehman, Ronda P345
Lehman, Samuel P671
Lehman, Terry L. E98
Lehmann, Daniel John A235
Lehmann, Frauke W251
Lehmann, Gail A1040
Lehmann, Gail E499
Lehmkuhl, Gregory E9
Lehmus, Matti W427
Lehner, Friedrich W628
Lehner, Ulrich W199
Lehnertz, Rod P612
Lehti, Matti W247
Lehtoranta, Ari W348
Lei, Bangjing W663
Lei, Xiaoyi W528
Leibholz, Dan A81
Leibinger-Kammueller, Nicola W543
Leibler, Kenneth R. A380
Leibold, Carla A. A307
Leibold, Carla A. E133
Leibowitz, Arthur N. (Abbie) E436
Leibowitz, Shelley B. A713
Leibson, Marie T. A845
Leibson, Marie T. E395
Leichtner, Scott J P241
Leide, Dominic E473
Leiden, Jeffrey M. A1089
Leidwinger, Kevin James A1065
Leighton, Allan W160
Leighton, Colleen W80
Leighton, F. Thomson E12
Leighty, Scott P50

Leinbach, Tracy A. A503
Leinbach, Tracy A. A1087
Leinenbach, Keith A. A472
Leinenbach, Keith A. E230
Leininger, Edward A. E184
Leinonen, Jukka W594
Leitch, Glenn R. A534
Leite, Sharon M. E305
Leith, Rob A. G. W426
Leitl, Christoph W453
Leitzell, Jeffrey R. A375
Leland, D. Mark E171
Leland, D. Mark E391
Leland, David A231
Lelieveld, Rob J. W. W442
Lema, Eduardo Perez de W382
LeMahieu, Kevin M. A125
LeMahieu, Kevin M. E52
Lemaitre, Daniel T. E233
LeMaitre, George W. E297
Lemaitre, Phillippe E249
Lemane, Thierry W238
Lemann, Paulo Alberto W40
Lemarchand, Agnes W165
Lemarchand, Agnes W554
Lemarié, Marie W213
Lemasney, Mark A436
LeMasters, Robb A. E70
Lemay, Stephane W480
Lemek, Brian J. A913
Lemek, Brian J. E427
Lemercier, Jean-Luc A361
Lemierre, Jean W104
Lemierre, Jean W613
Lemieux, Catherine A399
LeMieux, George S. E212
LeMire, Anne M. A68
Lemke, Eric T. A703
Lemke, Eric T. E327
Lemke, Kevin D. A37
Lemke, Kevin D. E14
Lemmon, Mark D. E57
Lemoine, Bernard W213
Lemoine, David A. E277
Lemoine, Mathilde W125
Lemon, Paulette A527
Lemonis, Marcus A. A195
Lemppenau, Joachim W639
Lempres, Elizabeth C. A465
Lempres, Elizabeth C. W262
Lempres, Michael T. A937
Lempres, Michael T. E441
Lenehan, Pamela F. E347
Lenehan, William H. A654
Lenehan, William H. E217
Leng, Xuesong W663
Lengler, Peter W517
Lenhard, Felix W642
Lenhardt, David K. A209
Leniski, Stephanie R. A618
Leniski, Stephanie R. E290
Lenman, Alasdair W662
Lennartz-Pipenbacher, Ulrike W198
Lenner, Marc J. A1086
Lenner, Marc J. E516
Lennon, Carolan W21
Lennon, Gary W419
Lenny, Richard H. A286
Lenny, Richard H. A553
Lenny, Richard H. A675

Lentsch, William P. A323
Lentz, Dennis W273
Lentz, James E. A639
Lentz, Mary L. A554
Lentz, Mary L. E268
Lenz, Michael C. A405
Leodler, Kathy D. E490
Leombruno, Todd M. A804
Leon, Ernesto Zedillo Ponce de A37
Leon, Jonathan A. A794
Leonard, Christopher A389
Leonard, Christopher P219
Leonard, Colin M. E283
Leonard, David J. A357
Leonard, Deborah L. A400
Leonard, Edmund T. E69
Leonard, James C. A410
Leonard, Jeffery A. E13
Leonard, John M. A576
Leonard, Keith R. A573
Leonard, Robert M. A1043
Leonard, Thomas C. E286
Leonard, Travis E. E260
Leonardi, Phil P398
Leonardi, Thomas B. A1037
Leone, Deborah R. A787
Leone, Flavia W623
Leonetti, Olivier C. A1148
Leonetti, Olivier C. W327
Leonetti, Olivier C. W209
Leong, Chris W524
Leong, Dennis W377
Leong, Horn Kee W649
Leong, Justin E417
Leong, Kwok Nyem W484
Leonsis, Theodore J. A62
Leonti, Joseph R. A804
Leopold, Diane G. A1094
Leopold, Diane G. A340
Leopold, Diane G. A659
Leost, Jacques W161
Lepage, Philippe W225
Lepage, Solenne W22
Lepasoon, Karin W548
Lepetit, Marie-Christine W215
Lepinay, Philippe W601
Lepine, Beverley A5
Leppänen, Heikki W348
Leppert, Edward J. A854
Leppert, Thomas C. A438
Lepsøe, Birthe Cecilie W558
Lequient, Frederic E519
Lerberghe, Rose-Marie Van W107
Lerberghe, Rose-Marie Van W127
Lerman, Bradley E. A677
Lerner, Bruce A. A521
Lerner, Caryn A. W287
Lerner, Ida W204
Lerner, Joseph C. A372
Lerner, Joseph C. E167
Lerner, Scott E. E50
Lerner, Steven J. A1086
Lerner, Steven J. E521
Lerner, Yishai A588
Leroux, Monique F. W31
Leroux, Monique F. W99
Leroux, Monique F. W168
Leroux, Sylvain W122
Leroy, Didier W616
Leroy, Dominique A992

COMBINED HOOVER'S HANDBOOK INDEX OF EXECUTIVES

A = AMERICAN BUSINESS
E = EMERGING COMPANIES
P = PRIVATE COMPANIES
W = WORLD BUSINESSS

Leroy, Dominique W199
Leroy, Dominique W165
LeRoy, Spencer A774
Lesar, David J. A218
Lesavoy, Bernard M. E156
Lescoeur, Bruno W215
Lesjak, Catherine A. A462
Lesjak, Catherine A. A458
Lesler, Michael E364
Leslie, Nadine A854
Lesny, Maciej W389
Lessard, Laurier James E67
Lester, George W. A207
Lester, Harry T. A1033
Lester, Harry T. E493
Lester, Jeff P104
Lester, Matthew W89
Lester, Susan E. A800
Letelier, Mauricio Baeza W314
Leten, Ronnie W4
Leten, Ronnie W228
Letham, Dennis J. A1005
Letham, Dennis J. E180
Letier, A. Scott A1142
Leto, Francis J. A1138
Leto, Francis J. E544
Lett, J. David A472
Lett, J. David E230
Letta, Enrico W486
Lettieri, Richard J. E190
Letwin, Stephen J. J. E253
Leu, Karen A187
Leue, Torsten W269
Leue, Torsten W586
Leukert, Bernd W195
Leung, Andrew Kwan Yuen W179
Leung, Andrew Wing Lok W268
Leung, Antony Kam Chung W138
Leung, Don T.P. E323
Leung, Sandra ("Sandy") A178
Leung, Simon Y. A999
Leupold, Samuel W222
Leupold, Samuel Georg Friedrich W523
Leupp, Jay Paul E247
Leuschen, David M. E169
Levatich, Matthew S. A366
Levendos, Christopher (Chris) D. A301
Levenhagen, Eric E471
Levenick, Stuart L. A485
Levenick, Stuart L. A371
Levens, Jerry L. A495
Levenson, Bruce E481
Levenson, Robert J. E374
Levenson, Rodger A1138
Levenson, Rodger E544
Lévêque, Didier W127
Levesque, Julie W420
Levesque, Paul E543
Levi, Barbara W499
LeVier, Jack K. A796
Levin, Eric J. A1106
Levin, Joseph A696
Levin, Joseph E261

Levin, Justine P569
Levin, Uri W311
Levine, Jeremy S. E386
Levine, Paul M. A1149
Levine, Peter P655
LeVine, Suzan W486
Levine, Uri W304
Levingston, Charles D. A350
Levingston, Charles D. E148
Levinson, Andrew J. E54
Levinson, Arthur D. A89
Levinson, Sara L. A654
Levitt, Brian M. A919
Levitt, Brian M. W611
Levitt, Randall J. E79
Levorato, Claudio W627
Levy, Alan J. A573
Levy, Avraham W311
Levy, Carlos W266
Levy, Caroline E88
Levy, Ellen D. E531
Levy, Grant A. E10
Lévy, Jean-Bernard W215
Levy, Jeffrey M. A280
Levy, Jeffrey M. E113
Levy, Maurice W486
Levy, Michael T. E301
Levy, Ofer W78
Levy, Paul S. A184
Levy, Reynold A431
Levy, Reynold E205
Levy, Susan C. A748
Levy, Tao E312
Lew, Indu P472
Lewent, Judy C. A716
Lewiner, Colette W107
Lewiner, Colette W215
Lewiner, Colette W161
Lewis-Hall, Freda C. A821
Lewis, Aaron E455
Lewis, Adam M. E383
Lewis, Alton B. E199
Lewis, Aylwin B. A660
Lewis, Aylwin B. A1099
Lewis, Cindi H. A71
Lewis, Cindi H. E29
Lewis, Cindy K. E8
Lewis, Clinton A. A568
Lewis, Clunet R. E471
Lewis, Dave A817
Lewis, Fred J. E79
Lewis, George R. W360
Lewis, Gregory P. A530
Lewis, Holden A394
Lewis, Jim W. E291
Lewis, Joan M. E308
Lewis, John D. A435
Lewis, John D. E210
Lewis, Jonathan W228
Lewis, Karla R. A887
Lewis, Karla R. A483
Lewis, Kevin A. W30
Lewis, Lee A516
Lewis, Lemuel E. A338
Lewis, M. Scott A497
Lewis, Margaret G. A401
Lewis, Margaret G. E530
Lewis, Mark G. E61
Lewis, Martha S. E452
Lewis, Mitchell B. E234

Lewis, Oliver E. A271
Lewis, Oliver E. E109
Lewis, Patricia L. A1075
Lewis, Patricia L. A622
Lewis, Patrick W364
Lewis, Patrick W364
Lewis, Raquelle W. A218
Lewis, Ric W360
Lewis, Rich A130
Lewis, Ronald J. A123
Lewis, Sara Grootwassink A1127
Lewis, Sara Grootwassink A452
Lewis, Scott R. A502
Lewis, Sheri A112
Lewis, Sian W164
Lewis, Stephen W596
Lewis, Stuart Wilson W195
Lewis, Tom A397
Lewis, Tom E187
Lewis, W. Ashton A1033
Lewis, W. Ashton E492
Lewis, William J. A531
Lewis, William J. E259
Lewis, William M. A16
Lewnes, Ann A15
Ley, Alma Lily A796
Ley, James P177
Leysen, Thomas W623
Leyva, Mauricio A600
Lheureux, Pascal W174
Lhoest, Frank W655
Li, Adrian David Man-kiu W80
Li, An W529
Li, An W530
Li, Arthur Kwok Cheung W80
Li, Aubrey Kwok Sing W355
Li, Aubrey Kwok-sing W80
Li, Baizheng W100
Li, Buhai W272
Li, Buqing W664
Li, Celina P406
Li, Changqing W663
Li, Chaochun W144
Li, Chong W152
Li, Chujun W88
Li, Daniel Dong Hui W256
Li, Daocheng W516
Li, David Kwok-po W144
Li, David Kwok-po W80
Li, Dazhuang W34
Li, Defang W145
Li, Dong Sheng W597
Li, Dongxiang W528
Li, Fei W477
Li, Fei-Fei A1047
Li, Fei-Fei W95
Li, Feng W274
Li, Fengbao W98
Li, Fushen W152
Li, Fushen W151
Li, Gang W139
Li, Godwin Chi Chung W268
Li, Guoan W179
Li, Guodong W139
Li, Guohui W148
Li, Guoqiang W663
Li, Haifeng W291
Li, Hongshuan W261
Li, Hongwu W644
Li, Hua W327

Li, Huagang W268
Li, Hualin W355
Li, Huidi W143
Li, Jennifer Xin-Zhe W6
Li, Jennifer Xinzhe W242
Li, Jennifer Xinzhe W286
Li, Jiamin W466
Li, Jian W663
Li, Jianmin W291
Li, Jianqiang W307
Li, Jianxiong W431
Li, Jianying W574
Li, Jiashi W150
Li, Jifeng W140
Li, Jinfen W268
Li, Jing W662
Li, Jingchao W100
Li, Jingren W356
Li, Jipeng W656
Li, Jun W153
Li, Kun W662
Li, Li W274
Li, Li W559
Li, Liangfu W656
Li, Maoguang W272
Li, Meocre Kwon-wing W80
Li, Miao W152
Li, Min W202
Li, Ming W529
Li, Ming W100
Li, Mingbo W98
Li, Mingguang W142
Li, Natasha E49
Li, Pengyun W291
Li, Qian W117
Li, Qiangqiang W152
Li, Qin W572
Li, Qingping W156
Li, Qingwen W153
Li, Qiqiang W431
Li, Quan W431
Li, Quancai W664
Li, Qunfeng W40
Li, Robin Yanhong W67
Li, Ronghua W143
Li, Ruoshan W512
Li, Samson Kai-cheong W80
Li, Sen W138
Li, Shan W176
Li, Shaozhong W572
Li, Sheng W529
Li, Shipeng W268
Li, Shipeng W660
Li, Shu Fu W256
Li, Shuhua W144
Li, Shuqing W291
Li, Stephen Charles Kwok-sze W80
Li, Susan A689
Li, Susan J. A34
Li, Tao W150
Li, Tongbin W150
Li, Victor Tzar Kuoi W286
Li, Wanjun W261
Li, Wei W542
Li, Wei W529
Li, Wei W660
Li, Weijian W603
Li, Xianglu W431
Li, Xiaobo W40
Li, Xiaojia E311

A = AMERICAN BUSINESS
E = EMERGING COMPANIES
P = PRIVATE COMPANIES
W = WORLD BUSINESSS

Li, Xiaojian W528
Li, Xiaosheng W147
Li, Xin W148
Li, Xinbo W140
Li, Xingchun W291
Li, Xiuhua W256
Li, Xiyong W660
Li, Xuan W106
Li, Yantao W106
Li, Ying W664
Li, Ying W663
Li, Yong W158
Li, Yonglin W146
Li, Yongzhao W117
Li, Yongzhong W530
Li, Yugang W275
Li, Yun W138
Li, Yunhua W656
Li, Zhen W37
Li, Zheng W178
Li, Zheng W533
Li, Zhengmao W151
Li, Zhi W655
Li, Zhihuang W656
Li, Zhiming W149
Li, Zhongwu W37
Li, Zixue W664
Li, Zongjian W431
Lian, Yongmei W529
Liang, Aishi W142
Liang, Aishi W466
Liang, Baojun W151
Liang, Charles E472
Liang, Chuangshun W137
Liang, Daguang W40
Liang, Guokun W173
Liang, Haishan W268
Liang, Hong W145
Liang, Hongliu W608
Liang, Janet A591
Liang, Janet A638
Liang, Janet P294
Liang, Jie W326
Liang, Liang W663
Liang, Qing W326
Liang, Victor Zhixiang W67
Liang, Weibin W529
Liang, Wengen W516
Liang, Xinjun W248
Liang, Yongming W140
Liang, Zaizhong W516
Liang, Zhongtai W327
Liao, Daniel A78
Liao, Daniel E383
Liao, David Yi Chien W268
Liao, Edward P511
Liao, Jianfeng W575
Liao, Jianwen W152
Liao, Jianxin W662
Liao, Jianxiong W263
Liao, Jie W656
Liao, Jinwun W168
Liao, Lin W301
Liao, Lujiang W534

Liao, Xingeng W326
Liao, Yixin W656
Liao, Zihping W168
Liarokapis, Georges W358
Liautaud, Bernard W517
Liaw, Jeffrey E120
Liaw, Marvin W583
Liaw, Y.H. W583
Libarle, Daniel G. A381
Liberman, Margaret R. E295
Libertino, John P306
Liberto, Diana Louise E106
Libman, Brian L. E190
Libnic, Samuel W70
Libonate, Mark P49
Libs, Gary L. A1115
Libs, Gary L. E533
LiCalsi, Michael E232
Licata, Joseph G. A914
Liceaga, Juan Carlos Rebollo W295
Licence, Stephen W360
Lich, Brad A. A354
Licht, Kris W490
Lichtendahl, Kenneth C. A240
Liddell, Katrina A892
Liddicoat, John W393
Lidefelt, Jon W579
Lieb, Eckhard W196
Liebelt, Graeme R. W63
Lieber, Robert C. A1046
Lieberman, Gerald M. W598
Liebert, Rebecca B. A298
Lieblein, Grace D. A530
Lieblein, Grace D. A69
Lieblong, Alex R. A524
Lieblong, Alex R. E258
Liebman, Eric E451
Liedberg, Douglas H. A313
Liegel, Matthew A. A996
Lien, Michael Jown Leam W628
Lientz, James R. A574
Liepe, Andreas W96
Liepitz, Karl A. A679
Lies, Michel M W666
Lievonen, Matti W554
Lifford, Pamela A993
Lifshatz, Stephen J. E147
Lifshitz, Yaacov W312
Lifton, Richard P. W502
Liggett, Emily M. E504
Lighte, Peter Rupert A857
Lightsey, Charles R. A414
Lightsey, Charles R. E193
Ligocki, Kathleen A. A840
Ligocki, Kathleen A. A622
Liguori, Thomas A118
Like, Steven K. E85
Likosar, Jeffrey A16
Lilek, JoAnn Sannasardo E19
Liljedal, Sara Hagg W60
Lillevang, Marianne W330
Lilleyman, Greg W246
Lillie, Brian J. E305
Lillie, Charisse R. A383
Lillikas, Yiorgos W50
Lillis, Terrance J. A248
Lim, Anthony Weng Kin W190
Lim, Beng Choon W286
Lim, Eric Jin Huei W628
Lim, Ho Kee W322

Lim, Hong Tat W380
Lim, Hwee Hua W322
Lim, Hyun-Seung W352
Lim, Khiang Tong W463
Lim, Lean See W286
Lim, Michael Choo San W456
Lim, Olivier Tse Ghow W190
Lima, Armando Zagalo de A841
Lima, Tito L. A259
Lima, Tito L. E103
Liman, Ulrich W174
Limbeck, Reiner van W510
Limber, Joseph M. E545
Limcaoco, Jose Teodoro K. W85
Limoges, Andrew A1071
Limpongpan, Sathit W352
Limskul, Arunporn W352
Lin, Bough W51
Lin, C.F. W252
Lin, Chenghong W140
Lin, Ching-Hua W596
Lin, Chong W291
Lin, Chris Horng-Dar W583
Lin, Chuang-I (Christopher) A878
Lin, Chuang-I (Christopher) E409
Lin, Dairen W142
Lin, Fang W655
Lin, Feng (Richard) A878
Lin, Feng (Richard) E409
Lin, Frank W636
Lin, Frank F.C. W650
Lin, Guangnan W169
Lin, Henry W650
Lin, Hongfu W663
Lin, Hongying W663
Lin, Howard W252
Lin, Hsien-Ming W650
Lin, J.K. W583
Lin, Jen-Jen Chang W206
Lin, Jingzhen W105
Lin, Judy E472
Lin, Junjie W656
Lin, Manjun W139
Lin, Mao W655
Lin, Mingsong W169
Lin, Paul A878
Lin, Paul E409
Lin, Ruijin W656
Lin, Sandra Beach A59
Lin, Sarena S. W95
Lin, Shengde W257
Lin, Shuiqing W663
Lin, Sui W268
Lin, Syaru Shirley W590
Lin, Tao W655
Lin, Tengjiao W575
Lin, Tingyi W145
Lin, Weiqing W663
Lin, William W109
Lin, Xiaochun W150
Lin, Xiaofeng W144
Lin, Yihui W575
Lin, Zhangguo W272
Lin, Zhiquan W142
Linares, Carlos A237
Lincoln, Blanche Lambert A371
Lindahl, Richard S. E157
Lindberg, Eric J. E242
Lindburg, Roy G. E433
Linde, Tamara Louise A858

Lindelauf, Leo W489
Lindenbaum, Matthew A. A329
Lindenmuth, Gregory D. A152
Linder, Theresa E117
Lindfors, Lars Peter W427
Lindgren, Bengt Erik W579
Lindholm, Charlotta W548
Lindner, Carl H. A64
Lindner, Patrick A1125
Lindner, Richard G. A274
Lindner, Russel C. A401
Lindner, S. Craig A64
Lindner, Thomas W586
Lindow, John P. A666
Lindquist, Scott R. A258
Lindsay-wood, Elizabeth P251
Lindsay, Denise E321
Lindsay, Donald R. W382
Lindsey, George W. E358
Lindstrom, Carol E38
Lindstrom, David E. A704
Lindstrom, David E. E328
Lindwall, Dan W579
Lindwall, Pauline W390
Linebarger, Norman Thomas A306
Linehan, Karen W515
Lines, James K. E451
Ling, Curtis E314
Ling, Hai A670
Ling, Ke W257
Ling, Yiqun W146
Ling, Zhenwen W533
Ling, Zhongqiu W292
Liniger, David L. (Dave) E410
Liniger, Gail E. A410
Link, Janet M. A962
Link, Linda A927
Link, Linda E435
Link, Margaret A. A679
Linnartz, Stephanie C. A526
Linnartz, Stephanie C. A1059
Linnen, Edward P. A116
Linnenbringer, Jean A261
Lins, Clarissa W49
Linton, Joy W116
Linton, Paul E224
Linton, Thomas K. W366
Linton, William W216
Liollio, Constantine S. A496
Liotta, Gary P. A439
Lipar, Eric E299
Lipar, Jack E299
Lipkin, Gerald H. A396
Lipkin, Gerald H. A400
Lipkin, Gerald H. E187
Lipowsky, Ursula W269
Lippert, Jason D. E293
Lippincott, Robert E287
Lippoldt, Darin M. E346
Lipsitz, Michael A915
Lipson, Jeffrey A. E245
Lipson, Nancy A737
Lipstein, Robert J. A923
Lipstein, Robert J. E433
Lipstein, Steven H. A54
Lira, Alma P401
Lis, Gregorio Maranon y Bertran de W169
Lisbjerg, Michael Abildgaard W632
Lisenby, Jeffrey P. A847

COMBINED HOOVER'S HANDBOOK INDEX OF EXECUTIVES

A = AMERICAN BUSINESS
E = EMERGING COMPANIES
P = PRIVATE COMPANIES
W = WORLD BUSINESSS

Liseno, Katherine J. A396
Liseno, Katherine J. E187
Lisin, Yury Viktorovich W617
Lisowski, Jason J. A432
Liss, Samuel G. E520
Lissalde, Frederic B. A173
Lisson, Kathryn Mary W487
List, Teri L. A315
List, Teri L. A701
List, Teri L. A1096
Lister, Paul W55
Lister, Philip M. A547
Listerman, Devin W. E185
Listner, Michael E364
Litchfield, Caroline A684
Litchfield, Steven G. E314
Lith, Karen T. Van A101
Litinsky, James H. E334
Litsey, Jana J. A545
Little, Joshua Eric A685
Little, Mark W573
Little, Mark M. A81
Little, Pamela A. A913
Little, Pamela A. E427
Little, Patricia A. A673
Little, Patricia A. A1055
Little, R. Parrish A528
Little, R. Parrish E258
Little, Sonya C. A496
Little, T. Mitch E250
Little, Teri A. A90
Little, Teri A. A607
Little, Thomas Mitchell A656
Littlefair, Andrew J. A516
Littlefield, Christopher J. A846
Littlejohn, Kimberly K. E515
Littlejohn, Melanie E372
Littlejohns, Barry B. E83
Littleton, Gayle A383
Littman, Dan R. A821
Littman, Owen S. E125
Littner, Leslie W78
Littreal, William B. A1033
Littreal, William B. E492
Litvack, Karina A. W227
Liu, Aijun W140
Liu, Benren W248
Liu, Bing W528
Liu, Chang W431
Liu, Chang M. A211
Liu, Chang M. E84
Liu, Changqing W239
Liu, Changyue W150
Liu, Chenggang W105
Liu, Chenglong W356
Liu, Chengyu W284
Liu, Chongsong W431
Liu, Chun W636
Liu, Chunkai W662
Liu, Daojun W516
Liu, Daokun W608
Liu, David Haifeng W236
Liu, Debin W431
Liu, Deborah (Deb) A571

Liu, Don H. A997
Liu, Don H. A574
Liu, Dunlei W274
Liu, Erfei W326
Liu, Fang W138
Liu, Fanglai W608
Liu, Fangyun W326
Liu, Feng W656
Liu, Gang W153
Liu, Gang W356
Liu, Genle W189
Liu, Guangxin W663
Liu, Guiqing W151
Liu, Guoyue W256
Liu, Henry Yuhong W480
Liu, Hong W472
Liu, Hong W656
Liu, Hongbin W146
Liu, Hongfeng W106
Liu, Hongyu W142
Liu, Hua W516
Liu, I-Ming (Vincent) A878
Liu, I-Ming (Vincent) E409
Liu, Jack C. A351
Liu, Jack C. E150
Liu, Jean W338
Liu, Jean Qing W202
Liu, Jialin W236
Liu, Jian W274
Liu, Jian W272
Liu, Jian W660
Liu, Jianhui W100
Liu, Jin W105
Liu, Jing W327
Liu, Jingdong W575
Liu, Jipeng W153
Liu, Jizhen W291
Liu, John D. A1129
Liu, Jun W362
Liu, Jun W136
Liu, Juncai W477
Liu, Liange W105
Liu, Maoxun W138
Liu, Mark W583
Liu, Mingsheng W528
Liu, Ning W142
Liu, Ping W477
Liu, Pingping A1145
Liu, Qian W261
Liu, Qianhan W274
Liu, Qingliang W142
Liu, Quancheng W189
Liu, Ranxing W291
Liu, Richard Qiangdong W324
Liu, Ruchen W146
Liu, Sai Fei W534
Liu, Sara E472
Liu, Shen W100
Liu, Shiping W574
Liu, Shuwei W263
Liu, Shuwei W152
Liu, Tally C. E472
Liu, Tiantian W40
Liu, Ting Y. A211
Liu, Ting Y. E84
Liu, Tracy E3
Liu, Tsu-Jae King A560
Liu, Wei W291
Liu, Wei W142
Liu, Wenhong W663

Liu, Wensheng W477
Liu, Xia A1114
Liu, Xiang W138
Liu, Xianhua W466
Liu, Xiao W152
Liu, Xiao Feng W355
Liu, Xiaodan W145
Liu, Xiaodong W106
Liu, Xiaoqiang W528
Liu, Xiaoyong W148
Liu, Xiaozhi W40
Liu, Xiaozhi W328
Liu, Xike W326
Liu, Xin W533
Liu, Xing W636
Liu, Xuefen W274
Liu, Xuehai W256
Liu, Yan W256
Liu, Yanping W529
Liu, Yaowu W136
Liu, Ye W533
Liu, Yexi P462
Liu, Yi W542
Liu, Yingchuan W477
Liu, Yonghao W431
Liu, Yongzhuo W139
Liu, Yuanman W254
Liu, Yuezhen W466
Liu, Yunhong W529
Liu, Zhengchang W146
Liu, Zhihao W663
Liu, Zhonghai W327
Liu, Zongwen W528
Liuson, Julia E75
Liveris, Andrew N. A565
Livermore, Ann M. A1069
Livermore, Ann M. A867
Livermore, Ann M. A514
Livfors, Mia Brunell W277
Livingston, I. Scott A939
Livingston, Ian W179
Livingston, Ian W422
Livingston, Ian Paul A911
Livingston, James G. A398
Livingston, Mark E398
Livingston, Philip B. E409
Livingston, Robert A. W80
Livingston, Robert A. A907
Livingstone, Catherine W164
Lizardi, Rafael R. A1010
Lizaur, Jose Ignacio Perez W265
Lizcano, Gonzalo de la Hoz W87
Ljung, Roger W579
Ljungberg, Erik W579
Llado, George E94
Llechu, Armando P308
Lleras, Jose Antonio Vargas W220
Llewellyn, Rania W358
Llorens, Juan Pi W68
Llosa, Reynaldo W174
Lloveras, Maria Teresa Garcia-Mila W71
Lloveras, Teresa Garcia-Mila W493
Lloyd-Smith, Malcolm E346
Lloyd, Anne H. E275
Lloyd, George E425
Lloyd, Jonathan W323
Lloyd, Karole F. A24
Lloyd, Meaghan E497
Lloyd, Michael A. E506

Lloyd, Richard H. E336
Lloyd, Robert W. E68
Lo, Andrew Tak Shing A573
Lo, John Shek Hon W596
Lo, Peter Chi Lik W148
Lo, Peter Chi Lik W372
Lo, Raymond W51
Lo, Renee Wonlai E278
Lo, Vincent Hong Sui W268
Lo, Wei-Jen W583
Lo, Winston Yau-lai W80
Loacker, Stefan W580
Loacker, Stefan W580
Loacker, Stefan W642
Loader, Adrian W283
Loader, Enos L. E189
Loaiza, Monica W643
Loan, Charles C. Van A555
Loan, Charles C. Van E269
Lobach, David M. E156
Lobacheva, Ekaterina W655
Lober, Ralph J. E117
Lobo, Kevin A. A804
Lobo, Kevin A. A981
Locascio, Dirk J. A1083
LoCascio, T. S. A424
LoCascio, T. S. E200
Locatelli, Rossella W310
Loch, James J. E140
Lochen, Richard S. A816
Locke, Anna T. E454
Locke, Jace D P216
Locke, Lori C. A332
Lockhart, Dennis P. A574
Lockhart, Dennis P. A399
Lockhart, Michael D. A747
Lockhart, Nancy H. O. W646
Lockhart, Stephen H. A707
Lockwood, Kristina E239
Locoh-Donou, Francois A198
Locy, Peter R. A214
Loddesol, Lars Aa. W562
Lodge, Jane Ann W191
Lodge, Timothy J. A352
Loeb, Gary H A573
Loeb, Marshall A. E151
Loeffler, Lance A494
Loeffler, Martin H. A79
Loeffler, Nancy B. A956
Loeger, Julie A. A357
Loera, Alfredo W266
Loescher, Peter W593
Loewe, Nancy S. A1127
Lofficial, Xavier W548
Loffler, Carmen W171
Loften, Gina L. E500
Lofton, Adrienne A34
Lofton, Kevin E. A895
Lofton, Kevin E. A473
Lofton, Kevin E. W393
Loftus, John Richardson E168
Logan, Ann E423
Logan, Barry S. A1111
Loganadhan, Vinodh W235
Logue, Daniel V. E484
Loh, Gordon A821
Lohani, Rachit E374
Lohawatanakul, Chingchai W137
Lohneiss, Herbert W3
Lohr, Walter G. A315

COMBINED HOOVER'S HANDBOOK INDEX OF EXECUTIVES

A = AMERICAN BUSINESS
E = EMERGING COMPANIES
P = PRIVATE COMPANIES
W = WORLD BUSINESSS

Loire, Bernard W490
Lokey, James W. E114
Lollgen, Frank W95
Lomba, Jaime Terceiro W87
Lombard, Gerhard E129
Lombard, Marie-Christine W635
Lombard, Shelly C. A148
Lombardi, Brandon F. A959
Lombardi, Christy M. E113
Lombardi, Leonard V. A418
Lombardi, Leonard V. E195
Lombardi, Michele W157
Lomelin, Carlos Vicente Salazar W69
Lomeo, Jody L. E175
London, Sarah M. A216
London, Terry E. E284
Lonegro, Frank A. A145
Lonergan, Edward F. A795
Lonergan, Robert A. A103
Long, Andrew G. A794
Long, Annabelle Yu A993
Long, David H. A380
Long, Donald J. A741
Long, Donald J. E349
Long, Eric D. E514
Long, Gary J. A392
Long, Gary J. E183
Long, Justin M. A213
Long, Letitia A. A992
Long, Michael J. A97
Long, Michael J. A73
Long, Suzette M. A210
Long, Thomas E. A1008
Long, Thomas E. A369
Long, Thomas E. E514
Long, William C P490
Longacre, Doug A428
Longe, Thomas J. A524
Longe, Thomas J. E258
Longenecker, John P. E369
Longenecker, Thomas D. A788
Longenecker, Thomas D. E366
Longhi, Mario A1054
Longhofer, T. Luke A421
Longhofer, T. Luke E198
Longino, Lisa A296
Longley, S. Catherine A192
Longman, Gary L. E97
Longo, Joseph A237
Longo, Michael E. E254
Longobardi, Sara M. A814
Longobardi, Sara M. E379
Lønnum, Tor Magne W558
Loo, Koen Van W200
Loomis, Edward P. E108
Looney, Bernard W109
Loope, Andrew E. E247
Loosli, Hansueli W581
Loper, D. Shane A496
Lopes, Alexsandro Broedel W315
Lopez-Balboa, Francisco J. A1071
Lopez, Alejandro Arango W210
Lopez, Andres A. A114
Lopez, Andres A. A764

Lopez, Belen Garijo W68
Lopez, Daniel Alcain A112
Lopez, David R. A125
Lopez, David R. E52
Lopez, Esteban E5
Lopez, Fermin P498
Lopez, Frank E66
Lopez, George A. E262
Lopez, Gerald B P401
Lopez, Gerardo I. A735
Lopez, Gerardo I. A213
Lopez, Gerardo I. E412
Lopez, Jorge A680
Lopez, Jorge P343
Lopez, Jose Maria Alvarez-Pallete W593
Lopez, Miguel A. E420
Lopez, Patricia E. A92
Lopez, Rafael de Juan W169
Lora, Melissa B. A594
Lora, Melissa B. A286
Loranger, Steven R. A361
Lorberbaum, Jeffrey S. A706
Lorch, Nicole S. A425
Lorch, Nicole S. E201
Lord, Hambleton A191
Lord, Hambleton E77
Lord, L. Jack A852
Lord, L. Jack E399
Lord, Patrick J. A619
Lord, Phillippe A687
Lord, Rachel A160
Lord, Robert W. E190
Loree, James M. A1129
Lorenston, Jeffery B. A427
Lorenston, Jeffery B. E203
Lorentzen, Kyle D. A279
Lorentzen, Oivind E144
Lorenz, Lorrie E111
Lorenz, William Kent A416
Lorenzatto, Rudimar Andreis W468
Lorenzen, Jeffrey D. A60
Lorenzini, Pedro Paulo Giubbina W315
Lorenzo, Juan Ramon Jimenez W73
Lores, Enrique J. A538
Lores, Enrique J. A807
Loretta, David E147
Loretz-Congdon, Stacy A639
Lorey, Brandon Craig E149
Lorey, David P. E185
Lorig, Brian W. A607
Lorne, Simon M. E483
Lortz, Andre A221
Lortz, Andre P113
Losch, William C. A641
Losch, William C. E304
Loscher, Peter W351
Loseth, Tore W227
Losh, J. Michael A666
Losh, J. Michael W44
Losinski, Adam E455
Losquadro, Geraldine (Gerri) W233
Lostetter, Vicki A1125
Lott, Charles E. E85
Lott, James J. A12
Lott, James J. E4
Lott, Tommy W. A214
Lotvin, Alan M. A311
Lou, Dongyang W141
Lou, Jianchang W275

Lou, Qiliang W179
Louden, Steve E423
Loudermilk, J. Matthew (Joey) A24
Loudermilk, Robert C. (Robin) A468
Loudon, Bridget W596
Lougheed, James E314
Loughery, Robert G. E98
Loughlin, Suzanne E420
Loughran, Barbara L. A580
Louichareon, Benja W352
Louie, Linda H. A76
Louis, Harald W510
Lounsbury, Loren H. A428
Lourd, Bryan E261
Loureiro, Guilherme W643
Loureiro, Joao Manuel de Matos W70
Lousada, Max A1106
Loutfy, N. W8
Louwhoff, Roel W561
Love, Charles R. A953
Love, Charles R. E455
Love, John H. A66
Love, John H. E25
Love, John P. E509
Love, John P. E510
Love, John P. E509
Love, Lisa Anne A240
Love, Michael A. E64
Lovejoy, David R. A425
Lovejoy, David R. E201
Lovejoy, Kristin G. A340
Lovelace, Rob A197
Lovelace, Rob P103
Loven, Lotta W579
Loveridge, Anne W419
Lovett, Laurie A742
Lovik, Kenneth J. A425
Lovik, Kenneth J. E201
Loving, Richard W. E70
Lovinger, John P. E102
Lovins, Gregory S. A114
Lovoi, John V. E250
Lovold, Maria Ervik W204
Low-Friedrich, Iris W251
Low, Check Kian A180
Low, Russell J. E47
Low, Sin Leng W357
Lowder, James K. A32
Lowder, W. Chester E515
Lowe, Alan S. E305
Lowe, Carol P. A364
Lowe, Eugene J. E188
Lowe, Harold E. E336
Lowe, John E. A826
Lowe, Kenneth W. A332
Lowe, LeAngela W. E40
Lowe, Rebekah M. A528
Lowe, Rebekah M. E258
Lowenthal, Albert G. E363
Lowenthal, Robert S. E363
Lower, Harold E. A493
Lower, Harold E. E243
Lower, Joseph T. A109
Lowery, Donna T. A414
Lowery, Donna T. E193
Lowery, Frederick M. A349
Lowery, Norman D. A422
Lowery, Norman L. A422
Lowman, Teresita M. A694
Lown, Christian M. A450

Lowrey, Charles F. A856
Lowry, Jennifer E. E337
Lowry, Michael H. E76
Lowry, Michael Wayne A794
Lowry, Robert T. E191
Lowth, Simon W114
Lox, Egbert W623
Loy, Bertrand E165
Loy, Paul Ho Sing A617
Loy, Paul Ho Sing E289
Loyland, Karna A37
Loyland, Karna E14
Loyo, Eduardo Henrique de Mello Motta W69
Lozano, Marcelo Zambrano W131
Lozano, Monica C. A997
Lozano, Monica C. A89
Lozano, Monica C. A128
Lozano, Rafael Garza W131
Lozano, Rogelio Zambrano W131
Lu, Ao W140
Lu, Boqing W529
Lu, Caijuan W261
Lu, Curtis P. E224
Lu, Ding E370
Lu, Fang Ming W240
Lu, Fei W291
Lu, Feiying E323
Lu, Gary W168
Lu, Hong Bing W534
Lu, Hsu-Tung W530
Lu, Jie W140
Lu, Jinhai W356
Lu, Keh-Shew E143
Lu, Lucy E522
Lu, Meiyi Feng W141
Lu, Ming W481
Lu, Ning W145
Lu, Pengjun W636
Lu, Qi W517
Lu, Qiaoling W145
Lu, Ruby Rong A1145
Lu, Ruby Rong W626
Lu, Shan W152
Lu, Shan W596
Lu, Sidney W284
Lu, Wei W140
Lu, Weixiong W142
Lu, Wenwu W644
Lu, Xiaoma W575
Lu, Xiaoqiang W146
Lu, Xiongwen W88
Lu, Xueling A1145
Lu, Yan W362
Lu, Yaozhong W466
Lu, Yongzhen W301
Lu, Zhongming W254
Lu, Zhongnian W140
Luallen, Eugenia Crittenden "Crit" A283
Luan, Baoxing W256
Lubek, David W127
Lubel, Kimberly S. A1124
Lubel, Kimberly S. A809
Lubik, Thomas A. A401
Lublin, Jason A367
Lublin, Scott A691
Lublin, Scott E323
Lubner, Clive E190
Lubow, Stuart H. A328

COMBINED HOOVER'S HANDBOOK INDEX OF EXECUTIVES

A = AMERICAN BUSINESS
E = EMERGING COMPANIES
P = PRIVATE COMPANIES
W = WORLD BUSINESSS

Luca, Guerrino De A742
Lucarelli, Lisa M. A1043
Lucas-Bull, Wendy Elizabeth W8
Lucas, David H. E190
Lucas, Emily P678
Lucas, Hal M. E177
Lucas, Richard M. E531
Lucchese, Cynthia L. E119
Luce, Graham N. A159
Lucet, Catherine W127
Lucey, John W. E384
Lucey, Kevin W191
Lucey, Matthew C. A809
Lucey, Matthew C. E374
Luchangco, Eric Roberto M. W85
Lucht, David G. A642
Lucht, David G. E304
Luciano, Juan R. A635
Luciano, Juan R. A94
Lucier, Gregory T. E83
Luckshire, Daniel J. E440
Lucky, Donald C.I. E337
Lucky, James L. E43
Lucore, George R. E172
Lucsok, Anna E547
Luczo, Stephen (Steve) J. A713
Luczo, Stephen (Steve) J. A105
Luddy, Frederic B. A931
Ludeman, Daniel A977
Ludeman, Daniel E464
Ludwick, Andrew K. A1148
Ludwig, A Lesile A350
Ludwig, A Lesile E148
Ludwig, Edward J. A311
Ludwig, Edward J. A175
Ludwig, Helmuth W279
Ludwig, Jane C. E185
Ludwig, Jeffrey G. A703
Ludwig, Jeffrey G. E327
Ludwig, West A418
Luebbers, Kevin M. E67
Luedke, William T. A852
Luedke, William T. E399
Luff, Nick L. W504
Luffey, Gary A788
Luffey, Gary E364
Luge, Ingo W602
Luha, Eugen-Gheorghe W207
Luhabe, Wendy N. W167
Luis, Patrick A. E90
Luis, Victor E137
Lukander, Jenni W443
Luke, Donald L. E264
Luke, Richard P376
Lukinovich, David J. E279
Lukins, Scott B. A1099
Lumali, Ergun W395
Lummus, Dewayne A60
Luna, Gina A. E423
Lunak, Leslie N. A135
Lund-Andersen, Sally W558
Lund, Helge W109
Lund, Jens H. W205
Lund, Randal L. A271

Lund, Randal L. E109
Lundberg, Fredrik W548
Lundberg, Fredrik W579
Lunde, Marit E144
Lundgren, John F. A1096
Lundgren, Tamara L. A909
Lundgren, Tamara L. E430
Lundgren, Terry J. A850
Lundgren, Terry J. A400
Lundmark, Pekka W443
Lundquist, Andrew D. A288
Lundquist, Bo W277
Lundquist, Nicholas J. A394
Lundstedt, Martin W641
Lundstrom, Paul R. W242
Luning, Christopher Paul E174
Luo, Gang W662
Luo, Guiqing W292
Luo, Jianchuan W88
Luo, Laijun W150
Luo, Liang W144
Luo, Meijian W149
Luo, Rong W67
Luo, Sheng W257
Luo, Wenjun W528
Luo, Xiaoqian W291
Luo, Yan W153
Lupica, John J. W154
Lupoi, Alberto W392
Lupone, E. Robert A1012
Luquette, Gary P. E91
Lurie, Glenn A116
Lurker, Nancy A756
Lurker, Nancy P404
Luscan, Philippe W515
Lusco, C. Matthew A884
Lusk, Stephen W161
Lussier, Joseph R. A372
Lussier, Joseph R. E166
Luster, Alexandra M. E302
Lustig, Neil A924
Lusztyn, Marek W86
Lute, Jane H. A1061
Lute, Jane H. A662
Lutes, Christopher T. A219
Luth, Roseanne E134
Luthar, Vikram A94
Luther, Annette W502
Luthi, Francesca L. A103
Lutnick, Howard W. E347
Lutoff-Perlo, Lisa A110
Luts, Erik W336
Lutsey, Meisha A189
Lutz, Gary B. E206
Lutz, Klaus Josef W98
Lutz, Marcos Marinho A298
Lutz, Marcos Marinho W622
Lux, Andrew L. E42
Lux, Marshall J. A732
Lux, Melinda Davis A1064
Lux, Melinda Davis E509
Luzzi, Federico Ferro W592
Lv, Bo W466
Lv, Dapeng W145
Lv, Gang W307
Lv, Lianggong W145
Lv, Ming W528
Lv, Wenhan W656
Lv, Xiangyang W117
Lv, Xianliang W37

Lv, Xiaoping W254
Lv, Yuegang W256
Lv, Zhiren W256
Lv, Zhiwei W257
Lyall, J. Wade E447
Lyash, Jeff P68
Lyash, Jeffrey J. A1006
Lybarger, Stanley A. A167
Lybarger, Stanley A. E64
Lycouris, John C. E144
Lydon, Thomas F. E514
Lyga, Joseph A143
Lyga, Joseph E57
Lykins, Gregory B. A415
Lykins, Gregory B. E194
Lyle, David B. A574
Lyle, Mike Vacy W164
Lyle, Peter F. E247
Lyles, Lester L. A595
Lynch, Catherine A. E378
Lynch, Christopher W648
Lynch, Christopher S. A296
Lynch, Christopher S. A1003
Lynch, G. Patrick E352
Lynch, Karen S. A311
Lynch, Katie P382
Lynch, Kevin J. A396
Lynch, Kevin J. E187
Lynch, Kevin J. E77
Lynch, Marlon P615
Lynch, Michael J. A57
Lynch, Nnenna E62
Lynch, Robert P. A72
Lynch, Robert P. E29
Lynch, Thomas P586
Lynch, Thomas J. A108
Lynch, Thomas J. A306
Lynch, Thomas J. W590
Lynch, Timothy R. A500
Lynch, Timothy R. E246
Lynn, Jesse A. A432
Lynn, Jesse A. A1142
Lynton, Carol ("Lili") E227
Lynton, Michael M. A1106
Lynton, Michael M. E34
Lynton, Michael M. E65
Lyon, Andres Lyon W41
Lyon, Jeffrey S. A510
Lyon, Jeffrey S. E252
Lyon, Joseph Douglas E121
Lyon, Shawn M. A717
Lyon, William H. A998
Lyons, Bill E333
Lyons, Billy J. A774
Lyons, Billy J. E360
Lyons, Blake A399
Lyons, Charles A979
Lyons, Daniel E. W299
Lyons, Gary A. E346
Lyons, Irving F. A377
Lyons, Kevin D. E185
Lyons, Mark Donald W50
Lyons, Martin J. A54
Lyons, Michael P. A834
Lyons, Nicholas W471
Lyons, Peter D. A57
Lyons, Robert C. A799
Lyons, Thomas M. A854
Lyski, James A205
Lysyj, Lesya E65

Lyu, Fangming W284
Lyu, Ruizhi W148

M

M., Gustavo Marturet A52
Ma, Changhai W644
Ma, Connie W583
Ma, Gloria Sau Kuen W572
Ma, Guangyuan W516
Ma, Huateng W596
Ma, Jiaji W100
Ma, Jianchun W528
Ma, Jiangsheng W88
Ma, Jingan W291
Ma, Jisiang W169
Ma, Li W272
Ma, Li W542
Ma, Lishan W572
Ma, Mingzhe W472
Ma, Shiheng W173
Ma, Stephen W441
Ma, Xiaoyi W596
Ma, Xiaoyun W524
Ma, Xuezheng W362
Ma, Xulun W150
Ma, Yaotian W431
Ma, Yongsheng W145
Ma, Yuanxing W98
Ma, Zhengang W292
Ma, Zhihe W272
Ma, Zhixia W572
Maas-Brunner, Melanie W93
Mabaso-Koyana, S. N. W414
Mabelane, B. P. W518
Mabry, James C. A888
Mabry, James C. E414
Mabus, Raymond E. A313
Mabus, Raymond E. A518
Macadam, Stephen E. A1087
Macali, Ralph D. A393
Macali, Ralph D. E184
Macaskill, Bridget A. A588
Macciocchi, Vincent F. A94
MacDonald, Andrew A1052
MacDonald, Anne E65
MacDonald, Brian W573
MacDonald, Deborah A. A605
Macdonald, John A1111
MacDonald, Michael R. A1055
MacDonald, Neil B. A514
MacDonald, Ryan S. E63
MacDougall, Bennett A854
Maceda, Jason S. E235
Macedo, Paulo Jose de Ribeiro Moita de W70
MacFarlane, Charles S. E367
Macfarlane, John T. W63
MacGibbon, Alan N. W611
MacGillivray, Corey M. A444
MacGillivray, Robin Greenway E444
MacGregor, Catherine W225
Machado, Luis Francisco E490
Machas, Evelina Vougessis A513
Machell, Simon W574
Machen, Robert P35
Machenil, Lars W103
Macheras, Ann B. A401

COMBINED HOOVER'S HANDBOOK INDEX OF EXECUTIVES

A = AMERICAN BUSINESS
E = EMERGING COMPANIES
P = PRIVATE COMPANIES
W = WORLD BUSINESSS

Machler, Monica W666
Machler, Stefan W580
Machtmes, Todd A912
Machuca, Luis F. A1057
Machuel, Denis A612
Macia, Seraina (Maag) W176
macias, Elmer Franco W266
Maciel, Andre A610
Maciel, Antonio W383
MacInnes, Glenn I. A1113
MacIntosh, Britta E22
Mack-Askew, Tracy A271
Mack-Askew, Tracy E109
Mack, Amy E418
Mack, Dennis E177
Mack, Dennis J. A555
Mack, Dennis J. E269
Mack, Mary T. A1115
Mack, Michael P688
Mack, Michael J. A313
Mack, Robert P. A835
Mack, Tina E455
Mackay, A. D. David A447
Mackay, Allan David A254
MacKay, Craig C. A377
MacKay, Gregory S. A196
MacKay, Gregory S. E78
Mackay, Iain W258
MacKay, Kimberly Banks E534
Mackay, Leo S. A54
Mackay, Leo S. A267
Mackay, Martin W. E94
Mackay, Robert N. A307
Mackay, Robert N. E133
Mackay, Timothy R. E298
Macke, John F. A681
Macke, John F. E318
Macke, Kevin M. A1056
Macke, Kevin M. E505
Macken, Patrick W. E420
Mackenna, Francisco Perez W70
MacKenzie, Alexander R. (Rod) A821
Mackenzie, Amanda W371
MacKenzie, Amanda W371
Mackenzie, Andrew W533
Mackenzie, Don A180
Mackenzie, Don W113
MacKenzie, Iain E261
MacKenzie, Jonathan B. E316
MacKenzie, Ken N. W101
Mackenzie, Mindy A279
Mackey, Catherine J. E45
Mackey, Edward F. A175
Mackiw, Christine I. W571
MacLauchlan, Jeffrey D. A189
Maclean, Elaine W21
MacLellan, Robert F. A991
MacLellan, Robert F. E379
MacLennan, David W. A210
MacLennan, David W. A358
MacLeod, David W245
MacLeod, Fiona W157
MacLeod, Robert J. W328
MacLeod, Sharon W480

Maclin, S. Todd A604
MacMillan, Catherine Cope A1119
MacMillan, Stephen (Steve) P. A522
Macnab, Craig A69
Macnab, Craig E524
Macnaughton, Mike P516
MacNicholas, Garry W262
Macomber, Sasha G. A881
Macosko, David R. E529
MacPhail, Keith A. W133
Macpherson, D. G. A568
Macpherson, Donald G. A485
MacPherson, Kerrie D. A280
MacPherson, Kerrie D. E113
MacQuillan, Sandra A710
MacQuillan, Sandra E497
MacRae, Penelope W419
Macricostas, Constantine S. E383
Macricostas, George E383
MacSwain, Claudia N. A401
MacSween, Micheal R. W573
MacVay, Lauren M. A398
Madan, Charly W79
Madati, Kilandigalu M. E539
Maddalena, Stephen J. E102
Madden, Anne T. A458
Madden, Anne T. A530
Madden, Donald V P625
Madden, Margaret M. A821
Madden, Teresa S. E119
Madden, Teresa S. W218
Maddock, Ernest E. A118
Maddock, Ernest E. E485
Maddock, Ernest E. E504
Maddox, Michael J. A301
Maddox, Michael J. E131
Maddux, Franklin W. W249
Maddy, H. Charles A981
Maddy, H. Charles E469
Madea, Ann A938
Madea, Ann E442
Madelain, Michel W138
Mader, Jeffrey E471
Madere, Consuelo E. W451
Madero, Roger Saldana W131
Madhavan, Kalyan A397
Madhavan, Kalyan E187
Madhavan, S. W296
Madhavpeddi, Kalidas V. W260
Madina, Carlos W132
Madison, G. W. A539
Madison, George W. A881
Madoff, Paula E288
Madoff, Paula E493
Madoff, Paula B. W262
Madoff, Paula B. W480
Madon, Cyrus A180
Madon, Cyrus W113
Madonna, Harry D. A891
Madonna, John W. A316
Madre, Armelle de W600
Madsen, Jorn W31
Madsen, Michael A530
Madsen, Sarah E. A1065
Madsen, Thomas Lindegaard W2
Madsen, Toni H W446
Madson, Patrick J. A741
Madson, Patrick J. E349
Maduck, Sean E121
Mady, Mohamed H. Al W519

Maeda, Kaori W278
Maeda, Koichi W182
Maeda, Masahiko W614
Maeda, Masahiko W616
Maeda, Yuko W51
Maerki, Hans Ulrich W580
Maes, Benoit W107
Maestri, Luca A89
Maffei, Gregory B. A941
Maffei, Gregory B. A224
Maffei, Gregory B. A1149
Maffei, Gregory B. A633
Maffei, Gregory B. A641
Maffei, Gregory B. A871
Maffei, Gregory B. A872
Maffei, Gregory B. A633
Maffei, Gregory B. E300
Maganov, Ravil W476
Magee, Brona W526
Magee, Christine W596
Magee, Christine W399
Magee, Michael M. A554
Magee, Michael M. E269
Magennis, Elizabeth A287
Magennis, Elizabeth E115
Maggini, Joseph L. E321
Maggio, Paula C. A694
Maggioncalda, Jeffrey Nacey A984
Maggioncalda, Jeffrey Nacey E476
Maggs, Thomas O. A1043
Magid, Brent M. E295
Magid, Syvia L. E56
Magier, Eugene M. E351
Magistretti, Elisabetta W392
Magne, Christian W22
Magner, Marjorie A43
Magnin, Gérard W215
Magnin, Shelly Dumas A918
Magnoni, Ruggero W167
Magnus, Birger W562
Magnuson, Michele M. A532
Magnuson, Michele M. E259
Magnusson, Bo W579
Magstadt, Brian J. E444
Maguire, Andy W21
Maguire, Joanne M. A279
Mahajan, Manmohan A1101
Mahan, James S. A641
Mahan, James S. E304
Mahan, Lucy A428
Mahawongtikul, Pannalin W484
Mahbubani, Kishore W666
Mahe, Isabel Ge A964
Mahendra-Rajah, Prashanth A483
Mahendra-Rajah, Prashanth A81
Maher, Christopher D. A768
Maher, Christopher D. E359
Maher, Katherine A716
Maher, Mary Lou W119
Maher, Michael W. A745
Maher, Tina J. A422
Maheras, Thomas G. A330
Maheshwari, Anurag A791
Maheshwari, Sanjeev W561
Maheshwari, Sunita W271
Mahjour, Morteza W159
Mahlan, Deirdre A604
Mahmoodzadegan, Navid E330
Mahmoud, Tirad W8
Mahon, Anita E179

Mahon, Janice K. E511
Mahon, Kenneth J. A328
Mahon, Kenneth J. A396
Mahon, Kenneth J. E187
Mahon, Paul A. W262
Mahoney, David L. E121
Mahoney, John J. A187
Mahoney, Kevin P. A950
Mahoney, Michael F. A175
Mahoney, Michael F. A142
Mahoney, Paul E. E91
Mahoney, R. Scott A112
Mahoney, Richard S. E32
Mahoney, Sean O. W46
Mahoney, Sean O. W45
Mahoney, Shelagh E. A372
Mahoney, Shelagh E. E167
Mahoney, Tammy A650
Mahoney, Tammy E305
Mahoney, Timothy O. (Tim) A530
Mahtani, Kavita A539
Mai, Boliang W141
Mai, Jackson W206
Mai, Yanzhou W151
Maida, Robert P. E18
Maidment, Karen E. W611
Maier, Henry J. A900
Maier, Lothar E214
Maier, Stéphane E297
Mailloux, Robert D. A530
Main, Ann B. A378
Main, Richard W. A372
Main, Richard W. E166
Main, Susan L. E483
Main, Timothy L. A870
Main, Timothy R.M. E68
Mainer, Matthew J. A838
Maines, Robert J. A395
Maines, Robert J. E186
Maio, Keith D. A1151
Maio, Peter V. A1086
Maio, Peter V. E516
Maioli, Giampiero W174
Mair, Scott E420
Maisey, Simon E493
Maitland, Alister W380
Maiuri, Louis D. A973
Maiwurm, James J. A913
Maiwurm, James J. E427
Maiziere, Andreas De W234
Majarian, Andriana D. E90
Majima, Hironori W609
Majni, J Christopher P338
Majocha, Mark W617
Major, John E. E303
Major, Sean D. A30
Majoras, Deborah P. A850
Majoras, Deborah P. A1085
Majors, Charles H. A66
Majors, Charles H. E25
Majors, Michael C. A478
Majumder, I. Bobby E63
Mak, Celia Sze Man W236
Mak, Sze Man W663
Makalima, Linda W426
Makara, Richard E80
Makela, Jan A458
Makhmudova, Nigyar W187
Maki-Kala, Jyrki W427
Makihara, Jun A825

COMBINED HOOVER'S HANDBOOK INDEX OF EXECUTIVES

A = AMERICAN BUSINESS
E = EMERGING COMPANIES
P = PRIVATE COMPANIES
W = WORLD BUSINESSS

Makino, Akiji W183
Makino, Shinya W394
Makino, Yuko W462
Makiura, Shinji W659
Makris, George A. A938
Makris, George A. E442
Maksimow, Andre A168
Maksimow, Andre P89
Makwana, P. Mpho W426
Malady, Kyle A1088
Malady, Kyle E138
Malamut, Richard E107
Maland, Jerry P. A378
Malavasi, Ivan W627
Malave, Jesus (Jay) A643
Malcarney, Kristin A400
Malchow, Joseph I. E163
Malcolm, Gregory A269
Malcolm, Mark M. A460
Malcolm, Robert M. A512
Malcolm, Steven J. A783
Malcolm, Steven J. A167
Malcolm, Steven J. E64
Malcolmson, Robert W99
Maldonado, Javier A915
Maldonado, Luis Santiago Perdomo W210
Maleh, Paul A. E126
Malek, Barry E102
Maleti, Joe E46
Maletz, Mark Clifford W69
Malherbe, Josua W167
Malhotra, Pehlaj W287
Malhotra, Raghu A670
Malhotra, Sanjiv W561
Malik, Hasan A587
Malik, Muhammad Shahbaz E226
Malik, Rajiv A1093
Malkoski, Kristine K. A735
Mallela, Ravi E350
Mallesch, Eileen A. A410
Mallesch, Eileen A. A176
Mallet, Thierry W565
Mallett, Conrad L. A622
Malloch-Brown, Lord W311
Mallon, Jennifer L. E452
Mallon, Liam M. A388
Mallon, Mark E282
Malmberg, Juho W348
Malone, Dan E. E13
Malone, David J. A441
Malone, David J. E212
Malone, David P. A530
Malone, David P. E258
Malone, Evan D. A941
Malone, Evan D. A633
Malone, Evan Daniel A871
Malone, Evan Daniel A872
Malone, Evan Daniel A633
Malone, Farrell J. A788
Malone, Farrell J. E364
Malone, John C. A633
Malone, John C. A633
Malone, John C. A332

Malone, John C. A871
Malone, John C. A872
Malone, John C. E300
Malone, Mary Alice Dorrance A195
Malone, Michael D. A718
Malone, Michael D. E531
Malone, Michael D. E335
Malone, Michael W. A195
Malone, Mona W82
Malone, Robert A. A494
Malone, Robert A. E483
Malone, Steve V. A401
Maloney, James P. E316
Maloney, Patrick J. E333
Malrieu, Francoise W225
Maltbie, John L P176
Maltezos, Louis P. E22
Malungani, Mangalani Peter W310
Malyshev, Sergey W410
Malzahn, Daniel D. A762
Mamik, Aneek S. A781
Mamilli, Wafaa A1153
Mamilli, Wafaa A434
Man-bun, Brian David Li W80
Manabe, Masaaki W281
Manager, Vada O. E517
Manase, Zodwa Penelope W558
Mancho, Francisco Javier de Paz W593
Mancini, Joseph E400
Mancini, Massimo W592
Mancuso, Robert J. E354
Mancuso, Salvatore A47
Mandarich, David D. A652
Mandell, Brian M. A319
Manders, Matthew G. A239
Mandeville, Jean F.H.P. E141
Mandinach, Barry M. E528
Mandine, Beatrice W459
Manditch, Douglas C. A439
Mandraffino, Erika W227
Manes, Paola W627
Manfredonia, Donald L. A430
Mang, Thomas W192
Mangale, Alpheus W559
Mangan, Michael D. A673
Manganiello, Anthony A1095
Manganiello, Anthony P677
Mangano, Robert F. A617
Mangano, Robert F. E289
Mangione, Robert P521
Mangkhalathanakun, Paphon W603
Manifold, Albert W374
Manifold, Albert W178
Manigan, Mark P472
Manire, Ross W. A1148
Manire, Ross W. A82
Manjarrez, Marcela A373
Manjarrez, Marcela E168
Manley, John W596
Manley, John L. A1136
Manley, Justin A742
Manley, Justin P393
Manley, Kelly W157
Manley, Michael A342
Manley, Michael A109
Manley, Michael W562
Manley, Michael R. E1
Mann, Chris P185
Mann, Elizabeth E520
Mann, Erica L. A597

Mann, Jeffifer K. A1065
Mann, Jeffifer K. E509
Mann, Jennifer K. A266
Mann, Lindley S. E421
Mann, Richard L P658
Mannelly, Matthew A958
Mannen, Maryann T. A795
Mannen, Maryann T. A657
Mannen, Maryann T. A717
Manner, Carrie Eglinton E415
Manning, Jennifer D. A264
Manning, Robert A. W122
Manning, Robert J. A962
Manning, Thomas J. A279
Manolis, Eva E183
Manolis, Eva E281
Manone, Vito S. E190
Manoogian, Richard A. A666
Manos, Kristen L. A602
Manriquez, Jaime E428
Manseau, James J. A328
Mansfield, Keith A188
Mansfield, Keith E69
Mansfield, Michael J. A223
Mansfield, William P. A487
Mansour, Matt W487
Mansouri, Saeed Al W205
Manspile, Randal C. A401
Mansueto, Joe E333
Mantas, Jesus B. A158
Mantia, Linda P. A677
Mantilla, Luis Suarez de Lezo W423
Mantilla, Luis Suarez de Lezo W493
Mantinan, Jose Manuel Loureda W493
Mantlo, Bronwen L. A635
Mantua, Philip J. A913
Mantua, Philip J. E427
Manturov, Denis V. W474
Mantz, Constantine A P1
Manuele, Cynthia M. A1033
Manvitz, Ted A945
Manvitz, Ted E450
Manwani, Harish A1129
Manwani, Harish A473
Manwani, Harish A742
Manwell, Jason L. E190
Manz, Klint D. E507
Manzano, Stephen J. E31
Manzi, Jim P. A1027
Manzi, Rosina A439
Manzoni, John W201
Mao, Jidong W528
Mao, Jingwen W663
Mao, Juan W150
Mao, Qiwei W292
Mao, Robert Yu Lang E161
Mao, Weijian W292
Mao, Ying W275
Mao, Zhanhong W375
Mao, Zhihong W239
Maples, John T P509
Maples, Rick E. A424
Maples, Rick E. E200
Mapp, Harry L. A207
Maquaire, Stephane W127
Mara, Shaun P. E443
Maraganore, John M. W585
Marakby, Sherif S. W379
Maramag, Angela Pilar B. W85
Maramotti, Ignazio W177

Marani, Ohad W79
Marbach, Carl B. A1032
Marberger, David S. A286
Marcal, Rodrigo W383
MarcAurele, Joseph J. A1108
Marcel, Dominique W213
March, Kevin P. A90
Marchand, Chantale E409
Marchand, Paul A223
Marchesi, Vincent T. E178
Marchetti, Michael E430
Marchetti, Page W. A401
Marchetti, Walkiria Schirrmeister W69
Marchi, Alberto W222
Marchiniak, Jenny P327
Marchioni, John J. A927
Marchioni, John J. E435
Marcial, Maria Theresa D. W85
Marco, Lori J. A534
Marcoccia, Loretta W84
Marcogliese, Richard J. A321
Marcogliese, Richard J. W133
Marcon, Martha E. A685
Marconi, Luis G. E25
Marcote, Flora Perez W300
Marcotte, Louis W308
Marcoux, Isabelle W480
Marcuccilli, James C. A975
Marcus, Gill W558
Marcus, Gill W260
Marcus, Gisele A. A427
Marcus, Gisele A. E204
Marcus, Jeffrey B. A399
Marcus, Joel S. E15
Marcus, Scott E529
Marcuse, Ivan A547
Marcussen, Michala W548
Marcy, Charles F. E50
Maready, Kimberly S. A771
Marecic, Thomas C. A74
Maree, Jacko W559
Mareine, Philippe W61
Marek, Kelly J. E127
Mareuse, Olivier W631
Margetts, Robert John A548
Margolis, Daniel E155
Margolis, Joseph D. (Joe) E280
Margolis, Joseph D. (Joe) E180
Margulies, Anne H. A917
Marhenke, Michael C. A427
Marhenke, Michael C. E203
Mariani, Martin A. A1038
Mariani, Martin A. E496
Mariani, Pedro Henrique A123
Maric, Miran A99
Maricondo, Peter E. E510
Marie, Fernando Fort W174
Marien, Philippe W161
Marin, Alfredo Castelo W382
Marin, Juan Guitard W75
Marin, Valero W493
Marinello, Anthony J. A1043
Marinello, Kathryn V. A287
Marinello, Kathryn V. W641
Mariner, Jonathan D. A900
Mariner, Jonathan D. A1050
Marini-Portugal, Luis W495
Marino, Ricardo Villela W315
Marino, Ricardo Villela W314
Marino, Robert J. E260

COMBINED HOOVER'S HANDBOOK INDEX OF EXECUTIVES

A = AMERICAN BUSINESS
E = EMERGING COMPANIES
P = PRIVATE COMPANIES
W = WORLD BUSINESSS

Marino, Roger M. E481
Marino, Vincent James A864
Marion, John C. E336
Marioneaux, Stephanie J. A1033
Marioneaux, Stephanie J. E493
Mariotti, Marco A825
Maris, Stacey S. A105
Marischen, James M. (Jim) A977
Marischen, James M. (Jim) E464
Maritz, Philip F. A99
Mariucci, Anne L. A998
Mark, Richard A. A1093
Mark, Richard A. E234
Mark, Richard J. A1003
Mark, Richard J. A54
Markee, Richard L. E209
Markel, Anthony F. A659
Markel, Steven A. A659
Markell, Peter K. A352
Markelov, Vitaly A. W474
Markelov, Vitaly A. W256
Markley, John D. (Jay) A224
Markoe, Lynda A148
Markov, Vladimir K. W474
Markowitz, Sean N. A225
Marks, Howard S. W112
Marks, Judith Fran A791
Marks, Stephanie D. A332
Marks, Tom E177
Markus, Maura A. A977
Markus, Maura A. E464
Markwell, David W371
Markwood, Julie R. A981
Markwood, Julie R. E469
Marlatt, Geoffrey T. A794
Marley, Brian T. A10
Marlow, Stephen V. E349
Marmol, Guillermo G. (Gil) A443
Maro, Hideharu W609
Marone, Anthony F. E62
Maroney, Patrick F. A1066
Maroone, Michael E. A208
Marquardt, Jan-Willem W196
Marquardt, Jane P326
Marquardt, Rachelle E480
Marquardt, Rolf W579
Marques, Ana Paula Garrido de Pina W212
Marques, Miguel Athayde W254
Marquette, Travis A187
Marquette, Vanessa W526
Marquez, Antonio F. A350
Marquez, Antonio F. E148
Marquez, Felipe Gonzalez W423
Marquez, Ramon Martin Chavez W76
Marr, Christopher P. E461
Marr, David P. W651
Marr, John S. E502
Marra, David W491
Marrazzo, Samuel D. E193
Marrazzo, William J. A1054
Marren, John W. A18
Marria, Mohit A231
Marriner, Kirsten M. A254

Marriott, David S. A660
Marriott, Peter Ralph W648
Marroco, Tadeu Luiz W111
Marrodan, Carlos Losada W423
Marron, Jose W266
Marrs, Anna Elizabeth A62
Mars, Patrick J. E43
Marsac, Cecile Tandeau De W550
Marsh, Andrew S. A371
Marsh, Laurie M. A358
Marsh, Linda E33
Marsh, Linda E225
Marsh, Martha H. A361
Marsh, Mary W288
Marsh, Stephen P. A373
Marsh, Stephen P. E168
Marsh, William E72
Marsh, William C. E156
Marshall, Carianne A1106
Marshall, Christopher A718
Marshall, Christopher E335
Marshall, David M. A399
Marshall, Ernest W. A890
Marshall, Ernest W. E416
Marshall, Jay A548
Marshall, Jay P272
Marshall, Joseph W. E440
Marshall, Joseph W. E227
Marshall, Lynette P612
Marshall, Ruth Ann A286
Marshall, Ruth Ann A477
Marshall, Ruth Ann A885
Marshall, Ryan R. A862
Marshall, Ryan R. E210
Marshall, Tucker H. A947
Marsili, Daniel B. A269
Marson, Ann Marie E287
Marte, Mario J. A155
Marte, Mario J. A231
Martell, Angel Santodomingo W72
Martell, Keith G. W451
Martello, Joseph A. E34
Martello, Wan Ling A1052
Martello, Wan Ling W29
Martello, Wan Ling W562
Martens, Herbert R. E397
Martens, Philip R. A486
Martha, Geoffrey S. W393
Martich, Rick E249
Martin-Flickinger, Gerri K. A919
Martin-Lof, Sverker W548
Martin, Andy W364
Martin, Bob L. A1018
Martin, Bradley W235
Martin, Bradley Paul L. W231
Martin, Cathy W550
Martin, Christopher A854
Martin, Christopher A396
Martin, Christopher E187
Martin, Dalmacio D. W99
Martin, Dennis J. E188
Martin, Derek A167
Martin, Derek E64
Martin, Edward C. A66
Martin, Edward C. E25
Martin, Elizabeth E43
Martin, Eric J. A1065
Martin, George K. A454
Martin, J. Landis A301
Martin, James W500

Martin, James W499
Martin, Jared E111
Martin, Jay S. E158
Martin, Jeff M. E90
Martin, Jeffrey W. A929
Martin, Jeffrey Wayne E279
Martin, John J. A427
Martin, John J. E203
Martin, Jonathan P. A401
Martin, Kevin J. A298
Martin, Louis A1068
Martin, Lynn C. A561
Martin, M. John A316
Martin, Maria Fuencisla Gomez W73
Martin, Marissa S. A181
Martin, Mary Beth A64
Martin, Matthew A. A401
Martin, Matthew G. T. A417
Martin, Michael A. E352
Martin, Neil S. A867
Martin, Oscar Fanjul A662
Martin, Pascal W495
Martin, Paul E. A795
Martin, R. Brad A405
Martin, Robert N. A652
Martin, Robert W. A1028
Martin, Rodney O. A1098
Martin, Ronald C. E357
Martin, Rosemary W637
Martin, Steve W. A909
Martin, Tami T. E474
Martin, Thomas (Tom) A. A605
Martin, Thomas C. A422
Martin, William G. E428
Martin, William Scott A125
Martin, William Scott E52
Martineau, Phillip M. A39
Martinek, Charles A. E351
Martinek, Kenneth A. E351
Martinelli, Maurizio W631
Martines, Arnold D. A219
Martinetto, Joseph R. A919
Martinez, Alberto Torrado W73
Martinez, Amparo Moraleda W554
Martinez, Armando Martinez W295
Martinez, Carintia E331
Martinez, Guillermo Ortiz W69
Martinez, Jose Javier Fernandez W423
Martinez, Jose Manuel Martinez W71
Martinez, Jose Manuel Martinez W382
Martinez, Lisa P308
Martinez, Luis Hernando de Larramendi W382
Martinez, Maria A244
Martinez, Maria A677
Martinez, Maria Amparo Moraleda W24
Martinez, Melquiades (Mel) R. A763
Martinez, Mike P128
Martinez, Susana A1144
Martino, Antonio A937
Martino, Antonio E441
Martins, Alex P611
Martins, Izilda P. A116
Martinsen, Sten Roar W448
Martire, Frank R. A726
Marton, Szilvia Pinczesne W207
Martore, Gracia C. A1071
Martore, Gracia C. A778
Martore, Gracia C. A1125
Marty, Rudolf W34

Marty, Steve P516
Martynov, Viktor G. W474
Martz, Bennett Bradford A1066
Martz, Gary R. A489
Martz, Walter C. A913
Martz, Walter C. E427
Marugame, Hideya W330
Marumoto, Akira W388
Marushack, Joseph (Joe) E352
Maruszewski, Mark E462
Maruyama, Heiji W658
Maruyama, Masatoshi W389
Maruyama, Yoshimichi W527
Marwala, Tshilidzi W426
Marx, Geoffrey P431
Marx, Kerstin W199
Marzouq, Hamada A. Al W18
Mas, Jorge A668
Mas, Jose Ramon A668
Masai, Takako W82
Masai, Takako W400
Masanovich, Matti M. A1004
Mascarenas, Paul A. A1073
Mascarenas, Paul A. A780
Mascaro, Daniel P. A851
Masciantonio, Ronald James E209
Maseda, Miguel Valls W423
Maselli, Alessandro E83
Mashelkar, Raghunath A. W491
Mashinski, Carla S. E397
Mashinsky, Kristine M. E212
Masiello, Wendy Lee Motlong A595
Masih, Ashish E159
Masilela, Elias W558
Masiyiwa, Strive A730
Masiyiwa, Strive W626
Maslov, Sergey Vladimirovich W476
Maslyaev, Ivan W476
Masola, Diego W84
Mason, A. Craig A592
Mason, Austen D. A282
Mason, Barbara F. W84
Mason, Caren L. E460
Mason, Debby D P351
Mason, J. Thomas E306
Mason, Jo A284
Mason, Jo P158
Mason, John B. E156
Mason, Jonny W179
Mason, Joyce J. E229
Mason, Karol A289
Mason, Mark K. A527
Mason, Mark L. A246
Mason, Mike A635
Mason, Robert E. A418
Mason, Sidney D. A207
Mason, Stephen M. A201
Mason, Thomas P. A369
Mason, Thomas P. E514
Mason, William W358
Masotti, Massimo W627
Masrani, Bharat B. A919
Masrani, Bharat B. W611
Massanelli, Stephen C. A938
Massanelli, Stephen C. E442
Massanet, Francisco Miguel Reynes W423
Massaro, George E. E94
Massaro, Joseph R. A112
Massaro, Joseph R. W46

COMBINED HOOVER'S HANDBOOK INDEX OF EXECUTIVES

A = AMERICAN BUSINESS
E = EMERGING COMPANIES
P = PRIVATE COMPANIES
W = WORLD BUSINESSS

Masse, William D. E537
Massee, Mark H. E108
Massengill, Matthew E. A1122
Masseroli, Mario A825
Masset, Christian W215
Massey, C. Dandridge A884
Massey, Mary P516
Massey, Paul J. E382
Massiani, Luis A1113
Massignon, Jean-Baptiste W123
Masson, Michel Le W174
Massood, Michael A271
Massood, Michael E110
Massoomi, Mani A398
Mast, Darryl E. E326
Mastalerz, Jaroslaw W389
Mastantuono, Gina A931
Masterman, Andrew V. E66
Masters, Blythe S. J. W2
Masterson, Christopher J. E232
Mastin, Celeste Beeks E226
Mastorides, Arist R. E260
Mastro, Mary Lou P210
Mastropaolo, Michael E234
Masuda, Hiroya W319
Masuda, Hiroya W319
Masuda, Hiroya W319
Masuda, Hitoshi W449
Masuda, Kenichi W110
Masuda, Koichi W182
Masuda, Kuniaki W402
Masuda, Takashi W434
Masukawa, Michio W659
Masuko, Jiro W604
Mata, Jorge Pedro Jaime Sendra W265
Mata, Miguel W73
Matarranz, Victor A915
Matas, Barbara R. E448
Matchett, Geraldine W7
Mateev, Nikolai Ivanovich W576
Mateo, Alan V. E519
Matergia, Ralph A. E354
Matharu, Taptesh K. A911
Mather, Ann A730
Mather, Ann A45
Mather, Courtney R. A735
Matherly, Laura Kay E342
Mathers, David R. W176
Matheson, James D. A945
Matheson, James D. E450
Matheson, Les W419
Matheson, Monique S. A743
Mathew, Dennis A45
Mathew, Prakash E349
Mathew, Sara A973
Mathew, Sara A450
Mathew, Sara E145
Mathew, Sara W490
Mathews, Ben J.S. W109
Mathews, Denise R. A605
Mathews, Michael S. A37
Mathews, Michael S. E14
Matheys, Heidi J. E517
Mathieu, Michel W174

Mathis, Brian P486
Mathis, Vincent W. E468
Mathison, Lora P401
Mathrani, Sandeep L. A326
Matin, Arshad E38
Matinez, Maria Amparo Moraleda W638
Matis, Greg A562
Matis, Greg P278
Matis, Nina B. E426
Matlock, Robin L. E336
Matooane, Mantsika A. W426
Matos, Nuno W289
Matos, Sabina A971
Matos, Sabina P537
Matosevic, Josef E249
Matschullat, Robert W. A1096
Matsokhin, Boris E181
Matson, David I. A136
Matson, Kenneth J. A478
Matsubara, Keiji W270
Matsubara, Takehisa W83
Matsubayashi, Shigeyuki W297
Matsuda, Chieko W581
Matsuda, Chieko W343
Matsuda, Tomoharu W333
Matsuda, Yuzuru W354
Matsui, Connie L. E244
Matsui, Masaki W565
Matsui, Shinobu W465
Matsui, Takeshi W462
Matsui, Toru W408
Matsui, Yasushi W193
Matsukura, Hajime W425
Matsumoto, Colbert M. A219
Matsumoto, Hideharu W568
Matsumoto, Kazuhiro W464
Matsumoto, Masayoshi W567
Matsumoto, Masayuki W570
Matsumoto, Milton W69
Matsumoto, Oki A670
Matsumoto, Raymond A119
Matsumoto, Raymond E48
Matsumoto, Ryu W439
Matsumoto, Sachio W370
Matsumoto, Tadashi W402
Matsumura, Mikio W331
Matsumura, Takao W331
Matsunaga, Yosuke W436
Matsuno, Hiroyasu W21
Matsuo, Yoshiro W462
Matsushima, Jun W330
Matsushita, Isao W570
Matsushita, Masaki W267
Matsutani, Yukio W462
Matsuyama, Satohiko W658
Matsuzaka, Hidetaka W418
Matsuzaki, Koichi W330
Matsuzaki, Masatoshi W370
Matsuzaki, Satoru W460
Matsuzaki, Takashi W183
Matt, Peter R. A277
Mattei, Jean-Louis W347
Matteo, Jim P458
Matter, John P. E480
Mattera, Vincent D. E266
Matteson, Mark R. E117
Matteson, Timothy J. A617
Matteson, Timothy J. E289
Mattheus, Daniela W162

Matthews, Beveryly Kay A984
Matthews, Beveryly Kay E476
Matthews, Charles W. A305
Matthews, Darryl E497
Matthews, David E392
Matthews, E. Warren A207
Matthews, Ina Michelle A283
Matthews, Kade L. A421
Matthews, Kade L. E198
Matthews, Norman S. E242
Matthews, Phil P678
Matthews, Tanya E149
Matthews, Timothy A. E443
Matthews, William E. A955
Matthews, William E. E456
Mattimore, Karen A530
Mattingly, Mack F. E42
Mattis, James N. A460
Mattke, Timothy J. A694
Mattlin, Julie A. A251
Mattlin, Julie A. E100
Mattson, Eric L. A755
Mattson, George N. A323
Mattson, W. Patrick E288
Matturri, Alexander J. E87
Matula, Alan D. A60
Matula, Alan D. E532
Matula, Kristopher J. A166
Matus, Kristi E17
Matus, Kristi Ann A377
Matus, Kristi Ann E91
Matute, Rafael W643
Matytsyn, Alexander W476
Matyumza, Nomgando Nomalungelo Angelina W559
Matyumza, Nomgando Nomalungelo Angelina W518
Matz, Marilyn E485
Matz, R. Kevin A364
Mau, Vladimir A. W474
Mauch, Robert P. A73
Mauer, Ryan M. A1107
Mauge, Jacques W238
Maugeri, Maria Rosaria W627
Maun, Marc C. A167
Maun, Marc C. E64
Maure, Nicolas W492
Maurer, Daniel R. A261
Maurer, John A. A443
Maurer, Mark J. A979
Maurer, Matthias W280
Maurer, Thomas P. A799
Mauricio, Maxine L. A364
Mauricio, Maxine L. E355
Mauriello, Susan P177
Maurizio, Poletto W229
Mauro, Anthony A1093
Mauro, Beatrice Weder di W621
Mavoides, Peter M. E173
Maw, Scott Harlan A232
Mawakana, Tekedra A571
Mawson, Simon John W464
Maxfield, Sylvia A152
Maxson, Hilary W39
Maxwell, David G. A487
May, Alan Richard A514
May, Christopher J. A57
May, Devon E. A55
May, Floyd O'Lander E436
May, Gary S. A625

May, James A739
May, James M. A436
May, John Charles A320
May, Lee P168
May, Martin P. E451
May, Patrick E313
May, Stefan W207
May, Teresa M. E27
May, Timothy P639
Mayall, Wendy W471
Mayans, Rolando A378
Mayer, Anton W379
Mayer, Bethany Jean A619
Mayer, Bethany Jean A929
Mayer, David E336
Mayer, Jessica L. A201
Mayer, Marissa A. A1104
Mayer, Michael G. A414
Mayer, Michael G. E191
Mayes, Derrick B. E373
Mayfield, Pinkie D. E67
Mayhew, Nicholas John W180
Mayhew, Nicholas John W179
Maynadier, Patrick D. de A237
Maynard-Elliott, Nichelle A1142
Maynard, Easter A. A1042
Maynard, Michael G. A1132
Maynard, Michael G. E539
Mayo, Heather L. E242
Mayo, Marc M. A408
Mayo, Stephen L. A684
Mayopoulos, Timothy J. A920
Mayopoulos, Timothy J. E627
Mayor-Mora, Enrique A205
Mayoras, Richard Michael E170
Mayrhuber, Wolfgang W196
Mays, Gregory E471
Mays, Randall T. A641
Mayson, Howard J. A792
Mazaltarim, Daniel W511
Mazany, Terry A399
Mazdyasni, Matthew E33
Mazelsky, Jonathan J. E263
Maziol, Eric W348
Mazoyer, Jean-Paul W174
Mazumdar-Shaw, Kiran W304
Mazur, Ilan W78
Mazur, John J. A596
Mazur, John J. E286
Mazza, Janice Marinelli A742
Mazza, Joseph P. A596
Mazza, Joseph P. E286
Mazza, Larry F. E336
Mazza, Matt E34
Mazzarella, Kathleen M. A239
Mazzarella, Kathleen M. E487
Mazzarella, Kathleen M. A1110
Mazzarella, Maria W310
Mazzei, Angelo E517
Mazzella, Joseph A811
Mazzella, Joseph E377
Mazzilli, Ines W54
Mazzoli, Enea W627
Mazzucato, Mariana W222
Mbanda, Laurent P156
McAdam, Timothy E13
McAllister, Andrew S. A401
McAllister, Nancy A814
McAllister, Nancy E378
McAllister, Nancy E379

COMBINED HOOVER'S HANDBOOK INDEX OF EXECUTIVES

A = AMERICAN BUSINESS
E = EMERGING COMPANIES
P = PRIVATE COMPANIES
W = WORLD BUSINESSS

McAllister, Singleton B. E96
McAlmont, Shaun E. A173
McAlmont, Shaun E. E295
McAndrews, Brian P. A231
McAndrews, Brian P. E221
McAndrews, Brian T. E242
McAndrews, Michael S. E472
McAneny, Deborah H. A588
McAneny, Deborah H. E288
McArdle, Janine J. E33
McArthur, John H. W346
McArthur, Susan J. W263
McAtee, David R. A105
McAteer, Thomas J. E291
McAvity, Malcolm E144
McAvoy, John A290
McAvoy, John A289
McBain, Fiona C. W179
McBee, Richard E457
McBreen, Michael F. E278
McBride, Daniel G. E119
McBride, Douglas J. A474
McBride, Douglas J. E230
McBride, Dwight A289
McBride, Lura E. A1065
McBride, Shelley A. E274
McBride, Suzanne E. A942
McCabe, Brian K. A954
McCabe, John J. A439
McCabe, Michael I. E462
McCabe, Robert A. A829
McCabe, Robert A. E385
McCabe, Thomas E. E70
McCaffery, Michael G. A761
McCaffrey, Mark E234
McCague, Elizabeth (Beth) A. A72
McCague, Elizabeth (Beth) A. E29
McCahill, Francis X. E512
McCahon, Jane W. A1001
McCain, Ellis L. "Lon" A226
McCall, Jeff J. A629
McCallion, Anne D. A811
McCallion, Anne D. E377
McCallion, John D. A691
McCallister, Michael B. A410
McCallister, Michael B. A105
McCallister, Michael B. A1153
McCallister, Terry D. E397
McCallum, G. D. W580
McCalman, Jennifer L. A512
McCambridge, David J. E352
McCamey, William R. E41
McCamic, Jay T. A1115
McCamic, Jay T. E533
McCanless, Ross William (Bill) A647
McCann, Carolyn W648
McCann, Christopher G. E1
McCann, James F. E1
McCann, Michael M. E301
McCann, Patrick J. A106
McCann, Patrick J. E40
McCanna, Lawrence E. A940
McCardle.III, James T. E420
Mccarley, Kirk P178

McCarrier, Deanna K. E156
McCarroll, Elizabeth M. A711
McCarter, Patrick R. A279
McCarthy, Aaron D. W379
McCarthy, Christine M. A335
McCarthy, Christine M. A850
McCarthy, Colm W464
Mccarthy, Cormac Michael W191
McCarthy, Cornelius P. E317
McCarthy, Daniel J. A292
McCarthy, Deborah J. E537
McCarthy, Gloria M. A85
Mccarthy, James P. E311
McCarthy, Karen E. W507
McCarthy, Kevin S. A832
McCarthy, Kevin S. A833
McCarthy, Malcolm Christopher W138
McCarthy, Margaret (Meg) A59
McCarthy, Margaret M. A660
McCarthy, Margaret M. A176
McCarthy, Margaret M. A413
McCarthy, Marie J. A192
McCarthy, Mary Pat A700
McCarthy, Michael R. A1061
McCarthy, Michelle M. E319
Mccarthy, Paul M. E311
McCarthy, Ryan D. A189
McCarthy, Thomas A. A927
McCarthy, Thomas A. E435
McCartney, Twyla E189
McCarty, Richard A. E357
McCarvel, Thomas J. E149
McCaskey, James J. E326
McCasland, Tom H. A125
McCasland, Tom H. E52
McCaslin, James A. A57
McCaslin, Jocelyn E477
McCaw, Maureen W573
McCaw, Susan E10
McClain, Darren P639
McClain, Gerald K. E247
McClain, Gretchen W. A74
McClain, Gretchen W. A171
McClanahan, David M. A868
McClanathan, Joseph W. A182
McClanathan, Joseph W. A624
McClane, Matthew T. A596
McClane, Matthew T. E286
McClellan, Laurie E. E117
McClellan, Mark B. A585
McClellan, Mark B. A239
McClellan, Michael R. A747
McClellan, Stephen R. A483
McClelland, Bruce William E420
McClelland, David W. A446
McClelland, W Kent P498
McClenahan, Tom E312
McClimon, David S. A1144
McClincy, Christopher J. A386
McClintock, Robert J. E388
McClone, Dustin J. A741
McClone, Dustin J. E349
McCloy, Fiona P345
McClure, Beverley J. A531
McClure, Charles G. A345
McClure, Charles G. A343
McClure, Kathleen R. W10
McClure, Melinda H. E268
McClure, Teri Plummer A438
McClure, Teri Plummer A583

McClure, Teri Plummer A629
McClure, Teri Plummer E234
McColgan, Michael J. A367
McColl, John S. E124
McCollam, Sharon L. A35
McCollister, Rolfe Hood A188
McCollister, Rolfe Hood E69
McCollom, Mark R. A454
McCollum, Mark A. A656
McCollum, Mark A. A1124
McComb, G. Scott E247
McCombe, Mark S. A160
McComish, Christopher J. A910
McConeghy, Daniel C. W327
McConie, Jay P. A430
McConn, Ann M. A37
McConn, Ann M. E14
McConnell, Brian P. E455
McConnell, Gregory A. E96
McConnell, Julia A1125
McConnell, Rick M. E147
Mcconville, James W471
McConville, Jim W64
McCool, Jim W116
McCool, John E35
McCool, Robert J. A475
McCormack, Pamela A616
McCormick, Christopher J. A631
McCormick, Christopher J. A157
McCormick, Mary E. E151
McCormick, Robert J. A1043
McCormick, Thomas E. E397
McCormick, Tracy S. A704
McCormick, Tracy S. E328
McCourt, Marion A882
McCourt, Martin E532
McCourt, MaryFrances A78
McCourt, Thomas A. E282
McCowan, Debra E247
McCoy, Albert E. A329
Mccoy, Daniel P P166
McCoy, Dustan E. A452
McCoy, Michael R. A118
McCoy, Michael T. A199
McCoy, Sarah (Sally) Gaines E115
McCoy, Sherilyn S. A981
McCoy, Sherilyn S. A604
McCoy, Sherilyn S. W57
McCracken, Brendan M. A792
McCracken, Nicola W191
McCracken, Robert E. A617
McCracken, Robert E. E289
McCrary, Charles D. A884
McCray, Ronald D. A688
McCray, Ronald D. E323
McCrea, Marshall S. A369
McCreary, Lynn S. E350
McCree, Donald H. A248
McCreight, David W. A205
McCrink, Gerald A400
McCrory, Paul W111
McCrostie, Pip W385
McCulloch, Anne Segrest A398
McCullough, Gary E. A277
McCullough, Mark C. A59
McCurdy, Kay W. A455
McCurdy, Meghan A400
McCurdy, Michael W. A181
McCurry, James Kyle A427

McCurry, James Kyle E204
Mccuskey, Kenneth D P189
McDaniel, Cara A1086
McDaniel, Cara E521
McDaniel, Connie D. A477
McDaniel, Jerry L. A703
McDaniel, Jerry L. E327
McDaniel, Raymond W. A711
McDaniel, Suzan A586
McDearman, John C. A1132
McDearman, John C. E539
McDermott, Melissa E517
McDermott, Michael J. E420
McDermott, William R. A931
McDermott, William R. E547
McDevitt, Sean M. A145
McDevitt, William H. A130
McDew, Darren W. A6
McDonagh, Brendan W21
McDonagh, Francesca Jane W81
McDonagh, John E19
McDonald, Andrew L. A270
McDonald, Andrew L. E109
McDonald, Bryan D. A510
McDonald, Bryan D. E252
McDonald, Calvin R. A335
McDonald, Charles B. E72
McDonald, James O. A422
McDonald, Michael J. E190
McDonald, R. Bruce A313
McDonald, Rebecca Middleton E113
McDonald, Steven D. E90
McDonald, Wesley S. E539
McDonald, William J. A541
McDonell, Jason B. A17
McDonie, Patrick J. A995
McDonnell, Eileen C. A1076
McDonnell, Jeffrey M. A703
McDonnell, Jeffrey M. E327
McDonnell, Karl E467
McDonnell, Kevin E8
McDonnell, Matthew E61
McDonnell, Michael R. A158
McDonogh, Dermot A132
McDonough, Paul H. A261
McDorman, Diane H. A401
McDougall, Duane C. A166
McDowell, Mary T. E45
McDowell, Monte E315
McDowell, Ronda M. A913
McDowell, Ronda M. E427
McDowell, Scott E. A666
McElfresh, Jeff A105
McElhennon, Stephen H. A391
McElroy, David H. A65
McElroy, David H. W50
McEntee, James J. A1014
McEntee, James J. E488
McEvoy, M. Kevin A364
McEvoy, Robert A. A888
McEwan, Bill W351
McEwan, Ross W419
McFadden, Eliza E468
McFadden, Eve M. A989
McFarland, Clyde E. A1033
McFarland, Clyde E. E492
McFarland, F.K. A528
McFarland, F.K. E258
McFarland, Joseph (Joe) M. A647
McFarland, Katharina G. A920

HOOVER'S HANDBOOK OF EMERGING COMPANIES 2023 663

COMBINED HOOVER'S HANDBOOK INDEX OF EXECUTIVES

A = AMERICAN BUSINESS
E = EMERGING COMPANIES
P = PRIVATE COMPANIES
W = WORLD BUSINESSS

McFarland, R. William W235
McFarlane, John W648
McFarlane, John W89
McFerran, Michael R. E34
McFetridge, Adriane A1120
McFetridge, Adriane E535
McGarey, Jennifer C. A752
McGarry, Martha E. A788
McGarry, Michael H. A840
McGarry, Michael H. A1073
McGarry, Michael H. W536
McGarry, Steven J. A944
McGarry, Steven J. E450
McGarvie, Blythe J. A950
McGarvie, Blythe J. A643
McGaw, Richard W80
McGeary, Roderick C. A796
McGeary, Roderick C. A876
McGeary, Roderick C. A244
McGee, Eric A543
McGee, Grant B. A604
McGee, Henry W. A73
McGee, Jeninne C. A895
McGee, Richard K. A832
McGee, Richard K. A833
McGee, Susan B. E234
McGehee, Julie E431
McGeorge, W. Scott A938
McGeorge, W. Scott E442
McGettrick, Mark F. A794
Mcghee, Craig P123
McGhee, James E. A283
McGibney, Robert V. A594
McGill, Stephen C. E30
McGill, William Brett E310
McGill, William H. E310
McGill, Yvonne A90
McGill, Yvonne A322
McGilvray, Aaron M. A215
McGimpsey, Thomas O. E6
McGinness, Janet L. A670
McGinnis, Bradley F. E96
McGinnis, John T. A655
McGivney, Mark C. A662
McGlade, David P. A942
McGlade, John E. A483
McGlinchey, David A959
McGloin, William A453
McGlynn, Lorelei A917
McGlynn, Margaret G. A1089
McGookey, James E. A251
McGookey, James E. E100
McGough, Thomas M. (Tom) A286
McGovern, Gail J. A343
McGovern, Gail J. A345
McGovern, Gail J. A807
McGovern, Jeanne A548
McGovern, John F. A596
McGovern, John F. E286
McGovern, Lawrence D. A509
McGovern, Lawrence D. E251
McGovern, Michael Y. E72
McGowan, Christopher J. A166
McGowan, Edward J. E12

McGowan, Mark P. E162
Mcgowan, Murray W298
McGranahan, J. Russell E212
McGraner, Matt E348
McGrath, Albert G. E539
McGrath, Judith A. A50
McGrath, Rebecca J. W377
McGrath, Sheila A485
McGraw, E. Robinson A888
McGraw, E. Robinson E413
McGraw, Harold W. (Terry) A791
McGraw, Thomas C. A1038
McGraw, Thomas C. E496
Mcgreevey, Gregory G. A574
McGregor, George P512
McGregor, Jay E. E344
McGregor, Scott A. A90
McGrew, Matthew R. A315
McGuiness, Jeffrey R. E532
McGuire, David M. A958
McGuire, David M. E456
McGuire, Don A108
McGuire, Francis P. W295
McGuire, Timothy I. A336
McGuire, Tom W84
McGuirk, Patrick M. A435
McGuirk, Patrick M. A129
McGuirk, Patrick M. E210
McGuirt, Milford W. A920
McHale, Brian K. E69
McHale, Judith A. A518
McHale, Judith A. A802
McHargue, Rodger Allen A422
McHenry, Daniel J. A491
McHugh, James A292
McHugh, James A384
McHugh, Julie H. E282
McHugh, Richard E98
McIlwraith, John C E321
McInerney, Ryan A1096
McInerney, Thomas J. A470
McInnes, Ross W225
McIntire, Lee A. A792
McIntosh, Colleen M. A311
McIntosh, Sandy W596
McIntyre, Bridget F. W18
McIntyre, Geraldine Penny A864
McIntyre, Jennifer A. (Jen) A1075
McIntyre, Kenneth A. E347
McIntyre, Pamela A. W120
McIntyre, Shauna F. A639
McKay, David I. W507
Mckay, Douglas W419
McKay, H. Lamar A86
McKay, Lamar W178
McKay, Matthew J. A643
McKay, Michael H. E117
McKay, Tim S. W120
McKeag, Bryan R. A507
McKeag, Bryan R. E248
McKechnie, Mark E3
McKee, Daniel A971
McKee, Daniel P537
McKee, E. Marie A347
McKee, Lynn B. A1138
McKee, Lynn B. E544
McKee, Michael D. A413
McKee, Michael D. E412
McKelvey, James Morgan A162
McKendry, William D. A71

McKendry, William D. E29
McKenna, Dennis F. E393
McKenna, Frank J. W120
McKenna, Frank J. W112
McKenna, John M. A1033
McKenna, Judith A1104
McKenna, Michelle E543
McKenna, Siobhan Louise W651
McKenna, Trent T. E111
McKenney, Michael J. E286
McKenney, Richard P. A1082
McKenney, Richard P. A1079
McKenney, Richard P. W570
McKenney, Thomas P. E189
McKenzie, Diana L. A1089
McKenzie, Diana L. A691
McKenzie, John F. E351
McKenzie, Jonathan M. W133
McKeon, Brian P. E263
McKeon, Simon W500
McKeon, Simon W419
McKeon, Simon W499
McKeon, Timothy M. A494
McKeough, Kathleen E. A1108
McKernan, Thomas V. A413
Mckey, William P166
McKibben, Timothy J. E76
McKibben, Tracy B. A546
McKibben, Tracy B. A358
McKiernan, Anthony A671
McKillican, Rebecca W420
McKim, Tony C. E192
McKinley, Janet P586
McKinney-James, Rose A696
McKinney, Cassandra M. A274
McKinney, Greg A134
McKinney, Greg E54
McKinney, James J. A599
McKinney, Sean P. E99
McKinstry, Nancy A6
McKinstry, Nancy W10
McKissack, Eric T. A396
McKissack, Eric T. E186
McKnight, Andrew A. E334
McKnight, Gary C. A305
McKnight, William F. A753
McKoy, Philip G. A806
McLain, Kevin E360
McLain, Timothy S. A803
McLain, Timothy S. E371
McLain, William T. A354
McLallen, Walter F. E305
McLamb, Michael H. E310
McLaren, John B. E471
McLaren, K. Louise W570
McLarty, Thomas F. A1061
McLauchlin, Tracy A. E264
McLaughlin, Edward Grunde (Ed) A670
McLaughlin, Gregory T. E412
McLaughlin, Lawrence J. A393
McLaughlin, Mark D. A867
McLaughlin, Neal T. A1057
McLaughlin, Philip E517
McLaughlin, Robert M. A145
McLaughlin, Ronald Mitchell A411
McLaughlin, Sarah W81
McLaughlin, Thomas M. A860
McLay, Kathryn A1104
McLean, Benjamin J. A1053

McLean, Christine N. W235
McLean, Emmett E. E315
McLean, Hugh H. A774
McLean, Hugh H. E360
McLean, John A. A1032
McLean, Kerry J. A571
McLean, Margaret B. E500
McLean, Scott J. A1151
McLeod, E. Douglas A68
McLeod, E. Douglas A722
McLindon, Andrew D. A188
McLindon, Andrew D. E69
McLintock, Michael W55
Mclnness, Ross W511
McLoughlin, Christine F. W574
McLoughlin, Dennis E369
McLoughlin, Karen A. A155
McLoughlin, Keith R. A195
Mclsaac, Graham A. W287
McMahon, Brien J. A874
McMahon, Daniel K. E245
McMahon, Dirk C. A1075
McMahon, Lisa G. E537
McMahon, Robert W. A27
McMahon, Thomas H. E242
McMahon, Vincent K. E543
McManus, John M. A696
McMaster, Herbert Raymond E547
McMath, Gaye M. W260
McMichael, Bryan E106
Mcmillan, Lee P2
McMillan, Lorna W157
McMillan, Wayde D. E276
McMillon, C. Douglas (Doug) A1104
Mcmonagle, Richard A1009
Mcmonagle, Richard P563
Mcmorris, Marc F. E183
McMullen, Elizabeth A. A118
McMullen, Michael R. A27
McMullen, W. Rodney A1091
McMullen, W. Rodney A240
McMullen, W. Rodney A611
McMurray, Kurston Patrick A741
McMurray, Louis C. E90
McMurray, Michael C. W374
McMurray, Scott E421
McMurray, Sean Patrick A1118
McMurray, Sean Patrick E533
McMurry, Fred A. A414
McMurry, Fred A. E193
McNab, Paul E523
McNabb, Frederick William A565
McNabb, Frederick William A1075
McNally, Michael W548
McNally, Michael F. E301
McNamara, J. Paul A1063
McNamara, J. Paul E508
McNamara, John W. A490
McNamara, Kevin M. A1049
McNamara, Mary W462
McNamara, Michael M. A207
McNamara, Michael S. E525
McNamara, Robert A. A580
McNamara, William P. A187
McNeal, Glenda G. A745
McNeal, Gwyn G. E180
McNeely, Joseph E. A82
McNeely, Richard A337
McNeil, Jeffrey E163
McNeilage, Hazel M. A886

COMBINED HOOVER'S HANDBOOK INDEX OF EXECUTIVES

```
A = AMERICAN BUSINESS
E = EMERGING COMPANIES
P = PRIVATE COMPANIES
W = WORLD BUSINESSS
```

McNeill, Kevin B. E402
McNeill, W. David E372
McNerney, Robert A854
McNitt, Peter B. A774
McPartland, James E. (Bo) A478
McPeek, Jennifer J. E87
McPhail, Richard V. A526
McPhaill, Kevin J. A935
McPhaill, Kevin J. E439
McPhee, Sarah W562
McPherson, Amy A864
McPherson, Charles W. A955
McPherson, Charles W. E456
McPherson, John D. A304
McPherson, John R. A277
McPherson, Kevin M. E311
McPherson, Philip J. E56
McPherson, Scott E. A818
McQuade, Barbara L. A545
McQuade, Joseph E. A499
McQuade, Joseph E. E246
McQuade, Kathryn A. B. A47
McQuillen, David W463
McRae, Brent E340
McRae, Eric S. A427
McRae, Eric S. E204
McRae, Lawrence D. A298
McRae, Robert G. E436
McRaven, William H. A288
McReynolds, John W. A369
McRobert, Michael P. E315
McSally, Michael J. A367
McSharry, Heather Ann W178
McSherry, Melissa K. A878
McSherry, Melissa K. A879
McSween, W. Scott A186
McSweeney, Erin L. W242
Mctaggart, Douglas F. W574
McTear, Paul H. E237
McVey, J. Kyle A421
McVey, J. Kyle E197
McVey, Keshmira P90
McVey, Richard M. E311
McWaters, Kimberly J. A812
McWhinney, Deborah D. A173
McWhinney, Deborah D. A911
McWhorter, Dorri E239
McWilliams, Judith P176
McWilliams, Vicki D. E495
Md, A Brent Eastman P488
Md, Ananias Diokno P691
Md, Bruce H Hamory A458
Md, Bruce H Hamory P236
Md, Dan Blue P483
Md, David Wood P72
Md, Gordon Hunt A982
Md, Gordon Hunt P550
Md, James M Orsini P644
Md, Linda Butler P462
Md, Norman Rizk A961
Md, Norman Rizk P531
Md, Steve Keuer P123
Mead, Mike A261
Mead, Steven J. A191

Mead, Steven J. E77
Meade, Christopher J. A160
Meador, David E. A343
Meadow, Patricia T. A400
Meagher, Laura C. A1091
Meakins, Ian W170
Meaney, James W170
Meaney, Susan A213
Meaney, William L. A973
Means, William L. E147
Mears, Michael N. A929
Mears, Michael N. A325
Meates, Helen T. E388
Mechetti, Carlos W132
Mecke, Stephen C. E461
Meddings, Richard W176
Meddings, Richard W618
Medeiros, Carlos Henrique Senna W630
Medeiros, Karen P239
Meden, Scott A. A745
Medhat, Parham A650
Medhat, Parham E305
Medhus, Tore W558
Medici, Ugo W177
Medina, Dionisio Garza W131
Medina, Gualberto (Gil) A749
Medina, Joseph H P401
Medina, Manuel Hidalgo A178
Medina, Sergio Mauricio Menendez W131
Medina, Victor W410
Meditz, John C. E221
Medler, Linda R. A834
Medley, Mark B. A282
Medlicott, Stella W228
Medline, Michael W216
Medori, Rene A737
Medori, Rene W635
medrano, Jose G. Aguilera W266
Meduski, Mary E. E72
Medvedev, Alexander Ivanovich W256
Medvedev, Yuri M. W329
Medvedovsky, Maxim W323
Mee, Loh Sook W261
Mee, Michael F. A638
Meegan, John P. A753
Meehan, Thalia A191
Meehan, Thalia E77
Meeker, Mary A162
Meeks, Elsie M. A398
Meeks, James E. E120
Meffert, Walt P363
Mefford, Jeffrey S. A703
Mefford, Jeffrey S. E327
Mega, Jessica L. A315
Megalou, Christos Ioannis W473
Megarbane, Fabrice W358
Meguro, Hiroshi W408
Mehan, Daniel Joseph W240
Mehdi, Yusuf I. A1082
Mehlman, Anne E130
Mehmel, Robert F. E242
Mehos, Manuel J. A1086
Mehos, Manuel J. E521
Mehra, Jyoti A619
Mehra, Sachin A912
Mehra, Sachin A670
Mehra, Vineet E305
Mehrabian, Robert E483

Mehran, Alexander R. A402
Mehrotra, Sanjay A700
Mehrotra, Sanjay A214
Mehta, Aman W588
Mehta, Harmeen W371
Mehta, Manish A160
Mehta, Sanjay E485
Mehta, Satish A231
Mehta, Siddharth N. A42
Mehta, Siddharth N. A749
Mehta, Siddharth N. "Bobby" A588
Mehta, Tarak W6
Mei-Pochtler, Antonella W486
Mei-Pochtler, Antonella W54
Mei, Claire A547
Meier, Keith A103
Meier, Richard A. E61
Meier, Stephanie E61
Meikle, Scott Gerald A619
Meiklejohn, Mark J. A181
Meiler, Paula J. E132
Meilstrup, Eric J. E293
Meindl, Edward E313
Meiras, Inigo W169
Meirovitz, Hagit W312
Meisinger, Chad L. E340
Meister, Doris P. A651
Meister, Keith A. A696
Meister, Paul M. E31
Meister, Paul M. W45
Meister, Paul M. W46
Meixelsperger, Mary E. E517
Mejdell, Dag W448
Mejia, Luis Alberto Moreno W244
Mejias, Antonio Huertas W382
Mejorada, Enrique Castillo Sanchez A953
Mejorada, Enrique Castillo Sanchez W27
Meldrum, Guy W111
Meledandri, Chris W433
Melej, Cristian A. A519
Melej, Cristian A. E256
Melikyan, Gennady W521
Melin, Alf W590
Melincoff, Gwen A. E107
Meline, David W. A76
Meline, David W. W7
Melito, David P. A985
Mellander, Carl W228
Melle, Patrice M. Le A347
Mellini, Paul V. E473
Mello, Guilherme (Gui) Nebel de A1086
Mello, Manuel Alfredo da Cunha Jose de W70
Mello, Paul P. A400
Mello, Wilson W323
Melnick, Gregg A. A148
Melnick, Paul C. E97
Melo, Leila Cristiane Barboza Braga de W315
Melo, Pedro Augusto de W72
Melone, Anthony J. A301
Meloy, Mark J. A416
Meloy, Matthew J. A995
Melton, Stephen A. A71
Melton, Stephen A. E29
Meltzer, Carol A5
Meltzer, Neil P504

Meltzer, Seth A976
Melucci, Jeffrey P. A604
Melville, David R. A188
Melville, David R. E69
Melville, Randolph W. E234
Melville, Randolph W. E426
Melvin, George A927
Melvin, George E435
Melvin, Leland D. E70
Melvin, Vincent P. A97
Melwani, Prakash A. E130
Memioglu, Erol W621
Memioglu, Erol W346
Menard, Peter M. E143
Menchelli, Irzio Pinasco W174
Mencini, Frank C. A441
Mencini, Frank C. E212
Mencoff, Samuel M. A799
Mendel, John William A643
Mendelsohn, Nicola S. W201
Mendelson, Avner A1086
Mendelson, Avner E516
Mendenhall, Dudley W. E218
Mendes, Paul M. W120
Mendez-Andino, Jose L. A795
Mendez, Angel L. E448
Mendez, Norma Isaura Castaneda W265
Mendillo, Jane L. A466
Mendivil, Paulino J. Rodriguez W27
Mendizabal, Cristina Garmendia W169
Mendoza, Estelito P. W514
Mendoza, Letitia A23
Mendoza, Maria Teresa Pulido W87
Menendez-Cambo, Patricia A385
Menendez, Ana M. A1111
Menezes, Ivan M. A993
Menezes, Ivan M. W201
Meng, Cai W142
Meng, Jing W140
Meng, Jinsong W37
Meng, Qingsheng W148
Meng, Sen W140
Meng, Xiangsheng W574
Meng, Yan W172
Menges, Kathrin W14
Mengi, Cem W26
Mengucci, John S. A189
Menke, Sean E. A1110
Menne, Simone W277
Menne, Simone W327
Menne, Simone W198
Mennen, Justin L. A895
Menneto, Steven D. A835
Menon, Ajay A828
Menon, Viju S. A981
Mensah, Nana A316
Menshikov, Sergey N. W474
Menshikov, Sergey N. W256
Mente, Michael E418
Mentis, Angela W419
Menzaghi, Frédérique E80
Menzel, Harald W192
Meo, Francesco De W251
Meo, Luca de W492
Meo, Luca De W592
Mera, Francisco Jose Riberas de W593
Merad, Abdellah W523
Mercado, Pablo G. E111
Merchant, Rahul N. A612

HOOVER'S HANDBOOK OF EMERGING COMPANIES 2023

COMBINED HOOVER'S HANDBOOK INDEX OF EXECUTIVES

A = AMERICAN BUSINESS
E = EMERGING COMPANIES
P = PRIVATE COMPANIES
W = WORLD BUSINESSS

Mercier, Daniel W193
Mercier, Johanna A473
Mercier, Johanna E346
Mercier, John M. A138
Mercier, John M. E55
Mercier, Matthew E141
Merck, Peter Emanuel W397
Merckle, Ludwig W273
Merckle, Tobias W273
Merdian, Charles E299
Meredith, Christine A976
Meredith, David L. A889
Meredith, David L. E414
Meredith, Ian T. A175
Meredith, Todd J. E247
Merigold, Catharine E8
Merin, Mitchell M. W571
Merino, Bruce A. A1053
Merkatoris, Susan L. A741
Merkatoris, Susan L. E349
Merkel, Michael T A222
Merkel, Michael T P114
Merkel, Stephen M. E347
Merkens, Hermann Josef W3
Merkt, Steven T. W590
Merlo, Silvia W363
Merrifield, Gary A. A880
Merrifield, Gary A. E412
Merrifield, Stacy E222
Merrill, Allan P. A450
Merriman, Ronald L. E412
Merrin, Patrice W260
Merritt, David C. A224
Merritt, David C. A998
Merriwether, Cambrea R. A214
Merriwether, Deidra C. A1127
Merriwether, Deidra C. A485
Merrywell, Christopher M. A270
Merrywell, Christopher M. E109
Merten, Jesse E. A42
Mervine, Edward A. E372
Merwe, Daniel Maree Van der W562
Merwe, Hans van der W558
Merwe, Kathryn van der W63
Merz, Albrecht W98
Merz, Martina W641
Merz, Martina W196
Merz, Martina W602
Mesa, Manuel J. Perez de la E5
Mesa, Manuel J. Perez de la E389
Meschewski, Jennifer A742
Meservey, Lulu C. A13
Meshari, Ahmad W486
Meshel, Jeffrey Wayne A936
Meshel, Jeffrey Wayne E441
Mesick, Ralph M. A423
Mesler, Amanda W422
Mesquita, Jorge S. A710
Mesquita, Jorge S. A541
Messemer, Annette W548
Messemer, Deborah M. A807
Messenberg, Shmuel W410
Messer, Bridget W574
Messer, Raymond F. E463

Messersmith, Amy B. A184
Messier, Luc W550
Messina, Carlo W310
Messing, Barbara H. E368
Messmer, Harold M. A898
Messner, Timothy A. A333
Mestrallet, Gérard W548
Mestrallet, Gérard W565
Meswani, Hital R. W491
Meswani, Nikhil R. W491
Metcalf-Kupres, Kimberley A790
Metcalf, James S. A1005
Metcalf, John E340
Metcalf, Leo T. A958
Metcalf, Leo T. E456
Metcalf, Nicole A556
Metcalf, Nicole E270
Metcalfe, G. Joe W260
Metcalfe, Ronald A. E470
Meter, Valerie J. Van A399
Meth, Thomas E169
Methvin, Stacy P. A830
Mettee, Michael M. A395
Mettee, Michael M. E185
Mettler, Christopher J. A932
Mettler, Christopher J. E436
Metz, Adam L. A788
Metz, Adam L. E365
Metz, Christopher T. E90
Metz, Gunnar W98
Metz, Robert de W199
Meunier, Bernard W429
Meunier, Bertrand W61
Meurice, Eric W623
Meurs, Bert van W351
Meuse, David R. A966
Meuse, David R. E274
Mexia, Antonio Luis Guerra Nunes W70
Mey, Jozef De W18
Meyer, Barry M. A14
Meyer, David M. A487
Meyer, Derek A101
Meyer, James (Jim) E. A224
Meyer, James (Jim) E. A941
Meyer, Jill P. A240
Meyer, John T. E486
Meyer, Marc W61
Meyer, Melody W109
Meyer, Melody B. A755
Meyer, Melody B. A8
Meyer, Michael J. A190
Meyner, Michael J. E73
Meyer, Perry L. A235
Meyer, Perry L. E356
Meyer, Thomas D. E455
Meyer, Timothy L. E114
Meyer, Tobias W198
Meyercord, F. Duffield A810
Meyercord, F. Duffield E375
Meyercord, Wade F. A697
Meyerdirk, Elizabeth Miin W528
Meyerhoeffer, Jason A. A398
Meyers, Brian K. E302
Meyers, Charles J. A377
Meyers, Francoise Bettencourt W358
Meyers, Jean-Victor W358
Meyers, Kenneth F. A986
Meyers, Nicolas W358
Meyers, Terence B. A693

Meyling, Marie-Helene W215
Meyrowitz, Carol A1030
Mezeul, Patricia A439
Mezger, Jeffrey T. A594
Mgoduso, Thandeka Nozipho W558
Mhatre, Nitin J. A152
Mhatre, Rohin E415
Mi, Dabin W291
Miaja, Rafael Robles W35
Miao, Gang W528
Miau, Feng-Chiang W128
Miau, Matthew A999
Mibe, Toshihiro W285
Miceli, Paul J A616
Michael, Aaron A812
Michael, Edward L. E406
Michael, Jonathan E. A896
Michael, Jonathan E. E422
Michael, Macht W644
Michael, Mark C. A913
Michael, Mark C. E427
Michael, Ralph S. A252
Michael, Robert A. A8
Michaels, Barry D. E547
Michaels, Paul S. A600
Michas, Alexis P. A173
Michas, Alexis P. E380
Michaud, Anik W39
Michaud, Bruno W294
Michaud, Thomas B. A977
Michaud, Thomas B. E464
Michel, Berangere W364
Michel, Berangere W364
Michel, Gilles W554
Michel, Gilles W631
Michel, John M. A527
Michel, Serge W631
Michel, Stephane W613
Michel, Todd A. A251
Michel, Todd A. E100
Micheletti, Andrew J. A119
Micheletti, Andrew J. E48
Michels, David P. A605
Michels, Douglas A. E534
Michelson, Michael W. A505
Michelson, Michael W. A1150
Michi, Ayumi W538
Micklem, Mark C. A913
Micklem, Mark C. E427
Micklewright, Scott W. A702
Micklewright, Scott W. E325
Middleton, Daina E370
Middleton, Suzanne O. E279
Midgley, Clare P569
Midkiff, H. Marvin A207
Midler, Laurence H. A213
Midseim, Anne-Lene W448
Midteide, Thomas W204
Miebach, Michael A670
Miedler, Andrew T. A586
Mielak, Gary P210
Miele, Laura A363
Mielke, Daniela A. A1014
Mielke, Daniela A. E488
Mielle, Dominique E411
Miels, Luke W258
Might, Thomas O. E72
Migita, Akio W437
Miglani, Nalin E179
Migliorino, Anthony V. E401

Mignone, Roberto A. W598
Migoya, Alfonso Gonzalez W244
Miguel, Jose Marcos Ramirez W265
Miguel, Josu Jon Imaz San W493
Mihalik, Trevor I. A929
Mihaljevic, Tomislav A458
Mihaylo, Steven G. E129
Mii, Y.J. W583
Mikalsen, Wenche W558
Mikami, Takeshi W570
Mikami, Yasuaki W460
Mikan, G. Mike A110
Mikasa, Yuji W436
Mike, Kanetsugu W405
Mike, Kanetsugu W407
Mikells, Kathryn A. A502
Mikells, Kathryn A. A388
Mikes, Ellie L. A452
Mikes, Suzanne E117
Mikhailova, Elena V. W474
Mikhailova, Elena Vladimirovna W256
Mikhalenko, Vyacheslav A. W474
Miki, Takayuki W409
Mikitani, Hiroshi W487
Mikkelson, Adam P. E312
Mikkilineni, Krishna A530
Mikogami, Daisuke W566
Mikoshiba, Toshiaki W285
Mikuen, Scott T. A613
Milanes, Douglas J. A316
Milano, Todd A. E467
Milavsky, Elizabeth A. E371
Milbourne, Robert H. E91
Milchovich, Raymond J. A349
Milek, John J. A394
Miles, Allen J. E537
Miles, Amy E. A1018
Miles, Amy E. A747
Miles, Amy E. A76
Miles, David W. E540
Miles, Gene E. E196
Miles, Mark W. A153
Miles, Randall D. E180
Miles, Rudolph M. A563
Milewski, Frank C. A1033
Miley, Nate P166
Milgrim, Brett N. A184
Milgrim, Brett N. E381
Milikin, Maurice Anthony W40
Millage, Timothy R. E295
Millard, Robert B. A613
Millard, Robert B. E176
Miller, A. Fred A397
Miller, A. Fred E187
Miller, Adam A971
Miller, Adam P537
Miller, Alan B. A1076
Miller, Alexey Borisovich W474
Miller, Alexey Borisovich W256
Miller, Amber A296
Miller, Andrew E281
Miller, Ann M. A743
Miller, Barry E. E158
Miller, Brian E57
Miller, Brian K. E502
Miller, Bruce W182
Miller, Bruce E. E401
Miller, C. Richard A401
Miller, Cecil R. A592
Miller, Cheryl S. A1050

COMBINED HOOVER'S HANDBOOK INDEX OF EXECUTIVES

A = AMERICAN BUSINESS
E = EMERGING COMPANIES
P = PRIVATE COMPANIES
W = WORLD BUSINESSS

Miller, Cheryl S. E88
Miller, Cindy J. A1054
Miller, Craig A136
Miller, D. Byrd A803
Miller, D. Byrd E371
Miller, David E234
Miller, David W311
Miller, David B. A719
Miller, David B. E362
Miller, David J. E155
Miller, Debra B. A138
Miller, Debra B. E55
Miller, Dennis E. E356
Miller, Douglas C. E126
Miller, Dwight A. A703
Miller, Dwight A. E327
Miller, Elizabeth A98
Miller, Elizabeth E36
Miller, Frank C. A490
Miller, Gina Byrne A722
Miller, Gragg E. A510
Miller, Gragg E. E252
Miller, Greg E455
Miller, Heidi G. A434
Miller, Irene Ruth W300
Miller, Irene Ruth W611
Miller, James A72
Miller, James E29
Miller, James H. A23
Miller, James H. A303
Miller, James O. A251
Miller, James O. E100
Miller, Jamie S. A867
Miller, Janet L. A252
Miller, Jeffrey A. A931
Miller, Jeffrey Allen A494
Miller, Jennifer L. E22
Miller, Jody Greenstone A643
Miller, John M. A902
Miller, Jonathan Frank A570
Miller, Jonathan Frank A742
Miller, Jonathan Frank E547
Miller, Jonathan Frank E12
Miller, Joseph A289
Miller, Joseph A290
Miller, Justin A112
Miller, Justin E58
Miller, Klaus W269
Miller, Kristine E. E72
Miller, Kurt G. E454
Miller, Lawrence E219
Miller, Liz A971
Miller, Liz P538
Miller, Marc D. A1076
Miller, Maribess L. A536
Miller, Maribess L. A1040
Miller, Maribess L. E499
Miller, Mark K. E235
Miller, Mary John A984
Miller, Mary John E476
Miller, Matthew A. E189
Miller, Matthew R. A803
Miller, Matthew R. E371
Miller, Melissa M. A95

Miller, Meredith E19
Miller, Michael B. E142
Miller, Michael R. E293
Miller, Michael T. E274
Miller, Quincy L. A352
Miller, Redonda G. A73
Miller, Richard P. A196
Miller, Richard P. E78
Miller, Robert G. E175
Miller, Russ A300
Miller, S. P. W414
Miller, Shannon A580
Miller, Sharon A. A860
Miller, Steven A239
Miller, Steven E111
Miller, Steven D. A1142
Miller, Stuart A. A629
Miller, Ted C. A945
Miller, Ted C. E451
Miller, Thomas L. E223
Miller, Timothy Alexander W31
Miller, Tina A639
Miller, Victor J. A530
Miller, William I. A306
Miller, William P. A57
Millerchip, Gary A611
Milleri, Francesco W231
Milleson, John R. E149
Millett, Mark D. A975
Millham, Brian A912
Millican, Steve F. E307
Milligan, George D. A1118
Milligan, George D. A1065
Milligan, George D. E533
Milligan, Sandra A787
Milligan, Stephen D. A905
Milligan, Stephen D. E45
Millington, Nicholas E452
Millner, Thomas L. A155
Millon, Jean-Pierre A311
Millones, Peter J. A170
Mills, Cheryl D. A160
Mills, Claire A400
Mills, Drake A788
Mills, Drake E364
Mills, Elliot A129
Mills, Gary R. A419
Mills, Howard D. A470
Mills, Jeannette M. A1006
Mills, Karena E102
Mills, Linda A. A65
Mills, Linda A. A723
Mills, Robert D. A1035
Mills, Robert D. E50
Mills, Robin W170
Mills, Scott M. A846
Mills, Stephen C. A927
Mills, Stephen C. E435
Mills, Steven A. A662
Mills, Steven W. A722
Millwood, Timothy A26
Milos, Charles D. A722
Milstein, Jed M. A99
Milton, John D. E222
Milton, Mark A. A592
Milton, Robert A. E10
Mims, Verett E441
Mimura, Akio W606
Mimura, Koichi W392
Minagawa, Makoto W278

Minaka, Masatsugu W183
Minakata, Takeshi W343
Minakawa, Tsuyoshi W26
Minami, Masahiro W494
Minami, Naohiro W321
Minami, Shinsuke W313
Minamide, Masanori W417
Minamide, Masao W83
Minas, Mauricio Machado de W69
Minato, Alan P176
Minaya, Jose A711
Minc, Alain W169
Minegishi, Masumi W490
Minemura, Ryuji W181
Mineno, Yoshihiro W183
Minetti, Carlos M. A330
Ming, Dong W141
Ming, Guoqing W268
Ming, Guozhen W268
Ming, Jenny J. A631
Ming, Patrick Huen Wing W70
Mingle, Robyn T. A279
Mingo, Felix de Vicente W73
Mingot, Antoni Peris W423
Minich, Lawrence J. E173
Minicucci, Benito A34
Minière, Dominique W215
Minieri, Joanne M. E527
Minihan, Kenneth A. E309
Mininberg, Julien R. A958
Mink, Kim Ann A354
Mink, Kim Ann W357
Minkel, Kimberley A. E175
Minner, G. William E219
Minnich, Brandt N. A685
Minnich, George E. A26
Minniear, Stephanie E455
Minnifield, Franky A283
Minnix, Lanesha T. A358
Minnix, Lanesha T. E6
Minogue, Michael R. E277
Minoia, Nicholas A287
Minoia, Nicholas E115
Minor, Glenda J. E430
Minteer, Robert J. A401
Minter, Travis A. E452
Mintz, Jack M. W299
Mintzer, Jennifer Francis E423
Minyard, Katherine L. A792
Minzberg, Samuel W287
Miosi, Salvatore A. A694
Miotto, Michael P. E128
Mirabile, Jennifer A192
Miralles, Albert J. A214
Miramontes, Louis P. A639
Miramontes, Louis P. A895
Miranda, Gerardo Jofre W172
Mire, Michael W64
Mires, Charles D. E97
Miron, Paulo Sergio W315
Miron, Robert J. A332
Miron, Steven A. A332
Miron, Steven A. A224
Mironenkov, Anton W655
Mirtillo, Nunzio W228
Mirviss, Jeffrey B. A175
Mirza, Jawaid A. W232
Misa, James F. Di E113
Misasi, Ryan J. A392
Misasi, Ryan J. E183

Miscik, Jami A713
Miscik, Judith A. A538
Miscik, Judith A. A466
Misheff, Donald T. A432
Mishima, Shin W329
Mishra, Deepak A825
Miskel, Christopher C. A455
Miskell, Eileen C. A554
Miskell, Eileen C. E268
Misra, Kabir W29
Missad, Matthew J. A1053
Missad, Matthew J. A555
Missad, Matthew J. E269
Missling, Jeffrey R. E349
Mistretta, Nancy G. A539
Mistysyn, Allen J. A933
Mita, Mayo W462
Mitachi, Takashi W606
Mitachi, Takashi W487
Mitachi, Takashi W566
Mitani, Eiichiro W402
Mitarai, Fujio W123
Mitau, Lee R. E226
Mitchell-Thomas, Kamilah E313
Mitchell, Adrian V. A962
Mitchell, Adrian V. A654
Mitchell, Adrienne P590
Mitchell, Arthur M. W347
Mitchell, Arthur M. W570
Mitchell, Bryant A441
Mitchell, Bryant E212
Mitchell, E. Gay W122
Mitchell, Guy W. A190
Mitchell, Guy W. E73
Mitchell, H. Elizabeth A927
Mitchell, H. Elizabeth E435
Mitchell, James Gordon W596
Mitchell, James R. A528
Mitchell, John C. A724
Mitchell, Kate D. A984
Mitchell, Kate D. E476
Mitchell, Kevin J. A826
Mitchell, Kevin J. A319
Mitchell, Kevin J. E382
Mitchell, Lee A. A472
Mitchell, Lee A. E230
Mitchell, M. Christian A797
Mitchell, M. Christian A1121
Mitchell, M. Christian E368
Mitchell, Maureen B. A1113
Mitchell, R. Brian A478
Mitchell, Robbin A608
Mitchell, Robbin E387
Mitchell, Royce W. A830
Mitchell, Samuel E. E517
Mitchell, Stephen Ray E518
Mitchell, Steven R. E462
Mitchell, Terence J. A691
Mitchell, Terence J. E323
Mitchell, Thomas E. A414
Mitchell, Thomas E. E193
Mitchell, Thomas J. E495
Mitchelmore, Lorraine A225
Mitchelmore, Lorraine W83
Mitchelmore, Lorraine W573
Mitchill, Neil G. A877
Mitchko-Beale, Stephanie A223
Mito, Nobuaki W565
Mitomo, Toshimoto W557
Mitrova, Tatiana W523

COMBINED HOOVER'S HANDBOOK INDEX OF EXECUTIVES

A = AMERICAN BUSINESS
E = EMERGING COMPANIES
P = PRIVATE COMPANIES
W = WORLD BUSINESSS

Mitsunari, Miki W657
Mitsuoka, Ryuichi W417
Mitsuya, Yuko W193
Mitsuya, Yuko W223
Mitsuya, Yuko W253
Mittal, Aditya W49
Mittal, Lakshmi N. A481
Mittal, Lakshmi N. W49
Mittal, Som E179
Mitterbauer, Peter W453
Mitts, Brian E348
Mitts, Heath A. W590
Mitzman, Robert J. E173
Miura, Atsunori W65
Miura, Hiroyoshi W26
Miura, Kunio W345
Miura, Satoshi W436
Miura, Satoshi W278
Miura, Toshiharu W527
Miya, Kenji W181
Miyabe, Yoshiyuki W465
Miyagawa, Tadashi W462
Miyahara, Hideo W462
Miyahara, Hiroyuki W267
Miyahara, Ikuko W604
Miyaji, Shinji W18
Miyajima, Takeshi W576
Miyajima, Tsukasa W181
Miyakawa, Junichi W550
Miyama, Minako W181
Miyamoto, Shigeru W433
Miyamoto, Yoichi W535
Miyanaga, Kenichi W408
Miyanaga, Masato W155
Miyanaga, Shunichi W405
Miyanaga, Shunichi W402
Miyanaga, Shunichi W403
Miyanoya, Atsushi W81
Miyashita, Moni E244
Miyashita, Yutaka W407
Miyata, Atsushi W407
Miyata, Hirohiko W408
Miyata, Hiromi W576
Miyata, Tomohide W223
Miyata, Yasuhiro W567
Miyauchi, Ken W550
Miyauchi, Koji W515
Miyazaki, Kenji W313
Miyazaki, Tsuyoshi W536
Miyoshi, Junko W316
Miyoshi, Kenji W316
Miyoshi, Toshiya W343
Mizel, Courtney L. A652
Mizel, Larry A. A652
Miziolek, Aleksandra ("Aleks") A1004
Mizrahi, Rafael Moises Kalach W35
Mizuguchi, Makoto W345
Mizuhara, Kiyoshi W347
Mizui, Toshiyuki W173
Mizuma, Katsuyuki W564
Mizumoto, Lance A. A423
Mizuno, Yasuhide W285
Mizuno, Yojiro W614
Mizuta, Hiroyuki W44

Mizutani, Hitoshi W155
Mjoli-Mncube, Nonhlanhla S. W8
Mkhize, Zamani Moses W518
Mkhwanazi, Themba M. W39
Mlinar, Michael P. E322
Mlotek, Mark E. A917
Mminele, Daniel W558
Mnookin, Allison A648
Mo, Bin W173
Mo, Yong W528
Mo, Youjian W274
Moag, Anthony G A1026
Moag, Anthony G P620
Mobley, Daniel W201
Moch, Nicolas W547
Mochet, Jean-Paul W127
Mochizuki, Mikio W612
Mock, James M. E380
Mockard, Jeanne L. A367
Mockler, Patrick E. A188
Mockler, Patrick E. E69
Modeski, Michael E366
Modise, Punkie E. W7
Modjtabai, Avid A118
Modruson, Frank Blaise A1148
Mody, Zia W286
Moehn, Michael L. A54
Moelis, Kenneth D. E330
Moeller, Jon R. A850
Moen, Anne Sigrun W204
Moes, Jeffrey B. E190
Moeseke, Hilde Van A486
Moffa, Dominic A458
Moffa, Dominic P236
Moffat, Nikki W99
Moffatt, James S. A423
Moffatt, Laurie Norton A152
Moffett, David M. A304
Moffett, David M. A807
Mogford, John W101
Mogg, Jim W. A783
Mogharbel, Khaled Al W523
Moglia, Giovanni Gionata Massimiliano W592
Moglia, Peter M. E15
Moh, Christine Suat Moi W286
Mohabeer, Dominique W96
Mohammad, Shamim A1068
Mohammad, Shamim A205
Mohan, Bi Joy W370
Mohapatra, Surya N. A625
Moharram, Shereef E114
Mohebbi, Afshin E141
Mohney, Jeffrey M. E469
Mohr, Gavin A. A555
Mohr, Gavin A. E269
Mohr, John P. A663
Mohr, Marshall L. A572
Mohr, Marshall L. E519
Mohr, Pauline F. M. van der Meer A1093
Moir, A. W8
Moir, Maxine A398
Moise, Anson M. A287
Moise, Anson M. E115
Moise, Philip H. E122
Moison, Franck J. A1069
Moison, Franck J. A497
Mok, Chung Fu W362
Mok, Tony W57

Mokari, Atabak E121
Mokate, Renosi Denise W558
Mokhele, K. D. K. W414
Mokoena, C. K. W518
Mokrysz, Teresa W389
Mol, Pim W W86
Moldovan, Kristopher E. A1097
Molefe, T. B. L. W414
Molepske, Michael B. A125
Molepske, Michael B. E52
Moles, Robert T. A509
Moles, Robert T. E251
Molewski, Michael D. E24
Molhem, Khalid Abdullah Al W520
Molina, Gloria A301
Molina, Gloria P171
Molina, Gustavo A397
Molina, Gustavo E187
Molina, V. Sue E546
Molinari, Luna W625
Molinaro, Marcus J P206
Molinini, Michael L. E96
Moll, James D. E98
Moll, Sandra J. E291
Mollenkopf, John C. E33
Mollenkopf, Steven M. A164
Mollenkopf, Steven M. A867
Moller, Jorgen W205
Mollerstad, Hilde W228
Mollet, Chris P210
Mollins, Sean Michael A888
Molloy, John P. A716
Molloy, Lawrence (Chip) P. A959
Molluso, Joseph E527
Molnar, Gary F. W133
Molnar, Jozsef W412
Moloko, Sello W8
Moloney, Daniel M. E546
Moloney, Herbert W. E295
Moloney, Jacqueline F. A372
Moloney, Jacqueline F. E167
Moloney, Jacqueline F. E329
Moloney, John W191
Molope, C. W. N. W414
Moltke, James von W195
Molvar, Roger H. A800
Molvar, Roger H. E199
Momen, Ronnie A627
Momper, Gilles W27
Momper, Matthew J. E274
Monaco, Al A1127
Monaco, Frank J. A393
Monaco, Frank J. E184
Monaco, Jason P. A958
Monaco, Michael P. E159
Monaghan, John W245
Monaghan, Matthew (Matt) E. A986
Monaghan, Thomas A223
Monahan, Elizabeth F P198
Monahan, Thomas L. E493
Moncada, George S. E311
Moncayo, Amelia A400
Monceau, Evelyn du W554
Mondardini, Monica W174
Mondello, Mark T. A578
Mondre, Gregory K. A716
Monesmith, Heath B. W209
Monette, Cory R. E164
Money, Elizabeth A. A378
Money, Laura A. W572

Mong, David Tak-yeung W80
Mongeau, Claude A747
Mongeau, Claude W611
Mongeau, Claude W133
Mongia, Nandini A855
Mongillo, Stephen A. A549
Monheit, Barry M. E25
Monie, Alain A23
Moniz, Ernest J. A952
Monnas, Giovanna Kampouri W489
Monroe, Charles R. A546
Monser, Edward L. A30
Monserrat, Alvaro J. A923
Monserrat, Alvaro J. E433
Monson, Kevin W. A704
Monson, Kevin W. E328
Montag, Bernhard W545
Montagnani, Maria Lillà W627
Montague, Adrian W548
Montana, Gregory G. (Greg) A408
Montanaro, Craig L. A596
Montanaro, Craig L. E286
Montanaro, Leopold W. A596
Montanaro, Leopold W. E286
Montanez, Alma Rosa A911
Montano, Juan M. A890
Montano, Juan M. E416
Montano, Michael A1047
Montano, Thomas B. A536
Montecalvo, David A. E534
Montecinos, Jose Miranda W220
Monteiro, Antonio Victor Martin W70
Monteiro, Antonio Vitor Martins W71
Montemagno, Thomas A224
Montemayor, David Juan Villarreal W265
Montemayor, Jaime A465
Montemayor, Jose O. A258
Montero, Juan M. A1033
Montero, Juan M. E493
Montes, Alfredo Villegas W70
Montes, Antonio Pardo de Santayana W72
Montesano, Hwa Jin Song W370
Montesano, Jin Song W658
Montesi, Corliss J. A613
Montesquiou, Bertrand de W125
Montford, John T. A956
Montgomery, Brian D. A874
Montgomery, Christopher P596
Montgomery, Darrell B. E271
Montgomery, David A. A188
Montgomery, David A. E69
Montgomery, Kendall E340
Montgomery, Michael E350
Montgomery, Neela A645
Montgomery, Norman J. A418
Montgomery, Norman J. E195
Montgomery, Robert G. E443
Montgomery, Thomas M. A74
Montgomery, William C. A374
Montiel, Maritza G. A272
Montiel, Maritza G. A673
Montier, Patrick W524
Montinola, Aurelio R. W85
Montlivault, Stephane de A791
Montmerle, Bruno W238
Montouche, Thierry W161
Montross, Scott J. E353
Montull, Daniel Javier Servitje W265

COMBINED HOOVER'S HANDBOOK INDEX OF EXECUTIVES

A = AMERICAN BUSINESS
E = EMERGING COMPANIES
P = PRIVATE COMPANIES
W = WORLD BUSINESSS

Monzon, Gilberto A836
Moody-Byrd, Gail E242
Moody-Dahlberg, Frances Anne A68
Moody-Dahlberg, Frances Anne A722
Moody, Ann M. A722
Moody, Brent L. A195
Moody, H. Craig E434
Moody, John S. E217
Moody, Robert L. A722
Moody, Ross R. A722
Moody, Ross R. A68
Moolji, Sanjay A1039
Moolji, Sanjay P628
Moon, Youngme E. A670
Moon, Youngme E. W626
Mooney, Andrew W116
Mooney, Beth E. A105
Mooney, Beth E. A444
Mooney, Beth E. W10
Mooney, Howard F. A415
Mooney, Howard F. E194
Mooney, Kerri A. A191
Mooney, Kerri A. E77
Mooney, P. Kelly A687
Moore, Andrew E49
Moore, Bennie R. A401
Moore, Brandon John E227
Moore, Charles O. E326
Moore, Christine P174
Moore, Christine M. A274
Moore, Christopher T. A478
Moore, Claiborne "Clay" L. A747
Moore, Clint E310
Moore, Clyde R. A611
Moore, Constance B. E247
Moore, Constance B. E495
Moore, Corey E. E279
Moore, Danny D. E185
Moore, Daryl D. A772
Moore, David T. E243
Moore, Ed P462
Moore, Eddie N. A794
Moore, Edward W. A907
Moore, Frederick V. A688
Moore, Frederick V. E323
Moore, Gary B. A607
Moore, Gregory J. A318
Moore, H. Lynn E502
Moore, H. Phillip A741
Moore, H. Phillip E349
Moore, Jack B. A595
Moore, Jack B. A767
Moore, Johnnie E. A401
Moore, Lena P61
Moore, Maurice E. E337
Moore, Patrick J. A94
Moore, Patrick J. E160
Moore, Patrick Q. A570
Moore, Patrick R. E341
Moore, Pattye L. A783
Moore, Preston A788
Moore, Preston E364
Moore, Randall L. E489
Moore, Renee A414

Moore, Renee E193
Moore, Richard H. A414
Moore, Richard H. E191
Moore, Robert Scott A32
Moore, Roger H. E116
Moore, Roy E. E5
Moore, Seth A. E368
Moore, Stephanie Zapata A1097
Moore, Stephen J. E301
Moore, Stephen M E171
Moore, Suzanne E189
Moore, Terry A. A393
Moore, Terry A. E184
Moore, Thomas L. E433
Moore, Wes E239
Moorhead, Daniel J. E547
Moorhead, John ("Jay") U. A5
Moorman, Charles Wick A230
Moorman, Charles Wick A786
Moorthy, Ganesh A697
Moosmayer, Klaus W449
Moot, Guy A1106
Moquin, Jeffrey P486
Mora, Elizabeth A. E330
Mora, Hanne de W430
Mora, Hanne de W641
Mora, Richard S. E163
Morabito, Paula A787
Moraes, Pedro Luiz Bodin de W315
Moragne, John D. E67
Morais, Diane E. A43
Moraleda, Amparo W2
Morales, Alfonso Gomez W73
Morales, Angel L. W495
Morales, David P687
Morales, Gustavo Arriagada W314
Morales, Maria Guadalupe W643
Morales, Ramiro Gerardo Villarreal W131
Morales, Vincent J. A840
Moran, Kevin Patrick E518
Moran, Robert F. A497
Moran, Thomas E. W209
Moranishi, Susan P166
Morano, Susan E3
Morano, Vittorio Pignatti W392
Moranville, Guy de Selliers de W18
Morara, Pier Luigi W627
Mordell, Mark D. E46
More, Daniel B. E446
Morea, Donna S. A920
Morea, Donna S. A1042
Morea, Joseph L. E270
Morefield, Diane M. E120
Morehead, Max C. E526
Moreira, John M. A380
Morel, Donald Eugene E278
Morel, Donald Eugene E83
Morel, Gilles A1129
Moreland, W. Benjamin A301
Morellini, Stefano W177
Moreno, Ana Cristina Peralta W69
moreno, Angel Losada W266
Moreno, Carlos Mario Giraldo W127
Moreno, Francisco W631
Moreno, Hector Maria Colonques W71
Moreno, John F. E397
Moreno, Juan Antonio Gonzalez W265
Moreno, Julian Acuna W314
Moreno, Luis Alberto A342

Moret, Blake D. A901
Moret, Blake D. E402
Moreto, Edson Marcelo W69
Moretti, Marella W592
Morfit, Mason A912
Morford, Craig S. A388
Morgado, Robert J. A14
Morgan-D'Amelio, Karen E. E420
Morgan-Silvester, Sarah A. W122
Morgan, Barlow A889
Morgan, Barlow E414
Morgan, Bartow A888
Morgan, Bartow E414
Morgan, Bennett J. E228
Morgan, Bruce W. D. W37
Morgan, Denise E546
Morgan, Gerald R. E217
Morgan, Glen W. A214
Morgan, Hugh A400
Morgan, James C. A90
Morgan, James H. A266
Morgan, John K. A1118
Morgan, Michael C. A605
Morgan, R. Scott A1033
Morgan, R. Scott E493
Morgan, Sandra Douglass A407
Morgan, Tony K. A954
Morgan, Wesley A. E515
Morgan, William J. E381
Morganroth, Greg S. E212
Morgon, Virginie W358
Mori, Hiroshi W407
Mori, Kazuhiko W297
Mori, Keiichi W336
Mori, Kimitaka W568
Mori, Masakatsu W343
Mori, Nobuchika A24
Mori, Nozomu W331
Mori, Shunzo W536
Mori, Takahiro W437
Mori, Yoshihiro W184
Morial, Marc H. A898
Moriani, Diva W54
Moriarty, Clodagh W318
Moriarty, Edmond N. A95
Moriarty, Rowland T. E126
Morici, John F. E16
Moridaira, Takayuki W455
Moriguchi, Yuko W454
Morikawa, Noriko W403
Morikis, John G. A447
Morikis, John G. A933
Morillo, Daniel A785
Morimoto, David S. A219
Morin, Francois W50
Morin, Marie-Lucie W572
Morin, Rene E451
Morinaka, Kanaya W581
Morioka, Kenji W316
Morisaki, Kazuto W345
Morishita, Yoshihito W607
Morissette, Benoit W308
Morita, Mamoru W279
Morita, Takayuki W425
Moriwaki, Yoichi W606
Moriya, Hidekdi W464
Moriya, Seiji W607
Moriyama, Masahiko W581
Moriyama, Masayuki W347
Morken, CeCelia A1115

Moro, Masahiro W389
morodo, Valentin Diez W266
Morohashi, Masahiro W26
Moroka, Kgomotso Ditsebe W559
Moroney, Simon E. W449
Morooka, Reiji W566
Morozov, Alexander W521
Morparia, Kalpana A825
Morral, Peter A485
Morris, Adrian W597
Morris, Brad P2
Morris, Brenda I. E65
Morris, Christine W611
Morris, David N358
Morris, David W662
Morris, David C. W579
Morris, David R. A878
Morris, David R. E409
Morris, Dawn C. E23
Morris, Debra L. E419
Morris, Edna K. A1035
Morris, Gregory A. A94
Morris, Gregory K. E376
Morris, James G. A199
Morris, James T. A359
Morris, James T. A951
Morris, Jason M. A747
Morris, Jennifer W246
Morris, John C. A627
Morris, John J. A1110
Morris, Leslie Wims A576
Morris, Maria R. A911
Morris, Maria R. A1115
Morris, Mary Catherine (Cathy) A97
Morris, Michael A1151
Morris, Michael G. A140
Morris, Michael G. A502
Morris, Robert T. E538
Morris, Steven M. A958
Morris, Steven M. E456
Morris, Susan A35
Morris, Ted A. A723
Morris, Victor P93
Morris, W. Howard A795
Morris, W. Howard E528
Morrish, Jon W273
Morrison, Dale F. A567
Morrison, Daniel A191
Morrison, Daniel E77
Morrison, Denise M. A870
Morrison, Denise M. A691
Morrison, Denise M. A1096
Morrison, Gregory B. A1086
Morrison, Gregory B. E425
Morrison, Gregory B. E521
Morrison, Harold L. A659
Morrison, Karen A490
Morrison, Maureen F. A99
Morrison, Patricia B. A142
Morrison, Scott C. A123
Morrison, Ward M. E410
Morrison, William D. E364
Morrison, William T. A1033
Morrison, William T. E493
Morrissette, Harris V. A1044
Morrissey, John J. A554
Morrissey, John J. E268
Morrissey, Joseph T. A787
Morrissey, Michael A853
Morrissey, Michael J. A927

HOOVER'S HANDBOOK OF EMERGING COMPANIES 2023

COMBINED HOOVER'S HANDBOOK INDEX OF EXECUTIVES

A = AMERICAN BUSINESS
E = EMERGING COMPANIES
P = PRIVATE COMPANIES
W = WORLD BUSINESSS

Morrissey, Michael J. E435
Morrissey, Michael M. E177
Morrow, Brian R. A905
Morrow, George J. E346
Morrow, George J. E16
Morrow, J. Barry E302
Morse, David L. A298
Morse, John B. A23
Morse, Laurence C. A1113
Morse, Robert Randolph A78
Morstofolini, Ernestina W177
Morton, James O'Shanna A554
Morton, James O'Shanna E268
Morton, Thomas E477
Morzaria, Tushar W109
Morzaria, Tushar W360
Morzaria, Tushar W89
Mosbacher, Robert A. A325
Mosca, Fabrizio W310
Mosch, Peter W61
Mosch, Peter W640
Moscho, Harold P602
Mosebrook, Jeffrey E278
Moser, Christopher A757
Moser, Scott L. A519
Moser, Scott L. E256
Moses, Jon J. E480
Moses, Marc W91
Moshier, Howard C. A1144
Mosich, Nicholas A. A119
Mosich, Nicholas A. E48
Moskalenko, Anatoly W476
Moskowitz, Amy P366
Moskowitz, Joseph L. A24
Moskowitz, Raina E175
Mosley, Daniel L. A150
Moss, Aaron D. A359
Moss, Aaron D. A951
Moss, Arvid W448
Moss, Bob L. A1111
Moss, Jeff W167
Moss, Patricia L. A679
Moss, Patricia L. A426
Moss, Patricia L. E202
Moss, Richard D. E540
Mossberg, Anna W581
Mossberg, Anna W579
Mosser, Patricia W445
Mosso, Robert B. E99
Moster, Steven W. E85
Moszkowski, Guy A915
Moszkowski, Neal E408
Mothner, Jonathan S. A985
Motl, Christopher J. A1113
Motlagh, Katherine E134
Motley, David L. A441
Motley, David L. E266
Motley, David L. E212
Motoi, Chie W515
Motta, Milena Teresa W310
Mottershead, Chris W328
Mottola, Frank E474
Mottram, Heidi W135
Moug, Kevin G. E367

Moukheibir, Catherine E282
Moul, Donald A. A1006
Moulin, Emmanuel W601
Moulin, Richard T. du E370
Moulonguet, Thierry W631
Mount, Melinda J. A221
Mountain, James R. A96
Moura, Gabriel Amado de W314
Moura, Julio W132
Mouras, Gregory T. E437
Mouri, Naohiro A65
Mourick, Mark Van E340
Mowat, David W596
Mowat, David W358
Mowbray, Kevin D. E295
Mowery, Theodore W. A702
Mowery, Theodore W. E326
Mowry, Meagan M. E108
Moxley, James R. A454
Moxley, Michael E235
Moy, Alicia E. A129
Moyer, Albert J. E314
Moyer, Glenn E. A1078
Moyer, Glenn E. E513
Moyer, James C. E331
Moyer, K. Leon A1078
Moyer, K. Leon E513
Moynihan, Brian T. A128
Moynot, Alain W165
Moyo, Dambisa F. A4
Moyo, Dambisa F. A230
Moyo, Dambisa F. W89
Mozingo, Caterina Ardon E315
Mozos, Jose Vicente de los W492
Mrkonic, George R. A111
Mrkonic, George R. A1055
Mroz, Carolyn M. E69
Mroz, Richard S. A396
Mroz, Richard S. E187
Mu, Tiejian W37
Mu, Xuan W291
Mucci, Martin A726
Mucic, Luka W273
Mucic, Luka W517
Mucke, Gabriele W415
Muckenhirn, Keith E32
Mudge, Richard R. E188
Mudick, Stephanie B. A800
Mudick, Stephanie B. A1014
Mudick, Stephanie B. E488
Mueck, Jutta W586
Muehlbauer, James L. A1068
Muehlemann, Werner W308
Muehlen, Constance E. von A34
Muehlhauser, Regina E350
Mueller, Brian R. E61
Mueller, Edward A. A677
Mueller, Karl W. A773
Mueller, Ken P453
Mueller, Klaus-Peter W251
Mueller, Meg R. A454
Mueller, Michael W358
Mueller, Otto W586
Mueller, Patricia H. A905
Mueller, Perry A852
Mueller, Perry E399
Mueller, Ralf W196
Mueller, Thomas A W86
Mueller, Werner W234
Mueller, Wolfgang W61

Muenz, David J. W333
Muffly, James L. E336
Mugiishi, Mark A423
Mugino, Hidenori W281
Muhaidib, Sulaiman Abdulkader Al W520
Muhart, Matthew P510
Muhlen, Alexander von zur W195
Muhsin, Bilal E312
Muhtadie, Fayez S. E212
Muir, Glenn P. E415
Muirhead, Christian A367
Mujica, Fernando Borja W73
Mujumdar, Shveta A718
Mujumdar, Shveta E335
Mukai, Chiaki W253
Mukai, Chiaki W333
Mukai, Takeshi W389
Mukhamadeev, Georgy Rashitovich W575
Mukhamedov, Leonid W524
Mukherjee, Anindita A710
Mukherjee, Sanjoy W233
Mulcahey, Terri L. A812
Mulcahy, Anne A585
Mulcahy, Anne A1132
Mulcahy, Anne A648
Mulcahy, David S. A60
Mulder, Susan R. A610
Muldoon, Fiona W81
Muldowney, Michael P. A1087
Mulhern, Carmel W164
Mulhern, Mark F. A561
Mulhern, Timothy W. A1013
Mulia, Salvatore F. E348
Mullaney, Patrick G. A489
Mullen, Dennis M. E50
Mullen, James C. A1027
Mullen, John Patrick W596
Mullen, Joyce A. A558
Mullen, Joyce A. E491
Mullen, Mark A45
Mullen, Patrick J. A810
Mullen, Patrick J. E376
Mullen, Walter Jack A134
Mullen, Walter Jack E54
Muller, Edward R. E8
Muller, Frans W351
Muller, Josef M. A303
Muller, Klaus-Peter W162
Muller, Luis A. E107
Muller, Michael W510
Muller, Udo W14
Mullery, Stephen P. A395
Mullery, Stephen P. E186
Mullet, Matthew D. E223
Mullican, Michael P. A10
Mulligan, Donal L. E161
Mulligan, John J. A997
Mulligan, John J. A675
Mulligan, Lawrence P. E293
Mulligan, Margaret J. W122
Mulligan, Richard C. A158
Mulligan, Sharmila A288
Mulligan, William C. A1013
Mullin, Hadley E418
Mullin, Thomas P. A926
Mullineaux, Donald J. A397
Mullings, Grace A. A1034
Mullings, Paul E. A28

Mullinix, Mark M. A401
Mullins, Eric D. A288
Mullins, Eric D. A1085
Mullins, James A917
Mulller, Jurgen W517
Mulloy, William Patrick A890
Mulloy, William Patrick E416
Mulroney, Brian A161
Mulrow, William J. A289
Mulrow, William J. A290
Mulye, Vishakha V. W296
Mumenthaler, Christian W580
Mumford, Lisa A874
Munaiz, Manuel Moreu W295
Munakata, Naoko W417
Munce, Claudia Fan A155
Munck, Johnny W348
Muncrief, Richard E. A325
Mundkur, Christine A. A201
Mundra, Hari L. W296
Mundy, Robert P. A799
Munekata, Hisako W83
Muney, Alan M. A239
Munfakh, Antoine G. E472
Munger, Charles T. A300
Munger, Charles T. A151
Munn, William J. A727
Munn, William J. E345
Munnings, Roger Llewelyn W476
Munnings, Roger Llewelyn W410
Munoz, Carmen W493
Munoz, David Ibarra W35
Munoz, Elena Leon W295
Munoz, Feliciano Gonzalez W283
Munoz, George A47
Munoz, George A660
Muñoz, José A548
Munoz, Oscar A213
Munoz, Oscar A912
Munte, Heribert Padrol W423
Munyantwali, Swithin J. W8
Muoio, Salvatore E301
Mupita, R. T. W414
Murabayashi, Shigeru W21
Murabito, John M. A239
Murabito, John M. E540
Murai, Jun W487
Murakami, Diane W. A219
Murakami, Ippei W44
Murakami, Kazuya W432
Murakami, Nobuhiko W616
Murakami, Takao W582
Muraki, Atsuko W316
Muraki, Atsuko W565
Muramoto, Morihiro W181
Muramoto, Shinichi W336
Murano, Elsa A. A534
Muransky, Edward W A393
Muransky, Edward W E184
Murao, Kazutoshi W462
Muraro, Robert M. A995
Murasawa, Atsushi W657
Murase, Masayoshi W437
Murase, Yukio W329
Murata, Nanako W297
Murata, Toshihiko W453
Murata, Tsuneo W417
Murata, Yoshiyuki W185
Muratore, Emiliano W73
Muratta, Lori M. E437

COMBINED HOOVER'S HANDBOOK INDEX OF EXECUTIVES

A = AMERICAN BUSINESS
E = EMERGING COMPANIES
P = PRIVATE COMPANIES
W = WORLD BUSINESSS

Murayama, Seiichi W223
Murdoch, James Rupert A1007
Murdoch, K. Rupert A738
Murdoch, K. Rupert A447
Murdoch, Lachlan K. A447
Murdoch, Lachlan K. A738
Murdock, Daniel C. A272
Murdock, Tyson E247
Muriel, Rodolfo Garcia W131
Murkovic, Bertina W640
Murphy-Chutorian, Douglas E436
Murphy, Andrew W364
Murphy, Andrew J. A882
Murphy, Brian Daniel E25
Murphy, Brian William A271
Murphy, Brian William E109
Murphy, Christopher J. A1
Murphy, Conor A176
Murphy, Conor W191
Murphy, Devin Ignatius E382
Murphy, Diana M. A988
Murphy, Diana M. A620
Murphy, Diana M. E479
Murphy, Dominic P. A1102
Murphy, Donal W191
Murphy, Edward F. A1151
Murphy, Emily W. E315
Murphy, Frances M. E144
Murphy, Gerry W179
Murphy, Gregory E. A927
Murphy, Gregory E. E435
Murphy, Gregory J. A759
Murphy, J. Andrew A951
Murphy, J. Andrew A359
Murphy, James W111
Murphy, John A264
Murphy, John J. E165
Murphy, John Raymond A765
Murphy, John Raymond E469
Murphy, Joseph M. A768
Murphy, Joseph M. E359
Murphy, Karen P236
Murphy, Ken W597
Murphy, Kevin W240
Murphy, Kevin C. A1
Murphy, Kevin S. A860
Murphy, Lila A. Manassa E238
Murphy, Mark E P526
Murphy, Mark J. A700
Murphy, Matthew D. E65
Murphy, Michael P500
Murphy, Michael R. W50
Murphy, Pam A902
Murphy, Patrick M. E138
Murphy, Peter E. E308
Murphy, Raymond G. E278
Murphy, Richard B. A1133
Murphy, Richard B. E541
Murphy, Robert B. (Bob) A902
Murphy, Robert Madison A719
Murphy, Sarah Rae A244
Murphy, Senan W178
Murphy, Stephen W122
Murphy, Stephen V. A430

Murphy, Susan G. A507
Murphy, Susan G. E248
Murphy, Thomas D. A350
Murphy, Thomas D. E148
Murphy, Thomas J. A98
Murphy, Thomas J. E36
Murphy, Thomas P. E459
Murphy, Thomas S. A151
Murphy, Timothy (Tim) H. A670
Murphy, Timothy J. W590
Murphy, Timothy R. A1056
Murphy, Timothy R. E505
Murphy, Wendy P613
Murray, Alan J. A764
Murray, Dennis E. A251
Murray, Dennis E. E100
Murray, Donald A. W122
Murray, Eileen K. W290
Murray, John G. E423
Murray, John G. E270
Murray, Katie W425
Murray, Katie W423
Murray, Kevin A398
Murray, Mark A. A345
Murray, Mark A. A343
Murray, Mark C. A215
Murray, Michael J. A536
Murray, Neil A588
Murray, Patrick R. W218
Murray, Sheila A. W99
Murray, Stephen M. A1091
Murray, Valerie O. A854
Murray, Vanda W116
Murray, William E43
Murrells, Steve W160
Murren, Heather Hay A407
Murria, Vinodka W116
Murski, Mark Wilhelm A226
Murthy, Mala A112
Murti, Arjun N. A288
Muruzabal, Claudio A846
Musa, Sam P449
Musalem, Alberto G. A450
Musca, Xavier W174
Muscato, Nick E20
Muscato, Stephen J. A1097
Muschong, Lisa A. A345
Muschong, Lisa A. A343
Muse, Scott H. E40
Musk, Elon R. A367
Musk, Elon R. A1007
Musk, Kimbal A1007
Muslah, Mansour Al W486
Musser, Eric S. A298
Musser, Jeffrey S. A386
Musslewhite, Robert W. E123
Musson, Karen E90
Mutch, Marcy D. A426
Mutch, Marcy D. E202
Muto, Koichi W278
Muzio, Frank S. A854
Muzio, Gaetano J. A874
Myers, Adam P84
Myers, Curtis J. A454
Myers, Dale S. A860
Myers, Daniel P. E90
Myers, Franklin E111
Myers, Johnny R. A72
Myers, Johnny R. E29
Myers, Keith G. E300

Myers, Larry W. E206
Myers, Marie A607
Myers, Marie E. A538
Myers, Michael P336
Myers, Richard B. E334
Myers, Robert F. E382
Myers, Timothy D. A130
Myers, Timothy Donald A95
Myers, Tyler K. E452
Myerson, Toby S. W407
Mylavarapu, Swati E239
Myles, Jenni A595
Mylod, Robert J. A169
Mynatt, Cynthia L. E515
Myong, Anne E16
Myrick, Tracy A345
Myrick, Tracy A343
Mytilinaios, Stefanos N. W33

N

N., Sreedhar W165
Na, Pengjie W662
Na, Wu Beng W463
Nabel, Elizabeth G. W393
Nabel, Gary J. E440
Nachbar, Moacir W69
Nachmias, Stuart A289
Nacht, Gabe E477
Nachtsheim, Jami K. Dover A573
Nackel, John G. E376
Nada, Hari W441
Nadeau, Bertin F. W571
Nadeau, Gerard (Gerry) F. A554
Nadeau, Gerard (Gerry) F. E268
Nadeau, Marie-Jose W225
Nadella, Satya A701
Nadella, Satya A964
Nadkarni, Gurudatta A289
Naef, Angela W490
Naese, Marc P419
Naffakh, Sami W490
Naftaly, Robert A1052
Naftaly, Robert P637
Nag, Nabanita C. A747
Nagahori, Kazumasa W417
Nagai, Koji W445
Nagai, Mikito W604
Nagai, Motoo W441
Nagai, Seiko W455
Nagamatsu, Fumihiko W527
Nagamori, Shigenobu W432
Nagano, Katsuya W279
Nagano, Minoru W449
Nagano, Satoshi W603
Nagano, Tsuyoshi W253
Nagano, Tsuyoshi W605
Nagao, Masahiko W577
Nagao, Yutaka W659
Nagaoka, Hiroshi W405
Nagaoka, Susumu W65
Nagara, Hajime W345
Nagasawa, Hitoshi W440
Nagasawa, Jun W402
Nagase, Toshiya W185
Nagashima, Hidemi W269
Nagashima, Iwao W407
Nagashima, Yukiko W321

Nagata, Mitsuhiro W581
Nagata, Ryoko W285
Nagataki, Kenichi W568
Nagatomi, Koji W408
Nagayama, Yoshiaki W1
Nagel, Alberto W391
Nagel, Richard J. E525
Nagel, Vernon J. E49
Naghibi, Christopher M. A423
Naghibi, Christopher M. E199
Nagle, Bruce H. A411
Nagle, Gary W260
Nagler, Lorna E. A1055
Nagler, Lorna E. E254
Naguib, Hatem H. E140
Nagy, Leslie K. A1110
Nahmad, Aaron J. A1111
Nahmad, Albert H. A1111
Nahmad, Henry M. E177
Naidoo, Dhanasagree W8
Naik, Rajan S. A716
Naim, Moises A23
Naing, Johshua E. W399
Nair, Balan A224
Nair, Hari N. A764
Nair, Leena W114
Nair, Radhakrishnan W296
Naito, Fumio W331
Naito, Tadaaki W440
Najera, Noe S. A532
Najera, Noe S. E259
Naka, Hiroyuki W316
Nakabayashi, Mieko W609
Nakada, Koichi W281
Nakagawa, Akira W42
Nakagawa, Roger T P96
Nakagawa, Yoichi W270
Nakagawa, Yutaka W530
Nakaguro, Kunio W441
Nakahama, Fumitaka W407
Nakahara, Asuka A272
Nakahara, Toshiya W223
Nakahata, Hidenobu W279
Nakahira, Yuko W400
Nakai, Kamezou W270
Nakai, Kazumasa W408
Nakai, Yoshihiro W527
Nakai, Yoshikazu W402
Nakajima, Isao W608
Nakajima, Masahiro W278
Nakajima, Masaki W566
Nakajima, Norio W417
Nakajima, Shigeru W567
Nakajima, Yoshimi W527
Nakamori, Makiko W316
Nakamoto, David P133
Nakamoto, Gary G. A913
Nakamoto, Gary G. E427
Nakamura, Atsushi W292
Nakamura, Jon A1038
Nakamura, Jon E496
Nakamura, Kazuya W281
Nakamura, Ken W1
Nakamura, Kuniharu W425
Nakamura, Kuniharu W536
Nakamura, Kuniharu W566
Nakamura, Mamiko W515
Nakamura, Masaru W436
Nakamura, Shigeharu W539
Nakamura, Tomomi W564

COMBINED HOOVER'S HANDBOOK INDEX OF EXECUTIVES

A = AMERICAN BUSINESS
E = EMERGING COMPANIES
P = PRIVATE COMPANIES
W = WORLD BUSINESSS

Nakamura, Toyoaki W82
Nakamura, Yoshihiko W405
Nakane, Takeshi W432
Nakane, Taketo W278
Nakanishi, Katsunori W539
Nakanishi, Katsuya W402
Nakashima, Toru W569
Nakata, Naofumi W26
Nakata, Takuya W658
Nakatani, Hiroshi W334
Nakayama, Kozue W313
Nakayama, Kozue W589
Nakayama, Shigeo W434
Nakayama, Tsunehiro W409
Nakazawa, Hiroshi W281
Nakazawa, Keiji W319
Nakyva, Maarit W340
Nalamasu, Omkaram A90
NaLamlieng, Chumpol W540
Nallen, John P. A447
Nally, Dennis M. A73
Nally, Dennis M. A713
Nally, Michael T. A840
Nam, Ickhyun W205
Nam, Young-Woo W366
Nambo, Masaru W253
Nambu, Masamitsu W181
Nambu, Toshikazu W566
Namdar, Frank A1057
Namekata, Yoichi W576
Namenye, Andrew J. E293
Namkung, James W. A561
Namvar, Ali A232
Namwong, Pornpen W540
Nanaumi, Shigeki W603
Nanavaty, Maulik A175
Nanbu, Masami W292
Nance, Frederick R. A907
Nance, James E. E515
Nance, Mark L. E1
Nance, Richard H. E527
Nance, Steven W. A792
Nanda, Nikhil W353
Nanji, Farhad A811
Nanji, Farhad E377
Nannetti, Paul W123
Nanninga, Stephan W116
Nanthawithaya, Arthid W541
Naouri, Jean-Charles W127
Napoli, Silvio W522
Napoli, Silvio W209
Napolitano, Janet E547
Napolitano, Vincent J. E288
Napp, Marc P510
Nappier, Herbert C. A468
Naqi, Anne M. E171
Naqvi, Saiyid T. A450
Nara, Michihiro W455
Nara, Tomoaki W319
naranjo, Guillermo Garcia W266
Narasimhan, Laxman A964
Narasimhan, Laxman A1088
Narasimhan, Laxman W490
Narasimhan, Shekar E67

Narasimhan, Vasant W449
Narayan, Ramani E352
Narayanan, Vanitha W523
Narayandas, Das E17
Narayen, Shantanu A821
Narayen, Shantanu A15
Narbut, Laurance E. E56
Nardecchia, Christopher (Chris) A902
Nardelli, Robert L. E70
Nardi, Barak W312
Narendra, Siva G. A398
Narendran, T. V. W588
Nargolwala, Kai S. W176
Nargolwala, Kaikhushru Shiavax W481
Narikawa, Michael E147
Narita, Susumu W42
Nark, Ted C. E31
Narron, James D. A402
Narula, Sanjeev A1093
Narutowicz, Anthony J. E69
Nasca, David J. A396
Nasca, David J. E175
Nasca, David J. E187
Nascimento, Renato Barbosa do W315
Nash, Chantelle R. E149
Nash, Michael B. E62
Nash, Peter Stanley W648
Nash, Sarah E. A140
Nash, William D. A205
Nasi, Alessandro W158
Nasi, Alessandro W235
Nasikkol, Tekin W602
Nason, Jennifer W500
Nason, Jennifer W499
Nassau, Henry N. E62
Nasser, Jacques A. A447
Nassetta, Christopher J. A518
Nassetta, Christopher J. E123
Nassy, Michael G. E227
Nastanski, Cynthia A. A817
Natale, Joseph M. W611
Natale, Patricia M. A554
Natale, Patricia M. E268
Natalone, John E34
Natarajan, Prabu A920
Natarajan, Rajesh E247
Nathan, Gilbert E. A411
Nattar, Ibrahim EL E162
Nauen, Andreas W544
Naughton, Mark P. E49
Naughton, Todd R. A1148
Naumann, Susan W390
Naus, Harold W306
Navarro, Alberto W266
Navarro, Imelda A563
Navarro, Isabel María Aguilera W131
Naveda, Alfonso Botin-Sanz de Sautuola y W87
Naveda, Marcelino Botin-Sanz de Sautuola y W87
Navitskas, Allison S. A951
Navitskas, Allison S. E454
Nawa, Takashi W555
Nawabi, Wahid E8
Nawana, Namal A522
Nayager, Dayalan W201
Nayak, Chitra W304
Nayar, Arun A895
Nayar, Deepak E303
Naylor, Derek E455

Naylor, Jeffrey G. A338
Naylor, Jeffrey G. A985
Naylor, Jeffrey G. A1112
Naylor, Maile A159
Nayyar, Nayaki R. A999
Nayyar, Sandeep E392
Nazemetz, Patricia M. A1144
Nazmiev, Eduard E181
Nazzaro, Frank A450
Nazzi, Gianfranco W598
Neal-Graves, Lisa E266
Neal, Diane L. A465
Neal, Gary D. E58
Neal, J. Scott A959
Neal, James R. E545
Neal, Kara Gae E153
Neal, Michael A. A591
Neal, Shana C. A147
Neal, Shana C. A794
Neal, Stephen C. A761
Neal, Steven A927
Neal, Steven E435
Nealon, Thomas (Tom) A10
Nearhos, Barry R. E319
Neary, Heather L. E173
Neary, John P. E128
Neate, James W84
Nebbia, Luciano W310
NeCastro, Timothy G. E171
Neczypor, Christopher A638
Nedeljkovic, Milan W96
Nedelman, Jeffrey A513
Needham, Daniel E333
Needham, Laura W371
Needham, Wendy B. A468
Neel, Lynne M. E156
Neeleman, Stephen D. E247
Neely, Kay C. E441
Neff, R. Matthew E273
Negishi, Akio W394
Negre, Jolene E. A335
Negron, Eduardo J. A836
Negus, Warwick Martin W85
Nehra, John M. A318
Neike, Cedrik W543
Neikirk, Christopher R. A747
Neikirk, Kenneth E. E250
Neil, Jennifer M. E389
Neiles, Byron C. W218
Neill, Lori E455
Neilon, Jay M. A891
Neilson, Derek W157
Neiss, Chad E. E158
Nejade, Henri W109
Nekipelov, Aleksandr Dmitrievich W617
Nekoshima, Akio W334
Nel, Frikkie W562
Nel, Maria W562
Nell, Steven E. A167
Nell, Steven E. E64
Nelles, Philip W171
Nelligan, Hanna Olivia A235
Nelly, Christian M. A374
Nelms, David W. A214
Nelson, Adam D. A1040
Nelson, Adam D. E499
Nelson, Amy H. A86
Nelson, Amy H. E250
Nelson, Andrew C. E279

Nelson, Brandon A583
Nelson, Brendan R. W109
Nelson, Brian Charles E83
Nelson, Carl A. E5
Nelson, Carol K. A398
Nelson, Cary R. E149
Nelson, Charles P. A1098
Nelson, Christopher C. A145
Nelson, Christopher J. A207
Nelson, David D. A1118
Nelson, David D. E533
Nelson, Deana P306
Nelson, Dionne E124
Nelson, Elizabeth W443
Nelson, Erin Mulligan E447
Nelson, F. Eric A1115
Nelson, F. Eric E533
Nelson, Gary Wendel E220
Nelson, Georgia R. A123
Nelson, Georgia R. A306
Nelson, Heather P571
Nelson, James L. A1142
Nelson, James L. E232
Nelson, James Larry A231
Nelson, James W. A399
Nelson, Jane E. A737
Nelson, John P. E30
Nelson, Jonathan B. A778
Nelson, Kelly R. E336
Nelson, Kimberly A. A269
Nelson, Kimberly A. A306
Nelson, Kimberly K. E457
Nelson, Krystal M. E352
Nelson, Mark A. A230
Nelson, Mark W. A992
Nelson, Melissa P132
Nelson, Ronald A. A1119
Nelson, Ronald L. A802
Nelson, Ronald L. A497
Nelson, Sally I. A397
Nelson, Sally I. E187
Nelson, Shawn E305
Nelson, Stephen E. E240
Nelson, Thomas C. A1146
Nelson, William R. A890
Nelson, William R. E416
Nemat, Claudia W24
Nemat, Claudia W199
Nemerov, Jackwyn L. A1030
Nemerson, Steven P476
Nemeth, Andy L. E373
Nemeth, Julio N. E65
Nemeth, Matthew A400
Nemeth, Terezia C. E15
Nemirovsky, Julian E440
Nemser, Earl H. E279
Nenadyshina, Viktoriya W256
Neo, Bock Cheng W463
Neo, Boon Siong W464
Neoh, Anthony Francis W301
Neoh, Anthony Francis W156
Neppl, John W. A185
Nerenhausen, Frank R. A789
Neri, Antonio F. A85
Neri, Antonio F. A514
Nerland, Paul P169
Nesbitt, Martin H. A231
Nesbitt, Martin H. A218
Nesbitt, Martin H. A56
Nesi, Victor J. A977

COMBINED HOOVER'S HANDBOOK INDEX OF EXECUTIVES

A = AMERICAN BUSINESS
E = EMERGING COMPANIES
P = PRIVATE COMPANIES
W = WORLD BUSINESSS

Nesi, Victor J. E464
Nesle, Alban de Mailly W65
Nesmes, Anne-Francoise W170
Ness, W. Denman Van E545
Nesselroad, Mark R. A1063
Nesselroad, Mark R. E508
Nesselrode, John M. E338
Nestegard, Susan K. A534
Neto, Joao Cox W468
Neto, Jorge Novis W314
Neto, Jose Ramos Rocha W69
Neto, Jose Virgilio Vita W315
Neto, Oscar de Paula Bernardes A715
Neto, Otavio Lopes Castello Branco W622
Nettie, Norman V. E283
Nettig, Walter W633
Nettles, Cory L. A101
Nettles, Michelle S. A655
Nettles, Patrick H. E47
Nettles, William E. E368
Netto, Alberto Monteiro de Queiroz W72
Netzer, Thomas A1112
Neu, Richard W. A545
Neuber, Friedel W270
Neuenschwander, Jean-Daniel W91
Neugent, Gerard D. A60
Neuhoff, Elizabeth R. E212
Neukom, William H. E216
Neumann, Horst W61
Neumann, Jens W270
Neumann, Kristin W109
Neumann, Spencer Adam A730
Neumann, Spencer Adam A15
Neumayer, Elliott A1121
Neumeister, Ulrich W390
Neupaver, Albert J. A1099
Neupel, Joachim W3
Neupert, Peter M. A615
Neuss, Sabine W171
Neuville, Colette W61
Nevatia, Puneet A191
Nevatia, Puneet E77
Neve, Laurinda M. A555
Neve, Laurinda M. E269
Nevels, James E. A1125
Nevels, James E. A37
Nevens, T. Michael A729
Neves, Eduardo W314
Neves, Joao Carvalho das W212
Nevin, Darius G. E14
Nevin, Michael A549
Nevinny, Corinne H. E277
Nevistic, Vesna W167
Newbern, Thomas B. A111
Newbigging, Alex W323
Newbigging, David Alexander W322
Newborn, Andrea R. A10
Newcomb, Anita Gentle A650
Newcomb, Anita Gentle E305
Newcomb, Robert T. A418
Newcomer, David A. E61
Newcomer, Lee N. E106

Newcomer, Peter D P664
Newell, Donna M. A12
Newell, Donna M. E4
Newell, Eric R. A378
Newell, Roberto W643
Newfield, Richard U. A722
Newfield, Richard U. E339
Newhall, Charles W. E474
Newham, Paul W85
Newhouse, Michael A. A224
Newlands, William (" Bill") A534
Newlands, William A. A291
Newlin, Karl W. A348
Newlin, Karl W. A345
Newlin, Stephen D. A1075
Newlin, Stephen D. A789
Newman, Brian A1069
Newman, Katherine G. A87
Newman, Mark E. A224
Newman, Randy L. A37
Newman, Randy L. E14
Newman, Stan E517
Newmyer, Joyce P6
Newsom, Cory T. A950
Newsom, Cory T. E454
Newsom, Mikella D. A950
Newsom, Mikella D. E454
Newsom, Richard W. A283
Newsome, Earl A145
Newsome, Paul P408
Newstead, Jennifer G. A689
Newton, Charles E106
Newton, Howell W. E237
Newton, Kimberley A. A157
Newton, Lloyd W. A613
Neylan, Kevin M. A396
Neylan, Kevin M. E187
Neymon, Denys W565
Ng, Daryl Win Kong W80
Ng, Dominic A351
Ng, Dominic E150
Ng, Estella Yi Kum W173
Ng, Jimmy Keng Joo W190
Ng, Kenneth Sing Yip W268
Ng, Kenneth Yu Lam W150
Ng, Wendy A400
Ng, Yuk Keung W663
Ngamsopee, Kannika W541
Ngau, Jonathan W. E297
Ngim, Andrew F. E509
Ngim, Andrew F. E510
Ngim, Andrew F. E509
Ngo, A. Catherine A219
Nguyen, C. Kim A401
Nguyen, Nam Tran E228
Nguyen, Robert Long E509
Nguyen, Robert Long E509
Nguyen, Robert Long E510
Nguyen, Xuong A979
Ni, Defeng W275
Ni, Jinmei W275
Ni, Shoumin W291
Ni, Xiangyang A1093
Niane, Aminata W61
Niblock, Robert A. A288
Niblock, Robert A. A834
Nibuya, Susumu W297
Niccol, Brian R. A594
Niccol, Brian R. A232
Nichol, Carrie A. A1150

Nicholas, Heidi A. A441
Nicholas, Heidi A. E212
Nicholas, James B. A816
Nicholas, Susan Y. E158
Nicholls, Matthew A448
Nicholls, Timothy S. A568
Nichols, George A886
Nichols, George A890
Nichols, George E416
Nichols, Robert A. A880
Nichols, Robert A. E412
Nichols, Thomas C. A516
Nichols, Victor K. A129
Nichols, W. Robert A516
Nicholson, Cynthia S. A927
Nicholson, Cynthia S. E435
Nicholson, E. Allen A308
Nicholson, E. Allen E133
Nicholson, Robert B. A617
Nicholson, Robert B. E289
Nicholson, Susan A. A910
Nickelson, Harvey J. E428
Nickey, Susan D. E245
Nickl, Wolfgang W95
Nickle, E. Glen E368
Nickles, Allen R. A251
Nickles, Allen R. E100
Nickles, Donald L. A1085
Nickles, Robert C. A421
Nickles, Robert C. E198
Nickolas, James A.J. A663
Nickolds, Paula W318
Nicol, Sylvie W276
Nicolas, Ernest A902
Nicolas, Ronald J. A796
Nicolas, Ronald J. E368
Nicolelli, Maurizio E179
Nicolet, Patrick W123
Nicoletti, Ralph J. A455
Nicosia, Darlene A443
Niederauer, Duncan L. A878
Niederauer, Duncan L. A431
Niederauer, Duncan L. A879
Niederauer, Duncan L. E205
Niedzwiecki, Kristen E455
Niehaus, Charles D. A844
Niehaus, Charles D. E394
Niehaus, Christopher J. E530
Niekamp, Cynthia A. A123
Niekamp, Cynthia A. W379
Nielsen, David J. E368
Nielsen, Jane Hamilton A710
Nielsen, Johanna A743
Nielsen, Kurt Anker W632
Nielsen, Mark D. A453
Nielsen, Raymond A. A329
Nielsen, Sarah N. A394
Nielsen, T. Tod E134
Niemiec, David W. E253
Niemloy, Phawana W79
Nienen, Marge P121
Nierenberg, Michael E347
Nieto, Carlos Andres Santos W210
Nieto, Luis P. A909
Nietzel, Alfred A. E91
Nieuwdorp, Roel W18
Niggli, Michael R. A823
Nightingale, Anthony W481
Nightingale, Anthony J. L. W323
Nightingale, Timothy P. A192

Nigon, Richard J. E352
Nigrin, Daniel P326
Nigro, James M. A617
Nigro, James M. E289
Nihot, Dailah W442
Niimi, Tsutomu W329
Niino, Takashi W425
Niinuma, Hiroshi W565
Niisato, Shinji W81
Nikkaku, Akihiro W610
Niland, Barbara A. E70
Nilekani, Nandan M. W304
Niljianskul, Chokechai W77
Nilsson, Jannicke W227
Nilsson, Thomas W60
Nimbley, Thomas J. A809
Nimbley, Thomas J. E374
Nimetz, Warren J. A1076
Nimmanhaeminda, Tarrin W540
Nimocks, Suzanne P. A792
Nimocks, Suzanne P. A795
Nimocks, Suzanne P. W49
Ning, Gaoning W236
Ninno, Giulio Del W482
Ninomiya, Hitomi W464
Nip, Yun Wing W144
Nisen, Perry W598
Nish, David W638
Nish, David Thomas W289
Nishi, Hirokazu W65
Nishi, Motohiro W533
Nishida, Mitsuo W567
Nishihara, Motoo W425
Nishihata, Kazuhiro W451
Nishii, Shigeru W281
Nishijima, Takashi W417
Nishikawa, Katsuyuki W533
Nishikawa, Kazunobu W418
Nishikawa, Kuniko W266
Nishimura, Akira W567
Nishimura, Atsuko W582
Nishimura, Keisuke W343
Nishimura, Shingo W223
Nishino, Hiroshi W297
Nishioka, Keiko W292
Nishioka, Seiichiro W223
Nishita, Akira W281
Nishita, Naoki W449
Nishitani, Jumpei W464
Nishiura, Yuji W370
Nishizawa, Nobuhiro W331
Nisita, Vittorio A787
Nisivoccia, Raymond E193
Nissen, James A P426
Nissen, John Ted E195
Niswonger, Jason R. E274
Nitcher, Eric W109
Nitzani, Yosef W410
Niu, Diana W641
Niu, Dongxiao W189
Niubo, Antonio Brufau W423
Niubo, Antonio Brufau W493
Nivens, Margaret P546
Nix, Craig L. A417
Nix, Jerry W. E425
Nix, William K. A958
Nix, William K. E456
Nixon, Christine A296
Nixon, Dennis E. A563
Nixon, Gordon M. A160

COMBINED HOOVER'S HANDBOOK INDEX OF EXECUTIVES

A = AMERICAN BUSINESS
E = EMERGING COMPANIES
P = PRIVATE COMPANIES
W = WORLD BUSINESSS

Nixon, Gordon M. W99
Nixon, Gordon M. W646
Nixon, John D. E527
Nixon, Ronald T. E300
Nixon, Torran B. A1057
Njau, Caroline P119
Nkeli, Mpho Elizabeth Kolekile W518
Nkosi, Sipho Abednego W518
Nkuhlu, Mfundo W426
Nobel, Paul M. A868
Noble, Craig W112
Noble, Jeremy A. A659
Noble, Walt P372
Nocella, Andrew P. A1062
Noda, Seiko W65
Noda, Yumiko W297
Noerremark, Henrik W632
Nogami, Masayuki W454
Noge, Emi W576
Nogimori, Masafumi W409
Noglows, William P. E303
Noguchi, Mikio W494
Nogueira, Andre W323
Noh, Geum-Sun W352
Noh, Jin-Ho W652
Nohara, Sawako W494
Nohira, Akinobu W453
Noji, Kunio W465
Nolan, James M A493
Nolan, James M E243
Nolan, Joseph R. A380
Nolan, Michael J. A406
Nolan, Peter J. A14
Nolan, Philip O. A189
Noland, Brian A1006
Nolens, Geraldine W623
Nolop, Bruce P. A662
Noma, Yoshinobu W609
Nomoto, Hirofumi W407
Nomura, Takao W330
Nonnenmacher, Rolf W171
Nonnenmacher, Rolf W174
Noonan, Aletha C. A214
Noonan, Anne P. E469
Noonan, Jack E333
Noonan, Thomas E. A561
Noone, John E. A702
Noone, John E. E326
Noons, Mary E. A1108
Noordende, Sander van't A20
Noordhoek, Jeffrey R. A727
Noordhoek, Jeffrey R. E345
Nooyi, Indra K. A50
Nooyi, Indra K. W351
Norcia, Gerardo A344
Norcia, Gerardo A343
Norcross, Gary A. A408
Nord, David G. A909
Nord, Matthew H. A999
Nord, Thomas C. E538
Nordberg, Bert W4
Nordberg, Bert W231
Norden, Gregory A1153
Norden, Gregory E425

Nordh, Hilde Vestheim W448
Nordhagen, Arlen D. E340
Nordholm, Bradford T. A395
Nordholm, Bradford T. E186
Nordin, Diane C. A391
Nordin, Diane C. A846
Nordmann, Dirk W171
Nordstrom, Erik B. A745
Nordstrom, Gunilla W4
Nordstrom, James F. A745
Nordstrom, Lars G. W446
Nordstrom, Peter E. A745
Noreck, Daniel T. E481
Noreus, Martin W579
Norgaard, Birgit Woidemann W205
Norgaard, Mariann W348
Norgeot, Peter S. A371
Noriega, Alfonso de Angoitia W265
Norman, Archie W385
Norman, Jessica K. E268
Norman, Kathy E189
Norman, William J. A153
Norment, Thomas K. A1033
Norment, Thomas K. E493
Normoyle, Helen W21
Noronha, Marcelo de Araujo W69
Norrington, Lorrie M. A269
Norrington, Lorrie M. E45
Norris, Brian A574
Norris, Craig A1098
Norris, David A37
Norris, David E14
Norris, Gina A. E160
Norris, John R. E487
Norris, Ralph W245
Norrod, Forrest Eugene A18
North, B. J. E388
North, John F. E292
North, Michael P. E20
Northcutt, R. Bruce A1124
Norton, Bradley S. A1004
Norton, David K. A814
Norton, David K. E379
Norton, G. Anthony E340
Norton, Johna L. A635
Norton, Larry A. A563
Norton, Nancy A. A405
Norton, Pierce H. A783
Norton, Susan A. E192
Norup, Keld W330
Norwalk, Leslie V. E346
Norwitt, Richard Adam A79
Norwood, Anthony E426
Norwood, Felicia F. A1115
Norwood, Felicia F. A85
Nosal, Ed A399
Noseworthy, John H. A1075
Noski, Charles H. A170
Noski, Charles H. A514
Nosko, Roland W15
Nota, Pieter W96
Notaras, Martha E370
Notebaert, Nicolas W635
Notebaert, Richard C. A59
Notebaert, Richard C. W44
Noteboom, Ben J. W16
Noth, Thomas W586
Noto, Anthony A448
Noto, Lucio A. A825
Nottebohm, Olivia E34

Nouchi, Yuzo W402
Nourry, Philippe W213
Noursalehi, Saum E368
Novacek, Jorie L. E172
Novaes, Djalma A302
Novak, Alexander W506
Novak, Alexander V. W474
Novak, Christy H. A754
Novak, David W495
Novak, David C. A272
Novak, Jonathan A296
Novakovic, Phebe N. A591
Novakovic, Phebe N. A460
Novara, Paula E232
Novich, Neil S. A485
Novich, Neil S. A145
Novich, Neil S. E255
Novick, Steve P138
Novo, Guillermo A840
Novogradac, Barbara J. A898
Nowak, Bogden A181
Nowell, Lionel L. A358
Nowell, Lionel L. A128
Nowell, Lionel L. A1012
Nowlan, Kevin A. A173
Nowlin, James T. A401
Nowotne, Doreen W109
Noyce, James W. A1065
Noyce, James W. A1118
Noyce, James W. E533
Noyer, Christian W104
Noyer, Christian W480
Noyes, Mark A290
Noyes, Mark A289
Noyori, Ryoji W610
Noznesky, Justin J. E43
Nuchjalearn, Weidt W352
Nudi, Jonathon J. A465
Nugent, Sean P. E412
Nukk-Freeman, Katherin A287
Nukk-Freeman, Katherin E115
Numata, S. Mae Fujita A271
Numata, S. Mae Fujita E109
Nunes, Adolfo Mesquita W254
Nunes, Regina Helena Jorge W295
Nunez, Carlos W266
Nunez, Diana P138
Nunez, Maria Eugenia de la Fuente W73
Nungester, Paul D. A844
Nungester, Paul D. E394
Nunley, P. A.L. A401
Nunn, Charlie W371
Nunnelly, Gary S. A843
Nunnelly, Gary S. E393
Nuno, Hugo J. A423
Nuno, Hugo J. E199
Nunokawa, Yoshikazu W607
Nursalim, Cherie W486
Nusse, Roeland E59
Nussel, Manfred W98
Nusterer, Norbert A306
Nutting, Ron P456
Nutzenberger, Stefanie W129
Nuxoll, Erin A166
Nuzzo, James A224
Nuzzolo, Agostino W592
Nwamu, Chonda J. E57
Nwankwo, Evans N. A64
Nyasulu, Hixonia W39

Nyberg, Bruce E. A435
Nyberg, Bruce E. E210
Nyberg, Carl W427
Nyblad, Nels W. E96
Nyce, Chad D. E302
Nyce, Chad D. E467
Nydick, Jay S. E426
Nye, C. Howard A663
Nye, C. Howard A460
Nyegaard, Peter W446
Nyembezi-Heita, Nonkululeko Merina Cheryl W39
Nyembezi-Heita, Nonkululeko Merina Cheryl W559
Nyffeler, Paul W631
Nyhus, Rhonda G. E338
Nylund, Arne Sigve W227
Nyman, Eric A503
Nyman, Per Olof W579
Nyman, Sven W548
Nyman, Torbjorn W228

O

O'Boyle, Carolyn L. E65
O'Boyle, Fergal J. E46
O'Boyle, Thomas R. A337
O'Brian, Kate E432
O'Brien, Ann W21
O'Brien, Christopher J. (Chris) A900
O'Brien, Dana C. A776
O'Brien, Dana C. E463
O'Brien, Daniel F. A554
O'Brien, Daniel F. E268
O'Brien, Deirdre A89
O'Brien, Donna M. A440
O'Brien, James J. A354
O'Brien, James J. A541
O'Brien, John R. E175
O'Brien, Joseph J. A913
O'Brien, Joseph J. E427
O'Brien, Michael W80
O'Brien, Michael J. A778
O'Brien, Patrick D. A681
O'Brien, Patrick D. E318
O'Brien, Raymond Vincent A308
O'Brien, Raymond Vincent E133
O'Brien, Thomas M. A420
O'Brien, Thomas M. A976
O'Brien, Thomas M. E197
O'Brien, Thomas M. E527
O'Brien, Timothy P. E190
O'Brien, William K. E319
O'Byrne, Barry W289
O'Byrne, Kevin W318
O'Byrne, Kevin W135
O'Callaghan, Cathy A444
O'Callaghan, Jeremiah Alphonsus W323
O'Connell, Diarmuid B. A313
O'Connell, Don E93
O'Connell, Katrina A1018
O'connell, Tim P141
O'connor, John A974
O'connor, John P539
O'Connor, John J. E297
O'Connor, John P. W260
O'Connor, Kevin J. A207

COMBINED HOOVER'S HANDBOOK INDEX OF EXECUTIVES

A = AMERICAN BUSINESS
E = EMERGING COMPANIES
P = PRIVATE COMPANIES
W = WORLD BUSINESSS

O'Connor, Kevin M. A328
O'Connor, Matt A197
O'Connor, Matt P103
O'Connor, Michael John W570
O'Connor, Sandie A132
O'Connor, Sean M. A979
O'Connor, Shawn E444
O'Connor, Shirin E337
O'Connor, Stephen W288
O'Connor, Thomas L. A809
O'Conor, Raymond F. A98
O'Conor, Raymond F. E36
O'Daniel, Julie M. E517
O'Day, Daniel P. A473
O'Day, Susan Perry A554
O'Day, Susan Perry E268
O'Dell, Richard D. E426
O'Donnell-Tormey, Jill E106
O'Donnell, John Andy E72
O'Donnell, Kevin J. W491
O'Donnell, Kristin Dempsey E190
O'Donnell, Lord W112
O'Donovan, James J. A732
O'Dowd, Kevin M. E453
O'Dowd, Sarah A. A619
O'Dwyer, Fergal W21
O'Farrell, Susan C. E297
O'farrill, Romulo W266
O'flaherty, Michael P. E61
O'Grady, Brendan P. W598
O'Grady, Michael G. A748
O'Grady, Myles W81
O'Hagan, Sarah Robb A583
O'Halloran, Brendan J. A138
O'Halloran, Brendan J. E55
O'Hanley, Ronald P. A1079
O'Hanley, Ronald P. A973
O'Hara, Laura P. A651
O'hearn, Patricia P140
O'Herlihy, Christopher A. A553
O'Herlihy, Christopher A. A666
O'Higgins, John W328
O'Kane, Michael T. A581
O'Keef, Robert F. A485
O'Keefe, Dan E. E153
O'Keeffe, John W201
O'Leary, Christopher D. A1001
O'Leary, Daniel E529
O'Leary, Daniel J. E260
O'Leary, Denise M. A56
O'Leary, Denise M. W393
O'Leary, Dennis V. E223
O'Leary, John C.G. W590
O'Leary, Joseph D. A959
O'mahony, Stephen P472
O'Malley, Kevin Patrick E351
O'Malley, Paul W164
O'Meara, Christina B. A913
O'Meara, Christina B. E427
O'nan, Stephen B A222
O'nan, Stephen B P114
O'neal, Dennis A. A429
O'Neal, E. Stanley A95
O'Neal, Gloria A. A72

O'Neal, Gloria A. E29
O'Neal, John L. A1125
O'Neil, James F. A432
O'Neil, Mark F. A205
O'Neill, Alison E475
O'Neill, Christopher (Chris) R. A1019
O'Neill, Claire A767
O'Neill, Daniel K. A429
O'Neill, Heidi A743
O'Neill, Lisa M. A617
O'Neill, Lisa M. E290
O'Neill, Michael W362
O'Neill, Michael J. A62
O'Neill, Myles A635
O'Quinn, Daniel E430
O'Rear, Keith J. A1127
O'Reilly, David W111
O'Reilly, David E. A765
O'Reilly, Larry A765
O'Reilly, Michael A659
O'Rourke, James C. A714
O'Rourke, James Calvin E491
O'Shaughnessy, Robert T. A862
O'Shaughnessy, Tim J. E393
O'Shaughnessy, William J. A870
O'Shea, Ana Patricia Botin-Sanz de Sautuola y A264
O'Shea, Ana Patricia Botin-Sanz de Sautuola y W75
O'Shea, Chris W135
O'Shea, Des W79
O'Shea, Javier Botin-Sanz de Sautuola y W76
O'Sullivan, Colleen M. A1148
O'Sullivan, Kieran M. E293
O'Sullivan, Michael A187
O'Sullivan, Sean P. A973
O'Sullivan, Stephanie L. A546
O'Toole, Amie Thuener A745
O'Toole, Beverly L. A480
O'Toole, Richard L. A1113
O'Toole, Timothy T. A359
O'Toole, Timothy T. A951
O'Brien, Gregory P. A588
O'Brien, MaryJo E357
O'Brien, Richard T. A1139
O'Bryan, Jennie A200
O'Bryan, Jennie E79
O'Callahan, Elizabeth M. A729
O'Connor, Kevin C. E537
O'Connor, Timothy A1139
O'Connor, Tonia E546
O'Dell, Timothy T. E91
O'Dowd, Sarah E261
O'Haver, Cort L. A1057
O'Hayer, Matthew E529
O'Hearn, Stephen T. A886
O'Kane, Nicholas W377
O'Keeffe, Patrick E472
O'Kelly, Ciaran E513
O'Leary, James A184
O'Malley, Peter J. E56
O'Mullane, John A825
O'Neil, Charles M. E246
O'Neill, Elizabeth A631
O'Neill, Kevin M. A458
O'Neill, Mark A. E149
O'Neill, Michelle A37
O'Neill, Robert E. A803
O'Neill, Robert E. E371

O'Neill, Tony W39
O'Reagan, Richard A. A666
O'Reilly, Christine W101
O'Reilly, Christine W63
O'Reilly, James F. A315
O'Reilly, Lindsay W90
O'Rourke, Catheryn W490
O'Sullivan, Paul D. W63
Oakes, Greg E83
Oakes, Patrick T. A106
Oakland, Steven A443
Oakley, Clark A1132
Oakley, Clark E539
Oates-Forney, Tamla D. A1110
Oates-Forney, Tamla D. E469
Oates, James M. A977
Oates, James M. E464
Oatman, Heather Marie E507
Obara, Shinobu W81
Obata, Yasuhiko W441
Obayashi, Hiroshi W402
Obayashi, Takeo W453
Oberg, Jay K. A274
Oberg, Kathleen K. A15
Oberg, Kathleen K. A660
Oberhausen, Stephanie P617
Oberlerchner, Fritz W562
Oberlin, Beat W91
Obermann, Rene W24
Obermeyer, James A. E72
Oberschmidleitner, Alois Johann W453
Oberst, Stephen J. A773
Oberton, Karleen M. A74
Oberton, Karleen M. A522
Obey, Willie P. A880
Obey, Willie P. E412
Obi, Michael A259
Obi, Michael E103
Oblak, Stephen A1112
Obregon-Jimenez, Rebeca E214
Ocampo, Marie Josephine M. W85
Ocana, Ann M P498
Ochi, Howard P482
Ochi, Toshiki W407
Ochiai, Hiroyuki W432
Ochiai, Seiichi W394
Ochrym, Natalie A. W571
Ochs, Wes E452
Ockers, Thomas P241
Oconnor, Caitlin A971
Oconnor, Caitlin P537
Odagiri, Junko W82
Odaira, Takashi W313
Oddestad, Lars W446
Oddleifson, Christopher A554
Oddleifson, Christopher E268
Odegaard, Richard P247
Odell, Michael R. A687
Odendaal, Hein W562
Odendaal, Lisa W462
Odgers, David A1056
Odgers, David E505
Odierno, Raymond T. A790
Odland, Steve A465
Oduor-Otieno, Martin W559
Oehler, Heinz W633
Oelrich, Friedrich W192
Oelrich, Stefan W95
Oesterle, Stephen N. A142
Oestmann, Jeffrey E236

Oestreicher, David A991
Oeter, Dietmar W397
Oeters, William E. A207
Oetterli, Thomas W522
Ofer, IDAN W410
Ofer, Liora W410
Ofer, Yehuda W410
Off, George W. A1001
Offer, Scott W242
Offereins, Diane E. A176
Ogami, Tetsuaki W436
Ogasawara, Takeshi W576
Ogawa, Hiromichi W455
Ogawa, Hiroyuki W347
Ogawa, Michiko W389
Ogawa, Shinsuke W608
Ogawa, Shoji W445
Ogawa, Tetsuo A1034
Ogawa, Yoichiro W285
Ogbechie, Angela E137
Ogden, George E. A809
Ogi, Akira W278
Ogilvie, Marran H. E217
Ogilvie, Thomas W198
Ogiso, Satoshi W278
Ogle, David A. A945
Ogle, David A. E451
Oglesby, Charles R. E310
Oglesby, Richard A. A106
Ognall, Andrew H. A1057
Ogren, Dan P366
Ogryzlo, Tom E43
Oguchi, Shimpei W582
Ogunlesi, Adebayo O. A480
Ogura, Ritsuo W408
Ogurek, Markus R. A279
Oguz, Bulent W26
Oguz, Orkun W26
Oh, Christine Y. E362
Oh, Gyutaeg W335
Oh, Irene H. A351
Oh, Irene H. E150
Oh, Joyce P251
Oh, Tony D. A1098
Oh, Yoon Ah E. E362
Ohannessian, Dikran W570
Ohara, Hiroyuki W155
Ohashi, Shigeki W28
Ohashi, Tetsuji W50
Ohashi, Tetsuji W658
Ohashi, Tetsuji W347
Ohgo, Naoki W581
Ohkubo, Shinichi W609
Ohkubo, Tetsuo W570
Ohlhaver, Peggy A797
Ohlhaver, Peggy E368
Ohlmeyer, Harm W14
Ohlsson-Leijon, Anna W60
Ohnishi, Tadashi W281
Ohno, Kotaro W17
Ohr, Eugene M. W294
Ohsberg, Ronald S. A1108
Ohta, Jun W569
Ohtsu, Keiji W285
Ohya, Mitsuo W610
Oie, Yuji W357
Oikawa, Hisahiko W494
Oilfield, David W371
Ojeisekhoba, Moses W580
Oka, Masaaki W568

HOOVER'S HANDBOOK OF EMERGING COMPANIES 2023

COMBINED HOOVER'S HANDBOOK INDEX OF EXECUTIVES

A = AMERICAN BUSINESS
E = EMERGING COMPANIES
P = PRIVATE COMPANIES
W = WORLD BUSINESSS

Oka, Masashi W425
Oka, Toshiko W557
Oka, Toshiko W223
Okabe, Nobuhiro E297
Okada, Akihioko W451
Okada, Kenji W606
Okada, Motoya W17
Okada, Yoshifumi W65
Okafuji, Masahiro W316
Okamatsu, Nobuhiko W454
Okamoto, Masahiko W610
Okamoto, Shigeaki W321
Okamoto, Tsuyoshi W319
Okamoto, Tsuyoshi W51
Okawa, Junko W336
Okawa, Katsuyoshi W453
Okazaki, Takeshi W237
Oken, Marc D. A662
Okhuijsen, Dennis A45
Oki, Kazuaki W550
Okihara, Takamune W331
Okina, Yuri W110
Okina, Yuri W387
Okitsu, Masahiro W530
Okkerse, Liesbet W336
Oklak, Dennis D. A1046
Okomo-Okello, Francis W8
Okonjo-Iweala, Ngozi A1047
Okorie, Eboh Duke A976
Okray, Thomas (Tom) B. W209
Oku, Masayuki W80
Okuda, Kentaro W445
Okumura, Mikio W555
Okuyama, Emiko W1
Olafson, Harlee N. A1118
Olafson, Harlee N. E533
Olague, Michael W. A935
Olague, Michael W. E439
Olaizola, Juan A915
Olano, Antonio Miguel-Romero de W382
Olanoff, Lawrence S. E282
Olayan, Hutham S. W112
Olayan, Khaled Suliman W520
Olcott, George W343
Olczak, Jacek A825
Old, William A. A337
Oldenberg, Mark C. E98
Oldenburg, Phyllis E61
Oldham, Paul E6
Oleas, Jurg W283
Olefson, Jonathan A986
Oleksiak, Peter B. A343
Oler, Debra S. E389
Olesky, Lee E493
Olevson, Jimmy E307
Olian, Judy D. E34
Olin, John A. A1099
Olinde, Thomas H. A496
Oliphant, Aradhna M. A418
Oliphant, Aradhna M. E195
Oliphant, Mark J. E291
Oliva, Lisa T. A401
Olivan, Javier A689

Oliveira, Aurelio Ricardo Bustilho de W220
Oliveira, Carlos Alberto Pereira de W468
Oliveira, Rafael A610
Oliveira, Raul Catarino Galamba de W68
Oliveira, Ronald E. E46
Oliver, Eric Lee E487
Oliver, George R. A877
Oliver, George R. W327
Oliver, Katherine E2
Oliver, Kirk R P639
Oliver, Kirk R. E171
Oliver, Mary Patricia A251
Oliver, Mary Patricia E100
Oliver, Stephen E. E204
Oliver, Timothy C. A726
Oliver, U. Starr A1033
Oliver, U. Starr E492
Olivera, Armando J. A289
Olivera, Armando J. A438
Olivera, Armando J. A290
Olivera, Armando J. A629
Oliveras, Gregory A742
Oliveras, Gregory P393
Olivier, Daniel L. A1144
Olivier, Gaelle W187
Olivier, Gaelle W548
Olivier, Gregoire W562
Oliviera, Ramon de W65
Olivieri, Fernando Angel Gonzalez W131
Ollagnier, Jean-Marc W10
Olle, Laura Newman E159
Olli, Amy Fliegelman A1098
Ollmann, Michael W269
Olmstead, Diane E180
Olosky, Michael E444
Olsavsky, Brian T. A50
Olsen, Denise A. E134
Olsen, Jens Peter Due W204
Olsen, Jonathan S. E280
Olsen, Kathleen E238
Olsen, Kevin M. E145
Olsen, Michael E. A45
Olson, Bart R. A800
Olson, Eric T. A1059
Olson, Jennifer E16
Olson, Jon A. A18
Olson, Luke E210
Olson, Paul L.H. E165
Olson, Peter E141
Olson, Richard M. E491
Olson, Ronald L. A151
Olson, Scott A175
Olson, Tagar C. A718
Olson, Tagar C. E335
Olson, Tim E98
Olson, Timothy J. W50
Olsson, Magnus W548
Olsson, Mikael W597
Olstad, Ellen Merete W448
Olszewski, Daniel P. A416
Olszewski, Grzegorz W86
Olvera, Jane A308
Olvera, Jane E134
Omalley, Ed P392
Oman, Mark C. A413
Oman, Robert M. A1034

Oman, Robert M. E493
Ommen, Nick J.M. van E530
Ommeren, Ruud van W123
Omoteyama, Kyoko W26
Omran, Mohammed Omran Al W520
Omtvedt, Craig P. A790
Omtvedt, Craig P. A286
Omura, Yukiko W288
Onaran, Cemal W618
Ondrof, Thomas Gerard (Tom) A92
Oneglia, Raymond R. A1046
Onen, Kudret W346
Onetto, Marc A. W242
Ong, Estrellita V. W99
Ongaro, Claudio Giovanni Ezio W592
Ongpin, Roberto V. W514
Onishi, Akira W614
Onishi, Hiroyuki W370
Onishi, Masanobu W535
Onishi, Shoichiro W607
Onishi, Tadashi W394
Onishi, Yasuo W65
Ono, Hiromichi W608
Ono, Mitsuru W388
Ono, Naoki W404
Ono, Naotake W237
Ono, Sadahiro W604
Ono, Taneki W319
Onodera, Yoshikazu W1
Onorato, Joseph A. A706
Onozawa, Yasuo W409
Onuki, Tetsuo W564
Onuki, Yuji W455
Onyia, Jude E346
Ooi, Sang Kuang W464
Oomi, Hideto W44
Oommen, Dilip W49
Oorlog, Jonathan W. ("Butch") A876
Oosterman, Wade A1001
Oosterman, Wade W99
Opedal, Anders W227
Opfermann, Andreas W369
Opfermann, Sibylle Daunis W165
Oplinger, William F. A37
Opp, Arlene R. E336
Opp, Joan C. A398
Oppel, Raymond A687
Oppenheimer, Deanna W. W597
Oppenheimer, Peter A481
Opstad, Alexander W204
Oracion, Laurie S. A279
Oran, Baris A493
Oran, Baris W267
Orban, George P. A905
Orban, Paul W. A333
Orcel, Andrea W625
Ordan, Mark S. A203
Orders, Amanda E66
Orders, James B. E454
Ordus, John P. A1035
Orem, Anita E58
Orenes, Francisco Jose Marco W382
Oreshkin, Maksim W521
Orestis, John C. E350
Orie, James G. A441
Orie, James G. E212
Orii, Masako W453
Oringer, Jonathan (Jon) E438
Orlando, Anthony J. A620
Orlando, Matthew A585

Orlando, Steven J. A707
Orlen, Gregg F. E537
Orlev, Arieh W410
Orleyn, Thandi W558
Orlopp, Bettina W162
Orman, Ellen A400
Orman, Gregory J. E315
Ormaza, Xabier Sagredo W295
Orndorff, Robert L. A913
Orndorff, Robert L. E427
Oro, Sachiko W454
Oropeza, Octavio Romero W470
Orr, Barry H. A507
Orr, Barry H. E248
Orr, Mark A492
Orr, Mark P248
Orr, R. Douglas E207
Orr, Robert Jeffrey W262
Orr, Robert Jeffrey W480
Orrego, Eduardo Ebensperger W70
Orrico, Brent A. A136
Orsen, Melissa J. E453
Orsi, Christina P. E175
Orsinger, Michel W585
Orsini, Frank C. A622
Orson, Marshall D P193
Ortberg, Robert K. A877
Ortberg, Robert K. W46
Ortberg, Robert K. W45
Ortega, Steven L. E297
Ortenzio, Robert A. A925
Ortenzio, Rocco A. A925
Orthwein, Peter B. A1028
Ortiz-izquierdo, Jose W266
Ortiz, Inigo Perez E236
Ortiz, Juan Carlos Andrade W232
Ortiz, Mauricio A. A274
Ortmanns, Stefan E91
Ortmanns, Thomas W3
Ortner, Reinhard W633
Ortolf, Tom A. A333
Orvos, Adam M. A905
Osaki, Atsushi W564
Osaki, Yoshimi W454
Osar, Karen R. A1113
Osawa, Masakazu W407
Osborn, Cathleen M. E529
Osborn, David P. A240
Osborn, Wayne G. W644
Osborn, William W. A398
Osborne, Matthew A. A352
Osborne, Richard J. E245
Osborne, Ronald W. W571
Osborne, William H. E404
Oscher, Ronald J. A74
Osdell, J. Garrett Van E116
Osgood, Jonathan E. A444
Osgood, Steven G. E246
Osgood, Steven G. E340
Osher, Jeffrey B. E239
Osherova, Maria A1106
Oshima, Masahiko W569
Oshimi, Yoshikazu W330
Oshita, Hajime W325
Osmonov, Asylbek A852
Osmonov, Asylbek E399
Osnoss, Joseph A477
Osono, Emi W606
Osorio, Luiz Eduardo Froes do Amaral W630

A = AMERICAN BUSINESS
E = EMERGING COMPANIES
P = PRIVATE COMPANIES
W = WORLD BUSINESSS

Ossadnik, Victoria E. W369
Osswald, Oliver W283
Ostberg, Par W548
Ostenbridge, Paul Van A271
Ostenbridge, Paul Van E110
Osterhout, Jeannette E361
Osterloh, Bernd W640
Ostertag, Benoit W492
Osterweil, Jody P639
Ostfeld, Scott D. A286
Ostroff, Dawn A802
Ostroff, Dawn A14
Ostrover, Bruce E366
Ostrowsky, Barry H. A858
Osugi, Kazuhito W266
Osuna, Masako W281
Osvald, Hakan W60
Osvaldik, Peter A992
Oswald, Gerhard W517
Oswald, Kathy A508
Oswald, Kathy P260
Oswald, Lisa S. A311
Oswalt, Hal W. A308
Oswalt, Hal W. E134
Ota, Hiroko W223
Ota, Hiroshi W334
Ota, Katsuyuki W223
Ota, Saedene K. A219
Ota, Yoshitsugu W534
Otaki, Seiichi W1
Otani, Tomoki W659
Otis, Clarence A399
Otis, Clarence A1088
Otis, Clarence A1037
Otis, Clarence A1091
Otis, LeAndra E455
Otomo, Hirotsugu W185
Otomo, Ken W417
Otsuka, Hidemitsu W180
Otsuka, Ichiro W462
Otsuka, Iwao W316
Otsuka, Jiro W453
Otsuka, Norio W553
Otsuka, Norio W582
Otsuka, Toru W445
Ott, Dennis H. A401
Ott, Robert J. W590
Ottaway, Andrew W. A435
Ottaway, Andrew W. E210
Ottel, Robert W639
Otten, Anthony L. E365
Ottersgard, Lars A721
Ottersgard, Lars W548
Ottinger, Eric H. A617
Ottinger, Eric H. E290
Otto, Deb A37
Otto, Deb E14
Ottolenghi, Les E468
Ottolino, Alfred J. A860
Ou, Aimin W239
Ou, Xueming W173
Ouart, Patrick W565
Ouchi, Atsushi W209
Ouchi, Yoshiaki W223

Ouchida, Michael P275
Oudea, Frederic W548
Oudeman, Marjan W554
Oughtred, A. Winn E363
Outland, John H. E232
Outlaw, James M. A1044
Ouvrier-Buffet, Gerard W174
Ouyang, Hui W472
Ovelmen, Karyn F. W49
Ovenden, James A. A435
Ovenden, James A. E210
Overall, Laura W157
Overbaugh, Christie Q. E434
Overbaugh, Jason G. E434
Overbey, Cecil E. A771
Overby, Brian A37
Overby, Brian E14

Ø

Øverland, Erling W558

O

Overlock, Willard J. E176
Overly, Jeffrey M. A818
Overs, Robert C. E247
Overstrom, Alex A834
Ovesen, Jesper W548
Ovrum, Margareth W227

Ø

Øvrum, Margareth W591

O

Owen, Andrea (Andi) A998
Owen, Gregory J. A722
Owen, Jan L. E336
Owen, Jeffery C. A336
Owen, John B. A330
Owen, Katherine Ann E355
Owen, Kenneth F. E536
Owen, Randel G. E207
Owen, Terry M. A394
Owens, Angela A56
Owens, Ashley P671
Owens, B. Craig A303
Owens, Charles E. E117
Owens, Edward P. E282
Owens, George Tracy E514
Owens, J. Michael W122
Owens, Lester J. A1115
Owens, Matthew R. E101
Owens, Mike A1034
Owens, Patricia L. A981
Owens, Patricia L. E469
Owens, R.V. A1033
Owens, R.V. E493
Owens, Robert W. A475
Owens, Thomas C. A1044

Owens, William F. E188
Owens, William L. A98
Owens, William L. E36
Oxley, Stephen W328
Oxley, Timothy M. E313
Oyabu, Chiho W82
Oyagi, Shigeo W607
Oyama, Akira W496
Oyama, Kazuya W570
Oyama, Kiichiro W293
Oyamada, Takashi W402
Oyler, W. Kenneth A890
Oyler, W. Kenneth E416
Oyolu, Chukwuemeka A. W374
Oz, Ran W78
Ozaki, Yoshinori W534
Ozan, Kevin M. A675
Ozan, Terrence R. A1013
Ozan, Terry W123
Ozark, Timothy K. A1
Ozawa, Toshihito W403
Ozawa, Yoshiro W417
Ozburn, Sue E83
Ozdemir, Yusuf W198
Ozen, Sait Ergun W618
Ozgen, Mustafa A. E423
Ozimek, Michael M. A1043
Ozsoy, Mevhibe Canan W618
Ozsuca, Ebru W619
Ozuah, Phillip A788
Ozus, K. Atil W26
Ozzie, Raymond E. A514

P

P.Y., Hacina W548
Pa'erhati, Maimaitiyiming W656
Paalvast, Edwin W351
Paasch, Dagmar W510
Paasschen, Frits D. van A1132
Paatelainen, Seppo W340
Paatero-Kaarnakari, Maria W247
Paavola, Teppo W13
Pacchioni, Milo W627
Pace, Brandon A627
Pace, Gary W. E369
Pace, Nicholas J. A794
Pace, Peter E405
Pace, Robert J. A898
Pace, Stephen J. E147
Pacelli, Steven R. E138
Pacha, Theodore H. A515
Pachman, Matthew E224
Pacilio, Michael J. A347
Pack, Michael E. A789
Packer, Paul E547
Paco, Oscar Romero De W251
Pacyna, Michael J. E190
Padbury, Mary W164
Paddon, Patrick E. E76
Paden, Frank L. E117
Padgett, Martin A. E206
Padilla, Raul A828
Padmanabhan, Srikanth A624
Padmanabhan, Srikanth A306
Padnos, Douglas B. A653
Padoan, Pietro Carlo W625
Padovani, Laura W89

Paech, Udo W280
Paefgen, Franz-Joseph W61
Paek, Nack Y. E323
Paes, Guilherme da Costa W69
Paese, Joseph L. A702
Paese, Joseph L. E326
Pagano, Helena J. W572
Pagano, Vincent A226
Page, Bradley D. E384
Page, David C. A818
Page, G. Ruffner A955
Page, G. Ruffner E456
Page, Gregory R. A320
Page, Gregory R. A4
Page, Gregory R. A298
Page, Gregory R. W209
Page, James H. A192
Page, Justine F. A180
Page, Lawrence A45
Page, Roxanne M. E96
Page, Stacey M. A519
Page, Stacey M. E256
Page, Stephen W618
Page, Stephen F. E8
Paglia, John Kenneth E444
Paglia, Louis J. W50
Pagliarini, Elizabeth A423
Pagliarini, Elizabeth E199
Pagliaro, Renato W391
Pagliuca, Stephen G. E266
Pagnutti, Louis P. W99
Pahk, Hee-Jae W478
Pahwa, Jagdeep A116
Pai, Lisa Kim A531
Pai, Lisa Kim E259
Pai, Satish W7
Paiano, Robert W. A502
Paik, Woo-Hyun W366
Pain, Mark A. W662
Paine, Gary D. E247
Paine, Lynn Sharp W61
Paine, Tim W499
Painter, Jeff E81
Painter, Jennifer Hankes E38
Painter, Jonathan W. E286
Painter, Robert E497
Pairitz, Peter L. A532
Pairitz, Peter L. E259
Paisley, Christopher B. A377
Paiva, Maria Luiza de Oliveira Pinto e W630
Paiz, Salvador W643
Paja, David W46
Paker, Can W26
Paker, Nafiz Can W267
Palacherla, Neelima P176
Palacios, Lorraine A397
Palacios, Lorraine E187
Palacios, Maria de Lourdes Melgar W73
Paladino, Christopher J. E453
Paladino, Mary E383
Paladino, Steven A917
Palagiano, Vincent F. A329
Palandjian, Leon A. A191
Palandjian, Leon A. E77
Palau-Hernandez, Margarita A1142
Palazzo, Dominic M. E340
Palecka, Peter W347
Palermo, Frank J. A910
Paley, Eric B. E489

COMBINED HOOVER'S HANDBOOK INDEX OF EXECUTIVES

A = AMERICAN BUSINESS
E = EMERGING COMPANIES
P = PRIVATE COMPANIES
W = WORLD BUSINESSS

Palfreyman, J. A. W579
Palin, Carrie A729
Paliwal, Dinesh C. A877
Palkhiwala, Akash A867
Pallot, Mark A465
Palmby, Paul L. E61
Palme, Marion W515
Palmer, Anthony J. A512
Palmer, Cheryl M. E50
Palmer, Christopher G. A397
Palmer, Christopher G. E187
Palmer, Duncan J. A790
Palmer, Elizabeth A296
Palmer, Eric P. A239
Palmer, John R.V. W382
Palmer, John W. E63
Palmer, Kerri A. A944
Palmer, Kerri A. E450
Palmer, R. Alan E117
Palmer, Richard Keith W562
Palmer, Sheryl D. A998
Palmer, Thomas R. A736
Palmer, Thomas W. E172
Palmer, Vicki R. A424
Palmer, Vicki R. E200
Palmieri, Jane M. A962
Palmieri, Matthew J. E512
Palmieri, Paul E. E371
Palmore, Roderick A. A483
Palmore, Roderick A. E87
Palomares, Carlos E413
Palomarez, Javier A. A668
Palombella, Vito J. E475
Palombo, Grace M. W262
Palsule, Himanshu E92
Palt, Alexandra W358
Paltrowitz, Jason L. E366
Palumbo, Christopher J. A401
Palus, Jean-Francois W338
Palzer, Stefan W429
Pamer-Wieser, Charlotte W449
Pamon, Steve E543
Pan, Gang W307
Pan, Jibo A397
Pan, Jibo E187
Pan, Jie W663
Pan, Jinfeng W106
Pan, Jiuwen W529
Pan, Nicholas D. Le W119
Pan, Richard W480
Pan, Wayne T. E436
Pan, Xiaotao W292
Pan, Xiaoyong W542
Pan, Zhaoguo W660
Pan, Zhengqi W141
Pan, Zhihua W477
Panagos, Costa A576
Panay, Panos E452
Panayiotou, Stacey J. A123
Panayiotou, Stacey J. Valy A486
Panayotopoulos, Dimitri W111
Panda, Debasish W561
Pandey, Dheeraj A15
Pandit, Vikram S. E179

Pando, Antonio Cosio W35
Panepinto, Stephen A397
Panepinto, Stephen E187
Panetta, Leon E. A786
Panfil, Derek A157
Pang, Lianyi W603
Pang, Simon A878
Pang, Simon E409
Pang, Y. K. W323
Pangalos, Menelas W57
Pangaribuan, Binsar W483
Pangburn, James Walter A68
Pangburn, Marc E245
Paniagua, Angel Jesus Acebes W295
Panich, Vicharn W541
Panikar, John M. W369
Paniry, Rina A965
Paniry, Rina E462
Panizza, Pablo W40
Pannu, Geraldine A878
Pannu, Geraldine E409
Panossian, Hratch W119
Panpothong, Anuttara W79
Pansa, Alessandro W363
Pant, Vandita W101
Pantelidis, Jim W295
Pantilione, Nicholas J. E371
Pantilione, Vito S. E371
Panuccio, Susan A738
Panyarachun, Anand W541
Panyarachun, Disathat W484
Pao, Yi Hsin W240
Paoli, Alberto de W219
Paoli, Mary De W570
Papa, Mark G. W523
Papadimitriou, Georgios W254
Papadopoulo, Nicolas W50
Papadopoulos, Stelios A158
Papadopoulos, Stelios E177
Papagaryfallou, Lazaros A. W33
Papanikolaou, Yianna W647
Papapostolou, Ted A549
Papastavrou, Jason D. A493
Pape, Jacques Le W22
Paperin, Stewart J. A96
Papermaster, Mark D. A18
Papin, Jeremie W441
Papirnik, Vladimira W336
Pappas, Bill A691
Pappas, Christopher D. A432
Pappas, Christopher D. A1075
Paquette, Michael S. A367
Paquette, Sylvie W308
Paquin, Natalye A1078
Paquin, Natalye E513
Paracchini, Alberto J. A188
Paracchini, Alberto J. E71
Parady, Steven N. E192
Parahus, Robert A1032
Paral, Jason E. E169
Parameswaran, Prabha A269
Paranjpe, Nitin W274
Paranjpe, Nitin W626
Paraskevopoulos, Nikolaos W280
Parasnis, Abhay E145
Paravicini, Lukas W297
Parcella, Gabriela Franco E486
Parcher, Charles A. A251
Parcher, Charles A. E100
Parchinski, Kathleen P217

Pardee, Charles A1139
Pardo, Felipe Bayon W210
Pardo, Jaime Chico W265
Pardo, Marcela Leonor Jimenez W314
Pardun, Thomas E. E314
Pare, Denis W193
Pare, Robert W420
Pareigat, Thomas G. A1014
Pareigat, Thomas G. E488
Parekh, Bobby W304
Parekh, Salil W304
Parekh, Salil W123
Parekh, Sandeep W271
Parent, Ghislain W420
Parent, Ken A159
Parent, Louise M. A1153
Parent, Louise M. A408
Parent, Marc W596
Parente, John A280
Parente, John E113
Parfet, Donald R. A666
Parfet, Donald R. A902
Parham, Richelle P. A155
Parham, Richelle P. A615
Parija, Soubhagya P386
Parikh, Amit E239
Parikh, Neha A208
Parikh, Shailee E299
Parimore, Robert A. E190
Parini, Michael J. A1089
Paris, Michel M. W61
Paris, Roberto de Jesus W69
Parish, Douglas J. A175
Parish, Douglas J. E66
Parisi, Erika K. A596
Parisi, Erika K. E286
Parisi, James E. E87
Parisi, Joseph A287
Parisi, Joseph E115
Parisot, Laurence W215
Park, Ansoon W537
Park, Anthony J. A406
Park, Chan-Hi W352
Park, Chan-Il W335
Park, David X. A119
Park, David X. E48
Park, David Y. E462
Park, Gee-Won W205
Park, Hong Kyun E375
Park, Hyo-Sung W352
Park, Jeff E398
Park, John J. E530
Park, Jong-Bae W352
Park, Jong-Ook W352
Park, Jung Ho W546
Park, Kimberly E121
Park, Kyong-Hoon W652
Park, Linda J. A361
Park, Min S. A498
Park, Myung Ja E362
Park, Oh-Soo W513
Park, Sang-Yong W652
Park, Seong-Won W366
Park, Steve K. E362
Park, Sung-hyung W537
Park, Taemin W50
Park, Winnie A338
Park, Young W323
Parker, Allen W. A1149
Parker, Anthony W. E232

Parker, Ava L. A787
Parker, Ava L. A668
Parker, Ava L. E397
Parker, C. Scott E443
Parker, Christine W648
Parker, Diane W. E489
Parker, Elton C. E280
Parker, George G. C. A431
Parker, George G. C. E205
Parker, Herbert K. A57
Parker, Jill E57
Parker, Jon C. E489
Parker, Kellie W500
Parker, Mark G. A335
Parker, Mark G. A743
Parker, P.W. (Bill) A985
Parker, Paul A254
Parker, Steve E19
Parker, Stuart B. A599
Parker, Stuart B. E247
Parker, Ted E. A414
Parker, Ted E. E193
Parker, Zachary C. E143
Parkerson, Michael A1014
Parkerson, Michael P570
Parkes, David W66
Parkhill, Karen L. A62
Parkhill, Karen L. W393
Parkinson, John W. E117
Parks, Delbert R. A940
Parks, Douglas L. A466
Parks, Kenneth Scott A795
Parks, Robert A729
Parks, Robert Ralph W541
Parlato, Francesco W363
Parmar, Manish E413
Parmenter, Darren E. A516
Parmentier, Jennifer A. A804
Parmer, Elizabeth E213
Parod, Richard W. E13
Parr, Jeremy W323
Parr, Ross H. A771
Parra, Carolina W122
Parrett, William G. A786
Parrett, William G. A161
Parrillo, Sandra Glaser A1108
Parris, Colin J. W46
Parris, Colin J. W45
Parrish, Benjamin F. A1035
Parrish, Harlan C. E190
Parrish, M. Lynn A283
Parrish, Mark W. A1093
Parrotte, Dianne M. E105
Parsey, Merdad V. A473
Parsley, E. William A834
Parson, Rosemary A1118
Parson, Rosemary E533
Parsons, Guy P. C. W662
Parsons, J. Pat A213
Parsons, James M. E301
Parsons, Raymond Whitmore Knighton W558
Parsons, Richard D. A620
Parsons, Suzan P671
Partain, Nathan I. E367
Partee, Brian K. A717
Parthemore, Eric A979
Partin, Robert Lee E57
Partlow, Robert E240
Partovi, Shez W351

COMBINED HOOVER'S HANDBOOK INDEX OF EXECUTIVES

```
A = AMERICAN BUSINESS
E = EMERGING COMPANIES
P = PRIVATE COMPANIES
W = WORLD BUSINESSS
```

Partridge, John M. A239
Partridge, Laila S. A191
Partridge, Laila S. E77
Partridge, Matthew M. E19
Pas, Aaron J. A28
Paschal, John E353
Paschke, Brett L. E147
Pascuzzi, Steve P185
Pashaev, Oleg W476
Pasquale, Douglas M. E486
Pasquariello, Maria Antonietta W627
Pasquesi, John M. W50
Pasquier, Bernard W314
Pasricha, Atul W441
Passafiume, Philip A853
Passos, Murilo Cesar Lemos dos Santos W630
Pasternak, Assaf W312
Pastides, Harris A988
Pastides, Harris E479
Pastor, Louis J. A1141
Pastore, Daniel Sposito W315
Patafio, Frank P. A749
Patanaphakdee, Parinya W352
Patel, Ajit A. E323
Patel, Akash J. A958
Patel, Akash J. E456
Patel, Bhavesh V. (Bob) A494
Patel, Chintu E31
Patel, Chirag E31
Patel, Gautam E31
Patel, H. D. A958
Patel, H. D. E456
Patel, Jaymin B. A958
Patel, Jaymin B. E68
Patel, Jeetendra I. A588
Patel, Kavita K. E436
Patel, Ketul J P264
Patel, Kiran M. A607
Patel, Malay W271
Patel, Nadir W122
Patel, Nikul E447
Patel, Nir A457
Patel, Pritesh E517
Patel, Raj E510
Patel, Sudhirkumar C. E492
Patel, Zarin W364
Pateman, Steve W81
Patent, Robert C. A691
Patent, Robert C. E323
Paterson, Iain W412
Paterson, Nigel W179
Patolawala, Monish D. A4
Patouhas, John S. A1004
Patriarca, Michael M. A1120
Patriarca, Michael M. E535
Patricio, Miguel A610
Patrick, Ryan P134
Patrick, Stephen C. A97
Patrickson, David Gallagher W132
Patrizio, Mapelli W451
Patrushev, Dmitry N. W474
Patry, Dean P40
Pats, Jean-Claude W168

Patsalos-Fox, Michael A267
Patsley, Pamela H. A1010
Patsley, Pamela H. A600
Patten, Randy L. A1065
Patterson, Chad M. E138
Patterson, David A. A1033
Patterson, David A. E492
Patterson, Elizabeth T. A1033
Patterson, Elizabeth T. E493
Patterson, Julien G. E62
Patterson, L Brooks P174
Patterson, Lynn K. W84
Patterson, Mark R. A528
Patterson, Mark R. E141
Patterson, Robert M. A490
Patterson, Roger P658
Patterson, Simon A322
Patterson, Simon W597
Patterson, Thomas L. E227
Patterson, William D. E337
Pattison, Lindsay W654
Patton, Charles A. A1042
Patton, Charles R. A59
Patton, Charles R. A401
Patton, Charles R. E463
Patton, Cynthia M. A76
Patton, Cynthia M. A788
Patton, James Anthony A1132
Patton, James Anthony E539
Patton, R. David A706
Patton, Robin Van P156
Paul, Alison Kenney A989
Paul, Barbara N. A747
Paul, David C. E233
Paul, H. Edward A643
Paul, Holly E224
Paul, Joseph R. E136
Paul, Stefan W355
Paula, Jefferson de W49
Pauldine, David J. E407
Paull, David Z. A393
Paull, David Z. E184
Paull, Kimberly A971
Paull, Kimberly P537
Paull, Matthew H. A30
Pauls, Douglas J. A135
Pauls, John C. A1056
Pauls, John C. E505
Paulsen, Thomas W. W87
Paup, Mark A. A753
Paus, William W547
Pavitt, James L. A189
Pawlenty, Timothy J. E450
Paxton, Christine Poland A718
Paxton, Christine Poland E335
Paxton, Stuart P310
Payan, Herve W61
Payan, Juan Manuel Rojas W210
Payne, Clifton A. A492
Payne, Clifton A. E243
Payne, David L. A1119
Payne, James P. A68
Payne, John W.R. E524
Payne, Lisa A. A902
Payne, Lisa A. A666
Payne, Richard B. A1115
Payne, Steven M. E233
Payne, Ulice A443
Payne, Ulice A655
Payne, Ulice A1114

Payne, W. Joseph E11
Payne, William A. A500
Payne, William A. E246
Payson, Norman C. E398
Payton, Robert P210
Payuhanaveechai, Chatchai W334
Payumo, Gerardo C. W514
Paz, George A530
Paz, George A857
Pe, Marc D Williams A1009
Pe, Marc D Williams P563
Peach, Richard D. E430
Peacock, David A. A977
Peacock, David A. E464
Peacock, Jonathan M. A112
Peacock, Karen E145
Peacock, Lynne W509
Peacor, Melissa S P175
Peak, Scott A225
Pearce, Charles A. E128
Pearce, Don E131
Pearce, Stephen W. W39
Pearce, Stephen W. W66
Pearce, Warren W. E274
Pearl, Michael C. E514
Pears, Jonathan W471
Pearse, Robert G. E131
Pearson, David T. E295
Pearson, J F P575
Pearson, John W198
Pearson, Lori W112
Pearson, Mark A377
Pearson, Mark E17
Pease, Alexander W. A1125
Pease, Flavia H. E94
Peck, Casey L. A515
Peck, Charles H. A181
Peck, Gary M. E336
Peck, Kristin C. A160
Peck, Kristin C. A1153
Peck, Laura A254
Peck, Thomas R. A989
Pecor, Raymond C. A280
Pecor, Raymond C. E113
Pecoraro, Lucette A400
Pédamon, Bernard W22
Pedersen, Brandon S. A386
Pedersen, Bret Allen E168
Pedersen, John A136
Pederson, E. J. A68
Pederson, E. J. A722
Pederson, Robin E374
Pedini, Claire W165
Pedro, Claudia San A167
Pedro, Claudia San E64
Pedroni, Marco W627
Pedroso, Luis M. A372
Pedroso, Luis M. E167
Peed, R. Daniel A1066
Peek, Mark S. E497
Peeler, D. Randolph E341
Peeples, William R. E114
Peer, Quinten W655
Peereboom, Paulo A989
Peery, R. Wade A395
Peery, R. Wade E185
Pefanis, Harry N. A833
Pefanis, Harry N. A832
Pegula, Kim S. A892
Pehrsson, Biljana W579

Peiffer, Garry L. A717
Peiler, Mark E. E63
Peirano, Cristian W73
Peiros, Lawrence S. E391
Peirson, James W157
Peiser, Robert A. E515
Pejic, Klementina W581
Pekala, Joseph S. A794
Pekofske, Dan A716
Pelata, Patrick W511
Peled, Erfat W78
Pelisson, Gilles C. W10
Pelkey, Sean R. A304
Pelkowski, Julie Marie E172
Pell, Michael P. A397
Pellegrini, Mirella W222
Pellegrino, Frank G. E98
Pellegrino, Nancy D. A528
Pellerin, Fleur W524
Pelletan, Jerome W357
Pelletier, Liane J. A386
Pelletier, Liane J. E221
Pelletier, Megan A528
Pelletier, Megan E258
Pellicioli, Lorenzo W54
Pelligrino, Joseph P. E297
Pelling, S. C. W579
Pelosi, Janine E547
Pelosi, Peggie J. E180
Pelouch, Miroslav W207
Pelton, Janet S. E357
Peltz, Nelson W626
Peluso, Michelle A. A743
Pemberton, Jill M. E491
Pena, Austin E62
Pena, Julio V. A52
Pena, Luis W266
Pena, Mardelle W. E528
Pena, Rafael Espino de la W470
Penafiel, Juan Edgardo Goldenberg W217
Penafiel, Juan Edgardo Goldenberg W41
Penchienati-Bosetta, Veronique W187
Pendarvis, David B. E417
Pendergast, Christopher A917
Pendley, David R. E97
Penegor, Todd Allan A123
Penfield, Susan L. A171
Peng, Feng W100
Peng, Guoquan W291
Peng, Heping W307
Peng, Jiangling W656
Peng, Jianjun W139
Peng, Kaiyu W100
Peng, Philip W650
Peng, Victor A18
Peng, Victor A607
Peng, Wei W150
Peng, Xingyu W291
Peng, Yanxiang W156
Peng, Yi W137
Peng, Yulong W431
Penha, Alex E43
Pénicaud, Muriel A655
Penicaud, Pierre W486
Penido, Jose Luciano Duarte W630
Penker, Heimo W453
Penland, Joe E. A214
Penn, Andrew R. W595

HOOVER'S HANDBOOK OF EMERGING COMPANIES 2023

COMBINED HOOVER'S HANDBOOK INDEX OF EXECUTIVES

```
A = AMERICAN BUSINESS
E = EMERGING COMPANIES
P = PRIVATE COMPANIES
W = WORLD BUSINESSS
```

Penn, Laurence E155
Penn, Ronda M. A66
Penn, Ronda M. E25
Penner, Gregory B. A1104
Penner, Michael D. W84
Penner, Shawn D. A378
Penner, Timothy H. W308
Penney, Robert P110
Pennington, Brooks M. E90
Pennington, Penelope A586
Pennoni, Celestino R. E371
Penny, Gareth Peter W410
Penny, J. Scott E68
Penrose, Karen W85
Penrose, Sheila A. A588
Penske, Gregory W. A812
Penske, Roger S. A812
Pentland, Louise W279
Pentz, Markwart von A320
Peon, Lorenzo W266
Pepin, Normand W294
Pepy, Guilaume W565
Pepy, Guillaume A224
Pera, Robert J. E503
Peraino, Vito C. A64
Perakis-Valat, Alexis W358
Percy-Robb, Michael I. W570
Pereda, Maria Dolores Herrera W295
Pereira, Alexandre Gomes W630
Pereira, Daniella W162
Pereira, George A400
Pereira, George M. A797
Pereira, George M. E368
Pereira, Jaime A475
Pereira, John M. A181
Pereira, Kelly W507
Pereira, Rodrigo de Mesquita W468
Pereira, Ronaldo Iabrudi dos Santos W127
Perelman, Robert A616
Peres, Nechemia (Chemi) J. W598
Perez-Alvarado, Gilda E62
Perez-Hickman, Fernando E348
Perez-Tenessa, Alejandro A367
Perez, Arturo Manuel Fernandez W265
Perez, Beatriz R. A845
Perez, Beatriz R. A485
Perez, Beatriz R. E395
Perez, Charles A. Ruys de A1121
Perez, Javier A670
Perez, Jose Luis del Valle W11
Perez, Jose Luis del Valle W280
Perez, Jose Manuel Inchausti W382
Perez, Jose Maria Abril W593
Perez, Juan Pedro Santa Maria W73
Perez, Juan R. A512
Perez, Laree E. A663
Perez, Maripaz P202
Perez, Rey A722
Pérez, Sonia A. A496
Perez, Vicente S. W100
Perez, William D. E284
Perica, Adrian W202
Perillat, Christophe W630

Périllat, Christophe W27
Perisich, John M. E397
Perisutti, Stephen J. A933
Perkins, Abbey A979
Perkins, Bruce D. E20
Perkins, James W. E223
Perkins, Joe Bob A995
Perkins, Michael L. A1115
Perkins, Michael L. E533
Perkins, Miles S. E223
Perkins, Noelle J. A1075
Perkins, Paul P218
Perkins, Rodney E223
Perkins, Scott Redvers W651
Perko, Thomas L. A1099
Perl, Lionel W18
Perlman, Dana M. A765
Perlman, Jacob H. A224
Perlmutter, Roger M. A684
Perlowitz, Jeffrey A. A811
Perlowitz, Jeffrey A. E377
Permet, Robert P368
Pernot, Laurance W165
Perochena, Antonio del Valle A188
Perochena, Antonio del Valle E71
Perold, Jacques P. A42
Perold, Jacques P. E336
Perotti, Daniel S. A811
Perotti, Daniel S. E378
Perotti, Daniel S. E377
Perotti, William L. A305
Perpall, Frederick A405
Perpall, Frederick A965
Perpall, Frederick E462
Perra, Alexandre W215
Perrault, Paul A. A181
Perreault, Roger A1054
Perreiah, Diana B. A95
Perret, Jean-Dominique W495
Perrette, Jean-Briac A332
Perrier, Yves W174
Perrin, Maria P265
Perro, Richard P. A430
Perrotti, Roberto W54
Perrotty, P. Sue E232
Perry, Alan W. A190
Perry, Alan W. E73
Perry, Barry W. A97
Perry, Brian E. E319
Perry, Carol P543
Perry, Christopher J. A1133
Perry, Christopher J. E541
Perry, Curtis J. A889
Perry, Curtis J. E414
Perry, David T. A752
Perry, Debra J. A103
Perry, Dexter V. A414
Perry, Dexter V. E191
Perry, Jacob W410
Perry, James B. E227
Perry, James Richard A369
Perry, Jeffery S. A447
Perry, Jodi L. A876
Perry, Joseph J. A329
Perry, Karl E P59
Perry, Kirk L. A947
Perry, Kristy E57
Perry, Marie L. E38
Perry, Mark L. A761
Perry, Matthew D. E545

Perry, Ruth R. E223
Perry, William Wesley E229
Persaud, Andre A894
Perschke, Daniel W. E431
Pershing, John E. W122
Persichetti, Chris J. E23
Personne, Eric W492
Persson, Fredrik W4
Persson, Goran W579
Persson, Karl-Johan W277
Persson, Stefan Renee W277
Pertchik, Jonathan M. E423
Pertz, Douglas A. A17
Peru, Ramiro G. A85
Peschard, Guillermo W643
Pesendorfer, Josef W453
Pesgens, Suzanne P304
Peshkin, John R. A862
Pesicka, Edward A. A793
Pessah, David E234
Pessina, Stefano A1101
Pessoa, Ana Paula A738
Pessoa, Ana Paula W635
Pessoa, Ana Paula W176
Pessoa, Rogerio Cavalcanti de Albuquerque W69
Petach, Ann Marie A588
Pete, Clint J. E93
Petelle, James F. E275
Peter, Henry W580
Peter, Henry W580
Peter, Nicolas W96
Peterffy, Thomas E279
Peterffy, William E279
Peterman, Carla A823
Peterman, Robert H. A845
Peterman, Robert H. E395
Peterman, Tamara M. A1056
Peterman, Tamara M. E505
Petermann, Christopher D. A596
Petermann, Christopher D. E286
Peters, Allan E405
Peters, Allen T. A1053
Peters, Bradley P. A1118
Peters, Bradley P. E533
Peters, Carter M. E243
Peters, Claire W651
Peters, Frederick C. (Ted) E374
Peters, Gregory K. A730
Peters, James W. A1129
Peters, John S. E76
Peters, Joshua J. E153
Peters, Lauren B. A1094
Peters, Len A734
Peters, Len P389
Peters, Luther A306
Peters, Rebecca A761
Peters, Richard W3
Peters, Scott M. A885
Peters, Sharon A223
Peters, Susan P. A645
Peters, Valerie A. A776
Petersen, Gary R. A832
Petersen, Gary R. A833
Petersen, Jacob E297
Petersen, Kaj W348
Petersen, Mads Boye E370
Peterside, Atedo W559
Petersmeyer, Gary S. E119
Peterson, Adam K. A727

Peterson, Adam K. E345
Peterson, Allison A864
Peterson, Bradley J. A721
Peterson, Christopher H. A159
Peterson, Christopher H. A735
Peterson, David K. A207
Peterson, David R. W295
Peterson, Douglas L. A911
Peterson, Jason E170
Peterson, Joel E57
Peterson, Joel E. A259
Peterson, Joel E. E103
Peterson, Justin E493
Peterson, Kurt A1023
Peterson, Kurt P606
Peterson, Laura J. E11
Peterson, Marissa T. A541
Peterson, Mark P30
Peterson, Mary Todd E113
Peterson, Matthew J. A1076
Peterson, Richard D A221
Peterson, Richard D P113
Peterson, Richard D. E512
Peterson, Robert L. A767
Peterson, Roger P90
Peterson, Sandra E. A701
Peterson, Stacy E539
Peterson, Steve A301
Peterson, Steve E131
Peticov, Glaucimar W69
Petizio, Robert P167
Petkovich, Jacob R. E373
Petmecky, William M. A359
Petram, Hans Dieter W586
Petrarca, Mark A. E490
Petrelli, Paul O. W571
Petrie, Michael J. A681
Petrie, Michael J. E318
Petrillo, Louis T. W50
Petrino, Richard A62
Petro, Andrea E411
Petro, Randall R. A685
Petro, Thomas M. A1078
Petro, Thomas M. E513
Petrovic, Shacey E276
Petrucci, Angela N. A722
Petrucci, Angela N. E339
Petrucelli, Bryan P. E287
Petterson, Lars W548
Petti, Filippo P398
Pettie, Mark A1113
Pettigrew, Jim W21
Pettigrew, Jim W157
Pettigrew, John W422
Pettit, C.D. Baer E335
Pettiti, Gianluca A1027
Petty, Brian P. E189
Petty, Gary Wayne A945
Petty, Gary Wayne E451
Petty, Miltom E. A642
Petty, Miltom E. E304
Petz, Heidi G. A933
Peuch, Olivier Le W523
Peugeot, Robert W511
Peugeot, Robert W238
Peugeot, Robert W562
Peugeot, Thierry W238
Peverett, Jane L. W119
Peyrelevade, Jean W344
peza, Pablo De la W266

COMBINED HOOVER'S HANDBOOK INDEX OF EXECUTIVES

A = AMERICAN BUSINESS
E = EMERGING COMPANIES
P = PRIVATE COMPANIES
W = WORLD BUSINESSS

Pfalzgraf, David R. E175
Pfau, Lorenz W171
Pfeifer, John C. A789
Pfeiffer, Gary M. A870
Pfeiffer, Gerald E. A504
Pfeiffer, Philip J. A1085
Pfeiffer, Wendy M. E405
Pfeil, Keith W. E233
Pferdehirt, Douglas J. W590
Pfinsgraff, Martin A834
Pfister, Bruno W526
Pflederer, Kent A. A799
Pflimlin, Thierry W613
Pforzheimer, Carl Andrew A1083
Phairatphiboon, Virat W79
Pham, Thuan A1052
Phan, Steven Swee Kim W628
Pharaon, Fadi W228
Pharr, Brett L. A688
Pharr, Brett L. E323
Phegley, R. Lee A574
Phelan, David C. A973
Phelan, John W. A515
Phelan, Kenneth J. A545
Phelan, Kevin C. E270
Phelps, W. Bruce E246
Philip, Edward M. A1062
Philipovitch, Kerry E472
Philippe, Herve W637
Philipps, Kate W511
Philipps, Roberto Oscar W132
Philips, Kathleen A1149
Phillippy, Robert J. E287
Phillips, Carrie P646
Phillips, Charles E. A62
Phillips, Charles E. A802
Phillips, Christopher E102
Phillips, Daniel R. E372
Phillips, David C. E321
Phillips, David P. A860
Phillips, Holly L. E440
Phillips, Jeanne L. A719
Phillips, Joelle J. A200
Phillips, Joelle J. E79
Phillips, John T. E54
Phillips, Joy Lambert A496
Phillips, Joyce Ann A426
Phillips, Joyce Ann E202
Phillips, Kenneth A. E354
Phillips, Kevin M. E308
Phillips, Nancy R. A802
Phillips, Ottis H. A945
Phillips, Ottis H. E451
Phillips, Robert L. W122
Phillips, Ronald L. A989
Phipps, Chad F. A1150
Phipps, Gilliam D. A959
Phipps, Terry S. E222
Phlegar, Charles D P676
Phokasub, Yol W541
Phornprapha, Phornthep W77
Phutrakul, Tanate W306
Phyfer, Cheri M. A447
Pi, Anrong W136

Pi, Nick A843
Pi, Nick E392
Piacenza, Bruno W277
Piacquad, David A. A76
Pianalto, Sandra A857
Pianalto, Sandra A947
Pianalto, Sandra A209
Piasecki, Nicole W. A1127
Piasecki, Nicole W. W66
Piazza, Samuel A. Di A848
Piazza, Samuel A. Di A588
Picat, Maxime W562
Picaud, Geraldine W303
Picaud, Geraldine W283
Picca, Bruno W310
Picchi, Nicla W627
Piccinno, Emanuele W227
Piccirillo, Charles S. A981
Piccirillo, Charles S. E469
Pichai, Sundar A44
Pichayanan, Danucha W484
Piche, Catherine A301
Piche, Pierre W480
Pichel, Logan M. A890
Pichel, Logan M. E416
Pichelli, Aldo (Al) E483
Pichette, Patrick A1047
Pichler, Barbara W229
Pichon, Emily E. A618
Pichon, Emily E. E290
Pichottka, Andrea W277
Pick, Edward N. A713
Pickard, Ann D. A595
Pickel, Michael W269
Pickens, Kenneth M. E452
Pickerell, Blair C. A846
Pickering, Anthony B. A510
Pickering, Anthony B. E252
Pickering, Christine L. A496
Pickett, Denise A62
Pickett, Denise W596
Pickle, Elaine E91
Pickles, David R. E489
Picknelly, Paul C. E537
Pickney, Roderick A. E67
Pictet, Guillaume W167
Piech, Hans Michel W61
Piech, Hans Michel W640
Piepszak, Jennifer A. A591
Pierce, Glenn F. E529
Pierce, Joseph A. A305
Pierce, Joseph G. (Joe) E223
Pierce, Lacey A. E113
Pierce, Patrick D. E113
Pierce, Sandra E. A545
Pierce, Sandra E. A813
Pierce, Sandra E. A57
Pierce, Tera P138
Pierdicchi, Maria W625
Pierer, Heinrich V. W346
Pierre, G. Trent E455
Pierre, Sharon St P366
Pierschbacher, John L. E30
Pierson, Paul J. A422
Pierson, R. Hunter E391
Pierson, Rose Z. A230
Piesik, Margaret R. E223
Pietikainen, Sirpa W348
Pietrandrea, Brian P. E171
Pietrangelo, Michael A. E512

Pietranton, Anthony F. A1115
Pietranton, Anthony F. E533
Pietri, Antonio J. E39
Pietrzak, John E91
Piette, Barbara A. E401
Pigg, Joseph E. A207
Pignuolo, Charles J. A190
Pignuolo, Charles J. E73
Pigott, John M. A796
Pigott, Mark C. A796
Pigott, Robert T. A213
Pijor, David W. E227
Pike, Lynn A. A62
Pike, Thomas H. A663
Pilastri, Stefano W177
Pilmer, Donald A774
Pilmer, Donald E360
Pilnick, Gary H. A597
Pimentel, Armando A436
Pimentel, Armando A70
Pimentel, Richard E114
Pin, Tan Yam W261
Pinard, Jean-Paul W456
Pinatel, Bernard W613
Pinault, Francois-Henri W338
Pinczuk, Ana G. W46
Pinczuk, Ana G. W45
Pineda, Patricia Salas A631
Pineda, Patricia Salas A778
Pineres, Ernesto Gutierrez de W210
Pingclasai, Jrarat W352
Pinheiro, Brian E350
Pinkerton, Mac S. A900
Pinner, Ernest S. A955
Pinner, Ernest S. E456
Pinoncely, Gilles W127
Pinsupa, Noppadol W484
Pinter, Jozef W229
Pinto, Ari W78
Pinto, Carlos W254
Pinto, Daniel E. A591
Pinto, Helena Sofia Silva Borges Salgado Fonseca Cerveira W212
Pinto, John J. A732
Pinto, Marcio Percival Alves W324
Pintoff, Craig A. A1071
Pintoff, Scott E311
Pintozzi, John C. A42
Piper, Michael S. E219
Pipes, Kristy M. A20
Pipes, Kristy M. E179
Pippins, Dakota A. A534
Piquemal, Thomas W215
Piramal, Swati A. W231
Pires, Luciano Siani A715
Pires, Luciano Siani W630
Piret, Claude W199
Pirie, Ellen P177
Pirishi, Ersi W358
Pirondini, Andrea W482
Pirotte, Olivier W565
Pirro, Nicholas J P174
Pisani, Alberto Maria W310
Pisano, Paulo A170
Pischetsrieder, Bernd W395
Pischinger, Wolfgang W453
Pistelli, Lapo W227
Pistorio, Pasquale W61
Pita, George L. A792
Pitchford, Lloyd W116

Pitkethly, Graeme W626
Pitman, Elizabeth N. E315
Pitofsky, David B. A738
Pitoniak, Edward Baltazar E524
Pitt, Douglas M. A488
Pitt, Justin D. A282
Pittard, Patrick S. A638
Pittard, Ray W617
Pittelkow, Charles R. E480
Pitters, Ron A120
Pitters, Ron E48
Pittman, John C. E156
Pittman, Paul A. E185
Pittman, Steuart P166
Pitts, Gregory C. A845
Pitts, Gregory C. E395
Pivirotto, Charles J. A596
Pivirotto, Charles J. E286
Piwnica, Carole W515
Piyajitti, Supa W541
Pizarro, Pedro J. A359
Pizarro, Pedro J. A951
Pizzinatto, Rodrigo de Almeida W622
Pizzo, Kristine P386
Place, Nick L. A175
Place, Nick L. E66
Placek, Richard C. E537
Plafker, Jed A. A448
Plaines, Stephanie A254
Plaines, Stephanie A742
Plam, Kathleen P132
Plank, Kevin A. A1059
Plansky, Michael C. E440
Planson, Steven J. E184
Plant, John C. A666
Plant, John C. A578
Planta, Andreas von W449
Plante, Gilles W36
Plante, Robert A. A810
Plante, Robert A. E375
Plassat, Georges W125
Plastinina, Nina W410
Plater, Michael A. E302
Plath, Claudia W129
Plath, Thomas J. A568
Platov, Pavel W410
Platt, Alison W597
Platt, Gillian L. W178
Platt, Ira A208
Platt, James W44
Platt, Tracy L. A221
Platteeuw, Filip W623
Plattner, Hasso W517
Platzer, Wilbert L. E404
Plazas, Hernando Ramirez W210
Pleasant, Dan M. A66
Pleasant, Dan M. E25
Plecki, Robert F. A415
Plecki, Robert F. E194
Pleines, Thomas W68
Pleininger, Johann W458
Plemmons, Gregory B. A771
Plenborg, Thomas W205
Plessis-Belair, Michel W480
Plessis, Jan du W114
Plessis, Johann du W562
Plevneliev, Rosen E423
Plew, Daniel P. Van A882
Plewman, Patrick T. A870
Plimpton, Tara Ann A885

COMBINED HOOVER'S HANDBOOK INDEX OF EXECUTIVES

A = AMERICAN BUSINESS
E = EMERGING COMPANIES
P = PRIVATE COMPANIES
W = WORLD BUSINESSS

Plisinski, Michael P. E362
Ploeg, Julia Vander E180
Ploey, Wouter De W104
Ploog, Jens W129
Ploss, Ines W273
Ploss, Reinhard W303
Plotkin, Ben A. A977
Plotkin, Ben A. E464
Plottke, Ulrich W415
Plourd, Martin E. E114
Plourde, Real W31
Plueger, John L. E10
Plum, Brian K. E62
Plumart, Marc W550
Plumb, Spencer G. E81
Plummer, James D. E75
Plummer, Michelle M. E240
Plummer, Tammy L. E192
Plummer, William B. A477
Plummer, William B. A1110
Plump, Andrew W585
Plunkett, Debora A. A189
Plunkett, Debora A. E319
Plush, Gerald P. A52
Pluss, Steven A941
Plust, Steven A485
Pluta, Thomas E493
Plyler, R. Scott E452
Poarch, Donald L. A556
Poarch, Donald L. E270
Poblador, Alexander J. W514
Pobo, Angel W613
Pochowicz, Jeffrey J. A675
Podolskaya, Natalia W476
Podolsky, Daniel K. A27
Podzimek, Cheryl Beranek E101
Poe, Alfred E50
Poelvoorde, Geert Van W49
Poenitske, Jason P P405
Poetsch, Hans Dieter W61
Poff, Brian E5
Poffinberger, Aaron M. E149
Pohl, Paul R. E537
Pohlad, Robert C. A818
Pohle, Richard A545
Pohlman, Kevin M. A806
Pohlman, Thomas H. E30
Pohls, Rene W207
Poindexter, Philip S. A978
Poindexter, Philip S. E465
Poitevint, Alec L. A1066
Pojamarnpornchai, Ronnakitt W117
Poladian, Avedick B. A767
Polan, Mary Lake E406
Polen, Thomas E. A147
Polet, Robert B. A825
Poletaev, Maxim W410
Polewaczyk, James F. E263
Policarpo, Michael D. E525
Policicchio, Betsy A742
Policicchio, Betsy P393
Policinski, Christopher J. A534
Policinski, Christopher J. A1139
Polito, Karyn A152

Polius, Olivia D. A386
Polk, Dennis J. A999
Polk, Dennis J. A287
Polk, Dennis J. E486
Polk, James C. A129
Polk, Michael A645
Polk, Michael B. A269
Pollack, Dennis E401
Pollack, Jonathan Lee E62
Pollack, Kenneth L. A28
Pollack, Martha A565
Pollak, Andrea W269
Pollard, Robert E. E401
Pollitt, Byron H. A1099
Pollitzer, Adam S. E350
Pollock, John W471
Pollok, John C. A955
Pollok, John C. E456
Polohakul, Ampol W334
Poloncarz, Mark P169
Poloni, Lara A20
Poloz, Stephen S. W218
Polsky, Barbara S. A797
Polsky, Barbara S. E368
Polsky, Lisa A693
Polster, Bryan C. E46
Polyakov, Andrey Aleksandrovich W506
Polymeropoulos, Mihael H. E518
Polzer, Robert J. A1153
Pomeroy, Brian W487
Pomodoro, Livia W310
Pompa, Mark A. A364
Pond, Ayoka P63
Ponder, Mark G. A373
Ponder, Mark G. E168
Pongritsakda, Wiwat W117
Pont, Eleuthere I. Du A1138
Pont, Eleuthere I. Du E544
Pont, Eleuthère I. du A349
Pontoppidan, Caroline W1
Pontzer, Deborah Dick A259
Pontzer, Deborah Dick E103
Poohkay, Brent W451
Poole, Edward A958
Poole, Edward E456
Pooler, Joseph W. E105
Poolthong, Yaowalak W352
Poomsurakul, Yuthasakk W117
Poon, Chiu Kwok W572
Poon, Christine A. A882
Poon, Christine A. A856
Poon, Christine A. A934
Poon, Joseph C.H. A211
Poon, Joseph C.H. E84
Poonen, Sanjay W351
Poongkumarn, Prasert W137
Pope, Daniel M. E502
Pope, Darren W157
Pope, Janet W371
Pope, John C. A1110
Pope, John C. A610
Pope, Lawrence J. A494
Pope, Maria M. A1057
Pope, Richard E. E470
Pope, Stephanie F. A164
Popelier, Luc W336
Poplin, Chris M. E515
Popov, Anatoly W521
Popovici, Silviu A817
Poppe, Patricia K. A823

Poppe, Patricia K. A1129
Poppe, Patricia K. A294
Poppe, Patricia K. A256
Poppen, Joel L. A700
Poppen, Lauren E480
Pops, Richard F. E346
Popwell, David T. A424
Popwell, David T. E200
Porat, Ruth A161
Porat, Ruth M. A45
Porcella, Kelly Amanda A616
Porcelli, Frank A450
Pordage, Simon M. W63
Pordon, Anthony R. A812
Porges, David L. A740
Porksen, Niels A26
Poroch, David P. A471
Porrino, Peter Richard A65
Porsche, Ferdinand Oliver W640
Porsche, Wolfgang W640
Port, Barry R. E164
Portalatin, Julio A. A973
Porteous, David L. A545
Porter, Alan W374
Porter, Andy P569
Porter, Brian J. W84
Porter, Christopher W. E514
Porter, Hector Fernandez W643
Porter, J. Chester E301
Porter, Jonathan A32
Porter, Kelly E292
Porter, Roger B. A799
Porter, Roger B. E180
Porter, Stuart E91
Portigliatti, Maude W168
Portney, Emily H. E311
Portnoy, Adam D. E423
Portnoy, Adam D. E270
Porwal, Hemant A1117
Posard, Matthew L. E244
Posey, Bruce K. E405
Posey, Richard E. E494
Poshyanonda, Pipatpong W334
Posner, Brian S. W50
Posner, Christopher E80
Possne, Anna W579
Post, Denny Marie E529
Post, Herschel W19
Post, Joachim W96
Poste, George E178
Postma, Richard L. A653
Potanin, Vladimir O. W410
Potes, Eric E102
Potes, Kelly J. E96
Potier, Benoit W357
Potier, Benoit W543
Potier, Helene Auriol W511
Poton, Eric W631
Potraffke, Roger E185
Potsch, Hans Dieter W640
Pott, Jeff W57
Pott, Richard W174
Pottorff, Gary W P399
Potts, Daniel W. A12
Potts, Daniel W. E4
Potvin, Jacques W294
Pou, William Know A955
Pou, William Know E456
Poukens, Pierre A548
Poul, Mojdeh A962

Poul, Mojdeh A4
Poulakidas, Dean Michael E538
Poulliot, Brian A159
Poulton, Cheryl E247
Pound, Theodore F. A218
Poupart-Lafarge, Henri W548
Pouraghabagher, Setareh A966
Pourbaix, Alexander J. W133
Pourre, Catherine W174
Poussot, Bernard J. W502
Pouyanne, Patrick W613
Powar, N. W8
Powar, Rahul W160
Powell, Aaron M. A934
Powell, Bradley S. A386
Powell, Carolyn A854
Powell, Curtis N. A1043
Powell, Fred M. E32
Powell, Jeffrey L. E286
Powell, Jeffrey S. A259
Powell, Jeffrey S. E103
Powell, Jerome H. A403
Powell, Kendall J. (Ken) W393
Powell, Kristin Y. A528
Powell, Kristin Y. E258
Powell, Mike W240
Powell, Nicholas (Nick) A1075
Powell, Rice W251
Powell, Rice W249
Powell, Scott E. A1115
Powell, Shelley W573
Powell, Steven D. A359
Powell, Steven D. A951
Powell, Thomas E. E484
Powell, Willa P467
Powell, Willie E512
Power, Andrew P. E141
Power, Una M. W84
Powers, Brian E. E127
Powers, David E137
Powers, John J. A415
Powers, John J. E194
Powers, Richard T. E173
Powers, Robert D. A32
Powers, Scott F. A108
Powers, Scott F. A862
Powers, Scott F. W572
Powlus, Lee C. A814
Powlus, Lee C. E379
Pownall, Lindsey W597
Powrie, Raymond P104
Poynot, Steven M. E79
Pozen, Robert C. A742
Pozez, Norman R. A350
Pozez, Norman R. E148
Pozzi, James Edward A67
Prabhu, Krish A. A914
Prado, Belen Moscoso Del W550
Prado, Jose Luis A534
Prado, Jose Luis A749
Pragada, Robert V. A580
Pragada, Robert V. W209
Prager, Richard L. E311
Pragnell, Michael W635
Prahm, Jeremy E. E190
Prakash, Shailesh E344
Pramaggiore, Anne R. A400
Pramanik, Amal W169
Pramanik, Bhaskar W561
Prame, Thomas M. A532

682

HOOVER'S HANDBOOK OF EMERGING COMPANIES 2023

COMBINED HOOVER'S HANDBOOK INDEX OF EXECUTIVES

A = AMERICAN BUSINESS
E = EMERGING COMPANIES
P = PRIVATE COMPANIES
W = WORLD BUSINESSS

Prame, Thomas M. E259
Prange, Karen N. E43
Prasad, Ashwin W597
Prasad, P. M. S. W491
Prashad, Louise W201
Prasitsirigul, Sayam W79
Pratcher, Tyson A. E190
Pratt, Charlotte A190
Pratt, Charlotte E73
Pratt, Gordon G. E301
Pratt, Marcel S A251
Pratt, Marcel S P137
Pratt, Roger E441
Pravda, Ricardo E83
Praw, Albert Z. A594
Prawer, Arik Y. A1149
Praylo, Paul W. A763
Precinct, Rodney Ellis P170
Precourt, Walter F. A714
Preete, Kerry J. A1075
Pregenzer, John W. E40
Preiser, David A. A763
Preiser, David A. E260
Preiss, Frederick E43
Preisser, Brenna A182
Premo, Mark A854
Premo, Mark P446
Premutico, Mauro E511
Prendergast, Mark P245
Prescott, Edward S. A401
Prescott, Gordon A152
Prescott, Thomas M. E16
Presley, John A945
Presley, John E451
Press, Donna G Orender Senior V P429
Press, Eric L. A87
Press, Eric L. A16
Press, Henry Hughes Senior V P429
Press, Jeff Monday V P429
Press, Michael Holsher Senior V P437
Press, Richard S. E238
Press, Robert J Combs Senior V P429
Press, Ronald E Price Senior V P429
Press, Will Mann V P429
Pressler, Paul S. A356
Pressnall, Kellie E492
Prestidge, Corey G. A516
Preston, Margaret Mary V. A791
Preston, Margaret Mary V. A673
Preston, Tracy M. A497
Pretlow, Paula B. A1132
Pretorius, Stepehn W654
Pretorius, Sy P421
Prettejohn, Nick W371
Preuss, Caroline J. W260
Preusse, Mary Hogan E141
Preusse, Mary Hogan E412
Prevoznik, Michael E. A870
Priami, Stephane W174
Pribyl, Brian M. A722
Price, Arthur J. A188
Price, Arthur J. E69
Price, David N. E111
Price, Harriet B. A419

Price, John Wiley P168
Price, Lord Mark W161
Price, Mark Philip W161
Price, Michael H. A681
Price, Michael H. E317
Price, Paula A. A178
Price, Paula A. A318
Price, Paula A. W10
Price, Penry W. A237
Price, Richard W39
Price, Scott A. A1069
Price, T. Michael A418
Price, T. Michael E195
Price, Teddy R. A880
Price, Teddy R. E412
Price, Timothy R. W287
Price, Timothy R. W235
Prichard, J. Robert S. W646
Priebe, Stephen M. A978
Priebe, Stephen M. E465
Priest, Steve A357
Priestly, Kay G. W591
Prieto, Domingo Valdes W220
Prieur, C. James A52
Prieur, C. James W382
Prime, Joshua E. A631
Prince, Charles A585
Prince, David W13
Prince, David A A507
Prince, David A E248
Prince, Scott S. A87
Prindiville, Mark A42
Pringpong, Sriprabha W352
Pringuet, Pierre W123
Prinner, John P245
Prinz, Brian E425
Prising, Jonas A608
Prising, Jonas A655
Pritchard, Beth M. W371
Pritchard, Sandy Kinney W21
Pritchett, Wendell E. A1032
Pritzker, Penny S. A701
Privitera, Salvatore E42
Priyadarshi, Sudhanshu A600
Prober, Charles E430
Probert, Todd A189
Probst, Redgie James A868
Probst, Sonia M. A753
Proch, Michel-Alain W486
Proch, Michel-Alain W61
Prochaska, Joseph J. A988
Prochaska, Joseph J. E479
Procope, Jonelle A941
Procter, H. Palmer A71
Procter, H. Palmer E28
Proctor, Georganne C. A881
Proctor, Gregory S. A1115
Proctor, Gregory S. E533
Proctor, H. Palmer E68
Proctor, Hawthorne L. A958
Proffitt, Joshua L. E300
Profusek, Robert A. A1085
Progler, Christopher J. E383
Proietti, Joseph T. A333
Prokopanko, James T. A1139
Prokopanko, James T. A885
Prommool, Terdkiat W484
Proost, Robert L. A134
Proost, Robert L. E54
Propheter, Gary L. E57

Prosser, David J. W310
Prosser, Joseph P564
Prot, Baudouin W338
Prot, Baudouin W631
Prouve, Cedric A620
Provancher, Jennifer L. E480
Provencher, Janice E58
Provoost, Rudy W495
Provost, Eric W358
Prozes, Andrew E493
Prudenti, A. Gail A135
Pruett, Steven J. A939
Pruis, Dirk J. E322
Pruitt, J. Scott A826
Pruitt, J. Scott E382
Pruitt, Kristin L. A618
Pruitt, Kristin L. E290
Pruitt, William D. E357
Prukbamroong, Surachai W79
Pruner, Alexandra D. A832
Pruner, Alexandra D. A833
Pruner, Alexandra D. A757
Pruzan, Jonathan M. A713
Pryor, D. Scott A995
Pryor, Felecia J. E302
Pryor, Juliette W. A468
Pryor, Juliette Williams A35
Pryor, Paula A. E531
Psaltis, Vassilios E. W33
Psihas, Julian Jorge Lazalde A953
Ptacin, Brogan M. A188
Ptacin, Brogan M. E71
Pucci, Paolo E534
Pucci, Sabrina W54
Pucel, Kenneth J. A835
Puckett, A. Lynne A659
Puckett, A. Lynne A215
Puckett, Karen A. A371
Puckett, Richard H. A1044
Pudipeddi, Raj E16
Puech, Olivier A69
Pueyo, Pilar A191
Pueyo, Pilar E77
Puffer, Manfred W303
Pugh, Andrea A788
Pugh, Andrea E366
Pugh, Michael W. E181
Pugliese, John A854
Pugliese, Stephanie A1059
Pugliese, Stephanie L. A447
Pulido, Jaime Saenz de Tejada W618
Pulido, Jaime Saenz de Tejada W68
Pullin, Dennis W. E255
Pulomena, John A143
Pulomena, John E57
Pulomena, John P357
Pultri, Alessandro W227
Puma, Grace A997
Puma, Mary G. E47
Pumpian, Ann P500
Puno, Reynato S. W514
Puntillo, Anthony M. E191
Purcell, Cailin P589
Purcell, Cynthia D. A136
Purcell, Thomas H. E268
Purdy, Graham A. E501
Puri, Ajay K. A761
Puri, Anil K. E129
Purisima, Cesar Velasquez W85
Purisima, Cesar Velasquez W20

Purkey, Tom P594
Pursell, David A. A86
Purtill, Sabra A65
Purtill, Sabra A296
Purvis, Michael J. E522
Purvis, Tom A938
Purvis, Tom E442
Puryear, Pamela A958
Pusateri, Keith P345
Pusey, Leigh Ann A635
Pusey, Stephen C. A453
Pushis, Glenn A. A975
Pushor, Kathleen S. A558
Put, Dirk Van de A709
Putin, Mikhail E. W474
Putnam, Angela L. A772
Putnam, James S. A648
Putnam, Michael R. E308
Putnam, Nancy C. E506
Putz, Alexander W397
Putz, Lasse W129
Putzier, Jeffrey K. E30
Putziger, Michael T. A372
Putziger, Michael T. E167
Puyfontaine, Arnaud Roy de W592
Puyfontaine, Arnaud Roy de W637
Puyol, Antonio Abruna W174
Puzey, Mark R. W260
Pyatt, Jeffrey B. E67
Pyle, Thomas F. E284
Pyo, Hyun-Myung W352
Pyott, David E. I. E61
Pyott, David E. I. W351

Q

Qadri, Ashfaq E49
Qi, Dapeng W144
Qi, Weidong W656
Qi, Xingli W141
Qian, Daqun W268
Qian, Jun W326
Qiao, Jian W362
Qiao, Song W362
Qin, Lihong W372
Qin, Tongzhou W375
Qin, Xuetang W248
Qin, Yanpo W660
Qiu, Fasen W145
Qiu, Hai W663
Qiu, Xiangmin W307
Qiu, Xueqin W98
Qiu, Yibo W275
Qiu, Yinfu W100
Qiu, Zhi Zhong W158
Qiu, Zongjie W158
Qu, Bo W189
Qu, Hongkun W644
Qu, Ming E370
Qu, Qing W542
Qu, Yonghai W144
Quade, Bradley A. A416
Quader, Syed Maqbul W486
Quagliano, Michael E451
Quah, Poh Keat W484
Quah, Wee Ghee W464
Quaid, John J. A717
Quaid, Michael E64

HOOVER'S HANDBOOK OF EMERGING COMPANIES 2023

COMBINED HOOVER'S HANDBOOK INDEX OF EXECUTIVES

A = AMERICAN BUSINESS
E = EMERGING COMPANIES
P = PRIVATE COMPANIES
W = WORLD BUSINESSS

Qualls, John E57
Quan, Patrick F P586
Quandel, Noble C. A702
Quandel, Noble C. E326
Quandt, Stefan W96
Quarles, Christa S. A604
Quarta, Roberto W654
Quarta, Roberto W495
Quateman, Lisa G. A1121
Quatrochi, Christopher K. E344
Quayle, R.D. (Dan) A208
Quazzo, Stephen R. E382
Qubein, Nido R. A1042
Que, Dongwu W152
Queenan, Daniel G. A213
Quek, Leng Chan W286
Quek, Sean Kon W286
Quelch, John Anthony A52
Quental, Marina Barrenne de Artagao W630
Querner, Immo W586
Query, K. Rex A759
Quesenbery, Christy F. E526
Quesnel, Olivier W235
Quick, Christopher C. E527
Quick, Janet A507
Quick, Janet E248
Quick, Peter A430
Quigley, Robert J. A874
Quigley, Timothy P511
Quill, John W. A52
Quillen, Michael J. A663
Quincey, James A264
Quincey, James A821
Quiniones, Gil C. A383
Quinlan, Joseph "Larry" A931
Quinlan, Larry A170
Quinlan, Michael T. A249
Quinlan, Michael T. E99
Quinn, Brian P356
Quinn, Bridget K. A1129
Quinn, George W580
Quinn, George W666
Quinn, Jason P W7
Quinn, Jessica Lieberman A62
Quinn, Katherine B. A895
Quinn, Kevin G. A507
Quinn, Kevin G. E248
Quinn, Matthew E81
Quinn, Michael J. E420
Quinn, Noel W289
Quinn, Peter W191
Quinn, R. Patrick A732
Quinn, Ryan S. E381
Quinn, Stephen D. A491
Quinn, Stephen D. A1151
Quinn, T. Kyle A796
Quinn, Thomas R. A788
Quinn, Thomas R. E365
Quinn, William G. E254
Quintana, Julio M. A737
Quintana, Marie A1003
Quintero, Guillermo W506
Quinton, Robert E57

Quintos, Karen H. A306
Quirk, Kathleen L. A452
Quirk, Raymond R. A406
Quiros, Carlos Espinosa de los Monteros Bernaldo de W300
Quiroz, Fernando W266
Quist, Adam George E434
Quist, S. Andrew E434
Quist, Scott M. E434
Qureshi, Rima A670
Qureshi, Rima A1088
Qutub, Robert (Bob) W491

R

R.n., Ann Cella P522
R.Ph., William C. Irwin E420
Raabe, Christian W397
Raas, Fredy W398
Rabb, Robert M. E336
Rabbatts, Heather W56
Rabbitt, Linda D. A401
Rabe, Thomas W14
Rabinovitch, Gabrielle A807
Rabinowicz, Daniel W31
Rabl-Stadler, Helga W453
Raborn, Richard H. E13
Rabun, Daniel W. A86
Rabun, Daniel W. E91
Rachou, Nathalie W631
Racioppi, Michael A917
Radakovich, Lynn Vojvodich A170
Radakovich, Lynn Vojvodich A444
Radakovich, Lynn Vojvodich A322
Rademacher, Randy D. E11
Rader, Chris P. A523
Rader, Chris P. E257
Radhakrishnan, Ranjay W490
Radigan, Kevin E503
Radke, Robin M. E322
Rado, Nicholas J. E470
Radtke, Duane C. A325
Radway, Robert E. W579
Rady, Ernest S. E397
Rady, Paul M. E33
Radzan, Vinay W271
Radziwill, John A979
Rael, Felipe A. A397
Rael, Felipe A. E187
Raether, Paul E. E66
Raets, Laurent W623
Rafael, Elizabeth (Betsy) E45
Raff, Beryl B. A10
Raff, Robert A962
Raffa, Kathy A. A350
Raffa, Kathy A. E148
Raffaeli, C. Cathleen A396
Raffaeli, C. Cathleen E187
Rafferty, Emily K. A401
Rafferty, Emily K. E388
Rafferty, Michael P. A1040
Rafferty, Michael P. E499
Raffo, Christopher R. E114
Rafkin, Scott W641
Ragatz, Erik D. E242
Ragauss, Peter A. A1131
Ragauss, Peter A. A86
Ragavan, Chetlur S. A261

Ragen, York A. E228
Raghavan, Prabhakar A45
Raghuram, Rangarajan A1098
Ragnhall, Hans W548
Ragsdale, Bruce E261
Ragues, V. M. W414
Ragusa, Elysia Holt A1008
Raha, Samraat S. A27
Rahe, Maribeth S. A420
Rahe, Maribeth S. E116
Rahe, Maribeth S. E197
Rahilly, Ita M. A1033
Rahilly, Sean E162
Rahim, Rami E45
Rahman, Jill A. A153
Rahman, Nazneen W57
Rahmani, Valerie W491
Rahmstrom, Mats W60
Rai, Ankor E179
Rai, Pushpendra W561
Raia, Steven P. E490
Raich, Jeffrey E330
Raifeld, Pavel E272
Raigoso, Aitor Moso W295
Raikes, Jeffrey S. A300
Raim, Ellen E344
Raina, Robin E153
Rainbolt, David E. A125
Rainbolt, David E. E52
Rainbolt, H. E. A125
Rainbolt, H. E. E52
Raines, Monica E5
Rainey, Joe D. A494
Rainey, John David A1104
Rainko, Kelly D. E532
Rainwater, Keith S. A395
Rainwater, Keith S. E185
Raisbeck, David W. A354
Raiss, Sarah E. A277
Raiss, Sarah E. W371
Raja, Mukund C. E492
Raja, Prabu G. A90
Rajamannar, Raja A841
Rajamannar, Raja A670
Rajan, Arun A900
Rajaram, Gokul E489
Rajaram, Gokul E386
Rajeh, Maamoun W50
Rajkumar, Amanda W14
Rajlin, Juan A140
Raju, Robin M. A377
Rak, Vlad A326
Rakolta, John E9
Rakshit, Arup W271
Rales, Mitchell P. A315
Rales, Steven M. A315
Ralhan, Sameer A224
Ralli, Georges W631
Ralli, Georges W125
Ralls-Morrison, Desiree A675
Ralls-Morrison, Desiree A326
Ralston, Dianne B. W523
Rama, Hasmukh P. E492
Ramaker, David B. A681
Ramaker, David B. E318
Ramakrishna, Sudhakar E451
Raman, Sundar W170
Ramanantsoa, Bernard W459
Ramanathan, Guru E342
Ramarch, Suchat W484

Ramaswamy, Ganesh A121
Ramaswamy, Ganesh A120
Ramaswamy, Sreeganesh W327
Rambeau, Jon A613
Ramesh, Aparna A395
Ramesh, Aparna E186
Ramier, Greg W371
Ramirez, Austin M. A772
Ramirez, Claudia Sender W283
Ramirez, Elisa Zuniga A816
Ramirez, Jaime A. A604
Ramirez, Jorge Oscar A400
Ramirez, Maria Fiorini A691
Ramirez, Maria Fiorini E323
Ramirez, Pamela I. A478
ramirez, Roberto Hernandez W266
Ramirez, Shanna P143
Ramm-Schmidt, Christian W247
Ramo, Joshua Cooper A405
Ramo, Joshua Cooper A964
Ramon, David A. E228
Ramon, Ramon Adell W423
Ramos, A Kenneth E90
Ramos, Daniel E14
Ramos, Denise L. A128
Ramos, Denise L. A877
Ramos, Denise L. A826
Ramos, Dioscoro I. W100
Ramos, Jose Maldonado W68
Ramos, Maria W561
Ramos, Maria W167
Ramos, Mauricio A224
Ramos, Raul R. E207
Ramos, Richard T. A703
Ramos, Richard T. E327
Ramrath, Joseph R. A499
Ramsay, Caroline W16
Ramsay, Norrie C. W133
Ramsden, Jonathan E. A157
Ramseier, Roland W631
Ramser, Mark Russell A803
Ramser, Mark Russell E371
Ramsey, Chris A. A472
Ramsey, Chris A. E230
Ramsey, James B. E457
Ramsey, Matthew S. A369
Ramsey, Samuel T. A945
Ramsey, Samuel T. E450
Ramsey, Tom P170
Ramu, Raymond R. E426
Ramyarupa, Apichart W77
Rana, Harpreet E413
Rancourt, Wayne M. A166
Rand, Alison S. A845
Rand, Alison S. E395
Rand, Edward L. A847
Randall, Catherine J. A32
Randall, Christopher S. A722
Randall, Christopher S. E339
Randall, Elizabeth Ellen A271
Randall, Elizabeth Ellen E110
Randall, H. Douglas A1108
Randall, Jane L. E455
Randel, Don M. A258
Randel, Johnny D. E462
Randle, Stuart A. A145
Randle, Stuart A. E484
Randolph, Amy L. A415
Randolph, Amy L. E194
Ranelli, John R. E90

COMBINED HOOVER'S HANDBOOK INDEX OF EXECUTIVES

A = AMERICAN BUSINESS
E = EMERGING COMPANIES
P = PRIVATE COMPANIES
W = WORLD BUSINESSS

Raney, Steven M. A876
Ranganathan, Madhu E12
Ranger, Michael W. A290
Ranger, Michael W. A289
Rango, Robert A. A607
Rangsiyopash, Roongrote W540
Ranhoff, David A. E163
Rank, Norbert W61
Rankin, David H. A922
Rankin, Devina A. A1110
Rankin, Frank A. E515
Rankin, James A524
Rankin, James E258
Rankin, Patrick Keith A116
Rankowitz, Michael L. E522
Ranttila, Michael C. E326
Ranzini, Stephen Lange E512
Rao, Dana A15
Rao, Karthik A742
Rao, Roberto W479
Rao, U.B. Pravin W304
Rao, Venkat Dhenuvakonda A256
Rao, Venkat Dhenuvakonda A294
Raoult, Frédérique W565
Rapanos, Vasileios T. W33
Raphael, Carol A917
Rapino, Michael A941
Rapino, Michael A641
Rapley, David E. A872
Rapley, David E. A633
Rapley, David E. A633
Rapoport, Iuri W69
Rapp, Edward J. A8
Rapp, George S. E53
Rapp, Karen M. A697
Rapp, Roxy H. E46
Rapp, W. Randall A301
Rapp, W. Randall E131
Rappa, Salvatore E388
Rappaport, Alan H. E525
Rappe, Kristine A. E532
Rariy, Roman V. E154
Rasche, Charlotte M. A852
Rasche, Charlotte M. E399
Rascoff, Spencer M. A1149
Rash, Matthew P P42
Raskind, Peter E. A198
Rasmuson, Kelly E. A398
Rasmussen, Daniel J. E97
Rasmussen, Jorgen Huno W632
Rasmussen, Melissa E341
Rasmussen, Stephen S. A59
Rasmussen, Teresa J. E226
Rasmussen, Torsten Erik W632
Rasmussen, Vibeke Storm W348
Rassieur, Benjamin F. A276
Rassmussen, Anne P423
Rassy, Manfred W415
Rastetter, William H. E346
Rataj, Susan H. A27
Ratcliffe, David M. A1042
Rath, Henry E475
Rath, John F. A617
Rath, John F. E289

Rath, Kimberly K. A727
Rath, Kimberly K. E345
Rathgeber, John F. W50
Ratinoff, Edward J. A120
Ratinoff, Edward J. E48
Ratnakar, Raj A349
Ratner-Salzberg, Deborah E79
Rattanapian, Chongrak W334
Rattanasombat, Buranin W484
Ratterman, Joseph (Joe) P. E87
Rattray, Sandy C. E336
Ratzan, Brian K. E443
Rau, John P. A1136
Rau, Raghavendra E546
Rau, Sally E77
Rauch, Douglas Gregory A959
Rauckman, Kevin S. A301
Rauckman, Kevin S. E131
Raup, Chuck A512
Rausas, Christophe Pelissie du W635
Rausch, Timothy S. A1006
Ravich, Jess M. A5
Ravine, Harris E76
Rawji, Irfhan A. W122
Rawlinson, David J. A871
Rawlinson, David L. A330
Rawls, Chad A938
Rawls, Chad E442
Rawls, Michael R. A718
Rawls, Michael R. E335
Ray, Adam A223
Ray, Barry S. A704
Ray, Barry S. E328
Ray, Bradford T. E301
Ray, Caroline B. A56
Ray, Eric R. A874
Ray, James R. E297
Ray, Joel P462
Ray, Michael C. A1122
Ray, Neville R. A992
Raybaud, Maria Elena Antolin W295
Rayman, Reed B. A16
Raymer, Rick A982
Raymond, Anne L. E462
Raymond, John T. A741
Raymond, John T. A833
Raymond, John T. A832
Raymond, Mary Jane E266
Raymond, Philip C. A32
Raymond, Stephanie R. A841
Raymund, Steven A. A578
Raymund, Steven A. A1118
Rayno, Peter J. A372
Rayno, Peter J. E167
Raynor, Brett E. E62
Razak, Saad Abdul W205
Razon-Feingold, Halli E348
Rea, Timothy A587
Read, C. Jack A248
Read, Colin L. A98
Read, Colin L. E36
Read, Mark W654
Read, Michael G. A237
Read, Nicholas Jonathan A170
Read, Nick W637
Read, Paul A655
Read, Rory P. W362
Read, S. MacGregor E242
Ready, William J. A108
Ready, William J. A1132

Ready, William J. E386
Reagan, James C. A920
Reagan, Ronald R. A436
Reardon, Aaron P177
Reardon, Martine W216
Reardon, Nancy A. A157
Reasoner, Mark A. E25
Reaud, Reagan A. A214
Reaud, Wayne A. A548
Reaume, Marty M. E457
Rebecchini, Clemente W54
Rebel, Brad A134
Rebel, Brad E54
Rebelez, Darren M. A209
Rebellius, Matthias W543
Rebelo, Sergio Tavares W325
Reber, Brett A. A378
Reber, John M. E98
Rebsamen, C B P308
Rebsch, Gary P366
Recer, James A1086
Recer, James E521
Rechsteiner, Michael W581
Recordon, Luc W88
Recto, Eric O. W514
Rector, Susan D. A815
Redd, Ershel C. A995
Reddin, Matthew S. A938
Reddin, Matthew S. E442
Reddin, Thomas J. A99
Reddoch, James E425
Reddy, Avinash A328
Reddy, Christine A145
Reddy, John P. E253
Reddy, Madhukar E314
Reddy, Sundeep G. A912
Redfern, David W258
Redington, Dan E420
Redman, Monte N. A396
Redman, Monte N. E187
Redmann, Tom E63
Redmond, Andrea A42
Redstone, Shari E. A802
Redwine, Farrell B. A745
Redzic, Ognjen A103
Reece, H. Wade A531
Reece, Joseph E. A726
Reece, Paris Gary A652
Reed-Klages, Debra L. A210
Reed-Klages, Debra L. A643
Reed, Brian K. E158
Reed, Colin V. A424
Reed, Colin V. E200
Reed, Cory J. A320
Reed, David A. E293
Reed, David W. E6
Reed, Debra L. A230
Reed, Edwin C. A396
Reed, Edwin C. E187
Reed, Glenn P498
Reed, Glenn P270
Reed, Glenn W. A774
Reed, James D. E515
Reed, Jason C. E441
Reed, JoAnn A. A69
Reed, John W515
Reed, Kimberly A. W585
Reed, Marcy L. A951
Reed, Matthew D. E108
Reed, Michael P. A1138

Reed, Michael P. E544
Reed, Monica P. A573
Reed, Robert Lee E111
Reed, Scott A. A937
Reed, Scott A. E441
Reed, Stephanie P481
Reed, Steven William A532
Reed, Steven William E259
Reed, Susan P167
Reed, W. Earl E300
Reed, Willie M. A1153
Reeder, Joe R. A913
Reeder, Joe R. E427
Reel, Jerry R. E61
Reel, Stephanie P618
Reents, Scott T. A8
Rees, Andrew E130
Rees, Dan W84
Rees, Joanna E183
Rees, Mike W306
Reese, C. Richard E94
Reese, David M. A76
Reese, J. Mitchell E411
Reeson, Terrance J. E388
Reeve, Abba E102
Reeve, Pamela D. A. A69
Reeves, Charles N. A704
Reeves, Charles N. E328
Reeves, Eric A. A83
Reeves, Kevin R. A815
Regan, Barry J. E138
Regan, John F. A596
Regan, John F. E286
Regan, Timothy E145
Regan, Timothy J A1026
Regan, Timothy J P620
Regent, Aaron W. W451
Regent, Aaron W. W84
Regitz, Christine W517
Reglin, David C. A555
Reglin, David C. E269
Regnery, David S. W617
Regnier, Mike C. W662
Rego, Francisco Teixeira W254
Rego, Vagner W60
Rehder, Jeffrey Allen E340
Rehder, W.M. Henning W390
Reibel, Jeffrey T. E300
Reibersdorfer, Guenther W627
Reic, Iskra W57
Reich, Jonathan E547
Reich, Robert M. A918
Reich, Sandra W62
Reich, Victoria J. A358
Reich, Victoria J. A557
Reichanthal, Max Alan E221
Reichelderfer, Brenda L. E188
Reichin, Michael C. A427
Reichin, Michael C. E203
Reichstetter, Arthur C. A605
Reichstul, Henri Philippe W493
Reid, Alan McWilliams A914
Reid, Bill W651
Reid, Carol L. A372
Reid, Carol L. E167
Reid, Carter M. A340
Reid, Ian M. W122
Reid, James E235
Reid, Rachel A1098
Reid, Richard W56

HOOVER'S HANDBOOK OF EMERGING COMPANIES 2023

COMBINED HOOVER'S HANDBOOK INDEX OF EXECUTIVES

A = AMERICAN BUSINESS
E = EMERGING COMPANIES
P = PRIVATE COMPANIES
W = WORLD BUSINESSS

Reid, Sean P. A28
Reid, Thomas J. A272
Reid, William P. A364
Reiff, Melissa E175
Reilly, Brian Patrick A231
Reilly, David B. A499
Reilly, David B. E246
Reilly, John P. A231
Reilly, Joseph B. E400
Reilly, Michael A52
Reilly, Paul C. A876
Reilly, Paul J. A103
Reilly, Rob W654
Reilly, Robert Q. A834
Reilly, Thomas E80
Reilly, Wendell S. E68
Reiman, Jason A512
Reimann, Kathryn A627
Reimer, Hagen W543
Reinbold-Knape, Petra W95
Reinbold-Knape, Petra W174
Reiner, Andres D. E374
Reiner, Gary M. A514
Reiner, Gary M. A246
Reiners, Derek S. A741
Reinertsen, Inge W558
Reinhardsen, Jon Erik W594
Reinhardsen, Jon Erik W227
Reinhardt, Jason E305
Reinhardt, Joerg W449
Reinhardt, Max E369
Reinhardt, William A691
Reinhardt, William E323
Reinhart, Ariane W171
Reinhart, Charles A. E369
Reinoso, Sonsoles Rubio W295
Reis, Danny van der E34
Reis, Jose Vieira dos W70
Reiser, Michele W637
Reisman, Richard J. A98
Reisman, Richard J. E36
Reiss, Dale Anne A1046
Reitan, Torgrim W227
Reiter, Joakim W637
Reithofer, Norbert W96
Reithofer, Norbert W543
Reitsma, Raymond E. A681
Reitsma, Raymond E. E317
Reitzes, Mark T. A753
Reitzle, Wolfgang W171
Rekow, E. Dianne A917
Relic, Zelko E16
Reller, Tami L. E457
Remes, Seppo Juha W476
Remling, Jennifer W654
Remmler, Peter W602
Remnant, Philip J. W481
Remolona, Eli M. W85
Remondi, John F. A723
Ren, Jidong W150
Ren, Jun W574
Ren, Maohui W292
Ren, Ruijie W239
Ren, Tianbao W375

Ren, Xiaochang W153
Ren, Yuxin W596
Renard, Jean-Baptiste W427
Renda, Benedetto W177
Renda, Larree M. A209
Renda, Larree M. A905
Rendell, Edward G. E232
Rendle, Linda J. A254
Rendle, Linda J. A1096
Rendle, Steven E. A1091
Rendle, Steven E. A155
Renduchintala, Venkata S.M. W10
Renfrew, Bill A428
Renfro, LaVonda A1086
Renfro, LaVonda E521
Renna, Michael J. E453
Renne, Louise A249
Renne, Louise P126
Rennick, Charles D. E481
Rennick, Gavin W523
Rennie, David W430
Renninger, Richard L. A316
Renovales, Jaime Perez W75
Rensburg, Ihronn W8
Rensmon, Patrick D. E149
Rentler, Barbara A905
Renuart, Victor Eugene E242
Renwick, Glenn M. A1075
Reny, Luc W480
Repenning, Brent R. E136
Repko, John P. A65
Replogle, Roger W. A402
Repo, Susan E328
Repplier, Colleen C. E287
Represas, Carlos E. W580
Rerkpiboon, Auttapol W484
Resendez, Roberto R. A563
Reses, Jacqueline Dawn A367
Reske, James R. A418
Reske, James R. E195
Resnick, Andrea Shaw A993
Ressler, Antony P. E34
Restel, Anthony J. A424
Restel, Anthony J. E200
Restrepo, Robert P. A896
Restrepo, Robert P. A470
Restrepo, Robert P. E422
Retort, Vincent E305
Reu-Narvaez, Tanya A878
Reu-Narvaez, Tanya A879
Reuss, Mark L. A466
Revai, Erik Z. A402
Revel-Muroz, Pavel Aleksandrovich W617
Rex, Anne G. A82
Rex, Elly Smedegaard W632
Rex, John F. A1075
Rey, David A. E183
Reyes, Alejandro P270
Reyes, Cecilia W442
Reyes, Luis A. A432
Reyes, Marcelo W132
Reyes, Timothy D. A37
Reynal, Vicente A56
Reyneveld, Willy E517
Reynolds, Alan D. E190
Reynolds, Catherine B. A460
Reynolds, Catherine M. A256
Reynolds, Christopher P. A956
Reynolds, Craig B. E312

Reynolds, Daniel G. E76
Reynolds, E. Leland E195
Reynolds, Emily J. A395
Reynolds, Emily J. E185
Reynolds, Eric H. A254
Reynolds, Frederic G. A877
Reynolds, Fredric G. E386
Reynolds, John B. A134
Reynolds, John B. E54
Reynolds, John R. A438
Reynolds, Katherine M. A125
Reynolds, Katherine M. E52
Reynolds, Loretta E. A1082
Reynolds, Marshall T. E470
Reynolds, Marshall T. E199
Reynolds, Mathew E61
Reynolds, Paula Rosput A462
Reynolds, Paula Rosput W422
Reynolds, Paula Rosput W109
Reynolds, Randolph N. E62
Rhea, John B. A973
Rhea, John B. E280
Rheaume, Lindsey S A350
Rheaume, Lindsey S E148
Rhee, Don E375
Rhee, Frank S. E323
Rhenman, Torkel W374
Rhinehart, Mary K. W178
Rhino, Christian W389
Rhoades, David A292
Rhoades, Ronald E. E97
Rhoads, Ann D. E233
Rhoads, Ann D. E406
Rhodes, Ann Marie A515
Rhodes, James H. A860
Rhodes, Linda A1153
Rhodes, Matthew (Matt) E174
Rhodes, Nicholas Peter W128
Rhodes, Sheri E214
Rhodes, Thomas W. A1053
Rhodes, William C. A111
Rhodes, William C. A336
Rhyu, James Jeaho E468
Rial, Sergio A. L. A323
Rial, Sergio A. L. W75
Rial, Sergio Agapito Lires W72
Riazi, Atefeh A680
Riazi, Atefeh P343
Ribar, Monika W196
Ribeiro, Joaquin J. W176
Riboud, Franck W187
Ricard, Alexandre W358
Ricard, Denis W294
Riccardi, Daniela W338
Ricci, Giuseppe W227
Riccobono, Richard M. E199
Rice, Andre A258
Rice, Dame Susan E166
Rice, Dame Susan W318
Rice, David P61
Rice, Derica W. A178
Rice, Derica W. A997
Rice, Derica W. A335
Rice, Derica W. A203
Rice, E. John A785
Rice, Edward S. A613
Rice, J. Bernard E538
Rice, Jill M. A136
Rice, John Daniel W649
Rice, John E. E531

Rice, John G. A65
Rice, John G. A121
Rice, John G. A120
Rice, John McCune E321
Rice, Linda Johnson A1007
Rice, Linda Johnson A778
Rice, Linda Johnson E162
Rice, Michael J. A788
Rice, Michael J. E366
Rice, Rex D. E184
Rice, Thomas A796
Rice, Thomas E368
Rice, Valerie Montgomery A1075
Rich, Brian F. A256
Rich, Brian F. A294
Rich, Melinda R. A651
Rich, Melinda R. E532
Rich, Michael A398
Rich, Mindy P462
Rich, Ronald K. A422
Richard, Mark J. A494
Richard, Oliver G. (Rick) A59
Richard, Oliver G. (Rick) A226
Richard, Patrick W635
Richard, Robert A. A344
Richard, Ronald B. E157
Richard, Stephane W459
Richards, Belinda W471
Richards, David Z. E99
Richards, Emmet C. A167
Richards, Emmet C. E64
Richards, Jay D. A135
Richards, Jerald W. E391
Richards, Mark W. A814
Richards, Mark W. E379
Richards, R. Ryan A1151
Richards, Thomas E. A749
Richardson, Andrew C. E19
Richardson, Andrew C. E426
Richardson, Brian J. A1078
Richardson, Brian J. E513
Richardson, Carol W287
Richardson, James H. E15
Richardson, John M. A164
Richardson, John M. A292
Richardson, John M. E70
Richardson, Julie G. W621
Richardson, Karen A. W109
Richardson, Nina L. A893
Richardson, Nina L. E107
Richardson, Scott A. A215
Richardson, Stephen A. E15
Richardson, Yolonda C. E330
Richardville, Craig P505
Richelieu, William A. (Tony) A594
Richenhagen, Martin H. A840
Richenhagen, Martin H. W369
Richer, Clare S. A846
Richerson, H. Elmer A1132
Richerson, H. Elmer E539
Riches, Lucinda J. W178
Richey, Ellen E239
Richie, Laurel J. A503
Richie, Laurel J. A985
Richison, Chad E374
Richlovsky, Thomas A. A1064
Richlovsky, Thomas A. E509
Richman, Frederick A. A898
Richmond, Brent E. A1115
Richmond, Brent E. E533

A = AMERICAN BUSINESS
E = EMERGING COMPANIES
P = PRIVATE COMPANIES
W = WORLD BUSINESSS

Richmond, Lauren E. E190
Richstone, Ellen B. E365
Richter, Bret E547
Richter, Dennis E185
Richter, Glenn R. A567
Richter, John P145
Richter, Steven G. E537
Richter, Tangela S. A1115
Richter, Tangela S. A62
Richtor, Vaughn Nigel W603
Rickard, David A. A1083
Rickard, Jason E282
Ricke, Sadia W548
Ricker, Bob P462
Rickertsen, Carl J. A153
Ricketts, Carlton A. A199
Ricketts, Peter W225
Ricketts, Todd M. A919
Ricks, David A. A15
Ricks, David A. A635
Ricks, Ron A956
Ricks, Thomas G. A792
Ricupati, Agostino E119
Riddick, Frank A. E543
Riddle, Timothy J. A1039
Riddle, Timothy J. E498
Rideout, Jeffrey A. E20
Rider, Matthew J. W16
Ridge, Steven D. A340
Ridinger, Richard W109
Ridings, Thomas J. E34
Ridley, Fred S. A965
Ridley, Fred S. E462
Ridolfi, Robert N. E53
Rieb, Markus W415
Riebe, Clay A1086
Riebe, Clay E521
Riedel, George A. A221
Riedel, Peter W273
Riedl, Melanie W303
Riefler, Linda H. A304
Riefler, Linda H. E336
Riegel, Steve Brian A235
Rieger, Ralf W586
Riel, Pierre A300
Riel, Susan G. A350
Riel, Susan G. E148
Rielly, John P. E253
Rieman, Deborah D. A298
Riemer, Hans P366
Riesbeck, Richard L. E506
Riese, Ulf W579
Riesterer, Terry L. A902
Riffle, Christopher J. E204
Rifkin, Daniel M. A287
Rifkin, Daniel M. E115
Rigail, Anne W601
Rigatti, Maria A951
Rigatti, Maria A359
Rigby, Joseph M. A340
Rigby, Joseph M. E453
Rigby, Robert M. A397
Rigby, Robert M. E187
Rigel, H. Edward E507

Riggenberg, Jason T. A1144
Riggle, Carrie L. A418
Riggle, Carrie L. E195
Riggs, Kristen A512
Riggs, R. Lane A1085
Riggs, Rory B. E425
Righetti, Ottorino W177
Righini, Elisabetta W627
Rignac, Jean-Paul W215
Rijsseghem, Christine Van W336
Rijswijk, Steven van W306
Riker, Leslie A. E189
Riksen, R. Todd A958
Riley, Brandon W596
Riley, Brian M. A398
Riley, Bryant R. E49
Riley, Bryant R. E219
Riley, Christiana W195
Riley, Darryl P. E260
Riley, Deon N. A140
Riley, Gillian W84
Riley, H. Sanford W122
Riley, Kevin L. E246
Riley, Kevin P. A426
Riley, Kevin P. E202
Riley, Paul A825
Riley, Richard T. E145
Riley, Robert E. A1131
Riley, Susan J. E147
Riley, Wayne Joseph A505
Rimer, Barbara K. A24
Rimmer, Nneka Louise A292
Rimmer, Nneka Louise E161
Rindone, Raymond J. A124
Rine, James D. A1056
Rine, James D. E505
Rinehart, Charles R. A671
Riney, Stephen J. A86
Ring, David V. A106
Ring, David V. E40
Ring, Timothy M. A870
Ring, Timothy M. A147
Ringel, Johannes W234
Ringenbach, John P. A1013
Ringler, G.F. (Rick) E213
Ringrose, Kate W135
Rinker, Douglas C. E149
Rinn, Russell B. A975
Rinne, Kristin S. W228
Rio, Ana Marie del E268
Riojas, Rogelio E452
Riolacci, Pierre-Francois W225
Riolacci, Pierre-François W22
Riordan, Christine M. E410
Riordan, Kevin F. A136
Rios, Cesar W174
Rios, Gonzalo E43
Rios, Susan P401
Ripa, Anders W228
Ripa, Elisabetta W594
Ripley, Christopher S. A939
Ripley, Rosemary L. W274
Ripoll, Jacques W174
Rippe, Stephen N. E397
Rippert, Andrew T. W50
Risa, Einar W558
Risch, Frank A. A830
Rise, Hans Christian W446
Rishi, Girish D. A558
Rishton, John W626

Risk-McElroy, Stephanie M. E421
Risk, Bonita Pauline E421
Riske, Gordon W60
Riskey, Mary K. A1048
Risley, Angie W318
Rispoli, Michael J. E347
Ristuben, Steve P134
Ritchie, Bradford E. A981
Ritchie, Bradford E. E469
Ritchie, James Joseph E287
Ritchie, Mary C. W295
Ritenour, Jeffrey L. A325
Ritrievi, Rory G. A702
Ritrievi, Rory G. E325
Rittapirom, Thaweelap W77
Rittenmeyer, Ronald A. A1003
Ritter, C. Dowd A32
Ritter, Geralyn S. A787
Ritter, Gordon E519
Ritter, Louisa G. E287
Ritter, Stephen J. E328
Ritter, William D. A885
Ritterbusch, Todd A1040
Ritterbusch, Todd E499
Ritterbush, David W. E443
Rittstieg, Andreas W109
Ritzman, Steven K. A429
Ritzmann, William F. A251
Ritzmann, William F. E100
Rivard, Line W399
Rivas, Lee E408
Rivas, Maria E119
Rivas, Patricio W132
Rivas, Sindy P436
Rivaz, Vincent de W215
Rive, Ernesto Dalle W627
Rive, Ernesto Dalle W627
Rivera, Alfredo A846
Rivera, Carlos Abrams- A610
Rivera, Carlos Abrams- E160
Rivera, Efrain A588
Rivera, Frederick B. A510
Rivera, Frederick B. E252
Rivera, Sandra A377
Rivera, Sandra A560
Rivera, Steven H. E298
Rivers, Robert F. A351
Rivet, Simon W399
Rivett, Phil W561
Rivinius, Jessica P354
Rivkin, Robert S. A1062
Rizik, Matthew A900
Rizvi, Abid E360
Rizza, Franco W73
Rizzardi, Russell W. A1119
Rizzo, Alessandro Minuto W363
Rizzo, James G. A143
Rizzo, James G. E57
Rizzo, Mario A42
Rizzuti, Edward T. E13
Ro, Sung-Tae W652
Roach, David P. E507
Roach, Quentin A1083
Robards, Thomas F. E155
Robb, Gary Charles E121
Robb, Jeffrey A. E132
Robb, Karl E170
Robbiati, Tarek A514
Robbins, Bradford B. E485
Robbins, Brian K. E210

Robbins, Charles H. A244
Robbins, Charles H. A160
Robbins, Ira D. A1086
Robbins, Ira D. E516
Robbins, Kenneth B P255
Robbins, Kris A. A1056
Robbins, Kris A. E505
Robbins, Kristina A426
Robbins, Kristina E202
Robbins, Paige K. A485
Robbins, Spencer B. A143
Robbins, Spencer B. E57
Robel, Charles J. E234
Roberson, Charles D. E291
Roberson, Robin A125
Roberson, Robin E52
Robert, Arnaud W515
Roberts, A. Craig A492
Roberts, A. Craig E243
Roberts, Brett A. E128
Roberts, Brian L. A272
Roberts, Carol L. A1091
Roberts, Carol L. A37
Roberts, Daniel G. A814
Roberts, Daniel G. E379
Roberts, Daryl A59
Roberts, David B. E297
Roberts, Debbie S. A896
Roberts, Debbie S. E422
Roberts, Eiry W. E346
Roberts, G. H. W116
Roberts, Gregory N. A5
Roberts, Janice M. A1148
Roberts, John N. A543
Roberts, Kenneth E. A639
Roberts, Michael A539
Roberts, Michael J. A650
Roberts, Rebecca B. A8
Roberts, S. Elaine A966
Roberts, Shelley W170
Roberts, Simon W318
Roberts, Timothy D. A826
Roberts, Timothy D. A319
Roberts, Timothy D. E382
Roberts, Tristram W90
Roberts, Tristram W89
Roberts, Wayne A. A587
Robertson, Alicia A188
Robertson, Alicia E69
Robertson, Brian A539
Robertson, Christy E214
Robertson, Cliff A P479
Robertson, Elizabeth W. A1033
Robertson, Elizabeth W. E493
Robertson, Gregory A188
Robertson, Gregory E69
Robertson, Julie J. A376
Robertson, Peter James A580
Robertson, Peter James W518
Robertson, Simon M. E176
Robertson, Steve P255
Robertson, Thomas S. A203
Robeson, Robin E. E243
Robeson, Rose M. A1131
Robeson, Rose M. E33
Robillard, Donald F. A225
Robinette, Gary E. E447
Robino, David J. A639
Robins, Ronald A. (Rocky) A157
Robins, Scott L. A184

COMBINED HOOVER'S HANDBOOK INDEX OF EXECUTIVES

A = AMERICAN BUSINESS
E = EMERGING COMPANIES
P = PRIVATE COMPANIES
W = WORLD BUSINESSS

Robinson, Anne W422
Robinson, Barry C. A441
Robinson, Barry C. E212
Robinson, Cathy Marie A989
Robinson, Dashiell I. A881
Robinson, David C. A502
Robinson, Denise P589
Robinson, Donald T. E336
Robinson, Dorothy P695
Robinson, Elizabeth E. Beshel A1037
Robinson, Elizabeth E. Beshel A132
Robinson, Graham N. A752
Robinson, James A. A797
Robinson, James A. E368
Robinson, Jodi A224
Robinson, Joseph R. A1115
Robinson, Joseph R. E533
Robinson, Kenneth B. A767
Robinson, Kenneth B. E374
Robinson, Lori J. A216
Robinson, Michael A301
Robinson, Michael E131
Robinson, Patricia B. E494
Robinson, Paul M. A1106
Robinson, Peter M. E509
Robinson, Peter M. E510
Robinson, Peter M. E509
Robinson, R. Bruce E19
Robinson, Ray M. A56
Robinson, Rebecca K. A1151
Robinson, Ronald A. E13
Robinson, Stephen C. E224
Robinson, V. Daniel A724
Robison, Dennis C. A953
Robison, Dennis C. E455
Robison, Jennifer L. E382
Robison, Kim E. A1107
Robison, M. LaVoy A872
Robison, Mark Andrew A844
Robison, Mark Andrew E394
Robo, James L. A543
Robredo, Rafael Miranda W112
Robson-Capps, Teresa W157
Robson, Jeremy W574
Robusto, Dino E. A258
Roby, Anne K. W369
Rocca, Marília Artimonte W72
Rocchetta, Oddone Incisa della W157
Roch, Lewis M. E81
Rocha, Elaine A. A296
Rocha, Oscar Gonzalez A953
Rocha, Vitor W351
Roche, Brian P285
Roche, John C. A499
Roche, Max W213
Roche, Mike W377
Roche, Mike W644
Roche, Robert P. E32
Roche, Talbott L. A363
Roche, Vincent T. A81
Rochet, Lubomira A600
Rochet, Lubomira W548
Rochon, Thomas R. A1033
Rochow, Garrick J. A294

Rochow, Garrick J. A256
Rock, Jennifer A. A1149
Rock, Robert H. E404
Rocker, Kenyatta G. (Kenny) A1061
Rocker, Tchernavia A1059
Rocks, Patti Temple A774
Rocks, Patti Temple E360
Rockwell, Edward E170
Roddenberry, Stephen K. A1136
Rode, Paul A. E57
Roden, Laura A509
Roden, Laura E251
Rodgers, Elliott D. A443
Rodgers, Elliott D. A631
Rodgers, Thomas L. A677
Rodgers, Thurman John E163
Rodino, Jeffrey M. E373
Rodkin, Gary M. A673
Rodler, Friedrich W229
Rodrigues, Alvaro Felipe Rizzi W315
Rodrigues, Andre Luis Teixeira W315
Rodrigues, Daniel A. A373
Rodrigues, Daniel A. E168
Rodrigues, Frederico Trajano Inacio W315
Rodrigues, Michael J. E357
Rodriguez, Adrian A402
Rodriguez, Carlos A. A108
Rodriguez, David A. A478
Rodriguez, Eduardo A. A783
Rodriguez, Florentino Perez W11
Rodriguez, Javier J. A317
Rodriguez, Javier J. A473
Rodriguez, Jessica A187
Rodriguez, Jose Luis Negro W71
Rodriguez, Jose Mauricio W76
Rodriguez, Jose R. E397
Rodríguez, José R. A836
Rodríguez, Manuel Sánchez A391
Rodriguez, Maria Soledad Perez W11
Rodriguez, Milagros E517
Rodriguez, Oscar W266
Rodriguez, Sean A399
Rodriguez, Thomas Stanley Heather W265
Rodriguez, Yolanda P270
Rodriquez, David E27
Roe, Michelle M. E325
Roe, Scott A. A993
Roedel, Kathryn (Kathy) V. E228
Roedel, Richard W. E66
Roeder, Helene von W397
Roeder, Roshan S. A752
Roepke, Susan E. E291
Roethel, Peter A400
Roethlisberger, Benhard W631
Roetlin, Tony A515
Roewe, Randy A421
Roewe, Randy E197
Roffler, Michael J. A431
Roffler, Michael J. E205
Rogachey, Denis W476
Rogan, Tim E. A806
Rogelstad, Timothy J. E367
Roger, Bruno W123
Roger, Francois W492
Roger, Francois-Xavier W429
Rogers, Alexander H. A867
Rogers, Brian C. A877
Rogers, Brian C. A647

Rogers, Dawn A821
Rogers, Dawn A349
Rogers, Hartley R. E244
Rogers, Jenifer Simms W408
Rogers, Jenifer Simms W441
Rogers, Jenifer Simms W334
Rogers, Jenifer Simms W528
Rogers, John W654
Rogers, John F.W. A480
Rogers, John W. A743
Rogers, John W. A675
Rogers, Kathleen A. A397
Rogers, Kristi Marie E405
Rogers, Mark N. A78
Rogers, Mary Jo E452
Rogers, Matthew C. A383
Rogers, Michael John E175
Rogers, Mike A167
Rogers, Mike E64
Rogers, Mike W425
Rogers, Mike W423
Rogers, Randy P555
Rogers, Rich P444
Rogers, Robert Wade A547
Rogers, Sandra Phillips A224
Rogers, W. Allen E275
Rogers, William H. A1042
Rogers, William H. A399
Rogerson, Craig A. A841
Rogge, Karen M. E362
Roggemann, Gerhard W270
Rogowski, Michael W586
Roh, Yong-hoon W537
Rohde, Horst W234
Rohde, Wolfgang W483
Rohkamm, Eckhard W586
Rohleder, Stephen J. A267
Rohler, Klaus-Peter W33
Rohman, Thomas P. A106
Rohman, Thomas P. E40
Rohner, Urs W176
Rohner, Urs W258
Rohr, Karl von W195
Rohrer, Katherine T. (Kathy) A24
Rohrig, Beate W15
Rohrs, Thomas M. E6
Rohrs, Thomas M. E261
Roizen, J. Heidi E280
Rojas, German Eduardo Quintero W210
Rojas, Gonzalo Alberto Perez W76
Rojas, Jose Calderon W27
Rojas, Jose Fernando Calderon W244
Rojas, Jurgen Gerardo Loeber W210
Rojas, Mauricio Rosillo W76
Rojas, Rogelio M. Rebolledo W265
Rojek, Kenneth J P393
Rojeski, Karen A691
Rojeski, Karen E323
Roks, Edwin E483
Rolland, Marc W550
Rollen, Ola W632
Rolling, Mark C. A343
Rollins, Annette F. A106
Rollins, Edward C. E57
Rollins, Gary W. E424
Rollins, James D. A190
Rollins, James D. E73
Rollins, Pamela R. E425
Rollison, Marvin L P218

Rolston, Sharon L. W364
Romagnoli, Ilaria W592
Romain, Kenneth G. St. E389
Romaine, Mark A. A475
Romaine, Stephen S. A1033
Roman, Brian A1093
Roman, David W362
Roman, Derrick A. A279
Roman, Eugene E170
Roman, Martin W633
Roman, Michael F. A4
Roman, Michael F. A6
Roman, Richard A. E353
Romanet, Augustin de W526
Romanko, Michael F. E209
Romano, Kelly A. A1054
Romano, Kelly A. E145
Romanowski, Paul J. A536
Romanowski, Roman W395
Romasco, Robert G. E19
Rome, Amanda A1139
Romeo, Fabio W482
Romeo, Fabio Ignazio W482
Rometty, Virginia M. A591
Romig, Shirley E305
Romine, Warren N. E215
Romm, Adria Alpert A332
Romm, Sylvia P50
Romney, Edgar E19
Romney, Ronna E. A707
Romo, Tammy A956
Romo, Tammy A1003
Romojaro, Jaime Guardiola W71
Rompaey, Yves Van W623
Romrell, Larry E. A871
Romrell, Larry E. A872
Romrell, Larry E. A633
Romrell, Larry E. A633
Ronca, Giovanni W592
Roncey, Frank W104
Ronde, Pascal E107
Rondinone, Ralph E523
Ronen, Nechama W78
Rongkavilit, Chokechai P671
Ronner, Markus W621
Ronning, Roger W594
Ronson, Lisa W162
Roobeek, Annemieke J.M. W344
Rood, John D. A407
Rooij, Frank de A825
Rooney, David C. E343
Rooney, Robert P. A713
Rooney, Robert R. W218
Rooney, Thomas P. E204
Roos, John V. A912
Roos, John V. W488
Roos, Murray E493
Root, M. Darren A472
Root, M. Darren E230
Roper, Pamela F. E124
Ropiecki, Gary L. E512
Ropp, Steven R. A515
Roquemaurel, Gérald de W127
Rorsgard, Veronica W548
Rorsted, Kasper Bo W430
Rorsted, Kasper Bo W14
Ros, Viv Da W37
Rosa, David J. A572
Rosamilia, Thomas W. A902
Rosano, Lawrence A732

COMBINED HOOVER'S HANDBOOK INDEX OF EXECUTIVES

A = AMERICAN BUSINESS
E = EMERGING COMPANIES
P = PRIVATE COMPANIES
W = WORLD BUSINESSS

Rosar, C. Alan E81
Rosario, Ramon R. del W85
Rosati, Mario M. A914
Rosato, David A152
Rosato, R. David A814
Rosato, R. David E379
Rosborough, Mark N. E192
Rose-Slade, Alison W425
Rose-Slade, Alison W423
Rose, Carlton E. E302
Rose, Cindy W654
Rose, Clayton S. A128
Rose, Crystal K. A219
Rose, Dennis E. A844
Rose, Dennis E. E394
Rose, Gary A. E321
Rose, Jody A. A191
Rose, Jody A. E77
Rose, Karl W458
Rose, Kelly B. A288
Rose, Matthew K. A438
Rose, Matthew K. A105
Rose, Nathaniel J. E245
Rose, Patricia A. A192
Rose, Shawn W84
Rose, Tyler H. E419
Rose, Tyler H. E287
Rose, Wolfgang W270
Roseborough, Teresa Wynn A526
Roseborough, Teresa Wynn A502
Rosen, Andrea S. W382
Rosen, Elaine D. A103
Rosen, Julie B. A140
Rosen, Lawrence W198
Rosen, Mickie W85
Rosen, Steven H. E127
Rosenbach, Thomas P. A653
Rosenbaum, David A. A176
Rosenbaum, Randall A971
Rosenbaum, Randall P537
Rosenberg, Joachim W641
Rosenberg, Mitchell M. A423
Rosenberg, Mitchell M. E199
Rosenberg, Nick A691
Rosenberg, Nick E323
Rosenberg, Ralph F. E288
Rosenberg, Scott E423
Rosenberg, Steven P. A1008
Rosenberger, Geoffrey H. E67
Rosenblatt, David S. A1047
Rosenblatt, David S. E261
Rosenblatt, Sidney D. E511
Rosenblum, David L. A497
Rosenblum, Hanoch W410
Rosenblum, Jay E. A103
Rosenbury, Tim E243
Rosencrants, Thomas G. E42
Rosendal, Jari W427
Rosenfeld, Edward R. A864
Rosenfeld, Eric S. E370
Rosenfeld, Irene B. A867
Rosenfeld, Klaus W544
Rosenfeld, Klaus W171
Rosenfeld, Ronald A. A732

Rosengren, Bjorn W6
Rosenstein, Beryl A1019
Rosenstein, Beryl P587
Rosensweig, Daniel L. (Dan) A15
Rosenthal, Alan B. E229
Rosenthal, Bennett E34
Rosenthal, Bennett E49
Rosenthal, Craig L. E57
Rosenthal, Dale S. A679
Rosenthal, Gary L. E72
Rosenthal, John L. A176
Rosenthal, John L. A176
Rosenthal, Michael E334
Rosenthal, Norman L. A455
Rosenthaler, Albert E. A871
Rosenthaler, Albert E. A633
Rosenthaler, Albert E. E300
Rosgaard, Ole G. A489
Rosier, William Grady A763
Rosiles, Adrian Otero W84
Rosinus, Michael F. E46
Roskovich, Charles B. A860
Rosler, Philipp W545
Roslund, Loredana W228
Rosman, Adam L. A434
Rosmarin, Adam W93
Rosner, Elimelech E247
Ross, C. Duane E291
Ross, Cathy D. A123
Roß, Heinz Peter W586
Ross, Jack J. E411
Ross, Jessica P. E221
Ross, John A941
Ross, Jonathan W.R. E108
Ross, Kimberly A. A239
Ross, Kimberly A. W430
Ross, Larry W. A524
Ross, Larry W. E258
Ross, Patricia "Patty" M. E344
Ross, Robert W. E475
Ross, Steven D. A618
Ross, Steven D. E290
Ross, Susan Williamson A763
Ross, Yolanda P345
Rossen, Jeremy D. E547
Rossi, Francesco S. (Frank) A810
Rossi, Francesco S. (Frank) E376
Rossi, Jack E199
Rossi, James L. A249
Rossi, James L. E99
Rossi, Jerome R. E9
Rossi, Mario W581
Rossi, Roberto W479
Rossi, Roberto Angelini W41
Rossi, Roberto Angelini W217
Rossi, Salvatore W592
Rossi, Simone W215
Rossin, Thomas E. A923
Rossin, Thomas E. E433
Rosso, Richard A287
Rossotti, Charles O. A171
Rost, Nicholas E374
Rostan, Richard H. A386
Rostrup, Jorgen C. Arentz W594
Rota, Kerim W26
Roth, Colin P223
Roth, David A95
Roth, Heidi Rena E287
Roth, Irit W79
Roth, Jean-Pierre W580

Roth, R. Lawrence E363
Roth, Ronald G. E101
Rothberg, Richard J. A322
Rothensteiner, Walter W627
Rothermel, Daniel K. A307
Rothermel, Daniel K. E133
Rothermel, Paige P84
Rothkopf, Jack E. E401
Rothman, Paul B. A684
Rothman, Thomas E. A170
Rothrock, Ray A. E423
Rothschild, Alexandre De W107
Rothschild, David de W127
Rothschild, Lynn Forester de A620
Rothstein, Bruce E72
Rothstein, Sharon A162
Rothstein, Stuart A. A87
Rotsch, Friederike W517
Rotsztain, Diego A. A979
Rott, Roland A458
Rottenberg, Julie B. A1096
Rotter, Franz W639
Roualet, Mark C. A460
Roughead, Gary A752
Roughton-Smith, Stephen W81
Rouis, Jonathan F. E364
Rounce, Justin W590
Roupie, Christophe E311
Rourke, Mark B. A917
Roush, John A. E297
Roush, John A. E6
Roussat, Olivier W107
Rousseau, Henri- Paul A915
Rousseau, Jean M P178
Rousseau, Laurent W526
Roussel, Olivier W165
Roussel, Stephane W637
Roussis, Theodoros W336
Roussy, Delphine W168
Rouvitha-Panou, Irene C. W231
Roux, David J. A175
Roverato, Jean-Francois W213
Rovig, Joseph W. A754
Rovinescu, Calin W99
Rovinescu, Calin W84
Rowe-Straker, Annmarie A400
Rowe, Jane W218
Rowe, R. Scott A868
Rowe, S. Jane W611
Rowe, Sharon H. A250
Rowe, Sharon H. E99
Rowe, Steve W385
Rowe, Zane C. A1098
Rowinsky, Eric K. A158
Rowland, Michael W647
Rowland, Sandra E. A790
Rowland, Stephen Eric E147
Rowland, Suzanne B. A924
Rowles, Michael A641
Rowley, Richard B. E364
Roxbury, Jennifer A. E156
Roy, J. Steven E361
Roy, Michael K. Le A653
Roy, Michel W193
Roy, Nilanjan W304
Roy, Peter A. A1068
Roy, Rob E477
Roy, Sumit E412
Royal, Pamela J. A340
Royer, David L. E91

Royere, Jean-Marc de W357
Rozado, Carmen Fernandez W11
Rozado, Maria del Carmen Fernandez W212
Rozanski, Horacio D. A660
Rozanski, Horacio D. A171
Roze, Frederic W358
Rubananko, Yoram A300
Rubash, Mark J. A573
Rubel, Matthew E. E285
Rubenstein, David M. A203
Rubenstein, William S. A135
Ruberg, David C. E141
Ruberti, Alexandre E88
Rubin, Diane A423
Rubin, Diane E199
Rubin, Elana W596
Rubin, Jonathan E474
Rubin, Slava A1111
Rubinson, Lewis P467
Rubinstein, Jerold H. E514
Rubinstein, Jonathan J. A50
Rubiolo, Juan Ignacio A23
Rubsamen-Schaeff, Helga W397
Rucheton, Philippe W200
Rucinski, Bruce E19
Ruck, Myles J. D. W559
Rucker, Kim K.W. A538
Rucker, Kim K.W. A657
Rucker, Kim K.W. A215
Rudd, Amber W135
Rudd, R. Matthew W122
Rudd, W. Troy A20
Ruddy, Benjamin G. E149
Ruddy, Jordan B. E62
Rude, Maureen J. E149
Rudisill, Philip M. A1033
Rudisill, Philip M. E492
Rudloff, Hans-Joerg W506
Rudnick, Ellen A. A806
Rudnick, Ellen A. A773
Rudolph, Michael E307
Rudy, Thomas L. E98
Rue, William M. A927
Rue, William M. E435
Rueda, Delfin W442
Rueger, Thomas V. A1033
Rueger, Thomas V. E492
Ruegger, Philip T. A1037
Ruelas-Hashimoto, Tracy E428
Ruemmler, Kathryn H. A480
Ruenthip, Tinakorn W136
Ruesterholz, Virginia P. A502
Rufart, Victor W161
Ruff, Ellen T. E174
Ruffel, Charles A. A919
Rugge, Nathan A927
Rugge, Nathan E435
Ruggeri, Rachel A964
Ruggieri, John T. A1108
Ruggiero, Mark J. A554
Ruggiero, Mark J. E268
Ruggles, Lisa C. E123
Ruh, William A. W379
Ruhl, Joseph A. E364
Ruhlman, Jon Ryan E393
Ruhlman, Robert G. E393
Ruijter, Ignace de W623
Ruisanchez, Raul Jacob A953
Ruiz-Tagle, Carlos Hurtado W217

COMBINED HOOVER'S HANDBOOK INDEX OF EXECUTIVES

A = AMERICAN BUSINESS
E = EMERGING COMPANIES
P = PRIVATE COMPANIES
W = WORLD BUSINESSS

Ruiz, Christian A223
Ruiz, Gisel E529
Ruiz, Jesus W643
Ruiz, Paulo W209
Ruiz, Thomas E271
Rukwied, Joachim W98
Rull, Arlyn P355
Rull, Steven M. A188
Rull, Steven M. E71
Rullo, Steven M. W262
Rumbolz, Michael D. E524
Rumeu, Jaime Alvarez de las Asturias Bohorques W382
Rummelhoff, Irene W448
Rummelhoff, Irene W227
Rummelt, Andreas W57
Rumsey, Jennifer W. A306
Rumsey, Jennifer W. E255
Runevad, Anders W632
Runevad, Anders W524
Runge, Marschall S. A636
Runge, William Henry A706
Runion, Christopher S. E181
Runje, Zeljko W506
Runkle, Matthew J.K. A226
Ruotsala, Matti W247
Rupert, Anton W167
Rupert, Jan W167
Rupert, Johann W167
Rupp, Joseph D. A760
Rupp, Joseph D. A764
Rupp, Lorie K. A417
Ruppel, Chris E239
Ruppel, John J. A704
Ruppel, John J. E328
Ruppert, Bradley A. E293
Ruppert, Craig A. A913
Ruppert, Craig A. E427
Ruschell, Joseph M. A541
Rusckowski, Stephen H. A870
Rush, Blair T. E98
Rush, David E. A184
Rush, Jean E5
Rush, Stephen F. A1111
Rushing, Rodney E. A932
Rushing, Rodney E. E436
Ruslim, Michael Dharmawan W464
Russ, Benjamin E. A227
Russell, Cornelius J. E192
Russell, Duncan W16
Russell, Erin L. E286
Russell, Erin L. E154
Russell, Frederick L. E287
Russell, Heather J. E493
Russell, James E297
Russell, John G. A256
Russell, John G. A294
Russell, Joyce E88
Russell, Kenneth D. A516
Russell, Kevin E181
Russell, Kimberly Adams A1043
Russell, Leigh-Ann W109
Russell, Michael E. (Mike) A305
Russell, Nancy D. W262

Russell, Paula A795
Russell, Randy T. E515
Russell, Sarah W446
Russell, Scott W517
Russell, Stuart J. W308
Russell, Vernon A. E515
Russo, Arthur R. A311
Russo, Karla M. A397
Russo, Marc S. A707
Russo, Michael J. A440
Russo, Patricia F. A684
Russo, Patricia F. A514
Russo, Patricia F. A466
Russo, Roberto W157
Russwurm, Siegfried W602
Rust, Bradley M. A472
Rust, Bradley M. E230
Rust, Edward Barry A210
Rust, Glenn W. E526
Rust, Michael T. A890
Rust, Michael T. E416
Rust, Patsy I. E307
Ruth, James R. (Jim) E168
Ruth, Jon M. E275
Ruth, Kim A. A1040
Ruth, Kim A. E498
Rutherford, Jamey Traywick A10
Rutherford, John R. A374
Rutherford, Linda Burke A305
Rutherford, William B. A505
Rutishauser, Lucy A. A939
Rutkowski, Joseph A. E275
Rutledge, Elizabeth A62
Rutledge, Thomas M. A223
Ruttanaporn, Supapun W137
Rutten, Giel A78
Ruttledge, Michael A248
Rutz, Michael P. E303
Ruud, David S. A344
Ruud, Yngve W355
Ruxandra, Oana A1106
Ruxandra, Oana E418
Ruyter, Finn Bjorn W228
Ruzicka, John J. A421
Ruzicka, John J. E197
Ryan-Berman, Bridget M. A99
Ryan, Arthur F. A882
Ryan, Carrie W. E115
Ryan, Christina M A472
Ryan, Christina M E230
Ryan, Christopher James E291
Ryan, Daniel J. E15
Ryan, Edward A. A679
Ryan, James C. A772
Ryan, James C. E237
Ryan, James M. A381
Ryan, Jason M. A218
Ryan, John P188
Ryan, John R. A418
Ryan, Kara Gostenhofer A218
Ryan, Kathleen A. A1108
Ryan, Kimberly K. E255
Ryan, Mark W191
Ryan, Michael P398
Ryan, Michael P. A791
Ryan, Patrick L. E193
Ryan, Patrick Louis A749
Ryan, Patrick M. E193
Ryan, Paul D. A447
Ryan, Peter J P519

Ryan, Ronald E77
Ryan, T. Timothy A915
Ryan, T. Timothy W262
Ryan, T. Timothy W480
Ryan, Thomas M. E388
Ryan, Thomas M. E209
Ryback, Andrew J. E388
Rybar, Ronald K. E189
Rychlak, Lawrence E409
Rydberg-Dumont, Josephine W548
Ryder, David P673
Ryder, Thomas O'Neal A50
Rydin, Charlotte W579
Ryerkerk, Lori J. A215
Ryerkerk, Lori J. W209
Rykhus, Daniel A. A426
Rykhus, Daniel A. E202
Ryman, Craig W85
Rystedt, Fredrik W231
Ryu, Young Sang W546
Rzonca, Noriko W173

S

S, Mary Beth Claus P386
S., Ravi Kumar W304
Saab, Joseph R. A568
Saad, Bader M. Al W395
Saadeh-Jajeh, Diana A457
Sabag, Mark W598
Sabaini, Patricio Gomez W220
Sabanci, Erol W26
Sabanci, Erol W267
Sabanci, Guler W267
Sabanci, Serra W267
Sabanci, Sevil Sabanci W267
Sabanovic, Ruza W594
Sabat, Joseph W. A393
Sabat, Joseph W. E184
Sabater, Carlos A. A595
Sabater, Carlos A. E389
Sabater, Guillermo W73
Sabatini, Gino M. E530
Sabbatini, Brian P671
Sabelhaus, Melanie R. E146
Sabeti, Pardis C. A315
Sabhasri, Chayodom W484
Sabherwal, Ajay E224
Sabia, James A. A291
Sabia, Maureen J. W122
Sabin, Brian E517
Sabin, Ralph C. E199
Sabloff, Anne M. E311
Sabloff, Barry M. E311
Sabo, Elias J. E115
Saccaro, James K. A142
Sacchi, Diana E249
Sacchi, Guido F. A477
Sacchi, Laurent W187
Sachar, Sanjiv W271
Sachdev, Amit K. A1089
Sacher, Andrea W95
Sachs, Bruce I. A1089
Sachse, David R. A125
Sachse, David R. E52
Sachtleben-Reimann, Katja W586
Sack, James M. A763
Sacks, Ian E408

Sacks, Ian E247
Sacristan, Carlos Ruiz A953
Sada, Armando Garza W131
Sada, Armando Garza W27
Sadana, Anshul E35
Sadana, Sumit A700
Sadasivam, Shaker E266
Sadeghian, Christopher K. A914
Sadler, Jason D. A239
Sadler, Robert E. A651
Sadolin, Annette W205
Sadoun, Arthur W486
Sadove, Stephen I. A269
Sadove, Stephen I. A92
Sadowski, John D. A913
Sadowski, John D. E427
Sadowski, Peter E32
Sadowski, Peter T. A407
Sadygov, Famil K. W474
Sadygov, Famil K. W256
Saechao, Cynthia P639
Saeger, Terry M. E307
Saegusa, Yukari A289
Saehelin, Tobias B. W355
Saejima, Naoki W581
Saeki, Kaname W316
Saeki, Yasumitsu W439
Saenz, Denise P180
Saenz, Luis A971
Saenz, Luis P537
Sæther, Glenn W558
Saez, Baruc W314
Safady, Edward Z. A852
Safady, Edward Z. E399
Saffer, Lori Polep P161
Saffrett, John W27
Saga, Kosuke W576
Sagalyn, Lynne B. E62
Sagan, Leo R. E537
Sagan, Paul L. A1098
Sagara, Kevin C. A929
Sagara, Masayuki W454
Sagartz, John E. E273
Sagehorn, David M. A26
Sagehorn, David M. E96
Sagiya, Mari W402
Sagliocca, Andrew C. E173
Sagripanti, Mary A. E532
Saha, Saugata A911
Sahagun, Fernando Benjamin Ruiz W73
Sahashi, Toshiyuki W567
Sahlstrand, Catharina Belfrage W579
Sahney, Nitin E179
Saia, Andrea Lynn E16
Saich, John A. A926
Saida, Kunitaro W123
Saideman, Susan G. A237
Saigh, Alexandre Teixeira de Assumpcao W622
Saik, Walker F. E389
Saiki, Akitaka W402
Saiki, Mitsushi W607
Saiki, Naoko W553
Saiki, Naoko W347
Sailer, Daniel E81
Sailer, Ryan A1059
Saillant, Paul du W231
Saines, Ian M. E10
Saint-Affrique, Antoine de W187

COMBINED HOOVER'S HANDBOOK INDEX OF EXECUTIVES

A = AMERICAN BUSINESS
E = EMERGING COMPANIES
P = PRIVATE COMPANIES
W = WORLD BUSINESSS

Saint-Aignan, Patrick de A973
Saint-Exupery, Jacques de W562
Saint-Geours, Frederic W238
Saint-Geours, Frederic W127
Saint, Frederick (Fred) G. E123
Saintil, Merline A136
Saintil, Merline A999
Saito, Hitoshi W608
Saito, Kinji W577
Saito, Kiyomi W330
Saito, Mitsuru W434
Saito, Noboru W589
Saito, Ryoichi W334
Saito, Shinichi W570
Saito, Takahiro W533
Saito, Takeshi W223
Saito, Tamotsu W319
Saito, Tamotsu W330
Saito, Toshihide W155
Saito, Yasushi W336
Saito, Yoji W402
Saitoh, Yasuhiko W536
Saiyegh, Merza Hassan Al W205
Saiz, Emilio de Eusebio W73
Sajdak, Guida R. E537
Sajeski, Jon C. E441
Saka, Mao A1034
Saka, Tamer W267
Sakaguchi, Masatoshi W83
Sakai, Akira W281
Sakai, Ichiro W389
Sakai, Kazunori W609
Sakai, Kunihiko W285
Sakai, Noriaki W297
Sakai, Takako W432
Sakai, Toshikazu W534
Sakai, Toshiyuki W454
Sakaki, Junichi W26
Sakakibara, Hiroshi W402
Sakakibara, Sadayuki W331
Sakamoto, Hideyuki W441
Sakamoto, Hideyuki W405
Sakamoto, Kevin E57
Sakamoto, Shuichi W51
Sakamoto, Yoshiyuki W566
Sakamura, Ken W439
Sakane, Masahiro W330
Sakata, Seiji W496
Sakellariou, Anastasia Ch. W33
Sakellaris, George P. E22
Sakita, Kaoru W50
Sakkab, Nabil Y. A47
Saklad, Joseph H. E448
Sakon, Yuji W392
Saksena, Asheesh A1018
Sakuma, Hidetoshi W137
Sakurada, Katsura W451
Sakurada, Kengo W555
Sakuragi, Kimie W313
Sakurai, Eriko W333
Sakurai, Eriko W570
Sakurai, Makoto W82
Sakurai, Naoya W612
Sakurai, Shigeyuki W582

Sala, Umberto della A595
Salakas, Nikolaos V. W33
Salakhutdinov, Vladimir W655
Salamone, Denis J. A651
Salanger, Matthew J. A724
Salazar, Bryon C. A880
Salazar, Bryon C. E412
Salazar, John P. A397
Salazar, John P. E187
Salazar, Lisa M. A175
Salazar, Lisa M. E66
Salazar, Tammi R. A880
Salazar, Tammi R. E412
Saleh, Gholam M. E340
Saleh, Mark D. E111
Saleki-Gerhardt, Azita A8
Saleki-Gerhardt, Azita E166
Salem-Jackson, Kim E12
Salem, Matthew A. E288
Salem, Paul J. A696
Salen, Kristina M. A941
Salerno, Frederic V. A561
Salerno, Frederic V. E12
Salerno, Lawrence G. E418
Salesky, Bryan S. A834
Saliba, N. W8
Salice, Thomas P. E325
Saligram, Ravichandra K. A237
Saligram, Ravichandra K. A735
Salinas, Jerry A305
Salins, Peter D A974
Salins, Peter D P539
Salka, Susan R. A677
Sallade, Peter E181
Salles, Joao Moreira W315
Salles, Pedro Moreira W315
Sallnow-Smith, Nicholas Robert W180
Sallouti, Roberto Balls W69
Sallstrom, Mikael W641
Salmirs, Scott B. A10
Salmon, Scott E445
Salmon, Sean W393
Salmon, Thomas E. A772
Salomon, Christophe W600
Salsberg, Eric W235
Salter, Dean W596
Saltich, Daniel J P498
Saltzman, David E347
Salute, Richard J. E348
Salvador, Luc-Francois W123
Salvador, Scot R. A1043
Salvadori, Daniel Gesua Sive A6
Salvati, Michael E. A87
Salvato, Alfred P620
Salvatore, Bryan J. A499
Salvino, Michael J. A349
Salyers, David G. A955
Salyers, David G. E456
Salzman, Marian A825
Sam, Elizabeth W334
Samad, Sam A. A870
Samad, Sam A. E263
Samalapa, Tida W334
Samant, Rahul D. A323
Samant, Shashank A770
Samaram, Maris W541
Samarasekera, Indira V. W379
Samarasekera, Indira V. W308
Samardzich, Barb J. W15
Samath, Jamie E. A573

Sambra, Bernardo W174
Samet, Zipora W79
Samhan, Mohammed Abdulrehman Al W520
Sami, Peter W86
Sami, Sabir A1146
Sammons, John F. A954
Sampang, Anna A1034
Sample, John G. A196
Sample, John G. E79
Sampsell, David H. E140
Sampson, Jennifer H. A274
Sampson, John M. A342
Sams, Louise S. A425
Sams, Louise S. E123
Samson, Clement W193
Samson, Marvin S E32
Samstag, Karl W453
Samuels, Ivanetta Davis E20
Samuels, Theodore R. A178
Samuels, Theodore R. A216
Samuelsen, Stian Tegler W204
Samuelson, Errol G. A1149
Samuelson, Jonas W4
Samujh, Nishlan W311
Samura, Shunichi W576
Sanada, Yukimitsu W417
Sanborn, Cynthia (Cindy) M. A747
Sanborn, H. Scott A500
Sanborn, H. Scott E246
Sanborn, Richard M. A373
Sanborn, Richard M. E168
Sanborn, Scott A627
Sanchez-Incera, Bernardo W27
Sanchez-Real, Jose Ignacio Comenge W161
Sanchez, Adalio T. A118
Sanchez, Alejandro "Alex" M. A1043
sanchez, Angel Cordova W266
Sanchez, Antonio R. A563
Sanchez, Carlos E517
Sanchez, Daniel E. A332
Sanchez, Francisco J. A94
Sanchez, Frederic W459
Sanchez, Monique A5
Sanchez, Perfecto E481
Sanchez, Robert A288
Sanchez, Robert A290
Sanchez, Robert E. A909
Sanchez, Robert E. A1010
Sand, Michael R. E490
Sandberg, Cecilia W60
Sandberg, Rebecca B. A1048
Sandberg, Sheryl K. A689
Sandbrook, William J. E111
Sande, Marc Van W623
Sandeen, Mark P11
Sander, Hans-Werner W192
Sander, Louise W579
Sander, Mark G. A772
Sandercock, Brett E417
Sanders, A. Shane A315
Sanders, Carol P. A416
Sanders, Carol P. W491
Sanders, Corey Ian A696
Sanders, Dan J. A959
Sanders, Dax A. A605
Sanders, Dena E338
Sanders, Duane A. A599

Sanders, E. Lawrence E113
Sanders, John H. E354
Sanders, Sabrina A105
Sanders, W. Reid A1048
Sanders, W. Reid A485
Sandgaard, Thomas E547
Sandgren, James A. A772
Sandhar, Karamjit S. W133
Sandler, Debra A. A94
Sandler, Debra A. A336
Sandler, Debra A. A600
Sandlin, Robert E. E222
Sandman, Dan D. A717
Sandri, Fabio A828
Sandri, Marcio A. A795
Sandrock, Alfred W. E529
Sands, Anita M. A931
Sands, Richard A291
Sands, Robert A291
Sandstrom, Katherine M. E152
Sandvik, Helvi K. A34
Sanford, Glenn Darrel E180
Sanford, Linda Szabat A570
Sanford, Linda Szabat A290
Sanford, Linda Szabat A289
Sang, Mun Shin W365
Sang, Seung YI W513
Sanger, Bertrand W88
Sanghi, Steve A697
Sanghrajka, Jayesh W304
Sanghvi, Sanjiv A130
Sangiovanni-Vincentelli, Alberto E75
Sangkram, Rungroj W484
Sanglard, Paul-Andre W88
Sanguinetti, Kevin A392
Sanguinetti, Kevin E183
Sani, Suresh L. A1086
Sani, Suresh L. E516
Sanibell, Ozlen W26
Sanint, Gabriel Jaramillo W131
Sanjines, Javier G. Astaburuaga W274
Sanjines, Javier Gerardo Astaburuaga W244
Sankaran, Vivek A817
Sankaran, Vivek A35
Sankarlingam, Velchamy E547
Sankey, Vernon W61
Sanner, J. Michael E54
Sanodo, Raquel P271
Sanphasitvong, Umroong W117
Sans, Paul A400
Sansbury, Bryan E299
Sansone, Christopher R. E271
Sansone, Judith S. A989
Sansone, Thomas A. A578
Santacroce, Kevin L. A328
Santamaria, Mary Catherine Elizabeth P. W85
Santana, Maria Helena dos Santos Fernandes de W315
Santana, Megan D. A1078
Santana, Megan D. E513
Santana, Rafael A1037
Santana, Rafael A1099
Santana, Ralph E. A336
Santangelo, Andreana A500
Santangelo, Andreana E246
Santangelo, Joseph A. A724
Santaniello, Daniel J. E190
Santarosa, Romolo C. A498

COMBINED HOOVER'S HANDBOOK INDEX OF EXECUTIVES

A = AMERICAN BUSINESS
E = EMERGING COMPANIES
P = PRIVATE COMPANIES
W = WORLD BUSINESSS

Santelli, Jonathan N. A876
Santi, E. Scott A485
Santi, E. Scott A553
Santi, Roque A. A120
Santi, Roque A. E48
Santiago, Carmelo L. W514
Santiago, Helen S. E98
Santilli, Paula A817
Santilli, Paula A526
Santini, Gino E107
Santner, Friedrich W229
Santomassimo, Michael P. A1115
Santomero, Anthony M. W491
Santona, Gloria W44
Santora, Greg J. E16
Santoro, Nicholas E347
Santos, Bernerd Da A23
Santos, Edwin J. A1108
Santos, Esteban A76
Santos, Jose Soares dos W325
Santos, Marcos Antonio Molina dos W383
Santos, Maria Aparecida Pascoal Marcal dos W383
Santos, Marlene M. A823
Santos, Pedro Soares dos W324
Santos, Renato Monteiro dos W69
Santos, Ricardo Florence dos W383
Santos, Rodrigo W95
Santos, Tomás Milmo W131
Sanusi, S. L. A. M. W414
Sanz, Carlos Gustavo Cano W210
Sanz, Francisco Javier Garcia W280
Sanz, Francisco Javier Garcia W61
Sanzone, ToniAnn E530
Sanzone, Virginia E262
Saperstein, Andrew M. A713
Sapienza, Paola W592
Sapiro, Miriam E. W196
Saporito, Francesco W627
Sapoznik, Andre W315
Sapp, Betty J. A123
Saptharishi, Mahesh A716
Saputo, Lino A. W420
Saran, Atul E157
Sarandos, Theodore A. A730
Sarangi, Umesh Chandra W271
Sarasin, Arsa W137
Sarasin, Arsa W540
Sarasin, Eric G. W86
Sarasin, Pow W334
Sarasin, Pow W137
Sarbekian, Fran P498
Sardon, Francisco W84
Sargen, Gregory P. E45
Sargent, Dale P682
Sargent, Richard C. E506
Sargent, Ronald L. A611
Sargent, Ronald L. A1115
Sargent, Ronald L. E209
Sargent, Timothy Willis E506
Sarin, Aradhana W57
Sarin, Arun A919
Sarin, Arun E91

Sarin, Arun W10
Sarker, Ari A670
Sarlat-Depotte, Veronique W492
Sarma, Chander P. E61
Sarma, Karthik R. A116
Sarnoff, Ann M. A807
Sarnoff, Dafna E81
Sarofim, Christopher B. A599
Saroukos, Constantine W585
Sarowitz, Steven I. E374
Sarrafian, Zareh H. A797
Sarrafian, Zareh H. A477
Sarrafian, Zareh H. E368
Sarsam, Tony B. A958
Sarsynski, Elaine A. A531
Sarsynski, Elaine A. A470
Sartain, Elizabeth P. (Libby) A655
Sartore, David E. A397
Sarup, Deepak W541
Sarup, S. W8
Sarver, M. Adam A419
Sasa, Seiichi W110
Sasae, Kenichiro W253
Sasae, Kenichiro W405
Sasae, Kenichiro W50
Sasagawa, Atsushi W453
Sasajima, Kazuyuki W181
Sasaki, Hitoshi W400
Sasaki, Junko W270
Sasaki, Makiko W449
Sasaki, Mami W184
Sasaki, Michio W607
Sasaki, Sadao W607
Sasaki, Shigeo W331
Sasaki, Teruyuki W407
Sasaki, Tomohiko W42
Sasaki, Toshihiko W297
Sasaki, Yasushi W81
Sasayama, Shinichi W608
Sass, Allan E229
Sassenfeld, Peter W280
Sasser, Alison L. A687
Sasser, Bob A337
Sassoon, James Meyer W323
Sastre, Maria A. A765
Sastre, Maria A. A465
Sasturain, Juan Ignacio Cirac W593
Satake, Akira W319
Satake, Noriyuki W253
Satake, Yasumine W576
Satchi-Fainaro, Ronit W598
Sathyanarayanan, Bala V. A489
Sato, Atsuko W319
Sato, Hidehiko W494
Sato, Hirofumi W608
Sato, Hiroshi W567
Sato, Hiroyuki W612
Sato, Kiyoshi W389
Sato, Koji W184
Sato, Makoto W408
Sato, Masahiko W26
Sato, Minoru W603
Sato, Motomu W81
Sato, Mototsugu W465
Sato, Naoki W437
Sato, Rieko W182
Sato, Samuel M. E147
Sato, Seiji W336
Sato, Shigeki W589
Sato, Shinichi W432

Sato, Shinji W267
Sato, Toshimi W453
Sato, Yoshio W155
Sato, Yoshio W568
Sato, Yumiko W462
Satriano, Pietro A205
Satterfield, Adam N. A771
Satterlee, Scott A. A394
Satterthwaite, Livingston L. A306
Sattgast, Rich A971
Sattgast, Rich P537
Sattler, Thomas E480
Saturno, Terry R. E364
Satvat, Ali J. E106
Satz, Devin E227
Sauber, Franziska Tschudi W580
Sauder, Kevin J. E184
Sauer, Michael D. E166
Saueressig, Thomas W517
Sauerland, Frank W199
Sauerland, John Peter A851
Saugier, Jean-Marc W490
Saun, Bruce Van A711
Saun, Bruce Van A248
Saunders, Anne G. E344
Saunders, Brenton L. E57
Saunders, F. R. E205
Saunders, Mitchell C. E41
Saunier, Thomas W526
Sautel, Stephen D. E173
Sauter, Dennis Charles E348
Sauvageau, Yvon W294
Savage, E. Jean A1125
Savage, Jeffrey S. A1139
Savage, Sheri L. E504
Savarese, Lawrence J. A732
Savart, Michel W127
Savatyugin, Alexei W329
Saville, Kendell J. A5
Saville, Paul C. A762
Savitskaya, Elena W410
Savoie, Andree W420
Savoy, Brian D. A348
Savoy, Brian D. A347
Savoy, Michelle R. W358
Saw, Choo Boon W495
Sawa, Masahiko W297
Sawada, Jun W439
Sawada, Michitaka W333
Sawada, Michitaka W347
Sawada, Michitaka W465
Sawada, Satoru W608
Sawers, John W109
Sawhney, Ash E153
Sawhney, Inderpreet E255
Sawhney, Inderpreet W304
Sawiris, Nassef W15
Sawyer, John E. E206
Sawyer, Robert W371
Sawyers, Charles L. W449
Saxon, Helena W548
Saxon, Ulrika W4
Sayde, Maurice H. W77
Sayed, Khaled Mohamed Ebrahim Al W631
Sayer, Patrick W631
Sayer, Patrick W495
Sayiner, Necip E392
Sayles, David B. A96
Sayman, Ersan E210

Sayward, Shelley E82
Sazdanoff, Catherine A. E321
Sbordone, Argia M. A400
Sbraire, Jean-Pierre W613
Scacco, Gustave "Gus" . J. E364
Scadina, Mark R. E183
Scaff, David H. E190
Scaglione, Diego Anthony A770
Scalia, Chris A512
Scalzo, Joseph E. E443
Scaminace, Joseph M. A242
Scaminace, Joseph M. A804
Scangos, George A. A27
Scanlan, Agnes Bundy A1042
Scanlan, Agnes Bundy E34
Scanlan, Agnes Bundy E408
Scanlon, George P. A620
Scanlon, Jennifer F. A747
Scanlon, John P110
Scanlon, Meghan A175
Scannell, John R. A651
Scannell, Timothy J. A981
Scannell, Timothy J. E276
Scannell, William F. A322
Scarborough, Dean A. A486
Scarborough, Joel P. A478
Scarfo, Anthony E420
Scarlett, Catherine M. A724
Scarlett, Kathleen (Kamy) A155
Scaroni, Paolo W631
Scarpelli, Cassiano Ricardo W69
Scavilla, Daniel T. E233
Scavuzzo, Tony E243
Scearcy, Lynda B. A935
Scearcy, Lynda B. E439
Sceppaguercio, Maria A600
Scerch, Andrea A670
Sceti, Elio Leoni A610
Sceti, Elio Leoni W40
Schaaf, Brian E. A446
Schaaff, Tim W557
Schaapveld, Alexandra W548
Schachenhofer, Nicole W458
Schacht, Horst Joachim W355
Schachtel, John D. E413
Schack, Wesley W. von E483
Schade, Christian S. E278
Schadler, Alletta M. E99
Schadler, Charles F. A555
Schadler, Charles F. E269
Schaefer, Charles H. E240
Schaefer, John H. A83
Schaefer, Roland W192
Schaeffer, Melissa A30
Schaeffer, Melissa W617
Schaeffer, Scott F. E268
Schaeffler, George F.W. W171
Schaeffler, Maria-Elisabeth W171
Schaeppi, Urs W581
Schaeufele, Eugen W192
Schafer, Klaus O. W174
Schafer, Markus W395
Schaferkordt, Anke A1112
Schaferkordt, Anke W96
Schaferkordt, Anke W93
Schaffner, Jerry L. A516
Schaffner, Rick P73
Schalekamp, William A. A592
Schalk, Sammy A. A953
Schalk, Sammy A. E455

COMBINED HOOVER'S HANDBOOK INDEX OF EXECUTIVES

A = AMERICAN BUSINESS
E = EMERGING COMPANIES
P = PRIVATE COMPANIES
W = WORLD BUSINESSS

Schaller, Bart A985
Schaller, Hans-Karl W639
Schaller, Heinrich W639
Schalliol, Charles E. A427
Schalliol, Charles E. E203
Schalow, Laurie A232
Schapiro, Mary L. A713
Schapiro, Mary L. A311
Schapiro, Morton O. A662
Schapiro, Richard M. A707
Schar, Gretchen W. A240
Scharf, Charles W. A701
Scharf, Charles W. A1115
Scharwath, Tim W198
Schat, Sipko N. W86
Schatz, Jacob J. A363
Schaubach, Dwight C. A1033
Schaubach, Dwight C. E493
Schaubeck, Patricia M. A328
Schaubert, Sharon A. A703
Schaubert, Sharon A. E327
Schauerman, John P. E397
Schaufler, Thomas W162
Schaumburg, Anne C. A757
Schaupp, William E. A210
Schechter, Adam H. A615
Schechter, Joshua A. A148
Schechter, Lori A. A677
Schechter, Robert P. E402
Schechtman, Natalie S. A17
Scheffer, Henk W49
Scheffer, Jaap de Hoop W22
Scheid, John Stephen A927
Scheid, John Stephen E435
Scheid, Steven L. E350
Scheidegger, Urs W522
Scheider, Wolf-Henning W168
Scheiderer, Frank W15
Scheidreiter, Gerhard W639
Scheidt, Herbert J. W642
Scheinkestel, Nora L. W596
Scheinkestel, Nora L. W648
Scheinman, Daniel E35
Scheinman, Daniel E547
Scheirer, Mark W. A504
Scheiwe, Steven D. A718
Scheiwe, Steven D. E335
Schell, Brian N. E87
Schellekens, Ronald Adrianus Wilhelmus A817
Schellemans, Denise W93
Scheller, Eric A. E514
Scheller, Gregor W98
Schemm, Dennis Charles E494
Schena, Joseph J. E443
Schenck, A. William A1039
Schenck, A. William E498
Schenk, Daniel W91
Schenk, Dieter W249
Schenkel, Scott F. A729
Scheopner, Michael E. E291
Schepper, Kurt De W18
Scherer, Barbara V. E32
Scherer, Barbara V. E504

Scherer, Christian W24
Scherer, Mary C. A201
Scherger, Stephen R. A486
Schermer, Gregory P. E295
Schermer, Robert E. E321
Schermerhorn, Todd C. A1037
Scherping, Katherine Lee E501
Scherr, Stephen M. A513
Scheske, Ronald W. E469
Scheub, Todd M. E191
Schickli, K. Dillon A195
Schierhorn, Joseph M. E352
Schievelbein, Thomas C. A546
Schiff, Charles O. A240
Schiff, Thomas Reid A240
Schifter, Richard P. A648
Schilk, Wolfgang W661
Schiller, Xaver W398
Schilling, Brian R. E98
Schilling, Chris A92
Schillinger, Doug K. E57
Schillo, Heike W192
Schiminski, Siegmund W192
Schimmel, Lawrence E397
Schindler, Alfred N. W523
Schindler, Marcus W450
Schindler, Ozzie A. E512
Schindler, Philipp A45
Schioldager, Amy L. A296
Schipper, Heiko W95
Schippers, Harrie C.A.M. A796
Schipporeit, Erhard W510
Schipporeit, Erhard W269
Schipporeit, Erhard W586
Schiraldi, Richard J. A844
Schiraldi, Richard J. E394
Schirmer-Mosset, Elisabeth W91
Schirripa, John T. E336
Schlabach, Freeman D. E223
Schlackman, Scott D. E316
Schlagbauer, Joerg W61
Schlanger, Daniel K. A301
Schlanger, David J. E398
Schlarbaum, Jeffrey T. E291
Schlecht, Richard W. E147
Schlecht, Stephen L. E147
Schleifer, Leonard S. A882
Schleper, Denny P146
Schlesinger, Allyson A271
Schlesinger, Allyson E109
Schlesinger, Sarah J. E272
Schleweis, Helmut W192
Schlichting, Nancy M. A1102
Schlichting, Nancy M. A142
Schlifske, John Edward A608
Schlitz, Lei Z. A94
Schlogel, Vania E. A124
Schlonsky, Michael Allen (Mike) A157
Schlossberg, Andrew R. A573
Schlosser, John W. A605
Schlosstein, Ralph L. E176
Schlotman, J. Michael A597
Schlueter, Tom E455
Schmaltz, Dana L. E531
Schmanske, Mary V. A625
Schmeling, Judy A. E292
Schmeling, Judy K. A209
Schmid, Hannes W628
Schmid, Martin W580
Schmid, Martin W580

Schmid, Michael W389
Schmidhuber, Roland W453
Schmidt-KieBling, Michael W95
Schmidt, Barry A492
Schmidt, Barry P248
Schmidt, Cathleen A. A191
Schmidt, Cathleen A. E77
Schmidt, Christoph W96
Schmidt, Colleen A45
Schmidt, Darryl A125
Schmidt, Darryl E52
Schmidt, David G. E33
Schmidt, Erika L. E204
Schmidt, James F. E525
Schmidt, John K. A507
Schmidt, John K. E248
Schmidt, Kay E83
Schmidt, Kurt T. A195
Schmidt, Mikael W231
Schmidt, Robert R. E406
Schmidt, Stefan W96
Schmidt, Stephen J. E532
Schmidt, Timothy L. A856
Schmidt, William H. E169
Schmitt, Becky A267
Schmitt, Bernhard W203
Schmitt, Brian D. E108
Schmitt, Christophe W238
Schmitt, Heinz W273
Schmitt, James C. A515
Schmittmann, Stefan W389
Schmittroth, Sabine U. W162
Schmitz, Andreas W207
Schmitz, Christoph W207
Schmitz, Eloise E. A373
Schmitz, Eloise E. E168
Schmitz, Jochen W545
Schmitz, Martin J. A507
Schmitz, Martin J. E248
Schmitz, Rolf Martin W207
Schmoke, Kurt L. A911
Schmoock, David W362
Schmuck, Harry W. E117
Schmueckle, Henry T. E274
Schmukler, Louis S. A178
Schnabel, Susan C. A45
Schnautz, Thomas W. A747
Schneck-Last, Vivian C. A945
Schneck-Last, Vivian C. E450
Schneck, Karen A400
Schneeberger, Carol A. A815
Schneider-Maunoury, Frederic J. M. W52
Schneider, Barry T. A975
Schneider, David E409
Schneider, David E67
Schneider, Donald R. A432
Schneider, Etienne W49
Schneider, Frank W62
Schneider, Joseph P. E456
Schneider, Louisa Serene E366
Schneider, Malinda L. E190
Schneider, Michael W644
Schneider, Paul J. A918
Schneider, Peter W192
Schneider, Peter W. A845
Schneider, Peter W. E395
Schneider, Ruy Flaks W468
Schneider, Ryan M. A878
Schneider, Ryan M. A879

Schneider, Ryan M. A85
Schneider, Sven W303
Schneider, Terrence G. E140
Schneider, Thomas W. E372
Schneider, Todd M. A242
Schneider, Ulf Mark W429
Schnel, Jonah F. A124
Schnepp, Gilles W515
Schnepp, Gilles W187
Schnepp, Gilles W165
Schnewlin, Frank W580
Schnewlin, Frank W580
Schnewlin, Frank W642
Schnitzer, Alan D. A1037
Schnoor, Anya M. W84
Schnuck, Todd R. A276
Schnupp, Diane D. E287
Schnur, Jamie M. E293
Schnur, Steven W. E146
Schnyder, Marc W34
Schoch, Manfred W96
Schoels, Peter A435
Schoels, Peter E210
Schoen, Anthony A. E206
Schoen, Hans J. W. W442
Schoen, Steven B. A400
Schoenberger, Erika J. E136
Schoenfeld, Jeffrey E322
Schoenfelder, Joerg W171
Schoenhals, Marvin N. (Skip) A1138
Schoenhals, Marvin N. (Skip) E544
Schoerner, Peter W234
Schoewe, Thomas M. A752
Schoewe, Thomas M. A466
Scholhamer, James P. (Jim) E504
Scholin, Margo S. A397
Scholin, Margo S. E187
Scholtz, Juergen W303
Scholz, Philipp W277
Scholz, Stefan W171
Schomburger, Jeffrey K. A1050
Schoneman, Debbra L. E387
Schoner, Tina R. A489
Schonhardt, Conny W640
Schooler, Rick P308
Schools, Timothy K. A199
Schools, Timothy K. E79
Schoonman, Gerbert G. E253
Schopp, Alvyn A. E33
Schoppert, Wendy L. A770
Schoppert, Wendy Lee A157
Schorling, Melker W277
Schorna, Angela W458
Schorr, Lawrence J. A326
Schot, Abraham W533
Schott, Jennifer K. A553
Schott, John H. A981
Schott, John H. E469
Schottenstein, Robert H. E306
Schottenstein, Robert H. E274
Schrader, William R. A381
Schraeder, Werner W273
Schrag, Laura Alvarez A271
Schrag, Laura Alvarez E109
Schramm, Jude A. A410
Schraudenbach, John F. E361
Schraut, Josef W98
Schreck, Eric W. A1043
Schreier, Richard J. E30
Schreier, Thomas S. E387

COMBINED HOOVER'S HANDBOOK INDEX OF EXECUTIVES

A = AMERICAN BUSINESS
E = EMERGING COMPANIES
P = PRIVATE COMPANIES
W = WORLD BUSINESSS

Schreiner, James A. E329
Schreiner, Jeff A1023
Schreiner, Jeff P606
Schreiner, Linda V. A107
Schreiner, Linda V. E40
Schreuder, Jana A612
Schreyer, Edward J. A1040
Schreyer, Edward J. E499
Schrider, Daniel J. A913
Schrider, Daniel J. E427
Schriesheim, Robert A. A942
Schriesheim, Robert A. E260
Schrimsher, Neil A. A806
Schrock, Donald E. E314
Schrock, Michael V. E39
Schroede, A. D. A539
Schroeder, Aaron M. A979
Schroeder, Alice D. W481
Schroeder, Gerhard W506
Schroeder, Jeffrey M. A685
Schroeder, Lothar M. W199
Schroeder, Mark A. A472
Schroeder, Mark A. E230
Schroeder, Mark S. A615
Schroeder, Matthew A894
Schroeter, Martin J. A612
Schrum, Roger P. A950
Schudel, Hans Ulrich W91
Schueler, Kevin P581
Schueller, Stephan W3
Schueneman, Diane Lynn W91
Schueneman, Diane Lynn W89
Schuetz, Alexander E249
Schuh, Michele A428
Schuhmacher, Dirk W510
Schuhmacher, Erich W129
Schuit, Jan W603
Schuler, Cherie A398
Schuler, Eric W631
Schuler, Richard J. A860
Schuler, Roland W98
Schuler, Stacie E236
Schuler, Steven T. A1118
Schuler, Steven T. E533
Schuler, Tina W127
Schuller, Daniel J. E174
Schulman, Daniel H. A1088
Schulman, Daniel H. A807
Schulte, David J. E536
Schulte, Stefan W198
Schultek, Thomas W62
Schulten, Andre A850
Schultz, Howard A964
Schultz, John F. A1057
Schultz, John F. A514
Schultz, Kare A567
Schultz, Kare W598
Schultz, Lisa J. A1086
Schultz, Lisa J. E516
Schultz, Majken W188
Schultz, Regis W127
Schultz, Renee R. E378
Schultz, Robert F. A703
Schultz, Robert F. E327
Schultz, Wesley E. E356
Schultz, Yvette K. E33
Schulz, David S. A1117
Schulz, Ekkehard D. W270
Schulz, Fred W207
Schulz, Jurgen W129
Schulz, Mark A. A796
Schulz, Thomas W448
Schulze, Richard M. A155
Schulzendorf, Kerstin W303
Schum, Ellen M. E50
Schumacher, Alan H. A35
Schumacher, Hein W626
Schumacher, Laura J. A460
Schumacher, Patrick M. A776
Schumacher, Paul T. A450
Schumacher, Wolf W3
Schuman, Mark A. A60
Schuman, Susan A802
Schumann, Mariel von W544
Schumann, William H. A118
Schupp, Rudy E. A740
Schurr, Daniel William A235
Schurz, Todd F. A1
Schussel, Wolfgang W476
Schuster, Michael W229
Schutt, Aaron M. E352
Schutt, Daniel W. E507
Schutte, John L. A978
Schutte, John L. E465
Schutter, George A483
Schutter, George P243
Schuyler, Matthew W. A518
Schwab-Pomerantz, Carrie P487
Schwab, Charles R. A919
Schwab, Peter W639
Schwab, Susan C. A210
Schwab, Susan C. A660
Schwab, Susan C. A405
Schwabero, Mark D. A1
Schwakopf, Terry A136
Schwalb, Rolf-Dieter W53
Schwan, Severin W176
Schwan, Severin W502
Schwartz, Barry F. E227
Schwartz, Brad E. A401
Schwartz, Brad E. A1033
Schwartz, Brad E. E492
Schwartz, Christy A785
Schwartz, Elliot E34
Schwartz, Eric I. E278
Schwartz, Faith A. A881
Schwartz, Greg M. A1149
Schwartz, Greg M. E81
Schwartz, Harold E. A693
Schwartz, Harvey M. A203
Schwartz, James P166
Schwartz, Jeffery D. A673
Schwartz, Lawrence W. E227
Schwartz, Margie E517
Schwartz, Mel P681
Schwartz, Michael A. E348
Schwartz, Phillip S. E24
Schwartz, Raphe P120
Schwartz, Steven J. E79
Schwarz-Schütte, Patrick W390
schwarz, Christian Gunther W328
Schwarz, Jean-Francois W88
Schwarz, Peter W234
Schwarz, Ronald E. A617

Schwarz, Ronald E. E289
Schwarzenbauer, Peter W61
Schwarzer, Daniela W104
Schwarzman, Stephen A. A161
Schwarzwaelder, Steven B. A364
Schweitzer, Jeffrey M. A1078
Schweitzer, Jeffrey M. E513
Schweitzer, Louis W631
Schweitzer, Pascal A1099
Schweizer, Kaspar W91
Schwenger, Thomas D. E519
Schwertz, Rolf W62
Schwieterman, Dale E81
Schwieters, John T. A315
Schwimmer, Howard E419
Schwister, Rob A37
Schwister, Rob E14
Schwizer, Paola W177
Sciammas, Maurice E331
Scicluna, Martin W318
Sciuto, Joe P446
Scobie, Carolyn W487
Scocchia, Cristina W231
Scopellite, Steven M. A768
Scopellite, Steven M. E359
Scott, Andrew W654
Scott, Bertram L. A147
Scott, Bertram L. A647
Scott, Bertram L. A377
Scott, Cheryl E398
Scott, Cochran A. E489
Scott, Emily Allinder P68
Scott, Evan T. A643
Scott, James E. E280
Scott, James R. A426
Scott, James R. E202
Scott, Jonathan R. A426
Scott, Jonathan R. E202
Scott, Kevin W562
Scott, Kimberly A490
Scott, Leo H. A207
Scott, Lorrie D. E391
Scott, Nicholas N. A259
Scott, Nicholas N. E103
Scott, Peter M. E146
Scott, Raymond E. A622
Scott, Rob G. W644
Scott, Robert H. E46
Scott, Ryan E175
Scott, Sandra K. E221
Scott, Stuart A543
Scott, Tracy J. E63
Scovanner, Douglas A. A857
Scovill, J. Bradley E98
Scoville, Adam Lindquist E410
Scp, Katrina R Redmond A355
Scp, Katrina R Redmond P209
Screen, Chris W85
Screven, Edward A786
Scrivanich, Luke M. E523
Scroggs, Jennifer A844
Scroggs, Jennifer E394
Scruby, H. David E19
Scruggs, Frank P. A1042
Scudder, Michael L. A773
Sculley, Sheryl L. A694
Scully, Josep P. A138
Scully, Josep P. E55
Scully, Robert W. A1153
Scully, Robert W. W154

Scully, Thomas A. A926
Scurlock, Eva D. E298
Scurlock, J. Matthew A1008
Seabrook, Daniela W351
Seager, Richard B. A259
Seager, Richard B. E103
Seah, Peter Lim Huat W190
Seale, Margaret Leone W648
Seaman, Bradley S. A975
Seams, Christopher A. E362
Sear, Steven M. A323
Searby, Sean E19
Seard-mccormick, Ellicia A389
Seard-mccormick, Ellicia P219
Searle, Charles St. Leger W597
Sears, Christine A1042
Sears, Janice L. E280
Sears, Thea R. E136
Seaton, David T. A288
Seaton, David T. A715
Seaton, Elizabeth Whitehead A271
Seaton, Elizabeth Whitehead E109
Seaton, Mark Edward A413
Seaver, Derrick P176
Seaver, R. Arthur E454
Seavers, Dean L. A74
Seawell, A. Brooke A761
Sebastian, Teresa Mosley A23
Sebold, Edward A612
Sebra, James J. E268
Sebree, Jolyn J. E260
Sécheval, Helman le Pas de W631
Sechin, Igor W505
Second, Adolph M Orlando P604
Secor, Mark E. A532
Secor, Mark E. E259
Secor, Thomas N. E355
Secrest, Brent B. A374
Sederstrom, Nneka O P260
Sedgwick, David M. E164
Sedgwick, David M. E81
Sedgwick, Karen L. A929
Sedlak, Thomas E304
Sedlarcik, Frank A565
See-Yan, Lin W261
Seedorf, Herman L. A809
Seeger, Britta W395
Seeger, David W. A888
Seeger, Laureen E. A62
Seeger, Laureen E. E224
Seeger, William E262
Seeger, Zvezdana W510
Seegmiller, Dwight O. A515
Seelemann-Wandtke, Nicole W199
Seendripu, Kishore E314
Seetharam, Anil E5
Seewald, Russell E57
Sefzik, Peter L. A274
Segal, Alfredo Cutiel Ergas W70
Segal, Eric Andrew A788
Segal, Eric Andrew E366
Segal, Hugh D. W571
Segal, Julian W37
Segal, Michael S. E129
Segal, Ned D. A1047
Segal, Susan L. W84
Segalen, Loiek W601
Sege, Ronald A. E503
Segedi, Bryan A1120
Segedi, Bryan E535

COMBINED HOOVER'S HANDBOOK INDEX OF EXECUTIVES

A = AMERICAN BUSINESS
E = EMERGING COMPANIES
P = PRIVATE COMPANIES
W = WORLD BUSINESSS

Seger, Clint P81
Seger, Thomas W. A472
Seger, Thomas W. E230
Segers, Dennis E370
Segert, Robert E. E170
Segovia, Armando J. Garcia W131
Segovia, Elizabeth E92
Segundo, Karen de W207
Sehm, Silke W269
Seibel, Douglas Arthur A12
Seibel, Douglas Arthur E4
Seibel, Michael E145
Seibert, Gregg A. E173
Seibert, Steven M. A715
Seidenberg, Beth C. E398
Seidenberg, Martin W509
Seidenburg, J. Douglas A414
Seidenburg, J. Douglas E193
Seidler, Lee J. E190
Seidman-Becker, Caryn A526
Seidman, Christine E. A684
Seidman, Leslie F. A462
Seidman, Leslie F. A711
Seif, Margaret K. A81
Seifert, Caroline W162
Seifert, James J. E356
Seifert, Kathi P. A636
Seifert, Martin Frank E236
Seiffert, Ronald J. A753
Seifried, Edmond J. E301
Seifter, Lowell A. A724
Seiler, David R. A416
Seiler, Joseph C. E301
Seiler, Martina W277
Seishima, Takayuki W566
Seith, Douglas J. E43
Seitz, Kenneth A. W451
Sekhri, Paul J. E519
Seki, Hideaki W279
Seki, Hiroyuki W407
Seki, Jun W432
Seki, Mitsuyoshi W659
Seki, Miwa W185
Sekiguchi, Hiroyuki W608
Sekiguchi, Kenji W464
Sekiguchi, Ko W462
Sekiguchi, Nobuko W345
Sekiguchi, Takeshi W535
Sekine, Aiko W460
Sekine, Masahiro W539
Seko, Tomoaki W515
Seksay, Edward H. A554
Seksay, Edward H. E268
Selander, Robert W. E247
Seleznev, Kirill Gennadievich W256
Selig, Stefan M. E426
Seligman, Mark W425
Seligman, Mark W423
Seligman, Naomi O. A786
Seligman, Nicole A802
Seligman, Nicole W654
Seligman, Sandra A976
Seligsohn, Sherwin I. E511
Selleck, Erin A627

Sellers, Anne E. A681
Sellers, Anne E. E318
Sellers, Mary E. A129
Sellers, Thomas P251
Sellner, Georg W192
Seltz, Judi A615
Selvakesari, Anand A246
Selvaraj, Shelly R. E138
Selzer, Lawrence A. A1127
Seman, Julie A. A845
Seman, Julie A. E395
Semler, Herbert J. E436
Semlitsch, Jaan Ivar W204
Semple, Alan G. E72
Semple, Frank M. A657
Semple, Frank M. A717
Sen, Laura J. A187
Sen, Michael W251
Sen, Semih A1015
Sen, Semih P574
Sena, Peter P. A952
Senaha, Ayano W490
Senard, Jean-Dominique W165
Senard, Jean-Dominique W441
Senard, Jean-Dominique W492
Senda, Tetsuya W319
Senda, Tetsuya W319
Senda, Yoshiharu W357
Sender, Claudia Ramirez W593
Senectaire, Christian W515
Seng, Koh Beng W261
Senge, James Scott E153
Senger-Weiss, Elisabeth Krainer W229
Senger, Joseph A. A311
Senior, Bruce Mc Donald Md P93
Senior, Doctor Brent Powers P315
Senior, Greg G Maxwell A230
Senior, Greg G Maxwell P117
Senior, J Craig Baker P33
Senior, Jared W Heald P218
Senior, Jay Robaidek P664
Senior, Jill C Anderson P386
Senior, Robert Lovett P625
Senior, Timothy F Sullivan P426
Senior, William H Dunn P283
Senk, Glen T. E239
Senn, Hernan Somerville W220
Senner, Christopher J. E177
Sennesael, Kris A942
Sennett, Marjorie T. E105
Sensel, Robert D. E189
Sensing, J. Steven A909
Senthilkumar, Santhanakrishnan A132
Seo, Nam-Jong W335
Seong, Si-Heon W352
Seppi, Brandy A. E470
Sepulveda, Carlos M. A1040
Sepulveda, Carlos M. E499
Sepulveda, Eli A836
Sequeira, Ramona A361
Sera, Jean M. A116
Serafin, Zig A711
Serafini-Lamanna, Tony E321
Serck-Hanssen, Harald W204
Serdyukov, Valery Pavlovich W256
Serebryannikov, Sergey Vladimirovich W476
Sereda, Mikhail Leonidovich W474
Sereda, Mikhail Leonidovich W256
Sereinig, Johann W633

Sergel, Richard P. A973
Serhan, Samir J. A30
Serianni, Charles F. A892
Serio, Gregory V. A874
Serizawa, Yu W492
Serizay, Alexandra W550
Serna, Ed P565
Serna, Juan Manuel Gonzalez W295
Seroussi, Yair W78
Serow, Erika E292
Serra, Eileen M. A198
Serrado, Francisco Javier W80
Serrao, Darren C. A286
Servitje, Andres Obregon W265
Servitje, Luis Jorba W265
Servitje, Marina De Tavira W265
Servitje, Mauricio Jorba W265
Servitje, Nicolas Mariscal W265
Servitje, Raul Ignacio Obregon W265
Servranckx, Jean-Louis W213
Seseri, Rudina A651
Seshadri, Raj A876
Seshadri, Raj A670
Seshasayee, Ramaswami E404
Setas, Miguel Nuno Simoes Nunes Ferreira W212
Seth, Alpna E59
Seth, Basant W561
Sethavaravichit, Thidarat W79
Sethna, Meenal A. E303
Sethov, Inger W448
Setiadharma, Budi W464
Setnes, Magne W274
Seto, Jacqueline A. E504
Seto, Kinya W370
Seton, Michael A. E441
Settersten, Scott M. A1055
Settle, John H. A66
Settle, John H. E25
Setty, Challa Sreenivasulu W561
Setubal, Alfredo Egydio W315
Setubal, Roberto Egydio W315
Setzer, Nikolai W171
Seurkamp, Aaron A853
Severino, Jean-Michel W187
Severino, Jean-Michel W168
Severino, Jean-Michel W459
Severino, Michael E. A112
Sevillia, Olivier W123
Sewalls, Travis P478
Seward, Gregory W. A642
Seward, Gregory W. E304
Sewell, Collin P274
Sewell, David A400
Sewell, David B. A548
Sewell, David B. A1125
Sewell, Michael J. A240
Sewing, Christian W195
Sexton, Heidi J. E452
Sexton, John Patrick E87
Sexton, O. Griffith E244
Sexton, Robert F. A396
Sexton, Robert F. E186
Seybold, David J. E500
Seydoux, Henri W523
Seymour, David A56
Seyrek, N. Burak W619
Seze, Amaury de W125
Seze, Amaury de W480
Seze, Amaury de W565

Sezen, Yalcin W619
Sezgin, Muammer Cuneyt W618
Sferruzza, Hilla A687
Sgaglione, Lucille T. A149
Sgro, David D. E370
Sgro, Gianfranco W355
Sha, Zhenquan W533
Shackelton, Christopher S. E292
Shackleford, Robert Mitchell A32
Shackley, Brian E8
Shackouls, Bobby S. A832
Shackouls, Bobby S. A833
Shad, Harold William E222
Shadbolt, Nicola W245
Shadman, Mehri A1059
Shaeff, Julie S. E111
Shaevsky, Mark P691
Shafer, D. Brent A142
Shafer, David Brent A221
Shaffer, Charles M. A923
Shaffer, Charles M. A433
Shaffer, Dennis G. A251
Shaffer, Dennis G. E100
Shaffer, Oren G. A493
Shaffer, Rhonda E58
Shaffer, Robert A410
Shaffer, Stefan L. E117
Shaffer, Timothy H. A393
Shaffer, Timothy H. E184
Shafik, Baroness Nemat W543
Shagley, Richard J. A422
Shah, Aarti S. A635
Shah, Aarti S. A761
Shah, Jai A624
Shah, Jai A666
Shah, Jayendrakumar J. E492
Shah, Mahendra R. E492
Shah, Meena J. E492
Shah, Mihir A588
Shah, Minesh A148
Shah, Namita W613
Shah, Neal H. A830
Shah, Nikita E31
Shah, Niraj A1112
Shah, Sachin G. A60
Shah, Sachin G. W112
Shah, Taalib W90
Shah, Vivek E547
Shahar, Shai E214
Shahbaz, Shahzad A. W33
Shaheen, Gabriel L. A975
Shaheen, George T. A729
Shaheen, George T. E239
Shaikh, Mohammad E400
Shalett, Lisa M. A811
Shalett, Lisa M. E377
Shambaugh, Shawn C. E517
Shamburger, Julie N. A954
Shammo, Francis J. A1079
Shan, Helen E170
Shan, Shulan W34
Shan, Weijian W29
Shanafelt, Armen B. E475
Shanahan, James E212
Shanahan, Lauri M. E137
Shanahan, Patrick M. A625
Shands, H. J. A954
Shane, David N. A681
Shane, David N. E318
Shane, Steven R. A920

COMBINED HOOVER'S HANDBOOK INDEX OF EXECUTIVES

A = AMERICAN BUSINESS
E = EMERGING COMPANIES
P = PRIVATE COMPANIES
W = WORLD BUSINESSS

Shaner, William E166
Shang, Xiaofeng W664
Shang, Xiaoke W656
Shang, Xingwu W239
Shang, Yu W572
Shani, Shaul E420
Shank, Suzanne F. A900
Shank, Suzanne F. A294
Shank, Suzanne F. A256
Shankar, Krishnamurthy W304
Shankar, Ramakrishna A1056
Shankar, Ramakrishna E505
Shankar, Sailaja K. A173
Shankland, Martin W14
Shanklin, Ana Leonor Revenga W69
Shanks, Earl C. E227
Shanks, Eugene B. W154
Shanks, Scott P548
Shanks, Virginia E. A47
Shannahan, Andrew A513
Shannon, Margaret B. A868
Shannon, Michael J. E404
Shannon, Nancy A289
Shannon, Roger D. E291
Shao, Guanglu W151
Shao, Min W138
Shao, Mingtian W528
Shao, Mingxiao W372
Shao, Renciou W168
Shao, Ruiqing W292
Shao, Wence W100
Shao, Zhemin W529
Shao, Zili A1145
Shao, Zili W212
Shapard, Robert S. A625
Shaper, C. Park A605
Shapira, Adrianne A608
Shapiro, Edward L. A1062
Shapiro, Glenn T. A42
Shapiro, Mark A367
Shapiro, Mark L. A150
Shapiro, Paul E. A1032
Shapiro, Robert E368
Shapiro, Stephen W90
Shapiro, Stephen W89
Shapland, George T. A415
Shapland, George T. E194
Shara, Thomas J. A616
Shara, Thomas J. E289
Sharbutt, David E. A69
Share, Gregory M. E287
Sharett, Anthony M. A688
Sharett, Anthony M. E323
Sharieff, Ghazala P489
Sharkey, John F. E372
Sharma, Rajesh A86
Sharma, Ruby E344
Sharma, V. K. W588
Sharma, Vismay W358
Sharma, Vivek A583
Sharman, Sandy W119
Sharp, Christopher E141
Sharp, Douglas J. A573
Sharp, Elizabeth A. E25

Sharp, Evan E386
Sharp, Kenneth P. A349
Sharp, Michael J P451
Sharp, Michael J. A581
Sharp, Robert P. A493
Sharp, Robert P. E243
Sharp, Shalini A788
Sharp, Shalini E346
Sharpe, Anita A251
Sharpe, Anita P137
Sharpe, Maria Renna E299
Sharpe, Matthew P. A531
Sharpe, Robert F. A70
Sharples, Brian H. A43
Sharples, Brian H. E234
Sharps, Robert W. A991
Sharritts, Jeffery S. A244
Shasta, Theodore E. A671
Shasta, Theodore E. W154
Shatalov, Sergey W476
Shatkus, John A. A888
Shatsky, Pavel Olegovich W476
Shattock, Matthew J. A1091
Shattock, Matthew J. A254
Shattuck, Katherine W. E98
Shattuck, Mayo A. A198
Shattuck, Mayo A. A1018
Shaughnessy, Maura A23
Shavel, Lee M. E520
Shaver, David C. A1065
Shaver, David C. E509
Shaver, Matthew A. E515
Shaver, Tina M. A844
Shaver, Tina M. E394
Shaw, Alan H. A747
Shaw, Brian Gordon A792
Shaw, Christi A112
Shaw, Daniel L. A396
Shaw, Daniel L. E186
Shaw, Daren J. E164
Shaw, Harold H P334
Shaw, Jeffrey C. A367
Shaw, Jennifer A163
Shaw, Jennifer P87
Shaw, Ruth G. A343
Shaw, Ruth G. A345
Shaw, Scott M. E302
Shaw, Theresa A. A54
Shaw, Thomas J. E418
Shaw, Wayne E. W133
Shaw, William J. A203
Shay, Scott A. A936
Shay, Scott A. E440
Shea, Brian T. A70
Shea, Brian T. A408
Shea, E. Stewart A424
Shea, E. Stewart E200
Shea, Peter O. A407
Shea, William E. E1
Sheahan, Denis K. A191
Sheahan, Denis K. E77
Sheahan, Richard Casey E284
Shean, Christopher W. A872
Shean, Christopher W. A633
Shear, Neal A. A225
Shearer, Robert K. A237
Shearer, Robert M. A767
Sheares, Bradley T. A917
Shebik, Steven E. A261
Shedlin, Gary S. A160

Sheedy, Robert Joseph E242
Sheehan, Andrew T. E407
Sheehan, Anne A1094
Sheehan, James N. A534
Sheehan, Jeannine E271
Sheehy, Kim E477
Sheere, Jane W113
Sheets, Jeffrey E402
Sheets, Jeffrey Wayne A1124
Sheets, Jeffrey Wayne W523
Sheffield, Chaney M. A153
Sheffield, Holly R. E119
Sheffield, Scott D. A830
Sheffield, Scott D. A1131
Sheflett, George Cody A845
Sheflett, George Cody E395
Sheft, Robert E240
Sheidler, Jack W A472
Sheidler, Jack W E230
Sheikh, Sana P245
Sheinwald, Nigel A573
Sheinwald, Nigel W533
Shek, Abraham Lai Him W173
Shekhter, Elaina E170
Shekhterman, Igor W655
Sheldon, Michael J. E50
Sheldon, Todd N. A862
Shell, Jeffrey (Jeff) A272
Shellberg, Jeffrey D. A175
Shellberg, Jeffrey D. E66
Shelley, Stephen W371
Shelton, Kenneth A. E134
Shelton, Kirk M. A754
Shen, Baowei W98
Shen, Bingxi W301
Shen, Bo W530
Shen, Changchun W37
Shen, Dou W67
Shen, Eric Ya W636
Shen, Jianlin W662
Shen, Jinjun W140
Shen, Jinjun W663
Shen, Jyunde W168
Shen, Norman Jen-Lin E370
Shen, Si W301
Shen, Weitao W656
Shen, Wunjhong W168
Shen, Xianfeng W98
Shen, Xiaosu W512
Shen, Xiong W603
Shen, Yaohua W656
Shen, Yifeng W656
Sheng, Ruisheng W472
Shepard, Darren A. A59
Shepherd, J. Michael A402
Shepherd, Jeffrey (Jeff) W. A17
Shepherd, Joel R. A66
Shepherd, Joel R. E25
Sheppard, Jack C. E371
Sheppeck, Bryan E77
Sherbet, Eric M. A576
Sherbin, David M. W46
Sherburne, Jane C. A539
Sherburne, Jane C. E483
Sheresky, Michael James E480
Sheridan, Edwin A. E38
Sheridan, Robert G. A196
Sheridan, Robert G. E78
Sheridan, Robert K. A519
Sheridan, Robert K. E256

Sheriff, Karen W99
Sherman, A. Haag A516
Sherman, Darrell C. A998
Sherman, Floyd F. E381
Sherman, Jennifer L. E188
Sherman, Jolene E295
Sherman, Jonathon A. E43
Sherman, Merrill W. A181
Sherman, Patrick A. A427
Sherman, Patrick A. E203
Sherman, Scott A400
Sherr, Richard A1030
Sherrill, Gregg M. A42
Sherrill, Stephen C. E50
Sherry, Ann W419
Sherwin, Stephen A. A158
Sherwin, Stephen A. E346
Shetzline, Michael E282
Shewmake, Donna G. E526
Shi, Christiana Smith A1069
Shi, Christiana Smith A710
Shi, Dai W236
Shi, Dan W146
Shi, Fang W307
Shi, Hong W106
Shi, Hongyu W431
Shi, Jianzhong W179
Shi, Jun W326
Shi, Lan W141
Shi, Lei W136
Shi, Parker L. A351
Shi, Parker L. E150
Shi, Shouming W139
Shi, Yifeng W662
Shi, Zhengfeng W529
Shiba, Yojiro W434
Shiba, Yojiro W110
Shiba, Yoshitaka W407
Shibagaki, Takahiro W182
Shibasaki, Hiroko W389
Shibasaki, Kenichi W659
Shibata, Hisashi W539
Shibata, Koichiro W345
Shibata, Misuzu W555
Shibata, Mitsuyoshi W313
Shibata, Satoru W433
Shiel, James G. A149
Shields, Maria T. E32
Shiely, John S. A790
Shiff, Susan E80
Shiffman, Gary A. E471
Shifman, Frances B. A922
Shigeji, Yoshinobu W582
Shigemori, Takashi W565
Shigemura, Dean Y. A129
Shigenaga, Dean A. E15
Shigeno, Tomihei W663
Shigeta, Tetsuya W408
Shigitani, Ayumi W608
Shih, Clara A964
Shih, Lee Chien W261
Shih, Stan W584
Shih, Stan W650
Shih, Stone W650
Shih, Tsan-Ming W252
Shih, Willy C. W242
Shiina, Hideki W223
Shileny, Lisa A. A515
Shilling, Randy L. A747
Shilling, Steven R. A259

COMBINED HOOVER'S HANDBOOK INDEX OF EXECUTIVES

A = AMERICAN BUSINESS
E = EMERGING COMPANIES
P = PRIVATE COMPANIES
W = WORLD BUSINESSS

Shilling, Steven R. E103
Shillingburg, Stephanie E E181
Shim, Sam Sang-Koo E323
Shimada, Akira W439
Shimada, Koichi W28
Shimada, Taro W612
Shimamoto, Kazuaki W449
Shimamoto, Yasuji W331
Shimamura, Hidehiko W334
Shimamura, Takuya W18
Shimao, Tadashi W155
Shimazaki, Noriaki W445
Shimazu, Hisatomo W410
Shimba, Jun W550
Shimer, Julie A. E312
Shimizu, Hiroshi W436
Shimizu, Keita W464
Shimizu, Motoaki W535
Shimokawa, Hiroyoshi W334
Shimonishi, Keisuke W185
Shimonomura, Hiroaki W454
Shin, Jong-Gyun W513
Shin, Seiichi W25
Shin, Steve A78
Shin, Yong Sin E362
Shinbo, Katsuyoshi W570
Shinder, Marcella A205
Shindo, Fumio W455
Shindo, Kosei W437
Shindo, Nakaba W659
Shindo, Satoshi W449
Shindo, Tetsuhiko W313
Shing, Yvonne Mo Han W148
Shingai, Yasushi W182
Shingai, Yasushi W407
Shinkawa, Asa W607
Shinkawa, Asa W433
Shinn, Mee Nam W367
Shinobe, Osamu W333
Shinohara, Hidenori W568
Shinohara, Naoyuki W403
Shinohara, Yukihiro W193
Shinoyama, Yoichi W270
Shinozaki, Tadayoshi W137
Shintaku, Masaaki W237
Shintaku, Yutaro W354
Shiono, Noriko W343
Shiota, Ko W433
Shipley, Caroline C. A196
Shipley, Caroline C. E78
Shipley, Kenneth E. E296
Shipp, Earl W422
Shipp, Earl L. A776
Shirai, Toshiyuki W417
Shirai, Yusuke W413
Shiraishi, Isao W534
Shirakawa, Hiroshi W181
Shiraki, Yukiyasu W329
Shiratori, Kazuo W293
Shirayama, Masaki W567
Shirey, Terry A. A1151
Shirley, Donald R. A799
Shirley, Edward D. A989
Shirley, Natalie A125

Shirley, Natalie E52
Shirley, Soderman P446
Shitara, Motofumi W658
Shitgasornpongse, Supot W117
Shito, Atsushi W1
Shiu, Ian Sai Cheung W128
Shivananda, Sripada A807
Shive, Dunia A. A604
Shivers, Edward T. A860
Shlomi, Irit W79
Shmatko, Sergey Ivanovich W476
Shmerling, Michael D. A889
Shmerling, Michael D. E414
Shnayder, Boris E170
Shobuda, Kiyotaka W388
Shoda, Takashi W184
Shoemaker, Anthony A600
Shoemaker, Scott E271
Shoji, Hiroshi W181
Shoji, Kuniko W392
Shoji, Tetsuya W321
Shon, Larry D. De A502
Shook, Kevin M. A848
Shoptaw, Robert L. A938
Shoptaw, Robert L. E442
Shoquist, Debora A761
Short, Andrea G. A1
Short, Johnathan H. A561
Short, Michael John (Mike) A900
Short, Mike E57
Short, Robert D. E527
Shortt, James W. E372
Shotoku, Ayako W465
Shott, Nicholas W471
Shotts, Philip G. A269
Shotwell, David F. A1057
Shotwell, Gwynne E. A835
Shou, Donghua W145
Shoukry, Paul A876
Shouraboura, Nadia W655
Shouvlin, Patrick J. A176
Shoven, John B. E75
Shrader, Ralph W. A171
Shreiner, Kurt A. A106
Shrewsberry, John R. A1115
Shrewsbury, Ronda Weybrigth A1
Shribman, Daniel E50
Shriram, Kavitark Ram A45
Shrishrimal, Sumi E138
Shroff, Mohak A357
Shropshire, Kenneth L. E330
Shropshire, Tom W201
Shroyer, Christopher M. A415
Shroyer, Christopher M. E194
Shu, Ungyong W182
Shu, Ungyong W553
Shu, Yinbiao W291
Shuda, Scott A. E271
Shudo, Kuniyuki W570
Shueh, Stephen E53
Shuenyane, Khumo L W311
Shufeldt, R. Charles A106
Shuler, James E517
Shulkin, Boris W379
Shulman, Becky S. A688
Shulman, Becky S. E323
Shulman, Douglas H. A781
Shulman, Jonathan I A152
Shults, Kristen S. E536
Shumate, Alex A947

Shumate, Alex E134
Shumway, Jeffery A558
Shuster, Bradley M. A650
Shuster, Bradley M. E350
Shuster, Bradley M. E305
Shuster, Richard A1015
Shuster, Richard P571
Shute, Todd W287
Shuto, Kazuhiko W610
Shuttleworth, Julie W246
Shvarts, Evgeny W410
Shvets, Nikolay Nikolayevich W476
Shvetsov, Sergei W521
Shy, Jiaw-Hwang W206
Si, Wei W663
Sia, Joyce Ming Kuang W628
Siatis, Perry C. A8
Sibanda, Lindiwe Majele W430
Sibbern, Bjorn A721
Sibblies, Beverley A. A330
Sibeko, Thulani W559
Sibenac, Lisa A231
Sibiya, Philisiwe G. W311
Sibley, Tarrant L. A503
Sicchitano, Kenton J. A81
Siciliano, F. Daniel A398
Sickler, John N. E512
Sickmeyer, Tyler E304
Sicupira, Cecilia W40
Siddiqui, Fahim A526
Siddiqui, Masroor Taale A738
Siddiqui, Omer P192
Sidhu, Jay S. A307
Sidhu, Jay S. E132
Sidhu, Samvir S. A307
Sidhu, Samvir S. E133
Sidwell, David H. W154
Siebert, John M. E475
Siebert, Kevin Christopher E523
Siedel, Richard W. E270
Siegel, David A652
Siegel, David N. E471
Siegel, Kenneth I. A645
Siegel, Kenneth I. A258
Siegel, Laurie A. A650
Siegel, Matthew E452
Siegel, Susan E. E16
Siegel, Todd E. E473
Siegel, Walter A917
Siegert, Nancy L P360
Siegmund, Jan A267
Siekerka, Michele N. A248
Siekerka, Michele N. A575
Sielak, George P43
Siemens, Nathalie von W545
Siemens, Nathalie von W231
Siemens, Nathalie von W543
Siemers, William R. E17
Sierau, Ullrich W510
Sierotko, Walter A854
Sierra, Antonio Lorenzo W493
Sierra, Jose Arnau W300
Sierra, Luis M. A975
Sievers, Dirk W602
Sievert, Christian W277
Sievert, G. Michael A992
Sievewright, Sandra L. A143
Sievewright, Sandra L. E56
Sieving, Charles E. A436
Sieving, Charles E. A739

Siewart, Patrick T. A114
Siewert, Patrick T. A710
Sigal, Charles Elliott E475
Sight, James W. E242
Sigi, Thomas W61
Sigismondi, Laurent W203
Sigmund, Michael W543
Signore, Gianni Del E370
Signorello, Christopher J. A1143
Sijbesma, Feike W626
Sijbesma, Feike W351
Sijbrand, Jan W21
Sikka, Vishal A786
Sikka, Vishal W96
Sikka, Vishal W258
Sikorski, Fred J. E306
Sikorski, Ralf W510
Silagy, Eric E. A740
Silagy, Eric E. A436
Silberman, Robert S. E467
Silbermann, Benjamin E386
Silcock, Christopher W. A518
Silfen, Jane E382
Silguy, Yves-Thibault de W373
Silguy, Yves-Thibault de W554
Silguy, Yves-Thibault de W329
Silguy, Yves-Thibault de W635
Silha, Roman W398
Silitch, Nicholas C. A856
Sill, Garrett S. E434
Silliman, Craig L. A1088
Silva, Diane J. A372
Silva, Diane J. E167
Silva, Dorothea D. E90
Silva, Enrique A879
Silva, Enrique (Rick) A878
Silva, Filipe W254
Silva, Francisco de Assis e W323
Silva, Janet De W308
Silva, Joao Carlos Gomes da W69
Silva, Kevin A. A1098
Silva, Luis Maria Viana Palha da W212
Silva, Marcelo Gasparino da W630
Silva, Miguel Eduardo Padilla W244
Silva, Nelson W170
Silva, Nelson L. C. W451
Silva, Paul M. A1089
Silva, Paulo Cesar de Souza e W468
Silva, Rodrigo Costa Lima e W468
Silvent, Karima W65
Silver, Caroline A561
Silver, Caroline W374
Silver, Jonathan W422
Silverman, Alan H. E190
Silverman, Daniel C P504
Silverman, David A79
Silverman, David S. E506
Silverman, Deven P394
Silverman, Frank B. A1043
Silverman, Joshua (Josh) E175
Silverman, Louis E. E460
Silvernail, Andrew K. A981
Silverton, Michael J. W377
Sim, Brandon E33
Sim, Edward (Eddie) H. A1076
Sim, Judith E216
Sim, Kenneth E33
Simard, Curtis C. A138
Simard, Curtis C. E55
Simard, Regis W258

COMBINED HOOVER'S HANDBOOK INDEX OF EXECUTIVES

A = AMERICAN BUSINESS
E = EMERGING COMPANIES
P = PRIVATE COMPANIES
W = WORLD BUSINESSS

Simasathien, Panas W540
Simeone, Jill E175
Simhandl, Martin W633
Siminoff, Ellen F. E480
Simkowitz, Daniel A. A713
Simm, Daryl A778
Simmonds, Andy W618
Simmonds, David B. W262
Simmonds, Ian A941
Simmonds, Robert C. W99
Simmonds, Sidney G. E227
Simmons, Gary K. A1085
Simmons, Harris H. A1151
Simmons, Linda H. A500
Simmons, Linda H. E246
Simmons, Peggy I. A167
Simmons, Peggy I. E64
Simmons, Sabrina L. A1132
Simmons, Timothy W. E433
Simms, Erin P529
Simms, James A. E525
Simola, Jozsef Farkas W412
Simon, Dorothea W543
Simon, Henry W466
Simon, Isabelle W600
Simon, John F. A67
Simon, John R. A823
Simon, Joseph W. E330
Simon, Lynn T. A282
Simon, Mindy F. W44
Simon, Ronald I. E155
Simon, Stefan W195
Simon, William S. A316
Simon, William S. A497
Simonds, Michael Q. A1079
Simone, Nicolas W468
Simoneau, Brianne L. A1144
Simonelli, Charlotte C. A878
Simonelli, Charlotte C. A879
Simonelli, Lorenzo A120
Simonelli, Lorenzo A121
Simoni, Renzo W581
Simonich, Brent B. A648
Simons, Doyle R. A434
Simons, James R. E407
Simons, Jennifer L. A415
Simons, Jennifer L. E194
Simonson, Richard A. A363
Simonyan, Rair Rairovich W617
Simor, Andras W229
Simpson-Taylor, Kathleen A5
Simpson, John C. A880
Simpson, John C. E412
Simpson, John William W179
Simpson, Mandy W36
Simpson, Peter W364
Simpson, Peter W364
Simpson, Shelley A543
Simril, Kenneth M. A185
Sims, Beth W. A395
Sims, Beth W. E185
Sims, Frank L. E453
Sims, Gary L. A704
Sims, Gary L. E328

Sims, Randy D. A221
Sims, Savalle C. A332
Sims, Todd D. E50
Simsek, Sahismail W619
Simuro, Frank A. E123
Sinai, Todd M. E411
Sinapi-Thomas, Lucia W123
Sinclair, Christopher A. W490
Sinclair, Jack L. A959
Sinclair, Michael J. A519
Sinclair, Michael J. E256
Sinclair, Stuart William W371
Sindel, Mehmet W26
Sinden, Janice A652
Sindhvananda, Kamthon W540
Sing, George L. A882
Singer, Aaron K. E98
Singer, David V. A182
Singer, David V. A818
Singer, Frederick W308
Singer, Gerhard W458
Singer, Harry A251
Singer, Harry E100
Singer, Maria R. A1076
Singer, Robert S. A600
Singer, Roger M. W233
Singh-Bushell, Ekta E500
Singh, Akshay W495
Singh, Bijay W203
Singh, Gagan P336
Singh, Harmit J. A631
Singh, Inder W487
Singh, Jesse G. E49
Singh, Manjit W572
Singh, Manoj P. A349
Singh, Mohit A227
Singh, Prahlad R. A80
Singh, Prahlad R. E380
Singh, Rajinder P. A135
Singh, Rakesh W271
Singh, Ranjit W21
Singh, Robin E57
Singh, S. Steven A1107
Singh, Shiv A1071
Singh, Sumeet A823
Singh, Sumit A231
Singisetti, Ravi Kumar A267
Singletary, Richard L. E489
Singleton, Denise R. A826
Singleton, Dennis E. E141
Singleton, Jake E285
Singleton, James L. A1117
Singleton, John Knox E247
Singleton, Philip Austin E361
Singleton, Sean A1107
Sinha, Chandan W561
Sink, Brandon J. A647
Siong, Neo Boon W261
Sipes, Kevin D. A890
Sipes, Kevin D. E416
Sipf, Eric D. E206
Siplin, Victoria P P174
Siragusa, Stefano W592
Siraj, Faisal W495
Sirhal, Mara A148
Sirichatchai, Somkiat W334
Sirisamphand, Thosaporn W541
Sirisumphand, Thosaporn W484
Sirman, Lori A788
Sirman, Lori E364

Sirodom, Kulpatra W541
Sirota, Marc A45
Sirpilla, John A. E293
Sirucic, Enver W93
Sisco, Cynthia A596
Sisco, Cynthia E286
Sishuba-Bonoyi, P. T. W414
Sisitsky, Todd B. A576
Sistine, Peter J. Van A125
Sistine, Peter J. Van E52
Sisto, Carlo Alberto W157
Sit, Roger J. A545
Sita, Veresh A116
Sitherwood, Suzanne A37
Sithi-Amnuai, Piti W77
Sitman, Robert E62
Sitorus, Martua W649
Sitterman, Gidon W410
Siu, Francis Wai Keung W156
Siu, Hera K. A483
Siu, Wing A143
Siu, Wing E57
Sivanesan, Janaki E173
Sivaram, Srinivasan (Siva) A1122
Siver, Darrin C. A796
Sivignon, Pierre-Jean W125
Sivils, James L. E243
Sixt, Frank J. W133
Sjoqvist, Nikolaj H. A1110
Sjostedt, Eva-Lotta W398
Skaaret, Heidi W562
Skaggs, Robert C. A343
Skaggs, Robert C. A345
Skaggs, Stephen A. E266
Skains, Thomas E. A347
Skains, Thomas E. A1042
Skala, P. Justin A1146
Skarie, David P. A838
Skarjune, Dolores L. A478
Skaugen, Grace Reksten E388
Skeans, Tracy L. A1146
Skeie, Svein W227
Skelly, Jonathan E49
Skelly, Noreen E. E117
Skerritt, Susan E. A280
Skerritt, Susan E. E113
Skiadas, Anthony T. A1088
Skidmore, Constance E. E111
Skidmore, David K. A982
Skidmore, Douglas S. A240
Skidmore, William J. E326
Skillings, Colleen R. E356
Skillman, Rebecca S. A772
Skinner, Deborah E. A392
Skinner, Deborah E. E183
Skinner, Frances A. A815
Skinner, James A. A1102
Skinner, James E. A95
Skinner, Jann W487
Skinner, Todd C. E493
Skipworth, Michael J. E539
Skirnick, Gabriella N. E234
Skjaervik, Rita W594
Skjerven, Wendy C. A1037
Sklar, Joel A130
Skoff, Herbert W453
Skoglund, Ake W579
Skoglund, William B. A774
Skoglund, William B. E360
Skogman, Kyle D. A1065

Skolds, John L. A740
Skonnard, Aaron B. A1151
Skorobogatova, Olga W521
Skory, John E P575
Skotdal, Andrew P. E103
Skou, Soren W443
Skou, Soren W1
Skouen, Petter W347
Skoufalos, Ioannis E260
Skovronsky, Daniel M. A635
Skudutis, Tommy J. W379
Skule, Jeremy A721
Skurbe, Barton E260
Skuthan, Frank J. E364
Skvortsova, Elena W458
Skyba, Karl W633
Skyler, Jay S. E138
Slack, David A226
Slack, David A225
Slade, Rachel W419
Sladek, Maureen A620
Slader, Lindsay A. E336
Slager, Donald W. A663
Slamon, Dennis J. E61
Slane, Kevin A913
Slane, Kevin E427
Slape, Nick W159
Slark, Martin P. A749
Slate, MaryEmily A759
Slater, Austin J. E113
Slater, Catherine I. A764
Slater, Jennifer E517
Slater, Richard W626
Slater, Rodney E. A1088
Slater, Todd A. A776
Slatoff, Karl E480
Slattery, Geraldine W101
Slattery, John A462
Slaven, John A37
Sledd, Robert C. A793
Sledd, Robert C. E389
Sleeper, Nathan K. A145
Sleeth, Shaun P336
Slemmer, Carol L. E189
Slessor, Michael D. E214
Slevinski, Danette L P644
Sleyster, Scott G. A856
Slicer, Mark E362
Slifer, Rodney E. E19
Slifka, Eric S. A475
Slifka, Richard A475
Slim, Vanessa Hajj W35
Sliney, David D. A977
Sliney, David D. E464
Sloan, Jeffrey S. A477
Sloan, Nicolette A130
Sloan, O. Temple A414
Sloan, O. Temple E191
Sloan, Thomas G. A415
Sloan, Thomas G. E194
Sloan, Wayne R. E291
Sloane, Barry E348
Sloat, Julia A. A59
Slocum, Michael S. A198
Slone, Reuben E. A17
Slonski, Joel H. E111
Slosar, John Robert W287
Slosar, John Robert W128
Slotkin, Judy A941
Slotnik, Joseph J. A181

COMBINED HOOVER'S HANDBOOK INDEX OF EXECUTIVES

```
A = AMERICAN BUSINESS
E = EMERGING COMPANIES
P = PRIVATE COMPANIES
W = WORLD BUSINESSS
```

Sloves, Andrew E347
Sloves, Evan A244
Slusher, John F. A743
Slusky, Alexander R. E77
Slutzky, Paul E240
Sluyter, Kent A856
Smach, Thomas J. E130
Smaczny, Tomasz W128
Smaghi, Lorenzo Bini W548
Smail, David W. A16
Small, Albert H. A1063
Small, Albert H. E508
Small, Gary M. A844
Small, Gary M. E394
Small, Ian S. E305
Small, Martin J. A160
Small, Michael J. A773
Small, Penelope Chalmers W565
Smalley, Gary G. A1046
Smalley, Robert W. E149
Smart, Jill B. A1136
Smart, Jill B. E170
Smeaton, Paul W574
Smedegaard, Elly W632
Smedegaard, Niels W205
Smernoff, Christopher E155
Smestad, Jennifer O. E367
Smet, Bart De W18
Smet, John P586
Smiddy, Craig R. A773
Smiles, Peter W487
Smiley, Carl W562
Smiley, Terry A32
Smirl, Richard W. E528
Smit, Ben W558
Smit, Kornelis (Neil) A867
Smith-Gander, Diane L. W644
Smith, Abbie J. A909
Smith, Alan A296
Smith, Alma Wheeler E512
Smith, Alvin L. E111
Smith, Amy M. A258
Smith, Andrea B. A505
Smith, Ania E539
Smith, Arthur L. E128
Smith, Barbara M. A922
Smith, Barbara R. A277
Smith, Barbara R. A274
Smith, Barry M. E164
Smith, Barry M. E376
Smith, Bob L. E237
Smith, Bradford L. A701
Smith, Bradford L. A730
Smith, Bradley Scott (Brad) E374
Smith, Brandon B. A235
Smith, Brandon B. A1004
Smith, Brian A168
Smith, Brian P89
Smith, Brian W161
Smith, Brian J. A618
Smith, Brian J. E290
Smith, Bryan E. A721
Smith, Bryan Scott A948
Smith, Carey A. A951

Smith, Carey A. A359
Smith, Carla J. W308
Smith, Catherine R. A840
Smith, Cathy R. A142
Smith, Christopher A678
Smith, Christopher E261
Smith, Christopher P337
Smith, Christopher W623
Smith, Christopher M. E406
Smith, Clifford T. A252
Smith, Clinton P670
Smith, Craig S. A660
Smith, Craige L. A1063
Smith, Craige L. E508
Smith, Dan F. E307
Smith, Daniel E. E19
Smith, Daniel T. A795
Smith, Dannette L. A1075
Smith, David A P375
Smith, David A. E490
Smith, David B. A553
Smith, David B. A749
Smith, David Bruton A948
Smith, David C P672
Smith, David D. A939
Smith, Dennis P. A401
Smith, Donald R. A719
Smith, Donald R. E185
Smith, Douglas E. E171
Smith, Douglas I. A528
Smith, Dwight E. A815
Smith, Dwight E. A966
Smith, E. Follin A909
Smith, Edgar R. E199
Smith, Edward Royal E169
Smith, Elizabeth A. A518
Smith, Ellen M. A710
Smith, Emily C. E161
Smith, Eric W487
Smith, Franz P520
Smith, Fred Julius E117
Smith, Frederick G. A939
Smith, Frederick W. A404
Smith, G. Stacy A556
Smith, G. Stacy E270
Smith, George R. E247
Smith, Gerald B. A783
Smith, Gerald B. W209
Smith, Geraud E517
Smith, Gerry W362
Smith, Gerry P. A97
Smith, Gerry P. A770
Smith, Glyn Michael W159
Smith, Gordon A. A591
Smith, Greg C. A813
Smith, Gregory A A857
Smith, Gregory C. A622
Smith, Gregory D. A560
Smith, Gregory D. A55
Smith, Gregory L. A719
Smith, Gregory M. A810
Smith, Gregory M. E376
Smith, Gregory S. E485
Smith, Gregory S. W15
Smith, Gunner A795
Smith, Hatton C. V. A932
Smith, Hatton C. V. E436
Smith, Hillary B. E407
Smith, Howard W. E531
Smith, Ian W157

Smith, Ian G. E81
Smith, J. David E234
Smith, J. Duncan A939
Smith, J. Eric W580
Smith, Jack E517
Smith, James C. A821
Smith, Jeffrey C. A703
Smith, Jeffrey C. E327
Smith, Jeffrey P. A1135
Smith, Jeffrey V P176
Smith, Jeffrey W. A1006
Smith, Jennifer A. A1151
Smith, Jennifer Carr W651
Smith, Jennifer LD E58
Smith, Jill D. E39
Smith, Jill D. E408
Smith, Joanne D. A323
Smith, John F. A57
Smith, Juletta M. A311
Smith, Julie Anne E178
Smith, Kara Gaughen A519
Smith, Kara Gaughen E256
Smith, Karen L. E32
Smith, Kathleen C. A747
Smith, Kenneth E. A138
Smith, Kenneth E. E55
Smith, Kenneth W. A392
Smith, Kenneth W. E183
Smith, Kenneth Wm. A188
Smith, Kenneth Wm. E69
Smith, Kevin W504
Smith, Kevin Gene A258
Smith, Kirin M. E127
Smith, Kris W573
Smith, Lee Matthew A435
Smith, Lee Matthew E210
Smith, Marcus G. A948
Smith, Marcus L. E336
Smith, Mark W561
Smith, Mark A. A306
Smith, Mark L. E206
Smith, Matthew K. A427
Smith, Matthew K. E204
Smith, Michael A. A1148
Smith, Michael C. A1055
Smith, Michael L. A425
Smith, Michael L. E201
Smith, Michael R. A860
Smith, Michael R. A673
Smith, Michael T. E483
Smith, Murray D. A1131
Smith, Nancy A. A638
Smith, Oliver Pierce A741
Smith, Oliver Pierce E349
Smith, Patti Gates E156
Smith, Paul A931
Smith, Peter F. A259
Smith, Peter F. E103
Smith, Philip Andrew A979
Smith, Philip R. E537
Smith, Philip W. A810
Smith, Philip W. E376
Smith, Phillip R. A218
Smith, Preston L. A954
Smith, R. Sharon A52
Smith, Ramsey D. A470
Smith, Rebecca S. A574
Smith, Reese L. A829
Smith, Reese L. E385
Smith, Richard A. A781

Smith, Richard D. E18
Smith, Richard P. A1038
Smith, Richard P. E495
Smith, Richard W. A405
Smith, Richard W. E420
Smith, Robert E350
Smith, Robert E. A940
Smith, Robert E. A460
Smith, Rodney M. A69
Smith, Ronald G. A885
Smith, Ross S. W287
Smith, Ryan R. E293
Smith, Salaam Coleman A1019
Smith, Salaam Coleman E386
Smith, Sally J. A534
Smith, Sally J. A37
Smith, Sally J. E14
Smith, Sally J. E140
Smith, Sandy A. E287
Smith, Scott A927
Smith, Scott E435
Smith, Scott Andrew A1093
Smith, Scott K. A554
Smith, Scott K. E268
Smith, Serene M. E410
Smith, Shannon Lee A67
Smith, Sherrese M. E72
Smith, Sherry M. A320
Smith, Sherry M. A878
Smith, Sherry M. A879
Smith, Sherry M. E387
Smith, Stacy J. E45
Smith, Stephen B. A200
Smith, Stephen B. E80
Smith, Stephen Joseph A1086
Smith, Steven E299
Smith, Stuart G. E192
Smith, Tracey A. E321
Smith, Valerie A. A858
Smith, W. Brett E514
Smith, Wayne T. A282
Smith, Wayne T. A30
Smith, William A. A888
Smith, William A. A605
Smith, William G. A196
Smith, William G. A952
Smith, William G. E79
Smith, William L. A823
Smith, Zeke W. A32
Smitherman, Barry T. A218
Smithers, Paul E. E271
Smithson, Michael F. A1046
Smithwick, Michael P487
Smits-Nusteling, Carla W443
Smits, Hans N.J. W344
Smits, Steven J. A641
Smits, Steven J. E304
Smittcamp, William S. E90
Smoke, Tony A32
Smolik, Brent J. A656
Smucker, Mark T. A604
Smucker, Mark T. A947
Smucker, Richard K. A947
Smucker, Timothy P. A947
Smul, Spencer G. A620
Smyth, Margaret M. E175
Smyth, Margaret Mary A453
Smyth, Maureen A717
Snabe, Jim Hagemann W1
Snabe, Jim Hagemann W33

HOOVER'S HANDBOOK OF EMERGING COMPANIES 2023
699

COMBINED HOOVER'S HANDBOOK INDEX OF EXECUTIVES

A = AMERICAN BUSINESS
E = EMERGING COMPANIES
P = PRIVATE COMPANIES
W = WORLD BUSINESSS

Snabe, Jim Hagemann W543
Snapp, David H. E291
Snapper, Suzanne D. E164
Snead, Thomas G. A107
Snead, Thomas G. E40
Snedker, Steen W330
Snee, James P. A534
Snee, James P. A892
Sneed, Michael E. A1112
Sneed, Paula A. A919
Snell, Richard S. A374
Snider, Michael E299
Snider, Steven E81
Sniezek, Roger W162
Snipe, Alexander E195
Snively, Joshua A. A955
Snively, Joshua A. E456
Snodgrass, Tedd P90
Snodgres, Jon K. E415
Snoke, Glenn W. A788
Snoke, Glenn W. E366
Snow, John W. E35
Snow, Michael E347
Snowden, Mark D E340
Snowden, Raymond Ward A472
Snowden, Raymond Ward E230
Snowe, Olympia J. A991
Snyder, Angela M. A454
Snyder, Barbara R. A851
Snyder, Barbara R. A602
Snyder, Donald D. A1120
Snyder, Donald D. E535
Snyder, Donald D. E477
Snyder, Lila J. A862
Snyder, Mark E244
Snyder, Nicholas John E175
Snyder, Ryan E315
Snyder, Scott A. A454
Snyder, Thomas G A250
Snyder, Thomas G P135
So, Jack Chak-Kwong W19
So, Jack Chak-Kwong W128
Soaries, DeForest Blake A396
Soaries, DeForest Blake E187
Soaries, DeForest Blake E268
Sobel, Brian M. A130
Sobel, Jonathan S. A516
Sobers, Patrick G. A722
Sobers, Patrick G. E339
Sobeske, Jim E455
Sobey, Frank C. W216
Sobey, John R. W216
Sobey, Karl R. W216
Sobey, Paul D. W216
Sobey, Robert G. C. W216
Sobrinho, Jose Batista W323
Sobrinho, Omar Carneiro da Cunha W468
Sobti, Sanjiv A135
Soderberg, Carl J. A192
Soderbery, Robert W. A1122
Soderstrom, Johanna W427
Soebhektie, Agoest W483
Soga, Takaya W440

Soh, Kian Tiong W190
Soh, Simon E199
Soh, Vincent W463
Sohi, Mohsen M. A121
Sohi, Mohsen M. A120
Sohn, Sung Won A1120
Sohn, Sung Won E535
Sohn, Tae-Seung W652
Sohn, Young K. E75
Soiland, Marlene K. A381
Soirat, Arnaud W500
Soirat, Arnaud W499
Soistman, Francis S. E154
Sokmen, Virma W661
Sokolich, Mark A287
Sokolich, Mark E115
Sola, Jure A914
Sola, Lester P355
Sola, Mario Rotllant W161
Solash, Todd A296
Solaun, Xabier Viteri W295
Sole, Jordi Gual W229
Solender, Elizabeth A788
Solender, Elizabeth E364
Soler, Jaime W132
Solhaug, Eli W204
Soliday, Lance A. A385
Solis, Marissa E116
Solis, Oscar Von Hauske W35
Solls, Mark A. E280
Solomin, Vyacheslav W410
Solomon, Darlene J. S. E355
Solomon, Darren C. W574
Solomon, David M. A480
Solomon, Glenn A785
Solomon, Jeffrey M. E125
Solomon, Joanne E523
Solomon, Lawrence F. E170
Solomon, Lee J. A16
Solomon, Lesley P188
Solomon, Liliana W398
Solomon, Stuart B. W335
Solomont, Alan D. A112
Soltau, Jill A. A956
Soltau, Jill A. A111
Soltesz, James A A350
Soltesz, James A E148
Solvay, Jean-Marie W554
Somasundaram, Sivasankaran E91
Sombutsiri, Sirichai W541
Somerhalder, John W. A432
Somerset, Gary P449
Sommella, Vincent E3
Sommer, Oliver H. E175
Sommerfeld, Jim P581
Sommo, Christine A400
Son, Masayoshi W550
Sondhi, Samrat E180
Sonenshine, Jacob A423
Sonenshine, Jacob E199
Song, Bo W189
Song, Ding W533
Song, Guangju W477
Song, Hongjiong W662
Song, Jianhua W301
Song, Jie W106
Song, Jingshang W291
Song, Jun W173
Song, Kangle W156
Song, Ling W140

Song, Shuguang W150
Song, Tao W173
Song, Zhiyi W291
Sonmez, Zafer W620
Sonn, Heather W562
Sonnen, Anne C. W262
Sonnenberg, Steven A. A975
Sonnenfeld, Jeffrey A. A629
Sono, Mari W445
Sonoki, Hiroshi W65
Sonsteby, Charles (Chuck) M. A316
Sonsteby, Charles (Chuck) M. E517
Sontag, Michael C. E397
Sonthalia, Rajeev W523
Sonu, Suk-Ho W335
Soo, Hoi-Lun W180
Soo, Hoi-Lun W179
Soo, Kim Wai W36
Sood, Sanjay A214
Sood, Sapna W385
Sooy, Thomas C A958
Sooy, Thomas C E456
Sopher, Jerry S. E69
Sophonpanich, Chartsiri W77
Sopp, Mark W. A595
Soran, Philip E. E387
Soran, Philip E. E457
Sorbara, N. W377
Sorensen, Donna J. A865
Sorensen, Donna J. E403
Sorensen, Gregory W545
Sorensen, Hanne Birgitte Breinbjerg W587
Sorensen, Hanne Birgitte Breinbjerg W283
Sørensen, Harvey R. A378
Sørensen, Lars Rebien A1027
Sørensen, Lars Rebien W231
Sorensen, Torben Ballegaard W4
Sorensen, Vagn Ove W158
Sorenson, Arne M. A701
Sorenson, John Bradley A175
Sorenson, Kory W471
Sorenson, Kory W526
Sorfleet, Diana B. A304
Sorgi, Vincent A841
Soriano, Cesar M. E154
Soriano, Lidio V. A836
Soriot, Pascal W57
Soritsch-Renier, Ursula W165
Soroye, Olumide E520
Sorrentini, Lucy A271
Sorrentini, Lucy E109
Sorrentino, Frank A287
Sorrentino, Frank E115
Sosebee, Jane S. E195
Sosland, L. Joshua A1056
Sosland, L. Joshua E505
Sossen, Andrew Jay A965
Sossen, Andrew Jay E462
Sota, Ivan De La W33
Soting, Kjell-Ake W228
Soto, Alexandra W398
Soto, Benjamin M A350
Soto, Benjamin M E148
Soto, Cristobal Ortega W314
Soto, Juan Carlos Alvarez de A915
Soto, Myrna M. A294
Soto, Myrna M. A256
Soto, Myrna M. A836

Sotoodeh, John A124
Souan, Ryan E436
Soucie, Keith N. A372
Soucie, Keith N. E167
Souda, Nobuyuki W293
Souders, Donald E. E510
Soukenik, Amber B. Wallace A393
Soukenik, Amber B. Wallace E184
Soule, David B. E192
Souleles, Thomas S. A799
Sounillac, Jean-Pierre W238
Sourisse, Pascal W492
Sourisse, Pascal W635
Sourisse, Pascale W600
Sousa, Emma de A558
Sousa, Gregory E364
Soussan, Jean-Manuel W107
Soutchay, Bock E517
South, Martin A662
Souza, Alvaro Antonio Cardoso de W72
Souza, Alvaro Cardoso de W76
Souza, Andre Nogueira de A828
Souza, Diane W515
Souza, Errol De A425
Souza, Flavio Augusto Aguiar de W315
Sova, Gary E82
Sowazi, N. L. W414
Sozen, Suleyman W618
Spade, David W. A427
Spade, David W. E203
Spaggiari, Corrado W177
Spain, Mark W81
Spain, Michael H. A1033
Spainhour, Sterling A. E237
Spair, Ronald H. A454
Spalti, Dieter W283
Spaly, Brian A. E49
Spann, Rick A237
Spanos, Mike A817
Spar, Debora L. A1027
Sparby, David M. A679
Sparda, Edward L. A519
Sparda, Edward L. E256
Spark, Frances R. A28
Sparkman, Ricky D. A282
Sparks, C. Todd A1040
Sparks, C. Todd E499
Sparks, Carl D. E120
Sparks, Daniel Paul E315
Sparks, David E. A702
Sparks, David E. E326
Sparks, Edwin C. A224
Sparks, Larry J. E261
Sparks, Monica L. A800
Sparks, Scotty Andrew E250
Spaseska, Aleksandra W644
Spatz, David M. E56
Spaude, Robin E236
Spaulding, Miranda J. E149
Speaker, Andrew R. E450
Spears, Alan M. E421
Spears, Kirsten M. A180
Spears, Michael P. E277
Specht, William A. A702
Specht, William A. E326
Special, Frederick Khouri Evp P227
Special, Jay Cole P685
Specker, Steven R. A952
Specter, Eric M. E209
Spector, Adam A448

COMBINED HOOVER'S HANDBOOK INDEX OF EXECUTIVES

A = AMERICAN BUSINESS
E = EMERGING COMPANIES
P = PRIVATE COMPANIES
W = WORLD BUSINESSS

Spector, David A. A811
Spector, David A. E377
Spector, David A. E378
Speed, James Herbert E280
Speed, Kevin P56
Speed, Leland R. E151
Speetzen, Michael T. A835
Spehar, Danielle E9
Spehar, Edward A176
Spehar, Edward A176
Speirs, Belinda W574
Spek, Hanspeter W390
Spellacy, Suzanne M. E356
Spence, Patrick E452
Spence, Robert E447
Spence, Timothy N. A410
Spence, William H. A1131
Spencer, Larry O. A1129
Spencer, Matthew J. A475
Spencer, Ronald B. A981
Spencer, Ronald B. E469
Spencer, Simon A207
Spengler, Richard S. A575
Speranza, Emanuela A74
Speranzo, Anthony J. E408
Sperling, Scott M. A1027
Speroni, Stefano W227
Spiegel, Eric A. A342
Spiegel, Noel J. A874
Spiegel, Reuven A321
Spieker, Marc W207
Spielman, Cheryl D E336
Spielmann, Brian D. A416
Spielrein, Eric W490
Spierkel, Gregory W524
Spierkel, Gregory M.E. A796
Spierkel, Gregory M.E. A696
Spiess, Lukas W91
Spiess, Paul D. A352
Spiesshofer, Ulrich W523
Spiesshofer, Ulrich W303
Spillane, Michael E65
Spillenkothen, Richard A915
Spillman, Scott E63
Spillum, Martin W347
Spilman, Robert H. A340
Spilman, Vance H. E62
Spinale, Joseph W P526
Spinelli, Tony A810
Spinelli, Tony E376
Spinetta, Jean-Cyril W22
Spinosa, Frank Anthony A848
Spira, Joel E221
Spiro, Martin F. E24
Spiten, Ingjerd Blekeli W204
Spitz, David J. E92
Spitz, Verena W93
Spitznogle, Gary O. A59
Spivey, Leslie Scott A397
Splaine, Thomas F. A617
Splaine, Thomas F. E289
Splinter, Michael R. A721
Splinter, Michael R. W584
Spoelberch, Gregoire de W40

Spoerl, Joseph E455
Spoerry, Robert F. E325
Spofford, Claire E297
Spohr, Carsten W415
Spohr, Carsten W196
Sponaugle, Stephen J. A397
Spoo, Sibylle W199
Spoon, Alan G. A315
Spoon, Alan G. E261
Spooner, William A P500
Spradley, Suzanne P392
Spradlin, Shane M. A812
Spratt, Randall N. A818
Spray, Stephen M. A240
Sprecher, Jeffrey C. A561
Sprieser, Judith A. A561
Sprieser, Judith A. A42
Sprieser, Judith A. A735
Spriggs, Rodney E304
Spring, Antony (Tony) A654
Spring, Donald J. A703
Spring, Donald J. E327
Spring, Maria F. A722
Spring, Maria F. E339
Spring, Stevie W160
Springer, Gerhard W563
Springer, Hermann W234
Springer, Jack D. E308
Springer, Jon W. E512
Springer, Mary Beth E90
Springs, Albert A. E452
Springs, Jack L. E452
Sprink, Eric M. E103
Sprink, John A528
Sprink, John E258
Spruell, Byron W44
Sprules, Karl E17
Sprunger, Kerry E223
Sprunk, Eric D. A465
Spurgeon, Nicky W364
Spurlin, Sharon E450
Spurling, David A. A510
Spurling, David A. E252
Squeri, Stephen J. A62
Squires, James A. A747
Squires, Keith P615
Squires, Nelson J. A1117
Squires, Paul M. A922
Sr, Johannes Britz Int P665
Sreeram, Attiganal N. A342
Srethapramotaya, Virojn W79
Srichaiya, Veerapat W352
Sridharan, Karthik A768
Sridharan, Karthik E359
Srihong, Teeranun W334
Srinivasa, Parthasarathy E172
Srinivasan, Krishnakumar E41
Srinivasan, LaVerne Evans E480
Srinivasan, Magesh A224
Srinivasan, Mallika A26
Srinivasan, Mallika W588
Sripratak, Adirek W136
Sripratak, Adirek W117
Sriram, B. W296
Srivanich, Payong W352
Srivanich, Payong W484
Srivastava, Raman W262
Srivastava, Sapna E272
Srivorasart, Rungson W603
Srukhosit, Narongdech W484

Staats, Aaron C. von E402
Stabile, Sophie W550
Stach, Leigh Ann E114
Stachelhaus, Regine W174
Stacherski, Kenneth A458
Stachura, Paul M. A966
Stack, David M. E369
Stack, Donald L. E235
Stack, Edward W. A326
Stack, John James A43
Stack, John James W229
Stackhouse, Julie L. A938
Stackhouse, Julie L. E442
Stackley, Sean J. A613
Stacy, Michelle V. E281
Stadelhofer, Juergen W234
Stadigh, Kari W443
Stadigh, Kari W446
Stadler, Elisabeth W458
Stadler, Elisabeth W639
Stadler, Elisabeth W633
Stadler, Rupert W61
Stadtler, Dj P378
Staehelin, Tobias B. W522
Stafeil, Jeffrey M. A95
Stafeil, Jeffrey M. W15
Staff, Joel V. A605
Staffeldt, Erik E250
Staffieri, Michael D. A318
Stafford, Harrison A852
Stafford, Harrison E399
Stafford, Ingrid S. A1133
Stafford, Ingrid S. E541
Stafford, Ron E338
Stafford, Ryan K. E303
Stafford, William P. A419
Stager, Nancy Huntington A352
Stagliano, Joseph R. A724
Staglin, Garen K. A984
Staglin, Garen K. E476
Stahl, Jack L. A1068
Stahl, Jack L. E83
Stahl, Murray E487
Stahl, Murray E221
Stahl, Neil A882
Stahl, Stephanie A338
Stahl, Stephanie A735
Stahlberg, Christian W427
Stahlin, Paul V. A749
Stahlkopf, Dev A701
Stahlkopf, Dev A244
Staiblin, Jasmin W666
Staiblin, Jasmin W504
Stainthorpe, Mark A. W120
Stake, James B. A900
Stake, James B. E367
Stakias, G. Michael E145
Staley, Gary E523
Staley, Jes W89
Stalick, Theodore R. A685
Stalker, Ian E43
Stalker, Robin J. W162
Stall, Gabriele Katharina W390
Stall, John A. A740
Stallings, James B. A408
Stallings, Robert W. A1008
Stallings, Wendy T. A771
Stallworth, John L. A988
Stallworth, John L. E479

Stalnecker, Susan M. A625
Stamens, Karine W511
Stamm, K. Brad E184
Stamoulis, Christiana A522
Stamoulis, Christiana E267
Stamps, Sheila A. A576
Stanbrook, Steven P. A491
Stanbrook, Steven P. W298
Stancombe, Chris W123
Stander, Deon M. A114
Stanek, Mary Ellen A1114
Stangl, Sandra N. A1018
Staniforth, Karen A895
Stanik, John S. A441
Stanik, John S. E212
Stankey, John T. A105
Stanleick, Andrew Roy E57
Stanley, Deirdre A290
Stanley, Deirdre A620
Stanley, Deirdre A289
Stanley, Robert A941
Stanley, Stephen E P42
Stanoch, Ruth E. A704
Stanoch, Ruth E. E328
Stansbury, Christopher (Chris) D. A97
Stansbury, Christopher (Chris) D. A649
Stansbury, Christopher (Chris) D. A872
Stansfield, George A377
Stansfield, George W65
Stanton, Brent M. A401
Stanton, Cheryl A. E63
Stanton, John W. A300
Stanton, John W. A701
Stanton, Jonathan W298
Stanton, Katie W637
Stanton, Kevin A670
Stanton, Philip H. A1099
Stanton, Thomas R. A190
Stanton, Thomas R. E73
Stanwood, Michael P226
Stapleton, Charles D. E136
Stapleton, John P. A466
Star, James A. A231
Stara, Friedrich W633
Starace, Francesco W219
Starace, Francesco W222
Stark, David M. W598
Stark, Derek W. A811
Stark, Derek W. E378
Stark, Derek W. E377
Stark, Juergen M. E501
Stark, Paul J. A251
Stark, Paul J. E100
Stark, Sandy A964
Starkey, Adria D. E190
Starks, Daniel J. A6
Starnes, Clarke R. A1042
Starnes, W. Stancil A847
Starr, Lisa Hoffman P515
Starrett, Peter M. E210
Starrett, Peter M. E64
Stars, Hauke W355
Stars, Hauke W510
Staszak, Catherine M. E69
Stata, Ray A81
States, Lauren C. A1113
Stathoulopoulos, Paul N. A575
Staton, Daniel C. A96

COMBINED HOOVER'S HANDBOOK INDEX OF EXECUTIVES

A = AMERICAN BUSINESS
E = EMERGING COMPANIES
P = PRIVATE COMPANIES
W = WORLD BUSINESSS

Staub, Julie P602
Staub, Susan A389
Staub, Susan P219
Staub, Zeno W642
Stauffer, Jeffrey S E158
Stausholm, Jakob W500
Stausholm, Jakob W499
Stavridis, James G. E216
Stavropoulos, Nickolas A372
Stavropoulos, Nickolas E167
Stavropoulos, Nickolas E22
Stavros, Christopher G. E307
Stawski, Waldemar W389
Stead, Jimmy A305
Steans, Jennifer W. A1086
Steans, Jennifer W. E516
Stebbins, Paul H. A1136
Stech, Brian E501
Stecher, David E271
Stecher, Kenneth W. A240
Steck, Brian A228
Steck, Debra Lynn E223
Steck, Heike W517
Steck, Kevin P543
Steckelberg, Kelly E547
Stecko, Paul T. A799
Steddum, Chris E487
Steegen, An W623
Steel, John H. E506
Steel, Robert K. A460
Steele, Barry G. E271
Steele, Gail P166
Steele, John F. A240
Steele, Lauren C. A266
Steele, Robert A159
Steele, Robert A. A153
Steele, Robert A. A735
Steele, Sally A. A280
Steele, Sally A. E113
Steele, Toni S. E217
Steelhammer, Robert A852
Steelhammer, Robert E399
Steenbergen, Ewout L. A911
Steeneck, Craig D. E260
Steenland, Douglas M. A56
Steenland, Douglas M. A518
Steenrod, Mitchell D. A205
Steer, Randolph C. E59
Steer, Robert L. A922
Steere, Brian A971
Steere, Brian P537
Stefan, Dorfler W229
Stefanelli, Maria Alessandra W310
Stefani, Alexander A650
Stefani, Alexander E305
Stefanini, Pierluigi W627
Stefanini, Pierluigi W627
Stefansic, Robert J. A557
Stefanski, Ben S. A1013
Stefanski, Marc A. A1013
Stefanucci, Anne Marie A430
Steffens, Greg A. A953
Steffens, Greg A. E455
Stehlik, Christine P241

Steib, Michael F. A43
Steigerwalt, Eric T. A176
Steigerwalt, Eric T. A176
Steijaert, Manu A675
Steilemann, Markus W174
Steimberg, Amichai A607
Steimer, Olivier W154
Steimer, Olivier W88
Stein, Clint E. A270
Stein, Clint E. E109
Stein, David L. A101
Stein, Elliot H. E57
Stein, Jeffrey Scott A52
Stein, Jeffrey Scott A493
Stein, Jonathan C. E253
Stein, Kevin A329
Stein, Laura A710
Stein, Martin E. E222
Stein, Matt E189
Stein, Michael M. E229
Stein, Randy I. E529
Stein, Richard L. A410
Stein, Robert W. A103
Stein, Steven H. E267
Steinbarger, George E313
Steinberg, Joseph S. A581
Steinberg, Joseph S. E529
Steinberg, Marc S. E386
Steinberger, Eric P50
Steinbock, Gerd W270
Steinborn, Brigit W543
Steinemann, Jurgen B. W398
Steiner, Arnold L. A774
Steiner, David P. A405
Steiner, Deborah L P451
Steiner, Eddie L. E132
Steiner, Jeffrey B. A616
Steiner, Mitchell S. E522
Steiner, Paul A. A276
Steinert, Earl A. A488
Steinert, Langley E81
Steines, Ann Munson A745
Steinfort, Rebecca Lee E340
Steinhart, Ronald G. A813
Steinhoff, Bruno Ewald W562
Steinhorst, Ulrike W631
Steinke, Bruce A. A54
Steinke, Craig A. A184
Steinke, Katherine A. A398
Steinmeier, Richard A648
Steinour, Stephen D. A545
Steinour, Stephen D. A140
Steinwert, Kent A. A392
Steinwert, Kent A. E183
Stelben, John J. E154
Stella, Bruno W220
Stelling, James P. A67
Stelling, Kessel D. A471
Stelling, Kessel D. A987
Stelling, Kessel D. E478
Stelly, Donald D. E300
Stelzer, Laurie D. E475
Stemler, Kerry M. A1115
Stemler, Kerry M. E533
Stemler, Steven R. E206
Stempien, Catherine S. A112
Stemple, Lloyd E372
Stendahl, Lea P544
Stengel, Scott A. A43
Stengel, William P. A468

Stengele, Helmut W517
Stenger, Thomas P. A530
Stenger, Thomas P. E258
Stenqvist, Lars W641
Stenson, Brian A974
Stenson, Brian P539
Stenstadvold, Halvor W562
Stephen, James C. E532
Stephens, Gary W. E357
Stephens, Gina E46
Stephens, Jeffrey R. E434
Stephens, John J. A452
Stephens, Kevin A. A301
Stephens, Steve Dan A1151
Stephenson, Aaron A225
Stephenson, Aaron A226
Stephenson, Carol M. A466
Stephenson, Gordon Sheridan A1149
Stephenson, Jim P627
Stephenson, Mona Abutaleb A913
Stephenson, Mona Abutaleb E427
Stephenson, Randall L. A1104
Stephenson, Scott G. A858
Stepnowski, Amy A502
Sterin, Steven M. A349
Sterling, Brian R. E387
Sterling, Jacob Andersen W2
Sterling, Michelle M. E142
Stern, Alfred W458
Stern, James A. A1048
Stern, Sadie M. E138
Stern, Walter A52
Stern, Walter P31
Stern, William H. A72
Stern, William H. E29
Sternlicht, Barry S. A620
Sternlicht, Barry S. A965
Sternlicht, Barry S. E462
Sterrett, Stephen E. A153
Sterrs, Lawrence J. A192
Stetelman, Andrew D. A414
Stetelman, Andrew D. E193
Stetson, Jennifer C. E235
Stevanovic, Andreja E407
Steven-Waiss, Kelley E214
Steven, James A1106
Stevens, Anne L. W39
Stevens, Charles K. A354
Stevens, Charles K. A1005
Stevens, Charles K. A666
Stevens, Charles K. W242
Stevens, Daniel L. E199
Stevens, Edward E284
Stevens, Glenn H. A979
Stevens, Glenn R. W377
Stevens, Jennifer L. E190
Stevens, Jon I A163
Stevens, Jon I P86
Stevens, Lisa W44
Stevens, Mark A. A761
Stevens, Melissa S. A410
Stevens, Raymond C. A315
Stevens, Robert J. A991
Stevens, Susan F. A1057
Stevens, Tim E407
Stevens, Wayne A. A1044
Stevenson, Gary R. E287
Stevenson, Katharine Berghuis W119
Stevenson, Kimberly S. E520
Stevenson, Kimberly S. E329

Stevenson, Roberton James E5
Stevenson, Ruth A722
Stevenson, Ruth E339
Stevenson, Tim E221
Stevison, James M. E319
Stewart, Alan W597
Stewart, Alan J. H. W201
Stewart, Bonita C. E137
Stewart, Cecelia D. A424
Stewart, Cecelia D. E200
Stewart, Charles A45
Stewart, Derrick J. A772
Stewart, Donald A. W570
Stewart, Frank A. E372
Stewart, James P57
Stewart, James R. A703
Stewart, James R. E327
Stewart, Jeffrey R. A8
Stewart, Julia A. A114
Stewart, Kelly J. A401
Stewart, Laura Lee E452
Stewart, Lee C. E174
Stewart, Lisa A. E536
Stewart, Louis P139
Stewart, Lucas E323
Stewart, Mark W562
Stewart, Marta R. A934
Stewart, Michael G. E315
Stewart, Michael J. A427
Stewart, Michael J. E203
Stewart, Michelle R. A354
Stewart, Misako A130
Stewart, Niccole E217
Stewart, Randy R. A1151
Stewart, Samanta Hegedus E242
Stewart, Shelley A791
Stewart, Stacey D. E378
Stewart, Sue S. A196
Stewart, Sue S. E78
Stewart, Vincent R. A595
Stice, J. Michael A657
Stice, J. Michael A717
Stice, Travis D. E409
Stickels, Eric E. A280
Stickels, Eric E. E112
Stiefler, Jeffrey E. A408
Stiehle, Thomas E. A546
Stiepleman, David A941
Stiers, Mark W. A345
Stigers, Michael (Mike) C. A1068
Stigers, Thomas s M. A1125
Still, Debra W. A231
Stilwell, McDavid E106
Stimoniaris, Athanasios W640
Stinnett, Thomas Clay A978
Stinnett, Thomas Clay E465
Stinson-Milienu, Karen Lee A422
Stipancich, John K. A904
Stiritz, William P. A838
Stirling, Amy W157
Stirling, Lisa A631
Stith, Thomas A. A771
Stithit, Wuttikorn W484
Stjernholm, Helena W641
Stjernholm, Helena W228
Stock, Alan J. A12
Stock, Alan J. E4
Stock, Elane B. A1146
Stock, Elane B. W490
Stockert, David P. E146

```
A = AMERICAN BUSINESS
E = EMERGING COMPANIES
P = PRIVATE COMPANIES
W = WORLD BUSINESSS
```

Stockfish, Devin W. A1127
Stockton, Angie A742
Stockton, Angie P393
Stockton, Dmitri L. A997
Stockton, Dmitri L. A320
Stockton, Dmitri L. A909
Stockton, Dmitri L. A1125
Stockton, Kevin A. A282
Stockton, Michael W P383
Stoddard, Daniel G. A340
Stoddart, Richard S. A503
Stoehr, David L. A1133
Stoehr, David L. E541
Stoffels, Paul W351
Stogner, Grey A301
Stogner, Grey E131
Stokely, John D. E149
Stokely, John E. E389
Stokely, John E. E308
Stokes, Eric E353
Stokes, Nicole S. A71
Stokes, Nicole S. E29
Stokes, Russell A462
Stokes, Russell A1069
Stokes, William W. E62
Stoliar, Gabriel A252
Stoll, Jérôme W490
Stolly, Timothy J. E428
Stolper, Mark D. E106
Stolzer, Daniel R. A454
Stolzman, Marc D. E418
Stone, Alan J. A196
Stone, Alan J. E78
Stone, Andrew P. A881
Stone, Ian Charles W597
Stone, Jeff P175
Stone, Joseph V. E113
Stone, Larry D. A326
Stone, Loren R. "Bob" A1144
Stone, Michael J. A896
Stone, Michael J. E422
Stone, Paul E. A513
Stone, R. Dary E124
Stone, R. Gregg A191
Stone, R. Gregg E77
Stone, Randy A349
Stone, Scott B. A989
Stone, Susan A. A258
Stone, William Gordon E142
Stoneberg, Peter B. E287
Stonehill, Charles G. T. A377
Stonehill, Charles G. T. E17
Stonehocker, Tim A599
Stoner, Christy D. E515
Stoner, Floyd E. A788
Stoner, Floyd E. E366
Stoner, Roberta B P257
Stones, Charles A. A395
Stones, Charles A. E186
Stonesifer, Patricia Q. A50
Stonestreet, Dana L. A528
Stonestreet, Dana L. E258
Stoney, Michael John E490
Stoops, Pamela S. E421

Stoots, Brad E153
Stopczynski, Pawel W86
Stops, Wendy W164
Stops, Wendy W162
Storch, Gerald L. A178
Storchak, Sergey A. W329
Storey, Barry L. A988
Storey, Barry L. E479
Stork, David G. A639
Stork, Johannes M. C. W52
Stork, Kendall E. A688
Stork, Kendall E. E323
Storl, Michael W15
Storm, Kees J. W344
Storms, Tim J. A1008
Storrie, Colin W651
Storruste, Heidi W562
Story, Amanda G. E62
Story, Susan N. A340
Story, Susan N. A737
Story, Susan N. A876
Stothfang, Marc W174
Stotlar, Douglas W. A888
Stotlar, Douglas W. A20
Stott, John P. A94
Stouder, Jeffrey K. E296
Stoufflet, Stéphane W490
Stough, Michael D. A401
Stout, David M. A578
Stout, John T. A82
Stover, David L. A86
Stovesand, Kirk B. E114
Stovsky, Richard P. E159
Stowe, Barry W666
Stowe, Jay P285
Stoyles, Lyndall W596
Stoyles, Lyndall W37
Straarup, Peter W188
Straber, Renee A666
Straberg, Hans W60
Strable-Soethout, Deanna D. A846
Strache, Andreas W196
Straehle, Joachim H. W86
Strah, Kenneth A. A432
Strah, Steven E. A432
Strahlman, Ellen R. A47
Strain, Denise A430
Strain, John E297
Strain, Kevin D. W572
Straka, Patrick J. E97
Strakosch, Gregory E481
Stramaglia, Michael P. W570
Strand, Carina W579
Strand, Ina W31
Strandberg, Steven F. E129
Strange, J. Leland E122
Strange, Sterling T. E526
Strank, Dame Angela W504
Strasser, Arnaud Daniel Charles Walter Joachim W127
Strasser, Roland W93
Strassheim, Dale S. A504
Stratton, John G. A460
Stratton, John G. A6
Stratton, John G. A453
Straub, Francis X. A259
Straub, Francis X. E103
Straubel, Jeffrey B. A1007
Strauch, Roger A. E96
Strausbaugh, Samuel S. A844

Strausbaugh, Samuel S. E394
Strauss, Christi W646
Strauss, Cindy P446
Strauss, Mark F. A454
Strauss, Toby W360
Strazik, Scott A462
Street, Chad C. A283
Streeter, Stephanie A. A1122
Strei, Katherine E157
Streibel-Zarfl, Ingrid W93
Streibich, Karl-Heinz W545
Streibich, Karl-Heinz W415
Streibich, Karl-Heinz W199
Streit, Clara C. W642
Streit, Clara Christina F. T. W325
Streit, Clara Christina F. T. W442
Streit, Kurt W631
Stricker, Robert A531
Strickland, Hoyt J. A68
Strickland, Jill P452
Strimbu, William J. A441
Strimbu, William J. E212
Stringer, David A428
Stringer, Scott A250
Stringer, Scott P135
Stringfield, JoAnne E376
Strobeck, Matthew W. E406
Strobel, Martin W64
Strobel, Pamela B. A553
Strohm, Jean-Luc W88
Strohmeyer, Karl A377
Strom, Arlene W573
Strom, Jeff A166
Stromberg, Charlotte W548
Stromberg, William J. A458
Stromberg, William J. A991
Stromer, Michael A583
Strong-Treister, Diane W. A249
Strong-Treister, Diane W. E99
Strong, Anthony D. E368
Strong, Dana A272
Strong, George G. E129
Strong, John A. E382
Strong, Robert S. A945
Strong, Robert S. E450
Strong, Ryan A428
Strong, Stewart W. E43
Stronks, Timothy J. E114
Strotbek, Axel W61
Stroup, John S. A1004
Strube, Juergen W270
Strutz, Eric W288
Strydesky, John E. E193
Stryker, David M. A547
Stryker, Ronda E. A981
Stuard, William S. A397
Stuart, Cindy P264
Stuart, Sandra W287
Stuart, Susan S. A747
Stuart, T. Brent E207
Stuart, Timothy E. A892
Stubblefield, Michael A112
Stubbs, P. Scott E180
Stubler, Jerome W225
Stucki, Aaron K. W590
Studenmund, Jaynie M. A797
Studenmund, Jaynie M. E368
Studenmund, Jaynie M. E179
Studer, Martine W165
Studer, Michael T. E162

Stuijt, Janet W442
Stulac-motzel, Wendy Chief Ambulatory Populat ion P260
Stumbo, Kevin J. A282
Stumper, Klaus W280
Stuntz, Linda G. A359
Stuntz, Linda G. A951
Sturgeon, Dione R. E517
Sturgeon, James L. A214
Sturgess, Kate A951
Sturm, Stephan W196
Sturm, Stephan W251
Sturm, Stephan W249
Sturrock, A. Troy A369
Stutzman, Paul P245
Styczynski, Tomasz W86
Stymiest, Barbara W646
Stymiest, Barbara G. W572
Stypulkowski, Cezary W389
Styslinger, Lee J. A885
Su, Hengxuan W142
Su, Li W660
Su, Lisa T. A244
Su, Lisa T. A18
Su, May E362
Su, Rubo W173
Su, Shaojun W145
Su, Xianglin W140
Su, Zimeng W516
Suarez, Jaime A825
Suarez, Oscar A52
Subotovsky, Santiago E547
Subramaniam, Rajesh A404
Subramaniam, Shivan S. A248
Subramanian, Bala A1069
Subramanian, Bala W351
Subramanian, Guhan A643
Subramoney, S. W518
Subramoney, Stanley S. W426
Sucharczuk, Guy A279
Suchodolski, Keith A596
Suchodolski, Keith E286
Suchy, Daniel R. E111
Suckale, Margret W273
Suckale, Margret W199
Suckale, Margret W303
Suda, Miyako W394
Sudduth, Scott E107
Sudhof, Thomas C. W515
Suess, Calvin A392
Suess, Calvin E183
Suess, Gregory E547
Suever, Catherine A. A557
Sufrategui, Jose Ramon Martinez W71
Suga, Masahiko W534
Suga, Yasuo W610
Sugar, Patrick D. E426
Sugar, Ronald D. A76
Sugar, Ronald D. A230
Sugar, Ronald D. A89
Sugar, Ronald D. A1052
Sugarman, Gary L. E301
Sugarman, Jay E426
Sugata, Shiro W659
Sugawara, Etsuko W81
Sugawara, Ikuro W253
Sugawara, Ikuro W279
Sugawara, Ikuro W616
Sugg, Laura A. A858
Suggs, Denis E373

COMBINED HOOVER'S HANDBOOK INDEX OF EXECUTIVES

A = AMERICAN BUSINESS
E = EMERGING COMPANIES
P = PRIVATE COMPANIES
W = WORLD BUSINESSS

Suggs, Leo H. A771
Suggs, Mark A. E340
Suggs, Sean M. A889
Suggs, Sean M. E414
Sughrue, John T. A1086
Sughrue, John T. E521
Sugi, Hikaru W404
Sugiarto, Prijono W464
Sugihara, Tomoka W357
Sugimori, Masato W389
Sugimori, Tsutomu W223
Sugimoto, Seigo W253
Sugimoto, Yasushi W331
Sugita, Koji W410
Sugita, Masahiro W1
Sugita, Mitsuhide W539
Sugita, Naoto W83
Sugiura, Masakazu W292
Sugiura, Tsuyoshi W418
Sugrañes, Rosa A424
Sugrañes, Rosa E200
Sugrue, Kristyn M. A159
Suh, Chris A363
Suh, Donghee W365
Suing, Clifford C. A706
Sujjapongse, Somchai W352
Sukeno, Kenji W253
Sukhanunth, Sansana W334
Sukhov, Gennady W474
Sukhov, Gennady W256
Suksawang, Sumalee W352
Sulaiman, Norazzah W495
Suleiman, Ezra W565
Sulentic, Robert E. A213
Sulerzyski, Charles W. A815
Sullivan, Andrew A856
Sullivan, Angus W164
Sullivan, Arthur E401
Sullivan, Caroline A711
Sullivan, Charles E. E537
Sullivan, Daniel A400
Sullivan, Daniel G. A399
Sullivan, Daniel J. A917
Sullivan, Daniel J. A351
Sullivan, Frank C. A907
Sullivan, Gary M. A321
Sullivan, Gregory B. A208
Sullivan, Heidi C. A685
Sullivan, James E A1021
Sullivan, James E P593
Sullivan, James M. A924
Sullivan, Jeffrey M. E461
Sullivan, John A300
Sullivan, John J. A191
Sullivan, John J. E77
Sullivan, Kathryn D. A568
Sullivan, Kevin F. E242
Sullivan, Lenore M. E391
Sullivan, Louis W. E157
Sullivan, Marianne E378
Sullivan, Martha N. A114
Sullivan, Melody J. A395
Sullivan, Melody J. E185
Sullivan, Michael J. A499

Sullivan, Michael J. E246
Sullivan, Nora B. E175
Sullivan, Owen J. A726
Sullivan, Paul J. A187
Sullivan, Richard L. E210
Sullivan, Sean S. A941
Sullivan, Shawn T. A519
Sullivan, Shawn T. E256
Sullivan, Stuart P P503
Sullivan, William E. E134
Sullivan, William G. E311
Sully, Raef M. W451
Sulpizio, Christel A915
Sulpizio, Richard E417
Sult, John R. A1097
Sultana, Keith A. W617
Sultemeier, Chris T. A1144
Sultemeier, Chris T. E146
Sultzbaugh, Marc P340
Sulzberger, Gabrielle A670
Sumar, Nageeb P223
Sumi, Shuzo W557
Sumi, Shuzo W614
Sumino, Toshiaki W181
Sumitomo, Yasuhiko W65
Summe, Gregory L. A112
Summe, Gregory L. A973
Summers, Lawrence (Larry) Henry A162
Summers, Markus A. A401
Summers, William B. A907
Summy, Amy B. A615
Sumner, Randee Nichole A776
Sumoski, David A. A759
Sun, Anthony E105
Sun, Chengming W142
Sun, Chengyu W662
Sun, Cui W147
Sun, Dahong W153
Sun, Danmei W533
Sun, Daoju W431
Sun, David P. W128
Sun, Dennis Tai-Lun W180
Sun, Fujie W158
Sun, Hongbin W572
Sun, Jane Jie W20
Sun, Jianyi W472
Sun, Juyi W257
Sun, Maolin W100
Sun, Peijian W145
Sun, Richard A211
Sun, Richard E84
Sun, Ridong W528
Sun, Ruiwen W144
Sun, Shaojun W644
Sun, Shu W202
Sun, Tong W529
Sun, Weimin W574
Sun, Wende W663
Sun, Xiaoning W236
Sun, Yongcai W178
Sun, Yongxing W189
Sun, Yu W104
Sun, Yun W106
Sun, Yunchi W139
Sundaram, D. W304
Sundaram, Easwaran A1118
Sundaram, Easwaran E451
Sundaram, Mani E12
Sundberg, Matti W548

Sunderland, Steven G. A336
Sung, Christina Wen-chi E143
Sung, Jae-ho W537
Sung, Sik Hwang W365
Sung, Tae-Yoon W352
Sunkle, David C. E393
Sunshine, Eugene S. E87
Sunshine, Eugene S. W50
Suntrapak, Todd P671
Sununu, John E. A175
Supinit, Vijit W603
Suppa, Jerry E397
Suquet, Jose S. A885
Suquet, José S. A399
Suranjan, Magesvaran E532
Suraphongchai, Vichit W541
Surdykowski, Andrew J. A561
Suresh, Subra A538
Surface, Carol A. W393
Surgner, W. Hildebrandt A47
Suri, Rajeev A981
Surjaudaja, Pramukti W464
Surma, John P. A858
Surma, John P. A657
Surma, John P. A717
Surma, John P. W617
Surowka, Pawel W86
Susan, Schmidt P446
Susca, Vito A936
Susca, Vito E440
Suskind, Dennis A. A328
Susman, Sally A821
Susman, Sally W654
Suss, Eric M. E79
Sussman, Elliot J. A1076
Sussman, Lester M. A351
Sussman, Lester M. E150
Sustana, Mark A629
Sutanto, Suryo W483
Sutaria, Saumya A1003
Sutaris, Joseph E. A280
Sutaris, Joseph E. E112
Sutcliffe, James H. W571
Suter, Kelly A. E490
Sutera, Albert J P580
Sutherland, David S. A1073
Sutherland, David S. W299
Sutherland, John Wesley A641
Sutherland, John Wesley E304
Sutherland, L. Frederick A289
Sutherland, L. Frederick A290
Sutherland, Peter Dennis W346
Sutherland, Susan A. A402
Sutherlin, Michael W. E430
Suthiwart-Narueput, Sethaput W603
Sutil, Lucia Santa Cruz W73
Sutil, Vicky A321
Sutivong, Pramon W540
Suto, Hideho W603
Sutter-Rudisser, Michele F. W229
Suttles, Douglas J. A792
Sutton, Doniel N. A905
Sutton, Ellen P401
Sutton, Joseph W. E22
Sutton, Marina Park A509
Sutton, Marina Park E251
Sutton, Mark S. A568
Sutton, Mark S. A611
Sutton, Patricia A P7
Sutton, Scott McDougald A776

Sutula, Stanley J. A269
Suwa, Takako W319
Suwaidi, Eissa Mohammed Al W47
Suwinski, Jan H. A1028
Suzuki, Asako W285
Suzuki, Hitoshi W82
Suzuki, Kenji W83
Suzuki, Kenji W25
Suzuki, Koichi W1
Suzuki, Masafumi W285
Suzuki, Masako W319
Suzuki, Miyuki A1122
Suzuki, Nobuya W281
Suzuki, Nobuya W394
Suzuki, Norimasa W21
Suzuki, Tatsuya W434
Suzuki, Teruo W370
Suzuki, Toshiaki W577
Suzuki, Toshihiro W577
Suzuki, Toshio W1
Suzuki, Yasunobu W404
Suzuki, Yoichi W330
Suzuki, Yoko W110
Suzuki, Yoshiteru W460
Svahn, Helene W395
Svanberg, Carl-Henric W641
Svanberg, Louise W231
Svarva, Olaug W204
Svelto, Anna Chiara W222
Svenson, Jennifer A138
Svenson, Jennifer E55
Svensson, Ake A804
Svensson, Örjan W231
Svensson, Roger W228
Svensson, Ulrik W196
Svider, Raymond A45
Svider, Raymond A231
Svoboda, Frank M. A478
Svoboda, Kurt W627
Swager, Karen A714
Swain, Carol E348
Swain, Clinton M. A1132
Swain, Clinton M. E539
Swain, Susan M. A332
Swainson, John A. A918
Swalling, John C. E352
Swan, Mara E. E66
Swan, Robert Holmes A357
Swanback, Michelle E500
Swanson, Al A832
Swanson, Al A832
Swanson, Brian A119
Swanson, Brian E48
Swaringen, S. Todd E515
Swarovski, Christoph W458
Swartout, Steven H. A196
Swartout, Steven H. E78
Swartz, Alexander T. A401
Swartz, Jan G. A696
Swartz, Kevin L. E30
Swartz, Richard S. E337
Swartz, Robin E529
Swartz, Russell C. A359
Swartzendruber, Kevin E444
Swedish, Joseph R. A565
Swedish, Joseph R. A214
Swedjemark, Theodor W6
Sweeney, Anne M. A730
Sweeney, Eileen W123
Sweeney, Gary D. A1133

COMBINED HOOVER'S HANDBOOK INDEX OF EXECUTIVES

A = AMERICAN BUSINESS
E = EMERGING COMPANIES
P = PRIVATE COMPANIES
W = WORLD BUSINESSS

Sweeney, Gary D. E541
Sweeney, James E. E452
Sweeney, Joseph E. A70
Sweeney, Kevin M. E537
Sweet, Julie Spellman W10
Sweet, Leah E234
Sweet, Schuyler Wallace E506
Sweitzer, Brandon W. W235
Sweitzer, Caesar F. A303
Swenson, Michael L. E98
Swets, Jon W. A653
Swick, Stephen L. A59
Swieringa, John W. A333
Swift, Christopher J. A502
Swift, Christopher J. A248
Swift, Malcolm S. A673
Swift, Micheal A P177
Swinbank, Joseph B. A214
Swindells, Matthew W162
Swinson, Stephen K. A301
Swinson, Stephen K. E131
Swinton, Carolyn P444
Swire, Barnaby N. W579
Swire, J. S. W580
Swire, Merlin Bingham W579
Swire, Merlin Bingham W128
Swire, S. C. W580
Swisher, Daniel N. E121
Switz, Robert E. A700
Switzer, John A. A528
Switzer, John A. E258
Switzer, Matthew A. A845
Switzer, Matthew A. E395
Swoboda, Marco W276
Swoish, Tom E455
Swords, Sheridan C. A783
Swyers, Steven O. A531
Swygert, John W. E360
Sy, Teresita T. W100
Syal, Rajeev A545
Sykes, Nancy E. A952
Sykes, Ollin B. E93
Sylvain, Jereme E138
Sylvest, Camilla W450
Sylvester, Edward B. A1119
Sylvester, Maryrose T. A1110
Symancyk, James Kevin A140
Symonds, Jonathan W258
Symson, Adam P. E431
Syphax, Scott C. A398
Syquia, Juan Carlos L. W85
Syu, Jyongci W169
Syu, Mingsing W168
Szablak, Chester J. A372
Szablak, Chester J. E167
Szczuk, Jason A168
Szczuk, Jason P89
Szczurek, Michal Jan W603
Sze, Julia W. E85
Sze, Julia W. E501
Sze, Mei Ming W248
Sze, Robert Tsai-To W180
Sze, Robert Tsai-To W179
Szelag, Grzegorz W631

Szews, Charles L. A277
Szews, Charles L. A491
Szkutak, Thomas J. A571
Szlezak, Andrzej W325
Szlosek, Thomas A. A112
Szlosek, Thomas A. E283
Szmagala, Taras G. W209
Sznewajs, John G. A666
Sznewajs, John G. A294
Sznewajs, John G. A256
Sznewajs, Robert D. A124
Szomburg, Jan W389
Szostak, M. Anne E263
Szubinski, Clinton A687
Szurek, Paul E. E217
Szydlowski, Norman J. E171
Szyman, Catherine M. A361
Szymanczyk, Michael E. A340
Szymanski, David M. A770

T

T., Thomas Mathew W358
Taaveniku, Arja W579
Tabacco, Joseph J. E368
Tabaka, William L. A539
Tabata, Takuji W1
Tabbutt, Mark N. A1107
Taber, Afshin A400
Tabernero, Jordi Garcia W423
Tabron, La June Montgomery A597
Tacchetti, Gregory A. A966
Taccone, Anthony R. E236
Tachibana, Atsushi W319
Tachibana, Sakie Fukushima W44
Tachouet, Matthew P670
Tackett, Shane R. A34
Tada, Takayasu W281
Taddese, Menassie A1093
Tadeu, Ricardo W40
Tadlock, Stephen E72
Tadokoro, Takeshi W330
Tadolini, Barbara W627
Tadros, Alain W399
Tadros, Ramy A691
Taftali, A. Umit W661
Tagawa, Joji W492
Tagawa, Joji W405
Tagawa, Joji W441
Tagawa, Toshikazu W156
Taggart, Harriett Tee A499
Taglieri, Lina W646
Tago, Hideto W539
Taguchi, Kenichi W21
Taguchi, Sachio W81
Tahara, Keisuke W179
Tai, Jackson Pei A636
Tai, Jackson Pei A670
Tai, Jackson Pei W290
Tai, Jeng-wu W284
Tai, Pin A211
Tai, Pin E84
Taiclet, James D. A643
Taillandier-Thomas, Patrice W347
Taira, Tom A208
Taishido, Atsuko W581
Tait, Matthew A. E308
Taittinger, Anne-Claire W601

Taittinger, Anne-Claire W125
Taka, Iwao W539
Takada, Yoshihisa W330
Takada, Yoshimasa W281
Takagi, Shuichi W462
Takahara, Takahisa W445
Takahashi, Atsushi W81
Takahashi, Chie W576
Takahashi, Kyohei W387
Takahashi, Makoto W336
Takahashi, Masahiro W81
Takahashi, Shinichi W313
Takahashi, Shinya W433
Takahashi, Shojiro W533
Takahashi, Yasuhide W454
Takahashi, Yoshinori W278
Takakura, Toru W570
Takamaki, Heikki W340
Takamatsu, Kazuko W331
Takami, Kazunori W608
Takano, Hiromitsu W604
Takase, Hideaki W407
Takashi, Hirose W437
Takashima, Hideya W603
Takashima, Makoto W570
Takata, Kenji W316
Takatsu, Norio W137
Takaura, Hideo W607
Takayama, Yasuko W137
Takayama, Yasuko W173
Takayanagi, Nobuhiro W404
Takayanagi, Ryutaro W403
Takeda, Junko W173
Takeda, Kazuhiko W404
Takegawa, Keiko W527
Takeguchi, Fumitoshi W462
Takei, Tsutomu W266
Takemasu, Yoshiaki W408
Takenaka, Heizo W460
Takeoka, Yaeko W405
Takeshima, Masayuki W454
Takeshita, Noriaki W565
Taketa, Richard H. E370
Taketomi, Masao W181
Takeuchi, Akira W404
Takeuchi, Kei W184
Takeuchi, Keisuke W319
Takeuchi, Kohei W285
Takeuchi, Minako W533
Takeuchi, Tetsuo W316
Takeuchi, Toshiaki W333
Takeuchi, Toshie W28
Takeuchi, Yutaka W439
Taki, Layth E547
Takiguchi, Yurina W538
Takimoto, Johei W400
Takvam, Martha W347
Talamo, Yolanda W274
Talarico, Nick P199
Talbot, Randall H. A1107
Talbot, Siobhan W178
Talintyre, April W462
Talisman, Jonathan A150
Tall, Macky W420
Tallapragada, Srinivas A912
Tallapragada, Srinivas E234
Tallett, Elizabeth E. A846
Tallett, Elizabeth E. A85
Talley, Kevin C. E5
Talley, Michael A. E512

Talma, Arja W340
Talone, Joao Luis Ramalho de Carvalho W212
Talton, Sheila G. A320
Talton, Sheila G. A989
Talvitie, Kristian E402
Talwalkar, Abhijit Y. A18
Talwalkar, Abhijit Y. A619
Talwalkar, Abhijit Y. W590
Talwar, Harit A670
Tam, Danny Kam Wah W240
Tamayo, Arturo Condo W76
Tamayo, Carlos G. A381
Tamberlane, John A936
Tamberlane, John E440
Tambor, Richard N. E361
Tamburi, Giovanni W482
Tamer, Ford G. E485
Tamme, Susan Stout A890
Tamme, Susan Stout E416
Tamone, Tanya E420
Tamoud, Mourad W524
Tamsons, Asa W228
Tamsons, Asa W157
Tamura, Hisashi W576
Tamura, Koji W405
Tamura, Mayumi W370
Tamura, Mayumi W535
Tamura, Yasuro W581
Tamura, Yoshiaki W181
Tan, Benjamin A P625
Tan, Charles Keng Lock W36
Tan, Choon Hin W628
Tan, Christina E144
Tan, Colin Kwang Chuan A1145
Tan, Colin Tiang Soon W649
Tan, Cynthia Guan Hiang W463
Tan, Darren Siew Peng W463
Tan, Desney E417
Tan, Edmundo L. W100
Tan, Farid E323
Tan, Fiona A1112
Tan, Hock E. A179
Tan, Irving A962
Tan, Josefina N. W100
Tan, Lay Koon W242
Tan, Lip-Bu W524
Tan, Marc W190
Tan, May Siew Boi W382
Tan, Nestor V. W99
Tan, Peter Moo Tan W628
Tan, Philip Chen Chong W79
Tan, Serena Mei Shwen W156
Tan, Shunlong W656
Tan, Xiaogang W153
Tan, Xiaosheng W153
Tan, Xuguang W644
Tanabe, Barbara J. A129
Tanabe, Eiichi W440
Tanaka, Kazuhiro W155
Tanaka, Kouji W570
Tanaka, Norihiko W659
Tanaka, Norikazu W402
Tanaka, Satoshi W527
Tanaka, Satoshi W436
Tanaka, Seiichi W552
Tanaka, Shigeyoshi W582
Tanaka, Susumu W319
Tanaka, Takashi W336
Tanaka, Tatsuo W180

HOOVER'S HANDBOOK OF EMERGING COMPANIES 2023

COMBINED HOOVER'S HANDBOOK INDEX OF EXECUTIVES

A = AMERICAN BUSINESS
E = EMERGING COMPANIES
P = PRIVATE COMPANIES
W = WORLD BUSINESSS

Tanaka, Toshihiro W325
Tanaka, Toshiki W28
Tanaka, Toshizo W123
Tanaka, Tsutomu W552
Tancongco, Federico P. W100
Tanda, Stephan B. A557
Taneja, Rajat A1096
Taneja, Rajat E336
Taneja, Vaibhav A1007
Tanemura, Ronald K. A941
Tang, Anthony M. A211
Tang, Anthony M. E84
Tang, David W561
Tang, Fei W534
Tang, Francis E143
Tang, Frank Kui W10
Tang, Henry W80
Tang, Jiang W156
Tang, Jianhua W292
Tang, Mei W117
Tang, Michael A27
Tang, Na W148
Tang, Shihui W542
Tang, Shoulian W106
Tang, Vance W348
Tang, Vance W. E27
Tang, Vance W. E111
Tang, Wan Mui W240
Tang, Wing Chew W484
Tang, Xiaodong W326
Tang, Xin W142
Tang, Xiuguo W516
Tang, Ya W516
Tang, Yizhi W636
Tangen, Blake P581
Tango, Yasutake W454
Tangtatswas, Singh W77
Tani, Sadafumi W496
Tanigaki, Kunio W319
Taniguchi, Masako W449
Taniguchi, Shinichi W155
Taniguchi, Shoji W460
Tanikawa, Kei W44
Tanimoto, Hideo W356
Tanimura, Keizo W50
Taniyama, Jirou W582
Tanizaki, Katsunori W569
Tanji, Kenneth Y. A856
Tanji, Kevin E546
Tank, Stacey W274
Tanna, Catherine W101
Tanner, Bruce L. A69
Tanner, Bruce L. A1042
Tanner, Dallas B. E280
Tanner, David A. E350
Tanner, Hans Christoph W203
Tanner, Kirk A817
Tanner, Lindsay W574
Tanner, Reed J. A1115
Tanner, Reed J. E533
Tannowa, Tsutomu W336
Tannuzzo, Gene R. A895
Tanous, James J. E18
Tanski, Ronald J. A256

Tanski, Ronald J. A294
Tantakasem, Piti W603
Tanthuwanit, Sumate W541
Tantisawetrat, Yokporn W541
Tantivejkul, Sumet W540
Tantivorawong, Apisak W352
Tao, Ran W148
Tao, Xinliang W512
Tapases, Christos A. E537
Tapiero, Jacques A673
Tapnack, Alan W310
Tapscott, James F. A774
Tapscott, James F. E360
Tarantino, Laura A650
Tarantino, Laura E305
Taranto, Eric R. E329
Taranto, Joseph V. W232
Tarbutton, Charles K. A471
Tardan, Francois E357
Tardif, Pierre W193
Tarpey, Mia A296
Tarullo, Daniel K. A403
Tarver, Edward J. E195
Tarvin, Julie L. A563
Tarvin, Michael E. A926
Tasaka, Takayuki W462
Tascarella, Ronald A. E372
Tashima, Yuko W137
Tashiro, Yuko W658
Tashita, Kayo W267
Tashma, Lauren S. A486
Tasman, Norman A978
Tasman, Norman E465
Tastad, Carolyn M. A597
Tata, Jimmy W271
Tata, Ratan N. W588
Tate, Jeffrey L. A545
Tate, Jeffrey L. A624
Tate, Masafumi W184
Tateishi, Noboru W441
Tatsiy, Vladimir Vitalyevich W476
Tatsuoka, Tsuneyoshi W402
Tatsuoka, Tsuneyoshi W51
Tatterson, William Mark A1063
Tatterson, William Mark E508
Tatum, Demitrios P172
Tatum, Lisa M. Skeete A981
Tatum, Mark A. A466
Taubert, Jennifer L. A585
Taubert, Jennifer L. A675
Taubitz, Fredricka A774
Taubman, Paul J. E388
Taubman, Robert S. A274
Tauzin, W. J. E300
Tavares, Carlos W562
Tavares, Carlos W24
Tavares, Diogo Mendonca Rodrigues W254
Tavenner, Marilyn B. A926
Tawes, Michael C. E452
Taxay, Marc E35
Taxil, Christian W215
Tay, Ah Lek W484
Tay, Julie E16
Tay, Kah Chye W649
Tay, Talal E113
Tayano, Ken W183
Taylor-Broughton, Christine B. A276
Taylor, Aileen W289
Taylor, Ann W601

Taylor, Anne A491
Taylor, Beth A. E273
Taylor, Bret A1047
Taylor, Colleen A647
Taylor, Cynthia B. A105
Taylor, Daniel J. A696
Taylor, David S. A850
Taylor, David S. A323
Taylor, Del Mar Deeni E384
Taylor, Diana L. A246
Taylor, Diana L. W112
Taylor, Douglas C. A252
Taylor, Emily A336
Taylor, Frederick L. A414
Taylor, Frederick L. E191
Taylor, Gary E411
Taylor, Jack T. A929
Taylor, Jack T. A719
Taylor, Jason L. A145
Taylor, Joanne W37
Taylor, Jodi L. A947
Taylor, John A. A485
Taylor, John T. E301
Taylor, Johnny C. A1143
Taylor, Jonathan W116
Taylor, Julia A. E480
Taylor, K. Jon A432
Taylor, Kathleen W13
Taylor, Kathleen P. W507
Taylor, Keisha E431
Taylor, Keith D. A377
Taylor, Larry P145
Taylor, Leo P585
Taylor, Michael J. A489
Taylor, Michael J. E221
Taylor, Michael L. A427
Taylor, Michael L. E204
Taylor, Michelle E242
Taylor, Milbrey Rennie A430
Taylor, Nancy M. E490
Taylor, Nathaniel H. A1083
Taylor, Nicole C. A402
Taylor, Paul W. A800
Taylor, Peter J. A359
Taylor, Peter J. A951
Taylor, R. Eugene A948
Taylor, R. Eugene A424
Taylor, R. Eugene E200
Taylor, Rhonda M. A336
Taylor, Robert C. A516
Taylor, Ronald R. E417
Taylor, Rory E43
Taylor, Scott C. E547
Taylor, Scott C. E387
Taylor, Sharon C. W559
Taylor, Sharon L. E221
Taylor, Steven A788
Taylor, Steven E364
Taylor, Stuart A. A123
Taylor, Stuart A. E255
Taylor, Sue A166
Taylor, Teresa A. A992
Taylor, Thomas V. E210
Taylor, Thomas V. E341
Taylor, Vincent A1098
Taynton, Philis P177
Tayon, James E. E25
Teagle, Walter C. A430
Teague, A. James A374
Tebbe, Brad M. E186

Tebbe, Keith E185
Tebbe, Mark A. E162
Techasarintr, Padoong W117
Tecotzky, Mark E155
Tedbury, Andrew W116
Tedesco, James P167
Tedesco, Maria P. A106
Tedesco, Maria P. E40
Teepsuwan, Veraphan W79
Teets, John Christopher E11
Teets, Richard P. A975
Teffner, Carrie W. A349
Tegan, Jennifer T. A1033
Teglia, Karin Gustafson A1133
Teglia, Karin Gustafson E541
Teh, Hong Piow W484
Teh, Kok Peng W464
Tehle, David M. A1083
Tehle, David M. E341
Tehrani, Sean P462
Teich, Andrew C. A893
Teichgraeber, Gretchen G. E215
Teixeira, Kay P327
Teixeira, Rui Manuel Rodrigues Lopes W212
Tejada, Jennifer G. A620
Tejada, Jose-Miguel A1135
Tejagupta, Pongpinit W79
Tejera, Federico J. Gonzalez W550
Tejera, Pablo Isla Alvarez de W300
Tejerina, Isabel Garcia W295
Tejima, Tatsuya W270
Tekorius, Lorie L. E13
Telesmanic, Robert A267
Telesz, Scott E. E253
Tellem, Nancy A900
Tellem, Nancy A742
Telles, Marcel Herrmann W40
Tellez, Cora M. A797
Tellez, Cora M. E368
Tellock, Glen E. A1114
Temperley, Dessi W161
Temperley, Dessislava A825
Tempini, Giovanni Gorno W592
Temple-Boyer, Heloise W338
Temple, Christopher M. A833
Temple, Christopher M. A832
Temple, Michael G. A853
Templeman-Jones, Anne W164
Templeton, Lauren C. W235
Templeton, Mark B. E35
Templeton, Richard K. A1010
Templin, Donald C. A1098
Templin, Mark S. A1034
Tena, Antonio Basolas W423
Tena, Nemesio Fernandez-Cuesta Luca de W423
Tendil, Claude W526
Teng, Chin-Chi E75
Teng, Chung-Yi W128
Teng, Jiao W106
Teng, Soon Lang W463
Teng, Yu W291
Teng, Zhenyu W663
Tengel, Jeffrey (Jeff) J. A554
Tengel, Jeffrey (Jeff) J. A814
Tengel, Jeffrey (Jeff) J. E268
Tengel, Jeffrey (Jeff) J. E379
Tennant, Joan Lamm A52
Tenner, Mandy E19

A = AMERICAN BUSINESS
E = EMERGING COMPANIES
P = PRIVATE COMPANIES
W = WORLD BUSINESSS

Tennican, Liz E217
Tennyson, Steve W82
Teno, Andrew J. A432
Teo, Chiang Liang W495
Teo, Kim Yong W649
Teo, La-Mei W649
Teo, Lay Lim W628
Teo, Swee-Lian W20
Teofilo, Joanie Cahill A496
Teoh, Chia-Yin W190
Teoh, Su Yin W156
Teplukhin, Pavel Mikhailovich W476
Terabatake, Masamichi W321
Terada, Masahiro W538
Teraguchi, Tomoyuki W445
Terahata, Masashi W325
Terakawa, Akira W387
Teramoto, Yoshihiro W582
Teran, Antonio Puron Mier y W73
Terasaka, Koji W155
Terasawa, Eisuke W538
Terbsiri, Atikom W484
Tercinier, Louis W174
Terekhov, Alexander Pavlovich W476
Terner, Franck W22
Terracina, Roy D. E514
Terrano, Janine T. A271
Terrano, Janine T. E109
Terraz, Nicolas W613
Terre, Joan-David Grima W11
Terrell, Frederick O. A802
Terrell, Frederick O. A132
Terrell, Scott E219
Terreson, Douglas T. A826
Terrill, Christopher S. A879
Terrill, Christopher S. A878
Terrillion, Scott M. E80
Terry, Alison W246
Terry, Hilliard C. A1057
Terry, Hilliard C. A99
Terry, Hilliard C. E513
Terry, Mark Aaron A1064
Terry, Mark Aaron E509
Terry, Robert J. A942
Terry, Thomas S. A1056
Terry, Thomas S. E505
Tersigni, Anthony R. E408
Teruel, Javier G. A742
Terui, Keikou W110
Terwiesch, Peter W6
Terwindt, Steven W109
Terzariol, Giulio W33
Terzich, Michael H. A1148
Tese, Vincent A561
Teshima, Nobuyuki W405
Teshima, Toshihiro W555
Teshirogi, Isao W18
Tesija, Kathryn A. A254
Tesija, Kathryn A. W651
Teslyk, Kevin W84
Tessel, Marianna A571
Tessel, Marianna A244
Tessier-Lavigne, Marc A882
Tessier-Lavigne, Marc A401

Tessier, Claude W31
Testa, Christopher P. A1068
Testa, Daniel M. E227
Testa, William A. A399
Testerman, Christopher R P174
Teter, Timothy S. A761
Tetu, Louis W31
Teubner, Russell W. A938
Teubner, Russell W. E442
Teuscher, Stephan W198
Tewell, Dennis W31
Tewes, Timothy A. A727
Tewes, Timothy A. E345
Tewksbury, Theodore L. E314
Textor, Donald F. A376
Teyssen, Johannes W109
Thabet, Pierre W420
Thai-Tang, Hau N. A444
Thai-Tang, Hau N. A173
Thain, John A. A1052
Thajchayapong, Pairash W334
Thakar, Sumedh S. E405
Thakrar, Rakesh W471
Thalberg, Marisa F. A647
Thaler, Warren S. E16
Thallinger, Gunther W33
Tham, Sai Choy W190
Thaman, Michael H. A934
Thamsirisup, Wanna W79
Thanasorn, Phaphatsorn W117
Thanattrai, Phonganant W79
Thanavaranit, Potjanee W79
Thansathit, Suvarn W77
Tharp, Morris A. A935
Tharp, Morris A. E439
Thatcher, Laura G. A904
Thau, Andrew A124
Thavisin, Phongsthorn W484
Thaxton, Gregory A. E287
Thaxton, Kirk W. A421
Thaxton, Kirk W. E198
Thayer, Jennifer E. A531
Thaysen, Jacob A27
Thebault, J. Brian A927
Thebault, J. Brian E435
Thedford, Donald W. A954
Theiler, Jeffrey N. E384
Theiler, Jeffrey R. A880
Theiler, Jeffrey R. E412
Theilmann, Michael T. A35
Thein, Kim Mon W36
Theine, Mark D. E384
Theisen, Randall S. A1120
Theisen, Randall S. E535
Theisen, Sonja Anne A688
Theisen, Sonja Anne E323
Theissig, Bettina W187
Thelen, Bruce E471
Thelen, Daniel W397
Thelen, Simon W397
Themelis, Nicholas E311
Theobald, Stephen P. E531
Theodore, Phillip L. A893
Theodoredis, Roger E. A232
Theodosopoulos, Nikos E35
Theofilaktidis, Maria W84
Theologides, Stergios A391
Theophilus, Nicole B. A1099
Thepaut, Eric Francis Yves A175
Therady, Agnes P229

Therivel, Laurent C. A1001
Theroux, Stephen R. A138
Theroux, Stephen R. E55
Thiam, Tidjane W338
Thian, Fui Ming (Catherine) A878
Thian, Fui Ming (Catherine) E410
Thibaudet, Philippe W165
Thibault, Dean R. E291
Thibault, Francois W398
Thibault, Rene E. W283
Thiede, Dirk W277
Thiede, Jeffrey S. A679
Thiel, John W. A448
Thiel, Lynn M. A816
Thielen, Bruce J. E338
Thierer, Mark A. A330
Thiers, Bernard P. A706
Thigpen, Mary ("Mimi") E. A531
Thigpen, Mary ("Mimi") E. A478
Thigpen, Mary ("Mimi") E. E259
Thijs, Johan W336
Thoele, Larry J. A620
Thoma, Jeanne A. E45
Thomas, Andrea B. E316
Thomas, Bill W159
Thomas, Cheryl L. A1085
Thomas, Corey E. A648
Thomas, Daniel J. A926
Thomas, Daphyne S. E181
Thomas, David A. A343
Thomas, David A. A345
Thomas, David M. A570
Thomas, David M. A447
Thomas, Deborah M. A645
Thomas, Eira M. W573
Thomas, Francis M. E433
Thomas, Gareth W160
Thomas, J. Darrell W111
Thomas, Jeffrey K. A401
Thomas, John M. A1006
Thomas, John T. E384
Thomas, Kenneth H. E351
Thomas, Lee M A298
Thomas, Linda C. E352
Thomas, Lizanne A106
Thomas, Michael E217
Thomas, Michael H. E274
Thomas, Patrick W328
Thomas, Patrick W492
Thomas, Patrick W167
Thomas, Patrick W. W174
Thomas, Paul L. E338
Thomas, Peter R. S. W310
Thomas, Peter T. A153
Thomas, Philip W84
Thomas, Ralf P. W543
Thomas, Ralf P. W545
Thomas, Richard C. A797
Thomas, Richard C. E368
Thomas, Shundrawn A. A886
Thomas, Tom E477
Thomas, William R. A755
Thomas, William R. E160
Thomason, Keith P594
Thomasson, Virginia C. A414
Thomasson, Virginia C. E191
Thompson, Alfred F. E326
Thompson, C. Reynolds E315
Thompson, Cary H. A407
Thompson, Christopher M. T. A580

Thompson, Clare W374
Thompson, Daniel C. E206
Thompson, David K. A880
Thompson, David K. E412
Thompson, Don L. A880
Thompson, Don L. E412
Thompson, Donald A749
Thompson, Donald H. A939
Thompson, Dorothy C. W209
Thompson, Erik Dahl A685
Thompson, Fiona W574
Thompson, G. Kennedy A829
Thompson, G. Kennedy E385
Thompson, G. Kennedy E275
Thompson, H. Brian A813
Thompson, J. Kenneth A830
Thompson, J. Kenneth A34
Thompson, James W274
Thompson, James H. A867
Thompson, James Kirk A543
Thompson, Jane J. A723
Thompson, Jeff P231
Thompson, Jeffrey R. A199
Thompson, John R. A743
Thompson, John R. A747
Thompson, John Wendell A701
Thompson, Kathy C. A978
Thompson, Kathy C. E465
Thompson, Kelly Ann A423
Thompson, Kevin L. A800
Thompson, Larry E. A396
Thompson, Larry E. E187
Thompson, Laura K. A1118
Thompson, Laura K. A804
Thompson, Marcy J. A950
Thompson, Mark W451
Thompson, Mark E. A545
Thompson, Mark G. A207
Thompson, Marsha L. E340
Thompson, Matt P271
Thompson, Michael L. A242
Thompson, Paul W. A841
Thompson, Richard B. A393
Thompson, Richard B. E184
Thompson, Robert P246
Thompson, Samme L. A69
Thompson, Simon W509
Thompson, Simon W499
Thompson, Stephen A516
Thompson, Sue P280
Thompson, Thomas N. A1042
Thompson, Tommy G. E384
Thompson, Travis J. E260
Thompson, Warren M. A818
Thompson, Warren M. E146
Thompson, William A. A287
Thompson, William A. E115
Thompson, William C. E430
Thomsen, Jorn Ankaer W632
Thomsen, Kim Hvid W632
Thomsen, Laurie J. A1037
Thomson, Justin A991
Thomson, Kathy R. E287
Thomson, L. Barry W84
Thomson, Laurie R. A485
Thomson, Louise W419
Thomson, Phil W258
Thomson, Robert J. A738
Thong, Yaw Hong W484
Thongyai, Peekthong W484

COMBINED HOOVER'S HANDBOOK INDEX OF EXECUTIVES

A = AMERICAN BUSINESS
E = EMERGING COMPANIES
P = PRIVATE COMPANIES
W = WORLD BUSINESSS

Thor, Wieslaw W389
Thoralfsson, Barbara Milian W231
Thoralfsson, Barbara Milian W4
Thormann, Dominique W490
Thorn, Bruce K. A157
Thornal, Kevin R. A522
Thornberry, Richard G. A873
Thornburg, Eric W. E446
Thornburgh, Richard E. A911
Thorne, Rosemary P. W554
Thornes, Sverre W347
Thornton, Felicia D. E210
Thornton, John Lawson A444
Thornton, Leslie T P687
Thornton, Matthew A301
Thornton, Matthew A934
Thorson, John A. A1119
Throener, Kevin J. A235
Throsby, Tim W89
Thuestad, John G. W448
Thuillier, Lawrence (Larry) J. A741
Thulin, Inge G. A684
Thulin, Niclas W231
Thurber, Lynn C. E146
Thurmond, Richard B. A1033
Thurmond, Richard B. E493
Thyen, Christopher J. E287
Thygesen, Henriette Hallberg W1
Tian, Bo W138
Tian, Guoli W138
Tian, Hui W660
Tian, Jingqi W256
Tian, Suning W362
Tian, Xin W272
Tian, Yong W88
Tian, Yongzhong W662
Tian, Zhaohua W660
Tian, Zhiping W652
Tiarks, Roy H. A396
Tiarks, Roy H. E186
Tibbetts, Shawn J. E35
Tibi, Valerie Della Puppa W613
Tice, Gary L. A423
Tice, Gary L. E199
Tickles, Chuck P218
Tidwell, Kay L. E420
Tieanworn, Min W137
Tieben, Stefan W398
Tielsch, Monika W395
Tienghongsakiul, Lawan W117
Tierney, Brian X. A59
Tietz, Christopher G. A200
Tietz, Christopher G. E79
Tiffany, Patricia A439
Tighe, Jan E. A548
Tighe, Jan E. A481
Tighlaline, Fatima W357
Tilden, Bradley D. A34
Tilden, Bradley D. A745
Tilford, Thomas B. A1099
Till, James M. A153
Tillage, Keith A188
Tillage, Keith E69
Tillett, G. Douglas A399

Tillett, Ronald L. A106
Tillett, Ronald L. E40
Tillman, Audrey Boone A24
Tillman, Lee M. A656
Tilly, Edward T. E87
Tilmant, Michel J. W104
Tilton, David A458
Tilton, David P236
Tilton, Glenn F. A826
Tilton, Glenn F. A8
Tily, Gil Coleman A78
Timanus, H. E. A852
Timanus, H. E. E399
Timm, Bryan L. A1057
Timm, Jill A608
Timm, Stepen J. A877
Timmerman, Douglas R. A43
Timmermans, Jesse E418
Timms, Geoffrey J. W360
Timperman, Jurgen A207
Timur, Hakan W267
Timuray, Serpil W187
Tindal, Bruce B. E192
Tiner, John W176
Ting, Lee Sen W362
Tinggren, Jurgen W327
Tingley, Sandy P446
Tió, José R. Coleman A836
Tio, Romano E63
Tippit, James P. A556
Tippit, James P. E270
Tippy, Courtney A. A1110
Tipton, J. Stephen A524
Tipton, J. Stephen E258
Tiradnakorn, Tara W603
Tirador, Gabriel A685
Tirawattanagool, Nopporn W79
Tirinnanzi, Martha A561
Tirpak, Bradley M. E56
Tisch, Alexander A645
Tisch, Andrew H. A645
Tisch, Andrew H. A258
Tisch, Benjamin J. A258
Tisch, James S. A258
Tisch, James S. A462
Tisch, James S. A645
Tisch, Jonathan M. A645
Tisdel, Gregory A. E104
Tishman, Daniel R. A20
Tison, Stuart E166
Tissue, Robert S. A981
Tissue, Robert S. E469
Titasattavorakul, Piyawat W117
Titi, Fani W311
Titi, Fani W310
Titinger, Jorge E47
Titinger, Jorge L. E107
Titinger, Jorge Luis E214
Titinger, Jorge Luis E261
Titov, Vasily Nikolaevich W476
Titterto, Charles F. A774
Titus, Brian A298
Titus, Danny L. E357
Titus, Martin E A1031
Titus, Martin E P623
Tjan, Ivo A. E134
Toalson, Michael L. E526
Tobe, Tomoko W336
Tobias, Paul D. A741
Tobias, Paul D. E349

Tobimatsu, Junichi W413
Tobin, James R. E233
Tobin, Richard Joseph A342
Tocci, Nathalie W227
Tocio, Mary Ann A187
Toczydlowski, Gregory C. A1037
Toda, Kazuhide W436
Todaro, Richard L. E50
Todd, Lauren K. E22
Todd, Roderick M. E195
Todd, Stephen M. A342
Todd, Stephen M. E91
Todgham, Paul D. E105
Todhanakasem, Kittiya W352
Todman, Michael A. A710
Todman, Michael A. A857
Todman, Michael A. A207
Todorcevski, Zlatko W162
Todoroki, Masahiko W536
Todorov, Pierre W215
Toellner, Ann P656
Toenjes-Werner, Elke W395
Toepfer, Thomas W174
Toft, Hans W348
Togashi, Brandon E340
Togawa, Masanori W182
Tojo, Noriko W462
Tojo, Takashi W581
Tokarev, Nikolay Petrovich W617
Tokioka, Dana M. A129
Tokita, Takahito W253
Tokuhira, Tsukasa W657
Tokunaga, Setsuo W403
Tokunaga, Toshiaki W279
Tokuno, Mariko W659
Tokuno, Mariko W404
Tokuoka, Yuji W181
Tokura, Masakazu W565
Tol, Maurits van W328
Toledo, Phil De A197
Toledo, Phil De P103
Toll, Robert I. A1032
Tolla, John A120
Tolla, John E48
Tolle, Rolf Albert Wilhelm W487
Tolliver, Paula C. A573
Tolliver, Paula C. A900
Tolman, Sarah E. E192
Tolot, Jérôme W565
Tolson, Aaron C. E154
Tolson, Laurie Z. A321
Tolson, Susan M. E480
Tomao, Alessandro W72
Tomasevic, Josip T. A26
Tomasky, Susan A858
Tomasky, Susan A657
Tomasky, Susan P33
Tomaszewski, Jeffery S. A950
Tomazoni, Gilberto A828
Tomazoni, Gilberto W323
Tomb, Matthew C. A418
Tomb, Matthew C. E195
Tombar, Tymothi O. E72
Tomczuk, Marek W86
Tomczyk, Fredric J. E87
Tome, Carol B. A1088
Tome, Carol B. A1069
Tometich, Andrew E. E404
Tomii, Satoshi W319
Tominaga, Hiroshi W616

Tomioka, Yasuyuki W439
Tomita, Tetsuro W208
Tomita, Tetsuro W223
Tomita, Tetsuro W437
Tomiyama, Yuji W353
Tomlin, Dervla W262
Tomlin, Laura M. E431
Tomlin, Robert Michael W456
Tomnitz, Donald J. E213
Tomoda, Shigeru W330
Tomono, Hiroshi W331
Tomono, Hiroshi W565
Tompkins, Bonnie M. E336
Tomsic, Steven A447
Tondi, Francesca W625
Tondreau, Pamela L. E161
Tonelli, Fulvio W8
Toney, Charles A685
Tong, Carlson W561
Tong, Chris A995
Tong, Guohua W152
Tong, Hon-shing W80
Tong, Judy Wenhong W29
Tong, Richard E357
Tong, Ronald Wui Tung W173
Tong, Tao Sang W596
Tonge, Eoin W385
Tonina, Norman J. E204
Tonjes, Bernd W234
Tønnesen, Erik Edvard W558
Tonnison, John A. A1083
Tononi, Massimo W482
Tonosu, Kaori W319
Toogood, Jane E. W328
Toohey, Robert A42
Tookes, Hansel E. A909
Tookes, Hansel E. A298
Toole, Gasper L. E433
Toole, Samara E49
Tooley, David J. A953
Tooley, David J. E455
Toothaker, Bradley J. A618
Toothaker, Bradley J. E290
Toothaker, Scott G. A138
Toothaker, Scott G. E55
Topalian, Leon J. A759
Tope, Chad J. A722
Topel, Karin W199
Topete, Xavier Garcia de Quevedo A953
Topol, Eric J. E138
Topsch, Edgar W277
Torabi, Peymon S. E191
Torbakhov, Alexander W655
Torbett, H. Lindsey A880
Torbett, H. Lindsey E412
Torchio, Louis J. A753
Toretti, Christine J. A910
Torgeby, Johan A721
Torgeby, Johan W547
Torgerson, William G. E314
Torgow, Gary H. A545
Torgow, Gary H. A343
Torgow, Gary H. A345
Torigoe, Nobuhiro W281
Torii, Shingo W183
Torley, Helen I. E244
Tormoen, Sandra L. A401
Torno, Vitaliano A764
Tornos, Ivan A1150
Torrallardona, Maria Isabel Mata W265

COMBINED HOOVER'S HANDBOOK INDEX OF EXECUTIVES

A = AMERICAN BUSINESS
E = EMERGING COMPANIES
P = PRIVATE COMPANIES
W = WORLD BUSINESSS

Torrecillas, Jose Miguel Andres W68
Torrego, Agustin Batuecas W11
Torres, Daria Stacy-Walls A271
Torres, Daria Stacy-Walls E110
Torres, Denice M. E475
Torres, Emilio Saracho Rodriguez de W300
Torres, Grace C. A768
Torres, Grace C. E359
Torres, Issac P. A1
Torres, Juan Romero W131
Torres, Rafael E503
Torres, Rosangela Buzanelli W468
Torres, Russell A604
Torres, Sherice R. A17
Torrion, Philippe W215
Torroella, Jose Ignacio Mariscal W265
Torronen, Rauno W340
Torstendahl, Mats W547
Toruner, Yaman W26
Tory, Jennifer W99
Toscano, Kristine H. A176
Tostivin, Jean-Claude W161
Totoki, Hiroki W557
Totoki, Hiroki W490
Totta, DeAnn M. E315
Toubro, Per Alling W188
Touche, Ricardo Guajardo W27
Touche, Ricardo Guajardo W265
Touche, Ricardo Guajardo W244
Tourangeau, Serge W193
Tournay, Philippe W554
Tov, Imri W78
Tower, Marcus R. A747
Townes-Whitley, Toni A834
Townes-Whitley, Toni A657
Townes-Whitley, Toni A721
Townsell, Donna J. A524
Townsell, Donna J. E258
Townsend, ?Frances F. W154
Townsend, Christopher G. W33
Townsend, Frances Fragos A13
Townsend, Frances Fragos A452
Townsend, Kent G. A199
Toy, David A. A1083
Toya, Tomoki W576
Toyama, Kazuhiko W465
Toyama, Ryoko W609
Toyoda, Akio W193
Toyoda, Akio W616
Toyoda, Masakazu W441
Toyoda, Tetsuro W614
Toyoma, Makoto W357
Toyoshima, Masakazu W293
Toyoshima, Naoyuki W357
Tozer, Theodore W. A811
Tozer, Theodore W. E377
Tracey, Bernard M P521
Tracey, C. Lynn E223
Tracey, Patricia A. A1073
Traeger, Norman L. E306
Trager, A. Scott A890
Trager, A. Scott E416
Trager, Kusman Andrew A890

Trager, Kusman Andrew E416
Trager, Steven E. A890
Trager, Steven E. E416
Train, Michael (Mike) H. A365
Trainor, Christopher H. E255
Trakulhoon, Vipoota W352
Tran, Kelvin V. W611
Tran, Khanh T. A886
Tran, Tuan A538
Transier, William L. E250
Trapp, Jacqueline A359
Trappey, Ann Forte A523
Trappey, Ann Forte E257
Trappier, Eric W601
Traquina, Perry M. A713
Traquina, Perry M. A42
Traquina, Perry M. A357
Trattner, Cathrine W458
Traub, Robert T. E404
Trautman, David L. A803
Trautman, David L. E371
Travis, Nigel A17
Travis, Thomas L. E54
Travis, Tracey T. A620
Travis, Tracey T. A689
Travis, Tracey T. W10
Travisano, Jacqueline A. A110
Tray, Thomas E267
Treadway, Charles "Chuck" L. A279
Treadwell, David L. A435
Treadwell, David L. E210
Treanor, John F. A1108
Trease, Sandra A. Van A373
Trease, Sandra A. Van E168
Treece, Christopher G. A935
Treece, Christopher G. E439
Treff, Douglas J. E130
Trefzger, Detlef W355
Tremblay, Dale W. A1008
Tremblay, Michel W294
Trencher, Eliott E287
Trent, Keith A951
Trent, Keith A359
Trent, Thad A780
Tretiak, Gregory D. W263
Tretiak, Gregory D. W480
Trevino, Lorenzo H. Zambrano W266
Trevino, Maria Dolores Dancausa W87
Trevisan, Jason E81
Trezise, Scott A. A649
Tribbett, Charles A. A749
Tribolati, John H. A591
Triche, Debbie B. A880
Triche, Debbie B. E412
Trick, David A52
Trickett, Jeremy W. W262
Trickett, Mariya K. W46
Tricoire, Jean-Pascal A867
Tricoire, Jean-Pascal W524
Trigg, Donald D. A221
Trigg, Shane E34
Trilling, Sara A964
Trimble, James M. E101
Trimble, William C. E150
Trione, Victor S. A650
Trione, Victor S. E305
Tripeny, R. Tony A298
Triplett, Michael W. A239
Tripodi, Blair E312
Tripodi, Joseph V. A1099

Tritton, Mark J. A745
Trittschuh, Larry E247
Trius, Vincent A828
Trivedi, Ashok E313
Trivedi, Yogendra P. W491
Trochu, Cynthia Hoff A1010
Troendle, August J. E317
Trogele, Ulrich G. E26
Troiano, John G. E361
Trojan, Gregory A. A209
Troska, Hubertus W395
Trotta, James A401
Trotter, Johnny E. A421
Trotter, Johnny E. E198
Trousdale, Bill E471
Troyer, Trent B. E189
Trubeck, William L. A216
Trudeau, Mark C. W590
Trudel, Stephane W31
Trudell, Cynthia M. W122
Trudell, Cynthia M. W491
True, Simon W471
Trueman, John F. W288
Truex, Ronald D. A618
Truex, Ronald D. E290
Trujillo, David I. A1052
Trundle, Stephen E13
Truntschnig, Hannes W562
Trunzo, Anthony L. A893
Truscott, William F. A70
Trutna, Thomas P. A175
Trutna, Thomas P. E66
Tryder, David E. A500
Tryder, David E. E246
Tryforos, Thomas N. E128
Tryforos, Thomas N. E120
Tryniski, Mark E. A280
Tryniski, Mark E. E112
Tsai, Chen-Chiu W128
Tsai, Cheng-Ta W128
Tsai, Chi-Wen W51
Tsai, Daniel W252
Tsai, Fei-Long W206
Tsai, Hong-Tu W128
Tsai, Hsiang-Hsin W128
Tsai, John W449
Tsai, Joseph Chung W29
Tsai, Lih-Shyng (Rick L.) A619
Tsai, Michael Kuo-Chih E143
Tsai, Michael Kuo-Chih W650
Tsai, Richard M. W252
Tsai, Tsung-Hsien W128
Tsai, Yi E547
Tsang, Christopher Hing Keung W268
Tsay, Caroline J. A264
Tsay, Caroline J. E333
Tschage, Uwe W162
Tschudi, Franziska W580
Tschudin, Marie-France W65
Tschutscher, Klaus W580
Tse, Alan K. L. A588
Tse, Aloysius Hau Yin W151
Tse, Aloysius Hau Yin W158
Tse, Andy Po Shing W456
Tse, Chi Wai W572
Tse, Edmund Sze-Wing W19
Tse, Wai Wah W139
Tseng, F.C. W584
Tseng, Jih-Hsiung W206
Tseng, Saria E331

Tshabalala, B. S. W414
Tshabalala, Simpiwe K. W559
Tshutscher, Klaus W580
Tsien, Matthew A26
Tsien, Matthew A466
Tsien, Samuel N. W463
Tsimbinos, Steven James A768
Tsimbinos, Steven James E359
Tsingos, Christine A. E362
Tsitsiragos, Dimitris C. W33
Tsokova, Olga A431
Tsokova, Olga E205
Tsonos, William C. A181
Tsourapas, Panagiotis A269
Tsubouchi, Kazuto W539
Tsubume, Hiroyuki W316
Tsuchiya, Hiroshi W582
Tsuchiya, Masato W26
Tsuchiya, Michihiro W567
Tsuchiya, Mitsuru W181
Tsuchiya, Satoshi W454
Tsuda, Junji W357
Tsue, May Sik Yu W158
Tsuemura, Shuji W281
Tsuga, Kazuhiro W465
Tsui, Cyrus E370
Tsuji, Koichi W407
Tsuji, Yoshiyuki W26
Tsujimura, Hideo W334
Tsukamoto, Takashi W17
Tsukiyama, Keitaro W407
Tsukui, Susumu W334
Tsuma, Glen T. E76
Tsunakawa, Satoshi W612
Tsushima, Yasushi W345
Tsutsui, Yoshinobu W436
Tsutsui, Yoshinobu W465
Tsutsui, Yoshinobu W570
Tsutsumi, Tomoaki W576
Tsutsumi, Yoshito W535
Tu, Amy A1050
Tu, Dongyang W326
Tu, Huabin W356
Tu, Shutian W326
Tuan, Mei-Mei H. A1014
Tuan, Mei-Mei H. E488
Tuan, Sherman E472
Tubbs, Abram A400
Tucci, Joseph M. A716
Tuchinda, Pornsanong W79
Tuchman, Kenneth D. E500
Tucker, Aaron E510
Tucker, Daniel S. A471
Tucker, David W. E5
Tucker, Douglas J. A703
Tucker, Douglas J. E327
Tucker, Mark E. W289
Tucker, Sara Martinez A59
Tucker, Steven B. A945
Tucker, Steven B. E451
Tucker, Weston E62
Tuder, Irma L. A932
Tuder, Irma L. E436
Tueffers, Mark H. E223
Tuer, David A. W120
Tufano, Paul J. E485
Tufekcioglu, Metin W620
Tuggle, Clyde C. A471
Tulananda, Deja W77
Tulaney, Thomas P. A816

COMBINED HOOVER'S HANDBOOK INDEX OF EXECUTIVES

A = AMERICAN BUSINESS
E = EMERGING COMPANIES
P = PRIVATE COMPANIES
W = WORLD BUSINESSS

Tulenko, Stephen A711
Tullier, Kelly Mahon A1096
Tullio, David M. A753
Tully, Daniel A. A397
Tully, William P. E286
Tumilty, Mike W471
Tumolo, Louis E420
Tumpalan, Ferdinand A. W514
Tumpel-Gugerell, Gertrude W162
Tumpel-Gugerell, Gertrude W458
Tumsavas, Fusun W619
Tung, Chee Chen W128
Tung, Chee Hwa W29
Tung, Joseph W51
Tung, Savio Wai-Hok W105
Tungesvik, Geir W227
Tunnell, Richard T P644
Tuomas, Kerttu W348
Tuozzolo, Claudio E525
Tupper, Colleen E60
Tupper, Colleen E107
Turcke, Maryann A942
Turcke, Maryann A453
Turcke, Maryann W507
Turcotte, Benoit W193
Turcotte, Brian K. E221
Turcotte, Denis A. E236
Turcotte, Martine W119
Turcotte, Martine W216
Turcu, Anemona W646
Tureli, Rahim Askin W619
Tureman, Shawn I. A747
Turicchi, R. Scott E547
Turk, Carolyn J. E326
Turley, James S. A752
Turley, James S. A246
Turley, James S. A366
Turman, John Michael E372
Turnbull, Cheryl L. E242
Turner, Bradford R. A735
Turner, Brent E300
Turner, Brent E219
Turner, Brian Kevin A35
Turner, Cathy W371
Turner, Charles L. E452
Turner, Chris A10
Turner, Chris A1146
Turner, David G. A1138
Turner, David G. E544
Turner, David J. A884
Turner, David T. E246
Turner, Harold W. A880
Turner, Harold W. E412
Turner, James W481
Turner, James S. A200
Turner, James S. E79
Turner, Jim L. A303
Turner, John B. E358
Turner, John C. E234
Turner, John M. A884
Turner, John T. A477
Turner, Joseph W. A488
Turner, Kathy V. E263
Turner, Keene S. A373

Turner, Keene S. E168
Turner, Leagh E. W382
Turner, Leslie M. A432
Turner, M. Terry A829
Turner, M. Terry E385
Turner, Mark A. A1138
Turner, Mark A. E544
Turner, Michael L. A1078
Turner, Michael L. E513
Turner, Michelle L. A613
Turner, Mike A492
Turner, Mike P248
Turner, Mike W89
Turner, Patricia L. A768
Turner, Patricia L. E359
Turner, Quint O. E11
Turner, Reginald M. A666
Turner, Reginald M. A274
Turner, Robert W. E23
Turner, Rosemary A719
Turner, William P312
Turner, William H. E191
Turner, William V. A488
Turney, Sharen J. A10
Turney, Sharen J. E374
Turpen, John G. A556
Turpen, John G. E270
Turpen, Michael C. A167
Turpen, Michael C. E64
Turrini, Adriano W627
Turrini, Régis W215
Turtz, Evan M. W617
Tusa, David P. E437
Tutcher, Dan C. W218
Tuten, Steve P285
Tutkovics, Julie C. A545
Tutor, Ronald N. A1046
Tuttle, John A561
Tutton, Christopher J. E218
Tuwaijir, Mohammed Mazyed Al W520
Tuzun, Tayfun W82
Tveter, Eric J. A430
Twarozynski, James J. A555
Twarozynski, James J. E269
Twedt, Jill A166
Tweed, Dale E43
Tweedy, Jeffrey C. A10
Tweedy, Robyn P381
Twigge, Giovani E263
Twigger, Liam A. W260
Twinem, Mary J. E517
Twomey, Cormac J. A287
Ty, Arthur Vy W399
Tyler, Antony Nigel W128
Tyler, Breck W. A1044
Tyler, Brian S. A677
Tyler, Brian S. A892
Tyler, Ian Paul W66
Tyler, Jason J. A748
Tyler, Laura W101
Tyler, Lauren M. A39
Tyler, Michele L. E391
Tyler, Staci H. E151
Tyree, Anthony E. E316
Tysen, Atticus A745
Tysoe, Ronald W. A242
Tyson, Barbara A. A1050
Tyson, Dylan A856
Tyson, Dylan A855
Tyson, John H. A1049

Tyson, John R. A1050
Tyson, Mitchell G. E383
Tyus, Derek L. E532
Tzanakaki, Eirini E. W33
Tzitzon, Nicholas A931
Tzoumakas, Kimberly J. E106

U

Uang, Du-Tsuen W51
Ubben, Jeffrey W. A388
Ubben, Jeffrey W. E169
Ube, Fumio W81
Ubertalli, Niccolo W661
Ubinas, Luis Antonio A105
Ubinas, Luis Antonio A363
Uchibori, Takeo W266
Uchibori, Tamio W370
Uchida, Kanitsu W184
Uchida, Ken W330
Uchida, Makoto W441
Uchida, T. Christopher E370
Uchida, Takashi W608
Uchikami, Kazuhiro W253
Uchikawa, Jun W570
Uchimura, Hiroshi W336
Uchinaga, Yukako W439
Uchiyama, Hideyo W555
Uchiyamada, Takeshi W408
Uchiyamada, Takeshi W616
Udd, Ragnar W101
Udell, C. Robert E116
Udvar-Hazy, Steven F. E10
Uebber, Bodo W15
Ueberroth, Heidi J. A363
Ueda, Hiroshi W565
Ueda, Keisuke W576
Ueda, Takashi W409
Uehara, Hirohisa W581
Uehara, Karen K.L. W218
Uehara, Keiko W604
Ueki, Eiji W82
Uematsu, Takayuki W173
Uemura, Kyoko W550
Ueno, Hiroaki W400
Ueno, Sayu W408
Ueno, Shingo W566
Ueno, Susumu W536
Uffer, Fabian W526
Uggla, Ane Maersk Mc-Kinney W1
Uggla, Lance A670
Uggla, Robert Mærsk W2
Uhde, Philip E279
Uhl, Jessica W532
Uhl, Jessica R. A481
Uhlmann, Paul A1056
Uhlmann, Paul E505
Uitto, Tommi W443
Ujiie, Teruhiko W1
Ulatowski, Daniel A. E128
Ulbrich, Christian A588
Ulissi, Roberto W227
Ullal, Jayshree E35
Ullastres, Demetrio W213
Ullem, Scott B. A361
Ullem, Scott B. A153
Ullmann, Michael H. A585
Ullmer, Michael James W651

Ulm, Scott J. A96
Ulmer, Fran A428
Ulmer, Gregory M. A643
Ulrich, Jing W14
Ulusu, Atilla W620
Umanoff, Adam S. A951
Umanoff, Adam S. A359
Umbgrove, Johannes Herman Frederik G. W33
Umeda, Hirokazu W465
Umeyama, Katsuhiro W433
Umphrey, Sheila G. A214
Umpleby, D. James A230
Umpleby, Donald James (Jim) A210
Unakul, Snoh W540
Unanue, Carlos A. A836
Underberg, Sharon E. E263
Underhill, Kimberly K. A443
Underwood, April A1149
Underwood, Baxter R. E471
Underwood, Neil L. A641
Underwood, Neil L. E304
Ung, Swee-Im W603
Unger, Kathryn Graves A507
Unger, Kathryn Graves E248
Unger, Laura S. A723
Unger, Laura Simone W445
Ungerleider, Howard I. A342
Ungerleider, Howard I. A612
Uniacke, Kaysie E234
Unis, Gregory A1094
Uno, Motoaki W408
Unoura, Hiroo W403
Unruch, Joel W10
Unruh, Jess E239
Unruh, Marcy E517
Unverferth, R. Steven E507
Uotani, Yoshihiro W555
Upadhyay, Suketu P. A1150
Upperman, Dorothy A868
Upshaw, Alfonse L. E438
Upshaw, Donnie S. E539
Upson, Jill S. A981
Upson, Jill S. E469
Upton, Jerome T. A470
Urakawa, Tatsuya W185
Urano, Kuniko W437
Urbain, Xavier A643
Urban, Brett E66
Urban, David J. E527
Urban, Franz W633
Urban, Michael A999
Urban, Philip H. A927
Urban, Philip H. E435
Urbanski, Joseph E222
Urbaszek, Marcin A485
Urcola, Maria Rotondo W593
Urdang, E. Scott E227
Ure, Michael P. E536
Ureta, Antonio W132
Ureta, Fernando Concha W314
Uribe, Claudia Echavarria W76
Uribe, Esteban Piedrahita W210
Uribe, Gonzalo A604
Uribe, Jaime Caballero W210
Uribe, Jorge A. A465
Uribe, Jorge A. A557
Uribe, Juan Carlos Mora W76
Uribe, Maria Cristina Arrastia W76

COMBINED HOOVER'S HANDBOOK INDEX OF EXECUTIVES

A = AMERICAN BUSINESS
E = EMERGING COMPANIES
P = PRIVATE COMPANIES
W = WORLD BUSINESSS

Uribe, Mayra P174
Uribe, Rodrigo Prieto W76
Uridil, Nancy E. A397
Uriu, Michiaki W357
Urkiel, William S. A303
Urness, Todd B. A175
Urness, Todd B. E66
Urrutia, Manuel Enrique Bezanilla W41
Ursat, Xavier W215
Uruma, Kei W402
Urushi, Shihoko W319
Usategui, Mary E397
Usdan, Robert I. A691
Usdan, Robert I. E323
Ushijima, Shin W436
Ushio, Yoko W1
Uslu, Ismail E458
Usmani, A. W8
Usmanov, Ildus Shagalievich W575
Usui, Yasunori W576
Utermark, D. Chad A760
Uthayophas, Siribunchong W541
Uthra, Sandeep E79
Utsubo, Seiichiro W394
Utter, Lynn M. A638
Utterback, Cynthia A. E149
Utz, John A. A101
Uyeda, Allen B. A423
Uzawa, Ayumi W612
Uzun, Ali Tarik W346

V

V, Gary Delanois Senior P1
V, Gregory A Beck A222
V, Gregory A Beck P114
V, Todd S Werner Junior P7
V, Tyrone Jeffers P519
Vaart, Sandra D. Van der A615
Vaccariello, Caroline Saylor E393
Vacheron, Terry A573
Vachris, Roland M. A300
Vadakumcherry, Sebastian A35
Vadakumcherry, Sebastian P15
Vadala, Shawn P. E325
Vadlamannati, Ramaprasad A840
Vadon, Mark C. A871
Vagelos, P. Roy A882
Vagt, Robert F. A605
Vagt, Robert F. E171
Vahedi, Vahid A619
Vahey, Walter G. E485
Vahradian, Robert E299
Vahrenholt, Fritz W62
Vaivao, Ivan P498
Vajda, Devit P151
Valavanis, Spero W. A532
Valavanis, Spero W. E259
Valcarce, Mario W132
Valderrama, Magdalena Sofia Salarich Fernandez de W73

Valdes, Clemente Ismael Reyes Retana W265
Valdes, Michael E180
Valdespino, Ricardo W643
Valdez, Armando P150
Valdez, Arthur L. A17
Vale, Michael G. A4
Vale, Michael G. E491
Valencia, Antonio G. A313
Valencia, Jaime Estevez W70
Valente, Denise Aguiar Alvarez W69
Valenti, Douglas E407
Valenti, Samuel A57
Valentin, Helle W510
Valentine, Andre S. A287
Valentine, Brian A. A82
Valenzuela, Fernando Porcile W172
Valenzuela, Steve E14
Valeriani, Nicholas J. A361
Valette, Jean-Michel E65
Valgiurata, Lucio Zanon di W177
Valine, Yousef A. A642
Valine, Yousef A. E304
Valk, Eric van der E360
Valkov, Anton W655
Valla, Natacha W526
Valla, Natacha W373
Vallacchi, Grace M. A768
Vallacchi, Grace M. E359
Valle, Diego Della W373
Valle, Gustavo Carlos A710
Valle, Margherita Della W637
Valle, Margherita Della W490
Vallebueno, Carlos W266
Vallee, Philippe W600
Vallee, Roy A. A402
Valles, Noe G. A951
Valles, Noe G. E454
Vanacker, Peter E.V. W427
Vanacker, Peter E.V. W374
Vanaria, Raymond J. E401
Vanaselja, Siim A. W262
Vanaselja, Siim A. W480
Vance, Brian L. A510
Vance, Brian L. E252
Vance, James J. A397
Vance, Katisha T. A848
Vance, Tyler A. A134
Vance, Tyler A. E54
Vandal, Thierry W507
Vandebroek, Sophie V. E263
Vandenberghe, James H. A345
Vandenberghe, James H. A343
Vanderhaegen, Frederic A112
Vanderlaan, Meg P375
Vandermeulen, Johan W111
Vanderslice, Elizabeth W. A18
VanGelder, Kim E. A411
Vanhaelst, Bruno W550
Vanhevel, Jan A. W33
VanHimbergen, Robert M. E255
Vanlaeys, Antoine W358
Vanni, Enrico W449
Vanssay, Annick de W550
VanWees, Jason E483
Vanzo, Kendra L. A772
Vara, Armando Antonio Martins W70
Vara, Raymond P. A129
Varadarajan, Seshasayee (Sesha) A619
Varallo, Deborah A1132

Varallo, Deborah E539
Vareberg, Terje W562
Varela, Tomas W618
Varela, Virginia A. A398
Varenne, Francois de W526
Varga, Paul C. A654
Vargo, Ronald P. E170
Varin, Philippe W238
Varin, Philippe W215
Varischetti, Nicholas D. E156
Varischetti, Peter C. A259
Varischetti, Peter C. E103
Varma, Atul E244
Varma, Jay E440
Varma, Rishi A. A514
Varnado, Anddria Clack-Rogers A1057
Varnell, John W235
Varner, Chilton D. E68
Varnholt, Burkhard P. W86
Varon, Leslie F. A619
Varon, Leslie F. E244
Varsellona, Maria W626
Varsellona, Maria W6
Varwijk, Erik F. W22
Varwijk, Erik F. W344
Vasantasingh, Chulasingh W352
Vasconcellos, William Cruz de A828
Vasconcelos, Thomaz de Mello Paes de W70
Vascsinec, Gina A1148
Vasella, Daniel L. A62
Vasella, Daniel L. A818
Vasilieva, Elena Alexandrovna W474
Vasilogiannaki, Athina W637
Vasos, Todd J. A602
Vasos, Todd J. A336
Vasquez, Christann M. E247
Vasquez, Gaddi H. A359
Vasquez, Ricardo W419
Vassalluzzo, Joseph S. A770
Vassalluzzo, Scott J. E128
Vasseur, Denis Le W480
Vassiliadis, Michael W93
Vassiliadis, Michael W277
Vassiliou, Konstantinos V. W231
Vassoille, Jocelyne W635
Vastrup, Claus W188
Vaswani, Ashok W89
Vatnick, Silvina W76
Vaughan, J. David E372
Vaughan, Richard C. A671
Vaughan, Therese M. A65
Vaughan, Therese M. A1118
Vaughan, Therese M. E533
Vaughan, Therese M. E520
Vaughn-Furlow, Rebecca N. A1044
Vaughn, D Blayne P405
Vaughn, Mark J. E136
Vaughn, Nooshin A548
Vaught, Lori E372
Vauth, Robin W E160
Vautrinot, Suzanne M. A1115
Vautrinot, Suzanne M. A304
Vautrinot, Suzanne M. A358
Vazquez, Carlos J. A836
Vazquez, Carlos J. A396
Vazquez, Carlos J. E187
Vazquez, Raul A571
Veal, Jimmy D. A72
Veal, Jimmy D. E29

Veasey, Ashley W84
Vecchio, Jennifer A187
Vecchio, Leonardo del W231
Vecchione, Kenneth A. A1120
Vecchione, Kenneth A. E535
Vedie, Simone W174
Vedrine, Hubert W373
Vedyakhin, Alexander W521
Veeger, Noud W348
Veer, Jeroen van der W227
Vega, Blanca Trevino de W643
Vega, Ralph de la A62
Vegara, David W618
Veiel, Eric L. A991
Veiga-Pestana, Miguel W490
Veihmeyer, John B. A444
Veitch, Jonathan E423
Vejjajiva, Athasit W137
Vekich, Michael M. E63
Velasco, Ernesto Vega W35
velasco, German Larrea mota W266
Velasco, German Larrea Mota A953
Velasco, Ignacio Garralda Ruiz de W219
Velasco, Roque W643
Velay-Borrini, Patricia W486
Velez, Cecilia Maria White W210
Velez, Luis Guillermo Echeverri W210
Vella, Francesco W627
Vellano, Enrico W235
Velli, Joseph Mark A267
Vellios, Thomas G. E209
Vels, Michael W216
Veluswamy, Leslie A328
Veluswamy, Leslie E19
Vemana, Prat A453
Vemuri, Ashok A611
Ven, Michael G. Van de A274
Vena, V. James A405
Vena, Vincenzo J. A1061
Venable, Cheryl L. A399
Venable, Jerry P295
Venables, Thomas R. A554
Venables, Thomas R. E268
Venegas, Edmundo Miguel Vallejo W265
Venegas, J. Enrique E338
Veneman, Ann M. W430
Venet, Francois W357
Venezia, Patrick A1021
Venezia, Patrick P593
Venkatachari, Dilip A1082
Venkatakrishnan, C. S. W89
Venkatakrishnan, C. S. W90
Venkatesan, Ravi W279
Vennam, Rajesh A316
Ventress, Peter W116
Ventura, Robert J. A418
Ventura, Robert J. E195
Venturelli, Larry M. A486
Venturi, Marco Giuseppe W627
Venturoni, Guido W363
Venugopal, B W561
Verbaeten, Tom W157
Verbrugge, Joseph A. A941
Verbrugge, Joseph A. E468
Verdecanna, Pebbie A1098
Verdejo, Fernando Mata W382
Verdes, Marcelino Fernandez W280
Verduin, Patricia D. A269

COMBINED HOOVER'S HANDBOOK INDEX OF EXECUTIVES

A = AMERICAN BUSINESS
E = EMERGING COMPANIES
P = PRIVATE COMPANIES
W = WORLD BUSINESSS

Verenes, J. Chris E433
Vergara, Emerson Bastian W314
Vergara, Rodrigo Montes W73
Verger, Frederic W511
Verghese, Sunny George W456
Vergis, Janet S. A237
Vergis, Janet S. W598
Vergnano, Mark P. W327
Verhagen, Herna W351
Verhagen, Herna W306
Verity, William W. A64
Verkhov, Vyacheslav W476
Verma, Richard R. A991
Verma, Vikas E274
Verma, Vikram E77
Vermeir, Raphael Loius L. W227
Vermeulen, Patrick W623
Vermillion, Teresa M. A776
Vermooten, Adrian W559
Vernaillen, Hilde W627
Verneuille, Janet T. A430
Vernick, Robert A. E156
Vernon, W. Anthony A673
Verplancke, Jan Paul Marie Francis W69
Verret, David E. E304
Verrier, James R. A804
Verrier, Sandrine W104
Verschuren, Annette M. W120
Verstreken, Jan A522
Verwaayen, Bernardus Johannes Maria E12
Vescovi, Ana Paula Vitali Janes W622
Vespoli, L L P575
Vessey, Rupert A178
Vessey, Rupert E59
Vestberg, Hans E. A160
Vestjens, Roel A490
Vetras, Daniel P. E46
Vetter, David R. A999
Vetter, Galen G. A37
Vetter, Galen G. E14
Vettese, Frank W507
Vezina, Ann F. A999
Vezina, Ann F. A287
Vezina, Yves W399
Vial, Martine W492
Viale, Enrico W220
Viana-baptista, Antonio Pedro de Carvalho W325
Viani, Ede Ilson W72
Viani, Giovanni W177
Vice, John H. W559
Vicente, Carlos Rey de W72
Vicente, Ignacio Martín San W493
Vicente, Manuel Domingos W70
Vick, Marsha A423
Vick, Marsha E199
Vickers, Selwyn M. A32
Victor, Diane de Saint W298
Victor, Paul W518
Vidalis, Efthimios O. W33
Vidarte, Susana Rodriguez W69
Videtto, Emily E27

Vidman, Moshe W79
Viehbacher, Christopher A. A158
Vieira, Donna F. A944
Vieira, Donna F. E450
Vieitas, Deborah Stern W72
Viera, Paul E. E480
Viets, Joshua J. A227
Vieweg, Cecilia W4
Vignial, Antoine W165
Vij, Sandeep S. E266
Vijayaraghavan, Ravi K. E32
Vila, Carlos Torres W68
Vilain, Michele W107
Vilanek, Christoph W129
Vilca, Lina Vingerhoets A953
Vilcek, HelenBeth Garofalo E190
Viljoen, Natascha W39
Villa, Gabriele W391
Villa, Giovanna W661
Villa, Norma P639
Villano, John L. E425
Villar, Salvador W266
Villarreal, Jose H. A1061
Villasana, George A. A99
Villela, Ana Lucia de Mattos Barretto
Villela W315
Villeneuve, Costanza Esclapon de W222
Villeneuve, Nadia A207
Villepin, Clement de W600
Villota, Maxime W215
Vinaiphat, Premrutai W484
Vinals, Jose W561
Vince, Robin A132
Vincent, Anton V. A568
Vincent, Brad A. A167
Vincent, Brad A. E64
Vincent, Frederic W492
Vincent, Marie Claire W266
Vincent, Mary L. A527
Vincent, Richard A. E247
Vincent, Ronald E129
Vincent, Suzanne M A586
Vincent, Suzanne M P292
Vinci, Francesco Saverio W391
Vinci, Gerald F. E96
Vinciarelli, Patrizio E525
Vinciquerra, Anthony J. A867
Vinck, Karel W623
Vines, Timothy A885
Vinese, Eric Philippe W168
Vinet, Pascal W357
Viniar, David A. A481
Vinokur, Svetlana E188
Viola, Michael T. A556
Viola, Michael T. E527
Viola, Michael T. E270
Viola, Vincent J. E527
Vipperman, Robert P21
Virnig, Kenneth E147
Viron, Francoise de W554
Viscasillas, Pilar Perales W382
Visedpaitoon, Pong W136
Viselli, Joseph E490
Visher, Carole W523
Viswanathan, Rajagopal W84
Viswanathan, Sowmya P527
Viswanathan, Subramaniam ("Subra") A231
Vitale, Angelo A900

Vitale, Diana W303
Vitale, Nancy E529
Vitale, Robert V. A838
Vitale, Robert V. E161
Vitale, Robert V. E57
Vitalone, Britt J. A677
Vithoulkas, John A P170
Vitosh, Bruce A. E340
Vittal, Ireena W201
Vittal, Ireena W170
Vittorio, Michael N. A815
Vivaldi, Carlo W661
Vivek, Vibhu E77
Viyugin, Oleg W506
Vladimirovna, Zavaleeva Elena W506
Vlatkovich, Mychal P134
Vlerick, Philippe W336
Vo-Quang, Edouard W480
Vobejda, Susan E489
Vodopija, Jad W101
Voegele, Michael A825
Voellmin, Dieter W91
Vogel, Carl E. A941
Vogel, Kimberley H. A1038
Vogel, Kimberley H. E496
Vogel, Roland W269
Vogelbaum, Martin E80
Vogelsang, Harald W192
Voges, William J. A422
Vogt, Mark A. A890
Vogt, Mark A. E416
Vogt, Susan L.N. E437
Vohs, Christopher J. E63
Voigtlander, Christian B. E262
Voiland, Eugene E517
Voinovich, Michael C. E326
Voisin, Jean-Baptiste W373
Vokey, Sheila W80
Volas, Gerald (Jerry) E494
Volchyok, Leon E62
Vold, Irene W594
Volent, Paula J. E336
Volikova, Svetlana W655
Volk, David J. A175
Volk, David J. E66
Volk, Sergey W410
Volke, Robert J. E254
Volkens, Bettina W196
Volkmann, Elke W171
Volkmer, Bart E. E145
Vollaro, John D. W50
Vollmer, Jason L. A679
Volpe, Sandra M. A892
Volpert, Verena W602
Volpetti, Stefano A825
Volpi, Michelangelo A. E452
Volpini, Adriano Cabral W315
Vondran, Steven O. A69
Vong, John E33
Voorhees, Steven C. A1042
Vorholt, Jeffrey J. E11
Vorsheck, Elizabeth Hirt E172
Vos, Glen De W46
Vosburg, Craig E. A670
Voscherau, Eggert W280
Voser, Peter R. A565
Voser, Peter R. W6
Voskuil, Steven E. A512
Voskuil, Steven E. A140
Voss, Donald R. A527

Voss, Susan E. A1065
Voss, William Bradley A1040
Voss, William Bradley E499
Voss, William R. A958
Voss, Zeb A692
Voss, Zeb P352
Vot, Denis Le W492
Votek, Glenn A. A83
Vounatsos, Michel E381
Vousden, Karen H. A178
Voyack, Frank A747
Voyles, Robb L. A494
Vpof, Chad T Lefteris P462
Vrablec, Mark J. A95
Vradenburg, Steve E83
Vranos, Michael W. E155
Vrecko, Marc W631
Vuillod, Veronique W161
Vulgamott, Brent A. E25
VunCannon, Tony J. A528
VunCannon, Tony J. E258
Vyugin, Oleg Vyacheslavovich W617

W

Waal, Philippe de W174
Waas, Franz W191
Waayenburg, Hans Van W123
Wacha, Bruce C. E50
Wacharapong, Poomchai W79
Wacklon, D. E. A288
Wacksman, Jeremy A1149
Waddell, Frederick H. A8
Waddell, Frederick H. A565
Waddell, Frederick H. A399
Waddell, M. Keith A898
Wade-Gery, Laura W364
Wade-Gery, Laura W360
Wade, Anne K. E469
Wade, Claude A65
Wade, Janie E408
Wade, M. Andrew E42
Wade, Randall A741
Wade, Tim W157
Wadecki, I. Marie E25
Wadhwani, David A15
Wadhwani, Sunil E313
Wadsworth, Con L. E463
Waecker, Max W61
Waersted, Gunn W594
Waersted, Gunn W446
Waga, Masayuki W555
Wagers, Thomas B. E338
Waghray, Ajay A823
Wagler, Theresa E. A975
Wagler, Tyson J A472
Wagler, Tyson J E230
Wagner-Fleming, Susan A578
Wagner, Andreas W510
Wagner, Charles F. A1089
Wagner, Cortney Ann A235
Wagner, Donald A. A1106
Wagner, Donald S. E147
Wagner, Harvey L P575
Wagner, Harvey L P351
Wagner, Harvey L P425
Wagner, Helmut W3
Wagner, Mark C. E158

COMBINED HOOVER'S HANDBOOK INDEX OF EXECUTIVES

```
A = AMERICAN BUSINESS
E = EMERGING COMPANIES
P = PRIVATE COMPANIES
W = WORLD BUSINESSS
```

Wagner, Markus W415
Wagner, Matthew D. A195
Wagner, Matthew P. A800
Wagner, Patricia K. E397
Wagner, Patrick J. A656
Wagner, Renate W33
Wagner, Renate W625
Wagner, Richard T. E275
Wagner, Robert J. A125
Wagner, Robert J. E52
Wagner, Susan L. A89
Wagner, Susan L. A160
Wagner, Thomas A513
Wagner, William E537
Wagner, William J. E537
Wagner, William M. E81
Wagner, William R. E12
Wagoner, G. Richard A573
Wahl, Kim W204
Wahlroos, Bjorn W446
Wahlstrom, Mats E106
Wai, Tan Tat W380
Wainer, Andrea F. A6
Wainscott, James L. A804
Wainscott, James L. A304
Waite, Simon W662
Waite, Thomas G. E467
Waitman, Ted E218
Wajner, Matthew F. A413
Wajnert, Thomas C. A650
Wajnert, Thomas C. E305
Wajsgras, David C. E663
Wakabayashi, Tatsuo W404
Wako, Masahiro W1
Walbaum, Marie-Francoise W601
Walbridge, Morgan E49
Walburger, Corbin A962
Walcott, Jill A. A653
Walcott, Peter W. E165
Waldeck, Phil A856
Walden, Dana A641
Walders, William P257
Waldheim, William S. E514
Waldman, Eyal P340
Waldo, Robert A. E462
Waldron, John E. A480
Waldron, John F. A530
Waldron, John R. E102
Wales, Kim A575
Walkden, Pamela W76
Walke, Megan A. E255
Walker-Lee, Robin A364
Walker, Al A288
Walker, Algernon P130
Walker, Andrew W60
Walker, Annette M P524
Walker, Brian C. A1053
Walker, Brooks P487
Walker, Chris L. E68
Walker, Christine L. A432
Walker, Cynthia L. A929
Walker, Cyrus D. E260
Walker, Daniel H. E376
Walker, Daniel K. A393

Walker, Darren A818
Walker, Darren A162
Walker, David C. E298
Walker, Frank L. E279
Walker, Harry M. A1044
Walker, James B. W176
Walker, John A. E117
Walker, John B. E307
Walker, John D. E90
Walker, John F. E195
Walker, John H. A760
Walker, John H. A764
Walker, John H. A791
Walker, Jonathan E34
Walker, Karen A636
Walker, Kenneth G. A393
Walker, Kent John A45
Walker, Kevin P. A955
Walker, Kevin P. E456
Walker, Kimberly G. A276
Walker, Kumi D. E306
Walker, Lauren E316
Walker, Lisa E455
Walker, Mark S. E213
Walker, Roberto A846
Walker, Scott P692
Walker, Steven G. A853
Walker, Steven R. A774
Walker, Taylor A1132
Walker, Taylor E539
Walker, Terry L. A427
Walker, Terry L. E203
Walker, Tristan A443
Walker, W. Henry A393
Walker, William M. E531
Wall, Brett W393
Wall, Daniel R. A386
Wall, John M. E75
Wall, Oliver W81
Wall, Peter A. A460
Wall, Peter R. A929
Wallace, Carol P. E446
Wallace, Michael K. A125
Wallace, Michael K. E52
Wallace, Mike W235
Wallace, Noel R. A269
Wallace, Richard P. A607
Wallace, Timothy G. E114
Wallace, Vanessa M. W644
Wallace, William "Wally" A788
Wallace, William "Wally" E364
Wallace, William Scott A189
Wallach, Matthew J. E519
Wallbaum, Elisabeth W207
Wallenberg, Jacob A721
Wallenberg, Jacob W228
Wallenberg, Jacob W6
Wallenberg, Marcus W57
Wallenberg, Marcus W548
Wallenberg, Marcus W4
Wallenberg, Natalia W351
Wallenberg, Peter W60
Waller, John W245
Waller, Kathy N. A323
Wallerstein, David A M W596
Wallimann, Regula W13
Wallin, Kim A969
Wallin, Kim P535
Wallin, Peter W548
Wallin, Ulrich W586

Walling, Kevin R. A512
Wallingford, Judith E. E350
Wallis, David E443
Wallis, David E. E336
Wallis, Tim R. A1065
Wallis, Tim R. E509
Wallman, Richard F. A904
Wallman, Richard F. E94
Walmsley, Emma N. A701
Walmsley, Emma N. W258
Walsh, Brendan E314
Walsh, Brian E. W263
Walsh, Derrick K. A120
Walsh, Derrick K. E48
Walsh, Eugene J. E190
Walsh, Jane C. A191
Walsh, Jane C. E77
Walsh, John E. A768
Walsh, John E. E359
Walsh, John L. A1054
Walsh, Kenneth M. E149
Walsh, Malacky E311
Walsh, Matthew M. A787
Walsh, Meghan P260
Walsh, Nancy A. E457
Walsh, Patricia J. A296
Walsh, Paul S. A405
Walsh, Paul S. A675
Walsh, Paul Steven W170
Walsh, Richard Joe A1085
Walsh, Sam M. C. W260
Walsh, Samuel W408
Walsh, Timothy A. A67
Walsh, William J. E204
Walt, Amy A294
Walter, Gérard W127
Walter, Jordan E234
Walter, Luc A80
Walter, W. Edward A70
Walters, Andrew F. E446
Walters, Elizabeth J. (Lisa) E459
Walters, Judy A. A685
Walters, Kathleen A. A578
Walters, Kelly S P579
Walters, Kirk W. A814
Walters, Kirk W. A651
Walters, Kirk W. E379
Walters, Mimi K. E50
Walters, Robert D. A900
Walters, Sarah W133
Walterskirchen, Herbert W453
Walthall, Leonard L. E23
Walthall, Todd E17
Walti, Beat W205
Walton, Andrew W371
Walton, S. Robson (Rob) A1104
Walton, Steuart L. A1104
Walton, Thomas W.H. A799
Walton, William H. E222
Waltz, William E. E39
Walz, Brian K. A82
Walz, Steven A. E428
Wampler, Keith L. A107
Wampler, Keith L. E40
Wampler, Kevin S. A337
Wan, Hongwei W648
Wan, Long W648
Wan, Lynn Tiew Leng W456
Wan, Peter Kam To W148
Wan, Shuei-Ping W206

Wan, Yong W189
Wanblad, Duncan Graham W39
Wanczyk, Stefan E298
Wandell, Keith E. A313
Wandell, Keith E. A342
Waneka, Jeffrey J. E337
Wang, Aiguo W528
Wang, Aiqing W307
Wang, Alice H. A1145
Wang, Bairong W301
Wang, Baojun W37
Wang, Bin W150
Wang, Bin W142
Wang, Bing W104
Wang, Bo W326
Wang, Botang W169
Wang, Caiyun W307
Wang, Chang W608
Wang, Changhui W656
Wang, Cheng W40
Wang, Chenxi A679
Wang, Chenyang W106
Wang, Chiwei W326
Wang, Chuan W139
Wang, Chuanfu W117
Wang, Chuncheng W148
Wang, Chunyao W660
Wang, Dajyun W169
Wang, Dashu W291
Wang, David E129
Wang, David H. E3
Wang, Dong W256
Wang, Dongjin W158
Wang, Elaine Yee Ning W268
Wang, Fawen W263
Wang, Feng W326
Wang, Fengying W261
Wang, Gaofei W202
Wang, Gary Pak-Ling W180
Wang, Gary Pak-Ling W179
Wang, Haifeng W152
Wang, Haifeng W67
Wang, Haihuai W138
Wang, Haiwu W152
Wang, Hang W431
Wang, Hao W138
Wang, Ho-min W537
Wang, Hongfei W327
Wang, Hsuehming W151
Wang, Huacheng W146
Wang, Huimin A361
Wang, J.C. W206
Wang, J.K. W583
Wang, Jane J. A258
Wang, Jane J. A645
Wang, Jian E3
Wang, Jian W136
Wang, Jian W512
Wang, Jianchao W40
Wang, Jianhua W38
Wang, Jianli W656
Wang, Jianping W146
Wang, Jianxun W239
Wang, Jingwu W301
Wang, Jinkuan W528
Wang, Jiouhong W169
Wang, Juan W88
Wang, Judy E370
Wang, Jun W34
Wang, Jun W153

HOOVER'S HANDBOOK OF EMERGING COMPANIES 2023

COMBINED HOOVER'S HANDBOOK INDEX OF EXECUTIVES

A = AMERICAN BUSINESS
E = EMERGING COMPANIES
P = PRIVATE COMPANIES
W = WORLD BUSINESSS

Wang, Junhui W142
Wang, Junhui W152
Wang, Keqin W268
Wang, Kui W291
Wang, Leon W57
Wang, Li W608
Wang, Li W644
Wang, Li-Ling W128
Wang, Liang W466
Wang, Lijun W239
Wang, Luning W662
Wang, Mengde W572
Wang, Mingzhe W236
Wang, Nongsheng W608
Wang, Peihua W268
Wang, Peiwen W528
Wang, Peng W660
Wang, Pengfei W40
Wang, Qi W104
Wang, Qin W655
Wang, Qiying W662
Wang, Qiying W189
Wang, Qunbin W248
Wang, Ren W140
Wang, Ruijian W239
Wang, Ruolin W660
Wang, Shaojun W173
Wang, Shihtong W168
Wang, Shiqi W147
Wang, Shouye W148
Wang, Shudong W137
Wang, Songlin W275
Wang, Tayu W145
Wang, Tianguang W257
Wang, Tingge W662
Wang, Tongzhou W138
Wang, Wanglin W38
Wang, Warton A1145
Wang, Wei W140
Wang, Wei-Chung A780
Wang, Weiming W274
Wang, Wen W327
Wang, Wenxue W140
Wang, Wenzhang W137
Wang, Xi W142
Wang, Xiangdong W528
Wang, Xiangming W148
Wang, Xiangxi W149
Wang, Xianzhu W375
Wang, Xiaobo W291
Wang, Xiaochu W152
Wang, Xiaochu W151
Wang, Xiaodong W529
Wang, Xiaogang W307
Wang, Xiaohua W263
Wang, Xiaoling W574
Wang, Xiaoqing W142
Wang, Xiaoqiu W292
Wang, Xiaoqiu W512
Wang, Xiaosong W254
Wang, Xiaowei W356
Wang, Xiaowen W533
Wang, Xiaoyan W362
Wang, Xingzhong W149

Wang, Xinhua W656
Wang, Xinhua W147
Wang, Xinming W140
Wang, Xiqing W608
Wang, Xiuming W146
Wang, Y. L. W583
Wang, Yaling W656
Wang, Yang W257
Wang, Yanhui W153
Wang, Yanhui W656
Wang, Yidong W37
Wang, Yihuai W140
Wang, Yijiang W533
Wang, Yong W257
Wang, Yong W662
Wang, Yongbin W138
Wang, Yongjian W472
Wang, Yougui W144
Wang, Yu Ling E340
Wang, Yuechun W542
Wang, Yuhang W143
Wang, Yuqi W136
Wang, Yusuo W202
Wang, Zhen W117
Wang, Zhen W88
Wang, Zhen-Wei W530
Wang, Zhenhua W254
Wang, Zhibing W655
Wang, Zhijian W644
Wang, Zhiliang W472
Wang, Zhixue W150
Wang, Zhongzhu W431
Wang, Zihao W656
Wang, Zongming W169
Wanitschek, Gottfried W627
Wanitschek, Gottfried W563
Wankel, Sibylle W96
Wanker, Siegfried W562
Wann, Robert A732
Wanstrath, Kenenth T. E185
Wanzer, Dara A125
Wanzer, Dara E52
Warburton, Sharon W644
Warch, John E. E425
Ward, Anne Sempowski E518
Ward, Barbara K. W37
Ward, Brian P. E67
Ward, Charles G. A1087
Ward, Chris W273
Ward, Doris M A249
Ward, Doris M P126
Ward, Elizabeth A. A499
Ward, F. Stephen E192
Ward, Greg C. W377
Ward, Gregory A. A398
Ward, James H. A575
Ward, Jeffery L. A417
Ward, Jeffrey C. E426
Ward, Jill A. E147
Ward, Laysha L. A1062
Ward, Marce E. E76
Ward, Michael J. A834
Ward, Patrick J. A1138
Ward, Patrick J. A298
Ward, Patrick J. E544
Ward, Patrick J. W242
Ward, Susan F. E426
Ward, Tamara A195
Warden, Derek P.B. E260
Warden, Kathy J. A684

Warden, Kathy J. A752
Wardle, Clare W161
Ware, Bruce E61
Ware, Lauren E. A401
Ware, Todd P. A396
Ware, Todd P. E186
Warford, Dustin A509
Warford, Dustin E251
Wargo, J. David A332
Wargo, J. David E300
Wargo, Kyle R. A951
Wargo, Kyle R. E454
Waring, Thomas H. E175
Warmbold, Benita M. W84
Warne, Peter H. W377
Warne, Teresa A P32
Warner, Bradford H. A198
Warner, Cynthia J. A230
Warner, Cynthia J. A929
Warner, Elizabeth P103
Warner, Gerard ("Jerry") H. E119
Warner, Jane L. A1005
Warner, Jane L. A182
Warner, Jennifer P453
Warner, Lara J. W176
Warner, Louise W37
Warner, Louise W31
Warner, Michelle M. E330
Warnica, Kimberly O. A656
Warnig, Matias W329
Warnig, Matias W617
Warnig, Matthias W506
Warnke, Karl J. E135
Warnock, John E. A15
Warren, Burney S. A722
Warren, Burney S. E339
Warren, Denise W. A998
Warren, Jim P225
Warren, Kelcy L. A369
Warren, Kevin M. A434
Warren, Michael A180
Warren, Michael J. E531
Warren, Thomas K. A408
Warren, Todd A952
Warren, W. Michael A853
Warrior, Padmasree A701
Warsh, Kevin M. A1069
Warzala, Richard S. E18
Wasantapruek, Don W484
Waschbichler, Werner W98
Wasechek, Wayne E391
Washburn, Christopher L. A830
Washburne, Ray W. A982
Washington, A. Eugene A585
Washington, Akihiko A349
Washington, Donald W. A523
Washington, Donald W. E257
Washington, Gregory N. A911
Washington, Herbert L. A651
Washington, Lisa E268
Washington, Paul E. A556
Washington, Paul E. E270
Washington, Robin L. A912
Washington, Robin L. A45
Washington, Robin L. A530
Washington, Rose M. A167
Washington, Rose M. E64
Washington, Vanessa L. A423
Washington, Zuhairah Scott E209
Washlow, Sally A. E365

Wasmer, Martin M. E190
Wassenaar, Yvonne E215
Wasser, Marilyn J. A878
Wasser, Marilyn J. A879
Wasserman, Frederick Gerald E143
Wasserman, Yuval E261
Wasserman, Zachary J. A545
Wassersug, Mark P. A561
Wassmer, Michael J. A198
Wasteson, Martin W579
Wasti, Rashid W646
Wastler, Ernst W251
Wat, Joey A1145
Watabe, Nobuhiko W389
Watabiki, Mariko W370
Watahiki, Manriko W612
Watanabe, Akihiro W612
Watanabe, Dai W353
Watanabe, Hayao W603
Watanabe, Hideaki W441
Watanabe, Hiroshi W460
Watanabe, Hiroshi W404
Watanabe, Hiroyuki W17
Watanabe, Katsuaki W658
Watanabe, Katsuaki W567
Watanabe, Kazunori W402
Watanabe, Kenji W434
Watanabe, Kensaku W581
Watanabe, Koichiro W181
Watanabe, Koichiro W439
Watanabe, Masakazu W81
Watanabe, Masazumi W82
Watanabe, Osamu W253
Watanabe, Osamu R. E330
Watanabe, Shinjiro W392
Watanabe, Shuichi W392
Watanabe, Tatsuya W334
Watanagase, Tarisa W408
Watari, Chiharu W209
Watase, Hiromi W539
Watcharananan, Arunee W136
Waterhouse, Deborah W258
Waterhouse, Kevin C. E173
Waterman, Bruce G. A792
Waters, Andy D. A283
Waters, Gregory L. A780
Waters, Kathleen A. A317
Waters, Martin P. A1094
Waters, Ralph W245
Waters, Ronald V. A447
Waters, Ronald V. E374
Waters, Samuel D. E149
Waterston, Maureen A625
Watjen, Thomas R. W481
Watkins, Gretchen H. A715
Watkins, James Arthur W322
Watkins, James M. E64
Watkins, Latriece A641
Watkins, Mark R. E326
Watkins, Teresa E239
Watkins, Tracy E. E98
Watkins, Walter C. E423
Watkins, William D. W242
Watkoske, Daniel J. A1086
Watsa, Benjamin P. W235
Watsa, V. Prem W235
Watson, Ann A510
Watson, Ann E252
Watson, Daniel E. E57
Watson, David N. A78

COMBINED HOOVER'S HANDBOOK INDEX OF EXECUTIVES

A = AMERICAN BUSINESS
E = EMERGING COMPANIES
P = PRIVATE COMPANIES
W = WORLD BUSINESSS

Watson, David N. A272
Watson, Emma W338
Watson, Gerald W471
Watson, Lucas E. A485
Watson, Max P. A491
Watson, Michael J. A1110
Watson, Patricia A. A902
Watson, Peter G. A489
Watson, Richard K. W260
Watson, Robin A530
Watson, Secil Tabli A130
Watson, Wendy A. A248
Watt, Andrew E. E467
Watt, John H. A724
Wattana, Waewalai W603
Wattanasiritham, Jada W541
Wattanavrangkul, Kobkarn W334
Wattenbarger, Michael D. E5
Watters, James H. E67
Watters, Joseph (Joe) A. E310
Watterson, Andrew M. A956
Watts, Claudius E. A279
Watts, David W85
Watts, Garry W161
Watts, J. C. E374
Watts, Jeffery M. A394
Watts, Myles James A396
Watts, Myles James E186
Watts, R. Andrew E68
Watzinger, Gerhard E313
Waugh, Seth H. A448
Waun, Thomas J. E5
Wawrin, Stephen R. E173
Wawroski, Judith I. A563
Waxman, Alan A941
Way, B. I. W377
Way, Edward Yung Do W128
Way, John A. E400
Way, T. Lawrence A307
Way, T. Lawrence E133
Waycaster, Bill W. A319
Waycaster, C. Mitchell A888
Waycaster, C. Mitchell E414
Wayland, Joseph F. W154
Wayne, Donald C. A868
Wayne, Richard E350
Ways-Ruart, Paul Cornet de W40
Waysand, Claire W225
Wear, Diane T. A1006
Weatherall, Percy W323
Weaver, Amy E. A675
Weaver, Amy E. A912
Weaver, Fawn A367
Weaver, Gregory G. A1088
Weaver, James C. A594
Weaver, Jeff A927
Weaver, Jeff E435
Weaver, Judith A. E158
Weaver, Linford A788
Weaver, Linford E366
Weaver, Scott D. E160
Weaver, Susan T. E5
Webb, Carl B. A516
Webb, David A. A446

Webb, Doug W328
Webb, Helen W160
Webb, Jack H. A724
Webb, James R. A295
Webb, Justin T. A702
Webb, Justin T. E325
Webb, Kris W162
Webb, Larry R. A240
Webb, Maynard G. A912
Webb, Maynard G. A1096
Webb, Michael W287
Webb, Michael R. W451
Webb, Phillip M. A32
Webb, Thomas J. E367
Webb, Winifred E34
Webb, Winifred Markus A10
Weber, Alfred J. A1033
Weber, Axel A. W621
Weber, Christina W196
Weber, Christophe W585
Weber, Del B P410
Weber, Emily P339
Weber, Frank W96
Weber, Frank W395
Weber, Fred E34
Weber, Guglielmo W310
Weber, James H. A274
Weber, Jason H. A12
Weber, Jason H. E4
Weber, John A. W233
Weber, Juergen W196
Weber, Mark D. E188
Weber, Matthias W580
Weber, Robert C. E260
Weber, Stephen B. A845
Weber, Stephen B. E395
Weber, Steven P. E183
Webster, Patrick M. A1053
Webster, Ranson W. A509
Webster, Ranson W. E251
Webster, William E. A347
Wechsler, George J. E76
Weck, Pierre J.P De A128
Weckenbrock, Michael B. A531
Weckert, Leah W162
Weckes, Marion W510
Weckesser, Stefanie W198
Weddell, Steven M. E297
Weddle, Mary K. A1063
Weddle, Mary K. E508
Wedel, Gregory G. A125
Wedel, Gregory G. E52
Wee, Ee Cheong W628
Wee, Ee Lim W628
Wee, Lee Seng W261
Wee, Susie A81
Weed, Keith W318
Weed, Keith W654
Weeks, Harry Odell E433
Weeks, Jason A515
Weeks, Terri-Lee W84
Weeks, Wendell P. A298
Weeks, Wendell P. A50
Weese, David H. de A493
Weger, David S. E76
Weger, Hans S. E461
Wehmann, James M. E183
Wehmer, Edward J. A1133
Wehmer, Edward J. E541
Wehner, David M. A689

Wehrle, Richard J. E13
Wehrwein, Sven A. E43
Wehrwein, Sven A. E457
Wehrwein, Sven A. E400
Wei, Anxiang W608
Wei, C.C. W583
Wei, Chuanjun W257
Wei, Cilin W169
Wei, Ciouruei W168
Wei, Huaning W372
Wei, Jianjun W261
Wei, Kechao W528
Wei, Keliang W139
Wei, Mei W257
Wei, Shuanglai W106
Wei, Weifeng W138
Wei, Xinjiang W153
Wei, Yong W512
Wei, Yong W663
Weideman, William H. A776
Weidemanis, Joakim A315
Weidemeyer, Thomas H. A1110
Weidemeyer, Thomas H. A757
Weigand, David E472
Weight, Joel E368
Weigl, Gunter W14
Weikel, Mark J. A1035
Weil, Edward M. E232
Weil, Kelley E. A167
Weil, Kelley E. E64
Weil, Meredith S. A1013
Weil, Stephan W640
Weiland, Ed P483
Weiler, Melissa V. A581
Weill, Sanford I. W346
Weill, Veronique W631
Weimer, Charles A428
Weimin, Shi A1039
Weimin, Shi P628
Weinberg, David B. A264
Weinberg, John A. A401
Weinberg, John S. A444
Weinberg, John S. E176
Weinberg, Serge W515
Weinberger, Mark A. A585
Weinberger, Mark A. A691
Weiner, Daniel E444
Weiner, David A616
Weiner, Michael D. A95
Weiner, Michael D. E34
Weiner, Russell J. A254
Weinert, Dean W. E421
Weinert, Robin S. E421
Weinfurter, Daniel P192
Weingarten, Steven J. A910
Weinreich, Birgit W196
Weinstein, Andrew B. E436
Weinstein, Donald P. A108
Weinstein, Glen D. E281
Weinstein, James P382
Weinstock, Craig L. A754
Weir, Daniel F. A1013
Weir, Derek W159
Weir, Helen W351
Weisbarth, Michael A. E393
Weisbord, Robert D. A939
Weisel, Thomas W. A977
Weisel, Thomas W. E464
Weisenburger, Randall E334
Weisenburger, Randall J. A1085

Weisler, Dion J. A1027
Weisler, Dion J. A560
Weisler, Dion J. W101
Weisner, Aimee S. E460
Weiss, Aaron E471
Weiss, Andrea M. A148
Weiss, Andrea M. A765
Weiss, Arthur A. E471
Weiss, Daniel K. A1115
Weiss, Daniel K. E533
Weiss, Jerry A450
Weiss, Jonathan G. A1115
Weiss, Mark A. A64
Weiss, Richard A. E384
Weiss, Robert S. E119
Weiss, Shimon W410
Weissbeck, Ralf W13
Weissburg, Martin W641
Weissenberger-Eibl, Marion W273
Weissenfluh, Franziska von W631
Weisser, Alberto A818
Weisser, Alberto W95
Weisser, Alberto W369
Weissl, Josef W453
Weissman, Ayako Hirota W612
Weissmann, Thomas C. W34
Weitchner, Meir W78
Weitz, Mark E50
Weitz, Ron P169
Weitz, Wallace R. A151
Weitz, Wallace R. E72
Weitzel, Harry P. A374
Weitzman, Debbie A201
Weitzman, Howard E49
Welborn, Robert S. A755
Welborn, Wesley Miller A945
Welborn, Wesley Miller E451
Welch, Brian P176
Welch, Deborah P527
Welch, James L. A918
Welch, John K. A546
Welch, Joshua G. E23
Welch, M. Scott A618
Welch, M. Scott E290
Welch, M. Scott E373
Welch, Michael A99
Welch, Robert W597
Weldon, Raymond F. E436
Weldon, William C. A311
Weldon, William C. W235
Welinder, Margareta W277
Welland, Shamus E. W382
Wellauer, Thomas W580
Wellauer, Thomas W16
Wellborn, Gayle E247
Wellborn, W. Christopher A706
Weller, Greg E445
Weller, Sara W371
Weller, Sara W114
Wellink, Nout W301
Wellman, Kristine M. A224
Wells, Charles R. E319
Wells, Darren R. A483
Wells, David B. E489
Wells, Donna C. E329
Wells, Gregory L. E526
Wells, Ian W246
Wells, James Kent A656
Wells, Jason P. A218
Wells, Michael W481

COMBINED HOOVER'S HANDBOOK INDEX OF EXECUTIVES

A = AMERICAN BUSINESS
E = EMERGING COMPANIES
P = PRIVATE COMPANIES
W = WORLD BUSINESSS

Wells, Nadya W521
Wells, Paul R. A853
Wells, Richard W662
Wells, Steven A. E102
Welsh, Beth A810
Welsh, Beth E376
Welsh, John E. E300
Welsh, Mark A. A752
Welsh, W. Russell E338
Welt, Philip S. A149
Welters, Anthony A473
Welters, Anthony A645
Welters, Anthony A203
Welty, Jonathan D. A397
Weltzien, Lourdes G. E321
Wemmer, Dieter W621
Wemyss, W. J. W580
Wen, Daocai W644
Wen, Dongfen W158
Wen, Limin W147
Wendeling-Schröder, Ulrike W586
Wendell, Amy A. A142
Wendell, Amy A. A522
Wendell, Peter C. A684
Wendler, Daniel W242
Wendler, Olaf W280
Wendling, Brian J. A633
Wendling, Brian J. A633
Wendling, Brian J. A871
Wendling, Brian J. E300
Weng, Deh-Yen W128
Weng, Yingjun W140
Wengel, Kathryn E. A615
Wenger, E. Philip A454
Wenick, Mark A393
Wenick, Mark E184
Wenig, Devin N. A466
Wenkoff, Carman R. A336
Wenner, David L. E50
Wennes, Timothy A915
Wenning, Joachim W415
Wenning, Werner W586
Wenning, Werner W543
Wennink, Peter T. F. M. W52
Wentworth, Lynn A. A486
Wentworth, Lynn A. E134
Wentworth, Timothy C. A239
Wenzel, Abby M. E232
Wenzel, Brian J. A985
Werber, Merryl E. E287
Werblo, Jackelyn E P92
Weresch, Werner W640
Werkema, Gordon A399
Werner-Dietz, Stephanie W443
Werner, Hiltrud Dorothea W640
Werner, Johannes W192
Werner, William C. A158
Wernette, Gregory A. E298
Werth, Frank W174
Wertheim, Aviram W410
Wertheim, Moshe W410
Wesch, David E142
Wesdorp, Kees W351
Wesner, Sarah E46

Wess, Mark P444
Wessel, Michael R. A483
Wessel, Rick L. E207
West, Bradley R. E381
West, Brian J. A164
West, Catherine G. A198
West, Christopher D. E540
West, Daniel E. E388
West, David J. E443
West, Duncan G. W574
West, Fay E404
West, George Vincent E210
West, J. Robinson W493
West, Joe F. A214
West, Lance N. E190
West, Mary Beth A35
West, Mary Beth A503
West, Mary Beth A647
West, Michael A711
West, Mindy K. A938
West, Mindy K. A719
West, Mindy K. E442
West, Nadja Y. A585
West, Nadja Y. A1003
West, Nadja Y. A760
West, Roderick K. A371
West, Tony A1052
West, William Corey A786
Westacott, Jennifer W644
Westbrook, C. Hunter A528
Westbrook, C. Hunter E258
Westbrook, Kelvin R. A992
Westbrook, Kelvin R. A715
Westbrook, Kelvin R. A94
Westbrook, L. Andrew A955
Westbrook, L. Andrew E456
Westby, Sharon Alberta E421
Westerhold, Mary J. A427
Westerhold, Mary J. E204
Westerholt, Thomas Schmall-Von W640
Westerkamp, Richard F. A401
Westerlund, David A. A1139
Westermann, Donald M. A352
Westhoff, Frank W162
Westlake, Lisa S. W379
Westley, kevin Anthony W287
Weston, Bradley Morgan E65
Weston, Galen G. W371
Weston, Galen G. W646
Weston, George Garfield W55
Weston, Marc A P189
Weston, W. Galen W646
Westphal, Mark W. A838
Westphal, Rouven W517
Westra, Richard L. A311
Westrick, Karl J P327
Westrick, Thomas J. A458
Westwell, Stephen W518
Wetherbee, Margaret E222
Wetmore, Jonathan R. W299
Wetscherek, Ewald W627
Wettergren, Björn W642
Wetzel, Gus S. E246
Wetzel, M. Lynn E421
Wetzel, Paul M. A176
Wetzko, Manuela W398
Wexler, Lawrence S. E501
Weyers, Robert J. A741
Weyers, Robert J. E349

Weymouth, David Avery W462
Weymouth, Katharine B. A892
Weymouth, Katharine B. E72
Whalen, David G. E389
Whalen, James F. E79
Whalen, Julie P. A1132
Whalen, Julie P. A385
Whaley, Keith E. A945
Whaley, Keith E. E451
Whall, Timothy J. E14
Whang, Scott Yoon-Suk A530
Whang, Scott Yoon-Suk E258
Wharton, Scott W164
Wheat, Bill W. A536
Wheatley, Christine S. A611
Wheatley, T. Alan A541
Wheaton, Kingsley W111
Wheeler, Adam P. A95
Wheeler, Brad A. E274
Wheeler, Bradford J. A311
Wheeler, Carrie A. A338
Wheeler, Carrie A. A785
Wheeler, Graeme W138
Wheeler, Richard T. A1033
Wheeler, Richard T. E493
Wheeler, Scott T. E123
Wheeler, William J. E176
Whelan, James KC W311
Whelan, Mark W63
Whelan, Mark David W36
Whelan, Robert M. E39
Whelan, Ronald P. E450
Whetstone, Rachel A730
Wheway, Scott W135
Wheway, Scott W371
Whiddon, Thomas E. A338
Whiddon, Thomas E. A950
Whip, Jennifer R. A435
Whip, Jennifer R. E210
Whipple, John F. A280
Whipple, John F. E113
Whipple, Josh A477
Whipple, Ross M. A134
Whipple, Ross M. E54
Whisler, J. Steven A182
Whisler, J. Steven A304
Whiston, William E. A1113
Whitaker, Charles N. (Charlie) A47
Whitaker, Jerry R. A924
Whitbread, Jasmine M. W654
Whitbread, Jasmine M. W561
Whitbread, Jasmine M. W167
Whitcomb, Gary D. E54
Whitcutt, Peter W39
White, Albert G. (Al) E119
White, Andrea Lynn A470
White, Anne E. A635
White, Brian C. E214
White, Craig M. E153
White, Daniel J. A251
White, Daniel J. E100
White, Darryl W82
White, Don A811
White, Don E377
White, Duane E. A507
White, Duane E. E248
White, G. Clark A995
White, Gary G. A1063
White, Gary G. E508
White, Geoff A35

White, George Burton A648
White, Gregory A. A192
White, James C. A556
White, James C. E270
White, James D. E443
White, Jeffrey R. E457
White, Julia W517
White, Katherine E. A772
White, Lisa A. A401
White, Lisa M. A1057
White, Lori E223
White, Marvin L. E157
White, Matthew A. E122
White, Matthew J. W369
White, Michael D. A1129
White, Michael D. A604
White, Michael D. A128
White, Miles D. A675
White, Noel A1049
White, Randall W. E153
White, Rebecca E310
White, Richard A439
White, Rob L. A656
White, Robert John (Bob) W393
White, Robert S. E43
White, Sharon E. W364
White, Sharon E. W364
White, Stephen C. W662
White, Stephen W. E360
White, Steve G. A188
White, Steve G. E69
White, Steven A. A485
White, Steven A. A534
White, Teresa A988
White, Teresa E479
White, Thomas M. E463
White, Tony L. W617
White, William J. A52
Whited, Elizabeth F. (Beth) A907
Whited, Elizabeth F. (Beth) A1061
Whiteford, Grace Puma A788
Whitehead, Dane E. A656
Whitehouse, Aaron M. E175
Whitehurst, Bradford D. E514
Whitehurst, James M. A1063
Whiteing, David W561
Whitelaw, Mary W21
Whitesell, Patrick A367
Whitesell, Patrick A1059
Whiteside, Jeff E180
Whitfield, Fred Alan A765
Whitfield, Jo W160
Whitfield, Rob W164
Whitford, Thomas K. A539
Whiting, Donald J. E24
Whiting, Susan D. A599
Whitley, David A971
Whitley, David P537
Whitley, George P. A1033
Whitley, George P. E492
Whitley, M. Lee A120
Whitley, Sarah J. M. W487
Whitlock, Gary L E169
Whitlock, Paul W462
Whitman, Margaret C. A466
Whitman, Margaret C. A850
Whitman, Robert A. E126
Whitmire, Brett R. E143
Whitmire, Yuki A1097
Whitmore, Justin A600

COMBINED HOOVER'S HANDBOOK INDEX OF EXECUTIVES

```
A = AMERICAN BUSINESS
E = EMERGING COMPANIES
P = PRIVATE COMPANIES
W = WORLD BUSINESSS
```

Whitney, Grant E471
Whitney, Kenneth C. E388
Whitson, Jerry E. A825
Whittemore, George R. E526
Whittemore, Kent G. A1066
Whitten, Anthony Charles A322
Whittington, Marna C. A826
Whittle, John E216
Whonder, Carmencita N. M. A87
Whynott, Paul A985
Whynott, Paul D. A400
Whyte, Gregory J. E412
Wibergh, Johan E497
Wibulswasdi, Chaiyawat W137
Wichlacz, Lee E249
Wichmann, David S. A175
Wichterich, Michael A227
Wicke, Jan Martin W280
Wicker-Miurin, Field W104
Wicker-Miurin, Fields W481
Wicker-Miurin, Jane Fields W526
Wicker, Dennis A. A414
Wicker, Dennis A. A266
Wicker, Dennis A. E191
Wicker, K. Wayne E452
Wicki, Andreas E369
Wickramasinghe, Mahes S. W122
Wicks, Pippa W160
Widder, Kenneth J. E406
Wideman, Elizabeth A272
Widerlite, Paula P323
Widmann, Amir E504
Widmann, Michael E451
Wiebe, Robert W371
Wiechmann, Andrew C. E335
Wieczorek, Roman W548
Wiedenfels, Gunnar A332
Wiedenfels, Gunnar W517
Wiedlea, John T. E469
Wiedman, Mark K. A160
Wiegel, Molly Kelly E67
Wiehart, Gerd W633
Wiehoff, John P. A835
Wiehoff, John P. A1082
Wiele, Thomas R. A515
Wienbar, Sharon L. A893
Wiens, Joel H. E421
Wierenga, Peter D. E322
Wierod, Morten W6
Wiersma, Lonna L. A681
Wiersma, Lonna L. E317
Wierzbowski, Marek W389
Wiese, Christo W562
Wiese, Edward A. A991
Wiese, Jacob W562
Wiese, Judith W543
Wiese, Peter G. A1038
Wiese, Peter G. E495
Wieser, Florian W129
Wieser, James L. E191
Wiessman, David A321
Wiestler, Otmar D. W95
Wiggers, Edilson W69
Wiggins, Keith E83

Wight, David G. E352
Wigley, Stephen R. E107
Wiiliams, R. Sanders A615
Wiinholt, Marianne W448
Wijers, Hans G. J. W306
Wijk, Leo M. van W489
Wijk, Leo van W22
Wijkstrom, Joakim E518
Wijnberg, Sandra S. A108
Wijnberg, Sandra S. A991
Wijnberg, Sandra S. A267
Wikramanayake, Shemara R. W377
Wilbur, Cristina A. W502
Wilbur, Norman G. E434
Wilburn, Tyree G. E300
Wilcher, LaJuana S. A395
Wilcher, LaJuana S. E186
Wilcox, Edward Earl A796
Wilcox, Edward Earl E368
Wilcox, Frank C. E512
Wilcox, Mark A. A927
Wilcox, Mark A. E435
Wilcox, Tyler J. A815
Wild, Geoffrey E329
Wildberger, Karsten W207
Wildberger, Karsten W129
Wilde, Erik E228
Wilde, Frederic de A825
Wilde, Lisa de W596
Wilde, Peter W86
Wilde, Peter O. A181
Wilder, Livnat Ein-Shay W79
Wilder, Michael L. A401
Wilderotter, Mary Agnes A300
Wilds, Eric J. W379
Wildstein, Harris A891
Wileke, Kina W641
Wilensky, Gail R. A1075
Wilensky, Gail R. A870
Wilentz, Joel M. E512
Wiley, Becky E102
Wiley, Robert G. A399
Wilhelm, Harald W395
Wilkens, Deborah W207
Wilkerson, Aubrey Michael (Mike) E181
Wilkerson, Vicki A389
Wilkerson, Vicki P219
Wilkes, David S. A142
Wilkes, David S. A986
Wilkin, Carolyn A. W308
Wilkin, Laura E270
Wilkins, Aaron E353
Wilkins, Carleton Richard A496
Wilkins, Charles L. A1113
Wilkins, David H. A1065
Wilkins, David H. E509
Wilkins, Joseph D. E406
Wilkins, Michael W487
Wilkins, Michael T. A1065
Wilkins, Rayford A1085
Wilkins, Rayford A713
Wilkins, Rayford A210
Wilkinson, Geoffrey C. A519
Wilkinson, Geoffrey C. E256
Wilkinson, Peter J. A615
Wilkinson, Stefanie W101
Wilkinson, Walter H. E232
Wilkison, Rodney R. E236
Wilks, Jeffrey S. A1086

Wilks, Jeffrey S. E516
Will, Angelika W398
Will, W. Anthony A776
Willard, Howard A. E101
Wille, Bart W49
Wille, Scott R. A35
Willett, Joseph Timothy E397
Willett, Robert J. E105
Willetts, David A549
Willi, René A917
Williams, Alicia A399
Williams, Andy E61
Williams, Anre D. A62
Williams, Anthony E12
Williams, Ashbel C. A196
Williams, Ashbel C. E79
Williams, Ashley H. A1013
Williams, Ather A1115
Williams, Barbara S. E515
Williams, Brian R. A840
Williams, Bridget P598
Williams, Careina D. E81
Williams, Carol A. A776
Williams, Christopher J. A1061
Williams, Christopher J. A254
Williams, Christopher J. A70
Williams, Clay C. A754
Williams, Coram W13
Williams, Craig Anthony A198
Williams, Darren K. A1063
Williams, Darren K. E508
Williams, David R. E129
Williams, Derek G. E117
Williams, Donald Richard A845
Williams, Donald Richard E395
Williams, Douglas L. A106
Williams, Edward E. E173
Williams, Ena A209
Williams, Ernest A927
Williams, Ernest E435
Williams, Felicia A878
Williams, Felicia A879
Williams, Felicia E321
Williams, Frederica M. A380
Williams, G. Rainey A125
Williams, G. Rainey E52
Williams, Glenn J. A845
Williams, Glenn J. E395
Williams, H. James A282
Williams, Jack P. A388
Williams, Janice L. A350
Williams, Janice L. E148
Williams, Jeffrey A. E23
Williams, Jeffrey E. A89
Williams, Jennifer D. E408
Williams, Joe L. E221
Williams, John A774
Williams, John E360
Williams, John W646
Williams, John B. A101
Williams, John C. A402
Williams, John D. A795
Williams, John E. A214
Williams, John M. A138
Williams, John M. E55
Williams, Joseph R. E102
Williams, Julie A52
Williams, Julie P31
Williams, Julie F A65
Williams, Julie F P34

Williams, Karen J. A401
Williams, Keith W364
Williams, Keith W509
Williams, Kim A1127
Williams, Kim A1139
Williams, Kim E431
Williams, Kristen Williams E369
Williams, Kristina K. A397
Williams, L. Denise A408
Williams, Leroy J. A1056
Williams, Leroy J. E505
Williams, Marsha C. A410
Williams, Melvin D. A432
Williams, Michael J. A879
Williams, Michael J. A878
Williams, Mikel H. E50
Williams, Mitch W495
Williams, Nigel W164
Williams, Noel B. A625
Williams, Pamela J P511
Williams, Patricia M. A500
Williams, Patricia M. E246
Williams, Patrick F. E460
Williams, Paul S. E11
Williams, Polly W618
Williams, R. Sanders A76
Williams, Randa Duncan A374
Williams, Richard T. A266
Williams, Richard T. A528
Williams, Richard T. E258
Williams, Robert E57
Williams, Ronald A. A62
Williams, Ronald A. A164
Williams, Ronald A. A585
Williams, Scott K. E147
Williams, Shawn D. A656
Williams, Sherry E19
Williams, Sidney S. A1086
Williams, Sidney S. E516
Williams, Stephanie N. A823
Williams, Steven W. A37
Williams, Susan Slavik A485
Williams, Thomas J. A498
Williams, Thomas L. A483
Williams, Thomas L. A804
Williams, Tiffany A. E190
Williams, Timothy E518
Williams, Timothy V. E92
Williams, Toby J. E374
Williams, Valerie M. A343
Williams, Valerie M. A778
Williams, Valerie M. A345
Williams, Valerie M. A325
Williams, Vanessa P. A532
Williams, Vanessa P. E259
Williams, Vicki A83
Williams, Warner E517
Williams, William L. A641
Williams, William L. E304
Williams, William Mark A889
Williams, William Mark E414
Williamson, Charles R. A796
Williamson, Keith H. A841
Williamson, Mats W548
Williamson, Philip C. E457
Williamson, Randall S. E274
Williamson, Sarah K. E176
Williamson, Stephen A1027
Williamson, Stephen A567
Willie, Kerry T. A395

COMBINED HOOVER'S HANDBOOK INDEX OF EXECUTIVES

```
A = AMERICAN BUSINESS
E = EMERGING COMPANIES
P = PRIVATE COMPANIES
W = WORLD BUSINESSS
```

Willie, Kerry T. E186
Willingham, Edward L. A401
Willingham, John A. E181
Willis, Angel Shelton A924
Willis, Austin C. E538
Willis, Austin Chandler E538
Willis, Charles F. E538
Willis, Gregory B. E10
Willmott, Greg W662
Willner, Morris E35
Willoughby, Dawn C. A947
Willoughby, Dawn C. A567
Willoughby, Dawn C. W590
Wills, Kevin G. A92
Wills, Phillip R. E227
Willsey, Lance E178
Willy, W. Sean W596
Wilm, Renee L. A633
Wilm, Renee L. A871
Wilm, Renee L. E300
Wilmington, Mark V. E97
Wilmot, Damian W. A500
Wilmot, Damian W. A809
Wilmot, Damian W. E246
Wilmott, Timothy J. A316
Wilson-Thompson, Kathleen A1007
Wilson-Thompson, Kathleen A677
Wilson, Alan D. A991
Wilson, Alan D. A1125
Wilson, Amy E. A342
Wilson, Andrew A363
Wilson, Anthony L. A952
Wilson, Benjamin F. A823
Wilson, Cameron W246
Wilson, Charles Joseph A205
Wilson, Darryl L. A740
Wilson, Darryl L. W209
Wilson, David K. A602
Wilson, Dow R. A27
Wilson, Dwayne A. A557
Wilson, Dwayne A. A303
Wilson, Dwayne A. E463
Wilson, Frank Anders (Andy) E355
Wilson, Frederick R. E175
Wilson, James N. E121
Wilson, Jeffrey L. E99
Wilson, Joan M. W571
Wilson, John W245
Wilson, John F. E424
Wilson, John H. E160
Wilson, Josh M. E206
Wilson, Joshua J. E430
Wilson, Julia W91
Wilson, Kendrick R. E176
Wilson, Kenneth S. A578
Wilson, Kerry Dale E388
Wilson, Kurt P285
Wilson, Lena W425
Wilson, Lena W423
Wilson, Lonny D. E54
Wilson, Malcolm A493
Wilson, Mark W371
Wilson, Mark Andrew A160
Wilson, Michael A. E30

Wilson, Michael M. W573
Wilson, Michelle D. E543
Wilson, Michelle D. E501
Wilson, Millar A52
Wilson, Nicholas J P625
Wilson, Nicole H P174
Wilson, Nigel D. W360
Wilson, Richad W462
Wilson, Robert W. W570
Wilson, Sherwood G P676
Wilson, Stephen P. E293
Wilson, Stephen R. A546
Wilson, Stephenie M. E189
Wilson, Steven K. E242
Wilson, Thomas A.S. A848
Wilson, Thomas J. A42
Wilson, Thomas L. A752
Wilson, Timothy W. A393
Wilson, Virginia M. A207
Wilson, Virginia M. E94
Wilson, Wayne R. E308
Wilson, William E. A214
Wilt, Toby S. A200
Wilt, Toby S. E80
Wiltse, Steven M. E227
Wilver, Peter M. A142
Wimbush, F. Blair A107
Wimbush, F. Blair E40
Wimmer, Andreas W33
Wimpfheimer, Andrew T. E366
Winckler, Georg W627
Windes, Rick A. A953
Windes, Rick A. E455
Windhaus, Donna P79
Windley, John F. A955
Windley, John F. E456
Windsor, Jason W64
Windt, Katja W198
Wine, Scott W. A1082
Wine, Scott W. W157
Wineman, Benjamin A976
Wines, Lynne A135
Winfrey, Christopher L. A223
Wing, Allison M. A209
Wingate, Phyllis Ellen E455
Winges, M. Bradley A516
Wingo, Bill P293
Wingo, M. Scot E92
Winkeljohann, Norbert W95
Winkelmann, Thomas A583
Winkleblack, Arthur B. A237
Winkleblack, Arthur B. A92
Winkler, Annette W357
Winkler, Annette W492
Winkler, Jason J. A716
Winkler, Peter W633
Winlof, Kerstin W579
Winn, James C. E526
Winn, Penny W37
Winnefeld, James A. A877
Winship, Henry W. (Jay) A900
Winship, Henry W. (Jay) A185
Winstel, John D. A317
Winston, Benjamin ("Ben") S. A696
Winston, Mary A. A232
Winston, Roy E369
Wintemute, Eric G. E26
Winter, Benjamin A. A625
Winter, Jaap W489
Winter, Matthew E. A16

Winter, Matthew E. A502
Winter, Michael R. E18
Winter, P. Clinton A1063
Winter, P. Clinton E508
Winterbottom, Brad L. A1118
Winterbottom, Brad L. E533
Winters, Bill W561
Winters, Chad R. E534
Winters, James E484
Winters, Richard E218
Winters, William T. W449
Wiren, Marco W443
Wiren, Marco W427
Wiriaatmadja, Rachmat W483
Wirsbinski, Carol Ann E101
Wirsch, Manfred W398
Wirth, Michael K. A230
Wise, Andrew W93
Wise, Andrew J. A98
Wise, Andrew J. E36
Wise, Bonnie M P170
Wise, Deanna A137
Wise, Deanna P59
Wise, Murray R. E185
Wise, R. Halsey A221
Wise, R. Halsey E39
Wise, Stephen H. E406
Wisecup, Reyne K. A394
Wiseman, Eric C. A239
Wiseman, Garry R. E344
Wiser, Ron G. A397
Wiser, Ron G. E187
Wishart, Ben W351
Wishnick, Ross E53
Wishom, Andrea E386
Wisk, Mariana A103
Wisneski, Frank V. E22
Wisniecka, Joanna A400
Wisniowski, Dorothy A108
Wissmann, Matthias W196
Witczak, Eric J. A741
Witczak, Eric J. E349
Witherington, Philip J. W382
Withers, Dean W. E181
Withrow, Terrance P. E357
Witmer, Meryl B. A151
Witney, Frank R. E381
Witoonchart, Gasinee W77
Witt, Alan S. A1033
Witt, Alan S. E493
Witt, John W323
Witt, Marshall W. A999
Witt, Mary John A889
Witt, Mary John E414
Witte, Jan D. De E278
Witte, Jan De E417
Witte, Paul J. E421
Wittekind, Beverly B. E164
Wittemans, Marc W336
Wittenschlaeger, Thomas E218
Witter, Frank W640
Witter, Jonathan W. A944
Witter, Jonathan W. E450
Witteveen, Nicole E9
Wittig, Martin C. W355
Wittig, Thomas W96
Wittman, Vanessa A. A170
Wittmann, Stefan W162
Wittmeyer, Michael R. A5
Witty, Andrew P. A1075

Witty, Peter N. E72
Witynski, Michael A. A337
Witz, Jennifer C. A941
Witz, Pascale E381
Wlodarczyk, Francis S. A902
Wo, C. Scott A423
Wo, Robert W. A129
Wodopia, Franz-josef W234
Woehrl, Dagmar G W86
Woelfer, W. Todd A1028
Woelke, Sylvia W129
Woelkers, Paul C. E190
Woertz, Patricia A. A850
Woertz, Patricia A. A4
Wohl, Richard H. A308
Wohl, Richard H. E133
Wojahn, Jeffrey E. E101
Wojcicki, Susan D. A912
Wojtowicz, Jean L. A425
Wojtowicz, Jean L. A427
Wojtowicz, Jean L. E201
Wojtowicz, Jean L. E203
Wolberg, Kirsten O. A945
Wolberg, Kirsten O. E450
Wolberg, Kirsten O. E147
Wolberg, Lyle A976
Wolf, Alex E34
Wolf, Bryan E477
Wolf, Chris A37
Wolf, Chris E14
Wolf, Christina A. A1117
Wolf, Dale B. A707
Wolf, Dale B. E154
Wolf, George J. A691
Wolf, George J. E323
Wolf, Kenneth E. E342
Wolf, Mark D. E463
Wolf, Reinhard W98
Wolf, Siegfried W171
Wolf, Siegfried W563
Wolf, Timothy V. A1139
Wolfe, Andrew L. E501
Wolfe, Brian J. E271
Wolfe, Cindy A134
Wolfe, Cindy E54
Wolfe, Joseph C. A747
Wolfe, Serena A83
Wolfe, Stephen P322
Wolfe, Stephen A. A418
Wolfe, Stephen A. E195
Wolfe, Steven C. E313
Wolfenbarger, Janet Carol A20
Wolff, Anne Clarke A80
Wolff, Jared M. A124
Wolfgring, Alexander W625
Wolfrath, Stephen R. A895
Wolfshohl, Candace K. A305
Wolin, Harry A. A18
Wolk, Joseph A585
Wolkoff, Neal L. E366
Wollam, Becky W364
Wolle, Joerg W355
Wolman, Alexander L. A401
Wolpert, Geoffrey A. A945
Wolpert, Geoffrey A. E451
Wolsfeld, Matthew C. E352
Woltosz, Walter S. E444
Woltz, H. O. E275
Womack, Christopher C. A573
Womack, Christopher C. A952

COMBINED HOOVER'S HANDBOOK INDEX OF EXECUTIVES

A = AMERICAN BUSINESS
E = EMERGING COMPANIES
P = PRIVATE COMPANIES
W = WORLD BUSINESSS

Womack, Christopher C. A471
Womack, Christopher C. E174
Wondeh, Inez A1119
Wonderling, Robert C. A1078
Wonderling, Robert C. E513
Wong, Allan Chi-yun W80
Wong, Andrea L. A871
Wong, Andrea L. A633
Wong, Andrea L. A633
Wong, Anselm E283
Wong, Anthony T. A398
Wong, David Shou-Yeh W179
Wong, David Shou-Yeh W179
Wong, Derek Hon-Hing W179
Wong, Grace W143
Wong, Gregory E407
Wong, Harold Tsu-Hing W179
Wong, Heng Tew W456
Wong, Hoi Ming A785
Wong, Hon-Hing W179
Wong, Irwin A211
Wong, Irwin E84
Wong, Janet S. E169
Wong, Janet S. E305
Wong, Jeanette W621
Wong, Jeanette W481
Wong, Jennifer (Jen) L. A330
Wong, Kan Seng W628
Wong, Kennedy Ying Ho W144
Wong, M. Victoria A244
Wong, May Kay W268
Wong, Peter Tung Shun W128
Wong, Peter Tung Shun W286
Wong, R. Wai A747
Wong, Raymond L.M. A39
Wong, Rosanna Yick-ming W287
Wong, Vivian A. E492
Wong, Wai Ming W362
Wong, Wai Ming W151
Wong, Zongbin W168
Wongsmith, Nampung W117
Wongsuwan, Phatcharavat W117
Wongtrakool, Bonnie M. A1121
Wongtschowski, Pedro W622
Woo, Byoung-Kwon W652
Woo, Carolyn Y. W44
Woo, Chia-Wei W362
Woo, Liyuan E57
Woo, Melissa P356
Woo, Nam K. W366
Woo, Nam-Sung W513
Wood, Adam A950
Wood, Amy C. E99
Wood, Andrea W596
Wood, Anthony E423
Wood, Brent W. E151
Wood, Carrie E490
Wood, Catherine E348
Wood, Cheryl B. A845
Wood, Cheryl B. E395
Wood, Chester A. A1044
Wood, E. Jenner A468
Wood, E. Jenner A952
Wood, F. Lewis A1033

Wood, F. Lewis E493
Wood, Gregory S. E382
Wood, Larry L. A361
Wood, Leanne W637
Wood, Paul A237
Wood, Phoebe A. A573
Wood, Phoebe A. A841
Wood, Phoebe A. A830
Wood, Phoebe A. A624
Wood, Renee K. E117
Wood, Robert L. A1075
Wood, Robert L. W369
Wood, Roger J. A182
Wood, Tony W422
Wood, Tony W258
Woodall, James W. (Woody) A408
Woodall, Robert L. A95
Woodburn, Charles W66
Woodhouse, Hope B. A485
Woodhouse, Hope B. A1048
Woodring, Greig A. A502
Woodruff, Carolyn J. E62
Woodrum, Douglas N. E56
Woodrum, James D. A799
Woods, Candace J. A856
Woods, Candace J. A855
Woods, Catherine W371
Woods, Catherine W371
Woods, Charles Scott A1044
Woods, Darren W. A388
Woods, Edgar L. E452
Woods, Eugene A1015
Woods, Eugene A155
Woods, Eugene P571
Woods, Gordon T. A935
Woods, Gordon T. E439
Woods, John F. A248
Woods, Karen B. A420
Woods, Karen B. E197
Woods, M. Troy A477
Woods, Michael W. A772
Woods, Ngaire W500
Woods, Ngaire W499
Woods, Robert F. A349
Woods, Thomas D. A128
Woodside, David B. A138
Woodside, David B. E55
Woodson, Bret A. E540
Wooldridge, Michael G. A1053
Woolley, Kenneth M. E180
Woolson, Dan E262
Woolstenhulme, Micah A1065
Woon, Tracey Kim Hong W628
Wootton, Charles A. E192
Woram, Brian J. A594
Worden, Anita R. A372
Worden, Anita R. E167
Work, Robert O. A877
Workman, John L. E188
Works, David A1083
Worman, Douglas M. A258
Wormoudt, Mardi P177
Wormsley, David W260
Wornham, Thomas V. E397
Worobel, Ryan P683
Woronoff, Michael A. E15
Worrell, Beth R. E372
Worsoe-Petersen, Lars W4
Wortberg, Ernst J. W62
Worth, Philip Jason A1118

Worth, Philip Jason E533
Wortham, Lee C. E175
Worthington, Robert T. A681
Worthington, Robert T. E318
Wortmann-Kool, Coerien M. W16
Worzel, Kenneth J. A745
Woste, Ewald W207
Wothe, Mike E381
Woyner, Jeanine E61
Woys, James E. A707
Woytera, Chun W157
Wray, Peter H. E181
Wray, William K. A1108
Wren, John D. A778
Wright, Adam L. A823
Wright, Andrea T. E67
Wright, Andrew W288
Wright, Andrew P.C. A660
Wright, Bryan P. A292
Wright, Christopher A904
Wright, Cornell W99
Wright, David B. E520
Wright, Deborah Patricia W72
Wright, Dickerson E357
Wright, Doreen A. E130
Wright, Doug A530
Wright, Emory M. E16
Wright, Gregory S. E141
Wright, Jacqueline E178
Wright, James W517
Wright, James M. A369
Wright, John W. E470
Wright, Joseph T. A816
Wright, Julia E91
Wright, Kelly D. A717
Wright, Kristen C. A111
Wright, Laura H. A256
Wright, Laura H. A294
Wright, Laura H. W590
Wright, Lori A797
Wright, Lori P419
Wright, Lori A P218
Wright, Lori A. A797
Wright, Lori A. E368
Wright, MaryAnn A491
Wright, MaryAnn A700
Wright, Pamela Mars W274
Wright, Patrick W419
Wright, Richard M. A1138
Wright, Richard M. E544
Wright, Robert A. W80
Wright, Robert G. A321
Wright, Robert R. A386
Wright, Scott J. A547
Wright, Terry J. A401
Wrighton, Mark S. A298
Wrozek, Robert E102
Wskeland, Oddgeir A377
Wskeland, Oddgeir P217
Wu, Bilei W239
Wu, Bin W40
Wu, Bingqi W148
Wu, Changqi W268
Wu, Charles F. E340
Wu, Chengye W472
Wu, Chih-Wei A843
Wu, Chih-Wei E393
Wu, Chung-Wei A785
Wu, Dawei W173
Wu, Dinggang W542

Wu, Donghua W326
Wu, Dongying W100
Wu, Fei W533
Wu, Gangping W472
Wu, Guangqi W158
Wu, Guohong W662
Wu, Heping W608
Wu, Honghui W663
Wu, Hongwei W644
Wu, James W650
Wu, Jian-Hsing W128
Wu, Jian-Li W206
Wu, Jianbin W144
Wu, Jianing W152
Wu, Jianing W146
Wu, Jianing W398
Wu, Jianjun W148
Wu, Jie W656
Wu, Jie W575
Wu, Jiejiang W656
Wu, Jiesi W150
Wu, Jun W148
Wu, Jundong W664
Wu, Junhao W145
Wu, Kuan-Her W206
Wu, Liqun W139
Wu, Maggie Wei W29
Wu, Michael W583
Wu, Michael C. A140
Wu, Michael Wei Kuo W268
Wu, Michael Wei Kuo W323
Wu, Peter A211
Wu, Peter E84
Wu, Ping W248
Wu, Pingan W140
Wu, Po W145
Wu, Po-Hsuan W530
Wu, Qiang W256
Wu, Qiuting W98
Wu, Rui W202
Wu, Sanqiang W141
Wu, Simone E14
Wu, Tang-Chieh W128
Wu, Tien W51
Wu, Wayne A843
Wu, Wayne E393
Wu, Xiangdong W140
Wu, Xiangjiang W301
Wu, Xiangqian W660
Wu, Xiaogen W152
Wu, Xiaoming W40
Wu, Xiaonan W158
Wu, Yajun W372
Wu, Yibing W362
Wu, Yiming W144
Wu, Yingxiang W150
Wu, Yuci W284
Wu, Yuejie W291
Wu, Yunxuan W656
Wu, Zhenqin W142
Wu, Zhijie W261
Wu, Zhong W275
Wu, Zhongbing W140
Wuerffel, Nathaniel A400
Wuerst, Alexander W192
Wulff, Henrik W450
Wulfsohn, Bryan A693
Wulfsohn, Loren W288
Wunderlich, Gary K. E50
Wunning, Steven H. A934

COMBINED HOOVER'S HANDBOOK INDEX OF EXECUTIVES

A = AMERICAN BUSINESS
E = EMERGING COMPANIES
P = PRIVATE COMPANIES
W = WORLD BUSINESSS

Wunning, Steven H. E469
Wurster, Richard A. A919
Wurth, Michel W49
Wurz, Isolde W602
Wyant, Jill S. A342
Wyatt, Ben W500
Wyatt, Douglas Vincent A815
Wyatt, E. Lee A570
Wyatt, John H. A962
Wyatt, Tim A226
Wycoff, Terrill L. E30
Wydock, Edward J. A134
Wydock, Edward J. E54
Wyk, Rene van W8
Wyk, Steven C. Van A886
Wylie, Scott C. E206
Wyman, Kenneth R. E18
Wynd, Colin A400
Wynne, Eileen E331
Wyrsch, Martha Brown A868
Wyrsch, Martha Brown A413
Wyrsch, Martha Brown W422
Wyshner, David B. A612
Wyss, Hans W34
Wyszomierski, Jack L. E545
Wyszomierski, Jack L. E178
Wyszomierski, Jack L. E445

X

Xi, Dan W597
Xi, Guohua W156
Xi, Juntong W529
Xi, You W257
Xia, Aidong W291
Xia, Dawei W575
Xia, Haijun W139
Xia, Howard H. E266
Xia, Qing W291
Xia, Qinglong W158
Xia, Xiaoyue W664
Xia, Yang W138
Xia, Yu W355
Xia, Zuoquan W117
Xian, Ming E316
Xiang, Bing W372
Xiang, Guodong W603
Xiang, Hong W144
Xiang, Wenbo W516
Xiang, Yinan E3
Xiao, Chuangying W256
Xiao, Deming E331
Xiao, Ji W292
Xiao, Jingqin W656
Xiao, Mingfu W37
Xiao, Quan W140
Xiao, Wei W656
Xiao, Xiangning W256
Xiao, Xiao W144
Xiao, Xinfang W528
Xiao, Yaomeng W660
Xiao, Youliang W516

Xie, Bing W150
Xie, Daxiong W664
Xie, Dong W152
Xie, Ji W148
Xie, Jichuan W140
Xie, Jilong W178
Xie, Jiren W472
Xie, Juzhi W268
Xie, Ken E216
Xie, Ling W292
Xie, Michael E216
Xie, Rong W88
Xie, Shuorong W608
Xie, Shutai W173
Xie, Weiming W662
Xie, Weizhi W158
Xie, Xionghui W663
Xie, Yiqun W150
Xie, Yonglin W472
Xie, Yun W291
Xin, Dinghua W146
Xin, Dinghua W179
Xin, Jie W152
Xin, Keng W530
Xin, Qi W326
Xin, Xin W533
Xin, Zhonghua W136
Xing, Jian W141
Xing, Yi W477
Xing, Ziwen W263
Xiong, Bo W141
Xiong, Yan W301
Xiu, Long W147
Xu, Bin W272
Xu, Chenye W596
Xu, David Peng W202
Xu, Dingbo W356
Xu, Dingbo W324
Xu, Erming W151
Xu, Fanggen W662
Xu, Feng W528
Xu, Haifeng W291
Xu, Haigen W239
Xu, Hong W574
Xu, Hui W261
Xu, Jacky Yu W636
Xu, Jiajun W257
Xu, Jiana W655
Xu, Jiandong W138
Xu, Jianhua W139
Xu, Jianxin W529
Xu, Jinwu W528
Xu, Jinwu W156
Xu, Keqiang W158
Xu, Kuiru W663
Xu, Lei W324
Xu, Linhua W292
Xu, Lirong W173
Xu, Mengzhou W291
Xu, Min E3
Xu, Mingjun W149
Xu, Minjing W575
Xu, Qian W257
Xu, Qian W137
Xu, Qiang W663
Xu, Qiang W663
Xu, Sandy Ran W324
Xu, Shancheng W149
Xu, Shouben W301
Xu, Sunqing W529

Xu, Tao W106
Xu, Toby Hong W29
Xu, Tony A689
Xu, Wen W139
Xu, Wenhui W144
Xu, Wuqi W608
Xu, Xiangwu W139
Xu, Xiaojun W139
Xu, Xiaoxi W656
Xu, Xing W140
Xu, Xinyu W644
Xu, Yang A457
Xu, Yangping W106
Xu, Yinfei W274
Xu, Yongbin W663
Xu, Yongjun W142
Xu, Youli W530
Xu, Younong W534
Xu, Yuguang W662
Xu, Zheng W529
Xu, Zhibin W431
Xu, Zhigang W431
Xu, Zhiguo W140
Xu, Ziyang W664
Xue, Yan W603

Y

Ya-Qin, Zhang W246
Yabe, Takeshi W65
Yabokla, Erica A961
Yabokla, Erica P531
Yabu, Yukiko W185
Yabuki, Jeffery W. W507
Yabunaka, Mitoji W402
Yacob, Ezra Y. A375
Yadav, Sujata A352
Yadav, Sunil A693
Yagi, Makoto W436
Yagi, Minoru W539
Yago, Natsunosuke W564
Yaguchi, Norihiko W582
Yahes, Jarrod E438
Yajnik, Sanjiv A198
Yajnik, Sanjiv A213
Yakovlev, Vadim W256
Yaku, Toshikazu W569
Yalcin, Gamze W619
Yale, Phyllis R. A318
Yale, Phyllis R. A178
Yamabe, Dayna P586
Yamada, Akira W449
Yamada, Aya W432
Yamada, Kathy E79
Yamada, Meyumi W527
Yamada, Meyumi W555
Yamada, Noboru W657
Yamada, Shigeru W173
Yamada, Shinnosuke W581
Yamada, Tatsumi W400
Yamada, Tomoki W410
Yamada, Yasuko W293
Yamadera, Masahiko W659
Yamaguchi, Goro W336
Yamaguchi, Goro W356
Yamaguchi, Hiroyuki W607
Yamaguchi, Masato W181
Yamaguchi, Mitsugu W345

Yamaguchi, Naohiro W313
Yamaguchi, Nobuaki W570
Yamaguchi, Satoshi W313
Yamaguchi, Shigeki W451
Yamaguchi, Toshiaki W184
Yamai, Lisa W577
Yamaji, Toru W535
Yamakoshi, Koji W44
Yamamoto, Akiko W454
Yamamoto, Atsushi W582
Yamamoto, Fumiaki W534
Yamamoto, Hidehiro W281
Yamamoto, Katsutoshi W83
Yamamoto, Katsuya W334
Yamamoto, Keiji W336
Yamamoto, Kensei W316
Yamamoto, Kenzo W568
Yamamoto, Kenzo W110
Yamamoto, Kenzo W319
Yamamoto, Masami W325
Yamamoto, Masami W253
Yamamoto, Shigeo W297
Yamamoto, Takashi W409
Yamamoto, Takatoshi W279
Yamamoto, Takatoshi W417
Yamamoto, Yasuo W405
Yamamoto, Yoshihisa W25
Yamana, Kazuaki W405
Yamana, Shoei W589
Yamanaka, Masashi (Mik) A812
Yamanishi, Tetsuji W589
Yamasaki, Brian Y. A807
Yamasaki, Kiyomi W137
Yamasaki, Toru W515
Yamashiro, Yukihiko W319
Yamashita, Kazuhito W321
Yamashita, Koji W410
Yamashita, Masahiro W65
Yamashita, Mitsuhiko W587
Yamashita, Shuji W281
Yamashita, Takashi W570
Yamashita, Toru W568
Yamashita, Yoshinori W496
Yamashita, Yukihiro W577
Yamato, Kenichi W407
Yamato, Shiro W65
Yamauchi, Chizuru W436
Yamauchi, Junko W410
Yamauchi, Kazunori W394
Yamauchi, Masaki W494
Yamauchi, Masaki W659
Yamauchi, Takashi W582
Yamaura, Masai W1
Yamazaki, Hisashi W319
Yamazaki, Hisashi W566
Yamazaki, Kei W292
Yamazaki, Masao W433
Yamazaki, Shohei W441
Yamazaki, Shozo W570
Yan, Aizhong W398
Yan, Andrew Y. W248
Yan, Andrew Y. W148
Yan, Chao W662
Yan, Christine Y. A780
Yan, Jian Guo W144
Yan, Jianbo W644
Yan, Jun W106
Yan, Ming W153
Yan, Xiaojiang W179
Yan, Yan W150

COMBINED HOOVER'S HANDBOOK INDEX OF EXECUTIVES

A = AMERICAN BUSINESS
E = EMERGING COMPANIES
P = PRIVATE COMPANIES
W = WORLD BUSINESSS

Yan, Ye W144
Yanagi, Hiroyuki W18
Yanagi, Hiroyuki W343
Yanagi, Hiroyuki W402
Yanagi, Masanori W570
Yanagida, Naoki W555
Yanagisawa, Yasunobu W316
Yanai, Kazumi W237
Yanai, Koji W237
Yanai, Shiomo E31
Yanai, Shlomo A825
Yanai, Tadashi W237
Yanase, Goro W612
Yancopoulos, George D. A882
Yaney, Brad A938
Yaney, Brad E442
Yang, Baizhang W275
Yang, Bingsheng W136
Yang, Chengjun W327
Yang, Congsen W141
Yang, Donghao W636
Yang, Erzhu W173
Yang, Fang W431
Yang, Geoffrey Y. A448
Yang, Guang W574
Yang, Guipeng W100
Yang, Guofeng W136
Yang, Haisheng W528
Yang, Heng-Hwa W206
Yang, Huiyan W173
Yang, Jackie E370
Yang, Jerry W29
Yang, Jian W256
Yang, Jianghong W656
Yang, Jianjun W663
Yang, Jie W143
Yang, Jigang W466
Yang, Jin W542
Yang, Jiping W149
Yang, Jun W542
Yang, Jun W608
Yang, Kai W663
Yang, KP E370
Yang, Lin W236
Yang, Liu W327
Yang, Liuyong W275
Yang, Lvbo W529
Yang, Marjorie Mun Tak W287
Yang, Michael M. A498
Yang, Mulin W100
Yang, Phoebe L. A458
Yang, Qiang W143
Yang, Shicheng W173
Yang, Siu Shun W301
Yang, Siu Shun W597
Yang, Tianping W142
Yang, Timothy D. E307
Yang, Vivian W. E489
Yang, Weimin W257
Yang, Weiqiao W528
Yang, Wendy W. E137
Yang, William Wang A1145
Yang, Xiangdong W106
Yang, Xianghong W292

Yang, Xiao W239
Yang, Xiaoping W472
Yang, Xiaoping W156
Yang, Xinguo W662
Yang, Yada W375
Yang, Yi W431
Yang, Yong W662
Yang, Yongchao W173
Yang, Yongqing W136
Yang, Yuanqing W67
Yang, Yuanqing W362
Yang, Yun W158
Yang, Zheng W431
Yang, Zhengfan E3
Yang, Zhenghong W662
Yang, Zhengwen W37
Yang, Zhicheng W173
Yang, Zhiguang W142
Yang, Zhijian W172
Yang, Zhijuan W261
Yang, Ziying W173
Yankevich, Alexey W256
Yannaccone, Susan A879
Yannaccone, Susan A878
Yano, Harumi W319
Yao, Bo W472
Yao, Chuanda W516
Yao, Daochun W608
Yao, Jun W533
Yao, Ke W326
Yao, Linlong W88
Yao, Lushi W608
Yao, Minfang W529
Yao, Xu-Jie W128
Yao, Yanmin W138
Yao, Yong W150
Yao, Zhihua W662
Yapp, Alison W170
Yaqub, Beel W358
Yarad, Stephen D. A693
Yarbrough, James D. A68
Yarckin, Jeffrey S. E19
Yardley, James C. A929
Yared, Rana E493
Yarlagadda, Choudhary A231
Yaroslavsky, Zev A301
Yaroslavsky, Zev P171
Yarrington, Patricia E. A402
Yarrington, Patricia E. A643
Yaryan, Kevin Andrew E186
Yasinsky, John B. A1040
Yasinsky, John B. E498
Yastine, Barbara A. A845
Yastine, Barbara A. A1151
Yastine, Barbara A. E395
Yasuda, Masamichi W407
Yasuda, Mitsuharu W449
Yasuda, Takao W464
Yasuda, Yuko W417
Yasui, Hajime W533
Yasui, Mikiya W82
Yasunaga, Tatsuo W408
Yasuoka, Sadako W434
Yatabe, Yasushi W223
Yatabe, Yoichiro W405
Yates, Abigail K. A321
Yates, Lloyd M. A662
Yates, Timothy T. A279
Yates, William G. A1044
Yawman, David A817

Yazaki, Toshiyuki W319
Yazdi, Cynthia M. A716
Ybarra, Paco A246
Ye, Cai W291
Ye, Guohua W34
Ye, Haiqiang W533
Ye, Jianping W172
Ye, Lin W100
Ye, Xiaojie W98
Ye, Yanliu W655
Yeager, Jeff A397
Yeager, Jeff E187
Yeager, Rande Keith A773
Yealy, Donald A1080
Yealy, Donald P667
Yeaman, Eric K. A34
Yeap, Geoffrey W583
Yearley, Douglas C. A1032
Yearout, Suzanne S. E372
Yearwood, John W591
Yeary, Frank D. A560
Yeary, Frank D. A807
Yee, Yang Chiah E392
Yeghyayan, Silva A888
Yeh, Jeffrey A878
Yeh, Jeffrey E409
Yeh, Kung-Liang W252
Yehia, Samer Haj W79
Yell, Ieda Gomes W165
Yellen, Janet L. A403
Yellin, Jonathan D. E126
Yelmenoglu, Ibrahim W620
Yemin, Ezra Uzi A321
Yen, Yun E224
Yeo, Alvin Khirn Hai W628
Yeo, Eun-Jung W352
Yeo, George Yong-Boon W19
Yeo, Mee Sook W367
Yeo, Teng Yang W649
Yeoh, Chin Kee W484
Yeoh, Francis Sock Ping W287
Yeoh, Patrick W464
Yeoh, Peter W463
Yerger, Ann A148
Yerks, Austin J. E144
Yeshaya, Sharon A713
Yesho, LaDawn D. A910
Yeu, Lin Elizabeth E460
Yeung, Alex Sau Hung W257
Yeung, Ann Yun Chi Kung W104
Yeung, Jason Chi Wai W151
Yeung, Ka Wai Andy A1145
Yeung, Kwok Keung W173
Yeung, William Chu Kwong E161
Yezhkov, Sergey E170
Yi, Baohou W137
Yi, Lian W512
Yi, Sang A1150
Yi, Sang-Seung W294
Yi, Sunny W537
Yi, Xiaogang W516
Yi, Zuo W292
Yildirim, Arda W620
Yildiz, Beril A567
Yin, Charles Chuanli W659
Yin, Hongxia W529
Yin, Huijun W148
Yin, Keding W529
Yin, Peter E420
Yin, Shiming W533

Yin, Sisong W397
Yin, Tian W100
Yin, Yande W292
Yin, Zhaolin W145
Yip, Amy W481
Yip, Wai Ming W236
Yiu, Stephen K.W. W143
Yocum, Arlene M. A252
Yocum, Deb P543
Yoda, Toshihide W392
Yoder, Sheldon E. A515
Yoh, Caren C. A440
Yohanan, Robert R. A188
Yohanan, Robert R. E71
Yohannes, Daniel A342
Yohannes, Daniel A1139
Yokoo, Keisuke W496
Yokota, Noriya W343
Yokota, Shinichi W83
Yokotani, Kazuya W418
Yokoyama, Kiichi W603
Yokoyama, Shuichi W407
Yoler, Laurie J. A237
Yonamine, Paul K. A219
Yonamine, Paul K. W528
Yonebayashi, Akira W65
Yonehana, Tetsuya W407
Yonemoto, Tsutomu W137
Yonemura, Toshiro W527
Yong, Michael W252
Yongpisanpop, Ampa W117
Yoo, C.S. W583
Yoo, H. Julie A401
Yoo, Julien E234
Yoon, Bu-Geun W513
Yoon, Chi-Won W294
Yoon, Dong-Min W513
Yoon, Jaewon W537
Yoon, Jin-Soo W335
Yoon, Jong-Kyoo W335
Yoon, Ki Won E362
Yoon, Tae-Sik A95
Yoon, Youngmin W546
Yoritomi, Toshiya W293
York, Douglas A. E206
York, James R. E275
York, Jeffrey E242
York, Jill E. A774
York, Jill E. E360
York, Shaun E219
Yoshida, Akio W17
Yoshida, Haruyuki W353
Yoshida, Katsuhiko W334
Yoshida, Kenichiro W557
Yoshida, Masatake W253
Yoshida, Moritaka W25
Yoshida, Motokazu W278
Yoshida, Naoki W464
Yoshida, Satoshi W370
Yoshida, Shuichi W439
Yoshihara, Hiroaki W279
Yoshihashi, Mitsuru W83
Yoshii, Keiichi W184
Yoshikawa, Hiroaki W21
Yoshikawa, Hiroshi W515
Yoshikawa, Hiroshi W437
Yoshikawa, Masahiro W405
Yoshikawa, Masato W353
Yoshimaru, Yukiko W527
Yoshimatsu, Masuo W110

COMBINED HOOVER'S HANDBOOK INDEX OF EXECUTIVES

A = AMERICAN BUSINESS
E = EMERGING COMPANIES
P = PRIVATE COMPANIES
W = WORLD BUSINESSS

Yoshimi, Tsuyoshi W110
Yoshimoto, Kazumi W439
Yoshimura, Kazuyuki W336
Yoshimura, Takuya W433
Yoshimura, Yasunori W464
Yoshinaga, Kunimitsu W657
Yoshinaga, Minoru W610
Yoshino, Shigehiro W607
Yoshizawa, Chisato W253
Yoshizawa, Kazuhiro W185
Yost, Joseph P. A486
Yost, Mark H. E447
Yost, R. David A662
Yost, R. David A128
You, Harry L. A180
You, Yalin W356
Youman, Robert W. E191
Young-Gardey, Margo E19
Young-Scrivner, Annie A1146
Young, Andrew A198
Young, Brian D. E507
Young, Brian S. E355
Young, Charles D. E280
Young, Charles D. E210
Young, Charles E. E450
Young, Christopher D. A62
Young, Christopher H. A671
Young, Daniel T. A483
Young, Dona D. W16
Young, Dona Davis A443
Young, Donald M. A16
Young, Douglas L. A145
Young, Ho Lee W513
Young, J. Robert E19
Young, James Douglas E450
Young, Jay A958
Young, Jay P518
Young, John D. W327
Young, John F. A383
Young, Julie M. A259
Young, Julie M. E103
Young, Kenneth E49
Young, Kenneth M. (Kenny) E219
Young, Larry D. A600
Young, Lina A. A373
Young, Lina A. E168
Young, Mark R. A1151
Young, Mary Maurice A988
Young, Mary Maurice E479
Young, Micah E312
Young, Nicolas E348
Young, Norbert W. E301
Young, Ray G. A94
Young, Ray G. A568
Young, Steven K. A348
Young, Steven K. A347
Young, Terrance P249
Young, Terrance A. A392
Young, Terrance A. E183
Young, Theodore B. E144
Young, Tobi M. Edwards A494
Young, Tracie A. A891
Young, Wai Chow (Albert) E33
Young, William John E450

Young, William L. W308
Young, Willian L. W379
Younger, Simon P. W299
Youngworth, Jacqueline M. A519
Youngworth, Jacqueline M. E256
Yousaf, Mohammad E350
Youssouf, Emily Ann A811
Youssouf, Emily Ann E377
Yowan, David L. A723
Yrarrazaval, Pedro Silva W314
Ytterberg, Jan W641
Yu, Baocai W145
Yu, Carolyn M. E509
Yu, Carolyn M. E509
Yu, Carolyn M. E510
Yu, Carrie W17
Yu, David E234
Yu, Dingming W662
Yu, Doug W583
Yu, Gary E143
Yu, Gideon A498
Yu, Guangming W663
Yu, Hailong W397
Yu, Handu W268
Yu, Hansheng W88
Yu, Hee-Yol W352
Yu, Herman W67
Yu, Jiannan W431
Yu, Jiehui W603
Yu, K. Peony E460
Yu, Lawrence Kam Kee W139
Yu, Li A843
Yu, Li E392
Yu, Liang W152
Yu, Meng W575
Yu, Miao W268
Yu, Sara Siying W29
Yu, Shen-Fu W51
Yu, Shui W40
Yu, Tong W326
Yu, Vernon D. W218
Yu, Weiqiao W139
Yu, Yajing W656
Yu, Yang W156
Yu, Yuxian W656
Yu, Zhongliang W148
Yu, Zhuoping W644
Yuan, Baoyin W147
Yuan, Changqing W142
Yuan, Dakang W140
Yuan, Eric S. E547
Yuan, Guoqiang W149
Yuan, Honglin W144
Yuan, Hongming W644
Yuan, Renjun W663
Yuan, Shengzhou W529
Yuan, Shu W104
Yuasa, Takayuki W605
Yuasa, Toru W253
Yuce, Burcu Civelek W26
Yudd, Charles P320
Yue, Xuguang W34
Yue, Ying W261
Yue, Yuanbin W144
Yuen, Aiken A1145
Yuen, Loretta W463
Yuen, Nicole E279
Yumoto, Shoichi W267
Yun, Ju-Hwa W513
Yung, Mark T. A800

Yunker, Craig A1033
Yurconic, John T. E156
Yurdum, Sema W618
Yusuf, Kareem A893
Yuthavong, Yongyuth W334
Yuvienco, Maria Dolores B. W85
Yzaguirre, M. Max A650
Yzaguirre, M. Max E305

Z

zabalegui, Carlos Gonzalez W266
Zabel, Brian P. E204
Zabel, Steven A. A1079
Zabriskie, Katheryn M. E113
Zacarias, Celina L. E114
Zacariassen, Christian P378
Zaccardo, Jennifer E204
Zaccaro, Joanne Caruso A580
Zachary, Jennifer L. A684
Zachert, Matthias W543
Zachman, Brian A185
Zacur, Mark P. A793
Zadoks, Jeff A. A838
Zaffino, Peter S. A295
Zaffino, Peter S. A65
Zagorski, Judy A1054
Zagra, Levent W620
Zaheer, Srilata E226
Zahl, Brendan W. A722
Zahl, Brendan W. E339
Zaimler, Kivanc W267
Zainulbhai, Adil W491
Zaitzeff, Michael A. A152
Zajicek, Hubert W639
Zakas, Marietta Edmunds A106
Zakharova, Marianna Aleksandrovna W410
Zakrowski, Donald A. A635
Zalaznick, Lauren A742
Zales, Samuel E81
Zalik, David E240
Zallie, James P. A557
Zalm, Gerrit W533
Zalman, David A852
Zalman, David E399
Zalotrawala, Tabassum S. A232
Zaman, Neil E75
Zamarin, Chad J. A1131
Zamarro, Christina L. A613
Zambanini, Adam Dante E494
Zambelli, Rossana W627
Zamboni, Daniele W310
Zambrano, Cesar Augusto Montemayor W73
Zambrano, Ian Christian Armstrong W131
Zammit, Patrick A999
Zampi, Jason A. A747
Zamuner, Valery W31
Zanata, Alberto W4
Zanavich, W Marie P610
Zancanaro, Gilles W161
Zancani, Alexandre Grossmann W315
Zander, Brian E530
Zandi, Mark M. A694
Zane, Ellen M. A175
Zane, Ellen M. A985

Zangardi, John A. E405
Zanghi, Phyllis J. A60
Zanias, Georgios P. W231
Zanichelli, Rossano W177
Zanin, Ryan A. A391
Zanin, Ryan A. W647
Zannino, Richard F. A620
Zannino, Richard F. E360
Zannino, Richard F. E261
Zano, Yaakov W311
Zanten, Frank van W351
Zanten, Frank van W116
Zapanti, Maria W473
Zapatero, Francisco Jesus Moza W73
Zapico, David A. A74
Zapolsky, David A. A50
Zappa, Janice E428
Zappa, Michael P184
Zappia, Andrea W231
Zaramella, Luca A709
Zarcone, Dominick P. A643
Zarcone, Dominick P. E228
Zarcone, Donna F. A239
Zarcone, Donna F. A214
Zarin, Larry E2
Zarmi, Sigal A16
Zarmi, Sigal E234
Zaror, Jorge Selume W314
Zarri, Francesca W227
Zarrilli, Stephen T. E233
Zarrilli, Stephen T. E528
Zaslav, David M. A332
Zaslav, David M. A941
Zatta, Jayson M. A1115
Zatta, Jayson M. E533
Zaunbrecher, Susan B. A410
Zausmer, Adam E411
Zavadil, Bill E409
Zavaglia, Joseph P. E223
Zaveri, Bhavesh W271
Zayicek, Beth A. A574
Zazworsky, Leon A803
Zazworsky, Leon E371
Zbanek, Cathy W. A1013
Zebula, Charles E. A59
Zecca, John A. A721
Zech, Gretchen K. A97
Zecher, Linda Kay A503
Zechmeister, Michael P. A900
Zeder, Franz W631
Zeffiro, A. Mark E40
Zehnder-Lai, Eunice W203
Zeidel, Darren W44
Zeidler, Susanne W251
Zeile, Art A722
Zeile, Art E339
Zeiler, Julie E281
Zeisel, Karin W229
Zeisser, Michael P. A627
Zelenzcuk, Nicholas W358
Zelkova, Larisa W410
Zelkowicz, Stephen J. E144
Zelleke, Andargachew S. A191
Zelleke, Andargachew S. E77
Zellner, Theo W192
Zelnick, Strauss A965
Zelnick, Strauss E462
Zelnick, Strauss E480
Zember, Dennis J. A845
Zember, Dennis J. A71

COMBINED HOOVER'S HANDBOOK INDEX OF EXECUTIVES

```
A = AMERICAN BUSINESS
E = EMERGING COMPANIES
P = PRIVATE COMPANIES
W = WORLD BUSINESSS
```

Zember, Dennis J. E395
Zember, Dennis J. E28
Zemljak, Renee E. A792
Zemlyak, James M. A977
Zemlyak, James M. E464
Zeng, Gang W397
Zeng, Han W141
Zeng, Jian W656
Zeng, Min W326
Zeng, Ming W372
Zeng, Saixing W512
Zeng, Yangfeng W656
Zeng, Yuan W656
Zenkner, Marcelo Barbosa de Castro W468
Zenner, Patrick J. E534
Zentmyer, Hugh J. E333
Zentner, Quentin W471
Zenuk, Mark N. A185
Zerbe, Glenn H E356
Zerbs, Michael W84
Zerhouni, Elias A. A315
Zerhouni, Mohammed (Rally) G. E446
Zerza, Armin A14
Zettl, Albert W207
Zhai, Yalin W145
Zhang, Baoying W152
Zhang, Bo W153
Zhang, Bo W663
Zhang, Bo W141
Zhang, Bob Bo W202
Zhang, Bowen W355
Zhang, Changyan W149
Zhang, Cheng W147
Zhang, Chengjie W137
Zhang, Chuanchang W660
Zhang, Chunxia W375
Zhang, Daniel Yong W29
Zhang, Daniel Yong W202
Zhang, Dawei W148
Zhang, Deyong W153
Zhang, Dingming W212
Zhang, Duanqing W663
Zhang, Fengshan W466
Zhang, Gelin W291
Zhang, Guijin W528
Zhang, Guohua W239
Zhang, Haitao W292
Zhang, Hong W136
Zhang, Hong W431
Zhang, Hongjun W37
Zhang, Jian W140
Zhang, Jianbing W326
Zhang, Jianfeng W152
Zhang, Jianhua W326
Zhang, Jianping W292
Zhang, Jianping W172
Zhang, Jianzhong W272
Zhang, Jiawei W140
Zhang, Jie W301
Zhang, Jindong W574
Zhang, Jinglei W141
Zhang, Jingzhong W356
Zhang, Jun W292

Zhang, Jundu W263
Zhang, Junping W307
Zhang, Juntian W656
Zhang, Ke W137
Zhang, Kehua W88
Zhang, Kejian W148
Zhang, Kevin W583
Zhang, Kui W326
Zhang, Lan W128
Zhang, Liang W148
Zhang, Liangfu W644
Zhang, Lianqi W533
Zhang, Lin W156
Zhang, Lin W142
Zhang, Ling W656
Zhang, Maohan W375
Zhang, Mei W533
Zhang, Mengxing W397
Zhang, Min A1145
Zhang, Min W138
Zhang, Min W117
Zhang, Min W575
Zhang, Minggui W431
Zhang, Mingwen W172
Zhang, Pang W324
Zhang, Peng W291
Zhang, Qi W138
Zhang, Qianchun W375
Zhang, Qiang W572
Zhang, Qiang W327
Zhang, Qiaoqiao W137
Zhang, Quan W644
Zhang, Ruilian W141
Zhang, Runsheng W528
Zhang, Shaofeng W145
Zhang, Shaoping W137
Zhang, Shengman W248
Zhang, Shiping W141
Zhang, Shuili W656
Zhang, Songsheng W173
Zhang, Sufang W664
Zhang, Wangjin W472
Zhang, Wanshun W477
Zhang, Wei W477
Zhang, Wei W301
Zhang, Wei W263
Zhang, Wei W142
Zhang, Weidong W145
Zhang, Weijiong W292
Zhang, Weiwu W301
Zhang, Wenwu W301
Zhang, Xialong W596
Zhang, Xiang E297
Zhang, Xianzhi W291
Zhang, Xiaofeng W375
Zhang, Xiaojun W291
Zhang, Xiaolong W542
Zhang, Xiaolu W472
Zhang, Xiaorong W40
Zhang, Xinling W307
Zhang, Xinmin W106
Zhang, Xinning W178
Zhang, Ya-Qin W654
Zhang, Yan W529
Zhang, Yandi W397
Zhang, Yanhua W477
Zhang, Yaoyuan W173
Zhang, Yi W140
Zhang, Yi W144
Zhang, Yichen W152

Zhang, Yiguang W528
Zhang, Yuanhan W145
Zhang, Yueduan W656
Zhang, Yuexia W141
Zhang, Yuliang W529
Zhang, Yuming W533
Zhang, Yun W529
Zhang, Yunyan W40
Zhang, Yuxing W98
Zhang, Yuzhu W272
Zhang, Yuzhuo W146
Zhang, Zhengao W477
Zhang, Zhengrong W150
Zhang, Zhenhao W144
Zhang, Zhicheng W663
Zhang, Zhiguo W145
Zhang, Zhiqiang W291
Zhang, Zhixiao W140
Zhang, Zhiyong W151
Zhang, Zhongyi W608
Zhang, Zijuan W256
Zhang, Zuoxue W663
Zhao, Bingxiang W148
Zhao, Buyu W40
Zhao, Chengxia W307
Zhao, Dachun W143
Zhao, Dengshan W146
Zhao, Dong W143
Zhao, Guixiang W326
Zhao, Guoqing W261
Zhao, Hongjing W140
Zhao, Hu W179
Zhao, Huifang W644
Zhao, Ji E370
Zhao, Junwu W292
Zhao, Kexiong W656
Zhao, Keyu W291
Zhao, Minge W100
Zhao, Ping W291
Zhao, Qilin W542
Zhao, Qingchun W660
Zhao, Rongzhe W137
Zhao, Songzheng W528
Zhao, Weilin W136
Zhao, Xi'an W138
Zhao, Ying W307
Zhao, Yong W542
Zhao, Yonglu W656
Zhe, Sun W148
Zhen, Marianne E272
Zhen, Tracey A654
Zhen, Wang W526
Zheng, Baohua P486
Zheng, Bing W663
Zheng, Changhong W138
Zheng, Chengliang W529
Zheng, Falong W528
Zheng, Ganshu W656
Zheng, Gaoqing W326
Zheng, Guoyu W301
Zheng, Jessie Junfang W29
Zheng, Jianhua W529
Zheng, Kai W660
Zheng, Michael A397
Zheng, Michael E187
Zheng, Nanyan W636
Zheng, Peiming A791
Zheng, Shuliang W141
Zheng, Wei W431
Zheng, Xingang W275

Zheng, Yanli W140
Zheng, Yongda W655
Zheng, Youcheng W663
Zhong, Changhao W575
Zhong, Lixin W292
Zhong, Lixin W512
Zhong, Ruiming W147
Zhong, Wei W254
Zhong, Wei W148
Zhong, Wenxu W355
Zhong, Xiangqun W104
Zhong, Zhengqiang W356
Zhou, Changjiang W138
Zhou, Da W327
Zhou, Dayu W149
Zhou, Dekang W372
Zhou, Donghui W145
Zhou, Dongli W477
Zhou, Fang W656
Zhou, Hong W660
Zhou, Hua W516
Zhou, Hui W291
Zhou, Jeff E331
Zhou, Jichang W398
Zhou, Jing W542
Zhou, Jun W608
Zhou, Jun W530
Zhou, Langhui W292
Zhou, Linlin W248
Zhou, Ping W529
Zhou, Xuedong W88
Zhou, Yali W140
Zhou, Yalin W117
Zhou, Yifeng W656
Zhou, Yingqi W292
Zhou, Zhiping W153
Zhou, Zhonghui W173
Zhu, Daqing W291
Zhu, Guang W663
Zhu, Hanming W88
Zhu, Hexin W156
Zhu, Hongbiao W138
Zhu, Huaming W272
Zhu, Huarong W153
Zhu, Huijun W98
Zhu, Jia W572
Zhu, Jinmei W533
Zhu, Jiusheng W152
Zhu, Kebing W151
Zhu, Kebing W152
Zhu, Keshi W38
Zhu, Limin W660
Zhu, Linan W362
Zhu, Min W151
Zhu, Ning W327
Zhu, Peili W512
Zhu, Qixin W239
Zhu, Rongbin W575
Zhu, Rongen W292
Zhu, Runzhou W34
Zhu, Shaofang W375
Zhu, Shengtao W140
Zhu, Stephen Jingshi W202
Zhu, Tong W291
Zhu, Weimin W664
Zhu, Wenkai W142
Zhu, Xingwen W326
Zhu, Xu W152
Zhu, Yingfeng W603
Zhu, Yong W603

COMBINED HOOVER'S HANDBOOK INDEX OF EXECUTIVES

```
A = AMERICAN BUSINESS
E = EMERGING COMPANIES
P = PRIVATE COMPANIES
W = WORLD BUSINESSS
```

Zhu, Yonghong W88
Zhu, Yonghong W145
Zhu, Youchun W292
Zhu, Yuanchao W179
Zhu, Yueliang W256
Zhu, Zengjin W254
Zhu, Zhaokai W529
Zhu, Zhengfu W477
Zhu, Zhiqiang W141
Zhuang, Jiansheng W664
Zhuang, Jingxiong W292
Zhuang, Shangbiao W146
Zhuo, Alan Yue W202
Zi, Xunting W662
Zichlinskey, Nir W78
Zicht, J. Philip E81
Ziebell, Mark R. E45
Ziegler, Alexandre W511
Ziegler, Ann E. A1083
Ziegler, Ann E. A497
Ziegler, Marie Z. A865
Ziegler, Marie Z. E403
Zieglgansberger, J. Drew W133
Zielke, Martin W389
Ziemba, Lawrence Michael A832
Ziemba, Lawrence Michael A809
Ziemba, Lawrence Michael A833
Ziemer, James L. A1012
Ziemer, James L. A1028
Zierer, Werner W96
Zife, Aryeh W410
Ziffer, Jack A P61
Zijderveld, Jan W351
Zilberfarb, Ben-Zion W312
Zillmer, John J. A304
Zillmer, John J. A358
Zillmer, John J. A92
Ziman, Richard S. E419
Zimino, Henrik W348
Zimlich, Joseph C. E206
Zimmer, James E. A427
Zimmer, James E. E204
Zimmer, Jeffrey J. A96
Zimmer, Silke W398
Zimmerer, Maximilian W415
Zimmerly, Ronald L. E326
Zimmerman, Arnold E501
Zimmerman, Charles H. A1078
Zimmerman, Charles H. E513
Zimmerman, Lawrence A. W46
Zimmerman, Michael J. A977
Zimmerman, Michael J. E464
Zimmerman, Roger L. E158
Zimmermann, Norbertz W453
Zimpfer, Matthew J. A261
Zindel, Christoph W545
Zinger, Benjamin W410
Zingoni, Maria Victoria W493
Zink, Charles L P429
Zink, Gregory L. E348
Zink, Linda M. E443
Zink, Ryan M. E235
Zinn, Daniel E366
Zinsner, David A. A560

Zinsou-Derlin, Lionel W187
Zinsou-Derlin, Lionel W61
Zinterhofer, Eric L. A224
Zippelius, Peter E83
Zipperle, Cynthia Hillebrand A541
Zipse, Oliver W96
Zirakparvar, M. Esmail E26
Zises, Selig A. E173
Zitterow, David M. (Dave) A392
Zitterow, David M. (Dave) E183
Zitzelsberger, Roman W395
Zitzner, Duane E. A999
Ziv, Omer W79
Ziviani, Nivio W468
Zlatkis, Bella W521
Zlatkus, Lizebeth H. A688
Zlatkus, Lizebeth H. E323
Zlotnicka, Eva T. E169
Zmigrosky, P. Matt E409
Zmitrovich, Joseph T. E149
Zmitrowicz, Magdalena W86
Zobel, Inigo U. W514
Zodl, Helmut A458
Zoellick, Robert B. A1047
Zoellner, Brian E338
Zoghbi, Huda Y. A882
Zohar, Shlomo A321
Zoino, Christine A. A757
Zoiss, Edward J. A613
Zollar, Alfred W. A565
Zollar, Alfred W. A858
Zollar, Alfred W. A721
Zollar, Alfred W. A132
Zollars, William D. A221
Zommer, Nathan E303
Zong, Wenlong W291
Zong, Yixiang W261
Zoon, Kathryn C. E157
Zoppo, Maria Cristina W310
Zoretic, Richard C. A707
Zorn, Rebecca E. A478
Zorrilla, Enrique W266
Zou, Hongying W397
Zou, Jixin W88
Zou, Laichang W663
Zou, Shaorong W655
Zovighian, Bernard J. A361
Zu, Sijie W512
Zuber, Maria T. A1012
Zuber, Maria T. A128
Zuber, Paul A. E260
Zubiria, Eugenio W266
Zubkov, Viktor A. W474
Zubretsky, Joseph M. A707
Zubrow, Barry L. W119
Zucaro, Aldo C. A773
Zucchelli, Mario W627
Zucchelli, Mario W627
Zuccotti, Patricia L. A180
Zuccotti, Patricia L. W113
Zucker, Gillian B. E260
Zucker, Scott E493
Zuckerberg, Mark A689
Zuckerman, Steven J. A307
Zuckerman, Steven J. E133
Zuckert, Michael S. A984
Zuckert, Michael S. E476
Zuehlke, Oliver W95
Zuehls, Dale S. A531
Zuehls, Dale S. E259

Zuhl, Colleen A. A1028
Zukauckas, Linda K. A742
Zukunft, Gunnar W543
Zullinger, Joel R. A788
Zullinger, Joel R. E365
Zulueta, Alfonso G. A635
Zulueta, Alfonso G. A986
Zuo, Min W530
Zuppas, Eleni Nitsa E519
Zuraitis, Marita A248
Zuraitis, Marita A531
Zurbay, Donald J. A806
Zurbuegg, Peter W34
Zurfluh, Tammy E61
Zurkamer, Andrea E. A504
Zurquiyah-Rousset, Sophie W591
Zurquiyah, Sophie W511
Zvi, Shmuel Ben W79
Zwiener, David K. A1099
Zygocki, Rhonda I. W133
Zyl, Johan van W562